Colli
ENGLIS
DICTIONARY

Published by Collins
An imprint of HarperCollins Publishers
Westerhill Road
Bishopbriggs
Glasgow G64 2QT

www.collinsdictionary.com

Typeset by Davidson Publishing Solutions

Printed in Italia by Grafica Veneta
ISBN 978-2-32101-792-9

La présente édition est diffusée par les Dictionnaires Le Robert.

A catalogue record for this book is available from the British Library.

If you would like to comment on any aspect of this book, please contact us at the given address or online.
E-mail: dictionaries@harpercollins.co.uk
facebook.com/collinsdictionary
@collinsdict

Acknowledgements
We would like to thank those authors and publishers who kindly gave permission for copyright material to be used in the Collins Corpus. We would also like to thank Times Newspapers Ltd for providing valuable data.

This book is produced from independently certified FSC™ paper to ensure responsible forest management.

For more information visit: www.harpercollins.co.uk/green

Préface

Cette édition du *Collins English Dictionary* est l'outil idéal pour tous les étudiants de l'enseignement du secondaire et supérieur qui sont amenés à passer des examens d'anglais.

Dictionnaire unilingue non encyclopédique, le *Collins English Dictionary* est autorisé pour les épreuves du baccalauréat des spécialités *Langues, Littératures et Civilisations étrangères* (LLCER) et *Anglais monde contemporain* (AMC) et pour les épreuves d'anglais de certains BTS tertiaires (MCO, SAM, GPME, CI).

D'un format pratique, le *Collins English Dictionary* permet de trouver rapidement tous les mots et les expressions nécessaires non seulement à la compréhension, mais aussi au résumé et au commentaire de documents relatifs aux thématiques des programmes scolaires.

Tout le vocabulaire courant, ainsi que celui de la presse et de la littérature, y est défini de façon claire et concise. Les principaux noms propres, y compris ceux de personnages fictifs ou légendaires, sont également présentés. Les définitions s'accompagnent de plusieurs types d'informations essentielles pour bien comprendre et maîtriser ce vocabulaire.

• Les **temps primitifs des verbes irréguliers, les pluriels irréguliers, les comparatifs et superlatifs irréguliers** ainsi que ceux des adjectifs et des adverbes courts sont rappelés pour éviter toute erreur.

• Les **marques de domaine** (*architecture, économie, médecine,* etc.) délimitent les contextes d'emploi et permettent d'utiliser le mot juste en fonction du document étudié.

• Des **milliers d'exemples et de collocations** (mots qui se trouvent régulièrement associés) fournissent des contextes typiques, faciles à mémoriser et à réutiliser.

• Les **locutions et expressions figurées** sont mises en relief et clairement définies, afin d'écarter toute interprétation fautive que produirait un « mot à mot » et d'aider à s'exprimer de façon idiomatique.

Préface

• Les **registres de langue** (*littéraire, argotique, familier, vieilli*) sont précisés pour assurer l'emploi du mot correct en fonction du contexte et prévenir les ruptures de style.

• Des **marques** (*anglais britannique, écossais, irlandais, américain, canadien, australien, néo-zélandais,* etc.) précisent les régions et pays où certains mots et expressions sont en usage.

• Des **remarques étymologiques** éclairent l'origine des mots (*latin, grec, ancien français, vieil anglais, espagnol, arabe,* etc.) et de certaines expressions figurées.

• Enfin, de **nombreuses notes d'usage** alertent sur des mots ou des tournures à éviter. D'autres notes pointent des constructions grammaticales importantes ou mettent en lumière les différences sémantiques entre quasi-synonymes.

Ce contenu très riche offre aux étudiants les moyens d'améliorer leurs compétences linguistiques et d'enrichir leur culture personnelle, clés de la réussite à l'examen.

Les dictionnaires Le Robert

Comment utiliser ce dictionnaire

Les mots-vedettes

Ils sont présentés en gras et par ordre alphabétique.

abbey

Les homographes sont suivis d'un numéro en exposant. Ex. :

abbot
abbreviate
ABC^1
ABC^2
abdicate

Les verbes à particule et les composés

Ils sont présentés à leur place alphabétique pour les trouver rapidement. Ex. :

breakfast *n* **1** the first meal of the day ▹ *vb* **2** to eat breakfast [BREAK + FAST^2]
break in *vb* **1** to enter a building illegally, esp. by force **2** to interrupt **3** to accustom (a person or animal) to normal duties or practice **4** to use or wear (new shoes or new equipment) until comfortable or running smoothly ▹ *n* **break-in** **5** the act of illegally entering a building, esp. by thieves
breaking point *n* the point at which something or someone gives way under strain
breakneck *adj* (of speed or pace) excessively fast and dangerous
break off *vb* **1** to sever or detach **2** to end (a relationship or association) **3** to stop abruptly

Les variantes orthographiques

Elles sont présentées derrière la graphie principale. Ex. :

adrenalin *or* **adrenaline**

Notez que si les suffixes **-ize** des verbes et **-ization** des noms sont les plus courants, leurs variantes **-ise** et **-isation** sont également tout à fait acceptables.

Comment utiliser ce dictionnaire

La prononciation

Elle n'est indiquée, entre parenthèses, que pour les mots difficiles à prononcer.
La syllabe accentuée est en gras. Ex. :

antipodes (an-**tip**-pod-deez)

Les catégories grammaticales

Elles apparaissent sous forme abrégée, en italique. Ex. :

ablaze *adj*

Lorsqu'un mot a plusieurs catégories grammaticales, le changement de catégorie est signalé par un triangle éclairé et chaque catégorie est suivie d'un chiffre arabe. Ex. :

adept *adj* 1 proficient in some requiring skill ▷ *n* 2 a person skilled in something

Lorsque la définition s'applique à toutes les catégories grammaticales, celles-ci sont présentées ensemble. Ex. :

awash *adv, adj* washed over by water

Formes irrégulières

Les formes irrégulières ou inattendues des verbes, noms, adjectifs et adverbes sont présentées en gras. Ex. :

begin *vb* **-ginning, -gan, -gun**
regret *vb* **-gretting, -gretted**
anniversary *n, pl* **-ries**
angry *adj* **-grier, -griest**
well *adv* **better, best**

Les sens

Les différents sens des mots sont introduits par des chiffres arabes. Ex. :

absorb *vb* **1** to soak up a liquid **2** to engage the interest of someone **3** to receive the force of an impact ...

Comment utiliser ce dictionnaire

Expressions idiomatiques

Elles apparaissent en gras, précédées d'un chiffre arabe. Ex. :

hand ... **22 keep one's hand in** to continue to practise something
23 (near) at hand very close
24 on hand close by; available

Les dérivés

Les dérivés du mot-vedette sont présentés en gras à la fin de l'article principal, accompagnés de leur catégorie grammaticale. Ex. :

absurd *adj* obviously senseless or illogical; ridiculous [Latin *absurdus*] **absurdity** *n* **absurdly** *adv*

Lorsque le sens d'un dérivé n'est pas donné, c'est qu'il peut être facilement déduit de la définition du mot-vedette ou d'un autre dérivé.

Les notes d'usage

Elles sont clairement signalées par la marque USAGE. Ex. :

USAGE The phrase *with bated breath* is sometimes wrongly spelled *with baited breath*.

Contents

EDITORIAL STAFF
Ian Brookes
Andrew Delahunty
Alice Grandison
Andrew Holmes
Mary O'Neill

SUPPLEMENT
Elizabeth Walter and Kate Woodford

FOR THE PUBLISHER
Gerry Breslin
Kerry Ferguson

Foreword

The purpose of Collins Dictionaries is simple: to take as sharp and as true a picture of language as possible. In order to stay at the forefront of language developments we have an extensive reading, listening and viewing programme, taking in broadcasts, websites and publications from around the globe. These are fed into our monitoring system, an unparalleled 4.5 billion-word analytical database: the Collins Corpus. By analysing this data, Collins editors are able to build up a picture of the vocabulary of today, and how it is being used.

Now Collins has another important word-tracking resource. When we launched Collins Dictionary online in 2012, we invited word lovers across the globe to contribute new words and help us make our word collection process truly democratic. By 2019, we had received well over 20,000 suggestions, opening up whole new worlds of words and areas of language for the editors to consider.

Everyone is welcome to join us in the home of living English by contributing new words and meanings at www.collinsdictionary.com, where we celebrate the extraordinary breadth and changing nature of English worldwide.

Using this dictionary

Main entry words printed in large bold type, eg

abbey

All main entry words, including abbreviations and combining forms, in one alphabetical sequence, eg

abbot
abbreviate
ABC[1]
ABC[2]
abdicate

Variant spellings shown in full, eg

adrenalin *or* **adrenaline**

Note: where the spellings **-ize** and **-ization** are used at the end of a word, the alternative forms **-ise** and **-isation** are equally acceptable.

Pronunciations given in brackets for words that are difficult or confusing; the word is respelt as it is pronounced, with the stressed syllable in bold type, eg

antipodes (an-**tip**-pod-deez)

Parts of speech shown in italics as an abbreviation, eg

ablaze *adj*

When a word can be used as more than one part of speech, the change of part of speech is shown after an arrow, eg

adept *adj* 1 proficient in something requiring skill ▷ *n* 2 a person skilled in something

Parts of speech may be combined for words, eg

awash *adv, adj* washed over by water

Using this dictionary

Irregular parts or confusing forms of verbs, nouns, adjectives, and adverbs shown in bold type, eg

> **begin** *vb* **-ginning, -gan, -gun**
> **regret** *vb* **-gretting, -gretted**
> **anniversary** *n, pl* **-ries**
> **angry** *adj* **-grier, -griest**
> **well** *adv* **better, best**

Meanings separated by numbers, eg

> **absorb** *vb* **1** to soak up a liquid **2** to engage the interest of someone **3** to receive the force of an impact ...

Phrases and idioms are included in the meanings of the main entry word, eg

> **hand** ... **22 keep one's hand in** to continue to practise something **23 (near) at hand** very close **24 on hand** close by; available

Related words shown in the same paragraph as the main entry word, eg

> **absurd** *adj* obviously senseless or illogical; ridiculous [Latin *absurdus*] **absurdity** *n* **absurdly** *adv*

Note: where the meaning of a related word is not given, it may be understood from the main entry word, or from another related word.

Usage notes introduced by the label USAGE, eg

> **USAGE** The phrase *with bated breath* is sometimes wrongly spelled *with baited breath*.

Abbreviations used in this dictionary

Abbrev	abbreviation	*geom*	geometry
AD	anno Domini	*interj*	interjection
adj	adjective	*masc*	masculine
adv	adverb	*med*	medicine
anthropol	anthropology	*meteorol*	meteorology
archaeol	archaeology	*myth*	mythology
archit	architecture	*n*	noun
astrol	astrology	N	North
astron	astronomy	*naut*	nautical
Austral	Australia(n)	NZ	New Zealand
bacteriol	bacteriology	*ornithol*	ornithology
BC	before Christ	*pathol*	pathology
biochem	biochemistry	*pharmacol*	pharmacology
biol	biology	*photog*	photography
Brit	British	*physiol*	physiology
Canad	Canadian	*pl*	plural
cap	capital(s)	*prep*	preposition
chem	chemistry	*pron*	pronoun
conj	conjuction	*psychol*	psychology
crystallog	crystallography	RC	Roman Catholic
E	East	S	South
econ	economics	*Scot*	Scottish
eg	for example	*sing*	singular
esp.	especially	*sociol*	sociology
etc.	et cetera	*theol*	theology
fem	feminine	US	United States
foll	followed	*vb*	verb
geog	geography	W	West
geol	geology	*zool*	zoology

Aa

a *or* **A** *n, pl* **a's, A's** *or* **As 1** the first letter of the English alphabet **2 from A to B** from one place to another: *I just want a car that takes me from A to B* **3 from A to Z** from start to finish
a *adj (indefinite article)* **1** used preceding a singular count noun that has not been mentioned before: *a book*; *a great shame* **2** used preceding a noun or adjective of quantity: *a litre of wine*; *a great amount has been written*; *I swim a lot and walk much more* **3** each or every; per: *I saw him once a week for six weeks*
A 1 *music* the sixth note of the scale of C major **2** ampere(s) **3** atomic: *an A-bomb*
Å angstrom unit
a- *or before a vowel* **an-** *prefix* not or without: *atonal*; *asexual*; *anaemia* [Greek]
A1, A-1 *or* **A-one** *adj informal* first-class, excellent
A4 *n* a standard paper size, 297 × 210 mm
AA 1 Alcoholics Anonymous **2** (in Britain and South Africa) Automobile Association
AAA *Brit* (formerly) Amateur Athletic Association
A & R artists and repertoire
aardvark *n* a S African anteater with long ears and snout [obsolete Afrikaans: earth pig]
AB 1 able-bodied seaman **2** Alberta
ab- *prefix* away from or opposite to: *abnormal* [Latin]
aback *adv* **taken aback** startled or disconcerted
abacus (ab-a-cuss) *n* a counting device consisting of a frame holding beads on metal rods [Latin]
abaft *adv, adj naut* closer to the stern of a ship [Old English *be* by + *æftan* behind]
abalone (ab-a-**lone**-ee) *n* an edible sea creature with a shell lined with mother-of-pearl [American Spanish *abulón*]
abandon *vb* **1** to desert or leave: *he had already abandoned his first wife* **2** to give up completely: *did you abandon all attempts at contact with the boy?* **3** to give oneself over completely to an emotion ▷ *n* **4 with abandon** uninhibitedly and without restraint [Old French *a bandon* under one's control] **abandonment** *n*
abandoned *adj* **1** no longer used or occupied: *four people were found dead in an abandoned vehicle* **2** wild and uninhibited: *that fluffy abandoned laugh*
abase *vb* **abasing, abased** > **abase oneself** to make oneself humble [Old French *abaissier*] **abasement** *n*
abashed *adj* embarrassed and ashamed [Old French *esbair* to be astonished]
abate *vb* **abating, abated** to make or become less strong: *the tension has abated in recent months* [Old French *abatre* to beat down] **abatement** *n*
abattoir (ab-a-twahr) *n* a slaughterhouse [French *abattre* to fell]
abbacy *n, pl* **-cies** the office or jurisdiction of an abbot or abbess [Church Latin *abbatia*]
abbé (ab-bay) *n* a French abbot or other cleric
abbess *n* the nun in charge of a convent [Church Latin *abbatissa*]
abbey *n* **1** a church associated with a community of monks or nuns **2** a community of monks or nuns **3** a building inhabited by monks or nuns [Church Latin *abbatia* ABBACY]
abbot *n* the head of an abbey of monks [Aramaic *abbā* father]
abbreviate *vb* **-ating, -ated 1** to shorten a word by leaving out some letters **2** to cut short [Latin *brevis* brief] **abbreviation** *n*
ABC[1] *n* **1** the alphabet **2** an alphabetical guide **3** the basics of something
ABC[2] Australian Broadcasting Corporation
abdicate *vb* **-cating, -cated 1** to give up the throne formally **2** to give up one's responsibilities [Latin *abdicare* to disclaim] **abdication** *n*
abdomen *n* the part of the body that contains the stomach and intestines [Latin] **abdominal** *adj*
abdominoplasty *n* the surgical removal of excess skin and fat from the abdomen
abduct *vb* to remove (a person) by force; kidnap [Latin *abducere* to lead away] **abduction** *n* **abductor** *n*
abeam *adv, adj* at right angles to the length of a ship or aircraft
Aberdeen Angus *n* a black hornless breed of beef cattle originating in Scotland
aberrant *adj* not normal, accurate, or correct: *aberrant behaviour*
aberration *n* **1** a sudden change from what is normal, accurate, or correct **2** a brief lapse in control of one's thoughts or feelings: *he suddenly had a mental aberration* [Latin *aberrare* to wander away]
abet *vb* **abetting, abetted** to help or encourage in wrongdoing [Old French *abeter* to lure on]
abeyance *n* **in abeyance** put aside temporarily [Old French *abeance*, literally: a gaping after]
abhor *vb* **-horring, -horred** to detest utterly [Latin *abhorrere* to shudder at]
abhorrent *adj* hateful or disgusting **abhorrence** *n*
abide *vb* **1** to tolerate: *I can't abide stupid people* **2** to last or exist for a long time: *these instincts, while subdued in the individual, may abide in the race* **3 abide by** to act in accordance with: *we must abide by the findings of the report* **4** *archaic* to live [Old English *ābīdan*, from *a-* (intensive) + *bīdan* to wait]
abiding *adj* lasting for ever: *an abiding interest in history*
ability *n, pl* **-ties 1** possession of the necessary skill or power to do something **2** great skill or competence: *his ability as a speaker was legendary* [Latin *habilitas*]
abject *adj* **1** utterly miserable: *his mother grew up in abject poverty* **2** lacking all self-respect [Latin *abjectus* thrown away] **abjectly** *adv*
abjure *vb* **-juring, -jured** to renounce or deny under oath [Latin *abjurare*] **abjuration** *n*
ablation *n* **1** the surgical removal of an organ or part **2** the wearing away of a rock or glacier **3** the melting of a part, such as the heat shield of a space re-entry vehicle [Latin *ablatus* carried away]

a

ablaze *adj* **1** on fire **2** brightly illuminated: *the sky was ablaze with the stars shining bright* **3** emotionally aroused: *his eyes were ablaze with anger*

able *adj* **1** having the necessary power, skill, or opportunity to do something **2** capable or talented [Latin *habilis* easy to hold]

-able *adj suffix* able to be acted upon as specified: *washable* [Latin *-abilis, -ibilis*] **-ably** *suffix forming adverbs* **-ability** *suffix forming nouns*

able-bodied *adj* **1** strong and healthy **2** not having a physical disability

> **USAGE** When talking about people who do not have a disability, the term *non-disabled* is preferred.

able-bodied seaman *or* **able seaman** *n* a seaman who is trained in certain skills

abled *adj* having a range of physical powers as specified: *less abled; differently abled*

ableism (ay-bel-iz-zum) *n* discrimination against people with disabilities

able rating *n* (in Britain) a seaman of the lowest rank in a navy

ablutions *pl n* the act of washing: *after the nightly ablutions, I settled down to read* [Latin *abluere* to wash away]

ably *adv* competently or skilfully

ABM antiballistic missile

abnegation *n* the act of giving something up [Latin *abnegare* to deny]

abnormal *adj* differing from the usual or typical **abnormality** *n* **abnormally** *adv*

aboard *adv, adj, prep* on, in, onto, or into (a ship, plane, or train)

abode *n* one's home [from ABIDE]

abolish *vb* to do away with (laws, regulations, or customs) [Latin *abolere* to destroy]

abolition *n* **1** the act of doing away with something: *the abolition of the death penalty* **2 Abolition** the ending of slavery **abolitionist** *n, adj*

A-bomb *n* short for **atomic bomb**

abominable *adj* very bad or unpleasant: *I think that what is being done here is utterly abominable* **abominably** *adv*

abominable snowman *n* a large creature, like a man or an ape, that is said to live in the Himalayas [translation of Tibetan *metohkangmi* foul snowman]

abominate *vb* **-nating, -nated** to dislike intensely [Latin *abominari* to regard as an ill omen] **abomination** *n*

aboriginal *adj* existing in a place from the earliest known period [Latin *aborigines* the name of the inhabitants of Latium in pre-Roman times]

Aboriginal *adj* of or relating to the peoples who inhabited Australia before the arrival of European settlers

Aborigine *n sometimes offensive* a member or descendant of any of the peoples who were already living in Australia before the arrival of European settlers

> **USAGE** The noun *Aborigine* is sometimes considered offensive. It is better to use the term *Aboriginal people* or *Indigenous people*.

abort *vb* **1** (of a pregnancy) to end before the fetus is viable **2** to perform an abortion on a pregnant woman **3** to end a plan or process before completion [Latin *abortare*]

abortion *n* **1** an operation to end pregnancy **2** the premature ending of a pregnancy when a fetus is expelled from the womb before it can live independently **3** the failure of a mission or project **4** *offensive* something that is grotesque **abortionist** *n*

abortion pill *n* a drug used to terminate a pregnancy in its earliest stage

abortive *adj* failing to achieve its purpose

abound *vb* **1** to exist in large numbers **2 abound in** to have a large number of [Latin *abundare* to overflow]

about *prep* **1** relating to or concerning **2** near to **3** carried on: *I haven't any money about me* **4** on every side of ▹ *adv* **5** near in number, time, or degree; approximately **6** nearby **7** here and there: *there were some fifteen other people scattered about on the first floor* **8** all around; on every side **9** in or to the opposite direction **10** in rotation: *turn and turn about* **11** used to indicate understatement: *it's about time somebody told the truth on that subject* **12 about to** on the point of; intending to: *she was about to get in the car* **13 not about to** determined not to: *we're not about to help her out* ▹ *adj* **14** active: *he was off the premises well before anyone was up and about* [Old English *abūtan, onbūtan* on the outside of]

about-turn *or US* **about-face** *n* **1** a complete change of opinion or direction **2** a reversal of the direction in which one is facing

above *prep* **1** higher than; over **2** greater than in quantity or degree: *above average* **3** superior to or higher than in quality, rank, or ability **4** too high-minded for: *she considered herself above the task of working* **5** too respected for; beyond: *his fleet was above suspicion* **6** too difficult to be understood by: *a discussion that was way above my head* **7** louder or higher than (other noise) **8** in preference to **9 above all** most of all; especially ▹ *adv* **10** in or to a higher place: *the hills above* **11** in a previous place (in something written or printed) **12** higher in rank or position ▹ *n* **13 the above** something previously mentioned ▹ *adj* **14** appearing in a previous place (in something written or printed): *for a copy of the free brochure write to the above address* [Old English *abufan*]

above board *adj* completely honest and open

abracadabra *n* a word used by conjurors when performing a magic trick [Latin]

abrasion *n* **1** a scraped area on the skin; graze **2** *geog* the erosion of rock by rock fragments scratching and scraping it [Latin *abradere* to scrape away]

abrasive *adj* **1** rude and unpleasant in manner **2** tending to rub or scrape; rough ▹ *n* **3** a substance used for cleaning, smoothing, or polishing

abreast *adj* **1** alongside each other and facing in the same direction: *the two cars were abreast* **2 abreast of** up to date with

abridge *vb* **abridging, abridged** to shorten a written work by taking out parts [Late Latin *abbreviare*] **abridgment** *or* **abridgement** *n*

abroad *adv* **1** to or in a foreign country **2** generally known or felt: *there is a new spirit abroad*

a

abrogate *vb* **-gating, -gated** to cancel (a law or an agreement) formally [from Latin *ab-* away + *rogare* to propose a law] **abrogation** *n*
abrupt *adj* **1** sudden or unexpected: *an abrupt departure* **2** rather rude in speech or manner [Latin *abruptus* broken off] **abruptly** *adv* **abruptness** *n*
abs *pl n* abdominal muscles
abscess (ab-sess) *n* **1** a swelling containing pus as a result of inflammation ▷ *vb* **2** to form a swelling containing pus [Latin *abscessus* literally: a throwing off] **abscessed** *adj*
abscissa *n, pl* **-scissas** *or* **-scissae** *maths* (in a two-dimensional system of Cartesian coordinates) the distance from the vertical axis measured parallel to the horizontal axis [New Latin *linea abscissa* a cut-off line]
abscond *vb* to run away unexpectedly [Latin *abscondere* to conceal]
abseil (ab-sale) *vb* **1** to go down a steep drop by a rope fastened at the top and tied around one's body ▷ *n* **2** an instance of abseiling [German *abseilen*]
absence *n* **1** the state of being away **2** the time during which a person or thing is away **3** the fact of being without something
absent *adj* **1** not present in a place or situation **2** lacking **3** not paying attention ▷ *vb* **4 absent oneself** to stay away [Latin *absens*] **absently** *adv*
absentee *n* a person who should be present but is not
absenteeism *n* persistent absence from work or school
absent-minded *adj* inattentive or forgetful **absent-mindedly** *adv*
absinthe *n* a strong, green, alcoholic drink, originally containing wormwood [Greek *apsinthion* wormwood]
absolute *adj* **1** total and complete: *he ordered an immediate and absolute ceasefire* **2** with unrestricted power and authority: *she has absolute control with fifty per cent of the shares* **3** undoubted or certain: *I was telling the absolute truth* **4** not dependent on or relative to anything else **5** pure; unmixed: *absolute alcohol* ▷ *n* **6** a principle or rule believed to be unfailingly correct **7 the Absolute** *philosophy* that which is totally unconditioned, perfect, or complete [Latin *absolutus*]
absolutely *adv* **1** completely or perfectly ▷ *interj* **2** yes indeed, certainly
absolute majority *n* a number of votes totalling over 50 per cent, such as the total number of votes that beats the combined opposition
absolute pitch *n* the ability to identify the pitch of a note, or to sing a given note, without reference to one previously sounded
absolute zero *n physics* the lowest temperature theoretically possible, at which the particles that make up matter would be at rest: equivalent to -273.15°C or -459.67°F
absolution *n Christianity* a formal forgiveness of sin pronounced by a priest
absolutism *n* a political system in which a monarch or dictator has unrestricted power
absolve *vb* **-solving, -solved** to declare to be free from blame or sin [Latin *absolvere*]
absorb *vb* **1** to soak up a liquid **2** to engage the interest of someone **3** to receive the force of an impact **4** *physics* to take in radiant energy and retain it **5** to take in or incorporate: *this country has absorbed almost one million refugees* [Latin *absorbere* to suck] **absorbent** *adj* **absorbing** *adj*
absorption *n* **1** the process of absorbing something or the state of being absorbed **2** *physiol* the process by which nutrients enter the tissues of an animal or a plant **absorptive** *adj*
abstain *vb* **1** (usually foll. by *from*) to choose not to do or partake of something: *you will be asked to abstain from food prior to your general anaesthetic* **2** to choose not to vote [Latin *abstinere*] **abstainer** *n*
abstemious (ab-steem-ee-uss) *adj* taking very little alcohol or food [Latin *abstemius*] **abstemiously** *adv* **abstemiousness** *n*
abstention *n* **1** the formal act of not voting **2** the act of abstaining from something, such as drinking alcohol
abstinence *n* the practice of choosing not to do something one would like **abstinent** *adj*
abstract *adj* **1** referring to ideas or qualities rather than material objects: *an abstract noun* **2** not applied or practical; theoretical: *he was frustrated by the highly abstract mathematics being taught* **3** of art in which the subject is represented by shapes and patterns rather than by a realistic likeness ▷ *n* **4** a summary **5** an abstract painting or sculpture **6** an abstract word or idea **7 in the abstract** without referring to specific circumstances ▷ *vb* **8** to summarize **9** to remove or extract [Latin *abstractus* drawn off]
abstracted *adj* lost in thought; preoccupied **abstractedly** *adv*
abstraction *n* **1** a general idea rather than a specific example: *these absurd philosophical abstractions continued to bother him* **2** the quality of being abstract or abstracted
abstruse *adj* not easy to understand [Latin *abstrusus* concealed]
absurd *adj* obviously senseless or illogical; ridiculous [Latin *absurdus*] **absurdity** *n* **absurdly** *adv*
abundance *n* **1** a great amount **2** degree of plentifulness **3 in abundance** in great amounts: *they had fish and fruit in abundance* [Latin *abundare* to abound] **abundant** *adj*
abundantly *adv* **1** very: *he made his disagreement with the prime minister abundantly clear* **2** plentifully; in abundance
abuse *n* **1** prolonged ill-treatment of or violence towards someone: *child abuse* **2** insulting comments **3** improper use: *an abuse of power* ▷ *vb* **abusing, abused 4** to take advantage of dishonestly: *these two ministers had abused their position for financial gain* **5** to ill-treat violently or sexually: *he had been sexually abused as a child* **6** to speak insultingly or cruelly to [Latin *abuti* to misuse] **abuser** *n*
abusive *adj* **1** rude or insulting: *he was alleged to have used abusive language towards spectators* **2** involving cruelty and ill-treatment: *an abusive relationship* **abusively** *adv*
abut *vb* **abutting, abutted** to be next to or touching [Old French *abouter*]

a

abutment *n* a construction that supports the end of a bridge

abysmal *adj informal* extremely bad [Medieval Latin *abysmus* abyss] **abysmally** *adv*

abyss *n* **1** a very deep hole in the ground **2** a frightening or threatening situation: *the abyss of revolution and war ahead* [Greek *abussos* bottomless]

Ac *chem* actinium

AC **1** alternating current **2** athletic club

a/c **1** account **2** account current

acacia (a-**kay**-sha) *n* a shrub or tree with small yellow or white flowers [Greek *akakia*]

academic *adj* **1** relating to a college or university **2** (of pupils) having an aptitude for study **3** relating to studies such as languages and pure science rather than technical or professional studies **4** of theoretical interest only: *the argument is academic* ▷ *n* **5** a member of the teaching or research staff of a college or university **academically** *adv*

academy *n, pl* **-mies** **1** a society for the advancement of literature, art, or science **2** a school for training in a particular skill: *sixteen hundred students would also spend their first year at the military academy* **3** a secondary school [Greek *akadēmeia* the place where Plato taught]

Acadian *adj* **1** denoting or relating to Acadia or its inhabitants ▷ *n* **2** any of the early French settlers in Nova Scotia ▷ See also **Cajun**

acanthus *n* **1** a plant with large spiny leaves and spikes of white or purplish flowers **2** a carved ornament based on the leaves of the acanthus plant [Greek *akantha* thorn]

ACAS (in Britain) Advisory Conciliation and Arbitration Service

ACC (in New Zealand) Accident Compensation Corporation

acc. **1** *grammar* accusative **2** account

accede *vb* **-ceding, -ceded** > **accede to** **1** to agree to **2** to take up (an office or position): *he acceded to the throne after his Irish exile* [Latin *accedere*]

accelerando *adv music* with increasing speed [Italian]

accelerate *vb* **-ating, -ated** **1** to move or cause to move more quickly **2** to cause to happen sooner than expected [Latin *accelerare*]

acceleration *n* **1** the act of increasing speed **2** the rate of increase of speed or the rate of change of velocity

accelerator *n* **1** a pedal in a motor vehicle that is pressed to increase speed **2** *physics* a machine for increasing the speed and energy of charged particles

accent *n* **1** the distinctive style of pronunciation of a person or group from a particular area, country, or social background **2** a mark used in writing to indicate the prominence of a syllable or the way a vowel is pronounced **3** particular emphasis: *there will be an accent on sport and many will enjoy rowing* **4** the stress on a syllable or musical note ▷ *vb* **5** to lay particular emphasis on [Latin *accentus*]

accentuate *vb* **-ating, -ated** to stress or emphasize **accentuation** *n*

accept *vb* **1** to take or receive something offered **2** to agree to **3** to consider something as true **4** to tolerate or resign oneself to **5** to take on the responsibilities of: *he asked if I would become his assistant and I accepted that position* **6** to receive someone into a community or group **7** to receive something as adequate or valid [Latin *acceptare*]

acceptable *adj* **1** able to be endured; tolerable: *in war killing is acceptable* **2** good enough; adequate: *he found the article acceptable* **acceptability** *n* **acceptably** *adv*

acceptance *n* **1** the act of accepting something **2** favourable reception **3** belief or agreement

accepted *adj* commonly approved or recognized: *the accepted wisdom about old age*

access *n* **1** a means of approaching or entering a place **2** the condition of allowing entry, for example entry to a building by wheelchairs or prams **3** the right or opportunity to use something or enter a place: *the bourgeoisie gained access to political power* **4** the opportunity or right to see or approach someone: *my ex-wife sabotages my access to the children* ▷ *vb* **5** to obtain (information) from a computer [Latin *accedere* to accede]

accessible *adj* **1** easy to approach, enter, or use **2** easy to understand: *the most accessible opera by Wagner* **accessibility** *n*

accession *n* the act of taking up an office or position: *the 40th anniversary of her accession to the throne*

accessory *n, pl* **-ries** **1** a supplementary part or object **2** a small item, such as a bag or belt, worn or carried by someone to complete his or her outfit **3** a person who is involved in a crime but who was not present when it took place [Late Latin *accessorius*]

access road *n* a road providing a way to a particular place or on to a motorway

access time *n* the time required to retrieve a piece of stored information from a computer's memory

accident *n* **1** an unpleasant event that causes damage, injury, or death **2** an unforeseen event or one without apparent cause: *they had met in town by accident* [Latin *accidere* to happen]

accidental *adj* **1** occurring by chance or unintentionally ▷ *n* **2** *music* a symbol denoting a sharp, flat, or natural that is not a part of the key signature **accidentally** *adv*

accident-prone *adj* (of a person) often involved in accidents

acclaim *vb* **1** to applaud or praise: *the highly acclaimed children's TV series* **2** to acknowledge publicly: *he was immediately acclaimed the new prime minister* ▷ *n* **3** an enthusiastic expression of approval [Latin *acclamare*]

acclamation *n* **1** an enthusiastic reception or display of approval **2** *Canad* an instance of being elected without opposition **3** **by acclamation** by a majority without a ballot

acclimatize *or* **-tise** *vb* **-tizing, -tized** *or* **-tising, -tised** to adapt to a new climate or environment **acclimatization** *or* **-tisation** *n*

accolade *n* **1** an award, praise, or honour **2** a touch on the shoulder with a sword conferring a knighthood [Latin *ad-* to + *collum* neck]

accommodate *vb* **-dating, -dated** **1** to provide with lodgings **2** to have room for **3** to do a favour for **4** to adjust or become adjusted; to adapt [Latin *accommodare*]

accommodating *adj* willing to help; obliging

accommodation *n* a place in which to sleep, live, or work

accommodation address *n Brit* an address on letters to a person who cannot or does not wish to receive mail at a permanent address

accompaniment *n* **1** something that accompanies something else **2** *music* a supporting part for an instrument, a band, or an orchestra

accompanist *n* a person who plays a musical accompaniment

accompany *vb* **-nies, -nying, -nied** **1** to go with (someone) **2** to happen or exist at the same time as **3** to provide a musical accompaniment for [Old French *accompaignier*]

accomplice *n* a person who helps someone else commit a crime [Late Latin *complex* partner]

accomplish *vb* **1** to manage to do; achieve: *most infants accomplish it immediately* **2** to complete [Latin *complere* to fill up]

accomplished *adj* **1** expert or proficient: *an accomplished liar* **2** successfully completed

accomplishment *n* **1** the successful completion of something **2** something successfully completed **3** (*often pl*) personal abilities or skills

accord *n* **1** agreement or harmony **2** a formal agreement between groups or nations: *the Paris peace accords* **3** **of one's own accord** voluntarily or willingly **4** **with one accord** unanimously ▷ *vb* **5** to grant: *she was at last accorded her true status* **6** **accord with** to fit in with or be consistent with [Latin *ad-* to + *cor* heart]

accordance *n* **in accordance with** conforming to or according to: *food is prepared in accordance with Jewish laws*

according *adv* **1** **according to** **A** as stated by: *according to her, they were once engaged* **B** in conformity with: *work hours varied according to the tides* **2** **according as** depending on whether

accordingly *adv* **1** in an appropriate manner **2** consequently

accordion *n* a box-shaped musical instrument played by moving the two sides apart and together, and pressing a keyboard or buttons to produce the notes [German *Akkordion*] **accordionist** *n*

accost *vb* to approach, stop, and speak to (someone) rudely or aggressively [Latin *ad-* to + *costa* side, rib]

account *n* **1** a report or description **2** an arrangement for a financial institution to look after one's money **3** a statement of financial transactions with the resulting balance **4** part or behalf: *I am sorry that you suffered on my account* **5** **call someone to account** to demand an explanation from someone **6** **give a good** *or* **bad account of oneself** to perform well or fail to perform well **7** **of no account** of little importance or value **8** **on account of** because of **9** **take account of** *or* **take into account** to take into consideration; allow for ▷ *vb* **10** to consider as: *the evening was accounted a major step forward by all concerned* [Old French *acont*]

accountable *adj* responsible to someone or for some action **accountability** *n*

accountant *n* a person who maintains and audits business accounts **accountancy** *n*

account for *vb* **1** to give reasons for **2** to explain or count up what has been spent

accounting *n* the skill or practice of maintaining and auditing business accounts

accoutrements (ak-**koo**-tra-ments) *or US* **accouterments** (ak-**koo**-ter-ments) *pl n* clothing and equipment for a particular activity [Old French *accoustrer* to equip]

accredit *vb* **1** to give official recognition to **2** to send (a diplomat) with official credentials to a particular country **3** to certify as meeting required standards **4** to attribute (a quality or an action) to (a person) [French *accréditer*] **accreditation** *n*

accretion (ak-**kree**-shun) *n* **1** a gradual increase in size, through growth or addition **2** something added, such as an extra layer [Latin *accretio*]

accrue *vb* **-cruing, -crued** **1** (of money or interest) to increase gradually over a period of time **2** **accrue to** to fall naturally to: *some advantage must accrue to the weaker party* [Latin *accrescere*]

accumulate *vb* **-lating, -lated** to gather together in an increasing quantity; collect [Latin *accumulare* to heap up] **accumulative** *adj*

accumulation *n* **1** something that has been collected **2** the collecting together of things

accumulator *n* **1** *Brit & Austral* a rechargeable device for storing electrical energy **2** *Brit horse racing* a collective bet on successive races, with both stake and winnings being carried forward to accumulate progressively

accuracy *n* faithful representation of the truth: *care is taken to ensure the accuracy of the content*

accurate *adj* faithfully representing the truth: *all the information was accurate* [Latin *accurare* to perform with care] **accurately** *adv*

accursed (a-**curse**-id) *adj* **1** under a curse **2** hateful or detestable

accusation *n* **1** an allegation that a person is guilty of some wrongdoing **2** a formal charge brought against a person **accusatory** *adj*

accusative *n grammar* a grammatical case in some languages that identifies the direct object of a verb

accuse *vb* **-cusing, -cused** to charge a person with wrongdoing [Latin *accūsāre*] **accuser** *n* **accusing** *adj* **accusingly** *adv*

accused *n* **the accused** *law* the defendant appearing on a criminal charge

accustom *vb* **accustom oneself to** to become familiar with or used to from habit or experience [Old French *acostumer*]

accustomed *adj* **1** usual or customary: *he parked his motorcycle in its accustomed place* **2** **accustomed to** **A** used to **B** in the habit of

ace *n* **1** a playing card with one symbol on it **2** *informal* an expert: *an American stock car ace* **3** *tennis* a winning serve that the opponent fails to reach **4** a fighter pilot who has destroyed several enemy aircraft ▷ *adj* **5** *informal* superb or excellent: *an ace skateboarder* [Latin *as* a unit]

acerbic (ass-**sir**-bik) *adj* harsh or bitter: *an acerbic critic* [Latin *acerbus* sharp, sour]

acerbity *n, pl* **-ties 1** bitter speech or temper **2** bitterness of taste

acetaldehyde (ass-it-**tal**-dee-hide) *n chem* a colourless volatile liquid, used as a solvent

acetate (**ass**-it-tate) *n* **1** *chem* any salt or ester of acetic acid **2** Also: **acetate rayon** a synthetic textile fibre made from cellulose acetate

acetic (ass-**see**-tik) *adj chem* of, containing, or producing acetic acid or vinegar [Latin *acetum* vinegar]

acetic acid *n chem* a strong-smelling colourless liquid used to make vinegar

acetone (**ass**-it-tone) *n chem* a strong-smelling colourless liquid used as a solvent for paints and lacquers

acetylene (ass-**set**-ill-een) *n chem* a colourless soluble flammable gas used in welding metals

ache *vb* **aching, ached 1** to feel or be the source of a continuous dull pain **2** to suffer mental anguish ▷ *n* **3** a continuous dull pain [Old English *ācan*]

achieve *vb* **achieving, achieved** to gain by hard work or effort [Old French *achever* to bring to an end] **achiever** *n*

achievement *n* **1** something that has been accomplished by hard work, ability, or heroism **2** the successful completion of something

Achilles heel (ak-**kill**-eez) *n* a small but fatal weakness [*Achilles* in Greek mythology was killed by an arrow in his unprotected heel]

Achilles tendon *n* the fibrous cord that connects the muscles of the calf to the heel bone

achromatic *adj* **1** without colour **2** refracting light without breaking it up into its component colours **3** *music* involving no sharps or flats **achromatically** *adv*

acid *n* **1** *chem* one of a class of compounds, corrosive and sour when dissolved in water, that combine with a base to form a salt **2** *slang* LSD **3** a sour-tasting substance ▷ *adj* **4** *chem* of, from, or containing acid **5** sharp or sour in taste **6** sharp in speech or manner [Latin *acidus*] **acidly** *adv*

Acid House *or* **Acid** *n* a type of funk-based, electronically edited dance music of the late 1980s, which has hypnotic sound effects and which is associated with the use of the drug ecstasy [*acid* (LSD) + *House* music]

acidic *adj* containing acid

acidify *vb* **-fies, -fying, -fied** to convert into acid **acidification** *n*

acidity *n* **1** the quality of being acid **2** the amount of acid in a solution

acid rain *n* rain containing pollutants released into the atmosphere by burning coal or oil

acid reflux *n* the regurgitation of stomach acid into the oesophagus, causing heartburn

acid test *n* a rigorous and conclusive test of worth or value [from the testing of gold with nitric acid]

acknowledge *vb* **-edging, -edged 1** to recognize or admit the truth of a statement **2** to show recognition of a person by a greeting or glance **3** to make known that a message or letter has been received **4** to express gratitude for (a favour or compliment) [Old English *oncnāwan* to recognize]

acknowledgment *or* **acknowledgement** *n* **1** the act of acknowledging something or someone **2** something done or given as an expression of gratitude

acme (**ak**-mee) *n* the highest point of achievement or excellence [Greek *akmē*]

acne (**ak**-nee) *n* a skin disease in which pus-filled spots form on the face [New Latin]

acolyte *n* **1** a follower or attendant **2** *Christianity* a person who assists a priest [Greek *akolouthos*]

aconite *n* **1** a poisonous plant with hoodlike flowers **2** dried aconite root, used as a narcotic [Greek *akoniton*]

acorn *n* the fruit of the oak tree, consisting of a smooth nut in a cuplike base [Old English *æcern*]

acoustic *adj* **1** of sound, hearing, or acoustics **2** (of a musical instrument) without electronic amplification **3** designed to absorb sound: *acoustic tiles* [Greek *akouein* to hear] **acoustically** *adv*

acoustics *n* **1** the scientific study of sound ▷ *pl n* **2** the characteristics of a room or auditorium determining how well sound can be heard within it

acquaint *vb* **acquaint with** to make (someone) familiar with [Latin *accognoscere* to know well]

acquaintance *n* **1** a person whom one knows slightly **2** slight knowledge of a person or subject **3 make the acquaintance of** to come into social contact with **4** the people one knows: *an actress of my acquaintance*

acquainted *adj* **1** on terms of familiarity but not intimacy **2 acquainted with** familiar with: *she became acquainted with the classics of Chinese literature*

acquiesce (ak-wee-**ess**) *vb* **-escing, -esced** to agree to what someone wants [Latin *acquiescere*] **acquiescence** *n* **acquiescent** *adj*

> **USAGE** The use of *to* after *acquiesce* was formerly regarded as incorrect, but is now acceptable.

acquire *vb* **-quiring, -quired** to get or develop (something such as an object, trait, or ability) [Latin *acquirere*] **acquirement** *n*

acquired taste *n* **1** a liking for something at first considered unpleasant **2** the thing liked

acquisition *n* **1** something acquired, often to add to a collection **2** the act of acquiring something

acquisitive *adj* eager to gain material possessions **acquisitively** *adv* **acquisitiveness** *n*

acquit *vb* **-quitting, -quitted 1** to pronounce someone not guilty: *he's been acquitted of negligence* **2** to behave in a particular way: *she acquitted herself well in the meeting* [Old French *aquiter*] **acquittal** *n*

acre *n* **1** a unit of area equal to 4840 square yards (4046.86 square metres) **2 acres** *informal* a large amount: *acres of skin* [Old English *æcer*]

acreage (**ake**-er-rij) *n* land area in acres

acrid (**ak**-rid) *adj* **1** unpleasantly strong-smelling **2** sharp in speech or manner [Latin *acer* sharp, sour] **acridity** *n* **acridly** *adv*

acrimony *n* bitterness and resentment felt about something [Latin *acrimonia*] **acrimonious** *adj*

acrobat *n* an entertainer who performs gymnastic feats requiring skill, agility, and balance [Greek *akrobatēs* one who walks on tiptoe] **acrobatic** *adj* **acrobatically** *adv*

acrobatics *pl n* the skills or feats of an acrobat

acronym *n* a word made from the initial letters of other words, for example UNESCO for the *United Nations Educational, Scientific, and Cultural Organization* [Greek *akros* outermost + *onoma* name]
acrophobia *n* abnormal fear of being at a great height [Greek *akron* summit + *phobos* fear]
acropolis (a-crop-pol-liss) *n* the citadel of an ancient Greek city [Greek *akros* highest + *polis* city]
across *prep* **1** from one side to the other side of **2** on or at the other side of ▷ *adv* **3** from one side to the other **4** on or to the other side [Old French *a croix* crosswise]
across-the-board *adj* affecting everyone in a particular group or place equally: *across-the-board tax cuts*
acrostic *n* a number of lines of writing, such as a poem, in which the first or last letters form a word or proverb [Greek *akros* outermost + *stikhos* line of verse]
acrylic *adj* **1** made of acrylic ▷ *n* **2** a man-made fibre used for clothes and blankets **3** a kind of paint made from acrylic acid [Latin *acer* sharp + *olere* to smell]
acrylic acid *n chem* a strong-smelling colourless corrosive liquid
acrylic resin *n chem* any of a group of polymers of acrylic acid, used as synthetic rubbers, in paints, and as plastics
act *n* **1** something done **2** a formal decision reached or law passed by a law-making body: *an act of parliament* **3** a major division of a play or opera **4** a short performance, such as a sketch or dance **5** a pretended attitude: *she appeared calm but it was just an act* **6 get in on the act** *informal* to become involved in something in order to share the benefit **7 get one's act together** *informal* to organize oneself ▷ *vb* **8** to do something **9** to perform (a part or role) in a play, film, or broadcast **10** to present (a play) on stage **11 act for** to be a substitute for: *Mr Lewis was acting for the head of the department* **12 act as** to serve the function of: *she is acting as my bodyguard* **13** to behave: *she acts as though she really hates you* **14** to behave in an unnatural way ▷ See also **act up** [Latin *actum* a thing done]
ACT Australian Capital Territory
acting *n* **1** the art of an actor ▷ *adj* **2** temporarily performing the duties of: *the acting president has declared a state of emergency*
actinide series *n chem* a series of 15 radioactive elements with increasing atomic numbers from actinium to lawrencium
actinium *n chem* a radioactive element of the actinide series, occurring as a decay product of uranium. Symbol: **Ac** [Greek *aktis* ray]
action *n* **1** doing something for a particular purpose **2** something done on a particular occasion **3** a lawsuit **4** movement during some physical activity **5** the operating mechanism in a gun or machine **6** the way in which something operates or works **7** *slang* the main activity in a place **8** the events that form the plot of a story or play **9** activity, force, or energy **10** a minor battle **11 actions** behaviour **12 out of action** not functioning
actionable *adj law* giving grounds for legal action
action painting *n* an art form in which paint is thrown, smeared, dripped, or spattered on the canvas
action replay *n* the rerunning of a small section of a television film or tape, for example of a sporting event
action stations *pl n* the positions taken up by individuals in preparation for battle or for some other activity
activate *vb* **-vating, -vated 1** to make something active **2** *physics* to make something radioactive **3** *chem* to increase the rate of a reaction **activation** *n*
active *adj* **1** busy and energetic **2** energetically involved in or working hard for: *active in the peace movement* **3** happening now and energetically: *the plan is under active discussion* **4** functioning or causing a reaction: *the active ingredient is held within the capsule* **5** (of a volcano) erupting periodically **6** *grammar* denoting a form of a verb used to indicate that the subject is performing the action, for example *kicked* in *The boy kicked the football* ▷ *n* **7** *grammar* the active form of a verb **actively** *adv*
active list *n military* a list of officers available for full duty
active service *n* military duty in an operational area
activist *n* a person who works energetically to achieve political or social goals **activism** *n*
activity *n* **1** the state of being active **2** lively movement **3** *pl* **-ties** any specific action or pursuit: *he was engaged in political activities abroad*
act of God *n law* a sudden occurrence caused by natural forces, such as a flood
actor *n* a person who acts in a play, film, or broadcast
actress *n* a female actor
actual *adj* existing in reality or as a matter of fact [Latin *actus* act]

> **USAGE** The excessive use of *actual* and *actually* should be avoided. They are unnecessary in sentences such as *in actual fact, he is forty-two*, and *he did actually go to the play but did not enjoy it.*

actuality *n, pl* **-ties** reality
actually *adv* as an actual fact; really
actuary *n, pl* **-aries** a person qualified to calculate commercial risks and probabilities involving uncertain future events, esp. in such contexts as life assurance [Latin *actuarius* one who keeps accounts] **actuarial** *adj*
actuate *vb* **-ating, -ated 1** to start up a mechanical device **2** to motivate someone [Medieval Latin *actuare*]
act up *vb informal* to behave in a troublesome way
acuity (ak-kew-it-ee) *n* keenness of vision or thought [Latin *acutus* acute]
acumen (ak-yew-men) *n* the ability to make good decisions [Latin: sharpness]
acupuncture *n* a medical treatment involving the insertion of needles at various parts of the body to stimulate the nerve impulses [Latin *acus* needle + PUNCTURE] **acupuncturist** *n*

acute *adj* **1** severe or intense: *acute staff shortages* **2** penetrating in perception or insight **3** sensitive or keen: *it was amazing how acute your hearing got in the bush* **4** (of a disease) sudden and severe **5** *maths* (of an angle) of less than 90° **6** (of a hospital or bed) intended to accommodate short-term patients ▹ *n* **7** an acute accent [Latin *acutus*] **acutely** *adv* **acuteness** *n*

acute accent *n* the mark (´), used in some languages to indicate that the vowel over which it is placed is pronounced in a certain way

ad *n informal* an advertisement

AD (indicating years numbered from the supposed year of the birth of Christ) in the year of the Lord [Latin *anno Domini*]

ad- *prefix* **1** to or towards: *adverb* **2** near or next to: *adrenal* [Latin]

Ada *n* a high-level computer programming language, used esp. for military systems [after *Ada*, Countess of Lovelace, pioneer in computer programming]

adage (ad-ij) *n* a traditional saying that is generally accepted as being true [Latin *adagium*]

adagietto *music* ▹ *adv* **1** slowly, but more quickly than adagio ▹ *n, pl* **-tos** **2** a movement or piece to be performed fairly slowly

adagio (ad-**dahj**-yo) *music* ▹ *adv* **1** slowly ▹ *n, pl* **-gios** **2** a movement or piece to be performed slowly [Italian]

Adam *n* **1** *Bible* the first man created by God **2** **not know someone from Adam** to not know someone at all

adamant *adj* unshakable in determination or purpose [Greek *adamas* unconquerable] **adamantly** *adv*

Adam's apple *n* the projecting lump of thyroid cartilage at the front of a person's neck

adapt *vb* **1** to adjust (something or oneself) to different conditions **2** to change something to suit a new purpose [Latin *adaptare*] **adaptable** *adj* **adaptability** *n*

adaptation *n* **1** something that is produced by adapting something else: *a TV adaptation of a Victorian novel* **2** the act of adapting

adaptor *or* **adapter** *n* **1** a device used to connect several electrical appliances to a single socket **2** any device for connecting two parts of different sizes or types

ADC aide-de-camp

add *vb* **1** to combine (numbers or quantities) so as to make a larger number or quantity **2** to join something to something else so as to increase its size, effect, or scope: *these new rules will add an extra burden on already overworked officials* **3** to say or write something further **4** **add in** to include ▹ See also **add up** [Latin *addere*]

addendum *n, pl* **-da** something added on, esp. an appendix to a book or magazine

adder *n* a small poisonous snake with a black zigzag pattern along the back [Old English *nǣdre*]

addict *n* **1** a person who is unable to stop taking narcotic drugs **2** *informal* a person who is devoted to something: *he's a telly addict* [Latin *addictus* given over] **addictive** *adj*

addicted *adj* **1** dependent on a narcotic drug **2** *informal* devoted to something: *I'm a news freak and addicted to BBC Breakfast News* **addiction** *n*

addition *n* **1** the act of adding **2** a person or thing that is added **3** a mathematical operation in which the total of two or more numbers or quantities is calculated **4** **in addition (to)** besides; as well (as) **additional** *adj* **additionally** *adv*

additive *n* any substance added to something, such as food, to improve it or prevent deterioration

addled *adj* **1** confused or unable to think clearly **2** (of eggs) rotten [Old English *adela* filth]

add-on *n* a feature that can be added to a standard model to give increased benefits

address *n* **1** the place at which someone lives **2** the conventional form by which the location of a building is described **3** a formal speech **4** *computers* **A** a number giving the location of a piece of stored information **B** a series of characters that represents a location on the internet ▹ *vb* **5** to mark (a letter or parcel) with an address **6** to speak to **7** to direct one's attention to (a problem or an issue) **8** **address oneself to** **A** to speak or write to **B** to apply oneself to: *we have got to address ourselves properly to this problem* [Latin *ad-* to + *directus* direct]

addressee *n* a person to whom a letter or parcel is addressed

adduce *vb* **-ducing, -duced** to mention something as evidence [Latin *adducere* to lead to]

add up *vb* **1** to calculate the total of (two or more numbers or quantities) **2** *informal* to make sense: *there's something about it that doesn't add up* **3** **add up to** to amount to

adenoidal *adj* having a nasal voice or impaired breathing because of enlarged adenoids

adenoids (**ad**-in-oidz) *pl n* a mass of tissue at the back of the throat [Greek *adenoeidēs* glandular]

adept *adj* **1** proficient in something requiring skill ▹ *n* **2** a person skilled in something [Latin *adipisci* to attain] **adeptness** *n*

adequate *adj* just enough in amount or just good enough in quality [Latin *ad-* to + *aequus* equal] **adequacy** *n* **adequately** *adv*

à deux (ah **duh**) *adj, adv* of or for two people [French]

ADHD *med* attention deficit hyperactivity disorder

adhere *vb* **-hering, -hered** **1** to stick to **2** to act according to (a rule or agreement) **3** to be a loyal supporter of (something) [Latin *adhaerere*]

USAGE See at **adhesion**.

adherent *n* **1** a supporter or follower ▹ *adj* **2** sticking or attached **adherence** *n*

adhesion *n* **1** the quality or condition of sticking together **2** *pathol* the joining together of two structures or parts of the body that are normally separate, for example after surgery

USAGE *Adhesion* is preferred when talking about sticking or holding fast in a physical sense. *Adherence* is preferred when talking about attachment to a political party, cause, etc.

adhesive *n* **1** a substance used for sticking things together ▹ *adj* **2** able or designed to stick to things

ad hoc *adj, adv* for a particular purpose only [Latin: to this]
adieu (a-**dew**) *interj, n, pl* **adieux** *or* **adieus** (a-**dewz**) goodbye [French]
ad infinitum *adv* endlessly: *we would not be able to sustain the currency ad infinitum* [Latin]
adipose *adj* of or containing fat; fatty: *adipose tissue* [Latin *adeps* fat]
adj. adjective
adjacent *adj* **1** near or next: *the schools were adjacent but there were separate doors* **2** *geom* (of a side of a right-angled triangle) lying between a specified angle and the right angle [Latin *ad-* near + *jacere* to lie]
adjective *n* a word that adds information about a noun or pronoun [Latin *nomen adjectivum* attributive noun] **adjectival** *adj*
adjoin *vb* to be next to and joined onto **adjoining** *adj*
adjourn *vb* **1** to close a court at the end of a session **2** to postpone or be postponed temporarily **3** *informal* to go elsewhere: *can we adjourn to the dining room?* [Old French *ajourner* to defer to an arranged day] **adjournment** *n*
adjudge *vb* **-judging, -judged** to declare someone to be something specified: *my wife was adjudged to be the guilty party*
adjudicate *vb* **-cating, -cated 1** to give a formal decision on a dispute **2** to serve as a judge, for example in a competition [Latin *adjudicare*] **adjudication** *n* **adjudicator** *n*
adjunct *n* **1** something added that is not essential **2** a person who is subordinate to another [Latin *adjunctus* adjoined]
adjure *vb* **-juring, -jured 1** to command someone to do something **2** to appeal earnestly to someone [Latin *adjurare*] **adjuration** *n*
adjust *vb* **1** to adapt to a new environment **2** to alter slightly, so as to be accurate or suitable **3** *insurance* to determine the amount payable in settlement of a claim [Old French *adjuster*] **adjustable** *adj* **adjuster** *n*
adjustment *n* **1** a slight alteration **2** the act of adjusting
adjutant (aj-oo-tant) *n* an officer in an army who acts as administrative assistant to a superior [Latin *adjutare* to aid]
ad-lib *vb* **-libbing, -libbed 1** to improvise a speech or piece of music without preparation ▷ *adj* **2** improvised: *ad-lib studio chat* ▷ *n* **3** an improvised remark ▷ *adv* **ad lib 4** spontaneously or freely [short for Latin *ad libitum*, literally: according to pleasure]
Adm. Admiral
adman *n, pl* **-men** *informal* a person who works in advertising
admin *n informal* administration
administer *vb* **1** to manage (an organization or estate) **2** to organize and put into practice: *anyone can learn to administer the test procedure* **3** to give medicine to someone **4** to supervise the taking of (an oath) [Latin *administrare*]
administrate *vb* **-trating, -trated** to manage an organization
administration *n* **1** management of the affairs of an organization **2** the people who administer an organization **3** a government: *the first non-communist administration in the country's history* **4** the act of administering something, such as medicine or an oath **administrative** *adj*
administrator *n* a person who administers an organization or estate
admirable (ad-mer-a-bl) *adj* deserving or inspiring admiration: *the boldness of the undertaking is admirable* **admirably** *adv*
admiral *n* **1** Also called: **admiral of the fleet** a naval officer of the highest rank **2** any of various brightly coloured butterflies [Arabic *amīr-al* commander of]
Admiralty *n Brit* the former government department in charge of the Royal Navy
admire *vb* **-miring, -mired** to respect and approve of (a person or thing) [Latin *admirari* to wonder at] **admiration** *n* **admirer** *n* **admiring** *adj* **admiringly** *adv*
admissible *adj law* allowed to be brought as evidence in court
admission *n* **1** permission or the right to enter **2** permission to join an organization **3** the price charged for entrance **4** a confession: *she was, by her own admission, not educated*
admit *vb* **-mitting, -mitted 1** to confess or acknowledge (a crime or mistake) **2** to concede (the truth of something) **3** to allow (someone) to enter **4** to take (someone) in to a hospital for treatment: *he was admitted for tests* **5 admit to** to allow someone to participate in something **6 admit of** to allow for: *these rules admit of no violation* [Latin *admittere*]
admittance *n* **1** the right to enter **2** the act of entering a place
admittedly *adv* it must be agreed: *my research is admittedly incomplete*
admixture *n* **1** a mixture **2** an ingredient
admonish *vb* to reprimand sternly [Latin *admonere*] **admonition** *n* **admonitory** *adj*
ad nauseam (ad **naw**-zee-am) *adv* to a boring or sickening extent: *she went on and on ad nauseam about her divorce* [Latin: to (the point of) nausea]
ado *n* fuss: *without further ado* [Middle English *at do* a to-do]
adobe (ad-**oh**-bee) *n* **1** a sun-dried brick **2** the claylike material from which such bricks are made **3** a building made of such bricks [Spanish]
adolescence *n* the period between puberty and adulthood [Latin *adolescere* to grow up]
adolescent *adj* **1** of or relating to adolescence **2** *informal* (of behaviour) immature ▷ *n* **3** an adolescent person
Adonis *n* a handsome young man [name of a handsome youth in Greek myth]
adopt *vb* **1** *law* to take someone else's child as one's own **2** to choose (a plan or method) **3** to choose (a country or name) to be one's own [Latin *adoptare*] **adoptee** *n* **adoption** *n*
adoptive *adj* **1** acquired or related by adoption: *an adoptive father* **2** of or relating to adoption
adorable *adj* very attractive; lovable
adore *vb* **adoring, adored 1** to love intensely or deeply **2** *informal* to like very much: *I adore being in the country* **3** to worship a god with religious rites

[Latin *adorare*] **adoration** *n* **adoring** *adj* **adoringly** *adv*

adorn *vb* to decorate; increase the beauty of [Latin *adornare*] **adornment** *n*

adrenal (ad-reen-al) *adj anatomy* **1** on or near the kidneys **2** of or relating to the adrenal glands [Latin *ad-* near + *renes* kidneys]

adrenal glands *pl n anatomy* two endocrine glands covering the upper surface of the kidneys

adrenalin *or* **adrenaline** *n biochem* a hormone secreted by the adrenal gland in response to stress. It increases heart rate, pulse rate, and blood pressure

adrift *adj, adv* **1** drifting **2** without a clear purpose **3** *informal* off course, wrong: *it was obvious that something had gone adrift*

adroit *adj* quick and skilful in how one behaves or thinks [French *à droit* rightly] **adroitly** *adv* **adroitness** *n*

adsorb *vb* (of a gas or vapour) to condense and form a thin film on a surface [Latin *ad-* to + *sorbere* to drink in] **adsorbent** *adj* **adsorption** *n*

ADT Atlantic Daylight Time

adulation *n* uncritical admiration [Latin *adulari* to flatter]

adult *n* **1** a mature fully grown person, animal, or plant ▹ *adj* **2** having reached maturity; fully developed **3** suitable for or typical of adult people: *she had very adult features* **4** sexually explicit: *adult films* [Latin *adultus* grown up] **adulthood** *n*

adulterate *vb* **-ating, -ated** to spoil something by adding inferior material [Latin *adulterare*] **adulteration** *n*

adulterer *or fem* **adulteress** *n* a person who has committed adultery

adultery *n, pl* **-teries** sexual unfaithfulness of a husband or wife [Latin *adulterium*] **adulterous** *adj*

adv. adverb

advance *vb* **-vancing, -vanced** **1** to go or bring forward **2** to make progress: *this student has advanced in reading and writing* **3** to further a cause: *an association founded to advance the interests of ex-soldiers* **4** **advance on** to move towards someone in a threatening manner **5** to present an idea for consideration **6** to lend a sum of money ▹ *n* **7** a forward movement **8** improvement or progress: *the greatest advance in modern medicine* **9** a loan of money **10** a payment made before it is legally due **11** an increase in price: *any advance on fifty pounds?* **12** **in advance** beforehand: *you have to pay in advance* **13** **in advance of** ahead of in time or development ▹ *adj* **14** done or happening before an event: *advance warning* ▹ See also **advances** [Latin *abante* from before]

advanced *adj* **1** at a late stage in development **2** not elementary: *he was taking the advanced class in economics*

Advanced level *n Brit* a formal name for **A level**

advancement *n* promotion in rank or status

advances *pl n* approaches made to a person with the hope of starting a romantic or sexual relationship

advantage *n* **1** a more favourable position or state **2** benefit or profit: *they could make this work to their advantage* **3** *tennis* the point scored after deuce **4** **take advantage of** **A** to use a person unfairly **B** to use an opportunity **5** **to advantage** to good effect: *her hair was shaped to display to advantage her superb neck* [Latin *abante* from before]

advantaged *adj* in a superior social or financial position

advantageous *adj* likely to bring benefits **advantageously** *adv*

advection *n physics* the transferring of heat in a horizontal stream of gas [Latin *ad-* to + *vehere* to carry]

advent *n* an arrival: *the advent of the personal computer* [Latin *ad-* to + *venire* to come]

Advent *n Christianity* the season that includes the four Sundays before Christmas

Adventist *n* a member of a Christian group that believes in the imminent return of Christ

adventitious *adj* added or appearing accidentally [Latin *adventicius* coming from outside]

adventure *n* **1** a risky undertaking, the ending of which is uncertain: *our African adventure* **2** exciting or unexpected events [Latin *advenire* to happen to (someone), arrive]

adventure playground *n Brit, Austral & NZ* a playground for children that contains building materials and other equipment to build with or climb on

adventurer *or fem* **adventuress** *n* **1** a person who seeks money or power by unscrupulous means **2** a person who seeks adventure

adventurism *n* recklessness in politics or finance

adventurous *adj* daring or enterprising

adverb *n* a word that modifies a sentence, verb, adverb, or adjective, for example *easily, very,* and *happily* in *They could easily envy the very happily married couple* [Latin *adverbium,* literally: added word] **adverbial** *adj*

adversary (ad-verse-er-ree) *n, pl* **-saries** an opponent in a fight, disagreement, or sporting contest [Latin *adversus* against]

adverse *adj* **1** unfavourable to one's interests: *adverse effects* **2** antagonistic or hostile [Latin *ad-* towards + *vertere* to turn] **adversely** *adv*

adversity *n, pl* **-ties** very difficult or hard circumstances

advert *n informal* an advertisement

advertise *vb* **-tising, -tised** **1** to present or praise (goods or a service) to the public, in order to encourage sales **2** to make (a vacancy, an event, or an article for sale) publicly known [Latin *advertere* to turn one's attention to] **advertiser** *n* **advertising** *n*

advertisement *n* any public announcement designed to sell goods or publicize an event

advertorial *n* advertising material presented under the guise of editorial material [from *advert* + (*edit*)*orial*]

advice *n* **1** recommendation as to an appropriate choice of action **2** formal notification of facts [Latin *ad* to + *visum* view]

advisable *adj* sensible and likely to achieve the desired result **advisability** *n*

advise *vb* **-vising, -vised** **1** to offer advice to **2** to inform or notify [Latin *ad-* to + *videre* to see] **adviser** *or* **advisor** *n*

advised *adj* thought-out: *ill-advised*
advisedly (ad-vize-id-lee) *adv* deliberately; after careful consideration: *I use the word advisedly*
advisory *adj* **1** able to offer advice ▷ *n, pl* **-ries** **2** a statement giving advice or a warning **3** a person or organization that gives advice: *the Prime Minister's media advisory*
advocaat *n* a liqueur with a raw egg base [Dutch]
advocacy *n* active support of a cause or course of action
advocate *vb* **-cating, -cated 1** to recommend a course of action publicly ▷ *n* **2** a person who upholds or defends a cause or course of action **3** a person who speaks on behalf of another in a court of law **4** *Scots law* a barrister [Latin *advocare* to call, summon]
adware *n computers* **1** software that collects information about a user's browsing patterns in order to display relevant advertisements **2** software that is produced with advertisements embedded within it
adze *or US* **adz** *n* a tool with a blade at right angles to the handle, used for shaping timber [Old English *adesa*]
aegis (ee-jiss) *n* **under the aegis of** with the sponsorship or protection of [Greek *aigis* shield of Zeus]
aeolian harp (ee-**oh**-lee-an) *n* a musical instrument that produces sounds when the wind passes over its strings [after *Aeolus*, god of winds in Greek myth]
aeon *or US* **eon** (ee-on) *n* **1** an immeasurably long period of time **2** the longest division of geological time [Greek *aiōn*]
aerate *vb* **-ating, -ated** to put gas into a liquid, for example when making a fizzy drink **aeration** *n*
aerial *n* **1** the metal pole or wire on a television or radio which transmits or receives signals ▷ *adj* **2** in, from, or operating in the air **3** extending high into the air **4** of or relating to aircraft [Greek *aēr* air]
aerial top dressing *n* spreading of fertilizer from an aeroplane onto remote areas
aero-, aeri- *or* **aer-** *combining form* **1** relating to aircraft **2** relating to air, atmosphere, or gas [Greek *aēr* air]
aerobatics *n* spectacular manoeuvres, such as loops or rolls, performed by aircraft [AERO- + (ACRO)ATICS]
aerobe *n biol* an organism that requires oxygen to survive [Greek *aēr* air + *bios* life]
aerobic *adj* designed for or relating to aerobics: *aerobic exercise*
aerobics *n* exercises to increase the amount of oxygen in the blood and strengthen the heart and lungs
aerodrome *n* a small airport
aerodynamics *n* the study of how air flows around moving objects **aerodynamic** *adj* **aerodynamicist** *n*
aero engine *n* an engine for an aircraft
aerofoil *n* a part of an aircraft, such as the wing, designed to give lift in flight
aerogram *n* an airmail letter on a single sheet of light paper that seals to form an envelope
aeronautics *n* the study or practice of flight through the air **aeronautical** *adj*
aeroplane *or US & Canad* **airplane** *n* a heavier-than-air powered flying vehicle with fixed wings [AERO- + Greek *planos* wandering]
aerosol *n* a small metal pressurized can from which a substance can be dispensed in a fine spray [AERO- + SOL(UTION)]
aerospace *n* **1** the earth's atmosphere and space beyond ▷ *adj* **2** of rockets or space vehicles: *the aerospace industry*
aesthete *or US* **esthete** (**eess**-theet) *n* a person who has or who pretends to have a highly developed appreciation of beauty
aesthetic *or US* **esthetic** (iss-**thet**-ik) *adj* **1** relating to the appreciation of art and beauty ▷ *n* **2** a principle or set of principles relating to the appreciation of art and beauty [Greek *aisthanomai* to perceive, feel] **aesthetically** *or US* **esthetically** *adv* **aestheticism** *or US* **estheticism** *n*
aesthetics *or US* **esthetics** *n* **1** the branch of philosophy concerned with the study of the concepts of beauty and taste **2** the study of the rules and principles of art
aether *n* same as **ether** (senses 2, 3)
aetiology (ee-tee-**ol**-a-jee) *n* same as **etiology**
a.f. audio frequency
afar *n* **from afar** from or at a great distance
affable *adj* showing warmth and friendliness [Latin *affabilis*] **affability** *n* **affably** *adv*
affair *n* **1** an event or happening: *the Watergate affair* **2** a sexual relationship outside marriage **3** a thing to be done or attended to: *my wife's career is her own affair* **4** something previously specified: *lunch was a subdued affair* [Old French *à faire* to do]
affairs *pl n* **1** personal or business interests **2** matters of public interest: *foreign affairs*
affect[1] *vb* **1** to influence (someone or something): *the very difficult conditions continued to affect our performance* **2** (of pain or disease) to attack: *the virus can spread to affect the heart muscle* **3** to move someone emotionally: *the experience has affected him deeply* [Latin *afficere*]
affect[2] *vb* **1** to put on a show of: *she affects a certain disinterest* **2** to wear or use by preference: *he likes to be called Captain John and affects a nautical cap* [Latin *affectare* to strive after]
affectation *n* an attitude or manner put on to impress others
affected *adj* **1** behaving or speaking in a manner put on to impress others **2** pretended: *an affected indifference*
affecting *adj* arousing feelings of pity; moving
affection *n* **1** fondness or tenderness for a person or thing **2 affections** feelings of love; emotions: *I was angry with her for playing with their affections*
affectionate *adj* having or displaying tenderness, affection, or warmth **affectionately** *adv*
affectless *adj* **1** showing no emotion or concern for others **2** not causing any emotion: *an affectless novel*
affianced (af-**fie**-anst) *adj old-fashioned* engaged to be married [Medieval Latin *affidare* to trust (oneself) to]

a

affidavit (af-fid-**dave**-it) *n law* a written statement made under oath [Medieval Latin, literally: he declares on oath]
affiliate *vb* **-ating, -ated 1** (of a group) to link up with a larger group ▷ *n* **2** a person or organization that is affiliated with another [Medieval Latin *affiliatus* adopted as a son] **affiliation** *n*
affinity *n, pl* **-ties 1** a feeling of closeness to and understanding of a person **2** a close similarity in appearance, structure, or quality **3** a chemical attraction [Latin *affinis* bordering on, related]
affirm *vb* **1** to declare to be true **2** to state clearly one's support for (an idea or belief) [Latin *ad-* to + *firmare* to make firm] **affirmation** *n*
affirmative *adj* **1** indicating agreement: *an affirmative answer* ▷ *n* **2** a word or phrase indicating agreement, such as *yes*
affix *vb* **1** to attach or fasten ▷ *n* **2** a word or syllable added to a word to produce a derived or inflected form, such as *-ment* in *establishment* [Medieval Latin *affixare*]
afflict *vb* to cause someone suffering or unhappiness [Latin *affligere* to knock against]
affliction *n* **1** something that causes physical or mental suffering **2** a condition of great distress or suffering
affluent *adj* having plenty of money [Latin *ad-* to + *fluere* to flow] **affluence** *n*
affluent society *n* a society in which the material benefits of prosperity are widely available
afford *vb* **1 can afford** to be able to do or spare something without risking financial difficulties or undesirable consequences: *she can't afford to be choosy* **2** to give or supply: *afford me an opportunity to judge for myself* [Old English *geforthian* to further, promote] **affordable** *adj* **affordability** *n*
afforest *vb* to plant trees on [Medieval Latin *afforestare*] **afforestation** *n*
affray *n Brit, Austral & NZ* a noisy fight in a public place [Vulgar Latin *exfridare* (unattested) to break the peace]
affront *n* **1** a deliberate insult ▷ *vb* **2** to hurt someone's pride or dignity [Old French *afronter* to strike in the face]
afghan *n NZ* a type of biscuit
Afghan *adj* **1** of Afghanistan ▷ *n* **2** a person from Afghanistan **3** the language of Afghanistan
Afghan hound *n* a large slim dog with long silky hair
aficionado (af-fish-yo-**nah**-do) *n, pl* **-dos** an enthusiastic fan of a sport or interest [Spanish]
afield *adv* **far afield** far away: *they used to travel as far afield as Hungary*
aflame *adv, adj* **1** in flames **2** deeply aroused: *his face was aflame with self-contempt and embarrassment*
afloat *adj* **1** floating **2** free of debt: *his goal is to keep the company afloat* **3** aboard ship ▷ *adv* **4** floating **5** free of debt **6** aboard ship; at sea
afoot *adj, adv* happening; in operation: *I had no suspicion of what was afoot*
afore *adv, prep, conj old-fashioned or dialect* before
aforementioned *adj* mentioned before
aforesaid *adj* referred to previously
aforethought *adj* premeditated: *malice aforethought*
a fortiori (eh for-tee-or-rye) *adv* for similar but more convincing reasons [Latin]
afraid *adj* **1** feeling fear or apprehension **2** regretful: *I'm afraid I lost my temper* [Middle English *affraied*]
afresh *adv* once more
African *adj* **1** of Africa ▷ *n* **2** a person from Africa
Africana *pl n* objects of cultural or historical interest from Africa
African-American *n* **1** an American of African descent ▷ *adj* **2** of African-Americans, their history, or their culture
Africander *n* a breed of humpbacked cattle originally from southern Africa [Afrikaans *Afrikander*]
African time *n S African slang* unpunctuality
African violet *n* a flowering house plant with pink or purple flowers and hairy leaves
Afrikaans *n* one of the official languages of South Africa, descended from Dutch [Dutch]
Afrikaner *n* a White South African whose native language is Afrikaans
Afro *n, pl* **-ros** a full, rounded hairstyle
Afro- *combining form* indicating Africa or African: *Afro-Caribbean*
aft *adv, adj* at or towards the rear of a ship or aircraft [shortened from ABAFT]
after *prep* **1** following in time or place **2** in pursuit of: *he was after my mother's jewellery* **3** concerning: *she asked after Laura* **4** considering: *you seem all right after what happened last night* **5** next in excellence or importance to **6** in imitation of; in the manner of **7** in accordance with: *a man after his own heart* **8** with the same name as: *the street is named after the designer of the church* **9** US past (the hour of): *fifteen after twelve* **10 after all A** in spite of everything: *I was, after all, a suspect* **B** in spite of expectations or efforts **11 after you** please go before me ▷ *adv* **12** at a later time; afterwards ▷ *conj* **13** at a time later than the time when: *she arrived after the reading had begun* ▷ *adj* **14** *naut* further aft: *the after cabin* [Old English *æfter*]
afterbirth *n* the placenta and fetal membranes expelled from the mother's womb after childbirth
aftercare *n* **1** the help and support given to a person discharged from a hospital or prison **2** the regular care required to keep something in good condition
afterdamp *n* a poisonous gas formed after the explosion of firedamp in a coal mine
aftereffect *n* any result occurring some time after its cause
afterglow *n* **1** the glow left after the source of a light has disappeared, for example after sunset **2** a pleasant feeling remaining after an enjoyable experience
afterlife *n* life after death
aftermath *n* effects or results of an event considered collectively: *the aftermath of the weekend violence* [*after* + Old English *mæth* a mowing]
afternoon *n* the period between noon and evening
afterpains *pl n* pains caused by contraction of a woman's womb after childbirth

afters *n informal* the sweet course of a meal
aftersales *n* any customer service that follows the sale of a product **after-sales** *adj*
aftershave *n* a scented lotion applied to a man's face after shaving
aftershock *n* one of a series of minor tremors occurring after the main shock of an earthquake
aftertaste *n* a taste that lingers on after eating or drinking
afterthought *n* **1** something thought of after the opportunity to use it has passed **2** an addition to something already completed
afterwards *or* **afterward** *adv* later [Old English *æfterweard*]
Ag *chem* silver [Latin *argentum*]
again *adv* **1** another or a second time: *I want to look at that atlas again* **2** once more in a previously experienced state or condition: *he pictured her again as she used to be* **3** in addition to the original amount: *twice as much again* **4** on the other hand **5** moreover or furthermore: *she is talented and, again, hard-working* **6 again and again** continually or repeatedly [Old English *ongegn* opposite to]
against *prep* **1** standing or leaning beside: *she leaned against a tree* **2** opposed to or in disagreement with **3** in contrast to: *his complexion was a sickly white against the black stubble of his beard* **4** coming in contact with: *rain rattled against the window* **5** having an unfavourable effect on: *the system works against you when you don't have money* **6** as a protection from: *a safeguard against bacteria* **7** in exchange for or in return for: *the dollar has gained very slightly against the yen* **8 as against** as opposed to; as compared with [Middle English *ageines*]
agape *adj* **1** (of the mouth) wide open **2** (of a person) very surprised
agar (ayg-ar) *or* **agar-agar** *n* a jelly-like substance obtained from seaweed and used as a thickener in food [Malay]
agaric *n* any fungus with gills on the underside of the cap, such as a mushroom [Greek *agarikon*]
agate (ag-git) *n* a hard semiprecious form of quartz with striped colouring [Greek *akhatēs*]
agave (a-**gave**-vee) *n* a tropical American plant with tall flower stalks and thick leaves [Greek *agauos* illustrious]
age *n* **1** the length of time that a person or thing has existed **2** a period or state of human life **3** the latter part of human life **4** a period of history marked by some feature **5 ages** *informal* a long time **6 come of age** to become legally responsible for one's actions (usually at 18 years) ▷ *vb* **ageing** *or* **aging, aged 7** to become old: *skin type changes as one ages* **8** to appear or cause to appear older: *the years had not aged her in any way* [Latin *aetas*]
aged *adj* **1** (ay-jid) advanced in years; old **2** (rhymes with **raged**) being at the age of: *a girl aged thirteen is missing*
ageing *or* **aging** *n* **1** the fact or process of growing old ▷ *adj* **2** becoming or appearing older
ageism *or* **agism** *n* discrimination against people on the grounds of age **ageist** *or* **agist** *n, adj*
ageless *adj* **1** apparently never growing old **2** seeming to have existed for ever; eternal: *an ageless profession*
agency *n, pl* **-cies 1** an organization providing a specific service: *an advertising agency* **2** the business or functions of an agent **3** action or power by which something happens: *the intervention of a human agency in the sequence of events* [Latin *agere* to do]
agenda *n* **1** a schedule or list of items to be attended to, for example at a meeting **2** *US & Canad* an appointment diary with room for storing addresses, telephone numbers, etc. [Latin: things to be done]
agent *n* **1** a person who arranges business for other people, esp. for actors or singers **2** a spy **3** a substance which causes change in other substances: *an emulsifying agent* **4** someone or something which causes an effect: *the agent of change*
agent provocateur (azh-on prov-vok-at-**tur**) *n, pl* **agents provocateurs** (azh-on prov-vok-at-**tur**) a person employed by the authorities to tempt people to commit illegal acts and so be discredited or punished [French]
age-old *adj* very old; ancient
agglomerate *vb* **-ating, -ated 1** to form or be formed into a mass ▷ *n* **2** a volcanic rock consisting of fused angular fragments of rock [Latin *agglomerare*]
agglomeration *n* a confused mass or cluster
agglutinate *vb* **-nating, -nated** to stick as if with glue [Latin *agglutinare*] **agglutination** *n*
aggrandize *or* **-dise** *vb* **-dizing, -dized** *or* **-dising, -dised** to make greater in size, power, or rank [Old French *aggrandir*] **aggrandizement** *or* **-disement** *n*
aggravate *vb* **-vating, -vated 1** to make (a disease, situation, or problem) worse **2** *informal* to annoy [Latin *aggravare* to make heavier] **aggravating** *adj* **aggravation** *n*
aggravated *adj law* (of a criminal offence) made more serious by its circumstances
aggregate *n* **1** an amount or total formed from separate units **2** *geol* a rock, such as granite, consisting of a mixture of minerals **3** the sand and stone mixed with cement and water to make concrete ▷ *adj* **4** formed of separate units collected into a whole ▷ *vb* **-gating, -gated 5** to combine or be combined into a whole **6** to amount to (a particular number) [Latin *aggregare* to add to a flock or herd] **aggregation** *n*
aggression *n* **1** violent and hostile behaviour **2** an unprovoked attack [Latin *aggredi* to attack] **aggressor** *n*
aggressive *adj* **1** full of anger or hostility **2** forceful or determined: *an aggressive salesman* **aggressively** *adv* **aggressiveness** *n*
aggrieved *adj* upset and angry [Latin *aggravare* to aggravate]
aggro *slang* ▷ *n* **1** *Brit, Austral & NZ* aggressive behaviour ▷ *adj* **2** *Austral* angry and aggressive [from *aggravation*]
aghast *adj* overcome with amazement or horror [Old English *gæstan* to frighten]
agile *adj* **1** quick in movement; nimble **2** mentally quick or acute [Latin *agilis*] **agility** *n*
agin *prep dialect* against or opposed to: *he gave the usual line of talk agin the government* [obsolete *again* against]

a

a

agitate *vb* **-tating, -tated 1** to excite, disturb, or trouble **2** to shake or stir (a liquid) **3** to attempt to stir up public opinion for or against something [Latin *agitare*] **agitated** *adj* **agitatedly** *adv* **agitation** *n* **agitator** *n*
agitprop *n* political agitation and propaganda [Russian *Agitpropbyuro*]
aglitter *adj* sparkling or glittering
aglow *adj* glowing
aglu *or* **agloo** *n Canad* a breathing hole made in ice by a seal [Inuit]
AGM annual general meeting
agnostic *n* **1** a person who believes that it is impossible to know whether God exists **2** a person who claims that the answer to some specific question cannot be known with certainty ▷ *adj* **3** of or relating to agnostics [A- + *gnostic* having knowledge] **agnosticism** *n*
ago *adv* in the past: *fifty years ago* [Old English *āgān* to pass away]

> **USAGE** The use of *ago* with *since* (*it's ten years ago since he wrote the novel*) is redundant and should be avoided: *it's ten years since he wrote the novel.*

agog *adj* eager or curious: *Marcia would be agog to hear his news* [Old French *en gogues* in merriments]
agonize *or* **-nise** *vb* **-nizing, -nized** *or* **-nising, -nised 1** to worry greatly **2** to suffer agony **agonizing** *or* **-nising** *adj* **agonizingly** *or* **-nisingly** *adv*
agony *n, pl* **-nies** acute physical or mental pain [Greek *agōnia* struggle]
agony aunt *n* a person who replies to readers' letters in an agony column
agony column *n* a newspaper or magazine feature offering advice on readers' personal problems
agoraphobia *n* a pathological fear of being in public places [Greek *agora* marketplace + *phobos* fear] **agoraphobic** *adj, n*
AGR advanced gas-cooled reactor
agrarian *adj* of or relating to land or agriculture [Latin *ager* field] **agrarianism** *n*
agree *vb* **agreeing, agreed 1** to be of the same opinion **2** to give assent; consent **3** to be consistent **4 agree on** to reach a joint decision about: *the ministers agreed on a strategy* **5 agree with** to be agreeable or suitable to (one's health or appearance): *marriage and motherhood must agree with you* **6** to concede: *the unions have agreed that the results of appraisal are relevant* **7** *grammar* to be the same in number, gender, and case as a connected word [Old French *a gre* at will]
agreeable *adj* **1** pleasant and enjoyable **2** prepared to consent: *I cannot say that she was agreeable to the project but she was resigned* **agreeably** *adv*
agreement *n* **1** the act or state of agreeing **2** a legally enforceable contract
agribusiness *n* **1** the use of intensive methods to increase profits in agriculture **2** all of the businesses that process, distribute, and support farm products [*agri(culture) + business*]
agriculture *n* the rearing of crops and livestock; farming [Latin *ager* field + *cultura* cultivation] **agricultural** *adj* **agriculturalist** *n*
agrimony *n* a plant with small yellow flowers and bitter-tasting bristly fruits [Greek *argemōnē* poppy]
agrochemical *n* a chemical used in agriculture
agrodolce (ag-gro-**dole**-chay) *n* an Italian sweet-and-sour sauce [Italian]
agronomy (ag-**ron**-om-mee) *n* the science of land cultivation, soil management, and crop production [Greek *agros* field + *nemein* to manage] **agronomist** *n*
aground *adv* onto the bottom of shallow water: *they felt a jolt as the ship ran aground*
ague (**aig**-yew) *n* **1** *old-fashioned* malarial fever with shivering **2** a fit of shivering [Old French *(fievre) ague* acute fever]
ah *interj* an exclamation expressing pleasure, pain, sympathy, etc.
aha *interj* an exclamation expressing triumph, surprise, etc.
ahead *adv* **1** at or in the front; before **2** forwards: *go straight ahead* **3 get ahead** to achieve success: *I was young and hungry to get ahead* ▷ *adj* **4** in a leading position: *he is ahead in the polls*
ahem *interj* a clearing of the throat, used to attract attention or express doubt
ahi *n* another name for **yellowfin tuna** [Hawaiian]
ahoy *interj naut* a shout made to call a ship or to attract attention
AI 1 artificial insemination **2** artificial intelligence
aid *n* **1** money, equipment, or services provided for people in need; assistance **2** a person or device that helps or assists ▷ *vb* **3** to help financially or in other ways [Latin *adjutare* to help]
Aid *or* **-aid** *combining form* denoting a charitable organization that raises money for a particular cause: *Band Aid*
AID (formerly) artificial insemination by donor
aide *n* an assistant: *a senior aide to the Prime Minister*
aide-de-camp (aid-de-**kom**) *n, pl* **aides-de-camp** (aid-de-**kom**) a military officer serving as personal assistant to a senior [French: camp assistant]
AIDS acquired immunodeficiency syndrome: a viral disease that destroys the body's ability to fight infection
AIH artificial insemination by husband
ail *vb literary* **1** to trouble or afflict **2** to feel unwell [Old English *eglan*]
aileron (**ale**-er-on) *n* a hinged flap on the back of an aircraft wing which controls rolling [French *aile* wing]
ailing *adj* unwell or unsuccessful over a long period: *an ailing company*
ailment *n* a slight illness
aim *vb* **1** to point (a weapon or missile) or direct (a blow or remark) at a particular person or object **2** to propose or intend: *they aim to provide full and equal rights to all groups* ▷ *n* **3** the action of directing something at an object **4** intention or purpose **5 take aim** to point a weapon or missile at a person or object [Latin *aestimare* to estimate]
aimless *adj* having no purpose or direction **aimlessly** *adv*
ain't *not standard* am not, is not, are not, have not, or has not: *it ain't fair*

air *n* **1** the mixture of gases that forms the earth's atmosphere. It consists chiefly of nitrogen, oxygen, argon, and carbon dioxide **2** the space above and around the earth; sky. Related adjective: **aerial** **3** a distinctive quality, appearance, or manner: *I thought he had an air of elegance and celebrity about him* **4** a simple tune **5** transportation in aircraft: *I went off to Italy by air and train* **6** **in the air** in circulation; current: *a sense of expectation is in the air* **7** **into thin air** leaving no trace behind **8** **on the air** in the act of broadcasting on radio or television **9** **up in the air** uncertain ▷ *vb* **10** to make known publicly: *these issues will be aired at a ministerial meeting* **11** to expose to air to dry or ventilate **12** (of a television or radio programme) to be broadcast ▷ See also **airs** [Greek *aēr*]

airbag *n* a safety device in a car, consisting of a bag that inflates automatically in an accident to protect the driver or passenger

air base *n* a centre from which military aircraft operate

airborne *adj* **1** carried by air **2** (of aircraft) flying; in the air

air brake *n* a brake in heavy vehicles that is operated by compressed air

airbrush *n* **1** an atomizer which sprays paint by means of compressed air ▷ *vb* **2** to paint using an airbrush **3** to improve the image of (a person or thing) by hiding defects beneath a bland exterior

air chief marshal *n* a very senior officer in an air force

air commodore *n* a senior officer in an air force

air conditioning *n* a system for controlling the temperature and humidity of the air in a building **air-conditioned** *adj* **air conditioner** *n*

aircraft *n, pl* **-craft** any machine capable of flying, such as a glider or aeroplane

aircraft carrier *n* a warship with a long flat deck for the launching and landing of aircraft

aircraftman *or fem* **aircraftwoman** *n, pl* **-men** *or* **-women** a serviceman or servicewoman of the most junior rank in an air force

air cushion *n* **1** an inflatable cushion **2** the pocket of air that supports a hovercraft

Airedale *n* a large terrier with rough tan-coloured hair and a black patch covering most of the back

airfield *n* a place where aircraft can land and take off

air force *n* the branch of a nation's armed services that is responsible for air warfare

air gun *n* a gun fired by means of compressed air

airhead *n slang* a person who is stupid or incapable of serious thought

air hostess *n chiefly Brit old-fashioned* a female flight attendant on an airline

airily *adv* in a light-hearted and casual manner

airing *n* **1** exposure to air or warmth for drying or ventilation **2** exposure to public debate: *both these notions got an airing during the campaign*

airing cupboard *n* a heated cupboard in which laundry is aired and kept dry

airless *adj* lacking fresh air; stuffy

air letter *n* same as **aerogram**

airlift *n* **1** the transportation by air of troops or cargo when other routes are blocked ▷ *vb* **2** to transport by an airlift

airline *n* an organization that provides scheduled flights for passengers or cargo

airliner *n* a large passenger aircraft

airlock *n* **1** a bubble of air blocking the flow of liquid in a pipe **2** an airtight chamber between places that do not have the same air pressure, such as in a spacecraft or submarine

airmail *n* **1** the system of sending mail by aircraft **2** mail sent by aircraft

airman *or fem* **airwoman** *n, pl* **-men** *or* **-women** a person serving in an air force

air marshal *n* **1** a senior Royal Air Force officer of equivalent rank to a vice admiral in the Royal Navy **2** the rank of a Royal New Zealand Air Force officer when Chief of the Defence Force

Air Miles *pl n* points awarded on buying flight tickets and certain other products which can be used to pay for other flights

airplane *n US & Canad* an aeroplane

airplay *n* the broadcast performances of a record on radio

air pocket *n* a small descending air current that causes an aircraft to lose height suddenly

airport *n* a landing and taking-off area for civil aircraft, with facilities for aircraft maintenance and passenger arrival and departure

air pump *n* a device for pumping air into or out of something

air rage *n* aggressive behaviour by an airline passenger that endangers the safety of the crew and other passengers

air raid *n* an attack by enemy aircraft in which bombs are dropped

air rifle *n* a rifle fired by means of compressed air

airs *pl n* manners put on to impress people: *we're poor and we never put on airs*

airship *n* a lighter-than-air self-propelled aircraft

airsick *adj* nauseated from travelling in an aircraft

airside *n* the part of an airport nearest the aircraft

airspace *n* the atmosphere above a particular country, regarded as its territory

airspeed *n* the speed of an aircraft relative to the air in which it moves

airstrip *n* a cleared area for the landing and taking-off of aircraft

air terminal *n* a building in a city from which air passengers are transported to an airport

airtight *adj* **1** sealed so that air cannot enter **2** having no weak points: *your reasoning is airtight and your evidence sound*

airtime *n* the time allocated to a particular programme, topic, or type of material on radio or television

air vice-marshal *n* a senior officer in an air force

airwaves *pl n informal* radio waves used in radio and television broadcasting

airway *n* an air route used regularly by aircraft

airworthy *adj* (of an aircraft) safe to fly **airworthiness** *n*

airy *adj* **airier, airiest 1** spacious and well ventilated **2** light-hearted and casual **3** having little basis in reality; fanciful: *airy assurances*
aisle (rhymes with **mile**) *n* a passageway separating seating areas in a church, theatre, or train, or separating rows of shelves in a supermarket [Latin *ala* wing]
aitchbone *n* a cut of beef from the rump bone [Middle English *nache-bone*]
ajar *adj, adv* (of a door) slightly open [Old English *cierran* to turn]
AK Alaska
AK-47 *n trademark* same as **Kalashnikov**
aka also known as
akimbo *adv* **(with) arms akimbo** with hands on hips and elbows turned outwards [Middle English *in kenebowe* in keen (ie sharp) bow]
akin *adj* **akin to** similar or very close to: *the technique is akin to impressionist painting*
Al *chem* aluminium
AL Alabama
à la *prep* in the manner or style of: *laced with Gothic allusion à la David Lynch* [French]
alabaster *n* a kind of white stone used for making statues and vases [Greek *alabastros*]
à la carte *adj, adv* (of a menu) having dishes individually priced [French]
alacrity *n* speed or eagerness: *I accepted the invitation with alacrity* [Latin *alacer* lively]
à la mode *adj* fashionable [French]
alarm *n* **1** fear aroused by awareness of danger **2** a noise warning of danger: *there had been no time to put on life jackets or to sound the alarm* **3** a device that transmits a warning **4** short for **alarm clock** ▷ *vb* **5** to fill with fear **6** to fit or activate a burglar alarm on (a house, car, etc.) [Old Italian *all'arme* to arms] **alarming** *adj*
alarm clock *n* a clock that sounds at a set time to wake a person up
alarmist *n* **1** a person who alarms others needlessly ▷ *adj* **2** causing needless alarm
alas *adv* **1** unfortunately or regrettably: *the answer, alas, is that they cannot get any for the moment* ▷ *interj* **2** *old-fashioned* an exclamation of grief or alarm [Old French *ha las!*]
alb *n* a long white linen robe worn by a Christian priest [Latin *albus* white]
albacore *n* a tuna found in warm seas which is valued as a food fish [Arabic *al-bakrah*]
Albanian *adj* **1** of Albania ▷ *n* **2** a person from Albania **3** the language of Albania
albatross *n* **1** a large sea bird with very long wings **2** *golf* a score of three strokes under par for a hole [Portuguese *alcatraz* pelican]
albeit *conj* even though: *these effects occur, albeit to a lesser degree* [Middle English *al be it* although it be (that)]
albino *n, pl* **-nos** a person or animal with white or almost white hair and skin and pinkish eyes [Latin *albus* white] **albinism** *n*
Albion *n poetic* Britain or England [Latin]
album *n* **1** a book with blank pages, for keeping photographs or stamps in **2** a collection of recordings released as a single item [Latin: blank tablet]
albumen *n* **1** egg white **2** *biochem* same as **albumin** [Latin *albus* white]
albumin *or* **albumen** *n biochem* a water-soluble protein found in blood plasma, egg white, milk, and muscle
alchemy *n* a medieval form of chemistry concerned with trying to change base metals into gold and to find an elixir to prolong life indefinitely [Arabic *al* the + *kīmiyā'* transmutation] **alchemist** *n*
alcohol *n* **1** a colourless flammable liquid present in intoxicating drinks **2** intoxicating drinks generally [Arabic *al-kuhl* powdered antimony]
alcohol-free *adj* **1** (of beer or wine) containing only a trace of alcohol **2** (of a period of time) during which no alcohol is taken: *an alcohol-free evening*
alcoholic *n* **1** a person who is addicted to alcohol ▷ *adj* **2** of or relating to alcohol
alcoholism *n* a condition in which dependence on alcohol harms a person's health and everyday life
alcopop *n informal* an alcoholic drink that tastes like a soft drink
alcove *n* a recess in the wall of a room [Arabic *al-qubbah* the vault]
aldehyde *n chem* any organic compound containing the group –CHO, derived from alcohol by oxidation [New Latin *al(cohol) dehyd(rogenatum)* dehydrogenated alcohol]
alder *n* a tree with toothed leaves and conelike fruits, often found in damp places [Old English *alor*]
alderman *n, pl* **-men 1** (formerly, in England and Wales) a senior member of a local council, elected by other councillors **2** (in the US, Canada and Australia) a member of the governing body of a city [Old English *ealdor* chief + *mann* man]
ale *n* **1** a beer fermented in an open vessel using yeasts that rise to the top of the brew **2** (formerly) an alcoholic drink that is unflavoured by hops **3** *Brit* another word for **beer** [Old English *alu, ealu*]
alehouse *n old-fashioned* a public house
alembic *n* **1** an obsolete type of container used for distillation **2** anything that distils or purifies things [Arabic *al-anbīq* the still]
alert *adj* **1** watchful and attentive **2 alert to** aware of ▷ *n* **3** a warning or the period during which a warning remains in effect **4 on the alert** watchful ▷ *vb* **5** to warn of danger **6** to make aware of a fact [Italian *all'erta* on the watch] **alertness** *n*
A level *n* **1** *Brit* the advanced level of a subject taken for the General Certificate of Education **2** a pass in a subject at A level
Alexander technique *n* a technique for improving posture by becoming more aware of it [after Frederick Matthias *Alexander*, Australian actor]
alfalfa *n* a plant widely used for feeding farm animals [Arabic *al-fasfasah*]
alfresco *adj, adv* in the open air [Italian: in the cool]

algae (al-jee) *pl n, sing* **alga** (al-ga) plants which grow in water or moist ground, and which have no true stems, roots, or leaves [Latin *alga* seaweed]

algebra *n* a branch of mathematics in which symbols are used to represent numbers [Arabic *al-jabr* the reunion of broken parts] **algebraic** *adj*

ALGOL *n* an early computer programming language designed for mathematical and scientific purposes [*alg(orithmic) o(riented) l(anguage)*]

Algonquin *or* **Algonkin** *n* **1** a member of a Native American people formerly living along the St Lawrence and Ottawa Rivers in Canada **2** the language of this people

algorism *n* the Arabic or decimal system of counting [from *al-Khuwārizmi*, 9th-century Persian mathematician]

algorithm *n* a logical arithmetical or computational procedure for solving problems [changed from ALGORISM]

alias *adv* **1** also known as: *Iris florentina, alias orris root* ▹ *n, pl* **-ases 2** a false name [Latin: otherwise]

alibi *n, pl* **-bis 1** *law* a plea of being somewhere else when a crime was committed **2** *informal* an excuse ▹ *vb* **-biing, -bied 3** to provide someone with an alibi [Latin: elsewhere]

Alice band *n* a band worn across the head to hold the hair back from the face

alien *adj* **1** foreign **2** from another world **3 alien to** repugnant or opposed to: *these methods are alien to the world of politics* ▹ *n* **4** a person who is a citizen of a country other than the one in which he or she lives **5** a being from another world **6** a person who does not seem to fit in with his or her environment [Latin *alienus*]

alienable *adj law* able to be transferred to another owner

alienate *vb* **-ating, -ated 1** to cause (a friend) to become unfriendly or hostile **2** to cause (someone) to feel that he or she does not belong somewhere **3** *law* to transfer the ownership of property to another person **alienation** *n*

alight[1] *vb* **alighting, alighted** *or* **alit 1** to step out of a vehicle or off a horse: *we alighted on Vladivostok station* **2** to land: *we saw thirty goldfinches alighting on the ledge* [Old English *ālīhtan*]

alight[2] *adj, adv* **1** on fire **2** illuminated: *the lamp on the desk was alight*

align (a-line) *vb* **1** to bring (a person or group) into agreement with the policy of another **2** to place (two objects) in a particular position in relation to each other [Old French *à ligne* into line] **alignment** *n*

alike *adj* **1** similar: *they were thought to be very alike* ▹ *adv* **2** in the same way: *they even dressed alike* **3** considered together: *players and spectators alike* [Old English *gelīc*]

alimentary *adj* of or relating to nutrition

alimentary canal *n* the tubular passage in the body through which food is passed and digested

alimony *n law* an allowance paid under a court order by one spouse to another after separation [Latin *alimonia* sustenance]

A-line *adj* (of a skirt) slightly flared

aliphatic *adj chem* (of an organic compound) having an open chain structure [Greek *aleiphar* oil]

aliquant *adj maths* denoting or belonging to a number that is not an exact divisor of a given number [Latin *aliquantus* somewhat]

aliquot *adj maths* denoting or belonging to an exact divisor of a number [Latin: several]

A list *n* **1** the most socially desirable category ▹ *adj* **A-list 2** of the most socially desirable category: *an A-list event*

alive *adj* **1** living; having life **2** in existence: *he said that he would keep the company alive, no matter what* **3** lively **4 alive to** aware of **5 alive with** swarming with: *the rocky shoreline was alive with birds* [Old English *on līfe* in life]

alkali (alk-a-lie) *n chem* a substance that combines with acid and neutralizes it to form a salt [Arabic *al-qili* the ashes (of saltwort)]

alkaline *adj chem* having the properties of or containing an alkali **alkalinity** *n*

alkaloid *n chem* any of a group of organic compounds containing nitrogen. Many are poisonous and some are used as drugs

alkane *n chem* any saturated hydrocarbon with the general formula C_nH_{2n+2}

alkene *n chem* any unsaturated hydrocarbon with the general formula C_nH_{2n}

all *determiner* **1** the whole quantity or number (of): *all the banks agree; we're all to blame* **2** every one of a class: *almost all animals sneeze* ▹ *adj* **3** the greatest possible: *in all seriousness* **4** any whatever: *I'm leaving out all question of motive for the time being* **5 all along** since the beginning **6 all but** nearly **7 all in all** everything considered **8 all over A** finished **B** everywhere in or on: *we send them all over the world* **C** *informal* typically: *that's him all over* **9 all the** so much (more or less) than otherwise: *the need for new drugs is all the more important* **10 at all** used for emphasis: *my throat's no better at all* **11 be all for** *informal* to be strongly in favour of **12 for all** in spite of: *for all his cynicism, he's at heart a closet idealist* **13 in all** altogether: *there were five in all* ▹ *adv* **14** (in scores of games) each: *the score was two all* ▹ *n* **15 give one's all** to make the greatest possible effort [Old English *eall*]

Allah *n* the name of God in Islam

allay *vb* to reduce (fear, doubt, or anger) [Old English *ālecgan* to put down]

all clear *n* a signal indicating that danger is over

allegation *n* an unproved assertion or accusation

allege *vb* **-leging, -leged** to state without proof [Latin *allegare* to dispatch on a mission]

alleged *adj* stated but not proved: *the spot where the alleged crime took place* **allegedly** (al-lej-id-lee) *adv*

allegiance *n* loyalty or dedication to a person, cause, or belief [Old French *lige* liege]

allegory *n, pl* **-ries** a story, poem, or picture with an underlying meaning as well as the literal one [Greek *allēgorein* to speak figuratively] **allegorical** *adj* **allegorize** *or* **-rise** *vb*

allegretto *music* ▹ *adv* **1** fairly quickly or briskly ▹ *n, pl* **-tos 2** a piece or passage to be performed fairly quickly or briskly [Italian]

allegro *music* ▹ *adv* **1** in a brisk lively manner ▹ *n, pl* **-gros 2** a piece or passage to be performed in a brisk lively manner [Italian]

allele (al-**leel**) *n* any of two or more genes that are responsible for alternative characteristics, such as smooth or wrinkled seeds in peas
alleluia *interj* praise the Lord! [Hebrew *halleluyah*]
allergen (al-ler-jen) *n* a substance capable of causing an allergic reaction **allergenic** *adj*
allergic *adj* **1** having or caused by an allergy **2 allergic to** *informal* having a strong dislike of: *father and son seemed to have been allergic to each other from the start*
allergy *n, pl* **-gies 1** extreme sensitivity to a substance such as a food or pollen, which causes the body to react to any contact with it **2** *informal* a strong dislike for something [Greek *allos* other + *ergon* activity]
alleviate *vb* **-ating, -ated** to lessen (pain or suffering) [Latin *levis* light] **alleviation** *n*
USAGE See at **ameliorate**.
alley *n* **1** a narrow passage between or behind buildings **2 A** a building containing lanes for tenpin bowling **B** a long narrow wooden lane down which the ball is rolled in tenpin bowling **3** a path in a garden, often lined with trees [Old French *alee*]
alleyway *n* a narrow passage with buildings or walls on both sides
all found *adv* (of charges for accommodation) including meals, heating, and other living expenses
Allhallows *n* same as **All Saints' Day**
alliance *n* **1** the state of being allied **2** a formal relationship between two or more countries or political parties to work together **3** the countries or parties involved [Old French *alier* to ally]
allied *adj* **1** united by a common aim or common characteristics: *the allied areas of telepathy and clairvoyance* **2 Allied** relating to the countries that fought against Germany and Japan in the Second World War: *the Allied bombing of German cities*
alligator *n* a large reptile of the southern US, similar to the crocodile but with a shorter broader snout [Spanish *el lagarto* the lizard]
all in *adj* **1** *informal* exhausted **2** (of wrestling) with no style forbidden ▷ *adv* **3** with all expenses included
alliteration *n* the use of the same sound at the start of words occurring together, as in *round the rugged rock the ragged rascal ran* [Latin *litera* letter] **alliterative** *adj*
allocate *vb* **-cating, -cated** to assign to someone or for a particular purpose [Latin *locus* a place] **allocation** *n*
allopathy (al-**lop**-ath-ee) *n* *med* an orthodox method of treating disease, by using drugs that produce an effect opposite to the effect of the disease being treated, as contrasted with homeopathy [Greek *allos* other + *pathos* suffering] **allopathic** *adj*
allot *vb* **-lotting, -lotted** to assign as a share or for a particular purpose [Old French *lot* portion]
allotment *n* **1** *Brit* a small piece of land rented by a person to grow vegetables on **2** a portion allotted **3** distribution
allotrope *n* *chem* any of two or more physical forms in which an element can exist
allotropy *n* *chem* the existence of an element in two or more physical forms [Greek *allos* other + *tropos* manner] **allotropic** *adj*
all-out *adj informal* using one's maximum powers: *an all-out attack on inflation*
allow *vb* **1** to permit someone to do something **2** to set aside: *I allowed plenty of time* **3** to acknowledge (a point or claim) **4 allow for** to take into account [Late Latin *allaudare* to extol] **allowable** *adj*
allowance *n* **1** an amount of money given at regular intervals **2** (in Britain) an amount of a person's income that is not subject to income tax **3 make allowances for A** to treat or judge someone less severely because he or she has special problems **B** to take into account in one's plans
alloy *n* **1** a mixture of two or more metals ▷ *vb* **2** to mix metals in order to obtain a substance with a desired property [Latin *alligare* to bind]
all-purpose *adj* useful for many purposes
all right *adj* **1** acceptable or satisfactory: *is everything all right?* **2** unharmed; safe: *I'm going to check if he's all right* ▷ *interj* **3** an expression of approval or agreement ▷ *adv* **4** satisfactorily **5** safely **6** without doubt: *it was her all right*
USAGE See at **alright**.
all-round *adj* **1** having many skills; versatile: *an all-round player* **2** of broad scope; comprehensive: *we cannot do without up-to-date and all-round training*
all-rounder *n* a person with many skills and abilities
All Saints' Day *n* a Christian festival celebrated on November 1 to honour all the saints
All Souls' Day *n* *RC Church* a day of prayer (November 2) for the dead in purgatory
allspice *n* a spice used in cooking, which comes from the berries of a tropical American tree
all-time *adj informal* unsurpassed at a particular time: *one of boxing's all-time greats*
allude *vb* **-luding, -luded** > **allude to** to refer indirectly to [Latin *alludere*]
USAGE Avoid confusion with **elude**.
allure *n* attractiveness or appeal [Old French *alurer* to lure]
alluring *adj* extremely attractive
allusion *n* an indirect reference
alluvial *adj* **1** of or relating to alluvium ▷ *n* **2** same as **alluvium**
alluvium *n, pl* **-via** a fertile soil consisting of mud, silt, and sand deposited by flowing water [Latin]
ally *n, pl* **-lies 1** a country, person, or group with an agreement to support another ▷ *vb* **-lies, -lying, -lied 2 ally oneself with** to agree to support another country, person, or group [Latin *ligare* to bind]
alma mater *n* the school, college, or university that one attended [Latin: bountiful mother]
almanac *n* a yearly calendar with detailed information on matters like anniversaries and phases of the moon [Late Greek *almenikhiaka*]
almighty *adj* **1** having power over everything **2** *informal* very great: *there was an almighty bang* ▷ *n* **3 the Almighty** God

almond *n* an edible oval nut with a yellowish-brown shell, which grows on a small tree [Greek *amugdalē*]

almoner *n Brit* a former name for a hospital social worker [Old French *almosne* alms]

almost *adv* very nearly

alms (**ahmz**) *pl n old-fashioned* donations of money or goods to poor people [Greek *eleēmosunē* pity]

almshouse *n Brit* (formerly) a house, financed by charity, which offered accommodation to poor people

aloe *n* **1** a plant with fleshy spiny leaves **2 aloes** a bitter drug made from aloe leaves [Greek]

aloe vera *n* a plant producing a juice which is used to treat skin and hair

aloft *adv* **1** in the air **2** *naut* in the rigging of a ship [Old Norse *ā lopt*]

alone *adj* **1** without anyone or anything else ▹ *adv* **2** without anyone or anything else **3 leave someone** *or* **something alone** to refrain from annoying someone or interfering with something **4 let alone** not to mention: *it looked inconceivable that he could run again, let alone be elected* [Old English *al one* all (entirely) one]

along *prep* **1** over part or all of the length of: *we were going along the railway tracks* ▹ *adv* **2** moving forward: *they were roaring along at 40mph* **3** in company with another or others: *let them go along for the ride* **4 along with** together with: *I'm including the good days along with the bad* [Old English *andlang*]

USAGE See at **plus**.

alongside *prep* **1** close beside ▹ *adv* **2** near the side of something

aloof *adj* distant or haughty in manner [obsolete *a loof* to windward]

alopecia (al-loh-**pee**-sha) *n* loss of hair, usually due to illness [Greek *alōpekia* mange in foxes]

aloud *adv* in an audible voice

alp *n* **1** a high mountain **2 the Alps** a high mountain range in S central Europe [Latin *Alpes*]

alpaca *n* **1** a South American mammal related to the llama, with dark shaggy hair **2** wool or cloth made from this hair [indigenous S American word *allpaca*]

alpenstock *n* a strong stick with an iron tip used by hikers and mountain climbers [German]

alpha *n* **1** the first letter in the Greek alphabet (Α, α) **2** *Brit* the highest grade in an examination or for a piece of academic work **3 alpha and omega** the first and last

alphabet *n* a set of letters in fixed conventional order, used in a writing system [*alpha* + *beta*, the first two letters of the Greek alphabet]

alphabetical *adj* in the conventional order of the letters of an alphabet **alphabetically** *adv*

alphabetize *or* **-ise** *vb* **-izing, -ized** *or* **-ising, -ised** to put in alphabetical order **alphabetization** *or* **-isation** *n*

alphanumeric *adj* consisting of alphabetical and numerical symbols

alpha particle *n physics* a positively charged particle, emitted during some radioactive transformations

alpha ray *n physics* a stream of alpha particles

alpine *adj* **1** of high mountains **2 Alpine** of the Alps ▹ *n* **3** a plant grown on or native to mountains

alpinist *n* a mountain climber

already *adv* **1** before the present time **2** before an implied or expected time

alright *adj, interj, adv not standard* same as **all right**

USAGE The form *alright*, though very common, is still considered by many people to be wrong or less acceptable than *all right*.

Alsatian *n* a large wolflike dog

also *adv* in addition; too [Old English *alswā*]

also-ran *n* a loser in a race, competition, or election

Alta. Alberta

altar *n* **1** the table used for Communion in Christian churches **2** a raised structure on which sacrifices are offered and religious rites performed [Latin *altus* high]

altarpiece *n* a painting or a decorated screen set above and behind the altar in a Christian church

alter *vb* to make or become different; change [Latin *alter* other]

alteration *n* a change or modification

altercation *n* a noisy argument [Latin *altercari* to quarrel]

alter ego *n* **1** a hidden side to one's personality **2** a very close friend [Latin: other self]

alternate *vb* **-nating, -nated 1** to occur by turns **2** to interchange regularly or in succession ▹ *adj* **3** occurring by turns **4** every second (one) of a series: *alternate days* **5** being a second choice [Latin *alternare*] **alternately** *adv* **alternation** *n*

alternate angles *pl n geom* two angles at opposite ends and on opposite sides of a line intersecting two other lines

alternating current *n* an electric current that reverses direction at frequent regular intervals

alternative *n* **1** a possibility of choice between two or more things **2** either or any of such choices ▹ *adj* **3** presenting a choice between two or more possibilities **4** of a lifestyle, etc. that is less conventional or materialistic than is usual **alternatively** *adv*

alternative energy *n* a form of energy obtained from natural resources like waves and wind

alternative medicine *n* the treatment of disease by unconventional methods like homeopathy, and involving attention to the patient's emotional wellbeing

alternator *n* an electrical machine that generates an alternating current

although *conj* in spite of the fact that

altimeter (al-**tim**-it-er) *n* an instrument that measures altitude [Latin *altus* high + -METER]

altitude *n* height, esp. above sea level [Latin *altus* high, deep]

alto *n, pl* **-tos 1** short for **contralto 2** the highest adult male voice **3** a singer with an alto voice **4** a musical instrument, for instance a saxophone, that is the second or third highest in its family ▹ *adj* **5** denoting such an instrument, singer, or voice: *an alto flute* [Italian: high]

altogether *adv* **1** completely: *an altogether different message* **2** on the whole: *this is not altogether a bad thing* **3** in total: *altogether, 25 aircraft took part* ▹ *n* **4 in the altogether** *informal* naked

altruism *n* unselfish concern for the welfare of others [Italian *altrui* others] **altruist** *n* **altruistic** *adj*

a

alum *n chem* a double sulphate of aluminium and potassium, used in manufacturing and in medicine [Latin *alumen*]
aluminium *or US & Canad* **aluminum** *n chem* a light malleable silvery-white metallic element that does not rust. Symbol: **Al**
aluminize *or* **-ise** *vb* **-nizing, -nized** *or* **-nising, -nised** to cover with aluminium
alumnus (al-**lumm**-nuss) *or fem* **alumna** (al-**lumm**-na) *n, pl* **-ni** (-nie) *or* **-nae** (-nee) *chiefly US & Canad* a graduate of a school or college [Latin: nursling, pupil]
alveolus (al-**vee**-ol-luss) *n, pl* **-li** (-lie) any small pit, cavity, or saclike dilation, such as a honeycomb cell, a tooth socket, or the tiny air sacs in the lungs [Latin: a little hollow]
always *adv* **1** without exception: *she was always at the top of her form in school work* **2** continually: *you're always shouting or whining* **3** in any case: *they're all adults, they can always say no* [Old English *ealne weg* all the way]
alyssum *n* a garden plant with clusters of small white flowers [Greek *alussos* curing rabies]
Alzheimer's disease (**alts**-hime-erz) *n* a disorder of the brain resulting in a progressive decline in intellectual and physical abilities and eventual dementia [after A. *Alzheimer*, German physician]
am *vb* (*with "I" as subject*) a form of the present tense of **be** [Old English *eam*]
Am *chem* americium
AM **1** amplitude modulation **2** (in Britain) Member of the National Assembly for Wales
Am. America(n)
a.m. before noon [Latin *ante meridiem*]
amah *n* (in E Asia, formerly) a nurse or maidservant [Portuguese *ama*]
amakwerekwere *n S African informal, derogatory* a term used by Black people to refer to foreign Africans [from Xhosa *ama*, a plural prefix, + *kwerekwere* imitative of unintelligible sound]
amalgam *n* **1** a blend or combination **2** an alloy of mercury with another metal: *dental amalgam* [Medieval Latin *amalgama*]
amalgamate *vb* **-mating, -mated 1** to combine or unite **2** to alloy (a metal) with mercury **amalgamation** *n*
amandla (a-**mand**-la) *n S African* a political slogan calling for power to the Black population [Nguni (language group of southern Africa): power]
amanuensis (am-man-yew-**en**-siss) *n, pl* **-ses** (-seez) a person who copies manuscripts or takes dictation [Latin *servus a manu* slave at hand]
amaranth *n* **1** *poetic* an imaginary flower that never fades **2** a lily-like plant with small green, red, or purple flowers [Greek *a-* not + *marainein* to fade]
amaretti *pl n* Italian almond biscuits [Italian *amaro* bitter]
amaryllis *n* a lily-like plant with large red or white flowers and a long stalk [*Amaryllis*, Greek name for a shepherdess]
amass *vb* to accumulate or collect: *the desire to amass wealth* [Latin *ad-* to + *massa* mass]
amateur *n* **1** a person who engages in a sport or other activity as a pastime rather than as a profession **2** a person unskilled in a subject or activity ▷ *adj* **3** doing something out of interest, not for money **4** amateurish [Latin *amator* lover] **amateurism** *n*
amateurish *adj* lacking skill
amatory *adj* of or relating to romantic or sexual love [Latin *amare* to love]
amaut *or* **amowt** *n Canad* a hood on an Inuit woman's parka for carrying a child
amaze *vb* **amazing, amazed** to fill with surprise; astonish [Old English *āmasian*] **amazement** *n* **amazing** *adj* **amazingly** *adv*
Amazon *n* **1** a strong and powerful woman **2** *Greek myth* one of a race of women warriors of Scythia [Greek] **Amazonian** *adj*
ambassador *n* **1** a diplomat of the highest rank, sent to another country as permanent representative of his or her own country **2** a representative or messenger: *he saw himself as an ambassador for the game* [Old Provençal *ambaisador*] **ambassadorial** *adj*
amber *n* **1** a yellow translucent fossilized resin, used in jewellery ▷ *adj* **2** brownish-yellow [Arabic *'anbar* ambergris]
ambergris (**am**-ber-greece) *n* a waxy substance secreted by the sperm whale, which is used in making perfumes [Old French *ambre gris* grey amber]
ambidextrous *adj* able to use both hands with equal ease [Latin *ambi-* both + *dexter* right hand]
ambience *or* **ambiance** *n* the atmosphere of a place
ambient *adj* **1** surrounding: *low ambient temperatures* **2** creating a relaxing atmosphere: *ambient music* [Latin *ambi-* round + *ire* to go]
ambiguity *n, pl* **-ties 1** the possibility of interpreting an expression in more than one way **2** an ambiguous situation or expression: *the ambiguities of feminine identity*
ambiguous *adj* having more than one possible interpretation [Latin *ambigere* to go around] **ambiguously** *adv*
ambit *n* limits or boundary [Latin *ambire* to go round]
ambition *n* **1** strong desire for success **2** something so desired; a goal [Latin *ambitio* a going round (of candidates)]
ambitious *adj* **1** having a strong desire for success **2** requiring great effort or ability: *ambitious plans*
ambivalence (am-**biv**-a-lenss) *n* the state of feeling two conflicting emotions at the same time **ambivalent** *adj*
amble *vb* **-bling, -bled 1** to walk at a leisurely pace ▷ *n* **2** a leisurely walk or pace [Latin *ambulare* to walk]
ambrosia *n* **1** something delightful to taste or smell **2** *classical myth* the food of the gods [Greek: immortality]
ambulance *n* a motor vehicle designed to carry sick or injured people [Latin *ambulare* to walk]
ambulatory *adj* **1** of or relating to walking **2** able to walk ▷ *n, pl* **-ries 3** a place for walking in, such as a cloister
ambush *n* **1** the act of waiting in a concealed position to make a surprise attack **2** an attack

from such a position ▷ *vb* **3** to attack suddenly from a concealed position [Old French *embuschier* to position in ambush]

ameliorate (am-**meal**-yor-rate) *vb* **-rating, -rated** to make (something) better [Latin *melior* better] **amelioration** *n*

USAGE *Ameliorate* is often wrongly used where *alleviate* is meant. *Ameliorate* should be used to mean 'improve', not 'make easier to bear', so one should talk about *alleviating* pain or hardship, not *ameliorating* it.

amen *interj* so be it: used at the end of a prayer [Hebrew: certainly]

amenable (a-**mean**-a-bl) *adj* likely or willing to cooperate [Latin *minare* to drive (cattle)]

amend *vb* to make small changes to something such as a piece of writing or a contract, in order to improve it: *he has amended the basic design* [Old French *amender*]

amendment *n* an improvement or correction

amends *pl n* **make amends for** to compensate for some injury or insult

amenity *n, pl* **-ties** a useful or enjoyable feature: *all kinds of amenities including horse riding and golf* [Latin *amoenus* agreeable]

amenorrhoea *or esp US* **amenorrhea** (aim-men-or-**ree**-a) *n* abnormal absence of menstruation [Greek *a-* not + *mēn* month + *rhein* to flow]

Amen-Ra *n* an Egyptian god with a ram's head

American *adj* **1** of the United States of America or the American continent ▷ *n* **2** a person from the United States of America or the American continent

American football *n* a game similar to rugby, played by two teams of eleven players

American Indian *n* same as **Native American**

USAGE The term *American Indian* is still acceptable and is used by indigenous people themselves. However, the most widely accepted phrase in general use is *Native American*.

Americanism *n* an expression or custom that is characteristic of the people of the United States

Americanize *or* **-ise** *vb* **-izing, -ized** *or* **-ising, -ised** to make American in outlook or form

americium *n chem* a white metallic element artificially produced from plutonium. Symbol: **Am** [from *America* (where it was first produced)]

amethyst (am-myth-ist) *n* **1** a purple or violet variety of quartz used as a gemstone ▷ *adj* **2** purple or violet [Greek *amethustos* not drunken]

Amex (**aah**-mex) **1** *trademark* American Express **2** American Stock Exchange

Amharic *n* the official language of Ethiopia

amiable *adj* having a pleasant nature; friendly [Latin *amicus* friend] **amiability** *n* **amiably** *adv*

amicable *adj* characterized by friendliness: *ideally the parting should be amicable* [Latin *amicus* friend] **amicability** *n* **amicably** *adv*

amid *or* **amidst** *prep* in the middle of; among [Old English *on middan* in the middle]

amide *n chem* **1** any organic compound containing the group $-CONH_2$ **2** an inorganic compound having the general formula $M(NH_2)_x$, where M is a metal atom [from *ammonia*]

amidships *adv naut* at, near, or towards the centre of a ship

amine (am-**mean**) *n chem* an organic base formed by replacing one or more of the hydrogen atoms of ammonia by organic groups [from *ammonium*]

amino acid (am-**mean**-oh) *n chem* any of a group of organic compounds containing the **amino** group, $-NH_2$, and one or more carboxyl groups, $-COOH$, esp. one that is a component of protein

amir (am-**meer**) *n* same as **emir** [Arabic]

amiss *adv* **1** wrongly or badly: *anxious not to tread amiss* **2** **take something amiss** to be offended by something ▷ *adj* **3** wrong or faulty [Middle English *a mis*, from *mis* wrong]

amity *n formal* friendship [from Latin *amicus* friend]

ammeter *n* an instrument for measuring an electric current in amperes [*am(pere)* + -METER]

ammo *n informal* ammunition

ammonia *n* **1** a colourless strong-smelling gas containing hydrogen and nitrogen **2** a solution of this in water [ultimately from a substance found near the shrine of the Roman-Egyptian god Jupiter *Ammon*]

ammonite *n* the fossilized spiral shell of an extinct sea creature [Medieval Latin *cornu Ammonis* horn of Ammon]

ammonium *adj chem* of or containing the chemical group NH_4- or the ion NH_4^+

ammunition *n* **1** bullets, bombs, and shells that can be fired from or as a weapon **2** facts that can be used in an argument [Latin *munitio* fortification]

amnesia *n* a partial or total loss of memory [Greek: forgetfulness] **amnesiac** *adj, n*

amnesty *n, pl* **-ties** **1** a general pardon for offences against a government **2** a period during which a law is suspended, to allow people to confess to crime or give up weapons without fear of prosecution [Greek *a-* not + *mnasthai* to remember]

amniocentesis *n, pl* **-ses** removal of amniotic fluid from the womb of a pregnant woman in order to detect possible abnormalities in the fetus [*amnion* + Greek *kentēsis* a pricking]

amnion *n, pl* **-nia** the innermost of two membranes enclosing an embryo [Greek: a little lamb] **amniotic** *adj*

amniotic fluid *n* the fluid surrounding the fetus in the womb

amoeba *or US* **ameba** (am-**mee**-ba) *n, pl* **-bae** (-bee) *or* **-bas** a microscopic single-cell creature that is able to change its shape [Greek *ameibein* to change]

amok *or* **amuck** *adv* **run amok** to run about in a violent frenzy [Malay *amoq* furious assault]

among *or* **amongst** *prep* **1** in the midst of: *she decided to dwell among the Greeks* **2** in the group, class, or number of: *he is among the top trainers* **3** to each of: *the stakes should be divided among the players* **4** with one another within a group: *sort it out among yourselves* [Old English *amang*]

USAGE See at **between**.

a

a

amoral (aim-mor-ral) *adj* without moral standards or principles **amorality** *n*

> **USAGE** *Amoral* is often wrongly used where *immoral* is meant. *Immoral* should be used to talk about the breaking of moral rules, *amoral* about people who have no moral code or about places or situations where moral considerations do not apply.

amorous *adj* feeling, displaying, or relating to sexual love or desire [Latin *amor* love]

amorphous *adj* **1** lacking a definite shape **2** of no recognizable character or type [Greek *a-* not + *morphē* shape]

amortize *or* **-tise** *vb* **-tizing, -tized** *or* **-tising, -tised** *finance* to pay off (a debt) gradually by periodic transfers to a sinking fund [Latin *ad* to + *mors* death]

amount *n* **1** extent or quantity ▷ *vb* **2 amount to** to be equal or add up to [Old French *amonter* to go up]

> **USAGE** The use of a plural noun after *amount of (an amount of bananas; the amount of refugees)* should be avoided: *a quantity of bananas; the number of refugees.*

amour *n* a secret love affair [Latin *amor* love]

amour-propre (am-moor-**prop**-ra) *n* self-esteem

amp *n* **1** an ampere **2** *informal* an amplifier

amperage *n* the strength of an electric current measured in amperes

ampere (am-pair) *n* the basic unit of electric current [after A. M. *Ampère*, French physicist & mathematician]

ampersand *n* the character &, meaning *and* [shortened from *and per se and*, that is, the symbol & by itself (represents) *and*]

amphetamine (am-**fet**-am-mean) *n* a drug used as a stimulant [shortened from chemical name]

amphibian *n* **1** an animal, such as a newt, frog, or toad, that lives on land but breeds in water **2** a vehicle that can travel on both water and land

amphibious *adj* **1** living or operating both on land and in or on water **2** relating to a military attack launched from the sea against a shore [Greek *amphibios* having a double life]

amphitheatre *or US* **amphitheater** *n* a circular or oval building without a roof, in which tiers of seats rise from a central open arena [Greek *amphitheatron*]

amphora (am-for-ra) *n, pl* **-phorae** (-for-ree) an ancient Greek or Roman jar with two handles and a narrow neck [Greek *amphi-* on both sides + *phoreus* bearer]

ample *adj* **1** more than sufficient: *there is already ample evidence* **2** large: *ample helpings of stewed pomegranates and pears* [Latin *amplus*]

amplifier *n* an electronic device used to increase the strength of a current or sound signal

amplify *vb* **-fies, -fying, -fied 1** *electronics* to increase the strength of (a current or sound signal) **2** to explain in more detail **3** to increase the size, extent, or effect of [Latin *amplificare*] **amplification** *n*

amplitude *n* **1** greatness of extent **2** *physics* the maximum displacement from the zero or mean position of a wave or oscillation [Latin *amplus* spacious]

amplitude modulation *n electronics* a method of transmitting information using radio waves in which the amplitude of the carrier wave is varied in accordance with the amplitude of the input signal

amply *adv* fully or generously: *she was amply rewarded for it*

ampoule *or US* **ampule** *n med* a small glass container in which liquids for injection are sealed [French]

ampulla *n, pl* **-pullae 1** *anatomy* the dilated end part of certain tubes in the body **2** *Christianity* a container for the wine and water, or the oil, used in church [Latin]

amputate *vb* **-tating, -tated** to cut off (a limb or part of a limb) for medical reasons [Latin *am-* around + *putare* to prune] **amputation** *n*

amputee *n* a person who has had a limb amputated

amuck *adv* same as **amok**

amulet *n* a trinket or jewel worn as a protection against evil [Latin *amuletum*]

amuse *vb* **amusing, amused 1** to cause to laugh or smile **2** to entertain or keep interested [Old French *amuser* to cause to be idle] **amusing** *adj* **amusingly** *adv*

amusement *n* **1** the state of being amused **2** something that amuses or entertains someone

amusement arcade *n Brit* a covered area with coin-operated electronic game machines

amusement park *n* a large open-air entertainment area with rides and stalls

amylase *n* an enzyme present in saliva that helps to change starch into sugar

an *adj (indefinite article)* same as **a**: used before an initial vowel sound: *an old man; an hour* [Old English *ān* one]

> **USAGE** *An* was formerly often used before words that begin with *h* and are unstressed on the first syllable: *an hotel; an historic meeting:* sometimes the initial *h* was not pronounced. This usage is now becoming obsolete.

an- *prefix* See **a-**

Anabaptist *n* **1** a member of a 16th-century Protestant movement that believed in adult baptism ▷ *adj* **2** of this movement [Late Greek *anabaptizein* to baptize again]

anabolic steroid *n* a synthetic steroid hormone used to stimulate muscle and bone growth

anabolism *n biol* a metabolic process in which body tissues are synthesized from food [Greek *anabolē* a rising up]

anachronism (an-**nak**-kron-iz-zum) *n* **1** the representation of something in a historical context in which it could not have occurred or existed **2** a person or thing that seems to belong to another time [Greek *ana* against + *khronos* time] **anachronistic** *adj*

anaconda *n* a large S American snake which squeezes its prey to death [probably from Sinhalese *henakandayā* whip snake]

anaemia *or US* **anemia** (an-**neem**-ee-a) *n* a deficiency of red blood cells or their haemoglobin content, resulting in paleness and lack of energy [Greek *an* without + *haima* blood]

anaemic *or US* **anemic** *adj* **1** having anaemia **2** pale and sickly-looking **3** lacking vitality
anaerobe *n biol* an organism that does not require oxygen [Greek *an* not + *aēr* air + *bios* life] **anaerobic** *adj*
anaesthesia *or US* **anesthesia** (an-niss-**theez**-ee-a) *n* loss of bodily feeling caused by disease or accident or by drugs such as ether: called **general anaesthesia** when consciousness is lost and **local anaesthesia** when only a specific area of the body is involved [Greek]
anaesthetic *or US* **anesthetic** (an-niss-**thet**-ik) *n* **1** a substance that causes anaesthesia ▷ *adj* **2** causing anaesthesia
anaesthetist (an-**neess**-thet-ist) *n Brit* a doctor who administers anaesthetics
anaesthetize, anaesthetise *or US* **anesthetize** *vb* **-tizing, -tized** *or* **-tising, -tised** to cause to feel no pain by administering an anaesthetic
anagram *n* a word or phrase made by rearranging the letters of another word or phrase [Greek *anagrammatizein* to transpose letters]
anal (ain-al) *adj* **1** of or relating to the anus **2** short for **anal-retentive** [New Latin *analis*]
analgesia *n* the absence of pain [Greek]
analgesic (an-nal-**jeez**-ik) *n* **1** a drug that relieves pain ▷ *adj* **2** pain-relieving: *an analgesic balm*
analog *n* same as **analogue**

> **USAGE** The spelling *analog* is a US variant of *analogue* in all its senses, and is also the generally preferred spelling in the computer industry.

analogize *or* **-gise** *vb* **-gizing, -gized** *or* **-gising, -gised 1** to use analogy in argument **2** to reveal analogy between (one thing and another)
analogous *adj* similar in some respects [Greek *analogos* proportionate]

> **USAGE** The use of *with* after *analogous* should be avoided: *swimming has no event that is analogous to* (not *with*) *the 100 metres in athletics.*

analogue *or US* **analog** *n* **1** a physical object or quantity used to measure or represent another quantity **2** something that is analogous to something else ▷ *adj* **3** displaying information by means of a dial: *analogue speedometers*

> **USAGE** See at **analog**.

analogy *n, pl* **-gies 1** a similarity, usually in a limited number of features **2** a comparison made to show such a similarity [Greek *analogia*] **analogical** *adj*
anal-retentive *adj* (of a person) excessively fussy and concerned with order and minute details
analyse *or US* **-lyze** (an-nal-lize) *vb* **-lysing, -lysed** *or* **-lyzing, -lyzed 1** to examine (something) in detail in order to discover its meaning or essential features **2** to break (something) down into its components **3** to psychoanalyse (someone)
analysis (an-**nal**-liss-iss) *n, pl* **-ses** (-seez) **1** the separation of a whole into its parts for study or interpretation **2** a statement of the results of this **3** short for **psychoanalysis** [Greek *analusis* a dissolving]
analyst *n* **1** a person who is skilled in analysis' **2** a psychoanalyst
analytical *or* **analytic** *adj* relating to or using analysis **analytically** *adv*
anaphylactic shock *n* a severe, sometimes fatal, reaction to a substance to which a person has an extreme sensitivity, often involving respiratory difficulty and circulation failure [Greek *ana* again + *phulaxis* guarding]
anarchism *n* a doctrine advocating the abolition of government and its replacement by a social system based on voluntary cooperation
anarchist *n* **1** a person who advocates anarchism **2** a person who causes disorder or upheaval **anarchistic** *adj*
anarchy (**an**-ark-ee) *n* **1** general lawlessness and disorder **2** the absence of government [Greek *an* without + *arkh-* leader] **anarchic** *adj*
anastigmat *n* a lens corrected for astigmatism **anastigmatic** *adj*
anathema (an-**nath**-im-a) *n* a detested person or thing: *the very colour was anathema to her* [Greek: something accursed]
anathematize *or* **-tise** *vb* **-tizing, -tized** *or* **-tising, -tised** to curse: *he anathematized the world in general*
anatomist *n* an expert in anatomy
anatomy *n, pl* **-mies 1** the science of the physical structure of animals and plants **2** the structure of an animal or plant **3** *informal* a person's body: *the male anatomy* **4** a detailed analysis: *an anatomy of the massacre* [Greek *ana* up + *temnein* to cut] **anatomical** *adj*
ANC African National Congress
ancestor *n* **1** a person in former times from whom one is descended **2** a forerunner: *the immediate ancestor of rock and roll is rhythm and blues* [Latin *antecedere* to go before]
ancestral *adj* of or inherited from ancestors
ancestry *n, pl* **-tries 1** family descent: *of Japanese ancestry* **2** origin or roots: *a vehicle whose ancestry dated back to the 1950s*
anchor *n* **1** a hooked device attached to a boat by a cable and dropped overboard to fasten the boat to the sea bottom **2** a source of stability or security: *a spiritual anchor* **3 anchors** *slang* the brakes of a motor vehicle: *he rammed on the anchors* ▷ *vb* **4** to use an anchor to hold (a boat) in one place **5** to fasten securely: *we anchored his wheelchair to a rock* [Greek *ankura*]
anchorage *n* a place where boats can be anchored
anchor ice *n Canad* ice that forms at the bottom of a lake or river
anchorite *n* a person who chooses to live in isolation for religious reasons [Greek *anakhōrein* to retire]
anchorman *or* **anchorwoman** *n, pl* **-men** *or* **-women 1** a broadcaster in a central studio, who links up and presents items from outside camera units and reporters in other studios **2** the last person to compete in a relay team
anchovy (**an**-chov-ee) *n, pl* **-vies** a small marine food fish with a salty taste [Spanish *anchova*]
ancien régime (on-syan ray-**zheem**) *n* **1** the political and social system of France before the 1789 Revolution **2** a former political system [French: old regime]

a

ancient *adj* **1** dating from very long ago **2** very old **3** of the far past, esp. before the collapse of the Western Roman Empire (476 AD) ▷ *n* **4 ancients** people who lived very long ago, such as the Romans and Greeks [Latin *ante* before]

a

ancillary *adj* **1** supporting the main work of an organization: *hospital ancillary workers* **2** used as an extra or supplement: *I had a small ancillary sleeping tent* [Latin *ancilla* female servant]

and *conj* **1** in addition to: *plants and birds* **2** as a consequence: *she fell downstairs and broke her neck* **3** afterwards: *she excused herself and left* **4** used for emphasis or to indicate repetition or continuity: *they called again and again* **5** used to express a contrast between instances of something: *there are jobs and jobs* **6** *informal* used in place of *to* in infinitives after verbs such as *try, go,* and *come*: *come and see us again* [Old English]

USAGE See at **try**.

andante (an-**dan**-tay) *music* ▷ *adv* **1** moderately slowly ▷ *n* **2** a passage or piece to be performed moderately slowly [Italian *andare* to walk]

andantino (an-dan-**tee**-no) *music* ▷ *adv* **1** slightly faster than andante ▷ *n, pl* **-nos 2** a passage or piece to be performed in this way

andiron *n* either of a pair of metal stands for supporting logs in a fireplace [Old French *andier*]

and/or *conj not standard* either one or the other or both

> **USAGE** Many people think that *and/or* is only acceptable in legal and commercial contexts. In other contexts, it is better to use *or both*: *many drinkers lose their jobs or their driving licences or both* (not *their jobs and/or their driving licences*).

androgen *n* any of the steroids that promote the development of male sexual organs and certain male sexual characteristics [Greek *anēr* man + *-gen* (suffix) producing]

androgynous *adj* having both male and female characteristics [Greek *anēr* man + *gunē* woman]

android *n* a robot resembling a human being [Late Greek *androeidēs* manlike]

andrology (an-**drol**-la-jee) *n* the branch of medicine concerned with diseases and conditions specific to men [Greek *anēr* man + -LOGY] **andrologist** *n*

anecdote *n* a short amusing account of an incident [Greek *anekdotos* not published] **anecdotal** *adj*

anemia *n US* same as **anaemia**

anemometer *n* an instrument for recording wind speed

anemone (an-**nem**-on-ee) *n* a flowering plant with white, purple, or red flowers [Greek: windflower]

aneroid barometer *n* a device for measuring air pressure, consisting of a partially evacuated chamber, in which variations in pressure cause a pointer on the lid to move [Greek *a* not + *nēros* wet]

anesthesia *n US* same as **anaesthesia**

aneurysm *or* **aneurism** (an-new-riz-zum) *n med* a permanent swelling of a blood vessel [Greek *aneurunein* to dilate]

anew *adv* **1** once more **2** in a different way

angel *n* **1** a spiritual being believed to be an attendant or messenger of God **2** a conventional representation of an angel as a human being with wings **3** *informal* a person who is kind, pure, or beautiful **4** *informal* an investor in a theatrical production [Greek *angelos* messenger]

angel cake *or esp US* **angel food cake** *n* a very light sponge cake

angelfish *n, pl* **-fish** *or* **-fishes** a South American aquarium fish with large fins

angelic *adj* **1** very kind, pure, or beautiful **2** of or relating to angels **angelically** *adv*

angelica (an-**jell**-ik-a) *n* a plant whose candied stalks are used in cookery [Medieval Latin *(herba) angelica* angelic herb]

Angelus (**an**-jell-uss) *n RC Church* **1** prayers recited in the morning, at midday, and in the evening **2** the bell signalling the times of these prayers [Latin *Angelus domini nuntiavit Mariae* the angel of the Lord brought tidings to Mary]

anger *n* **1** a feeling of extreme annoyance or displeasure ▷ *vb* **2** to make (someone) angry [Old Norse *angr* grief]

angina (an-**jine**-a) *or* **angina pectoris** (**peck**-tor-riss) *n* a sudden intense pain in the chest caused by a momentary lack of adequate blood supply to the heart muscle [Greek *ankhonē* a strangling]

angle[1] *n* **1** the space between or shape formed by two straight lines or surfaces that meet **2** the divergence between two such lines or surfaces, measured in degrees **3** a recess or corner **4** point of view ▷ *vb* **-gling, -gled 5** to move in or place at an angle **6** to write (an article) from a particular point of view [Latin *angulus* corner]

angle[2] *vb* **-gling, -gled 1** to fish with a hook and line **2 angle for** to try to get by hinting: *he's just angling for sympathy* [Old English *angul* fish-hook]

angler *n* a person who fishes with a hook and line

Angles *pl n* a race from N Germany who settled in E and N England in the 5th and 6th centuries AD [Latin *Anglus* a person from Angul, Germany]

Anglican *adj* **1** of or relating to the Church of England ▷ *n* **2** a member of the Anglican Church [Latin *Anglicus* English, of the Angles] **Anglicanism** *n*

Anglicism *n* an expression or custom that is peculiar to the English

anglicize *or* **-cise** *vb* **-cizing, -cized** *or* **-cising, -cised** to make or become English in outlook or form

angling *n* the art or sport of fishing with a hook and line

Anglo *n, pl* **-glos 1** *US* a White inhabitant of the US who is not of Latin extraction **2** *Canad* an English-speaking Canadian

Anglo- *combining form* English or British: *the history of Anglo-German relations* [Medieval Latin *Anglii* the English]

Anglo-French *adj* **1** of England and France **2** of the Anglo-French language ▷ *n* **3** the Norman-French language of medieval England

Anglo-Indian *adj* **1** of England and India **2** denoting or relating to Anglo-Indians ▷ *n* **3** a person of mixed English and Indian descent

4 an English person who has lived for a long time in India
Anglo-Norman *adj* **1** of or relating to the Norman conquerors of England or their language ▹ *n* **2** a Norman inhabitant of England after 1066 **3** the Anglo-French language
Anglophile *n* a person who admires England or the English
Anglo-Saxon *n* **1** a member of any of the West Germanic tribes that settled in Britain from the 5th century AD **2** any White person whose native language is English **3** same as **Old English** **4** *informal* plain, blunt, and often rude English ▹ *adj* **5** of the Anglo-Saxons or the Old English language **6** of the White Protestant culture of Britain and the US
angora *n* **1** a variety of goat, cat, or rabbit with long silky hair **2** the hair of the angora goat or rabbit **3** cloth made from this hair [*Angora*, former name of Ankara, in Turkey]
Angostura Bitters *pl n trademark* a bitter tonic, used as a flavouring in alcoholic drinks [from *Angostura* in Venezuela]
angry *adj* **-grier, -griest** **1** feeling or expressing annoyance or rage **2** severely inflamed: *he had angry welts on his forehead* **3** dark and stormy: *angry waves* **angrily** *adv*

USAGE It was formerly considered incorrect to talk about being *angry at* a person, but this use is now acceptable.

angst *n* a feeling of anxiety [German]
angstrom *n* a unit of length equal to 10^{-10} metre, used to measure wavelengths [after Anders J. *Ångström*, Swedish physicist]
anguish *n* great mental pain [Latin *angustus* narrow]
anguished *adj* feeling or showing great mental pain: *anguished cries*
angular *adj* **1** lean and bony: *his angular face* **2** having an angle or angles **3** measured by an angle: *angular momentum* **angularity** *n*
anhydride *n chem* a substance that combines with water to form an acid
anhydrous *adj chem* containing no water [Greek *an* without + *hudōr* water]
anil *n* a West Indian shrub which is a source of indigo [Arabic *an-nīl*, the indigo]
aniline *n chem* a colourless oily poisonous liquid, obtained from coal tar and used for making dyes, plastics, and explosives
animal *n* **1** *zool* any living being that is capable of voluntary movement and possesses specialized sense organs **2** any living being other than a human being **3** any living being with four legs **4** a cruel or coarse person **5** *facetious* a person or thing: *there's no such animal* ▹ *adj* **6** of or from animals **7** of or relating to physical needs or desires [Latin *animalis* (adjective) living, breathing]
animalcule *n* a microscopic animal
animal husbandry *n* the science of breeding, rearing, and caring for farm animals
animalism *n* **1** preoccupation with physical matters; sensuality **2** the doctrine that human beings lack a spiritual nature
animality *n* **1** the animal instincts of human beings **2** the state of being an animal
animalize *or* **-ise** *vb* **-izing, -ized** *or* **-ising, -ised** to make (a person) brutal or sensual
animal magnetism *n* the quality of being sexually attractive
animal rights *pl n* the rights of animals to be protected from human abuse
animal spirits *pl n* outgoing and boisterous enthusiasm [from a vital force once supposed to be dispatched by the brain to all points of the body]
animate *vb* **-mating, -mated** **1** to give life to **2** to make lively **3** to produce (a story) as an animated cartoon ▹ *adj* **4** having life [Latin *anima* breath, spirit]
animated *adj* **1** interesting and lively **2** (of a cartoon) made by using animation **animatedly** *adv*
animated cartoon *n* a film produced by photographing a series of gradually changing drawings, which give the illusion of movement when the series is projected rapidly
animation *n* **1** the techniques used in the production of animated cartoons **2** an animated cartoon **3** liveliness and enthusiasm: *there's an animation in her that is new*
animator *n* a person who makes animated cartoons
animism *n* the belief that natural objects possess souls [Latin *anima* breath, spirit] **animist** *n, adj* **animistic** *adj*
animosity *n, pl* **-ties** a powerful dislike or hostility [see ANIMUS]
animus *n* intense dislike; hatred [Latin: mind, spirit]
anion (an-eye-on) *n* an ion with negative charge [Greek *ana-* up + *ienai* to go] **anionic** *adj*
anise (an-niss) *n* a Mediterranean plant with liquorice-flavoured seeds [Greek *anison*]
aniseed *n* the liquorice-flavoured seeds of the anise plant, used for flavouring
ankh *n* a T-shaped cross with a loop on the top, which symbolized eternal life in ancient Egypt [Egyptian *'nh* life, soul]
ankle *n* **1** the joint connecting the leg and the foot **2** the part of the leg just above the foot [Old Norse]
anklet *n* an ornamental chain worn round the ankle
ankylosis (ang-kill-**loh**-siss) *n* abnormal immobility of a joint, caused by a fibrous growth within the joint [Greek *ankuloun* to crook]
anna *n* a former Indian coin worth one sixteenth of a rupee [Hindi *ānā*]
annals *pl n* **1** yearly records of events **2** regular reports of the work of a society or other organization [Latin *(libri) annales* yearly (books)] **annalist** *n*
anneal *vb* to toughen (glass or metal) by heat treatment [Old English *onǣlan*]
annelid *n* a worm with a segmented body, such as the earthworm [Latin *anulus* ring]
annex *vb* **1** to seize (territory) by conquest or occupation **2** to take without permission **3** to join or add (something) to something larger [Latin *annectere* to attach to] **annexation** *n*
annexe *or esp US* **annex** *n* **1** an extension to a main building **2** a building used as an addition to a main one nearby

annihilate *vb* **-lating, -lated 1** to destroy (a place or a group of people) completely **2** *informal* to defeat totally in an argument or a contest [Latin *nihil* nothing] **annihilation** *n*

anniversary *n, pl* **-ries 1** the date on which an event, such as a wedding, occurred in some previous year **2** the celebration of this [Latin *annus* year + *vertere* to turn]

anno Domini *adv* in the year of our Lord

annotate *vb* **-tating, -tated** to add critical or explanatory notes to a written work [Latin *nota* mark] **annotation** *n*

announce *vb* **-nouncing, -nounced 1** to make known publicly **2** to proclaim **3** to declare the arrival of (a person) **4** to be a sign of: *snowdrops announced the arrival of spring* [Latin *annuntiare*] **announcement** *n*

announcer *n* a person who introduces programmes on radio or television

annoy *vb* **1** to irritate or displease **2** to harass sexually [Latin *in odio (esse)* (to be) hated] **annoyance** *n* **annoying** *adj*

annual *adj* **1** occurring or done once a year: *the union's annual conference* **2** lasting for a year: *the annual subscription* ▷ *n* **3** a plant that completes its life cycle in one year **4** a book published once every year [Latin *annus* year] **annually** *adv*

annualize *or* **-ise** *vb* **-izing, -ized** *or* **-ising, -ised** to calculate (a rate) for or as if for a year

annuity *n, pl* **-ties** a fixed sum payable at specified intervals over a period [Latin *annuus* annual]

annul *vb* **-nulling, -nulled** to declare (a contract or marriage) invalid [Latin *nullus* not any]

annular (an-new-lar) *adj* ring-shaped [Latin *anulus* ring]

annular eclipse *n* an eclipse of the sun in which a ring of sunlight can be seen surrounding the shadow of the moon

annulate (an-new-lit) *adj* having, composed of, or marked with rings [Latin *anulus* ring]

annulment *n* the formal declaration that a contract or marriage is invalid

Annunciation *n Christianity* **1 the Annunciation** the announcement by the angel Gabriel to the Virgin Mary of her conception of Christ **2** the festival commemorating this, on March 25 (Lady Day) [Latin *annuntiare* to announce]

anode *n electronics* the positive electrode in an electrolytic cell or in an electronic valve [Greek *anodos* a way up]

anodize *or* **-dise** *vb* **-dizing, -dized** *or* **-dising, -dised** *chem* to coat (a metal) with a protective oxide film by electrolysis

anodyne *n* **1** something that relieves pain or distress ▷ *adj* **2** bland or dull **3** capable of relieving pain or distress [Greek *an-* without + *odunē* pain]

anoint *vb* to smear with oil as a sign of consecration [Latin *inunguere*]

anointing of the sick *n RC Church* a sacrament in which a person who is dying is anointed by a priest

anomalous *adj* different from the normal or usual order or type [Greek *an-* not + *homalos* even]

anomaly (an-nom-a-lee) *n, pl* **-lies** something that deviates from the normal; an irregularity

anomie *or* **anomy** (an-oh-mee) *n sociol* lack of social or moral standards [Greek *a-* without + *nomos* law]

anon *adv old-fashioned or informal* soon: *you shall see him anon* [Old English *on āne* in one, that is, immediately]

anon. anonymous

anonymize *or* **-ise** *vb* **-izing, -ized** *or* **-ising, -ised** to organize in a way that preserves anonymity: *anonymized customer data*

anonymous *adj* **1** by someone whose name is unknown or withheld: *an anonymous letter* **2** having no known name: *an anonymous writer* **3** lacking distinguishing characteristics: *an anonymous little town* **4 Anonymous** of an organization that helps applicants who remain anonymous: *Alcoholics Anonymous* [Greek *an-* without + *onoma* name] **anonymity** *n*

anorak *n* **1** a waterproof hip-length jacket with a hood **2** *Brit informal* a socially inept person with a hobby considered to be boring [Greenland Inuktitut *ánorâq*]

anorexia *or* **anorexia nervosa** *n* a mental health condition characterized by fear of gaining weight and refusal to eat [Greek *an-* without + *orexis* appetite] **anorexic** *adj, n*

another *adj* **1** one more: *they don't have the right to demand another chance* **2** different: *you'll have to find another excuse* ▷ *pron* **3** one more: *help yourself to another* **4** a different one: *one way or another* [originally *an other*]

answer *vb* **1** to reply or respond (to) by word or act **2** to be responsible (to a person) **3** to reply correctly to (a question) **4** to respond or react: *a dog that answers to the name of Pugg* **5** to meet the requirements of **6** to give a defence of (a charge) ▷ *n* **7** a reply to a question, request, letter, or article **8** a solution to a problem **9** a reaction or response [Old English *andswaru*]

answerable *adj* **answerable for** *or* **to** responsible for or accountable to

answer back *vb* to reply rudely (to)

answering machine *n* a device for answering a telephone automatically and recording messages

ant *n* a small often wingless insect, living in highly organized colonies [Old English *ǣmette*]

antacid *chem* ▷ *n* **1** a substance used to treat acidity in the stomach ▷ *adj* **2** having the properties of this substance

antagonism *n* openly expressed hostility

antagonist *n* an opponent or adversary **antagonistic** *adj*

antagonize *or* **-nise** *vb* **-nizing, -nized** *or* **-nising, -nised** to arouse hostility in: *it was not prudent to antagonize a hired killer* [Greek *anti-* against + *agōn* contest]

antalkali (ant-alk-a-lie) *n chem* a substance that neutralizes alkalis

Antarctic *n* **1 the Antarctic** the area around the South Pole ▷ *adj* **2** of this region [Greek *antarktikos*]

Antarctic Circle *n* the imaginary circle around the earth at latitude 66° 32′ S

ante *n* **1** the stake put up before the deal in poker by the players **2** *informal* a sum of money representing a person's share **3 up the ante**

informal to increase the costs or risks involved in an action ▷ *vb* **-teing, -ted** *or* **-teed 4** to place (one's stake) in poker **5 ante up** *informal* to pay [Latin: before]

ante- *prefix* before in time or position: *antediluvian*; *antechamber* [Latin]

anteater *n* a mammal with a long snout used for eating termites

antecedent *n* **1** an event or circumstance that happens or exists before another **2** *grammar* a word or phrase to which a relative pronoun, such as *who*, refers **3 antecedents** a person's ancestors and past history ▷ *adj* **4** preceding in time or order [Latin *antecedere* to go before]

antechamber *n* an anteroom

antedate *vb* **-dating, -dated 1** to be or occur at an earlier date than **2** to give (something) a date that is earlier than the actual date

antediluvian *adj* **1** belonging to the ages before the biblical Flood **2** old-fashioned [Latin *ante-* before + *diluvium* flood]

antelope *n, pl* **-lopes** *or* **-lope** any of a group of graceful deerlike mammals of Africa and Asia, which have long legs and horns [Late Greek *antholops* a legendary beast]

antenatal *adj* before birth; during pregnancy: *an antenatal clinic*

antenna *n* **1** *pl* **-nae** one of a pair of mobile feelers on the heads of insects, lobsters, and certain other creatures **2** *pl* **-nas** an aerial: *TV antennas* [Latin: sail yard]

antepenultimate *adj* **1** third from last ▷ *n* **2** anything that is third from last

ante-post *adj Brit* (of a bet) placed before the runners in a race are confirmed

anterior *adj* **1** at or towards the front **2** earlier [Latin]

anteroom *n* a small room leading into a larger room, often used as a waiting room

anthem *n* **1** a song of loyalty or devotion: *a national anthem* **2** a piece of music for a choir, usually set to words from the Bible [Late Latin *antiphona* antiphon]

anther *n botany* the part of the stamen of a flower which contains the pollen [Greek *anthos* flower]

ant hill *n* a mound of soil built by ants around the entrance to their nest

anthology *n, pl* **-gies** a collection of poems or other literary pieces by various authors [Greek *anthos* flower + *legein* to collect] **anthologist** *n*

anthracite *n* a hard coal that burns slowly with little smoke or flame but intense heat [Greek *anthrax* coal]

anthrax *n* a dangerous infectious disease of cattle and sheep, which can be passed to humans [Greek: carbuncle]

anthropocentric *adj* regarding the human being as the most important factor in the universe [Greek *anthrōpos* human being + Latin *centrum* centre]

anthropoid *adj* **1** resembling a human being ▷ *n* **2** an ape, such as the chimpanzee, that resembles a human being

anthropology *n* the study of human origins, institutions, and beliefs [Greek *anthrōpos* human being + *logos* word] **anthropological** *adj* **anthropologist** *n*

anthropomorphism *n* the attribution of human form or personality to a god, animal, or object **anthropomorphic** *adj*

anthropomorphous *adj* shaped like a human being [Greek *anthrōpos* human being + *morphē* form]

anti *informal* ▷ *adj* **1** opposed to a party, policy, or attitude ▷ *n* **2** an opponent of a party, policy, or attitude

anti- *prefix* **1** against or opposed to: *antiwar* **2** opposite to: *anticlimax* **3** counteracting or neutralizing: *antifreeze* [Greek]

anti-aircraft *adj* for defence against aircraft attack

antiballistic missile *n* a missile designed to destroy a ballistic missile in flight

antibiotic *n* **1** a chemical substance capable of destroying bacteria ▷ *adj* **2** of or relating to antibiotics

antibody *n, pl* **-bodies** a protein produced in the blood which destroys bacteria

Antichrist *n* **1** *New Testament* the chief enemy of Christ **2** an enemy of Christ or Christianity

anticipate *vb* **-pating, -pated 1** to foresee and act in advance of: *he anticipated some probing questions* **2** to look forward to **3** to make use of (something, such as one's salary) before receiving it **4** to mention (part of a story) before its proper time [Latin *ante-* before + *capere* to take] **anticipatory** *adj*

> **USAGE** The use of *anticipate* to mean *expect* should be avoided.

anticipation *n* the act of anticipating; expectation, premonition, or foresight: *smiling in happy anticipation*

anticlerical *adj* opposed to the power and influence of the clergy in politics

anticlimax *n* a disappointing conclusion to a series of events **anticlimactic** *adj*

anticline *n geol* a fold of rock raised up into a broad arch so that the strata slope down on both sides

anticlockwise *adv, adj* in the opposite direction to the rotation of the hands of a clock

anticoagulant (an-tee-koh-**ag**-yew-lant) *n* a substance that prevents the clotting of blood

antics *pl n* absurd acts or postures [Italian *antico* something grotesque (from fantastic carvings found in ruins of ancient Rome)]

anticyclone *n meteorol* an area of moving air of high pressure in which the winds rotate outwards

antidepressant *n* **1** a drug used to treat depression ▷ *adj* **2** of or relating to such a drug

antidote *n* **1** *med* a substance that counteracts a poison **2** anything that counteracts a harmful condition: *exercise may be a good antidote to insomnia* [Greek *anti-* against + *didonai* to give]

antifreeze *n* a liquid added to water to lower its freezing point, used in the radiator of a motor vehicle to prevent freezing

antigen (**an**-tee-jen) *n* a substance, usually a toxin, that causes the body to produce antibodies [*anti(body)* + *-gen* (suffix) producing]

antihero *n, pl* **-roes** a central character in a novel, play, or film, who lacks the traditional heroic virtues

a

antihistamine *n* a drug that neutralizes the effects of histamine, used in the treatment of allergies
antiknock *n* a substance added to motor fuel to reduce knocking in the engine caused by too rapid combustion
antilogarithm *n maths* a number corresponding to a given logarithm
antimacassar *n* a cloth put over the back of a chair to prevent it getting dirty [*anti-* + *Macassar (oil)*]
antimatter *n physics* a form of matter composed of antiparticles
antimony (an-tim-mon-ee) *n chem* a silvery-white metallic element that is added to alloys to increase their strength. Symbol: **Sb** [Medieval Latin *antimonium*]
antinomy (an-tin-nom-ee) *n, pl* **-mies** contradiction between two laws or principles that are reasonable in themselves [Greek *anti-* against + *nomos* law]
antinovel *n* a type of prose fiction in which conventional elements of the novel are rejected
antinuclear *adj* opposed to nuclear weapons or nuclear power
antioxidant *n chem* a substance that slows down the process of oxidation
antiparticle *n physics* an elementary particle that has the same mass as its corresponding particle, but opposite charge and opposite magnetism
antipasto *n, pl* **-tos** an appetizer in an Italian meal [Italian: before food]
antipathy (an-tip-a-thee) *n* a feeling of strong dislike or hostility [Greek *anti-* against + *patheia* feeling] **antipathetic** *adj*
antipersonnel *adj* (of weapons or bombs) designed to be used against people rather than equipment
antiperspirant *n* a substance applied to the skin to reduce or prevent perspiration
antiphon *n* a hymn sung in alternate parts by two groups of singers [Greek *anti-* against + *phōnē* sound]
antipodes (an-tip-pod-deez) *pl n* **1** any two places that are situated diametrically opposite one another on the earth's surface **2 the Antipodes** *Brit* Australia and New Zealand [Greek plural of *antipous* having the feet opposite] **antipodean** *adj*
antipope *n* a pope set up in opposition to the one chosen by church laws
antipyretic *adj* **1** reducing fever ▷ *n* **2** a drug that reduces fever
antiquarian *adj* **1** collecting or dealing with antiquities or rare books ▷ *n* **2** an antiquary
antiquary *n, pl* **-quaries** a person who collects, deals in, or studies antiques or ancient works of art
antiquated *adj* obsolete or old-fashioned [Latin *antiquus* ancient]
antique *n* **1** a decorative object or piece of furniture, of an earlier period, that is valued for its beauty, workmanship, and age ▷ *adj* **2** made in an earlier period **3** *informal* old-fashioned [Latin *antiquus* ancient]
antiquity *n, pl* **-ties** **1** great age **2** the far distant past **3 antiquities** objects dating from ancient times
antiracism *n* the policy of challenging racism or promoting racial tolerance **antiracist** *n, adj*
antirrhinum *n* a two-lipped flower of various colours, such as the snapdragon [Greek *anti-* like, imitating + *rhis* nose]
antiscorbutic *adj* preventing or curing scurvy
anti-Semitic *adj* discriminating against Jews **anti-Semite** *n* **anti-Semitism** *n*
antiseptic *adj* **1** preventing infection by killing germs ▷ *n* **2** an antiseptic substance
antiserum *n* blood serum containing antibodies used to treat or provide immunity to a disease
antishake *adj* (of photographic equipment) reducing the blurring caused by movement of the person taking a photograph
antisocial *adj* **1** avoiding the company of other people **2** (of behaviour) annoying or harmful to other people
antistatic *adj* reducing the effects of static electricity
antitank *adj* (of weapons) designed to destroy military tanks
antithesis (an-tith-iss-iss) *n, pl* **-ses** (-seez) **1** the exact opposite **2** *rhetoric* the placing together of contrasting ideas or words to produce an effect of balance, such as *where gods command, mere mortals must obey* [Greek *anti-* against + *tithenai* to place] **antithetical** *adj*
antitoxin *n* an antibody that acts against a toxin **antitoxic** *adj*
antitrades *pl n* winds blowing in the opposite direction from and above the trade winds
antitrust *adj US, Austral & S African* (of laws) opposing business monopolies
antivirus *adj* **1** relating to software designed to protect computer files from viruses ▷ *n* **2** such a piece of software
antler *n* one of a pair of branched horns on the heads of male deer [Old French *antoillier*]
antonym *n* a word that means the opposite of another [Greek *anti-* opposite + *onoma* name]
antrum *n, pl* **-tra** *anatomy* a natural cavity, esp. in a bone [Latin: cave]
Anubis *n* an Egyptian god with a jackal's head
anus (ain-uss) *n* the opening at the end of the alimentary canal, through which faeces are discharged [Latin]
anvil *n* a heavy iron block on which metals are hammered into particular shapes [Old English *anfealt*]
anxiety *n, pl* **-ties** **1** a state of uneasiness about what may happen **2** eagerness: *she was uneasy with his mixture of diffidence and anxiety to please* **3** *psychol* a state of intense worry
anxious *adj* **1** worried and tense **2** causing anxiety: *he was anxious about the enormity of the task ahead* **3** intensely desiring: *both sides were anxious for a deal* [Latin *anxius*] **anxiously** *adv*
any *determiner* **1** one, some, or several, no matter how much or what kind: *the jar opener fits over the top of any bottle or jar; have you left me any?* **2** even the smallest amount or even one: *we can't answer any questions; don't give her any* **3** whatever or

whichever: *police may board any bus or train* **4** an indefinite or unlimited amount or number: *he would sign cheques for any amount of money* ▷ *adv* **5** to even the smallest extent: *the outcome wouldn't have been any different* [Old English *ǣnig*]

anybody *pron* same as **anyone**

anyhow *adv* same as **anyway**

anyone *pron* **1** any person: *is anyone there?* **2** a person of any importance: *is he anyone?*

anything *pron* **1** any object, event, or action whatever: *they'll do anything to please you* ▷ *adv* **2** in any way: *it is not a computer nor anything like a computer* **3 anything but** not at all: *the result is anything but simple*

anyway *adv* **1** at any rate; nevertheless **2** in any manner **3** carelessly

anywhere *adv* **1** in, at, or to any place **2 get anywhere** to be successful: *we will not get anywhere by being negative*

Anzac *n* (in the First World War) a soldier serving with the Australian and New Zealand Army Corps

Anzac biscuit *n Austral & NZ* a sweet biscuit containing oats, coconut, and syrup

Anzac Day April 25, a public holiday in Australia and New Zealand commemorating the Anzac landing at Gallipoli in 1915

AOB (on the agenda for a meeting) any other business

aorta (eh-**or**-ta) *n* the main artery of the body, which carries oxygen-rich blood from the heart [Greek *aortē* something lifted]

apace *adv literary* quickly: *repairs to the grid continued apace*

Apache *n, pl* **Apaches** *or* **Apache** a member of a Native American people of the southwestern US and N Mexico [Mexican Spanish]

apart *adj, adv* **1** to or in pieces: *he took a couple of cars apart and rebuilt them* **2** separate in time, place, or position: *my father and myself stood slightly apart from them* **3** individual or distinct: *a nation apart* **4** not being taken into account: *early timing difficulties apart, they encountered few problems* **5 apart from** other than: *apart from searching the house there is little more we can do* [Old French *a part* at (the) side]

apartheid *n* (formerly) the official government policy of racial segregation in South Africa [Afrikaans *apart* + *-heid* -hood]

apartment *n* **1** any room in a building, usually one of several forming a suite, used as living accommodation **2** *chiefly US & Canad* a set of rooms forming a home within a building usually incorporating other similar homes. Also called (Brit): **flat** [French *appartement*]

apathy *n* lack of interest or enthusiasm [Greek *a-* without + *pathos* feeling] **apathetic** *adj*

apatosaurus *n* a very large plant-eating four-footed dinosaur that had a long neck and long tail [Greek *apatē* deceit + *sauros* lizard]

ape *n* **1** an animal, such as a chimpanzee or gorilla, which is closely related to human beings and the monkeys, and which has no tail **2** a stupid, clumsy, or ugly man ▷ *vb* **aping, aped 3** to imitate [Old English *apa*] **apelike** *adj*

apeman *n, pl* **-men** an extinct primate thought to have been the forerunner of true humans

aperient (ap-**peer**-ee-ent) *med* ▷ *adj* **1** having a mild laxative effect ▷ *n* **2** a mild laxative [Latin *aperire* to open]

aperitif (ap-per-rit-**teef**) *n* an alcoholic drink taken before a meal [French]

aperture *n* **1** a hole or opening **2** an opening in a camera or telescope that controls the amount of light entering it [Latin *aperire* to open]

apex *n* the highest point [Latin: point]

APEX Advance Purchase Excursion: a reduced fare for journeys by air or rail booked a specified period in advance

aphasia *n* a disorder of the central nervous system that affects the ability to use and understand words [Greek *a-* not + *phanai* to speak]

aphelion (ap-**heel**-lee-on) *n, pl* **-lia** (-lee-a) *astron* the point in the orbit of a planet or comet when it is farthest from the sun [Greek *apo-* from + *hēlios* sun]

aphid (**eh**-fid) *or* **aphis** (**eh**-fiss) *n, pl* **aphids** *or* **aphides** (**eh**-fid-deez) a small insect which feeds by sucking the juices from plants [New Latin]

aphorism *n* a short clever saying expressing a general truth [Greek *aphorizein* to define]

aphrodisiac (af-roh-**diz**-zee-ak) *n* **1** a substance that arouses sexual desire ▷ *adj* **2** arousing sexual desire [Greek *aphrodisios* belonging to *Aphrodite*, goddess of love]

Aphrodite *n Greek myth* the goddess of love

apiary (**ape**-yar-ee) *n, pl* **-aries** a place where bees are kept [Latin *apis* bee] **apiarist** *n*

apical (**ape**-ik-kl) *adj* of, at, or being an apex

apiculture *n* the breeding and care of bees [Latin *apis* bee + CULTURE] **apiculturist** *n*

apiece *adv* each: *they had another cocktail apiece and then went down to dinner*

apish (**ape**-ish) *adj* **1** stupid or foolish **2** resembling an ape

aplenty *adj, adv* in plenty: *a match with goals aplenty*

aplomb (ap-**plom**) *n* calm self-possession [French: uprightness]

apocalypse *n* **1** the end of the world **2** an event of great destructive violence [Greek *apo-* away + *kaluptein* to hide] **apocalyptic** *adj*

Apocalypse *n* **the Apocalypse** *Bible* the Book of Revelation, the last book of the New Testament

Apocrypha (ap-**pok**-rif-fa) *pl n* **the Apocrypha** the 14 books included as an appendix to the Old Testament, which are not accepted as part of the Hebrew scriptures [Late Latin *apocrypha (scripta)* hidden (writings), from Greek *apokruptein* to hide away]

apocryphal *adj* of questionable authenticity: *the paranoid and clearly apocryphal story*

apogee (**ap**-oh-jee) *n* **1** *astron* the point in its orbit around the earth when the moon or a satellite is farthest from the earth **2** the highest point: *the concept found its apogee in Renaissance Italy* [Greek *apogaios* away from the earth]

apolitical *adj* not concerned with political matters

Apollo *n classical myth* the god of the sun, music, and medicine

apologetic *adj* showing or expressing regret **apologetically** *adv*

apologetics *n* the branch of theology concerned with the reasoned defence of Christianity
apologia *n* a formal written defence of a cause
apologist *n* a person who offers a formal defence of a cause
apologize *or* **-gise** *vb* **-gizing, -gized** *or* **-gising, -gised** to say that one is sorry for some wrongdoing
apology *n, pl* **-gies 1** an expression of regret for some wrongdoing **2** same as **apologia 3 an apology for** a poor example of: *an apology for a man* [Greek *apologia* a verbal defence, speech]
apophthegm (ap-poth-em) *n* a short clever saying expressing a general truth [Greek *apophthengesthai* to speak frankly]
apoplectic *adj* **1** of apoplexy **2** *informal* furious
apoplexy *n med* a stroke [Greek *apoplēssein* to cripple by a stroke]
apostasy (ap-**poss**-stass-ee) *n, pl* **-sies** abandonment of one's religious faith, political party, or cause [Greek *apostasis* desertion]
apostate *n* **1** a person who has abandoned his or her religion, political party, or cause ▷ *adj* **2** guilty of apostasy
a posteriori (**eh** poss-steer-ee-**or**-rye) *adj logic* involving reasoning from effect to cause [Latin: from the latter]
apostle *n* **1** *Christianity* one of the twelve disciples chosen by Christ to preach his gospel **2** an ardent supporter of a cause or movement [Greek *apostolos* a messenger]
apostolic (ap-poss-**stoll**-ik) *adj* **1** of or relating to the Apostles or their teachings **2** of or relating to the pope
Apostolic See *n* the see of the pope, at Rome
apostrophe¹ (ap-**poss**-trof-fee) *n* the punctuation mark (') used to indicate the omission of a letter or letters, such as *he's* for *he has* or *he is*, and to form the possessive, as in *John's father* [Greek *apostrephein* to turn away]
apostrophe² *n rhetoric* a digression from a speech to address an imaginary or absent person or thing [Greek: a turning away]
apostrophize *or* **-phise** *vb* **-phizing, -phized** *or* **-phising, -phised** *rhetoric* to address an apostrophe to
apothecary *n, pl* **-caries** *old-fashioned* a chemist [Late Latin *apothecarius* warehouseman]
apotheosis (ap-poth-ee-**oh**-siss) *n, pl* **-ses** (-seez) **1** a perfect example: *it was the apotheosis of elitism* **2** elevation to the rank of a god [Greek]
app *n* a computer program designed for a particular purpose, esp. one for use on a mobile device
appal *or US* **appall** *vb* **-palling, -palled** to fill with horror; terrify [Old French *appalir* to turn pale]
appalling *adj* **1** causing dismay, horror, or revulsion **2** very bad **appallingly** *adv*
apparatus *n* **1** a collection of equipment used for a particular purpose **2** any complicated device, system, or organization: *the whole apparatus of law enforcement* [Latin]
apparel (ap-**par**-rel) *n old-fashioned* clothing [Latin *parare* to prepare]
apparent *adj* **1** readily seen or understood; obvious **2** seeming as opposed to real: *he frowned in apparent bewilderment* [Latin *apparere* to appear]
apparently *adv*
apparition *n* a ghost or ghostlike figure [Latin *apparere* to appear]
appeal *vb* **1** to make an earnest request **2 appeal to** to attract, please, or interest **3** *law* to apply to a higher court to review (a case or issue decided by a lower court) **4** to resort to a higher authority to change a decision **5** to call on in support of an earnest request: *he appealed for volunteers to help in relief work* **6** *cricket* to request the umpire to declare a batsman out ▷ *n* **7** an earnest request for money or help **8** the power to attract, please, or interest people **9** *law* a request for a review of a lower court's decision by a higher court **10** an application to a higher authority to change a decision that has been made **11** *cricket* a request to the umpire to declare the batsman out [Latin *appellare* to entreat]
appealing *adj* attractive or pleasing
appear *vb* **1** to come into sight **2** to seem: *it appears that no one survived the crash* **3** to come into existence: *a rash and small sores appeared around the shoulder and neck* **4** to perform: *she hadn't appeared in a film for almost fifty years* **5** to be present in court before a magistrate or judge: *two men have appeared in court in London charged with conspiracy* **6** to be published or become available: *both books appeared in 1934* [Latin *apparere*]
appearance *n* **1** a sudden or unexpected arrival of someone or something at a place **2** the introduction or invention of something: *the appearance of smartphones* **3** an act or instance of appearing: *it will be her fiftieth appearance for her country* **4** the way a person or thing looks: *I spotted a man of extraordinary appearance* **5 keep up appearances** to maintain the public impression of wellbeing or normality **6 put in an appearance** to attend an event briefly **7 to all appearances** apparently: *to all appearances they seemed enthralled by what she was saying*
appease *vb* **-peasing, -peased 1** to pacify (someone) by yielding to his or her demands **2** to satisfy or relieve (a feeling) [Old French *apaisier*]
appeasement *n*
appellant *law* ▷ *n* **1** a person who appeals to a higher court to review the decision of a lower court ▷ *adj* **2** same as **appellate**
appellate (ap-**pell**-it) *adj law* **1** of appeals **2** (of a tribunal) having the power to review appeals
appellation *n formal* a name or title
append *vb formal* to add as a supplement: *a series of notes appended to his translation of the poems* [Latin *pendere* to hang]
appendage *n* a secondary part attached to a main part
appendicectomy *or esp US, Canad & Austral* **appendectomy** *n, pl* **-mies** surgical removal of the appendix [*appendix* + Greek *tomē* a cutting]
appendicitis *n* inflammation of the appendix, causing abdominal pain
appendix (ap-**pen**-dix) *n, pl* **-dices** (-diss-seez) *or* **-dixes 1** separate additional material at the end of a book **2** *anatomy* a short thin tube, closed at one end and attached to the large intestine at the other end [Latin]

appertain *vb* **appertain to** to belong to, relate to, or be connected with [Latin *ad-* to + *pertinere* to pertain]

appetence *or* **appetency** *n, pl* **-tences** *or* **-tencies** a craving or desire [Latin *appetentia*]

appetite *n* **1** a desire for food or drink **2** a liking or willingness: *he had an insatiable appetite for publicity* [Latin *appetere* to desire ardently]

appetizer *or* **-iser** *n* a small amount of food or drink taken at the start of a meal to stimulate the appetite

appetizing *or* **-ising** *adj* stimulating the appetite; looking or smelling delicious

applaud *vb* **1** to show approval of by clapping one's hands **2** to express approval of: *we applaud her determination and ambition* [Latin *applaudere*]

applause *n* appreciation shown by clapping one's hands

apple *n* **1** a round firm fruit with red, yellow, or green skin and crisp whitish flesh, that grows on trees **2 apple of one's eye** a person that one loves very much [Old English *æppel*]

apple-pie order *n* **in apple-pie order** *informal* very tidy

applet *n* a computing program that runs within a page on the internet [*app(lication program)* + *-let* small or lesser]

appliance *n* a machine or device that has a specific function

applicable *adj* appropriate or relevant

applicant *n* a person who applies for something, such as a job or grant

application *n* **1** a formal request, for example for a job **2** the act of applying something to a particular use: *you can make practical application of this knowledge to everyday living* **3** concentrated effort: *success would depend on their talent and application* **4** the act of putting something, such as a lotion or paint, onto a surface **5** Also called: **application programme** a computer program designed for a particular purpose

applicator *n* a device for applying cosmetics, medication, or some other substance

applied *adj* put to practical use: *applied mathematics*

appliqué (ap-**plee**-kay) *n* a kind of decoration in which one material is cut out and sewn or fixed onto another [French: applied]

apply *vb* **-plies, -plying, -plied 1** to make a formal request for something, such as a job or a loan **2** to put to practical use: *he applied his calligrapher's skill* **3** to put onto a surface: *the hand lotion should be applied whenever possible throughout the day* **4** to be relevant or appropriate: *he had been involved in research applied to flying wing aircraft* **5 apply oneself** to concentrate one's efforts or faculties [Latin *applicare* to attach to]

appoint *vb* **1** to assign officially to a job or position **2** to fix or decide (a time or place for an event) **3** to equip or furnish: *it was a beautifully appointed room with rows and rows of books* [Old French *apointer* to put into a good state] **appointee** *n*

appointment *n* **1** an arrangement to meet a person **2** the act of placing someone in a job or position **3** the person appointed **4** the job or position to which a person is appointed **5 appointments** fixtures or fittings

apportion *vb* to divide out in shares

apposite *adj* suitable or appropriate: *an apposite saying* [Latin *ad-* near + *ponere* to put]

apposition *n* a grammatical construction in which a noun or group of words is placed after another to modify its meaning, for example *my friend the mayor*

appraisal *n* an assessment of the worth or quality of a person or thing

appraise *vb* **-praising, -praised** to assess the worth, value, or quality of [Old French *aprisier*]

> **USAGE** *Appraise* is sometimes wrongly used where *apprise* is meant: *they had been apprised* (not *appraised*) *of my arrival*.

appreciable *adj* enough to be noticed; significant **appreciably** *adv*

appreciate *vb* **-ating, -ated 1** to value highly: *we appreciate his music but can't afford £400 a seat* **2** to be aware of and understand: *I can fully appreciate how desperate you must feel* **3** to feel grateful for: *we do appreciate all you do for us* **4** to increase in value [Latin *pretium* price]

appreciation *n* **1** gratitude **2** awareness and understanding of a problem or difficulty **3** sensitive recognition of good qualities, as in art **4** an increase in value

appreciative *adj* feeling or expressing appreciation **appreciatively** *adv*

apprehend *vb* **1** to arrest and take into custody **2** to grasp (something) mentally; understand [Latin *apprehendere* to lay hold of]

apprehension *n* **1** anxiety or dread **2** the act of arresting **3** understanding

apprehensive *adj* fearful or anxious about the future

apprentice *n* **1** someone who works for a skilled person for a fixed period in order to learn his or her trade ▹ *vb* **-ticing, -ticed 2** to take or place as an apprentice [Old French *aprendre* to learn] **apprenticeship** *n*

apprise *or* **-prize** *vb* **-prising, -prised** *or* **-prizing, -prized** to make aware: *I needed to apprise the students of the dangers that may be involved* [French *apprendre* to teach; learn]

> **USAGE** See at **appraise**.

appro *n* **on appro** *informal* on approval

approach *vb* **1** to come close or closer to **2** to make a proposal or suggestion to **3** to begin to deal with (a matter) ▹ *n* **4** the act of coming close or closer **5** a proposal or suggestion made to a person **6** the way or means of reaching a place; access **7** a way of dealing with a matter **8** an approximation **9** the course followed by an aircraft preparing for landing [Latin *ad-* to + *prope* near] **approachable** *adj*

approach road *n* a smaller road leading into a major road

approbation *n* approval

appropriate *adj* **1** right or suitable ▹ *vb* **-ating, -ated 2** to take for one's own use without permission **3** to put (money) aside for a particular purpose [Latin *ad-* to + *proprius* one's own] **appropriately** *adv*

appropriation *n* **1** the act of putting money aside for a particular purpose **2** money put aside for a particular purpose

a

approval *n* **1** consent **2** a favourable opinion **3 on approval** (of articles for sale) with an option to be returned without payment if unsatisfactory: *each volume in the collection will be sent to you on approval*

approve *vb* **-proving, -proved 1 approve of** to consider fair, good, or right **2** to authorize or agree to [Latin *approbare*]

approx. approximate or approximately

approximate *adj* **1** almost but not quite exact ▷ *vb* **-mating, -mated 2 approximate to A** to come close to **B** to be almost the same as [Latin *ad-* to + *proximus* nearest] **approximately** *adv* **approximation** *n*

appurtenances *pl n* minor or additional features or possessions [Old French *apartenance* secondary thing]

APR annual percentage rate

Apr. April

après-ski (ap-ray-**skee**) *n* social activities after a day's skiing

apricot *n* **1** a yellowish-orange juicy fruit which resembles a small peach ▷ *adj* **2** yellowish-orange [Latin *praecox* early-ripening]

April *n* the fourth month of the year [Latin *Aprilis*]

April fool *n* a victim of a practical joke played on April 1 (**April Fools' Day** *or* **All Fools' Day**)

a priori (eh pry-or-**rye**) *adj logic* involving reasoning from cause to effect [Latin: from the previous]

apron *n* **1** a garment worn over the front of the body to protect one's clothes **2** a hard-surfaced area at an airport or hangar for manoeuvring and loading aircraft **3** the part of a stage extending in front of the curtain **4 tied to someone's apron strings** dependent on or dominated by someone [Old French *naperon* little cloth]

apropos (ap-prop-**poh**) *adj* **1** appropriate ▷ *adv* **2** by the way; incidentally **3 apropos of** with regard to [French *à propos* to the purpose]

apse *n* an arched or domed recess at the east end of a church [Greek *apsis* a fitting together]

apsis (**ap**-siss) *n, pl* **apsides** (ap-**sid**-deez) *astron* either of two points lying at the extremities of the elliptical orbit of a planet or satellite [see APSE]

apt *adj* **1** having a specified tendency: *they are apt to bend the rules* **2** suitable or appropriate **3** quick to learn: *she was turning out to be a more apt pupil than he had expected* [Latin *aptus* fitting] **aptly** *adv* **aptness** *n*

apteryx *n* same as **kiwi** (sense 1) [Greek *a-* without + *pteron* wing]

aptitude *n* natural tendency or ability

aqua *adj* short for **aquamarine** [Latin: water]

aqua fortis *n obsolete* nitric acid [Latin: strong water]

aqualung *n* an apparatus for breathing underwater, consisting of a mouthpiece attached to air cylinders

aquamarine *n* **1** a clear greenish-blue gemstone ▷ *adj* **2** greenish-blue [Latin *aqua marina* sea water]

aquaplane *n* **1** a board on which a person stands to be towed by a motorboat for sport ▷ *vb* **-planing, -planed 2** to ride on an aquaplane **3** (of a motor vehicle) to skim uncontrollably on a thin film of water

aqua regia (ak-wa **reej**-ya) *n* a mixture of nitric acid and hydrochloric acid [New Latin: royal water; referring to its use in dissolving gold, the royal metal]

aquarium *n, pl* **aquariums** *or* **aquaria 1** a tank in which fish and other underwater creatures are kept **2** a building containing such tanks [Latin *aquarius* relating to water]

Aquarius *n astrol* the eleventh sign of the zodiac: the Water Carrier [Latin]

aquatic *adj* **1** growing or living in water **2** *sport* performed in or on water ▷ *n* **3** an aquatic animal or plant **4 aquatics** water sports [Latin *aqua* water]

aquatint *n* a print like a watercolour, produced by etching copper with acid [Italian *acqua tinta* dyed water]

aqua vitae (ak-wa **vee**-tie) *n old-fashioned* brandy [Medieval Latin: water of life]

aqueduct *n* a structure, often a bridge, that carries water across a valley or river [Latin *aqua* water + *ducere* to convey]

aqueous *adj* **1** of, like, or containing water **2** produced by the action of water [Latin *aqua* water]

aqueous humour *n physiol* the watery fluid in the eyeball, between the cornea and the lens

aquifer *n* a deposit of rock, such as sandstone, containing water that can be used to supply wells [Latin *aqua* water + *ferre* to carry]

aquiline *adj* **1** (of a nose) curved like an eagle's beak **2** of or like an eagle [Latin *aquila* eagle]

Ar *chem* argon

AR Arkansas

Arab *n* **1** a member of a Semitic people originally from Arabia ▷ *adj* **2** of the Arabs [Arabic *'Arab*]

arabesque (ar-ab-**besk**) *n* **1** a ballet position in which one leg is raised behind and the arms are extended **2** *arts* an elaborate design of intertwined leaves, flowers, and scrolls **3** an ornate piece of music [Italian *arabesco* in the Arabic style]

Arabian *adj* **1** of Arabia or the Arabs ▷ *n* **2** same as **Arab**

Arabic *n* **1** the language of the Arabs ▷ *adj* **2** of this language, the Arabs, or Arabia

Arabic numerals *pl n* the symbols 1, 2, 3, 4, 5, 6, 7, 8, 9, 0, used to represent numbers

arable *adj* (of land) suitable for growing crops on [Latin *arare* to plough]

arachnid (ar-**rak**-nid) *n* an eight-legged insect-like creature, such as a spider, scorpion, or tick [Greek *arakhnē* spider]

arak *n* same as **arrack**

Aramaic *n* an ancient Semitic language spoken in parts of Syria and the Lebanon

Aran *adj* (of knitwear) knitted in a complicated pattern traditional to the Aran Islands off the west coast of Ireland

arbiter *n* **1** a person empowered to judge in a dispute **2** a person with influential opinions about something: *the customer must be the ultimate arbiter of quality*

arbitrary *adj* **1** not done according to any plan or for any particular reason **2** without

consideration for the wishes of others: *the arbitrary power of the king* **arbitrarily** *adv*
arbitrate *vb* **-trating, -trated** to settle (a dispute) by arbitration [Latin *arbitrari* to give judgment] **arbitrator** *n*
arbitration *n* the hearing and settlement of a dispute by an impartial referee chosen by both sides
arbor[1] *n US* same as **arbour**
arbor[2] *n* a revolving shaft or axle in a machine [Latin: tree]
arboreal (ahr-**bore**-ee-al) *adj* **1** of or resembling a tree **2** living in or among trees
arboretum (ahr-bore-**ee**-tum) *n, pl* **-ta** (-ta) a botanical garden where rare trees or shrubs are cultivated [Latin *arbor* tree]
arboriculture *n* the cultivation of trees or shrubs [Latin *arbor* tree + CULTURE]
arbor vitae (ahr-bore **vee**-tie) *n* an evergreen tree [New Latin: tree of life]
arbour *or US* **arbor** *n* a shelter in a garden shaded by trees or climbing plants [Latin *herba* grass]
arbutus (ar-**byew**-tuss) *n* an evergreen shrub with berries like strawberries [Latin]
arc *n* **1** something curved in shape **2** *maths* a section of a circle or other curve **3** *electronics* a stream of very bright light that forms when an electric current flows across a small gap between two electrodes ▷ *vb* **4** to form an arc [Latin *arcus* bow, arch]
ARC AIDS-related complex: relatively mild symptoms suffered in the early stages of infection with the AIDS virus
arcade *n* **1** a covered passageway lined with shops **2** a set of arches and their supporting columns [Latin *arcus* bow, arch]
Arcadian *literary* ▷ *adj* **1** rural, in an idealized way ▷ *n* **2** a person who leads a quiet simple country life [*Arcadia*, rural district of Ancient Greece]
arcane *adj* very mysterious [Latin *arcanus* secret]
arch[1] *n* **1** a curved structure that spans an opening or supports a bridge or roof **2** something curved **3** the curved lower part of the foot ▷ *vb* **4** to form an arch [Latin *arcus* bow, arc]
arch[2] *adj* **1** knowing or superior **2** coyly playful: *she gave him an arch smile* [independent use of ARCH-] **archly** *adv*
arch- *or* **archi-** *combining form* chief or principal: *archbishop; archenemy* [Greek *arkhein* to rule]
archaeobotany *n* the study of plant remains found at archaeological sites **archaeobotanist** *n*
archaeology *or* **archeology** *n* the study of ancient cultures by the scientific analysis of physical remains [Greek *arkhaiologia* study of what is ancient] **archaeological** *or* **archeological** *adj* **archaeologist** *or* **archeologist** *n*
archaeopteryx *n* an extinct primitive bird with teeth, a long tail, and well-developed wings [Greek *arkhaios* ancient + *pterux* winged creature]
archaeozoology *n* the study of animal remains found at archaeological sites **archaeozoologist** *n*
archaic (ark-**kay**-ik) *adj* **1** of a much earlier period **2** out of date or old-fashioned **3** (of a word or phrase) no longer in everyday use [Greek *arkhē* beginning] **archaically** *adv*
archaism (**ark**-kay-iz-zum) *n* an archaic word or style **archaistic** *adj*
archangel (**ark**-ain-jell) *n* an angel of the highest rank
archbishop *n* a bishop of the highest rank
archbishopric *n* the rank, office, or diocese of an archbishop
archdeacon *n* a church official ranking just below a bishop **archdeaconry** *n*
archdiocese *n* the diocese of an archbishop
archduchess *n* **1** a woman who holds the rank of archduke **2** the wife or widow of an archduke
archduchy *n, pl* **-duchies** the territory ruled by an archduke or archduchess
archduke *n* a duke of high rank, esp. one from Austria
archenemy *n, pl* **-mies** a chief enemy
archeology *n* same as **archaeology**
archer *n* a person who shoots with a bow and arrow [Latin *arcus* bow]
archery *n* the art or sport of shooting with a bow and arrow
archetype (**ark**-ee-type) *n* **1** a perfect or typical specimen **2** an original model; prototype [Greek *arkhetupos* first-moulded] **archetypal** *adj*
archidiaconal (ark-ee-die-**ak**-on-al) *adj* of an archdeacon or his office
archiepiscopal (ark-ee-ip-**piss**-kop-al) *adj* of an archbishop or his office
Archimedes' principle (ark-ee-**mee**-deez) *n physics* the principle that the apparent loss in weight of an object immersed in a fluid is equal to the weight of the displaced fluid [after *Archimedes*, Greek mathematician & physicist]
archipelago (ark-ee-**pel**-a-go) *n, pl* **-gos** **1** a group of islands **2** a sea full of small islands [Greek *arkhi-* chief + *pelagos* sea]
architect *n* **1** a person qualified to design and supervise the construction of buildings **2** any planner or creator: *you will be the architect of your own future* [Greek *arkhi-* chief + *tektōn* workman]
architecture *n* **1** the style in which a building is designed and built: *Gothic architecture* **2** the science of designing and constructing buildings **3** the structure or design of anything: *computer architecture* **architectural** *adj*
architrave (**ark**-ee-trave) *n archit* **1** a beam that rests on top of columns **2** a moulding around a doorway or window opening [Italian, from *arch-* + *trave* beam]
archive (**ark**-ive) *n* **1** a place where records or documents are kept **2** **archives** a collection of records or documents **3** *computers* data moved to a disk or directory for long-term storage ▷ *vb* **4** to store in an archive
archivist (**ark**-iv-ist) *n* a person in charge of archives
archway *n* a passageway under an arch
arctic *adj informal* very cold; freezing
Arctic *n* **1** **the Arctic** the area around the North Pole ▷ *adj* **2** of this region [Greek *arktikos* northern, literally: pertaining to (the constellation of) the Bear]
Arctic Circle *n* the imaginary circle around the earth at latitude 66° 32′ N

arctic hare *n* a large hare of the Canadian Arctic whose fur turns white in winter
arctic willow *n* a low-growing shrub of the Canadian Arctic
arc welding *n* a technique in which metal is welded by heat generated by an electric arc
ardent *adj* **1** passionate **2** intensely enthusiastic [Latin *ardere* to burn] **ardently** *adv*
ardour *or US* **ardor** *n* **1** emotional warmth; passion **2** intense enthusiasm [Latin *ardere* to burn]
arduous *adj* difficult to accomplish; strenuous [Latin *arduus* steep, difficult]
are[1] *vb* the plural form of the present tense of **be**: used as the singular form with *you* [Old English *aron*]
are[2] *n* a unit of measure equal to one hundred square metres [Latin *area* piece of ground]
area *n* **1** a section, part, or region **2** a part having a specified function: *reception area* **3** the size of a two-dimensional surface **4** a subject field: *the area of literature* **5** a sunken area giving access to a basement **6** any flat, curved, or irregular expanse of a surface **7** range or scope [Latin: level ground, threshing floor]
area school *n NZ* a school in a rural area that includes primary and post-primary classes
arena *n* **1** a seated enclosure where sports events take place **2** the area of an ancient Roman amphitheatre where gladiators fought **3** a sphere of intense activity: *the political arena* [Latin *harena* sand]
aren't are not
areola *n, pl* **-lae** *or* **-las** a small circular area, such as the coloured ring around the human nipple [Latin]
Ares *n Greek myth* the god of war
arête *n* a sharp ridge separating valleys [French: fishbone]
Argentine *or* **Argentinian** *adj* **1** of Argentina ▷ *n* **2** a person from Argentina
argon *n chem* an unreactive odourless element of the rare gas series, forming almost 1 per cent of the atmosphere. Symbol: **Ar** [Greek *argos* inactive]
argosy *n, pl* **-sies** *old-fashioned or poetic* a large merchant ship, or a fleet of such ships [Italian *Ragusea (nave)* (ship) of Ragusa, a former name for Dubrovnik]
argot (ahr-go) *n* slang or jargon peculiar to a particular group [French]
argue *vb* **-guing, -gued 1** to try to prove by presenting reasons **2** to debate **3** to quarrel **4** to persuade: *we argued her out of going* **5** to suggest: *her looks argue despair* [Latin *arguere* to make clear, accuse] **arguable** *adj* **arguably** *adv*
argument *n* **1** a quarrel **2** a discussion **3** a point presented to support or oppose a proposition
argumentation *n* the process of reasoning methodically
argumentative *adj* likely to argue
argy-bargy *or* **argie-bargie** *n, pl* **-bargies** *Brit informal* a squabbling argument [Scots]
aria (ah-ree-a) *n* an elaborate song for solo voice in an opera or choral work [Italian]
arid *adj* **1** having little or no rain **2** uninteresting [Latin *aridus*] **aridity** *n*
Aries *n astrol* the first sign of the zodiac: the Ram [Latin]
aright *adv* correctly or properly
arise *vb* **arising, arose, arisen 1** to come into being: *the opportunity for action did not arise* **2** to come into notice: *people can seek answers to their problems as and when they arise* **3 arise from** to happen as a result of **4** *old-fashioned* to get or stand up [Old English *ārīsan*]
aristocracy *n, pl* **-cies 1** a class of people of high social rank **2** government by this class **3** a group of people considered to be outstanding in a particular sphere of activity [Greek *aristos* best + *kratein* to rule]
aristocrat *n* a member of the aristocracy
aristocratic *adj* **1** of the aristocracy **2** grand or elegant
Aristotelian (ar-riss-tot-**eel**-ee-an) *adj* of Aristotle, 4th-century BC Greek philosopher, or his philosophy
arithmetic *n* **1** the branch of mathematics concerned with numerical calculations, such as addition, subtraction, multiplication, and division **2** calculations involving numerical operations **3** knowledge of or skill in arithmetic: *even simple arithmetic was beyond him* ▷ *adj also* **arithmetical 4** of or using arithmetic [Greek *arithmos* number] **arithmetically** *adv* **arithmetician** *n*
arithmetic mean *n* the average value of a set of terms, expressed as their sum divided by their number: *the arithmetic mean of 3, 4, and 8 is 5*
arithmetic progression *n* a sequence, each term of which differs from the preceding term by a constant amount, such as 3, 6, 9, 12
ark *n Bible* the boat built by Noah, which survived the Flood [Latin *arca* box, chest]
Ark *n Judaism* **1** Also called: **Holy Ark** the cupboard in a synagogue in which the Torah scrolls are kept **2** Also called: **Ark of the Covenant** a chest containing the laws of the Jewish religion, regarded as the most sacred symbol of God's presence among the Hebrew people
arm[1] *n* **1** (in humans, apes, and monkeys) either of the upper limbs from the shoulder to the wrist **2** the sleeve of a garment **3** the side of a chair on which one's arm can rest **4** a subdivision or section of an organization: *the London-based arm of a Swiss bank* **5** something resembling an arm in appearance or function: *the arm of a record player* **6** power or authority: *the long arm of the law* **7 arm in arm** with arms linked **8 at arm's length** at a distance **9 with open arms** with warmth and hospitality [Old English]
arm[2] *vb* **1** to supply with weapons **2** to prepare (an explosive device) for use **3** to provide (a person or thing) with something that strengthens, or protects: *you will be armed with all the information you will ever need* ▷ See also **arms** [Latin *arma* arms, equipment] **armed** *adj*
armada *n* **1** a large number of ships **2 the Armada** the great fleet sent by Spain against England in 1588 [Medieval Latin *armata* fleet, armed forces]
armadillo *n, pl* **-los** a small S American burrowing mammal covered in strong bony plates [Spanish *armado* armed (man)]

Armageddon *n* **1** *New Testament* the final battle between good and evil at the end of the world **2** a catastrophic and extremely destructive conflict [Hebrew *har megiddōn*, mountain district of *Megiddo* (in N Palestine)]

armament *n* **1** **armaments** the weapon equipment of a military vehicle, ship, or aircraft **2** preparation for war [Latin *armamenta* equipment]

armature *n* **1** a revolving structure in an electric motor or generator, wound with the coils that carry the current **2** *sculpture* a framework to support the clay or other material used in modelling [Latin *armātūra* armour, equipment]

armchair *n* **1** an upholstered chair with side supports for the arms ▷ *adj* **2** taking no active part: *we are, on the whole, a nation of armchair athletes*

armed forces *pl n* all the military forces of a nation or nations

armful *n* as much as can be held in the arms: *armfuls of lovely flowers*

armhole *n* the opening in a piece of clothing through which the arm passes

armistice (arm-miss-stiss) *n* an agreement between opposing armies to stop fighting [Latin *arma* arms + *sistere* to stop]

Armistice Day *n* the anniversary of the signing of the armistice that ended the First World War, on November 11, 1918

armlet *n* a band or bracelet worn around the arm

armorial *adj* of or relating to heraldry or heraldic arms

armour *or US* **armor** *n* **1** metal clothing worn by medieval warriors for protection in battle **2** *military* armoured fighting vehicles in general **3** the protective metal plates on a tank or warship **4** protective covering, such as the shell of certain animals **5** a quality or attitude that gives protection ▷ *vb* **6** to equip or cover with armour [Latin *armātūra* armour, equipment]

armoured *or US* **armored** *adj* **1** having a protective covering **2** consisting of armoured vehicles: *an armoured brigade*

armourer *or US* **armorer** *n* **1** a person who makes or mends arms and armour **2** a person in charge of small arms in a military unit

armour plate *n* a tough heavy steel for protecting warships and vehicles **armour-plated** *adj*

armoury *or US* **armory** *n, pl* **-mouries** *or* **-mories** **1** a secure storage place for weapons **2** military supplies **3** resources on which to draw: *modern medicine has a large armoury of drugs for the treatment of illness*

armpit *n* **1** the hollow beneath the arm where it joins the shoulder **2** *slang* an extremely unpleasant place: *the armpit of the Mediterranean*

armrest *n* the part of a chair or sofa that supports the arm

arms *pl n* **1** weapons collectively **2** military exploits: *prowess in arms* **3** the heraldic symbols of a family or state **4** **take up arms** to prepare to fight **5** **under arms** armed and prepared for war **6** **up in arms** prepared to protest strongly

army *n, pl* **-mies** **1** the military land forces of a nation **2** a large number of people or animals [Medieval Latin *armata* armed forces]

aroha *n NZ* love, compassion, or affection [Māori]

aroma *n* **1** a distinctive pleasant smell **2** a subtle pervasive quality or atmosphere [Greek: spice]

aromatherapy *n* the use of fragrant essential oils as a treatment in alternative medicine, often to relieve tension

aromatic *adj* **1** having a distinctive pleasant smell **2** *chem* (of an organic compound) having an unsaturated ring of atoms, usually six carbon atoms ▷ *n* **3** something, such as a plant or drug, that gives off a fragrant smell

arose *vb* the past tense of **arise**

around *prep* **1** situated at various points in: *cameramen were positioned around the auditorium* **2** from place to place in: *he had spent twenty-five minutes driving around Amsterdam* **3** somewhere in or near **4** approximately in: *around 1980* ▷ *adv* **5** in all directions from a point of reference: *there wasn't a house for miles around* **6** in the vicinity, esp. restlessly but idly: *I couldn't hang around too long* **7** in no particular place or direction: *a few tropical fish tanks dotted around* **8** *informal* present in some unknown or unspecified place **9** *informal* available: *these laptops have been around for several years* **10** **have been around** *informal* to have gained considerable experience of a worldly or social nature

> **USAGE** In American English, *around* is usually used instead of *round* in adverbial and prepositional senses, except in a few fixed phrases such as *all year round*. The use of *around* in adverbial senses is less common in British English.

arouse *vb* **arousing, aroused** **1** to produce (a reaction, emotion, or response) **2** to awaken from sleep **arousal** *n*

arpeggio (arp-pej-ee-oh) *n, pl* **-gios** a chord whose notes are played or sung in rapid succession [Italian]

arquebus (ark-wee-bus) *n* a portable long-barrelled gun dating from the 15th century [Middle Dutch *hakebusse* hook gun]

arrack *or* **arak** *n* a coarse alcoholic drink distilled in some Asian countries from grain or rice [Arabic *'araq* sweat, sweet juice]

arraign (ar-rain) *vb* **1** to bring (a prisoner) before a court to answer a charge **2** to accuse [Old French *araisnier* to accuse] **arraignment** *n*

arrange *vb* **-ranging, -ranged** **1** to plan in advance: *my parents had arranged a surprise party* **2** to arrive at an agreement: *they had arranged to go to the cinema* **3** to put into a proper or systematic order **4** to adapt (a musical composition) for performance in a certain way [Old French *a-* to + *rangier* to put in a row, range]

arrangement *n* **1** a preparation or plan made for an event: *travel arrangements* **2** an agreement or a plan to do something **3** a thing composed of various ordered parts: *a flower arrangement* **4** the form in which things are arranged **5** an adaptation of a piece of music for performance in a different way

arrant *adj* utter or downright: *that's the most arrant nonsense I've ever heard* [Middle English variant of *errant* (wandering, vagabond)]

a

arras *n* a tapestry wall-hanging [*Arras*, a town in N France]
array *n* **1** an impressive display or collection **2** an orderly arrangement, such as of troops in battle order **3** *computers* a data structure in which elements may be located by index numbers **4** *poetic* rich clothing ▷ *vb* **5** to arrange in order **6** to dress in rich clothing [Old French *arayer* to arrange]
arrears *pl n* **1** money owed **2 in arrears** late in paying a debt [Latin *ad* to + *retro* backwards]
arrest *vb* **1** to take (a person) into custody **2** to slow or stop the development of **3** to catch and hold (one's attention) ▷ *n* **4** the act of taking a person into custody **5 under arrest** being held in custody by the police **6** the slowing or stopping of something: *a cardiac arrest* [Latin *ad* at, to + *restare* to stand firm, stop]
arresting *adj* attracting attention; striking
arrival *n* **1** the act of arriving **2** a person or thing that has just arrived **3** *informal* a recently born baby
arrive *vb* **-riving, -rived 1** to reach a place or destination **2 arrive at** to come to (a conclusion, idea, or decision) **3** to occur: *the crisis he predicted then has now arrived* **4** *informal* to be born **5** *informal* to attain success [Latin *ad* to + *ripa* river bank]
arrivederci (ar-reeve-a-**der**-chee) *interj* goodbye [Italian]
arrogant *adj* having an exaggerated opinion of one's own importance or ability [Latin *arrogare* to claim as one's own] **arrogance** *n* **arrogantly** *adv*
arrogate *vb* **-gating, -gated** to claim or seize without justification [Latin *arrogare*] **arrogation** *n*
arrow *n* **1** a long slender pointed weapon, with feathers at one end, that is shot from a bow **2** an arrow-shaped sign or symbol used to show the direction to a place [Old English *arwe*]
arrowhead *n* the pointed tip of an arrow
arrowroot *n* an easily digestible starch obtained from the root of a West Indian plant
arse *or US & Canad* **ass** *n vulgar slang* the buttocks or anus [Old English *ærs*]
arsehole *or US & Canad* **asshole** *n vulgar slang* **1** the anus **2** a stupid or annoying person
arsenal *n* **1** a building in which arms and ammunition are made or stored **2** a store of anything regarded as weapons: *this new weapon in the medical arsenal* [Arabic *dār* house + *sin'ah* manufacture]
arsenic *n* **1** a toxic metalloid element. Symbol: **As 2** a nontechnical name for **arsenic trioxide**, a highly poisonous compound used as a rat poison and insecticide ▷ *adj also* **arsenical 3** of or containing arsenic [Syriac *zarnīg*]
arson *n* the crime of intentionally setting fire to property [Latin *ardere* to burn] **arsonist** *n*
art *n* **1** the creation of works of beauty or other special significance **2** works of art collectively **3** human creativity as distinguished from nature **4** skill: *she was still new to the art of bargaining* **5** any branch of the visual arts, esp. painting **6 get something down to a fine art** to become proficient at something through practice ▷ See also **arts** [Latin *ars* craftsmanship]
Art Deco (art **deck**-oh) *n* a style of design, at its height in the 1930s, characterized by geometrical shapes [French *art décoratif*]
artefact *or* **artifact** *n* something made by human beings, such as a tool or a work of art [Latin *ars* skill + *facere* to make]
Artemis *n Greek myth* the goddess of hunting
arterial *adj* **1** of or affecting an artery **2** being a major route: *an arterial road*
arteriosclerosis (art-ear-ee-oh-skler-**oh**-siss) *n* thickening and loss of elasticity of the walls of the arteries. Nontechnical name: **hardening of the arteries**
artery *n, pl* **-teries 1** any of the tubes that carry oxygenated blood from the heart to various parts of the body **2** a major road or means of communication [Latin *arteria*]
artesian well (art-**teez**-yan) *n* a well receiving water from a higher altitude, so the water is forced to flow upwards [from Old French *Arteis* Artois (in N France) where such wells were common]
Artex *n trademark Brit* a type of coating for walls and ceilings that gives a textured finish
art form *n* a recognized mode or medium of artistic expression
artful *adj* **1** cunning **2** skilful in achieving a desired end **artfully** *adv*
arthritis *n* inflammation of a joint or joints, causing pain and stiffness [Greek *arthron* joint] **arthritic** *adj, n*
arthropod *n* a creature, such as an insect or a spider, which has jointed legs and a hard case on its body [Greek *arthron* joint + *pous* foot]
artic *n Brit informal* an articulated lorry
artichoke *n* **1** Also called: **globe artichoke** the flower head of a thistle-like plant, cooked as a vegetable **2** same as **Jerusalem artichoke** [Arabic *al-kharshūf*]
article *n* **1** a written composition in a magazine or newspaper **2** an item or object **3** a clause in a written document **4** *grammar* any of the words *a*, *an*, or *the* [Latin *articulus* small joint]
articled *adj* bound by a written contract, such as one that governs a period of training: *an articled clerk*
articular *adj* of or relating to joints [Latin *articulus* small joint]
articulate *adj* **1** able to express oneself fluently and coherently **2** distinct, clear, or definite: *his amiable and articulate campaign attracted support* **3** *zool* possessing joints ▷ *vb* **-lating, -lated 4** to speak clearly and distinctly **5** to express coherently in words [Latin *articulare* to divide into joints] **articulately** *adv*
articulated lorry *n* a large lorry in two separate sections connected by a pivoted bar
articulation *n* **1** the expressing of an idea in words **2** the process of articulating a speech sound or the sound so produced **3** a being jointed together **4** *zool* a joint between bones or arthropod segments
artifact *n* same as **artefact**
artifice *n* **1** a clever trick **2** skill or cleverness [Latin *ars* skill + *facere* to make]
artificer (art-**tiff**-iss-er) *n* a skilled craftsman

artificial *adj* **1** man-made; not occurring naturally **2** made in imitation of a natural product: *artificial flavourings* **3** not sincere [Latin *artificialis* belonging to art] **artificiality** *n* **artificially** *adv*
artificial insemination *n* introduction of semen into the womb by means other than sexual intercourse
artificial intelligence *n* the branch of computer science aiming to produce machines which can imitate intelligent human behaviour
artificial respiration *n* any method of restarting a person's breathing after it has stopped
artillery *n* **1** large-calibre guns **2** military units specializing in the use of such guns [Old French *artillier* to equip with weapons]
artisan *n* a skilled workman; craftsman [French] **artisanal** *adj*
artist *n* **1** a person who produces works of art such as paintings or sculpture **2** a person who is skilled at something **3** same as **artiste** **artistic** *adj* **artistically** *adv*
artiste *n* a professional entertainer such as a singer or dancer
artistry *n* **1** artistic ability **2** great skill
artless *adj* **1** free from deceit or cunning: *artless generosity* **2** natural or unpretentious **artlessly** *adv*
Art Nouveau (ahr noo-**voh**) *n* a style of art and architecture of the 1890s, characterized by sinuous outlines and stylized natural forms [French: new art]
arts *pl n* **1 the arts** the nonscientific branches of knowledge **2** See **fine art** **3** cunning schemes
artwork *n* all the photographs and illustrations in a publication
arty *adj* **artier, artiest** *informal* having an affected interest in art **artiness** *n*
arum lily *n* a plant with a white funnel-shaped leaf surrounding a yellow spike of flowers
Aryan (air-ree-an) *n* **1** (in Nazi ideology) a non-Jewish person of the Nordic type **2** a person supposedly descended from the Indo-Europeans ▷ *adj* **3** of Aryans [Sanskrit *ārya* of noble birth]
as *conj* **1** while or when: *he arrived just as the band finished the song* **2** in the way that: *they had talked and laughed as only the best of friends can* **3** that which; what: *George did as he was asked* **4** (of) which fact or event (referring to the previous statement): *to become wise, as we all know, is not easy* **5 as it were** in a way; in a manner of speaking: *he was, as it were, on probation* **6** since; seeing that **7** for instance ▷ *adv, conj* **8** used to indicate amount or extent in comparisons: *he was as fat as his mum and dad* ▷ *prep* **9** in the role of; being: *my task, as his physician, is to do the best that I can* **10 as for** *or* **to** with reference to **11 as if** *or* **though** as it would be if: *she felt as if she had been run over by a bulldozer* **12 as (it) is** in the existing state of affairs [Old English *alswā* likewise]

USAGE See at **like**[1].

As *chem* arsenic
ASA **1** (in Britain) Amateur Swimming Association **2** (in Britain) Advertising Standards Authority
asafoetida *n* a strong-smelling plant resin used as a spice in Eastern cookery [Medieval Latin *asa* gum + Latin *foetidus* evil-smelling]
a.s.a.p. as soon as possible
asbestos *n* a fibrous mineral which does not burn, formerly widely used as a heat-resistant material [Greek: inextinguishable]
asbestosis *n* inflammation of the lungs resulting from inhalation of asbestos fibre
ascend *vb* **1** to go or move up **2** to slope upwards **3 ascend the throne** to become king or queen [Latin *ascendere*]
ascendancy *or* **ascendance** *n* the condition of being dominant: *when hardliners were in the ascendancy last winter*
ascendant *or* **ascendent** *adj* **1** dominant or influential ▷ *n* **2** *astrol* the sign of the zodiac that is rising on the eastern horizon at a particular moment **3 in the ascendant** increasing in power or influence
ascension *n* the act of ascending
Ascension Day *n Christianity* the 40th day after Easter, when the Ascension of Christ into Heaven is celebrated
ascent *n* **1** the act of ascending **2** an upward slope
ascertain *vb* to find out definitely [Old French *acertener* to make certain] **ascertainment** *n*
ascetic (ass-**set**-tik) *n* **1** a person who abstains from worldly comforts and pleasures ▷ *adj* **2** rigidly abstinent and self-denying [Greek *askētikos*]
ASCII (**ass**-kee) *n* a code for transmitting data between computers [*A(merican) S(tandard) C(ode for) I(nformation) I(nterchange)*]
ascorbic acid (ass-**core**-bik) *n* a vitamin that occurs in citrus fruits, tomatoes, and green vegetables, and which prevents and cures scurvy. Also called: **vitamin C** [A- + SCORBUTIC]
ascribe *vb* **-cribing, -cribed** **1** to attribute, as to a particular origin: *headaches which may be ascribed to stress* **2** to consider that (a particular quality) is possessed by something or someone: *specific human qualities are ascribed to each of the four elements* [Latin *ad* in addition + *scribere* to write] **ascription** *n*

USAGE *Ascribe* is sometimes used where *subscribe* is meant: *I do not subscribe* (not *ascribe*) *to this view.*

aseptic (eh-**sep**-tik) *adj* free from harmful bacteria
asexual (eh-**sex**-yew-al) *adj* **1** having no apparent sex or sex organs **2** (of reproduction) not involving sexual activity **3** (of a person) not sexually attracted to other people **asexually** *adv*
ash[1] *n* **1** the powdery substance formed when something is burnt **2** fine particles of lava thrown out by an erupting volcano [Old English *æsce*]
ash[2] *n* a tree with grey bark and winged seeds [Old English *æsc*]
ashamed *adj* **1** overcome with shame or remorse **2** unwilling through fear of humiliation or shame: *she'd be ashamed to admit to jealousy* [Old English *āscamod*]
ash can *n US* a dustbin

ashen *adj* pale with shock
ashes *pl n* **1** remains after burning **2** the remains of a human body after cremation
Ashes *pl n* **the Ashes** a cricket trophy competed for by England and Australia since 1882 [from a mock obituary of English cricket after a great Australian victory]
ashlar *or* **ashler** *n* **1** a square block of cut stone for use in building **2** a thin dressed stone used to face a wall [Old French *aisselier* crossbeam]
ashore *adv* towards or on land
ashram *n* a religious retreat where a Hindu holy man lives [Sanskrit *āśrama*]
ashtray *n* a dish for tobacco ash and cigarette ends
Ash Wednesday *n* the first day of Lent, named from the Christian custom of sprinkling ashes on penitents' heads
ashy *adj* **ashier, ashiest 1** pale greyish **2** covered with ash
Asian *adj* **1** of Asia **2** *Brit* of the Indian subcontinent ▷ *n* **3** a person from Asia **4** *Brit* a person from the Indian subcontinent or a descendant of one

USAGE The use of *Asian* or *Asiatic* as a noun can be offensive and should be avoided.

Asian pear *n* an apple-shaped pear with crisp juicy flesh
Asiatic *adj* Asian

USAGE See at **Asian**.

aside *adv* **1** to one side **2** out of other people's hearing: *her mother took her aside for a serious talk* **3** out of mind: *she pushed aside her fears of being beaten or killed* **4** into reserve: *a certain amount must also be put aside for defence and government* ▷ *n* **5** a remark not meant to be heard by everyone present **6** a remark that is not connected with the subject being discussed
asinine (ass-in-nine) *adj* **1** obstinate or stupid **2** of or like an ass [Latin *asinus* ass]
ask *vb* **1** to say or write (something) in a form that requires an answer: *I asked him his name; 'do you think we'll have trouble landing?' he asked* **2** to make a request or demand: *the chairman asked for a show of hands* **3** to invite **4** to inquire about: *I pretended to be lost and asked for directions* **5** to expect: *is that too much to ask?* [Old English *āscian*]
ask after *vb* to make polite inquiries about the health of: *he asked after you*
askance (ass-kanss) *adv* **look askance at A** to look at with an oblique glance **B** to regard with suspicion [origin unknown]
askew *adv, adj* towards one side; crooked
ask for *vb* **1** to seek to speak to **2** to request **3** *informal* to behave in a manner that is regarded as inviting (something): *you were asking for trouble there*
asking price *n* the price suggested by a seller
aslant *adv* **1** at a slant ▷ *prep* **2** slanting across
asleep *adj* **1** in or into a state of sleep **2** (of limbs) numb **3** *informal* not listening or paying attention
ASLEF (in Britain) Associated Society of Locomotive Engineers and Firemen
AS level *n* **1** *Brit* the advanced subsidiary level of a subject taken for the General Certificate of Education, having a smaller content than the advanced level **2** a pass in a subject at AS level
asp *n* a small viper of S Europe [Greek *aspis*]
asparagus *n* the young shoots of a plant of the lily family, which can be cooked and eaten [Greek *asparagos*]
aspartame *n* an artificial sweetener
aspect *n* **1** a distinct feature or element in a problem or situation **2** a position facing a particular direction: *the room's east-facing aspect* **3** appearance or look: *a room with a somewhat gloomy aspect* [Latin *ad-* to, at + *specere* to look]
aspen *n* a poplar tree whose leaves quiver in the wind [Old English *æspe*]
Asperger syndrome *or* **Asperger's syndrome** *n* a form of autism in which the person affected has limited but obsessive interests [after H. *Asperger*, physician]
asperity (ass-per-rit-ee) *n, pl* **-ties** roughness or sharpness of temper [Latin *asper* rough]
aspersion *n* **cast aspersions on** to make disparaging or malicious remarks about [Latin *aspergere* to sprinkle]
asphalt *n* **1** a black tarlike substance used in road-surfacing and roofing materials ▷ *vb* **2** to cover with asphalt [Greek *asphaltos*, probably from *a-* not + *sphallein* to cause to fall; referring to its use as a binding agent]
asphodel *n* a plant with clusters of yellow or white flowers
asphyxia (ass-fix-ee-a) *n* unconsciousness or death caused by lack of oxygen [Greek *a-* without + *sphuxis* pulse]
asphyxiate *vb* **-ating, -ated** to smother or suffocate **asphyxiation** *n*
aspic *n* a savoury jelly based on meat or fish stock, used as a mould for meat or vegetables [French]
aspidistra *n* a house plant with long tapered evergreen leaves [Greek *aspis* shield]
aspirant *n* a person who aspires, such as to a powerful position
aspirate *phonetics* ▷ *vb* **-rating, -rated 1** to pronounce (a word or syllable) with an initial *h* ▷ *n* **2** the sound represented in English and several other languages as *h*
aspiration *n* **1** a strong desire or aim **2** *phonetics* the pronunciation of an aspirated consonant **aspirational** *adj*
aspirator *n* a device for removing fluids from a body cavity by suction
aspire *vb* **-piring, -pired** to yearn for something or hope to do or be something: *it struck him as bizarre that somebody could aspire to be a dental technician* [Latin *aspirare* to breathe upon] **aspiring** *adj*
aspirin *n, pl* **-rin** *or* **-rins 1** a drug used to relieve pain and fever **2** a tablet of aspirin [German]
ass[1] *n* **1** a mammal resembling the horse but with longer ears **2** a foolish person [Old English *assa*]
ass[2] *n US & Canad vulgar slang* same as **arse** [Old English *ærs*]
assagai *n* same as **assegai**
assail *vb* **1** to attack violently **2** to criticize strongly **3** to disturb: *he was assailed by a dizzy sensation* [Latin *assilire* to leap on] **assailant** *n*

assassin *n* a murderer of a prominent person [Arabic *hashshāshīn*, plural of *hashshāsh* one who eats hashish]
assassinate *vb* **-nating, -nated** to murder (a prominent person) **assassination** *n*
assault *n* **1** a violent attack, either physical or verbal ▷ *vb* **2** to attack violently [Old French *asaut*]
assault and battery *n criminal law* a threat of attack to another person followed by actual attack
assault course *n* an obstacle course designed to give soldiers practice in negotiating hazards
assay *vb* **1** to analyse (a substance, such as gold) to find out how pure it is ▷ *n* **2** an analysis of the purity of an ore or precious metal [Old French *assai*]
assegai *or* **assagai** *n, pl* **-gais** a sharp light spear used in southern Africa [Arabic *az zaghayah*]
assemblage *n* **1** a collection or group of things **2** the act of assembling
assemble *vb* **-bling, -bled 1** to collect or gather together **2** to put together the parts of (a machine) [Old French *assembler*]
assembler *n* **1** a person or thing that assembles **2** a computer program that converts a set of low-level symbolic data into machine language
assembly *n, pl* **-blies 1** a number of people gathered together for a meeting **2** a group of people who meet regularly to make decisions or laws for a particular region or country: *the National Assembly for Wales* **3** the act of assembling
assembly line *n* a sequence of machines and workers in a factory assembling a product
assemblyman *or fem* **assemblywoman** *n, pl* **-men** *or* **-women** a member of a legislative assembly
assent *n* **1** agreement, consent ▷ *vb* **2** to agree [Latin *assentiri*]
assert *vb* **1** to state or declare **2** to insist upon (one's rights, etc.) **3 assert oneself** to speak and act forcefully [Latin *asserere* to join to oneself]
assertion *n* **1** a positive statement, usually made without evidence **2** the act of asserting
assertive *adj* confident and direct in dealing with others **assertively** *adv* **assertiveness** *n*
assess *vb* **1** to judge the worth or importance of **2** to estimate the value of (income or property) for taxation purposes [Latin *assidere* to sit beside] **assessment** *n*
assessor *n* **1** a person who values property for taxation or insurance purposes **2** a person with technical expertise called in to advise a court **3** a person who evaluates the merits of something
asset *n* **1** a thing or person that is valuable or useful **2** any property owned by a person or company [Latin *ad-* to + *satis* enough]
asset-stripping *n commerce* the practice of taking over a failing company at a low price and then selling the assets piecemeal **asset-stripper** *n*
asseverate *vb* **-ating, -ated** *formal* to declare solemnly [Latin *asseverare* to do (something) earnestly] **asseveration** *n*
assiduous *adj* **1** hard-working **2** done with care [Latin *assidere* to sit beside] **assiduity** *n* **assiduously** *adv*
assign *vb* **1** to select (someone) for a post or task **2** to give a task or duty (to someone) **3** to attribute to a specified cause **4** to set apart (a place or time) for a particular function or event: *to assign a day for the meeting* **5** *law* to transfer (one's right, interest, or title to property) to someone else [Latin *assignare*]
assignation (ass-sig-**nay**-shun) *n* a secret arrangement to meet, esp. one between lovers [Latin *assignatio* a marking out]
assignment *n* **1** something that has been assigned, such as a task **2** the act of assigning **3** *law* the transfer to another person of a right, interest, or title to property
assimilate *vb* **-lating, -lated 1** to learn and understand (information) thoroughly **2** to adjust or become adjusted: *they became assimilated to German culture* **3** to absorb (food) [Latin *ad-* to + *similis* like] **assimilable** *adj* **assimilation** *n*
assist *vb* **1** to give help or support ▷ *n* **2** *sport* a pass by a player which enables another player to score a goal [Latin *assistere* to stand by]
assistance *n* help or support
assistant *n* **1** a helper or subordinate **2** same as **shop assistant** ▷ *adj* **3** junior or deputy: *assistant manager*
assistant referee *n soccer* the official name for **linesman** (sense 1)
assizes *pl n Brit* (formerly in England and Wales) the sessions of the principal court in each county [Latin *assidere* to sit beside]
assoc. association
associate *vb* **-ating, -ated 1** to connect in the mind **2** to mix socially: *addicts are driven to associate with criminals* **3 be associated** *or* **associate oneself with** to be involved with (a group) because of shared views: *she had long been associated with the far right* ▷ *n* **4** a partner in business **5** a companion or friend ▷ *adj* **6** having partial rights or subordinate status: *an associate member* **7** joined with in business: *an associate director* [Latin *ad-* to + *sociare* to join]
association *n* **1** a group of people with a common interest **2** the act of associating or the state of being associated **3** friendship: *their association still had to remain a secret* **4** a mental connection of ideas or feelings: *the place contained associations for her*
association football *n* same as **soccer**
associative *adj maths* (of an operation such as multiplication or addition) producing the same answer regardless of the way the elements are grouped, for example $(2 \times 3) \times 4 = 2 \times (3 \times 4)$
assonance *n* the rhyming of vowel sounds but not consonants, as in *time* and *light* [Latin *assonare* to sound]
assorted *adj* **1** consisting of various kinds mixed together **2** matched: *an ill-assorted childless couple* [Old French *assorter*]
assortment *n* a collection of various things or sorts
asst assistant
assuage (ass-**wage**) *vb* **-suaging, -suaged** to relieve (grief, pain, or thirst) [Latin *suavis* pleasant]
assume *vb* **-suming, -sumed 1** to take to be true without proof **2** to undertake or take on: *every*

general staff officer was able to assume control of the army **3** to make a pretence of: *the man had assumed a debonair attitude* **4** to take on: *her eyes assumed a scared haunted look* [Latin *ad-* to + *sumere* to take up]

a

assumed name *n* a false name used by someone to disguise his or her identity

assuming *conj* if it is assumed or taken for granted: *assuming the first two phases were successful, the third phase would follow*

assumption *n* **1** something that is taken for granted **2** the act of assuming power or possession [Latin *assumptio* a taking up]

Assumption *n Christianity* the taking up of the Virgin Mary into heaven when her earthly life was ended

assurance *n* **1** a statement or assertion intended to inspire confidence **2** feeling of confidence; certainty **3** insurance that provides for events that are certain to happen, such as death

assure *vb* **-suring, -sured 1** to promise or guarantee **2** to convince: *they assured me that they had not seen the document* **3** to make (something) certain **4** *chiefly Brit* to insure against loss of life [Latin *ad-* to + *securus* secure]

assured *adj* **1** confident or self-assured **2** certain to happen **3** *chiefly Brit* insured **assuredly** (a-**sure**-id-lee) *adv*

Assyrian *n* an inhabitant of ancient Assyria, a kingdom of Mesopotamia

AST Atlantic Standard Time

astatine *n chem* a radioactive element occurring naturally in minute amounts or artificially produced by bombarding bismuth with alpha particles. Symbol: **At** [Greek *astatos* unstable]

aster *n* a plant with white, blue, purple, or pink daisy-like flowers [Greek: star]

asterisk *n* **1** a star-shaped character (*) used in printing or writing to indicate a footnote, etc. ▹ *vb* **2** to mark with an asterisk [Greek *asteriskos* a small star]

astern *adv, adj naut* **1** at or towards the stern of a ship **2** backwards **3** behind a vessel

asteroid *n* any of the small planets that orbit the sun between Mars and Jupiter [Greek *asteroeidēs* starlike]

asthma (**ass**-ma) *n* an illness causing difficulty in breathing [Greek] **asthmatic** *adj, n*

astigmatic *adj* relating to or affected with astigmatism [Greek *a-* without + *stigma* spot, focus]

astigmatism (eh-**stig**-mat-tiz-zum) *n* a defect of a lens, esp. of the eye, causing it not to focus properly

astir *adj* **1** out of bed **2** in motion

astonish *vb* to surprise greatly [Latin *ex-* out + *tonare* to thunder] **astonishing** *adj* **astonishment** *n*

astound *vb* to overwhelm with amazement [Old French *estoner*] **astounding** *adj*

astraddle *prep* astride

astrakhan *n* **1** a fur made of the dark curly fleece of lambs from Astrakhan in Russia **2** a cloth resembling this

astral *adj* **1** relating to or resembling the stars **2** of the spirit world [Greek *astron* star]

astray *adj, adv* out of the right or expected way [Old French *estraier* to stray]

astride *adj* **1** with a leg on either side **2** with legs far apart ▹ *prep* **3** with a leg on either side of

astringent *adj* **1** causing contraction of body tissue **2** checking the flow of blood from a cut **3** severe or harsh ▹ *n* **4** an astringent drug or lotion [Latin *astringens* drawing together] **astringency** *n*

astro- *combining form* indicating a star or stars: *astrology* [Greek]

astrolabe *n* an instrument formerly used to measure the altitude of stars and planets [Greek *astron* star + *lambanein* to take]

astrology *n* the study of the alleged influence of the stars, planets, sun, and moon on human affairs [Greek *astron* star + *logos* word, account] **astrologer** *or* **astrologist** *n* **astrological** *adj*

astronaut *n* a person trained for travelling in space [Greek *astron* star + *nautēs* sailor]

astronautics *n* the science and technology of space flight **astronautical** *adj*

astronomical *or* **astronomic** *adj* **1** enormously large **2** of astronomy **astronomically** *adv*

astronomical unit *n* a unit of distance equal to the average distance between the earth and the sun (1.495×10^{11}m)

astronomy *n* the scientific study of heavenly bodies [Greek *astron* star + *nomos* law] **astronomer** *n*

astrophysics *n* the study of the physical and chemical properties of celestial bodies **astrophysical** *adj* **astrophysicist** *n*

Astroturf *n trademark* a brand of artificial grass [from the *Astro(dome)*, sports stadium where it was first used + *turf*]

astute *adj* quick to notice or understand [Latin *astutus*] **astutely** *adv* **astuteness** *n*

asunder *adv, adj literary* into parts or pieces; apart

asylum *n* **1** refuge granted to a political refugee from a foreign country **2** (formerly) a psychiatric hospital [Greek *asulon*]

asymmetric bars (ass-sim-**met**-rik, ay-sim-**met**-rik) *pl n gymnastics* a pair of bars parallel to each other but at different heights, used for various exercises

asymmetry *n* lack of symmetry **asymmetric** *or* **asymmetrical** *adj*

asymptote (**ass**-im-tote) *n* a straight line that is closely approached but never met by a curve [Greek *asumptōtos* not falling together] **asymptotic** *adj*

at *prep* **1** indicating location or position: *she had planted a vegetable garden at the back* **2** towards; in the direction of: *she was staring at the wall behind him* **3** indicating position in time: *we arrived at 12.30* **4** engaged in: *the innocent laughter of children at play* **5** during the passing of: *she works at night as a nurse's aide* **6** for; in exchange for: *crude oil is selling at its lowest price since September* **7** indicating the object of an emotion: *I'm angry at you because you were rude to me* [Old English *æt*]

At *chem* astatine

at. **1** atmosphere **2** atomic

atavism (**at**-a-viz-zum) *n* **1** the recurrence of primitive characteristics that were present in distant ancestors but not in more recent ones **2** reversion to a former type [Latin *atavus* great-grandfather's grandfather, ancestor] **atavistic** *adj*

ataxia *n pathol* lack of muscular coordination [Greek] **ataxic** *adj*

ate *vb* the past tense of **eat**

atelier (at-tell-yay) *n* an artist's studio

atheism (aith-ee-iz-zum) *n* the belief that there is no God [Greek *a-* without + *theos* god] **atheist** *n*

Athena *or* **Athene** *n Greek myth* the goddess of wisdom

atherosclerosis *n, pl* **-ses** a disease in which deposits of fat cause the walls of the arteries to thicken [Greek *athērōma* tumour + SCLEROSIS] **atherosclerotic** *adj*

athlete *n* **1** a person trained to compete in sports or exercises **2** *chiefly Brit* a competitor in track-and-field events [Greek *athlos* a contest]

athlete's foot *n* a fungal infection of the skin of the foot

athletic *adj* **1** physically fit or strong **2** of or for an athlete or athletics **athletically** *adv* **athleticism** *n*

athletics *pl n Brit & Austral* track-and-field events

at-home *n Brit & Austral* a social gathering in a person's home

athwart *prep* **1** across ▷ *adv* **2** transversely; from one side to another

atigi (at-uh-gee) *n* a type of parka worn by the Inuit in Canada

Atlantic *adj* of the Atlantic Ocean, the world's second largest ocean, bounded by the Arctic, the Antarctic, America, and Europe and Africa [Greek *(pelagos) Atlantikos* (the sea) of Atlas (so called because it lay beyond the Atlas Mountains)]

Atlanticism *n* belief in close economic and military cooperation between Europe and the United States **Atlanticist** *n*

Atlantis *n* (in ancient legend) a continent said to have sunk beneath the Atlantic west of Gibraltar

atlas *n* a book of maps [because *Atlas*, a Titan in Greek mythology, was shown supporting the heavens in 16th-century books of maps]

ATM *n* the US term for **cash dispenser** [*a(utomated) t(eller) m(achine)*]

atmosphere *n* **1** the mass of gases surrounding the earth or any other heavenly body **2** the air in a particular place **3** a pervasive feeling or mood: *the atmosphere was tense* **4** a unit of pressure equal to the normal pressure of the air at sea level [Greek *atmos* vapour + *sphaira* sphere] **atmospheric** *adj* **atmospherically** *adv*

atmospherics *pl n* radio interference caused by electrical disturbance in the atmosphere

atoll *n* a circular coral reef surrounding a lagoon [*atollon*, native name in the Maldive Islands]

atom *n* **1** **A** the smallest quantity of an element which can take part in a chemical reaction **B** this entity as a source of nuclear energy **2** a very small amount [Greek *atomos* that cannot be divided]

atom bomb *n* same as **atomic bomb**

atomic *adj* **1** of or using atomic bombs or atomic energy **2** of atoms **atomically** *adv*

atomic bomb *or* **atom bomb** *n* a type of bomb in which the energy is provided by nuclear fission

atomic energy *n* same as **nuclear energy**

atomic mass unit *n* a unit of mass that is equal to one twelfth of the mass of an atom of carbon-12

atomic number *n* the number of protons in the nucleus of an atom of an element

atomic theory *n* any theory in which matter is regarded as consisting of atoms

atomic weight *n* the ratio of the average mass per atom of an element to one twelfth of the mass of an atom of carbon-12

atomize *or* **-ise** *vb* **-izing, -ized** *or* **-ising, -ised** **1** to separate into free atoms **2** to reduce to fine particles or spray **3** to destroy by nuclear weapons

atomizer *or* **-iser** *n* a device for reducing a liquid to a fine spray

atonal (eh-tone-al) *adj* (of music) not written in an established key **atonality** *n*

atone *vb* **atoning, atoned** to make amends (for a sin, crime, or wrongdoing)

atonement *n* **1** something done to make amends for wrongdoing **2** *Christian theol* the reconciliation of humankind with God through the sacrificial death of Christ [Middle English *at onement* in harmony]

atop *prep* on top of

atrium *n, pl* **atria** **1** *anatomy* the upper chamber of each half of the heart **2** a central hall that extends through several storeys in a modern building **3** the open main court of an ancient Roman house [Latin] **atrial** *adj*

atrocious *adj* **1** extremely cruel or wicked **2** horrifying or shocking **3** *informal* very bad [Latin *atrox* dreadful] **atrociously** *adv*

atrocity *n* **1** behaviour that is wicked or cruel **2** *pl* **-ties** an act of extreme cruelty

atrophy (at-trof-fee) *n, pl* **-phies** **1** a wasting away of a physical organ or part **2** a failure to grow ▷ *vb* **-phies, -phying, -phied** **3** to waste away [Greek *atrophos* ill-fed]

atropine *n* a poisonous alkaloid obtained from deadly nightshade [New Latin *atropa* deadly nightshade]

attach *vb* **1** to join, fasten, or connect **2** to attribute or ascribe: *he attaches particular importance to the proposed sale* **3** **attach oneself** *or* **be attached to** to become associated with or join [Old French *atachier*]

attaché (at-tash-shay) *n* a specialist attached to a diplomatic mission [French]

attaché case *n* a flat rectangular briefcase for carrying papers

attached *adj* **1** married, engaged, or in an exclusive sexual relationship **2** **attached to** fond of

attachment *n* **1** affection or regard for **2** an accessory that can be fitted to a device to change what it can do **3** a computer file sent with an email message

attack *vb* **1** to launch a physical assault (against) **2** to criticize vehemently **3** to set about (a job or problem) with vigour **4** to affect adversely: BSE *attacks the animal's brain* **5** to take the initiative in a game or sport ▷ *n* **6** the act of attacking **7** any sudden appearance of a disease or symptoms: *a bad attack of mumps* [Old Italian *attaccare*] **attacker** *n*

attain *vb* **1** to manage to do or get (something): *the country attained economic growth* **2** to reach [Latin *attingere*] **attainable** *adj*

attainment *n* an achievement or the act of achieving something

attar *n* a perfume made from damask roses [Persian *'atir* perfumed]

attempt *vb* **1** to make an effort (to do or achieve something); try ▷ *n* **2** an endeavour to achieve something; effort **3** **attempt on someone's life** an attack on someone with the intention to kill [Latin *attemptare*]

> **USAGE** *Attempt* should not be used in the passive when followed by an infinitive: *attempts were made to find a solution* (not *a solution was attempted to be found*).

attend *vb* **1** to be present at (an event) **2** to go regularly to a school, college, etc. **3** to look after: *the actors lounged in their canvas chairs, attended by sycophants* **4** to pay attention **5** **attend to** to apply oneself to: *I've a few things I must attend to* [Latin *attendere* to stretch towards]

attendance *n* **1** the act of attending **2** the number of people present **3** regularity in attending

attendant *n* **1** a person who assists, guides, or provides a service ▷ *adj* **2** associated: *nuclear power and its attendant dangers* **3** being in attendance

attendee *n* a person who is present at a specified event

attention *n* **1** concentrated direction of the mind **2** consideration, notice, or observation **3** detailed care or treatment **4** the alert position in military drill **5** **attentions** acts of courtesy: *the attentions of men seemed to embarrass her*

attentive *adj* **1** paying close attention **2** considerately helpful: *at society parties he is attentive to his wife* **attentively** *adv* **attentiveness** *n*

attenuated *adj* **1** weakened **2** thin and extended [Latin *attenuare* to weaken] **attenuation** *n*

attest *vb* **1** to affirm or prove the truth of **2** to bear witness to (an act or event) [Latin *testari* to bear witness] **attestation** *n*

attested *adj Brit* (of cattle) certified to be free from a disease, such as tuberculosis

attic *n* a space or room within the roof of a house [from the *Attic* style of architecture]

attire *n* clothes, esp. fine or formal ones [Old French *atirier* to put in order]

attired *adj* dressed in a specified way

attitude *n* **1** the way a person thinks and behaves **2** a position of the body **3** *informal* a hostile manner **4** the orientation of an aircraft or spacecraft in relation to some plane or direction [Latin *aptus* apt]

attitudinize *or* **-nise** *vb* **-nizing, -nized** *or* **-nising, -nised** to adopt a pose or opinion for effect

attorney *n* **1** a person legally appointed to act for another **2** *US* a lawyer [Old French *atourner* to direct to]

attorney general *n, pl* **attorneys general** *or* **attorney generals** a chief law officer of some governments

attract *vb* **1** to arouse the interest or admiration of **2** (of a magnet) to draw (something) closer by exerting a force on it [Latin *attrahere* to draw towards]

attraction *n* **1** the act or quality of attracting **2** an interesting or desirable feature: *the attractions of working abroad* **3** an object or place that people visit for interest: *this carefully preserved tourist attraction* **4** (of a magnet) a force by which one object attracts another

attractive *adj* appealing to the senses or mind **attractively** *adv* **attractiveness** *n*

attribute *vb* **-uting, -uted** **1** **attribute to** to regard as belonging to or produced by: *a play attributed to William Shakespeare* ▷ *n* **2** a quality or feature belonging to or representative of a person or thing [Latin *attribuere* to associate with] **attributable** *adj* **attribution** *n*

attributive *adj grammar* (of an adjective) coming before the noun modified

attrition *n* constant wearing down to weaken or destroy: *a war of attrition* [Latin *atterere* to weaken]

attune *vb* **-tuning, -tuned** to adjust or accustom (a person or thing)

ATV all-terrain vehicle: a vehicle with wheels designed to travel on rough ground

atypical (eh-**tip**-ik-kl) *adj* not typical **atypically** *adv*

Au *chem* gold [Latin *aurum*]

aubergine (**oh**-bur-zheen) *n Brit* the dark purple fruit of a tropical plant, cooked and eaten as a vegetable [French, from Arabic *al-bādindjān*]

aubrietia (aw-**bree**-sha) *n* a trailing purple-flowered rock plant [after Claude *Aubriet*, painter of flowers and animals]

auburn *adj* (of hair) reddish-brown [(originally meaning: blond) Latin *albus* white]

auction *n* **1** a public sale at which articles are sold to the highest bidder ▷ *vb* **2** to sell by auction [Latin *auctio* an increasing]

auctioneer *n* a person who conducts an auction

audacious *adj* **1** recklessly bold or daring **2** impudent or presumptuous [Latin *audax* bold] **audacity** *n*

audible *adj* loud enough to be heard [Latin *audire* to hear] **audibility** *n* **audibly** *adv*

audience *n* **1** a group of spectators or listeners at a concert or play **2** the people reached by a book, film, or radio or television programme **3** a formal interview [Latin *audire* to hear]

audio *adj* **1** of or relating to sound or hearing **2** of or for the transmission or reproduction of sound [Latin *audire* to hear]

audiobook *n* a reading of a book recorded on tape, CD, or digital formats

audio frequency *n* a frequency in the range 20 hertz to 20 000 hertz, audible to the human ear

audiometer (aw-dee-**om**-it-er) *n* an instrument for testing hearing

audiotypist *n* a typist trained to type from a dictating machine **audiotyping** *n*

audiovisual *adj* involving both hearing and sight: *audiovisual teaching aids*

audit *n* **1** an official inspection of business accounts, conducted by an independent qualified accountant **2** any thoroughgoing assessment or review: *an audit of their lifestyle* ▷ *vb* **auditing,**

audited 3 to examine (business accounts) officially [Latin *audire* to hear]
audition *n* 1 a test of a performer's or musician's ability for a particular role or job ▷ *vb* 2 to test or be tested in an audition [Latin *audire* to hear]
auditor *n* a person qualified to audit accounts [Latin *auditor* a hearer]
auditorium *n, pl* **-toriums** *or* **-toria** 1 the area of a concert hall or theatre in which the audience sits 2 *US & Canad* a building for public meetings [Latin]
auditory *adj* of or relating to hearing [Latin *audire* to hear]
au fait (oh **fay**) *adj* 1 (usually foll. by *with*) fully informed (about) 2 expert [French: to the point]
auf Wiedersehen (owf **vee**-der-zay-en) *interj* goodbye [German]
Aug. August
Augean (aw-**jee**-an) *adj* extremely dirty or corrupt [from *Augeas*, in Greek mythology, king whose filthy stables Hercules cleaned in one day]
auger *n* a pointed tool for boring holes [Old English *nafugār* nave (ie hub of a wheel) spear]
aught *pron old-fashioned or literary* anything whatever: *for aught I know* [Old English *āwiht*]
augment *vb* to make or become greater in number or strength [Latin *augere* to increase] **augmentation** *n*
augmented reality *n* an artificial environment created through the combination of real-world and computer-generated data
au gratin (oh **grat**-tan) *adj* cooked with a topping of breadcrumbs and sometimes cheese [French]
augur *vb* to be a good or bad sign of future events: *a double fault on the opening point did not augur well* [Latin: diviner of omens]
augury *n* 1 the foretelling of the future 2 *pl* **-ries** an omen
august *adj* dignified and imposing [Latin *augustus*]
August *n* the eighth month of the year [Latin, after the emperor *Augustus*]
Augustan *adj* 1 of the Roman emperor Augustus Caesar or the poets writing during his reign 2 of any literary period noted for refinement and classicism
auk *n* a northern sea bird with a heavy body, short wings, and black-and-white plumage [Old Norse *ālka*]
auld lang syne *n* times past [Scots, literally: old long since]
aunt *n* 1 a sister of one's father or mother 2 the wife of one's uncle 3 a child's term of address for a female friend of the parents [Latin *amita* a father's sister]
auntie *or* **aunty** *n, pl* **-ies** *informal* an aunt
Aunt Sally *n, pl* **-lies** 1 a figure used in fairgrounds as a target 2 any target for insults or criticism
au pair *n* a young foreign person, typically a woman, who helps with childcare and housework in return for board and lodging [French]
aura *n, pl* **auras** *or* **aurae** 1 a distinctive air or quality associated with a person or thing 2 any invisible emanation [Greek: breeze]
aural *adj* of or using the ears or hearing [Latin *auris* ear] **aurally** *adv*
aureate *adj literary* 1 covered with gold 2 (of a style of writing or speaking) excessively elaborate [Latin *aurum* gold]
aureole *or* **aureola** *n* 1 a ring of light surrounding the head of a figure represented as holy; halo 2 the sun's corona, visible as a faint halo during eclipses [Latin *aurum* gold]
au revoir (oh riv-**vwahr**) *interj* goodbye [French]
auric *adj* of or containing gold in the trivalent state [Latin *aurum* gold]
auricle *n* 1 the upper chamber of the heart 2 the outer part of the ear [Latin *auris* ear] **auricular** *adj*
auricula *n, pl* **-lae** *or* **-las** an alpine primrose with leaves shaped like a bear's ear [Latin *auris* ear]
auriferous *adj* containing gold [Latin *aurum* gold + *ferre* to bear]
aurochs *n, pl* **-rochs** a recently extinct European wild ox [German]
aurora *n, pl* **-ras** *or* **-rae** 1 an atmospheric phenomenon of bands of light sometimes seen in the polar regions 2 *poetic* the dawn [Latin: dawn]
aurora australis *n* the aurora seen around the South Pole [New Latin: southern aurora]
aurora borealis *n* the aurora seen around the North Pole [New Latin: northern aurora]
auscultation *n* the listening to of the internal sounds of the body, usually with a stethoscope, to help with medical diagnosis [Latin *auscultare* to listen attentively]
auspices (aw-spiss-siz) *pl n* **under the auspices of** with the support and approval of [Latin *auspicium* augury from birds]
auspicious *adj* showing the signs of future success

> **USAGE** The use of *auspicious* to mean 'very special' (as in *this auspicious occasion*) should be avoided.

Aussie *n, adj informal* Australian
austere *adj* 1 stern or severe: *his austere and serious attitude to events* 2 self-disciplined or ascetic: *an extraordinarily austere and puritanical organization* 3 severely simple or plain: *the austere backdrop of grey* [Greek *austēros* astringent]
austerity *n, pl* **-ties** 1 the state of being austere 2 reduced availability of luxuries and consumer goods
austral *adj* of or from the south [Latin *auster* the south wind]
Austral. 1 Australasia 2 Australia(n)
Australasian *adj* of Australia, New Zealand, and neighbouring islands
Australia Day *n* public holiday in Australia on January 26
Australian *adj* 1 of Australia ▷ *n* 2 a person from Australia
Austrian *adj* 1 of Austria ▷ *n* 2 a person from Austria
autarchy (aw-tar-kee) *n, pl* **-chies** absolute power or autocracy [Greek *autarkhia*]
autarky (aw-tar-kee) *n, pl* **-kies** a policy of economic self-sufficiency [Greek *autarkeia*]
authentic *adj* 1 of undisputed origin or authorship; genuine 2 reliable or accurate

a

3 *music* using period instruments, scores, and playing techniques [Greek *authentikos*] **authentically** *adv* **authenticity** *n*

authenticate *vb* **-cating, -cated** to establish as genuine **authentication** *n*

author *n* **1** a person who writes a book, article, or other written work **2** an originator or creator [Latin *auctor*]

authoritarian *adj* **1** insisting on strict obedience to authority ▷ *n* **2** a person who insists on strict obedience to authority **authoritarianism** *n*

authoritative *adj* **1** recognized as being reliable: *the authoritative book on Shakespeare* **2** possessing authority; official **authoritatively** *adv*

authority *n, pl* **-ties 1** the power to command, control, or judge others **2** a person or group with this power: *a third escapee turned himself in to the authorities* **3** a decision-making organization or government department: *the local authority* **4** an expert in a particular field **5** official permission: *she had no authority to negotiate* **6** a position that has the power to command, control, or judge others: *people in authority* **7 on good authority** from reliable evidence **8** confidence resulting from expertise [Latin *auctor* author]

authorize *or* **-ise** *vb* **-izing, -ized** *or* **-ising, -ised 1** to give authority to **2** to give official permission for **authorization** *or* **-isation** *n*

Authorized Version *n* **the Authorized Version** an English translation of the Bible published in 1611

authorship *n* **1** the origin or originator of a written work or plan **2** the profession of writing

autism *n psychiatry* a developmental condition characterized by difficulties in responding to and communicating with other people [Greek *autos* self] **autistic** *adj*

auto *n, pl* **-tos** *US & Canad informal* short for **automobile**

auto- *or sometimes before a vowel* **aut-** *combining form* **1** self; of or by the same one: *autobiography* **2** self-propelling: *automobile* [Greek *autos* self]

autobahn *n* a motorway in German-speaking countries [German, from *Auto* car + *Bahn* road]

autobiography *n, pl* **-phies** an account of a person's life written by that person **autobiographer** *n* **autobiographical** *adj*

autoclave *n* an apparatus for sterilizing objects by steam under pressure [AUTO- + Latin *clavis* key]

autocracy *n, pl* **-cies** government by an individual with unrestricted authority

autocrat *n* **1** a ruler with absolute authority **2** a dictatorial person [AUTO- + Greek *kratos* power] **autocratic** *adj* **autocratically** *adv*

autocross *n* a sport in which cars race over a circuit of rough grass

Autocue *n trademark* an electronic television prompting device displaying a speaker's script, unseen by the audience

auto-da-fé (aw-toe-da-**fay**) *n, pl* **autos-da-fé 1** *history* the ceremonial passing of sentence on heretics by the Spanish Inquisition **2** the burning to death of heretics [Portuguese, literally: act of the faith]

autofocus *n* a camera system in which the lens is focused automatically

autogiro *or* **autogyro** *n, pl* **-ros** a self-propelled aircraft resembling a helicopter but with an unpowered rotor

autograph *n* **1** a handwritten signature of a famous person ▷ *vb* **2** to write one's signature on or in [AUTO- + Greek *graphein* to write]

automat *n US* a vending machine

automate *vb* **-mating, -mated** to make (a manufacturing process) automatic

automatic *adj* **1** (of a device or mechanism) able to activate or regulate itself **2** (of a process) performed by automatic equipment **3** done without conscious thought **4** (of a firearm) utilizing some of the force of each explosion to reload and fire continuously **5** occurring as a necessary consequence: *the certificate itself carries no automatic legal benefits* ▷ *n* **6** an automatic firearm **7** a motor vehicle with automatic transmission [Greek *automatos* acting independently] **automatically** *adv*

automatic pilot *n* **1** a device that automatically maintains an aircraft on a preset course **2 on automatic pilot** repeating an action or process without thought

automatic transmission *n* a transmission system in a motor vehicle in which the gears change automatically

automation *n* the use of automatic, often electronic, methods to control industrial processes

automaton *n, pl* **-tons** *or* **-ta 1** a mechanical device operating under its own power **2** a person who acts mechanically [Greek *automatos* spontaneous]

automobile *n US & Canad* a car

automotive *adj* **1** relating to motor vehicles **2** self-propelling

autonomous *adj* **1** having self-government **2** independent of others [AUTO- + Greek *nomos* law]

autonomy *n, pl* **-mies 1** the right or state of self-government **2** freedom to determine one's own actions and behaviour [Greek *autonomia*]

autopilot *n* an automatic pilot

autopsy *n, pl* **-sies** examination of a corpse to determine the cause of death [Greek *autopsia* seeing with one's own eyes]

autoroute *n* a motorway in French-speaking countries [French, from *auto* car + *route* road]

autostrada *n* a motorway in Italian-speaking countries [Italian, from *auto* car + *strada* road]

autosuggestion *n* a process in which a person unconsciously supplies the means of influencing his or her own behaviour or beliefs

autumn *n* **1** the season of the year between summer and winter **2** a period of late maturity followed by a decline [Latin *autumnus*] **autumnal** *adj*

aux. auxiliary

auxiliaries *pl n* foreign troops serving another nation

auxiliary *adj* **1** secondary or supplementary **2** supporting ▷ *n, pl* **-ries 3** a person or thing that supports or supplements [Latin *auxilium* help]

auxiliary verb *n* a verb used to indicate the tense, voice, or mood of another verb, such as *will* in *I will go*

AV (of the Bible) Authorized Version
av. **1** average **2** avoirdupois
avail *vb* **1** to be of use, advantage, or assistance (to) **2 avail oneself of** to make use of ▹ *n* **3** use or advantage: *to no avail* [Latin *valere* to be strong]
available *adj* **1** obtainable or accessible **2** able to be contacted and willing to talk: *a spokesman insisted she was not available for comment* **availability** *n* **availably** *adv*
avalanche *n* **1** a fall of large masses of snow and ice down a mountain **2** a sudden or overwhelming quantity of anything [French]
avant-garde (av-ong-**gard**) *n* **1** those artists, writers, or musicians whose techniques and ideas are in advance of those generally accepted ▹ *adj* **2** using ideas or techniques in advance of those generally accepted [French: vanguard]
avarice (av-a-riss) *n* extreme greed for wealth [Latin *avere* to crave] **avaricious** *adj*
avast *interj naut* stop! cease! [probably Dutch *hou'vast* hold fast]
avatar *n* **1** *Hinduism* the appearance of a god in human or animal form **2** a movable image that represents a person in a virtual environment, such as an online role-playing game [Sanskrit *avatāra* a going down]
Ave (ah-vay) *or* **Ave Maria** (ma-ree-a) *n* same as **Hail Mary** [Latin: hail, Mary!]
Ave. avenue
avenge *vb* **avenging, avenged** to inflict a punishment in retaliation for (harm done) or on behalf of (the person harmed) [Latin *vindicare*] **avenger** *n*

USAGE The use of *avenge* with a reflexive pronoun was formerly considered incorrect, but is now acceptable: *she avenged herself on the man who killed her daughter.*

avenue *n* **1** a wide street **2** a road bordered by two rows of trees **3** a line of approach: *the United States was exhausting every avenue to achieve a diplomatic solution* [French, from *avenir* to come to]
aver (av-**vur**) *vb* **averring, averred** to state to be true [Latin *verus* true] **averment** *n*
average *n* **1** the typical or normal amount or quality **2** the result obtained by adding the numbers or quantities in a set and dividing the total by the number of members in the set **3 on average** usually or typically ▹ *adj* **4** usual or typical **5** calculated as an average **6** mediocre or inferior ▹ *vb* **-aging, -aged 7** to calculate or estimate the average of **8** to amount to or be on average [Middle English *averay* loss arising from damage to ships, ultimately from Arabic *awār* damage]
averse *adj* opposed: *he's not averse to publicity, of the right kind* [Latin *avertere* to turn from]
aversion *n* **1** extreme dislike or disinclination **2** a person or thing that arouses this
avert *vb* **1** to turn away: *he had to avert his eyes* **2** to ward off: *a final attempt to avert war* [Latin *avertere* to turn from]
Avesta *n* a collection of sacred writings of Zoroastrianism
avian (aiv-ee-an) *adj* of or like a bird: *the treatment of avian diseases* [Latin *avis* bird]
avian flu *n* another name for **bird flu** [Latin *avis* bird]
aviary *n, pl* **aviaries** a large enclosure in which birds are kept [Latin *avis* bird]
aviation *n* the art or science of flying aircraft [Latin *avis* bird]
aviator *or fem* **aviatrix** *n old-fashioned* the pilot of an aircraft
avid *adj* **1** very keen or enthusiastic: *she is an avid football fan* **2** eager: *avid for economic development* [Latin *avere* to long for] **avidity** *n* **avidly** *adv*
avocado *n, pl* **-dos** a pear-shaped tropical fruit with a leathery green skin and greenish-yellow flesh [Spanish *aguacate*]
avocation *n* **1** *Brit, Austral & NZ old-fashioned* a person's regular job **2** *formal* a hobby [Latin *avocare* to distract]
avocet *n* a long-legged shore bird with a long slender upward-curving bill [Italian *avocetta*]
avoid *vb* **1** to refrain from doing **2** to prevent from happening **3** to keep out of the way of [Old French *esvuidier*] **avoidable** *adj* **avoidably** *adv* **avoidance** *n*
avoirdupois *or* **avoirdupois weight** (av-er-de-**poise**) *n* a system of weights based on the pound, which contains 16 ounces [Old French *aver de peis* goods of weight]
avow *vb* **1** to state or affirm **2** to admit openly [Latin *advocare* to call upon] **avowal** *n* **avowed** *adj* **avowedly** (a-vow-id-lee) *adv*
avuncular *adj* (of a man) friendly, helpful, and caring towards someone younger [Latin *avunculus* (maternal) uncle]
await *vb* **1** to wait for **2** to be in store for
awake *adj* **1** not sleeping **2** alert or aware: *awake to the danger* ▹ *vb* **awaking, awoke** *or* **awaked, awoken** *or* **awaked 3** to emerge or rouse from sleep **4** to become or cause to become alert [Old English *awacan*]

USAGE See at **wake**[1].

awaken *vb* **1** to awake **2** to cause to be aware of: *anxieties awakened by reunification*
awakening *n* the start of a feeling or awareness in someone: *a picture of an emotional awakening*
award *vb* **1** to give (something) for merit **2** *law* to declare to be entitled, such as by decision of a court ▹ *n* **3** something awarded, such as a prize **4** *law* the decision of an arbitrator or court [Old French *eswarder* to decide after investigation]
aware *adj* **1 aware of** knowing about: *he's at least aware of the problem* **2** informed: *they are becoming more politically aware every day* [Old English *gewær*] **awareness** *n*
awash *adv, adj* washed over by water
away *adv* **1** from a particular place: *I saw them walk away and felt absolutely desolated* **2** in or to another, a usual, or a proper place: *he decided to put the car away in the garage* **3** at a distance: *keep away from the windows* **4** out of existence: *the pillars rotted away* **5** indicating motion or distance from a normal or proper place: *the girl shook her head and looked away* **6** continuously: *he continued to scribble away* ▹ *adj* **7** not present: *she had been away from home for years* **8** distant: *the castle was farther away than he had thought* **9** *sport* played on an opponent's ground [Old English *on weg* on way]
awayday *n* a day trip taken for pleasure [from *awayday ticket* a special-rate day return by train]

a

awe *n* **1** wonder and respect mixed with dread ▷ *vb* **awing, awed 2** to inspire with reverence or dread [Old Norse *agi*]
aweigh *adj naut* (of an anchor) no longer hooked into the bottom
awesome *adj* **1** inspiring or displaying awe **2** *slang* excellent or outstanding
awestruck *adj* overcome or filled with awe
awful *adj* **1** very bad or unpleasant **2** *informal* considerable or great: *that's an awful lot of money, isn't it?* **3** *obsolete* inspiring reverence or dread ▷ *adv* **4** *not standard* very: *I'm working awful hard on my lines*
awfully *adv* **1** in an unpleasant way **2** *informal* very: *we were both awfully busy*
awhile *adv* for a brief period
awkward *adj* **1** clumsy or ungainly **2** embarrassed: *he was awkward and nervous around girls* **3** difficult to deal with: *the lawyer was in an awkward situation* **4** difficult to use or handle: *it was small but heavy enough to make it awkward to carry* **5** embarrassing: *there were several moments of awkward silence* [Old Norse *öfugr* turned the wrong way round] **awkwardly** *adv* **awkwardness** *n*
awl *n* a pointed hand tool for piercing wood, leather, etc. [Old English *ǣl*]
awn *n* any of the bristles growing from the flowering parts of certain grasses and cereals [Old English *agen* ear of grain]
awning *n* a canvas roof supported by a frame to give protection against the weather [origin unknown]
awoke *vb* a past tense and (now rare or dialectal) past participle of **awake**
awoken *vb* a past participle of **awake**
AWOL (eh-woll) *adj military* absent without leave but without intending to desert
awry (a-rye) *adv, adj* **1** with a twist to one side; askew: *my neck was really awry after the journey* **2** amiss or faulty: *if a gear gets stuck, the whole system goes awry* [Middle English *on wry*]
axe *or US* **ax** *n, pl* **axes 1** a hand tool with one side of its head sharpened to a cutting edge, used for felling trees and splitting timber **2 an axe to grind** a favourite topic one wishes to promote **3** *informal* a severe cut in spending or in the number of staff employed ▷ *vb* **axing, axed 4** *informal* to dismiss (employees), restrict (expenditure), or terminate (a project) [Old English *æx*]
axes¹ *n* the plural of **axis**
axes² *n* the plural of **axe**
axial *adj* **1** forming or of an axis **2** in, on, or along an axis **axially** *adv*
axil *n* the angle where the stalk of a leaf joins a stem [Latin *axilla* armpit]
axiom *n* **1** a generally accepted principle **2** a self-evident statement [Greek *axios* worthy]
axiomatic *adj* **1** containing axioms **2** self-evident or obvious **axiomatically** *adv*
axis (ax-iss) *n, pl* **axes** (ax-eez) **1** a real or imaginary line about which a body can rotate or about which an object or geometrical construction is symmetrical **2** one of two or three reference lines used in coordinate geometry to locate a point in a plane or in space [Latin]
axle *n* a shaft on which a wheel or pair of wheels revolves [Old Norse *öxull*]
axolotl *n* an aquatic salamander of N America [Mexican Indian: water doll]
ayah *n* (in parts of the former British Empire) a maidservant or nursemaid [Hindi *āyā*]
ayatollah *n* one of a class of Islamic religious leaders in Iran [Arabic *aya* sign + *allah* God]
aye *or* **ay** *interj* **1** *Brit, Austral & NZ* yes ▷ *n* **2** an affirmative vote or voter [probably from *I*, expressing assent]
Ayrshire *n* one of a breed of brown-and-white dairy cattle [*Ayrshire*, county of Scotland]
AZ Arizona
azalea (az-zale-ya) *n* a garden shrub grown for its showy flowers [Greek *azaleos* dry]
azimuth *n* **1** the arc of the sky between the zenith and the horizon **2** *surveying* the horizontal angle of a bearing measured clockwise from the north [Arabic *as-samt* the path]
Aztec *n* **1** a member of a Mexican Indian race who established a great empire, overthrown by the Spanish in the early 16th century **2** the language of the Aztecs ▷ *adj* **3** of the Aztecs or their language [*Aztlan*, their traditional place of origin, literally: near the cranes]
azure *n* **1** the deep blue colour of a clear blue sky **2** *poetic* a clear blue sky ▷ *adj* **3** deep blue [Arabic *lāzaward* lapis lazuli]

Bb

b *or* **B** *n, pl* **b's, B's** *or* **Bs 1** the second letter of the English alphabet **2 from A to B** See **a** (sense 2)
b *cricket* **A** bowled **B** bye
B 1 *music* the seventh note of the scale of C major **2** the second in a series, class, or rank **3** *chem* boron **4** *chess* bishop
b. born
B2B business-to-business; denoting trade between commercial organizations rather than between businesses and private customers
Ba *chem* barium
BA 1 Bachelor of Arts **2** British Airways
baa *vb* **baaing, baaed 1** (of a sheep) to make a characteristic bleating sound ▷ *n* **2** the cry made by a sheep
baas *n S African offensive* a boss [Afrikaans]
baaskap *n* (in South Africa) control by White people of non-White people [Afrikaans]
babaco *n* a greenish-yellow egg-shaped fruit
babble *vb* **-bling, -bled 1** to talk in a quick, foolish, or muddled way **2** to make meaningless sounds: *children first gurgle and babble at random* **3** to disclose secrets carelessly **4** *literary* (of streams) to make a low murmuring sound ▷ *n* **5** muddled or foolish speech **6** a murmuring sound [probably imitative] **babbler** *n* **babbling** *n*
babe *n* **1** a baby **2 babe in arms** *informal* a naive or inexperienced person **3** *informal* an attractive person, esp. a young woman
babel (babe-el) *n* **1** a confusion of noises or voices **2** a scene of noise and confusion [from the confusion of languages on the tower of *Babel* (Genesis 11:1–10)]
babiche *n Canad* thongs or lacings of rawhide
baboon *n* a medium-sized monkey with a long face, large teeth, and a fairly long tail [Middle English *babewyn* gargoyle]
baby *n, pl* **-bies 1** a newborn child **2** the youngest or smallest of a family or group **3** a recently born animal **4** an immature person **5** *slang* a sweetheart **6** a project of personal concern **7 be left holding the baby** to be left with a responsibility ▷ *adj* **8** comparatively small of its type: *baby carrots* ▷ *vb* **-bies, -bying, -bied 9** to treat like a baby [probably childish reduplication] **babyhood** *n* **babyish** *adj*
baby bonus *n Canad informal* a regular government payment to the parents of children up to a certain age
baby-sit *vb* **-sitting, -sat** to act or work as a baby-sitter **baby-sitting** *n, adj*
baby-sitter *n* a person who takes care of a child while the parents are out
baccalaureate (back-a-law-ree-it) *n* the university degree of Bachelor of Arts [Medieval Latin *baccalarius* bachelor]
baccarat (back-a-rah) *n* a card game in which two or more punters gamble against the banker [French *baccara*]
bacchanalian (back-a-nail-ee-an) *adj literary* (of a party) unrestrained and involving a great deal of drinking and sometimes sexual activity [from *Bacchus*, Greek & Roman god of wine]
Bacchus *n classical myth* the god of wine; Dionysus
baccy *n Brit informal* tobacco
bach (batch) NZ ▷ *n* **1** a small holiday cottage ▷ *vb* **2** to look after oneself when one's spouse is away
bachelor *n* **1** an unmarried man **2** a person who holds a first degree from a university or college [Old French *bacheler* youth, squire]
bachelorhood *n*
Bachelor of Arts *n* a person with a first degree from a university or college, usually in the arts
bacillary *adj* of or caused by bacilli
bacillus (bass-ill-luss) *n, pl* **-li** (-lie) a rod-shaped bacterium, esp. one causing disease [Latin *baculum* walking stick]
back *n* **1** the rear part of the human body, from the neck to the pelvis **2** the spinal column **3** the part or side of an object opposite the front **4** the part of anything less often seen or used **5** *ball games* a defensive player or position **6 at the back of one's mind** not in one's conscious thoughts **7 behind someone's back** secretly or deceitfully **8 put** *or* **get someone's back up** to annoy someone **9 turn one's back on someone** to refuse to help someone ▷ *vb* **10** to move or cause to move backwards **11** to provide money for (a person or enterprise) **12** to bet on the success of: *to back a horse* **13** to provide (a pop singer) with a musical accompaniment **14** (foll. by *on* or *onto*) to have the back facing (towards): *his garden backs onto a school* **15** (of the wind) to change direction anticlockwise ▷ *adj* **16** situated behind: *back garden* **17** owing from an earlier date: *back rent* **18** remote: *a back road* ▷ *adv* **19** at, to, or towards the rear **20** to or towards the original starting point or condition: *I went back home* **21** in reply or retaliation: *to hit someone back* **22** in concealment or reserve: *to keep something back* **23 back and forth** to and fro **24 back to front A** in reverse **B** in disorder ▷ See also **back down, back off** *etc.* [Old English *bæc*]
backbencher *n* a Member of Parliament who does not hold office in the government or opposition
backbite *vb* **-biting, -bit, -bitten** *or* **-bit** to talk spitefully about an absent person **backbiter** *n*
back boiler *n Brit* a tank at the back of a fireplace for heating water
backbone *n* **1** the spinal column **2** strength of character **3** the part of something that gives it strength: *they formed the backbone of the regiment*
back-breaking *adj* (of work) exhausting
backburn *Austral & NZ* ▷ *vb* **1** to clear (an area of bush) by creating a fire that burns in the opposite direction from the wind **2** to prevent a bush fire from spreading by clearing an area of land in front of it ▷ *n* **3** the act or result of backburning

b

back catalogue *n* a musician's previous recordings, as opposed to their current recordings
backchat *n informal* impudent replies
backcloth *n* a painted curtain at the back of a stage set. Also called: **backdrop**
backcomb *vb* to comb (the hair) towards the roots to give more bulk to a hairstyle
back country *n Austral & NZ* land far away from settled areas
backdate *vb* **-dating, -dated** to make (a document or arrangement) effective from a date earlier than its completion
back door *n* a means of entry to a job or position that is secret or obtained through influence
back down *vb* to withdraw an earlier claim
backer *n* a person who gives financial or other support
backfire *vb* **-firing, -fired 1** (of a plan or scheme) to fail to have the desired effect **2** (of an internal-combustion engine) to make a loud noise as a result of an explosion of unburnt gases in the exhaust system
backgammon *n* a game for two people played on a board with pieces moved according to throws of the dice [*back* + obsolete *gammon* game]
background *n* **1** the events or circumstances that help to explain something **2** a person's social class, education, or experience **3** the part of a scene furthest from the viewer **4** an inconspicuous position: *in the background* **5** the space behind the chief figures or objects in a picture
backhand *tennis & squash etc.* ▷ *adj* **1** (of a stroke) made from across the body with the back of the hand facing the direction of the stroke ▷ *n* **2** a backhand stroke
backhanded *adj* **1** (of a blow or shot) performed with the arm moving from across the body **2** ambiguous or implying criticism: *a backhanded compliment*
backhander *n* **1** *slang* a bribe **2** a backhanded stroke or blow
backing *n* **1** support **2** something that forms or strengthens the back of something **3** musical accompaniment for a pop singer
backing dog *n* NZ a dog that moves a flock of sheep by jumping on their backs
backlash *n* **1** a sudden and adverse reaction **2** a recoil between interacting badly fitting parts in machinery
backlog *n* an accumulation of things to be dealt with
backlot *n* an area outside a film or television studio used for outdoor filming
back number *n* **1** an old issue of a newspaper or magazine **2** *informal* a person or thing considered to be old-fashioned
back off *vb* **1** to retreat **2** to abandon an intention or objective
back office *n* **1** the administrative staff of a financial institution or other business ▷ *adj* **back-office 2** of or relating to such staff: *back-office operations*
back out *vb* (often foll. by *of*) to withdraw from (an agreement)
backpack *n* **1** a rucksack ▷ *vb* **2** to go hiking or travelling with a backpack **backpacker** *n*
back passage *n* the rectum
back-pedal *vb* **-pedalling, -pedalled** *or US* **-pedaling, -pedaled** to retract or modify a previous opinion or statement
back room *n* **1** a place where secret research or planning is done ▷ *adj* **back-room 2** of or relating to secret research or planning: *back-room boys*
back seat *n informal* a less important or responsible position: *lyricism took a back seat to drama*
back-seat driver *n informal* a person who offers unwanted advice
backside *n informal* the buttocks
backslide *vb* **-sliding, -slid** to relapse into former bad habits or vices **backslider** *n*
backspace *vb* **-spacing, -spaced** to move a typewriter carriage or computer cursor backwards
backspin *n sport* a backward spin given to a ball to reduce its speed at impact
backstabbing *n* treacherous actions or remarks that are likely to cause harm to a person **backstabber** *n* **backstab** *vb*
backstage *adv* **1** behind the stage in a theatre ▷ *adj* **2** situated backstage
backstairs *or* **backstair** *adj* underhand: *backstairs gossip*
backstreet *n* **1** a street in a town far from the main roads ▷ *adj* **2** denoting secret or illegal activities: *a backstreet abortion*
backstroke *n swimming* a stroke performed on the back, using backward circular strokes of each arm
backtrack *vb* **1** to go back along the same route one has just travelled **2** to retract or reverse one's opinion or policy
back up *vb* **1** to support **2** *computers* to make a copy of (a data file), esp. as a security copy **3** (of traffic) to become jammed behind an obstruction ▷ *n* **backup 4** support or reinforcement **5** a reserve or substitute ▷ *adj* **backup 6** able to be substituted: *a backup copy*
backward *adj* **1** directed towards the rear **2** *sometimes offensive* slow in physical or material development **3** reluctant or bashful ▷ *adv* **4** same as **backwards backwardness** *n*
backwards *or* **backward** *adv* **1** towards the rear **2** with the back foremost **3** in the reverse of the usual direction **4** into a worse state: *the Gothic novel's been going backwards since Radcliffe* **5 bend over backwards** *informal* to make a special effort to please someone
backwash *n* **1** water washed backwards by the motion of oars or a ship **2** an unpleasant aftereffect of an event or situation
backwater *n* **1** an isolated or backward place or condition **2** a body of stagnant water connected to a river
backwoods *pl n* **1** any remote, sparsely populated place **2** partially cleared, sparsely populated forests **backwoodsman** *n*
back yard *n* **1** a yard at the back of a house, etc. **2 in one's own back yard A** close at hand **B** involving or implicating one

bacon *n* **1** meat from the back and sides of a pig, dried, salted, and often smoked **2** **bring home the bacon** *informal* **a** to achieve success **b** to provide material support [Old French]

BACS Bankers' Automated Clearing System: a method of making payments directly to a creditor's bank

bacteria *pl n, sing* **-rium** a large group of microorganisms, many of which cause disease [Greek *baktron* rod] **bacterial** *adj*

bacteriology *n* the study of bacteria **bacteriologist** *n*

Bactrian camel *n* a two-humped camel [*Bactria*, ancient country of Asia]

bad *adj* **worse, worst** **1** not good; of poor quality **2** lacking skill or talent: *I'm so bad at that sort of thing* **3** harmful: *smoking is bad for you* **4** evil or immoral **5** naughty or mischievous **6** rotten or decayed: *a bad egg* **7** severe: *a bad headache* **8** incorrect or faulty: *bad grammar* **9** sorry or upset: *I feel bad about saying no* **10** unfavourable or distressing: *bad news* **11** offensive or unpleasant: *bad language* **12** not valid: *a bad cheque* **13** not recoverable: *a bad debt* **14** **badder, baddest** *slang* good; excellent **15** **not bad** *or* **not so bad** *informal* fairly good **16** **too bad** *informal* (often used dismissively) regrettable ▷ *n* **17** unfortunate or unpleasant events: *you've got to take the good with the bad* ▷ *adv* **18** *not standard* badly: *to want something bad* [Middle English] **badness** *n*

bad blood *n* a feeling of intense hatred or hostility between people

bade *or* **bad** *vb* a past tense of **bid**

badge *n* **1** a distinguishing emblem or mark worn to show membership or achievement **2** any revealing feature or mark [Old French *bage*]

badger *n* **1** a stocky burrowing mammal with a black and white striped head ▷ *vb* **2** to pester or harass [probably from *badge*]

badinage (**bad**-in-nahzh) *n* playful and witty conversation [French]

badly *adv* **worse, worst** **1** poorly; inadequately **2** unfavourably: *our plan worked out badly* **3** severely: *badly damaged* **4** very much: *he badly needed to improve his image* **5** **badly off** poor

badminton *n* a game played with rackets and a shuttlecock which is hit back and forth across a high net [*Badminton* House, Glos]

Bafana Bafana (bah-**fan**-na) *pl n S African* the South African national soccer team [from Nguni (language group of southern Africa) *bafana* the boys]

baffle *vb* **-fling, -fled** **1** to perplex ▷ *n* **2** a mechanical device to limit or regulate the flow of fluid, light, or sound [origin unknown] **bafflement** *n* **baffling** *adj*

bag *n* **1** a flexible container with an opening at one end **2** the contents of such a container **3** a piece of luggage **4** a handbag **5** a loose fold of skin under the eyes **6** any sac in the body of an animal **7** *derogatory slang* an ugly or bad-tempered woman: *an old bag* **8** the amount of game taken by a hunter **9** **in the bag** *slang* assured of succeeding ▷ *vb* **bagging, bagged** **10** to put into a bag **11** to bulge or cause to bulge **12** to capture or kill, as in hunting **13** *informal* to succeed in securing: *he bagged the best chair* ▷ See also **bags** [probably Old Norse *baggi*]

bagatelle *n* **1** something of little value **2** a board game in which balls are struck into holes **3** a short piece of music [French]

bagel (**bay**-gl) *n* a hard ring-shaped bread roll [Yiddish *beygel*]

baggage *n* **1** suitcases packed for a journey **2** an army's portable equipment **3** *informal* previous knowledge or experience that may have an influence in new circumstances: *cultural baggage* [Old French *bagage*]

baggy *adj* **-gier, -giest** (of clothes) hanging loosely **bagginess** *n*

bag lady *n* a homeless woman who carries around all her possessions in shopping bags

bagpipes *pl n* a musical wind instrument in which sounds are produced in reed pipes by air from an inflated bag

bags *pl n* **1** *informal* a lot ▷ *interj* **2** Also: **bags I** *children's slang Brit & NZ* an indication of the desire to do, be, or have something

bah *interj* an expression of contempt or disgust

bail[1] *law* ▷ *n* **1** a sum of money deposited with the court as security for a person's reappearance in court **2** the person giving such security **3** **jump bail** to fail to reappear in court after bail has been paid **4** **stand** *or* **go bail** to act as surety for someone ▷ *vb* **5** (foll. by *out*) to obtain the release of (a person) from custody by depositing money with the court [Old French: custody]

bail[2] *or* **bale** *vb* **bail out** to remove water from (a boat). See also **bail out** [Old French *baille* bucket]

bail[3] *n* **1** *cricket* either of two small wooden bars across the tops of the stumps **2** a partition between stalls in a stable or barn **3** *Austral & NZ* a framework in a cow shed used to secure the head of a cow during milking **4** a movable bar on a typewriter that holds the paper against the roller [Old French *baile* stake]

bailey *n* the outermost wall or court of a castle [Old French *baille* enclosed court]

Bailey bridge *n* a temporary bridge that can be rapidly assembled [after Sir Donald Coleman *Bailey*, its designer]

bailiff *n* **1** *Brit* a sheriff's officer who serves writs and summonses **2** the agent of a landlord or landowner [Old French *baillif*]

bailiwick *n* **1** *law* the area over which a bailiff has power **2** a person's special field of interest [*bailie* magistrate + obsolete *wick* district]

bail out *or* **bale out** *vb* **1** to help (a person or organization) out of a predicament **2** to make an emergency parachute jump from an aircraft

bail up *vb* **1** *Austral & NZ informal* to confine (a cow) or (of a cow) to be confined by the head in a bail. See **bail**[3] **2** *Austral history* (of a bushranger) to hold under guard in order to rob **3** *Austral* to submit to robbery without offering resistance **4** *Austral informal* to accost or detain, esp. in conversation

bain-marie (ban-mar-**ee**) *n, pl* **bains-marie** a container for holding hot water, in which sauces and other dishes are gently cooked or kept warm [French: bath of Mary]

bairn *n Scot & N English* a child [Old English *bearn*]

b

bait *n* **1** something edible fixed to a hook or in a trap to attract fish or animals **2** an enticement ▹ *vb* **3** to put a piece of food on or in (a hook or trap) **4** to persecute or tease **5** to set dogs upon (a bear or badger) [Old Norse *beita* to hunt]

USAGE The phrase *with bated breath* is sometimes wrongly spelled *with baited breath*.

b

baize *n* a feltlike woollen fabric, usually green, which is used for the tops of billiard and card tables [Old French *bai* reddish-brown]
bake *vb* **baking, baked 1** to cook by dry heat in an oven **2** to cook bread, pastry, or cakes **3** to make or become hardened by heat **4** *informal* to be extremely hot [Old English *bacan*]
bakeapple *n* cloudberry
baked beans *pl n* haricot beans, baked and tinned in tomato sauce
Bakelite (**bake**-a-lite) *n trademark* any of a class of resins used as electric insulators and for making plastics [after L. H. *Baekeland*, inventor]
bakeoff *n* a baking competition
baker *n* a person who makes or sells bread, cakes, etc.
baker's dozen *n* thirteen
bakery *n, pl* **-eries** a place where bread, cakes, etc. are made or sold
baking powder *n* a powdered mixture that contains sodium bicarbonate and cream of tartar: used in baking as a raising agent
bakkie (**buck**-ee) *n S African* a small truck with an enclosed cab and an open goods area at the back [Afrikaans *bak* container]
baksheesh *n* (in some Eastern countries) money given as a tip or present [Persian *bakhshīsh*]
Balaclava *or* **Balaclava helmet** *n* a close-fitting woollen hood that covers the ears and neck [after *Balaklava*, in the Crimea]
balalaika *n* a Russian musical instrument with a triangular body and three strings [Russian]
balance *n* **1** stability of mind or body: *lose one's balance* **2** a state of being in balance **3** harmony in the parts of a whole **4** the power to influence or control: *the balance of power* **5** something that remains: *the balance of what you owe* **6** *accounting* **A** the matching of debit and credit totals in an account **B** a difference between such totals **7** a weighing device **8 in the balance** in an undecided condition **9 on balance** after weighing up all the factors ▹ *vb* **-ancing, -anced 10** to weigh in or as if in a balance **11** to be or come into equilibrium **12** to bring into or hold in equilibrium **13** to compare the relative weight or importance of **14** to arrange so as to create a state of harmony **15** *accounting* to compare or equalize the credit and debit totals of (an account) [Latin *bilanx* having two scales]
balance of payments *n* the difference in value between a nation's total payments to foreign countries and its total receipts from foreign countries
balance of power *n* the equal distribution of military and economic power among countries
balance of trade *n* the difference in value between exports and imports of goods
balance sheet *n* a statement that shows the financial position of a business
balcony *n, pl* **-nies 1** a platform projecting from a building with a balustrade along its outer edge, often with access from a door **2** an upper tier of seats in a theatre or cinema [Italian *balcone*]
bald *adj* **1** having no hair or fur, esp. of a man having no hair on the scalp **2** lacking natural covering **3** plain or blunt: *the bald facts* **4** (of a tyre) having a worn tread [Middle English *ballede*] **baldly** *adv* **baldness** *n*
balderdash *n* stupid or illogical talk [origin unknown]
balding *adj* becoming bald
bale[1] *n* **1** a large bundle of hay or goods bound by ropes or wires for storage or transportation ▹ *vb* **baling, baled 2** to make (hay) or put (goods) into a bale or bales [Old High German *balla* ball]
bale[2] *vb* **baling, baled** same as **bail**[2]
baleen *n* whalebone [Latin *balaena* whale]
baleen whale *n* same as **whalebone whale**
baleful *adj* harmful, menacing, or vindictive **balefully** *adv*
bale out *vb* same as **bail out**
balk *or* **baulk** *vb* **1** to stop short: *the horse balked at the jump* **2** to recoil: *France balked at the parliament having a veto* **3** to thwart, check, or foil: *he was balked in his plans* [Old English *balca* ridge]
Balkan *adj* of any of the countries of the Balkan Peninsula in SE Europe, between the Adriatic and Aegean Seas
ball[1] *n* **1** a spherical or nearly spherical mass: *a ball of wool* **2** a round or roundish object used in various games **3** a single delivery of the ball in a game **4** any more or less rounded part of the body: *the ball of the foot* **5 have the ball at one's feet** to have the chance of doing something **6 on the ball** *informal* alert; informed **7 play ball** *informal* to cooperate **8 set** *or* **keep the ball rolling** to initiate or maintain the progress of an action, discussion, or project ▹ *vb* **9** to form into a ball ▹ See also **balls, balls-up** [Old Norse *böllr*]
ball[2] *n* **1** a lavish or formal social function for dancing **2 have a ball** *informal* to have a very enjoyable time [Late Latin *ballare* to dance]
ballad *n* **1** a narrative song or poem often with a chorus that is repeated **2** a slow sentimental song [Old Provençal *balada* song accompanying a dance]
ballade *n* **1** *prosody* a verse form consisting of three stanzas and an envoy, all ending with the same line **2** *music* a romantic instrumental composition
ball-and-socket joint *n anatomy* a joint in which a rounded head fits into a rounded cavity, allowing a wide range of movement
ballast *n* **1** a substance, such as sand, used to stabilize a ship when it is not carrying cargo **2** crushed rock used for the foundation of a road or railway track ▹ *vb* **3** to give stability or weight to [probably Low German]
ball bearing *n* **1** an arrangement of steel balls placed between moving parts of a machine in order to reduce friction **2** a metal ball used in such an arrangement
ball boy *or* **ball girl** *n* (in tennis) a person who retrieves balls that go out of play

ball cock *n* a device consisting of a floating ball and valve for regulating the flow of liquid into a tank or cistern

ballerina *n* a female ballet dancer [Italian]

ballet *n* **1** a classical style of expressive dancing based on precise conventional steps **2** a theatrical representation of a story performed by ballet dancers [Italian *balletto* a little dance] **balletic** *adj*

ball game *n* **1** a game played with a ball **2** *US & Canad* a game of baseball **3** *informal* a state of affairs: *a whole new ball game*

ballistic missile *n* a launched weapon which is guided automatically in flight but falls freely at its target

ballistics *n* the study of the flight of projectiles, often in relation to firearms [Greek *ballein* to throw] **ballistic** *adj*

balloon *n* **1** an inflatable rubber bag used as a plaything or party decoration **2** a large bag inflated with a lighter-than-air gas, designed to rise and float in the atmosphere with a basket for carrying passengers **3** an outline containing the words or thoughts of a character in a cartoon ▷ *vb* **4** to fly in a balloon **5** to swell or increase rapidly in size: *the cost of health care has ballooned* [Italian dialect *ballone* ball] **balloonist** *n*

ballot *n* **1** the practice of selecting a representative or course of action by voting **2** the number of votes cast in an election **3** the actual vote or paper indicating a person's choice ▷ *vb* **-loting, -loted 4** to vote or ask for a vote from: *we balloted the members on this issue* **5** to vote for or decide on something by ballot [Italian *ballotta* a little ball]

ballot box *n* a box into which voting papers are dropped on completion

ballot paper *n* a paper used for voting

ballpark *n* **1** *US & Canad* a stadium used for baseball games **2** *informal* approximate range: *in the right ballpark*

ballpoint *or* **ballpoint pen** *n* a pen which has a small ball bearing as a writing point

ballroom *n* a large hall for dancing

ballroom dancing *n* social dancing in couples to music in conventional rhythms, such as the waltz

balls *pl n slang* **1** the testicles **2** nonsense **3** courage and determination **ballsy** *adj*

balls-up *slang* ▷ *n* **1** something botched or muddled ▷ *vb* **balls up 2** to muddle or botch

bally *adj, adv Brit old-fashioned slang* extreme or extremely: *a bally nuisance*; *he's too bally charming for his own good*

ballyhoo *n informal* unnecessary or exaggerated fuss [origin unknown]

balm *n* **1** an aromatic substance obtained from certain tropical trees and used for healing and soothing **2** something comforting or soothing: *her calmness was like a balm to my troubled mind* **3** an aromatic herb, lemon balm [Latin *balsamum* balsam]

balmy *adj* **balmier, balmiest 1** (of weather) mild and pleasant **2** same as **barmy**

baloney *or* **boloney** *n informal* nonsense [*Bologna* (sausage)]

balsa (**bawl**-sa) *n* **1** a tree of tropical America which yields light wood **2** Also: **balsawood** the light wood of this tree, used for making rafts, models, etc. [Spanish: raft]

balsam *n* **1** an aromatic resin obtained from various trees and shrubs and used in medicines and perfumes **2** any plant yielding balsam **3** a flowering plant, such as busy lizzie [Greek *balsamon*]

balti (**bawl**-tee, **bol**-tee) *n* a spicy Indian dish served in a metal dish [Urdu: pail]

Baltic (**bawl**-tik) *adj* of the Baltic Sea in N Europe or the states bordering it

baluster *n* a set of posts supporting a rail [French *balustre*]

balustrade *n* an ornamental rail supported by a set of posts [French]

bamboo *n* a tall treelike tropical grass with hollow stems which are used to make canes, furniture, etc. [probably from Malay *bambu*]

bamboozle *vb* **-zling, -zled** *informal* **1** to cheat; mislead **2** to confuse [origin unknown] **bamboozlement** *n*

BAME Black, Asian, and minority ethnic

ban *vb* **banning, banned 1** to prohibit or forbid officially ▷ *n* **2** an official prohibition [Old English *bannan* to proclaim]

banal (ban-**nahl**) *adj* lacking originality [Old French: common to all] **banality** *n*

banana *n* a crescent-shaped fruit that grows on a tropical or subtropical treelike plant [Spanish or Portuguese, of African origin]

banana republic *n derogatory* a small politically unstable country whose economy is dominated by foreign interests

band¹ *n* **1** a group of musicians playing together, esp. on brass or percussion instruments **2** a group of people having a common purpose: *a band of revolutionaries* ▷ *vb* **3** (foll. by *together*) to unite [French *bande*]

band² *n* **1** a strip of some material, used to hold objects together: *a rubber band* **2** a strip of fabric used as an ornament or to reinforce clothing **3** a stripe of contrasting colour or texture **4** a driving belt in machinery **5** *physics* a range of frequencies or wavelengths between two limits ▷ *vb* **6** to fasten or mark with a band [Old French *bende*]

bandage *n* **1** a piece of material used to dress a wound or wrap an injured limb ▷ *vb* **-daging, -daged 2** to cover or wrap with a bandage [French *bande* strip]

bandanna *or* **bandana** *n* a large brightly-coloured handkerchief or neckerchief [Hindi *bāndhnū* tie-dyeing]

B & B bed and breakfast

bandbox *n* a lightweight usually cylindrical box for hats

bandeau (**ban**-doe) *n, pl* **-deaux** (-doze) a narrow ribbon worn round the head [French]

banderole *n* **1** a narrow flag usually with forked ends **2** a ribbon-like scroll bearing an inscription [Old French]

bandicoot *n* **1** an Australian marsupial with a long pointed muzzle and a long tail **2** **bandicoot rat** any of three burrowing rats of S and SE Asia [Telugu (language of SE India) *pandikokku*]

bandit *n* a robber, esp. a member of an armed gang [Italian *bandito*] **banditry** *n*
bandmaster *n* the conductor of a band
bandolier *n* a shoulder belt with small pockets for cartridges [Old French *bandouliere*]
band saw *n* a power-operated saw consisting of an endless toothed metal band running over two wheels
bandsman *n, pl* **-men** a player in a musical band
bandstand *n* a roofed outdoor platform for a band
bandwagon *n* **jump** *or* **climb on the bandwagon** to join a popular party or movement that seems assured of success
bandwidth *n* the range of frequencies used for transmitting electronic information
bandy *adj* **-dier, -diest 1** Also: **bandy-legged** having legs curved outwards at the knees **2** (of legs) curved outwards at the knees ▷ *vb* **-dies, -dying, -died 3** to exchange (words), sometimes in a heated manner **4 bandy about** to use (a name, term, etc.) frequently [probably from Old French *bander* to hit back and forth]
bane *n* a person or thing that causes misery or distress: *the bane of my life* [Old English *bana*] **baneful** *adj*
bang *n* **1** a short loud explosive noise, such as the report of a gun **2** a hard blow or loud knock **3** *vulgar slang* an act of sexual intercourse **4 with a bang** successfully: *the party went with a bang* ▷ *vb* **5** to hit or knock, esp. with a loud noise **6** to close (a door) noisily **7** to make or cause to make a loud noise, as of an explosion **8** *vulgar slang* to have sexual intercourse with ▷ *adv* **9** with a sudden impact: *the car drove bang into a lamppost* **10** precisely: *bang in the middle* [Old Norse *bang*, *banga* hammer]
banger *n* **1** *Brit & Austral informal* an old decrepit car **2** *slang* a sausage **3** a firework that explodes loudly
Bangladeshi *adj* **1** of Bangladesh ▷ *n* **2** a person from Bangladesh
bangle *n* a bracelet worn round the arm or sometimes round the ankle [Hindi *bangrī*]
banian *n* same as **banyan**
banish *vb* **1** to send into exile **2** to drive away: *it's the only way to banish weeds from the garden* [Old French *banir*] **banishment** *n*
banisters *or* **bannisters** *pl n* the railing and supporting balusters on a staircase [altered from BALUSTER]
banjo *n, pl* **-jos** *or* **-joes** a stringed musical instrument with a long neck and a circular drumlike body [US pronunciation of earlier *bandore*] **banjoist** *n*
bank[1] *n* **1** an institution offering services, such as the safekeeping and lending of money at interest **2** the building used by such an institution **3** the funds held by a banker or dealer in some gambling games **4** any supply, store, or reserve: *a data bank* ▷ *vb* **5** to deposit (cash or a cheque) in a bank **6** to transact business with a bank ▷ See also **bank on** [probably from Italian *banca* bench, moneychanger's table]
bank[2] *n* **1** a long raised mass, esp. of earth **2** a slope, as of a hill **3** the sloping side and ground on either side of a river ▷ *vb* **4** to form into a bank or mound **5** to cover (a fire) with ashes and fuel so that it will burn slowly **6** (of an aircraft) to tip to one side in turning [Scandinavian]
bank[3] *n* **1** an arrangement of similar objects in a row or in tiers ▷ *vb* **2** to arrange in a bank [Old French *banc* bench]
bankable *adj* likely to ensure financial success: *a bankable star* **bankability** *n*
bank account *n* an arrangement whereby a customer deposits money at a bank and may withdraw it when it is needed
bank card *n* any plastic card issued by a bank, such as a debit card or cheque card
banker[1] *n* **1** a person who owns or manages a bank **2** the keeper of the bank in various gambling games
banker[2] *n Austral & NZ informal* a stream almost overflowing its banks: *the creek was running a banker*
banker's order *n* same as **standing order** (sense 1)
bank holiday *n* (in Britain) a public holiday when banks are closed by law
banking *n* the business engaged in by a bank
bank machine *n chiefly Canad* same as **cash dispenser**
banknote *n* a piece of paper money issued by a central bank
bank on *vb* to rely on
bankrupt *n* **1** a person, declared by a court to be unable to pay his or her debts, whose property is sold and the proceeds distributed among the creditors **2** a person no longer having a particular quality: *a spiritual bankrupt* ▷ *adj* **3** declared insolvent **4** financially ruined **5** no longer having a particular quality: *morally bankrupt* ▷ *vb* **6** to make bankrupt [Old Italian *banca* BANK[1] + *rotta* broken] **bankruptcy** *n*
banksia *n* an Australian evergreen tree or shrub
banner *n* **1** a long strip of material displaying a slogan, advertisement, etc. **2** a placard carried in a demonstration **3** Also called: **banner headline** a large headline in a newspaper extending across the page **4** an advertisement, often animated, that extends across the width of a web page [Old French *baniere*]
bannock *n Scot* a round flat cake made from oatmeal or barley [Old English *bannuc*]
banns *pl n* the public announcement of an intended marriage [plural of obsolete *bann* proclamation]
banquet *n* **1** an elaborate formal dinner often followed by speeches ▷ *vb* **-queting, -queted 2** to hold or take part in a banquet [Italian *banco* a table]
banshee *n* (in Irish folklore) a female spirit whose wailing warns of a coming death [Irish Gaelic *bean sídhe* woman of the fairy mound]
bantam *n* **1** a small breed of domestic fowl **2** a small but aggressive person [after *Bantam*, village in Java, said to be the original home of this fowl]
bantamweight *n* a professional boxer weighing up to 118 lb (53.5 kg) or an amateur weighing up to 119 lb (54 kg)
banter *vb* **1** to tease jokingly ▷ *n* **2** teasing or joking conversation [origin unknown]

Bantu *n* **1** a group of languages of Africa **2** *pl* **-tu** *or* **-tus** *offensive* a Black speaker of a Bantu language ▹ *adj* **3** of the Bantu languages [Bantu *Ba-ntu* people]

Bantustan *n S African offensive* a former name for **homeland** (sense 2)

banyan *or* **banian** *n* an Indian tree whose branches grow down into the soil forming additional trunks [Hindi *baniyā*]

baobab (bay-oh-bab) *n* an African tree with a massive grey trunk, short angular branches, and large pulpy fruit [probably from a native African word]

bap *n Brit* a large soft bread roll [origin unknown]

baptism *n* a Christian religious rite in which a person is immersed in or sprinkled with water as a sign of being cleansed from sin and accepted as a member of the Church **baptismal** *adj*

baptism of fire *n* **1** any introductory ordeal **2** a soldier's first experience of battle

Baptist *n* **1** a member of a Protestant denomination that believes in the necessity of adult baptism by immersion **2 the Baptist** John the Baptist ▹ *adj* **3** of the Baptist Church

baptize *or* **-tise** *vb* **-tizing, -tized** *or* **-tising, -tised** **1** *Christianity* to immerse (a person) in water or sprinkle water on (him or her) as part of the rite of baptism **2** to give a name to [Greek *baptein* to bathe, dip]

bar[1] *n* **1** a rigid usually straight length of metal, wood, etc. used as a barrier or structural part **2** a solid usually rectangular block of any material: *a bar of soap* **3** anything that obstructs or prevents: *a bar to women's mobility* **4** a counter or room where alcoholic drinks are served **5** a narrow band or stripe, as of colour or light **6** a heating element in an electric fire **7** See **Bar** **8** the place in a court of law where the accused stands during trial **9** *music* a group of beats that is repeated with a consistent rhythm throughout a piece of music **10** *football etc.* same as **crossbar** **11** *heraldry* a narrow horizontal line across a shield **12 behind bars** in prison ▹ *vb* **barring, barred** **13** to secure with a bar: *to bar the door* **14** to obstruct: *the fallen tree barred the road* **15** to exclude: *he was barred from membership of the club* **16** to mark with a bar or bars ▹ *prep* **17** except for [Old French *barre*]

bar[2] *n* a unit of pressure equal to 10^5 newtons per square metre [Greek *baros* weight]

Bar *n* **1 the Bar** barristers collectively **2 be called to the Bar** *Brit* to become a barrister

barachois (ba-rush-wah) *n* (in the Atlantic Provinces of Canada) a shallow lagoon formed by a sand bar

barb *n* **1** a cutting remark **2** a point facing in the opposite direction to the main point of a fish-hook, harpoon, etc. **3** a beardlike growth, hair, or projection ▹ *vb* **4** to provide with a barb or barbs [Latin *barba* beard] **barbed** *adj*

barbarian *n* **1** a member of a primitive or uncivilized people **2** a coarse or vicious person ▹ *adj* **3** uncivilized or brutal

barbaric *adj* primitive or brutal

barbarism *n* **1** a brutal, coarse, or ignorant act **2** the condition of being backward, coarse, or ignorant **3** a substandard word or expression

barbarity *n, pl* **-ties** **1** the state of being barbaric or barbarous **2** a vicious act

barbarous *adj* **1** uncivilized: *a barbarous and uninhabitable jungle* **2** brutal or cruel: *the barbarous tortures inflicted on them* [Greek *barbaros* barbarian, non-Greek]

barbecue *n* **1** a grill on which food is cooked over hot charcoal, usually out of doors **2** food cooked over hot charcoal, usually out of doors **3** a party or picnic at which barbecued food is served ▹ *vb* **-cuing, -cued** **4** to cook on a grill, usually over charcoal [American Spanish *barbacoa* frame made of sticks]

barbed wire *n* strong wire with sharp points protruding at close intervals

barbel *n* **1** a long thin growth that hangs from the jaws of certain fishes, such as the carp **2** a freshwater fish with such a growth [Latin *barba* beard]

barbell *n* a long metal rod to which heavy discs are attached at each end for weightlifting

barber *n* a person whose business is cutting men's hair and shaving beards [Latin *barba* beard]

barberry *n, pl* **-ries** a shrub with orange or red berries [Arabic *barbāris*]

barbican *n* a walled defence to protect a gate or drawbridge of a fortification [Old French *barbacane*]

barbiturate *n* a derivative of barbituric acid used in medicine as a sedative

barbituric acid *n* a crystalline solid used in the preparation of barbiturate drugs [German *Barbitursäure*]

Barbour *n trademark Brit* a waterproof waxed jacket

barcarole *or* **barcarolle** *n* **1** a Venetian boat song **2** an instrumental composition resembling this [French]

bar chart *or* **bar graph** *n* a diagram consisting of vertical or horizontal bars whose lengths are proportional to amounts or quantities

bar code *n* an arrangement of numbers and parallel lines on a package, which can be electronically scanned at a checkout to give the price of the goods

bard *n* **1** *archaic or literary* a poet **2 A** (formerly) an ancient Celtic poet **B** a poet who wins a verse competition at a Welsh eisteddfod **3 the Bard** William Shakespeare, English playwright and poet [Scottish Gaelic]

bare *adj* **1** unclothed: used esp. of a part of the body **2** without the natural, conventional, or usual covering: *bare trees* **3** lacking appropriate furnishings, etc.: *a bare room* **4** simple: *the bare facts* **5** just sufficient: *the bare minimum* ▹ *vb* **baring, bared** **6** to uncover [Old English *bær*] **bareness** *n*

bareback *adj, adv* (of horse-riding) without a saddle

bare-faced *or* **barefaced** *adj* obvious or shameless: *a bare-faced lie*

barefoot *or* **barefooted** *adj, adv* with the feet uncovered

bareheaded *adj, adv* with the head uncovered

bare-knuckle *adj* **1** without boxing gloves **2** aggressive and without reservations

b

barely *adv* **1** only just: *barely enough* **2** scantily: *barely furnished*
USAGE See at **hardly**.
bargain *n* **1** an agreement establishing what each party will give, receive, or perform in a transaction **2** something acquired or received in such an agreement **3** something bought or offered at a low price **4 drive a hard bargain** to forcefully pursue one's own profit in a transaction **5 into the bargain** besides ▷ *vb* **6** to negotiate the terms of an agreement or transaction [Old French *bargaigne*]
bargain for *vb* to anticipate
bargain on *vb* to rely or depend on
barge *n* **1** a flat-bottomed boat, used for transporting freight, esp. on canals **2** a boat, often decorated, used in pageants, etc. ▷ *vb* **barging, barged** *informal* **3** (foll. by *into*) to bump into **4** to push one's way violently **5** (foll. by *into* or *in*) to interrupt rudely: *he barged into our conversation* [Medieval Latin *barga*]
bargee *n Brit* a person in charge of a barge
bargepole *n* **1** a long pole used to propel a barge **2 not touch with a bargepole** *informal* to refuse to have anything to do with
bariatric *adj* of or relating to the treatment of obesity: *bariatric surgery* [Greek *baros* weight + *iatrikos* of healing]
barista (bar-**ee**-sta) *n* a person who makes and sells coffee in a coffee bar
baritone *n* **1** the second lowest adult male voice **2** a singer with such a voice [Greek *barus* low + *tonos* tone]
barium (**bare**-ee-um) *n chem* a soft silvery-white metallic chemical element. Symbol: **Ba** [Greek *barus* heavy]
barium meal *n* a preparation of barium sulphate, which is opaque to X-rays, used in X-ray examination of the alimentary canal
bark[1] *n* **1** the loud harsh cry of a dog or certain other animals ▷ *vb* **2** (of a dog or other animal) to make its typical cry **3** to shout in an angry tone: *he barked an order* **4 bark up the wrong tree** *informal* to misdirect one's attention or efforts [Old English *beorcan*]
bark[2] *n* **1** an outer protective layer of dead corklike cells on the trunks of trees ▷ *vb* **2** to scrape or rub off (skin), as in an injury **3** to remove the bark from (a tree) [Old Norse *börkr*]
barker *n* a person at a fairground who loudly addresses passers-by to attract customers
barking *adj slang* mad or crazy
barley *n* **1** a tall grasslike plant with dense bristly flower spikes, widely cultivated for grain **2** the grain of this grass used in making beer and whisky and for soups [Old English *bere*]
barleycorn *n* a grain of barley, or barley itself
barley sugar *n* a brittle clear amber-coloured sweet
barley water *n* a drink made from an infusion of barley
barm *n* the yeasty froth on fermenting malt liquors [Old English *bearm*]
barmaid *n* a woman who serves in a pub
barman *n, pl* **-men** a man who serves in a pub
bar mitzvah *Judaism* ▷ *n* **1** a ceremony marking the 13th birthday of a boy and his assumption of religious obligations ▷ *adj* **2** (of a Jewish boy) having undergone this ceremony [Hebrew: son of the law]
barmy *adj* **-mier, -miest** *slang* foolish or slightly crazy: *a barmy idea* [originally, full of BARM, frothing, excited]
barn *n* a large farm outbuilding, chiefly for storing grain, but also for livestock [Old English *bere* barley + *ærn* room]
barnacle *n* a marine shellfish that lives attached to rocks, ship bottoms, etc. [Old French *bernac*] **barnacled** *adj*
barnacle goose *n* a goose with a black-and-white head and body [it was formerly believed that the goose developed from a shellfish]
barn dance *n* **1** *US & Canad* a party with square-dancing **2** *Brit* a progressive round country dance
barney *n informal* a noisy fight or argument [origin unknown]
barn owl *n* an owl with a pale brown-and-white plumage and a heart-shaped face
barnstorm *vb* **1** *chiefly US & Canad* to tour rural districts making speeches in a political campaign **2** to tour rural districts putting on shows **barnstorming** *n, adj*
barnyard *n* a yard adjoining a barn
barograph *n meteorol* a barometer that automatically keeps a record of changes in atmospheric pressure [Greek *baros* weight + *graphein* to write]
barometer *n* an instrument for measuring atmospheric pressure, used to determine weather or altitude changes [Greek *baros* weight + *metron* measure] **barometric** *adj*
baron *n* **1** a member of the lowest rank of nobility in the British Isles **2** a powerful businessman or financier: *a press baron* [Old French] **baronial** *adj*
baroness *n* **1** a woman holding the rank of baron **2** the wife or widow of a baron
baronet *n* a commoner who holds the lowest hereditary British title **baronetcy** *n*
barony *n, pl* **-nies** the domain or rank of a baron
baroque (bar-**rock**) *n* **1** a highly ornate style of architecture and art, popular in Europe from the late 16th to the early 18th century **2** a highly ornamented 17th-century style of music ▷ *adj* **3** ornate in style [French from Portuguese *barroco* imperfectly shaped pearl]
barque (**bark**) *n* **1** a sailing ship, esp. one with three masts **2** *poetic* any boat [Old Provençal *barca*]
barrack[1] *vb* to house (soldiers) in barracks
barrack[2] *vb* **1** *Brit, Austral & NZ informal* to criticize loudly or shout against (a team or speaker) **2** *Austral & NZ* (foll. by *for*) to shout encouragement for (a team) [Irish: to boast]
barracks *pl n* **1** a building or group of buildings used to accommodate military personnel **2** a large and bleak building [French *baraque*]
barracuda (bar-rack-**kew**-da) *n, pl* **-da** *or* **-das** a tropical fish which feeds on other fishes [American Spanish]
barrage (**bar**-rahzh) *n* **1** a continuous delivery of questions, complaints, etc. **2** *military* the continuous firing of artillery over a wide area

3 a construction built across a river to control the water level [French *barrer* to obstruct]

barrage balloon *n* a balloon tethered by cables, often with net suspended from it, used to deter low-flying air attack

barramundi *n* an edible Australian fish

barre (bar) *n* a rail at hip height used for ballet practice [French]

barrel *n* **1** a cylindrical container, usually with rounded sides and flat ends, and held together by metal hoops **2** a unit of capacity of varying amount in different industries **3** the tube through which the bullet of a firearm is fired **4 over a barrel** *informal* powerless ▷ *vb* **-relling, -relled** *or US* **-reling, -reled 5** to put into a barrel or barrels [Old French *baril*]

barrel organ *n* a musical instrument played by turning a handle

barren *adj* **1** incapable of producing offspring **2** unable to support the growth of crops, fruit, etc.: *barren land* **3** unprofitable or unsuccessful: *the team has had a barren season* **4** dull [Old French *brahain*] **barrenness** *n*

barricade *n* **1** a barrier, esp. one erected hastily for defence ▷ *vb* **-cading, -caded 2** to erect a barricade across (an entrance) [Old French *barrique* a barrel]

barrier *n* **1** anything that blocks a way or separates, such as a gate **2** anything that prevents progress: *a barrier of distrust* **3** anything that separates or hinders union: *a language barrier* [Old French *barre* bar]

barrier cream *n* a cream used to protect the skin

barrier reef *n* a long narrow ridge of coral, separated from the shore by deep water

barring *prep* unless something occurs; except for

barrister *n* a lawyer who is qualified to plead in the higher courts [from BAR¹]

barrow¹ *n* **1** same as **wheelbarrow 2** a handcart used by street traders [Old English *bearwe*]

barrow² *n* a heap of earth placed over a prehistoric tomb [Old English *beorg*]

barrow boy *n Brit* a man who sells goods from a barrow

Bart. Baronet

bartender *n* a person who serves drinks behind a bar

barter *vb* **1** to trade goods or services in exchange for other goods or services, rather than for money ▷ *n* **2** trade by the exchange of goods [Old French *barater* to cheat]

baryon (bar-ree-on) *n* an elementary particle that has a mass greater than or equal to that of the proton [Greek *barus* heavy]

baryta (bar-rite-a) *n* a compound of barium, such as barium oxide [Greek *barus* heavy]

barytes (bar-rite-eez) *n* a colourless or white mineral: a source of barium [Greek *barus* heavy]

basal *adj* **1** at, of, or constituting a base **2** fundamental

basal metabolic rate *n* the amount of energy consumed by an animal's body at rest

basalt (bass-awlt) *n* a dark volcanic rock [Greek *basanitēs* touchstone] **basaltic** *adj*

bascule *n* a drawbridge that operates by a counterbalanced weight [French: seesaw]

base¹ *n* **1** the bottom or supporting part of anything **2** the fundamental principle or part: *agriculture was the economic base of the city's growth* **3** a centre of operations, organization, or supply **4** a starting point: *the new discovery became the base for further research* **5** the main ingredient of a mixture: *to use rice as a base in cookery* **6** *chem* a compound that combines with an acid to form a salt **7** the lower side or face of a geometric construction **8** *maths* the number of units in a counting system that is equivalent to one in the next higher counting place: *10 is the base of the decimal system* **9** a starting or finishing point in any of various games ▷ *vb* **basing, based 10** (foll. by *on* or *upon*) to use as a basis for **11** (foll. by *at* or *in*) to station, post, or place [Latin *basis* pedestal]

base² *adj* **1** dishonourable or immoral: *base motives* **2** of inferior quality or value: *a base coin* **3** debased; counterfeit: *base currency* [Late Latin *bassus* of low height]

baseball *n* **1** a team game in which the object is to score runs by batting the ball and running round all four bases **2** the ball used in this game

baseless *adj* not based on fact

baseline *n* **1** a value or starting point on an imaginary scale with which other things are compared **2** a line at each end of a tennis court that marks the limit of play

baseliner *n tennis* a player who plays most of his or her shots from the back of court

basement *n* a partly or wholly underground storey of a building

base metal *n* a common metal such as copper or lead, that is not a precious metal

base rate *n* **1** the rate of interest used by a bank as a basis for its lending rates **2** the rate at which the Bank of England lends to other financial organizations, which effectively controls interest rates throughout the UK

bases¹ *n* the plural of **basis**

bases² *n* the plural of **base¹**

bash *informal* ▷ *vb* **1** to strike violently or crushingly **2** (foll. by *into*) to crash into ▷ *n* **3** a heavy blow **4 have a bash** *informal* to make an attempt [origin unknown]

bashful *adj* shy or modest [*bash*, short for ABASH] **bashfully** *adv*

-bashing *combining form informal* **A** indicating a malicious attack on members of a group: *union-bashing* **B** indicating an activity undertaken energetically: *Bible-bashing* **-basher** *combining form*

basic *adj* **1** of or forming a base or basis **2** elementary or simple: *a few basic facts* **3** excluding additions or extras: *basic pay* **4** *chem* of or containing a base ▷ *n* **5 basics** fundamental principles, facts, etc. **basically** *adv*

BASIC *n* a computer programming language that uses common English terms [*b(eginner's) a(ll-purpose) s(ymbolic) i(nstruction) c(ode)*]

basic slag *n* a slag produced in steel-making, containing calcium phosphate

basil *n* an aromatic herb used for seasoning food [Greek *basilikos* royal]

basilica *n* **1** a Roman building, used for public administration, which is rectangular with two aisles and a rounded end **2** a Christian church of similar design [Greek *basilikē oikia* the king's house]

basilisk *n* (in classical legend) a serpent that could kill by its breath or glance [Greek *basiliskos* royal child]

basin *n* **1** a round wide container open at the top **2** the amount a basin will hold **3** a washbasin or sink **4** any partially enclosed area of water where ships or boats may be moored **5** the catchment area of a particular river **6** a depression in the earth's surface [Old French *bacin*]

basis *n, pl* **bases** **1** something that underlies, supports, or is essential to an idea, belief, etc. **2** a principle on which something depends [Greek: step]

bask *vb* (foll. by *in*) **1** to lie in or be exposed (to pleasant warmth or sunshine) **2** to enjoy (approval or favourable conditions) [Old Norse *bathask* to bathe]

basket *n* **1** a container made of interwoven strips of wood or cane **2** the amount a basket will hold **3** *basketball* **A** the high horizontal hoop through which a player must throw the ball to score points **B** a point scored in this way [Middle English]

basketball *n* a team game in which points are scored by throwing the ball through a high horizontal hoop

basket weave *n* a weave of yarns, resembling that of a basket

basketwork *n* same as **wickerwork**

basking shark *n* a very large plankton-eating shark, which often floats at the sea surface

basmati rice *n* a variety of long-grain rice with slender aromatic grains, used for savoury dishes [Hindi: aromatic]

basque *n* a tight-fitting bodice for women [origin unknown]

Basque *n* **1** a member of a people living in the W Pyrenees in France and Spain **2** the language of the Basques ▷ *adj* **3** of the Basques [Latin *Vasco*]

bas-relief *n* sculpture in which the figures project slightly from the background [Italian *basso rilievo*]

bass[1] (base) *n* **1** the lowest adult male voice **2** a singer with such a voice **3** *informal* same as **bass guitar** or **double bass** ▷ *adj* **4** of the lowest range of musical notes: *the system is engineered to give good bass sound from very small speakers* **5** denoting a musical instrument that is lowest or second lowest in pitch in its family: *bass trombone* **6** of or relating to a bass guitar or double bass: *the band is unusual in that it has two bass players* **7** of or written for a singer with the lowest adult male voice: *the bass soloist in next week's performance of Handel's 'Messiah'* [Middle English *bas*]

bass[2] (rhymes with **gas**) *n* **1** any of various Australian freshwater and sea fish **2** a European spiny-finned freshwater fish [Middle English]

bass clef (base) *n* the clef that establishes F a fifth below middle C on the fourth line of the staff

bass drum (base) *n* a large drum of low pitch

basset hound *n* a smooth-haired dog with short legs and long ears [French *bas* low]

bass guitar (base) *n* an electric guitar with the same pitch and tuning as a double bass

bassinet *n* a wickerwork or wooden cradle or pram, usually hooded [French: little basin]

basso *n, pl* **-sos** *or* **-si** a singer with a bass voice [Late Latin *bassus* low]

bassoon *n* a woodwind instrument that produces a range of low sounds [Italian *basso* deep] **bassoonist** *n*

bastard *n* **1** *informal, derogatory* an obnoxious or despicable person **2** *old-fashioned or offensive* a person born of parents not married to each other **3** *informal* something extremely difficult or unpleasant ▷ *adj* **4** *old-fashioned or offensive* illegitimate by birth **5** counterfeit; spurious [Old French *bastart*] **bastardy** *n*

bastardize *or* **-ise** *vb* **-izing, -ized** *or* **-ising, -ised** **1** to debase **2** *old-fashioned or offensive* to declare illegitimate

baste[1] *vb* **basting, basted** to sew with loose temporary stitches [Old French *bastir* to build]

baste[2] *vb* **basting, basted** to moisten (meat) during cooking with hot fat [origin unknown]

baste[3] *vb* **basting, basted** to thrash [origin unknown]

bastinado *n, pl* **-does** **1** a punishment or torture by beating on the soles of the feet with a stick ▷ *vb* **-doing, -doed** **2** to beat (a person) in this way [Spanish *baston* stick]

bastion *n* **1** a projecting part of a fortification **2** a thing or person regarded as defending a principle or way of life: *a bastion of anti-communism* [French *bastille* fortress]

bat[1] *n* **1** any of various types of club used to hit the ball in certain sports **2** *cricket* a batsman **3 off one's own bat** **A** of one's own accord **B** by one's own unaided efforts ▷ *vb* **batting, batted** **4** to strike with or as if with a bat **5** *cricket etc.* to take a turn at batting [Old English *batt* club]

bat[2] *n* **1** a nocturnal mouselike flying animal with leathery wings **2 blind as a bat** having extremely poor eyesight [Scandinavian]

bat[3] *vb* **batting, batted** **1** to flutter (one's eyelids) **2 not bat an eyelid** *informal* to show no surprise [probably from obsolete *bate* flutter, beat]

batch *n* **1** a group of similar objects or people dispatched or dealt with at the same time **2** the bread, cakes, etc. produced at one baking ▷ *vb* **3** to group (items) for efficient processing [Middle English *bache*]

batch processing *n* a system by which the computer programs of several users are submitted as a single batch

bated *adj* **with bated breath** in suspense or fear

bath *n* **1** a large container in which to wash the body **2** the act of washing in such a container **3** the amount of water in a bath **4 baths** a public swimming pool **5** **A** a liquid in which something is immersed as part of a chemical process, such as developing photographs **B** the vessel containing such a liquid ▷ *vb* **6** *Brit* to wash in a bath [Old English *bæth*]

Bath chair *n* *old-fashioned* a wheelchair for invalids

bath cube *n* a cube of soluble scented material for use in a bath

bathe *vb* **bathing, bathed 1** to swim in open water for pleasure **2** to apply liquid to (the skin or a wound) in order to cleanse or soothe **3** *chiefly US & Canad* to wash in a bath **4** to spread over: *bathed in moonlight* ▷ *n* **5** *Brit* a swim in open water [Old English *bathian*] **bather** *n*

bathos (**bay**-thoss) *n* a sudden ludicrous descent from exalted to ordinary matters in speech or writing [Greek: depth] **bathetic** *adj*

bathrobe *n* **1** a loose-fitting garment for wear before or after a bath or swimming **2** *US & Canad* a dressing gown

bathroom *n* **1** a room with a bath or shower, washbasin, and toilet **2** *US & Canad* a toilet

bathyscaph *or* **bathyscaphe** *n* a deep-sea diving vessel for observation [Greek *bathus* deep + *skaphē* light boat]

bathysphere *n* a strong steel deep-sea diving sphere, lowered by cable [Greek *bathus* deep + *sphere*]

batik (bat-**teek**) *n* **A** a process of printing fabric in which areas not to be dyed are covered by wax **B** fabric printed in this way [Javanese: painted]

batman *n, pl* **-men** an officer's servant in the armed forces [Old French *bat* packsaddle]

baton *n* **1** a thin stick used by the conductor of an orchestra or choir **2** *athletics* a short bar transferred from one runner to another in a relay race **3** a police officer's truncheon **4** a short stick or something shaped like one [French]

baton round *n* same as **plastic bullet**

bats *adj old-fashioned, informal* mad or eccentric

batsman *n, pl* **-men** *cricket etc.* a player who bats or specializes in batting

battalion *n* a military unit comprised of three or more companies [French *bataillon*]

batten[1] *n* **1** a strip of wood used to strengthen something or make it secure **2** a strip of wood used for holding a tarpaulin in place over a hatch on a ship ▷ *vb* **3** to strengthen or fasten with battens [French *bâton* stick]

batten[2] *vb* (foll. by *on*) to thrive at the expense of (someone else) [probably from Old Norse *batna* to improve]

batter[1] *vb* **1** to hit repeatedly **2** to damage or injure, as by blows, heavy wear, etc. **3** to subject (someone, usually a close relative) to repeated physical violence [Middle English *bateren*] **battered** *adj* **batterer** *n* **battering** *n*

batter[2] *n* a mixture of flour, eggs, and milk, used in cooking [Middle English *bater*]

batter[3] *n baseball etc.* a player who bats

battering ram *n* (esp. formerly) a large beam used to break down fortifications

battery *n, pl* **-teries 1** two or more primary cells connected to provide a source of electric current **2** a number of similar things occurring together: *a battery of questions* **3** *criminal law* unlawful beating or wounding of a person **4** *chiefly Brit* a series of cages for intensive rearing of poultry **5** a fortified structure on which artillery is mounted ▷ *adj* **6** kept in a series of cages for intensive rearing: *battery hens* [Latin *battuere* to beat]

battle *n* **1** a fight between large armed forces **2** conflict or struggle ▷ *vb* **-tling, -tled 3** to fight in or as if in military combat: *shop stewards battling to improve conditions at work* **4** to struggle: *she battled through the crowd* [Latin *battuere* to beat]

battle-axe *n* **1** *informal, derogatory* a domineering woman **2** (formerly) a large broad-headed axe

battle cruiser *n* a high-speed warship with lighter armour than a battleship, but of the same size

battle cry *n* **1** a slogan used to rally the supporters of a campaign, movement, etc. **2** a shout uttered by soldiers going into battle

battledore *n* **1** Also called: **battledore and shuttlecock** an ancient racket game **2** a light racket used in this game [Middle English *batyldoure*]

battledress *n* the ordinary uniform of a soldier

battlefield *or* **battleground** *n* the place where a battle is fought

battlement *n* a wall with gaps, originally for firing through [Old French *bataille* battle]

battle royal *n* **1** a fight involving many combatants **2** a long violent argument

battleship *n* a large heavily armoured warship

batty *adj* **-tier, -tiest** *slang* **1** slightly crazy **2** eccentric: *a batty scientist* [from BAT[2]]

bauble *n* **1** a trinket of little value **2** a small round ornament hung from a branch of a Christmas tree [Old French *baubel* plaything]

baud *n* a unit used to measure the speed of transmission of electronic data [after J. M. E. *Baudot*, inventor]

bauera *n* small evergreen Australian shrub

Bauhaus (**bow**-house) *adj* of a school of architecture and applied arts in Germany in the 1920s and 30s characterized by a functionalist approach to design [German: building house]

baulk *vb, n* same as **balk**

bauxite *n* a claylike substance that is the chief source of aluminium [*(Les) Baux* in southern France, where originally found]

bawdy *adj* **bawdier, bawdiest** (of language, writing, etc.) containing humorous references to sex [Old French *baud* merry] **bawdily** *adv* **bawdiness** *n*

bawdyhouse *n archaic* a brothel

bawl *vb* **1** to cry noisily **2** to shout loudly ▷ *n* **3** a loud shout or cry [imitative] **bawling** *n*

bay[1] *n* a stretch of shoreline that curves inwards [Old French *baie*]

bay[2] *n* **1** a recess in a wall **2** an area set aside for a particular purpose: *a sick bay; a loading bay* **3** same as **bay window 4** an area off a road in which vehicles may park or unload **5** a compartment in an aircraft: *the bomb bay* [Old French *baee* gap]

bay[3] *n* **1** a deep howl of a hound or wolf **2 at bay A** forced to turn and face attackers: *the stag at bay* **B** at a safe distance: *to keep his mind blank and his despair at bay* ▷ *vb* **3** to howl in deep prolonged tones [Old French *abaiier* to bark]

bay[4] *n* **1** a Mediterranean laurel tree with glossy aromatic leaves **2 bays** a wreath of bay leaves [Latin *baca* berry]

bay[5] *adj* **1** reddish-brown ▷ *n* **2** a reddish-brown horse [Latin *badius*]

bayberry *n, pl* **-ries** a tropical American tree that yields an oil used in making bay rum. Also: **bay**

bay leaf *n* the dried leaf of a laurel, used for flavouring in cooking

bayonet *n* **1** a blade that can be attached to the end of a rifle and used as a weapon ▷ *vb* **-neting, -neted** *or* **-netting, -netted 2** to stab or kill with a bayonet [*Bayonne*, a port in France, where it originated]
bay rum *n* an aromatic liquid, used in medicines and cosmetics, which was originally obtained by distilling bayberry leaves with rum
bay window *n* a window projecting from a wall
bazaar *n* **1** a sale, esp. one in aid of charity **2** (esp. in Arab countries) a market area, esp. a street of small stalls [Persian *bāzār*]
bazooka *n* a portable rocket launcher that fires a projectile capable of piercing armour [after a pipe instrument devised by an American comedian]
BB *Brit* Boys' Brigade
BBC British Broadcasting Corporation
BBQ barbecue
BC 1 (indicating years numbered back from the supposed year of the birth of Christ) before Christ **2** British Columbia
BCE (used, esp. by non-Christians, in numbering years BC) before Common Era
BCG *trademark* Bacillus Calmette-Guérin (antituberculosis vaccine)
BD Bachelor of Divinity
BDS Bachelor of Dental Surgery
be *vb present sing 1st person* **am**, *2nd person* **are**, *3rd person* **is**, *present pl* **are**, *past sing 1st person* **was**, *2nd person* **were**, *3rd person* **was**, *past pl* **were**, *present participle* **being**, *past participle* **been 1** to exist; live: *I think, therefore I am* **2** to pay a visit; go: *have you been to Spain?* **3** to take place: *my birthday was last Thursday* **4** used as a linking verb between the subject of a sentence and its complement: *Shamin is a musician; honey is sweet; the dance is on Saturday* **5** forms the progressive present tense: *the man is running* **6** forms the passive voice of all transitive verbs: *a good film is being shown on television tomorrow* **7** expresses intention, expectation, or obligation: *the president is to arrive at 9.30* [Old English *bēon*]
Be *chem* beryllium
BE Bachelor of Engineering
be- *prefix* **1** to surround or cover: *befog* **2** to affect completely: *bedazzle* **3** to consider as or cause to be: *befriend* **4** to provide or cover with: *bejewel* **5** (*from verbs*) at, for, against, on, or over: *bewail* [Old English *be-*, *bi-* by]
beach *n* **1** an area of sand or pebbles sloping down to the sea or a lake ▷ *vb* **2** to run or haul (a boat) onto a beach [origin unknown]
beachcomber *n* a person who searches shore debris for anything of worth
beachhead *n military* an area of shore captured by an attacking army, on which troops and equipment are landed
beacon *n* **1** a signal fire or light on a hill or tower, used formerly as a warning of invasion **2** a lighthouse **3** a radio or other signal marking a flight course in air navigation **4** same as **Belisha beacon** [Old English *beacen* sign]
bead *n* **1** a small pierced piece of glass, wood, or plastic that may be strung with others to form a necklace, rosary, etc. **2** a small drop of moisture **3** a small metal knob acting as the sight of a firearm ▷ *vb* **4** to decorate with beads [Old English *bed* prayer] **beaded** *adj*
beading *n* a narrow rounded strip of moulding used for edging furniture
beadle *n* **1** *Brit* (formerly) a minor parish official who acted as an usher **2** *Scot* a church official who attends the minister [Old English *bydel*]
beady *adj* **beadier, beadiest** small, round, and glittering: *beady eyes*
beagle *n* a small hound with a smooth coat, short legs, and drooping ears [origin unknown]
beak¹ *n* **1** the projecting horny jaws of a bird **2** *slang* a person's nose [Latin *beccus*] **beaky** *adj*
beak² *n Brit, Austral & NZ slang* a judge, magistrate, or headmaster [originally thieves' jargon]
beaker *n* **1** a tall drinking cup **2** a lipped glass container used in laboratories [Old Norse *bikarr*]
beam *n* **1** a broad smile **2** a ray of light **3** a narrow flow of electromagnetic radiation or particles: *an electron beam* **4** a long thick piece of wood, metal, etc. used in building **5** the central shaft of a plough to which all the main parts are attached **6** the breadth of a ship at its widest part **7 off (the) beam** *informal* mistaken or irrelevant ▷ *vb* **8** to smile broadly **9** to send out or radiate **10** to divert or aim (a radio signal, light, etc.) in a certain direction: *the concert was beamed live from Geneva* [Old English]
beam-ends *pl n* **on one's beam-ends** out of money
bean *n* **1** the seed or pod of various climbing plants, eaten as a vegetable **2** any of various beanlike seeds, such as coffee **3 full of beans** *informal* full of energy and vitality **4 not have a bean** *slang* to be without money [Old English *bēan*]
beanbag *n* **1** a small cloth bag filled with dried beans and thrown in games **2** a very large cushion filled with polystyrene granules and used as a seat
bean curd *n* same as **tofu**
beanfeast *n Brit informal* any festive or merry occasion
beanie *n Brit, Austral & NZ* a close-fitting woollen hat
beano *n, pl* **beanos** *Brit old-fashioned slang* a celebration or party
beanpole *n slang* a tall thin person
beansprout *n* a small edible shoot grown from a bean seed, often used in Chinese dishes
bear¹ *vb* **bearing, bore, borne 1** to support or hold up **2** to bring: *to bear gifts* **3** to accept the responsibility of: *to bear a heavier burden of taxation* **4** to give birth to **5** to produce by natural growth: *to bear fruit* **6** to tolerate or endure **7** to stand up to; sustain: *his story does not bear scrutiny* **8** to hold in the mind: *to bear a grudge* **9** to show or be marked with: *he still bears the scars* **10** to have, be, or stand in (relation or comparison): *her account bears no relation to the facts* **11** to move in a specified direction: *bear left* **12 bring to bear** to bring into effect ▷ See also **bear down on, bear on** *etc.* [Old English *beran*]

USAGE When *bear* means 'give birth to', the past participle used to form the passive voice can be either *born* or *borne*. When it is followed by the preposition *by*, *borne* should be used: *babies borne by American surrogates*. In all other cases the past participle should be *born*: *I was born in Glasgow; the baby born to hairdresser Maxine*.

bear² *n, pl* **bears** *or* **bear 1** a large heavily-built mammal with a long shaggy coat **2** a bearlike animal, such as the koala **3** an ill-mannered person **4** *Stock Exchange* a person who sells shares in anticipation of falling prices to make a profit on repurchase **5 like a bear with a sore head** *informal* bad-tempered, irritable [Old English *bera*]

bearable *adj* endurable; tolerable

bear-baiting *n history* an entertainment in which dogs attacked a chained bear

beard *n* **1** the hair growing on the lower parts of a man's face **2** any similar growth in animals ▷ *vb* **3** to oppose boldly: *I bearded my formidable employer in her den* [Old English] **bearded** *adj*

bear down on *vb* **1** to press down on **2** to approach (someone) in a determined manner

bearer *n* **1** a person or thing that carries, presents, or upholds something **2** a person who presents a note or bill for payment

bear hug *n* a rough tight embrace

bearing *n* **1** (foll. by *on* or *upon*) relevance to: *it has no bearing on this problem* **2** a part of a machine supporting another part, and usually reducing friction **3** the act of producing fruit or young **4** a person's general social conduct **5** the angular direction of a point measured from a known position **6** the position, as of a ship, fixed with reference to two or more known points **7 bearings** a sense of one's relative position: *I lost my bearings in the dark* **8** *heraldry* a device on a heraldic shield

bear on *vb* to be relevant to

bear out *vb* to show to be truthful: *the witness will bear me out*

bearskin *n* **1** the pelt of a bear **2** a tall fur helmet worn by certain British Army regiments

bear up *vb* to cope with hardships: *they are bearing up well under the pressure*

bear with *vb* to be patient with

beast *n* **1** a large wild animal **2** a brutal or uncivilized person **3** savage nature or characteristics: *the beast in man* [Latin *bestia*]

beastly *adj* **-lier, -liest** *informal* unpleasant; disagreeable

beat *vb* **beating, beat, beaten** *or* **beat 1** to strike with a series of violent blows **2** to move (wings) up and down **3** to throb rhythmically **4** *cookery* to stir or whisk vigorously **5** to shape (metal) by repeated blows **6** *music* to indicate (time) by one's hand or a baton **7** to produce (a sound) by striking a drum **8** to overcome or defeat: *he was determined to beat his illness* **9** to form (a path or track) by repeated use **10** to arrive, achieve, or finish before (someone or something): *she beat her team mate fair and square* **11** (foll. by *back, down* or *off* etc.) to drive, push, or thrust **12** to scour (woodlands or undergrowth) to rouse game for shooting **13** *slang* to puzzle or baffle: *it beats me* ▷ *n* **14** a stroke or blow **15** the sound made by a stroke or blow **16** a regular throb **17** an assigned route, as of a police officer **18** the basic rhythmic unit in a piece of music **19** pop or rock music characterized by a heavy rhythmic beat ▷ *adj* **20** *slang* totally exhausted ▷ See also **beat down, beat up** [Old English *bēatan*] **beating** *n*

beatbox *n* **1** a drum machine ▷ *vb* **2** to simulate percussion instruments with the voice, esp. in hip-hop music **beatboxing** *n*

beat down *vb* **1** (of the sun) to shine intensely **2** *informal* to force or persuade (a seller) to accept a lower price

beater *n* **1** a device used for beating: *a carpet beater* **2** a person who rouses wild game

beatific *adj literary* **1** displaying great happiness **2** having a divine aura [Latin *beatus*]

beatify (bee-at-if-fie) *vb* **-fies, -fying, -fied 1** *RC Church* to declare (a deceased person) to be among the blessed in heaven: the first step towards canonization **2** to make extremely happy **beatification** *n*

beatitude *n* supreme blessedness or happiness [Latin *beatitudo*]

Beatitude *n Christianity* any of the blessings on the poor, meek, etc., in the Sermon on the Mount

Beat movement *n* a group of US writers who emerged in the 1950s, noted for their rejection of the social and political systems of the West and their espousal of alternative lifestyles

beatnik *n* a young person in the late 1950s who rebelled against conventional attitudes and styles of dress [BEAT (noun) + -NIK]

beat up *informal* ▷ *vb* **1** to inflict severe physical damage on (someone) by striking or kicking repeatedly ▷ *n* **2** *Austral & NZ* a small matter deliberately exaggerated ▷ *adj* **beat-up 3** dilapidated

beau (boh) *n, pl* **beaux** *or* **beaus** (bohz) **1** *chiefly US* a boyfriend **2** a man who is greatly concerned with his appearance [French]

Beaufort scale *n meteorol* a scale for measuring wind speeds, ranging from 0 (calm) to 12 (hurricane) [after Sir Francis *Beaufort*, who devised it]

Beaujolais *n* a red or white wine from southern Burgundy in France

beauteous *adj poetic* beautiful

beautician *n* a person who works in a beauty salon

beautiful *adj* **1** very attractive to look at **2** highly enjoyable; very pleasant **beautifully** *adv*

beautify *vb* **-fies, -fying, -fied** to make beautiful **beautification** *n*

beauty *n, pl* **-ties 1** the combination of all the qualities of a person or thing that delight the senses and mind **2** a very attractive woman **3** *informal* an outstanding example of its kind **4** *informal* an advantageous feature: *the beauty of this job is the short hours* [Latin *bellus* handsome]

beauty queen *n* a woman who has been judged the most beautiful in a contest

beauty salon *or* **beauty parlour** *n* an establishment that provides services such as hairdressing, facial treatment, and massage

beauty spot *n* **1** a place of outstanding beauty **2** a small dark-coloured spot formerly worn on a woman's face as decoration

beaver *n* **1** a large amphibious rodent with soft brown fur, a broad flat tail, and webbed hind feet

2 its fur 3 a tall hat made of this fur ▷ *vb* 4 **beaver away** to work very hard and steadily [Old English *beofor*]
bebop *n* same as **bop** [imitative of the rhythm]
becalmed *adj* (of a sailing ship) motionless through lack of wind
became *vb* the past tense of **become**
because *conj* 1 on account of the fact that: *because it's so cold we'll go home* 2 **because of** on account of: *I lost my job because of her* [Middle English *bi cause*]
USAGE See at **reason.**
bechamel sauce (bay-sham-**ell**) *n* a thick white sauce flavoured with onion and seasonings [after the Marquis of *Béchamel*, its inventor]
beck[1] *n* **at someone's beck and call** having to be constantly available to do as someone asks [Middle English *becnen* to beckon]
beck[2] *n* (in N England) a stream [Old English *becc*]
beckon *vb* 1 to summon with a gesture 2 to lure: *fame beckoned* [Old English *bīecnan*]
become *vb* **-coming, -came, -come** 1 to come to be: *she became Prime Minister in 2016* 2 (foll. by *of*) to happen to: *what became of him?* 3 to suit: *that dress becomes you* [Old English *becuman* happen]
becoming *adj* suitable or appropriate: *his conduct was not becoming to the rank of officer*
becquerel (beck-a-**rell**) *n* the SI unit of activity of a radioactive source [after A. H. *Becquerel*, physicist]
bed *n* 1 a piece of furniture on which to sleep 2 a plot of ground in which plants are grown 3 the bottom of a river, lake, or sea 4 any underlying structure or part 5 a layer of rock 6 **get out of bed on the wrong side** *informal* to begin the day in a bad mood 7 **go to bed with** to have sexual intercourse with ▷ *vb* **bedding, bedded** 8 (foll. by *down*) to go to or put into a place to sleep or rest 9 to have sexual intercourse with 10 to place firmly into position: *the poles were bedded in concrete* 11 *geol* to form or be arranged in a distinct layer 12 to plant in a bed of soil [Old English *bedd*]
BEd Bachelor of Education
bed and breakfast *n chiefly Brit* overnight accommodation and breakfast
bedaub *vb* to smear over with something sticky or dirty
bedbug *n* a small blood-sucking wingless insect that infests dirty houses
bedclothes *pl n* coverings for a bed
bedding *n* 1 bedclothes, sometimes with a mattress 2 litter, such as straw, for animals 3 the distinct layered deposits of rocks
bedeck *vb* to cover with decorations
bedevil (bid-**dev**-ill) *vb* **-illing, -illed** *or US* **-iling, -iled** 1 to harass or torment 2 to throw into confusion **bedevilment** *n*
bedfellow *n* 1 a temporary associate 2 a person with whom one shares a bed
bedlam *n* a noisy confused situation [from Hospital of St Mary of *Bethlehem*, a former psychiatric hospital in London]
bed linen *n* sheets and pillowcases for a bed
Bedouin *n* 1 *pl* **-ins** *or* **-in** a nomadic Arab tribesman of the deserts of Arabia, Jordan, and Syria 2 a wanderer [Arabic *badw* desert]
bedpan *n* a shallow container used as a toilet by people who are not well enough to leave bed
bedraggled *adj* with hair or clothing that is untidy, wet, or dirty
bedridden *adj* unable to leave bed because of illness
bedrock *n* 1 the solid rock beneath the surface soil 2 basic principles or facts
bedroom *n* 1 a room used for sleeping ▷ *adj* 2 containing references to sex: *a bedroom comedy*
Beds Bedfordshire
bedside *n* 1 the area beside a bed ▷ *adj* 2 placed at or near the side of the bed: *the bedside table*
bedsit *or* **bedsitter** *n* a furnished sitting room with a bed
bedsore *n* an ulcer on the skin, caused by a lengthy period of lying in bed due to illness
bedspread *n* a top cover on a bed
bedstead *n* the framework of a bed
bedstraw *n* a plant with small white or yellow flowers
bed-wetting *n* involuntarily urinating in bed
bee[1] *n* 1 a four-winged insect that collects nectar and pollen to make honey and wax 2 **have a bee in one's bonnet** to be obsessed with an idea [Old English *bīo*]
bee[2] *n* a social gathering to carry out a communal task: *quilting bee* [probably from Old English *bēn* boon]
Beeb *n* **the Beeb** *Brit informal* the BBC
beech *n* 1 a tree with smooth greyish bark 2 the hard wood of this tree 3 See **copper beech** [Old English *bēce*]
beechnut *n* the small brown triangular edible nut of the beech tree
beef *n* 1 the flesh of a cow, bull, or ox 2 *slang* a complaint ▷ *vb* 3 *slang* to complain ▷ See also **beef up** [Old French *boef*, from Latin *bos* ox]
beefburger *n* a flat fried or grilled cake of minced beef; hamburger
beefcake *n slang* men displayed for their muscular bodies, esp. in photographs
beefeater *n* a yeoman warder of the Tower of London
beef tea *n* a drink made by boiling pieces of lean beef
beef tomato *or* **beefsteak tomato** *n* a type of large fleshy tomato
beef up *vb informal* to strengthen
beefy *adj* **beefier, beefiest** 1 *informal* muscular 2 like beef **beefiness** *n*
beehive *n* a structure in which bees are housed
beekeeper *n* a person who keeps bees for their honey **beekeeping** *n*
beeline *n* **make a beeline for** to speedily take the most direct route to
Beelzebub (bee-**ell**-zib-bub) *n* Satan or any devil [Hebrew *bá'al zebūb*, literally: lord of flies]
been *vb* the past participle of **be**
beep *n* 1 a high-pitched sound, like that of a car horn or some electronic devices ▷ *vb* 2 to make or cause to make such a noise [imitative]
beer *n* 1 an alcoholic drink brewed from malt, sugar, hops, and water 2 a glass, can, or bottle containing this drink [Old English *beor*]
beer and skittles *n informal* enjoyment or pleasure

beer parlour *n Canad* a licensed place in which beer is sold and drunk
beery *adj* **beerier, beeriest** smelling or tasting of beer
beeswax *n* **1** a wax produced by honeybees for making honeycombs **2** this wax after refining, used in polishes, etc.
beet *n* a plant with an edible root and leaves, such as the sugar beet and beetroot [Old English *bēte*]
beetle[1] *n* **1** an insect with a hard wing-case closed over its back for protection ▷ *vb* **-tling, -tled** **2** (foll. by *along* or *off* etc.) *informal* to scuttle or scurry [Old English *bitela*]
beetle[2] *vb* **-tling, -tled** to overhang; jut: *the eaves of the roof beetled out over the windows* [origin unknown] **beetling** *adj*
beetle-browed *adj* having bushy or overhanging eyebrows
beetroot *n* a variety of the beet plant with a dark red root that may be eaten as a vegetable, in salads, or pickled
beet sugar *n* the sucrose obtained from sugar beet
befall *vb* **-falling, -fell, -fallen** *archaic or literary* to happen to [Old English *befeallan*]
befit *vb* **-fitting, -fitted** to be appropriate to or suitable for **befitting** *adj*
before *conj* **1** earlier than the time when **2** rather than: *she'll resign before she agrees to it* ▷ *prep* **3** preceding in space or time; in front of; ahead of: *they stood before the altar* **4** in the presence of: *to be brought before a judge* **5** in preference to: *to put friendship before money* ▷ *adv* **6** previously **7** in front [Old English *beforan*]
beforehand *adj, adv* early; in advance
befriend *vb* to become a friend to
befuddled *adj* stupefied or confused, as through alcoholic drink
beg *vb* **begging, begged** **1** to ask for money or food in the street **2** to ask formally, humbly, or earnestly: *I beg forgiveness; I beg to differ* **3** **beg the question** **A** to put forward an argument that assumes the very point it is supposed to establish, or that depends on some other questionable assumption **B** *not standard* to suggest that a question needs to be asked **4** **go begging** to be unwanted or unused [probably from Old English *bedecian*]

> **USAGE** The use of *beg the question* to mean 'to suggest that a question needs to be asked' is considered by some people to be incorrect.

began *vb* the past tense of **begin**
beget *vb* **-getting, -got** *or* **-gat, -gotten** *or* **-got** *old-fashioned* **1** to cause or create: *repetition begets boredom* **2** to father [Old English *begietan*]
beggar *n* **1** a person who lives by begging **2** *chiefly Brit* a fellow: *lucky beggar!* ▷ *vb* **3** **beggar description** to be impossible to describe **beggarly** *adj*
begin *vb* **-ginning, -gan, -gun** **1** to start (something) **2** to bring or come into being **3** to start to say or speak **4** to have the least capacity to do something: *it doesn't even begin to address the problem* [Old English *beginnan*] **beginner** *n*
beginner's luck *n* exceptional luck supposed to attend a beginner
beginning *n* **1** a start **2** **beginnings** an early part or stage **3** the place where or time when something starts **4** an origin; source
begone *interj* go away!
begonia *n* a tropical plant with ornamental leaves and waxy flowers [after Michel *Bégon*, patron of science]
begot *vb* a past tense and past participle of **beget**
begotten *vb* a past participle of **beget**
begrudge *vb* **-grudging, -grudged** **1** to envy (someone) the possession of something **2** to give or allow unwillingly: *he begrudged her an apology*
beguile (big-**gile**) *vb* **-guiling, -guiled** to charm (someone) into doing something he or she would not normally do
beguiling *adj* charming, often in a deceptive way
beguine (big-**geen**) *n* **1** a dance of South American origin **2** music for this dance [French *béguin* flirtation]
begum (**bay**-gum) *n* (in certain Muslim countries) a woman of high rank [Turkish *begim*]
begun *vb* the past participle of **begin**
behalf *n* **on** *or US & Canad* **in behalf of** in the interest of or for the benefit of [Old English *be* by + *halfe* side]
behave *vb* **-having, -haved** **1** to act or function in a particular way **2** to conduct oneself in a particular way: *the baby behaved very well* **3** to conduct oneself properly [Middle English]
behaviour *or US* **behavior** *n* **1** manner of behaving **2** *psychol* the response of an organism to a stimulus **behavioural** *or US* **behavioral** *adj*
behavioural science *n* the scientific study of the behaviour of organisms
behaviourism *or US* **behaviorism** *n* a school of psychology that regards objective observation of the behaviour of organisms as the only valid subject for study **behaviourist** *or US* **behaviorist** *adj, n*
behead *vb* to remove the head from [Old English *behēafdian*]
beheld *vb* the past of **behold**
behemoth (bee-**hee**-moth) *n* a huge person or thing [Hebrew *bĕhēmāh* beast, name given to a huge beast in the Bible (Job 40:15)]
behest *n* an order or earnest request: *I came at her behest* [Old English *behǣs*]
behind *prep* **1** in or to a position further back than **2** in the past in relation to: *I want to leave the past behind me* **3** late according to: *running behind schedule* **4** concerning the circumstances surrounding: *the reasons behind his departure* **5** supporting: *I'm right behind you in your application* ▷ *adv* **6** in or to a position further back **7** remaining after someone's departure: *she left her books behind* **8** in arrears: *to fall behind with payments* ▷ *adj* **9** in a position further back ▷ *n* **10** *informal* the buttocks [Old English *behindan*]
behindhand *adj, adv* **1** in arrears **2** backward **3** late
behold *vb* **-holding, -held** *archaic or literary* to look (at); observe [Old English *bihealdan*] **beholder** *n*
beholden *adj* indebted; obliged: *I am beholden to you*

behove *vb* **-hoving, -hoved** *archaic* to be necessary or fitting for: *it behoves me to warn you* [Old English *behōfian*]

beige *adj* pale creamy-brown [Old French]

being *n* **1** the state or fact of existing **2** essential nature; self **3** something that exists or is thought to exist: *a being from outer space* **4** a human being

b

bejewelled *or US* **bejeweled** *adj* decorated with jewels

bel *n* a unit for comparing two power levels or measuring the intensity of a sound, equal to 10 decibels [after A. G. *Bell*, scientist]

belabour *or US* **belabor** *vb* to attack verbally or physically

belated *adj* late or too late: *belated greetings* **belatedly** *adv*

belay *vb* **-laying, -layed 1** *naut* to secure (a line) to a pin or cleat **2** *naut* to stop **3** *mountaineering* to secure (a climber) by fixing a rope round a rock or piton [Old English *belecgan*]

belch *vb* **1** to expel wind from the stomach noisily through the mouth **2** to expel or be expelled forcefully: *smoke belching from factory chimneys* ▷ *n* **3** an act of belching [Old English *bialcan*]

beleaguered *adj* **1** struggling against difficulties or criticism: *the country's beleaguered health system* **2** besieged by an enemy: *a ship bringing food to the beleaguered capital of Monrovia* [BE- + obsolete *leaguer* a siege]

belfry *n, pl* **-fries 1** the part of a tower or steeple in which bells are hung **2** a tower or steeple [Germanic]

Belgian *adj* **1** of Belgium ▷ *n* **2** a person from Belgium

belgium sausage *n Austral & NZ* a large smooth bland sausage

Belial (bee-lee-al) *n* the devil or Satan [Hebrew *belīyya'al* worthless]

belie *vb* **-lying, -lied 1** to show to be untrue: *the facts belied the theory* **2** to misrepresent: *the score belied the closeness of the match* **3** to fail to justify: *the promises were soon belied* [Old English *belēogan*]

belief *n* **1** trust or confidence: *belief in the free market* **2** opinion; conviction: *it's my firm belief* **3** a principle, etc., accepted as true, often without proof **4** religious faith

believe *vb* **-lieving, -lieved 1** to accept as true or real: *I believe God exists* **2** to think, assume, or suppose: *I believe you know my father* **3** to accept the statement or opinion of (a person) as true **4** to have religious faith **5 believe in** to be convinced of the truth or existence of: *I don't believe in ghosts* [Old English *beliefan*] **believable** *adj* **believer** *n*

Belisha beacon (bill-lee-sha) *n Brit* a flashing orange globe mounted on a striped post, indicating a pedestrian crossing [after L. Hore-*Belisha*, politician]

belittle *vb* **-tling, -tled** to treat (something or someone) as having little value or importance

bell *n* **1** a hollow, usually metal, cup-shaped instrument that emits a ringing sound when struck **2** the sound made by such an instrument **3** an electrical device that rings or buzzes as a signal **4** something shaped like a bell **5** *Brit slang* a telephone call **6 ring a bell** to sound familiar; recall to the mind something previously experienced [Old English *belle*]

belladonna *n* **1** a drug obtained from deadly nightshade **2** same as **deadly nightshade** [Italian, literally: beautiful lady; supposed to refer to its use as a cosmetic]

bell-bottoms *pl n* trousers that flare from the knee **bell-bottomed** *adj*

belle *n* a beautiful woman, esp. the most attractive woman at a function: *the belle of the ball* [French]

belles-lettres (bell-let-tra) *n* literary works, particularly essays and poetry [French]

bellicose *adj* warlike; aggressive [Latin *bellum* war]

belligerence *n* the act or quality of being belligerent or warlike

belligerent *adj* **1** marked by readiness to fight **2** relating to or engaged in war ▷ *n* **3** a person or country engaged in war [Latin *bellum* war + *gerere* to wage]

bell jar *n* a bell-shaped glass cover used to protect flower arrangements or cover apparatus to confine gases in experiments

bellow *vb* **1** to make a loud deep cry like that of a bull **2** to shout in anger ▷ *n* **3** the characteristic noise of a bull **4** a loud deep roar [probably from Old English *bylgan*]

bellows *n* **1** a device consisting of an air chamber with flexible sides that is used to create and direct a stream of air **2** a flexible corrugated part, such as that connecting the lens system of some cameras to the body [plural of Old English *belig* belly]

bell pull *n* a handle or cord pulled to operate a bell

bell push *n* a button pressed to operate an electric bell

bell-ringer *n* a person who rings church bells or musical handbells **bell-ringing** *n*

bells and whistles *pl n* attractive but nonessential additional features [from the bells and whistles which used to decorate fairground organs]

belly *n, pl* **-lies 1** the part of the body of a vertebrate containing the intestines and other organs **2** the stomach **3** the front, lower, or inner part of something **4 go belly up** *informal* to die, fail, or end ▷ *vb* **-lies, -lying, -lied 5** to swell out; bulge [Old English *belig*]

bellyache *n* **1** *informal* a pain in the abdomen ▷ *vb* **-aching, -ached 2** *slang* to complain repeatedly

bellybutton *n informal* the navel

belly dance *n* **1** a sensuous dance performed by women, with undulating movements of the abdomen ▷ *vb* **belly-dance, -dancing, -danced 2** to dance thus **belly dancer** *n*

belly flop *n* **1** a dive into water in which the body lands horizontally ▷ *vb* **belly-flop, -flopping, -flopped 2** to perform a belly flop

bellyful *n* **1** *slang* more than one can tolerate **2** as much as one wants or can eat

belly laugh *n* a loud deep hearty laugh

belong *vb* **1** (foll. by *to*) to be the property of **2** (foll. by *to*) to be bound to (a person, organization, etc.) by ties of affection, association, membership, etc.: *the nations concerned belonged to NATO* **3** (foll. by *to, under* or *with* etc.) to be classified with: *it belongs to a different class of comets* **4** (foll. by *to*) to be a part of: *this lid belongs to that tin* **5** to have a proper or usual place **6** *informal* to be acceptable, esp. socially [Middle English *belongen*]

belonging *n* a secure relationship: *they have a strong sense of belonging*

belongings *pl n* the things that a person owns or has with him or her

beloved *adj* **1** dearly loved ▷ *n* **2** a person who is dearly loved

below *prep* **1** at or to a position lower than; under **2** less than **3** unworthy of; beneath ▷ *adv* **4** at or to a lower position **5** at a later place in something written **6** *archaic* on earth or in hell [Middle English *bilooghe*]

belt *n* **1** a band of leather or cloth worn around the waist **2** an area where a specific thing is found; zone: *a belt of high pressure* **3** same as **seat belt** **4** a band of flexible material between rotating shafts or pulleys to transfer motion or transmit goods: *a fan belt; a conveyer belt* **5** *informal* a sharp blow **6** **below the belt** *informal* unscrupulous or cowardly **7** **tighten one's belt** to reduce expenditure **8** **under one's belt** as part of one's experience: *he had a string of successes under his belt* ▷ *vb* **9** to fasten with or as if with a belt **10** to hit with a belt **11** *slang* to give (someone) a sharp blow **12** (foll. by *along*) *slang* to move very fast [Old English]

belter *n slang* an outstanding person or event: *a belter of a match*

belt out *vb informal* to sing (a song) loudly

belt up *vb* **1** *slang* to stop talking **2** to fasten with a belt

beluga (bill-loo-ga) *n* a large white sturgeon of the Black and Caspian Seas, from which caviar and isinglass are obtained [Russian *byeluga*]

belvedere *n* a building designed and situated to look out on pleasant scenery [Italian: beautiful sight]

BEM British Empire Medal

bemoan *vb* to lament: *he's always bemoaning his fate*

bemused *adj* puzzled or confused

ben *n Scot & Irish* a mountain peak: *Ben Lomond* [Gaelic *beinn*]

bench *n* **1** a long seat for more than one person **2** **the bench** **A** a judge or magistrate sitting in court **B** judges or magistrates collectively **3** a long and strong worktable [Old English *benc*]

benchmark *n* **1** a mark on a fixed object, used as a reference point in surveying **2** a criterion by which to measure something: *the speech was a benchmark of his commitment*

bench press *n* an exercise in which a person pushes a barbell upwards while lying flat on a bench

bend[1] *vb* **bending, bent** **1** to form a curve **2** to turn from a particular direction: *the road bends right* **3** (often foll. by *down* etc.) to incline the body **4** to submit: *to bend before public opinion* **5** to turn or direct (one's eyes, steps, or attention) **6** **bend someone's ear** *informal* to complain (to someone) for a long time **7** **bend the rules** *informal* to ignore or change rules to suit oneself ▷ *n* **8** a curved part **9** the act of bending **10** **round the bend** *Brit slang* mad [Old English *bendan*] **bendy** *adj*

bend[2] *n heraldry* a diagonal line across a shield [Old English: a band, strip]

bender *n informal* **1** a drinking bout **2** a shelter made from plastic sheeting and woven branches

bends *pl n* **the bends** *informal* decompression sickness

bend sinister *n heraldry* a diagonal line across a shield, indicating a bastard line

beneath *prep* **1** below; under **2** too trivial for: *beneath his dignity* ▷ *adv* **3** below; underneath [Old English *beneothan*]

Benedictine *n* **1** a monk or nun of the Christian order of Saint Benedict **2** a liqueur first made by Benedictine monks ▷ *adj* **3** of Saint Benedict or his order

benediction *n* **1** a prayer for divine blessing **2** a Roman Catholic service in which the congregation is blessed with the sacrament [Latin *benedictio*] **benedictory** *adj*

benefaction *n* **1** the act of doing good, particularly donating to charity **2** the donation or help given [Latin *bene* well + *facere* to do]

benefactor *or fem* **benefactress** *n* a person who supports a person or institution by giving money

benefice *n Christianity* a Church office that provides its holder with an income [Latin *beneficium* benefit]

beneficent (bin-eff-iss-ent) *adj* charitable; generous [Latin *beneficus*] **beneficence** *n*

beneficial *adj* helpful or advantageous [Latin *beneficium* kindness]

beneficiary *n, pl* **-ciaries** **1** a person who gains or benefits **2** *law* a person entitled to receive funds or property under a trust, will, etc.

benefit *n* **1** something that improves or promotes **2** advantage or sake: *I'm doing this for your benefit* **3** a payment made by an institution or government to a person who is ill, unemployed, etc. **4** a theatrical performance or sports event to raise money for a charity ▷ *vb* **-fiting, -fited** *or US* **-fitting, -fitted** **5** to do or receive good; profit [Latin *bene facere* to do well]

benefit society *n US* same as **friendly society**

benevolence *n* **1** inclination to do good **2** an act of kindness **benevolent** *adj*

Bengali *n* **1** a member of a people living chiefly in Bangladesh and West Bengal **2** the language of this people ▷ *adj* **3** of Bengal or the Bengalis

benighted *adj* lacking cultural, moral, or intellectual enlightenment

benign (bin-nine) *adj* **1** showing kindliness **2** favourable: *a stroke of benign fate* **3** *pathol* (of a tumour, etc.) able to be controlled [Latin *benignus*] **benignly** *adv*

benignant *adj* **1** kind or gracious **2** same as **benign** (senses 2, 3) **benignancy** *n*

benignity (bin-nig-nit-tee) *n* kindliness

bent *adj* **1** not straight; curved **2** *slang* **A** dishonest; corrupt: *bent officials* **B** *Brit & Austral offensive slang* homosexual **3** **bent on** determined to pursue (a course of action) ▷ *n* **4** personal inclination or aptitude: *he had a strong practical bent in his nature*

Benthamism *n* the utilitarian philosophy of Jeremy Bentham, which holds that the ultimate goal of society should be to promote the greatest happiness of the greatest number **Benthamite** *n, adj*

bento *or* **bento box** *n* a thin box, made of plastic or lacquered wood, divided into compartments, which contain small separate dishes comprising a Japanese meal, esp. lunch [Japanese *bento* box lunch]

b

bentwood *n* **1** wood bent in moulds, used mainly for furniture ▷ *adj* **2** made from such wood: *a bentwood chair*

benumb *vb* **1** to make numb or powerless **2** to stupefy (the mind, senses, will, etc.): *the work benumbed their minds and crushed their spirits*

benzene *n* a flammable poisonous liquid used as a solvent, insecticide, etc. [from *benzoin*, a fragrant resin from certain Asiatic trees]

benzine *n* a volatile liquid obtained from coal tar and used as a solvent

bequeath *vb* **1** *law* to dispose of (property) as in a will **2** to hand down: *the author bequeaths no solutions* [Old English *becwethan*]

bequest *n* **1** the act of gifting money or property in a will **2** money or property that has been gifted in a will

berate *vb* **-rating, -rated** to scold harshly

Berber *n* **1** a member of a Muslim people of N Africa **2** the language of this people ▷ *adj* **3** of the Berbers

berberis *n* a shrub with red berries [Medieval Latin]

berceuse (bare-**suhz**) *n* **1** a lullaby **2** an instrumental piece suggestive of this [French]

bereaved *adj* having recently lost a close relative or friend through death [Old English *bereafian* to deprive] **bereavement** *n*

bereft *adj* (foll. by *of*) deprived: *a government bereft of ideas*

beret (ber-ray) *n* a round flat close-fitting brimless cap [French]

berg[1] *n* short for **iceberg**

berg[2] *n S African* a mountain

bergamot *n* **1** a small Asian tree with sour pear-shaped fruit **2 essence of bergamot** a fragrant essential oil from the fruit rind of this plant, used in perfumery [French *bergamote*]

beri-beri *n* a disease caused by a dietary deficiency of thiamine (vitamin B_1) [Sinhalese]

berk *or* **burk** *n Brit, Austral & NZ slang* a stupid person; fool [*Berkshire Hunt*, rhyming slang for the taboo word *cunt*]

berkelium *n chem* an artificial radioactive element. Symbol: **Bk** [after *Berkeley*, California, where it was discovered]

Berks Berkshire

berm *n NZ* a narrow grass strip between the road and the footpath in a residential area

Bermuda shorts *pl n* shorts that come down to the knees [after *Bermudas*, islands in NW Atlantic]

Bernoulli principle *n physics* the principle that the pressure in a moving fluid becomes less as the speed rises [after Daniel *Bernoulli*, mathematician & physicist]

berry *n, pl* **-ries** a small round fruit that grows on bushes or trees and is often edible [Old English *berie*]

berserk *adj* **go berserk** to become violent or destructive [Icelandic *björn* bear + *serkr* shirt]

berth *n* **1** a bunk in a ship or train **2** *naut* a place assigned to a ship at a mooring **3** *naut* sufficient room for a ship to manoeuvre **4 give a wide berth to** to keep clear of ▷ *vb* **5** *naut* to dock (a ship) **6** to provide with a sleeping place **7** *naut* to pick up a mooring in an anchorage [probably from BEAR[1]]

beryl *n* a transparent hard mineral, used as a source of beryllium and as a gemstone [Greek *bērullos*]

beryllium *n* a toxic silvery-white metallic element. Symbol: **Be** [Greek *bērullos*]

beseech *vb* **-seeching, -sought** *or* **-seeched** to ask earnestly; beg [Middle English; see BE-, SEEK]

beset *vb* **-setting, -set 1** to trouble or harass constantly **2** to surround or attack from all sides

beside *prep* **1** next to; at, by, or to the side of **2** as compared with **3** away from: *beside the point* **4 beside oneself** overwhelmed; overwrought: *beside oneself with grief* ▷ *adv* **5** at, by, to, or along the side of something or someone [Old English *be sīdan*]

besides *adv* **1** in addition ▷ *prep* **2** apart from; even considering ▷ *conj* **3** anyway; moreover

besiege *vb* **-sieging, -sieged 1** to surround with military forces to bring about surrender **2** to hem in **3** to overwhelm, as with requests

besmirch *vb* to tarnish (someone's name or reputation)

besom *n* a broom made of a bundle of twigs tied to a handle [Old English *besma*]

besotted *adj* **1** having an irrational passion for a person or thing **2** stupefied with alcohol

besought *vb* a past of **beseech**

bespatter *vb* **1** to splash with dirty water **2** to dishonour or slander

bespeak *vb* **-speaking, -spoke, -spoken** *or* **-spoke 1** to indicate or suggest: *imitation bespeaks admiration* **2** to engage or ask for in advance: *she was bespoke to a family in the town*

bespectacled *adj* wearing spectacles

bespoke *adj chiefly Brit* **1** (esp. of a suit) made to the customer's specifications **2** making or selling such suits: *a bespoke tailor*

best *adj* **1** the superlative of **good 2** most excellent of a particular group, category, etc. **3** most suitable, desirable, etc. ▷ *adv* **4** the superlative of **well**[1] **5** in a manner surpassing all others; most attractively, etc. ▷ *n* **6 the best** the most outstanding or excellent person, thing, or group in a category **7** the utmost effort: *I did my best* **8** a person's finest clothes **9 at best A** in the most favourable interpretation **B** under the most favourable conditions **10 for the best A** for an ultimately good outcome **B** with good intentions **11 get the best of** to defeat or outwit **12 make the best of** to cope as well as possible with ▷ *vb* **13** to defeat [Old English *betst*]

bestial *adj* **1** brutal or savage **2** of or relating to a beast [Latin *bestia* beast]

bestiality *n, pl* **-ties 1** brutal behaviour, character, or action **2** sexual activity between a person and an animal

bestiary *n, pl* **-aries** a medieval collection of descriptions of animals

bestie *n slang* one's best friend

bestir *vb* **-stirring, -stirred** to cause (oneself) to become active

best man *n* the male attendant of the bridegroom at a wedding

bestow *vb* to present (a gift) or confer (an honour) **bestowal** *n*

bestrew *vb* **-strewing, -strewed, -strewn** *or* **-strewed** to scatter or lie scattered over (a surface)

bestride *vb* **-striding, -strode, -stridden** to have or put a leg on either side of

bestseller *n* a book or other product that has sold in great numbers **bestselling** *adj*

bet *n* **1** the act of staking a sum of money or other stake on the outcome of an event **2** the stake risked **3** a course of action: *your best bet is to go by train* **4** *informal* an opinion: *my bet is that you've been up to no good* ▷ *vb* **betting, bet** *or* **betted 5** to make or place a bet with (someone) **6** to stake (money, etc.) in a bet **7** *informal* to predict (a certain outcome): *I bet she doesn't turn up* **8 you bet** *informal* of course [probably short for *abet*]

beta *n* **1** the second letter in the Greek alphabet (Β, β) **2** the second in a group or series

beta-blocker *n* a drug that decreases the activity of the heart: used in the treatment of high blood pressure and angina pectoris

betacarotene *n biochem* the most important form of the plant pigment carotene, which occurs in milk, vegetables, and other foods and, when eaten by humans and animals, is converted in the body to vitamin A

betake *vb* **-taking, -took, -taken** > **betake oneself** *formal* to go or move: *he betook himself to the public house*

beta particle *n* a high-speed electron or positron emitted by a nucleus during radioactive decay or nuclear fission

betatron *n* a type of particle accelerator for producing high-energy beams of electrons

betel (bee-tl) *n* an Asian climbing plant, the leaves and nuts of which can be chewed [Malayalam (language of SW India) *vettila*]

bête noire (bet **nwahr**) *n, pl* **bêtes noires** a person or thing that one particularly dislikes or dreads [French, literally: black beast]

betide *vb* **-tiding, -tided** to happen or happen to: *woe betide us if we're not ready on time* [BE- + obsolete *tide* to happen]

betoken *vb* to indicate; signify

betray *vb* **1** to hand over or expose (one's nation, friend, etc.) treacherously to an enemy **2** to disclose (a secret or confidence) treacherously **3** to reveal unintentionally: *his singing voice betrays his origins* [Latin *tradere* to hand over] **betrayal** *n* **betrayer** *n*

betroth *vb archaic* to promise to marry or to give in marriage [Middle English *betreuthen*] **betrothal** *n*

betrothed *old-fashioned* ▷ *adj* **1** engaged to be married ▷ *n* **2** the person to whom one is engaged

better *adj* **1** the comparative of **good 2** more excellent than others **3** more suitable, attractive, etc. **4** improved or fully recovered in health **5 the better part of** a large part of ▷ *adv* **6** the comparative of **well' 7** in a more excellent manner **8** in or to a greater degree **9 better off** in more favourable circumstances, esp. financially **10 had better** would be sensible, etc. to: *I had better be off* ▷ *n* **11 the better** something that is the more excellent, useful, etc. of two such things **12 betters** people who are one's superiors, esp. in social standing **13 get the better of** to defeat or outwit ▷ *vb* **14** to improve upon [Old English *betera*]

better half *n humorous* one's spouse

betterment *n* improvement

better-off *adj* reasonably wealthy: *Catalonia aims to attract better-off tourists*

betting shop *n* (in Britain) a licensed bookmaker's premises not on a racecourse

between *prep* **1** at a point intermediate to two other points in space, time, etc. **2** in combination; together: *between them, they saved enough money to buy a car* **3** confined to: *between you and me* **4** indicating a linking relation or comparison **5** indicating alternatives, strictly only two alternatives ▷ *adv also* **in between 6** between one specified thing and another [Old English *betwēonum*]

> **USAGE** After *distribute* and words with a similar meaning, *among* should be used rather than *between*: *this enterprise issued shares which were distributed among its workers.*

betwixt *prep, adv* **1** *archaic* between **2 betwixt and between** in an intermediate or indecisive position

bevel *n* **1** a slanting edge ▷ *vb* **-elling, -elled** *or US* **-eling, -eled 2** to be inclined; slope **3** to cut a bevel on (a piece of timber, etc.) [Old French *baer* to gape]

bevel gear *n* a toothed gear meshed with another at an angle to it

beverage *n* any drink other than water [Old French *bevrage*]

bevvy *n, pl* **-vies** *dialect* **1** an alcoholic drink **2** a session of drinking [probably from Old French *bevee, buvee* drinking]

bevy *n, pl* **bevies** a flock; a group [origin unknown]

bewail *vb* to express great sorrow over; lament

beware *vb* **-waring, -wared** (often foll. by *of*) to be wary (of); be on one's guard (against) [*be* (imperative) + obsolete *war* wary]

bewilder *vb* to confuse utterly; puzzle [BE- + obsolete *wilder* to lose one's way] **bewildering** *adj* **bewilderment** *n*

bewitch *vb* **1** to attract and fascinate **2** to cast a spell over [Middle English *bewicchen*] **bewitching** *adj*

bey *n* **1** (in modern Turkey) a title of address, corresponding to *Mr* **2** (in the Ottoman Empire) a title given to provincial governors [Turkish: lord]

beyond *prep* **1** at or to a point on the other side of: *beyond those hills* **2** outside the limits or scope of ▷ *adv* **3** at or to the other or far side of something

4 outside the limits of something ▷ *n* **5 the beyond** the unknown, esp. life after death [Old English *begeondan*]
bezel *n* **1** the sloping edge of a cutting tool **2** the slanting face of a cut gem **3** a groove holding a gem, watch crystal, etc. **4** the outer frame of a computer screen, mobile phone, or other electronic device [French *biseau*] **bezelless** *adj*
bezique *n* a card game for two or more players [French *bésigue*]
B/F *or* **b/f** *accounting* brought forward
BFPO British Forces Post Office
Bh *chem* bohrium
Bhagavad-Gita (bug-a-vad-**geet**-a) *n* a sacred Hindu text composed about 200 BC [Sanskrit: song of the Blessed One]
bhaji *n, pl* **bhaji** *or* **bhajis** an Indian savoury made of chopped vegetables mixed in a spiced batter and deep-fried [Hindi]
bhang *n* a preparation of Indian hemp used as a narcotic and intoxicant [Hindi]
bhangra *n* a type of traditional Punjabi folk music combined with elements of Western pop music [Hindi]
bhp brake horsepower
Bi *chem* bismuth
bi- *combining form* **1** having two: *bifocal* **2** occurring or lasting for two: *biennial* **3** on both sides, directions, etc.: *bilateral* **4** occurring twice during: *biweekly* **5** *chem* **A** denoting a compound containing two identical cyclical hydrocarbon systems: *biphenyl* **B** indicating an acid salt of a dibasic acid: *sodium bicarbonate* [Latin *bis* twice]
biannual *adj* occurring twice a year **biannually** *adv*
bias *n* **1** mental tendency, esp. prejudice **2** a diagonal cut across the weave of a fabric **3** *bowls* a bulge or weight inside one side of a bowl that causes it to roll in a curve ▷ *vb* **-asing, -ased** *or* **-assing, -assed 4** to cause to have a bias; prejudice [Old French *biais*] **biased** *or* **biassed** *adj*
bias binding *n* a strip of material used for binding hems
biaxial *adj* (esp. of a crystal) having two axes
bib *n* **1** a piece of cloth or plastic worn to protect a very young child's clothes while eating **2** the upper front part of some aprons, dungarees, etc. [Middle English *bibben* to drink]
bibcock *n* a tap with a nozzle bent downwards
bibelot (**bib**-loh) *n* an attractive or curious trinket [Old French *beubelet*]
bibl. 1 bibliographical **2** bibliography
Bible *n* **1 the Bible** the sacred writings of the Christian religion, comprising the Old and New Testaments **2 bible** a book regarded as authoritative: *this guide has long been regarded as the hill walkers' bible* [Greek *biblion* book] **biblical** *adj*
Bible Belt *n* those states of the S US where Protestant fundamentalism is dominant
bibliography *n, pl* **-phies 1** a list of books on a subject or by a particular author **2** a list of sources used in a book, etc. **3** the study of the history, etc., of literary material [Greek *biblion* book + *graphein* to write] **bibliographer** *n*
bibliophile *n* a person who collects or is fond of books [Greek *biblion* book + *philos* loving]
bibulous *adj literary* addicted to alcohol [Latin *bibere* to drink]
bicameral *adj* (of a legislature) consisting of two chambers [BI- + Latin *camera* chamber]
bicarb *n* short for **bicarbonate of soda**
bicarbonate *n* a salt of carbonic acid
bicarbonate of soda *n* sodium bicarbonate used as medicine or a raising agent in baking
bicentenary *or US* **bicentennial** *adj* **1** marking a 200th anniversary ▷ *n, pl* **-naries 2** a 200th anniversary
biceps *n, pl* **-ceps** *anatomy* a muscle with two origins, esp. the muscle that flexes the forearm [BI- + Latin *caput* head]
bicker *vb* to argue over petty matters; squabble [origin unknown]
bickie *or* **bikkie** *n informal* a biscuit
bicuspid *adj* **1** having two points ▷ *n* **2** a bicuspid tooth
bicycle *n* **1** a vehicle with a metal frame and two wheels, one behind the other, pedalled by the rider ▷ *vb* **-cling, -cled 2** to ride a bicycle [BI- + Greek *kuklos* wheel]
bid *vb* **bidding, bad, bade** *or* **bid, bidden** *or* **bid 1** to offer (an amount) in an attempt to buy something **2** to say (a greeting): *to bid farewell* **3** to order: *do as you are bid!* **4** *bridge etc.* to declare how many tricks one expects to make ▷ *n* **5 A** an offer of a specified amount **B** the price offered **6 A** the quoting by a seller of a price **B** the price quoted **7** an attempt, esp. to attain power **8** *bridge etc.* the number of tricks a player undertakes to make [Old English *biddan*] **bidder** *n*
biddable *adj* obedient
bidding *n* **1** an order or command: *she had done his bidding* **2** an invitation; summons: *he knew to knock and wait for bidding before he entered* **3** the bids in an auction, card game, etc.
biddy *n, pl* **-dies** *informal, derogatory* a woman, esp. an old gossipy one [pet form of *Bridget*]
biddy-bid *or* **biddy-biddy** *n, pl* **-bids** *or* **-biddies** NZ a low-growing plant with hooked burrs
bide *vb* **biding, bided** *or* **bode, bided 1** *archaic or dialect* to remain **2 bide one's time** to wait patiently for an opportunity [Old English *bīdan*]
bidet (**bee**-day) *n* a small low basin for washing the genital area [French: small horse]
biennial *adj* **1** occurring every two years ▷ *n* **2** a plant that completes its life cycle in two years
bier *n* a stand on which a corpse or a coffin rests before burial [Old English *bǣr*]
biff *slang* ▷ *n* **1** a blow with the fist ▷ *vb* **2** to give (someone) such a blow [probably imitative]
bifid *adj* divided into two by a cleft in the middle [BI- + Latin *findere* to split]
bifocal *adj* having two different focuses, esp. (of a lens) permitting near and distant vision
bifocals *pl n* a pair of spectacles with bifocal lenses
bifurcate *vb* **-cating, -cated 1** to fork into two branches ▷ *adj* **2** forked into two branches [BI- + Latin *furca* fork] **bifurcation** *n*
big *adj* **bigger, biggest 1** of great or considerable size, weight, number, or capacity **2** having great significance; important **3** important through having power, wealth, etc. **4 A** elder: *my big brother*

B grown-up 5 generous: *that's very big of you* 6 extravagant; boastful: *big talk* 7 **too big for one's boots** conceited; unduly self-confident 8 in an advanced stage of pregnancy: *big with child* 9 **in a big way** in a very grand or enthusiastic way ▷ *adv informal* 10 boastfully; pretentiously: *he talks big* 11 on a grand scale: *think big* [origin unknown]

bigamy *n* the crime of marrying a person while still legally married to someone else [BI- + Greek *gamos* marriage] **bigamist** *n* **bigamous** *adj*

big-bang theory *n* a cosmological theory that suggests that the universe was created as the result of a massive explosion

Big Brother *n* a person or organization that exercises total dictatorial control [from the novel *1984* by George Orwell]

big business *n* large commercial organizations collectively

big data *n* data held in such large amounts that it can be difficult to process

big end *n* the larger end of a connecting rod in an internal-combustion engine

big game *n* large animals that are hunted or fished for sport

bighead *n informal* a conceited person **big-headed** *adj*

bight *n* 1 a long curved shoreline 2 the slack part or a loop in a rope [Old English *byht*]

big name *informal* ▷ *n* 1 a famous person ▷ *adj* **big-name** 2 famous

bigot *n* a person who is intolerant, esp. regarding religion, politics, or race [Old French] **bigoted** *adj* **bigotry** *n*

big shot *n informal* an important person

Big Smoke *n* **the Big Smoke** *informal* a big city, esp. London

big stick *n informal* force or the threat of force

big time *n* **the big time** *informal* the highest level of a profession, esp. entertainment **big-timer** *n*

big top *n informal* the main tent of a circus

bigwig *n informal* an important person

bijou (bee-zhoo) *n, pl* **-joux** (-zhooz) 1 something small and delicately worked ▷ *adj* 2 small but tasteful: *a bijou residence* [French: a jewel]

bike *n informal* a bicycle or motorcycle

biker *n informal* a person who rides a motorcycle

biker jacket *n* a short, close-fitting leather jacket often worn by motorcyclists

bikini *n* a woman's brief two-piece swimming costume [after *Bikini* atoll, from a comparison between the devastating effect of the atom-bomb test and the effect caused by women wearing bikinis]

bilateral *adj* affecting or undertaken by two parties; mutual

bilberry *n, pl* **-ries** a blue or blackish edible berry that grows on a shrub [probably Scandinavian]

bilby *n, pl* **-bies** an Australian marsupial with long pointed ears and grey fur

bile *n* 1 a greenish fluid secreted by the liver to aid digestion of fats 2 irritability or peevishness [Latin *bilis*]

bilge *n* 1 *informal* nonsense 2 *naut* the bottom of a ship's hull 3 the dirty water that collects in a ship's bilge [probably variant of *bulge*]

bilharzia (bill-**hart**-see-a) *n* a disease caused by infestation of the body with blood flukes [after T. *Bilharz*, who discovered the blood fluke]

biliary *adj* of bile, the ducts that convey bile, or the gall bladder

bilingual *adj* 1 able to speak two languages 2 expressed in two languages **bilingualism** *n*

bilious *adj* 1 nauseous; sick: *a bilious attack* 2 *informal* bad-tempered; irritable: *the regime's most persistent and bilious critic* 3 (of a colour) harsh and offensive [Latin *biliosus* full of bile]

bilk *vb* to cheat or deceive, esp. to avoid making payment to [perhaps variant of *balk*] **bilker** *n*

bill[1] *n* 1 a statement of money owed for goods or services supplied 2 a draft of a proposed new law presented to a law-making body 3 a printed notice or advertisement 4 *US & Canad* a piece of paper money; note 5 any list of items, events, etc., such as a theatre programme ▷ *vb* 6 to send or present an account for payment to (a person) 7 to advertise by posters 8 to schedule as a future programme: *next week they will discuss what are billed as new ideas for economic reform* 9 **fit** *or* **fill the bill** *informal* to be suitable or adequate [Late Latin *bulla* document]

bill[2] *n* 1 the projecting jaws of a bird; beak ▷ *vb* 2 **bill and coo** (of lovers) to kiss and whisper amorously [Old English *bile*]

billabong *n Austral* a pool in the bed of a stream with an interrupted water flow [Aboriginal]

billboard *n* a hoarding

billet[1] *vb* **-leting, -leted** 1 to assign a lodging to (a soldier) ▷ *n* 2 accommodation, esp. for a soldier, in civilian lodgings 3 *Austral & NZ* a person who is billeted [Old French *billette*, from *bulle* a document]

billet[2] *n* 1 a chunk of wood, esp. for fuel 2 a small bar of iron or steel [Old French *billette* a little log]

billet-doux (bill-ee-**doo**) *n, pl* **billets-doux** (bill-ee-**dooz**) *old-fashioned or humorous* a love letter [French: a sweet letter]

billhook *n* a tool with a hooked blade, used for chopping, etc.

billiards *n* a game in which a long cue is used to propel balls on a table [Old French *billard* curved stick]

billion *n, pl* **-lions** *or* **-lion** 1 one thousand million: 1 000 000 000 or 10^9 2 (in Britain, originally) one million million: 1 000 000 000 000 or 10^{12} 3 (*often pl*) *informal* an extremely large but unspecified number: *billions of dollars* [French] **billionth** *adj, n*

billionaire *n* a person who has money or property worth at least a billion pounds, dollars, etc.

bill of exchange *n* a document instructing a third party to pay a stated sum at a designated date or on demand

bill of fare *n* a menu

bill of health *n* 1 a certificate that confirms the health of a ship's company 2 **clean bill of health** *informal* A a good report of one's physical condition B a favourable account of a person's or a company's financial position

bill of lading *n* a document containing full particulars of goods shipped

b

billow *n* **1** a large sea wave **2** a swelling or surging mass, as of smoke or sound ▷ *vb* **3** to rise up or swell out [Old Norse *bylgja*] **billowing** *adj, n* **billowy** *adj*

billy *or* **billycan** *n, pl* **-lies** *or* **-lycans** a metal can or pot for boiling water, etc. over a campfire [Scots *billypot*]

b

billy goat *n* a male goat

biltong *n S African* strips of meat dried and cured in the sun [Afrikaans]

bimbo *n, pl* **-bos** *informal, offensive* an attractive but empty-headed young woman [Italian: little child]

bimetallic *adj* consisting of two metals

bimetallism *n* the use of two metals, esp. gold and silver, in fixed relative values as the standard of value and currency **bimetallist** *n*

bin *n* **1** a container for rubbish, etc. **2** a large container for storing something in bulk, such as coal, grain, or bottled wine ▷ *vb* **binning, binned** **3** to put in a rubbish bin: *I bin my junk mail without reading it* [Old English *binne* basket]

binary (**bine**-a-ree) *adj* **1** composed of two parts **2** *maths & computers* of or expressed in a system with two as its base **3** *chem* containing atoms of two different elements ▷ *n, pl* **-ries** **4** something composed of two parts [Late Latin *binarius*]

binary star *n* a system of two stars revolving around a common centre of gravity

bind *vb* **binding, bound** **1** to make secure, such as with a rope **2** to unite with emotional ties or commitment **3** to place (someone) under legal or moral obligation **4** to place under certain constraints: *bound by the rules* **5** to stick together or cause to stick: *egg binds fat and flour* **6** to enclose and fasten (the pages of a book) between covers **7** to provide (a garment) with an edging **8** (foll. by *up*) to bandage ▷ *n* **9** *informal* a difficult or annoying situation [Old English *bindan*]

binder *n* **1** a firm cover for holding loose sheets of paper together **2** a person who binds books **3** something used to fasten or tie, such as rope or twine **4** *obsolete* a machine for cutting and binding grain into sheaves

bindery *n, pl* **-eries** a place in which books are bound

binding *n* **1** anything that binds or fastens **2** the covering of a book ▷ *adj* **3** imposing an obligation or duty

bind over *vb* to place (a person) under a legal obligation, esp. to keep the peace

bindweed *n* a plant that twines around a support

binge *n informal* **1** a bout of excessive eating or drinking **2** excessive indulgence in anything [probably dialect: to soak]

binge drinking *n* the practice of drinking excessive amounts of alcohol regularly

bingo *n* a gambling game in which numbers called out are covered by players on their individual cards. The first to cover a given arrangement is the winner [origin unknown]

binnacle *n* a housing for a ship's compass [Late Latin *habitaculum* dwelling-place]

binocular *adj* involving or intended for both eyes: *binocular vision* [BI- + Latin *oculus* eye]

binoculars *pl n* an optical instrument for use with both eyes, consisting of two small telescopes joined together

binomial *n* **1** a mathematical expression consisting of two terms, such as $3x + 2y$ ▷ *adj* **2** referring to two names or terms [BI- + Latin *nomen* name]

binomial theorem *n* a general mathematical formula that expresses any power of a binomial without multiplying out, as in $(a+b)^2=a^2+2ab+b^2$

bio- *combining form* **1** indicating life or living organisms: *biogenesis* **2** indicating a human life or career: *biography* [Greek *bios* life]

bioastronautics *n* the study of the effects of space flight on living organisms

biochemistry *n* the study of the chemical compounds, reactions, etc., occurring in living organisms **biochemical** *adj* **biochemist** *n*

biocide *n* a substance used to destroy living things [BIO- + Latin *caedere* to kill]

biocoenosis *or US* **biocenosis** (bye-oh-see-**no**-siss) *n* the relationships between animals and plants subsisting together [BIO- + Greek *koinōsis* sharing]

biodegradable *adj* (of sewage and packaging) capable of being decomposed by natural means **biodegradability** *n*

biodiesel *n* a biofuel intended for use in diesel engines

biodiversity *n* the existence of a wide variety of plant and animal species in their natural environments

bioengineering *n* the design and manufacture of aids, such as artificial limbs, to help people with disabilities

biofuel *n* fuel derived from renewable biological resources

biogas *n* gaseous fuel produced by the fermentation of organic waste

biogenesis *n* the principle that a living organism must originate from a similar parent organism

biogenic (bye-oh-**jen**-ik) *adj* originating from a living organism

biography *n, pl* **-phies** **1** an account of a person's life by another person **2** such accounts collectively [BIO- + Greek *graphein* to write] **biographer** *n* **biographical** *adj*

biol. **1** biological **2** biology

biological *adj* **1** of or relating to biology **2** (of a detergent) containing enzymes that remove natural stains, such as blood or grass **biologically** *adv*

biological clock *n* an inherent timing mechanism that controls the rhythmic repetition of processes in living organisms, such as sleeping

biological control *n* the control of destructive organisms, esp. insects, by nonchemical means, such as introducing a natural predator of the pest

biological warfare *n* the use of living organisms or their toxic products to induce death or incapacity in humans

biology *n* the study of living organisms **biologist** *n*

biomass *n* the total number of living organisms in a given area
biomechanics *n* the study of the mechanics of the movement of living organisms
biomedicine *n* **1** the medical and biological study of the effects of unusual environmental stress **2** the study of herbal remedies
biometric *adj* relating to the analysis of biological data using mathematical and statistical methods, esp. for purposes of identification: *biometric passport*
biometry *or* **biometrics** *n* the analysis of biological data using mathematical and statistical methods, esp. for purposes of identification
bionic *adj* **1** of or relating to bionics **2** (in science fiction) having physical functions augmented by electronic equipment [BIO- + *(electro)nic*]
bionics *n* **1** the study of biological functions in order to develop electronic equipment that operates similarly **2** the replacement of limbs or body parts by artificial electronically powered parts
biophysics *n* the physics of biological processes and the application of methods used in physics to biology **biophysical** *adj* **biophysicist** *n*
biopic (bye-oh-pick) *n informal* a film based on the life of a famous person [*bio(graphical)* + *pic(ture)*]
biopsy *n, pl* **-sies** examination of tissue from a living body to determine the cause or extent of a disease [BIO- + Greek *opsis* sight]
biorhythm *n* a complex recurring pattern of physiological states, believed to affect physical, emotional, and mental states
bioscope *n* **1** a kind of early film projector **2** *S African* a cinema
biosphere *n* the part of the earth's surface and atmosphere inhabited by living things
biosynthesis *n* the formation of complex compounds by living organisms **biosynthetic** *adj*
biotech *n* short for **biotechnology**
biotechnology *n* the use of microorganisms, such as cells or bacteria, in industry and technology
bioterrorism *n* the use of viruses, bacteria, etc. by terrorists **bioterrorist** *n*
biotin *n* a vitamin of the B complex, abundant in egg yolk and liver [Greek *biotē* life]
bipartisan *adj* consisting of or supported by two political parties
bipartite *adj* **1** consisting of or having two parts **2** affecting or made by two parties: *a bipartite agreement*
biped (bye-ped) *n* **1** any animal with two feet ▷ *adj also* **bipedal** **2** having two feet [BI- + Latin *pes* foot]
biplane *n* an aeroplane with two sets of wings, one above the other
bipolar *adj* **1** having two poles **2** having two extremes **3** *psychiatry* having bipolar disorder **bipolarity** *n*
bipolar disorder *n psychiatry* a condition characterized by an alternation between extreme euphoria and deep depression
birch *n* **1** a tree with thin peeling bark and hard close-grained wood **2** **the birch** a bundle of birch twigs or a birch rod used, esp. formerly, for flogging offenders ▷ *vb* **3** to flog with the birch [Old English *bierce*]
bird *n* **1** a two-legged creature with feathers and wings, which lays eggs and can usually fly. Related adjective: **avian** **2** *Brit slang, sometimes offensive* a girl or young woman **3** *informal* a person: *he's a rare bird* **4** **a bird in the hand** something definite or certain **5** **birds of a feather** people with the same ideas or interests **6** **kill two birds with one stone** to accomplish two things with one action [Old English *bridd*]
bird flu *n* a form of influenza occurring in poultry caused by a virus capable of spreading to humans
birdie *n* **1** *informal* a bird **2** *golf* a score of one stroke under par for a hole
birdlime *n* a sticky substance smeared on twigs to catch small birds
bird of paradise *n* a songbird of New Guinea, the male of which has brilliantly coloured plumage
bird of prey *n* a bird, such as a hawk or owl, that hunts other animals for food
birdseed *n* a mixture of various kinds of seeds for feeding cage birds
bird's-eye view *n* **1** a view seen from above **2** a general or overall impression of something
bird-watcher *n* a person who studies wild birds in their natural surroundings
biretta *n RC Church* a stiff square clerical cap [Italian *berretta*]
Biro *n, pl* **-ros** *trademark* a kind of ballpoint pen
birth *n* **1** the process of bearing young; childbirth **2** the act of being born **3** the beginning of something; origin **4** ancestry: *of noble birth* **5** **give birth to** **A** to bear (offspring) **B** to produce or originate (an idea, plan, etc.) [Old Norse *byrth*]
birth certificate *n* an official form stating the time and place of a person's birth
birth control *n* limitation of child-bearing by means of contraception
birthday *n* **1** an anniversary of the day of one's birth **2** the day on which a person was born
birthmark *n* a blemish on the skin formed before birth
birth mother *n* the woman who gives birth to a child, regardless of whether she is the genetic mother or subsequently brings up the child
birthplace *n* the place where someone was born or where something originated
birth rate *n* the ratio of live births to population, usually expressed per 1000 population per year
birthright *n* privileges or possessions that a person has or is believed to be entitled to as soon as he or she is born
biscuit *n* **1** a small flat dry sweet or plain cake **2** porcelain that has been fired but not glazed ▷ *adj* **3** pale brown or yellowish-grey [Old French *(pain) bescuit* twice-cooked (bread)]
bisect *vb* **1** *maths* to divide into two equal parts **2** to cut or split into two [BI- + Latin *secare* to cut] **bisection** *n*
bisexual *adj* **1** sexually attracted to both men and women **2** showing characteristics of both sexes ▷ *n* **3** a bisexual person **bisexuality** *n*
bishop *n* **1** a member of clergy having spiritual and administrative powers over a diocese

2 a chess piece capable of moving diagonally [Greek *episkopos* overseer]
bishopric *n* the see, diocese, or office of a bishop
bismuth *n chem* a brittle pinkish-white metallic element. Some compounds are used in alloys and in medicine. Symbol: **Bi** [German *Wismut*]
bison *n, pl* **-son** an animal of the cattle family with a massive head, shaggy forequarters, and a humped back [Germanic]

b

bisque[1] *n* a thick rich soup made from shellfish [French]
bisque[2] *adj* **1** pink-to-yellowish-tan ▷ *n* **2** *ceramics* same as **biscuit** (sense 2) [shortened from *biscuit*]
bistable *adj* (of an electronic system) having two stable states
bistro *n, pl* **-tros** a small restaurant [French]
bit[1] *n* **1** a small piece, portion, or quantity **2** a short time or distance **3 a bit** rather; somewhat: *a bit stupid* **4 a bit of** rather: *a bit of a fool* **5 bit by bit** gradually **6 do one's bit** to make one's expected contribution [Old English *bite* action of biting]
bit[2] *n* **1** a metal mouthpiece on a bridle for controlling a horse **2** a cutting or drilling tool, part, or head in a brace, drill, etc. [Old English *bita*]
bit[3] *vb* the past tense of **bite**
bit[4] *n maths & computers* **1** a single digit of binary notation, represented either by 0 or by 1 **2** the smallest unit of information, indicating the presence or absence of a single feature [*b(inary + dig)it*]
bitch *n* **1** a female dog, fox, or wolf **2** *derogatory slang* a malicious or spiteful woman **3** *informal* a difficult situation or problem ▷ *vb* **4** *informal* to complain; grumble [Old English *bicce*]
bitchy *adj* **bitchier, bitchiest** *informal* spiteful or malicious **bitchiness** *n*
bitcoin *n* a form of digital currency that is created, held, and exchanged electronically
bite *vb* **biting, bit, bitten 1** to grip, cut off, or tear with the teeth or jaws **2** (of animals or insects) to injure by puncturing (the skin) with the teeth or fangs **3** (of corrosive material) to eat away or into **4** to smart or cause to smart; sting **5** *angling* (of a fish) to take the bait or lure **6** to take firm hold of or act effectively upon: *turn the screw till it bites the wood* **7** *slang* to annoy or worry: *what's biting her?* ▷ *n* **8** the act of biting **9** a thing or amount bitten off **10** a wound or sting inflicted by biting **11** *angling* an attempt by a fish to take the bait or lure **12** a snack **13** a stinging or smarting sensation [Old English *bītan*] **biter** *n*
biting *adj* **1** piercing; keen: *a biting wind* **2** sarcastic; incisive
bitmap *n computers* a picture created by colour or shading on a visual display unit
bit part *n* a very small acting role with few lines to speak
bitstream *n computers* a sequence of digital data transmitted electronically
bitten *vb* the past participle of **bite**
bitter *adj* **1** having an unpalatable harsh taste, as the peel of an orange **2** showing or caused by hostility or resentment **3** difficult to accept: *a bitter blow* **4** sarcastic: *bitter words* **5** bitingly cold: *a bitter night* ▷ *n* **6** *Brit* beer with a slightly bitter taste [Old English *biter*] **bitterly** *adv* **bitterness** *n*
bittern *n* a large wading marsh bird with a booming call [Old French *butor*]
bitters *pl n* bitter-tasting spirits flavoured with plant extracts
bittersweet *adj* **1** tasting of or being a mixture of bitterness and sweetness **2** pleasant but tinged with sadness
bitty *adj* **-tier, -tiest** lacking unity; disjointed **bittiness** *n*
bitumen *n* a sticky or solid substance that occurs naturally in asphalt and tar and is used in road surfacing [Latin] **bituminous** *adj*
bituminous coal *n* a soft black coal that burns with a smoky yellow flame
bivalve *n* **1** a sea creature, such as an oyster or mussel, that has a shell consisting of two hinged valves and breathes through gills ▷ *adj* **2** of these molluscs
bivouac *n* **1** a temporary camp, as used by soldiers or mountaineers ▷ *vb* **-acking, -acked 2** to make a temporary camp [French]
biz *n informal* business
bizarre *adj* odd or unusual, esp. in an interesting or amusing way [Italian *bizzarro* capricious]
Bk *chem* berkelium
BL 1 *chiefly Brit* Bachelor of Law **2** Bachelor of Letters **3** Barrister-at-Law
blab *vb* **blabbing, blabbed** to divulge (secrets) indiscreetly [Germanic]
blabber *n* **1** a person who blabs ▷ *vb* **2** to talk without thinking [Middle English *blabberen*]
black *adj* **1** having no hue, owing to the absorption of all or almost all light; of the colour of coal **2** without light **3** without hope; gloomy: *the future looked black* **4** dirty or soiled **5** angry or resentful: *black looks* **6** unpleasant in a cynical or macabre manner: *black comedy* **7** (of coffee or tea) without milk or cream **8** wicked or harmful: *a black lie* ▷ *n* **9** the darkest colour; the colour of coal **10** a dye or pigment producing this colour **11** black clothing, worn esp. in mourning: *she was in black, as though in mourning* **12** complete darkness: *the black of the night* **13 in the black** in credit or without debt ▷ *vb* **14** same as **blacken 15** to polish (shoes or boots) with blacking **16** *Brit, Austral & NZ* (of trade unionists) to organize a boycott of (specified goods, work, etc.) ▷ See also **blackout** [Old English *blæc*] **blackness** *n* **blackish** *adj*
Black *adj* **1** (of a person) belonging to a race of people with dark skins **2** of or relating to a Black person or Black people ▷ *n* **3** *offensive* a member of a race of people with dark skins

> **USAGE** Talking about *a Black* or *Blacks* is considered offensive and it is better to talk about *a Black person* or *Black people*.

black-and-blue *adj* (of the skin) bruised, as from a beating
black-and-white *n* **1** a photograph, film, etc., in black, white, and shades of grey, rather than in colour **2 in black and white A** in print or writing **B** in extremes: *he always sees things in black and white*
black-backed gull *n* a large common black-and-white European gull

blackball[1] *vb* **1** to vote against **2** to exclude (someone) from a group, etc. [from *black ball*, used formerly to veto]

blackball[2] *n NZ* a hard boiled sweet with black-and-white stripes

black bear *n* **1** a bear inhabiting forests of North America **2** a bear of central and E Asia

black belt *n judo & karate etc.* **A** a black belt that signifies that the wearer has reached a high standard in a martial art **B** a person entitled to wear this

blackberry *n, pl* **-ries** a small blackish edible fruit that grows on a woody bush with thorny stems. Also called: **bramble**

BlackBerry *n, pl* **-ries** *trademark* a brand of smartphone

blackbird *n* a common European thrush, the male of which has black plumage and a yellow bill

blackboard *n* a hard or rigid surface made of a smooth usually dark substance, used for writing or drawing on with chalk, esp. in teaching

black box *n informal* a flight recorder

blackcap *n* a brownish-grey warbler, the male of which has a black crown

blackcock *n* the male of the black grouse

Black Country *n* **the Black Country** the formerly heavily industrialized West Midlands of England

blackcurrant *n* a very small blackish edible fruit that grows in bunches on a bush

blackdamp *n* air that is low in oxygen content and high in carbon dioxide as a result of an explosion in a mine

Black Death *n* **the Black Death** a form of bubonic plague in Europe and Asia during the 14th century

black economy *n Brit, Austral & NZ* that portion of the income of a nation that remains illegally undeclared

blacken *vb* **1** to make or become black or dirty **2** to damage (someone's reputation); discredit: *they planned to blacken my father's name*

black eye *n* bruising round the eye

Black Friar *n* a Dominican friar

blackguard (**blag**-gard) *n* an unprincipled contemptible person [originally, lowest group at court]

blackhead *n* **1** a black-tipped plug of fatty matter clogging a pore of the skin **2** a bird with black plumage on the head

black hole *n astron* a region of space resulting from the collapse of a star and surrounded by a gravitational field from which neither matter nor radiation can escape

black ice *n* a thin transparent layer of new ice on a road

blacking *n* any preparation for giving a black finish to shoes, metals, etc.

blackjack[1] *n* pontoon or a similar card game [*black* + *jack* (the knave)]

blackjack[2] *n chiefly US & Canad* a truncheon of leather-covered lead with a flexible shaft [*black* + *jack* (implement)]

black lead *n* same as **graphite**

blackleg *n Brit* **1** a person who continues to work or does another's job during a strike ▷ *vb* **-legging, -legged 2** to refuse to join a strike

blacklist *n* **1** a list of people or organizations considered untrustworthy or disloyal ▷ *vb* **2** to put (someone) on a blacklist

black magic *n* magic used for evil purposes

blackmail *n* **1** the act of attempting to obtain money by threatening to reveal shameful information **2** the use of unfair pressure in an attempt to influence someone ▷ *vb* **3** to obtain or attempt to obtain money by intimidation **4** to attempt to influence (a person) by unfair pressure [*black* + Old English *māl* terms]
blackmailer *n*

Black Maria (mar-**rye**-a) *n* a police van for transporting prisoners

black mark *n* a discredit noted against someone

black market *n* a place or a system for buying or selling goods or currencies illegally, esp. in violation of controls or rationing
black marketeer *n*

black mass *n* a blasphemous travesty of the Christian Mass, used in black magic

blackout *n* **1** (in wartime) the putting out or hiding of all lights as a precaution against a night air attack **2** a momentary loss of consciousness, vision, or memory **3** a temporary electrical power failure **4** the prevention of information broadcasts: *a news blackout* ▷ *vb* **black out 5** to put out (lights) **6** to lose vision, consciousness, or memory temporarily **7** to stop (news, a television programme, etc.) from being broadcast

black pepper *n* a dark-coloured hot seasoning made from the dried berries and husks of the pepper plant

Black Power *n* a movement of Black people to obtain equality with White people

black pudding *n Brit* a black sausage made from pig's blood, suet, etc.

Black Rod *n* (in Britain) the chief usher of the House of Lords and of the Order of the Garter

black sheep *n* a person who is regarded as a disgrace or failure by his or her family or peer group

Blackshirt *n* a member of the Italian Fascist party before and during the Second World War

blacksmith *n* a person who works iron with a furnace, anvil, and hammer

black spot *n* **1** a place on a road where accidents frequently occur **2** an area where a particular situation is exceptionally bad: *an unemployment black spot*

blackthorn *n* a thorny shrub with black twigs, white flowers, and small sour plumlike fruits

black tie *n* **1** a black bow tie worn with a dinner jacket ▷ *adj* **black-tie 2** denoting an occasion when a dinner jacket should be worn

Black Watch *n* **the Black Watch** an infantry unit in the British Army, formerly a separate regiment but now part of the Royal Regiment of Scotland

black widow *n* an American spider, the female of which is highly venomous and commonly eats its mate

bladder *n* **1** *anatomy* a membranous sac, usually containing liquid, esp. the urinary bladder **2** a hollow bag made of leather, etc. which becomes round when filled with air or liquid **3** a hollow saclike part in certain plants, such as seaweed [Old English *blǣdre*] **bladdery** *adj*

blade *n* **1** the part of a sharp weapon, tool, or knife, that forms the cutting edge **2** the thin flattish part of a propeller, oar, or fan **3** the flattened part of a leaf, sepal, or petal **4** the long narrow leaf of a grass or related plant [Old English *blæd*]

b

blag *vb* **blagging, blagged** *Brit slang* **1** to obtain by wheedling or cadging **2** to steal or rob [origin unknown]

blame *vb* **blaming, blamed 1** to consider (someone) responsible for: *I blame her for the failure* **2** (foll. by *on*) to put responsibility for (something) on (someone): *she blames the failure on me* **3 be to blame** to be at fault ▷ *n* **4** responsibility for something that is wrong: *they must take the blame for the failure* **5** an expression of condemnation: *analysts lay the blame on party activists* [Late Latin *blasphemare* to blaspheme] **blamable** *or* **blameable** *adj* **blameless** *adj*

blameworthy *adj* deserving blame **blameworthiness** *n*

blanch *vb* **1** to whiten **2** to become pale, as with sickness or fear **3** to prepare (meat or vegetables) by plunging them in boiling water **4** to cause (celery, chicory, etc.) to grow white from lack of light [Old French *blanc* white]

blancmange (blam-**monzh**) *n* a jelly-like dessert of milk, stiffened usually with cornflour [Old French *blanc manger* white food]

bland *adj* **1** dull and uninteresting: *the bland predictability of the film* **2** (of food, drink, etc.) flavourless **3** smooth in manner: *he looked at his visitor with a bland smile* [Latin *blandus* flattering] **blandly** *adv*

blandish *vb* to persuade by mild flattery; coax [Latin *blandiri*]

blandishments *pl n* flattery intended to coax or cajole

blank *adj* **1** (of a writing surface) not written on **2** (of a form, etc.) with spaces left for details to be filled in **3** without ornament or break: *a blank wall* **4** empty or void: *a blank space* **5** showing no interest or expression: *a blank look* **6** lacking ideas or inspiration: *his mind went blank* ▷ *n* **7** an empty space **8** an empty space for writing in **9** the condition of not understanding: *my mind went a complete blank* **10** a mark, often a dash, in place of a word **11** same as **blank cartridge 12 draw a blank** to get no results from something ▷ *vb* **13** (foll. by *out*) to cross out, blot, or obscure **14 blank something out** to refuse to think about something; clear something from one's mind **15** *slang* to ignore: *the crowd blanked her for the first four numbers* [Old French *blanc* white] **blankly** *adv*

blank cartridge *n* a cartridge containing powder but no bullet

blank cheque *n* **1** a signed cheque on which the amount payable has not been specified **2** complete freedom of action

blanket *n* **1** a large piece of thick cloth for use as a bed covering **2** a concealing cover, as of smoke, leaves, or snow ▷ *adj* **3** applying to or covering a wide group or variety of people, conditions, situations, etc.: *a blanket ban on all supporters travelling to away matches* ▷ *vb* **-keting, -keted 4** to cover as if with a blanket **5** to cover a wide area of; give blanket coverage to [Old French *blancquete*]

blanket stitch *n* a strong reinforcing stitch for the edges of blankets

blank verse *n* unrhymed verse

blare *vb* **blaring, blared 1** to sound loudly and harshly **2** to proclaim loudly: *the newspaper headlines blared the news* ▷ *n* **3** a loud harsh noise [Middle Dutch *bleren*]

blarney *n* flattering talk [after the *Blarney* Stone in SW Ireland, said to endow whoever kisses it with skill in flattery]

blasé (**blah**-zay) *adj* indifferent or bored, esp. through familiarity [French]

blaspheme *vb* **-pheming, -phemed 1** to speak disrespectfully of (God or sacred things) **2** to utter curses [Greek *blasphēmos* evil-speaking] **blasphemer** *n*

blasphemy *n, pl* **-mies** behaviour or language that shows disrespect for God or sacred things **blasphemous** *adj*

blast *n* **1** an explosion, such as that caused by dynamite **2** the charge used in a single explosion **3** a sudden strong gust of wind or air **4** a sudden loud sound, such as that made by a trumpet **5** a violent verbal outburst, esp. critical **6** *slang* a very enjoyable or thrilling experience: *the party was a blast* **7 at full blast** at maximum speed, volume, etc. ▷ *interj* **8** *slang* an exclamation of annoyance ▷ *vb* **9** to blow up (a rock, tunnel, etc.) with explosives **10** to make or cause to make a loud harsh noise **11** to criticize severely [Old English *blǣst*]

blasted *adj, adv slang* extreme or extremely: *a blasted idiot*

blast furnace *n* a furnace for smelting using a blast of preheated air

blastoff *n* **1** the launching of a rocket under its own power ▷ *vb* **blast off 2** (of a rocket) to be launched

blatant (**blay**-tant) *adj* **1** glaringly obvious: *a blatant lie* **2** offensively noticeable: *their blatant disregard for my feelings* [coined by Edmund Spenser, poet] **blatantly** *adv*

blather *vb, n* same as **blether**

blaze[1] *n* **1** a strong fire or flame **2** a very bright light or glare **3** an outburst (of passion, patriotism, etc.) ▷ *vb* **blazing, blazed 4** to burn fiercely **5** to shine brightly **6** to become stirred, as with anger or excitement **7 blaze away** to shoot continuously ▷ See also **blazes** [Old English *blæse*]

blaze[2] *n* **1** a mark, usually indicating a path, made on a tree **2** a light-coloured marking on the face of an animal ▷ *vb* **blazing, blazed 3** to mark (a tree, path, etc.) with a blaze **4 blaze a trail** to explore new territories, areas of knowledge, etc. [probably from Middle Low German *bles* white marking]

blaze³ *vb* **blazing, blazed** > **blaze something abroad** to make something widely known [Middle Dutch *blāsen*]
blazer *n* a fairly lightweight jacket, often in the colours of a sports club, school, etc.
blazes *pl n slang, euphemistic* hell
blazon *vb* **1** to proclaim publicly: *the newspaper photographs were blazoned on the front pages* **2** *heraldry* to describe or colour (heraldic arms) conventionally ▷ *n* **3** *heraldry* a coat of arms [Old French *blason* coat of arms]
bleach *vb* **1** to make or become white or colourless by exposure to sunlight, or by the action of chemical agents ▷ *n* **2** a bleaching agent [Old English *blǣcan*]
bleaching powder *n* a white powder consisting of chlorinated calcium hydroxide
bleak *adj* **1** exposed and barren **2** cold and raw **3** offering little hope; dismal: *a bleak future* [Old English *blāc* pale] **bleakly** *adv* **bleakness** *n*
bleary *adj* **blearier, bleariest 1** with eyes dimmed, by tears or tiredness: *a few bleary hacks* **2** indistinct or unclear **blearily** *adv*
bleary-eyed *or* **blear-eyed** *adj* with eyes blurred, such as with old age or after waking
bleat *vb* **1** (of a sheep, goat, or calf) to utter its plaintive cry **2** to whine ▷ *n* **3** the characteristic cry of sheep, goats, and calves **4** a weak complaint or whine [Old English *blǣtan*]
bleed *vb* **bleeding, bled 1** to lose or emit blood **2** to remove or draw blood from (a person or animal) **3** (of plants) to exude (sap or resin), esp. from a cut **4** *informal* to obtain money, etc., from (someone), esp. by extortion **5** to draw liquid or gas from (a container or enclosed system) **6 my heart bleeds for you** I am sorry for you: often used ironically [Old English *blēdan*]
bleeding *adj, adv Brit slang* extreme or extremely: *a bleeding fool*
bleep *n* **1** a short high-pitched signal made by an electronic device **2** same as **bleeper** ▷ *vb* **3** to make a bleeping signal **4** to call (someone) by means of a bleeper [imitative]
bleeper *n* a small portable radio receiver that makes a bleeping signal
blemish *n* **1** a defect; flaw; stain ▷ *vb* **2** to spoil or tarnish [Old French *blemir* to make pale]
blench *vb* to shy away, as in fear [Old English *blencan* to deceive]
blend *vb* **1** to mix or mingle (components) **2** to mix (different varieties of tea, whisky, etc.) **3** to look good together; harmonize **4** (esp. of colours) to shade gradually into each other ▷ *n* **5** a mixture produced by blending [Old English *blandan*]
blende *n* a mineral consisting mainly of zinc sulphide: the chief source of zinc
blended family *n* a family consisting of two parents along with the children of their former relationships
blender *n* an electrical kitchen appliance for pureeing vegetables, etc.
blenny *n, pl* **-nies** a small fish of coastal waters with a tapering scaleless body and long fins [Greek *blennos* slime]
bless *vb* **blessing, blessed** *or* **blest 1** to make holy by means of a religious rite **2** to give honour or glory to (a person or thing) as holy **3** to call upon God to protect **4** to worship or adore (God) **5 be blessed with** to be endowed with: *she is blessed with immense energy* **6 bless me!** an exclamation of surprise **7 bless you!** said to a person who has just sneezed [Old English *blǣdsian* to sprinkle with sacrificial blood]
blessed *adj* **1** made holy **2** *RC Church* (of a person) beatified by the pope **3** bringing great happiness or good fortune: *he was blessed with good looks* **4** *euphemistic* damned: *I'm blessed if I know*
blessing *n* **1** the act of invoking divine protection or aid **2** approval; good wishes **3** a happy event
blest *vb* a past of **bless**
blether *Scot* ▷ *vb* **1** to speak foolishly at length ▷ *n* **2** foolish talk **3** a person who blethers [Old Norse *blathr* nonsense]
blew *vb* the past tense of **blow¹**
blight *n* **1** a person or thing that spoils or prevents growth **2** any plant disease characterized by withering and shrivelling without rotting **3** a fungus or insect that causes blight in plants **4** an ugly urban district ▷ *vb* **5** to cause to suffer a blight **6** to frustrate or disappoint: *blighted love* **7** to destroy: *the event blighted her life* [origin unknown]
blighter *n Brit, Austral & NZ informal* a despicable or irritating person or thing
Blighty *n Brit, Austral & NZ slang* **1** (used esp. by troops serving abroad) Britain; home **2** *pl* **Blighties** (esp. in the First World War) a wound that causes the recipient to be sent home to Britain [Hindi *bilāyatī* foreign land]
blimey *interj Brit & NZ slang* an exclamation of surprise or annoyance [short for *gorblimey* God blind me]
blimp¹ *n* **1** a small nonrigid airship **2** *films* a soundproof cover fixed over a camera during shooting [probably from *(type) B-limp*]
blimp² *n chiefly Brit* a person who is stupidly complacent and reactionary. Also called: **Colonel Blimp** [a cartoon character]
blind *adj* **1** unable to see **2** unable or unwilling to understand: *she is blind to his faults* **3** not determined by reason: *blind hatred* **4** acting or performed without control or preparation **5** done without being able to see, relying on instruments for information **6** hidden from sight: *a blind corner* **7** closed at one end: *a blind alley* **8** completely lacking awareness or consciousness: *a blind stupor* **9** having no openings: *a blind wall* ▷ *adv* **10** without being able to see ahead or using only instruments: *flying blind* **11** without adequate information: *we bought the house blind* **12 blind drunk** *informal* very drunk ▷ *vb* **13** to deprive of sight permanently or temporarily **14** to deprive of good sense, reason, or judgment **15** to darken; conceal **16** to overwhelm by showing detailed knowledge: *he tried to blind us with science* ▷ *n* **17** a shade for a window **18** any obstruction or hindrance to sight, light, or air **19** a person, action, or thing that serves to deceive or conceal the truth [Old English] **blinding** *adj* **blindly** *adv* **blindness** *n*
USAGE See at **disabled**.

blind alley *n* **1** an alley open at one end only **2** *informal* a situation in which no further progress can be made

blind date *n informal* a prearranged social meeting between two people who have not met before

blindfold *vb* **1** to prevent (a person or animal) from seeing by covering the eyes ▷ *n* **2** a piece of cloth used to cover the eyes ▷ *adj, adv* **3** having the eyes covered with a cloth [Old English *blindfellian* to strike blind]

blind man's buff *n* a game in which a blindfolded person tries to catch and identify the other players [obsolete *buff* a blow]

blind spot *n* **1** a small oval-shaped area of the retina which is unable to see **2** a place where vision is obscured **3** a subject about which a person is ignorant or prejudiced

blindworm *n* same as **slowworm**

bling *adj informal* **1** flashy, ostentatious, glitzy, etc. ▷ *n* **2** ostentatious jewellery

blink *vb* **1** to close and immediately reopen (the eyes), usually involuntarily **2** to shine intermittently or unsteadily ▷ *n* **3** the act or an instance of blinking **4** a glance; glimpse **5 on the blink** *slang* not working properly [variant of BLENCH]

blinker *vb* **1** to provide (a horse) with blinkers **2** to obscure or be obscured with or as with blinkers

blinkered *adj* **1** considering only a narrow point of view **2** (of a horse) wearing blinkers

blinkers *pl n Brit & Austral* leather side pieces attached to a horse's bridle to prevent sideways vision

blinking *adj, adv informal* extreme or extremely: *a blinking idiot*

blip *n* **1** a repetitive sound, such as the kind produced by an electronic device **2** the spot of light on a radar screen indicating the position of an object **3** a temporary irregularity in the performance of something [imitative]

bliss *n* **1** perfect happiness; serene joy **2** the joy of heaven [Old English *blīths*] **blissful** *adj* **blissfully** *adv*

B list *n* **1** a category slightly below the most socially desirable ▷ *adj* **B-list 2** of the category slightly below the most socially desirable: *B-list celebrities*

blister *n* **1** a small bubble on the skin filled with a watery fluid **2** a swelling containing air or liquid, such as on a painted surface ▷ *vb* **3** to have or cause to have blisters **4** to attack verbally with great scorn [Old French *blestre*] **blistering** *adj*

blithe *adj* **1** heedless; casual and indifferent **2** very happy or cheerful [Old English *blīthe*] **blithely** *adv*

blithering *adj informal* stupid; foolish: *you blithering idiot* [variant of *blethering*]

BLitt Bachelor of Letters [Latin *Baccalaureus Litterarum*]

blitz *n* **1** a violent and sustained attack by enemy aircraft **2** any intensive attack or concerted effort ▷ *vb* **3** to attack suddenly and intensively [see BLITZKRIEG]

Blitz *n* **the Blitz** the systematic bombing of Britain in 1940–41 by the German Air Force

blitzkrieg *n* a swift intensive military attack designed to defeat the opposition quickly [German: lightning war]

blizzard *n* a blinding storm of wind and snow [origin unknown]

bloat *vb* **1** to cause to swell, as with a liquid or air **2** to cause to be puffed up, as with conceit **3** to cure (fish, esp. herring) by half drying in smoke [Old Norse *blautr* soaked] **bloated** *adj*

bloater *n Brit* a herring that has been salted in brine, smoked, and cured

blob *n* **1** a soft mass or drop **2** a spot of colour, ink, etc. **3** an indistinct or shapeless form or object [imitative]

bloc *n* a group of people or countries combined by a common interest [French]

block *n* **1** a large solid piece of wood, stone, etc. **2** such a piece on which particular tasks may be done, as chopping, cutting, etc. **3** a large building of offices, flats, etc. **4** a group of buildings in a city bounded by intersecting streets on each side **5** an obstruction or hindrance: *a writer with a block* **6** one of a set of wooden or plastic cubes as a child's toy **7** *slang* a person's head **8** a piece of wood, metal, etc., engraved for printing **9** a casing housing one or more freely rotating pulleys. See also **block and tackle 10** a quantity considered as a single unit ▷ *vb* **11** to obstruct or impede by introducing an obstacle: *lorry drivers had blocked the routes to Paris* **12** to impede, retard, or prevent (an action or procedure) **13** to stamp (a title or design) on (a book cover, etc.) **14** *cricket* to play (a ball) defensively ▷ See also **block out** [Dutch *blok*] **blockage** *n*

blockade *n* **1** *military* the closing off of a port or region to prevent the passage of goods ▷ *vb* **-ading, -aded 2** to impose a blockade on

block and tackle *n* a hoisting device in which a rope or chain is passed around a pair of blocks containing one or more pulleys

blockboard *n* a type of plywood consisting of strips of wood sandwiched between layers of veneer

blockbuster *n informal* **1** a film, novel, etc. that has been or is expected to be highly successful **2** a large bomb used to demolish extensive areas

blockhead *n* a stupid person **blockheaded** *adj*

blockie *n Austral* an owner of a small property, esp. a farm

block letter *n* a plain capital letter. Also called: **block capital**

block out *vb* **1** to plan or describe (something) in a general fashion **2** to prevent the entry or consideration of (something)

blog *n* **1** a journal written online and accessible to users of the internet. Full name: **weblog** ▷ *vb* **blogging, blogged 2** to write a blog **blogger** *n* **blogging** *n*

blogosphere *n informal* a collective term for the weblogs on the internet

bloke *n Brit, Austral & NZ informal* a man [Shelta] **blokeish** *or* **blokey** *adj*

blonde *or masc* **blond** *adj* **1** (of hair) fair **2** (of a person) having fair hair and a light complexion ▷ *n* **3** a person having light-coloured hair and skin [Old French] **blondeness** *or masc* **blondness** *n*
blood *n* **1** a reddish fluid in vertebrates that is pumped by the heart through the arteries and veins. Related adjective: **haemal** **2** bloodshed, esp. when resulting in murder: *they were responsible for the spilling of blood throughout the country* **3** lifeblood **4** relationship through being of the same family, race, or kind; kinship **5** **the blood** royal or noble descent: *a prince of the blood* **6** **flesh and blood** **A** near kindred or kinship, esp. that between a parent and child **B** human nature: *it's more than flesh and blood can stand* **7** **in one's blood** as a natural or inherited characteristic or talent **8** newcomers viewed as an invigorating force: *new blood* **9** **in cold blood** showing no passion; ruthlessly **10** **make one's blood boil** to cause one to be angry or indignant **11** **make one's blood run cold** to fill one with horror ▷ *vb* **12** *hunting* to cause (young hounds) to taste the blood of a freshly killed quarry **13** to initiate (a person) to war or hunting [Old English *blōd*]
blood-and-thunder *adj* denoting melodramatic behaviour
blood bank *n* a place where blood is stored until required for transfusion
blood bath *n* a massacre
blood brother *n* a man or boy who has sworn to treat another as his brother, often in a ceremony in which their blood is mingled
blood count *n* determination of the number of red and white blood corpuscles in a specific sample of blood
blood-curdling *or* **bloodcurdling** *adj* terrifying
blood donor *n* a person who gives blood to be used for transfusion
blood group *n* any one of the various groups into which human blood is classified
blood heat *n* the normal temperature of the human body, 98.4°F or 37°C
bloodhound *n* a large hound, formerly used in tracking and police work
bloodless *adj* **1** without blood: *bloodless surgery* **2** conducted without violence: *a bloodless coup* **3** anaemic-looking; pale **4** lacking vitality; lifeless: *the bloodless ambience of supermarkets*
blood-letting *n* **1** bloodshed, esp. in a feud **2** the former medical practice of removing blood
bloodlust *n* a desire for violence and carnage
blood money *n* **1** money obtained by ruthlessly sacrificing others **2** money paid to a hired murderer **3** compensation paid to the relatives of a murdered person
blood orange *n* a variety of orange, the pulp of which is dark red when ripe
blood poisoning *n* same as **septicaemia**
blood pressure *n* the pressure exerted by the blood on the inner walls of the blood vessels
blood relation *or* **blood relative** *n* a person related by birth
bloodshed *n* slaughter; killing
bloodshot *adj* (of an eye) inflamed
blood sport *n* any sport involving the killing of an animal
bloodstained *adj* discoloured with blood
bloodstock *n* thoroughbred horses
bloodstream *n* the flow of blood through the vessels of a living body
bloodsucker *n* **1** an animal that sucks blood, esp. a leech **2** *informal* a person who preys upon another person, esp. by extorting money
bloodthirsty *adj* **-thirstier, -thirstiest** taking pleasure in bloodshed or violence
blood vessel *n* a tube through which blood travels in the body
bloody *adj* **bloodier, bloodiest** **1** covered with blood **2** marked by much killing and bloodshed: *a bloody war* **3** cruel or murderous: *a bloody tyrant* ▷ *adj, adv* **4** *slang* extreme or extremely: *a bloody fool; a bloody good idea* ▷ *vb* **bloodies, bloodying, bloodied** **5** to stain with blood
Bloody Caesar *n* a drink consisting of vodka, juice made from clams and tomatoes, Worcester sauce, and Tabasco
Bloody Mary *n* a drink consisting of tomato juice and vodka
bloody-minded *adj Brit & NZ informal* deliberately obstructive and unhelpful
bloom *n* **1** a blossom on a flowering plant **2** the state or period when flowers open **3** a healthy or flourishing condition; prime **4** a youthful or healthy glow **5** a fine whitish coating on the surface of fruits or leaves ▷ *vb* **6** (of flowers) to open **7** to bear flowers **8** to flourish or grow **9** to be in a healthy, glowing condition [Germanic]
bloomer *n Brit informal* a stupid mistake; blunder [from BLOOMING]
bloomers *pl n* **1** *informal* women's baggy knickers **2** (formerly) loose trousers gathered at the knee, worn by women [after Mrs A. *Bloomer*, social reformer]
blooming *adv, adj Brit informal* extreme or extremely: *blooming painful* [euphemistic for *bloody*]
blossom *n* **1** the flower or flowers of a plant, esp. producing edible fruit **2** the period of flowering ▷ *vb* **3** (of plants) to flower **4** to come to a promising stage [Old English *blōstm*]
blot *n* **1** a stain or spot, esp. of ink **2** something that spoils **3** a stain on one's character ▷ *vb* **blotting, blotted** **4** to stain or spot **5** to cause a blemish in or on: *he blotted his copybook by missing a penalty* **6** to soak up (excess ink, etc.) by using blotting paper **7** **blot out** **A** to darken or hide completely: *the mist blotted out the sea* **B** to block from one's mind: *to blot out the memories* [Germanic]
blotch *n* **1** an irregular spot or discoloration ▷ *vb* **2** to become or cause to become marked by such discoloration [probably from *botch*, influenced by *blot*] **blotchy** *adj*
blotter *n* a sheet of blotting paper
blotting paper *n* a soft absorbent paper, used for soaking up surplus ink
blotto *adj Brit, Austral & NZ slang* extremely drunk [from *blot* (verb)]
blouse *n* **1** a woman's shirtlike garment **2** a waist-length belted jacket worn by soldiers ▷ *vb* **blousing, bloused** **3** to hang or cause to hang in full loose folds [French]

blouson (**blew**-zon) *n* a short loose jacket with a tight-fitting waist [French]

blow[1] *vb* **blowing, blew, blown 1** (of a current of air, the wind, etc.) to be or cause to be in motion **2** to move or be carried by or as if by wind **3** to expel (air, etc.) through the mouth or nose **4** to breathe hard; pant **5** to inflate with air or the breath **6** (of wind, etc.) to make a roaring sound **7** to cause (a musical instrument) to sound by forcing air into it **8** (often foll. by *up*, *down* or *in* etc.) to explode, break, or disintegrate completely **9** *electronics* (of a fuse or valve) to burn out because of excessive current **10** to shape (glass, etc.) by forcing air or gas through the material when molten **11** *slang* to spend (money) freely **12** *slang* to use (an opportunity) ineffectively **13** *slang* to expose or betray (a secret) **14** *past participle* **blowed** *informal* same as **damn 15 blow hot and cold** *informal* to keep changing one's attitude towards someone or something **16 blow one's top** *informal* to lose one's temper ▷ *n* **17** the act or an instance of blowing **18** the sound produced by blowing **19** a blast of air or wind **20** *Brit slang* cannabis ▷ See also **blow away, blow out** *etc.* [Old English *blāwan*]

blow[2] *n* **1** a powerful or heavy stroke with the fist, a weapon, etc. **2** a sudden setback: *the scheme was dealt a blow by the introduction of martial law* **3** an attacking action: *a blow for freedom* **4 come to blows** **A** to fight **B** to result in a fight [probably Germanic]

blow away *vb slang* **1** to kill by shooting **2** to defeat utterly

blow-by-blow *adj* explained in great detail: *a blow-by-blow account*

blow-dry *vb* **-dries, -drying, -dried 1** to style (the hair) while drying it with a hand-held hair dryer ▷ *n* **2** this method of styling hair

blower *n* **1** a mechanical device, such as a fan, that blows **2** *informal* a telephone

blowfly *n, pl* **-flies** a fly that lays its eggs in meat

blowhole *n* **1** the nostril of a whale **2** a hole in ice through which seals, etc. breathe **3** a vent for air or gas **4** *geol* a hole in a cliff top leading to a sea cave

blowie *n Austral informal* a bluebottle

blown *vb* a past participle of **blow**[1]

blow out *vb* **1** (of a flame) to extinguish or be extinguished **2** (of a tyre) to puncture suddenly **3** (of an oil or gas well) to lose oil or gas in an uncontrolled manner ▷ *n* **blowout 4** a sudden burst in a tyre **5** the uncontrolled escape of oil or gas from a well **6** *slang* a large filling meal **7** *Austral* a sudden large increase

blow over *vb* **1** to be forgotten **2** to cease or be finished: *the crisis blew over*

blowpipe *n* **1** a long tube from which poisoned darts, etc. are shot by blowing **2** a tube for blowing air into a flame to intensify its heat **3** an iron pipe used to blow glass into shape

blowsy *adj* **blowsier, blowsiest 1** (of a woman) untidy in appearance **2** (of a woman) ruddy in complexion [dialect *blowze* beggar girl]

blowtorch *or* **blowlamp** *n* a small burner that produces a very hot flame, used to remove old paint, soften metal, etc.

blow up *vb* **1** to explode or cause to explode **2** to inflate with air **3** to increase the importance of (something): *an affair blown up out of all proportion* **4** *informal* to lose one's temper **5** *informal* to reprimand (someone) **6** *informal* to enlarge (a photograph) **7** to come into existence with sudden force: *a crisis had blown up* ▷ *n* **blow-up 8** *informal* an enlarged photograph

blowy *adj* **blowier, blowiest** windy

blubber *n* **1** the fatty tissue of aquatic mammals such as the whale **2** *informal* flabby body fat ▷ *vb* **3** to sob without restraint [probably imitative]

bludge *Austral & NZ informal* ▷ *vb* **bludging, bludged 1** (foll. by *on*) to scrounge from **2** to evade work ▷ *n* **3** a very easy task

bludgeon *n* **1** a stout heavy club, typically thicker at one end ▷ *vb* **2** to hit as if with a bludgeon **3** to force; bully; coerce [origin unknown]

blue *n* **1** the colour of a clear unclouded sky **2** anything blue, such as blue clothing or blue paint: *she is clothed in blue* **3** a sportsperson who represents or has represented Oxford or Cambridge University **4** *Brit informal* a Tory **5** *Austral & NZ slang* an argument or fight **6** Also: **bluey** *Austral & NZ slang* a court summons **7** *Austral & NZ informal* a mistake **8 out of the blue** unexpectedly ▷ *adj* **bluer, bluest 9** of the colour blue; of the colour of a clear unclouded sky **10** (of the flesh) having a purple tinge from cold **11** depressed or unhappy **12** pornographic: *blue movies* ▷ *vb* **blueing** *or* **bluing, blued 13** to make or become blue or bluer **14** *old-fashioned, informal* to spend extravagantly or wastefully: *I consoled myself by blueing my royalty cheque* ▷ See also **blues** [Old French *bleu*] **blueness** *n*

blue baby *n* a baby born with a bluish tinge to the skin because of lack of oxygen in the blood

bluebell *n* a woodland plant with blue bell-shaped flowers

blueberry *n, pl* **-ries** a very small blackish edible fruit that grows on a North American shrub

bluebird *n* a North American songbird with a blue plumage

blue blood *n* royal or aristocratic descent

bluebook *n* **1** (in Britain) a government publication, usually the report of a commission **2** (in Canada) an annual statement of government accounts

bluebottle *n* **1** a large fly with a dark-blue body; blowfly **2** *Austral & NZ informal* a Portuguese man-of-war

blue cheese *n* cheese containing a blue mould, such as Stilton or Danish blue

blue chip *n* **1** *finance* a stock considered reliable ▷ *adj* **blue-chip 2** denoting something considered to be a valuable asset

blue-collar *adj* denoting manual industrial workers

blue-eyed boy *n informal* a favourite

blue funk *n slang* a state of great terror

blue heeler *n Austral & NZ informal* a dog that controls cattle by biting their heels

bluenose *n* **1** *US slang* a puritanical or prudish person **2** Also: **bluenoser** (*sometimes cap*) *Canad informal* a native or inhabitant of Nova Scotia

blue pencil *n* **1** deletion or alteration of the contents of a book or other work ▷ *vb* **blue-pencil, -cilling, -cilled** *or US* **-ciling, -ciled 2** to alter or delete parts of (a book, film, etc.)

blue peter *n* a signal flag of blue with a white square at the centre, displayed by a vessel about to leave port

blueprint *n* **1** an original description of a plan or idea that explains how it is expected to work **2** a photographic print of plans, technical drawings, etc. consisting of white lines on a blue background

blue ribbon *n* **1** a badge awarded as the first prize in a competition **2** (in Britain) a badge of blue silk worn by members of the Order of the Garter

blues *pl n* **the blues 1** a feeling of depression or deep unhappiness **2** a type of folk song originating among Black Americans

blue-screen *adj* relating to a film technique in which actors are filmed against a blue screen so that special effects can be added later

blue-sky *adj* of research done for theoretical reasons rather than for practical application

bluestocking *n usually derogatory* a scholarly or intellectual woman [from the blue worsted stockings worn by members of an 18th-century literary society]

bluetit *n* a small European bird with a blue crown, wings, and tail and yellow underparts

bluetongue *n* an Australian lizard with a blue tongue

Bluetooth *n trademark* a short-range radio technology that allows wireless communication between computers, mobile phones, etc.

blue whale *n* a very large bluish-grey whale: the largest mammal

bluff[1] *vb* **1** to pretend to be confident in order to influence (someone) ▷ *n* **2** deliberate deception to create the impression of a strong position **3 call someone's bluff** to challenge someone to give proof of his or her claims [Dutch *bluffen* to boast]

bluff[2] *n* **1** a steep promontory, bank, or cliff **2** *Canad* a clump of trees on the prairie; copse ▷ *adj* **3** good-naturedly frank and hearty [probably from Middle Dutch *blaf* broad]

bluish *or* **blueish** *adj* slightly blue

blunder *n* **1** a stupid or clumsy mistake ▷ *vb* **2** to make stupid or clumsy mistakes **3** to act clumsily; stumble [Scandinavian] **blundering** *n, adj*

blunderbuss *n* an obsolete gun with wide barrel and flared muzzle [Dutch *donderbus* thunder gun]

blunt *adj* **1** (esp. of a knife) lacking sharpness **2** not having a sharp edge or point: *a blunt instrument* **3** (of people, manner of speaking, etc.) straightforward and uncomplicated ▷ *vb* **4** to make less sharp **5** to diminish the sensitivity or perception of: *prison life has blunted his mind* [Scandinavian] **bluntly** *adv*

blur *vb* **blurring, blurred 1** to make or become vague or less distinct **2** to smear or smudge **3** to make (the judgment, memory, or perception) less clear; dim ▷ *n* **4** something vague, hazy, or indistinct **5** a smear or smudge [perhaps variant of *blear*] **blurred** *adj* **blurry** *adj*

blurb *n* a promotional description, such as on the jackets of books [coined by G. Burgess, humorist & illustrator]

blurt *vb* (foll. by *out*) to utter suddenly and involuntarily [probably imitative]

blush *vb* **1** to become suddenly red in the face, esp. from embarrassment or shame ▷ *n* **2** a sudden reddening of the face, esp. from embarrassment or shame **3** a rosy glow **4** same as **rosé** [Old English *blӯscan*]

blusher *n* a cosmetic applied to the cheeks to give a rosy colour

bluster *vb* **1** to speak loudly or in a bullying way **2** (of the wind) to be gusty ▷ *n* **3** empty threats or protests [probably from Middle Low German *blüsteren* to blow violently] **blustery** *adj*

BM 1 Bachelor of Medicine **2** British Museum

BMA British Medical Association

BMI body mass index: an index used to indicate whether or not a person is a healthy weight for his or her height

B-movie *n* a film originally made as a supporting film, now considered a genre in its own right

BMR basal metabolic rate

BMus Bachelor of Music

BMX *n* **1** bicycle motocross: stunt riding over an obstacle course on a bicycle **2** a bicycle designed for bicycle motocross

BO 1 *informal* body odour **2** box office

boa *n* **1** a large nonvenomous snake of Central and South America that kills its prey by constriction **2** a long thin scarf of feathers or fur [Latin]

boab (**boh**-ab) *n Austral informal* short for **baobab**

boa constrictor *n* a very large snake of tropical America and the West Indies that kills its prey by constriction

boar *n* **1** an uncastrated male pig **2** a wild pig [Old English *bār*]

board *n* **1** a long wide flat piece of sawn timber **2** a smaller flat piece of rigid material for a specific purpose: *ironing board* **3 A** a group of people who officially administer a company, trust, etc. **B** any other official group, such as examiners or interviewers **4** a person's meals, provided regularly for money **5** stiff cardboard or similar material, used for the outside covers of a book **6** a flat thin rectangular sheet of composite material, such as chipboard **7** *naut* the side of a ship **8** a portable surface for indoor games such as chess or backgammon **9 go by the board** *informal* to be in disuse, neglected, or lost **10 on board** on or in a ship, aeroplane, etc. ▷ *vb* **11** to go aboard (a train or other vehicle) **12** to attack (a ship) by forcing one's way aboard **13** (foll. by *up* or *in* etc.) to cover with boards **14** to receive meals and lodging in return for money **15 board out** to arrange for (someone, esp. a child) to receive food and lodging away from home **16** (in ice hockey and box lacrosse) to bodycheck an opponent against the boards ▷ See also **boards** [Old English *bord*]

boarder *n Brit* a pupil who lives at school during term time

boarding *n* **1** the act of embarking on an aircraft, train, ship, etc. **2** a structure of boards **3** timber boards collectively **4** (in ice hockey and box lacrosse) an act of bodychecking an opponent against the boards

boarding house *n* a private house that provides accommodation and meals for paying guests

boarding school *n* a school providing living accommodation for pupils

b

boardroom *n* a room where the board of directors of a company meets

boards *pl n* **1** a wooden wall forming the enclosure in which ice hockey or box lacrosse is played **2 the boards** the stage

boast *vb* **1** to speak in excessively proud terms of one's possessions, talents, etc. **2** to possess (something to be proud of): *a team which boasts five current world record holders* ▹ *n* **3** a bragging statement **4** something that is bragged about: *this proved to be a false boast* [origin unknown]

boastful *adj* tending to boast

boat *n* **1** a small vessel propelled by oars, paddle, sails, or motor **2** *informal* a ship **3** See **gravy boat, sauce boat 4 in the same boat** sharing the same problems **5 miss the boat** to lose an opportunity **6 rock the boat** *informal* to cause a disturbance in the existing situation ▹ *vb* **7** to travel or go in a boat, esp. as recreation [Old English *bāt*]

boater *n* a stiff straw hat with a straight brim and flat crown

boathouse *n* a shelter by the edge of a river, lake, etc., for housing boats

boating *n* rowing, sailing, or cruising in boats as a form of recreation

boatman *n, pl* **-men** a man who works on, hires out, or repairs boats

boatswain (boh-sn) *n naut* same as **bosun**

boat train *n* a train scheduled to take passengers to or from a particular ship

bob¹ *vb* **bobbing, bobbed 1** to move or cause to move up and down repeatedly, such as while floating in water **2** to move or cause to move with a short abrupt movement, esp. of the head **3 bob up** to appear or emerge suddenly ▹ *n* **4** a short abrupt movement, as of the head [origin unknown]

bob² *n* **1** a hairstyle in which the hair is cut short evenly all round the head **2** a dangling weight on a pendulum or plumb line ▹ *vb* **bobbing, bobbed 3** to cut (the hair) in a bob [Middle English *bobbe* bunch of flowers]

bob³ *n, pl* **bob** *Brit, Austral & NZ informal* (formerly) a shilling: *two bob* [origin unknown]

bobbejaan *n S African* **1** a baboon **2** a large black spider **3** a monkey wrench [Afrikaans]

bobbin *n* a reel on which thread or yarn is wound [Old French *bobine*]

bobble *n* **1** a tufted ball, usually woollen, that is used for decoration ▹ *vb* **-bling, -bled 2** (of a ball) to bounce erratically because of an uneven playing surface [from BOB¹]

bobby *n, pl* **-bies** *Brit informal* a British police officer [after *Robert* Peel, who set up the Metropolitan Police Force]

bobby pin *n US, Canad, Austral & NZ* a metal hairpin

bobotie (ba-**boot**-ee) *n S African* a traditional Cape dish of curried minced meat [probably from Malay]

bobsleigh *n* **1** a sledge for racing down a steeply banked ice-covered run ▹ *vb* **2** to ride on a bobsleigh

bobtail *n* **1** a docked tail **2** an animal with such a tail ▹ *adj also* **bobtailed 3** having the tail cut short

bocconcini (bok-on-**chee**-nee) *pl n* small bite-sized pieces of mozzarella cheese [Italian]

Boche (**bosh**) *n derogatory slang* a German, esp. a German soldier [French]

bod *n informal* **1** a person: *he's a senior marketing bod* **2** short for **body** (sense 1) [short for *body*]

bode¹ *vb* **boding, boded** to be an omen of (good or ill); portend [Old English *bodian*]

bode² *vb* a past tense of **bide**

bodega *n* a shop in a Spanish-speaking country that sells wine [Spanish]

bodge *vb* **bodging, bodged** *Brit, Austral & NZ informal* to make a mess of; botch

bodice *n* **1** the upper part of a dress, from the shoulder to the waist **2** a tight-fitting corset worn laced over a blouse, or (formerly) as a woman's undergarment [originally Scots *bodies*, plural of *body*]

bodily *adj* **1** relating to the human body ▹ *adv* **2** by taking hold of the body: *he threw him bodily from the platform* **3** in person; in the flesh

bodkin *n* a blunt large-eyed needle [origin unknown]

body *n, pl* **bodies 1** the entire physical structure of an animal or human. Related adjective: **corporal 2** the trunk or torso **3** a corpse **4** a group regarded as a single entity: *a local voluntary body* **5** the main part of anything: *the body of a car* **6** a separate mass of water or land **7** the flesh as opposed to the spirit **8** fullness in the appearance of the hair **9** the characteristic full quality of certain wines **10** *informal* a person: *all the important bodies from the council were present* **11** a woman's one-piece undergarment **12 keep body and soul together** to manage to survive [Old English *bodig*]

bodyboard *n* a small polystyrene surfboard **bodyboarder** *n*

body building *n* regular exercising designed to enlarge the muscles

bodycheck *ice hockey etc.* ▹ *n* **1** obstruction of another player ▹ *vb* **2** to deliver a bodycheck to (an opponent)

bodyguard *n* a person or group of people employed to protect someone

body language *n* the communication of one's thoughts or feelings by the position or movements of one's body rather than by words

body mass index *n* See **BMI**

body politic *n* **the body politic** the people of a nation or the nation itself considered as a political entity

body search *n* **1** a search by police, customs officials, etc., that involves examination of a prisoner's or suspect's bodily orifices ▹ *vb* **body-search 2** to search (a prisoner or suspect) in this manner

body shop *n* a repair yard for vehicle bodywork

body snatcher *n* (formerly) a person who robbed graves and sold the corpses for dissection

body stocking *n* **1** a one-piece undergarment for women, covering the torso **2** a tightly-fitting garment covering the whole of the body, worn esp. for dancing or exercising
body warmer *n* a sleeveless quilted jerkin, worn as an outer garment
bodywork *n* the external shell of a motor vehicle
Boer *n* a descendant of any of the Dutch or Huguenot colonists who settled in South Africa [Dutch]
boere- *combining form S African* rustic or country-style [from Afrikaans *boer* a farmer]
boeremeisie (**boor**-a-may-see) *n S African* a country girl of Afrikaans stock
boereseun (**boor**-a-see-oon) *n S African* a country boy of Afrikaans stock
boerewors (**boor**-a-vorss) *n S African* a traditional home-made farmer's sausage
boffin *n old-fashioned, informal* a scientist or expert [origin unknown]
bog *n* **1** a wet spongy area of land **2** *slang* a toilet [Gaelic *bogach* swamp] **boggy** *adj* **bogginess** *n*
bog down *vb* **bogging, bogged** to impede physically or mentally
bogey *or* **bogy** *n* **1** an evil or mischievous spirit **2** something that worries or annoys **3** *golf* a score of one stroke over par on a hole **4** *slang* a piece of dried mucus from the nose [probably obsolete *bug* an evil spirit]
bogeyman *n, pl* **-men** a frightening person, real or imaginary, used as a threat, esp. to children
boggle *vb* **-gling, -gled 1** to be surprised, confused, or alarmed: *the mind boggles at the idea* **2** to hesitate or be evasive when confronted with a problem [probably Scots]
bogie *or* **bogy** *n* an assembly of wheels forming a pivoted support at either end of a railway coach [origin unknown]
bogle (**boh**-gul) *n* a rhythmic dance performed to ragga music [origin unknown]
bog-standard *adj Brit & Irish slang* completely ordinary; run-of-the-mill
bogus (**boh**-guss) *adj* not genuine [origin unknown]
bogy *n, pl* **-gies** same as **bogey** or **bogie**
bohemian *n* **1** a person, esp. an artist or writer, who lives an unconventional life ▷ *adj* **2** unconventional in appearance, behaviour, etc. **bohemianism** *n*
bohrium *n chem* an element artificially produced in minute quantities. Symbol: **Bh** [after N. Bohr, physicist]
boil[1] *vb* **1** to change or cause to change from a liquid to a vapour so rapidly that bubbles of vapour are formed in the liquid **2** to reach or cause to reach boiling point **3** to cook or be cooked by the process of boiling **4** to bubble and be agitated like something boiling: *the sea was boiling* **5** to be extremely angry ▷ *n* **6** the state or action of boiling ▷ See also **boil away, boil down, boil over** [Latin *bullire* to bubble]
boil[2] *n* a red painful swelling with a hard pus-filled core caused by infection of the skin [Old English *bȳle*]
boil away *vb* to cause (liquid) to evaporate completely by boiling or (of liquid) to evaporate completely
boil down *vb* **1** to reduce or be reduced in quantity by boiling **2 boil down to** to be the essential element in
boiler *n* **1** a closed vessel in which water is heated to provide steam to drive machinery **2** a domestic device to provide hot water, esp. for central heating
boilermaker *n* a person who works with metal in heavy industry
boilerplate *n* a standard text, esp. for a contract or letter, that can be modified to cover different situations
boiler suit *n Brit* a one-piece overall
boiling point *n* **1** the temperature at which a liquid boils **2** *informal* the condition of being angered or highly excited
boil over *vb* **1** to overflow or cause to overflow while boiling **2** to burst out in anger or excitement
boisterous *adj* **1** noisy and lively; unruly **2** (of the sea, etc.) turbulent or stormy [Middle English *boistuous*]
bold *adj* **1** courageous, confident, and fearless **2** immodest or impudent: *she gave him a bold look* **3** *Irish* (of a child) naughty; badly behaved **4** standing out distinctly; conspicuous: *a figure carved in bold relief* [Old English *beald*] **boldly** *adv* **boldness** *n*
bole *n* the trunk of a tree [Old Norse *bolr*]
bolero *n, pl* **-ros 1** a Spanish dance, usually in triple time **2** music for this dance **3** a short open jacket not reaching the waist [Spanish]
boll *n* the rounded seed capsule of flax, cotton, etc. [Dutch *bolle*]
bollard *n* **1** *Brit & Austral* a small post marking a kerb or traffic island or barring cars from entering **2** a strong wooden or metal post on a wharf, quay, etc., used for securing mooring lines [perhaps from *bole*]
bollocks *vulgar slang* ▷ *pl n* **1** the testicles ▷ *n* **2** nonsense; rubbish ▷ *interj* **3** an exclamation of annoyance, disbelief, etc. [Old English *beallucas*]
Bolshevik *n* **1** (formerly) a Russian Communist **2** any Communist **3** *informal, derogatory* any political radical, esp. a revolutionary [Russian *Bol'shevik* majority] **Bolshevism** *n* **Bolshevist** *adj, n*
bolshie *or* **bolshy** *Brit & NZ informal* ▷ *adj* **1** difficult to manage; rebellious **2** politically radical or left-wing ▷ *n, pl* **-shies 3** any political radical [from BOLSHEVIK]
bolster *vb* **1** to support or strengthen: *the government were unwilling to bolster sterling* ▷ *n* **2** a long narrow pillow **3** any pad or support [Old English]
bolt[1] *n* **1** a bar that can be slid into a socket to lock a door, gate, etc. **2** a metal rod or pin that has a head and a screw thread to take a nut **3** a flash (of lightning) **4** a sudden movement, esp. in order to escape **5** an arrow, esp. for a crossbow **6 a bolt from the blue** a sudden, unexpected, and usually unwelcome event **7 shoot one's bolt** to exhaust one's efforts ▷ *vb* **8** to run away

suddenly **9** to secure or lock with or as if with a bolt **10** to attach firmly (one thing to another) by means of a nut and bolt **11** to eat hurriedly: *bolting your food may lead to indigestion* **12** (of a horse) to run away without control **13** (of vegetables) to produce flowers and seeds too soon ▹ *adv* **14 bolt upright** stiff and rigid [Old English: arrow]

b

bolt² *or* **boult** *vb* **1** to pass (flour, a powder, etc.) through a sieve **2** to examine and separate [Old French *bulter*]

bolt hole *n* a place of escape

bomb *n* **1** a hollow projectile containing explosive, incendiary, or other destructive substance **2** an object in which an explosive device has been planted: *a car bomb* **3** *chiefly Brit slang* a large sum of money: *it cost a bomb* **4** *slang* a disastrous failure: *the new play was a total bomb* **5 like a bomb** *informal* with great speed or success **6 the bomb** a hydrogen or an atom bomb considered as the ultimate destructive weapon ▹ *vb* **7** to attack with a bomb or bombs; drop bombs (on) **8** (foll. by *along*) *informal* to move or drive very quickly **9** *slang* to fail disastrously ▹ See also **bomb out** [Greek *bombos* booming noise] **bombing** *n*

bombard *vb* **1** to attack with concentrated artillery fire or bombs **2** to attack persistently **3** to attack verbally, esp. with questions **4** *physics* to direct high-energy particles or photons against (atoms, nuclei, etc.) [Old French *bombarde* stone-throwing cannon] **bombardment** *n*

bombardier *n* **1** *Brit* a noncommissioned rank in the Royal Artillery **2** *US* the member of a bomber aircrew responsible for releasing the bombs

Bombardier *n Canad trademark* a snow tractor, usually having caterpillar tracks at the rear and skis at the front

bombast *n* pompous and flowery language [Medieval Latin *bombax* cotton] **bombastic** *adj*

Bombay duck *n* a fish that is eaten dried with curry dishes as a savoury [through association with *Bombay* (now Mumbai), port in India]

bombazine *n* a twill fabric, usually of silk and worsted, formerly worn dyed black for mourning [Latin *bombyx* silk]

bomber *n* **1** a military aircraft designed to carry out bombing missions **2** a person who plants bombs

bomb out *vb informal* to fail disastrously

bombshell *n* a shocking or unwelcome surprise

bona fide (bone-a **fide**-ee) *adj* **1** genuine: *a bona fide manuscript* **2** undertaken in good faith: *a bona fide agreement* [Latin]

bonanza *n* **1** sudden and unexpected luck or wealth **2** *US & Canad* a mine or vein rich in ore [Spanish: calm sea, hence, good luck]

bonbon *n* a sweet [French]

bond *n* **1** something that binds, fastens, or holds together **2** something that brings or holds people together; tie: *a bond of friendship* **3 bonds** something that restrains or imprisons **4** a written or spoken agreement, esp. a promise: *a marriage bond* **5** *chem* a means by which atoms are combined in a molecule **6** *finance* a certificate of debt issued in order to raise funds **7** *S African* the conditional pledging of property, esp. a house, as security for the repayment of a loan **8** *law* a written acknowledgment of an obligation to pay a sum or to perform a contract **9 in bond** *commerce* securely stored until duty is paid ▹ *vb* **10** to hold or be held together; bind **11** to form a friendship **12** to put or hold (goods) in bond [Old Norse *band*]

bondage *n* **1** a sexual practice in which one partner is tied or chained up **2** slavery **3** subjection to some influence or duty

bonded *adj* **1** *finance* consisting of, secured by, or operating under a bond or bonds **2** *commerce* in bond

bond paper *n* superior quality writing paper

bone *n* **1** any of the various structures that make up the skeleton in most vertebrates **2** the porous rigid tissue of which these parts are made **3** something consisting of bone or a bonelike substance **4 bones** the human skeleton **5** a thin strip of plastic, etc. used to stiffen corsets and brassieres **6 close to** *or* **near the bone** risqué or indecent **7 have a bone to pick** to have grounds for a quarrel **8 make no bones about A** to be direct and candid about **B** to have no scruples about **9 the bare bones** the essentials ▹ *vb* **boning, boned 10** to remove the bones from (meat for cooking, etc.) **11** to stiffen (a corset, etc.) by inserting bones ▹ See also **bone up on** [Old English *bān*] **boneless** *adj*

bone china *n* a type of fine porcelain containing powdered bone

bone-dry *adj informal* completely dry

bone-idle *adj* extremely lazy

bone meal *n* dried and ground animal bones, used as a fertilizer or in stock feeds

boneshaker *n slang* a decrepit or rickety vehicle

bone up on *vb informal* to study intensively

bonfire *n* a large outdoor fire [Middle English *bone-fire*, from the use of bones as fuel]

bongo *n, pl* **-gos** *or* **-goes** a small bucket-shaped drum, usually one of a pair, played by beating with the fingers [American Spanish]

bonhomie (bon-om-**mee**) *n* exuberant friendliness [French]

bonito (ba-**nee**-toh) *n, pl* **-os 1** a small tunny-like marine food fish **2** a related fish, whose flesh is dried and flaked and used in Japanese cookery

bonk *vb informal* **1** to have sexual intercourse **2** to hit [probably imitative] **bonking** *n*

bonkers *adj Brit, Austral & NZ slang* mad; crazy [origin unknown]

bon mot (bon **moh**) *n, pl* **bons mots** a clever and fitting remark [French, literally: good word]

bonnet *n* **1** *Brit* the hinged metal cover over a motor vehicle's engine **2** any of various hats tied with ribbons under the chin **3** (in Scotland) a soft cloth cap [Old French *bonet*]

bonny *adj* **-nier, -niest 1** *Scot & N English dialect* beautiful: *a bonny lass* **2** good or fine [Latin *bonus*]

bonsai *n, pl* **-sai** an ornamental tree or shrub grown in a small shallow pot in order to stunt its growth [Japanese *bon* bowl + *sai* to plant]

bonsela (bon-**sell**-a) *n S African informal* a small gift of money [Zulu *ibanselo* gift]

bonus *n* something given, paid, or received above what is due or expected [Latin: good]

bon voyage *interj* a phrase used to wish a traveller a pleasant journey [French]

bony *adj* **bonier, boniest 1** resembling or consisting of bone **2** thin **3** having many bones

boo *interj* **1** a shout uttered to express dissatisfaction or contempt **2** an exclamation uttered to startle someone ▹ *vb* **booing, booed 3** to shout 'boo' at (someone or something) as an expression of disapproval

boob *slang* ▹ *n* **1** *Brit, Austral & NZ* an embarrassing mistake; blunder **2** a female breast **3** *Austral* a prison ▹ *vb* **4** *Brit, Austral & NZ* to make a blunder [from *booby*]

boobook (boo-book) *n* a small spotted Australian brown owl

booby *n, pl* **-bies 1** *old-fashioned* an ignorant or foolish person **2** a tropical marine bird related to the gannet [Latin *balbus* stammering]

booby prize *n* a mock prize given to the person with the lowest score in a competition

booby trap *n* **1** a hidden explosive device primed so as to be set off by an unsuspecting victim **2** a trap for an unsuspecting person, esp. one intended as a practical joke

boodle *n slang* money or valuables, esp. when stolen, counterfeit, or used as a bribe [Dutch *boedel* possessions]

boogie *vb* **-gieing, -gied** *slang* to dance to fast pop music [origin unknown]

boogie board *n* another name for **bodyboard**

boogie-woogie *n* a style of piano jazz using blues harmonies [perhaps imitative]

boohai *n NZ informal* **1** a very remote area **2 up the boohai** very mistaken or astray [from the remote township of *Puhoi*]

boohoo *vb* **-hooing, -hooed 1** to sob or pretend to sob noisily ▹ *n, pl* **-hoos 2** distressed or pretended sobbing

book *n* **1** a number of printed pages bound together along one edge and protected by covers **2** a written work or composition, such as a novel **3** a number of sheets of paper bound together: *an account book* **4 books** a record of the transactions of a business or society **5** the libretto of an opera or musical **6** a major division of a written composition, such as of a long novel or of the Bible **7** a number of tickets, stamps, etc. fastened together along one edge **8** a record of betting transactions **9 a closed book** a subject that is beyond comprehension: *art remains a closed book to him* **10 bring to book** to reprimand or require (someone) to give an explanation of his or her conduct **11 by the book** according to the rules **12 in someone's good** *or* **bad books** regarded by someone with favour or disfavour **13 throw the book at someone A** to charge someone with every relevant offence **B** to inflict the most severe punishment on someone ▹ *vb* **14** to reserve (a place, passage, etc.) or engage the services of (someone) in advance **15** (of a police officer) to take the name and address of (a person) for an alleged offence with a view to prosecution **16** (of a football referee) to take the name of (a player) who has broken the rules seriously ▹ See also **book in** [Old English *bōc*]

bookcase *n* a piece of furniture containing shelves for books

book club *n* a club that sells books at low prices to members, usually by mail order

book end *n* one of a pair of supports for holding a row of books upright

bookie *n informal* short for **bookmaker**

book in *vb chiefly Brit & NZ* to register one's arrival at a hotel

booking *n* **1** *Brit, Austral & NZ* a reservation, as of a table or seat **2** *theatre* an engagement of a performer

bookish *adj* **1** fond of reading; studious **2** forming opinions through reading rather than experience

book-keeping *n* the skill or occupation of systematically recording business transactions **book-keeper** *n*

booklet *n* a thin book with paper covers

bookmaker *n* a person who as an occupation accepts bets, esp. on horse racing **bookmaking** *n*

bookmark *n* **1** a strip of some material put between the pages of a book to mark a place **2** an identifier put on a website that enables the user to return to it quickly and easily ▹ *vb* **3** to identify and store (a website) so that one can return to it quickly and easily

bookstall *n* a stall or stand where periodicals, newspapers, or books are sold

bookworm *n* **1** a person devoted to reading **2** a small insect that feeds on the binding paste of books

Boolean algebra (boo-lee-an) *n* a system of symbolic logic devised to codify nonmathematical logical operations: used in computers [after George *Boole*, mathematician]

boom¹ *vb* **1** to make a loud deep echoing sound **2** to prosper vigorously and rapidly: *business boomed* ▹ *n* **3** a loud deep echoing sound **4** a period of high economic growth [imitative]

boom² *n* **1** *naut* a spar to which the foot of a sail is fastened to control its position **2** a pole carrying an overhead microphone and projected over a film or television set **3** a barrier across a waterway [Dutch: tree]

boomer *n Austral* a large male kangaroo

boomerang *n* **1** a curved wooden missile of Aboriginal Australians which can be made to return to the thrower **2** an action or statement that recoils on its originator ▹ *vb* **3** (of a plan) to recoil unexpectedly, harming its originator [Aboriginal]

boomslang *n* a large greenish venomous tree-living snake of southern Africa [Afrikaans]

boon¹ *n* something extremely useful, helpful, or beneficial [Old Norse *bōn* request]

boon² *adj* close or intimate: *boon companion* [Latin *bonus* good]

boongary (**boong**-gar-ree) *n* a tree kangaroo of NE Queensland, Australia

boor *n* an ill-mannered, clumsy, or insensitive person [Old English *gebūr* dweller, farmer] **boorish** *adj*

boost *n* **1** encouragement or help: *a boost to morale* **2** an upward thrust or push **3** an increase or rise ▹ *vb* **4** to encourage or improve: *to boost morale*

b

5 to cause to rise; increase: *we significantly boosted our market share* **6** to advertise on a big scale [origin unknown]

booster *n* **1** a supplementary injection of a vaccine given to ensure that the first injection will remain effective **2** a radio-frequency amplifier to strengthen signals **3** the first stage of a multistage rocket

boot[1] *n* **1** an outer covering for the foot that extends above the ankle **2** *Brit* an enclosed compartment of a car for holding luggage **3** *informal* a kick: *he gave the door a boot* **4 lick someone's boots** to behave flatteringly towards someone **5 put the boot in** *slang* **A** to kick a person when already down **B** to finish something off with unnecessary brutality **6 the boot** *slang* dismissal from employment ▷ *vb* **7** to kick **8** to start up (a computer) **9 boot out** *informal* **A** to eject forcibly **B** to dismiss from employment [Middle English *bote*]

boot[2] *n* **to boot** as well; in addition [Old English *bōt* compensation]

boot camp *n* a centre for juvenile offenders, with strict discipline and hard physical exercise

bootee *n* a soft boot for a baby, esp. a knitted one

booth *n, pl* **booths 1** a small partially enclosed cubicle **2** a stall, esp. a temporary one at a fair or market [Scandinavian]

bootleg *vb* **-legging, -legged 1** to make, carry, or sell (illicit goods, esp. alcohol) ▷ *adj* **2** produced, distributed, or sold illicitly ▷ *n* **3** something that is produced, distributed, or sold illicitly [smugglers carried bottles of liquor concealed in their boots] **bootlegger** *n*

bootless *adj* of little or no use; vain; fruitless [Old English *bōtlēas*]

bootlicker *n informal* a person who seeks favour by grovelling to someone in authority

booty[1] *n, pl* **-ties** any valuable article or articles obtained as plunder [Old French *butin*]

booty[2] *n, pl* **-ties** *slang* the buttocks [from *butt* the buttocks]

booze *informal* ▷ *n* **1** alcoholic drink ▷ *vb* **boozing, boozed 2** to drink alcohol, esp. in excess [Middle Dutch *būsen*] **boozy** *adj*

booze bus *n Austral & NZ informal* a mobile police unit used to conduct drug and alcohol tests on drivers

boozer *n informal* **1** a person who is fond of drinking **2** *Brit, Austral & NZ* a bar or pub

booze-up *n Brit, Austral & NZ slang* a drinking spree

bop *n* **1** a form of jazz with complex rhythms and harmonies ▷ *vb* **bopping, bopped 2** *informal* to dance to pop music [from BEBOP] **bopper** *n*

bora *n Austral* an Aboriginal ceremony [from a native Australian language]

boracic *adj* same as **boric**

borage *n* a Mediterranean plant with star-shaped blue flowers [Arabic *abū 'āraq* literally: father of sweat]

borax *n* a white mineral in crystalline form used in making glass, soap, etc. [Persian *būrah*]

Bordeaux *n* a red or white wine produced around Bordeaux in SW France

border *n* **1** the dividing line between political or geographic regions **2** a band or margin around or along the edge of something **3** a design around the edge of something **4** a narrow strip of ground planted with flowers or shrubs: *a herbaceous border* ▷ *vb* **5** to provide with a border **6 A** to be adjacent to; lie along the boundary of **B** to be nearly the same as; verge on: *a story that borders on the unbelievable* [Old French *bort* side of a ship]

borderland *n* **1** land located on or near a boundary **2** an indeterminate state or condition

borderline *n* **1** a dividing line **2** an indeterminate position between two conditions: *the borderline between love and friendship* ▷ *adj* **3** on the edge of one category and verging on another: *a borderline failure*

Borders *pl n* **the Borders** the area straddling the border between England and Scotland

bore[1] *vb* **boring, bored 1** to produce (a hole) with a drill, etc. **2** to produce (a tunnel, mine shaft, etc.) by drilling ▷ *n* **3** a hole or tunnel in the ground drilled in search of minerals, oil, etc. **4 A** the hollow of a gun barrel **B** the diameter of this hollow; calibre [Old English *borian*]

bore[2] *vb* **boring, bored 1** to tire or make weary by being dull, repetitious, or uninteresting ▷ *n* **2** a dull or repetitious person, activity, or state [origin unknown] **bored** *adj* **boring** *adj*

bore[3] *n* a high wave moving up a narrow estuary, caused by the tide [Old Norse *bāra*]

bore[4] *vb* the past tense of **bear**[1]

boreal forest (bore-ee-al) *n* the forest of northern latitudes, esp. in Scandinavia, Canada, and Siberia, consisting mainly of spruce and pine [Latin *boreas* the north wind]

boredom *n* the state of being bored

boree (baw-ree) *n Austral* same as **myall**

boric *adj* of or containing boron

boric acid *n* a white soluble crystalline solid used as a mild antiseptic

born *vb* **1** a past participle of **bear**[1] **2 not have been born yesterday** not to be gullible or foolish ▷ *adj* **3** possessing certain qualities from birth: *a born musician* **4** being in a particular social status at birth: *ignobly born*

> **USAGE** Care should be taken not to use *born* where *borne* is intended: *he had borne* (not *born*) *his ordeal with great courage: the following points should be borne in mind.*

born-again *adj* **1** having experienced conversion, esp. to evangelical Christianity **2** showing the enthusiasm of someone newly converted to any cause: *a born-again romantic* ▷ *n* **3** a person with fervent enthusiasm for a newfound cause

borne *vb* a past participle of **bear**[1]

> **USAGE** See at **born**.

boron *n chem* a hard almost colourless crystalline metalloid element that is used in hardening steel. Symbol: **B** [*bor(ax)* + *(carb)on*]

boronia *n* an Australian aromatic flowering shrub

borough *n* **1** a town, esp. (in Britain) one that forms the constituency of an MP or that was originally incorporated by royal charter **2** any of the constituent divisions of Greater London or New York City [Old English *burg*]

borrow *vb* **1** to obtain (something, such as money) on the understanding that it will be returned to the lender **2** to adopt (ideas, words, etc.) from another source [Old English *borgian*] **borrower** *n* **borrowing** *n*

USAGE The use of *off* after *borrow* was formerly considered incorrect, but is now acceptable in informal contexts.

borscht *or* **borsch** *n* a Russian soup based on beetroot [Russian *borshch*]

borstal *n* (formerly, in Britain) a prison for offenders aged 15 to 21 [after *Borstal*, village in Kent where the first institution was founded]

borzoi *n* a tall dog with a narrow head and a long coat [Russian: swift]

bosh *n Brit, Austral & NZ informal* meaningless talk or opinions; nonsense [Turkish *boş* empty]

Bosnian *adj* **1** from Bosnia ▷ *n* **2** a person from Bosnia

bosom *n* **1** the chest or breast of a person, esp. the female breasts **2** a protective centre or part: *the bosom of the family* **3** the breast considered as the seat of emotions ▷ *adj* **4** very dear: *a bosom friend* [Old English *bōsm*]

boss[1] *informal* ▷ *n* **1** a person in charge of or employing others ▷ *vb* **2** to employ, supervise, or be in charge of **3** **boss around** *or* **about** to be domineering or overbearing towards [Dutch *baas* master]

boss[2] *n* a raised knob or stud, esp. an ornamental one on a vault, shield, etc. [Old French *boce*]

bossa nova *n* **1** a dance similar to the samba, originating in Brazil **2** music for this dance [Portuguese]

bossy *adj* **bossier, bossiest** *informal* domineering, overbearing, or authoritarian **bossiness** *n*

bosun *or* **boatswain** (**boh**-sn) *n* an officer who is responsible for the maintenance of a ship and its equipment

bot *n* a computer program that carries out tasks for other programs or users [short for *robot*]

bot. **1** botanical **2** botany

botany *n, pl* **-nies** the study of plants, including their classification, structure, etc. [Greek *botanē* plant] **botanical** *or* **botanic** *adj* **botanist** *n*

botch *vb* **1** to spoil through clumsiness or ineptitude **2** to repair badly or clumsily ▷ *n also* **botch-up** **3** a badly done piece of work or repair [origin unknown]

both *adj* **1** two considered together: *both parents were killed during the war* ▷ *pron* **2** two considered together: *both are to blame* ▷ *conj* **3** not just one but also the other of two (people or things): *both she and her sister enjoyed the show* [Old Norse *bāthir*]

bother *vb* **1** to take the time or trouble: *don't bother to come with me* **2** to give annoyance, pain, or trouble to **3** to trouble (a person) by repeatedly disturbing; pester ▷ *n* **4** a state of worry, trouble, or confusion **5** a person or thing that causes fuss, trouble, or annoyance **6** *informal* a disturbance or fight: *a spot of bother* ▷ *interj* **7** *Brit, Austral & NZ* an exclamation of slight annoyance [origin unknown]

bothersome *adj* causing bother

bothy *n, pl* **bothies** *chiefly Scot* **1** a hut used for temporary shelter **2** (formerly) a farm worker's quarters [perhaps from *booth*]

Botox *n trademark* **1** a preparation of botulinum toxin used to treat muscle spasm and to remove wrinkles ▷ *vb* **2** to apply Botox to (a person or a part of the body) [from BOT(ULINUM) (T)OX(IN)]

bottle *n* **1** a container, often of glass and usually cylindrical with a narrow neck, for holding liquids **2** the amount such a container will hold **3** *Brit slang* courage; nerve: *you don't have the bottle* **4** **the bottle** *informal* drinking of alcohol, esp. to excess ▷ *vb* **-tling, -tled** **5** to put or place in a bottle or bottles ▷ See also **bottle up** [Late Latin *buttis* cask]

bottle bank *n* a large container into which members of the public can throw glass bottles and jars for recycling

bottle-feed *vb* **-feeding, -fed** to feed (a baby) with milk from a bottle

bottle-green *adj* dark green

bottleneck *n* **1** a narrow stretch of road or a junction at which traffic is or may be held up **2** something that holds up progress

bottlenose dolphin *n* a grey or greenish dolphin with a bottle-shaped snout

bottle party *n* a party to which guests bring drink

bottler *n Austral & NZ old-fashioned, informal* an exceptional person or thing

bottle shop *n Austral & NZ* a shop licensed to sell alcohol for drinking elsewhere

bottle store *n S African* a shop licensed to sell alcohol for drinking elsewhere

bottle tree *n* an Australian tree with a bottle-shaped swollen trunk

bottle up *vb* to restrain (powerful emotion)

bottom *n* **1** the lowest, deepest, or farthest removed part of a thing: *the bottom of a hill* **2** the least important or successful position: *the bottom of a class* **3** the ground underneath a sea, lake, or river **4** the underneath part of a thing **5** the buttocks **6** **at bottom** in reality; basically **7** **be at the bottom of** to be the ultimate cause of **8** **get to the bottom of** to discover the real truth about ▷ *adj* **9** lowest or last [Old English *botm*]

bottomless *adj* **1** unlimited; inexhaustible: *bottomless resources* **2** very deep: *bottomless valleys*

bottom line *n* **1** the conclusion or main point of a process, discussion, etc. **2** the last line of a financial statement that shows the net profit or loss of a company or organization

bottom out *vb* to reach the lowest point and level out: *consumer spending has bottomed out*

botulism *n* severe food poisoning resulting from the toxin **botulin**, produced in imperfectly preserved food [Latin *botulus* sausage]

bouclé *n* a curled or looped yarn or fabric giving a thick knobbly effect [French: curly]

boudoir (**boo**-dwahr) *n* a woman's bedroom or private sitting room [French, literally: room for sulking in]

bouffant (**boof**-fong) *adj* (of a hairstyle) having extra height and width through backcombing [French *bouffer* to puff up]

bougainvillea *n* a tropical climbing plant with flowers surrounded by showy red or purple bracts [after L. A. de *Bougainville*, navigator]

b

bough *n* any of the main branches of a tree [Old English *bōg* arm, twig]
bought *vb* the past of **buy**
bouillon (**boo**-yon) *n* a thin clear broth or stock [French *bouillir* to boil]
boulder *n* a smooth rounded mass of rock shaped by erosion [Scandinavian]
boulder clay *n* an unstratified glacial deposit of fine clay, boulders, and pebbles
boules (**bool**) *n* a game, popular in France, in which metal bowls are thrown to land as close as possible to a target ball [French: balls]
boulevard *n* a wide usually tree-lined road in a city [Middle Dutch *bolwerc* bulwark; because originally often built on the ruins of an old rampart]
boult *vb* same as **bolt²**
bounce *vb* **bouncing, bounced 1** (of a ball, etc.) to rebound from an impact **2** to cause (a ball, etc.) to hit a solid surface and spring back **3** to move or cause to move suddenly; spring: *I bounced down the stairs* **4** *slang* (of a bank) to send (a cheque) back or (of a cheque) to be sent back unredeemed because of lack of funds in the account ▷ *n* **5** the action of rebounding from an impact **6** a leap or jump **7** springiness **8** *informal* vitality; vigour **9** *informal* a temporary increase or rise: *a sales bounce* [probably imitative] **bouncy** *adj*
bounce back *vb* to recover one's health, good spirits, confidence, etc., easily
bouncer *n* **1** *slang* a person employed at a nightclub, etc. to prevent unwanted people from entering and to eject drunks or troublemakers **2** *cricket* a ball bowled so that it bounces high on pitching
bouncing *adj* vigorous and robust: *a bouncing baby*
bouncy castle *n* a very large inflatable model, usually of a castle, on which children may bounce at fairs, etc.
bound¹ *vb* **1** the past of **bind** ▷ *adj* **2** tied as if with a rope **3** restricted or confined: *housebound* **4** certain: *it's bound to happen* **5** compelled or obliged: *they agreed to be bound by the board's recommendations* **6** (of a book) secured within a cover or binding **7 bound up with** closely or inextricably linked with
bound² *vb* **1** to move forwards by leaps or jumps **2** to bounce; spring away from an impact ▷ *n* **3** a jump upwards or forwards **4** a bounce, as of a ball [Old French *bondir*]
bound³ *vb* **1** to place restrictions on; limit: *bounded by tradition* **2** to form a boundary of ▷ *n* **3** See **bounds** [Old French *bonde*] **boundless** *adj*
bound⁴ *adj* going or intending to go towards: *homeward bound* [Old Norse *buinn*, past participle of *būa* prepare]
boundary *n, pl* **-ries 1** something that indicates the farthest limit, such as of an area **2** *cricket* **A** the marked limit of the playing area **B** a stroke that hits the ball beyond this limit, scoring four or six runs
bounden *adj old-fashioned* morally obligatory: *bounden duty*
bounder *n old-fashioned Brit slang* a morally reprehensible person; cad
bounds *pl n* **1** a limit; boundary: *their jealousy knows no bounds* **2** something that restricts or controls, esp. the standards of a society: *within the bounds of good taste*
bountiful *or* **bounteous** *adj literary* **1** plentiful; ample: *a bountiful harvest* **2** giving freely; generous
bounty *n, pl* **-ties 1** *literary* generosity; liberality **2** something provided in generous amounts: *nature's bounty* **3** a reward or premium by a government [Latin *bonus* good]
bouquet *n* **1** a bunch of flowers, esp. a large carefully arranged one **2** the aroma of wine [French: thicket]
bouquet garni *n, pl* **bouquets garnis** a bunch of herbs tied together and used for flavouring soups, stews, or stocks [French]
bourbon (**bur**-bn) *n* a whiskey distilled, chiefly in the US, from maize [after *Bourbon* county, Kentucky, where it was first made]
bourgeois (**boor**-zhwah) *often derogatory* ▷ *adj* **1** characteristic of or comprising the middle class **2** conservative or materialistic in outlook **3** (in Marxist thought) dominated by capitalism ▷ *n, pl* **-geois 4** a member of the middle class, esp. one regarded as being conservative and materialistic [Old French *borjois* citizen]
bourgeoisie (boor-zhwah-**zee**) *n* **the bourgeoisie 1** the middle classes **2** (in Marxist thought) the capitalist ruling class
bourn *n chiefly S Eng* a stream [Old French *bodne* limit]
bourrée (**boor**-ray) *n* **1** a traditional French dance in fast duple time **2** music for this dance [French]
Bourse (**boorss**) *n* a stock exchange, esp. of Paris [French: purse]
bout *n* **1 A** a period of time spent doing something, such as drinking alcohol **B** a period of illness: *a bad bout of flu* **2** a boxing, wrestling, or fencing match [obsolete *bought* turn]
boutique *n* a small shop, esp. one that sells fashionable clothes [French]
boutique hotel *n* a small, high-quality, fashionable hotel
bouzouki *n* a Greek long-necked stringed musical instrument related to the mandolin [Modern Greek]
bovine *adj* **1** of or relating to cattle **2** dull, sluggish, or ugly [Latin *bos* ox]
bow¹ (rhymes with **cow**) *vb* **1** to lower (one's head) or bend (one's knee or body) as a sign of respect, greeting, agreement, or shame **2** to comply or accept: *bow to the inevitable* **3 bow and scrape** to behave in a slavish manner ▷ *n* **4** a lowering or bending of the head or body as a mark of respect, etc. **5 take a bow** to acknowledge applause ▷ See also **bow out** [Old English *būgan*]
bow² (rhymes with **know**) *n* **1** a decorative knot usually having two loops and two loose ends **2** a long stick across which are stretched strands of horsehair, used for playing a violin, viola, cello, etc. **3** a weapon for shooting arrows, consisting of an arch of flexible wood, plastic, etc. bent by a string fastened at each end **4** something that is curved, bent, or arched

▹ *vb* **5** to form or cause to form a curve or curves [Old English *boga* arch, bow]

bow³ (rhymes with **cow**) *n* **1** *chiefly naut* the front end or part of a vessel **2** *rowing* the oarsman at the bow [probably Low German *boog*]

bowdlerize *or* **-ise** *vb* **-izing, -ized** *or* **-ising, -ised** to remove passages or words regarded as indecent from (a play, novel, etc.) [after Thomas *Bowdler*, editor who expurgated Shakespeare] **bowdlerization** *or* **-isation** *n*

bowel *n* **1** an intestine, esp. the large intestine in humans **2 bowels** entrails **3 bowels** the innermost part: *the bowels of the earth* [Latin *botellus* a little sausage]

bower *n* a shady leafy shelter in a wood or garden [Old English *būr* dwelling]

bowerbird *n* a brightly coloured songbird of Australia and New Guinea

bowie knife *n* a stout hunting knife [after Jim *Bowie*, Texan adventurer]

bowl¹ *n* **1** a round container open at the top, used for holding liquid or serving food **2** the amount a bowl will hold **3** the hollow part of an object, esp. of a spoon or tobacco pipe [Old English *bolla*]

bowl² *n* **1** **A** a wooden ball used in the game of bowls **B** a large heavy ball with holes for gripping used in the game of bowling ▹ *vb* **2** to roll smoothly or cause to roll smoothly along the ground **3** *cricket* **A** to send (a ball) from one's hand towards the batsman **B** Also: **bowl out** to dismiss (a batsman) by delivering a ball that breaks his wicket **4** to play bowls **5 bowl along** to move easily and rapidly, as in a car ▹ See also **bowl over, bowls** [French *boule*]

bow-legged *adj* having legs that curve outwards at the knees

bowler¹ *n* **1** a person who bowls in cricket **2** a player at the game of bowls

bowler² *n* a stiff felt hat with a rounded crown and narrow curved brim [after John *Bowler*, hatter]

bowline *n naut* **1** a line used to keep the sail taut against the wind **2** a knot used for securing a loop that will not slip at the end of a piece of rope [probably from Middle Low German *bōlīne*]

bowling *n* **1** a game in which a heavy ball is rolled down a long narrow alley at a group of wooden pins **2** *cricket* the act of delivering the ball to the batsman

bowl over *vb* **1** *informal* to surprise (a person) greatly, in a pleasant way **2** to knock down

bowls *n* a game played on a very smooth area of grass in which opponents roll biased wooden bowls as near a small bowl (the jack) as possible

bow out *vb* to retire or withdraw gracefully

bowsprit *n naut* a spar projecting from the bow of a sailing ship [Middle Low German *bōch* BOW³ + *sprēt* pole]

bowstring *n* the string of an archer's bow

bow tie *n* a man's tie in the form of a bow

bow window *n* a curved bay window

bow-wow *n* **1** a child's word for **dog** **2** an imitation of the bark of a dog

box¹ *n* **1** a container with a firm base and sides and sometimes a removable or hinged lid **2** the contents of such a container **3** a separate compartment for a small group of people, as in a theatre **4** a compartment for a horse in a stable or a vehicle **5** a section of printed matter on a page, enclosed by lines or a border **6** a central agency to which mail is addressed and from which it is collected or redistributed: *a post-office box* **7** same as **penalty box** **8 the box** *Brit informal* television ▹ *vb* **9** to put into a box ▹ See also **box in** [Greek *puxos* BOX³] **boxlike** *adj*

box² *vb* **1** to fight (an opponent) in a boxing match **2** to engage in boxing **3** to hit (esp. a person's ears) with the fist ▹ *n* **4** a punch with the fist, esp. on the ear [origin unknown]

box³ *n* a slow-growing evergreen tree or shrub with small shiny leaves [Greek *puxos*]

boxer *n* **1** a person who boxes **2** a medium-sized dog with smooth hair and a short nose

boxer shorts *or* **boxers** *pl n* men's underpants shaped like shorts but with a front opening

box girder *n* a girder that is hollow and square or rectangular in shape

box in *vb* to prevent from moving freely; confine

boxing *n* the act, art, or profession of fighting with the fists

Boxing Day *n* the first day after Christmas (in Britain, traditionally and strictly, the first weekday), observed as a holiday [from the former custom of giving Christmas boxes to tradesmen on this day]

box jellyfish *n* a highly venomous jellyfish with a cuboid body that lives in Australian tropical waters

box junction *n* (in Britain) a road junction marked with yellow crisscross lines which vehicles may only enter when their exit is clear

box lacrosse *n Canad* lacrosse played indoors

box number *n* a number used as an address for mail, esp. one used by a newspaper for replies to an advertisement

box office *n* **1** an office at a theatre, cinema, etc. where tickets are sold **2** the public appeal of an actor or production ▹ *adj* **box-office** **3** relating to the sales at the box office: *a box-office success*

box pleat *n* a flat double pleat made by folding under the fabric on either side of it

boxroom *n* a small room in which boxes, cases, etc. may be stored

box set *n* **1** a collection of items of the same type, packaged together for sale in a presentation box **2** a set of episodes of a television series made available to watch or listen to at the same time

box spring *n* a coiled spring contained in a boxlike frame, used for mattresses, chairs, etc.

boxwood *n* the hard yellow wood of the box tree, used to make tool handles, etc. See **box³**

boy *n* **1** a male child **2** a man regarded as immature or inexperienced **3** *S African offensive* a Black male servant [origin unknown] **boyhood** *n* **boyish** *adj*

boycott *vb* **1** to refuse to deal with (an organization or country) as a protest against its actions or policy ▹ *n* **2** an instance or the use of boycotting [after Captain *Boycott*, Irish land agent, a victim of such practices for refusing to reduce rents]

boyfriend *n* a male friend with whom a person is romantically or sexually involved
Boyle's law *n* the principle that the pressure of a gas varies inversely with its volume at constant temperature [after Robert *Boyle*, scientist]
Boy Scout *n* another name for **Scout**
BP 1 blood pressure **2** British Pharmacopoeia
bpi bits per inch (used of a computer tape or disk surface)
Bq *physics* becquerel
Br *chem* bromine
Br. 1 Breton **2** Britain **3** British
bra *n* a woman's undergarment for covering and supporting the breasts [from *brassiere*]
braaivleis (brye-flayss) *S African* ▷ *n* **1** a grill on which food is cooked over hot charcoal, usually outdoors **2** an outdoor party at which food like this is served ▷ *vb* **3** to cook (food) in this way. Also: **braai** [Afrikaans]
brace *n* **1** something that steadies, binds, or holds up another thing **2** a beam or prop, used to stiffen a framework **3** a hand tool for drilling holes **4** a pair, esp. of game birds **5** either of a pair of characters, { }, used for connecting lines of printing or writing **6** See **braces** ▷ *vb* **bracing, braced 7** to steady or prepare (oneself) before an impact **8** to provide, strengthen, or fit with a brace [Latin *bracchia* arms]
brace and bit *n* a hand tool for boring holes, consisting of a cranked handle into which a drilling bit is inserted
bracelet *n* an ornamental chain or band worn around the arm or wrist [Latin *bracchium* arm]
bracelets *pl n slang* handcuffs
braces *pl n* **1** *Brit & NZ* a pair of straps worn over the shoulders for holding up the trousers **2** an appliance of metal bands and wires for correcting unevenness of teeth
brachiopod (brake-ee-oh-pod) *n* an invertebrate sea animal with a shell consisting of two valves [Greek *brakhiōn* arm + *pous* foot]
brachium (brake-ee-um) *n, pl* **brachia** (brake-ee-a) *anatomy* the arm, esp. the upper part [Latin *bracchium* arm]
bracing *adj* refreshing: *the bracing climate*
bracken *n* **1** a fern with large fronds **2** a clump of these ferns [Scandinavian]
bracket *n* **1** a pair of characters, [ ], ( ), or { }, used to enclose a section of writing or printing **2** a group or category falling within certain defined limits: *the lower income bracket* **3** an L-shaped or other support fixed to a wall to hold a shelf, etc. ▷ *vb* **-eting, -eted 4** to put (written or printed matter) in brackets **5** to group or class together [Latin *braca* breeches]
brackish *adj* (of water) slightly salty [Middle Dutch *brac*]
bract *n* a leaf, usually small and scaly, growing at the base of a flower [Latin *bractea* thin metal plate]
brad *n* a small tapered nail with a small head [Old English *brord* point]
brae *n Scot* a hill or slope [Middle English *bra*]
brag *vb* **bragging, bragged 1** to speak arrogantly and boastfully ▷ *n* **2** boastful talk or behaviour **3** a card game similar to poker [origin unknown]
braggart *n* a person who boasts loudly or exaggeratedly
Brahma *n* **1** a Hindu god, the Creator **2** same as **Brahman** (sense 2)
Brahman *n, pl* **-mans 1** Also: **Brahmin** a member of the highest or priestly caste in the Hindu caste system **2** *Hinduism* the ultimate and impersonal divine reality of the universe [Sanskrit: prayer] **Brahmanic** *adj*
braid *vb* **1** to interweave (hair, thread, etc.) **2** to decorate with an ornamental trim or border ▷ *n* **3** a length of hair that has been braided **4** narrow ornamental tape of woven silk, wool, etc. [Old English *bregdan*] **braiding** *n*
Braille *n* a system of writing for blind people consisting of raised dots interpreted by touch [after Louis *Braille*, its inventor]
brain *n* **1** the soft mass of nervous tissue within the skull of vertebrates that controls and coordinates the nervous system **2** (*often pl*) *informal* intellectual ability: *he's got brains* **3** *informal* an intelligent person **4 on the brain** *informal* constantly in mind: *I had that song on the brain* **5 the brains** *informal* a person who plans and organizes something: *the brains behind the bid* ▷ *vb* **6** *slang* to hit (someone) hard on the head [Old English *brægen*]
brainchild *n informal* an idea or plan produced by creative thought
braindead *adj* **1** having suffered brain death **2** *informal* stupid
brain death *n* complete stoppage of breathing due to irreparable brain damage
brain drain *n informal* the emigration of scientists, technologists, academics, etc.
brainfood *n* any foodstuff containing nutrients thought to promote brain function
brainless *adj* stupid or foolish
brainstorm *n* **1** *informal* a sudden mental aberration **2** a session of intensive discussion to solve problems **3** *informal* same as **brainwave**
brainstorming *n* a thorough discussion to solve problems or create ideas
brains trust *n* a group of knowledgeable people who discuss topics in public or on radio or television
brain-teaser *n informal* a difficult problem
brainwash *vb* to cause (a person) to alter his or her beliefs, by methods based on isolation, sleeplessness, etc. **brainwashing** *n*
brainwave *n informal* a sudden idea or inspiration
brain wave *n* a fluctuation of electrical potential in the brain
brainy *adj* **brainier, brainiest** *informal* clever; intelligent
braise *vb* **braising, braised** to cook (food) slowly in a closed pan with a small amount of liquid [Old French *brese* live coals]
brak[1] (bruck) *n S African* a crossbred dog; mongrel [Dutch]
brak[2] (bruck) *adj S African* (of water) slightly salty; brackish [Afrikaans]
brake[1] *n* **1** a device for slowing or stopping a vehicle **2** something that slows down or stops progress: *he put a brake on my enthusiasm* ▷ *vb* **braking, braked 3** to slow down or cause to

slow down, by or as if by using a brake [Middle Dutch *braeke*]

brake² *n Brit* an area of dense undergrowth; thicket [Old English *bracu*]

brake horsepower *n* the rate at which an engine does work, measured by the resistance of an applied brake

brake light *n* a red light at the rear of a motor vehicle that lights up when the brakes are applied

brake shoe *n* a curved metal casting that acts as a brake on a wheel

bramble *n* **1** a prickly plant or shrub such as the blackberry **2** *Scot, N English & NZ* a blackberry [Old English *brǣmbel*] **brambly** *adj*

bran *n* husks of cereal grain separated from the flour [Old French]

branch *n* **1** a secondary woody stem extending from the trunk or main branch of a tree **2** one of a number of shops, offices, or groups that belongs to a central organization: *she was transferred to their Japanese branch* **3** a subdivision or subsidiary section of something larger or more complex: *branches of learning* ▷ *vb* **4** to divide, then develop in different directions [Late Latin *branca* paw] **branchlike** *adj*

branch off *vb* to diverge from the main way, road, topic, etc.

branch out *vb* to expand or extend one's interests

brand *n* **1** a particular product or a characteristic that identifies a particular producer **2** a trade name or trademark **3** a particular kind or variety **4** an identifying mark made, usually by burning, on the skin of animals as a proof of ownership **5** an iron used for branding animals **6** a mark of disgrace **7** *archaic or poetic* a flaming torch ▷ *vb* **8** to label, burn, or mark with or as if with a brand **9** to label (someone): *he was branded a war criminal* [Old English: fire]

brandish *vb* to wave (a weapon, etc.) in a triumphant or threatening way [Old French *brandir*]

brand-new *adj* absolutely new

brandy *n, pl* **-dies** an alcoholic spirit distilled from wine [Dutch *brandewijn*]

brandy snap *n* a crisp sweet biscuit, rolled into a cylinder

brash *adj* **1** tastelessly or offensively loud, or showy: *brash modernization* **2** impudent or bold: *I thought it was very brash of her to ask me* [origin unknown] **brashness** *n*

brass *n* **1** an alloy of copper and zinc **2** an object, ornament, or utensil made of brass **3** **A** the large family of wind instruments including the trumpet, trombone, etc. made of brass **B** instruments of this family forming a section in an orchestra **4** same as **top brass** **5** *N English dialect* money **6** *Brit* an engraved brass memorial tablet in a church **7** *informal* bold self-confidence; nerve [Old English *bræs*]

brass band *n* a group of musicians playing brass and percussion instruments

brasserie *n* a bar or restaurant serving drinks and cheap meals [French *brasser* to stir]

brass hat *n Brit informal* a top-ranking official, esp. a military officer

brassica *n* any plant of the cabbage and turnip family [Latin: cabbage]

brassiere *n* same as **bra** [French]

brass rubbing *n* an impression of an engraved brass tablet made by rubbing a paper placed over it with heelball or chalk

brass tacks *pl n* **get down to brass tacks** *informal* to discuss the realities of a situation

brassy *adj* **brassier, brassiest** **1** brazen or flashy **2** like brass, esp. in colour **3** (of sound) harsh and strident

brat *n* a child, esp. one who is unruly [origin unknown]

bravado *n* an outward display of self-confidence [Spanish *bravada*]

brave *adj* **1** having or displaying courage, resolution, or daring **2** fine; splendid: *a brave sight* ▷ *n* **3** *old-fashioned* a warrior of a Native American tribe of N America ▷ *vb* **braving, braved** **4** to confront with resolution or courage: *she braved the 21 miles of Lake Tahoe* [Italian *bravo*] **bravery** *n*

bravo *interj* **1** well done! ▷ *n* **2** *pl* **-vos** a cry of 'bravo' **3** *pl* **-voes** *or* **-vos** a hired killer or assassin [Italian]

bravura *n* **1** a display of boldness or daring **2** *music* brilliance of execution [Italian]

brawl *n* **1** a loud disagreement or fight ▷ *vb* **2** to quarrel or fight noisily [probably from Dutch *brallen* to boast]

brawn *n* **1** strong well-developed muscles **2** physical strength **3** *Brit & NZ* a seasoned jellied loaf made from the head of a pig [Old French *braon* meat] **brawny** *adj*

bray *vb* **1** (of a donkey) to utter its characteristic loud harsh sound **2** to utter something with a loud harsh sound ▷ *n* **3** the loud harsh sound uttered by a donkey **4** a similar loud sound [Old French *braire*]

braze *vb* **brazing, brazed** to join (two metal surfaces) by fusing brass between them [Old French: to burn]

brazen *adj* **1** shameless and bold **2** made of or resembling brass **3** having a ringing metallic sound ▷ *vb* **4** **brazen it out** to face and overcome a difficult or embarrassing situation boldly or shamelessly **brazenly** *adv*

brazier¹ (bray-zee-er) *n* a portable metal container for burning charcoal or coal [French *braise* live coals]

brazier² *n* a worker in brass

brazil *n* **1** the red wood of various tropical trees of America **2** same as **brazil nut** [Old Spanish *brasa* glowing coals; referring to the redness of the wood]

Brazilian *adj* **1** of Brazil ▷ *n* **2** a person from Brazil

brazil nut *n* a large three-sided nut of a tropical American tree

breach *n* **1** a breaking of a promise, obligation, etc. **2** any serious disagreement or separation **3** a crack, break, or gap ▷ *vb* **4** to break (a promise, law, etc.) **5** to break through or make an opening or hole in [Old English *bræc*]

USAGE See at **breech**.

breach of promise *n* *law* (formerly) failure to carry out one's promise to marry

b

breach of the peace *n law* an offence against public order causing an unnecessary disturbance of the peace

bread *n* **1** a food made from a dough of flour or meal mixed with water or milk, usually raised with yeast and then baked **2** necessary food **3** *slang* money ▷ *vb* **4** to cover (food) with breadcrumbs before cooking [Old English *brēad*]

bread and butter *n informal* a means of support; livelihood

breadboard *n* **1** a wooden board on which bread is sliced **2** an experimental arrangement of electronic circuits

breadfruit *n, pl* **-fruits** *or* **-fruit** a tree of the Pacific Islands, whose edible round fruit has a texture like bread when baked

breadline *n* **on the breadline** impoverished; living at subsistence level

breadth *n* **1** the extent or measurement of something from side to side **2** openness and lack of restriction, esp. of viewpoint or interest; liberality [Old English *brād* broad]

breadwinner *n* a person supporting a family with his or her earnings

break *vb* **breaking, broke, broken 1** to separate or become separated into two or more pieces **2** to damage or become damaged so as not to work **3** to burst or cut the surface of (skin) **4** to fracture (a bone) in (a limb, etc.) **5** to fail to observe (an agreement, promise, or law): *they broke their promise* **6** to reveal or be revealed: *she broke the news gently* **7** (foll. by *with*) to separate oneself from **8** to discontinue or become discontinued: *to break a journey* **9** to bring or come to an end: *the winter weather broke at last* **10** to weaken or overwhelm or be weakened or overwhelmed, as in spirit: *he felt his life was broken by his illness* **11** to cut through or penetrate: *silence broken by shouts* **12** to improve on or surpass: *she broke three world records* **13** (often foll. by *in*) to accustom (a horse) to the bridle and saddle, to being ridden, etc. **14** (foll. by *of*) to cause (a person) to give up (a habit): *this cure will break you of smoking* **15** to weaken the impact or force of: *this net will break his fall* **16** to decipher: *to break a code* **17** to lose the order of: *to break ranks* **18** to reduce to poverty or the state of bankruptcy **19** to come into being: *light broke over the mountains* **20** (foll. by *into*) **A** to burst into (song, laughter, etc.) **B** to change to (a faster pace) **21** to open with explosives: *to break a safe* **22** **A** (of waves) to strike violently against **B** (of waves) to collapse into foam or surf **23** *snooker* to scatter the balls at the start of a game **24** *boxing & wrestling* (of two fighters) to separate from a clinch **25** (of the male voice) to undergo a change in register, quality, and range at puberty **26** to interrupt the flow of current in (an electrical circuit) **27 break camp** to pack up and leave a camp **28 break even** to make neither a profit nor a loss **29 break the mould** to make a change that breaks an established habit or pattern ▷ *n* **30** the act or result of breaking; fracture **31** a brief rest **32** a sudden rush, esp. to escape: *they made a sudden break for freedom* **33** any sudden interruption in a continuous action **34** *Brit & NZ* a short period between classes at school **35** a (short) holiday **36** *informal* a fortunate opportunity, esp. to prove oneself **37** *informal* a piece of good or bad luck **38** *billiards & snooker* a series of successful shots during one turn **39** *snooker* the opening shot that scatters the placed balls **40** a discontinuity in an electrical circuit **41 break of day** the dawn ▷ See also **breakaway, break down** *etc.* [Old English *brecan*] **breakable** *adj*

breakage *n* **1** the act or result of breaking **2** compensation or allowance for goods damaged while in use, transit, etc.

breakaway *n* **1** loss or withdrawal of a group of members from an association, club, etc. **2** *Austral* a stampede of cattle, esp. at the smell of water ▷ *adj* **3** dissenting: *a breakaway faction* ▷ *vb* **break away 4** to leave hastily or escape **5** to withdraw or quit

break dance *n* **1** an acrobatic dance style associated with hip-hop music, originating in the 1980s ▷ *vb* **break-dance, -dancing, -danced 2** to perform a break dance **break dancing** *n*

break down *vb* **1** to cease to function; become ineffective **2** to give way to strong emotion or tears **3** to crush or destroy **4** to have a nervous breakdown **5** to separate into component parts: *with exercise the body breaks down fat to use as fuel* **6** to separate or cause to separate into simpler chemical elements; decompose **7** to analyse or be subjected to analysis ▷ *n* **breakdown 8** an act or instance of breaking down; collapse **9** same as **nervous breakdown 10** an analysis of something into its parts

breaker *n* **1** a large sea wave with a white crest or one that breaks into foam on the shore **2** a Citizens' Band radio operator

breakfast *n* **1** the first meal of the day ▷ *vb* **2** to eat breakfast [BREAK + FAST²]

break in *vb* **1** to enter a building illegally, esp. by force **2** to interrupt **3** to accustom (a person or animal) to normal duties or practice **4** to use or wear (new shoes or new equipment) until comfortable or running smoothly ▷ *n* **break-in 5** the act of illegally entering a building, esp. by thieves

breaking point *n* the point at which something or someone gives way under strain

breakneck *adj* (of speed or pace) excessively fast and dangerous

break off *vb* **1** to sever or detach **2** to end (a relationship or association) **3** to stop abruptly

break out *vb* **1** to begin or arise suddenly: *fighting broke out between the two factions* **2** to make an escape, esp. from prison **3 break out in** to erupt in (a rash or spots) ▷ *n* **break-out 4** an escape, esp. from prison

break through *vb* **1** to penetrate **2** to achieve success after lengthy efforts ▷ *n* **breakthrough 3** a significant development or discovery

break up *vb* **1** to separate or cause to separate **2** to put an end to (a relationship) or (of a relationship) to come to an end **3** to dissolve or cause to dissolve: *the meeting broke up at noon* **4** *Brit* (of a school) to close for the holidays ▷ *n* **break-up 5** a separation or disintegration

breakwater *n* a massive wall built out into the sea to protect a shore or harbour from the force of waves

bream *n, pl* **bream** **1** a freshwater fish covered with silvery scales **2** a food fish of European seas **3** a food fish of Australasian seas [Old French *bresme*]

breast *n* **1** either of the two soft fleshy milk-secreting glands on a woman's chest **2** the front part of the body from the neck to the abdomen; chest **3** the corresponding part in certain other mammals **4** the source of human emotions **5** the part of a garment that covers the breast **6** **make a clean breast of something** to divulge truths about oneself ▷ *vb literary* **7** to reach the summit of: *breasting the mountain top* **8** to confront boldly; face: *breast the storm* [Old English *brēost*]

breastbone *n* same as **sternum**

breast-feed *vb* **-feeding, -fed** to feed (a baby) with milk from the breast; suckle

breastplate *n* a piece of armour covering the chest

breaststroke *n* a swimming stroke in which the arms are extended in front of the head and swept back on either side

breastwork *n fortifications* a temporary defensive work, usually breast-high

breath *n* **1** the taking in and letting out of air during breathing **2** a single instance of this **3** the air taken in or let out during breathing **4** the vapour, heat, or odour of air breathed out **5** a slight gust of air **6** a short pause or rest **7** a suggestion or slight evidence; suspicion: *trembling at the least breath of scandal* **8** a whisper or soft sound **9** **catch one's breath** **A** to rest until breathing is normal **B** to stop breathing momentarily from excitement, fear, etc. **10** **out of breath** gasping for air after exertion **11** **save one's breath** to avoid useless talk **12** **take someone's breath away** to overwhelm someone with surprise, etc. **13** **under one's breath** in a quiet voice or whisper [Old English *brǣth*]

breathable *adj* **1** (of air) fit to be breathed **2** (of material) allowing air to pass through so that perspiration can evaporate

Breathalyser *or* **-lyzer** *n Brit trademark* a device for estimating the amount of alcohol in the breath [*breath* + *(an)alyser*] **breathalyse** *or* **-lyze** *vb*

breathe *vb* **breathing, breathed** **1** to take in oxygen and give out carbon dioxide; respire **2** to exist; be alive **3** to rest to regain breath or composure **4** (esp. of air) to blow lightly **5** to exhale or emit: *the dragon breathed fire* **6** to impart; instil: *a change that breathed new life into Polish industry* **7** to speak softly; whisper **8** **breathe again** *or* **freely** *or* **easily** to feel relief **9** **breathe one's last** to die

breather *n informal* a short pause for rest

breathing *n* **1** the passage of air into and out of the lungs to supply the body with oxygen **2** the sound this makes

breathing space *n* a short period during which a difficult situation temporarily becomes less severe: *the cut in interest rates creates a breathing space for struggling businesses*

breathless *adj* **1** out of breath; gasping, etc. **2** holding one's breath or having it taken away by excitement, etc. **3** (esp. of the atmosphere) motionless and stifling **breathlessness** *n*

breathtaking *adj* causing awe or excitement

breath test *n* a chemical test of a driver's breath to determine the amount of alcohol consumed

bred *vb* the past of **breed**

bredie (**breed**-ee) *n S African* a meat and vegetable stew [Portuguese *bredo* ragout]

breech *n* **1** the buttocks **2** the part of a firearm behind the barrel [Old English *brēc*, plural of *brōc* leg covering]

> **USAGE** *Breech* is sometimes wrongly used as a verb where *breach* is meant: *the barrier/agreement was breached* (not *breeched*).

breech delivery *n* birth of a baby with the feet or buttocks appearing first

breeches *pl n* trousers extending to the knee or just below, worn for riding, etc.

breeches buoy *n* a pulley device with a life buoy and pair of breeches attached, which is used as a means of transference between ships or rescue from the sea

breed *vb* **breeding, bred** **1** to produce new or improved strains of (domestic animals and plants) **2** to produce or cause to produce by mating **3** to bear (offspring) **4** to bring up; raise: *she was city bred* **5** to produce or be produced: *the agreement bred confidence between the two* ▷ *n* **6** a group of animals, esp. domestic animals, within a species, that have certain clearly defined characteristics **7** a kind, sort, or group: *he was a gentleman, a breed not greatly admired* **8** a lineage or race [Old English *brēdan*] **breeder** *n*

breeder reactor *n* a nuclear reactor that produces more fissionable material than it uses

breeding *n* **1** the process of producing plants or animals by controlled methods of reproduction **2** the process of bearing offspring **3** the result of good upbringing or training

breeze[1] *n* **1** a gentle or light wind **2** *informal* an easy task ▷ *vb* **breezing, breezed** **3** to move quickly or casually: *he breezed into the room* [probably from Old Spanish *briza*]

breeze[2] *n* ashes of coal, coke, or charcoal [French *braise* live coals]

breeze block *n* a light building brick made from the ashes of coal, coke, etc. bonded together by cement

breezy *adj* **breezier, breeziest** **1** fresh; windy **2** casual or carefree

brekky *n, pl* **-ies** *slang* breakfast

Bren gun *n* an air-cooled gas-operated light machine gun [after *Br(no)*, Czech Republic, and *En(field)*, England, where it was made]

brent *or esp US* **brant** *n* a small goose with dark grey plumage and a short neck

brethren *pl n archaic* a plural of **brother**

> **USAGE** This plural of *brother*, which has existed since at least 1200 AD, is now archaic in English. It is, however, used between fellow members of a religious group or order, or sometimes between fellow members of a group, political party, or community with shared interests: *Baker's Republican brethren; his sporting brethren.*

Breton *adj* **1** of Brittany ▷ *n* **2** a person from Brittany **3** the Celtic language of Brittany

breve *n* an accent (˘) placed over a vowel to indicate that it is short or is pronounced in a specified way [Latin *brevis* short]

breviary *n, pl* **-ries** *RC Church* a book of psalms, hymns, prayers, etc., to be recited daily [Latin *brevis* short]

brevity *n* **1** a short duration; brief time **2** lack of verbosity [Latin *brevitas*]

brew *vb* **1** to make (beer, ale, etc.) from malt and other ingredients by steeping, boiling, and fermentation **2** to prepare (a drink, such as tea) by infusing **3** to devise or plan: *to brew a plot* **4** to be in the process of being brewed **5** to be about to happen or forming: *a rebellion was brewing* ▷ *n* **6** a beverage produced by brewing, esp. tea or beer **7** an instance of brewing: *last year's brew* [Old English *brēowan*] **brewer** *n*

brewery *n, pl* **-eries** a place where beer, ale, etc., is brewed

Brexit *n* the withdrawal of the United Kingdom from the European Union in March 2019 [BR(ITISH) + EXIT]

briar[1] *or* **brier** *n* **1** a shrub of S Europe, with a hard woody root (briarroot) **2** a tobacco pipe made from this root [French *bruyère*]

briar[2] *n* same as **briar**[1]

bribe *vb* **bribing, bribed 1** to promise, offer, or give something, often illegally, to (a person) to receive services or gain influence ▷ *n* **2** a reward, such as money or favour, given or offered for this purpose [Old French *briber* to beg] **bribery** *n*

bric-a-brac *n* miscellaneous small ornamental objects [French]

brick *n* **1** a rectangular block of baked or dried clay, used in building construction **2** the material used to make such blocks **3** any rectangular block: *a brick of ice cream* **4** bricks collectively **5** *informal* a reliable, trustworthy, or helpful person **6 drop a brick** *Brit & NZ informal* to make a tactless or indiscreet remark ▷ *vb* **7** (foll. by *in*, *up* or *over*) to construct, line, pave, fill, or wall up with bricks: *they bricked up access to the historic pillar* [Middle Dutch *bricke*]

brickbat *n* **1** blunt criticism **2** a piece of brick used as a weapon [BRICK + BAT[1]]

bricklayer *n* a person who builds with bricks

brick-red *adj* reddish-brown

bridal *adj* of a bride or a wedding [Old English *brȳdealu* bride ale]

bride *n* a woman who has just been or is about to be married [Old English *brȳd*]

bridegroom *n* a man who has just been or is about to be married [Old English *brȳdguma*]

bridesmaid *n* a girl or young woman who attends a bride at her wedding

bridge[1] *n* **1** a structure that provides a way over a railway, river, etc. **2** a platform from which a ship is piloted and navigated **3** the hard ridge at the upper part of the nose **4** a dental plate containing artificial teeth that is secured to natural teeth **5** a piece of wood supporting the strings of a violin, guitar, etc. ▷ *vb* **bridging, bridged 6** to build or provide a bridge over (something) **7** to connect or reduce the distance between: *talks aimed at bridging the gap between the two sides* [Old English *brycg*]

bridge[2] *n* a card game for four players, based on whist, in which the trump suit is decided by bidding between the players [origin unknown]

bridgehead *n military* a fortified or defensive position at the end of a bridge nearest to the enemy

bridgework *n* a partial denture attached to the surrounding teeth

bridging loan *n* a loan made to cover the period between two transactions, such as the buying of another house before the sale of the first is completed

bridle *n* **1** headgear for controlling a horse, consisting of straps and a bit and reins **2** something that curbs or restrains ▷ *vb* **-dling, -dled 3** to show anger or indignation: *he bridled at the suggestion that he should resign* **4** to put a bridle on (a horse) **5** to restrain; curb [Old English *brigdels*]

bridle path *n* a path suitable for riding or leading horses

Brie (**bree**) *n* a soft creamy white cheese [*Brie*, region in N France]

brief *adj* **1** short in duration **2** short in length or extent; scanty: *a brief bikini* **3** terse or concise ▷ *n* **4** a condensed statement or written synopsis **5** *law* a document containing all the facts and points of law of a case by which a solicitor instructs a barrister to represent a client **6** *RC Church* a papal letter that is less formal than a bull **7** Also called: **briefing** instructions **8 hold a brief for** to argue for; champion **9 in brief** in short; to sum up ▷ *vb* **10** to prepare or instruct (someone) by giving a summary of relevant facts **11** *English law* **A** to instruct (a barrister) by brief **B** to retain (a barrister) as counsel [Latin *brevis*] **briefly** *adv*

briefcase *n* a flat portable case for carrying papers, books, etc.

briefs *pl n* men's or women's underpants without legs

brier[1] *or* **briar** *n* any of various thorny shrubs or other plants, such as the sweetbrier [Old English *brēr*, *brǣr*]

brier[2] *n* same as **briar**[1]

brig[1] *n naut* a two-masted square-rigged ship [from BRIGANTINE]

brig[2] *n Scot & N English* a bridge

Brig. Brigadier

brigade *n* **1** a military formation smaller than a division and usually commanded by a brigadier **2** a group of people organized for a certain task: *a rescue brigade* [Old French]

brigadier *n* a senior officer in an army, usually commanding a brigade

brigalow *n Austral* a type of acacia tree [from a native Australian language]

brigand *n* a bandit, esp. a member of a gang operating in mountainous areas [Old French]

brigantine *n* a two-masted sailing ship [Old Italian *brigantino* pirate ship]

bright *adj* **1** emitting or reflecting much light; shining **2** (of colours) intense or vivid **3** full of promise: *a bright future* **4** lively or cheerful

5 quick-witted or clever ▷ *adv* 6 brightly: *the light burned bright in his office* [Old English *beorht*] **brightly** *adv* **brightness** *n*

brighten *vb* 1 to make or become bright or brighter 2 to make or become cheerful

brill *n, pl* **brill** *or* **brills** a European flatfish similar to the turbot [probably Cornish *brȳthel* mackerel]

brilliance *or* **brilliancy** *n* 1 great brightness 2 excellence in physical or mental ability 3 splendour

brilliant *adj* 1 shining with light; sparkling 2 (of a colour) vivid 3 splendid; magnificent: *a brilliant show* 4 of outstanding intelligence or intellect ▷ *n* 5 a diamond cut with many facets to increase its sparkle [French *brillant* shining]

brilliantine *n* a perfumed oil used to make the hair smooth and shiny [French]

brim *n* 1 the upper rim of a cup, bowl, etc. 2 a projecting edge of a hat ▷ *vb* **brimming, brimmed** 3 to be full to the brim: *he saw the tears that brimmed in her eyes* [Middle High German *brem*] **brimless** *adj*

brimful *adj* (foll. by *of*) completely filled with

brimstone *n obsolete* sulphur [Old English *brynstān*]

brindled *adj* brown or grey streaked with a darker colour: *a brindled dog* [Middle English *brended*]

brine *n* 1 a strong solution of salt and water, used for pickling 2 *literary* the sea or its water [Old English *brīne*]

bring *vb* **bringing, brought** 1 to carry, convey, or take (something or someone) to a designated place or person 2 to cause to happen: *responsibility brings maturity* 3 to cause to come to mind: *it brought back memories* 4 to cause to be in a certain state, position, etc.: *the punch brought him to his knees* 5 to make (oneself): *she couldn't bring herself to do it* 6 to sell for: *the painting brought a large sum* 7 *law* A to institute (proceedings, charges, etc.) B to put (evidence, etc.) before a tribunal ▷ See also **bring about, bring down** *etc.* [Old English *bringan*]

bring about *vb* to cause to happen: *a late harvest brought about by bad weather*

bring-and-buy sale *n Brit & NZ* an informal sale, often for charity, to which people bring items for sale and buy those that others have brought

bring down *vb* to cause to fall

bring forth *vb* to give birth to

bring forward *vb* 1 to move (a meeting or event) to an earlier date or time 2 to present or introduce (a subject) for discussion 3 *accounting* to transfer (a sum) to the top of the next page or column

bring in *vb* 1 to yield (income, profit, or cash) 2 to introduce (a legislative bill, etc.) 3 to return (a verdict)

bring off *vb* to succeed in achieving (something difficult)

bring out *vb* 1 to produce, publish, or have (a book) published 2 to expose, reveal, or cause to be seen: *he brought out the best in me* 3 (foll. by *in*) to cause (a person) to become covered with (a rash, spots, etc.)

bring over *vb* to cause (a person) to change allegiances

bring round *vb* 1 to restore (a person) to consciousness after a faint 2 to convince (another person) of an opinion or point of view

bring to *vb* to restore (a person) to consciousness: *the smelling salts brought her to*

bring up *vb* 1 to care for and train (a child); rear 2 to raise (a subject) for discussion; mention 3 to vomit (food)

brinjal *n S African & Indian* a dark purple tropical fruit, cooked and eaten as a vegetable [Portuguese *berinjela*]

brink *n* 1 the edge or border of a steep place 2 the land at the edge of a body of water 3 **on the brink of** very near; on the point of: *on the brink of disaster* [Middle Dutch *brinc*]

brinkmanship *n* the practice of pressing a dangerous situation to the limit of safety in order to win an advantage

briny *adj* **brinier, briniest** 1 of or like brine; salty ▷ *n* 2 **the briny** *informal* the sea

brio *n* liveliness; vigour [Italian]

briquette *n* a small brick made of compressed coal dust, used for fuel [French]

brisk *adj* 1 lively and quick; vigorous: *brisk trade* 2 invigorating or sharp: *brisk weather* 3 practical and businesslike: *his manner was brisk* [probably variant of BRUSQUE] **briskly** *adv*

brisket *n* beef from the breast of a cow [probably Scandinavian]

brisling *n* same as **sprat** [Norwegian]

bristle *n* 1 any short stiff hair, such as on a pig's back 2 something resembling these hairs: *toothbrush bristle* ▷ *vb* **-tling, -tled** 3 to stand up or cause to stand up like bristles 4 to show anger or indignation: *she bristled at the suggestion* 5 to be thickly covered or set: *the hedges bristled with blossom* [Old English *byrst*] **bristly** *adj*

Brit *n informal* a British person

Brit. 1 Britain 2 British

Britannia *n* a female warrior carrying a trident and wearing a helmet, personifying Great Britain

Britannia metal *n* an alloy of tin with antimony and copper

Britannic *adj* of Britain; British: *Her Britannic Majesty*

britches *pl n* same as **breeches**

British *adj* 1 of Britain or the British Commonwealth 2 denoting the English language as spoken and written in Britain ▷ *pl n* 3 **the British** the people of Britain

British Summer Time *n* a time set one hour ahead of Greenwich Mean Time: used in Britain from the end of March to the end of October, providing an extra hour of daylight in the evening. Abbrev: **BST**

Briton *n* 1 a native or inhabitant of Britain 2 *history* any of the early Celtic inhabitants of S Britain [of Celtic origin]

brittle *adj* 1 easily cracked or broken; fragile 2 curt or irritable: *a brittle reply* 3 hard or sharp in quality: *a brittle laugh* [Old English *brēotan* to break] **brittly** *adv*

broach *vb* 1 to initiate or introduce (a topic) for discussion 2 to tap or pierce (a container) to

b

b

draw off (a liquid) **3** to open in order to begin to use ▹ *n* **4** a spit for roasting meat [Latin *brochus* projecting]

broad *adj* **1** having great breadth or width **2** of vast extent: *broad plains* **3** not detailed; general **4** clear and open: *broad daylight* **5** obvious: *broad hints* **6** tolerant: *a broad view* **7** extensive: *broad support* **8** vulgar or coarse **9** strongly marked: *he spoke broad Australian English* ▹ *n* **10** *slang, chiefly US & Canad* a woman **11** **the Broads** in East Anglia, a group of shallow lakes connected by a network of rivers [Old English *brād*] **broadly** *adv*

B-road *n* a secondary road in Britain

broadband *n* a telecommunications technique that uses a wide range of frequencies to allow messages to be sent simultaneously

broad bean *n* the large edible flattened seed of a Eurasian bean plant

broadcast *n* **1** a transmission or programme on radio or television ▹ *vb* **-casting, -cast** *or* **-casted** **2** to transmit (announcements or programmes) on radio or television **3** to take part in a radio or television programme **4** to make widely known throughout an area: *to broadcast news* **5** to scatter (seed, etc.) **broadcaster** *n* **broadcasting** *n*

broaden *vb* to make or become broad or broader; widen

broad gauge *n* a railway track with a greater distance between the lines than the standard gauge of 56½ inches

broad-leaved *adj* denoting trees other than conifers; having broad rather than needle-shaped leaves

broadloom *adj* of or designating carpets woven on a wide loom

broad-minded *adj* **1** tolerant of opposing viewpoints; liberal **2** not easily shocked

broadsheet *n* a newspaper in a large format

broadside *n* **1** a strong or abusive verbal or written attack **2** *naval* the simultaneous firing of all the guns on one side of a ship **3** *naut* the entire side of a ship ▹ *adv* **4** with a broader side facing an object

broadsword *n* a broad-bladed sword used for cutting rather than stabbing

brocade *n* **1** a rich fabric woven with a raised design ▹ *vb* **-cading, -caded** **2** to weave with such a design [Spanish *brocado*]

broccoli *n* a variety of cabbage with greenish flower heads [Italian]

brochette (brosh-ett) *n* a skewer used for holding pieces of meat or vegetables while grilling [Old French *brochete*]

brochure *n* a pamphlet or booklet, esp. one containing introductory information or advertising [French]

broderie anglaise *n* open embroidery on white cotton, fine linen, etc. [French: English embroidery]

broekies (brook-eez) *pl n S African informal* underpants [Afrikaans]

brogue¹ *n* a sturdy walking shoe, often with ornamental perforations [Irish Gaelic *bróg*]

brogue² *n* a broad gentle-sounding dialectal accent, esp. that used by the Irish in speaking English [origin unknown]

broil *vb* same as **grill** (sense 1) [Old French *bruillir*]

broiler *n* a young tender chicken suitable for roasting

broke *vb* **1** the past tense of **break** ▹ *adj* **2** *informal* having no money

broken *vb* **1** the past participle of **break** ▹ *adj* **2** fractured, smashed, or splintered **3** interrupted; disturbed: *broken sleep* **4** not functioning **5** (of a promise or contract) violated; infringed **6** (of the speech of a foreigner) imperfectly spoken: *broken English* **7** Also: **broken-in** made tame by training **8** exhausted or weakened, as through ill-health or misfortune

broken chord *n* same as **arpeggio**

broken-down *adj* **1** worn out, as by age or long use; dilapidated **2** not in working order

brokenhearted *adj* overwhelmed by grief or disappointment

broken home *n* a family that does not live together because the parents are separated or divorced

broker *n* **1** an agent who buys or sells goods, securities, etc.: *an insurance broker* **2** a person who deals in second-hand goods [Anglo-French *brocour* broacher]

brokerage *n* commission charged by a broker

broker-dealer *n* same as **stockbroker**

brolga *n* a large grey Australian crane with a trumpeting call. Also called: **native companion**

brolly *n, pl* **-lies** *Brit, Austral & NZ informal* an umbrella

bromance *n informal* a close, non-sexual friendship between two men

bromide *n* **1** *chem* any compound of bromine with another element or radical **2** a dose of sodium or potassium bromide given as a sedative **3** a boring, meaningless, or obvious remark

bromide paper *n* a type of photographic paper coated with an emulsion of silver bromide

bromine *n chem* a dark red liquid chemical element that gives off a pungent vapour. Symbol: **Br** [Greek *brōmos* bad smell]

bronchial *adj* of or relating to both of the bronchi or the smaller tubes into which they divide

bronchiole *n* any of the smallest bronchial tubes

bronchitis *n* inflammation of the bronchial tubes, causing coughing and difficulty in breathing

bronchus (bronk-uss) *n, pl* **bronchi** (bronk-eye) either of the two main branches of the windpipe [Greek *bronkhos*]

bronco *n, pl* **-cos** (in the US and Canada) a wild or partially tamed horse [Mexican Spanish]

brontosaurus *n* a former name for **apatosaurus**

bronze *n* **1** an alloy of copper and smaller proportions of tin **2** a statue, medal, or other object made of bronze ▹ *adj* **3** made of or resembling bronze **4** yellowish-brown ▹ *vb* **bronzing, bronzed** **5** (esp. of the skin) to make or become brown; tan [Italian *bronzo*]

Bronze Age *n* a phase of human culture, lasting in Britain from about 2000 to 500 BC during which weapons and tools were made of bronze

bronze medal *n* a medal of bronze awarded to a competitor who comes third in a contest or race

brooch *n* an ornament with a hinged pin and catch, worn fastened to clothing [Old French *broche*]

brood *n* **1** a number of young animals, esp. birds, produced at one hatching **2** all the children in a family: often used jokingly ▷ *vb* **3** (of a bird) to sit on or hatch eggs **4** to think long and unhappily about something: *he brooded on his failure to avert the confrontation* [Old English *brōd*] **brooding** *n, adj*

broody *adj* **broodier, broodiest 1** moody; introspective **2** (of poultry) wishing to sit on or hatch eggs **3** *informal* (of a woman) wishing to have a baby

brook[1] *n* a natural freshwater stream [Old English *brōc*]

brook[2] *vb* to bear; tolerate: *she would brook no opposition* [Old English *brūcan*]

broom *n* **1** a type of long-handled sweeping brush **2** a yellow-flowered shrub **3 a new broom** a newly appointed official, etc., eager to make radical changes [Old English *brōm*]

broomstick *n* the long handle of a broom

bros. *or* **Bros.** brothers

broth *n* a soup made by boiling meat, vegetables, etc. in water [Old English]

brothel *n* a house where men pay to have sexual intercourse with prostitutes [short for *brothel-house*, from Middle English *brothel* useless person]

brother *n* **1** a man or boy with the same parents as another person. Related adjective: **fraternal** **2** a man belonging to the same group, trade union, etc. as another or others; fellow member **3** comrade; friend **4** *Christianity* a member of a male religious order [Old English *brōthor*]

brotherhood *n* **1** fellowship **2** an association, such as a trade union **3** the state of being a brother

brother-in-law *n, pl* **brothers-in-law 1** the brother of one's wife or husband **2** the husband of one's sibling

brotherly *adj* of or like a brother, esp. in showing loyalty and affection

brougham (brew-am) *n* a horse-drawn closed carriage with a raised open driver's seat in front [after Lord *Brougham*]

brought *vb* the past of **bring**

brouhaha *n* loud confused noise [French]

brow *n* **1** the part of the face from the eyes to the hairline; forehead **2** same as **eyebrow** **3** the jutting top of a hill [Old English *brū*]

browbeat *vb* **-beating, -beat, -beaten** to frighten (someone) with threats

brown *adj* **1** of the colour of wood or the earth **2** (of bread) made from wheatmeal or wholemeal flour **3** deeply tanned ▷ *n* **4** the colour of wood or the earth **5** anything brown, such as brown paint or brown clothing: *clad in brown* ▷ *vb* **6** to make or become brown or browner, for example as a result of cooking [Old English *brūn*] **brownish** *adj*

brown bear *n* a large ferocious brownish bear of N America, Europe, and Asia

brown coal *n* same as **lignite**

browned-off *adj informal, chiefly Brit* thoroughly bored and depressed

brownfield *adj* relating to an urban area which has previously been built on: *brownfield sites*

Brownian motion *n physics* the random movement of particles in a fluid, caused by continuous bombardment from molecules of the fluid [after Robert *Brown*, physicist]

brownie *n* **1** (in folklore) an elf said to do helpful work, esp. household chores, at night **2** a small square nutty chocolate cake

Brownie Guide *or* **Brownie** *n* a member of the junior branch of the Guides

Brownie point *n* a notional mark to one's credit for being seen to do the right thing

browning *n Brit* a substance used to darken gravies

brown paper *n* a kind of coarse unbleached paper used for wrapping

brown rice *n* unpolished rice, in which the grains retain the outer yellowish-brown layer (bran)

Brown Shirt *n* **1** (in Nazi Germany) a storm trooper **2** a member of any fascist party or group

brown trout *n* a common brownish trout

browse *vb* **browsing, browsed 1** to look through (a book or articles for sale) in a casual leisurely manner **2** *computers* to read hypertext, esp. on the internet **3** (of deer, goats, etc.) to feed upon vegetation by continual nibbling ▷ *n* **4** an instance of browsing [French *broust* bud]

browser *n computers* a software package that enables a user to read hypertext, esp. on the internet

brucellosis *n* an infectious disease of cattle, goats, and pigs, caused by bacteria and transmittable to humans [after Sir David *Bruce*, bacteriologist]

bruise *vb* **bruising, bruised 1** to injure (body tissue) without breaking the skin, usually with discoloration, or (of body tissue) to be injured in this way **2** to hurt (someone's feelings) **3** to damage (fruit) ▷ *n* **4** a bodily injury without a break in the skin, usually with discoloration [Old English *brȳsan*]

bruiser *n informal* a strong tough person, esp. a boxer or a bully

brumby *n, pl* **-bies** *Austral* **1** a wild horse **2** an unruly person [origin unknown]

brunch *n* a meal eaten late in the morning, combining breakfast with lunch [BR(EAKFAST) + (L)UNCH]

brunette *n* a woman with dark brown hair [French]

brunt *n* the main force or shock of a blow, attack, etc.: *the town bore the brunt of the earthquake*

bruschetta (broo-**sket**-ta) *n* an Italian open sandwich of toasted bread topped with olive oil and tomatoes, olives, etc. [Italian]

brush[1] *n* **1** a device made of bristles, hairs, wires, etc. set into a firm back or handle: used to apply paint, groom the hair, etc. **2** the act of brushing **3** a brief encounter, esp. an unfriendly one **4** the bushy tail of a fox **5** an electric conductor, esp. one made of carbon, that conveys current between stationary and rotating parts of a generator, motor, etc. ▷ *vb* **6** to clean, scrub, or paint with a brush **7** to apply or remove with a brush or brushing movement **8** to touch lightly and briefly ▹ See also **brush aside, brush off, brush up** [Old French *broisse*]

brush² *n* a thick growth of shrubs and small trees; scrub [Old French *broce*]

brush aside *or* **brush away** *vb* to dismiss (a suggestion or an idea) without consideration; disregard

brushed *adj textiles* treated with a brushing process to raise the nap and give a softer and warmer finish: *brushed nylon*

brush off *slang* ▹ *vb* **1** to dismiss and ignore (a person), esp. curtly ▹ *n* **brushoff 2 give someone the brushoff** to reject someone

brush turkey *n* a bird of New Guinea and Australia resembling the domestic fowl, with black plumage

brush up *vb* **1** (often foll. by *on*) to refresh one's knowledge or memory of (a subject) ▹ *n* **brush-up 2** *Brit* the act of tidying one's appearance: *have a wash and brush-up*

brushwood *n* **1** cut or broken-off tree branches, twigs, etc. **2** same as **brush²**

brushwork *n* a characteristic manner of applying paint with a brush: *Rembrandt's brushwork*

brusque *adj* blunt or curt in manner or speech [Italian *brusco* sour] **brusquely** *adv* **brusqueness** *n*

Brussels sprout *n* a vegetable like a tiny cabbage

brut (broot) *adj* (of champagne or sparkling wine) very dry

brutal *adj* **1** cruel; vicious; savage **2** harsh or severe **3** extremely honest or frank in speech or manner **brutality** *n* **brutally** *adv*

brutalism *n* an austere architectural style of the 1950s and 1960s, characterized by the use of exposed concrete and angular shapes

brutalize *or* **-ise** *vb* **-izing, -ized** *or* **-ising, -ised 1** to make or become brutal **2** to treat (someone) brutally **brutalization** *or* **-isation** *n*

brute *n* **1** a brutal person **2** any animal that is not a human; beast ▹ *adj* **3** wholly instinctive or physical, like that of an animal: *cricket is not a game of brute force* **4** without reason or intelligence **5** coarse and grossly sensual [Latin *brutus* irrational]

brutish *adj* **1** of or resembling a brute; animal **2** coarse; cruel; stupid

bryony *n, pl* **-nies** a herbaceous climbing plant with greenish flowers and red or black berries [Greek *bruōnia*]

Brythonic (brith-on-ik) *n* **1** the S group of Celtic languages, consisting of Welsh, Cornish, and Breton ▹ *adj* **2** of this group of languages [Welsh *Brython* Celt]

BS 1 Bachelor of Surgery **2** British Standard(s)

BSc Bachelor of Science

BSE bovine spongiform encephalopathy: a fatal virus disease of cattle

BSI British Standards Institution

BSL British Sign Language

BST British Summer Time

Bt Baronet

BT British Telecom

btu *or* **BThU** British thermal unit

BTW by the way

bubble *n* **1** a small globule of air or a gas in a liquid or a solid **2** a thin film of liquid forming a ball around air or a gas: *a soap bubble* **3** a dome, esp. a transparent glass or plastic one **4** an unreliable scheme or enterprise ▹ *vb* **-bling, -bled 5** to form bubbles **6** to move or flow with a gurgling sound **7 bubble over** to express an emotion freely: *she was bubbling over with excitement* [probably Scandinavian]

bubble and squeak *n Brit, Austral & NZ* a dish of boiled cabbage and potatoes fried together

bubble bath *n* **1** a substance used to scent, soften, and foam in bath water **2** a bath with such a substance

bubble car *n Brit* a small car of the 1950s with a transparent bubble-shaped top

bubble gum *n* a type of chewing gum that can be blown into large bubbles

bubble wrap *n* a type of polythene wrapping containing many small air pockets, used to protect breakable goods

bubbly *adj* **-blier, -bliest 1** lively; animated; excited **2** full of or resembling bubbles ▹ *n* **3** *informal* champagne

bubo (byew-boh) *n, pl* **-boes** *pathol* inflammation and swelling of a lymph node, esp. in the armpit or groin [Greek *boubōn* groin] **bubonic** (bew-bonn-ik) *adj*

bubonic plague *n* an acute infectious disease characterized by the formation of buboes

buccaneer *n* a pirate, esp. in the Caribbean in the 17th and 18th centuries [French *boucanier*]

buck¹ *n* **1** the male of the goat, hare, kangaroo, rabbit, and reindeer **2** *archaic* a spirited young man **3** the act of bucking ▹ *vb* **4** (of a horse or other animal) to jump vertically, with legs stiff and back arched **5** (of a horse, etc.) to throw (its rider) by bucking **6** *informal* to resist or oppose obstinately: *bucking the system* ▹ See also **buck up** [Old English *bucca* he-goat]

buck² *n US, Canad, Austral & NZ informal* a dollar [origin unknown]

buck³ *n* **pass the buck** *informal* to shift blame or responsibility onto another [probably from *buckhorn knife,* placed before a player in poker to indicate that he was the next dealer]

bucket *n* **1** an open-topped cylindrical container with a handle **2** the amount a bucket will hold **3** a bucket-like part of a machine, such as the scoop on a mechanical shovel **4 kick the bucket** *slang* to die ▹ *vb* **-eting, -eted 5** (often foll. by *down*) (of rain) to fall very heavily [Old English *būc*]

bucket list *n informal* a list of things one wants to experience before one dies

bucket shop *n* **1** *chiefly Brit* a travel agency specializing in cheap airline tickets **2** an unregistered firm of stockbrokers that engages in fraudulent speculation

buckle *n* **1** a clasp for fastening together two loose ends, esp. of a belt or strap ▹ *vb* **-ling, -led 2** to fasten or be fastened with a buckle **3** to bend or cause to bend out of shape, esp. as a result of pressure or heat [Latin *buccula* cheek strap]

buckle down *vb* to apply oneself with determination

buckler *n* a small round shield worn on the forearm [Old French *bocler*]

Bucks Buckinghamshire
buckshee *adj Brit slang* without charge; free [from BAKSHEESH]
buckshot *n* large lead pellets used for hunting game
buckskin *n* **1** a strong greyish-yellow suede leather, originally made from deerskin **2 buckskins** trousers made of buckskin
buckteeth *pl n* projecting upper front teeth **buck-toothed** *adj*
buckthorn *n* a thorny shrub whose berries were formerly used as a purgative
buck up *vb informal* **1** to make or become more cheerful or confident **2** to make haste
buckwheat *n* **1** a type of small black seed used as animal fodder and in making flour **2** the flour obtained from such seeds [Middle Dutch *boecweite*]
bucolic (byew-**koll**-ik) *adj* **1** of the countryside or country life; rustic **2** of or relating to shepherds; pastoral ▷ *n* **3** a pastoral poem [Greek *boukolos* cowherd]
bud *n* **1** a swelling on the stem of a plant that develops into a flower or leaf **2** a partially opened flower: *rosebud* **3** any small budlike outgrowth: *taste buds* **4 nip something in the bud** to put an end to something in its initial stages ▷ *vb* **budding, budded 5** (of plants and some animals) to produce buds **6** *horticulture* to graft (a bud) from one plant onto another [Middle English *budde*]
Buddhism *n* a religion founded by the Buddha that teaches that all suffering can be brought to an end by overcoming greed, hatred, and delusion **Buddhist** *n, adj*
budding *adj* beginning to develop or grow: *a budding actor*
buddleia *n* a shrub which has long spikes of purple flowers [after A. *Buddle*, botanist]
buddy *n, pl* **-dies 1** *chiefly US & Canad informal* a friend **2** a volunteer who helps and supports a person with a chronic illness ▷ *vb* **-dies, -dying, -died 3** to act as a buddy to (a person with a chronic illness) [probably variant of BROTHER]
budge *vb* **budging, budged 1** to move slightly: *he refuses to budge off that chair* **2** to change or cause to change opinions: *nothing would budge her from this idea* [Old French *bouger*]
budgerigar *n* a small cage bird bred in many different-coloured varieties [Aboriginal]
budget *n* **1** a plan of expected income and expenditure over a specified period **2** the total amount of money allocated for a specific purpose during a specified period ▷ *adj* **3** inexpensive: *a budget hotel* ▷ *vb* **-eting, -eted 4** to enter or provide for in a budget **5** to plan the expenditure of (money or time) [Latin *bulga* leather pouch] **budgetary** *adj*
Budget *n* **the Budget** an annual estimate of British government expenditures and revenues and the financial plans for the following financial year
budget deficit *n* the amount by which government spending exceeds income from taxation, etc.
budgie *n informal* same as **budgerigar**
buff[1] *n* **1** a soft thick flexible undyed leather **2** a cloth or pad of material used for polishing **3 in the buff** *informal* completely naked ▷ *adj* **4** dull yellowish-brown **5** *informal* physically fit and attractive ▷ *vb* **6** to clean or polish (a metal, floor, shoes, etc.) with a buff [Late Latin *bufalus* buffalo]
buff[2] *n informal* an expert on or devotee of a given subject: *an opera buff* [from the buff-coloured uniforms worn by volunteer firefighters in New York City]
buffalo *n, pl* **-loes** *or* **-lo 1** a type of cattle with upward-curving horns **2** same as **water buffalo 3** *US & Canad* a bison [Greek *bous* ox]
buffer[1] *n* **1** one of a pair of spring-loaded steel pads at the ends of railway vehicles and railway tracks that reduces shock on impact **2** a person or thing that lessens shock or protects from damaging impact, circumstances, etc. **3** *chem* **A** a substance added to a solution to resist changes in its acidity or alkalinity **B** Also called: **buffer solution** a solution containing such a substance **4** *computers* a memory device for temporarily storing data ▷ *vb* **5** to cushion; provide a buffer for **6** *computers* to store (data) temporarily in a buffer [from BUFFET[2]]
buffer[2] *n Brit informal* a stupid or bumbling person, esp. a man: *an old buffer* [origin unknown]
buffer state *n* a small and usually neutral state between two rival powers
buffer zone *n* an area lying between two states, providing each with protection from the other
buffet[1] (**boof**-fay, **buff**-ay) *n* **1** a counter where light refreshments are served **2** a meal at which guests help themselves from a number of dishes [French]
buffet[2] (**buff**-it) *vb* **-feting, -feted 1** to knock against or about; batter: *the ship was buffeted by strong winds* **2** to hit, esp. with the fist ▷ *n* **3** a blow, esp. with the fist [Old French *buffeter*]
buffet car (**boof**-fay) *n Brit* a railway coach where light refreshments are served
buffoon *n* a person who amuses others by silly behaviour [Latin *bufo* toad] **buffoonery** *n*
bug *n* **1** any of various insects having piercing and sucking mouthparts **2** *chiefly US & Canad* any insect **3** *informal* a minor illness caused by a germ or virus **4** *informal* a small error, esp. in a computer or computer program **5** *informal* an obsessive idea or hobby **6** *informal* a concealed microphone used for recording conversations in spying **7** *Austral* a flattish edible shellfish ▷ *vb* **bugging, bugged** *informal* **8** to irritate or upset (someone) **9** to conceal a microphone in (a room or telephone) [origin unknown]
bugbear *n* a thing that causes obsessive anxiety [obsolete *bug* an evil spirit + BEAR[2]]
bugger *n* **1** *slang* a person or thing considered to be unpleasant or difficult **2** *slang* a humorous or affectionate term for someone: *a friendly little bugger* **3** *offensive* a person who practises anal intercourse ▷ *vb* **4** *slang* to tire; weary **5** *offensive* to practise anal intercourse with ▷ *interj* **6** *slang* an exclamation of annoyance or disappointment [Medieval Latin *Bulgarus* Bulgarian heretic]
bugger about *or* **bugger around** *vb Brit slang* **1** to fool about and waste time **2** to create

difficulties for: *they really buggered me about when I tried to get my money back*

bugger off *vb Brit slang* to go away; depart

bugger up *vb Brit slang* to spoil or ruin (something)

buggery *n* anal intercourse

buggy *n, pl* **-gies** **1** a light horse-drawn carriage having two or four wheels **2** a lightweight folding pram for babies or young children [origin unknown]

b

bugle *music* ▷ *n* **1** a brass instrument used chiefly for military calls ▷ *vb* **-gling, -gled** **2** to play or sound (on) a bugle [short for *bugle horn* ox horn, from Latin *buculus* bullock] **bugler** *n*

build *vb* **building, built** **1** to make or construct by joining parts or materials: *more than 100 bypasses have been built in the past decade* **2** to establish and develop: *it took ten years to build the business* **3** to make in a particular way or for a particular purpose: *she's built for speed, not stamina* **4** (often foll. by *up*) to increase in intensity ▷ *n* **5** physical form, figure, or proportions: *he has an athletic build* [Old English *byldan*]

builder *n* a person who constructs houses and other buildings

building *n* **1** a structure, such as a house, with a roof and walls **2** the business of building houses, etc.

building society *n* (in the UK) a cooperative banking enterprise where money can be invested and mortgage loans made available. Since 1986 they have been empowered to offer banking services

build up *vb* **1** to construct (something) gradually, systematically, and in stages **2** to increase by degrees: *he steadily built up a power base* **3** to prepare for or gradually approach a climax ▷ *n* **build-up** **4** a progressive increase in number or size: *the build-up of industry* **5** a gradual approach to a climax **6** extravagant publicity or praise, esp. as a campaign

built *vb* the past of **build**

built-in *adj* **1** included as an essential part: *a built-in cupboard* **2** essential: *a built-in instinct*

built-up *adj* **1** having many buildings: *a built-up area* **2** increased by the addition of parts: *built-up heels*

bulb *n* **1** same as **light bulb** **2** the onion-shaped base of the stem of some plants, which sends down roots **3** a plant, such as a daffodil, which grows from a bulb **4** any bulb-shaped thing [Greek *bolbos* onion] **bulbous** *adj*

Bulgarian *adj* **1** of Bulgaria ▷ *n* **2** a person from Bulgaria **3** the language of Bulgaria

bulge *n* **1** a swelling or an outward curve on a normally flat surface **2** a sudden increase in number, esp. of population ▷ *vb* **bulging, bulged** **3** to swell outwards [Latin *bulga* bag] **bulging** *adj*

bulimia *n* a mental health condition characterized by a compulsion to purge oneself of the food one has eaten [Greek *bous* ox + *limos* hunger] **bulimic** *adj, n*

bulk *n* **1** volume or size, esp. when great **2** the main part: *he spends the bulk of his time abroad* **3** a large body, esp. of a person **4** the part of food which passes unabsorbed through the digestive system **5** **in bulk** in large quantities: *how frequently do you buy food in bulk for your family?* ▷ *vb* **6** **bulk large** to be or seem important or prominent [Old Norse *bulki* cargo]

USAGE The use of a plural noun after *bulk* was formerly considered incorrect, but is now acceptable.

bulk buying *n* the purchase of goods in large amounts, often at reduced prices

bulkhead *n* any upright partition in a ship or aeroplane [probably from Old Norse *bálkr* partition + HEAD]

bulky *adj* **bulkier, bulkiest** very large and massive, esp. so as to be unwieldy **bulkiness** *n*

bull¹ *n* **1** a male of domestic cattle, esp. one that is sexually mature **2** the male of various other animals including the elephant and whale **3** a very large, strong, or aggressive person **4** *Stock Exchange* a speculator who buys in anticipation of rising prices in order to make a profit on resale **5** *chiefly Brit* same as **bull's-eye** (senses 1, 2) **6** **like a bull in a china shop** clumsy **7** **take the bull by the horns** to face and tackle a difficulty without shirking [Old English *bula*]

bull² *n* a ludicrously self-contradictory or nonsensical statement [origin unknown]

bull³ *n* a formal document issued by the pope [Latin *bulla* round object]

bull bars *pl n* a large protective metal grille on the front of some vehicles, esp. four-wheel-drive vehicles

bulldog *n* a thickset dog with a broad head and a muscular body

bulldog clip *n* a clip for holding papers together, consisting of two metal clamps and a spring

bulldoze *vb* **-dozing, -dozed** **1** to move, demolish, or flatten with a bulldozer **2** *informal* to coerce (someone) into doing something by intimidation [origin unknown]

bulldozer *n* a powerful tractor fitted with caterpillar tracks and a blade at the front, used for moving earth

bullet *n* a small metallic missile used as the projectile of a gun or rifle [French *boulette* little ball]

bulletin *n* **1** a broadcast summary of the news **2** an official statement on a matter of public interest **3** a periodical published by an organization for its members [Italian *bulla* papal edict]

bulletin board *n* **1** *US* same as **notice board** **2** *computers* a type of data-exchange system by which messages can be sent and read

bullet point *n* one of a series of important items for discussion or action in a document, usually marked by a square or round symbol

bullfight *n* a public show, popular in Spain, in which a matador baits and usually kills a bull in an arena **bullfighter** *n* **bullfighting** *n*

bullfinch *n* a common European songbird with a black head and, in the male, a pinkish breast

bullfrog *n* any of various large frogs having a loud deep croak

bullion *n* gold or silver in the form of bars and ingots [Anglo-French: mint]

bull-necked *adj* having a short thick neck

bullock *n* a gelded bull; steer [Old English *bulluc*]

bullring *n* an arena for staging bullfights
bull's-eye *n* **1** the small central disc of a target or a dartboard **2** a shot hitting this **3** *informal* something that exactly achieves its aim **4** a peppermint-flavoured boiled sweet **5** a small circular window **6** a thick disc of glass set into a ship's deck, etc. to admit light **7** the glass boss at the centre of a sheet of blown glass **8** **A** a convex lens used as a condenser **B** a lamp or lantern containing such a lens
bullshit *slang* ▷ *n* **1** exaggerated or foolish talk; nonsense ▷ *vb* **-shitting, -shitted 2** to talk bullshit to: *don't bullshit me*
bull terrier *n* a terrier with a muscular body and a short smooth coat
bully *n, pl* **-lies 1** a person who repeatedly hurts, persecutes, or intimidates other people ▷ *vb* **-lies, -lying, -lied 2** to hurt, intimidate, or persecute (another person) ▷ *interj* **3** **bully for you** *informal* well done! bravo!: now usually used sarcastically [originally, sweetheart, fine fellow, swaggering coward, probably from Middle Dutch *boele* lover]
bully beef *n* canned corned beef [French *bœuf bouilli* boiled beef]
bully-off *hockey* ▷ *n* **1** the method of restarting play in which two opposing players stand with the ball between them and strike their sticks together three times before trying to hit the ball ▷ *vb* **bully off 2** to restart play with a bully-off [origin unknown]
bulrush *n* **1** a tall reedlike marsh plant with brown spiky flowers **2** *Bible* same as **papyrus** (sense 1) [Middle English *bulrish*]
bulwark *n* **1** a wall or similar structure used as a fortification; rampart **2** a person or thing acting as a defence [Middle High German *bolwerk*]
bum[1] *n Brit, Austral & NZ slang* the buttocks or anus [origin unknown]
bum[2] *informal* ▷ *n* **1** a disreputable loafer or idler **2** a tramp; hobo ▷ *vb* **bumming, bummed 3** to get by begging; cadge: *to bum a lift* **4** **bum around** to spend time to no good purpose; loaf ▷ *adj* **5** of poor quality; useless: *he hit a bum note* [probably from German *bummeln* to loaf]
bumbag *n* a small bag worn on a belt around the waist
bumble *vb* **-bling, -bled 1** to speak or do in a clumsy, muddled, or inefficient way **2** to move in a clumsy or unsteady way [origin unknown] **bumbling** *adj, n*
bumblebee *n* a large hairy bee [obsolete *bumble* to buzz]
bumf *or* **bumph** *n Brit, Austral & NZ* **1** *informal* official documents or forms **2** *slang* toilet paper [short for *bumfodder*]
bump *vb* **1** to knock or strike (someone or something) with a jolt **2** to travel or proceed in jerks and jolts **3** to hurt by knocking ▷ *n* **4** an impact; knock; jolt; collision **5** a dull thud from an impact or collision **6** a lump on the body caused by a blow **7** a raised uneven part, such as on a road surface ▷ See also **bump into, bump off, bump up** [probably imitative] **bumpy** *adj*
bumper[1] *n* a horizontal bar attached to the front and rear of a vehicle to protect against damage from impact
bumper[2] *n* **1** a glass or tankard, filled to the brim, esp. as a toast **2** an unusually large or fine example of something ▷ *adj* **3** unusually large, fine, or abundant: *a bumper crop* [probably obsolete *bump* to bulge]
bumph *n* same as **bumf**
bump into *vb informal* to meet (someone) by chance
bumpkin *n* an awkward simple rustic person: *a country bumpkin* [probably from Dutch]
bump off *vb slang* to murder (someone)
bumptious *adj* offensively self-assertive or conceited [probably *bump* + *fractious*]
bump up *vb informal* to increase (prices) by a large amount
bun *n* **1** a small sweetened bread roll, often containing currants or spices **2** a small round cake **3** a hairstyle in which long hair is gathered into a bun shape at the back of the head [origin unknown]
bunch *n* **1** a number of things growing, fastened, or grouped together: *a bunch of grapes; a bunch of keys* **2** a collection; group: *a bunch of queries* **3** a group or company: *a bunch of cowards* ▷ *vb* **4** to group or be grouped into a bunch [origin unknown]
bundle *n* **1** a number of things or a quantity of material gathered or loosely bound together: *a bundle of sticks* **2** something wrapped or tied for carrying; package **3** a number of different items sold as a single package **4** *biol* a collection of strands of specialized tissue such as nerve fibres **5** *botany* a strand of conducting tissue within plants ▷ *vb* **-dling, -dled 6** (foll. by *out, off* or *into* etc.) to cause (someone) to go, esp. roughly or unceremoniously: *she bundled them unceremoniously out into the garden* **7** to push or throw (something), esp. in a quick untidy way: *the soiled items were bundled into a black plastic bag* **8** to sell (different items) together as a single package [probably from Middle Dutch *bundel*]
bundle up *vb* to make (something) into a bundle or bundles
bundu *n S African & Zimbabwean slang* a largely uninhabited wild region far from towns [from a Bantu language]
bun fight *n Brit, Austral & NZ slang* a tea party
bung *n* **1** a stopper, esp. of cork or rubber, used to close something such as a cask or flask **2** same as **bunghole** ▷ *vb* **3** (foll. by *up*) *informal* to close or seal (something) with or as if with a bung **4** *Brit, Austral & NZ slang* to throw (something) somewhere in a careless manner; sling [Middle Dutch *bonghe*]
bungalow *n* a one-storey house [Hindi *banglā* (house) of Bengali type]
bungee jumping *or* **bungy jumping** *n* a sport in which a person jumps from a high bridge, tower, etc., to which he or she is connected by a rubber rope [from *bungie*, slang word for India rubber]
bunghole *n* a hole in a cask or barrel through which liquid can be drained
bungle *vb* **-gling, -gled 1** to spoil (an operation) through clumsiness or incompetence; botch ▷ *n* **2** a clumsy or unsuccessful performance; blunder [origin unknown] **bungler** *n* **bungling** *adj, n*

bunion *n* an inflamed swelling of the first joint of the big toe [origin unknown]
bunk[1] *n* **1** a narrow shelflike bed fixed along a wall, esp. in a caravan or ship **2** same as **bunk bed** [probably from *bunker*]
bunk[2] *n informal* same as **bunkum**
bunk[3] *n* **do a bunk 1** *Brit, Austral & NZ slang* to make a hurried and secret departure **2** *chiefly NZ & S African* to be absent without permission [origin unknown]
bunk bed *n* one of a pair of beds constructed one above the other to save space
bunker *n* **1** an obstacle on a golf course, usually a sand-filled hollow bordered by a ridge **2** an underground shelter **3** a large storage container for coal, etc. [Scots *bonkar*]
bunkum *n* empty talk; nonsense [after *Buncombe*, North Carolina, alluded to in an inane speech by its Congressional representative]
bunny *n, pl* **-nies** a child's word for **rabbit** [Scottish Gaelic *bun* rabbit's tail]
bunny girl *n* a night-club hostess whose costume includes a rabbit-like tail and ears
Bunsen burner *n* a gas burner consisting of a metal tube with an adjustable air valve at the base [after R. W. *Bunsen*, chemist]
bunting[1] *n* decorative flags, pennants, and streamers [origin unknown]
bunting[2] *n* a songbird with a short stout bill [origin unknown]
bunya *n* a tall dome-shaped Australian coniferous tree
bunyip *n Austral* a legendary monster said to live in swamps and lakes [from a native Australian language]
buoy *n* **1** a brightly coloured floating object anchored to the sea bed for marking moorings, navigable channels, or obstructions in the water ▷ *vb* **2** (foll. by *up*) to prevent from sinking: *the life belt buoyed him up* **3** to raise the spirits of; hearten: *exports are on the increase, buoyed by a weak dollar* **4** *naut* to mark (a channel or obstruction) with a buoy or buoys [probably Germanic]
buoyant *adj* **1** able to float in or rise to the surface of a liquid **2** (of a liquid or gas) able to keep a body afloat **3** thriving: *a buoyant economy* **4** cheerful or resilient **buoyancy** *n*
bur *or* **burr** *n* **1** a seed case or flower head with hooks or prickles **2** any plant that produces burs [probably from Old Norse]
burble *vb* **-bling, -bled 1** to make or utter with a bubbling sound; gurgle **2** to talk quickly and excitedly [probably imitative]
burbot *n, pl* **-bots** *or* **-bot** a freshwater fish of the cod family that has barbels around its mouth [Old French *bourbotte*]
burden[1] *n* **1** something that is carried; load **2** something that is difficult to bear. ▷ Related adjective: **onerous** ▷ *vb* **3** to put or impose a burden on; load **4** to weigh down; oppress [Old English *byrthen*] **burdensome** *adj*
burden[2] *n* **1** a line of words recurring at the end of each verse of a song **2** the theme of a speech, book, etc. [Old French *bourdon* droning sound]
burdock *n* a weed with large heart-shaped leaves and burlike fruits [BUR + DOCK[4]]
bureau (byew-roe) *n, pl* **-reaus** *or* **-reaux** (-rose) **1** an office or agency, esp. one providing services for the public **2** *US* a government department **3** *chiefly Brit* a writing desk with pigeonholes and drawers against which the writing surface can be closed when not in use **4** *US* a chest of drawers [French]
bureaucracy *n, pl* **-cies 1** a rigid system of administration based upon organization into bureaus, division of labour, a hierarchy of authority, etc. **2** government by such a system **3** government officials collectively **4** any administration in which action is impeded by unnecessary official procedures
bureaucrat *n* **1** an official in a bureaucracy **2** an official who adheres rigidly to bureaucracy **bureaucratic** *adj*
bureau de change *n* a place where foreign currencies can be exchanged [French]
burette *or US* **buret** *n* a graduated glass tube with a stopcock on one end for dispensing known volumes of fluids [Old French *buire* ewer]
burgeon *vb* to develop or grow rapidly; flourish [Old French *burjon*]
burger *n informal* short for **hamburger**
burgh *n* (in Scotland until 1975) a town with a degree of self-government [Scots form of *borough*]
burgher *n archaic* a respectable citizen, esp. in medieval Europe [German *Bürger* or Dutch *burger*]
burglar *n* a person who illegally enters a property to commit a crime [Medieval Latin *burglator*]
burglary *n, pl* **-ries** the crime of entering a building as a trespasser to commit theft or another offence
burgle *vb* **-gling, -gled** to break into (a house, shop, etc.)
burgomaster *n* the chief magistrate of a town in Austria, Belgium, Germany, or the Netherlands [Dutch *burgemeester*]
Burgundy *n* **1** a red or white wine produced in the Burgundy region, around Dijon in France ▷ *adj* **burgundy 2** dark purplish-red
burial *n* the burying of a dead body
burin (byoor-in) *n* a steel chisel used for engraving metal, wood, or marble [French]
burk *n Brit slang* same as **berk**
burka *n* same as **burqa**
burl *or* **birl** *n informal* **1** *Scot, Austral & NZ* an attempt; try: *give it a burl* **2** *Austral & NZ* a ride in a car [from Scots *birl* to spin or turn]
burlesque *n* **1** an artistic work, esp. literary or dramatic, satirizing a subject by caricaturing it **2** *US & Canad theatre* a bawdy comedy show of the late 19th and early 20th centuries ▷ *adj* **3** of or characteristic of a burlesque [Italian *burla* a jest]
burly *adj* **-lier, -liest** large and thick of build; sturdy [Germanic]
burn[1] *vb* **burning, burnt** *or* **burned 1** to be or set on fire **2** to destroy or be destroyed by fire **3** to damage, injure, or mark by heat: *he burnt his hand* **4** to die or put to death by fire **5** to be or feel hot: *my forehead is burning* **6** to smart or cause to smart: *brandy burns your throat* **7** to feel strong emotion, esp. anger or passion **8** to use for the purposes of light, heat, or power: *to burn coal* **9** to form by or as if by fire: *to burn a hole* **10** to char or become

charred: *the toast is burning* **11** to copy information onto (a compact disc) **12 burn one's bridges** *or* **boats** to commit oneself to a particular course of action with no possibility of turning back **13 burn one's fingers** to suffer from having meddled or interfered ▷ *n* **14** an injury caused by exposure to heat, electrical, chemical, or radioactive agents **15** a mark caused by burning ▷ See also **burn out** [Old English *beornan*]

burn² *n Scot & N English* a small stream [Old English *burna*]

burner *n* the part of a stove or lamp that produces flame or heat

burning *adj* **1** intense; passionate **2** urgent; crucial: *a burning problem*

burning glass *n* a convex lens for concentrating the sun's rays to produce fire

burnish *vb* to make or become shiny or smooth by friction; polish [Old French *brunir* to make brown]

burnous *n* a long circular cloak with a hood, worn esp. by Arabs [Arabic *burnus*]

burn out *vb* **1** to become or cause to become inoperative as a result of heat or friction: *the clutch burnt out* ▷ *n* **burnout 2** total exhaustion and inability to work effectively as a result of excessive demands or overwork

burnt *vb* **1** a past of **burn¹** ▷ *adj* **2** affected by or as if by burning; charred

burp *n* **1** *informal* a belch ▷ *vb* **2** *informal* to belch **3** to cause (a baby) to belch [imitative]

burqa *or* **burka** *n* a long enveloping garment worn by some Muslim women in public, covering all but the wearer's eyes [from Arabic]

burr *n* **1** the soft trilling sound given to the letter (r) in some English dialects **2** a whirring or humming sound **3** a rough edge left on metal or paper after cutting **4** a small hand-operated drill [origin unknown]

burrawang *n* an Australian plant with fern-like flowers and an edible nut

burrow *n* **1** a hole dug in the ground by a rabbit or other small animal ▷ *vb* **2** to dig (a tunnel or hole) in, through, or under ground **3** to move through a place by or as if by digging **4** to delve deeply: *he burrowed into his coat pocket* **5** to live in or as if in a burrow [probably variant of *borough*]

bursar *n* a treasurer of a school, college, or university [Medieval Latin *bursarius* keeper of the purse]

bursary *n, pl* **-ries 1** a scholarship or grant awarded esp. in Scottish and New Zealand schools and universities **2** *NZ* a state examination for senior pupils at secondary school

burst *vb* **bursting, burst 1** to break or cause to break open or apart suddenly and noisily; explode **2** to come or go suddenly and forcibly: *he burst into the room* **3** to be full to the point of breaking open: *bursting at the seams* **4** (foll. by *into*) to give vent to (something) suddenly or loudly: *she burst into song* ▷ *n* **5** an instance of breaking open suddenly; explosion **6** a break; breach: *there was a burst in the pipe* **7** a sudden increase of effort; spurt: *a burst of speed* **8** a sudden and violent occurrence or outbreak: *a burst of applause* [Old English *berstan*]

burton *n* **go for a burton** *Brit & NZ slang* **A** to be broken, useless, or lost **B** to die [origin unknown]

bury *vb* **buries, burying, buried 1** to place (a corpse) in a grave **2** to place (something) in the earth and cover it with soil **3** to cover (something) from sight; hide **4** to occupy (oneself) with deep concentration: *he buried himself in his work* **5** to dismiss (a feeling) from the mind: *they decided to bury any hard feelings* [Old English *byrgan*]

bus *n* **1** a large motor vehicle designed to carry passengers between stopping places along a regular route **2** *informal* a car or aircraft that is old and shaky **3** *electronics & computers* an electrical conductor used to make a common connection between several circuits ▷ *vb* **bussing, bussed** *or* **busing, bused 4** to travel or transport by bus **5** *chiefly US & Canad* to transport (children) by bus from one area to another in order to create racially integrated schools [short for OMNIBUS]

busby *n, pl* **-bies** a tall fur helmet worn by certain British soldiers [origin unknown]

bush¹ *n* **1** a dense woody plant, smaller than a tree, with many branches; shrub **2** a dense cluster of such shrubs; thicket **3** something resembling a bush, esp. in density: *a bush of hair* **4 the bush** an uncultivated area covered with trees or shrubs in Australia, Africa, New Zealand, and Canada **5** *Canad* an area on a farm on which timber is grown and cut **6 beat about the bush** to avoid the point at issue [Germanic]

bush² *n* **1** a thin metal sleeve or tubular lining serving as a bearing ▷ *vb* **2** to fit a bush to (a casing or bearing) [Middle Dutch *busse* box]

bushbaby *n, pl* **-babies** a small agile tree-living mammal with large eyes and a long tail

bushed *adj informal* extremely tired; exhausted

bushel *n Brit* an obsolete unit of dry or liquid measure equal to 8 gallons (36.4 litres) [Old French *boissel*]

bush jacket *n* a casual jacket with four patch pockets and a belt

bush line *n Canad* an airline operating in the bush country of Canada's northern regions

bush lot *n Canad* same as **bush¹** (sense 5)

bushman *n, pl* **-men** *Austral & NZ* a person who lives or travels in the bush

Bushman *n, pl* **-men** a member of a hunting and gathering people of southern Africa [Afrikaans *boschjesman*]

bush pilot *n Canad* a pilot who operates a plane in the bush country

bush sickness *n NZ* a disease of animals caused by mineral deficiency in old bush country **bush-sick** *adj*

bush telegraph *n* a means of spreading rumour or gossip

bush tucker *n Austral* **A** any wild animal, insect, plant, etc., traditionally used as food by Aboriginal Australians **B** a style of cooking using these ingredients

bushveld *n S African* bushy countryside [Afrikaans]

bushwalking *n Austral* the leisure activity of walking in the bush **bushwalker** *n*

bushy *adj* **bushier, bushiest 1** (of hair) thick and shaggy **2** covered or overgrown with bushes

business *n* **1** the purchase and sale of goods and services **2** a commercial or industrial establishment **3** a trade or profession **4** commercial activity: *the two countries should do business with each other* **5** proper or rightful concern or responsibility: *mind your own business* **6** an affair; matter: *it's a dreadful business* **7** serious work or activity: *get down to business* **8** a difficult or complicated matter: *it's a business trying to see him* **9 mean business** to be in earnest [Old English *bisignis* care, attentiveness]

businesslike *adj* efficient and methodical

businessman *or fem* **businesswoman** *n, pl* **-men** *or* **-women** a person engaged in commercial or industrial business, usually an owner or executive

businessperson *n, pl* **-people** *or* **-persons** a person engaged in commercial or industrial business, usually an owner or executive

business rate *n* a tax levied on businesses, based on the value of their premises

business school *n* an institution that offers courses to managers in aspects of business, such as marketing, finance, and law

busker *n* a person who entertains for money in streets, stations, etc. [perhaps from Spanish *buscar* to look for] **busk** *vb*

busman's holiday *n informal* a holiday spent doing the same as one does at work

bust[1] *n* **1** a woman's bosom **2** a sculpture of the head, shoulders, and upper chest of a person [Italian *busto* a sculpture]

bust[2] *informal* ▷ *vb* **busting, busted** *or* **bust 1** to burst or break **2** (of the police) to raid or search (a place) or arrest (someone) **3** *US & Canad* to demote in military rank ▷ *adj* **4** broken **5 go bust** to become bankrupt [from *burst*]

bustard *n* a bird with a long strong legs, a heavy body, a long neck, and speckled plumage

bustle[1] *vb* **-tling, -tled 1** (often foll. by *about*) to hurry with a great show of energy or activity ▷ *n* **2** energetic and noisy activity [probably obsolete *buskle* to prepare] **bustling** *adj*

bustle[2] *n* a cushion or framework worn by women in the late 19th century at the back in order to expand the skirt [origin unknown]

bust-up *informal* ▷ *n* **1** a serious quarrel, esp. one ending a relationship **2** *Brit, Austral & NZ* a disturbance or brawl ▷ *vb* **bust up 3** to quarrel and part **4** to disrupt (a meeting), esp. violently

busy *adj* **busier, busiest 1** actively or fully engaged; occupied **2** crowded with or characterized by activity **3** (of a telephone line) in use; engaged ▷ *vb* **busies, busying, busied 4** to make or keep (someone, esp. oneself) busy; occupy [Old English *bisig*] **busily** *adv*

busybody *n, pl* **-bodies** a meddlesome, prying, or officious person

but *conj* **1** contrary to expectation: *he cut his hand but didn't cry* **2** in contrast; on the contrary: *I like seafood but my husband doesn't* **3** other than: *we can't do anything but wait* **4** without it happening: *we never go out but it rains* ▷ *prep* **5** except: *they saved all but one* **6 but for** were it not for: *but for you, we couldn't have managed* ▷ *adv* **7** only: *I can but try; he was but a child* ▷ *n* **8** an objection: *ifs and buts* [Old English *būtan* without, except]

but and ben *n Scot* a two-roomed cottage consisting of an outer room (**but**) and an inner room (**ben**) [Old English *būtan* outside + *binnan* inside]

butane (**byew**-tane) *n* a colourless gas used in the manufacture of rubber and fuels [from *butyl*]

butch *adj slang* (of a woman or man) markedly or aggressively masculine [from *butcher*]

butcher *n* **1** a person who sells meat **2** a person who kills animals for meat **3** a brutal murderer ▷ *vb* **4** to kill and prepare (animals) for meat **5** to kill (people) at random or brutally **6** to make a mess of; botch [Old French *bouchier*]

butcherbird *n* an Australian magpie that impales its prey on thorns

butchery *n, pl* **-eries 1** senseless slaughter **2** the business of a butcher

butler *n* the head manservant of a household, in charge of the wines, table, etc. [Old French *bouteille* bottle]

butt[1] *n* **1** the thicker or blunt end of something, such as the stock of a rifle **2** the unused end of a cigarette or cigar; stub **3** *chiefly US & Canad slang* the buttocks [Middle English]

butt[2] *n* **1** a person or thing that is the target of ridicule or teasing **2** *shooting & archery* **A** a mound of earth behind the target **B butts** the target range [Old French *but*]

butt[3] *vb* **1** to strike (something or someone) with the head or horns **2** (foll. by *in* or *into*) to intrude, esp. into a conversation; interfere ▷ *n* **3** a blow with the head or horns [Old French *boter*]

butt[4] *n* a large cask for collecting or storing liquids [Late Latin *buttis* cask]

butte (**byewt**) *n US & Canad* an isolated steep flat-topped hill [Old French *bute* mound behind a target]

butter *n* **1** an edible fatty yellow solid made from cream by churning **2** any substance with a butter-like consistency, such as peanut butter ▷ *vb* **3** to put butter on or in (something) ▷ See also **butter up** [Greek *bous* cow + *turos* cheese] **buttery** *adj*

butter bean *n* a large pale flat edible bean

buttercup *n* a small bright yellow flower

butterfingers *n informal* a person who drops things by mistake or fails to catch things

butterflies *pl n informal* a nervous feeling in the stomach

butterfly *n, pl* **-flies 1** an insect with a slender body and brightly coloured wings **2** a swimming stroke in which the arms are plunged forward together in large circular movements **3** a person who never settles with one interest or occupation for long [Old English *buttorflēoge*]

butterfly nut *n* same as **wing nut**

buttermilk *n* the sourish liquid remaining after the butter has been separated from milk

butterscotch *n* a hard brittle toffee made with butter, brown sugar, etc.

butter up *vb* to flatter

buttery *n, pl* **-teries** *Brit* (in some universities) a room in which food and drink are sold to students [Latin *butta* cask]

buttock *n* **1** either of the two large fleshy masses that form the human rump **2** the corresponding part in some mammals [perhaps from Old English *buttuc* round slope]

button *n* **1** a disc or knob of plastic, wood, etc., attached to a garment, which fastens two surfaces together by passing through a buttonhole **2** a small disc that operates a door bell or machine when pressed **3** a small round object, such as a sweet or badge ▷ *vb* **4** to fasten (a garment) with a button or buttons [Old French *boton*]

buttonhole *n* **1** a slit in a garment through which a button is passed to fasten two surfaces together **2** a flower worn pinned to the lapel or in the buttonhole ▷ *vb* **-holing, -holed 3** to detain (a person) in conversation

button mushroom *n* an unripe mushroom

button up *vb* **1** to fasten (a garment) with a button or buttons **2** *informal* to conclude (business) satisfactorily: *we've got it all buttoned up*

buttress *n* **1** a construction, usually of brick or stone, built to support a wall **2** any support or prop ▷ *vb* **3** to support (a wall) with a buttress **4** to support or sustain: *his observations are buttressed by the most recent scholarly research* [Old French *bouter* to thrust]

butty *n, pl* **-ties** *chiefly N English dialect* a sandwich: *a jam butty* [from *buttered (bread)*]

butyl (**byew**-tile) *adj* of or containing any of four isomeric forms of the group C_4H_9–: *butyl rubber* [Latin *butyrum* butter]

buxom *adj* (of a woman) healthily plump, attractive, and full-bosomed [Middle English *buhsum* compliant]

buy *vb* **buying, bought 1** to acquire (something) by paying a sum of money for it; purchase **2** to be capable of purchasing: *money can't buy love* **3** to acquire by any exchange or sacrifice: *the rise in interest rates was just to buy time until the weekend* **4** to bribe (someone) **5** *slang* to accept (something) as true **6** (foll. by *into*) to purchase shares of (a company) ▷ *n* **7** a purchase: *a good buy* ▷ See also **buy in, buy into** *etc.* [Old English *bycgan*]

USAGE The use of *off* after *buy* as in *I bought this off my neighbour* was formerly considered incorrect, but is now acceptable in informal contexts.

buyer *n* **1** a person who buys; customer **2** a person employed to buy merchandise for a shop or factory

buy in *vb* to purchase (goods) in large quantities

buy into *vb* to agree with (an argument or theory)

buy off *vb* to pay (someone) to drop a charge or end opposition

buy-out *n* **1** the purchase of a company, often by its former employees ▷ *vb* **buy out 2** to purchase the ownership of a company or property from (someone)

buy up *vb* **1** to purchase all that is available of (something) **2** to purchase a controlling interest in (a company)

buzz *n* **1** a rapidly vibrating humming sound, such as of a bee **2** a low sound, such as of many voices in conversation **3** *informal* a telephone call **4** *informal* a sense of excitement ▷ *vb* **5** to make a vibrating sound like that of a prolonged *z* **6** (of a place) to be filled with an air of excitement: *the city buzzed with the news* **7** to summon (someone) with a buzzer **8** *informal* to fly an aircraft very low over (people, buildings, or another aircraft) **9 buzz about** *or* **around** to move around quickly and busily [imitative]

buzzard *n* a bird of prey with broad wings and tail and a soaring flight [Latin *buteo* hawk]

buzzer *n* an electronic device that produces a buzzing sound as a signal

buzzkill *or* **buzzkiller** *n informal* someone or something that stops people from enjoying themselves

buzz off *vb Brit & Austral informal* to go away; depart

buzz word *n informal* a word, originally from a particular jargon, which becomes a popular vogue word

by *prep* **1** used to indicate the performer of the action of a passive verb: *seeds eaten by the birds* **2** used to indicate the person responsible for a creative work: *three songs by Britten* **3** via; through: *enter by the back door* **4** used to indicate a means used: *he frightened her by hiding behind the door* **5** beside; next to; near: *a tree by the stream* **6** passing the position of; past: *I drove by the place where she works* **7** not later than; before: *return the books by Tuesday* **8** used to indicate extent: *it is hotter by five degrees* **9** multiplied by: *four by three equals twelve* **10** during the passing of: *by night* **11** placed between measurements of the various dimensions of something: *a plank fourteen inches by seven* ▷ *adv* **12** near: *the house is close by* **13** away; aside: *he put some money by each week* **14** passing a point near something; past: *he drove by* ▷ *n, pl* **byes 15** same as **bye**[1] [Old English *bī*]

by and by *adv* presently or eventually

by and large *adv* in general; on the whole

bye[1] *n* **1** *sport* the status of a player or team who wins a preliminary round by virtue of having no opponent **2** *cricket* a run scored off a ball not struck by the batsman **3 by the bye** incidentally; by the way [variant of *by*]

bye[2] *or* **bye-bye** *interj informal* goodbye

by-election *or* **bye-election** *n* an election held during the life of a parliament to fill a vacant seat

bygone *adj* past; former: *a bygone age*

bygones *pl n* **let bygones be bygones** to agree to forget past quarrels

bylaw *or* **bye-law** *n* a rule made by a local authority [probably Scandinavian]

by-line *n* **1** a line under the title of an article in a newspaper or magazine, giving the author's name **2** same as **touchline**

BYO *or* **BYOG** *n Austral & NZ* an unlicensed restaurant at which diners may bring their own alcoholic drink [*bring your own (grog)*]

bypass *n* **1** a main road built to avoid a city **2** a secondary pipe, channel, or appliance through which the flow of a substance, such as gas or electricity, is redirected **3** a surgical operation in which the blood flow is redirected away from a diseased or blocked part of the heart ▷ *vb* **4** to go around or avoid (a city, obstruction, problem, etc.) **5** to proceed without reference to (regulations or a superior); get round; avoid

b

by-play *n* secondary action in a play, carried on apart while the main action proceeds
by-product *n* **1** a secondary or incidental product of a manufacturing process **2** a side effect
byre *n Brit* a shelter for cows [Old English *bȳre*]
byroad *n* a secondary or side road
bystander *n* a person present but not involved; onlooker; spectator
byte *n computers* a group of bits processed as one unit of data [origin unknown]
byway *n* a secondary or side road, esp. in the country
byword *n* **1** a person or thing regarded as a perfect example of something: *their name is a byword for quality* **2** a common saying; proverb
Byzantine *adj* **1** of Byzantium, an ancient Greek city on the Bosphorus **2** of the Byzantine Empire, the continuation of the Roman Empire in the East **3** of the style of architecture developed in the Byzantine Empire, with massive domes, rounded arches, and mosaics **4** (of attitudes, methods, etc.) inflexible or complicated ▷ *n* **5** an inhabitant of Byzantium

Cc

C 1 centi- 2 *cricket* caught 3 cubic 4 the speed of light in free space

C 1 *music* the first note of a major scale containing no sharps or flats (**C major**) 2 *chem* carbon 3 Celsius 4 centigrade 5 century: C20 6 coulomb 7 the Roman numeral for 100 8 a high-level computer programming language

c. (used preceding a date) about: *c. 1800* [Latin *circa*]

Ca *chem* calcium

CA 1 California 2 Central America 3 Chartered Accountant

ca. (used preceding a date) about: *ca. 1930* [Latin *circa*]

cab *n* 1 a taxi 2 the enclosed driver's compartment of a lorry, bus, or train [from *cabriolet*]

cabal (kab-**bal**) *n* 1 a small group of political plotters 2 a secret plot or conspiracy [French *cabale*]

cabaret (**kab**-a-ray) *n* 1 a floor show of dancing and singing at a nightclub or restaurant 2 a place providing such entertainment [French: tavern]

cabbage *n* 1 a vegetable with a large head of green or reddish-purple leaves 2 *informal, offensive* a person who is unable to move or think, as a result of brain damage [Norman French *caboche* head]

cabbage tree *n NZ* a palm-like tree with a bare trunk and spiky leaves

cabbage white *n* a large white butterfly whose larvae feed on cabbage leaves

cabbie *or* **cabby** *n, pl* **-bies** *informal* a taxi driver

caber *n Scot* a heavy section of trimmed tree trunk tossed in competition at Highland games [Gaelic *cabar* pole]

Cabernet Sauvignon (**kab**-er-nay **so**-veen-yon) *n* a dry red wine produced in the Bordeaux region of France and elsewhere [French]

cabin *n* 1 a room used as living quarters in a ship or boat 2 a small simple dwelling: *a log cabin* 3 the enclosed part of an aircraft in which the passengers or crew sit [Late Latin *capanna* hut]

cabin boy *n* a boy who waits on the officers and passengers of a ship

cabin cruiser *n* a motorboat with a cabin

cabinet *n* a piece of furniture containing shelves, cupboards, or drawers for storage or display: *a filing cabinet; a cocktail cabinet* [Old French *cabine* cabin]

Cabinet *n* a committee of senior government ministers or advisers to a president

cabinet-maker *n* a person who makes fine furniture **cabinet-making** *n*

cabin fever *n chiefly Canad* acute depression resulting from being isolated or sharing cramped quarters

cable *n* 1 a strong thick rope of twisted hemp or wire 2 a bundle of wires covered with plastic or rubber that conducts electricity 3 a telegram sent abroad by submarine cable or telephone line 4 Also called: **cable stitch** a knitted design which resembles a twisted rope 5 short for **cable television** ▷ *vb* **-bling, -bled** 6 to send (someone) a message by cable [Late Latin *capulum* halter]

cable car *n* a vehicle that is pulled up a steep slope by a moving cable

cable television *n* a television service in which the subscriber's television is connected to a central receiver by cable

caboodle *n* **the whole caboodle** *informal* the whole lot [origin unknown]

caboose *n* 1 *US & Canad* a railway car at the rear of a train, used as quarters for the crew 2 *Canad* a mobile building used as a cookhouse or bunkhouse for a work crew [Dutch *cabūse*]

cabriolet (kab-ree-oh-**lay**) *n* a small two-wheeled horse-drawn carriage with a folding hood [French: a little skip; referring to the lightness of movement]

cacao (kak-**kah**-oh) *n* a tropical American tree with seed pods (**cacao beans**) from which cocoa and chocolate are prepared [Mexican Indian *cacauatl* cacao beans]

cachalot *n* the sperm whale [Portuguese *cachalote*]

cache (**kash**) *n* a hidden store of weapons, provisions, or treasure [French *cacher* to hide]

cachet (**kash**-shay) *n* prestige or distinction: *a Mercedes carries a certain cachet* [French]

cachou *n* a lozenge eaten to sweeten the breath [Malay *kāchu*]

cack-handed *adj informal* clumsy: *I open cans in a very cack-handed way* [dialect *cack* excrement]

cackle *vb* **-ling, -led** 1 to laugh shrilly 2 (of a hen) to squawk with shrill broken notes ▷ *n* 3 the sound of cackling [probably imitative] **cackling** *adj*

cacophony (kak-**koff**-on-ee) *n* harsh discordant sound: *a cacophony of barking* [Greek *kakos* bad + *phōnē* sound] **cacophonous** *adj*

cactus *n, pl* **-tuses** *or* **-ti** a thick fleshy desert plant with spines but no leaves [Greek *kaktos* type of thistle]

cad *n old-fashioned, informal* a man who behaves dishonourably [from *caddie*] **caddish** *adj*

cadaver (kad-**dav**-ver) *n* *med* a corpse [Latin]

cadaverous *adj* pale, thin, and haggard

caddie *n* 1 a person who carries a golfer's clubs ▷ *vb* **-dying, -died** 2 to act as a caddie [from *cadet*]

caddis fly *n* an insect whose larva (the **caddis worm**) lives underwater in a protective case of silk, sand, and stones

caddy[1] *n, pl* **-dies** *chiefly Brit* a small container for tea [Malay *kati*]

caddy[2] *n, pl* **-dies**, *vb* **-dies, -dying, -died** same as **caddie**

cadence (**kade**-enss) *n* 1 the rise and fall in the pitch of the voice 2 the close of a musical phrase [Latin *cadere* to fall]

cadenza *n* a complex solo passage in a piece of music [Italian]

cadet *n* a young person training for the armed forces or the police [French]

cadge *vb* **cadging, cadged** *informal* to get (something) from someone by taking advantage of his or her generosity [origin unknown] **cadger** *n*
cadi *n* a judge in a Muslim community [Arabic *qādī* judge]
cadmium *n chem* a bluish-white metallic element found in zinc ores and used in electroplating and alloys. Symbol: **Cd** [Latin *cadmia* zinc ore]
cadre (**kah**-der) *n* a small group of people selected and trained to form the core of a political organization or military unit [Latin *quadrum* square]
caecum *or US* **cecum** (**seek**-um) *n, pl* **-ca** (-ka) the pouch at the beginning of the large intestine [short for Latin *intestinum caecum* blind intestine]
Caenozoic *adj* same as **Cenozoic**
Caerphilly *n* a creamy white mild-flavoured cheese
Caesar (**seez**-ar) *n* **1** a Roman emperor **2** any emperor or dictator **3** short for **Caesar salad**
Caesarean, Caesarian *or US* **Cesarean** (siz-**zair**-ee-an) *n* short for **Caesarean section**
Caesarean section *n* surgical incision into the womb in order to deliver a baby [from the belief that Julius Caesar was delivered in this way]
Caesar salad *n* a salad of lettuce, cheese, and croutons with a dressing of olive oil, garlic, and lemon juice [after *Caesar* Cardini, its inventor]
caesium *or US* **cesium** *n chem* a silvery-white metallic element used in photocells. Symbol: **Cs** [Latin *caesius* bluish-grey]
caesura (siz-**your**-ra) *n, pl* **-ras** *or* **-rae** (-ree) a pause in a line of verse [Latin: a cutting]
café *n* **1** a small or inexpensive restaurant that serves drinks and snacks or light meals **2** *S African* a corner shop [French]
cafeteria *n* a self-service restaurant [American Spanish: coffee shop]
caff *n slang* a café
caffeine *n* a stimulant found in tea, coffee, and cocoa [German *Kaffee* coffee]
caftan *n* same as **kaftan**
cage *n* **1** an enclosure made of bars or wires, for keeping birds or animals in **2** the enclosed platform of a lift in a mine ▷ *vb* **caging, caged** **3** to confine in a cage [Latin *cavea* enclosure] **caged** *adj*
cagey *adj* **cagier, cagiest** *informal* reluctant to go into details; wary: *he is cagey about what he paid for the business* [origin unknown] **cagily** *adv*
cagoule (kag-**gool**) *n Brit* a lightweight hooded waterproof jacket [French]
cahoots *pl n* **in cahoots** *informal* conspiring together: *the loan sharks were in cahoots with the home-improvement companies* [origin unknown]
caiman *n, pl* **-mans** same as **cayman**
cairn *n* a mound of stones erected as a memorial or marker [Gaelic *carn*]
cairngorm *n* a smoky yellow or brown quartz gemstone [*Cairn Gorm* (blue cairn), mountain in Scotland]
caisson (**kayss**-on) *n* a watertight chamber used to carry out construction work under water [French]
cajole *vb* **-joling, -joled** to persuade by flattery; coax: *he allowed himself to be cajoled into staying on* [French *cajoler*] **cajolery** *n*
Cajun *n* **1** a native of Louisiana descended from 18th-century Acadian immigrants **2** the dialect of French spoken by such people **3** the music of this ethnic group ▷ *adj* **4** denoting or relating to such people, their language, or their music [from Acadian]
cake *n* **1** a sweet food baked from a mixture of flour, sugar, eggs, etc. **2** a flat compact mass of something: *a cake of soap* **3 have one's cake and eat it** to enjoy both of two incompatible alternatives **4 piece of cake** *informal* something that is easy to do **5 sell like hot cakes** *informal* to be sold very quickly: *commercial novels sell like hot cakes* ▷ *vb* **caking, caked** **6** to form into a hardened mass or crust: *her hair was caked with grease and dust* [Old Norse *kaka*]
cakewalk *n informal* a task that is easy to accomplish [originally the name of a dance for which a *cake* was awarded as a prize]
cal. calorie (small)
Cal. **1** Calorie (large) **2** California
calabash *n* **1** a large round gourd that grows on a tropical American tree **2** a bowl made from the dried hollow shell of a calabash [obsolete French *calabasse*]
calabrese (kal-lab-**bray**-zee) *n* a kind of green sprouting broccoli [Italian: from *Calabria* (region of SW Italy)]
calamari *n* squid cooked for eating, esp cut into rings and fried in batter [from Italian, plural of *calamaro* squid]
calamine *n* a pink powder consisting chiefly of zinc oxide, used to make soothing skin lotions and ointments [Medieval Latin *calamina*]
calamitous *adj* resulting in or from disaster: *the country's calamitous economic decline*
calamity *n, pl* **-ties** a disaster or misfortune [Latin *calamitas*]
calcareous (kal-**care**-ee-uss) *adj* of or containing calcium carbonate [Latin *calx* lime]
calciferol *n* a substance found in fish oils and used in the treatment of rickets. Also called: **vitamin D_2** [*calcif(erous + ergost)erol*, a substance in plants that is a source of vitamin D]
calciferous *adj* producing salts of calcium, esp. calcium carbonate
calcify *vb* **-fies, -fying, -fied** to harden by the depositing of calcium salts [Latin *calx* lime] **calcification** *n*
calcine *vb* **-cining, -cined** to oxidize (a substance) by heating [Medieval Latin *calcinare* to heat] **calcination** *n*
calcite *n* a colourless or white form of calcium carbonate
calcium *n chem* a soft silvery-white metallic element found in bones, teeth, limestone, and chalk. Symbol: **Ca** [Latin *calx* lime]
calcium carbonate *n* a white crystalline salt found in limestone, chalk, and pearl, used to make cement
calcium hydroxide *n* a white crystalline alkali used to make mortar and soften water
calcium oxide *n* same as **quicklime**

calculable *adj* able to be computed or estimated
calculate *vb* **-lating, -lated 1** to solve or find out by a mathematical procedure or by reasoning **2** to aim to have a particular effect: *this ad campaign is calculated to offend* [Latin *calculare*, from *calculus* pebble used as a counter]
calculated *adj* **1** undertaken after considering the likelihood of success: *a calculated gamble* **2** carefully planned: *a calculated and callous murder*
calculating *adj* selfishly scheming
calculation *n* **1** the act or result of calculating **2** selfish scheming: *there was an element of calculation in her insistence on arriving after dark*
calculator *n* a small electronic device for doing mathematical calculations
calculus *n* **1** the branch of mathematics dealing with infinitesimal changes to a variable number or quantity **2** *pl* **-li** *pathol* same as **stone** (sense 7) [Latin: pebble]
Caledonian *adj* Scottish [from *Caledonia*, the Roman name for Scotland]
calendar *n* **1** a chart showing a year divided up into months, weeks, and days **2** a system for determining the beginning, length, and divisions of years: *the Jewish calendar* **3** a schedule of events or appointments: *concerts were an important part of the social calendar of the Venetian nobility* [Latin *kalendae* the calends]
calender *n* **1** a machine in which paper or cloth is smoothed by passing it between rollers ▷ *vb* **2** to smooth in such a machine [French *calandre*]
calends *or* **kalends** *pl n* (in the ancient Roman calendar) the first day of each month [Latin *kalendae*]
calendula *n* a plant with orange-and-yellow rayed flowers [Medieval Latin]
calf[1] *n, pl* **calves 1** a young cow, bull, elephant, whale, or seal **2** same as **calfskin** [Old English *cealf*]
calf[2] *n, pl* **calves** the back of the leg between the ankle and the knee [Old Norse *kālfi*]
calf love *n* adolescent infatuation
calfskin *n* fine leather made from the skin of a calf
calibrate *vb* **-brating, -brated** to mark the scale or check the accuracy of (a measuring instrument) **calibration** *n*
calibre *or US* **caliber** (**kal**-lib-ber) *n* **1** a person's ability or worth: *a poet of Wordsworth's calibre* **2** the diameter of the bore of a gun or of a shell or bullet [Arabic *qālib* shoemaker's last, mould]
calico *n* a white or unbleached cotton fabric [*Calicut*, town in India]
californium *n chem* a radioactive metallic element produced artificially. Symbol: **Cf** [after the University of *California*, where it was discovered]
caliper *n US* same as **calliper**
caliph *n Islam* the title of the successors of Mohammed as rulers of the Islamic world [Arabic *khalīfa* successor]
caliphate *n* the office, jurisdiction, or reign of a caliph
calisthenics *n* same as **callisthenics**
call *vb* **1** to name: *a town called Eyemouth* **2** to describe (someone or something) as being: *they called him a Hitler* **3** to speak loudly so as to attract attention **4** to telephone: *he left a message for Lynch to call him* **5** to summon: *a doctor must be called immediately* **6** to pay someone a visit: *the social worker called and she didn't answer the door* **7** to arrange: *the meeting was called for the lunch hour* **8 call someone's bluff** See **bluff**[1] (sense 3) ▷ *n* **9** a cry or shout **10** the cry made by a bird or animal **11** a communication by telephone **12** a short visit: *I paid a call on an old friend* **13** a summons or invitation: *the police and fire brigade continued to respond to calls* **14** need, demand, or desire: *a call for economic sanctions* **15** allure or fascination: *the call of the open road* **16 on call** available when summoned: *there's a doctor on call in town* ▷ See also **call for, call in** *etc.* [Old English *ceallian*] **caller** *n*
call box *n* a soundproof enclosure for a public telephone
call centre *n Brit, Austral & NZ* an office where staff carry out an organization's telephone transactions
call for *vb* **1** to require: *appendicitis calls for removal of the appendix* **2** to come and fetch
call girl *n* a prostitute with whom appointments are made by telephone
calligraphy *n* beautiful handwriting [Greek *kallos* beauty + -GRAPHY] **calligrapher** *n* **calligraphic** *adj*
call in *vb* **1** to summon to one's assistance: *she called in a contractor to make the necessary repairs* **2** to pay a brief visit **3** to demand payment of (a loan): *if the share price continues to drop, some banks may call in their loans*
calling *n* **1** a strong urge to follow a particular profession or occupation, esp. a caring one **2** a profession or occupation, esp. a caring one
Calliope *n Greek myth* the Muse of epic poetry
calliper *or US* **caliper** *n* **1** a metal splint for supporting the leg **2** a measuring instrument consisting of two steel legs hinged together [variant of *calibre*]
callisthenics *or* **calisthenics** *n* light exercises designed to promote general fitness [Greek *kalli-* beautiful + *sthenos* strength] **callisthenic** *or* **calisthenic** *adj*
call off *vb* **1** to cancel or abandon: *the strike has now been called off* **2** to order (a dog or a person) to stop attacking someone
call on *or* **call upon** *vb* to make an appeal or request to: *church leaders called on political leaders to resume the discussions*
callous *adj* showing no concern for other people's feelings [Latin *callosus*] **callously** *adv* **callousness** *n*
calloused *adj* covered in calluses
call out *vb* **1** to shout loudly **2** to summon to one's assistance: *the army and air force have been called out to help drop food packets* **3** to order (workers) to strike
callow *adj* young and inexperienced: *a callow youth* [Old English *calu*]
call up *vb* **1** to summon for active military service **2** to cause one to remember ▷ *n* **call-up 3** a general order to report for military service
callus *n, pl* **-luses** an area of hard or thickened skin on the hand or foot [Latin *callum* hardened skin]

calm *adj* **1** not showing or not feeling agitation or excitement **2** not ruffled by the wind: *a flat calm sea* **3** (of weather) windless ▷ *n* **4** a peaceful state ▷ *vb* **5** (often foll. by *down*) to make or become calm [Late Latin *cauma* heat, hence a rest during the heat of the day] **calmly** *adv* **calmness** *n*

Calor Gas *n trademark Brit* butane gas liquefied under pressure in portable containers for domestic use

caloric (kal-or-ik) *adj* of heat or calories

calorie *n* **1** a unit of measure for the energy value of food **2** Also: **small calorie** the quantity of heat required to raise the temperature of 1 gram of water by 1°C [Latin *calor* heat]

Calorie *n* **1** Also: **large calorie** a unit of heat, equal to one thousand calories **2** the amount of a food capable of producing one calorie of energy

calorific *adj* of calories or heat

calumniate *vb* **-ating, -ated** to make false or malicious statements about (someone)

calumny *n, pl* **-nies** a false or malicious statement; slander [Latin *calumnia* slander]

Calvary *n Christianity* the place just outside the walls of Jerusalem where Jesus Christ was crucified [Latin *calvaria* skull]

calve *vb* **calving, calved** to give birth to a calf

calves *n* the plural of **calf**[1]

Calvinism *n* the theological system of Calvin, the 16th-century French theologian, stressing predestination and salvation solely by God's grace **Calvinist** *n, adj* **Calvinistic** *adj*

calypso *n, pl* **-sos** a West Indian song with improvised topical lyrics [probably from *Calypso*, sea nymph in Greek mythology]

calyx (kale-ix) *n, pl* **calyxes** *or* **calyces** (kal-iss-seez) the outer leaves that protect the developing bud of a flower [Latin: shell, husk]

calzone (kal-zone-ee) *n* a folded pizza filled with cheese, tomatoes, etc.

cam *n* a part of an engine that converts a circular motion into a to-and-fro motion [Dutch *kam* comb]

camaraderie *n* familiarity and trust between friends [French]

camber *n* a slight upward curve to the centre of a road surface [Latin *camurus* curved]

Cambodian *adj* **1** of Cambodia ▷ *n* **2** a person from Cambodia

Cambrian *adj geol* of the period of geological time about 600 million years ago

cambric *n* a fine white linen fabric [Flemish *Kamerijk* Cambrai]

Cambs Cambridgeshire

camcorder *n* a combined portable video camera and recorder

came *vb* the past tense of **come**

camel *n* either of two humped mammals, the dromedary and Bactrian camel, that can survive long periods without food or water in desert regions [Greek *kamēlos*]

camellia (kam-meal-ya) *n* an ornamental shrub with glossy leaves and white, pink, or red flowers [after G. J. *Kamel*, Jesuit missionary]

camel's hair *or* **camelhair** *n* soft cloth, usually tan in colour, which is made from camel's hair and is used to make coats

Camembert (kam-mem-bare) *n* a soft creamy cheese [*Camembert*, village in Normandy]

cameo *n, pl* **cameos** **1** a brooch or ring with a profile head carved in relief **2** a small but important part in a film or play played by a well-known actor or actress [Italian *cammeo*]

camera *n* **1** a piece of equipment used for taking photographs, video, or film **2** **in camera** in private [Greek *kamara* vault]

cameraman *n, pl* **-men** a person who operates a camera for television or cinema

camera obscura *n* a darkened room with an opening through which images of outside objects are projected onto a flat surface [New Latin]

camera phone *n* a mobile phone incorporating a digital camera

camiknickers *pl n Brit* a woman's undergarment consisting of knickers attached to a camisole top

camisole *n* a woman's bodice-like garment with shoulder straps [French]

camomile *or* **chamomile** (kam-mo-mile) *n* a sweet-smelling plant used to make herbal tea [Greek *khamaimēlon* earth-apple (referring to the scent of the flowers)]

camouflage (kam-moo-flahzh) *n* **1** the use of natural surroundings or artificial aids to conceal or disguise something ▷ *vb* **-flaging, -flaged** **2** to conceal by camouflage [French]

camp[1] *n* **1** a place where people stay in tents **2** a collection of huts and other buildings used as temporary lodgings for military troops or for prisoners of war **3** a group that supports a particular doctrine: *the socialist camp* ▷ *vb* **4** to stay in a camp [Latin *campus* field] **camper** *n* **camping** *n*

camp[2] *informal* ▷ *adj* **1** effeminate; affected in mannerisms or dress **2** consciously artificial, vulgar, or mannered ▷ *vb* **3** **camp it up** to behave in a camp manner [origin unknown]

campaign *n* **1** a series of coordinated activities designed to achieve a goal **2** *military* a number of operations aimed at achieving a single objective ▷ *vb* **3** to take part in a campaign: *he paid tribute to all those who'd campaigned for his release* [Latin *campus* field] **campaigner** *n*

campanile (camp-an-neel-lee) *n* a bell tower, usually one not attached to another building [Italian]

campanology *n* the art of ringing bells [Late Latin *campana* bell] **campanologist** *n*

campanula *n* a plant with blue or white bell-shaped flowers [New Latin: a little bell]

camp bed *n* a lightweight folding bed

camp follower *n* **1** a person who supports a particular group or organization without being a member of it **2** a civilian who unofficially provides services to military personnel

camphor *n* a sweet-smelling crystalline substance obtained from the wood of the **camphor tree**, which is used medicinally and in mothballs [Arabic *kāfūr*]

camphorated *adj* impregnated with camphor

campion *n* a red, pink, or white European wild flower [origin unknown]

camp oven *n Austral & NZ* a heavy metal pot or box with a lid, used for baking over an open fire

camp site *n* a place where people can stay in tents

campus *n, pl* **-puses** the grounds and buildings of a university or college [Latin: field]

camshaft *n* a part of an engine consisting of a rod to which cams are attached

can[1] *vb, past tense* **could** **1** be able to: *make sure he can breathe easily* **2** be allowed to: *you can swim in the large pool* [Old English *cunnan*]

USAGE See at **may**[1].

can[2] *n* **1** a metal container, usually sealed, for food or liquids ▷ *vb* **canning, canned** **2** to put (something) into a can [Old English *canne*]

Can. **1** Canada **2** Canadian

Canada Day *n* (in Canada) July 1, a public holiday marking the anniversary of the day in 1867 when Canada became a dominion

Canada goose *n* a greyish-brown North American goose with a black neck and head

Canada jay *n* a grey jay of northern N America, notorious for stealing

Canadian *adj* **1** of Canada ▷ *n* **2** a person from Canada

Canadiana *pl n* objects relating to Canadian history and culture

Canadian football *n* a game like American football played on a grass field between teams of 12 players

Canadianism *n* **1** the Canadian national character or spirit **2** a linguistic feature peculiar to Canada or Canadians

Canadianize *or* **-ise** *vb* **-izing, -ized** *or* **-ising, -ised** to make Canadian

Canadian Shield *n* the wide area of Precambrian rock extending over most of central and E Canada: rich in minerals

Canadien *or fem* **Canadienne** (kan-ad-**ee**-en) *n* a French Canadian [French: Canadian]

canaille (kan-**nye**) *n* the masses or rabble [French, from Italian *canaglia* pack of dogs]

canal *n* **1** an artificial waterway constructed for navigation or irrigation **2** a passage or duct in a person's body: *the alimentary canal* [Latin *canna* reed]

canalize *or* **-lise** *vb* **-lizing, -lized** *or* **-lising, -lised** **1** to give direction to (a feeling or activity) **2** to convert into a canal **canalization** *or* **-lisation** *n*

canapé (**kan**-nap-pay) *n* a small piece of bread or toast spread with a savoury topping [French: sofa]

canard *n* a false report [French: a duck]

canary *n, pl* **-naries** a small yellow songbird often kept as a pet

canasta *n* a card game like rummy, played with two packs of cards [Spanish: basket (because two packs, or a basketful, of cards are required)]

cancan *n* a lively high-kicking dance performed by a female group [French]

cancel *vb* **-celling, -celled** *or US* **-celing, -celed** **1** to stop (something that has been arranged) from taking place **2** to mark (a cheque or stamp) with an official stamp to prevent further use **3** **cancel out** to make ineffective by having the opposite effect: *economic vulnerability cancels out any possible political gain* [Late Latin *cancellare* to strike out, make like a lattice] **cancellation** *n*

cancer *n* **1** a serious disease resulting from a malignant growth or tumour, caused by abnormal and uncontrolled cell division **2** a malignant growth or tumour **3** an evil influence that spreads dangerously: *their country would remain a cancer of instability* [Latin: crab, creeping tumour] **cancerous** *adj*

Cancer *n* **1** *astrol* the fourth sign of the zodiac; the Crab **2** **tropic of Cancer** See **tropic** (sense 1) [Latin]

C

candela (kan-**dee**-la) *n* the SI unit of luminous intensity (the amount of light a source gives off in a given direction) [Latin: candle]

candelabrum *or* **candelabra** *n, pl* **-bra, -brums** *or* **-bras** a large branched holder for candles or overhead lights [Latin *candela* candle]

candid *adj* honest and straightforward in speech or behaviour [Latin *candere* to be white] **candidly** *adv*

candidate *n* **1** a person seeking a job or position **2** a person taking an examination **3** a person or thing regarded as suitable or likely for a particular fate or position: *someone who smokes, drinks, or eats too much is a candidate for heart disease* [Latin *candidatus* clothed in white] **candidacy** *or* **candidature** *n*

candied *adj* coated with or cooked in sugar: *candied peel*

candle *n* **1** a stick or block of wax or tallow surrounding a wick, which is burned to produce light **2** **burn the candle at both ends** to exhaust oneself by doing too much [Latin *candela*]

candlelight *n* the light from a candle or candles **candlelit** *adj*

Candlemas *n* *Christianity* February 2, the Feast of the Purification of the Virgin Mary

candlepower *n* the luminous intensity of a source of light: now expressed in candelas

candlestick *or* **candleholder** *n* a holder for a candle

candlewick *n* cotton with a tufted pattern, used to make bedspreads and dressing gowns

candour *or US* **candor** *n* honesty and straightforwardness of speech or behaviour [Latin *candor*]

candy *n, pl* **-dies** *chiefly US & Canad* a sweet or sweets [Arabic *qand* cane sugar]

candyfloss *n Brit* a light fluffy mass of spun sugar, held on a stick

candy-striped *adj* having narrow coloured stripes on a white background

candytuft *n* a garden plant with clusters of white, pink, or purple flowers

cane *n* **1** the long flexible stems of the bamboo or any similar plant **2** strips of such stems, woven to make wickerwork **3** a bamboo stem tied to a garden plant to support it **4** a flexible rod used to beat someone **5** a slender walking stick ▷ *vb* **caning, caned** **6** to beat with a cane [Greek *kanna*]

cane sugar *n* the sugar that is obtained from sugar cane

cane toad *n* a large toad used to control insects and other pests of sugar cane plantations

canine (**kay**-nine) *adj* **1** of or like a dog ▷ *n* **2** a sharp-pointed tooth between the incisors and the molars [Latin *canis* dog]

canister *n* a metal container for dry food [Latin *canistrum* basket woven from reeds]
canker *n* **1** an ulceration or ulcerous disease **2** something evil that spreads and corrupts [Latin *cancer* crab, creeping tumour]
cannabis *n* a drug obtained from the dried leaves and flowers of the hemp plant [Greek *kannabis*]
canned *adj* **1** preserved in a can **2** *informal* recorded in advance: *canned carols*

C

cannelloni *or* **canneloni** *pl n* tubular pieces of pasta filled with meat or cheese [Italian]
cannery *n, pl* **-neries** a place where foods are canned
cannibal *n* **1** a person who eats human flesh **2** an animal that eats the flesh of other animals of its kind [Spanish *Canibales* natives of Cuba and Haiti] **cannibalism** *n*
cannibalize *or* **-ise** *vb* **-izing, -ized** *or* **-ising, -ised** to use parts from (one machine or vehicle) to repair another
canning *n* the process of sealing food in cans to preserve it
cannon *n, pl* **-nons** *or* **-non 1** a large gun consisting of a metal tube mounted on a carriage, formerly used in battles **2** an automatic aircraft gun **3** *billiards* a shot in which the cue ball strikes two balls successively ▷ *vb* **4 cannon into** to collide with [Italian *canna* tube]
cannonade *n* continuous heavy gunfire
cannonball *n* a heavy metal ball fired from a cannon
cannon fodder *n* men regarded as expendable in war
cannot *vb* can not
canny *adj* **-nier, -niest** shrewd or cautious [from *can* (in the sense: to know how)] **cannily** *adv*
canoe *n* a light narrow open boat, propelled by one or more paddles [Carib] **canoeist** *n*
canoeing *n* the sport of rowing or racing in a canoe
canon[1] *n* a priest serving in a cathedral [Late Latin *canonicus* person living under a rule]
canon[2] *n* **1** *Christianity* a Church decree regulating morals or religious practices **2** a general rule or standard: *the Marx-Engels canon* **3** a list of the works of an author that are accepted as authentic: *the Yeats canon* **4** a piece of music in which a melody in one part is taken up in one or more other parts successively [Greek *kanōn* rule]
canonical *adj* **1** conforming with canon law **2** included in a canon of writings
canonical hour *n* *RC Church* one of the seven prayer times appointed for each day
canonicals *pl n* the official clothes worn by clergy when taking services
canonize *or* **-ise** *vb* **-izing, -ized** *or* **-ising, -ised** *RC Church* to declare (a dead person) to be a saint **canonization** *or* **-isation** *n*
canon law *n* the body of laws of a Christian Church
canoodle *vb* **-dling, -dled** *slang* to kiss and cuddle [origin unknown]
canopied *adj* covered with a canopy: *canopied niches*
canopy *n, pl* **-pies 1** an ornamental awning above a bed or throne **2** a rooflike covering over an altar, niche, or door **3** any large or wide covering: *the thick forest canopy* **4** the part of a parachute that opens out **5** the transparent hood of an aircraft cockpit [Greek *kōnōpeion* bed with a mosquito net]
cant[1] *n* **1** insincere talk concerning religion or morals **2** specialized vocabulary of a particular group, such as thieves or lawyers ▷ *vb* **3** to use cant: *canting hypocrites* [probably from Latin *cantare* to sing]
cant[2] *n* **1** a tilted position ▷ *vb* **2** to tilt or overturn: *the engine was canted to one side* [perhaps from Latin *canthus* iron hoop round a wheel]
can't *vb* can not
cantabile (kan-**tah**-bill-lay) *adv* *music* in a singing style, flowingly and melodiously [Italian]
cantaloupe *or* **cantaloup** *n* *Brit* a kind of melon with sweet-tasting orange flesh [*Cantaluppi*, near Rome, where first cultivated in Europe]
cantankerous *adj* quarrelsome or bad-tempered [origin unknown]
cantata (kan-**tah**-ta) *n* a musical setting of a text, consisting of arias, duets, and choruses [Italian]
canteen *n* **1** a restaurant attached to a workplace or school **2** a box containing a set of cutlery [Italian *cantina* wine cellar]
canter *n* **1** a gait of horses that is faster than a trot but slower than a gallop ▷ *vb* **2** (of a horse) to move at a canter [short for *Canterbury trot*, the pace at which pilgrims rode to Canterbury]
canticle *n* a short hymn with words from the Bible [Latin *canticulum*]
cantilever *n* a beam or girder fixed at one end only [origin unknown]
cantilever bridge *n* a bridge made of two cantilevers which meet in the middle
canto (**kan**-toe) *n, pl* **-tos** a main division of a long poem [Italian: song]
canton *n* a political division of a country, such as Switzerland [Old French: corner]
Cantonese *adj* **1** of Canton, a port in SE China ▷ *n* **2** *pl* **-nese** a person from Canton **3** the Chinese dialect of Canton
cantonment (kan-**toon**-ment) *n* a permanent military camp in British India [Old French *canton* corner]
cantor *n* *Judaism* a man employed to lead synagogue services [Latin: singer]
Canuck *n, adj* *US & Canad informal* Canadian [origin unknown]
canvas *n* **1** a heavy cloth of cotton, hemp, or jute, used to make tents and sails and for painting on in oils **2** an oil painting done on canvas **3 under canvas** in a tent: *sleeping under canvas* [Latin *cannabis* hemp]
canvass *vb* **1** to try to persuade (people) to vote for a particular candidate or party in an election **2** to find out the opinions of (people) by conducting a survey ▷ *n* **3** the activity of canvassing [probably from obsolete sense of *canvas* (to toss someone in a canvas sheet, hence, to criticize)] **canvasser** *n* **canvassing** *n*
canyon *n* a deep narrow steep-sided valley [Spanish *cañon*]
canyoning *n* the sport of travelling down a river

situated in a canyon by a variety of means including scrambling, swimming, and abseiling
caoutchouc (cow-chook) *n* same as **rubber**[1] (sense 1) [from indigenous S American word]
cap *n* **1** a soft close-fitting covering for the head **2** *sport* a cap given to someone selected for a national team **3** a small flat lid: *petrol cap* **4** a small amount of explosive enclosed in paper and used in a toy gun **5** a contraceptive device placed over the mouth of the womb **6** an upper financial limit **7 cap in hand** humbly ▷ *vb* **capping, capped 8** to cover or top with something: *a thick cover of snow capped the cars* **9** *sport* to select (a player) for a national team: *Australia's most capped player* **10** to impose an upper level on (a tax): *charge capping* **11** *informal* to outdo or excel: *capping anecdote with anecdote* [Late Latin *cappa* hood]
CAP (in the EU) Common Agricultural Policy
cap. capital
capability *n, pl* **-ties** the ability or skill to do something
capable *adj* **1** having the ability or skill to do something: *a side capable of winning the championship* **2** competent and efficient: *capable high achievers* [Latin *capere* to take] **capably** *adv*
capacious *adj* having a large capacity or area [Latin *capere* to take]
capacitance *n physics* **1** the ability of a capacitor to store electrical charge **2** a measure of this
capacitor *n physics* a device for storing a charge of electricity
capacity *n, pl* **-ties 1** the ability to contain, absorb, or hold something **2** the maximum amount something can contain or absorb: *filled to capacity* **3** the ability to do something: *his capacity to elicit great loyalty* **4** a position or function: *acting in an official capacity* **5** the maximum output of which an industry or factory is capable: *the refinery had a capacity of three hundred thousand barrels a day* **6** *physics* same as **capacitance** ▷ *adj* **7** of the maximum amount or number possible: *a capacity crowd* [Latin *capere* to take]
caparisoned (kap-**par**-riss-sond) *adj* (esp. of a horse) magnificently decorated or dressed [Old Spanish *caparazón* saddlecloth]
cape[1] *n* a short sleeveless cloak [Late Latin *cappa*]
cape[2] *n* a large piece of land that juts out into the sea [Latin *caput* head]
Cape *n* **the Cape 1** the Cape of Good Hope **2** the SW region of South Africa's Cape Province
caper *n* **1** a high-spirited escapade ▷ *vb* **2** to skip about light-heartedly [probably from CAPRIOLE]
capercaillie *or* **capercailzie** (kap-per-**kale**-yee) *n* a large black European woodland grouse [Scottish Gaelic *capull coille* horse of the woods]
capers *pl n* the pickled flower buds of a Mediterranean shrub, used in making sauces [Greek *kapparis* caper plant]
capillarity *n physics* a phenomenon caused by surface tension that results in the surface of a liquid rising or falling in contact with a solid
capillary (kap-**pill**-a-ree) *n, pl* **-laries 1** *anatomy* one of the very fine blood vessels linking the arteries and the veins ▷ *adj* **2** (of a tube) having a fine bore **3** *anatomy* of the capillaries [Latin *capillus* hair]
capital[1] *n* **1** the chief city of a country, where the government meets **2** the total wealth owned or used in business by an individual or group **3** wealth used to produce more wealth by investment **4 make capital out of** to gain advantage from: *to make political capital out of the hostage situation* **5** a capital letter ▷ *adj* **6** *law* involving or punishable by death: *a capital offence* **7** denoting the large letter used as the initial letter in a sentence, personal name, or place name **8** *Brit, Austral & NZ old-fashioned* excellent or first-rate: *a capital dinner* [Latin *caput* head]
capital[2] *n* the top part of a column or pillar [Old French *capitel*, from Latin *caput* head]
capital gain *n* profit from the sale of an asset
capital goods *pl n econ* goods that are themselves utilized in the production of other goods
capitalism *n* an economic system based on the private ownership of industry
capitalist *adj* **1** based on or supporting capitalism: *capitalist countries* ▷ *n* **2** a supporter of capitalism **3** a person who owns a business **capitalistic** *adj*
capitalize *or* **-ise** *vb* **-izing, -ized** *or* **-ising, -ised 1 capitalize on** to take advantage of: *to capitalize on the available opportunities* **2** to write or print (words) in capital letters **3** to convert (debt or earnings) into capital stock **capitalization** *or* **-isation** *n*
capital levy *n* a tax on capital or property as contrasted with a tax on income
capitally *adv old-fashioned* in an excellent manner; admirably
capital punishment *n* the punishment of death for committing a serious crime
capital stock *n* **1** the value of the total shares that a company can issue **2** the total capital existing in an economy at a particular time
capitation *n* a tax of a fixed amount per person [Latin *caput* head]
capitulate *vb* **-lating, -lated** to surrender under agreed conditions [Medieval Latin *capitulare* to draw up under headings] **capitulation** *n*
capo *n, pl* **-pos** a device fitted across the strings of a guitar or similar instrument so as to raise the pitch [Italian *capo tasto* head stop]
capoeira (kap-poo-**eer**-a) *n* a combination of martial art and dance, which originated among African slaves in 19th-century Brazil [from Portuguese]
capon (**kay**-pon) *n* a castrated cock fowl fattened for eating [Latin *capo*]
caponata (kap-a-**nah**-ta) *n* a dish of fried seasoned aubergine and other vegetables, served as an appetizer [Italian]
cappuccino (kap-poo-**cheen**-oh) *n, pl* **-nos** coffee with steamed milk, usually sprinkled with powdered chocolate [Italian]
caprice (kap-**reess**) *n* **1** a sudden change of attitude or behaviour **2** a tendency to have such changes [Italian *capriccio* a shiver, caprice]
capricious *adj* having a tendency to sudden unpredictable changes of attitude or behaviour **capriciously** *adv*
Capricorn *n* **1** *astrol* the tenth sign of the zodiac; the Goat **2 tropic of Capricorn** See **tropic** (sense 1) [Latin *caper* goat + *cornu* horn]

C

capriole *n* **1** an upward but not forward leap made by a horse ▹ *vb* **-oling, -oled 2** to perform a capriole [Latin *capreolus*, *caper* goat]
caps. capital letters
capsicum *n* a kind of pepper used as a vegetable or ground to produce a spice [Latin *capsa* box]
capsize *vb* **-sizing, -sized** (of a boat) to overturn accidentally [origin unknown]
capstan *n* a vertical rotating cylinder round which a ship's rope or cable is wound [Old Provençal *cabestan*]
capstone *n* same as **copestone** (sense 2)
capsule *n* **1** a soluble gelatine case containing a dose of medicine **2** *botany* a plant's seed case that opens when ripe **3** *anatomy* a membrane or sac surrounding an organ or part **4** See **space capsule** ▹ *adj* **5** very concise: *capsule courses* [Latin *capsa* box]
capsulize *or* **-ise** *vb* **-izing, -ized** *or* **-ising, -ised 1** to state (information) in a highly condensed form **2** to enclose in a capsule
Capt. Captain
captain *n* **1** the person in charge of a ship, boat, or civil aircraft **2** a middle-ranking naval officer **3** a junior officer in the army **4** the leader of a team or group ▹ *vb* **5** to be captain of [Latin *caput* head] **captaincy** *n*
captcha *n* a test designed to determine whether a computer user is a person or a machine [from *c*ompletely *a*utomated *p*ublic *T*uring Test to tell *c*omputers and *h*umans *a*part]
caption *n* **1** a title, brief explanation, or comment accompanying a picture or cartoon ▹ *vb* **2** to provide with a caption [Latin *captio* a seizing]
captious *adj* tending to make trivial criticisms [Latin *captio* a seizing]
captivate *vb* **-vating, -vated** to attract and hold the attention of; enchant [Latin *captivus* captive] **captivating** *adj*
captive *n* **1** a person who is kept in confinement ▹ *adj* **2** kept in confinement **3** (of an audience) unable to leave [Latin *captivus*]
captivity *n* the state of being kept in confinement
captor *n* a person who captures a person or animal
capture *vb* **-turing, -tured 1** to take by force **2** to succeed in representing (something elusive) in words, pictures, or music: *today's newspapers capture the mood of the nation* **3** *physics* (of an atomic nucleus) to acquire (an additional particle) ▹ *n* **4** the act of capturing or the state of being captured [Latin *capere* to take]
capuchin (kap-yew-chin) *n* a S American monkey with a cowl of thick hair on the top of its head [Italian *cappuccio* hood]
Capuchin *n* **1** a friar belonging to a branch of the Franciscan Order founded in 1525 ▹ *adj* **2** of this order [Italian *cappuccio* hood]
capybara *n* the largest living rodent, found in S America
car *n* **1** a motorized road vehicle designed to carry a small number of people **2** the passenger compartment of a cable car, airship, lift, or balloon **3** *US & Canad* a railway carriage [Latin *carra*, *carrum* two-wheeled wagon]
caracal *n* a lynx with reddish fur, which inhabits deserts of N Africa and S Asia [Turkish *kara kūlāk* black ear]
carafe (kar-raff) *n* a wide-mouthed bottle for water or wine [Arabic *gharrāfah* vessel]
carambola *n* a yellow edible star-shaped fruit that grows on a Brazilian tree [Spanish]
caramel *n* **1** a chewy sweet made from sugar and milk **2** burnt sugar, used for colouring and flavouring food [French]
caramelize *or* **-ise** *vb* **-izing, -ized** *or* **-ising, -ised** to turn into caramel
carapace *n* the thick hard upper shell of tortoises and crustaceans [Spanish *carapacho*]
carat *n* **1** a unit of weight of precious stones, equal to 0.20 grams **2** a measure of the purity of gold in an alloy, expressed as the number of parts of gold in 24 parts of the alloy [Arabic *qīrāt* weight of four grains]
caravan *n* **1** a large enclosed vehicle designed to be pulled by a car or horse and equipped to be lived in **2** (in some Eastern countries) a company of traders or other travellers journeying together [Persian *kārwān*]
caravanning *n* travelling or holidaying in a caravan
caravanserai *n* (in some Eastern countries, esp. formerly) a large inn enclosing a courtyard, providing accommodation for caravans [Persian *kārwānsarāī* caravan inn]
caraway *n* a Eurasian plant with seeds that are used as a spice in cooking [Arabic *karawyā*]
carb *n informal* short for **carbohydrate**
carbide *n chem* a compound of carbon with a metal
carbine *n* a type of light rifle [French *carabine*]
carbohydrate *n* any of a large group of energy-producing compounds, including sugars and starches, that contain carbon, hydrogen, and oxygen
carbolic acid *n* a disinfectant derived from coal tar
carbon *n* **1** a nonmetallic element occurring in three forms, charcoal, graphite, and diamond, and present in all organic compounds. Symbol: **C 2** short for **carbon paper** or **carbon copy** [Latin *carbo* charcoal]
carbonaceous *adj* of, resembling, or containing carbon
carbonate *n* a salt or ester of carbonic acid
carbonated *adj* (of a drink) containing carbon dioxide; fizzy
carbon black *n* powdered carbon produced by partial burning of natural gas or petroleum, used in pigments and ink
carbon capture *n* the capture of carbon dioxide in the atmosphere, intended to prevent climate change
carbon copy *n* **1** a duplicate obtained by using carbon paper **2** *informal* a person or thing that is identical or very similar to another
carbon dating *n* a technique for finding the age of organic materials, such as wood, based on their content of radioactive carbon
carbon dioxide *n* a colourless odourless incombustible gas formed during breathing,

and used in fire extinguishers and in making fizzy drinks
carbon footprint *n* a measure of the amount of carbon dioxide released into the atmosphere through a single endeavour or through the activities of a person, company, etc. over a given period
carbonic *adj* containing carbon
carbonic acid *n* a weak acid formed when carbon dioxide combines with water
carboniferous *adj* yielding coal or carbon
Carboniferous *adj geol* of the period of geological time about 330 million years ago, during which coal seams were formed
carbonize *or* **-ise** *vb* **-izing, -ized** *or* **-ising, -ised** **1** to turn into carbon as a result of partial burning **2** to coat (a substance) with carbon **carbonization** *or* **-isation** *n*
carbon monoxide *n* a colourless odourless poisonous gas formed by the incomplete burning of carbon compounds; part of the gases that come from a vehicle's exhaust
carbon-neutral *adj* not affecting the overall volume of carbon dioxide in the atmosphere
carbon offset *n* a compensatory measure made by an individual or company for carbon emissions, such as tree planting
carbon paper *n* a thin sheet of paper coated on one side with a dark waxy pigment, containing carbon, used to make a duplicate of something as it is typed or written
carbon tax *n* a tax on the emissions caused by the burning of coal, gas, and oil, aimed at reducing the production of greenhouse gases
carbon tetrachloride *n* a colourless nonflammable liquid used as a solvent, cleaning fluid, and insecticide
car boot sale *n* a sale of goods from car boots in a site hired for the occasion
Carborundum *n trademark* an abrasive material consisting of silicon carbide
carboxyl group *or* **carboxyl radical** *n chem* the chemical group –COOH: the functional group in organic acids
carboy *n* a large bottle protected by a basket or box [Persian *qarāba*]
carbuncle *n* a large painful swelling under the skin like a boil [Latin *carbo* coal]
carburettor *or US & Canad* **carburetor** *n* a device in an internal-combustion engine that mixes petrol with air and regulates the intake of the mixture into the engine
carcass *or* **carcase** *n* **1** the dead body of an animal **2** *informal* a person's body: *ask that person to move his carcass* [Old French *carcasse*]
carcinogen *n* a substance that produces cancer [Greek *karkinos* cancer] **carcinogenic** *adj*
carcinoma *n, pl* **-mas** *or* **-mata** a malignant tumour [Greek *karkinos* cancer]
card[1] *n* **1** a piece of stiff paper or thin cardboard used for reference, identification, or sending greetings or messages: *a business card; a Christmas card* **2** one of a set of small pieces of cardboard, marked with figures or symbols, used for playing games or for fortune-telling **3** a small rectangle of stiff plastic used for identification or for making financial transactions: *a library card; a charge card* **4** *old-fashioned, informal* a witty or eccentric person ▷ See also **cards** [Greek *khartēs* leaf of papyrus]
card[2] *n* **1** a machine or tool for combing fibres of cotton or wool to disentangle them before spinning ▷ *vb* **2** to process with such a machine or tool [Latin *carduus* thistle]
cardamom *n* a spice that is obtained from the seeds of a tropical plant [Greek *kardamon* cress + *amōmon* an Indian spice]
cardboard *n* a thin stiff board made from paper pulp
card-carrying *adj* being an official member of an organization: *a card-carrying Conservative*
cardholder *n* a person who owns a credit or debit card
cardiac *adj* of or relating to the heart [Greek *kardia* heart]
cardigan *n* a knitted jacket [after 7th Earl of *Cardigan*]
cardinal *n* **1** any of the high-ranking clergymen of the Roman Catholic Church who elect the pope and act as his chief counsellors ▷ *adj* **2** fundamentally important; principal [Latin *cardo* hinge]
cardinal number *n* a number denoting quantity but not order in a group, for example one, two, or three
cardinal points *pl n* the four main points of the compass: north, south, east, and west
cardinal virtues *pl n* the most important moral qualities, traditionally justice, prudence, temperance, and fortitude
card index *n* an index in which each item is separately listed on systematically arranged cards
cardiogram *n* an electrocardiogram. See **electrocardiograph**
cardiograph *n* an electrocardiograph **cardiographer** *n* **cardiography** *n*
cardiology *n* the branch of medicine dealing with the heart and its diseases **cardiologist** *n*
cardiothoracic *adj* of or relating to the heart or the chest
cardiovascular *adj* of or relating to the heart and the blood vessels
cards *n* **1** any game played with cards, or card games generally **2 lay one's cards on the table** to declare one's intentions openly **3 on the cards** likely to take place: *a military coup was on the cards* **4 play one's cards right** to handle a situation cleverly
cardsharp *or* **cardsharper** *n* a professional card player who cheats
card vote *n Brit & NZ* a vote by delegates in which each delegate's vote counts as a vote by all his or her constituents
care *vb* **caring, cared 1** to be worried or concerned: *he does not care what people think about him* **2** to like (to do something): *anybody care to go out?* **3 care for A** to look after or provide for: *it is still largely women who care for dependent family members* **B** to like or be fond of: *he did not care for his concentration to be disturbed; I don't suppose you could ever care for me seriously* **4 I couldn't care less** I am completely

C

indifferent ▷ *n* **5** careful or serious attention; caution: *treat all raw meat with extreme care to avoid food poisoning* **6** protection or charge: *the children are now in the care of a state orphanage* **7** trouble or worry: *his mind turned towards money cares* **8 care of** (written on envelopes) at the address of **9 in** *or* **into care** *Brit & NZ* (of a child) made the legal responsibility of a local authority or the state by order of a court **10 take care** to be careful **11 take care of** to look after: *women have to take greater care of themselves during pregnancy* [Old English *cearian*]

careen *vb* to tilt over to one side [Latin *carina* keel]

career *n* **1** the series of jobs in a profession or occupation that a person has through his or her life: *a career in child psychology* **2** the part of a person's life spent in a particular occupation or type of work: *a school career punctuated with exams* ▷ *vb* **3** to rush in an uncontrolled way ▷ *adj* **4** having chosen to dedicate his or her life to a particular occupation: *a career soldier* [Latin *carrus* two-wheeled wagon]

careerist *n* a person who seeks to advance his or her career by any means possible **careerism** *n*

carefree *adj* without worry or responsibility

careful *adj* **1** cautious in attitude or action **2** very exact and thorough **carefully** *adv* **carefulness** *n*

careless *adj* **1** done or acting with insufficient attention **2** unconcerned in attitude or action **carelessly** *adv* **carelessness** *n*

carer *n* a person who looks after someone who is ill or old, often a relative: *the group offers support for the carers of those with dementia*

caress *n* **1** a gentle affectionate touch or embrace ▷ *vb* **2** to touch gently and affectionately [Latin *carus* dear]

caret (**kar**-ret) *n* a symbol (‸) indicating a place in written or printed matter where something is to be inserted [Latin: there is missing]

caretaker *n* **1** a person employed to look after a place or thing ▷ *adj* **2** performing the duties of an office temporarily: *a caretaker administration*

careworn *adj* showing signs of stress or worry

cargo *n, pl* **-goes** *or esp US* **-gos** goods carried by a ship, aircraft, or other vehicle [Spanish *cargar* to load]

cargo pants *or* **cargo trousers** *pl n* loose trousers with a large external pocket on the side of each leg

Carib *n* **1** *pl* **-ibs** *or* **-ib** a member of a group of Native American peoples of NE South America and the S West Indies **2** any of the languages of these peoples [Spanish *Caribe*]

Caribbean *adj* of the Caribbean Sea, bounded by Central America, South America, and the West Indies, or the surrounding countries and islands

caribou *n, pl* **-bou** *or* **-bous** a large North American reindeer [from a Native American language]

caricature *n* **1** a drawing or description of a person which exaggerates characteristic features for comic effect **2** a description or explanation of something that is so exaggerated or over-simplified that it is difficult to take seriously: *the classic caricature of the henpecked husband* ▷ *vb* **-turing, -tured 3** to make a caricature of [Italian *caricatura* a distortion]

caries (**care**-reez) *n* tooth decay [Latin: decay]

carillon (kar-**rill**-yon) *n* **1** a set of bells hung in a tower and played either from a keyboard or mechanically **2** a tune played on such bells [French]

caring *adj* **1** feeling or showing care and compassion for other people **2** of or relating to professional social or medical care: *the caring professions*

carjack *vb* to attack (a driver in a car) in order to rob the driver or to steal the car for another crime [CAR + (HI)JACK]

cark *vb* **cark it** *Austral & NZ slang* to die

Carmelite *n* **1** a Christian friar or nun belonging to the order of Our Lady of Carmel ▷ *adj* **2** of this order [after Mount *Carmel*, in Palestine, where the order was founded]

carminative *adj* **1** able to relieve flatulence ▷ *n* **2** a carminative drug [Latin *carminare* to card wool, comb out]

carmine *adj* vivid red [Arabic *qirmiz* kermes]

carnage *n* extensive slaughter of people [Latin *caro* flesh]

carnal *adj* of a sexual or sensual nature: *carnal knowledge* [Latin *caro* flesh] **carnality** *n*

carnation *n* a cultivated plant with clove-scented white, pink, or red flowers [Latin *caro* flesh]

carnelian *n* a reddish-yellow variety of chalcedony, used as a gemstone [Old French *corneline*]

carnet (**kar**-nay) *n* a customs licence permitting motorists to take their cars across certain frontiers [French: notebook]

carnival *n* **1** a festive period with processions, music, and dancing in the street **2** a travelling funfair [Old Italian *carnelevare* a removing of meat (referring to the Lenten fast)]

carnivore (**car**-niv-vore) *n* **1** a meat-eating animal **2** *informal* an aggressively ambitious person [Latin *caro* flesh + *vorare* to consume] **carnivorous** (car-**niv**-or-uss) *adj*

carob *n* the pod of a Mediterranean tree, used as a chocolate substitute [Arabic *al kharrūbah*]

carol *n* **1** a joyful religious song sung at Christmas ▷ *vb* **-olling, -olled** *or US* **-oling, -oled 2** to sing carols **3** to sing joyfully [Old French]

carotene *n* *biochem* any of four orange-red hydrocarbons, found in many plants, converted to vitamin A in the liver [from Latin *carota* carrot]

carotid (kar-**rot**-id) *n* **1** either of the two arteries that supply blood to the head and neck ▷ *adj* **2** of either of these arteries [Greek *karoun* to stupefy; so named because pressure on them produced unconsciousness]

carousal *n* a merry drinking party

carouse *vb* **-rousing, -roused** to have a merry drinking party: *carousing with friends* [German *(trinken) gar aus* (to drink) right out]

carousel (kar-roo-**sell**) *n* **1** a revolving conveyor for luggage at an airport or for slides for a projector **2** *US & Canad* a merry-go-round [Italian *carosello*]

carp[1] *n, pl* **carp** *or* **carps** a large freshwater food fish [Old French *carpe*]

carp[2] *vb* to complain or find fault [Old Norse *karpa* to boast] **carping** *adj, n*

carpaccio (kar-patch-ee-oh) *n* an Italian dish of thin slices of raw meat or fish [Italian]
carpal *n* a wrist bone [Greek *karpos* wrist]
car park *n* an area or building reserved for parking cars
carpel *n* the female reproductive organ of a flowering plant [Greek *karpos* fruit]
carpenter *n* a person who makes or repairs wooden structures [Latin *carpentarius* wagon-maker]
carpentry *n* the skill or work of a carpenter
carpet *n* **1** a heavy fabric for covering floors **2** a covering like a carpet: *a carpet of leaves* **3 on the carpet** *informal* being or about to be reprimanded **4 sweep something under the carpet** to conceal or keep silent about something that one does not want to be discovered ▷ *vb* **-peting, -peted 5** to cover with a carpet or a covering like a carpet [Latin *carpere* to pluck, card]
carpetbag *n* a travelling bag made of carpeting
carpetbagger *n* **1** a politician who seeks office in a place where he or she has no connections **2** *Brit* a person who makes a short-term investment in a mutual savings or life-assurance organization in order to benefit from free shares issued following the organization's conversion to a public limited company
carpeting *n* carpet material or carpets in general
carpet snake *n* a large nonvenomous Australian snake with a carpet-like pattern on its back
car phone *n* a telephone that operates by cellular radio for use in a car
carport *n* a shelter for a car, consisting of a roof supported by posts
carpus *n, pl* **-pi** the set of eight bones of the human wrist [Greek *karpos*]
carrageen *n* an edible red seaweed of North America and N Europe [*Carragheen*, near Waterford, Ireland]
carriage *n* **1** *Brit, Austral & NZ* one of the sections of a train for passengers **2** the way a person holds and moves his or her head and body **3** a four-wheeled horse-drawn passenger vehicle **4** the moving part of a machine, such as a typewriter, that supports and shifts another part **5** the charge made for conveying goods [Old French *cariage*]
carriage clock *n* a style of portable clock, originally used by travellers
carriageway *n* **1** *Brit* the part of a road along which traffic passes in one direction: *the westbound carriageway of the M4* **2** *NZ* the part of a road used by vehicles
carrier *n* **1** a person, vehicle, or organization that carries something: *armoured personnel carriers* **2** a person or animal that, without suffering from a disease, is capable of transmitting it to others **3** short for **aircraft carrier**
carrier bag *n Brit* a large plastic or paper bag for carrying shopping
carrier pigeon *n* a homing pigeon used for carrying messages
carrion *n* dead and rotting flesh [Latin *caro* flesh]
carrion crow *n* a scavenging European crow with a completely black plumage and bill
carrot *n* **1** a long tapering orange root vegetable **2** something offered as an incentive [Greek *karōton*]
carroty *adj* (of hair) reddish-orange
carry *vb* **-ries, -rying, -ried 1** to take from one place to another **2** to have with one habitually, for example in one's pocket or handbag: *to carry a donor card* **3** to transmit or be transmitted: *to carry disease* **4** to have as a factor or result: *the offence carries a maximum penalty of seven years in prison* **5** to be pregnant with: *she is carrying her third child* **6** to hold (one's head or body) in a specified manner: *she walked out, carrying her head high* **7** to secure the adoption of (a bill or motion): *the resolution was carried by fewer than twenty votes* **8** (of a newspaper or television or radio station) to include in the contents: *several papers carried front-page pictures of the Russian president* **9** *maths* to transfer (a number) from one column of figures to the next **10** to travel a certain distance or reach a specified point: *his faint voice carried no farther than the front few rows* **11 carry the can** *informal* to take all the blame for something ▷ See also **carry away, carry forward** *etc.* [Latin *carrum* transport wagon]
carry away *vb* **be** *or* **get carried away** to be engrossed in or fascinated by something to the point of losing self-control: *he could be carried away by his own rhetoric*
carrycot *n* a light portable bed for a baby, with handles and a hood, which usually also serves as the body of a pram
carry forward *vb* to transfer (an amount) to the next column, page, or accounting period
carry off *vb* **1** to lift and take (someone or something) away: *the German striker was carried off after snapping an Achilles tendon* **2** to win: *who will carry off this year's honours is unclear* **3** to handle (a situation) successfully: *he had the presence and social ability to carry off the job* **4** to cause to die: *the circulatory disorder which carried off other members of his family*
carry on *vb* **1** to continue: *we'll carry on exactly where we left off* **2** to do, run, or take part in: *the vast trade carried on in the city* **3** *informal* to cause a fuss: *I don't want to carry on and make a big scene* ▷ *n* **carry-on 4** *informal, chiefly Brit* a fuss
carry out *vb* **1** to follow (an order or instruction) **2** to accomplish (a task): *to carry out repairs*
carry over *vb* to extend from one period or situation into another: *major debts carried over from last year*
carry through *vb* to bring to completion: *these are difficult policies to carry through*
carsick *adj* nauseated from riding in a car
cart *n* **1** an open horse-drawn vehicle, usually with two wheels, used to carry goods or passengers **2** any small vehicle that is pulled or pushed by hand ▷ *vb* **3** to carry, usually with some effort: *men carted bricks and tiles and wooden boards* ▷ See also **cart off** [Old Norse *kartr*]
carte blanche *n* complete authority: *she's got carte blanche to redecorate* [French: blank paper]
cartel *n* an association of competing firms formed in order to fix prices [German *Kartell*]
Cartesian *adj* of René Descartes, 17th-century French philosopher and mathematician, or his works [*Cartesius*, Latin form of Descartes]

Cartesian coordinates *pl n* a set of numbers that determine the location of a point in a plane or in space by its distance from two fixed intersecting lines
carthorse *n* a large heavily built horse kept for pulling carts or for farm work
Carthusian *n* **1** a Christian monk or nun belonging to a strict monastic order founded in 1084 ▷ *adj* **2** of this order [Latin *Carthusia* Chartreuse, near Grenoble]
cartilage (**kar**-till-ij) *n* a strong flexible tissue forming part of the skeleton [Latin *cartilago*] **cartilaginous** *adj*
cart off *vb* to take (someone) somewhere forcefully: *we had been carted off to the security police building*
cartography *n* the art of making maps or charts [French *carte* map, chart] **cartographer** *n* **cartographic** *adj*
carton *n* **1** a cardboard box or container **2** a container of waxed paper in which drinks are sold [Italian *carta* card]
cartoon *n* **1** a humorous or satirical drawing in a newspaper or magazine **2** same as **comic strip** **3** same as **animated cartoon** [Italian *cartone* pasteboard] **cartoonist** *n*
cartouche (kah-**toosh**) *n* **1** an ornamental tablet or panel in the form of a scroll **2** (in ancient Egypt) an oblong or oval figure containing royal or divine names [French: scroll, cartridge]
cartridge *n* **1** a metal casing containing an explosive charge and bullet for a gun **2** the part of the pick-up of a record player that converts the movements of the stylus into electrical signals **3** a sealed container of film or tape, or ink for a printer or pen [from French *cartouche*]
cartridge belt *n* a belt with loops or pockets for holding cartridges
cartridge clip *n* a metallic container holding cartridges for an automatic gun
cartridge paper *n* a type of heavy rough drawing paper
cartwheel *n* **1** a sideways somersault supported by the hands with legs outstretched **2** the large spoked wheel of a cart
carve *vb* **carving, carved 1** to cut in order to form something: *carving wood* **2** to form (something) by cutting: *the statue which was carved by Michelangelo* **3** to slice (cooked meat) ▷ See also **carve out, carve up** [Old English *ceorfan*] **carver** *n*
carve out *vb informal* to make or create: *to carve out a political career*
carvery *n, pl* **-veries** a restaurant where customers pay a set price for unrestricted helpings of carved meat and other food
carve up *vb* **1** to divide or share out: *in 1795, Poland was carved up between three empires* ▷ *n* **carve-up** **2** the division or sharing out of something: *a territorial carve-up*
carving *n* a figure or design produced by carving stone or wood
carving knife *n* a long-bladed knife for carving cooked meat
carwash *n* a place fitted with equipment for automatically washing cars
caryatid (kar-ree-**at**-id) *n* a supporting column in the shape of a female figure [Greek *Karuatides* priestesses of Artemis at *Karuai* (Caryae), in Laconia]
Casanova *n* a promiscuous man [after Giovanni *Casanova*, Italian adventurer]
casbah *n* the citadel of a North African city [Arabic *kasba* citadel]
cascade *n* **1** a waterfall or series of waterfalls over rocks **2** something flowing or falling like a waterfall: *a cascade of luxuriant hair* ▷ *vb* **-cading, -caded 3** to flow or fall in a cascade: *rays of sunshine cascaded down* [Italian *cascare* to fall]
cascading style sheet *n computers* a file recording style details, such as fonts, colours, etc., that ensures style is consistent over all the pages of a website
cascara *n* the bark of a N American shrub, used as a laxative [Spanish: bark]
case[1] *n* **1** a single instance or example of something: *cases of teenage pregnancies* **2** a matter for discussion: *the case before the Ethics Committee* **3** a specific condition or state of affairs: *a sudden-death play-off in the case of a draw* **4** a set of arguments supporting an action or cause: *I put my case before them* **5** a person or problem dealt with by a doctor, social worker, or solicitor **6 A** an action or lawsuit: *a rape case* **B** the evidence offered in court to support a claim: *he will try to show that the case against his client is largely circumstantial* **7** *grammar* a form of a noun, pronoun, or adjective showing its relation to other words in the sentence: *the accusative case* **8** *informal* an amusingly eccentric person **9 in any case** no matter what **10 in case** so as to allow for the possibility that: *the President has ordered a medical team to stand by in case hostages are released* **11 in case of** in the event of: *in case of a future conflict* [Old English *casus* (grammatical) case, associated with Old French *cas* a happening; both from Latin *cadere* to fall]
case[2] *n* **1** a container, such as a box or chest **2** a suitcase **3** a protective outer covering ▷ *vb* **casing, cased 4** *slang* to inspect carefully (a place one plans to rob) [Latin *capsa* box]
case-hardened *adj* having been made callous by experience: *a case-hardened senior policewoman*
case history *n* a record of a person's background or medical history
casein *n* a protein found in milk, which forms the basis of cheese [Latin *caseus* cheese]
case law *n* law established by following judicial decisions made in earlier cases
caseload *n* the number of cases that someone like a doctor or social worker deals with at any one time
casement *n* a window that is hinged on one side [probably from Old French *encassement* frame]
case-sensitive *adj* distinguishing between upper-case and lower-case letters: *your password is case-sensitive*
case study *n* an analysis of a group or person in order to make generalizations about a larger group or society as a whole
casework *n* social work based on close study of the personal histories and circumstances of individuals and families **caseworker** *n*
cash *n* **1** money in the form of banknotes and coins **2** *informal* money: *strapped for cash* ▷ *adj*

3 of, for, or paid in cash: *cash hand-outs* ▷ *vb* **4** to obtain or pay banknotes or coins for (a cheque or postal order) ▷ See also **cash in on** [Old Italian *cassa* money box] **cashless** *adj*
cash-and-carry *adj* operating on a basis of cash payment for goods that are taken away by the purchaser: *the cash-and-carry wholesalers*
cashback *n* **1** a discount offered in return for immediate payment **2** a service by which a customer in a shop can draw out cash on a debit card
cash-book *n accounting* a journal in which all money transactions are recorded
cash card *n* a card issued by a bank or other financial institution which can be inserted into a cash dispenser in order to obtain money
cash crop *n* a crop produced for sale rather than for subsistence
cash desk *n* a counter or till in a shop where purchases are paid for
cash discount *n* a discount granted to a purchaser who pays within a specified period
cash dispenser *n* a computerized device which supplies cash when a special card is inserted and the user's code number keyed in
cashew *n* an edible kidney-shaped nut [indigenous S American word *acajú*]
cash flow *n* the movement of money into and out of a business
cashier[1] *n* a person responsible for handling cash in a bank, shop, or other business [French *casse* money chest]
cashier[2] *vb* to dismiss with dishonour from the armed forces [Latin *quassare* to QUASH]
cash in on *vb informal* to gain profit or advantage from: *trying to cash in on the dispute*
cashmere *n* a very fine soft wool obtained from goats [from *Kashmir*, in SW central Asia]
cash on delivery *n* a system involving cash payment to the carrier on delivery of merchandise. Abbrev: **COD**
cashpoint *n Brit* same as **cash dispenser**
cash register *n* a till that has a mechanism for displaying and adding the prices of the goods sold
casing *n* a protective case or covering
casino *n, pl* **-nos** a public building or room where gambling games are played [Italian]
cask *n* **1** a strong barrel used to hold alcoholic drink **2** *Austral* a cubic carton containing wine, with a tap for dispensing [Spanish *casco* helmet]
casket *n* **1** a small box for valuables **2** *US* a coffin [probably from Old French *cassette* little box]
Cassandra *n* someone whose prophecies of doom are unheeded [Trojan prophetess in Greek mythology]
cassava *n* a starch obtained from the root of a tropical American plant, used to make tapioca [West Indian *caçábi*]
casserole *n* **1** a covered dish in which food is cooked slowly, usually in an oven, and served **2** a dish cooked and served in this way: *beef casserole* ▷ *vb* **-roling, -roled 3** to cook in a casserole [French]
cassette *n* a plastic case containing a reel of film or magnetic tape [French: little box]
cassia *n* **1** a tropical plant whose pods yield a mild laxative **2 cassia bark** a cinnamon-like spice obtained from the bark of a tropical Asian tree [Greek *kasia*]
cassock *n* an ankle-length garment, usually black, worn by some Christian priests [Italian *casacca* a long coat]
cassowary *n, pl* **-waries** a large flightless bird of Australia and New Guinea [Malay *kĕsuari*]
cast *n* **1** the actors in a play collectively **2 A** an object made of material that has been shaped, while molten, by a mould **B** the mould used to shape such an object **3** *surgery* a rigid casing made of plaster of Paris for immobilizing broken bones while they heal **4** a sort, kind, or style: *people of an academic cast of mind* **5** a slight squint in the eye ▷ *vb* **casting, cast 6** to select (an actor) to play a part in a play or film **7** to give or deposit (a vote) **8** to express (doubts or aspersions) **9** to cause to appear: *a shadow cast by the grandstand; the gloom cast by the recession* **10 A** to shape (molten material) by pouring it into a mould **B** to make (an object) by such a process **11** to throw (a fishing line) into the water **12** to throw with force: *cast into a bonfire* **13** to direct (a glance): *he cast his eye over the horse-chestnut trees* **14** to roll or throw (a dice) **15 cast aside** to abandon or reject: *cast aside by her lover* **16 cast a spell A** to perform magic **B** to have an irresistible influence ▷ See also **cast around, cast back** *etc.* [Old Norse *kasta*]
castanets *pl n* a musical instrument, used by Spanish dancers, consisting of curved pieces of hollow wood, held between the fingers and thumb and clicked together [Spanish *castañeta*, from *castaña* chestnut]
cast around *or* **cast about** *vb* to make a mental or visual search: *he cast around for a job*
castaway *n* a person who has been shipwrecked
cast back *vb* to turn (the mind) to the past
cast down *vb* to make (a person) feel discouraged or dejected
caste *n* **1** any of the four major hereditary classes into which Hindu society is divided **2** social rank [Latin *castus* pure, not polluted]
castellated *adj* having turrets and battlements, like a castle [Medieval Latin *castellare* to fortify as a castle]
caster *n* same as **castor**
caster sugar *n* finely ground white sugar
castigate *vb* **-gating, -gated** to find fault with or reprimand (a person) harshly [Latin *castigare* to correct] **castigation** *n*
casting *n* an object that has been cast in metal from a mould
casting vote *n* the deciding vote used by the chairperson of a meeting when an equal number of votes are cast on each side
cast iron *n* **1** iron containing so much carbon that it is brittle and must be cast into shape rather than wrought ▷ *adj* **cast-iron 2** made of cast iron **3** definite or unchallengeable: *cast-iron guarantees*
castle *n* **1** a large fortified building or set of buildings, often built as a residence for a ruler or nobleman in medieval Europe **2** same as **rook**[2] [Latin: castellum]

castle in the air *or* **in Spain** *n* a hope or desire unlikely to be realized

cast-off *adj* **1** discarded because no longer wanted or needed: *cast-off clothing* ▷ *n* **2** a person or thing that has been discarded because no longer wanted or needed ▷ *vb* **cast off 3** to discard (something no longer wanted or needed) **4** to untie a ship from a dock **5** to knot and remove (a row of stitches, esp. the final row) from the needle in knitting

C

cast on *vb* to make (a row of stitches) on the needle in knitting

castor *n* a small swivelling wheel fixed to a piece of furniture to enable it to be moved easily in any direction

castor oil *n* an oil obtained from the seeds of an Indian plant, used as a lubricant and purgative

castrate *vb* **-trating, -trated 1** to remove the testicles of **2** to deprive of vigour or masculinity [Latin *castrare*] **castration** *n*

castrato *n, pl* **-ti** *or* **-tos** (in 17th- and 18th-century opera) a male singer whose testicles were removed before puberty, allowing the retention of a soprano or alto voice [Italian]

casual *adj* **1** being or seeming careless or nonchalant: *she was casual about security* **2** occasional or irregular: *casual workers* **3** shallow or superficial: *casual relationships* **4** for informal wear: *a casual jacket* **5** happening by chance or without planning: *a casual comment* ▷ *n* **6** an occasional worker [Latin *casus* event, chance] **casually** *adv*

casuals *pl n* informal clothing

casualty *n, pl* **-ties 1** a person who is killed or injured in an accident or war **2** the hospital department where victims of accidents are given emergency treatment **3** a person or thing that has suffered as the result of a particular event or circumstance: *583 job losses with significant casualties among public-sector employees*

casuarina (kass-yew-a-**reen**-a) *n* an Australian tree with jointed green branches [from Malay *kĕsuari*, referring to the resemblance of the branches to the feathers of the cassowary]

casuistry *n* reasoning that is misleading or oversubtle [Latin *casus* case] **casuist** *n*

cat *n* **1** a small domesticated mammal with thick soft fur and whiskers **2** a wild animal related to the cat, such as the lynx, lion, or tiger. Related adjective: **feline 3 let the cat out of the bag** to disclose a secret **4 raining cats and dogs** raining very heavily **5 set the cat among the pigeons** to stir up trouble [Latin *cattus*] **catlike** *adj*

catabolism *n biol* a metabolic process in which complex molecules are broken down into simple ones with the release of energy [Greek *kata-* down + *ballein* to throw] **catabolic** *adj*

cataclysm (**kat**-a-kliz-zum) *n* **1** a violent upheaval of a social, political, or military nature: *the cataclysm of the Second World War* **2** a disaster such as an earthquake or a flood [Greek *katakluzein* to flood] **cataclysmic** *adj*

catacombs (**kat**-a-koomz) *pl n* an underground burial place consisting of tunnels with side recesses for tombs [Late Latin *catacumbas* cemetery near Rome]

catafalque (**kat**-a-falk) *n* a raised platform on which a body lies in state before or during a funeral [Italian *catafalco*]

Catalan *adj* **1** of Catalonia ▷ *n* **2** a language of Catalonia in NE Spain **3** a person from Catalonia

catalepsy *n* a trancelike state in which the body is rigid [Greek *katalēpsis* a seizing] **cataleptic** *adj*

catalogue *or US* **catalog** *n* **1** a book containing details of items for sale **2** a list of all the books of a library **3** a list of events, qualities, or things considered as a group: *a catalogue of killings* ▷ *vb* **-loguing, -logued** *or* **-loging, -loged 4** to enter (an item) in a catalogue **5** to list a series of (events, qualities, or things): *the report catalogues two decades of human-rights violations* [Greek *katalegein* to list] **cataloguer** *n*

catalpa *n* a tree of N America and Asia with bell-shaped whitish flowers [Carolina Creek (a Native American language) *kutuhlpa* winged head]

catalyse *or US* **-lyze** *vb* **-lysing, -lysed** *or* **-lyzing, -lyzed** to influence (a chemical reaction) by catalysis

catalysis *n* acceleration of a chemical reaction by the action of a catalyst [Greek *kataluein* to dissolve] **catalytic** *adj*

catalyst *n* **1** a substance that speeds up a chemical reaction without itself undergoing any permanent chemical change **2** a person or thing that causes an important change to take place: *a catalyst for peace*

catalytic converter *n* a device which uses catalysts to reduce the quantity of poisonous substances emitted by the exhaust of a motor vehicle

catalytic cracker *n* a unit in an oil refinery in which mineral oils are converted into fuels by a catalytic process

catamaran *n* a boat with twin parallel hulls [Tamil *kattumaram* tied timber]

catamite *n* a boy kept for sexual purposes [Latin *Catamitus*, variant of *Ganymedes* Ganymede, cupbearer to the gods in Greek mythology]

catapult *n* **1** a Y-shaped device with a loop of elastic fastened to the ends of the prongs, used by children for firing stones **2** a device used to launch aircraft from a warship ▷ *vb* **3** to shoot forwards or upwards violently: *traffic catapulted forward with a roar* **4** to cause (someone) suddenly to be in a particular situation: *catapulted to stardom* [Greek *kata-* down + *pallein* to hurl]

cataract *n* **1** *pathol* **A** a condition in which the lens of the eye becomes partially or totally opaque **B** the opaque area **2** a large waterfall [Greek *katarassein* to dash down]

catarrh (kat-**tar**) *n* excessive mucus in the nose and throat, often experienced during or following a cold [Greek *katarrhein* to flow down] **catarrhal** *adj*

catastrophe (kat-**ass**-trof-fee) *n* a great and sudden disaster or misfortune [Greek *katastrephein* to overturn] **catastrophic** *adj*

catatonia *n* a state of muscular rigidity and stupor, sometimes found in schizophrenia [Greek *kata-* down + *tonos* tension] **catatonic** *adj*

cat burglar *n* a burglar who enters buildings by climbing through upper windows

catcall *n* a shrill whistle or cry of disapproval or derision
catch *vb* **catching, caught 1** to seize and hold **2** to capture (a person or a fish or animal) **3** to surprise in an act: *two boys were caught stealing* **4** to reach (a bus, train, or plane) in time to board it **5** to see or hear: *you'll have to be quick if you want to catch her DJ-ing* **6** to be infected with (an illness) **7** to entangle or become entangled **8** to attract (someone's attention, imagination, or interest) **9** to comprehend or make out: *you have to work hard to catch his tone and meaning* **10** to reproduce (a quality) accurately in a work of art **11** (of a fire) to start burning **12** *cricket* to dismiss (a batsman) by catching a ball struck by him or her before it touches the ground **13 catch at A** to attempt to grasp **B** to take advantage of (an opportunity) **14 catch it** *informal* to be punished ▷ *n* **15** a device such as a hook, for fastening a door, window, or box **16** the total number of fish caught **17** *informal* a concealed or unforeseen drawback **18** an emotional break in the voice **19** *informal* a person considered worth having as a husband or wife **20** *cricket* the act of catching a ball struck by a batsman before it touches the ground, resulting in him or her being out ▷ See also **catch on, catch out, catch up** [Latin *capere* to seize]
catch-22 *n* a situation in which a person is frustrated by a set of circumstances that prevent any attempt to escape from them [from the title of a novel by J Heller]
catchcry *n, pl* **-cries** *Austral* a well-known, frequently used phrase, esp one associated with a particular group
catching *adj* infectious
catchment *n* **1** a structure in which water is collected **2** all the people served by a school or hospital in a particular catchment area
catchment area *n* **1** the area of land draining into a river, basin, or reservoir **2** the area served by a particular school or hospital
catch on *vb informal* **1** to become popular or fashionable **2** to understand: *I was slow to catch on to what she was trying to tell me*
catch out *vb informal, chiefly Brit* to trap (someone) in an error or a lie
catchpenny *adj Brit* designed to have instant appeal without regard for quality
catch phrase *n* a well-known phrase or slogan associated with a particular entertainer or other celebrity
catch up *vb* **1 be caught up in** to be unwillingly or accidentally involved in: *hundreds of civilians have been caught up in the clashes* **2 catch up on** *or* **with** to bring (something) up to date: *he had a lot of paperwork to catch up on* **3 catch up with** to reach or pass (someone or something): *she ran to catch up with him* ▷ *n* **catch-up 4** a meeting held in order to bring someone up to date with developments **5** a facility for watching a television programme after it has been broadcast **6 play catch-up** *informal* to attempt to match a standard set by another person or organization
catchword *n* a well-known and frequently used phrase or slogan
catchy *adj* **catchier, catchiest** (of a tune) pleasant and easily remembered
catechism (kat-tik-kiz-zum) *n* instruction on the doctrine of a Christian Church by a series of questions and answers [Greek *katēkhizein* to catechize]
catechize *or* **-echise** *vb* **-echizing, -echized** *or* **-echising, -echised 1** to instruct in Christianity using a catechism **2** to question (someone) thoroughly [Greek *katēkhizein*] **catechist** *n*
categorical *or* **categoric** *adj* absolutely clear and certain: *he was categorical in his denial* **categorically** *adv*
categorize *or* **-rise** *vb* **-rizing, -rized** *or* **-rising, -rised** to put in a category **categorization** *or* **-risation** *n*
category *n, pl* **-ries** a class or group of things or people with some quality or qualities in common [Greek *katēgoria* assertion]
cater *vb* **1** to provide what is needed or wanted: *operating theatres that can cater for open-heart surgery* **2** to provide food or services: *chef is pleased to cater for vegetarians and vegans* [Anglo-Norman *acater* to buy]
caterer *n* a person whose job is to provide food for social events such as parties and weddings
catering *n* the supplying of food for a social event
caterpillar *n* **1** the wormlike larva of a butterfly or moth **2** *trademark* Also: **caterpillar track** an endless track, driven by cogged wheels, used to propel a heavy vehicle such as a bulldozer [probably from Old French *catepelose* hairy cat]
caterwaul *vb* **1** to make a yowling noise like a cat ▷ *n* **2** such a noise [imitative]
catfish *n, pl* **-fish** *or* **-fishes** a freshwater fish with whisker-like barbels around the mouth
catgut *n* a strong cord made from dried animals' intestines, used to string musical instruments and sports rackets
catharsis (kath-thar-siss) *n* **1** the relief of strong suppressed emotions, for example through drama or psychoanalysis **2** evacuation of the bowels, esp. with the use of a laxative [Greek *kathairein* to purge, purify]
cathartic *adj* **1** causing catharsis ▷ *n* **2** a drug that causes catharsis
Cathay *n* a literary or archaic name for China [Medieval Latin *Cataya*]
cathedral *n* the principal church of a diocese [Greek *kathedra* seat]
Catherine wheel *n* a firework that rotates, producing sparks and coloured flame [after St *Catherine* of Alexandria, martyred on a spiked wheel]
catheter (kath-it-er) *n* a slender flexible tube inserted into a body cavity to drain fluid [Greek *kathienai* to insert]
cathode *n electronics* the negative electrode in an electrolytic cell or in an electronic valve or tube [Greek *kathodos* a descent]
cathode rays *pl n* a stream of electrons emitted from the surface of a cathode in a valve
cathode-ray tube *n* a valve in which a beam of electrons is focused onto a fluorescent screen to produce a visible image, used in television receivers and visual display units

catholic *adj* (of tastes or interests) covering a wide range [Greek *katholikos* universal]
Catholic *Christianity* ▷ *adj* **1** of the Roman Catholic Church ▷ *n* **2** a member of the Roman Catholic Church **Catholicism** *n*
cation (kat-eye-on) *n* a positively charged ion [Greek *kata-* down + *ienai* to go]
catkin *n* a drooping flower spike found on trees such as the birch, hazel, and willow [obsolete Dutch *katteken* kitten]
catmint *n* a Eurasian plant with scented leaves that attract cats. Also: **catnip**
catnap *n* **1** a short sleep or doze ▷ *vb* **-napping, -napped 2** to sleep or doze for a short time or intermittently
cat-o'-nine-tails *n, pl* **-tails** a rope whip with nine knotted thongs, formerly used to inflict floggings as a punishment
cat's cradle *n* a game played by making patterns with a loop of string between the fingers
Catseyes *pl n trademark Brit, Austral & NZ* glass reflectors set into the road at intervals to indicate traffic lanes by reflecting light from vehicles' headlights
cat's paw *n* a person used by someone else to do unpleasant things for him or her [from the tale of a monkey who used a cat's paw to draw chestnuts out of a fire]
cattle *pl n* domesticated cows and bulls. Related adjective: **bovine** [Old French *chatel* chattel]
cattle-cake *n* concentrated food for cattle in the form of cakelike blocks
cattle-grid *or NZ* **cattle-stop** *n* a grid covering a hole dug in a road to prevent livestock crossing while allowing vehicles to pass unhindered
catty *adj* **-tier, -tiest** *informal* spiteful: *her remarks were amusing and only slightly catty* **cattiness** *n*
catwalk *n* **1** a narrow pathway over the stage of a theatre or along a bridge **2** a narrow platform where models display clothes in a fashion show
Caucasian *or* **Caucasoid** *adj* **1** of the predominantly light-skinned supposed racial group of humankind ▷ *n* **2** a member of this group
caucus *n, pl* **-cuses 1** a local committee or faction of a political party **2** a political meeting to decide future plans **3** *NZ* a formal meeting of all MPs of one party [probably of Native American origin]
caudal *adj zool* at or near the tail or back part of an animal's body [Latin *cauda* tail]
caught *vb* the past of **catch**
caul *n anatomy* a membrane sometimes covering a child's head at birth [Old French *calotte* close-fitting cap]
cauldron *or* **caldron** *n* a large pot used for boiling [Latin *caldarium* hot bath]
cauliflower *n* a vegetable with a large head of white flower buds surrounded by green leaves [Italian *caoli fiori* cabbage flowers]
cauliflower ear *n* permanent swelling and distortion of the ear, caused by repeated blows usually received in boxing
caulk *vb* to fill in (cracks) with paste or some other material [Latin *calcare* to trample]
causal *adj* of or being a cause: *a causal connection* **causally** *adv*
causation *or* **causality** *n* **1** the production of an effect by a cause **2** the relationship of cause and effect
causative *adj* producing an effect: *bright lights seem to be a causative factor in some migraines*
cause *n* **1** something that produces a particular effect **2** grounds for action; justification: *there is cause for concern* **3** an aim or principle which an individual or group is interested in and supports: *the Socialist cause* ▷ *vb* **causing, caused 4** to be the cause of [Latin *causa*] **causeless** *adj*
cause célèbre (kawz sill-leb-ra) *n, pl* **causes célèbres** (kawz sill-leb-raz) a controversial legal case, issue, or person [French]
causeway *n* a raised path or road across water or marshland [Middle English *cauciwey* paved way]
caustic *adj* **1** capable of burning or corroding by chemical action: *caustic soda* **2** bitter and sarcastic: *caustic critics* ▷ *n* **3** *chem* a caustic substance [Greek *kaiein* to burn] **caustically** *adv*
caustic soda *n* same as **sodium hydroxide**
cauterize *or* **-ise** *vb* **-izing, -ized** *or* **-ising, -ised** to burn (a wound) with heat or a caustic agent to prevent infection [Greek *kaiein* to burn] **cauterization** *or* **-isation** *n*
caution *n* **1** care or prudence, esp. in the face of danger **2** warning: *a word of caution* **3** *law, chiefly Brit* a formal warning given to a person suspected of an offence ▷ *vb* **4** to warn or advise: *he cautioned against an abrupt turnaround* [Latin *cautio*] **cautionary** *adj*
cautious *adj* showing or having caution **cautiously** *adv*
cavalcade *n* a procession of people on horseback or in cars [Italian *cavalcare* to ride on horseback]
cavalier *adj* **1** showing haughty disregard; offhand ▷ *n* **2** *old-fashioned* a gallant or courtly gentleman [Late Latin *caballarius* rider]
Cavalier *n* a supporter of Charles I during the English Civil War
cavalry *n* the part of an army originally mounted on horseback, but now often using fast armoured vehicles [Italian *cavaliere* horseman] **cavalryman** *n*
cave *n* a hollow in the side of a hill or cliff, or underground [Latin *cavus* hollow]
caveat (kav-vee-at) *n* **1** *law* a formal notice requesting the court not to take a certain action without warning the person lodging the caveat **2** a caution [Latin: let him beware]
cave in *vb* **1** to collapse inwards **2** *informal* to yield completely under pressure: *the government caved in to the revolutionaries' demands* ▷ *n* **cave-in 3** the sudden collapse of a roof or piece of ground
caveman *n, pl* **-men 1** a prehistoric cave dweller **2** *informal* a man who is primitive or brutal in behaviour
cavern *n* a large cave [Latin *cavus* hollow]
cavernous *adj* like a cavern in vastness, depth, or hollowness: *the cavernous building*
caviar *or* **caviare** *n* the salted roe of the sturgeon, regarded as a delicacy and usually served as an appetizer [Turkish *havyār*]
cavil *vb* **-illing, -illed** *or US* **-iling, -iled 1** to raise annoying petty objections ▷ *n* **2** a petty objection [Latin *cavillari* to jeer]

caving *n* the sport of climbing in and exploring caves **caver** *n*
cavity *n, pl* **-ties** **1** a hollow space **2** *dentistry* a decayed area on a tooth [Latin *cavus* hollow]
cavort *vb* to skip about; caper
caw *n* **1** the cry of a crow, rook, or raven ▷ *vb* **2** to make this cry [imitative]
cay *n* a small low island or bank of sand and coral fragments [Spanish *cayo*]
cayenne pepper *or* **cayenne** *n* a very hot red spice made from the dried seeds of capsicums [indigenous S American word *quiynha*]
cayman *or* **caiman** *n, pl* **-mans** a tropical American reptile similar to an alligator [Carib]
CB **1** Citizens' Band **2** Commander of the Order of the Bath
CBC Canadian Broadcasting Corporation
CBE Commander of the Order of the British Empire (a Brit. title)
CBI Confederation of British Industry
cc *or* **c.c.** **1** carbon copy **2** (in South Africa) closed corporation **3** cubic centimetre
CC **1** County Council **2** Cricket Club
CCS cascading style sheet
CCTV closed-circuit television
cd candela
Cd *chem* cadmium
CD compact disc
CDI compact disc interactive: a system for storing a mix of software, data, audio, and compressed video for interactive use under processor control
Cdn. Canadian
CD player *n* a device for playing compact discs
Cdr Commander
CD-R compact disc recordable
CD-ROM compact disc read-only memory: a compact disc used with a computer system as a read-only optical disc
CD-RW compact disc rewritable
CDT Central Daylight Time
CD-video *n* a compact-disc player that, when connected to a television and a hi-fi, produces high-quality stereo sound and synchronized pictures from a compact disc
Ce *chem* cerium
CE (used, esp. by non-Christians, in numbering years AD) Common Era
cease *vb* **ceasing, ceased** **1** to bring or come to an end ▷ *n* **2** **without cease** without stopping [Latin *cessare*]
ceasefire *n* a temporary period of truce
ceaseless *adj* without stopping **ceaselessly** *adv*
cedar *n* **1** a coniferous tree with needle-like evergreen leaves and barrel-shaped cones **2** the sweet-smelling wood of this tree [Greek *kedros*]
cede *vb* **ceding, ceded** to transfer or surrender (territory or legal rights) [Latin *cedere* to yield]
cedilla *n* a character (¸) placed underneath a *c*, esp. in French or Portuguese, indicating that it is to be pronounced (s), not (k) [Spanish: little *z*]
ceilidh (**kay**-lee) *n* an informal social gathering in Scotland or Ireland with folk music and country dancing [Gaelic]
ceiling *n* **1** the inner upper surface of a room **2** an upper limit set on something such as a payment or salary **3** the upper altitude to which an aircraft can climb [origin unknown]
celandine *n* a wild plant with yellow flowers [Greek *khelidōn* swallow; the plant's season was believed to parallel the migration of swallows]
celebrant *n* a person who performs or takes part in a religious ceremony
celebrate *vb* **-brating, -brated** **1** to hold festivities: *let's celebrate!* **2** to hold festivities to mark (a happy event, birthday, or anniversary) **3** to perform (a solemn or religious ceremony) **4** to praise publicly: *the novel is justly celebrated as a masterpiece* [Latin *celeber* numerous, renowned] **celebration** *n* **celebratory** *adj*
celebrated *adj* well known: *the celebrated musician*
celebrity *n, pl* **-ties** **1** a famous person **2** the state of being famous
celeriac (sill-**ler**-ree-ak) *n* a variety of celery with a large turnip-like root
celerity (sill-**ler**-rit-tee) *n formal* swiftness [Latin *celeritas*]
celery *n* a vegetable with long green crisp edible stalks [Greek *selinon* parsley]
celesta *n* an instrument like a small piano in which key-operated hammers strike metal plates [French *céleste* heavenly]
celestial *adj* **1** heavenly or divine: *celestial music* **2** of or relating to the sky or space: *celestial objects such as pulsars and quasars* [Latin *caelum* heaven]
celestial equator *n* an imaginary circle lying on the celestial sphere in a plane perpendicular to the earth's axis
celestial sphere *n* an imaginary sphere of infinitely large radius enclosing the universe
celibate *adj* **1** unmarried or abstaining from sex, esp. because of a religious vow of chastity ▷ *n* **2** a celibate person [Latin *caelebs* unmarried] **celibacy** *n*
cell *n* **1** *biol* the smallest unit of an organism that is able to function independently **2** a small simple room in a prison, convent, or monastery **3** any small compartment, such as a cell of a honeycomb **4** a small group operating as the core of a larger organization: *Communist cells* **5** a device that produces electrical energy by chemical action **6** *US & Canad* a cellular phone [Latin *cella* room, storeroom]
cellar *n* **1** an underground room, usually used for storage **2** a place where wine is stored **3** a stock of bottled wines [Latin *cellarium* food store]
cellarage *n* **1** the area of a cellar **2** a charge for storing goods in a cellar
cello (**chell**-oh) *n, pl* **-los** a large low-pitched musical instrument of the violin family, held between the knees and played with a bow [short for *violoncello*] **cellist** *n*
Cellophane *n trademark* a thin transparent material made from cellulose that is used as a protective wrapping, esp. for food [*cellulose* + Greek *phainein* to shine, appear]
cellular *adj* **1** of, consisting of, or resembling a cell or cells: *cellular changes* **2** woven with an open texture: *cellular blankets* **3** designed for or using cellular radio: *cellular phones*
cellular radio *n* radio communication, used esp. in mobile phones, based on a network of

transmitters each serving a small area known as a cell
cellulite *n* fat deposits under the skin alleged to resist dieting
celluloid *n* **1** a kind of plastic made from cellulose nitrate and camphor, used to make toys and, formerly, photographic film **2** the cinema or films generally: *a Shakespeare play committed to celluloid*
cellulose *n* the main constituent of plant cell walls, used in making paper, rayon, and plastics

C

cellulose acetate *n* a nonflammable material used to make film, lacquers, and artificial fibres
cellulose nitrate *n* a compound used in plastics, lacquers, and explosives
Celsius *adj* denoting a measurement on the Celsius scale [after Anders *Celsius*, astronomer who invented it]
Celsius scale *n* a scale of temperature in which 0° represents the melting point of ice and 100° represents the boiling point of water
Celt (**kelt**) *n* **1** a person from Scotland, Ireland, Wales, Cornwall, or Brittany **2** a member of a people who inhabited Britain, Gaul, and Spain in pre-Roman times [Latin *Celtae* the Celts]
Celtic (**kel**-tik, **sel**-tik) *n* **1** a group of languages that includes Gaelic, Welsh, and Breton ▷ *adj* **2** of the Celts or the Celtic languages
cement *n* **1 A** a fine grey powder made of limestone and clay, mixed with water and sand to make mortar or concrete **B** mortar or concrete **2** something that unites, binds, or joins things or people: *bone cement; the cement of fear and hatred of the Left* **3** *dentistry* a material used for filling teeth ▷ *vb* **4** to join, bind, or cover with cement **5** to make (a relationship) stronger: *this would cement a firm alliance between the army and rebels* [Latin *caementum* stone from the quarry]
cemetery *n, pl* **-teries** a place where dead people are buried: *a military cemetery* [Greek *koimētērion* room for sleeping]
cenotaph *n* a monument honouring soldiers who died in a war [Greek *kenos* empty + *taphos* tomb]
Cenozoic *or* **Caenozoic** (see-no-**zoh**-ik) *adj geol* of the most recent geological era, beginning 65 million years ago, characterized by the development and increase of the mammals [Greek *kainos* recent + *zōion* animal]
censer *n* a container for burning incense
censor *n* **1** a person authorized to examine films, letters, or publications, in order to ban or cut anything considered obscene or objectionable ▷ *vb* **2** to ban or cut portions of (a film, letter, or publication) [Latin *censere* to consider]
censorious *adj* harshly critical
censorship *n* the practice or policy of censoring films, letters, or publications
censure *n* **1** severe disapproval ▷ *vb* **-suring, -sured 2** to criticize (someone or something) severely [Latin *censere* to assess]
census *n, pl* **-suses** an official periodic count of a population including such information as sex, age, and occupation [Latin *censere* to assess]
cent *n* a monetary unit worth one hundredth of the main unit of currency in many countries [Latin *centum* hundred]
cent. **1** central **2** century
centaur *n Greek myth* a creature with the head, arms, and torso of a man, and the lower body and legs of a horse [Greek *kentauros*]
centavo *n, pl* **-vos** a monetary unit worth one hundredth of the main unit of currency in many Latin American countries [Spanish: one hundredth part]
centenarian *n* a person who is at least 100 years old
centenary (sen-**teen**-a-ree) *n, pl* **-naries** *chiefly Brit* a 100th anniversary or the celebration of one. US equivalent: **centennial** [Latin *centum* hundred]
center *n, vb US* same as **centre**
centesimal *n* **1** one hundredth ▷ *adj* **2** of or divided into hundredths [Latin *centum* hundred]
centi- *prefix* **1** denoting one hundredth: *centimetre* **2** denoting one hundred: *centipede* [Latin *centum* hundred]
centigrade *adj* same as **Celsius**

> **USAGE** Although still used in meteorology, *centigrade*, when indicating the Celsius scale of temperature, is now usually avoided in other scientific contexts because of its possible confusion with the hundredth part of a grade.

centigram *or* **centigramme** *n* one hundredth of a gram
centilitre *or US* **centiliter** *n* a measure of volume equivalent to one hundredth of a litre
centime (**son**-teem) *n* a monetary unit worth one hundredth of the main unit of currency in a number of countries [Latin *centum* hundred]
centimetre *or US* **centimeter** *n* a unit of length equal to one hundredth of a metre
centipede *n* a small wormlike creature with many legs
central *adj* **1** of, at, or forming the centre of something: *eastern and central parts of the country* **2** main or principal: *a central issue* **centrally** *adv* **centrality** *n*
central bank *n* a national bank that acts as the government's banker, controls credit, and issues currency
Central European Time *n* the standard time adopted by Western European countries one hour ahead of Greenwich Mean Time, corresponding to British Summer Time. Abbrev: **CET**
central government *n* the government of a whole country, as opposed to the smaller organizations that govern counties, towns, and districts
central heating *n* a system for heating a building by means of radiators or air vents connected to a central source of heat **centrally heated** *adj*
centralism *n* the principle of bringing a country or an organization under central control **centralist** *adj*
centralize *or* **-ise** *vb* **-izing, -ized** *or* **-ising, -ised** to bring (a country or an organization) under central control **centralization** *or* **-isation** *n*
central locking *n* a system by which all the doors of a motor vehicle are locked automatically when the driver's door is locked manually
central nervous system *n* the part of the nervous system of vertebrates that consists of the brain and spinal cord

central processing unit *n* the part of a computer that controls all the other parts
central reservation *n Brit & NZ* the strip that separates the two sides of a motorway or dual carriageway
centre *or US* **center** *n* **1** the middle point or part of something **2** a place where a specified activity takes place: *a shopping centre* **3** a person or thing that is a focus of interest: *the centre of a long-running dispute* **4** a place of activity or influence: *the parliament building was the centre of resistance* **5** a political party or group that favours moderation **6** *sport* a player who plays in the middle of the field rather than on a wing ▷ *vb* **-tring, -tred** *or US* **-tering, -tered 7** to put in the centre of something **8 centre on** to have as a centre or main theme: *the summit is expected to centre on expanding the role of the UN* [Greek *kentron* needle, sharp point]
centreboard *or US* **centerboard** *n* a supplementary keel for a sailing boat or dinghy
centrefold *or US* **centerfold** *n* a large coloured illustration, often a photograph of a naked or scantily dressed person, folded to form the centre pages of a magazine
centre forward *n sport* the middle player in the forward line of a team
centre half *or* **centre back** *n soccer* a defender who plays in the middle of the defence
centre of gravity *n* the point in an object around which its mass is evenly distributed
centre pass *n hockey* a push or hit made in any direction to start the game
centrepiece *or US* **centerpiece** *n* **1** the most important item of a group of things: *she was the centrepiece of this conference* **2** an ornament for the centre of a table
centrifugal (sent-**riff**-few-gl) *adj* **1** moving or tending to move away from a centre **2** of or operated by centrifugal force: *centrifugal extractors* [Greek *kentron* centre + Latin *fugere* to flee]
centrifugal force *n* a force that acts outwards on any body that rotates or moves along a curved path
centrifuge *n* a machine that separates substances by the action of centrifugal force
centripetal (sent-**rip**-it-al) *adj* moving or tending to move towards a centre [Greek *kentron* centre + Latin *petere* to seek]
centripetal force *n* a force that acts inwards on any body that rotates or moves along a curved path
centrist *n* a person who holds moderate political views
centurion *n* (in ancient Rome) the officer in command of a century [Latin *centurio*]
century *n, pl* **-ries 1** a period of 100 years **2** a score of 100 runs in cricket **3** (in ancient Rome) a unit of foot soldiers, originally consisting of 100 men [Latin *centuria*]
CEO chief executive officer
cephalopod (**seff**-a-loh-pod) *n* a sea mollusc with a head and tentacles, such as the octopus [Greek *kephalē* head + *pous* foot]
ceramic *n* **1** a hard brittle material made by heating clay to a very high temperature **2** an object made of this material ▷ *adj* **3** made of ceramic: *ceramic tiles* [Greek *keramos* potter's clay]
ceramics *n* the art of producing ceramic objects **ceramicist** *or* **ceramist** *n*
Cerberus (**sir**-ber-uss) *n Greek myth* a three-headed dog who guarded the entrance to Hades
cere *n* a soft waxy swelling, containing the nostrils, at the base of the upper beak of a parrot [Latin *cera* wax]
cereal *n* **1** any grass that produces an edible grain, such as oat, wheat, or rice **2** the grain produced by such a plant **3** a breakfast food made from this grain, usually eaten mixed with milk [Latin *cerealis* concerning agriculture]
cerebellum (serr-rib-**bell**-lum) *n, pl* **-lums** *or* **-la** (-la) the back part of the brain, which controls balance and muscular coordination [Latin]
cerebral (**serr**-rib-ral) *adj* **1** of the brain: *a cerebral haemorrhage* **2** involving intelligence rather than emotions or instinct: *the cerebral joys of the literary world*
cerebral palsy *n* a condition in which the limbs and muscles are permanently weak, caused by damage to the brain
cerebrate (**serr**-rib-rate) *vb* **-brating, -brated** *usually facetious* to use the mind; think **cerebration** *n*
cerebrospinal *adj* of the brain and spinal cord: *a sample of cerebrospinal fluid*
cerebrovascular (serr-rib-roh-**vass**-kew-lar) *adj* of the blood vessels and blood supply of the brain
cerebrum (**serr**-rib-rum) *n, pl* **-brums** *or* **-bra** (-bra) the main part of the human brain, associated with thought, emotion, and personality [Latin: the brain]
ceremonial *adj* **1** of ceremony or ritual ▷ *n* **2** a system of formal rites; ritual **ceremonially** *adv*
ceremonious *adj* excessively polite or formal **ceremoniously** *adv*
ceremony *n, pl* **-nies 1** a formal act or ritual performed for a special occasion: *a wedding ceremony* **2** formally polite behaviour **3 stand on ceremony** to insist on or act with excessive formality [Latin *caerimonia* what is sacred]
Ceres *n* the Roman goddess of agriculture
cerise (ser-**reess**) *adj* cherry-red [French: cherry]
cerium *n chem* a steel-grey metallic element found only in combination with other elements. Symbol: **Ce** [from *Ceres* (an asteroid)]
CERN Conseil Européen pour la Recherche Nucléaire: a European organization for research in high-energy particle physics
cert *n* **a dead cert** *informal* something that is certain to happen or to be successful
cert. certificate
certain *adj* **1** positive and confident about something: *he was certain they would agree* **2** definitely known: *it is by no means certain the tomb still exists* **3** sure or bound: *the cuts are certain to go ahead* **4** some but not much: *a certain amount* **5** particular: *certain aspects* **6** named but not known: *a running commentary by a certain Mr Fox* **7 for certain** without doubt [Latin *certus* sure]
certainly *adv* without doubt: *he will certainly be back*
certainty *n* **1** the condition of being certain **2** *pl* **-ties** something established as inevitable

certifiable *adj* considered to be legally insane
certificate *n* an official document stating the details of something such as birth, death, or completion of an academic course [Old French *certifier* to certify]
certified *adj* holding or guaranteed by a certificate: *a certified acupuncturist*
certify *vb* **-fies, -fying, -fied 1** to confirm or attest to **2** to guarantee (that certain required standards have been met) **3** to declare legally insane [Latin *certus* certain + *facere* to make] **certification** *n*
certitude *n formal* confidence or certainty
cervical smear *n med* a smear taken from the neck (cervix) of the womb for detection of cancer
cervix *n, pl* **cervixes** *or* **cervices 1** the lower part of the womb that extends into the vagina **2** *anatomy* the neck [Latin] **cervical** *adj*
cesium *n US* same as **caesium**
cessation *n* an ending or pause: *a cessation of hostilities* [Latin *cessare* to be idle]
cession *n* the act of ceding territory or legal rights [Latin *cedere* to yield]
cesspool *or* **cesspit** *n* a covered tank or pit for collecting and storing sewage or waste water [Old French *souspirail* air vent]
CET Central European Time
cetacean (sit-**tay**-shun) *n* a sea creature such as a whale or dolphin, which belongs to a family of fish-shaped mammals and breathes through a blowhole [Greek *kētos* whale]
cetane (**see**-tane) *n* a colourless liquid hydrocarbon, used as a solvent [Latin *cetus* whale]
cetane number *n* a measure of the quality of a diesel fuel expressed as the percentage of cetane in it
cf compare [Latin *confer*]
Cf *chem* californium
CF Canadian Forces
CFB Canadian Forces Base
CFC chlorofluorocarbon
CFL Canadian Football League
CFS chronic fatigue syndrome
cg centigram
CGI computer-generated image(s)
cgs units *pl n* a metric system of units based on the centimetre, gram, and second: for scientific and technical purposes, replaced by SI units
CH Companion of Honour (a Brit. title)
ch. 1 chapter **2** church
Chablis (**shab**-lee) *n* a dry white wine made around Chablis, France
cha-cha *or* **cha-cha-cha** *n* **1** a modern ballroom dance from Latin America **2** music for this dance [American (Cuban) Spanish]
chaconne *n* a musical form consisting of a set of variations on a repeated melodic bass line
chad *n* the small pieces removed during the punching of holes in punch cards, printer paper, etc.
chafe *vb* **chafing, chafed 1** to make sore or worn by rubbing **2** to be annoyed or impatient: *she chafes against the restrictions of her small-town community* [Old French *chaufer* to warm]
chafer *n* a large slow-moving beetle [Old English *ceafor*]
chaff¹ *n* **1** grain husks separated from the seeds during threshing **2** something of little worth; rubbish: *you had to be a very perceptive listener to sort the wheat from the chaff of his discourse* [Old English *ceaf*]
chaff² *vb* to tease good-naturedly [probably slang variant of *chafe*]
chaffinch *n* a small European songbird with black-and-white wings and, in the male, a reddish body and blue-grey head [Old English *ceaf* CHAFF¹ + *finc* finch]
chafing dish *n* a dish with a heating apparatus beneath it, for cooking or keeping food warm at the table
chagrin (**shag**-grin) *n* a feeling of annoyance and disappointment [French]
chagrined *adj* annoyed and disappointed
chain *n* **1** a flexible length of metal links, used for fastening, binding, or connecting, or in jewellery **2 chains** anything that restricts or restrains someone: *bound by the chains of duty* **3** a series of connected facts or events **4** a number of establishments, such as hotels or shops, that have the same owner or management **5** *chem* a number of atoms or groups bonded together so that the resulting molecule, ion, or radical resembles a chain **6** a row of mountains or islands ▷ *vb* **7** to restrict, fasten, or bind with or as if with a chain: *the demonstrators chained themselves to railings* [Latin *catena*]
chain gang *n US* a group of convicted prisoners chained together
chain letter *n* a letter, often with a request for or promise of money, that is sent to many people who are asked to send copies to other people
chain mail *n* same as **mail²**
chain reaction *n* **1** a series of events, each of which causes the next **2** a chemical or nuclear reaction in which the product of one step triggers the following step
chain saw *n* a motor-driven saw in which the cutting teeth form links in a continuous chain
chain-smoke *vb* **-smoking, -smoked** to smoke continuously, lighting one cigarette from the preceding one **chain smoker** *n*
chair *n* **1** a seat with a back and four legs, for one person to sit on **2** an official position of authority or the person holding it: *the chair of the Security Council* **3** a professorship **4 in the chair** presiding over a meeting **5 the chair** *informal* the electric chair ▷ *vb* **6** to preside over (a meeting) [Greek *kathedra*]
chairlift *n* a series of chairs suspended from a moving cable for carrying people up a slope
chairman *or fem* **chairwoman** *n, pl* **-men** *or* **-women** a person who is in charge of a company's board of directors or a meeting **chairmanship** *n*

> **USAGE** *Chairman* can seem inappropriate when applied to a woman, while *chairwoman* can be offensive. *Chair* and *chairperson* can be applied to either a man or a woman; *chair* is generally preferred to *chairperson*.

chaise (**shaze**) *n* a light horse-drawn carriage with two wheels [French]

chaise longue (long) *n, pl* **chaise longues** *or* **chaises longues** a couch with a back and a single armrest [French]

chalcedony (kal-**sed**-don-ee) *n, pl* **-nies** a form of quartz composed of very fine crystals, often greyish or blue in colour [Greek *khalkēdōn* a precious stone]

chalet *n* **1** a type of Swiss wooden house with a steeply sloping roof **2** a similar house used as a ski lodge or holiday home [French]

chalice (**chal**-liss) *n* **1** *poetic* a drinking cup or goblet **2** *Christianity* a gold or silver goblet containing the wine at communion [Latin *calix* cup]

chalk *n* **1** a soft white rock consisting of calcium carbonate **2** a piece of chalk, either white or coloured, used for writing and drawing on blackboards **3 as different as chalk and cheese** *informal* totally different **4 not by a long chalk** *informal* by no means: *you haven't finished by a long chalk* ▷ *vb* **5** to draw or mark with chalk [Latin *calx* limestone] **chalky** *adj*

chalk up *vb informal* **1** to score or register: *the home side chalked up a 9–1 victory* **2** to charge or credit (money) to an account

challenge *n* **1** a demanding or stimulating situation **2** a call to engage in a contest, fight, or argument **3** a questioning of a statement or fact **4** a demand by a sentry for identification or a password **5** *law* a formal objection to a juror ▷ *vb* **-lenging, -lenged 6** to invite or call (someone) to take part in a contest, fight, or argument **7** to call (a decision or action) into question **8** to order (a person) to stop and be identified **9** *law* to make formal objection to (a juror) [Latin *calumnia* calumny] **challenger** *n* **challenging** *adj*

challenged *adj* disabled or disadvantaged as specified: *physically challenged performers*

chalybeate (kal-**lib**-bee-it) *adj* containing or impregnated with iron salts: *a natural chalybeate spring rises at the edge of the lake* [Greek *khalups* iron]

chamber *n* **1** a meeting hall, usually one used for a legislative or judicial assembly **2** a room equipped for a particular purpose: *a decompression chamber* **3** a legislative or judicial assembly: *the Senate, the upper chamber of Canada's parliament* **4** *old-fashioned or poetic* a room in a house, esp. a bedroom **5** a compartment or cavity: *the heart chambers* **6** a compartment for a cartridge or shell in a gun ▷ See also **chambers** [Greek *kamara* vault]

chamberlain *n history* an officer who managed the household of a king or nobleman [Old French *chamberlayn*]

chambermaid *n* a woman employed to clean bedrooms in a hotel

chamber music *n* classical music to be performed by a small group of musicians

Chamber of Commerce *n* an organization of local business people to promote, regulate, and protect their interests

chamber pot *n* a bowl for urine, formerly used in bedrooms

chambers *pl n* **1** a judge's room for hearing private cases not taken in open court **2** (in England) the set of rooms used as offices by a barrister

chameleon (kam-**meal**-yon) *n* a small lizard with long legs that is able to change colour to blend in with its surroundings [Greek *khamai* on the ground + *leōn* lion]

chamfer (**cham**-fer) *n* **1** a bevelled surface at an edge or corner ▷ *vb* **2** to cut a chamfer on or in [Old French *chant* edge + *fraindre* to break]

chamois *n, pl* **-ois 1** (**sham**-wah) a small mountain antelope of Europe and SW Asia **2** (**sham**-ee) a soft suede leather made from the skin of this animal or from sheep or goats **3** (**sham**-ee) Also: **chamois leather, shammy, chammy** a piece of such leather or similar material, used for cleaning and polishing [Old French]

chamomile (**kam**-mo-mile) *n* same as **camomile**

champ[1] *vb* **1** to chew noisily **2 champ at the bit** *informal* to be restless or impatient to do something [probably imitative]

champ[2] *n informal* short for **champion** (sense 1)

champagne *n* **1** a white sparkling wine produced around Reims and Épernay, France ▷ *adj* **2** denoting a luxurious lifestyle: *a champagne capitalist* [Champagne, region of France]

champers (**sham**-perz) *n slang* champagne

champion *n* **1** a person, plant, or animal that has defeated all others in a competition: *the Olympic 100 metres champion* **2** someone who defends a person or cause: *a champion of the downtrodden* ▷ *vb* **3** to support: *he unceasingly championed equal rights and opportunities* ▷ *adj* **4** *N English dialect* excellent [Latin *campus* field] **championship** *n*

chance *n* **1** the extent to which something is likely to happen; probability **2** an opportunity or occasion to do something: *a chance to escape rural poverty* **3** a risk or gamble: *the government is not in the mood to take any more chances* **4** the unknown and unpredictable element that causes something to happen in one way rather than another: *in Buddhism there is no such thing as chance or coincidence* **5 by chance** without planning: *by chance she met an old school friend* **6 on the off chance** acting on the slight possibility: *he had called on the agents on the off chance that he might learn something of value* ▷ *vb* **chancing, chanced 7** to risk or hazard: *a few picnickers chanced the perilous footpath* **8** to do something without planning to: *I chanced to look down* **9 chance on** *or* **upon** to discover by accident: *I chanced upon a copy of this book* [Latin *cadere* to occur]

chancel *n* the part of a church containing the altar and choir [Latin *cancelli* lattice]

chancellery *or* **chancellory** *n, pl* **-leries** *or* **-lories 1** *Brit & Austral* the residence or office of a chancellor **2** *US* the office of an embassy or consulate [Anglo-French *chancellerie*]

chancellor *n* **1** the head of government in several European countries **2** *US* the president of a university **3** *Brit, Austral & Canad* the honorary head of a university [Late Latin *cancellarius* porter] **chancellorship** *n*

Chancellor of the Exchequer *n Brit* the cabinet minister responsible for finance

Chancery *n* (in England) the Lord Chancellor's court, a division of the High Court of Justice [shortened from CHANCELLERY]

chancre (shang-ker) *n pathol* a painless ulcer that develops as a primary symptom of syphilis [French]
chancy *adj* **chancier, chanciest** *informal* uncertain or risky
chandelier (shan-dill-eer) *n* an ornamental hanging light with branches and holders for several candles or bulbs [French]
chandler *n* a dealer in a specified trade or merchandise: *a ship's chandler* [Old French *chandelier* dealer in candles] **chandlery** *n*

C

change *n* **1** the fact of becoming different **2** variety or novelty: *they wanted to print some good news for a change* **3** a different set, esp. of clothes **4** money exchanged for its equivalent in a larger denomination or in a different currency **5** the balance of money when the amount paid is larger than the amount due **6** coins of a small denomination ▷ *vb* **changing, changed 7** to make or become different **8** to replace with or exchange for another: *the Swedish Communist Party changed its name to the Left Party* **9** to give and receive (something) in return: *slaves and masters changed places* **10** to give or receive (money) in exchange for its equivalent sum in a smaller denomination or different currency **11** to put on other clothes **12** to get off one bus, train, or airliner, and onto another: *there's no direct train, so you'll need to change at York* ▷ See also **change down, changeover, change up** [Latin *cambire* to exchange, barter] **changeless** *adj*
changeable *adj* changing often **changeability** *n*
change down *vb* to select a lower gear when driving
changeling *n* a child believed to have been exchanged by fairies for the parents' real child
change of life *n* the menopause
changeover *n* **1** a complete change from one system, attitude, or product to another ▷ *vb* **change over 2** to swap places or activities: *the train crews changed over at the frontier*
change up *vb* to select a higher gear when driving
channel *n* **1** a band of radio frequencies assigned for the broadcasting of a radio or television signal **2** a path for an electrical signal or computer data **3** a means of access or communication: *reports coming through diplomatic channels* **4** a broad strait connecting two areas of sea **5** the bed or course of a river, stream, or canal **6** a navigable course through an area of water **7** a groove ▷ *vb* **-nelling, -nelled** *or US* **-neling, -neled 8** to direct or convey through a channel or channels: *tunnels that channel the pilgrims into the area; to channel funds abroad* [Latin *canalis* pipe, conduit]
Channel *n* **the Channel** the English Channel
channel-hop *vb* **-hopping, -hopped** to change television channels repeatedly using a remote control device
chant *vb* **1** to repeat (a slogan) over and over **2** to sing or recite (a psalm) ▷ *n* **3** a rhythmic or repetitious slogan repeated over and over, usually by more than one person **4** a religious song with a short simple melody in which several words or syllables are sung on one note [Latin *canere* to sing]
chanter *n* the pipe on a set of bagpipes on which the melody is played
chanticleer *n* a name for a cock, used in fables [Old French *chanter cler* to sing clearly]
chanty *n, pl* **-ties** same as **shanty²**
Chanukah *or* **Hanukkah** (hah-na-ka) *n* an eight-day Jewish festival, held in December, commemorating the rededication of the temple by Judas Maccabaeus [Hebrew]
chaos *n* complete disorder or confusion [Greek *khaos*] **chaotic** *adj* **chaotically** *adv*
chap *n informal* a man or boy [from Old English *cēapman* pedlar]
chapati *or* **chapatti** *n* (in Indian cookery) a kind of flat thin unleavened bread [Hindi]
chapel *n* **1** a place of worship with its own altar, in a church or cathedral **2** a similar place of worship in a large house or institution **3** (in England and Wales) a Nonconformist place of worship **4** (in Scotland) a Roman Catholic church **5** the members of a trade union in a newspaper office, printing house, or publishing firm [Latin *cappa* cloak: originally the sanctuary where the cloak of St Martin was kept]
chaperone (shap-per-rone) *n* **1** an older person who accompanies and supervises a young person or young people on social occasions ▷ *vb* **-oning, -oned 2** to act as a chaperone to [Old French *chape* hood]
chaplain *n* a member of the Christian clergy attached to a chapel, military body, or institution [Late Latin *cappella* chapel] **chaplaincy** *n*
chaplet *n* a garland worn on the head [Old French *chapelet*]
chapped *adj* (of the skin) raw and cracked, through exposure to cold [probably Germanic]
chappie *n informal* a man or boy
chaps *pl n* leather leggings without a seat, worn by cowboys [shortened from Spanish *chaparejos*]
chapter *n* **1** a division of a book **2** a period in a life or history: *the latest chapter in the long and complex tale of British brewing* **3** a sequence of events: *a chapter of accidents* **4** a branch of some societies or clubs **5** a group of the canons of a cathedral **6 chapter and verse** exact authority for an action or statement [Latin *caput* head]
char¹ *vb* **charring, charred** to blacken by partial burning [short for *charcoal*]
char² *Brit informal* ▷ *n* **1** short for **charwoman** ▷ *vb* **charring, charred 2** to clean other people's houses as a job [Old English *cerr* turn of work]
char³ *n Brit old-fashioned slang* tea [Chinese *ch'a*]
char⁴ *n, pl* **char** *or* **chars** a troutlike fish of cold lakes and northern seas [origin unknown]
charabanc (shar-rab-bang) *n Brit obsolete* a coach for sightseeing [French: wagon with seats]
character *n* **1** the combination of qualities distinguishing an individual person, group of people, or place: *the unique charm and character of this historic town* **2** a distinguishing quality or characteristic: *bodily movements of a deliberate character* **3** reputation, esp. good reputation: *a man of my Dad's character and standing in the community* **4** an attractively unusual or interesting quality: *the little town was full of life and character* **5** a person represented in a play, film, or story **6** an unusual

or amusing person: *quite a character* **7** *informal* a person: *a flamboyant character* **8** a single letter, numeral, or symbol used in writing or printing **9 in** *or* **out of character** typical *or* not typical of the apparent character of a person [Greek *kharaktēr* engraver's tool] **characterless** *adj*

character assassination *n* an attempt to destroy someone's good reputation by slander or deliberate misrepresentation of his or her views: *he described the accusation as 'an appalling piece of character assassination'*

characteristic *n* **1** a distinguishing feature or quality **2** *maths* the integral part of a logarithm: *the characteristic of 2.4771 is 2* ▷ *adj* **3** typical or representative of someone or something: *the prime minister fought with characteristic passion* **characteristically** *adv*

characterization *or* **-isation** *n* **1** the description or portrayal of a person by an actor or writer: *a novel full of rich characterization and complex plotting* **2** the act or an instance of characterizing

characterize *or* **-ise** *vb* **-izing, -ized** *or* **-ising, -ised** **1** to be a characteristic of: *the violence that characterized the demonstrations* **2** to describe: *we have made what I would characterize as outstanding progress*

charade (shar-**rahd**) *n* an absurd pretence [French]

charades *n* a game in which one team acts out each syllable of a word or phrase, which the other team has to guess

charcoal *n* **1** a black form of carbon made by partially burning wood or other organic matter **2** a stick of this used for drawing **3** a drawing done in charcoal ▷ *adj* **4** Also: **charcoal-grey** very dark grey [origin unknown]

Chardonnay (**shar**-don-nay) *n* a white wine produced in the Burgundy region of France and elsewhere [French]

charge *vb* **charging, charged** **1** to ask (an amount of money) as a price **2** to enter a debit against a person's account for (a purchase) **3** to accuse (someone) formally of a crime in a court of law **4** to make a rush at or sudden attack upon **5** to fill (a glass) **6** to cause (an accumulator or capacitor) to take and store electricity **7** to fill or saturate with liquid or gas: *old mine workings charged with foul gas* **8** to fill with a feeling or mood: *the emotionally charged atmosphere* **9** *formal* to command or assign: *the president has charged his foreign minister with trying to open talks* ▷ *n* **10** a price charged for something; cost **11** a formal accusation of a crime in a court of law **12** an onrush or attack **13** custody or guardianship: *in the charge of the police* **14** a person or thing committed to someone's care: *a nanny reported the father of one of her charges to social workers* **15** **A** a cartridge or shell **B** the explosive required to fire a gun **16** *physics* **A** the attribute of matter responsible for all electrical phenomena, existing in two forms, positive and negative **B** the total amount of electricity stored in a capacitor or an accumulator **17 in charge of** in control of and responsible for: *in charge of defence and foreign affairs* [Old French *chargier* to load]

chargeable *adj* **1** liable to be taxed or charged **2** liable to result in a legal charge

charge card *n* a card issued by a chain store, shop, or organization, that enables customers to obtain goods and services for which they pay later

chargé d'affaires (**shar**-zhay daf-**fair**) *n, pl* **chargés d'affaires** (**shar**-zhay daf-**fair**) **1** the temporary head of a diplomatic mission in the absence of the ambassador or minister **2** the head of a small or unimportant diplomatic mission [French]

charge hand *n* a workman ranked just below a foreman

charge nurse *n* a nurse in charge of a hospital ward

charger *n* **1** a device for charging a battery **2** (in the Middle Ages) a warhorse

char-grilled *adj* (of food) grilled over charcoal

chariot *n* a two-wheeled horse-drawn vehicle used in ancient times for wars and races [Old French *char* car]

charioteer *n* a chariot driver

charisma (kar-**rizz**-ma) *n* the quality or power of an individual to attract, influence, or inspire people [Greek *kharis* grace, favour] **charismatic** (kar-rizz-**mat**-ik) *adj*

charismatic movement *n* *Christianity* a group that believes in divine gifts such as instantaneous healing and uttering unintelligible sounds while in a religious ecstasy

charitable *adj* **1** kind or lenient in one's attitude towards others **2** of or for charity: *a charitable organization* **charitably** *adv*

charity *n* **1** *pl* **-ties** an organization set up to provide help to those in need **2** the giving of help, such as money or food, to those in need **3** help given to those in need; alms **4** a kindly attitude towards people [Latin *caritas* affection]

charlady *n, pl* **-ladies** *Brit* same as **charwoman**

charlatan (**shar**-lat-tan) *n* a person who claims expertise that he or she does not have [Italian *ciarlare* to chatter]

Charles' law *n* *physics* the principle that the volume of a gas varies in proportion to its temperature at constant pressure [after Jacques *Charles*, physicist]

charleston *n* a lively dance of the 1920s [after *Charleston*, South Carolina]

charlie *n* *Brit old-fashioned, informal* a fool

charlock *n* a weed with hairy leaves and yellow flowers [Old English *cerlic*]

charlotte *n* a dessert made with fruit and bread or cake crumbs: *apple charlotte* [French]

charm *n* **1** the quality of attracting, fascinating, or delighting people **2** a trinket worn on a bracelet **3** a small object worn for supposed magical powers **4** a magic spell ▷ *vb* **5** to attract, fascinate, or delight **6** to influence or obtain by personal charm: *you can easily be charmed into changing your mind* **7** to protect as if by magic: *a charmed life* [Latin *carmen* song] **charmer** *n* **charmless** *adj*

charming *adj* delightful or attractive **charmingly** *adv*

charm offensive *n* a concentrated attempt to gain favour by being helpful and obliging

charnel house *n* (formerly) a building or vault for the bones of the dead [Latin *carnalis* fleshly]

charollais (sharr-ol-lay) *n* a breed of large white beef cattle [Monts du *Charollais*, E France]
chart *n* **1** a graph, table, or sheet of information in the form of a diagram **2** a map of the sea or the stars **3 the charts** *informal* the weekly lists of the bestselling pop records or the most popular videos ▹ *vb* **4** to plot the course of **5** to make a chart of **6** to appear in the pop charts [Greek *khartēs* papyrus]

C

charter *n* **1** a formal document granting or demanding certain rights or liberties: *a children's charter* **2** the fundamental principles of an organization: *the UN Charter* **3** the hire or lease of transportation for private use ▹ *vb* **4** to lease or hire by charter **5** to grant a charter to [Latin *charta* leaf of papyrus]
chartered accountant *n* an accountant who has passed the examinations of the Institute of Chartered Accountants
Chartism *n* *English history* a movement (1838–48) for social and political reforms, demand for which was presented to Parliament in charters **Chartist** *n, adj*
chartreuse (shar-truhz) *n* a green or yellow liqueur made from herbs [after *La Grande Chartreuse*, monastery near Grenoble, where the liqueur is produced]
charwoman *n, pl* **-women** *Brit* a woman whose job is to clean other people's houses
chary (chair-ee) *adj* **charier, chariest** wary or careful: *chary of interfering* [Old English *cearig*]
Charybdis (kar-rib-diss) *n* **1** a ship-devouring monster in classical mythology, identified with a whirlpool off the coast of Sicily **2 between Scylla and Charybdis** See **Scylla**
chase[1] *vb* **chasing, chased 1** to pursue (a person or animal) persistently or quickly **2** to force (a person or animal) to leave a place **3** *informal* to court (someone) in an unsubtle manner **4** *informal* to rush or run: *chasing around the world* **5** *informal* to pursue (something or someone) energetically in order to obtain results or information ▹ *n* **6** the act or an instance of chasing a person or animal [Latin *capere* to take]
chase[2] *vb* **chasing, chased** to engrave or emboss (metal) [Old French *enchasser*]
chaser *n* a drink drunk after another of a different kind, for example beer after whisky
chasm (kaz-zum) *n* **1** a very deep crack in the ground **2** a wide difference in interests or feelings: *a deep chasm separating science from politics* [Greek *khasma*]
chassis (shass-ee) *n, pl* **chassis** (shass-eez) the steel frame, wheels, and mechanical parts of a vehicle [French]
chaste *adj* **1** abstaining from sex outside marriage or from all sexual intercourse **2** (of conduct or speech) pure, decent, or modest: *a chaste kiss on the forehead* **3** simple in style: *chaste furniture* [Latin *castus* pure] **chastely** *adv* **chastity** *n*
chasten (chase-en) *vb* to subdue (someone) by criticism [Latin *castigare*]
chastise *vb* **-tising, -tised 1** to scold severely **2** *old-fashioned* to punish by beating [Middle English *chastisen*] **chastisement** *n*
chasuble (chazz-yew-bl) *n* *Christianity* a long sleeveless robe worn by a priest when celebrating Mass [Late Latin *casubla* garment with a hood]
chat *n* **1** an informal conversation **2** the activity of exchanging short messages using a computer or mobile phone ▹ *vb* **chatting, chatted 3** to have an informal conversation **4** to exchange short messages using a computer or mobile phone ▹ See also **chat up** [short for *chatter*]
chateau (shat-toe) *n, pl* **-teaux** (-toe) *or* **-teaus** a French country house or castle [French]
chatelaine (shat-tell-lane) *n* (formerly) the mistress of a large house or castle [French]
chatline *n* a telephone service enabling callers to join in general conversation with each other
chatroom *n* a site on the internet where several connected users can exchange messages in real time
chat show *n* a television or radio show in which guests are interviewed informally
chattels *pl n old-fashioned* possessions [Old French *chatel* personal property]
chatter *vb* **1** to speak quickly and continuously about unimportant things **2** (of birds or monkeys) to make rapid repetitive high-pitched noises **3** (of the teeth) to click together rapidly through cold or fear ▹ *n* **4** idle talk or gossip **5** the high-pitched repetitive noise made by a bird or monkey [imitative]
chatterbox *n informal* a person who talks a great deal, usually about unimportant things
chattering classes *n* **the chattering classes** *informal, often derogatory* the members of the educated sections of society who enjoy discussion of political, social, and cultural issues
chatty *adj* **-tier, -tiest 1** (of a person) fond of friendly, informal conversation; talkative **2** (of a letter) informal and friendly; gossipy
chat up *vb Brit & Austral informal* to talk flirtatiously to (someone) with a view to starting a romantic or sexual relationship
chauffeur *or fem* **chauffeuse** *n* **1** a person employed to drive a car for someone ▹ *vb* **2** to act as driver for (someone) [French: stoker]
chauvinism (show-vin-iz-zum) *n* an irrational belief that one's own country, race, group, or sex is superior: *male chauvinism* [after Nicolas *Chauvin*, French soldier under Napoleon] **chauvinist** *n, adj* **chauvinistic** *adj*
chav *n Brit slang, derogatory* a young working-class person who dresses in casual sports clothes
cheap *adj* **1** costing relatively little; inexpensive **2** of poor quality; shoddy: *planks of cheap, splintery pine* **3** not valued highly; not worth much: *promises are cheap* **4** *informal* mean or despicable: *a cheap jibe* ▹ *n* **5 on the cheap** *Brit informal* at a low cost ▹ *adv* **6** at a low cost [Old English *ceap* barter, price] **cheaply** *adv* **cheapness** *n*
cheapen *vb* **1** to lower the reputation of; degrade **2** to reduce the price of
cheap-jack *n informal* a person who sells cheap and shoddy goods
cheapskate *n informal* a miserly person
cheat *vb* **1** to defraud: *he cheated her out of millions* **2** to act dishonestly in order to gain some advantage or profit **3 cheat on** *informal* to be

unfaithful to (one's spouse or lover) ▹ *n* **4** a person who cheats **5** a fraud or deception [short for *escheat*]

check *vb* **1** to examine, investigate, or make an inquiry into **2** to slow the growth or progress of **3** to stop abruptly **4** to correspond or agree: *that all checks with our data here* ▹ *n* **5** a test to ensure accuracy or progress **6** a means to ensure against fraud or error **7** a break in progress; stoppage **8** *US* same as **cheque** **9** *chiefly US & Canad* the bill in a restaurant **10** a pattern of squares or crossed lines **11** a single square in such a pattern **12** *chess* the state or position of a king under direct attack **13 in check** under control or restraint ▹ *interj* **14** *chiefly US & Canad* an expression of agreement ▹ See also **check in**, **check out** *etc.* [Old French *eschec* a check at chess]

checked *adj* having a pattern of squares

checker *n US & Canad* **1** same as **chequer** **2** same as **draughtsman** (sense 3)

checkered *adj US & Canad* same as **chequered**

checkers *n US & Canad* same as **draughts**

check in *vb* **1 A** to register one's arrival at a hotel or airport **B** to register the arrival of (guests or passengers) at a hotel or airport ▹ *n* **check-in** **2 A** the formal registration of arrival at a hotel or airport **B** the place where one registers one's arrival at a hotel or airport

check list *n* a list to be referred to for identification or verification

checkmate *n* **1** *chess* the winning position in which an opponent's king is under attack and unable to escape **2** utter defeat ▹ *vb* **-mating, -mated** **3** *chess* to place the king of (one's opponent) in checkmate **4** to thwart or defeat [Arabic *shāh māt* the king is dead]

check out *vb* **1** to pay the bill and leave a hotel **2** to investigate, examine, or look at: *he asked if he could check out the old man's theory; start the evening off by checking out one of the in bars in the city* ▹ *n* **checkout** **3** a counter in a supermarket, where customers pay

checkpoint *n* a place where vehicles or travellers are stopped for identification or inspection

checkup *n* a thorough examination to see if a person or thing is in good condition

check up on *vb* to investigate the background of

Cheddar *n* a firm orange or yellowy-white cheese [*Cheddar*, village in Somerset, where it was originally made]

cheek *n* **1** either side of the face below the eye **2** *informal* impudence, boldness, or lack of respect **3** *informal* a buttock **4 cheek by jowl** close together **5 turn the other cheek** to refuse to retaliate ▹ *vb* **6** *Brit, Austral & NZ informal* to speak or behave disrespectfully to someone [Old English *ceace*]

cheekbone *n* the bone at the top of the cheek, just below the eye

cheeky *adj* **cheekier, cheekiest** disrespectful; impudent **cheekily** *adv* **cheekiness** *n*

cheep *n* **1** the short weak high-pitched cry of a young bird ▹ *vb* **2** to utter a cheep [imitative]

cheer *vb* **1** to applaud or encourage with shouts **2 cheer up** to make or become happy or hopeful; comfort or be comforted ▹ *n* **3** a shout of applause or encouragement **4** a feeling of cheerfulness: *the news brought little cheer* [Middle English (in the sense: face, welcoming aspect), from Greek *kara* head]

cheerful *adj* **1** having a happy disposition **2** pleasantly bright: *a cheerful colour* **3** ungrudging: *a cheerful giver* **cheerfully** *adv* **cheerfulness** *n*

cheerio *interj* **1** *informal* a farewell greeting ▹ *n* **2** *Austral & NZ* a small red cocktail sausage

cheerleader *n* a person who leads a crowd in cheers, usually at sports events

cheerless *adj* dreary or gloomy

cheers *interj informal, chiefly Brit* **1** a drinking toast **2** a farewell greeting **3** an expression of gratitude

cheery *adj* **cheerier, cheeriest** cheerful **cheerily** *adv*

cheese[1] *n* **1** a food made from coagulated milk curd **2** a block of this [Latin *caseus*]

cheese[2] *n* **big cheese** *slang* an important person [perhaps from Hindi *chiz* thing]

cheeseburger *n* a hamburger with a slice of cheese melted on top of it

cheesecake *n* **1** a dessert with a biscuit-crumb base covered with a sweet cream-cheese mixture and sometimes with a fruit topping **2** *slang* magazine photographs of naked or scantily dressed women

cheesecloth *n* a light, loosely woven cotton cloth

cheesed off *adj Brit, Austral & NZ slang* bored, disgusted, or angry [origin unknown]

cheeseparing *adj* **1** mean or miserly ▹ *n* **2** meanness or miserliness

cheesy *adj* **cheesier, cheesiest** **1** like cheese **2** *informal* (of a smile) broad but possibly insincere **3** *informal* in poor taste: *a cheesy game show*

cheetah *n* a large fast-running wild cat of Africa and SW Asia, which has a light brown coat with black spots [Hindi *cītā*]

chef *n* a cook, usually the head cook, in a restaurant or hotel [French]

chef-d'oeuvre (shay-**durv**) *n, pl* **chefs-d'oeuvre** (shay-**durv**) a masterpiece [French]

Chelsea Pensioner *n* an inhabitant of the Chelsea Royal Hospital in SW London, a home for old and infirm soldiers

chem. **1** chemical **2** chemist **3** chemistry

chemical *n* **1** any substance used in or resulting from a reaction involving changes to atoms or molecules ▹ *adj* **2** of or used in chemistry **3** of, made from, or using chemicals: *a chemical additive found in many foods* **chemically** *adv*

chemical engineering *n* the applications of chemistry in industrial processes **chemical engineer** *n*

chemical warfare *n* warfare using weapons such as gases and poisons

chemin de fer (shem-**man** de fair) *n* a gambling game, a variation of baccarat [French: railway, referring to the fast tempo of the game]

chemise (shem-**meez**) *n* a woman's old-fashioned loose-fitting slip or dress [Late Latin *camisa*]

chemist *n* **1** *Brit, Austral & NZ* a shop selling medicines and cosmetics **2** *Brit, Austral & NZ* a

C

qualified dispenser of prescribed medicines **3** a specialist in chemistry [Medieval Latin *alchimista* alchemist]

chemistry *n* the branch of science concerned with the composition, properties, and reactions of substances

chemo *n informal* short for **chemotherapy**

chemotherapy (kee-moh-**ther**-a-pee) *n* the treatment of disease, often cancer, by means of chemicals

C

chenille (shen-**neel**) *n* **1** a thick soft tufty yarn **2** a fabric made of this [French]

cheque *or US* **check** *n* a written order to someone's bank to pay money from his or her account to the person to whom the cheque is made out [from *check* (in the sense: means of verification)]

cheque book *n* a book of detachable blank cheques issued by a bank

cheque card *n Brit* a plastic card issued by a bank guaranteeing payment of a customer's cheques

chequer *or US* **checker** *n* a piece used in Chinese chequers. See also **chequers** [Middle English: chessboard]

chequered *or US* **checkered** *adj* **1** marked by varied fortunes: *a chequered career* **2** marked with alternating squares of colour

chequered flag *n* the black-and-white checked flag traditionally shown to the winner and all finishers at the end of a motor race by a senior race official

chequers *or US* **checkers** *n* the game of draughts

cherish *vb* **1** to cling to (an idea or feeling): *cherished notions* **2** to care for [Latin *carus* dear]

Cherokee *n* **1** a member of a Native American people, formerly of the Appalachian mountains, now living chiefly in Oklahoma **2** the language of this people

cheroot (sher-**root**) *n* a cigar with both ends cut off squarely [Tamil *curuttu* curl, roll]

cherry *n, pl* **-ries 1** a small round soft fruit with red or blackish skin and a hard stone **2** the tree on which this fruit grows ▷ *adj* **3** deep red: *cherry lips* [Greek *kerasios*]

cherry tomato *n* a miniature tomato, slightly bigger than a cherry

cherub *n, pl* **cherubs** *or* (for sense 1) **cherubim 1** *Christianity* an angel, often represented as a winged child **2** an innocent or sweet child [Hebrew *kĕrūbh*] **cherubic** (chair-**roo**-bik) *adj*

chervil *n* an aniseed-flavoured herb [Old English *cerfelle*]

Cheshire cheese *n* a mild white or pale orange cheese with a crumbly texture

chess *n* a game of skill for two players using a chessboard on which chessmen are moved, with the object of checkmating the opponent's king [Old French *esches*, plural of *eschec* check]

chessboard *n* a square board divided into 64 squares of two alternating colours, for playing chess

chessman *n, pl* **-men** a piece used in chess [Middle English *chessemeyne* chess company]

chest *n* **1** the front of the body, from the neck to the waist **2 get something off one's chest** *informal* to unburden oneself of worries or secrets by talking about them **3** a heavy box for storage or shipping: *a tea chest* [Greek *kistē* box]

chesterfield *n* **1** a large couch with high padded sides and back **2** *Canad* any sofa or couch [after a 19th-century Earl of *Chesterfield*]

chestnut *n* **1** a reddish-brown edible nut **2** the tree that this nut grows on **3** a horse of a reddish-brown colour **4** *informal* an old or stale joke ▷ *adj* **5** dark reddish-brown: *chestnut hair* [Greek *kastanea*]

chest of drawers *n* a piece of furniture consisting of a set of drawers in a frame

chesty *adj* **chestier, chestiest** *Brit informal* having or symptomatic of chest disease: *chesty colds* **chestiness** *n*

cheval glass (shev-**val**) *n* a full-length mirror mounted so as to swivel within a frame [French *cheval* support (literally: horse)]

chevalier (shev-a-**leer**) *n* **1** a member of the French Legion of Honour **2** a chivalrous man [Medieval Latin *caballarius* horseman]

Cheviot *n* a large British sheep with a heavy medium-length fleece [*Cheviot* Hills on borders of England & Scotland]

chevron (**shev**-ron) *n* a V-shaped pattern, such as those worn on the sleeve of a military uniform to indicate rank [Old French]

chew *vb* **1** to work the jaws and teeth in order to grind (food) ▷ *n* **2** the act of chewing **3** something that is chewed, such as a sweet or a piece of tobacco [Old English *ceowan*]

chewing gum *n* a flavoured gum which is chewed but not swallowed

chew over *vb* to consider carefully

chewy *adj* **chewier, chewiest** of a consistency requiring a lot of chewing

chez (**shay**) *prep* at the home of [French]

chianti (kee-**ant**-ee) *n* a dry red wine produced in Tuscany, Italy

chiaroscuro (kee-ah-roh-**skew**-roh) *n, pl* **-ros** the distribution of light and shade in a picture [Italian *chiaro* clear + *oscuro* obscure]

chic (**sheek**) *adj* **1** stylish or elegant ▷ *n* **2** stylishness or elegance [French]

chicane (shik-**kane**) *n* an obstacle placed on a motor-racing circuit to slow the cars down [French *chicaner* to quibble]

chicanery *n* trickery or deception

chick *n* **1** a baby bird, esp. a domestic fowl **2** *slang, sometimes offensive* a young woman [short for *chicken*]

chicken *n* **1** a domestic fowl bred for its flesh or eggs **2** the flesh of this bird used for food **3** *slang* a coward ▷ *adj* **4** *slang* cowardly [Old English *ciecen*]

chicken feed *n slang* a trifling amount of money

chicken-hearted *adj* easily frightened; cowardly

chicken out *vb informal* to fail to do something through cowardice

chickenpox *n* an infectious viral disease, usually affecting children, which produces an itchy rash

chicken wire *n* wire netting

chickpea *n* an edible hard yellow pealike seed [Latin *cicer*]

chickweed *n* a common garden weed with small white flowers
chicory *n* **1** a plant grown for its leaves, which are used in salads, and for its roots **2** the root of this plant, roasted, dried, and used as a coffee substitute [Greek *kikhōrion*]
chide *vb* **chiding, chided** *or* **chid** *old-fashioned* to rebuke or scold [Old English *cīdan*]
chief *n* **1** the head of a group or body of people **2** the head of a tribe ▷ *adj* **3** most important: *the chief suspects* **4** highest in rank: *the Chief Constable* [Latin *caput* head]
chiefly *adv* **1** especially or essentially **2** mainly or mostly
chief petty officer *n* a senior noncommissioned officer in a navy
chieftain *n* the leader of a tribe or clan [Late Latin *capitaneus* commander]
chief technician *n* a noncommissioned officer in the Royal Air Force
chiffchaff *n* a European warbler with a yellowish-brown plumage [imitative]
chiffon (**shif**-fon) *n* a fine see-through fabric of silk or nylon [French *chiffe* rag]
chiffonier *or* **chiffonnier** (shiff-on-**near**) *n* **1** a tall elegant chest of drawers **2** a wide low open-fronted cabinet [French]
chignon (**sheen**-yon) *n* a roll or knot of long hair pinned up at the back of the head [French]
chigoe (**chig**-go) *n* a tropical flea that burrows into the skin. Also: **chigger** [Carib *chigo*]
chihuahua (chee-**wah**-wah) *n* a tiny short-haired dog, originally from Mexico [after *Chihuahua*, state in Mexico]
chilblain *n* an inflammation of the fingers or toes, caused by exposure to cold [CHILL (noun) + *blain* a blister]
child *n, pl* **children 1** a young human being; boy or girl **2** a son or daughter. Related adjective: **filial 3** a childish or immature person **4** the product of an influence or environment: *a child of the Army* **5 with child** *old-fashioned* pregnant [Old English *cild*] **childless** *adj* **childlessness** *n*
childbearing *n* **1** the process of giving birth to a child ▷ *adj* **2 of childbearing age** of an age when women are able to give birth to children
child benefit *n Brit* a regular government payment to parents of children up to a certain age
childbirth *n* the act of giving birth to a child. Related adjective: **natal**
childhood *n* the time or condition of being a child
childish *adj* **1** immature or silly: *childish fighting over who did what* **2** of or like a child: *childish illnesses*
childlike *adj* like a child, for example in being innocent or trustful
child minder *n* a person who looks after children whose parents are working
children *n* the plural of **child**
child's play *n informal* something that is easy to do
chill *n* **1** a feverish cold **2** a moderate coldness **3** a feeling of coldness resulting from a cold or damp environment or from sudden fear ▷ *vb* **4** to make (something) cool or cold: *chilled white wine* **5** to cause (someone) to feel cold or frightened **6** *informal* to relax or calm oneself ▷ *adj* **7** unpleasantly cold: *chill winds* [Old English *ciele*] **chilling** *adj* **chillingly** *adv*
chilled *or* **chilled-out** *adj informal* relaxed or easy-going in character or behaviour
chiller *n* **1** short for **spine-chiller 2** a cooling or refrigerating device
chilli *or* **chili** *n* **1** *pl* **chillies** *or* **chilies** the small red or green hot-tasting pod of a type of capsicum, used in cookery, often in powdered form **2** short for **chilli con carne** [Mexican Indian]
chilli con carne *n* a highly seasoned Mexican dish of meat, onions, beans, and chilli powder [Spanish: chilli with meat]
chill out *informal* ▷ *vb* **1** to relax, esp. after energetic dancing or hard work ▷ *adj* **chill-out 2** suitable for relaxation after energetic dancing: *a chill-out area*
chilly *adj* **-lier, -liest 1** feeling or causing to feel moderately cold **2** without warmth; unfriendly: *a chilly reception*
chilly bin *n NZ informal* a portable insulated container for packing food and drink in ice
Chiltern Hundreds *pl n* (in Britain) a nominal office for which an MP applies in order to resign his or her seat
chime *n* **1** the musical ringing sound made by a bell or clock ▷ *vb* **chiming, chimed 2** (of a bell) to make a clear musical ringing sound **3** (of a clock) to indicate (the time) by chiming [Latin *cymbalum* cymbal]
chime in *vb* to say something just after someone else has spoken
chimera (kime-**meer**-a) *n* **1** a wild and unrealistic dream or idea **2** *Greek myth* a fire-breathing monster with the head of a lion, body of a goat, and tail of a serpent [Greek *khimaira* she-goat]
chimerical *adj* wildly fanciful or imaginary
chime with *vb* to agree or be consistent with
chimney *n* a hollow vertical structure that carries smoke or steam away from a fire or engine [Greek *kaminos* oven]
chimney breast *n* the walls surrounding the base of a chimney or fireplace
chimneypot *n* a short pipe on the top of a chimney
chimney stack *n* the part of a chimney sticking up above a roof
chimney sweep *n* a person who cleans soot from chimneys
chimp *n informal* short for **chimpanzee**
chimpanzee *n* an intelligent small black ape of central W Africa [African dialect]
chin *n* the front part of the face below the mouth [Old English *cinn*]
china[1] *n* **1** ceramic ware of a type originally from China **2** dishes or ornamental objects made of china [Persian *chīnī*]
china[2] *n Brit & S African informal* a friend or companion [from cockney rhyming slang *china plate* mate]
china clay *n* same as **kaolin**
Chinaman *n, pl* **-men** *archaic or offensive* a native or inhabitant of China

Chinatown *n* a section of a town or city outside China with a mainly Chinese population
chinchilla *n* **1** a small S American rodent bred in captivity for its soft silvery-grey fur **2** the fur of this animal [Spanish]
chine *n* **1** a cut of meat including part of the backbone ▷ *vb* **chining, chined 2** to cut (meat) along the backbone [Old French *eschine*]
Chinese *adj* **1** of China ▷ *n* **2** *pl* **-nese** a person from China or a descendant of one **3** any of the languages of China
Chinese chequers *n* a game played with marbles or pegs on a six-pointed star-shaped board
Chinese lantern *n* a collapsible lantern made of thin paper
Chinese leaves *pl n* the edible leaves of a Chinese cabbage
Chinese puzzle *n* a complicated puzzle or problem
chink[1] *n* a small narrow opening: *a chink of light* [Old English *cine* crack]
chink[2] *vb* **1** to make a light ringing sound ▷ *n* **2** a light ringing sound [imitative]
chinless wonder *n Brit informal* a person, usually upper-class, lacking strength of character
chinoiserie (sheen-**wahz**-a-ree) *n* **1** a style of decorative art based on imitations of Chinese motifs **2** objects in this style [French *chinois* Chinese]
Chinook *n* **1** *pl* **-nook** *or* **-nooks** a member of a Native American people of the Pacific coast of N America **2** the language of this people
Chinook salmon *n* a Pacific salmon valued as a food fish
chinos (**chee**-nohz) *pl n* trousers made of a kind of hard-wearing cotton [*chino*, the cloth; origin unknown]
chintz *n* a printed patterned cotton fabric with a glazed finish, used for curtains and chair coverings [Hindi *chīnt*]
chintzy *adj* **chintzier, chintziest 1** of or covered with chintz **2** (of a room or house) decorated in an excessively fussy or twee way
chinwag *n Brit, Austral & NZ informal* a chat
chip *n* **1** a thin strip of potato fried in deep fat **2** *US, Canad, Austral & NZ* a potato crisp **3** *electronics* a tiny wafer of semiconductor material, such as silicon, processed to form an integrated circuit **4** a counter used to represent money in gambling games **5** a small piece removed by chopping, cutting, or breaking **6** a mark left where a small piece has been broken off something **7 chip off the old block** *informal* a person who resembles one of his or her parents in personality **8 have a chip on one's shoulder** *informal* to be resentful or bear a grudge **9 when the chips are down** *informal* at a time of crisis ▷ *vb* **chipping, chipped 10** to break small pieces from [Old English *cipp*]
chip and PIN *n* a system for authorizing credit- or debit-card payment requiring the purchaser to enter a personal identification number
chipboard *n* thin rigid board made of compressed wood particles
chip in *vb informal* **1** to contribute to a common fund **2** to interrupt with a remark
chipmunk *n* a squirrel-like striped burrowing rodent of North America and Asia [from a Native American language]
chipolata *n chiefly Brit* a small sausage [Italian *cipolla* onion]
Chippendale *adj* (of furniture) by or in the style of Thomas Chippendale, with Chinese and Gothic motifs, curved legs, and massive carving
chipset *n* a group of integrated circuits on the motherboard of a computer that controls the flow of data and instructions
chiropody (kir-**rop**-pod-ee) *n* the treatment of minor foot complaints like corns **chiropodist** *n*
chiropractic (kire-oh-**prak**-tik) *n* a system of treating bodily disorders by manipulation of the spine [Greek *kheir* hand + *praktikos* practical] **chiropractor** *n*
chirp *vb* **1** (of some birds and insects) to make a short high-pitched sound **2** *Brit, Austral & NZ* to speak in a lively fashion ▷ *n* **3** a chirping sound [imitative]
chirpy *adj* **chirpier, chirpiest** *informal* lively and cheerful **chirpiness** *n*
chirrup *vb* **1** (of some birds) to chirp repeatedly ▷ *n* **2** a chirruping sound [variant of *chirp*]
chisel *n* **1** a metal tool with a sharp end for shaping wood or stone ▷ *vb* **-elling, -elled** *or US* **-eling, -eled 2** to carve or form with a chisel [Latin *caesus* cut]
chiselled *or US* **chiseled** *adj* finely or sharply formed: *chiselled angular features*
chit *n* a short official note, such as a memorandum, requisition, or receipt. Also: **chitty** [Hindi *cittha* note]
chitchat *n* chat or gossip
chitin (**kite**-in) *n* the tough substance forming the outer layer of the bodies of arthropods [Greek *khitōn* tunic]
chitterlings *pl n* the intestines of a pig or other animal prepared as food [origin unknown]
chivalrous *adj* gallant or courteous **chivalrously** *adv*
chivalry *n* **1** courteous behaviour, esp. by men towards women **2** the medieval system and principles of knighthood [Old French *chevalier* knight] **chivalric** *adj*
chives *pl n* the long slender hollow leaves of a small Eurasian plant, used in cooking for their onion-like flavour [Latin *caepa* onion]
chivvy *vb* **-vies, -vying, -vied** *Brit* to harass or nag [probably from *Chevy Chase*, a Scottish ballad]
chlamydia (klam-**mid**-ee-a) *n* a sexually transmitted disease caused by a parasitic bacterium [Greek *khlamus* mantle]
chloral hydrate *n* a colourless crystalline solid used as a sedative
chlorate *n chem* any salt containing the ion ClO_3^-
chloride *n chem* **1** any compound of chlorine and another element and radical **2** any salt or ester of hydrochloric acid
chlorinate *vb* **-ating, -ated 1** to disinfect (water) with chlorine **2** *chem* to combine or treat (a substance) with chlorine: *chlorinated hydrocarbons* **chlorination** *n*
chlorine *n* a poisonous strong-smelling greenish-yellow gaseous element, used in water

purification and as a disinfectant, and, combined with sodium, to make common salt. Symbol: **Cl**

chloro- *combining form* green [Greek *khlōros*]

chlorofluorocarbon *n chem* any of various gaseous compounds of carbon, hydrogen, chlorine, and fluorine, used as refrigerants and aerosol propellants, some of which break down the ozone in the atmosphere

chloroform *n* a sweet-smelling liquid, used as a solvent and cleansing agent, and formerly as an anaesthetic [CHLORO- + *formyl*: see FORMIC ACID]

chlorophyll *or US* **chlorophyl** *n* the green colouring matter of plants, which enables them to convert sunlight into energy [CHLORO- + Greek *phullon* leaf]

chloroplast *n biol* one of the parts of a plant cell that contains chlorophyll [CHLORO- + Greek *plastos* formed]

chock *n* **1** a block or wedge of wood used to prevent the sliding or rolling of a heavy object ▹ *vb* **2** to fit with or secure by a chock [origin unknown]

chock-a-block *adj* filled to capacity

chock-full *adj* completely full

chocolate *n* **1** a food made from roasted ground cacao seeds, usually sweetened and flavoured **2** a sweet or drink made from this ▹ *adj* **3** deep brown [Aztec *xocolatl*] **chocolaty** *adj*

choice *n* **1** the act of choosing or selecting **2** the opportunity or power of choosing: *parental choice* **3** a person or thing chosen or that may be chosen: *the president's choice as the new head of the CIA* **4** an alternative action or possibility: *they had no choice but to accept* **5** a range from which to select: *a choice of weapons* ▹ *adj* **6** of high quality: *choice government jobs* **7** carefully chosen: *a few choice words* **8** vulgar: *choice language* [Old French *choisir* to choose]

choir *n* **1** an organized group of singers, usually for singing in church **2** the part of a church, in front of the altar, occupied by the choir [Latin *chorus*]

choirboy *n* a boy who sings in a church choir

choke *vb* **choking, choked 1** to hinder or stop the breathing of (a person or animal) by strangling or smothering **2** to have trouble in breathing, swallowing, or speaking **3** to block or clog up: *the old narrow streets become choked to a standstill* **4** to hinder the growth of: *weeds would outgrow and choke the rice crop* ▹ *n* **5** a device in a vehicle's engine that enriches the petrol-air mixture by reducing the air supply [Old English *ācēocian*]

choke back *vb* to suppress (tears or anger)

choked *adj informal* disappointed or angry: *I still feel choked about him leaving*

choker *n* a tight-fitting necklace

choke up *vb* **1** to block completely **2 choked up** *informal* overcome with emotion

choko *n, pl* **-kos** *Austral & NZ* the pear-shaped fruit of a tropical American vine, eaten as a vegetable [Brazilian Indian]

choler (**kol**-ler) *n archaic* anger or bad temper [Greek *kholē* bile]

cholera (**kol**-ler-a) *n* a serious infectious disease causing severe diarrhoea and stomach cramps, caught from contaminated water or food [Greek *kholē* bile]

choleric *adj* bad-tempered

cholesterol (kol-**lest**-er-oll) *n* a fatty alcohol found in all animal fats, tissues, and fluids, an excess of which is thought to contribute to heart and artery disease [Greek *kholē* bile + *stereos* solid]

chomp *vb* to chew (food) noisily

chook *n informal, chiefly Austral & NZ* a hen or chicken

choose *vb* **choosing, chose, chosen 1** to select (a person, thing, or course of action) from a number of alternatives **2** to like or please: *when she did choose to reveal her secret, the group were initially hushed* **3** to consider it desirable or proper: *I don't choose to read that sort of book* [Old English *ceosan*]

choosy *adj* **choosier, choosiest** *informal* fussy; hard to please

chop[1] *vb* **chopping, chopped 1** (often foll. by *down* or *off*) to cut (something) with a blow from an axe or other sharp tool **2** to cut into pieces **3** *boxing & karate* to hit (an opponent) with a short sharp blow **4** *Brit, Austral & NZ informal* to dispense with or reduce **5** *sport* to hit (a ball) sharply downwards ▹ *n* **6** a cutting blow **7** a slice of mutton, lamb, or pork, usually including a rib **8** *sport* a sharp downward blow or stroke **9 the chop** *slang* dismissal from employment [variant of *chap*: see CHAPPED]

chop[2] *vb* **chopping, chopped 1 chop and change** to change one's mind repeatedly **2 chop logic** to use excessively subtle or involved argument [Old English *ceapian* to barter]

chop chop *adv slang* quickly

chopper *n* **1** *informal* a helicopter **2** *chiefly Brit* a small hand axe **3** a butcher's cleaver **4** a type of bicycle or motorcycle with very high handlebars **5** *NZ* a child's bicycle

choppy *adj* **-pier, -piest** (of the sea) fairly rough **choppiness** *n*

chops *pl n Brit, Austral & NZ informal* **1** the jaws or cheeks **2 lick one's chops** to anticipate something with pleasure [origin unknown]

chopsticks *pl n* a pair of thin sticks of ivory, wood, or plastic, used for eating Chinese or other East Asian food [pidgin English, from Chinese]

chop suey *n* a Chinese-style dish of chopped meat, bean sprouts, and other vegetables in a sauce [Chinese *tsap sui* odds and ends]

choral *adj* of or for a choir

chorale (kor-**rahl**) *n* **1** a slow stately hymn tune **2** *chiefly US* a choir or chorus [German *Choralgesang* choral song]

chord[1] *n* **1** *maths* a straight line connecting two points on a curve **2** *anatomy* same as **cord 3 strike** *or* **touch a chord** to bring about an emotional response, usually of sympathy [Greek *khordē* string]

chord[2] *n* the simultaneous sounding of three or more musical notes [short for *accord*]

chordate *n* any animal that has a long fibrous rod just above the gut to support the body, such as the vertebrates

chore *n* **1** a small routine task **2** an unpleasant task [Old English *cerr* a turn of work]

C

chorea (kor-ree-a) *n* a disorder of the nervous system characterized by uncontrollable brief jerky movements [Greek *khoreia* dance]
choreograph *vb* to compose the steps and dances for (a piece of music or ballet)
choreography *n* **1** the composition of steps and movements for ballet and other dancing **2** the steps and movements of a ballet or dance [Greek *khoreia* dance + -GRAPHY] **choreographer** *n* **choreographic** *adj*
chorister *n* a singer in a church choir
chortle *vb* **-tling, -tled 1** to chuckle with amusement ▷ *n* **2** an amused chuckle [coined by Lewis Carroll]
chorus *n, pl* **-ruses 1** a large choir **2** a piece of music to be sung by a large choir **3** a part of a song repeated after each verse **4** something expressed by many people at once: *a chorus of boos* **5** the noise made by a group of birds or small animals: *the dawn chorus* **6** a group of singers or dancers who perform together in a show **7** (in ancient Greece) a group of actors who commented on the action of a play **8** (in Elizabethan drama) the actor who spoke the prologue and epilogue **9 in chorus** in unison ▷ *vb* **10** to sing or say together [Greek *khoros*]
chorus girl *n* a young woman who dances or sings in the chorus of a show or film
chose *vb* the past tense of **choose**
chosen *vb* **1** the past participle of **choose** ▷ *adj* **2** selected for some special quality: *the chosen one*
chough (chuff) *n* a large black bird of the crow family [origin unknown]
choux pastry (shoo) *n* a very light pastry made with eggs [French *pâte choux* cabbage dough]
chow *n* **1** a thick-coated dog with a curled tail, originally from China **2** *informal* food [pidgin English]
chowder *n* a thick soup containing clams or fish [French *chaudière* kettle]
chow mein *n* a Chinese-American dish consisting of chopped meat or vegetables fried with noodles [from Chinese]
chrism *n* consecrated oil used for anointing in some churches [Greek *khriein* to anoint]
Christ *n* **1** Jesus of Nazareth (Jesus Christ), regarded by Christians as the Messiah of Old Testament prophecies **2** the Messiah of Old Testament prophecies **3** an image or picture of Christ ▷ *interj* **4** *taboo slang* an oath expressing annoyance or surprise [Greek *khristos* anointed one]
christen *vb* **1** same as **baptize 2** to give a name to (a person or thing) **3** *informal* to use for the first time [Old English *cristnian*] **christening** *n*
Christendom *n* all Christian people or countries
Christian *n* **1** a person who believes in and follows Jesus Christ **2** *informal* a person who displays the virtues of kindness and mercy encouraged in the teachings of Jesus Christ ▷ *adj* **3** of Jesus Christ, Christians, or Christianity **4** kind or good
Christian Era *n* the period beginning with the year of Christ's birth
Christianity *n* **1** the religion based on the life and teachings of Christ **2** Christian beliefs or practices **3** same as **Christendom**
Christianize *or* **-ise** *vb* **-izing, -ized** *or* **-ising, -ised 1** to convert to Christianity **2** to fill with Christian principles, spirit, or outlook **Christianization** *or* **-isation** *n*
Christian name *n* a personal name formally given to Christians at baptism: loosely used to mean a person's first name

> **USAGE** The alternatives *first name*, *forename*, and *given name*, which do not refer to a particular faith, and are therefore more inclusive, are now usually preferred to *Christian name* in general use.

Christian Science *n* the religious system founded by Mary Baker Eddy (1866), which emphasizes spiritual regeneration and healing through prayer **Christian Scientist** *n*
Christmas *n* **1 A** a Christian festival commemorating the birth of Christ, held by most Churches to have occurred on December 25 **B** Also: **Christmas Day** December 25, as a day of secular celebrations when gifts and greetings are exchanged ▷ *adj* **2** connected with or taking place at the time of year when this festival is celebrated: *the Christmas holidays* [Old English *Crīstes mæsse* Mass of Christ] **Christmassy** *adj*
Christmas box *n* a tip or present given at Christmas, esp. to postmen or tradesmen
Christmas Eve *n* the evening or the whole day before Christmas Day
Christmas pudding *n Brit & Austral* a rich steamed pudding containing suet, dried fruit, and spices
Christmas rose *n* an evergreen plant with white or pink winter-blooming flowers
Christmas tree *n* an evergreen tree or an imitation of one, decorated as part of Christmas celebrations
chromate *n chem* any salt or ester of chromic acid
chromatic *adj* **1** of or in colour or colours **2** *music* **A** involving the sharpening or flattening of notes or the use of such notes **B** of the chromatic scale [Greek *khrōma* colour] **chromatically** *adv*
chromatics *n* the science of colour
chromatic scale *n* a twelve-note scale including all the semitones of the octave
chromatin *n biochem* the part of the nucleus of a cell that forms the chromosomes and can easily be dyed [from *chrome*]
chromatography *n* the technique of separating and analysing the components of a mixture of liquids or gases by slowly passing it through an adsorbing material [Greek *khrōma* colour + -GRAPHY]
chrome *n* **1** same as **chromium 2** anything plated with chromium ▷ *vb* **chroming, chromed 3** to plate with chromium [Greek *khrōma* colour]
chromite *n* a brownish-black mineral which is the only commercial source of chromium
chromium *n chem* a hard grey metallic element, used in steel alloys and electroplating to increase hardness and corrosion resistance. Symbol: **Cr** [from *chrome*]
chromosome *n* any of the microscopic rod-shaped structures that appear in a cell nucleus during cell division, consisting of units (genes) that are responsible for the transmission

of hereditary characteristics [Greek *khrōma* colour + *sōma* body]
chromosphere *n* a gaseous layer of the sun's atmosphere extending from the photosphere to the corona
chronic *adj* **1** (of a disease) developing slowly or lasting for a long time **2** (of a bad habit or bad behaviour) having continued for a long time; habitual: *chronic drug addiction* **3** very serious or severe: *chronic food shortages* **4** *Brit, Austral & NZ informal* very bad: *the play was chronic* [Greek *khronos* time] **chronically** *adv*
chronic fatigue syndrome *n* a condition characterized by painful muscles and general weakness sometimes persisting long after a viral illness
chronicle *n* **1** a record of events in chronological order ▷ *vb* **-cling, -cled 2** to record in or as if in a chronicle [Greek *khronika* annals] **chronicler** *n*
chronological *adj* **1** (of a sequence of events) arranged in order of occurrence **2** relating to chronology **chronologically** *adv*
chronology *n, pl* **-gies 1** the arrangement of dates or events in order of occurrence **2** the determining of the proper sequence of past events **3** a table of events arranged in order of occurrence [Greek *khronos* time + -LOGY] **chronologist** *n*
chronometer *n* a timepiece designed to be accurate in all conditions [Greek *khronos* time + -METER]
chrysalis (**kriss**-a-liss) *n* an insect in the stage between larva and adult, when it is in a cocoon [Greek *khrusos* gold]
chrysanthemum *n* a garden plant with large round flowers made up of many petals [Greek *khrusos* gold + *anthemon* flower]
chub *n, pl* **chub** *or* **chubs** a common freshwater game fish of the carp family with a dark greenish body [origin unknown]
chubby *adj* **-bier, -biest** plump and round [perhaps from *chub*] **chubbiness** *n*
chuck[1] *vb* **1** *informal* to throw carelessly **2** *informal* (sometimes foll. by *in* or *up*) to give up; reject: *he chucked in his job* **3** to pat (someone) affectionately under the chin **4** *Austral & NZ informal* to vomit ▷ *n* **5** a throw or toss **6** a pat under the chin ▷ See also **chuck off, chuck out** [origin unknown]
chuck[2] *n* **1** Also: **chuck steak** a cut of beef from the neck to the shoulder blade **2** a device that holds a workpiece in a lathe or a tool in a drill [variant of *chock*]
chuck[3] *n W Canad* **1** a large body of water **2** Also: **saltchuck** the sea [Chinook]
chuckle *vb* **-ling, -led 1** to laugh softly or to oneself ▷ *n* **2** a partly suppressed laugh [probably from *chuck* cluck]
chuck off *vb* (often foll. by *at*) *Austral & NZ informal* to abuse or make fun of
chuck out *vb informal* to throw out
chuddies *pl n Indian informal* underpants
chuff *vb* to move while making a puffing sound, as a steam engine [imitative]
chuffed *adj informal* pleased or delighted: *I suppose you're feeling pretty chuffed* [origin unknown]
chug *n* **1** a short dull sound like the noise of an engine ▷ *vb* **chugging, chugged 2** (esp. of an engine) to operate or move with this sound: *lorries chug past* [imitative]
chukka *or* **chukker** *n polo* a period of continuous play, usually 7½ minutes [Hindi *cakkar*]
chum *n* **1** *informal* a close friend ▷ *vb* **chumming, chummed 2 chum up with** to form a close friendship with [probably from *chamber fellow*]
chummy *adj* **-mier, -miest** *informal* friendly **chummily** *adv* **chumminess** *n*
chump *n* **1** *informal* a stupid person **2** a thick piece of meat [origin unknown]
chunder *vb slang, chiefly Austral* to vomit [origin unknown]
chunk *n* **1** a thick solid piece of something **2** a considerable amount [variant of CHUCK[2]]
chunky *adj* **chunkier, chunkiest 1** thick and short **2** containing thick pieces **3** *chiefly Brit* (of clothes, esp. knitwear) made of thick bulky material **chunkiness** *n*
church *n* **1** a building for public Christian worship **2** religious services held in a church **3** a particular Christian denomination **4** Christians collectively **5** the clergy as distinguished from the laity **6 Church** institutional religion as a political or social force: *conflict between Church and State* [Greek *kuriakon (dōma)* the Lord's (house)]
churchgoer *n* a person who attends church regularly
churchman *n, pl* **-men** a clergyman
Church of England *n* the reformed established state Church in England, with the sovereign as its temporal head
Church of Scotland *n* the established Presbyterian church in Scotland
churchwarden *n* **1** *Church of England & Episcopal Church* a lay assistant of a parish priest **2** an old-fashioned long-stemmed tobacco pipe made of clay
churchyard *n* the grounds round a church, used as a graveyard
churl *n* **1** a surly ill-bred person **2** *archaic* a farm labourer [Old English *ceorl*]
churlish *adj* surly and rude
churn *n* **1** a machine in which cream is shaken to make butter **2** a large container for milk ▷ *vb* **3** to stir (milk or cream) vigorously in order to make butter **4** to move about violently: *a hot tub of churning water* [Old English *ciern*]
churn out *vb informal* to produce (something) rapidly and in large numbers
chute[1] (**shoot**) *n* a steep sloping channel or passage down which things may be dropped [Old French *cheoite* fallen]
chute[2] *n informal* short for **parachute**
chutney *n* a pickle of Indian origin, made from fruit, vinegar, spices, and sugar: *mango chutney* [Hindi *catni*]
chutzpah (**hoots**-pa) *n informal* unashamed self-confidence; impudence [Yiddish]
chyle *n* a milky fluid formed in the small intestine during digestion [Greek *khulos* juice]
chyme *n* the thick fluid mass of partially digested food that leaves the stomach [Greek *khumos* juice]

chypre (**sheep**-ra) *n* a perfume made from sandalwood [French: Cyprus]
Ci curie
CI Channel Islands
CIA Central Intelligence Agency; a US bureau responsible for espionage and intelligence activities
ciabatta (cha-**bat**-ta) *n* a type of bread made with olive oil [Italian: slipper]
cicada (sik-**kah**-da) *n* a large broad insect, found in hot countries, that makes a high-pitched drone [Latin]
cicatrix (**sik**-a-trix) *n, pl* **cicatrices** (sik-a-**trice**-eez) the tissue that forms in a wound during healing; scar [Latin: scar]
cicerone (siss-a-**rone**-ee) *n, pl* **-nes** *or* **-ni** *literary* a person who guides and informs sightseers [after *Cicero*, Roman orator]
CID (in Britain) Criminal Investigation Department; the detective division of a police force
cider *n* an alcoholic drink made from fermented apple juice [Hebrew *shēkhār* strong drink]
cigar *n* a tube-like roll of cured tobacco leaves for smoking [Spanish *cigarro*]
cigarette *n* a thin roll of shredded tobacco in thin paper, for smoking [French: a little cigar]
ciggie *or* **ciggy** *n, pl* **-ies** *informal* a cigarette
cilantro (sil-**lan**-tro) *n chiefly US & Canad* a European plant, cultivated for its aromatic seeds and leaves, used in flavouring foods. Also called: **coriander** [Spanish]
cilium *n, pl* **cilia** *biol* **1** any of the short threads projecting from a cell or organism, whose rhythmic beating causes movement **2** an eyelash [Latin] **ciliary** *adj*
C in C *military* Commander in Chief
cinch (**sinch**) *n* **1** *informal* an easy task **2** *slang* a certainty [Spanish *cincha* saddle girth]
cinchona (sing-**kone**-a) *n* **1** a South American tree or shrub with medicinal bark **2** its dried bark, which yields quinine **3** a drug made from cinchona bark [after the Countess of *Chinchón*]
cincture *n literary* something, such as a belt or girdle, that goes around another thing [Latin *cingere* to gird]
cinder *n* **1** a piece of material that will not burn, left after burning coal or wood **2 cinders** ashes [Old English *sinder*]
Cinderella *n* a poor, neglected, or unsuccessful person or thing [after *Cinderella*, the heroine of a fairy tale]
cinema *n* **1** a place designed for showing films **2 the cinema** **A** the art or business of making films **B** films collectively [Greek *kinēma* motion] **cinematic** *adj*
cinematography *n* the technique of making films: *he won an Oscar for his stunning cinematography* [CINEMA + -GRAPHY] **cinematographer** *n* **cinematographic** *adj*
cineraria *n* a garden plant with daisy-like flowers [Latin *cinis* ashes]
cinerarium *n, pl* **-raria** a place for keeping the ashes of the dead after cremation [Latin *cinerarius* relating to ashes] **cinerary** *adj*
cinnabar *n* **1** a heavy red mineral containing mercury **2** a large red-and-black European moth [Greek *kinnabari*]
cinnamon *n* the spice obtained from the aromatic bark of a tropical Asian tree [Hebrew *qinnamown*]
cinquefoil *n* **1** a plant with five-lobed compound leaves **2** an ornamental carving in the form of five arcs arranged in a circle [Latin *quinquefolium* plant with five leaves]
Cinque Ports *pl n* an association of ports on the SE coast of England, with certain ancient duties and privileges
cipher *or* **cypher** (**sife**-er) *n* **1** a method of secret writing using substitution of letters according to a key **2** a secret message **3** the key to a secret message **4** a person or thing of no importance **5** *obsolete* the numeral zero ▷ *vb* **6** to put (a message) into secret writing [Arabic *sifr* zero]
circa (**sir**-ka) *prep* (used with a date) approximately; about: *circa 1788* [Latin]
circadian *adj* of biological processes that occur regularly at 24-hour intervals [Latin *circa* about + *dies* day]
circle *n* **1** a curved line surrounding a central point, every point of the line being the same distance from the centre **2** the figure enclosed by such a curve **3** something formed or arranged in the shape of a circle: *they ran round in little circles* **4** a group of people sharing an interest, activity, or upbringing: *his judgment is well respected in diplomatic circles* **5** *theatre* the section of seats above the main level of the auditorium **6** a process or chain of events or parts that forms a connected whole; cycle **7 come full circle** to arrive back at one's starting point ▷ *vb* **-cling, -cled 8** to move in a circle (around) **9** to enclose in a circle [Latin *circus*]
circlet *n* a small circle or ring, esp. a circular ornament worn on the head [Old French *cerclet* little circle]
circuit *n* **1** a complete route or course, esp. one that is circular or that lies around an object **2** a complete path through which an electric current can flow **3 A** a periodical journey around an area, as made by judges or salespeople **B** the places visited on such a journey **4** a motor-racing track **5** *sport* a series of tournaments in which the same players regularly take part: *the professional golf circuit* **6** a number of theatres or cinemas under one management [Latin *circum* around + *ire* to go]
circuit breaker *n* a device that stops the flow of current in an electrical circuit if there is a fault
circuitous (sir-**kew**-it-uss) *adj* indirect and lengthy: *a circuitous route*
circuitry (**sir**-kit-tree) *n* **1** the design of an electrical circuit **2** the system of circuits used in an electronic device
circular *adj* **1** of or in the shape of a circle **2** travelling in a circle **3** (of an argument) not valid because a statement is used to prove the conclusion and the conclusion to prove the statement **4** (of letters or announcements) intended for general distribution ▷ *n* **5** a letter or advertisement sent to a large number of people at the same time **circularity** *n*

circularize *or* **-ise** *vb* **-izing, -ized** *or* **-ising, -ised** to distribute circulars to
circular saw *n* a power-driven saw in which a circular disc with a toothed edge is rotated at high speed
circulate *vb* **-lating, -lated 1** to send, go, or pass from place to place or person to person: *rumours were circulating that he was about to resign* **2** to move through a circuit or system, returning to the starting point: *regular exercise keeps the blood circulating around the body* **3** to move around the guests at a party, talking to different people: *it wasn't like her not to circulate among all the guests* [Latin *circulari*] **circulatory** *adj*
circulation *n* **1** the flow of blood from the heart through the arteries, and then back through the veins to the heart, where the cycle is renewed **2** the number of copies of a newspaper or magazine that are sold **3** the distribution of newspapers or magazines **4** sending or moving around: *the circulation of air* **5 in circulation A** (of currency) being used by the public **B** (of people) active in a social or business context
circum- *prefix* around; on all sides: *circumlocution* [Latin]
circumcise *vb* **-cising, -cised 1** to remove the foreskin of (a male) **2** to cut or remove the clitoris of (a female) **3** to perform such an operation as a religious rite on (someone) [Latin CIRCUM- + *caedere* to cut] **circumcision** *n*
circumference *n* **1** the boundary of a specific area or figure, esp. of a circle **2** the distance round this [Latin CIRCUM- + *ferre* to bear] **circumferential** *adj*
circumflex *n* a mark (^) placed over a vowel to show that it is pronounced in a particular way, for instance as a long vowel in French [Latin CIRCUM- + *flectere* to bend]
circumlocution *n* **1** an indirect way of saying something **2** an indirect expression **circumlocutory** *adj*
circumnavigate *vb* **-gating, -gated** to sail, fly, or walk right around **circumnavigation** *n*
circumscribe *vb* **-scribing, -scribed 1** *formal* to limit or restrict within certain boundaries: *the President's powers are circumscribed by the Constitution* **2** *geom* to draw a geometric figure around (another figure) so that the two are in contact but do not intersect [Latin CIRCUM- + *scribere* to write] **circumscription** *n*
circumspect *adj* cautious and careful not to take risks [Latin CIRCUM- + *specere* to look] **circumspection** *n* **circumspectly** *adv*
circumstance *n* **1** an occurrence or condition that accompanies or influences a person or event **2** unplanned events and situations which cannot be controlled: *a victim of circumstance* **3 pomp and circumstance** formal display or ceremony **4 under** *or* **in no circumstances** in no case; never **5 under the circumstances** because of conditions [Latin CIRCUM- + *stare* to stand]
circumstantial *adj* **1** (of evidence) strongly suggesting something but not proving it **2** fully detailed
circumstantiate *vb* **-ating, -ated** to prove by giving details
circumvent *vb formal* **1** to avoid or get round (a rule, restriction, etc.) **2** to outwit (a person) [Latin CIRCUM- + *venire* to come] **circumvention** *n*
circus *n, pl* **-cuses 1** a travelling company of entertainers such as acrobats, clowns, trapeze artists, and trained animals **2** a public performance given by such a company **3** *Brit* an open place in a town where several streets meet **4** *informal* a hectic or well-published situation: *her second marriage turned into a media circus* **5** (in ancient Rome) an open-air stadium for chariot races or public games **6** a travelling group of professional sportspeople: *the Formula One circus* [Greek *kirkos* ring]
cirque (**sirk**) *n* a steep-sided semicircular hollow found in mountainous areas
cirrhosis (sir-**roh**-siss) *n* a chronic progressive disease of the liver, often caused by drinking too much alcohol [Greek *kirrhos* orange-coloured]
cirrocumulus (sirr-oh-**kew**-myew-luss) *n, pl* **-li** (-lie) a high cloud of ice crystals grouped into small separate globular masses
cirrostratus (sirr-oh-**strah**-tuss) *n, pl* **-ti** (-tie) a uniform layer of cloud above about 6000 metres
cirrus *n, pl* **-ri 1** a thin wispy cloud found at high altitudes **2** a plant tendril **3** a slender tentacle in certain sea creatures [Latin: curl]
cis *adj* short for **cisgender**
CIS Commonwealth of Independent States
cisalpine *adj* on this (the southern) side of the Alps, as viewed from Rome
cisco *n, pl* **-coes** *or* **-cos** a whitefish, esp. the lake herring of cold deep lakes of North America [from a Native American language]
cisgender *adj* having a gender identity that fully corresponds to the gender assigned to one at birth
cissy *n, pl* **-sies**, *adj* same as **sissy**
Cistercian *n* **1** a Christian monk or nun belonging to an especially strict Benedictine order ▷ *adj* **2** of or relating to this order [*Cîteaux*, original home of the order]
cistern *n* **1** a water tank, esp. one which holds water for flushing a toilet **2** an underground reservoir [Latin *cista* box]
citadel *n* a fortress in a city [Latin *civitas*]
citation *n* **1** an official commendation or award, esp. for bravery **2** the quoting of a book or author **3** a quotation
cite *vb* **citing, cited 1** to quote or refer to (a passage, book, or author) **2** to bring forward as proof **3** to summon to appear before a court of law **4** to mention or commend (someone) for outstanding bravery **5** to enumerate: *the president cited the wonders of the American family* [Old French *citer* to summon]
citified *adj often derogatory* having the customs, manners, or dress of city people
citizen *n* **1** a native or naturalized member of a state or nation **2** an inhabitant of a city or town
citizenry *n* citizens collectively
Citizens' Band *n* a range of radio frequencies for use by the public for private communication
citizenship *n* the condition or status of a citizen, with its rights and duties
citrate *n* any salt or ester of citric acid

C

citric *adj* of or derived from citrus fruits or citric acid
citric acid *n* a weak acid found especially in citrus fruits and used as a flavouring (E330)
citron *n* **1** a lemon-like fruit of a small Asian tree **2** the candied rind of this fruit, for decorating foods [Latin *citrus* citrus tree]
citronella *n* **1** a tropical Asian grass with lemon-scented leaves **2** the aromatic oil obtained from this grass
citrus fruit *n* a juicy, sharp-tasting fruit such as an orange, lemon, or lime [Latin *citrus* citrus tree]
city *n, pl* **cities 1** any large town **2** (in Britain) a town that has received this title from the Crown **3** the people of a city collectively **4** (in the US and Canada) a large town with its own government established by charter from the state or provincial government [Latin *civis* citizen]
City *n* **the City** *Brit* **1** the area in central London in which the United Kingdom's major financial business is transacted **2** the various financial institutions in this area
city editor *n* **1** *Brit* (on a newspaper) the editor in charge of business news **2** *US & Canad* (on a newspaper) the editor in charge of local news
city-state *n history* a state consisting of a sovereign city and its dependencies
civet (**siv**-vit) *n* **1** a spotted catlike mammal of Africa and S Asia **2** the musky fluid produced by this animal, used in perfumes [Arabic *zabād* civet perfume]
civic *adj* of a city or citizens **civically** *adv*
civic centre *n Brit & NZ* a complex of public buildings, including recreational facilities and offices of local government
civics *n* the study of the rights and responsibilities of citizenship
civil *adj* **1** of or occurring within the state or between citizens: *civil unrest* **2** of or relating to the citizen as an individual: *civil rights* **3** not part of the military, legal, or religious structures of a country: *civil aviation* **4** polite or courteous: *he seemed very civil and listened politely* [Latin *civis* citizen] **civilly** *adv*
civil defence *n* the organizing of civilians to deal with enemy attacks and natural disasters
civil disobedience *n* nonviolent protest, such as a refusal to obey laws or pay taxes
civil engineer *n* a person qualified to design and construct public works, such as roads or bridges **civil engineering** *n*
civilian *n* **1** a person who is not a member of the armed forces or police ▷ *adj* **2** not relating to the armed forces or police: *civilian clothes*
civility *n, pl* **-ties 1** polite or courteous behaviour **2 civilities** polite words or actions
civilization *or* **-lisation** *n* **1** the total culture and way of life of a particular people, nation, region, or period **2** a human society that has a complex cultural, political, and legal organization **3** the races collectively who have achieved such a state **4** cities or populated areas, as contrasted with sparsely inhabited areas **5** intellectual, cultural, and moral refinement
civilize *or* **-lise** *vb* **-lizing, -lized** *or* **-lising, -lised 1** to bring out of barbarism into a state of civilization **2** to refine, educate, or enlighten **civilized** *or* **-lised** *adj*
civil law *n* **1** the law of a state, relating to private and civilian affairs **2** a system of law based on that of ancient Rome
civil liberties *pl n* a person's rights to freedom of speech and action
civil list *n* (in Britain) the annual amount given by Parliament to the royal household and the royal family
civil marriage *n law* a marriage performed by an official other than a member of the clergy
civil partnership *n* a legal union, similar to a marriage, usually between two people of the same sex
civil rights *pl n* the personal rights of the individual citizen to have equal treatment and equal opportunities
civil servant *n* a member of the civil service
civil service *n* the service responsible for the public administration of the government of a country
civil war *n* war between people of the same country
civvies *pl n Brit, Austral & NZ slang* civilian clothes as opposed to uniform
civvy street *n slang* civilian life
CJD Creutzfeldt-Jakob disease: a fatal virus disease that affects the central nervous system
cl centilitre
Cl *chem* chlorine
clack *n* **1** the sound made by two hard objects striking each other ▷ *vb* **2** to make this sound [imitative]
clad *vb* a past of **clothe**
cladding *n* **1** the material used to cover the outside of a building **2** a protective metal coating attached to another metal [special use of CLAD]
cladistics *n* a method of grouping animals by measurable likenesses [Greek *klados* branch]
claim *vb* **1** to assert as a fact: *he had claimed to be too ill to return* **2** to demand as a right or as one's property: *you can claim housing benefit to help pay your rent* **3** to call for or need: *this problem claims our attention* **4** to cause the death of: *violence which has claimed at least fifty lives* **5** to succeed in obtaining; win: *she claimed her fifth European tour victory with a closing round of 64* ▷ *n* **6** an assertion of something as true or real **7** an assertion of a right; a demand for something as due **8** a right or just title to something: *a claim to fame* **9** anything that is claimed, such as a piece of land staked out by a miner **10 A** a demand for payment in connection with an insurance policy **B** the sum of money demanded [Latin *clamare* to shout] **claimant** *n*
clairvoyance *n* the alleged power of perceiving things beyond the natural range of the senses [French: clear-seeing]
clairvoyant *n* **1** a person claiming to have the power to foretell future events ▷ *adj* **2** of or possessing clairvoyance
clam *n* an edible shellfish with a hinged shell. See also **clam up** [earlier *clamshell* shell that clamps]
clamber *vb* **1** to climb awkwardly, using hands and feet ▷ *n* **2** a climb performed in this manner [probably variant of *climb*]

clammy *adj* **-mier, -miest** unpleasantly moist and sticky [Old English *clǣman* to smear] **clammily** *adv* **clamminess** *n*

clamour *or US* **clamor** *n* **1** a loud protest **2** a loud and persistent noise or outcry ▷ *vb* **3** **clamour for** to demand noisily **4** to make a loud noise or outcry [Latin *clamare* to cry out] **clamorous** *adj*

clamp[1] *n* **1** a mechanical device with movable jaws for holding things together tightly **2** See **wheel clamp** ▷ *vb* **3** to fix or fasten with a clamp **4** to immobilize (a car) by means of a wheel clamp [Dutch or Low German *klamp*]

clamp[2] *n* a mound of a harvested root crop, covered with straw and earth to protect it from winter weather [Middle Dutch *klamp* heap]

clamp down *vb* **1** **clamp down on** **A** to become stricter about **B** to suppress (something regarded as undesirable) ▷ *n* **clampdown** **2** a sudden restriction placed on an activity

clam up *vb* **clamming, clammed** *informal* to keep or become silent

clan *n* **1** a group of families with a common surname and a common ancestor, esp. among Scottish Highlanders **2** an extended family related by ancestry or marriage: *America's leading political clan, the Kennedys* **3** a group of people with common characteristics, aims, or interests [Scottish Gaelic *clann*] **clansman** *or fem* **clanswoman** *n*

clandestine *adj formal* secret and concealed: *a base for clandestine activities* [Latin *clam* secretly] **clandestinely** *adv*

clang *vb* **1** to make a loud ringing noise, as metal does when it is struck ▷ *n* **2** a ringing metallic noise [Latin *clangere*]

clanger *n* **drop a clanger** *informal* to make a very noticeable mistake

clangour *or US* **clangor** *n* a loud continuous clanging sound [Latin *clangor*] **clangorous** *adj*

clank *n* **1** an abrupt harsh metallic sound ▷ *vb* **2** to make such a sound [imitative]

clannish *adj* (of a group) tending to exclude outsiders: *the villagers can be very clannish*

clap[1] *vb* **clapping, clapped** **1** to applaud by striking the palms of one's hands sharply together **2** to place or put quickly or forcibly: *in former times he would have been clapped in irons or shot* **3** to strike (a person) lightly with an open hand as in greeting **4** to make a sharp abrupt sound like two objects being struck together **5** **clap eyes on** *informal* to catch sight of ▷ *n* **6** the act or sound of clapping **7** a sharp abrupt sound, esp. of thunder **8** a light blow [Old English *clæppan*]

clap[2] *n slang* gonorrhoea [Old French *clapier* brothel]

clapped out *adj informal* worn out; dilapidated

clapper *n* **1** a small piece of metal hanging inside a bell, which causes it to sound when struck against the side **2** **like the clappers** *Brit informal* extremely quickly: *he left, pedalling like the clappers*

clapperboard *n* a pair of hinged boards clapped together during film shooting to help in synchronizing sound and picture

claptrap *n informal* foolish or pretentious talk: *pseudo-intellectual claptrap*

claque *n formal* **1** a group of people hired to applaud **2** a group of fawning admirers [French *claquer* to clap]

claret (**klar**-rit) *n* **1** a dry red wine, esp. one from Bordeaux ▷ *adj* **2** purplish-red [Latin *clarus* clear]

clarify *vb* **-fies, -fying, -fied** **1** to make or become clear or easy to understand **2** to make or become free of impurities, esp. by heating: *clarified butter* [Latin *clarus* clear + *facere* to make] **clarification** *n*

clarinet *n* a keyed woodwind instrument with a single reed [French *clarinette*] **clarinettist** *n*

clarion *n* **1** an obsolete high-pitched trumpet **2** its sound [Latin *clarus* clear]

clarion call *n* strong encouragement to do something

clarity *n* clearness [Latin *claritas*]

clash *vb* **1** to come into conflict **2** to be incompatible **3** (of dates or events) to coincide **4** (of colours or styles) to look ugly or incompatible together: *patterned fabrics which combine seemingly clashing shades to great effect* **5** to make a loud harsh sound, esp. by striking together ▷ *n* **6** a collision or conflict **7** a loud harsh noise [imitative]

clasp *n* **1** a fastening, such as a catch or hook, for holding things together **2** a firm grasp or embrace ▷ *vb* **3** to grasp or embrace tightly **4** to fasten together with a clasp [origin unknown]

clasp knife *n* a large knife with blades which fold into the handle

class *n* **1** a group of people sharing a similar social and economic position **2** the system of dividing society into such groups **3** a group of people or things sharing a common characteristic **4** **A** a group of pupils or students who are taught together **B** a meeting of a group of students for tuition **5** a standard of quality or attainment: *second class* **6** *informal* excellence or elegance, esp. in dress, design, or behaviour: *a full-bodied red wine with real class* **7** *biol* one of the groups into which a phylum is divided, containing one or more orders **8** **in a class of its own** *or* **in a class by oneself** without an equal for ability, talent, etc. ▷ *adj* **9** *informal* excellent, skilful, or stylish: *a class act* ▷ *vb* **10** to place in a class [Latin *classis* class, rank]

class-conscious *adj* aware of belonging to a particular social rank

classic *adj* **1** serving as a standard or model of its kind; typical: *it is a classic symptom of iron deficiency* **2** of lasting interest or significance because of excellence: *the classic work on Central America* **3** characterized by simplicity and purity of form: *a classic suit* ▷ *n* **4** an author, artist, or work of art of the highest excellence **5** a creation or work considered as definitive [Latin *classicus* of the first rank]

classical *adj* **1** of or in a restrained conservative style: *it had been built in the 18th century in a severely classical style* **2** *music* **A** in a style or from a period marked by stability of form, intellectualism, and restraint **B** denoting serious art or music in general **3** of or influenced by ancient Greek and Roman culture **4** of the form of a language historically used for formal and literary purposes: *classical Chinese* **5** (of an education)

C

based on the humanities and the study of Latin and Greek **classically** *adv*

classic car *n chiefly Brit* a car that is more than 25 years old

classicism *n* **1** an artistic style based on Greek and Roman models, showing emotional restraint and regularity of form **2** knowledge of the culture of ancient Greece and Rome **classicist** *n*

classics *pl n* **1** the study of ancient Greek and Roman literature and culture **2 the classics** **A** those works of literature regarded as great or lasting **B** the ancient Greek and Latin languages

classification *n* **1** placing things systematically in categories **2** a division or category in a classifying system [French] **classificatory** *adj*

classified *adj* **1** arranged according to some system of classification **2** *government* (of information) not available to people outside a restricted group, esp. for reasons of national security

classify *vb* **-fies, -fying, -fied** **1** to arrange or order by classes **2** *government* to declare (information) to be officially secret **classifiable** *adj*

classless *adj* **1** not belonging to a class **2** distinguished by the absence of economic or social distinctions: *a classless society*

classmate *n* a friend or contemporary in the same class of a school

classroom *n* a room in a school where lessons take place

classy *adj* **classier, classiest** *informal* stylish and sophisticated **classiness** *n*

clatter *vb* **1** to make a rattling noise, as when hard objects hit each other ▷ *n* **2** a rattling sound or noise [Old English *clatrung* clattering]

clause *n* **1** a section of a legal document such as a will or contract **2** *grammar* a group of words, consisting of a subject and a predicate including a finite verb, that does not necessarily constitute a sentence [Latin *clausula* conclusion] **clausal** *adj*

claustrophobia *n* an abnormal fear of being in a confined space [Latin *claustrum* cloister + -PHOBIA] **claustrophobic** *adj*

clavichord *n* an early keyboard instrument with a very soft tone [Latin *clavis* key + *chorda* string]

clavicle *n* either of the two bones connecting the shoulder blades with the upper part of the breastbone; the collarbone [Latin *clavis* key]

claw *n* **1** a curved pointed nail on the foot of birds, some reptiles, and certain mammals **2** a similar part in some invertebrates, such as a crab's pincer ▷ *vb* **3** to scrape, tear, or dig with claws or nails: *she clawed his face with her fingernails* **4** to achieve (something) only after overcoming great difficulties: *he clawed his way to power and wealth; settlers attempting to claw a living from the desert* [Old English *clawu*]

claw back *vb* **1** to get back (something) with difficulty **2** to recover (a part of a grant or allowance) in the form of a tax or financial penalty

clay *n* **1** a very fine-grained earth, soft when moist and hardening when baked, used to make bricks and pottery **2** earth or mud **3** *poetic* the material of the human body [Old English *clǣg*] **clayey, clayish** *or* **claylike** *adj*

claymore *n* a large two-edged broadsword used formerly by Scottish Highlanders [Gaelic *claidheamh mōr* great sword]

clay pigeon *n* a disc of baked clay hurled into the air from a machine as a target for shooting

CLC Canadian Labour Congress

clean *adj* **1** free from dirt or impurities: *clean water* **2** habitually hygienic and neat **3** morally sound: *clean living* **4** without objectionable language or obscenity: *good clean fun* **5** without anything in it or on it: *a clean sheet of paper* **6** causing little contamination or pollution: *rape seed oil may provide a clean alternative to petrol* **7** recently washed; fresh **8** thorough or complete: *a clean break with the past* **9** skilful and done without fumbling; dexterous: *a clean catch* **10** *sport* played fairly and without fouls **11** free from dishonesty or corruption: *clean government* **12** simple and streamlined in design: *the clean lines and colourful simplicity of these ceramics* **13** (esp. of a driving licence) showing or having no record of offences **14** *slang* **A** innocent **B** not carrying illegal drugs, weapons, etc. ▷ *vb* **15** to make or become free of dirt: *he wanted to help me clean the room* ▷ *adv* **16** in a clean way **17** *not standard* completely: *she clean forgot to face the camera* **18 come clean** *informal* to make a revelation or confession ▷ *n* **19** the act or an instance of cleaning: *the fridge could do with a clean* ▷ See also **clean up** [Old English *clǣne*]

clean-cut *adj* **1** clearly outlined **2** wholesome in appearance

cleaner *n* **1** a person, device, or substance that removes dirt **2** a shop or firm that provides a dry-cleaning service **3 take someone to the cleaners** *informal* to rob or defraud someone

cleanly (**kleen**-lee) *adv* **1** easily or smoothly **2** in a fair manner ▷ *adj* (**klen**-lee) **-lier, -liest** **3** habitually clean or neat **cleanliness** *n*

cleanse *vb* **cleansing, cleansed** **1** to remove dirt from **2** to remove evil or guilt from **cleanser** *n*

clean-shaven *adj* (of men) having the facial hair shaved off

clean sheet *n sport* an instance of conceding no goals or points in a match

clean-tech *informal* ▷ *adj* **1** using clean technology ▷ *n* **2** same as **clean technology**

clean technology *n* techniques that minimize the damage caused to the environment as a result of manufacturing processes

clean up *vb* **1** to make (something) free from dirt **2** to make tidy or presentable **3** to rid (a place) of undesirable people or conditions **4** *informal* to make a great profit ▷ *n* **cleanup** **5** the process of cleaning up

clear *adj* **1** free from doubt or confusion: *clear evidence of police thuggery* **2** certain in the mind; sure: *I am still not clear about what they can and cannot do* **3** easy to see or hear; distinct **4** perceptive; alert: *clear thinking* **5** evident or obvious: *it is not clear how she died* **6** transparent: *clear glass doors* **7** free from darkness or obscurity; bright **8** (of sounds or the voice) not harsh or hoarse **9** even and pure in tone or colour **10** free of obstruction; open: *a clear path runs under the trees* **11** (of weather) free from dullness or clouds **12** without blemish or defect: *a clear skin* **13** free of suspicion, guilt, or blame: *a clear conscience* **14** (of money) without deduction; net **15** free from debt or obligation **16** without qualification or limitation; complete: *a clear lead* ▷ *adv* **17** in a clear or distinct manner **18** completely **19 clear of** out of the way of: *once we were clear of the harbour we headed east* ▷ *n* **20 in the clear** free of suspicion, guilt, or blame ▷ *vb* **21** to free from doubt or confusion **22** to rid of objects or obstructions **23** to make or form (a path) by removing obstructions **24** to move or pass by or over without contact: *he cleared the fence easily* **25** to make or become free from darkness or obscurity **26** to rid (one's throat) of phlegm **27 A** (of the weather) to become free from dullness, fog, or rain **B** (of mist or fog) to disappear **28** (of a cheque) to pass through one's bank and be charged against one's account **29** to free from impurity or blemish **30** to obtain or give (clearance) **31** to prove (someone) innocent of a crime or mistake **32** to permit (someone) to see or handle classified information **33** to make or gain (money) as profit **34** to discharge or settle (a debt) **35 clear the air** to sort out a misunderstanding ▷ See also **clear away, clear off** *etc.* [Latin *clarus*] **clearly** *adv*

clearance *n* **1** the act of clearing: *slum clearance* **2** permission for a vehicle or passengers to proceed **3** official permission to have access to secret information or areas **4** space between two parts in motion

clearance sale *n* a sale in which a shop sells off unwanted goods at reduced prices

clear away *vb* to remove (dishes, etc.) from the table after a meal

clear-cut *adj* **1** easy to distinguish or understand: *there is no clear-cut distinction between safe and unsafe areas of the city* **2** clearly outlined

clearing *n* an area with few or no trees or shrubs in wooded or overgrown land

clearing bank *n* (in Britain) any bank that makes use of the central clearing house in London

clearing house *n* **1** *banking* an institution where cheques and other commercial papers drawn on member banks are cancelled against each other so that only net balances are payable **2** a central agency for the collection and distribution of information or materials

clear off *vb informal* to go away: often used as a command

clear out *vb* **1** to remove and sort the contents of (a room or container) **2** *informal* to go away: often used as a command ▷ *n* **clear-out 3** an act of clearing someone or something out

clear up *vb* **1** to put (a place or thing that is disordered) in order **2** to explain or solve (a mystery or misunderstanding) **3** (of an illness) to become better **4** (of the weather) to become brighter

clearway *n Brit & Austral* a stretch of road on which motorists may stop only in an emergency

cleat *n* **1** a wedge-shaped block attached to a structure to act as a support **2** a piece of wood or iron with two projecting ends round which ropes are fastened [Germanic]

cleavage *n* **1** the space between a woman's breasts, as revealed by a low-cut dress **2** a division or split **3** (of crystals) the act of splitting or the tendency to split along definite planes so as to make smooth surfaces

cleave[1] *vb* **cleaving, cleft, cleaved** *or* **clove, cleft, cleaved** *or* **cloven 1** to split apart: *cleave the stone along the fissures* **2** to make by or as if by cutting: *a two-lane highway that cleaved its way through the northern extremities of the Everglades* [Old English *clēofan*]

cleave[2] *vb* **cleaving, cleaved** to cling or stick: *a farmhouse cleaved to the hill* [Old English *cleofian*]

cleaver *n* a heavy knife with a square blade, used for chopping meat

cleavers *n* a plant with small white flowers and sticky fruits [Old English *clīfe*]

clef *n music* a symbol placed at the beginning of each stave indicating the pitch of the music written after it [French]

cleft *n* **1** a narrow opening in a rock **2** an indentation or split ▷ *adj* **3 in a cleft stick** in a very difficult position ▷ *vb* **4** a past of **cleave**[1]

cleft lip *n* a slight split in the mid line of the upper lip

cleft palate *n* a congenital crack in the mid line of the hard palate

clematis *n* a climbing plant grown for its large colourful flowers [Greek *klēma* vine twig]

clemency *n* mercy

clement *adj* **1** (of the weather) mild **2** merciful [Latin *clemens* mild]

clementine *n* a citrus fruit resembling a tangerine [French]

clench *vb* **1** to close or squeeze together (the teeth or a fist) tightly **2** to grasp or grip firmly ▷ *n* **3** a firm grasp or grip [Old English *beclencan*]

clerestory (clear-store-ee) *n, pl* **-ries** a row of windows in the upper part of the wall of the nave of a church above the roof of the aisle [*clear + storey*] **clerestoried** *adj*

clergy *n, pl* **-gies** priests and religious ministers as a group, esp. in the Christian Church [see CLERK]

clergyman *or fem* **clergywoman** *n, pl* **-men** *or* **-women** a member of the clergy

cleric *n* a member of the clergy

clerical *adj* **1** of clerks or office work: *a clerical job* **2** of or associated with the clergy: *a Lebanese clerical leader*

clerical collar *n* a stiff white collar with no opening at the front, worn by the clergy in certain Churches

clerihew *n* a form of comic or satiric verse, consisting of two couplets and containing the name of a well-known person [after E. *Clerihew* Bentley, who invented it]

clerk *n* **1** an employee in an office, bank, or court who keeps records, files, and accounts **2** *US & Canad* a hotel receptionist **3** *archaic* a scholar ▷ *vb* **4** to work as a clerk [Greek *klērikos* cleric, from *klēros* heritage] **clerkship** *n*

clever *adj* **1** displaying sharp intelligence or mental alertness **2** skilful with one's hands **3** smart in a superficial way **4** *Brit informal* sly or cunning [Middle English *cliver*]
cleverly *adv* **cleverness** *n*

clianthus *n* a plant of Australia and New Zealand with clusters of ornamental scarlet flowers [probably from Greek *kleos* glory + *anthos* flower]

cliché (**klee**-shay) *n* an expression or idea that is no longer effective because of overuse [French] **clichéd** *or* **cliché'd** *adj*

click *n* **1** a short light often metallic sound ▷ *vb* **2** to make a clicking sound: *cameras clicked and whirred* **3** Also: **click on** *computers* to press and release (a button on a mouse) or select (a particular function) by pressing and releasing a button on a mouse **4** *informal* to become suddenly clear: *it wasn't until I saw the photograph that everything clicked into place* **5** *slang* (of two people) to get on well together: *I met him at a dinner party and we clicked straight away* **6** *slang* to be a great success: *the film cost so much that if it hadn't clicked at the box office we'd have been totally wiped out* [imitative]

clickbait *n informal* a link on a website that is intended to lure the user to another website

client *n* **1** someone who uses the services of a professional person or organization **2** a customer **3** *computers* a program or work station that requests data from a server [Latin *cliens* retainer]

clientele (klee-on-**tell**) *n* customers or clients collectively

cliff *n* a steep rock face, esp. along the seashore [Old English *clif*]

cliffhanger *n* a film, game, etc. which is exciting and full of suspense because its outcome is uncertain **cliffhanging** *adj*

climacteric *n* **1** same as **menopause** **2** the period in the life of a man corresponding to the menopause, during which sexual drive and fertility diminish [Greek *klimakter* rung of a ladder]

climate *n* **1** the typical weather conditions of an area **2** an area with a particular kind of climate **3** a prevailing trend: *the current economic climate* [Greek *klima* inclination, region] **climatic** *adj* **climatically** *adv*

> **USAGE** *Climatic* is sometimes wrongly used where *climactic* is meant. *Climatic* should be used to talk about things relating to climate; *climactic* is used to describe something which forms a climax.

climate change *n* the long-term shift in the world's weather patterns and temperatures

climax *n* **1** the most intense or highest point of an experience or of a series of events: *a striking climax to the year's efforts to promote tourism* **2** a decisive moment in a dramatic or other work: *the film has a climax set atop a gale-swept lighthouse* **3** an orgasm ▷ *vb* **4** to reach or bring to a climax [Greek *klimax* ladder] **climactic** *adj*

climb *vb* **1** to go up or ascend (stairs, a mountain, etc.) **2** to move or go with difficulty: *she climbed through a window* **3** to rise to a higher point or intensity: *I grew increasingly delirious as my temperature climbed* **4** to increase in value or amount: *the number could eventually climb to half-a-million* **5** to ascend in social position: *he climbed the ranks of the organization* **6** (of plants) to grow upwards by twining, using tendrils or suckers **7** to incline or slope upwards: *the road climbed up through the foothills* **8** **climb into** *informal* to put on or get into: *I climbed into the van* ▷ *n* **9** the act or an instance of climbing **10** a place or thing to be climbed, esp. a route in mountaineering [Old English *climban*] **climbable** *adj* **climber** *n* **climbing** *n, adj*

climb down *vb* **1** to retreat (from an opinion or position) ▷ *n* **climb-down** **2** a retreat from an opinion or position

clime *n poetic* a region or its climate

clinch *vb* **1** to settle (an argument or agreement) decisively **2** to secure (a nail) by bending the protruding point over **3** to engage in a clinch, as in boxing or wrestling ▷ *n* **4** the act of clinching **5** *boxing & wrestling* a movement in which one or both competitors hold on to the other to avoid punches or regain wind **6** *slang* a lovers' embrace [variant of *clench*]

clincher *n informal* something decisive, such as a fact, argument, or point scored

cling *vb* **clinging, clung** **1** (often foll. by *to*) to hold fast or stick closely (to something) **2** to be emotionally overdependent on **3** to continue to do or believe in: *he clings to the belief that people are capable of change* [Old English *clingan*] **clinging** *or* **clingy** *adj*

clingfilm *n Brit* a thin polythene material used for wrapping food

clinic *n* **1** a place in which outpatients are given medical treatment or advice **2** a similar place staffed by specialist physicians or surgeons: *I have an antenatal clinic on Friday afternoon* **3** *Brit & NZ* a private hospital or nursing home **4** the teaching of medicine to students at the bedside [Greek *klinē* bed]

clinical *adj* **1** of or relating to the observation and treatment of patients directly: *clinical trials of a new drug* **2** of or relating to a clinic **3** logical and unemotional: *they have a somewhat clinical attitude to their children's upbringing* **4** (of a room or buildings) plain, simple, and usually unattractive **clinically** *adv*

clinical thermometer *n* a thermometer for measuring the temperature of the body

clink[1] *vb* **1** to make a light sharp metallic sound ▷ *n* **2** such a sound [perhaps from Middle Dutch *klinken*]

clink[2] *n slang* prison [after *Clink*, a former prison in London]

clinker *n* the fused coal left over in a fire or furnace [Dutch *klinker* a type of brick]

clinker-built *adj* (of a boat or ship) with a hull made from overlapping planks [obsolete *clinker* a nailing together, probably from *clinch*]

Clio *n Greek myth* the Muse of history

clip[1] *vb* **clipping, clipped** **1** to cut or trim with scissors or shears **2** to remove a short section from (a film or newspaper) **3** *Brit & Austral* to punch a hole in (something, esp. a ticket) **4** *informal* to strike with a sharp, often slanting, blow **5** to shorten (a word) **6** *slang* to obtain (money) by cheating ▷ *n* **7** the act of clipping **8** a short extract from a film **9** something that has been clipped **10** *informal* a sharp, often slanting, blow: *a clip on the ear* **11** *informal* speed: *proceeding at a smart clip* **12** *Austral & NZ* the total quantity of wool shorn, as in one place or season [Old Norse *klippa* to cut]

C

clip² *n* **1** a device for attaching or holding things together **2** an article of jewellery that can be clipped onto a dress or hat **3** short for **paperclip** or **cartridge clip** ▷ *vb* **clipping, clipped 4** to attach or hold together with a clip [Old English *clyppan* to embrace]

clipboard *n* **1** a portable writing board with a clip at the top for holding paper **2** *computers* a temporary storage area for holding text or graphics that have been cut or copied from a document

clip joint *n slang* a nightclub in which customers are overcharged

clipped *adj* (of speech) abrupt, clearly pronounced, and using as few words as possible

clipper *n* a fast commercial sailing ship

clippers *pl n* a tool used for clipping and cutting

clipping *n* something cut out, esp. an article from a newspaper

clique (**kleek**) *n* a small exclusive group of friends or associates [French] **cliquey, cliquy** *or* **cliquish** *adj*

clit *n taboo slang* short for **clitoris**

clitoris (**klit**-or-riss) *n* a small sexually sensitive organ at the front of the vulva [Greek *kleitoris*] **clitoral** *adj*

Cllr councillor

cloaca (kloh-**ake**-a) *n, pl* **-cae** a cavity in most animals, except higher mammals, into which the alimentary canal and the genital and urinary ducts open [Latin: sewer]

cloak *n* **1** a loose sleeveless outer garment, fastened at the throat and falling straight from the shoulders **2** something that covers or conceals ▷ *vb* **3** to hide or disguise **4** to cover with or as if with a cloak [Medieval Latin *clocca* cloak, bell]

cloak-and-dagger *adj* of or involving mystery and secrecy

cloakroom *n* **1** a room in which coats may be left temporarily **2** *Brit euphemistic* a toilet

clobber¹ *vb informal* **1** to batter **2** to defeat utterly **3** to criticize severely [origin unknown]

clobber² *n Brit, Austral & NZ informal* personal belongings, such as clothes [origin unknown]

cloche (**klosh**) *n* **1** *Brit, Austral & NZ* a small glass or plastic cover for protecting young plants **2** a woman's close-fitting hat [French: bell]

clock¹ *n* **1** a device for showing the time, either through pointers that revolve over a numbered dial, or through a display of figures **2** a device with a dial for recording or measuring **3** the downy head of a dandelion that has gone to seed **4** short for **time clock 5** *informal* same as **speedometer** or **mileometer 6** *Brit slang* the face **7 round the clock** all day and all night ▷ *vb* **8** to record (time) with a stopwatch, esp. in the calculation of speed **9** *Brit, Austral & NZ slang* to strike, esp. on the face or head **10** *informal* to turn back the mileometer on (a car) illegally so that its mileage appears less **11** *Brit slang* to see or notice [Medieval Latin *clocca* bell]

clock² *n* an ornamental design on the side of a sock [origin unknown]

clock in *or* **clock on** *vb* to register one's arrival at work on an automatic time recorder

clock out *or* **clock off** *vb* to register one's departure from work on an automatic time recorder

clock up *vb* to record or reach (a total): *he has now clocked up over 500 games for the club*

clockwise *adv, adj* in the direction in which the hands of a clock rotate

clockwork *n* **1** a mechanism similar to that of a spring-driven clock, as in a wind-up toy **2 like clockwork** with complete regularity and precision

clod *n* **1** a lump of earth or clay **2** *Brit, Austral & NZ* a dull or stupid person [Old English] **cloddish** *adj*

clodhopper *n informal* **1** a clumsy person **2 clodhoppers** large heavy shoes

clog *vb* **clogging, clogged 1** to obstruct or become obstructed with thick or sticky matter **2** to encumber **3** to stick in a mass ▷ *n* **4** a wooden or wooden-soled shoe [origin unknown]

cloisonné (klwah-**zon**-nay) *n* a design made by filling in a wire outline with coloured enamel [French]

cloister *n* **1** a covered pillared walkway within a religious building **2** a place of religious seclusion, such as a monastery ▷ *vb* **3** to confine or seclude in or as if in a monastery [Medieval Latin *claustrum* monastic cell, from Latin *claudere* to close]

cloistered *adj* sheltered or protected

clomp *n, vb* same as **clump** (senses 2, 3)

clone *n* **1** a group of organisms or cells of the same genetic constitution that have been reproduced asexually from a single plant or animal **2** *informal* a person who closely resembles another **3** *slang* a mobile phone that has been given the electronic identity of an existing mobile phone, so that calls made on it are charged to that owner ▷ *vb* **cloning, cloned 4** to produce as a clone **5** *informal* to produce near copies of (a person) **6** *slang* to give (a mobile phone) the electronic identity of an existing mobile phone so that calls made on it are charged to that owner [Greek *klōn* twig, shoot] **cloning** *n*

clonk *vb* **1** to make a loud dull thud **2** *informal* to hit ▷ *n* **3** a loud thud [imitative]

close¹ *vb* **closing, closed 1** to shut: *he lay back and closed his eyes* **2** to bar, obstruct, or fill up (an entrance, a hole, etc.): *the blockades had closed major roads, railways, and border crossings* **3** to cease or cause to cease giving service: *both stores closed at 9 p.m.*; *the Shipping Company closed its offices in Bangkok* **4** to end; terminate: *'Never,' she said, so firmly that it closed the subject* **5** (of agreements or deals) to complete or be completed successfully **6** to come closer (to): *she was still in second place but closing fast on the leader* **7** to take hold: *his small fingers closed around the coin* **8** *Stock Exchange* to have a value at the end of a day's trading, as specified: *the pound closed four-and-a-half cents higher* **9** to join the ends or edges of something: *to close a circuit* ▷ *n* **10** the act of closing **11** the end or conclusion: *the close of play* **12** (rhymes with **dose**) *Brit* a courtyard or quadrangle enclosed by buildings **13** *Scot* the entry from the street to a tenement building ▷ See also **close down, close in** *etc.* [Latin *claudere*]

C

close² *adj* **1** near in space or time **2** intimate: *we were such close friends in those days* **3** near in relationship: *the dead woman seems to have had no close relatives* **4** careful, strict, or searching: *their research will not stand up to close scrutiny* **5** having the parts near together: *a close formation* **6** near to the surface; short: *an NCO's haircut, cropped close on top, shaved clean at sides and back* **7** almost equal: *a close game* **8** not deviating or varying greatly from something: *a close resemblance* **9** confined or enclosed **10** oppressive, heavy, or airless: *damp, close weather* **11** strictly guarded: *he had been placed in close arrest* **12** secretive or reticent **13** miserly; not generous **14** restricted as to public admission or membership ▷ *adv* **15** closely; tightly **16** near or in proximity [Old French *clos*] **closely** *adv* **closeness** *n*

closed *adj* **1** blocked against entry **2** only admitting a selected group of people; exclusive: *he had a fairly closed circle of friends* **3** not open to question or debate **4** *maths* **A** (of a curve or surface) completely enclosing an area or volume **B** (of a set) made up of members on which a specific operation, such as addition, gives as its result another existing member of the set

closed circuit *n* a complete electrical circuit through which current can flow

closed-circuit television *n* a television system used within a limited area such as a building

closed corporation *n chiefly S African* a business whose shares are owned by a small number of persons

close down *vb* **1** to stop operating or working: *the factory closed down many years ago* ▷ *n* **close-down** **2** *Brit & NZ radio & television* the end of a period of broadcasting

closed shop *n Brit, Austral & NZ* (formerly) a place of work in which all workers had to belong to a particular trade union

close harmony *n* a type of singing in which all parts except the bass lie close together

close in *vb* **1** (of days) to become shorter with the approach of winter **2** **close in on** to advance on so as to encircle or surround

close quarters *pl n* **at close quarters** **A** engaged in hand-to-hand combat **B** very near together

close season *n* **1** the period of the year when it is illegal to kill certain game or fish **2** *sport* the period of the year when there is no domestic competition

close shave *n informal* a narrow escape

closet *n* **1** *US & Austral* a small cupboard **2** a small private room **3** short for **water closet** **4** **in the closet** *informal* not openly acknowledging one's sexual orientation ▷ *adj* **5** private or secret: *a closet fan of horror films* ▷ *vb* **-eting, -eted** **6** to shut away in private, esp. in order to talk: *he was closeted with the President* [Old French *clos* enclosure]

close-up *n* **1** a photograph or film or television shot taken at close range **2** a detailed or intimate view or examination ▷ *vb* **close up** **3** to shut entirely: *every other shop front seemed to be closed up* **4** to draw together: *the ranks closed up and marched on* **5** (of wounds) to heal completely

close with *vb* to engage in battle with (an enemy)

closure *n* **1** the act of closing or the state of being closed **2** something that closes or shuts **3** a procedure by which a debate may be stopped and an immediate vote taken **4** *chiefly US* **A** a resolution of a significant event or relationship in a person's life **B** the sense of contentment experienced after such a resolution

clot *n* **1** a soft thick lump formed from liquid **2** *informal* a stupid person ▷ *vb* **clotting, clotted** **3** to form soft thick lumps [Old English *clott*]

cloth *n, pl* **cloths** **1** a fabric formed by weaving, felting, or knitting fibres **2** a piece of such fabric used for a particular purpose **3** **the cloth** the clergy [Old English *clāth*]

clothe *vb* **clothing, clothed** *or* **clad** **1** to put clothes on **2** to provide with clothes **3** to cover or envelop (something) so as to change its appearance: *a small valley clothed in thick woodland* [Old English *clāthian*]

clothes *pl n* **1** articles of dress **2** *chiefly Brit* short for **bedclothes** [Old English *clāthas*, plural of *clāth* cloth]

clotheshorse *n* **1** a frame on which to hang laundry for drying or airing **2** a person who is extremely concerned with his or her appearance

clothesline *n* a piece of rope from which clean washing is hung to dry

clothes peg *n* a small wooden or plastic clip for attaching washing to a clothesline

clothier *n* a person who makes or sells clothes or cloth

clothing *n* **1** garments collectively **2** something that covers or clothes

clotted cream *n Brit* a thick cream made from scalded milk

cloud *n* **1** a mass of water or ice particles visible in the sky **2** a floating mass of smoke, dust, etc. **3** a large number of insects or other small animals in flight **4** something that darkens, threatens, or carries gloom **5** **in the clouds** not in contact with reality **6** **on cloud nine** *informal* elated; very happy **7** **the cloud** a network of remote computers that can be accessed via the internet on a temporary basis **8** **under a cloud** **A** under reproach or suspicion **B** in a state of gloom or bad temper ▷ *vb* **9** to make or become more difficult to see through: *my glasses kept clouding up; mud clouded the water* **10** to confuse or impair: *her judgment was no longer clouded by alcohol* **11** to make or become gloomy or depressed: *bereavement clouded the last years of his life* ▷ See also **cloud over** [Old English *clūd* rock, hill] **cloudless** *adj*

cloudburst *n* a heavy fall of rain

cloud chamber *n physics* an apparatus for detecting high-energy particles by observing their tracks through a chamber containing a supersaturated vapour

cloud computing *n* a system in which services stored on the internet are accessible to users on a temporary basis

cloud-cuckoo-land *n* a place of fantasy or impractical ideas

cloud over *vb* **1** (of the sky or weather) to become cloudy: *it was clouding over and we thought it would rain* **2** (of a person's face or eyes) to suddenly look gloomy or depressed: *Grace's face clouded over and she turned away*

cloudy *adj* **cloudier, cloudiest 1** covered with cloud or clouds **2** (of liquids) opaque or muddy **3** confused or unclear **cloudily** *adv* **cloudiness** *n*

clout *n* **1** *informal* a fairly hard blow **2** power or influence ▷ *vb* **3** *informal* to hit hard [Old English *clūt* piece of cloth]

clove¹ *n* a dried closed flower bud of a tropical tree, used as a spice [Latin *clavus* nail]

clove² *n* a segment of a bulb of garlic [Old English *clufu* bulb]

clove³ *vb* a past tense of **cleave¹**

clove hitch *n* a knot used to fasten a rope to a spar or a larger rope

cloven *vb* **1** a past participle of **cleave¹** ▷ *adj* **2** split or divided

cloven hoof *or* **cloven foot** *n* the divided hoof of a pig, goat, cow, or deer

clover *n* **1** a plant with three-lobed leaves and dense flower heads **2** **in clover** *informal* in ease or luxury [Old English *clāfre*]

clown *n* **1** a comic entertainer, usually bizarrely dressed and made up, appearing in the circus **2** an amusing person **3** a clumsy rude person ▷ *vb* **4** to behave foolishly **5** to perform as a clown [origin unknown] **clownish** *adj*

cloying *adj* so sweet or pleasurable that it ultimately becomes sickly: *cloying sentimentality* [Middle English *cloy* originally to nail, hence, to obstruct] **cloyingly** *adv*

club *n* **1** a group or association of people with common aims or interests **2** the building used by such a group **3** a stout stick used as a weapon **4** a stick or bat used to strike the ball in various sports, esp. golf **5** an establishment where people go to drink and dance, esp. late in the evening **6** a building in which members go to meet, dine, read, etc. **7** *chiefly Brit* an organization, esp. in a shop, set up as a means of saving **8** a playing card marked with one or more black trefoil symbols **9** short for **Indian club** ▷ *vb* **clubbing, clubbed 10** to beat with a club **11** **club together** to combine resources or efforts for a common purpose [Old Norse *klubba*]

club class *n* **1** a class of air travel which is less luxurious than first class but more luxurious than economy class ▷ *adj* **club-class 2** of this class of air travel

club foot *n* a congenital deformity of the foot

clubhouse *n* the premises of a sports or other club, esp. a golf club

club root *n* a fungal disease of cabbages and related plants, in which the roots become thickened and distorted

cluck *n* **1** the low clicking noise made by a hen ▷ *vb* **2** (of a hen) to make a clicking sound **3** to express (a feeling) by making a similar sound: *the landlady was clucking feverishly behind them* [imitative]

clue *n* **1** something that helps to solve a problem or unravel a mystery **2** **not have a clue** **A** to be completely baffled **B** to be ignorant or incompetent [variant of *clew* ball of thread]

clued-up *adj informal* shrewd and well-informed

clueless *adj slang* helpless or stupid

clump *n* **1** a small group of things or people together **2** a dull heavy tread ▷ *vb* **3** to walk or tread heavily **4** to form into clumps [Old English *clympe*] **clumpy** *adj*

clumsy *adj* **-sier, -siest 1** lacking in skill or physical coordination: *an extraordinarily clumsy player* **2** badly made or done **3** said or done without thought or tact: *I took the clumsy hint and left* [Middle English *clumse* to benumb] **clumsily** *adv* **clumsiness** *n*

clung *vb* the past of **cling**

clunk *n* **1** a dull metallic sound ▷ *vb* **2** to make such a sound [imitative]

cluster *n* **1** a number of things growing, fastened, or occurring close together **2** a number of people or things grouped together ▷ *vb* **3** to gather or be gathered in clusters [Old English *clyster*]

clutch¹ *vb* **1** to seize with or as if with hands or claws **2** to grasp or hold firmly **3** **clutch at** to attempt to get hold or possession of ▷ *n* **4** a device that enables two revolving shafts to be joined or disconnected, esp. one that transmits the drive from the engine to the gearbox in a vehicle **5** the pedal that operates the clutch in a car **6** a firm grasp **7** **clutches** **A** hands or claws in the act of clutching: *a photo of a red salmon escaping the clutches of a bear cub* **B** power or control: *rescued from the clutches of the Gestapo* [Old English *clyccan*]

clutch² *n* **1** a set of eggs laid at the same time **2** a group, bunch, or cluster: *a clutch of gloomy economic reports* [Old Norse *klekja* to hatch]

clutch bag *n* a handbag without handles

clutter *vb* **1** to scatter objects about (a place) in an untidy manner ▷ *n* **2** an untidy heap or mass of objects **3** a state of untidiness [Middle English *clotter*]

Clydesdale *n* a heavy powerful carthorse, originally from Scotland

cm centimetre

Cm *chem* curium

Cmdr Commander

Cn *chem* copernicium

CND Campaign for Nuclear Disarmament

CNS *biol* central nervous system

Co *chem* cobalt

CO **1** Colorado **2** Commanding Officer

Co.¹ *or* **co.** **1** Company **2** **and co.** *informal* and the rest of them: *Harold and co.*

Co.² County

co- *prefix* **1** together; joint or jointly: *coproduction* **2** indicating partnership or equality: *co-star; copilot* **3** to the same or a similar degree: *coextend* **4** (in mathematics and astronomy) of the complement of an angle: *cosecant* [Latin; see COM-]

c/o **1** care of **2** *accounting* carried over

coach *n* **1** a large comfortable single-decker bus used for sightseeing or long-distance travel **2** a railway carriage **3** a large four-wheeled enclosed carriage, usually horse-drawn **4** a trainer or instructor: *the coach of the Mexican national team* **5** a tutor who prepares students for examinations ▷ *vb* **6** to train or teach [from *Kocs*, village in Hungary where horse-drawn coaches were first made] **coaching** *n*

coachman *n, pl* **-men** the driver of a horse-drawn coach or carriage
coachwork *n* the body of a car
coagulate (koh-ag-yew-late) *vb* **-lating, -lated** to change from a liquid into a soft semisolid mass; clot [Latin *coagulare*] **coagulant** *n* **coagulation** *n*
coal *n* **1** a compact black or dark brown rock consisting largely of carbon formed from partially decomposed vegetation: a fuel and a source of coke, coal gas, and coal tar **2** one or more lumps of coal **3 coals to Newcastle** something supplied to a place where it is already plentiful [Old English *col*]
coalesce (koh-a-less) *vb* **-lescing, -lesced** to unite or come together in one body or mass [Latin *co-* together + *alescere* to increase] **coalescence** *n* **coalescent** *adj*
coalface *n* the exposed seam of coal in a mine
coalfield *n* an area rich in deposits of coal
coal gas *n* a mixture of gases produced by the distillation of bituminous coal and used for heating and lighting
coalition (koh-a-lish-un) *n* a temporary alliance, esp. between political parties [Latin *coalescere* to coalesce]
coal scuttle *n* a container for holding coal for a domestic fire
coal tar *n* a black tar, produced by the distillation of bituminous coal, used for making drugs and chemical products
coal tit *n* a small songbird with a black head with a white patch on the nape
coaming *n* a raised frame round a ship's hatchway for keeping out water [origin unknown]
coarse *adj* **1** rough in texture or structure **2** unrefined or indecent: *coarse humour* **3** of inferior quality [origin unknown] **coarsely** *adv* **coarseness** *n*
coarse fish *n Brit* a freshwater fish that is not of the salmon family **coarse fishing** *n*
coarsen *vb* to make or become coarse
coast *n* **1** the place where the land meets the sea **2 the coast is clear** *informal* the obstacles or dangers are gone ▷ *vb* **3** to move by momentum or force of gravity, without the use of power **4** to proceed without great effort: *they coasted to a 31–9 win in the pairs* [Latin *costa* side, rib] **coastal** *adj*
coaster *n* **1** a small mat placed under a bottle or glass to protect a table **2** *Brit* a small ship used for coastal trade
coastguard *n* **1** an organization which aids shipping, saves lives at sea, and prevents smuggling **2** a member of such an organization
coastline *n* the outline of a coast
coat *n* **1** an outer garment with sleeves, covering the body from the shoulders to below the waist **2** the hair, wool, or fur of an animal **3** any layer that covers a surface ▷ *vb* **4** to cover with a layer [Old French *cote*]
coat hanger *n* a curved piece of wood, wire, or plastic, fitted with a hook and used to hang up clothes
coating *n* a layer or film spread over a surface: *a thick coating of breadcrumbs*
coat of arms *n* the heraldic emblem of a family or organization
coat of mail *n history* a protective garment made of linked metal rings or plates
coax *vb* **1** to persuade (someone) gently **2** to obtain (something) by persistent coaxing **3** to work on (something) carefully and patiently so as to make it function as desired: *I watched him coax the last few drops of beer out of his glass* [obsolete *cokes* a fool]
coaxial (koh-ax-ee-al) *adj* **1** *electronics* (of a cable) transmitting by means of two concentric conductors separated by an insulator **2** having a common axis
cob *n* **1** a male swan **2** a thickset type of horse **3** the stalk of an ear of maize **4** *Brit & Austral* a round loaf of bread **5** *Brit* a hazel tree or hazelnut [origin unknown]
cobalt *n chem* a brittle hard silvery-white metallic element used in alloys. Symbol: **Co** [Middle High German *kobolt* goblin; from the miners' belief that goblins placed it in the silver ore]
cobber *n Austral & NZ informal* a friend [dialect *cob* to take a liking to someone]
cobble *n* a cobblestone
cobbled *adj* (of a street or road) paved with cobblestones
cobbler *n* a person who makes or mends shoes [origin unknown]
cobblers *pl n Brit, Austral & NZ slang* nonsense [rhyming slang *cobblers' awls* balls]
cobblestone *n* a rounded stone used for paving [from *cob*]
cobble together *vb* **-bling, -bled** to put together clumsily: *a coalition cobbled together from parties with widely differing aims*
cobia (koh-bee-a) *n* a large dark-striped game fish of tropical and subtropical seas
COBOL *n* a high-level computer programming language designed for general commercial use [*co(mmon) b(usiness) o(riented) l(anguage)*]
cobra *n* a highly venomous hooded snake of tropical Africa and Asia [Latin *colubra* snake]
cobweb *n* **1** a web spun by certain spiders **2** a single thread of such a web [Old English *(ātor)coppe* spider] **cobwebbed** *adj* **cobwebby** *adj*
cobwebs *pl n* mustiness, confusion, or obscurity: *her election dusted away the cobwebs that normally surround the presidency*
coca *n* the dried leaves of a S American shrub which contain cocaine [indigenous S American word *kúka*]
Coca-Cola *n trademark* a carbonated soft drink
cocaine *n* an addictive drug derived from coca leaves, used as a narcotic and local anaesthetic
coccyx (kok-six) *n, pl* **coccyges** (kok-sije-eez) *anatomy* a small triangular bone at the base of the spine in human beings and some apes [Greek *kokkux* cuckoo, from its likeness to a cuckoo's beak] **coccygeal** *adj*
cochineal *n* a scarlet dye obtained from a Mexican insect, used for colouring food [Greek *kokkos* kermes berry]
cochlea (kok-lee-a) *n, pl* **-leae** (-lee-ee) *anatomy* the spiral tube in the internal ear, which converts sound vibrations into nerve impulses [Greek *kokhlias* snail] **cochlear** *adj*

cock *n* **1** a male bird, esp. of domestic fowl **2** a stopcock **3** *taboo slang* a penis **4** the hammer of a gun **5** *Brit informal* friend: used as a term of address ▷ *vb* **6** to draw back the hammer of (a gun) so that it is ready to fire **7** to lift and turn (part of the body) in a particular direction ▷ See also **cockup** [Old English *cocc*]

cockabully *n* a small freshwater fish of New Zealand [Māori *kokopu*]

cockade *n* a feather or rosette worn on the hat as a badge [French *coq* cock]

cock-a-hoop *adj Brit, Austral & NZ* in very high spirits [origin unknown]

cock-a-leekie *n* a Scottish soup of chicken boiled with leeks

cock-and-bull story *n informal* an obviously improbable story, esp. one used as an excuse

cockatiel *n* a crested Australian parrot with a greyish-brown and yellow plumage

cockatoo *n, pl* **-toos** a light-coloured crested parrot of Australia and E Asia [Malay *kakatua*]

cockatrice *n* a legendary monster that could kill with a glance [Late Latin *calcatrix* trampler]

cockchafer *n* a large flying beetle [COCK + *chafer* beetle]

cocked hat *n* **1** a hat with three corners and a turned-up brim **2** **knock into a cocked hat** *slang* to outdo or defeat

cockerel *n* a young domestic cock, less than a year old

cocker spaniel *n* a small spaniel [from *cocking* hunting woodcocks]

cockeyed *adj informal* **1** crooked or askew **2** foolish or absurd **3** cross-eyed

cockfight *n* a fight between two gamecocks fitted with sharp metal spurs

cockie *or* **cocky** *n, pl* **-kies** *Austral & NZ informal* a cockatoo

cockle *n* **1** an edible bivalve shellfish **2** its shell **3** **warm the cockles of one's heart** to make one feel happy [Greek *konkhule* mussel]

cockleshell *n* **1** the rounded shell of the cockle **2** a small light boat

cockney *n* **1** a native of London, esp. of its East End **2** the urban dialect of London or its East End ▷ *adj* **3** characteristic of cockneys or their dialect [Middle English *cokeney* cock's egg, later applied contemptuously to townsmen]

cockpit *n* **1** the compartment in an aircraft for the pilot and crew **2** the driver's compartment in a racing car **3** *naut* a space in a small vessel containing the wheel and tiller **4** the site of many battles or conflicts: *the south of the country is a cockpit of conflicting interests* **5** an enclosure used for cockfights

cockroach *n* a beetle-like insect that is a household pest [Spanish *cucaracha*]

cockscomb *n* same as **coxcomb**

cocksure *adj* overconfident or arrogant [origin unknown]

cocktail *n* **1** a mixed alcoholic drink **2** an appetizer of seafood or mixed fruits **3** any combination of diverse elements: *Central America was a cocktail of death, poverty, and destruction* [origin unknown]

cockup *Brit & Austral slang* ▷ *n* **1** something done badly ▷ *vb* **cock up** **2** to ruin or spoil

cocky *adj* **cockier, cockiest** excessively proud of oneself **cockily** *adv* **cockiness** *n*

coco *n, pl* **-cos** the coconut palm [Portuguese: grimace; from the likeness of the three holes of the nut to a face]

cocoa *or* **cacao** *n* **1** a powder made by roasting and grinding cocoa beans **2** a hot or cold drink made from cocoa powder [from CACAO]

cocoa bean *n* a cacao seed

cocoa butter *n* a fatty solid obtained from cocoa beans and used for confectionery and toiletries

coconut *n* **1** the fruit of a type of palm tree (**coconut palm**), which has a thick fibrous oval husk and a thin hard shell enclosing edible white flesh. The hollow centre is filled with a milky fluid (**coconut milk**) **2** the flesh of the coconut

coconut matting *n* coarse matting made from the husk of the coconut

cocoon *n* **1** a silky protective covering produced by a silkworm or other insect larva, in which the pupa develops **2** a protective covering ▷ *vb* **3** to wrap in or protect as if in a cocoon [Provençal *coucoun* eggshell]

cocotte *n* a small fireproof dish in which individual portions of food are cooked and served [French]

cod[1] *n, pl* **cod** *or* **cods** a large food fish [probably Germanic]

cod[2] *adj Brit slang* having the character of an imitation or parody: *the chorus were dressed in exuberant cod-medieval costumes* [origin unknown]

COD cash (in the US, collect) on delivery

coda (**kode**-a) *n music* the final part of a musical movement or work [Italian: tail]

coddle *vb* **-dling, -dled** **1** to pamper or overprotect **2** to cook (eggs) in water just below boiling point [origin unknown]

code *n* **1** a system of letters, symbols, or prearranged signals, by which information can be communicated secretly or briefly **2** a set of principles or rules: *a code of practice* **3** a system of letters or digits used for identification purposes: *area code; tax code* ▷ *vb* **coding, coded** **4** to translate or arrange into a code **5** to write computer programs [Latin *codex* book, wooden block]

codeine (**kode**-een) *n* a drug made mainly from morphine, used as a painkiller and sedative [Greek *kōdeia* head of a poppy]

codex (**koh**-dex) *n, pl* **-dices** (-diss-seez) a volume of manuscripts of an ancient text [Latin: wooden block, book]

codfish *n, pl* **-fish** *or* **-fishes** a cod

codger *n Brit, Austral & NZ informal* an old man [probably variant of *cadger*]

codicil (**cod**-iss-ill) *n law* an addition to a will [from CODEX]

codify (**kode**-if-fie) *vb* **-fies, -fying, -fied** to organize or collect together (rules or procedures) systematically **codification** *n*

codling *n* a young cod

cod-liver oil *n* an oil extracted from fish, rich in vitamins A and D

codpiece *n history* a bag covering the male genitals, attached to breeches [obsolete *cod* scrotum]

codswallop *n Brit, Austral & NZ slang* nonsense [origin unknown]
coeducation *n* the education of boys and girls together **coeducational** *adj*
coefficient *n* **1** *maths* a number or constant placed before and multiplying another quantity: *the coefficient of the term 3xyz is 3* **2** *physics* a number or constant used to calculate the behaviour of a given substance under specified conditions

C

coelacanth (seel-a-kanth) *n* a primitive marine fish, thought to be extinct until a living specimen was discovered in 1938 [Greek *koilos* hollow + *akanthos* spine]
coelenterate (seel-**lent**-a-rate) *n* any invertebrate that has a saclike body with a single opening, such as a jellyfish or coral [Greek *koilos* hollow + *enteron* intestine]
coeliac *or US* **celiac** *n* **1** a person who has coeliac disease ▷ *adj* **2** of or related to the abdomen [Greek *koilia* belly]
coeliac disease (**seel**-ee-ak) *n* a disease which makes the digestion of food difficult [Greek *koilia* belly]
coenobite (**seen**-oh-bite) *n* a member of a religious order in a monastic community [Greek *koinos* common + *bios* life]
coequal *adj, n* equal
coerce (koh-**urss**) *vb* **-ercing, -erced** to compel or force [Latin *co-* together + *arcere* to enclose] **coercion** *n*
coercive *adj* using force or authority to make a person do something against his or her will
coeval (koh-**eev**-al) *adj* **1** contemporary ▷ *n* **2** a contemporary [Latin *co-* together + *aevum* age] **coevally** *adv*
coexist *vb* **1** to exist together at the same time or in the same place **2** to exist together in peace despite differences **coexistence** *n* **coexistent** *adj*
coextensive *adj* covering the same area, either literally or figuratively: *the concepts of 'the nation' and 'the people' are not coextensive*
C of E Church of England
coffee *n* **1** a drink made from the roasted and ground seeds of a tall tropical shrub **2** Also called: **coffee beans** the beanlike seeds of this shrub **3** the shrub yielding these seeds ▷ *adj* **4** medium-brown [Turkish *kahve*, from Arabic *qahwah* coffee, wine]
coffee bar *n* a café; snack bar
coffee house *n* a place where coffee is served, esp. one that was a fashionable meeting place in 18th-century London
coffee mill *n* a machine for grinding roasted coffee beans
coffee table *n* a small low table
coffee-table book *n* a large expensive illustrated book
coffer *n* **1** a chest for storing valuables **2 coffers** a store of money **3** an ornamental sunken panel in a ceiling or dome [Greek *kophinos* basket]
cofferdam *n* a watertight enclosure pumped dry to enable construction work or ship repairs to be done
coffered *adj* (of a ceiling or dome) decorated with ornamental sunken panels
coffin *n* a box in which a corpse is buried or cremated [Latin *cophinus* basket]
cog *n* **1** one of the teeth on the rim of a gearwheel **2** a gearwheel, esp. a small one **3** an unimportant person in a large organization or process [Scandinavian]
cogent (**koh**-jent) *adj* forcefully convincing [Latin *co-* together + *agere* to drive] **cogency** *n*
cogitate (**koj**-it-tate) *vb* **-tating, -tated** to think deeply about (something) [Latin *cogitare*] **cogitation** *n* **cogitative** *adj*
cognac (**kon**-yak) *n* high-quality French brandy
cognate *adj* **1** derived from a common original form: *cognate languages* **2** related to or descended from a common ancestor ▷ *n* **3** a cognate word or language **4** a relative [Latin *co-* same + *gnatus* born] **cognation** *n*
cognition *n formal* **1** the processes of getting knowledge, including perception, intuition, and reasoning **2** the results of such a process [Latin *cognoscere* to learn] **cognitive** *adj*
cognizance *or* **cognisance** *n formal* **1** knowledge or understanding **2 take cognizance of** to take notice of **3** the range or scope of knowledge or understanding [Latin *cognoscere* to learn] **cognizant** *or* **cognisant** *adj*
cognomen (kog-**noh**-men) *n, pl* **-nomens** *or* **-nomina** (-**nom**-min-a) *formal* **1** a nickname **2** a surname **3** an ancient Roman's third name or nickname [Latin: additional name]
cognoscenti (kon-yo-**shen**-tee) *pl n, sing* **-te** (-tee) connoisseurs [obsolete Italian]
cogwheel *n* same as **gearwheel**
cohabit *vb* to live together as a couple without being married [Latin *co-* together + *habitare* to live] **cohabitation** *n*
cohabitee *n* a person who lives with, and has a sexual and romantic relationship with, someone to whom he or she is not married
cohere *vb* **-hering, -hered 1** to hold or stick firmly together **2** to be logically connected or consistent [Latin *co-* together + *haerere* to cling]
coherent *adj* **1** logical and consistent **2** capable of intelligible speech **3** cohering or sticking together **4** *physics* (of two or more waves) having the same frequency and a constant fixed phase difference **coherence** *n*
cohesion *n* **1** sticking together **2** *physics* the force that holds together the atoms or molecules in a solid or liquid **cohesive** *adj*
cohort *n* **1** a band of associates **2** a tenth part of an ancient Roman Legion [Latin *cohors* yard, company of soldiers]
coif *n* **1** a close-fitting cap worn in the Middle Ages **2** a hairstyle ▷ *vb* **coiffing, coiffed 3** to arrange (the hair) [Late Latin *cofea* helmet, cap]
coiffeur (kwah-**fur**) *or fem* **coiffeuse** (kwah-**furz**) *n* a hairdresser [French]
coiffure (kwah-**fyoor**) *n* a hairstyle [French]
coil[1] *vb* **1** to wind or be wound into loops **2** to move in a winding course ▷ *n* **3** something wound in a connected series of loops **4** a single loop of such a series **5** a contraceptive device in the shape of a coil, inserted in the womb **6** an electrical conductor wound into a spiral, to provide inductance [Old French *coillir* to collect together]

coil² *n* **mortal coil** the troubles of the world [coined by William Shakespeare]

coin *n* **1** a metal disc used as money **2** metal currency collectively ▷ *vb* **3** to invent (a new word or phrase) **4** to make or stamp (coins) **5 coin it in** *or* **coin money** *informal* to make money rapidly [Latin *cuneus* wedge]

coinage *n* **1** coins collectively **2** the currency of a country **3** a newly invented word or phrase **4** the act of coining

coincide *vb* **-ciding, -cided 1** to happen at the same time **2** to agree or correspond exactly: *what she had said coincided exactly with his own thinking* **3** to occupy the same place in space [Latin *co-* together + *incidere* to occur]

coincidence *n* **1** a chance occurrence of simultaneous or apparently connected events **2** a coinciding

coincident *adj* **1** having the same position in space or time **2 coincident with** in exact agreement with

coincidental *adj* resulting from coincidence; not intentional **coincidentally** *adv*

coir *n* coconut fibre, used in making rope and matting [Malayalam (a language of SW India) *kāyar* rope]

coitus (**koh**-it-uss) *or* **coition** (koh-**ish**-un) *n* sexual intercourse [Latin *coire* to meet] **coital** *adj*

coke¹ *n* **1** a solid fuel left after gas has been distilled from coal ▷ *vb* **coking, coked 2** to become or convert into coke [probably dialect *colk* core]

coke² *n slang* cocaine

Coke *n trademark* short for **Coca-Cola**

col *n* the lowest point of a ridge connecting two mountain peaks [French: neck]

Col. Colonel

cola *n* **1** a soft drink flavoured with an extract from the nuts of a tropical tree **2** the W African tree whose nuts contain this extract [probably variant of W African *kolo* nut]

colander *n* a bowl with a perforated bottom for straining or rinsing foods [Latin *colum* sieve]

cold *adj* **1** low in temperature: *the cold March wind; cans of cold beer* **2** not hot enough: *eat your food before it gets cold!* **3** lacking in affection or enthusiasm **4** not affected by emotion: *the cold truth* **5** dead **6** (of a trail or scent in hunting) faint **7** (of a colour) giving the impression of coldness **8** *slang* unconscious **9** *informal* (of a seeker) far from the object of a search **10** denoting the contacting of potential customers without previously approaching them to establish their interest: *cold mailing* **11 cold comfort** little or no comfort **12 have** *or* **get cold feet** to be or become fearful or reluctant **13 in cold blood** deliberately and without mercy **14 leave someone cold** *informal* to fail to excite or impress someone **15 throw cold water on** *informal* to discourage ▷ *n* **16** the absence of heat **17** a viral infection of the nose and throat characterized by catarrh and sneezing **18** the sensation caused by loss or lack of heat **19 (out) in the cold** *informal* neglected or ignored ▷ *adv* **20** *informal* unrehearsed or unprepared: *he played his part cold* [Old English *ceald*] **coldly** *adv* **coldness** *n*

cold-blooded *adj* **1** callous or cruel **2** *zool* (of all animals except birds and mammals) having a body temperature that varies according to the temperature of the surroundings

cold chisel *n* a toughened steel chisel

cold cream *n* a creamy preparation used for softening and cleansing the skin

cold frame *n* an unheated wooden frame with a glass top, used to protect young plants

cold front *n meteorol* the boundary line between a warm air mass and the cold air pushing it from beneath and behind

cold-hearted *adj* lacking in feeling or warmth **cold-heartedness** *n*

cold shoulder *informal* ▷ *n* **1 give someone the cold shoulder** to snub someone ▷ *vb* **cold-shoulder 2** to treat with indifference

cold snap *n* a short period of cold and frosty weather

cold sore *n* a cluster of blisters near the lips, caused by a virus

cold storage *n* **1** the storage of things in a refrigerated place **2** *informal* a state of temporary disuse: *the idea has been in cold storage ever since*

cold sweat *n informal* coldness and sweating as a bodily reaction to fear or nervousness

cold turkey *n slang* a method of curing drug addiction by the sudden withdrawal of all doses

cold war *n* a state of political hostility between two countries without actual warfare

cole *n* any of various plants such as the cabbage and rape [Latin *caulis* cabbage]

coleslaw *n* a salad dish of shredded raw cabbage in a dressing [Dutch *koolsalade* cabbage salad]

coley *n Brit* an edible fish with white or grey flesh [perhaps from *coalfish*]

colic *n* severe pains in the stomach and bowels [Greek *kolon* COLON²] **colicky** *adj*

colitis (koh-**lie**-tiss) *n* inflammation of the colon, usually causing diarrhoea and lower abdominal pain

collaborate *vb* **-rating, -rated 1** to work with another or others on a joint project **2** to cooperate with an enemy invader [Latin *com-* together + *laborare* to work] **collaboration** *n* **collaborative** *adj* **collaborator** *n*

collage (**kol**-lahzh) *n* **1** an art form in which various materials or objects are glued onto a surface to make a picture **2** a picture made in this way **3** a work, such as a piece of music, created by combining unrelated styles [French] **collagist** *n*

collagen *n* a protein found in cartilage and bone that yields gelatine when boiled [Greek *kolla* glue]

collapse *vb* **-lapsing, -lapsed 1** to fall down or cave in suddenly **2** to fail completely: *a package holiday company which collapsed last year* **3** to fall down from lack of strength, exhaustion, or illness: *he collapsed with an asthma attack* **4** to sit down and rest because of tiredness or lack of energy: *she collapsed in front of the telly when she got home* **5** to fold compactly, esp. for storage ▷ *n* **6** the act of falling down or falling to pieces **7** a sudden failure or breakdown [Latin *collabi* to fall in ruins]

collapsible *adj* able to be folded up for storage
collar *n* **1** the part of a garment round the neck **2** a band of leather, rope, or metal placed around an animal's neck **3** *biol* a ringlike marking around the neck of a bird or animal **4** a cut of meat, esp. bacon, from the neck of an animal **5** a ring or band around a pipe, rod, or shaft ▷ *vb Brit, Austral & NZ informal* **6** to seize; arrest **7** to catch in order to speak to **8** to take for oneself [Latin *collum* neck]
collarbone *n* same as **clavicle**
collate *vb* **-lating, -lated 1** to examine and compare carefully **2** to gather together and put in order [Latin *com-* together + *latus* brought] **collator** *n*
collateral *n* **1** security pledged for the repayment of a loan **2** a person, animal, or plant descended from the same ancestor as another but through a different line ▷ *adj* **3** descended from a common ancestor but through different lines **4** additional but subordinate: *a spokeswoman said that there was no collateral information to dispute the assurances the government had been given* **5** situated or running side by side: *collateral ridges of mountains* [Latin *com-* together + *lateralis* of the side]
collateral damage *n military* unintentional civilian casualties or damage to civilian property caused by military action: *to minimize collateral damage maximum precision in bombing is required*
collation *n* **1** the act or result of collating **2** *formal* a light meal
colleague *n* a fellow worker, esp. in a profession [Latin *collega*]
collect[1] *vb* **1** to gather together or be gathered together **2** to gather (objects, such as stamps) as a hobby or for study **3** to go to a place to fetch (a person or thing) **4** to receive payments of (taxes, dues, or contributions) **5** to regain control of (oneself or one's emotions) [Latin *com-* together + *legere* to gather]
collect[2] *n Christianity* a short prayer said during certain church services [Medieval Latin *oratio ad collectam* prayer at the assembly]
collected *adj* **1** calm and self-controlled **2** brought together into one book or set of books: *the collected works of Dickens*
collection *n* **1** things collected or accumulated **2** a group of people **3** the act or process of collecting **4** a selection of clothes usually presented by a particular designer **5** a sum of money collected, as in church **6** a regular removal of letters from a postbox
collective *adj* **1** done by or characteristic of individuals acting as a group: *the army's collective wisdom regarding peacekeeping* ▷ *n* **2** a group of people working together on an enterprise and sharing the benefits from it **collectively** *adv*
collective bargaining *n* negotiation between a trade union and an employer on the wages and working conditions of the employees
collective noun *n* a noun that is singular in form but that refers to a group of people or things, as *crowd* or *army*

> **USAGE** Collective nouns are usually used with singular verbs: *the family is on holiday; General Motors is mounting a big sales campaign.* In British usage, however, plural verbs are sometimes employed in this context, esp. where reference is being made to a collection of individual objects or people rather than to the group as a unit: *the family are all on holiday.* Care should be taken that the same collective noun is not treated as both singular and plural in the same sentence: *the family is well and sends its best wishes* or *the family are all well and send their best wishes*, but not *the family is well and send their best wishes.*

collectivism *n* the theory that the state should own all means of production **collectivist** *adj*
collectivize *or* **-vise** *vb* **-vizing, -vized** *or* **-vising, -vised** to organize according to the theory of collectivism **collectivization** *or* **-visation** *n*
collector *n* **1** a person who collects objects as a hobby **2** a person employed to collect debts, rents, or tickets
collector's item *n* an object highly valued by collectors for its beauty or rarity
colleen *n Irish* a girl [Irish Gaelic *cailín*]
college *n* **1** an institution of higher or further education that is not a university **2** a self-governing section of certain universities **3** *Brit & NZ* a name given to some secondary schools **4** an organized body of people with specific rights and duties: *the president is elected by an electoral college* **5** a body organized within a particular profession, concerned with regulating standards **6** the staff and students of a college [Latin *collega* colleague]
collegian *n* a member of a college
collegiate *adj* **1** of a college or college students **2** (of a university) composed of various colleges
collide *vb* **-liding, -lided 1** to crash together violently **2** to conflict or disagree [Latin *com-* together + *laedere* to strike]
collie *n* a silky-haired dog used for herding sheep and cattle [Scots, probably from earlier *colie* black]
collier *n chiefly Brit* **1** a coal miner **2** a ship designed to carry coal
colliery *n, pl* **-lieries** *chiefly Brit* a coal mine and its buildings
collision *n* **1** a violent crash between moving objects **2** the conflict of opposed ideas or wishes [Latin *collidere* to collide]
collision course *n* **1** a trajectory of movement likely to result in a collision **2** a course of action likely to result in a serious disagreement or confrontation: *the union is on an inevitable collision course with the government*
collocate *vb* **-cating, -cated** (of words) to occur together regularly **collocation** *n*
colloid *n* a mixture of particles of one substance suspended in a different substance [Greek *kolla* glue] **colloidal** *adj*
collop *n* a small slice of meat [Scandinavian]
colloquial *adj* suitable for informal speech or writing **colloquially** *adv*
colloquialism *n* **1** a colloquial word or phrase **2** the use of colloquial words and phrases
colloquium *n, pl* **-quiums** *or* **-quia** an academic conference or seminar [Latin; see COLLOQUY]
colloquy *n, pl* **-quies** *formal* a conversation or conference [Latin *com-* together + *loqui* to speak] **colloquist** *n*

collude *vb* **-luding, -luded** to cooperate secretly or dishonestly with someone [Latin *colludere* to conspire]
collusion *n* secret or illegal agreement or cooperation **collusive** *adj*
collywobbles *pl n slang* **1** an intense feeling of nervousness **2** an upset stomach [probably from *colic* + *wobble*]
cologne *n* a perfumed toilet water [*Cologne*, Germany, where it was first manufactured]
colon[1] *n, pl* **-lons** the punctuation mark (:) used before an explanation or an example, a list, or an extended quotation [Greek *kōlon* limb, clause]
colon[2] *n, pl* **-lons** *or* **-la** the part of the large intestine connected to the rectum [Greek *kolon* large intestine] **colonic** *adj*
colonel *n* a senior commissioned officer in the army or air force [Old Italian *colonnello* column of soldiers] **colonelcy** *n*
colonial *adj* **1** of or inhabiting a colony or colonies **2** of a style of architecture popular in North America in the 17th and 18th centuries: *a colonial mansion* **3** of a style of architecture popular in Australia when it was a colony of Britain ▷ *n* **4** an inhabitant of a colony
colonial goose *n NZ old-fashioned* stuffed roast mutton
colonialism *n* the policy of acquiring and maintaining colonies, esp. for exploitation **colonialist** *n, adj*
colonist *n* a settler in or inhabitant of a colony
colonize *or* **-nise** *vb* **-nizing, -nized** *or* **-nising, -nised** **1** to establish a colony in (an area) **2** to settle in (an area) as colonists **colonization** *or* **-nisation** *n*
colonnade *n* a row of evenly spaced columns, usually supporting a roof [French *colonne* column] **colonnaded** *adj*
colony *n, pl* **-nies** **1** a group of people who settle in a new country but remain under the rule of their homeland **2** the territory occupied by such a settlement **3** a group of people with the same nationality or interests, forming a community in a particular place: *an artists' colony* **4** *zool* a group of the same type of animal or plant living or growing together **5** *bacteriol* a group of microorganisms when grown on a culture medium [Latin *colere* to cultivate, inhabit]
colophon *n* a publisher's symbol on a book [Greek *kolophōn* a finishing stroke]
color *n, vb US* same as **colour**
Colorado beetle *n* a black-and-yellow beetle that is a serious pest of potatoes [*Colorado*, state of central US]
coloration *or* **colouration** *n* arrangement of colours: *a red coloration of the eyes*
coloratura *n music* **1** a part for a solo singer which has much complicated ornamentation of the basic melody **2** a soprano who specializes in such music [obsolete Italian, literally: colouring]
colossal *adj* **1** very large in size: *the turbulent rivers and colossal mountains of New Zealand* **2** very serious or significant: *a colossal legal blunder*
colossus *n, pl* **-si** *or* **-suses** **1** a very large statue **2** a huge or important person or thing [Greek *kolossos*]
colostomy *n, pl* **-mies** an operation to form an opening from the colon onto the surface of the body, for emptying the bowel [COLON[2] + Greek *stoma* mouth]
colour *or US* **color** *n* **1** a property of things that results from the particular wavelengths of light which they reflect or give out, producing a sensation in the eye **2** a colour, such as a red or green, that possesses hue, as opposed to black, white, or grey **3** a substance, such as a dye, that gives colour **4** the skin complexion of a person **5** the use of all the colours in painting, drawing, or photography **6** the distinctive tone of a musical sound **7** details which give vividness or authenticity: *I walked the streets and absorbed the local colour* **8** semblance or pretext: *under colour of* ▷ *vb* **9** to apply colour to (something) **10** to influence or distort: *anger coloured her judgment* **11** to become red in the face, esp. when embarrassed or annoyed **12** to give a convincing appearance to: *he coloured his account of what had happened* ▷ See also **colours** [Latin *color*]
colour bar *n* racial discrimination, esp. by White people against non-White people
colour-blind *adj* **1** unable to distinguish between certain colours, esp. red and green **2** not discriminating on grounds of skin colour: *colour-blind policies* **colour blindness** *n*
coloured *or US* **colored** *adj* **1** having a colour or colours other than black or white: *coloured glass bottles; a peach-coloured outfit with matching hat* **2** *old-fashioned, offensive* (of a person) not White
Coloured *or US* **Colored** *S African* ▷ *n* **1** a person of racially mixed parentage or descent ▷ *adj* **2** of mixed White and non-White parentage
colourful *or US* **colorful** *adj* **1** with bright or richly varied colours **2** vivid or distinctive in character
colouring *or US* **coloring** *n* **1** the application of colour **2** something added to give colour **3** appearance with regard to shade and colour **4** the colour of a person's complexion
colourless *or US* **colorless** *adj* **1** without colour: *a colourless gas* **2** dull and uninteresting: *a colourless personality* **3** grey or pallid in tone or hue: *a watery sun hung low in the colourless sky*
colours *or US* **colors** *pl n* **1** the flag of a country, regiment, or ship **2** *Brit sport* a badge or other symbol showing membership of a team, esp. at a school or college **3** **nail one's colours to the mast** to commit oneself publicly to a course of action **4** **show one's true colours** to display one's true nature or character
colour sergeant *n* a sergeant who carries the regimental, battalion, or national colours
colour supplement *n Brit* an illustrated magazine accompanying a newspaper
colt *n* **1** a young male horse or pony **2** *sport* a young and inexperienced player [Old English: young ass]
coltsfoot *n, pl* **-foots** a weed with yellow flowers and heart-shaped leaves
columbine *n* a plant that has brightly coloured flowers with five spurred petals [Medieval Latin *columbina herba* dovelike plant]
column *n* **1** an upright pillar usually having a cylindrical shaft, a base, and a capital **2** a form or structure in the shape of a column: *a column of*

smoke **3** a vertical division of a page of text, esp. in a newspaper or dictionary **4** a regular feature in a paper: *a cookery column* **5** a vertical arrangement of numbers **6** *military* a narrow formation in which individuals or units follow one behind the other [Latin *columna*] **columnar** *adj*

columnist *n* a journalist who writes a regular feature in a newspaper

com- *or* **con-** *prefix* used with a main word to mean together; with; jointly: *commingle* [Latin, from *cum* with]

C

coma *n* a state of unconsciousness from which a person cannot be aroused, caused by injury, disease, or drugs [Greek *kōma* heavy sleep]

Comanche (kom-**man**-chee) *n, pl* **-ches** *or* **-che** a member of a Native American people, formerly living in the plains to the east of the Rockies, now chiefly in Oklahoma

comatose *adj* **1** in a coma **2** sound asleep

comb *n* **1** a toothed instrument for disentangling or arranging hair **2** a tool or machine that cleans and straightens wool or cotton **3** a fleshy serrated crest on the head of a domestic fowl **4** a honeycomb ▹ *vb* **5** to use a comb on **6** to search with great care: *police combed the streets for the missing girl* [Old English *camb*]

combat *n* **1** a fight or struggle ▹ *vb* **-bating, -bated 2** to fight: *a coordinated approach to combating the growing drugs problem* [Latin *com-* with + *battuere* to beat] **combative** *adj*

combatant *n* **1** a person taking part in a combat ▹ *adj* **2** engaged in or ready for combat

combat trousers *or* **combats** *pl n* loose casual trousers with large pockets on the sides of the legs

combe *n* same as **coomb**

comber *n* a long curling wave

combination *n* **1** the act of combining or state of being combined **2** people or things combined **3** the set of numbers or letters that opens a combination lock **4** a motorcycle with a sidecar **5** *maths* an arrangement of the members of a set into specified groups without regard to order in the group

combination lock *n* a lock that can only be opened when a set of dials is turned to show a specific sequence of numbers or letters

combinations *pl n Brit* a one-piece undergarment with long sleeves and legs

combine *vb* **-bining, -bined 1** to join together **2** to form a chemical compound ▹ *n* **3** an association of people or firms for a common purpose **4** short for **combine harvester** [Latin *com-* together + *bini* two by two]

combine harvester *n* a machine used to reap and thresh grain in one process

combings *pl n* the loose hair or fibres removed by combing, esp. from animals

combining form *n* a part of a word that occurs only as part of a compound word, such as *anthropo-* in *anthropology*

combo *n, pl* **-bos** a small group of jazz musicians

combustible *adj* capable of igniting and burning easily

combustion *n* **1** the process of burning **2** a chemical reaction in which a substance combines with oxygen to produce heat and light [Latin *comburere* to burn up]

come *vb* **coming, came, come 1** to move towards a place considered near to the speaker or hearer: *come and see me as soon as you can* **2** to arrive or reach: *turn left and continue until you come to a cattle-grid; he came to Britain in the 1920s* **3** to occur: *Christmas comes but once a year* **4** to happen as a result: *no good will come of this* **5** to occur to the mind: *the truth suddenly came to me* **6** to reach a specified point, state, or situation: *a dull brown dress that came down to my ankles; he'd come to a decision* **7** to be produced: *it also comes in other colours* **8 come from** to be or have been a resident or native (of): *my mother comes from Greenock* **9** to become: *it was like a dream come true* **10** *slang* to have an orgasm **11** *Brit & NZ informal* to play the part of: *don't come the innocent with me* **12** (*subjunctive use*) when a specified time arrives: *come next August* **13 as ... as they come** the most characteristic example of a type: *he's an arrogant swine and as devious as they come* **14 come again?** *informal* what did you say? **15 come to light** to be revealed ▹ *interj* **16** an exclamation expressing annoyance or impatience: *come now!* ▹ See also **come about, come across** *etc.* [Old English *cuman*]

come about *vb* to happen

come across *vb* **1** to meet or find by accident **2** to communicate the intended meaning or impression **3 come across as** to give a certain impression

come at *vb* to attack: *he came at me with an axe*

comeback *n informal* **1** a return to a former position or status **2** a response or retaliation ▹ *vb* **come back 3** to return, esp. to the memory **4** to become fashionable again

come between *vb* to cause the estrangement or separation of (two people)

come by *vb* to find or obtain, esp. accidentally: *Graham filled him in on how he came by the envelope*

comedian *or fem* **comedienne** *n* **1** an entertainer who tells jokes **2** a person who performs in comedy

comedown *n* **1** a decline in status or prosperity **2** *informal* a disappointment ▹ *vb* **come down 3** (of prices) to become lower **4** to reach a decision: *a 1989 court ruling came down in favour of three councils who wanted Sunday trading banned* **5** to be handed down by tradition or inheritance **6 come down in the world** to lose status or prosperity **7 come down on** to reprimand sharply **8 come down to** to amount to: *at the end the case came down to the one simple issue* **9 come down with** to begin to suffer from (illness)

comedy *n, pl* **-dies 1** a humorous film, play, or broadcast **2** such works as a genre **3** the humorous aspect of life or of events **4** (in classical literature) a play that ends happily [Greek *kōmos* village festival + *aeidein* to sing]

come forward *vb* **1** to offer one's services **2** to present oneself

come-hither *adj informal* flirtatious and seductive: *a come-hither look*

come in *vb* **1** to prove to be: *it came in useful* **2** to become fashionable or seasonable **3** to finish a race (in a certain position) **4** to be received: *reports of more deaths came in today* **5** (of money) to be received as income **6** to be involved in a situation: *where do I come in?* **7 come in for** to be the object of: *she came in for a lot of criticism*

come into *vb* **1** to enter **2** to inherit

comely *adj* **-lier, -liest** *old-fashioned* good-looking [Old English *cȳmlīc* beautiful] **comeliness** *n*

come of *vb* to result from: *nothing came of it*

come off *vb* **1** to emerge from a situation in a certain position: *the people who have come off worst are the poorest in society* **2** *informal* to take place **3** to have the intended effect: *it was a gamble that didn't come off*

come-on *n* **1** *informal* a lure or enticement ▷ *vb* **come on 2** (of power or water) to start running or functioning **3** to make progress: *my plants are coming on nicely* **4** to begin: *I think I've got a cold coming on* **5** to make an entrance on stage **6** to make a certain impression: *he comes on like a hard man* **7 come on to** *informal* to make sexual advances to

come out *vb* **1** to be made public or revealed: *it was only then that the truth came out* **2** to be published or put on sale: *their latest album came out last month* **3** Also: **come out of the closet** to reveal something formerly concealed, esp. that one is not heterosexual **4** *chiefly Brit* to go on strike **5** to declare oneself: *the report has come out in favour of maintaining child benefit* **6** to end up or turn out: *this wine consistently came out top in our tastings; the figures came out exactly right* **7** to enter society formally **8 come out in** to become covered with (a rash or spots) **9 come out with** to say or disclose: *she came out with a remark that left me speechless*

come over *vb* **1** to influence or affect: *I don't know what's come over me* **2** to communicate the intended meaning or impression **3** to give a certain impression **4** to change sides or opinions **5** *informal* to feel a particular sensation: *it makes him come over slightly queasy*

come round *vb* **1** to recover consciousness **2** to change one's opinion

comestibles *pl n* food [Latin *comedere* to eat up]

comet *n* a heavenly body that travels round the sun, leaving a long bright trail behind it [Greek *komētēs* long-haired]

come through *vb* to survive or endure (an illness or difficult situation) successfully

come to *vb* **1** to regain consciousness **2** to amount to (a total figure)

come up *vb* **1** to be mentioned or arise: *we hope that the difficulties that have arisen in the past will not keep coming up* **2** to be about to happen: *the club has important games coming up* **3 come up against** to come into conflict with **4 come up in the world** to rise in status **5 come up to** to meet a standard **6 come up with** to produce or propose: *he has a knack for coming up with great ideas*

come upon *vb* to meet or encounter unexpectedly

comeuppance *n informal* deserved punishment [from *come up* (in the sense: to appear before a court)]

comfit *n* a sugar-coated sweet [Latin *confectum* something prepared]

comfort *n* **1** a state of physical ease or well-being **2** relief from suffering or grief **3** a person or thing that brings ease **4 comforts** things that make life easier or more pleasant: *the comforts of home* ▷ *vb* **5** to soothe or console **6** to bring physical ease to [Latin *con-* (intensive) + *fortis* strong] **comforting** *adj*

comfortable *adj* **1** giving comfort; relaxing **2** free from trouble or pain **3** *informal* well-off financially **4** not afraid or embarrassed: *he was not comfortable expressing sympathy* **comfortably** *adv*

comforter *n* **1** a person or thing that comforts **2** a baby's dummy **3** *Brit* a woollen scarf

comfrey *n* a tall plant with bell-shaped blue, purple, or white flowers [Latin *conferva* water plant]

comfy *adj* **-fier, -fiest** *informal* comfortable

comic *adj* **1** humorous; funny **2** of or relating to comedy ▷ *n* **3** a comedian **4** a magazine containing comic strips [Greek *kōmikos*]

comical *adj* causing amusement, often because of being ludicrous or ridiculous: *an enthusiasm comical to behold* **comically** *adv*

comic opera *n* an opera with speech and singing that tells an amusing story

comic strip *n* a sequence of drawings in a newspaper or magazine, telling a humorous story or an adventure

coming *adj* **1** (of time or events) approaching or next: *in the coming weeks* **2** likely to be important in the future: *he was regarded as a coming man at the Foreign Office* **3 have it coming to one** *informal* to deserve what one is about to suffer ▷ *n* **4** arrival or approach

comity *n, pl* **-ties** *formal* friendly politeness, esp. between different countries [Latin *comis* affable]

comma *n* the punctuation mark (,) indicating a slight pause and used where there is a list of items or to separate the parts of a sentence [Greek *komma* clause]

command *vb* **1** to order or compel **2** to have authority over **3** to deserve and get: *a public figure who commands almost universal respect* **4** to look down over: *the house commands a magnificent view of the sea and the islands* ▷ *n* **5** an authoritative instruction that something must be done **6** the authority to command **7** knowledge; control: *a fluent command of French* **8** a military or naval unit with a specific function **9** *computers* a part of a program consisting of a coded instruction to the computer to perform a specified function [Latin *com-* (intensive) + *mandare* to order]

commandant *n* an officer in charge of a place or group of people

commandeer *vb* **1** to seize for military use **2** to take as if by right: *he commandeered the one waiting taxi outside the station* [Afrikaans *kommandeer*]

commander *n* **1** an officer in command of a military group or operation **2** a middle-ranking naval officer **3** a high-ranking member of some orders of knights

commander-in-chief *n, pl* **commanders-in-chief** the supreme commander of a nation's armed forces

commanding *adj* **1** being in charge: *the commanding officer* **2** in a position or situation where success looks certain: *a commanding lead* **3** having the air of authority: *a commanding voice* **4** having a wide view

commandment *n* a divine command, esp. one of the Ten Commandments in the Old Testament
commando *n, pl* **-dos** *or* **-does** **A** a military unit trained to make swift raids in enemy territory **B** a member of such a unit [Dutch *commando* command]
commedia dell'arte (kom-**made**-ee-a dell-**art**-tay) *n* a form of improvised comedy popular in Italy in the 16th century, with stock characters and a stereotyped plot [Italian]
commemorate *vb* **-rating, -rated** to honour or keep alive the memory of: *a series of events to commemorate the end of the Second World War* [Latin *com-* (intensive) + *memorare* to remind] **commemoration** *n* **commemorative** *adj*
commence *vb* **-mencing, -menced** to begin [Latin *com-* (intensive) + *initiare* to begin]
commencement *n* **1** the beginning; start **2** *US & Canad* a graduation ceremony
commend *vb* **1** to praise in a formal manner: *the judge commended her bravery* **2** to recommend: *he commended the scheme warmly* **3** to entrust: *I commend my child to your care* [Latin *com-* (intensive) + *mandare* to entrust] **commendable** *adj* **commendation** *n*
commensurable *adj* **1** measurable by the same standards **2** *maths* **A** having a common factor **B** having units of the same dimensions and being related by whole numbers **commensurability** *n*
commensurate *adj* **1** corresponding in degree, size, or value **2** commensurable [Latin *com-* same + *mensurare* to measure]
comment *n* **1** a remark, criticism, or observation **2** a situation or event that expresses some feeling: *a sad comment on the nature of many relationships* **3** talk or gossip **4** a note explaining or criticizing a passage in a text **5** **no comment** I decline to say anything about the matter ▷ *vb* **6** to remark or express an opinion [Latin *commentum* invention]
commentariat *n* the journalists and broadcasters who analyse and comment on current affairs [from COMMENTATOR + PROLETARIAT]
commentary *n, pl* **-taries** **1** a spoken accompaniment to an event, broadcast, or film **2** a series of explanatory notes on a subject
commentate *vb* **-tating, -tated** to act as a commentator

> **USAGE** The verb *commentate*, derived from *commentator*, is sometimes used as a synonym for *comment on* or *provide a commentary for*. It is not yet fully accepted as standard, though widespread in sports reporting and journalism.

commentator *n* **1** a person who provides a spoken commentary for a broadcast, esp. of a sporting event **2** an expert who reports on and analyses a particular subject
commerce *n* **1** the buying and selling of goods and services **2** *literary* social relations [Latin *commercium*]
commercial *adj* **1** of or engaged in commerce: *commercial exploitation of sport* **2** sponsored or paid for by an advertiser: *commercial radio* **3** having profit as the main aim: *this is a more commercial, accessible album than its predecessor* ▷ *n* **4** a radio or television advertisement
commercialism *n* **1** the principles and practices of commerce **2** exclusive or inappropriate emphasis on profit
commercialize *or* **-ise** *vb* **-izing, -ized** *or* **-ising, -ised** **1** to make commercial **2** to exploit for profit, esp. at the expense of quality **commercialization** *or* **-isation** *n*
commercial traveller *n* a travelling salesperson
commie *n, pl* **-mies**, *adj humorous, derogatory* Communist
commingle *vb* **-gling, -gled** to mix or be mixed
commis (**kom**-iss, **kom**-ee) *adj Brit* (of a waiter or chef) apprentice: *the commis chef* [French]
commiserate *vb* **-ating, -ated** (usually foll. by *with*) to express sympathy or pity (for) [Latin *com-* together + *miserari* to bewail] **commiseration** *n*
commissar *n* (formerly) an official responsible for political education in Communist countries
commissariat *n* a military department in charge of food supplies [Medieval Latin *commissarius* commissary]
commissary *n, pl* **-saries** **1** *US* a shop supplying food or equipment, as in a military camp **2** a representative or deputy [Medieval Latin *commissarius* official in charge]
commission *n* **1** an order for a piece of work, esp. a work of art or a piece of writing **2** a duty given to a person or group to perform **3** the fee or percentage paid to a salesperson for each sale made **4** a group of people appointed to perform certain duties: *a new parliamentary commission on defence* **5** the act of committing a sin or crime **6** *military* the rank or authority officially given to an officer **7** authority to perform certain duties **8** **in** *or* **out of commission** in *or* not in working order ▷ *vb* **9** to place an order for: *a report commissioned by the United Nations; a new work commissioned by the BBC Symphony Orchestra* **10** *military* to give a commission to **11** to prepare (a ship) for active service **12** to grant authority to [Latin *committere* to commit]
commissionaire *n chiefly Brit* a uniformed doorman at a hotel, theatre, or cinema [French]
commissioned officer *n* a military officer holding a rank by a commission
commissioner *n* **1** an appointed official in a government department or other organization **2** a member of a commission
commit *vb* **-mitting, -mitted** **1** to perform (a crime or error) **2** to hand over or allocate: *a marked reluctance to commit new money to business* **3** to pledge to a cause or a course of action **4** to send (someone) to prison or hospital **5** **commit to memory** to memorize **6** **commit to paper** to write down [Latin *committere* to join]
commitment *n* **1** dedication to a cause or principle **2** an obligation, responsibility, or promise that restricts freedom of action **3** the act of committing or state of being committed
committal *n* the official consignment of a person to a prison or psychiatric hospital
committed *adj* having pledged oneself to a particular belief or course of action: *a committed pacifist*

committee *n* a group of people appointed to perform a specified service or function [Middle English *committen* to entrust]
commode *n* **1** a chair with a hinged flap concealing a chamber pot **2** a chest of drawers [French]
commodious *adj* with plenty of space [Latin *commodus* convenient]
commodity *n, pl* **-ties** something that can be bought or sold [Latin *commoditas* suitability]
commodore *n* **1** *Brit* a senior commissioned officer in the navy **2** the president of a yacht club [probably from Dutch *commandeur*]
common *adj* **1** frequently encountered: *a fairly common plant; this disease is most common in kittens and young cats* **2** widespread among people in general: *common practice* **3** belonging to two or more people: *we share common interests* **4** belonging to the whole community: *common property* **5** low-class, vulgar, or coarse **6** *maths* belonging to two or more: *the lowest common denominator* **7** not belonging to the upper classes: *the common people* **8 common or garden** *informal* ordinary ▷ *n* **9** a piece of open land belonging to all the members of a community **10 in common** shared, in joint use ▷ See also **Commons** [Latin *communis* general] **commonly** *adv*
commonality *n, pl* **-ties** **1** the sharing of common attributes **2** the ordinary people
commonalty *n, pl* **-ties** **1** the ordinary people **2** the members of an incorporated society
common cold *n* same as **cold** (sense 17)
commoner *n* a person who does not belong to the nobility
common fraction *n* same as **simple fraction**
common law *n* **1** law based on judges' decisions and custom, as distinct from written laws ▷ *adj* **common-law** **2** (of a relationship) regarded as a marriage through being long-standing
Common Market *n* a former name for **European Union**
commonplace *adj* **1** so common or frequent as not to be worth commenting on: *foreign holidays have now become commonplace* **2** dull or unoriginal: *a commonplace observation* ▷ *n* **3** a cliché **4** an ordinary thing [translation of Latin *locus communis* argument of wide application]
common room *n chiefly Brit & Austral* a sitting room for students or staff in schools or colleges
commons *pl n* **1** *Brit* shared food or rations **2 short commons** reduced rations
Commons *n* **the Commons** same as **House of Commons**
common sense *n* **1** good practical understanding ▷ *adj* **common-sense** **2** inspired by or displaying this
common time *n music* a time signature with four crotchet beats to the bar; four-four time: *a dance in common time*
commonwealth *n* the people of a state or nation viewed politically
Commonwealth *n* **the Commonwealth** **A** Official name: **the Commonwealth of Nations** an association of sovereign states that are or at some time have been ruled by Britain **B** the official title of the federated states of Australia
commotion *n* noisy disturbance [Latin *com-* (intensive) + *movere* to move]
communal *adj* **1** belonging to or used by a community as a whole **2** of a commune **communally** *adv*
commune[1] *n* **1** a group of people living together and sharing possessions and responsibilities **2** the smallest district of local government in Belgium, France, Italy, and Switzerland [Latin *communia* things held in common]
commune[2] *vb* **-muning, -muned** > **commune with** **A** to experience strong emotion for: *communing with nature* **B** to talk intimately with [Old French *comuner* to hold in common]
communicable *adj* **1** capable of being communicated **2** (of a disease) capable of being passed on easily
communicant *n Christianity* a person who receives Communion
communicate *vb* **-cating, -cated** **1** to exchange (thoughts) or make known (information or feelings) by speech, writing, or other means **2** (usually foll. by *to*) to transmit (to): *the reaction of the rapturous audience communicated itself to the performers* **3** to have a sympathetic mutual understanding **4** *Christianity* to receive Communion [Latin *communicare* to share] **communicator** *n* **communicative** *adj*
communicating *adj* making or having a direct connection from one room to another: *the suite is made up of three communicating rooms; the communicating door*
communication *n* **1** the exchange of information, ideas, or feelings **2** something communicated, such as a message **3 communications** means of travelling or sending messages
communication cord *n Brit* a chain in a train which may be pulled by a passenger to stop the train in an emergency
communion *n* **1** a sharing of thoughts, emotions, or beliefs **2 communion with** strong feelings for: *private communion with nature* **3** a religious group with shared beliefs and practices: *the Anglican communion* [Latin *communis* common]
Communion *n Christianity* **1** a ritual commemorating Christ's Last Supper by the consecration of bread and wine **2** the consecrated bread and wine. Also called: **Holy Communion**
communiqué (kom-mune-ik-kay) *n* an official announcement [French]
communism *n* the belief that private ownership should be abolished and all work and property should be shared by the community [French *communisme*] **communist** *n, adj*
Communism *n* **1** a political movement based upon the writings of Karl Marx that advocates communism **2** the political and social system established in countries with a ruling Communist Party **Communist** *n, adj*
community *n, pl* **-ties** **1** all the people living in one district **2** a group of people with shared origins or interests: *the local Jewish community* **3** a group of countries with certain interests in common **4** the public; society **5** a group of

interdependent plants and animals inhabiting the same region [Latin *communis* common]

community centre *n* a building used by a community for social gatherings or activities

community charge *n* a poll tax which was levied in Scotland from 1989 until 1993 and in England and Wales from 1990 until 1993

community college *n US & Canad* a nonresidential college offering two-year courses of study

community service *n* organized unpaid work intended for the good of the community: often used as a punishment for minor criminals

commutative *adj maths* giving the same result irrespective of the order of the numbers or symbols

commutator *n* a device used to change alternating electric current into direct current

commute *vb* **-muting, -muted 1** to travel some distance regularly between one's home and one's place of work **2** *law* to reduce (a sentence) to one less severe **3** to substitute **4** to pay (an annuity or pension) at one time, instead of in instalments ▷ *n* **5** a journey made by commuting [Latin *com-* mutually + *mutare* to change] **commutable** *adj* **commutation** *n*

commuter *n* a person who regularly travels a considerable distance to work

compact[1] *adj* **1** closely packed together **2** neatly fitted into a restricted space **3** concise; brief ▷ *vb* **4** to pack closely together ▷ *n* **5** a small flat case containing a mirror and face powder [Latin *com-* together + *pangere* to fasten] **compactly** *adv* **compactness** *n*

compact[2] *n* a contract or agreement [Latin *com-* together + *pacisci* to contract]

compact disc *n* a small digital audio disc on which the sound is read by an optical laser system

companion *n* **1** a person who associates with or accompanies someone: *a travelling companion* **2** (esp. formerly) a woman paid to live or travel with another woman **3** a guidebook or handbook **4** one of a pair [Late Latin *companio* one who eats bread with another] **companionship** *n*

companionable *adj* friendly and pleasant to be with **companionably** *adv*

companionway *n* a ladder from one deck to another in a ship

company *n, pl* **-nies 1** a business organization **2** a group of actors **3** a small unit of troops **4** the officers and crew of a ship **5** the fact of being with someone: *I enjoy her company* **6** a number of people gathered together **7** a guest or guests **8** a person's associates **9 keep someone company** to accompany someone **10 part company** to disagree or separate [see COMPANION]

company sergeant-major *n military* the senior noncommissioned officer in a company

comparable *adj* **1** worthy of comparison **2** able to be compared (with) **comparability** *n*

comparative *adj* **1** relative: *despite the importance of his discoveries, he died in comparative poverty* **2** involving comparison: *comparative religion* **3** *grammar* the form of an adjective or adverb that indicates that the quality denoted is possessed to a greater extent. In English the comparative is marked by the suffix *-er* or the word *more* ▷ *n* **4** the comparative form of an adjective or adverb **comparatively** *adv*

compare *vb* **-paring, -pared 1** to examine in order to observe resemblances or differences: *the survey compared the health of three groups of children* **2 compare to** to declare to be like: *one ambulance driver compared the carnage to an air crash* **3** (usually foll. by *with*) to resemble: *his storytelling compares with the likes of Le Carré* **4** to bear a specified relation when examined: *this full-flavoured white wine compares favourably with more expensive French wines* **5 compare notes** to exchange opinions ▷ *n* **6 beyond compare** without equal [Latin *com-* together + *par* equal]

comparison *n* **1** a comparing or being compared **2** likeness or similarity: *there is no comparison at all between her and Catherine* **3** *grammar* the positive, comparative, and superlative forms of an adjective or adverb **4 in comparison to** *or* **with** compared to **5 bear** *or* **stand comparison with** to be able to be compared with (something else), esp. favourably: *his half-dozen best novels can stand comparison with anyone's*

compartment *n* **1** one of the sections into which a railway carriage is sometimes divided **2** a separate section: *filing the information away in some compartment of his mind* **3** a small storage space: *the ice-making compartment of the fridge* [French *compartiment*]

compartmentalize *or* **-ise** *vb* **-izing, -ized** *or* **-ising, -ised** to put into categories or sections

compass *n* **1** an instrument for finding direction, with a magnetized needle which points to magnetic north **2** limits or range: *within the compass of a normal-sized book such a comprehensive survey is not possible* **3 compasses** an instrument used for drawing circles or measuring distances, that consists of two arms, joined at one end [Latin *com-* together + *passus* step]

compassion *n* a feeling of distress and pity for the suffering or misfortune of another [Latin *com-* with + *pati* to suffer]

compassionate *adj* showing or having compassion **compassionately** *adv*

compassionate leave *n* leave from work granted on the grounds of family illness or bereavement

compatible *adj* **1** able to exist together harmoniously **2** consistent: *his evidence is fully compatible with the other data* **3** (of pieces of equipment) capable of being used together [Late Latin *compati* to suffer with] **compatibility** *n*

compatriot *n* a fellow countryman or countrywoman [French *compatriote*]

compel *vb* **-pelling, -pelled 1** to force (to be or do something) **2** to obtain by force: *his performance compelled attention* [Latin *com-* together + *pellere* to drive]

compelling *adj* **1** arousing strong interest: *a compelling new novel* **2** convincing: *compelling evidence*

compendious *adj* brief but comprehensive

compendium *n, pl* **-diums** *or* **-dia** **1** *Brit* a selection of different table games in one container **2** a concise but comprehensive summary [Latin: a saving, literally: something weighed]

compensate *vb* **-sating, -sated** **1** to make amends to (someone), esp. for loss or injury **2** to cancel out the effects of (something): *the car's nifty handling fails to compensate for its many flaws* **3** to serve as compensation for (injury or loss) [Latin *compensare*] **compensatory** *adj*

compensation *n* **1** payment made as reparation for loss or injury **2** the act of making amends for something

compere *Brit, Austral & NZ* ▷ *n* **1** a person who introduces a stage, radio, or television show ▷ *vb* **-pering, -pered** **2** to be the compere of [French: godfather]

compete *vb* **-peting, -peted** **1** to take part in (a contest or competition) **2** to strive (to achieve something or to be successful): *able to compete on the international market* [Latin *com-* together + *petere* to seek]

competence *or* **competency** *n* **1** the ability to do something well or effectively **2** a sufficient income to live on **3** the state of being legally competent or qualified

competent *adj* **1** having sufficient skill or knowledge: *he was a very competent engineer* **2** suitable or sufficient for the purpose: *it was a competent performance, but hardly a remarkable one* **3** having valid legal authority: *lawful detention after conviction by a competent court* [Latin *competens*]

competition *n* **1** the act of competing; rivalry: *competition for places was keen* **2** an event in which people compete **3** the opposition offered by competitors **4** people against whom one competes

competitive *adj* **1** involving rivalry: *the increasingly competitive computer industry* **2** characterized by an urge to compete: *her naturally competitive spirit* **3** of good enough value to be successful against commercial rivals: *we offer worldwide flights at competitive prices* **competitiveness** *n*

competitor *n* a person, team, or firm that competes

compile *vb* **-piling, -piled** **1** to collect and arrange (information) from various sources **2** *computers* to convert (commands for a computer) from the language used by the person using it into machine code suitable for the computer, using a compiler [Latin *com-* together + *pilare* to thrust down, pack] **compilation** *n*

compiler *n* **1** a person who compiles information **2** a computer program that converts a high-level programming language into the machine language used by a computer

complacency *n* extreme self-satisfaction **complacent** *adj* **complacently** *adv*

complain *vb* **1** to express resentment or displeasure **2** **complain of** to state that one is suffering from (a pain or illness): *she complained of breathing trouble and chest pains* **3** to make a formal protest: *he complained to the police about his rowdy neighbours* [Latin *com-* (intensive) + *plangere* to bewail]

complainant *n* *law* a plaintiff

complaint *n* **1** the act of complaining **2** a reason for complaining **3** a mild illness **4** a formal protest

complaisant (kom-**play**-zant) *adj* willing to please or oblige [Latin *complacere* to please greatly] **complaisance** *n*

complement *n* **1** a person or thing that completes something **2** a complete amount or number: *a full complement of staff nurses and care assistants* **3** the officers and crew needed to man a ship **4** *grammar* a word or words added to the verb to complete the meaning of the predicate in a sentence, as *a fool* in *He is a fool* or *that he would come* in *I hoped that he would come* **5** *maths* the angle that when added to a specified angle produces a right angle ▷ *vb* **6** to complete or form a complement to [Latin *com-* (intensive) + *plere* to fill]

USAGE Avoid confusion with **compliment**.

complementary *adj* **1** forming a complete or balanced whole **2** forming a complement

complementary medicine *n* same as **alternative medicine**

complete *adj* **1** thorough; absolute: *it was a complete shambles* **2** perfect in quality or kind: *he is the complete modern footballer* **3** finished **4** having all the necessary parts **5** **complete with** having as an extra feature or part: *a mansion complete with swimming pool* ▷ *vb* **-pleting, -pleted** **6** to finish **7** to make whole or perfect [Latin *complere* to fill up] **completely** *adv* **completion** *n*

complex *adj* **1** made up of interconnected parts **2** intricate or complicated **3** *maths* of or involving complex numbers ▷ *n* **4** a whole made up of related parts: *a leisure complex including a gymnasium, squash courts, and a 20-metre swimming pool* **5** *psychoanalysis* a group of unconscious feelings that influences a person's behaviour **6** *informal* an obsession or phobia: *I have never had a complex about my height* [Latin *com-* together + *plectere* to braid]

USAGE *Complex* is sometimes used where *complicated* is meant. *Complex* should be used to say only that something consists of several parts rather than that, because something consists of many parts, it is difficult to understand or analyse.

complex fraction *n* *maths* a fraction in which the numerator or denominator or both contain fractions

complexion *n* **1** the colour and general appearance of the skin of a person's face **2** character or nature: *the political complexion of the government* [Latin *complexio* a combination]

complexity *n, pl* **-ties** **1** the state or quality of being intricate or complex **2** something complicated

complex number *n* any number of the form $a + bi$, where a and b are real numbers and $i = \sqrt{-1}$

compliance *n* **1** complying **2** a tendency to do what others want **compliant** *adj*

complicate *vb* **-cating, -cated** to make or become complex or difficult to deal with [Latin *complicare* to fold together]

complicated *adj* difficult to understand or deal with

USAGE See at **complex**.

C

complication *n* **1** something that makes a situation more difficult to deal with: *an added complication is the growing concern for the environment* **2** a medical condition arising as a consequence of another

complicit *adj* involved with others in an undesirable or illegal activity: *the government was complicit in abuses of human rights*

complicity *n, pl* **-ties** the fact of being an accomplice in a crime

compliment *n* **1** an expression of praise **2 compliments** formal greetings ▹ *vb* **3** to express admiration for [Italian *complimento*]

USAGE Avoid confusion with **complement**.

complimentary *adj* **1** expressing praise **2** free of charge: *a complimentary drink*

comply *vb* **-plies, -plying, -plied** to act in accordance (with a rule, order, or request) [Spanish *cumplir* to complete]

component *n* **1** a constituent part or feature of a whole **2** *maths* one of a set of two or more vectors whose resultant is a given vector ▹ *adj* **3** forming or functioning as a part or feature: *over 60 component parts* [Latin *componere* to put together]

comport *vb formal* **1 comport oneself** to behave in a specified way **2 comport with** to suit or be appropriate to [Latin *comportare* to collect] **comportment** *n*

compose *vb* **-posing, -posed 1** to put together or make up **2** to be the component elements of **3** to create (a musical or literary work) **4** to calm (oneself) **5** to arrange artistically **6** *printing* to set up (type) [Latin *componere* to put in place]

composed *adj* (of people) in control of their feelings

composer *n* a person who writes music

composite *adj* **1** made up of separate parts **2** (of a plant) with flower heads made up of many small flowers, such as the dandelion **3** *maths* capable of being factorized: *a composite function* ▹ *n* **4** something composed of separate parts **5** a composite plant [Latin *compositus* well arranged]

Composite *adj* of a style of classical architecture which combines elements of the Ionic and Corinthian styles

composite school *n Canad* a secondary school that offers both academic courses and vocational training

composition *n* **1** the act of putting together or composing **2** something composed **3** the things or parts which make up a whole **4** a work of music, art, or literature **5** the harmonious arrangement of the parts of a work of art **6** a written exercise; an essay **7** *printing* the act or technique of setting up type

compositor *n* a person who arranges type for printing

compos mentis *adj* sane [Latin]

compost *n* **1** a mixture of decaying plants and manure, used as a fertilizer **2** soil mixed with fertilizer, used for growing plants ▹ *vb* **3** to make (vegetable matter) into compost [Latin *compositus* put together]

composure *n* the state of being calm or unworried

compote *n* fruit stewed with sugar or in a syrup [French]

compound[1] *n* **1** *chem* a substance that contains atoms of two or more chemical elements held together by chemical bonds **2** any combination of two or more parts, features, or qualities **3** a word formed from two existing words or combining forms ▹ *vb* **4** to combine so as to create a compound **5** to make by combining parts or features: *the film's score is compounded from surging strings, a heavenly chorus, and jazzy saxophones* **6** to intensify by an added element: *the problems of undertaking relief work are compounded by continuing civil war* **7** *law* to agree not to prosecute in return for payment: *to compound a crime* ▹ *adj* **8** composed of two or more parts or elements **9** *music* with a time in which the number of beats per bar is a multiple of three: *such tunes are usually in a form of compound time, for example six-four* [Latin *componere* to put in order] **compoundable** *adj*

compound[2] *n* a fenced enclosure containing buildings, such as a camp for prisoners of war [Malay *kampong* village]

compound fracture *n* a fracture in which the broken bone pierces the skin

compound interest *n* interest paid on a sum and its accumulated interest

comprehend *vb* **1** to understand **2** to include [Latin *comprehendere*] **comprehensible** *adj*

comprehension *n* **1** understanding **2** inclusion

comprehensive *adj* **1** of broad scope or content **2** (of car insurance) providing protection against most risks, including third-party liability, fire, theft, and damage **3** *Brit* of the comprehensive school system ▹ *n* **4** *Brit* a comprehensive school

comprehensive school *n Brit* a secondary school for children of all abilities

compress *vb* **1** to squeeze together **2** to condense ▹ *n* **3** a cloth or pad applied firmly to some part of the body to cool inflammation or relieve pain [Latin *comprimere*]

compression *n* **1** the act of compressing **2** the reduction in volume and increase in pressure of the fuel mixture in an internal-combustion engine before ignition

compressor *n* a device that compresses a gas

comprise *vb* **-prising, -prised 1** to be made up of: *the group comprised six French diplomats, five Italians, and three Bulgarians* **2** to form or make up: *women comprised 57 per cent of all employees, but less than 10 per cent of managers* [French *compris* included]

USAGE The use of *of* after *comprise* should be avoided: *the library comprises* (not *comprises of*) *500 000 books and manuscripts.*

compromise (kom-prom-mize) *n* **1** settlement of a dispute by concessions on each side: *everyone pleaded for compromise; the compromise was only reached after hours of hard bargaining* **2** the terms of such a settlement **3** something midway between different things ▹ *vb* **-mising, -mised 4** to settle (a dispute) by making concessions **5** to put (oneself or another person) in a dishonourable position ▹ *adj* **6** being, or having the nature of, a compromise: *a compromise solution* [Latin *compromittere* to promise at the same time] **compromising** *adj*

comptroller *n* a financial controller

compulsion *n* **1** an irresistible urge to perform some action **2** compelling or being compelled [Latin *compellere* to compel]
compulsive *adj* **1** resulting from or acting from a compulsion **2** irresistible or absorbing **compulsively** *adv*
compulsory *adj* required by regulations or laws
compulsory purchase *n* the enforced purchase of a property by a local authority or government department
compunction *n* a feeling of guilt or regret [Latin *compungere* to sting]
computation *n* a calculation involving numbers or quantities **computational** *adj*
compute *vb* **-puting, -puted** to calculate (an answer or result), often by using a computer [Latin *computare*]
computer *n* an electronic device that processes data according to a set of instructions
computer game *n* an electronic game played by manipulating an input device in response to the graphics on a computer screen
computerize *or* **-ise** *vb* **-izing, -ized** *or* **-ising, -ised** **1** to equip with a computer **2** to control or perform (operations) by means of a computer **computerization** *or* **-isation** *n*
computing *n* **1** the activity of using computers and writing programs for them **2** the study of computers and their application
comrade *n* **1** a fellow member of a union or a socialist political party **2** a companion [French *camarade*] **comradely** *adj* **comradeship** *n*
con[1] *informal* ▷ *n* **1** same as **confidence trick** ▷ *vb* **conning, conned** **2** to swindle or defraud
con[2] *n* See **pros and cons** [Latin *contra* against]
con[3] *n slang* a convict
Con *politics* Conservative
con- *prefix* See **com-**
concatenation *n formal* a series of linked events [Latin *com-* together + *catena* chain]
concave *adj* curving inwards like the inside surface of a ball [Latin *concavus* arched] **concavity** *n*
conceal *vb* **1** to cover and hide **2** to keep secret [Latin *com-* (intensive) + *celare* to hide] **concealment** *n*
concede *vb* **-ceding, -ceded** **1** to admit (something) as true or correct **2** to give up or grant (something, such as a right) **3** to acknowledge defeat in (a contest or argument) [Latin *concedere*]
conceit *n* **1** an excessively high opinion of oneself **2** *literary* a far-fetched or clever comparison [see CONCEIVE]
conceited *adj* having an excessively high opinion of oneself **conceitedness** *n*
conceivable *adj* capable of being understood, believed, or imagined **conceivably** *adv*
conceive *vb* **-ceiving, -ceived** **1** to imagine or think **2** to consider in a certain way: *we must do what we conceive to be right* **3** to form in the mind **4** to become pregnant [Latin *concipere* to take in]
concentrate *vb* **-trating, -trated** **1** to focus all one's attention, thoughts, or efforts on something: *she tried hard to concentrate, but her mind kept flashing back to the previous night* **2** to bring or come together in large numbers or amounts in one place: *a flawed system that concentrates power in the hands of the few* **3** to make (a liquid) stronger by removing water from it ▷ *n* **4** a concentrated substance [Latin *com-* same + *centrum* centre] **concentrated** *adj*
concentration *n* **1** intense mental application **2** the act of concentrating **3** something that is concentrated **4** the amount or proportion of a substance in a mixture or solution
concentration camp *n* a prison camp for civilian prisoners, as in Nazi Germany
concentric *adj* having the same centre: *concentric circles* [Latin *com-* same + *centrum* centre]
concept *n* an abstract or general idea: *one of the basic concepts of quantum theory* [Latin *concipere* to conceive]
conception *n* **1** a notion, idea, or plan **2** the fertilization of an egg by a sperm in the Fallopian tube followed by implantation in the womb **3** origin or beginning: *the gap between the conception of an invention and its production* [Latin *concipere* to conceive]
conceptual *adj* of or based on concepts
conceptualize *or* **-ise** *vb* **-izing, -ized** *or* **-ising, -ised** to form a concept or idea of **conceptualization** *or* **-isation** *n*
concern *n* **1** anxiety or worry: *the current concern over teenage pregnancies* **2** something that is of interest or importance to a person **3** regard or interest: *a scrupulous concern for client confidentiality* **4** a business or firm ▷ *vb* **5** to worry or make anxious **6** to involve or interest: *he had converted the building into flats without concerning himself with the niceties of planning permission* **7** to be relevant or important to [Latin *com-* together + *cernere* to sift]
concerned *adj* **1** interested or involved: *I have spoken to the person concerned and she has no recollection of saying such a thing* **2** worried or anxious: *we are increasingly concerned for her safety*
concerning *prep* about; regarding
concert *n* **1** a performance of music by players or singers in front of an audience **2 in concert** **A** working together **B** (of musicians or singers) performing live [Latin *com-* together + *certare* strive]
concerted *adj* decided or planned by mutual agreement: *a concerted effort*
concertina *n* **1** a small musical instrument similar to an accordion ▷ *vb* **-naing, -naed** **2** to collapse or fold up like a concertina [from *concert*]
concerto (kon-**chair**-toe) *n, pl* **-tos** *or* **-ti** (-tee) a large-scale composition for an orchestra and one or more soloists [Italian]
concert pitch *n* the internationally agreed pitch to which concert instruments are tuned for performance
concession *n* **1** any grant of rights, land, or property by a government, local authority, or company **2** a reduction in price for a certain category of person: *fare concessions for senior citizens* **3** the act of yielding or conceding **4** something conceded **5** *Canad* **A** a land subdivision in a township survey **B** same as **concession road** [Latin *concedere* to concede] **concessionary** *adj*
concessionaire *n* someone who holds a concession

C

concession road *n Canad* one of a series of roads separating concessions in a township

conch *n, pl* **conchs** *or* **conches** **1** a marine mollusc with a large brightly coloured spiral shell **2** its shell [Greek *konkhē* shellfish]

concierge (kon-see-**airzh**) *n* (esp. in France) a caretaker in a block of flats [French]

conciliate *vb* **-ating, -ated** to try to end a disagreement with or pacify (someone) [Latin *conciliare* to bring together] **conciliator** *n*

C

conciliation *n* **1** the act of conciliating **2** a method of helping the parties in a dispute to reach agreement, esp. divorcing or separating couples to part amicably

conciliatory *adj* intended to end a disagreement

concise *adj* brief and to the point [Latin *concidere* to cut short] **concisely** *adv* **conciseness** *or* **concision** *n*

conclave *n* **1** a secret meeting **2** *RC Church* a private meeting of cardinals to elect a new pope [Latin *clavis* key]

conclude *vb* **-cluding, -cluded** **1** to decide by reasoning: *a police investigation concluded that no crime had been committed* **2** to come or bring to an end: *the festival concludes on December 19th* **3** to arrange or settle finally: *officials have refused to comment on the failure to conclude an agreement* [Latin *concludere*]

conclusion *n* **1** a final decision, opinion, or judgment based on reasoning: *the obvious conclusion is that something is being covered up* **2** end or ending **3** outcome or result: *if you take that strategy to its logical conclusion you end up with communism* **4** **in conclusion** finally **5** **jump to conclusions** to come to a conclusion too quickly, without sufficient thought or evidence

conclusive *adj* putting an end to doubt: *there is no conclusive proof of this* **conclusively** *adv*

concoct *vb* **1** to make by combining different ingredients **2** to invent or make up (a story or plan) [Latin *coquere* to cook] **concoction** *n*

concomitant *adj* **1** existing or along with (something else): *the concomitant health gains* ▷ *n* **2** something that is concomitant [Latin *com-* with + *comes* companion]

concord *n* **1** agreement or harmony **2** peaceful relations between nations **3** *music* a harmonious combination of musical notes [Latin *com-* same + *cor* heart] **concordant** *adj*

concordance *n* **1** a state of harmony or agreement **2** an alphabetical list of words in a text, with the context and often the meaning

concordat *n formal* a treaty or agreement, such as one between the Vatican and another state [Latin *concordatum* something agreed]

concourse *n* **1** a large open space in a public place, where people can meet: *a crowded concourse at Heathrow Airport* **2** a crowd [Latin *concurrere* to run together]

concrete *n* **1** a building material made of cement, sand, stone, and water that hardens to a stonelike mass ▷ *vb* **-creting, -creted** **2** to cover with concrete ▷ *adj* **3** made of concrete **4** specific as opposed to general **5** relating to things that can be perceived by the senses, as opposed to abstractions [Latin *concrescere* to grow together]

concretion *n* **1** a solidified mass **2** the act of solidifying

concubine (kon-kew-bine) *n* **1** *archaic* a woman cohabiting with a man **2** a secondary wife in polygamous societies [Latin *concumbere* to lie together] **concubinage** *n*

concupiscence (kon-**kew**-piss-enss) *n formal* strong sexual desire [Latin *concupiscere* to covet] **concupiscent** *adj*

concur *vb* **-curring, -curred** to agree; be in accord [Latin *concurrere* to run together]

concurrence *n* **1** agreement **2** simultaneous occurrence

concurrent *adj* **1** taking place at the same time or place **2** meeting at, approaching, or having a common point: *concurrent lines* **3** in agreement **concurrently** *adv*

concuss *vb* to injure (the brain) by a fall or blow [Latin *concutere* to disturb greatly]

concussion *n* **1** a brain injury caused by a blow or fall, usually resulting in loss of consciousness **2** violent shaking

condemn *vb* **1** to express strong disapproval of **2** to pronounce sentence on in a court of law **3** to force into a particular state: *a system that condemns most of our youngsters to failure* **4** to judge or declare (something) unfit for use **5** to indicate the guilt of: *everything the man had said condemned him, morally if not technically* [Latin *condemnare*] **condemnation** *n* **condemnatory** *adj*

condensation *n* **1** anything that has condensed from a vapour, esp. on a window **2** the act of condensing, or the state of being condensed

condense *vb* **-densing, -densed** **1** to express in fewer words **2** to increase the density of; concentrate **3** to change from a gas to a liquid or solid [Latin *condensare*]

condensed milk *n* milk thickened by evaporation, with sugar added

condenser *n* **1** an apparatus for reducing gases to their liquid or solid form by the removal of heat **2** same as **capacitor** **3** a lens that concentrates light

condescend *vb* **1** to behave patronizingly towards (one's supposed inferiors) **2** to do something as if it were beneath one's dignity [Church Latin *condescendere*] **condescending** *adj* **condescension** *n*

condiment *n* any seasoning for food, such as salt, pepper, or sauces [Latin *condire* to pickle]

condition *n* **1** a particular state of being: *the human condition; the van is in very poor condition* **2** **conditions** circumstances: *worsening weather conditions; the government pledged to improve living and working conditions* **3** a necessary requirement for something else to happen: *food is a necessary condition for survival* **4** a restriction or a qualification **5** a term of an agreement: *the conditions of the lease are set out* **6** state of physical fitness, esp. good health: *she is in a serious condition in hospital; out of condition* **7** an ailment: *a heart condition* **8** **on condition that** provided that ▷ *vb* **9** to accustom or alter the reaction of (a person or animal) to a particular stimulus or situation **10** to treat with a conditioner **11** to make fit or healthy **12** to influence or determine the form that something takes: *he argued that the failure of Latin American industry was conditioned by international economic structures* [Latin *con-* together + *dicere* to say] **conditioning** *n, adj*

conditional *adj* **1** depending on other factors **2** *grammar* expressing a condition on which something else depends, for example 'If he comes' is a conditional clause in the sentence 'If he comes I shall go'

conditioner *n* a thick liquid used when washing to make hair or clothes feel softer

condo *n, pl* **-dos** *US & Canad informal* a condominium building or apartment

condolence *n* sympathy expressed for someone in grief or pain [Latin *com-* together + *dolere* to grieve] **condole** *vb*

condom *n* a rubber sheath worn on the penis or in the vagina during sexual intercourse to prevent conception or infection [origin unknown]

condominium *n, pl* **-ums 1** *Austral, US & Canad* **A** an apartment building in which each apartment is individually owned **B** an apartment in such a building **2** joint rule of a state by two or more other states [Latin *com-* together + *dominium* ownership]

condone *vb* **-doning, -doned** to overlook or forgive (an offence or wrongdoing) [Latin *com-* (intensive) + *donare* to donate]

condor *n* a very large rare S American vulture [indigenous S American word *kuntur*]

conducive *adj* (often foll. by *to*) likely to lead to or produce (a result) [Latin *com-* together + *ducere* to lead]

conduct *n* **1** behaviour **2** the management or handling of an activity or business ▷ *vb* **3** to carry out: *the police are conducting an investigation into the affair* **4 conduct oneself** to behave (oneself) **5** to control (an orchestra or choir) by the movements of the hands or a baton **6** to accompany and guide (people or a party): *a conducted tour* **7** to transmit (heat or electricity) [Latin *com-* together + *ducere* to lead]

conductance *n* the ability of a specified body to conduct electricity

conduction *n* the transmission of heat or electricity

conductivity *n* the property of transmitting heat, electricity, or sound

conductor *n* **1** a person who conducts an orchestra or choir **2** an official on a bus who collects fares **3** *US, Canad & NZ* a railway official in charge of a train **4** something that conducts electricity or heat **conductress** *fem n*

conduit (kon-dew-it) *n* **1** a route or system for transferring things from one place to another: *a conduit for sending money to the United States* **2** a channel or tube for carrying a fluid or electrical cables **3** a means of access or communication [Latin *conducere* to lead]

cone *n* **1** a geometric solid consisting of a circular or oval base, tapering to a point **2** a cone-shaped wafer shell used to contain ice cream **3** the scaly fruit of a conifer tree **4** *Brit, Austral & NZ* a plastic cone used as a temporary traffic marker on roads **5** a type of cell in the retina, sensitive to colour and bright light [Greek *kōnus* pine cone, geometrical cone]

coney *n* same as **cony**

confab *n informal* a conversation

confabulation *n formal* a conversation [Latin *confabulari* to talk together]

confection *n* **1** any sweet food, such as a cake or a sweet **2** *old-fashioned* an elaborate piece of clothing [Latin *confectio* a preparing]

confectioner *n* a person who makes or sells confectionery

confectionery *n, pl* **-eries 1** sweets and chocolates collectively: *a drop in confectionery sales* **2** the art or business of a confectioner

confederacy *n, pl* **-cies** a union of states or people joined for a common purpose [Late Latin *confoederatio* agreement] **confederal** *adj*

confederate *n* **1** a state or individual that is part of a confederacy **2** an accomplice or conspirator ▷ *adj* **3** united; allied ▷ *vb* **-ating, -ated 4** to unite in a confederacy [Late Latin *confoederare* to unite by a league]

Confederate *adj* of or supporting those American states which withdrew from the USA in 1860–61, leading to the American Civil War

confederation *n* **1** a union or alliance of states or groups **2** confederating or being confederated **3** a federation

confer *vb* **-ferring, -ferred 1** to discuss together **2** to grant or give: *the power conferred by wealth* [Latin *com-* together + *ferre* to bring] **conferment** *n* **conferrable** *adj*

conference *n* a meeting for formal consultation or discussion [Medieval Latin *conferentia*]

confess *vb* **1** to admit (a fault or crime) **2** to admit to be true, esp. reluctantly **3** *Christianity* to declare (one's sins) to God or to a priest, so as to obtain forgiveness [Latin *confiteri* to admit]

confession *n* **1** something confessed **2** an admission of one's faults, sins, or crimes **3 confession of faith** a formal public statement of religious beliefs

confessional *n* **1** *Christianity* a small room or enclosed stall in a church where a priest hears confessions ▷ *adj* **2** of or suited to a confession

confessor *n* **1** *Christianity* a priest who hears confessions and gives spiritual advice **2** *history* a person who demonstrates their Christian religious faith by the holiness of their life: *Edward the Confessor*

confetti *n* small pieces of coloured paper thrown at weddings [Italian]

confidant *or fem* **confidante** *n* a person to whom private matters are confided [French *confident*]

confide *vb* **-fiding, -fided 1 confide in** to tell (something to someone) in confidence **2** *formal* to entrust into another's keeping [Latin *confidere*]

confidence *n* **1** trust in a person or thing **2** belief in one's own abilities **3** trust or a trustful relationship: *she won first the confidence, then the admiration, of her bosses* **4** something confided, such as a secret **5 in confidence** as a secret

confidence trick *n* a swindle in which the swindler gains the victim's trust in order to cheat him or her

C

confident *adj* **1** having or showing certainty: *we are now confident that this technique works* **2** sure of oneself [Latin *confidere* to have complete trust in] **confidently** *adv*
confidential *adj* **1** spoken or given in confidence **2** entrusted with another's secret affairs: *a confidential secretary* **3** suggestive of intimacy: *a halting, confidential manner* **confidentiality** *n* **confidentially** *adv*
C
confiding *adj* trusting: *a close and confiding relationship* **confidingly** *adv*
configuration *n* **1** the arrangement of the parts of something **2** the form or outline of such an arrangement [Late Latin *configurare* to model on something]
configure *vb* **-guring, -gured** *computers* to set up (a piece of hardware or software) so that it is ready for use
confine *vb* **-fining, -fined 1** to keep within bounds **2** to restrict the free movement of: *a nasty dose of flu which confined her to bed for days* ▷ *n* **3 confines** boundaries or limits [Latin *finis* boundary]
confinement *n* **1** being confined **2** the period of childbirth
confirm *vb* **1** to prove to be true or valid **2** to reaffirm (something), so as to make (it) more definite: *she confirmed that she is about to resign as leader of the council* **3** to strengthen: *this cruise confirmed my first impressions of the boat's performance* **4** to formally make valid **5** *Christianity* to administer the rite of confirmation to [Latin *confirmare*]
confirmation *n* **1** the act of confirming **2** something that confirms **3** a rite in several Christian churches that admits a baptized person to full church membership
confirmed *adj* long-established in a habit or condition: *a confirmed bachelor*
confiscate *vb* **-cating, -cated** to seize (property) by authority [Latin *confiscare* to seize for the public treasury] **confiscation** *n*
conflagration *n* a large destructive fire [Latin *com-* (intensive) + *flagrare* to burn]
conflate *vb* **-flating, -flated** to combine or blend into a whole [Latin *conflare* to blow together] **conflation** *n*
conflict *n* **1** opposition between ideas or interests **2** a struggle or battle ▷ *vb* **3** to be incompatible [Latin *confligere* to combat] **conflicting** *adj*
confluence *n* **1** a place where rivers flow into one another **2** a gathering [Latin *confluere* to flow together] **confluent** *adj*
conform *vb* **1** to comply with accepted standards, rules, or customs **2** (usually foll. by *with*) to be like or in accordance with: *people tend to absorb ideas that conform with their existing beliefs, and reject those that do not* [Latin *confirmare* to strengthen]
conformation *n* **1** the general shape of an object **2** the arrangement of the parts of an object
conformist *adj* **1** A (of a person) behaving or thinking like most other people rather than in an original or unconventional way: *a shy and conformist type of boy* B (of an organization or society) expecting everyone to behave in the same way: *the school was a dull, conformist place for staff and students alike* ▷ *n* **2** a person who behaves or thinks like most other people rather than in an original or unconventional way
conformity *n, pl* **-ities 1** compliance in actions or behaviour with certain accepted rules, customs, or standards **2** likeness
confound *vb* **1** to astound or bewilder **2** to fail to distinguish between **3 confound it!** damn it! [Latin *confundere* to mingle, pour together]
confounded *adj* **1** *informal* damned: *what a confounded nuisance!* **2** bewildered; confused: *her silent, utterly confounded daughter*
confrere (kon-frair) *n* a colleague: *their Gallic confreres* [Medieval Latin *confrater*]
confront *vb* **1** (of a problem or task) to present itself to **2** to meet face to face in hostility or defiance **3** to present (someone) with something, esp. in order to accuse or criticize: *she finally confronted him with her suspicions* [Latin *com-* together + *frons* forehead]
confrontation *n* a serious argument or fight
Confucianism *n* the teachings of Confucius (551–479 BC), the ancient Chinese philosopher, which emphasize moral order **Confucian** *n, adj* **Confucianist** *n*
confuse *vb* **-fusing, -fused 1** to fail to distinguish between (one thing and another) **2** to perplex or disconcert **3** to make unclear: *he confused his talk with irrelevant detail* **4** to throw into disorder [Latin *confundere* to pour together] **confusing** *adj* **confusingly** *adv*
confused *adj* **1** lacking a clear understanding of something **2** disordered and difficult to understand or make sense of: *a confused dream*
confusion *n* **1** mistaking one person or thing for another **2** bewilderment **3** lack of clarity **4** disorder
confute *vb* **-futing, -futed** to prove to be wrong [Latin *confutare* to check, silence] **confutation** *n*
conga *n* **1** a Latin American dance performed by a number of people in single file **2** a large single-headed drum played with the hands ▷ *vb* **-gaing, -gaed 3** to dance the conga [from American Spanish]
congeal *vb* to change from a liquid to a semisolid state [Latin *com-* together + *gelare* to freeze]
congenial *adj* **1** friendly, pleasant, or agreeable: *she found the Botanic Gardens a most congenial place for strolling* **2** having a similar disposition or tastes [*con-* (same) + *genial*] **congeniality** *n*
congenital *adj* (of an abnormal condition) existing at birth but not inherited: *congenital heart disease* [Latin *con-* together + *genitus* born] **congenitally** *adv*
conger *n* a large sea eel [Greek *gongros*]
congested *adj* **1** crowded to excess **2** clogged or blocked [Latin *congerere* to pile up] **congestion** *n*
conglomerate *n* **1** a large corporation made up of many different companies **2** a thing composed of several different elements **3** a type of rock consisting of rounded pebbles or fragments held together by silica or clay ▷ *vb* **-ating, -ated 4** to form into a mass ▷ *adj* **5** made up of several different elements **6** (of rock) consisting of rounded pebbles or fragments held together by silica or clay [Latin *conglomerare* to roll up] **conglomeration** *n*

congratulate *vb* **-lating, -lated 1** to express one's pleasure to (a person) at his or her success or good fortune **2 congratulate oneself** to consider oneself clever or fortunate (as a result of): *she congratulated herself on her own business acumen* [Latin *congratulari*] **congratulatory** *adj*

congratulations *pl n, interj* expressions of pleasure or joy on another's success or good fortune

congregate *vb* **-gating, -gated** to collect together in or as a crowd [Latin *congregare* to collect into a flock]

congregation *n* a group of worshippers **congregational** *adj*

Congregationalism *n* a system of Protestant church government in which each church is self-governing **Congregationalist** *adj, n*

congress *n* a formal meeting of representatives for discussion [Latin *com-* together + *gradi* to walk] **congressional** *adj*

Congress *n* the federal legislature of the US, consisting of the House of Representatives and the Senate **Congressional** *adj* **Congressman** *or fem* **Congresswoman** *n*

congruent *adj* **1** agreeing or corresponding **2** *geom* identical in shape and size: *congruent triangles* [Latin *congruere* to agree] **congruence** *n*

congruous *adj formal* **1** appropriate or in keeping: *an elegant, though not altogether congruous, wing was added to the house in 1735* **2** corresponding or agreeing: *this finding is congruous with Adam's 1982 study* [Latin *congruere* to agree] **congruity** *n*

conical *adj* in the shape of a cone

conic section *n* a figure, either a circle, ellipse, parabola, or hyperbola, formed by the intersection of a plane and a cone

conifer *n* a tree or shrub bearing cones and evergreen leaves, such as the fir or larch [Latin *conus* cone + *ferre* to bear] **coniferous** *adj*

conjecture *n* **1** the formation of conclusions from incomplete evidence **2** a guess ▷ *vb* **-turing, -tured 3** to form (an opinion or conclusion) from incomplete evidence [Latin *conjicere* to throw together] **conjectural** *adj*

conjoin *vb* to join or become joined

conjoined twins *pl n* twins born joined together at some part of the body

conjugal (kon-jew-gal) *adj* of marriage: *conjugal rights* [Latin *conjunx* wife or husband]

conjugate *vb* (kon-jew-gate) **-gating, -gated 1** *grammar* to give the inflections of (a verb) **2** (of a verb) to undergo inflection according to a specific set of rules **3** *formal* to combine: *a country in which conjugating Marxism with Christianity has actually been tried* ▷ *n* (kon-jew-git) **4** *formal* something formed by conjugation: *haemoglobin is a conjugate of a protein with an iron-containing pigment* [Latin *com-* together + *jugare* to connect]

conjugation *n* **1** *grammar* **A** inflection of a verb for person, number, tense, voice, and mood **B** the complete set of the inflections of a given verb **2** a joining

conjunction *n* **1** joining together **2** simultaneous occurrence of events **3** a word or group of words that connects words, phrases, or clauses; for example *and*, *if*, and *but* **4** *astron* the apparent nearness of two heavenly bodies to each other **conjunctional** *adj*

conjunctiva *n, pl* **-vas** *or* **-vae** the delicate mucous membrane that covers the eyeball and inner eyelid [New Latin *membrana conjunctiva* the conjunctive membrane] **conjunctival** *adj*

conjunctive *adj* **1** joining or joined **2** used as a conjunction: *a conjunctive adverb* ▷ *n* **3** a word or words used as a conjunction [Latin *conjungere* to join]

conjunctivitis *n* inflammation of the conjunctiva

conjuncture *n* a combination of events, esp. one that leads to a crisis

conjure *vb* **-juring, -jured 1** to make (something) appear, as if by magic **2** to perform tricks that appear to be magic **3** to summon (a spirit or demon) by magic **4** *formal or literary* to appeal earnestly to: *I conjure you by all which you profess: answer me!* [Latin *conjurare* to swear together] **conjuring** *n*

conjure up *vb* **1** to create an image in the mind: *the name Versailles conjures up a past of sumptuous grandeur* **2** to produce as if from nowhere: *he conjured up a fabulous opening goal*

conjuror *or* **conjurer** *n* a person who performs magic tricks for people's entertainment

conk *Brit, Austral & NZ slang* ▷ *n* **1** the head or nose ▷ *vb* **2** to strike (someone) on the head or nose [probably changed from *conch*]

conker *n* same as **horse chestnut** (sense 2)

conkers *n Brit* a game in which a player swings a horse chestnut (conker), threaded onto a string, against that of another player to try to break it [dialect *conker* snail shell, originally used in the game]

conk out *vb informal* **1** (of a machine or car) to break down **2** to become tired or fall asleep suddenly [origin unknown]

con man *n informal* a person who swindles someone by means of a confidence trick

connect *vb* **1** to link or be linked: *high blood pressure is closely connected to heart disease* **2** to put into telephone communication with **3** (of two public vehicles) to have the arrival of one timed to occur just before the departure of the other, for the convenience of passengers **4** to associate in the mind: *he had always connected sex with violence and attacks rather than loving and concern* **5** to relate by birth or marriage: *she was distantly connected with the Wedgwood family* [Latin *connectere* to bind together] **connective** *adj*

connection *or* **connexion** *n* **1** a relationship or association **2** a link or bond **3** a link between two components in an electric circuit **4 A** an opportunity to transfer from one public vehicle to another **B** the vehicle scheduled to provide such an opportunity **5** an influential acquaintance **6** a relative **7** logical sequence in thought or expression **8** a telephone link **9** *slang* a supplier of illegal drugs, such as heroin **10 in connection with** with reference to: *a number of people have been arrested in connection with the explosion*

connective tissue *n* body tissue that supports organs, fills the spaces between them, and forms tendons and ligaments

conning tower *n* the raised observation tower containing the periscope on a submarine [*con* to steer a ship]

connivance *n* encouragement or permission of wrongdoing

connive *vb* **-niving, -nived 1 connive at** to allow or encourage (wrongdoing) by ignoring it **2** to conspire [Latin *connivere* to blink, hence, leave uncensured]

C

connoisseur (kon-noss-sir) *n* a person with special knowledge of the arts, food, or drink [French]

connotation *n* an additional meaning or association implied by a word: *the German term carries a connotation of elitism* [Latin *con-* together + *notare* to mark, note] **connote** *vb*

connubial (kon-new-bee-al) *adj formal* of marriage: *connubial bliss* [Latin *conubium* marriage]

conquer *vb* **1** to defeat (an opponent or opponents) **2** to overcome (a difficulty or feeling) **3** to gain possession of (a place) by force or war [Latin *conquirere* to search for] **conquering** *adj* **conqueror** *n*

conquest *n* **1** the act of conquering **2** a person or thing that has been conquered **3** a person whose affections have been won

conquistador *n, pl* **-dors** *or* **-dores** one of the Spanish conquerors of Mexico and Peru in the 16th century [Spanish: conqueror]

Cons. Conservative

consanguineous *adj formal* related by birth [Latin *con-* with + *sanguis* blood] **consanguinity** *n*

conscience *n* **1** the sense of right and wrong that governs a person's thoughts and actions **2** a feeling of guilt: *he showed no hint of conscience over the suffering he had inflicted* **3 in (all) conscience** in fairness **4 on one's conscience** causing feelings of guilt [Latin *conscire* to know]

conscience-stricken *adj* feeling guilty because of having done something wrong

conscientious *adj* **1** painstaking or thorough in one's work **2** governed by conscience **conscientiously** *adv* **conscientiousness** *n*

conscientious objector *n* a person who refuses to serve in the armed forces on moral or religious grounds

conscious *adj* **1** alert and awake **2** aware of one's surroundings and of oneself **3** aware (of something): *he was conscious of a need to urinate* **4** deliberate or intentional: *a conscious attempt* **5** of the part of the mind that is aware of a person's self, surroundings, and thoughts, and that to a certain extent determines choices of action ▷ *n* **6** the conscious part of the mind [Latin *com-* with + *scire* to know] **consciously** *adv* **consciousness** *n*

conscript *n* **1** a person who is enrolled for compulsory military service ▷ *vb* **2** to enrol (someone) for compulsory military service [Latin *conscriptus* enrolled]

conscription *n* compulsory military service

consecrate *vb* **-crating, -crated 1** to make or declare sacred or for religious use **2** to devote or dedicate (something) to a specific purpose **3** *Christianity* to sanctify (bread and wine) to be received as the body and blood of Christ [Latin *consecrare*] **consecration** *n*

consecutive *adj* following in order without interruption: *three consecutive nights of rioting* [Latin *consequi* to pursue] **consecutively** *adv*

consensus *n* general or widespread agreement [Latin *consentire* to agree]

> **USAGE** Since *consensus* refers to a collective opinion, the words *of opinion* in the phrase *consensus of opinion* are redundant and should therefore be avoided.

consent *n* **1** agreement, permission, or approval **2 age of consent** the age at which sexual intercourse is permitted by law ▷ *vb* **3** to permit or agree (to) [Latin *consentire* to agree] **consenting** *adj*

consequence *n* **1** a logical result or effect **2** significance or importance: *we said little of consequence to each other; a woman of little consequence* **3 in consequence** as a result **4 take the consequences** to accept whatever results from one's actions

consequent *adj* **1** following as an effect **2** following as a logical conclusion [Latin *consequens* following closely]

> **USAGE** See at **consequential.**

consequential *adj* **1** important or significant **2** following as a result

> **USAGE** Although both *consequential* and *consequent* can refer to something that happens as the result of something else, *consequent* is more common in this sense in modern English: *the new measures were put into effect, and the consequent protest led to the dismissal of those responsible.*

consequently *adv* as a result; therefore

conservancy *n* environmental conservation

conservation *n* **1** protection and careful management of the environment and natural resources **2** protection from change, loss, or injury **3** *physics* the principle that the quantity of a specified aspect of a system, such as momentum or charge, remains constant **conservationist** *n*

conservative *adj* **1** favouring the preservation of established customs and values, and opposing change **2** moderate or cautious: *a conservative estimate* **3** conventional in style: *people in this area are conservative in their tastes* ▷ *n* **4** a conservative person **conservatism** *n*

Conservative *adj* **1** of or supporting the Conservative Party, the major right-wing political party in Britain, which believes in private enterprise and capitalism **2** of or supporting a similar right-wing party in other countries ▷ *n* **3** a supporter or member of the Conservative Party

conservatoire (kon-serv-a-twahr) *n* a school of music [French]

conservatory *n, pl* **-tories 1** a greenhouse attached to a house **2** a conservatoire

conserve *vb* **-serving, -served 1** to protect from harm, decay, or loss **2** to preserve (fruit or other food) with sugar ▷ *n* **3** fruit preserved by cooking in sugar [Latin *conservare* to keep safe]

consider *vb* **1** to be of the opinion that **2** to think carefully about (a problem or decision) **3** to bear in mind: *Corsica is well worth considering for those* *seeking a peaceful holiday in beautiful surroundings* **4** to have regard for or care about: *you must try to consider other people's feelings more* **5** to discuss (something) in order to make a decision **6** to look at: *he considered her and she forced herself to sit calmly under his gaze* [Latin *considerare* to inspect closely]

considerable *adj* **1** large enough to reckon with: *a considerable number of people* **2** a lot of: *he was in considerable pain* **considerably** *adv*

considerate *adj* thoughtful towards other people

consideration *n* **1** careful thought **2** a fact to be taken into account when making a decision **3** thoughtfulness for other people **4** payment for a service **5 take into consideration** to bear in mind **6 under consideration** being currently discussed

considered *adj* **1** presented or thought out with care: *a considered opinion* **2** thought of in a specified way: *highly considered*

considering *conj, prep* **1** taking (a specified fact) into account: *considering the mileage the car had done, it was lasting well* ▷ *adv* **2** *informal* taking into account the circumstances: *it's not bad considering*

consign *vb* **1** to give into the care or charge of **2** to put irrevocably: *those events have been consigned to history* **3** to put (in a specified place or situation): *only a few months ago such demands would have consigned the student leaders to prisons and labour camps* **4** to address or deliver (goods): *a cargo of oil drilling equipment consigned to Saudi Arabia* [Latin *consignare* to put one's seal to, sign] **consignee** *n* **consignor** *n*

consignment *n* **1** a shipment of goods **2** the act or an instance of consigning: *the goods are sent to Hong Kong for onward consignment to customers in the area*

consist *vb* **1 consist of** to be made up of: *a match consists of seven games* **2 consist in** to have as its main or only part: *their religion consists only in going to church* [Latin *consistere* to stand firm]

consistency *n, pl* **-encies 1** degree of thickness or smoothness **2** being consistent

consistent *adj* **1** holding to the same principles **2** in agreement **consistently** *adv*

consolation *n* **1** a person or thing that is a comfort in a time of sadness or distress **2** a consoling or being consoled

consolation prize *n* something given to console the loser of a game

console[1] *vb* **-soling, -soled** to comfort (someone) in sadness or distress [Latin *consolari*] **consolable** *adj*

console[2] *n* **1** a panel of controls for electronic equipment **2** a cabinet for a television or audio equipment **3** an ornamental bracket used to support a wall fixture **4** the desklike case of an organ, containing the pedals, stops, and keys [Old French *consolateur* one that provides support]

consolidate *vb* **-dating, -dated 1** to make or become stronger or more stable **2** to combine into a whole [Latin *consolidare* to make firm] **consolidation** *n* **consolidator** *n*

consommé (kon-som-may) *n* a thin clear meat soup [French]

consonance *n formal* agreement or harmony

consonant *n* **1 A** a speech sound made by partially or completely blocking the breath streams, for example *b* or *f* **B** a letter representing this ▷ *adj* **2 consonant with** in keeping or agreement with: *an individualistic style of religion, more consonant with liberal society* **3** harmonious: *this highly dissonant chord is followed by a more consonant one* [Latin *consonare* to sound at the same time]

consort *vb* **1 consort with** to keep company with ▷ *n* **2** a husband or wife of a reigning monarch **3** a small group of voices or instruments [Latin *consors* partner]

consortium *n, pl* **-tia** an association of business firms [Latin: partnership]

conspectus *n formal* a survey or summary [Latin: a viewing]

conspicuous *adj* **1** clearly visible **2** noteworthy or striking: *conspicuous bravery* [Latin *conspicuus*] **conspicuously** *adv*

conspiracy *n, pl* **-cies 1** a secret plan to carry out an illegal or harmful act **2** the act of making such plans

conspire *vb* **-spiring, -spired 1** to plan a crime together in secret **2** to act together as if by design: *the weather and the recession conspired to hit wine production and sales* [Latin *conspirare* to plot together] **conspirator** *n* **conspiratorial** *adj*

constable *n* a police officer of the lowest rank [Late Latin *comes stabuli* officer in charge of the stable]

constabulary *n, pl* **-laries** *chiefly Brit* the police force of an area

constant *adj* **1** continuous: *she has endured constant criticism, mockery, and humiliation* **2** unchanging: *the average speed of the winds remained constant over this period* **3** faithful ▷ *n* **4** *maths & physics* a quantity or number which remains invariable: *the velocity of light is a constant* **5** something that is unchanging [Latin *constare* to be steadfast] **constancy** *n* **constantly** *adv*

constellation *n* **1** a group of stars which form a pattern and are given a name **2** a group of people or things: *the constellation of favourable circumstances* [Latin *com-* together + *stella* star]

consternation *n* a feeling of anxiety or dismay

constipated *adj* unable to empty one's bowels [Latin *constipare* to press closely together]

constipation *n* a condition in which emptying one's bowels is difficult

constituency *n, pl* **-cies 1** the area represented by a Member of Parliament **2** the voters in such an area

constituent *n* **1** a person living in an MP's constituency **2** a component part ▷ *adj* **3** forming part of a whole: *the constituent parts of the universe* **4** having the power to make or change a constitution of a state: *a constituent assembly* [Latin *constituere* to constitute]

constitute *vb* **-tuting, -tuted 1** to form or make up: *the amazing range of crags that constitute the Eglwyseg Mountains* **2** to set up (an institution) formally [Latin *com-* (intensive) + *statuere* to place]

constitution *n* **1** the principles on which a state is governed **2 the Constitution** (in certain countries) the statute embodying such principles **3** a person's state of health **4** the make-up or structure of something: *changes in the very constitution of society*

constitutional *adj* **1** of a constitution **2** authorized by or in accordance with the Constitution of a nation: *constitutional monarchy* **3** inherent in the nature of a person or thing: *a constitutional sensitivity to cold* ▷ *n* **4** a regular walk taken for the good of one's health **constitutionally** *adv*

constitutive *adj* **1** forming a part of something **2** with the power to appoint or establish

C

constrain *vb* **1** to compel or force: *he felt constrained to apologize* **2** to limit, restrict, or inhibit: *the mobility of workers is constrained by the serious housing shortage* [Latin *constringere* to bind together]

constrained *adj* embarrassed or unnatural: *his constrained expression*

constraint *n* **1** something that limits a person's freedom of action **2** repression of natural feelings **3** a forced unnatural manner

constrict *vb* **1** to make smaller or narrower by squeezing **2** to limit or restrict [Latin *constringere* to tie up together] **constrictive** *adj*

constriction *n* **1** a feeling of tightness in some part of the body, such as the chest **2** a narrowing **3** something that constricts

constrictor *n* **1** a snake that coils around and squeezes its prey to kill it **2** a muscle that contracts an opening

construct *vb* **1** to build or put together **2** *geom* to draw (a figure) to specified requirements **3** to compose (an argument or sentence) ▷ *n* **4** a complex idea resulting from the combination of simpler ideas **5** something formulated or built systematically [Latin *construere* to build] **constructor** *n*

construction *n* **1** the act of constructing or manner in which a thing is constructed **2** something that has been constructed **3** the business or work of building houses or other structures **4** *formal* an interpretation: *the financial markets will put the worst possible construction on any piece of news which might affect them* **5** *grammar* the way in which words are arranged in a sentence, clause, or phrase **constructional** *adj*

constructive *adj* **1** useful and helpful: *constructive criticism* **2** *law* deduced by inference; not openly expressed **constructively** *adv*

construe *vb* **-struing, -strued 1** to interpret the meaning of (something): *her indifference was construed as rudeness* **2** to analyse the grammatical structure of (a sentence) **3** to combine (words) grammatically **4** *old-fashioned* to translate literally [Latin *construere* to build]

consul *n* **1** an official representing a state in a foreign country **2** one of the two chief magistrates in ancient Rome [Latin] **consular** *adj* **consulship** *n*

consulate *n* **1** the workplace and official home of a consul **2** the position or period of office of a consul

consult *vb* **1** to ask advice from or discuss matters with (someone): *he never consults his wife about what he's about to do* **2** to refer to for information: *she consulted the map again* [Latin *consultare*]

consultant *n* **1** a specialist doctor with a senior position in a hospital **2** a specialist who gives expert professional advice **consultancy** *n*

consultation *n* **1** the act of consulting **2** a meeting for discussion or the seeking of advice **consultative** *adj*

consulting *adj* acting as an adviser on professional matters: *consulting engineers*

consulting room *n* a room in which a doctor sees patients

consume *vb* **-suming, -sumed 1** to eat or drink **2** to use up **3** to destroy: *the ship blew up and was consumed by flames* **4** to obsess: *he was consumed with jealousy over the ending of their affair* [Latin *com-* (intensive) + *sumere* to take up] **consumable** *adj* **consuming** *adj*

consumer *n* a person who buys goods or uses services

consumer durables *pl n* manufactured products that have a relatively long life, such as cars or televisions

consumer goods *pl n* goods bought for personal needs rather than those required for the production of other goods or services

consumerism *n* **1** the belief that a high level of consumer spending is desirable and beneficial to the economy: *the obsessive consumerism of the 80s* **2** protection of the rights of consumers

consummate *vb* (kon-sum-mate) **-mating, -mated 1** to make (a marriage) legal by sexual intercourse **2** to complete or fulfil ▷ *adj* (kon-**sum**-mit) **3** supremely skilled: *a consummate craftsman* **4** complete or extreme: *consummate skill; consummate ignorance* [Latin *consummare* to complete] **consummation** *n*

consumption *n* **1** the quantity of something consumed or used: *for such a powerful car, fuel consumption is modest* **2** the act of eating or drinking something: *this meat is unfit for human consumption* **3** *econ* purchase of goods and services for personal use **4** *old-fashioned* tuberculosis of the lungs

consumptive *adj* **1** wasteful or destructive **2** of tuberculosis of the lungs ▷ *n* **3** a person with tuberculosis of the lungs

cont. continued

contact *n* **1** the state or act of communication: *the airport lost contact with the plane shortly before the crash* **2** the state or act of touching: *rugby is a game of hard physical contact* **3** an acquaintance who might be useful in business **4** a connection between two electrical conductors in a circuit **5** a person who has been exposed to a contagious disease ▷ *vb* **6** to come or be in communication or touch with [Latin *contingere* to touch on all sides] **contactless** *adj*

contact lens *n* a small lens placed on the eyeball to correct defective vision

contagion *n* **1** the passing on of disease by contact **2** a contagious disease **3** a corrupting influence that tends to spread [Latin *contagio* infection]

contagious *adj* **1** (of a disease) capable of being passed on by contact **2** (of a person) capable of passing on a transmissible disease **3** spreading from person to person: *contagious enthusiasm*

contain *vb* **1** to hold or be capable of holding: *the bag contained a selection of men's clothing* **2** to have as one of its ingredients or constituents: *tea and* *coffee both contain appreciable amounts of caffeine* **3** to consist of: *the book contains 13 very different and largely separate chapters* **4** to check or restrain (feelings or behaviour) **5** to prevent from spreading or going beyond fixed limits: *the blockade was too weak to contain the French fleet* [Latin *continere*] **containable** *adj*

container *n* **1** an object used to hold or store things in **2** a large standard-sized box for transporting cargo by lorry or ship

containerize *or* **-ise** *vb* **-izing, -ized** *or* **-ising, -ised** **1** to pack (cargo) in large standard-sized containers **2** to fit (a port, ship, or lorry) to carry goods in standard-sized containers **containerization** *or* **-isation** *n*

containment *n* the prevention of the spread of something harmful

contaminate *vb* **-nating, -nated** **1** to make impure; pollute **2** to make radioactive [Latin *contaminare* to defile] **contaminant** *n* **contamination** *n*

contemplate *vb* **-plating, -plated** **1** to think deeply about **2** to consider as a possibility **3** to look at thoughtfully **4** to meditate [Latin *contemplare*] **contemplation** *n*

contemplative *adj* **1** of or given to contemplation ▷ *n* **2** a person dedicated to religious contemplation

contemporaneous *adj* happening at the same time **contemporaneity** *n*

contemporary *adj* **1** existing or occurring at the present time **2** living or occurring in the same period **3** modern in style or fashion **4** of approximately the same age ▷ *n, pl* **-raries** **5** a person or thing living at the same time or of approximately the same age as another [Latin *com-* together + *temporarius* relating to time]

USAGE Since *contemporary* can mean either of the same period or of the present period, it is best to avoid this word where ambiguity might arise, as in *a production of* Othello *in contemporary dress. Modern dress* or *Elizabethan dress* can be used in such contexts to avoid ambiguity.

contempt *n* **1** scorn **2** **hold in contempt** to scorn or despise **3** deliberate disrespect for the authority of a court of law: *contempt of court* [Latin *contemnere* to scorn]

contemptible *adj* deserving to be despised or hated: *a contemptible lack of courage*

contemptuous *adj* showing or feeling strong dislike or disrespect **contemptuously** *adv*

contend *vb* **1** **contend with** to deal with **2** to assert **3** to compete or fight **4** to argue earnestly [Latin *contendere* to strive] **contender** *n*

content[1] *n* **1** **contents** everything inside a container **2** **contents** a list of chapters at the front of a book **3** the meaning or substance of a piece of writing, often as distinguished from its style or form **4** the information presented on a website **5** the amount of a substance contained in a mixture: *the water vapour content of the atmosphere* [Latin *contentus* contained]

content[2] *adj* **1** satisfied with things as they are **2** willing to accept a situation or a proposed course of action ▷ *vb* **3** to satisfy (oneself or another person) ▷ *n* **4** peace of mind [Latin *contentus* contented, having restrained desires] **contentment** *n*

contented *adj* satisfied with one's situation or life **contentedly** *adv* **contentedness** *n*

contention *n* **1** disagreement or dispute **2** a point asserted in argument **3** **bone of contention** a point of dispute [Latin *contentio*]

contentious *adj* **1** causing disagreement **2** tending to quarrel **contentiousness** *n*

contest *n* **1** a game or match in which people or teams compete **2** a struggle for power or control ▷ *vb* **3** to dispute: *he has said he will not contest the verdict* **4** to take part in (a contest or struggle for power): *all parties which meet the legal requirements will be allowed to contest the election* [Latin *contestari* to introduce a lawsuit] **contestable** *adj*

contestant *n* a person who takes part in a contest

context *n* **1** the circumstances relevant to an event or fact **2** the words before and after a word or passage in a piece of writing that contribute to its meaning: *taken out of context, lines like these sound ridiculous, but, as part of a scrupulously written play, they are just right* [Latin *com-* together + *texere* to weave] **contextual** *adj*

contiguous *adj formal* very near or touching [Latin *contiguus*]

continent[1] *n* one of the earth's large landmasses (Asia, Australia, Africa, Europe, North and South America, and Antarctica) [Latin *terra continens* continuous land] **continental** *adj*

continent[2] *adj* **1** able to control one's bladder and bowels **2** sexually restrained [Latin *continere* to contain, retain] **continence** *n*

Continent *n* **the Continent** the mainland of Europe as distinct from the British Isles **Continental** *adj*

continental breakfast *n* a light breakfast of coffee and rolls

continental climate *n* a climate with hot summers, cold winters, and little rainfall, typical of the interior of a continent

continental drift *n geol* the theory that the earth's continents drift gradually over the surface of the planet, due to currents in its mantle

continental quilt *n Brit* a large quilt used as a bed cover in place of the top sheet and blankets

continental shelf *n* the gently sloping shallow sea bed surrounding a continent

contingency *n, pl* **-cies** **1** an unknown or unforeseen future event or condition **2** something dependent on a possible future event

contingent *n* **1** a group of people with a common interest, that represents a larger group: *a contingent of European scientists* **2** a military group that is part of a larger force: *the force includes a contingent of the Foreign Legion* ▷ *adj* **3** (foll. by *on* or *upon*) dependent on (something uncertain) **4** happening by chance [Latin *contingere* to touch, befall]

continual *adj* **1** occurring without interruption **2** recurring frequently [Latin *continuus* uninterrupted] **continually** *adv*

USAGE See at **continuous**.

continuance *n* **1** the act of continuing **2** duration

continuation *n* **1** the act of continuing **2** a part or thing added, such as a sequel **3** a renewal of an interrupted action or process

continue *vb* **-tinuing, -tinued 1** to remain or cause to remain in a particular condition or place **2** to carry on (doing something): *we continued kissing; heavy fighting continued until Thursday afternoon* **3** to resume after an interruption: *we'll continue after lunch* **4** to go on to a further place: *the road continues on up the hill* [Latin *continuare* to join together]

C

continuity *n, pl* **-ties 1** a smooth development or sequence **2** the arrangement of scenes in a film so that they follow each other logically and without breaks

continuo *n, pl* **-tinuos** *music* a continuous bass accompaniment played usually on a keyboard instrument [Italian]

continuous *adj* **1** without end: *a continuous process* **2** not having any breaks or gaps in it: *a continuous line of boats; continuous rain* [Latin *continuus*] **continuously** *adv*

> **USAGE** Both *continual* and *continuous* can be used to say that something continues without interruption, but only *continual* can correctly be used to say that something keeps happening repeatedly.

continuum *n, pl* **-tinua** *or* **-tinuums** a continuous series or whole, no part of which is noticeably different from the parts immediately next to it, although the ends or extremes of it are very different from each other: *the continuum from minor misbehaviour to major crime* [Latin]

contort *vb* to twist or bend out of shape [Latin *contortus* intricate] **contortion** *n*

contortionist *n* a performer who contorts his or her body to entertain others

contour *n* **1** an outline **2** same as **contour line** ▷ *vb* **3** to shape so as to form or follow the contour of something [Italian *contornare* to sketch]

contour line *n* a line on a map or chart joining points of equal height or depth

contra- *prefix* **1** against or contrasting: *contraceptive* **2** (in music) lower in pitch: *contrabass* [Latin *contra* against]

contraband *n* **1** smuggled goods ▷ *adj* **2** (of goods) smuggled [Spanish *contrabanda*]

contraception *n* the deliberate use of artificial or natural means to prevent pregnancy [CONTRA- + CONCEPTION]

contraceptive *n* **1** a device, such as a condom, that is used to prevent pregnancy ▷ *adj* **2** providing or relating to contraception: *the contraceptive pill*

contract *n* **1** a formal agreement between two or more parties **2** a document setting out a formal agreement ▷ *vb* **3** to make a formal agreement with (a person or company) to do or deliver (something) **4** to enter into (a relationship or marriage) formally: *to contract a marriage without the approval of one's guardian* **5** to make or become smaller, narrower, or shorter **6** to become affected by (an illness) **7** to draw (muscles) together or (of muscles) to be drawn together **8** to shorten (a word or phrase) by omitting letters or syllables, usually indicated in writing by an apostrophe [Latin *contractus* agreement] **contractible** *adj*

contract bridge *n* the most common variety of bridge, in which only tricks bid and won count towards the game

contraction *n* **1** a contracting or being contracted **2** a shortening of a word or group of words, often marked by an apostrophe, for example *I've come* for *I have come* **3 contractions** *med* temporary shortening and tensing of the uterus during pregnancy and labour

contractor *n* a person or firm that supplies materials or labour for other companies

contract out *vb Brit* to agree not to take part in a scheme

contractual *adj* of or in the nature of a contract

contradict *vb* **1** to declare the opposite of (a statement) to be true **2** (of a fact or statement) to suggest that (another fact or statement) is wrong [Latin *contra-* against + *dicere* to speak] **contradiction** *n*

contradictory *adj* (of facts or statements) inconsistent

contradistinction *n* a distinction made by contrasting different qualities **contradistinctive** *adj*

contraflow *n* a flow of road traffic going alongside but in an opposite direction to the usual flow

contralto *n, pl* **-tos** *or* **-ti 1** the lowest female voice **2** a singer with such a voice [Italian]

contraption *n informal* a strange-looking device or gadget [origin unknown]

contrapuntal *adj music* of or in counterpoint [Italian *contrappunto* counterpoint]

contrariwise *adv* **1** from a contrasting point of view **2** in the opposite way

contrary *n, pl* **-ries 1 on** *or* **to the contrary** in opposition to what has just been said or implied ▷ *adj* **2** opposed; completely different: *a contrary view, based on equally good information* **3** perverse; obstinate **4** (of the wind) unfavourable ▷ *adv* **contrary to 5** in opposition or contrast to: *contrary to popular belief* **6** in conflict with: *contrary to nature* [Latin *contrarius* opposite] **contrariness** *n*

contrast *n* **1** a difference which is clearly seen when two things are compared **2** a person or thing showing differences when compared with another **3** the degree of difference between the colours in a photograph or television picture ▷ *vb* **4** to compare or be compared in order to show the differences between (things): *he contrasts that society with contemporary America* **5 contrast with** to be very different from: *her speed of reaction contrasted with her husband's vagueness* [Latin *contra-* against + *stare* to stand] **contrasting** *adj*

contravene *vb* **-vening, -vened** *formal* to break (a rule or law) [Latin *contra-* against + *venire* to come] **contravention** *n*

contretemps (kon-tra-tahn) *n, pl* **-temps** an embarrassing minor disagreement [French]

contribute *vb* **-buting, -buted** (often foll. by *to*) **1** to give (support or money) for a common purpose or fund **2** to supply (ideas or opinions)

3 contribute to to be partly responsible for: *his own unconvincing play contributed to his defeat* **4** to write (an article) for a publication [Latin *contribuere* to collect] **contribution** *n* **contributory** *adj* **contributor** *n*

contrite *adj* full of guilt or regret [Latin *contritus* worn out] **contritely** *adv* **contrition** *n*

contrivance *n* **1** an ingenious device **2** an elaborate or deceitful plan **3** the act or power of contriving

contrive *vb* **-triving, -trived 1** to make happen: *he had already contrived the murder of King Alexander* **2** to devise or construct ingeniously: *he contrived a plausible reason to fly back to London; he contrived a hook from a bent nail* [Old French *controver*]

control *n* **1** power to direct something: *the province is mostly under guerrilla control* **2** a curb or check: *import controls* **3 controls** instruments used to operate a machine **4** a standard of comparison used in an experiment **5** an experiment used to verify another by having all aspects identical except for the one that is being tested ▷ *vb* **-trolling, -trolled 6** to have power over: *the gland which controls the body's metabolic rate* **7** to limit or restrain: *he could not control his jealousy* **8** to regulate or operate (a machine) **9** to restrict the authorized supply of (certain drugs) [Old French *conteroller* to regulate] **controllable** *adj*

controller *n* **1** a person who is in charge **2** a person in charge of the financial aspects of a business

control tower *n* a tall building at an airport from which air traffic is controlled

controversy *n, pl* **-sies** argument or debate concerning a matter about which there is strong disagreement [Latin *contra-* against + *vertere* to turn] **controversial** *adj*

contumacy (kon-tume-mass-ee) *n, pl* **-cies** *literary* obstinate disobedience [Latin *contumax* obstinate] **contumacious** (kon-tume-**may**-shuss) *adj*

contumely (kon-tume-mill-ee) *n, pl* **-lies** *literary* **1** scornful or insulting treatment **2** a humiliating insult [Latin *contumelia*]

contusion *n formal* a bruise [Latin *contusus* bruised] **contuse** *vb*

conundrum *n* **1** a puzzling question or problem **2** a riddle whose answer contains a pun [origin unknown]

conurbation *n* a large heavily populated urban area formed by the growth and merging of towns [Latin *con-* together + *urbs* city]

convalesce *vb* **-lescing, -lesced** to recover health after an illness or operation [Latin *com-* (intensive) + *valescere* to grow strong]

convalescence *n* **1** gradual return to health after illness or an operation **2** the period during which such recovery occurs **convalescent** *n, adj*

convection *n* the transmission of heat caused by movement of molecules from cool regions to warmer regions of lower density [Latin *convehere* to bring together]

convector *n* a heating device which gives out hot air

convene *vb* **-vening, -vened** to gather or summon for a formal meeting [Latin *convenire* to assemble]

convener *or* **convenor** *n* a person who calls or chairs a meeting: *the shop stewards' convener at the factory* **convenership** *or* **convenorship** *n*

convenience *n* **1** the quality of being suitable or convenient **2 at your convenience** at a time suitable to you **3** an object that is useful: *a house with every modern convenience* **4** *euphemistic, chiefly Brit* a public toilet

convenience food *n* food that needs little preparation and can be used at any time

convenient *adj* **1** suitable or opportune **2** easy to use **3** nearby [Latin *convenire* to be in accord with]

convent *n* **1** a building where nuns live **2** a school in which the teachers are nuns **3** a community of nuns [Latin *conventus* meeting]

conventicle *n history* a secret or unauthorized religious meeting [Latin *conventiculum*]

convention *n* **1** the established view of what is thought to be proper behaviour **2** an accepted rule or method: *a convention used by printers* **3** a formal agreement or contract between people and nations **4** a large formal assembly of a group with common interests [Latin *conventio* an assembling]

conventional *adj* **1** following the accepted customs and lacking originality **2** established by accepted usage or general agreement **3** (of weapons or warfare) not nuclear **conventionally** *adv*

conventionality *n, pl* **-ties 1** the quality of being conventional **2** something conventional

conventionalize *or* **-ise** *vb* **-izing, -ized** *or* **-ising, -ised** to make conventional

converge *vb* **-verging, -verged 1** to move towards or meet at the same point **2** (of opinions or effects) to move towards a shared conclusion or result [Latin *com-* together + *vergere* to incline] **convergence** *n* **convergent** *adj*

conversant *adj* **conversant with** having knowledge or experience of [Latin *conversari* to keep company with]

conversation *n* informal talk between two or more people

conversational *adj* **1** of or used in conversation: *conversational French* **2** resembling informal spoken language: *the author's easy, conversational style*

conversationalist *n* a person with a specified ability at conversation: *a brilliant conversationalist*

conversation piece *n* something, such as an unusual object, that provokes conversation

converse[1] *vb* **-versing, -versed** to have a conversation [Latin *conversari* to keep company with]

converse[2] *adj* **1** reversed or opposite ▷ *n* **2** a statement or idea that is the opposite of another [Latin *conversus* turned around] **conversely** *adv*

conversion *n* **1** a change or adaptation **2** *maths* a calculation in which a weight, volume, or distance is worked out in a different system of measurement: *the conversion from Fahrenheit to Celsius* **3** a change to another belief or religion **4** *rugby* a score made after a try by kicking the ball over the crossbar from a place kick [Latin *conversio* a turning around]

convert *vb* **1** to change or adapt **2** to cause (someone) to change in opinion or belief **3** to change (a measurement) from one system of units to another **4** to change (money) into a different currency **5** *rugby* to make a conversion after (a try) ▷ *n* **6** a person who has been converted to another belief or religion [Latin *convertere* to turn around, alter] **converter** *or* **convertor** *n*

convertible *adj* **1** capable of being converted **2** *finance* (of a currency) freely exchangeable into other currencies ▷ *n* **3** a car with a folding or removable roof

C

convex *adj* curving outwards like the outside surface of a ball [Latin *convexus* vaulted, rounded] **convexity** *n*

convey *vb* **1** to communicate (information) **2** to carry or transport from one place to another **3** (of a channel or path) to transfer or transmit **4** *law* to transfer (the title to property) [Old French *conveier*] **conveyable** *adj* **conveyor** *n*

conveyance *n* **1** *old-fashioned* a vehicle **2** *law* **A** a transfer of the legal title to property **B** the document effecting such a transfer **3** the act of conveying: *the conveyance of cycles on peak hour trains* **conveyancer** *n*

conveyancing *n* the branch of law dealing with the transfer of ownership of property

conveyor belt *n* an endless moving belt driven by rollers and used to transport objects, esp. in a factory

convict *vb* **1** to declare (someone) guilty of an offence ▷ *n* **2** a person serving a prison sentence [Latin *convictus* convicted]

conviction *n* **1** a firmly held belief or opinion **2** an instance of being found guilty of a crime: *he had several convictions for petty theft* **3** a convincing or being convinced **4 carry conviction** to be convincing

convince *vb* **-vincing, -vinced** to persuade by argument or evidence [Latin *convincere* to demonstrate incontrovertibly] **convinced** *adj* **convincible** *adj* **convincing** *adj*

convivial *adj* sociable or lively: *a convivial atmosphere; convivial company* [Late Latin *convivialis*] **conviviality** *n*

convocation *n formal* a large formal meeting

convoke *vb* **-voking, -voked** *formal* to call together [Latin *convocare*]

convoluted *adj* **1** coiled or twisted **2** (of an argument or sentence) complex and difficult to understand

convolution *n* **1** a coil or twist **2** an intricate or confused matter or condition **3** a convex fold in the surface of the brain

convolvulus *n, pl* **-luses** *or* **-li** a twining plant with funnel-shaped flowers and triangular leaves [Latin: bindweed]

convoy *n* a group of vehicles or ships travelling together [Old French *convoier* to convey]

convulse *vb* **-vulsing, -vulsed 1** to shake or agitate violently **2** (of muscles) to undergo violent spasms **3** *informal* to be overcome (with laughter or rage) **4** to disrupt the normal running of: *student riots have convulsed India* [Latin *con-* together + *vellere* to pluck, pull] **convulsive** *adj*

convulsion *n* **1** a violent muscular spasm **2** a violent upheaval **3 convulsions** *informal* uncontrollable laughter: *I was in convulsions*

cony *or* **coney** *n, pl* **-nies** *or* **-neys** *Brit* **1** a rabbit **2** rabbit fur [Latin *cuniculus* rabbit]

coo *vb* **cooing, cooed 1** (of a dove or pigeon) to make a soft murmuring sound **2 bill and coo** to murmur softly or lovingly ▷ *n* **3** a cooing sound ▷ *interj* **4** *Brit slang* an exclamation of surprise or amazement [imitative] **cooing** *adj, n*

cooee *interj* **1** *Brit, Austral & NZ* a call used to attract attention **2** *Austral & NZ* **within cooee** within calling distance: *the school was within cooee of our house* [Aboriginal]

cook *vb* **1** to prepare (food) by heating or (of food) to be prepared in this way **2** *slang* to alter or falsify (figures or accounts): *she had cooked the books* ▷ *n* **3** a person who prepares food for eating ▷ See also **cook up** [Latin *coquere*]

cook-chill *n* a method of food preparation used by caterers, in which cooked dishes are chilled rapidly and reheated as required

cooker *n* **1** *chiefly Brit* an apparatus for cooking heated by gas or electricity **2** *Brit* an apple suitable for cooking but not for eating raw

cookery *n* the art or practice of cooking. Related adjective: **culinary**

cookery book *or* **cookbook** *n* a book containing recipes for cooking

cookie *n, pl* **cookies 1** *US & Canad* a biscuit **2 that's the way the cookie crumbles** *informal* that is how things inevitably are **3** *informal* a person: *a real tough cookie* **4** *computers* a piece of data downloaded from a website to a user's computer, allowing the user to be identified on future visits to the website [Dutch *koekje* little cake]

cook up *vb* to invent (a story or scheme)

cool *adj* **1** moderately cold: *it should be served cool, even chilled* **2** comfortably free of heat: *it was one of the few cool days that summer* **3** calm and unemotional: *a cool head* **4** indifferent or unfriendly: *the idea met with a cool response* **5** calmly impudent **6** *informal* (of a large sum of money) without exaggeration: *a cool million* **7** *informal* sophisticated or elegant **8** (of a colour) having violet, blue, or green predominating **9** *informal* excellent; marvellous ▷ *vb* **10** to make or become cooler **11** to calm down ▷ *n* **12** coolness: *in the cool of the evening* **13** *slang* calmness; composure: *he lost his cool and wantonly kicked the ball away* [Old English *cōl*] **coolly** *adv* **coolness** *n*

coolant *n* a fluid used to cool machinery while it is working

cool drink *n S African* a soft drink

cooler *n* a container for making or keeping things cool

coolibah *n* an Australian eucalypt that grows beside rivers [Aboriginal]

coolie *n old-fashioned, offensive* an unskilled E Asian labourer [Hindi *kulī*]

cooling tower *n* a tall hollow structure in a factory or power station, inside which hot water cools as it trickles down

coomb *or* **coombe** *n* a short valley or deep hollow [Old English *cumb*]

coon *n* **1** *informal* short for **raccoon** **2** *offensive slang* a Black person of African origin or a member of an Australian Aboriginal people **3** *S African offensive* a person of mixed race

coop[1] *n* **1** a cage or pen for poultry or small animals ▹ *vb* **2 coop up** to confine in a restricted place [Latin *cupa* basket, cask]
coop[2] *or* **co-op** (koh-op) *n Brit, Austral & NZ* a cooperative society or a shop run by a cooperative society
cooper *n* a person who makes or repairs barrels or casks [see COOP[1]]
cooperate *or* **co-operate** *vb* **1** to work or act together **2** to assist or be willing to assist [Latin *co-* with + *operari* to work] **cooperation** *or* **co-operation** *n*
cooperative *or* **co-operative** *adj* **1** willing to cooperate **2** (of an enterprise or farm) owned and managed collectively ▹ *n* **3** a cooperative organization
cooperative society *n* a commercial enterprise owned and run by customers or workers, in which the profits are shared among the members
coopt *or* **co-opt** (koh-opt) *vb* to add (someone) to a group by the agreement of the existing members [Latin *cooptare* to choose, elect]
coordinate *or* **co-ordinate** *vb* **-nating, -nated** **1** to bring together and cause to work together efficiently ▹ *n* **2** *maths* any of a set of numbers defining the location of a point with reference to a system of axes ▹ *adj* **3** of or involving coordination **4** of or involving the use of coordinates: *coordinate geometry* [Latin *co-* together + *ordinatio* arranging] **coordination** *or* **co-ordination** *n* **coordinator** *or* **co-ordinator** *n*
coordinates *or* **co-ordinates** *pl n* clothes designed to be worn together
coot *n* **1** a small black water bird **2** *Brit, Austral & NZ* a foolish person [probably Low German]
cop *slang* ▹ *n* **1** a police officer **2 not much cop** of little value or worth ▹ *vb* **copping, copped** **3** to take or seize **4 cop it** to get into trouble or be punished: *he copped it after he was spotted driving a car without a seat belt* ▹ See also **cop out** [perhaps from Old French *caper* to seize]
copal *n* a resin used in varnishes
copartner *n* a partner or associate **copartnership** *n*
cope[1] *vb* **coping, coped** **1** to deal successfully (with): *well-nourished people cope better with stress* **2** to tolerate or endure: *the ability to cope with his pain* [Old French *coper* to strike, cut]
cope[2] *n* a large ceremonial cloak worn by some Christian priests [Late Latin *cappa* hooded cloak]
cope[3] *vb* **coping, coped** to provide (a wall) with a coping [probably from French *couper* to cut]
copeck *n* same as **kopeck**
Copernican (kop-per-nik-an) *adj* of the theory that the earth and the planets rotate round the sun [after N. *Copernicus*, astronomer]
copernicium *n chem* a highly radioactive element that is produced synthetically. Symbol: **Cn** [after N. *Copernicus*, astronomer]
copestone *n* **1** Also called: **coping stone** a stone used to form a coping **2** the stone at the top of a building or wall
copier *n* a person or machine that copies
copilot *n* the second pilot of an aircraft
coping *n* a layer of rounded or sloping bricks on the top of a wall
coping saw *n* a handsaw with a U-shaped frame, used for cutting curves in wood
copious (kope-ee-uss) *adj* existing or produced in large quantities [Latin *copiosus*] **copiously** *adv*
cop out *slang* ▹ *vb* **1** to avoid taking responsibility or committing oneself ▹ *n* **cop-out** **2** a way or an instance of avoiding responsibility or commitment [probably from COP]
copper[1] *n* **1** a soft reddish metallic element, used in such alloys as brass and bronze. Symbol: **Cu** **2** *informal* any copper or bronze coin **3** *chiefly Brit* a large metal container used to boil water ▹ *adj* **4** reddish-brown [Latin *Cyprium aes* Cyprian metal, from Greek *Kupris* Cyprus]
copper[2] *n Brit slang* a police officer [from COP (verb)]
copper beech *n* a European beech with reddish leaves
copper-bottomed *adj* financially reliable [from the practice of coating the bottom of ships with copper to prevent the timbers rotting]
copperhead *n* a poisonous snake with a reddish-brown head
copperplate *n* **1** an elegant handwriting style **2** a polished copper plate engraved for printing **3** a print taken from such a plate
copper sulphate *n* a blue crystalline copper salt used in electroplating and in plant sprays
coppice *n* a small group of trees or bushes growing close together [Old French *copeiz*]
copra *n* the dried oil-yielding kernel of the coconut [Malayalam (a language of SW India) *koppara* coconut]
copse *n* same as **coppice**
Copt *n* **1** a member of the Coptic Church, a part of the Christian Church which was founded in Egypt **2** an Egyptian descended from the ancient Egyptians [Coptic *kyptios* Egyptian]
Coptic *n* **1** the language of the Copts, descended from Ancient Egyptian and surviving only in the Coptic Church ▹ *adj* **2** of the Copts or the Coptic Church
copula *n, pl* **-las** *or* **-lae** a verb, such as *be*, that is used to link the subject with the complement of a sentence, as in *he became king* [Latin: bond]
copulate *vb* **-lating, -lated** to have sexual intercourse [Latin *copulare* to join together] **copulation** *n*
copy *n, pl* **copies** **1** a thing made to look exactly like another **2** a single specimen of a book, magazine, or record of which there are many others exactly the same: *my copy of 'Death on the Nile'* **3** written material for printing **4** the text of an advertisement **5** *journalism informal* suitable material for an article: *disasters are always good copy* ▹ *vb* **copies, copying, copied** **6** to make a copy (of) **7** to act or try to be like another [Latin *copia* abundance]
copybook *n* **1** a book of specimens of handwriting for imitation **2 blot one's copybook** *informal* to spoil one's reputation by a mistake or indiscretion ▹ *adj* **3** done exactly according to the rules **4** trite or unoriginal
copycat *n informal* a person who imitates or copies someone

copyist *n* **1** a person who makes written copies **2** an imitator: *although the songs are derivative, it is unfair to dismiss the band as mere copyists*
copyright *n* **1** the exclusive legal right to reproduce and control an original literary, musical, or artistic work ▷ *vb* **2** to take out a copyright on ▷ *adj* **3** protected by copyright
copy typist *n* a typist who types from written or typed drafts rather than dictation
copywriter *n* a person employed to write advertising copy
coquette *n* a woman who flirts [French] **coquetry** *n* **coquettish** *adj*
coracle *n* a small round boat made of wicker covered with skins [Welsh *corwgl*]
coral *n* **1** the stony substance formed by the skeletons of marine animals called polyps, often forming an island or reef **2** any of the polyps whose skeletons form coral ▷ *adj* **3** orange-pink [Greek *korallion*]
cor anglais *n, pl* **cors anglais** *music* an alto woodwind instrument of the oboe family [French: English horn]
corbel *n archit* a stone or timber support sticking out of a wall [Old French: a little raven]
corbie *n Scot* a raven or crow [Latin *corvus*]
cord *n* **1** string or thin rope made of twisted strands **2** *anatomy* a structure in the body resembling a rope: *the vocal cords* **3** a ribbed fabric like corduroy **4** *US, Canad, Austral & NZ* an electrical flex **5** a unit for measuring cut wood, equal to 128 cubic feet ▷ *adj* **6** (of fabric) ribbed ▷ See also **cords** [Greek *khordē*]
cordate *adj* heart-shaped
corded *adj* **1** tied or fastened with cord **2** (of a fabric) ribbed: *white corded silk* **3** (of muscles) standing out like cords
cordial *adj* **1** warm and friendly: *a cordial atmosphere* **2** heartfelt or sincere: *I developed a cordial dislike for the place* ▷ *n* **3** a drink with a fruit base: *lime cordial* [Latin *cor* heart] **cordially** *adv*
cordiality *n* warmth of feeling
cordite *n* a smokeless explosive used in guns and bombs [from *cord*, because of its stringy appearance]
cordless *adj* (of an electrical appliance such as a kettle or telephone) powered by an internal battery or kept in a holder which is connected to the mains, so that there is no cable connecting the appliance itself to the electrical mains
cordon *n* **1** a chain of police, soldiers, or vehicles guarding an area **2** an ornamental braid or ribbon **3** *horticulture* a fruit tree trained to grow as a single stem bearing fruit ▷ *vb* **4** **cordon off** to put or form a cordon round [Old French: a little cord]
cordon bleu (**bluh**) *adj* (of cookery or cooks) of the highest standard: *a cordon bleu chef* [French: blue ribbon]
cordon sanitaire *n* **1** a line of buffer states shielding a country **2** a guarded line isolating an infected area [French, literally: sanitary line]
cords *pl n* trousers made of corduroy
corduroy *n* a heavy cotton fabric with a velvety ribbed surface [origin unknown]
corduroys *pl n* trousers made of corduroy
core *n* **1** the central part of certain fleshy fruits, containing the seeds **2** the central or essential part of something: *the historic core of the city* **3** a piece of magnetic soft iron inside an electromagnet or transformer **4** *geol* the central part of the earth **5** a cylindrical sample of rock or soil, obtained by the use of a hollow drill **6** *physics* the region of a nuclear reactor containing the fissionable material **7** the main internal memory of a computer ▷ *vb* **coring, cored** **8** to remove the core from (fruit) [origin unknown]
corella *n* a white Australian cockatoo
co-respondent *n* a person with whom someone being sued for divorce is claimed to have committed adultery
corgi *n* a short-legged sturdy dog [Welsh *cor* dwarf + *ci* dog]
coriander *n* a European plant, cultivated for its aromatic seeds and leaves, used in flavouring foods [Greek *koriannon*]
Corinthian *adj* **1** of Corinth, a port in S Greece **2** of a style of classical architecture characterized by a bell-shaped capital with carved leaf-shaped ornaments ▷ *n* **3** a person from Corinth
cork *n* **1** the thick light porous outer bark of a Mediterranean oak **2** a piece of cork used as a stopper **3** *botany* the outer bark of a woody plant ▷ *vb* **4** to stop up (a bottle) with a cork [probably from Arabic *qurq*]
corkage *n* a charge made at a restaurant for serving wine bought elsewhere
corked *adj* (of wine) spoiled through being stored in a bottle with a decayed cork
corker *n old-fashioned slang* a splendid or outstanding person or thing
corkscrew *n* **1** a device for pulling corks from bottles, usually consisting of a pointed metal spiral attached to a handle ▷ *adj* **2** like a corkscrew in shape ▷ *vb* **3** to move in a spiral or zigzag course
corm *n* the scaly bulblike underground stem of certain plants [Greek *kormos* tree trunk]
cormorant *n* a large dark-coloured long-necked sea bird [Old French *corp* raven + *-mareng* of the sea]
corn[1] *n* **1** a cereal plant such as wheat, oats, or barley **2** the grain of such plants **3** *US, Canad, Austral & NZ* maize **4** *slang* something unoriginal or oversentimental [Old English]
corn[2] *n* a painful hardening of the skin around a central point in the foot, caused by pressure [Latin *cornu* horn]
corn circle *n* same as **crop circle**
corncob *n* the core of an ear of maize, to which the kernels are attached
corncrake *n* a brown bird with a harsh grating cry
cornea (**korn-ee-a**) *n* the transparent membrane covering the eyeball [Latin *cornu* horn] **corneal** *adj*
corned beef *n* cooked beef preserved in salt
cornelian *n* same as **carnelian**
corner *n* **1** the place or angle formed by the meeting of two converging lines or surfaces **2** the space within the angle formed, as in a room **3** the place where two streets meet

4 a sharp bend in a road 5 a remote place: *far-flung corners of the world* 6 any secluded or private place 7 *sport* a free kick or shot taken from the corner of the field 8 **cut corners** to take the shortest or easiest way at the expense of high standards 9 **turn the corner** to pass the critical point of an illness or a difficult time ▹ *adj* 10 on or in a corner: *a corner seat* ▹ *vb* 11 to force (a person or animal) into a difficult or inescapable position 12 (of a vehicle or its driver) to turn a corner 13 to obtain a monopoly of [Latin *cornu* point, horn]

corner shop *n* a small general shop serving a neighbourhood

cornerstone *n* 1 an indispensable part or basis: *the food we eat is one of the cornerstones of good health* 2 a stone at the corner of a wall

cornet *n* 1 a brass instrument of the trumpet family 2 *Brit* a cone-shaped ice-cream wafer [Latin *cornu* horn] **cornetist** *n*

corn exchange *n* a building where corn is bought and sold

cornflakes *pl n* a breakfast cereal made from toasted maize

cornflour *n* 1 a fine maize flour, used for thickening sauces 2 NZ a fine wheat flour

cornflower *n* a small plant with blue flowers

cornice (korn-iss) *n* 1 a decorative moulding round the top of a wall or building 2 *archit* the projecting mouldings at the top of a column [Old French]

Cornish *adj* 1 of Cornwall ▹ *n* 2 a Celtic language of Cornwall ▹ *pl n* 3 **the Cornish** the people of Cornwall

Cornish pasty *n* a pastry case with a filling of meat and vegetables

cornucopia (korn-yew-**kope**-ee-a) *n* 1 a great abundance: *a cornucopia of rewards* 2 a symbol of plenty, consisting of a horn overflowing with fruit and flowers [Latin *cornu copiae* horn of plenty]

corny *adj* **cornier, corniest** *slang* unoriginal or oversentimental

corolla *n* the petals of a flower collectively [Latin: garland]

corollary (kor-**oll**-a-ree) *n, pl* **-laries** 1 a proposition that follows directly from another that has been proved 2 a natural consequence [Latin *corollarium* money paid for a garland]

corona (kor-**rone**-a) *n, pl* **-nas** *or* **-nae** (-nee) 1 a circle of light around a luminous body, usually the moon 2 the outermost part of the sun's atmosphere, visible as a faint halo during a total eclipse 3 a long cigar with blunt ends 4 *botany* a crownlike part of some flowers on top of the seed or on the inner side of the corolla 5 *physics* an electrical glow appearing around the surface of a charged conductor [Latin: crown]

coronary (**kor**-ron-a-ree) *adj* 1 *anatomy* of the arteries that supply blood to the heart ▹ *n, pl* **-naries** 2 a coronary thrombosis [Latin *coronarius* belonging to a wreath or crown]

coronary thrombosis *n* a condition where the blood flow to the heart is blocked by a clot in a coronary artery

coronation *n* the ceremony of crowning a monarch [Latin *coronare* to crown]

coronavirus *n* a type of airborne virus accounting for 10–30% of all colds [from its corona-like appearance under an electron microscope]

coroner *n* a public official responsible for the investigation of violent, sudden, or suspicious deaths [Anglo-French *corouner*]

coronet *n* 1 a small crown worn by princes or peers 2 a band of jewels worn as a headdress [Old French *coronete*]

corpora *pl n* the plural of **corpus**

corporal[1] *n* a noncommissioned officer in an army [Old French *caporal*, from Latin *caput* head]

corporal[2] *adj* of the body [Latin *corpus* body]

corporal punishment *n* physical punishment, such as caning

corporate *adj* 1 relating to business corporations: *corporate finance* 2 shared by a group 3 forming a corporation; incorporated [Latin *corpus* body]

corporation *n* 1 a large business or company 2 a city or town council 3 *informal* a large paunch **corporative** *adj*

corporatism *n* organization of a state on the lines of a business enterprise, with substantial government management of the economy

corporeal (kore-**pore**-ee-al) *adj* of the physical world rather than the spiritual [Latin *corpus* body]

corps (**kore**) *n, pl* **corps** 1 a military unit with a specific function: *medical corps* 2 an organized body of people: *the diplomatic corps* [French]

corps de ballet *n* the members of a ballet company [French]

corpse *n* a dead body, esp. of a human being [Latin *corpus*]

corpulent *adj* fat or plump [Latin *corpulentus*] **corpulence** *n*

corpus *n, pl* **-pora** a collection of writings, such as one by a single author or on a specific topic: *the corpus of Marxist theory* [Latin: body]

corpuscle *n* a red blood cell (see **erythrocyte**) or white blood cell (see **leucocyte**) [Latin *corpusculum* a little body] **corpuscular** *adj*

corral *US & Canad* ▹ *n* 1 an enclosure for cattle or horses ▹ *vb* **-ralling, -ralled** 2 to put in a corral [Spanish]

corrasion *n* *geol* erosion of rocks caused by fragments transported over them by water, wind, or ice [Latin *corradere* to scrape together]

correct *adj* 1 free from error; true: *the correct answer* 2 in conformity with accepted standards: *in most cultures there is a strong sense of correct sexual conduct* ▹ *vb* 3 to make free from or put right errors 4 to indicate the errors in (something) 5 to rebuke or punish in order to improve: *I stand corrected* 6 to make conform to a standard [Latin *corrigere* to make straight] **correctly** *adv* **correctness** *n*

correction *n* 1 an act or instance of correcting 2 an alteration correcting something: *corrections to the second proofs* 3 a reproof or punishment **correctional** *adj*

corrective *adj* intended to put right something that is wrong: *corrective action*

correlate *vb* **-lating, -lated** 1 to place or be placed in a mutual relationship: *water consumption is closely correlated to the number of people living in a house*

C

▷ *n* **2** either of two things mutually related **correlation** *n*

correlative *adj* **1** having a mutual relationship **2** *grammar* (of words, usually conjunctions) corresponding to each other and occurring regularly together, for example *neither* and *nor*

correspond *vb* **1** to be consistent or compatible (with) **2** to be similar (to) **3** to communicate (with) by letter [Latin *com-* together + *respondere* to respond] **corresponding** *adj* **correspondingly** *adv*

correspondence *n* **1** communication by letters **2** the letters exchanged in this way **3** relationship or similarity

correspondence course *n* a course of study conducted by post

correspondent *n* **1** a person who communicates by letter **2** a person employed by a newspaper or news service to report on a special subject or from a foreign country

corridor *n* **1** a passage in a building or a train **2** a strip of land or airspace that provides access through the territory of a foreign country **3 corridors of power** the higher levels of government or the Civil Service [Old Italian *corridore*, literally: place for running]

corrie *n* (in Scotland) a circular hollow on the side of a hill [Gaelic *coire* cauldron]

corrigendum (kor-rij-**end**-um) *n, pl* **-da** (-da) **1** an error to be corrected **2** a slip of paper inserted into a book after printing, listing corrections [Latin: that which is to be corrected]

corroborate *vb* **-rating, -rated** to support (a fact or opinion) by giving proof [Latin *com-* (intensive) + *roborare* to make strong] **corroboration** *n* **corroborative** *adj*

corroboree *n Austral* **1** an Aboriginal gathering or dance of festive or warlike character **2** *informal* any noisy gathering [Aboriginal]

corrode *vb* **-roding, -roded 1** to eat away or be eaten away by chemical action or rusting **2** to destroy gradually: *rumours corroding the public's affection for the royal family* [Latin *corrodere* to gnaw to pieces]

corrosion *n* **1** the process by which something, esp. a metal, is corroded **2** the result of corrosion **corrosive** *adj*

corrugate *vb* **-gating, -gated** to fold into alternate grooves and ridges [Latin *corrugare*] **corrugation** *n*

corrugated iron *n* a thin sheet of iron or steel, formed with alternating ridges and troughs

corrupt *adj* **1** open to or involving bribery or other dishonest practices: *corrupt practices* **2** morally depraved **3** (of a text or data) made unreliable by errors or alterations ▷ *vb* **4** to make corrupt [Latin *corruptus* spoiled] **corruptive** *adj*

corruptible *adj* capable of being corrupted

corruption *n* **1** dishonesty and illegal behaviour **2** the act of corrupting morally or sexually **3** the process of rotting or decaying **4** an unintentional or unauthorized alteration in a text or data **5** an altered form of a word

corsage (kore-**sahzh**) *n* a small bouquet worn on the bodice of a dress [Old French *cors* body]

corsair *n* **1** a pirate **2** a pirate ship **3** a privateer [Old French *corsaire*]

corse *n archaic* a corpse

corselet *n* **1** a woman's one-piece undergarment, combining corset and bra **2** a piece of armour to cover the trunk [Old French *cors* bodice]

corset *n* **1** a close-fitting undergarment worn by women to shape the torso **2** a similar garment worn by either sex to support and protect the back [Old French: a little bodice] **corsetry** *n*

cortege (kore-**tayzh**) *n* a funeral procession [Italian *corteggio*]

cortex (**kore**-tex) *n, pl* **-tices** (-tiss-seez) *anatomy* the outer layer of the brain or some other internal organ [Latin: bark, outer layer] **cortical** *adj*

cortisone *n* a steroid hormone used in treating rheumatoid arthritis, allergies, and skin diseases [*corticosterone*, a hormone]

corundum *n* a hard mineral used as an abrasive, of which the ruby and white sapphire are precious forms [Tamil *kuruntam*]

coruscate *vb* **-cating, -cated** *formal* to emit flashes of light; sparkle [Latin *coruscare* to flash] **coruscating** *adj* **coruscation** *n*

corvette *n* a lightly armed escort warship [perhaps from Middle Dutch *corf*]

corymb *n botany* a flat-topped flower cluster with the stems growing progressively shorter towards the centre [Greek *korumbos* cluster]

cos[1] *or* **cos lettuce** *n* a lettuce with a long slender head and crisp leaves [after *Kos*, the Aegean island of its origin]

cos[2] cosine

cosec (**koh**-sek) cosecant

cosecant (koh-**seek**-ant) *n* (in trigonometry) the ratio of the length of the hypotenuse to that of the opposite side in a right-angled triangle

cosh *chiefly Brit* ▷ *n* **1** a heavy blunt weapon, often made of hard rubber ▷ *vb* **2** to hit on the head with a cosh [Romany *kosh*]

cosignatory *n, pl* **-ries** a person or country that signs a document jointly with others

cosine (**koh**-sine) *n* (in trigonometry) the ratio of the length of the adjacent side to that of the hypotenuse in a right-angled triangle [see co-, SINE]

cosmetic *n* **1** anything applied to the face or body in order to improve the appearance ▷ *adj* **2** done or used to improve the appearance of the face or body **3** improving in appearance only: *glossy brochures are part of a cosmetic exercise* [Greek *kosmētikos*, from *kosmein* to arrange]

cosmetic surgery *n* surgery performed to improve the appearance, rather than for medical reasons

cosmic *adj* **1** of or relating to the whole universe: *the cosmic order* **2** occurring in or coming from outer space: *cosmic dust*

cosmogony *n, pl* **-nies** the study of the origin of the universe [Greek *kosmos* world + *gonos* creation]

cosmology *n* the study of the origin and nature of the universe [Greek *kosmos* world + -LOGY] **cosmological** *adj* **cosmologist** *n*

cosmonaut *n* the Russian name for an astronaut [Russian *kosmonavt*, from Greek *kosmos* universe + *nautēs* sailor]

cosmopolitan *adj* **1** composed of people or elements from many different countries or cultures **2** having lived and travelled in many countries **3** sophisticated and cultured ▷ *n* **4** a cosmopolitan person [Greek *kosmos* world + *politēs* citizen] **cosmopolitanism** *n*

cosmos *n* the universe considered as an ordered system [Greek *kosmos* order]

Cossack *n* **1** a member of a S Russian people, famous as horsemen and dancers ▷ *adj* **2** of the Cossacks: *a Cossack dance* [Russian *kazak* vagabond]

cosset *vb* **-seting, -seted** to pamper or pet [origin unknown]

cossie (koz-ee) *n informal* a swimming costume

cost *n* **1** the amount of money, time, or energy required to obtain or produce something **2** suffering or sacrifice: *these were crucial truths which rugby never grasped, to its cost* **3** the amount paid for a commodity by its seller: *to sell at cost* **4 costs** *law* the expenses of a lawsuit **5 at all costs** regardless of any cost or effort involved **6 at the cost of** at the expense of losing: *they eventually triumphed, but at the cost of many lives* ▷ *vb* **costing, cost 7** to be obtained or obtainable in exchange for: *calls cost 45p a minute* **8** to involve the loss or sacrifice of: *a fall which almost cost him his life* **9 costing, costed** to estimate the cost of producing (something) [Latin *constare* to stand at, cost]

cost accounting *n* the recording and controlling of all the costs involved in running a business **cost accountant** *n*

costal *adj* of the ribs

cost-effective *adj* providing adequate financial return in relation to outlay

costermonger *n Brit* a person who sells fruit and vegetables from a barrow in the street [*costard* a kind of apple + *monger* trader]

costive *adj old-fashioned* having or causing constipation [Old French *costivé*]

costly *adj* **-lier, -liest 1** expensive **2** involving great loss or sacrifice: *a bitter and costly war* **costliness** *n*

cost of living *n* the average cost of the basic necessities of life, such as food, housing, and clothing

costume *n* **1** a style of dressing, including all the clothes and accessories, typical of a particular country or period **2** the clothes worn by an actor or performer: *a jester's costume* **3** short for **swimming costume** ▷ *vb* **-tuming, -tumed 4** to provide with a costume: *she was costumed by many of the great Hollywood designers* [Italian: dress, custom] **costumed** *adj*

costume jewellery *n* inexpensive but attractive jewellery

costumier *n* a maker or supplier of theatrical or fancy dress costumes

cosy *or US* **cozy** *adj* **-sier, -siest** *or US* **-zier, -ziest 1** warm and snug **2** intimate and friendly: *a cosy chat* ▷ *n, pl* **-sies** *or US* **-zies 3** a cover for keeping things warm: *a tea cosy* [Scots] **cosiness** *or US* **coziness** *n*

cot¹ *n* **1** a bed with high sides for a baby or very young child **2** a small portable bed [Hindi *khāt* bedstead]

cot² *n* **1** *literary or archaic* a small cottage **2** a cote [Old English]

cot³ cotangent

cotangent *n* (in trigonometry) the ratio of the length of the adjacent side to that of the opposite side in a right-angled triangle

cot death *n* the unexplained sudden death of a baby while asleep

cote *or* **cot** *n* a small shelter for birds or animals [Old English]

coterie (kote-er-ee) *n* a small exclusive group of friends or people with common interests [French]

cotoneaster (kot-tone-ee-ass-ter) *n* a garden shrub with red berries

cottage *n* a small simple house, usually in the country [from COT²] **cottager** *n*

cottage cheese *n* a mild soft white cheese made from skimmed milk curds

cottage industry *n* a craft industry in which employees work at home

cottage pie *n* a dish of minced meat topped with mashed potato

cottaging *n Brit, Austral & NZ* homosexual activity between men in a public lavatory [from *cottage* (in the sense: a public lavatory)]

cotter¹ *n machinery* a bolt or wedge that is used to secure parts of machinery [Middle English *cotterel*]

cotter² *n Scot history* a farm labourer occupying a cottage and land rent-free [see COT²]

cotter pin *n machinery* a split pin used to hold parts together and fastened by having the ends spread apart after it is inserted

cotton *n* **1** the soft white downy fibre surrounding the seeds of a plant grown in warm climates, used to make cloth and thread **2** cloth or thread made from cotton fibres [Arabic *qutn*] **cottony** *adj*

cotton bud *n* a small stick with cotton wool tips used for cleaning the ears, applying make-up, etc.

cotton on *vb informal* to understand or realize the meaning (of): *it has taken the world 20 years to cotton on to this idea*

cotton wool *n chiefly Brit* absorbent fluffy cotton, used for surgical dressings and to apply creams to the skin

cotyledon (kot-ill-ee-don) *n* the first leaf produced by a plant embryo [Greek *kotulē* cup]

couch *n* **1** a piece of upholstered furniture for seating more than one person **2** a bed on which patients of a doctor or a psychoanalyst lie during examination or treatment ▷ *vb* **3** to express in a particular style of language: *a proclamation couched in splendidly archaic phraseology* **4** *archaic* (of an animal) to crouch, as when preparing to leap [Old French *coucher* to lay down]

couchette (koo-shett) *n* a bed converted from seats on a train or ship [French]

couch grass *n* a grassy weed which spreads quickly

couch potato *n slang* a physically lazy person, esp. one who spends most of the day in front of the television

cougan *n Austral slang* a drunk and rowdy person

cougar (koo-gar) *n* same as **puma** [from indigenous S American word]

cough *vb* **1** to expel air abruptly and noisily from the lungs **2** (of an engine or other machine) to make a sound similar to this ▷ *n* **3** an act or sound of coughing **4** an illness which causes frequent coughing [Old English *cohhetten*]
cough up *vb* **1** to give up (money or information) **2** to bring up into the mouth by coughing: *to cough up blood*
could *vb* **1** used to make the past tense of **can**[1] **2** used to make the subjunctive mood of **can**[1], esp. in polite requests or conditional sentences: *could I have a word with you, please?* **3** used to indicate the suggestion of a course of action: *we could make a fortune from selling players, but that would not be in the long-term interests of the club* **4** used to indicate a possibility: *it could simply be a spelling mistake* [Old English *cūthe*]
couldn't could not
coulis (**koo**-lee) *n* a thin purée of vegetables or fruit, usually served as a sauce surrounding a dish: *rum truffle cake with raspberry coulis* [French: purée]
coulomb (**koo**-lom) *n* the SI unit of electric charge [after C. A. de *Coulomb*, physicist]
coulter (**kole**-ter) *n* a vertical blade on a plough in front of the ploughshare [Latin *culter* ploughshare, knife]
council *n* **1** a group meeting for discussion or consultation **2** a legislative or advisory body: *the United Nations Security Council* **3** *Brit* the local governing authority of a town or county **4** *Austral* the local governing authority of a district or shire ▷ *adj* **5** of or provided by a local council: *a council house* [Latin *concilium* assembly]
USAGE Avoid confusion with **counsel**.
councillor *or US* **councilor** *n* a member of a council
USAGE Avoid confusion with **counsellor**.
council tax *n* (in Britain) a tax based on the relative value of property, levied to fund local council services
counsel *n* **1** advice or guidance **2** discussion or consultation: *when it was over they took counsel of their consciences* **3** a barrister or group of barristers who conduct cases in court and advise on legal matters ▷ *vb* **-selling, -selled** *or US* **-seling, -seled** **4** to give advice or guidance to **5** to recommend or urge [Latin *consilium* deliberating body] **counselling** *or US* **counseling** *n*
USAGE Avoid confusion with **council**.
counsellor *or US* **counselor** *n* **1** an adviser **2** *US* a lawyer who conducts cases in court
USAGE Avoid confusion with **councillor**.
count[1] *vb* **1** to say numbers in ascending order up to and including: *count from one to ten* **2** to add up or check (each thing in a group) in order to find the total: *she counted the money she had left* **3** to be important: *it's the thought that counts* **4** to consider: *she can count herself lucky* **5** to take into account or include: *the time he'd spent in prison on remand counted towards his sentence* **6 not counting** excluding **7** *music* to keep time by counting beats ▷ *n* **8** the act of counting **9** the number reached by counting: *a high pollen count* **10** *law* one of a number of charges **11 keep** *or* **lose count** to keep or fail to keep an accurate record of items or events **12 out for the count** unconscious ▷ See also **count against, countdown** *etc.* [Latin *computare* to calculate] **countable** *adj*
count[2] *n* a middle-ranking European nobleman [Latin *comes* associate]
count against *vb* to have an effect or influence that makes something more unlikely: *his age counts against him getting promotion*
countdown *n* the act of counting backwards to zero to time exactly an operation such as the launching of a rocket
countenance *n* **1** *literary* the face or facial expression ▷ *vb* **-nancing, -nanced** **2** to support or tolerate [Latin *continentia* restraint, control]
counter[1] *n* **1** a long flat surface in a bank or shop, on which business is transacted **2** a small flat disc used in board games **3** a disc or token used as an imitation coin **4 under the counter** (of the sale of goods) illegal [Latin *computare* to compute]
counter[2] *n* an apparatus for counting things
counter[3] *vb* **1** to say or do (something) in retaliation or response **2** to oppose or act against **3** to return the attack of (an opponent) ▷ *adv* **4** in an opposite or opposing direction or manner **5 run counter to** to be in direct contrast with ▷ *adj* **6** opposing or opposite ▷ *n* **7** something that is contrary or opposite to something else **8** an opposing action **9** a return attack, such as a blow in boxing [Latin *contra* against]
counter- *prefix* **1** against or opposite: *counterattack* **2** complementary or corresponding: *counterpart* [Latin *contra*]
counteract *vb* to act against or neutralize **counteraction** *n* **counteractive** *adj*
counterattack *n* **1** an attack in response to an attack ▷ *vb* **2** to make a counterattack (against)
counterbalance *n* **1** a weight or influence that balances or neutralizes another ▷ *vb* **-ancing, -anced** **2** to act as a counterbalance to
counterbid *n* a bid made in response to a bid from another party, offering more favourable terms to the seller
counterblast *n* an aggressive response to a verbal attack
counterclockwise *adv, adj US & Canad* same as **anticlockwise**
counterespionage *n* activities to counteract enemy espionage
counterfeit *adj* **1** made in imitation of something genuine with the intent to deceive or defraud: *counterfeit currency* **2** pretended: *counterfeit friendship* ▷ *n* **3** an imitation designed to deceive or defraud ▷ *vb* **4** to make a fraudulent imitation of **5** to feign: *surprise is an easy emotion to counterfeit* [Old French *contrefait*]
counterfoil *n Brit* the part of a cheque or receipt kept as a record
counterintelligence *n* activities designed to frustrate enemy espionage
countermand *vb* to cancel (a previous order) [Old French *contremander*]
countermeasure *n* an action taken to counteract some other action
counterpane *n* a bed covering [Medieval Latin *culcita puncta* quilted mattress]

counterpart *n* **1** a person or thing complementary to or corresponding to another **2** a duplicate of a legal document
counterpoint *n* **1** the harmonious combining of two or more parts or melodies **2** a melody or part combined in this way ▷ *vb* **3** to set in contrast [Old French *contrepoint* an accompaniment set against the notes of a melody]
counterpoise *vb* **-poising, -poised** to oppose with something of equal weight or effect: *counterpoising humour and horror*
counterproductive *adj* having an effect opposite to the one intended
countersign *vb* **1** to sign (a document already signed by another) as confirmation ▷ *n* **2** the signature so written
countersink *vb* **-sinking, -sank, -sunk** to drive (a screw) into a shaped hole so that its head is below the surface
countertenor *n* **1** an adult male voice with an alto range **2** a singer with such a voice
counterterrorism *n* activities intended to prevent terrorist acts or to eradicate terrorist groups **counterterrorist** *adj*
countess *n* **1** a woman holding the rank of count or earl **2** the wife or widow of a count or earl
countless *adj* too many to count
count noun *n* a noun that may be preceded by an indefinite article and can be used in the plural, such as *telephone* or *thing*
count on *vb* to rely or depend on
count out *vb* **1** to exclude **2** to declare (a boxer) defeated when he or she has not risen from the floor within ten seconds
countrified *adj* having an appearance or manner associated with the countryside rather than a town
country *n, pl* **-tries 1** an area distinguished by its people, culture, language, or government **2** the territory of a nation or state **3** the people of a nation or state **4** the part of the land that is away from cities or industrial areas **5** a person's native land **6** same as **country and western 7 across country** not keeping to roads **8 go to the country** *Brit & NZ* to dissolve Parliament and hold a general election [Medieval Latin *contrata (terra)* (land) lying opposite]
country and western *or* **country music** *n* popular music based on American White folk music
country club *n* a club in the country, which has sporting and social facilities
country dance *n* a type of British folk dance performed in rows or circles
countryman *or fem* **countrywoman** *n, pl* **-men** *or* **-women 1** a person from one's own country **2** *Brit, Austral & NZ* a person who lives in the country
countryside *n* land away from the cities
county *n, pl* **-ties 1** (in some countries) a division of a country ▷ *adj* **2** *Brit informal* upper-class [Old French *conté* land belonging to a count]
coup (koo) *n* **1** a brilliant and successful action **2** a coup d'état [French]
coup de grâce (koo de grahss) *n, pl* **coups de grâce** (koo de grahss) a final or decisive action [French]
coup d'état (koo day-tah) *n, pl* **coups d'état** (kooz day-tah) a sudden violent or illegal overthrow of a government [French]
coupé (koo-pay) *n* a sports car with two doors and a sloping fixed roof [French *carrosse coupé* cut-off carriage]
couple *n* **1** two people who are married, living together, or having a sexual relationship **2** two partners in a dance or game **3 a couple of A** a pair of: *a couple of guys* **B** *informal* a few: *a couple of weeks* ▷ *pron* **4 a couple A** two **B** *informal* a few: *give him a couple* ▷ *vb* **-pling, -pled 5** to connect or link: *an ingrained sense of shame, coupled with a fear of ridicule* **6** *literary* to have sexual intercourse [Latin *copula* a bond]
couplet *n* two successive lines of verse, usually rhyming and of the same metre
coupling *n* a device for connecting things, such as railway cars or trucks
coupon *n* **1** a piece of paper entitling the holder to a discount or free gift **2** a detachable slip that can be used as a commercial order form **3** *Brit* a detachable entry form for a competition [Old French *colpon* piece cut off]
courage *n* **1** the ability to face danger or pain without fear **2 the courage of one's convictions** the confidence to act according to one's beliefs [Latin *cor* heart]
courageous *adj* showing courage **courageously** *adv*
courgette *n* a type of small vegetable marrow [French]
courier *n* **1** a person who looks after and guides travellers **2** a person paid to deliver urgent messages or parcels ▷ *vb* **3** to transport (a message or parcel) by courier [Latin *currere* to run]
course *n* **1** a complete series of lessons or lectures: *a training course* **2** a sequence of medical treatment prescribed for a period of time: *a course of antibiotics* **3** an onward movement in time or space: *during the course of his career he worked with many leading actors* **4** a route or direction taken: *the ships were blown off course by a gale* **5** the path or channel along which a river moves **6** an area on which a sport is played or a race is held: *a golf course* **7** any of the successive parts of a meal **8** a continuous, usually horizontal layer of building material, such as bricks or tiles, at one level in a building **9** a mode of conduct or action: *the safest course of action was to do nothing* **10** the natural development of a sequence of events: *allow the fever to run its course* **11** a period of time: *over the course of the last two years* **12 as a matter of course** as a natural or normal consequence or event **13 in the course of** in the process of **14 in due course** at the natural or appropriate time **15 of course A** (*adv*) as expected; naturally **B** (*interj*) certainly; definitely ▷ *vb* **coursing, coursed 16** (of a liquid) to run swiftly **17** to hunt with hounds that follow the quarry by sight and not scent [Latin *cursus* a running]
coursebook *n* a book that is used as part of an educational course
courser[1] *n* **1** a person who courses hounds **2** a hound trained for coursing
courser[2] *n literary* a swift horse; steed [Old French *coursier*]

coursework *n* work done by a student and assessed as part of an educational course
coursing *n* hunting with hounds trained to hunt game by sight
court *n* **1** *law* **A** a judicial body that hears and makes decisions on legal cases **B** the room or building in which such a body meets **2** a marked area used for playing a racket game **3** an area of ground wholly or partly surrounded by walls or buildings **4** a name given to some short streets, blocks of flats, or large country houses as a part of their address: *Carlton Court* **5** the residence or retinue of a sovereign **6** any formal assembly held by a sovereign **7 go to court** to take legal action **8 hold court** to preside over a group of admirers **9 out of court** without a trial or legal case **10 pay court to** to give flattering attention to ▷ *vb* **11** to attempt to gain the love of **12** to pay attention to (someone) in order to gain favour **13** to try to obtain (something): *he has not courted controversy, but he has certainly attracted it* **14** to make oneself open or vulnerable to: *courting disaster* [Latin *cohors* cohort]
court card *n* (in a pack of playing cards) a king, queen, or jack [earlier *coat-card*, from the decorative coats worn by the figures depicted]
courteous *adj* polite and considerate in manner [Middle English *corteis* with courtly manners] **courteously** *adv* **courteousness** *n*
courtesan (**kore**-tiz-**zan**) *n history* a mistress or high-class prostitute [Old French *courtisane*]
courtesy *n, pl* **-sies 1** politeness; good manners **2** a courteous act or remark **3 by courtesy of** with the consent of [Old French *corteis* courteous]
courthouse *n* a public building in which courts of law are held
courtier *n* an attendant at a royal court
courtly *adj* **-lier, -liest 1** ceremoniously polite **2** of or suitable for a royal court **courtliness** *n*
court martial *n, pl* **court martials** *or* **courts martial 1** the trial of a member of the armed forces charged with breaking military law ▷ *vb* **court-martial, -tialling, -tialled** *or US* **-tialing, -tialed 2** to try by court martial
courtship *n* the courting of an intended spouse or mate
court shoe *n* a low-cut shoe for women, without laces or straps
courtyard *n* an open area of ground surrounded by walls or buildings
couscous (**kooss**-kooss) *n* **1** a type of semolina used in North African cookery **2** a spicy North African dish, consisting of steamed semolina served with a stew [Arabic *kouskous*]
cousin *n* the child of one's aunt or uncle. Also called: **first cousin** [Latin *consobrinus*]
couture (koo-**toor**) *n* **1** high-fashion designing and dressmaking ▷ *adj* **2** relating to high fashion design and dressmaking: *couture clothes* [French: sewing]
couturier *n* a person who designs fashion clothes for women [French]
covalency *or US* **covalence** *n chem* **1** the ability to form a bond in which two atoms share a pair of electrons **2** the number of covalent bonds which a particular atom can make with others **covalent** *adj*
cove[1] *n* a small bay or inlet [Old English *cofa*]
cove[2] *n old-fashioned slang* a fellow; chap [probably from Romany *kova*]
coven (**kuv**-ven) *n* a meeting of witches [Latin *convenire* to come together]
covenant (**kuv**-ven-ant) *n* **1** *chiefly Brit* a formal agreement to make an annual payment to charity **2** *law* a formal sealed agreement **3** *Bible* God's promise to the Israelites and their commitment to worship him alone ▷ *vb* **4** to agree by a legal covenant [Latin *convenire* to come together, agree] **covenanter** *n*
Covenanter *n Scot history* a person upholding either of two 17th-century covenants to establish and defend Presbyterianism
Coventry *n* **send someone to Coventry** to punish someone by refusing to speak to him or her [after *Coventry*, England]
cover *vb* **1** to place something over so as to protect or conceal **2** to put a garment on; clothe **3** to extend over or lie thickly on the surface of: *the ground was covered with dry leaves* **4** (sometimes foll. by *up*) to screen or conceal; hide from view **5** to travel over **6** to protect (an individual or group) by taking up a position from which fire may be returned if those being protected are fired upon **7** to keep a gun aimed at **8 A** to insure against loss or risk **B** to provide for (loss or risk) by insurance **9** to include or deal with: *the course covers accounting, economics, statistics, law, and computer applications* **10** to act as reporter or photographer on (a news event) for a newspaper or magazine **11** (of a sum of money) to be enough to pay for (something) **12** *music* to record a cover version of **13** *sport* to guard or obstruct (an opponent, team-mate, or area) **14 cover for** to deputize for (a person) **15** (foll. by *for* or *up for*) to provide an alibi (for): *can my men count on your friends at City Hall to cover for us?* ▷ *n* **16** anything which covers **17** a blanket or bedspread **18** the outside of a book or magazine **19** a pretext or disguise: *he claimed UN resolutions were being used as a cover for planned American aggression* **20** an envelope or other postal wrapping: *under plain cover* **21** an individual table setting **22** insurance **23** a cover version **24 the covers** *cricket* the area roughly at right angles to the pitch on the off side and about halfway to the boundary **25 break cover** to come out from a shelter or hiding place **26 take cover** to make for a place of safety or shelter **27 under cover** protected or in secret ▷ See also **cover-up** [Latin *cooperire* to cover completely] **covering** *adj, n*
coverage *n journalism* the amount of reporting given to a subject or event
cover charge *n* a fixed service charge added to the bill in a restaurant
cover girl *n* an attractive woman whose picture appears on the cover of a magazine
covering letter *n* an accompanying letter sent as an explanation
coverlet *n* same as **bedspread**
cover note *n Brit & Austral* a temporary certificate from an insurance company giving proof of a current policy
covert *adj* **1** concealed or secret ▷ *n* **2** a thicket or woodland providing shelter for game **3** *ornithol*

any of the small feathers on the wings and tail of a bird that surround the bases of the larger feathers [Old French: covered] **covertly** *adv*
cover-up *n* **1** concealment or attempted concealment of a mistake or crime ▷ *vb* **cover up** **2** to cover completely **3** to attempt to conceal (a mistake or crime)
cover version *n* a version by a different artist of a previously recorded musical item
covet *vb* **-eting, -eted** to long to possess (something, esp. something belonging to another person) [Latin *cupiditas* cupidity]
covetous *adj* jealously longing to possess something **covetously** *adv* **covetousness** *n*
covey (kuv-vee) *n* **1** a small flock of grouse or partridge **2** a small group of people [Old French *cover* to sit on, hatch]
cow[1] *n* **1** the mature female of cattle **2** the mature female of various other mammals, such as the elephant or whale **3** *not in technical use* any domestic species of cattle **4** *informal, offensive* a disagreeable woman [Old English *cū*]
cow[2] *vb* to frighten or subdue with threats [Old Norse *kūga* to oppress]
coward *n* a person who is easily frightened and avoids dangerous or difficult situations [Latin *cauda* tail] **cowardly** *adj*
cowardice *n* lack of courage
cowbell *n* a bell hung around a cow's neck
cowboy *n* **1** (in the US and Canada) a ranch worker who herds and tends cattle, usually on horseback **2** a conventional character of Wild West folklore or films **3** *Brit, Austral & NZ informal* an irresponsible or unscrupulous worker or businessperson **cowgirl** *fem n*
cowcatcher *n US & Canad* a fender on the front of a locomotive to clear the track of animals or other obstructions
cow cocky *n Austral & NZ* a one-man dairy farmer
cower *vb* to cringe or shrink in fear [Middle Low German *kūren* to lie in wait]
cowl *n* **1** a loose hood **2** a monk's hooded robe **3** a cover fitted to a chimney to increase ventilation and prevent draughts [Latin *cucullus* hood] **cowled** *adj*
cowlick *n* a tuft of hair over the forehead
cowling *n* a streamlined detachable metal covering around an engine
co-worker *n* a fellow worker: *these habits can drive your boss and co-workers crazy*
cow parsley *n* a hedgerow plant with umbrella-shaped clusters of white flowers
cowpat *n* a pool of cow dung
cowpox *n* a contagious disease of cows, the virus of which is used to make smallpox vaccine
cowrie *n, pl* **-ries** the glossy brightly-marked shell of a marine mollusc [Hindi *kaurī*]
cowslip *n* a European wild plant with yellow flowers [Old English *cūslyppe*, from *cū* cow + *slyppe* slime, dung]
cox *n* **1** a coxswain ▷ *vb* **2** to act as coxswain of (a boat)
coxcomb *or* **cockscomb** *n* **1** the comb of a domestic cock **2** *archaic* a conceited dandy
coxswain (kok-sn) *n* the person who steers a lifeboat or rowing boat [*cock* a ship's boat + SWAIN]
coy *adj* **1** affectedly shy and modest **2** unwilling to give information [Latin *quietus* quiet] **coyly** *adv* **coyness** *n*
coyote (koy-ote-ee) *n, pl* **-otes** *or* **-ote** a small wolf of the deserts and prairies of North America [Mexican Indian *coyotl*]
coypu *n, pl* **-pus** *or* **-pu** a beaver-like amphibious rodent, bred for its fur [from a Native American language]
cozen *vb literary* to cheat or trick [originally a cant term] **cozenage** *n*
Cpl Corporal
CPR cardiopulmonary resuscitation: a medical technique for reviving someone whose heart has stopped beating
CPU *computers* central processing unit
Cr *chem* chromium
crab *n* **1** an edible shellfish with five pairs of legs, the first pair modified into pincers **2** short for **crab louse** **3** **catch a crab** *rowing* to make a stroke in which the oar misses the water or digs too deeply, causing the rower to fall backwards [Old English *crabba*]
crab apple *n* a kind of small sour apple
crabbed *adj* **1** (of handwriting) cramped and hard to read **2** bad-tempered [probably from *crab*, because of its sideways movement & *crab apple*, because of its sourness]
crabby *adj* **-bier, -biest** bad-tempered
crab louse *n* a parasitic louse living in the pubic area of humans
crack *vb* **1** to break or split without complete separation of the parts **2** to break with a sudden sharp sound **3** to make or cause to make a sudden sharp sound: *the coachman cracked his whip* **4** (of the voice) to become harsh or change pitch suddenly **5** *informal* to fail or break down: *she had cracked under the strain of losing her job* **6** to yield or cease to resist: *he had cracked under torture* **7** to hit with a forceful or resounding blow **8** to break into or force open: *it'll take me longer if I have to crack the safe myself* **9** to solve or decipher (a code or problem) **10** *informal* to tell (a joke) **11** to break (a molecule) into smaller molecules or radicals by heat or catalysis as in the distillation of petroleum **12** to open (a bottle) for drinking **13** **crack it** *informal* to achieve something ▷ *n* **14** a sudden sharp noise **15** a break or fracture without complete separation of the two parts **16** a narrow opening or fissure **17** *informal* a sharp blow **18** **crack of dawn** daybreak **19** a broken or cracked tone of voice **20** *informal* an attempt **21** *informal* a gibe or joke **22** *slang* a highly addictive form of cocaine **23** *chiefly Irish informal* fun; informal entertainment **24** **a fair crack of the whip** *informal* a fair chance or opportunity ▷ *adj* **25** *slang* first-class or excellent: *crack troops* ▷ See also **crack down, crack up** [Old English *cracian*]
crackbrained *adj* idiotic or crazy: *a crackbrained scheme*
crack down *vb* **1** **crack down on** to take severe measures against ▷ *n* **crackdown** **2** severe or repressive measures
cracked *adj* **1** damaged by cracking **2** harsh-sounding **3** *informal* crazy

C

cracked wheat *n* whole wheat cracked between rollers so that it will cook more quickly
cracker *n* **1** a thin crisp unsweetened biscuit **2** a decorated cardboard tube, pulled apart with a bang, containing a paper hat and a joke or a toy **3** a small explosive firework **4** *slang* an excellent or notable thing or person
crackers *adj Brit & NZ slang* mad
cracking *adj* **1 get cracking** *informal* to start doing something immediately **2 a cracking pace** *informal* a high speed ▷ *adv, adj* **3** *Brit informal* first-class: *five cracking good saves* ▷ *n* **4** the oil-refining process in which heavy oils are broken down into smaller molecules by heat or catalysis
crackle *vb* **-ling, -led 1** to make small sharp popping noises ▷ *n* **2** a crackling sound **crackly** *adj*
crackling *n* **1** a series of small sharp popping noises **2** the crisp browned skin of roast pork
crackpot *informal* ▷ *n* **1** an eccentric person ▷ *adj* **2** eccentric: *crackpot philosophies*
crack up *vb* **1** *informal* to have an emotional breakdown **2** to begin to break into pieces: *there are worrying reports of buildings cracking up as the earth dries out and foundations move* **3 not all it is cracked up to be** *informal* not as good as people have claimed it to be ▷ *n* **crackup 4** *informal* an emotional breakdown
-cracy *combining form* indicating a type of government or rule: *plutocracy; mobocracy*. See also **-crat** [Greek *kratos* power]
cradle *n* **1** a baby's bed on rockers **2** a place where something originates: *the cradle of civilization* **3** a supporting framework or structure **4** a platform or trolley in which workmen are suspended on the side of a building or ship ▷ *vb* **-dling, -dled 5** to hold gently as if in a cradle [Old English *cradol*]
cradle-snatcher *n informal* a person who marries or has a sexual relationship with someone much younger than himself or herself
craft *n* **1** an occupation requiring skill or manual dexterity **2** skill or ability **3** cunning or guile **4** *pl* **craft** a boat, ship, aircraft, or spacecraft ▷ *vb* **5** to make skilfully [Old English *cræft* skill, strength]
craftsman *or fem* **craftswoman** *n, pl* **-men** *or* **-women 1** a skilled worker **2** a skilled artist **craftsmanship** *n*
crafty *adj* **-tier, -tiest** skilled in deception **craftily** *adv* **craftiness** *n*
crag *n* a steep rugged rock or peak [Celtic] **craggy** *adj*
craic *n* an Irish spelling of **crack** (sense 23)
crake *n zool* a bird of the rail family, such as the corncrake [Old Norse *krāka* crow or *krākr* raven]
cram *vb* **cramming, crammed 1** to force (more people or things) into (a place) than it can hold **2** to eat or feed to excess **3** *chiefly Brit* to study hard just before an examination [Old English *crammian*]
crammer *n* a person or school that prepares pupils for an examination
cramp¹ *n* **1** a sudden painful contraction of a muscle **2** temporary stiffness of a muscle group from overexertion: *writer's cramp* **3** severe stomach pain **4** a clamp for holding masonry or timber together ▷ *vb* **5** to affect with a cramp [Old French *crampe*]
cramp² *vb* **1** to confine or restrict **2 cramp someone's style** *informal* to prevent someone from impressing another person or from behaving naturally: *shyness will cramp their style* [Middle Dutch *crampe* hook]
cramped *adj* **1** closed in **2** (of handwriting) small and irregular
crampon *n* a spiked iron plate strapped to a boot for climbing on ice [French]
cranberry *n, pl* **-ries** a sour edible red berry [Low German *kraanbere* crane berry]
crane *n* **1** a machine for lifting and moving heavy objects, usually by suspending them from a movable projecting arm **2** a large wading bird with a long neck and legs ▷ *vb* **craning, craned 3** to stretch out (the neck) in order to see something [Old English *cran*]
crane fly *n* a fly with long legs, slender wings, and a narrow body
cranesbill *n* a plant with pink or purple flowers
cranial *adj* of or relating to the skull
craniology *n* the scientific study of the human skull [Greek *kranion* skull + -LOGY]
cranium *n, pl* **-niums** *or* **-nia** *anatomy* **1** the skull **2** the part of the skull that encloses the brain [Greek *kranion*]
crank *n* **1** a device for transmitting or converting motion, consisting of an arm projecting at right angles from a shaft **2** a handle incorporating a crank, used to start an engine or motor **3** *informal* an eccentric or odd person ▷ *vb* **4** to turn with a crank **5** to start (an engine) with a crank [Old English *cranc*]
crankcase *n* the metal case that encloses the crankshaft in an internal-combustion engine
crankpin *n* a short cylindrical pin in a crankshaft, to which the connecting rod is attached
crankshaft *n* a shaft with one or more cranks, to which the connecting rods are attached
cranky *adj* **-kier, -kiest** *informal* **1** eccentric **2** bad-tempered **crankiness** *n*
cranny *n, pl* **-nies** a narrow opening [Old French *cran*]
crap¹ *slang* ▷ *n* **1** nonsense **2** junk **3** *taboo* faeces ▷ *vb* **crapping, crapped 4** *taboo* to defecate [Middle English *crappe* chaff] **crappy** *adj*
crap² *n* same as **craps**
crape *n* same as **crepe**
craps *n* **1** a gambling game played with two dice **2 shoot craps** to play this game [probably from *crabs* lowest throw at dice]
crapulent *or* **crapulous** *adj literary* given to or resulting from excessive eating or drinking [Latin *crapula* drunkenness] **crapulence** *n*
crash *n* **1** a collision involving a vehicle or vehicles **2** a sudden descent of an aircraft as a result of which it crashes **3** a sudden loud noise **4** a breaking and falling to pieces **5** the sudden collapse of a business or stock exchange ▷ *vb* **6** to cause (a vehicle or aircraft) to collide with another vehicle, the ground, or some other object or (of vehicles or aircraft) to be involved

in a collision **7** to make or cause to make a loud smashing noise **8** to drop with force and break into pieces with a loud noise **9** to break or smash into pieces with a loud noise **10** (of a business or stock exchange) to collapse or fail suddenly **11** to move violently or noisily **12** (of a computer system or program) to fail suddenly because of a malfunction **13** *Brit & Austral informal* to gate-crash ▷ *adj* **14** requiring or using great effort in order to achieve results quickly: *a crash course* [probably Middle English *crasen* to smash + *dasshen* to strike]

crash barrier *n* a safety barrier along the centre of a motorway, around a racetrack, or at the side of a dangerous road

crash dive *n* **1** a sudden steep emergency dive by a submarine ▷ *vb* **crash-dive, -diving, -dived 2** to perform a crash dive

crash helmet *n* a helmet worn by motorcyclists to protect the head in case of a crash

crashing *adj informal* extreme: *a crashing bore*

crash-land *vb* (of an aircraft) to land in an emergency, causing damage **crash-landing** *n*

crash out *vb informal* **1** to go to sleep or become unconscious **2** to be eliminated from a competition in a way that brings disgrace or embarrassment

crash team *n* a medical team with special equipment who can arrive quickly to treat a patient having a heart attack

crass *adj* stupid and insensitive: *the enquiry is crass and naive* [Latin *crassus* thick] **crassly** *adv* **crassness** *n*

-crat *combining form* indicating a supporter or member of a particular form of government: *autocrat; democrat* [Greek *-kratēs*] **-cratic** *or* **-cratical** *combining form*

crate *n* **1** a large container made of wooden slats, used for packing goods **2** *slang* an old car or aeroplane ▷ *vb* **crating, crated 3** to put in a crate [Latin *cratis* wickerwork] **crateful** *n*

crater *n* **1** the bowl-shaped opening in a volcano or a geyser **2** a cavity made by the impact of a meteorite or an explosion **3** a roughly circular cavity on the surface of the moon and some planets ▷ *vb* **4** to make or form craters in (a surface, such as the ground) [Greek *kratēr* mixing bowl] **cratered** *adj*

cravat *n* a scarf worn round the neck instead of a tie [French *cravate*]

crave *vb* **craving, craved 1** to desire intensely: *a vulnerable, unhappy girl who craved affection* **2** *formal* to beg or plead for: *may I crave your lordship's indulgence?* [Old English *crafian*] **craving** *n*

craven *adj* **1** cowardly ▷ *n* **2** a coward [Middle English *cravant*]

craw *n* **1** the crop of a bird **2** the stomach of an animal **3 stick in one's craw** *informal* to be difficult for one to agree with or accept [Middle English]

crawfish *n, pl* **-fish** *or* **-fishes** same as **crayfish**

crawl *vb* **1** to move on one's hands and knees **2** (of insects, worms, or snakes) to creep slowly **3** to move very slowly **4** to act in a servile manner **5** to be or feel as if covered with crawling creatures: *the kind of smile that made your hair stand on end and your flesh crawl* ▷ *n* **6** a slow creeping pace or motion **7** *swimming* a stroke in which the feet are kicked like paddles while each arm in turn reaches forward and pulls back through the water [probably from Old Norse *krafla*]

crayfish *or esp US* **crawfish** *n, pl* **-fish** *or* **-fishes** an edible shellfish like a lobster [Old French *crevice* crab]

crayon *n* **1** a small stick or pencil of coloured wax or clay ▷ *vb* **2** to draw or colour with a crayon [Latin *creta* chalk]

craze *n* **1** a short-lived fashion or enthusiasm ▷ *vb* **crazing, crazed 2** to make mad **3** *ceramics & metallurgy* to develop or cause to develop fine cracks: *you must prevent the drill crazing the glazed surface of the tile* [probably from Old Norse]

crazed *adj* **1** wild and uncontrolled in behaviour **2** (of porcelain) having fine cracks

crazy *adj* **-zier, -ziest** *informal* **1** ridiculous **2 crazy about** extremely fond of: *he was crazy about me* **3** extremely annoyed or upset **crazily** *adv* **craziness** *n*

crazy paving *n Brit, Austral & NZ* a form of paving on a path, made of irregular slabs of stone

creak *vb* **1** to make or move with a harsh squeaking sound ▷ *n* **2** a harsh squeaking sound [imitative] **creaky** *adj* **creakiness** *n*

cream *n* **1** the fatty part of milk, which rises to the top **2** a cosmetic or medication that resembles cream in consistency **3** any of various foods resembling or containing cream **4** the best part of something **5 cream sherry** a full-bodied sweet sherry ▷ *adj* **6** yellowish-white ▷ *vb* **7** to beat (foodstuffs) to a light creamy consistency **8** to remove the cream from (milk) **9** to prepare or cook (foodstuffs) with cream or milk **10 cream off** to take away the best part of [Late Latin *cramum*] **creamy** *adj*

cream cheese *n* a type of very rich soft white cheese

creamer *n chiefly Brit* a powdered milk substitute for coffee

creamery *n, pl* **-eries** a place where dairy products are made or sold

cream of tartar *n* a purified form of the tartar produced in wine-making, an ingredient in baking powder

crease *n* **1** a line made by folding or pressing **2** a wrinkle or furrow, esp. on the face **3** *cricket* any of four lines near each wicket marking positions for the bowler or batsman ▷ *vb* **creasing, creased 4** to make or become wrinkled or furrowed [Middle English *crēst*] **creasy** *adj*

create *vb* **-ating, -ated 1** to cause to come into existence **2** to be the cause of **3** to appoint to a new rank or position **4** *Brit slang* to make an angry fuss [Latin *creare*]

creation *n* **1** a creating or being created **2** something brought into existence or created

Creation *n Christianity* **1** God's act of bringing the universe into being **2** the universe as thus brought into being by God

creationism *n* the doctrine that ascribes the origins of all things to God's acts of creation rather than to evolution **creationist** *n, adj*

creative *adj* **1** having the ability to create **2** imaginative or inventive ▷ *n* **3** a creative person, esp. one who devises advertising campaigns **creativity** *n*

creator *n* a person who creates

Creator *n* **the Creator** God

creature *n* **1** an animal, bird, or fish **2** a person **3** a person or thing controlled by another

crèche *n* **1** a day nursery for very young children **2** a supervised play area provided for young children for short periods [French]

C

cred *n slang* short for **street cred**

credence (**kreed**-enss) *n* belief in the truth or accuracy of a statement: *the question is, how much credence to give to their accounts?* [Latin *credere* to believe]

credentials *pl n* **1** something that entitles a person to credit or confidence **2** a document giving evidence of the bearer's identity or qualifications

credibility gap *n* the difference between claims or statements made and the true facts

credible *adj* **1** capable of being believed; convincing: *there is no credible evidence* **2** trustworthy or reliable: *the latest claim is the only one to involve a credible witness* [Latin *credere* to believe] **credibility** *n*

credit *n* **1** **A** the system of allowing customers to receive goods or services before payment **B** the time allowed for paying for such goods or services **2** a reputation for trustworthiness in paying debts **3** **A** the positive balance in a person's bank account **B** the sum of money that a bank makes available to a client in excess of any deposit **4** a sum of money or equivalent purchasing power, available for a person's use **5** *accounting* **A** acknowledgment of a sum of money by entry on the right-hand side of an account **B** an entry or total of entries on this side **6** praise or approval, as for an achievement or quality: *you must give her credit for her perseverance* **7** a person or thing who is a source of praise or approval: *she is a credit to her family* **8** influence or reputation based on the good opinion of others: *he acquired credit within the community* **9** belief or confidence in someone or something: *this theory is now gaining credit among the scientific community* **10** *education* **A** distinction awarded to an examination candidate obtaining good marks **B** certification that a section of an examination syllabus has been satisfactorily completed **11** **on credit** with payment to be made at a future date ▷ *vb* **-iting, -ited** **12** *accounting* **A** to enter (an item) as a credit in an account **B** to acknowledge (a payer) by making such an entry **13** **credit with** to give credit for: *credit us with some intelligence* **14** to believe ▷ See also **credits** [Latin *credere* to believe]

creditable *adj* deserving praise or honour **creditably** *adv*

credit account *n Brit* a credit system in which shops allow customers to obtain goods and services before payment

credit card *n* a card issued by banks or shops, allowing the holder to buy on credit

credit crunch *n* a period during which there is a sudden reduction in the availability of credit from banks, mortgage lenders, etc.

creditor *n* a person or company to whom money is owed

credit rating *n* an evaluation of the ability of a person or business to repay money lent

credits *pl n* a list of people responsible for the production of a film, programme, or record

creditworthy *adj* (of a person or a business) regarded as deserving credit on the basis of earning power and previous record of debt repayment **creditworthiness** *n*

credo *n, pl* **-dos** a creed

credulity *n* willingness to believe something on little evidence

credulous *adj* **1** too willing to believe: *he has convinced only a few credulous American intellectuals* **2** arising from or showing credulity: *credulous optimism* [Latin *credere* to believe]

creed *n* **1** a system of beliefs or principles **2** a formal statement of the essential parts of Christian belief [Latin *credo* I believe]

creek *n* **1** a narrow inlet or bay **2** *US, Canad, Austral & NZ* a small stream or tributary **3** **up the creek** *slang* in a difficult position [Old Norse *kriki* nook]

creel *n* a wickerwork basket used by fishermen [Scots]

creep *vb* **creeping, crept** **1** to move quietly and cautiously **2** to crawl with the body near to or touching the ground **3** to have the sensation of something crawling over the skin, from fear or disgust: *she makes my flesh creep* **4** (of plants) to grow along the ground or over rocks ▷ *n* **5** a creeping movement **6** *slang* an obnoxious or servile person [Old English *crēopan*]

creeper *n* **1** a plant, such as ivy, that grows by creeping **2** *US & Canad* same as **tree creeper**

creeps *pl n* **give someone the creeps** to give someone a feeling of fear or disgust

creepy *adj* **creepier, creepiest** *informal* causing a feeling of fear or disgust **creepiness** *n*

creepy-crawly *n, pl* **-crawlies** *Brit informal* a small crawling creature

cremate *vb* **-mating, -mated** to burn (a corpse) to ash [Latin *cremare*] **cremation** *n*

crematorium *n, pl* **-riums** *or* **-ria** a building where corpses are cremated

crème de la crème *n* the very best: *the crème de la crème of cities* [French]

crème de menthe *n* a liqueur flavoured with peppermint [French]

crenellated *or US* **crenelated** *adj* having battlements [Late Latin *crena* a notch] **crenellation** *or US* **crenelation** *n*

creole *n* **1** a language developed from a mixture of different languages which has become the main language of a place ▷ *adj* **2** of or relating to a creole [Spanish]

Creole *n* **1** (in the West Indies and Latin America) a native-born person of mixed European and African descent **2** (in the Gulf States of the US) a native-born person of French descent **3** the French creole spoken in the Gulf States ▷ *adj* **4** of or relating to any of these peoples: *Creole cooking*

creosote *n* **1** a thick dark liquid made from coal tar and used for preserving wood **2** a colourless liquid made from wood tar and used as an

antiseptic ▷ *vb* **-soting, -soted 3** to treat with creosote [Greek *kreas* flesh + *sōtēr* preserver]
crepe (krayp) *n* **1** a thin light fabric with a crinkled texture **2** a very thin pancake, often folded around a filling **3** a type of rubber with a wrinkled surface, used for the soles of shoes [French]
crepe paper *n* paper with a crinkled texture, used for decorations
crept *vb* the past of **creep**
crepuscular *adj* **1** of or like twilight **2** (of animals) active at twilight [Latin *crepusculum* dusk]
Cres. Crescent
crescendo (krish-**end**-oh) *n, pl* **-dos 1** a gradual increase in loudness **2** a musical passage that gradually gets louder ▷ *adv* **3** gradually getting louder [Italian]
crescent *n* **1** the curved shape of the moon when in its first or last quarter **2** *chiefly Brit & NZ* a crescent-shaped street ▷ *adj* **3** crescent-shaped [Latin *crescere* to grow]
cress *n* a plant with strong-tasting leaves, used in salads and as a garnish [Old English *cressa*]
crest *n* **1** the top of a mountain, hill, or wave **2** a tuft or growth of feathers or skin on the top of a bird's or animal's head **3** a heraldic design or figure used on a coat of arms and elsewhere **4** an ornamental plume or emblem on top of a helmet ▷ *vb* **5** to come or rise to a high point **6** to lie at the top of **7** to reach the top of (a hill or wave) [Latin *crista*] **crested** *adj*
crestfallen *adj* disappointed or disheartened
Cretaceous *adj geol* of the period of geological time about 135 million years ago, at the end of which the dinosaurs died out [Latin *creta* chalk]
cretin *n* **1** *offensive* a very stupid person **2** *not in technical use, old-fashioned* a person with learning difficulties and physical disabilities because of a thyroid deficiency [French from Latin *Christianus* Christian, alluding to the humanity of such people despite their disabilities] **cretinism** *n* **cretinous** *adj*
cretonne *n* a heavy printed cotton or linen fabric, used in furnishings [French]
crevasse *n* a deep open crack in a glacier [French]
crevice *n* a narrow crack or gap in rock [Latin *crepare* to crack]
crew[1] *n* **1** the people who serve on or operate a ship, boat, or aircraft **2** a group of people working together: *a film crew* **3** *informal* any group of people ▷ *vb* **4** to serve as a crew member on a ship or boat [Middle English *crue* reinforcement, from Latin *crescere* to increase]
crew[2] *vb archaic* a past of **crow**[2]
crew cut *n* a closely cut haircut for men
crewel *n* a loosely twisted worsted yarn, used in embroidery [origin unknown] **crewelwork** *n*
crew neck *n* a plain round neckline **crew-neck** *or* **crew-necked** *adj*
crib *n* **1** a piece of writing stolen from elsewhere **2** a translation or list of answers used by students, often dishonestly **3** a baby's cradle **4** a rack or manger for fodder **5** a model of the manger scene at Bethlehem **6** short for **cribbage** **7** *NZ* a small holiday house ▷ *vb* **cribbing, cribbed 8** to copy (someone's work) dishonestly **9** to confine in a small space [Old English *cribb*]
cribbage *n* a card game for two to four players, who each try to win a set number of points before the others [origin unknown]
crib sheet *n* **1** a sheet containing notes on a subject, used as a study aid **2** a sheet with information on a complicated topic, used in a debate
crib-wall *n NZ* a retaining wall built against an earth bank
crick *informal* ▷ *n* **1** a painful muscle spasm or cramp in the neck or back ▷ *vb* **2** to cause a crick in [origin unknown]
cricket[1] *n* **1** a game played by two teams of eleven players using a ball, bats, and wickets **2 not cricket** *informal* not fair play [Old French *criquet* wicket] **cricketer** *n*
cricket[2] *n* a jumping insect like a grasshopper, which produces a chirping sound by rubbing together its forewings [Old French *criquer* to creak, imitative]
cried *vb* the past of **cry**
crier *n* an official who makes public announcements
crime *n* **1** an act prohibited and punished by law **2** unlawful acts collectively **3** *informal* a disgraceful act: *to be a woman writing rock music is neither a crime against nature nor a freakish rarity* [Latin *crimen*]
criminal *n* **1** a person guilty of a crime ▷ *adj* **2** of or relating to crime or its punishment **3** *informal* senseless or disgraceful: *a criminal waste of money* **criminally** *adv* **criminality** *n*
criminalize *or* **-ise** *vb* **-izing, -ized** *or* **-ising, -ised 1** to make (an action or activity) criminal **2** to treat (a person) as a criminal
criminology *n* the scientific study of crime [Latin *crimen* crime + -LOGY] **criminologist** *n*
crimp *vb* **1** to fold or press into ridges **2** to curl (hair) tightly with curling tongs **3** *chiefly US informal* to restrict or hinder: *a slowdown in the US economy could crimp some big Swedish concerns' profits* ▷ *n* **4** the act or result of crimping [Old English *crympan*]
Crimplene *n trademark* a crease-resistant synthetic fabric
crimson *adj* deep purplish-red [Arabic *qirmizi* kermes (dried bodies of insects used to make a red dye)]
cringe *vb* **cringing, cringed 1** to shrink or flinch in fear: *he cringed and shrank against the wall* **2** to behave in a submissive or timid way: *an organization that tends to cringe before political authority* **3** *informal* to be very embarrassed: *I cringe every time I see that old photo of me* ▷ *n* **4** the act of cringing [Old English *cringan* to yield in battle]
crinkle *vb* **-kling, -kled 1** to become slightly creased or folded ▷ *n* **2** a crease or fold [Old English *crincan* to bend] **crinkly** *adj*
crinoline *n* a petticoat stiffened with hoops to make the skirt stand out [Latin *crinis* hair + *lino* flax]
cripple *n* **1** *offensive* a person who is unable to walk or walk easily **2** *offensive* a person who is or seems

deficient in some way: *an emotional cripple* ▷ *vb* **-pling, -pled 3** to disable (someone) **4** to damage (something) [Old English *crypel*] **crippled** *adj* **crippling** *adj*

crisis *n, pl* **-ses 1** a crucial stage or turning point in the course of anything **2** a time of extreme trouble or danger [Greek *krisis* decision]

crisp *adj* **1** fresh and firm: *a crisp green salad* **2** dry and brittle: *bake until crisp and golden brown* **3** clean and neat: *crisp white cotton* **4** (of weather) cold but invigorating: *a crisp autumn day* **5** clear and sharp: *the telescope is able to provide crisp images of distant galaxies* **6** lively or brisk: *the service is crisp and efficient* ▷ *n* **7** *Brit* a very thin slice of potato fried till crunchy ▷ *vb* **8** to make or become crisp [Latin *crispus* curled] **crisply** *adv* **crispness** *n*

C

crispbread *n* a thin dry biscuit made of wheat or rye

crispy *adj* **crispier, crispiest** hard and crunchy **crispiness** *n*

crisscross *vb* **1** to move in or mark with a crosswise pattern ▷ *adj* **2** (of lines) crossing one another in different directions

criterion *n, pl* **-ria** *or* **-rions** a standard by which something can be judged or decided [Greek *kritērion*]

> **USAGE** *Criteria*, the plural of *criterion*, is not acceptable as a singular noun: *this criterion is not valid; these criteria are not valid.*

critic *n* **1** a professional judge of art, music, or literature **2** a person who finds fault and criticizes [Greek *kritēs* judge]

critical *adj* **1** very important or dangerous: *this was a critical moment in her career* **2** so seriously ill or injured as to be in danger of dying: *he is in a critical condition in hospital* **3** fault-finding or disparaging: *the article is highly critical of the government* **4** examining and judging analytically and without bias: *he submitted the plans to critical examination* **5** of a critic or criticism **6** *physics* denoting a constant value at which the properties of a system undergo an abrupt change: *the critical temperature above which the material loses its superconductivity* **7** (of a nuclear power station or reactor) having reached a state in which a nuclear chain reaction becomes self-sustaining **critically** *adv*

criticism *n* **1** fault-finding or censure **2** an analysis of a work of art or literature **3** the occupation of a critic **4** a work that sets out to analyse

criticize *or* **-cise** *vb* **-cizing, -cized** *or* **-cising, -cised 1** to find fault with **2** to analyse (something)

critique *n* **1** a critical essay or commentary **2** the act or art of criticizing [French]

croak *vb* **1** (of a frog or crow) to make a low hoarse cry **2** to utter or speak with a croak **3** *slang* to die ▷ *n* **4** a low hoarse sound [Old English *crācettan*] **croaky** *adj*

Croatian (kroh-**ay**-shun) *adj* **1** of Croatia ▷ *n* **2** a person from Croatia **3** the dialect of Serbo-Croat spoken in Croatia

crochet (**kroh**-shay) *vb* **-cheting, -cheted 1** to make (a piece of needlework) by looping and intertwining thread with a hooked needle ▷ *n* **2** work made by crocheting [French: small hook]

crock[1] *n* an earthenware pot or jar [Old English *crocc* pot]

crock[2] *n* **old crock** *Brit, Austral & NZ slang* a person or thing that is old or broken-down [Scots]

crockery *n* china dishes or earthenware vessels collectively

crocodile *n* **1** a large amphibious tropical reptile with a tapering snout **2** *Brit, Austral & NZ informal* a line of people, esp. schoolchildren, walking two by two [Greek *krokodeilos* lizard]

crocodile tears *pl n* an insincere show of grief [from the belief that crocodiles wept over their prey to lure further victims]

crocus *n, pl* **-cuses** a plant with white, yellow, or purple flowers in spring [Greek *krokos* saffron]

croft *n* a small farm worked by one family in Scotland [Old English] **crofter** *n* **crofting** *adj, n*

croissant (**krwah**-son) *n* a flaky crescent-shaped bread roll [French]

cromlech *n Brit* **1** a circle of prehistoric standing stones **2** *not in technical use* a dolmen [Welsh]

crone *n* a witchlike old woman [Old French *carogne* carrion]

crony *n, pl* **-nies** a close friend [Greek *khronios* long-lasting]

crook *n* **1** *informal* a dishonest person **2** a bent or curved place or thing: *she held the puppy in the crook of her arm* **3** a bishop's or shepherd's staff with a hooked end ▷ *adj* **4** *Austral & NZ informal* **A** ill **B** of poor quality **C** unpleasant; bad **5 go (off) crook** *Austral & NZ informal* to lose one's temper **6 go crook at** *or* **on** *Austral & NZ informal* to rebuke or upbraid ▷ *vb* **7** to bend or curve [Old Norse *krokr* hook]

crooked *adj* **1** bent or twisted **2** set at an angle **3** *informal* dishonest or illegal **crookedly** *adv* **crookedness** *n*

croon *vb* to sing, hum, or speak in a soft low tone [Middle Dutch *crōnen* to groan] **crooner** *n*

crop *n* **1** a cultivated plant, such as a cereal, vegetable, or fruit plant **2** the season's total yield of farm produce **3** any group of things appearing at one time: *a remarkable crop of new Scottish plays* **4** the handle of a whip **5** short for **riding crop** **6** a pouchlike part of the gullet of a bird, in which food is stored or prepared for digestion **7** a short cropped hairstyle ▷ *vb* **cropping, cropped 8** to cut (something) very short **9** to produce or harvest as a crop **10** (of animals) to feed on (grass) **11** to clip part of (the ear or ears) of (an animal), esp. for identification ▷ See also **crop up** [Old English *cropp*]

crop circle *n* a pattern made up of ring shapes formed by the unexplained flattening of cereals growing in a field

cropper *n* **come a cropper** *informal* **A** to fail completely **B** to fall heavily

crop top *n* a short T-shirt or vest that reveals the wearer's midriff

crop up *vb informal* to occur or appear unexpectedly

croquet (**kroh**-kay) *n* a game played on a lawn in which balls are hit through hoops [French]

croquette (kroh-**kett**) *n* a fried cake of mashed potato, meat, or fish [French]

crosier *n* same as **crozier**

cross *vb* **1** to move or go across (something): *she crossed the street to the gallery* **2** to meet and pass: *further south, the way is crossed by Brewer Street* **3** *Brit & NZ* to draw two parallel lines across (a cheque) and so make it payable only into a bank account **4** to mark with a cross or crosses **5** to cancel or delete with a cross or with lines: *she crossed out the first three words* **6** to place across or crosswise: *he sat down and crossed his legs* **7** to make the sign of the cross upon as a blessing **8** to annoy or anger (someone) by challenging or opposing their wishes and plans **9** to interbreed or cross-fertilize **10** *football* to pass (the ball) from a wing to the middle of the field **11** (of each of two letters or messages) to be sent before the other is received **12** (of telephone lines) to interfere with each other so that several callers are connected together at one time **13** **cross one's fingers** to fold one finger across another in the hope of bringing good luck **14** **cross one's heart** to promise by making the sign of a cross over one's heart **15** **cross one's mind** to occur to one briefly or suddenly ▷ *n* **16** a structure, symbol, or mark consisting of two intersecting lines **17** an upright post with a bar across it, used in ancient times as a means of execution **18** a representation of the Cross on which Jesus Christ was executed as an emblem of Christianity **19** a symbol (×) used as a signature or error mark **20** **the sign of the cross** a sign made with the hand by some Christians to represent the Cross **21** a medal or monument in the shape of a cross **22** the place in a town or village where a cross has been set up **23** *biol* **A** the process of crossing; hybridization **B** a hybrid **24** a mixture of two things **25** a hindrance or misfortune: *we've all got our own cross to bear* **26** *football* a pass of the ball from a wing to the middle of the field ▷ *adj* **27** angry **28** lying or placed across: *a cross beam* [Latin *crux*] **crossly** *adv* **crossness** *n*

Cross *n* **the Cross** **A** the cross on which Jesus Christ was crucified **B** Christianity

cross- *combining form* **1** indicating action from one individual or group to another: *cross-cultural*; *cross-refer* **2** indicating movement or position across something: *crosscurrent*; *crosstalk* **3** indicating a crosslike figure or intersection: *crossbones*

crossbar *n* **1** a horizontal beam across a pair of goalposts **2** the horizontal bar on a man's bicycle

cross-bench *n Brit* a seat in Parliament for a member belonging to neither the government nor the opposition **cross-bencher** *n*

crossbill *n* a finch that has a bill with crossed tips

crossbow *n* a weapon consisting of a bow fixed across a wooden stock, which releases an arrow when the trigger is pulled

crossbreed *vb* **-breeding, -bred** **1** to produce (a hybrid animal or plant) by crossing two different species ▷ *n* **2** a hybrid animal or plant

crosscheck *vb* **1** to check the accuracy of (something) by using a different method ▷ *n* **2** a crosschecking

cross-country *adj, adv* **1** by way of open country or fields ▷ *n* **2** a long race held over open ground

crosscut *vb* **-cutting, -cut** **1** to cut across ▷ *adj* **2** cut across ▷ *n* **3** a transverse cut or course

cross-examine *vb* **-examining, -examined** **1** *law* to question (a witness for the opposing side) in order to check his or her testimony **2** to question closely or relentlessly **cross-examination** *n* **cross-examiner** *n*

cross-eyed *adj* with one or both eyes turning inwards towards the nose

cross-fertilize *or* **-lise** *vb* **-lizing, -lized** *or* **-lising, -lised** to fertilize (an animal or plant) by fusion of male and female reproductive cells from different individuals of the same species **cross-fertilization** *or* **-lisation** *n*

crossfire *n* **1** *military* gunfire crossing another line of fire **2** a lively exchange of ideas or opinions

crosshatch *vb drawing* to shade with two or more sets of parallel lines that cross one another

crossing *n* **1** a place where a street, railway, or river may be crossed **2** the place where one thing crosses another **3** a journey across water

cross-legged *adj* sitting with the legs bent and the knees pointing outwards

crossover *n* a combination of two different styles, esp. of music or fashion

crosspatch *n informal* a bad-tempered person [*cross* + obsolete *patch* fool]

cross-ply *adj* (of a tyre) having the fabric cords in the outer casing running diagonally to stiffen the sidewalls

cross-purposes *pl n* **at cross-purposes** misunderstanding each other in a discussion

cross-question *vb* to cross-examine

cross-refer *vb* **-referring, -referred** to refer from one part of something to another

cross-reference *n* **1** a reference within a text to another part of the text ▷ *vb* **-referencing, -referenced** **2** to cross-refer

crossroad *n US & Canad* **1** a road that crosses another road **2** a road that connects one main road to another

crossroads *n* **1** the point at which roads cross one another **2** **at the crossroads** at the point at which an important choice has to be made

cross section *n* **1** *maths* a surface formed by cutting across a solid, usually at right angles to its longest axis **2** a random sample regarded as representative: *a cross section of society* **cross-sectional** *adj*

cross-stitch *n* an embroidery stitch made from two crossing stitches

crosstalk *n* **1** *Brit* rapid or witty talk **2** unwanted signals transferred between communication channels

crosswalk *n US & Canad* a place marked where pedestrians may cross a road

crosswise *or* **crossways** *adj, adv* **1** across: *slice the celery crosswise* **2** in the shape of a cross

crossword puzzle *or* **crossword** *n* a puzzle in which vertically and horizontally crossing words suggested by clues are written into a grid of squares

crotch *n* **1** the forked part of the human body between the legs **2** the corresponding part of a pair of trousers or pants **3** any forked part formed by the joining of two things: *the crotch of the tree* [probably variant of CRUTCH] **crotched** *adj*

crotchet *n music* a note having the time value of a quarter of a semibreve [Old French *crochet* little hook]
crotchety *adj informal* bad-tempered
crouch *vb* **1** to bend low with the legs and body pulled close together ▷ *n* **2** this position [Old French *crochir* to become bent like a hook]
croup¹ (**kroop**) *n* a throat disease of children, with a hoarse cough and laboured breathing [Middle English: to cry hoarsely, probably imitative]
croup² (**kroop**) *n* the hindquarters of a horse [Old French *croupe*]
croupier (**kroop-ee-ay**) *n* a person who collects bets and pays out winnings at a gambling table [French]
crouton *n* a small piece of fried or toasted bread served in soup [French]
crow¹ *n* **1** a large black bird with a harsh call **2 as the crow flies** in a straight line [Old English *crāwa*]
crow² *vb* **1** *past tense* **crowed** *or* **crew** (of a cock) to utter a shrill squawking sound **2** to boast about one's superiority **3** (of a baby) to utter cries of pleasure ▷ *n* **4** a crowing sound [Old English *crāwan*]
crowbar *n* a heavy iron bar used as a lever
crowd *n* **1** a large number of things or people gathered together **2** a particular group of people: *we got to know a French crowd from Lyons* **3 the crowd** the masses ▷ *vb* **4** to gather together in large numbers **5** to press together into a confined space **6** to fill or occupy fully **7** *informal* to make (someone) uncomfortable by coming too close [Old English *crūdan*] **crowded** *adj*
crowdfunding *n* the practice of funding a project by getting small donations from many supporters, often via the internet
crowd-pleaser *n* a person or thing that appeals to a large proportion of an audience **crowd-pleasing** *adj*
crowdsourcing *n* the use of many disparate people as contributors to a project, esp. via the internet
crown *n* **1** a monarch's ornamental headdress, usually made of gold and jewels **2** a wreath for the head, given as an honour **3** the highest or central point of something arched or curved: *the crown of the head* **4 A** the enamel-covered part of a tooth projecting beyond the gum **B** a substitute crown, usually of gold or porcelain, fitted over a decayed or broken tooth **5** a former British coin worth 25 pence (five shillings) **6** the outstanding quality or achievement: *the last piece is the crown of the evening* ▷ *vb* **7** to put a crown on the head of (someone) to proclaim him or her monarch **8** to put on the top of **9** to reward **10** to form the topmost part of **11** to put the finishing touch to (a series of events): *she crowned a superb display with three goals* **12** to attach a crown to (a tooth) **13** *Brit, Austral & NZ slang* to hit over the head **14** *draughts* to promote (a draught) to a king by placing another draught on top of it [Greek *korōnē*]
Crown *n* **the Crown** the power or institution of the monarchy
crown colony *n* a British colony controlled by the Crown
crown court *n* a local criminal court in England and Wales
Crown Derby *n* a type of fine porcelain made at Derby
crown jewels *pl n* the jewellery used by a sovereign on ceremonial occasions
crown-of-thorns *n* a starfish with a spiny outer covering that feeds on living coral
crown prince *n* the male heir to a sovereign throne **crown princess** *n*
crow's feet *pl n* wrinkles at the outer corners of the eye
crow's nest *n* a lookout platform fixed at the top of a ship's mast
crozier *or* **crosier** *n* a hooked staff carried by bishops as a symbol of office [Old French *crossier* staff-bearer]
crucial *adj* **1** of exceptional importance **2** *Brit slang* very good [Latin *crux* cross] **crucially** *adv*
cruciate *adj* shaped or arranged like a cross [Latin *crux* cross] **cruciately** *adv*
cruciate ligament *n anatomy* either of a pair of ligaments that cross each other in the knee
crucible *n* a pot in which metals or other substances are melted [Medieval Latin *crucibulum* night lamp]
crucifix *n* a model cross with a figure of Christ upon it [Church Latin *crucifixus* the crucified Christ]
crucifixion *n* a method of execution by fastening to a cross, normally by the hands and feet
Crucifixion *n Christianity* **1 the Crucifixion** the crucifying of Christ **2** a representation of this
cruciform *adj* shaped like a cross
crucify *vb* **-fies, -fying, -fied 1** to put to death by crucifixion **2** to treat cruelly **3** *slang* to defeat or ridicule totally [Latin *crux* cross + *figere* to fasten]
crud *n slang* a sticky or encrusted substance [earlier form of CURD] **cruddy** *adj*
crude *adj* **1** rough and simple: *crude farm implements* **2** tasteless or vulgar **3** in a natural or unrefined state ▷ *n* **4** short for **crude oil** [Latin *crudus* bloody, raw] **crudely** *adv* **crudity** *or* **crudeness** *n*
crude oil *n* unrefined petroleum
crudités (**crew-dit-tay**) *pl n* a selection of raw vegetables often served with a variety of dips before a meal [French *crudité* rawness]
cruel *adj* **1** deliberately causing pain without pity **2** causing pain or suffering [Latin *crudelis*] **cruelly** *adv* **cruelty** *n*
cruet *n* **1** a small container for pepper, salt, etc., at table **2** a set of such containers on a stand [Old French *crue* flask]
cruise *n* **1** a sail taken for pleasure, stopping at various places ▷ *vb* **cruising, cruised 2** to sail about from place to place for pleasure **3** (of a vehicle, aircraft, or ship) to travel at a moderate and efficient speed **4** to proceed steadily or easily: *they cruised into the final of the qualifying competition* [Dutch *kruisen* to cross]
cruise missile *n* a low-flying subsonic missile that is guided throughout its flight
cruiser *n* **1** a large fast warship armed with medium-calibre weapons **2** Also called: **cabin cruiser** a motorboat with a cabin
cruiserweight *n* a professional boxer weighing up to 195 pounds (88.5 kg)

crumb *n* **1** a small fragment of bread or other dry food **2** a small bit or scrap: *a crumb of comfort* [Old English *cruma*]
crumble *vb* **-bling, -bled 1** to break into crumbs or fragments **2** to fall apart or decay ▷ *n* **3** a baked pudding consisting of stewed fruit with a crumbly topping: *rhubarb crumble* **crumbly** *adj* **crumbliness** *n*
crumby *adj* **crumbier, crumbiest 1** full of crumbs **2** same as **crummy**
crummy *adj* **-mier, -miest** *slang* **1** of very bad quality: *a crummy hotel* **2** unwell: *I felt really crummy* [variant spelling of *crumby*]
crumpet *n* **1** a light soft yeast cake, eaten buttered **2** *chiefly Brit slang, sometimes offensive* attractive women collectively [origin unknown]
crumple *vb* **-pling, -pled 1** to crush or become crushed into untidy wrinkles or creases **2** to collapse in an untidy heap: *her father lay crumpled on the floor* ▷ *n* **3** an untidy crease or wrinkle [obsolete *crump* to bend] **crumply** *adj*
crunch *vb* **1** to bite or chew with a noisy crushing sound **2** to make a crisp or brittle sound ▷ *n* **3** a crunching sound **4 the crunch** *informal* the critical moment or situation [imitative] **crunchy** *adj* **crunchiness** *n*
crupper *n* **1** a strap that passes from the back of a saddle under a horse's tail **2** the horse's rump [Old French *crupiere*]
crusade *n* **1** any of the medieval military expeditions undertaken by European Christians to recapture the Holy Land from the Muslims **2** a vigorous campaign in favour of a cause ▷ *vb* **-sading, -saded 3** to take part in a crusade [Latin *crux* cross] **crusader** *n*
cruse *n* a small earthenware container for liquids [Old English *crūse*]
crush *vb* **1** to press or squeeze so as to injure, break, or put out of shape **2** to break or grind into small pieces **3** to control or subdue by force **4** to extract (liquid) by pressing: *crush a clove of garlic* **5** to defeat or humiliate utterly **6** to crowd together ▷ *n* **7** a dense crowd **8** the act of crushing **9** *informal* an infatuation: *I had a teenage crush on my French teacher* **10** a drink made by crushing fruit: *orange crush* [Old French *croissir*]
crush barrier *n* a barrier put up to separate sections of large crowds and prevent crushing
crust *n* **1** the hard outer part of bread **2** the baked shell of a pie or tart **3** any hard outer layer: *a thin crust of snow* **4** the solid outer shell of the earth ▷ *vb* **5** to cover with or form a crust [Latin *crusta* hard surface, rind]
crustacean *n* **1** an animal with a hard outer shell and several pairs of legs, which usually lives in water, such as a crab or lobster ▷ *adj* **2** of crustaceans [Latin *crusta* shell]
crusty *adj* **crustier, crustiest 1** having a crust **2** rude or irritable **crustiness** *n*
crutch *n* **1** a long staff with a rest for the armpit, used to support the weight of the body **2** something that supports **3** *Brit* same as **crotch** (sense 1) [Old English *crycc*]
crutchings *pl n Austral & NZ* the wool clipped from a sheep's hindquarters
crux *n, pl* **cruxes** *or* **cruces** a crucial or decisive point [Latin: cross]
cry *vb* **cries, crying, cried 1** to shed tears **2** to make a loud vocal sound, usually to express pain or fear or to appeal for help **3** to utter loudly or shout **4** (of an animal or bird) to utter loud characteristic sounds **5 cry for** to appeal urgently for ▷ *n, pl* **cries 6** a fit of weeping **7** the act or sound of crying **8** the characteristic utterance of an animal or bird **9** an urgent appeal: *a cry for help* **10** a public demand: *a cry for more law and order on the streets* **11 a far cry from** something very different from **12 in full cry** **A** in eager pursuit **B** in the middle of talking or doing something ▷ See also **cry off** [Old French *crier*]
crying *adj* **a crying shame** something that demands immediate attention
cry off *vb informal* to withdraw from an arrangement
cryogenics *n* the branch of physics concerned with very low temperatures and their effects [Greek *kruos* cold + *-genēs* born] **cryogenic** *adj*
crypt *n* a vault or underground chamber, such as one beneath a church, used as a burial place [Greek *kruptē*]
cryptic *adj* having a hidden or secret meaning; puzzling: *no-one knew what he meant by that cryptic remark* [Greek *kruptos* concealed] **cryptically** *adv*
cryptogam *n botany* a plant that reproduces by spores not seeds [Greek *kruptos* hidden + *gamos* marriage]
cryptography *n* the art of writing in and deciphering codes [Greek *kruptos* hidden + -GRAPHY] **cryptographer** *n* **cryptographic** *adj*
crystal *n* **1** a solid with a regular internal structure and symmetrical arrangement of faces **2** a single grain of a crystalline substance **3** a very clear and brilliant glass **4** something made of crystal **5** crystal glass articles collectively **6** *electronics* a crystalline element used in certain electronic devices, such as a detector or oscillator ▷ *adj* **7** bright and clear: *the crystal waters of the pool* [Greek *krustallos* ice, crystal]
crystal ball *n* the glass globe used in crystal gazing
crystal gazing *n* **1** the act of staring into a crystal ball, supposedly in order to see future events **2** the act of trying to foresee or predict **crystal gazer** *n*
crystalline *adj* **1** of or like crystal or crystals **2** clear
crystallize, crystalize *or* **-ise** *vb* **-izing, -ized** *or* **-ising, -ised 1** to make or become definite **2** to form into crystals **3** to preserve (fruit) in sugar **crystallization, crystalization** *or* **-isation** *n*
crystallography *n* the science of crystal structure
crystalloid *n* a substance that in solution can pass through a membrane
crystal meth *n informal* crystal methamphetamine, a concentrated and highly potent form of methamphetamine with dangerous side effects
Cs *chem* caesium
CSA (in Britain) Child Support Agency

CSE (formerly, in Britain) Certificate of Secondary Education: an examination the first grade pass of which was an equivalent to a GCE O level
CS gas *n* a gas causing tears and painful breathing, used to control civil disturbances [initials of its US inventors, Ben Carson and Roger Staughton]
CST Central Standard Time
CT Connecticut
CT scanner *n* an X-ray machine that can produce cross-sectional images of the soft tissues [*c(omputerized) t(omography) scanner*]
CTV Canadian Television (Network Limited)
Cu *chem* copper [Late Latin *cuprum*]
cu. cubic
cub *n* **1** the young of certain mammals, such as the lion or bear **2** a young or inexperienced person ▷ *vb* **cubbing, cubbed 3** to give birth to (cubs) [origin unknown]
Cub *n* short for **Cub Scout**
Cuban *adj* **1** from Cuba ▷ *n* **2** a person from Cuba
cubbyhole *n* a small enclosed space or room [dialect *cub* cattle pen]
cube *n* **1** an object with six equal square faces **2** the product obtained by multiplying a number by itself twice: *the cube of 2 is 8* ▷ *vb* **cubing, cubed 3** to find the cube of (a number) **4** to cut into cubes [Greek *kubos*]
cube root *n* the number or quantity whose cube is a given number or quantity: *2 is the cube root of 8*
cubic *adj* **1 a** having three dimensions **b** having the same volume as a cube with length, width, and depth each measuring the given unit: *a cubic metre* **2** having the shape of a cube **3** *maths* involving the cubes of numbers
cubicle *n* an enclosed part of a large room, screened for privacy [Latin *cubiculum*]
cubic measure *n* a system of units for the measurement of volumes
cubism *n* a style of art, begun in the early 20th century, in which objects are represented by geometrical shapes **cubist** *adj, n*
cubit *n* an ancient measure of length based on the length of the forearm [Latin *cubitum* elbow, cubit]
cuboid *adj* **1** shaped like a cube ▷ *n* **2** *maths* a geometric solid whose six faces are rectangles
Cub Scout *or* **Cub** *n* a member of a junior branch of the Scout Association
cuckold *literary or old-fashioned* ▷ *n* **1** a man whose spouse has been unfaithful to him ▷ *vb* **2** to make a cuckold of [Middle English *cukeweld*]
cuckoo *n, pl* **cuckoos 1** a migratory bird with a characteristic two-note call, noted for laying its eggs in the nests of other birds ▷ *adj* **2** *informal* mad or foolish [Old French *cucu*, imitative]
cuckoopint *n* a plant with arrow-shaped leaves, purple flowers, and red berries
cuckoo spit *n* a white frothy mass produced on plants by the larvae of some insects
cucumber *n* **1** a long fruit with thin green rind and crisp white flesh, used in salads **2 as cool as a cucumber** calm and self-possessed [Latin *cucumis*]
cud *n* **1** partially digested food which a ruminant brings back into its mouth to chew again **2 chew the cud** to think deeply [Old English *cudu*]
cuddle *vb* **-dling, -dled 1** to hug or embrace fondly **2 cuddle up** to lie close and snug ▷ *n* **3** a fond hug [origin unknown] **cuddly** *adj*
cudgel *n* a short thick stick used as a weapon [Old English *cycgel*]
cue[1] *n* **1** a signal to an actor or musician to begin speaking or playing **2** a signal or reminder **3 on cue** at the right moment ▷ *vb* **cueing, cued 4** to give a cue to [perhaps from the letter *q*, used in an actor's script to represent Latin *quando* when]
cue[2] *n* **1** a long tapering stick used to hit the balls in billiards, snooker, or pool ▷ *vb* **cueing, cued 2** to hit (a ball) with a cue [variant of QUEUE]
cue ball *n snooker* the ball struck by the cue, as distinguished from the object balls
cuff[1] *n* **1** the end of a sleeve **2** *US, Canad, Austral & NZ* a turn-up on trousers **3 off the cuff** *informal* impromptu: *he delivers many speeches off the cuff* [Middle English *cuffe* glove]
cuff[2] *Brit, Austral & NZ* ▷ *vb* **1** to strike with an open hand ▷ *n* **2** a blow with an open hand [origin unknown]
cuff link *n* one of a pair of decorative fastenings for shirt cuffs
cuisine (quiz-zeen) *n* **1** a style of cooking: *Italian cuisine* **2** the range of food served in a restaurant [French]
cul-de-sac *n, pl* **culs-de-sac** *or* **cul-de-sacs** a road with one end blocked off [French: bottom of the bag]
culinary *adj* of the kitchen or cookery [Latin *culina* kitchen]
cull *vb* **1** to choose or gather **2** to remove or kill (the inferior or surplus animals) from a herd ▷ *n* **3** the act of culling [Latin *colligere* to gather together]
culminate *vb* **-nating, -nated** to reach the highest point or climax: *the parade culminated in a memorial service* [Latin *culmen* top] **culmination** *n*
culottes *pl n* women's flared trousers cut to look like a skirt [French]
culpable *adj* deserving blame [Latin *culpa* fault] **culpability** *n*
culprit *n* the person guilty of an offence or misdeed [Anglo-French *culpable* guilty + *prit* ready]
cult *n* **1** a specific system of religious worship **2** a sect devoted to the beliefs of a cult **3** devoted attachment to a person, idea, or activity **4** a popular fashion: *the bungee-jumping cult* ▷ *adj* **5** very popular among a limited group of people: *a cult TV series* [Latin *cultus* cultivation, refinement]
cultish *adj* intended to appeal to a small group of fashionable people
cultivate *vb* **-vating, -vated 1** to prepare (land) to grow crops **2** to grow (plants) **3** to develop or improve (something) by giving special attention to it: *he tried to cultivate a reputation for fairness* **4** to try to develop a friendship with (a person) [Latin *colere* to till]
cultivated *adj* well-educated: *a civilized and cultivated man*
cultivation *n* **1** the act of cultivating **2** culture or refinement
cultivator *n* a farm implement used to break up soil and remove weeds

culture *n* **1** the ideas, customs, and art of a particular society **2** a particular civilization at a particular period **3** a developed understanding of the arts **4** the cultivation and rearing of plants or animals **5** a growth of bacteria for study ▹ *vb* **-turing, -tured 6** to grow (bacteria) in a special medium [Latin *colere* to till] **cultural** *adj*

cultured *adj* **1** showing good taste or manners **2** artificially grown or synthesized

cultured pearl *n* a pearl artificially grown in an oyster shell

culture shock *n sociol* the feelings of isolation and anxiety experienced by a person on first coming into contact with a culture very different from his or her own

culvert *n* a drain or pipe that crosses under a road or railway [origin unknown]

cum *prep* with: *a small living-cum-dining room* [Latin]

cumbersome *or* **cumbrous** *adj* **1** awkward because of size or shape **2** difficult because of complexity: *the cumbersome appeals procedure*

cumin *or* **cummin** *n* **1** the spicy-smelling seeds of a Mediterranean herb, used in cooking **2** the plant from which these seeds are obtained [Greek *kuminon*]

cummerbund *n* a wide sash worn round the waist, esp. with a dinner jacket [Hindi *kamarband*, from Persian *kamar* loins + *band* band]

cumquat *n* same as **kumquat**

cumulative (kew-myew-la-tiv) *adj* growing in amount, strength, or effect by small steps: *the cumulative effect of twelve years of war*

cumulus (kew-myew-luss) *n, pl* **-li** (-lie) a thick or billowing white or dark grey cloud [Latin: mass]

cuneiform (**kew**-nif-form) *n* **1** an ancient system of writing using wedge-shaped characters ▹ *adj* **2** written in cuneiform [Latin *cuneus* wedge]

cunjevoi *n Austral* **1** a plant of tropical Asia and Australia with small flowers, cultivated for its edible rhizome **2** a sea squirt

cunnilingus *n* the kissing and licking of a woman's genitals by her sexual partner [Latin *cunnus* vulva + *lingere* to lick]

cunning *adj* **1** clever at deceiving **2** made with skill ▹ *n* **3** cleverness at deceiving **4** skill or ingenuity [Old English *cunnende*]

cunt *n taboo slang* **1** the female genitals **2** *derogatory* a stupid or obnoxious person [Middle English]

cup *n* **1** a small bowl-shaped drinking container with a handle **2** the contents of a cup **3** something shaped like a cup: *a bra with padded cups* **4** a cup-shaped trophy awarded as a prize **5** a sporting contest in which a cup is awarded to the winner **6** a mixed drink with fruit juice or wine as a base: *claret cup* **7** one's lot in life: *his cup of bitterness was full to overflowing* **8 someone's cup of tea** *informal* someone's chosen or preferred thing ▹ *vb* **cupping, cupped 9** to form (the hands) into the shape of a cup **10** to hold in cupped hands [Old English *cuppe*]

cupboard *n* a piece of furniture or a recess with a door, for storage

cupboard love *n* a show of love put on in order to gain something

Cup Final *n* **1** the annual final of the FA or Scottish Cup soccer competition **2** the final of any cup competition

Cupid *n* **1** the Roman god of love, represented as a winged boy with a bow and arrow **2** a picture or statue of Cupid [Latin *cupido* desire]

cupidity (kew-**pid**-it-ee) *n formal* strong desire for wealth or possessions [Latin *cupere* to long for]

cupola (**kew**-pol-la) *n* **1** a domed roof or ceiling **2** a small dome on the top of a roof **3** an armoured revolving gun turret on a warship [Latin *cupa* tub]

cupreous (**kew**-pree-uss) *adj* of or containing copper [Latin *cuprum* copper]

cupric (**kew**-prick) *adj* of or containing copper in the divalent state

cupronickel (kew-proh-**nik**-el) *n* a copper alloy containing up to 40 per cent nickel

cup tie *n Brit sport* an eliminating match between two teams in a cup competition

cur *n* **1** a vicious mongrel dog **2** a contemptible person [Middle English *kurdogge*]

curable *adj* capable of being cured **curability** *n*

curaçao (**kew**-rah-so) *n* an orange-flavoured liqueur

curacy (**kew**-rah-see) *n, pl* **-cies** the work or position of a curate

curare (kew-**rah**-ree) *n* a poisonous resin obtained from a South American tree, used as a muscle relaxant in medicine [Carib *kurari*]

curate[1] (**kyoor**-it) *n* a member of the clergy who assists a vicar or parish priest [Medieval Latin *cura* spiritual oversight]

curate[2] (kew-**rate**) *vb* **1** to be the curator of (a museum or art gallery) **2** to organize, arrange, and present (a cultural event)

curative *adj* **1** able to cure ▹ *n* **2** something able to cure

curator *n* the person in charge of a museum or art gallery [Latin: one who cares] **curatorial** *adj* **curatorship** *n*

curb *n* **1** something that restrains or holds back **2** a horse's bit with an attached chain or strap, used to check the horse **3** a raised edge that strengthens or encloses ▹ *vb* **4** to control or restrain ▹ See also **kerb** [Latin *curvus* curved]

curcumin *n* a yellow pigment, present in turmeric, that is an antioxidant and has anti-inflammatory properties

curd *n* **1** coagulated milk, used in making cheese or as a food **2** any similar substance: *bean curd* [origin unknown]

curd cheese *n* a mild smooth white cheese made from skimmed milk curds

curdle *vb* **-dling, -dled 1** to turn into curd; coagulate **2 make someone's blood curdle** to fill someone with horror

cure *vb* **curing, cured 1** to get rid of (an ailment or problem) **2** to restore (someone) to health **3** to preserve (meat or fish) by salting or smoking **4** to preserve (leather or tobacco) by drying **5** to vulcanize (rubber) ▹ *n* **6** a restoration to health **7** medical treatment that restores health **8** a means of restoring health or improving a situation **9** a curacy [Latin *cura* care]

C

cure-all *n* something supposed to cure all ailments or problems
curette *or* **curet** *n* **1** a surgical instrument for scraping tissue from body cavities ▷ *vb* **-retting, -retted 2** to scrape with a curette [French] **curettage** *n*
curfew *n* **1** a law which states that people must stay inside their houses after a specific time at night **2** the time set as a deadline by such a law **3** *history* the ringing of a bell at a fixed time, as a signal for putting out fires and lights [Old French *cuevrefeu* cover the fire]
Curia *n, pl* **-riae** the court and government of the Roman Catholic Church [Latin] **curial** *adj*
curie *n* the standard unit of radioactivity [after Pierre *Curie*, French physicist]
curio (kew-ree-oh) *n, pl* **-rios** a rare or unusual thing valued as a collector's item [from *curiosity*]
curiosity *n, pl* **-ties 1** eagerness to know or find out **2** a rare or unusual thing
curious *adj* **1** eager to learn or know **2** eager to find out private details **3** unusual or peculiar [Latin *curiosus* taking pains over something] **curiously** *adv*
curium (kew-ree-um) *n chem* a silvery-white metallic radioactive element artificially produced from plutonium. Symbol: **Cm** [after Pierre & Marie *Curie*, French physicists]
curl *vb* **1** to twist (hair) or (of hair) to grow in coils or ringlets **2** to twist into a spiral or curve **3** to play the game of curling **4 curl one's lip** to show contempt by raising a corner of the lip ▷ *n* **5** a coil of hair **6** a curved or spiral shape ▷ See also **curl up** [probably from Middle Dutch *crullen*] **curly** *adj*
curler *n* **1** a pin or small tube for curling hair **2** a person who plays curling
curlew *n* a large wading bird with a long downward-curving bill [Old French *corlieu*]
curlicue *n* an intricate ornamental curl or twist [*curly* + CUE²]
curling *n* a game played on ice, in which heavy stones with handles are slid towards a target circle
curl up *vb* **1** to lie or sit with legs drawn up **2** to be embarrassed or horrified
curmudgeon *n* a bad-tempered or mean person [origin unknown] **curmudgeonly** *adj*
currajong *n* same as **kurrajong**
currant *n* **1** a small dried seedless raisin **2** a small round acid berry, such as the redcurrant [earlier *rayson of Corannte* raisin of Corinth]
currawong *n* an Australian songbird [Aboriginal]
currency *n, pl* **-cies 1** the system of money or the actual coins and banknotes in use in a particular country **2** general acceptance or use: *ideas that had gained currency during the early 1960s* [Latin *currere* to run, flow]
current *adj* **1** of the immediate present: *current affairs; the current economic climate* **2** most recent or up-to-date: *the current edition* **3** commonly accepted: *current thinking on this issue* **4** circulating and valid at present: *current coins* ▷ *n* **5** a flow of water or air in a particular direction **6** *physics* a flow or rate of flow of electric charge through a conductor **7** a general trend or drift: *two opposing currents of thought* [Latin *currere* to run, flow] **currently** *adv*
current account *n* a bank account from which money may be drawn at any time using a chequebook or debit card
curriculum *n, pl* **-la** *or* **-lums 1** all the courses of study offered by a school or college **2** a course of study in one subject at a school or college: *the history curriculum* [Latin: course] **curricular** *adj*
curriculum vitae (vee-tie) *n, pl* **curricula vitae** an outline of someone's educational and professional history, prepared for job applications [Latin: the course of one's life]
curry¹ *n, pl* **-ries 1** a dish of Indian origin consisting of meat or vegetables in a hot spicy sauce **2** curry seasoning or sauce **3 curry powder** a mixture of spices for making curry ▷ *vb* **-ries, -rying, -ried 4** to prepare (food) with curry powder [Tamil *kari* sauce, relish]
curry² *vb* **-ries, -rying, -ried 1** to groom (a horse) **2** to dress (leather) after it has been tanned **3 curry favour** to ingratiate oneself with an important person [Old French *correer* to make ready]
currycomb *n* a ridged comb used for grooming horses
curse *vb* **cursing, cursed 1** to swear or swear at (someone) **2** to call on supernatural powers to bring harm to (someone or something) ▷ *n* **3** a profane or obscene expression, usually of anger **4** an appeal to a supernatural power for harm to come to a person **5** harm resulting from a curse **6** something that causes great trouble or harm **7 the curse** *informal* menstruation or a menstrual period [Old English *cursian*]
cursed *adj* **1** under a curse **2 cursed with** having (something unfortunate or unwanted): *the player has been cursed with injuries this season*
cursive *adj* **1** of handwriting or print in which letters are joined in a flowing style ▷ *n* **2** a cursive letter or printing type [Medieval Latin *cursivus* running]
cursor *n* **1** a movable shape, typically a flashing bar or underline, that shows a specific position on a computer screen **2** the sliding part of a slide rule or other measuring instrument
cursory *adj* hasty and usually superficial [Late Latin *cursorius* of running] **cursorily** *adv*
curt *adj* so blunt and brief as to be rude [Latin *curtus* cut short] **curtly** *adv* **curtness** *n*
curtail *vb* **1** to cut short: *the opening round was curtailed by heavy rain* **2** to restrict: *a plan to curtail drinks advertising* [obsolete *curtal* to dock] **curtailment** *n*
curtain *n* **1** a piece of material hung at an opening or window to shut out light or to provide privacy **2** a hanging cloth that conceals all or part of a theatre stage from the audience **3** the end of a scene or a performance in the theatre, marked by the fall or closing of the curtain **4** the rise or opening of the curtain at the start of a performance **5** something forming a barrier or screen: *a curtain of rain* ▷ *vb* **6** to shut off or conceal with a curtain **7** to provide with curtains [Late Latin *cortina*]

curtain call *n theatre* a return to the stage by performers to receive applause
curtain-raiser *n* **1** *theatre* a short play performed before the main play **2** a minor event happening before a major one
curtains *pl n informal* death or ruin; the end
curtsy *or* **curtsey** *n, pl* **-sies** *or* **-seys 1** a woman's formal gesture of respect made by bending the knees and bowing the head ▷ *vb* **-sies, -sying, -sied** *or* **-seys, -seying, -seyed 2** to make a curtsy [variant of *courtesy*]
curvaceous *adj informal* having a curved shapely body
curvature *n* the state or degree of being curved
curve *n* **1** a continuously bending line with no straight parts **2** something that curves or is curved **3** curvature **4** *maths* a system of points whose coordinates satisfy a given equation **5** a line representing data on a graph ▷ *vb* **curving, curved 6** to form into or move in a curve [Latin *curvare* to bend] **curvy** *adj*
curvet *n* **1** a horse's low leap with all four feet off the ground ▷ *vb* **-vetting, -vetted** *or* **-veting, -veted 2** to make such a leap [Latin *curvare* to bend]
curvilinear *adj* consisting of or bounded by a curved line
cuscus *n, pl* **-cuses** a large nocturnal possum of N Australia and New Guinea [probably from a native word in New Guinea]
cushion *n* **1** a bag filled with a soft material, used to make a seat more comfortable **2** something that provides comfort or absorbs shock **3** the resilient felt-covered rim of a billiard table ▷ *vb* **4** to protect from injury or shock **5** to lessen the effects of **6** to provide with cushions [Latin *culcita* mattress] **cushiony** *adj*
cushy *adj* **cushier, cushiest** *informal* easy: *a cushy job* [Hindi *khush* pleasant]
cusp *n* **1** a small point on the grinding or chewing surface of a tooth **2** a point where two curves meet **3** *astrol* any division between houses or signs of the zodiac **4** *astron* either of the points of a crescent moon **5 on the cusp** at the point of moving from one state into another: *on the cusp of middle age* [Latin *cuspis* pointed end]
cuss *informal* ▷ *n* **1** a curse or oath **2** an annoying person ▷ *vb* **3** to swear or swear at
cussed (kuss-id) *adj informal* **1** obstinate: *the older she got the more cussed she became* **2** same as **cursed cussedness** *n*
custard *n* **1** a sauce made of milk and sugar thickened with cornflour **2** a baked sweetened mixture of eggs and milk [Middle English *crustade* kind of pie]
custodian *n* the person in charge of a public building **custodianship** *n*
custody *n, pl* **-dies 1** the act of keeping safe **2** imprisonment prior to being tried [Latin *custos* guard, defender] **custodial** *adj*
custom *n* **1** a long-established activity, action, or festivity: *the custom of serving port after dinner* **2** the long-established habits or traditions of a society **3** a usual practice or habit: *she held his hand more tightly than was her custom in public* **4** regular use of a shop or business ▷ *adj* **5** made to the specifications of an individual customer: *a custom car; custom-tailored suits* ▷ See also **customs** [Latin *consuetudo*]
customary *adj* **1** usual **2** established by custom **customarily** *adv* **customariness** *n*
custom-built *or* **-made** *adj* made according to the specifications of an individual customer
customer *n* **1** a person who buys goods or services **2** *informal* a person with whom one has to deal: *a tricky customer*
custom house *n* a government office where customs are collected
customize *or* **-ise** *vb* **-izing, -ized** *or* **-ising, -ised** to make (something) according to a customer's individual requirements
customs *n* **1** duty charged on imports or exports **2** the government department responsible for collecting this **3** the area at a port, airport, or border where baggage and freight are examined for dutiable goods
cut *vb* **cutting, cut 1** to open up or penetrate (a person or thing) with a sharp instrument **2** (of a sharp instrument) to penetrate or open up (a person or thing) **3** to divide or be divided with or as if with a sharp instrument **4** to trim **5** to abridge or shorten **6** to reduce or restrict: *cut your intake of fried foods* **7** to form or shape by cutting **8** to reap or mow **9** *sport* to hit (the ball) so that it spins and swerves **10** to hurt the feelings of (a person): *her rudeness cut me to the core* **11** *informal* to pretend not to recognize **12** *informal* to absent oneself from without permission: *he found the course boring, and was soon cutting classes* **13** to stop (doing something): *cut the nonsense* **14** to dilute or adulterate: *heroin cut with talcum powder* **15** to make a sharp or sudden change in direction: *the path cuts to the right just after you pass the quarry* **16** to grow (teeth) through the gums **17** *films* **A** to call a halt to a shooting sequence **B cut to** to move quickly to (another scene) **18** *films* to edit (film) **19** to switch off (a light or engine) **20** to make (a commercial recording): *he cut his first solo album in 1971* **21** *cards* **A** to divide (the pack) at random into two parts after shuffling **B** to pick cards from a spread pack to decide the dealer or who plays first **22 cut a dash** to make a stylish impression **23 cut a person dead** *informal* to ignore a person completely **24 cut and run** *informal* to escape quickly from a difficult situation **25 cut both ways A** to have both good and bad effects **B** to serve both sides of an argument **26 cut it fine** *informal* to allow little margin of time or space **27 cut no ice** *informal* to fail to make an impression **28 cut one's teeth on** *informal* to get experience from ▷ *n* **29** the act of cutting **30** a stroke or incision made by cutting **31** a piece cut off **32** a channel or path cut or hollowed out **33** a reduction: *a pay cut* **34** a deletion in a text, film, or play **35** *informal* a portion or share **36** the style in which hair or a garment is cut **37** a direct route; short cut **38** *sport* a stroke which makes the ball spin and swerve **39** *films* an immediate transition from one shot to the next **40** *Brit* a canal **41 a cut above** *informal* superior to; better than ▷ *adj* **42** made or shaped by cutting **43** reduced by cutting: *the shop has hundreds of suits, all at cut prices* **44** adulterated or diluted **45 cut**

and dried *informal* settled in advance ▷ See also **cut across, cutback** *etc.* [probably from Old Norse]

cut across *vb* **1** to go against (ordinary restrictions or expectations): *this dilemma has cut across class divisions* **2** to cross or traverse

cutaneous (kew-**tane**-ee-uss) *adj* of the skin [Latin *cutis* skin]

cutaway *adj* (of a drawing or model) having part of the outside omitted to reveal the inside

C

cutback *n* **1** a decrease or reduction ▷ *vb* **cut back** **2** to shorten by cutting **3** (often foll. by *on*) to make a reduction: *we may cut back on other expenditure*

cut down *vb* **1** to fell **2** (often foll. by *on*) to make a reduction: *cut down on the amount of salt you eat* **3** to kill **4 cut someone down to size** to cause someone to feel less important or to be less conceited

cute *adj* **1** appealing or attractive **2** *informal* clever or shrewd [from ACUTE] **cuteness** *n*

cut glass *n* **1** glass with patterns cut into the surface ▷ *adj* **cut-glass** **2** upper-class; refined: *Victoria with her cut-glass accent*

cuticle (**kew**-tik-kl) *n* **1** hardened skin round the base of a fingernail or toenail **2** same as **epidermis** [Latin *cuticula* skin]

cut in *vb* **1** to interrupt **2** to move in front of another vehicle, leaving too little space

cutlass *n* a curved one-edged sword formerly used by sailors [French *coutelas*]

cutler *n* a person who makes or sells cutlery [Latin *culter* knife]

cutlery *n* knives, forks, and spoons, used for eating

cutlet *n* **1** a small piece of meat taken from the neck or ribs **2** a flat croquette of chopped meat or fish [Old French *costelette* a little rib]

cut off *vb* **1** to remove or separate by cutting **2** to stop the supply of **3** to interrupt (a person who is speaking), esp. during a telephone conversation **4** to bring to an end **5** to disinherit: *cut off without a penny* **6** to intercept so as to prevent retreat or escape ▷ *n* **cutoff** **7** the point at which something is cut off; limit **8** *chiefly US* a short cut **9** a device to stop the flow of a fluid in a pipe

cut out *vb* **1** to shape by cutting **2** to delete or remove **3** *informal* to stop doing (something) **4** (of an engine) to cease to operate suddenly **5** (of an electrical device) to switch off, usually automatically **6 be cut out for** to be suited or equipped for: *you're not cut out for this job* **7 have one's work cut out** to have as much work as one can manage ▷ *n* **cutout** **8** a device that automatically switches off a circuit or engine as a safety device **9** something that has been cut out from something else

cut-price *or esp US* **cut-rate** *adj* **1** at a reduced price **2** offering goods or services at prices below the standard price

cutter *n* **1** a person or tool that cuts **2** a small f ast boat

cut-throat *adj* **1** fierce or ruthless in competition: *the cut-throat world of international finance* **2** (of a card game) played by three people: *cut-throat poker* ▷ *n* **3** a murderer **4** *Brit & NZ* a razor with a long blade that folds into its handle

cutting *n* **1** an article cut from a newspaper or magazine **2** a piece cut from a plant for rooting or grafting **3** a passage cut through high ground for a road or railway **4** the editing process of a film ▷ *adj* **5** (of a remark) likely to hurt the feelings **6** keen; piercing: *a cutting wind* **7** designed for cutting: *the hatchet's blade is largely stone, but its cutting edge is made of copper*

cutting edge *n* the leading position in any field; forefront: *the cutting edge of space technology*

cuttlefish *n, pl* **-fish** *or* **-fishes** a flat squidlike mollusc which squirts an inky fluid when in danger [Old English *cudele*]

cut up *vb* **1** to cut into pieces **2** *informal* (of a driver) to overtake or pull in front of (another driver) in a dangerous manner **3 be cut up** *informal* to be very upset **4 cut up rough** *Brit informal* to become angry or violent

CV curriculum vitae

cwm (**koom**) *n* (in Wales) a valley [Welsh]

cwt hundredweight

cyan *adj* deep bluish-green [Greek *kuanos* dark blue]

cyanic acid *n* a colourless poisonous volatile liquid acid

cyanide *n* any of a number of highly poisonous substances containing a carbon-nitrogen group of atoms

cyanogen *n* a poisonous colourless flammable gas [Greek *kuanos* dark blue]

cyanosis *n pathol* a blue discoloration of the skin, caused by a deficiency of oxygen in the blood [Greek *kuanos* dark blue]

cyber- *combining form* indicating computers: *cyberspace* [from CYBERNETICS]

cyberattack *n* an attempt to cause damage or disruption by interfering with a computer system

cyberbully *n* a person who bullies another person via electronic technology such as mobile phones and social media

cybercafé *n* a café equipped with computer equipment which customers can use to access the internet [CYBER- + CAFÉ]

cybercrime *n* crime committed by means of computers or the internet

cybernetics *n* the branch of science in which electronic and mechanical systems are studied and compared to biological systems [Greek *kubernētēs* steersman] **cybernetic** *adj*

cyberspace *n* the hypothetical environment which contains all the data stored in computers [CYBER- + SPACE]

cybersquatting *n* the practice of registering an internet domain name that is likely to be wanted by another person or organization in the hope that it can be sold to them for a profit **cybersquatter** *n*

cyberterrorism *n* the unlawful and politically motivated use of computer technology to cause fear, disruption, or financial loss **cyberterrorist** *n*

cyclamen (**sik**-la-men) *n* a plant with white, pink, or red flowers, with turned-back petals [Greek *kuklaminos*]

cycle *vb* **-cling, -cled** **1** to ride a bicycle **2** to occur in cycles ▷ *n* **3** *Brit, Austral & NZ* a bicycle **4** *US* a motorcycle **5** a complete series of recurring events **6** the time taken or needed for one such series **7** a single complete movement in an electrical, electronic, or mechanical process **8** a set of plays, songs, or poems about a figure or event [Greek *kuklos*] **cycling** *n*

cyclical *or* **cyclic** *adj* **1** occurring in cycles **2** *chem* (of an organic compound) containing a closed ring of atoms

cyclist *n* a person who rides a bicycle

cyclo- *or before a vowel* **cycl-** *combining form* **1** indicating a circle or ring: *cyclotron* **2** *chem* denoting a cyclical compound: *cyclopropane* [Greek *kuklos* cycle]

cyclometer (sike-**lom**-it-er) *n* a device that records the number of revolutions made by a wheel and the distance travelled

cyclone *n* **1** a body of moving air below normal atmospheric pressure, which often brings rain **2** a violent tropical storm [Greek *kuklōn* a turning around] **cyclonic** *adj*

cyclopedia *or* **cyclopaedia** *n* same as **encyclopedia**

Cyclops *n, pl* **Cyclopes** *or* **Cyclopses** *classical myth* one of a race of giants having a single eye in the middle of the forehead [Greek *Kuklōps* round eye]

cyclotron *n* an apparatus, used in atomic research, which accelerates charged particles by means of a strong vertical magnetic field

cyder *n* same as **cider**

cygnet *n* a young swan [Latin *cygnus* swan]

cylinder *n* **1** a solid or hollow body with circular equal ends and straight parallel sides **2** a container or other object shaped like a cylinder **3** the chamber in an internal-combustion engine within which the piston moves **4** the rotating mechanism of a revolver, containing cartridge chambers [Greek *kulindein* to roll] **cylindrical** *adj*

cymbal *n* a percussion instrument consisting of a round brass plate which is struck against another or hit with a stick [Greek *kumbē* something hollow] **cymbalist** *n*

cyme *n botany* a flower cluster which has a single flower on the end of each stem and of which the central flower blooms first [Greek *kuma* anything swollen] **cymose** *adj*

Cymric (**kim**-rik) *adj* **1** of Wales ▷*n* **2** the Celtic language of Wales

cynic (**sin**-ik) *n* a person who believes that people always act selfishly [Greek *kuōn* dog]

Cynic *n* a member of an ancient Greek philosophical school that had contempt for worldly things **Cynicism** *n*

cynical *adj* **1** believing that people always act selfishly **2** sarcastic or sneering **cynically** *adv*

cynicism *n* the attitude or beliefs of a cynic

cynosure (**sin**-oh-zyure) *n literary* a centre of interest or attention [Greek *Kunosoura* dog's tail (name of the constellation of Ursa Minor)]

cypher (**sife**-er) *n, vb* same as **cipher**

cypress *n* **1** an evergreen tree with dark green leaves **2** the wood of this tree [Greek *kuparissos*]

Cypriot *adj* **1** of Cyprus ▷*n* **2** a person from Cyprus **3** the dialect of Greek spoken in Cyprus

Cyrillic *adj* of the Slavic alphabet devised supposedly by Saint Cyril, now used primarily for Russian and Bulgarian

cyst (**sist**) *n* **1** *pathol* an abnormal membranous sac containing fluid or diseased matter **2** *anatomy* any normal sac in the body [Greek *kustis* pouch, bag]

cystic fibrosis *n* a congenital disease, usually affecting young children, which causes breathing disorders and malfunctioning of the pancreas

cystitis (siss-**tite**-iss) *n* inflammation of the bladder, causing a desire to urinate frequently, accompanied by a burning sensation

-cyte *combining form* indicating a cell: *leucocyte* [Greek *kutos* vessel]

cytology (site-**ol**-a-jee) *n* the study of plant and animal cells **cytological** *adj* **cytologically** *adv* **cytologist** *n*

cytoplasm *n* the protoplasm of a cell excluding the nucleus **cytoplasmic** *adj*

czar (**zahr**) *n* same as **tsar**

Czech *adj* **1** of the Czech Republic ▷*n* **2** a person from the Czech Republic **3** the language of the Czech Republic

Dd

d 1 *physics* density 2 deci-
D 1 *music* the second note of the scale of C major 2 *chem* deuterium 3 the Roman numeral for 500
d. 1 *Brit & NZ* (before decimalization) penny *or* pennies 2 died 3 daughter
dab[1] *vb* **dabbing, dabbed** 1 to pat lightly and quickly 2 to apply with short tapping strokes: *dabbing antiseptic on cuts* ▷ *n* 3 a small amount of something soft or moist 4 a light stroke or tap 5 **dabs** *slang, chiefly Brit* fingerprints [imitative]
dab[2] *n* a small European flatfish covered with rough toothed scales [Anglo-French *dabbe*]
dabble *vb* **-bling, -bled** 1 to be involved in an activity in a superficial way: *she dabbles in right-wing politics* 2 to splash (one's toes or fingers) in water [probably from Dutch *dabbelen*] **dabbler** *n*
dab hand *n informal* a person who is particularly skilled at something: *a dab hand with a needle and thread* [origin unknown]
dace *n, pl* **dace** *or* **daces** a European freshwater fish of the carp family [Old French *dars* dart]
dachshund *n* a small dog with short legs and a long body [German *Dachs* badger + *Hund* dog]
dactyl *n prosody* a metrical foot of three syllables, one long followed by two short [Greek *daktulos* finger, comparing the finger's three joints to the three syllables] **dactylic** *adj*
dad *or* **daddy** *n informal* father [from child's *da da*]
Dada *or* **Dadaism** *n* an art movement of the early 20th century that systematically used arbitrary and absurd concepts [French: hobbyhorse] **Dadaist** *n, adj*
daddy-longlegs *n informal* 1 *Brit* crane fly 2 a small web-spinning spider with long legs
dado (day-doe) *n, pl* **-does** *or* **-dos** 1 the lower part of an interior wall, often separated by a rail, that is decorated differently from the upper part 2 *archit* the part of a pedestal between the base and the cornice [Italian: die, die-shaped pedestal]
daemon (deem-on) *n* same as **demon**
daffodil *n* 1 a spring plant with yellow trumpet-shaped flowers ▷ *adj* 2 brilliant yellow [variant of Latin *asphodelus* asphodel]
daft *adj informal, chiefly Brit* 1 foolish or crazy 2 **daft about** very enthusiastic about: *he's daft about football* [Old English *gedæfte* gentle, foolish]
dag *Austral & NZ* ▷ *n* 1 the dried dung on a sheep's rear 2 *informal* an amusing person ▷ *pl n* 3 **rattle one's dags** *informal* hurry up ▷ *vb* 4 to remove the dags from a sheep [origin unknown]
dagga (duhh-a) *n S African* a local name for marijuana [probably from Khoikhoi *daxa*]
dagger *n* 1 a short knifelike weapon with a double-edged pointed blade 2 a character (†) used to indicate a cross-reference 3 **at daggers drawn** in a state of open hostility 4 **look daggers** to glare with hostility [origin unknown]
daggy *adj* **-gier, -giest** *Austral & NZ informal* 1 untidy; dishevelled 2 eccentric
daguerreotype (dag-gair-oh-type) *n* a type of early photograph produced on chemically treated silver [after L. *Daguerre*, its inventor]
dahlia (day-lya) *n* a garden plant with showy flowers [after Anders *Dahl*, botanist]
Dáil Éireann (doil air-in) *or* **Dáil** *n* (in the Republic of Ireland) the lower chamber of parliament [Irish *dáil* assembly + *Éireann* of Ireland]
daily *adj* 1 occurring every day or every weekday: *there have been daily airdrops of food, blankets, and water* 2 of or relating to a single day or to one day at a time: *her home help comes in on a daily basis; exercise has become part of our daily lives* ▷ *adv* 3 every day ▷ *n, pl* **-lies** 4 *Brit & Austral* a daily newspaper 5 *Brit informal* a person employed to keep someone's house clean [Old English *dæglic*]
dainty *adj* **-tier, -tiest** 1 delicate, pretty, or elegant: *dainty little pink shoes* ▷ *n, pl* **-ties** 2 *Brit* a small choice cake or sweet [Old French *deintié*] **daintily** *adv*
daiquiri (dak-eer-ee) *n, pl* **-ris** an iced drink containing rum, lime juice, and sugar [after *Daiquiri*, town in Cuba]
dairy *n, pl* **dairies** 1 a company or shop that sells milk and milk products 2 a place where milk and cream are stored or made into butter and cheese 3 food containing milk or milk products: *I can't eat dairy* 4 *NZ* a small shop selling groceries and milk often outside normal trading hours ▷ *adj* 5 of milk or milk products: *dairy produce* [Old English *dǣge* servant girl]
dairy cattle *n* cows reared mainly for their milk
dairy farm *n* a farm where cows are kept mainly for their milk
dairymaid *n Brit, Austral & NZ archaic* a woman employed to milk cows
dairyman *n Brit, Austral & S African* a man employed to look after cows
dais (day-iss) *n* a raised platform in a hall or meeting place used by a speaker [Old French *deis*]
daisy *n, pl* **-sies** a small low-growing flower with a yellow centre and pinkish-white petals [Old English *dægesēge* day's eye]
daisy chain *n* a string of daisies joined together by their stems to make a necklace
daisywheel *n* a flat disc in a computer printer with radiating spokes for printing characters
dal[1] *n* same as **dhal**
dal[2] decalitre(s)
Dalai Lama *n* the chief lama and (until 1959) ruler of Tibet
dale *n* an open valley [Old English *dæl*]
dalliance *n old-fashioned* flirtation
dally *vb* **-lies, -lying, -lied** 1 *old-fashioned* to waste time or dawdle 2 **dally with** to deal frivolously with: *to dally with someone's affections* [Anglo-French *dalier* to gossip]
Dalmatian *n* a large dog with a smooth white coat and black spots
dam[1] *n* 1 a barrier built across a river to create a lake 2 a lake created by such a barrier ▷ *vb*

damming, dammed **3** to block up (a river) by a dam [probably from Middle Low German]

dam² *n* the female parent of an animal such as a sheep or horse [variant of *dame*]

dam³ decametre(s)

damage *vb* **-aging, -aged** **1** to harm or injure ▷ *n* **2** injury or harm caused to a person or thing **3** *informal* cost: *what's the damage?* [Latin *damnum* injury, loss] **damaging** *adj*

damages *pl n law* money awarded as compensation for injury or loss

damask *n* a heavy fabric with a pattern woven into it, used for tablecloths, curtains, etc. [*Damascus*, where fabric originally made]

dame *n slang* a woman [Latin *domina* lady]

Dame *n* (in Britain) the title of a woman who has been awarded the Order of the British Empire or another order of chivalry

damn *interj* **1** *slang* an exclamation of annoyance ▷ *adv* **2** *slang* Also: **damned** extremely ▷ *adj* **3** *slang* Also: **damned** extreme: *a damn nuisance* ▷ *vb* **4** to condemn as bad or worthless **5** to curse **6** (of God) to condemn to hell or eternal punishment **7** to prove (someone) guilty **8** **damn with faint praise** to praise so unenthusiastically that the effect is condemnation ▷ *n* **9** **not give a damn** *informal* not to care [Latin *damnum* loss, injury] **damning** *adj*

damnable *adj* very unpleasant or annoying **damnably** *adv*

damnation *interj* **1** an exclamation of anger ▷ *n* **2** *theol* eternal punishment

damned *adj* **1** condemned to hell ▷ *adv, adj slang* **2** extreme or extremely: *a damned good try* **3** used to indicate amazement or refusal: *I'm damned if I'll do it!*

damnedest *n* **do one's damnedest** *informal* to do one's best: *I'm doing my damnedest to make myself clear*

damp *adj* **1** slightly wet ▷ *n* **2** slight wetness; moisture ▷ *vb* **3** to make slightly wet **4** **damp down** **A** to reduce the intensity of (someone's emotions or reactions): *they attempted to damp down protests* **B** to reduce the flow of air to (a fire) to make it burn more slowly [Middle Low German: steam] **damply** *adv* **dampness** *n*

dampcourse *or* **damp-proof course** *n* a layer of waterproof material built into the base of a wall to prevent moisture rising

dampen *vb* **1** to reduce the intensity of **2** to make damp

damper *n* **1** **put a damper on** to produce a depressing or inhibiting effect on **2** a movable plate to regulate the draught in a stove or furnace **3** the pad in a piano or harpsichord that deadens the vibration of each string as its key is released **4** *chiefly Austral & NZ* any of various unleavened loaves and scones, typically cooked on an open fire

damsel *n archaic or poetic* a young woman [Old French *damoisele*]

damson *n* a small blue-black edible plumlike fruit that grows on a tree [Latin *prunum damascenum* Damascus plum]

dan *n judo & karate* **1** any of the ten black-belt grades of proficiency **2** a competitor entitled to dan grading [Japanese]

dance *vb* **dancing, danced** **1** to move the feet and body rhythmically in time to music **2** to perform (a particular dance): *to dance a tango* **3** to skip or leap **4** to move in a rhythmic way: *their reflection danced in the black waters* **5** **dance attendance on someone** to carry out someone's slightest wish in an overeager manner ▷ *n* **6** a social meeting arranged for dancing **7** a series of rhythmic steps and movements in time to music **8** a piece of music in the rhythm of a particular dance [Old French *dancier*] **dancer** *n* **dancing** *n, adj*

dance floor *n* an area of a nightclub, etc. that is set aside for dancing

dancehall *n* a style of dance-oriented reggae

D and C *n med* dilatation of the cervix and curettage of the uterus: a minor operation to clear the womb or remove tissue for diagnosis

dandelion *n* a wild plant with yellow rayed flowers and deeply notched leaves [Old French *dent de lion* tooth of a lion, referring to its leaves]

dander *n* **get one's dander up** *Brit, Austral & NZ slang* to become angry [from *dandruff*]

dandified *adj* dressed like or resembling a dandy

dandle *vb* **-dling, -dled** to move (a young child) up and down on one's knee [origin unknown]

dandruff *n* loose scales of dry dead skin shed from the scalp [origin unknown]

dandy *n, pl* **-dies** **1** a man who is greatly concerned with the elegance of his appearance ▷ *adj* **-dier, -diest** **2** *informal* very good or fine [origin unknown]

dandy-brush *n* a stiff brush used for grooming a horse

Dane *n* a person from Denmark

danger *n* **1** the possibility that someone may be injured or killed **2** someone or something that may cause injury or harm **3** a likelihood that something unpleasant will happen: *the danger of flooding* [Middle English *daunger* power, hence power to inflict injury]

danger money *n* extra money paid to compensate for the risks involved in dangerous work

dangerous *adj* likely or able to cause injury or harm **dangerously** *adv*

dangle *vb* **-gling, -gled** **1** to hang loosely **2** to display (something attractive) as an enticement [probably imitative]

Danish *adj* **1** of Denmark ▷ *n* **2** the language of Denmark

Danish blue *n* a white cheese with blue veins and a strong flavour

Danish pastry *n* a rich puff pastry filled with apple, almond paste, etc. and topped with icing

dank *adj* (esp. of cellars or caves) unpleasantly damp and chilly [probably from Old Norse]

dapper *adj* (of a man) neat in appearance and slight in build [Middle Dutch]

dappled *adj* **1** marked with spots of a different colour; mottled **2** covered in patches of light and shadow [origin unknown]

dapple-grey *n* a horse with a grey coat and darker-coloured spots

Darby and Joan *n chiefly Brit* a happily married elderly couple [couple in 18th-century ballad]

dare *vb* **daring, dared** **1** to be courageous enough to try (to do something) **2** to challenge (someone) to do something risky **3 I dare say A** it is quite possible **B** probably ▷ *n* **4** a challenge to do something risky [Old English *durran*]

USAGE When used negatively or interrogatively, *dare* does not usually add *-s: he dare not come; dare she come?* When used negatively in the past tense, however, *dare* usually adds *-d: he dared not come.*

daredevil *n* **1** a recklessly bold person ▷ *adj* **2** recklessly bold or daring

daring *adj* **1** willing to do things that may be dangerous ▷ *n* **2** the courage to do things that may be dangerous **daringly** *adv*

dark *adj* **1** having little or no light **2** (of a colour) reflecting little light: *dark brown* **3** (of hair or skin) brown or black **4** (of thoughts or ideas) gloomy or sad **5** sinister or evil: *a dark deed* **6** sullen or angry: *a dark scowl* **7** secret or mysterious: *keep it dark* ▷ *n* **8** absence of light; darkness **9** night or nightfall **10 in the dark** in ignorance [Old English *deorc*] **darkly** *adv* **darkness** *n*

dark age *n* a period of ignorance or barbarism

Dark Ages *pl n* the period of European history between 500 and 1000 AD

darken *vb* **1** to make or become dark or darker **2** to make gloomy, angry, or sad

dark horse *n* a person who reveals little about himself or herself, esp. someone who has unexpected talents

darkroom *n* a darkened room in which photographic film is developed

darling *n* **1** a person very much loved: used as a term of address **2** a favourite: *the darling of the gossip columns* ▷ *adj* **3** beloved **4** pleasing: *a darling film* [Old English *dēorling*]

darmstadtium *n* a radioactive element produced synthetically in small quantities. Symbol: **Ds** [after *Darmstadt*, the city in Germany]

darn¹ *vb* **1** to mend a hole in (a knitted garment) with a series of interwoven stitches ▷ *n* **2** a patch of darned work on a garment [origin unknown]

darn² *interj, adj, adv, vb, n euphemistic* same as **damn**

darnel *n* a weed that grows in grain fields [origin unknown]

dart *n* **1** a small narrow pointed missile that is thrown or shot, as in the game of darts **2** a sudden quick movement **3** a tapered tuck made in dressmaking ▷ *vb* **4** to move or throw swiftly and suddenly [Germanic] **darting** *adj*

dartboard *n* a circular board used as the target in the game of darts

darts *n* a game in which darts are thrown at a dartboard

Darwinism *or* **Darwinian theory** *n* the theory of the origin of animal and plant species by evolution [after Charles *Darwin*, English naturalist] **Darwinian** *adj, n* **Darwinist** *n, adj*

dash *vb* **1** to move hastily; rush **2** to hurl; crash: *deep-sea rollers dashing spray over jagged rocks* **3** to frustrate: *prospects for peace have been dashed* ▷ *n* **4** a sudden quick movement **5** a small amount: *a dash of milk* **6** a mixture of style and courage: *the commander's dash did not impress him* **7** the punctuation mark (—), used to indicate a change of subject **8** the symbol (–), used in combination with the symbol *dot* (.) in Morse code ▷ See also **dash off** [Middle English *daschen, dassen*]

dashboard *n* the instrument panel in a car, boat, or aircraft

dasher *n Canad* one of the boards surrounding an ice-hockey rink

dashing *adj* stylish and attractive: *a splendidly dashing character*

dash off *vb* to write down or finish off hastily

dassie *n S African* a hyrax, esp. a rock hyrax [Afrikaans]

dastardly *adj old-fashioned* mean and cowardly [Middle English *dastard* dullard]

dasyure (dass-ee-your) *n* a small marsupial of Australia, New Guinea, and adjacent islands

dat. dative

data *n* **1** a series of observations, measurements, or facts; information **2** the numbers, digits, characters, and symbols operated on by a computer [Latin: (things) given]

USAGE Although *data* is now usually treated as a singular noun, it was originally a plural and is still treated as such in much scientific and technical writing.

database *n* **1** a store of information in a form that can be easily handled by a computer **2** a large store of information: *a database of knowledge*

data capture *n* a process for converting information into a form that can be handled by a computer

data processing *n* a sequence of operations performed on data, esp. by a computer, in order to extract or interpret information

date¹ *n* **1** a specified day of the month **2** the particular day or year when an event happened **3 A** an appointment, esp. with a person to whom one is romantically or sexually attached **B** the person with whom the appointment is made **4 to date** up to now ▷ *vb* **dating, dated 5** to mark (a letter, cheque, etc.) with the date **6** to assign a date of occurrence or creation to **7** to reveal the age of: *that dress dates her* **8** to make or become old-fashioned: *it's the freshest look this year but may date quickly* **9** *informal, chiefly US & Canad* to be a boyfriend or girlfriend of **10 date from** *or* **date back to** to have originated at (a specified time) [Latin *dare* to give, as in *epistula data Romae* letter handed over at Rome]

USAGE See at **year**.

date² *n* the dark-brown, sweet-tasting fruit of the date palm [Greek *daktulos* finger]

dated *adj* unfashionable; outmoded

dateless *adj* likely to remain fashionable or interesting regardless of age

dateline *n journalism* information placed at the top of an article stating the time and place the article was written

Date Line *n* short for **International Date Line**

date palm *n* a tall palm grown in tropical regions for its fruit

date rape *n* the act of someone raping a person while they are on a date together

dative *n grammar* the grammatical case in certain languages that expresses the indirect object [Latin *dativus*]

datum *n, pl* **-ta** a single piece of information usually in the form of a fact or statistic [Latin: something given]
daub *vb* **1** to smear (paint or mud) quickly or carelessly over a surface **2** to paint (a picture) clumsily or badly ▷ *n* **3** a crude or badly done painting: *a typical child's daub* [Old French *dauber* to paint]
daughter *n* **1** a female child **2** a girl or woman who comes from a certain place or is connected with a certain thing: *a daughter of the church* ▷ *adj* **3** *biol* denoting a cell, chromosome, etc. produced by the division of one of its own kind **4** *physics* (of a nuclide) formed from another nuclide by radioactive decay [Old English *dohtor*] **daughterly** *adj*
daughter-in-law *n, pl* **daughters-in-law** the wife of one's son or daughter
daunting *adj* intimidating or worrying: *this project grows more daunting every day* [Latin *domitare* to tame]
dauntless *adj* fearless; not discouraged
dauphin (daw-fin) *n* (formerly) the eldest son of the king of France [Old French: originally a family name]
davenport *n* **1** *chiefly Brit* a writing desk with drawers at the side **2** *Austral, US & Canad* a large sofa [sense 1 supposedly after Captain *Davenport*, who commissioned the first ones]
davit (dav-vit) *n* a crane, usually one of a pair, on the side of a ship for lowering or hoisting a lifeboat [Anglo-French *daviot*, from *Davi* David]
Davy Jones's locker *n* the ocean's bottom, regarded as the grave of those lost or buried at sea [origin unknown]
Davy lamp *n* same as **safety lamp** [after Sir Humphrey *Davy*, chemist]
dawdle *vb* **-dling, -dled** to walk slowly or lag behind [origin unknown]
dawn *n* **1** daybreak **2** the beginning of something ▷ *vb* **3** to begin to grow light after the night **4** to begin to develop or appear **5 dawn on** *or* **upon** to become apparent (to someone) [Old English *dagian* to dawn]
dawn chorus *n* the singing of birds at dawn
day *n* **1** the period of 24 hours from one midnight to the next **2** the period of light between sunrise and sunset **3** the part of a day occupied with regular activity, esp. work **4** a period or point in time: *in days gone by; in Shakespeare's day* **5** a day of special observance: *Christmas Day* **6** a time of success or recognition: *his day will come* **7 all in a day's work** part of one's normal activity **8 at the end of the day** in the final reckoning **9 call it a day** to stop work or other activity **10 day in, day out** every day without changing **11 that'll be the day** **A** that is most unlikely to happen **B** I look forward to that. ▷ Related adjective: **diurnal** [Old English *dæg*]
daybreak *n* the time in the morning when light first appears
daycare *n* care that is provided during the working day for people who cannot look after themselves, such as young children or people who are ill
day centre *n* a place that provides care where elderly or disabled people can spend the day
daydream *n* **1** a pleasant fantasy indulged in while awake ▷ *vb* **2** to indulge in idle fantasy **daydreamer** *n*
Day-Glo *adj* (of a colour) luminous in daylight: *Day-Glo pink* [from a trade name for a brand of fluorescent paint]
daylight *n* **1** light from the sun **2** daytime **3** daybreak **4 see daylight** to realize that the end of a difficult task is approaching ▷ See also **daylights**
daylight robbery *n informal* blatant overcharging
daylights *pl n informal* **1 beat the living daylights out of someone** to beat someone soundly **2 scare the living daylights out of someone** to frighten someone greatly
daylight-saving time *n* time set one hour ahead of the local standard time, to provide extra daylight in the evening in summer
Day of Atonement *n* same as **Yom Kippur**
day release *n Brit* a system whereby workers go to college one day a week for vocational training
day return *n* a reduced fare for a train or bus journey travelling both ways in one day
day room *n* a communal living room in a hospital or similar institution
daytime *n* the time from sunrise to sunset
day-to-day *adj* routine; everyday
daze *vb* **dazing, dazed** **1** to cause to be in a state of confusion or shock ▷ *n* **2** a state of confusion or shock: *in a daze* [Old Norse *dasa*] **dazed** *adj*
dazzle *vb* **-zling, -zled** **1** to impress greatly: *she was dazzled by his wit* **2** to blind for a short time by sudden excessive light: *he passed two cars and they dazzled him with their headlights* ▷ *n* **3** bright light that dazzles [from *daze*] **dazzling** *adj* **dazzlingly** *adv*
dB *or* **db** decibel(s)
Db *chem* dubnium
DBE Dame (Commander of the Order) of the British Empire
DC **1** direct current **2** District of Columbia
DD Doctor of Divinity
D-day *n* the day selected for the start of some operation [after *D(ay)-day*, the day of the Allied invasion of Europe on June 6, 1944]
DDS *or* **DDSc** Doctor of Dental Surgery *or* Science
DDT *n* dichlorodiphenyltrichloroethane; an insecticide, now banned in many countries
DE Delaware
de- *prefix* **1** indicating removal: *dethrone* **2** indicating reversal: *declassify* **3** indicating departure from: *decamp* [Latin]
deacon *n Christianity* **1** (in episcopal churches) an ordained minister ranking immediately below a priest **2** (in some Protestant churches) a lay official who assists the minister [Greek *diakonos* servant]
deactivate *vb* **-vating, -vated** to make (a bomb or other explosive device) harmless
dead *adj* **1** no longer alive **2** no longer in use or finished: *a dead language; a dead match* **3** unresponsive **4** (of a limb) numb **5** complete or absolute: *there was dead silence* **6** *informal* very tired **7** (of a place) lacking activity **8** *electronics* **A** drained of electric charge **B** not connected to a source of electric charge **9** *sport* (of a ball) out

of play **10 dead from the neck up** *informal* stupid **11 dead to the world** *informal* fast asleep ▷ *n* **12** a period during which coldness or darkness is most intense: *the dead of winter* ▷ *adv* **13** *informal* extremely: *dead easy* **14** suddenly and abruptly: *stop dead* **15 dead on** exactly right [Old English *dēad*]

deadbeat *n informal* a lazy or socially undesirable person

dead beat *adj informal* exhausted

dead duck *n slang* something that is doomed to failure

d

deaden *vb* to make (something) less intense: *drugs deaden the pain; heavy curtains deadened the echo* **deadening** *adj*

dead end *n* **1** a cul-de-sac **2** a situation in which further progress is impossible: *efforts to free the hostages had reached a dead end*

deadhead *n US & Canad* **1** *informal* a person who does not pay on a bus, at a game, etc. **2** *informal* a commercial vehicle travelling empty **3** *slang* a dull person **4** a totally or partially submerged log floating in a lake

dead heat *n* a tie for first place between two or more participants in a race or contest

dead letter *n* **1** a letter that cannot be delivered or returned due to lack of information **2** a law or rule that is no longer enforced

deadline *n* a time or date by which a job or task must be completed

deadlock *n* a point in a dispute at which no agreement can be reached

deadlocked *adj* having reached a deadlock

dead loss *n informal* a useless person or thing

deadly *adj* **-lier, -liest 1** likely to cause death: *deadly poison* **2** *informal* extremely boring ▷ *adv, adj* **3** like or suggestive of death: *deadly pale* ▷ *adv* **4** extremely: *she was being deadly serious*

deadly nightshade *n* a poisonous plant with purple bell-shaped flowers and black berries

dead man's handle *or* **dead man's pedal** *n* a safety device which only allows equipment to operate when a handle or pedal is being pressed

dead march *n* solemn funeral music played to accompany a procession

dead-nettle *n* a plant with leaves like nettles but without stinging hairs

deadpan *adj* **1** deliberately emotionless ▷ *adv* **2** in a deliberately emotionless manner

dead reckoning *n* a method of establishing one's position using the distance and direction travelled

dead set *adv* firmly decided: *he is dead set on leaving*

dead soldier *or* **dead marine** *n informal* an empty beer or spirit bottle

dead weight *n* **1** a heavy weight or load **2** the difference between the loaded and the unloaded weights of a ship

dead wood *n informal* people or things that are no longer useful

deaf *adj* **1** unable to hear **2 deaf to** refusing to listen or take notice of [Old English *dēaf*] **deafness** *n*

USAGE See at **disabled**.

deaf-and-dumb *adj old-fashioned, offensive* unable to hear or speak

deafblind *adj* unable to hear or see

deafen *vb* to make deaf, esp. momentarily by a loud noise **deafening** *adj*

deaf-mute *n old-fashioned, offensive* a person who is unable to hear or speak

deal¹ *n* **1** an agreement or transaction **2** a particular type of treatment received: *a fair deal* **3** a large amount: *the land alone is worth a good deal* **4** *cards* a player's turn to distribute the cards **5 big deal** *slang* an important matter: often used sarcastically ▷ *vb* **dealing, dealt** (**delt**) **6** to inflict (a blow) on **7** *slang* to sell any illegal drug **8 deal in** to engage in commercially **9 deal out** to apportion or distribute ▷ See also **deal with** [Old English *dǣlan*]

deal² *n* **1** a plank of softwood timber **2** the sawn wood of various coniferous trees [Middle Low German *dele* plank]

dealbreaker *n informal* an issue that prevents an agreement from being reached or that nullifies an existing agreement

dealer *n* **1** a person or organization whose business involves buying and selling things **2** *slang* a person who sells illegal drugs **3** *cards* the person who distributes the cards

dealings *pl n* business relations with a person or organization

dealt *vb* the past of **deal¹**

deal with *vb* **1** to take action on: *he was not competent to deal with the legal aspects* **2** to be concerned with: *I do not wish to deal with specifics* **3** to do business with

dean *n* **1** the chief administrative official of a college or university faculty **2** *chiefly Church of England* the chief administrator of a cathedral or collegiate church [Late Latin *decanus* one set over ten people]

deanery *n, pl* **-eries 1** a place where a dean lives **2** the parishes presided over by a rural dean

dear *n* **1** (often used in direct address) someone regarded with affection ▷ *adj* **2** beloved; precious **3 A** highly priced **B** charging high prices **4** a form of address used at the beginning of a letter before the name of the recipient: *Dear Mr Anderson* **5 dear to** important or close to ▷ *interj* **6** an exclamation of surprise or dismay: *oh dear, I've broken it* ▷ *adv* **7** dearly: *her errors have cost her dear* [Old English *dēore*] **dearly** *adv*

dearth (**dirth**) *n* an inadequate amount; scarcity [Middle English *derthe*]

death *n* **1** the permanent end of life in a person or animal **2** an instance of this: *his sudden death* **3** ending or destruction **4 at death's door** likely to die soon **5 catch one's death (of cold)** *informal* to contract a severe cold **6 like death warmed up** *informal* looking or feeling very ill or very tired **7 put to death** to execute **8 to death A** until dead **B** very much: *I had probably scared him to death* [Old English *dēath*]

deathbed *n* the bed in which a person dies or is about to die

deathblow *n* a thing or event that destroys hope

death certificate *n* a document signed by a doctor certifying the death of a person and stating the cause of death if known

death duty *n* (in Britain) the former name for **inheritance tax**

death knell *n* something that heralds death or destruction
deathless *adj* everlasting because of fine qualities: *highbrow, deathless, and often endless prose*
deathly *adj* **1** resembling death: *a deathly pallor* **2** deadly
death mask *n* a cast taken from the face of a person who has recently died
death rate *n* the ratio of deaths in an area or group to the population of that area or group
death row *n US* part of a prison where convicts awaiting execution are imprisoned
death's-head *n* a human skull or a picture of one used to represent death or danger
death trap *n* a place or vehicle considered very unsafe
death warrant *n* **1** the official authorization for carrying out a sentence of death **2 sign one's (own) death warrant** to cause one's own destruction
deathwatch beetle *n* a beetle that bores into wood and produces a tapping sound
deb *n informal* a debutante
debacle (day-**bah**-kl) *n* something that ends in a disastrous failure, esp. because it has not been properly planned [French]
debar *vb* **-barring, -barred** to prevent (someone) from doing something
USAGE See at **disbar.**
debase *vb* **-basing, -based** to lower in quality, character, or value [see DE-, BASE²] **debasement** *n*
debatable *adj* not absolutely certain: *her motives are highly debatable*
debate *n* **1** a discussion **2** a formal discussion, as in a parliament, in which opposing arguments are put forward ▷ *vb* **-bating, -bated 3** to discuss (something) formally **4** to consider (possible courses of action) [Old French *debatre*]
debauch (dib-**bawch**) *vb* to make someone bad or corrupt, esp. sexually [Old French *desbaucher* to corrupt]
debauched *adj* immoral; sexually corrupt
debauchery *n* excessive drunkenness or sexual activity
debenture *n* a long-term bond, bearing fixed interest and usually unsecured, issued by a company or governmental agency [Latin *debentur mihi* there are owed to me] **debentured** *adj*
debenture stock *n* shares issued by a company, guaranteeing a fixed return at regular intervals
debilitate *vb* **-tating, -tated** to make gradually weaker [Latin *debilis* weak] **debilitating** *adj* **debilitation** *n*
debility *n, pl* **-ties** a state of weakness, esp. caused by illness
debit *n* **1** the money, or a record of the money, withdrawn from a person's bank account **2** *accounting* **A** acknowledgment of a sum owing by entry on the left side of an account **B** an entry or the total of entries on this side ▷ *vb* **-iting, -ited 3** to charge (an account) with a debt: *they had debited our account* **4** *accounting* to record (an item) as a debit in an account [Latin *debitum* debt]
debit card *n* a card issued by a bank or other financial institution enabling customers to pay for goods by inserting it into a computer-controlled device at the place of sale, which is connected through the telephone network to the financial institution
debonair *or* **debonnaire** *adj* (of a man) confident, charming, and well-dressed [Old French]
debouch *vb* **1** (esp. of troops) to move into a more open space **2** (of a river, glacier, etc.) to flow into a larger area or body [Old French *dé-* from + *bouche* mouth] **debouchment** *n*
debrief *vb* to interrogate (a soldier, diplomat, astronaut, etc.) on the completion of a mission **debriefing** *n*
debris (**deb**-ree) *n* **1** fragments of something destroyed; rubble **2** a mass of loose stones and earth [French]
debt *n* **1** a sum of money owed **2 bad debt** a debt that is unlikely to be paid **3 in debt** owing money **4 in someone's debt** grateful to someone for his or her help: *I couldn't have managed without you – I'm in your debt* [Latin *debitum*]
debt of honour *n* a debt that is morally but not legally binding
debtor *n* a person who owes money
debug *vb* **-bugging, -bugged** *informal* **1** to locate and remove defects in (a computer program) **2** to remove concealed microphones from (a room or telephone)
debunk *vb informal* to expose the falseness of: *many commonly held myths are debunked by the book* [DE- + BUNK²] **debunker** *n*
debut (**day**-byoo) *n* the first public appearance of a performer [French]
debutante (**day**-byoo-tont) *n* a young upper-class woman who is formally presented to society [French]
Dec. December
decade *n* a period of ten years [Greek *deka* ten]
decadence (**deck**-a-denss) *n* a decline in morality or culture [Medieval Latin *decadentia* a falling away] **decadent** *adj*
decaf (**dee**-kaf) *informal* ▷ *n* **1** decaffeinated coffee ▷ *adj* **2** decaffeinated
decaffeinated (dee-**kaf**-fin-ate-id) *adj* with the caffeine removed: *decaffeinated tea*
decagon *n geom* a figure with ten sides [Greek *deka* ten + *gōnia* angle] **decagonal** *adj*
decahedron (deck-a-**heed**-ron) *n* a solid figure with ten plane faces [Greek *deka* ten + *hedra* base] **decahedral** *adj*
decalitre *or US* **decaliter** *n* a measure of volume equivalent to 10 litres
Decalogue *n* same as **Ten Commandments** [Greek *deka* ten + *logos* word]
decametre *or US* **decameter** *n* a unit of length equal to ten metres
decamp *vb* to leave secretly or suddenly
decant *vb* **1** to pour (a liquid, esp. wine) from one container to another **2** *chiefly Brit* to rehouse (people) while their homes are being renovated [Medieval Latin *de-* from + *canthus* spout, rim]
decanter *n* a stoppered bottle into which a drink is poured for serving
decapitate *vb* **-tating, -tated** to behead [Latin *de-* from + *caput* head] **decapitation** *n*

d

decapod *n* **1** a creature, such as a crab, with five pairs of walking limbs **2** a creature, such as a squid, with eight short tentacles and two longer ones [Greek *deka* ten + *pous* foot]

decarbonize *or* **-ise** *vb* **-izing, -ized** *or* **-ising, -ised** to remove carbon from (an internal-combustion engine) **decarbonization** *or* **-isation** *n*

decathlon *n* an athletic contest in which each athlete competes in ten different events [Greek *deka* ten + *athlon* contest] **decathlete** *n*

decay *vb* **1** to decline gradually in health, prosperity, or quality **2** to rot or cause to rot **3** *physics* (of an atomic nucleus) to undergo radioactive disintegration ▷ *n* **4** the process of something rotting: *too much sugar can cause tooth decay* **5** the state brought about by this process **6** *physics* disintegration of a nucleus, occurring spontaneously or as a result of electron capture [Latin *de-* from + *cadere* to fall]

d

decease *n formal* death [Latin *decedere* to depart]

deceased *formal* ▷ *adj* **1** dead ▷ *n* **2** a dead person: *the deceased*

deceit *n* behaviour intended to deceive

deceitful *adj* full of deceit

deceive *vb* **-ceiving, -ceived 1** to mislead by lying **2 deceive oneself** to refuse to acknowledge something one knows to be true **3** to be unfaithful to (one's sexual partner) [Latin *decipere* to ensnare, cheat]

decelerate *vb* **-ating, -ated** to slow down [DE- + (AC)CELERATE] **deceleration** *n*

December *n* the twelfth month of the year [Latin: the tenth month (the Roman year originally began with March)]

decencies *pl n* generally accepted standards of good behaviour

decency *n* conformity to the prevailing standards of what is right

decennial *adj* **1** lasting for ten years **2** occurring every ten years

decent *adj* **1** conforming to an acceptable standard or quality: *a decent living wage; she's made a few decent films* **2** polite or respectable: *he's a decent man* **3** fitting or proper: *that's the decent thing to do* **4** conforming to conventions of sexual behaviour **5** *informal* kind; generous: *she was pretty decent to me* [Latin *decens* suitable] **decently** *adv*

decentralize *or* **-ise** *vb* **-izing, -ized** *or* **-ising, -ised** to reorganize into smaller local units **decentralization** *or* **-isation** *n*

deception *n* **1** the act of deceiving someone or the state of being deceived **2** something that deceives; trick

deceptive *adj* likely or designed to deceive **deceptively** *adv* **deceptiveness** *n*

deci- *combining form* denoting one tenth: *decimetre* [Latin *decimus* tenth]

decibel *n* a unit for comparing two power levels or measuring the intensity of a sound [DECI- + BEL]

decide *vb* **-ciding, -cided 1** to reach a decision: *we must decide on suitable action; he decided to stay on* **2** to cause to reach a decision **3** to settle (a question): *possible profits decided the issue* **4** to influence the outcome of (a contest) decisively: *the goal that decided the match came just before half-time* [Latin *decidere* to cut off]

decided *adj* **1** definite or noticeable: *a decided improvement* **2** strong and definite: *he has decided views on the matter* **decidedly** *adv*

deciduous *adj* **1** (of a tree) shedding all leaves annually **2** (of antlers or teeth) being shed at the end of a period of growth [Latin *deciduus* falling off]

decilitre *or US* **deciliter** *n* a measure of volume equivalent to one tenth of a litre

decimal *n* **1** a fraction written in the form of a dot followed by one or more numbers, for example .2 = $^2/_{10}$ ▷ *adj* **2** relating to or using powers of ten **3** expressed as a decimal [Latin *decima* a tenth]

decimal currency *n* a system of currency in which the units are parts or powers of ten

decimalize *or* **-ise** *vb* **-izing, -ized** *or* **-ising, -ised** to change (a system or number) to the decimal system **decimalization** *or* **-isation** *n*

decimal point *n* the dot between the unit and the fraction of a number in the decimal system

decimal system *n* a number system with a base of ten, in which numbers are expressed by combinations of the digits 0 to 9

decimate *vb* **-mating, -mated** to destroy or kill a large proportion of [Latin *decimare*] **decimation** *n*

> **USAGE** You would talk about the whole of something being *decimated*, not a part: *disease decimated the population*, not *disease decimated most of the population*.

decimetre *or US* **decimeter** *n* a unit of length equal to one tenth of a metre

decipher *vb* **1** to make out the meaning of (something obscure or illegible) **2** to convert from code into plain text **decipherable** *adj*

decision *n* **1** a choice or judgment made about something **2** the act of making up one's mind **3** the ability to make quick and definite decisions [Latin *decisio* a cutting off]

decisive *adj* **1** having great influence on the result of something: *the decisive goal was scored in the closing minutes* **2** having the ability to make quick decisions **decisively** *adv* **decisiveness** *n*

deck *n* **1** an area of a ship that forms a floor, at any level **2** a similar area in a bus **3** same as **tape deck 4** *US & Austral* a pack of playing cards **5 clear the decks** *informal* to prepare for action, as by removing obstacles ▷ *vb* **6** *slang* to knock (a person) to the ground [Middle Dutch *dec* a covering]

deck chair *n* a folding chair with a wooden frame and a canvas seat

decking *n* a wooden deck or platform, esp. one in a garden for deck chairs, etc.

deckle edge *n* a rough edge on paper, often left as ornamentation [the *deckle* is the frame that holds the pulp in paper making] **deckle-edged** *adj*

deck out *vb* to make more attractive by decorating: *the village was decked out in the blue-and-white flags*

declaim *vb* **1** to speak loudly and dramatically **2 declaim against** to protest against loudly and publicly [Latin *declamare*] **declamation** *n* **declamatory** *adj*

declaration *n* **1** a firm, emphatic statement **2** an official announcement or statement **declaratory** *adj*

declare *vb* **-claring, -clared 1** to state firmly and forcefully **2** to announce publicly or officially: *a state of emergency has been declared* **3** to state officially that (someone or something) is as specified: *he was declared fit to play* **4** to acknowledge (dutiable goods or income) for tax purposes **5** *cards* to decide (the trump suit) by making the winning bid **6** *cricket* to bring an innings to an end before the last batsman is out **7 declare for** *or* **against** to state one's support or opposition for something [Latin *declarare* to make clear]

declassify *vb* **-fies, -fying, -fied** to state officially that (information or a document) is no longer secret **declassification** *n*

declension *n grammar* changes in the form of nouns, pronouns, or adjectives to show case, number, and gender [Latin *declinatio* a bending aside, hence variation]

declination *n* **1** *astron* the angular distance of a star or planet north or south from the celestial equator **2** the angle made by a compass needle with the direction of the geographical north pole

decline *vb* **-clining, -clined 1** to become smaller, weaker, or less important **2** to politely refuse to accept or do (something) **3** *grammar* to list the inflections of (a noun, pronoun, or adjective) ▷ *n* **4** a gradual weakening or loss [Latin *declinare* to bend away]

declivity *n, pl* **-ties** a downward slope [Latin *declivitas*] **declivitous** *adj*

declutch *vb* to disengage the clutch of a motor vehicle

decoct *vb* to extract the essence from (a substance) by boiling [Latin *decoquere* to boil down] **decoction** *n*

decode *vb* **-coding, -coded** to convert from code into ordinary language **decoder** *n*

decoke *vb* **-coking, -coked** same as **decarbonize**

décolletage (day-kol-**tahzh**) *n* a low-cut dress or neckline [French]

décolleté (day-**kol**-tay) *adj* **1** (of a woman's garment) low-cut ▷ *n* **2** a low-cut neckline [French]

decommission *vb* to dismantle or remove from service (a nuclear reactor, weapon, ship, etc. which is no longer required)

decompose *vb* **-posing, -posed 1** to rot **2** to break up or separate into constituent parts **decomposition** *n*

decompress *vb* **1** to free from pressure **2** to return (a diver) to normal atmospheric pressure **decompression** *n*

decompression sickness *n* a disorder characterized by severe pain and difficulty in breathing caused by a sudden and sustained change in atmospheric pressure

decongestant *n* a drug that relieves nasal congestion

decontaminate *vb* **-nating, -nated** to make (a place or object) safe by removing poisons, radioactivity, etc. **decontamination** *n*

decor (**day**-core) *n* a style or scheme of interior decoration and furnishings in a room or house [French]

decorate *vb* **-rating, -rated 1** to make more attractive by adding some ornament or colour **2** to paint or wallpaper **3** to confer a mark of distinction, esp. a medal, upon [Latin *decorare*] **decorative** *adj* **decorator** *n*

Decorated style *or* **Decorated architecture** *n* a 14th-century style of English architecture characterized by the ogee arch, geometrical tracery, and floral decoration

decoration *n* **1** an addition that makes something more attractive or ornate **2** the way in which a room or building is decorated **3** something, esp. a medal, conferred as a mark of honour

decorous (**deck**-or-uss) *adj* polite, calm, and sensible in behaviour [Latin *decorus*] **decorously** *adv* **decorousness** *n*

decorum (dik-**core**-um) *n* polite and socially correct behaviour

decoy *n* **1** a person or thing used to lure someone into danger **2** an image of a bird or animal, used to lure game into a trap or within shooting range ▷ *vb* **3** to lure into danger by means of a decoy [probably from Dutch *de kooi* the cage]

decrease *vb* **-creasing, -creased 1** to make or become less in size, strength, or quantity ▷ *n* **2** a lessening; reduction **3** the amount by which something has been diminished [Latin *decrescere* to grow less] **decreasing** *adj* **decreasingly** *adv*

decree *n* **1** a law made by someone in authority **2** a judgment of a court ▷ *vb* **decreeing, decreed 3** to order by decree [Latin *decretum* ordinance]

decree absolute *n* the final decree in divorce proceedings, which leaves the parties free to remarry

decree nisi *n* a provisional decree in divorce proceedings, which will later be made absolute unless cause is shown why it should not [Latin *nisi* unless]

decrepit *adj* weakened or worn out by age or long use [Latin *crepare* to creak] **decrepitude** *n*

decretal *n RC Church* a papal decree [Late Latin *decretalis*]

decry *vb* **-cries, -crying, -cried** to express open disapproval of [Old French *descrier*]

decrypt *vb* **1** to decode (a message) with or without previous knowledge of its key **2** to make intelligible (a television or other signal) that has been deliberately distorted for transmission ▷ See also **encrypt** [DE- + (EN)CRYPT] **decryption** *n*

dedicate *vb* **-cating, -cated 1** to devote (oneself or one's time) wholly to a special purpose or cause **2** to inscribe or address (a book, piece of music, etc.) to someone as a token of affection or respect **3** to play (a record) on radio for someone as a greeting **4** to set apart for sacred uses [Latin *dedicare* to announce]

dedicated *adj* **1** devoted to a particular purpose or cause **2** *computers* designed to fulfil one function

dedication *n* **1** wholehearted devotion **2** an inscription in a book dedicating it to a person

deduce *vb* **-ducing, -duced** to reach (a conclusion) by reasoning from evidence; work out [Latin *de-* away + *ducere* to lead] **deducible** *adj*

deduct *vb* to subtract (a number, quantity, or part) [Latin *deducere* to deduce]

deductible *adj* **1** capable of being deducted **2** *US* tax-deductible

deduction *n* **1** the act or process of subtracting **2** something that is deducted **3** *logic* **A** a process of reasoning by which a conclusion necessarily follows from a set of general premises **B** a conclusion reached by this process **deductive** *adj*

deed *n* **1** something that is done **2** a notable achievement **3** action as opposed to words **4** *law* a legal document, esp. one concerning the ownership of property [Old English *dēd*]

deed box *n* a strong box in which deeds and other documents are kept

deed poll *n law* a deed made by one party only, esp. to change one's name

deejay *n informal* a disc jockey [from the initials DJ]

deem *vb* to judge or consider: *common sense is deemed to be a virtue* [Old English *dēman*]

deep *adj* **1** extending or situated far down from a surface: *a deep ditch* **2** extending or situated far inwards, backwards, or sideways **3** of a specified dimension downwards, inwards, or backwards: *six metres deep* **4** coming from or penetrating to a great depth **5** difficult to understand **6** of great intensity: *deep doubts* **7 deep in** totally absorbed in: *deep in conversation* **8** (of a colour) intense or dark **9** low in pitch: *a deep laugh* **10 go off the deep end** *informal* to lose one's temper **11 in deep water** *informal* in a tricky position or in trouble ▷ *n* **12** any deep place on land or under water **13 the deep A** *poetic* the ocean **B** *cricket* the area of the field relatively far from the pitch **14** the most profound, intense, or central part: *the deep of winter* ▷ *adv* **15** late: *deep into the night* **16** profoundly or intensely: *deep down I was afraid it was all my fault* [Old English *dēop*] **deeply** *adv*

deepen *vb* to make or become deeper or more intense

deep-freeze *n* **1** same as **freezer** ▷ *vb* **-freezing, -froze, -frozen 2** to freeze or keep in a deep-freeze

deep-fry *vb* **-fries, -frying, -fried** to cook in hot oil deep enough to completely cover the food

deep-laid *adj* (of a plan) carefully worked out and kept secret

deep-rooted *or* **deep-seated** *adj* (of ideas, beliefs, etc.) firmly fixed or held

deep-vein thrombosis *n* a blood clot in one of the major veins, usually in the legs or pelvis

deer *n, pl* **deer** *or* **deers** a large hoofed mammal [Old English *dēor* beast]

deerstalker *n* a cloth hat with peaks at the front and back and earflaps

de-escalate *vb* to reduce the intensity of (a problem or situation) **de-escalation** *n*

def *adj* **deffer, deffest** *slang* very good [perhaps from *definitive*]

deface *vb* **-facing, -faced** to deliberately spoil the surface or appearance of **defacement** *n*

de facto *adv* **1** in fact ▷ *adj* **2** existing in fact, whether legally recognized or not [Latin]

defalcate *vb* **-cating, -cated** *law* to make wrong use of funds entrusted to one [Medieval Latin *defalcare* to cut off] **defalcation** *n*

defame *vb* **-faming, -famed** to attack the good reputation of [Latin *diffamare* to spread by unfavourable report] **defamation** *n* **defamatory** (dif-**fam**-a-tree) *adj*

default *n* **1** a failure to do something, esp. to meet a financial obligation or to appear in court **2** an instruction to a computer to select a particular option unless the user specifies otherwise **3 by default** happening because something else has not happened: *they gained a colony by default because no other European power wanted it* **4 in default of** in the absence of ▷ *vb* **5** to fail to fulfil an obligation, esp. to make payment when due [Old French *defaillir* to fail] **defaulter** *n*

defeat *vb* **1** to win a victory over **2** to thwart or frustrate: *this accident has defeated all his hopes of winning* ▷ *n* **3** the act of defeating or state of being defeated [Old French *desfaire* to undo, ruin]

defeatism *n* a ready acceptance or expectation of defeat **defeatist** *n, adj*

defecate *vb* **-cating, -cated** to discharge waste from the body through the anus [Latin *defaecare*] **defecation** *n*

defect *n* **1** an imperfection or blemish ▷ *vb* **2** to desert one's country or cause to join the opposing forces [Latin *deficere* to forsake, fail] **defection** *n* **defector** *n*

defective *adj* imperfect or faulty: *defective hearing*

defence *or US* **defense** *n* **1** resistance against attack **2** something that provides such resistance **3** an argument or piece of writing in support of something that has been criticized or questioned **4** a country's military resources **5** *law* a defendant's denial of the truth of a charge **6** *law* the defendant and his or her legal advisers collectively **7** *sport* the players in a team whose function is to prevent the opposing team from scoring **8 defences** fortifications [Latin *defendere* to defend] **defenceless** *or US* **defenseless** *adj*

defend *vb* **1** to protect from harm or danger **2** to support in the face of criticism: *I spoke up to defend her* **3** to represent (a defendant) in court **4** to protect (a title or championship) against a challenge [Latin *defendere* to ward off] **defender** *n*

defendant *n* a person accused of a crime

defensible *adj* capable of being defended because believed to be right **defensibility** *n*

defensive *adj* **1** intended for defence **2** guarding against criticism or exposure of one's failings: *he can be highly defensive and wary* ▷ *n* **3 on the defensive** in a position of defence, as in being ready to reject criticism **defensively** *adv*

defer[1] *vb* **-ferring, -ferred** to delay until a future time; postpone: *payment was deferred indefinitely* [Old French *differer* to be different, postpone] **deferment** *or* **deferral** *n*

defer[2] *vb* **-ferring, -ferred** > **defer to** to submit to or comply with the wishes or judgments (of): *I defer to your superior knowledge* [Latin *deferre* to bear down]

deference *n* polite and respectful behaviour

deferential *adj* showing respect **deferentially** *adv*

defiance *n* open resistance to authority or opposition **defiant** *adj*

defibrillator *n med* an apparatus for stopping fibrillation of the heart by application of an electric current

deficiency *n, pl* **-cies 1** the state of being deficient **2** a lack or shortage

deficiency disease *n* any condition, such as scurvy, caused by a lack of vitamins or other essential substances

deficient *adj* **1** lacking something essential **2** inadequate in quantity or quality [Latin *deficere* to fall short]

deficit *n* the amount by which a sum is lower than that expected or required [Latin: there is lacking]

defile[1] *vb* **-filing, -filed 1** to make foul or dirty **2** to make unfit for ceremonial use [Old French *defouler* to trample underfoot, abuse] **defilement** *n*

defile[2] *n* a narrow pass or gorge: *the sandy defile of Wadi Rum* [French *défiler* to file off]

define *vb* **-fining, -fined 1** to describe the nature of **2** to state precisely the meaning of **3** to show clearly the outline of: *the picture was sharp and cleanly defined* **4** to fix with precision; specify: *define one's duties* [Latin *definire* to set bounds to] **definable** *adj*

definite *adj* **1** firm, clear, and precise: *I have very definite views on this subject* **2** having precise limits or boundaries **3** known for certain: *it's definite that they have won* [Latin *definitus* limited, distinct] **definitely** *adv*

definite article *n grammar* the word 'the'

definition *n* **1** a statement of the meaning of a word or phrase **2** a description of the essential qualities of something **3** the quality of being clear and distinct **4** sharpness of outline

definitive *adj* **1** final and unable to be questioned or altered: *a definitive verdict* **2** most complete, or the best of its kind: *the book was hailed as the definitive Dickens biography* **definitively** *adv*

deflate *vb* **-flating, -flated 1** to collapse or cause to collapse through the release of gas **2** to take away the self-esteem or conceit from **3** to cause deflation of (an economy) [DE- + (IN)FLATE]

deflation *n* **1** *econ* a reduction in economic activity resulting in lower levels of output and investment **2** a feeling of sadness following excitement **deflationary** *adj*

deflect *vb* to turn or cause to turn aside from a course [Latin *deflectere*] **deflection** *n* **deflector** *n*

deflower *vb literary* to deprive (a woman) of her virginity

defoliate *vb* **-ating, -ated** to deprive (a plant) of its leaves [Latin *de-* from + *folium* leaf] **defoliant** *n* **defoliation** *n*

deforestation *n* the cutting down or destruction of forests

deform *vb* to put (something) out of shape or spoil its appearance [Latin *de-* from + *forma* shape beauty]

deformed *adj* disfigured or misshapen

deformity *n, pl* **-ties 1** *pathol* a distortion of an organ or part **2** the state of being deformed

defraud *vb* to cheat out of money, property, or a right to do something

defray *vb* to provide money to cover costs or expenses [Old French *deffroier* to pay expenses] **defrayal** *n*

defrock *vb* to deprive (a priest) of ecclesiastical status

defrost *vb* **1** to make or become free of frost or ice **2** to thaw (frozen food) by removing from a deep-freeze

deft *adj* quick and skilful in movement; dexterous [Middle English variant of *daft* (in the sense: gentle)] **deftly** *adv* **deftness** *n*

defunct *adj* no longer existing or working properly [Latin *defungi* to discharge (one's obligations), die]

defuse *or US sometimes* **defuze** *vb* **-fusing, -fused** *or* **-fuzing, -fuzed 1** to remove the fuse of (an explosive device) **2** to reduce the tension in (a difficult situation): *I said it in a bid to defuse the situation*

USAGE Avoid confusion with **diffuse**.

defy *vb* **-fies, -fying, -fied 1** to resist openly and boldly **2** to elude in a baffling way: *his actions defy explanation* **3** *formal* to challenge (someone to do something) [Old French *desfier*]

degenerate *adj* **1** having deteriorated to a lower mental, moral, or physical level ▷ *n* **2** a degenerate person ▷ *vb* **-ating, -ated 3** to become degenerate [Latin *degener* departing from its kind, ignoble] **degeneracy** *n*

degeneration *n* **1** the process of degenerating **2** *biol* the loss of specialization or function by organisms

degenerative *adj* (of a disease or condition) getting steadily worse

degrade *vb* **-grading, -graded 1** to reduce to dishonour or disgrace **2** to reduce in status or quality **3** *chem* to decompose into atoms or smaller molecules [Latin *de-* from + *gradus* rank, degree] **degradation** *n* **degrading** *adj*

degree *n* **1** a stage in a scale of relative amount or intensity: *this task involved a greater degree of responsibility* **2** an academic award given by a university or college on successful completion of a course **3** *grammar* any of the forms of an adjective used to indicate relative amount or intensity **4** a unit of temperature. Symbol: ° **5** a measure of angle equal to one three-hundred-and-sixtieth of the circumference of a circle. Symbol: ° **6** a unit of latitude or longitude. Symbol: ° **7 by degrees** little by little; gradually [Latin *de-* down + *gradus* step]

dehisce *vb* **-hiscing, -hisced** (of the seed capsules of some plants) to burst open spontaneously [Latin *dehiscere* to split open] **dehiscence** *n* **dehiscent** *adj*

dehumanize *or* **-ise** *vb* **-izing, -ized** *or* **-ising, -ised 1** to deprive of the qualities thought of as being best in human beings, such as kindness **2** to make (an activity) mechanical or routine **dehumanization** *or* **-isation** *n*

dehydrate *vb* **-drating, -drated 1** to remove water from (food) in order to preserve it **2 be dehydrated** (of a person) to be weak or ill through losing too much water from the body **dehydration** *n*

de-ice *vb* **de-icing, de-iced** to free of ice **de-icer** *n*

deify (day-if-fie) *vb* **-fies, -fying, -fied** to treat or worship (someone or something) as a god [Latin *deus* god + *facere* to make] **deification** *n*

deign (dane) *vb* to do something that one considers beneath one's dignity: *she did not deign to reply* [Latin *dignari* to consider worthy]

deindustrialization *or* **-isation** *n* a decline in the importance of a country's manufacturing industry

d

deism (dee-iz-zum) *n* belief in the existence of God based only on natural reason, without reference to revelation **deist** *n, adj* **deistic** *adj*
deity (dee-it-ee) *n, pl* **-ties 1** a god or goddess **2** the state of being divine [Latin *deus* god]
Deity *n* **the Deity** God
déjà vu (day-zhah voo) *n* a feeling of having experienced before something that is happening at the present moment [French: already seen]
dejected *adj* in low spirits; downhearted [Latin *deicere* to cast down] **dejectedly** *adv* **dejection** *n*
de jure *adv* according to law [Latin]
deke *Canad slang* ▷ *vb* **deking, deked 1** (in ice hockey or box lacrosse) to draw (a defending player) out of position by faking a shot or movement ▷ *n* **2** such a shot or movement [from *decoy*]
dekko *n* **have a dekko** *Brit, Austral & NZ slang* to have a look [Hindi *dekhnā* to see]
delay *vb* **1** to put (something) off to a later time **2** to slow up or cause to be late **3** **A** to hesitate in doing something **B** to deliberately take longer than necessary to do something ▷ *n* **4** the act of delaying **5** a period of inactivity or waiting before something happens or continues [Old French *des-* off + *laier* to leave]
delectable *adj* delightful or very attractive [Latin *delectare* to delight]
delectation *n formal* great pleasure and enjoyment
delegate *n* **1** a person chosen to represent others at a conference or meeting ▷ *vb* **-gating, -gated 2** to entrust (duties or powers) to another person **3** to appoint as a representative [Latin *delegare* to send on a mission]
delegation *n* **1** a group chosen to represent others **2** the act of delegating
delete *vb* **-leting, -leted** to remove or cross out (something printed or written) [Latin *delere*] **deletion** *n*
deleterious (del-lit-eer-ee-uss) *adj formal* harmful or injurious [Greek *dēlētērios*]
Delft *n* tin-glazed earthenware which originated in Delft the Netherlands, typically with blue decoration on a white ground. Also: **delftware**
deli *n informal* short for **delicatessen**
deliberate *adj* **1** carefully thought out in advance; intentional **2** careful and unhurried: *a deliberate gait* ▷ *vb* **-ating, -ated 3** to consider (something) deeply; think over [Latin *deliberare* to consider well] **deliberately** *adv* **deliberative** *adj*
deliberation *n* **1** careful consideration **2** calmness and absence of hurry **3** **deliberations** formal discussions
delicacy *n, pl* **-cies 1** fine or subtle quality, construction, etc.: *delicacy of craftsmanship* **2** fragile or graceful beauty **3** something that is considered particularly nice to eat **4** frail health **5** refinement of feeling, manner, or appreciation: *the delicacy of the orchestra's playing* **6** need for careful or tactful treatment
delicate *adj* **1** fine or subtle in quality or workmanship **2** having a fragile beauty **3** (of colour, smell, or taste) pleasantly subtle **4** easily damaged; fragile **5** precise or sensitive in action: *the delicate digestive system* **6** requiring tact: *a delicate matter* **7** showing consideration for the feelings of other people [Latin *delicatus* affording pleasure] **delicately** *adv*
delicatessen *n* a shop selling unusual or imported foods, often already cooked or prepared [German *Delikatessen* delicacies]
delicious *adj* **1** very appealing to taste or smell **2** extremely enjoyable [Latin *deliciae* delights] **deliciously** *adv*
delight *n* **1** extreme pleasure **2** something or someone that causes this ▷ *vb* **3** to please greatly **4** **delight in** to take great pleasure in [Latin *delectare* to please] **delightful** *adj* **delightfully** *adv*
delighted *adj* greatly pleased
delimit *vb* **-iting, -ited** to mark or lay down the limits of **delimitation** *n*
delineate (dill-lin-ee-ate) *vb* **-ating, -ated 1** to show by drawing **2** to describe in words [Latin *delineare* to sketch out] **delineation** *n*
delinquent *n* **1** someone, esp. a young person, who breaks the law ▷ *adj* **2** repeatedly breaking the law [Latin *delinquens* offending] **delinquency** *n*
deliquesce *vb* **-quescing, -quesced** (esp. of certain salts) to dissolve in water absorbed from the air [Latin *deliquescere* to melt away] **deliquescence** *n* **deliquescent** *adj*
delirious *adj* **1** having delirium **2** wildly excited and happy **deliriously** *adv*
delirium *n* **1** a state of excitement and mental confusion, often with hallucinations **2** violent excitement [Latin: madness]
delirium tremens (trem-enz) *n* a severe condition characterized by delirium and trembling, caused by chronic alcoholism [New Latin: trembling delirium]
deliver *vb* **1** to carry (goods or mail) to a destination **2** to hand over: *the tenants were asked to deliver up their keys* **3** to aid in the birth of (offspring) **4** to present (a lecture or speech) **5** to release or rescue (from captivity or danger) **6** to strike (a blow) suddenly **7** *informal* Also: **deliver the goods** to produce something promised [Latin *de-* from + *liberare* to free] **deliverance** *n*
delivery *n, pl* **-eries 1** **A** the act of delivering goods or mail **B** something that is delivered **2** the act of giving birth to a baby **3** manner or style in public speaking: *her delivery was clear and humorous* **4** *cricket* the act or manner of bowling a ball **5** *S African* a semi-official slogan for the provision of services to previously disadvantaged communities
dell *n chiefly Brit* a small wooded hollow [Old English]
delouse *vb* **-lousing, -loused** to rid (a person or animal) of lice
Delphic *adj* obscure or ambiguous, like the ancient Greek oracle at Delphi
delphinium *n, pl* **-iums** *or* **-ia** a large garden plant with spikes of blue flowers [Greek *delphis* dolphin]
delta *n* **1** the fourth letter in the Greek alphabet (Δ, δ) **2** the flat area at the mouth of some rivers where the main stream splits up into several branches
delude *vb* **-luding, -luded** to make someone believe something that is not true [Latin *deludere*]
deluge (del-lyooj) *n* **1** a great flood of water **2** torrential rain **3** an overwhelming number

▷ *vb* **-uging, -uged 4** to flood **5.** to overwhelm [Latin *diluere* to wash away]

Deluge *n* **the Deluge** same as the **Flood**

delusion *n* **1** a mistaken idea or belief **2** the state of being deluded **delusive** *adj* **delusory** *adj*

de luxe *adj* rich or sumptuous; superior in quality: *a de luxe hotel* [French]

delve *vb* **delving, delved 1** to research deeply or intensively (for information) **2** *old-fashioned* to dig [Old English *delfan*]

demagnetize *or* **-ise** *vb* **-izing, -ized** *or* **-ising, -ised** to remove magnetic properties **demagnetization** *or* **-isation** *n*

demagogue *or US sometimes* **demagog** *n* a political agitator who attempts to win support by appealing to the prejudice and passions of the mob [Greek *dēmagōgos* people's leader] **demagogic** *adj* **demagogy** *n*

demand *vb* **1** to request forcefully **2** to require as just, urgent, etc.: *the situation demands intervention* **3** to claim as a right ▷ *n* **4** a forceful request **5** something that requires special effort or sacrifice: *demands upon one's time* **6** *econ* willingness and ability to purchase goods and services **7 in demand** sought after; popular **8 on demand** as soon as requested: *the funds will be available on demand* [Latin *demandare* to commit to]

demanding *adj* requiring a lot of skill, time, or effort: *a demanding relationship*

demarcation *n* the act of establishing limits or boundaries, esp. between the work performed by members of different trade unions [Spanish *demarcar* to appoint the boundaries of]

demean *vb* **1** to undermine the status or dignity of (someone or something) **2 demean oneself** to do something unworthy of one's status or character: *there is no doubt that he will lose face with the boss by having to demean himself in this way* [DE- + MEAN²]

demeanour *or US* **demeanor** *n* the way a person behaves [Old French *de-* (intensive) + *mener* to lead]

demented *adj* having a severe mental illness [Late Latin *dementare* to drive mad] **dementedly** *adv*

dementia (dim-men-sha) *n* a state of serious mental deterioration [Latin: madness]

demerara sugar *n* brown crystallized cane sugar from the West Indies [after *Demerara*, a region of Guyana]

demerit *n* **1** a fault or disadvantage **2** *US & Canad* a mark given against a student for failure or misconduct

demesne (dim-mane) *n* **1** land surrounding a house or manor **2** *property law* the possession of one's own property or land **3** a region or district; domain [Old French *demeine*]

Demeter *n Greek myth* the goddess of agriculture

demi- *combining form* **1** half: *demirelief* **2** of less than full size, status, or rank: *demigod* [Latin *dimidius* half]

demigod *n* **1 A** a being who is part mortal, part god **B** a lesser deity **2** a godlike person

demijohn *n* a large bottle with a short narrow neck, often encased in wickerwork [probably from French *dame-jeanne*]

demilitarize *or* **-rise** *vb* **-rizing, -rized** *or* **-rising, -rised** to remove all military forces from (an area): *demilitarized zone* **demilitarization** *or* **-risation** *n*

demimonde *n* **1** (esp. in the 19th century) a class of women considered to be outside respectable society because of promiscuity **2** any group considered not wholly respectable [French: half-world]

demise *n* **1** the eventual failure of something originally successful **2** *euphemistic, formal* death **3** *property law* a transfer of an estate by lease ▷ *vb* **-mising, -mised 4** *property law* to transfer for a limited period; lease [Old French *demis* dismissed]

demi-sec *adj* (of wines) medium-sweet

demisemiquaver *n music* a note with the time value of one thirty-second of a semibreve

demist *vb* to make or become free of condensation **demister** *n*

demo *n, pl* **-os** *informal* **1** short for **demonstration** (sense 1) **2** a demonstration record or tape

demob *vb* **-mobbing, -mobbed** *Brit, Austral & NZ informal* to demobilize

demobilize *or* **-lise** *vb* **-lizing, -lized** *or* **-lising, -lised** to release from the armed forces **demobilization** *or* **-lisation** *n*

democracy *n, pl* **-cies 1** a system of government or organization in which the citizens or members choose leaders or make other important decisions by voting **2** a country in which the citizens choose their government by voting [Greek *dēmokratia*]

democrat *n* a person who believes in democracy

Democrat *n US politics* a member or supporter of the Democratic Party, the more liberal of the two main political parties in the US **Democratic** *adj*

democratic *adj* of or relating to a country, organization, or system in which leaders are chosen or decisions are made by voting **democratically** *adv*

demodulation *n electronics* the process by which an output wave or signal is obtained having the characteristics of the original modulating wave or signal

demographic *adj* **1** of or relating to population statistics ▷ *n* **2** a group of people within a population who share a particular characteristic: *the female demographic*

demography *n* the study of population statistics, such as births and deaths [Greek *dēmos* the populace + -GRAPHY]

demolish *vb* **1** to tear down or break up (buildings) **2** to put an end to; destroy: *I demolished her argument in seconds* **3** *facetious* to eat up: *he demolished the whole cake* [Latin *demoliri* to throw down] **demolisher** *n* **demolition** *n*

demon *n* **1** an evil spirit **2** a person, obsession, etc., thought of as evil or persistently tormenting **3** a person extremely skilful in or devoted to a given activity: *a demon at pool* [Greek *daimōn* spirit, fate] **demonic** *adj*

demonetize *or* **-tise** *vb* **-tizing, -tized** *or* **-tising, -tised** to withdraw from use as currency **demonetization** *or* **-tisation** *n*

demoniac *or* **demoniacal** *adj* **1** appearing to be possessed by a devil **2** suggesting inner possession or inspiration: *the demoniac fire of genius* **3** frantic or frenzied: *demoniac activity* **demoniacally** *adv*

demonize *or* **-ise** *vb* **-izing, -ized** *or* **-ising, -ised** **1** to make into a demon **2** to describe as evil or guilty: *America is demonized by many in France*
demonolatry *n* the worship of demons [*demon* + Greek *latreia* worship]
demonology *n* the study of demons or demonic beliefs [*demon* + -LOGY]
demonstrable *adj* able to be proved **demonstrably** *adv*
demonstrate *vb* **-strating, -strated 1** to show or prove by reasoning or evidence **2** to display and explain the workings of (a machine, product, etc.) **3** to reveal the existence of: *the adult literacy campaign demonstrated the scale of educational deprivation* **4** to show support or opposition by public parades or rallies [Latin *demonstrare* to point out]
demonstration *n* **1** a march or public meeting to demonstrate opposition to something or support for something **2** an explanation, display, or experiment showing how something works **3** proof or evidence leading to proof
demonstrative *adj* **1** tending to show one's feelings freely and openly **2** *grammar* denoting a word used to point out the person or thing referred to, such as *this* and *those* **3 demonstrative of** giving proof of **demonstratively** *adv*
demonstrator *n* **1** a person who demonstrates how a device or machine works **2** a person who takes part in a public demonstration
demoralize *or* **-ise** *vb* **-izing, -ized** *or* **-ising, -ised** to deprive (someone) of confidence or enthusiasm: *she had been demoralized and had just given up* **demoralization** *or* **-isation** *n*
demote *vb* **-moting, -moted** to lower in rank or position [DE- + (PRO)MOTE] **demotion** *n*
demotic *adj* of or relating to the common people [Greek *dēmotikos*]
demur *vb* **-murring, -murred 1** to show reluctance; object ▷ *n* **2 without demur** without objecting [Latin *demorari* to linger]
demure *adj* quiet, reserved, and rather shy [perhaps from Old French *demorer* to delay, linger] **demurely** *adv* **demureness** *n*
demutualize *or* **-ise** *vb* **-izing, -ized** *or* **-ising, -ised** (of a mutual savings or life-assurance organization) to convert to a public limited company **demutualization** *or* **-isation** *n*
demystify *vb* **-fies, -fying, -fied** to remove the mystery from: *he attempted to demystify the contemporary jargon of psychology* **demystification** *n*
den *n* **1** the home of a wild animal; lair **2** *chiefly US* a small secluded room in a home, often used for a hobby **3** a place where people indulge in criminal or immoral activities: *a den of iniquity* [Old English *denn*]
denarius (din-air-ee-uss) *n, pl* **-narii** (-nair-ee-eye) a silver coin of ancient Rome, often called a penny in translation [Latin]
denary (dean-a-ree) *adj* calculated by tens; decimal [Latin *denarius*]
denationalize *or* **-ise** *vb* **-izing, -ized** *or* **-ising, -ised** to transfer (an industry or a service) from public to private ownership **denationalization** *or* **-isation** *n*
denature *vb* **-turing, -tured 1** to change the nature of **2** to make (alcohol) unfit to drink by adding another substance
dendrology *n* the study of trees [Greek *dendron* tree + -LOGY]
dene *or* **dean** *n chiefly Brit* a narrow wooded valley
dengue (deng-gee) *n* a viral disease transmitted by mosquitoes, characterized by headache, fever, pains in the joints, and a rash [probably of African origin]
denial *n* **1** a statement that something is not true **2** a rejection of a request **3** *psychol* a process by which painful thoughts are not permitted into the consciousness
denier (den-yer) *n* a unit of weight used to measure the fineness of silk and man-made fibres [Old French: coin]
denigrate *vb* **-grating, -grated** to criticize (someone or something) unfairly [Latin *denigrare* to make very black] **denigration** *n* **denigrator** *n*
denim *n* **1** a hard-wearing cotton fabric used for jeans, skirts, etc. **2 denims** jeans made of denim [French *(serge) de Nîmes* (serge) of Nîmes, in S France]
denizen *n* **1** a person, animal, or plant that lives or grows in a particular place **2** an animal or plant established in a place to which it is not native [Old French *denzein*]
denominate *vb* **-nating, -nated** to give a specific name to; designate [Latin *denominare*]
denomination *n* **1** a group which has slightly different beliefs from other groups within the same faith **2** a unit in a system of weights, values, or measures: *coins of small denomination have been withdrawn* **3** a name given to a class or group; classification **denominational** *adj*
denominator *n* the number below the line in a fraction, as 8 in $^{7}/_{8}$
denote *vb* **-noting, -noted 1** to be a sign or indication of: *these contracts denote movement on the widest possible scale* **2** (of a word or phrase) to have as a literal or obvious meaning [Latin *denotare* to mark] **denotation** *n*
denouement (day-noo-mon) *n* the final outcome or solution in a play or other work [French]
denounce *vb* **-nouncing, -nounced 1** to condemn openly or vehemently **2** to give information against [Latin *denuntiare* to make an official proclamation, threaten]
dense *adj* **1** thickly crowded or closely packed **2** difficult to see through: *dense clouds of smoke* **3** *informal* stupid or dull **4** (of a film, book, etc.) difficult to follow or understand: *the content should be neither too dense nor too abstract* [Latin *densus* thick] **densely** *adv*
density *n, pl* **-ties 1** the degree to which something is filled or occupied: *an average population density* **2** *physics* a measure of the compactness of a substance, expressed as its mass per unit volume **3** a measure of a physical quantity per unit of length, area, or volume
dent *n* **1** a hollow in the surface of something ▷ *vb* **2** to make a dent in [variant of *dint*]
dental *adj* of or relating to the teeth or dentistry [Latin *dens* tooth]

dental floss *n* a waxed thread used to remove particles of food from between the teeth
dental surgeon *n* same as **dentist**
dentate *adj* having teeth or toothlike notches [Latin *dentatus*]
dentifrice (den-tif-riss) *n* paste or powder for cleaning the teeth [Latin *dens* tooth + *fricare* to rub]
dentine (den-teen) *n* the hard dense tissue that forms the bulk of a tooth [Latin *dens* tooth]
dentist *n* a person qualified to practise dentistry [French *dentiste*]
dentistry *n* the branch of medicine concerned with the teeth and gums
dentition *n* the typical arrangement, type, and number of teeth in a species [Latin *dentitio* a teething]
denture *n (often pl)* a partial or full set of artificial teeth [French *dent* tooth]
denude *vb* **-nuding, -nuded 1** to make bare; strip: *the atrocious weather denuded the trees* **2** *geol* to expose (rock) by the erosion of the layers above
denudation *n*
denumerable *adj maths* countable
denunciation *n* open condemnation; denouncing [Latin *denuntiare* to proclaim]
deny *vb* **-nies, -nying, -nied 1** to declare (a statement) to be untrue **2** to refuse to give or allow: *we have been denied permission* **3** to refuse to acknowledge: *the baron denied his wicked son* [Latin *denegare*]
deodar *n* a Himalayan cedar with drooping branches [Hindi]
deodorant *n* a substance applied to the body to prevent or disguise the odour of perspiration
deodorize *or* **-ise** *vb* **-izing, -ized** *or* **-ising, -ised** to remove or disguise the odour of **deodorization** *or* **-isation** *n*
deoxyribonucleic acid *n* same as **DNA**
depart *vb* **1** to leave **2** to differ or deviate: *to depart from the original concept* [Old French *departir*]
departed *adj euphemistic* dead
department *n* **1** a specialized division of a large business organization, hospital, university, etc. **2** a major subdivision of the administration of a government **3** an administrative division in several countries, such as France **4** *informal* a specialized sphere of activity: *wine-making is my wife's department* [French *département*]
departmental *adj*
department store *n* a large shop divided into departments selling many kinds of goods
departure *n* **1** the act of departing **2** a divergence from previous custom, rule, etc. **3** a course of action or venture: *the album represents a new departure for them*
depend *vb* **depend on** **A** to put trust (in); rely (on) **B** to be influenced or determined (by): *the answer depends on four main issues* **C** to rely (on) for income or support [Latin *dependere* to hang from]
dependable *adj* reliable and trustworthy
dependability *n* **dependably** *adv*
dependant *n* a person who depends on another for financial support
USAGE Avoid confusion with **dependent**.
dependence *n* **1** the state of relying on something in order to be able to survive or operate properly **2** reliance or trust: *they had a bond between them of mutual dependence and trust*
dependency *n, pl* **-cies 1** a territory subject to a state on which it does not border **2** *psychol* overreliance on another person or on a drug
dependent *adj* **1** depending on a person or thing for aid or support **2** **dependent on** *or* **upon** influenced or conditioned by
USAGE Avoid confusion with **dependant**.
depict *vb* **1** to represent by drawing, painting, etc. **2** to describe in words [Latin *depingere*] **depiction** *n*
depilatory (dip-pill-a-tree) *adj* **1** able or serving to remove hair ▷ *n, pl* **-ries 2** a chemical used to remove hair [Latin *depilare* to pull out the hair]
deplete *vb* **-pleting, -pleted 1** to use up (supplies or money) **2** to reduce in number [Latin *deplere* to empty out] **depletion** *n*
deplorable *adj* very bad or unpleasant
deplorably *adv*
deplore *vb* **-ploring, -plored** to express or feel strong disapproval of [Latin *deplorare* to weep bitterly]
deploy *vb* to organize (troops or resources) into a position ready for immediate and effective action [Latin *displicare* to unfold] **deployment** *n*
deponent *n law* a person who makes a statement on oath [Latin *deponens* putting down]
depopulate *vb* **-lating, -lated** to cause to be reduced in population **depopulation** *n*
deport *vb* **1** to remove forcibly from a country **2** **deport oneself** to behave in a specified manner [Latin *deportare* to carry away, banish]
deportation *n* the act of expelling someone from a country
deportee *n* a person deported or awaiting deportation
deportment *n* the way in which a person moves and stands: *she had the manners and deportment of a great lady* [Old French *deporter* to conduct (oneself)]
depose *vb* **-posing, -posed 1** to remove from an office or position of power **2** *law* to testify on oath [Latin *deponere* to put aside]
deposit *vb* **-iting, -ited 1** to put down **2** to entrust (money or valuables) for safekeeping **3** to place (money) in a bank account or other savings account **4** to lay down naturally: *the river deposits silt* ▷ *n* **5** a sum of money placed in a bank account or other savings account **6** money given in part payment for goods or services **7** an amount of a substance left on a surface as a result of a chemical or geological process [Latin *depositus* put down]
deposit account *n Brit* a bank account that earns interest
depositary *n, pl* **-taries** a person or group to whom something is entrusted for safety
deposition *n* **1** *law* the sworn statement of a witness used in court in his or her absence **2** the act of deposing **3** the act of depositing **4** something deposited [Late Latin *depositio* a laying down, testimony]
depositor *n* a person who places or has money on deposit in a bank or similar organization: *panic-stricken depositors*
depository *n, pl* **-ries 1** a store where furniture, valuables, etc. can be kept for safety **2** same as **depositary**

depot (dep-oh) *n* **1** a place where goods and vehicles are kept when not in use **2** *US, Canad & NZ* a bus or railway station [French]
depraved *adj* morally bad; corrupt [Latin *depravare* to distort, corrupt]
depravity *n, pl* **-ties** moral corruption
deprecate *vb* **-cating, -cated** to express disapproval of [Latin *deprecari* to avert, ward off] **deprecation** *n* **deprecatory** *adj*
USAGE Avoid confusion with **depreciate.**
depreciate *vb* **-ating, -ated 1** to decline in value or price **2** to deride or criticize [Latin *de-* down + *pretium* price] **depreciatory** *adj*
USAGE Avoid confusion with **deprecate.**
depreciation *n* **1** *accounting* the reduction in value of a fixed asset through use, obsolescence, etc. **2** a decrease in the exchange value of a currency **3** the act or an instance of belittling
depredation *n* plundering; pillage [Latin *depraedare* to pillage]
depress *vb* **1** to make sad and gloomy **2** to lower (prices) **3** to push down [Old French *depresser*] **depressing** *adj* **depressingly** *adv*
depressant *adj* **1** *med* able to reduce nervous or functional activity; sedative ▷ *n* **2** a depressant drug
depressed *adj* **1** (of a person) having depression **2** low in spirits; downcast **3** suffering from economic hardship, such as unemployment: *the current depressed conditions* **4** pressed down or flattened
depression *n* **1** a mental health condition in which a person has feelings of gloom and inadequacy **2** an economic condition in which there is substantial unemployment, low output and low investment; slump **3** *meteorol* a mass of air below normal atmospheric pressure, which often causes rain **4** a sunken place
Depression *n* **the Depression** the worldwide economic depression of the early 1930s
depressive *adj* **1** causing sadness and lack of energy **2** subject to periods of depression
deprive *vb* **-priving, -prived** > **deprive of** to prevent from having or enjoying [Latin *de-* from + *privare* to deprive of] **deprivation** *n*
deprived *adj* lacking adequate living conditions, education, etc.: *deprived ghettos*
dept department
depth *n* **1** the distance downwards, backwards, or inwards **2** intensity of emotion or feeling **3** the quality of having a high degree of knowledge, insight, and understanding **4** intensity of colour **5** lowness of pitch **6 depths A** a remote inaccessible region: *the depths of the forest* **B** the most severe part: *the depths of depression* **C** a low moral state **7 out of one's depth A** in water deeper than one is tall **B** beyond the range of one's competence or understanding [Middle English *dep* deep]
depth charge *n* a bomb used to attack submarines that explodes at a preset depth of water
deputation *n* a body of people appointed to represent others
depute *vb* **-puting, -puted** to appoint (someone) to act on one's behalf [Late Latin *deputare* to assign, allot]
deputize *or* **-tise** *vb* **-tizing, -tized** *or* **-tising, -tised** (usually foll. by *for*) to act as deputy
deputy *n, pl* **-ties** a person appointed to act on behalf of another [Old French *deputer* to appoint]
derail *vb* to cause (a train or tram) to go off the rails **derailment** *n*
derailleur (dee-rail-yer) *n* a type of gear-change mechanism for bicycles
deranged *adj* **1** mad, or behaving in a wild and uncontrolled way **2** in a state of disorder [from Old French *desrengier* to disorder, disturb] **derangement** *n*
derby *n, pl* **-bies** *US & Canad* a bowler hat
Derby *n, pl* **-bies 1 the Derby** an annual horse race for three-year-olds, run at Epsom Downs, Surrey **2 local derby** a sporting event between teams from the same area [after the Earl of *Derby*, who founded the race in 1780]
deregulate *vb* **-lating, -lated** to remove regulations or controls from **deregulation** *n*
derelict *adj* **1** abandoned or unused and falling into ruins ▷ *n* **2** a social outcast or vagrant [Latin *derelinquere* to abandon]
dereliction *n* **1** the state of being abandoned **2 dereliction of duty** wilful neglect of one's duty
derestrict *vb Brit, Austral & NZ* to make (a road) free from speed limits **derestriction** *n*
deride *vb* **-riding, -rided** to speak of or treat with contempt or ridicule [Latin *deridere* to laugh at, scorn] **derision** *n*
de rigueur (de rig-gur) *adj* required by fashion [French, literally: of strictness]
derisive *adj* mocking or scornful **derisively** *adv*
derisory *adj* too small or inadequate to be considered seriously: *the shareholders have dismissed the offer as derisory*
derivation *n* the origin or descent of something, such as a word
derivative *adj* **1** based on other sources; not original ▷ *n* **2** a word, idea, etc., that is derived from another **3** *maths* the rate of change of one quantity with respect to another
derive *vb* **-riving, -rived** to draw or be drawn (from) in source or origin [Old French *deriver* to spring from]
dermatitis *n* inflammation of the skin [Greek *derma* skin]
dermatology *n* the branch of medicine concerned with the skin [Greek *derma* skin + -LOGY] **dermatologist** *n*
derogate *vb* **-gating, -gated** > **derogate from** to cause to seem inferior; detract from [Latin *derogare* to diminish] **derogation** *n*
derogatory (dir-rog-a-tree) *adj* expressing or showing a low opinion of someone or something
derrick *n* **1** a simple crane that has lifting tackle slung from a boom **2** the framework erected over an oil well to enable drill tubes to be raised and lowered [after *Derrick*, famous hangman]
derring-do *n archaic or literary* a daring spirit or deed [Middle English *durring don* daring to do]
derv *n Brit* diesel oil, when used for road transport [*d(iesel) e(ngine) r(oad) v(ehicle)*]
dervish *n* a member of a Muslim religious order noted for a frenzied, ecstatic, whirling dance [Persian *darvīsh* mendicant monk]

desalination *n* the process of removing salt, esp. from sea water

descale *vb* to remove the hard coating which sometimes forms inside kettles, pipes, etc.

descant *n* **1** a tune played or sung above a basic melody ▹ *adj* **2** of the highest member in a family of musical instruments: *a descant clarinet* [Latin *dis-* apart + *cantus* song]

descend *vb* **1** to move down (a slope, staircase, etc.) **2** to move or fall to a lower level, pitch, etc. **3 be descended from** to be connected by a blood relationship to **4 descend on** to visit unexpectedly **5 descend to** to stoop to (unworthy behaviour) [Latin *descendere*]

descendant *n* a person or animal descended from an individual, race, or species

descendent *adj* descending

descent *n* **1** the act of descending **2** a downward slope **3** a path or way leading downwards **4** derivation from an ancestor; family origin **5** a decline or degeneration

describe *vb* **-scribing, -scribed 1** to give an account of (something or someone) in words **2** to trace the outline of (a circle, etc.) [Latin *describere* to copy off, write out]

description *n* **1** a statement or account that describes someone or something **2** the act of describing **3** sort, kind, or variety: *antiques of every description*

descriptive *adj* describing something: *it was a very descriptive account of the play* **descriptively** *adv*

descry *vb* **-scries, -scrying, -scried 1** to catch sight of **2** to discover by looking carefully [Old French *descrier* to proclaim]

desecrate *vb* **-crating, -crated** to violate the sacred character of (an object or place) [DE- + (CON)SECRATE] **desecration** *n*

desegregate *vb* **-gating, -gated** to end racial segregation in (a school or other public institution) **desegregation** *n*

deselect *vb* **1** to cancel (a highlighted selection of data) on a computer screen **2** *Brit politics* (of a constituency organization) to refuse to select (an MP) for re-election **deselection** *n*

desensitize *or* **-tise** *vb* **-tizing, -tized** *or* **-tising, -tised** to make insensitive or less sensitive: *the patient was desensitized to the allergen; to desensitize photographic film*

desert¹ *n* a region that has little or no vegetation because of low rainfall [Church Latin *desertum*]

desert² *vb* **1** to abandon (a person or place) without intending to return **2** *chiefly military* to leave (a post or duty) with no intention of returning [Latin *deserere*] **deserted** *adj* **deserter** *n* **desertion** *n*

desertification *n* a process by which fertile land turns into desert

desert island *n* a small uninhabited island in the tropics

deserts *pl n* **get one's just deserts** to get the punishment one deserves [Old French *deserte* something deserved]

deserve *vb* **-serving, -served** to be entitled to or worthy of [Latin *deservire* to serve devotedly]

deserved *adj* rightfully earned **deservedly** (diz-**zerv**-id-lee) *adv*

deserving *adj* worthy of a reward, help, or praise

deshabille (day-zab-**beel**) *or* **dishabille** *n* the state of being partly dressed [French *déshabillé*]

desi *Indian* ▹ *adj* **1** indigenous or local ▹ *n* **2** *informal* a person considered to be of South Asian origin [Hindi]

desiccate *vb* **-cating, -cated** to remove most of the water from; dry [Latin *desiccare* to dry up] **desiccated** *adj* **desiccation** *n*

design *vb* **1** to work out the structure or form of (something), by making a sketch or plans **2** to plan and make (something) artistically **3** to intend (something) for a specific purpose: *the move is designed to reduce travelling costs* ▹ *n* **4** a sketch, plan, or preliminary drawing **5** the arrangement or features of an artistic or decorative work: *he built it to his own design* **6** a finished artistic or decorative creation **7** the art of designing **8** an intention; purpose **9 have designs on** to plot to gain possession of [Latin *designare* to mark out, describe]

designate (**dez**-zig-nate) *vb* **-nating, -nated 1** to give a name to or describe as: *vessels sunk during battle are designated as war graves* **2** to select (someone) for an office or duty; appoint ▹ *adj* **3** appointed, but not yet in office: *a Prime Minister designate* [Latin *designatus* marked out]

designated driver *n* a person who volunteers not to drink alcohol at a social event, in order to drive people who have been drinking

designation *n* **1** something that designates, such as a name **2** the act of designating

designedly (dee-**zine**-id-lee) *adv* by intention

designer *n* **1** a person who draws up original sketches or plans from which things are made ▹ *adj* **2** designed by a well-known fashion designer: *a wardrobe full of designer clothes* **3** having an appearance of fashionable trendiness: *designer stubble*

designing *adj* cunning and scheming

desirable *adj* **1** worth having or doing: *a desirable lifestyle* **2** arousing sexual desire **desirability** *n* **desirably** *adv*

desire *vb* **-siring, -sired 1** to want very much **2** *formal* to request: *we desire your company at the wedding of our daughter* ▹ *n* **3** a wish or longing **4** sexual appetite **5** a person or thing that is desired [Latin *desiderare*]

desirous *adj* (usually foll. by *of*) having a desire for: *deeply desirous of regaining the leadership*

desist *vb* to stop doing: *please desist from talking* [Latin *desistere*]

desk *n* **1** a piece of furniture with a writing surface and usually drawers **2** a service counter in a public building, such as a hotel **3** the section of a newspaper or television station responsible for a particular subject: *the picture desk* [Medieval Latin *desca* table]

deskill *vb* **1** to mechanize or computerize (a job) thereby reducing the skill required to do it **2** to deprive (employees) of the opportunity to use their skills **deskilling** *n*

desktop *n* **1** the main screen display on a personal computer **2** a personal computer that is small enough to use at a desk ▹ *adj* **3** (esp. of a computer system) for use at a desk

d

desktop publishing *n* a system that uses computer software to combine text and graphics to produce professional-looking material for publication

desolate *adj* **1** uninhabited and bleak **2** made uninhabitable; devastated **3** without friends, hope, or encouragement **4** gloomy or dismal; depressing ▷ *vb* **-lating, -lated 5** to deprive of inhabitants **6** to make barren; devastate **7** to make wretched or forlorn [Latin *desolare* to leave alone] **desolately** *adv* **desolateness** *n*

desolation *n* **1** ruin or devastation **2** solitary misery; wretchedness

despair *n* **1** total loss of hope ▷ *vb* **2** to lose or give up hope: *we must not despair of finding a peaceful solution* [Old French *despoir* hopelessness]

despatch *vb, n* same as **dispatch**

desperado *n, pl* **-does** *or* **-dos** a reckless person ready to commit any violent illegal act [probably pseudo-Spanish]

desperate *adj* **1** willing to do anything to improve one's situation **2** (of an action) undertaken as a last resort **3** very grave: *in desperate agony* **4** having a great need or desire: *I was desperate for a child* [Latin *desperare* to have no hope] **desperately** *adv*

desperation *n* **1** desperate recklessness **2** the state of being desperate

despicable *adj* deserving contempt **despicably** *adv*

despise *vb* **-pising, -pised** to look down on with contempt [Latin *despicere* to look down]

despite *prep* in spite of [Old French *despit*]

despoil *vb formal* to plunder [Latin *despoliare*] **despoliation** *n*

despondent *adj* dejected or depressed [Latin *despondere* to lose heart] **despondency** *n* **despondently** *adv*

despot *n* any person in power who acts tyrannically [Greek *despotēs* lord, master] **despotic** *adj* **despotically** *adv*

despotism *n* **1** absolute or tyrannical government **2** tyrannical behaviour

dessert *n* the sweet course served at the end of a meal [French]

dessertspoon *n* a spoon between a tablespoon and a teaspoon in size

destabilize *or* **-lise** *vb* **-lizing, -lized** *or* **-lising, -lised** to make or become unstable or less stable **destabilization** *or* **-lisation** *n*

destination *n* the place to which someone or something is going

destined (dess-tinnd) *adj* **1** certain to be or do something: *the school is destined to close this summer* **2** heading towards a specific destination: *some of the oil was destined for Eastern Europe* [Latin *destinare* to appoint]

destiny *n, pl* **-nies 1** the future destined for a person or thing **2** the predetermined course of events **3** the power that predetermines the course of events [Old French *destinee*]

destitute *adj* lacking the means to live; totally impoverished [Latin *destituere* to leave alone] **destitution** *n*

de-stress *vb* to become or cause to become less stressed or anxious

destroy *vb* **1** to ruin; demolish **2** to put an end to **3** to kill (an animal) **4** to crush or defeat [Latin *destruere* to pull down]

destroyer *n* **1** a small heavily armed warship **2** a person or thing that destroys

destructible *adj* capable of being destroyed

destruction *n* **1** the act of destroying something or state of being destroyed **2** a cause of ruin [Latin *destructio* a pulling down]

destructive *adj* **1** causing or capable of causing harm, damage, or injury **2** intended to discredit, esp. without positive suggestions or help: *destructive speeches against the platform* **destructively** *adv*

desuetude (diss-syoo-it-tude) *n formal* the condition of not being in use [Latin *desuescere* to lay aside a habit]

desultory (dez-zl-tree) *adj* **1** passing or jumping from one thing to another; disconnected: *desultory conversation* **2** occurring in a random way: *a desultory thought* [Latin *de-* from + *salire* to jump] **desultorily** *adv*

detach *vb* **1** to disengage and separate **2** *military* to send (a regiment, officer, etc.) on a special assignment [Old French *destachier*] **detachable** *adj*

detached *adj* **1** *Brit, Austral & S African* separate or standing apart: *a detached farmhouse* **2** showing no emotional involvement: *she continued to watch him in her grave and detached manner*

detachment *n* **1** the state of not being personally involved in something **2** *military* a small group of soldiers separated from the main group

detail *n* **1** an item that is considered separately **2** an item considered to be unimportant: *a mere detail* **3** treatment of individual parts: *the census provides a considerable amount of detail* **4** a small section of a work of art often enlarged to make the smaller features more distinct **5** *chiefly military* **A** personnel assigned a specific duty **B** the duty **6 in detail** including all the important particulars ▷ *vb* **7** to list fully **8** *chiefly military* to select (personnel) for a specific duty [Old French *detailler* to cut in pieces]

detailed *adj* having many details

detain *vb* **1** to delay (someone) **2** to force (someone) to stay: *the police detained him for questioning* [Latin *detinere*] **detainee** *n* **detainment** *n*

detect *vb* **1** to perceive or notice: *to detect a note of sarcasm* **2** to discover the existence or presence of: *to detect alcohol in the blood* [Latin *detegere* to uncover] **detectable** *adj* **detector** *n*

detection *n* **1** the act of noticing, discovering, or sensing something **2** the act or process of extracting information

detective *n* **A** a police officer who investigates crimes **B** same as **private detective**

detente (day-tont) *n* the easing of tension between nations [French]

detention *n* **1** imprisonment, esp. of a suspect awaiting trial **2** a form of punishment in which a pupil is detained after school

detention centre *n* a place where asylum seekers, illegal immigrants, or people awaiting trial may be detained for short periods by order of a court

deter *vb* **-terring, -terred** to discourage or prevent someone from doing something by instilling fear or doubt in them [Latin *deterrere*]

detergent *n* **1** a chemical substance used for washing clothes, dishes, etc. ▷ *adj* **2** having cleansing power [Latin *detergens* wiping off]

deteriorate *vb* **-rating, -rated** to become worse [Latin *deterior* worse] **deterioration** *n*

determinant *adj* **1** serving to determine or affect ▷ *n* **2** a factor that controls or influences what will happen **3** *maths* a square array of elements that represents the sum of certain products of these elements

determinate *adj* definitely limited or fixed

determination *n* **1** the condition of being determined; resoluteness **2** the act of making a decision

determine *vb* **-mining, -mined 1** to settle (an argument or a question) conclusively **2** to find out the facts about (something): *the tests determined it was in fact cancer* **3** to fix in scope, extent, etc.: *to determine the degree of the problem* **4** to make a decision [Latin *determinare* to set boundaries to]

determined *adj* firmly decided **determinedly** *adv*

determiner *n* *grammar* a word, such as a number, article, or personal pronoun, that determines the meaning of a noun phrase

determinism *n* the theory that human choice is not free, but is decided by past events **determinist** *n, adj*

deterrent *n* **1** something that deters **2** a weapon or set of weapons held by one country to deter another country attacking ▷ *adj* **3** tending to deter [Latin *deterrens* hindering] **deterrence** *n*

detest *vb* to dislike intensely [Latin *detestari*] **detestable** *adj*

detestation *n* intense hatred

dethrone *vb* **-throning, -throned** to remove from a throne or deprive of any high position **dethronement** *n*

detonate *vb* **-nating, -nated** to make (an explosive device) explode or (of an explosive device) to explode [Latin *detonare* to thunder down] **detonation** *n*

detonator *n* a small amount of explosive or a device used to set off an explosion

detour *n* a deviation from a direct route or course of action [French]

detoxify *vb* **-fies, -fying, -fied** to remove poison from **detoxification** *n*

detract *vb* **detract from** to make (something) seem less good, valuable, or impressive: *I wouldn't want to detract from your triumph* [Latin *detrahere* to pull away, disparage] **detraction** *n* **detractor** *n*

> **USAGE** *Detract* is sometimes wrongly used where *distract* is meant: *a noise distracted* (not *detracted) my attention.*

detriment *n* disadvantage or damage [Latin *detrimentum* a rubbing off] **detrimental** *adj* **detrimentally** *adv*

detritus (dit-**trite**-uss) *n* **1** a loose mass of stones and silt worn away from rocks **2** debris [Latin: a rubbing away] **detrital** *adj*

de trop (de **troh**) *adj* unwanted or unwelcome: *I know when I'm de trop, so I'll leave you two together* [French]

detumescence *n* the subsidence of a swelling [Latin *detumescere* to cease swelling]

deuce (**dyewss**) *n* **1** *tennis* a tied score that requires one player to gain two successive points to win the game **2** a playing card or dice with two spots [Latin *duo* two]

deus ex machina *n* an unlikely development introduced into a play or film to resolve the plot

deuterium *n* a stable isotope of hydrogen. Symbol: **D**, **^{2}H** [Greek *deuteros* second]

deuterium oxide *n* same as **heavy water**

Deutschmark (**doytch**-mark) *or* **Deutsche Mark** (**doytch**-a) *n* a former monetary unit of Germany [German: German mark]

deutzia (**dyewt**-see-a) *n* a shrub with clusters of pink or white flowers

devalue *vb* **-valuing, -valued 1** to reduce the exchange value of (a currency) **2** to reduce the value of (something or someone) **devaluation** *n*

devastate *vb* **-tating, -tated** to damage (a place) severely or destroy it [Latin *devastare*] **devastation** *n*

devastated *adj* shocked and extremely upset **devastating** *adj* **devastatingly** *adv*

develop *vb* **1** to grow or bring to a later, more elaborate, or more advanced stage **2** to come or bring into existence: *the country has developed a consumer society* **3** to make or become gradually clearer or more widely known **4** to follow as a result of something: *Cubism developed from attempts to give painting a more intellectual concept of form* **5** to contract (an illness) **6** to improve the value or change the use of (land) **7** to exploit the natural resources of (a country or region) **8** *photog* to treat (a photographic plate or film) to produce a visible image [Old French *desveloper* to unwrap]

developer *n* **1** a person who develops property **2** *photog* a chemical used to develop photographic film

developing country *n* a poor or nonindustrial country that is seeking to develop its resources by industrialization

development *n* **1** the process of growing or developing **2** the product of developing **3** an event or incident that changes a situation **4** an area of land that has been developed **developmental** *adj*

development area *n* (in Britain) an area which has experienced economic depression and which is given government assistance to establish new industry

deviant *adj* **1** deviating from what is considered acceptable behaviour ▷ *n* **2** a person whose behaviour deviates from what is considered to be acceptable **deviance** *n*

deviate *vb* **-ating, -ated 1** to differ from others in belief or thought **2** to depart from one's usual or previous behaviour [Late Latin *deviare* to turn aside from the direct road] **deviation** *n*

device *n* **1** a machine or tool used for a particular purpose **2** *euphemistic* a bomb **3** a scheme or plan **4** a design or emblem **5 leave someone to his** *or* **her own devices** to leave someone alone to do as

he or she wishes [Old French *devis* contrivance + *devise* intention]
devil *n* **1** *theol* **the Devil** the chief spirit of evil and enemy of God **2** any evil spirit **3** a person regarded as wicked **4** a person: *lucky devil* **5** a person regarded as daring: *be a devil!* **6** *informal* something difficult or annoying **7 between the devil and the deep blue sea** between equally undesirable alternatives **8 give the devil his due** to acknowledge the talent or success of an unpleasant person **9 talk of the devil!** used when an absent person who has been the subject of conversation arrives unexpectedly **10 the devil** used as an exclamation to show surprise or annoyance: *what the devil is she doing here?* ▷ *vb* **-villing, -villed** *or US* **-viling, -viled 11** to prepare (food) by coating with a highly flavoured spiced mixture **12** *chiefly Brit* to do routine literary work for a lawyer or author [Greek *diabolos* enemy, accuser]
devilish *adj* **1** of or like a devil; fiendish ▷ *adv, adj* **2** *informal, old-fashioned* extreme or extremely: *devilish good food* **devilishly** *adv*
devil-may-care *adj* happy-go-lucky; reckless
devilment *n* mischievous conduct
devilry *n* **1** reckless fun or mischief **2** wickedness
devil's advocate *n* a person who takes an opposing or unpopular point of view for the sake of argument
devious *adj* **1** insincere and dishonest **2** (of a route or course of action) indirect [Latin *devius* lying to one side of the road] **deviously** *adv*
devise *vb* **-vising, -vised** to work out (something) in one's mind [Old French *deviser* to divide]
devoid *adj* **devoid of** completely lacking in a particular quality: *she was a woman totally devoid of humour* [Old French *devoider* to remove]
devolution *n* a transfer of authority from a central government to regional governments [Medieval Latin *devolutio* a rolling down] **devolutionist** *n, adj*
devolve *vb* **-volving, -volved** to pass or cause to pass to a successor or substitute, as duties or power [Latin *devolvere* to roll down]
Devon *n* a breed of large red cattle originally from Devon
Devonian *adj* **1** *geol* of the period of geological time about 405 million years ago **2** of or relating to Devon
devote *vb* **-voting, -voted** to apply or dedicate (one's time, money, or effort) to a particular purpose [Latin *devovere* to vow]
devoted *adj* feeling or demonstrating loyalty or devotion: *he was clearly devoted to his family* **devotedly** *adv*
devotee (dev-vote-**tee**) *n* **1** a person fanatically enthusiastic about a subject or activity **2** a zealous follower of a religion
devotion *n* **1** strong attachment to or affection for someone or something **2** religious zeal; piety **3 devotions** religious observance or prayers **devotional** *adj*
devour *vb* **1** to eat up greedily **2** to engulf and destroy **3** to read avidly [Latin *devorare* to gulp down] **devouring** *adj*
devout *adj* **1** deeply religious **2** sincere; heartfelt: *a devout confession* [Latin *devotus* faithful] **devoutly** *adv*
dew *n* drops of water that form on the ground or on a cool surface at night from vapour in the air [Old English *dēaw*] **dewy** *adj*
dewberry *n, pl* **-berries** a type of bramble with blue-black fruits
dewclaw *n* a nonfunctional claw on a dog's leg
Dewey Decimal System *n* a system of library book classification with ten main subject classes [after Melvil *Dewey*, educator]
dewlap *n* a loose fold of skin hanging under the throat in cattle, dogs, etc. [Middle English *dew* + *lap* hanging flap]
dew-worm *n US & Canad* a large earthworm used as fishing bait
dewy-eyed *adj* innocent and inexperienced
dexter *adj* of or on the right side of a shield, etc., from the bearer's point of view [Latin]
dexterity *n* **1** skill in using one's hands **2** mental quickness [Latin *dexteritas* aptness, readiness]
dexterous *adj* possessing or done with dexterity **dexterously** *adv*
dextrin *or* **dextrine** *n* a sticky substance obtained from starch: used as a thickening agent in food [French *dextrine*]
dextrose *n* a glucose occurring in fruit, honey, and in the blood of animals
DFC (in Britain) Distinguished Flying Cross
dg decigram
dhal *or* **dal** *n* **1** the nutritious pealike seed of a tropical shrub **2** a curry made from lentils or other pulses [Hindi *dāl*]
dharma *n* **1** *Hinduism* moral law or behaviour **2** *Buddhism* ideal truth [Sanskrit]
dhoti *n, pl* **-tis** a long loincloth worn by men in India [Hindi]
DI 1 *Brit* Detective Inspector **2** Donor Insemination: a method of making a woman pregnant by transferring sperm from a man other than her husband or regular partner using artificial means
di- *prefix* **1** twice; two; double: *dicotyledon* **2** containing two specified atoms or groups of atoms: *carbon dioxide* [Greek]
diabetes (die-a-**beet**-eez) *n* a medical condition in which the body is unable to control the level of sugar in the blood [Greek: a passing through]
diabetic *n* **1** a person who has diabetes ▷ *adj* **2** of or having diabetes **3** suitable for people who have diabetes: *diabetic chocolate*
diabolic *adj* of the Devil; satanic [Greek *diabolos* devil]
diabolical *adj* **1** *informal* unpleasant or annoying: *the weather was diabolical* **2** *informal* extreme: *diabolical cheek* **3** same as **diabolic** **diabolically** *adv*
diabolism *n* **A** witchcraft or sorcery **B** worship of devils **diabolist** *n*
diaconate *n* the position or period of office of a deacon [Late Latin *diaconatus*] **diaconal** *adj*
diacritic *n* a sign placed above or below a character or letter to indicate phonetic value or stress [Greek *diakritikos* serving to distinguish]

diadem *n old-fashioned* a small jewelled crown or headband, usually worn by royalty: *a gold diadem* [Greek: royal headdress]

diaeresis *or esp US* **dieresis** (die-**air**-iss-iss) *n, pl* **-ses** (-seez) the mark (¨) placed over the second of two adjacent vowels to indicate that it is to be pronounced separately, as in naïve [Greek: a division]

diagnose *vb* **-nosing, -nosed** to determine by diagnosis

diagnosis (die-ag-**no**-siss) *n, pl* **-ses** (-seez) the discovery and identification of diseases from the examination of symptoms [Greek: a distinguishing] **diagnostic** *adj*

diagonal *adj* **1** *maths* connecting any two vertices in a polygon that are not adjacent **2** slanting ▷ *n* **3** a diagonal line, plane, or pattern [Greek *dia-* through + *gōnia* angle] **diagonally** *adv*

diagram *n* a sketch or plan showing the form or workings of something [Greek *diagraphein* to mark out] **diagrammatic** *adj*

dial *n* **1** the face of a clock or watch, marked with divisions representing units of time **2** the graduated disc on a measuring instrument **3** the control on a radio or television set used to change the station **4** a numbered disc on the front of some telephones ▷ *vb* **dialling, dialled** *or US* **dialing, dialed 5** to try to establish a telephone connection with (someone) by operating the dial or buttons on a telephone [Latin *dies* day]

dialect *n* a form of a language spoken in a particular geographical area [Greek *dialektos* speech, dialect] **dialectal** *adj*

dialectic *n* **1** logical debate by question and answer to resolve differences between two views **2** the art of logical argument [Greek *dialektikē (tekhnē)* (the art) of argument] **dialectical** *adj*

dialling tone *or US, Canad, Austral & NZ* **dial tone** *n* a continuous sound heard on picking up a telephone receiver, indicating that a number can be dialled

dialogue *or US sometimes* **dialog** *n* **1** conversation between two people **2** a conversation in a literary or dramatic work **3** a discussion between representatives of two nations or groups [Greek *dia-* between + *legein* to speak]

dialysis (die-**al**-iss-iss) *n, pl* **-ses** (-seez) **1** *med* the filtering of blood through a semipermeable membrane to remove waste products **2** the separation of the particles in a solution by filtering through a semipermeable membrane [Greek *dialuein* to tear apart, dissolve] **dialyser** *or US* **-lyzer** *n* **dialytic** *adj*

diamagnetism *n* the phenomenon exhibited by substances that are repelled by both poles of a magnet

diamanté (die-a-**man**-tee) *adj* decorated with glittering bits of material, such as sequins [French]

diameter *n* **A** a straight line through the centre of a circle or sphere **B** the length of such a line [Greek *dia-* through + *metron* measure]

diametric *or* **diametrical** *adj* **1** of or relating to a diameter **2** completely opposed: *the diametric opposition of the two camps* **diametrically** *adv*

diamond *n* **1** a usually colourless exceptionally hard precious stone of crystallized carbon **2** *geom* a figure with four sides of equal length forming two acute and two obtuse angles **3** a playing card marked with one or more red diamond-shaped symbols **4** *baseball* the playing field ▷ *adj* **5** (of an anniversary) the sixtieth: *diamond wedding* [Latin *adamas* the hardest iron or steel, diamond]

Diana *n* the Roman goddess of hunting

diapason (die-a-**pay**-zon) *n music* **1** either of two stops found throughout the range of a pipe organ **2** the range of an instrument or voice [Greek *dia pasōn* through all (the notes)]

diaper *n US & Canad* a nappy [Medieval Greek *diaspros* pure white]

diaphanous (die-**af**-fan-uss) *adj* (of fabrics) fine and translucent [Greek *diaphanēs* transparent]

diaphoretic *n* **1** a drug that causes perspiration or sweat ▷ *adj* **2** relating to or causing perspiration or sweat

diaphragm (**die**-a-fram) *n* **1** *anatomy* the muscular partition that separates the abdominal cavity and chest cavity **2** same as **cap** (sense 5) **3** a device to control the amount of light entering an optical instrument **4** a thin vibrating disc which converts sound to electricity or vice versa, as in a microphone or loudspeaker [Greek *dia-* across + *phragma* fence]

diapositive *n* a positive transparency; slide

diarist *n* a person who writes a diary that is subsequently published

diarrhoea *or esp US* **diarrhea** (die-a-**ree**-a) *n* frequent discharge of abnormally liquid faeces [Greek *dia-* through + *rhein* to flow]

diary *n, pl* **-ries 1** a book containing a record of daily events, appointments, or observations **2** a written record of daily events, appointments, or observations [Latin *dies* day]

Diaspora (die-**ass**-spore-a) *n* **1** the dispersion of the Jews after the Babylonian conquest of Palestine **2** a dispersion of people originally belonging to one nation [Greek: a scattering]

diastase (**die**-ass-stayss) *n* an enzyme that converts starch into sugar [Greek *diastasis* a separation] **diastasic** *adj*

diastole (die-**ass**-stoh-lee) *n* dilation of the chambers of the heart **diastolic** *adj*

diatom *n* a microscopic unicellular alga [Greek *diatomos* cut in two]

diatomic *adj* containing two atoms

diatonic *adj* of or relating to any scale of five tones and two semitones produced by playing the white keys of a keyboard instrument [Greek *diatonos* extending]

diatribe *n* a bitter critical attack [Greek *dia-* through + *tribein* to rub]

dibble *n* a small hand tool used to make holes in the ground for bulbs, seeds, or roots [origin unknown]

dice *n, pl* **dice 1** a small cube, each of whose sides has a different number of spots (1 to 6), used in games of chance ▷ *vb* **dicing, diced 2** to cut (food) into small cubes **3 dice with death** to take a risk [originally plural of DIE²]

dicey *adj* **dicier, diciest** *informal* dangerous or tricky

d

dichotomy (die-kot-a-mee) *n, pl* **-mies** division into two opposed groups or parts [Greek *dicha* in two + *temnein* to cut] **dichotomous** *adj*

> **USAGE** *Dichotomy* should always refer to a division of some kind into two groups. It is sometimes used to refer to a puzzling situation which seems to involve a contradiction, but this use is generally thought to be incorrect.

dichromatic *adj* having two colours [Greek *di-* double + *khrōma* colour]

d

dick *n slang* **1** *vulgar* a penis **2 clever dick** an opinionated person [*Dick* familiar form of *Richard*]

dickens *n* **the dickens** *informal* used as an exclamation to show surprise, confusion, or annoyance: *what the dickens do you think you're doing?* [from the name *Dickens*]

Dickensian *adj* **1** of Charles Dickens (1812–70), British novelist **2** denoting poverty, distress, and exploitation, as depicted in the novels of Dickens

dicky¹ *n, pl* **dickies** *informal* a false shirt front [from *Dick*, name]

dicky² *adj* **dickier, dickiest** *Brit & NZ informal* shaky or weak: *a dicky heart* [origin unknown]

dicky-bird *n* a child's word for a bird

dicky-bow *n Brit informal* a bow tie

dicotyledon (die-kot-ill-**leed**-on) *n* a flowering plant with two seed leaves

dictate *vb* **-tating, -tated 1** to say (words) aloud for another person to transcribe **2** to seek to impose one's will on others ▷ *n* **3** an authoritative command **4** a guiding principle: *the dictates of reason* [Latin *dictare* to say repeatedly]

dictation *n* **1** the act of dictating words to be taken down in writing **2** the words dictated

dictator *n* **1** a ruler who has complete power **2** a person who behaves in a tyrannical manner **dictatorship** *n*

dictatorial *adj* **1** of or pertaining to a dictator **2** tyrannical; overbearing **dictatorially** *adv*

diction *n* the manner of pronouncing words and sounds [Latin *dicere* to speak]

dictionary *n, pl* **-aries 1 A** a book that consists of an alphabetical list of words with their meanings **B** a similar book giving equivalent words in two languages **2** a reference book listing terms and giving information about a particular subject [Late Latin *dictio* word]

dictum *n, pl* **-tums** *or* **-ta 1** a formal statement; pronouncement **2** a popular saying or maxim [Latin]

did *vb* the past tense of **do¹**

didactic *adj* intended to teach or instruct people: *an Impressionist work can be as didactic in its way as a sermon* [Greek *didaktikos* skilled in teaching] **didactically** *adv* **didacticism** *n*

diddle *vb* **-dling, -dled** *informal* to swindle [Jeremy *Diddler*, a scrounger in a 19th-century play] **diddler** *n*

didgeridoo *n* an Australian Aboriginal deep-toned wind instrument [imitative]

didn't did not

die¹ *vb* **dying, died 1** (of a person, animal, or plant) to cease all biological activity permanently **2** (of something inanimate) to cease to exist **3** to lose strength, power, or energy by degrees **4** to stop working: *the engine died* **5 be dying** to be eager (for something or to do something) **6 be dying of** *informal* to be nearly overcome with (laughter, boredom, etc.) **7 die hard** to change or disappear only slowly: *old loyalties die hard* **8 to die for** *informal* highly desirable: *a salary to die for* ▷ See also **die down, die out** [Old English *dīegan*]

> **USAGE** It was formerly considered incorrect to use the preposition *from* after *die*, but *of* and *from* are now both acceptable: *he died of/from his injuries.*

die² *n* **1** a shaped block used to cut or form metal **2** a casting mould **3** same as **dice** (sense 1) **4 the die is cast** an irrevocable decision has been taken [Latin *dare* to give, play]

die down *vb* **1** to lose strength or power by degrees **2** to become calm: *the storm has died down now*

die-hard *or* **diehard** *n* a person who resists change

dieldrin *n* a highly toxic crystalline insecticide

dielectric *n* **1** a substance of very low electrical conductivity; insulator ▷ *adj* **2** having the properties of a dielectric [Greek *dia-* through + ELECTRIC]

die out *or* **die off** *vb* to become extinct or disappear after a gradual decline

dieresis (die-air-iss-iss) *n, pl* **-ses** (-seez) same as **diaeresis**

diesel *n* **1** same as **diesel engine 2** a vehicle driven by a diesel engine **3** *informal* diesel oil [after R. *Diesel*, engineer]

diesel-electric *n* a locomotive with a diesel engine driving an electric generator

diesel engine *n* an internal-combustion engine in which oil is ignited by compression

diesel oil *or* **diesel fuel** *n* a fuel obtained from petroleum distillation, used in diesel engines

diet¹ *n* **1** the food that a person or animal regularly eats **2** a specific allowance or selection of food, to control weight or for health reasons: *a high-fibre diet* ▷ *vb* **3** to follow a special diet so as to lose weight ▷ *adj* **4** suitable for eating with a weight-reduction diet: *diet soft drinks* [Greek *diaita* mode of living] **dietary** *adj* **dieter** *n*

diet² *n* a legislative assembly in some countries [Medieval Latin *dieta* public meeting]

dietary fibre *n* the roughage in fruits and vegetables that aids digestion

dietetic *adj* prepared for special dietary requirements

dietetics *n* the study of diet, nutrition, and the preparation of food

dietician *n* a person qualified to advise people about healthy eating

differ *vb* **1** to be dissimilar in quality, nature, or degree **2** to disagree [Latin *differre* to scatter, be different]

difference *n* **1** the state or quality of being unlike **2** a disagreement or argument **3** the result of the subtraction of one number or quantity from another **4 make a difference** to have an effect **5 split the difference A** to compromise **B** to divide a remainder equally

different *adj* **1** partly or completely unlike **2** new or unusual **3** not identical or the same;

other: *he wears a different tie every day* **differently** *adv*

> **USAGE** The constructions *different from, different to,* and *different than* are all found in the works of writers of English during the past. Nowadays, however, the most widely acceptable preposition to use after *different* is *from. Different to* is common in British English, but is considered by some people to be incorrect, or less acceptable. *Different than* is a standard construction in American English. As, however, this idiom is not regarded as totally acceptable in British usage, it is preferable either to use *different from: this result is only slightly different from that obtained in the US* or to rephrase the sentence: *this result differs only slightly from that in the US.*

differential *adj* **1** of, relating to, or using a difference **2** *maths* involving differentials ▹ *n* **3** a factor that differentiates between two comparable things **4** *maths* a minute difference between values in a scale **5** *chiefly Brit* the difference between rates of pay for different types of labour, esp. within a company or industry

differential calculus *n* the branch of mathematics concerned with derivatives and differentials

differential gear *n* the gear in the driving axle of a road vehicle that permits one driving wheel to rotate faster than the other when cornering

differentiate *vb* **-ating, -ated 1** to perceive or show the difference (between) **2** to make (one thing) distinct from other such things **3** *maths* to determine the derivative of a function or variable **differentiation** *n*

difficult *adj* **1** not easy to do, understand, or solve **2** not easily pleased or satisfied: *a difficult patient* **3** full of hardships or trials: *he had recently had a difficult time with his job as a self-employed builder*

difficulty *n, pl* **-ties 1** the state or quality of being difficult **2** a task or problem that is hard to deal with **3** a troublesome or embarrassing situation: *in financial difficulties* **4** an objection or obstacle: *you're just making difficulties* **5** lack of ease; awkwardness: *she could run only with difficulty* [Latin *difficultas*]

diffident *adj* lacking self-confidence; shy [Latin *dis-* not + *fidere* to trust] **diffidence** *n* **diffidently** *adv*

diffract *vb* to cause to undergo diffraction **diffractive** *adj*

diffraction *n* **1** *physics* a deviation in the direction of a wave at the edge of an obstacle in its path **2** the formation of light and dark fringes by the passage of light through a small aperture [Latin *diffringere* to shatter]

diffuse *vb* **-fusing, -fused 1** to spread over a wide area **2** *physics* to cause to undergo diffusion ▹ *adj* **3** spread out over a wide area **4** lacking conciseness [Latin *diffusus* spread abroad] **diffuser** *n* **diffusible** *adj*

> **USAGE** Avoid confusion with **defuse.**

diffusion *n* **1** the act of diffusing or the fact of being diffused; dispersion **2** *physics* the random thermal motion of atoms and molecules in gases, liquids, and some solids **3** *physics* the transmission or reflection of light, in which the radiation is scattered in many directions

dig *vb* **digging, dug 1** to cut into, break up, and turn over or remove (earth), esp. with a spade **2** to excavate (a hole or tunnel) by digging, usually with an implement or (of animals) with claws **3** to obtain by digging: *dig out potatoes* **4** to find by effort or searching: *she dug out a torch from her bag* **5** *informal* to like or understand **6** (foll. by *in* or *into*) to thrust or jab ▹ *n* **7** the act of digging **8** an archaeological excavation **9** a thrust or poke **10** a cutting remark ▹ See also **dig in** [Middle English *diggen*]

d

digest *vb* **1** to subject (food) to a process of digestion **2** to absorb mentally ▹ *n* **3** a shortened version of a book, report, or article [Latin *digerere* to divide] **digestible** *adj*

digestion *n* **1** the process of breaking down food into easily absorbed substances **2** the body's system for doing this

digestive *adj* relating to digestion

digger *n* a machine used for excavation

dig in *vb* **1** to mix (compost or fertilizer) into the soil by digging **2** to begin to eat vigorously **3** *informal* (of soldiers) to dig a trench and prepare for an enemy attack **4 dig one's heels in** *informal* to refuse to move or be persuaded

digit (**dij**-it) *n* **1** a finger or toe **2** any numeral from 0 to 9 [Latin *digitus* toe, finger]

digital *adj* **1** displaying information as numbers rather than with a dial **2** representing data as a series of numerical values **3** of or possessing digits **digitally** *adv*

digital clock *or* **digital watch** *n* a clock or watch in which the time is indicated by digits rather than by hands on a dial

digitalis *n* a drug made from foxglove leaves: used as a heart stimulant [Latin: relating to a finger (from the shape of the foxglove flowers)]

digitate *adj* **1** (of leaves) having leaflets in the form of a spread hand **2** (of animals) having digits

digitize *or* **-ise** *vb* **-izing, -ized** *or* **-ising, -ised** to transcribe (data) into a digital form for processing by a computer **digitization** *or* **-isation** *n* **digitizer** *or* **-iser** *n*

dignified *adj* calm, impressive, and worthy of respect

dignify *vb* **-fies, -fying, -fied 1** to add distinction to: *the meeting was dignified by the minister* **2** to add a semblance of dignity to by the use of a pretentious name or title: *she dignifies every plant with its Latin name* [Latin *dignus* worthy + *facere* to make]

dignitary *n, pl* **-taries** a person of high official position or rank

dignity *n, pl* **-ties 1** serious, calm, and controlled behaviour or manner **2** the quality of being worthy of honour **3** sense of self-importance: *he considered the job beneath his dignity* [Latin *dignus* worthy]

digraph *n* two letters used to represent a single sound, such as *gh* in *tough*

digress *vb* to depart from the main subject in speech or writing [Latin *digressus* turned aside] **digression** *n*

digs *pl n Brit, Austral & S African informal* lodgings [from *diggings*, perhaps referring to where one digs or works]

dihedral *adj* having or formed by two intersecting planes

dilapidated *adj* (of a building) having fallen into ruin [Latin *dilapidare* to waste] **dilapidation** *n*

dilate *vb* **-lating, -lated** to make or become wider or larger: *her eyes dilated in the dark* [Latin *dilatare* to spread out] **dilation** *or* **dilatation** *n*

dilatory (dill-a-tree) *adj* tending or intended to waste time [Late Latin *dilatorius*] **dilatorily** *adv* **dilatoriness** *n*

d

dildo *n, pl* **-dos** an object used as a substitute for an erect penis [origin unknown]

dilemma *n* a situation offering a choice between two equally undesirable alternatives [Greek *di-* double + *lēmma* proposition]

> **USAGE** The use of *dilemma* to refer to a problem that seems incapable of a solution is considered by some people to be incorrect.

dilettante (dill-it-tan-tee) *n, pl* **-tantes** *or* **-tanti** a person whose interest in a subject is superficial rather than serious [Italian] **dilettantism** *n*

diligent *adj* **1** careful and persevering in carrying out tasks or duties **2** carried out with care and perseverance: *a diligent approach to work* [Latin *diligere* to value] **diligence** *n* **diligently** *adv*

dill *n* a sweet-smelling herb used for flavouring [Old English *dile*]

dilly-dally *vb* **-lies, -lying, -lied** *Brit, Austral & NZ informal* to dawdle or waste time [reduplication of *dally*]

dilute *vb* **-luting, -luted 1** to make (a liquid) less concentrated by adding water or another liquid **2** to make (someone's power, idea, or role) weaker or less effective: *socialists used their majority in parliament to dilute legislation crucial to developing a market economy* ▷ *adj* **3** *chem* (of a solution) having a low concentration [Latin *diluere*] **dilution** *n*

diluvian *or* **diluvial** *adj* of a flood, esp. the great Flood described in the Old Testament [Latin *diluere* to wash away]

dim *adj* **dimmer, dimmest 1** badly lit **2** not clearly seen; faint: *a dim figure in the doorway* **3** not seeing clearly: *eyes dim with tears* **4** *informal* mentally dull **5** not clear in the mind; obscure: *a dim awareness* **6** lacking in brightness or lustre: *a dim colour* **7 take a dim view of** to disapprove of ▷ *vb* **dimming, dimmed 8** to become or cause to become dim **9** to cause to seem less bright **10** *US & Canad* same as **dip** (sense 4) [Old English *dimm*] **dimly** *adv* **dimness** *n*

dime *n* a coin of the US and Canada worth ten cents [Latin *decem* ten]

dimension *n* **1** an aspect or factor: *the attack brought a whole new dimension to the bombing campaign* **2 dimensions** scope or extent **3** (*often pl*) a measurement of the size of something in a particular direction [Latin *dimensio* an extent] **dimensional** *adj*

dimer *n chem* a molecule made up of two identical molecules bonded together

diminish *vb* **1** to make or become smaller, fewer, or less **2** *music* to decrease (a minor interval) by a semitone **3** to reduce in authority or status [Latin *deminuere* to make smaller + archaic *minish* to lessen]

diminuendo *music* ▷ *n, pl* **-dos 1** **A** a gradual decrease in loudness **B** a passage which gradually decreases in loudness ▷ *adv* **2** gradually decreasing in loudness [Italian]

diminution *n* reduction in size, volume, intensity, or importance [Latin *deminutio*]

diminutive *adj* **1** very small; tiny **2** *grammar* **A** denoting an affix added to a word to convey the meaning *small* or *unimportant* or to express affection, as for example, the suffix *-ette* in French **B** denoting a word formed by the addition of a diminutive affix ▷ *n* **3** *grammar* a diminutive word or affix **diminutiveness** *n*

dimmer *n* **1** a device for dimming an electric light **2** *US* **A** a dipped headlight on a road vehicle **B** a parking light on a car

dimple *n* **1** a small natural dent on the cheeks or chin ▷ *vb* **-pling, -pled 2** to produce dimples by smiling [Middle English *dympull*]

dimwit *n informal* a stupid person **dim-witted** *adj*

din *n* **1** a loud unpleasant confused noise ▷ *vb* **dinning, dinned 2 din something into someone** to instil something into someone by constant repetition [Old English *dynn*]

dinar (dee-nahr) *n* a monetary unit of various Balkan, Middle Eastern, and North African countries [Latin *denarius* a Roman coin]

dine *vb* **dining, dined 1** to eat dinner **2 dine on** *or* **off** to make one's meal of: *the guests dined on roast beef* [Old French *disner*]

diner *n* **1** a person eating a meal in a restaurant **2** *chiefly US & Canad* a small cheap restaurant **3** short for **dining car**

dinette *n* an alcove or small area for use as a dining room

ding *n informal* a small dent in a vehicle

ding-dong *n* **1** the sound of a bell **2** *Brit informal* a violent exchange of blows or words [imitative]

dinges (ding-uss) *n S African informal* a jocular word for something whose name is unknown or forgotten; thingumabob [Dutch *ding* thing]

dinghy (ding-ee, ding-gee) *n, pl* **-ghies** a small boat, powered by sail, oars, or outboard motor [Hindi or Bengali *dingi*]

dingle *n* a small wooded hollow or valley [origin unknown]

dingo *n, pl* **-goes** an Australian native wild dog [Aboriginal]

dingy (din-jee) *adj* **-gier, -giest 1** *Brit, Austral & NZ* dull, neglected, and drab: *he waited in this dingy little outer office* **2** shabby and discoloured: *she was wearing dingy white overalls* [origin unknown] **dinginess** *n*

dining car *n* a railway coach in which meals are served

dining room *n* a room where meals are eaten

dinkum *adj Austral & NZ informal* genuine or right: *a fair dinkum offer* [English dialect: work]

dinky *adj* **dinkier, dinkiest** *chiefly Brit informal* small and neat; dainty [dialect *dink* neat]

dinky-di *adj Austral informal* typical [variant of DINKUM]

dinner *n* **1** the main meal of the day, eaten either in the evening or at midday **2** a formal social

occasion at which an evening meal is served [Old French *disner* to dine]
dinner jacket *n* a man's semiformal black evening jacket without tails
dinner service *n* a set of matching dishes suitable for serving a meal
dinosaur *n* any of a large order of extinct prehistoric reptiles many of which were gigantic [Greek *deinos* fearful + *sauros* lizard]
dint *n* **by dint of** by means of: *by dint of their own efforts* [Old English *dynt* a blow]
diocesan *adj* of or relating to a diocese
diocese (**die**-a-siss) *n* the district over which a bishop has control [Greek *dioikēsis* administration]
diode *n* **1** a semiconductor device for converting alternating current to direct current **2** an electronic valve with two electrodes between which a current can flow only in one direction [Greek *di-* double + *hodos* a way, road]
dioecious (die-**eesh**-uss) *adj* (of plants) having the male and female reproductive organs on separate plants [Greek *di-* twice + *oikia* house]
Dionysian (die-on-**niz**-zee-an) *adj* wild or orgiastic [from *Dionysus*, Greek god of wine]
Dionysus *n Greek myth* the god of wine
dioptre *or US* **diopter** (die-**op**-ter) *n* a unit for measuring the refractive power of a lens [Greek *dia-* through + *opsesthai* to see]
diorama *n* **1** a miniature three-dimensional scene, in which models of figures are seen against a background **2** a picture made up of illuminated translucent curtains, viewed through an aperture [Greek *dia-* through + *horama* view]
dioxide *n* an oxide containing two oxygen atoms per molecule
dip *vb* **dipping, dipped 1** to plunge or be plunged quickly or briefly into a liquid **2** to put one's hands into something, esp. to obtain an object: *she dipped into her handbag looking for change* **3** to slope downwards **4** to switch (car headlights) from the main to the lower beam **5** to undergo a slight decline, esp. temporarily: *sales dipped in November* **6** to immerse (farm animals) briefly in a chemical to rid them of insects **7** to lower or be lowered briefly: *she dipped her knee in a curtsy* ▹ *n* **8** the act of dipping **9** a brief swim **10** a liquid chemical in which farm animals are dipped **11** a depression, esp. in a landscape **12** a momentary sinking down **13** a creamy mixture into which pieces of food are dipped before being eaten ▹ See also **dip into** [Old English *dyppan*]
Dip Ed (in Britain) Diploma in Education
diphtheria (dif-**theer**-ree-a) *n* a contagious disease producing fever and difficulty in breathing and swallowing [Greek *diphthera* leather; from the membrane that forms in the throat]
diphthong *n* a vowel sound, occupying a single syllable, in which the speaker's tongue moves continuously from one position to another, as in the pronunciation of *a* in *late* [Greek *di-* double + *phthongos* sound]
dip into *vb* **1** to draw upon: *he dipped into his savings* **2** to read passages at random from (a book or journal)
diploid *adj biol* denoting a cell or organism with pairs of homologous chromosomes [Greek *di-* double + *-ploos* -fold]
diploma *n* a document conferring a qualification or recording successful completion of a course of study [Latin: official document, literally: letter folded double]
diplomacy *n* **1** the conduct of the relations between nations by peaceful means **2** skill in the management of international relations **3** tact or skill in dealing with people
diplomat *n* an official, such as an ambassador, engaged in diplomacy
diplomatic *adj* **1** of or relating to diplomacy **2** skilled in negotiating between nations **3** tactful in dealing with people [French *diplomatique* concerning the documents of diplomacy; see DIPLOMA] **diplomatically** *adv*
diplomatic immunity *n* the freedom from legal action and exemption from taxation which diplomats have in the country where they are working
dipole *n* **1** two equal but opposite electric charges or magnetic poles separated by a small distance **2** a molecule that has two such charges or poles **dipolar** *adj*
dipper *n* **1** a ladle used for dipping **2** a songbird that inhabits fast-flowing streams
diprotodont (die-**pro**-toe-dont) *n* a marsupial with fewer than three upper incisor teeth on each side of the jaw
dipsomania *n* a compulsive desire to drink alcoholic beverages [Greek *dipsa* thirst + *mania* madness] **dipsomaniac** *n, adj*
dipstick *n* a rod with notches on it dipped into a container to indicate the fluid level
dip switch *n* a device for dipping headlights on a vehicle
dipterous *adj* having two wings or winglike parts [Greek *dipteros* two-winged]
diptych (**dip**-tik) *n* a painting on two hinged panels [Greek *di-* double + *ptuchē* a panel]
dire *adj* disastrous, urgent, or terrible: *he was now in dire financial straits* [Latin *dirus* ominous]
direct *adj* **1** shortest; straight: *a direct route* **2** without intervening people: *they secretly arranged direct links to their commanders* **3** honest; frank: *he was polite but very direct* **4** diametric: *the direct opposite* **5** in an unbroken line of descent: *a direct descendant* ▹ *adv* **6** directly; straight ▹ *vb* **7** to conduct or control the affairs of **8** to give orders with authority to (a person or group) **9** to tell (someone) the way to a place **10** to address (a letter, parcel, etc.) **11** to address (a look or remark) at someone: *the look she directed at him was one of unconcealed hatred* **12 A** to provide guidance to (actors, cameramen, etc.) in (a play or film) **B** to supervise the making or staging of (a film or play) [Latin *dirigere* to guide] **directness** *n*
direct access *n* a method of reading data from a computer file without reading through the file from the beginning
direct current *n* an electric current that flows in one direction only
direct debit *n* an order given to a bank or other financial institution by an account holder to pay

an amount of money from the account to a specified person or company at regular intervals

direction *n* **1** the course or line along which a person or thing moves, points, or lies **2** management or guidance: *the campaign was successful under his direction* **3** the work of a stage or film director

directional *adj* **1** of or showing direction **2** *electronics* (of an aerial) transmitting or receiving radio waves more effectively in some directions than in others

d

directions *pl n* instructions for doing something or for reaching a place

directive *n* an instruction; order

directly *adv* **1** in a direct manner **2** at once; without delay **3** immediately or very soon: *I'll do that directly* ▷ *conj* **4** as soon as: *we left directly the money arrived*

direct message *n* (on a social network) a message that can be read only by one or more named recipients

direct object *n grammar* a noun, pronoun, or noun phrase denoting the person or thing receiving the direct action of a verb. For example, *a book* in *They bought Anne a book*

director *n* **1** a person or thing that directs or controls **2** a member of the governing board of a business, trust, etc. **3** the person responsible for the artistic and technical aspects of the making of a film or television programme **directorial** *adj* **directorship** *n*

directorate *n* **1** a board of directors **2** the position of director

director-general *n, pl* **directors-general** a person in overall charge of certain large organizations

directory *n, pl* **-ries 1** a book listing names, addresses, and telephone numbers of individuals or business companies **2** *computers* an area of a disk containing the names and locations of the files it currently holds

direct speech *n* the reporting of what someone has said by quoting the exact words

direct tax *n* a tax paid by the person or organization on which it is levied

dirge *n* **1** a chant of lamentation for the dead **2** any mournful song [Latin *dirige* direct (imperative), opening word of antiphon used in the office of the dead]

dirigible (dir-rij-jib-bl) *adj* **1** able to be steered ▷ *n* **2** same as **airship** [Latin *dirigere* to direct]

dirk *n* a dagger, formerly worn by Scottish Highlanders [Scots *durk*]

dirndl *n* **1** a woman's dress with a full gathered skirt and fitted bodice **2** a gathered skirt of this kind [from German]

dirt *n* **1** any unclean substance, such as mud; filth **2** loose earth; soil **3** packed earth, cinders, etc., used to make a racetrack **4** obscene speech or writing **5** *informal* harmful gossip [Old Norse *drit* excrement]

dirt-cheap *adj, adv* at an extremely low price

dirt-poor *adj chiefly US* extremely poor

dirt track *n* a racetrack made of packed earth or cinders

dirty *adj* **dirtier, dirtiest 1** covered or marked with dirt; filthy **2** causing one to become grimy: *a dirty job* **3** (of a colour) not clear and bright **4** unfair, dishonest, or unkind: *dirty tricks* **5 A** obscene: *dirty jokes* **B** sexually clandestine: *a dirty weekend* **6** revealing dislike or anger: *a dirty look* **7** (of weather) rainy or stormy **8 dirty work** unpleasant or illicit activity ▷ *n* **9 do the dirty on** *informal* to behave meanly towards ▷ *vb* **dirties, dirtying, dirtied 10** to make dirty; soil **dirtiness** *n*

dirty bomb *n informal* a bomb made from nuclear waste combined with conventional explosives that is capable of spreading radioactive material over a wide area

dis *vb* **disses, dissing, dissed** *slang, chiefly US* same as **diss**

dis- *prefix* **1** indicating reversal: *disconnect* **2** indicating negation or lack: *dissimilar; disgrace* **3** indicating removal or release: *disembowel*

disability *n, pl* **-ties 1** a physical or mental condition or illness that restricts a person in his or her ability to move or use his or her senses **2** something that disables someone

disable *vb* **-abling, -abled 1** to cause a person to be restricted in his or her ability to move or use the senses **2** to switch off (a device or computer program) **disablement** *n*

disabled *adj* having a physical or mental condition that restricts one's ability to move or use one's senses

> **USAGE** The use of *the disabled, the blind,* etc. can be offensive and should be avoided. Instead you should talk about *people with disabilities, blind people,* etc.

disabuse *vb* **-abusing, -abused** to rid (someone) of a mistaken idea: *Krysia felt unable to disabuse him of his prejudices*

disaccharide (die-sack-a-ride) *n* a sugar, such as sucrose, whose molecules consist of two linked monosaccharides

disadvantage *n* **1** an unfavourable or harmful circumstance **2 at a disadvantage** in a less favourable position than other people: *he continued to insist that he was at a disadvantage at the hearings* **disadvantageous** *adj*

disadvantaged *adj* socially or economically deprived

disaffected *adj* having lost loyalty to or affection for someone or something; alienated: *three million disaffected voters* **disaffection** *n*

disagree *vb* **-greeing, -greed 1** to have differing opinions or argue about (something) **2** to fail to correspond; conflict **3** to cause physical discomfort to: *curry disagrees with me*

disagreeable *adj* **1** (of an incident or situation) unpleasant **2** (of a person) bad-tempered or disobliging **disagreeably** *adv*

disagreement *n* **1** refusal or failure to agree **2** a difference between results, totals, etc., which shows that they cannot all be true **3** an argument

disallow *vb* to reject as untrue or invalid; cancel

disappear *vb* **1** to cease to be visible; vanish **2** to go away or become lost, esp. without explanation **3** to cease to exist: *the pain has disappeared* **disappearance** *n*

disappoint *vb* **1** to fail to meet the expectations or hopes of; let down **2** to prevent the fulfilment of (a plan, etc.); frustrate [Old French *desapointier*] **disappointed** *adj* **disappointing** *adj*
disappointment *n* **1** the feeling of being disappointed **2** a person or thing that disappoints
disapprobation *n* disapproval
disapprove *vb* **-proving, -proved** to consider wrong or bad **disapproval** *n* **disapproving** *adj*
disarm *vb* **1** to deprive of weapons **2** to win the confidence or affection of **3** (of a country) to decrease the size and capability of one's armed forces
disarmament *n* the reduction of fighting capability by a country
disarming *adj* removing hostility or suspicion **disarmingly** *adv*
disarrange *vb* **-ranging, -ranged** to throw into disorder **disarrangement** *n*
disarray *n* **1** confusion and lack of discipline **2** extreme untidiness ▷ *vb* **3** to throw into confusion
disassociate *vb* **-ating, -ated** same as **dissociate** **disassociation** *n*
disaster *n* **1** an accident that causes great distress or destruction **2** something, such as a project, that fails or has been ruined [Italian *disastro*] **disastrous** *adj* **disastrously** *adv*
disavow *vb* to deny connection with or responsibility for (something) **disavowal** *n*
disband *vb* to stop or cause to stop functioning as a unit or group **disbandment** *n*
disbar *vb* **-barring, -barred** to deprive (a barrister) of the right to practise

> **USAGE** *Disbar* is sometimes wrongly used where *debar* is meant: *he was debarred* (not *disbarred*) *from attending meetings.*

disbelieve *vb* **-lieving, -lieved** **1** to reject (a person or statement) as being untruthful **2 disbelieve in** to have no faith or belief in: *to disbelieve in the supernatural* **disbelief** *n*
disburse *vb* **-bursing, -bursed** to pay out [Old French *desborser*] **disbursement** *n*

> **USAGE** *Disburse* is sometimes wrongly used where *disperse* is meant: *the police used water cannon to disperse* (not *disburse*) *the crowd.*

disc *n* **1** a flat circular object **2** a sound recording made on such an object **3** *anatomy* a circular flat structure in the body, esp. between the vertebrae **4** *computers* same as **disk** [Latin *discus* discus]
discard *vb* to get rid of (something or someone) as useless or undesirable [DIS- + *card* (the playing card)]
disc brake *n* a brake in which two pads rub against a flat disc
discern *vb* to see or be aware of (something) clearly [Latin *discernere* to divide] **discernible** *adj*
discerning *adj* having or showing good judgment **discernment** *n*
discharge *vb* **-charging, -charged** **1** to release or allow to go **2** to dismiss (someone) from duty or employment **3** to fire (a gun) **4** to cause to pour forth: *the scar was red and swollen and began to discharge pus* **5** to remove (the cargo) from a boat, etc.; unload **6** to meet the demands of (a duty or responsibility) **7** to relieve oneself of (a debt) **8** *physics* to take or supply electrical current from (a cell or battery) ▷ *n* **9** something that is discharged **10** dismissal or release from an office, job, etc. **11** a pouring out of a fluid; emission **12** *physics* a conduction of electricity through a gas
disciple (diss-sipe-pl) *n* **1** a follower of the doctrines of a teacher **2** *Christianity* one of the personal followers of Christ during his earthly life [Latin *discipulus* pupil]
disciplinarian *n* a person who practises strict discipline
disciplinary *adj* of or imposing discipline; corrective
discipline *n* **1** the practice of imposing strict rules of behaviour on other people **2** the ability to behave and work in a controlled manner **3** a particular area of academic study ▷ *vb* **-plining, -plined** **4** to improve or attempt to improve the behaviour of (oneself or someone else) by training or rules **5** to punish [Latin *disciplina* teaching]
disciplined *adj* able to behave and work in a controlled way
disc jockey *n* a person who announces and plays recorded pop records on a radio programme or at a disco
disclaim *vb* **1** to deny (responsibility for or knowledge of something) **2** to give up (any claim to)
disclaimer *n* a statement denying responsibility for or knowledge of something
disclose *vb* **-closing, -closed** **1** to make (information) known **2** to allow to be seen: *she agreed to disclose the contents of the box* **disclosure** *n*
disco *n, pl* **-cos** **1** a nightclub for dancing to amplified pop records **2** an occasion at which people dance to amplified pop records **3** mobile equipment for providing music for a disco [from DISCOTHEQUE]
discography *n, pl* **-phies** a classified list of sound recordings
discolour *or US* **discolor** *vb* to change in colour; to fade or stain **discoloration** *n*
discomfit *vb* **-fiting, -fited** to make uneasy or confused [Old French *desconfire* to destroy] **discomfiture** *n*
discomfort *n* **1** a mild pain **2** a feeling of worry or embarrassment **3 discomforts** conditions that cause physical uncomfortableness: *the physical discomforts of pregnancy*
discommode *vb* **-moding, -moded** to cause inconvenience [DIS- + obsolete *commode* to suit] **discommodious** *adj*
discompose *vb* **-posing, -posed** to disturb or upset someone **discomposure** *n*
disconcert *vb* to disturb the confidence or self-possession of; upset, embarrass, or take aback **disconcerting** *adj*
disconnect *vb* **1** to undo or break the connection between (two things) **2** to stop the supply of (gas or electricity to a building) ▷ *n* **3** a lack of connection; disconnection: *a disconnect between political discourse and the public* **disconnection** *n*
disconnected *adj* (of speech or ideas) not logically connected

d

disconsolate *adj* sad beyond comfort [Medieval Latin *disconsolatus*] **disconsolately** *adv*
discontent *n* lack of contentment, as with one's condition or lot in life **discontented** *adj* **discontentedly** *adv*
discontinue *vb* **-nuing, -nued** to come or bring to an end; stop
discontinuous *adj* characterized by interruptions; intermittent **discontinuity** *n*
discord *n* **1** lack of agreement or harmony between people **2** harsh confused sounds **3** a combination of musical notes that lacks harmony [Latin *discors* at variance]
discordant *adj* **1** at variance; disagreeing **2** harsh in sound; inharmonious **discordance** *n*
discotheque *n* same as **disco** [French]
discount *vb* **1** to leave (something) out of account as being unreliable, prejudiced, or irrelevant **2** to deduct (an amount or percentage) from the price of something ▷ *n* **3** a deduction from the full amount of a price **4 at a discount** below the regular price
discountenance *vb* **-nancing, -nanced** to make (someone) ashamed or confused
discourage *vb* **-raging, -raged 1** to deprive of the will or enthusiasm to persist in something **2** to oppose by expressing disapproval **discouragement** *n* **discouraging** *adj*
discourse *n* **1** conversation **2** a formal treatment of a subject in speech or writing ▷ *vb* **-coursing, -coursed 3** to speak or write (about) at length [Medieval Latin *discursus* argument]
discourteous *adj* showing bad manners; rude **discourteously** *adv* **discourtesy** *n*
discover *vb* **1** to be the first to find or find out about **2** to learn about for the first time **3** to find after study or search **discoverer** *n*
discovery *n, pl* **-veries 1** the act of discovering **2** a person, place, or thing that has been discovered
discredit *vb* **-diting, -dited 1** to damage the reputation of (someone) **2** to cause (an idea) to be disbelieved or distrusted ▷ *n* **3** something that causes disgrace **discreditable** *adj*
discreet *adj* **1** careful to avoid embarrassment when dealing with secret or private matters **2** unobtrusive: *there was a discreet entrance down a side alley* [Old French *discret*] **discreetly** *adv*

USAGE Avoid confusion with **discrete**.

discrepancy *n, pl* **-cies** a conflict or variation between facts, figures, or claims [Latin *discrepare* to differ in sound] **discrepant** *adj*

USAGE *Discrepancy* is sometimes wrongly used where *disparity* is meant. A *discrepancy* exists between things which ought to be the same; it can be small but is usually significant. A *disparity* is a large difference between measurable things such as age, rank, or wages.

discrete *adj* separate or distinct [Latin *discretus* separated] **discreteness** *n*

USAGE Avoid confusion with **discreet**.

discretion (diss-kresh-on) *n* **1** the quality of behaving so as to avoid social embarrassment or distress **2** freedom or authority to make judgments and to act as one sees fit: *at his discretion* **discretionary** *adj*
discriminate *vb* **-nating, -nated 1** to make a distinction against or in favour of a particular person or group **2** to recognize or understand a difference: *to discriminate between right and wrong* [Latin *discriminare* to divide] **discriminating** *adj*
discrimination *n* **1** unfair treatment of a person, racial group, or minority **2** subtle appreciation in matters of taste **3** the ability to see fine distinctions
discriminatory *adj* based on prejudice
discursive *adj* passing from one topic to another [Latin *discursus* a running to and fro]
discus *n athletics* a disc-shaped object with a heavy middle, thrown by athletes [Greek *diskos*]
discuss *vb* **1** to consider (something) by talking it over **2** to treat (a subject) in speech or writing [Latin *discutere* to dash to pieces] **discussion** *n*
disdain *n* **1** a feeling of superiority and dislike; contempt ▷ *vb* **2** to refuse or reject with disdain: *he disdained domestic conventions* [Old French *desdeign*] **disdainful** *adj* **disdainfully** *adv*
disease *n* an unhealthy condition in a person, animal, or plant which is caused by bacteria or infection [Old French *desaise*] **diseased** *adj*
diseconomy *n econ* a disadvantage, such as higher costs, resulting from the scale on which a business operates
disembark *vb* to land or cause to land from a ship, aircraft, or other vehicle **disembarkation** *n*
disembodied *adj* **1** lacking a body **2** seeming not to be attached to or come from anyone **disembodiment** *n*
disembowel *vb* **-elling, -elled** *or US* **-eling, -eled** to remove the entrails of **disembowelment** *n*
disempower *vb* to deprive (a person) of power or authority **disempowerment** *n*
disenchanted *adj* disappointed and disillusioned (with something) **disenchantment** *n*
disenfranchise *vb* **-chising, -chised** to deprive (someone) of the right to vote or of other rights of citizenship
disengage *vb* **-gaging, -gaged 1** to release from a connection **2** *military* to withdraw from close action **disengagement** *n*
disentangle *vb* **-gling, -gled 1** to release from entanglement or confusion **2** to unravel or work out **disentanglement** *n*
disequilibrium *n* a loss or absence of stability or balance
disestablish *vb* to deprive (a church or religion) of established status **disestablishment** *n*
disfavour *or US* **disfavor** *n* **1** disapproval or dislike **2** the state of being disapproved of or disliked
disfigure *vb* **-guring, -gured** to spoil the appearance or shape of **disfigurement** *n*
disfranchise *vb* **-chising, -chised** same as **disenfranchise**
disgorge *vb* **-gorging, -gorged 1** to vomit **2** to discharge (contents)
disgrace *n* **1** a condition of shame, loss of reputation, or dishonour **2** a shameful person or thing **3** exclusion from confidence or trust: *he was sent home in disgrace* ▷ *vb* **-gracing, -graced 4** to bring shame upon (oneself or others) **disgraceful** *adj* **disgracefully** *adv*

disgruntled *adj* sulky or discontented: *the disgruntled home supporters* [DIS- + obsolete *gruntle* to complain] **disgruntlement** *n*
disguise *vb* **-guising, -guised 1** to change the appearance or manner in order to conceal the identity of (someone or something) **2** to misrepresent (something) in order to obscure its actual nature or meaning ▷ *n* **3** a mask, costume, or manner that disguises **4** the state of being disguised [Old French *desguisier*] **disguised** *adj*
disgust *n* **1** a great loathing or distaste ▷ *vb* **2** to sicken or fill with loathing [Old French *desgouster* to sicken] **disgusted** *adj* **disgusting** *adj*
dish *n* **1** a container used for holding or serving food, esp. an open shallow container **2** the food in a dish **3** a particular kind of food **4** short for **dish aerial 5** *informal* an attractive person ▷ See also **dish out, dish up** [Old English *disc*]
dishabille (diss-a-**beel**) *n* same as **deshabille**
dish aerial *n* a large disc-shaped aerial with a concave reflector, used to receive signals in radar, radio telescopes, and satellite broadcasting
disharmony *n* lack of agreement or harmony **disharmonious** *adj*
dishcloth *n* a cloth for washing dishes
dishearten *vb* to weaken or destroy the hope, courage, or enthusiasm of **disheartened** *adj* **disheartening** *adj*
dishevelled *or US* **disheveled** *adj* (of a person's hair, clothes, or general appearance) disordered and untidy [Old French *deschevelé*]
dishonest *adj* not honest or fair **dishonestly** *adv* **dishonesty** *n*
dishonour *or US* **dishonor** *vb* **1** to treat with disrespect **2** to refuse to pay (a cheque) ▷ *n* **3** a lack of honour or respect **4** a state of shame or disgrace **5** something that causes a loss of honour **dishonourable** *or US* **dishonorable** *adj* **dishonourably** *or US* **dishonorably** *adv*
dish out *vb* **1** to distribute **2 dish it out** to inflict punishment
dish up *vb* to serve (food)
dishwasher *n* a machine for washing and drying dishes, cutlery, etc.
dishwater *n* **1** water in which dishes have been washed **2 like dishwater** (of tea) very weak
dishy *adj* **dishier, dishiest** *informal* good-looking
disillusion *vb* **1** to destroy the illusions or false ideas of (someone) ▷ *n also* **disillusionment 2** the state of being disillusioned
disillusioned *adj* disappointed at finding out reality does not match one's ideals
disincentive *n* something that discourages someone from behaving or acting in a particular way
disinclined *adj* unwilling or reluctant **disinclination** *n*
disinfect *vb* to rid of harmful germs by cleaning with a chemical substance **disinfection** *n*
disinfectant *n* a substance that destroys harmful germs
disinformation *n* false information intended to mislead
disingenuous *adj* dishonest and insincere **disingenuously** *adv*
disinherit *vb* **-iting, -ited** *law* to deprive (an heir) of inheritance **disinheritance** *n*
disintegrate *vb* **-grating, -grated 1** to lose cohesion; break up: *the business disintegrated* **2** (of an object) to break into fragments; shatter **3** *physics* **A** to undergo nuclear fission or include nuclear fission in **B** same as **decay** (sense 3) **disintegration** *n*
disinter *vb* **-terring, -terred 1** to dig up **2** to bring to light; expose
disinterested *adj* **1** free from bias; objective **2** feeling or showing a lack of interest; uninterested **disinterest** *n*

> **USAGE** Many people consider that the use of *disinterested* to mean not interested is incorrect and that *uninterested* should be used.

disjointed *adj* having no coherence; disconnected: *a disjointed conversation*
disjunctive *adj* serving to disconnect or separate
disk *n* **1** *chiefly US & Canad* same as **disc 2** *computers* a storage device, consisting of a stack of plates coated with a magnetic layer, which rotates rapidly as a single unit [see DISC]
disk drive *n* the controller and mechanism for reading and writing data on computer disks
dislike *vb* **-liking, -liked 1** to consider unpleasant or disagreeable ▷ *n* **2** a feeling of not liking something or someone
dislocate *vb* **-cating, -cated 1** to displace (a bone or joint) from its normal position **2** to disrupt or shift out of place **dislocation** *n*
dislodge *vb* **-lodging, -lodged** to remove (something) from a previously fixed position
disloyal *adj* not loyal; deserting one's allegiance or duty **disloyalty** *n*
dismal *adj* **1** gloomy and depressing **2** *informal* of poor quality [Medieval Latin *dies mali* unlucky days] **dismally** *adv*
dismantle *vb* **-tling, -tled 1** to take apart piece by piece **2** to cause (an organization or political system) to stop functioning by gradually reducing its power or purpose [Old French *desmanteler*]
dismay *vb* **1** to fill with alarm or depression ▷ *n* **2** a feeling of alarm or depression [Old French *des-* (intensive) + *esmayer* to frighten]
dismember *vb* **1** to remove the limbs of **2** to cut to pieces **dismemberment** *n*
dismiss *vb* **1** to remove (an employee) from a job **2** to allow (someone) to leave **3** to put out of one's mind; no longer think about **4** (of a judge) to state that (a case) will not be brought to trial **5** *cricket* to bowl out (a side) for a particular number of runs [Latin *dis-* from + *mittere* to send] **dismissal** *n* **dismissive** *adj*
dismount *vb* to get off a horse or bicycle
disobedient *adj* refusing to obey **disobedience** *n*
disobey *vb* to neglect or refuse to obey (a person or an order)
disobliging *adj* unwilling to help
disorder *n* **1** a state of untidiness and disorganization **2** public violence or rioting **3** an illness **disordered** *adj*
disorderly *adj* **1** untidy and disorganized **2** uncontrolled; unruly **3** *law* violating public peace
disorganize *or* **-ise** *vb* **-izing, -ized** *or* **-ising, -ised** to disrupt the arrangement or system of **disorganization** *or* **-isation** *n*

disorientate *or* **disorient** *vb* **-tating, -tated** *or* **-enting, -ented** to cause (someone) to lose his or her bearings **disorientation** *n*
disown *vb* to deny any connection with (someone)
disparage *vb* **-aging, -aged** to speak contemptuously of [Old French *desparagier*] **disparagement** *n* **disparaging** *adj*
disparate *adj* utterly different in kind [Latin *disparare* to divide] **disparity** *n*
USAGE See at **discrepancy**.
dispassionate *adj* not influenced by emotion; objective **dispassionately** *adv*
dispatch *or* **despatch** *vb* **1** to send off to a destination or to perform a task **2** to carry out (a duty or task) promptly **3** to murder ▷ *n* **4** an official communication or report, sent in haste **5** a report sent to a newspaper by a correspondent **6** murder **7 with dispatch** quickly [Italian *dispacciare*]
dispatch rider *n Brit, Austral & NZ* a motorcyclist who carries dispatches
dispel *vb* **-pelling, -pelled** to disperse or drive away [Latin *dispellere*]
dispensable *adj* not essential; expendable
dispensary *n, pl* **-ries** a place where medicine is prepared and given out
dispensation *n* **1** the act of distributing or dispensing **2** *chiefly RC Church* permission to dispense with an obligation of church law **3** any exemption from an obligation **4** the ordering of life and events by God
dispense *vb* **-pensing, -pensed 1** to distribute in portions **2** to prepare and distribute (medicine) **3** to administer (the law, etc.) **4 dispense with** to do away with or manage without [Latin *dispendere* to weigh out] **dispenser** *n*
USAGE *Dispense with* is sometimes wrongly used where *dispose of* is meant: *this task can be disposed of* (not *dispensed with*) *quickly and easily.*
dispensing optician *n* See **optician** (sense 2)
disperse *vb* **-persing, -persed 1** to scatter over a wide area **2** to leave or cause to leave a gathering: *police dispersed rioters* **3** to separate (light) into its different wavelengths **4** to separate (particles) throughout a solid, liquid, or gas [Latin *dispergere* to scatter widely] **dispersal** *or* **dispersion** *n*
USAGE See at **disburse**.
dispirit *vb* to make downhearted **dispirited** *adj* **dispiriting** *adj*
displace *vb* **-placing, -placed 1** to move (something) from its usual place **2** to remove (someone) from a post or position of authority
displaced person *n* a person forced from his or her home or country, esp. by war or revolution
displacement *n* **1** the act of displacing **2** *physics* the weight or volume of liquid displaced by an object submerged or floating in it **3** *maths* the distance measured in a particular direction from a reference point. Symbol: *s*
display *vb* **1** to show **2** to reveal or make evident: *to display anger* ▷ *n* **3** the act of exhibiting or displaying **4** something displayed **5** an exhibition **6** *electronics* a device capable of representing information visually, as on a screen **7** *zool* a pattern of behaviour by which an animal attracts attention while courting, defending its territory, etc. [Anglo-French *despleier* to unfold]
displease *vb* **-pleasing, -pleased** to annoy or offend (someone) **displeasure** *n*
disport *vb* **disport oneself** to indulge oneself in pleasure [Anglo-French *desporter*]
disposable *adj* **1** designed for disposal after use: *disposable cups* **2** available for use if needed: *disposable capital*
disposal *n* **1** the act or means of getting rid of something **2 at one's disposal** available for use
dispose *vb* **-posing, -posed 1 dispose of A** to throw away **B** to give, sell, or transfer to another **C** to deal with or settle: *I disposed of that problem right away* **D** to kill **2** to arrange or place in a particular way: *around them are disposed the moulded masks of witch doctors* [Latin *disponere* to set in different places]
USAGE See at **dispense**.
disposed *adj* **1** willing or eager (to do something): *few would feel disposed to fault his judgment* **2** having an inclination as specified (towards someone or something): *my people aren't too well disposed towards defectors*
disposition *n* **1** a person's usual temperament **2** a tendency or habit **3** arrangement; layout
dispossess *vb* to deprive (someone) of (a possession) **dispossessed** *adj* **dispossession** *n*
disproportion *n* lack of proportion or equality
disproportionate *adj* out of proportion **disproportionately** *adv*
disprove *vb* **-proving, -proved** to show (an assertion or claim) to be incorrect
dispute *n* **1** a disagreement between workers and their employer **2** an argument between two or more people **3 beyond dispute** unable to be questioned or denied: *it's beyond dispute that tensions already existed between them* ▷ *vb* **-puting, -puted 4** to argue or quarrel about (something) **5** to doubt the validity of **6** to fight over possession of [Latin *disputare* to discuss] **disputation** *n* **disputatious** *adj*
disqualify *vb* **-fies, -fying, -fied 1** to officially ban (someone) from doing something: *he was disqualified from driving for ten years* **2** to make ineligible, as for entry to an examination **disqualification** *n*
disquiet *n* **1** a feeling of anxiety or uneasiness ▷ *vb* **2** to make (someone) anxious **disquieting** *adj* **disquietude** *n*
disquisition *n* a formal written or oral examination of a subject
disregard *vb* **1** to give little or no attention to; ignore ▷ *n* **2** lack of attention or respect
disrepair *n* the condition of being worn out or in poor working order
disreputable *adj* having or causing a bad reputation **disreputably** *adv*
disrepute *n* a loss or lack of good reputation
disrespect *n* contempt or lack of respect **disrespectful** *adj*
disrobe *vb* **-robing, -robed** *literary* to undress
disrupt *vb* to interrupt the progress of [Latin *disruptus* burst asunder] **disruption** *n* **disruptive** *adj*
diss *vb slang, chiefly US* to treat (a person) with contempt [from DISRESPECT]

dissatisfied *adj* displeased or discontented **dissatisfaction** *n*

dissect *vb* **1** to cut open (a corpse) to examine it **2** to examine critically and minutely: *the above conclusion causes one to dissect that policy more closely* [Latin *dissecare*] **dissection** *n*

dissemble *vb* **-bling, -bled** to conceal one's real motives or emotions by pretence [Latin *dissimulare*] **dissembler** *n*

disseminate *vb* **-nating, -nated** to spread (information, ideas, etc.) widely [Latin *disseminare*] **dissemination** *n*

dissension *n* disagreement and argument [Latin *dissentire* to dissent]

dissent *vb* **1** to disagree **2** *Christianity* to reject the doctrines of an established church ▷ *n* **3** a disagreement **4** *Christianity* separation from an established church [Latin *dissentire* to disagree] **dissenter** *n* **dissenting** *adj*

Dissenter *n Christianity, chiefly Brit* a Protestant who refuses to conform to the established church

dissentient *adj* dissenting from the opinion of the majority

dissertation *n* **1** a written thesis, usually required for a higher degree **2** a long formal speech [Latin *dissertare* to debate]

disservice *n* a harmful action

dissident *n* **1** a person who disagrees with a government or a powerful organization ▷ *adj* **2** disagreeing or dissenting [Latin *dissidere* to be remote from] **dissidence** *n*

dissimilar *adj* not alike; different **dissimilarity** *n*

dissimulate *vb* **-lating, -lated** to conceal one's real feelings by pretence **dissimulation** *n*

dissipate *vb* **-pating, -pated 1** to waste or squander **2** to scatter or break up [Latin *dissipare* to disperse]

dissipated *adj* showing signs of overindulgence in alcohol or other physical pleasures

dissipation *n* **1** the process of dissipating **2** unrestrained indulgence in physical pleasures

dissociate *vb* **-ciating, -ciated 1 dissociate oneself from** to deny or break an association with (a person or organization) **2** to regard or treat as separate **dissociation** *n*

dissoluble *adj* same as **soluble** [Latin *dissolubilis*] **dissolubility** *n*

dissolute *adj* leading an immoral life [Latin *dissolutus* loose]

dissolution *n* **1** the act of officially breaking up an organization or institution **2** the act of officially ending a formal agreement, such as a marriage **3** the formal ending of a meeting or assembly, such as a Parliament

dissolve *vb* **-solving, -solved 1** to become or cause to become liquid; melt **2** to officially break up (an organization or institution) **3** to formally end: *the campaign started as soon as Parliament was dissolved last month* **4** to collapse emotionally: *she dissolved in loud tears* **5** *films & television* to fade out one scene and replace with another to make two scenes merge imperceptibly [Latin *dissolvere* to make loose]

dissonance *n* a lack of agreement or harmony between things: *this dissonance of colours* **dissonant** *adj*

dissuade *vb* **-suading, -suaded** to deter (someone) by persuasion from doing something or believing in something [Latin *dissuadere*] **dissuasion** *n*

dissyllable *or* **disyllable** *n* a word of two syllables **dissyllabic** *or* **disyllabic** *adj*

distaff *n* the rod on which flax is wound for spinning [Old English *distæf*]

distaff side *n* the female side of a family

distance *n* **1** the space between two points or places **2** the state of being apart **3** a distant place **4** remoteness in manner **5 the distance** the most distant part of the visible scene **6 go the distance A** *boxing* to complete a bout without being knocked out **B** to complete an assigned task or responsibility **7 keep one's distance** to maintain a reserved attitude to another person ▷ *vb* **-tancing, -tanced 8 distance oneself from** *or* **be distanced from** to separate oneself or be separated mentally from

distance learning *n* a teaching system involving video, audio, and written material for studying at home

distant *adj* **1** far-off; remote **2** far apart **3** separated by a specified distance: *five kilometres distant* **4** apart in relationship: *a distant cousin* **5** going to a faraway place **6** remote in manner; aloof **7** abstracted: *a distant look entered her eyes* [Latin *dis-* apart + *stare* to stand] **distantly** *adv*

distaste *n* a dislike of something offensive

distasteful *adj* unpleasant or offensive **distastefulness** *n*

distemper[1] *n* a highly contagious viral disease that can affect young dogs [Latin *dis-* apart + *temperare* to regulate]

distemper[2] *n* **1** paint mixed with water, glue, etc. which is used for painting walls ▷ *vb* **2** to paint with distemper [Latin *dis-* (intensive) + *temperare* to mingle]

distend *vb* to expand by pressure from within; swell [Latin *distendere*] **distensible** *adj* **distension** *n*

distich (diss-stick) *n prosody* a unit of two verse lines [Greek *di-* two + *stikhos* row, line]

distil *or US* **distill** *vb* **-tilling, -tilled 1** to subject to or obtain by distillation **2** to give off (a substance) in drops **3** to extract the essence of [Latin *de-* down + *stillare* to drip]

distillation *n* **1** the process of evaporating a liquid and condensing its vapour **2** Also: **distillate** a concentrated essence

distiller *n* a person or company that makes spirits

distillery *n, pl* **-eries** a place where alcoholic drinks are made by distillation

distinct *adj* **1** not the same; different: *these two areas produce wines with distinct characteristics* **2** clearly seen, heard, or recognized: *it is not possible to draw a distinct line between the two categories; there's a distinct smell of burning* **3** clear and definite: *there is a distinct possibility of rain* **4** obvious: *a distinct improvement* [Latin *distinctus*] **distinctly** *adv*

distinction *n* **1** the act of distinguishing or differentiating **2** a distinguishing feature **3** the state of being different or distinguishable **4** special honour, recognition, or fame **5** excellence of character **6** a symbol of honour or rank

distinctive *adj* easily recognizable; characteristic **distinctively** *adv* **distinctiveness** *n*

distingué (diss-**tang**-gay) *adj* distinguished or noble [French]

distinguish *vb* **1** to make, show, or recognize a difference: *I have tried to distinguish between fact and theory* **2** to be a distinctive feature of: *what distinguishes the good teenage reader from the less competent one?* **3** to make out by hearing, seeing, or tasting: *she listened but could distinguish nothing except the urgency of their discussion* **4 distinguish oneself** to make oneself noteworthy [Latin *distinguere* to separate] **distinguishable** *adj* **distinguishing** *adj*

d

distinguished *adj* **1** dignified in appearance or behaviour **2** highly respected: *a distinguished historian*

distort *vb* **1** to alter or misrepresent (facts) **2** to twist out of shape; deform **3** *electronics* to reproduce or amplify (a signal) inaccurately [Latin *distorquere* to turn different ways] **distorted** *adj* **distortion** *n*

distract *vb* **1** to draw (a person or his or her attention) away from something **2** to amuse or entertain [Latin *distrahere* to pull in different directions]

USAGE See at **detract**.

distracted *adj* unable to concentrate because one's mind is on other things

distraction *n* **1** something that diverts the attention **2** something that serves as an entertainment **3** mental turmoil

distrain *vb law* to seize (personal property) to enforce payment of a debt [Latin *di-* apart + *stringere* to draw tight] **distraint** *n*

distrait (diss-**tray**) *adj* absent-minded or abstracted [French]

distraught (diss-**trawt**) *adj* upset or agitated [obsolete *distract*]

distress *n* **1** extreme unhappiness or worry **2** great physical pain **3** financial trouble **4 in distress** in dire need of help ▷ *vb* **5** to upset badly [Latin *districtus* divided in mind] **distressing** *adj* **distressingly** *adv*

distressed *adj* **1** much troubled; upset **2** in great physical pain **3** in financial difficulties **4** (of furniture or fabric) having signs of ageing artificially applied

distributary *n, pl* **-taries** one of several outlet streams draining a river, esp. on a delta

distribute *vb* **-uting, -uted 1** to hand out or deliver (leaflets, mail, etc.) **2** to share (something) among the members of a particular group [Latin *distribuere*]

distribution *n* **1** the delivering of leaflets, mail, etc., to individual people or organizations **2** the sharing out of something among a particular group **3** the arrangement or spread of anything over an area, space, or period of time: *the unequal distribution of wealth* **4** *commerce* the process of satisfying the demand for goods and services

distributive *adj* **1** of or relating to distribution **2** *maths* of the rule that the same result is produced when multiplication is performed on a set of numbers as when performed on the members of the set individually

distributor *n* **1** a wholesaler who distributes goods to retailers in a specific area **2** the device in a petrol engine that sends the electric current to the sparking plugs

district *n* **1** an area of land regarded as an administrative or geographical unit **2** an area which has recognizable or special features: *an upper-class residential district* [Medieval Latin *districtus* area of jurisdiction]

district court judge *n Austral & NZ* a judge presiding over a lower court

district nurse *n* (in Britain) a nurse who attends to patients in their homes within a particular district

distrust *vb* **1** to regard as untrustworthy ▷ *n* **2** a feeling of suspicion or doubt **distrustful** *adj*

disturb *vb* **1** to intrude on; interrupt **2** to upset or worry **3** to disarrange; muddle **4** to inconvenience [Latin *disturbare*] **disturbing** *adj* **disturbingly** *adv*

disturbance *n* **1** an interruption or intrusion **2** an unruly outburst in public

disturbed *adj psychiatry* emotionally upset, troubled, or maladjusted

disunite *vb* **-niting, -nited** to cause disagreement among **disunion** *n* **disunity** *n*

disuse *n* the state of being neglected or no longer used; neglect

disused *adj* no longer used

disyllable *n* same as **dissyllable**

ditch *n* **1** a narrow channel dug in the earth for drainage or irrigation ▷ *vb* **2** *slang* to abandon or discard: *she ditched her boyfriend last month* [Old English *dīc*]

dither *vb* **1** *chiefly Brit & NZ* to be uncertain or indecisive ▷ *n* **2** *chiefly Brit* a state of indecision or agitation [Middle English *didder*] **ditherer** *n* **dithery** *adj*

dithyramb *n* (in ancient Greece) a passionate choral hymn in honour of Dionysus [Greek *dithurambos*] **dithyrambic** *adj*

ditto *n, pl* **-tos 1** the above; the same: used in lists to avoid repetition, and represented by the mark (") placed under the thing repeated ▷ *adv* **2** in the same way [Italian (dialect) *detto* said]

ditty *n, pl* **-ties** a short simple song or poem [Latin *dictare* to say repeatedly]

ditzy *or* **ditsy** *adj* **ditzier, ditziest** *or* **ditsier, ditsiest** *slang* silly and scatterbrained [perhaps from DOTTY + DIZZY]

diuretic (die-yoor-**et**-ik) *n* a drug that increases the flow of urine [Greek *dia-* through + *ourein* to urinate]

diurnal (die-**urn**-al) *adj* **1** happening during the day or daily **2** (of animals) active during the day [Latin *diurnus*]

diva *n, pl* **-vas** *or* **-ve** a distinguished female singer; prima donna [Latin: a goddess]

divalent *adj chem* having two valencies or a valency of two **divalency** *n*

divan *n* **A** a low bed with a thick base under the mattress **B** a couch with no back or arms [Turkish *dīvān*]

dive *vb* **diving, dived** *or US* **dove, dived 1** to plunge headfirst into water **2** (of a submarine or diver) to submerge under water **3** (of a bird or aircraft) to fly in a steep nose-down descending path **4** to move quickly in a specified direction: *he dived for the door* **5 dive in** *or* **into** **A** to put (one's hand) quickly or forcefully into **B** to start doing (something) enthusiastically ▷ *n* **6** a headlong plunge into water **7** the act of diving **8** a steep nose-down descent of a bird or aircraft **9** *slang* a disreputable bar or club [Old English *dȳfan*]

dive bomber *n* a military aircraft designed to release bombs on a target during a dive **dive-bomb** *vb*

diver *n* **1** a person who works or explores underwater **2** a person who dives for sport **3** a large diving bird of northern oceans with a straight pointed bill and webbed feet

diverge *vb* **-verging, -verged** **1** to separate and go in different directions **2** to be at variance; differ: *the two books diverge in setting and in style* **3** to deviate (from a prescribed course) [Latin *dis-* apart + *vergere* to turn] **divergence** *n* **divergent** *adj*

diverse *adj* **1** having variety; assorted **2** different in kind [Latin *diversus* turned in different directions]

diversify *vb* **-fies, -fying, -fied** **1** to create different forms of; vary **2** (of an enterprise) to vary (products or operations) in order to expand or reduce the risk of loss [Latin *diversus* different + *facere* to make] **diversification** *n*

diversion *n* **1** *chiefly Brit* an official detour used by traffic when a main route is closed **2** something that distracts someone's attention or concentration **3** the act of diverting from a specified course **4** a pleasant or amusing pastime or activity **diversionary** *adj*

diversity *n* **1** the quality of being different or varied **2** a point of difference

divert *vb* **1** to change the course or direction of (traffic) **2** to distract the attention of **3** to entertain or amuse [Latin *divertere* to turn aside]

diverticulitis *n* inflammation of pouches in the wall of the colon, causing lower abdominal pain [Latin *deverticulum* path, track]

divertimento *n, pl* **-ti** a piece of entertaining music in several movements [Italian]

divest *vb* **1** to strip (of clothes) **2** to deprive of a role, function, or quality: *the chairman felt duty-bound to stay with the company after it was divested of all its aviation interests* [earlier *devest*]

divide *vb* **-viding, -vided** **1** to separate into parts **2** to share or be shared out in parts **3** to disagree or cause to disagree: *experts are divided over the plan* **4** to keep apart or be a boundary between **5** to categorize or classify **6** to calculate how many times one number can be contained in another ▷ *n* **7** a division or split **8** *chiefly US & Canad* an area of high ground separating drainage basins [Latin *dividere* to force apart]

dividend *n* **1** a portion of a company's profits paid to its shareholders **2** an extra benefit: *Saudi progressives saw a dividend to the crisis* **3** *maths* a number to be divided by another number [Latin *dividendum* what is to be divided]

divider *n* a screen placed so as to divide a room into separate areas

dividers *pl n* compasses with two pointed arms, used for measuring or dividing lines

divination *n* the art of discovering future events as though by supernatural powers

divine *adj* **1** of God or a god **2** godlike **3** *informal* splendid or perfect ▷ *n* **4** a priest who is learned in theology ▷ *vb* **-vining, -vined** **5** to discover (something) by intuition or guessing [Latin *divus* a god] **divinely** *adv* **diviner** *n*

diving bell *n* a diving apparatus with an open bottom, supplied with compressed air from above

diving board *n* a platform from which swimmers may dive

diving suit *n* a waterproof suit used for diving with a detachable helmet and an air supply

divining rod *n* a forked twig said to move when held over ground in which water or metal is to be found

divinity *n, pl* **-ties** **1** the study of religion **2** a god or goddess **3** the state of being divine

divisible *adj* capable of being divided **divisibility** *n*

division *n* **1** the separation of something into two or more distinct parts **2** the act of dividing or sharing out **3** one of the parts into which something is divided **4** the mathematical operation of dividing **5** a difference of opinion **6** a part of an organization that has been made into a unit for administrative or other reasons **7** a formal vote in Parliament **8** one of the groups of teams that make up a football or other sports league **9** *army* a major formation containing the necessary arms to sustain independent combat **10** *biol* one of the major groups into which the plant kingdom is divided, corresponding to a phylum [Latin *dividere* to divide] **divisional** *adj*

division sign *n* the symbol ÷, placed between two numbers to indicate that the first number should be divided by the second, as in $12 \div 6 = 2$

divisive (div-**vice**-iv) *adj* tending to cause disagreement: *she played an important role in defusing potentially divisive issues*

divisor *n* a number to be divided into another number

divorce *n* **1** the legal ending of a marriage **2** a separation, esp. one that is permanent ▷ *vb* **-vorcing, -vorced** **3** to separate or be separated by divorce **4** to remove or separate [Latin *divertere* to separate]

divorcee *or masc* **divorcé** *n* a person who is divorced

divot *n* a small piece of turf

divulge *vb* **-vulging, -vulged** to make known: *I am not permitted to divulge his name* [Latin *divulgare*] **divulgence** *n*

divvy[1] *vb* **-vies, -vying, -vied** > **divvy up** *informal* to divide and share

divvy[2] *n, pl* **-vies** *Brit dialect* a stupid person

Diwali (duh-**wah**-lee) *n* an annual Hindu festival honouring Lakshmi, the goddess of wealth

Dixie *n* the southern states of the US. Also called: **Dixieland** [origin unknown]

DIY *or* **d.i.y.** *Brit, Austral & NZ* do-it-yourself

dizzy *adj* **-zier, -ziest** **1** feeling giddy **2** unable to think clearly; confused **3** tending to cause giddiness or confusion ▷ *vb* **-zies, -zying, -zied** **4** to cause to feel giddy or confused [Old English *dysig* silly] **dizzily** *adv* **dizziness** *n*

d

DJ *or* **dj** **1** disc jockey **2** *Brit* dinner jacket
djinni *or* **djinny** *n, pl* **djinn** same as **jinni**
dl decilitre(s)
DLitt *or* **DLit** **1** Doctor of Letters **2** Doctor of Literature [Latin *Doctor Litterarum*]
DLL *computers* dynamic link library: a set of programs that can be activated and then discarded by other programs
dm decimetre(s)
DM direct message
DMus Doctor of Music
DNA deoxyribonucleic acid, the main constituent of the chromosomes of all organisms
DNA fingerprinting *or* **DNA profiling** *n* same as **genetic fingerprinting**
D-notice *n Brit & Austral* an official notice sent to newspapers prohibiting the publication of certain security information [from their administrative classification letter]
do[1] *vb* **does, doing, did, done** **1** to perform or complete (a deed or action): *we do a fair amount of entertaining* **2** to be adequate: *it's not what I wanted but it will have to do* **3** to provide: *this hotel only does bed and breakfast* **4** to make tidy or elegant: *he watched her do her hair* **5** to improve: *that style does nothing for you* **6** to find an answer to (a problem or puzzle) **7** to conduct oneself: *do as you want* **8** to cause or produce: *herbal teas have active ingredients that can do good* **9** to give or grant: *do me a favour* **10** to work at as a course of study or a job **11** to mimic **12** to achieve a particular speed, amount, or rate: *this computer system can do 40 different cross checks; this car will do 120 mph* **13 A** used to form questions: *do you like it?* **B** used to intensify positive statements and commands: *tensions do exist* **C** used to form negative statements or commands: *do not talk while I'm talking!* **D** used to replace an earlier verb: *she exercises much more than I do* **14** *informal* to visit (a place) as a tourist: *we plan to do the States this year* **15** *slang* to serve (a period of time) as a prison sentence **16** *informal* to cheat or rob: *I was done out of ten pounds* **17** *slang* **A** to arrest **B** to convict of a crime: *he was done for burglary* **18** *slang, chiefly Brit* to assault **19** *slang* to take or use (drugs) **20** **make do** to manage with whatever is available ▷ *n, pl* **dos** *or* **do's** **21** *informal, chiefly Brit & NZ* a party or other social event **22** **do's and don'ts** *informal* rules ▷ See also **do away with, do by** *etc.* [Old English *dōn*]
do[2] *n, pl* **dos** *music* same as **doh**
do away with *vb* to get rid of (someone or something)
Doberman pinscher *or* **Doberman** *n* a large dog with a glossy black-and-tan coat [after L. *Dobermann*, dog breeder]
dob in *vb* **dobbing, dobbed** *Austral & NZ informal* **1** to inform against **2** to contribute to a fund
do by *vb* to treat in the manner specified: *he felt badly done by*
doc *n informal* same as **doctor**
DOC (in New Zealand) Department of Conservation
docile *adj* (of a person or animal) easily controlled [Latin *docilis* easily taught] **docilely** *adv* **docility** *n*
dock[1] *n* **1** an enclosed area of water where ships are loaded, unloaded, or repaired **2** a wharf or pier ▷ *vb* **3** to moor or be moored at a dock **4** to link (two spacecraft) or (of two spacecraft) to be linked together in space [Middle Dutch *docke*]
dock[2] *vb* **1** to deduct (an amount) from (a person's wages) **2** to remove part of (an animal's tail) by cutting through the bone [Middle English *dok*]
dock[3] *n* an enclosed space in a court of law where the accused person sits or stands [Flemish *dok* sty]
dock[4] *n* a weed with broad leaves [Old English *docce*]
docker *n Brit* a person employed to load and unload ships
docket *chiefly Brit* ▷ *n* **1** a label on a package or other delivery, stating contents, delivery instructions, etc. ▷ *vb* **-eting, -eted** **2** to fix a docket to (a package or other delivery) [origin unknown]
dockyard *n* a place where ships are built or repaired
Doc Martens *pl n trademark* a brand of lace-up boots with thick lightweight resistant soles
doctor *n* **1** a person licensed to practise medicine **2** a person who has been awarded a doctorate **3** *chiefly US & Canad* a person licensed to practise dentistry or veterinary medicine ▷ *vb* **4** to change in order to deceive: *she confessed to having doctored the figures* **5** to poison or drug (food or drink) **6** to castrate (an animal) [Latin: teacher] **doctoral** *adj*
doctorate *n* the highest academic degree in any field of knowledge
doctrinaire *adj* stubbornly insistent on the application of a theory without regard to practicality
doctrine (**dock**-trin) *n* **1** a body of teachings of a religious, political, or philosophical group **2** a principle or body of principles that is taught or advocated [Latin *doctrina* teaching] **doctrinal** *adj*
docudrama *n* a film or television programme based on true events, presented in a dramatized form
document *n* **1** a piece of paper that provides an official record of something **2** an item of text or graphics that is stored as a file on a computer ▷ *vb* **3** to record or report (something) in detail **4** to support (a claim) with evidence [Latin *documentum* a lesson]
documentary *n, pl* **-ries** **1** a film or television programme presenting the facts about a particular subject ▷ *adj* **2** of or based on documents: *vital documentary evidence has been found*
documentation *n* documents supplied as proof or evidence of something
docu-soap *n* a television documentary series presenting the lives of the people filmed as entertainment
dodder *vb* to move unsteadily [variant of earlier *dadder*] **dodderer** *n* **doddery** *adj*
doddle *n Brit, Austral & NZ informal* something easily accomplished: *the test turned out to be a doddle* [origin unknown]
dodecagon (doe-**deck**-a-gon) *n* a polygon with twelve sides [Greek *dōdeka* twelve + *gōnia* angle]
dodecahedron (doe-deck-a-**heed**-ron) *n* a solid figure with twelve plane faces

dodge *vb* **dodging, dodged 1** to avoid being hit, caught, or seen by moving suddenly **2** to evade by cleverness or trickery: *the Government will not be able to dodge the issue* ▷ *n* **3** a cunning and deceitful trick [origin unknown]
Dodgem *n trademark* a small electric car driven and bumped against similar cars in a rink at a funfair
dodger *n* a person who evades a duty or obligation
dodgy *adj* **dodgier, dodgiest** *Brit, Austral & NZ informal* **1** dangerous, risky, or unreliable: *he's in a very dodgy political position* **2** untrustworthy: *they considered him a very dodgy character*
dodo *n, pl* **dodos** *or* **dodoes 1** a large extinct bird that could not fly **2 as dead as a dodo** no longer existing [Portuguese *duodo* stupid]
do down *vb* to belittle or humiliate: *the moderate constructionist does not wish to do science down*
doe *n, pl* **does** *or* **doe** the female of the deer, hare, or rabbit [Old English *dā*]
doek (rhymes with **book**) *n S African informal* a square of cloth worn on the head by women [Afrikaans]
doer *n* an active or energetic person
does *vb* third person singular of the present tense of **do'**
doff *vb* to take off or lift (one's hat) in salutation [Old English *dōn of*]
do for *vb informal* **1** to cause the ruin, death, or defeat of: *I'm done for if this error comes to light* **2** to do housework for **3 do well for oneself** to thrive or succeed
dog *n* **1** a domesticated canine mammal occurring in many different breeds **2** any other member of the dog family, such as the dingo or coyote. Related adjective: **canine 3** the male of animals of the dog family **4** *informal* a person: *you lucky dog!* **5** *US & Canad informal* something unsatisfactory or inferior **6 a dog's life** a wretched existence **7 dog eat dog** ruthless competition **8 like a dog's dinner** dressed smartly and ostentatiously ▷ *vb* **dogging, dogged 9** to follow (someone) closely **10** to trouble: *dogged by ill health* ▷ See also **dogs** [Old English *docga*]
dog box *n Austral & NZ informal* same as **doghouse**
dogcart *n* a light horse-drawn two-wheeled cart
dog collar *n* **1** a collar for a dog **2** *informal* a clerical collar
dog days *pl n Brit, Austral & NZ* the hottest period of the summer [in ancient times reckoned from the heliacal rising of the Dog Star]
doge (doje) *n* (formerly) the chief magistrate of Venice or Genoa [Latin *dux* leader]
dog-eared *adj* **1** (of a book) having pages folded down at the corner **2** shabby or worn
dog-end *n Brit, Austral & NZ informal* a cigarette end
dogfight *n* **1** close-quarters combat between fighter aircraft **2** any rough fight
dogfish *n, pl* **-fish** *or* **-fishes** a small shark
dogged (dog-gid) *adj* obstinately determined **doggedly** *adv* **doggedness** *n*
doggerel *n* poorly written, usually comic, verse [Middle English *dogerel* worthless]
doggo *adv* **lie doggo** *informal* to hide and keep quiet [probably from *dog*]
doggy *or* **doggie** *n, pl* **-gies 1** a child's word for a dog ▷ *adj* **-gier, -giest 2** of or like a dog **3** fond of dogs: *I suppose dogs are all right but doggy folk can be real bores*
doggy bag *n* a bag in which leftovers from a meal may be taken away, supposedly for the diner's dog
doghouse *n* **1** *US & Canad* a kennel **2 in the doghouse** *informal* in disfavour
dogie, dogy *or* **dogey** (dohg-ee) *n, pl* **-gies** *or* **-geys** *US & Canad* a motherless calf [from *dough-guts*, because they were fed on flour-and-water paste]
dog in the manger *n* a person who prevents others from using something he or she has no use for
dogleg *n* a sharp bend
dogma *n* a doctrine or system of doctrines proclaimed by authority as true [Greek: opinion]
dogmatic *adj* habitually stating one's opinions in a forceful or arrogant manner **dogmatically** *adv* **dogmatism** *n*
do-gooder *n informal* a well-intentioned but naive or impractical person
dog paddle *n* a swimming stroke in which the hands are paddled in imitation of a swimming dog. Also called: **doggy paddle**
dogs *pl n* **1 the dogs** *Brit & Austral informal* greyhound racing **2 go to the dogs** *informal* to go to ruin physically or morally **3 let sleeping dogs lie** to leave things undisturbed
dogsbody *n, pl* **-bodies** *informal* a person who carries out boring or unimportant tasks for others
dog-tired *adj informal* exhausted
dogwatch *n* either of two watches aboard ship, from four to six pm or from six to eight pm
doh *or* **do** *n music* (in tonic sol-fa) the first note of any ascending major scale
doily *or* **doyley** *n, pl* **-lies** *or* **-leys** a decorative lacelike paper mat laid on a plate [after Doily, a London draper]
do in *vb slang* **1** to kill **2** to exhaust
doings *pl n* **1** deeds or actions: *her brother's doings upset her terribly* ▷ *n* **2** *informal* anything of which the name is not known or is left unsaid: *do you have the doings to open this?*
do-it-yourself *n* the practice of constructing and repairing things oneself
Dolby *n trademark* **1** a system used in tape recorders which reduces noise level on recorded or broadcast sound **2** a system used in cinemas and television sets which provides surround sound
doldrums *n* **the doldrums 1 A** a feeling of depression **B** a state of inactivity **2** a belt of sea along the equator noted for absence of winds [probably from Old English *dol* dull]
dole *n* **1 the dole** *Brit, Austral & NZ informal* money received from the state while unemployed **2 on the dole** *Brit, Austral & NZ informal* receiving benefit while unemployed ▷ *vb* **doling, doled 3 dole out** to distribute in small quantities [Old English *dāl* share]
dole bludger *n Austral & NZ informal* a person who chooses to live off unemployment benefit

d

doleful *adj* dreary or mournful [from Latin *dolere* to lament] **dolefully** *adv* **dolefulness** *n*

doll *n* **1** a small model of a human being, used as a toy **2** *slang* a pretty girl or young woman [probably from Doll, pet name for *Dorothy*]

dollar *n* the standard monetary unit of various countries [Low German *daler*]

dollop *n informal* an amount of food served in a lump: *he shook the bottle and added a large dollop of ketchup* [origin unknown]

doll up *vb* **get dolled up** *slang* to dress (oneself) in a stylish or showy manner

d

dolly *n, pl* **-lies 1** a child's word for a **doll** (sense 1) **2** *films & television* a wheeled support on which a camera may be mounted **3** Also called: **dolly bird** *old-fashioned slang, chiefly Brit* an attractive and fashionable girl

dolman sleeve *n* a sleeve that is very wide at the armhole and tapers to a tight wrist [Turkish *dolaman* a winding round]

dolmen *n* a prehistoric monument consisting of a horizontal stone supported by vertical stones, thought to be a tomb [French]

dolomite *n* a mineral consisting of calcium magnesium carbonate [after Déodat de *Dolomieu*, mineralogist]

dolphin *n* a sea mammal of the whale family, with a long pointed snout [Greek *delphis*]

dolt *n* a stupid person [probably related to Old English *dol* stupid] **doltish** *adj*

domain *n* **1** a particular area of activity or interest **2** land under one ruler or government **3** a group of computers that have the same suffix in their names on the internet, specifying the country, type of institution, etc. where they are located **4** *NZ* a public park [French *domaine*]

dome *n* **1** a rounded roof built on a circular base **2** something shaped like this [Latin *domus* house]

domed *adj* shaped like a dome

domestic *adj* **1** of one's own country or a specific country: *the domestic economy was generally better* **2** of the home or family **3** enjoying home or family life: *she was never a very domestic sort of person* **4** intended for use in the home: *the kitchen was equipped with all the latest domestic appliances* **5** (of an animal) bred or kept as a pet or for the supply of food ▷ *n* **6** a household servant [Latin *domesticus* belonging to the house] **domestically** *adv*

domesticate *vb* **-cating, -cated 1** to bring or keep (wild animals or plants) under control or cultivation **2** to accustom (someone) to home life **domestication** *n*

domesticity *n, pl* **-ties 1** home life **2** devotion to home life

domestic science *n* the study of cooking, needlework, and other household skills

domicile (dom-miss-ile) *n* **1** *formal* a person's regular dwelling place **2** *law* the country in which a person has his or her permanent legal residence [Latin *domus* house] **domiciliary** *adj*

domiciled *adj* living or established in a particular place: *the holding company was domiciled in Bermuda*

dominant *adj* **1** having control, authority, or influence: *a dominant leader* **2** main or chief: *coal is still, worldwide, the dominant fuel* **3** *genetics* (in a pair of genes) designating the gene that produces a particular character in an organism **dominance** *n*

dominate *vb* **-nating, -nated 1** to control or govern **2** to tower above (surroundings): *the building had been designed to dominate the city skyscape* **3** to predominate in [Latin *dominari* to be lord over] **dominating** *adj* **domination** *n*

dominee (doom-in-nee) *n S African* a minister of the Dutch Reformed Church [Dutch, from Latin *dominus* master]

domineering *adj* acting arrogantly or tyrannically [Dutch *domineren*]

Dominican *n* **1** a friar or nun of the Christian order founded by Saint Dominic ▷ *adj* **2** of the Dominican order

dominion *n* **1** control or authority **2** the land governed by one ruler or government **3** (formerly) a self-governing division of the British Empire [Latin *dominium* ownership]

domino[1] *n, pl* **-noes** a small rectangular block marked with dots, used in dominoes [Italian, perhaps from *domino!* master!, said by the winner]

domino[2] *n, pl* **-noes** *or* **-nos** a large hooded cloak worn with an eye mask at a masquerade [Latin *dominus* lord, master]

dominoes *n* a game in which dominoes with matching halves are laid together

don[1] *vb* **donning, donned** to put on (clothing) [Middle English]

don[2] *n* **1** *Brit* a member of the teaching staff at a university or college **2** a Spanish gentleman or nobleman **3** (in the Mafia) the head of a family [Latin *dominus* lord]

donate *vb* **-nating, -nated** to give (something) to a charity or other organization

donation *n* **1** the act of donating **2** a contribution to a charity or other organization [Latin *donum* gift]

donder *S African slang* ▷ *vb* **1** to beat (someone) up ▷ *n* **2** a wretch; swine [Dutch *donderen* to swear, bully]

done *vb* **1** the past participle of **do[1]** ▷ *interj* **2** an expression of agreement: *£60 seems reasonable, done!* ▷ *adj* **3** (of a task) completed **4** (of food) cooked enough **5** used up: *the milk is done* **6** *Brit, Austral & NZ* socially acceptable: *the done thing* **7** *informal* cheated or tricked **8** **done in** *or* **up** *informal* exhausted

doner kebab *n* a dish of grilled minced lamb, served in a split slice of unleavened bread [Turkish *döner* rotating]

dongle *n computers* a plug-in device that allows a computer user to access the internet via mobile broadband

donjon *n* the heavily fortified central tower of a castle [archaic variant of *dungeon*]

Don Juan *n* a successful seducer of women [after the legendary Spanish philanderer]

donkey *n* **1** a long-eared member of the horse family **2** a person who is considered to be stupid or stubborn [origin unknown]

donkey jacket *n Brit, Austral & NZ* a man's thick hip-length jacket with a waterproof panel across the shoulders

donkey's years *pl n informal* a long time

donkey-work *n* uninteresting groundwork
donnish *adj* resembling a university don; pedantic or fussy
donor *n* **1** *med* a person who gives blood or organs for use in the treatment of another person **2** a person who makes a donation [Latin *donare* to give]
donor card *n* a card carried by someone to show that the body parts specified may be used for transplants after the person's death
Don Quixote (don kee-**hoe**-tee) *n* an impractical idealist [after the hero of Miguel de Cervantes' novel *Don Quixote de la Mancha*]
don't do not
doodle *vb* **-dling, -dled 1** to scribble or draw aimlessly ▷ *n* **2** a shape or picture drawn aimlessly [originally, a foolish person]
doom *n* **1** death or a terrible fate ▷ *vb* **2** to destine or condemn to death or a terrible fate [Old English *dōm*]
doomsday *or* **domesday** *n* **1** the day on which the Last Judgment will occur **2** any dreaded day [Old English *dōmes dæg* Judgment Day]
doona *n Austral* a large quilt used as a bed cover in place of the top sheet and blankets
door *n* **1** a hinged or sliding panel for closing the entrance to a building, room, or cupboard **2** a doorway or entrance **3** a means of access or escape: *the door to happiness* **4 lay something at someone's door** to blame someone for something **5 out of doors** in the open air [Old English *duru*]
doorjamb *n* one of the two vertical posts that form the sides of a door frame. Also called: **doorpost**
doorman *n, pl* **-men** a man employed to be on duty at the main entrance of a large building
doormat *n* **1** a mat, placed at an entrance, for wiping dirt from shoes **2** *informal* a person who offers little resistance to being treated badly
doorstep *n* **1** a step in front of a door **2** *informal* a thick slice of bread
doorstop *n* a heavy object or one fixed to the floor, which prevents a door from closing or from striking a wall
door-to-door *adj* **1** (of selling) from one house to the next **2** (of a journey) direct
doorway *n* an opening into a building or room
doosra *n cricket* a delivery bowled by an off-spinner that turns the opposite way from an off-break [Urdu, Hindi]
dop *n S African informal* a tot or small drink, usually alcoholic [Afrikaans]
dope *n* **1** *slang* an illegal drug, such as cannabis **2** a drug administered to a person or animal to affect performance in a race or other sporting competition **3** *informal* a slow-witted person **4** *informal* confidential information **5** a thick liquid, such as a lubricant ▷ *vb* **doping, doped 6** to administer a drug to [Dutch *doop* sauce]
dopey *or* **dopy** *adj* **dopier, dopiest 1** *informal* half-asleep, as when under the influence of a drug **2** *slang* silly
doppelgänger (**dop**-pl-geng-er) *n legend* a ghostly duplicate of a living person [German *Doppelgänger* double-goer]
Doppler effect *n* a change in the apparent frequency of a sound or light wave as a result of relative motion between the observer and the source [after C. J. *Doppler*, physicist]
dorba *n Austral informal* a stupid, inept, or clumsy person
Doric *adj* **1** of a style of classical architecture characterized by a heavy fluted column and a simple capital ▷ *n* **2** a rustic dialect, esp. a Scots one [*Doris*, in ancient Greece]
dormant *adj* **1** temporarily quiet, inactive, or not being used **2** *biol* alive but in a resting condition [Latin *dormire* to sleep] **dormancy** *n*
dormer *or* **dormer window** *n* a window that is built upright in a sloping roof [Latin *dormitorium* dormitory]
dormitory *n, pl* **-ries 1** a large room, esp. at a school, containing several beds **2** a building, esp. at a college, providing living accommodation ▷ *adj* **3** *Brit & Austral* denoting an area from which most of the residents commute to work: *the swelling suburban dormitory areas* [Latin *dormitorium*, from *dormire* to sleep]
Dormobile *n trademark* a vanlike vehicle specially equipped for living in while travelling
dormouse *n, pl* **-mice** a small rodent resembling a mouse with a furry tail [origin unknown]
dorp *n S African* a small town or village [Dutch]
dorsal *adj anatomy & zool* of or on the back [Latin *dorsum* back]
dory *n, pl* **-ries** a spiny-finned food fish. Also called: **John Dory** [French *dorée* gilded]
DOS *computers* disk operating system
dose *n* **1** a specific quantity of a medicine taken at one time **2** *informal* something unpleasant to experience: *a dose of the cold* **3** the total energy of radiation absorbed **4** *slang* a sexually transmitted infection ▷ *vb* **dosing, dosed 5** to administer a quantity of medicine to (someone) [Greek *dosis* a giving] **dosage** *n*
dosh *n slang* money
dosing strip *n* (in New Zealand) an area for treating dogs suspected of having hydatid disease
doss *slang* ▷ *vb* **1 doss down** to sleep on a makeshift bed **2** to pass time aimlessly: *I doss around a lot* ▷ *n* **3** a task requiring little effort [origin unknown]
dosshouse *n slang* a cheap lodging house for homeless people
dossier (**doss**-ee-ay) *n* a collection of papers about a subject or person [French]
dot *n* **1** a small round mark **2** the small round mark used to represent the short sound in Morse code **3 on the dot** at exactly the arranged time ▷ *vb* **dotting, dotted 4** to mark with a dot **5** to scatter or intersperse: *there are numerous churches dotted around Rome* **6 dot one's i's and cross one's t's** *informal* to pay meticulous attention to detail [Old English *dott* head of a boil]
dotage *n* feebleness of mind as a result of old age [Middle English *doten* to dote]
dotard *n* a person who is feeble-minded through old age
dotcom *or* **dot.com** *n* a company that conducts most of its business on the internet [from *.com*,

the domain name suffix of businesses trading on the internet]

dote *vb* **doting, doted** > **dote on** *or* **upon** to love (someone or something) to an excessive degree [Middle English *doten*] **doting** *adj*

dotterel *n* a shore bird with reddish-brown underparts and white bands around the head and neck [Middle English *dotrelle*]

dottle *n* the tobacco left in a pipe after smoking [obsolete *dot* lump]

dotty *adj* **-tier, -tiest** *slang* slightly crazy [from *dot*] **dottiness** *n*

d

double *adj* **1** as much again in size, strength, number, etc.: *a double scotch* **2** composed of two equal or similar parts **3** designed for two users: *a double bed* **4** folded in half: *the blanket had been folded double* **5** stooping: *she was bent double over the flower bed* **6** ambiguous: *a double meaning* **7** false, deceitful, or hypocritical: *double standards* **8** *music* (of an instrument) sounding an octave lower: *a double bass* ▷ *adv* **9** twice over: *that's double the amount requested* ▷ *n* **10** twice the size, strength, number, etc. **11** a double measure of spirits **12** a person who closely resembles another person **13** a bet on two horses in different races in which any winnings from the first race are placed on the horse in the later race **14 at** *or* **on the double** quickly or immediately ▷ *vb* **-bling, -bled 15** to make or become twice as much **16** to bend or fold so that one part covers another **17** to play two parts or serve two roles **18** to turn sharply **19** *bridge* to make a call that will double certain scoring points if the preceding bid becomes the contract **20 double for** to act as substitute for ▷ See also **double back, doubles, double up** [Latin *duplus* twofold] **doubler** *n*

double agent *n* a spy employed by two enemy countries at the same time

double back *vb* to go back in the opposite direction: *I doubled back searching for the track*

double-barrelled *or US* **-barreled** *adj* **1** (of a gun) having two barrels **2** *Brit* (of a surname) having hyphenated parts

double bass *n* a stringed instrument, the largest and lowest member of the violin family

double-breasted *adj* (of a garment) having overlapping fronts

double-check *vb* to make certain by checking again

double chin *n* a fold of fat under the chin

double cream *n Brit & Austral* thick cream with a high fat content

double-cross *vb* **1** to cheat or betray ▷ *n* **2** an instance of double-crossing

double-dealing *n* treacherous or deceitful behaviour

double-decker *n* **1** *chiefly Brit* a bus with two passenger decks one on top of the other ▷ *adj* **2** *informal* having two layers: *a double-decker sandwich*

double-double *n* **1** *chiefly US & Canad basketball* the feat of scoring 10 or more in each of two classes of quantifiable positive action (such as points, assists, rebounds, etc.) **2** *Canad* a cup of coffee served with two helpings of cream and sugar

double Dutch *n informal* speech or writing that is difficult to understand: *it was double Dutch to me*

double-edged *adj* **1** (of a remark) malicious in intent though apparently complimentary **2** (of a knife) having a cutting edge on either side of the blade

double entendre (**doob**-bl on-**tond**-ra) *n* a word or phrase with two interpretations, esp. with one meaning that is rude [obsolete French]

double entry *n* a book-keeping system in which a transaction is entered as a debit in one account and as a credit in another

double glazing *n* a window consisting of two layers of glass separated by a space, fitted to reduce heat loss

double Gloucester (**glost**-er) *n* a smooth orange-red cheese with a mild flavour

double-jointed *adj* (of a person) having unusually flexible joints

double knitting *n* a medium thickness of knitting wool

double negative *n* a grammatical construction, considered incorrect, in which two negatives are used where one is needed, for example *I wouldn't never have believed it*

double-park *vb* to park (a vehicle) alongside another vehicle, causing an obstruction

double pneumonia *n* pneumonia affecting both lungs

double-quick *adj* **1** very quick ▷ *adv* **2** in a very quick manner

doubles *n* a game between two pairs of players

double standard *n* a set of principles that allows greater freedom to one person or group than to another

doublet (**dub**-lit) *n history* a man's close-fitting jacket, with or without sleeves [Old French]

double take *n* a delayed reaction by a person to a remark or situation: *she did a double take when he said he was leaving*

double talk *n* deceptive or ambiguous talk

doublethink *n* the acceptance of conflicting facts or principles at the same time

double time *n* **1** *Brit, Austral & NZ* a doubled wage rate sometimes paid for overtime work **2** *music* two beats per bar

double up *vb* **1** to bend or cause to bend in two: *she was doubled up with stomach cramps* **2** to share with other people: *we only took two cars, so we had to double up*

double whammy *n informal* a devastating setback made up of two elements

doubloon *n* a former Spanish gold coin [Spanish *doblón*]

doubly *adv* **1** to or in a greater degree, quantity, or measure: *I have to be doubly careful* **2** in two ways: *the defence debate was doubly complicated*

doubt *n* **1** uncertainty about the truth, facts, or existence of something **2** an unresolved difficulty or point **3 give someone the benefit of the doubt** to accept that someone is speaking the truth **4 no doubt** almost certainly ▷ *vb* **5** to be inclined to disbelieve: *I doubt that we are late* **6** to distrust or be suspicious of: *he doubted their motives* [Latin *dubitare* to hesitate] **doubter** *n*

USAGE Where a clause follows *doubt* in a positive sentence, it was formerly considered correct to use *whether*: (*I doubt whether he will come*), but now *if* and *that* are also acceptable. In negative statements, *doubt* is followed by *that*: *I do not doubt that he is telling the truth*. In such sentences, *but* (*I do not doubt but that he is telling the truth*) is redundant.

doubtful *adj* **1** unlikely or improbable: *it's doubtful that I will marry again* **2** unsure or uncertain: *I was doubtful about some of his ideas* **doubtfully** *adv* **doubtfulness** *n*

USAGE It was formerly considered correct to use *whether* after *doubtful* (*it is doubtful whether he will come*), but now *if* and *that* are also acceptable.

doubtless *adv* probably or almost certainly: *somebody will know and doubtless somebody will ring us*

douche (**doosh**) *n* **1** a stream of water directed onto or into the body for cleansing or medical purposes **2** an instrument for applying a douche ▷ *vb* **douching, douched 3** to cleanse or treat by means of a douche [French]

dough *n* **1** a thick mixture of flour and water or milk, used for making bread, pastry, or biscuits **2** *slang* money [Old English *dāg*]

doughnut *n* a small cake of sweetened dough cooked in hot fat

doughty (**dowt**-ee) *adj* **-tier, -tiest** *old-fashioned* brave and determined [Old English *dohtig*]

do up *vb* **1** to wrap and make into a bundle: *he did up the parcel* **2** to fasten: *to do up one's blouse* **3** to renovate or redecorate

dour (**doo**-er, **dow**-er) *adj* sullen and unfriendly [probably from Latin *durus* hard] **dourness** *n*

douse *or* **dowse** (rhymes with **mouse**) *vb* **dousing, doused** *or* **dowsing, dowsed 1** to drench with water or other liquid **2** to put out (a light) [origin unknown]

dove *n* **1** a bird with a heavy body, small head, and short legs **2** *politics* a person opposed to war [Old English *dūfe*]

dovecote *or* **dovecot** *n* a box, shelter, or part of a house built for doves or pigeons to live in

dove-grey *adj* greyish-brown

dovetail *n* **1** Also called: **dovetail joint** a wedge-shaped joint used to fit two pieces of wood tightly together ▷ *vb* **2** to fit together closely or neatly: *her resignation dovetails well with the new structure*

dowager *n* a woman possessing property or a title obtained from her dead husband [Old French *douagiere*]

dowdy *adj* **-dier, -diest** wearing dull and unfashionable clothes [Middle English *dowd* slut] **dowdily** *adv* **dowdiness** *n*

dowel *n* a wooden or metal peg that fits into two corresponding holes to join larger pieces of wood or metal together [Middle Low German *dövel* plug]

dower *n* **1** the life interest in a part of her husband's estate allotted to a widow by law **2** *archaic* a dowry [Latin *dos* gift]

dower house *n* a house for the use of a widow, often on her deceased husband's estate

do with *vb* **1 could do with** need or would benefit from: *I could do with some royal treatment* **2 have to do with** to be associated with: *his illness has a lot to do with his failing the exam* **3 to do with** concerning; related to: *this book has to do with the occult*

do without *vb* to manage without

down[1] *prep* **1** from a higher to a lower position in or on **2** at a lower or further level or position on, in, or along: *I wandered down the corridor* ▷ *adv* **3** at or to a lower level or position: *he bent down* **4** indicating lowering or destruction: *to bring down an aircraft* **5** indicating intensity or completion: *calm down and mind your manners* **6** immediately: *cash down* **7** on paper: *she copied it down* **8** away from a more important place: *she came down from head office* **9** reduced to a state of lack: *he was down to his last pound* **10** lacking a specified amount: *down several pounds* **11** lower in price **12** from an earlier to a later time: *the ring was handed down from my grandmother* **13** to a finer state: *to grind down* **14** *sport* being a specified number of points or goals behind an opponent **15** (of a person) being inactive, owing to illness: *down with the cold* ▷ *adj* **16** depressed or unhappy: *she seems very down today* ▷ *vb* **17** *informal* to eat or drink quickly **18** to fell (someone or something) ▷ *n* **19 have a down on** *informal* to feel hostile towards: *you seem to have a down on the family tonight* [Old English *dūne* from the hill]

down[2] *n* soft fine feathers [Old Norse *dūnn*] **downy** *adj*

down-and-out *n* **1** a person who is homeless and destitute ▷ *adj* **2** without any means of support; destitute

downbeat *adj informal* **1** depressed or gloomy: *she was in one of her downbeat moods* **2** casual and restrained: *the chairman's statement was decidedly downbeat* ▷ *n* **3** *music* the first beat of a bar

downcast *adj* **1** sad and dejected **2** (of the eyes) directed downwards

downer *n slang* **1** a barbiturate, tranquillizer, or narcotic **2 on a downer** in a state of depression

downfall *n* **1** a sudden loss of position or reputation **2** the cause of this

downgrade *vb* **-grading, -graded** to reduce in importance or value

downhearted *adj* sad and discouraged

downhill *adj* **1** going or sloping down ▷ *adv* **2** towards the bottom of a hill **3 go downhill** *informal* to deteriorate

Downing Street *n* the British prime minister or the British government [after the street in London which contains the official residence of the prime minister and the chancellor of the exchequer]

download *vb* **1** to transfer (data) from the memory of one computer to that of another ▷ *n* **2** a file transferred in this way

down-market *adj* cheap, popular, and of poor quality

down payment *n* the deposit paid on an item purchased on hire-purchase, mortgage, etc.: *an initial down payment is usually required*

downpour *n* a heavy continuous fall of rain

downright *adv* **1** extremely: *it's just downright cruel* ▷ *adj* **2** absolute; utter: *Crozier is a downright thief*

down-river *adj, adv* nearer the mouth of a river

downs *pl n* an area of low grassy hills, esp. in S England
downshifting *n* the practice of simplifying one's lifestyle and becoming less materialistic
downside *n* the disadvantageous aspect of a situation: *the downside of capitalism*
downsize *vb* **1** to reduce the number of people employed by (a company) **2** to reduce the size of or produce a smaller version of (something)
Down's syndrome *or esp US, Canad & Austral* **Down syndrome** *n pathol* a congenital condition characterized by learning difficulties and physical differences, such as shorter stature [after John *Langdon-Down*, physician]
downstairs *adv* **1** down the stairs; to or on a lower floor ▷ *n* **2** a lower or ground floor
downstream *adv, adj* in or towards the lower part of a stream; with the current
downtime *n commerce* time during which a computer or other machine is not working
down-to-earth *adj* sensible or practical
downtown *chiefly US, Canad & NZ* ▷ *n* **1** the central or lower part of a city, esp. the main commercial area ▷ *adv* **2** towards, to, or into this area
downtrodden *adj* oppressed and lacking the will to resist
downturn *n* a drop in the success of an economy or a business
down under *informal* ▷ *n* **1** Australia or New Zealand ▷ *adv* **2** in or to Australia or New Zealand
downward *adj* **1** descending from a higher to a lower level, condition, or position ▷ *adv* **2** same as **downwards** **downwardly** *adv*
downwards *or* **downward** *adv* **1** from a higher to a lower level, condition, or position **2** from an earlier time or source to a later one
downwind *adv, adj* in the same direction towards which the wind is blowing; with the wind from behind
dowry *n, pl* **-ries** the property brought by a woman to her husband at marriage [Latin *dos*]
dowse (rhymes with **cows**) *vb* **dowsing, dowsed** to search for underground water or minerals using a divining rod [origin unknown] **dowser** *n*
doxology *n, pl* **-gies** *Christianity* a hymn or verse of praise to God [Greek *doxologos* uttering praise]
doyen (doy-en) *or fem* **doyenne** (doy-en) *n* the senior member of a group, profession, or society [French]
doze *vb* **dozing, dozed** **1** to sleep lightly or for a short period **2** **doze off** to fall into a light sleep ▷ *n* **3** a short sleep [probably from Old Norse *dūs* lull]
dozen *adj, n* twelve [Latin *duodecim*] **dozenth** *adj*
dozy *adj* **dozier, doziest** **1** feeling sleepy **2** *Brit informal* stupid and slow-witted
DP displaced person
DPB (in New Zealand) Domestic Purposes Benefit
dpi *computers* dots per inch: a measure of the clarity of a printed image
DPP (in Britain) Director of Public Prosecutions
Dr **1** Doctor **2** Drive
drab *adj* **drabber, drabbest** **1** dull and dreary **2** light olive-brown [Old French *drap* cloth] **drabness** *n*
drachm (**dram**) *n Brit* a unit of liquid measure equal to one eighth of a fluid ounce (3.55 ml) [variant of DRAM]
drachma *n, pl* **-mas** *or* **-mae** a former monetary unit of Greece [Greek *drakhmē* a handful]
draconian *adj* severe or harsh: *draconian measures were taken by the government* [after *Draco*, Athenian statesman]
draft *n* **1** a preliminary outline of a letter, book, or speech **2** a written order for payment of money by a bank **3** *US & Austral* selection for compulsory military service ▷ *vb* **4** to write a preliminary outline of a letter, book, or speech **5** to send (personnel) from one place to another to carry out a specific job **6** *chiefly US* to select for compulsory military service ▷ *n, vb* **7** *US* same as **draught** [variant of DRAUGHT]
drag *vb* **dragging, dragged** **1** to pull with force along the ground **2** to trail on the ground **3** to persuade (someone) to go somewhere: *he didn't want to come so I had to drag him along* **4** to move (oneself) slowly and with difficulty: *I had to drag myself out of bed this morning* **5** to linger behind: *she dragged along behind her mother* **6** to search (a river) with a dragnet or hook **7** to draw (on a cigarette) **8** *computers* to move (a graphics image) from one place to another on the screen by manipulating a mouse with its button held down **9** **drag away** *or* **from** to force (oneself) to come away from something interesting: *I was completely spellbound and couldn't drag myself away from the film* **10** **drag on** *or* **out** to last or be prolonged tediously: *winter dragged on* **11** **drag one's feet** *informal* to act with deliberate slowness ▷ *n* **12** a person or thing that slows up progress **13** *informal* a tedious or boring thing: *it was a drag having to walk two miles to the station every day* **14** *informal* a draw on a cigarette **15** an implement, such as a dragnet, used for dragging **16** *aeronautics* the resistance to the motion of a body passing through air **17** **in drag** (of a man) wearing women's clothes, usually as a form of entertainment ▷ See also **drag up** [Old English *dragan* to draw]
draggle *vb* **-gling, -gled** to make or become wet or dirty by trailing on the ground [Middle English]
dragnet *n* a net used to scour the bottom of a pond or river when searching for something
dragoman *n, pl* **-mans** *or* **-men** (in some Middle Eastern countries) a professional interpreter or guide [Arabic *targumān*]
dragon *n* **1** a mythical monster that resembles a large fire-breathing lizard **2** *informal, derogatory* a fierce woman **3** **chase the dragon** *slang* to smoke opium or heroin [Greek *drakōn*]
dragonfly *n, pl* **-flies** a brightly coloured insect with a long slender body and two pairs of wings
dragoon *n* **1** a heavily armed cavalryman ▷ *vb* **2** to coerce or force: *we were dragooned into participating* [French *dragon*]
drag race *n* a race in which specially built or modified cars or motorcycles are timed over a measured course **drag racing** *n*
drag up *vb informal* to revive (an unpleasant fact or story)
drain *n* **1** a pipe that carries off water or sewage **2** a cause of a continuous reduction in energy or

resources: *the expansion will be a drain on resources* **3** a metal grid on a road or pavement through which rainwater flows **4 down the drain** wasted ▷ *vb* **5** to draw off or remove (liquid) from **6** to flow (away) or filter (off) **7** to dry or be emptied as a result of liquid running off or flowing away **8** to drink the entire contents of (a glass or cup) **9** to make constant demands on (energy or resources); exhaust **10** (of a river) to carry off the surface water from (an area) [Old English *drēahnian*]

drainage *n* **1** a system of pipes, drains, or ditches used to drain water or other liquids **2** the process or a method of draining

draining board *n* a grooved surface at the side of a sink, used for draining washed dishes

drainpipe *n* a pipe for carrying off rainwater or sewage

drake *n* the male of a duck [origin unknown]

dram *n* **1** a small amount of spirits, such as whisky **2** a unit of weight equal to one sixteenth of an ounce (avoirdupois) [Greek *drakhmē*; see DRACHMA]

drama *n* **1** a serious play for theatre, television, or radio **2** plays in general, as a form of literature **3** the art of writing, producing, or acting in a play **4** a situation that is exciting or highly emotional [Greek: something performed]

dramatic *adj* **1** of or relating to drama **2** like a drama in suddenness or effectiveness: *the government's plan has had a dramatic effect on employment in television* **3** acting or performed in a flamboyant way: *he spread his hands in a dramatic gesture of helplessness* **dramatically** *adv*

dramatics *n* **1** the art of acting or producing plays ▷ *pl n* **2** exaggerated, theatrical behaviour

dramatis personae (**drah**-mat-tiss per-**soh**-nigh) *pl n* the characters in a play [New Latin]

dramatist *n* a playwright: *Austria's greatest living dramatist*

dramatize *or* **-tise** *vb* **-tizing, -tized** *or* **-tising, -tised 1** to rewrite (a book or story) in a form suitable for performing on stage **2** to express (something) in a dramatic or exaggerated way: *he dramatizes his illness* **dramatization** *or* **-tisation** *n*

drank *vb* the past tense of **drink**

drape *vb* **draping, draped 1** to cover with material or fabric **2** to hang or arrange in folds **3** to place casually: *he draped his arm across the back of the seat* ▷ See also **drapes** [Old French *draper*]

draper *n Brit* a person who sells fabrics and sewing materials

drapery *n, pl* **-peries 1** fabric or clothing arranged and draped **2** fabrics and cloth collectively

drapes *pl n Austral, NZ, US & Canad* material hung at an opening or window to shut out light or to provide privacy; curtains

drastic *adj* strong and severe: *the police are taking drastic measures against car thieves* [Greek *drastikos*] **drastically** *adv*

drat *interj slang* an exclamation of annoyance [probably alteration of *God rot*]

draught *or US* **draft** *n* **1** a current of cold air, usually one coming into a room or vehicle **2** a portion of liquid to be drunk, esp. a dose of medicine **3** a gulp or swallow: *she took a deep draught then a sip* **4** one of the flat discs used in the game of draughts. US and Canad equivalent: **checker 5 feel the draught** to be short of money **6 on draught** (of beer) drawn from a cask ▷ *adj* **7** (of an animal) used for pulling heavy loads: *horses are specialized draught animals* [probably Old Norse *drahtr*]

draught beer *n* beer stored in a cask

draughtboard *n* a square board divided into 64 squares, used for playing draughts

draughts *n* a game for two players using a draughtboard and 12 draughtsmen each [plural of *draught* (in obsolete sense: a chess move)]

draughtsman *or US* **draftsman** *n, pl* **-men 1** a person employed to prepare detailed scale drawings of equipment, machinery, or buildings **2** a person skilled in drawing **3** *Brit* a flat disc used in the game of draughts. US and Canad equivalent: **checker draughtsmanship** *n*

draughty *or US* **drafty** *adj* **draughtier, draughtiest** *or US* **draftier, draftiest** exposed to draughts of air **draughtily** *adv* **draughtiness** *n*

draw *vb* **drawing, drew, drawn 1** to sketch (a picture, pattern, or diagram) with a pen or pencil **2** to cause (a person or thing) to move closer or further away from a place by pulling **3** to bring, take, or pull (something) out of a container: *he drew a gun and laid it on the table* **4** to take (something) from a particular source: *the inhabitants drew water from the well two miles away* **5** to move in a specified direction: *she drew alongside me* **6** to attract: *she drew enthusiastic audiences from all over the country* **7** to formulate or decide: *he drew similar conclusions* **8** to cause to flow: *the barman nodded and drew two pints* **9** to choose or be given by lottery: *Brazil have drawn Spain in the semi-final* **10** (of two teams or contestants) to finish a game with an equal number of points **11** *archery* to bend (a bow) by pulling the string **12** to cause (pus) to discharge from an abscess or wound ▷ *n* **13** a raffle or lottery **14** *informal* a person, place, show, or event that attracts a large audience **15** a contest or game ending in a tie ▷ See also **drawback, draw in** *etc.* [Old English *dragan*]

drawback *n* **1** a disadvantage or hindrance ▷ *vb* **draw back 2** to move backwards: *the girl drew back as though in pain* **3** to turn aside from an undertaking: *the prime minister drew back from his original intention*

drawbridge *n* a bridge that may be raised to prevent access or to enable vessels to pass

drawer *n* **1** a sliding box-shaped part of a piece of furniture used for storage **2** a person or thing that draws

drawers *pl n old-fashioned* an undergarment worn on the lower part of the body

draw in *vb* **1** (of a train) to arrive at a station **2 the nights are drawing in** the hours of daylight are becoming shorter

drawing *n* **1** a picture or plan made by means of lines on a surface **2** the art of making drawings

drawing pin *n Brit & NZ* a short tack with a broad smooth head used for fastening papers to a drawing board or other surface

drawing room *n* a room where visitors are received and entertained

drawl *vb* **1** to speak slowly with long vowel sounds ▷ *n* **2** the way of speech of someone who drawls [probably frequentative of *draw*] **drawling** *adj*

drawn *vb* **1** the past participle of **draw** ▷ *adj* **2** haggard, tired, or tense in appearance

draw off *vb* to cause (a liquid) to flow from something

draw on *vb* **1** to make use of from a source or fund: *they are able to draw on a repertoire of around 400 songs* **2** (of a period of time) to come near or pass by: *summer draws on; time draws on*

d

draw out *vb* **1** (of a train) to leave a station **2** to encourage (someone) to talk freely: *therapy groups will continue to draw her out* **3 draw out of** to find out (information) from

drawstring *n* a cord run through a hem around an opening, so that when it is pulled tighter, the opening closes

draw up *vb* **1** to prepare and write out: *the signatories drew up a draft agreement* **2** (of a vehicle) to come to a halt

dray *n* a low cart used for carrying heavy loads [Old English *dræge* dragnet]

dread *vb* **1** to anticipate with apprehension or terror ▷ *n* **2** great fear [Old English *ondrǣdan*]

dreadful *adj* **1** extremely disagreeable or shocking **2** extreme: *there were dreadful delays* **dreadfully** *adv*

dreadlocks *pl n* hair worn in the Rastafarian style of tightly curled strands

dreadnought *n* a type of battleship with heavy guns

dream *n* **1** an imagined series of events experienced in the mind while asleep **2** a daydream: *she escaped into dreams of the perfect job* **3** a goal or aim: *unity has been their constant dream* **4** a wonderful person or thing: *her house is a dream* ▷ *vb* **dreaming, dreamed** *or* **dreamt 5** to experience (a dream) **6** to indulge in daydreams **7** to be unrealistic: *you're dreaming if you think we can win* **8 dream of** to consider the possibility of: *she would not dream of taking his advice* **9 dream of** *or* **about** to have an image of or fantasy about: *they often dream about what life will be like for them on the outside* ▷ *adj* **10** beautiful or pleasing: *a dream kitchen* [Old English *drēam* song] **dreamer** *n*

dream team *n informal* a group of people regarded as having the perfect combination of talents

dream ticket *n* a combination of two people, esp. candidates in an election, that is considered to be ideal

dream up *vb* to formulate in the imagination: *a character dreamed up by a scriptwriter*

dreamy *adj* **dreamier, dreamiest 1** vague or impractical: *she was wild-eyed and dreamy* **2** relaxing or gentle: *I felt this dreamy contentment* **3** *informal* wonderful or impressive: *he drives a dreamy Jaguar* **dreamily** *adv* **dreaminess** *n*

dreary *adj* **drearier, dreariest** dull or uninteresting: *there are long streets of dreary red houses spreading everywhere* [Old English *drēorig* gory] **drearily** *adv* **dreariness** *n*

dredge[1] *n* **1** a machine used to scoop or suck up silt or mud from a river bed or harbour ▷ *vb* **dredging, dredged 2** to remove silt or mud from (a river bed or harbour) by means of a dredge **3** to search for (a submerged object) with or as if with a dredge [origin unknown] **dredger** *n*

dredge[2] *vb* **dredging, dredged** to sprinkle (food) with a substance, such as flour [Old French *dragie*] **dredger** *n*

dredge up *vb informal* to remember (something obscure or half-forgotten): *I didn't retain you to dredge up unfortunate incidents from my past*

dregs *pl n* **1** solid particles that settle at the bottom of some liquids **2 the dregs** the worst or most despised elements: *the dregs of colonial society* [Old Norse *dregg*]

drench *vb* **1** to make completely wet **2** to give medicine to (an animal) [Old English *drencan* to cause to drink] **drenching** *n, adj*

Dresden *or* **Dresden china** *n* delicate and decorative porcelain made near Dresden, Germany

dress *n* **1** a one-piece garment with a skirt and bodice and sometimes sleeves **2** complete style of clothing: *contemporary dress* ▷ *adj* **3** suitable for a formal occasion: *he was wearing a dress shirt* ▷ *vb* **4** to put clothes on **5** to put on formal clothes **6** to apply protective covering to (a wound) **7** to cover (a salad) with dressing **8** to prepare (meat, poultry, or fish) for selling or cooking by cleaning or gutting **9** to put a finish on (the surface of stone, metal, or other building material) ▷ See also **dress up** [Old French *drecier* to arrange]

dressage (**dress**-ahzh) *n* **A** the method of training horses to perform manoeuvres as a display of obedience **B** the manoeuvres performed [French]

dress circle *n* the first gallery in a theatre

dress code *n* a set of rules regarding the style of dress acceptable in an office, restaurant, etc.

dresser[1] *n* **1** a piece of furniture with shelves and cupboards, used for storing or displaying dishes **2** *US* a chest of drawers [Old French *drecier* to arrange]

dresser[2] *n* **1** a person who dresses in a specified way: *Lars was a meticulous, elegant dresser* **2** *theatre* a person employed to assist performers with their costumes

dressing *n* **1** a sauce for food: *salad dressing* **2** *US & Canad* same as **stuffing** (sense 1) **3** a covering for a wound **4** manure or fertilizer spread on land **5** a gluey material used for stiffening paper, textiles, etc.

dressing-down *n informal* a severe reprimand

dressing gown *n* a loose-fitting garment worn over one's pyjamas or nightdress

dressing room *n* a room used for changing clothes and applying make-up, esp. a backstage room in a theatre

dressing table *n* a piece of bedroom furniture with a mirror and a set of drawers

dressmaker *n* a person who makes clothes for women **dressmaking** *n*

dress rehearsal *n* **1** the last rehearsal of a play, opera, or show using costumes, lighting, and other effects **2** any full-scale practice: *astronauts are in the midst of a two-day dress rehearsal of their launch countdown*

dress shirt *n* a man's evening shirt, worn as part of formal evening dress
dress suit *n* a man's evening suit
dress up *vb* **1** to put on glamorous or stylish clothes **2** to put fancy dress on: *the guests dressed up like cowboys* **3** to disguise (something) to make it more attractive or acceptable: *the offer was simply an old one dressed up in new terms*
dressy *adj* **dressier, dressiest 1** (of clothes or occasions) elegant **2** (of people) dressing stylishly **dressiness** *n*
drew *vb* the past tense of **draw**
drey *or* **dray** *n Brit & Austral* a squirrel's nest [origin unknown]
dribble *vb* **-bling, -bled 1** to flow or allow to flow in a thin stream or drops **2** to allow saliva to trickle from the mouth **3** (in football, hockey, etc.) to propel (the ball) by kicking or tapping in quick succession ▷ *n* **4** a small quantity of liquid falling in drops or flowing in a thin stream **5** a small supply: *there's only a dribble of milk left* **6** an act or instance of dribbling [obsolete *drib*, variant of *drip*] **dribbler** *n*
dribs and drabs *pl n informal* small occasional amounts
dried *vb* the past of **dry**
drier[1] *adj* a comparative of **dry**
drier[2] *n* same as **dryer**[1]
driest *adj* a superlative of **dry**
drift *vb* **1** to be carried along by currents of air or water **2** to move aimlessly from one place or activity to another **3** to wander away from a fixed course or point **4** (of snow) to pile up in heaps ▷ *n* **5** something piled up by the wind or current, as a snowdrift **6** a general movement or development: *there has been a drift away from family control* **7** the main point of an argument or speech: *I was beginning to get his drift* **8** the extent to which a vessel or aircraft is driven off course by winds, etc. **9** a current of water created by the wind [Old Norse]
drifter *n* **1** a person who moves aimlessly from place to place **2** a boat used for drift-net fishing
drift net *n* a fishing net that is allowed to drift with the tide
driftwood *n* wood floating on or washed ashore by the sea
drill[1] *n* **1** a machine or tool for boring holes **2** *military* training in procedures or movements, as for parades **3** strict and often repetitious training **4** *informal* correct procedure: *he knows the drill as well as anybody* ▷ *vb* **5** to bore a hole in (something) with or as if with a drill **6** to instruct or be instructed in military procedures or movements **7** to teach by rigorous exercises or training [Middle Dutch *drillen*]
drill[2] *n* **1** a machine for planting seeds in rows **2** a furrow in which seeds are sown **3** a row of seeds planted by means of a drill ▷ *vb* **4** to plant (seeds) by means of a drill [origin unknown]
drill[3] *n* a hard-wearing cotton cloth, used for uniforms [German *Drillich*]
drill[4] *n* a W African monkey, related to the mandrill [from a West African word]
drilling platform *n* an offshore structure that supports a drilling rig
drilling rig *n* the complete machinery, equipment, and structures needed to drill an offshore oil well
drily *or* **dryly** *adv* in a dry manner
drink *vb* **drinking, drank, drunk 1** to swallow (a liquid) **2** to consume alcohol, esp. to excess **3** to bring (oneself) into a specified condition by consuming alcohol: *he drank himself senseless every night* **4 drink someone's health** to wish someone health or happiness with a toast **5 drink in** to pay close attention to: *I drank in what the speaker said* **6 drink to** to drink a toast to: *I drank to their engagement* ▷ *n* **7** liquid suitable for drinking **8** a portion of liquid for drinking **9** alcohol, or the habit of drinking too much of it [Old English *drincan*] **drinkable** *adj* **drinker** *n*
drink-driving *adj* of or relating to driving a car after drinking alcohol: *a drink-driving offence*
drip *vb* **dripping, dripped 1** to fall or let fall in drops ▷ *n* **2** a drop of liquid **3** the falling of drops of liquid **4** the sound made by falling drops **5** *informal* a weak or foolish person **6** *med* a device that administers a liquid drop by drop into a vein [Old English *dryppan*]
drip-dry *adj* **1** (of clothes or fabrics) designed to dry without creases if hung up when wet ▷ *vb* **-dries, -drying, -dried 2** to dry or become dry thus
drip-feed *vb* **-feeding, -fed 1** to feed (someone) a liquid drop by drop, usually through a vein ▷ *n* **drip feed 2** same as **drip** (sense 6)
dripping *n* the fat that comes from meat while it is being roasted
drive *vb* **driving, drove, driven 1** to guide the movement of (a vehicle) **2** to transport or be transported in a vehicle **3** to goad into a specified state: *the black despair that finally drove her to suicide* **4** to push or propel: *he drove the nail into the wall with a hammer* **5** *sport* to hit (a ball) very hard and straight **6** *golf* to strike (the ball) with a driver **7** to chase (game) from cover **8 drive home** to make (a point) clearly understood by emphasis ▷ *n* **9** a journey in a driven vehicle **10** a road for vehicles, esp. a private road leading to a house **11** a special effort made by a group of people for a particular purpose: *a charity drive* **12** energy, ambition, or initiative **13** *psychol* a motive or interest: *sex drive* **14** a sustained and powerful military offensive **15** the means by which power is transmitted in a machine **16** *sport* a hard straight shot or stroke [Old English *drīfan*]
drive at *vb* to intend or mean: *he had no idea what she was driving at*
drive-by *n informal* an incident in which a person is shot at by a person in a moving vehicle
drive-in *n* **1** a cinema, restaurant, etc. offering a service where people remain in their cars while using the service provided ▷ *adj* **2** denoting a cinema, etc. of this kind
drivel *n* **1** foolish talk ▷ *vb* **-velling, -velled** *or US* **-veling, -veled 2** to speak foolishly **3** to allow (saliva) to flow from the mouth [Old English *dreflian* to slaver]
driven *vb* the past participle of **drive**

driver *n* **1** a person who drives a vehicle **2** *golf* a long-shafted club with a large head and steep face, used for tee shots **driverless** *adj*

driver's licence *n Canad & Austral* an official document authorizing a person to drive a motor vehicle. Also called (in Britain and certain other countries): **driving licence**

drive-through *or* **drive-thru** *n* **1** a takeaway restaurant, bank, etc., designed so that customers can use it without leaving their cars ▷ *adj* **2** denoting a restaurant, etc. of this kind

d

drive-time *n* **1** the time of day when many people are driving to or from work, considered as a broadcasting slot ▷ *adj* **2** of this time of day: *the daily drive-time show*

driveway *n* a path for vehicles connecting a building to a public road

driving licence *n* an official document authorizing a person to drive a motor vehicle

drizzle *n* **1** very light rain ▷ *vb* **-zling, -zled** **2** to rain lightly [Old English *drēosan* to fall] **drizzly** *adj*

droll *adj* quaintly amusing [French *drôle* scamp] **drollery** *n* **drolly** *adv*

dromedary (drom-mid-er-ee) *n, pl* **-daries** a camel with a single hump [Greek *dromas* running]

drone[1] *n* **1** a male honeybee **2** a person who lives off the work of others **3** a pilotless remote-controlled aircraft [Old English *drān*]

drone[2] *vb* **droning, droned** **1** to make a monotonous low dull sound **2** **drone on** to talk in a monotonous tone without stopping ▷ *n* **3** a monotonous low dull sound **4** a single-reed pipe in a set of bagpipes [related to DRONE[1]]

drongo *n, pl* **-gos** a tropical songbird with a glossy black plumage, a forked tail, and a stout bill

drool *vb* **1** **drool over** to show excessive enthusiasm for or pleasure in **2** same as **drivel** (senses 2, 3) [probably alteration of DRIVEL]

droop *vb* **1** to sag, as from weakness or lack of support **2** to be overcome by weariness: *her eyelids drooped as if she were falling asleep* [Old Norse *drūpa*] **drooping** *adj*

droopy *adj* **droopier, droopiest** hanging or sagging downwards: *a droopy moustache*

drop *vb* **dropping, dropped** **1** to fall or allow (something) to fall vertically **2** to decrease in amount, strength, or value **3** to fall to the ground, as from exhaustion **4** to sink to a lower position, as on a scale **5** to mention casually: *she dropped a hint* **6** to set down (passengers or goods): *can you drop me at the hotel?* **7** *informal* to send: *drop me a letter* **8** to discontinue: *can we drop the subject?* **9** *informal* to be no longer friendly with: *I dropped him when I discovered his political views* **10** to leave out in speaking: *she has a tendency to drop her h's* **11** (of animals) to give birth to (offspring) **12** *sport* to omit (a player) from a team **13** to lose (a game or point) **14** **drop back** to progress more slowly than other people going in the same direction **15** **drop in** *or* **by** *informal* to pay someone a casual visit ▷ *n* **16** a small quantity of liquid forming a round shape **17** a small quantity of liquid **18** a small round sweet: *a lemon drop* **19** a decrease in amount, strength, or value **20** the vertical distance that anything may fall **21** the act of unloading troops or supplies by parachute ▷ See also **drop off, dropout, drops** [Old English *dropian*]

drop curtain *n theatre* a curtain that can be raised and lowered onto the stage

drop kick *n* a kick in certain sports such as rugby, in which the ball is dropped and kicked as it bounces from the ground

droplet *n* a very small drop of liquid

drop off *vb* **1** to set down (passengers or goods) **2** to fall asleep **3** to decrease or decline: *sales dropped off during our period of transition*

dropout *n* **1** a person who rejects conventional society **2** a student who does not complete a course of study ▷ *vb* **drop out** **3** to abandon or withdraw (from an institution or group)

dropper *n* a small tube with a rubber part at one end for drawing up and dispensing drops of liquid

droppings *pl n* the dung of certain animals, such as rabbits or birds

drops *pl n* any liquid medication applied by means of a dropper

drop scone *n* a flat spongy cake made by dropping a spoonful of batter on a hot griddle

dropsy *n* an illness in which watery fluid collects in the body [Middle English *ydropesie*, from Greek *hudōr* water] **dropsical** *adj*

drosky *or* **droshky** *n, pl* **-kies** an open four-wheeled carriage, formerly used in Russia [Russian *drozhki*]

dross *n* **1** the scum formed on the surfaces of molten metals **2** anything of inferior quality: *we can't publish this dross* [Old English *drōs* dregs]

drought (rhymes with **out**) *n* a prolonged period of time during which no rain falls [Old English *drūgoth*]

drove[1] *vb* the past tense of **drive**

drove[2] *n* **1** a herd of livestock being driven together **2** a moving crowd of people [Old English *drāf* herd]

drover *n* a person who drives sheep or cattle

drown *vb* **1** to die or kill by immersion in liquid **2** to drench thoroughly **3** to make (a sound) impossible to hear by making a loud noise [probably from Old English *druncnian*]

drowse *vb* **drowsing, drowsed** to be sleepy, dull, or sluggish [probably from Old English *drūsian* to sink]

drowsy *adj* **drowsier, drowsiest** **1** feeling sleepy **2** peaceful and quiet: *row upon row of windows looked out over drowsy parkland* **drowsily** *adv* **drowsiness** *n*

drubbing *n* an utter defeat, as in a contest: *the Communists received a drubbing* [probably from Arabic *dáraba* to beat]

drudge *n* **1** a person who works hard at an uninteresting task ▷ *vb* **drudging, drudged** **2** to work at such tasks [origin unknown]

drudgery *n* uninteresting work that must be done

drug *n* **1** any substance used in the treatment, prevention, or diagnosis of disease **2** a chemical substance, such as a narcotic, taken for the effects it produces ▷ *vb* **drugging, drugged** **3** to administer a drug to (a person or animal) in order to induce sleepiness or unconsciousness

4 to mix a drug with (food or drink): *who drugged my wine?* [Old French *drogue*]
drug addict *n* a person who is dependent on narcotic drugs
druggist *n US & Canad* a pharmacist
drugstore *n US & Canad* a pharmacy where a wide variety of goods are available
Druid *n* a member of an ancient order of Celtic priests [Latin *druides*] **Druidic** *or* **Druidical** *adj*
drum *n* **1** a percussion instrument sounded by striking a skin stretched across the opening of a hollow cylinder **2** the sound produced by a drum **3** an object shaped like a drum: *an oil drum* **4** same as **eardrum** ▷ *vb* **drumming, drummed 5** to play (music) on a drum **6** to tap rhythmically or regularly: *he drummed his fingers on the desk* **7** to fix in someone's mind by constant repetition: *my father always drummed into us how privileged we were* ▷ See also **drum up** [Middle Dutch *tromme*] **drummer** *n*
drumbeat *n* the sound made by beating a drum
drumhead *n* the part of a drum that is struck
drum machine *n* a synthesizer programmed to reproduce the sound of percussion instruments
drum major *n* the noncommissioned officer in the army who is in command of the drums and the band when paraded together
drum majorette *n* a girl who marches at the head of a procession, twirling a baton
drumstick *n* **1** a stick used for playing a drum **2** the lower joint of the leg of a cooked fowl
drum up *vb* to obtain (support or business) by making requests or canvassing
drunk *vb* **1** the past participle of **drink** ▷ *adj* **2** intoxicated with alcohol to the extent of losing control over normal functions **3** overwhelmed by strong influence or emotion: *they are drunk with joy at their unexpected victory* ▷ *n* **4** a person who is drunk or drinks habitually to excess [Old English *druncen*, past participle of *drincan* to drink]
drunkard *n* a person who is frequently or habitually drunk
drunken *adj* **1** intoxicated with alcohol **2** habitually drunk **3** caused by or relating to alcoholic intoxication: *a drunken argument* **drunkenly** *adv* **drunkenness** *n*
drupe *n* a fleshy fruit with a stone, such as the peach or cherry [Greek *druppa* olive]
dry *adj* **drier, driest** *or* **dryer, dryest 1** lacking moisture **2** having little or no rainfall **3** having the water drained away or evaporated: *a dry gully for the most part of the year* **4** not providing milk: *a dry cow* **5** (of the eyes) free from tears **6** *Brit, Austral & NZ informal* thirsty **7** eaten without butter or jam: *a dry cracker* **8** (of wine) not sweet **9** dull and uninteresting: *a dry subject* **10** (of humour) subtle and sarcastic **11** prohibiting the sale of alcoholic liquor: *a dry district* ▷ *vb* **dries, drying, dried 12** to make or become dry **13** to preserve (food) by removing the moisture ▷ See also **dry out, dry up** [Old English *drȳge*] **dryness** *n*
dryad *n, pl* **dryads** *or* **dryades** (dry-ad-deez) *Greek myth* a wood nymph [Greek *druas*]
dry battery *n* an electric battery composed of dry cells
dry cell *n* an electric cell in which the electrolyte is in the form of a paste to prevent it from spilling
dry-clean *vb* to clean (clothes, etc.) with a solvent other than water **dry-cleaner** *n* **dry-cleaning** *n*
dry dock *n* a dock that can be pumped dry to permit work on a ship's bottom
dryer[1] *n* any device that removes moisture by heating or by hot air
dryer[2] *adj* same as **drier**[1]
dry ice *n* solid carbon dioxide used as a refrigerant
dryly *adv* same as **drily**
dry out *vb* **1** to make or become dry **2** to undergo or cause to undergo treatment for alcoholism or drug addiction
dry rot *n* **1** crumbling and drying of timber, caused by certain fungi **2** a fungus causing this decay
dry run *n informal* a rehearsal
dry stock *n NZ* cattle raised for meat
dry-stone *adj* (of a wall) made without mortar
dry up *vb* **1** to make or become dry **2** to dry (dishes, cutlery, etc.) with a tea towel after they have been washed **3** (of a resource) to come to an end **4** *informal* to stop speaking: *she suddenly dried up in the middle of her speech*
Ds *chem* darmstadtium
DSC *Brit military* Distinguished Service Cross
DSO *Brit military* Distinguished Service Order
DTP *computers* desktop publishing
DT's *informal* delirium tremens
dual *adj* having two parts, functions, or aspects: *dual controls; dual nationality* [Latin *duo* two] **duality** *n*
dual carriageway *n Brit, Austral & NZ* a road with a central strip of grass or concrete to separate traffic travelling in opposite directions
dub[1] *vb* **dubbing, dubbed** to give (a person or place) a name or nickname: *he is dubbed a racist despite his strong denials* [Old English *dubbian*]
dub[2] *vb* **dubbing, dubbed 1** to provide (a film) with a new soundtrack in a different language **2** to provide (a film or tape) with a soundtrack ▷ *n* **3** *music* a style of reggae record production involving exaggeration of instrumental parts, echo, etc. [shortened from DOUBLE]
dubbin *n* a kind of thick grease applied to leather to soften it and make it waterproof [*dub* to dress leather]
dubious (dew-bee-uss) *adj* **1** not entirely honest, safe, or reliable: *this allegation was at best dubious and at worst an outright fabrication* **2** unsure or undecided: *she felt dubious about the entire proposition* **3** of doubtful quality or worth: *she had the dubious honour of being taken for his mother* [Latin *dubius* wavering] **dubiety** (dew-by-it-ee) *n* **dubiously** *adv*
dubnium *n chem* an element produced in minute quantities by bombarding plutonium with high-energy neon ions. Symbol: **Db** [after *Dubna* in Russia, where it was first reported]
ducal (duke-al) *adj* of a duke
ducat (duck-it) *n* a former European gold or silver coin [Old Italian *ducato*]
duchess *n* **1** a woman who holds the rank of duke **2** the wife or widow of a duke [Old French *duchesse*]
duchy *n, pl* **duchies** the area of land owned or ruled by a duke or duchess [Old French *duche*]

duck[1] *n, pl* **ducks** *or* **duck** **1** a water bird with short legs, webbed feet, and a broad blunt bill **2** the flesh of this bird used for food **3** the female of such a bird **4** *cricket* a score of nothing **5** **like water off a duck's back** without effect: *I reprimanded him but it was like water off a duck's back* [Old English *dūce*]

duck[2] *vb* **1** to move (the head or body) quickly downwards, to escape being seen or avoid a blow **2** to plunge suddenly under water **3** *informal* to dodge (a duty or responsibility) [Middle English]

d

duck-billed platypus *n* See **platypus**

duckling *n* a young duck

ducks and drakes *n* **1** a game in which a flat stone is bounced across the surface of water **2** **play ducks and drakes with** *informal* to use recklessly: *he has played ducks and drakes with his life*

duct *n* **1** a tube, pipe, or channel through which liquid or gas is sent **2** a tube in the body through which liquid such as tears or bile can pass [Latin *ducere* to lead]

ductile *adj* (of a metal) able to be shaped into sheets or drawn out into threads [Latin *ductilis*] **ductility** *n*

dud *informal* ▷ *n* **1** an ineffectual person or thing: *they had the foresight to pick on someone who was not a total dud* ▷ *adj* **2** bad or useless: *a dud cheque* [origin unknown]

dude *n informal* **1** *US & Canad* a man: *a fair-haired dude in his late twenties* **2** *chiefly US & Canad old-fashioned* a dandy **3** *Western US & Canad* a city dweller who spends his or her holiday on a ranch [origin unknown]

dudgeon *n* **in high dudgeon** angry or resentful: *the scientist departed in high dudgeon* [origin unknown]

due *adj* **1** expected to happen, be done, or arrive at a particular time: *he is due to return on Thursday* **2** immediately payable: *the balance is now due* **3** owed as a debt: *they finally agreed to pay her the money she was due* **4** fitting or proper: *he was found guilty of driving without due care and attention* **5** **due to** happening or existing as a direct result of someone or something else: *the cause of death was chronic kidney failure due to diabetes* ▷ *n* **6** something that is owed or required **7** **give someone his** *or* **her due** to acknowledge someone's good points: *I'll give him his due, he's resourceful* ▷ *adv* **8** directly or exactly: *due west* [Latin *debere* to owe]

> **USAGE** The use of *due to* as a compound preposition *(the performance has been cancelled due to bad weather)* was formerly considered incorrect, but is now acceptable.

duel *n* **1** a formal fight between two people using guns, swords, or other weapons to settle a quarrel ▷ *vb* **duelling, duelled** *or US* **dueling, dueled** **2** to fight in a duel [Latin *duellum*, poetical variant of *bellum* war] **duellist** *or US* **duelist** *n*

duenna *n* (esp. in Spain) an elderly woman acting as chaperone to girls [Spanish *dueña*]

dues *pl n* membership fees paid to a club or organization: *union dues*

duet *n* a piece of music sung or played by two people [Latin *duo* two] **duettist** *n*

duff *adj* **1** *chiefly Brit informal* broken or useless: *my car had a duff clutch* ▷ *vb* **2** *golf informal* to bungle (a shot) **3** **duff up** *Brit slang* to beat (someone) severely [probably from *duffer*]

duffel *or* **duffle** *n* same as **duffel coat** [after *Duffel*, Belgian town]

duffel bag *n* a cylinder-shaped canvas bag fastened with a drawstring

duffel coat *n* a wool coat usually with a hood and fastened with toggles

duffer *n informal* a dull or incompetent person [origin unknown]

dug[1] *vb* the past of **dig**

dug[2] *n* a teat or udder of a female animal [Scandinavian]

dugite (**doo**-gyte) *n* a medium-sized Australian venomous snake

dugong *n* a whalelike mammal found in tropical waters [Malay *duyong*]

dugout *n* **1** a canoe made by hollowing out a log **2** *Brit* (at a sports ground) the covered bench where managers and substitutes sit **3** *military* a covered shelter dug in the ground to provide protection

duiker *or* **duyker** (**dike**-er) *n, pl* **-kers** *or* **-ker** a small African antelope [Dutch: diver]

du jour (doo **zhoor**) *adj informal* currently fashionable [French, literally: of the day]

duke *n* **1** a nobleman of the highest rank **2** the prince or ruler of a small principality or duchy [Latin *dux* leader] **dukedom** *n*

dulcet (**dull**-sit) *adj* (of a sound) soothing or pleasant: *she smiled and, in dulcet tones, told me I would be next* [Latin *dulcis* sweet]

dulcimer *n* a tuned percussion instrument consisting of a set of strings stretched over a sounding board and struck with hammers [Old French *doulcemer*]

dull *adj* **1** not interesting: *the finished article would make dull reading* **2** slow to learn or understand **3** (of an ache) not intense: *I have a dull ache in the middle of my back* **4** (of weather) not bright or clear **5** not lively or energetic: *she appeared, looking dull and apathetic* **6** (of colour) lacking brilliance **7** (of the blade of a knife) not sharp **8** (of a sound) not loud or clear: *his head fell back to the carpet with a dull thud* ▷ *vb* **9** to make or become dull [Old English *dol*] **dullness** *n* **dully** *adv*

dullard *n old-fashioned* a dull or stupid person

dulse *n* a seaweed with large red edible fronds [Irish *duilesc* seaweed]

duly *adv* **1** in a proper manner: *my permit was duly stamped* **2** at the proper time: *the photographer duly arrived*

dumb *adj* **1** *offensive* lacking the power to speak **2** lacking the power of human speech: *the event was denounced as cruelty to dumb animals* **3** temporarily unable to speak: *I was struck dumb when I heard the news* **4** done or performed without speech: *I looked at her in dumb puzzlement* **5** *informal* stupid or slow to understand ▷ See also **dumb down** [Old English] **dumbly** *adv*

dumbbell *n* **1** a short bar with a heavy ball or disc at either end, used for physical exercise **2** *slang, chiefly US & Canad* a stupid person

dumb down *vb* to make (something) less intellectually demanding or sophisticated: *a move to dumb down its news coverage*

dumbfounded *adj* speechless with amazement: *she sat open-mouthed and dumbfounded* [*dumb* + *(con)found*]

dumb show *n* meaningful gestures without speech

dumbstruck *adj* temporarily speechless through shock or surprise

dumb terminal *n* another name for **work station** (sense 2)

dumbwaiter *n* **1** a lift for carrying food, etc. from one floor of a building to another **2** *Brit* **A** a stand placed near a dining table to hold food **B** a revolving circular tray placed on a table to hold food

dumdum *or* **dumdum bullet** *n* a soft-nosed bullet that expands on impact and causes large and serious wounds [after *Dum-Dum*, town near Calcutta where originally made]

dummy *n, pl* **-mies 1** a large model that looks like a human being, used for displaying clothes in a shop, as a target, etc. **2** a copy of an object, often lacking some essential feature of the original **3** *slang* a stupid person **4** *bridge* **A** the hand exposed on the table by the declarer's partner and played by the declarer **B** the declarer's partner **5** a rubber teat for babies to suck ▷ *adj* **6** imitation or substitute: *you can train them with dummy bombs and live ammunition* [from *dumb*]

dummy run *n* a practice or test carried out to test if any problems remain: *we'll do a dummy run on the file to see if the program works*

dump *vb* **1** to drop or let fall in a careless manner: *he dumped the books on the bed* **2** *informal* to abandon (someone or something) without proper care: *the unwanted babies were dumped in orphanages* **3** to dispose of (nuclear waste) **4** *commerce* to sell (goods) in bulk and at low prices, usually in another country, in order to keep prices high in the home market **5** *computers* to record (the contents of the memory) on a storage device at a series of points during a computer run ▷ *n* **6** a place where rubbish is left **7** *informal* a dirty, unattractive place: *you're hardly in this dump out of choice* **8** *military* a place where weapons or supplies are stored [probably from Old Norse]

dumpling *n* **1** a small ball of dough cooked and served with stew **2** a round pastry case filled with fruit: *an apple dumpling* [obsolete *dump* lump]

dumps *pl n* **down in the dumps** *informal* feeling depressed and miserable [probably from Middle Dutch *domp* haze]

dumpy *adj* **dumpier, dumpiest** short and plump [perhaps related to DUMPLING]

dun[1] *vb* **dunning, dunned 1** to press (a debtor) for payment ▷ *n* **2** a demand for payment [origin unknown]

dun[2] *adj* brownish-grey [Old English *dunn*]

dunce *n Brit, Austral & NZ* a person who is stupid or slow to learn [*Dunses*, term of ridicule applied to the followers of John *Duns Scotus*, scholastic theologian]

dunderhead *n Brit, Austral & NZ* a slow-witted person [probably from Dutch *donder* thunder + HEAD]

dune *n* a mound or ridge of drifted sand [Middle Dutch]

dung *n* the faeces from large animals [Old English: prison]

dungarees *pl n* trousers with a bib attached [*Dungrī*, district of Bombay, where the fabric used originated]

dungeon *n* a prison cell, often underground [Old French *donjon*]

dunghill *n* a heap of dung

dunk *vb* **1** to dip (a biscuit or piece of bread) in a drink or soup before eating it **2** to put (something) in liquid: *dunk the garment in the dye for 15 minutes* **3** *basketball* to drop (the ball) through the hoop after having leapt high enough to have the hands above the rim ▷ *n* **4** *basketball* a scoring shot in which one player drops the ball through the hoop after having leapt high enough to have the hands above the rim [Old High German *dunkōn*]

dunlin *n* a small sandpiper, of northern and arctic regions, with a brown back and a black breast [from DUN[2]]

dunnock *n* same as **hedge sparrow** [from DUN[2]]

dunny *n, pl* **-nies** *Austral & NZ informal* a toilet [of obscure origin]

duo *n, pl* **duos 1** two singers or musicians who sing or play music together as a pair **2** *informal* two people who have something in common or do something together: *when they're together they make an impressive duo* [Latin: two]

duodecimal *adj* relating to twelve or twelfths [Latin *duodecim* twelve]

duodenum (dew-oh-**deen**-um) *n* the first part of the small intestine, just below the stomach [Medieval Latin *intestinum duodenum digitorum* intestine of twelve fingers' length] **duodenal** *adj*

duologue *or US sometimes* **duolog** *n* a part or all of a play in which the speaking roles are limited to two actors [DUO + (MONO)LOGUE]

DUP (in Northern Ireland) Democratic Unionist Party

dupe *vb* **duping, duped 1** to deceive or cheat: *you duped me into doing exactly what you wanted* ▷ *n* **2** a person who is easily deceived [French]

duple *adj* **1** same as **double 2** *music* having two beats in a bar [Latin *duplus* double]

duplex *n* **1** *US & Canad* **A** an apartment on two floors **B** *US & Austral* a semidetached house ▷ *adj* **2** having two parts [Latin: twofold]

duplicate *adj* **1** copied exactly from an original: *he had a duplicate key to the front door* ▷ *n* **2** an exact copy **3 in duplicate** in two exact copies: *submit the draft in duplicate, please* ▷ *vb* **-cating, -cated 4** to make an exact copy of **5** to do again (something that has already been done) [Latin *duplicare* to double] **duplication** *n* **duplicator** *n*

duplicity *n* deceitful behaviour: *he is a man of duplicity, who turns things to his advantage* [Old French *duplicite*]

durable *adj* strong and long-lasting: *the car's body was made of a light but durable plastic* [Latin *durare* to last] **durability** *n*

durable goods *pl n* goods that do not require frequent replacement. Also called: **durables**

duration *n* the length of time that something lasts [Latin *durare* to last]

durbar *n* **A** (formerly) the court of a native ruler or a governor in India **B** a reception at such a court [Hindi *darbār*]

d

duress *n* physical or moral pressure used to force someone to do something: *confessions obtained under duress* [Latin *durus* hard]

during *prep* throughout or within the limit of (a period of time) [Latin *durare* to last]

dusk *n* the time just before nightfall when it is almost dark [Old English *dox*]

dusky *adj* **duskier, duskiest 1** dark in colour: *her gold earrings gleamed against her dusky cheeks* **2** dim or shadowy: *the dusky room was crowded with absurd objects* **duskily** *adv* **duskiness** *n*

dust *n* **1** small dry particles of earth, sand, or dirt **2 bite the dust A** to stop functioning: *my television has finally bitten the dust* **B** to fall down dead **3 shake the dust off one's feet** to depart angrily **4 throw dust in someone's eyes** to confuse or mislead someone ▷ *vb* **5** to remove dust from (furniture) by wiping **6** to sprinkle (something) with a powdery substance: *serve dusted with brown sugar and cinnamon* [Old English *dūst*]

dustbin *n* a large, usually cylindrical, container for household rubbish

dust bowl *n* a dry area in which the surface soil is exposed to wind erosion

dustcart *n chiefly Brit & NZ* a lorry for collecting household rubbish

dust cover *n* **1** same as **dustsheet 2** same as **dust jacket**

duster *n* a cloth used for dusting

dust jacket *or* **dust cover** *n* a removable paper cover used to protect a book

dustman *n, pl* **-men** *Brit* a man whose job is to collect household rubbish

dust mite *n* one of two varieties of mites that feed on shed human skin cells and whose excrement is a household allergen

dustpan *n* a short-handled shovel into which dust is swept from floors

dustsheet *or* **dust cover** *n* a large cloth cover used to protect furniture from dust

dust-up *n informal* a fight or argument

dusty *adj* **dustier, dustiest 1** covered with dust **2** (of a colour) tinged with grey

Dutch *adj* **1** of the Netherlands ▷ *n* **2** the language of the Netherlands ▷ *pl n* **3 the Dutch** the people of the Netherlands ▷ *adv* **4 go Dutch** *informal* to share expenses equally, for example in a restaurant

Dutch auction *n* an auction in which the price is lowered by stages until a buyer is found

Dutch barn *n Brit* a farm building with a steel frame and a curved roof

Dutch courage *n* false courage gained from drinking alcohol

Dutch elm disease *n* a fungal disease of elm trees

Dutchman *or fem* **Dutchwoman** *n, pl* **-men** *or* **-women** a person from the Netherlands

Dutch oven *n* **1** an iron or earthenware container with a lid, used for stews, etc. **2** a metal box, open in front, for cooking in front of an open fire

Dutch treat *n informal* an outing where each person pays his or her own expenses

Dutch uncle *n informal* a person who criticizes or scolds frankly and severely

dutiable *adj* (of goods) requiring payment of duty

dutiful *adj* doing what is expected: *she is a responsible and dutiful mother* **dutifully** *adv*

duty *n, pl* **-ties 1** the work performed as part of one's job: *it is his duty to supervise the memorial services* **2** a obligation to fulfil one's responsibilities: *it's my duty as a doctor to keep it confidential* **3** a government tax on imports **4 on** *or* **off duty** at (*or* not at) work [Anglo-French *dueté*]

duty-bound *adj* morally obliged to do something: *we are duty-bound to take whatever measures are necessary*

duty-free *adj, adv* with exemption from customs or excise duties

duty-free shop *n* a shop, esp. at an airport, that sells duty-free goods

duvet (doo-vay) *n* same as **continental quilt** [French]

DVD Digital Versatile *or* Video Disk: a type of compact disc that can store large amounts of video and audio information

DVLA *Brit* Driver and Vehicle Licensing Agency

DVT deep-vein thrombosis

dwaal *n S African* a state of absent-mindedness; a daze [Afrikaans]

dwang *n NZ & S African* a short piece of wood inserted in a timber-framed wall

dwarf *vb* **1** to cause (someone or something) to seem small by being much larger ▷ *adj* **2** (of an animal or plant) much below the average size for the species: *a dwarf evergreen shrub* ▷ *n, pl* **dwarfs** *or* **dwarves 3** a person who is smaller than average size as a result of a medical condition **4** (in folklore) a small ugly manlike creature, often possessing magical powers [Old English *dweorg*]

dwarf planet *n* any celestial body orbiting the sun within the solar system, larger than a satellite but smaller than a planet

dwell *vb* **dwelling, dwelt** *or* **dwelled** *formal, literary* to live as a permanent resident [Old English *dwellan* to seduce, get lost] **dweller** *n*

dwelling *n formal, literary* a place of residence

dwell on *or* **dwell upon** *vb* to think, speak, or write at length about (something)

dwindle *vb* **-dling, -dled** to grow less in size, strength, or number [Old English *dwīnan*]

Dy *chem* dysprosium

dye *n* **1** a colouring substance **2** the colour produced by dyeing ▷ *vb* **dyeing, dyed 3** to colour (hair or fabric) by applying a dye [Old English *dēag*] **dyer** *n*

dyed-in-the-wool *adj* having strong and unchanging attitudes or opinions: *he's a dyed-in-the-wool communist*

dying *vb* **1** the present participle of **die**[1] ▷ *adj* **2** occurring at the moment of death: *in accordance with his dying wish* **3** (of a person or animal) very ill and likely to die soon **4** becoming less important or less current: *coal mining is a dying industry*

dyke[1] *or esp US* **dike** *n* **1** a wall built to prevent flooding **2** a ditch **3** *Scot* a dry-stone wall [Old English *dic* ditch]

dyke[2] *or* **dike** *n offensive slang* a lesbian [origin unknown]

dynamic *adj* **1** (of a person) full of energy, ambition, or new ideas **2** relating to a force of society, history, or the mind that produces a change: *the government needs a more dynamic policy towards the environment* **3** *physics* relating to energy or forces that produce motion [Greek *dunamis* power] **dynamically** *adv*

dynamics *n* **1** the branch of mechanics concerned with the forces that change or produce the motions of bodies ▷ *pl n* **2** those forces that produce change in any field or system **3** *music* the various degrees of loudness called for in a performance

dynamism *n* great energy or enthusiasm

dynamite *n* **1** an explosive made of nitroglycerine **2** *informal* a dangerous or exciting person or thing: *she's still dynamite* ▷ *vb* **-miting, -mited 3** to mine or blow (something) up with dynamite [Greek *dunamis* power]

dynamo *n, pl* **-mos** a device for converting mechanical energy into electricity [short for *dynamoelectric machine*]

dynamoelectric *adj* of the conversion of mechanical energy into electricity or vice versa

dynamometer (dine-a-**mom**-it-er) *n* an instrument for measuring mechanical power or force

dynast *n* a hereditary ruler [Greek *dunasthai* to be powerful]

dynasty *n, pl* **-ties 1** a series of rulers or influential people from the same family **2** a period of time during which a country is ruled by the same family [Greek *dunastēs* dynast] **dynastic** *adj*

dysentery *n* infection of the intestine which causes severe diarrhoea [Greek *dusentera* bad bowels]

dysfunction *n* **1** *med* any disturbance or abnormality in the function of an organ or part **2** (esp. of a family) failure to show the characteristics or fulfil the purposes accepted as normal or beneficial **dysfunctional** *adj*

dyslexia *n* a developmental disorder that causes learning difficulty with reading, writing, and numeracy [Greek *dus-* not + *lexis* word] **dyslexic** *adj, n*

dysmenorrhoea *or esp US* **dysmenorrhea** *n* painful or difficult menstruation [Greek *dus-* bad + *rhoia* a flowing]

dyspepsia *n* indigestion [Greek *dus-* bad + *pepsis* digestion] **dyspeptic** *adj, n*

dysprosium *n chem* a metallic element of the lanthanide series. Symbol: **Dy** [Greek *dusprositos* difficult to get near]

dystrophy (**diss**-trof-fee) *n* See **muscular dystrophy** [Greek *dus-* not + *trophē* food]

d

Ee

e *maths* a number used as the base of natural logarithms. Approximate value: 2.718 282...

E **1** *music* the third note of the scale of C major **2** East(ern) **3** English **4** *physics* **A** energy **B** electromotive force **5** *slang* the drug ecstasy or an ecstasy tablet

e- *prefix* electronic: *e-card; e-banking*

E- *prefix* used with a number following it to indicate that something, such as a food additive, conforms to an EU standard

each *adj* **1** every one of two or more people or things considered individually: *each year* ▷ *pron* **2** every one of two or more people or things: *each had been given one room to design* ▷ *adv* **3** for, to, or from each person or thing: *twenty pounds each* **4 each other** (of two or more people) each one to or at the other or others; one another: *they stared at each other* [Old English *ǣlc*]

> **USAGE** *Each* is a singular pronoun and should be used with a singular form of a verb: *each of the candidates was* (not *were*) *interviewed separately.* See also at **either**.

eager *adj* very keen to have or do something [Latin *acer* sharp, keen] **eagerly** *adv* **eagerness** *n*

eagle *n* **1** a large bird of prey with broad wings and strong soaring flight **2** *golf* a score of two strokes under par for a hole [Latin *aquila*]

eagle-eyed *adj* having very sharp eyesight

eaglet *n* a young eagle

ear[1] *n* **1** the part of the body with which a person or animal hears **2** the external visible part of the ear **3** the ability to hear musical and other sounds and interpret them accurately: *a good ear for languages* **4** willingness to listen: *they are always willing to lend an ear* **5 be all ears** to be prepared to listen attentively to something **6 fall on deaf ears** to be ignored: *his words fell on deaf ears* **7 in one ear and out the other** heard but quickly forgotten or ignored **8 out on one's ear** *informal* dismissed suddenly and unpleasantly **9 play by ear** to play without written music **10 play it by ear** *informal* to make up one's plan of action as one goes along **11 turn a deaf ear to** to be deliberately unresponsive to: *many countries have turned a deaf ear to their cries for help* **12 up to one's ears in** *informal* deeply involved in [Old English *ēare*]

ear[2] *n* the part of a cereal plant, such as wheat or barley, that contains the seeds [Old English *ēar*]

earache *n* pain in the ear

earbash *vb Brit, Austral & NZ informal* to talk incessantly **earbashing** *n*

eardrum *n* the thin membrane separating the external ear from the middle ear

earful *n informal* a scolding or telling-off

earl *n* (in Britain) a nobleman ranking below a marquess and above a viscount [Old English *eorl*] **earldom** *n*

Earl Grey *n* a variety of China tea flavoured with oil of bergamot

ear lobe *n* the soft hanging lowest part of the human ear

early *adj* **-lier, -liest 1** before the correct or expected time **2** in the first part of a period of time: *early April* **3** near the beginning of the development or history of something: *early Britain was very primitive; early models of this car rust easily* ▷ *adv* **4** occurring or arriving before the correct or expected time **5** in the first part of a period of time **6** near the beginning of the development or history of something: *early in the war* [Old English *ǣrlīce*]

Early English *n* a style of architecture used in England in the 12th and 13th centuries, characterized by narrow pointed arches and ornamental intersecting stonework in windows

earmark *vb* **1** to set (something) aside for a specific purpose ▷ *n* **2** a feature that enables the nature of something to be identified: *it had all the earmarks of a disaster*

earn *vb* **1** to gain or be paid (money) in return for work **2** to acquire or deserve through one's behaviour or action: *you've earned a good night's sleep* **3** to make (money) as interest or profit: *her savings earned 8% interest* [Old English *earnian*] **earner** *n*

earnest *adj* **1** serious and sincere, often excessively so ▷ *n* **2 in earnest** with serious or sincere intentions [Old English *eornost*] **earnestly** *adv* **earnestness** *n*

earnings *pl n* money earned

earphones *pl n* a piece of equipment worn over or inside the ears to allow a person to listen to recorded music without anyone else hearing it

ear-piercing *adj* extremely loud or shrill

earplug *n* a piece of soft material placed in the ear to keep out noise or water

earring *n* a piece of jewellery worn attached to the ear

earshot *n* the range within which a sound can be heard: *out of earshot*

ear-splitting *adj* extremely loud or shrill

earth *n* **1** (*sometimes cap*) the planet that we live on, the third planet from the sun, the only one on which life is known to exist. Related adjective: **terrestrial 2** the part of the surface of this planet that is not water **3** the soil in which plants grow **4** the hole in which a fox lives **5** a wire in a piece of electrical equipment through which electricity can escape into the ground if a fault develops **6 come down to earth** to return to reality from a daydream or fantasy **7 on earth** used for emphasis: *what on earth happened?* ▷ *vb* **8** to fit (a piece of electrical equipment) with an earth [Old English *eorthe*]

earthbound *adj* **1** unable to leave the surface of the earth **2** lacking in imagination

earthen *adj* made of earth or baked clay: *an earthen floor*

earthenware *n* dishes and other objects made of baked clay: *an earthenware flowerpot*

earthly *adj* **-lier, -liest 1** of life on earth as opposed to any heavenly or spiritual state **2** *informal* conceivable or possible: *what earthly reason would they have for lying?*

earthquake *n* a series of vibrations at the earth's surface caused by movement of the earth's crust

earth science *n* any science, such as geology, concerned with the structure, age, etc., of the earth

earth-shattering *adj* very surprising or shocking: *an earth-shattering event*

earthwards *adv* towards the earth

earthwork *n* **1** excavation of earth, as in engineering construction **2** a fortification made of earth

earthworm *n* a common worm that burrows in the soil

earthy *adj* **earthier, earthiest 1** open and direct in the treatment of sex, excretion, etc. **2** of or like earth: *earthy colours* **earthiness** *n*

earwig *n* a thin brown insect with pincers at the tip of its abdomen [Old English *ēarwicga*, from *ēare* ear + *wicga* beetle]

ease *n* **1** lack of difficulty **2** freedom from discomfort or worry **3** rest, leisure, or relaxation **4** freedom from poverty: *a life of leisure and ease* **5 at ease A** *military* (of a soldier) standing in a relaxed position with the feet apart **B** in a relaxed attitude or frame of mind ▷ *vb* **easing, eased 6** to make or become less difficult or severe: *the pain gradually eased* **7** to move into or out of a place or situation slowly and carefully **8 ease off** *or* **up** to lessen or cause to lessen in severity, pressure, tension, or strain: *the rain eased off* [Old French *aise*]

easel *n* a frame on legs, used for supporting an artist's canvas or a display [Dutch *ezel* ass]

easily *adv* **1** without difficulty **2** without doubt; by far: *easily the most senior Chinese leader to visit the West*

USAGE See at **easy**.

east *n* **1** one of the four cardinal points of the compass, at 90° clockwise from north **2** the direction along a line of latitude towards the sunrise **3 the east** any area lying in or towards the east ▷ *adj* **4** situated in, moving towards, or facing the east **5** (esp. of the wind) from the east ▷ *adv* **6** in, to, or towards the east [Old English *ēast*]

East *n* **1 the East A** the southern and eastern parts of Asia **B** (esp. formerly) the countries in Eastern Europe and Asia which are or have been under Communist rule ▷ *adj* **2** of or denoting the eastern part of a country or region

eastbound *adj* going towards the east

Easter *n* **1** *Christianity* a festival commemorating the Resurrection of Christ ▷ *adj* **2** taking place at the time of the year when this festival is celebrated: *the Easter weekend* [Old English *ēastre*]

Easter egg *n* a chocolate egg given at Easter

easterly *adj* **1** of or in the east ▷ *adv, adj* **2** towards the east **3** from the east: *an easterly breeze*

eastern *adj* **1** situated in or towards the east **2** facing or moving towards the east **3** (*sometimes cap*) of or characteristic of the east or East **easternmost** *adj*

Easterner *n* a person from the east of a country or region

eastern hemisphere *n* the half of the globe that contains Europe, Asia, Africa, and Australia

eastings *pl n* a series of numbers in a grid reference indicating the distance eastwards from a given meridian

eastward *adj, adv also* **eastwards 1** towards the east ▷ *n* **2** the eastward part or direction

easy *adj* **easier, easiest 1** not difficult; simple: *the house is easy to keep clean* **2** free from pain, care, or anxiety: *an easy life* **3** tolerant and undemanding; easy-going **4** defenceless or readily fooled: *easy prey* **5** moderate and not involving any great effort: *an easy ride* **6** *informal* ready to fall in with any suggestion made: *he wanted to do something and I was easy about it* **7** *informal* pleasant and not involving any great effort to enjoy: *easy on the eye* ▷ *adv* **8 go easy on A** to avoid using too much of: *he'd tried to go easy on the engines* **B** to treat less severely than is deserved: *go easy on him, he's just a kid* **9 take it easy** to relax and avoid stress or undue hurry [Old French *aisié*] **easiness** *n*

USAGE *Easy* should only be used as an adverb in certain set phrases: *to take it easy; easy does it*. Where a fixed expression is not involved, the usual adverbial form of *easy* is preferred: *this polish goes on more easily* (not *easier*) *than the other.*

easy chair *n* a comfortable upholstered armchair

easy-going *adj* relaxed in manner or attitude; very tolerant

eat *vb* **eating, ate, eaten 1** to take (food) into the mouth and swallow it **2** to have a meal: *sometimes we eat out of doors* **3** *informal* to make anxious or worried: *what's eating you?* **4 eat away** *or* **into** *or* **up** to destroy or use up partly or wholly: *inflation ate into the firm's profits* ▷ See also **eat out, eat up** [Old English *etan*] **eater** *n*

eatable *adj* fit or suitable for eating

eating *n* **1** food in relation to its quality or taste: *these add up to lots of vitamins and minerals, and good eating* ▷ *adj* **2** suitable for eating uncooked: *eating apples*

eat out *vb* to eat at a restaurant

eat up *vb* **1** to eat or consume entirely: *eat up these potatoes* **2** *informal* to affect severely: *I was eaten up by jealousy*

eau de Cologne (oh de kol-lone) *n* full form of **cologne** [French: water of Cologne]

eau de vie (oh de vee) *n* brandy or a similar alcoholic drink [French: water of life]

eaves *pl n* the edge of a sloping roof that overhangs the walls [Old English *efes*]

eavesdrop *vb* **-dropping, -dropped** to listen secretly to a private conversation [Old English *yfesdrype* water dripping from the eaves] **eavesdropper** *n*

eavestrough *n Canad* a gutter at the eaves of a building

e-banking *n* the use of the internet for banking transactions

ebb *vb* **1** (of the sea or the tide) to flow back from its highest point **2** to fall away or decline: *her anger ebbed away* ▷ *n* **3** the flowing back of the tide from high to low water **4 at a low ebb** in a weak state: *her creativity was at a low ebb* [Old English *ebba* ebb-tide]

Ebola virus disease (i-boh-la) *n* a severe infectious disease characterized by fever, vomiting, and internal bleeding [after the *Ebola* River in Democratic Republic of Congo, where an outbreak occurred in 1976]

ebony *n* **1** a very hard dark-coloured wood used to make furniture, etc. ▷ *adj* **2** very deep black [Greek *ebenos*]

e-book *n* **1** a book in electronic form ▷ *vb* **2** to book (tickets, appointments, etc.) through the internet

e

ebullient *adj* full of enthusiasm or excitement [Latin *ebullire* to bubble forth, be boisterous] **ebullience** *n*

EC 1 European Commission **2** European Community: a former name for the European Union

eccentric *adj* **1** unconventional or odd **2** (of circles) not having the same centre ▷ *n* **3** a person who behaves unconventionally or oddly [Greek *ek-* away from + *kentron* centre] **eccentrically** *adv*

eccentricity *n* **1** unconventional or odd behaviour **2** *pl* **-ties** an unconventional or odd habit or act

ecclesiastic *n* **1** a member of the Christian clergy ▷ *adj* **2** of or relating to the Christian Church or its clergy [Greek *ekklēsia* assembly]

ecclesiastical *adj* of or relating to the Christian Church or its clergy

ECG electrocardiogram

echelon (esh-a-lon) *n* **1** a level of power or responsibility: *the upper echelons of society* **2** *military* a formation in which units follow one another but are spaced out sideways to allow each a line of fire ahead [French *échelon* rung of a ladder]

echidna (ik-kid-na) *n, pl* **-nas, -nae** (-nee) an Australian spiny egg-laying mammal. Also called: **spiny anteater**

echinoderm (ik-kine-oh-durm) *n* a sea creature with a five-part symmetrical body, such as a starfish or sea urchin [Greek *ekhinos* sea urchin + *derma* skin]

echo *n, pl* **-oes 1 A** the reflection of sound by a solid object **B** a sound reflected by a solid object **2** a repetition or imitation of someone else's opinions **3** something that brings back memories: *an echo of the past* **4** the signal reflected back to a radar transmitter by an object ▷ *vb* **-oing, -oed 5** (of a sound) to be reflected off an object in such a way that it can be heard again **6** (of a place) to be filled with a sound and its echoes: *the church echoed with singing* **7** (of people) to repeat or imitate (what someone else has said): *his conclusion echoed that of Jung* [Greek *ēkhō*] **echoing** *adj*

echo chamber *n* a room with walls that reflect sound, used to create an echo effect

echolocation *n* the discovery of an object's position by measuring the time taken for an echo to return from it

echo sounder *n* a navigation device that determines depth by measuring the time taken for a pulse of sound to reach the sea bed and for the echo to return

e-cigarette *n* an electronic vaporizer that simulates the effect of smoking. Often shortened to: **e-cig**

éclair *n* a finger-shaped cake of choux pastry, filled with cream and coated with chocolate [French: lightning (probably because it does not last long)]

eclampsia *n pathol* a serious condition that can develop towards the end of a pregnancy, causing high blood pressure, swelling, and convulsions

eclectic *adj* **1** composed of elements selected from a wide range of styles, ideas, or sources: *the contenders for this year's Turner Prize are an eclectic bunch* **2** selecting elements from a wide range of styles, ideas, or sources: *an eclectic approach that takes the best from all schools of psychology* ▷ *n* **3** a person who takes an eclectic approach [Greek *eklegein* to select] **eclecticism** *n*

eclipse *n* **1** the obscuring of reflected light from a celestial body as it passes through the shadow of another; a **lunar eclipse** occurs when the moon passes through the shadow of the earth **2** a loss of importance, power, or fame: *communism eventually went into eclipse* ▷ *vb* **eclipsing, eclipsed 3** to overshadow or surpass **4** (of a star or planet) to hide (another planet or star) from view [Greek *ekleipsis* a forsaking]

ecliptic *n astron* the great circle on the celestial sphere representing the apparent annual path of the sun relative to the stars

eco- *combining form* denoting ecology or ecological: *ecotourism*

E.coli (ee-koal-eye) *n* a common bacterium often found in the intestines [shortened from *Escherichia coli*, after Theodor Escherich, paediatrician]

ecological *adj* **1** of or relating to ecology **2** tending or intended to benefit or protect the environment: *an ecological approach to agriculture* **ecologically** *adv*

ecology *n* the study of the relationships between people, animals, and plants, and their environment [Greek *oikos* house] **ecologist** *n*

e-commerce *or* **ecommerce** *n* business transactions conducted on the internet

econ. economy

economic *adj* **1** of or relating to an economy or economics **2** *Brit & Austral* capable of being produced or operated for profit **3** *informal* inexpensive or cheap

economical *adj* **1** not requiring a lot of money to use: *low fuel consumption makes this car very economical* **2** (of a person) spending money carefully and sensibly **3** using no more time, effort, or resources than is necessary **4 economical with the truth** *euphemistic* deliberately withholding information **economically** *adv*

economics *n* **1** the study of the production and consumption of goods and services and the commercial activities of a society ▷ *pl n* **2** financial aspects: *the economics of health care*

economist *n* a person who specializes in economics

economize *or* **-mise** *vb* **-mizing, -mized** *or* **-mising, -mised** to reduce expense or waste: *people are being advised to economize on fuel use*

economy *n, pl* **-mies 1** the system by which the production, distribution, and consumption of goods and services is organized in a country or community: *the rural economy* **2** the ability of a country to generate wealth through business and industry: *unless the economy improves, more jobs will be lost* **3** careful use of money or resources to save expense, time, or energy **4** an instance of this: *we can make economies by reusing envelopes* ▷ *adj* **5** denoting a class of air travel that is cheaper than first-class **6** offering a larger quantity for a lower price: *an economy pack* [Greek *oikos* house + *nemein* to manage]

economy-class syndrome *n* a deep-vein thrombosis that has developed in the legs or pelvis of a person travelling for a long time in cramped conditions [reference to the restricted legroom of cheaper seats on passenger aircraft]

economy of scale *n econ* a fall in average costs resulting from an increase in the scale of production

ecosystem *n ecology* the system of relationships between animals and plants and their environment

ecoterrorism *n* the use of violence in order to achieve environmentalist aims [from *eco-* + *terrorism*]

ecoterrorist *n* a person who uses violence in order to achieve environmentalist aims [from *eco-* + *terrorist*]

ecotourism *n* tourism designed to contribute to the protection of the environment or at least minimize damage to it **ecotourist** *n*

ecru *adj* pale creamy-brown [French]

ecstasy *n, pl* **-sies 1** a state of extreme delight or joy **2** *slang* a strong drug that acts as a stimulant and can cause hallucinations [Greek *ekstasis* displacement, trance] **ecstatic** *adj* **ecstatically** *adv*

ECT electroconvulsive therapy: the treatment of depression and some other mental health problems by passing a current of electricity through the brain, producing a convulsion

ectomorph *n physiol* a person with a thin body build. See also **endomorph, mesomorph** [Greek *ektos* outside + *morphē* shape] **ectomorphic** *adj*

ectopic *adj med* (of an organ or other body part) congenitally displaced or abnormally positioned [Greek *ektopos* out of position]

ectoplasm *n* (in spiritualism) the substance that supposedly is emitted from the body of a medium during a trance [Greek *ektos* outside + *plasma* something moulded]

ecumenical *adj* **1** of or relating to the Christian Church throughout the world **2** tending to promote unity among Christian churches [Greek *oikoumenikos* of the inhabited world]

ecumenism *or* **ecumenicism** *n* the aim of unity among Christian churches throughout the world

eczema (**ek**-sim-a, ig-**zeem**-a) *n pathol* a condition in which the skin becomes inflamed and itchy [Greek *ek-* out + *zein* to boil]

ed. 1 edition **2** editor

Edam *n* a round yellow Dutch cheese with a red waxy covering [after *Edam*, in Holland]

eddo (**ed**-doh) *n, pl* **eddoes** same as **taro**

eddy *n, pl* **-dies 1** a circular movement of air, water, or smoke ▷ *vb* **-dies, -dying, -died 2** to move with a gentle circular motion; swirl gently [probably from Old Norse]

edelweiss (**ade**-el-vice) *n* a small white alpine flower [German: noble white]

edema (id-**deem**-a) *n, pl* **-mata** same as **oedema**

Eden *n* **1** Also called: **Garden of Eden** *Bible* the garden in which Adam and Eve were placed at the Creation **2** a place of great delight or contentment [Hebrew *'ēdhen* place of pleasure]

edentate *n* **1** a mammal with few or no teeth, such as an armadillo or a sloth ▷ *adj* **2** denoting such a mammal [Latin *edentatus* lacking teeth]

edge *n* **1** a border or line where something ends or begins: *the edge of the city* **2** a line along which two faces or surfaces of a solid meet **3** the sharp cutting side of a blade **4** keenness, sharpness, or urgency: *there was a nervous edge to his voice* **5 have the edge on** to have a slight advantage over **6 on edge** nervous and irritable **7 set someone's teeth on edge** to make someone acutely irritated ▷ *vb* **edging, edged 8** to make, form, or be an edge or border for: *a pillow edged with lace* **9** to move very gradually in a particular direction: *I edged through to the front of the crowd* [Old English *ecg*]

edgeways *or esp US & Canad* **edgewise** *adv* **1** with the edge forwards or uppermost **2 get a word in edgeways** to interrupt a conversation in which someone else is talking continuously

edging *n* anything placed along an edge for decoration

edgy *adj* **edgier, edgiest** nervous, irritable, or anxious **edginess** *n*

edible *adj* fit to be eaten; eatable [Latin *edere* to eat] **edibility** *n*

edict (**ee**-dikt) *n* a decree or order given by any authority [Latin *edicere* to declare]

edifice (**ed**-if-iss) *n* **1** a large or impressive building **2** an elaborate system of beliefs and institutions: *the entire crumbling edifice of a former superpower* [Latin *aedificare* to build]

edify (**ed**-if-fie) *vb* **-fies, -fying, -fied** to inform or instruct (someone) with a view to improving his or her morals or understanding [Latin *aedificare* to build] **edification** *n* **edifying** *adj*

edit *vb* **editing, edited 1** to prepare (text) for publication by checking and improving its accuracy or clarity **2** to be in charge of (a newspaper or magazine) **3** to prepare (a film, television or radio programme, etc.) by rearranging or selecting material **4 edit out** to remove (a section) from a text, film, etc.

edition *n* **1** a particular version of a book, newspaper, or magazine produced at one time: *the revised paperback edition* **2** a single television or radio programme which forms part of a series: *the first edition goes on the air in 30 minutes*

editor *n* **1** a person who edits **2** a person in overall charge of a newspaper or magazine **3** a person in charge of one section of a newspaper or magazine: *the Political Editor* **4** a person in overall control of a television or radio programme [Latin *edere* to publish] **editorship** *n*

editorial *n* **1** an article in a newspaper expressing the opinion of the editor or publishers ▷ *adj* **2** of

editing or editors: *an editorial meeting* **3** relating to the contents and opinions of a magazine or newspaper: *the paper's editorial policy* **editorially** *adv*
EDT Eastern Daylight Time
educate *vb* **-cating, -cated 1** to teach (someone) over a long period of time so that he or she acquires knowledge and understanding of a range of subjects **2** to send (someone) to a particular educational establishment: *he was educated at a boarding school in Switzerland* **3** to teach (someone) about a particular matter: *a campaign to educate people to the dangers of smoking* [Latin *educare* to rear, educate] **educative** *adj*

e

educated *adj* **1** having an education, esp. a good one **2** displaying culture, taste, and knowledge **3 educated guess** a guess that is based on experience
education *n* **1** the process of acquiring knowledge and understanding **2** knowledge and understanding acquired through study and training: *education is the key to a good job* **3** the process of teaching, esp. at a school, college, or university **4** the theory of teaching and learning **educational** *adj* **educationally** *adv* **educationalist** *or* **educationist** *n*
Edwardian *adj* of or in the reign of King Edward VII of Great Britain and Ireland (1901–10)
EEC European Economic Community: a former name for the European Union
EEG electroencephalogram
eel *n* a slimy snakelike fish [Old English *ǣl*]
e'er *adv poetic* short for **ever**
eerie *adj* **eerier, eeriest** strange and frightening [probably from Old English *earg* cowardly] **eerily** *adv*
efface *vb* **-facing, -faced 1** to obliterate or make dim: *nothing effaced the memory* **2** to rub out or erase **3 efface oneself** to make oneself inconspicuous [French *effacer* to obliterate the face] **effacement** *n*
effect *n* **1** a change or state of affairs caused by something or someone: *the gales have had a serious effect on the crops* **2** power to influence or produce a result: *antibiotics have no effect on viruses – they only work against bacteria* **3** the condition of being operative: *a new law has come into effect* **4** the overall impression: *the whole effect is one of luxury* **5** basic meaning or purpose: *words to that effect* **6** an impression, usually a contrived one: *he paused for effect* **7** a physical phenomenon: *the greenhouse effect* **8 in effect** for all practical purposes: *in effect he has no choice* **9 take effect** to begin to produce results ▷ *vb* **10** to cause (something) to take place: *a peace treaty was effected* [Latin *efficere* to accomplish]
effective *adj* **1** producing a desired result: *polio's spread was checked by the creation of an effective vaccine in the 1950s* **2** officially coming into operation: *the new rates become effective at the end of May* **3** impressive: *a highly effective speech* **4** in reality, although not officially or in theory: *he is in effective control of the company* **effectively** *adv* **effectiveness** *n*
effects *pl n* **1** personal belongings **2** lighting, sounds, etc., to accompany a stage, film, or broadcast production
effectual *adj* **1** producing the intended result **2** (of a document, etc.) having legal force **effectually** *adv*
effeminate *adj* (of a man) displaying characteristics regarded as typical of a woman [Latin *femina* woman] **effeminacy** *n*
effervescent *adj* **1** (of a liquid) giving off bubbles of gas **2** (of a person) lively and enthusiastic [Latin *effervescere* to foam up] **effervescence** *n*
effete (if-**feet**) *adj* weak, powerless, and decadent [Latin *effetus* exhausted by bearing young]
efficacious *adj* producing the intended result [Latin *efficere* to achieve] **efficacy** *n*
efficient *adj* working or producing effectively without wasting effort, energy, or money [Latin *efficiens* effecting] **efficiency** *n* **efficiently** *adv*
effigy (**ef**-fij-ee) *n, pl* **-gies 1** a statue or carving of someone, often as a memorial: *a 14th-century wooden effigy of a knight* **2** a crude representation of someone, used as a focus for contempt: *an effigy of the president was set on fire* [Latin *effingere* to portray]
efflorescence *n* **1** the blooming of flowers on a plant **2** a brief period of high-quality artistic activity [Latin *efflorescere* to blossom]
effluent *n* liquid discharged as waste, for instance from a factory or sewage works [Latin *effluere* to flow out]
effluvium *n, pl* **-via** an unpleasant smell, such as the smell of decaying matter [Latin: a flowing out]
efflux *n* **1** the process of flowing out **2** something that flows out
effort *n* **1** physical or mental energy needed to do something **2** a determined attempt to do something **3** an achievement or creation: *his earliest literary efforts* [Latin *fortis* strong] **effortless** *adj* **effortlessly** *adv*
effrontery *n* insolence or boldness [Late Latin *effrons* putting forth one's forehead]
effusion *n* **1** an unrestrained verbal expression of emotions or ideas **2** a sudden pouring out: *small effusions of blood* [Latin *effundere* to shed]
effusive *adj* enthusiastically showing pleasure, gratitude, or approval **effusively** *adv* **effusiveness** *n*
EFL English as a Foreign Language
EFTA European Free Trade Association
EFTPOS electronic funds transfer at point of sale
eg *or* **e.g.** for example [Latin *exempli gratia*]
egalitarian *adj* **1** expressing or supporting the idea that all people should be equal ▷ *n* **2** a person who believes that all people should be equal [French *égal* equal] **egalitarianism** *n*
egg *n* **1** the oval or round object laid by the females of birds, reptiles, and other creatures, containing a developing embryo **2** a hen's egg used for food **3** a type of cell produced in the body of a female animal which can develop into a baby if fertilized by a male reproductive cell **4 have egg on one's face** *informal* to have been made to look ridiculous **5 put all one's eggs in one basket** to rely entirely on one action or decision, with no alternative in case of failure [Old Norse]
egg cup *n* a small cup for holding a boiled egg
egghead *n informal* an intellectual person

eggnog *n* a drink made of raw eggs, milk, sugar, spice, and brandy or rum [*egg* + *nog* strong ale]
egg on *vb* to encourage (someone) to do something foolish or daring [Old English *eggian*]
eggplant *n US, Canad, Austral & NZ* a dark purple tropical fruit, cooked and eaten as a vegetable
eggshell *n* **1** the hard porous outer layer of a bird's egg ▹ *adj* **2** (of paint) having a very slight sheen
ego *n, pl* **egos** **1** the part of a person's self that is able to recognize that person as being distinct from other people and things **2** a person's opinion of his or her own worth: *as well as the physical injuries, there were one or two bruised egos* [Latin: I]
egocentric *adj* thinking only of one's own interests and feelings **egocentricity** *n*
Egoli (eh-**goh**-li) *n* an informal name for Johannesburg [from Zulu *eGoli* place of gold]
egomania *n* an obsessive concern with fulfilling one's own needs and desires, regardless of the effect on other people **egomaniac** *n*
egotism *or* **egoism** *n* concern only for one's own interests and feelings **egotist** *or* **egoist** *n* **egotistical, egoistical, egotistic** *or* **egoistic** *adj*
ego trip *n informal* something that a person does in order to boost his or her self-image
egregious (ig-**greej**-uss) *adj* shockingly bad: *egregious government waste* [Latin *egregius* outstanding (literally: standing out from the herd)]
egress (**ee**-gress) *n formal* **1** the act of going out **2** a way out or exit [Latin *egredi* to come out]
egret (**ee**-grit) *n* a wading bird like a heron, with long white feathery plumes [Old French *aigrette*]
Egyptian *adj* **1** of Egypt **2** of the ancient Egyptians ▹ *n* **3** a person from Egypt **4** a member of an ancient people who established an advanced civilization in Egypt **5** the language of the ancient Egyptians
Egyptology *n* the study of the culture of ancient Egypt **Egyptologist** *n*
eh *interj* **1** an exclamation used to ask for repetition or confirmation **2** *Canad & E Scot* a filler phrase used to make a pause in speaking, or add slight emphasis: *it's broken, eh, so I can't play for six weeks*
eider *or* **eider duck** *n* a large sea duck of the N hemisphere [Old Norse *æthr*]
eiderdown *n* a thick warm cover for a bed, filled with soft feathers, originally the breast feathers of the female eider duck
Eid-ul-Adha (**eed**-ool-**ah**-da) *n* an annual Muslim festival, marking the end of the pilgrimage to Mecca [from Arabic *id ul adha* festival of sacrifice]
Eid-ul-Fitr (**eed**-ool-**feet**-er) *n* an annual Muslim festival, marking the end of Ramadan [from Arabic *id ul fitr* festival of fast-breaking]
eight *n* **1** the cardinal number that is the sum of one and seven **2** a numeral, 8 or VIII, representing this number **3** something representing or consisting of eight units **4** *rowing* **A** a light narrow boat rowed by eight people **B** the crew of such a boat ▹ *adj* **5** amounting to eight: *eight apples* [Old English *eahta*] **eighth** *adj, n*
eighteen *n* **1** the cardinal number that is the sum of ten and eight **2** a numeral, 18 or XVIII, representing this number **3** something representing or consisting of 18 units ▹ *adj* **4** amounting to eighteen: *eighteen months* **eighteenth** *adj, n*
eightfold *adj* **1** having eight times as many or as much **2** composed of eight parts ▹ *adv* **3** by eight times as many or as much
eightsome reel *n* a lively Scottish country dance for eight people
eighty *n, pl* **eighties** **1** the cardinal number that is the product of ten and eight **2** a numeral, 80 or LXXX, representing this number **3** something representing or consisting of 80 units ▹ *adj* **4** amounting to eighty: *eighty miles* **eightieth** *adj, n*
eina (**ay**-na) *interj S African* an exclamation of pain [Khoikhoi]
einsteinium *n chem* a radioactive metallic element artificially produced from plutonium. Symbol: **Es** [after Albert *Einstein*, physicist]
Éire *n* Ireland or the Republic of Ireland [Irish Gaelic]
EIS Educational Institute of Scotland
eisteddfod (ice-**sted**-fod) *n* a Welsh festival with competitions in music, poetry, drama, and art [Welsh: session]
either *adj, pron* **1** one or the other (of two): *we were offered either fish or beef* **2** both one and the other: *we sat at either end of a long sofa* ▹ *conj* **3** used preceding two or more possibilities joined by *or*: *it must be stored either in the fridge or in a cool place* ▹ *adv* **4** likewise: *I don't eat meat and my husband doesn't either* **5** used to qualify or modify a previous statement: *he wasn't exactly ugly, but he wasn't handsome either* [Old English *ǣgther*]

> **USAGE** *Either* should be followed by a singular verb: *either is good; either of these books is useful*. Care should be taken to avoid ambiguity when using *either* to mean *both* or *each*, as in the following sentence: *a ship could be moored on either side of the channel*. Agreement between the verb and its subject in *either...or...* constructions follows the pattern given for *neither...nor...* See at **neither**.

ejaculate *vb* **-lating, -lated** **1** to discharge semen from the penis while having an orgasm **2** *literary* to say or shout suddenly [Latin *ejaculari* to hurl out] **ejaculation** *n* **ejaculatory** *adj*
eject *vb* **1** to push or send out forcefully **2** to compel (someone) to leave a place or position **3** to leave an aircraft rapidly in mid-flight, using an ejector seat [Latin *ejicere*] **ejection** *n* **ejector** *n*
ejector seat *or* **ejection seat** *n* a seat in a military aircraft that throws the pilot out in an emergency
eke out *vb* **eking, eked** **1** to make (a supply) last for a long time by using as little as possible **2** to manage to sustain (a living) despite having barely enough food or money [obsolete *eke* to enlarge]
elaborate *adj* **1** very complex because of having many different parts: *elaborate equipment* **2** having a very complicated design: *elaborate embroidery*

▷ *vb* **-rating, -rated 3 elaborate on** to describe in more detail: *he did not elaborate on his plans* **4** to develop (a plan or theory) in detail [Latin *elaborare* to take pains] **elaborately** *adv* **elaboration** *n*

élan (ale-an) *n* style and liveliness [French]

eland (eel-and) *n* a large spiral-horned antelope of southern Africa [Dutch: elk]

elapse *vb* **elapsing, elapsed** (of time) to pass by [Latin *elabi* to slip away]

elastane *n* a synthetic fibre that is able to return to its original shape after being stretched

elastic *adj* **1** capable of returning to its original shape after stretching, compression, or other distortion **2** capable of being adapted to meet the demands of a particular situation: *an elastic interpretation of the law* **3** made of elastic ▷ *n* **4** tape, cord, or fabric containing flexible rubber [Greek *elastikos* propellent] **elastically** *adv* **elasticated** *adj* **elasticity** *n*

elastic band *n* a rubber band

elated *adj* extremely happy and excited [Latin *elatus* carried away] **elatedly** *adv*

elation *n* a feeling of great happiness and excitement

elbow *n* **1** the joint between the upper arm and the forearm **2** the part of a garment that covers the elbow ▷ *vb* **3** to push with one's elbow or elbows: *she elbowed him aside; he elbowed his way to the bar* [Old English *elnboga*]

elbow grease *n facetious* vigorous physical labour, esp. hard rubbing

elbow room *n* sufficient scope to move or to function

elder[1] *adj* **1** (of one of two people) born earlier ▷ *n* **2** an older person: *have some respect for your elders* **3** a senior member of a tribe, who has authority **4** (in certain Protestant Churches) a member of the church who has certain administrative, teaching, or preaching powers [Old English *eldra*]

elder[2] *n* a shrub or small tree with clusters of small white flowers and dark purple berries [Old English *ellern*]

elderberry *n, pl* **-ries 1** the fruit of the elder **2** same as **elder**[2]

elderly *adj* **1** rather old ▷ *pl n* **2 the elderly** old people

elder statesman *n* a respected influential older person, esp. a politician

eldest *adj* (of a person, esp. a child) oldest [Old English *eldesta*]

El Dorado (el dor-**rah**-doe) *n* **1** a fabled city in South America, supposedly rich in treasure **2** Also: **eldorado** any place of great riches or fabulous opportunity [Spanish: the golden (place)]

eldritch *adj poetic Scot* unearthly or weird [origin unknown]

elect *vb* **1** to choose (someone) to fill a position by voting for him or her: *she was elected President in 1990* **2** to choose or decide: *those who elected to stay* ▷ *adj* **3** voted into office but not yet having taken over from the current office-bearer: *the President elect* ▷ *pl n* **4 the elect** any group of people specially chosen for some privilege [Latin *eligere* to select] **electable** *adj*

election *n* **1 A** a process whereby people vote for a person or party to fill a position: *last month's presidential election* **B** short for **general election** **2** the gaining of political power or taking up of a position in an organization as a result of being voted for: *he will be seeking election as the President of Romania*

electioneering *n* the act of taking an active part in a political campaign, for example by canvassing

elective *adj* **1** of or based on selection by vote: *an elective office* **2** not compulsory or necessary: *an elective hysterectomy*

elector *n* **1** someone who is eligible to vote in an election **2** (in the Holy Roman Empire) any of the German princes who were entitled to elect a new emperor: *the Elector of Hanover*

electoral *adj* of or relating to elections: *the electoral system* **electorally** *adv*

electoral register *n* the official list of all the people in an area who are eligible to vote in elections

electorate *n* **1** all the people in an area or country who have the right to vote in an election **2** the rank or territory of an elector of the Holy Roman Empire

electric *adj* **1** produced by, transmitting, or powered by electricity: *an electric fire* **2** very tense or exciting: *the atmosphere was electric* ▷ *n* **3 electrics** *Brit* an electric circuit or electric appliances [Greek *ēlektron* amber (because friction causes amber to become electrically charged)]

USAGE See at **electronic.**

electrical *adj* of or relating to electricity **electrically** *adv*

USAGE See at **electronic.**

electrical engineering *n* the branch of engineering concerned with practical applications of electricity and electronics **electrical engineer** *n*

electric blanket *n* a blanket fitted with an electric heating element, used to warm a bed

electric chair *n* (in the US) a chair for executing criminals by passing a strong electric current through them

electric eel *n* an eel-like South American freshwater fish, which can stun or kill its prey with a powerful electric shock

electric field *n physics* a region of space surrounding a charged particle within which another charged particle experiences a force

electric guitar *n* an electrically amplified guitar

electrician *n* a person trained to install and repair electrical equipment

electricity *n* **1** a form of energy associated with stationary or moving electrons, ions, or other charged particles **2** the supply of electricity to houses, factories, etc., for heating, lighting, etc.

electric shock *n* pain and muscular spasms caused by an electric current passing through the body

electrify *vb* **-fies, -fying, -fied 1** to adapt or equip (a system or device) to work by electricity: *the whole track has now been electrified* **2** to provide (an area) with electricity **3** to startle or excite intensely **electrification** *n*

electrifying *adj* very exciting and surprising

electro- *combining form* electric or electrically: *electroconvulsive* [Greek *ēlektron* amber; see ELECTRIC]

electrocardiograph *n* an instrument for making tracings (**electrocardiograms**) recording the electrical activity of the heart

electrocute *vb* **-cuting, -cuted** to kill or injure by an electric shock [ELECTRO- + (EXE)CUTE] **electrocution** *n*

electrode *n* a small piece of metal used to take an electric current to or from a power source, piece of equipment, or living body

electrodynamics *n* the branch of physics concerned with the interactions between electrical and mechanical forces

electroencephalograph (ill-lek-tro-en-**sef**-a-loh-graf) *n* an instrument for making tracings (**electroencephalograms**) recording the electrical activity of the brain

electrolysis (ill-lek-**troll**-iss-iss) *n* **1** the process of passing an electric current through a liquid in order to produce a chemical reaction in the liquid **2** the destruction of living tissue, such as hair roots, by an electric current

electrolyte *n* a solution or molten substance that conducts electricity **electrolytic** *adj*

electromagnet *n* a magnet consisting of a coil of wire wound round an iron core through which a current is passed

electromagnetic *adj* **1** of or operated by an electromagnet **2** of or relating to electromagnetism **electromagnetically** *adv*

electromagnetism *n* magnetism produced by an electric current

electromotive *adj physics* of or producing an electric current

electromotive force *n physics* **1** a source of energy that can cause current to flow in an electrical circuit **2** the rate at which energy is drawn from such a source when a unit of current flows through the circuit, measured in volts

electron *n physics* an elementary particle in all atoms that has a negative electric charge

electronegative *adj physics* **1** having a negative electric charge **2** tending to gain or attract electrons

electronic *adj* **1** (of a device, circuit, or system) containing transistors, silicon chips, etc., which control the current passing through it **2** making use of electronic systems: *electronic surveillance devices* **electronically** *adv*

> **USAGE** *Electronic* refers to equipment, such as television sets, computers, etc., in which the current is controlled by transistors, valves, and similar components. *Electrical* is used in a more general sense to refer to the use of electricity as a whole as opposed to other forms of energy: *electrical engineering; an electrical appliance*. *Electric* can be used interchangeably with *electrical*, but is often restricted to the description of particular devices or to concepts relating to the flow of current: *electric fire; electric charge*.

electronic ink *n* a material used in e-readers, consisting of black particles suspended in white fluid which become visible in response to an electronic charge

electronic publishing *n* the publication of information in formats that can be accessed by computers

electronics *n* the technology concerned with the development, behaviour, and applications of devices and circuits

electron microscope *n* a powerful microscope that uses electrons, rather than light, to produce a magnified image

electronvolt *n physics* a unit of energy equal to the work done on an electron accelerated through a potential difference of 1 volt

electroplate *vb* **-plating, -plated 1** to coat (an object) with metal by dipping it in a special liquid through which an electric current is passed ▷ *n* **2** electroplated articles collectively

electropositive *adj physics* **1** having a positive electric charge **2** tending to release electrons

electrostatics *n* the branch of physics concerned with static electricity **electrostatic** *adj*

elegant *adj* **1** attractive and graceful or stylish **2** cleverly simple and clear: *an elegant summary* [Latin *elegans* tasteful] **elegance** *n* **elegantly** *adv*

elegiac *adj literary* sad, mournful, or plaintive

elegy (**el**-lij-ee) *n, pl* **-gies** a mournful poem or song, esp. a lament for the dead [Greek *elegos* lament]

> **USAGE** Avoid confusion with **eulogy**.

element *n* **1** one of the fundamental components making up a whole **2** *chem* any of the known substances that cannot be separated into simpler substances by chemical means **3** a distinguishable section of a social group: *liberal elements in Polish society* **4** a degree: *an element of truth* **5** a metal part in an electrical device, such as a kettle, that changes the electric current into heat **6** one of the four substances (earth, air, water, and fire) formerly believed to make up the universe **7** *maths* any of the members of a set **8** **in one's element** in a situation in which one is happy and at ease: *she was in her element behind the wheel* **9** **elements** **A** the basic principles of something **B** weather conditions, esp. wind, rain, and cold: *only 200 braved the elements* [Latin *elementum*]

elemental *adj* of or like basic and powerful natural forces or passions

elementary *adj* **1** simple, basic, and straightforward: *elementary precautions* **2** involving only the most basic principles of a subject: *elementary mathematics*

elementary particle *n physics* any of several entities, such as electrons, neutrons, or protons, that are less complex than atoms

elementary school *n* **1** *Brit* a former name for **primary school** **2** *US & Canad* a state school for the first six to eight years of a child's education

elephant *n* **1** a very large four-legged animal that has a very long flexible nose called a trunk, large ears, and two ivory tusks, and lives in Africa or India **2** **elephant in the room** an obvious truth deliberately ignored by all parties in a situation [Greek *elephas*]

elephantiasis (el-lee-fan-tie-a-siss) *n pathol* a skin disease, caused by parasitic worms, in which the affected parts of the body become extremely enlarged

elephantine *adj* like an elephant, esp. in being huge, clumsy, or ponderous

elevate *vb* **-vating, -vated 1** to raise in rank or status: *he had elevated flirting to an art form* **2** to lift to a higher place: *this action elevates the upper back* [Latin *elevare*]

elevated *adj* **1** higher than normal: *elevated cholesterol levels* **2** (of ideas or pursuits) on a high intellectual or moral level: *elevated discussions about postmodernism* **3** (of land or part of a building) higher than the surrounding area

elevation *n* **1** the act of elevating someone or something: *his elevation to the peerage* **2** height above sea level **3** a raised area **4** a scale drawing of one side of a building

elevator *n* **1** *Austral, US & Canad* a lift for carrying people **2** a mechanical hoist

eleven *n* **1** the cardinal number that is the sum of ten and one **2** a numeral, 11 or XI, representing this number **3** something representing or consisting of 11 units **4** a team of 11 players in football, cricket, etc. ▷ *adj* **5** amounting to eleven: *eleven years* [Old English *endleofan*] **eleventh** *adj, n*

eleven-plus *n* (in Britain, esp. formerly) an examination taken by children aged 10 or 11 that determines the type of secondary education they will be given

elevenses *pl n Brit, Austral, S African & NZ informal* a mid-morning snack

eleventh hour *n* **1** the latest possible time ▷ *adj* **eleventh-hour 2** done at the latest possible time: *an eleventh-hour rescue*

elf *n, pl* **elves** (in folklore) a small mischievous fairy [Old English *ælf*]

elfin *adj* **1** small and delicate: *her elfin features* **2** of or relating to elves

elicit *vb* **1** to bring about (a response or reaction): *her remarks elicited a sharp retort* **2** to draw out (information) from someone: *a phone call elicited the fact that she had just awakened* [Latin *elicere*]

elide *vb* **eliding, elided** to omit (a syllable or vowel) from a spoken word [Latin *elidere* to knock]

eligible *adj* **1** meeting the requirements or qualifications needed: *he may be eligible for free legal services* **2** *old-fashioned* desirable as a spouse [Latin *eligere* to elect] **eligibility** *n*

eliminate *vb* **-nating, -nated 1** to get rid of (something or someone unwanted, unnecessary, or not meeting the requirements needed): *he can be eliminated from the list of suspects* **2** to remove (a competitor or team) from a contest, esp. following a defeat: *they were eliminated in the third round* **3** *slang* to murder in cold blood: *Stalin had thousands of his former comrades eliminated* [Latin *eliminare* to turn out of the house] **elimination** *n*

> **USAGE** *Eliminate* is sometimes wrongly used to talk about avoiding the repetition of something undesirable: *we must prevent* (not *eliminate*) *further mistakes of this kind.*

elision *n* omission of a syllable or vowel from a spoken word [Latin *elidere* to elide]

elite (ill-eet) *n* the most powerful, rich, or gifted members of a group or community

elitism *n* **1** the belief that society should be governed by a small group of people who are superior to everyone else **2** pride in being part of an elite **elitist** *n, adj*

elixir (ill-ix-er) *n* **1** an imaginary substance that is supposed to be capable of prolonging life and changing base metals into gold **2** a liquid medicine mixed with syrup [Arabic *al iksīr*]

Elizabethan *adj* **1** of or in the reign of Queen Elizabeth I of England (1558–1603) ▷ *n* **2** a person who lived during the reign of Queen Elizabeth I

elk *n* a very large deer of N Europe and Asia with broad flat antlers

ellipse *n* an oval shape resembling a flattened circle

ellipsis (ill-lip-siss) *n, pl* **-ses** (-seez) **1** the omission of a word or words from a sentence **2** *printing* three dots (...) indicating an omission [Greek *elleipein* to leave out]

ellipsoid *n geom* a surface whose plane sections are ellipses or circles

elliptical *or* **elliptic** *adj* **1** oval-shaped **2** (of speech or writing) obscure or ambiguous

> **USAGE** The use of *elliptical* to mean *circumlocutory* should be avoided as it may be interpreted wrongly as meaning *condensed* or *concise*.

elm *n* **1** a tall tree with broad leaves **2** the hard heavy wood of this tree [Old English]

elocution *n* the art of speaking clearly in public [Latin *e-* out + *loqui* to speak] **elocutionist** *n*

elongate (eel-long-gate) *vb* **-gating, -gated** to make or become longer [Latin *e-* away + *longe* (adverb) far] **elongation** *n*

elope *vb* **eloping, eloped** (of two people) to run away secretly to get married [Anglo-French *aloper*] **elopement** *n*

eloquence *n* the ability to speak or write in a skilful and convincing way

eloquent *adj* **1** (of speech or writing) fluent and persuasive **2** (of a person) able to speak in a fluent and persuasive manner **3** visibly or vividly expressive: *he raised an eloquent eyebrow* [Latin *e-* out + *loqui* to speak] **eloquently** *adv*

else *adv* **1** in addition or more: *what else do you want to know?* **2** other or different: *it was unlike anything else that had happened* **3 or else A** if not, then: *tell us soon or else we shall go mad* **B** *informal* or something terrible will result: used as a threat: *do it our way or else* [Old English *elles*]

elsewhere *adv* in or to another place

ELT English Language Teaching

elucidate *vb* **-dating, -dated** to make (something obscure or difficult) clear [Late Latin *elucidare* to enlighten] **elucidation** *n*

elude *vb* **eluding, eluded 1** to avoid or escape from (someone or something) **2** to fail to be understood or remembered by: *the mysteries of commerce elude me* [Latin *eludere* to deceive]

> **USAGE** *Elude* is sometimes wrongly used where *allude* is meant: *he was alluding* (not *eluding*) *to his previous visit to the city.*

elusive *adj* **1** difficult to find or catch **2** difficult to remember or describe **elusiveness** *n*

> **USAGE** See at **illusory**.

elver *n* a young eel [variant of *eelfare* eel-journey]
elves *n* the plural of **elf**
Elysium (ill-liz-zee-um) *n* **1** *Greek myth* the dwelling place of the blessed after death **2** a state or place of perfect bliss [Greek *ēlusion pedion* blessed fields] **Elysian** *adj*
emaciated (im-mace-ee-ate-id) *adj* extremely thin through illness or lack of food [Latin *macer* thin] **emaciation** *n*
email *or* **e-mail** (ee-mail) *n* **1** the transmission of messages from one computer terminal to another ▷ *vb* **2** to contact (a person) by email **3** to send (a message) by email
emanate (em-a-nate) *vb* **-nating, -nated** to come or seem to come from someone or something: *an aura of power emanated from him* [Latin *emanare* to flow out] **emanation** *n*
emancipate *vb* **-pating, -pated** to free from social, political, or legal restrictions [Latin *emancipare* to give independence (to a son)] **emancipation** *n*
emasculate *vb* **-lating, -lated** to deprive of power or strength [Latin *emasculare* to remove the testicles of] **emasculation** *n*
embalm *vb* to preserve (a corpse) by the use of chemicals and oils [Old French *embaumer*]
embankment *n* a man-made ridge of earth or stone that carries a road or railway or prevents a river or lake from overflowing
embargo *n, pl* **-goes** **1** an order by a government or international body prohibiting trade with a country: *America lifted its trade embargo on China* ▷ *vb* **-going, -goed** **2** to place an official prohibition on [Spanish]
embark *vb* **1** to go on board a ship or aircraft **2 embark on** to begin (a new project or venture) [Old Provençal *embarcar*] **embarkation** *n*
embarrass *vb* **1** to make (someone) feel shy, ashamed, or guilty about something **2** to cause political problems for (a government or party) **3** to cause to have financial difficulties [Italian *imbarrare* to confine within bars] **embarrassed** *adj* **embarrassing** *adj* **embarrassingly** *adv* **embarrassment** *n*
embassy *n, pl* **-sies** **1** the residence or place of business of an ambassador **2** an ambassador and his or her assistants and staff [Old Provençal *ambaisada*]
embattled *adj* **1** (of a country) involved in fighting a war, esp. when surrounded by enemies **2** facing many problems and difficulties: *the embattled Mayor*
embed *vb* **-bedding, -bedded** **1** to fix firmly in a surrounding solid mass: *the boy has shrapnel embedded in his spine* **2** to fix (an attitude or idea) in a society or in someone's mind: *corruption was deeply embedded in the ruling party*
embellish *vb* **1** to make (something) more attractive by adding decorations **2** to make (a story) more interesting by adding details which may not be true [Old French *embelir*] **embellishment** *n*
ember *n* a smouldering piece of coal or wood remaining after a fire has died [Old English *ǣmyrge*]
embezzle *vb* **-zling, -zled** to steal (money that belongs to the company or organization that one works for) [Anglo-French *embeseiller* to destroy] **embezzlement** *n* **embezzler** *n*
embittered *adj* feeling anger and despair as a result of misfortune: *embittered by poverty* **embitterment** *n*
emblazon (im-blaze-on) *vb* **1** to decorate with a coat of arms, slogan, etc.: *a jacket emblazoned with his band's name* **2** to proclaim or publicize: *I am not sure he would want his name emblazoned in my column*
emblem *n* an object or design chosen to symbolize an organization or idea [Greek *emblēma* insertion] **emblematic** *adj*
embody *vb* **-bodies, -bodying, -bodied** **1** to be an example of or express (an idea or other abstract concept) **2** to include as part of a whole: *the proposal has been embodied in a draft resolution* **embodiment** *n*
embolden *vb* to make bold
embolism *n pathol* the blocking of a blood vessel by a blood clot, air bubble, etc.
embolus *n, pl* **-li** *pathol* a blood clot, air bubble, or other stoppage that blocks a small blood vessel [Greek *embolos* stopper]
emboss *vb* to mould or carve a decoration on (a surface) so that it stands out from the surface [Old French *embocer*]
embrace *vb* **-bracing, -braced** **1** to clasp (someone) with one's arms as an expression of affection or a greeting **2** to accept eagerly: *he has embraced the Islamic faith* **3** to include or be made up of: *a church that embraces two cultures* ▷ *n* **4** an act of embracing [Latin *im-* in + *bracchia* arms]
embrasure *n* **1** an opening for a door or window which is wider on the inside of the wall than on the outside **2** an opening in a battlement or wall, for shooting through [French]
embrocation *n* a lotion rubbed into the skin to ease sore muscles [Greek *brokhē* a moistening]
embroider *vb* **1** to do decorative needlework on (a piece of cloth or a garment) **2** to add imaginary details to (a story) [Old French *embroder*] **embroiderer** *n*
embroidery *n* **1** decorative needlework, usually on cloth or canvas **2** the act of adding imaginary details to a story
embroil *vb* to involve (oneself or another person) in problems or difficulties [French *embrouiller*] **embroilment** *n*
embryo (em-bree-oh) *n, pl* **-bryos** **1** an unborn animal or human being in the early stages of development, in humans up to approximately the end of the second month of pregnancy **2** something in an early stage of development: *the embryo of a serious comic novel* [Greek *embruon*]
embryology *n* the scientific study of embryos
embryonic *adj* **1** of or relating to an embryo **2** in an early stage
emend *vb* to make corrections or improvements to (a text) [Latin *e-* out + *mendum* a mistake] **emendation** *n*
emerald *n* **1** a green transparent variety of beryl highly valued as a gem ▷ *adj* **2** bright green [Greek *smaragdos*]
Emerald Isle *n poetic* Ireland
emerge *vb* **emerging, emerged** **1** to come into view out of something: *a man emerged from the*

shadows **2** to come out of a particular state of mind or way of existence: *she emerged from the trance* **3** to come to the end of a particular event or situation: *no party emerged from the election with a clear majority* **4** to become apparent, esp. as the result of a discussion or investigation: *it emerged that he had made up much of his CV to get a job as a teacher* **5** to come into existence over a long period of time: *a new style of dance music emerged in the late 1980s* [Latin *emergere* to rise up from]
emergence *n* **emergent** *adj*

emergency *n, pl* **-cies 1** an unforeseen or sudden occurrence, esp. of danger demanding immediate action **2 state of emergency** a time of crisis, declared by a government, during which normal laws and civil rights can be suspended ▹ *adj* **3** for use in an emergency: *the emergency exit* **4** made necessary because of an emergency: *emergency surgery*

emeritus (im-**mer**-rit-uss) *adj* retired, but retaining one's title on an honorary basis: *a professor emeritus* [Latin *merere* to deserve]

emery *n* a hard greyish-black mineral used for smoothing and polishing [Greek *smuris* powder for rubbing]

emery board *n* a strip of cardboard coated with crushed emery, for filing one's fingernails

emetic (im-**met**-ik) *n* **1** a substance that causes vomiting ▹ *adj* **2** causing vomiting [Greek *emetikos*]

EMF electromotive force

emigrate *vb* **-grating, -grated** to leave one's native country to settle in another country [Latin *emigrare*] **emigrant** *n, adj* **emigration** *n*

émigré (em-mig-gray) *n* someone who has left his or her native country for political reasons [French]

eminence *n* **1** the state of being well-known and well-respected **2** a piece of high ground

Eminence *n* **Your** *or* **His Eminence** a title used to address or refer to a cardinal

éminence grise (em-in-nonss **greez**) *n, pl* **éminences grises** a person who wields power and influence unofficially [French, literally: grey eminence, originally applied to Père Joseph, secretary of Cardinal Richelieu]

eminent *adj* well-known and well-respected [Latin *eminere* to stand out]

eminently *adv* extremely: *eminently sensible*

emir (em-**meer**) *n* an independent ruler in the Islamic world [Arabic *'amīr* commander]
emirate *n*

emissary *n, pl* **-saries** an agent sent on a mission by a government or head of state [Latin *emissarius*]

emission *n* **1** the act of giving out heat, light, a smell, etc. **2** energy or a substance given out by something: *exhaust emissions from motor vehicles*

emit *vb* **emitting, emitted 1** to give or send forth (heat, light, a smell, etc.) **2** to produce (a sound) [Latin *emittere* to send out]

Emmental (em-men-tahl) *n* a hard Swiss cheese with holes in it [after *Emmenthal*, valley in Switzerland]

emoji (im-**moh**-jee) *n* a small image used in electronic messaging to express an idea or emotion [Japanese *e* picture + *moji* letter]

emollient *adj* **1** (of skin cream or lotion) having a softening effect **2** helping to avoid confrontation; calming: *his emollient political style* ▹ *n* **3** a cream or lotion that softens the skin [Latin *emollire* to soften]

emolument *n* fees or wages from employment [Latin *emolumentum* benefit; originally, fee paid to a miller]

emote *vb* **emoting, emoted** to display exaggerated emotion, as if acting

emoticon (im-**mote**-ik-kon) *n* a series of symbols used in electronic messaging to express an idea or emotion [EMOT(ION) + ICON]

emotion *n* **1** any strong feeling, such as joy or fear **2** the part of a person's character based on feelings rather than thought: *the conflict between emotion and logic* [Latin *emovere* to disturb]

emotional *adj* **1** of or relating to the emotions: *emotional abuse* **2** influenced by feelings rather than rational thinking: *he was too emotional to be a good doctor* **3** appealing to the emotions: *emotional appeals for public support* **4** showing one's feelings openly, esp. when upset: *he became very emotional and burst into tears* **emotionalism** *n* **emotionally** *adv*

emotive *adj* tending or designed to arouse emotion

> **USAGE** *Emotional* is preferred to *emotive* when describing a display of emotion: *he was given an emotional* (not *emotive*) *welcome.*

empathize *or* **-thise** *vb* **-thizing, -thized** *or* **-thising, -thised** (often foll. by *with*) to sense and understand someone else's feelings as if they were one's own

empathy *n* the ability to sense and understand someone else's feelings as if they were one's own [Greek *empatheia* affection, passion]
empathic *adj*

emperor *n* a man who rules an empire [Latin *imperare* to command]

emperor penguin *n* a very large Antarctic penguin with orange-yellow patches on its neck

emphasis *n, pl* **-ses 1** special importance or significance given to something, such as an object or idea **2** stress on a particular syllable, word, or phrase in speaking [Greek]

emphasize *or* **-sise** *vb* **-sizing, -sized** *or* **-sising, -sised** to give emphasis or prominence to: *to emphasize her loyalty*

emphatic *adj* **1** expressed, spoken, or done forcefully: *an emphatic denial of the allegations* **2** forceful and positive: *he was emphatic about his desire for peace talks* [Greek *emphainein* to display]
emphatically *adv*

emphysema (em-fiss-**see**-ma) *n pathol* a condition in which the air sacs of the lungs are grossly enlarged, causing breathlessness [Greek *emphusēma* a swelling up]

empire *n* **1** a group of countries under the rule of a single person or sovereign state **2** a large industrial organization that is controlled by one person: *the heiress to a jewellery empire* [Latin *imperare* to command]

empire-builder *n informal* a person who seeks extra power by increasing the number of his or her staff **empire-building** *n, adj*

empirical *adj* derived from experiment, experience, and observation rather than from theory or logic: *there is no empirical data to support this claim* [Greek *empeirikos* practised] **empirically** *adv*
empiricism *n philosophy* the doctrine that all knowledge derives from experience **empiricist** *n*
emplacement *n* a prepared position for an artillery gun
employ *vb* **1** to hire (someone) to do work in return for money **2** to keep busy or occupy: *she was busily employed cutting the grass* **3** to use as a means: *you can employ various methods to cut your heating bills* ▷ *n* **4 in the employ of** doing regular paid work for: *he is in the employ of The Sunday Times* [Old French *emploier*] **employable** *adj*
employee *or US* **employe** *n* a person who is hired to work for someone in return for payment
employer *n* a person or company that employs workers
employment *n* **1** the act of employing or state of being employed **2** a person's work or occupation **3** the availability of jobs for the population of a town, country, etc.: *the party's commitment to full employment*
emporium *n, pl* **-riums** *or* **-ria** *old-fashioned* a large retail shop with a wide variety of merchandise [Latin, from Greek *emporos* merchant]
empower *vb* to give (someone) the power or authority to do something
empowerment *n* **1** the giving or delegation of power; authority **2** *S African* a semi-official slogan for the empowering of previously disadvantaged populations
empress *n* **1** a woman who rules an empire **2** the wife or widow of an emperor [Latin *imperatrix*]
empty *adj* **-tier, -tiest 1** containing nothing **2** without inhabitants; unoccupied **3** without purpose, substance, or value: *he contemplated yet another empty weekend* **4** insincere or trivial: *empty words* **5** *informal* drained of energy or emotion **6** *maths & logic* (of a set or class) containing no members ▷ *vb* **-ties, -tying, -tied 7** to make or become empty **8** to remove from something: *they emptied out the remains of the tin of paint* ▷ *n, pl* **-ties 9** an empty container, esp. a bottle [Old English *ǣmtig*] **emptiness** *n*
empty-handed *adj* having gained nothing: *the robbers ran off empty-handed*
empty-headed *adj* silly or incapable of serious thought
empyrean (em-pie-**ree**-an) *n poetic* the sky or the heavens [Greek *empuros* fiery]
EMS European Monetary System: the system enabling some EU members to coordinate their exchange rates
emu *n* a large Australian long-legged bird that cannot fly [Portuguese *ema* ostrich]
EMU 1 European Monetary Union **2** Economic and Monetary Union
emulate *vb* **-lating, -lated** to imitate (someone) in an attempt to do as well as or better than him or her [Latin *aemulus* competing with] **emulation** *n* **emulator** *n*
emulsifier *n* a substance that helps to combine two liquids, esp. a water-based liquid and an oil
emulsify *vb* **-fies, -fying, -fied** to make or form into an emulsion
emulsion *n* **1** a mixture of two liquids in which particles of one are suspended evenly throughout the other **2** *photog* a light-sensitive coating for photographic film **3** a type of water-based paint [Latin *emulgere* to milk out]
enable *vb* **-abling, -abled 1** to provide (someone) with the means or opportunity to do something **2** to make possible: *to enable the best possible chance of cure*
enabling act *n* a legislative act giving certain powers to a person or organization
enact *vb* **1** to establish by law: *plans to enact a bill of rights* **2** to perform (a story or play) by acting **enactment** *n*
enamel *n* **1** a coloured glassy coating on the surface of articles made of metal, glass, or pottery **2** an enamel-like paint or varnish **3** the hard white substance that covers teeth ▷ *vb* **-elling, -elled** *or US* **-eling, -eled 4** to decorate or cover with enamel [Old French *esmail*]
enamoured *or US* **enamored** *adj* **enamoured of A** in love with **B** very fond of and impressed by: *he is not enamoured of Hollywood* [Latin *amor* love]
en bloc (on **blok**) *adv* as a whole; all together [French]
enc. 1 enclosed **2** enclosure
encamp *vb formal* to set up a camp **encampment** *n*
encapsulate *vb* **-lating, -lated 1** to put in a concise form; summarize **2** to enclose in, or as if in, a capsule **encapsulation** *n*
encase *vb* **-casing, -cased** to enclose or cover completely: *her arms were encased in plaster* **encasement** *n*
encephalitis (en-sef-a-**lite**-iss) *n* inflammation of the brain [Greek *en-* in + *kephalē* head] **encephalitic** *adj*
encephalogram *n* an electroencephalogram [Greek *en-* in + *kephalē* head + *gramma* drawing]
enchant *vb* **1** to delight and fascinate **2** to cast a spell on [Latin *incantare* to chant a spell] **enchanted** *adj* **enchantment** *n* **enchanter** *or fem* **enchantress** *n*
enchilada (en-chill-**lah**-da) *n* a Mexican dish consisting of a tortilla filled with meat, served with chilli sauce
encircle *vb* **-cling, -cled** to form a circle round **encirclement** *n*
enclave *n* a part of a country entirely surrounded by foreign territory: *a Spanish enclave* [Latin *in-* in + *clavis* key]
enclose *vb* **-closing, -closed 1** to surround completely: *the house enclosed a courtyard* **2** to include along with something else: *he enclosed a letter with the parcel*
enclosed *adj* kept separate from the normal everyday activities of the outside world: *an enclosed community of nuns*
enclosure *n* **1** an area of land enclosed by a fence, wall, or hedge **2** something, such as a cheque, enclosed with a letter
encode *vb* **-coding, -coded** to convert (a message) into code
encomium *n* a formal expression of praise [Latin]

e

encompass *vb* **1** to enclose within a circle; surround **2** to include all of: *the programme encompasses the visual arts, music, literature, and drama*

encore *interj* **1** again: used by an audience to demand a short extra performance ▹ *n* **2** an extra song or piece performed at a concert in response to enthusiastic demand from the audience [French]

encounter *vb* **1** to meet (someone) unexpectedly **2** to be faced with: *he had rarely encountered such suffering* **3** to meet (an opponent or enemy) in a competition or battle ▹ *n* **4** a casual or unexpected meeting **5** a game or battle: *a fierce encounter between the army and armed rebels* [Latin *in-* in + *contra* against, opposite]

e

encourage *vb* **-raging, -raged 1** to give (someone) the confidence to do something **2** to stimulate (something or someone) by approval or help [French *encourager*] **encouragement** *n* **encouraging** *adj*

encroach *vb* to intrude gradually on someone's rights or on a piece of land [Old French *encrochier* to seize] **encroachment** *n*

encrust *vb* to cover (a surface) with a layer of something, such as jewels or ice **encrustation** *n*

encrypt *vb* to put (a message or data) into a coded form [Greek *en-* in + *kruptos* hidden] **encryption** *n*

encumber *vb* **1** to hinder or impede: *neither was greatly encumbered with social engagements* **2** to burden with a load or with debts [Old French *en-* into + *combre* a barrier]

encumbrance *n* something that impedes or is burdensome

encyclical (en-**sik**-lik-kl) *n* a letter sent by the pope to all Roman Catholic bishops [Greek *kuklos* circle]

encyclopedia *or* **encyclopaedia** *n* a book or set of books, often in alphabetical order, containing facts about many different subjects or about one particular subject [Greek *enkuklios* general + *paideia* education]

encyclopedic *or* **encyclopaedic** *adj* (of knowledge or information) very full and thorough; comprehensive

end *n* **1** one of the two extreme points of something such as a road **2** the surface at one of the two extreme points of an object: *a pencil with a rubber at one end* **3** the extreme extent or limit of something: *the end of the runway* **4** the most distant place or time that can be imagined: *the ends of the earth* **5** the act or an instance of stopping doing something or stopping something from continuing: *I want to put an end to all the gossip* **6** the last part of something: *at the end of the story* **7** a remnant or fragment: *cigarette ends* **8** death or destruction **9** the purpose of an action: *he will only use you to achieve his own ends* **10** *sport* either of the two defended areas of a playing field **11 in the end** finally **12 make ends meet** to have just enough money to meet one's needs **13 no end** used for emphasis: *these moments give me no end of trouble* **14 on end** *informal* without pause or interruption: *for months on end* **15 the end** *slang* the worst, esp. beyond the limits of endurance ▹ *vb* **16** to bring or come to a finish **17 end it all** *informal* to die by suicide ▹ See also **end up** [Old English *ende*]

endanger *vb* to put in danger

endangered *adj* (of a species of animal) in danger of becoming extinct

endear *vb* to cause to be liked: *his wit endeared him to a great many people* **endearing** *adj*

endearment *n* an affectionate word or phrase

endeavour *or US* **endeavor** *formal* ▹ *vb* **1** to try (to do something) ▹ *n* **2** an effort to do something [Middle English *endeveren*]

endemic *adj* present within a localized area or only found in a particular group of people: *he found 100 species of plant endemic to that ridge* [Greek *en-* in + *dēmos* the people]

ending *n* **1** the last part or conclusion of something: *the film has a happy ending* **2** the tip or end of something: *nerve endings*

endive *n* a plant with crisp curly leaves, used in salads [Old French]

endless *adj* **1** having no end; eternal or infinite **2** continuing too long or continually recurring: *an endless stream of visitors* **endlessly** *adv*

endmost *adj* nearest the end

endocrine *adj* of or denoting a gland that secretes hormones directly into the bloodstream, or a hormone secreted by such a gland [Greek *endon* within + *krinein* to separate]

endogenous (en-**dodge**-in-uss) *adj biol* developing or originating from within

endometrium (end-oh-**meet**-tree-um) *n* the mucous membrane lining the womb [Greek *endon* within + *mētra* womb] **endometrial** *adj*

endomorph *n physiol* a person with a fat and heavy body build. See also **ectomorph**, **mesomorph** [Greek *endon* within + *morphē* shape] **endomorphic** *adj*

endorphin *n* any of a group of chemicals found in the brain, which have an effect similar to morphine

endorsation *n Canad* approval or support

endorse *vb* **-dorsing, -dorsed 1** to give approval or support to **2** to sign the back of (a cheque) to specify the payee **3** *chiefly Brit* to record a conviction on (a driving licence) [Old French *endosser* to put on the back] **endorsement** *n*

endoscope *n med* a long slender medical instrument used for examining the interior of hollow organs **endoscopy** *n*

endoskeleton *n zool* an internal skeleton, such as the bony skeleton of vertebrates

endothermic *adj* (of a chemical reaction) involving or requiring the absorption of heat

endow *vb* **1** to provide with a source of permanent income, esp. by leaving money in a will **2 endowed with** provided with or possessing (a quality or talent) [Old French *endouer*]

endowment *n* **1** the money given to an institution, such as a hospital **2** a natural talent or quality

endowment assurance *or* **endowment insurance** *n* a kind of life insurance that pays a specified sum directly to the policyholder at a designated date or to his or her beneficiary should he or she die before this date

endpaper *n* either of two leaves at the front and back of a book pasted to the inside of the cover

end product *n* the final result of a process
end up *vb* **1** to arrive at a place by a roundabout route or without intending to: *the van somehow ended up in Bordeaux* **2** to arrive at a particular condition or situation without expecting to: *I thought I was going to hate it, but I ended up enjoying myself*
endurance *n* the ability to withstand prolonged hardship
endure *vb* **-during, -dured 1** to bear (hardship) patiently **2** to tolerate or put up with: *I cannot endure your disloyalty any longer* **3** to last for a long time [Latin *indurare* to harden] **endurable** *adj*
enduring *adj* long-lasting
end user *n* the person for whom a product or service is designed
endways *or esp US & Canad* **endwise** *adv* having the end forwards or upwards
enema (en-im-a) *n med* a quantity of fluid inserted into the rectum to empty the bowels, for example before an operation [Greek: injection]
enemy *n, pl* **-mies 1** a person who is hostile or opposed to a person, group, or idea **2** a hostile nation or people **3** something that harms or opposes something: *oil is an enemy of the environment.* ▹ Related adjective: **inimical** ▹ *adj* **4** of or belonging to an enemy: *enemy troops* [Latin *inimicus* hostile]
energetic *adj* **1** having or showing energy and enthusiasm: *an energetic campaigner for democracy* **2** involving a lot of movement and physical effort: *energetic exercise* **energetically** *adv*
energize *or* **-gise** *vb* **-gizing, -gized** *or* **-gising, -gised** to stimulate or enliven
energy *n, pl* **-gies 1** capacity for intense activity; vigour **2** intensity or vitality of action or expression; forcefulness **3** *physics* the capacity to do work and overcome resistance **4** a source of power, such as electricity [Greek *energeia* activity]
energy drink *n* a soft drink designed to boost the drinker's energy levels
enervate *vb* **-vating, -vated** to deprive of strength or vitality [Latin *enervare* to remove the nerves from] **enervating** *adj* **enervation** *n*
enfant terrible (on-fon ter-reeb-la) *n, pl* **enfants terribles** a talented but unconventional or indiscreet person [French, literally: terrible child]
enfeeble *vb* **-bling, -bled** to make (someone or something) weak
enfilade *military* ▹ *n* **1** a burst of gunfire sweeping from end to end along a line of troops ▹ *vb* **-lading, -laded 2** to attack with an enfilade [French *enfiler* to thread on string]
enfold *vb* **1** to cover (something) by, or as if by, wrapping something round it: *darkness enfolded the city* **2** to embrace or hug
enforce *vb* **-forcing, -forced 1** to ensure that (a law or decision) is obeyed **2** to impose (obedience) by, or as if by, force **enforceable** *adj* **enforcement** *n*
enfranchise *vb* **-chising, -chised** to grant (a person or group of people) the right to vote **enfranchisement** *n*
Eng. 1 England **2** English
engage *vb* **-gaging, -gaged 1** Also: **be engaged** (usually foll. by *in*) to take part or participate: *he engaged in criminal and illegal acts; they were engaged in espionage* **2** to involve (a person or his or her attention) intensely: *there's nothing to engage the intellect in this film* **3** to employ (someone) to do something **4** to promise (to do something) **5** *military* to begin a battle with **6** to bring (part of a machine or other mechanism) into operation, esp. by causing components to interlock **7 engage in conversation** to start a conversation with [Old French *en-* in + *gage* a pledge]
engaged *adj* **1** having made a promise to get married **2** *Brit* (of a telephone line or a toilet) already being used
engagement *n* **1** a business or social appointment **2** the period when a couple has agreed to get married but the wedding has not yet taken place **3** a limited period of employment, esp. in the performing arts **4** a battle
engagement ring *n* a ring worn by someone who is engaged to be married
engaging *adj* pleasant and charming **engagingly** *adv*
engender *vb* to produce (a particular feeling, atmosphere, or situation) [Latin *ingenerare*]
engine *n* **1** any machine designed to convert energy into mechanical work, esp. one used to power a vehicle **2** a railway locomotive [Latin *ingenium* nature, talent]
engineer *n* **1** a person trained in any branch of engineering **2** a person who repairs and maintains mechanical or electrical devices **3** a soldier trained in engineering and construction work **4** an officer responsible for a ship's engines **5** *US & Canad* a train driver ▹ *vb* **6** to cause or plan (an event or situation) in a clever or devious manner **7** to design or construct as a professional engineer
engineering *n* the profession of applying scientific principles to the design and construction of engines, cars, buildings, bridges, roads, and electrical machines
English *adj* **1** of England or the English language ▹ *n* **2** the principal language of Britain, Ireland, Australia, New Zealand, the US, Canada, and several other countries ▹ *pl n* **3 the English** the people of England
English breakfast *n* a breakfast including cooked food, such as bacon and eggs
Englishman *or fem* **Englishwoman** *n, pl* **-men** *or* **-women** a person from England
engorge *vb* **-gorging, -gorged** *pathol* to clog or become clogged with blood **engorgement** *n*
engrave *vb* **-graving, -graved 1** to carve or etch a design or inscription into (a surface) **2** to print (designs or characters) from a plate into which they have been cut or etched **3** to fix deeply or permanently in the mind [*en-* in + obsolete *grave* to carve] **engraver** *n*
engraving *n* **1** a printing surface that has been engraved **2** a print made from this
engross (en-groce) *vb* to occupy the attention of (someone) completely [*en-* in + Latin *grossus* thick] **engrossing** *adj*

e

engulf *vb* **1** to immerse, plunge, or swallow up: *engulfed by flames* **2** to overwhelm: *a terrible fear engulfed her*

enhance *vb* **-hancing, -hanced** to improve or increase in quality, value, or power: *grilling on the barbecue enhances the flavour* [Old French *enhaucier*] **enhancement** *n* **enhancer** *n*

enigma *n* something or someone that is mysterious or puzzling [Greek *ainissesthai* to speak in riddles] **enigmatic** *adj* **enigmatically** *adv*

enjoin *vb* **1** to order (someone) to do something **2** to impose (a particular kind of behaviour) on someone: *the sect enjoins poverty on its members* **3** *law* to prohibit (someone) from doing something by an injunction [Old French *enjoindre*]

e

enjoy *vb* **1** to receive pleasure from **2** to have or experience (something, esp. something good): *many older people enjoy excellent health* **3 enjoy oneself** to have a good time [Old French *enjoir*] **enjoyable** *adj* **enjoyably** *adv* **enjoyment** *n*

enlarge *vb* **-larging, -larged 1** to make or grow larger **2 enlarge on** to speak or write about in greater detail **enlargement** *n* **enlarger** *n*

enlighten *vb* to give information or understanding to **enlightening** *adj*

enlightened *adj* **1** rational and having beneficial effects: *an enlightened approach to social welfare* **2** (of a person) tolerant and unprejudiced

enlightenment *n* the act of enlightening or the state of being enlightened

enlist *vb* **1** to enter the armed forces **2** to obtain (someone's help or support) **enlistment** *n*

enlisted *adj* (of a man or woman in the US Army or Navy) being below the rank of an officer

enliven *vb* to make lively, cheerful, or bright **enlivening** *adj*

en masse (on **mass**) *adv* all together; as a group [French]

enmeshed *adj* deeply involved: *enmeshed in turmoil*

enmity *n* a feeling of hostility or ill will [Latin *inimicus* hostile]

ennoble *vb* **-bling, -bled 1** to make (someone) a member of the nobility **2** to make (someone or his or her life) noble or dignified: *poverty does not ennoble people*

ennui (on-**nwee**) *n literary* boredom and dissatisfaction resulting from lack of activity or excitement [French]

enormity *n* **1** extreme wickedness **2** *pl* **-ties** an act of great wickedness **3** the vastness or extent of a problem or difficulty

> **USAGE** In modern English, it is common to talk about the *enormity* of something such as a task or a problem, but one should not talk about the *enormity* of an object or area: *distribution is a problem because of India's enormous size* (not *India's enormity*).

enormous *adj* unusually large in size, extent, or degree [Latin *e-* out of, away from + *norma* rule, pattern] **enormously** *adv*

enough *adj* **1** as much or as many as necessary **2 that's enough!** used to stop someone behaving in a particular way ▷ *pron* **3** an adequate amount or number: *I don't know enough about the subject to be able to speak about it* ▷ *adv* **4** as much as necessary **5** fairly or quite: *that's a common enough experience* **6** very: used to give emphasis to the preceding word: *funnily enough, I wasn't alarmed* **7** just adequately: *he sang well enough* [Old English *genōh*]

en passant (on pass-**on**) *adv* in passing: *references made en passant* [French]

enquire *vb* **-quiring, -quired** same as **inquire** **enquiry** *n*

enrage *vb* **-raging, -raged** to make extremely angry

enraptured *adj* filled with delight and fascination

enrich *vb* **1** to improve or increase the quality or value of: *his poetry has vastly enriched the English language* **2** to improve in nutritional value, colour, or flavour: *a sauce enriched with beer* **3** to make wealthy or wealthier **enriched** *adj* **enrichment** *n*

enrol *or US* **enroll** *vb* **-rolling, -rolled** to become or cause to become a member **enrolment** *or US* **enrollment** *n*

en route (on **root**) *adv* on or along the way [French]

ensconce *vb* **-sconcing, -sconced** to settle firmly or comfortably [Middle English *en-* in + *sconce* fortification]

ensemble (on-**som**-bl) *n* **1** all the parts of something considered as a whole **2** the complete outfit of clothes a person is wearing **3** a group of musicians or actors performing together **4** *music* a passage in which all or most of the performers are playing or singing at once [French: together]

enshrine *vb* **-shrining, -shrined** to contain and protect (an idea or right) in a society, legal system, etc.: *the university's independence is enshrined in its charter*

enshroud *vb* to cover or hide (an object) completely, as if by draping something over it: *fog enshrouded the forest*

ensign *n* **1** a flag flown by a ship to indicate its nationality **2** any flag or banner **3** (in the US Navy) a commissioned officer of the lowest rank **4** (formerly, in the British infantry) a commissioned officer of the lowest rank [Latin *insignia* badges]

enslave *vb* **-slaving, -slaved** to make a slave of (someone) **enslavement** *n*

ensnare *vb* **-snaring, -snared 1** to trap or gain power over (someone) by dishonest or underhand means **2** to catch (an animal) in a snare

ensue *vb* **-suing, -sued 1** to happen next **2** to occur as a consequence: *if glaucoma is not treated, blindness can ensue* [Latin *in-* in + *sequi* to follow] **ensuing** *adj*

en suite (on **sweet**) *adj, adv* (of a bathroom) connected to a bedroom and entered directly from it: *an en-suite bathroom; a room with a bathroom en suite* [French, literally: in sequence]

ensure *or esp US* **insure** *vb* **-suring, -sured 1** to make certain: *we must ensure that similar accidents do not happen again* **2** to make safe or protect: *female athletes should take extra iron to ensure against anaemia*

ENT *med* ear, nose, and throat

entablature *n archit* the part of a classical building supported by the columns, consisting of an architrave, a frieze, and a cornice [Italian *intavolatura* something put on a table, hence, something laid flat]

entail *vb* **1** to bring about or impose inevitably: *he wasn't ready for all that marriage entails* **2** *Brit, Austral & NZ property law* to restrict the ability to inherit (a piece of property) to designated heirs [Middle English *en-* in + *taille* limitation]

entangle *vb* **-gling, -gled 1** to catch very firmly in something, such as a net or wire: *a fishing line had entangled his legs* **2** to involve in a complicated series of problems or difficulties: *he entangles himself in contradictions* **3** to involve in a troublesome relationship: *Harvey soon got entangled with a certain Miss Gilmour* **entanglement** *n*

entente (on-tont) *n* short for **entente cordiale** [French: understanding]

entente cordiale (cord-ee-**ahl**) *n* a friendly understanding between two or more countries [French: cordial understanding]

enter *vb* **1** to come or go into (a particular place): *he entered the room* **2** to join (a party or organization) **3** to become involved in or take part in: *1500 schools entered the competition* **4** to become suddenly present or noticeable in: *a note of anxiety entered his voice* **5** to record (an item) in a journal or list **6** *theatre* to come on stage: used as a stage direction: *enter Joseph* **7** to begin (a new process or period of time): *the occupation of the square has entered its eleventh day* [Latin *intrare*]

enteric (en-**ter**-ik) *adj* of the intestines [Greek *enteron* intestine]

enter into *vb* **1** to be an important factor in (a situation or plan): *money doesn't enter into it: it's a matter of principle* **2** to start to do or be involved in (a process or series of events): *the government will not enter into negotiations with terrorists*

enteritis (en-ter-**rite**-iss) *n* inflammation of the small intestine

enterprise *n* **1** a business firm **2** a project or undertaking, esp. one that requires boldness or effort **3** boldness and energy [Old French *entreprendre* to undertake]

enterprising *adj* full of boldness and initiative **enterprisingly** *adv*

entertain *vb* **1** to provide amusement for (a person or audience) **2** to show hospitality to (guests) **3** to consider (an idea or suggestion) [Old French *entre-* mutually + *tenir* to hold]

entertainer *n* a person who entertains, esp. professionally

entertaining *adj* **1** interesting, amusing, and enjoyable ▷ *n* **2** the provision of hospitality to guests: *the smart kitchen is perfect for entertaining*

entertainment *n* **1** enjoyment and interest: *a match of top-quality entertainment and goals* **2** an act or show that entertains, or such acts and shows collectively

enthral *or US* **enthrall** (en-**thrawl**) *vb* **-thralling, -thralled** to hold the attention or interest of **enthralling** *adj* **enthralment** *or US* **enthrallment** *n*

enthrone *vb* **-throning, -throned 1** to place (a person) on a throne in a ceremony to mark the beginning of his or her new role as a monarch or bishop **2** to give an important or prominent position to (something): *she will always be enthroned in my heart* **enthronement** *n*

enthuse *vb* **-thusing, -thused** to feel or cause to feel enthusiasm

enthusiasm *n* ardent and lively interest or eagerness: *your enthusiasm for literature* [Greek *enthousiazein* to be possessed by a god]

enthusiast *n* a person who is very interested in and keen on something **enthusiastic** *adj* **enthusiastically** *adv*

entice *vb* **-ticing, -ticed** to attract (someone) away from one place or activity to another [Old French *enticier*] **enticement** *n* **enticing** *adj*

entire *adj* made up of or involving all of something, including every detail, part, or aspect [Latin *integer* whole] **entirely** *adv*

entirety *n, pl* **-ties 1** all of a person or thing: *you must follow this diet for the entirety of your life* **2 in its entirety** as a whole

entitle *vb* **-tling, -tled 1** to give (someone) the right to do or have something **2** to give a name or title to (a book or film) **entitlement** *n*

entity *n, pl* **-ties** something that exists in its own right and not merely as part of a bigger thing [Latin *esse* to be]

entomb *vb* **1** to place (a corpse) in a tomb **2** to bury or trap: *Ernest Shackleton's ship, Endurance, became entombed in ice* **entombment** *n*

entomology *n* the study of insects [Greek *entomon* insect] **entomological** *adj* **entomologist** *n*

entourage (on-toor-ahzh) *n* a group of people who assist or travel with an important or well-known person [French *entourer* to surround]

entozoon (en-toe-**zoe**-on) *n, pl* **-zoa** (-**zoe**-a) a parasite, such as a tapeworm, that lives inside another animal

entrails *pl n* **1** the internal organs of a person or animal; intestines **2** the innermost parts of anything [Latin *interanea* intestines]

entrance[1] *n* **1** something, such as a door or gate, through which it is possible to enter a place **2** the act of coming into a place, esp. with reference to the way in which it is done: *she made a sudden startling entrance* **3** *theatre* the act of appearing on stage **4** the right to enter a place: *he refused her entrance because she was carrying her Scottie dog* **5** ability or permission to join or become involved with a group or organization: *entrance to the profession should be open to men and women alike* ▷ *adj* **6** necessary in order to enter something: *they have paid entrance fees for English-language courses*

entrance[2] *vb* **-trancing, -tranced** to fill with delight **entrancement** *n* **entrancing** *adj*

entrant *n* a person who enters a university, competition, etc.

entrap *vb* **-trapping, -trapped 1** to trick (someone) into danger or difficulty **2** to catch in a trap **entrapment** *n*

entreat *vb* to ask (someone) earnestly to do something [Old French *entraiter*]

entreaty *n, pl* **-treaties** an earnest request or plea

entrecote (on-tra-coat) *n* a steak of beef cut from between the ribs [French]

entrée (**on**-tray) *n* **1** the right to enter a place **2** a dish served before a main course **3** *chiefly US* the main course [French]

entrench *vb* **1** to fix or establish firmly: *the habit had become entrenched* **2** *military* to fortify (a position) by digging trenches around it **entrenchment** *n*

entrepreneur *n* the owner of a business who attempts to make money by risk and initiative [French] **entrepreneurial** *adj*

entropy (en-trop-ee) *n* **1** *formal* lack of pattern or organization **2** *physics* a thermodynamic quantity that represents the amount of energy present in a system that cannot be converted into work because it is tied up in the atomic structure of the system [Greek *entropē* a turning towards]

e

entrust *vb* **1** to give (someone) a duty or responsibility: *Miss Conway, who was entrusted with the child's education* **2** to put (something) into the care of someone: *he stole all the money we had entrusted to him*

> **USAGE** It is usually considered incorrect to talk about *entrusting* someone *to do* something: *the army cannot be trusted* (not *entrusted*) *to carry out orders*.

entry *n, pl* **-tries** **1** something, such as a door or gate, through which it is possible to enter a place **2** the act of coming in to a place, esp. with reference to the way in which it is done **3** the right to enter a place: *he was often refused entry to Boston's bars because he looked so young* **4** the act of joining an organization or group: *Poland's entry into the EU* **5** a brief note, article, or group of figures in a diary, book, or computer file **6** a quiz form, painting, etc., submitted in an attempt to win a competition **7** a person, horse, car, etc., entering a competition ▹ *adj* **8** necessary in order to enter something: *entry fee*

entwine *vb* **-twining, -twined** to twist together or round something else

E number *n* any of a series of numbers with the prefix E- indicating a specific food additive recognized by the EU

enumerate *vb* **-ating, -ated** **1** to name or list one by one **2** to count **3** *Canad* to include in the voting list for an area [Latin *e-* out + *numerare* to count] **enumeration** *n* **enumerator** *n*

enunciate *vb* **-ating, -ated** **1** to pronounce (words) clearly **2** to state precisely or formally [Latin *enuntiare* to declare] **enunciation** *n*

enuresis (en-yoo-**reece**-iss) *n* involuntary urination, esp. during sleep [Greek *en-* in + *ouron* urine]

envelop *vb* to cover, surround, or enclose [Old French *envoluper*] **envelopment** *n*

envelope *n* **1** a flat covering of paper, that can be sealed, used to enclose a letter, etc. **2** any covering, wrapper, or enclosing structure: *an envelope of filo pastry* **3** *geom* a curve that is tangential to each one of a group of curves [French *envelopper* to wrap round]

enviable *adj* so desirable or fortunate that it is likely to cause envy **enviably** *adv*

envious *adj* feeling, showing, or resulting from envy **enviously** *adv*

environment (en-**vire**-on-ment) *n* **1** the surroundings in which a person, animal, or plant lives **2** *ecology* **the environment** the natural world of land, sea, air, plants, and animals: *nuclear waste must be prevented from leaking into the environment* [French *environs* surroundings] **environmental** *adj*

environmentalist *n* a person concerned with the protection and preservation of the natural environment

environs *pl n* a surrounding area, esp. the outskirts of a city

envisage *or US* **envision** *vb* **-aging, -aged** *or* **-ioning, -ioned** to believe to be possible or likely in the future: *the commission envisages a mix of government and private funding* [French *en-* in + *visage* face]

> **USAGE** It was formerly considered incorrect to use a clause after *envisage* as in *it is envisaged that the new centre will cost £40 million*, but this use is now acceptable.

envoy *n* **1** a messenger or representative **2** a diplomat ranking next below an ambassador [French *envoyer* to send]

envy *n, pl* **-vies** **1** a feeling of discontent aroused by someone else's possessions, achievements, or qualities **2** something that causes envy: *their standards are the envy of the world* ▹ *vb* **-vies, -vying, -vied** **3** to wish that one had the possessions, achievements, or qualities of (someone else) [Latin *invidia*] **envyingly** *adv*

enzyme *n* any of a group of complex proteins that act as catalysts in specific biochemical reactions [Greek *en-* in + *zumē* leaven] **enzymatic** *adj*

Eocene (**ee**-oh-seen) *adj* of the epoch of geological time about 55 million years ago [Greek *ēōs* dawn + *kainos* new]

Eolithic *adj* of the early period of the Stone Age, when crude stone tools were used

EP *n* an extended-play single, one of the formats in which music is sold, usually comprising four or five tracks

epaulette *n* a piece of ornamental material on the shoulder of a garment, esp. a military uniform [French]

épée (**ep**-pay) *n* a straight-bladed sword used in fencing

ephedrine (**eff**-fid-dreen) *n* an alkaloid used for the treatment of asthma and hay fever [*Ephedra*, genus of plants which produce it]

ephemera (if-**fem**-a-ra) *pl n* items designed to last only for a short time, such as programmes or posters

ephemeral *adj* lasting only for a short time [Greek *hēmera* day]

epic *n* **1** a long exciting book, poem, or film, usually telling of heroic deeds **2** a long narrative poem telling of the deeds of a legendary hero ▹ *adj* **3** very large or grand: *a professional feud of epic proportions* [Greek *epos* word, song]

epicene *adj* (esp. of a man) having characteristics or features that are not definitely male or female [Greek *epikoinos* common to many]

epicentre *or US* **epicenter** *n* the point on the earth's surface immediately above the origin of an earthquake [Greek *epi* above + *kentron* point]

epicure *n* a person who enjoys good food and drink [after *Epicurus*, Greek philosopher, who held that pleasure is the highest good] **epicurism** *n*

epicurean *adj* **1** devoted to sensual pleasures, esp. food and drink ▷ *n* **2** same as **epicure** **epicureanism** *n*

epidemic *n* **1** a widespread occurrence of a disease **2** a rapid development or spread of something: *the epidemic of childhood obesity* ▷ *adj* **3** (esp. of a disease) affecting many people in an area: *stress has now reached epidemic proportions* [Greek *epi* among + *dēmos* people]

epidemiology (ep-pid-deem-ee-**ol**-a-jee) *n* the branch of medical science concerned with the occurrence and control of diseases in populations **epidemiologist** *n*

epidermis *n* the thin protective outer layer of the skin [Greek *epi* upon + *derma* skin] **epidermal** *adj*

epidural (ep-pid-**dure**-al) *adj* **1** on or over the outermost membrane covering the brain and spinal cord (**dura mater**) ▷ *n* **2** **A** an injection of anaesthetic into the space outside the outermost membrane enveloping the spinal cord **B** anaesthesia produced by this method [from *dura mater*]

epiglottis *n* a thin flap of cartilage at the back of the mouth that covers the entrance to the larynx during swallowing [Greek *epi* upon + *glōtta* tongue]

epigram *n* **1** a witty remark **2** a short poem with a witty ending [Greek *epi* upon + *graphein* to write] **epigrammatic** *adj*

epigraph *n* **1** a quotation at the beginning of a book **2** an inscription on a monument or building [Greek *epi* upon + *graphein* to write]

epilepsy *n* a disorder of the central nervous system which causes periodic loss of consciousness and sometimes convulsions [Greek *epi* upon + *lambanein* to take]

epileptic *adj* **1** of or having epilepsy ▷ *n* **2** *sometimes offensive* a person who has epilepsy

> **USAGE** The use of *epileptic* as a noun can be offensive and should be avoided. Instead you should talk about *a person with epilepsy*.

epilogue *n* a short concluding passage or speech at the end of a book or play [Greek *epi* upon + *logos* word, speech]

epiphany (ip-**piff**-a-nee) *n, pl* **-nies** a moment of great or sudden revelation [Greek *epiphaneia* an appearing]

Epiphany *n, pl* **-nies** a Christian festival held on January 6 commemorating, in the Western church, the manifestation of Christ to the Magi and, in the Eastern church, the baptism of Christ

episcopacy (ip-**piss**-kop-a-see) *n Christianity* **1** government of a Church by bishops **2** *pl* **-cies** same as **episcopate**

episcopal (ip-**piss**-kop-al) *adj Christianity* of or relating to bishops [Greek *episkopos* overseer]

Episcopal Church *n* (in Scotland and the US) a self-governing branch of the Anglican Church

episcopalian *adj also* **episcopal** *Christianity* **1** practising or advocating Church government by bishops ▷ *n* **2** an advocate of such Church government

Episcopalian (ip-piss-kop-**pale**-ee-an) *adj* **1** of or relating to the Episcopal Church ▷ *n* **2** a member of this Church **Episcopalianism** *n*

episcopate (ip-**piss**-kop-it) *n Christianity* **1** the office, status, or term of office of a bishop **2** bishops collectively

episiotomy (ip-peez-ee-**ot**-tom-ee) *n, pl* **-tomies** an operation involving cutting into the area between the genitals and the anus sometimes performed during childbirth to make the birth easier

episode *n* **1** an event or series of events **2** any of the sections into which a novel or a television or radio serial is divided [Greek *epi* in addition + *eisodios* coming in]

episodic *adj* **1** resembling or relating to an episode **2** occurring at irregular and infrequent intervals

epistemology (ip-iss-stem-**ol**-a-jee) *n* the theory of knowledge, esp. the critical study of its validity, methods, and scope [Greek *epistēmē* knowledge] **epistemological** *adj* **epistemologist** *n*

epistle *n* **1** *formal or humorous* a letter **2** a literary work in letter form, esp. a poem [Greek *epistolē*]

Epistle *n New Testament* any of the letters written by the apostles

epistolary *adj* **1** of or relating to letters **2** (of a novel) presented in the form of a series of letters

epitaph *n* **1** a commemorative inscription on a tombstone **2** a commemorative speech or written passage [Greek *epi* upon + *taphos* tomb]

epithelium *n, pl* **-lia** *anatomy* a cellular tissue covering the external and internal surfaces of the body [Greek *epi* upon + *thēlē* nipple] **epithelial** *adj*

epithet *n* a word or short phrase used to describe someone or something: *these tracks truly deserve that overworked epithet 'classic'* [Greek *epitithenai* to add]

epitome (ip-**pit**-a-mee) *n* **1** a person or thing that is a typical example of a characteristic or class: *the epitome of rural tranquillity* **2** a summary, esp. of a written work [Greek *epitemnein* to abridge]

epitomize *or* **-mise** *vb* **-mizing, -mized** *or* **-mising, -mised** to be or make a perfect or typical example of

EPNS electroplated nickel silver

epoch (**ee**-pok) *n* **1** a long period of time marked by some predominant characteristic: *the cold-war epoch* **2** the beginning of a new or distinctive period: *the invention of nuclear weapons marked an epoch in the history of warfare* **3** *geol* a unit of time within a period during which a series of rocks is formed [Greek *epokhē* cessation] **epochal** *adj*

epoch-making *adj* very important or significant

eponymous (ip-**pon**-im-uss) *adj* **1** (of a person) being the person after whom a literary work, film, etc., is named: *the eponymous heroine in the film of Jane Eyre* **2** (of a literary work, film, etc.) named after its central character or creator: *The Stooges' eponymous debut album* [Greek *epōnumos* giving a significant name]

epoxy *chem* ▷ *adj* **1** of or containing an oxygen atom joined to two different groups that are themselves joined to other groups **2** of or consisting of an epoxy resin ▷ *n, pl* **epoxies** **3** an epoxy resin [Greek *epi* upon + OXY(GEN)]

epoxy resin *n* a tough resistant thermosetting synthetic resin, used in laminates and adhesives

EPROM *n computers* erasable programmable read-only memory: a storage device that can be reprogrammed to hold different data

Epsom salts *pl n* a medicinal preparation of hydrated magnesium sulphate, used to empty the bowels [after *Epsom*, a town in England]

equable (ek-wab-bl) *adj* **1** even-tempered and reasonable **2** (of a climate) not varying much throughout the year, and neither very hot nor very cold [Latin *aequabilis*] **equably** *adv*

equal *adj* **1** identical in size, quantity, degree, or intensity **2** having identical privileges, rights, or status **3** applying in the same way to all people or in all circumstances: *equal rights* **4 equal to** having the necessary strength, ability, or means for: *she was equal to any test the corporation put to her* ▷ *n* **5** a person or thing equal to another ▷ *vb* **equalling, equalled** *or US* **equaling, equaled 6** to be equal to; match **7** to make or do something equal to: *he has equalled his world record in the men's 100 metres* [Latin *aequalis*] **equally** *adv*

> **USAGE** The use of *more equal* as in *from now on their relationship will be a more equal one* is acceptable in modern English usage. *Equally* is preferred to *equally as* in sentences such as *reassuring the victims is equally important. Just as* is preferred to *equally as* in sentences such as *their surprise was just as great as his.*

equality *n, pl* **-ties** the state of being equal

equalize *or* **-ise** *vb* **-izing, -ized** *or* **-ising, -ised 1** to make equal or uniform **2** (in a sport) to reach the same score as one's opponent or opponents **equalization** *or* **-isation** *n* **equalizer** *or* **-iser** *n*

equal opportunity *n* the offering of employment or promotion equally to all, without discrimination as to sex, race, colour, etc.

equanimity *n* calmness of mind or temper; composure [Latin *aequus* even + *animus* mind, spirit]

equate *vb* **equating, equated 1** to make or regard as equivalent **2** *maths* to form an equation from **equatable** *adj*

equation *n* **1** a mathematical statement that two expressions are equal **2** a situation or problem in which a number of different factors need to be considered: *this plan leaves human nature out of the equation* **3** the act of equating **4** *chem* a representation of a chemical reaction using symbols of the elements

equator *n* an imaginary circle around the earth at an equal distance from the North Pole and the South Pole [Medieval Latin *(circulus) aequator (diei et noctis)* (circle) that equalizes (the day and night)]

equatorial *adj* of, like, or existing at or near the equator

equerry (ek-kwer-ee) *n, pl* **-ries** *Brit* an officer of the royal household who acts as a personal attendant to a member of the royal family [Old French *escuirie* group of squires]

equestrian *adj* **1** of or relating to horses and riding **2** on horseback: *an equestrian statue of the Queen* [Latin *equus* horse] **equestrianism** *n*

equidistant *adj* equally distant

equilateral *adj* **1** having all sides of equal length ▷ *n* **2** a geometric figure having all sides of equal length

equilibrium *n, pl* **-ria 1** a stable condition in which forces cancel one another **2** a state of mental and emotional balance; composure [Latin *aequi-* equal + *libra* balance]

equine *adj* of or like a horse [Latin *equus* horse]

equinoctial *adj* **1** relating to or occurring at an equinox ▷ *n* **2** a storm at or near an equinox

equinox *n* either of the two occasions when day and night are of equal length, around March 21 and September 23 [Latin *aequi-* equal + *nox* night]

equip *vb* **equipping, equipped 1** to provide with supplies, components, etc.: *the car comes equipped with a catalytic converter* **2** to provide with abilities, understanding, etc.: *stress is something we are all equipped to cope with* [Old French *eschiper* to fit out (a ship)]

equipment *n* **1** a set of tools or devices used for a particular purpose: *communications equipment* **2** an act of equipping

equipoise *n* the state of being perfectly balanced; equilibrium

equitable *adj* fair and reasonable **equitably** *adv*

equitation *n* the study of riding and horsemanship [Latin *equitare* to ride]

equities *pl n* same as **ordinary shares**

equity *n, pl* **-ties 1** the quality of being impartial; fairness **2** *law* a system of using principles of natural justice and fair conduct to reach a judgment when common law is inadequate or inappropriate **3** the difference in value between a person's debts and the value of the property on which they are secured: *negative equity* [Latin *aequus* level, equal]

Equity *n Brit, Austral & NZ* the actors' trade union

equivalent *n* **1** something that has the same use or function as something else: *Denmark's equivalent to Silicon Valley* ▷ *adj* **2** equal in value, quantity, significance, etc. **3** having the same or a similar effect or meaning [Latin *aequi-* equal + *valere* to be worth] **equivalence** *n*

equivocal *adj* **1** capable of varying interpretations; ambiguous **2** deliberately misleading or vague **3** of doubtful character or sincerity: *the party's commitment to genuine reform is equivocal* [Latin *aequi-* equal + *vox* voice] **equivocally** *adv*

equivocate *vb* **-cating, -cated** to use vague or ambiguous language in order to deceive someone or to avoid telling the truth **equivocation** *n* **equivocator** *n*

er *interj* a sound made when hesitating in speech

Er *chem* erbium

ER Queen Elizabeth [Latin *Elizabeth Regina*]

era *n* **1** a period of time considered as distinctive; epoch **2** an extended period of time measured from a fixed point: *the Communist era* **3** *geol* a major division of time [Latin *aera* counters, pieces of brass money]

eradicate *vb* **-cating, -cated** to destroy or get rid of completely: *measures to eradicate racism* [Latin *e-* out + *radix* root] **eradicable** *adj* **eradication** *n* **eradicator** *n*

erase *vb* **erasing, erased 1** to destroy all traces of: *he could not erase the memory of his earlier defeat* **2** to rub or wipe out (something written) **3** to remove sound or information from (a magnetic tape or disk) [Latin *e-* out + *radere* to scrape] **erasable** *adj*

eraser *n* an object, such as a piece of rubber, for erasing something written

erasure *n* **1** an erasing **2** the place or mark where something has been erased

Erato *n Greek myth* the Muse of love poetry

erbium *n chem* a soft silvery-white element of the lanthanide series of metals. Symbol: **Er** [after *Ytterby*, Sweden, where is was first found]

ere *conj, prep poetic* before [Old English *ǣr*]

e-reader *n* a portable device that allows users to download and read texts in electronic form

erect *vb* **1** to build **2** to raise to an upright position **3** to found or form: *the caricature of socialism erected by Lenin* ▷ *adj* **4** upright in posture or position **5** *physiol* (of the penis, clitoris, or nipples) firm or rigid after swelling with blood, esp. as a result of sexual excitement [Latin *erigere* to set up] **erection** *n*

erectile *adj physiol* (of an organ, such as the penis) capable of becoming erect

eremite (air-rim-mite) *n* a Christian hermit [Greek *erēmos* lonely]

ergo *conj* therefore [Latin]

ergonomic *adj* **1** designed to minimize effort and discomfort **2** of or relating to ergonomics

ergonomics *n* the study of the relationship between workers and their environment [Greek *ergon* work + (ECO)NOMICS]

ergot *n* **1** a disease of a cereal, such as rye, caused by a fungus **2** the dried fungus used in medicine [French: spur (of a cock)]

Erin *n archaic or poetic* Ireland [Irish Gaelic *Éirinn*]

ermine *n, pl* **-mines** *or* **-mine 1** the stoat in northern regions, where it has a white winter coat **2** the fur of this animal, used to trim state robes of judges, nobles, etc. [Medieval Latin *Armenius (mus)* Armenian (mouse)]

erne *or* **ern** *n* a fish-eating sea eagle [Old English *earn*]

Ernie *n* (in Britain) a machine that randomly selects winning numbers of Premium Bonds [acronym of Electronic Random Number Indicator Equipment]

erode *vb* **eroding, eroded 1** to wear down or away **2** to deteriorate or cause to deteriorate [Latin *e-* away + *rodere* to gnaw]

erogenous (ir-roj-in-uss) *adj* sensitive to sexual stimulation: *an erogenous zone* [Greek *erōs* love + *-genēs* born]

erosion *n* **1** the wearing away of rocks or soil by the action of water, ice, or wind **2** a gradual lessening or reduction: *an erosion of national sovereignty* **erosive** *or* **erosional** *adj*

erotic *adj* of, concerning, or arousing sexual desire or giving sexual pleasure [Greek *erōs* love] **erotically** *adv*

erotica *pl n* explicitly sexual literature or art

eroticism *n* **1** erotic quality or nature **2** the use of sexually arousing symbolism in literature or art **3** sexual excitement or desire

err *vb* **1** to make a mistake **2** to sin [Latin *errare*]

errand *n* **1** a short trip to get or do something for someone **2 run an errand** to make such a trip [Old English *ǣrende*]

errant *adj* **1** behaving in a way considered to be unacceptable: *an errant schoolboy* **2** *old-fashioned or literary* wandering in search of adventure: *a knight errant* [Latin *iter* journey] **errantry** *n*

erratic *adj* **1** irregular or unpredictable: *his increasingly erratic behaviour* ▷ *n* **2** *geol* a rock that has been transported by glacial action [Latin *errare* to wander] **erratically** *adv*

erratum *n, pl* **-ta** an error in writing or printing [Latin]

erroneous *adj* based on or containing an error or errors; incorrect **erroneously** *adv*

error *n* **1** a mistake, inaccuracy, or misjudgment **2** the act or state of being wrong or making a misjudgment: *the plane was shot down in error* **3** the amount by which the actual value of a quantity might differ from an estimate: *a 3% margin of error* [Latin]

ersatz (air-zats) *adj* made in imitation of something more expensive: *ersatz coffee* [German *ersetzen* to substitute]

Erse *n, adj* Irish Gaelic [Lowland Scots *Erisch* Irish]

erstwhile *adj* **1** former ▷ *adv* **2** *archaic* formerly

eruct *or* **eructate** *vb formal* to belch [Latin *e-* out + *ructare* to belch] **eructation** *n*

erudite (air-rude-ite) *adj* having or showing great academic knowledge [Latin *erudire* to polish] **erudition** *n*

erupt *vb* **1** (of a volcano) to throw out molten lava, ash, and steam in a sudden and violent way **2** to burst forth suddenly and violently: *riots erupted across the country* **3** (of a group of people) to suddenly become angry and aggressive: *the meeting erupted in fury* **4** (of a blemish) to appear on the skin [Latin *e-* out + *rumpere* to burst] **eruptive** *adj* **eruption** *n*

erysipelas (air-riss-sip-ill-ass) *n* an acute disease of the skin, with fever and raised purplish patches [Greek *erusi-* red + *-pelas* skin]

erythrocyte (ir-rith-roe-site) *n* a red blood cell that transports oxygen through the body [Greek *eruthros* red + *kutos* hollow vessel]

Es *chem* einsteinium

escalate *vb* **-lating, -lated** to increase or be increased in size, seriousness, or intensity [from *escalator*] **escalation** *n*

escalator *n* a moving staircase consisting of stair treads fixed to a conveyor belt [Latin *scala* ladder]

escalope (ess-kal-lop) *n* a thin slice of meat, usually veal [Old French: shell]

escapade *n* a mischievous act or adventure [French]

escape *vb* **-caping, -caped 1** to get away or break free from (confinement) **2** to manage to avoid (something dangerous, unpleasant, or difficult) **3** (of gases, liquids, etc.) to leak gradually **4** to elude; be forgotten by: *those little round cakes whose name escapes me* ▷ *n* **5** the act of escaping or state of having escaped **6** a way of avoiding something difficult, dangerous, or unpleasant: *his frequent illnesses provided an escape from intolerable stress* **7** a means of relaxation or relief: *he found temporary escape through the local cinema* **8** a leakage of gas or liquid [Late Latin *e-* out + *cappa* cloak]

escapee *n* a person who has escaped, esp. from prison

e

escapement *n* the mechanism in a clock or watch which connects the hands to the pendulum or balance

escape road *n* a small road leading off a steep hill, into which a car can be driven if the brakes fail

escape velocity *n* the minimum velocity necessary for a particle, space vehicle, etc. to escape from the gravitational field of the earth or other celestial body

escapism *n* an inclination to retreat from unpleasant reality, for example through fantasy **escapist** *n, adj*

escapologist *n* an entertainer who specializes in freeing himself or herself from chains, ropes, etc. **escapology** *n*

e

escarpment *n* the long continuous steep face of a ridge or mountain [French *escarpement*]

eschatology (ess-cat-**tol**-a-jee) *n* the branch of theology concerned with the end of the world [Greek *eskhatos* last] **eschatological** *adj*

escheat (iss-**cheat**) *law* ▷ *n* **1** (formerly) the return of property to the state in the absence of legal heirs **2** the property so reverting ▷ *vb* **3** to obtain (land) by escheat [Old French *escheoir* to fall to the lot of]

eschew (iss-**chew**) *vb* to avoid doing or being involved in (something disliked or harmful) [Old French *eschiver*] **eschewal** *n*

escort *n* **1** people or vehicles accompanying another to protect or guard them **2** a person who accompanies someone of the opposite sex on a social occasion ▷ *vb* **3** to act as an escort to [French *escorte*]

escritoire (ess-kree-**twahr**) *n* a writing desk with compartments and drawers [Medieval Latin *scriptorium* writing room in a monastery]

escudo (ess-**kew**-doe) *n, pl* **-dos** a former monetary unit of Portugal [Spanish: shield]

esculent *formal* ▷ *adj* **1** edible ▷ *n* **2** any edible substance [Latin *esculentus* good to eat]

escutcheon *n* **1** a shield displaying a coat of arms **2 blot on one's escutcheon** a stain on one's honour [Latin *scutum* shield]

Eskimo *sometimes offensive* ▷ *n* **1** *pl* **-mos** *or* **-mo** a member of a group of peoples who live in N Canada, Greenland, Alaska, and E Siberia **2** a language of these peoples ▷ *adj* **3** of these peoples [Algonquian *esquimawes*]

> **USAGE** *Eskimo* is considered by many people to be offensive.The peoples native to the area from western Greenland to NW Canada prefer to be called *Inuit*.

ESN *Brit* educationally subnormal; formerly used to designate a child of limited intelligence who needs special schooling

esoteric (ee-so-**ter**-rik) *adj* understood by only a small number of people, esp. because they have special knowledge [Greek *esōterō* inner] **esoterically** *adv*

ESP extrasensory perception

esp. especially

espadrille (ess-pad-**drill**) *n* a light canvas shoe with a braided cord sole [French]

espalier (ess-**pal**-yer) *n* **1** a shrub or fruit tree trained to grow flat **2** the trellis on which such plants are grown [French]

esparto *or* **esparto grass** *n, pl* **-tos** any of various grasses of S Europe and N Africa, used to make ropes, mats, etc. [Greek *spartos* a kind of rush]

especial *adj formal* same as **special** [Latin *specialis* individual]

> **USAGE** *Especial* and *especially* have a more limited use than *special* and *specially. Special* is preferred to *especial* when the sense is one of being out of the ordinary: *a special lesson; he has been specially trained. Special* is also used when something is referred to as being for a particular purpose: *the word was specially underlined for you.* Where an idea of pre-eminence or individuality is involved, either *especial* or *special* may be used: *he is my especial* (or *special*) *friend; he is especially* (or *specially*) *good at his job.* In informal English, however, *special* is usually preferred in all contexts.

especially *adv* **1** particularly: *people are dying, especially children and babies* **2** more than usually: *an especially virulent disease*

Esperanto *n* an international artificial language [literally: the one who hopes, pseudonym of Dr L. L. Zamenhof, its Polish inventor] **Esperantist** *n, adj*

espionage (ess-pyon-ahzh) *n* **1** the use of spies to obtain secret information, esp. by governments **2** the act of spying [French *espionnage*]

esplanade *n* a long open level stretch of ground, esp. beside the seashore or in front of a fortified place [French]

espousal *n* **1** adoption or support: *his espousal of the free market* **2** *old-fashioned* a marriage or engagement ceremony

espouse *vb* **-pousing, -poused 1** to adopt or give support to (a cause, ideal, etc.) **2** *old-fashioned* (esp. of a man) to marry [Latin *sponsare*]

espresso *n, pl* **-sos** coffee made by forcing steam or boiling water through ground coffee [Italian: pressed]

esprit (ess-**pree**) *n* spirit, liveliness, or wit [French]

esprit de corps (de **kore**) *n* consciousness of and pride in belonging to a particular group [French]

espy *vb* **espies, espying, espied** to catch sight of [Old French *espier*]

Esq. esquire

esquire *n* **1** *chiefly Brit* a title of respect placed after a man's name and usually shortened to *Esq.*: *I Davies, Esquire* **2** (in medieval times) the attendant of a knight [Late Latin *scutarius* shield bearer]

essay *n* **1** a short literary composition on a single subject **2** a short piece of writing on a subject done as an exercise by a student **3** an attempt ▷ *vb* **4** *formal* to attempt: *he essayed a faint smile* [Old French *essai* an attempt]

essayist *n* a person who writes essays

essence *n* **1** the most important and distinctive feature of something, which determines its identity **2** a concentrated liquid used to flavour food **3 in essence** essentially **4 of the essence** vitally important [Latin *esse* to be]

essential *adj* **1** vitally important; absolutely necessary: *it is essential to get this finished on time*

2 basic or fundamental: *she translated the essential points of the lecture into English* ▷ *n* 3 something fundamental or indispensable **essentially** *adv*

essential oil *n* any of various volatile oils in plants, which have the odour or flavour of the plant from which they are extracted

EST 1 Eastern Standard Time 2 electric-shock treatment

est. 1 established 2 estimate(d)

establish *vb* 1 to create or set up (an organization, link, etc.): *the regime wants to establish better relations with neighbouring countries* 2 to become firmly associated with a particular activity or reputation: *the play that established him as a major dramatist* 3 to prove: *a test to establish if your baby has any chromosomal disorder* 4 to cause (a principle) to be accepted: *our study establishes the case for further research* [Latin *stabilis* firm, stable]

Established Church *n* a church, such as the Church of England, that is recognized as the official church of a country

establishment *n* 1 the act of establishing or state of being established 2 A a business organization or other institution B a place of business 3 the people employed by an organization

Establishment *n* **the Establishment** a group of people having authority within a society: usually seen as conservative

estate *n* 1 a large piece of landed property, esp. in the country 2 *Brit & Austral* a large area of land with houses or factories built on it: *an industrial estate* 3 *law* property or possessions, esp. of a deceased person 4 *history* any of the orders or classes making up a society [Latin *status* condition]

estate agent *n Brit & Austral* a person whose job is to help people buy and sell houses and other property

estate car *n Brit* a car which has a long body with a door at the back end and luggage space behind the rear seats

estate duty *n* a former name for **inheritance tax**

esteem *n* 1 admiration and respect ▷ *vb* 2 to have great respect or high regard for (someone) 3 *formal* to judge or consider: *I should esteem it a kindness* [Latin *aestimare* to assess the worth of] **esteemed** *adj*

ester *n chem* a compound produced by the reaction between an acid and an alcohol [German]

estimable *adj* worthy of respect

estimate *vb* **-mating, -mated** 1 to form an approximate idea of (size, cost, etc.); calculate roughly 2 to form an opinion about; judge 3 to submit an approximate price for a job to a prospective client ▷ *n* 4 an approximate calculation 5 a statement of the likely charge for certain work 6 an opinion [Latin *aestimare* to assess the worth of] **estimator** *n*

estimation *n* 1 a considered opinion; judgment: *overall, he went up in my estimation* 2 the act of estimating

Estonian *adj* 1 from Estonia ▷ *n* 2 a person from Estonia

estranged *adj* 1 no longer living with one's husband or wife: *his estranged wife* 2 having quarrelled and lost touch with one's family or friends: *I am estranged from my son* [from Latin *extraneus* foreign] **estrangement** *n*

estuary *n, pl* **-aries** the widening channel of a river where it nears the sea [Latin *aestus* tide] **estuarine** *adj*

ET *Brit* Employment Training: (formerly) a government scheme offering training in technology and business skills for unemployed people

ETA estimated time of arrival

et al. 1 and elsewhere 2 and others [(sense 1) Latin *et alibi*; (sense 2) Latin *et alii*]

etc. et cetera

et cetera *or* **etcetera** (et **set**-ra) *adv* 1 and the rest; and others; or the like 2 and so forth [Latin *et* and + *cetera* the other (things)]

> **USAGE** It is unnecessary to use *and* before *etc.* as *etc.* (*et cetera*) already means *and other things.* The repetition of *etc.*, as in *he brought paper, ink, notebooks, etc., etc.*, is avoided except in informal contexts.

etceteras *pl n* miscellaneous extra things or people

etch *vb* 1 to wear away the surface of (a metal, glass, etc.) by the action of an acid 2 to cut (a design or pattern) into a printing plate with acid 3 to imprint vividly: *the scene is etched on my mind* [Dutch *etsen*] **etcher** *n*

etching *n* 1 the art or process of preparing or printing etched designs 2 a print made from an etched plate

eternal *adj* 1 without beginning or end; lasting for ever 2 unchanged by time: *eternal truths* 3 seemingly unceasing: *his eternal whingeing* 4 of or like God or a god: *the Eternal Buddha* [Latin *aeternus*] **eternally** *adv*

eternal triangle *n* an emotional or sexual relationship in which there are conflicts involving three people

eternity *n, pl* **-ties** 1 endless or infinite time 2 a seemingly endless period of time: *it seemed an eternity before he could feel his heart beating again* 3 the timeless existence after death 4 the state of being eternal

eternity ring *n* a ring given as a token of lasting affection, esp. one set all around with stones to symbolize continuity

ethane *n* a flammable gaseous alkane obtained from natural gas and petroleum: used as a fuel [from *ethyl*]

ethanoic acid *n* same as **acetic acid**

ethanol *n* same as **alcohol** (sense 1)

ethene *n* same as **ethylene**

ether *n* 1 a colourless sweet-smelling liquid used as a solvent and anaesthetic 2 the substance formerly believed to fill all space and to transmit electromagnetic waves 3 the upper regions of the atmosphere; clear sky ▷ Also (for senses 2 and 3): **aether** [Greek *aithein* to burn]

ethereal (eth-**eer**-ee-al) *adj* 1 extremely delicate or refined 2 heavenly or spiritual [Greek *aithēr* ether] **ethereally** *adv*

ethic *n* a moral principle or set of moral values held by an individual or group [Greek *ēthos* custom]

ethical *adj* **1** of or based on a system of moral beliefs about right and wrong **2** in accordance with principles of professional conduct **3** of or relating to ethics **ethically** *adv*

ethics *pl n* **1** a code of behaviour, esp. of a particular group, profession, or individual: *business ethics* **2** the moral fitness of a decision, course of action, etc. ▷ *n* **3** the study of the moral value of human conduct

Ethiopian *adj* **1** of Ethiopia ▷ *n* **2** a person from Ethiopia

e

ethnic *or* **ethnical** *adj* **1** of or relating to a human group with racial, religious, and linguistic characteristics in common **2** characteristic of another culture, esp. a peasant one: *ethnic foodstuffs* [Greek *ethnos* race] **ethnically** *adv*

ethnic cleansing *n* the practice, by the dominant ethnic group in an area, of removing other ethnic groups by expulsion or extermination

ethnocentric *adj* of or relating to the belief that one's own nation, culture, or group is intrinsically superior **ethnocentricity** *n*

ethnology *n* the branch of anthropology that deals with races and peoples and their relations to one another **ethnological** *adj* **ethnologist** *n*

ethos (eeth-oss) *n* the distinctive spirit and attitudes of a people, culture, etc. [Greek]

ethyl (eth-ill) *adj* of, consisting of, or containing the monovalent group C_2H_5– [from *ether*]

ethyl alcohol *n* same as **alcohol** (sense 1)

ethylene *or* **ethene** *n* a colourless flammable gaseous alkene used to make polythene and other chemicals

etiolate (ee-tee-oh-late) *vb* **-lating, -lated** **1** *formal* to become or cause to become weak **2** *botany* to make a green plant paler through lack of sunlight [French *étioler* to make pale] **etiolation** *n*

etiology *n, pl* **-gies** **1** the study of causation **2** the study of the cause of diseases [Greek *aitia* cause + -LOGY] **etiological** *adj*

etiquette *n* **1** the customs or rules of behaviour regarded as correct in social life **2** a conventional code of practice in certain professions [French]

étude (ay-tewd) *n music* a short composition for a solo instrument, esp. intended to be played as an exercise or to demonstrate virtuosity [French: study]

etymology *n, pl* **-gies** **1** the study of the sources and development of words **2** an account of the source and development of a word [Greek *etumon* basic meaning + -LOGY] **etymological** *adj* **etymologist** *n*

Eu *chem* europium

EU European Union

eucalyptus *or* **eucalypt** *n, pl* **-lyptuses, -lyptus** *or* **-lypts** any of a mostly Australian genus of trees, widely cultivated for timber and gum, and for the medicinal oil in their leaves (**eucalyptus oil**) [Greek *eu-* well + *kaluptos* covered]

Eucharist (yew-kar-ist) *n* **1** the Christian sacrament commemorating Christ's Last Supper by the consecration of bread and wine **2** the consecrated elements of bread and wine [Greek *eukharistos* thankful] **Eucharistic** *adj*

Euclidean *or* **Euclidian** (yew-klid-ee-an) *adj* denoting a system of geometry based on the rules of Euclid, 3rd-century BC Greek mathematician

eugenics (yew-jen-iks) *n* the study of methods of improving the human race, esp. by selective breeding [Greek *eugenēs* well-born] **eugenic** *adj* **eugenically** *adv* **eugenicist** *n*

eulogize *or* **-gise** *vb* **-gizing, -gized** *or* **-gising, -gised** to praise (a person or thing) highly in speech or writing **eulogistic** *adj*

eulogy *n, pl* **-gies** **1** a speech or piece of writing praising a person or thing, esp. a person who has recently died **2** high praise [Greek *eulogia* praise]
USAGE Avoid confusion with **elegy**.

eunuch *n* a man who has been castrated, esp. (formerly) a guard in a harem [Greek *eunoukhos* bedchamber attendant]

euphemism *n* an inoffensive word or phrase substituted for one considered offensive or upsetting, such as *departed* for *dead* [Greek *eu-* well + *phēmē* speech] **euphemistic** *adj* **euphemistically** *adv*

euphonious *adj* pleasing to the ear

euphonium *n* a brass musical instrument with four valves, resembling a small tuba [*euph(ony + harm)onium*]

euphony *n, pl* **-nies** a pleasing sound, esp. in speech [Greek *eu-* well + *phōnē* voice]

euphoria *n* a feeling of great but often unjustified or exaggerated happiness [Greek *eu-* well + *pherein* to bear] **euphoric** *adj*

Eur. **1** Europe **2** European

Eurasian *adj* **1** of Europe and Asia **2** of mixed European and Asian descent ▷ *n* **3** a person of mixed European and Asian descent

eureka (yew-reek-a) *interj* an exclamation of triumph on discovering or solving something [Greek *heurēka* I have found (it)]

euro *n, pl* **euros** the unit of the European Union's single currency

Euro- *combining form* Europe or European

Eurocentric *adj* chiefly concerned with Europe and European culture: *a Eurocentric view of British history*

Euroland *or* **Eurozone** *n* the geographical area containing the countries that have joined the European single currency

European *adj* **1** of Europe ▷ *n* **2** a person from Europe **3** a person of European descent **4** an advocate of closer links between the countries of Europe, esp. those in the European Union **Europeanism** *n*

European Community *or* **European Economic Community** *n* former names for **European Union**

European Union *n* an economic organization of European states, which have some shared monetary, social, and political goals

Europhile (you-roh-file) *n* **1** a person who admires Europe or the European Union ▷ *adj* **2** marked by admiration of Europe or the European Union

europium *n chem* a silvery-white element of the lanthanide series. Symbol: **Eu** [after *Europe*]
Eurozone *n* same as **Euroland**
Eustachian tube *n* a tube that connects the middle ear with the pharynx and equalizes the pressure between the two sides of the eardrum [after Bartolomeo *Eustachio*, anatomist]
Euterpe *n Greek myth* the Muse of lyric poetry
euthanasia *n* the act of killing someone painlessly, esp. to relieve suffering from an incurable illness [Greek: easy death]
euthanize *or* **-nise** *vb* **-nizing, -nized** *or* **-nising, -nised** to kill (a person or animal) painlessly, esp. to relieve suffering from an incurable illness. Also (Austral): **euthanaze** [back formation from EUTHANASIA]
eV electronvolt
evacuate *vb* **-ating, -ated 1** to send away from a dangerous place to a safe place: *200 people were evacuated from their homes because of the floods* **2** to empty (a place) of people because it has become dangerous: *the entire street was evacuated until the fire was put out* **3** *physiol* to discharge waste from the body [Latin *evacuare* to empty] **evacuation** *n* **evacuee** *n*
evade *vb* **evading, evaded 1** to get away from or avoid (imprisonment, captors, etc.) **2** to get around, shirk, or dodge (the law, a duty, etc.) **3** to avoid answering (a question) [Latin *evadere* to go forth]
evaluate *vb* **-ating, -ated** to find or judge the quality or value of (something) [French *évaluer*] **evaluation** *n*
evanesce *vb* **-nescing, -nesced** *formal* to fade gradually from sight [Latin *evanescere*]
evanescent *adj formal* quickly fading away; ephemeral or transitory **evanescence** *n*
evangelical *adj* **1** of or following from the Christian Gospels **2** of certain Protestant sects which emphasize salvation through faith alone and a belief in the absolute authority of the Bible **3** displaying missionary zeal in promoting something ▷ *n* **4** a member of an evangelical sect [Greek *evangelion* good news] **evangelicalism** *n* **evangelically** *adv*
evangelism *n* the practice of spreading the Christian gospel
evangelist *n Christianity* a preacher, sometimes itinerant **evangelistic** *adj*
Evangelist *n Christianity* any of the writers of the Gospels: Matthew, Mark, Luke, or John
evangelize *or* **-lise** *vb* **-lizing, -lized** *or* **-lising, -lised** to preach the Christian gospel (to) **evangelization** *or* **-lisation** *n*
evaporate *vb* **-rating, -rated 1** to change from a liquid or solid to a vapour **2** to become less and less and finally disappear: *faith in the government evaporated rapidly after the election* [Latin *e-* out + *vapor* steam] **evaporable** *adj* **evaporation** *n*
evaporated milk *n* thick unsweetened tinned milk from which some of the water has been removed
evasion *n* **1** the act of evading something, esp. a duty or responsibility, by cunning or illegal means: *tax evasion* **2** cunning or deception used to dodge a question, duty, etc.
evasive *adj* **1** seeking to evade; not straightforward: *an evasive answer* **2** avoiding or seeking to avoid trouble or difficulties: *evasive action* **evasively** *adv*
eve *n* **1** the evening or day before some special event **2** the period immediately before an event: *on the eve of the Second World War* **3** *poetic or old-fashioned* evening [variant of EVEN²]
Eve *n Bible* the first woman, created by God from Adam's rib
even¹ *adj* **1** level and regular; flat **2** on the same level: *make sure the surfaces are even with one another* **3** regular and unvarying: *an even pace* **4** equally balanced between two sides **5** equal in number, quantity, etc. **6** (of a number) divisible by two **7** denoting alternatives, events, etc., that have an equal probability: *they have a more than even chance of winning the next election* **8** having scored the same number of points **9 even money** *or* **evens** a bet in which the winnings are exactly the same as the amount staked **10 get even with** *informal* to exact revenge on; settle accounts with ▷ *adv* **11** used to suggest that the content of a statement is unexpected or paradoxical: *it's chilly in Nova Scotia, even in August* **12** used to intensify a comparative adjective or adverb: *an even greater demand* **13** used to introduce a word that is stronger and more accurate than one already used: *a normal, even inevitable aspect of ageing* **14** used preceding a hypothesis to emphasize that whether or not the condition is fulfilled, the statement remains valid: *the remark didn't call for an answer even if he could have thought of one* **15 even so** in spite of any assertion to the contrary; nevertheless **16 even though** despite the fact that ▷ See also **even out, even up** [Old English *efen*] **evenly** *adv* **evenness** *n*
even² *n poetic or old-fashioned* **1** eve **2** evening [Old English *ǣfen*]
even-handed *adj* fair; impartial
evening *n* **1** the latter part of the day, esp. from late afternoon until nightfall ▷ *adj* **2** of or in the evening: *the evening meal* [Old English *ǣfnung*]
evening class *n Brit, Austral & NZ* an educational class for adults, held during the evening
evening dress *n* clothes for a formal occasion during the evening
evening primrose *n* a plant with yellow flowers that open in the evening
evening star *n* a planet, usually Venus, seen shining brightly just after sunset
even out *vb* to make or become even, by the removal of bumps, inequalities, etc.
evensong *n Church of England* the daily evening service. Also called: **Evening Prayer**
event *n* **1** anything that takes place, esp. something important **2** a planned and organized occasion: *the wedding was one of the social events of the year* **3** any one contest in a sporting programme **4 in any event** *or* **at all events** whatever happens **5 in the event** when it came to the actual or final outcome: *in the event, neither of them turned up* **6 in the event of** if (such a thing) happens **7 in the event that** if it should happen that [Latin *evenire* to happen]
even-tempered *adj* calm and not easily angered

eventful *adj* full of exciting or important incidents
eventide *n archaic or poetic* evening
eventing *n Brit, Austral & NZ* riding competitions (esp. **three-day events**), usually involving cross-country riding, jumping, and dressage
eventual *adj* happening or being achieved at the end of a situation or process: *the Fascists' eventual victory in the Spanish Civil War* **eventually** *adv*
eventuality *n, pl* **-ties** a possible occurrence or result: *I was utterly unprepared for such an eventuality*
even up *vb* to make or become equal
ever *adv* **1** at any time: *it was the fourth fastest time ever* **2** always: *ever present* **3** used to give emphasis: *tell him to put to sea as soon as ever he can* **4 ever so** *or* **ever such** *informal, chiefly Brit* used to give emphasis: *I'm ever so sorry* [Old English *ǣfre*]
evergreen *adj* **1** (of certain trees and shrubs) bearing foliage throughout the year ▷ *n* **2** an evergreen tree or shrub
everlasting *adj* **1** never coming to an end; eternal **2** lasting so long or occurring so often as to become tedious **everlastingly** *adv*
evermore *adv* all time to come
every *adj* **1** each without exception: *they were winning every battle* **2** the greatest or best possible: *there is every reason to believe in the sincerity of their commitment* **3** each: *every 20 years* **4 every bit as** *informal* just as: *she's every bit as clever as you* **5 every other** each alternate: *every other month* [Old English *ǣfre* ever + *ǣlc* each]
everybody *pron* every person; everyone
USAGE See at **everyone**.
everyday *adj* **1** commonplace or usual **2** happening each day **3** suitable for or used on ordinary days
Everyman *n* the ordinary person; common man [after the central figure in a medieval morality play]
everyone *pron* every person; everybody
USAGE *Everyone* and *everybody* are interchangeable, as are *no one* and *nobody*, and *someone* and *somebody*. Care should be taken to distinguish between *everyone* and *someone* as single words and *every one* and *some one* as two words, the latter form correctly being used to refer to each individual person or thing in a particular group: *every one of them is wrong.*
everything *pron* **1** the whole; all things: *everything had been carefully packed* **2** the thing that is most important: *work was everything to her*
everywhere *adv* to or in all parts or places
evict *vb* to expel (someone) legally from his or her home or land [Latin *evincere* to vanquish utterly] **eviction** *n*
evidence *n* **1** something which provides ground for belief or disbelief: *there is no evidence that depression is inherited* **2** *law* matter produced before a court of law in an attempt to prove or disprove a point in issue **3 in evidence** on display; apparent ▷ *vb* **-dencing, -denced 4** to show clearly; demonstrate: *you evidenced no talent for music*
evident *adj* easy to see or understand [Latin *videre* to see] **evidently** *adv*
evidential *adj* of, serving as, or based on evidence **evidentially** *adv*
evil *n* **1** a force or power that brings about wickedness and harm: *the battle between good and evil* **2** a wicked or morally wrong act or thing: *the evil of racism* ▷ *adj* **3** (of a person) deliberately causing great harm and misery; wicked: *an evil dictator* **4** (of an act, idea, etc.) causing great harm and misery; morally wrong: *what you did was deeply evil* **5** very unpleasant: *it was fascinating to see people vanish as if we had some very evil smell* [Old English *yfel*] **evilly** *adv*
evildoer *n* a person who does evil **evildoing** *n*
evil eye *n* **the evil eye** a look superstitiously supposed to have the power of inflicting harm
evince *vb* **evincing, evinced** *formal* to show or display (a quality or feeling) clearly: *a humility which he had never evinced in earlier days* [Latin *evincere* to overcome]
USAGE *Evince* is sometimes wrongly used where *evoke* is meant: *the proposal evoked* (not *evinced*) *a storm of protest.*
eviscerate *vb* **-ating, -ated** to remove the internal organs of; disembowel [Latin *e-* out + *viscera* entrails] **evisceration** *n*
evocation *n* the act of evoking **evocative** *adj*
evoke *vb* **evoking, evoked 1** to call or summon up (a memory or feeling) from the past **2** to provoke or bring about: *his sacking evoked a huge public protest* [Latin *evocare* to call forth]
USAGE See at **evince** and **invoke**.
evolution *n* **1** *biol* a gradual change in the characteristics of a population of animals or plants over successive generations **2** a gradual development, esp. to a more complex form [Latin *evolutio* an unrolling] **evolutionary** *adj*
evolve *vb* **evolving, evolved 1** to develop gradually **2** (of animal or plant species) to undergo evolution [Latin *evolvere* to unfold]
e-voting *n* the application of electronic technology to cast and count votes in an election
ewe *n* a female sheep [Old English *ēowu*]
ewer *n* a large jug with a wide mouth [Latin *aqua* water]
ex[1] *prep finance* excluding or without: *ex dividend* [Latin: out of, from]
ex[2] *n, pl* **exes** *informal* one's former wife, husband, or romantic partner
ex- *prefix* **1** out of, outside, or from: *exit* **2** former: *his famous ex-wife* [Latin]
exacerbate (ig-zass-er-bate) *vb* **-bating, -bated** to make (pain, emotion, or a situation) worse [Latin *acerbus* bitter] **exacerbation** *n*
exact *adj* **1** correct in every detail; strictly accurate **2** precise, as opposed to approximate **3** based on measurement and the formulation of laws: *forecasting floods is not an exact science* ▷ *vb* **4** to obtain or demand as a right, esp. through force or strength: *the rebels called for revenge to be exacted for the killings* [Latin *exigere* to demand]
exacting *adj* making rigorous or excessive demands
exaction *n formal* **1** the act of obtaining or demanding money as a right **2** a sum or payment exacted
exactitude *n* the quality of being exact; precision

exactly *adv* **1** with complete accuracy and precision: *I don't know exactly where they live* **2** in every respect: *he looks exactly like his father* ▷ *interj* **3** just so! precisely!

exaggerate *vb* **-rating, -rated 1** to regard or represent as greater than is true **2** to make greater or more noticeable [Latin *exaggerare* to heap up] **exaggerated** *adj* **exaggeratedly** *adv* **exaggeration** *n*

exalt *vb* **1** to praise highly **2** to raise to a higher rank [Latin *exaltare* to raise] **exalted** *adj* **exaltation** *n*

> **USAGE** *Exalt* is sometimes wrongly used where *exult* is meant: *he was exulting* (not *exalting*) *in his win earlier that day.*

exam *n* short for **examination**

examination *n* **1** the act of examining **2** *education* exercises, questions, or tasks set to test a person's knowledge and skill **3** *med* physical inspection of a patient **4** *law* the formal questioning of a person on oath

examine *vb* **-mining, -mined 1** to inspect carefully or in detail; investigate **2** *education* to test the knowledge of (a candidate) in (a subject) **3** *med* to investigate the state of health of (a patient) **4** *law* to formally question (someone) on oath [Latin *examinare* to weigh] **examinee** *n* **examiner** *n*

example *n* **1** a specimen that is typical of its group; sample: *a fine example of Georgian architecture* **2** a particular event, object, or person that demonstrates a point or supports an argument, theory, etc.: *Germany is a good example of how federalism works in practice* **3** a person, action, or thing that is worthy of imitation **4** a punishment or the person punished regarded as a warning to others **5 for example** as an illustration [Latin *exemplum*]

exasperate *vb* **-rating, -rated** to cause great irritation to [Latin *exasperare* to make rough] **exasperated** *adj* **exasperating** *adj* **exasperation** *n*

ex cathedra *adj, adv* **1** with the authority of one's official position **2** *RC Church* (of doctrines of faith or morals) defined by the pope as infallibly true [Latin: from the chair]

excavate *vb* **-vating, -vated 1** to unearth (buried objects) methodically to discover information about the past **2** to make a hole in something by digging into it or hollowing it out: *one kind of shrimp excavates a hole for itself* [Latin *excavare* to make hollow] **excavation** *n* **excavator** *n*

exceed *vb* **1** to be greater in degree or quantity **2** to go beyond the limit of (a restriction) [Latin *excedere* to go beyond]

exceedingly *adv* very; extremely

excel *vb* **-celling, -celled 1** to be better than; surpass **2 excel in** *or* **at** to be outstandingly good at [Latin *excellere* to rise up]

excellence *n* the quality of being exceptionally good

Excellency *or* **Excellence** *n, pl* **-lencies** *or* **-lences** > **Your** *or* **His** *or* **Her Excellency** a title used to address a high-ranking official, such as an ambassador

excellent *adj* exceptionally good; outstanding

except *prep* **1** Also: **except for** not including; apart from: *everyone except Jill laughed* **2 except that** but for the fact that ▷ *vb* **3** to leave out or exclude [Latin *excipere* to take out]

excepting *prep* except

> **USAGE** The use of *excepting* is considered by many people to be acceptable only after *not, only, always,* or *without*. Elsewhere *except* is preferred: *every country agreed to the proposal except* (not *excepting*) *Spain; he was well again except for* (not *excepting*) *a slight pain in his chest.*

exception *n* **1** anything excluded from or not conforming to a general rule or classification **2 take exception to** to make objections to

exceptionable *adj* open to objection

exceptional *adj* **1** forming an exception **2** having much more than average intelligence, ability, or skill **exceptionally** *adv*

excerpt *n* **1** a passage taken from a book, speech, etc.; extract ▷ *vb* **2** to take a passage from a book, speech, etc. [Latin *excerptum* (something) picked out]

excess *n* **1** the state or act of going beyond normal or permitted limits **2** an immoderate or abnormal amount **3** the amount, number, etc., by which one thing exceeds another **4** behaviour regarded as too extreme or immoral to be acceptable: *a life of sex, drugs, and drunken excess* **5 excesses** acts or actions that are unacceptably cruel or immoral: *one of the bloodiest excesses of a dictatorial regime* **6 in excess of** more than **7 to excess** to an extreme or unhealthy extent: *he had started to drink to excess* ▷ *adj* **8** more than normal, necessary, or permitted: *excess fat* [Latin *excedere* to go beyond] **excessive** *adj* **excessively** *adv*

excess luggage *or* **excess baggage** *n* luggage that is more in weight or number of pieces than is allowed by one's terms of travel with an airline, etc.

exchange *vb* **-changing, -changed 1** (of two or more people, governments, etc.) to give each other (something similar) at the same time: *they nervously exchanged smiles* **2** to replace (one thing) with another, esp. to replace unsatisfactory goods: *could I exchange this for a larger size, please?* ▷ *n* **3** the act of exchanging **4** anything given or received as an equivalent or substitute for something else **5** an argument **6** Also called: **telephone exchange** a centre in which telephone lines are interconnected **7** a place where securities or commodities are traded, esp. by brokers or merchants **8** a transfer of sums of money of equivalent value, as between different currencies **9** the system by which commercial debts are settled, esp. by bills of exchange, without direct payment of money [Latin *cambire* to barter] **exchangeable** *adj*

exchange rate *n* the rate at which the currency unit of one country may be exchanged for that of another

Exchequer *n* *government* (in Britain and certain other countries) the accounting department of the Treasury [Old French *eschequier* counting table]

excise[1] *n* **1** a tax on goods, such as alcoholic drinks, produced for the home market **2** *Brit* that section of the government service responsible for the collection of excise, now the Board of Customs and Excise [Latin *assidere* to sit beside, assist in judging]

excise[2] *vb* **-cising, -cised 1** to delete a passage from a book **2** to remove an organ or part surgically [Latin *excidere* to cut down] **excision** *n*

exciseman *n, pl* **-men** *Brit* (formerly) a government agent who collected excise and prevented smuggling

excitable *adj* nervous and easily excited **excitability** *n*

excite *vb* **-citing, -cited 1** to make (a person) feel so happy that he or she is unable to relax because he or she is looking forward eagerly to something: *he was excited at the long-awaited arrival of a son* **2** to cause or arouse (an emotion, response, etc.): *the idea strongly excited his interest* **3** to arouse sexually **4** *physiol* to cause a response in (an organ, tissue, or part) **5** *physics* to raise (an atom, molecule, etc.) to a higher energy level [Latin *exciere* to stimulate] **excited** *adj* **excitedly** *adv*

excitement *n* **1** the state of being excited **2** a person or thing that excites

exciting *adj* causing excitement; stirring; stimulating **excitingly** *adv*

exclaim *vb* to cry out or speak suddenly or excitedly, as from surprise, delight, horror, etc. [Latin *exclamare*]

exclamation *n* **1** an abrupt or excited cry or utterance **2** the act of exclaiming **exclamatory** *adj*

exclamation mark *or US* **exclamation point** *n* the punctuation mark (!) used after exclamations and forceful commands

exclude *vb* **-cluding, -cluded 1** to keep out; prevent from entering **2** to leave out of consideration [Latin *excludere*] **exclusion** *n*

excluding *prep* excepting

exclusive *adj* **1** excluding or incompatible with anything else: *these two theories are mutually exclusive* **2** not shared: *exclusive rights* **3** used or lived in by a privileged minority, esp. a fashionable clique: *an exclusive skiing resort* **4** not including the numbers, dates, etc., mentioned **5 exclusive of** except for; not taking account of **6 exclusive to** limited to; found only in ▷ *n* **7** a story reported in only one newspaper **exclusively** *adv* **exclusivity** *or* **exclusiveness** *n*

excommunicate *vb* **-cating, -cated** *Christianity* to expel (someone) from membership of a church and ban him or her from taking part in its services [Late Latin *excommunicare* to exclude from the community] **excommunication** *n*

excoriate *vb* **-ating, -ated 1** *literary* to censure severely **2** to strip skin from (a person or animal) [Late Latin *excoriare* to strip, flay] **excoriation** *n*

excrement *n* waste matter discharged from the body; faeces [Latin *excernere* to sift, excrete] **excremental** *adj*

excrescence *n* something that protrudes, esp. an outgrowth from a part of the body [Latin *excrescrere* to grow out] **excrescent** *adj*

excreta (ik-skree-ta) *pl n* urine and faeces discharged from the body

excrete *vb* **-creting, -creted** to discharge waste matter, such as urine, sweat, or faeces, from the body [Latin *excernere* to discharge] **excretion** *n* **excretory** *adj*

excruciating *adj* **1** unbearably painful; agonizing **2** hard to bear: *never had an afternoon passed with such excruciating slowness* [Latin *excruciare* to torture] **excruciatingly** *adv*

exculpate *vb* **-pating, -pated** to free from blame or guilt [Latin *ex* from + *culpa* fault]

excursion *n* a short outward and return journey, esp. for sightseeing, etc.; outing [Latin *excurrere* to run out]

excuse *n* **1** an explanation offered to justify an action which has been criticized or as a reason for not fulfilling an obligation, etc. ▷ *vb* **-cusing, -cused 2** to put forward a reason or justification for (an action, fault, or offending person) **3** to pardon (a person) or overlook (a fault) **4** to free (someone) from having to carry out a task, obligation, etc.: *a doctor's letter excusing him from games at school* **5** to allow to leave **6 be excused** *euphemistic* to go to the toilet **7 excuse me!** an expression used to catch someone's attention or to apologize for an interruption, disagreement, etc. [Latin *ex* out + *causa* cause, accusation] **excusable** *adj*

ex-directory *adj Brit & NZ* not listed in a telephone directory by request

execrable (eks-sik-rab-bl) *adj* of very poor quality [see EXECRATE] **execrably** *adv*

execrate *vb* **-crating, -crated 1** to feel and express loathing and hatred of (someone or something) **2** to curse (a person or thing) [Latin *exsecrari* to curse] **execration** *n*

executable *computers* ▷ *adj* **1** (of a program) able to be run ▷ *n* **2** a file containing a program that will run as soon as it is opened

execute *vb* **-cuting, -cuted 1** to put (a condemned person) to death **2** to carry out or accomplish **3** to produce or create (a work of art) **4** *law* to render (a deed) effective, for example by signing it **5** to carry out the terms of (a contract, will, etc.) [Old French *executer*] **executer** *n*

execution *n* **1** the act of executing **2** the carrying out or undergoing of a sentence of death **3** the manner in which something is performed; technique

executioner *n* a person whose job is to kill people who have been sentenced to death

executive *n* **1** a person or group responsible for the administration of a project or business **2** the branch of government responsible for carrying out laws, decrees, etc. ▷ *adj* **3** having the function of carrying plans, orders, laws, etc., into effect: *the executive producer* **4** of or for executives: *the executive car park* **5** *informal* very expensive or exclusive: *executive cars*

executor *or fem* **executrix** *n law* a person appointed by someone to ensure that the conditions set out in his or her will are carried out **executorial** *adj*

exegesis (eks-sij-jee-siss) *n, pl* **-ses** (-seez) explanation of a text, esp. of the Bible [Greek *exēgeisthai* to interpret]

exemplar *n* **1** a person or thing to be copied; model **2** a typical specimen; example [Latin *exemplum* example]

exemplary *adj* **1** so good as to be an example worthy of imitation **2** (of a punishment) extremely harsh, so as to discourage others from committing a similar crime

exemplify *vb* **-fies, -fying, -fied 1** to show by example **2** to serve as an example of [Latin *exemplum* example + *facere* to make] **exemplification** *n*

exempt *adj* **1** not subject to an obligation, tax, etc. ▷ *vb* **2** to release (someone) from an obligation, tax, etc. [Latin *exemptus* removed] **exemption** *n*

exequies (eks-sik-weez) *pl n, sing* **-quy** funeral rites [Latin *exequiae*]

exercise *n* **1** physical exertion, esp. for training or keeping fit **2** an activity planned to achieve a particular purpose: *the group's meeting was mainly an exercise in mutual reassurance* **3** a set of movements, tasks, etc., designed to improve or test one's ability or fitness **4** the use or practice of (a right, power, or authority) **5** *military* a manoeuvre or simulated combat operation ▷ *vb* **-cising, -cised 6** to put into use; make use of: *we urge all governments involved to exercise restraint* **7** to take exercise or perform exercises **8** to practise using in order to develop or train: *to exercise one's voice* **9** to worry or vex: *the government has been exercised by the threat from international criminal groups* **10** *military* to carry out simulated combat, manoeuvres, etc. [Latin *exercere* to drill] **exerciser** *n*

exert *vb* **1** to use influence, authority, etc. forcefully or effectively **2 exert oneself** to make a special effort [Latin *exserere* to thrust out]

exertion *n* **1** effort or exercise, esp. physical effort: *the sudden exertion of running for a bus* **2** the act or an instance of using one's influence, powers, or authority: *the exertion of parental authority*

exeunt (eks-see-unt) they go out: used as a stage direction [Latin]

exfoliate *vb* **-ating, -ated 1** to peel off in scales or layers **2** to remove dead cells from the skin by washing with a granular cosmetic preparation **exfoliation** *n*

ex-gratia (eks-gray-sha) *adj* given as a favour where no legal obligation exists: *an ex-gratia payment* [New Latin: out of kindness]

exhale *vb* **-haling, -haled 1** to expel breath or smoke from the lungs; breathe out **2** to give off or be given off as gas, fumes, etc.: *the crater exhaled smoke* [Latin *exhalare*] **exhalation** *n*

exhaust *vb* **1** to tire out **2** to use up totally **3** to discuss (a topic) so thoroughly that no more remains to be said ▷ *n* **4** gases ejected from an engine as waste products **5** the parts of an engine through which waste gases pass [Latin *exhaurire* to draw out] **exhausted** *adj* **exhaustible** *adj*

exhaustion *n* **1** extreme tiredness **2** the act of exhausting or state of being exhausted

exhaustive *adj* very thorough; comprehensive **exhaustively** *adv*

exhibit *vb* **1** to display (a work of art) to the public **2** to show (a quality or feeling): *they exhibited extraordinary courage* ▷ *n* **3** an object exhibited to the public **4** *law* a document or object produced in court as evidence [Latin *exhibere* to hold forth] **exhibitor** *n*

exhibition *n* **1** a public display of art, skills, etc. **2** the act of exhibiting or the state of being exhibited: *an exhibition of bad temper* **3 make an exhibition of oneself** to behave so foolishly that one attracts public attention

exhibitionism *n* **1** a compulsive desire to attract attention to oneself **2** a compulsive desire to expose one's genitals publicly **exhibitionist** *n*

exhilarate *vb* **-rating, -rated** to make (someone) feel lively and cheerful [Latin *exhilarare*] **exhilaration** *n*

exhilarating *adj* causing strong feelings of excitement and happiness

exhort *vb formal* to urge (someone) earnestly [Latin *exhortari*] **exhortation** *n*

exhume (ig-zyume) *vb* **-huming, -humed** *formal* to dig up something buried, esp. a corpse [Latin *ex* out + *humus* the ground] **exhumation** *n*

exigency *n, pl* **-gencies** *formal* **1** an urgent demand or need **2** an emergency [Latin *exigere* to require] **exigent** *adj*

exiguous *adj formal* scanty or meagre [Latin *exiguus*] **exiguity** *n*

exile *n* **1** a prolonged, usually enforced absence from one's country **2** a person banished or living away from his or her country ▷ *vb* **-iling, -iled 3** to expel (someone) from his or her country; banish [Latin *exsilium*]

exist *vb* **1** to have being or reality; be: *does God exist?* **2** to only just be able to keep oneself alive, esp. because of poverty or hunger **3** to be living; live **4** to be present under specified conditions or in a specified place [Latin *exsistere* to step forth] **existing** *adj*

existence *n* **1** the fact or state of being real, live, or actual **2** a way of life, esp. a poor or hungry one **3** everything that exists **existent** *adj*

existential *adj* **1** of or relating to existence, esp. human existence **2** of or relating to existentialism

existentialism *n* a philosophical movement stressing personal experience and responsibility of the individual, who is seen as a free agent **existentialist** *adj, n*

exit *n* **1** a way out **2** the act of going out **3** *theatre* the act of going offstage **4** *Brit & Austral* a point at which vehicles may leave a motorway ▷ *vb* **exiting, exited 5** to go away or out; depart **6** *theatre* he or she goes offstage: used as a stage direction: *exit bleeding from the room* [Latin *exire* to go out]

exocrine *adj* of or denoting a gland, such as the sweat gland, that discharges its product through a duct [Greek *exō* outside + *krinein* to separate]

exodus (eks-so-duss) *n* the departure of a large number of people [Greek *ex* out + *hodos* way]

Exodus *n Bible* the second book of the Old Testament, containing a description of the departure of the Israelites from Egypt

ex officio (eks off-fish-ee-oh) *adv, adj* by right of position or office [Latin]

e

exonerate *vb* **-ating, -ated** to clear (someone) of blame or a criminal charge [Latin *exonerare* to free from a burden] **exoneration** *n*

exorbitant *adj* (of prices, demands, etc.) excessively great or high: *an exorbitant rent* [Latin *ex* out, away + *orbita* track] **exorbitantly** *adv*

exorcize *or* **-cise** *vb* **-cizing, -cized** *or* **-cising, -cised** to expel (evil spirits) by prayers and religious rites [Greek *ex* out + *horkos* oath] **exorcism** *n* **exorcist** *n*

exoskeleton *n zool* the protective or supporting structure covering the outside of the body of many animals, for example insects or crabs

e

exothermic *adj* (of a chemical reaction) involving or leading to the giving off of heat

exotic *adj* **1** having a strange allure or beauty **2** originating in a foreign country; not native ▷ *n* **3** a non-native plant [Greek *exō* outside] **exotically** *adv*

exotica *pl n* exotic objects, esp. as a collection

expand *vb* **1** to make or become greater in extent, size, or scope **2** to spread out; unfold **3 expand on** to go into more detail about (a story or subject) **4** to become increasingly relaxed, friendly, and talkative **5** *maths* to express a function or expression as the sum or product of terms [Latin *expandere* to spread out] **expandable** *adj*

expanse *n* an uninterrupted wide area; stretch: *a large expanse of water*

expansible *adj* able to expand or be expanded

expansion *n* **1** the act of expanding **2** an increase or development, esp. in the activities of a company

expansionism *n* the practice of expanding the economy or territory of a country **expansionist** *n, adj*

expansive *adj* **1** wide or extensive **2** friendly, open, and talkative **expansiveness** *n*

expat *adj, n* short for **expatriate**

expatiate (iks-pay-shee-ate) *vb* **-ating, -ated** > **expatiate on** *formal* to speak or write at length on (a subject) [Latin *exspatiari* to digress] **expatiation** *n*

expatriate (eks-pat-ree-it) *adj* **1** living away from one's native country: *an expatriate American* **2** exiled ▷ *n* **3** a person living away from his or her native country **4** an exile [Latin *ex* out, away + *patria* native land] **expatriation** *n*

expect *vb* **1** to regard as likely **2** to look forward to or be waiting for **3** to require (something) as an obligation: *he expects an answer by January* **4 be expecting** *informal* to be pregnant [Latin *exspectare* to watch for]

expectancy *n* **1** something expected, esp. on the basis of a norm: *a life expectancy of 78* **2** anticipation or expectation

expectant *adj* **1** expecting or hopeful **2 A** pregnant **B** being the partner of a woman who is pregnant: *an expectant father* **expectantly** *adv*

expectation *n* **1** the state of expecting or of being expected **2** something looked forward to, whether feared or hoped for **3** belief that someone should behave in a particular way: *women with expectations of old-fashioned gallantry*

expectorant *med* ▷ *adj* **1** helping to bring up phlegm from the respiratory passages ▷ *n* **2** an expectorant medicine

expectorate *vb* **-rating, -rated** *formal* to cough up and spit out (phlegm from the respiratory passages) [Latin *expectorare* to drive from the breast, expel] **expectoration** *n*

expediency *or* **expedience** *n, pl* **-encies** *or* **-ences** **1** the use of methods that are advantageous rather than fair or just **2** appropriateness or suitability

expedient (iks-pee-dee-ent) *n* **1** something that achieves a particular purpose: *income controls were used only as a short-term expedient* ▷ *adj* **2** useful or advantageous in a given situation: *they only talk about human rights when it is politically expedient* [Latin *expediens* setting free; see EXPEDITE]

expedite *vb* **-diting, -dited** *formal* **1** to hasten the progress of **2** to do quickly [Latin *expedire* to free the feet]

expedition *n* **1** an organized journey or voyage, esp. for exploration **2** the people and equipment comprising an expedition **3** a pleasure trip or excursion: *an expedition to the seaside* [Latin *expedire* to prepare, expedite] **expeditionary** *adj*

expeditious *adj* done quickly and efficiently

expel *vb* **-pelling, -pelled** **1** to drive out with force **2** to dismiss from a school, club, etc., permanently [Latin *expellere*]

expend *vb formal* to spend or use up (time, energy, or money) [Latin *expendere* to weigh out, pay]

expendable *adj* **1** not worth preserving **2** able to be sacrificed to achieve an objective, esp. a military one

expenditure *n* **1** something expended, esp. money **2** the amount expended

expense *n* **1** a particular payment of money; expenditure **2** the amount of money needed to buy or do something; cost **3 expenses** money spent in the performance of a job, etc. **4** something requiring money for its purchase or upkeep **5 at the expense of** to the detriment of [Latin *expensus* weighed out]

expense account *n* **1** an arrangement by which an employee's expenses are refunded by his or her employer **2** a record of such expenses

expensive *adj* costing a great deal of money **expensiveness** *n*

experience *n* **1** direct personal participation or observation of something: *his experience of prison life* **2** a particular incident, feeling, etc., that a person has undergone **3** accumulated knowledge, esp. of practical matters ▷ *vb* **-encing, -enced** **4** to participate in or undergo **5** to be moved by; feel [Latin *experiri* to prove]

experienced *adj* skilful or knowledgeable as a result of having done something many times before

experiential *adj philosophy* relating to or derived from experience

experiment *n* **1** a test or investigation to provide evidence for or against a theory: *a scientific experiment* **2** the trying out of a new idea or method ▷ *vb* **3** to carry out an experiment or experiments [Latin *experiri* to test] **experimentation** *n* **experimenter** *n*

experimental *adj* **1** relating to, based on, or having the nature of an experiment **2** trying out new ideas or methods **experimentally** *adv*

expert *n* **1** a person who has extensive skill or knowledge in a particular field ▷ *adj* **2** skilful or knowledgeable **3** of, involving, or done by an expert [Latin *expertus* known by experience] **expertly** *adv*

expertise (eks-per-**teez**) *n* special skill, knowledge, or judgment [French]

expiate *vb* **-ating, -ated** *formal* to make amends for (a sin or wrongdoing) [Latin *expiare*] **expiation** *n*

expiration *n* **1** the finish of something; expiry **2** the act, process, or sound of breathing out **expiratory** *adj*

expire *vb* **-piring, -pired 1** to finish or run out; come to an end **2** to breathe out air **3** to die [Latin *exspirare* to breathe out]

expiry *n, pl* **-ries** a coming to an end, esp. of the period of a contract

explain *vb* **1** to make something easily understandable, esp. by giving a clear and detailed account of it **2 explain oneself** to justify or attempt to justify oneself by giving reasons for one's actions **3 explain away** to offer excuses or reasons for (mistakes) [Latin *explanare* to flatten, make clear]

explanation *n* **1** the reason or reasons why a particular event or situation happened: *there is no reasonable explanation for her behaviour* **2** a detailed account or description: *a 90-minute explanation of his love of jazz*

explanatory *adj* serving or intended to serve as an explanation

expletive (iks-**plee**-tiv) *n* an exclamation or swearword expressing emotion rather than meaning [Latin *explere* to fill up]

explicable *adj* capable of being explained

explicate *vb* **-cating, -cated** *formal* to make clear; explain [Latin *explicare* to unfold] **explication** *n*

explicit *adj* **1** precisely and clearly expressed, leaving nothing to implication: *an explicit commitment to democracy* **2** leaving little to the imagination; graphically detailed: *the film contains some sexually explicit scenes* **3** (of a person) expressing something in a precise and clear way, so as to leave no doubt about what is meant [Latin *explicitus* unfolded] **explicitly** *adv*

explode *vb* **-ploding, -ploded 1** to burst with great violence; blow up **2** (of a gas) to undergo a sudden violent expansion as a result of a fast chemical or nuclear reaction **3** to react suddenly or violently with emotion **4** (esp. of a population) to increase rapidly **5** to show (a theory, etc.) to be baseless [Latin *explodere* to drive off by clapping]

exploit *vb* **1** to take advantage of (a person or situation) for one's own ends **2** to make the best use of ▷ *n* **3** a notable deed or feat [Old French: accomplishment] **exploitation** *n* **exploiter** *n*

exploitative *adj* tending to take advantage of a person or situation for one's own ends

explore *vb* **-ploring, -plored 1** to examine or investigate, esp. systematically **2** to travel into an unfamiliar region, esp. for scientific purposes [Latin *ex* out + *plorare* to cry aloud] **exploration** *n* **exploratory** *or* **explorative** *adj* **explorer** *n*

explosion *n* **1** an exploding **2** a violent release of energy resulting from a rapid chemical or nuclear reaction **3** a sudden or violent outburst of activity, noise, emotion, etc. **4** a rapid increase

explosive *adj* **1** able or likely to explode **2** potentially violent: *an explosive situation* ▷ *n* **3** a substance capable of exploding **explosiveness** *n*

expo *n, pl* **-pos** short for **exposition** (sense 3)

exponent *n* **1** a person who advocates an idea, cause, etc.: *an exponent of free speech* **2** a person who is a skilful performer of some activity: *one of the greatest modern exponents of the blues* **3** *maths* a number placed as a superscript to another number indicating how many times the number is to be used as a factor [Latin *exponere* to expound]

exponential *adj* **1** *maths* of or involving numbers raised to an exponent **2** *informal* very rapid **exponentially** *adv*

export *n* **1** the sale of goods and services to a foreign country: *a ban on the export of arms* **2 exports** goods or services sold to a foreign country ▷ *vb* **3** to sell (goods or services) or transport (goods) to a foreign country [Latin *exportare* to carry away] **exporter** *n*

expose *vb* **-posing, -posed 1** to uncover (something previously covered) **2** to reveal the truth about (someone or something), esp. when it is shocking or scandalous: *an MP whose private life was recently exposed in the press* **3** to leave (a person or thing) unprotected in a potentially harmful situation: *workers were exposed to relatively low doses of radiation* **4 expose someone to** to give someone an introduction to or experience of (something new) **5** *photog* to subject (a film) to light when using a camera **6 expose oneself** to display one's sexual organs in public [Latin *exponere* to set out]

exposé (iks-**pose**-ay) *n* the bringing of a scandal, crime, etc. to public notice [French]

exposed *adj* **1** not concealed; displayed for viewing: *the exposed soles of his shoes* **2** without shelter from the elements **3** vulnerable: *the enemy attacked our army's exposed flank*

exposition *n* **1** a systematic explanation of a subject **2** the act of expounding or setting out a viewpoint **3** a large public exhibition **4** *music* the first statement of the themes of a movement [Latin *exponere* to display]

expository *adj* explanatory

ex post facto *adj* having retrospective effect [Latin *ex* from + *post* afterwards + *factus* done]

expostulate *vb* **-lating, -lated** > **expostulate with** to reason or argue with, esp. in order to dissuade or as a protest [Latin *expostulare* to require] **expostulation** *n* **expostulatory** *adj*

exposure *n* **1** the state of being exposed to, or lacking protection from, something: *the body cannot cope with sudden exposure to stress* **2** the revealing of the truth about someone or something, esp. when it is shocking or scandalous: *the exposure of a loophole in the tax laws* **3** the harmful effect on a person's body caused by lack of shelter from the weather, esp. the cold **4** appearance before the public, as on television

5 *photog* **A** the act of exposing a film to light **B** an area on a film that has been exposed **6** *photog* **A** the intensity of light falling on a film multiplied by the time for which it is exposed **B** a combination of lens aperture and shutter speed used in taking a photograph

exposure meter *n photog* an instrument for measuring the intensity of light so that suitable camera settings can be chosen

expound *vb* to explain (a theory, belief, etc.) in detail [Latin *exponere* to set forth]

express *vb* **1** to state (an idea or feeling) in words; utter: *two record labels have expressed an interest in signing the band* **2** to show (an idea or feeling): *his body and demeanour expressed distrust* **3** to indicate through a symbol or formula **4** to squeeze out (juice, etc.) **5 express oneself** to communicate one's thoughts or ideas ▷ *adj* **6** explicitly stated **7** deliberate and specific: *she came with the express purpose of causing a row* **8** of or for rapid transportation of people, mail, etc. ▷ *n* **9** a fast train stopping at only a few stations **10** *chiefly US & Canad* a system for sending mail rapidly ▷ *adv* **11** using a system for rapid transportation of people, mail, etc.: *please send this letter express: it's very urgent!* [Latin *exprimere* to force out] **expressible** *adj*

expression *n* **1** the transforming of ideas into words **2** a showing of emotion without words **3** communication of emotion through music, painting, etc. **4** a look on the face that indicates mood or emotion **5** a particular phrase used conventionally to express something **6** *maths* a variable, function, or some combination of these **expressionless** *adj*

expressionism *n* an early 20th-century artistic and literary movement which sought to express emotions rather than to represent the physical world **expressionist** *n, adj*

expression mark *n music* one of a set of symbols indicating how a piece or passage is to be performed

expressive *adj* **1** of or full of expression **2 expressive of** showing or suggesting: *looks expressive of hatred and revenge*

expressly *adv* **1** definitely **2** deliberately and specifically

expressway *n chiefly US* a motorway

expropriate *vb* **-ating, -ated** *formal* (of a government or other official body) to take (money or property) away from its owners [Medieval Latin *expropriare* to deprive of possessions] **expropriation** *n* **expropriator** *n*

expulsion *n* the act of expelling or the fact of being expelled [Latin *expellere* to expel] **expulsive** *adj*

expunge (iks-sponge) *vb* **-punging, -punged** *formal* to remove all traces of: *he had tried to expunge his failure from his mind* [Latin *expungere* to blot out]

expurgate (eks-per-gate) *vb* **-gating, -gated** to amend (a piece of writing) by removing sections thought to be offensive [Latin *expurgare* to clean out] **expurgation** *n* **expurgator** *n*

exquisite *adj* **1** extremely beautiful or attractive **2** showing unusual delicacy and craftsmanship **3** sensitive or discriminating: *exquisite manners* **4** intensely felt: *exquisite joy* [Latin *exquisitus* excellent] **exquisitely** *adv*

ex-serviceman *or fem* **ex-servicewoman** *n, pl* **-men** *or* **-women** a person who has served in the armed forces

extant *adj* still in existence; surviving [Latin *exstans* standing out]

> **USAGE** *Extant* is sometimes wrongly used simply to say that something exists, without any connotation of survival: *plutonium is perhaps the deadliest element in existence* (not *the deadliest element extant*).

extemporaneous *adj* spoken or performed without preparation **extemporaneously** *adv*

extempore (iks-temp-or-ee) *adj, adv* without planning or preparation [Latin *ex tempore* instantaneously]

extemporize *or* **-rise** *vb* **-rizing, -rized** *or* **-rising, -rised** to perform or speak without preparation **extemporization** *or* **-risation** *n* **extemporizer** *or* **-riser** *n*

extend *vb* **1** to make bigger or longer than before: *they extended the house by building a conservatory* **2** to reach to a certain distance or in a certain direction: *the suburbs extend for many miles* **3** to last for a certain time: *in Norway maternity leave extends to 52 weeks* **4** to broaden the meaning or scope of: *the law was extended to ban all guns* **5** to make something exist or be valid for longer than before: *her visa was extended for three months* **6** to present or offer: *a tradition of extending asylum to refugees* **7** to straighten or stretch out (part of the body): *she extended a hand in welcome* **8 extend oneself** to make use of all one's ability or strength, often because forced to: *she'll have to really extend herself if she wants to win* [Latin *extendere* to stretch out] **extendable** *adj*

extended family *n* a social unit in which parents, children, grandparents, and other relatives live as a family unit

extensible *adj* capable of being extended

extension *n* **1** a room or rooms added to an existing building **2** a development that includes or affects more people or things than before: *an extension of democracy within the EU* **3** an additional telephone connected to the same line as another **4** an extra period of time in which something continues to exist or be valid: *an extension of the contract for another 2 years* ▷ *adj* **5** denoting something that can be extended or that extends another object: *an extension ladder* **6** of or relating to the provision of teaching and other facilities by a school or college to people who cannot attend full-time courses

extensive *adj* **1** covering a large area: *extensive moorland* **2** very great in effect: *the bomb caused extensive damage* **3** containing many details, ideas, or items on a particular subject: *an extensive collection of modern art* **extensively** *adv*

extensor *n* any muscle that stretches or extends an arm, leg, or other part of the body

extent *n* **1** the length, area, or size of something **2** the scale or seriousness of a situation or difficulty: *the extent of the damage* **3** the degree or amount to which something applies: *to a certain extent that's true*

extenuate *vb* **-ating, -ated** *formal* to make (an offence or fault) less blameworthy, by giving reasons that partly excuse it [Latin *extenuare* to make thin] **extenuating** *adj* **extenuation** *n*

exterior *n* **1** a part or surface that is on the outside **2** the outward appearance of a person: *Amir's grumpy exterior concealed a warm heart* **3** a film scene shot outside ▷ *adj* **4** of, situated on, or suitable for the outside **5** coming or acting from outside or abroad [Latin comparative of *exterus* on the outside]

exterior angle *n* an angle of a polygon contained between one side extended and the adjacent side

exterminate *vb* **-nating, -nated** to destroy (a group or type of people, animals, or plants) completely [Latin *exterminare* to drive away] **extermination** *n* **exterminator** *n*

external *adj* **1** of, situated on, or suitable for the outside: *there was damage to the house's external walls* **2** coming or acting from outside: *most ill health is caused by external influences* **3** of or involving foreign nations: *Hong Kong's external trade* **4** *anatomy* situated on or near the outside of the body: *the external ear* **5** brought into an organization to do a task which must be done impartially, esp. one involving testing or checking: *external examiners* **6** of or relating to someone taking a university course, but not attending a university: *an external degree* ▷ *n* **7 externals** obvious circumstances or aspects, esp. superficial ones: *despite the war, the externals of life in the city remain normal* [Latin *externus*] **externality** *n* **externally** *adv*

externalize *or* **-ise** *vb* **-izing, -ized** *or* **-ising, -ised** to express (thoughts or feelings) in words or actions **externalization** *or* **-isation** *n*

extinct *adj* **1** (of an animal or plant species) having died out **2** no longer in existence, esp. because of social changes: *shipbuilding is virtually extinct in Scotland* **3** (of a volcano) no longer liable to erupt [Latin *exstinguere* to extinguish]

extinction *n* **1** the dying out of a plant or animal species **2** the end of a particular way of life or type of activity

extinguish *vb* **1** to put out (a fire or light) **2** to remove or destroy entirely [Latin *exstinguere*] **extinguishable** *adj* **extinguisher** *n*

extirpate (eks-ter-pate) *vb* **-pating, -pated** to remove or destroy completely: *the Romans attempted to extirpate the Celtic religion* [Latin *exstirpare* to root out] **extirpation** *n*

extol *or US* **extoll** *vb* **-tolling, -tolled** to praise lavishly [Latin *extollere* to elevate]

extort *vb* to obtain (money or favours) by intimidation, violence, or the misuse of authority [Latin *extorquere* to wrest away] **extortion** *n*

extortionate *adj* (of prices, profits, etc.) much higher than is fair **extortionately** *adv*

extra *adj* **1** more than is usual, expected, or needed; additional ▷ *n* **2** a person or thing that is additional **3** something for which an additional charge is made **4** *films* a person temporarily engaged, usually for crowd scenes **5** *cricket* a run not scored from the bat **6** an additional edition of a newspaper ▷ *adv* **7** unusually; exceptionally [probably from *extraordinary*]

extra- *prefix* outside or beyond an area or scope: *extracellular; extraterrestrial* [Latin]

extract *vb* **1** to pull out or uproot by force **2** to remove from a container **3** to derive (pleasure, information, etc.) from some source **4** *informal* to obtain (money, information, etc.) from someone who is not willing to provide it: *a confession extracted by force* **5** to obtain (a substance) from a material or the ground by mining, distillation, digestion, etc.: *oil extracted from shale* **6** to copy out (an article, passage, etc.) from a publication ▷ *n* **7** something extracted, such as a passage from a book, etc. **8** a preparation containing the concentrated essence of a substance [Latin *extrahere* to draw out] **extractive** *adj* **extractor** *n*

> **USAGE** *Extract* is sometimes wrongly used where *extricate* would be better: *he will find it difficult extricating* (not *extracting*) *himself from this situation.*

extraction *n* **1** the act or an instance of extracting **2** the removal of a tooth by a dentist: *few patients need an extraction* **3** the origin or ancestry of a person: *he is of German extraction*

extractor fan *n* a fan used to remove stale air from a room

extracurricular *adj* not part of the normal courses taken by students: *her free time is devoted to extracurricular duties*

extradite *vb* **-diting, -dited** to hand over (an alleged offender) to the country where the crime took place for trial: *an agreement to extradite him to Hong Kong* [Latin *ex* away + *traditio* a handing over] **extraditable** *adj* **extradition** *n*

extrajudicial *adj* **1** outside the ordinary course of legal proceedings: *extrajudicial evidence* **2** beyond the jurisdiction or authority of the court: *an extrajudicial opinion*

extramarital *adj* occurring between a married person and a person other than his or her spouse: *an extramarital affair*

extramural *adj* connected with but outside the normal courses of a university or college [Latin *extra* beyond + *murus* wall]

extraneous (iks-train-ee-uss) *adj* not essential or relevant to the situation or subject being considered [Latin *extraneus* external]

extraordinary *adj* **1** very unusual or surprising: *the award of a Victoria Cross for an act of extraordinary bravery under hostile fire* **2** having some special or extreme quality: *an extraordinary first novel* **3** (of a meeting, ambassador, etc.) specially called or appointed to deal with one particular topic [Latin *extraordinarius* beyond what is usual] **extraordinarily** *adv*

extraordinary rendition *n* the process by which a country seizes a terrorist suspect and then transports him or her for interrogation to a country where due process of law is unlikely to be respected

extrapolate (iks-trap-a-late) *vb* **-lating, -lated** **1** to infer (something not known) from the known facts, using logic and reason **2** *maths* to estimate (the value of a function or measurement) beyond

e

the known values, by the extension of a curve [EXTRA- + *-polate*, as in *interpolate*] **extrapolation** *n*

extrasensory *adj* of or relating to extrasensory perception

extrasensory perception *n* the supposed ability to obtain information without the use of normal senses of sight, hearing, etc.

extravagant *adj* **1** spending more than is reasonable or affordable **2** costing more than is reasonable or affordable: *an extravagant gift* **3** going beyond usual or reasonable limits: *extravagant expectations* **4** (of behaviour or gestures) extreme, esp. in order to make a particular impression: *an extravagant display of affection* **5** very elaborate and impressive: *extravagant costumes* [Latin *extra* beyond + *vagari* to wander] **extravagance** *n*

e

extravaganza *n* **1** an elaborate and lavish entertainment **2** any fanciful display, literary composition, etc. [Italian: extravagance]

extravert *adj, n* same as **extrovert**

extreme *adj* **1** of a high or the highest degree or intensity **2** exceptionally severe or unusual: *people can survive extreme conditions* **3** (of an opinion, political group, etc.) beyond the limits regarded as acceptable; fanatical **4** farthest or outermost ▹ *n* **5** either of the two limits of a scale or range **6 go to extremes** to be unreasonable in speech or action **7 in the extreme** to the highest or furthest degree: *the effect was dramatic in the extreme* [Latin *extremus* outermost] **extremely** *adv*

extreme sport *n* any of various sports with a high risk of injury or death

extreme unction *n RC Church* a former name for **anointing of the sick**

extremist *n* **1** a person who favours or uses extreme or violent methods, esp. to bring about political change ▹ *adj* **2** holding extreme opinions or using extreme methods **extremism** *n*

extremity *n, pl* **-ties 1** the farthest point **2** an unacceptable or extreme nature or degree: *the extremity of his views alienated other nationalists* **3** an extreme condition, such as misfortune **4 extremities** hands and feet

extricate *vb* **-cating, -cated** to free from a difficult or complicated situation or place [Latin *extricare*] **extricable** *adj* **extrication** *n*
USAGE See at **extract**.

extrinsic *adj* **1** not an integral or essential part **2** originating or acting from outside [Latin *exter* outward + *secus* alongside] **extrinsically** *adv*

extroversion *n psychol* the directing of one's interests outwards, esp. towards making social contacts

extrovert *adj* **1** lively and outgoing **2** *psychol* concerned more with external reality than inner feelings ▹ *n* **3** a person who has these characteristics [*extro-* (variant of EXTRA-, contrasting with *intro-*) + Latin *vertere* to turn] **extroverted** *adj*

extrude *vb* **-truding, -truded 1** to squeeze or force out **2** to produce (moulded sections of plastic, metal, etc.) by forcing through a shaped die [Latin *extrudere* to thrust out] **extruded** *adj* **extrusion** *n*

exuberant *adj* **1** full of vigour and high spirits **2** (of vegetation) growing thickly; flourishing [Latin *exuberans* abounding] **exuberance** *n*

exude *vb* **-uding, -uded 1** (of a liquid or smell) to seep or flow out slowly and steadily **2** to seem to have (a quality or feeling) to a great degree: *the Chancellor exuded confidence* [Latin *exsudare*] **exudation** *n*

exult *vb* to be joyful or jubilant [Latin *exsultare* to jump for joy] **exultation** *n* **exultant** *adj*
USAGE See at **exalt**.

eye *n* **1** the organ of sight in humans and animals **2** the external part of an eye, often including the area around it **3** (*often pl*) the ability to see or record what is happening: *the eyes of an entire nation were upon us* **4** a look, glance, or gaze **5** attention or observation: *his new shirt caught my eye* **6** the ability to judge or appreciate something: *his shrewd eye for talent* **7** (*often pl*) opinion, judgment, or authority: *in the eyes of the law* **8** a dark spot on a potato from which new shoots can grow **9** a small hole, such as the one at the blunt end of a sewing needle **10** a small area of calm in the centre of a storm, hurricane, or tornado **11 all eyes** *informal* acutely vigilant **12 an eye for an eye** justice consisting of an equivalent action to the original wrong or harm **13 have eyes for** to be interested in **14 in one's mind's eye** imagined or remembered vividly **15 in the public eye** exposed to public curiosity **16 keep an eye on** to take care of **17 keep an eye open** *or* **out for** to watch with special attention for **18 keep one's eyes peeled** *or* **skinned** to watch vigilantly **19 look someone in the eye** to look openly and without embarrassment at someone **20 make eyes at someone** to look at someone in an obviously attracted manner **21 more than meets the eye** hidden motives, meanings, or facts **22 my eye!** *old-fashioned, informal* nonsense! **23 see eye to eye with** to agree with **24 set** *or* **lay** *or* **clap eyes on** to see: *I never laid eyes on him again* **25 turn a blind eye to** *or* **close one's eyes to** to pretend not to notice **26 up to one's eyes in** extremely busy with **27 with an eye to** with the intention of **28 with one's eyes open** in full knowledge of all the facts ▹ *vb* **eyeing** *or* **eying, eyed 29** to look at carefully or warily ▹ See also **eye up** [Old English *ēage*] **eyeless** *adj* **eyelike** *adj*

eyeball *n* **1** the entire ball-shaped part of the eye **2 eyeball to eyeball** in close confrontation ▹ *vb* **3** *slang* to stare at

eyebrow *n* **1** the bony ridge over each eye **2** the arch of hair on this ridge **3 raise an eyebrow** to show doubt or disapproval

eye candy *n slang* someone or something that is attractive to look at but otherwise not interesting

eye-catching *adj* very striking and tending to catch people's attention **eye-catcher** *n*

eye dog *n NZ* a dog trained to control sheep by staring at them

eyeful *n* **1** *slang* a good look at or view of something **2** *slang* an attractive sight, esp. a woman **3** an amount of liquid, dust, etc., that has got into someone's eye

eyeglass *n* a lens for aiding defective vision

eyelash *n* any of the short hairs that grow from the edge of the eyelids
eyelet *n* **1** a small hole for a lace or cord to be passed through **2** a small metal ring reinforcing such a hole
eyelevel *adj* level with a person's eyes: *an eyelevel oven*
eyelid *n* either of the two folds of skin that cover an eye when it is closed
eyeliner *n* a cosmetic used to outline the eyes
eye-opener *n informal* something startling or revealing
eyepiece *n* the lens in a microscope, telescope, etc., into which the person using it looks
eye shadow *n* a coloured cosmetic worn on the upper eyelids
eyesight *n* the ability to see: *poor eyesight*
eyesore *n* something very ugly
eyestrain *n* fatigue or irritation of the eyes, caused by tiredness or a failure to wear glasses
eyetooth *n, pl* **-teeth 1** either of the two canine teeth in the upper jaw **2 give one's eyeteeth for** to go to any lengths to achieve or obtain (something)
eye up *vb informal* to look at (someone) in a way that indicates sexual interest
eyewash *n* **1** a lotion for the eyes **2** *informal* nonsense; rubbish
eyewitness *n* a person present at an event who can describe what happened
eyrie *n* **1** the nest of an eagle, built in a high inaccessible place **2** any high isolated place [Latin *area* open field, hence, nest]

Ff

f

f[1] *physics* frequency
f[2]**, f/** *or* **f:** f-number
F 1 *music* the fourth note of the scale of C major **2** Fahrenheit **3** farad(s) **4** *chem* fluorine **5** *physics* force **6** franc(s)
f. *or* **F. 1** fathom(s) **2** female **3** *grammar* feminine **4** *pl* **ff.** following (page)
fa *n music* same as **fah**
FA (in Britain) Football Association
F.A.B. *interj Brit informal* an expression of agreement to, or acknowledgement of, a command [from British television series, *Thunderbirds*]
Fabian (**fay**-bee-an) *adj* **1** of the Fabian Society, which aims to establish socialism gradually and democratically ▹ *n* **2** a member of the Fabian Society [after *Fabius*, Roman general, who wore out Hannibal's strength while avoiding a pitched battle] **Fabianism** *n*
fable *n* **1** a short story, often one with animals as characters, that illustrates a moral **2** an unlikely story which is usually untrue **3** a story about mythical characters or events [Latin *fabula* story]
fabled *adj* well-known from anecdotes and stories rather than experience
Fablon *n trademark* a brand of adhesive-backed plastic used for covering surfaces
fabric *n* **1** any cloth made from yarn or fibres by weaving or knitting **2** the structure that holds a system together: *the fabric of society* **3** the walls, floor, and roof of a building [Latin *faber* craftsman]
fabricate *vb* **-cating, -cated 1** to invent (a story or lie): *fabricated reports about the opposition* **2** to make or build [Latin *fabrica* workshop] **fabrication** *n*
fabulous *adj* **1** *informal* extremely good **2** almost unbelievable: *a city of fabulous wealth* **3** told of in fables and legends: *a fabulous horned creature* [Latin *fabulosus* celebrated in fable] **fabulously** *adv*
facade (fass-**sahd**) *n* **1** the front of a building **2** a front or deceptive outer appearance
face *n* **1** the front of the head from the forehead to the lower jaw **2 A** one's expression: *as his eyes met hers his face sobered* **B** a distorted expression to show disgust or defiance: *she was pulling a face at him* **3** the front or main side of an object, building, etc. **4** the surface of a clock or watch that has the numbers or hands on it **5** the functional side of an object, such as a tool or playing card **6** the exposed area of a mine from which coal or metal can be mined **7** *Brit slang* a well-known or important person **8 in the face of** in spite of: *a determined character in the face of adversity* **9 lose face** to lose one's credibility **10 on the face of it** to all appearances **11 put a good** *or* **brave face on something** to maintain a cheerful appearance despite misfortune **12 save face** to keep one's good reputation **13 set one's face against** to oppose with determination **14 to someone's face** directly and openly ▹ *vb* **facing, faced 15** to look towards **16** to be opposite **17** to be confronted by: *they were faced with the prospect of high inflation* **18** to provide with a surface of a different material ▹ See also **face up to** [Latin *facies* form]
Facebook *n trademark* a popular social networking site
face card *n* a playing card showing a king, queen, or jack
faceless *adj* without individual identity or character: *faceless government officials*
face-lift *n* **1** cosmetic surgery for tightening sagging skin and smoothing wrinkles on the face **2** an outward improvement designed to give a more modern appearance: *the stadium was given a face-lift*
facer *n Brit old-fashioned, informal* a difficulty or problem
face-saving *adj* preventing damage to one's reputation **face-saver** *n*
facet *n* **1** an aspect of something, such as a personality **2** any of the surfaces of a cut gemstone [French *facette* little face]
FaceTime *n trademark* **1** a software application by which users can make video calls over the internet ▹ *vb* **-Timing, -Timed 2** to make a call by FaceTime
facetious (fass-**see**-shuss) *adj* joking, or trying to be amusing, esp. at inappropriate times [Old French *facetie* witticism] **facetiously** *adv*
face up to *vb* to accept (an unpleasant fact or reality)
face value *n* apparent worth or meaning: *only a fool would take it at face value*
facia (**fay**-shee-a) *n, pl* **-ciae** (-shee-ee) same as **fascia**
facial *adj* **1** of the face ▹ *n* **2** a beauty treatment for the face **facially** *adv*
facile (**fass**-ile) *adj* **1** (of a remark, argument, etc.) overly simple and showing lack of real thought **2** easily performed or achieved: *a facile winner of his only race this year* [Latin *facilis* easy]
facilitate *vb* **-tating, -tated** to make easier the progress of: *the agreement helped facilitate trade between the countries* **facilitation** *n*
facility *n, pl* **-ties 1 facilities** the means or equipment needed for an activity: *leisure and shopping facilities* **2** the ability to do things easily and well **3** skill or ease: *grown human beings can forget with remarkable facility* [Latin *facilis* easy]
facing *n* **1** a piece of material used esp. to conceal the seam of a garment **2 facings** contrasting collar and cuffs on a jacket **3** an outer layer of material applied to the surface of a wall
facsimile (fak-**sim**-ill-ee) *n* an exact copy [Latin *fac simile!* make something like it!]
fact *n* **1** an event or thing known to have happened or existed **2** a truth that can be proved from experience or observation **3** a piece of information **4 after** *or* **before the fact** *criminal law*

after or before the commission of the offence **5 as a matter of fact** *or* **in fact** in reality or actuality **6 fact of life** an inescapable truth, esp. an unpleasant one. See also **facts of life** [Latin *factum* something done]

faction *n* **1** a small group of people within a larger body, but differing from it in certain aims and ideas **2** strife within a group [Latin *factio* a making] **factional** *adj*

factious *adj* inclined to quarrel and cause divisions: *a factious political party is unelectable*

USAGE See at **fractious.**

factitious *adj* artificial rather than natural [Latin *facticius*]

factor *n* **1** an element that contributes to a result: *reliability was an important factor in the success of the car* **2** *maths* any whole number that will divide exactly into a given number, for example 2 and 3 are factors of 6 **3** a quantity by which an amount is multiplied or divided to become that number of times bigger or smaller: *production increased by a factor of 3* **4** *med* any of several substances that participate in the clotting of blood: *factor VIII* **5** a level on a scale of measurement: *sun cream with a protection factor of 30* **6** (in Scotland) the manager of an estate [Latin: one who acts]

USAGE *Factor* (sense 1) should only be used to refer to something which contributes to a result. It should not be used to refer to a part of something such as a plan or arrangement; instead a word such as *component* or *element* should be used.

factorial *maths* ▷ *n* **1** the product of all the whole numbers from one to a given whole number ▷ *adj* **2** of factorials or factors

factorize *or* **-rise** *vb* **-rizing, -rized** *or* **-rising, -rised** *maths* to resolve (a whole number) into factors **factorization** *or* **-risation** *n*

factory *n, pl* **-ries** a building where goods are manufactured in large quantities [Late Latin *factorium*, from *facere* to make]

factory farm *n Brit, Austral & NZ* a farm in which animals are given foods that increase the amount of meat, eggs, or milk they yield **factory farming** *n*

factory ship *n* a vessel that processes fish supplied by a fleet

factotum *n* a person employed to do all kinds of work [Latin *fac!* do! + *totum* all]

facts of life *pl n* the details of sexual behaviour and reproduction

factual *adj* concerning facts rather than opinions or theories: *a factual report* **factually** *adv*

faculty *n, pl* **-ties 1** one of the powers of the mind or body, such as memory, sight, or hearing **2** any ability or power, either inborn or acquired: *his faculties of reasoning were considerable* **3 a** a department within a university or college **b** its staff **c** *chiefly US & Canad* all the teaching staff of a university, school, or college [Latin *facultas* capability]

fad *n informal* **1** an intense but short-lived fashion: *the latest healthy-eating fad* **2** a personal whim [origin unknown] **faddish** *adj*

faddy *adj* **-dier, -diest** unreasonably fussy, particularly about food

fade *vb* **fading, faded 1** to lose brightness, colour, or strength **2 fade away** *or* **out** to vanish slowly [Middle English *fade* dull]

fade in *or* **fade out** *vb* (of vision or sound in a film or broadcast) to increase or decrease gradually

faeces *or esp US* **feces** (fee-seez) *pl n* bodily waste matter discharged through the anus [Latin: dregs] **faecal** *or esp US* **fecal** (fee-kl) *adj*

Faeroese *or* **Faroese** (fair-oh-eez) *adj* **1** of the Faeroes, islands in the N Atlantic ▷ *n* **2** *pl* **-ese** a person from the Faeroes **3** the language of the Faeroes

faff about *vb Brit & S African informal* to dither or fuss [origin unknown]

fag[1] *n informal* a boring or tiring task: *weeding was a fag* [origin unknown]

fag[2] *n slang* a cigarette [origin unknown]

fag[3] *n offensive slang, chiefly US & Canad* short for **faggot**[2]

fag end *n* **1** the last and worst part: *another dull game at the fag end of the football season* **2** *Brit & NZ informal* the stub of a cigarette

fagged *adj informal* exhausted by hard work. Also: **fagged out**

faggot[1] *or esp US* **fagot** *n* **1** *Brit, Austral & NZ* a ball of chopped liver bound with herbs and bread **2** a bundle of sticks [from Old French]

faggot[2] *n offensive slang* a homosexual man [special use of FAGGOT[1]]

fah *n music* (in tonic sol-fa) the fourth note of any ascending major scale

Fahrenheit (far-ren-hite) *adj* of or measured according to the scale of temperature in which 32° represents the melting point of ice and 212° the boiling point of water [after Gabriel *Fahrenheit*, physicist]

faïence (fie-ence) *n* tin-glazed earthenware [*Faenza*, N Italy, where made]

fail *vb* **1** to be unsuccessful in an attempt **2** to stop operating **3** to judge or be judged as being below the officially accepted standard required in a course or examination **4** to prove disappointing or useless to (someone): *the government has failed the homeless* **5** to neglect or be unable (to do something): *he failed to repair the car* **6** to go bankrupt ▷ *n* **7** a failure to attain the required standard **8 without fail a** regularly or without exception: *use this shampoo once a week without fail* **b** definitely: *they agreed to enforce the embargo without fail* [Latin *fallere* to disappoint]

failing *n* **1** a weak point ▷ *prep* **2 failing that** alternatively: *your doctor will normally be able to advise you or, failing that, one of the self-help agencies*

fail-safe *adj* **1** designed to return to a safe condition in the event of a failure or malfunction **2** safe from failure

failure *n* **1** the act or an instance of failing **2** someone or something that is unsuccessful: *he couldn't help but regard his own son as a failure* **3** the fact of something required or expected not being done or not happening: *his failure to appear at the meeting* **4** a halt in normal operation: *heart failure* **5** a decline or loss of something: *crop failure* **6** the fact of not reaching the required standard in an examination or test

fain *adv old-fashioned* gladly or willingly [Old English *fægen*]

faint *adj* **1** lacking clarity, brightness, or volume: *her voice was very faint* **2** feeling dizzy or weak **3** lacking conviction or force: *a faint attempt to smile* ▷ *vb* **4** to lose consciousness ▷ *n* **5** a sudden loss of consciousness [Old French *faindre* to be idle] **faintly** *adv*

faint-hearted *adj* lacking courage and confidence

fair[1] *adj* **1** reasonable and just: *a move towards fair trade* **2** in agreement with rules **3** light in colour: *her fair skin* **4** *old-fashioned* young and beautiful: *a fair maiden* **5** quite good: *a fair attempt at making a soufflé* **6** quite large: *they made a fair amount of money* **7** (of the tide or wind) favourable to the passage of a ship or plane **8** fine or cloudless **9 fair and square** in a correct or just way ▷ *adv* **10** in a fair way **11** absolutely or squarely: *he was caught fair off his guard* [Old English *fæger*] **fairness** *n*

fair[2] *n* **1** a travelling entertainment with sideshows, rides, and amusements **2** an exhibition of goods produced by a particular industry to promote business: *the Frankfurt book fair* [Latin *feriae* holidays]

fair copy *n* a neat copy, without mistakes or alterations, of a piece of writing

fair game *n* a person regarded as a justifiable target for criticism or ridicule

fairground *n* an open space used for a fair

fairing *n* a metal structure fitted around parts of an aircraft, car, etc., to reduce drag [*fair* to streamline]

Fair Isle *n* an intricate multicoloured knitted pattern [after one of the Shetland Islands where this type of pattern originated]

fairly *adv* **1** to a moderate degree or extent: *in the Philippines labour is fairly cheap* **2** to a great degree or extent: *the folder fairly bulged with documents* **3** as deserved: *the shares are fairly valued*

fair play *n* a conventional standard of honourable behaviour

fair sex *n* **the fair sex** *old-fashioned* women collectively

fair trade *n* the practice of buying goods from producers in the developing world at a guaranteed price

fairway *n* **1** (on a golf course) the mown areas between tees and greens **2** *naut* a part of a river or sea on which ships may sail

fair-weather *adj* not reliable in difficult situations: *a fair-weather friend*

fairy *n, pl* **fairies 1** an imaginary supernatural being with magical powers **2** *offensive slang* a homosexual man [Old French *faerie* fairyland, from *feie* fairy]

fairy bread *n Austral & NZ* white bread covered with small beads of brightly coloured sugar

fairy floss *n Austral* a light fluffy mass of spun sugar, held on a stick. Also called: **candy floss**

fairy godmother *n* a generous friend who appears unexpectedly and offers help in time of trouble

fairyland *n* **1** an imaginary place where fairies live **2** an enchanted or wonderful place

fairy lights *pl n* small coloured electric bulbs used as decoration, esp. on a Christmas tree

fairy penguin *n* a small penguin with a bluish head and back, found on the Australian coast

fairy ring *n* a ring of dark grass caused by fungi

fairy tale *or* **fairy story** *n* **1** a story about fairies or magical events **2** a highly improbable account: *his report was little more than a fairy tale* ▷ *adj* **fairy-tale 3** of or like a fairy tale: *a fairy-tale wedding* **4** highly improbable: *a fairy-tale account of his achievements*

fait accompli (fate ak-**kom**-plee) *n* something already done and beyond alteration: *they had to accept the invasion as a fait accompli* [French]

faith *n* **1** strong belief in something, esp. without proof **2** a specific system of religious beliefs **3** complete confidence or trust, such as in a person or remedy **4** allegiance to a person or cause **5 bad faith** dishonesty **6 good faith** honesty [Latin *fides* trust, confidence]

faithful *adj* **1** remaining true or loyal **2** maintaining sexual loyalty to one's lover or spouse **3** consistently reliable: *my old, but faithful, four-cylinder car* **4** accurate in detail: *a faithful translation of the book* ▷ *pl n* **the faithful 5 A** the believers in a religious faith **B** loyal followers **faithfully** *adv* **faithfulness** *n*

faith healing *n* treatment of a sick person through the power of religious faith **faith healer** *n*

faithless *adj* treacherous or disloyal

fajitas (fa-**hee**-taz) *pl n* a Mexican dish of soft tortillas wrapped around fried strips of meat or vegetables [Mexican Spanish]

fake *vb* **faking, faked 1** to cause (something not genuine) to appear real or more valuable by fraud **2** to pretend to have (an illness, emotion, etc.) ▷ *n* **3** an object, person, or act that is not genuine ▷ *adj* **4** not genuine: *fake fur* [probably from Italian *facciare* to make or do]

fakir (**fay**-keer) *n* **1** a Muslim religious ascetic who spurns worldly possessions **2** a Hindu holy man [Arabic *faqīr* poor]

falcon *n* a type of bird of prey that can be trained to hunt other birds and small animals [Late Latin *falco* hawk]

falconry *n* **1** the art of training falcons to hunt **2** the sport of hunting with falcons **falconer** *n*

fall *vb* **falling, fell, fallen 1** to descend by the force of gravity from a higher to a lower place **2** to drop suddenly from an upright position **3** to collapse to the ground **4** to become less or lower in number or quality: *inflation fell by one percentage point* **5** to slope downwards **6** to be badly wounded or killed **7** to give in to attack: *in 1939 Barcelona fell to the Nationalists* **8** to lose power or status **9** to pass into a specified condition: *I fell asleep* **10** to adopt a downhearted expression: *his face fell and he pouted like a child* **11** (of night or darkness) to begin **12** to occur at a specified time: *Christmas falls on a Sunday* **13** to give in to temptation or sin **14 fall apart A** to break owing to long use or poor construction: *the chassis is falling apart* **B** to become disorganized and ineffective: *since you resigned, the office has fallen apart* **15 fall short** to prove inadequate **16 fall short of** to fail to reach (a standard) ▷ *n* **17** an instance of falling

18 an amount of something, such as snow or soot, that has fallen **19** a decrease in value or number **20** a decline in status or importance: *the town's fall from prosperity* **21** a capture or overthrow: *the fall of Budapest in February 1945* **22** *wrestling* a scoring move, pinning both shoulders of one's opponent to the floor for a specified period **23** *chiefly US* autumn ▷ See also **fall about, fall away, falls** *etc.* [Old English *feallan*]

Fall *n* **the Fall** *theol* the state of mankind's innate sinfulness following Adam's sin of disobeying God

fall about *vb* to laugh uncontrollably

fallacy *n, pl* **-cies 1** an incorrect or misleading notion based on inaccurate facts or faulty reasoning: *the fallacy underlying the government's industrial policy* **2** reasoning that is unsound [Latin *fallere* to deceive] **fallacious** *adj*

fall away *vb* **1** to slope down: *the ground fell away sharply to the south* **2** to decrease in size or intensity: *obstacles to all-party talks are falling away with amazing speed*

fall back *vb* **1** to retreat **2 fall back on** to have to choose (a less acceptable alternative): *they had to fall back on other lines of defence*

fall behind *vb* **1** to fail to keep up **2** to be in arrears, such as with a payment

fall down *vb* **1** to drop suddenly or collapse **2** to fail to meet requirements **3** (of an argument or idea) to fail at a specific point: *in one area only did the case fall down*

fallen *vb* **1** the past participle of **fall** ▷ *adj* **2** *old-fashioned* (of a woman) having had sex outside marriage **3** killed in battle

fall for *vb* **1** to become strongly attracted to (someone) **2** to be deceived by (a lie or trick)

fall guy *n informal* **1** the victim of a confidence trick **2** a person who is publicly blamed for something, though it may not be his or her fault

fallible *adj* **1** (of a person) liable to make mistakes **2** capable of error: *our all-too-fallible economic indicators* [Latin *fallere* to deceive] **fallibility** *n*

fall in *vb* **1** to collapse **2** to get into line or formation in a display, march, or procession **3 fall in with A** to meet and join **B** to agree with or support (a person or a suggestion)

falling star *n informal* a meteor

fall off *vb* **1** to drop unintentionally to the ground from (a bicycle, horse, etc.) **2** to decrease in size or intensity: *demand for beef began to fall off*

fall on *vb* **1** to attack (an enemy) **2** to meet with (something unpleasant): *his family had fallen on hard times* **3** to affect: *a horrified hush fell on the company* **4 fall on one's feet** to emerge unexpectedly well from a difficult situation

Fallopian tube *n* either of a pair of slender tubes through which eggs pass from the ovaries to the uterus in female mammals [after Gabriello *Fallopio*, anatomist]

fallout *n* **1** radioactive material in the atmosphere following a nuclear explosion **2** unpleasant circumstances following an event: *the political fallout of the riots* ▷ *vb* **fall out 3** *informal* to disagree and quarrel: *I hope we don't fall out over this issue* **4** to leave a military formation

fallow¹ *adj* (of land) left unseeded after being ploughed to regain fertility for a future crop [Old English *fealga*]

fallow² *adj* light yellowish-brown [Old English *fealu*]

fallow deer *n* a deer that has a reddish coat with white spots in summer

falls *pl n* a waterfall

fall through *vb* to fail before completion: *his transfer deal fell through*

fall to *vb* **1** to become the responsibility of: *it fell to the Prime Minister to announce the plans* **2** to begin (some activity, such as eating, working, or fighting)

false *adj* **1** not in accordance with the truth or facts: *false allegations* **2** not real or genuine but intended to seem so: *false teeth* **3** misleading or deceptive: *their false promises* **4** forced or insincere: *false cheer* **5** based on mistaken ideas [Latin *falsus*] **falsely** *adv* **falseness** *n*

false alarm *n* a situation that appears to be dangerous but turns out not to be: *air-raid sirens sounded once but it turned out to be a false alarm*

falsehood *n* **1** the quality of being untrue **2** a lie

false pretences *pl n* **under false pretences** so as to mislead people about one's true intentions

false start *n athletics & swimming* an occasion when one competitor starts a race before the starter's signal has been given, which means that all competitors have to be recalled and the race restarted

falsetto *n, pl* **-tos** a voice pitch higher than one's normal range [Italian]

falsies *pl n informal* pads worn to exaggerate the size of a woman's breasts

falsify *vb* **-fies, -fying, -fied** to make (a report or evidence) false by alteration in order to deceive [Latin *falsus* false + *facere* to make] **falsification** *n*

falsity *n, pl* **-ties 1** the state of being false **2** a lie

falter *vb* **1** to be hesitant, weak, or unsure **2** (of a machine) to lose power or strength in an uneven way: *the engine began to falter and the plane lost height* **3** to speak nervously and without confidence **4** to stop moving smoothly and start moving unsteadily: *as he neared the house his steps faltered* [origin unknown] **faltering** *adj*

fame *n* the state of being widely known or recognized [Latin *fama* report]

famed *adj* extremely well-known: *a nation famed for its efficiency*

familial *adj formal* of or relating to the family

familiar *adj* **1** well-known **2** frequent or common: *it was a familiar argument* **3 familiar with** well acquainted with **4** friendly and informal **5** more intimate than is acceptable ▷ *n* **6** an animal or bird believed to share with a witch her supernatural powers **7** a friend [Latin *familia* family] **familiarly** *adv* **familiarity** *n*

familiarize *or* **-rise** *vb* **-rizing, -rized** *or* **-rising, -rised** to make (oneself or someone else) fully aware of a particular subject **familiarization** *or* **-risation** *n*

family *n, pl* **-lies 1** a social group consisting of parents and their offspring. Related adjective: **familial 2** one's wife or husband and one's children **3** one's children **4** a group descended from a common ancestor **5** all the people living together in one household **6** any group of related objects or beings: *a family of chemicals* **7** *biol* one of the groups into which an order is divided, containing one or more genera: *the cat family* ▷ *adj* **8** of or suitable for a family or any of its members: *films for a family audience* **9 in the family way** *informal* pregnant [Latin *familia*]

family doctor *n Brit, Austral & NZ informal* same as **general practitioner**

family man *n* **1** a man with a wife and children **2** a man who loves his family and spends a lot of time with them

family name *n* a surname, esp. when regarded as representing a family's good reputation

family planning *n* the control of the number of children in a family by the use of contraceptives

family tree *n* a chart showing the relationships between individuals in a family over many generations

famine *n* a severe shortage of food [Latin *fames* hunger]

famish *vb* **be famished** *or* **famishing** to be very hungry [Latin *fames* hunger]

famous *adj* known to or recognized by many people [Latin *famosus*]

famously *adv* **1** well-known: *her famously relaxed manner* **2** very well: *the two got on famously*

fan¹ *n* **1** any device for creating a current of air, esp. a rotating machine of blades attached to a central hub **2** a hand-held object, usually made of paper, which creates a draught of cool air when waved **3** something shaped like such a fan, such as the tail of certain birds ▷ *vb* **fanning, fanned 4** to create a draught of air in the direction of (someone or something) **5 fan out** to spread out in the shape of a fan: *the troops fanned out along the beach* [Latin *vannus*]

fan² *n* a person who admires or is enthusiastic about a pop star, actor, sport, or hobby: *he was a big fan of American football* [from *fanatic*]

fanatic *n* **1** a person whose enthusiasm for something, esp. a political or religious cause, is extreme **2** *informal* a person devoted to a particular hobby or pastime ▷ *adj also* **fanatical 3** excessively enthusiastic [Latin *fanaticus* belonging to a temple, hence, inspired by a god, frenzied] **fanatically** *adv* **fanaticism** *n*

fanbase *n* a body of admirers of a particular pop singer, sports team, etc.

fan belt *n* the belt that drives a cooling fan in a car engine

fancier *n* a person with a keen interest in the thing specified: *a pigeon fancier*

fanciful *adj* **1** not based on fact **2** made in a curious or imaginative way: *fanciful architecture* **3** guided by unrestrained imagination: *fanciful tales of fairy folk* **fancifully** *adv*

fan club *n* an organized group of admirers of a particular pop singer or star

fancy *adj* **-cier, -ciest 1** special, unusual, and elaborate **2** (often used ironically) superior in quality **3** (of a price) higher than expected ▷ *n, pl* **-cies 4** a sudden spontaneous idea **5** a sudden or irrational liking for a person or thing **6** *old-fashioned or literary* a person's imagination ▷ *vb* **-cies, -cying, -cied 7** *Brit informal* to be physically attracted to (another person) **8** *informal* to have a wish for **9** to picture in the imagination **10** to think or suppose: *I fancy I am redundant here* **11 fancy oneself** to have a high opinion of oneself ▷ *interj* **12** Also: **fancy that!** an exclamation of surprise [Middle English *fantsy*] **fancily** *adv*

fancy dress *n* clothing worn for a party at which people dress up to look like a particular animal or character

fancy-free *adj* free from commitments, esp. marriage

fancy goods *pl n* small decorative gifts

fancy man *n old-fashioned slang* a male lover

fancy woman *n old-fashioned slang* a female lover

fancywork *n* ornamental needlework

fandango *n, pl* **-gos 1** a lively Spanish dance **2** music for this dance [Spanish]

fanfare *n* a short rousing tune played on brass instruments [French]

fang *n* **1** the long pointed tooth of a poisonous snake through which poison is injected **2** the canine tooth of a meat-eating mammal [Old English: what is caught, prey]

fanjet *n* same as **turbofan**

fanlight *n* a semicircular window over a door or another window

fanny *n, pl* **-nies** *slang* **1** *Brit & Austral taboo* the female genitals **2** *chiefly US & Canad* the buttocks [origin unknown]

fantail *n* **1** a breed of domestic pigeon with a large tail like a fan **2** a fly-catching bird of Australia, New Zealand, and SE Asia with a broad fan-shaped tail

fantasia *n* **1** any musical work not composed in a strict form **2** a mixture of popular tunes arranged as a continuous whole [Italian: fancy]

fantasize *or* **-sise** *vb* **-sizing, -sized** *or* **-sising, -sised** to imagine pleasant but unlikely events

fantastic *adj* **1** *informal* excellent **2** *informal* very large in degree or amount: *a fantastic amount of money* **3** strange or exotic in appearance: *fantastic costumes* **4** difficult to believe or unlikely to happen **fantastically** *adv*

fantasy *n, pl* **-sies 1** a far-fetched idea **2** imagination unrestricted by reality **3** a daydream **4** fiction with a large fantasy content **5** *music* same as **fantasia** [Greek *phantazein* to make visible]

fan vaulting *n archit* vaulting with ribs that radiate like those of a fan from the top part of a pillar

fanzine (**fan**-zeen) *n* a magazine produced by fans of a specific interest, football club, etc., for fellow fans

FAQ *n computers* frequently asked question *or* questions: a document containing basic information on a particular subject

far *adv* **farther, farthest** *or* **further, furthest 1** at, to, or from a great distance **2** at or to a remote time: *as far back as 1984* **3** by a considerable degree: *far greater* **4 as far as A** to the degree or extent that **B** to the distance or place of **C** *informal* with reference to **5 by far** by a considerable margin **6 far and away** by a very great margin: *far and* *away the ugliest building in the city* **7 far and wide** in a great many places over a large area **8 go far A** to be successful **B** to be sufficient or last long: *her wages didn't go far* **9 go too far** to go beyond reasonable limits: *the press have gone too far this time* **10 so far A** up to the present moment **B** up to a certain point, extent, or degree ▷ *adj* **11** distant in space or time: *the far south* **12** extending a great distance **13** more distant: *over in the far corner* **14 far from** by no means: *the battle is far from over* [Old English *feorr*]

farad *n physics* the SI unit of electric capacitance [after Michael *Faraday*, physicist]

faraway *adj* **1** very distant **2** dreamy or absent-minded: *a faraway look in his eyes*

farce *n* **1** a humorous play involving characters in unlikely and ridiculous situations **2** the style of comedy of this kind **3** a ludicrous situation: *the game degenerated into farce* [Latin *farcire* to stuff, interpolate passages (in plays)] **farcical** *adj* **farcically** *adv*

fare *n* **1** the amount charged or paid for a journey in a bus, train, or plane **2** a paying passenger **3** a range of food and drink: *marvellous picnic fare* ▷ *vb* **faring, fared 4** to get on (in a specified way): *he fared well in the exam* [Old English *faran*]

Far East *n* the countries of E Asia **Far Eastern** *adj*

farewell *interj* **1** *old-fashioned* goodbye ▷ *n* **2** the act of saying goodbye and leaving ▷ *vb* **3** NZ to say goodbye ▷ *adj* **4** parting or closing: *the President's farewell speech*

far-fetched *adj* unlikely to be true

far-flung *adj* **1** distributed over a wide area **2** far distant or remote

farinaceous *adj* containing starch or having a starchy texture [Latin *far* coarse meal]

farm *n* **1** a tract of land, usually with a house and buildings, cultivated as a unit or used to rear livestock **2** a unit of land or water devoted to the growing or rearing of some particular type of fruit, animal, or fish: *a salmon farm; an ostrich farm* ▷ *vb* **3 A** to cultivate (land) **B** to rear (animals or fish) on a farm **4** to do agricultural work as a way of life **5** to collect and keep the profits from (a tax district or business) ▷ See also **farm out** [Old French *ferme* rented land]

farmed *adj* (of fish or game) reared on a farm rather than caught in the wild

farmer *n* a person who owns or manages a farm

farmers' market *n* a market at which farm produce is sold directly to the public by the producer

farm hand *n* a person who is hired to work on a farm

farmhouse *n* a house attached to a farm

farming *n* the business or skill of agriculture

farmland *n* land that is used for or suitable for farming

farm out *vb* **1** to send (work) to be done by another person or firm **2** (of the state) to put (a child) into the care of a private individual

farmstead *n* a farm and its main buildings

farmyard *n* the small area of land enclosed by or around the farm buildings

far-off *adj* distant in space or time: *a far-off land*

far-out *adj* **1** very unusual or strange: *the idea was so far-out it was ludicrous* **2** *informal* wonderful

farrago (far-rah-go) *n, pl* **-gos** *or* **-goes** a hotchpotch or mixture, esp. a ridiculous or unbelievable one: *a farrago of patriotic nonsense*

far-reaching *adj* extensive in influence, effect, or range

farrier *n chiefly Brit* a person who shoes horses [Latin *ferrarius* smith]

farrow *n* **1** a litter of piglets ▷ *vb* **2** (of a sow) to give birth to a litter [Old English *fearh*]

far-seeing *adj* having wise judgment

far-sighted *adj* **1** able to look forward and plan ahead **2** *US* long-sighted

fart *vulgar* ▷ *n* **1** an emission of intestinal gas from the anus ▷ *vb* **2** to break wind [Middle English *farten*]

farther *adv* **1** to or at a greater distance in space or time **2** in addition ▷ *adj* **3** more distant or remote in space or time [Middle English]

> **USAGE** *Farther, farthest, further,* and *furthest* can all be used to refer to literal distance, but *further* and *furthest* are regarded as more correct for figurative senses denoting greater or additional amount, time, etc.: *further to my letter. Further* and *furthest* are also preferred for figurative distance.

farthermost *adj* most distant or remote

farthest *adv* **1** to or at the greatest distance in space or time ▷ *adj* **2** most distant or remote in space or time [Middle English *ferthest*]

farthing *n* a former British coin worth a quarter of an old penny [Old English *fēorthing*]

farthingale *n* a hoop worn under skirts in the Elizabethan period [Old Spanish *verdugo* rod]

fasces (fass-eez) *pl n, sing* **-cis** (-siss) (in ancient Rome) a bundle of rods containing an axe with its blade pointing out; a symbol of a magistrate's power [Latin]

fascia *or* **facia** (fay-shee-a) *n, pl* **-ciae** (-shee-ee) **1** the flat surface above a shop window **2** *archit* a flat band or surface **3** *Brit* the outer panel which surrounds the instruments and dials of a motor vehicle **4** a detachable cover for a mobile phone [Latin: band]

fascinate *vb* **-nating, -nated** to attract and delight by arousing interest [Latin *fascinum* a bewitching] **fascinating** *adj* **fascinatingly** *adv* **fascination** *n*

> **USAGE** A person can be fascinated *by* or *with* another person or thing. It is correct to speak of someone's fascination *with* a person or thing; you can also say a person or thing has a fascination *for* someone.

Fascism (fash-iz-zum) *n* **1** the authoritarian and nationalistic political movement in Italy (1922–43) **2** any ideology or movement like this [Italian *fascio* political group] **Fascist** *n, adj*

fashion *n* **1** style in clothes, hairstyles, behaviour, etc., that is popular at a particular time **2** the way that something happens or is done: *conversing in a very animated fashion* **3 after a fashion** in some way, but not very well: *she apologized, after a fashion, for her haste* ▷ *vb* **4** to form, make, or shape: *he had fashioned a crude musical instrument* [Latin *facere* to make]

fashionable *adj* **1** popular with a lot of people at a particular time **2** popular among well-off or famous people: *the fashionable Côte d'Azur* **fashionably** *adv*

fast¹ *adj* **1** acting or moving quickly **2** accomplished in or lasting a short time **3** adapted to or allowing for rapid movement: *the fast lane* **4** (of a clock or watch) indicating a time in advance of the correct time **5** given to a life of expensive and exciting activities: *the desire for a fast life* **6** firmly fixed, fastened, or shut **7** (of colours and dyes) not likely to fade **8** *photog* (of film) very sensitive and able to be used in low-light conditions **9 fast friends** devoted and loyal friends **10 pull a fast one** *informal* to play an unscrupulous trick ▷ *adv* **11** quickly **12 fast asleep** in a deep sleep **13** firmly and tightly: *stuck fast* **14 play fast and loose** to behave in an insincere or unreliable manner [Old English *fæst* strong, tight]

fast² *vb* **1** to go without food for a period of time, esp. for religious reasons ▷ *n* **2** a period of fasting [Old English *fæstan*]

fast-breeder reactor *n* a nuclear reactor that produces more fissionable material (plutonium) than it consumes for the purposes of generating electricity

fasten *vb* **1** to make or become secure or joined **2** to close by fixing firmly in place or locking **3 fasten on A** to direct one's attention in a concentrated way towards: *the mind needs such imagery to fasten on to* **B** to take a firm hold on [Old English *fæstnian*] **fastener** *n*

fastening *n* something that fastens something, such as a clasp or lock

fast food *n* food, such as hamburgers, that is prepared and served very quickly

fastidious *adj* **1** paying great attention to neatness, detail, and order: *a fastidious dresser* **2** excessively concerned with cleanliness [Latin *fastidiosus* scornful] **fastidiously** *adv* **fastidiousness** *n*

fast lane *n* **1** the outside lane on a motorway for overtaking or travelling fast **2** *informal* the quickest but most competitive route to success: *the hectic pace of life in the corporate fast lane*

fastness *n Brit & Austral literary* a stronghold or safe place that is hard to get to

fast-track *adj* **1** taking the quickest but most competitive route to success or personal advancement: *a fast-track marketer's dream* ▷ *vb* **2** to speed up the progress of (a project or person)

fat *adj* **fatter, fattest 1** having more flesh on the body than is thought necessary or desirable; overweight **2** (of meat) containing a lot of fat **3** thick or wide: *his obligatory fat cigar* **4** profitable or productive: *fat years for the farmers are few and far between* **5 a fat chance** *slang* not much likelihood at all **6 a fat lot of good** *slang* not at all good or useful ▷ *n* **7** extra or unwanted flesh on the body **8** a greasy or oily substance obtained from animals or plants and used in cooking **9 the fat is in the fire** an action has been taken from which disastrous consequences are expected **10 the fat of the land** the best that is obtainable [Old English *fætt* crammed] **fatless** *adj* **fatness** *n*

fatal *adj* **1** resulting in death: *a fatal accident* **2** resulting in unfortunate consequences: *the consortium's second fatal mistake* [Latin *fatum* fate] **fatally** *adv*

fatalism *n* the belief that all events are decided in advance by God or Fate so that human beings are powerless to alter their destiny **fatalist** *n* **fatalistic** *adj* **fatalistically** *adv*

fatality *n, pl* **-ties** a death caused by an accident or disaster

fate *n* **1** the ultimate force that supposedly predetermines the course of events **2** the inevitable fortune that happens to a person or thing **3** death or downfall: *Custer met his fate at Little Bighorn* [Latin *fatum*]

fated *adj* **1** certain to be or do something: *he was always fated to be a musician* **2** doomed to death or destruction

fateful *adj* having important, and usually disastrous, consequences **fatefully** *adv*

Fates *pl n classical myth* the goddesses who control human destiny

fathead *n informal* a stupid person **fatheaded** *adj*

father *n* **1** a male parent **2** a person who founds a line or family; forefather **3** a man who starts, creates, or invents something: *the father of democracy in Costa Rica* **4** a leader of an association or council: *the city fathers* ▷ *vb* **5** (of a man) to be the biological cause of the conception and birth of (a child) [Old English *fæder*] **fatherhood** *n*

Father *n* **1** God **2** a title used for Christian priests **3** any of the early writers on Christian doctrine

Father Christmas *n* same as **Santa Claus**

father-in-law *n, pl* **fathers-in-law** the father of one's wife or husband

fatherland *n* a person's native country

fatherly *adj* kind or protective, like a father

Father's Day *n* a day celebrated in honour of fathers

fathom *n* **1** a unit of length, used in navigation, equal to six feet (1.83 metres) ▷ *vb* **2** to understand by thinking carefully about: *I couldn't fathom his intentions* [Old English *fæthm*] **fathomable** *adj*

fathomless *adj* too deep or difficult to fathom

fatigue (fat-eeg) *n* **1** extreme physical or mental tiredness **2** the weakening of a material caused by repeated stress or movement **3** the duties of a soldier that are not military **4 fatigues** a soldier's clothing for nonmilitary or battlefield duties ▷ *vb* **-tiguing, -tigued 5** to make or become weary or exhausted [Latin *fatigare* to tire]

fat stock *n* livestock fattened and ready for market

fatten *vb* to grow or cause to grow fat or fatter **fattening** *adj*

fatty *adj* **-tier, -tiest 1** containing or derived from fat **2** greasy or oily ▷ *n, pl* **-ties 3** *informal* a fat person

fatty acid *n* any of a class of organic acids some of which, such as stearic acid, are found in animal or vegetable fats

fatuity *n, pl* **-ties 1** foolish thoughtlessness **2** a fatuous remark

fatuous *adj* foolish, inappropriate, and showing no thought [Latin *fatuus*] **fatuously** *adv*

faucet (faw-set) *n* **1** a tap fitted to a barrel **2** *US & Canad* a tap [Old French *fausset*]
fault *n* **1** responsibility for something wrong **2** a defect or failing: *they shut the production line to remedy a fault* **3** a weakness in a person's character **4** *geol* a fracture in the earth's crust with displacement of the rocks on either side **5** *tennis & squash etc.* a serve that bounces outside the proper service court or fails to get over the net **6** (in showjumping) a penalty mark for failing to clear, or refusing, a fence **7 at fault** to be to blame for something wrong **8 find fault with** to seek out minor imperfections in **9 to a fault** more than is usual or necessary: *generous to a fault* ▷ *vb* **10** to criticize or blame **11** *geol* to undergo or cause to undergo a fault [Latin *fallere* to fail] **faultless** *adj* **faultlessly** *adv*
fault-finding *n* continual criticism
faulty *adj* **faultier, faultiest** badly designed or not working properly: *a faulty toaster*
faun *n* (in Roman legend) a creature with the head and torso of a man and the legs, ears, and horns of a goat [Latin *Faunus*, god of forests]
fauna *n, pl* **-nas** *or* **-nae** all the animal life of a given place or time: *the fauna of the Arctic* [Late Latin *Fauna*, a goddess of living things]
faux pas (foe **pah**) *n, pl* **faux pas** (foe **pahz**) a socially embarrassing action or mistake [French]
favour *or US* **favor** *n* **1** an approving attitude: *the company looked with favour on his plan* **2** an act done out of goodwill or generosity **3** bias at the expense of others: *his fellow customs officers, showing no favour, demanded to see his luggage* **4 in** *or* **out of favour** regarded with approval *or* disapproval **5 in favour of** **A** approving **B** to the benefit of ▷ *vb* **6** to prefer **7** to show bias towards (someone) at the expense of others: *parents sometimes favour the youngest child in the family* **8** to support or agree with (something): *he favours the abolition of capital punishment* [Latin *favere* to protect] **favoured** *or US* **favored** *adj*
favourable *or US* **favorable** *adj* **1** advantageous, encouraging, or promising: *a favourable climate for business expansion* **2** giving consent or approval **favourably** *or US* **favorably** *adv*
favourite *or US* **favorite** *adj* **1** most liked ▷ *n* **2** a person or thing regarded with especial preference or liking **3** *sport* a competitor thought likely to win [Latin *favere* to protect]
favouritism *or US* **favoritism** *n* the practice of giving special treatment to a person or group: *favouritism in the allocation of government posts*
fawn[1] *n* **1** a young deer aged under one year ▷ *adj* **2** pale greyish-brown [Latin *fetus* offspring]
fawn[2] *vb* **fawn on** **1** to seek attention from (someone) by insincere flattery: *it makes me sick to see the way you fawn on that awful woman* **2** (of a dog) to try to please (someone) by a show of extreme friendliness [Old English *fægnian* to be glad] **fawning** *adj*
fax *n* **1** an electronic system for transmitting an exact copy of a document **2** a document sent by this system **3** Also called: **fax machine, facsimile machine** a machine which transmits and receives exact copies of documents ▷ *vb* **4** to send (a document) by this system [short for *facsimile*]
fazed *adj* worried or disconcerted [Old English *fēsian*]
FBI (in the US) Federal Bureau of Investigation
FC (in Britain) Football Club
FD Defender of the Faith: the title of the British sovereign as head of the Church of England [Latin *Fidei Defensor*]
Fe *chem* iron [Latin *ferrum*]
fealty *n, pl* **-ties** (in feudal society) the loyalty sworn to a lord by his tenant or servant [Latin *fidelitas* fidelity]
fear *n* **1** a feeling of distress or alarm caused by danger or pain that is about to happen **2** something that causes fear **3** possibility or likelihood: *there is no fear of her agreeing to that* **4 no fear** *informal* certainly not ▷ *vb* **5** to be afraid of (someone or something) **6** *formal* to be sorry: *I fear the children were not very good yesterday* **7 fear for** to feel anxiety about [Old English *fǣr*] **fearless** *adj* **fearlessly** *adv*
fearful *adj* **1** afraid and full of fear **2** frightening or causing fear: *the ship hit a fearful storm* **3** *informal* very bad: *they were making a fearful noise* **fearfully** *adv*
fearsome *adj* terrible or frightening
feasible *adj* able to be done: *a manned journey to Mars is now feasible* [Anglo-French *faisable*] **feasibility** *n* **feasibly** *adv*
feast *n* **1** a large and special meal for many people **2** something extremely pleasing: *a feast of colour* **3** an annual religious celebration ▷ *vb* **4** to take part in a feast **5** to give a feast to **6 feast on** to eat a large amount of: *down come hundreds of vultures to feast on the remains* **7 feast one's eyes on** to look at (someone or something) with a great deal of attention and pleasure [Latin *festus* joyful]
Feast of Tabernacles *n* same as **Sukkoth**
feat *n* a remarkable, skilful, or daring action: *an extraordinary feat of engineering* [Anglo-French *fait*]
feather *n* **1** any of the flat light structures that form the plumage of birds, each consisting of a shaft with soft thin hairs on either side **2 feather in one's cap** a cause for pleasure at one's achievements ▷ *vb* **3** to fit, cover, or supply with feathers **4** *rowing* to turn an oar parallel to the water between strokes, in order to lessen wind resistance **5 feather one's nest** to collect possessions and money to make one's life comfortable, often dishonestly [Old English *fether*] **feathered** *adj* **feathery** *adj*
feather bed *n* **1** a mattress filled with feathers or down ▷ *vb* **featherbed, -bedding, -bedded** **2** to pamper or spoil (someone)
featherbedding *n* the practice of working in a factory or office deliberately slowly and inefficiently so that more workers are employed than are necessary
featherbrain *n* an empty-headed or forgetful person **featherbrained** *adj*
featherweight *n* **1** a professional or an amateur boxer weighing up to 126 pounds (57 kg) **2** something very light or of little importance
feature *n* **1 features** any one of the parts of the face, such as the nose, chin, or mouth **2** a prominent or distinctive part of something:

regular debates were a feature of our final year **3** the main film in a cinema programme **4** an item appearing regularly in a newspaper or magazine **5** a prominent story in a newspaper ▷ *vb* **-turing, -tured 6** to have as a feature or make a feature of: *this cooker features a fan-assisted oven* **7** to give special prominence to: *the film features James Mason as Rommel* [Anglo-French *feture*] **featureless** *adj*

Feb. February

febrile (**fee**-brile) *adj formal* **1** very active and nervous: *increasingly febrile activity at the Stock Exchange* **2** of or relating to fever [Latin *febris* fever]

February *n, pl* **-aries** the second month of the year [Latin *Februarius mensis* month of expiation]

f

feckless *adj* irresponsible and lacking character and determination: *her feckless brother was always in debt* [obsolete *feck* value, effect]

fecund *adj literary* **1** fertile or capable of producing many offspring **2** intellectually productive or creative: *an extraordinarily fecund year even by Mozart's standards* [Latin *fecundus*] **fecundity** *n*

fed *vb* the past of **feed**

federal *adj* **1** of a form of government in which power is divided between one central and several regional governments **2** of the central government of a federation **3** *Austral* of a style of house built around the time of Federation [Latin *foedus* league] **federalism** *n* **federalist** *n, adj*

Federal *adj* of or supporting the Union government during the American Civil War

Federal Government *n* the national government of a federated state, such as that of Canada located in Ottawa or of Australia in Canberra

federalize *or* **-lise** *vb* **-lizing, -lized** *or* **-lising, -lised 1** to unite in a federal union **2** to subject to federal control **federalization** *or* **-isation** *n*

federate *vb* **-rating, -rated** to unite in a federal union **federative** *adj*

federation *n* **1** the union of several provinces, states, etc. **2** any alliance or association of organizations which have freely joined together for a common purpose: *a federation of twenty regional unions*

fed up *adj informal* annoyed or bored

fee *n* **1** a charge paid to be allowed to do something: *many people resent the licence fee* **2** a payment asked by professional people for their services **3** *property law* an interest in land that can be inherited. The interest can be with unrestricted rights (**fee simple**) or restricted (**fee tail**) [Old French *fie*]

feeble *adj* **1** lacking in physical or mental strength **2** not effective or convincing: *feeble excuses for Scotland's latest defeat* [Old French *feble*] **feebly** *adv*

feeble-minded *adj* unable to think or understand effectively

feed *vb* **feeding, fed 1** to give food to (a person or an animal) **2** to give (something) as food: *people feeding bread to their cattle* **3** to eat food: *red squirrel feed in the pines* **4** to supply or prepare food for **5** to provide what is needed for the continued existence, operation, or growth of: *illustrations which will feed an older child's imagination; pools fed by waterfalls* ▷ *n* **6** the act of feeding **7** food, esp. that given to animals or babies **8** *Brit, Austral & NZ informal* a meal [Old English *fēdan*]

feedback *n* **1** information in response to an inquiry or experiment: *considerable feedback from the customers* **2** the return of part of the output of an electronic circuit to its input **3** the return of part of the sound output of a loudspeaker to the microphone, so that a high-pitched whine is produced

feeder *n* **1** a device used to feed an animal, child, or sick person **2** an animal or a person who feeds: *these larvae are voracious feeders* **3** a road, rail, or air service that links outlying areas to the main network **4** a tributary or channel of a river

feel *vb* **feeling, felt 1** to have a physical or emotional sensation of: *he felt a combination of shame and relief* **2** to become aware of or examine by touching **3** Also: **feel in one's bones** to sense by intuition **4** to believe or think: *I felt I got off pretty lightly* **5 feel for** to show compassion towards **6 feel like** to have an inclination for (something or doing something): *I feel like going to the cinema* **7 feel up to** to be fit enough for (something or doing something) ▷ *n* **8** the act of feeling **9** an impression: *all this mixing and matching has a French feel to it* **10** the sense of touch **11** an instinctive ability: *a feel for art* [Old English *fēlan*]

feeler *n* **1** an organ on an insect's head that is sensitive to touch **2 put out feelers** to make informal suggestions or remarks designed to probe the reactions of others

feeling *n* **1** an emotional reaction: *a feeling of discontent* **2 feelings** emotional sensitivity: *I don't want to hurt your feelings* **3** instinctive appreciation and understanding: *your feeling for language* **4** an intuitive understanding that cannot be explained: *I began to have a sinking feeling that I was not going to get rid of her* **5** opinion or view: *it was his feeling that the report was a misinterpretation of what had been said* **6** capacity for sympathy or affection: *moved by feeling for his fellow citizens* **7 A** the ability to experience physical sensations: *he has no feeling in his left arm* **B** the sensation so experienced **8** the impression or mood created by something: *a feeling of excitement in the air* **9 bad feeling** resentment or anger between people, for example after an argument or an injustice: *his refusal may have triggered bad feeling between the two men* **feelingly** *adv*

feet *n* **1** the plural of **foot 2 be run** *or* **rushed off one's feet** to be very busy **3 feet of clay** a weakness that is not widely known **4 have** *or* **keep one's feet on the ground** to be practical and reliable **5 put one's feet up** to take a rest **6 stand on one's own feet** to be independent **7 sweep off one's feet** to fill with enthusiasm

feign (**fane**) *vb* to pretend to experience (a particular feeling): *he didn't have to feign surprise* [Old French *feindre*] **feigned** *adj*

feint[1] (**faint**) *n* **1** a misleading movement designed to distract an opponent, such as in boxing or fencing ▷ *vb* **2** to make a feint [Old French *feindre* to feign]

feint[2] (**faint**) *n printing* paper that has pale lines across it for writing on [variant of *faint*]

feisty (fie-stee) *adj* **feistier, feistiest** *informal* **1** showing courage or spirit **2** *US & Canad* frisky **3** *US & Canad* irritable [from dialect *feist* small dog]
feldspar *or* **felspar** *n* a hard mineral that is the main constituent of igneous rocks [German *Feldspath*] **feldspathic** *or* **felspathic** *adj*
felicitations *pl n, interj* expressions of pleasure at someone's success or good fortune; congratulations
felicitous *adj* appropriate and well-chosen: *a felicitous combination of architectural styles*
felicity *n* **1** great happiness and pleasure **2** the quality of being pleasant or desirable: *small moments of architectural felicity amidst acres of monotony* **3** *pl* **-ties** an appropriate and well-chosen remark: *Nietzsche's verbal felicities are not lost in translation* [Latin *felicitas* happiness]
feline *adj* **1** of or belonging to the cat family **2** like a cat, esp. in stealth or grace ▷ *n* **3** any member of the cat family [Latin *feles* cat] **felinity** *n*
fell¹ *vb* the past tense of **fall**
fell² *vb* **1** to cut down (a tree) **2** to knock down (a person), esp. in a fight [Old English *fellan*]
fell³ *adj* **in one fell swoop** in one single action or on one single occasion: *they arrested all the hooligans in one fell swoop* [Middle English *fel*]
fell⁴ *n Scot & N English* a mountain, hill, or moor [Old Norse *fjall*]
fell⁵ *n* an animal's skin or hide with its hair [Old High German *fel* skin]
fellatio (fill-lay-shee-oh) *n* a sexual activity in which the penis is stimulated by the partner's mouth [Latin *fellare* to suck]
felloe *or* **felly** *n, pl* **-loes** *or* **-lies** a segment or the whole rim of a wooden wheel [Old English *felge*]
fellow *n* **1** a man or boy **2** a comrade or associate **3** a person in the same group or condition: *he earned the respect of his fellows at Dunkirk* **4** a member of the governing body at any of various universities or colleges **5** (in Britain) a postgraduate research student ▷ *adj* **6** in the same group or condition: *a conversation with a fellow passenger* [Old English *fēolaga*]
Fellow *n* a senior member of an academic institution
fellow feeling *n* sympathy existing between people who have shared similar experiences
fellowship *n* **1** the state of sharing mutual interests or activities **2** a society of people sharing mutual interests or activities **3** companionship or friendship **4** *education* a financed research post providing study facilities
fellow traveller *n history* a person who sympathized with the Communist Party but was not a member of it
felon *n criminal law* (formerly) a person who committed a serious crime [Old French: villain]
felony *n, pl* **-nies** *criminal law* (formerly) a serious crime, such as murder or arson **felonious** *adj*
felspar *n* same as **feldspar**
felt¹ *vb* the past of **feel**
felt² *n* a matted fabric of wool, made by working the fibres together under pressure [Old English]
felt-tip pen *n* a pen with a writing point made from pressed fibres
fem. **1** female **2** feminine
female *adj* **1** of the sex producing offspring **2** of or characteristic of a woman **3** (of reproductive organs such as the ovary and carpel) capable of producing reproductive cells (**gametes**) that are female **4** (of flowers) not having parts in which pollen is produced (**stamens**) **5** (of a mechanical component) having an opening into which a projecting male component can be fitted ▷ *n* **6** a female person, animal, or plant [Latin *femina* a woman]
feminine *adj* **1** possessing qualities considered typical of or appropriate to a woman **2** of women **3** *grammar* denoting a gender of nouns that includes some female animate things [Latin *femina* a woman] **femininity** *n*
feminism *n* a doctrine or movement that advocates equal rights for women **feminist** *n, adj*
femme fatale (**fam** fat-**tahl**) *n, pl* **femmes fatales** (**fam** fat-**tahlz**) an alluring or seductive woman who leads men into dangerous or difficult situations by her charm [French]
femto- *combining form* denoting 10^{-15}: *femtometer* [Danish *femten* fifteen]
femur (**fee**-mer) *n, pl* **femurs** *or* **femora** (**fee**-mer-ra) the thighbone [Latin: thigh] **femoral** *adj*
fen *n Brit* low-lying flat marshy land [Old English *fenn*]
fence *n* **1** a barrier that encloses an area such as a garden or field, usually made of posts connected by wire rails or boards **2** an obstacle for a horse to jump in steeplechasing or showjumping **3** *slang* a dealer in stolen property **4** *machinery* a guard or guide, esp. in a circular saw or plane **5** **(sit) on the fence** (to be) unwilling to commit oneself ▷ *vb* **fencing, fenced** **6** to construct a fence on or around (a piece of land) **7** **fence in** *or* **off** to close in *or* separate off with or as if with a fence **8** to fight using swords or foils **9** to argue cleverly but evasively: *they fenced for a while, weighing each other up* [Middle English *fens*, from *defens* defence]
fencing *n* **1** the sport of fighting with swords or foils **2** materials used for making fences
fend *vb* **1** **fend for oneself** to look after oneself; be independent **2** **fend off** to defend oneself against (verbal or physical attack) [Middle English *fenden*]
fender *n* **1** a low metal barrier that stops coals from falling out of a fireplace **2** a soft but solid object, such as a coil of rope, hung over the side of a vessel to prevent damage when docking **3** *US & Canad* the wing of a car
fenestration *n* the arrangement of windows in a building [Latin *fenestra* window]
feng shui (**fung shway**) *n* the Chinese art of deciding the best design or position of a grave, building, etc., in order to bring good luck [Chinese *feng* wind + *shui* water]
Fenian (**feen**-yan) *n* (formerly) a member of an Irish revolutionary organization founded to fight for an independent Ireland [after *Fianna*, legendary band of Irish warriors] **Fenianism** *n*
fenland *n Brit* an area of low-lying flat marshy land

fennel *n* a fragrant plant whose seeds, leaves, and root are used in cookery [Old English *fenol*]
fenugreek *n* a Mediterranean plant grown for its heavily scented seeds [Latin *faenum Graecum* Greek hay]
feoff (feef) *n* same as **fief** [Anglo-French]
feral *adj* **1** (of animals and plants) existing in a wild state, esp. after being domestic or cultivated **2** savage [Latin *ferus* savage]
ferment *n* **1** excitement and unrest caused by change or uncertainty **2** any substance, such as yeast, that causes fermentation ▷ *vb* **3** to undergo or cause to undergo fermentation [Latin *fermentum* yeast]
USAGE See at **foment**.

f

fermentation *n* a chemical reaction in which an organic molecule splits into simpler substances, esp. the conversion of sugar to ethyl alcohol by yeast
fermium *n chem* an element artificially produced by neutron bombardment of plutonium. Symbol: **Fm** [after Enrico *Fermi*, physicist]
fern *n* a flowerless plant with roots, stems, and long feathery leaves that reproduces by releasing spores [Old English *fearn*] **ferny** *adj*
ferocious *adj* savagely fierce or cruel [Latin *ferox*] **ferocity** *n*
ferret *n* **1** a small yellowish-white animal related to the weasel and bred for hunting rats and rabbits ▷ *vb* **-reting, -reted 2** to hunt rabbits or rats with ferrets **3** to search around **4 ferret out** **A** to drive from hiding **B** to find by determined investigation: *she could ferret out little knowledge of his background* [Latin *fur* thief]
ferric *adj* of or containing iron in the trivalent state [Latin *ferrum* iron]
Ferris wheel *n* a large vertical fairground wheel with hanging seats for riding on [after G. W. G. *Ferris*, American engineer]
ferroconcrete *n* same as **reinforced concrete**
ferrous *adj* of or containing iron in the divalent state [Latin *ferrum* iron]
ferruginous (fur-rooj-in-uss) *adj* (of a mineral or rock) containing iron [Latin *ferrum* iron]
ferrule *n* a metal ring or cap placed over the end of a stick for added strength [Latin *viria* bracelet]
ferry *n, pl* **-ries 1** a boat for transporting passengers and vehicles across a body of water, esp. as a regular service **2** such a service ▷ *vb* **-ries, -rying, -ried 3** to transport or go by ferry **4** to transport (passengers or goods) on a regular basis [Old English *ferian* to carry] **ferryman** *n*
fertile *adj* **1** capable of producing offspring, crops, or vegetation **2** *biol* capable of growth and development: *fertile seeds* **3** highly productive: *a fertile imagination* **4** *physics* (of a substance) able to be transformed into fissile or fissionable material [Latin *fertilis*] **fertility** *n*
fertilize *or* **-lise** *vb* **-lizing, -lized** *or* **-lising, -lised 1** to provide (an animal or plant) with sperm or pollen to bring about fertilization **2** to supply (soil) with nutrients **fertilization** *or* **-lisation** *n*
fertilizer *or* **-liser** *n* any substance, such as manure, added to soil to increase its productivity
fervent *or* **fervid** *adj* intensely sincere and passionate [Latin *fervere* to boil] **fervently** *adv*
fervour *or US* **fervor** *n* great intensity of feeling or belief [Latin *fervere* to boil]
fescue *n* a pasture and lawn grass with stiff narrow leaves [Old French *festu*]
fest *n* an event at which the emphasis is on a particular activity: *fashion fest* [German: festival]
fester *vb* **1** to grow worse and increasingly hostile: *the bitterness which had been festering beneath the surface* **2** (of a wound) to form pus **3** to rot and decay: *rubbish festered in the heat* [Old French *festre* suppurating sore]
festival *n* **1** an organized series of special events and performances: *the Edinburgh Festival* **2** a day or period set aside for celebration [Latin *festivus* joyful]
festive *adj* of or like a celebration [Latin *festivus* joyful]
festivity *n, pl* **-ties 1** happy celebration: *a spirit of joy and festivity* **2 festivities** celebrations
festoon *vb* **1** to drape with decorations: *Christmas trees festooned with fairy lights* ▷ *n* **2** a decorative chain of flowers or ribbons suspended in loops [Italian *festone* ornament for a feast]
feta *n* a white Greek cheese made from sheep's or goat's milk [Modern Greek]
fetal alcohol syndrome *n* a condition in newborn babies caused by excessive alcohol intake by the mother during pregnancy: characterized by retarded growth and mental disability
fetch[1] *vb* **1** to go after and bring back **2** to be sold for (a certain price): *Impressionist pictures fetch very high prices* **3** *informal* to give someone (a blow or slap) **4 fetch and carry** to perform menial tasks [Old English *feccan*]
fetch[2] *n* the ghost or apparition of a living person [origin unknown]
fetching *adj informal* attractive: *a fetching dress*
fetch up *vb* **1** *US & NZ informal* to arrive or end up **2** *slang* to vomit food
fete (fate) *n* **1** an event, usually outdoors, with stalls, competitions, etc., held to raise money for charity ▷ *vb* **feting, feted 2** to honour and entertain (someone) publicly: *the President was feted with an evening of music and dancing* [French]
fetid *or* **foetid** *adj* having a stale and unpleasant smell [Latin *fetere* to stink]
fetish *n* **1** **A** a form of behaviour in which a person derives sexual satisfaction from handling an object **B** any object that is involved in such behaviour **2** any object, activity, etc., to which one is excessively devoted: *cleanliness is almost a fetish with her* **3** an object that is believed to have magical powers [Portuguese *feitiço* sorcery] **fetishism** *n* **fetishist** *n*
fetlock *n* **1** the back part of a horse's leg, just behind the hoof **2** the tuft of hair growing from this part [Middle English *fetlak*]
fetter *n* **1 fetters** checks or restraints: *free from the fetters of religion* **2** a chain fixed around a prisoner's ankle ▷ *vb* **3** to prevent from behaving freely and naturally: *fettered by bureaucracy* **4** to tie up in fetters [Old English *fetor*]
fettle *n* **in fine fettle** in good spirits or health [Old English *fetel* belt]

fetus *or* **foetus** (fee-tuss) *n, pl* **-tuses** the embryo of a mammal in the later stages of development [Latin: offspring] **fetal** *or* **foetal** *adj*

feu *n Scots law* a right to the use of land in return for a fixed annual payment (**feu duty**) [Old French]

feud *n* **1** long and bitter hostility between two families, clans, or individuals ▹ *vb* **2** to carry on a feud [Old French *feide*]

feudal *adj* of or characteristic of feudalism [Medieval Latin *feudum* fief]

feudalism *n* the legal and social system in medieval Europe, in which people were given land and protection by a lord in return for which they worked and fought for him. Also called: **feudal system**

fever *n* **1** an abnormally high body temperature, accompanied by a fast pulse rate, shivering, and nausea. Related adjective: **febrile** **2** any disease characterized by a high temperature **3** intense nervous excitement: *she waited in a fever of anxiety* [Latin *febris*]

feverish *or* **fevered** *adj* **1** suffering from fever **2** in a state of nervous excitement: *a feverish scramble to buy shares* **feverishly** *adv*

fever pitch *n* a state of intense excitement

few *adj* **1** hardly any: *few homes had telephones in Paris in the 1930s* **2** **a few** a small number of: *a few days ago* **3** **a good few** *informal* several **4** **few and far between** scarce **5** **quite a few** *informal* several [Old English *fēawa*]

USAGE See at **less**.

fey *adj* **1** vague and whimsically strange **2** having the ability to look into the future [Old English *fæge* marked out for death]

fez *n, pl* **fezzes** a round red brimless hat with a flat top and a tassel hanging from it. Formerly worn by men in Turkey and some Arab countries [Turkish]

ff. and the following (pages, lines, etc.)

fiancé *or fem* **fiancée** (fee-on-say) *n* a person who is engaged to be married [Old French *fiancier* to promise, betroth]

fiasco *n, pl* **-cos** *or* **-coes** an action or attempt that fails completely in a ridiculous or disorganized way: *the invasion of Cuba ended in a fiasco* [Italian: flask; sense development obscure]

fiat (fie-at) *n* **1** an official order issued without the consultation of those expected to obey it: *the junta ruled by fiat* **2** official permission [Latin: let it be done]

fib *n* **1** a trivial and harmless lie ▹ *vb* **fibbing, fibbed** **2** to tell such a lie [origin unknown] **fibber** *n*

fibre *or US* **fiber** *n* **1** a natural or synthetic thread that may be spun into yarn **2** a threadlike animal or plant tissue: *a simple network of nerve fibres* **3** a fibrous substance that helps the body digest food: *fruits, vegetables, grains, lentils, and beans are high in fibre* **4** strength of character: *moral fibre* **5** essential substance or nature: *my every fibre sang out in sudden relief* [Latin *fibra* filament, entrails] **fibrous** *adj*

fibreboard *n* a building material made of compressed wood

fibreglass *n* **1** material consisting of matted fine glass fibres, used as insulation **2** a light strong material made by bonding fibreglass with a synthetic resin, used for boats and car bodies

fibre optics *n* the transmission of information by light along very thin flexible fibres of glass **fibre optic** *adj*

fibril (fibe-rill) *n* a small fibre

fibrillation *n* uncontrollable twitching of muscle fibres, esp. those of the heart

fibrin *n* a white insoluble elastic protein formed when blood clots

fibrinogen (fib-rin-no-jen) *n biol* a soluble plasma protein involved in blood clotting

fibro *n Austral* a mixture of cement and asbestos fibre, formerly used in building materials. Short for: **fibrocement**

fibroid (fibe-royd) *adj* **1** *anatomy* (of structures or tissues) containing or resembling fibres ▹ *n* **2** a harmless tumour composed of fibrous connective tissue

fibrosis (fibe-roh-siss) *n* the formation of an abnormal amount of fibrous tissue

fibrositis (fibe-roh-site-iss) *n* inflammation of fibrous tissue, esp. of the back muscles, causing pain and stiffness

fibula (fib-yew-la) *n, pl* **-lae** (-lee) *or* **-las** the outer and thinner of the two bones between the knee and ankle of the human leg [Latin: a clasp] **fibular** *adj*

fickle *adj* **1** changeable in purpose, affections, etc.: *notoriously fickle voters* **2** (of the weather) changing often and suddenly [Old English *ficol* deceitful] **fickleness** *n*

fiction *n* **1** literary works invented by the imagination, such as novels **2** an invented story or explanation: *the fiction that cricket is more noble than other sports* **3** *law* something assumed to be true for the sake of convenience, though probably false [Latin *fictio* a fashioning] **fictional** *adj*

fictionalize *or* **-lise** *vb* **-lizing, -lized** *or* **-lising, -lised** to make into fiction

fictitious *adj* **1** not genuine: *rumours of false accounting and fictitious loans had surrounded the bank for years* **2** of or in fiction

fiddle *n* **1** *informal or derogatory* the violin **2** a violin played as a folk instrument **3** *Brit & NZ informal* a dishonest action or scheme **4** **on the fiddle** *informal* engaged in an illegal or fraudulent undertaking **5** **fit as a fiddle** *informal* in very good health **6** **play second fiddle** *informal* to undertake a role that is less important or powerful than someone else's ▹ *vb* **-dling, -dled** **7** to play (a tune) on the fiddle **8** *informal* to do (something) by illegal or dishonest means **9** *informal* to falsify (accounts) **10** **fiddle with** to move or touch (something) restlessly or nervously **11** **fiddle about** *or* **around** *informal* to waste time [Old English *fithele*]

fiddle-faddle *interj old-fashioned* nonsense [reduplication of *fiddle*]

fiddler *n* **1** a person who plays the fiddle **2** a small burrowing crab **3** *informal* a person who dishonestly alters something or lies in order to get money

fiddlesticks *interj* an expression of annoyance or disagreement

f

fiddling *adj* small or unimportant

fiddly *adj* **-dlier, -dliest** small and awkward to do or handle

fidelity *n, pl* **-ties 1** faithfulness to one's spouse or lover **2** loyalty to a person, belief, or cause **3** accuracy in reporting detail: *an account of the invasion written with objectivity and fidelity* **4** *electronics* the degree to which an amplifier or radio accurately reproduces the input signal [Latin *fides* faith]

fidget *vb* **-dgeting, -dgeted 1** to move about restlessly **2 fidget with** to make restless or uneasy movements with (something): *he broke off, fidgeting with the papers, unable to meet their gaze* ▷ *n* **3** a person who fidgets **4 the fidgets** a state of restlessness: *these youngsters are very highly strung and tend to get the fidgets* [earlier *fidge*] **fidgety** *adj*

fiduciary (fid-**yewsh**-ya-ree) *law* ▷ *n* **1** a person bound to act for someone else's benefit, as a trustee ▷ *adj* **2** of or relating to a trust or trustee [Latin *fiducia* trust]

fie *interj obsolete or facetious* an exclamation of disapproval [Old French *fi*]

fief (**feef**) *n* (in feudal Europe) land granted by a lord in return for military service [Old French *fie*]

fiefdom *n* **1** (in Feudal Europe) the property owned by a lord **2** an area over which a person has influence or authority

field *n* **1** an area of uncultivated grassland; meadow **2** a piece of cleared land used for pasture or growing crops **3** a marked off area on which sports or athletic competitions are held **4** an area that is rich in minerals or other natural resources: *an oil field* **5 a** all the competitors in a competition **b** the competitors in a competition excluding the favourite **6** a battlefield **7** *cricket* the fielders collectively **8** a wide expanse of land covered by some substance such as snow or lava **9** an area of human activity or knowledge: *the most distinguished physicist in the field of quantum physics* **10** a place away from the laboratory or classroom where practical work is done **11** the surface or background of something, such as a flag **12** *physics* In full: **field of force** the region surrounding a body, such as a magnet, within which it can exert a force on another similar body not in contact with it **13 play the field** *informal* to have many romantic relationships ▷ *adj* **14** *military* of equipment or personnel for operations in the field: *field guns* ▷ *vb* **15** *sport* to catch or return (the ball) as a fielder **16** *sport* to send (a player or team) onto the field to play **17** *sport* (of a player or team) to act or take turn as a fielder or fielders **18** *informal* to deal successfully with (a question or remark) [Old English *feld*]

field day *n* **1** *informal* an opportunity or occasion for unrestrained action, esp. if previously denied or restricted: *the revelations gave the press a field day* **2** *military* a day devoted to manoeuvres or exercises

fielder *n sport* a member of the fielding side

field event *n* a competition, such as the discus, that takes place on a field as opposed to the track

fieldfare *n* a type of large thrush [Old English *feldefare*]

field glasses *pl n* binoculars

field hockey *n US & Canad* hockey played on a field, as distinguished from ice hockey

field marshal *n* an officer holding the highest rank in certain armies

fieldmouse *n, pl* **-mice** a nocturnal mouse that lives in woods and fields

field officer *n* an officer holding the rank of major, lieutenant colonel, or colonel

fieldsman *n, pl* **-men** *cricket* a fielder

field sports *pl n* sports carried on in the countryside, such as hunting or fishing

field trip *n* an expedition, esp. by students, to study something at first hand

fieldwork *n military* a temporary structure used in defending a place or position

field work *n* an investigation made in the field as opposed to the classroom or laboratory **field worker** *n*

fiend (**feend**) *n* **1** an evil spirit **2** a cruel or wicked person **3** *informal* a person who is extremely interested in or fond of something: *a fitness fiend* [Old English *fēond*] **fiendish** *adj* **fiendishly** *adv*

Fiend *n* **the Fiend** the devil

fierce *adj* **1** very aggressive or angry: *a fierce dog* **2** intense or strong: *a fierce wind* [Latin *ferus*] **fiercely** *adv*

fiery (**fire**-ee) *adj* **fierier, fieriest 1** consisting of or like fire: *a fiery explosion* **2** displaying strong passion, esp. anger: *a fiery speech* **3** (of food) very spicy **fierily** *adv* **fieriness** *n*

fiesta *n* (esp. in Spain and Latin America) a religious festival or carnival [Spanish]

FIFA (**fee**-fa) International Association Football Federation [French *Fédération Internationale de Football Association*]

fife *n* a small high-pitched flute, often used in military bands [Old High German *pfīfa*]

fifteen *n* **1** the cardinal number that is the sum of ten and five **2** a numeral, 15 or XV, representing this number **3** something representing or consisting of 15 units **4** a Rugby Union team ▷ *adj* **5** amounting to fifteen: *fifteen trees* **fifteenth** *adj, n*

fifth *adj* **1** of or being number five in a series **2** denoting the fifth from lowest (usually the highest) forward gear in a motor vehicle ▷ *n* **3** one of five equal parts of something **4** *music* the interval between one note and the note three-and-a-half tones higher or lower than it **5** the fifth from lowest (usually the highest) forward gear in a motor vehicle

fifth column *n* any group that secretly helps the enemies of its own country or organization **fifth columnist** *n*

fifty *n, pl* **-ties 1** the cardinal number that is the product of ten and five **2** a numeral, 50 or L, representing this number **3** something representing or consisting of 50 units ▷ *adj* **4** amounting to fifty: *fifty bodies* **fiftieth** *adj, n*

fifty-fifty *adj, adv informal* **1** in equal parts **2** just as likely to happen as not to happen: *a fifty-fifty chance of survival*

fig *n* **1** a soft sweet fruit full of tiny seeds, which grows on a tree **2 not care** *or* **give a fig** not to care at all: *he did not give a fig for his enemies* [Latin *ficus* fig tree]

fig. 1 figurative(ly) 2 figure

fight *vb* **fighting, fought** 1 to struggle against (an enemy) in battle or physical combat 2 to struggle to overcome or destroy: *to fight drug trafficking* 3 to carry on (a battle or contest) 4 to make (one's way) somewhere with difficulty: *they fought their way upstream* 5 **fight for** to uphold (a cause) by struggling: *fight for your rights* 6 **fight it out** to struggle or compete until a decisive result is obtained 7 **fight shy of** to avoid: *they fought shy of direct involvement in the conflict* ▷ *n* 8 a battle 9 a quarrel or contest 10 a boxing match 11 **put up a fight** to offer resistance [Old English *feohtan*] **fighting** *n*

fighter *n* 1 a professional boxer 2 a person who has determination 3 *military* an armed aircraft for destroying other aircraft

fighting chance *n* a slight chance of success dependent on a struggle

fight off *vb* 1 to drive away (an attacker) 2 to struggle to avoid: *to fight off infection*

fig leaf *n* 1 a representation of a leaf of the fig tree used in sculpture to cover the genitals of nude figures 2 anything used to conceal something thought to be shameful: *the agreement was a fig leaf for Hitler's violation of the treaty*

figment *n* **a figment of one's imagination** something nonexistent and only imagined by someone [Latin *fingere* to shape]

figuration *n* ornamentation

figurative *adj* 1 (of language) abstract, imaginative, or symbolic; not literal 2 (of art) involving realistic representation of people and things **figuratively** *adv*

figure *n* 1 a written symbol for a number 2 an amount expressed in numbers 3 **figures** calculations with numbers 4 visible shape or form; outline 5 a slim bodily shape: *it's not good for your figure* 6 a well-known person: *a public figure* 7 a representation in painting or sculpture, esp. of the human body 8 an illustration or diagram in a text 9 a decorative pattern 10 a fixed set of movements in dancing or skating 11 *geom* any combination of points, lines, curves, or planes 12 *music* a characteristic short pattern of notes 13 **figure of fun** a person who is often laughed at by other people ▷ *vb* **-uring, -ured** 14 to calculate (sums or amounts) 15 *US, Canad, Austral & NZ informal* to consider 16 to be included or play a part: *a house which figures in several of White's novels* 17 *informal* to be consistent with expectation: *he's a small-time crook, earns most of his cash as an informer. – That figures* [Latin *figura* a shape]

figured *adj* 1 decorated with a design: *a chair upholstered in figured velvet* 2 *music* ornamental

figurehead *n* 1 a person who is formally the head of a movement or an organization, but has no real authority 2 a carved bust on the bow of some sailing vessels

figure of speech *n* an expression, such as a simile, in which words do not have their literal meaning

figure out *vb informal* to work out, solve, or understand: *I can't figure him out*

figure skating *n* ice skating in which the skater traces outlines of selected patterns **figure skater** *n*

figurine *n* a small carved or moulded figure [French]

filament *n* 1 the thin wire inside a light bulb that emits light 2 *electronics* a high-resistance wire forming the cathode in some valves 3 a single strand of fibre 4 *botany* the stalk of a stamen [Latin *filum* thread] **filamentary** *adj*

filbert *n* the brown edible nuts of the hazel [after St *Philbert*, because the nuts are ripe around his feast day, August 22]

filch *vb* to steal in small amounts [Middle English *filchen* to steal, attack]

file[1] *n* 1 a folder or box used to keep documents in order 2 the documents, etc., kept in this way 3 documents or information about a specific subject or person: *the doctor handed him his file* 4 a line of people in marching formation, one behind another 5 *computers* an organized collection of related records 6 **on file** recorded for reference, as in a file ▷ *vb* **filing, filed** 7 to place (a document) in a file 8 to place (a legal document) on public or official record 9 to bring a lawsuit, esp. for divorce 10 to submit (a report or story) to a newspaper 11 to march or walk in a line [Latin *filum* a thread]

file[2] *n* 1 a hand tool consisting of a steel blade with small cutting teeth on its faces, used for shaping or smoothing ▷ *vb* **filing, filed** 2 to shape or smooth (a surface) with a file [Old English *fil*]

filial *adj* of or suitable to a son or daughter: *filial duty* [Latin *filius* son]

filibuster *n* 1 the process of obstructing legislation by means of long speeches so that time runs out and a vote cannot be taken 2 a legislator who engages in such obstruction ▷ *vb* 3 to obstruct (legislation) with such delaying tactics [probably from Dutch *vrijbuiter* pirate]

filigree *n* 1 delicate ornamental work of gold or silver wire ▷ *adj* 2 made of filigree [Latin *filum* thread + *granum* grain]

filings *pl n* shavings or particles removed by a file: *iron filings*

Filipino (fill-lip-**pee**-no) *adj* 1 of the Philippines ▷ *n, pl* **-nos** 2 Also (fem): **Filipina** a person from the Philippines

fill *vb* (often foll. by *up*) 1 to make or become full 2 to occupy the whole of: *their supporters filled the entire stand* 3 to plug (a gap or crevice) 4 to meet (a requirement or need) satisfactorily: *this book fills a major gap* 5 to cover (a page or blank space) with writing or drawing 6 to hold and perform the duties of (an office or position) 7 to appoint or elect an occupant to (an office or position) ▷ *n* 8 **one's fill** sufficient for one's needs or wants ▷ See also **fill in, fill out, fill up** [Old English *fyllan*]

filler *n* 1 a paste used for filling in cracks or holes in a surface before painting 2 *journalism* an item to fill space between more important articles

fillet *n* 1 a piece of boneless meat or fish 2 a thin strip of ribbon or lace worn in the hair or around the neck 3 *archit* a narrow flat moulding ▷ *vb* **-leting, -leted** 4 to cut or prepare (meat or fish) as a fillet [Latin *filum* thread]

fill in *vb* **1** to complete (a form) **2** to act as a substitute **3** to put material into (a hole) so as to make it level with a surface **4** *informal* to give (a person) fuller details

filling *n* **1** a substance or thing used to fill something: *a sandwich filling* **2** *dentistry* a substance that fills a gap or cavity of a tooth ▷ *adj* **3** (of food or a meal) substantial and satisfying

filling station *n chiefly Brit* a place where petrol and other supplies for motorists are sold

fillip *n* **1** something that adds stimulation or enjoyment **2** the action of holding a finger towards the palm with the thumb and suddenly releasing it with a snapping sound [imitative]

fill out *vb* **1** to fill in (a form or application) **2** to make or become plumper, thicker, or rounder **3** to make more substantial: *he filled out his speech with a few jokes*

fill up *vb* **1** to complete (a form or application) **2** to make or become full

filly *n, pl* **-lies** a young female horse [Old Norse *fylja*]

film *n* **1 A** a sequence of images projected onto a screen, creating the illusion of movement **B** a form of entertainment in such a sequence of images. ▷ Related adjective: **cinematic** **2** a thin flexible strip of cellulose coated with a photographic emulsion, used to make negatives and slides **3** a thin coating, covering, or layer: *a fine film of dust covered the floor* **4** a thin sheet of any material, as of plastic for packaging ▷ *vb* **5 A** to photograph with a movie or video camera **B** to make a film of (a screenplay or event) **6** **film over** to cover or become covered with a thin layer ▷ *adj* **7** of or relating to films or the cinema [Old English *filmen* membrane]

filmic *adj* of or suggestive of films or the cinema **filmically** *adv*

film star *n* a popular film actor or actress

filmy *adj* **filmier, filmiest** very thin and almost transparent: *a shirt of filmy black chiffon* **filmily** *adv* **filminess** *n*

filo *or* **filo pastry** (feel-o) *n* a type of flaky Greek pastry in very thin sheets [Modern Greek *phullon* leaf]

filter *n* **1** a substance, such as paper or sand, that allows fluid to pass but retains solid particles **2** any device containing such a substance, esp. a tip on the mouth end of a cigarette **3** any electronic or acoustic device that blocks signals of certain frequencies while allowing others to pass **4** a computer program that processes data in order to remove certain items: *a spam filter* **5** any transparent disc of gelatine or glass used to reduce the intensity of given frequencies from the light leaving a lamp or entering a camera **6** *Brit* a traffic signal which permits vehicles to turn either left or right when the main signals are red ▷ *vb* **7** Also: **filter out** to remove or separate (particles) from (a liquid or gas) by a filter **8** Also: **filter through** to pass through a filter or something like a filter [Medieval Latin *filtrum* piece of felt used as a filter]

filter out *or* **filter through** *vb* to become known gradually: *the crowd broke up when the news filtered through*

filter paper *n* a porous paper used for filtering liquids

filter tip *n* **1** an attachment to the mouth end of a cigarette for trapping impurities **2** a cigarette with such an attachment **filter-tipped** *adj*

filth *n* **1** disgusting dirt and muck **2** offensive material or language [Old English *fȳlth*] **filthiness** *n* **filthy** *adj*

filtrate *n* **1** a liquid or gas that has been filtered ▷ *vb* **-trating, -trated** **2** to filter [Medieval Latin *filtrare* to filter] **filtration** *n*

fin *n* **1** any of the winglike projections from a fish's body enabling it to balance and swim **2** *Brit* a vertical surface to which the rudder is attached at the rear of an aeroplane **3** a swimmer's flipper [Old English *finn*] **finned** *adj*

fin. **1** finance **2** financial

finagle (fin-nay-gl) *vb* **-gling, -gled** *informal* to use or achieve by craftiness or trickery [origin unknown]

final *adj* **1** of or occurring at the end; last **2** having no possibility of further discussion, action, or change: *a final decision* ▷ *n* **3** a deciding contest between the winners of previous rounds in a competition ▷ See also **finals** [Latin *finis* limit, boundary] **finality** *n* **finally** *adv*

finale (fin-nah-lee) *n* the concluding part of a dramatic performance or musical composition [Italian]

finalist *n* a contestant who has reached the last stage of a competition

finalize *or* **-lise** *vb* **-lizing, -lized** *or* **-lising, -lised** to put into final form; settle: *plans have yet to be finalized* **finalization** *or* **-lisation** *n*

> **USAGE** Although *finalize* has been in widespread use for some time, many speakers and writers still prefer to use *complete, conclude,* or *make final,* esp. in formal contexts.

finals *pl n* **1** the deciding part of a competition **2** *education Brit & S African* the last examinations in an academic course

finance *vb* **-nancing, -nanced** **1** to provide or obtain funds for (a project or large purchase) ▷ *n* **2** the system of money, credit, and investment **3** management of money, loans, or credits: *the dangerous political arena of public-sector finance* **4** funds or the provision of funds **5** **finances** money resources: *the company's crumbling finances* [Old French *finer* to end, settle by payment]

financial *adj* **1** of or relating to finance, finances, or people who manage money **2** *Austral & NZ informal* having ready money **financially** *adv*

financial year *n* any annual accounting period

financier *n* a person who is engaged in large-scale financial operations

finch *n* a small songbird with a short strong beak [Old English *finc*]

find *vb* **finding, found** **1** to discover by chance **2** to discover by search or effort **3** to realize or become aware: *I have found that if you make the effort then people will be more willing to help you* **4** to consider (someone or something) to have a particular quality: *his business partner had found that odd* **5** to experience (a particular feeling): *she found comfort in his words* **6** *law* to pronounce (the defendant) guilty or not guilty **7** to reach (a target) **8** to provide, esp. with difficulty: *we'll find room for you too* **9** **find one's feet** to become capable or confident ▷ *n* **10** a person or thing that is found, esp. a valuable discovery: *the archaeological find of the century* [Old English *findan*]

finder *n* **1** a small telescope fitted to a larger one **2** a person or thing that finds

finding *n* the conclusion reached after an inquiry or investigation

find out *vb* **1** to learn something that one did not already know **2** **find someone out** to discover that someone has been dishonest or deceitful

fine[1] *adj* **1** very good **2** superior in skill: *a fine doctor* **3** (of weather) clear and dry **4** *informal* quite well: *I felt fine* **5** satisfactory: *as far as we can tell, everything is fine* **6** of delicate or careful workmanship: *fine porcelain* **7** subtle: *too fine a distinction* **8** very thin or slender: *fine soft hair* **9** very small: *fine print* **10** (of edges or blades) sharp **11** fancy, showy, or smart **12** good-looking **13** *humorous* disappointing or terrible: *a fine mess!* ▷ *adv* **14** *informal* very well: *that's what we've always done, and it suits us just fine* ▷ *vb* **fining, fined 15** to make (something) finer or thinner **16** **fine down** to make (a theory or criticism) more precise or exact [Latin *finis* end, boundary, as in *finis honorum* the highest degree of honour] **finely** *adv*

fine[2] *n* **1** a payment imposed as a penalty ▷ *vb* **fining, fined 2** to impose a fine on [Old French *fin*]

fine art *n* **1** art produced chiefly to appeal to the sense of beauty **2** any of the fields in which such art is produced, such as painting, sculpture, and engraving

fine-drawn *adj* **1** (of arguments or distinctions) subtle **2** (of wire) drawn out until very fine

finery *n* elaborate or showy decoration, esp. clothing and jewellery: *the princess dressed up in her finery*

fines herbes (feenz **airb**) *pl n* finely chopped mixed herbs, used to flavour omelettes [French]

finespun *adj* **1** spun or drawn out to a fine thread **2** excessively subtle or concerned with minute detail: *a finespun theological debate*

finesse (fin-**ness**) *n* **1** elegant and delicate skill **2** subtlety and tact in handling difficult situations: *a lack of diplomatic finesse* **3** *bridge & whist* an attempt to win a trick when opponents hold a high card in the suit led by playing a lower card ▷ *vb* **-nessing, -nessed 4** to bring about with finesse **5** *bridge & whist* to play (a card) as a finesse [Old French]

fine-tooth comb *or* **fine-toothed comb** *n* **1** a comb with fine teeth set closely together **2** **go over with a fine-tooth comb** to examine very thoroughly

fine-tune *vb* **-tuning, -tuned** to make fine adjustments to (something) so that it works really well

finger *n* **1** one of the four long jointed parts of the hand **2** the part of a glove made to cover a finger **3** something that resembles a finger in shape or function **4** a quantity of liquid in a glass as deep as a finger is wide **5** **get** *or* **pull one's finger out** *Brit & NZ informal* to begin or speed up activity, esp. after initial delay **6** **put one's finger on** to identify precisely **7** **put the finger on** *informal* to inform on or identify, esp. for the police **8** **twist around one's little finger** to have easy and complete influence over ▷ *vb* **9** to touch or manipulate with the fingers; handle **10** to use one's fingers in playing (a musical instrument) **11** *informal, chiefly US* to identify as a criminal or suspect [Old English] **fingerless** *adj*

fingerboard *n* the long strip of hard wood on a violin, guitar, etc., upon which the strings are stopped by the fingers

finger bowl *n* a small bowl of water for rinsing the fingers at table during a meal, esp. at a formal dinner

fingering *n* **1** the technique of using one's fingers in playing a musical instrument **2** the numerals in a musical part indicating this

fingernail *n* a thin hard clear plate covering part of the upper surface of the end of each finger

fingerprint *n* **1** an impression of the pattern of ridges on the inner surface of the end of each finger and thumb ▷ *vb* **2** to take an inked impression of the fingerprints of (a person) **3** to take a sample of the DNA of (a person)

fingerstall *n* a protective covering for a finger

fingertip *n* **1** the end of a finger **2** **have at one's fingertips** to know thoroughly

finicky *or* **finicking** *adj* **1** extremely fussy **2** overelaborate or ornate: *finicky designer patterns* [earlier *finical*, from FINE[1]]

finis *n* the end: used at the end of books [Latin]

finish *vb* **1** to bring to an end; conclude or stop **2** to be at or come to the end; use up **3** to bring to a desired or complete condition **4** to put a particular surface texture on (wood, cloth, or metal) **5** **finish off** **A** to complete by doing the last part of: *she finished off her dissertation last week* **B** to destroy or defeat completely: *the physical demands of two young children nearly finished me off* **6** **finish with** to end a relationship with (someone) ▷ *n* **7** the final stage or part; end **8** death or absolute defeat **9** the surface texture of wood, cloth, or metal **10** a thing or event that completes [Latin *finire*]

finishing school *n* a private school for girls that teaches social skills and polite behaviour

finite (**fine**-ite) *adj* **1** having limits in size, space, or time: *finite supplies of fossil fuels* **2** *maths & logic* having a countable number of elements **3** *grammar* denoting any form of a verb inflected for person, number, and tense [Latin *finitus* limited]

Finn *n* a person from Finland

finnan haddock *or* **finnan haddie** *n* a smoked haddock [*Findon*, town near Aberdeen]

Finnish *adj* **1** of Finland ▷ *n* **2** the language of Finland

fino (**fee**-no) *n* a very dry sherry [Spanish: fine]

fiord (**fee**-ord) *n* same as **fjord**

fipple flute *n* an end-blown flute with a plug (**fipple**) at the mouthpiece, such as the recorder or flageolet

fir *n* a pyramid-shaped tree with needle-like leaves and erect cones [Old English *furh*]

fire *n* **1** the state of combustion producing heat, flames, and often smoke **2** burning coal or wood, esp. in a hearth to heat a room **3** a destructive uncontrolled burning that destroys buildings, crops, etc. **4** *Brit* an electric or gas device for heating a room **5** the act of shooting weapons **6** passion and enthusiasm: *her questions brought new fire to the debate* **7 catch fire** to start burning **8 on fire A** burning **B** ardent or eager **9 open fire** to start firing a gun, artillery, etc. **10 play with fire** to be involved in something risky **11 set fire to** *or* **set on fire A** to ignite **B** to arouse or excite **12 under fire** being attacked, such as by weapons or by harsh criticism ▷ *vb* **firing, fired 13** to discharge (a firearm) **14** to detonate (an explosive device) **15** *informal* to dismiss from employment **16** to ask (a lot of questions) quickly in succession **17** *ceramics* to bake in a kiln to harden the clay **18** to kindle or be kindled **19** (of an internal-combustion engine) to produce an electrical spark which causes the fuel to burn and the engine to start **20** to provide with fuel **21** to arouse to strong emotion: *he fired his team mates with enthusiasm* [Old English *fȳr*]

fire alarm *n* a device to give warning of fire

firearm *n* a weapon, such as a pistol, that fires bullets

fireball *n* **1** ball-shaped lightning **2** the hot ionized gas at the centre of a nuclear explosion **3** a large bright meteor **4** *slang* an energetic person

firebomb *n* a bomb that is designed to cause fires

firebrand *n* a person who arouses passionate political feelings, often causing trouble

firebreak *n* a strip of open land in a forest to stop the advance of a fire

firebrick *n* a heat-resistant brick, used for lining furnaces, flues, and fireplaces

fire brigade *n Brit & Austral* an organized body of firefighters

fire clay *n* a heat-resistant clay used in making firebricks and furnace linings

firecracker *n* a firework which produces a loud bang

firedamp *n Brit, Austral & NZ* an explosive mixture of hydrocarbons, chiefly methane, formed in coal mines

firedog *n* same as **andiron**

fire door *n* a door made of noncombustible material that prevents a fire spreading within a building

fire drill *n* a rehearsal of procedures for escape from a fire

fire-eater *n* a performer who pretends to swallow flaming rods

fire engine *n* a vehicle that carries firefighters and firefighting equipment to a fire

fire escape *n* a metal staircase or ladder on the outside of a building for escape in the event of fire

fire-extinguisher *n* a portable device for spraying water, foam, or powder to extinguish a fire

firefighter *n* a person whose job is to put out fires and rescue people endangered by them **firefighting** *adj, n*

firefly *n, pl* **-flies** a beetle that glows in the dark

fireguard *n* a screen made of wire mesh put before an open fire to protect against sparks

fire hall *n Canad* a fire station

fire hydrant *n* an outlet from a water main in the street, from which firefighters can draw water in an emergency

fire irons *pl n* a shovel, poker, and tongs for tending a domestic fire

fireman *n, pl* **-men 1** a male firefighter **2** (on steam trains) the person who stokes the fire

fireplace *n* an open recess at the base of a chimney for a fire; hearth

fireplug *n chiefly US & NZ* same as **fire hydrant**

fire power *n military* the amount of fire that can be delivered by a unit or weapon

fire raiser *n Brit* a person who deliberately sets fire to property **fire raising** *n*

fire ship *n history* a ship loaded with explosives, set on fire and left to drift among an enemy's warships

fireside *n* the hearth

fire station *n* a building where firefighting vehicles and equipment are stationed

firetrap *n* a building that would burn easily or one without fire escapes

firewall *n* software that prevents unauthorized access to a computer network from the internet

firewater *n informal* any alcoholic spirit

firework *n* a device containing chemicals that is ignited to produce coloured sparks and sometimes bangs

fireworks *pl n* **1** a show in which fireworks are let off **2** *informal* an outburst of temper **3** an exciting and impressive performance, speech, or piece of writing: *Dickens' verbal fireworks*

firie *n Austral informal* a firefighter

firing *n* **1** a discharge of a firearm **2** the process of baking ceramics in a kiln **3** something used as fuel

firing line *n* **1** *military* the positions from which fire is delivered **2** the leading or most vulnerable position in an activity: *the manager is in the firing line after a string of bad results*

firing squad *n* a group of soldiers appointed to shoot a condemned criminal dead

firkin *n* **1** a small wooden barrel or similar container **2** *Brit* a unit of capacity equal to nine gallons [Middle Dutch *vierde* fourth]

firm¹ *adj* **1** not soft or yielding to a touch or pressure **2** securely in position **3** definitely established: *a firm agreement* **4** having determination or strength: *if you are firm and consistent she will come to see things your way* ▷ *adv* **5 stand firm** to refuse to give in ▷ *vb* **6** to make or become firm: *to firm up flabby thighs* [Latin *firmus*] **firmly** *adv* **firmness** *n*

firm² *n* a business company [Spanish *firma* signature]

firmament *n literary* the sky or the heavens [Late Latin *firmamentum*]

first *adj* **1** earliest in time or order **2** rated, graded, or ranked above all other levels: *the First Lord of the Admiralty* **3** denoting the lowest forward gear in a motor vehicle **4** *music* denoting the highest voice part in a chorus or one of the sections of an orchestra: *the first violin* ▷ *n* **5** the person or thing coming before all others **6** the beginning or outset **7** *education, chiefly Brit* an honours degree of the highest class **8** the lowest forward gear in a motor vehicle ▷ *adv* **9** before anything else: *I would advise you to try surgery first* **10** for the first time: *this story first came to public attention in January 1984* [Old English *fyrest*]

first aid *n* immediate medical assistance given in an emergency

first-born *adj* **1** eldest of the children in a family ▷ *n* **2** the eldest child in a family

first class *n* **1** the class or grade of the best or highest value, rank, or quality ▷ *adj* **first-class** **2** of the best or highest class or grade **3** excellent **4** denoting the most comfortable class of accommodation in a hotel, aircraft, or train **5** denoting mail that is handled faster than second-class mail ▷ *adv* **first-class** **6** by first-class mail, transport, etc.

first-day cover *n philately* an envelope postmarked on the first day of the issue of its stamps

first-degree burn *n* a burn in which the skin surface is red and painful

first floor *n* **1** the storey of a building immediately above the one at ground level **2** US the storey at ground level

first-foot *Scot & NZ* ▷ *n* **1** the first person to enter a household in the New Year ▷ *vb* **2** to visit (someone) as first-foot **first-footing** *n*

first fruits *pl n* **1** the first results or profits of an undertaking **2** fruit that ripens first

first-hand *adj* **1** obtained directly from the original source ▷ *adv* **2** directly from the original source **3 at first hand** directly

First Lady *n* (in the US) the wife of the president

firstly *adv* same as **first** (sense 9)

first mate *n* an officer second in command to the captain of a merchant ship

First Minister *n* the chief minister of the Scottish Parliament, the Northern Ireland Assembly, or the National Assembly for Wales

First Nation *n* the indigenous people of a country

first night *n* the first public performance of a play or other production

first offender *n* a person convicted of a criminal offence for the first time

first officer *n* same as **first mate**

First Peoples *pl n Canad* a collective term for the Native Canadian peoples, the Inuit, and the Métis

first person *n* the form of a pronoun or verb used by the speaker to refer to himself or herself, or a group including himself or herself

first-person shooter *n* a computer game in which the player aims and shoots at targets, and the graphics displayed are seen from the viewpoint of the shooter

first-rate *adj* of the best quality; excellent

firth *n* a narrow inlet of the sea, esp. in Scotland [Old Norse *fjörthr* fjord]

fiscal *adj* **1** of or relating to government finances, esp. tax revenues ▷ *n* **2** (in Scotland) same as **procurator fiscal** [Latin *fiscalis* concerning the state treasury]

fish *n, pl* **fish** *or* **fishes** **1** a cold-blooded animal with a backbone, gills, and usually fins and a skin covered in scales, that lives in water. Related adjective: **piscine** **2** the flesh of fish used as food **3 cold fish** a person who shows little emotion **4 drink like a fish** to drink alcohol to excess **5 have other fish to fry** to have other more important concerns **6 like a fish out of water** ill at ease in an unfamiliar situation ▷ *vb* **7** to attempt to catch fish **8** to fish in (a particular area of water): *the first trawler to fish these waters* **9** to grope for and find with some difficulty: *he fished a cigarette from his pocket* **10 fish for** to seek (something) indirectly: *he was fishing for compliments* [Old English *fisc*]

fishcake *n* a fried flattened ball of flaked fish mixed with mashed potatoes

fisherman *n, pl* **-men** a person who fishes as a profession or for sport

fishery *n, pl* **-eries** **1 A** the industry of catching, processing, and selling fish **B** a place where this is carried on **2** a place where fish are reared

fish-eye lens *n photog* a lens with a highly curved front that covers almost 180°

fishfinger *n* an oblong piece of fish coated in breadcrumbs

fishing *n* the occupation of catching fish

fishing rod *n* a long tapered flexible pole for use with a fishing line and, usually, a reel

fishmeal *n* ground dried fish used as feed for farm animals or as a fertilizer

fishmonger *n chiefly Brit* a seller of fish

fishnet *n* an open mesh fabric resembling netting, sometimes used for tights or stockings

fishplate *n* a flat piece of metal joining one rail or beam to the next, esp. on railway tracks

fishwife *n, pl* **-wives** *derogatory* a coarse or bad-tempered woman with a loud voice

fishy *adj* **fishier, fishiest** **1** of or suggestive of fish **2** *informal* suspicious or questionable: *something a bit fishy about his explanation* **fishily** *adv*

fissile *adj* **1** capable of undergoing nuclear fission **2** tending to split

fission *n* **1** the act or process of splitting into parts **2** *biol* a form of asexual reproduction involving a division into two or more equal parts **3** the splitting of atomic nuclei with the release of a large amount of energy [Latin *fissio* a splitting] **fissionable** *adj*

fissure (fish-er) *n* any long narrow cleft or crack, esp. in a rock [Latin *fissus* split]

fist *n* a hand with the fingers clenched into the palm [Old English *fȳst*]

fisticuffs *pl n* fighting with the fists [probably from obsolete *fisty* with the fist + CUFF[2]]

fistula (fist-yew-la) *n pathol* a long narrow ulcer [Latin: tube, ulcer]

fit[1] *vb* **fitting, fitted** **1** to be appropriate or suitable for **2** to be of the correct size or shape (for) **3** to adjust in order to make appropriate **4** to try clothes on (someone) and note any adjustments needed **5** to make competent or ready: *the experience helped to fit him for the task* **6** to correspond with the facts or circumstances: *this part doesn't fit in with the* *rest of his theory* ▷ *adj* **fitter, fittest 7** appropriate **8** in good health **9** worthy or suitable: *houses fit for human habitation* **10** *slang* (of a person) sexually attractive ▷ *n* **11** the manner in which something fits: *the suit was an excellent fit* ▷ See also **fit in, fit out** [probably from Middle Dutch *vitten*] **fitly** *adv* **fitness** *n*

fit² *n* **1** a sudden attack or convulsion, such as an epileptic seizure **2** a sudden short burst or spell: *fits of laughter; a fit of pique* **3 in fits and starts** in spasmodic spells **4 have a fit** *informal* to become very angry [Old English *fitt* conflict]

fitful *adj* occurring in irregular spells **fitfully** *adv*

fit in *vb* **1** to give a place or time to (someone or something) **2** to belong or conform, esp. after adjustment

fitment *n* **1** an accessory attached to a machine **2** *chiefly Brit* a detachable part of the furnishings of a room

fit out *vb* to equip: *he started to fit out a ship in secret*

fitted *adj* **1** designed for excellent fit: *a fitted suit* **2** (of a carpet) covering a floor completely **3 A** (of furniture) built to fit a particular space **B** (of a kitchen, bathroom, etc.) having equipment and furniture built or selected to suit the measurements of the room **4** (of sheets) having ends that are elasticated to fit tightly over a mattress

fitter *n* **1** a person who is skilled in the installation and adjustment of machinery **2** a person who fits garments

fitting *adj* **1** appropriate or proper ▷ *n* **2** an accessory or part **3** the trying-on of clothes so that they can be adjusted to fit **4 fittings** furnishings or accessories in a building **fittingly** *adv*

five *n* **1** the cardinal number that is the sum of one and four **2** a numeral, 5 or V, representing this number **3** something representing or consisting of five units ▷ *adj* **4** amounting to five: *five years* ▷ See also **fives** [Old English *fīf*]

five-eighth *n* **1** *Austral* (in rugby) a player positioned between the scrum-half and the inside-centre **2** NZ (in rugby) either of two players positioned between the halfback and the centre

fivefold *adj* **1** having five times as many or as much **2** composed of five parts ▷ *adv* **3** by five times as many or as much

fivepins *n* a bowling game played esp. in Canada

fiver *n Brit, Austral & NZ informal* a five-pound or five-dollar note

fives *n* a ball game similar to squash but played with bats or the hands

fix *vb* **1** to make or become firm, stable, or secure **2** to repair **3** to attach or place permanently: *fix the mirror to the wall* **4** to settle definitely or decide upon: *the meeting is fixed for the 12th* **5** to direct (the eyes, etc.) steadily: *she fixed her eyes upon the jewels* **6** *informal* to unfairly influence the outcome of: *the fight was fixed by the promoter* **7** *informal* to put a stop to the activities of (someone): *the Party was determined to fix him* **8** *informal* to prepare: *let me fix you a drink* **9** *photog* to treat (a film, plate, or paper) with fixer to make the image permanent **10** to convert (atmospheric nitrogen) into nitrogen compounds **11** *slang* to inject a narcotic drug ▷ *n* **12** *informal* a difficult situation **13** the reckoning of a navigational position of a ship by radar, etc. **14** *slang* an injection of a narcotic ▷ See also **fix up** [Latin *fixus* fixed]

fixation *n* **1** an obsessive interest in something **2** *psychol* a strong attachment of a person to another person or an object in early life **3** *chem* the conversion of nitrogen in the air into a compound, esp. a fertilizer **fixated** *adj*

fixative *n* **1** a fluid sprayed over drawings to prevent smudging **2** a liquid used to hold objects, esp. dentures, in place **3** a substance added to a perfume to make it less volatile

fixed *adj* **1** attached or placed so as to be immovable **2** stable: *fixed rates* **3** unchanging and appearing artificial: *a fixed smile* **4** established as to relative position: *a fixed point* **5** always at the same time **6** (of ideas) firmly maintained **7** *informal* equipped or provided for, esp. with money or possessions **8** *informal* illegally arranged: *a fixed trial* **fixedly** (**fix**-id-lee) *adv*

fixed star *n* an extremely distant star that appears to be almost stationary

fixer *n* **1** a solution used in photographic development that fixes the image in place, preventing further chemical reactions **2** *slang* a person who makes arrangements, esp. illegally

fixity *n, pl* **-ties** the state or quality of a person's gaze, attitude, or concentration not changing or weakening: *a remarkable fixity of purpose*

fixture *n* **1** an object firmly fixed in place, esp. a household appliance **2** something or someone regarded as fixed in a particular place or position: *the regatta has become a fixture of the sporting calendar* **3 A** a sports match **B** the date of it

fix up *vb* **1** to arrange **2 fix up with** to provide with: *can you fix me up with tickets?*

fizz *vb* **1** to make a hissing or bubbling sound **2** (of a drink) to produce bubbles of carbon dioxide ▷ *n* **3** a hissing or bubbling sound **4** releasing of small bubbles of gas by a liquid **5** any effervescent drink [imitative] **fizzy** *adj* **fizziness** *n*

fizzle *vb* **-zling, -zled 1** to make a hissing or bubbling sound **2 fizzle out** *informal* to fail or die out, esp. after a promising start [probably from obsolete *fist* to break wind]

fjord (fee-**ord**) *n* a long narrow inlet of the sea between high cliffs, esp. in Norway [Norwegian, from Old Norse *fjörthr*]

Fl flerovium

FL Florida

fl. fluid

flab *n* unsightly or unwanted fat on the body [from *flabby*]

flabbergasted *adj informal* completely astonished [origin unknown]

flabby *adj* **-bier, -biest 1** having flabby flesh **2** loose or limp **3** weak and lacking purpose: *flabby hesitant leaders* [alteration of *flappy*, from *flap*] **flabbiness** *n*

flaccid (**flass**-id) *adj* soft and limp [Latin *flaccidus*] **flaccidity** *n*

flag¹ *n* **1** a piece of cloth often attached to a pole, used as an emblem or for signalling **2** an indicator built into a computer program to help determine whether a particular event has occurred ▷ *vb* **flagging, flagged 3** to mark with a tag or sticker **4** NZ to give up an activity **5 flag down** to signal (a vehicle) to stop **6 flag up** to bring (something) to someone's attention [origin unknown]

flag² *n* same as **iris** (sense 2) [origin unknown]

flag³ *vb* **flagging, flagged 1** to lose enthusiasm or energy **2** to become limp [origin unknown] **flagging** *adj*

flag⁴ *n* short for **flagstone**

flagellate *vb* (flaj-a-late) **-lating, -lated 1** to whip, esp. in religious penance or for sexual pleasure ▷ *adj* (**flaj**-a-lit) **2** possessing one or more flagella **3** like a whip [Latin *flagellare* to whip] **flagellation** *n*

flagellum (flaj-**jell**-lum) *n, pl* **-la** (-la) *or* **-lums 1** *biol* a long whiplike outgrowth that acts as an organ of movement **2** *botany* a long thin shoot or runner [Latin: a little whip]

flageolet (flaj-a-**let**) *n* a high-pitched musical instrument of the recorder family [French]

flagfall *n Austral* the minimum charge for hiring a taxi, to which the rate per kilometre is added

flagged *adj* paved with flagstones

flag of convenience *n* a foreign flag flown by a ship registered in that country to gain financial or legal advantage

flag of truce *n* a white flag indicating an invitation to an enemy to negotiate

flagon *n* **1** a large bottle of wine, cider, etc. **2** a narrow-necked jug for containing liquids [Late Latin *flasco* flask]

flagpole *or* **flagstaff** *n* a pole on which a flag is flown

flagrant (**flayg**-rant) *adj* openly outrageous: *flagrant violation of international law* [Latin *flagrare* to blaze, burn] **flagrancy** *n*

flagship *n* **1** a ship aboard which the commander of a fleet is quartered **2** the most important ship belonging to a shipping company **3** the most modern or impressive product or asset of an organization: *the company has opened its own flagship store*

flagstone *n* a flat slab of hard stone for paving [Old Norse *flaga* slab]

flag-waving *n informal* an emotional appeal to patriotic feeling

flail *n* **1** a tool formerly used for threshing grain by hand ▷ *vb* **2** to wave about wildly: *arms flailing, they staggered about* **3** to beat with or as if with a flail [Latin *flagellum* whip]

flair *n* **1** natural ability: *she has a flair for languages* **2** originality and stylishness: *to dress with flair* [French]

flak *n* **1** anti-aircraft fire **2** severe criticism: *most of the flak was directed at the umpire* [German *Fl(ieger)a(bwehr)k(anone)* aircraft defence gun]

flake¹ *n* **1** a small thin piece chipped off an object or substance **2** a small piece: *flakes of snow* **3** *slang* an eccentric or unreliable person ▷ *vb* **flaking, flaked 4** to peel or cause to peel off in flakes **5** to break into small thin pieces: *bake for 30 minutes, or until the fish is firm and flakes easily* [from Old Norse] **flaky** *adj*

flake² *n* (in Australia) the commercial name for the meat of the gummy shark

flake out *vb informal* to collapse or fall asleep from exhaustion

flak jacket *n* a reinforced sleeveless jacket for protection against gunfire or shrapnel

flambé (flahm-bay) *vb* **flambéing, flambéd** to cook or serve (food) in flaming brandy [French]

flamboyant *adj* **1** behaving in a very noticeable, extravagant way: *a flamboyant jazz pianist* **2** very bright and showy [French: flaming] **flamboyance** *n*

flame *n* **1** a hot luminous body of burning gas coming in flickering streams from burning material **2 flames** the state of burning: *half the building was in flames* **3** intense passion: *the flame of love* ▷ *vb* **flaming, flamed 4** to burn brightly **5** to become red or fiery: *colour flamed in Sally's cheeks* **6** to become angry or excited [Latin *flamma*]

flamenco *n, pl* **-cos 1** a rhythmic Spanish dance accompanied by a guitar and vocalist **2** music for this dance [Spanish]

flame-thrower *n* a weapon that ejects a stream or spray of burning fluid

flaming *adj* **1** burning with flames **2** glowing brightly **3** very angry and heated: *a flaming row* **4** *informal* extreme; damned: *what the flaming hell do you think you're doing?* ▷ *adv* **5** *informal* extremely; damned: *I was flaming mad about what happened*

flamingo *n, pl* **-gos** *or* **-goes** a large pink wading bird with a long neck and legs [Portuguese *flamengo*]

flammable *adj* easily set on fire; inflammable **flammability** *n*

> **USAGE** *Flammable* and *inflammable* are interchangeable when used of the properties of materials. *Flammable* is, however, often preferred for warning labels as there is less likelihood of misunderstanding (*inflammable* being sometimes taken to mean *not flammable*). *Inflammable* is preferred in figurative contexts: *this could prove to be an inflammable situation.*

flan *n* an open sweet or savoury tart [French]

flange *n* a projecting collar or rim on an object for strengthening it or for attaching it to another object [origin unknown]

flank *n* **1** the side of a man or animal between the ribs and the hip **2** a cut of beef from the flank **3** the side of a naval or military formation ▷ *vb* **4** to be positioned at the side of (a person or thing) [Old French *flanc*]

flannel *n* **1** *Brit* a small piece of towelling cloth used to wash the face **2** a soft light woollen fabric used for clothing **3 flannels** trousers made of flannel **4** *Brit informal* evasive talk that avoids giving any commitment or direct answer ▷ *vb* **-nelling, -nelled** *or US* **-neling, -neled 5** *Brit informal* to flatter or talk evasively [Welsh *gwlân* wool]

flannelette *n* a cotton imitation of flannel, used to make sheets and nightdresses

flap *vb* **flapping, flapped 1** to move backwards and forwards or up and down, like a bird's wings in flight ▷ *n* **2** the action of or noise made by flapping **3** a piece of material attached at one edge and usually used to cover an opening, such as on a pocket **4** a hinged section of an aircraft wing that is raised or lowered to control the aircraft's speed **5** *informal* a state of panic or agitation [probably imitative]

flapjack *n* **1** *Brit* a chewy biscuit made with rolled oats **2** *NZ* a small thick pancake

flapper *n* (in the 1920s) a lively young woman who dressed and behaved unconventionally

flare *vb* **flaring, flared 1** to burn with an unsteady or sudden bright flame **2** (of temper, violence, or trouble) to break out suddenly **3** to spread outwards from a narrow to a wider shape ▷ *n* **4** an unsteady flame **5** a sudden burst of flame **6 A** a blaze of light used to illuminate, signal distress, alert, etc. **B** the device producing such a blaze **7 flares** trousers with legs that flare out at the bottom [origin unknown] **flared** *adj*

flare up *vb* **1** to burst suddenly into fire **2** *informal* to burst into anger

flash *n* **1** a sudden short blaze of intense light or flame **2** a sudden occurrence of a particular emotion or experience: *a flash of anger* **3** a very brief time: *in a flash he was inside and locked the door behind him* **4** a short unscheduled news announcement **5** *Brit & Austral* an emblem on a uniform or vehicle to identify its military formation **6** *photog* short for **flashlight 7 flash in the pan** a project, person, etc., that enjoys only short-lived success ▷ *adj* **8** *informal* ostentatious or vulgar **9** brief and rapid: *a flash fire* ▷ *vb* **10** to burst or cause to burst suddenly into flame **11** to shine with a bright light suddenly or repeatedly **12** to move very fast **13** to come rapidly (into the mind or vision) **14 A** to signal very fast: *a warning was flashed onto a screen in the cockpit* **B** to signal by use of a light, such as car headlights **15** *informal* to display in a boastful and extravagant way: *flashing banknotes around* **16** *informal* to show briefly **17** *Brit slang* to expose oneself indecently [origin unknown] **flasher** *n*

flashback *n* a scene in a book, play, or film that shows earlier events

flash drive *n* a portable storage device such as a memory card

flash flood *n* a sudden short-lived flood

flashing *n* a weatherproof material used to cover the joins in a roof

flashlight *n* **1** *photog* a brief bright light emitted by a camera when taking a photograph **2** *chiefly US & Canad* a torch

flash mob *n* a group of people who arrange by phone or online to meet in a public place to stage a brief performance or stunt

flash point *n* **1** a critical time beyond which a situation will inevitably erupt into violence **2** the lowest temperature at which the vapour above a liquid can be ignited

flashy *adj* **flashier, flashiest** showy in a vulgar way: *a loud and flashy tie* **flashily** *adv* **flashiness** *n*

flask *n* **1** same as **vacuum flask 2** a small flat container for alcoholic drink designed to be carried in a pocket **3** a bottle with a narrow neck, esp. used in a laboratory [Medieval Latin *flasca, flasco*]

flat[1] *adj* **flatter, flattest 1** horizontal or level: *roofs are now flat instead of slanted* **2** even or smooth: *a flat surface* **3** lying stretched out at full length **4** (of a tyre) deflated **5** (of shoes) having an unraised heel **6** without qualification; total: *a flat rejection* **7** fixed: *a flat rate* **8** unexciting: *a picture curiously flat in tone* **9** without variation or emotion: *a flat voice* **10** (of drinks) no longer fizzy **11** (of a battery) fully discharged **12** (of paint) without gloss **13** *music* **A** denoting a note that has been lowered in pitch by one chromatic semitone: *B flat* **B** (of an instrument, voice, etc.) out of tune by being too low in pitch ▷ *adv* **14** in or into a level or flat position: *the boat was knocked almost flat* **15** completely: *flat broke* **16** exactly: *in three months flat* **17** *music* **A** lower than a standard pitch **B** too low in pitch: *singing flat* **18 fall flat (on one's face)** to fail to achieve a desired effect **19 flat out** *informal* with maximum speed and effort ▷ *n* **20** a flat object or part **21** low-lying land, esp. a marsh **22** a mud bank exposed at low tide **23** *music* **A** an accidental that lowers the pitch of a note by one semitone. Symbol: ♭ **B** a note affected by this accidental **24** *theatre* a wooden frame covered with painted canvas, used to form part of a stage setting **25** a punctured car tyre **26 the flat** *chiefly Brit* the season of flat racing [Old Norse *flatr*] **flatly** *adv*

flat[2] *n* **1** a set of rooms forming a home entirely on one floor of a building ▷ *vb* **flatting, flatted 2** *Austral & NZ* to share a flat **3 go flatting** *Austral & NZ* to leave home to share a flat [Old English *flett* floor, hall, house]

flatboat *n* a flat-bottomed boat for transporting goods on a canal

flatfish *n, pl* **-fish** *or* **-fishes** a sea fish, such as the sole, which has a flat body with both eyes on the uppermost side

flat-footed *adj* **1** having less than the usual degree of arching in the insteps of the feet **2** *informal* clumsy or insensitive

flathead *n* a common Australian flatfish

flatiron *n* (formerly) an iron for pressing clothes that was heated by being placed on a stove

flatlet *n Brit, Austral & S African* a small flat

flatmate *n* a person with whom one shares a flat

flat-pack *adj* (of furniture, etc.) supplied in pieces in a flat box for assembly by the buyer

flat racing *n* the racing of horses on racecourses without jumps

flatscreen *n* a slimline television set or computer monitor with a flat screen

flat spin *n* **1** an aircraft spin in which the longitudinal axis is more nearly horizontal than vertical **2** *informal* a state of confusion

flatten *vb* **1** to make or become flat or flatter **2** *informal* **A** to knock down or injure **B** to crush or subdue

flatter *vb* **1** to praise insincerely, esp. in order to win favour **2** to show to advantage: *she wore a simple green cotton dress which she knew flattered her* **3** to make (a person) appear more attractive than in reality: *a portrait that flattered him* **4** to cater to the vanity of (a person): *I was flattered by her praise* **5 flatter oneself** to believe, perhaps mistakenly, something good about oneself [Old French *flater* to lick, fawn upon] **flatterer** *n*

flattery *n, pl* **-teries** excessive or insincere praise

flattie *n NZ & S African informal* a flat tyre

flatulent *adj* suffering from or caused by too much gas in the stomach or intestines [Latin *flatus* blowing] **flatulence** *n*

flatworm *n* a worm, such as a tapeworm, with a flattened body

flaunt *vb* to display (oneself or one's possessions) arrogantly: *flaunting his new car* [origin unknown]

> **USAGE** *Flaunt* is sometimes wrongly used where *flout* is meant: *they must be prevented from flouting* (not *flaunting*) *the law.*

flautist (flaw-tist) *n* a flute player [Italian *flautista*]

flavour *or US* **flavor** *n* **1** taste perceived in food or liquid in the mouth **2** a distinctive quality or atmosphere: *Rome has its own particular flavour* ▹ *vb* **3** to give flavour to: *salmon flavoured with dill* [Old French *flaour*] **flavourless** *or US* **flavorless** *adj*

flavouring *or US* **flavoring** *n* a substance used to flavour food

flaw *n* **1** an imperfection or blemish **2** a mistake in something that makes it invalid: *a flaw in the system* [probably from Old Norse *flaga* stone slab] **flawed** *adj* **flawless** *adj*

flax *n* **1** a plant that has blue flowers and is cultivated for its seeds and the fibres of its stems **2** its fibres, made into linen fabrics **3** NZ a perennial plant producing a fibre that is used by Maoris for decorative work and weaving baskets [Old English *fleax*]

flaxen *adj* **1** of flax **2** (of hair) pale yellow

flay *vb* **1** to strip off the skin of, esp. by whipping **2** to criticize severely [Old English *flēan*]

flea *n* **1** a small wingless jumping insect feeding on the blood of mammals and birds **2 flea in one's ear** *informal* a sharp rebuke [Old English *flēah*]

fleabite *n* **1** the bite of a flea **2** a slight annoyance or discomfort

flea-bitten *adj* **1** bitten by or infested with fleas **2** *informal* shabby or decrepit: *a flea-bitten hotel*

flea market *n* an open-air market selling cheap second-hand goods

fleapit *n informal* a shabby cinema or theatre

fleck *n* **1** a small marking or streak **2** a small or tiny piece of something: *a fleck of grit* ▹ *vb* **3** to speckle: *a grey suit flecked with white* [probably from Old Norse *flekkr* stain, spot]

fled *vb* the past of **flee**

fledged *adj* **1** (of young birds) able to fly **2** qualified and competent: *a fully fledged doctor* [Old English *-flycge*, as in *unflycge* unfledged]

fledgling *or* **fledgeling** *n* **1** a young bird that has grown feathers ▹ *adj* **2** new or inexperienced: *her fledgling legal practice*

flee *vb* **fleeing, fled 1** to run away from (a place, danger, etc.) **2** to run or move quickly [Old English *flēon*]

fleece *n* **1** the coat of wool that covers a sheep **2** the wool removed from a sheep at one shearing **3** sheepskin or a fabric with soft pile, used as a lining for coats, etc. **4** *Brit* a jacket or top made of this fabric **5** a warm outdoor jacket or top made from a polyester fabric with a brushed nap ▹ *vb* **fleecing, fleeced 6** to defraud or overcharge **7** same as **shear** (sense 1) [Old English *flēos*]

fleecy *adj* **1** of or resembling fleece ▹ *n, pl* **-ies** **2** *NZ informal* a person who collects fleeces after shearing and prepares them for baling

fleet[1] *n* **1** a number of warships organized as a tactical unit **2** all the ships of a nation or company: *the British merchant fleet* **3** a number of vehicles under the same ownership [Old English *flēot* ship, flowing water]

fleet[2] *adj* rapid in movement [probably from Old English *flēotan* to float]

fleet chief petty officer *n* a noncommissioned officer in a navy

fleeting *adj* rapid and soon passing: *a fleeting moment* **fleetingly** *adv*

Fleet Street *n* **1** the street in London where many newspaper offices were formerly situated **2** British national newspapers collectively: *Fleet Street's obsession with the Royal Family*

Fleming *n* a person from Flanders or Flemish-speaking Belgium

Flemish *adj* **1** of Flanders, in Belgium ▹ *n* **2** one of the two official languages of Belgium ▹ *pl n* **3 the Flemish** people from Flanders or Flemish-speaking Belgium

flerovium *n chem* a synthetic element. Symbol: **Fl** [after G.N. *Flerov*, physicist]

flesh *n* **1** the soft part of the body of an animal or human, esp. muscular tissue. Related adjective: **carnal** **2** *informal* excess weight; fat **3** the meat of animals as opposed to that of fish or, sometimes, fowl **4** the thick soft part of a fruit or vegetable **5 the flesh** sexuality or sensuality: *pleasures of the flesh* **6 flesh and blood** human beings or human nature: *it is almost more than flesh and blood can bear* **7 in the flesh** in person; actually present **8 one's own flesh and blood** one's own family **9 press the flesh** *informal* to shake hands with large numbers of people, esp. in political campaigning [Old English *flǣsc*]

flesh-coloured *adj* resembling any shade of human skin

fleshly *adj* **-lier, -liest 1** relating to sexuality or sensuality **2** worldly as opposed to spiritual

flesh out *vb* to expand on or give more details to: *further meetings will be needed to flesh out the agreement*

fleshpots *pl n* places, such as brothels and strip clubs, where sexual desires are catered to [from the Biblical use as applied to Egypt (Exodus 16:3)]

flesh wound *n* a wound affecting superficial tissues

fleshy *adj* **fleshier, fleshiest 1** plump **2** resembling flesh **3** *botany* (of some fruits) thick and pulpy **fleshiness** *n*

fleur-de-lys *or* **fleur-de-lis** (flur-de-lee) *n, pl* **fleurs-de-lys** *or* **fleurs-de-lis** (flur-de-leez) a representation of a lily with three distinct petals [Old French *flor de lis* lily flower]

flew *vb* the past tense of **fly**[1]

flews *pl n* the fleshy hanging upper lip of a bloodhound or similar dog [origin unknown]

flex *n* **1** *Brit & Austral* a flexible insulated electric cable: *a coiled kettle flex* ▹ *vb* **2** to bend **3** to bend and stretch (a muscle) [Latin *flexus* bent, winding]

f

flexible *adj* **1** able to be bent easily without breaking **2** adaptable to changing circumstances: *flexible working arrangements* **flexibility** *n* **flexibly** *adv*
flexitime *n* a system permitting flexibility of working hours at the beginning or end of the day, provided an agreed total is worked
flibbertigibbet *n old-fashioned* an irresponsible, silly, gossipy person [origin unknown]
flick *vb* **1** to touch or move with the finger or hand in a quick jerky movement **2** to move with a short sudden movement, often repeatedly: *the windscreen wipers flicked back and forth* **3 flick through** to look at (a book or magazine) quickly or idly ▷ *n* **4** a tap or quick stroke **5 give the flick** *informal, chiefly Austral* to dismiss or reject [imitative]
flicker *vb* **1** to give out an unsteady or irregular light **2** to move quickly to and fro ▷ *n* **3** an unsteady or brief light **4** a brief or faint indication of emotion: *a flicker of fear in his voice* [Old English *flicorian*]
flick knife *n* a knife with a retractable blade that springs out when a button is pressed
flicks *pl n slang, old-fashioned* the cinema
flier *n* same as **flyer**
flight[1] *n* **1** a journey by aircraft **2** the act or manner of flying **3** a group of flying birds or aircraft **4** an aircraft flying on a scheduled journey **5** a set of stairs between one landing and the next **6 flight of fancy** an idea that is imaginative but not practical **7** small plastic or feather fins at the rear of an arrow or dart which make it stable in flight [Old English *flyht*]
flight[2] *n* **1** the act of running away, esp. from danger **2 put to flight** to cause to run away **3 take (to) flight** to run away [Old English *flyht* (unattested)]
flight attendant *n* a person who attends to the needs of passengers on a commercial flight
flight deck *n* **1** the crew compartment in an airliner **2** the upper deck of an aircraft carrier from which aircraft take off
flightless *adj* (of certain birds and insects) unable to fly
flight lieutenant *n* a junior commissioned officer in an air force
flight recorder *n* an electronic device in an aircraft for storing information concerning its performance in flight. It is often used to determine the cause of a crash. Also called: **black box**
flight sergeant *n* a noncommissioned officer in an air force
flighty *adj* **flightier, flightiest** frivolous and not very reliable or serious **flightiness** *n*
flimsy *adj* **-sier, -siest 1** not strong or substantial **2** light and thin: *a flimsy gauze mask* **3** not very convincing: *flimsy evidence* [origin unknown] **flimsily** *adv* **flimsiness** *n*
flinch *vb* **1** to draw back suddenly from pain or something unpleasant **2 flinch from** to avoid: *I wouldn't flinch from saying that to his face* [Old French *flenchir*]
fling *vb* **flinging, flung 1** to throw with force **2** to move or go hurriedly or violently: *she flung her arms open wide* **3** to put or send without warning: *they used to fling me in jail* **4** to put (something) somewhere hurriedly or carelessly **5 fling oneself into** to apply oneself with enthusiasm to ▷ *n* **6** a short spell of self-indulgent enjoyment **7** a brief romantic or sexual relationship **8** a vigorous Scottish country dance: *a Highland fling* [from Old Norse]
flint *n* **1** a very hard stone that produces sparks when struck with steel **2** any piece of flint, esp. one used as a primitive tool **3** a small piece of an iron alloy, used in cigarette lighters [Old English] **flinty** *adj*
flintlock *n* an obsolete gun in which the powder was lit by a spark produced by a flint
flip *vb* **flipping, flipped 1** to throw (something light or small) carelessly **2** to turn (something) over: *flip the fish on its back* **3** to turn (a device or machine) on or off by quickly pressing a switch **4** to throw (an object such as a coin) so that it turns in the air **5** to buy and sell an asset (often property) quickly for profit **6 flip through** to look at (a book or magazine) idly **7** Also: **flip one's lid** *slang* to fly into an emotional outburst ▷ *n* **8** a snap or tap, usually with the fingers ▷ *adj* **9** *informal* flippant or pert [probably imitative]
flipchart *n* a large pad of paper mounted on a stand, used in giving lectures, etc.
flip-flop *n* **1** *Brit & S African* a rubber-soled sandal attached to the foot by a thong between the big toe and the next toe **2** *informal* a reversal of opinion, policy, etc. ▷ *vb informal* **3** to reverse one's opinion, policy, etc. [reduplication of *flip*]
flippant *adj* treating serious matters with inappropriate light-heartedness or lack of respect [probably from *flip*] **flippancy** *n*
flipper *n* **1** the flat broad limb of seals, whales, and other aquatic animals specialized for swimming **2** either of a pair of rubber paddle-like devices worn on the feet as an aid in swimming
flirt *vb* **1** to behave as if sexually attracted to someone **2** (foll. by *with*) to consider lightly; toy with: *he had often flirted with the idea of emigrating* ▷ *n* **3** a person who flirts [origin unknown] **flirtation** *n* **flirtatious** *adj*
flit *vb* **flitting, flitted 1** to fly or move along rapidly and lightly **2** to pass quickly: *a shadow flitted across his face* **3** *Scot & N English dialect* to move house **4** *Brit informal* to leave hurriedly and stealthily in order to avoid debts ▷ *n* **5** the act of flitting **6 do a flit** *NZ informal* to abandon rented accommodation [Old Norse *flytja* to carry]
flitch *n* a side of pork salted and cured [Old English *flicce*]
flitter *vb rare* same as **flutter**
float *vb* **1** to rest on the surface of a fluid without sinking **2** to move lightly or freely across a surface or through air or water **3** to move about aimlessly, esp. in the mind: *a pleasant image floated into his mind* **4 A** to launch (a commercial enterprise, etc.) **B** to offer for sale on the stock market **5** *finance* to allow (a currency) to fluctuate against other currencies ▷ *n* **6** an inflatable object that helps people learning to swim stay afloat **7** *angling* an indicator attached to a baited line that moves when a fish bites **8** a long rigid boatlike structure,

of which there are usually two, attached to an aircraft instead of wheels so that it can land on and take off from water **9** a decorated lorry that is part of a procession **10** a small delivery vehicle: *a milk float* **11** *Austral & NZ* a vehicle for transporting horses **12** a sum of money used to cover small expenses or provide change **13** the hollow floating ball of a ball cock [Old English *flotian*]

floatation *n* same as **flotation**

floating *adj* **1** (of a population) moving about; not settled **2** (of an organ or part) displaced or abnormally movable: *a floating kidney* **3** (of a voter) not committed to one party **4** *finance* **A** (of capital) available for current use **B** (of a currency) free to fluctuate against other currencies

floating rib *n* a lower rib not attached to the breastbone

floats *pl n theatre* footlights

flocculent *adj* like tufts of wool [Latin *floccus* tuft of wool] **flocculence** *n*

flock[1] *n* **1** a group of animals of one kind, esp. sheep or birds **2** a large number of people **3** a congregation of Christians regarded as the responsibility of a member of the clergy ▷ *vb* **4** to gather together or move in large numbers [Old English *flocc*]

flock[2] *n* **1** waste from fabrics such as cotton or wool, used for stuffing mattresses ▷ *adj* **2** (of wallpaper) having a velvety raised pattern [Latin *floccus* tuft of wool]

floe *n* a sheet of floating ice [probably from Norwegian *flo* slab, layer]

flog *vb* **flogging, flogged 1** to beat harshly, esp. with a whip or stick **2** (sometimes foll. by *off*) *informal* to sell **3** *Austral & NZ informal* to steal **4 flog a dead horse** *chiefly Brit* to waste one's energy [probably from Latin *flagellare*] **flogging** *n*

flood *n* **1** an overflowing of water on an area that is normally dry **2** a large amount of water **3** the rising of the tide from low to high water. Related adjective: **diluvial, diluvian 4** a large amount: *a flood of letters* **5** *theatre* short for **floodlight** ▷ *vb* **6** to cover or become covered with water **7** to fill to overflowing **8** to put a large number of goods on sale on (a market) at the same time, often at a cheap price: *the US was flooded with cheap televisions* **9** to flow or surge: *the memories flooded back* **10** to supply excess petrol to (a petrol engine) so that it cannot work properly **11** to bleed profusely from the womb [Old English *flōd*] **flooding** *n*

Flood *n* **the Flood** *Old Testament* the flood from which Noah and his family and livestock were saved in the ark (Genesis 7–8)

floodgate *n* **1** a gate used to control the flow of water **2 floodgates** controls against an outpouring of emotion: *it had opened the floodgates of her anxiety*

floodlight *n* **1** a lamp that casts a broad intense light, used in the theatre or to illuminate sports grounds or the exterior of buildings ▷ *vb* **-lighting, -lit 2** to illuminate by floodlight

flood plain *n geog* a flat area bordering a river, made of sediment deposited during flooding

floor *n* **1** the lower surface of a room **2** a storey of a building **3** a flat bottom surface: *the ocean floor* **4** that part of a legislative hall in which debate is conducted **5** a minimum limit: *a wages floor for low-paid employees* **6 have the floor** to have the right to speak in a debate or discussion ▷ *vb* **7** to knock to the ground **8** *informal* to disconcert or defeat [Old English *flōr*]

floorboard *n* one of the boards forming a floor

floored *adj* covered with a floor: *an attic floored with pine planks*

flooring *n* **1** the material used in making a floor: *pine flooring* **2** a floor

floor plan *n* a scale drawing of the arrangement of rooms on one floor of a building

floor show *n* a series of entertainments, such as singing and dancing, in a nightclub

floozy, floozie *or* **floosie** *n, pl* **-zies** *or* **-sies** *slang, old-fashioned* a woman considered to be disreputable or immoral [origin unknown]

flop *vb* **flopping, flopped 1** to bend, fall, or collapse loosely or carelessly **2** *informal* to fail: *his first big film flopped* **3** to fall or move with a sudden noise ▷ *n* **4** *informal* a complete failure **5** the act of flopping [variant of *flap*] **floppy** *adj*

flora *n* all the plant life of a given place or time [*Flora*, Roman goddess of flowers]

floral *adj* decorated with or consisting of flowers or patterns of flowers

Florentine *adj* **1** of Florence, a city in central Italy ▷ *n* **2** a person from Florence

floret (**flaw**-ret) *n* a small flower forming part of a composite flower head [Old French *florete*]

floribunda *n* a type of rose whose flowers grow in large clusters [New Latin *floribundus* flowering freely]

florid *adj* **1** having a red or flushed complexion **2** very ornate and extravagant: *florid prose* [Latin *floridus* blooming]

florin *n* a former British, Australian, and New Zealand coin, equivalent to ten pence or twenty cents [Old Italian *fiorino* Florentine coin]

florist *n* a person or shop selling flowers

floss *n* **1** fine silky fibres, such as those obtained from silkworm cocoons **2** See **dental floss** ▷ *vb* **3** to clean (between the teeth) with dental floss [probably from Old French *flosche* down] **flossy** *adj*

flotation *or* **floatation** *n* the launching or financing of a commercial enterprise by bond or share issues

flotilla *n* a small fleet or a fleet of small ships [Spanish *flota* fleet]

flotsam *n* **1** floating wreckage from a ship **2 flotsam and jetsam A** odds and ends **B** *Brit* homeless or vagrant people [Anglo-French *floteson*]

flounce[1] *vb* **flouncing, flounced 1** to move or go with emphatic movements ▷ *n* **2** the act of flouncing [Scandinavian]

flounce[2] *n* an ornamental frill on a garment or tablecloth [Old French *froncir* to wrinkle]

flounder[1] *vb* **1** to struggle to move or stay upright, esp. in water or mud **2** to behave or speak in an awkward, confused way [probably a blend of FOUNDER + BLUNDER]

USAGE *Flounder* is sometimes wrongly used where *founder* is meant: *the project foundered* (not *floundered*) *because of a lack of funds.*

flounder² *n, pl* **-der** *or* **-ders** an edible flatfish [Scandinavian]

flour *n* **1** a powder prepared by grinding grain, esp. wheat ▷ *vb* **2** to sprinkle (food or utensils) with flour [Middle English *flur* 'flower', i.e. best part] **floury** *adj*

flourish *vb* **1** to be active, successful, or widespread; prosper **2** to be at the peak of development **3** to wave (something) dramatically ▷ *n* **4** a dramatic waving or sweeping movement: *she created a flourish with an imaginary wand* **5** an ornamental curly line in writing **6** a fancy or extravagant action or part of something: *he took his tie off with a flourish* [Latin *florere* to flower] **flourishing** *adj*

f

flout (rhymes with out) *vb* to deliberately disobey (a rule, law, etc.) [probably from Middle English *flouten* to play the flute]

USAGE See at **flaunt**.

flow *vb* **1** (of liquids) to move in a stream **2** (of blood, electricity, etc.) to circulate **3** to move steadily and smoothly: *a golf club with rich-looking cars flowing into it* **4** to be produced effortlessly: *words flowed from him in a steady stream* **5** to hang freely: *her hair loose and flowing down her back* **6** to be abundant: *at the buffet lunch, wine flowed like water* **7** (of tide water) to rise ▷ *n* **8** the act, rate, or manner of flowing: *the abundant flow of water through domestic sprinklers* **9** a continuous stream or discharge **10** the advancing of the tide [Old English *flōwan*]

flow chart *or* **flow sheet** *n* a diagram showing a sequence of operations in an industrial process, computer program, etc.

flower *n* **1** the part of a plant that is, usually, brightly coloured, and quickly fades, producing seeds **2** a plant grown for its colourful flowers. Related adjective: **floral** **3** the best or finest part: *in the flower of her youth* **4** **in flower** with flowers open ▷ *vb* **5** to produce flowers; bloom **6** to reach full growth or maturity: *liberty only flowers in times of peace* [Latin *flos*]

flowered *adj* decorated with flowers or a floral design

flowerpot *n* a pot in which plants are grown

flowery *adj* **1** decorated with flowers or floral patterns **2** (of language or style) containing elaborate literary expressions **floweriness** *n*

flown *vb* the past participle of **fly¹**

fl. oz. fluid ounce(s)

Flt Lt Flight Lieutenant

Flt Sgt Flight Sergeant

flu *n informal* short for **influenza**

fluctuate *vb* **-ating, -ated** to change frequently and erratically: *share prices fluctuated wildly throughout the day* [Latin *fluctus* a wave] **fluctuation** *n*

flue *n* a passage or pipe in a chimney, used to carry off smoke, gas, or hot air [origin unknown]

fluent *adj* **1** able to speak or write with ease: *they spoke fluent English; fluent in French* **2** spoken or written with ease [Latin *fluere* to flow] **fluency** *n* **fluently** *adv*

fluff *n* **1** soft light particles, such as the down of cotton or wool **2** *informal* a mistake, esp. in speaking or reading lines ▷ *vb* **3** to make or become soft and puffy **4** *informal* to make a mistake in performing [probably from earlier *flue* downy matter] **fluffy** *adj* **fluffiness** *n*

fluid *n* **1** a substance, such as a liquid or gas, that can flow and has no fixed shape ▷ *adj* **2** capable of flowing and easily changing shape **3** constantly changing or apt to change [Latin *fluere* to flow] **fluidity** *n*

fluid ounce *n* **1** *Brit* a unit of liquid measure equal to one twentieth of an Imperial pint (28.4 ml) **2** *US* a unit of liquid measure equal to one sixteenth of a US pint (29.6 ml)

fluke¹ *n* an accidental stroke of luck [origin unknown] **fluky** *adj*

fluke² *n* **1** the flat triangular point of an anchor **2** either of the two lobes of the tail of a whale [perhaps a special use of FLUKE³ (in the sense: a flounder, flatfish)]

fluke³ *n* any parasitic flatworm, such as the liver fluke [Old English *flōc*]

flume *n* **1** a narrow sloping channel for water **2** an enclosed water slide at a swimming pool

flummery *n informal* silly or trivial talk [Welsh *llymru*]

flummox *vb* to puzzle or confuse [origin unknown]

flung *vb* the past of **fling**

flunk *vb US, Canad, Austral, NZ & S African informal* to fail (an examination, course, etc.) [origin unknown]

flunky *or* **flunkey** *n, pl* **flunkies** *or* **flunkeys** **1** a manservant who wears ceremonial dress **2** a person who performs small unimportant tasks for a powerful or important person in the hope of being rewarded [origin unknown]

fluor (flew-or) *n* same as **fluorspar** [Latin: a flowing; so called from its use as a metallurgical flux]

fluoresce *vb* **-rescing, -resced** to exhibit fluorescence [back formation from FLUORESCENCE]

fluorescence *n* **1** *physics* the emission of light from atoms or molecules that are bombarded by particles, such as electrons, or by radiation from a separate source **2** the radiation emitted as a result of fluorescence [from *fluor*] **fluorescent** *adj*

fluorescent lamp *n* a lamp in which ultraviolet radiation from an electrical gas discharge causes a thin layer of phosphor on a tube's inside surface to fluoresce

fluoridate *vb* **-dating, -dated** to add fluoride to (water) as protection against tooth decay **fluoridation** *n*

fluoride *n chem* any compound containing fluorine and another element or radical

fluorinate *vb* **-nating, -nated** to treat or combine with fluorine **fluorination** *n*

fluorine *n chem* a poisonous strong-smelling pale yellow gas that is the most reactive of all the elements. Symbol: **F**

fluoroscopy (floor-oss-kop-ee) *n* same as **radioscopy**

fluorspar, fluor *or US & Canad* **fluorite** *n* a white or colourless mineral, consisting of calcium fluoride in crystalline form: the chief ore of fluorine

flurry *n, pl* **-ries 1** a short rush of vigorous activity or movement **2** a light gust of wind or rain, or fall of snow ▷ *vb* **-ries, -rying, -ried 3** to confuse or bewilder [obsolete *flurr* to scatter]

flush[1] *vb* **1** to blush or cause to blush **2** to send water quickly through (a pipe or a toilet) so as to clean it **3** to elate: *she was flushed with excitement* ▷ *n* **4** a rosy colour, esp. in the cheeks **5** a sudden flow, such as of water **6** a feeling of elation: *in the flush of victory* **7** freshness: *in the first flush of youth* [perhaps from FLUSH[3]] **flushed** *adj*

flush[2] *adj* **1** level with another surface **2** *informal* having plenty of money ▷ *adv* **3** so as to be level [probably from FLUSH[1] (in the sense: spring out)]

flush[3] *vb* to drive out of a hiding place [Middle English *flusshen*]

flush[4] *n* (in poker and similar games) a hand containing only one suit [Latin *fluxus* flux]

fluster *vb* **1** to make or become nervous or upset ▷ *n* **2** a nervous or upset state [from Old Norse]

flute *n* **1** a wind instrument consisting of a tube of wood or metal with holes in the side stopped either by the fingers or keys. The breath is directed across a mouth hole in the side **2** a tall narrow wineglass, used esp. for champagne ▷ *vb* **fluting, fluted 3** to utter in a high-pitched tone [Old French *flahute*] **fluty** *adj*

fluted *adj* having decorated grooves

fluting *n* a design or decoration of flutes on a column

flutter *vb* **1** to wave rapidly **2** (of birds or butterflies) to flap the wings **3** to move with an irregular motion **4** *pathol* (of the heart) to beat abnormally rapidly **5** to move about restlessly ▷ *n* **6** a quick flapping or vibrating motion **7** a state of nervous excitement or confusion **8** excited interest **9** *Brit informal* a modest bet **10** *pathol* an abnormally rapid beating of the heart **11** *electronics* a slow variation in pitch in a sound-reproducing system [Old English *floterian* to float to and fro]

fluvial (**flew**-vee-al) *adj* of or relating to a river [Latin *fluvius* river]

flux *n* **1** continuous change or instability **2** a flow or discharge **3** a substance mixed with a metal oxide to assist in fusion **4** *physics* **A** the rate of flow of particles, energy, or a fluid **B** the strength of a field in a given area: *magnetic flux* [Latin *fluxus* a flow]

fly[1] *vb* **flies, flying, flew, flown 1** to move through the air on wings or in an aircraft **2** to control the flight of (an aircraft) **3** to float, flutter, display, or be displayed in the air: *the Red Cross flag flew at each corner of the compound* **4** to transport or be transported through the air by aircraft, wind, etc. **5** to move very quickly or suddenly: *the front door flew open* **6** to pass quickly: *how time flies* **7** to escape from (an enemy or a place) **8 fly a kite** to release information or take a step in order to test public opinion **9 fly at** to attack (someone) **10 fly high** *informal* to have a high aim **11 let fly** *informal* to lose one's temper: *a young child letting fly at you in a sudden moment of temper* ▷ *n, pl* **flies 12** Also: **flies** a closure that conceals a zip, buttons, or other fastening, as on trousers **13** a flap forming the entrance to a tent **14 flies** *theatre* the space above the stage, used for storing scenery [Old English *flēogan*]

fly[2] *n, pl* **flies 1** a small insect with two pairs of wings **2** any of various similar but unrelated insects, such as the dragonfly **3** *angling* a lure made from a fish-hook attached with feathers to resemble a fly **4 fly in the ointment** *informal* a slight flaw that detracts from value or enjoyment **5 fly on the wall** a person who watches others, while not being noticed himself or herself **6 there are no flies on him** *or* **her** *informal* he *or* she is no fool [Old English *flēoge*]

fly[3] *adj slang, chiefly Brit* sharp and cunning [origin unknown]

flyaway *adj* **1** (of hair) very fine and soft **2** frivolous or light-hearted: *a flyaway remark*

flyblown *adj* **1** covered with blowfly eggs **2** in a dirty and bad condition

fly-by-night *informal* ▷ *adj* **1** unreliable or untrustworthy, esp. in money matters ▷ *n* **2** an untrustworthy person

flycatcher *n* a small insect-eating songbird

flyer *or* **flier** *n* **1** a small advertising leaflet **2** a person or thing that flies or moves very fast **3** *old-fashioned* an aircraft pilot

fly-fishing *n angling* fishing using artificial flies as lures

flying *n* **1** the act of piloting, navigating, or travelling in an aircraft ▷ *adj* **2** hurried and brief: *a flying visit* **3** fast or built for speed: *Australia's flying fullback* **4** hanging, waving, or floating freely: *flags flying proudly*

flying boat *n* a seaplane in which the fuselage consists of a hull that provides buoyancy

flying buttress *n* an arch and vertical column that supports a wall from the outside

flying colours *pl n* conspicuous success; triumph: *they passed with flying colours*

flying fish *n* a fish of warm and tropical seas, with winglike fins used for gliding above the water

flying fox *n* **1** a large fruit bat of tropical Africa and Asia **2** *Austral & NZ* a platform suspended from an overhead cable, used for transporting people or materials

flying officer *n* a junior commissioned officer in an air force

flying saucer *n* an unidentified disc-shaped flying object alleged to come from outer space

flying squad *n* a small group of police or soldiers ready to move into action quickly

flying start *n* **1** any promising beginning: *a flying start to the new financial year* **2** a start to a race in which the competitor is already travelling at speed as he or she passes the starting line

flyleaf *n, pl* **-leaves** the inner leaf of the endpaper of a book

flyover *n* an intersection of two roads at which one is carried over the other by a bridge

flypaper *n* paper with a sticky and poisonous coating, hung up to trap flies

fly-past *n* a ceremonial flight of aircraft over a given area

fly sheet *n* a piece of canvas drawn over the ridgepole of a tent to form an outer roof

fly spray *n* a liquid used to destroy flies, sprayed from an aerosol
flyweight *n* a professional or an amateur boxer weighing up to 112 pounds (51 kg)
flywheel *n* a heavy wheel that regulates the speed of a machine
Fm *chem* fermium
FM **1** frequency modulation **2** First Minister
f-number *n photog* the ratio of the effective diameter of a lens to its focal length
foal *n* **1** the young of a horse or related animal ▷ *vb* **2** to give birth to a foal [Old English *fola*]
foam *n* **1** a mass of small bubbles of gas formed on the surface of a liquid **2** frothy saliva **3** a light spongelike solid used for insulation, packing, etc. ▷ *vb* **4** to produce or cause to produce foam **5 foam at the mouth** to be very angry [Old English *fām*] **foamy** *adj*
fob *n* **1** a chain by which a pocket watch is attached to a waistcoat **2** a small pocket in a man's waistcoat, for holding a watch [Germanic]
f.o.b. *or* **FOB** *commerce* free on board
fob off *vb* **fobbing, fobbed 1** to pretend to satisfy (a person) with lies or excuses **2** to sell or pass off (inferior goods) as valuable [probably from German *foppen* to trick]
focal *adj* **1** of or relating to a focus **2** situated at or measured from the focus
focal length *n* the distance from the focal point of a lens or mirror to the surface of the mirror or the centre of the lens
focal point *n* **1** the point where the rays of light from a lens or mirror meet **2** the centre of attention or interest: *a focal point for the new high-technology industries*
focus (foe-kuss) *vb* **-cusing, -cused** *or* **-cussing, -cussed 1** to adjust one's eyes or an instrument on an object so that its image is clear **2** to concentrate ▷ *n, pl* **-cuses** *or* **-ci** (-sigh, -kye, -kee) **3** a point of convergence of light or sound waves, or a point from which they appear to diverge **4 in focus** (of an object or image being viewed) clear and sharp **5 out of focus** (of an object or image being viewed) blurred and fuzzy **6** same as **focal point** or **focal length 7** *optics* the state of an optical image when it is distinct or the state of an instrument producing this image **8** a point upon which attention or activity is concentrated: *the focus was on health and education* **9** *geom* a fixed reference point on the concave side of a conic section, used when defining its eccentricity [Latin: hearth, fireplace]
focus group *n* a group of people gathered by a market research company to discuss and assess a product or service
fodder *n* bulk feed for livestock, esp. hay or straw [Old English *fōdor*]
foe *n formal or literary* an enemy [Old English *fāh* hostile]
FoE *or* **FOE** Friends of the Earth
foetid *adj* same as **fetid**
foetus *n, pl* **-tuses** same as **fetus**
fog *n* **1** a mass of droplets of condensed water vapour suspended in the air, often greatly reducing visibility **2** *photog* a blurred area on a developed negative, print, or transparency ▷ *vb* **fogging, fogged 3** to envelop or become enveloped with or as if with fog [probably from Old Norse] **foggy** *adj*
fog bank *n* a distinct mass of fog, esp. at sea
fogbound *adj* prevented from operating by fog
fogey *or* **fogy** *n, pl* **-geys** *or* **-gies** an extremely old-fashioned person: *a stick-in-the-mud old fogey* [origin unknown] **fogeyish** *or* **fogyish** *adj*
foghorn *n* a large horn sounded at intervals as a warning to ships in fog
foible *n* a slight peculiarity or minor weakness: *he was intolerant of other people's foibles* [obsolete French form of *faible* feeble]
foil¹ *vb* to baffle or frustrate (a person or an attempt) [Middle English *foilen* to trample]
foil² *n* **1** metal in the form of very thin sheets **2** a person or thing setting off another thing to advantage: *mint sauce is an excellent foil to lamb* [Latin *folia* leaves]
foil³ *n* a light slender flexible sword tipped by a button, used in fencing [origin unknown]
foist *vb* **foist on** to force (someone) to have or experience (something): *the tough economic policies which have been foisted on the developing world* [probably from obsolete Dutch *vuisten* to enclose in one's hand]
fold¹ *vb* **1** to bend double so that one part covers another **2** to bring together and intertwine (the arms or legs) **3 fold up** to enclose in a surrounding material **4** *literary* to clasp (a person) in one's arms **5** Also: **fold in** to mix (ingredients) by gently turning one over the other with a spoon **6** *informal* (of a business, organization, or project) to fail or go bankrupt ▷ *n* **7** a piece or section that has been folded **8** a mark, crease, or hollow made by folding **9** a bend in stratified rocks that results from movements within the earth's crust [Old English *fealdan*]
fold² *n* **1** *Brit, Austral & S African* a small enclosure for sheep **2** a church or the members of it [Old English *falod*]
folder *n* **1** a binder or file for holding loose papers **2** an area of a computer disk which contains one or more files or other folders
folding door *n* a door with two or more vertical hinged leaves that can be folded one against another
foliaceous *adj* **1** like a leaf **2** *geol* consisting of thin layers [Latin *foliaceus*]
foliage *n* **1** the green leaves of a plant **2** leaves together with the stems, twigs, and branches they are attached to, esp. when used for decoration [Old French *fuellage*]
foliation *n* **1** *botany* **A** the process of producing leaves **B** the state of being in leaf **2** a leaflike decoration
folio *n, pl* **-lios 1** a sheet of paper folded in half to make two leaves for a book **2** a book of the largest common size made up of such sheets **3 A** a leaf of paper numbered on the front side only **B** the page number of a book **4** NZ a collection of related material ▷ *adj* **5** of or made in the largest book size, common esp. in early centuries of European printing: *the entire series is being reissued, several in the original folio format* [Latin *in folio* in a leaf]

folk *pl n* **1** people in general, esp. those of a particular group or class: *ordinary folk* **2** Also: **folks** *informal* members of one's family; relatives ▷ *n* **3** *informal* short for **folk music** **4** a people or tribe ▷ *adj* **5** originating from or traditional to the common people of a country: *folk art* [Old English *folc*]

folk dance *n* **1** a traditional country dance **2** music for such a dance

folk etymology *n* the gradual change in the form of a word through the influence of a more familiar word, as for example *crayfish* from its Middle English form *crevis*

folklore *n* the traditional beliefs of a people as expressed in stories and songs

folk music *n* **1** music that is passed on from generation to generation **2** a piece written in the style of this music

folk song *n* **1** a song handed down among the common people **2** a modern song like this **folk singer** *n*

folksy *adj* **-sier, -siest** simple and unpretentious, sometimes in an artificial way

follicle *n* any small sac or cavity in the body, esp. one from which a hair grows [Latin *folliculus* small bag] **follicular** *adj*

follow *vb* **1** to go or come after **2** to accompany: *he followed Isabel everywhere* **3** to be a logical or natural consequence of **4** to keep to the course or track of **5** to act in accordance with: *follow the rules below and it will help you a great deal* **6** to accept the ideas or beliefs of **7** to understand (an explanation) **8** to have a keen interest in: *he's followed the singer's career for more than 25 years* **9** to choose to receive messages or blogs posted online by (a particular person) ▷ See also **follow-on, follow through, follow up** [Old English *folgian*]

follower *n* **1** a person who accepts the teachings of another: *a follower of Nietzsche* **2** a supporter, such as of a sport or team

following *adj* **1** about to be mentioned **2** next in time **3** (of winds or currents) moving in the same direction as a vessel ▷ *prep* **4** as a result of: *uncertainty following the collapse of communism* ▷ *n* **5** a group of supporters or enthusiasts

> **USAGE** The use of *following* to mean 'as a result of' is very common in journalism, but should be avoided in other kinds of writing.

follow-on *cricket* ▷ *n* **1** an immediate second innings forced on a team scoring a prescribed number of runs fewer than its opponents in the first innings ▷ *vb* **follow on** **2** to play a follow-on: *England had to follow on*

follow through *vb* **1** to continue an action or series of actions until finished **2** *sport* to continue a stroke, kick, etc., after striking the ball ▷ *n* **follow-through** **3** *sport* continuation of a kick, stroke, etc., after striking the ball: *try to keep your follow-through as low as possible*

follow up *vb* **1** to investigate (a person, evidence, etc.) closely **2** to continue (action) after a beginning, esp. to increase its effect ▷ *n* **follow-up** **3** something done to reinforce an initial action: *a routine follow-up to his operation*

folly *n, pl* **-lies** **1** the quality of being foolish **2** a foolish action, idea, etc. **3** an imitation castle, temple, etc., built as a decoration in a large garden or park [Old French *folie* madness]

foment (foam-**ent**) *vb* to encourage or stir up (trouble) [Latin *fomentum* a poultice] **fomentation** *n*

> **USAGE** Both *foment* and *ferment* can be used to talk about stirring up trouble: *he was accused of fomenting/fermenting unrest*. Only *ferment* can be used intransitively or as a noun: *his anger continued to ferment* (not *foment*); *rural areas were unaffected by the ferment in the cities*.

fond *adj* **1** **fond of** having a liking for **2** loving and affectionate: *his fond parents* **3** (of hopes or wishes) cherished but unlikely to be realized [Middle English *fonnen* to be foolish] **fondly** *adv* **fondness** *n*

fondant *n* (a sweet made from) a thick flavoured paste of sugar and water [French]

fondle *vb* **-dling, -dled** to touch or stroke tenderly [obsolete *fond* to fondle]

fondue *n* a Swiss dish, consisting of melted cheese into which small pieces of bread are dipped [French: melted]

font[1] *n* a large bowl in a church for baptismal water [Latin *fons* fountain]

font[2] *n printing* a complete set of type of one style and size [Old French *fonte* a founding, casting]

fontanelle *or esp US* **fontanel** *n anatomy* a soft membranous gap between the bones of a baby's skull [Old French *fontanele* a little spring]

food *n* any substance that can be taken into the body by a living organism and changed into energy and body tissue. Related adjective: **gastronomic** [Old English *fōda*]

foodbank *n* a charity that provides food to people in financial trouble

food chain *n ecology* a series of organisms in a community, each member of which feeds on another in the chain and is in turn eaten

food group *n* any of the categories into which different foods may be placed according to the type of nourishment they supply

foodie *n informal* a person with a keen interest in food and cookery

food poisoning *n* an acute illness caused by food that is contaminated by bacteria

food processor *n* a machine for chopping, mixing, or liquidizing food

foodstuff *n* any substance that can be used as food

fool[1] *n* **1** a person who lacks sense or judgment **2** a person who is made to appear ridiculous **3** (formerly) a professional jester living in a royal or noble household **4** **play** *or* **act the fool** to deliberately act foolishly ▷ *vb* **5** to deceive (someone), esp. in order to make them look ridiculous **6** **fool around** *or* **about with** *informal* to act or play with irresponsibly or aimlessly **7** to speak or act in a playful or jesting manner [Latin *follis* bellows]

fool[2] *n chiefly Brit* a dessert made from a puree of fruit with cream [perhaps from FOOL[1]]

foolery *n* foolish behaviour

foolhardy *adj* **-hardier, -hardiest** recklessly adventurous [Old French *fol* foolish + *hardi* bold] **foolhardily** *adv* **foolhardiness** *n*

f

foolish *adj* very silly, unwise, or absurd **foolishly** *adv* **foolishness** *n*
foolproof *adj informal* **1** incapable of going wrong; infallible: *a foolproof identification system* **2** (of machines, etc.) guaranteed to function as intended despite human misuse or error
fool's errand *n* a fruitless undertaking
fool's gold *n* a yellow-coloured mineral, such as pyrite, that is sometimes mistaken for gold
fool's paradise *n* a state of happiness based on false hopes or beliefs
foosball *n US & Canad* a game in which opponents on either side of a purpose-built table attempt to strike a ball into the other side's goal by moving horizontal bars with miniatures of footballers attached
foot *n, pl* **feet 1** the part of the leg below the ankle joint that is in contact with the ground during standing and walking **2** the part of a garment covering a foot **3** a unit of length equal to 12 inches (0.3048 metre) **4** the bottom, base, or lower end of something: *at the foot of the hill; the foot of the page* **5** *old-fashioned* infantry **6** *prosody* a group of two or more syllables in which one syllable has the major stress, forming the basic unit of poetic rhythm **7 one foot in the grave** *informal* near to death **8 on foot** walking **9 put one's best foot forward** to try to do one's best **10 put one's foot down** *informal* to act firmly **11 put one's foot in it** *informal* to make an embarrassing and tactless mistake **12 under foot** on the ground ▷ *vb* **13 foot it** *informal* to travel on foot **14 foot the bill** to pay the entire cost of something ▷ See also **feet** [Old English *fōt*] **footless** *adj*

> **USAGE** In front of another noun, the plural for the unit of length is *foot: a 20-foot putt; his 70-foot ketch.* Foot can also be used instead of *feet* when mentioning a quantity and in front of words like *tall: four foot of snow; he is at least six foot tall.*

footage *n* **1** a length of film **2** the sequences of filmed material: *footage of refugees leaving the city*
foot-and-mouth disease *n* a highly infectious viral disease of cattle, pigs, sheep, and goats, in which blisters form in the mouth and on the feet
football *n* **1** any of various games played with a ball in which two teams compete to kick, head, or propel the ball into each other's goal **2** the ball used in any of these games **footballer** *n*
football pools *pl n* same as **pools**
footbridge *n* a narrow bridge for the use of pedestrians
footfall *n* the sound of a footstep
foothills *pl n* relatively low hills at the foot of a mountain
foothold *n* **1** a secure position from which further progress may be made: *a firm foothold in Europe's telecommunications market* **2** a ledge or other place where a foot can be securely positioned, as during climbing
footing *n* **1** basis or foundation: *on a sound financial footing* **2** the relationship between two people or groups: *on an equal footing* **3** a secure grip by or for the feet
footle *vb* **-ling, -led** *chiefly Brit informal* to loiter aimlessly [probably from French *foutre* to copulate with] **footling** *adj*
footlights *pl n theatre* lights set in a row along the front of the stage floor
footloose *adj* free to go or do as one wishes
footman *n, pl* **-men** a male servant in uniform
footnote *n* a note printed at the bottom of a page
footpad *n old-fashioned* a highwayman, on foot rather than horseback
footpath *n* **1** a narrow path for walkers only **2** *Austral* a raised space alongside a road, for pedestrians
footplate *n chiefly Brit* a platform in the cab of a steam locomotive on which the crew stand to operate the controls
footprint *n* **1** an indentation or outline of the foot on a surface **2** the shape and size of the area something occupies: *enlarging the footprint of the building* **3** impact on the environment
footsie *n informal* flirtation involving the touching together of feet
footsore *adj* having sore or tired feet, esp. from much walking
footstep *n* **1** a step in walking **2** the sound made by walking **3** a footmark **4 follow in someone's footsteps** to continue the example of another
footstool *n* a low stool used for supporting the feet of a seated person
footwear *n* anything worn to cover the feet
footwork *n* the way in which the feet are used, for example in sports or dancing: *nimble footwork*
fop *n* a man who is excessively concerned with fashion [perhaps from Middle English *foppe* fool] **foppery** *n* **foppish** *adj*
for *prep* **1** directed or belonging to: *a bottle of beer for himself* **2** to the advantage of: *he spelt it out for her* **3** in the direction of: *he headed for the door* **4** over a span of (time or distance): *she considered him coolly for a moment* **5** in favour of: *support for the war* **6** in order to get: *for a bit of company* **7** designed to meet the needs of: *the instructions are for right-handed players* **8** at a cost of: *two dishes for one* **9** in place of: *she had to substitute for her mother because they woke late* **10** because of: *dancing for joy* **11** regarding the usual characteristics of: *unusually warm for the time of year* **12** concerning: *our idea for the last scene* **13** as being: *do you take me for an idiot?* **14** at (a specified time): *multiparty elections are planned for next year* **15** to do or take part in: *two guests for dinner* **16** in the duty or task of: *that's for you to decide* **17** in relation to; as it affects: *it's too hard for me* **18** in order to preserve or retain: *fighting for survival* **19** as a direct equivalent to: *word for word* **20** in order to become or enter: *training for the priesthood* **21** in exchange for: *the cash was used to pay for food, shelter, and medical supplies* **22 for all** See **all** (sense 12) **23 for it** *Brit & Austral informal* liable for punishment or blame: *you'll be for it if you get caught* ▷ *conj* **24** *formal* because or seeing that: *implausibility cries aloud, and this is a pity, for much of the narrative is entertaining* [Old English]
forage (for-ridge) *vb* **-aging, -aged 1** to search for food **2** to obtain (something) by searching about: *she foraged for her shoes* ▷ *n* **3** food for horses or

cattle, esp. hay or straw **4** the act of searching for food or provisions [Old French *fourrage*]

forage cap *n* a cap with a flat round crown and a visor, worn by soldiers when not in battle or on parade

foramen (for-ray-men) *n, pl* **-ramina** (-ram-in-a) *or* **-ramens** *anatomy* a natural hole, esp. one in a bone through which nerves pass [Latin]

forasmuch as *conj old-fashioned or law* seeing that or since

foray *n* **1** a short raid or incursion **2** a first attempt or new undertaking: *his first foray into films* [Middle English *forrayen* to pillage]

forbade *or* **forbad** *vb* the past tense of **forbid**

forbear[1] *vb* **-bearing, -bore, -borne** to cease or refrain (from doing something) [Old English *forberan*] **forbearance** *n*

forbear[2] *n* same as **forebear**

forbid *vb* **-bidding, -bade** *or* **-bad, -bidden** *or* **-bid** to prohibit or refuse to allow [Old English *forbēodan*]

> **USAGE** It was formerly considered incorrect to talk of *forbidding* someone *from* doing something, but in modern usage either *from* or *to* can be used: *he was forbidden from entering/to enter the building.*

forbidding *adj* severe and threatening in appearance or manner: *a very large and forbidding building*

forbore *vb* the past tense of **forbear**[1]

forborne *vb* the past participle of **forbear**[1]

force[1] *n* **1** strength or power: *the force of the impact had thrown him into the fireplace* **2** exertion or the use of exertion against a person or thing that resists: *they used force and repression against those who opposed their policies* **3** *physics* an influence that changes a body from a state of rest to one of motion or changes its rate of motion. Symbol: F **4 A** intellectual or moral influence: *the Superintendent acknowledged the force of the Chief Constable's argument* **B** a person or thing with such influence: *the major force behind the group's success* **5** drive or intensity: *she reacted with frightening speed and force* **6** a group of people organized for particular duties or tasks: *a UN peacekeeping force* **7 in force A** (of a law) having legal validity **B** in great strength or numbers ▷ *vb* **forcing, forced** **8** to compel (a person, group, etc.) to do something through effort, superior strength, etc.: *forced into an arranged marriage* **9** to acquire or produce through effort, superior strength, etc.: *I forced a smile* **10** to propel or drive despite resistance **11** to break down or open (a lock, door, etc.) **12** to impose or inflict: *a series of opposition strikes forced the appointment of a coalition government* **13** to cause (plants or farm animals) to grow at an increased rate [Latin *fortis* strong]

force[2] *n* (in N England) a waterfall [Old Norse *fors*]

forced *adj* **1** done because of force: *forced labour* **2** false or unnatural: *forced jollity* **3** due to an emergency: *a forced landing*

force-feed *vb* **-feeding, -fed** to force (a person or animal) to swallow food

forceful *adj* **1** strong, emphatic, and confident: *a forceful speech* **2** effective **forcefully** *adv*

forcemeat *n* a mixture of chopped ingredients used for stuffing [from *force* (see FARCE) + *meat*]

forceps *n, pl* **-ceps** a surgical instrument in the form of a pair of pincers [Latin *formus* hot + *capere* to seize]

forcible *adj* **1** involving physical force **2** convincing or effective: *a strong shrewd mind and a steady forcible manner* **forcibly** *adv*

ford *n* **1** a shallow area in a river that can be crossed by car, on horseback, etc. ▷ *vb* **2** to cross (a river) over a shallow area [Old English] **fordable** *adj*

fore *adj* **1** at, in, or towards the front: *the fore foot* ▷ *n* **2** the front part **3 fore and aft** located at both ends of a vessel: *two double cabins fore and aft* **4 to the fore** to the front or prominent position ▷ *interj* **5** a golfer's shouted warning to a person in the path of a flying ball [Old English]

fore- *prefix* **1** before in time or rank: *foregoing* **2** at or near the front: *foreground* [Old English]

forearm[1] *n* the part of the arm from the elbow to the wrist

forearm[2] *vb* to prepare or arm beforehand

forebear *or* **forbear** *n* an ancestor

foreboding *n* a strong feeling that something bad is about to happen

forecast *vb* **-casting, -cast** *or* **-casted** **1** to predict or calculate (weather, events, etc.), in advance ▷ *n* **2** a statement predicting the weather **3** a prediction **forecaster** *n*

forecastle, fo'c's'le *or* **fo'c'sle** (foke-sl) *n* the raised front part of a ship

foreclose *vb* **-closing, -closed** *law* to take possession of property bought with borrowed money because repayment has not been made: *the banks have been reluctant to foreclose on troubled borrowers* [Old French *for-* out + *clore* to close] **foreclosure** *n*

forecourt *n* a courtyard in front of a building, such as one in a filling station

forefather *n* an ancestor

forefinger *n* the finger next to the thumb. Also called: **index finger**

forefoot *n, pl* **-feet** either of the front feet of an animal

forefront *n* **1** the most active or prominent position: *at the forefront of medical research* **2** the very front

foregather *or* **forgather** *vb* to gather together or assemble

forego[1] *vb* **-going, -went, -gone** to precede in time, place, etc. [Old English *foregān*]

forego[2] *vb* **-going, -went, -gone** same as **forgo**

foregoing *adj* (esp. of writing or speech) going before; preceding

foregone conclusion *n* an inevitable result

foreground *n* **1** the part of a view, esp. in a picture, nearest the viewer **2** an important or prominent position

forehand *tennis & squash etc.* ▷ *adj* **1** (of a stroke) made so that the racket is held with the wrist facing the direction of play ▷ *n* **2** a forehand stroke

forehead *n* the part of the face between the natural hairline and the eyes [Old English *forhēafod*]

foreign *adj* **1** of, located in, or coming from another country, area, or people **2** dealing or

concerned with another country, area, or people: *the Foreign Minister* **3** not familiar; strange **4** in an abnormal place or position: *a foreign body in the food* [Latin *foris* outside]
foreigner *n* **1** a person from a foreign country **2** an outsider
foreign minister *or* **foreign secretary** *n* (in Britain) a cabinet minister who is responsible for a country's dealings with other countries
foreign office *n* (in Britain) a ministry that is concerned with a country's dealings with other countries
foreknowledge *n* knowledge of something before it actually happens
foreleg *n* either of the front legs of an animal
forelock *n* a lock of hair growing or falling over the forehead
foreman *n, pl* **-men** **1** a person who supervises other workers **2** *law* the leader of a jury
foremast *n* the mast nearest the bow of a ship
foremost *adj* **1** first in time, place, or importance: *Germany's foremost conductor* ▷ *adv* **2** first in time, place, or importance [Old English *formest*, from *forma* first]
forename *n* first name
forenoon *n* the daylight hours before noon
forensic (for-**ren**-sik) *adj* used in or connected with a court of law [Latin *forensis* public] **forensically** *adv*
forensic medicine *n* the application of medical knowledge for the purposes of the law, such as in determining the cause of death
foreordain *vb* to determine (events, etc.) in the future
forepaw *n* either of the front feet of a land mammal that does not have hooves
foreplay *n* sexual stimulation before intercourse
forerunner *n* **1** a person or thing that existed or happened before another and is similar in some way: *a forerunner of the surrealist painters* **2** a person or thing that is a sign of what will happen in the future
foresail *n* the main sail on the foremast of a ship
foresee *vb* **-seeing, -saw, -seen** to see or know beforehand **foreseeable** *adj*
foreshadow *vb* to show, indicate, or suggest in advance
foreshore *n* the part of the shore between high- and low-tide marks
foreshorten *vb* to see or draw (an object) from such an angle that it appears to be shorter than it really is
foresight *n* **1** the ability to anticipate and provide for future needs **2** the front sight on a firearm
foreskin *n* *anatomy* the fold of skin covering the tip of the penis
forest *n* **1** a large wooded area with a thick growth of trees and plants **2** a group of narrow or tall objects standing upright: *a forest of waving arms* **3** NZ an area planted with pines or other trees that are not native to the country [Medieval Latin *forestis* unfenced woodland, from Latin *foris* outside] **forested** *adj*
forestall *vb* to delay, stop, or guard against beforehand: *an action forestalling any further talks* [Middle English *forestallen* to waylay]
forestation *n* the planting of trees over a wide area
forester *n* a person skilled in forestry or in charge of a forest
forestry *n* the science or skill of growing and maintaining trees in a forest, esp. to obtain wood
foretaste *n* an early but limited experience of something to come
foretell *vb* **-telling, -told** *literary* to correctly predict (an event, a result, etc.) beforehand
forethought *n* thoughtful planning for future events: *a little forethought can avoid a lot of problems later*
foretoken *n* a sign of a future event
for ever *or* **forever** *adv* **1** without end **2** at all times **3** *informal* for a long time: *I could go on for ever about similar incidents*
forewarn *vb* to warn beforehand
foreword *n* an introductory statement to a book
forfeit (**for**-fit) *n* **1** something lost or given up as a penalty for a fault, mistake, etc. ▷ *vb* **2** to lose as a forfeit ▷ *adj* **3** lost as a forfeit [Old French *forfet* offence] **forfeiture** *n*
forgather *vb* same as **foregather**
forgave *vb* the past tense of **forgive**
forge[1] *n* **1** a place in which metal is worked by heating and hammering; smithy **2** a furnace used for heating metal ▷ *vb* **forging, forged** **3** to shape (metal) by heating and hammering **4** to make a fraudulent imitation of (a signature, money, a painting, etc.) **5** to create (an alliance, relationship, etc.) [Old French *forgier* to construct] **forger** *n*
forge[2] *vb* **forging, forged** **1** to move at a steady pace **2** **forge ahead** to increase speed or progress; take the lead [origin unknown]
forgery *n, pl* **-geries** **1** an illegal copy of a painting, banknote, antique, etc. **2** the crime of making a fraudulent imitation
forget *vb* **-getting, -got, -gotten** **1** to fail to remember (someone or something once known) **2** to neglect, either by mistake or on purpose **3** to leave behind by mistake **4** **forget oneself** to act in an uncharacteristically unrestrained or unacceptable manner: *behave yourself or I might forget myself and slap your wrists* [Old English *forgietan*] **forgettable** *adj*
forgetful *adj* **1** tending to forget **2** **forgetful of** inattentive to or neglectful of: *Fiona, forgetful of the time, was still in bed* **forgetfully** *adv*
forget-me-not *n* a low-growing plant with clusters of small blue flowers
forgive *vb* **-giving, -gave, -given** **1** to stop feeling anger and resentment towards (a person) or at (an action that has caused upset or harm) **2** to pardon (a mistake) **3** to free from (a debt) [Old English *forgiefan*]
forgiveness *n* the act of forgiving or the state of being forgiven
forgiving *adj* willing to forgive
forgo *or* **forego** *vb* **-going, -went, -gone** to give up or do without [Old English *forgān*]
forgot *vb* **1** the past tense of **forget** **2** *old-fashioned or dialect* a past participle of **forget**
forgotten *vb* a past participle of **forget**

fork *n* **1** a small tool with long thin prongs on the end of a handle, used for lifting food to the mouth **2** a larger similar-shaped gardening tool, used for lifting or digging **3 forks** the part of a bicycle that links the handlebars to the front wheel **4 A** (of a road, river, etc.) a division into two or more branches **B** the point where the division begins **C** such a branch ▷ *vb* **5** to pick up, dig, etc., with a fork **6** to be divided into two or more branches **7** to take one or other branch at a fork in a road, etc. [Latin *furca*]
forked *adj* **1** having a fork or forklike parts **2** zigzag: *forked lightning*
fork-lift truck *n* a vehicle with two moveable arms at the front that can be raised and lowered for transporting and unloading goods
fork out *vb slang* to pay, esp. with reluctance
forlorn *adj* **1** lonely, unhappy, and uncared-for **2** (of a place) having a deserted appearance **3** desperate and without any expectation of success: *a final, apparently forlorn attempt to save the war-torn country* [Old English *forloren* lost] **forlornly** *adv*
forlorn hope *n* **1** a hopeless enterprise **2** a faint hope [changed (by folk etymology) from Dutch *verloren hoop* lost troop]
form *n* **1** the shape or appearance of something **2** a visible person or animal **3** the particular mode in which a thing or person appears: *wood in the form of paper* **4** a type or kind: *shells were used as a form of currency* **5** physical or mental condition **6** a printed document, esp. one with spaces in which to fill details or answers **7** the previous record of a horse, athlete, etc. **8** *Brit slang* a criminal record **9** *education, chiefly Brit & NZ* a group of children who are taught together **10** manners and etiquette: *it is considered bad form not to wear a tie* **11** the structure and arrangement of a work of art or piece of writing as distinguished from its content **12** a bench **13** a hare's nest **14** any of the various ways in which a word may be spelt or inflected ▷ *vb* **15** to give shape to or take shape, esp. a particular shape **16** to come or bring into existence: *glaciers dammed the valley bottoms with debris behind which lakes have formed* **17** to make or construct or be made or constructed **18** to train or mould by instruction or example **19** to acquire or develop: *they've formed this impression; we formed a bond* **20** to be an element of: *they had formed part of a special murder unit* [Latin *forma* shape, model]
formal *adj* **1** of or following established conventions: *formal talks; a formal announcement* **2** characterized by conventional forms of ceremony and behaviour: *a small formal dinner party* **3** suitable for occasions organized according to conventional ceremony: *formal cocktail frocks* **4** methodical and organized: *a formal approach* **5** (of education and training) given officially at a school, college, etc.: *he had no formal training in maths* **6** symmetrical in form: *a formal garden* **7** relating to the form or structure of something as distinguished from its substance or content: *they addressed the formal elements of the structure of police work* **8** *philosophy* logically deductive rather than based on facts and observation [Latin *formalis*] **formally** *adv*
formaldehyde (for-**mal**-de-hide) *n* a colourless poisonous strong-smelling gas, used as formalin and in synthetic resins. Also: **methanal** [*form(ic) + aldehyde*]
formalin *n* a solution of formaldehyde in water, used as a disinfectant and as a preservative for biological specimens
formalism *n* concern with outward appearances and structure at the expense of content **formalist** *n*
formality *n, pl* **-ties 1** something done as a requirement of custom or good manners: *he dealt with the formalities regarding the cremation* **2** a necessary procedure without real effect: *trials were often a mere formality with the verdict decided beforehand* **3** strict observance of ceremony
formalize *or* **-ise** *vb* **-izing, -ized** *or* **-ising, -ised 1** to make official or valid **2** to give a definite form to **formalization** *or* **-isation** *n*
format *n* **1** the shape, size, and general appearance of a publication **2** style or arrangement, such as of a television programme: *a chat-show format* **3** *computers* the arrangement of data on disk or magnetic tape to comply with a computer's input device ▷ *vb* **-matting, -matted 4** to arrange in a specified format [Latin *formatus* formed]
formation *n* **1** the act of having or taking form or existence **2** something that is formed **3** the manner in which something is arranged **4** an arrangement of people or things acting as a unit, such as a troop of soldiers **5** a series of rocks or clouds of a particular structure or shape
formative *adj* **1** of or relating to formation, development, or growth: *formative years at school* **2** shaping or moulding: *the formative influence on his life*
former *adj* **1** belonging to or occurring in an earlier time: *a grotesque parody of a former greatness* **2** having been at a previous time: *the former prime minister* ▷ *n* **3 the former** the first or first mentioned of two
formerly *adv* in the past
Formica *n trademark* a hard laminated plastic used esp. for heat-resistant surfaces
formic acid *n* an acid derived from ants [Latin *formica* ant]
formidable *adj* **1** frightening because very difficult to deal with or overcome: *the Finnish winter presents formidable problems to drivers* **2** extremely impressive: *a formidable Juventus squad* [Latin *formido* fear] **formidably** *adv*
formless *adj* without a definite shape or form
formula (**form**-yew-la) *n, pl* **-las** *or* **-lae** (-lee) **1** a group of letters, numbers, or other symbols which represents a mathematical or scientific rule **2** a plan or set of rules for doing or producing something: *a formula for peace in the Middle East* **3** an established form of words, as used in religious ceremonies, legal proceedings, etc. **4** a powder used to make a milky drink for babies **5** *motor racing* the category in which a car competes, judged according to various criteria including engine size [Latin *forma* form] **formulaic** *adj*

formulary *n, pl* **-laries** a book of prescribed formulas
formulate *vb* **-lating, -lated 1** to express in a formula **2** to plan or describe precisely and clearly: *formulate a regional energy strategy* **formulation** *n*
fornicate *vb* **-cating, -cated** to have sexual intercourse without being married [Latin *fornix* vault, brothel situated therein] **fornicator** *n*
fornication *n* voluntary sexual intercourse outside marriage
forsake *vb* **-saking, -sook, -saken 1** to withdraw support or friendship from **2** to give up (something valued or enjoyed) [Old English *forsacan*]
forsooth *adv old-fashioned* in truth or indeed [Old English *forsōth*]
forswear *vb* **-swearing, -swore, -sworn 1** to reject or renounce with determination **2** to testify falsely in a court of law [Old English *forswearian*]
forsythia (for-**syth**-ee-a) *n* a shrub with yellow flowers which appear in spring before the leaves [after William *Forsyth*, botanist]
fort *n* **1** a fortified building or position **2 hold the fort** *informal* to keep things in operation during someone's absence [Latin *fortis* strong]
forte[1] (for-tay) *n* something at which a person excels: *cooking is his forte* [Latin *fortis* strong]
forte[2] *adv music* loudly [Italian]
forth *adv* **1** *formal or old-fashioned* forward, out, or away: *running back and forth across the street; Christopher Columbus set forth on his epic voyage of discovery* **2 and so forth** and so on [Old English]
forthcoming *adj* **1** about to appear or happen: *the forthcoming elections* **2** given or made available **3** (of a person) willing to give information
forthright *adj* direct and outspoken
forthwith *adv* at once
fortification *n* **1** the act of fortifying **2 fortifications** walls, mounds, etc., used to strengthen the defences of a place
fortified wine *n* wine mixed with a small amount of brandy or alcohol, such as port or sherry
fortify *vb* **-fies, -fying, -fied 1** to make (a place) defensible, such as by building walls **2** to strengthen physically, mentally, or morally: *the news fortified their resolve to succeed* **3** to increase the nutritious value of (a food), such as by adding vitamins [Latin *fortis* strong + *facere* to make]
fortissimo *adv music* very loudly [Italian]
fortitude *n* calm and patient courage in trouble or pain [Latin *fortitudo* courage]
fortnight *n* a period of 14 consecutive days [Old English *fēowertīene niht* fourteen nights]
fortnightly *chiefly Brit* ▷ *adj* **1** occurring or appearing once each fortnight ▷ *adv* **2** once a fortnight
fortress *n* a large fort or fortified town [Latin *fortis* strong]
fortuitous (for-**tyew**-it-uss) *adj* happening by chance, esp. by a lucky chance [Latin *fortuitus*] **fortuitously** *adv*
fortunate *adj* **1** having good luck **2** occurring by good luck **fortunately** *adv*
fortune *n* **1** a very large sum of money **2** luck, esp. when favourable **3** (*often pl*) a person's destiny **4** a power regarded as being responsible for human affairs **5** wealth or material prosperity [Latin *fors* chance]
fortune-teller *n* a person who claims to predict events in other people's lives
forty *n, pl* **-ties 1** the cardinal number that is the product of ten and four **2** a numeral, 40 or XL, representing this number **3** something representing or consisting of 40 units ▷ *adj* **4** amounting to forty: *forty pages* **fortieth** *adj, n*
forty-ninth parallel *n Canad informal* the border with the USA, which is in part delineated by the parallel line of latitude at 49°N
forty winks *n informal* a short light sleep
forum *n* **1** a meeting or medium for the open discussion of subjects of public interest **2** (in ancient Roman cities) an open space serving as a marketplace and centre of public business **3** (in South Africa) a pressure group of leaders and representatives [Latin]
forward *adj* **1** directed or moving ahead **2** at, in, or near the front **3** overfamiliar or disrespectful **4** well developed or advanced **5** of or relating to the future or favouring change ▷ *n* **6** an attacking player in any of various sports, such as soccer ▷ *adv* **7** same as **forwards** ▷ *vb* **8** to send (a letter, etc.) on to an ultimate destination **9** to advance or promote: *the veneer of street credibility he had used to forward his career* [Old English *foreweard*]
forwards *or* **forward** *adv* **1** towards or at a place ahead or in advance, esp. in space but also in time **2** towards the front
fosse *or* **foss** *n* a ditch or moat, esp. one dug as a fortification [Latin *fossa*]
fossick *vb Austral & NZ* **1** to search for gold or precious stones in abandoned workings, rivers, etc. **2** to search for, through, or in something; to forage [probably from English dialect *fussock* to bustle about]
fossil *n* **1** remains of a plant or animal that existed in a past geological age, occurring in the form of mineralized bones, shells, etc. ▷ *adj* **2** of, like, or being a fossil [Latin *fossilis* dug up]
fossil fuel *n* fuel, such as coal or oil, formed from the decayed remains of prehistoric animals and plants
fossilize *or* **-ise** *vb* **-izing, -ized** *or* **-ising, -ised 1** to convert or be converted into a fossil **2** to become out-of-date or inflexible: *fossilized political attitudes*
foster *adj* **1** of or involved in the bringing up of a child not one's own: *foster care* ▷ *vb* **2** to bring up (a child not one's own) **3** to promote the growth or development of: *Catherine fostered knowledge and patronized the arts* [Old English *fōstrian* to feed] **fostering** *n*
fought *vb* the past of **fight**
foul *adj* **1** offensive or loathsome: *a foul deed* **2** stinking or dirty **3** full of dirt or offensive matter **4** (of language) obscene or vulgar **5** unfair: *by fair or foul means* **6** (of weather) unpleasant **7** very bad-tempered and irritable: *he was in a foul mood* **8** *informal* disgustingly bad ▷ *n* **9** *sport* a violation of the rules ▷ *vb* **10** to make

dirty or polluted **11** to make or become entangled **12** to make or become clogged **13** *sport* to commit a foul against (an opponent) ▷ *adv* **14 fall foul of** to come into conflict with [Old English *fūl*]

foul-mouthed *adj* habitually using swearwords and bad language

foul play *n* **1** violent activity, esp. murder **2** a violation of the rules in a game

foul up *vb* **1** *informal* to mismanage or bungle **2** to contaminate **3** to block or choke ▷ *n* **foul-up 4** a state of disorder resulting from mistakes or carelessness: *a foul-up by their computers*

found¹ *vb* the past of **find**

found² *vb* **1** to bring into being or establish (something, such as an institution) **2** to lay the foundation of **3 founded on** to have a basis in: *a political system founded on fear* [Latin *fundus* bottom] **founder** *n* **founding** *adj*

found³ *vb* **1** to cast (metal or glass) by melting and pouring into a mould **2** to make (articles) in this way [Latin *fundere* to melt] **founder** *n*

foundation *n* **1** the basic experience, idea, or attitude on which a way of life or belief is based: *respect for the law is the foundation of commercial society* **2** a construction below the ground that distributes the load of a building, wall, etc. **3** the base on which something stands **4** the act of founding **5** an endowment for the support of an institution, such as a college **6** an institution supported by an endowment **7** a cosmetic used as a base for make-up

foundation stone *n* a stone laid at a ceremony to mark the foundation of a new building

founder *vb* **1** to break down or fail: *his negotiations have foundered on economic grounds* **2** (of a ship) to sink **3** to sink into or become stuck in soft ground **4** (of a horse) to stumble or go lame [Old French *fondrer* to submerge]

> **USAGE** *Founder* is sometimes wrongly used where *flounder* is meant: *this unexpected turn of events left him floundering* (not *foundering*).

foundling *n chiefly Brit* an abandoned baby whose parents are not known [Middle English *foundeling*]

foundry *n, pl* **-ries** a place where metal is melted and cast

fount¹ *n* **1** *poetic* a spring or fountain **2** a source or supply: *a fount of knowledge* [from *fountain*]

fount² *n printing, chiefly Brit* same as **font²**

fountain *n* **1** an ornamental feature in a pool or lake consisting of a jet of water forced into the air by a pump **2** a jet or spray of water **3** a natural spring of water **4** a source or supply: *a fountain of many new ideas about the causes of cancer* **5** a cascade of sparks, lava, etc. [Latin *fons* spring]

fountainhead *n* a principal or original source

fountain pen *n* a pen supplied with ink from a container inside it

four *n* **1** the cardinal number that is the sum of one and three **2** a numeral, 4 or IV, representing this number **3** something representing or consisting of four units **4** *cricket* a score of four runs, obtained by hitting the ball so that it crosses the boundary after hitting the ground **5** *rowing* **A** a rowing boat propelled by four oarsmen **B** the crew of such a rowing boat ▷ *adj* **6** amounting to four: *four zones* [Old English *fēower*]

four-by-four *n* a vehicle with four-wheel drive

fourfold *adj* **1** having four times as many or as much **2** composed of four parts ▷ *adv* **3** by four times as many or as much

four-in-hand *n* a carriage drawn by four horses and driven by one driver

four-letter word *n* any of several short English words referring to sex or excrement: regarded generally as offensive or obscene

four-poster *n* a bed with posts at each corner supporting a canopy and curtains

fourscore *adj old-fashioned* eighty

foursome *n* **1** a group of four people **2** *golf* a game between two pairs of players

foursquare *adv* **1** squarely or firmly ▷ *adj* **2** solid and strong **3** forthright and uncompromising

four-stroke *adj* designating an internal-combustion engine in which the piston makes four strokes for every explosion

fourteen *n* **1** the cardinal number that is the sum of ten and four **2** a numeral, 14 or XIV, representing this number **3** something representing or consisting of 14 units ▷ *adj* **4** amounting to fourteen: *fourteen points* **fourteenth** *adj, n*

fourth *adj* **1** of or being number four in a series **2** denoting the fourth from lowest forward gear in a motor vehicle ▷ *n* **3** the fourth from lowest forward gear in a motor vehicle

fourth dimension *n* **1** the dimension of time, which in addition to three spatial dimensions specifies the position of a point or particle **2** the concept in science fiction of an extra dimension **fourth-dimensional** *adj*

fourth estate *n* the press

four-wheel drive *n* a system in a vehicle in which all four wheels are connected to the source of power

fowl *n* **1** a domesticated bird such as a hen **2** any other bird that is used as food or hunted as game **3** the meat of fowl **4** *old-fashioned* a bird ▷ *vb* **5** to hunt or snare wild birds [Old English *fugol*]

fox *n, pl* **foxes** *or* **fox 1** a doglike wild animal with a pointed muzzle and a bushy tail **2** its reddish-brown or grey fur **3** a person who is cunning and sly ▷ *vb* **4** *informal* to confuse or puzzle [Old English]

foxglove *n* a tall plant with purple or white flowers

foxhole *n military* a small pit dug to provide shelter against enemy fire

foxhound *n* a breed of short-haired terrier, originally kept for hunting foxes

fox-hunting *n* the activity of hunting foxes with hounds

foxtrot *n* **1** a ballroom dance with slow and quick steps **2** music for this ▷ *vb* **-trotting, -trotted 3** to perform this dance

foxy *adj* **foxier, foxiest 1** of or resembling a fox, esp. in craftiness **2** reddish-brown **foxily** *adv* **foxiness** *n*

foyer (foy-ay) *n* an entrance hall in a hotel, theatre, or cinema [French: fireplace]

fp forte-piano

f

FP 1 fire plug 2 freezing point
Fr 1 *Christianity* **A** Father **B** Frater 2 *chem* francium
fr. 1 franc 2 from
fracas (frak-ah) *n* a noisy quarrel or fight [French]
fracking *n* a method of extracting oil or gas from rock by forcing liquid at high pressure into the rock [from *fracture*]
fraction *n* **1** *maths* a numerical quantity that is not a whole number **2** any part or subdivision **3** a very small proportion or amount of something **4** *chem* a component of a mixture separated by distillation [Latin *fractus* broken] **fractional** *adj* **fractionally** *adv*
fractional distillation *or* **fractionation** *n chem* the process of separating the constituents of a liquid mixture by heating it and condensing the components separately according to their different boiling points
fractious *adj* (esp. of children) easily upset and angered, often due to tiredness [obsolete *fraction* discord]

> **USAGE** *Fractious* is sometimes wrongly used where *factious* is meant: *this factious* (not *fractious*) *dispute has split the party still further.*

fracture *n* **1** breaking, esp. the breaking or cracking of a bone ▷ *vb* **-turing, -tured 2** to break [Latin *frangere* to break] **fractural** *adj*
fragile *adj* **1** able to be broken or damaged easily **2** in a weakened physical state: *you're looking a bit fragile this morning* [Latin *fragilis*] **fragility** *n*
fragment *n* **1** a piece broken off **2** an incomplete piece: *fragments of information* ▷ *vb* **3** to break into small pieces or different parts [Latin *fragmentum*] **fragmentation** *n*
fragmentary *adj* made up of small or unconnected pieces: *fragmentary evidence to support his theory*
fragrance *n* **1** a pleasant smell **2** a perfume or scent
fragrant *adj* having a pleasant smell [Latin *fragrare* to emit a smell]
frail *adj* **1** physically weak and delicate **2** easily damaged: *the frail aircraft* **3** easily tempted [Old French *frele*]
frailty *n* **1** physical or moral weakness **2** *pl* **-ties** an inadequacy or fault resulting from moral weakness
frame *n* **1** an open structure that gives shape and support to something, such as a building **2** an enclosing case or border into which something is fitted: *the window frame* **3** the system around which something is built up: *caught up in the frame of the revolution* **4** the structure of the human body **5** one of a series of exposures on film used in making motion pictures **6** a television picture scanned by electron beams at a particular frequency **7** *snooker* **A** a single game in a match **B** a wooden triangle used to arrange the red balls in formation before the start of a game **8** short for **cold frame 9** *slang* a frame-up **10 frame of mind** a state of mind: *in a complacent frame of mind* ▷ *vb* **framing, framed 11** to construct by fitting parts together **12** to create and develop (plans or a policy) **13** to construct (a statement) in a particular kind of language **14** to provide or enclose with a frame **15** *slang* to conspire to incriminate (someone) on a false charge [Old English *framian* to avail]
frame of reference *n* **1** a set of standards that determines behaviour **2** any set of planes or curves, such as the three coordinate axes, used to locate a point in space
frame-up *n slang* a conspiracy to incriminate someone on a false charge
framework *n* **1** a particular set of beliefs, ideas, or rules referred to in order to solve a problem: *a moral framework* **2** a structure supporting something
franc *n* the standard monetary unit of Switzerland, various African countries, and formerly of France and Belgium [Latin *Rex Francorum* King of the Franks, inscribed on 14th-century francs]
franchise *n* **1** the right to vote, esp. for a member of parliament **2** any exemption, privilege, or right granted by a public authority **3 A** *commerce* authorization granted by a manufacturing or entertainment enterprise to market its products **B** an organization that receives such an authorization **4** a series of films, video games, etc that has a strong identity and lends itself to merchandising ▷ *vb* **-chising, -chised 5** *commerce, chiefly US & Canad* to grant (a person, firm, etc.) a franchise [Old French *franchir* to set free]
Franciscan *n* **1** a member of a Christian religious order of friars or nuns founded by Saint Francis of Assisi ▷ *adj* **2** of this order
francium *n chem* an unstable radioactive element of the alkali-metal group. Symbol: **Fr** [from *France*, because first found there]
Franco- *combining form* indicating France or French: *the Franco-Prussian war* [Medieval Latin *Francus*]
frangipani (fran-jee-**pah**-nee) *n* **1** an Australian evergreen tree with large yellow fragrant flowers **2** a tropical shrub with fragrant white or pink flowers
frank *adj* **1** honest and straightforward in speech or attitude ▷ *vb* **2** to put a mark on (a letter), ensuring free carriage ▷ *n* **3** an official mark stamped to a letter ensuring free delivery [Medieval Latin *francus* free] **frankly** *adv* **frankness** *n*
Frank *n* a member of the West Germanic peoples who in the late 4th century AD gradually conquered most of Gaul [Old English *Franca*]
Frankenstein *n* a creation or monster that brings disaster and is beyond the control of its creator. Also called: **Frankenstein's monster** [after Baron *Frankenstein*, who created a monster from parts of corpses in the novel by Mary Shelley]
frankfurter *n* a smoked sausage of pork or beef [short for German *Frankfurter Wurst* sausage from Frankfurt]
frankincense *n* an aromatic gum resin burnt as incense [Old French *franc* free, pure + *encens* incense]
Frankish *n* **1** the ancient West Germanic language of the Franks ▷ *adj* **2** of the Franks or their language

frantic *adj* **1** distracted with fear, pain, joy, etc. **2** hurried and disorganized: *frantic activity* [Latin *phreneticus* mad] **frantically** *adv*

frappé *adj* (esp. of drinks) chilled [French]

fraternal *adj* **1** of a brother; brotherly **2** designating twins that developed from two separate fertilized ova [Latin *frater* brother] **fraternally** *adv*

fraternity *n, pl* **-ties 1** a body of people united in interests, aims, etc. **2** friendship between groups of people **3** *US & Canad* a society of male students

fraternize *or* **-nise** *vb* **-nizing, -nized** *or* **-nising, -nised** to associate on friendly terms: *fraternizing with the customers is off-limits* **fraternization** *or* **-nisation** *n*

fratricide *n* **1** the act of killing one's brother **2** a person who kills his or her brother [Latin *frater* brother + *caedere* to kill] **fratricidal** *adj*

Frau (rhymes with **how**) *n, pl* **Frauen** *or* **Fraus** a German form of address equivalent to *Mrs* or *Ms* [German]

fraud *n* **1** deliberate deception or cheating intended to gain an advantage **2** an act of such deception **3** *informal* a person who acts in a false or deceitful way [Latin *fraus*]

fraudster *n* a person who commits a fraud; swindler

fraudulent *adj* **1** acting with intent to deceive **2** proceeding from fraud: *fraudulent income* [Latin *fraudulentus*] **fraudulence** *n*

fraught (**frawt**) *adj* **1 fraught with** involving or filled with: *we expected the trip to be fraught with difficulties* **2** tense or anxious [Middle Dutch *vrachten*]

Fräulein (**froy**-line) *n, pl* **-lein** *or* **-leins** a German form of address equivalent to *Miss* [German]

fray[1] *n* **1** *Brit, Austral & NZ* a noisy quarrel or brawl **2 the fray** any challenging conflict: *at the last minute a rival bidder entered the fray* [short for *affray*]

fray[2] *vb* **1** to wear away into loose threads, esp. at an edge **2** to make or become strained or irritated [French *frayer* to rub]

frazil (**fray**-zil) *n* small pieces of ice that form in water moving turbulently enough to prevent the formation of a sheet of ice [French *fraisil* cinders]

frazzle *n informal* the state of being exhausted: *worn to a frazzle* [probably from Middle English *faselen* to fray]

freak *n* **1** a person, animal, or plant that is abnormal or deformed **2** an object, event, etc., that is abnormal: *a statistical freak* **3** *informal* a person whose appearance or behaviour is very unusual **4** *informal* a person who is very enthusiastic about something specified: *a health freak* ▷ *adj* **5** abnormal or unusual: *a freak accident* [origin unknown] **freakish** *adj* **freaky** *adj*

freak out *vb informal* to be or cause to be in a heightened emotional state

freckle *n* **1** a small brownish spot on the skin ▷ *vb* **-ling, -led 2** to mark or become marked with freckles [Old Norse *freknur* freckles] **freckled** *adj*

free *adj* **freer, freest 1** able to act at will; not under compulsion or restraint **2** not enslaved or confined **3** (of a country) independent **4** (of a translation) not exact or literal **5** provided without charge: *free school meals* **6** not occupied or in use; available: *is this seat free?* **7** (of a person) not busy **8** open or available to all **9** not fixed or joined; loose: *the free end* **10** without obstruction or blockage: *the free flow of capital* **11** *chem* chemically uncombined: *free nitrogen* **12 free and easy** casual or tolerant **13 free from** not subject to: *free from surveillance* **14 free with** using or giving (something) a lot: *he was free with his tongue* **15 make free with** to behave too familiarly towards ▷ *adv* **16** in a free manner **17** without charge or cost ▷ *vb* **freeing, freed 18** to release or liberate **19** to remove obstructions or impediments from **20** to make available or usable: *capital freed by the local authority* **21 free of** *or* **from** to relieve or rid of (obstacles, pain, etc.) [Old English *frēo*] **freely** *adv*

-free *combining form* free from: *duty-free; gluten-free*

freebie *n slang* something provided without charge

freeboard *n* the space or distance between the deck of a vessel and the water line

freebooter *n* a pirate [Dutch *vrijbuit* booty]

freeborn *adj history* not born in slavery

Free Church *n chiefly Brit* any Protestant Church other than the Established Church

Freecycle *n trademark* **1** a network of citizens who promote recycling online by offering one another unwanted items free of charge ▷ *vb* **freecycle 2** to recycle (an unwanted item) by offering it free of charge

freediving *n* the sport or activity of diving without the aid of breathing apparatus

freedman *n, pl* **-men** *history* a man freed from slavery

freedom *n* **1** the state of being free, esp. to enjoy political and civil liberties **2** exemption or immunity: *freedom from government control* **3** liberation, such as from slavery **4** the right or privilege of unrestricted access: *freedom of the skies* **5** self-government or independence **6** the power to order one's own actions **7** ease or frankness of manner

free enterprise *n* an economic system in which commercial organizations compete for profit with little state control

free fall *n* **1** the part of a parachute descent before the parachute opens **2** free descent of a body in which gravity is the only force acting on it

free-for-all *n informal* a disorganized brawl or argument involving all those present

free hand *n* **1** unrestricted freedom to act: *the president must be able to deal with foreign hostilities with a free hand* ▷ *adj, adv* **freehand 2** (done) by hand without the use of guiding instruments

freehold *property law* ▷ *n* **1** tenure of property for life without restrictions ▷ *adj* **2** of or held by freehold **freeholder** *n*

free house *n Brit* a public house not bound to sell only one brewer's products

free kick *n soccer* an unopposed kick of the ball awarded for a foul or infringement

freelance *n* **1** a self-employed person doing specific pieces of work for various employers ▷ *vb* **-lancing, -lanced 2** to work as a freelance ▷ *adj, adv* **3** of or as a freelance [originally applied to a mercenary soldier]

freeloader *n slang* a person who habitually depends on others for food, accommodation, etc.

free love *n old-fashioned* the practice of having sexual relationships outside marriage, often several relationships at the same time

freeman *n, pl* **-men** a person who has been given the freedom of a city as an honour in return for public service

free-market *adj* denoting an economic system which allows supply and demand to regulate prices and wages

Freemason *n Also called* **Mason** a member of a widespread secret order whose members are pledged to help each other **Freemasonry** *n*

free-range *adj* kept or produced in natural conditions: *free-range eggs*

f

freesia *n* a plant with fragrant tubular flowers [after F. H. T. *Freese*, physician]

free space *n* a region that has no gravitational and electromagnetic fields

freestanding *adj* not attached to or supported by another object

freestyle *n* **1** a competition, such as in swimming, in which each participant may use a style of his or her choice **2** a style of wrestling in which fighters may use the legs as well as the upper body

freethinker *n* a person who forms his or her ideas independently of authority, esp. in matters of religion

free trade *n* international trade that is free of such government interference as protective tariffs and import quotas

free verse *n* unrhymed verse without a fixed rhythm

Freeview *n trademark* (in Britain) a free service providing digital terrestrial television

freeway *n US & Austral* a motorway

freewheel *vb* **1** to travel downhill on a bicycle without pedalling ▷ *n* **2** a device in the rear hub of a bicycle wheel that permits it to rotate freely while the pedals are stationary

freewheeling *adj* behaving in a relaxed spontaneous manner, without any long-term plans or commitments: *he had to change his freewheeling lifestyle after his son was born*

free will *n* **1** the ability to make a choice without outside coercion or pressure: *you walked in here of your own free will* **2** *philosophy* the belief that human behaviour is an expression of personal choice and is not determined by physical forces, Fate, or God

freeze *vb* **freezing, froze, frozen 1** to change from a liquid to a solid by the reduction of temperature, such as water to ice **2** to preserve (food) by subjection to extreme cold **3** to cover or become covered with ice **4** to fix fast or become fixed (to something) because of frost **5** to feel or cause to feel the effects of extreme cold **6** to die of extreme cold **7** to become motionless through fear, shock, etc. **8** to cause (moving film) to stop at a particular frame **9** to fix (prices, incomes, etc.) at a particular level **10** to forbid by law the exchange or collection of (loans, assets, etc.) ▷ *n* **11** the act of freezing or state of being frozen **12** *meteorol* a spell of temperatures below freezing point **13** the fixing of incomes, prices, etc. by legislation [Old English *frēosan*]

freeze-dry *vb* **-dries, -drying, -dried** to preserve (food) by rapid freezing and drying in a vacuum

freeze out *vb* to prevent (someone) from being involved in an activity, conversation, etc., by being unfriendly or reserved

freezer *n* an insulated cabinet for cold-storage of perishable foods

freezing *adj informal* very cold

freezing point *n* the temperature below which a liquid turns into a solid

freezing works *n Austral & NZ* a slaughterhouse at which animals are slaughtered and carcasses frozen, esp. for export

freight (frate) *n* **1 A** commercial transport of goods **B** the cargo transported **C** the cost of this **2** *chiefly Brit* a ship's cargo or part of it ▷ *vb* **3** to transport (goods) by freight **4** to load with goods for transport [Middle Dutch *vrecht*]

freighter *n* a ship or aircraft designed for transporting cargo

French *adj* **1** of France ▷ *n* **2** the official language of France and an official language of Switzerland, Belgium, Canada, and certain other countries ▷ *pl n* **3 the French** the people of France [Old English *Frencisc* French, Frankish]

French beans *pl n* green beans, the pods of which are eaten

French bread *n* white bread in a long thin crusty loaf

French Canadian *n* a Canadian citizen whose native language is French

French chalk *n* a variety of talc used to mark cloth or remove grease stains

French dressing *n* a salad dressing made from oil and vinegar with seasonings

French fries *pl n chiefly US & Canad* potato chips

French horn *n music* a valved brass wind instrument with a coiled tube

Frenchify *vb* **-fies, -fying, -fied** *informal* to make or become French in appearance, etc.

French letter *n Brit & NZ slang* a condom

Frenchman *or fem* **Frenchwoman** *n, pl* **-men** *or* **-women** a person from France

French polish *n* a shellac varnish for wood, giving a high gloss

French seam *n* a seam in which the edges are enclosed

French windows *pl n* a window extending to floor level, used as a door

frenetic (frin-net-ik) *adj* wild, excited, and uncontrolled [Greek *phrenitis* insanity] **frenetically** *adv*

frenzy *n, pl* **-zies 1** violent or wild and uncontrollable behaviour **2** excited or agitated activity: *a frenzy of speculation* [Late Latin *phrenesis* madness, from Greek *phren* mind] **frenzied** *adj*

frequency *n, pl* **-cies 1** the number of times that an event occurs within a given period **2** the state of being frequent **3** *physics* the number of times a wave repeats itself in a given time

frequency distribution *n* statistical data arranged to show the frequency with which the possible values of a variable occur

frequency modulation *n* a method of transmitting information by varying the frequency of the carrier wave in accordance with the amplitude of the input signal
frequent *adj* **1** happening often **2** habitual ▷ *vb* **3** to visit often: *a spa town frequented by the Prussian nobility* [Latin *frequens* numerous] **frequently** *adv*
frequentative *grammar* ▷ *adj* **1** denoting a verb or an affix meaning repeated action ▷ *n* **2** a frequentative verb or affix
fresco *n, pl* **-coes** *or* **-cos 1** a method of wall-painting using watercolours on wet plaster **2** a painting done in this way [Italian: fresh plaster]
fresh *adj* **1** newly made, acquired, etc. **2** not thought of before; novel: *fresh ideas* **3** most recent: *fresh allegations* **4** further or additional: *a fresh supply* **5** (of food) not canned or frozen **6** (of water) not salty **7** bright and clear: *a fresh morning* **8** (of a wind) cold and fairly strong **9** not tired; alert **10** not worn or faded: *the fresh colours of spring* **11** having a healthy or ruddy appearance **12** having recently come (from somewhere): *cakes fresh from the oven* **13** youthful or inexperienced **14** *informal* overfamiliar or disrespectful ▷ *adv* **15** recently: *a delicious fresh-baked cake* [Old English *fersc*] **freshly** *adv* **freshness** *n*
freshen *vb* **1** to make or become fresh or fresher **2** (of the wind) to become stronger **3 freshen up** to wash and tidy up one's appearance: *I'll go and freshen up*
fresher *or* **freshman** *n, pl* **-ers** *or* **-men** *Brit & US* a first-year student at college or university
freshet *n* **1** the sudden overflowing of a river **2** a stream of fresh water emptying into the sea
freshwater *adj* of or living in fresh water
fret¹ *vb* **fretting, fretted 1** to worry: *he would fret about the smallest of problems* **2** to rub or wear away **3** to feel or give annoyance ▷ *n* **4** a state of irritation or anxiety [Old English *fretan* to eat]
fret² *n* **1** a repetitive geometrical figure used for ornamentation ▷ *vb* **fretting, fretted 2** to ornament with fret or fretwork [Old French *frete* interlaced design used on a shield]
fret³ *n* a small metal bar set across the fingerboard of a musical instrument, such as a guitar, as a guide to fingering [origin unknown]
fretful *adj* irritable or upset **fretfully** *adv*
fret saw *n* a fine-toothed saw with a long thin narrow blade, used for cutting designs in thin wood or metal
fretwork *n* decorative geometrical carving in wood
Freudian (froy-dee-an) *adj* of or relating to Sigmund Freud (1856–1939), Austrian psychiatrist, or his ideas **Freudianism** *n*
Freudian slip *n* a slip of the tongue that may reveal an unconscious wish
Fri. Friday
friable (fry-a-bl) *adj* easily broken up [Latin *friare* to crumble] **friability** *n*
friar *n* a member of a male Roman Catholic religious order [Latin *frater* brother]
friar's balsam *n* a compound with a camphor-like smell, used as an inhalant to relieve bronchitis
friary *n, pl* **-aries** a house of friars
fricassee *n* stewed meat, esp. chicken or veal, served in a thick white sauce [Old French]
fricative *n* **1** a consonant produced by friction of breath through a partly closed mouth, such as (f) or (z) ▷ *adj* **2** relating to or being a fricative [Latin *fricare* to rub]
friction *n* **1** a resistance encountered when one body moves relative to another body with which it is in contact **2** the act of rubbing one object against another **3** disagreement or conflict [Latin *fricare* to rub] **frictional** *adj*
Friday *n* the sixth day of the week [Old English *Frīgedæg* day of Freya, Norse goddess]
fridge *n* a cabinet for keeping food and drink cool. In full: **refrigerator**
fried *vb* the past of **fry¹**
friend *n* **1** a person known well to another and regarded with liking, affection, and loyalty **2** an ally in a fight or cause **3** a patron or supporter: *our cause has many influential friends throughout Europe* **4 make friends (with)** to become friendly (with) ▷ *vb* **5** to add (a person) as a contact on a social networking site [Old English *frēond*] **friendless** *adj* **friendship** *n*
Friend *n* a member of the Society of Friends; Quaker
friendly *adj* **-lier, -liest 1** showing or expressing liking, goodwill, or trust **2** on the same side; not hostile **3** tending to help or support ▷ *n, pl* **-lies 4** *sport* a match played for its own sake and not as part of a competition **friendliness** *n*
-friendly *combining form* helpful, easy, or good for the person or thing specified: *a user-friendly computer system; the development of an environment-friendly weedkiller*
friendly society *n Brit* an association of people who pay regular dues in return for old-age pensions, sickness benefits, etc.
frier *n* a fryer
fries *pl n* short for **French fries**
Friesian (free-zhan) *n* any of several breeds of black-and-white dairy cattle
frieze (freeze) *n* **1** a sculptured or decorated band on a wall **2** *archit* the horizontal band between the architrave and cornice of a classical temple [French *frise*]
frigate (frig-it) *n* **1** a fast warship, smaller than a destroyer **2** a medium-sized warship of the 18th and 19th centuries [French *frégate*]
fright *n* **1** sudden fear or alarm **2** a sudden alarming shock **3** *informal* a very strange or unattractive person or thing [Old English *fryhto*]
frighten *vb* **1** to terrify or scare **2** to force (someone) to do something from fear **frightening** *adj*
frightful *adj* **1** very alarming or horrifying **2** annoying or disagreeable: *a frightful pair of socks* **3** *informal* extreme: *a frightful mess* **frightfully** *adv*
frigid (frij-id) *adj* **1** (esp. of a woman) lacking sexual responsiveness **2** very cold: *the frigid air* **3** formal or stiff in behaviour or temperament [Latin *frigidus* cold] **frigidity** *n*
frill *n* **1** a long narrow strip of fabric with many folds in it, attached at one edge of something as a decoration **2** an unnecessary part of something added to make it more attractive or interesting:

no fuss, no frills, just a purity of sound and clarity of vision [origin unknown] **frilly** *or* **frilled** *adj*

frilled lizard *n* a large tree-living Australian lizard with an erectile fold of skin around the neck

fringe *n* **1** *chiefly Brit* hair cut short and hanging over the forehead **2** an ornamental edge of hanging threads, tassels, etc. **3** an outer edge: *London's southern fringe* **4** the minor and less important parts of an activity or organization: *two agents on the fringes of espionage activity* **5** a small group of people within a larger body, but differing from it in certain aims and ideas: *the radical fringe of the Green Party* ▷ *adj* **6** (of theatre) unofficial or unconventional ▷ *vb* **fringing, fringed 7** to form a border for: *sandy paths fringing the water's edge* **8** to decorate with a fringe: *tinsel fringed the desk* [Latin *fimbria* fringe, border]

f

fringe benefit *n* a benefit given in addition to a regular salary or wage

fringed *adj* **1** (of clothes, curtains, etc.) decorated with a fringe **2** **fringed with** *or* **by** bordered with or by: *a field fringed with trees*

frippery *n, pl* **-peries 1** showy but useless ornamentation **2** unimportant or trivial matters [Old French *frepe* frill, rag]

Frisbee *n trademark* a light plastic disc thrown with a spinning motion for recreation

Frisian (free-zhan) *n* **1** a language spoken in the NW Netherlands **2** a speaker of this language ▷ *adj* **3** of this language or its speakers [Latin *Frisii* people of northern Germany]

frisk *vb* **1** to leap, move about, or act in a playful manner **2** *informal* to search (someone) by feeling for concealed weapons, etc. ▷ *n* **3** a playful movement **4** *informal* an instance of frisking a person [Old French *frisque*]

frisky *adj* **friskier, friskiest** lively, high-spirited, or playful **friskily** *adv*

frisson (freess-on) *n* a short sudden feeling of fear or excitement [French]

fritter *n* a piece of food, such as apple, that is dipped in batter and fried in deep fat [Latin *frigere* to fry]

fritter away *vb* to waste: *he did not fritter away his energy on trivialities* [obsolete *fitter* to break into small pieces]

frivolous *adj* **1** not serious or sensible in content, attitude, or behaviour **2** unworthy of serious or sensible treatment: *frivolous distractions* [Latin *frivolus*] **frivolity** *n*

frizz *vb* **1** (of hair) to form or cause (hair) to form tight curls ▷ *n* **2** hair that has been frizzed [French *friser* to curl] **frizzy** *adj*

frizzle[1] *vb* **-zling, -zled 1** to form (hair) into tight crisp curls ▷ *n* **2** a tight curl [probably related to Old English *frīs* curly]

frizzle[2] *vb* **-zling, -zled** to cook or heat until crisp or shrivelled up [probably blend of *fry + sizzle*]

frock *n old-fashioned* **1** a girl's or woman's dress **2** a loose garment, formerly worn by peasants [Old French *froc*]

frock coat *n* a man's skirted coat, as worn in the 19th century

frog[1] *n* **1** a smooth-skinned tailless amphibian with long back legs used for jumping **2** **a frog in one's throat** phlegm on the vocal cords, hindering speech [Old English *frogga*]

frog[2] *n* a military-style fastening on a coat consisting of a button and a loop [origin unknown] **frogging** *n*

frog[3] *n* horny material in the centre of the sole of a horse's foot [origin unknown]

frogman *n, pl* **-men** a swimmer equipped with a rubber suit, flippers, and breathing equipment for working underwater

frogmarch *n* **1** a method of carrying a resisting person in which each limb is held and the victim is face downwards ▷ *vb* **2** to carry in a frogmarch or cause to move forward unwillingly

frogspawn *n* a jelly-like substance containing a frog's eggs

frolic *vb* **-icking, -icked 1** to run and play in a lively way ▷ *n* **2** lively and merry behaviour **3** a light-hearted occasion [Dutch *vrolijk*]

frolicsome *adj* merry and playful

from *prep* **1** indicating the original location, situation, etc.: *from America* **2** in a period of time starting at: *from 1950 to the current year* **3** indicating the distance between two things or places: *60 miles from the Iraqi border* **4** indicating a lower amount: *from 5 to 6* **5** showing the model of: *drawn from life* **6** used with a verbal noun to denote prohibition, etc.: *she was banned from smoking at meetings* **7** because of: *five hundred horses collapsed from exhaustion* [Old English *fram*]

fromage frais (from-ahzh **fray**) *n* a low-fat soft cheese with a smooth light texture [French: fresh cheese]

frond *n* **1** the compound leaf of a fern **2** the leaf of a palm [Latin *frons*]

front *n* **1** that part or side that is forward, or most often seen or used **2** a position or place directly before or ahead **3** the beginning, opening, or first part **4** the position of leadership **5** a promenade at a seaside resort **6** *military* **A** the total area in which opposing armies face each other **B** the space in which a military unit is operating **7** *meteorol* the dividing line between two different air masses **8** an outward appearance: *he put on a bold front* **9** *informal* a business or other activity serving as a respectable cover for another, usually criminal, organization **10** Also called: **front man, front woman** a nominal leader of an organization **11** a particular field of activity: *on the economic front* **12** a group of people with a common goal: *the National Liberation Front* ▷ *adj* **13** of, at, or in the front ▷ *vb* **14** to face (onto) **15** to be a front of or for **16** to appear as a presenter in (a television show, etc) **17** to be the leader of (a band) on stage [Latin *frons* forehead, foremost part]

frontage *n* **1** the facade of a building or the front of a plot of ground **2** the extent of the front of a shop, plot of land, etc.

frontal *adj* **1** of, at, or in the front **2** of or relating to the forehead [Latin *frons* forehead]

front bench *n* (in Britain) the leadership of either the Government or Opposition in the

House of Commons or in various other legislative assemblies **front-bencher** *n*

frontier *n* **1** the region of a country bordering on another, or a line marking such a boundary **2** the edge of the settled area of a country **3 frontiers** the limit of knowledge in a particular field: *at that time, laser spectroscopy was on the frontiers of chemical research* [Old French *front* part which is opposite]

frontispiece *n* an illustration facing the title page of a book [Late Latin *frontispicium* facade]

frontrunner *n informal* the leader or a favoured contestant in a race or election

frosh *n US & Canad informal* a freshman

frost *n* **1** a white deposit of ice particles **2** an atmospheric temperature of below freezing point, producing this deposit ▷ *vb* **3** to cover with frost **4** to kill or damage (plants) with frost [Old English]

frostbite *n* destruction of tissues, esp. of the fingers, ears, toes, and nose, by freezing **frostbitten** *adj*

frosted *adj* (of glass) having the surface roughened so that it cannot be seen through clearly

frosting *n chiefly US & Canad* icing

frosty *adj* **frostier, frostiest 1** characterized by frost: *the frosty air* **2** covered by frost **3** unfriendly or disapproving: *a frosty reception from the bank manager* **frostily** *adv* **frostiness** *n*

froth *n* **1** a mass of small bubbles of air or a gas in a liquid **2** a mixture of saliva and air bubbles formed at the lips in certain diseases, such as rabies **3** trivial but superficially attractive ideas or entertainment ▷ *vb* **4** to produce or cause to produce froth [Old Norse *frotha*] **frothy** *adj*

frown *vb* **1** to wrinkle one's brows in worry, anger, or concentration **2 frown on** to disapprove of: *unnecessary waste is frowned on* ▷ *n* **3** the act of frowning **4** a look of disapproval or displeasure [Old French *froigner*]

frowsty *adj* **frowstier, frowstiest** *Brit* stale or musty [from *frowzy*]

frowzy *or* **frowsy** *adj* **frowzier, frowziest** *or* **frowsier, frowsiest 1** slovenly or unkempt in appearance **2** musty and stale [origin unknown]

froze *vb* the past tense of **freeze**

frozen *vb* **1** the past participle of **freeze** ▷ *adj* **2** turned into or covered with ice **3** killed or stiffened by extreme cold **4** (of food) preserved by a freezing process **5 A** (of prices or wages) officially fixed at a certain level **B** (of business assets) not convertible into cash **6** motionless: *she was frozen in horror*

FRS (in Britain) Fellow of the Royal Society

fructify *vb* **-fies, -fying, -fied** to bear or cause to bear fruit [Latin *fructus* fruit + *facere* to produce]

fructose *n* a crystalline sugar occurring in honey and many fruits [Latin *fructus* fruit]

frugal (froo-gl) *adj* **1** economical in the use of money or resources; thrifty **2** meagre and inexpensive: *a frugal meal* [Latin *frugi* useful, temperate] **frugality** *n* **frugally** *adv*

fruit *n* **1** any fleshy part of a plant that supports the seeds and is edible, such as the strawberry **2** *botany* the ripened ovary of a flowering plant, containing one or more seeds **3** any plant product useful to man, including grain and vegetables **4 fruits** the results of an action or effort, esp. if pleasant: *they have enjoyed the fruits of a complete victory* ▷ *vb* **5** to bear fruit [Latin *fructus* enjoyment, fruit]

fruiterer *n chiefly Brit & Austral* a person who sells fruit

fruit fly *n* **1** a small fly that feeds on and lays its eggs in plant tissues **2** a similar fly that feeds on plant sap, decaying fruit, etc., and is widely used in genetic experiments

fruitful *adj* **1** producing good and useful results: *a fruitful relationship* **2** bearing much fruit **fruitfully** *adv*

fruition (froo-ish-on) *n* **1** the fulfilment of something worked for or desired **2** the act or condition of bearing fruit [Latin *frui* to enjoy]

fruitless *adj* **1** producing nothing of value: *a fruitless debate* **2** without fruit **fruitlessly** *adv*

fruit machine *n Brit & NZ* a coin-operated gambling machine that pays out money when a particular combination of symbols, usually representing fruit, appears on a screen

fruit salad *or* **fruit cocktail** *n* a dish consisting of pieces of different kinds of fruit

fruit sugar *n* same as **fructose**

fruity *adj* **fruitier, fruitiest 1** of or like fruit **2** (of a voice) mellow or rich **3** *informal, chiefly Brit* referring humorously to things relating to sex **fruitiness** *n*

frump *n derogatory* a woman who dresses in a dull and old-fashioned way [Middle Dutch *verrompelen* to wrinkle] **frumpy** *or* **frumpish** *adj*

frustrate *vb* **-trating, -trated 1** to upset or anger (a person) by presenting difficulties that cannot be overcome: *his lack of ambition frustrated me* **2** to hinder or prevent (the efforts, plans, or desires of) [Latin *frustrare* to cheat] **frustrating** *adj* **frustration** *n*

frustrated *adj* dissatisfied or unfulfilled

frustum *n, pl* **-tums** *or* **-ta** *geom* the part of a solid, such as a cone or pyramid, contained between the base and a plane parallel to the base that intersects the solid [Latin: piece]

fry[1] *vb* **fries, frying, fried 1** to cook or be cooked in fat or oil, usually over direct heat ▷ *n, pl* **fries 2** Also: **fry-up** *informal* a dish of mixed fried food ▷ See also **fries** [Latin *frigere*] **fryer** *or* **frier** *n*

fry[2] *pl n* **1** the young of various species of fish **2** See **small fry** [Old French *freier* to spawn]

frying pan *n* **1** a long-handled shallow pan used for frying **2 out of the frying pan into the fire** from a bad situation to a worse one

FSH *biol* follicle-stimulating hormone: a hormone secreted by the pituitary gland

f-stop *n photog* any of the lens aperture settings of a camera

ft. foot or feet

ftp file transfer protocol: a standard protocol for transferring files across a network, esp. the internet

fuchsia (fyew-sha) *n* an ornamental shrub with hanging purple, red, or white flowers [after Leonhard *Fuchs*, botanist]

fuck *taboo* ▷ *vb* **1** to have sexual intercourse with (someone) ▷ *n* **2** an act of sexual intercourse **3** *slang* a partner in sexual intercourse **4 not give a fuck** not to care at all ▷ *interj* **5** *offensive* an expression of strong disgust or anger [Germanic] **fucking** *n, adj, adv*

fuck off *vb offensive, taboo* to go away

fuck up *vb offensive, taboo* to make a mess of (something)

fuddle *vb* **-dling, -dled 1** to cause to be confused or intoxicated ▷ *n* **2** a confused state [origin unknown] **fuddled** *adj*

fuddy-duddy *n, pl* **-dies** *informal* a person, esp. an elderly one, who is extremely conservative or dull [origin unknown]

fudge[1] *n* a soft sweet made from sugar, butter, and milk [origin unknown]

fudge[2] *vb* **fudging, fudged 1** to make (an issue or problem) less clear deliberately **2** to avoid making a firm statement or decision [origin unknown]

fuel *n* **1** any substance burned for heat or power, such as coal or petrol **2** the material that produces energy by fission in a nuclear reactor **3 add fuel to** to make (a difficult situation) worse ▷ *vb* **fuelling, fuelled** *or US* **fueling, fueled 4** to supply with or receive fuel **5** to intensify or make worse (a feeling or situation): *the move is bound to fuel speculation* [Old French *feu* fire]

fuel cell *n* a cell in which chemical energy is converted directly into electrical energy

fug *n chiefly Brit & NZ* a hot stale atmosphere [origin unknown] **fuggy** *adj*

fugitive (fyew-jit-iv) *n* **1** a person who flees, esp. from arrest or pursuit ▷ *adj* **2** fleeing **3** not permanent; fleeting [Latin *fugere* to take flight]

fugu *n* any of various marine pufferfish eaten in Japan once certain lethally poisonous parts have been removed [Japanese]

fugue (fyewg) *n* a musical form consisting of a theme repeated above or below the continuing first statement [French] **fugal** *adj*

Führer *n* a leader: the title used by Hitler as Nazi dictator [German]

-ful *adj suffix* **1** full of or characterized by: *painful; restful* **2** able or tending to: *useful* ▷ *n suffix* **3** as much as will fill the thing specified: *mouthful*

fulcrum *n, pl* **-crums** *or* **-cra** the pivot about which a lever turns [Latin: foot of a couch]

fulfil *or US* **fulfill** *vb* **-filling, -filled 1** to bring about the achievement of (a desire or promise) **2** to carry out (a request or order) **3** to satisfy (demands or conditions) **4 fulfil oneself** to achieve one's potential [Old English *fulfyllan*] **fulfilment** *or US* **fulfillment** *n*

full[1] *adj* **1** holding as much or as many as possible **2** abundant in supply: *full of enthusiasm* **3** having consumed enough food or drink **4** (of the face or figure) rounded or plump **5** complete: *the full amount* **6** with all privileges or rights: *full membership* **7** *music* powerful or rich in volume and sound **8** (of a garment) containing a large amount of fabric **9 full of** engrossed with: *she had been full of her own plans lately* **10 full of oneself** full of pride or conceit **11 full up** filled to capacity ▷ *adv* **12** completely or entirely **13** directly or right: *she hit him full in the face* **14 full well** very or extremely well: *we knew full well that she was watching every move we made* ▷ *n* **15 in full** without omitting or shortening **16 to the full** thoroughly or fully [Old English] **fullness** *or esp US* **fulness** *n*

full[2] *vb* to make (cloth) more compact during manufacture through shrinking and beating [Old French *fouler*]

fullback *n soccer, hockey & rugby* a defensive player

full-blooded *adj* **1** vigorous or enthusiastic **2** (esp. of horses) having ancestors of a single race or breed

full-blown *adj* fully developed

full board *n* the daily provision by a hotel of bed, breakfast, and midday and evening meals

full-bodied *adj* having a full rich flavour or quality: *a full-bodied vintage port*

fuller's earth *n* a natural absorbent clay used for fulling cloth

full-frontal *adj informal* exposing the genitals to full view

full house *n* **1** a theatre filled to capacity **2** (in bingo) the set of numbers needed to win

full-length *adj* **1** (of a mirror, portrait, etc.) showing the complete human figure **2** not abridged

full moon *n* the phase of the moon when it is visible as a fully illuminated disc

full-on *adj informal* complete; unrestrained: *full-on military intervention*

full-scale *adj* **1** (of a plan) of actual size **2** using all resources; all-out

full stop *n* the punctuation mark (.) used at the end of a sentence and after abbreviations. Also called (esp. US and Canad): **period**

full-time *adj* **1** for all of the normal working week: *a full-time job* ▷ *adv* **full time 2** on a full-time basis: *she worked full time until she was 72* ▷ *n* **full time 3** *soccer, rugby & hockey* the end of the game

full toss *or* **full pitch** *n cricket* a bowled ball that reaches the batsman without bouncing

fully *adv* **1** to the greatest degree or extent **2** amply or adequately **3** at least: *fully a hundred people*

fully-fashioned *adj* (of stockings or knitwear) shaped and seamed so as to fit closely

fulmar *n* a heavily-built Arctic sea bird with a short tail [Scandinavian]

fulminate *vb* **-nating, -nated** > **fulminate against** to criticize or denounce angrily [Latin *fulmen* lightning that strikes] **fulmination** *n*

fulsome *adj* **1** exaggerated and elaborate, and often sounding insincere: *fulsome praise* **2** *not standard* extremely complimentary

> **USAGE** The use of *fulsome* to mean 'extremely complimentary' is considered by some people to be incorrect, although it is widely encountered in journalism.

fumble *vb* **-bling, -bled 1** to use the hands clumsily or grope about blindly: *fumbling for a torch* **2** to say or do awkwardly ▷ *n* **3** the act of fumbling [probably Scandinavian]

fume *vb* **fuming, fumed 1** to be overcome with anger or fury **2** to give off (fumes) or (of fumes) to be given off, esp. during a chemical reaction **3** to treat with fumes ▷ *n* **4** (*often pl*) pungent or toxic vapour, gas, or smoke: *exhaust fumes* [Latin *fumus* smoke, vapour]

fumigate (fyew-mig-gate) *vb* **-gating, -gated** to treat (something contaminated) with fumes [Latin *fumus* smoke + *agere* to drive] **fumigation** *n*

fun *n* **1** pleasant, enjoyable, and light-hearted activity or amusement **2 for** *or* **in fun** for amusement or as a joke **3 make fun of** *or* **poke fun at** to ridicule or tease ▷ *adj* **4** (of a person) amusing and likeable **5** (of a place or activity) amusing and enjoyable [obsolete *fon* to make a fool of]

function *n* **1** the intended role or purpose of a person or thing **2** an official or formal social gathering **3** a factor, the precise nature of which depends upon another thing in some way: *muscle breakdown is a function of vitamin E deficiency* **4** *maths* a quantity, the value of which depends on the varying value of another quantity **5** a sequence of operations that a computer or calculator performs when a specified key is pressed ▷ *vb* **6** to operate or work **7 function as** to perform the action or role of (something or someone else) [Latin *functio*]

functional *adj* **1** of or performing a function **2** practical rather than decorative **3** in working order **4** *med* affecting a function of an organ without structural change **functionally** *adv*

functional food *n* a food containing additives which provide extra nutritional value. Also called: **nutraceutical**

functionalism *n* the theory that the form of a thing should be determined by its use **functionalist** *n, adj*

functionary *n, pl* **-aries** a person acting in an official capacity, such as for a government; official

fund *n* **1** a reserve of money set aside for a certain purpose **2** a supply or store of something ▷ *vb* **3** to provide money to **4** *finance* to convert (short-term debt) into long-term debt bearing fixed interest ▷ See also **funds** [Latin *fundus* the bottom, piece of land] **funder** *n*

fundamental *adj* **1** essential or primary: *fundamental mathematical concepts* **2** basic: *a fundamental error* ▷ *n* **3 fundamentals** the most important and basic parts of a subject or activity **4** the lowest note of a harmonic series **fundamentally** *adv*

fundamentalism *n* **1** *Christianity* the view that the Bible is literally true **2** *Islam* a movement favouring strict observance of Islamic law **fundamentalist** *n, adj*

fundamental particle *n physics* same as **elementary particle**

fundholding *n* the system in which general practitioners may choose to receive a fixed budget from which they pay for non-urgent hospital treatment and drug costs for patients

fundi (foon-dee) *n S African* an expert [Nguni (language group of southern Africa) *umfindisi*]

funding *n* **1** the provision of money for a project or organization **2** the amount of money provided

fundraiser *n* **1** a person involved in organizing fundraising activities **2** an event held to raise money for a cause

fundraising *n* **1** the activity involved in raising money for a cause ▷ *adj* **2** of, for, or relating to fundraising: *a fundraising walk*

funds *pl n* money that is readily available

funeral *n* **1** a ceremony at which a dead person is buried or cremated **2 it's your funeral** *informal* a mistake has been made and you alone will be responsible for its consequences ▷ *adj* **3** of or for a funeral [Latin *funus*] **funerary** *adj*

funeral director *n* an undertaker

funeral parlour *n* a place where the dead are prepared for burial or cremation

funereal (fyew-**neer**-ee-al) *adj* suggestive of a funeral; gloomy or sombre **funereally** *adv*

funfair *n Brit* an amusement park with machines to ride on and stalls

fungicide *n* a substance used to destroy fungi [FUNGUS + Latin *caedere* to kill]

fungoid *adj* resembling a fungus

fungous *adj* appearing suddenly and spreading quickly like a fungus

fungus *n, pl* **fungi** *or* **funguses** a plant without leaves, flowers, or roots, that reproduces by spores, including moulds, yeasts, and mushrooms [Latin] **fungal** *adj*

funicular (fyew-**nik**-yew-lar) *n* a railway up the side of a mountain, consisting of two cars at either end of a cable passing round a driving wheel at the summit. Also called: **funicular railway** [Latin *funis* rope]

funk[1] *old-fashioned Brit* ▷ *n* **1** a state of nervousness, fear, or depression **2** a coward ▷ *vb* **3** to avoid doing (something) through fear [origin unknown]

funk[2] *n* a type of dance music with a strong beat [from *funky*]

funky *adj* **-kier, -kiest** (of jazz or pop) having a strong beat [from obsolete *funk* to smoke tobacco, perhaps referring to music that is smelly, i.e. earthy]

funnel *n* **1** a tube with a wide mouth tapering to a small hole, used for pouring liquids into narrow openings **2** a chimney of a ship or steam train ▷ *vb* **-nelling, -nelled** *or US* **-neling, -neled 3** to move or cause to move through, or as if through, a funnel [Old Provençal *fonilh*]

funnel-web *n Austral* a large poisonous black spider that builds funnel-shaped webs

funny *adj* **-nier, -niest 1** causing amusement or laughter; humorous **2** peculiar or odd **3** *informal* faint or ill: *this smell is making me feel a bit funny* **4 funny business** *informal* suspicious or dubious behaviour **funnily** *adv* **funniness** *n*

funny bone *n* a sensitive area near the elbow where the nerve is close to the surface of the skin

fur *n* **1** the dense coat of fine silky hairs on many mammals **2** the skin of certain animals, with the hair left on **3** a garment made of fur **4 make the fur fly** to cause a scene or disturbance

f

5 *informal* a whitish coating on the tongue, caused by illness **6** *Brit* a deposit on the insides of water pipes or kettles, caused by hard water ▹ *vb* **furring, furred 7** Also: **fur up** to cover or become covered with a furlike deposit [Old French *fuerre* sheath]

furbelow *n old-fashioned* **1** a pleated or gathered piece of material used as a decoration on a woman's garment; ruffle **2 furbelows** showy ornamentation [French dialect *farbella* a frill]

furbish *vb formal* to brighten up or renovate [Old French *fourbir* to polish]

furcate *vb* **-cating, -cated 1** to divide into two parts ▹ *adj* **2** forked: *furcate branches* [Latin *furca* a fork] **furcation** *n*

f

Furies *pl n, sing* **Fury** *classical myth* the goddesses of vengeance, who pursued unpunished criminals

furious *adj* **1** extremely angry or annoyed **2** violent or unrestrained, such as in speed or energy: *fast and furious dance routines* **furiously** *adv*

furl *vb* to roll up (an umbrella, flag, or sail) neatly and securely [Old French *ferm* tight + *lier* to bind]

furlong *n* a unit of length equal to 220 yards (201.168 metres) [Old English *furlang*, from *furh* furrow + *lang* long]

furlough (fur-loh) *n* leave of absence from work or from military duty [Dutch *verlof*]

furnace *n* **1** an enclosed chamber in which heat is produced to destroy refuse or smelt ores **2** *informal* a very hot place [Latin *fornax*]

furnish *vb* **1** to provide (a house or room) with furniture, etc. **2** to supply or provide [Old French *fournir*] **furnished** *adj*

furnishings *pl n* furniture, carpets, and fittings with which a room or house is furnished

furniture *n* the large movable articles, such as chairs and tables, that equip a room or house [Old French *fournir* to equip]

furore (fyew-ror-ee) *n* a very angry or excited reaction by people to something: *the latest furore over executive pay* [Latin *furor* frenzy]

furrier *n* a person who makes or sells fur garments [Middle English *furour*]

furrow *n* **1** a long narrow trench made in the ground by a plough **2** any long deep groove, esp. a deep wrinkle on the forehead ▹ *vb* **3** to become wrinkled **4** to make furrows in (land) [Old English *furh*]

furry *adj* **-rier, -riest** like or covered with fur or something furlike

further *adv* **1** in addition **2** to a greater degree or extent **3** to or at a more advanced point **4** to or at a greater distance in time or space ▹ *adj* **5** additional **6** more distant or remote in time or space ▹ *vb* **7** to assist the progress of (something) [Old English *furthor*] **furtherance** *n*

USAGE See at **farther.**

further education *n* (in Britain, Australia, and South Africa) formal education beyond school other than at university

furthermore *adv* in addition

furthest *adv* **1** to the greatest degree or extent **2** to or at the greatest distance in time or space; farthest ▹ *adj* **3** most distant in time or space; farthest

furtive *adj* sly, cautious, and secretive [Latin *furtivus* stolen] **furtively** *adv*

fury *n, pl* **-ries 1** violent anger **2** uncontrolled violence: *the fury of the sea* **3** an outburst of violent anger **4** a person with a violent temper **5 like fury** *old-fashioned* with great energy, strength, or power [Latin *furere* to be furious]

Fury *n, pl* **-ries** See **Furies**

furze *n* gorse [Old English *fyrs*] **furzy** *adj*

fuse[1] *or US* **fuze** *n* **1** a lead containing an explosive for detonating a bomb ▹ *vb* **fusing, fused** *or US* **fuzing, fuzed 2** to equip with such a fuse [Latin *fusus* spindle]

fuse[2] *n* **1** a protective device for safeguarding electric circuits, containing a wire that melts and breaks the circuit when the current exceeds a certain value ▹ *vb* **fusing, fused 2** *Brit* to fail or cause to fail as a result of a fuse blowing **3** to equip (a plug or circuit) with a fuse **4** to join or become combined: *the two ideas fused in his mind* **5** to unite or become united by melting **6** to become or cause to become liquid, esp. by the action of heat [Latin *fusus* melted, cast]

fuselage (fyew-zill-lahzh) *n* the main body of an aircraft [French]

fusible *adj* capable of being melted

fusilier (fyew-zill-leer) *n* (formerly) an infantryman armed with a light musket: a term still used in the names of certain British regiments [French]

fusillade (fyew-zill-lade) *n* **1** a rapid continual discharge of firearms **2** a sudden outburst of criticism, questions, etc. [French *fusiller* to shoot]

fusilli (foo-zee-li) *n* pasta in the form of short spirals [Italian]

fusion *n* **1** the act or process of melting together **2** something produced by fusing **3** a kind of popular music that is a blend of two or more styles, such as jazz and funk **4** something new created by a mixture of qualities, ideas, or things **5** See **nuclear fusion** ▹ *adj* **6** relating to a style of cooking that combines traditional Western techniques and ingredients with those used in Eastern cuisine [Latin *fusio* a melting]

fuss *n* **1** needless activity and worry **2** complaint or objection: *it was silly to make a fuss over seating arrangements* **3** an exhibition of affection or admiration: *when I arrived my nephews made a big fuss of me* ▹ *vb* **4** to worry unnecessarily **5** to be excessively concerned over trivial matters **6** to bother (a person) **7 fuss over** to show great or excessive concern or affection for [origin unknown]

fusspot *n informal* a person who is difficult to please and complains often

fussy *adj* **fussier, fussiest 1** inclined to fuss **2** very particular about detail **3** overelaborate: *a fussy, overdecorated palace* **fussily** *adv*

fustian *n* **1** (formerly) a hard-wearing fabric of cotton mixed with flax or wool **2** pompous talk or writing [Old French *fustaigne*]

fusty *adj* **-tier, -tiest 1** smelling of damp or mould **2** old-fashioned [Middle English *fust* wine cask] **fustiness** *n*

futile (fyew-tile) *adj* **1** useless or having no chance of success **2** foolish and of no value:

her futile remarks began to annoy me [Latin *futtilis* pouring out easily] **futility** *n*

futon (foo-tonn) *n* a Japanese padded quilt, laid on the floor as a bed

future *n* **1** the time yet to come **2** undetermined events that will occur in that time **3** the condition of a person or thing at a later date **4** prospects: *he had faith in its future* **5** *grammar* a tense of verbs used when the action specified has not yet taken place **6** **in future** from now on ▷ *adj* **7** that is yet to come or be **8** of or expressing time yet to come **9** destined to become **10** *grammar* in or denoting the future as a tense of verbs ▷ See also **futures** [Latin *futurus* about to be]

future perfect *grammar* ▷ *adj* **1** denoting a tense of verbs describing an action that will have been performed by a certain time ▷ *n* **2** the future perfect tense

futures *pl n* commodities bought or sold at an agreed price for delivery at a specified future date

futurism *n* an early 20th-century artistic movement making use of the characteristics of the machine age **futurist** *n, adj*

futuristic *adj* **1** of design or technology that appears to belong to some future time **2** of futurism

futurity *n, pl* **-ties** **1** future **2** a future event

futurology *n* the study or prediction of the future of mankind

fuzz[1] *n* a mass or covering of fine or curly hairs, fibres, etc. [probably from Low German *fussig* loose]

fuzz[2] *n Brit, Austral & NZ slang* the police or a police officer [origin unknown]

fuzzy *adj* **fuzzier, fuzziest** **1** of, like, or covered with fuzz **2** unclear, blurred, or distorted: *just a few fuzzy pictures of the creature exist* **3** (of hair) tightly curled **fuzzily** *adv* **fuzziness** *n*

fwd forward

FX *films informal* special effects [a phonetic respelling of *effects*]

FYI for your information

f

Gg

g 1 gallon(s) 2 gram(s) 3 acceleration due to gravity
G 1 *music* the fifth note of the scale of C major 2 gravity 3 good 4 giga- 5 *slang* grand (a thousand pounds or dollars)
G7 Group of Seven: a group of seven nations whose leaders meet regularly to coordinate economic policy
G20 Group of Twenty (Finance Ministers and Central Bank Governors)
Ga *chem* gallium
GA Georgia
gab *informal* ▹ *vb* **gabbing, gabbed** 1 to talk a lot, esp. about unimportant things ▹ *n* 2 idle talk 3 **gift of the gab** the ability to talk easily and persuasively [probably from Irish Gaelic *gob* mouth]
gabardine *or* **gaberdine** *n* 1 a strong twill cloth used esp. for raincoats 2 a coat made of this cloth [Old French *gauvardine* pilgrim's garment]
gabble *vb* **-bling, -bled** 1 to speak rapidly and indistinctly: *the interviewee started to gabble furiously* ▹ *n* 2 rapid and indistinct speech [Middle Dutch *gabbelen*]
gable *n* the triangular upper part of a wall between the sloping ends of a ridged roof [probably from Old Norse *gafl*] **gabled** *adj*
gad *vb* **gadding, gadded** (foll. by *about* or *around*) to go about in search of pleasure [obsolete *gadling* companion]
gadabout *n informal* a person who restlessly seeks amusement
gadfly *n, pl* **-flies** 1 a large fly that bites livestock 2 a constantly irritating person [obsolete *gad* sting]
gadget *n* a small mechanical device or appliance [perhaps from French *gâchette* trigger] **gadgetry** *n*
gado-gado *n* an Indonesian dish of cooked mixed vegetables and hard-boiled eggs served with a peanut sauce [Bahasa Indonesia]
gadoid (**gay**-doid) *adj* 1 of or belonging to the cod family of marine fishes ▹ *n* 2 any gadoid fish [New Latin *gadus* cod]
gadolinium *n chem* a silvery-white metallic element of the rare-earth group. Symbol: **Gd** [after Johan *Gadolin*, mineralogist]
gadzooks *interj archaic* a mild oath [perhaps from *God's hooks* the nails of the cross, from *Gad*, archaic euphemism for *God*]
Gael (**gayl**) *n* a Gaelic-speaker of Scotland, Ireland, or the Isle of Man [Gaelic *Gaidheal*] **Gaeldom** *n*
Gaelic (**gal**-lik, **gay**-lik) *n* 1 any of the closely related Celtic languages of Scotland, Ireland, or the Isle of Man ▹ *adj* 2 of the Celtic people of Scotland, Ireland, or the Isle of Man, or their language
gaff[1] *n* 1 *angling* a pole with a hook attached for landing large fish 2 *naut* a spar hoisted to support a fore-and-aft sail [Provençal *gaf* boathook]
gaff[2] *n* **blow the gaff** *Brit slang* to give away a secret [origin unknown]
gaffe *n* something said or done that is socially upsetting or incorrect [French]
gaffer *n* 1 *informal, chiefly Brit* a boss or foreman 2 an old man: often used affectionately 3 *informal* the senior electrician on a television or film set [from *godfather*]
gag[1] *vb* **gagging, gagged** 1 to choke as if about to vomit or as if struggling for breath 2 to stop up (a person's mouth), usually with a piece of cloth, to prevent them from speaking or crying out 3 to deprive of free speech ▹ *n* 4 something, usually a piece of cloth, stuffed into or tied across the mouth 5 any restraint on free speech 6 a device for keeping the jaws apart: *a dentist's gag* [Middle English *gaggen*]
gag[2] *informal* ▹ *n* 1 a joke, usually one told by a professional comedian ▹ *vb* **gagging, gagged** 2 to tell jokes [origin unknown]
gaga (**gah**-gah) *adj informal* 1 confused and having some memory loss, esp. as a result of old age 2 foolishly doting: *she's gaga over him* [French]
gage[1] *n* (formerly) a glove or other object thrown down to indicate a challenge to fight [Old French]
gage[2] *n, vb* **gaging, gaged** *US* same as **gauge**
gaggle *n* 1 *informal* a group of people gathered together 2 a flock of geese [Germanic]
gaiety *n, pl* **-ties** 1 a state of lively good spirits 2 festivity; merrymaking
USAGE See at **gay**.
gaily *adv* 1 in a lively manner; cheerfully 2 with bright colours
gain *vb* 1 to acquire (something desirable) 2 to increase, improve, or advance: *wholesale prices gained 5.6 percent* 3 to get to; reach: *gaining the top of the hill* 4 (of a watch or clock) to become or be too fast 5 **gain on** to get nearer to or catch up on ▹ *n* 6 something won or acquired; profit; advantage: *a clear gain would result* 7 an increase in size or amount 8 *electronics* the ratio of the output signal of an amplifier to the input signal, usually measured in decibels [Old French *gaignier*]
gainful *adj* useful or profitable **gainfully** *adv*
gainsay *vb* **-saying, -said** *archaic or literary* to deny or contradict [Middle English *gainsaien*, from *gain-* against + *saien* to say]
gait *n* 1 manner of walking 2 (of horses and dogs) the pattern of footsteps at a particular speed, such as a trot [variant of *gate*]
gaiters *pl n* cloth or leather coverings for the legs or ankles [French *guêtre*]
gal *n informal* a girl
gala (**gah**-la) *n* 1 a special social occasion, esp. a special performance 2 *chiefly Brit* a sporting occasion with competitions in several events: *next week's sports gala* [Old French *galer* to make merry]
galactic *adj* of the Galaxy or other galaxies
galaxy *n, pl* **-axies** 1 a star system held together by gravitational attraction 2 a collection of

brilliant people or things: *a galaxy of legal talent* [Middle English (in the sense: the Milky Way); from Greek *gala* milk]
Galaxy *n* **the Galaxy** the spiral galaxy that contains the solar system. Also called: **Milky Way**
gale *n* **1** a strong wind, specifically one of force 8 on the Beaufort scale **2 gales** a loud outburst: *gales of laughter* [origin unknown]
galena *or* **galenite** *n* a soft bluish-grey mineral consisting of lead sulphide: the chief source of lead [Latin: lead ore]
Galia melon *n* a kind of melon with a raised network texture on the skin and sweet flesh
gall[1] (**gawl**) *n* **1** *informal* bold impudence: *she was stunned I had the gall to ask* **2** a feeling of great bitterness **3** *physiol obsolete* same as **bile** [Old Norse]
gall[2] (**gawl**) *vb* **1** to annoy or irritate **2** to make the skin sore by rubbing ▷ *n* **3** something that causes annoyance **4** a sore on the skin caused by rubbing [Germanic]
gall[3] (**gawl**) *n* an abnormal outgrowth on a tree or plant caused by parasites [Latin *galla*]
gallant *adj* **1** persistent and courageous in the face of overwhelming odds: *a gallant fight* **2** (of a man) making a show of polite attentiveness to women **3** having a reputation for bravery: *Police Medal for gallant and meritorious services* ▷ *n* **4** *history* a young man who tried to impress women with his fashionable clothes or daring acts [Old French *galer* to make merry] **gallantly** *adv*
gallantry *n* **1** showy, attentive treatment of women **2** great bravery in war or danger
gall bladder *n* a muscular sac, attached to the liver, that stores bile
galleon *n* a large three-masted sailing ship used from the 15th to the 18th centuries [Spanish *galeón*]
gallery *n, pl* **-leries 1** a room or building for displaying works of art **2** a balcony running along or around the inside wall of a church, hall, or other building **3** *theatre* **A** an upper floor that projects from the rear and contains the cheapest seats **B** the audience seated there **4** an underground passage in a mine or cave **5** a group of spectators, for instance at a golf match **6 play to the gallery** to try to gain approval by appealing to popular taste [Old French *galerie*]
galley *n* **1** the kitchen of a ship, boat, or aircraft **2** a ship propelled by oars or sails, used in ancient or medieval times [Old French *galie*]
galley slave *n* **1** a criminal or slave forced to row in a galley **2** *informal* a drudge
Gallic *adj* **1** French **2** of ancient Gaul or the Gauls
Gallicism *n* a word or idiom borrowed from French
gallinaceous *adj* of an order of birds, including poultry, pheasants, and grouse, that have a heavy rounded body [Latin *gallina* hen]
galling (**gawl**-ing) *adj* annoying or bitterly humiliating
gallium *n chem* a silvery metallic element used in high-temperature thermometers and low-melting alloys. Symbol: **Ga** [Latin *gallus* cock, translation of French *coq* in the name of its discoverer, *Lecoq* de Boisbaudran]
gallivant *vb* to go about in search of pleasure [perhaps from *gallant*]
gallon *n* **1** *Brit* a unit of liquid measure equal to 4.55 litres **2** *US* a unit of liquid measure equal to 3.79 litres [Old Northern French *galon*]
gallop *vb* **1** (of a horse) to run fast with a two-beat stride in which all four legs are off the ground at once **2** to ride (a horse) at a gallop **3** to move or progress rapidly ▷ *n* **4** the fast two-beat gait of horses **5** an instance of galloping [Old French *galoper*]
Galloway *n* a breed of black cattle originally bred in Galloway [after *Galloway*, district of SW Scotland]
gallows *n, pl* **-lowses** *or* **-lows 1** a wooden structure consisting of two upright posts with a crossbeam, used for hanging criminals **2 the gallows** execution by hanging [Old Norse *galgi*]
gallstone *n* a small hard mass formed in the gall bladder or its ducts
Gallup Poll *n* a sampling of the views of a representative cross section of the population, usually used to forecast voting [after G. H. *Gallup*, statistician]
galop *n* **1** a 19th-century dance in quick duple time **2** music for this dance [French]
galore *adj* in abundance: *there were bargains galore* [Irish Gaelic *go leór* to sufficiency]
galoshes *pl n Brit, Austral & NZ* a pair of waterproof overshoes [Old French *galoche* wooden shoe]
galumph *vb Brit, Austral & NZ informal* to leap or move about clumsily or joyfully [probably a blend of GALLOP + TRIUMPH]
galvanic *adj* **1** of or producing an electric current by chemical means, such as in a battery **2** *informal* stimulating, startling, or energetic
galvanize *or* **-nise** *vb* **-nizing, -nized** *or* **-nising, -nised 1** to stimulate into action **2** to cover (metal) with a protective zinc coating **3** to stimulate by an electric current [after Luigi *Galvani*, physiologist] **galvanization** *or* **-nisation** *n*
galvanometer *n* a sensitive instrument for detecting or measuring small electric currents
gambit *n* **1** an opening remark or action intended to gain an advantage **2** *chess* an opening move in which a piece, usually a pawn, is sacrificed to gain an advantageous position [Italian *gambetto* a tripping up]
gamble *vb* **-bling, -bled 1** to play games of chance to win money or prizes **2** to risk or bet (something) on the outcome of an event or sport **3 gamble away** to lose by gambling **4 gamble on** to act with the expectation of: *she has gambled on proving everyone wrong* ▷ *n* **5** a risky act or venture **6** a bet or wager [probably variant of GAME[1]] **gambler** *n* **gambling** *n*
gamboge (gam-**boje**) *n* a gum resin obtained from a tropical Asian tree, used as a yellow pigment and as a purgative [from *Cambodia*, where first found]
gambol *vb* **-bolling, -bolled** *or US* **-boling, -boled 1** to jump about playfully; frolic ▷ *n* **2** a playful jumping about; frolicking [French *gambade*]
game[1] *n* **1** an amusement for children **2** a competitive activity with rules **3** a single period of play in such an activity **4** (in some sports) the score needed to win **5** a single contest in a series;

match **6** short for **computer game** or **video game** **7** style or ability in playing a game: *in the second set his overall game improved markedly* **8** an activity that seems to operate according to unwritten rules: *the political game of power* **9** an activity undertaken in a spirit of playfulness: *people who regard life as a game* **10** wild animals, birds, or fish, hunted for sport or food **11** the flesh of such animals, used as food **12** an object of pursuit: *fair game* **13** *informal* a trick or scheme: *what's his game?* **14** **games** an event consisting of various sporting contests, usually in athletics: *Commonwealth Games* **15** **give the game away** to reveal one's intentions or a secret **16** **on the game** *slang* working as a prostitute **17** **play the game** to behave fairly **18** **the game is up** the scheme or trick has been found out and so cannot succeed ▷ *adj* **19** *informal* full of fighting spirit; plucky **20** *informal* prepared or willing: *I'm always game for a new sensation* ▷ *vb* **gaming, gamed** **21** to play games of chance for money; gamble **22** to play computer games [Old English *gamen*] **gamely** *adv* **gameness** *n*

game[2] *adj Brit, Austral & NZ* lame: *he had a game leg* [probably from Irish *cam* crooked]

gamekeeper *n Brit* a person employed to take care of game on an estate

game plan *n* **1** *US & Canad* a strategy for playing a particular game **2** any plan or strategy

gamer *n* a person who plays computer games

games console *n* an electronic device, linked to a television set, used for playing video games

gamesmanship *n informal* the art of winning by cunning practices without actually cheating

gamester *n* a gambler

gamete (gam-eet) *n* a cell that can fuse with another in reproduction [Greek *gametē* wife] **gametic** *or* **gametal** *adj*

gamey *or* **gamy** *adj* **gamier, gamiest** having the smell or flavour of game

gamin *n* a street urchin [French]

gamine (gam-een) *n* a slim and boyish girl or young woman [French]

gaming *n* gambling

gamma *n* the third letter in the Greek alphabet (Γ, γ)

gamma radiation *n* electromagnetic radiation of shorter wavelength and higher energy than X-rays

gamma rays *pl n* streams of gamma radiation

gammon *n* **1** cured or smoked ham **2** the hindquarter of a side of bacon [Old French *gambe* leg]

gammy *adj* **-mier, -miest** *Brit & NZ slang* (of the leg) lame [dialect variant of GAME²]

gamp *n Brit informal* an umbrella [after Mrs Gamp in Dickens' *Martin Chuzzlewit*]

gamut *n* **1** entire range or scale: *a rich gamut of facial expressions* **2** *music* **A** a scale **B** the whole range of notes [Medieval Latin, from *gamma*, the lowest note of the hexachord as established by Guido d'Arezzo + *ut* (now, *doh*), the first of the notes of the scale *ut, re, mi, fa, sol, la, si*]

gamy *adj* same as **gamey**

gander *n* **1** a male goose **2** *informal* a quick look: *have a gander* [Old English *gandra, ganra*]

gang[1] *n* **1** a group of people who go around together, often to commit crime **2** an organized group of workmen ▷ *vb* **3** to become or act as a gang ▷ See also **gang up on** [Old English: journey]

gang[2] *vb Scot* to go or walk [Old English *gangan*]

gangbang *n slang* sexual intercourse between a person and several men one after the other, esp. against the person's will

gangland *n* the criminal underworld

gangling *or* **gangly** *adj* lanky and awkward in movement [see GANG²]

ganglion *n, pl* **-glia** *or* **-glions** a collection of nerve cells outside the brain and spinal cord [Greek: cystic tumour] **ganglionic** *adj*

gangplank *n naut* a portable bridge for boarding and leaving a ship

gangrene *n* decay of body tissue caused by the blood supply being interrupted by disease or injury [Greek *gangraina* an eating sore] **gangrenous** *adj*

gangsta rap *n* a style of rap music originating from US Black street culture [phonetic rendering of GANGSTER]

gangster *n* a member of an organized gang of criminals **gangsterism** *n*

gangue *n* valueless material in an ore [German *Gang* vein of metal, course]

gang up on *or* **gang up against** *vb informal* to combine in a group against

gangway *n* **1** *Brit* an aisle between rows of seats **2** same as **gangplank** **3** an opening in a ship's side to take a gangplank

gannet *n* **1** a heavily built white sea bird **2** *Brit slang* a greedy person [Old English *ganot*]

ganoid *adj* **1** (of the scales of certain fishes) consisting of an inner bony layer covered with an enamel-like substance **2** (of a fish) having such scales ▷ *n* **3** a ganoid fish [Greek *ganos* brightness]

gantry *n, pl* **-tries** a large metal framework used to support something, such as a travelling crane, or to position a rocket on its launch pad [Latin *cantherius* supporting frame, pack ass]

gaol (jayl) *n, vb Brit & Austral* same as **jail** **gaoler** *n*

gap *n* **1** a break or opening in something **2** an interruption or interval **3** a difference in ideas or viewpoint: *the generation gap* [Old Norse: chasm] **gappy** *adj*

gape *vb* **gaping, gaped** **1** to stare in wonder with the mouth open **2** to open the mouth wide, as in yawning **3** to be or become wide open: *a hole gaped in the roof* [Old Norse *gapa*] **gaping** *adj*

gap year *n* a year's break between leaving school and starting further education

garage *n* **1** a building used to keep cars **2** a place where cars are repaired and petrol is sold ▷ *vb* **-aging, -aged** **3** to put or keep a car in a garage [French]

garage sale *n* a sale of household items held at a person's home, usually in the garage

garb *n* **1** clothes, usually the distinctive dress of an occupation or group: *modern military garb* ▷ *vb* **2** to clothe [Old French *garbe* graceful contour]

garbage *n* **1** *US, Austral & NZ* household waste **2** worthless rubbish or nonsense [probably from Anglo-French]

garbled *adj* (of a story, message, etc.) jumbled and confused [Old Italian *garbellare* to strain, sift]
garbo *n, pl* **-bos** *Austral informal* a person whose job is to collect household waste
garçon (garss-on) *n* a waiter [French]
garda *n, pl* **gardaí** a member of the police force of the Republic of Ireland [Irish Gaelic: guard]
garden *n* **1** an area of land usually next to a house, for growing flowers, fruit, or vegetables. Related adjective: **horticultural 2** Also: **gardens** a cultivated area of land open to the public: *Kensington Gardens* **3 lead someone up the garden path** *informal* to mislead or deceive someone ▷ *vb* **4** to work in or take care of a garden [Old French *gardin*] **gardener** *n* **gardening** *n*
garden centre *n* a place where plants and gardening tools and equipment are sold
garden city *n Brit* a planned town of limited size surrounded by countryside
gardenia (gar-deen-ya) *n* **1** a large fragrant waxy white flower **2** the evergreen shrub on which it grows [after Dr Alexander *Garden*, botanist]
gardening leave *n chiefly Brit informal* a period during which an employee who is about to leave a company continues to receive a salary but does not work
garfish *n* **1** a freshwater fish with a long body and very long toothed jaws **2** a sea fish with similar characteristics
gargantuan *adj* huge or enormous [after *Gargantua*, a giant in Rabelais' *Gargantua and Pantagruel*]

> **USAGE** Some people think that *gargantuan* should only be used to describe things connected with food: *a gargantuan meal; his gargantuan appetite.*

gargle *vb* **-gling, -gled 1** to rinse the mouth and throat with (a liquid) by slowly breathing out through the liquid ▷ *n* **2** the liquid used for gargling **3** the act or sound of gargling [Old French *gargouille* throat]
gargoyle *n* (on ancient buildings) a waterspout below the roof, carved in the form of a grotesque face or figure [Old French *gargouille* gargoyle, throat]
garish *adj* crudely bright or colourful [obsolete *gaure* to stare] **garishly** *adv* **garishness** *n*
garland *n* **1** a wreath of flowers and leaves worn round the head or neck or hung up ▷ *vb* **2** to decorate with a garland or garlands [Old French *garlande*]
garlic *n* the bulb of a plant of the onion family, with a strong taste and smell, made up of small segments which are used in cooking [Old English *gārlēac*] **garlicky** *adj*
garment *n* an article of clothing [Old French *garniment*]
garner *vb* to collect or gather: *the financial rewards garnered by his book* [Latin *granum* grain]
garnet *n* a red semiprecious gemstone [Old French *grenat* red, from *pome grenate* pomegranate]
garnish *vb* **1** to decorate (food) with something to add to its appearance or flavour ▷ *n* **2** a decoration for food [Old French *garnir* to adorn, equip]
garret *n* an attic in a house [Old French *garite* watchtower]
garrison *n* **1** soldiers who guard a base or fort **2** the place itself ▷ *vb* **3** to station (soldiers) in (a fort or base) [Old French *garir* to defend]
garrotte *or* **garotte** *n* **1** a Spanish method of execution by strangling **2** a cord, wire, or iron collar, used to strangle someone ▷ *vb* **-rotting, -rotted 3** to execute with a garrotte [Spanish *garrote*]
garrulous *adj* constantly chattering; talkative [Latin *garrire* to chatter] **garrulousness** *n*
garter *n* **1** a band, usually of elastic, worn round the leg to hold up a sock or stocking **2** *US & Canad* a suspender [Old French *gartier*]
Garter *n* **the Order of the Garter** the highest order of British knighthood
garter stitch *n* knitting in which all the rows are knitted in plain stitch
gas *n, pl* **gases** *or* **gasses 1** an airlike substance that is neither liquid nor solid at room temperature and atmospheric pressure **2** a fossil fuel in the form of a gas, used as a source of heat **3** an anaesthetic in the form of a gas **4** *mining* firedamp or the explosive mixture of firedamp and air **5** *US, Canad, Austral & NZ* petrol **6** a poisonous gas used in war **7** *informal* idle talk or boasting **8** *slang* an entertaining person or thing: *Monterey was a gas for musicians and fans alike* **9** *US informal* gas generated in the alimentary canal ▷ *vb* **gases** *or* **gasses, gassing, gassed 10** to subject to gas fumes so as to make unconscious or to suffocate **11** *informal* to talk a lot; chatter [coined from Greek *khaos* atmosphere]
gasbag *n informal* a person who talks too much
gas chamber *n* an airtight room which is filled with poison gas to kill people
gaseous (gass-ee-uss, gay-see-uss) *adj* of or like a gas
gash *n* **1** a long deep cut ▷ *vb* **2** to make a long deep cut in [Old French *garser* to scratch, wound]
gasholder *n* a large tank for storing gas before distributing it to users
gasify *vb* **-fies, -fying, -fied** to change into a gas **gasification** *n*
gasket *n* a piece of paper, rubber, or metal sandwiched between the faces of a metal joint to provide a seal [probably from French *garcette* rope's end]
gaslight *n* **1** a lamp in which light is produced by burning gas **2** the light produced by such a lamp
gasman *n, pl* **-men** a man employed to read household gas meters and install or repair gas fittings, etc.
gas mask *n* a mask fitted with a chemical filter to protect the wearer from breathing in harmful gases
gas meter *n* a device for measuring and recording the amount of gas passed through it
gasoline *or* **gasolene** *n US & Canad* petrol
gasometer (gas-som-it-er) *n* same as **gasholder**
gasp *vb* **1** to draw in the breath sharply or with difficulty **2** to utter breathlessly ▷ *n* **3** a short convulsive intake of breath [Old Norse *geispa* to yawn]
gas ring *n* a circular metal pipe with several holes in it fed with gas for cooking

gassy *adj* **-sier, -siest** filled with, containing, or like gas **gassiness** *n*
gastric *adj* of the stomach
gastric band *n* an adjustable band fitted inside the stomach to reduce its capacity as an aid to weight loss
gastric juice *n* a digestive fluid secreted by the stomach
gastric ulcer *n* an ulcer on the lining of the stomach
gastritis *n* inflammation of the lining of the stomach, causing vomiting or gastric ulcers
gastroenteritis *n* inflammation of the stomach and intestine, causing vomiting and diarrhoea
gastronomy *n* the art of good eating [Greek *gastēr* stomach + *nomos* law] **gastronomic** *adj*
gastropod *n* a mollusc, such as a snail or whelk, that has a single flat muscular foot, eyes on stalks, and usually a spiral shell [Greek *gastēr* stomach + *-podos* -footed]
gastropub *n* a pub that serves high-quality food
gasworks *n* a factory in which coal gas is made
gate *n* **1** a movable barrier, usually hinged, for closing an opening in a wall or fence **2 A** the number of people admitted to a sporting event or entertainment **B** the total entrance money received from them **3** an exit at an airport by which passengers get to an aircraft **4** *electronics* a circuit with one or more input terminals and one output terminal, the output being determined by the combination of input signals **5** a slotted metal frame that controls the positions of the gear lever in a motor vehicle [Old English *geat*]
gateau (gat-toe) *n, pl* **-teaux** (-toes) a large rich layered cake [French]
gate-crash *vb informal* to gain entry to (a party) without invitation **gate-crasher** *n*
gatehouse *n* a building at or above a gateway
gate-leg table *or* **gate-legged table** *n* a table with leaves supported by hinged legs that can swing back to let the leaves hang from the frame
gateway *n* **1** an entrance that may be closed by a gate **2** a means of entry or access: *his only gateway to the outside world* **3** *computers* hardware and software that connect incompatible computer networks, allowing them to communicate
gather *vb* **1** to come or bring together **2** to increase gradually in (pace, speed, or momentum) **3** to prepare oneself for a task or challenge by collecting one's thoughts, strength, or courage **4** to learn from information given; conclude: *this is pretty important, I gather* **5** to draw (fabric) into small folds or tucks **6** to pick or harvest (crops) ▹ *n* **7 gathers** small folds or tucks in fabric [Old English *gadrian*]
gathering *n* a group of people, usually meeting for some particular purpose: *the Braemar Highland Gathering*
GATT General Agreement on Tariffs and Trade: a former name for the World Trade Organization
gatvol (hhut-fol) *adj S African vulgar slang* annoyed; fed up [Afrikaans]
gauche (gohsh) *adj* socially awkward [French]
gaucho (gow-choh) *n, pl* **-chos** a cowboy of the South American pampas [American Spanish]
gaudy *adj* **gaudier, gaudiest** vulgarly bright or colourful [from *gaud* trinket] **gaudily** *adv* **gaudiness** *n*
gauge (gayj) *vb* **gauging, gauged 1** to estimate or judge (people's feelings or reactions) **2** to measure using a gauge ▹ *n* **3** an instrument for measuring quantities: *a petrol gauge* **4** a scale or standard of measurement **5** a standard for estimating people's feelings or reactions: *a gauge of public opinion* **6** the diameter of the barrel of a gun **7** the distance between the rails of a railway track [from Old French]
Gaul *n* a native of ancient Gaul
gaunt *adj* **1** bony and emaciated in appearance **2** (of a place) bleak or desolate: *the gaunt disused flour mill* [origin unknown] **gauntness** *n*
gauntlet[1] *n* **1** a long heavy protective glove **2** a medieval armoured glove **3 take up the gauntlet** to accept a challenge [Old French *gantelet*]
gauntlet[2] *n* **run the gauntlet** to be exposed to criticism or harsh treatment [Swedish *gatlopp* passageway]
gauss (rhymes with **mouse**) *n, pl* **gauss** the cgs unit of magnetic flux density [after K. F. *Gauss*, mathematician]
gauze *n* a transparent, loosely woven cloth, often used for surgical dressings [French *gaze*] **gauzy** *adj*
gave *vb* the past tense of **give**
gavel (gav-vl) *n* a small hammer used by a judge, auctioneer, or chairman to call for order or attention [origin unknown]
gavotte *n* **1** an old formal dance in quadruple time **2** music for this dance [French]
gawk *vb* **1** to stare stupidly ▹ *n* **2** a clumsy stupid person [Old Danish *gaukr*]
gawky *adj* **gawkier, gawkiest** clumsy and awkward
gawp *vb slang* to stare stupidly [Middle English *galpen*] **gawper** *n*
gay *adj* **1** homosexual **2** carefree and merry: *with gay abandon* **3** bright and cheerful: *smartly dressed in gay colours* ▹ *n* **4** a homosexual person [Old French *gai*]

> **USAGE** *Gayness* is the state of being homosexual. The noun which refers to the state of being carefree and merry is *gaiety*.

gaydar *n informal* the supposed ability of a homosexual person to determine whether or not another person is homosexual
gayness *n* homosexuality
gaze *vb* **gazing, gazed 1** to look long and steadily at someone or something ▹ *n* **2** a long steady look [Swedish dialect *gasa* to gape at]
gazebo (gaz-zee-boh) *n, pl* **-bos** a summerhouse or pavilion with a good view [perhaps a pseudo-Latin coinage based on *gaze*]
gazelle *n* a small graceful fawn-coloured antelope of Africa and Asia [Arabic *ghazāl*]
gazette *n* an official newspaper that gives lists of announcements, for instance in legal or military affairs [French]
gazetteer *n* a book or section of a book that lists and describes places
gazump *vb Brit & Austral informal* to raise the price of a house after agreeing a price verbally with an intending buyer [origin unknown]

gazunder *vb Brit informal* to reduce an offer on a house immediately before exchanging contracts, having earlier agreed a higher price with (the seller) **gazunderer** *n*

GB 1 Great Britain 2 Also: **Gb** gigabyte

GBH (in Britain and South Africa) grievous bodily harm

GC George Cross (a British award for bravery)

GCE 1 (formerly in Britain) General Certificate of Education 2 *informal* a pass in a GCE examination

GCSE 1 (in Britain) General Certificate of Secondary Education; an examination in specified subjects which replaced the GCE O level and CSE 2 *informal* a pass in a GCSE examination

Gd *chem* gadolinium

g'day *interj Austral & NZ informal* same as **good day**

GDP gross domestic product

Ge *chem* germanium

gear *n* 1 a set of toothed wheels that engages with another or with a rack in order to change the speed or direction of transmitted motion 2 a mechanism for transmitting motion by gears 3 the setting of a gear to suit engine speed or direction: *a higher gear; reverse gear* 4 clothing or personal belongings 5 equipment for a particular task: *police in riot gear* 6 **in** or **out of gear** with the gear mechanism engaged or disengaged ▷ *vb* 7 to prepare or organize for something: *to gear for war* ▷ See also **gear up** [Old Norse *gervi*]

gearbox *n* the metal casing enclosing a set of gears in a motor vehicle

gearing *n* a system of gears designed to transmit motion

gear lever *or US & Canad* **gearshift** *n* a lever used to engage or change gears in a motor vehicle

gear up *vb* to prepare for an activity: *to gear up for a massive relief operation*

gearwheel *n* one of the toothed wheels in the gears of a motor vehicle

gecko *n, pl* **geckos** a small tropical lizard [Malay *ge'kok*]

gee *interj US & Canad informal* a mild exclamation of surprise, admiration, etc. Also: **gee whizz** [euphemism for *Jesus*]

geebung (**gee**-bung) *n* 1 an Australian tree or shrub with an edible but tasteless fruit 2 the fruit of this tree

geek *n informal* 1 a person who is knowledgeable and enthusiastic about a specific subject 2 a boring and unattractive person [perhaps from Scottish *geck* fool] **geeky** *adj*

geelbek (**heel**-bek) *n S African* an edible marine fish with yellow jaws [Afrikaans *geel* yellow + *bek* mouth]

geese *n* the plural of **goose'**

geezer *n Brit, Austral & NZ informal* a man [probably dialect pronunciation of *guiser*, a mummer]

Geiger counter (**guy**-ger) *or* **Geiger-Müller counter** *n* an instrument for detecting and measuring radiation [after Hans *Geiger*, physicist]

geisha (**gay**-sha) *n* a professional female companion for men in Japan, trained in music, dancing, and conversation [Japanese]

gel (jell) *n* 1 a thick jelly-like substance, esp. one used to keep a hairstyle in shape ▷ *vb* **gelling, gelled** 2 to become a gel 3 same as **jell** 4 to apply gel to (one's hair) [from *gelatine*]

gelatine (**jell**-a-teen) *or* **gelatin** *n* a clear water-soluble protein made by boiling animal hides and bones, used in cooking, in glue, and in photographic film processes [Latin *gelare* to freeze]

gelatinous (jill-**at**-in-uss) *adj* with a thick, semiliquid consistency

geld *vb* **gelding, gelded** *or* **gelt** to castrate (a horse or other animal) [Old Norse *gelda*]

gelding *n* a castrated male horse [Old Norse *geldingr*]

gelignite *n* a type of dynamite used for blasting [GELATINE + Latin *ignis* fire]

gem *n* 1 a precious stone used for decoration. Related adjective: **lapidary** 2 a person or thing regarded as precious or special: *a perfect gem of a hotel* [Latin *gemma* bud, precious stone]

gemfish *n* an Australian food fish with a delicate flavour

Gemini *n astrol* the third sign of the zodiac; the Twins [Latin]

gemsbok (**hemss**-bok) *n S African* same as **oryx** [Afrikaans]

gemstone *n* a precious or semiprecious stone, esp. one which has been cut and polished

gen *n Brit, Austral & NZ informal* information: *I want to get as much gen as I can about the American market.* See also **gen up on** [from *gen(eral information)*]

Gen. General

gendarme (**zhahn**-darm) *n* a member of the French police force [French]

gender *n* 1 the state of being male or female with reference to socially and culturally defined characteristics of masculinity or femininity 2 the classification of nouns in certain languages as masculine, feminine, or neuter [Latin *genus* kind]

gender-neutral *adj* 1 suitable for any gender: *gender-neutral toys* 2 not referring to one gender only: *gender-neutral language*

gene (jean) *n* a unit composed of DNA forming part of a chromosome, by which inherited characteristics are transmitted from parent to offspring [German *Gen*]

genealogy (jean-ee-**al**-a-jee) *n* 1 the direct descent of an individual or group from an ancestor 2 *pl* **-gies** a chart showing the descent of an individual or group [Greek *genea* race] **genealogical** *adj* **genealogist** *n*

genera (**jen**-er-a) *n* a plural of **genus**

general *adj* 1 common or widespread: *general goodwill* 2 of, affecting, or including all or most of the members of a group 3 not specialized or specializing: *a general hospital* 4 including various or miscellaneous items: *general knowledge* 5 not definite; vague: *the examples used will give a general idea* 6 highest in authority or rank: *the club's general manager* ▷ *n* 7 a very senior military officer 8 **in general** generally; mostly or usually [Latin *generalis*]

general anaesthetic *n* a substance that causes general anaesthesia. See **anaesthesia**

general election *n* an election in which representatives are chosen in all constituencies of a state

generalissimo *n, pl* **-mos** a supreme commander of combined armed forces [Italian]
generality *n* **1** *pl* **-ties** a general principle or observation: *speaking in generalities* **2** *old-fashioned* the majority: *the generality of mankind*
generalization *or* **-lisation** *n* a principle or statement based on specific instances but applied generally: *the argument sinks to generalizations and name-calling*
generalize *or* **-lise** *vb* **-lizing, -lized** *or* **-lising, -lised** **1** to form general principles or conclusions from specific instances **2** to speak in generalities **3** to make widely used or known: *generalized violence*
generally *adv* **1** usually; as a rule: *these protests have generally been peaceful* **2** commonly or widely: *it's generally agreed he has performed well* **3** not specifically; broadly: *what are your thoughts generally about the war?*

g

general practitioner *n* a doctor who does not specialize but has a general medical practice in which he or she treats all illnesses
general-purpose *adj* having a variety of uses: *general-purpose cooking oil*
general staff *n* officers who assist commanders in the planning and execution of military operations
general strike *n* a strike by all or most of the workers of a country
generate *vb* **-rating, -rated** to produce or create [Latin *generare* to beget]
generation *n* **1** all the people of approximately the same age: *the younger generation* **2** a successive stage in descent of people or animals: *passed on from generation to generation* **3** the average time between two generations of a species, about 35 years for humans: *an alliance which has lasted a generation* **4** a specified stage of development: *the next generation of fighter aircraft* **5** production, esp. of electricity or heat
generation gap *n* the difference in outlook and the lack of understanding between people of different generations
generative *adj* capable of producing or originating something
generator *n* a device for converting mechanical energy into electrical energy
generic (jin-**ner**-ik) *adj* of a whole class, or group, or genus [Latin *genus* kind, race] **generically** *adv*
generous *adj* **1** ready to give freely; unselfish **2** free from pettiness in character and mind **3** large or plentiful: *a generous donation* [Latin *generosus* nobly born] **generously** *adv* **generosity** *n*
genesis (**jen**-iss-iss) *n, pl* **-ses** (-seez) the beginning or origin of anything [Greek]
Genesis *n Bible* the first book of the Old Testament, containing a description of the creation of the world
gene therapy *n genetics* the replacement or alteration of defective genes in order to prevent the occurrence of inherited diseases
genetic (jin-**net**-tik) *adj* of genetics, genes, or the origin of something [from *genesis*] **genetically** *adv*
genetically modified *adj* (of an organism) having DNA which has been altered for the purpose of improvement or correction of defects
genetic code *n biochem* the order in which the four nucleic acid bases of DNA are arranged in the molecule for transmitting genetic information to the cells
genetic engineering *n* alteration of the genetic structure of an organism in order to produce more desirable traits
genetic fingerprinting *n* the use of a person's unique pattern of DNA, which can be obtained from blood, saliva, or tissue, as a means of identification **genetic fingerprint** *n*
genetics *n* the study of heredity and variation in organisms **geneticist** *n*
genial (**jean**-ee-al) *adj* cheerful, easy-going, and friendly [Latin *genius* guardian deity] **geniality** *n* **genially** *adv*
genie (**jean**-ee) *n* (in fairy tales) a servant who appears by magic and fulfils a person's wishes [Arabic *jinni* demon]
genital *adj* of the sexual organs or reproduction [Latin *genitalis* concerning birth]
genitals *or* **genitalia** (jen-it-**ail**-ya) *pl n* the external sexual organs
genitive *n grammar* a grammatical case in some languages used to indicate a relation of ownership or association [Latin *genetivus* relating to birth]
genius (**jean**-yuss) *n, pl* **-uses** **1** a person with exceptional ability in a particular subject or activity **2** such ability **3** a person considered as exerting influence of a certain sort: *the evil genius behind the drug-smuggling empire* [Latin]
genocide (**jen**-no-side) *n* the deliberate killing of a people or nation [Greek *genos* race + Latin *caedere* to kill] **genocidal** *adj*
genome *n* **1** the full complement of genetic material within an organism **2** all the genes comprising a haploid set of chromosomes [from GENE + CHROMOSOME]
genomics *n* the branch of molecular genetics concerned with the study of genomes
genotoxic *adj* harmful to genetic material
genre (**zhahn**-ra) *n* **1** a kind or type of literary, musical, or artistic work: *the mystery and supernatural genres* **2** a kind of painting depicting incidents from everyday life [French]
gent *n Brit, Austral & NZ informal* short for **gentleman**
genteel *adj* **1** overly concerned with being polite **2** respectable, polite, and well-bred [French *gentil* well-born] **genteelly** *adv*
gentian (**jen**-shun) *n* a mountain plant with blue or purple flowers [Latin *gentiana*]
gentian violet *n* a violet-coloured solution used as an antiseptic and in the treatment of burns
Gentile *n* **1** a person who is not a Jew ▷ *adj* **2** not Jewish [Latin *gentilis* belonging to the same tribe]
gentility *n, pl* **-ties** **1** noble birth or ancestry **2** respectability and good manners [Old French *gentilite*]
gentle *adj* **1** kind and calm in character **2** temperate or moderate: *gentle autumn rain* **3** soft; not sharp or harsh: *gentle curves* [Latin *gentilis* belonging to the same family] **gentleness** *n* **gently** *adv*
gentlefolk *pl n old-fashioned* people regarded as being of good breeding

gentleman *n, pl* **-men 1** a cultured, courteous, and well-bred man **2** a man who comes from a family of high social position **3** a polite name for a man **gentlemanly** *adj*

gentrification *n* a process by which the character of a traditionally working-class area is made fashionable by middle-class people **gentrify** *vb*

gentry *n Brit old-fashioned* people just below the nobility in social rank [Old French *genterie*]

gents *n Brit & Austral informal* a men's public toilet

genuflect *vb* to bend the knee as a sign of reverence or deference, esp. in church [Latin *genu* knee + *flectere* to bend] **genuflection** *n*

genuine *adj* **1** real and exactly what it appears to be: *a genuine antique* **2** sincerely felt: *genuine concern* **3** (of a person) honest and without pretence [Latin *genuinus* inborn] **genuinely** *adv* **genuineness** *n*

gen up on *vb* **genning, genned** *Brit & Austral informal* to become, or make someone else, fully informed about

genus (jean-uss) *n, pl* **genera** *or* **genuses 1** *biol* one of the groups into which a family is divided, containing one or more species **2** a class or group [Latin: race]

geocentric *adj* **1** having the earth as a centre **2** measured as from the centre of the earth

geodesic *adj* **1** relating to the geometry of curved surfaces ▷ *n* **2** the shortest line between two points on a curved surface

geodesy *n* the study of the shape and size of the earth [Greek *gē* earth + *daiein* to divide]

geography *n* **1** the study of the earth's surface, including physical features, climate, and population **2** the physical features of a region [Greek *gē* earth + -GRAPHY] **geographer** *n* **geographical** *or* **geographic** *adj* **geographically** *adv*

geology *n* **1** the study of the origin, structure, and composition of the earth **2** the geological features of an area [Greek *gē* earth + -LOGY] **geological** *adj* **geologically** *adv* **geologist** *n*

geometric *or* **geometrical** *adj* **1** of geometry **2** consisting of shapes used in geometry, such as circles, triangles, and straight lines: *geometric design* **geometrically** *adv*

geometric progression *n* a sequence of numbers, each of which differs from the succeeding one by a constant ratio, for example 1, 2, 4, 8

geometry *n* the branch of mathematics concerned with points, lines, curves, and surfaces [Greek *geōmetrein* to measure the land] **geometrician** *n*

geophysics *n* the study of the earth's physical properties and the physical forces which affect it **geophysical** *adj* **geophysicist** *n*

Geordie *Brit* ▷ *n* **1** a person from Tyneside **2** the Tyneside dialect ▷ *adj* **3** of Tyneside: *a Geordie accent*

George Cross *n* a British award for bravery, usually awarded to civilians

georgette (jor-jet) *n* a thin crepe dress material [after Mme *Georgette*, a French dressmaker]

Georgian *adj* **1** of or in the reigns of any of the kings of Great Britain and Ireland called George **2** denoting a style of architecture or furniture prevalent in Britain in the 18th century: *an elegant Georgian terrace in Edinburgh*

geospatial *adj* of or relating to the relative position of things on the earth's surface

geostationary *adj* (of a satellite) orbiting so as to remain over the same point on the earth's surface

geotechnical *adj* relating to the application of technology to engineering problems caused by geological factors

geothermal *adj* of or using the heat in the earth's interior

geranium *n* a cultivated plant with scarlet, pink, or white flowers [Latin: cranesbill]

gerbil (jur-bill) *n* a small rodent with long back legs, often kept as a pet [French *gerbille*]

geriatric *adj* **1** of geriatrics or old people ▷ *n* **2** *old-fashioned, offensive* an older person

geriatrics *n* the branch of medicine concerned with illnesses affecting old people

germ *n* **1** a tiny living thing, esp. one that causes disease: *a diphtheria germ* **2** the beginning from which something may develop: *the germ of a book* [Latin *germen* sprout, seed]

German *adj* **1** of Germany ▷ *n* **2** a person from Germany **3** the official language of Germany, Austria, and parts of Switzerland

germane *adj* relevant: *the studies provided some evidence germane to these questions* [Latin *germanus* of the same race]

Germanic *n* **1** the ancient language from which English, German, and the Scandinavian languages developed ▷ *adj* **2** of this ancient language or the languages that developed from it **3** characteristic of German people or things: *Germanic-looking individuals*

germanium *n chem* a brittle grey metalloid element that is a semiconductor and is used in transistors. Symbol: **Ge** [after *Germany*]

German measles *n* same as **rubella**

German shepherd dog *n* same as **Alsatian**

germ cell *n* a sexual reproductive cell

germicide *n* a substance used to destroy germs [*germ* + Latin *caedere* to kill]

germinal *adj* **1** of or in the earliest stage of development: *the germinal phases of the case* **2** of germ cells

germinate *vb* **-nating, -nated** to grow or cause to grow [Latin *germinare* to sprout] **germination** *n*

germ warfare *n* the military use of disease-spreading bacteria against an enemy

gerontology *n* the scientific study of ageing and the problems of old people [Greek *gerōn* old man + -LOGY] **gerontologist** *n*

gerrymandering *n* the practice of dividing the constituencies of a voting area so as to give one party an unfair advantage [from Elbridge *Gerry*, US politician + *(sala)mander*, from the salamander-like outline of a reshaped electoral district]

gerund (jer-rund) *n* a noun formed from a verb, ending in *-ing*, denoting an action or state, for example *running* [Latin *gerundum* something to be carried on]

g

gesso (jess-oh) *n* plaster used for painting or in sculpture [Italian: chalk]
Gestapo *n* the secret state police of Nazi Germany [German *Ge(heime) Sta(ats)po(lizei)* secret state police]
gestation *n* **1** the process of carrying and developing babies in the womb during pregnancy, or the time during which this process takes place **2** the process of developing a plan or idea in the mind [Latin *gestare* to bear]
gesticulate *vb* **-lating, -lated** to make expressive movements with the hands and arms, usually while talking [Latin *gesticulari*] **gesticulation** *n*
gesture *n* **1** a movement of the hands, head, or body to express or emphasize an idea or emotion **2** something said or done to indicate intention, or as a formality: *a gesture of goodwill* ▷ *vb* **-turing, -tured 3** to make expressive movements with the hands and arms [Latin *gestus*]
get *vb* **getting, got 1** to come into possession of **2** to bring or fetch **3** to catch (an illness) **4** to become: *they get frustrated and angry* **5** to cause to be done or to happen: *he got a wart removed; to get steamed up* **6** to hear or understand: *did you get that joke?* **7** to reach (a place or point): *we could not get to the airport in time* **8** to catch (a bus or train) **9** to persuade: *she was trying to get him to give secrets away* **10** *informal* to annoy: *you know what really gets me?* **11** *informal* to baffle: *now you've got me* **12** *informal* to hit: *a bit of grenade got me on the left hip* **13** *informal* to be revenged on **14** *informal* to start: *we got talking about it; it got me thinking* ▷ *n* **15** *Brit slang* same as **git** ▷ See also **get about, get across** *etc.* [Old English *gietan*]
get about *or* **get around** *vb* **1** to be socially active **2** (of news or a rumour) to circulate
get across *vb* to make (something) understood
get at *vb* **1** to succeed in reaching or discovering: *the inquiry tried to get at the truth* **2** to imply or mean: *it is hard to see quite what he is getting at* **3** to annoy or criticize persistently: *people who know they're being got at*
get away *vb* **1** to escape or leave **2 get away with** to do (something wrong) without being caught or punished ▷ *interj* **3** an exclamation of disbelief ▷ *n* **getaway 4** the act of escaping, usually by criminals ▷ *adj* **getaway 5** used to escape: *the getaway car was abandoned*
get back *vb* **1** to have (something) returned to one **2** to return to a former state or activity: *get back to normal* **3 get back at** to retaliate against **4 get one's own back** *informal* to get one's revenge
get by *vb informal* to manage in spite of difficulties: *he saw for himself what people did to get by*
get in *vb* **1** to arrive **2** to be elected **3 get in on** to join in (an activity)
get off *vb* **1** to leave (a bus, train, etc.) **2** to escape the consequences of or punishment for an action: *the real culprits have got off scot-free* **3 get off with** *Brit & Austral informal* to begin a romantic or sexual relationship with
get on *vb* **1** to enter (a bus, train, etc.) **2** to have a friendly relationship: *he had a flair for getting on with people* **3** to grow old: *he was getting on in years* **4** (of time) to elapse: *the time was getting on* **5** to make progress: *how are the children getting on?* **6 get on with** to continue to do: *you can get on with whatever you were doing before* **7 getting on for** approaching (a time, age, or amount): *getting on for half a century ago*
get out *vb* **1** to leave or escape **2** to become known **3** to gain something of significance or value: *that's all I got out of it* **4 get out of** to avoid: *to get out of doing the dishes*
get over *vb* **1** to recover from (an illness or unhappy experience) **2** to overcome (a problem) **3 get over with** to bring (something necessary but unpleasant) to an end: *better to get it over with*
get round *vb* **1** to overcome (a problem or difficulty) **2** (of news or a rumour) to circulate **3** *informal* to gain the indulgence of (someone) by praise or flattery: *a child who learned to get round everybody and have her own way* **4 get round to** to come to (a task) eventually: *I will get round to paying the bill*
get through *vb* **1** to complete (a task or process) **2** to use up (money or supplies) **3** to succeed in (an examination or test) **4 get through to A** to succeed in making (someone) understand **B** to contact (someone) by telephone
get-together *n* **1** *informal* a small informal social gathering ▷ *vb* **get together 2** to meet socially or in order to have a discussion
get up *vb* **1** to get out of bed **2 get up to** *informal* to be involved in: *I don't know what those guys got up to down there* ▷ *n* **get-up 3** a costume or outfit
get-up-and-go *n informal* energy or drive
geyser (geez-er) *n* **1** a spring that discharges steam and hot water **2** *Brit & S African* a domestic gas water heater [Icelandic *Geysir*]
ghastly *adj* **-lier, -liest 1** *informal* very unpleasant **2** deathly pale **3** horrible: *a ghastly accident* [Old English *gāstlīc* spiritual]
ghat *n* (in India) **1** stairs leading down to a river **2** a place of cremation **3** a mountain pass [Hindi]
GHB gamma hydroxybutyrate: a substance with anaesthetic properties, used medically as a sedative and also as a recreational drug
ghee (gee) *n* clarified butter, used in Indian cookery [Hindi *ghī*]
gherkin *n* a small pickled cucumber [Dutch *agurkkijn*]
ghetto *n, pl* **-tos** *or* **-toes** an area that is inhabited by people of a particular race, religion, nationality, or class [Italian]
ghetto blaster *n informal* a large portable CD player or cassette recorder with built-in speakers
ghettoize *or* **-ise** *vb* **-izing, -ized** *or* **-ising, -ised** to confine (someone or something) to a particular area or category: *to ghettoize women as housewives* **ghettoization** *or* **-isation** *n*
ghillie *n* same as **gillie**
ghost *n* **1** the disembodied spirit of a dead person, supposed to haunt the living **2** a faint trace: *the ghost of a smile on his face* **3** a faint secondary image in an optical instrument or on a television screen ▷ *vb* **4** short for **ghostwrite** [Old English *gāst*]
ghost gum *n Austral* a eucalyptus with a white trunk and branches
ghostly *adj* **-lier, -liest** frightening in appearance or effect: *ghostly noises*

ghost town *n* a town that used to be busy but is now deserted
ghostwrite *vb* **-writing, -wrote, -written** to write (an article or book) on behalf of a person who is then credited as author **ghostwriter** *n*
ghoul (gool) *n* **1** a person who is interested in morbid or disgusting things **2** a demon that eats corpses [Arabic *ghūl*] **ghoulish** *adj* **ghoulishly** *adv*
GHQ *military* General Headquarters
GI[1] *n, pl* **GIs** *or* **GI's** *US informal* a soldier in the US Army [abbreviation of *government issue*]
GI[2] See **glycaemic index**
giant *n* **1** a mythical figure of superhuman size and strength **2** a person or thing of exceptional size, ability, or importance: *industrial giants* ▷ *adj* **3** remarkably large **4** (of an atom or ion or its structure) having large numbers of particles present in a crystal lattice, with each particle exerting a strong force of attraction on those near to it [Greek *gigas*]
giant panda *n* See **panda**
gibber[1] (jib-ber) *vb* to talk in a fast and unintelligible manner [imitative]
gibber[2] (gib-ber) *n Austral* **1** a boulder **2** barren land covered with stones [Aboriginal]
gibberish (jib-ber-rish) *n* rapid incomprehensible talk; nonsense
gibbet (jib-bit) *n* a gallows [Old French *gibet*]
gibbon (gib-bon) *n* a small agile ape of the forests of S Asia [French]
gibbous (gib-bus) *adj* (of the moon) more than half but less than fully illuminated [Latin *gibba* hump]
gibe (jibe) *n, vb* **gibing, gibed** same as **jibe**[1] [perhaps from Old French *giber* to treat roughly]
giblets (jib-lits) *pl n* the gizzard, liver, heart, and neck of a fowl [Old French *gibelet* stew of game birds]
gidday *or* **g'day** *interj Austral & NZ* a variant of **g'day**
giddy *adj* **-dier, -diest 1** feeling weak and unsteady on one's feet, as if about to faint **2** happy and excited: *a state of giddy expectation* [Old English *gydig* mad, frenzied, possessed by God] **giddiness** *n*
GIF *computers* **A** graphic interchange format: a standard compressed file format used for pictures **B** a picture held in this format
gift *n* **1** something given to someone: *a birthday gift* **2** a special ability or power: *a gift for caricature* [Old English: payment for a wife, dowry]
gifted *adj* having natural talent or aptitude: *that era's most gifted director*
giftwrap *vb* **-wrapping, -wrapped** to wrap (a gift) in decorative wrapping paper
gig[1] *n* **1** a single performance by jazz or pop musicians ▷ *vb* **gigging, gigged 2** to play gigs [origin unknown]
gig[2] *n* a light open two-wheeled one-horse carriage [origin unknown]
gig[3] *n computers informal* short for **gigabyte**
giga- *prefix* **1** denoting 10^9: *gigavolt* **2** *computers* denoting 2^{30}: *gigabyte* [Greek *gigas* giant]
gigabyte *n computers* one thousand and twenty-four megabytes
gigantic *adj* extremely large: *the most gigantic gold paperweight ever* [Greek *gigantikos*]
gig economy *n informal* an economy in which there are few permanent employees and most jobs are assigned to temporary or freelance workers
giggle *vb* **-gling, -gled 1** to laugh nervously or foolishly ▷ *n* **2** a nervous or foolish laugh **3** *informal* an amusing person or thing [imitative] **giggly** *adj*
gigolo (jig-a-lo) *n, pl* **-los** a man who is paid by an older woman to be her escort or lover [French]
gigot *n chiefly Brit* a leg of lamb or mutton [French]
gild *vb* **gilding, gilded** *or* **gilt 1** to cover with a thin layer of gold **2** to make (something) appear golden: *the morning sun gilded the hills* **3 gild the lily A** to adorn unnecessarily something already beautiful **B** to praise someone excessively [Old English *gyldan*]
gill (jill) *n* a unit of liquid measure equal to one quarter of a pint (0.14 litres) [Old French *gille* vat, tub]
gillie *or* **ghillie** *n Scot* an attendant or guide for hunting or fishing [Scottish Gaelic *gille* boy, servant]
gills (gillz) *pl n* the breathing organs of fish and other water creatures [from Old Norse]
gilt *vb* **1** a past of **gild** ▷ *adj* **2** covered with a thin layer of gold ▷ *n* **3** a thin layer of gold, used as decoration
gilt-edged *adj* denoting government securities on which interest payments and final repayments are guaranteed
gilts *pl n* gilt-edged securities
gimcrack (jim-krak) *adj* showy but cheap; shoddy [origin unknown]
gimlet (gim-let) *n* **1** a small hand tool with a pointed spiral tip, used for boring holes in wood ▷ *adj* **2** penetrating or piercing: *gimlet eyes* [Old French *guimbelet*]
gimmick *n informal* something designed to attract attention or publicity [origin unknown] **gimmickry** *n* **gimmicky** *adj*
gin[1] *n* an alcoholic drink distilled from malted grain and flavoured with juniper berries [Dutch *genever* juniper]
gin[2] *n* a noose of thin strong wire for catching small mammals [Middle English *gyn*]
ginger *n* **1** the root of a tropical plant, chopped or powdered and used as a spice, or sugared and eaten as a sweet ▷ *adj* **2** light reddish-brown: *ginger hair* [Old French *gingivre*] **gingery** *adj*
ginger ale *n* a nonalcoholic fizzy drink flavoured with ginger extract
ginger beer *n* a drink made by fermenting a mixture of syrup and root ginger
gingerbread *n* a moist brown cake flavoured with ginger
ginger group *n Brit, Austral & NZ* a group within a larger group that agitates for a more active policy
gingerly *adv* carefully or cautiously: *she sat gingerly on the edge of the chair* [perhaps from Old French *gensor* dainty]
ginger nut *or* **ginger snap** *n* a hard biscuit flavoured with ginger

gingham *n* a cotton fabric with a checked or striped design [Portuguese *guingão*]
gingivitis (jin-jiv-**vite**-iss) *n* inflammation of the gums [Latin *gingiva* gum]
ginormous *adj informal* very large [*gi(gantic) + (e)normous*]
gin rummy *n* a version of rummy in which a player may finish if the odd cards in his hand total less than ten points [GIN¹ + *rummy*]
ginseng (jin-seng) *n* the root of a plant of China and N America, believed to have tonic and energy-giving properties [Mandarin Chinese *jen shen*]
gip (jip) *n* same as **gyp**
Gipsy *n, pl* **-sies** same as **Gypsy**
giraffe *n* a cud-chewing African mammal with a very long neck and long legs and a spotted yellowy skin [Arabic *zarāfah*]
g
gird *vb* **girding, girded** *or* **girt 1** to put a belt or girdle around **2 gird (up) one's loins** to prepare oneself for action [Old English *gyrdan*]
girder *n* a large steel or iron beam used in the construction of bridges and buildings
girdle *n* **1** an elastic corset that covers the stomach and hips **2** anything that surrounds something or someone: *encased in a girdle of concrete* **3** *anatomy* an encircling arrangement of bones: *the shoulder girdle* ▷ *vb* **-dling, -dled 4** to surround: *a ring of volcanic ash girdling the earth* [Old English *gyrdel*]
girl *n* **1** a female child **2** a young woman [Middle English *girle*] **girlhood** *n* **girlish** *adj*
girlfriend *n* **1** a female friend with whom a person is romantically or sexually involved **2** any female friend
Girl Guide *n* a former name for **Guide**
girlie *adj informal* **1** featuring naked or scantily dressed women: *girlie magazines* **2** suited to or designed to appeal to young women: *a real girlie night out*
giro (jire-oh) *n, pl* **-ros 1** (in some countries) a system of transferring money within a bank or post office, directly from one account into another **2** *Brit informal* an unemployment or income support payment by giro cheque [Greek *guros* circuit]
girt *vb* a past of **gird**
girth *n* **1** the measurement around something **2** a band fastened round a horse's middle to keep the saddle in position [Old Norse *gjörth* belt]
gist (jist) *n* the main point or meaning of something: *the gist of the letter* [Anglo-French, as in *cest action gist en* this action consists in]
git *n Brit slang* a contemptible person [from *get* (in the sense: to beget, hence a bastard, fool)]
give *vb* **giving, gave, given 1** to present or hand (something) to someone **2** to pay (an amount of money) for a purchase **3** to grant or provide: *to give an answer* **4** to utter (a shout or cry) **5** to perform, make, or do: *the prime minister gave a speech* **6** to host (a party) **7** to sacrifice or devote: *comrades who gave their lives for their country* **8** to concede: *he was very efficient, I have to give him that* **9** to yield or break under pressure: *something has got to give* **10 give or take** plus or minus: *about one hundred metres, give or take five* ▷ *n* **11** a tendency to yield under pressure; elasticity ▷ See also **give away, give in** *etc.* [Old English *giefan*] **giver** *n*
give-and-take *n* **1** mutual concessions and cooperation **2** a smoothly flowing exchange of ideas and talk: *a relaxed give-and-take about their past involvement*
give away *vb* **1** to donate as a gift **2** to reveal (a secret) **3** to present (a bride) formally to her spouse in a marriage ceremony **4 give something away** NZ to give something up ▷ *n* **giveaway 5** something that reveals hidden feelings or intentions ▷ *adj* **giveaway 6** very cheap or free: *a giveaway rent*
give in *vb* to admit defeat
given *vb* **1** the past participle of **give** ▷ *adj* **2** specific or previously stated: *priorities within the given department* **3** to be assumed: *any given place on the earth* **4 given to** inclined to: *a man not given to undue optimism*
give off *vb* to send out (heat, light, or a smell)
give out *vb* **1** to hand out: *the bloke that was giving out those tickets* **2** to send out (heat, light, or a smell) **3** to make known: *the woman who gave out the news* **4** to fail: *the engine gave out*
give over *vb* **1** to set aside for a specific purpose: *the amount of space given over to advertisements* **2** *informal* to stop doing something annoying: *tell him to give over*
give up *vb* **1** to stop (doing something): *I did give up smoking* **2** to resign from (a job or position) **3** to admit defeat or failure **4** to abandon (hope) **5 give oneself up A** to surrender to the police or other authorities **B** to devote oneself completely: *she gave herself up to her work*
gizzard *n* the part of a bird's stomach in which hard food is broken up [Old French *guisier* fowl's liver]
glacé (glass-say) *adj* preserved in a thick sugary syrup: *glacé cherries* [French: iced]
glacial *adj* **1** of glaciers or ice **2** extremely cold **3** cold and unfriendly: *a glacial stare*
glacial period *n* same as **ice age**
glaciation *n* the process of covering part of the earth's surface with glaciers or masses of ice **glaciated** *adj*
glacier *n* a slowly moving mass of ice formed by an accumulation of snow [Latin *glacies* ice]
glad *adj* **gladder, gladdest 1** happy and pleased **2** very willing: *he was only too glad to help* **3** *archaic* causing happiness: *glad tidings* [Old English *glæd*] **gladly** *adv* **gladness** *n* **gladden** *vb*
glade *n* an open space in a forest: *a peaceful and sheltered glade* [origin unknown]
gladiator *n* (in ancient Rome) a man trained to fight in arenas to provide entertainment [Latin: swordsman] **gladiatorial** *adj*
gladiolus (glad-ee-**oh**-luss) *n, pl* **-li** (-lie) a garden plant with brightly coloured funnel-shaped flowers [Latin: a small sword]
glad rags *pl n informal* one's best clothes
gladsome *adj old-fashioned* joyous or cheerful
gladwrap *Austral, NZ & S African* ▷ *n* **1** *trademark* thin polythene material for wrapping ▷ *vb* **2** to wrap in gladwrap
glamorous *adj* attractive or fascinating

glamour *or US* **glamor** *n* exciting or alluring charm or beauty [Scots variant of *grammar* (hence a spell, because occult practices were popularly associated with learning)] **glamorize** *or* **-ise** *vb*

glance *n* **1** a quick look ▷ *vb* **glancing, glanced 2** to look quickly at something **3** to be deflected off an object at an oblique angle: *the ball glanced off a spectator* [Middle English *glacen* to strike obliquely] **glancing** *adj*

> **USAGE** *Glance* is sometimes wrongly used where *glimpse* is meant: *he caught a glimpse* (not *glance*) *of her making her way through the crowd.*

gland *n* **1** an organ that synthesizes and secretes chemical substances for the body to use or eliminate **2** a similar organ in plants [Latin *glans* acorn]

glandular *adj* of or affecting a gland or glands

glandular fever *n* an acute infectious viral disease that causes fever, sore throat, and painful swollen lymph nodes

glare *vb* **glaring, glared 1** to stare angrily **2** (of light or colour) to be too bright ▷ *n* **3** an angry stare **4** a dazzling light or brilliance **5 in the glare of publicity** receiving a lot of attention from the media or the public [Middle English]

glaring *adj* conspicuous or obvious: *glaring inconsistencies* **glaringly** *adv*

glasnost *n* a policy of public frankness and accountability, developed in the former Soviet Union in the 1980s under Mikhail Gorbachev [Russian: publicity, openness]

glass *n* **1** a hard brittle transparent solid, consisting of metal silicates or similar compounds **2** a drinking vessel made of glass **3** the amount contained in a drinking glass: *a glass of wine* **4** objects made of glass, such as drinking glasses and bowls [Old English *glæs*]

glass-blowing *n* the process of shaping a mass of molten glass by blowing air into it through a tube **glass-blower** *n*

glass ceiling *n* a situation in which progress, esp. promotion, appears to be possible, but restrictions or discrimination create a barrier that prevents it

glasses *pl n* a pair of lenses for correcting faulty vision, in a frame that rests on the nose and hooks behind the ears

glasshouse *n Brit & NZ* same as **greenhouse**

glassy *adj* **glassier, glassiest 1** smooth, clear, and shiny, like glass: *the glassy sea* **2** expressionless: *that glassy look*

Glaswegian (glaz-weej-an) *adj* **1** of Glasgow, a city in W Scotland ▷ *n* **2** a person from Glasgow **3** the Glasgow dialect

glaucoma *n* an eye disease in which increased pressure in the eyeball causes gradual loss of sight [Greek *glaukos* silvery, bluish-green]

glaze *vb* **glazing, glazed 1** to fit or cover with glass **2** to cover (a piece of pottery) with a protective shiny coating **3** to cover (food) with beaten egg or milk before cooking, in order to produce a shiny coating ▷ *n* **4** a protective shiny coating applied to a piece of pottery **5** a shiny coating of beaten egg or milk applied to food ▷ See also **glaze over** [Middle English *glasen*] **glazed** *adj* **glazing** *n*

glaze over *vb* to become dull through boredom or inattention: *the listener's eyes glaze over*

glazier *n* a person who fits windows or doors with glass

gleam *n* **1** a small beam or glow of light **2** a brief or dim indication: *a gleam of anticipation in his eye* ▷ *vb* **3** to shine [Old English *glǣm*] **gleaming** *adj*

glean *vb* **1** to gather (information) bit by bit **2** to gather the useful remnants of (a crop) after harvesting [Old French *glener*] **gleaner** *n*

gleanings *pl n* pieces of information that have been gleaned

glebe *n Brit & Austral* land granted to a member of the clergy as part of his or her benefice [Latin *glaeba*]

glee *n* great merriment or joy, esp. caused by the misfortune of another person [Old English *glēo*]

gleeful *adj* merry or joyful, esp. over someone else's mistake or misfortune **gleefully** *adv*

glen *n* a deep narrow mountain valley [Scottish Gaelic *gleann*]

glengarry *n, pl* **-ries** a brimless Scottish cap with a crease down the crown [after *Glengarry*, Scotland]

glib *adj* **glibber, glibbest** fluent and easy, often in an insincere or deceptive way: *there were no glib or easy answers* [probably from Middle Low German *glibberich* slippery] **glibly** *adv* **glibness** *n*

glide *vb* **gliding, glided 1** to move easily and smoothly **2** (of an aircraft) to land without engine power **3** to fly a glider **4** to float on currents of air [Old English *glīdan*]

glider *n* **1** an aircraft that does not use an engine, but flies by floating on air currents **2** *Austral* a flying phalanger

glide time *n NZ* same as **flexitime**

gliding *n* the sport of flying in a glider

glimmer *vb* **1** (of a light) to glow faintly or flickeringly ▷ *n* **2** a faint indication: *a glimmer of hope* **3** a glow or twinkle [Middle English]

glimpse *n* **1** a brief view: *a glimpse of a rare snow leopard* **2** a vague indication: *glimpses of insecurity* ▷ *vb* **glimpsing, glimpsed 3** to catch sight of momentarily [Germanic]

> **USAGE** *Glimpse* is sometimes wrongly used where *glance* is meant: *he gave a quick glance* (not *glimpse*) *at his watch.*

glint *vb* **1** to gleam brightly ▷ *n* **2** a bright gleam [probably from Old Norse]

glissade *n* **1** a gliding step in ballet **2** a controlled slide down a snow slope ▷ *vb* **-sading, -saded 3** to perform a glissade [French]

glissando *n, pl* **-dos** *music* a slide between two notes in which all intermediate notes are played [mock Italian, from French *glisser* to slide]

glisten *vb* (of a wet or glossy surface) to gleam by reflecting light: *sweat glistened above her eyes* [Old English *glisnian*]

glitch *n* a small problem that stops something from working properly [Yiddish *glitsh* a slip]

glitter *vb* **1** (of a surface) to reflect light in bright flashes **2** (of light) to be reflected in bright flashes **3** to be brilliant in a showy way: *she glitters socially* ▷ *n* **4** a sparkling light **5** superficial glamour: *the trappings and glitter of the European aristocracy* **6** tiny pieces of shiny decorative

material **7** *Canad* ice formed from freezing rain [Old Norse *glitra*] **glittering** *adj* **glittery** *adj*
glitzy *adj* **glitzier, glitziest** *slang* showily attractive [probably from German *glitzern* to glitter]
gloaming *n Scot poetic* twilight; dusk [Old English *glōmung*]
gloat *vb* to regard one's own good fortune or the misfortune of others with smug or malicious pleasure [probably Scandinavian]
glob *n informal* a rounded mass of thick fluid [probably from *globe*, influenced by *blob*]
global *adj* **1** of or applying to the whole earth: *global environmental problems* **2** of or applying to the whole of something: *a global total for local-authority revenue* **globally** *adv*
globalize *or* **-lise** *vb* **-izing, -ized** *or* **-ising, -ised** **1** to do business in countries all around the world **2** to put (something) into effect worldwide **globalization** *or* **-lisation** *n*

g

global village *n* the whole world considered as being a single community connected by modern telecommunications
global warming *n* an increase in the overall temperature worldwide believed to be caused by the greenhouse effect
globe *n* **1** a sphere on which a map of the world is drawn **2** **the globe** the earth **3** a spherical object, such as a glass lamp shade or fishbowl **4** *S African* an electric light bulb [Latin *globus*]
globetrotter *n* a habitual worldwide traveller **globetrotting** *n, adj*
globular *adj* shaped like a globe or globule
globule *n* a small round drop of liquid [Latin *globulus*]
globulin *n* a simple protein found in living tissue
glockenspiel *n* a percussion instrument consisting of tuned metal plates played with a pair of small hammers [German *Glocken* bells + *Spiel* play]
gloom *n* **1** depression or melancholy: *all doom and gloom* **2** partial or total darkness [Middle English *gloumben* to look sullen]
gloomy *adj* **gloomier, gloomiest** **1** despairing or sad **2** causing depression or gloom: *gloomy economic forecasts* **3** dark or dismal **gloomily** *adv*
gloop *or US* **glop** *n informal* any messy sticky fluid or substance [origin unknown] **gloopy** *or US* **gloppy** *adj*
glorify *vb* **-fies, -fying, -fied** **1** to make (something) seem more important than it really is: *the discussion forum is just a glorified noticeboard* **2** to praise: *few countries have glorified success in business more than the United States* **3** to worship (God) **glorification** *n*
glorious *adj* **1** brilliantly beautiful: *in glorious colour* **2** delightful or enjoyable: *the glorious summer weather* **3** having or full of glory: *glorious successes* **gloriously** *adv*
glory *n, pl* **-ries** **1** fame, praise, or honour: *tales of glory* **2** splendour: *the glory of the tropical day* **3** something worthy of praise: *the Lady Chapel is the great glory of Lichfield* **4** adoration or worship: *the greater glory of God* ▷ *vb* **-ries, -rying, -ried** **5** **glory in** to take great pleasure in: *the workers were glorying in their new-found freedom* [Latin *gloria*]
glory box *n Austral & NZ old-fashioned, informal* a box in which a young woman stores her trousseau
glory hole *n* an untidy cupboard or storeroom
Glos Gloucestershire
gloss[1] *n* **1** a bright shine on a surface **2** a superficially attractive appearance **3** a paint with a shiny finish **4** a cosmetic used to give a shiny appearance: *lip gloss* ▷ *vb* **5** to paint with gloss **6** **gloss over** to conceal (an error, failing, or awkward moment) by minimizing it: *don't try to gloss over bad news* [probably Scandinavian]
gloss[2] *n* **1** an explanatory comment added to the text of a book ▷ *vb* **2** to add a gloss or glosses to [Latin *glossa* unusual word requiring explanatory note]
glossary *n, pl* **-ries** an alphabetical list of technical or specialist words in a book, with explanations [Late Latin *glossarium*; see GLOSS[2]]
glossy *adj* **glossier, glossiest** **1** smooth and shiny: *glossy black hair* **2** superficially attractive or sophisticated: *his glossy Manhattan flat* **3** (of a magazine) produced on expensive shiny paper
glottal stop *n phonetics* a speech sound produced by tightly closing and then opening the glottis
glottis *n* the opening at the top of the windpipe, between the vocal cords [Greek *glōtta* tongue]
glove *n* **1** a shaped covering for the hand with individual sheaths for each finger and the thumb **2** a protective hand covering worn in sports such as boxing [Old English *glōfe*]
glove compartment *n* a small storage area in the dashboard of a car
gloved *adj* covered by a glove or gloves: *a gloved hand*
glow *n* **1** light produced as a result of great heat **2** a steady light without flames **3** brightness of complexion **4** a feeling of wellbeing or satisfaction ▷ *vb* **5** to produce a steady light without flames **6** to shine intensely **7** to experience a feeling of wellbeing or satisfaction: *she glowed with pleasure* **8** (of the complexion) to have a strong bright colour: *his pale face glowing at the recollection* [Old English *glōwan*]
glower (rhymes with **power**) *vb* **1** to stare angrily ▷ *n* **2** an angry stare [origin unknown]
glowing *adj* full of praise: *a glowing tribute*
glow-worm *n* a European beetle, the females and larvae of which have organs producing a soft greenish light
gloxinia *n* a plant with white, red, or purple bell-shaped flowers [after Benjamin P. *Gloxin*, botanist]
glucose *n* a white crystalline sugar found in plant and animal tissues [Greek *gleukos* sweet wine]
glue *n* **1** a substance used for sticking things together ▷ *vb* **gluing** *or* **glueing, glued** **2** to join or stick together with glue **3** **glued to** paying full attention to: *she lay on the sofa, glued to her phone* [Late Latin *glus*] **gluey** *adj*
glue ear *n* an accumulation of fluid in the middle ear of children, caused by infection and causing deafness
glue-sniffing *n* the practice of inhaling glue fumes to produce intoxicating or hallucinatory effects **glue-sniffer** *n*

glum *adj* **glummer, glummest** gloomy and quiet, usually because of a disappointment [variant of *gloom*] **glumly** *adv*
glut *n* **1** an excessive supply ▷ *vb* **glutting, glutted 2** to supply (a market) with a commodity in excess of the demand for it **3 glut oneself** to eat or drink more than one really needs [probably from Old French *gloutir* to swallow]
glute *n* short for **gluteus**
gluten (gloo-ten) *n* a sticky protein found in cereal grains, such as wheat [Latin: glue]
gluteus *or* **glutaeus** *n* any of the three muscles of the buttock [Greek *gloutos* rump]
glutinous (gloo-tin-uss) *adj* gluelike in texture
glutton *n* **1** someone who eats and drinks too much **2** a person who has a great capacity for something: *a glutton for work* [Latin *gluttire* to swallow] **gluttonous** *adj*
gluttony *n* the practice of eating too much
glycaemic index *or US* **glycemic index** *n* an index indicating the effects of various foods on blood sugar. Abbrev: **GI**
glycerine (gliss-ser-reen) *or* **glycerin** *n* a nontechnical name for **glycerol** [Greek *glukeros* sweet]
glycerol (gliss-ser-ol) *n* a colourless odourless syrupy liquid obtained from animal and vegetable fats, used as a solvent, antifreeze, and sweetener, and in explosives
glycogen (glike-oh-jen) *n* a starchlike carbohydrate stored in the liver and muscles of humans and animals
glycolysis (glike-kol-iss-iss) *n biochem* the breakdown of glucose by enzymes, with the release of energy
glyph (gliff) *n* **1** *archit* a carved channel or groove **2** a hieroglyphic symbol **3** a computer-generated character or symbol [French *glyphe*, from Greek *gluphē* carving]
gm gram
GM 1 genetically modified **2** *Brit* grant-maintained
G-man *n, pl* **G-men** *US slang* an FBI agent
GMB (in Britain) General, Municipal and Boilermakers (Trade Union)
GMO genetically modified organism
GMT Greenwich Mean Time
gnarled *adj* rough, twisted, and knobbly, usually through age
gnash *vb* to grind (the teeth) together in pain or anger [probably from Old Norse]
gnat *n* a small biting two-winged insect [Old English *gnætt*]
gnaw *vb* **1** to bite or chew constantly so as to wear away bit by bit **2 gnaw at** to cause constant distress or anxiety to: *uneasiness gnawed at his mind* [Old English *gnagan*] **gnawing** *adj*
gneiss *n* a coarse-grained layered metamorphic rock [German *Gneis*]
gnome *n* **1** an imaginary creature in fairy tales that looks like a little old man **2** a small statue of a gnome in a garden [French]
gnomic (no-mik) *adj literary* of or containing short clever sayings: *gnomic pronouncements*
Gnosticism (noss-tiss-siz-zum) *n* a religious movement involving belief in intuitive spiritual knowledge **Gnostic** *n, adj*
GNP gross national product
gnu (noo) *n, pl* **gnus** *or* **gnu** a sturdy African antelope with an oxlike head [Xhosa *nqu*]
go *vb* **goes, going, went, gone 1** to move or proceed to or from a place: *go forward* **2** to be in regular attendance at (work, church, or a place of learning) **3** to lead to a particular place: *the path that goes right along the bank* **4** to be kept in a particular place: *where does this go?* **5** to do or become as specified: *he went white; the gun went bang* **6** to be or continue to be in a specified state: *to go to sleep* **7** to operate or function: *the car wouldn't go* **8** to follow a specified course; fare: *I'd hate the meeting to go badly* **9** to be allotted to a particular purpose or recipient: *a third of the total budget goes on the army* **10** to be sold: *the portrait went for a fortune to a telephone bidder* **11** (of words or music) to be expressed or sung: *the song goes like this* **12** to fail or break down: *my eyesight is going; he was on lap 19 when the engine went* **13** to die: *she went quickly at the end* **14** to be spent or finished: *all tension and all hope had gone* **15** to proceed up to or beyond certain limits: *I think this is going too far* **16** to carry authority: *what Mummy says goes* **17** to endure or last out: *they go for eight or ten hours without resting* **18** *not standard* to say: *then she goes, 'shut up'* **19 anything goes** anything is acceptable **20 be going to** to intend or be about to: *he was afraid of what was going to happen next* **21 let go** to relax one's hold on; release **22 let oneself go A** to act in an uninhibited manner **B** to lose interest in one's appearance **23 to go** remaining: *two days to go till the holidays* ▷ *n, pl* **goes 24** an attempt: *he had a go at the furniture business* **25** a verbal or physical attack: *she couldn't resist having another go at me* **26** a turn to do something in a game: *'Your go now!' I shouted* **27** *informal* the quality of being active and energetic: *a grand old man, full of go and determination* **28 from the word go** *informal* from the very beginning **29 make a go of** *informal* to be successful in (a business venture or a relationship) **30 on the go** *informal* active and energetic ▷ See also **go about, go against** *etc.* [Old English *gān*]
go about *vb* **1** to tackle (a problem or task): *he went about it in the wrong way* **2** to busy oneself with: *people have been going about their business as usual*
goad *vb* **1** to provoke (someone) to take some kind of action, usually in anger ▷ *n* **2** something that provokes someone to take some kind of action **3** a sharp pointed stick for driving cattle [Old English *gād*]
go against *vb* **1** to conflict with (someone's wishes or beliefs) **2** to be unfavourable to (a person): *a referendum would almost certainly go against them*
go-ahead *n* **1 give the go-ahead** *informal* to give permission to proceed ▷ *adj* **2** enterprising or ambitious: *prosperous and go-ahead republics*
goal *n* **1** *sport* the space into which players try to propel the ball or puck to score **2** *sport* **A** a successful attempt at scoring **B** the score so made **3** an aim or purpose: *the goal is to get homeless people on their feet* [origin unknown] **goalless** *adj*

goalie *n informal* a goalkeeper
goalkeeper *n sport* a player whose duty is to prevent the ball or puck from entering the goal
goal line *n sport* the line marking each end of the pitch, on which the goals stand
goalpost *n* **1** either of two uprights supporting the crossbar of a goal **2 move the goalposts** to change the aims of an activity to ensure the desired results
goanna *n* a large Australian lizard [from IGUANA]
goat *n* **1** an agile cud-chewing mammal with hollow horns **2 act the goat** *informal* to behave in a silly manner **3 get someone's goat** *slang* to annoy someone [Old English *gāt*]
goatee *n* a small pointed beard that does not cover the cheeks
goatherd *n* a person who looks after a herd of goats
goatskin *n* leather made from the skin of a goat
goatsucker *n US & Canad* same as **nightjar**
go-away bird *n S African* a grey lourie [imitative]
gob[1] *n* a thick mass of a soft substance [Old French *gobe* lump]
gob[2] *n Brit, Austral & NZ slang* the mouth [origin unknown]
go back on *vb* to fail to fulfil (a promise): *he went back on his promise not to raise taxes*
gobbet *n* a chunk or lump [Old French *gobet*]
gobble[1] *vb* **-bling, -bled** to eat quickly and greedily [probably from GOB[1]]
gobble[2] *n* **1** the loud rapid gurgling sound made by a turkey ▷ *vb* **-bling, -bled 2** to make this sound [probably imitative]
gobbledegook *or* **gobbledygook** *n* pretentious or unintelligible language [whimsical formation from GOBBLE[2]]
gobbler *n informal* a turkey
go-between *n* a person who acts as a messenger between two people or groups
goblet *n* a drinking vessel with a base and stem but without handles [Old French *gobelet* a little cup]
goblin *n* a small grotesque creature in fairy tales that causes trouble for people [Old French]
gobshite *n Irish taboo slang* a stupid person [GOB[2] + *shite* excrement]
gobsmacked *adj Brit, Austral & NZ slang* astonished; astounded
goby *n, pl* **-by** *or* **-bies** a small spiny-finned fish [Latin *gobius* gudgeon]
go by *vb* **1** to pass: *as time goes by* **2** to be guided by: *if my experience is anything to go by*
go-cart *n* same as **go-kart**
god *n* **1** a supernatural being, worshipped as the controller of the universe or some aspect of life, or as the personification of some force **2** an image of such a being **3** a person or thing to which excessive attention is given: *the All Blacks are gods in New Zealand* **4 the gods** the top balcony in a theatre [Old English]
God *n* **1** the sole Supreme Being, Creator and ruler of all, in religions such as Christianity, Judaism, and Islam ▷ *interj* **2** an oath or exclamation of surprise or annoyance
godchild *n, pl* **-children** a person who is sponsored by godparents at baptism
goddaughter *n* a female godchild
goddess *n* a female god
godetia *n* a garden plant with showy flowers [after C. H. *Godet*, botanist]
godfather *n* **1** a male godparent **2** the head of a Mafia family or other criminal ring
God-fearing *adj* deeply religious
godforsaken *adj* desolate or dreary: *some godforsaken village in the Himalayas*
Godhead *n* the nature and condition of being God
godless *adj* **1** wicked or unprincipled **2** not religious **godlessness** *n*
godly *adj* **-lier, -liest** deeply religious **godliness** *n*
godmother *n* a female godparent
godparent *n* a person who promises at a person's baptism to look after his or her religious upbringing
godsend *n* a person or thing that comes unexpectedly but is very welcome
godson *n* a male godchild
Godspeed *interj* an expression of good wishes for a person's safe journey and success
goer *n* a person who attends something regularly: *a church goer*
go for *vb* **1** to choose: *any politician will go for the soft option* **2** *informal* to like very much **3** to attack **4** to apply equally to: *the same might go for the other woman*
go-getter *n informal* an ambitious enterprising person **go-getting** *adj*
gogga (hohh-a) *n S African informal* an insect [Nama (language of southern Africa) *xo xo*]
goggle *vb* **-gling, -gled** to stare with wide-open eyes. See also **goggles** [Middle English *gogelen* to look aside] **goggle-eyed** *adj*
gogglebox *n Brit slang* a television set
goggles *pl n* close-fitting protective spectacles
go-go *adj US & Canad informal* denoting a type of dancing performed to pop music by young women wearing few clothes
Goidelic *n* **1** the group of Celtic languages, consisting of Irish Gaelic, Scottish Gaelic, and Manx ▷ *adj* **2** of this group of languages [Old Irish *Goidel* Celt]
go in for *vb* **1** to enter (a competition) **2** to take up or take part in (an activity)
going *n* **1** the condition of the ground with regard to walking or riding: *the going for the cross-country is perfect* **2** *informal* speed or progress: *not bad going for a lad of 58* ▷ *adj* **3** thriving: *the racecourse was a going concern* **4** current or accepted: *this is the going rate for graduates*
going-over *n, pl* **goings-over** *informal* **1** a thorough examination or investigation **2** a physical beating
goings-on *pl n informal* mysterious or shady activities
go into *vb* to describe or investigate in detail
goitre *or US* **goiter** (goy-ter) *n pathol* a swelling of the thyroid gland in the neck [French]
go-kart *n* a small four-wheeled motor vehicle, used for racing
gold *n* **1** a bright yellow precious metal, used as a monetary standard and in jewellery and plating. Symbol: **Au 2** jewellery or coins made of this

metal **3** short for **gold medal** ▷ *adj* **4** deep yellow [Old English]

oldcrest *n* a small bird with a bright yellow-and-black crown

old-digger *n informal* someone who enters into a relationship with a more affluent person in order to get money or expensive things

old dust *n* **1** gold in the form of small particles or powder **2 like gold dust** in great demand because difficult to obtain: *kidney machines were like gold dust*

olden *adj* **1** made of gold: *golden bangles* **2** of the colour of gold: *golden corn* **3** *informal* very successful or destined for success: *the golden girl of British athletics* **4** excellent or valuable: *a golden opportunity for peace* **5** (of an anniversary) the fiftieth: *golden wedding; Golden Jubilee*

olden age *n* the most flourishing and outstanding period in the history of an art or nation: *the golden age of Dixieland jazz*

olden eagle *n* a large mountain eagle of the N hemisphere with golden-brown feathers

olden handshake *n informal* money given to an employee either on retirement or to compensate for loss of employment

olden hour *n* the first hour after a serious accident, when medical treatment for the victim is crucial

olden mean *n* the middle course between extremes

olden retriever *n* a retriever with silky wavy gold-coloured hair

oldenrod *n* a tall plant with spikes of small yellow flowers

olden rule *n* an important principle: *the golden rule is to start with the least difficult problems*

olden syrup *n* a light golden-coloured treacle used for sweetening food

olden wattle *n* an Australian plant with yellow flowers that yields a useful gum and bark

oldfinch *n* a European finch, the adult of which has yellow-and-black wings

oldfish *n, pl* **-fish** *or* **-fishes** a gold or orange-red freshwater fish, often kept as a pet

old foil *n* thin gold sheet that is thicker than gold leaf

old leaf *n* very thin gold sheet made by rolling or hammering gold and used for gilding

old medal *n* a medal made of gold, awarded to the winner of a race or competition

old-plated *adj* covered with a very thin coating of gold

old rush *n* a large-scale migration of people to a territory where gold has been found

oldsmith *n* a person who makes gold jewellery and other articles

old standard *n* a monetary system in which the basic currency unit equals a specified weight of gold

olf *n* **1** a game in which a ball is struck with clubs into a series of eighteen holes in a grassy course ▷ *vb* **2** to play golf [origin unknown] **golfer** *n*

olf club *n* **1** a long-shafted club used to strike a golf ball **2 A** an association of golf players **B** the premises of such an association

golf course *or* **golf links** *n* an area of ground laid out for golf

golly *interj* an exclamation of mild surprise [originally a euphemism for God]

gonad *n* an organ in which reproductive cells are produced, such as a testis or ovary [Greek *gonos* seed]

gondola *n* **1** a long narrow flat-bottomed boat with a high ornamented stem, traditionally used on the canals of Venice **2** a moving cabin suspended from a cable, used as a ski lift [Italian]

gondolier *n* a person who propels a gondola

gone *vb* **1** the past participle of **go** ▷ *adj* **2** no longer present or no longer in existence

goner *n slang* a person who is about to die or who is beyond help

gong *n* **1** a flat circular metal disc that is hit with a hammer to give out a loud sound **2** *Brit slang* a medal [Malay]

gonorrhoea *or esp US* **gonorrhea** (gon-or-ree-a) *n* a sexually transmitted disease that causes inflammation and a discharge from the genital organs [Greek *gonos* semen + *rhoia* flux]

goo *n informal* a sticky substance [origin unknown]

good *adj* **better, best 1** having admirable, pleasing, or superior qualities: *a good listener* **2** morally excellent; virtuous: *a good person* **3** beneficial: *exercise is good for the heart* **4** kindly or generous: *he is so good to us* **5** competent or talented: *she's good at physics* **6** obedient or well-behaved: *a good boy* **7** reliable or recommended: *a good make* **8** complete or thorough: *she went to have a good look round* **9** appropriate or opportune: *a good time to clear the air* **10** satisfying or enjoyable: *a good holiday* **11** newest or of the best quality: *keep the good dishes for guests* **12** fairly large, extensive, or long: *they contain a good amount of protein* **13 as good as** virtually or practically: *the war was as good as over* ▷ *n* **14** advantage or benefit: *what is the good of it all?* **15** positive moral qualities; virtue **16 for good** for ever; permanently: *his political career was over for good* ▷ See also **goods** [Old English *gōd*]

goodbye *interj* **1** an expression used on parting ▷ *n* **2** the act of saying goodbye: *he said his goodbyes* [from *God be with ye*]

good day *interj* an expression of greeting or farewell used during the day

good-for-nothing *n* **1** an irresponsible or worthless person ▷ *adj* **2** irresponsible or worthless

Good Friday *n Christianity* the Friday before Easter, observed as a commemoration of the Crucifixion of Jesus Christ

goodies *pl n* any things considered particularly desirable

good-looking *adj* handsome or pretty

goodly *adj* **-lier, -liest** fairly large: *a goodly number of children*

good morning *interj* an expression of greeting or farewell used in the morning

good-natured *adj* tolerant and kindly

goodness *n* **1** the quality of being good ▷ *interj* **2** an exclamation of surprise

g

good night *interj* an expression of farewell used in the evening or at night
goods *pl n* **1** articles produced to be sold: *consumer goods* **2** movable personal property: *houses and goods are insured from fire* **3 deliver the goods** *informal* to do what is expected or required **4 have the goods on someone** *US & Canad slang* to know something incriminating about someone
Good Samaritan *n* a person who helps someone in difficulty or distress [from a parable in Luke 10: 30–37]
good-tempered *adj* tolerant and kindly
good turn *n* a helpful and friendly act
goodwill *n* **1** kindly feelings towards other people **2** the popularity and good reputation of a well-established business, considered as a valuable asset
goody *interj* **1** a child's exclamation of pleasure ▷ *n, pl* **goodies** **2** *informal* the hero in a film or book. See **goodies**
goody-goody *informal* ▷ *n, pl* **-goodies** **1** a person who behaves well in order to please people in authority ▷ *adj* **2** behaving well in order to please people in authority
gooey *adj* **gooier, gooiest** *informal* **1** sticky, soft, and often sweet **2** sentimental: *one knows the whole gooey performance is an act*
goof *vb informal* **1** to bungle or botch **2 goof off** *US & Canad* to spend time in a lazy or foolish way: *he's goofing off on the Costa del Sol* [probably from dialect *goff* simpleton]
go off *vb* **1** to stop functioning: *the heating went off* **2** to make a sudden loud noise: *a bomb went off* **3** to occur as specified: *the actual launch went off perfectly* **4** *informal* (of food) to become stale or rotten **5** *Brit informal* to stop liking
goofy *adj* **goofier, goofiest** *informal* silly or ridiculous
google *vb* **1** to search for (something) on the internet using a search engine **2** to check the credentials of (someone) by searching for websites containing his or her name [from *Google*, a popular search engine on the internet]
googly *n, pl* **-lies** *cricket* a ball bowled like a leg break but spinning from off to leg on pitching [Australian English]
goon *n* **1** a stupid person **2** *US informal* a hired thug [dialect *gooney* fool; influenced by US cartoon character Alice the *goon*]
go on *vb* **1** to continue or proceed **2** to take place: *there's a war going on* **3** to talk at length and annoyingly
goosander *n* a duck of Europe and North America with a dark head and white body [probably from GOOSE¹ + Old Norse *önd* (genitive *andar*) duck]
goose¹ *n, pl* **geese** **1** a fairly large web-footed long-necked migratory bird **2** the female of such a bird **3** the flesh of the goose used for food **4** *informal* a silly person [Old English *gōs*]
goose² *vb* **goosing, goosed** *slang* to prod (someone) playfully in the bottom [from the jabbing of a goose's bill]
gooseberry *n, pl* **-ries** **1** a small edible green berry with tiny hairs on the skin **2 play gooseberry** *Brit & NZ informal* to be an unwanted single person accompanying a couple
goose flesh *n* the bumpy condition of the skin due to cold or fear, in which the muscles at the base of the hair follicles contract, making the hair bristle. Also: **goose pimples**
goose-step *vb* **-stepping, -stepped** to march raising the legs high alternately while keeping the legs straight
go out *vb* **1** to go to entertainments or social functions **2** to be extinguished or cease to function: *the lights went out* **3** (of information) to be released publicly **4** (of a broadcast) to be transmitted **5 go out with** to have a romantic relationship with
go over *vb* **1** to examine very carefully **2 go over to** to change to: *he went over to the Free Orthodox Churc*[h]
gopher (go-fer) *n* an American burrowing roden[t] with wide cheek pouches [origin unknown]
Gordian knot *n* **cut the Gordian knot** to solve a complicated problem by bold or forceful action [after *Gordius*, in Greek legend, who tied a knot that Alexander the Great cut with a sword]
gore¹ *n* blood shed from a wound [Old English *go*[*r*] dirt]
gore² *vb* **goring, gored** (of an animal) to pierce o[r] stab (a person or another animal) with a horn o[r] tusk [probably from Old English *gār* spear]
gore³ *n* a tapering piece of material in a garment sail, or umbrella [Old English *gāra*]
gorge *n* **1** a deep narrow steep-sided valley **2 one's gorge rises** one feels disgusted or nauseated ▷ *vb* **gorging, gorged** **3** Also: **gorge oneself** to eat greedily [Latin *gurges* whirlpool]
gorgeous *adj* **1** strikingly beautiful or attractive **2** *informal* warm, sunny, and very pleasant: *a gorgeous day* [Old French *gorgias* elegant]
gorgeously *adv*
Gorgon *n* **1** *Greek myth* one of three monstrous sisters who had live snakes for hair, and were so horrifying that anyone who looked at them was turned to stone **2** *informal, derogatory* a terrifying or repulsive woman [Greek *gorgos* terrible]
Gorgonzola *n* a sharp-flavoured blue-veined Italian cheese [after *Gorgonzola*, Italian town where it originated]
gorilla *n* a very large W African ape with coarse black hair [Greek *Gorillai*, an African tribe renowned for their hairy appearance]
gormless *adj Brit & NZ informal* stupid or dull-witted [obsolete *gaumless*]
go round *vb* to be sufficient: *there wasn't enough money to go round*
gorse *n* an evergreen shrub with small yellow flowers and prickles, which grows wild in the countryside [Old English *gors*]
gory *adj* **gorier, goriest** **1** horrific or bloodthirsty[:] *the gory details* **2** bloody: *gory remains*
gosh *interj* an exclamation of mild surprise or wonder [euphemistic for *God*]
goshawk *n* a large swift short-winged hawk [Old English *gōshafoc*]
gosling *n* a young goose [Old Norse *gæslingr*]
go-slow *n Brit & NZ* a deliberate slowing of the rate of production by workers as a tactic in industrial conflict

gospel *n* **1** *Christianity* **A** the teachings of Jesus Christ **B** the story of Christ's life and teachings **2** a doctrine held to be of great importance: *the gospel of self-help* **3** Also called: **gospel truth** unquestionable truth: *gross inaccuracies which are sometimes taken as gospel* ▷ *adj* **4** denoting a kind of religious music originating in the churches of the Black people in the Southern US [Old English *gōdspell*, from *gōd* good + *spell* message]

Gospel *n Christianity* any of the first four books of the New Testament, namely Matthew, Mark, Luke, and John, which tell the story of Jesus Christ

gossamer *n* **1** a very fine fabric **2** a filmy cobweb often seen on foliage or floating in the air [probably Middle English *gos* goose + *somer* summer; referring to *St Martin's summer*, a period in November when goose was eaten and cobwebs abounded]

gossip *n* **1** idle talk, usually about other people's private lives, esp. of a disapproving or malicious nature: *office gossip* **2** an informal conversation, esp. about other people's private lives: *to have a gossip and a giggle* **3** a person who habitually talks about other people, usually maliciously ▷ *vb* **4** to talk idly or maliciously, esp. about other people's private lives [Old English *godsibb* godparent, applied to a woman's female friends at the birth of a child] **gossipy** *adj*

got *vb* **1** the past of **get** **2** **have got** to possess **3** **have got to** must: *you have got to be prepared to work hard*

Gothic *adj* **1** of a style of architecture used in W Europe from the 12th to the 16th centuries, characterized by pointed arches, ribbed vaults, and flying buttresses **2** of a literary style featuring stories of gloom, horror, and the supernatural, popular in the late 18th century **3** of or in a heavy ornate script typeface ▷ *n* **4** Gothic architecture or art [Greek *Gothoi*]

go through *vb* **1** to experience (a difficult time or process) **2** to name or describe: *the president went through a list of government ministers* **3** to qualify for the next stage of a competition: *Belgium, Spain and Uruguay all went through from Group E* **4** to be approved: *the bill went through parliament* **5** **go through with** to bring to a successful conclusion, often by persistence

gotten *vb chiefly US* a past participle of **get**

gouache (goo-**ahsh**) *n* opaque watercolour paint bound with glue [French]

Gouda *n* a round mild-flavoured Dutch cheese

gouge (gowj) *vb* **gouging, gouged** **1** to scoop or force (something) out of its position **2** to cut (a hole or groove) in something with a pointed object ▷ *n* **3** a mark or groove made by gouging [French]

goulash (**goo**-lash) *n* a rich stew seasoned with paprika, originating in Hungary [Hungarian *gulyás hus* herdsman's meat]

gourd (goord) *n* **1** a large hard-shelled fruit similar to a cucumber or marrow **2** a container made from a dried gourd shell [Old French *gourde*]

gourmand (**goor**-mand) *n* a person devoted to eating and drinking, usually to excess [Old French *gourmant*]

gourmet (**goor**-may) *n* an expert on good food and drink [French]

gout (gowt) *n* a disease that causes painful inflammation of certain joints, for example of the big toe [Latin *gutta* a drop] **gouty** *adj*

govern *vb* **1** to direct and control the policy and affairs of (a country or an organization) **2** to control or determine: *the international organizations governing athletics and rugby* [Latin *gubernare* to steer] **governable** *adj*

governance *n* government, control, or authority

governess *n* a woman employed in a private household to teach the children

government *n* **1** the executive policy-making body of a country or state **2** the state and its administration: *the assembled heads of state and government* **3** the system by which a country or state is ruled: *the old hard-line government* **governmental** *adj*

governor *n* **1** the chief political administrator of a region, such as a US state or a colony. Related adjective: **gubernatorial** **2** *Brit* the senior administrator of a school, prison, or other institution **3** *Brit informal* one's employer or father **governorship** *n*

governor general *n, pl* **governors general** *or* **governor generals** the chief representative of the British government in a Commonwealth country

go with *vb* **1** to blend or harmonize with: *the style goes well with modern art* **2** to be linked with: *respect goes with age*

go without *vb* to be denied or deprived of: *no-one should go without food*

gown *n* **1** a woman's long formal dress **2** a surgeon's overall **3** a loose wide official robe worn by judges, lawyers, and academics [Late Latin *gunna* garment made of fur]

goy *n, pl* **goyim** *or* **goys** a Jewish word for a **Gentile** [Yiddish]

GP general practitioner

GPS Global Positioning System: a satellite-based navigation system

Graafian follicle *n anatomy* a cavity in the ovary that contains a developing egg cell [after R. de *Graaf*, anatomist]

grab *vb* **grabbing, grabbed** **1** to seize hold of **2** to take (food, drink, or rest) hurriedly **3** to take (an opportunity) eagerly **4** to seize illegally or unscrupulously: *land grabbing* **5** *informal* to interest or impress ▷ *n* **6** the act of grabbing [probably from Middle Dutch *grabben*]

grab bag *n* **1** a collection of miscellaneous things **2** *US, Canad & Austral* a bag from which gifts are drawn at random

grace *n* **1** elegance and beauty of movement, form, or expression **2** a pleasing or charming quality: *architecture with few redeeming graces* **3** courtesy or decency: *at least she had the grace to laugh* **4** a delay granted for the completion of a task or payment of a debt: *another year's grace* **5** *Christian theol* the free and unmerited favour of God shown towards humankind **6** a short prayer of thanks for a meal **7** **airs and graces** an affected manner **8** **with bad grace** unwillingly or grudgingly: *independence was granted with bad grace*

9 with good grace willingly or ungrudgingly: *to accept with good grace* ▷ *vb* **gracing, graced 10** to honour or favour: *graced by the presence of the ambassador* **11** to decorate or make more attractive: *bedsit walls graced by Che Guevara and James Dean* [Latin *gratia*]

Grace *n* **Your** *or* **His** *or* **Her Grace** a title used to address or refer to a duke, duchess, or archbishop

graceful *adj* having beauty of movement, style, or form **gracefully** *adv* **gracefulness** *n*

graceless *adj* **1** lacking elegance **2** lacking manners

grace note *n music* a note that ornaments a melody

Graces *pl n Greek myth* the three sister goddesses of charm and beauty

gracious *adj* **1** showing kindness and courtesy **2** characterized by elegance, ease, and indulgence: *gracious living* ▷ *interj* **3** an expression of mild surprise or wonder **graciously** *adv* **graciousness** *n*

g

gradation *n* **1** a series of systematic stages; gradual progression **2** a stage in such a series or progression **gradate** *vb*

grade *n* **1** a place on a scale of quality, rank, or size **2** a mark or rating indicating a student's level of achievement **3** a rank or level of importance in a company or organization **4** *US, Canad, Austral & S African* a class or year in a school **5 make the grade** *informal* to be successful by reaching a required standard ▷ *vb* **grading, graded 6** to arrange according to quality or rank: *passes are graded from A down to E* **7** to give a grade to: *students are graded by teachers based entirely on their coursework* [Latin *gradus* step]

gradient *n* **1** Also (esp. US): **grade** a sloping part of a railway, road, or path **2** Also (esp. US): **grade** a measure of the steepness of such a slope **3** a measure of the change in something, such as the angle of a curve, over a specified distance [Latin *gradiens* stepping]

gradual *adj* occurring, developing, or moving in small stages: *a gradual handover of power* [Latin *gradus* a step] **gradually** *adv*

gradualism *n* the policy of changing something gradually **gradualist** *adj*

graduate *n* **1** a person who holds a university or college degree **2** *US & Canad* a student who has completed a course of studies at a high school and received a diploma **3** same as **postgraduate** ▷ *vb* **-ating, -ated 4** to receive a degree or diploma **5** to change by degrees: *the winds graduate from tropical storms to cyclones* **6** to mark (a measuring flask or instrument) with units of measurement [Latin *gradus* a step]

graduation *n* **1** the act of graduating from university or college **2** *US & Canad* the act of graduating from high school **3** the ceremony at which degrees and diplomas are given to graduating students **4** a mark indicating measure on an instrument or container

Graeco-Roman *or esp US* **Greco-Roman** (greek-oh-**rome**-an) *adj* of, or showing the influence of, both Greek and Roman cultures

graffiti (graf-**fee**-tee) *n* drawings or words scribbled or sprayed on walls or posters [Italian: little scratches]

graft[1] *n* **1** *surgery* a piece of tissue transplanted to an area of the body in need of the tissue **2** a small piece of tissue from one plant that is joined to another plant so that they grow together as one ▷ *vb* **3** to transplant (tissue) to an area of the body in need of the tissue **4** to join (part of one plant) onto another plant so that they grow together as one **5** to attach or incorporate: *to graft Japanese production methods onto the American talent for innovation* [Greek *graphein* to write]

graft[2] *n* **1** *Brit informal* hard work **2** the practice of obtaining money by taking advantage of one's position ▷ *vb* **3** *informal* to work hard [origin unknown]

Grail *n* See **Holy Grail**

grain *n* **1** the small hard seedlike fruit of a cereal plant **2** a mass of such fruits gathered for food **3** cereal plants in general **4** a small hard particle: *a grain of salt* **5** a very small amount: *a grain of compassion* **6 A** the arrangement of the fibres, layers, or particles in wood, leather, or stone **B** the pattern or texture resulting from this **7 go against the grain** to be contrary to one's natural inclinations [Latin *granum*] **grainy** *adj*

gram *or* **gramme** *n* a metric unit of weight equal to one thousandth of a kilogram [Greek *gramma* small weight]

graminivorous *adj* (of an animal) grass-eating [Latin *gramen* grass + *vorare* to swallow]

grammar *n* **1** the rules of a language, that show how sentences are formed, or how words are inflected **2** the way in which grammar is used: *the teacher found errors of spelling and grammar* **3** a book on the rules of grammar [Greek *gramma* letter]

grammarian *n* a person who studies or writes about grammar for a living

grammar school *n* **1** *Brit* (esp. formerly) a secondary school for children of high academic ability **2** *US* same as **elementary school 3** *Austral* a private school, usually one controlled by a church

grammatical *adj* **1** of grammar **2** (of a sentence) following the rules of grammar **grammatically** *adv*

gramme *n* same as **gram**

gramophone *n* an old-fashioned type of record player [inversion of *phonogram*]

grampus *n, pl* **-puses** a dolphin-like mammal with a blunt snout [Old French *gras* fat + *pois* fish]

gran *n Brit, Austral & NZ informal* a grandmother

granary *n, pl* **-ries 1** a building for storing threshed grain **2** a region that produces a large amount of grain [Latin *granarium*]

Granary *adj trademark* (of bread or flour) containing malted wheat grain

grand *adj* **1** large or impressive in size or appearance; magnificent: *the grand hall* **2** ambitious or important: *grand themes* **3** dignified or haughty **4** *informal* excellent or wonderful **5** comprehensive or complete: *the grand total* ▷ *n* **6** *pl* **grand** *slang* a thousand pounds or dollars **7** short for **grand piano** [Latin *grandis*] **grandly** *adv*

grandad, granddad *or US* **granddaddy** *n, pl* **-dads** *or* **-daddies** *informal* a grandfather

grandchild *n, pl* **-children** a son or daughter of one's son or daughter

granddad *or US* **granddaddy** *n informal* See **grandad**

granddaughter *n* a daughter of one's son or daughter

grand duke *n* a prince or nobleman who rules a territory, state, or principality **grand duchess** *fem n* **grand duchy** *n*

grande dame (grond **dam**) *n* a woman regarded as the most prominent or respected member of her profession or group: *the grande dame of international fashion* [French]

grandee *n* **1** a high-ranking Spanish nobleman **2** a person who has a high rank or position: *the Party's grandees* [Spanish *grande*]

grandeur *n* **1** personal greatness, dignity, or nobility: *delusions of grandeur* **2** magnificence or splendour: *cathedral-like grandeur*

grandfather *n* the father of one's father or mother

grandfather clock *n* an old-fashioned clock in a tall wooden case that stands on the floor

grandiloquent *adj* using pompous or unnecessarily complicated language [Latin *grandiloquus*] **grandiloquence** *n*

grandiose *adj* impressive, or meant to impress: *grandiose plans for constructing a new stadium* [French]

grand jury *n law, chiefly US* a jury that investigates accusations of crime to decide whether the evidence is adequate to bring a prosecution

grandma *n informal* a grandmother. Also (old-fashioned): **grandmama**

grand mal *n* a form of epilepsy in which there is loss of consciousness and violent convulsions [French: great illness]

grandmaster *n* a person who is exceptionally good at a particular activity or skill, esp. chess

grandmother *n* the mother of one's father or mother

Grand National *n* an annual steeplechase for horses, run at Aintree, Liverpool

grandnephew *n* same as **great-nephew**

grandniece *n* same as **great-niece**

grand opera *n* an opera that has a serious plot and no spoken dialogue

grandpa *n informal* a grandfather. Also (old-fashioned): **grandpapa**

grandparent *n* the father or mother of one's father or mother

grand piano *n* a large piano in which the strings are arranged horizontally

Grand Prix (gron **pree**) *n* **1** an international formula motor race **2** a very important international competitive event in other sports, such as athletics [French: great prize]

grandsire *n old-fashioned* a grandfather

grand slam *n* **1** the achievement of winning all the games or major tournaments in a sport in one season **2** See **slam²**

grandson *n* a son of one's son or daughter

grandstand *n* the main block of seats giving the best view at a sports ground

grand tour *n* **1** (formerly) an extended tour of continental Europe **2** *informal* a tour of inspection: *a grand tour of the house*

grange *n Brit* a farmhouse or country house with its farm buildings [Anglo-French *graunge*]

granite (**gran**-nit) *n* a very hard rock consisting of quartz and feldspars that is widely used for building [Italian *granito* grained]

granivorous *adj* (of an animal) grain-eating [Latin *granum* grain + *vorare* to swallow]

granny *or* **grannie** *n, pl* **-nies** *informal* a grandmother

granny flat *n* a flat in or joined on to a house, suitable for an elderly relative to live in

granny knot *n* a reef knot with the ends crossed the wrong way, making it liable to slip or jam

grant *vb* **1** to give (a sum of money or a right) formally: *to grant a 38% pay rise*; *only the President can grant a pardon* **2** to consent to perform or fulfil: *granting the men's request for sanctuary* **3** to admit that (something) is true: *I grant that her claims must be true* **4** **take for granted** **A** to accept that something is true without requiring proof **B** to take advantage of (someone or something) without showing appreciation ▷ *n* **5** a sum of money provided by a government or public fund to a person or organization for a specific purpose: *student grants* [Old French *graunter*]

Granth (**grunt**) *n* the sacred scripture of the Sikhs [Hindi]

grant-maintained school *n Brit* a school funded directly by central government

granular *adj* of, like, or containing granules: *granular materials such as powders*

granulated *adj* (of sugar) in the form of coarse grains

granule *n* a small grain of something: *gravy granules* [Late Latin *granulum* a small grain]

grape *n* a small round sweet juicy fruit with a purple or green skin, which can be eaten raw, dried to make raisins, currants, or sultanas, or used to make wine [Old French *grape* bunch of grapes]

grapefruit *n, pl* **-fruit** *or* **-fruits** a large round yellow juicy citrus fruit with a slightly bitter taste

grapeshot *n* ammunition for cannons consisting of a cluster of iron balls that scatter after firing

grapevine *n* **1** a vine grown for its grapes **2** *informal* an unofficial means of passing on information from person to person: *he'd doubtless heard rumours on the grapevine*

graph *n* a diagram showing the relation between certain sets of numbers or quantities by means of a series of dots or lines plotted with reference to a set of axes [short for *graphic formula*]

-graph *combining form* **1** an instrument that writes or records: *tachograph* **2** a writing or record: *autograph* [Greek *graphein* to write] **-graphic** *or* **-graphical** *combining form* **-graphically** *combining form*

graphene *n* a very thin, strong material consisting of a single layer of carbon atoms arranged in a hexagonal pattern

graphic *adj* **1** vividly described: *a graphic account of her three days in captivity* **2** of the graphic arts: *graphic design* **3** Also: **graphical** *maths* of or using a graph: *a graphic presentation* [Greek *graphikos*] **graphically** *adv*

graphic arts *pl n* the visual arts based on drawing or the use of line
graphic novel *n* a novel in the form of a sequence of drawings with captions
graphics *n* **1** the art of drawing in accordance with mathematical rules ▷ *pl n* **2** the illustrations in a magazine or book, or in a television or film production **3** *computers* information displayed in the form of diagrams or graphs
graphite *n* a soft black form of carbon used in pencils, as a lubricant, and in some nuclear reactors [German *Graphit*]
graphology *n* the study of handwriting, usually to analyse the writer's character **graphologist** *n*
graph paper *n* paper printed with a design of small squares for drawing graphs or diagrams on
-graphy *combining form* **1** indicating a form of writing or representing things: *calligraphy*; *photography* **2** indicating an art or descriptive science: *choreography*; *topography* [Greek *graphein* to write]
grapnel *n* a device with several hooks at one end, which is used to grasp or secure an object, esp. in sailing [Old French *grapin* a little hook]
grapple *vb* **-pling, -pled** > **grapple with** **A** to try to cope with: *a difficult concept to grapple with* **B** to come to grips with (someone) in hand-to-hand combat [Old French *grappelle* a little hook]
grappling iron *n* same as **grapnel**
grasp *vb* **1** to grip firmly **2** to understand: *his failure to grasp the gravity of the crisis* ▷ *n* **3** a very firm grip **4** understanding or comprehension: *a good grasp of detail* **5** **within someone's grasp** almost certain to be accomplished or won: *she now has that prize within her grasp* [Low German *grapsen*]
grasping *adj* greedy for money
grass *n* **1** a very common green plant with jointed stems and long narrow leaves, eaten by animals such as sheep and cows, and used for lawns and sports fields **2** a particular kind of grass, such as bamboo **3** a lawn **4** *slang* marijuana **5** *Brit & Austral slang* a person who informs, usually on criminals ▷ *vb* **6** **grass on** *or* **up** *Brit slang* to inform on (someone) to the police or some other authority **7** **grass over** to cover with grass [Old English *græs*] **grassy** *adj*
grass hockey *n* (in W Canada) field hockey, as contrasted with ice hockey
grasshopper *n* an insect with long hind legs which it uses for leaping
grassland *n* **1** land covered with grass **2** pasture land
grass roots *pl n* **1** ordinary members of a group or organization, as distinct from its leaders ▷ *adj* **grassroots** **2** of the ordinary members of a group or organization: *the focus of a virulent grassroots campaign*
grass snake *n* a harmless snake with a brownish-green body
grass tree *n* an Australian plant with stiff grass-like leaves and small white flowers
grass widow *n* a woman whose spouse is regularly absent for a time [perhaps an allusion to a grass bed as representing an illicit relationship]
grate[1] *vb* **grating, grated** **1** to reduce to shreds by rubbing against a rough surface: *grated cheese* **2** to produce a harsh rasping sound by scraping against an object or surface: *the clutch plates grated* **3** **grate on** to annoy: *his manner always grated on me* [Old French *grater*]
grate[2] *n* **1** a framework of metal bars for holding coal or wood in a fireplace **2** same as **grating**[1] [Latin *cratis* hurdle]
grateful *adj* feeling or showing thanks [Latin *gratus*] **gratefully** *adv*
grater *n* a tool with a sharp surface for grating food
gratify *vb* **-fies, -fying, -fied** **1** to satisfy or please (someone) **2** to yield to (a desire or whim): *all his wishes were to be gratified* [Latin *gratus* grateful + *facere* to make] **gratification** *n*
grating[1] *n* a framework of metal bars covering an opening in a wall or in the ground
grating[2] *adj* **1** (of a sound) rough or unpleasant **2** annoying or irritating: *his cringing obsequiousness was grating*
gratis *adv, adj* without payment; free: *the gifts are gratis* [Latin]
gratitude *n* a feeling of being grateful for gifts or favours [Latin *gratus* grateful]
gratuitous (grat-**tyoo**-it-uss) *adj* **1** unjustified or unreasonable: *gratuitous violence* **2** given or received without charge or obligation: *his gratuitous voluntary services* [Latin *gratuitus*] **gratuitously** *adv*
gratuity (grat-**tyoo**-it-ee) *n, pl* **-ties** money given for services rendered; tip
grave[1] *adj* (rhymes with **save**) **1** serious and worrying: *grave concern* **2** serious and solemn in appearance or behaviour: *the woman looked grave and respectful* **3** (rhymes with **halve**) denoting an accent (`) over a vowel in some languages, such as French, which indicates that the vowel is pronounced in a particular way ▷ *n* (rhymes with **halve**) **4** a grave accent [Latin *gravis*] **gravely** *adv*
grave[2] (rhymes with **save**) *n* **1** a place where a dead person is buried. Related adjective: **sepulchral** **2** death: *she smoked herself to an early grave* **3** **make someone turn in his** *or* **her grave** to do something that would have shocked a person who is now dead [Old English *græf*]
gravel *n* **1** a mixture of rock fragments and pebbles that is coarser than sand **2** *pathol* small rough stones in the kidneys or bladder ▷ *vb* **-elling, -elled** *or US* **-eling, -eled** **3** to cover with gravel [Old French *gravele*]
gravelly *adj* **1** covered with gravel **2** (of a voice or sound) harsh and grating
graven image *n* *chiefly Bible* a carved image used as an idol
gravestone *n* a stone marking a grave
graveyard *n* a place where dead people are buried, esp. one by a church
graveyard slot *n* *television* the hours from late night until early morning when relatively few people are watching television
gravid (**grav**-id) *adj* *med* pregnant [Latin *gravis* heavy]
gravimeter (grav-**vim**-it-er) *n* **1** an instrument for measuring the force of gravity **2** an instrument for measuring relative density [French *gravimètre*]

gravitas (grav-vit-tass) *n* seriousness or solemnity [Latin: weight]
gravitate *vb* **-tating, -tated 1 gravitate towards** to be attracted or influenced by: *the mathematically inclined often gravitate towards computers* **2** *physics* to move under the influence of gravity
gravitation *n physics* **1** the force of attraction that bodies exert on one another as a result of their mass **2** the process or result of this interaction **gravitational** *adj*
gravity *n, pl* **-ties 1** *physics* **A** the force that attracts bodies towards the centre of the earth, a moon, or any planet **B** same as **gravitation** **2** seriousness or importance: *the gravity of the situation* **3** seriousness or solemnity of appearance or behaviour: *his priestly gravity* [Latin *gravitas* weight]
gravy *n, pl* **-vies A** the juices that come from meat during cooking **B** the sauce made by thickening and flavouring these juices [Old French *gravé*]
gravy boat *n* a small boat-shaped dish with a spout, used for serving gravy or sauce
gravy train *n slang* a job or scheme that produces a lot of money for little effort
gray *adj, n, vb chiefly US* grey
graze[1] *vb* **grazing, grazed A** (of an animal) to eat (grass or other growing plants) **B** to feed (animals) on grass or other growing plants [Old English *grasian*]
graze[2] *vb* **grazing, grazed 1** to break the skin of (a part of the body) by scraping **2** to brush against someone gently in passing ▷ *n* **3** an injury on the skin caused by scraping [probably a special use of GRAZE[1]]
grazier *n* a rancher or farmer who keeps cattle or sheep on grazing land
grazing *n* land where grass is grown for farm animals to feed upon
grease *n* **1** soft melted animal fat **2** a thick oily substance, such as the kind put on machine parts to make them work smoothly ▷ *vb* **greasing, greased 3** to apply grease to: *lightly grease a baking tin* **4 grease someone's palm** *slang* to bribe someone [Latin *crassus* thick]
greasepaint *n* theatrical make-up
greaseproof paper *n* any paper that is resistant to penetration by grease and oil, esp. one used for lining baking dishes or wrapping food
greasy *adj* **greasier, greasiest 1** covered with or containing grease **2** excessively pleasant or flattering in an insincere manner **greasiness** *n*
great *adj* **1** large in size **2** large in number or amount: *the great majority* **3** larger than others of its kind: *the great white whale* **4** extreme or more than usual: *great difficulty* **5** of importance or consequence: *a great discovery* **6** of exceptional talents or achievements: *a great artist* **7** skilful: *he's a great storyteller; they are great at problem solving* **8** *informal* excellent ▷ *n* **9 the greats** the most successful people in a particular field: *the all-time greats of golf* ▷ See also **Greats** [Old English *grēat*] **greatly** *adv* **greatness** *n*
great- *prefix* (in expressing relationship) one generation older or younger than: *great-grandmother*
great auk *n* an extinct large auk that could not fly
great-aunt *n* an aunt of one's father or mother
Great Britain *n* the mainland part of the British Isles; England, Scotland, and Wales
great circle *n maths* a circular section of a sphere that has a radius equal to the sphere's radius
greatcoat *n* a heavy overcoat
Great Dane *n* a very large dog with short smooth hair
great-nephew *n* a son of one's nephew or niece
great-niece *n* a daughter of one's nephew or niece
Greats *pl n* **1** the Honours course in classics, ancient history, and philosophy at Oxford University **2** the final examinations at the end of this course
great-uncle *n* an uncle of one's father or mother
Great War *n* same as **World War I**
greave *n* a piece of armour for the shin [Old French *greve*]
grebe *n* a diving water bird [French]
Grecian (gree-shan) *adj* of ancient Greece
greed *n* excessive desire for something, such as food or money
greedy *adj* **greedier, greediest** having an excessive desire for something, such as food or money: *greedy for personal possessions* [Old English *grǣdig*] **greedily** *adv*
Greek *adj* **1** of Greece ▷ *n* **2** a person from Greece **3** the language of Greece
Greek cross *n* a cross with each of the four arms of the same length
green *adj* **1** of a colour between yellow and blue; of the colour of grass **2** covered with grass, plants, or trees: *green fields* **3** of or concerned with conservation and improvement of the environment: used in a political context: *green issues* **4** (of fruit) fresh, raw, or unripe **5** pale and sick-looking **6** inexperienced or gullible **7 green with envy** very envious ▷ *n* **8** a colour between yellow and blue **9** anything green, such as green clothing or green ink: *printed in green* **10** a small area of grassy land: *the village green* **11** an area of smooth turf kept for a special purpose: *putting greens* **12 greens** the leaves and stems of certain plants, eaten as a vegetable: *turnip greens* **13 Green** a person who supports environmentalist issues [Old English *grēne*] **greenish** *or* **greeny** *adj* **greenness** *n*
green beans *pl n* long narrow green beans that are cooked and eaten as a vegetable
green belt *n* a protected zone of parkland or open country surrounding a town or city
green card *n* an official permit allowing the holder permanent residence and employment, issued to foreign nationals in the US
Green Cross Code *n Brit* a code for children giving rules on road safety
greenery *n* green leaves or growing plants: *lush greenery*
green-eyed monster *n* jealousy
greenfield *adj* relating to a rural area which has not previously been built on: *greenfield factory sites*
greenfinch *n* a European finch, the male of which has olive-green feathers
green fingers *pl n* skill in growing plants
greenfly *n, pl* **-flies** a green aphid commonly occurring as a pest on plants

g

greengage *n* a green sweet variety of plum [after Sir W. *Gage*, botanist]
greengrocer *n Brit & Austral* a shopkeeper who sells fruit and vegetables
greenhorn *n* an inexperienced person; novice [originally an animal with *green* (that is, young) horns]
greenhouse *n* **1** a building with glass walls and roof where plants are grown under controlled conditions ▷ *adj* **2** relating to or contributing to the greenhouse effect: *greenhouse gases such as carbon dioxide*
greenhouse effect *n* the gradual rise in temperature in the earth's atmosphere due to heat being absorbed from the sun and being trapped by gases such as carbon dioxide in the air around the earth
greenhouse gas *n* any gas that contributes to the greenhouse effect
greenkeeper *n* a person responsible for maintaining a golf course or bowling green
green light *n* **1** a signal to go **2** permission to proceed with a project ▷ *vb* **greenlight, -lighting, -lighted 3** to permit (a project) to proceed
green paper *n* a government document containing policy proposals to be discussed
green pepper *n* the green unripe fruit of the sweet pepper, eaten as a vegetable
greenroom *n* (esp. formerly) a backstage room in a theatre where performers rest or receive visitors
greenstick fracture *n* a fracture in which the bone is partly bent and splinters only on the outer side of the bend
greenstone *n NZ* a type of green jade used for Māori carvings and ornaments
greensward *n archaic or literary* an area of fresh green turf
green tea *n* tea made from leaves that have been dried quickly without fermenting
greenway *n US* a corridor of protected open space that is maintained for conservation, recreation, and non-motorized transportation
Greenwich Mean Time (gren-itch) *n* the local time of the 0° meridian passing through Greenwich, England: a basis for calculating times throughout most of the world. Abbrev: **GMT**
greet[1] *vb* **1** to address or meet with expressions of friendliness or welcome **2** to receive in a specified manner: *a direct request would be greeted coolly* **3** to be immediately noticeable to: *the scene of devastation which greeted him* [Old English *grētan*]
greet[2] *vb Scot* to weep [Old English *grætan*]
greeting *n* the act or words of welcoming on meeting
greetings *interj* an expression of friendly salutation
gregarious *adj* **1** enjoying the company of others **2** (of animals) living together in herds or in flocks [Latin *grex* flock]
Gregorian calendar *n* the revision of the calendar introduced in 1582 by Pope Gregory XIII and still widely used
Gregorian chant *n* same as **plainsong**
gremlin *n* an imaginary imp jokingly blamed for malfunctions in machinery [origin unknown]
grenade *n* a small bomb filled with explosive or gas, thrown by hand or fired from a rifle [Spanish *grenada* pomegranate]
grenadier *n military* **1** (in the British Army) a member of the senior regiment of infantry in the Household Brigade (the **Grenadier Guards**) **2** (formerly) a soldier trained to throw grenades [French]
grenadine (gren-a-**deen**) *n* a syrup made from pomegranate juice, often used as an ingredient in cocktails
grevillea *n* any of various Australian evergreen trees and shrubs [after C. F. *Greville*, botanist]
grew *vb* the past tense of **grow**
grey *or US* **gray** *adj* **1** of a colour between black and white; of the colour of ashes **2 A** (of hair) having partly turned white **B** (of a person) having grey hair **3** dismal, dark, or gloomy: *a grey and misty morning* **4** dull or boring: *in 1948 life generally was grey* ▷ *n* **5** a colour between black and white **6** anything grey, such as grey paint or grey clothing: *available in grey or brown* **7** a grey or whitish horse [Old English *grǣg*] **greyness** *n* **greyish** *adj*
grey area *n* a situation or area that has no clearly defined characteristics or that falls somewhere between two categories
greyed out *adj* (of a navigation button, menu item, etc. on a computer screen) not highlighted, indicating that the function is not available
Grey Friar *n* a Franciscan friar
greyhound *n* a tall slender dog that can run very fast and is used for racing
greying *adj* becoming grey: *greying hair*
greylag *or* **greylag goose** *n* a large grey Eurasian goose [GREY + LAG, because it migrates later than other species]
grey matter *n informal* intellect or brains: *those who don't have lots of grey matter*
grey squirrel *n* a grey-furred squirrel, native to E North America but now common in Britain
grid *n* **1** a network of crossing parallel lines on a map, plan, or graph paper for locating points **2 the grid** the national network of cables or pipes by which electricity, gas, or water is distributed **3** *electronics* an electrode that controls the flow of electrons between the cathode and anode of a valve [from *gridiron*]
griddle *n* a thick round iron plate placed on top of a cooker and used to cook food [Old French *gridil*]
gridiron *n* **1** a utensil of parallel metal bars, used to grill food **2 A** the field of play in American football **B** *informal* same as **American football** [Middle English *gredire*]
gridlock *n* **1** obstruction of traffic caused by queues of vehicles forming across junctions and so causing queues in intersecting streets **2** a point in a dispute at which no agreement can be reached: *political gridlock* ▷ *vb* **3** (of traffic) to obstruct (an area)
grid reference *n* a series of numbers indicating the location of a point on a map
grief *n* **1** deep or intense sorrow **2** *informal* trouble or annoyance: *people were giving me grief for leaving ten minutes early* **3 come to grief** to have an unfortunate or unsuccessful end or outcome

grief-stricken *adj* deeply affected by sorrow

grievance *n* **1** a real or imaginary cause for complaint **2** a feeling of resentment at having been unfairly treated

grieve *vb* **grieving, grieved** to feel or cause to feel great sorrow or distress [Old French *grever*] **grieved** *adj* **grieving** *adj*

grievous *adj* **1** very severe or painful: *grievous injuries* **2** very serious or worrying: *a grievous loss* **grievously** *adv*

grievous bodily harm *n criminal law* serious injury caused by one person to another

griffin, griffon *or* **gryphon** *n* a mythical winged monster with an eagle's head and a lion's body [Old French *grifon*]

griffon *n* **1** same as **griffin** **2** a large vulture with pale feathers and black wings **3** a small wire-haired breed of dog [French]

grill *vb* **1** to cook by direct heat under a grill or over a hot fire **2** *informal* to subject to relentless questioning: *the jury pool was grilled for signs of prejudice* ▷ *n* **3** a device on a cooker that radiates heat downwards for grilling food **4** a gridiron for cooking food **5** a dish of grilled food **6** See **grillroom** [Latin *craticula* fine wickerwork] **grilled** *adj* **grilling** *n*

grille *or* **grill** *n* a metal or wooden grating, used as a screen or partition [Latin *craticula* fine hurdlework]

grillroom *n* a restaurant specializing in grilled foods

grilse (grillss) *n, pl* **grilses** *or* **grilse** a salmon on its first return from the sea to fresh water [origin unknown]

grim *adj* **grimmer, grimmest** **1** unfavourable and worrying: *grim figures on unemployment* **2** harsh and unpleasant: *grim conditions in the detention centres* **3** stern or resolute: *a grim determination to fight on* **4** *informal* unpleasant or disagreeable [Old English *grimm*] **grimly** *adv* **grimness** *n*

grimace *n* **1** an ugly or distorted facial expression of disgust, pain, or displeasure ▷ *vb* **-macing, -maced** **2** to make a grimace [French]

grime *n* **1** ingrained dirt **2** a type of British rap music ▷ *vb* **griming, grimed** **3** to make very dirty: *sweat-grimed faces* [Middle Dutch] **grimy** *adj*

grin *vb* **grinning, grinned** **1** to smile broadly, showing one's teeth **2** **grin and bear it** *informal* to suffer hardship without complaint ▷ *n* **3** a broad smile [Old English *grennian*] **grinning** *adj*

grind *vb* **grinding, ground** **1** to reduce to small particles by pounding or rubbing: *grinding coffee* **2** to smooth, sharpen, or polish by friction **3** (of two objects) to scrape together with a harsh rasping sound **4** **an axe to grind** See **axe** (sense 2) **5** **grind one's teeth** to rub one's upper and lower teeth against each other, as if chewing **6** **grind to a halt** to come to an end or a standstill: *without enzymes life would grind to a halt* ▷ *n* **7** *informal* hard or tedious work: *the grind of everyday life* ▷ See also **grind down** [Old English *grindan*]

grind down *vb* to treat harshly so as to suppress resistance: *to grind down the opposition*

grinder *n* a device for grinding substances: *an electric coffee grinder*

grindstone *n* **1** a revolving stone disc used for sharpening, grinding, or polishing things **2** **keep one's nose to the grindstone** to work hard and steadily

grip *n* **1** a very tight hold: *he felt a grip at his throat* **2** the style or manner of holding something, such as a golf club or tennis racket **3** power or control over a situation, person, or activity: *rebel forces tighten their grip around the capital* **4** a travelling bag or holdall **5** a small bent clasp used to fasten the hair **6** a handle **7** a person who manoeuvres the cameras in a film or television studio **8** **get** *or* **come to grips with** to face up to and deal with (a problem or subject) ▷ *vb* **gripping, gripped** **9** to take a tight hold of **10** to affect strongly: *sudden panic gripped her* **11** to hold the interest or attention of: *gripped by the intensity of the film*; *the story gripped him* [Old English *gripe* grasp]

gripe *vb* **griping, griped** **1** *informal* to complain persistently **2** to cause sudden intense pain in the bowels ▷ *n* **3** *informal* a complaint **4** **the gripes** a sudden intense pain in the bowels [Old English *grīpan*]

grippe *n* a former name for **influenza** [French]

gripping *adj* very interesting and exciting: *a gripping story*

grisly *adj* **-lier, -liest** causing horror or dread: *grisly murders* [Old English *grislic*]

USAGE See at **grizzly**.

grist *n* **1** grain that is to be or that has been ground **2** **grist to the mill** anything that can be turned to profit or advantage [Old English *grīst*]

gristle *n* tough stringy animal tissue found in meat [Old English] **gristly** *adj*

grit *n* **1** small hard particles of sand, earth, or stone **2** courage and determination ▷ *vb* **gritting, gritted** **3** to cover (an icy road) with grit **4** **grit one's teeth** **A** to rub one's upper and lower teeth against each other, as if chewing **B** to decide to carry on in a difficult situation: *he urged the Cabinet to grit its teeth and continue cutting public spending* [Old English *grēot*]

grits *pl n* coarsely ground grain, a popular dish in the Southern US [Old English *grytt*]

gritter *n* a vehicle that spreads grit on the roads in icy weather

gritty *adj* **-tier, -tiest** **1** courageous and tough **2** covered with grit

grizzle *vb* **-zling, -zled** *Brit, Austral & NZ informal* to whine or complain [Germanic]

grizzled *adj* **1** (of hair) streaked or mixed with grey **2** (of a person) having grey hair

grizzly *n, pl* **-zlies** a large fierce greyish-brown bear of N America. In full: **grizzly bear**

USAGE *Grizzly* is sometimes wrongly used where *grisly* is meant: *a grisly* (not *grizzly*) *murder.*

groan *n* **1** a long deep cry of pain, grief, or disapproval **2** *informal* a grumble or complaint ▷ *vb* **3** to give a long deep cry of pain, grief, or disapproval **4** *informal* to complain or grumble **5** **groan under** to be weighed down by: *chemists' shelves groan under the weight of slimming aids* [Old English *grānian*] **groaning** *adj, n*

groat *n* a former British coin worth four old pennies [Middle Dutch *groot*]

groats *pl n* the crushed grain of various cereals [Old English *grot* particle]

g

grocer *n* a shopkeeper who sells food and other household supplies [Old French *grossier*]
groceries *pl n* food and other household supplies
grocery *n, pl* **-ceries** the business or premises of a grocer
grog *n* **1** an alcoholic drink, usually rum, diluted with water **2** *Brit, Austral & NZ informal* any alcoholic drink [after Old *Grog*, nickname of Edward Vernon, British admiral, who in 1740 issued naval rum diluted with water]
groggy *adj* **-gier, -giest** *informal* faint, weak, or dizzy
groin *n* **1** the part of the body where the abdomen joins the legs **2** *archit* a curved edge formed where two intersecting vaults meet [origin unknown]
grommet *n* **1** a rubber, plastic, or metal ring or eyelet **2** *med* a small tube inserted into the eardrum to drain fluid from the middle ear [obsolete French *gourmer* bridle]
groom *n* **1** a person employed to clean and look after horses **2** short for **bridegroom** ▷ *vb* **3** to clean and smarten (a horse or other animal) **4** to keep (oneself or one's appearance) clean and tidy: *carefully groomed hair* **5** to train (someone) for a particular task or occupation: *groomed for future leadership* [Middle English *grom* manservant] **grooming** *n*
groove *n* **1** a long narrow furrow cut into a surface **2** *informal* a pleasing rhythm [obsolete Dutch *groeve*] **grooved** *adj*
groovy *adj* **groovier, grooviest** *old-fashioned slang, often humorous* attractive, fashionable, or exciting
grope *vb* **groping, groped 1** to feel about uncertainly for something **2** to find (one's way) by groping **3** to search uncertainly for a solution or expression: *the new democracies are groping for stability* **4** *slang* to fondle (someone) in a rough sexual way ▷ *n* **5** an instance of groping [Old English *grāpian*]
gros point (groh point) *n* **1** a cross-stitch in embroidery **2** work done in this stitch [Old French: large point]
gross *adj* **1** outrageously wrong: *gross violations of human rights* **2** very coarse or vulgar: *gross bad taste* **3** *slang* disgusting or repulsive: *I think beards are gross* **4** repulsively fat **5** with no deductions for tax or the weight of the container; total: *gross income; a gross weight of 20 000 lbs* ▷ *n* **6** *pl* **gross** twelve dozen (144) **7** the entire amount or weight ▷ *vb* **8** to earn as total revenue, before deductions [Old French *gros* large] **grossly** *adv*
gross domestic product *n* the total value of all goods and services produced domestically by a nation during a year
gross national product *n* the total value of all final goods and services produced annually by a nation: equivalent to gross domestic product plus net investment income from abroad
gross profit *n accounting* the difference between total revenue from sales and the total cost of purchases or materials
grotesque (groh-tesk) *adj* **1** strangely distorted or bizarre: *a grotesque and pervasive personality cult* **2** ugly or repulsive ▷ *n* **3** a grotesque person or thing **4** an artistic style in which parts of human, animal, and plant forms are distorted and mixed, or a work of art in this style [Old Italian *(pittura) grottesca* cave (painting)] **grotesquely** *adv*
grotto *n, pl* **-toes** *or* **-tos** a small picturesque cave [Old Italian *grotta*]
grotty *adj* **-tier, -tiest** *Brit & NZ slang* **1** nasty or unattractive **2** in bad condition [from *grotesque*]
grouch *informal* ▷ *vb* **1** to complain or grumble ▷ *n* **2** a person who is always complaining **3** a persistent complaint [Old French *grouchier*]
grouchy *adj* **grouchier, grouchiest** bad-tempered
ground[1] *n* **1** the land surface **2** earth or soil **3** an area used for a particular purpose: *a cricket ground* **4** a matter for consideration or discussion: *there is no need to cover the same ground* **5** an advantage in an argument or competition: *neither side seems willing to give ground in this trial of strength* **6** the background colour of a painting **7** *US & Canad* an electrical earth **8** **grounds** **A** the land around a building **B** reason or justification: *the hostages should be freed on humanitarian grounds* **C** sediment or dregs: *coffee grounds* **9** **break new ground** to do something that has not been done before **10** **common ground** an agreed basis for identifying issues in an argument **11** **get something off the ground** to get something started: *to get the peace conference off the ground* **12** **into the ground** to exhaustion or excess: *he was running himself into the ground* **13** **suit someone down to the ground** *Brit informal* to be totally suitable or appropriate for someone ▷ *adj* **14** on the ground: *ground troops* ▷ *vb* **15** to confine (an aircraft or pilot) to the ground **16** *naut* to move (a ship) onto the bottom of shallow water, so that it cannot move **17** to instruct in the basics of a subject: *the student who is not grounded in the elements cannot understand the advanced teaching* **18** to provide a basis for; establish: *a scientifically grounded documentation* **19** to forbid (a child) to go out and enjoy himself or herself as a punishment **20** *US & Canad* to connect (a circuit or electrical device) to an earth [Old English *grund*]
ground[2] *vb* **1** the past of **grind** ▷ *adj* **2** reduced to fine particles by grinding: *ground glass*
ground bass *n music* a short melodic bass line that is repeated over and over again
ground beef *n* finely chopped beef, sometimes used to make hamburgers
ground-breaking *adj* innovative
ground control *n* the people and equipment on the ground that monitor the progress of aircraft or spacecraft
ground cover *n* dense low plants that spread over the surface of the ground
ground floor *n* the floor of a building that is level, or almost level, with the ground
grounding *n* a foundation, esp. the basic general knowledge of a subject
groundless *adj* without reason or justification: *the scare turned out to be groundless*
groundnut *n Brit* a peanut
ground rule *n* a basic rule or principle that applies to an activity: *the ground rules for bringing up children*
groundsel (grounce-el) *n* a yellow-flowered weed [Old English *grundeswelge*]

roundsheet *n* a waterproof sheet placed on the ground in a tent to keep out damp
roundsman *n, pl* **-men** a person employed to maintain a sports ground or park
roundswell *n* a rapidly developing general feeling or opinion
round water *n* water that has seeped through from the surface and is held underground
roundwork *n* preliminary work as a foundation or basis
roup *n* **1** a number of people or things considered as a unit **2** a small band of players or singers, esp. of popular music **3** an association of business firms that have the same owner **4** *chem* two or more atoms that are bound together in a molecule and behave as a single unit: *a methyl group* $-CH_3$ **5** *chem* a vertical column of elements in the periodic table that all have similar properties: *the halogen group* ▷ *vb* **6** to put into or form into a group [French *groupe*]
roup captain *n* a middle-ranking officer in some air forces
roupie *n slang* an ardent fan of a celebrity or of a sport or activity: *a polo groupie*
rouping *n* a set of people or organizations who act or work together to achieve a shared aim: *the main far-right grouping*
roup therapy *n psychol* the treatment of people by bringing them together to share their problems in group discussion
rouse[1] *n, pl* **grouse** **1** a game bird with a stocky body and feathered legs and feet **2** the flesh of this bird used for food [origin unknown]
rouse[2] *vb* **grousing, groused** **1** to complain or grumble ▷ *n* **2** a persistent complaint [origin unknown]
rouse[3] *adj Austral & NZ slang* fine or excellent [origin unknown]
rout *n* **1** a thin mortar for filling joints between tiles or masonry ▷ *vb* **2** to fill with grout [Old English *grūt*]
rove *n* a small wood or group of trees: *orange groves* [Old English *grāf*]
rovel (grov-el) *vb* **-elling, -elled** *or US* **-eling, -eled** **1** to behave excessively humbly towards someone, esp. a superior, in an attempt to win his or her favour **2** to crawl on the floor, often in search of something: *grovelling on the floor for missing cards* [Middle English *on grufe* on the face] **grovelling** *or US* **groveling** *adj, n*
row *vb* **growing, grew, grown** **1** (of a person or animal) to increase in size and develop physically **2** (of a plant) to exist and increase in size: *an ancient meadow where wild flowers grow* **3** to produce (a plant) by planting seeds, bulbs, or cuttings, and looking after it: *many farmers have expressed a wish to grow more cotton* **4** to let (one's hair or nails) develop: *to grow a beard* **5** to increase in size or degree: *the gulf between rich and poor is growing* **6** to originate or develop: *Melbourne grew from a sheep-farming outstation and occasional port to a city* **7** to become increasingly as specified: *as the night wore on the audience grew more intolerant* ▷ See also **grow on, grow out of** *etc.* [Old English *grōwan*] **growing** *adj* **grower** *n*
rowing pains *pl n* **1** pains in muscles or joints sometimes experienced by growing children **2** difficulties experienced in the early stages of a new enterprise
growl *vb* **1** (of a dog or other animal) to make a low rumbling sound, usually in anger **2** to say in a gruff or angry manner: *'You're late,' he growled* **3** to make a deep rumbling sound: *her stomach growled* ▷ *n* **4** the act or sound of growling [Old French *grouller* to grumble]
grown *adj* developed or advanced: *fully grown*; *a grown man*
grown-up *adj* **1** having reached maturity; adult **2** of or suitable for an adult ▷ *n* **3** an adult
grow on *vb* to become progressively more acceptable or pleasant to: *I didn't like that programme at first but it has grown on me*
grow-op *n Canad* a scheme to grow marijuana plants
grow out of *vb* to become too big or mature for: *I used to be into the fifties scene but grew out of it*
growth *n* **1** the process of growing **2** an increase in size, number, or significance: *the growth of drug trafficking* **3** something grown or growing: *a thick growth of ivy* **4** any abnormal tissue, such as a tumour ▷ *adj* **5** of or relating to growth: *growth hormone*
grow up *vb* to reach maturity; become adult
groyne *n* a wall or breakwater built out from a shore to control erosion [Old French *groign* snout]
grub *n* **1** *slang* food **2** the short legless larva of certain insects, such as beetles ▷ *vb* **grubbing, grubbed** **3** to search carefully for something by digging or by moving things about **4** **grub up** to dig (roots or plants) out of the ground [Germanic]
grubby *adj* **-bier, -biest** **1** rather dirty **2** unsavoury or morally unacceptable: *grubby activities* **grubbiness** *n*
grudge *n* **1** a persistent feeling of resentment against a person who has caused harm or upset ▷ *vb* **grudging, grudged** **2** to give unwillingly: *the rich men who grudged pennies for the poor* **3** to resent or envy the success or possessions of: *none of their guests grudged them this celebration* ▷ *adj* **4** planned or carried out in order to settle a grudge: *a grudge match* [Old French *grouchier* to grumble]
grudging *adj* felt or done unwillingly: *grudging admiration for his opponent* **grudgingly** *adv*
gruel *n* thin porridge made by boiling oatmeal in water or milk [Old French]
gruelling *or US* **grueling** *adj* extremely severe or tiring: *a gruelling journey* [obsolete *gruel* to punish]
gruesome *adj* inspiring horror and disgust [Scandinavian]
gruff *adj* **1** rough or surly in manner or speech **2** (of a voice) low and throaty [Germanic] **gruffly** *adv* **gruffness** *n*
grumble *vb* **-bling, -bled** **1** to complain in a nagging way: *his neighbour grumbled about the long wait* **2** to make low rumbling sounds: *the storm grumbled in the distance* ▷ *n* **3** a complaint **4** a low rumbling sound: *a distant grumble of artillery fire* [Middle Low German *grommelen*] **grumbling** *adj, n*
grumpy *adj* **grumpier, grumpiest** sulky and bad-tempered [imitative] **grumpily** *adv*
grunge *n* **1** a style of rock music with a fuzzy guitar sound **2** a deliberately untidy and

uncoordinated fashion style [from US slang: dirt, rubbish]
grungy *adj* **grungier, grungiest** *slang* **1** *chiefly US & Canad* squalid or seedy **2** (of pop music) characterized by a loud fuzzy guitar sound
grunt *vb* **1** to make a low short gruff noise, such as the sound made by a pig, or by a person to express annoyance **2** to express (something) gruffly: *he grunted his thanks* ▷ *n* **3** a low short gruff noise, such as the sound made by a pig, or by a person to express annoyance [Old English *grunnettan*]
Gruyère (**grew**-yair) *n* a hard flat pale yellow cheese with holes [after *Gruyère*, Switzerland, where it originated]
gryphon *n* same as **griffin**
GST (in Australia, New Zealand, and Canada) Goods and Services Tax
G-string *n* a strip of cloth worn between the legs and attached to a waistband
G-suit *n* a close-fitting pressurized garment that is worn by the crew of high-speed aircraft [from *g(ravity) suit*]
GT gran turismo: a touring car, usually a fast sports car with a hard fixed roof
guano (**gwah**-no) *n* the dried manure of sea birds, used as a fertilizer [indigenous S American word *huano* dung]
guarantee *n* **1** a formal assurance in writing that a product or service will meet certain standards or specifications **2** something that makes a specified condition or outcome certain: *there was no guarantee that there would not be another military coup* **3** same as **guaranty** ▷ *vb* **-teeing, -teed 4** to promise or make certain: *to guarantee absolute loyalty* **5** (of a company) to provide a guarantee in writing for (a product or service) **6** to take responsibility for the debts or obligations of (another person) [Germanic]
guarantor *n* a person who gives or is bound by a guarantee or guaranty
guaranty *n, pl* **-ties 1** a pledge of responsibility for fulfilling another person's obligations in case of that person's default **2** a thing given or taken as security for a guaranty
guard *vb* **1** to watch over or shield from danger or harm; protect: *US marines who guard the American embassy* **2** to keep watch over (a prisoner) to prevent escape **3** to protect (a right or privilege) **4** to take precautions: *to guard against a possible coup attempt* ▷ *n* **5** a person or group of people who protect or watch over people or things **6** *Brit, Austral & NZ* the official in charge of a train **7** a device or part of a machine designed to protect the user against injury **8** anything that provides protection: *a guard against future shocks* **9 off guard** having one's defences down; unprepared: *England were caught off guard as the Dutch struck two telling blows* **10 on guard** on duty to protect or watch over people or things **11 on one's guard** prepared to face danger or difficulties: *parents have been warned to be on their guard against kidnappers* **12 stand guard** (of a sentry) to keep watch [Old French *garder* to protect]
guarded *adj* cautious and avoiding any commitment: *a guarded welcome* **guardedly** *adv*
guardhouse *or* **guardroom** *n military* a military police office in which prisoners can be detained
guardian *n* **1** one who looks after, protects, or defends someone or something: *the nation's moral guardians* **2** someone legally appointed to manage the affairs of another person, such as a child or other vulnerable person **guardianship** *n*
guardsman *n, pl* **-men** *military* a member of a regiment responsible for ceremonial duties
guard's van *n Brit, Austral & NZ* a small railway carriage in which the guard travels
guava (**gwah**-va) *n* a round tropical fruit with yellow skin and pink pulp [from indigenous S American word]
gubernatorial *adj chiefly US* of or relating to a governor [Latin *gubernator* governor]
gudgeon[1] *n* a small slender European freshwater fish, used as bait by anglers [Old French *gougon*]
gudgeon[2] *n* the socket of a hinge, which fits round the pin [Old French *goujon*]
guelder rose (**geld**-er) *n* a Eurasian shrub with clusters of white flowers [from *Gelderland*, province of Holland]
Guernsey (**gurn**-zee) *n* a breed of dairy cattle that produces rich creamy milk, originating from Guernsey, in the Channel Islands
guerrilla *or* **guerilla** *n* a member of an irregular politically motivated, armed force that fights regular forces [Spanish]
guess *vb* **1** to form an estimate or conclusion about (something), without proper knowledge: *a competition to guess the weight of the cake* **2** to arrive at a correct estimate of (something) by guessing: *I had a notion that he guessed my thoughts* **3** *informal* to think or suppose: *I guess he must have been a great athlete* ▷ *n* **4** an estimate or conclusion arrived at by guessing: *we can hazard a guess at the answer* [probably from Old Norse]
guesswork *n* the process of arriving at conclusions or estimates by guessing
guest *n* **1** a person who receives hospitality at someone else's home **2** a person who is taken out socially by someone else who pays all the expenses **3** a performer or speaker taking part in an event, show, or programme by special invitation **4** a person who is staying in a hotel ▷ *vb* **5** to be a guest in an event, show, or programme: *she guested in concert with Kylie Minogue* [Old English *giest* guest, stranger, enemy]
guesthouse *n* a private home or boarding house offering accommodation
guest of honour *n* a famous or important person who is the most important guest at a dinner or other social occasion
guff *n Brit, Austral & NZ slang* ridiculous talk; nonsense [imitative]
guffaw *vb* **1** to laugh loudly and raucously ▷ *n* **2** loud raucous laugh [imitative]
GUI (**goo**-ee) *computers* graphical user interface
guidance *n* help, advice, or instruction, usually from someone more experienced or more qualified: *marriage guidance*
guide *n* **1** a person who conducts parties of tourists around places of interest, such as museums **2** a person who leads travellers to a

place, usually in a dangerous area: *a mountain guide* **3** something that can be used to gauge something or to help in planning one's actions: *starting salary was not an accurate guide to future earnings* **4** same as **guidebook 5** a book that explains the basics of a subject or skill: *a guide to higher education* ▷ *vb* **guiding, guided 6** to lead the way for (tourists or travellers) **7** to control the movement or course of; steer **8** to direct the affairs of (a person, team, or country): *he will stay with the club he guided to promotion to the First Division* **9** to influence (a person) in his or her actions or opinions: *to be guided by the law* [Germanic] **guiding** *adj*

Guide *n* a member of an organization for girls that encourages discipline and practical skills

guidebook *n* a book which gives tourist information on a place

guided missile *n* a missile whose course is controlled electronically

guide dog *n* a dog that has been trained to lead a blind person

guideline *n* a principle put forward to set standards or determine a course of action: *guidelines for arms exporting*

guild *n* **1** an organization or club for people with shared interests **2** (in Medieval Europe) an association of men in the same trade or craft [Old Norse *gildi*]

guilder *n, pl* **-ders** *or* **-der** a former monetary unit of the Netherlands [Middle Dutch *gulden*]

guildhall *n Brit* a hall where members of a guild meet

guile (gile) *n* craftiness or deviousness [Old French] **guileless** *adj*

guillemot (gil-lee-mot) *n* a northern oceanic black-and-white diving sea bird [French]

guillotine *n* **1** a device formerly used, esp. in France, for beheading people, consisting of a weighted blade between two upright posts, which was dropped on the neck **2** a device with a blade for cutting paper ▷ *vb* **-tining, -tined 3** to behead with a guillotine [after J. I. *Guillotin*, who advocated its use]

guilt *n* **1** the fact or state of having done wrong: *the court was unable to establish guilt* **2** remorse or self-reproach caused by feeling that one has done something wrong: *he feels no guilt about the planned cutbacks* [Old English *gylt*]

guiltless *adj* free of all responsibility for wrongdoing or crime; innocent

guilty *adj* **guiltier, guiltiest 1** *law* judged to have committed a crime: *she has been found guilty of drug trafficking* **2** responsible for doing something wrong: *students who are guilty of cheating* **3** showing, feeling, or indicating guilt: *guilty conscience* **guiltily** *adv*

guinea *n* a former British unit of currency worth £1.05 (21 shillings), sometimes still used in quoting professional fees [the coin was originally made of gold from Guinea]

guinea fowl *n* a domestic bird with a heavy rounded body and speckled feathers

guinea pig *n* **1** a tailless S American rodent, commonly kept as a pet or used in scientific experiments **2** a person used in an experiment [origin unknown]

guipure (geep-pure) *n* heavy lace that has its pattern connected by threads, rather than supported on a net mesh [French]

guise (rhymes with **size**) *n* **1** a false appearance: *in the guise of a wood-cutter* **2** general appearance or form: *haricot beans are best known in Britain in their popular guise of baked beans* [Old French]

guitar *n* a stringed instrument with a flat back and a long neck with a fretted fingerboard, which is played by plucking or strumming [Spanish *guitarra*] **guitarist** *n*

Gulag *n* a system or department that silences dissidents, esp. in the former Soviet Union [Russian *G(lavnoye) U(pravleniye Ispravitelno-Trudovykh) Lag(erei)* Main Administration for Corrective Labour Camps]

gulch *n US & Canad* a narrow ravine with a stream running through it [origin unknown]

gulf *n* **1** a large deep bay **2** something that divides or separates people, such as a lack of understanding: *gradually the gulf between father and son has lessened* [Greek *kolpos*]

Gulf War syndrome *n* a group of various debilitating symptoms experienced by many soldiers who served in the Gulf War of 1991, claimed to be associated with damage to the central nervous system

gull *n* a large sea bird with white feathers tipped with black or grey [Celtic]

gullet *n* the muscular tube through which food passes from the throat to the stomach [Latin *gula* throat]

gullible *adj* easily tricked; too trusting **gullibility** *n*

gully *or* **gulley** *n, pl* **-lies** *or* **-leys 1** a channel or small valley originally worn away by running water **2** *cricket* a fielding position on the off side, between the slips and point [French *goulet* neck of a bottle]

gulp *vb* **1** to swallow (a drink or food) rapidly in large mouthfuls **2** to gasp or breathe in violently, for example when nervous or when swimming **3 gulp back** to stifle or suppress: *he gulped back the tears as he said his goodbyes* ▷ *n* **4** the act of gulping **5** the quantity taken in a gulp [imitative]

gum¹ *n* **1** a sticky substance obtained from certain plants, which hardens on exposure to air and dissolves in water **2** a substance used for sticking things together **3** short for **chewing gum** or **bubble gum 4** *chiefly Brit* a gumdrop ▷ *vb* **gumming, gummed 5** to stick with gum ▷ See also **gum up** [Old French *gomme*]

gum² *n* the fleshy tissue that covers the bases of the teeth [Old English *gōma* jaw]

gum arabic *n* a gum obtained from certain acacia trees, used to make ink, food thickeners, and pills

gumboil *n* an abscess on the gum

gumboots *pl n Brit & NZ* long rubber boots, worn in wet or muddy conditions

gumdrop *n* a small hard fruit-flavoured jelly-like sweet

gummy¹ *adj* **-mier, -miest 1** sticky or tacky **2** producing gum

gummy² *adj* **-mier, -miest** toothless

gumption *n Brit & NZ informal* common sense or initiative [origin unknown]

gumtree *n* **1** any of various trees that yield gum, such as the eucalyptus **2 up a gumtree** *Brit & NZ informal* in an awkward position; in difficulties

gum up *vb* **gum up the works** *informal* to spoil a plan or hinder progress

gun *n* **1** a weapon with a metallic tube or barrel from which a missile is fired, usually by force of an explosion **2** a device used to force out (a substance, such as grease or paint) under pressure: *a spray gun* **3 jump the gun** *informal* to act prematurely **4 stick to one's guns** *informal* to stand by one's opinions or intentions in spite of opposition ▷ *vb* **gunning, gunned 5** to press hard on the accelerator of (a vehicle's engine) **6 gun down** to shoot (someone) with a gun ▷ *adj* **7** *NZ slang* expert: *a gun surfer* ▷ See also **gun for** [Middle English *gonne*]

gunboat *n* a small ship carrying mounted guns

g

gunboat diplomacy *n* diplomacy conducted by threats of military intervention

guncotton *n* a form of cellulose nitrate used as an explosive

gun dog *n* **1** a dog trained to locate or retrieve birds or animals that have been shot in a hunt **2** a dog belonging to any breed traditionally used for these activities

gunfire *n* the repeated firing of guns

gun for *vb informal* to search for (someone) in order to harm him or her in some way

gunge *n informal* a sticky or congealed substance [imitative] **gungy** *adj*

gunk *n informal* a slimy, oily, or dirty substance [perhaps imitative]

gunman *n, pl* **-men** a man who uses a gun to commit a crime

gunmetal *n* **1** a type of bronze containing copper, tin, and zinc ▷ *adj* **2** dark grey

gunnel (gun-nel) *n* same as **gunwale**

gunner *n* a member of the armed forces who works with, uses, or specializes in guns

gunnery *n* the art and science of the efficient design and use of large guns

gunny *n chiefly US* a coarse hard-wearing fabric, made from jute and used for sacks [Hindi *gōnī*]

gunpoint *n* **at gunpoint** being under or using the threat of being shot: *eight tourists have been kidnapped at gunpoint by unidentified men*

gunpowder *n* an explosive mixture of potassium nitrate, charcoal, and sulphur, used to make fireworks

gunrunning *n* the practice of smuggling guns and ammunition into a country **gunrunner** *n*

gunshot *n* **1** bullets fired from a gun **2** the sound of a gun being fired **3** the firing range of a gun: *within gunshot*

gunslinger *n slang* a person who can shoot very accurately and has been involved in many fights using guns, esp. in the frontier days of the American West

gunstock *n* the wooden handle to which the barrel of a rifle is attached

gunwale (gun-nel) *n naut* the top of the side of a ship [*wale*, ridge of planking originally supporting guns]

gunyah *n Austral* a hut or shelter in the bush [Aboriginal]

guppy *n, pl* **-pies** a small brightly coloured tropical fish, often kept in aquariums in people's homes [after R. J. L. *Guppy*, who gave specimens to the British Museum]

gurdwara (gurd-wah-ra) *n* a Sikh place of worship [from Punjabi]

gurgle *vb* **-gling, -gled 1** (of water) to make low bubbling noises when flowing **2** to make low throaty bubbling noises: *the baby gurgled in delight* ▷ *n* **3** the sound of gurgling [origin unknown]

Gurkha *n* **1** a member of a Hindu people living mainly in Nepal **2** a member of a Gurkha regiment in the Indian or British Army [Sanskrit]

gurnard *n, pl* **-nard** *or* **-nards** a sea fish with a spiny head and long finger-like pectoral fins [Old French *gornard* grunter]

guru *n* **1** a Hindu or Sikh religious teacher or leader **2** a leader or adviser of a person or group of people: *inside a team of advertising gurus are at work* [Hindi]

Guru Granth Sahib *n* same as **Granth**

gush *vb* **1** to pour out suddenly and profusely **2** to speak or behave in an overenthusiastic manner: *I'm not about to start gushing about raspberry coulis* ▷ *n* **3** a sudden large flow of liquid **4** a sudden surge of strong feeling: *she felt a gush of pure affection for her mother* [probably imitative]

gusher *n* **1** a person who gushes **2** a spurting oil well

gushing *adj* behaving in an overenthusiastic manner: *gushing television commentators*

gusset *n* a piece of material sewn into a garment to strengthen it [Old French *gousset*]

gust *n* **1** a sudden blast of wind **2** a sudden surge of strong feeling: *a gust of joviality* ▷ *vb* **3** to blow in gusts [Old Norse *gustr*] **gusty** *adj*

gusto *n* vigorous enjoyment: *we all sang with great gusto* [Spanish: taste]

gut *n* **1** same as **intestine 2** *slang* the belly; paunch **3** short for **catgut 4** a silky fibrous substance extracted from silkworms and used in the manufacture of fishing tackle ▷ *vb* **gutting, gutted 5** to remove the internal organs from (a dead animal or fish) **6** (of a fire) to destroy the inside of (a building): *a local pub was gutted* ▷ *adj* **7** *informal* basic, essential, or natural: *I have a gut feeling she's after something* ▷ See also **guts** [Old English *gutt*]

gutless *adj informal* lacking courage or determination

guts *pl n* **1** the internal organs of a person or an animal **2** courage, willpower, or daring **3** *informal* the inner or essential part: *the new roads have torn apart the guts of the city*

gutsy *adj* **gutsier, gutsiest** *slang* **1** bold or courageous: *the gutsy kid who lost a leg to cancer* **2** robust or vigorous: *a gutsy rendering of 'Bobby Shaftoe'*

gutta-percha *n* a whitish rubber substance, obtained from a tropical Asian tree and used in electrical insulation and dentistry [Malay *getah* gum + *percha* gumtree]

gutted *adj Brit, Austral & NZ informal* disappointed and upset: *the supporters will be absolutely gutted if the manager leaves the club*

gutter *n* **1** a channel on the roof of a building or alongside a kerb, used to collect and carry away rainwater **2** *tenpin bowling* one of the channels on either side of an alley **3 the gutter** a poverty-stricken, degraded, or criminal environment: *he dragged himself up from the gutter* ▷ *vb* **4** (of a candle) to flicker and be about to go out [Latin *gutta* a drop] **guttering** *n*

gutter press *n informal* the section of the popular press that concentrates on the sensational aspects of the news

guttersnipe *n Brit* a child who spends most of his or her time in the streets, usually in a slum area

guttural (gut-ter-al) *adj* **1** *phonetics* pronounced at the back of the throat **2** harsh-sounding [Latin *guttur* gullet]

guy[1] *n* **1** *informal* a man or boy **2** *informal* a person of either sex: *it's been very nice talking to you guys again* **3** *Brit* a crude model of Guy Fawkes, that is burnt on top of a bonfire on Guy Fawkes Day (November 5) [short for *Guy Fawkes*, who plotted to blow up the Houses of Parliament]

guy[2] *n* a rope or chain for steadying or securing something such as a tent. Also: **guyrope** [probably Low German]

guzzle *vb* **-zling, -zled** to eat or drink quickly or greedily: *the guests guzzled their way through squid with mushrooms* [origin unknown]

gybe *or* **jibe** (jibe) *naut* ▷ *vb* **gybing, gybed** *or* **jibing, jibed 1** (of a fore-and-aft sail) to swing suddenly from one side of a ship to the other **2** to change the course of (a ship) by letting the sail gybe ▷ *n* **3** an instance of gybing [obsolete Dutch *gijben*]

gym *n* short for **gymnasium** or **gymnastics**

gymkhana (jim-**kah**-na) *n Brit, Austral & NZ* an event in which horses and riders take part in various races and contests [Hindi *gend-khānā* ball house]

gymnasium *n* a large room containing equipment such as bars, weights, and ropes, for physical exercise [Greek *gumnazein* to exercise naked]

gymnast *n* a person who is skilled or trained in gymnastics

gymnastics *n* **1** practice or training in exercises that develop physical strength and agility ▷ *pl n* **2** such exercises **gymnastic** *adj*

gym shoes *pl n* same as **plimsolls**

gymslip *n* a tunic formerly worn by schoolgirls as part of school uniform

gynaecology *or US* **gynecology** (guy-nee-**kol**-la-jee) *n* the branch of medicine concerned with diseases and conditions specific to women [Greek *gunē* woman + -LOGY] **gynaecological** *or US* **gynecological** *adj* **gynaecologist** *or US* **gynecologist** *n*

gyp *or* **gip** *n* **give someone gyp** *Brit, Austral & NZ slang* to cause someone severe pain: *her back's still giving her gyp* [probably a contraction of *gee up!*]

gypsophila *n* a garden plant with small white flowers

gypsum *n* a mineral used in making plaster of Paris [Greek *gupsos*]

Gypsy *or* **Gipsy** *n, pl* **-sies** *sometimes offensive* a member of a travelling people scattered throughout Europe and North America; Romany [from *Egyptian*, since they were thought to have come originally from Egypt]

gyrate (jire-**rate**) *vb* **-rating, -rated** to turn round and round in a circle [Greek *guros* circle] **gyration** *n*

gyrfalcon (jur-fawl-kon) *n* a very large rare falcon of northern regions [Old French *gerfaucon*]

gyro *n, pl* **-ros** short for **gyroscope**

gyrocompass *n* a nonmagnetic compass that uses a motor-driven gyroscope to indicate true north [Greek *guros* circle + COMPASS]

gyroscope (jire-oh-skope) *n* a device containing a disc rotating on an axis that can turn freely in any direction, so that the disc maintains the same position regardless of the movement of the surrounding structure [Greek *guros* circle + *skopein* to watch] **gyroscopic** *adj*

Hh

H 1 *chem* hydrogen **2** *physics* henry
h. *or* **H. 1** height **2** hour
ha[1] *or* **hah** *interj* an exclamation expressing triumph, surprise, or scorn
ha[2] hectare
Ha *chem* hahnium
habeas corpus (**hay**-bee-ass **kor**-puss) *n law* a writ ordering a person to be brought before a judge, so as to decide whether his or her detention is lawful [Latin: you may have the body]
haberdasher *n Brit, Austral & NZ* a dealer in small articles used for sewing [Anglo-French *hapertas* small items of merchandise] **haberdashery** *n*
Haber process (**hah**-ber) *n chem* a method of making ammonia by reacting nitrogen with hydrogen at high pressure in the presence of a catalyst [after Fritz *Haber*, German chemist]
habiliments *pl n old-fashioned* clothes [Old French *habillement*]
habit *n* **1** a tendency to act in a particular way **2** established custom or use: *the English habit of taking tea in the afternoon* **3** an addiction to a drug **4** mental disposition or attitude: *deference was a deeply ingrained habit of mind* **5** the costume of a nun or monk **6** a woman's riding costume [Latin *habitus* custom]
habitable *adj* fit to be lived in **habitability** *n*
habitant *n* an early French settler in Canada or Louisiana or a descendant of one, esp. a farmer
habitat *n* the natural home of an animal or plant [Latin: it inhabits]
habitation *n* **1** occupation of a dwelling place: *unfit for human habitation* **2** *formal* a dwelling place
habit-forming *adj* tending to become a habit or addiction
habitual *adj* **1** done regularly and repeatedly: *habitual behaviour patterns* **2** by habit: *a habitual criminal* **habitually** *adv*
habituate *vb* **-ating, -ated** to accustom; get used to: *habituated to failure* **habituation** *n*
habitué (hab-**it**-yew-ay) *n* a frequent visitor to a place [French]
hachure (**hash**-yoor) *n* shading of short lines drawn on a map to indicate the degree of steepness of a hill [French]
hacienda (hass-ee-**end**-a) *n* (in Spanish-speaking countries) a ranch or large estate with a house on it [Spanish]
hack[1] *vb* **1** to chop roughly or violently **2** to cut and clear (a way) through undergrowth **3** (in sport) to foul (an opposing player) by kicking his or her shins **4** *Brit & NZ informal* to tolerate **5** to manipulate a computer program skilfully, esp. to gain unauthorized access to another computer system ▷ *n* **6** a cut or gash **7** a tool, such as a pick **8** a chopping blow **9** a kick on the shins, such as in rugby [Old English *haccian*] **hacker** *n* **hacking** *or* **hackery** *n*
hack[2] *n* **1** a writer or journalist who produces work fast and on a regular basis **2** a horse kept for riding, often one for hire **3** *Brit* a country ride on horseback ▷ *vb* **4** *Brit* to ride (a horse) cross-country for pleasure ▷ *adj* **5** unoriginal or of a low standard: *clumsily contrived hack verse* [short for *hackney*]
hacking *adj* (of a cough) dry, painful, and harsh-sounding
hacking jacket *n* a jacket with vents at the side and sloping pockets, originally designed for wearing on horseback
hackles *pl n* **1** the hairs or feathers on the back of the neck of certain animals or birds, which rise when they are angry **2 raise someone's hackles** to make someone feel angry or hostile [Middle English *hakell*]
hackney *n* **1** *Brit* a taxi **2** same as **hack**[2] (sense 2) [probably after *Hackney*, London, where horses were formerly raised]
hackneyed (**hak**-need) *adj* (of a word or phrase) unoriginal and overused
hacksaw *n* a small saw for cutting metal
had *vb* the past of **have**
haddock *n, pl* **-dock** a North Atlantic food fish [origin unknown]
hadedah *or* **hadeda** (**hah**-dee-dah) *n* a large grey-green S African ibis [imitative]
Hades (**hay**-deez) *n Greek myth* **1** the underworld home of the souls of the dead **2** the god of the underworld
Hadith (**had**-dith, hah-**deeth**) *n Islam* the body of tradition and legend about Mohammed and his followers, used as a basis of Islamic law [Arabic]
hadj *n* same as **hajj**
hadji *n, pl* **hadjis** same as **hajji**
hadn't had not
haemal *or US* **hemal** (**heem**-al) *adj* of the blood [Greek *haima* blood]
haematic *or US* **hematic** (hee-**mat**-ik) *adj* relating to or containing blood
haematite *or US* **hematite** *n* a type of iron ore which is reddish-brown when powdered
haematology *or US* **hematology** *n* the branch of medical science concerned with the blood [Greek *haima* blood + -LOGY] **haematologist** *or US* **hematologist** *n*
haemoglobin *or US* **hemoglobin** (hee-moh-**globe**-in) *n* a protein in red blood cells that carries oxygen from the lungs to the tissues [Greek *haima* blood + Latin *globus* ball]
haemophilia *or US* **hemophilia** (hee-moh-**fill**-lee-a) *n* a hereditary disorder, usually affecting males, in which the blood does not clot properly [Greek *haima* blood + *philos* loving] **haemophiliac** *n*
haemorrhage *or US* **hemorrhage** (**hem**-or-ij) *n* **1** heavy bleeding from ruptured blood vessels ▷ *vb* **-rhaging, -rhaged 2** to bleed heavily [Greek *haima* blood + *rhēgnunai* to burst]
haemorrhoids *or US* **hemorrhoids** (**hem**-or-oydz) *pl n pathol* swollen veins in the wall of the anus [Greek *haimorrhoos* discharging blood]
haere mai (**hire**-a-my) *interj NZ* an expression of greeting or welcome [Māori]

hafnium *n chem* a metallic element found in zirconium ores. Symbol: **Hf** [after *Hafnia*, Latin name of Copenhagen]
haft *n* the handle of an axe, knife, or dagger [Old English *hæft*]
hag *n* **1** an unpleasant or ugly old woman **2** a witch [Old English *hægtesse* witch] **haggish** *adj*
haggard *adj* looking tired and ill [Old French *hagard* wild]
haggis *n* a Scottish dish made from sheep's or calf's offal, oatmeal, suet, and seasonings boiled in a skin made from the animal's stomach [origin unknown]
haggle *vb* **-gling, -gled** to bargain or wrangle (over a price) [Scandinavian]
hagiography *n, pl* **-phies** the writing of lives of the saints [Greek *hagios* holy + *graphein* to write] **hagiographer** *n*
hagiology *n, pl* **-gies** literature about the lives and legends of saints [Greek *hagios* holy + -LOGY]
hag-ridden *adj* distressed or worried
hah *interj* same as **ha**[1]
ha-ha[1] *or* **haw-haw** *interj* a written representation of the sound of laughter
ha-ha[2] *n* a wall set in a ditch so as not to interrupt a view of the landscape [French]
hahnium *n chem* another name, not in technical use, for **dubnium**. Symbol: **Ha**
haiku (hie-koo) *n, pl* **-ku** a Japanese verse form in 17 syllables [Japanese]
hail[1] *n* **1** small pellets of ice falling from thunderclouds **2** words, ideas, missiles, etc., directed with force and in great quantity: *a hail of abuse* ▷ *vb* **3** to fall as hail: *it's hailing* **4** to fall like hail: *blows hailed down on him* [Old English *hægl*]
hail[2] *vb* **1** to call out to; greet: *a voice from behind hailed him* **2** to praise, acclaim, or acknowledge: *his crew had been hailed as heroes* **3** to stop (a taxi) by shouting or gesturing **4 hail from** to come originally from: *she hails from Nova Scotia* **5 within hailing distance** within hearing range ▷ *interj* **6** *poetic* an exclamation of greeting [Old Norse *heill* healthy]
hail-fellow-well-met *adj* genial and familiar in an offensive way
Hail Mary *n RC Church* a prayer to the Virgin Mary
hailstone *n* a pellet of hail
hailstorm *n* a storm during which hail falls
hair *n* **1** any of the threadlike outgrowths on the skin of mammals **2** a mass of such outgrowths, such as on a person's head or an animal's body **3** *botany* a threadlike growth from the outer layer of a plant **4** a very small distance or margin: *he missed death by a hair* **5 get in someone's hair** *informal* to annoy someone **6 hair of the dog** an alcoholic drink taken as a cure for a hangover **7 let one's hair down** to enjoy oneself without restraint **8 not turn a hair** to show no reaction **9 split hairs** to make petty and unnecessary distinctions [Old English *hær*] **hairless** *adj*
hairclip *n* a small clip used to hold the hair in place
haircut *n* **1** an instance of cutting the hair **2** the style in which hair has been cut **3** *Stock Exchange slang* a percentage of the value of an asset deducted to account for a possible fall in its value before it can be liquidated
hairdo *n, pl* **-dos** *informal* the style of a person's hair
hairdresser *n* **1** a person who cuts and styles hair. Related adjective: **tonsorial** **2** a hairdresser's premises **hairdressing** *n*
hairgrip *n chiefly Brit* a small bent clasp used to fasten the hair
hairline *n* **1** the edge of hair at the top of the forehead ▷ *adj* **2** very fine or narrow: *a hairline crack*
hairpiece *n* a section of false hair added to a person's real hair
hairpin *n* a thin U-shaped pin used to fasten the hair
hairpin bend *n* a bend in the road that curves very sharply
hair-raising *adj* very frightening or exciting
hair's-breadth *n* an extremely small margin or distance
hair shirt *n* a shirt made of horsehair cloth worn against the skin as a penance
hair slide *n* a decorative clasp used to fasten the hair
hairsplitting *n* **1** the act of making petty distinctions ▷ *adj* **2** characterized by petty distinctions
hairspring *n* a fine spring in some clocks and watches which regulates the timekeeping
hairstyle *n* the cut and arrangement of a person's hair **hairstylist** *n*
hair trigger *n* a trigger that responds to the slightest pressure
hairy *adj* **hairier, hairiest** **1** covered with hair **2** *slang* dangerous, exciting, and difficult **hairiness** *n*
hajj *or* **hadj** *n* the pilgrimage a Muslim makes to Mecca [Arabic]
hajji *or* **hadji** *n, pl* **hajjis** *or* **hadjis** a Muslim who has made a pilgrimage to Mecca
haka *n NZ* **1** a Māori war chant accompanied by actions **2** a similar chant by a sports team
hake *n, pl* **hake** *or* **hakes** **1** an edible fish of the cod family **2** *Austral* same as **barracuda** [origin unknown]
hakea (hah-kee-a) *n* an Australian tree or shrub with hard woody fruit
hakuna matata *interj African* no problem [from Swahili, there is no problem]
halal *or* **hallal** *n* meat from animals that have been slaughtered according to Muslim law [Arabic: lawful]
halberd *n history* a tall spear that includes an axe blade and a pick [Middle High German *helm* handle + *barde* axe]
halcyon (hal-see-on) *adj* **1** peaceful, gentle, and calm **2 halcyon days** a time, usually in the past, of greatest happiness or success [Greek *alkuōn* kingfisher]
hale *adj* healthy and robust: *hale and hearty* [Old English *hæl* whole]
half *n, pl* **halves** **1** either of two equal or corresponding parts that together make up a whole **2** the fraction equal to one divided by two **3** half a pint, esp. of beer **4** *sport* one of two equal periods of play in a game **5** a half-price ticket **6 by half** to an excessive degree: *too clever by half* **7 by halves** without being thorough: *in Italy they*

rarely do things by halves **8 go halves** to share expenses ▹ *adj* **9** denoting one of two equal parts: *a half chicken* ▹ *adv* **10** half in degree or quantity: *half as much* **11** partially; to an extent: *half hidden in the trees* **12 not half** *Brit informal* **A** very; indeed: *it isn't half hard to look at these charts* **B** yes, indeed [Old English *healf*]

half-and-half *adj* half one thing and half another thing

halfback *n rugby* a player positioned immediately behind the forwards

half-baked *adj informal* poorly planned: *half-baked policies*

half board *n Brit* the daily provision by a hotel of bed, breakfast, and evening meal

half-bottle *n* a bottle of spirits or wine that contains half the quantity of a standard bottle

half-breed *n offensive* a person whose parents are of different races

half-brother *n* the son of either one's mother or father by another partner

h

half-caste *n offensive* a person whose parents are of different races

half-cock *n* **go off at half-cock** *or* **half-cocked** to fail because of lack of preparation

half-crown *or* **half-a-crown** *n* a former British coin worth two shillings and sixpence ($12^1/_2$p)

half-cut *adj Brit slang* rather drunk

half-day *n* a day when one works only in the morning or only in the afternoon

half-dozen *n* six

half-hearted *adj* without enthusiasm or determination **half-heartedly** *adv*

half-hitch *n* a knot made by passing the end of a piece of rope around itself and through the loop so made

half-hour *n* **1** a period of 30 minutes **2** the point of time 30 minutes after the beginning of an hour **half-hourly** *adv, adj*

half-life *n* the time taken for radioactive material to lose half its radioactivity

half-light *n* a dim light, such as at dawn or dusk

half-mast *n* the halfway position of a flag on a mast as a sign of mourning

half measures *pl n* inadequate actions or solutions: *the education system cannot be reformed by half measures*

half-moon *n* **1** the moon when half its face is illuminated **2** the time at which a half-moon occurs **3** something shaped like a half-moon

half-nelson *n* a wrestling hold in which a wrestler places an arm under the opponent's arm from behind and exerts pressure with his or her palm on the back of the opponent's neck

halfpenny *or* **ha'penny** (**hayp**-nee) *n, pl* **-pennies** a former British coin worth half a penny

half-pie *adj NZ informal* badly planned; not properly thought out: *a half-pie scheme* [Māori *pai* good]

half-pipe *n* a structure with a U-shaped cross section, used in skateboarding, snowboarding, etc.

half-price *adj, adv* for half the normal price: *special half-price tickets; jeans bought half-price in a sale*

half-sister *n* the daughter of either one's mother or father by another partner

half term *n Brit education* a short holiday midway through a term

half-timbered *adj* (of a building) having an exposed timber framework filled with brick or plaster

half-time *n sport* an interval between the two halves of a game

half-title *n* the first right-hand page of a book, with only the title on it

halftone *n* a photographic illustration in which the image is composed of a large number of black and white dots

half-track *n* a vehicle with moving tracks on the rear wheels

half-truth *n* a partially true statement **half-true** *adj*

half volley *sport* ▹ *n* **1** a stroke or shot in which the ball is hit immediately after it bounces ▹ *vb* **half-volley 2** to hit or kick (a ball) immediately after it bounces

halfway *adv* **1** at or to half the distance **2** at or towards the middle of a period of time or of an event or process **3** rather: *halfway decent* **4 meet someone halfway** to compromise with someone ▹ *adj* **5** at the same distance from two points: *the halfway line*

halfway house *n* **1** a place to rest midway on a journey **2** the halfway stage in any process: *a halfway house between the theatre and cinema is possible*

halfwit *n* a foolish or inane person **halfwitted** *adj*

halibut *n* a large edible flatfish [Middle English *hali* holy (because it was eaten on holy days) + *butte* flatfish]

halitosis *n* bad-smelling breath [Latin *halitus* breath]

hall *n* **1** an entry area to other rooms in a house **2** a building or room for public meetings, dances, etc. **3** a residential building in a college or university **4** *Brit* a great house of an estate; manor **5** a large dining room in a college or university **6** the large room of a castle or stately home [Old English *heall*]

hallelujah, halleluiah (hal-ee-**loo**-ya) *or* **alleluia** *interj* an exclamation of praise to God [Hebrew *hellēl* to praise + *yāh* the Lord]

hallmark *n* **1** a typical feature: *secrecy became the hallmark of government* **2** *Brit* an official seal stamped on gold, silver, or platinum articles to guarantee purity and date of manufacture **3** a mark of authenticity or excellence ▹ *vb* **4** to stamp with a hallmark [after Goldsmiths' *Hall* in London, where items were stamped]

hallo *interj, n* same as **hello**

halloo *interj chiefly Brit* a shout used to call hounds at a hunt [perhaps variant of *hallow* to encourage hounds by shouting]

Halloumi *or* **Haloumi** *n* a salty white goat or sheep's cheese from Cyprus, usually eaten grilled [from Arabic *haluma* be mild]

hallowed *adj* **1** regarded as holy: *hallowed ground* **2** respected and revered because of age, importance, or reputation: *the hallowed pitch at Lord's* [Old English *hālgian* to consecrate]

Halloween *or* **Hallowe'en** *n* October 31, celebrated by children by dressing up as ghosts, witches, etc. [*all hallow even* all saints' eve]

hallucinate *vb* **-nating, -nated** to seem to see something that is not really there [Latin *alucinari*]
hallucination *n* the experience of seeming to see something that is not really there **hallucinatory** *adj*
hallucinogen *n* any drug that causes hallucinations **hallucinogenic** *adj*
hallway *n* an entrance area
halo (hay-loh) *n, pl* **-loes** *or* **-los** **1** a ring of light around the head of a sacred figure **2** a circle of refracted light around the sun or moon ▹ *vb* **-loes** *or* **-los, -loing, -loed** **3** to surround with a halo [Greek *halōs* circular threshing floor]
halogen (hal-oh-jen) *n chem* any of the nonmetallic chemical elements fluorine, chlorine, bromine, iodine, and astatine, which form salts when combined with metal [Greek *hals* salt + *-genēs* born]
halt *vb* **1** to come to a stop or bring (someone or something) to a stop ▹ *n* **2** a temporary standstill **3** a military command to stop **4** *chiefly Brit* a minor railway station without a building: *Deeside Halt* **5** **call a halt to** to put an end to [German *halten* to stop]
halter *n* **1** a strap around a horse's head with a rope to lead it with ▹ *vb* **2** to put a halter on (a horse) [Old English *hælfter*]
halterneck *n* a woman's top or dress which fastens behind the neck, leaving the back and arms bare
halting *adj* hesitant or uncertain: *she spoke halting Italian*
halve *vb* **halving, halved** **1** to divide (something) into two equal parts **2** to reduce (the size or amount of something) by half **3** *golf* to draw with one's opponent on (a hole or round)
halyard *n naut* a line for hoisting or lowering a ship's sail or flag [Middle English *halier*]
ham[1] *n* smoked or salted meat from a pig's thigh [Old English *hamm*]
ham[2] *n* **1** *informal* an amateur radio operator **2** *theatre informal* an actor who overacts and exaggerates the emotions and gestures of a part ▹ *adj* **3** (of actors or their performances) exaggerated and overstated ▹ *vb* **hamming, hammed** **4** **ham it up** *informal* to overact [special use of HAM[1]]
hamba *interj S African, usually offensive* go away [Nguni (language group of southern Africa): to go]
hamburger *n* a flat round of minced beef, often served in a bread roll [*Hamburger steak*, steak in the fashion of *Hamburg*, Germany]
ham-fisted *or* **ham-handed** *adj informal* very clumsy or awkward
hamlet *n* a small village [Old French *hamelet*]
hammer *n* **1** a hand tool consisting of a heavy metal head on the end of a handle, used for driving in nails, beating metal, etc. **2** the part of a gun that causes the bullet to shoot when the trigger is pulled **3** *athletics* **A** a heavy metal ball attached to a flexible wire: thrown in competitions **B** the sport of throwing the hammer **4** an auctioneer's mallet **5** the part of a piano that hits a string when a key is pressed **6** **come** *or* **go under the hammer** to be on sale at auction **7** **hammer and tongs** with great effort or energy ▹ *vb* **8** to hit with or as if with a hammer **9** *Brit* to criticize severely **10** *informal* to defeat heavily **11** to feel or sound like hammering: *his heart was hammering* **12** **hammer in** to force (facts or ideas) into someone through repetition **13** **hammer away at** to work at (something) constantly: *the paper hammered away at the same theme all the way through the campaign* ▹ See also **hammer out** [Old English *hamor*]
hammer and sickle *n* the emblem on the flag of the former Soviet Union, representing the industrial workers and the peasants
hammerhead *n* a shark with a wide flattened head
hammer out *vb* to produce (an agreement) with great effort
hammertoe *n* a condition in which the toe is permanently bent at the joint
hammock *n* a hanging bed made of canvas or net [Spanish *hamaca*]
hammy *n, pl* **-ies** *informal* a hamstring
hamper[1] *vb* to make it difficult for (someone or something) to move or progress [origin unknown]
hamper[2] *n* **1** a large basket with a lid **2** *Brit* a selection of food and drink packed as a gift [Middle English *hanaper* a small basket]
hamster *n* a small rodent with a stocky body, short tail, and cheek pouches [German]
hamstring *n* **1** one of the tendons at the back of the knee ▹ *vb* **-stringing, -strung** **2** to make it difficult for someone to take any action [*ham* (in the sense: leg)]
hand *n* **1** the part of the body at the end of the arm, consisting of a thumb, four fingers, and a palm. Related adjective: **manual** **2** a person's style of writing: *scrolls written in her own hand* **3** the influence a person or thing has over a particular situation: *the hand of the military in shaping policy was obvious* **4** a part in some activity: *I remember with gratitude Fortune's hand in starting my collection* **5** assistance: *give me a hand with the rice* **6** a round of applause: *give a big hand to the most exciting duo in the game* **7** consent to marry someone: *he asked for her hand in marriage* **8** a manual worker **9** a member of a ship's crew **10** a pointer on a dial or gauge, esp. on a clock **11** **A** the cards dealt in one round of a card game **B** one round of a card game **12** a position indicated by its location to the side of an object or the observer: *on the right hand* **13** a contrasting aspect or condition: *on the other hand* **14** source: *I had experienced at first hand many management styles* **15** a person who creates something: *a good hand at baking* **16** a unit of length equalling four inches, used for measuring the height of horses **17** **by hand** **A** by manual rather than mechanical means **B** by messenger: *the letter was delivered by hand* **18** **from hand to mouth** with no food or money in reserve: *living from hand to mouth* **19** **hand in glove** in close association **20** **hand over fist** steadily and quickly: *losing money hand over fist* **21** **in hand** **A** under control **B** receiving attention: *the business in hand* **C** available in reserve: *Pakistan have a game in hand* **22** **keep one's hand in** to continue to practise something **23** **(near) at hand** very close

24 on hand close by; available **25 out of hand** **A** beyond control **B** decisively, without possible reconsideration: *he dismissed the competition out of hand* **26 show one's hand** to reveal one's plans **27 to hand** accessible ▷ *vb* **28** to pass or give by the hand or hands **29 hand it to someone** to give credit to someone ▷ See also **hand down, hand on, hands** *etc.* [Old English] **handless** *adj*

handbag *n* a woman's small bag carried to contain personal articles

handball *n* a game in which two teams of seven players try to throw a ball into their opponent's goal

handbill *n* a small printed notice for distribution by hand

handbook *n* a reference manual giving practical information on a subject

handbrake *n* a brake in a motor vehicle operated by a hand lever

h & c hot and cold (water)

handcart *n* a simple cart pushed or pulled by hand, used for transporting goods

handcrafted *adj* made by handicraft

handcuff *n* **1 handcuffs** a linked pair of locking metal rings used for securing prisoners ▷ *vb* **2** to put handcuffs on (a person)

hand down *vb* **1** to pass on (knowledge, possessions, or skills) to a younger generation **2** to pass (outgrown clothes) on from one member of a family to a younger one **3** *US & Canad law* to announce (a verdict)

handful *n, pl* **-fuls 1** the amount that can be held in the hand **2** a small number: *a handful of parents* **3** *informal* a person or animal that is difficult to control: *as a child she was a real handful*

hand-held *adj* **1** held in position by the hand ▷ *n* **2** a device, such as a computer, that can be held in the hand

handicap *n* **1** *old-fashioned, offensive* a physical or mental disability **2** something that makes progress difficult **3 A** a contest in which competitors are given advantages or disadvantages in an attempt to equalize their chances **B** the advantage or disadvantage given **4** *golf* the number of strokes by which a player's averaged score exceeds par for the course ▷ *vb* **-capping, -capped 5** to make it difficult for (someone) to do something [probably *hand in cap,* a lottery game in which players drew forfeits from a cap]

handicapped *adj* *old-fashioned, offensive* having a physical or mental disability

> **USAGE** Many disabled people find the use of the word *handicapped* to describe them or their condition offensive. It is preferable to refer to someone as *having a disability* and to talk about *people with disabilities.*

handicraft *n* **1** a skill performed with the hands, such as weaving **2** the objects produced by people with such skills

handiwork *n* **1** the result of someone's work or activity **2** work produced by hand

handkerchief *n* a small square of fabric used to wipe the nose

handle *n* **1** the part of an object that is held or operated in order that it may be used **2** a small lever used to open and close a door or window **3** *slang* a person's name **4** a means of understanding or dealing with something: *trying to get a handle on why companies borrow money* **5 fly off the handle** *informal* to become suddenly extremely angry ▷ *vb* **-dling, -dled 6** to hold, move, operate, or touch with the hands **7** to have responsibility for: *she handles all their affairs personally* **8** to manage successfully: *I can handle this challenge* **9** to discuss (a subject) **10** to deal with in a specified way: *the affair was neatly handled* **11** to trade or deal in (specified merchandise): *we handle 1800 properties in Normandy* **12** to react or respond in a specified way to operation or control: *it's light and handles well* [Old English] **handling** *n*

handlebars *pl n* a metal tube with handles at each end, used for steering a bicycle or motorcycle

handler *n* **1** a person who trains and controls an animal **2** a person who handles something: *a baggage handler*

handmade *adj* made by hand, not by machine

handmaiden *or* **handmaid** *n* **1** *old-fashioned* a female servant **2** a person or thing that serves a useful but lesser purpose: *these policies resulted in agriculture becoming the poor handmaiden of industry*

hand-me-down *n informal* an item of clothing that someone has finished with and passed on to someone else

hand on *vb* to pass (something) to the next person in a succession

hand-out *n, pl* **hand-outs 1** clothing, food, or money given to a needy person **2** a leaflet, free sample, etc., given out to publicize something **3** a piece of written information given out to the audience at a talk, lecture, etc. ▷ *vb* **hand out 4** to distribute

hand over *vb* to give up possession of or transfer (something)

hand-pick *vb* to select (a person) with great care, such as for a special job **hand-picked** *adj*

handrail *n* a rail alongside a stairway, to provide support

hands *pl n* **1 change hands** to pass from the possession of one person to another **2 have one's hands full** to be completely occupied **3 in someone's hands** in someone's control or power: *that's in the hands of the courts* **4 off one's hands** no longer one's responsibility **5 on one's hands** for which one is responsible: *what a problem case I've got on my hands* **6 wash one's hands of** to have nothing more to do with **7 win hands down** to win easily

handset *n* **1** a telephone in which the mouthpiece and earpiece are contained in a single unit **2** a hand-held control for an electronic device

hands-free *adj, n* (of) a device allowing the user to make and receive telephone calls without holding the handset

handshake *n* the act of grasping and shaking a person's hand, such as in greeting or when agreeing on a deal

handsome *adj* **1** (esp. of a man) good-looking **2** (of a building, garden, etc.) large, well-made, and with an attractive appearance: *a handsome* *building* **3** (of an amount of money) generous or large: *a handsome dividend* [obsolete *handsom* easily handled] **handsomely** *adv*

hands-on *adj* involving practical experience of equipment: *Navy personnel joined the 1986 expedition for hands-on operating experience*

handspring *n* a gymnastic exercise in which a person leaps forwards or backwards into a handstand and then onto his or her feet

handstand *n* the act of supporting the body on the hands in an upside-down position

hand-to-hand *adj, adv* at close quarters, with fists or knives: *hand-to-hand combat; they fought hand-to-hand*

hand-to-mouth *adj, adv* with barely enough money or food to live on: *a hand-to-mouth existence; they lived hand-to-mouth*

handwork *n* work done by hand rather than by machine

handwriting *n* **1** writing by hand rather than by typing or printing **2** a person's characteristic writing style **handwritten** *adj*

handy *adj* **handier, handiest 1** conveniently within reach **2** easy to handle or use **3** good at manual work **handily** *adv*

handyman *n, pl* **-men** a man skilled at odd jobs

hang *vb* **hanging, hung 1** to fasten or be fastened from above **2** to place (something) in position, for instance by a hinge, so as to allow free movement: *to hang a door* **3** to be suspended so as to allow movement from the place where it is attached: *her long hair hung over her face* **4** to decorate with something suspended, such as pictures **5** (of cloth or clothing) to fall or flow in a particular way: *the fine gauge knit hangs loosely with graceful femininity* **6** *past tense & past participle* **hanged** to suspend or be suspended by the neck until dead **7** to hover: *clouds hung over the mountains* **8** to fasten to a wall: *to hang wallpaper* **9** to exhibit or be exhibited in an art gallery **10** *past tense & past participle* **hanged** *slang* to damn: used in mild curses or interjections **11 hang fire** to put off doing something **12 hang over** to threaten or overshadow: *the threat of war hung over the Middle East* ▷ *n* **13** the way in which something hangs **14 get the hang of something** *informal* to understand the technique of doing something ▷ See also **hang about, hang back** *etc.* [Old English *hangian*]

hang about *or* **hang around** *vb* **1** to stand about idly somewhere **2** (foll. by *with*) to spend a lot of time in the company (of someone)

hangar *n* a large building for storing aircraft [French: shed]

hang back *vb* to be reluctant to do something

hangdog *adj* dejected, ashamed, or guilty in appearance or manner

hanger *n* same as **coat hanger**

hanger-on *n, pl* **hangers-on** an unwanted follower, esp. of a rich or famous person

hang-glider *n* an unpowered aircraft consisting of a large cloth wing stretched over a light framework from which the pilot hangs in a harness **hang-gliding** *n*

hangi (hung-ee) *n* NZ **1** an open-air cooking pit **2** the food cooked in it **3** the social gathering at the resultant meal [Māori]

hanging *n* **1** the act or practice of putting a person to death by suspending the body by the neck **2** a large piece of cloth hung on a wall as a decoration

hanging valley *n geog* a tributary valley that enters a main valley high up because the main valley has been deepened through erosion by a glacier

hangman *n, pl* **-men** an official who carries out a sentence of hanging

hangnail *n* a piece of skin partly torn away from the base or side of a fingernail

hang on *vb* **1** *informal* to wait: *hang on a minute, will you?* **2** to continue or persist with effort or difficulty **3** to grasp or hold **4** to depend on: *a lot hangs on its success* **5** to listen attentively to: *she hangs on every word our leader says*

hang out *vb* **1** to suspend, be suspended, or lean **2** *informal* to live or spend a lot of time in a place: *fishermen hang out in waterfront bars* **3 let it all hang out** *slang, chiefly US* to relax completely; act or speak freely ▷ *n* **hang-out 4** *informal* a place where someone spends a lot of time

hangover *n* a feeling of sickness and headache after drinking too much alcohol

hang together *vb* **1** to be united **2** to be consistent: *the story simply did not hang together*

hang up *vb* **1** to replace (a telephone receiver) at the end of a conversation **2** to put on a hook or hanger ▷ *n* **hang-up 3** *informal* an emotional or psychological problem

hank *n* a loop or coil, esp. of yarn [from Old Norse]

hanker *vb* (foll. by *for* or *after*) to have a great desire for [probably from Dutch dialect *hankeren*] **hankering** *n*

hanky *or* **hankie** *n, pl* **hankies** *informal* short for **handkerchief**

hanky-panky *n informal* **1** casual sexual relations **2** mischievous behaviour [variant of *hocus-pocus*]

Hanoverian (han-no-veer-ee-an) *adj* of or relating to the British royal house ruling from 1714 to 1901 [after *Hanover*, Germany]

Hansard *n* the official report of the proceedings of the British or Canadian parliament [after L. *Hansard*, its original compiler]

Hanseatic League (han-see-at-ik) *n history* a commercial organization of towns in N Germany formed in the 14th century to protect and control trade

hansom *n* (formerly) a two-wheeled one-horse carriage with a fixed hood. Also called: **hansom cab** [after its designer J. A. *Hansom*]

Hants Hampshire

Hanukkah *n* same as **Chanukah**

haphazard *adj* not organized or planned [Old Norse *happ* chance, good luck + HAZARD] **haphazardly** *adv*

hapless *adj* unlucky: *the hapless victim of a misplaced murder attempt* [Old Norse *happ* chance, good luck]

haploid *adj biol* denoting a cell or organism with unpaired chromosomes [Greek *haplous* single]

haplotype *n genetics* a set of alleles inherited by an individual from a single parent

happen *vb* **1** to take place; occur **2** to chance (to be or do something): *I happen to know him* **3** to be the case, esp. by chance: *it happens that I know him* **4 happen to** (of some unforeseen event, such as death) to be the experience or fate of: *if anything happens to me you will know* [obsolete *hap*]

USAGE See at **occur**.

happening *n* an event that often occurs in a way that is unexpected or hard to explain: *some strange happenings in the village recently*

happy *adj* **-pier, -piest 1** feeling or expressing joy **2** causing joy or gladness: *the happiest day of my life* **3** fortunate or lucky: *it was a happy coincidence* **4** satisfied or content: *he seems happy to let things go on as they are* **5** willing: *I'll be happy to arrange a loan for you* [Old Norse *happ* chance, good luck] **happily** *adv* **happiness** *n*

happy-go-lucky *adj* carefree or easy-going

hara-kiri *n* (formerly, in Japan) ritual suicide by disembowelment when disgraced or under sentence of death [Japanese *hara* belly + *kiri* cut]

harangue *vb* **-ranguing, -rangued 1** to address (a person or group) in an angry or forcefully persuasive way ▷ *n* **2** a forceful or angry speech [Old Italian *aringa* public speech]

harass *vb* to trouble or annoy (someone) by repeated attacks, questions, or problems [French *harasser*] **harassed** *adj* **harassment** *n*

harbinger (har-binge-er) *n literary* a person or thing that announces or indicates the approach of something: *a harbinger of death* [Old French *herbergere*]

harbour *or US* **harbor** *n* **1** a sheltered port **2** a place of refuge or safety ▷ *vb* **3** to maintain secretly in the mind: *he might be harbouring a death wish* **4** to give shelter or protection to: *the government accused her of harbouring criminals* [Old English *herebeorg*, from *here* army + *beorg* shelter]

harbour master *n* an official in charge of a harbour

hard *adj* **1** firm, solid, or rigid **2** difficult to do or understand: *a hard sum* **3** showing or requiring a lot of effort or application: *hard work* **4** unkind or unfeeling: *she's very hard, no pity for anyone* **5** causing pain, sorrow, or hardship: *the hard life of a northern settler* **6** tough or violent: *a hard man* **7** forceful: *a hard knock* **8** cool or uncompromising: *we took a long hard look at our profit factor* **9** indisputable and proven to be true: *hard facts* **10** (of water) containing calcium salts which stop soap lathering freely **11** practical, shrewd, or calculating: *I am a hard businesswoman* **12** harsh: *hard light* **13** (of currency) high and stable in exchange value **14** (of alcoholic drink) being a spirit rather than a wine or beer **15** (of a drug) highly addictive **16** hard-core **17** *phonetics* denoting the consonants *c* and *g* when they are pronounced as in *cat* and *got* **18** politically extreme: *the hard left* **19 hard of hearing** slightly deaf **20 hard up** *informal* in need of money ▷ *adv* **21** with great energy or force: *they fought so hard and well in Spain* **22** with great intensity: *thinking hard about the conversation* **23 hard by** very close to: *Cleveland Place, hard by Bruntsfield Square* **24 hard put (to it)** scarcely having the capacity (to do something) ▷ *n* **25 have a hard on** *taboo slang* to have an erection of the penis [Old English *heard*] **hardness** *n*

hard-and-fast *adj* (of rules) fixed and not able to be changed

hardback *n* **1** a book with stiff covers ▷ *adj* **2** of or denoting a hardback

hardball *n US & Canad* **1** baseball as distinct from softball **2 play hardball** *informal* to act in a ruthless or uncompromising way

hard-bitten *adj informal* tough and determined

hardboard *n* stiff board made in thin sheets of compressed sawdust and wood pulp

hard-boiled *adj* **1** (of an egg) boiled until solid **2** *informal* tough, realistic, and unemotional

hard cash *n* money or payment in money, as opposed to payment by cheque, credit card, etc.

hard copy *n* computer output printed on paper

hardcore *n* **1** a style of rock music with short fast songs and little melody **2** a type of dance music with a very fast beat

hard core *n* **1** the members of a group who most resist change **2** broken stones used to form a foundation for a road ▷ *adj* **hard-core 3** (of pornography) showing sexual acts in explicit detail **4** extremely committed or fanatical: *a hard-core Communist*

hard disk *n computers* an inflexible disk in a sealed container

hard drive *n computers* the mechanism that handles the reading, writing, and storage of data on the hard disk

harden *vb* **1** to make or become hard; freeze, stiffen, or set **2** to make or become tough or unfeeling: *life in the camp had hardened her considerably* **3** to make or become stronger or firmer: *they hardened defences* **4** to make or become more determined or resolute: *the government has hardened its attitude to the crisis* **5** *commerce* (of prices or a market) to cease to fluctuate

hardened *adj* toughened by experience: *a hardened criminal*

hardfill *n NZ & S African* a stone waste material used for landscaping

hard-headed *adj* tough, realistic, or shrewd, esp. in business

hardhearted *adj* unsympathetic and uncaring

hardihood *n* courage or daring

hard labour *n* difficult and tiring physical work: used as a punishment for a crime in some countries

hard line *n* **1** an uncompromising policy: *a hard line on drugs* ▷ *adj* **hard-line 2** tough and uncompromising: *a hard-line attitude to the refugee problem* **hardliner** *n*

hardly *adv* **1** scarcely; barely: *he'd hardly sipped his whisky* **2** *humorous* not at all: *it was hardly in the Great Train Robbery league* **3** with difficulty: *their own families would hardly recognize them*

USAGE Since *hardly, scarcely*, and *barely* already have negative force, it is redundant to use another negative in the same clause: *he had hardly had* (not *he hadn't hardly had*) *time to think; there was scarcely any* (not *scarcely no*) *bread left.*

hard pad *n* (in dogs) an abnormal increase in the thickness of the foot pads: a sign of distemper

hard palate *n* the bony front part of the roof of the mouth

hard-pressed *adj* **1** under a great deal of strain and worry: *hard-pressed companies having to cut costs* **2** closely pursued

hard science *n* one of the natural or physical sciences, such as physics, chemistry, or biology

hard sell *n* an aggressive insistent technique of selling

hardship *n* **1** conditions of life that are difficult to endure **2** something that causes suffering

hard shoulder *n Brit & NZ* a surfaced verge running along the edge of a motorway and other roads for emergency stops

hardtack *n* a kind of hard saltless biscuit, formerly eaten by sailors

hardware *n* **1** metal tools or implements, esp. cutlery or cooking utensils **2** the physical equipment used in a computer system **3** heavy military equipment, such as tanks and missiles

hard-wired *adj* (of a circuit or instruction) permanently wired into a computer

hardwood *n* the wood of a deciduous tree such as oak, beech, or ash

hardy *adj* **-dier, -diest 1** able to stand difficult conditions **2** (of plants) able to live out of doors throughout the winter [Old French *hardi* emboldened] **hardiness** *n*

hare *n, pl* **hares** *or* **hare 1** a mammal like a large rabbit, with longer ears and legs ▷ *vb* **haring, hared 2** (foll. by *off* or *after*) *Brit & Austral informal* to run fast or wildly [Old English *hara*]

harebell *n* a blue bell-shaped flower

harebrained *adj* foolish or impractical: *harebrained schemes*

harelip *n offensive* an old-fashioned term for a **cleft lip**

harem *n* **A** (formerly) the part of a Muslim household reserved for wives and concubines **B** the women occupying this part of the house [Arabic *harīm* forbidden (place)]

haricot bean *or* **haricot** (**har**-rik-oh) *n* a white edible bean, which can be dried [French *haricot*]

harissa *n* a hot paste or sauce made from chilli peppers, tomatoes, spices, and olive oil, used in North African cuisine

hark *vb old-fashioned* to listen; pay attention: *hark, the cocks are crowing* [Old English *heorcnian*]

hark back *vb* to return (to an earlier subject in speech or thought): *he keeps harking back to his music-hall days*

harlequin *n* **1** *theatre* a stock comic character, usually wearing a diamond-patterned multicoloured costume and a black mask ▷ *adj* **2** in varied colours [Old French *Herlequin* leader of a band of demon horsemen]

harlequinade *n theatre* a play in which harlequin has a leading role

harlot *n literary* a prostitute [Old French *herlot* rascal] **harlotry** *n*

harm *vb* **1** to injure physically, morally, or mentally ▷ *n* **2** physical, moral, or mental injury [Old English *hearm*]

harmful *adj* causing or tending to cause harm, esp. to a person's health

harmless *adj* **1** safe to use, touch, or be near **2** unlikely to annoy or worry people: *a harmless habit*

harmonic *adj* **1** of, producing, or characterized by harmony; harmonious ▷ *n* **2** *music* an overtone of a musical note produced when that note is played, but not usually heard as a separate note ▷ See also **harmonics** [Latin *harmonicus* relating to harmony] **harmonically** *adv*

harmonica *n* a small wind instrument in which reeds enclosed in a narrow oblong box are made to vibrate by blowing and sucking

harmonics *n* the science of musical sounds

harmonious *adj* **1** (esp. of colours or sounds) consisting of parts which blend together well **2** showing agreement, peacefulness, and friendship: *a harmonious relationship* **3** tuneful or melodious

harmonium *n* a musical keyboard instrument in which air from pedal-operated bellows causes the reeds to vibrate

harmonize *or* **-nise** *vb* **-nizing, -nized** *or* **-nising, -nised 1** to sing or play in harmony, such as with another singer or player **2** to make or become harmonious

harmony *n, pl* **-nies 1** a state of peaceful agreement and cooperation **2** *music* a pleasant combination of two or more notes sounded at the same time **3** the way parts combine well together or into a whole [Greek *harmonia*]

harness *n* **1** an arrangement of straps for attaching a horse to a cart or plough **2** something resembling this, for attaching something to a person's body: *a parachute harness* **3 in harness** at one's routine work ▷ *vb* **4** to put a harness on (a horse or other animal) **5** to control something in order to make use of it: *learning to harness the power of your own mind* [Old French *harneis* baggage]

harp *n* **1** a large upright triangular stringed instrument played by plucking the strings with the fingers ▷ *vb* **2 harp on** to speak in a persistent and tedious manner (about a subject) [Old English *hearpe*] **harpist** *n*

harpoon *n* **1** a barbed spear attached to a long rope and thrown or fired when hunting whales, etc. ▷ *vb* **2** to spear with a harpoon [probably from Dutch *harpoen*]

harpsichord *n* a keyboard instrument, resembling a small piano, with strings that are plucked mechanically [Late Latin *harpa* harp + Latin *chorda* string] **harpsichordist** *n*

harpy *n, pl* **-pies** *derogatory* an unpleasant or greedy woman [from Greek *Harpuiai* the Harpies, literally: snatchers (mythical birdlike female monsters)]

harridan *n derogatory* a scolding old woman; nag [origin unknown]

harrier[1] *n* a cross-country runner [from *hare*]

harrier[2] *n* a bird of prey with broad wings and long legs and tail

harrow *n* **1** an implement used to break up clods of soil ▷ *vb* **2** to draw a harrow over (land) [from Old Norse]

harrowing *adj* very upsetting or disturbing

harry *vb* **-ries, -rying, -ried** to keep asking (someone) to do something; pester [Old English *hergian*]

harsh *adj* **1** severe and difficult to cope with: *harsh winters* **2** unkind and showing no understanding:

the judge was very harsh on the demonstrators **3** excessively hard, bright, or rough: *harsh sunlight* **4** (of sounds) unpleasant and grating [probably Scandinavian] **harshly** *adv* **harshness** *n*

hart *n, pl* **harts** *or* **hart** the male of the deer, esp. the red deer [Old English *heorot*]

hartebeest *n* a large African antelope with curved horns and a fawn-coloured coat [Dutch]

harum-scarum *adj* **1** reckless ▷ *adv* **2** recklessly ▷ *n* **3** an impetuous person [origin unknown]

harvest *n* **1** the gathering of a ripened crop **2** the crop itself **3** the season for gathering crops **4** the product of an effort or action ▷ *vb* **5** to gather (a ripened crop) **6** *chiefly US* to remove (an organ) from the body for transplantation [Old English *hærfest*]

harvester *n* **1** a harvesting machine, esp. a combine harvester **2** a person who harvests

harvest festival *n* **1** a Christian church service held every year to thank God for the harvest **2** any of various ceremonies celebrating the harvest in other religions

h

harvest moon *n* the full moon occurring nearest to the autumn equinox

harvest mouse *n* a very small reddish-brown mouse that lives in cornfields or hedgerows

has *vb* third person singular of the present tense of **have**

has-been *n informal* a person who is no longer popular or successful

hash¹ *n* **1** a dish of diced cooked meat, vegetables, etc., reheated: *corned-beef hash* **2** a reworking of old material **3** **make a hash of** *informal* to mess up or destroy [Old French *hacher* to chop up]

hash² *n slang* short for **hashish**

hash³ *or* **hashmark** *n* the character (#) used to precede a number

hash browns *pl n* diced boiled potatoes mixed with chopped onion, shaped into small cakes and fried until brown

hashish (**hash**-eesh) *n* a drug made from the hemp plant, smoked for its intoxicating effects [Arabic]

hashtag *n* (on the Twitter website) a word or phrase preceded by a hash, indicating the topic being discussed

hasn't has not

hasp *n* a clasp which fits over a staple and is secured by a pin, bolt, or padlock, used as a fastening [Old English *hæpse*]

hassium *n chem* an element synthetically produced in small quantities by high-energy ion bombardment. Symbol: **Hs** [Latin, from *Hesse*, the German state where it was discovered]

hassle *informal* ▷ *n* **1** a great deal of trouble **2** a prolonged argument ▷ *vb* **-sling, -sled** **3** to cause annoyance or trouble to (someone): *stop hassling me!* [origin unknown]

hassock *n* a cushion for kneeling on in church [Old English *hassuc* matted grass]

haste *n* **1** speed, esp. in an action **2** the act of hurrying in a careless manner **3** **make haste** to hurry or rush ▷ *vb* **hasting, hasted** **4** *poetic* to hasten [Old French]

hasten *vb* **1** to hurry or cause to hurry **2** to be anxious (to say something)

hasty *adj* **-tier, -tiest** **1** done or happening suddenly or quickly **2** done too quickly and without thought; rash **hastily** *adv*

hat *n* **1** a head covering, often with a brim, usually worn to give protection from the weather **2** *informal* a role or capacity: *I'm wearing my honorary consul's hat* **3** **keep something under one's hat** to keep something secret **4** **pass the hat round** to collect money for a cause **5** **take off one's hat to someone** to admire or congratulate someone [Old English *hætt*]

hatband *n* a band or ribbon around the base of the crown of a hat

hatch¹ *vb* **1** to cause (the young of various animals, esp. birds) to emerge from the egg or (of young birds, etc.) to emerge from the egg **2** (of eggs) to break and release the young animal within **3** to devise (a plot or plan) [Germanic]

hatch² *n* **1** a hinged door covering an opening in a floor or wall **2** **A** short for **hatchway** **B** a door in an aircraft or spacecraft **3** Also called: **serving hatch** an opening in a wall between a kitchen and a dining area **4** *informal* short for **hatchback** [Old English *hæcc*]

hatch³ *vb drawing & engraving etc.* to mark (a figure, etc.) with fine parallel or crossed lines to indicate shading [Old French *hacher* to chop] **hatching** *n*

hatchback *n* a car with a single lifting door in the rear

hatchet *n* **1** a short axe used for chopping wood, etc. **2** **bury the hatchet** to make peace or resolve a disagreement ▷ *adj* **3** narrow and sharp: *a hatchet face* [Old French *hachette*]

hatchet job *n informal* a malicious verbal or written attack

hatchet man *n informal* a person who carries out unpleasant tasks on behalf of an employer

hatchling *n* a young animal that has newly hatched from an egg

hatchway *n* an opening in the deck of a vessel to provide access below

hate *vb* **hating, hated** **1** to dislike (someone or something) intensely **2** to be unwilling (to do something): *I hate to trouble you* ▷ *n* **3** intense dislike **4** *informal* a person or thing that is hated: *my own pet hate is restaurants* [Old English *hatian*] **hater** *n*

hateful *adj* causing or deserving hate

Hathor *n* an Egyptian goddess of creation

hatred *n* intense dislike

hatter *n* **1** a person who makes and sells hats **2** **mad as a hatter** eccentric

hat trick *n* **1** *cricket* the achievement of a bowler in taking three wickets with three successive balls **2** any achievement of three successive goals, victories, etc.

hauberk *n history* a long sleeveless coat of mail [Old French *hauberc*]

haughty *adj* **-tier, -tiest** having or showing excessive pride or arrogance [Latin *altus* high] **haughtily** *adv* **haughtiness** *n*

haul *vb* **1** to drag or pull (something) with effort **2** to transport, such as in a lorry **3** *naut* to alter the course of (a vessel) ▷ *n* **4** the act of dragging with effort **5** a quantity of something obtained: *a good haul of fish; a huge haul of stolen goods*

6 long haul **A** a long journey **B** a long difficult process [Old French *haler*]

haulage *n* **1** the business of transporting goods **2** a charge for transporting goods

haulier *n Brit & Austral* a person or firm that transports goods by road

haulm (**hawm**) *n* the stalks of beans, peas, or potatoes collectively [Old English *healm*]

haunch *n* **1** the human hip or fleshy hindquarter of an animal **2** the leg and loin of an animal, used for food [Old French *hanche*]

haunt *vb* **1** to visit (a person or place) in the form of a ghost **2** to remain in the memory or thoughts of: *it was a belief which haunted her* **3** to visit (a place) frequently ▷ *n* **4** a place visited frequently [Old French *hanter*]

haunted *adj* **1** (of a place) frequented or visited by ghosts **2** (of a person) obsessed or worried

haunting *adj* having a quality of great beauty or sadness so as to be memorable: *a haunting melody*

hautboy (**oh-boy**) *n old-fashioned* an oboe [French *haut* high + *bois* wood]

haute couture (**oat** koo-**ture**) *n* high fashion [French]

hauteur (oat-**ur**) *n* haughtiness [French *haut* high]

Havana *n* a fine-quality hand-rolled cigar from Cuba

have *vb* **has, having, had 1** to possess: *he has a collection of classic cars; I have an iron constitution* **2** to receive, take, or obtain: *I had a long letter* **3** to hold in the mind: *she always had a yearning to be a schoolteacher* **4** to possess a knowledge of: *I have no German* **5** to experience or be affected by: *a good way to have a change* **6** to suffer from: *to have a blood pressure problem* **7** to gain control of or advantage over: *you have me on that point* **8** *slang* to cheat or outwit: *I've been had* **9** to show: *have mercy on me* **10** to take part in; hold: *I had a telephone conversation* **11** to cause to be done: *have my shoes mended by Friday* **12** to eat or drink **13** *taboo slang* to have sexual intercourse with **14** to tolerate or allow: *I won't have all this noise* **15** to receive as a guest: *we have visitors* **16** to be pregnant with or give birth to (offspring) **17** used to form past tenses: *I have gone; I had gone* **18 have had it** *informal* **A** to be exhausted or killed **B** to have lost one's last chance **19 have it off** *Brit taboo slang* to have sexual intercourse **20 have to** used to express compulsion or necessity: *you'd have to wait six months* ▷ *n* **21 haves** *informal* people who have wealth, security, etc.: *the haves and the have-nots* ▷ See also **have on, have out** *etc.* [Old English *habban*]

have-a-go *adj informal* (of people attempting arduous or brave tasks) brave or spirited: *have-a-go pensioner*

haven *n* **1** a place of safety **2** a harbour for shipping [Old English *hæfen*]

haven't have not

have on *vb* **1** to wear: *he had a pair of long trousers on* **2** to have a commitment: *what do you have on this afternoon?* **3** *informal* to trick or tease: *he's having you on* **4** to have (information, esp. when incriminating) about (a person): *she has something on him*

have out *vb* to settle (a matter), esp. by fighting or by frank discussion: *I went to Carl's office to have it out with him*

haver *vb* **1** *Scot & N English dialect* to talk nonsense **2** to be unsure and hesitant; dither [origin unknown]

haversack *n* a canvas bag carried on the back or shoulder [French *havresac*]

have up *vb* to bring to trial: *what, and get me had up for kidnapping?*

havoc *n* **1** *informal* chaos, disorder, and confusion **2 play havoc with** to cause a great deal of damage or confusion to [Old French *havot* pillage]

haw[1] *n* the fruit of the hawthorn [Old English *haga*]

haw[2] *vb* **hum** (*or* **hem**) **and haw** to hesitate in speaking [imitative]

hawk[1] *n* **1** a bird of prey with short rounded wings and a long tail **2** a supporter or advocate of warlike policies ▷ *vb* **3** to hunt with falcons or hawks [Old English *hafoc*] **hawkish** *adj* **hawklike** *adj*

hawk[2] *vb* to offer (goods) for sale in the street or door-to-door [from *hawker* pedlar]

hawk[3] *vb* **1** to clear the throat noisily **2** to force (phlegm) up from the throat [imitative]

hawker *n* a person who travels from place to place selling goods [probably from Middle Low German *hōken* to peddle]

hawk-eyed *adj* having extremely keen eyesight

hawser *n naut* a large heavy rope [Anglo-French *hauceour*]

hawthorn *n* a thorny tree or shrub with white or pink flowers and reddish fruits [Old English *haguthorn*]

hay *n* **1** grass cut and dried as fodder **2 hit the hay** *slang* to go to bed **3 make hay while the sun shines** to take full advantage of an opportunity [Old English *hieg*]

hay fever *n* an allergic reaction to pollen, which causes sneezing, runny nose, and watery eyes

haystack *or* **hayrick** *n* a large pile of hay built in the open and covered with thatch

haywire *adj* **go haywire** *informal* to stop functioning properly

hazard *n* **1** a thing likely to cause injury, loss, etc. **2** risk or likelihood of injury, loss, etc.: *evaluate the level of hazard in a situation* **3** *golf* an obstacle such as a bunker **4 at hazard** at risk ▷ *vb* **5** to risk: *hazarding the health of his crew* **6 hazard a guess** to make a guess [Arabic *az-zahr* the die]

hazard lights *or* **hazard warning lights** *pl n* the indicator lights on a motor vehicle when flashing simultaneously to indicate that the vehicle is stationary

hazardous *adj* involving great risk

haze *n* **1** *meteorol* reduced visibility as a result of condensed water vapour, dust, etc., in the air **2** confused or unclear understanding or feeling [from *hazy*]

hazel *n* **1** a shrub with edible rounded nuts ▷ *adj* **2** greenish-brown: *hazel eyes* [Old English *hæsel*]

hazelnut *n* the nut of a hazel shrub, which has a smooth shiny hard shell

hazy *adj* **-zier, -ziest 1** (of the sky or a view) unable to be seen clearly because of dust or heat

2 dim or vague: *my memory is a little hazy on this* [origin unknown] **hazily** *adv* **haziness** *n*

Hb haemoglobin

HB *Brit & Austral* (of pencil lead) hard-black: denoting a medium-hard lead

H-bomb *n* short for **hydrogen bomb**

HD high definition

HDD hard disk drive

he *pron* **1** (refers to) a male person or animal ▷ *n* **2** (refers to) a male person or animal: *a he-goat* [Old English *hē*]

> **USAGE** The use of *he* and other masculine pronouns to refer to an unspecified person or to people in general, as in *everybody can do as he likes in this country*, was formerly widespread. In modern usage, however, it is preferable to use gender-neutral alternatives such as *everybody can do as he or she likes in this country* or even *everybody can do as they like in this country*. The latter usage was formerly considered incorrect, but is now acceptable in all but the most formal contexts.

h

He *chem* helium

HE His *or* Her Excellency

head *n* **1** the upper or front part of the body that contains the brain, eyes, mouth, nose, and ears **2** a person's mind and mental abilities: *I haven't any head for figures* **3** the most forward part of a thing: *the head of a queue* **4** the highest part of a thing; upper end: *the head of the pass* **5** something resembling a head in form or function, such as the top of a tool **6** the position of leadership or command **7** the person commanding most authority within a group or an organization **8** *botany* the top part of a plant, where the leaves or flowers grow in a cluster **9** a culmination or crisis: *the matter came to a head in December 1928* **10** the froth on the top of a glass of beer **11** the pus-filled tip of a pimple or boil **12** part of a computer or tape recorder that can read, write, or erase information **13** the source of a river or stream **14** the side of a coin that usually bears a portrait of the head of a monarch, etc. **15** a headland or promontory: *Beachy Head* **16** pressure of water or steam in an enclosed space **17** *pl* **head** a person or animal considered as a unit: *the cost per head of Paris's refuse collection; six hundred head of cattle* **18** a headline or heading **19** *informal* short for **head teacher** **20** *informal* short for **headache** **21 give someone his** *or* **her head** to allow someone greater freedom or responsibility **22 go to one's head** **A** (of an alcoholic drink) to make one slightly drunk **B** to make one conceited: *success has gone to his head* **23 head over heels (in love)** very much (in love) **24 keep one's head** to remain calm **25 not make head nor tail of** not to understand (a problem, etc.) **26 off one's head** *slang* very foolish or mentally unstable **27 on one's own head** at one's own risk **28 over someone's head** **A** to a higher authority: *the taboo of going over the head of their immediate boss* **B** beyond a person's understanding **29 put our** *or* **your** *or* **their heads together** *informal* to consult together **30 turn someone's head** to make someone conceited ▷ *vb* **31** to be at the front or top of: *Barnes headed the list* **32** to be in charge of **33** (often foll. by *for*) to go or cause to go (towards): *to head for the Channel ports* **34** *soccer* to propel (the ball) by striking it with the head **35** to provide with a heading ▷ See also **head off**, **heads** [Old English *hēafod*]

headache *n* **1** a continuous pain in the head **2** *informal* any cause of worry, difficulty, or annoyance: *financial headaches*

head-banger *n Brit, Austral & NZ slang* **1** a person who shakes his or her head violently to the beat of heavy-metal music **2** a foolish or stupid person

headboard *n* a vertical board at the head of a bed

headdress *n* any decorative head covering

headed *adj* **1** having a head or heads: *two-headed; bald-headed* **2** having a heading: *headed notepaper*

header *n* **1** *soccer* the action of striking a ball with the head **2** *informal* a headlong fall or dive

headfirst *adv* **1** with the head foremost **2** quickly and without thinking carefully: *she jumped into marriage headfirst*

headgear *n* hats collectively

head-hunting *n* **1** (of companies) the practice of actively searching for new high-level personnel, often from rival companies **2** the practice among certain peoples of removing the heads of enemies they have killed and preserving them as trophies **head-hunter** *n*

heading *n* **1** a title for a page, chapter, etc. **2** a main division, such as of a speech **3** *mining* a horizontal tunnel

headland *n* a narrow area of land jutting out into a sea

headlight *or* **headlamp** *n* a powerful light on the front of a vehicle

headline *n* **1** a phrase in heavy large type at the top of a newspaper or magazine article indicating the subject **2 headlines** the main points of a television or radio news broadcast ▷ *vb* **-lining, -lined** **3** to provide with a headline **4** to be the main performer in (a show) **headliner** *n*

headlong *adv* **1** with the head foremost; headfirst **2** with great haste and without much thought: *they rushed headlong into buying a house* ▷ *adj* **3** hasty or reckless

headmaster *or fem* **headmistress** *n* the principal of a school

head off *vb* **1** to intercept and force to change direction: *police head off New Age travellers* **2** to prevent or avert: *trying to head off the prospect of civil war* **3** to depart or set out: *to head off to school*

head-on *adv, adj* **1** front foremost: *a head-on collision* **2** with directness or without compromise: *a head-on confrontation with the unions*

headphones *pl n* two small loudspeakers held against the ears, worn to listen to the radio or recorded music without other people hearing it

headquarters *pl n* any centre from which operations are directed

headroom *or* **headway** *n* the space below a roof or bridge which allows an object to pass or stay underneath it without touching it

heads *adv* with the side of a coin uppermost which has a portrait of a head on it

headship *n* the position or state of being a leader, esp. the head teacher of a school
headshrinker *n slang* a psychiatrist
headstall *n* the part of a bridle that fits round a horse's head
head start *n* an initial advantage in a competitive situation
headstone *n* a memorial stone at the head of a grave
headstrong *adj* determined to do something in one's own way and ignoring the advice of others
head teacher *n* the principal of a school
head-to-head *adv, adj informal* in direct competition
headwaters *pl n* the tributary streams of a river in the area in which it rises
headway *n* **1** progress towards achieving something: *have the police made any headway?* **2** motion forward: *we felt our way out to the open sea, barely making headway* **3** same as **headroom**
headwind *n* a wind blowing directly against the course of an aircraft or ship
heady *adj* **headier, headiest 1** (of an experience or period of time) extremely exciting **2** (of alcoholic drink, atmosphere, etc.) strongly affecting the physical senses: *a powerful, heady scent of cologne* **3** rash and impetuous
heal *vb* **1** (of a wound) to repair by natural processes, such as by scar formation **2** to restore (someone) to health **3** to repair (a rift in a personal relationship or an emotional wound) [Old English *hælan*] **healer** *n* **healing** *n, adj*
health *n* **1** the general condition of body and mind: *better health* **2** the state of being bodily and mentally vigorous and free from disease **3** the condition of an organization, society, etc.: *the economic health of the republics* [Old English *hǣlth*]
health camp *n NZ* a camp for children with health or behavioural problems
health centre *n Brit* the surgery and offices of the doctors in a district
health farm *n* a residential establishment for people wishing to improve their health by losing weight, exercising, etc.
health food *n* natural food, organically grown and free from additives
healthful *adj* same as **healthy** (senses 1, 2, 3)
health stamp *n NZ* a postage stamp with a small surcharge used to support health camps
health visitor *n* (in Britain) a nurse employed to visit people in their homes and give help and advice, esp to mothers of preschool children, people with disabilities, and elderly people
healthy *adj* **healthier, healthiest 1** having or showing good health **2** likely to produce good health: *healthy seaside air* **3** functioning well or being sound: *this is a very healthy business to be in* **4** *informal* considerable: *healthy profits* **5** sensible: *a healthy scepticism about his promises* **healthily** *adv* **healthiness** *n*
heap *n* **1** a pile of things lying one on top of another **2** (*often pl*) *informal* a large number or quantity ▹ *adv* **3 heaps** *informal* much: *he was heaps better* ▹ *vb* **4** to collect into a pile **5** to give freely (to): *film roles were heaped on her* [Old English *hēap*]
hear *vb* **hearing, heard 1** to perceive (a sound) with the sense of hearing **2** to listen to: *I didn't want to hear what he had to say* **3** to be informed (of something); receive information (about something): *I hear you mean to join the crusade* **4** *law* to give a hearing to (a case) **5 hear from** to receive a letter or telephone call from **6 hear! hear!** an exclamation of approval **7 hear of** to allow: *she wouldn't hear of it* [Old English *hieran*] **hearer** *n*
hearing *n* **1** the sense by which sound is perceived **2** an opportunity for someone to be listened to **3** the range within which sound can be heard; earshot **4** the investigation of a matter by a court of law
hearing aid *n* a small amplifier worn by a person with hearing difficulties in or behind the ear to improve his or her hearing
hearing dog *n* a dog that has been trained to help a deaf person by alerting him or her to various sounds
hearken *vb archaic* to listen [Old English *heorcnian*]
hearsay *n* gossip or rumour
hearse *n* a large car used to carry a coffin at a funeral [Latin *hirpex* harrow]
heart *n* **1** a hollow muscular organ whose contractions pump the blood throughout the body **2** this organ considered as the centre of emotions, esp. love **3** tenderness or pity: *my heart went out to her* **4** courage or spirit **5** the most central part or important part: *at the heart of Italian motor racing* **6** (of vegetables such as cabbage) the inner compact part **7** the breast: *she held him to her heart* **8** a shape representing the heart, with two rounded lobes at the top meeting in a point at the bottom **9 A** a red heart-shaped symbol on a playing card **B** a card with one or more of these symbols or (*when pl*) the suit of cards so marked **10 break someone's heart** to cause someone to grieve very deeply, esp. by ending a love affair **11 by heart** by memorizing **12 have a change of heart** to experience a profound change of outlook or attitude **13 have one's heart in one's mouth** to be full of apprehension, excitement, or fear **14 have the heart** to have the necessary will or callousness (to do something): *I didn't have the heart to tell him* **15 set one's heart on something** to have something as one's ambition **16 take heart** to become encouraged **17 take something to heart** to take something seriously or be upset about something **18 wear one's heart on one's sleeve** to show one's feelings openly **19 with all one's heart** deeply and sincerely [Old English *heorte*]
heartache *n* very great sadness and emotional suffering
heart attack *n* a sudden severe malfunction of the heart
heartbeat *n* one complete pulsation of the heart
heartbreak *n* intense and overwhelming grief, esp. after the end of a love affair **heartbreaking** *adj* **heartbroken** *adj*
heartburn *n* a burning sensation in the chest caused by indigestion
hearten *vb* to encourage or make cheerful **heartening** *adj*

heart failure *n* **1** a condition in which the heart is unable to pump an adequate amount of blood to the tissues **2** sudden stopping of the heartbeat, resulting in death

heartfelt *adj* sincerely and strongly felt: *heartfelt thanks*

hearth *n* **1** the floor of a fireplace **2** this as a symbol of the home [Old English *heorth*]

heartland *n* **1** the central region of a country or continent: *we headed west towards the heartland of Tibet* **2** the area where the thing specified is most common or strongest: *Germany's industrial heartland*

heartless *adj* unkind or cruel **heartlessly** *adv*

heart-rending *adj* causing great sadness and pity: *a heart-rending story*

hearts and minds *pl n* the collective trust or approval of a body of people such as a populace, esp. for a foreign military force: *we must win the hearts and minds of the people*

heart-searching *n* examination of one's feelings or conscience

h

heartstrings *pl n often facetious* deep emotions: *tugging at our heartstrings with pictures of suffering* [originally referring to the tendons supposed to support the heart]

heart-throb *n* a man, esp. a film or pop star, who is attractive to a lot of people

heart-to-heart *adj* **1** (of a talk) concerned with personal problems or intimate feelings ▷ *n* **2** an intimate conversation

heart-warming *adj* inspiring feelings of happiness: *the heart-warming spectacle of a family reunion*

heartwood *n* the central core of dark hard wood in tree trunks

hearty *adj* **heartier, heartiest 1** warm, friendly, and enthusiastic **2** strongly felt: *a hearty dislike* **3** (of a meal) substantial and nourishing **heartily** *adv*

heat *vb* **1** to make or become hot or warm ▷ *n* **2** the state of being hot **3** the energy transferred as a result of a difference in temperature. Related adjectives: **thermal, calorific 4** hot weather: *he loves the heat of Africa* **5** intensity of feeling: *the heat of their argument* **6** the most intense part: *in the heat of an election campaign* **7** pressure: *political heat on the government* **8** *sport* a preliminary eliminating contest in a competition **9 on** *or* **in heat** (of some female mammals) ready for mating [Old English *hǣtu*] **heating** *n*

heated *adj* impassioned or highly emotional: *a heated debate* **heatedly** *adv*

heater *n* a device for supplying heat

heath *n* **1** *Brit* a large open area, usually with sandy soil, low shrubs, and heather **2** a low-growing evergreen shrub with small bell-shaped pink or purple flowers [Old English *hǣth*]

heathen *old-fashioned* ▷ *n, pl* **-thens** *or* **-then 1** a person who does not believe in an established religion; pagan ▷ *adj* **2** of or relating to heathen peoples [Old English *hǣthen*]

heather *n* a shrub with small bell-shaped flowers growing on heaths and mountains [origin unknown]

Heath Robinson *adj* (of a mechanical device) absurdly complicated in design for a simple function [after William *Heath Robinson*, cartoonist]

heatstroke *n* same as **sunstroke**

heat wave *n* a spell of unusually hot weather

heave *vb* **heaving, heaved 1** to lift or move (something) with a great effort **2** to throw (something heavy) with effort **3** to utter (a sigh) noisily or unhappily **4** to rise and fall heavily **5** *past tense & past participle* **hove** *naut* **A** to move in a specified direction: *heave her bows around and head north* **B** (of a vessel) to pitch or roll **6** to vomit or retch ▷ *n* **7** the act of heaving [Old English *hebban*]

heaven *n* **1** (in some religions) the place where God is believed to live and where those leading good lives are believed to go when they die **2** a place or state of happiness **3 heavens** the sky **4** Also: **heavens** God or the gods, used in exclamatory phrases: *for heaven's sake!* [Old English *heofon*]

heavenly *adj* **1** *informal* wonderful or very enjoyable: *a heavenly meal* **2** of or occurring in space: *a heavenly body* **3** of or relating to heaven

heave to *vb* to stop (a ship) or (of a ship) to stop

heavy *adj* **heavier, heaviest 1** of comparatively great weight **2** with a relatively high density: *lead is a heavy metal* **3** great in degree or amount: *heavy traffic* **4** considerable: *heavy emphasis* **5** hard to fulfil: *an exceptionally heavy demand for this issue* **6** using or consuming a lot of something quickly: *a heavy drinker* **7** deep and loud: *heavy breathing* **8** clumsy and slow: *a heavy lumbering trot* **9** (of a movement or action) with great downward force or pressure: *a heavy blow with a club* **10** solid or fat: *mountain animals acquire a heavy layer of fat* **11** not easily digestible: *a heavy meal* **12** (of cakes or bread) insufficiently raised **13** (of soil) with a high clay content **14** sad or dejected: *you feel heavy or sad afterwards* **15** (of facial features) looking sad and tired **16** (of a situation) serious and causing anxiety or sadness **17** cloudy or overcast: *heavy clouds obscured the sun* **18** (of an industry) engaged in the large-scale manufacture of large objects or extraction of raw materials **19** *military* (of guns, etc.) large and powerful **20** dull and uninteresting: *Helen finds his friends very heavy going* **21** (of music, literature, etc.) difficult to understand or not immediately appealing **22** *slang* (of rock music) loud and having a powerful beat **23** *slang* using, or prepared to use, violence or brutality ▷ *n, pl* **heavies 24** *slang* a large strong man hired to threaten violence or deter others by his presence **25 A** a villainous role **B** an actor who plays such a part **26 the heavies** *informal* serious newspapers ▷ *adv* **27** heavily: *time hung heavy* [Old English *hefig*] **heavily** *adv* **heaviness** *n*

heavy-duty *adj* made to withstand hard wear, bad weather, etc.

heavy-handed *adj* acting forcefully and without care and thought

heavy-hearted *adj* sad and discouraged

heavy hydrogen *n* same as **deuterium**

heavy metal *n* a type of very loud rock music featuring guitar riffs
heavy water *n* water formed of oxygen and deuterium
heavyweight *n* **1** a professional boxer weighing over 195 pounds (88.5 kg) or an amateur weighing over 91 kg **2** a person who is heavier than average **3** *informal* an important or highly influential person
Heb. *or* **Hebr.** Hebrew (language)
Hebraic (hib-**ray**-ik) *adj* of the Hebrews or their language or culture
Hebrew *n* **1** the ancient language of the Hebrews, revived as the official language of Israel **2** a member of an ancient Semitic people; an Israelite ▷ *adj* **3** of the Hebrews or their language [Hebrew *'ibhrī* one from beyond (the river)]
heck *interj* a mild exclamation of surprise, irritation, etc. [euphemistic for *hell*]
heckle *vb* **-ling, -led** to interrupt (a public speaker) with comments, questions, or taunts [form of *hackle*] **heckler** *n*
hectare *n* a unit of measure equal to one hundred ares (10 000 square metres or 2.471 acres) [French]
hectic *adj* involving a lot of rushed activity [Greek *hektikos* hectic, consumptive]
hector *vb* **1** to bully or torment ▷ *n* **2** a blustering bully [after *Hector*, legendary Trojan warrior]
he'd he had *or* he would
hedge *n* **1** a row of shrubs or bushes forming a boundary **2** a barrier or protection against something, esp. against the risk of loss on an investment ▷ *vb* **hedging, hedged 3** to avoid making a decision by making noncommittal statements **4 hedge against** to guard against the risk of loss in (a bet or disagreement), by supporting the opposition as well [Old English *hecg*]
hedge fund *n finance* a speculative fund which offers substantial returns for high-risk investments
hedgehog *n* a small mammal with a protective covering of spines
hedgerow *n* a hedge of shrubs or low trees bordering a field
hedge sparrow *n* a small brownish songbird
hedonism *n* the doctrine that the pursuit of pleasure is the most important thing in life [Greek *hēdonē* pleasure] **hedonist** *n* **hedonistic** *adj*
heebie-jeebies *pl n* **the heebie-jeebies** *slang* nervous apprehension [coined by W. De Beck, cartoonist]
heed *formal* ▷ *n* **1** careful attention: *he must have taken heed of her warning* ▷ *vb* **2** to pay close attention to (a warning or piece of advice) [Old English *hēdan*]
heedless *adj* taking no notice; careless or thoughtless **heedlessly** *adv*
heehaw *interj* a representation of the braying sound of a donkey
heel¹ *n* **1** the back part of the foot **2** the part of a stocking or sock designed to fit the heel **3** the part of a shoe supporting the heel **4** *slang* a contemptible person **5 at one's heels** following closely behind one **6 down at heel** untidy and in poor condition **7 kick** *or* **cool one's heels** to be kept waiting **8 take to one's heels** to run off **9 to heel** under control, such as a dog walking by a person's heel ▷ *vb* **10** to repair or replace the heel of (a shoe or boot) [Old English *hēla*]
heel² *vb* to lean to one side [Old English *hieldan*]
heelball *n* **A** a mixture of beeswax and lampblack used by shoemakers **B** a similar substance used to take brass rubbings
heeler *n Austral & NZ* a dog that herds cattle by biting at their heels
hefty *adj* **heftier, heftiest** *informal* **1** large in size, weight, or amount **2** forceful and vigorous: *a hefty slap on the back* **3** involving a large amount of money: *a hefty fine*
hegemony (hig-**em**-on-ee) *n, pl* **-nies** domination of one state, country, or class within a group of others [Greek *hēgemonia*]
Hegira *n* the flight of Mohammed from Mecca to Medina in 622 AD, regarded as being the starting point of the Muslim era [Arabic *hijrah* flight]
heifer (**hef**-fer) *n* a young cow [Old English *heahfore*]
height *n* **1** the vertical distance from the bottom of something to the top **2** the vertical distance of a place above sea level **3** relatively great distance from bottom to top **4** the topmost point; summit **5** the period of greatest intensity: *the height of the shelling* **6** an extreme example: *the height of luxury* **7 heights** extremes: *dizzy heights of success* [Old English *hīehthu*]
heighten *vb* to make or become higher or more intense **heightened** *adj*
height of land *n US & Canad* a ridge of high ground dividing two river basins
heinous *adj* evil and shocking [Old French *haineus*]
heir *or fem* **heiress** *n* the person legally succeeding to the property of a deceased person [Latin *heres*]
heir apparent *n, pl* **heirs apparent 1** *law* a person whose right to succeed to certain property cannot be defeated **2** a person whose succession to a role or position is extremely likely: *heir apparent to the England captaincy*
heirloom *n* an object that has been in a family for generations [HEIR + *lome* tool]
heir presumptive *n property law* a person who expects to succeed to an estate but whose right may be defeated by the birth of an heir nearer in blood to the ancestor
heist *n slang* a robbery [from HOIST]
hejab *n* another spelling of **hijab**
held *vb* the past of **hold¹**
helical *adj* of or like a helix
helicopter *n* an aircraft, powered by rotating overhead blades, that is capable of hovering, vertical flight, and horizontal flight in any direction [Greek *helix* spiral + *pteron* wing]
helicopter parent *n* a parent who is excessively involved in all areas of his or her child's life [from the idea of a parent hovering over a child]
heliograph *n* an instrument with mirrors and a shutter used for sending messages in Morse code by reflecting the sun's rays [Greek *hēlios* sun + -GRAPHY]

heliotrope *n* a plant with small fragrant purple flowers [Greek *hēlios* sun + *trepein* to turn]
heliport *n* an airport for helicopters [*heli(copter)* + *port*]
helium (heel-ee-um) *n chem* a very light colourless odourless inert gas. Symbol: **He** [Greek *hēlios* sun, because first detected in the solar spectrum]
helix (heel-iks) *n, pl* **helices** (hell-iss-seez) *or* **helixes** a spiral [Greek: spiral]
hell *n* **1** (in Christianity and some other religions) the place or state of eternal punishment of the wicked after death **2** (in various religions and cultures) the abode of the spirits of the dead **3** *informal* a situation that causes suffering or extreme difficulty: *war is hell* **4 come hell or high water** *informal* whatever difficulties may arise **5 for the hell of it** *informal* for the fun of it **6 from hell** *informal* denoting a person or thing that is particularly bad or alarming: *the neighbour from hell* **7 give someone hell** *informal* **A** to give someone a severe reprimand or punishment **B** to be a torment to someone **8 hell for leather** at great speed **9 the hell** *informal* **A** used for emphasis: *what the hell* **B** an expression of strong disagreement: *the hell you do!* ▷ *interj* **10** *informal* an exclamation of anger or surprise [Old English]
he'll he will *or* he shall
hellbent *adj informal* rashly intent: *hellbent on revenge*
hellebore *n* a plant with white flowers that bloom in winter [Greek *helleboros*]
Hellene *n* a Greek
Hellenic *adj* **1** of the Greeks or their language **2** of or relating to ancient Greece during the classical period (776–323 BC)
Hellenism *n* **1** the principles and ideals of classical Greek civilization **2** the spirit or national character of the Greeks **Hellenist** *n*
Hellenistic *adj* of Greek civilization during the period 323–30 BC
hellfire *n* the torment of hell, imagined as eternal fire
hellish *adj informal* very unpleasant
hello, hallo *or* **hullo** *interj* **1** an expression of greeting or surprise **2** a call used to attract attention ▷ *n, pl* **-los 3** the act of saying 'hello' [French *holà*]
Hell's Angel *n* a member of a motorcycle gang noted for their lawless behaviour
helm *n* **1** *naut* the tiller or wheel for steering a ship **2 at the helm** in a position of leadership or control [Old English *helma*] **helmsman** *n*
helmet *n* a piece of protective headgear worn by motorcyclists, soldiers, police officers, divers, etc. [Old French]
helot *n* (in ancient Greece) a serf or slave [Greek *Heilōtes* serfs, literally: inhabitants of Helos]
help *vb* **1** to assist (someone to do something) **2** to contribute to: *to help Latin America's economies* **3** to improve a situation: *a felt or rubber underlay will help* **4 A** to refrain from: *I couldn't help feeling foolish* **B** to be responsible for: *you must not blame him, he simply can't help it* **5** to serve (a customer) **6 help oneself** to take something, esp. food or drink, for oneself, without being served ▷ *n* **7** the act of helping **8** a person or thing that helps, esp. a farm worker or domestic servant **9** a remedy: *there's no help for it* ▷ *interj* **10** used to call for assistance ▷ See also **help out** [Old English *helpan*] **helper** *n*
helpful *adj* giving help **helpfully** *adv* **helpfulness** *n*
helping *n* a single portion of food
helpless *adj* **1** unable to manage independently **2** made weak: *it reduced her to helpless laughter* **helplessly** *adv* **helplessness** *n*
helpline *n* a telephone line set aside for callers to contact an organization for help with a problem
helpmate *or* **helpmeet** *n* a companion and helper, esp. a husband or wife
help out *vb* to assist (someone) by sharing the burden or cost of something
helter-skelter *adj* **1** hurried or disorganized ▷ *adv* **2** in a hurried or disorganized manner ▷ *n* **3** *Brit* a high spiral slide at a fairground [probably imitative]
hem[1] *n* **1** the bottom edge of a garment, folded under and stitched down ▷ *vb* **hemming, hemmed 2** to provide (a garment) with a hem ▷ See also **hem in** [Old English *hemm*]
hem[2] *n* **1** a representation of the sound of clearing the throat, used to gain attention ▷ *vb* **hemming, hemmed 2** to make this sound **3 hem and haw** See **haw**[2]
he-man *n, pl* **-men** *informal* a strong man, esp. one who shows off his strength
hemi- *prefix* half: *hemisphere* [Greek]
hem in *vb* to surround and prevent from moving
hemipterous *or* **hemipteran** *adj* of an order of insects with sucking or piercing mouthparts [Greek *hēmi* half + *pteron* wing]
hemisphere *n* one half of a sphere, esp. of the earth (**northern** and **southern hemisphere**) or of the brain **hemispherical** *adj*
hemline *n* the level to which the hem of a skirt or dress hangs: *a mid-calf hemline*
hemlock *n* a poisonous drug derived from a plant with spotted stems and small white flowers [Old English *hymlic*]
hemp *n* **1** an Asian plant with tough fibres **2** the fibre of this plant, used to make canvas and rope **3** a narcotic drug obtained from this plant [Old English *hænep*] **hempen** *adj*
hen *n* the female of any bird, esp. the domestic fowl [Old English *henn*]
henbane *n* a poisonous plant with sticky hairy leaves
hence *adv* **1** for this reason; therefore **2** from this time: *two weeks hence* **3** *archaic* from here [Old English *hionane*]
henceforth *or* **henceforward** *adv* from now on
henchman *or fem* **henchwoman** *n, pl* **-men** *or* **-women** a person employed by someone powerful to carry out orders [Middle English *hengestman*]
henge *n* a circular monument, often containing a circle of stones, dating from the Neolithic and Bronze Ages [from *Stonehenge*]
henna *n* **1** a reddish dye, obtained from a shrub or tree of Asia and N Africa which is used to colour hair ▷ *vb* **2** to dye (the hair) with henna [Arabic *hinnā'*]

hen night *or* **hen party** *n informal* a party for women only, esp. held for a woman shortly before she is married
henpecked *adj* (of a man) harassed by the persistent nagging of his wife
henry *n, pl* **-ry, -ries** *or* **-rys** the SI unit of electric inductance [after Joseph *Henry*, physicist]
hepatic *adj* of the liver [Greek *hēpar* liver]
hepatitis *n* inflammation of the liver, causing fever, jaundice, and weakness
Hephaestus *n Greek myth* the god of fire
hepta- *combining form* seven: *heptameter*
heptagon *n geom* a figure with seven sides [Greek *heptagōnos* having seven angles] **heptagonal** *adj*
heptathlon *n* an athletic contest for women in which athletes compete in seven different events
her *pron* **1** (refers to) a female person or animal: *he loves her* **2** (refers to) things personified as feminine, such as ships and nations ▹ *adj* **3** of, belonging to, or associated with her: *her hair* [Old English *hire*]
USAGE See at **me**'.
Hera *or* **Here** *n Greek myth* the queen of the gods
herald *n* **1** a person who announces important news **2** *often literary* a forerunner ▹ *vb* **3** to announce or signal the approach of: *his arrival was heralded by excited barking* [Germanic] **heraldic** *adj*
heraldry *n, pl* **-ries** the study of coats of arms and family trees
herb *n* **1** an aromatic plant that is used for flavouring in cookery, and in medicine **2** *botany* a seed-bearing plant whose parts above ground die back at the end of the growing season [Latin *herba* grass, green plants] **herbal** *adj* **herby** *adj*
herbaceous *adj* designating plants that are soft-stemmed rather than woody
herbaceous border *n* a flower bed that contains perennials rather than annuals
herbage *n* herbaceous plants collectively, esp. those on which animals graze
herbalist *n* a person who grows or specializes in the use of medicinal herbs
herbicide *n* a substance used to destroy plants, esp. weeds [Latin *herba* plant + *caedere* to kill]
herbivore (**her**-biv-vore) *n* **1** an animal that feeds only on plants **2** *informal* a liberal or idealistic person [Latin *herba* plant + *vorare* to swallow] **herbivorous** (her-**biv**-or-uss) *adj*
herculean (her-kew-**lee**-an) *adj* **1** (of a task) requiring tremendous effort or strength **2** (*sometimes cap*) resembling Hercules, hero of classical myth, in strength or courage
herd *n* **1** a large group of mammals, esp. cattle, living and feeding together **2** *often derogatory* a large group of people ▹ *vb* **3** to collect or be collected into, or as if into, a herd [Old English *heord*]
herd instinct *n psychol* the inborn tendency to associate with others and follow the group's behaviour
herdsman *n, pl* **-men** *chiefly Brit* a man who looks after a herd of animals
here *adv* **1** in, at, or to this place, point, case, or respect: *I am pleased to be back here* **2** **here and there** at several places in or throughout an area **3** **here's to** a convention used in proposing a toast **4** **neither here nor there** of no relevance ▹ *n* **5** this place: *they leave here tonight* [Old English *hēr*]
hereabouts *or* **hereabout** *adv* in this region
hereafter *adv* **1** *formal or law* in a subsequent part of this document, matter, or case **2** at some time in the future ▹ *n* **3** **the hereafter** **A** life after death **B** the future
hereby *adv* (used in official statements and documents) by means of or as a result of this
hereditable *adj* same as **heritable**
hereditary *adj* **1** passed on genetically from one generation to another **2** *law* passed on to succeeding generations by inheritance
heredity (hir-**red**-it-ee) *n, pl* **-ties** the passing on from one generation to another of genetic factors that determine individual characteristics [Latin *hereditas* inheritance]
Hereford *n* a hardy breed of beef cattle which has a reddish body with white markings [after *Hereford*, English city]
herein *adv formal or law* in this place, matter, or document
hereinafter *adv formal or law* from this point on in this place, matter, or document
hereof *adv formal or law* of or concerning this
heresy (**herr**-iss-ee) *n, pl* **-sies** **1** an opinion contrary to the principles of a religion **2** any belief thought to be contrary to official or established theory [Greek *hairein* to choose]
heretic (**herr**-it-ik) *n* **1** *chiefly RC Church* a person who maintains beliefs contrary to the established teachings of the Church **2** a person who holds unorthodox opinions in any field **heretical** (hir-**ret**-ik-kl) *adj*
hereto *adv formal or law* to this place, matter, or document
heretofore *adv formal or law* until now
hereupon *adv* following immediately after this; at this stage
herewith *adv formal* together with this: *a schedule of the event is appended herewith*
heritable *adj* capable of being inherited
heritage *n* **1** something inherited at birth **2** anything that has been carried over from the past or handed down by tradition **3** the evidence of the past, such as historical sites, considered as the inheritance of present-day society
hermaphrodite (her-**maf**-roe-dite) *n* an animal, flower, or person that has both male and female reproductive organs [after *Hermaphroditus*, son of Hermes and Aphrodite, who merged with the nymph Salmacis to form one body] **hermaphroditic** *adj*
Hermes *n Greek myth* the messenger of the gods
hermetic *adj* sealed so as to be airtight [after the Greek god *Hermes Trismegistus*, traditionally the inventor of a magic seal] **hermetically** *adv*
hermit *n* a person living in solitude, esp. for religious reasons [Greek *erēmos* lonely]
hermitage *n* **1** the home of a hermit **2** any retreat
hermit crab *n* a small crab that lives in the empty shells of other shellfish

h

hernia *n* protrusion of an organ or part through the lining of the body cavity in which it is normally situated [Latin]

hero *n, pl* **-roes 1** the principal male character in a novel, play, etc. **2** a man of exceptional courage, nobility, etc. **3** a man who is idealized for having superior qualities in any field [Greek *hērōs*]

heroic *adj* **1** brave and courageous: *heroic work by the army engineers* **2** of, like, or befitting a hero **heroically** *adv*

heroics *pl n* behaviour or language considered too melodramatic or extravagant for the particular situation in which they are used

heroin *n* a highly addictive drug derived from morphine [probably from *hero,* referring to its aggrandizing effect on the personality]

heroine *n* **1** the principal female character in a novel, play, etc. **2** a woman of exceptional courage, nobility, etc. **3** a woman who is idealized for having superior qualities in any field

h

heroism (**herr**-oh-izz-um) *n* great courage and bravery

heron *n* a wading bird with a long neck, long legs, and grey or white feathers [Old French *hairon*]

heronry *n, pl* **-ries** a colony of breeding herons

hero worship *n* **1** admiration for heroes or idealized people ▷ *vb* **hero-worship, -shipping, -shipped** *or US* **-shiping, -shiped 2** to feel admiration or adulation for (someone)

herpes (**her**-peez) *n* any of several inflammatory skin diseases, including shingles and cold sores [Greek *herpein* to creep]

herpes simplex *n* an acute viral disease causing clusters of watery blisters [New Latin: simple herpes]

herpes zoster *n* same as **shingles** [New Latin: girdle herpes]

Herr (hair) *n, pl* **Herren** a German form of address equivalent to *Mr* [German]

herring *n, pl* **-rings** *or* **-ring** a food fish of northern seas, with a long silver-coloured body [Old English *hǣring*]

herringbone *n* a zigzag pattern consisting of short lines of V shapes

herring gull *n* a common gull that has white and grey feathers with black-tipped wings

hers *pron* **1** something belonging to her: *hers is the highest paid part-time job; the money which is rightfully hers* **2 of hers** belonging to her

herself *pron* **1 A** the reflexive form of *she* or *her*: *she busied herself with work* **B** used for emphasis: *none other than The Great Mother herself* **2** her normal self: *she hasn't been herself all week*

Herts Hertfordshire

hertz *n, pl* **hertz** the SI unit of frequency, equal to one cycle per second [after H. R. *Hertz,* physicist]

he's he is *or* he has

hESC human embryonic stem cell

hesitant *adj* doubtful and unsure in speech or action **hesitancy** *n* **hesitantly** *adv*

hesitate *vb* **-tating, -tated 1** to be slow and uncertain in acting **2** to be reluctant (to do something): *I hesitate to use the word 'squandered'* **3** to pause during speech because of uncertainty [Latin *haesitare*] **hesitation** *n*

hessian *n* a coarse jute fabric similar to sacking [after Hesse, Germany]

hetero- *combining form* other, another, or different: *heterosexual* [Greek *heteros* other]

heterodox *adj* different from established or accepted doctrines or beliefs [HETERO- + Greek *doxa* opinion] **heterodoxy** *n*

heterodyne *electronics* ▷ *vb* **-dyning, -dyned 1** to combine (two alternating signals) so as to produce two signals with frequencies corresponding to the sum and the difference of the original frequencies ▷ *adj* **2** produced or operating by heterodyning two signals [HETERO- + Greek *dunamis* power]

heterogeneous (het-er-oh-**jean**-ee-uss) *adj* varied in content; composed of different parts: *a heterogeneous collection of art* [HETERO- + Greek *genos* sort] **heterogeneity** *n*

heteromorphic *adj biol* **1** differing from the normal form **2** (esp. of insects) having different forms at different stages of the life cycle [HETERO- + Greek *morphē* form] **heteromorphism** *n*

heterosexual *n* **1** a person who is sexually attracted to members of the opposite sex ▷ *adj* **2** (of a person) sexually attracted to members of the opposite sex **3** (of a sexual relationship) between a man and a woman **heterosexuality** *n*

heterozygous *adj biol* having two different alleles of the same gene [HETERO- + Greek *zugōtos* yoked]

het up *adj informal* agitated or excited: *he was very het up about the traffic* [dialect for *heated*]

heuristic (hew-**rist**-ik) *adj* (of a method of teaching) allowing students to learn things for themselves by trial and error [Greek *heuriskein* to discover]

hew *vb* **hewing, hewed, hewed** *or* **hewn 1** to chop or cut with an axe **2** to carve (something) from a substance: *a tunnel hewn out of the living rock* [Old English *hēawan*]

hex *n* **1** short for **hexadecimal notation** ▷ *adj* **2** of or relating to hexadecimal notation: *hex code*

hexa- *combining form* six: *hexameter* [Greek *hex* six]

hexadecimal notation *n* a number system with a base of 16, the numbers 10–15 being represented by the letters A–F

hexagon *n geom* a figure with six sides **hexagonal** *adj*

hexagram *n geom* a star formed by extending the sides of a regular hexagon to meet at six points

hexameter (hek-**sam**-it-er) *n prosody* a verse line consisting of six metrical feet

hey *interj* **1** an expression of surprise or for catching attention **2 hey presto!** an exclamation used by conjurors at the climax of a trick [imitative]

heyday *n* the time of most power, popularity, or success: *the heyday of classical composition* [probably based on *hey*]

Hf *chem* hafnium

HFEA *Brit* Human Fertilization and Embryology Authority

Hg *chem* mercury

HGV (in Britain, formerly) heavy goods vehicle
HH **1** His (*or* Her) Highness **2** His Holiness (title of the pope)
hi *interj informal* hello [probably from *how are you?*]
HI Hawaii
hiatus (hie-**ay**-tuss) *n, pl* **-tuses** *or* **-tus** a pause or an interruption in continuity: *diplomatic relations restored after a four-year hiatus* [Latin: gap, cleft]
hiatus hernia *n* protrusion of the stomach through the diaphragm at the hole for the gullet
Hib *n* Haemophilus influenzae type b: a vaccine against a specific type of bacterial meningitis, administered to children under four years of age
hibernate *vb* **-nating, -nated** (of some animals) to pass the winter in a resting state in which heartbeat, temperature, and breathing rate are very low [Latin *hibernare* to spend the winter] **hibernation** *n*
Hibernia *n poetic* Ireland **Hibernian** *adj, n*
hibiscus *n, pl* **-cuses** a tropical plant with large brightly coloured flowers [Greek *hibiskos* marsh mallow]
hiccup *n* **1** a spasm of the breathing organs with a sharp coughlike sound **2 hiccups** the state of having such spasms **3** *informal* a minor difficulty ▷ *vb* **-cuping, -cuped** *or* **-cupping, -cupped** **4** to make a hiccup or hiccups. Also: **hiccough** [imitative]
hick *n US, Austral & NZ informal* an unsophisticated country person [after *Hick*, familiar form of *Richard*]
hickory *n, pl* **-ries** **1** a North American tree with edible nuts **2** the hard wood of this tree [Native American *pawcohiccora*]
hidden *vb* **1** a past participle of **hide**[1] ▷ *adj* **2** not easily noticed or obscure: *hidden dangers* **3** difficult to find
hidden agenda *n* a set of motives or intentions concealed from others who might object to them
hide[1] *vb* **hiding, hid, hidden** *or* **hid** **1** to conceal (oneself or an object) from view or discovery: *in an attempt to hide from his wife* **2** to keep (information or one's feelings) secret **3** to obscure or cover (something) from view: *the collar hid his face* ▷ *n* **4** *Brit* a place of concealment, disguised to appear as part of its surroundings, used by hunters, bird-watchers, etc. [Old English *hȳdan*]
hide[2] *n* the skin of an animal, either tanned or raw [Old English *hȳd*]
hide-and-seek *n* a game in which one player covers his or her eyes while the others hide, and that player then tries to find them
hideaway *n* a hiding place or secluded spot
hidebound *adj* restricted by petty rules and unwilling to accept new ideas
hideous (**hid**-ee-uss) *adj* extremely ugly or unpleasant [Old French *hisdos*]
hide-out *n* a hiding place
hiding[1] *n* **1** a state of concealment: *in hiding* **2 hiding place** a place of concealment
hiding[2] *n informal* a severe beating
hie *vb* **hieing** *or* **hying, hied** *archaic or poetic* to hurry [Old English *hīgian* to strive]
hierarchy (**hire**-ark-ee) *n, pl* **-chies** **1** a system of people or things arranged in a graded order **2 the hierarchy** the people in power in any organization [Late Greek *hierarkhēs* high priest] **hierarchical** *adj*
hieroglyphic (hire-oh-**gliff**-ik) *adj* **1** of or relating to a form of writing using picture symbols, as used in ancient Egypt ▷ *n also* **hieroglyph** **2** a symbol that is difficult to decipher **3** a picture or symbol representing an object, idea, or sound [Greek *hieros* holy + *gluphein* to carve]
hieroglyphics *n* **1** a form of writing, as used in ancient Egypt, in which pictures or symbols are used to represent objects, ideas, or sounds **2** writing that is difficult to decipher
hi-fi *n informal* **1** a set of high-quality sound-reproducing equipment **2** short for **high fidelity** ▷ *adj* **3** producing high-quality sound: *a hi-fi amplifier*
higgledy-piggledy *informal* ▷ *adj, adv* in a muddle [origin unknown]
high *adj* **1** being a relatively great distance from top to bottom: *a high stone wall* **2** being at a relatively great distance above sea level: *a high village* **3** being a specified distance from top to bottom: *three feet high* **4** coming up to a specified level: *waist-high* **5** being at its peak: *high summer* **6** of greater than average height: *a high ceiling* **7** greater than usual in intensity or amount: *high blood pressure; high fees* **8** (of a sound) acute in pitch **9** (of food) slightly decomposed, regarded as enhancing the flavour of game **10** towards the top of a scale of importance or quality: *high fashion* **11** intensely emotional: *high drama* **12** very cheerful: *high spirits* **13** *informal* under the influence of alcohol or drugs **14** luxurious or extravagant: *high life* **15** advanced in complexity: *high finance* **16** formal and elaborate: *High Mass* **17 high and dry** abandoned in a difficult situation **18 high and mighty** *informal* too confident and full of self-importance **19 high opinion** a favourable opinion ▷ *adv* **20** at or to a height: *flying high* ▷ *n* **21** a high level **22** same as **anticyclone** **23 on a high** *informal* **A** in a state of intoxication by alcohol or drugs **B** in a state of great excitement and happiness [Old English *hēah*]
High Arctic *n* the regions of Canada, esp. the northern islands, within the Arctic Circle
highball *n chiefly US* a long iced drink consisting of whisky with soda water or ginger ale
highbrow *often derogatory* ▷ *adj* **1** concerned with serious, intellectual subjects ▷ *n* **2** a person with such tastes
highchair *n* a long-legged chair with a table-like tray, used for a child at meal times
High Church *n* **1** the movement within the Church of England stressing the importance of ceremony and ritual ▷ *adj* **High-Church** **2** of or relating to this movement
high commissioner *n* the senior diplomatic representative sent by one Commonwealth country to another
high country *n* **the high country** NZ sheep pastures in the foothills of the Southern Alps
High Court *n* (in England, Wales, Australia, and New Zealand) the supreme court dealing with civil and criminal law cases

h

high definition *n* a digital technology that produces a television picture with superior definition to the standard
high-energy *adj* providing or inspiring a lot of energy: *a high-energy drink; a high-energy workout*
Higher *n* **1** (in Scotland) the advanced level of the Scottish Certificate of Education **2** a pass in a subject at this level: *she has got four Highers*
higher education *n* education at universities and colleges
higher-up *n informal* a person of higher rank
highest common factor *n* the largest number that divides equally into each member of a group of numbers
high explosive *n* an extremely powerful chemical explosive, such as TNT or gelignite
highfalutin (hie-fa-**loot**-in) *adj informal* (of behaviour) excessively grand or pompous [*-falutin* perhaps variant of *fluting*]
high fidelity *n* **1** the electronic reproduction of sound with little or no distortion ▷ *adj* **high-fidelity 2** able to produce sound with little or no distortion: *high-fidelity headphones*
high-five *n slang* a gesture of greeting or congratulation in which two people slap raised palms together
high-flown *adj* extravagant or pretentious: *high-flown language*
high-flyer *or* **high-flier** *n* **1** a person who is extremely ambitious **2** a person of great ability in a career **high-flying** *adj, n*
high frequency *n* a radio frequency between 30 and 3 megahertz
High German *n* the standard German language
high-handed *adj* using authority in an unnecessarily forceful way **high-handedness** *n*
high jump *n* **the high jump A** an athletic event in which competitors have to jump over a high bar **B** *Brit & Austral informal* a severe reprimand or punishment: *I was for the high jump again*
Highland *adj* of or denoting the Highlands, a mountainous region of NW Scotland **Highlander** *n*
Highland cattle *n* a breed of cattle with shaggy reddish-brown hair and long horns
Highland fling *n* an energetic Scottish solo dance
highlands *pl n* relatively high ground
high-level language *n* a computer programming language that is close to human language
highlight *n* **1** Also called: **high spot** the most exciting or memorable part of something **2** an area of the lightest tone in a painting or photograph **3** a lightened streak in the hair produced by bleaching ▷ *vb* **4** to give emphasis to: *the prime minister repeatedly highlighted the need for lower pay*
highlighter *n* **1** a cosmetic cream or powder applied to the face to highlight the cheekbones or eyes **2** a fluorescent felt-tip pen used as a marker to emphasize a section of text without obscuring it
highly *adv* **1** extremely: *highly desirable* **2** towards the top of a scale of importance, admiration, or respect: *highly paid doctors*
highly strung *or US & Canad* **high-strung** *adj* tense and easily upset
high-maintenance *adj* **1** (of a piece of equipment, motor vehicle, etc.) requiring regular maintenance to keep it in working order **2** *informal* (of a person) requiring a high level of care and attention; demanding
High Mass *n* a solemn and elaborate Mass
high-minded *adj* having high moral principles
Highness *n* (preceded by *Your, His* or *Her*) a title used to address or refer to a royal person
high-octane *adj* **1** (of petrol) having a high octane number **2** *informal* dynamic or intense: *a high-octane lifestyle*
high-pitched *adj* (of a sound, esp. a voice) pitched high in tone
high-powered *adj* **1** (of machinery or equipment) powerful, advanced, and sophisticated **2** important, successful, or influential: *a high-powered business contact*
high-pressure *adj informal* (of selling) persuasive in an aggressive and persistent manner
high priest *or fem* **high priestess** *n* the head of a cult or movement
high-rise *adj* **1** of or relating to a building that has many storeys: *a high-rise estate* ▷ *n* **2** a building that has many storeys
high-risk *adj* denoting a group or area that is particularly subject to a danger
highroad *n* a main road
high school *n* a secondary school
high seas *pl n* the open seas, which are outside the authority of any one nation
high season *n* the most popular time of year at a holiday resort, etc.
high-spirited *adj* lively and wishing to have fun and excitement
high street *n* the main street of a town, usually containing the most important shops
high tea *n Brit* an early evening meal consisting of a cooked dish, bread, cakes, and tea
high-tech *adj* same as **hi-tech**
high technology *n* any type of sophisticated industrial process, esp. one involving electronics
high-tension *adj* (of electricity cable) carrying a powerful current
high tide *n* the sea at its highest level on the coast
high time *adv informal* the latest possible time: *it's high time we mended that shelf*
high treason *n* a serious crime directly affecting a sovereign or state
high-water mark *n* **1** the level reached by sea water at high tide or a river in flood **2** the highest or most successful stage: *the premature high-water mark of his career*
highway *n* **1** a public road that everyone may use **2** *US, Canad, Austral & NZ* a main road, esp. one that connects towns
Highway Code *n* (in Britain) a booklet of regulations and recommendations for all road users
highwayman *n, pl* **-men** (formerly) a robber, usually on horseback, who held up travellers on public roads

hijab *or* **hejab** *n* a covering for the head and face, worn by some Muslim women [Arabic: curtain]
hijack *vb* **1** to seize control of or divert (a vehicle or aircraft) while travelling ▷ *n* **2** an instance of hijacking: *Indonesian ferry hijack ends* [origin unknown] **hijacker** *n*
hike *vb* **hiking, hiked 1** to walk a long way in the country, usually for pleasure **2** to raise (prices) **3** to pull up with a quick movement: *he hiked up his trouser legs* ▷ *n* **4** a long walk **5** a rise in price [origin unknown] **hiker** *n*
hilarious *adj* very funny [Greek *hilaros* cheerful] **hilariously** *adv* **hilarity** *n*
hill *n* **1** a natural elevation of the earth's surface, less high than a mountain **2** a heap or mound **3** an incline or slope [Old English *hyll*] **hilly** *adj*
hillbilly *n, pl* **-lies 1** *usually derogatory* an unsophisticated person from the mountainous areas in the southeastern US **2** same as **country and western** [*hill* + *Billy* (the nickname)]
hillock *n* a small hill or mound
hilt *n* **1** the handle or shaft of a sword, dagger, or knife **2 to the hilt** to the full: *he plays the role to the hilt* [Old English]
hilum *n, pl* **-la** *botany* a scar on a seed marking its point of attachment to the seed vessel [Latin: trifle]
him *pron* refers to a male person or animal: *I greeted him at the hotel; I must send him a note of congratulation* [Old English]
USAGE See at **me**[1].
himself *pron* **1 A** the reflexive form of *he* or *him*: *he secretly asked himself* **B** used for emphasis: *approved of by the Creator himself* **2** his normal self: *he was almost himself again*
hind[1] *adj* **hinder, hindmost** situated at the back: *a hind leg* [Old English *hindan* at the back]
hind[2] *n, pl* **hinds** *or* **hind** the female of the deer, esp. the red deer [Old English]
hinder[1] (hin-der) *vb* to get in the way of (someone or something) [Old English *hindrian*]
hinder[2] (hine-der) *adj* situated at the back [Old English]
Hindi *n* **1** a language or group of dialects of N central India **2** a formal literary dialect of this language, the official language of India [Old Persian *Hindu* the river Indus]
hindmost *adj* furthest back; last
hindquarters *pl n* the rear of a four-legged animal
hindrance *n* **1** an obstruction or snag **2** the act of hindering
hindsight *n* the ability to understand, after something has happened, what should have been done or what caused the event
Hindu *n, pl* **-dus 1** a person who practises Hinduism ▷ *adj* **2** of Hinduism
Hinduism *n* the dominant religion of India, which involves the worship of many gods and belief in reincarnation
Hindustani *n* a group of northern Indian languages that includes Hindi and Urdu
hinge *n* **1** a device for holding together two parts, such as a door and its frame, so that one can swing freely ▷ *vb* **hinging, hinged 2** to join or open (something) by means of a hinge **3 hinge on** to depend on: *billions of dollars of western aid hinged on the outcome of the talks* [probably Germanic] **hinged** *adj*
Hinglish *n* a variety of English incorporating elements of Hindi [blend of HINDI + ENGLISH]
hinny *n, pl* **-nies** the offspring of a male horse and a female donkey [Greek *hinnos*]
hint *n* **1** a suggestion given in an indirect or subtle manner **2** a helpful piece of advice **3** a small amount: *a hint of irony* ▷ *vb* **4** (sometimes foll. by *at*) to suggest indirectly: *a solution has been hinted at by a few politicians* [origin unknown]
hinterland *n* **1** land lying behind a coast or the shore of a river **2** an area near and dependent on a large city, esp. a port [German]
hip[1] *n* either side of the body below the waist and above the thigh [Old English *hype*]
hip[2] *n* the berry-like brightly coloured fruit of a rose bush. Also called: **rosehip** [Old English *hēope*]
hip[3] *interj* an exclamation used to introduce cheers: *hip, hip, hurrah* [origin unknown]
hip[4] *adj* **hipper, hippest** *slang* aware of or following the latest trends [variant of earlier *hep*]
hip bath *n* a portable bath in which the bather sits
hipbone *n* either of the two bones that form the sides of the pelvis
hip flask *n* a small metal flask for whisky, brandy, etc.
hip-hop *n* a US pop-culture movement originating in the 1980s, comprising rap music, graffiti, and break dancing
hippie *n* same as **hippy**[2]
hippo *n, pl* **-pos** *informal* short for **hippopotamus**
Hippocratic oath *n* an oath taken by a doctor to observe a code of medical ethics [after *Hippocrates*, Greek physician]
hippodrome *n* **1** a music hall, variety theatre, or circus **2** (in ancient Greece or Rome) an open-air course for horse and chariot races [Greek *hippos* horse + *dromos* race]
hippopotamus *n, pl* **-muses** *or* **-mi** a very large mammal with thick wrinkled skin and short legs, which lives around the rivers of tropical Africa [Greek *hippopotamos* river horse]
hippy[1] *adj* **-pier, -piest** *informal* having large hips
hippy[2] *or* **hippie** *n, pl* **-pies** (esp. during the 1960s) a person whose behaviour and dress imply a rejection of conventional values [from HIP[4]]
hipster *n* *informal* a person who believes he or she is following trends that are outside the mainstream
hipsters *pl n Brit* trousers cut so that the top encircles the hips
hire *vb* **hiring, hired 1** to acquire the temporary use of (a thing) or the services of (a person) in exchange for payment **2** to employ (a person) for wages **3** to provide (something) or the services of (oneself or others) for payment **4 hire out** *chiefly Brit* to pay independent contractors for (work to be done) ▷ *n* **5** the act of hiring **6 for hire** available to be hired [Old English *hӯrian*]
hireling *n derogatory* a person who works only for money

hire-purchase *n* a system in which a buyer takes possession of merchandise on payment of a deposit and completes the purchase by paying a series of instalments while the seller retains ownership until the final instalment is paid

hirsute (her-suit) *adj* hairy [Latin *hirsutus* shaggy]

his *adj* **1** of, belonging to, or associated with him: *his birthday* ▷ *pron* **2** something belonging to him: *his is on the left; that book is his* **3 of his** belonging to him [Old English]

Hispanic *adj* **1** of or derived from Spain or the Spanish ▷ *n* **2** *US* a US citizen of Spanish or Latin-American descent [Latin *Hispania* Spain]

hiss *n* **1** a sound like that of a prolonged *s* **2** such a sound as an expression of dislike or disapproval ▷ *vb* **3** to utter a hiss **4** to express with a hiss: *she hissed the name* **5** to show dislike or disapproval towards (a speaker or performer) by hissing [imitative]

hissy fit *n informal* a childish temper tantrum

h

histamine (hiss-ta-meen) *n* a chemical compound released by the body tissues in allergic reactions [Greek *histos* tissue + *amine*]

histogram *n* a statistical graph that represents the frequency of values of a quantity by vertical bars of varying heights and widths [probably *histo(ry)* + Greek *grammē* line]

histology *n* the study of the tissues of an animal or plant [Greek *histos* tissue + -LOGY]

historian *n* a person who writes or studies history

historic *adj* important in history, or likely to be seen as important in the future

> **USAGE** A distinction is usually made between *historic* (important, significant) and *historical* (pertaining to history): *a historic decision; a historical perspective*.

historical *adj* **1** occurring in the past **2** describing or representing situations or people that existed in the past: *a historical novel* **3** belonging to or typical of the study of history: *historical perspective* **historically** *adv*

> **USAGE** See at **historic**.

historicism *n* **1** the belief that natural laws govern historical events **2** excessive respect for historical institutions, such as traditions or laws

historicity *n* historical authenticity

historiographer *n* a historian employed to write the history of a group or public institution **historiography** *n*

history *n, pl* **-ries** **1** a record or account of past events and developments **2** all that is preserved of the past, esp. in written form **3** the study of interpreting past events **4** the past events or previous experiences of a place, thing, or person: *he knew the whole history of the place* **5** a play that depicts historical events [Greek *historia* inquiry]

histrionic *adj* **1** very dramatic and full of exaggerated emotion: *histrionic bursts of invective* ▷ *n* **2 histrionics** behaviour of this kind [Latin *histrio* actor] **histrionically** *adv*

hit *vb* **hitting, hit** **1** to strike or touch (a person or thing) forcefully **2** to come into violent contact with: *a helicopter hit a Volvo* **3** to propel (a ball) by striking **4** *cricket* to score (runs) **5** to affect (a person, place, or thing) badly: *the airline says that its revenue will be hit* **6** to reach (a point or place): *the city's crime level hit new heights* **7 hit the bottle** *slang* to start drinking excessive amounts of alcohol **8 hit the road** *informal* to set out on a journey ▷ *n* **9** an impact or collision **10** a shot or blow that reaches its target **11** *informal* a person or thing that gains wide appeal: *those early collections made her a hit with the club set* **12** a single visit to a website: *over 500,000 hits a day to its site* ▷ See also **hit off, hit on, hit out at** [Old English *hittan*]

hit-and-miss *adj informal* happening in an unplanned way: *farming can be very much a hit-and-miss affair*

hit-and-run *adj* denoting a motor-vehicle accident in which the driver does not stop to give assistance or inform the police

hitch *n* **1** a temporary or minor problem or difficulty **2** a knot that can be undone by pulling against the direction of the strain that holds it ▷ *vb* **3** *informal* **A** to obtain (a ride) by hitchhiking **B** to hitchhike **4** to fasten with a knot or tie **5 get hitched** *slang* to get married **6 hitch up** to pull up (one's trousers, etc.) with a quick jerk [origin unknown]

hitchhike *vb* **-hiking, -hiked** to travel by getting free lifts in motor vehicles **hitchhiker** *n*

hi-tech *adj* using sophisticated, esp. electronic, technology

hither *adv old-fashioned* to or towards this place: *come hither* [Old English *hider*]

hitherto *adv formal* until this time: *fundamental questions which have hitherto been ignored*

hit list *n informal* **1** a list of people to be murdered **2** a list of targets to be eliminated: *the Treasury draws up a hit list for spending cuts*

hit man *n* a person hired by terrorists or gangsters to murder someone

hit off *vb* **hit it off** *informal* to have a good relationship with someone

hit on *or* **hit upon** *vb* to think of (an idea or a solution)

hit-or-miss *adj informal* unplanned or unpredictable: *a hit-or-miss service*. Also: **hit-and-miss**

hit out at *vb* **1** to direct blows forcefully and vigorously at (someone) **2** to make a verbal attack upon (someone)

hit wicket *n cricket* a batsman breaking the wicket while playing a stroke and so being out

HIV human immunodeficiency virus, the cause of AIDS

hive *n* **1** a structure in which bees live **2 hive of activity** a busy place with many people working hard [Old English *hȳf*]

hive off *vb* **hiving, hived** to transfer (part of a business, esp. the profitable part of a nationalized industry) to new ownership

hives *n pathol* an allergic reaction in which itchy red or whitish raised patches develop on the skin [origin unknown]

HM (in Britain) Her (*or* His) Majesty

H.M.A.S. *or* **HMAS** (in Australia) Her (*or* His) Majesty's Australian Ship

HMI (in Britain) Her (*or* His) Majesty's Inspector; a government official who examines and supervises schools

hmm *interj* a sound made when considering or puzzling over something

HMRC (in Britain) Her (*or* His) Majesty's Revenue and Customs

H.M.S. *or* **HMS** (in Britain) Her (*or* His) Majesty's Ship

HMSO (in Britain) Her (*or* His) Majesty's Stationery Office

HNC (in Britain) Higher National Certificate; a qualification recognized by many national technical and professional institutions

HND (in Britain) Higher National Diploma; a qualification in a technical subject equivalent to an ordinary degree

ho *n US offensive slang* a woman [from Black or Southern US pronunciation of WHORE]

Ho *chem* holmium

hoar *n* short for **hoarfrost** [Old English *hār*]

hoard *n* **1** a store of money, food, etc., hidden away for future use ▷ *vb* **2** to save or store (money, food, etc.) [Old English *hord*] **hoarder** *n*

> **USAGE** *Hoard* is sometimes wrongly written where *horde* is meant: *hordes* (not *hoards*) *of tourists.*

hoarding *n* a large board at the side of a road, used for displaying advertising posters [Old French *hourd* palisade]

hoarfrost *n* a white layer of ice crystals formed on the ground by condensation at temperatures below freezing point

hoarse *adj* **1** (of a voice) rough and unclear through illness or too much shouting **2** having a rough and unclear voice [from Old Norse] **hoarsely** *adv* **hoarseness** *n*

hoary *adj* **hoarier, hoariest 1** having grey or white hair **2** very old: *a hoary old problem*

hoax *n* **1** a deception, esp. a practical joke ▷ *vb* **2** to deceive or play a joke on (someone) [probably from *hocus* to trick]

hob *n Brit* the flat top part of a cooker, or a separate flat surface, containing hotplates or burners [perhaps from *hub*]

hobble *vb* **-bling, -bled 1** to walk with a lame awkward movement **2** to tie the legs of (a horse) together in order to restrict its movement [probably from Low German]

hobby *n, pl* **-bies** an activity pursued in one's spare time for pleasure or relaxation [probably variant of the name *Robin*]

hobbyhorse *n* **1** a favourite topic about which a person likes to talk at every opportunity: *public transport is his hobbyhorse* **2** a toy consisting of a stick with a figure of a horse's head at one end **3** a figure of a horse attached to a performer's waist in a morris dance

hobgoblin *n* a small, mischievous creature in fairy stories [*hob*, variant of the name *Rob* + GOBLIN]

hobnail boots *pl n old-fashioned* heavy boots with short nails in the soles to lessen wear and tear [*hob* (in archaic sense: peg)]

hobnob *vb* **-nobbing, -nobbed** to socialize or talk informally: *hobnobbing with the rich* [*hob or nob* to drink to one another in turns]

hobo *n, pl* **-bos** *or* **-boes** *US, Canad, Austral & NZ* a tramp or vagrant [origin unknown]

Hobson's choice *n* the choice of taking what is offered or nothing at all [after Thomas *Hobson*, liveryman who gave his customers no choice]

hock[1] *n* the joint in the leg of a horse or similar animal that corresponds to the human ankle [Old English *hōhsinu* heel sinew]

hock[2] *n* a white wine from the German Rhine [German *Hochheimer*]

hock[3] *informal* ▷ *vb* **1** to pawn or pledge ▷ *n* **2 in hock A** in debt **B** in pawn [Dutch *hok* prison, debt]

hockey *n* **1** a game played on a field by two teams of 11 players who try to hit a ball into their opponents' goal using long sticks curved at the end **2** *US & Canad* ice hockey [origin unknown]

hocus-pocus *n informal* something said or done in order to confuse or trick someone [a dog Latin exclamation used by conjurors]

hod *n* an open metal or plastic box attached to a pole, for carrying bricks or mortar [Old French *hotte* pannier]

hodgepodge *n chiefly US & Canad* same as **hotchpotch**

Hodgkin's disease *n* a malignant disease that causes enlargement of the lymph nodes, spleen, and liver [after Thomas *Hodgkin*, physician]

hoe *n* **1** a long-handled implement used to loosen the soil or to weed ▷ *vb* **hoeing, hoed 2** to scrape or weed with a hoe [Germanic]

hog *n* **1** a castrated male pig **2** *US & Canad* any mammal of the pig family **3** *informal* a greedy person **4 go the whole hog** *slang* to do something in the most complete way possible ▷ *vb* **hogging, hogged 5** *slang* to take more than one's share of (something) [Old English *hogg*]

Hogmanay *n* New Year's Eve in Scotland [probably from Old French *aguillanneuf* a New Year's Eve gift]

hogshead *n* a large cask for storing alcoholic drinks [origin unknown]

hogwash *n informal* nonsense

ho-ho *interj* a written representation of the sound of a deep laugh

ho-hum *adj informal* uninteresting or mediocre: *a ho-hum performance*

hoick *vb* **1** to raise abruptly and sharply **2** NZ to clear the throat and spit [origin unknown]

hoi polloi *pl n* the ordinary people when compared to the rich or well-educated [Greek: the many]

hoisin *n* a sweet spicy sauce of soya beans, sugar, garlic, and vinegar, used in Chinese cookery [from Cantonese]

hoist *vb* **1** to raise or lift up, esp. by mechanical means ▷ *n* **2** any apparatus or device for lifting things [probably from Low German]

hoity-toity *adj informal* arrogant or haughty [obsolete *hoit* to romp]

hokey-pokey *n NZ* a brittle toffee sold in lumps

hokum *n slang, chiefly US & Canad* **1** nonsense; bunk **2** obvious sentimental material in a play or film [probably a blend of *hocus-pocus* + *bunkum*]

hold[1] *vb* **holding, held 1** to keep (an object or a person) with or within the hands or arms **2** to support: *a rope made from 1000 hairs would hold a large adult* **3** to maintain in a specified state or position: *his reputation continued to hold secure* **4** to have the capacity for: *trains designed to hold more than 400* **5** to set aside or reserve: *they will hold our tickets until tomorrow* **6** to restrain or keep back: *designed to hold dangerous criminals* **7** to remain unbroken: *if the elastic holds* **8** (of the weather) to remain dry and bright **9** to keep (the attention of): *a writer holds a reader by his temperament* **10** to arrange and cause to take place: *we must hold an inquiry* **11** to have the ownership or possession of: *she holds a degree in Egyptology* **12** to have responsibility for: *she cannot hold an elective office* **13** to be able to control the outward effects of drinking (alcohol): *he can't hold his drink* **14** to (cause to) remain committed to (a promise, etc.) **15** to claim or believe: *some Sufis hold that all religious leaders were prophets* **16** to remain valid or true: *the categories are not the same and equivalency does not hold* **17** to consider in a specified manner: *philosophies which we hold so dear* **18** to defend successfully: *the Russians were holding the Volga front* **19** *music* to sustain the sound of (a note) ▷ *n* **20** a way of holding something or the act of holding it **21** something to hold onto for support **22** controlling influence: *drugs will take a hold* **23 with no holds barred** with all limitations removed ▷ See also **hold back, hold down** *etc.* [Old English *healdan*] **holder** *n*

hold² *n* the space in a ship or aircraft for storing cargo or luggage [variant of *hole*]

holdall *n Brit* a large strong travelling bag

hold back *vb* **1** to restrain (someone) or refrain from doing something: *managers declined to hold back the crowds; buyers held back in the expectation of further price decreases* **2** to withhold: *holding back the wages*

hold down *vb* **1** to restrain or control (someone) **2** *informal* to manage to keep (a job) **3** to prevent (wages, prices, etc.) from rising much

hold forth *vb* to speak for a long time

hold in *vb* to control or conceal (one's feelings)

holding *n* **1** land held under a lease **2** property to which the holder has legal title, such as land, stocks, or shares

holding company *n* a company that holds the controlling shares in one or more other companies

holding paddock *n Austral & NZ* a paddock in which cattle or sheep are kept temporarily, such as when awaiting sale

hold off *vb* **1** to keep (an attacker or attacking force) at a distance **2** to put off (doing something): *he held off distributing weapons*

hold on *vb* **1** to maintain a firm grasp (of something or someone) **2** to wait, esp. on the telephone **3 hold on to** to keep: *he held on to his world No. 1 ranking*

hold out *vb* **1** to offer (something) **2** to last: *I could hold out until we return home* **3** to continue to stand firm and manage to resist opposition **4 hold out for** to wait patiently for (the fulfilment of one's wishes) **5 hold out on someone** *informal* to keep from telling someone some important information

hold over *vb* to postpone: *several cases had to be held over pending further investigation*

hold-up *n* **1** an armed robbery **2** a delay: *a traffic hold-up* ▷ *vb* **hold up 3** to delay **4** to support (an object) **5** to stop and rob (someone), using a weapon **6** to exhibit or present (something) as an example: *he was held up as a model professional*

hold with *vb* to approve of: *we don't hold with killing animals unless it provides food*

hole *n* **1** an area hollowed out in a solid **2** an opening in or through something **3** an animal's burrow **4** *informal* a fault or error: *this points to a very big hole in parliamentary security* **5** *informal* an unattractive town or other place **6** (on a golf course) any one of the divisions of a course (usually 18) represented by the distance between the tee and the sunken cup on the green into which the ball is to be played **7 in a hole** *slang* in a difficult and embarrassing situation **8 make a hole in** *informal* to use a great amount of (one's money or food supply) **9 pick holes in** to point out faults in ▷ *vb* **holing, holed 10** to make a hole or holes in (something) **11** to hit (a golf ball) into a hole. See **hole up** [Old English *hol*] **holey** *adj*

hole-and-corner *adj informal* furtive or secretive

hole in one *n golf* a shot from the tee that finishes in the hole

hole in the heart *n* a congenital defect of the heart, in which there is an abnormal opening in the partition between the left and right halves

hole up *vb informal* to go into hiding

Holi (holl-lee) *n* an annual Hindu spring festival, honouring Krishna

holiday *n* **1** a period of time spent away from home for enjoyment and relaxation **2** (*often pl*) *chiefly Brit & NZ* a period in which a break is taken from work or studies for rest or recreation **3** a day on which work is suspended by law or custom, such as a bank holiday ▷ *vb* **4** *chiefly Brit* to spend a holiday [Old English *hāligdæg* holy day]

holier-than-thou *adj* offensively self-righteous

Holiness *n* (preceded by *His* or *Your*) a title reserved for the pope

holism *n* **1** the view that a whole is greater than the sum of its parts **2** (in medicine) consideration of the complete person in the treatment of disease [Greek *holos* whole] **holistic** *adj*

hollandaise sauce *n* a rich sauce of egg yolks, butter, vinegar, and lemon juice [French *sauce hollandaise* Dutch sauce]

holler *informal* ▷ *vb* **1** to shout or yell ▷ *n* **2** a shout or yell [French *holà* stop!]

hollow *adj* **1** having a hole or space within; not solid: *a hollow tree* **2** curving inwards: *hollow cheeks* **3** (of sounds) as if echoing in a hollow place **4** without any real value or worth: *a hollow enterprise, lacking purpose, and lacking soul* ▷ *adv* **5 beat someone hollow** *Brit & NZ informal* to defeat someone thoroughly ▷ *n* **6** a cavity or space in something **7** a dip in the land ▷ *vb* **8** (often foll. by *out*) to form a hole or cavity in [Old English *holh* cave] **hollowly** *adv*

holly *n* an evergreen tree with prickly leaves and bright red berries, used for Christmas decorations [Old English *holegn*]

hollyhock *n* a tall garden plant with spikes of colourful flowers [*holy* + obsolete *hock* mallow]

holmium *n chem* a silver-white metallic element, the compounds of which are highly magnetic. Symbol: **Ho** [after *Holmia*, Latin name of Stockholm]

holm oak *n* an evergreen oak tree with prickly leaves like holly

holocaust *n* **1** destruction or loss of life on a massive scale **2 the Holocaust** mass murder of the Jews in Europe by the Nazis (1940–45) [Greek *holos* whole + *kaiein* to burn]

Holocene *adj* of the current geological epoch, which began about 10,000 years ago

hologram *n* a three-dimensional photographic image produced by means of a split laser beam [Greek *holos* whole + *grammē* line]

holograph *n* a book or document handwritten by its author [Greek *holos* whole + *graphein* to write]

holography *n* the science of using lasers to produce holograms [Greek *holos* whole + -GRAPHY] **holographic** *adj* **holographically** *adv*

hols *pl n Brit & S African informal* holidays

holster *n* a sheathlike leather case for a pistol, worn attached to a belt [Germanic]

holt *n* the lair of an otter [from HOLD²]

holy *adj* **-lier, -liest 1** of or associated with God or a deity **2** (of a person) religious and leading a virtuous life [Old English *hālig, hǣlig*] **holiness** *n*

Holy Communion *n Christianity* a church service in which people take bread and wine in remembrance of Christ's Last Supper and His atonement for the sins of the world

Holy Ghost *n* **the Holy Ghost** *Christianity* same as **Holy Spirit**

Holy Grail *n* **1 the Holy Grail** (in medieval legend) the bowl used by Jesus at the Last Supper **2** *informal* any ambition or goal [*grail* from Medieval Latin *gradalis* bowl]

Holy Land *n* **the Holy Land** Palestine

holy of holies *n* **1** any sacred place or a place considered as if it were sacred: *the holy of holies they called the Captain's Cabin* **2** the innermost chamber of a Jewish temple

holy orders *pl n* the status of an ordained Christian minister

Holy See *n* **the Holy See** *RC Church* the see of the pope as bishop of Rome

Holy Spirit *n* **the Holy Spirit** *Christianity* one of the three aspects of God

Holy Week *n Christianity* the week before Easter Sunday

homage *n* a public show of respect or honour towards someone or something: *the master's jazzy-classical homage to Gershwin* [Latin *homo* man]

homburg *n* a man's soft felt hat with a dented crown and a stiff upturned brim

home *n* **1** the place where one lives **2** the country or area of one's birth **3** a building or organization set up to care for people in a certain category, such as orphans or elderly people **4** the place where something is invented or started: *the home of the first aircraft* **5** *sport* a team's own ground: *the match is at home* **6** *baseball & rounders etc.* the objective towards which a player runs after striking the ball **7 at home A** in one's own home or country **B** at ease: *he felt more at home with the Russians* **C** receiving visitors ▷ *adj* **8** of one's home, birthplace, or native country **9** (of an activity) done in one's house: *home movies* **10** *sport* played on one's own ground: *a home game* **11 home and dry** *Brit slang* definitely safe or successful ▷ *adv* **12** to or at home: *I came home* **13** to or on the point: *the message struck home* **14** to the fullest extent: *they drove their spears home* **15 bring something home to someone** to make something clear to someone ▷ *vb* **homing, homed 16** (of birds) to return home accurately from a distance **17 home in on** to be directed towards (a goal or target) [Old English *hām*]

USAGE See at **hone.**

homeboy *n slang* **1** a close friend **2** a member of a gang

home-brew *n* beer or other alcoholic drink brewed at home

homecoming *n* a return home, esp. after a long absence

Home Counties *pl n* the counties surrounding London

home economics *n* the study of diet, budgeting, child care, and other subjects concerned with running a home

home farm *n Brit* a farm that belonged to and provided food for a large country house

Home Guard *n* a part-time military force of volunteers recruited for the defence of the United Kingdom in the Second World War

home help *n Brit, Austral & NZ* a person employed by a local authority to do housework in an elderly or disabled person's home

homeland *n* **1** the country from which the ancestors of a person or group came: *defending their homeland* **2** *S African* (formerly) an area reserved for occupation by a Black African people

homeless *adj* **1** having nowhere to live ▷ *pl n* **2 the homeless** people who have nowhere to live: *night shelters for the homeless* **homelessness** *n*

homely *adj* **-lier, -liest 1** simple, ordinary, and comfortable **2 A** *Brit* (of a person) warm and friendly **B** *chiefly US & Canad* (of a person) plain or unattractive **homeliness** *n*

home-made *adj* (esp. of foods) made at home or on the premises

Home Office *n Brit government* the department responsible for law and order, immigration, and other domestic affairs

homeopathy *or* **homoeopathy** (home-ee-**op**-ath-ee) *n* a method of treating disease by the use of small amounts of a drug that produces symptoms of the disease in healthy people [Greek *homoios* similar + *patheia* suffering] **homeopath** *or* **homoeopath** (**home**-ee-oh-path) *n* **homeopathic** *or* **homoeopathic** *adj*

homeostasis *or* **homoeostasis** (hom-ee-oh-**stass**-iss) *n* the tendency of an organism to achieve a stable metabolic state by compensating automatically for violent changes in the environment and other disruptions [Greek *homoios* similar + *stasis* a standing]

homeowner *n* a person who owns the home in which he or she lives

home page *n internet* the introductory information about a website with links to the information or services provided

h

Homeric (home-**mer**-rik) *adj* of or relating to Homer, Greek epic poet (circa 800 BC)
home rule *n* self-government in domestic affairs
Home Secretary *n Brit government* the head of the Home Office
homesick *adj* depressed by being away from home and family **homesickness** *n*
homespun *adj* (of philosophies or opinions) plain and unsophisticated
homestead *n* **1** a farmhouse and the adjoining land **2** (in the western US & Canada) a house and adjoining tract of land (originally often 160 acres) that was granted by the government for development as a farm
homesteader *n* (in the western US & Canada) a person who lives on and farms a homestead
homestead law *n* (in the western US & Canada) any of various laws granting certain privileges to owners of homesteads
home truths *pl n* unpleasant facts told to a person about himself or herself
home unit *n Austral & NZ* a self-contained residence that is part of a block of such residences
homeward *adj* **1** going home ▷ *adv also* **homewards** **2** towards home
homework *n* **1** school work done at home **2** research or preparation
homicide *n* **1** the act of killing someone **2** a person who kills someone [Latin *homo* man + *caedere* to kill] **homicidal** *adj*
homie *n slang, chiefly US* short for **homeboy**
homily *n, pl* **-lies** a moralizing talk or piece of writing [Greek *homilia* discourse] **homiletic** *adj*
homing *adj* **1** *zool* denoting the ability to return home after travelling great distances **2** (of a missile) capable of guiding itself onto a target
homing pigeon *n* a pigeon developed for its homing instinct, used for racing
hominid *n* **1** any member of the family of primates that includes modern humans and the extinct forerunners of humans ▷ *adj* **2** of or belonging to this family [Latin *homo* man]
hominoid *adj* **1** of or like a human; human-like ▷ *n* **2** a human-like animal [Latin *homo* man]
hominy *n chiefly US* coarsely ground maize prepared as a food by boiling in milk or water [probably from a Native American language]
homo[1] *n informal, offensive* short for **homosexual**
homo[2] *n Canad informal* homogenized milk
homo- *combining form* same or like: *homologous* [Greek *homos* same]
homogeneous (home-oh-**jean**-ee-uss) *adj* having parts or members which are all the same or which consist of only one substance: *the Arabs are not a single, homogeneous nation* [Greek *homos* same + *genos* kind] **homogeneity** *n*
homogenize *or* **-nise** *vb* **-nizing, -nized** *or* **-nising, -nised** **1** to break up the fat globules in (milk or cream) so that they are evenly distributed **2** to make different elements the same or similar: *homogenized products for a mass market*
homogenous (hom-**oj**-in-uss) *adj* having a similar structure because of common ancestry
homograph *n* a word spelt the same as another, but having a different meaning, such as *bear* (to carry) and *bear* (the animal) [Greek *homos* same + *graphein* to write]
homologous (hom-**ol**-log-uss) *adj* **1** having a related or similar position or structure **2** *biol* (of organs and parts) having the same origin but different functions: *the wing of a bat and the arm of a monkey are homologous* [Greek *homos* same + *logos* ratio]
homology (hom-**ol**-a-jee) *n* the condition of being homologous
homonym *n* a word pronounced and spelt the same as another, but having a different meaning, such as *novel* (a book) and *novel* (new)
homophobia *n* intense hatred or fear of homosexuals [*homo(sexual)* + *phobia*]
homophone *n* a word pronounced the same as another, but having a different meaning or spelling or both, such as *bear* and *bare* [Greek *homos* same + *phōnē* sound]
Homo sapiens (**home**-oh **sap**-ee-enz) *n* the name for modern humans as a species [Latin *homo* man + *sapiens* wise]
homosexual *n* **1** a person who is sexually attracted to members of the same sex ▷ *adj* **2** (of a person) sexually attracted to members of the same sex **3** (of a sexual relationship) between members of the same sex [Greek *homos* same] **homosexuality** *n*
homozygous *adj biol* having two identical alleles of the same gene [Greek *homos* same + *zugōtos* yoked]
homy *or esp US* **homey** *adj* **homier, homiest** like a home; pleasant and cosy
Hon. Honourable (title)
hone *vb* **honing, honed** **1** to develop and improve (a quality or ability): *a workshop to hone interview techniques* **2** to sharpen (a tool) ▷ *n* **3** a fine whetstone used for sharpening edged tools and knives [Old English *hān* stone]

> **USAGE** *Hone* is sometimes wrongly used where *home* is meant: *this device makes it easier to home in on* (not *hone in on*) *the target.*

honest *adj* **1** truthful and moral in behaviour; trustworthy **2** open and sincere in relationships and attitudes; without pretensions **3** gained or earned fairly: *an honest income* [Latin *honos* esteem]
honestly *adv* **1** in an honest manner **2** truly: *honestly, that's all I can recall*
honesty *n, pl* **-ties** **1** the quality of being truthful and trustworthy **2** a plant with flattened silvery pods which are used for indoor decoration
honey *n* **1** a sweet edible sticky substance made by bees from nectar **2** *chiefly US & Canad* a term of affection **3** *informal, chiefly US & Canad* something very good of its kind: *a honey of a picture about American family life* [Old English *huneg*]
honeybee *n* a bee widely domesticated as a source of honey and beeswax
honeycomb *n* a waxy structure, constructed by bees in a hive, that consists of many six-sided cells in which honey is stored
honeydew *n* a sugary substance excreted by aphids and similar insects
honeydew melon *n* a melon with yellow skin and sweet pale flesh
honeyed *adj poetic* flattering or soothing: *honeyed words*

honeymoon *n* **1** a holiday taken by a newly married couple **2** the early period of an undertaking or activity, such as the start of a new government's term of office, when an attitude of goodwill prevails ▷ *vb* **3** to take a honeymoon [traditionally, referring to the feelings of married couples as changing with the phases of the moon] **honeymooner** *n*

honeysuckle *n* a climbing shrub with sweet-smelling white, yellow, or pink flowers [Old English *hunigsūce*]

honeytrap *n Brit informal* a scheme in which a victim is lured into a compromising sexual situation that provides the opportunity for blackmail

hongi (hong-jee) *n* NZ a Māori greeting in which people touch noses

honk *n* **1** the sound made by a motor horn **2** the sound made by a goose ▷ *vb* **3** to make or cause (something) to make a honking sound

honky-tonk *n* **1** *US & Canad slang* a cheap disreputable nightclub or dance hall **2** a style of ragtime piano-playing, esp. on a tinny-sounding piano [rhyming compound based on HONK]

honorarium *n, pl* **-iums** *or* **-ia** a voluntary fee paid for a service which is usually free [Latin *honorarium (donum)* honorary gift]

honorary *adj* **A** held or given as a mark of respect, without the usual qualifications, payment, or work: *an honorary degree* **B** (of a secretary, treasurer, etc.) unpaid

honorific *adj* showing respect: *an honorific title*

honour *or US* **honor** *n* **1** allegiance to moral principles **2** a person's good reputation and the respect they are given by other people **3** **A** fame or glory **B** a person who wins fame or glory for his or her country, school, etc.: *he was an honour to his nation* **4** great respect or esteem, or an outward sign of this **5** a privilege or pleasure: *it was an honour to meet him* **6** *old-fashioned* a woman's virginity **7** *bridge & whist* any of the top four or five cards in a suit **8** *golf* the right to tee off first **9** **in honour of** out of respect for **10** **on one's honour** under a moral obligation ▷ *vb* **11** to hold someone in respect **12** to give (someone) special praise, attention, or an award **13** to accept and then pay (a cheque or bill) **14** to keep (one's promise); fulfil (a previous agreement) [Latin *honor* esteem]

Honour *n* (preceded by *Your*, *His* or *Her*) a title used to address or refer to certain judges

honourable *or US* **honorable** *adj* **1** principled **2** worthy of respect or esteem **honourably** *adv*

Honourable *adj* **the Honourable** a title of respect placed before a name: used of various officials, of the children of certain peers, and in Parliament by one member speaking of another

honours *or US* **honors** *pl n* **1** (in a university degree course) a rank or mark of the highest academic standard: *an honours degree* **2** observances of respect, esp. at a funeral **3** **do the honours** to serve as host or hostess by serving food or pouring drinks

hooch (rhymes with **smooch**) *n informal* alcoholic drink, esp. illegally distilled spirits [from a Native American language]

hood[1] *n* **1** a loose head covering either attached to a coat or made as a separate garment **2** *US, Canad & Austral* the bonnet of a car **3** the folding roof of a convertible car or a pram ▷ *vb* **4** to cover with or as if with a hood [Old English *hōd*] **hoodlike** *adj*

hood[2] *n slang* short for **hoodlum**

hooded *adj* **1** (of a garment) having a hood **2** (of eyes) having heavy eyelids that appear to be half-closed

hooded crow *n* a crow that has a grey body and black head, wings, and tail

hoodie *n informal* **1** a hooded sweatshirt **2** a young person who wears a hooded sweatshirt, regarded by some as a potential hooligan

hoodlum *n* a violent criminal, esp. one who is a member of a gang [origin unknown]

hoodoo *n, pl* **-doos** **1** *informal* bad luck **2** *informal* a person or thing that brings bad luck **3** *chiefly US* same as **voodoo**

hoodwink *vb* to trick or deceive [originally, to cover the eyes with a hood]

hooey *n slang* nonsense [origin unknown]

hoof *n, pl* **hooves** *or* **hoofs** **1** the horny covering of the end of the foot in the horse, deer, and certain other mammals **2** **on the hoof** **A** (of livestock) alive **B** in an impromptu way: *thinking on the hoof* ▷ *vb* **3** **hoof it** *slang* to walk [Old English *hōf*] **hoofed** *adj*

hoofer *n slang* a professional dancer

hoo-ha *n informal* a noisy commotion or fuss [origin unknown]

hook *n* **1** a curved piece of metal or plastic used to hang, hold, or pull something **2** something resembling a hook, such as a sharp bend in a river or a sharply curved strip of land **3** *boxing* a short swinging blow with the elbow bent **4** *cricket & golf* a shot that causes the ball to go to the player's left **5** **by hook or by crook** by any means: *get into the charts by hook or by crook* **6** **hook, line, and sinker** *informal* completely: *we fell for it hook, line, and sinker* **7** **let someone off the hook** *slang* to free someone from an obligation or a difficult situation **8** **sling one's hook** *Brit & Austral slang* to leave ▷ *vb* **9** to fasten with, or as if with, a hook **10** to catch (a fish) on a hook **11** *cricket & golf* to play (a ball) with a hook **12** *rugby* to obtain and pass (the ball) backwards from a scrum, using the feet [Old English *hōc*]

hookah *n* (esp. in Arab countries) a pipe for smoking marijuana or tobacco, with a long flexible stem connected to a container of water through which smoke is drawn and cooled [Arabic *huqqah*]

hooked *adj* **1** bent like a hook **2** (often foll. by *on*) **A** *slang* addicted (to): *hooked on drugs* **B** obsessed (with): *hooked on football*

hooker *n* **1** *slang* a prostitute **2** *rugby* a player who uses his feet to get the ball in a scrum

Hooke's law *n physics* the principle that a solid stretches or contracts in proportion to the force placed on it, within the limits of its elasticity [after Robert *Hooke*, physicist]

hook-up *n* the linking of broadcasting equipment or stations to transmit a special programme

hookworm *n* a blood-sucking worm with hooked mouthparts

hooligan *n slang* a young person who behaves in a noisy and violent way in public [origin unknown] **hooliganism** *n*

hoon *Austral & NZ slang* ▷ *n* **1** a loutish youth who drives irresponsibly ▷ *vb* **2** to drive irresponsibly

hoop *n* **1** a rigid circular band of metal, plastic, or wood **2** a child's toy shaped like a hoop and rolled on the ground or whirled around the body **3** *croquet* any of the iron arches through which the ball is driven **4** a large ring through which performers or animals jump **5 go** *or* **be put through the hoops** to go through an ordeal or test ▷ *vb* **6** to surround (something) with a hoop [Old English *hōp*] **hooped** *adj*

hoopla *n Brit & Austral* a fairground game in which hoops are thrown over objects in an attempt to win them

hoopoe (hoop-oo) *n* a bird with pinkish-brown plumage with black-and-white wings and a fanlike crest [imitative]

h

hoop pine *n* an Australian tree or shrub with flowers in dense spikes

hooray *interj, n* same as **hurrah**

Hooray Henry (hoo-ray) *n, pl* **Hooray Henries** *or* **-rys** *Brit informal* a young upper-class man with an affectedly loud and cheerful manner

hoot *n* **1** the sound of a car horn **2** the cry of an owl **3** a high-pitched noise showing disapproval **4** *informal* an amusing person or thing ▷ *vb* **5** *Brit* to blow (a car horn) **6** to make a hoot **7** to jeer or yell contemptuously at someone **8** to drive (speakers or performers on stage) off by hooting [imitative]

hooter *n chiefly Brit* **1** a device that hoots, such as a car horn **2** *slang* a nose

Hoover *n* **1** *trademark* a vacuum cleaner ▷ *vb* **hoover 2** to vacuum-clean (a carpet) **3** (often foll. by *up*) to devour (something) quickly and completely

hooves *n* a plural of **hoof**

hop[1] *vb* **hopping, hopped 1** to jump forwards or upwards on one foot **2** (of frogs, birds, etc.) to move forwards in short jumps **3** to jump over something **4** *informal* to move quickly (in, on, out of, etc.): *hop into bed* **5 hop it** *Brit & Austral slang* to go away ▷ *n* **6** an instance of hopping **7** *informal* an informal dance **8** *informal* a short journey, usually in an aircraft **9 on the hop** *informal* **A** active or busy: *he keeps me on the hop* **B** unawares or unprepared: *you caught me on the hop* [Old English *hoppian*]

hop[2] *n* a climbing plant with green conelike flowers. See also **hops** [Middle Dutch *hoppe*]

hope *vb* **hoping, hoped 1** to desire (something), usually with some possibility of fulfilment: *you would hope for their cooperation* **2** to trust or believe: *I hope I've arranged that* ▷ *n* **3** a feeling of desire for something, usually with confidence in the possibility of its fulfilment: *the news was greeted by some as hope for further interest rate cuts* **4** a reasonable ground for this feeling: *there is hope for you yet* **5** the person, thing, situation, or event that gives cause for hope or is desired: *the young are a symbol of hope for the future* [Old English *hopa*]

hopeful *adj* **1** having, inspiring, or expressing hope ▷ *n* **2** a person considered to be on the brink of success: *a young hopeful*

hopefully *adv* **1** in a hopeful manner **2** *informal* it is hoped: *hopefully I've got a long career ahead of me*

> **USAGE** The use of *hopefully* to mean *it is hoped* used to be considered incorrect by some people but has now become acceptable in informal contexts.

hopeless *adj* **1** having or offering no hope **2** impossible to solve **3** *informal* without skill or ability: *I'm hopeless at maths* **hopelessly** *adv* **hopelessness** *n*

hopper *n* a funnel-shaped device from which solid materials can be discharged into a receptacle below

hops *pl n* the dried flowers of the hop plant, used to give a bitter taste to beer

hopscotch *n* a children's game in which a player throws a stone to land in one of a pattern of squares marked on the ground and then hops over to it to pick it up [*hop* + obsolete *scotch* a line, scratch]

horde *n* a very large crowd, often frightening or unpleasant [Turkish *ordū* camp]

> **USAGE** *Horde* is sometimes wrongly written where *hoard* is meant: *a hoard* (not *horde*) *of gold coins.*

horehound *n* a plant that produces a bitter juice formerly used as a cough medicine [Old English *hārhūne*]

horizon *n* **1** the apparent line that divides the earth and the sky **2 horizons** the limits of a person's interests and activities: *seeking to broaden his horizons at college* **3 on the horizon** almost certainly going to happen or be done in the future: *a new type of computer is on the horizon* [Greek *horizein* to limit]

horizontal *adj* **1** flat and level with the ground or with a line considered as a base **2** affecting or happening at one level in a system or organization: *a horizontal division of labour* ▷ *n* **3** a horizontal plane, position, or line **horizontally** *adv*

hormone *n* **1** a chemical substance produced in an endocrine gland and transported in the blood to a certain tissue, on which it has a specific effect **2** a similar substance produced by a plant that is essential for growth **3** a synthetic substance having the same effects [Greek *hormōn*] **hormonal** *adj*

horn *n* **1** either of a pair of permanent bony outgrowths on the heads of animals such as cattle and antelopes **2** any hornlike projection, such as the eyestalk of a snail **3** the antler of a deer **4** the hard substance of which horns are made **5** a musical wind instrument made from horn **6** any musical instrument consisting of a pipe or tube of brass fitted with a mouthpiece **7** a device, such as on a vehicle, for producing a warning or signalling noise [Old English] **horned** *adj*

hornbeam *n* a tree with smooth grey bark

hornbill *n* a tropical bird with a bony growth on its large beak

hornblende *n* a green-to-black mineral containing aluminium, calcium, sodium, magnesium, and iron

hornet *n* **1** a large wasp that can inflict a severe sting **2 hornet's nest** a very unpleasant situation that is difficult to deal with: *you'll stir up a hornet's nest* [Old English *hyrnetu*]

horn of plenty *n* same as **cornucopia**

hornpipe *n* **1** a solo dance, traditionally performed by sailors **2** music for this dance

horny *adj* **hornier, horniest 1** of, like, or hard as horn **2** *slang* **A** sexually aroused **B** provoking sexual arousal **C** sexually eager

horology *n* the art of making clocks and watches or of measuring time [Greek *hōra* hour + -LOGY] **horological** *adj*

horoscope *n* **1** the prediction of a person's future based on the positions of the planets, sun, and moon at the time of birth **2** a diagram showing the positions of the planets, sun, and moon at a particular time and place [Greek *hōra* hour + *skopos* observer]

horrendous *adj* very unpleasant or shocking [Latin *horrendus* fearful]

horrible *adj* **1** disagreeable and unpleasant: *a horrible hotel room* **2** causing fear, shock, or disgust: *he died a horrible death* [Latin *horribilis*] **horribly** *adv*

horrid *adj* **1** disagreeable or unpleasant: *it had been a horrid day at school* **2** *informal* (of a person) unkind and nasty: *her horrid parents* [Latin *horridus* prickly]

horrific *adj* provoking horror: *horrific injuries* **horrifically** *adv*

horrify *vb* **-fies, -fying, -fied** to cause feelings of horror in (someone); shock (someone) greatly

horror *n* **1** extreme fear or terror **2** intense hatred: *she had a horror of violence* **3** a thing or person causing fear, loathing, or distaste ▷ *adj* **4** having a frightening subject, usually concerned with the supernatural: *a horror film* [Latin: a trembling with fear]

horrors *pl n* **the horrors** *slang* a fit of nervousness or anxiety

hors d'oeuvre (or **durv**) *n, pl* **hors d'oeuvre** *or* **hors d'oeuvres** (or **durv**) an appetizer, usually served before the main meal [French]

horse *n* **1** a four-footed mammal with hooves, a mane, and a tail, used for riding and pulling carts, etc. Related adjectives: **equestrian, equine 2** the adult male of this species; stallion **3** *gymnastics* a padded apparatus on legs, used for vaulting **4 be** *or* **get on one's high horse** *informal* to act in a haughty manner **5 the horses** *informal* horse races on which bets may be placed: *an occasional flutter on the horses* **6 the horse's mouth** the most reliable source: *I'll tell you straight from the horse's mouth* ▷ See also **horse around** [Old English *hors*]

horse around *or* **horse about** *vb informal* to play roughly or boisterously

horseback *n* a horse's back: *on horseback*

horsebox *n Brit, S African, NZ & Austral* a van or trailer used for transporting horses

horse brass *n* a decorative brass ornament, originally attached to a horse's harness

horse chestnut *n* **1** a tree with broad leaves and brown shiny inedible nuts enclosed in a spiky case **2** the nut of this tree

horseflesh *n* **1** horses collectively: *Ascot's annual parade of fashion and horseflesh* **2** the flesh of a horse as food

horsefly *n, pl* **-flies** a large fly which sucks the blood of horses, cattle, and people

horsehair *n* hair from the tail or mane of a horse, used in upholstery

horse laugh *n* a loud and coarse laugh

horseman *or fem* **horsewoman** *n, pl* **-men** *or* **-women 1** a person who is skilled in riding **2** a person riding a horse **horsemanship** *n*

horseplay *n* rough or rowdy play

horsepower *n* a unit of power (equivalent to 745.7 watts), used to measure the power of an engine

horseradish *n* a plant with a white strong-tasting root, which is used to make a sauce

horse sense *n* same as **common sense**

horseshoe *n* **1** a piece of iron shaped like a U, nailed to the bottom of a horse's hoof to protect the foot **2** an object of similar shape: often regarded as a symbol of good luck

horsetail *n* a plant with small dark toothlike leaves

horsewhip *n* **1** a whip with a long thong, used for managing horses ▷ *vb* **-whipping, -whipped 2** to beat (a person or animal) with such a whip

horsey *or* **horsy** *adj* **horsier, horsiest 1** of or relating to horses: *a horsey smell* **2** devoted to horses: *the horsey set* **3** like a horse: *a horsey face*

hortatory *or* **hortative** *adj formal* encouraging [Latin *hortari* to encourage]

horticulture *n* the art or science of cultivating gardens [Latin *hortus* garden + CULTURE] **horticultural** *adj* **horticulturalist** *or* **horticulturist** *n*

Horus *n* an Egyptian god with a falcon's head

hosanna *interj* an exclamation of praise to God [Hebrew *hōshi 'āh nnā* save now, we pray]

hose[1] *n* **1** a flexible pipe, for conveying a liquid or gas ▷ *vb* **hosing, hosed 2** to wash or water (a person or thing) with a hose [later use of HOSE[2]]

hose[2] *n* **1** *old-fashioned* stockings, socks, and tights collectively **2** *history* a man's garment covering the legs and reaching up to the waist [Old English *hosa*]

hoser *n* **1** *US slang* a person who swindles or deceives others **2** *Canad slang* an unsophisticated, esp. rural, person

hosiery *n* stockings, socks, and knitted underclothing collectively

hospice (hoss-piss) *n* **1** a nursing home that specializes in caring for the terminally ill **2** *archaic* a place of shelter for travellers, esp. one kept by a religious order [Latin *hospes* guest]

hospitable *adj* generous, friendly, and welcoming to guests or strangers: *charming and hospitable lodgings* [Medieval Latin *hospitare* to receive as a guest] **hospitably** *adv*.

hospital *n* an institution for the medical or psychiatric care and treatment of patients [Latin *hospes* guest]

hospitality *n, pl* **-ties** kindness in welcoming strangers or guests

hospitalize *or* **-lise** *vb* **-lizing, -lized** *or* **-lising, -lised** to admit or send (a person) into a hospital **hospitalization** *or* **-lisation** *n*

hospitaller *or US* **hospitaler** *n* a member of a religious order dedicated to hospital work, ambulance services, etc.

h

host¹ *n* **1** a person who receives or entertains guests, esp. in his or her own home **2** the organization or country providing the facilities for a function or event: *Rio de Janeiro, host of the 2016 Olympic Games* **3** the compere of a radio or television programme **4** *biol* an animal or plant in or on which a parasite lives **5** a computer connected to a network and providing facilities to other computers and their users **6** *old-fashioned* the owner or manager of an inn ▷ *vb* **7** to be the host of (a party, programme, or event): *he's hosting a radio show* [Latin *hospes* guest, host]

host² *n* a great number; multitude [Latin *hostis* stranger]

Host *n Christianity* the bread used in Holy Communion [Latin *hostia* victim]

hostage *n* a person who is illegally held prisoner until certain demands are met by other people [Old French *hoste* guest]

hostel *n* **1** a building providing overnight accommodation at a low cost for particular groups of people, such as the homeless **2** same as **youth hostel** **3** *Brit & NZ* a supervised lodging house for nurses, students, etc. [Medieval Latin *hospitale* hospice] **hosteller** *or US* **hosteler** *n*

hostelry *n, pl* **-ries** *archaic or facetious* an inn

hostel school *n Canad* same as **residential school**

hostess *n* **1** a woman who receives and entertains guests, esp. in her own house **2** a woman who receives and entertains patrons of a club, restaurant, or dance hall

hostile *adj* **1** unfriendly and aggressive **2** opposed (to): *hostile to the referendum* **3** relating to or involving the enemies of a country [Latin *hostis* enemy]

hostility *n, pl* **-ties** **1** unfriendly and aggressive feelings or behaviour **2** **hostilities** acts of warfare

hot *adj* **hotter, hottest** **1** having a relatively high temperature **2** having a temperature higher than desirable **3** spicy or causing a burning sensation on the tongue: *hot chillies* **4** (of a temper) quick to flare up **5** (of a contest or conflict) intense **6** recent or new: *hot from the press* **7** much favoured: *a hot favourite* **8** *informal* having a dangerously high level of radioactivity **9** *slang* stolen or otherwise illegally obtained **10** (of a colour) intense; striking: *hot pink* **11** following closely: *this album appeared hot on the heels of the debut smash* **12** *informal* dangerous or unpleasant: *they're making it hot for me here* **13** (in various games) very near the answer **14** **hot on** *informal* **A** strict about: *they are extremely hot on sloppy language* **B** particularly knowledgeable about **15** **hot under the collar** *informal* aroused with anger, annoyance, or resentment **16** **in hot water** *informal* in trouble ▷ See also **hot up** [Old English *hāt*] **hotly** *adv*

hot air *n informal* empty and usually boastful talk

hotbed *n* a place offering ideal conditions for the growth of an idea or activity: *a hotbed of resistance*

hot-blooded *adj* passionate or excitable

hot-button *adj informal* indicating a controversial subject that is likely to arouse strong emotions: *the hot-button issue of abortion*

hotchpotch *or esp US & Canad* **hodgepodge** *n* a jumbled mixture [Old French *hochepot* shake pot]

hot cross bun *n* a yeast bun marked with a cross and traditionally eaten on Good Friday

hot-desking *n* the practice of not assigning permanent desks in a workplace, so that employees may work at any available desk

hot dog *n* a long roll split lengthways with a hot sausage inside

hotel *n* a commercially run establishment providing lodging and meals for guests [French]

hotelier *n* an owner or manager of a hotel

hotfoot *adv* with all possible speed: *hotfoot to the accident*

hot-gospeller *n informal* a revivalist preacher with a highly enthusiastic delivery

hot-headed *adj* impetuous, rash, or hot-tempered **hot-headedness** *n*

hothouse *n* a greenhouse in which the temperature is maintained at a fixed level

hot key *n* a single key on a computer keyboard which provides a shortcut to a function in an application

hotline *n* a direct telephone link between heads of government for emergency use

hot money *n* capital that is transferred from one financial centre to another seeking the best opportunity for short-term gain

hotplate *n* **1** a heated metal surface on an electric cooker **2** a portable device on which food can be kept warm

hot pool *n NZ* a geothermally heated pool

hotpot *n* a casserole of meat and vegetables covered with a layer of potatoes

hot rod *n* a car with an engine that has been modified to produce increased power

hot seat *n* **1** *US slang* the electric chair **2** **in the hot seat** *informal* in a difficult and responsible position

hotspot *n* **1** a place where there is a lot of exciting activity or entertainment: *Birmingham's fashionable hot spots* **2** an area where there is fighting or political unrest: *a political hot spot in the Caucasus* **3** a small area of abnormally high temperature or radioactivity **4** a place (esp. a public building or commercial premises) offering a wireless internet connection

hot stuff *n informal* **1** a person, object, or activity considered attractive, exciting, or important: *they're still hot stuff* **2** pornographic or erotic books, plays, films, etc.

Hottentot *n offensive* same as **Khoikhoi** [origin unknown]

hotting *n Brit informal* the performing of high-speed stunts in a stolen car **hotter** *n*

hot tub *n* a large, often outdoor, bath filled with aerated water

hot up *vb* **hotting, hotted** *informal* to make or become more active and exciting

hot-water bottle *n* a rubber container, designed to be filled with hot water and used for warming a bed

hound *n* **1** a dog used for hunting: *to ride with the hounds* ▷ *vb* **2** to pursue, disturb, or criticize relentlessly: *hounded by the press* [Old English *hund*]

hour *n* **1** a period of time equal to 60 minutes; $^1/_{24}$ of a day **2** any of the points on the face of a clock or watch that indicate intervals of

60 minutes: *in my hurry I mistook the hour* **3** the time of day **4** the time allowed for, or used for, something: *a three-and-a-half-hour test* **5** the distance covered in an hour: *an hour from the heart of Tokyo* **6** a special moment: *the decisive hour* ▷ See also **hours** [Latin *hora*]

hourglass *n* a device consisting of two transparent sections linked by a narrow channel, containing a quantity of sand that takes an hour to trickle from one section to the other

houri *n, pl* **-ris** (in Muslim belief) any of the nymphs of Paradise [Arabic *haurā'* woman with dark eyes]

hourly *adj* **1** of, occurring, or done once every hour **2** measured by the hour: *hourly charges* **3** frequent ▷ *adv* **4** once every hour **5** by the hour: *hourly paid* **6** frequently **7** at any moment: *the arrival of the men was hourly expected*

hours *pl n* **1** an indefinite time: *they play on their bikes for hours* **2** a period regularly appointed for work or business **3** one's times of rising and going to bed: *you keep very late hours* **4** RC Church prayers recited at seven specified times of the day

Hours *pl n classical myth* the goddesses of the seasons

house *n* **1** a building used as a home; dwelling **2** the people in a house **3** a building for some specific purpose: *beach house* **4** a family or dynasty: *the House of Windsor* **5** a commercial company: *auction house* **6** a law-making body or the hall where it meets **7** a division of a large school: *he was captain of the house rugby team* **8** the audience in a theatre or cinema **9** *astrol* any of the 12 divisions of the zodiac **10** *informal* a brothel **11 get on like a house on fire** *informal* (of people) to get on very well together **12 on the house** (usually of drinks) paid for by the management **13 put one's house in order** to settle or organize one's affairs ▷ *adj* **14** (of wine) sold unnamed by a restaurant, at a lower price than wines specified on the wine list: *house red* ▷ *vb* **housing, housed 15** to give accommodation to **16** to contain or cover (something) [Old English *hūs*]

house arrest *n* confinement to one's own home rather than in prison

houseboat *n* a stationary boat used as a home

housebound *adj* unable to leave one's house, usually because of illness

housebreaking *n criminal law* the act of entering a building as a trespasser for an unlawful purpose **housebreaker** *n*

housecoat *n* a woman's loose robelike garment for indoor wear

housefly *n, pl* **-flies** a common fly often found in houses

household *n* **1** all the people living together in one house ▷ *adj* **2** relating to the running of a household: *household budget*

householder *n* a person who owns or rents a house

household name *or* **household word** *n* a person or thing that is very well known

housekeeper *n* a person employed to run someone else's household

housekeeping *n* **1** the running of a household **2** money allotted for this

house lights *pl n* the lights in the auditorium of a theatre or cinema

housemaid *n* (esp. formerly) a female servant employed to do housework

housemaid's knee *n* a fluid-filled swelling of the kneecap

houseman *n, pl* **-men** *med* a junior doctor in a hospital

house martin *n* a swallow with a slightly forked tail

House music *or* **House** *n* a type of dance music of the late 1980s, based on funk, with fragments of other recordings edited in electronically

House of Commons *n* (in Britain and Canada) the lower chamber of Parliament

House of Keys *n* the lower chamber of the law-making body of the Isle of Man

House of Lords *n* (in Britain) the upper chamber of Parliament, composed of the peers of the realm

House of Representatives *n* **1** (in the US) the lower chamber of Congress, or of many state legislatures **2** (in Australia) the lower chamber of Parliament **3** the sole chamber of New Zealand's Parliament

house party *n* **1** a party, usually in a country house, at which guests are invited to stay for several days **2** the guests who are invited

house-proud *adj* excessively concerned with the appearance, cleanliness, and tidiness of one's house

houseroom *n* **not give something houseroom** not to want to have something in one's house

house-train *vb* to train (a pet) to urinate and defecate outside

housewares *pl n US & Canad* kitchenware and other utensils for use in the home

house-warming *n* a party given after moving into a new home

housewife *n, pl* **-wives** a woman who runs her own household and does not have a paid job **housewifely** *adj*

housework *n* the work of running a home, such as cleaning, cooking, and shopping

housing *n* **1** houses collectively **2** the job of providing people with accommodation **3** a part designed to contain and support a component or mechanism: *the inspection panel set within the concrete housing*

hove *vb chiefly naut* a past of **heave**

hovea *n* an Australian plant with purple flowers

hovel *n* a small house or hut that is dirty or badly in need of repair [origin unknown]

hover *vb* **1** (of a bird, insect, or helicopter) to remain suspended in one place in the air **2** to linger uncertainly in a place **3** to be in an unsettled or uncertain situation or frame of mind: *hovering between two options* [Middle English *hoveren*]

hovercraft *n* a vehicle that is able to travel across both land and water on a cushion of air

how *adv* **1** in what way, by what means: *how did you spend the evening?; observing how elderly people coped* **2** to what extent: *they don't know how tough I am* **3** how good, how well, what ... like: *how good are the copies?; so that's how things are* **4** **how about?**

used to suggest something: *how about some tea?* **5 how are you?** what is your state of health? **6 how's that?** **A** what is your opinion?: *we'll go out for a late-night supper – how's that?* **B** *cricket* Also written: **howzat** (an appeal to the umpire) is the batsman out? [Old English *hu*]

howdah *n* a seat for riding on an elephant's back [Hindi *haudah*]

however *adv* **1** still; nevertheless: *the book does, however, almost get funny* **2** by whatever means: *get there however you can* **3** (*with an adjective or adverb*) no matter how: *however low we plunge, there is always hope*

howitzer *n* a large gun that fires shells at a steep angle [Czech *houfnice* stone-sling]

howl *n* **1** the long, loud wailing noise made by a wolf or dog **2** a similar cry of pain or sorrow **3** a loud burst of laughter ▷ *vb* **4** to express (something) in a howl or utter such cries **5** (of the wind, etc.) to make a wailing noise [Middle English *houlen*]

h

howl down *vb* to prevent (a speaker) from being heard by shouting disapprovingly

howler *n informal* a glaring mistake

howling *adj informal* great: *a howling success*

howzit *sentence substitute S African* an informal word for hello [from the phrase *how is it?*]

hoy *interj* a cry used to attract someone's attention [variant of *hey*]

hoyden *n old-fashioned* a wild boisterous girl; tomboy [perhaps from Middle Dutch *heidijn* heathen] **hoydenish** *adj*

HP *or* **h.p.** **1** *Brit* hire-purchase **2** horsepower

HQ *or* **h.q.** headquarters

hr hour

HRH Her (*or* His) Royal Highness

HRT **1** hormone replacement therapy **2** *Austral & NZ* high rising terminal

Hs *chem* hassium

HST (in Canada) Harmonized Sales Tax

HTML *n computers* hypertext markup language: a text description language that is used on the internet

HTTP *n computers* hypertext transfer protocol: a system of rules for transferring files on the internet

hub *n* **1** the central portion of a wheel, through which the axle passes **2** the central, most important, or active part of a place or organization **3** an airport, railway station, etc from which many services operate and connecting journeys can be made **4** a device for connecting computers in a network [probably variant of *hob*]

hubble-bubble *n* **1** same as **hookah** **2** *archaic* turmoil or confusion [imitative]

hubbub *n* **1** a confused noise of many voices **2** great confusion or excitement [probably from Irish *hooboobbes*]

hubby *n, pl* **-bies** *informal* a husband

hubcap *n* a metal disc that fits onto and protects the hub of a wheel, esp. on a car

hubris (**hew**-briss) *n formal* pride or arrogance [Greek] **hubristic** *adj*

huckster *n* **1** a person who uses aggressive methods of selling **2** *rare* a person who sells small articles or fruit in the street [probably from Middle Dutch *hoekster*]

huddle *n* **1** a small group of people or things standing or lying close together **2** **go into a huddle** *informal* to have a private conference ▷ *vb* **-dling, -dled** **3** (of a group of people) to crowd or nestle closely together **4** to curl up one's arms and legs close to one's body through cold or fear [origin unknown]

hue *n* **1** the feature of colour that enables an observer to classify it as red, blue, etc. **2** a shade of a colour [Old English *hīw* beauty]

hue and cry *n* a loud public outcry [Old French *hue* outcry]

huff *n* **1** a passing mood of anger or resentment: *in a huff* ▷ *vb* **2** to blow or puff heavily **3** *draughts* to remove (an opponent's draught) from the board for failure to make a capture **4** **huffing and puffing** empty threats or objections [imitative] **huffy** *adj* **huffily** *adv*

hug *vb* **hugging, hugged** **1** to clasp (someone or something) tightly, usually with affection **2** to keep close to (a shore or the kerb) ▷ *n* **3** a tight or fond embrace [probably Scandinavian]

huge *adj* extremely large [Old French *ahuge*] **hugely** *adv*

huggermugger *archaic* ▷ *n* **1** confusion or secrecy ▷ *adj, adv* **2** in confusion [origin unknown]

Huguenot (**hew**-gan-oh) *n* a French Calvinist of the 16th or 17th centuries [French]

huh *interj* an exclamation of derision, bewilderment, or inquiry

hui (**hoo**-ee) *n, pl* **huis** NZ **1** a Māori social gathering **2** a meeting to discuss Māori matters **3** any party [Māori]

hula *n* a Hawaiian dance performed by a woman [Hawaiian]

Hula Hoop *n trademark* a plastic hoop swung round the body by wiggling the hips

hulk *n* **1** the body of an abandoned ship **2** *derogatory* a large ungainly person or thing [Old English *hulc*]

hulking *adj* big and ungainly

hull *n* **1** the main body of a boat **2** the outer covering of a fruit or seed such as a pea or bean **3** the leaves round the stem of a strawberry, raspberry, or similar fruit ▷ *vb* **4** to remove the hulls from (fruit or seeds) [Old English *hulu*]

hullabaloo *n, pl* **-loos** a loud confused noise or commotion [*hallo* + Scots *baloo* lullaby]

hullo *interj, n* same as **hello**

hum *vb* **humming, hummed** **1** to make a low continuous vibrating sound **2** (of a person) to sing with the lips closed **3** to utter an indistinct sound when hesitating **4** *informal* to be in a state of feverish activity: *the town hums with activity and life* **5** *slang* to smell unpleasant **6** **hum and haw** See **haw**[2] ▷ *n* **7** a low continuous murmuring sound **8** an unpleasant smell ▷ *interj, n* **9** an indistinct sound of hesitation [imitative]

human *adj* **1** of or relating to people: *human occupants* **2** having the qualities of people as opposed to animals, divine beings, or machines: *human nature* **3** kind or considerate ▷ *n* **4** a human being [Latin *humanus*]

human being *n* a man, woman, or child
humane *adj* **1** showing kindness and sympathy **2** inflicting as little pain as possible: *a humane method of killing minke whales* **3** considered to have a civilizing effect on people: *the humane tradition of a literary education* [variant of *human*]
humanism *n* the rejection of religion in favour of a belief in the advancement of humanity by its own efforts **humanist** *n, adj* **humanistic** *adj*
humanitarian *adj* **1** having the interests of mankind at heart ▷ *n* **2** a person who has the interests of mankind at heart **humanitarianism** *n*
humanity *n, pl* **-ties 1** the human race **2** the quality of being human **3** kindness or mercy **4 humanities** the study of literature, philosophy, and the arts
humanize *or* **-ise** *vb* **-izing, -ized** *or* **-ising, -ised** to make human or humane **humanization** *or* **-isation** *n*
humankind *n* the human race; humanity
USAGE See at **mankind.**
humanly *adv* by human powers or means: *as fast as is humanly possible*
humanoid *adj* **1** like a human being in appearance ▷ *n* **2** (in science fiction) a robot or creature resembling a human being
human race *n* all men, women, and children collectively
human resources *pl n* **1** the people employed in an organization or for a service **2** (*functioning as sing*) the department in an organization that appoints or keeps records of employees
human rights *pl n* the basic rights of individuals to liberty, justice, etc.
humble *adj* **1** conscious of one's failings **2** modest and unpretentious: *humble domestic objects* **3** ordinary or not very important: *humble beginnings* ▷ *vb* **-bling, -bled 4** to cause to become humble; humiliate [Latin *humilis* low] **humbly** *adv*
humble pie *n* **eat humble pie** to be forced to behave humbly; be humiliated [earlier *an umble pie*, from *numbles* offal of a deer]
humbug *n* **1** *Brit* a hard peppermint sweet with a striped pattern **2** a speech or piece of writing that is obviously untrue, dishonest, or nonsense **3** a dishonest person [origin unknown]
humdinger *n slang* **1** something unusually large **2** an excellent person or thing [origin unknown]
humdrum *adj* ordinary, dull, and uninteresting [probably based on *hum*]
humerus (**hew**-mer-uss) *n, pl* **-meri** (-mer-rye) the bone from the shoulder to the elbow [Latin *umerus*] **humeral** *adj*
humid *adj* (of the weather) damp and warm [Latin *umidus*]
humidex (**hew**-mid-ex) *n Canad* a system of measuring discomfort showing the combined effect of humidity and temperature
humidify *vb* **-fies, -fying, -fied** to make the air in (a room) more humid or damp **humidifier** *n*
humidity *n* **1** dampness **2** a measure of the amount of moisture in the air
humiliate *vb* **-ating, -ated** to hurt the dignity or pride of: *the English cricket team was humiliated by Australia* [Latin *humilis* humble] **humiliating** *adj* **humiliation** *n*
humility *n* the quality of being humble and modest
hummingbird *n* a very small brightly-coloured American bird with a long slender bill, and powerful wings that hum as they vibrate
hummock *n* a very small hill or a mound [origin unknown]
hummus *n* a creamy dip originating in the Middle East, made from puréed chickpeas [from Turkish *humus*]
humongous a variant of **humungous**
humorist *n* a person who speaks or writes in a humorous way
humorous *adj* amusing, esp. in a witty or clever way **humorously** *adv*
humour *or US* **humor** *n* **1** the quality of being funny **2** the ability to appreciate or express things that are humorous: *a sense of humour* **3** situations, speech, or writings that are humorous **4** a state of mind; mood: *in astoundingly good humour* **5** *archaic* any of various fluids in the body: *aqueous humour* ▷ *vb* **6** to be kind and indulgent to: *he decided the patient needed to be humoured* [Latin *humor* liquid] **humourless** *adj*
hump *n* **1** a rounded lump on the ground **2** a rounded deformity of the back **3** a rounded lump on the back of a camel or related animal **4 the hump** *Brit informal* a fit of sulking: *you've got the hump today* ▷ *vb* **5** *slang* to carry or heave: *who would be responsible if they were injured humping heavy gear around?* [probably from *humpbacked*]
humpback *n* **1** same as **hunchback 2** Also called: **humpback whale** a large whalebone whale with a hump on its back **3** Also called: **humpback bridge** *Brit* a road bridge with a sharp slope on either side **humpbacked** *adj*
humph *interj* an exclamation of annoyance or scepticism
humungous *or esp US* **humongous** (hew-**mung**-gus) *adj informal* very large; enormous: *it was not a humungous box office hit* [probably from *huge + enormous*]
humus (**hew**-muss) *n* a dark brown or black mass of partially decomposed plant and animal matter in the soil [Latin: soil]
Humvee *n* a four-wheel drive military vehicle [h(igh-mobility) + m(ulti-purpose) v(ehicle) + -EE]
Hun *n, pl* **Huns** *or* **Hun 1** a member of any of several Asiatic peoples who invaded the Roman Empire in the 4th and 5th centuries AD **2** *offensive, informal* (esp. in World War I) a German [Old English *Hūnas*]
hunch *n* **1** a feeling or suspicion not based on facts: *she said that she had had a hunch that the coup would not succeed* **2** same as **hump** ▷ *vb* **3** to draw (oneself or one's shoulders) up or together [origin unknown]
hunchback *n old-fashioned, offensive* a person who has an abnormal curvature of the spine **hunchbacked** *adj*
hundred *n, pl* **-dreds** *or* **-dred 1** the cardinal number that is the product of ten and ten **2** a numeral, 100 or C, representing this number **3** (*often pl*) a large but unspecified number ▷ *adj* **4** amounting to a hundred: *a hundred yards* [Old English] **hundredth** *adj, n*

hundreds and thousands *pl n* tiny beads of coloured sugar, used in decorating cakes and sweets

hundredweight *n, pl* **-weights** *or* **-weight 1** *Brit* a unit of weight equal to 112 pounds or 50.802kg **2** *US & Canad* a unit of weight equal to 100 pounds or 45.359kg **3** a metric unit of weight equal to 50 kilograms

hung *vb* **1** the past of **hang** ▷ *adj* **2** (of a parliament or jury) with no side having a clear majority **3 hung over** *informal* suffering the effects of a hangover

USAGE When *hang* means 'execute', the past tense and past participle is *hanged* instead of *hung*.

Hungarian *adj* **1** of Hungary ▷ *n* **2** a person from Hungary **3** the language of Hungary

hunger *n* **1** a feeling of emptiness or weakness caused by lack of food **2** a lack of food that causes suffering or death: *refugees dying of hunger and disease* **3** desire or craving: *Europe's hunger for bullion* ▷ *vb* **4 hunger for** to have a great desire for [Old English *hungor*]

hunger strike *n* a refusal of all food, usually by a prisoner, as a means of protest

hungry *adj* **-grier, -griest 1** desiring food **2** (foll. by *for*) having a craving, desire, or need for: *hungry for revenge* **3** expressing greed, craving, or desire: *the media's hungry search for impact* **hungrily** *adv*

hunk *n* **1** a large piece: *a hunk of bread* **2** *slang* a well-built, sexually attractive man [probably related to Flemish *hunke*]

hunkers *pl n informal* haunches [origin unknown]

hunt *vb* **1** to seek out and kill (animals) for food or sport **2 hunt down** to track in an attempt to capture (someone): *hunting down villains* **3 hunt for** to search for: *Western companies are hunting for opportunities to invest* ▷ *n* **4** the act or an instance of hunting **5** a party organized for the pursuit of wild animals for sport **6** the members of such a party [Old English *huntian*] **hunting** *n*

huntaway *n* NZ a sheepdog trained to drive sheep by barking

hunter *n* **1** a person or animal that seeks out and kills or captures game **2** a person who looks carefully for something: *a house hunter* **3** a horse or dog bred for hunting **4** a watch with a hinged metal lid or case to protect the glass

hunter-gatherer *n* a member of a society that lives by hunting and gathering naturally occurring resources

huntsman *n, pl* **-men 1** a person who hunts **2** a person who trains hounds and manages them during a hunt

hurdle *n* **1** *athletics* one of a number of light barriers over which runners leap in certain events **2** a difficulty or problem: *the main technical hurdle is the environment* **3 hurdles** a race involving hurdles ▷ *vb* **-dling, -dled 4** to jump over (a hurdle or other obstacle) [Old English *hyrdel*] **hurdler** *n*

hurdy-gurdy *n, pl* **hurdy-gurdies** a mechanical musical instrument, such as a barrel organ [probably imitative]

hurl *vb* **1** to throw (something) with great force **2** to utter (something) with force; yell: *onlookers hurled abuse at them* [probably imitative]

hurling *or* **hurley** *n* a traditional Irish game resembling hockey

hurly-burly *n* great noise and activity; commotion [obsolete *hurling* uproar]

hurrah *or* **hooray** *interj, n* a cheer of joy or victory [probably from German *hurra*]

hurricane *n* a severe, often destructive storm, esp. a tropical cyclone [Spanish *huracán*]

hurricane lamp *n* a paraffin lamp with a glass covering

hurried *adj* done quickly or too quickly **hurriedly** *adv* **hurriedness** *n*

hurry *vb* **-ries, -rying, -ried 1** to move or act, or cause to move or act, in great haste: *the umpires hurried the players off the ground* **2** to speed up the completion or progress of: *eat a small snack rather than hurry a main meal* ▷ *n* **3** haste **4** urgency or eagerness **5 in a hurry** *informal* **A** easily: *a striking old guy, not the sort you'd forget in a hurry* **B** willingly: *he would not ease interest rates again in a hurry* [probably imitative]

hurt *vb* **hurting, hurt 1** to cause physical or mental injury to: *is she badly hurt?* **2** to cause someone to feel pain: *my head hurt* **3** *informal* to feel pain: *she was hurting* ▷ *n* **4** physical or mental pain or suffering ▷ *adj* **5** injured or pained: *his hurt head; a hurt expression* [Old French *hurter* to knock against] **hurtful** *adj*

hurtle *vb* **-ling, -led** to move very quickly or violently [Middle English *hurtlen*]

husband *n* **1** the man to whom a person is married ▷ *vb* **2** to use (resources, finances, etc.) economically [Old English *hūsbonda*]

husbandry *n* **1** the art or skill of farming **2** management of resources

hush *vb* **1** to make or be silent ▷ *n* **2** stillness or silence ▷ *interj* **3** a plea or demand for silence ▷ See also **hush up** [earlier *husht* quiet!] **hushed** *adj*

hush-hush *adj informal* (esp. of official work) secret and confidential

hush money *n slang* money given to a person to ensure that something is kept secret

hush up *vb* to suppress information or rumours about (something)

husk *n* **1** the outer covering of certain fruits and seeds ▷ *vb* **2** to remove the husk from [probably from Middle Dutch *hūs* house]

husky[1] *adj* **huskier, huskiest 1** (of a voice) slightly hoarse **2** *informal* (of a man) big and strong [probably from *husk*, from the toughness of a corn husk] **huskily** *adv*

husky[2] *n, pl* **huskies** an Arctic sledge dog with thick hair and a curled tail [probably based on *Eskimo*]

hussar (hoo-zar) *n history* a member of a light cavalry regiment [Hungarian *huszár*]

hussy *n, pl* **-sies** *old-fashioned, derogatory* a woman considered sexually immoral or improper [from *hussif* housewife]

hustings *pl n* the campaigns and speeches at a parliamentary election [Old Norse *hūsthing*, from *hūs* house + *thing* assembly]

hustle *vb* **-tling, -tled 1** to make (someone) move by pushing or jostling them: *he hustled her away* **2** to deal with (something) hurriedly: *they did not*

h

heedlessly hustle the tempo **3** *US & Canad slang* (of a prostitute) to solicit clients ▷ *n* **4** lively activity and excitement [Dutch *husselen* to shake]
hustler *n US informal* a person who tries to make money or gain an advantage from every situation, often by immoral or dishonest means
hut *n* a small house or shelter [French *hutte*]
hutch *n* a cage for small animals [Old French *huche*]
hyacinth *n* a plant with bell-shaped sweet-smelling flowers [Greek *huakinthos*]
hyaena *n* same as **hyena**
hybrid *n* **1** an animal or plant resulting from a cross between two different types of animal or plant **2** a vehicle that is powered by an internal-combustion engine and another source of power **3** anything that is a mixture of two different things ▷ *adj* **4** of mixed origin **5** (of a vehicle) powered by an internal-combustion engine and another source of power [Latin *hibrida*]
hybridize *or* **-dise** *vb* **-dizing, -dized** *or* **-dising, -dised** to produce or cause (species) to produce hybrids; crossbreed **hybridization** *or* **-disation** *n*
hydatid disease (**hide**-at-id) *n* a condition caused by the presence of bladder-like cysts (**hydatids**) in the liver, lungs, or brain [Greek *hudatis* watery sac]
hydra *n* **1** a mythical many-headed serpent **2** a persistent problem: *killing the hydra of drug production is impossible* **3** a microscopic freshwater creature with a slender tubular body and tentacles around the mouth [Greek *hudra* water serpent]
hydrangea *n* an ornamental shrub with large clusters of white, pink, or blue flowers [Greek *hudōr* water + *angeion* vessel]
hydrant *n* an outlet from a water main, from which water can be tapped for fighting fires
hydrate *chem* ▷ *n* **1** a compound containing water chemically combined with a substance: *chloral hydrate* ▷ *vb* **-drating, -drated 2** to treat or impregnate (a substance) with water **hydration** *n*
hydraulic *adj* operated by pressure transmitted through a pipe by a liquid, such as water or oil [Greek *hudōr* water + *aulos* pipe] **hydraulically** *adv*
hydraulics *n* the study of the mechanical properties of fluids as they apply to practical engineering
hydride *n chem* a compound of hydrogen with another element
hydro[1] *n, pl* **-dros** *Brit* a hotel offering facilities for hydropathic treatment
hydro[2] *adj* **1** short for **hydroelectric** ▷ *n* **2** *Canad* electricity as supplied to a residence, business, etc.
hydro- *or before a vowel* **hydr-** *combining form* **1** indicating water or fluid: *hydrodynamics* **2** *chem* indicating hydrogen in a chemical compound: *hydrochloric acid* [Greek *hudōr* water]
hydrocarbon *n chem* a compound containing only carbon and hydrogen
hydrocephalus *n* accumulation of fluid in the cavities of the brain, causing enlargement of the head in children [Greek *hudōr* water + *kephalē* head] **hydrocephalic** *adj*
hydrochloric acid *n chem* a solution of hydrogen chloride in water: a strong acid used in many industrial and laboratory processes
hydrodynamics *n* the branch of science concerned with the mechanical properties of fluids
hydroelectric *adj* **1** generated by the pressure of falling water: *hydroelectric power* **2** of the generation of electricity by water pressure: *a hydroelectric scheme* **hydroelectricity** *n*
hydrofoil *n* **1** a fast light vessel the hull of which is raised out of the water on one or more pairs of fins **2** any of these fins
hydrogen *n chem* a colourless gas that burns easily and is the lightest element in the universe. It occurs in water and in most organic compounds. Symbol: **H** [HYDRO- + *-gen* (producing); because its combustion produces water] **hydrogenous** *adj*
hydrogenate (hide-**roj**-in-nate) *vb* **-ating, -ated** *chem* to combine (a substance) with hydrogen: *hydrogenated vegetable oil* **hydrogenation** *n*
hydrogen bomb *n* an extremely powerful bomb in which energy is released by fusion of hydrogen nuclei to give helium nuclei
hydrogen peroxide *n* a colourless oily unstable liquid chemical used as a hair bleach and as an antiseptic
hydrogen sulphide *n* a colourless poisonous gas with an odour of rotten eggs
hydrography (hide-**rog**-ra-fee) *n* the study of the oceans, seas, and rivers **hydrographer** *n* **hydrographic** *adj*
hydrology *n* the study of the distribution, conservation, and use of the water of the earth and its atmosphere
hydrolysis (hide-**rol**-iss-iss) *n chem* a process of decomposition in which a compound reacts with water to produce other compounds [Greek *hudōr* water + *lusis* a loosening]
hydrometer (hide-**rom**-it-er) *n* an instrument for measuring the density of a liquid
hydropathy *n* a method of treating disease by the use of large quantities of water both internally and externally [Greek *hudōr* water + *patheia* suffering] **hydropathic** *adj*
hydrophilic *adj chem* tending to dissolve in or mix with water: *a hydrophilic layer*
hydrophobia *n* **1** same as **rabies 2** (esp. of a person with rabies) a fear of drinking fluids **hydrophobic** *adj*
hydroplane *n* **1** a motorboat that raises its hull out of the water at high speeds **2** a fin on the hull of a submarine for controlling its vertical motion
hydroponics *n* a method of growing plants in gravel, etc., through which water containing the necessary nutrients is pumped [HYDRO- + *(geo)ponics* science of agriculture]
hydrosphere *n* the watery part of the earth's surface
hydrostatics *n* the branch of science concerned with the properties and behaviour of fluids that are not in motion **hydrostatic** *adj*
hydrotherapy *n med* the treatment of certain diseases by exercise in water

hydrous *adj* containing water
hydroxide *n chem* a compound containing a hydroxyl group or ion
hydroxyl *adj chem* of or containing the monovalent group –OH or the ion OH^-: *forming a hydroxyl radical*
hyena *or* **hyaena** *n* a meat-eating doglike mammal of Africa and S Asia [Greek *hus* hog]
hygiene *n* **1** the principles and practices of health and cleanliness: *personal hygiene* **2** Also called: **hygienics** the science concerned with the maintenance of health [Greek *hugieinē*] **hygienic** *adj* **hygienically** *adv* **hygienist** *n*
hygrometer (hie-**grom**-it-er) *n* an instrument for measuring humidity [Greek *hugros* wet]
hygroscope *n* any device that indicates the humidity of the air without necessarily measuring it, such as an animal or vegetable fibre which contracts with moisture [Greek *hugros* wet + *skopein* to observe]
hygroscopic *adj* (of a substance) tending to absorb water from the air
hymen *n anatomy* a membrane that partly covers the entrance to the vagina and is usually ruptured when sexual intercourse takes place for the first time [Greek: membrane]
hymenopterous *adj* of or belonging to an order of insects with two pairs of membranous wings [Greek *humēn* membrane + *pteron* wing]
hymn *n* a Christian song of praise sung to God or a saint [Greek *humnos*]
hymnal *n* a book of hymns. Also: **hymn book**
hymnody *n* **1** the composition or singing of hymns **2** hymns collectively
hymnology *n* the study of hymn composition **hymnologist** *n*
hype *slang* ▷ *n* **1** intensive or exaggerated publicity or sales promotion ▷ *vb* **hyping, hyped 2** to market or promote (a commodity) using intensive or exaggerated publicity [origin unknown]
hyped up *adj old-fashioned slang* stimulated or excited by, or as if by, drugs
hyper *adj informal* overactive or overexcited
hyper- *prefix* above, over, or in excess: *hypercritical* [Greek *huper* over]
hyperactive *adj* (of a person) unable to relax and always in a state of restless activity
hyperbola (hie-**per**-bol-a) *n geom* a curve produced when a cone is cut by a plane at a steeper angle to its base than its side [Greek *huperbolē*]
hyperbole (hie-**per**-bol-ee) *n* a deliberate exaggeration of speech or writing used for effect, such as *he embraced her a thousand times* [Greek *huper* over + *ballein* to throw]
hyperbolic *or* **hyperbolical** *adj* **1** exaggerated **2** of a hyperbola or a hyperbole
hypercritical *adj* excessively critical
hyperglycaemia *or US* **hyperglycemia** (hie-per-glice-**seem**-ee-a) *n pathol* an abnormally large amount of sugar in the blood [Greek *huper* over + *glukus* sweet]
hyperlink *computers* ▷ *n* **1** a word, picture, etc., in a computer document on which a user may click to move to another part of the document or to another document ▷ *vb* **2** to link (files) in this way
hypermarket *n* a huge self-service store [translation of French *hypermarché*]
hypersensitive *adj* **1** unduly emotionally vulnerable **2** abnormally sensitive to an allergen, a drug, or high or low temperatures
hypersexual *adj* **1** excessively interested in sexual activity **2** inappropriately sexualized: *hypersexual and explicit portrayals of women*
hypersonic *adj* having a speed of at least five times the speed of sound
hypertension *n pathol* abnormally high blood pressure
hypertext *n* computer software and hardware that allows users to store and view text and move between related items easily
hypertrophy (hie-**per**-trof-fee) *n, pl* **-phies** enlargement of an organ or part resulting from an increase in the size of the cells [Greek *huper* over + *trophē* nourishment]
hyperventilation *n* an increase in the rate of breathing at rest, sometimes resulting in cramp and dizziness **hyperventilate** *vb*
hyphen *n* the punctuation mark (-), used to separate parts of compound words and between syllables of a word split between two consecutive lines [Greek *huphen* together]
hyphenate *vb* **-ating, -ated** to separate (words) with a hyphen **hyphenation** *n*
hyphenated *adj* having two words or syllables connected by a hyphen
hypnosis *n* an artificially induced state of relaxation in which the mind is more than usually receptive to suggestion
hypnotherapy *n* the use of hypnosis in the treatment of emotional and mental health problems **hypnotherapist** *n*
hypnotic *adj* **1** of or producing hypnosis or sleep **2** having an effect resembling hypnosis: *the film makes for hypnotic viewing* ▷ *n* **3** a drug that induces sleep [Greek *hupnos* sleep] **hypnotically** *adv*
hypnotism *n* the practice of or process of inducing hypnosis **hypnotist** *n*
hypnotize *or* **-tise** *vb* **-tizing, -tized** *or* **-tising, -tised 1** to induce hypnosis in (a person) **2** to hold the attention of (someone) completely; fascinate; mesmerize: *hypnotized by her beauty*
hypo- *or before a vowel* **hyp-** *prefix* beneath; less than: *hypodermic* [Greek *hupo* under]
hypoallergenic *adj* not likely to cause an allergic reaction
hypocaust *n* an ancient Roman heating system in which hot air circulated under the floor and between double walls [Latin *hypocaustum*, from Greek *hupokauston* room heated from below]
hypochondria *n* abnormal anxiety concerning one's health [Late Latin: abdomen, supposedly the seat of melancholy]
hypochondriac *n* a person abnormally concerned about his or her health
hypocrisy (hip-**ok**-rass-ee) *n, pl* **-sies 1** the practice of claiming to have standards or beliefs that are contrary to one's real character or actual behaviour **2** an act or instance of this

hypocrite (**hip**-oh-krit) *n* a person who pretends to be what he or she is not [Greek *hupokrinein* to pretend] **hypocritical** *adj*

hypodermic *adj* **1** used for injecting ▷ *n* **2** a hypodermic syringe or needle

hypodermic syringe *n* a syringe consisting of a hollow cylinder, a piston, and a hollow needle, used for withdrawing blood samples or injecting drugs under the skin

hypotension *n pathol* abnormally low blood pressure

hypotenuse (hie-**pot**-a-news) *n* the side in a right-angled triangle that is opposite the right angle [Greek *hupoteinousa grammē* subtending line]

hypothalamus *n, pl* **-mi** an area at the base of the brain, which controls hunger, thirst, and other functions

hypothermia *n pathol* an abnormally low body temperature, as a result of exposure to cold weather

hypothesis (hie-**poth**-iss-iss) *n, pl* **-ses** (-seez) a suggested explanation for a group of facts, accepted either as a basis for further verification or as likely to be true [Greek *hupotithenai* to propose, literally: put under] **hypothesize** *or* **-ise** *vb*

hypothetical *adj* based on assumption rather than fact or reality **hypothetically** *adv*

hyrax (**hire**-ax) *n, pl* **hyraxes** *or* **hyraces** (**hire**-a-seez) a genus of hoofed rodent-like animals

hyssop *n* **1** an aromatic plant used in herbal medicine **2** a Biblical plant, used for sprinkling in the ritual practices of the Hebrews [Greek *hussōpos*]

hysterectomy *n, pl* **-mies** surgical removal of the womb [Greek *hustera* womb + *tomē* a cutting]

hysteria *n* **1** a psychological disorder marked by emotional outbursts and, often, symptoms such as paralysis **2** any uncontrolled emotional state, such as of panic, anger, or excitement [Greek *hustera* womb, from the belief that hysteria in women originated in disorders of the womb]

hysteric *n* a hysterical person

hysterical *adj* **1** in a state of uncontrolled panic, anger, or excitement **2** *informal* wildly funny **hysterically** *adv*

hysterics *n* **1** an attack of hysteria **2** *informal* wild uncontrollable bursts of laughter

Hz hertz

Ii

i the imaginary number $\sqrt{-1}$
I[1] *pron* used by a speaker or writer to refer to himself or herself as the subject of a verb [Old English *ic*]
I[2] **1** *chem* iodine **2** the Roman numeral for one
I. **1** Independent **2** Institute **3** International **4** Island; Isle
IA Iowa
iamb (**eye**-am) *or* **iambus** *n, pl* **iambs** *or* **iambuses** *prosody* a metrical foot of two syllables, a short one followed by a long one [Greek *iambos*]
iambic (eye-**am**-bik) *prosody* ▷ *adj* **1** written in metrical units of one short and one long syllable ▷ *n* **2** an iambic foot, line, or stanza
Iberian *adj* **1** of Iberia, the peninsula made up of Spain and Portugal ▷ *n* **2** a person from Iberia
ibex (**ibe**-eks) *n, pl* **ibexes** *or* **ibex** a wild mountain goat with large backward-curving horns [Latin: chamois]
ibid. in the same place: used to refer to a book, page, or passage previously cited [Latin *ibidem*]
ibis (**ibe**-iss) *n, pl* **ibises** *or* **ibis** a large wading bird with a long thin curved bill [Egyptian *hby*]
Ibo (**ee**-boh) *n* **1** *pl* **Ibos** *or* **Ibo** a member of an African people of S Nigeria **2** their language
ICBM intercontinental ballistic missile
ice *n* **1** water that has frozen and become solid **2** *chiefly Brit* a portion of ice cream **3 break the ice** to relax the atmosphere, esp. between strangers **4 on ice** in readiness or reserve **5 on thin ice** in a dangerous situation: *he knew he was on thin ice* **6 the Ice** NZ *informal* Antarctica ▷ *vb* **icing, iced** **7** (foll. by *up* or *over*) to become covered with ice **8** to cover with icing **9** to cool or chill with ice [Old English *īs*]
ice age *n* any period of time during which a large part of the earth's surface was covered with ice, caused by the advance of glaciers
iceberg *n* **1** a large mass of ice floating in the sea **2 tip of the iceberg** the small visible part of a problem that is much larger [probably Middle Dutch *ijsberg* ice mountain]
iceberg lettuce *n* a type of lettuce with very crisp pale leaves tightly enfolded
iceboat *n* another name for **icebreaker**
icebox *n* **1** *US & Canad* a refrigerator **2** a compartment in a refrigerator for making or storing ice **3** a container packed with ice for keeping food and drink cold
icebreaker *n* a ship designed to break a channel through ice
icecap *n* a thick mass of glacial ice that permanently covers an area
ice cream *n* a sweet frozen food, made from cream, milk, or a custard base, flavoured in various ways
iced *adj* **1** served very cold **2** covered with icing
ice field *n* a large expanse of floating sea ice
ice floe *n* a sheet of ice floating in the sea
ice hockey *n* a game like hockey played on ice by two teams wearing skates
Icelander *n* a person from Iceland
Icelandic *adj* **1** of Iceland ▷ *n* **2** the official language of Iceland
ice lolly *n Brit informal* a water ice or an ice cream on a stick
ice pack *n* **1** a bag or folded cloth containing crushed ice, applied to a part of the body to reduce swelling **2** same as **pack ice**
ice skate *n* **1** a boot with a steel blade fitted to the sole which enables the wearer to glide over ice ▷ *vb* **ice-skate, -skating, -skated** **2** to glide over ice on ice skates **ice-skater** *n*
icewine *n Canad* a dessert wine made from grapes that have frozen before being harvested
I Ching *n* an ancient Chinese book of divination and a source of Confucian and Taoist philosophy
ichneumon (ik-**new**-mon) *n* a greyish-brown mongoose
ichthyology (ik-thi-**ol**-a-jee) *n* the study of fishes [Greek *ikhthus* fish + -LOGY] **ichthyological** *adj* **ichthyologist** *n*
icicle *n* a tapering spike of ice hanging where water has dripped [from ICE + Old English *gicel* icicle]
icing *n* **1** Also (esp. US and Canad.): **frosting** a mixture of sugar and water or egg whites used to cover and decorate cakes **2** the formation of ice on a ship or aircraft **3 icing on the cake** any unexpected extra or bonus
icing sugar *n* a very finely ground sugar used for making icing or sweets
icon *or* **ikon** *n* **1** a picture of Christ, the Virgin Mary, or a saint, venerated in the Orthodox Church **2** a picture on a computer screen representing a computer function that can be activated by moving the cursor over it **3** a person or thing regarded as a symbol of a belief or cultural movement: *a feminist icon* [Greek *eikōn* image]
iconoclast *n* **1** a person who attacks established or traditional ideas or principles **2** a destroyer of religious images or objects [Late Greek *eikōn* icon + *klastēs* breaker] **iconoclastic** *adj* **iconoclasm** *n*
icosahedron (ike-oh-sa-**heed**-ron) *n, pl* **-drons** *or* **-dra** (-dra) a solid figure with 20 faces [Greek *eikosi* twenty + *-edron* -sided]
icy *adj* **icier, iciest** **1** freezing or very cold **2** covered with ice: *an icy runway* **3** cold or reserved in manner **icily** *adv* **iciness** *n*
id *n psychoanalysis* the primitive instincts and energies in the unconscious mind that underlie all psychological impulses [Latin: it]
ID **1** Idaho **2** identification
Id. Idaho
I'd I had *or* I would
idea *n* **1** any product of mental activity; thought **2** a scheme, intention, or plan **3** the thought of something: *the idea excites me* **4** a belief or opinion **5** a vague notion; inkling: *they had no idea of the*

severity of my injuries **6** a person's conception of something: *his idea of integrity is not the same as mine* **7** aim or purpose: *the idea is to economize on transport* **8** *philosophy* (in Plato) a universal model of which all things in the same class are only imperfect imitations [Greek: model, outward appearance]

USAGE It is usually considered correct to say that someone has *the idea of doing* something, rather than *the idea to do* it: *he had the idea of taking* (not *the idea to take*) *a short holiday.*

ideal *n* **1** (*often pl*) a principle or model of ethical behaviour **2** a conception of something that is perfect **3** a person or thing considered to represent perfection **4** something existing only as an idea ▷ *adj* **5** most suitable: *the ideal person to head the delegation* **6** of, involving, or existing only as an idea; imaginary: *an ideal world* **ideally** *adv*

idealism *n* **1** belief in or striving towards ideals **2** the tendency to represent things in their ideal forms, rather than as they are **3** *philosophy* the doctrine that material objects and the external world do not exist in reality, but are creations of the mind **idealist** *n* **idealistic** *adj*

idealize *or* **-lise** *vb* **-lizing, -lized** *or* **-lising, -lised** to consider or represent (something) as ideal or more nearly perfect than is true **idealization** *or* **-lisation** *n*

idée fixe (ee-day **feeks**) *n, pl* **idées fixes** (ee-day **feeks**) an idea with which a person is obsessed [French]

idem *pron, adj* the same: used to refer to an article, chapter, or book already quoted [Latin]

identical *adj* **1** that is the same: *they got the identical motel room as last year* **2** exactly alike or equal **3** (of twins) developed from a single fertilized ovum that has split into two, and thus of the same sex and very much alike [Latin *idem* the same] **identically** *adv*

identification parade *n* a group of people, including one suspected of a crime, assembled to discover whether a witness can identify the suspect

identify *vb* **-fies, -fying, -fied 1** to prove or recognize as being a certain person or thing; determine the identity of **2** (often foll. by *with*) to understand and sympathize with a person or group because one regards oneself as being similar or similarly situated **3** to consider or treat as the same **4** to connect or associate closely: *he was closely identified with the community charge* **identifiable** *adj* **identification** *n*

Identikit *n* **1** *trademark* a composite picture, assembled from descriptions given, of a person wanted by the police ▷ *adj* **2** artificially created; formulaic: *an identikit pop group* **3** stereotypical: *the identikit tenacious lawyer*

identity *n, pl* **-ties 1** the state of being a specified person or thing: *the identity of his murderers was not immediately established* **2** the individual characteristics by which a person or thing is recognized **3** the state of being the same **4** *maths* Also called: **identity element** a member of a set that when combined with any other member of the set, leaves it unchanged: the identity for multiplication of numbers is 1 [Latin *idem* the same]

identity card *n* a card with a person's name, photograph, and other personal information on it

identity theft *n* the fraudulent use of another person's name and personal details to open a bank account, obtain credit, etc.

ideo- *combining form* of or indicating ideas: *ideology* [from French *idéo-*, from Greek *idea* idea]

ideogram *or* **ideograph** *n* a character or symbol that directly represents a concept or thing, rather than the sounds that form its name [Greek *idea* idea + *gramma* a drawing]

ideology *n, pl* **-gies** the body of ideas and beliefs of a person, group, or nation [from IDEO- + -LOGY] **ideological** *adj* **ideologically** *adv* **ideologist** *n*

ides *n* (in the ancient Roman calendar) the 15th day in March, May, July, and October and the 13th of the other months [Latin *idus*]

idiocy *n, pl* **-cies 1** utter stupidity **2** a foolish act or remark

idiom *n* **1** a group of words which, when used together, have a different meaning from the one suggested by the individual words, eg *it was raining cats and dogs* **2** linguistic usage that is grammatical and natural to native speakers **3** the characteristic vocabulary or usage of a person or group **4** the characteristic artistic style of an individual or school [Greek *idios* private, separate] **idiomatic** *adj*

idiosyncrasy *n, pl* **-sies** a personal peculiarity of mind, habit, or behaviour; quirk [Greek *idios* private, separate + *sunkrasis* mixture] **idiosyncratic** *adj*

idiot *n* **1** a foolish or senseless person **2** *old-fashioned, offensive* a person with severe learning difficulties [Greek *idiōtēs* private person, ignoramus] **idiotic** *adj* **idiotically** *adv*

idle *adj* **1** not doing anything **2** not operating or being used **3** not wanting to work; lazy **4** ineffective or useless: *it would be idle to look for a solution at this stage* **5** frivolous or trivial: *idle pleasures* **6** without basis; unfounded: *idle rumours* ▷ *vb* **idling, idled 7** (often foll. by *away*) to waste or pass (time) in idleness **8** (of an engine) to run at low speed without transmitting any power [Old English *īdel*] **idleness** *n* **idler** *n* **idly** *adv*

idol (**eye**-dl) *n* **1** an object of excessive devotion or admiration **2** an image of a god used as an object of worship [Greek *eidōlon* image]

idolatry (ide-**ol**-a-tree) *n* **1** the worship of idols **2** excessive devotion or reverence **idolater** *n* **idolatrous** *adj*

idolize *or* **-lise** *vb* **-lizing, -lized** *or* **-lising, -lised 1** to love or admire excessively **2** to worship as an idol **idolization** *or* **-lisation** *n*

idyll *or US sometimes* **idyl** (**id**-ill) *n* **1** a scene or time of peace and happiness **2** a poem or prose work describing a charming rural scene or episode [Greek *eidullion*] **idyllic** *adj*

i.e. that is to say [Latin *id est*]

IED improvised explosive device

if *conj* **1** in the event that, or on condition that: *if you work hard you'll succeed* **2** used to introduce an indirect question to which the answer is either *yes* or *no*; whether: *it doesn't matter if the play is any good or not* **3** even though: *a splendid if slightly* *decaying house* **4** used to introduce an unfulfilled wish, with *only*: *if only you had told her* ▷ *n* **5** a condition or stipulation: *there are no hidden ifs or buts* [Old English *gif*]

iffy *adj* **iffier, iffiest** *informal* full of uncertainty

igloo *n, pl* **-loos** a dome-shaped Inuit dwelling, built of blocks of solid snow [Inuktitut *igdlu*]

igneous (ig-nee-uss) *adj* **1** (of rocks) formed as molten rock cools and hardens **2** of or like fire [Latin *ignis* fire]

ignis fatuus (ig-niss **fat**-yew-uss) *n, pl* **ignes fatui** (ig-neez **fat**-yew-eye) same as **will-o'-the-wisp** [Medieval Latin, literally: foolish fire]

ignite *vb* **-niting, -nited 1** to catch fire **2** to set fire to [Latin *ignis* fire] **ignitable** *adj*

ignition *n* **1** the system used to ignite the fuel in an internal-combustion engine **2** an igniting or the process of igniting

ignoble *adj* **1** dishonourable **2** of humble origin or social status [Latin *in-* not + *nobilis* noble] **ignobly** *adv*

ignominy (ig-nom-in-ee) *n, pl* **-minies** disgrace or public shame: *the ignominy of being replaced* [Latin *ignominia* disgrace] **ignominious** *adj*

ignoramus *n, pl* **-muses** an ignorant person [Latin, literally: we have no knowledge of]

ignorance *n* lack of knowledge or education

ignorant *adj* **1** lacking in knowledge or education **2** rude through lack of knowledge of good manners: *an ignorant remark* **3 ignorant of** lacking in awareness or knowledge of: *ignorant of Asian culture*

ignore *vb* **-noring, -nored** to refuse to notice; disregard deliberately [Latin *ignorare* not to know]

iguana *n* a large tropical tree lizard of the W Indies and S America with a spiny back [indigenous S American word *iwana*]

ikebana (eek-a-**bah**-na) *n* the Japanese art of flower arrangement [Japanese]

ikon *n* same as **icon**

IL Illinois

il- *prefix* same as **in-**[1] or **in-**[2]

ileum *n* the third and lowest part of the small intestine [Latin: flank, groin]

ilex *n* **1** a genus of trees or shrubs that includes holly **2** same as **holm oak** [Latin]

ilium *n, pl* **-ia** the uppermost and widest of the three sections of the hipbone

ilk *n* a type or class: *three or four others of the same ilk* [Old English *ilca* the same family]

> **USAGE** Although the use of *ilk* to mean *a type or class* is sometimes condemned as being the result of a misunderstanding of a Scottish expression *of that ilk*, it is nevertheless well established and generally acceptable.

ill *adj* **worse, worst 1** not in good health **2** bad, harmful, or hostile: *ill effects* **3** promising an unfavourable outcome: *ill omen* **4 ill at ease** unable to relax ▷ *n* **5** evil or harm ▷ *adv* **6** badly, wrongly: *the title ill befits him* **7** with difficulty; hardly: *we can ill afford another scandal* [Old Norse *illr* bad]

ill. 1 illustrated **2** illustration

Ill. Illinois

I'll I will *or* I shall

ill-advised *adj* **1** (of a plan or action) badly thought out **2** (of a person) acting without reasonable care or thought

ill-bred *adj* lacking good manners **ill-breeding** *n*

ill-disposed *adj* unfriendly or unsympathetic

illegal *adj* against the law **illegally** *adv* **illegality** *n*

illegible *adj* unable to be read or deciphered **illegibility** *n*

illegitimate *adj* **1** born of parents who were not married to each other at the time **2** illegal; unlawful **illegitimacy** *n*

ill-fated *adj* doomed or unlucky

ill-favoured *adj* unattractive

ill-founded *adj* not based on proper proof or evidence

ill-gotten *adj* obtained dishonestly or illegally: *ill-gotten gains*

ill-health *n* the condition of being unwell

illiberal *adj* **1** narrow-minded or intolerant **2** not generous; mean **3** lacking in culture or refinement **illiberality** *n*

illicit *adj* **1** same as **illegal 2** forbidden or disapproved of by society: *an illicit kiss*

illiterate *adj* **1** unable to read and write **2** uneducated or ignorant: *linguistically illiterate* ▷ *n* **3** an illiterate person **illiteracy** *n*

ill-mannered *adj* having bad manners

illness *n* **1** a disease or indisposition **2** a state of ill health

illogical *adj* **1** senseless or unreasonable **2** not following logical principles **illogicality** *n* **illogically** *adv*

ill-starred *adj* very unlucky or unfortunate

ill-tempered *adj* having a bad temper

ill-timed *adj* done or happening at an unsuitable time

ill-treat *vb* to treat cruelly or harshly **ill-treatment** *n*

illuminant *n* **1** something that gives off light ▷ *adj* **2** giving off light

illuminate *vb* **-nating, -nated 1** to light up **2** to make easily understood; explain: *the report obscures rather than illuminates the most relevant facts* **3** to decorate with lights **4** to decorate (an initial letter or manuscript) with designs of gold, silver, or bright colours [Latin *illuminare* to light up] **illuminating** *adj* **illuminative** *adj*

illumination *n* **1** an illuminating or being illuminated **2** a source of light **3 illuminations** *chiefly Brit* lights used as decorations in streets or towns **4** the decoration in colours, gold, or silver used on some manuscripts

illumine *vb* **-mining, -mined** *literary* same as **illuminate**

illusion *n* **1** a false appearance or deceptive impression of reality: *her upswept hair gave the illusion of above average height* **2** a false or misleading idea or belief: *we may suffer from the illusion that we are special* [Latin *illusio* deceit]

illusionist *n* a conjuror

illusory *or* **illusive** *adj* seeming to be true, but actually false: *the economic benefits of such reforms were largely illusory*

> **USAGE** *Illusive* is sometimes wrongly used where *elusive* is meant: *they fought hard, but victory remained elusive* (not *illusive*).

illustrate *vb* **-trating, -trated 1** to clarify or explain by use of examples or comparisons **2** to provide (a book or text) with pictures **3** to be an example of [Latin *illustrare* to make light, explain] **illustrative** *adj* **illustrator** *n*
illustration *n* **1** a picture or diagram used to explain or decorate a text **2** an example: *an illustration of the brutality of the regime* **3** the art of illustrating
illustrious *adj* famous and distinguished [Latin *illustris* bright, famous]
ill will *n* unkind feeling; hostility
IM instant messaging
im- *prefix* same as **in-**[1] or **in-**[2]
I'm I am
image *n* **1** a mental picture of someone or something produced by the imagination or memory **2** the appearance or impression given to the public by a person or organization **3** a simile or metaphor **4** a representation of a person or thing in a work of art or literature **5** an optical reproduction of an object, formed by the lens of an eye or camera, or by a mirror **6** a person or thing that resembles another closely **7** a personification of a specified quality; epitome: *the image of good breeding* ▷ *vb* **imaging, imaged 8** to picture in the mind **9** to mirror or reflect an image of **10** to portray or describe [Latin *imago*]
imagery *n, pl* **-ries 1** figurative or descriptive language in a literary work **2** mental images **3** images collectively, esp. statues or carvings
imaginary *adj* **1** existing only in the imagination **2** *maths* relating to the square root of a negative number
imagination *n* **1** the faculty or action of producing mental images of what is not present or in one's experience **2** creative mental ability
imaginative *adj* **1** produced by or showing a creative imagination **2** having a vivid imagination
imagine *vb* **-ining, -ined 1** to form a mental image of **2** to think, believe, or guess: *I would imagine they'll be here soon* [Latin *imaginari*] **imaginable** *adj*
imaginings *pl n* speculative thoughts about what might be the case or what might happen; fantasies: *lurid imaginings*
imago (im-may-go) *n, pl* **imagoes** *or* **imagines** (im-maj-in-eez) a sexually mature adult insect [Latin: likeness]
imam *n Islam* **1** a leader of congregational prayer in a mosque **2** the title of some Muslim leaders [Arabic]
IMAX (eye-max) *n* a film projection process that produces an image ten times larger than standard
imbalance *n* a lack of balance, for instance in emphasis or proportion: *a chemical imbalance in the brain*
imbecile (im-biss-eel) *n* **1** *informal* an extremely stupid person **2** *psychol obsolete* a person of abnormally low intelligence ▷ *adj* **3** stupid or senseless: *imbecile fanaticism* [Latin *imbecillus* feeble] **imbecility** *n*
imbed *vb* **-bedding, -bedded** same as **embed**
imbibe *vb* **-bibing, -bibed** *formal* **1** to drink (alcoholic drinks) **2** to take in or assimilate (ideas): *values she had imbibed as a child* [Latin *imbibere*]
imbroglio (imb-role-ee-oh) *n, pl* **-glios** a confusing and complicated situation [Italian]
imbue *vb* **-buing, -bued** to fill or inspire (with ideals or principles) [Latin *imbuere* to stain]
IMF International Monetary Fund
imitate *vb* **-tating, -tated 1** to copy the manner or style of, or take as a model: *he remains rock's most imitated guitarist* **2** to mimic or impersonate, esp. for amusement **3** to make a copy or reproduction of; duplicate [Latin *imitari*] **imitable** *adj* **imitator** *n*
imitation *n* **1** a copy of an original or genuine article **2** an instance of imitating someone: *her Coward imitations were not the best thing she did* **3** behaviour modelled on the behaviour of someone else: *to learn by imitation* ▷ *adj* **4** made to resemble something which is usually superior or more expensive: *imitation leather*
imitative *adj* **1** imitating or tending to copy **2** copying or reproducing an original, esp. in an inferior manner: *imitative painting* **3** onomatopoeic
immaculate *adj* **1** completely clean or tidy: *an immaculate pinstripe suit* **2** completely flawless: *his equestrian pedigree is immaculate* [Latin *in-* not + *macula* blemish] **immaculately** *adv*
immanent *adj* **1** present within and throughout something **2** (of God) present throughout the universe [Latin *immanere* to remain in] **immanence** *n*
immaterial *adj* **1** of no real importance or relevance **2** not formed of matter
immature *adj* **1** not fully grown or developed **2** lacking wisdom, insight, or stability because of youth **immaturity** *n*
immeasurable *adj* too great to be measured **immeasurably** *adv*
immediate *adj* **1** taking place without delay: *an immediate cut in interest rates* **2** next or nearest in space, time, or relationship: *our immediate neighbour* **3** present; current: *they had no immediate plans to close it* [Latin *in-* not + *mediare* to be in the middle] **immediacy** *n* **immediately** *adv*
immemorial *adj* having existed or happened for longer than anyone can remember: *this has been the custom since time immemorial*
immense *adj* **1** huge or vast **2** *informal* very great [Latin *immensus* unmeasured] **immensely** *adv* **immensity** *n*
immerse *vb* **-mersing, -mersed 1** to plunge or dip into liquid **2** to involve deeply: *he immersed himself in the history of Rome* **3** to baptize by dipping the whole body into water [Latin *immergere*] **immersion** *n*
immersion heater *n* an electrical device in a domestic hot-water tank for heating water
immersive *adj* making one feel completely surrounded by and involved in something
immigrant *n* a person who comes to a foreign country in order to settle there
immigration *n* the act of coming to a foreign country in order to settle there [Latin *immigrare* to go into] **immigrate** *vb*

i

imminent *adj* likely to happen soon [Latin *imminere* to project over] **imminence** *n*
immiscible *adj* (of liquids) incapable of being mixed: *oil and water are immiscible* **immiscibility** *n*
immobile *adj* **1** not moving **2** not able to move or be moved **immobility** *n*
immobilize *or* **-lise** *vb* **-lizing, -lized** *or* **-lising, -lised** to make unable to move or work: *a device for immobilizing steering wheels* **immobilization** *or* **-lisation** *n*
immoderate *adj* excessive or unreasonable: *immoderate consumption of alcohol* **immoderately** *adv*
immodest *adj* **1** behaving in an indecent or improper manner **2** behaving in a boastful or conceited manner **immodesty** *n*
immolate *vb* **-lating, -lated** *literary* to kill or offer as a sacrifice, esp. by fire [Latin *immolare*] **immolation** *n*
immoral *adj* morally wrong; corrupt **immorality** *n*
immortal *adj* **1** not subject to death or decay **2** famous for all time **3** everlasting ▷ *n* **4** a person whose fame will last for all time **5** an immortal being **immortality** *n*
immortalize *or* **-ise** *vb* **-izing, -ized** *or* **-ising, -ised** **1** to give everlasting fame to: *a name immortalized by countless writers* **2** to give immortality to
immovable *or* **immoveable** *adj* **1** unable to be moved **2** unwilling to change one's opinions or beliefs **3** not affected by feeling; emotionless **4** unchanging **5** *law* (of property) consisting of land or houses **immovability** *or* **immoveability** *n* **immovably** *or* **immoveably** *adv*
immune *adj* **1** protected against a specific disease by inoculation or as the result of natural resistance **2** exempt from obligation or penalty **3 immune to** secure against: *football is not immune to economic recession* [Latin *immunis* exempt from a public service]
immune system *n* the mechanism by which a body reacts to foreign materials, involving the production of antibodies
immunity *n, pl* **-ties** **1** the ability of an organism to resist disease **2** freedom from prosecution, tax, etc.
immunize *or* **-nise** *vb* **-nizing, -nized** *or* **-nising, -nised** to make (someone) immune to a disease, esp. by inoculation **immunization** *or* **-nisation** *n*
immunodeficiency *n* a deficiency in or breakdown of a person's ability to fight diseases
immunology *n* the branch of medicine concerned with the study of immunity **immunological** *adj* **immunologist** *n*
immure *vb* **-muring, -mured** **1** *archaic or literary* to imprison **2** to shut (oneself) away from society [Latin *im-* in + *murus* wall]
immutable (im-mute-a-bl) *adj* unchangeable or unchanging: *the immutable sequence of night and day* **immutability** *n*
imp *n* **1** a small demon **2** a mischievous child [Old English *impa* bud, hence offspring, child]
imp. **1** imperative **2** imperfect
impact *n* **1** the effect or impression made by something **2** the act of one object striking another; collision **3** the force of a collision ▷ *vb* **4** to press firmly against or into **5 impact on** to have an effect on [Latin *impactus* pushed against] **impaction** *n*
impacted *adj* (of a tooth) unable to grow out because of being wedged against another tooth below the gum
impair *vb* to damage or weaken in strength or quality [Old French *empeirer* to make worse] **impairment** *n*
impala (imp-ah-la) *n, pl* **-las** *or* **-la** an African antelope with lyre-shaped horns [Zulu]
impale *vb* **-paling, -paled** to pierce through or fix with a sharp object: *they impaled his severed head on a spear* [Latin *im-* on + *palus* pole] **impalement** *n*
impalpable *adj formal* **1** not able to be felt by touching: *impalpable shadows* **2** difficult to understand **impalpability** *n*
impart *vb* **1** to communicate (information or knowledge) **2** to give (a specified quality): *flavouring to impart a sweet taste* [Latin *im-* in + *partire* to share]
impartial *adj* not favouring one side or the other **impartiality** *n* **impartially** *adv*
impassable *adj* (of terrain or roads) not able to be travelled through or over **impassability** *n*
impasse (am-pass) *n* a situation in which progress or escape is impossible [French]
impassible *adj* **1** *rare* not susceptible to pain or injury **2** impassive; unmoved **impassibility** *or* **impassibleness** *n*
impassioned *adj* full of emotion: *an impassioned plea to the United Nations*
impassive *adj* not showing or feeling emotion **impassively** *adv* **impassivity** *n*
impasto *n* the technique of applying paint thickly, so that brush marks are evident [Italian]
impatient *adj* **1** irritable at any delay or difficulty **2** restless to have or do something **impatience** *n* **impatiently** *adv*
impeach *vb* **1** *chiefly US* to charge (a public official) with an offence committed in office **2** *Brit & Austral criminal law* to accuse of treason or serious crime **3** to challenge or question (a person's honesty or honour) [Late Latin *impedicare* to entangle] **impeachable** *adj* **impeachment** *n*
impeccable *adj* without flaw or error: *impeccable manners* [Latin *in-* not + *peccare* to sin] **impeccably** *adv*
impecunious *adj formal* without money; penniless [Latin *in-* not + *pecuniosus* wealthy]
impedance (imp-eed-anss) *n electronics* the total effective resistance in an electric circuit to the flow of an alternating current
impede *vb* **-peding, -peded** to block or make progress or action difficult [Latin *impedire*]
impediment *n* **1** a hindrance or obstruction **2** a physical disability that makes speech or walking difficult
impel *vb* **-pelling, -pelled** **1** to urge or force (a person) to do something **2** to push, drive, or force into motion [Latin *impellere* to drive forward]
impending *adj* (esp. of something bad) about to happen [Latin *impendere* to overhang]
impenetrable *adj* **1** impossible to get through: *an impenetrable barrier* **2** impossible to understand **3** not receptive to ideas or influence: *impenetrable ignorance* **impenetrability** *n* **impenetrably** *adv*

impenitent *adj* not sorry or penitent **impenitence** *n*
imperative *adj* **1** extremely urgent; essential **2** commanding or authoritative: *an imperative tone of voice* **3** *grammar* denoting a mood of verbs used in commands ▷ *n* **4** *grammar* the imperative mood [Latin *imperare* to command]
imperceptible *adj* too slight, subtle, or gradual to be noticed **imperceptibly** *adv*
imperfect *adj* **1** having faults or errors **2** not complete **3** *grammar* denoting a tense of verbs describing continuous, incomplete, or repeated past actions ▷ *n* **4** *grammar* the imperfect tense **imperfectly** *adv*
imperfection *n* **1** the state of being imperfect **2** a fault or defect
imperial *adj* **1** of an empire, emperor, or empress **2** majestic; commanding **3** exercising supreme authority; imperious **4** (of weights or measures) conforming to the standards of a system formerly official in Great Britain ▷ *n* **5** a wine bottle holding the equivalent of eight normal bottles [Latin *imperium* authority]
imperialism *n* **1** the policy or practice of extending a country's influence over other territories by conquest, colonization, or economic domination **2** an imperial system, authority, or government **imperialist** *adj, n* **imperialistic** *adj*
imperil *vb* **-rilling, -rilled** *or US* **-riling, -riled** *formal* to put in danger
imperious *adj* used to being obeyed; domineering [Latin *imperium* power] **imperiously** *adv*
imperishable *adj* unable to disappear or be destroyed
impermanent *adj* not permanent; fleeting **impermanence** *n*
impermeable *adj* (of a substance) not allowing fluid to pass through: *an impermeable layer* **impermeability** *n*
impermissible *adj* not allowed
impersonal *adj* **1** without reference to any individual person; objective: *Buddhism began as a very impersonal doctrine* **2** without human warmth or sympathy: *an impersonal manner* **3** *grammar* **A** (of a verb) having no subject, as in *it is raining* **B** (of a pronoun) not referring to a person **impersonality** *n* **impersonally** *adv*
impersonate *vb* **-ating, -ated** **1** to pretend to be (another person) **2** to imitate the character or mannerisms of (another person) for entertainment **impersonation** *n* **impersonator** *n*
impertinent *adj* disrespectful or rude [Latin *impertinens* not belonging] **impertinence** *n*
imperturbable *adj* not easily upset; calm **imperturbability** *n* **imperturbably** *adv*
impervious *adj* **1** not letting water, etc. through **2** not influenced by a feeling, argument, etc.
impetigo (imp-it-**tie**-go) *n* a contagious skin disease causing spots or pimples [Latin: scabby eruption]
impetuous *adj* **1** acting without consideration **2** done rashly or hastily [Late Latin *impetuosus* violent] **impetuosity** *n*
impetus (imp-it-uss) *n, pl* **-tuses** **1** an incentive or impulse **2** *physics* the force that starts a body moving or that tends to resist changes in its speed or direction once it is moving [Latin: attack]
impi *n, pl* **-pi** *or* **-pies** a group of Zulu warriors [Nguni (language group of southern Africa) *impi*regiment, army]
impiety *n* lack of respect or religious reverence
impinge *vb* **-pinging, -pinged** (often foll. by *on*) to encroach (on), affect or restrict: *international economic forces impinging on the local economy* [Latin *impingere* to dash against] **impingement** *n*
impious (imp-e-uss) *adj* showing a lack of respect or religious reverence
impish *adj* mischievous **impishness** *n*
implacable *adj* **1** incapable of being appeased or pacified **2** unyielding **implacability** *n* **implacably** *adv*
implant *vb* **1** to fix firmly in the mind: *to implant sound moral principles* **2** to plant or embed **3** *surgery* to graft or insert (a tissue or hormone) into the body ▷ *n* **4** anything implanted in the body, such as a tissue graft **implantation** *n*
implausible *adj* not easy to believe **implausibility** *n*
implement *vb* **1** to carry out (instructions, etc.): *she refused to implement the agreed plan* ▷ *n* **2** a tool or other piece of equipment [Late Latin *implementum*, literally: a filling up] **implementation** *n*
implicate *vb* **-cating, -cated** **1** to show (someone) to be involved, esp. in a crime **2** to imply [Latin *implicare* to involve]
implication *n* **1** something that is suggested or implied **2** an act or instance of suggesting, implying, or being implied **3** a probable consequence (of something)
implicit *adj* **1** expressed indirectly: *an implicit agreement* **2** absolute and unquestioning: *implicit trust* **3** contained in, although not stated openly: *this view of the mind was implicit in all his work* [Latin *implicitus*] **implicitly** *adv*
implied *adj* hinted at or suggested: *an implied criticism*
implode *vb* **-ploding, -ploded** to collapse inwards [*im-* in + *(ex)plode*]
implore *vb* **-ploring, -plored** to beg desperately [Latin *implorare*]
imply *vb* **-plies, -plying, -plied** **1** to express or indicate by a hint; suggest **2** to suggest or involve as a necessary consequence: *a spending commitment implies a corresponding tax imposition* [Old French *emplier*]
USAGE See at **infer**.
impolite *adj* discourteous; rude **impoliteness** *n*
impolitic *adj* ill-advised; unwise
imponderable *adj* **1** unable to be weighed or assessed ▷ *n* **2** something difficult or impossible to assess
import *vb* **1** to bring in (goods) from another country **2** *formal* to signify; mean: *to import doom* ▷ *n* **3** something imported **4** *formal* importance: *his new work is of great import* **5** meaning **6** *informal* a sportsperson who is not native to the area where they play [Latin *importare* to carry in] **importer** *n* **importation** *n*
important *adj* **1** of great significance, value, or consequence **2** of social significance: *the second*

most important person in the government **3** of great concern: *it was important to me to know* [Medieval Latin *importare* to signify, from Latin: to carry in] **importance** *n* **importantly** *adv*

USAGE The use of *more importantly* as in *more importantly, the local council is opposed to this proposal* has become very common, but many people still prefer to use *more important*.

importunate *adj formal* persistent or demanding

importune *vb* **-tuning, -tuned** *formal* to harass with persistent requests [Latin *importunus* tiresome] **importunity** *n*

impose *vb* **-posing, -posed 1** to establish (a rule, condition, etc.) as something to be obeyed or complied with **2** to force (oneself) on others **3** *printing* to arrange (pages) in the correct order for printing **4** to pass off (something) deceptively on someone **5 impose on** to take advantage of (a person or quality): *she imposed on his kindness* [Latin *imponere* to place upon]

imposing *adj* grand or impressive: *an imposing building*

imposition *n* **1** the act of imposing **2** something imposed, esp. unfairly on someone **3** the arrangement of pages for printing **4** *old-fashioned* a task set as a school punishment

impossibility *n, pl* **-ties 1** the state or quality of being impossible **2** something that is impossible

impossible *adj* **1** not able to be done or to happen **2** absurd or unreasonable **3** *informal* intolerable or outrageous: *those children are impossible* **impossibly** *adv*

impostor *or* **imposter** *n* a person who cheats or swindles by pretending to be someone else [Late Latin *impostor* deceiver]

imposture *n formal* deception, esp. by pretending to be someone else

impotent (imp-a-tent) *adj* **1** not having the power to influence people or events **2** (of a man) incapable of sexual intercourse **impotence** *n*

impound *vb* **1** to take legal possession of; confiscate **2** to confine (an animal) in a pound

impoverish *vb* **1** to make (someone) poor **2** weaken the quality of something [Old French *empovrir*] **impoverished** *adj* **impoverishment** *n*

impracticable *adj* **1** not able to be put into practice **2** unsuitable for a desired use **impracticability** *n*

impractical *adj* **1** not sensible or workable: *the use of force was viewed as impractical* **2** not having practical skills **impracticality** *n*

imprecation *n formal* a curse [Latin *imprecari* to invoke] **imprecate** *vb*

imprecise *adj* inexact or inaccurate **imprecision** *n*

impregnable *adj* **1** unable to be broken into or taken by force: *an impregnable fortress* **2** unable to be affected or overcome: *a confident, impregnable person* [Old French *imprenable*] **impregnability** *n*

impregnate *vb* **-nating, -nated 1** to saturate, soak, or fill throughout **2** to make pregnant **3** to imbue or permeate: *the party has been impregnated with an enthusiasm for reform* [Latin *in-* in + *praegnans* pregnant] **impregnation** *n*

impresario *n, pl* **-sarios** a person who runs theatre performances, concerts, etc. [Italian]

impress *vb* **1** to make a strong, lasting, or favourable impression on: *he was impressed by the standard of play* **2** to stress or emphasize **3** to imprint or stamp by pressure: *a pattern impressed in paint on the rock* ▷ *n* **4** an impressing **5** a mark produced by impressing [Latin *imprimere* to press into] **impressible** *adj*

impression *n* **1** an effect produced in the mind by a person or thing: *she was keen to create a relaxed impression* **2** a vague idea or belief: *he only had a vague impression of how it worked* **3** a strong, favourable, or remarkable effect **4** an impersonation for entertainment **5** an imprint or mark produced by pressing **6** *printing* the number of copies of a publication printed at one time

impressionable *adj* easily impressed or influenced: *the promotion of smoking to the impressionable young* **impressionability** *n*

Impressionism *n* a style of painting developed in 19th-century France, with the aim of reproducing the immediate impression or mood of things, esp. the effects of light and atmosphere, rather than form or structure

impressionist *n* **1 Impressionist** an artist who painted in the style of Impressionism **2** a person who imitates the character or mannerisms of another person for entertainment

impressionistic *adj* **1 Impressionistic** of or about Impressionism **2** based on subjective observations or impressions rather than systematic study or facts: *Mitchell was making impressionistic documentaries*

impressive *adj* capable of impressing, esp. by size, magnificence, or importance **impressively** *adv*

imprimatur (imp-rim-**ah**-ter) *n* official approval for something to be printed, usually given by the Roman Catholic Church [New Latin: let it be printed]

imprint *n* **1** a mark or impression produced by pressing, printing, or stamping **2** the publisher's name and address, often with the date of publication, printed on the title page of a book ▷ *vb* **3** to produce (a mark) by pressing, printing, or stamping: *T-shirts imprinted with slogans* **4** to establish firmly; impress: *he couldn't dislodge the images imprinted on his brain*

imprison *vb* to confine in or as if in prison **imprisonment** *n*

improbable *adj* not likely or probable **improbability** *n* **improbably** *adv*

impromptu *adj* **1** without planning or preparation; improvised ▷ *adv* **2** in a spontaneous or improvised way: *he spoke impromptu* ▷ *n* **3** a short piece of instrumental music resembling improvisation **4** something that is impromptu [Latin *in promptu* in readiness]

improper *adj* **1** indecent **2** irregular or incorrect **improperly** *adv*

improper fraction *n* a fraction in which the numerator is greater than the denominator, as $^7/_6$

impropriety (imp-roe-**pry**-a-tee) *n, pl* **-ties** *formal* unsuitable or slightly improper behaviour

improve *vb* **-proving, -proved 1** to make or become better in quality **2 improve on** to achieve a better standard or quality in comparison with: *both had improved on their previous performance* [Anglo-French *emprouer* to turn to profit] **improvable** *adj*

improvement *n* **1** the act of improving or the state of being improved **2** a change that makes something better or adds to its value: *home improvements* **3** *Austral & NZ* a building on a piece of land, adding to its value

improvident *adj* **1** not providing for the future **2** incautious or rash **improvidence** *n*

improvise *vb* **-vising, -vised 1** to do or make quickly from whatever is available, without previous planning **2** to make up (a piece of music, speech, etc.) as one goes along [Latin *improvisus* unforeseen] **improvisation** *n*

imprudent *adj* not carefully thought out; rash **imprudence** *n*

impudent *adj* impertinent or insolent [Latin *impudens* shameless] **impudence** *n* **impudently** *adv*

impugn (imp-yoon) *vb formal* to challenge or attack as false [Latin *impugnare* to fight against] **impugnment** *n*

impulse *n* **1** a sudden desire or whim **2** an instinctive drive; urge: *the mothering impulse* **3** *physics* **A** the product of a force acting on a body and the time for which it acts **B** the change in the momentum of a body as a result of a force acting upon it **4** *physiol* a stimulus transmitted in a nerve or muscle [Latin *impulsus* incitement]

impulsive *adj* **1** tending to act without thinking first: *an impulsive man* **2** done without thinking first **3** forceful or impelling

impunity (imp-yoon-it-ee) *n* **with impunity** without punishment or unpleasant consequences [Latin *impunis* unpunished]

impure *adj* **1** having unwanted substances mixed in **2** immoral or obscene: *impure thoughts* **3** dirty or unclean

impurity *n, pl* **-ties 1** an impure element or thing: *impurities in the water* **2** the quality of being impure

impute *vb* **-puting, -puted 1** to attribute (blame or a crime) to a person **2** to attribute to a source or cause: *I impute your success to nepotism* [Latin *in-* in + *putare* to think] **imputation** *n*

in *prep* **1** inside; within: *in the room* **2** at a place where there is: *in the shade* **3** indicating a state, situation, or condition: *in silence* **4** when (a period of time) has elapsed: *come back in one year* **5** using: *written in code* **6** wearing: *the man in the blue suit* **7** with regard to (a specified activity or occupation): *in journalism* **8** while performing the action of: *in crossing the street he was run over* **9** having as purpose: *in honour of the president* **10** (of certain animals) pregnant with: *in calf* **11** into: *he fell in the water* **12 have it in one** to have the ability (to do something) **13 in that** *or* **in so far as** because or to the extent that: *it was of great help in that it gave me more confidence* ▷ *adv* **14** in or into a particular place; indoors: *come in* **15** at one's home or place of work: *he's not in at the moment* **16** in office or power: *the Conservatives got in at the last election* **17** so as to enclose: *block in* **18** (in certain games) so as to take one's turn of the play: *you have to get the other side out before you go in* **19** *Brit* (of a fire) alight **20** (*in combination*) indicating prolonged activity, esp. by a large number: *teach-in*; *sit-in* **21 have got it in for** *informal* to wish or intend harm towards **22 in for** about to experience (something, esp. something unpleasant): *they're in for a shock* **23 in on** acquainted with or sharing in: *I was in on all his plans* **24 in with** friendly with ▷ *adj* **25** fashionable; modish: *the in thing to do* ▷ *n* **26 ins and outs** the detailed points or facts (of a situation) [Old English]

In *chem* indium

IN Indiana

in. inch(es)

in-[1]**, il-, im-** *or* **ir-** *prefix* **A** not; non: *incredible*; *illegal*; *imperfect*; *irregular* **B** lack of: *inexperience* [Latin]

in-[2]**, il-, im-** *or* **ir-** *prefix* in; into; towards; within; on: *infiltrate* [from *in*]

inability *n* the fact of not being able to do something

in absentia *adv* in the absence of (someone indicated) [Latin]

inaccessible *adj* **1** impossible or very difficult to reach **2** unable to be used or seen: *his works are inaccessible to English-speaking readers* **3** difficult to understand or appreciate: *Webern's music is still considered inaccessible* **inaccessibility** *n*

inaccuracy *n, pl* **-cies 1** lack of accuracy; imprecision **2** an error or mistake **inaccurate** *adj*

inaction *n* lack of action; inertia

inactive *adj* **1** idle; not active **2** *chem* (of a substance) having little or no reactivity **inactivity** *n*

inadequacy *n, pl* **-cies 1** lack or shortage **2** the state of being or feeling inferior **3** a weakness or failing: *their own failures or inadequacies*

inadequate *adj* **1** not enough; insufficient **2** not good enough **inadequately** *adv*

inadmissible *adj* not allowable or acceptable

inadvertent *adj* done unintentionally **inadvertence** *n* **inadvertently** *adv*

inadvisable *adj* unwise; not sensible

inalienable *adj* not able to be taken away or transferred to another: *the inalienable rights of the citizen*

inamorata *or masc* **inamorato** *n, pl* **-tas** *or* **-tos** *literary* a sweetheart or lover [Italian *innamorata, innamorato*]

inane *adj* senseless or silly: *inane remarks* [Latin *inanis* empty] **inanity** *n*

inanimate *adj* lacking the qualities of living beings: *inanimate objects*

inanition *n formal* exhaustion or weakness, as from lack of food [Latin *inanis* empty]

inapplicable *adj* not suitable or relevant

inapposite *adj* not suitable or appropriate **inappositeness** *n*

inappropriate *adj* not suitable or proper **inappropriately** *adv*

inapt *adj* **1** not apt or fitting **2** lacking skill **inaptitude** *n*

inarticulate *adj* unable to express oneself clearly or well

inasmuch as *conj* **1** since; because **2** in so far as

inattentive *adj* not paying attention **inattention** *n*

inaudible *adj* not loud enough to be heard **inaudibly** *adv*

inaugural *adj* **1** of or for an inauguration ▷ *n* **2** *US* a speech made at an inauguration

inaugurate *vb* **-rating, -rated 1** to open or celebrate the first public use of ceremonially: *the newest electrified line was inaugurated today* **2** to formally establish (a new leader) in office **3** to begin officially or formally [Latin *inaugurare* to take omens, hence to install in office after taking auguries] **inauguration** *n* **inaugurator** *n*

inauspicious *adj* unlucky; suggesting an unfavourable outcome

inauthentic *adj* not genuine or real

inboard *adj* **1** (of a boat's motor or engine) situated within the hull **2** situated close to the fuselage of an aircraft ▷ *adv* **3** within the sides of, or towards the centre of, a vessel or aircraft

inborn *adj* existing from birth: *an inborn sense of optimism*

inbox *n* a folder in a computer mailbox in which incoming messages are stored

inbred *adj* **1** produced as a result of inbreeding **2** inborn or ingrained: *inbred good manners*

inbreed *vb* **-breeding, -bred** to breed from closely related individuals

inbreeding *n* breeding from closely related individuals

inbuilt *adj* (of a quality or feeling) present from the beginning: *an inbuilt prejudice*

Inc. *US & Austral* (of a company) incorporated

Inca *n* **1** *pl* **Inca** *or* **Incas** a member of a S American indigenous people whose empire, centred on Peru, lasted until the early 1530s **2** the language of this people

incalculable *adj* impossible to estimate or predict **incalculability** *n*

in camera *adv* in private session: *the proceedings were held in camera* [Latin]

incandescent *adj* **1** glowing with heat **2** (of artificial light) produced by a glowing filament [Latin *incandescere* to glow] **incandescence** *n*

incandescent lamp *n* a lamp that contains a filament which is electrically heated to incandescence

incantation *n* **1** ritual chanting of magic words or sounds **2** a magic spell [Latin *incantare* to repeat magic formulas] **incantatory** *adj*

incapable *adj* **1** helpless: *drunk and incapable* **2 incapable of** lacking the ability to

incapacitate *vb* **-tating, -tated** to deprive (a person) of strength, power, or ability; disable

incapacity *n, pl* **-ties 1** lack of power, strength, or ability **2** *law* legal disqualification or ineligibility

incarcerate *vb* **-rating, -rated** *formal* to confine or imprison [Latin *in-* in + *carcer* prison] **incarceration** *n*

incarnate *adj* **1** possessing human form: *a devil incarnate* **2** personified or typified: *stupidity incarnate* ▷ *vb* **-nating, -nated 3** to give a bodily or concrete form to **4** to be representative or typical of [Late Latin *incarnare* to make flesh]

incarnation *n* **1** the act of embodying or state of being embodied in human form **2** a person or thing that typifies some quality or idea

Incarnation *n* *Christian theol* God's coming to earth in human form as Jesus Christ

incautious *adj* (of a person or action) careless or rash

incendiary (in-**send**-ya-ree) *adj* **1** (of bombs, etc.) designed to cause fires **2** tending to create strife or violence **3** relating to the illegal burning of property or goods ▷ *n, pl* **-aries 4** a bomb that is designed to start fires **5** a person who illegally sets fire to property or goods [Latin *incendere* to kindle] **incendiarism** *n*

incense¹ *n* **1** an aromatic substance burnt for its fragrant odour, esp. in religious ceremonies **2** the odour or smoke so produced ▷ *vb* **-censing, -censed 3** to burn incense to (a deity) **4** to perfume or fumigate with incense [Church Latin *incensum*]

incense² *vb* **-censing, -censed** to make very angry [Latin *incensus* set on fire] **incensed** *adj*

incentive *n* **1** something that encourages effort or action **2** an additional payment made to employees to increase production ▷ *adj* **3** encouraging greater effort: *an incentive scheme for workers* [Latin *incentivus* setting the tune]

inception *n* the beginning of a project [Latin *incipere* to begin]

incessant *adj* never stopping [Latin *in-* not + *cessare* to cease] **incessantly** *adv*

incest *n* sexual intercourse between two people who are too closely related to marry [Latin *in-* not + *castus* chaste] **incestuous** *adj*

inch *n* **1** a unit of length equal to one twelfth of a foot (2.54cm) **2** *meteorol* the amount of rain or snow that would cover a surface to a depth of one inch **3** a very small distance, degree, or amount: *neither side was prepared to give an inch* **4 every inch** in every way: *she arrived looking every inch a star* **5 inch by inch** gradually **6 within an inch of one's life** almost to death ▷ *vb* **7** to move very slowly or gradually: *I inched my way to the bar* [Old English *ynce*]

inchoate (in-**koh**-ate) *adj formal* just begun and not yet properly developed [Latin *incohare* to make a beginning]

incidence *n* **1** extent or frequency of occurrence: *the rising incidence of car fires* **2** *physics* the arrival of a beam of light or particles at a surface **3** *geom* the partial overlapping of two figures or a figure and a line

incident *n* **1** an occurrence or event, esp. a minor one **2** a relatively insignificant event that might have serious consequences **3** a public disturbance ▷ *adj* **4** *physics* (of a beam of light or particles) arriving at or striking a surface **5 incident to** *formal* likely to occur in connection with: *the dangers are incident to a police officer's job* [Latin *incidere* to happen]

incidental *adj* **1** happening in connection with or resulting from something more important **2** secondary or minor: *incidental expenses* **incidentally** *adv*

incidental music *n* background music for a film or play

incidentals *pl n* minor expenses, events, or action
incinerate *vb* **-ating, -ated** to burn up completely [Latin *in-* to + *cinis* ashes] **incineration** *n*
incinerator *n* a furnace for burning rubbish
incipient *adj formal* just starting to be or happen [Latin *incipere* to begin]
incise *vb* **-cising, -cised** to cut into with a sharp tool [Latin *incidere* to cut into]
incision *n* a cut, esp. one made during a surgical operation
incisive *adj* direct and forceful: *witty and incisive comments*
incisor *n* a sharp cutting tooth at the front of the mouth
incite *vb* **-citing, -cited** to stir up or provoke to action [Latin *in-* in, on + *citare* to excite] **incitement** *n*
incivility *n, pl* **-ties 1** rudeness **2** an impolite act or remark
incl. 1 including **2** inclusive
inclement *adj formal* (of weather) stormy or severe **inclemency** *n*
inclination *n* **1** a liking, tendency, or preference: *he showed no inclination to change his routine* **2** the degree of slope from a horizontal or vertical plane **3** a slope or slant **4** *surveying* the angular distance of the horizon below the plane of observation
incline *vb* **-clining, -clined 1** to veer from a vertical or horizontal plane; slope or slant **2** to have or cause to have a certain tendency or disposition: *that does not incline me to think that you are right* **3** to bend or lower (part of the body, esp. the head) **4 incline one's ear** to listen favourably ▷ *n* **5** an inclined surface or slope [Latin *inclinare* to cause to lean] **inclined** *adj*
inclined plane *n* a sloping plane used to enable a load to be raised or lowered by pushing or sliding, which requires less force than lifting
include *vb* **-cluding, -cluded 1** to have as part of the whole **2** to put in as part of a set, group, or category [Latin *in-* in + *claudere* to close]
inclusion *n* **1** an including or being included **2** something included
inclusive *adj* **1** including everything: *capital inclusive of profit* **2** including the limits specified: *Monday to Friday inclusive* **3** comprehensive
incognito (in-kog-nee-toe) *adv, adj* **1** under an assumed name or appearance ▷ *n, pl* **-tos 2** a false identity **3** a person who is incognito [Latin *incognitus* unknown]
incognizant *adj* **incognizant of** unaware of **incognizance** *n*
incoherent *adj* **1** unable to express oneself clearly **2** not logically connected or ordered: *an incoherent argument* **incoherence** *n*
income *n* the total amount of money earned from work or obtained from other sources over a given period of time
income support *n chiefly Brit* an allowance paid to people with a very low income
income tax *n* a personal tax levied on annual income
incoming *adj* **1** about to arrive **2** about to come into office
incommensurable *adj* **1** not able to be judged, measured, or compared **2** *maths* not having a common divisor other than 1, such as 2 and $\sqrt{-5}$ **incommensurability** *n*
incommensurate *adj* **1** inadequate or disproportionate: *gains incommensurate with the risk involved* **2** incommensurable
incommode *vb* **-moding, -moded** *formal* to bother, disturb, or inconvenience [Latin *incommodus* inconvenient]
incommodious *adj formal* inconveniently small; cramped
incommunicado *adv, adj* not allowed to communicate with other people, for instance while in solitary confinement [Spanish *incomunicado*]
incomparable *adj* so excellent as to be beyond or above comparison **incomparably** *adv*
incompatible *adj* not able to exist together in harmony; conflicting or inconsistent **incompatibility** *n*
incompetent *adj* **1** not having the necessary ability or skill to do something **2** *law* not legally qualified: *an incompetent witness* ▷ *n* **3** an incompetent person **incompetence** *n*
incomplete *adj* not finished or whole
incomprehension *n* inability to understand **incomprehensible** *adj*
inconceivable *adj* so unlikely to be true as to be unthinkable **inconceivability** *n*
inconclusive *adj* not giving a final decision or result
incongruous *adj* out of place; inappropriate: *an incongruous figure among the tourists* **incongruously** *adv* **incongruity** *n*
inconnu (in-kon-new) *n Canad* a whitefish of Arctic waters [French, literally: unknown]
inconsequential *or* **inconsequent** *adj* **1** unimportant or insignificant **2** not following logically as a consequence **inconsequentially** *adv*
inconsiderable *adj* **1** not worth considering; insignificant **2 not inconsiderable** fairly large: *he gets not inconsiderable royalties from his musicals* **inconsiderably** *adv*
inconsiderate *adj* lacking in care or thought for others; thoughtless **inconsiderateness** *n*
inconsistent *adj* **1** unstable or changeable in behaviour or mood **2** containing contradictory elements: *an inconsistent argument* **3** not in accordance: *actions inconsistent with high office* **inconsistency** *n*
inconsolable *adj* very distressed **inconsolably** *adv*
inconspicuous *adj* not easily noticed or seen
inconstant *adj* **1** liable to change one's loyalties or opinions **2** variable: *their household income is inconstant* **inconstancy** *n*
incontestable *adj* impossible to deny or argue with
incontinent *adj* **1** unable to control the bladder and bowels **2** lacking self-restraint [Latin *in-* not + *continere* to restrain] **incontinence** *n*
incontrovertible *adj* absolutely certain; undeniable **incontrovertibly** *adv*
inconvenience *n* **1** a state or instance of trouble or difficulty ▷ *vb* **-iencing, -ienced 2** to cause trouble or difficulty to (someone) **inconvenient** *adj*

incorporate *vb* **-rating, -rated 1** to include or be included as part of a larger unit **2** to form a united whole or mass **3** to form into a corporation ▷ *adj* **4** incorporated [Latin *in-* in + *corpus* body] **incorporated** *adj* **incorporation** *n*
incorporeal (in-kore-pore-ee-al) *adj* without material form, substance, or existence
incorrect *adj* **1** wrong: *an incorrect answer* **2** not proper: *incorrect behaviour* **incorrectly** *adv*
incorrigible *adj* (of a person or behaviour) beyond correction or reform; incurably bad **incorrigibility** *n* **incorrigibly** *adv*
incorruptible *adj* **1** too honest to be bribed or corrupted **2** not prone to decay or disintegration **incorruptibility** *n*
increase *vb* **-creasing, -creased 1** to make or become greater in size, degree, or frequency ▷ *n* **2** a rise in size, degree, or frequency **3** the amount by which something increases **4 on the increase** becoming more common [Latin *in-* in + *crescere* to grow] **increasingly** *adv*
incredible *adj* **1** unbelievable **2** *informal* marvellous; amazing **incredibility** *n* **incredibly** *adv*
incredulity *n* unwillingness to believe
incredulous *adj* not prepared or willing to believe something
increment *n* **1** the amount by which something increases **2** a regular salary increase **3** *maths* a small positive or negative change in a variable or function [Latin *incrementum* increase] **incremental** *adj*
incriminate *vb* **-nating, -nated 1** to make (someone) seem guilty of a crime **2** to charge (someone) with a crime [Late Latin *incriminare* to accuse] **incrimination** *n* **incriminatory** *adj*
incrust *vb* same as **encrust**
incubate (in-cube-ate) *vb* **-bating, -bated 1** (of birds) to hatch (eggs) by sitting on them **2** to cause (bacteria) to develop, esp. in an incubator or culture medium **3** (of disease germs) to remain inactive in an animal or human before causing disease **4** to develop gradually [Latin *incubare*] **incubation** *n*
incubator *n* **1** *med* a heated enclosed apparatus for rearing premature babies **2** an apparatus for hatching birds' eggs or growing bacterial cultures
incubus (in-cube-uss) *n, pl* **-bi** *or* **-buses 1** a demon believed in folklore to have sexual intercourse with sleeping women **2** a nightmarish burden or worry [Latin *incubare* to lie upon]
inculcate *vb* **-cating, -cated** to fix in someone's mind by constant repetition [Latin *inculcare* to tread upon] **inculcation** *n*
inculpate *vb* **-pating, -pated** *formal* to incriminate [Latin *in-* on + *culpare* to blame]
incumbency *n, pl* **-cies** the office, duty, or tenure of an incumbent
incumbent *formal* ▷ *n* **1** a person who holds a particular office or position ▷ *adj* **2** morally binding as a duty: *it is incumbent on cricketers to respect the umpire's impartiality* [Latin *incumbere* to lie upon]
incur *vb* **-curring, -curred** to bring (something undesirable) upon oneself [Latin *incurrere* to run into]
incurable *adj* **1** not able to be cured: *an incurable tumour* **2** not able to be changed: *he is an incurable romantic* ▷ *n* **3** a person with an incurable disease **incurability** *n* **incurably** *adv*
incurious *adj* showing no curiosity or interest **incuriously** *adv*
incursion *n* **1** a sudden or brief invasion **2** an inroad or encroachment: *a successful incursion into the American book-shop market* [Latin *incursio* attack] **incursive** *adj*
ind. 1 independent **2** index **3** indicative **4** indirect **5** industrial
Ind. 1 Independent **2** India **3** Indian **4** Indiana **5** Indies
indaba (in-dah-ba) *n* **1** (among native peoples of southern Africa) a meeting to discuss a serious topic **2** *S African informal* a matter of concern or for discussion [Zulu]
indebted *adj* **1** owing gratitude for help or favours **2** owing money **indebtedness** *n*
indecent *adj* **1** morally or sexually offensive **2** unseemly or improper: *indecent haste* **indecency** *n* **indecently** *adv*
indecent assault *n* a sexual attack which does not include rape
indecent exposure *n* the crime of showing of one's genitals in public
indecipherable *adj* impossible to read
indecisive *adj* **1** unable to make decisions **2** not decisive or conclusive: *an indecisive argument* **indecision** *or* **indecisiveness** *n*
indeed *adv* **1** certainly; actually: *indeed, the sea featured heavily in his poems* **2** truly, very: *it has become a dangerous place indeed* **3** in fact; what is more: *it is necessary, indeed indispensable* ▷ *interj* **4** an expression of doubt or surprise
indefatigable *adj* never getting tired or giving up: *an indefatigable organizer* [Latin *in-* not + *defatigare*, from *fatigare* to tire] **indefatigably** *adv*
indefensible *adj* **1** (of behaviour or statements) unable to be justified or supported **2** (of places or buildings) impossible to defend against attack **indefensibility** *n*
indefinable *adj* difficult to describe or explain completely
indefinite *adj* **1** without exact limits: *an indefinite number* **2** vague or unclear **indefinitely** *adv*
indefinite article *n* *grammar* either of the words 'a' or 'an'
indelible *adj* **1** impossible to erase or remove **2** making indelible marks: *indelible ink* [Latin *in-* not + *delere* to destroy] **indelibly** *adv*
indelicate *adj* **1** offensive, embarrassing, or tasteless **2** coarse, crude, or rough **indelicacy** *n*
indemnify *vb* **-fies, -fying, -fied 1** to secure against loss, damage, or liability **2** to compensate for loss or damage **indemnification** *n*
indemnity *n, pl* **-ties 1** insurance against loss or damage **2** compensation for loss or damage **3** legal exemption from penalties incurred [Latin *in-* not + *damnum* damage]
indent *vb* **1** to start (a line of text) or position (a block of text) further from the margin than the main part of the text **2** to order (goods) using a special order form **3** to notch (an edge or border) **4** to write out (a document) in duplicate **5** to

bind (an apprentice) by indenture ▷ *n* **6** *chiefly Brit* an official order for goods, esp. foreign merchandise [Latin *in-* in + *dens* tooth]

indentation *n* **1** a hollow, notch, or cut, as on an edge or on a coastline **2** an indenting or being indented **3** Also: **indention** the leaving of space or the amount of space left between a margin and the start of an indented line

indenture *n* **1** a contract, esp. one binding an apprentice to his or her employer ▷ *vb* **-turing, -tured 2** to bind (an apprentice) by indenture **3** to enter into an agreement by indenture

independent *adj* **1** free from the influence or control of others **2** not dependent on anything else for function or validity **3** not relying on the support, esp. financial support, of others **4** capable of acting for oneself or on one's own **5** of or having a private income large enough to enable one to live without working: *independent means* **6** *maths* (of a variable) not dependent on another variable ▷ *n* **7** an independent person or thing **8** a politician who does not represent any political party **independence** *n* **independently** *adv*

independent school *n* a school that is neither financed nor controlled by the government or local authorities

in-depth *adj* detailed or thorough: *an in-depth analysis*

indescribable *adj* too intense or extreme for words **indescribably** *adv*

indestructible *adj* not able to be destroyed

indeterminate *adj* **1** uncertain in extent, amount, or nature **2** left doubtful; inconclusive: *an indeterminate reply* **3** *maths* **A** having no numerical meaning, as $^0/_0$ **B** (of an equation) having more than one variable and an unlimited number of solutions **indeterminable** *adj* **indeterminacy** *n*

index *n, pl* **-dexes** *or* **-dices 1** an alphabetical list of names or subjects dealt with in a book, indicating where they are referred to **2** a file or catalogue in a library which enables a book or reference to be found **3** a number indicating the level of wages or prices as compared with some standard value **4** an indication or sign: *national birth rate was once an index of military power* **5** *maths* **A** same as **exponent B** a superscript number placed to the left of a radical sign indicating the root to be extracted: *the index of* $\sqrt[3]{8}$ *is 3* **6** a number or ratio indicating a specific characteristic or property: *refractive index* ▷ *vb* **7** to put an index in (a book) **8** to enter (a word or item) in an index **9** to make index-linked [Latin: pointer]

indexation *or* **index-linking** *n* the act of making wages, pensions, or interest rates index-linked

index finger *n* the finger next to the thumb. Also called: **forefinger**

index-linked *adj* (of pensions, wages, or interest rates) rising and falling in line with the cost of living

Indiaman *n, pl* **-men** (formerly) a merchant ship engaged in trade with India

Indian *adj* **1** of India **2** of the original inhabitants of the American continent ▷ *n* **3** a person from India **4** a person descended from the original inhabitants of the American continent

Indian club *n* a heavy bottle-shaped club, usually swung in pairs for exercise

Indian corn *n* same as **maize**

Indian file *n* same as **single file**

Indian hemp *n* same as **hemp**

Indian ink *or esp US & Canad* **India ink** *n* a black ink made from a fine black soot

Indian summer *n* **1** a period of warm sunny weather in autumn **2** a period of tranquillity or of renewed productivity towards the end of a person's life or career

India paper *n* a thin soft opaque printing paper originally made in China and Japan

Indic *adj* **1** of a branch of Indo-European consisting of many of the languages of India, including Sanskrit, Hindi, and Urdu ▷ *n* **2** this group of languages

indicate *vb* **-cating, -cated 1** to be or give a sign or symptom of: *to concede 18 goals in 7 games indicates a serious malaise* **2** to point out or show **3** to state briefly **4** to switch on the indicators in a motor vehicle to show that one is changing direction **5** (of measuring instruments) to show a reading of **6** (*usually passive*) to recommend or require: *surgery seems to be indicated for this patient* [Latin *indicare*] **indication** *n*

indicative (in-**dik**-a-tiv) *adj* **1 indicative of** suggesting: *the symptoms aren't indicative of anything serious* **2** *grammar* denoting a mood of verbs used to make a statement ▷ *n* **3** *grammar* the indicative mood

indicator *n* **1** something that acts as a sign or indication: *an indicator of the moral decline of our society* **2** a device for indicating that a motor vehicle is about to turn left or right, esp. two pairs of lights that flash **3** an instrument, such as a gauge, that registers or measures something **4** *chem* a substance used to indicate the completion of a chemical reaction, usually by a change of colour

indices (**in**-diss-seez) *n* a plural of **index**

indict (in-**dite**) *vb* to charge (a person) formally with a crime, esp. in writing [Latin *in-* against + *dictare* to declare] **indictable** *adj*

indictment *n* **1** *criminal law* a formal charge of crime, esp. in writing: *the indictment contained three similar charges against each of the defendants* **2** a serious criticism: *a scathing indictment of faith healing*

indie *n informal* an independent record or film company

indifference *n* **1** lack of concern or interest: *elite indifference to mass opinion* **2** lack of importance: *a matter of indifference to me*

indifferent *adj* **1** showing no concern or interest: *he was indifferent to politics* **2** of only average standard or quality **3** not at all good: *she had starred in several very indifferent movies* **4** unimportant **5** showing or having no preferences [Latin *indifferens* making no distinction]

indigenous (in-**dij**-in-uss) *adj* originating or occurring naturally in a country or area: *the indigenous population is under threat* [Latin *indigenus*]

indigent *adj formal* so poor as to lack even necessities: *the indigent widow of a fellow writer* [Latin *indigere* to need] **indigence** *n*

indigestible *adj* difficult or impossible to digest **indigestibility** *n*
indigestion *n* difficulty in digesting food, accompanied by stomach pain, heartburn, and belching
indignant *adj* feeling or showing indignation [Latin *indignari* to be displeased with] **indignantly** *adv*
indignation *n* anger aroused by something felt to be unfair or wrong
indignity *n, pl* **-ties** embarrassing or humiliating treatment
indigo *adj* **1** deep violet-blue ▷ *n, pl* **-gos** *or* **-goes** **2** a dye of this colour originally obtained from plants [Spanish *indico*, from Greek *Indikos* of India]
indirect *adj* **1** done or caused by someone or something else: *indirect benefits* **2** not going in a direct course or line: *he took the indirect route home* **3** not coming straight to the point: *an indirect question* **indirectly** *adv*
indirect object *n grammar* the person or thing indirectly affected by the action of a verb and its direct object, as *John* in the sentence *I bought John a newspaper*
indirect speech *n* same as **reported speech**
indirect tax *n* a tax levied on goods or services which is paid indirectly by being added to the price
indiscernible *adj* not able or scarcely able to be seen
indiscipline *n* lack of discipline
indiscreet *adj* incautious or tactless in revealing secrets
indiscretion *n* **1** lack of discretion **2** an indiscreet act or remark
indiscriminate *adj* lacking discrimination or careful choice: *an indiscriminate bombing campaign* **indiscriminately** *adv* **indiscrimination** *n*
indispensable *adj* absolutely necessary: *an indispensable guide for any traveller* **indispensability** *n*
indisposed *adj* **1** sick or ill **2** unwilling [Latin *indispositus* disordered] **indisposition** *n*
indisputable *adj* beyond doubt
indissoluble *adj* permanent: *joining a political party is not an indissoluble marriage*
indistinct *adj* unable to be seen or heard clearly **indistinctly** *adv*
indistinguishable *adj* so similar as to be difficult to tell apart
indium *n chem* a rare soft silvery metallic element. Symbol: **In** [Latin *indicum* indigo]
individual *adj* **1** of, relating to, or meant for a single person or thing: *small sums from individual donors* **2** separate or distinct from others of its kind: *please mark the individual pages* **3** characterized by unusual and striking qualities ▷ *n* **4** a single person, esp. when regarded as distinct from others: *respect for the individual* **5** *informal* a person: *a most annoying individual* **6** *biol* a single animal or plant, esp. as distinct from a species [Latin *individuus* indivisible] **individually** *adv*
individualism *n* **1** the principle of leading one's life in one's own way **2** same as **laissez faire** **3** egotism **individualist** *n* **individualistic** *adj*
individuality *n, pl* **-ties** **1** distinctive or unique character or personality: *a house of great individuality* **2** the qualities that distinguish one person or thing from another **3** a separate existence
individualize *or* **-ise** *vb* **-izing, -ized** *or* **-ising, -ised** to make individual or distinctive in character
indivisible *adj* **1** unable to be divided **2** *maths* leaving a remainder when divided by a given number
indoctrinate *vb* **-nating, -nated** to teach (someone) systematically to accept a doctrine or opinion uncritically **indoctrination** *n*
Indo-European *adj* **1** of a family of languages spoken in most of Europe and much of Asia, including English, Russian, and Hindi ▷ *n* **2** the Indo-European family of languages
indolent *adj* lazy; idle [Latin *indolens* not feeling pain] **indolence** *n*
indomitable *adj* too strong to be defeated or discouraged: *an indomitable work ethic* [Latin *indomitus* untamable]
Indonesian *adj* **1** of Indonesia ▷ *n* **2** a person from Indonesia
indoor *adj* situated, happening, or used inside a building: *an indoor pool*
indoors *adv, adj* inside or into a building
indrawn *adj* drawn or pulled in: *he heard her indrawn breath*
indubitable (in-dew-bit-a-bl) *adj* beyond doubt; definite [Latin *in-* not + *dubitare* to doubt] **indubitably** *adv*
induce *vb* **-ducing, -duced** **1** to persuade or use influence on **2** to cause or bring about **3** *med* to cause (labour) to begin by the use of drugs or other means **4** *logic obsolete* to draw (a general conclusion) from particular instances **5** to produce (an electromotive force or electrical current) by induction **6** to transmit (magnetism) by induction [Latin *inducere* to lead in] **inducible** *adj*
inducement *n* **1** something that encourages someone to do something **2** the act of inducing
induct *vb* **1** to bring in formally or install in a job, rank, or position **2** to initiate in knowledge of (a group or profession): *boys are inducted into the world of men* [Latin *inductus* led in]
inductance *n* the property of an electric circuit as a result of which an electromotive force is created by a change of current in the same or in a neighbouring circuit
induction *n* **1** *logic* a process of reasoning by which a general conclusion is drawn from particular instances **2** *med* the process of inducing labour **3** the process by which electrical or magnetic properties are transferred, without physical contact, from one circuit or body to another **4** a formal introduction or entry into an office or position **5** (in an internal-combustion engine) the drawing in of mixed air and fuel from the carburettor to the cylinder **inductional** *adj*
induction coil *n* a transformer for producing a high voltage from a low voltage. It consists of a soft-iron core, a primary coil of few turns, and a concentric secondary coil of many turns
induction course *n* a training course to help familiarize someone with a new job

inductive *adj* **1** *logic* of or using induction: *inductive reasoning* **2** of or operated by electrical or magnetic induction
inductor *n* a device designed to create inductance in an electrical circuit
indulge *vb* **-dulging, -dulged 1** (often foll. by *in*) to yield to or gratify (a whim or desire for): *to indulge in new clothes* **2** to allow (someone) to have or do everything he or she wants: *he had given her too much, indulged her in everything* **3** to allow (oneself) the pleasure of something: *he indulged himself* **4** *informal* to take alcoholic drink [Latin *indulgere* to concede]
indulgence *n* **1** something that is allowed because it gives pleasure; extravagance **2** the act of indulging oneself or someone else **3** liberal or tolerant treatment **4** something granted as a favour or privilege **5** *RC Church* a remission of the temporal punishment for sin after its guilt has been forgiven
indulgent *adj* kind or lenient, often to excess **indulgently** *adv*
industrial *adj* **1** of, used in, or employed in industry **2** with an economy relying heavily on industry: *northern industrial cities*
industrial action *n* action, such as a strike or work-to-rule, by which workers complain about their conditions
industrial estate *n Brit, Austral, NZ & S African* an area of land set aside for factories and warehouses
industrialism *n* an organization of society characterized by large-scale manufacturing industry rather than trade or farming
industrialist *n* a person who owns or controls large amounts of money or property in industry
industrialize *or* **-lise** *vb* **-lizing, -lized** *or* **-lising, -lised** to develop industry on a large scale in (a country or region) **industrialization** *or* **-lisation** *n*
industrial relations *pl n* the relations between management and workers
Industrial Revolution *n* **the Industrial Revolution** the transformation in the 18th and 19th centuries of Britain and other countries into industrial nations
industrious *adj* hard-working
industry *n, pl* **-tries 1** the work and process involved in manufacture: *Japanese industry increased output considerably last year* **2** a branch of commercial enterprise concerned with the manufacture of a specified product: *the steel industry* **3** the quality of working hard [Latin *industrius* active]
Indy Car racing *n* a form of motor racing, chiefly in the US, around banked oval tracks [after the *Indianapolis 500* motor race]
inebriate *n* **1** a person who is habitually drunk ▷ *adj* **2** drunk, esp. habitually [Latin *ebrius* drunk] **inebriation** *n*
inebriated *adj* drunk
inedible *adj* not fit to be eaten
ineducable (in-**ed**-yuke-a-bl) *adj* considered incapable of being educated, esp. (formerly) on account of mental disability
ineffable *adj* too great or intense to be expressed in words [Latin *in-* not + *effabilis* utterable] **ineffably** *adv*
ineffective *adj* having no effect or an inadequate effect
ineffectual *adj* having no effect or an inadequate effect: *the raids were costly and ineffectual*
inefficient *adj* not performing a task or function to the best advantage **inefficiency** *n*
inelegant *adj* lacking elegance or refinement
ineligible *adj* not qualified for or entitled to something
ineluctable *adj formal* impossible to avoid: *the ineluctable collapse of the coalition* [Latin *in-* not + *eluctari* to escape]
inept *adj* **1** awkward, clumsy, or incompetent **2** not suitable or fitting; out of place [Latin *in-* not + *aptus* fitting] **ineptitude** *n*
inequable *adj* **1** unfair **2** not uniform
inequality *n, pl* **-ties 1** the state or quality of being unequal **2** an instance of this **3** lack of smoothness or regularity of a surface **4** *maths* a statement indicating that the value of one quantity or expression is not equal to another
inequitable *adj* unjust or unfair
inequity *n, pl* **-ties 1** injustice or unfairness **2** something which is unjust or unfair
ineradicable *adj* impossible to remove or root out: *an ineradicable sense of guilt*
inert *adj* **1** without the power to move or to resist motion **2** inactive or lifeless **3** having only a limited ability to react chemically [Latin *iners* unskilled]
inertia *n* **1** a feeling of unwillingness to do anything **2** *physics* the tendency of a body to remain still or continue moving unless a force is applied to it **inertial** *adj*
inescapable *adj* not able to be avoided
inessential *adj* **1** not necessary ▷ *n* **2** an unnecessary thing
inestimable *adj* too great to be calculated
inevitable *adj* **1** unavoidable; sure to happen **2** *informal* so regular as to be predictable: *the inevitable guitar solo* ▷ *n* **3** (often preceded by *the*) something that is unavoidable [Latin *in-* not + *evitare* to avoid] **inevitability** *n* **inevitably** *adv*
inexact *adj* not exact or accurate
inexcusable *adj* too bad to be justified or tolerated
inexhaustible *adj* incapable of being used up; endless
inexorable *adj* unable to be prevented from continuing or progressing: *an inexorable trend* [Latin *in-* not + *exorare* to prevail upon] **inexorably** *adv*
inexpensive *adj* not costing a lot of money
inexperienced *adj* having no knowledge or experience of a particular situation, activity, etc. **inexperience** *n*
inexpert *adj* lacking skill
inexpiable *adj* (of sin) incapable of being atoned for; unpardonable
inexplicable *adj* impossible to explain
inexpressible *adj* (of a feeling) too strong to be expressed in words
in extremis *adv* **1** in dire straits **2** at the point of death

inextricable *adj* **1** impossible to escape from: *an inextricable dilemma* **2** impossible to disentangle or separate: *an inextricable mass of twisted metal* **inextricably** *adv*

inf. **1** infantry **2** infinitive **3** informal **4** information

infallible *adj* **1** incapable of error **2** always successful: *an infallible cure* **3** (of the Pope, in Roman Catholic belief) incapable of error in setting forth matters of doctrine on faith and morals **infallibility** *n* **infallibly** *adv*

infamous (in-fam-uss) *adj* well-known for something bad

infamy *n, pl* **-mies** **1** the state of being infamous **2** an infamous act or event [Latin *infamis* of evil repute]

infancy *n, pl* **-cies** **1** the state or period of being an infant **2** an early stage of growth or development: *virtual reality is in its infancy* **3** *law* the state or period of being a minor

infant *n* **1** a very young child; baby **2** *law* same as **minor** (sense 4) **3** *Brit* a young school child ▷ *adj* **4** of, relating to, or designed for young children: *infant school* **5** in an early stage of development: *an infant democracy* [Latin *infans,* literally: speechless]

infanta *n* **1** (formerly) a daughter of a king of Spain or Portugal **2** the wife of an infante [Spanish and Portuguese]

infante *n* (formerly) any son of a king of Spain or Portugal, except the heir to the throne [Spanish and Portuguese]

infanticide *n* **1** the act of killing an infant **2** a person who kills an infant [INFANT + Latin *caedere* to kill]

infantile *adj* **1** childishly immature **2** of infants or infancy

infantile paralysis *n* same as **poliomyelitis**

infantry *n, pl* **-tries** soldiers who fight on foot [Italian *infanteria*]

infant school *n* (in England and Wales) a school for children aged between 5 and 7

infatuate *vb* **-ating, -ated** to inspire or fill with an intense and unreasoning passion [Latin *infatuare*] **infatuation** *n*

infatuated *adj* (often foll. by *with*) carried away by an intense and unreasoning passion for someone

infect *vb* **1** to contaminate (a person or thing) with a germ or virus or its consequent disease **2** to taint or contaminate **3** to affect with an opinion or feeling as if by contagion: *even she was infected by the excitement* [Latin *inficere* to stain]

infection *n* **1** an infectious disease **2** contamination of a person or thing by a germ or virus or its consequent disease

infectious *adj* **1** (of a disease) capable of being transmitted without actual contact **2** causing or transmitting infection **3** spreading from one person to another: *infectious laughter*

infectious mononucleosis *n* same as **glandular fever**

infelicity *n, pl* **-ties** *formal* **1** something, esp. a remark or expression, that is inapt **2** the state or quality of being unhappy or unfortunate **infelicitous** *adj*

infer *vb* **-ferring, -ferred** **1** to conclude by reasoning from evidence; deduce **2** *not standard* to imply or suggest [Latin *inferre* to bring into]

> **USAGE** The use of *infer* to mean *imply* is common in both speech and writing, but is regarded by many people as incorrect.

inference *n* **1** the act or process of reaching a conclusion by reasoning from evidence **2** an inferred conclusion or deduction

inferential *adj* of or based on inference

inferior *adj* **1** lower in quality, quantity, or usefulness **2** lower in rank, position, or status **3** of poor quality **4** lower in position **5** *printing* (of a character) printed at the foot of an ordinary character ▷ *n* **6** a person inferior to another, esp. in rank [Latin: lower] **inferiority** *n*

inferiority complex *n* *psychiatry* a disorder arising from a feeling of inferiority to others, characterized by aggressiveness or extreme shyness

infernal *adj* **1** of or relating to hell **2** *informal* irritating: *stop that infernal noise* [Latin *infernus* lower]

inferno *n, pl* **-nos** **1** an intense raging fire **2** a place or situation resembling hell, because it is crowded and noisy **3** **the inferno** hell [Late Latin *infernus* hell]

infertile *adj* **1** not capable of producing offspring **2** (of soil) not productive; barren **infertility** *n*

infest *vb* to inhabit or overrun (a place, plant, etc.) in unpleasantly large numbers: *the area was infested with moles* [Latin *infestare* to molest] **infestation** *n*

infidel *n* **1** a person who has no religious belief **2** a person who rejects a specific religion, esp. Christianity or Islam ▷ *adj* **3** of unbelievers or unbelief [Latin *infidelis* unfaithful]

infidelity *n, pl* **-ties** **1** sexual unfaithfulness to one's husband, wife, or lover **2** an act or instance of unfaithfulness

infield *n* **1** *cricket* the area of the field near the pitch **2** *baseball* the area of the playing field enclosed by the base lines **infielder** *n*

infighting *n* **1** rivalry or quarrelling between members of the same group or organization **2** *boxing* combat at close quarters

infiltrate *vb* **-trating, -trated** **1** to enter (an organization, area, etc.) gradually and in secret, so as to gain influence or control: *they infiltrated the party structure* **2** to pass (a liquid or gas) through (a substance) by filtering or (of a liquid or gas) to pass through (a substance) by filtering **infiltration** *n* **infiltrator** *n*

infinite (in-fin-it) *adj* **1** having no limits or boundaries in time, space, extent, or size **2** extremely or immeasurably great or numerous: *infinite wealth* **3** *maths* having an unlimited or uncountable number of digits, factors, or terms **infinitely** *adv*

infinitesimal *adj* **1** extremely small: *an infinitesimal risk* **2** *maths* of or involving a small change in the value of a variable that approaches zero as a limit ▷ *n* **3** *maths* an infinitesimal quantity

infinitive (in-fin-it-iv) *n* *grammar* a form of the verb which in most languages is not inflected for tense or person and is used without a particular subject: in English, the infinitive usually consists of the word *to* followed by the verb

infinitude *n literary* **1** the state or quality of being infinite **2** an infinite extent or quantity

infinity *n, pl* **-ties 1** an infinitely great number or amount **2** endless time, space, or quantity **3** *maths* the concept of a value greater than any finite numerical value

infirm *adj* physically or mentally weak, esp. from old age

infirmary *n, pl* **-ries** a place for the treatment of sick or injured people; hospital

infirmity *n, pl* **-ties 1** the state of being infirm **2** physical weakness or frailty

infix *vb* **1** to fix firmly in **2** to instil or impress on the mind by repetition **infixation** *or* **infixion** *n*

in flagrante delicto (in flag-grant-ee dee-lick-toe) *adv chiefly law* while committing the offence [Latin]

inflame *vb* **-flaming, -flamed 1** to make angry or excited **2** to increase or intensify; aggravate **3** to produce inflammation in or become inflamed **4** to set or be set on fire

inflammable *adj* **1** liable to catch fire **2** easily aroused to anger or passion **inflammability** *n*

USAGE See at **flammable**.

inflammation *n* **1** the reaction of living tissue to injury or infection, characterized by heat, redness, swelling, and pain **2** an inflaming or being inflamed

inflammatory *adj* **1** likely to provoke anger **2** characterized by or caused by inflammation

inflatable *adj* **1** capable of being inflated ▷ *n* **2** a plastic or rubber object which can be inflated

inflate *vb* **-flating, -flated 1** to expand or cause to expand by filling with gas or air **2** to give an impression of greater importance than is justified: *something to inflate their self-esteem* **3** to cause or undergo economic inflation [Latin *inflare* to blow into]

inflation *n* **1** an inflating or being inflated **2** *econ* a progressive increase in the general level of prices brought about by an increase in the amount of money in circulation or by increases in costs **3** *informal* the rate of increase of prices **inflationary** *adj*

inflect *vb* **1** to change (the voice) in tone or pitch **2** *grammar* to change (the form of a word) by inflection **3** to bend or curve [Latin *inflectere* to curve, alter] **inflective** *adj*

inflection *or* **inflexion** *n* **1** change in the pitch of the voice **2** *grammar* a change in the form of a word, signalling change in such grammatical functions as tense or number **3** an angle or bend **4** an inflecting or being inflected **5** *maths* a change in curvature from concave to convex or vice versa **inflectional** *or* **inflexional** *adj*

inflexible *adj* **1** unwilling to be persuaded; obstinate **2** (of a rule, etc.) firmly fixed: *inflexible schedules* **3** incapable of being bent: *inflexible joints* **inflexibility** *n*

inflict *vb* **1** to impose (something unpleasant) on **2** to deliver (a blow or wound) [Latin *infligere* to strike (something) against] **infliction** *n* **inflictor** *n*

in-flight *adj* happening or provided during flight in an aircraft: *in-flight meals*

inflorescence *n botany* **1** the part of a plant that consists of the flower-bearing stalks **2** the arrangement of the flowers on the stalks **3** the process of flowering; blossoming [Latin *in-* into + *florescere* to bloom]

inflow *n* **1** something, such as a liquid or gas, that flows in **2** the act of flowing in; influx

influence *n* **1** an effect of one person or thing on another **2** the power of a person or thing to have such an effect **3** power resulting from ability, wealth, or position **4** a person or thing with influence **5 under the influence** *informal* drunk ▷ *vb* **-encing, -enced 6** to have an effect upon (actions or events) **7** to persuade or induce [Latin *influere* to flow into]

influential *adj* having or exerting influence

influenza *n* a highly contagious viral disease characterized by fever, muscular pains, and catarrh [Italian: influence, hence incursion, epidemic]

influx *n* **1** the arrival or entry of many people or things **2** the act of flowing in [Latin *influere* to flow into]

info *n informal* short for **information**

inform *vb* **1** to give information to; tell: *he informed me that he would be free after lunch* **2** to make knowledgeable (about) or familiar (with): *he'll be informed of his rights* **3** to give incriminating information to the police **4** to impart some essential or formative characteristic to **5** to animate or inspire [Latin *informare* to describe] **informed** *adj*

informal *adj* **1** relaxed and friendly: *an informal interview* **2** appropriate to everyday life or use rather than formal occasions: *informal clothes* **3** (of speech or writing) appropriate to ordinary conversation rather than to formal written language **informality** *n* **informally** *adv*

informant *n* a person who gives information

information *n* **1** knowledge acquired in any manner; facts **2** *computers* **A** the meaning given to data by the way it is interpreted **B** same as **data** (sense 2)

information technology *n* the production, storage, and communication of information using computers and electronic technology

information theory *n* the study of the processes of communication and the transmission of information

informative *adj* giving useful information

informer *n* a person who informs to the police

infra dig *adj informal* beneath one's dignity [Latin *infra dignitatem*]

infrared *adj* **1** of or using rays with a wavelength just beyond the red end of the visible spectrum ▷ *n* **2** the infrared part of the spectrum [Latin *infra* beneath]

infrasonic *adj* having a frequency below the range audible to the human ear [Latin *infra* beneath]

infrasound *n* infrasonic waves

infrastructure *n* **1** the basic structure of an organization or system **2** the stock of facilities, services, and equipment in a country, including factories, roads, and schools, that are needed for it to function properly [Latin *infra* beneath]

infrequent *adj* not happening often **infrequently** *adv*

infringe *vb* **-fringing, -fringed 1** to violate or break (a law or agreement) **2 infringe on** *or* **upon** to encroach or trespass on: *the press infringed on their privacy* [Latin *infringere* to break off] **infringement** *n*

infuriate *vb* **-ating, -ated** to make very angry [Medieval Latin *infuriare*] **infuriating** *adj* **infuriatingly** *adv*

infuse *vb* **-fusing, -fused 1** to fill with (an emotion or quality) **2** to soak or be soaked in order to extract flavour [Latin *infundere* to pour into]

infusible *adj* unable to be fused or melted **infusibility** *n*

infusion *n* **1** the act of infusing **2** a liquid obtained by infusing

ingenious (in-**jean**-ee-uss) *adj* showing cleverness and originality: *a truly ingenious invention* [Latin *ingenium* natural ability]

ingenue (**an**-jay-new) *n* an innocent or inexperienced young woman, esp. as a role played by an actress [French]

ingenuity (in-jen-**new**-it-ee) *n* cleverness at inventing things [Latin *ingenuitas* a freeborn condition; meaning influenced by INGENIOUS]

ingenuous (in-**jen**-new-uss) *adj* **1** unsophisticated and trusting **2** frank and straightforward [Latin *ingenuus* freeborn, virtuous]

ingest *vb* to take (food or liquid) into the body [Latin *ingerere* to put into] **ingestion** *n*

ingle *n archaic or dialect* a fire in a room or a fireplace [probably Scottish Gaelic *aingeal* fire]

inglenook *n Brit* a corner by a fireplace

inglorious *adj* dishonourable or shameful

ingoing *adj* going in; entering

ingot *n* a piece of metal cast in a form suitable for storage, usually a bar [origin unknown]

ingrained *or* **engrained** *adj* **1** (of a habit, feeling, or belief) deeply impressed or instilled **2** (of dirt) worked into or through the fibre or pores [*dyed in grain* dyed with kermes through the fibre]

ingratiate *vb* **-ating, -ated** to act in order to bring (oneself) into favour (with someone) [Latin *in-* in + *gratia* favour] **ingratiating** *adj*

ingratitude *n* lack of gratitude or thanks

ingredient *n* a component of a mixture or compound, esp. in cooking [Latin *ingrediens* going into]

ingress *n formal* **1** the act of going or coming in **2** the right or permission to enter [Latin *ingressus*]

ingrowing *adj* (esp. of a toenail) growing abnormally into the flesh **ingrown** *adj*

inhabit *vb* to live or dwell in [Latin *inhabitare*] **inhabitable** *adj*

inhabitant *n* a person or animal that is a permanent resident of a particular place or region

inhalant (in-**hale**-ant) *n* a medicinal preparation inhaled to help breathing problems

inhale *vb* **-haling, -haled** to breathe in (air, smoke, or vapour) [Latin *in-* in + *halare* to breathe] **inhalation** *n*

inhaler *n* a container used to administer an inhalant

inharmonious *adj* lacking harmony; discordant; disagreeing

inhere *vb* **-hering, -hered** > **inhere in** to be an inseparable part (of) [Latin *inhaerere* to stick in]

inherent *adj* existing as an inseparable part **inherently** *adv*

inherit *vb* **1** to receive money, property, or a title from someone who has died **2** to receive (a characteristic) from an earlier generation by heredity **3** to receive (a position or situation) from a predecessor: *he inherited a mess* [Old French *enheriter*] **inheritor** *n*

inheritable *adj* **1** capable of being transmitted by heredity from one generation to a later one **2** capable of being inherited

inheritance *n* **1** *law* **A** hereditary succession to an estate or title **B** the right of an heir to succeed on the death of an ancestor **2** something inherited or to be inherited **3** the act of inheriting **4** the fact of receiving characteristics from an earlier generation by heredity

inheritance tax *n* (in Britain) a tax consisting of a percentage levied on the part of an inheritance that exceeds a specified allowance

inhibit *vb* **1** to restrain or hinder (an impulse or desire) **2** to prohibit or prevent: *an attempt to inhibit nuclear proliferation* **3** *chem* to stop, prevent, or decrease the rate of (a chemical reaction) [Latin *inhibere*] **inhibited** *adj* **inhibitor** *n*

inhibition *n* **1** *psychol* a feeling of fear or embarrassment that stops one from behaving naturally **2** an inhibiting or being inhibited **3** the process of stopping or retarding a chemical reaction

inhospitable *adj* **1** not welcoming; unfriendly **2** (of a place or climate) not easy to live in; harsh

inhuman *adj* **1** cruel or brutal **2** not human

inhumane *adj* extremely cruel or brutal

inhumanity *n, pl* **-ties 1** lack of kindness or compassion **2** an inhumane act

inimical *adj* **1** adverse or unfavourable: *inimical to change* **2** unfriendly or hostile [Latin *in-* not + *amicus* friendly]

inimitable *adj* impossible to imitate **inimitably** *adv*

iniquity *n, pl* **-ties 1** injustice or wickedness **2** a wicked act [Latin *iniquus* unfair] **iniquitous** *adj*

initial *adj* **1** of or at the beginning ▷ *n* **2** the first letter of a word, esp. a person's name **3** *printing* a large letter set at the beginning of a chapter or work ▷ *vb* **-tialling, -tialled** *or US* **-tialing, -tialed 4** to sign with one's initials, esp. to indicate approval [Latin *initium* beginning] **initially** *adv*

initiate *vb* **-ating, -ated 1** to begin or set going: *more women initiate divorce today* **2** to accept (new members) into a group, often through secret ceremonies **3** to teach the fundamentals of a skill or knowledge to (someone) ▷ *n* **4** a person who has been initiated, esp. recently **5** a beginner [Latin *initiare*] **initiation** *n* **initiator** *n*

initiative *n* **1** a first step; a commencing move: *a peace initiative* **2** the right or power to initiate something: *it forced local people to take the initiative* **3** enterprise: *the drive and initiative to create new* *products* **4 on one's own initiative** without being prompted

inject *vb* **1** *med* to put (a fluid) into the body with a syringe **2** to introduce (a new element): *to inject a dose of realism into the assessment* [Latin *injicere* to throw in] **injection** *n*

injudicious *adj* showing poor judgment; unwise

injunction *n* **1** *law* a court order not to do something **2** an authoritative command [Latin *injungere* to enjoin] **injunctive** *adj*

injure *vb* **-juring, -jured 1** to hurt physically or mentally **2** to do wrong to (a person), esp. by an injustice: *the injured party* **3** to damage: *an opportunity to injure your reputation* **injured** *adj*

injurious *adj* **1** causing harm **2** abusive, slanderous, or libellous

injury *n, pl* **-ries 1** physical hurt **2** a specific instance of this: *a leg injury* **3** harm done to the feelings **4** damage: *inflict no injury on the wealth of the nation* [Latin *injuria* injustice]

injury time *n sport* playing time added at the end of a match to compensate for time spent treating injured players. Also called: **stoppage time**

injustice *n* **1** unfairness **2** an unfair action

ink *n* **1** a black or coloured liquid used for printing, writing, and drawing **2** a dark brown fluid squirted for self-concealment by an octopus or cuttlefish **3** *informal* a tattoo or a series of tattoos ▷ *vb* **4** to mark or cover with ink **5 ink in** to arrange or confirm definitely [Old French *enque*]

inkling *n* a vague idea or suspicion [Middle English *inclen* to hint at]

inkstand *n* a stand or tray for holding writing tools and containers for ink

inkwell *n* a small container for ink, often fitted into the surface of a desk

inky *adj* **inkier, inkiest 1** dark or black, like ink **2** stained with ink **inkiness** *n*

inlaid *adj* **1** set in another material so that the surface is smooth, such as a design in wood **2** made in this way: *an inlaid table-top*

inland *adj* **1** of or in the interior of a country or region, away from a sea or border **2** *chiefly Brit* operating within a country or region; domestic: *inland trade* ▷ *n* **3** the interior of a country or region ▷ *adv* **4** towards or into the interior of a country or region

Inland Revenue *n* (in New Zealand and formerly in Britain) a government department that collects major direct taxes

in-law *n* **1** a relative by marriage ▷ *adj* **2** (*in combination*) related by marriage: *his brother-in-law*

inlay *vb* **-laying, -laid 1** to decorate (an article, esp. of furniture) by inserting pieces of wood, ivory, or metal so that the surfaces are smooth and flat ▷ *n* **2** decoration made by inlaying **3** an inlaid article **4** *dentistry* a filling shaped to fit a cavity

inlet *n* **1** a narrow strip of water extending from the sea into the land **2** a passage or valve through which a liquid or gas enters a machine

in-line skate *n* a type of roller skate in which the wheels are set in a single straight line

in loco parentis (par-rent-iss) in place of a parent: said of a person acting for a parent [Latin]

inmate *n* a person who is confined to an institution such as a prison or hospital

inmost *adj* same as **innermost**

inn *n* a pub or small hotel providing food and accommodation [Old English]

innards *pl n informal* **1** the internal organs of the body, esp. the entrails **2** the working parts of a machine [variant of *inwards*]

innate *adj* existing from birth, rather than acquired; inborn: *his innate decency* [Latin *innasci* to be born in] **innately** *adv*

inner *adj* **1** happening or located inside or further inside: *the door to the inner office* **2** of the mind or spirit: *her inner self* **3** exclusive or private: *the inner sanctum of the party secretariat* **4** more profound; less apparent: *the inner meaning* ▷ *n* **5** *archery* **A** the red innermost ring on a target **B** a shot which hits this ring

inner child *n psychol* the part of the psyche that retains the feelings as they were experienced in childhood

inner city *n* the parts of a city in or near its centre, where there are often social and economic problems

inner man *or fem* **inner woman** *n* **1** the mind or soul **2** *humorous* the stomach

innermost *adj* **1** most intimate or private: *innermost secrets* **2** furthest within

inner tube *n* an inflatable rubber tube inside a pneumatic tyre casing

inning *n baseball* a division of the game consisting of a turn at batting and a turn in the field for each side [Old English *innung* a going in]

innings *n* **1** *cricket* **A** the batting turn of a player or team **B** the runs scored during such a turn **2** a period of opportunity or action

innkeeper *n* an owner or manager of an inn

innocence *n* the quality or state of being innocent [Latin *innocentia* harmlessness]

innocent *adj* **1** not guilty of a particular crime **2** without experience of evil **3** harmless or innocuous **4 innocent of** without or lacking: *innocent of prejudice* ▷ *n* **5** an innocent person, esp. a young child or a naive adult **innocently** *adv*

innocuous *adj* having no adverse or harmful effect [Latin *innocuus*]

innovate *vb* **-vating, -vated** to introduce new ideas or methods [Latin *innovare* to renew] **innovative** *or* **innovatory** *adj* **innovator** *n*

innovation *n* **1** something newly introduced, such as a new method or device **2** the act of innovating

Innu *n* **1** a member of an Algonquian people living in Labrador and northern Quebec **2** the Algonquian language of this people

innuendo *n, pl* **-dos** *or* **-does** an indirect or subtle reference to something rude or unpleasant [Latin: by hinting]

Innuit (in-new-it) *n* same as **Inuit**

innumerable *adj* too many to be counted **innumerably** *adv*

innumerate *adj* having no understanding of mathematics or science **innumeracy** *n*

inoculate *vb* **-lating, -lated 1** to protect against disease by injecting with a vaccine **2** to introduce (microorganisms, esp. bacteria) into (a culture medium) [Latin *inoculare* to implant] **inoculation** *n*

inoffensive *adj* causing no harm or annoyance
inoperable *adj* *surgery* unable to be safely operated on: *an inoperable tumour*
inoperative *adj* not working or functioning: *continued shelling has rendered the ceasefire inoperative*
inopportune *adj* badly timed or inappropriate
inordinate *adj* **1** excessive: *an inordinate amount of time spent arguing* **2** unrestrained, as in behaviour or emotion: *inordinate anger* [Latin *inordinatus* disordered] **inordinately** *adv*
inorganic *adj* **1** not having the structure or characteristics of living organisms **2** *chem* of or denoting chemical compounds that do not contain carbon **3** not resulting from or produced by growth; artificial: *inorganic fertilizers*
inorganic chemistry *n* the branch of chemistry concerned with the elements and compounds which do not contain carbon
inpatient *n* a patient who stays in a hospital for treatment
input *n* **1** resources, such as money, labour, or power, put into a project **2** *computers* the data fed into a computer ▷ *vb* **-putting, -put 3** to enter (data) in a computer
inquest *n* **1** an official inquiry into an unexplained, sudden, or violent death, held by a coroner **2** *informal* an investigation or discussion [Latin *in-* into + *quaesitus* investigation]
inquietude *n formal* restlessness or anxiety
inquire *or* **enquire** *vb* **-quiring, -quired 1** to seek information (about) **2 inquire after** to ask about the health or progress of (a person) **3 inquire into** to make an investigation **4 inquire of** to ask (a person) for information: *I'll inquire of my aunt when she is coming* [Latin *inquirere*] **inquirer** *or* **enquirer** *n*
inquiry *or* **enquiry** *n, pl* **-ries 1** a question **2** an investigation
inquisition *n* **1** a thorough investigation **2** *archaic* a judicial or official inquiry **inquisitional** *adj*
Inquisition *n* *history* an organization within the Catholic Church (1232–1820) for suppressing heresy
inquisitive *adj* **1** excessively curious about other people's business **2** eager to learn **inquisitively** *adv* **inquisitiveness** *n*
inquisitor *n* **1** a person who inquires, esp. deeply or ruthlessly **2 Inquisitor** an officer of the Inquisition
inquisitorial *adj* **1** of or like an inquisition or an inquisitor **2** offensively curious **inquisitorially** *adv*
inquorate *adj* without enough people present to make a quorum
in re (in **ray**) *prep* in the matter of; concerning [Latin]
INRI Jesus of Nazareth, king of the Jews (the inscription placed over Christ's head during the Crucifixion) [Latin *Iesus Nazarenus Rex Iudaeorum*]
inroads *pl n* **make inroads into** to start affecting or reducing: *my gambling has made great inroads into my savings*
inrush *n* a sudden and overwhelming inward flow
ins. 1 inches **2** insurance
insane *adj* **1** mentally deranged **2** stupidly irresponsible: *acting on an insane impulse* **insanely** *adv*
insanitary *adj* dirty or unhealthy
insanity *n, pl* **-ties 1** the state of being insane **2** stupidity
insatiable (in-**saysh**-a-bl) *adj* impossible to satisfy **insatiability** *n* **insatiably** *adv*
inscribe *vb* **-scribing, -scribed 1** to mark or engrave with (words, symbols, or letters) **2** to write one's name, and sometimes a brief dedication, on (a book) before giving to someone **3** to enter (a name) on a list **4** *geom* to draw (a geometric construction) inside another construction so that the two are in contact at as many points as possible but do not intersect [Latin *inscribere*]
inscription *n* **1** something inscribed, esp. words carved or engraved on a coin, tomb, or ring **2** a signature or brief dedication in a book or on a work of art
inscrutable *adj* mysterious or enigmatic [Latin *in-* not + *scrutari* to examine] **inscrutability** *n*
insect *n* **1** a small animal that has six legs and usually has wings, such as an ant, fly, or butterfly **2** (loosely) any similar invertebrate, such as a spider, tick, or centipede [Latin *insectum* (animal that has been) cut into]
insecticide *n* a substance used to destroy insects [*insect* + Latin *caedere* to kill]
insectivore *n* **1** a small mammal, such as a hedgehog or a shrew, that eats invertebrates **2** a plant or animal that eats insects [*insect* + Latin *vorare* to swallow] **insectivorous** *adj*
insecure *adj* **1** anxious or uncertain **2** not adequately protected: *low-paid or insecure employment* **3** unstable or shaky **insecurity** *n*
inseminate *vb* **-nating, -nated** to impregnate (a female) with semen [Latin *in-* in + *semen* seed] **insemination** *n*
insensate *adj* **1** lacking sensation or consciousness **2** insensitive or unfeeling **3** foolish
insensible *adj* **1** unconscious **2** without feeling **3** imperceptible **4 insensible of** *or* **to** unaware of or indifferent to: *insensible to suffering* **insensibility** *n*
insensitive *adj* unaware of or ignoring other people's feelings **insensitivity** *n*
inseparable *adj* **1** constantly together because of mutual liking: *they became inseparable companions* **2** too closely connected to be separated **inseparably** *adv*
insert *vb* **1** to place or fit (something) inside something else **2** to introduce (a clause or comment) into text or a speech ▷ *n* **3** something inserted, esp. an advertisement in between the pages of a magazine [Latin *inserere* to plant in]
insertion *n* **1** the act of inserting **2** something inserted, such as an advertisement in a newspaper
in-service *adj* denoting training that is given to employees during the course of employment: *an in-service course*
inset *vb* **-setting, -set 1** to place in or within; insert ▷ *n* **2** something inserted **3** *printing* a small

map or diagram set within the borders of a larger one ▷ *adj* **4** decorated with something inserted

inshore *adj* **1** in or on the water, but close to the shore: *inshore fishermen* ▷ *adv, adj* **2** towards the shore from the water: *the boat was forced inshore; a strong wind blowing inshore*

inside *prep* **1** in or to the interior of: *a bomb had gone off inside the parliament building* **2** in a period of time less than: *they took the lead inside seven minutes* ▷ *adj* **3** on or of the inside: *an article on the paper's inside pages* **4** by or from someone within an organization, esp. illicitly: *inside information* **5** of or being the lane in a road which is nearer the side than other lanes going in the same direction: *all the lorries were in the inside lane* ▷ *adv* **6** on, in, or to the inside; indoors: *when the rain started we took our drinks inside* **7** *Brit, Austral & NZ slang* in or into prison ▷ *n* **8** the inner side, surface, or part of something **9 inside out** with the inside facing outwards **10 know inside out** to know thoroughly ▷ See also **insides**

USAGE See at **outside**.

inside job *n informal* a crime committed with the assistance of someone employed by or trusted by the victim

insider *n* a member of a group or organization who therefore has exclusive information about it

insider dealing *n* the illegal practice of a person on the stock exchange or in the civil service taking advantage of early confidential information in order to deal in shares for personal profit

insides *pl n informal* the stomach and bowels

insidious *adj* working in a subtle or apparently harmless way, but nevertheless dangerous or deadly: *an insidious virus* [Latin *insidiae* an ambush] **insidiously** *adv* **insidiousness** *n*

insight *n* **1** a penetrating understanding, as of a complex situation or problem **2** the ability to perceive clearly or deeply the inner nature of things

insignia (in-sig-nee-a) *n, pl* **-nias** *or* **-nia** a badge or emblem of membership, office, or honour [Latin: badges]

insignificant *adj* having little or no importance **insignificance** *n*

insincere *adj* pretending what one does not feel **insincerely** *adv* **insincerity** *n*

insinuate *vb* **-ating, -ated 1** to suggest indirectly by allusion, hints, or innuendo **2** to get (someone, esp. oneself) into a position by gradual manoeuvres: *she insinuated herself into the conversation* [Latin *insinuare* to wind one's way into]

insinuation *n* **1** an indirect or devious hint or suggestion **2** an act or the practice of insinuating

insipid *adj* **1** dull and boring **2** lacking flavour [Latin *in-* not + *sapidus* full of flavour] **insipidity** *n*

insist *vb* (often foll. by *on* or *upon*) **1** to make a determined demand (for): *he insisted on his rights* **2** to express a convinced belief (in) or assertion (of): *she insisted that she had been given permission* [Latin *insistere* to stand upon, urge]

insistent *adj* **1** making continual and persistent demands **2** demanding attention: *the chirruping of an insistent bird* **insistence** *n* **insistently** *adv*

in situ *adv, adj* in the original position [Latin]

in so far as *or* **insofar as** *prep* to the degree or extent that

insole *n* **1** the inner sole of a shoe or boot **2** a loose inner sole used to give extra warmth or to make a shoe fit

insolent *adj* rude and disrespectful [Latin *in-* not + *solere* to be accustomed] **insolence** *n* **insolently** *adv*

insoluble *adj* **1** impossible to solve **2** not able to be dissolved **insolubility** *n*

insolvent *adj* **1** unable to pay one's debts ▷ *n* **2** a person who is insolvent **insolvency** *n*

insomnia *n* inability to sleep [Latin *in-* not + *somnus* sleep] **insomniac** *n, adj*

insomuch *adv* **1** (foll. by *as* or *that*) to such an extent or degree **2** (foll. by *as*) because of the fact (that)

insouciant *adj* carefree or unconcerned [French] **insouciance** *n*

inspan *vb* **-spanning, -spanned** *chiefly S African* **1** to harness (animals) to (a vehicle); yoke **2** to press (people) into service [Middle Dutch *inspannen*]

inspect *vb* **1** to examine closely, esp. for faults or errors **2** to examine officially [Latin *inspicere*] **inspection** *n*

inspector *n* **1** an official who checks that things or places meet certain regulations and standards **2** a police officer ranking below a superintendent and above a sergeant

inspectorate *n* **1** a group of inspectors **2** the position or duties of an inspector

inspiration *n* **1** stimulation of the mind or feelings to activity or creativity **2** a person or thing that causes this state **3** an inspired idea or action **inspirational** *adj*

inspire *vb* **-spiring, -spired 1** to stimulate (a person) to activity or creativity **2** to arouse (an emotion or a reaction): *he inspires confidence* [Latin *in-* into + *spirare* to breathe]

inspired *adj* **1** brilliantly creative: *his most inspired compositions* **2** very clever and accurate: *an inspired guess*

inst. *old-fashioned* instant (this month)

instability *n* lack of steadiness or reliability

install *vb* **1** to put in and prepare (equipment) for use **2** to place (a person) formally in a position or rank **3** to settle (a person, esp. oneself) in a position or state: *Tony installed himself in an armchair* [Medieval Latin *installare*]

installation *n* **1** installing **2** equipment that has been installed **3** a place containing equipment for a particular purpose: *radar installation*

installment plan *n US* same as **hire-purchase**. Also (Canad): **instalment plan**

instalment *or US* **installment** *n* **1** one of the portions into which a debt is divided for payment at regular intervals **2** a portion of something that is issued, broadcast, or published in parts [probably from Old French *estal* something fixed]

instance *n* **1** a case or particular example **2** urgent request or order: *at the instance of* **3 for instance** as an example **4 in the first instance** in the first place; initially ▷ *vb* **-stancing, -stanced 5** to mention as an example [Latin *instantia* a being close upon]

instant *n* **1** a very brief time; moment **2** a particular moment: *at the same instant* ▷ *adj* **3** immediate **4** (of foods) able to be prepared very quickly and easily: *instant coffee* **5** urgent or pressing **6** of the present month: *a letter of the 7th instant* [Latin *instans* present, pressing closely]

instantaneous *adj* happening at once: *the applause was instantaneous* **instantaneously** *adv*

instantly *adv* immediately

instant message *n* **1** an electronic message sent in real time over a computer network ▷ *vb* **instant-message 2** to communicate with (another person) using such messages **instant messaging** *n*

instead *adv* **1** as a replacement or substitute for the person or thing mentioned **2 instead of** in place of or as an alternative to [*in stead* in place]

instep *n* **1** the middle part of the foot forming the arch between the ankle and toes **2** the part of a shoe or stocking covering this

instigate *vb* **-gating, -gated 1** to cause to happen: *to instigate rebellion* **2** to urge on to some action [Latin *instigare*] **instigation** *n* **instigator** *n*

instil *or US* **instill** *vb* **-stilling, -stilled 1** to introduce (an idea or feeling) gradually in someone's mind **2** *rare* to pour in or inject drop by drop [Latin *instillare* to pour in a drop at a time] **instillation** *n* **instiller** *n*

instinct *n* **1** the inborn tendency to behave in a particular way without the need for thought: *maternal instinct* **2** natural reaction: *my first instinct was to get out of the car* **3** intuition: *Mr Barr's mother said she knew by instinct that her son was safe* [Latin *instinctus* roused]

instinctive *or* **instinctual** *adj* done or happening without any logical thought: *an instinctive understanding of people* **instinctively** *or* **instinctually** *adv*

institute *n* **1** an organization set up for a specific purpose, esp. research or teaching **2** the building where such an organization is situated **3** a rule, custom, or precedent ▷ *vb* **-tuting, -tuted 4** to start or establish **5** to install in a position or office [Latin *instituere*, from *statuere* to place]

institution *n* **1** a large important organization such as a university or bank **2** an organization providing residential care for people with special needs **3** an established custom, law, or principle: *the institution of marriage* **4** *informal* a well-established person or feature: *the programme has become an institution* **5** an instituting or being instituted

institutional *adj* **1** of or relating to an institution: *institutional care* **2** dull, routine, and uniform: *institutional meals* **institutionalism** *n*

institutionalize *or* **-lise** *vb* **-lizing, -lized** *or* **-lising, -lised 1** (*often passive*) to subject (a person) to institutional life, often causing apathy and dependence on routine **2** to make or become an institution: *institutionalized religion* **3** to place in an institution

instruct *vb* **1** to order to do something **2** to teach (someone) how to do something **3** to brief (a solicitor or barrister) [Latin *instruere*]

instruction *n* **1** a direction or order **2** the process or act of teaching **instructional** *adj*

instructions *pl n* information on how to do or use something: *the plane had ignored instructions from air traffic controllers*

instructive *adj* informative or helpful

instructor *n* **1** a person who teaches something **2** *US & Canad* a college teacher ranking below assistant professor

instrument *n* **1** a tool or implement, esp. one used for precision work **2** *music* any of various devices that can be played to produce musical sounds **3** a measuring device to show height, speed, etc.: *the pilot's eyes never left his instruments* **4** *informal* a person used by another to gain an end **5** an important factor in something: *her evidence was an instrument in his arrest* **6** a formal legal document [Latin *instrumentum*]

instrumental *adj* **1** helping to cause **2** played by or composed for musical instruments **3** of or done with an instrument: *instrumental error*

instrumentalist *n* a person who plays a musical instrument

instrumentation *n* **1** a set of instruments in a car, etc. **2** the arrangement of music for instruments **3** the list of instruments needed for a piece of music

instrument panel *n* a panel holding the instruments in a vehicle or on a machine

insubordinate *adj* not submissive to authority **insubordination** *n*

insubstantial *adj* **1** flimsy, fine, or slight **2** imaginary or unreal

insufferable *adj* unbearable **insufferably** *adv*

insufficient *adj* not enough for a particular purpose **insufficiency** *n* **insufficiently** *adv*

insular *adj* **1** not open to change or new ideas: *theatre tradition become rather insular* **2** of or like an island [Latin *insula* island] **insularity** *n*

insulate *vb* **-lating, -lated 1** to prevent or reduce the transfer of electricity, heat, or sound by surrounding or lining with a nonconducting material **2** to isolate or set apart [Late Latin *insulatus* made into an island] **insulator** *n*

insulation *n* **1** material used to insulate something **2** the act of insulating

insulin (in-syoo-lin) *n* a hormone produced in the pancreas which controls the amount of sugar in the blood [Latin *insula* islet (of tissue in the pancreas)]

insult *vb* **1** to treat or speak to rudely: *they insulted us and even threatened to kill us* ▷ *n* **2** an offensive remark or action **3** a person or thing producing the effect of an insult: *their explanation is an insult to our intelligence* [Latin *insultare* to jump upon]

insuperable *adj* impossible to overcome; insurmountable **insuperability** *n*

insupportable *adj* **1** impossible to tolerate **2** incapable of being upheld or justified: *an insupportable accusation*

insurance *n* **1** the agreement by which one makes regular payments to a company who pay an agreed sum if damage, loss, or death occurs **2** the money paid for insurance or by an insurance company **3** a means of protection: *sensible insurance against heart attacks*

insurance policy *n* a contract of insurance

insure *vb* **-suring, -sured 1** to guarantee or protect (against risk or loss) **2** (often foll. by *against*) to issue (a person) with an insurance policy or take out an insurance policy (on): *the players were insured against accidents* **3** *chiefly US* same as **ensure insurable** *adj* **insurability** *n*

insured *n* **the insured** the person covered by an insurance policy

insurer *n* a person or company that sells insurance

insurgent *adj* **1** rebellious or in revolt against an established authority ▷ *n* **2** a person who takes part in a rebellion [Latin *insurgens* rising] **insurgency** *n*

insurmountable *adj* impossible to overcome: *insurmountable problems*

insurrection *n* the act of rebelling against an established authority [Latin *insurgere* to rise up] **insurrectionist** *n, adj*

int. 1 internal **2** Also: **Int** international

intact *adj* not changed or damaged in any way [Latin *intactus*]

intaglio (in-tah-lee-oh) *n, pl* **-lios** *or* **-li 1** a seal or gem decorated with an engraved design **2** an engraved design [Italian] **intagliated** *adj*

intake *n* **1** a thing or a quantity taken in: *an intake of students* **2** the act of taking in **3** the opening through which fluid or gas enters a pipe or engine

intangible *adj* **1** difficult for the mind to grasp: *intangible ideas* **2** incapable of being felt by touch **intangibility** *n*

integer *n* any positive or negative whole number or zero, as opposed to a number with fractions or decimals [Latin: untouched]

integral *adj* **1** being an essential part of a whole **2** whole or complete **3** *maths* **A** of or involving an integral **B** involving or being an integer ▷ *n* **4** *maths* the sum of a large number of minute quantities, summed either between stated limits (**definite integral**) or in the absence of limits (**indefinite integral**)

integral calculus *n* *maths* the branch of calculus concerned with the determination of integrals and their use in solving differential equations

integrand *n* *maths* a mathematical function to be integrated

integrate *vb* **-grating, -grated 1** to make or be made into a whole **2** to amalgamate (a racial or religious group) with an existing community **3** to designate (an institution) for use by all races or groups **4** *maths* to determine the integral of a function or variable [Latin *integrare*] **integration** *n*

integrated circuit *n* a tiny electronic circuit

integrity *n* **1** honesty **2** the quality of being whole or united: *respect for a state's territorial integrity* **3** the quality of being unharmed or sound: *the integrity of the cell membrane* [Latin *integritas*]

integument *n* any natural protective covering, such as a skin, rind, or shell [Latin *integumentum*]

intel *n informal* information collected by the military about the plans and movements of an enemy

intellect *n* **1** the ability to understand, think, and reason **2** a particular person's mind or intelligence, esp. a brilliant one: *his intellect is wasted on that job* **3** *informal* a person who has a brilliant mind [Latin *intellectus* comprehension]

intellectual *adj* **1** of, involving, or appealing to the intellect: *intellectual literature* **2** clever or intelligent ▷ *n* **3** a person who has a highly developed intellect **intellectuality** *n* **intellectually** *adv*

intelligence *n* **1** the ability to understand, learn, and think things out quickly **2** the collection of secret information, esp. for military purposes **3** a group or department collecting military information **4** *old-fashioned* news or information [Latin *intellegere* to understand, literally: to choose between]

intelligence quotient *n* a measure of the intelligence of a person calculated by dividing the person's mental age by his or her actual age and multiplying the result by 100. Abbrev: **IQ**

intelligent *adj* **1** having or showing intelligence: *an intelligent child; an intelligent guess* **2** (of a computerized device) able to initiate or modify action in the light of ongoing events **intelligently** *adv*

intelligent design *n* a theory that rejects the theory of natural selection, arguing for an intelligent cause in the form of a creator

intelligentsia *n* **the intelligentsia** the educated or intellectual people in a society [Russian *intelligentsiya*]

intelligible *adj* able to be understood **intelligibility** *n*

intemperate *adj* **1** unrestrained or uncontrolled: *intemperate remarks* **2** drinking alcohol too much or too often **3** extreme or severe: *an intemperate climate* **intemperance** *n*

intend *vb* **1** to propose or plan (something or to do something) **2** to have as one's purpose **3** to mean to express or indicate: *no criticism was intended* **4** (often foll. by *for*) to design or destine (for a certain purpose or person): *the plane was never intended for combat* [Latin *intendere* to stretch forth]

intended *adj* **1** planned or future ▷ *n* **2** *informal* a person whom one is to marry

intense *adj* **1** of very great force, strength, degree, or amount: *intense heat* **2** characterized by deep or forceful feelings: *an intense person* [Latin *intensus* stretched] **intensely** *adv* **intenseness** *n*

> **USAGE** *Intense* is sometimes wrongly used where *intensive* is meant: *the land is under intensive* (not *intense*) *cultivation. Intensely* is sometimes wrongly used where *intently* is meant: *he listened intently* (not *intensely*).

intensifier *n* a word, esp. an adjective or adverb, that intensifies the meaning of the word or phrase that it modifies, for example, *very* or *extremely*

intensify *vb* **-fies, -fying, -fied** to make or become intense or more intense **intensification** *n*

intensity *n, pl* **-ties 1** the state or quality of being intense **2** extreme force, degree, or amount **3** *physics* the amount or degree of strength of electricity, heat, light, or sound per unit area of volume

intensive *adj* **1** of or needing concentrated effort or resources: *intensive training* **2** using one specified factor more than others: *labour-intensive* **3** *agriculture* designed to increase production from a particular area: *intensive farming* **4** *grammar* (of a word) giving emphasis, for example, *very* in *the very same* **intensively** *adv* **intensiveness** *n*

USAGE See at **intense**.

intensive care *n* thorough, continuously supervised treatment of an acutely ill patient in a hospital

intent *n* **1** something that is intended **2** *law* the will or purpose to commit a crime: *loitering with intent* **3 to all intents and purposes** in almost every respect; virtually ▷ *adj* **4** having one's attention firmly fixed: *an intent look* **5 intent on** *or* **upon** strongly resolved on: *intent on winning the election* [Late Latin *intentus* aim] **intently** *adv* **intentness** *n*

USAGE See at **intense**.

intention *n* something intended; a plan, idea, or purpose: *he had no intention of resigning*

intentional *adj* done on purpose **intentionally** *adv*

inter (in-ter) *vb* **-terring, -terred** to bury (a corpse) [Latin *in-* into + *terra* earth]

inter- *prefix* **1** between or among: *international* **2** together, mutually, or reciprocally: *interdependent* [Latin]

interact *vb* to act on or in close relation with each other **interaction** *n* **interactive** *adj*

inter alia (in-ter ale-ya) *adv* among other things [Latin]

interbreed *vb* **-breeding, -bred 1** to breed within a related group so as to produce particular characteristics in the offspring **2** same as **crossbreed** (sense 1)

intercede *vb* **-ceding, -ceded 1** to plead in favour of **2** to act as a mediator in order to end a disagreement: *a police officer was watching the beatings without interceding* [Latin *inter-* between + *cedere* to move]

intercept *vb* **1** to stop or seize on the way from one place to another **2** *maths* to mark off or include (part of a line, curve, plane, or surface) between two points or lines ▷ *n* **3** *maths* **A** a point at which two figures intersect **B** the distance from the origin to the point at which a line, curve, or surface cuts a coordinate axis [Latin *intercipere* to seize before arrival] **interception** *n* **interceptor** *n*

intercession *n* **1** the act of interceding **2** a prayer offered to God on behalf of others **intercessor** *n*

interchange *vb* **-changing, -changed 1** to change places or cause to change places ▷ *n* **2** the act of interchanging **3** a motorway junction of interconnecting roads and bridges designed to prevent streams of traffic crossing one another **interchangeable** *adj* **interchangeably** *adv*

intercom *n* an internal communication system with loudspeakers [short for *intercommunication*]

intercommunicate *vb* **-cating, -cated 1** to communicate mutually **2** (of two rooms) to interconnect **intercommunication** *n*

intercommunion *n* association between Churches, involving mutual reception of Holy Communion

interconnect *vb* to connect with one another **interconnected** *adj* **interconnection** *n*

intercontinental *adj* travelling between or linking continents

intercourse *n* **1** the act of having sex **2** communication or dealings between individuals or groups [Latin *intercurrere* to run between]

interdenominational *adj* among or involving more than one denomination of the Christian Church

interdepartmental *adj* of or between different departments

interdependent *adj* dependent on one another **interdependence** *n*

interdict *n* **1** *law* an official prohibition or restraint **2** *RC Church* the exclusion of a person or place from certain sacraments, although not from communion ▷ *vb* **3** to prohibit or forbid [Latin *interdicere* to forbid] **interdiction** *n* **interdictory** *adj*

interdisciplinary *adj* involving more than one branch of learning

interest *n* **1** curiosity or concern about something or someone **2** the power of causing this: *to have great interest* **3** something in which one is interested; a hobby or pursuit **4** (*often pl*) advantage: *in one's own interests* **5** money paid for the use of credit or borrowed money: *she borrowed money at 25 per cent interest* **6** (*often pl*) a right, share, or claim, esp. in a business or property **7** (*often pl*) a group of people with common aims: *foreign interests* ▷ *vb* **8** to arouse the curiosity or concern of **9** to cause to become interested or involved in something [Latin: it concerns]

interested *adj* **1** showing or having interest **2** involved in or affected by: *a consultation paper sent to interested parties*

interest group *n* a group of persons who attempt to influence legislators on behalf of a particular interest

interesting *adj* causing interest **interestingly** *adv*

interface *n* **1** an area where two things interact or link: *the interface between Islamic culture and Western modernity* **2** an electrical circuit linking one device, esp. a computer, with another **3** the way that a piece of computer software appears to users, esp. in terms of being easy or difficult to operate **4** *physics & chem* a surface that forms the boundary between two liquids or chemical phases that cannot be mixed ▷ *vb* **-facing, -faced 5** to connect or be connected with by interface **interfacial** *adj*

interfacing *n* **1** a piece of fabric sewn beneath the facing of a garment to give shape and firmness **2** same as **interlining**

interfaith *adj* relating to, between, or involving different religions

interfere *vb* **-fering, -fered 1** to try to influence other people's affairs where one is not involved or wanted **2** *physics* to produce or cause to produce interference **3 interfere with A** to clash with or hinder: *I try not to let personal feelings interfere with my work* **B** *Brit, Austral & NZ euphemistic* to abuse sexually [Old French *s'entreferir* to collide] **interfering** *adj*

interference *n* **1** the act of interfering **2** any undesired signal that interferes with the reception of radio waves **3** *physics* the meeting of two waves which reinforce or neutralize each other depending on whether they are in or out of phase

interferon *n biochem* a protein made by cells that stops the development of an invading virus

interfuse *vb* **-fusing, -fused 1** to mix or become mixed **2** to blend or fuse together **interfusion** *n*

intergalactic *adj* occurring or located between different galaxies

interim *adj* **1** temporary or provisional: *an interim government* ▷ *n* **2 in the interim** during the intervening time [Latin: meanwhile]

interior *n* **1** a part or region that is on the inside: *the interior of the earth* **2** the inside of a building or room, with respect to design and decoration **3** the central area of a country or continent, furthest from the sea **4** a picture of the inside of a room or building ▷ *adj* **5** of, situated on, or suitable for the inside **6** mental or spiritual: *interior development* **7** coming or acting from within **8** of a nation's domestic affairs [Latin]

interior angle *n* an angle of a polygon contained between two adjacent sides

interior decoration *n* **1** the decoration and furnishings of the interior of a room or house **2** Also called: **interior design** the art or business of planning this **interior decorator** *n*

interj. interjection

interject *vb* to make (a remark) suddenly or as an interruption [Latin *interjicere* to place between]

interjection *n* a word or phrase which is used on its own and which expresses sudden emotion

interlace *vb* **-lacing, -laced** to join by lacing or weaving together: *interlaced fingers*

interlard *vb* to insert in or occur throughout: *to interlard one's writing with foreign phrases*

interlay *vb* **-laying, -laid** to insert (layers) between: *to interlay gold among the silver*

interleaf *n, pl* **-leaves** an extra leaf which is inserted

interleave *vb* **-leaving, -leaved** to insert, as blank leaves in a book, between other leaves

interleukin (in-ter-**loo**-kin) *n biochem* a substance obtained from white blood cells that stimulates their activity against infection and may be used to fight some forms of cancer

interline[1] *vb* **-lining, -lined** to write or print (matter) between the lines of (a text or book)

interline[2] *vb* **-lining, -lined** to provide (a part of a garment) with a second lining

interlining *n* the material used to interline parts of garments

interlink *vb* to connect together

interlock *vb* **1** to join or be joined firmly together ▷ *n* **2** a device used to prevent a mechanism from operating independently or unsafely

interlocutor (in-ter-**lock**-yew-ter) *n formal* a person who takes part in a conversation [Latin *inter-* between + *loqui* to talk]

interlocutory (in-ter-**lock**-yew-tree) *adj* **1** *law* pronounced during the course of legal proceedings; provisional: *an interlocutory injunction* **2** *formal* of dialogue; conversational

interloper (in-ter-lope-er) *n* a person in a place or situation where he or she has no right to be

interlude *n* **1** a period of time or different activity between longer periods or events **2 A** a pause between the acts of a play **B** a brief piece of music or other entertainment performed during this pause [Latin *inter-* between + *ludus* play]

intermarry *vb* **-ries, -rying, -ried 1** (of different races, religions, or social groups) to become connected by marriage **2** to marry within one's own family or tribe **intermarriage** *n*

intermediary *n, pl* **-aries 1** a person who tries to bring about agreement between others **2** a messenger ▷ *adj* **3** acting as an intermediary **4** intermediate

intermediate *adj* **1** occurring between two points or extremes **2** (of a class, course, etc.) suitable for learners with some level of skill or competence ▷ *n* **3** something intermediate **4** *chem* a substance formed between the first and final stages of a chemical process [Latin *inter-* between + *medius* middle] **intermediation** *n*

interment *n* a burial

intermezzo (in-ter-**met**-so) *n, pl* **-zos** *or* **-zi 1** a short piece of instrumental music performed between the acts of a play or opera **2 A** a short composition between two longer movements in an extended musical work **B** a similar composition intended for independent performance [Italian]

interminable *adj* seemingly endless because boring: *an interminable rambling anecdote* **interminably** *adv*

intermingle *vb* **-gling, -gled** to mix together

intermission *n* an interval between parts of a play, film, etc. [Latin *intermittere* to leave off, cease]

intermittent *adj* occurring at intervals **intermittently** *adv*

intern *vb* **1** to imprison, esp. during wartime ▷ *n* **2** a student or recent graduate receiving practical training in a working environment **3** *chiefly US* a trainee doctor in a hospital [Latin *internus* internal] **internment** *n*

internal *adj* **1** of, situated on, or suitable for the inside **2** *anatomy* affecting or relating to the inside of the body: *internal bleeding* **3** of a nation's domestic affairs: *internal politics* **4** coming or acting from within an organization: *an internal reorganization* **5** spiritual or mental: *internal conflict* [Latin *internus*] **internally** *adv*

internal-combustion engine *n* an engine in which power is produced by the explosion of a fuel-and-air mixture within the cylinders

international *adj* **1** of or involving two or more nations **2** controlling or legislating for several nations: *an international court* **3** available for use by all nations: *international waters* ▷ *n* **4** *sport* **A** a game or match between the national teams of different countries **B** a member of a national team **internationally** *adv*

International Date Line *n* the line approximately following the 180° meridian from Greenwich on the east side of which the date is one day earlier than on the west

internationalism *n* the ideal or practice of cooperation and understanding for the good of all nations **internationalist** *n*
International Phonetic Alphabet *n* a series of signs and letters for the representation of human speech sounds. Abbrev: **IPA**
International Style *or* **Modernism** *n* a 20th-century architectural style characterized by undecorated straight forms and the use of glass, steel, and reinforced concrete
internecine *adj formal* destructive to both sides: *internecine war* [Latin *internecare* to destroy]
internee *n* a person who is interned
internet *n (sometimes cap)* a large public access computer network linked to others worldwide
internet service provider *n* a business providing its customers with connection to the internet and other related services. Abbrev: **ISP**
internist *n chiefly US* a physician who specializes in internal medicine
interpenetrate *vb* **-trating, -trated 1** to penetrate (something) thoroughly **2** to penetrate each other or one another mutually **interpenetration** *n*
interpersonal *adj* of or relating to relationships between people: *interpersonal conflict at work*
interplanetary *adj* of or linking planets
interplay *n* the action and reaction of things upon each other
Interpol International Criminal Police Organization: an association of most national police forces, devoted chiefly to fighting international crime
interpolate (in-ter-pole-ate) *vb* **-lating, -lated 1** to insert (a comment or passage) into (a conversation or text) **2** *maths* to estimate (a value of a function) between the values already known [Latin *interpolare* to give a new appearance to] **interpolation** *n*
interpose *vb* **-posing, -posed 1** to place (something) between or among other things **2** to interrupt (with comments or questions) **3** to put forward so as to interrupt: *he ended the discussion by interposing a veto* [Latin *inter-* between + *ponere* to put] **interposition** *n*
interpret *vb* **1** to explain the meaning of **2** to work out the significance of: *his remarks were widely interpreted as a promise not to raise taxes* **3** to convey the meaning of (a poem, song, etc.) in performance **4** to act as an interpreter [Latin *interpretari*] **interpretive** *adj*
interpretation *n* **1** the act or result of interpreting or explaining **2** the particular way in which a performer expresses his or her view of a composition: *an interpretation of Mahler's fourth symphony* **3** explanation, as of a historical site, provided by the use of original objects, visual display material, etc.
interpreter *n* **1** a person who translates orally from one language into another **2** *computers* a program that translates a statement in a source program to machine language and executes it before translating and executing the next statement
interracial *adj* between or among people of different races
interregnum *n, pl* **-nums** *or* **-na** a period between the end of one ruler's reign and the beginning of the next [Latin *inter-* between + *regnum* reign] **interregnal** *adj*
interrelate *vb* **-lating, -lated** to connect (two or more things) or (of two or more things) to become connected to each other **interrelation** *n* **interrelationship** *n*
interrogate *vb* **-gating, -gated** to question (someone) closely [Latin *interrogare*] **interrogation** *n* **interrogator** *n*
interrogative (in-ter-rog-a-tiv) *adj* **1** used in asking a question: *an interrogative pronoun* **2** of or like a question: *an interrogative look* ▷ *n* **3** an interrogative word, phrase, sentence, or construction
interrogatory (in-ter-rog-a-tree) *adj* **1** expressing or involving a question ▷ *n, pl* **-tories 2** a question or interrogation
interrupt *vb* **1** to break into (a conversation or discussion) by questions or comment **2** to stop (a process or activity) temporarily [Latin *inter-* between + *rumpere* to break] **interrupted** *adj* **interruptive** *adj*
interrupter *or* **interruptor** *n* a device for opening and closing an electric circuit
interruption *n* **1** something that interrupts, such as a comment or question **2** an interval or intermission **3** the act of interrupting or the state of being interrupted
interscholastic *adj* occurring between two or more schools: *an interscholastic competition*
intersect *vb* **1** (of roads or lines) to cross (each other) **2** to divide or mark off (a place, area, or surface) by passing through or across [Latin *intersecare* to divide]
intersection *n* **1** a point at which things intersect, esp. a road junction **2** the act of intersecting or the state of being intersected **3** *maths* **A** a point or set of points common to two or more geometric figures **B** the set of elements that are common to two sets **intersectional** *adj*
intersex *adj* having both male and female, or neither uniquely male nor female, sexual characteristics
intersperse *vb* **-spersing, -spersed 1** to scatter among, between, or on **2** to mix (something) with other things scattered here and there [Latin *inter-* between + *spargere* to sprinkle] **interspersion** *n*
interstellar *adj* between or among stars
interstice (in-ter-stiss) *n (usually pl)* **1** a small gap or crack between things **2** *physics* the space between adjacent atoms in a crystal lattice [Latin *interstitium* interval]
intertwine *vb* **-twining, -twined** to twist together
interval *n* **1** the period of time between two events **2** *Brit & Austral* a short period between parts of a play, concert, etc. **3** *music* the difference of pitch between two notes **4 at intervals A** now and then: *turn the chicken at intervals* **B** with a certain amount of space between: *the poles were placed at intervals of twenty metres* [Latin *intervallum*, literally: space between two palisades]

intervene *vb* **-vening, -vened 1** (often foll. by *in*) to involve oneself in a situation, esp. to prevent conflict **2** to interrupt a conversation **3** to happen so as to stop something: *he hoped to play but a serious injury intervened* **4** to come or be among or between: *ten years had intervened since he had seen Joe* [Latin *intervenire* to come between]

intervention *n* the act of intervening, esp. to influence or alter a situation in some way **interventionist** *n, adj*

interview *n* **1** a formal discussion, esp. one in which an employer assesses a job applicant **2** a conversation in which a well-known person is asked about his or her views, career, etc., by a reporter ▷ *vb* **3** to question (someone) [Old French *entrevue*] **interviewee** *n* **interviewer** *n*

interwar *adj* of or happening in the period between World War I and World War II

interweave *vb* **-weaving, -wove** *or* **-weaved, -woven** *or* **-weaved** to weave together

intestate *adj* **1** (of a person) not having made a will ▷ *n* **2** a person who dies without having made a will [Latin *intestatus*] **intestacy** *n*

intestine *n* the part of the alimentary canal between the stomach and the anus. See **large intestine, small intestine** [Latin *intestinus* internal] **intestinal** *adj*

intifada (in-tiff-ah-da) *n* the Palestinian uprising against Israel in the West Bank and Gaza Strip [Arabic]

intimacy *n, pl* **-cies 1** close or warm friendship **2** (*often pl*) intimate words or acts within a close relationship

intimate¹ *adj* **1** characterized by a close or warm personal relationship: *an intimate friend* **2** deeply personal, private, or secret **3** (of knowledge) extensive and detailed **4** *euphemistic* having sexual relations **5** having a friendly quiet atmosphere: *an intimate nightclub* ▷ *n* **6** a close friend [Latin *intimus* innermost] **intimately** *adv*

intimate² *vb* **-mating, -mated** *formal* **1** to make (something) known in an indirect way: *he has intimated his intention to retire* **2** to announce [Late Latin *intimare* to proclaim] **intimation** *n*

intimidate *vb* **-dating, -dated** to subdue or influence (someone) through fear [Latin *in-* in + *timidus* fearful] **intimidating** *adj* **intimidation** *n*

into *prep* **1** to the inner part of: *they went into the house* **2** to the middle of so as to be surrounded by: *into the bushes* **3** against; up against: *he drove into a wall* **4** used to indicate the result of a change: *they turned the theatre into a garage* **5** *maths* used to indicate division: *three into six is two* **6** *informal* interested in: *I'm really into healthy food*

intolerable *adj* more than can be endured **intolerably** *adv*

intolerant *adj* refusing to accept practices and beliefs that differ from one's own **intolerance** *n*

intonation *n* **1** the sound pattern produced by variations in the voice **2** the act of intoning **3** *music* the ability to play or sing in tune **intonational** *adj*

intone *vb* **-toning, -toned 1** to speak or recite in a monotonous tone **2** to speak with a particular tone [Medieval Latin *intonare*]

in toto *adv* totally or entirely [Latin]

intoxicant *n* **1** something, such as an alcoholic drink, that causes intoxication ▷ *adj* **2** causing intoxication

intoxicate *vb* **-cating, -cated 1** (of an alcoholic drink) to make (a person) drunk **2** to stimulate or excite to a point beyond self-control [Latin *in-* in + *toxicum* poison] **intoxicated** *adj* **intoxicating** *adj*

intoxication *n* **1** the state of being drunk **2** great excitement and exhilaration

intractable *adj* **1** (of a person) difficult to influence or direct **2** (of a problem or illness) difficult to solve or cure **intractability** *n* **intractably** *adv*

intramural *adj chiefly US & Canad* operating within or involving those within a school or college: *intramural sports* [Latin *intra-* inside + *murus* wall]

intranet *n computers* an internal network that makes use of internet technology [*intra-* + INTERNET]

intransigent *adj* **1** refusing to change one's attitude ▷ *n* **2** an intransigent person, esp. in politics [Latin *in-* not + *transigere* to settle] **intransigence** *n*

intransitive *adj* (of a verb) not taking a direct object: *'to faint' is an intransitive verb* **intransitively** *adv*

intrapreneur *n Brit & US* a person who while remaining within a larger organization uses entrepreneurial skills to develop new services or systems as a subsidiary of the organization [*intra-* inside + *(entre)preneur*]

intrauterine *adj* situated within the womb [Latin *intra-* inside + *uterus* womb]

intrauterine device *n* a contraceptive device in the shape of a coil, inserted into the womb

intravenous (in-tra-vee-nuss) *adj anatomy* into a vein: *intravenous drug users* [Latin *intra-* inside + *vena* vein] **intravenously** *adv*

in-tray *n* a tray used in offices for incoming letters or documents requiring attention

intrepid *adj* fearless or bold [Latin *in-* not + *trepidus* fearful] **intrepidity** *n* **intrepidly** *adv*

intricate *adj* **1** difficult to sort out: *an intricate problem* **2** full of complicated detail: *intricate Arab mosaics* [Latin *intricare* to entangle] **intricacy** *n* **intricately** *adv*

intrigue *vb* **-triguing, -trigued 1** to make interested or curious: *a question which has intrigued him for years* **2** to plot secretly or dishonestly ▷ *n* **3** secret plotting **4** a secret love affair [French *intriguer*] **intriguing** *adj* **intriguingly** *adv*

intrinsic *adj* **1** essential to the real nature of a thing: *hedgerows are an intrinsic part of the countryside* **2** *anatomy* situated within or peculiar to a part: *intrinsic muscles* [Latin *intrinsecus* inwardly] **intrinsically** *adv*

intro *n, pl* **-tros** *informal* short for **introduction**

introduce *vb* **-ducing, -duced 1** to present (someone) by name (to another person) **2** to present (a radio or television programme) **3** to present for consideration or approval: *he introduced the bill to Parliament in 1967* **4** to bring into use: *they introduced a new system into our political life* **5** to insert **6 introduce to** to cause to experience for the first time: *his father introduced him to golf* **7 introduce with** to start: *he introduced his talk with some music* [Latin *introducere* to bring inside] **introducible** *adj*

introduction *n* **1** the act of introducing something or someone **2** a preliminary part, as of a book or musical composition **3** a book that explains the basic facts about a particular subject to a beginner **4** a presentation of one person to another or others
introductory *adj* serving as an introduction
introit *n* **1** *RC Church* a short prayer said or sung as the celebrant is entering the sanctuary to celebrate Mass **2** *Church of England* a hymn or psalm sung at the beginning of a service [Latin *introitus* entrance]
introspection *n* the examining of one's own thoughts, impressions, and feelings [Latin *introspicere* to look within] **introspective** *adj*
introversion *n psychol* the directing of interest inwards towards one's own thoughts and feelings rather than towards the external world or making social contacts
introvert *adj* **1** shy and quiet **2** *psychol* concerned more with inner feelings than with external reality ▷ *n* **3** such a person [Latin *intro-* inward + *vertere* to turn] **introverted** *adj*
intrude *vb* **-truding, -truded** to come in or join in without being invited [Latin *intrudere* to thrust in]
intruder *n* a person who enters a place without permission
intrusion *n* **1** the act of intruding; an unwelcome visit, etc.: *an intrusion into her private life* **2** *geol* **A** the forcing of molten rock into spaces in the overlying strata **B** molten rock formed in this way **intrusive** *adj*
intrust *vb* same as **entrust**
intuition *n* instinctive knowledge of or belief about something without conscious reasoning: *intuition told her something was wrong* [Latin *intueri* to gaze upon] **intuitional** *adj*
intuitive *adj* of, possessing, or resulting from intuition: *an intuitive understanding* **intuitively** *adv*
Inuit *n, pl* **-it** *or* **-its** an indigenous inhabitant of North America or Greenland [Inuktitut, plural of *inuk* person]
Inuk *n* a member of the Inuit people
Inuktitut *n* the language of the Inuit
inundate *vb* **-dating, -dated 1** to cover completely with water **2** to overwhelm, as if with a flood: *the police were inundated with calls* [Latin *inundare*] **inundation** *n*
inured *adj* able to tolerate something unpleasant because one has become accustomed to it: *he became inured to the casual brutality of his captors* [Middle English *enuren* to accustom] **inurement** *n*
invade *vb* **-vading, -vaded 1** to enter (a country or territory) by military force **2** to enter in large numbers: *the town was invaded by rugby supporters* **3** to disturb (privacy, etc.) [Latin *invadere*] **invader** *n*
invalid[1] *n* **1** a person who is weak or disabled by illness or injury ▷ *adj* **2** weak or disabled by illness or injury ▷ *vb* **3** *chiefly Brit* to dismiss (a soldier, etc.) from active service because of illness [Latin *in-* not + *validus* strong] **invalidism** *n*

> **USAGE** It is best to avoid using the term *invalid* when referring to people with chronic illnesses or disabilities.

invalid[2] *adj* **1** having no legal force: *an invalid cheque* **2** (of an argument, result, etc.) not valid because it has been based on a mistake **invalidity** *n* **invalidly** *adv*
invalidate *vb* **-dating, -dated 1** to make or show (an argument) to be invalid **2** to take away the legal force of (a contract) **invalidation** *n*
invaluable *adj* having great value that is impossible to calculate
invariable *adj* unchanging **invariably** *adv*
invasion *n* **1** the act of invading with armed forces **2** any intrusion: *an invasion of privacy* **invasive** *adj*
invective *n* abusive speech or writing [Late Latin *invectivus* scolding]
inveigh (in-**vay**) *vb* **inveigh against** *formal* to make harsh criticisms against [Latin *invehi*, literally: to be carried in, hence assail]
inveigle *vb* **-gling, -gled** to coax or manipulate (someone) into an action or situation [Old French *avogler* to blind, deceive] **inveiglement** *n*
invent *vb* **1** to think up or create (something new) **2** to make up (a story, excuse, etc.) [Latin *invenire* to find] **inventor** *n*
invention *n* **1** something that is invented **2** the act of inventing **3** creative power; inventive skill **4** *euphemistic* a lie: *his story is a malicious invention*
inventive *adj* creative and resourceful: *her inventive use of colour*
inventory (**in**-ven-tree) *n, pl* **-tories 1** a detailed list of the objects in a particular place ▷ *vb* **-tories, -torying, -toried 2** to make a list of [Medieval Latin *inventorium*]
inverse *adj* **1** opposite in effect, sequence, direction, etc. **2** *maths* linking two variables in such a way that one increases as the other decreases ▷ *n* **3** the exact opposite: *the inverse of this image* **4** *maths* an inverse element
inversion *n* **1** the act of inverting or state of being inverted **2** something inverted, esp. a reversal of order, functions, etc.: *an inversion of their previous relationship* **inversive** *adj*
invert *vb* **1** to turn upside down or inside out **2** to reverse in effect, sequence, or direction [Latin *in-* in + *vertere* to turn] **invertible** *adj*
invertebrate *n* **1** any animal without a backbone, such as an insect, worm, or octopus ▷ *adj* **2** of or designating invertebrates
inverted commas *pl n* same as **quotation marks**
invest *vb* **1** (often foll. by *in*) to put (money) into an enterprise with the expectation of profit **2** (often foll. by *in*) to devote (time or effort to a project) **3** to give power or authority to: *invested with the powers of government* **4** (often foll. by *in*) to install someone (in an official position) **5** (foll. by *with* or *in*) to credit or provide (a person with qualities): *he was invested with great common sense* **6 invest in** to buy: *she invested in some barbecue equipment* **7 invest with** *usually poetic* to cover, as if with a coat: *when spring invests the trees with leaves* [Medieval Latin *investire* to clothe] **investor** *n*
investigate *vb* **-gating, -gated** to inquire into (a situation or problem) thoroughly in order to discover the truth: *the police are currently investigating the case* [Latin *investigare* to search after] **investigative** *adj* **investigator** *n*

investigation *n* a careful search or examination in order to discover facts
investiture *n* the formal installation of a person in an office or rank
investment *n* **1** the act of investing **2** money invested **3** something in which money is invested
investment trust *n* a financial enterprise that invests its subscribed capital in a wide range of securities for its investors' benefit
inveterate *adj* **1** deep-rooted or ingrained: *an inveterate enemy of Marxism* **2** confirmed in a habit or practice: *an inveterate gambler* [Latin *inveteratus* of long standing] **inveteracy** *n*
invidious *adj* likely to cause resentment or unpopularity [Latin *invidia* envy]
invigilate (in-vij-il-late) *vb* **-lating, -lated** *Brit* to supervise people who are sitting an examination [Latin *invigilare* to watch over] **invigilation** *n* **invigilator** *n*
invigorate *vb* **-rating, -rated** to give energy to or refresh [Latin *in-* in + *vigor* vigour] **invigorating** *adj*
invincible *adj* incapable of being defeated: *an army of invincible strength* [Latin *in-* not + *vincere* to conquer] **invincibility** *n* **invincibly** *adv*
inviolable *adj* that must not be broken or violated: *an inviolable oath* **inviolability** *n*
inviolate *adj* free from harm or injury **inviolacy** *n*
invisible *adj* **1** not able to be seen by the eye: *invisible radiation* **2** concealed from sight **3** *econ* relating to services, such as insurance and freight, rather than goods: *invisible earnings* **invisibility** *n* **invisibly** *adv*
invitation *n* **1** a request to attend a dance, meal, etc. **2** the card or paper on which an invitation is written
invite *vb* **-viting, -vited 1** to ask (a person) in a friendly or polite way (to do something, attend an event, etc.) **2** to make a request for, esp. publicly or formally: *we invite applications for six scholarships* **3** to bring on or provoke: *his theory invites disaster* **4** to tempt ▷ *n* **5** *informal* an invitation [Latin *invitare*]
inviting *adj* tempting or attractive
in vitro *adv, adj* (of biological processes or reactions) happening outside the body of the organism in an artificial environment [New Latin, literally: in glass]
invocation *n* **1** the act of invoking **2** a prayer to God or another deity asking for help, forgiveness, etc. **invocatory** *adj*
invoice *n* **1** a bill for goods and services supplied ▷ *vb* **-voicing, -voiced 2** to present (a customer) with an invoice [Old French *envois*, plural of *envoi* message]
invoke *vb* **-voking, -voked 1** to put (a law or penalty) into use: *chapter 8 of the UN charter was invoked* **2** to bring about: *the hills invoked a feeling of serenity* **3** to call on (God or another deity) for help, inspiration, etc. **4** to summon (a spirit) by uttering magic words [Latin *invocare* to appeal to]

USAGE *Invoke* is sometimes wrongly used where *evoke* is meant: *this proposal evoked* (not *invoked*) *a strong reaction.*

involuntary *adj* **1** carried out without one's conscious wishes; unintentional **2** *physiol* (esp. of a movement or muscle) performed or acting without conscious control **involuntarily** *adv*
involute *adj also* **involuted 1** complex, intricate, or involved **2** rolled inwards or curled in a spiral ▷ *n* **3** *geom* the curve described by the free end of a thread as it is wound around another curve on the same plane [Latin *involutus*]
involve *vb* **-volving, -volved 1** to include as a necessary part **2** to have an effect on: *around fifty riders were involved and some were hurt* **3** to implicate: *several people were involved in the crime* **4** to make complicated: *the situation was further involved by her disappearance* [Latin *in-* in + *volvere* to roll] **involvement** *n*
involved *adj* **1** complicated **2 involved in** concerned in
invulnerable *adj* not able to be wounded or damaged **invulnerability** *n*
inward *adj* **1** directed towards the middle of something **2** situated within **3** of the mind or spirit: *inward meditation* **4** of one's own country or a specific country: *inward investment* ▷ *adv* **5** same as **inwards**
inwardly *adv* **1** within the private thoughts or feelings: *inwardly troubled, he kept smiling* **2** not aloud: *to laugh inwardly* **3** in or on the inside
inwards *or* **inward** *adv* towards the inside or middle of something
inwrought *adj* worked or woven into material, esp. decoratively
in-your-face *adj slang* aggressive and confrontational: *in-your-face advertising*
Io *chem* ionium
iodide *n chem* a compound containing an iodine atom, such as methyl iodide
iodine *n chem* a bluish-black element found in seaweed and used in medicine and in the manufacture of dyes. Symbol: **I** [Greek *iōdēs* rust-coloured, but mistakenly derived from *ion* violet]
iodize *or* **-dise** *vb* **-dizing, -dized** *or* **-dising, -dised** to treat with iodine **iodization** *or* **-disation** *n*
IOM Isle of Man
ion *n* an electrically charged atom or group of atoms formed by the loss or gain of one or more electrons [Greek, literally: going]
ion exchange *n* the process in which ions are exchanged between a solution and an insoluble solid. It is used to soften water
ionic *adj* of or in the form of ions
Ionic *adj* of a style of classical architecture characterized by fluted columns with scroll-like ornaments on the capital
ionize *or* **-ise** *vb* **-izing, -ized** *or* **-ising, -ised** to change or become changed into ions **ionization** *or* **-isation** *n*
ionosphere *n* a region of ionized layers of air in the earth's upper atmosphere, which reflects radio waves **ionospheric** *adj*
iota (eye-oh-ta) *n* **1** the ninth letter in the Greek alphabet (Ι, ι) **2** a very small amount: *I don't feel one iota of guilt*
IOU *n* a written promise or reminder to pay a debt [representing *I owe you*]

IOW Isle of Wight
IP *computers* internet protocol: a code used to label packets of data sent across the internet, identifying both the sending and the receiving computers
IPA International Phonetic Alphabet
IP address *computers* internet protocol address: a unique code that identifies each computer connected to the internet
ipecacuanha (ip-pee-kak-yew-**ann**-a) *or* **ipecac** (**ip**-pee-kak) *n* a drug made from the dried roots of a S American plant, used to cause vomiting [indigenous S American word *ipekaaguéne*]
iPod *n trademark* a small portable digital audio player capable of storing thousands of tracks in a variety of formats including MP3
ipso facto *adv* by that very fact or act [Latin]
IQ intelligence quotient
Ir *chem* iridium
IRA Irish Republican Army: a militant organization opposed to Northern Ireland remaining within the United Kingdom
Iranian *adj* **1** of Iran ▷ *n* **2** a person from Iran **3** a branch of the Indo-European family of languages, including Persian
Iraqi *adj* **1** of Iraq ▷ *n* **2** a person from Iraq
irascible *adj* easily angered [Latin *ira* anger] **irascibility** *n* **irascibly** *adv*
irate *adj* very angry [Latin *iratus* enraged]
ire *n literary* anger [Latin *ira*]
iridaceous (ir-rid-**day**-shuss) *adj* of or belonging to the iris family
iridescent (ir-rid-**ess**-ent) *adj* having shimmering changing colours like a rainbow [Latin *irid-* iris] **iridescence** *n*
iridium *n chem* a hard yellowish-white chemical element that occurs in platinum ores and is used as an alloy with platinum. Symbol: **Ir** [Latin *irid-* iris]
iris *n* **1** the coloured muscular membrane in the eye that surrounds and controls the size of the pupil **2** a tall plant with long pointed leaves and large flowers [Greek: rainbow]
Irish *adj* **1** of Ireland ▷ *n* **2** same as **Irish Gaelic** **3** the dialect of English spoken in Ireland ▷ *pl n* **4 the Irish** the people of Ireland
Irish coffee *n* hot coffee mixed with Irish whiskey and topped with double cream
Irish Gaelic *n* the Celtic language of Ireland
Irishman *or fem* **Irishwoman** *n, pl* **-men** *or* **-women** a person from Ireland
Irish moss *n* same as **carrageen**
irk *vb* to irritate or vex [Middle English *irken* to grow weary]
irksome *adj* annoying or tiresome
iron *n* **1** a strong silvery-white metallic element, widely used for structural and engineering purposes. Symbol: **Fe** **2** a tool made of iron **3** a small electrically heated device with a weighted flat bottom for pressing clothes **4** *golf* a club with an angled metal head **5** a splintlike support for a malformed leg **6** great strength or resolve: *a will of iron* **7 strike while the iron is hot** to act at a suitable moment ▷ *adj* **8** made of iron **9** very hard or merciless: *iron determination* **10** very strong: *an iron constitution* ▷ *vb* **11** to smooth (clothes or fabric) by removing (creases) with an iron ▷ See also **iron out, irons** [Old English *īren*]
Iron Age *n* a phase of human culture that began in the Middle East about 1100 BC, during which iron tools and weapons were used
ironbark *n* an Australian eucalyptus with hard rough bark
ironclad *adj* **1** covered or protected with iron: *an ironclad warship* **2** unable to be contradicted: *ironclad proof* ▷ *n* **3** *history* a large wooden 19th-century warship with armoured plating
Iron Curtain *n* (formerly) the guarded border between the countries of the Soviet bloc and the rest of Europe
ironic *or* **ironical** *adj* of, characterized by, or using irony **ironically** *adv*
ironing *n* clothes to be ironed
ironing board *n* a narrow cloth-covered board, usually with folding legs, on which to iron clothes
iron lung *n* an airtight metal cylinder enclosing the entire body up to the neck and providing artificial respiration
iron maiden *n* a medieval instrument of torture, consisting of a hinged case (often shaped in the form of a woman) lined with iron spikes
ironmaster *n Brit history* a manufacturer of iron
ironmonger *n Brit* a shopkeeper or shop dealing in hardware **ironmongery** *n*
iron out *vb* to settle (a problem or difficulty) through negotiation or discussion
iron pyrites *n* same as **pyrite**
iron rations *pl n* emergency food supplies, esp. for military personnel in action
irons *pl n* **1** fetters or chains **2 have several irons in the fire** to have several projects or plans at once
ironstone *n* **1** any rock consisting mainly of iron ore **2** a tough durable earthenware
ironwood *n* **1** any of various trees, such as hornbeam, with exceptionally hard wood **2** the wood of any of these trees
ironwork *n* work done in iron, esp. decorative work
ironworks *n* a building in which iron is smelted, cast, or wrought
irony *n, pl* **-nies** **1** the mildly sarcastic use of words to imply the opposite of what they normally mean **2** a situation or result that is the direct opposite of what was expected or intended [Greek *eirōneia*]
irradiate *vb* **-ating, -ated** **1** *physics* to subject to or treat with light or other electromagnetic radiation **2** to make clear or bright intellectually or spiritually **3** to light up; illuminate **irradiation** *n*
irrational *adj* **1** not based on logical reasoning **2** incapable of reasoning **3** *maths* (of an equation or expression) involving radicals or fractional exponents **irrationality** *n* **irrationally** *adv*
irrational number *n maths* any real number that cannot be expressed as the ratio of two integers, such as π
irreconcilable *adj* not able to be resolved or settled: *irreconcilable differences* **irreconcilability** *n*
irrecoverable *adj* not able to be recovered

irredeemable *adj* **1** not able to be reformed, improved, or corrected **2** (of bonds or shares) not able to be bought back directly or paid off **3** (of paper money) not able to be converted into coin **irredeemably** *adv*
irredentist *n* a person in favour of seizing territory that was once part of his or her country [Italian *irredenta*, from the phrase *Italia irredenta* Italy unredeemed] **irredentism** *n*
irreducible *adj* impossible to put in a reduced or simpler form **irreducibility** *n*
irrefutable *adj* impossible to deny or disprove
irregular *adj* **1** uneven in shape, position, arrangement, etc. **2** not conforming to accepted practice or routine **3** (of a word) not following the usual pattern of formation in a language **4** not occurring at expected or equal intervals: *an irregular pulse* **5** (of troops) not belonging to regular forces ▷ *n* **6** a soldier not in a regular army **irregularity** *n* **irregularly** *adv*
irrelevant *adj* not connected with the matter in hand **irrelevance** *or* **irrelevancy** *n*
irreligious *adj* **1** lacking religious faith **2** indifferent or opposed to religion
irremediable *adj* not able to be improved or cured
irremovable *adj* not able to be removed **irremovably** *adv*
irreparable *adj* not able to be repaired or put right: *irreparable damage to his reputation* **irreparably** *adv*
irreplaceable *adj* impossible to replace: *acres of irreplaceable moorland were devastated*
irrepressible *adj* not capable of being repressed, controlled, or restrained **irrepressibility** *n* **irrepressibly** *adv*
irreproachable *adj* blameless or faultless **irreproachability** *n*
irresistible *adj* **1** not able to be resisted or refused: *irresistible pressure from the financial markets* **2** extremely attractive: *an irresistible woman* **irresistibility** *n* **irresistibly** *adv*
irresolute *adj* unable to make decisions **irresolution** *n*
irrespective *adj* **irrespective of** without taking account of
irresponsible *adj* **1** not showing or done with due care for the consequences of one's actions or attitudes; reckless **2** not capable of accepting responsibility **irresponsibility** *n* **irresponsibly** *adv*
irretrievable *adj* impossible to put right or make good **irretrievability** *n* **irretrievably** *adv*
irreverence *n* **1** lack of due respect **2** a disrespectful remark or act **irreverent** *adj*
irreversible *adj* not able to be reversed or put right again: *irreversible loss of memory* **irreversibly** *adv*
irrevocable *adj* not possible to change or undo **irrevocably** *adv*
irrigate *vb* **-gating, -gated 1** to supply (land) with water through ditches or pipes in order to encourage the growth of crops **2** *med* to bathe (a wound or part of the body) [Latin *irrigare*] **irrigation** *n* **irrigator** *n*
irritable *adj* **1** easily annoyed or angered **2** *pathol* abnormally sensitive **3** *biol* (of all living organisms) capable of responding to such stimuli as heat, light, and touch **irritability** *n*
irritant *n* **1** something that annoys or irritates **2** a substance that causes a part of the body to become tender or inflamed ▷ *adj* **3** causing irritation
irritate *vb* **-tating, -tated 1** to annoy or anger (someone) **2** *pathol* to cause (an organ or part of the body) to become inflamed or tender **3** *biol* to stimulate (an organ) to respond in a characteristic manner [Latin *irritare* to provoke] **irritation** *n*
irrupt *vb* to enter forcibly or suddenly [Latin *irrumpere*] **irruption** *n* **irruptive** *adj*
is *vb* third person singular of the present tense of **be** [Old English]
ISA (**eye**-sa) *n* (in Britain) individual savings account
isallobar (ice-**sal**-oh-bar) *n* a line on a map connecting places with equal pressure changes [Greek *isos* equal + *allos* other + *baros* weight]
ISBN International Standard Book Number
isinglass (**ize**-ing-glass) *n* **1** a gelatine made from the air bladders of freshwater fish **2** same as **mica** [Middle Dutch *huysenblase* sturgeon bladder]
Isis *n* an Egyptian fertility goddess
Isl. **1** Island **2** Isle
Islam *n* **1** the Muslim religion teaching that there is only one God and that Mohammed is his prophet **2** Muslim countries and civilization [Arabic: surrender (to God)] **Islamic** *adj* **Islamist** *adj, n*
Islamic State *n* a militant organization whose aim is to create an Islamic caliphate in the Middle East and N Africa
island *n* **1** a piece of land that is completely surrounded by water **2** something isolated, detached, or surrounded **3** See **traffic island**. ▷ Related adjective: **insular** [Old English *īgland*]
islander *n* **1** a person who lives on an island **2** **Islander** NZ a Pacific Islander
isle *n* (except when part of a place name) a poetic name for an island
islet *n* a small island
ism *n informal, often derogatory* a doctrine, system, or practice, esp. one whose name ends in *-ism*, such as *communism* or *fascism*
-ism *n suffix* **1** indicating a political or religious belief: *socialism; Judaism* **2** indicating a characteristic quality: *heroism* **3** indicating an action: *exorcism* **4** indicating prejudice on the basis specified: *sexism*
isn't is not
iso- *or before a vowel* **is-** *combining form* equal or identical: *isomagnetic* [Greek *isos* equal]
isobar (**ice**-oh-bar) *n* **1** a line on a map connecting places of equal atmospheric pressure **2** *physics* any of two or more atoms that have the same mass number but different atomic numbers [Greek *isobarēs* of equal weight] **isobaric** *adj* **isobarism** *n*
isochronal *or* **isochronous** *adj* **1** equal in length of time **2** occurring at equal time intervals [Greek *isos* equal + *khronos* time] **isochronism** *n*
isohel *n* a line on a map connecting places with an equal period of sunshine [Greek *isos* equal + *hēlios* sun]

isohyet (ice-oh-hie-it) *n* a line on a map connecting places having equal rainfall [Greek *isos* equal + *huetos* rain]

isolate *vb* **-lating, -lated 1** to place apart or alone **2** *chem* to obtain (a substance) in an uncombined form **3** *med* to quarantine (a person or animal) with a contagious disease [Latin *insulatus*, literally: made into an island] **isolation** *n*

isomer (ice-oh-mer) *n chem* a substance whose molecules contain the same atoms as another but in a different arrangement **isomeric** *adj*

isometric *adj* **1** having equal dimensions or measurements **2** *physiol* relating to muscular contraction that does not produce shortening of the muscle **3** (of a three-dimensional drawing) having the three axes equally inclined and all lines drawn to scale [Greek *isometria* equal measurement] **isometrically** *adv*

isometrics *n* a system of isometric exercises

isomorphism *n* **1** *biol* similarity of form, as in different generations of the same life cycle **2** *chem* the existence of two or more substances of different composition in a similar crystalline form **3** *maths* a one-to-one correspondence between the elements of two or more sets **isomorph** *n* **isomorphic** *or* **isomorphous** *adj*

isosceles triangle (ice-soss-ill-eez) *n* a triangle with two sides of equal length [Greek *isos* equal + *skelos* leg]

isotherm (ice-oh-therm) *n* a line on a map linking places of equal temperature [Greek *isos* equal + *thermē* heat]

isotonic *adj* **1** *physiol* (of two or more muscles) having equal tension **2** (of a drink) designed to replace the fluid and salts lost from the body during exercise

isotope (ice-oh-tope) *n* one of two or more atoms with the same number of protons in the nucleus but a different number of neutrons [Greek *isos* equal + *topos* place] **isotopic** *adj* **isotopy** *n*

isotropic *or* **isotropous** *adj* having uniform physical properties, such as elasticity or conduction in all directions **isotropy** *n*

ISP internet service provider: a business providing its customers with connection to the internet

Israeli *adj* **1** of Israel ▷ *n, pl* **-lis** *or* **-li 2** a person from Israel

Israelite *n Bible* a member of the ethnic group claiming descent from Jacob; a Hebrew

issue *n* **1** a topic of interest or discussion **2** an important subject requiring a decision **3** a particular edition of a magazine or newspaper **4** a consequence or result **5** *law* the descendants of a person **6** the act of sending or giving out something **7** the act of emerging; outflow **8** something flowing out, such as a river **9 at issue A** under discussion **B** in disagreement **10 force the issue** to compel decision on some matter **11 join issue** to join in controversy **12 take issue** to disagree ▷ *vb* **-suing, -sued 13** to make (a statement, etc.) publicly **14** to supply officially (with) **15** to send out or distribute **16** to publish **17** to come forth or emerge [Old French *eissue* way out] **issuable** *adj*

isthmus (iss-muss) *n* a narrow strip of land connecting two relatively large land areas [Greek *isthmos*]

it *pron* **1** refers to a nonhuman, animal, plant, or inanimate thing, or sometimes to a small baby **2** refers to something unspecified or implied or to a previous or understood clause, phrase, or word: *I knew it* **3** used to represent human life or experience in respect of the present situation: *how's it going?* **4** used as the subject of impersonal verbs: *it is snowing*; *it's Friday* **5** *informal* the crucial or ultimate point: *the steering failed and I thought that was it* ▷ *n* **6** *informal* **A** sexual intercourse **B** sex appeal **7** a desirable quality or ability [Old English *hit*]

IT information technology

ITA initial teaching alphabet: a partly phonetic alphabet used to teach reading

Italian *adj* **1** of Italy ▷ *n* **2** a person from Italy **3** the official language of Italy and one of the official languages of Switzerland

Italianate *adj* Italian in style or character

italic *adj* **1** of a style of printing type in which the characters slant to the right ▷ *pl n* **2 italics** italic type or print, used for emphasis [Latin *Italicus* of Italy (where it was first used)]

italicize *or* **-cise** *vb* **-cizing, -cized** *or* **-cising, -cised** to print (text) in italic type **italicization** *or* **-cisation** *n*

itch *n* **1** a skin irritation causing a desire to scratch **2** a restless desire **3** any skin disorder, such as scabies, characterized by intense itching ▷ *vb* **4** to feel an irritating or tickling sensation **5** to have a restless desire (to do something): *they were itching to join the fight* [Old English *gīccean* to itch]

itchy *adj* **itchier, itchiest 1** having an itch **2 have itchy feet** to have a desire to travel **itchiness** *n*

it'd it would *or* it had

item *n* **1** a single thing in a list or collection **2** a piece of information: *a news item* **3** *accounting* an entry in an account **4** *informal* a couple [Latin: in like manner]

itemize *or* **-ise** *vb* **-izing, -ized** *or* **-ising, -ised** to put on a list or make a list of **itemization** *or* **-isation** *n*

iterate *vb* **-ating, -ated** to say or do again [Latin *iterum* again] **iteration** *n* **iterative** *adj*

itinerant *adj* **1** working for a short time in various places ▷ *n* **2** an itinerant worker or other person [Latin *iter* a journey]

itinerary *n, pl* **-aries 1** a detailed plan of a journey **2** a record of a journey **3** a guidebook for travellers

-itis *suffix forming nouns* indicating inflammation of a specified part: *tonsillitis* [Greek *-itēs* belonging to]

it'll it will *or* it shall

its *adj* **1** of or belonging to it: *its left rear wheel*; *I can see its logical consequence* ▷ *pron* **2** something belonging to it: *its is over there*

it's it is *or* it has

itself *pron* **1 A** the reflexive form of *it*: *the cat scratched itself* **B** used for emphasis: *even the money itself won't convince me* **2** its normal or usual self: *my parrot doesn't seem itself these days*

ITV (in Britain) Independent Television
IUD intrauterine device: a coil-shaped contraceptive fitted into the womb
I've I have
IVF in vitro fertilization
ivories *pl n slang* **1** the keys of a piano **2** the teeth **3** dice
ivory *n, pl* **-ries** **1** a hard smooth creamy white type of bone that makes up a major part of the tusks of elephants ▷ *adj* **2** yellowish-white [Latin *ebur*] **ivory-like** *adj*
ivory tower *n* remoteness from the realities of everyday life **ivory-towered** *adj*
IVR International Vehicle Registration
ivy *n, pl* **ivies** **1** a woody climbing or trailing plant with evergreen leaves and black berry-like fruits **2** any of various other climbing or creeping plants, such as the poison ivy [Old English *īfig*]
iwi (ee-wee) *n* NZ a Māori tribe [Māori]
ixia *n* a southern African plant of the iris family with showy ornamental funnel-shaped flowers [Greek *ixos* mistletoe]

Jj

J joule(s)
ja *interj S African* yes
jab *vb* **jabbing, jabbed 1** to poke sharply ▷ *n* **2** a quick short punch **3** *informal* an injection: *a flu jab* **4** a sharp poke [variant of *job*]
jabber *vb* **1** to speak very quickly and excitedly; chatter ▷ *n* **2** quick excited chatter [imitative]
jabiru *n* a large white-and-black Australian stork
jacaranda *n* a tropical American tree with sweet-smelling wood and pale purple flowers [from a Native American language]
jack *n* **1** a mechanical device used to raise a motor vehicle or other heavy object **2** a playing card with a picture of a pageboy on it **3** *bowls* a small white bowl at which the players aim their bowls **4** *electrical engineering* a socket into which a plug can be inserted **5** a flag flown at the bow of a ship, showing nationality **6** one of the pieces used in the game of jacks **7 every man jack** everyone without exception ▷ See also **jack in**, **jack up** [from short form of *John*]
jackal *n* a doglike wild animal of Africa and Asia, which feeds on the decaying flesh of dead animals [Persian *shagāl*]
jackanapes *n Brit* a mischievous child [literally: Jack of the ape, nickname of first Duke of Suffolk, whose badge showed an ape's ball and chain]
jackaroo *or* **jackeroo** *n, pl* **-roos** *Austral* a trainee on a sheep station [from *jack* man + *(kang)aroo*]
jackass *n* **1** a fool **2** a male donkey **3 laughing jackass** same as **kookaburra** [*jack* (male) + *ass*]
jackboot *n* **1** a leather military boot reaching up to the knee **2** brutal and authoritarian rule
jackdaw *n* a large black-and-grey crowlike bird of Europe and Asia [*jack* + *daw*, obsolete name for jackdaw]
jacket *n* **1** a short coat with a front opening and long sleeves **2** the skin of a potato **3** same as **dust jacket** [Old French *jaquet*]
jacket potato *n* a potato baked in its skin
Jack Frost *n* frost represented as a person
jack in *vb Brit slang* to abandon (an attempt or enterprise)
jack-in-the-box *n* a toy consisting of a box containing a figure on a compressed spring, which jumps out when the lid is opened
jackknife *vb* **-knifing, -knifed 1** (of an articulated lorry) to go out of control in such a way that the trailer swings round at a sharp angle to the cab ▷ *n, pl* **-knives 2** a knife with a blade that can be folded into the handle **3** a dive in which the diver bends at the waist in midair
jack of all trades *n, pl* **jacks of all trades** a person who can do many different kinds of work; handyman
jackpot *n* **1** the most valuable prize that can be won in a gambling game **2 hit the jackpot** *informal* to be very fortunate or very successful [probably from *jack* (playing card)]
jack rabbit *n* a hare of W North America with very long hind legs and large ears [*jackass-rabbit*, referring to its long ears]
Jack Tar *n chiefly literary* a sailor
jack up *vb* **1** to raise (a motor vehicle) with a jack **2** to increase (prices or salaries) **3** NZ *informal* to organize something through unorthodox channels ▷ *n* **jack-up 4** NZ *informal* something achieved dishonestly
Jacobean (jak-a-**bee**-an) *adj* of or in the reign of James I of England and Ireland (1603–25) [Latin *Jacobus* James]
Jacobite *n history* a supporter of James II and his descendants [Latin *Jacobus* James]
Jacquard (**jak**-ard) *n* a fabric with an intricate design incorporated into the weave [after J. M. *Jacquard*, its inventor]
Jacuzzi (jak-**oo**-zee) *n trademark* a large circular bath with a mechanism that swirls the water
jade *n* **1** an ornamental semiprecious stone, usually green in colour ▷ *adj* **2** bluish-green [obsolete Spanish *piedra de ijada* colic stone, because it was believed to cure colic]
jaded *adj* tired or bored from overindulgence or overwork
Jaffa *n Brit* a large thick-skinned orange [after *Jaffa*, port in W Israel]
jag[1] *n Scot informal* same as **jab** (sense 3) [origin unknown]
jag[2] *n slang* a period of uncontrolled indulgence in an activity: *all-night crying jags* [origin unknown]
jagged (**jag**-gid) *adj* having an uneven edge with sharp points [from *jag* a sharp point]
jaguar *n* a large wild cat of south and central America, with a spotted coat [from indigenous S American word]
jail *or* **gaol** *n* **1** a prison ▷ *vb* **2** to confine in prison [Old French *jaiole* cage]
jailbird *n informal* a person who is or has often been in jail
jailer *or* **gaoler** *n* a person in charge of a jail
jake *adj* **she's jake** *Austral & NZ slang* everything is under control [probably from the name *Jake*]
jalopy (jal-**lop**-ee) *n, pl* **-lopies** *informal* a dilapidated old car [origin unknown]
jam[1] *vb* **jamming, jammed 1** to wedge (an object) into a tight space or against another object: *the table was jammed against the wall* **2** to fill (a place) with people or vehicles: *the surrounding roads were jammed for miles* **3** to make or become stuck or locked: *the window was jammed open* **4** *radio* to prevent the clear reception of (radio communications) by transmitting other signals on the same wavelength **5** *slang* to play in a jam session **6 jam on the brakes** to apply the brakes of a vehicle very suddenly ▷ *n* **7** a situation where a large number of people or vehicles are crowded into a place: *a traffic jam* **8** *informal* a difficult situation: *you are in a bit of a jam* **9** same as **jam session** [probably imitative]
jam[2] *n* a food made from fruit boiled with sugar until the mixture sets, used for spreading on bread [perhaps from JAM[1] (the act of squeezing)]

Jamaican *adj* **1** of Jamaica ▹ *n* **2** a person from Jamaica
jamb *n* a side post of a doorframe or window frame [Old French *jambe* leg, jamb]
jamboree *n* a large gathering or celebration [origin unknown]
jammy *adj* **-mier, -miest 1** covered with or tasting like jam **2** *Brit slang* lucky: *jammy so-and-sos!*
jam-packed *adj* filled to capacity
jam session *n slang* an improvised performance by jazz or rock musicians [probably from JAM[1]]
Jan. January
Jandal *n trademark NZ* a rubber-soled sandal attached to the foot by a thong between the big toe and the next toe
jangle *vb* **-gling, -gled 1** to make a harsh unpleasant ringing noise **2** to produce an irritating or unpleasant effect on: *the caffeine in coffee can jangle the nerves* [Old French *jangler*]
janitor *n chiefly Scot, US & Canad* the caretaker of a school or other building [Latin: doorkeeper]
January *n* the first month of the year [Latin *Januarius*]
japan *n* **1** a glossy black lacquer, originally from E Asia, which is used on wood or metal ▹ *vb* **-panning, -panned 2** to varnish with japan
Japanese *adj* **1** of Japan ▹ *n* **2** *pl* **-nese** a person from Japan **3** the language of Japan
jape *n old-fashioned* a joke or prank [origin unknown]
japonica *n* **1** a Japanese shrub with red flowers and yellowish fruit **2** same as **camellia** [New Latin *Japonia* Japan]
jar[1] *n* **1** a wide-mouthed cylindrical glass container, used for storing food **2** *Brit informal* a glass of beer [Arabic *jarrah* large earthen vessel]
jar[2] *vb* **jarring, jarred 1** to have an irritating or unpleasant effect: *sometimes a light remark jarred on her father* **2** to be in disagreement or conflict: *their very different temperaments jarred* **3** to jolt or bump ▹ *n* **4** a jolt or shock [probably imitative]
jarring *adj*
jardiniere (zhah-din-**yair**) *n* an ornamental pot or stand for plants [French]
jargon *n* **1** specialized language relating to a particular subject, profession, or group **2** pretentious or unintelligible language [Old French]
jarrah *n* an Australian eucalypt yielding valuable timber
jasmine *n* a shrub or climbing plant with sweet-smelling flowers [Persian *yāsmīn*]
jasper *n* a kind of quartz, usually red in colour, which is used as a gemstone and for ornamental decoration [Greek *iaspis*]
jaundice *n* yellowing of the skin and the whites of the eyes, caused by an excess of bile pigments in the blood [French *jaune* yellow]
jaundiced *adj* **1** bitter or cynical: *the financial markets are taking a jaundiced view of the Government's motives* **2** having jaundice
jaunt *n* **1** a pleasure trip or outing ▹ *vb* **2** to go on a jaunt [origin unknown]
jaunty *adj* **-tier, -tiest 1** cheerful and energetic: *he managed to keep up a jaunty air* **2** smart and attractive: *a jaunty little hat* [French *gentil* noble]
jauntily *adv*
Java *n trademark* a computer programming language that is widely used on the internet [after *Java* coffee from the Indonesian island, allegedly drunk by its creators]
Javanese *adj* **1** of the island of Java, in Indonesia ▹ *n* **2** *pl* **-nese** a person from Java **3** the language of Java
javelin *n* a light spear thrown in a sports competition [Old French *javeline*]
jaw *n* **1** either of the bones that hold the teeth and frame the mouth **2** the lower part of the face below the mouth **3** *slang* a long chat ▹ *vb* **4** *slang* to have a long chat [probably Old French *joue* cheek]
jawbone *n* the bone in the lower jaw of a person or animal
ja well no fine *interj S African* used to indicate reluctant acceptance
jaws *pl n* **1** the mouth of a person or animal **2** the parts of a machine or tool that grip an object **3** the narrow opening of a gorge or valley **4** a dangerous or threatening position: *to snatch victory from the jaws of defeat*
jay *n* **1** a bird of Europe and Asia with a pinkish-brown body and blue-and-black wings **2** a N American bird with bright blue feathers [Old French *jai*]
jaywalking *n* crossing the road in a dangerous or careless manner [*jay* (in sense: a foolish person)]
jaywalker *n*
jazz *n* **1** a kind of popular music of African-American origin that has an exciting rhythm and often involves improvisation **2 and all that jazz** *slang* and other related things [origin unknown]
jazz up *vb informal* **1** to play (a piece of music) in a jazzy style **2** to make (something) appear more interesting or lively: *never seek to jazz up a plain story*
jazzy *adj* **-zier, -ziest 1** colourful and modern: *jazzy shop fronts* **2** of or like jazz
JCB *n trademark Brit* a large machine used in building, that has a shovel on the front and a digger arm on the back [initials of Joseph Cyril Bamford, its manufacturer]
jealous *adj* **1** suspicious or fearful of being displaced by a rival **2** envious: *I was jealous of the girls who had boyfriends* **3** resulting from jealousy: *my jealous tears* [Late Latin *zelus* emulation]
jealously *adv*
jealousy *n, pl* **-ousies** the state of or an instance of feeling jealous
jeans *pl n* casual denim trousers [from *jean fustian* fabric from Genoa]
Jeep *n trademark* a small road vehicle with four-wheel drive [perhaps *general-purpose (vehicle)*, influenced by Eugene the *Jeep*, creature in a comic strip]
jeer *vb* **1** to be derisive towards (someone) ▹ *n* **2** a cry of derision [origin unknown] **jeering** *adj, n*
jeggings *pl n* women's leggings designed to look like tight denim jeans [blend of *jeans* + *leggings*]
Jehovah *n* God [Hebrew *Yahweh*]
Jehovah's Witness *n* a member of a Christian Church whose followers believe that the end of the world is near

jejune *adj* **1** simple and unsophisticated **2** dull and uninteresting [Latin *jejunus* empty]
jejunum (jij-june-um) *n anatomy* the part of the small intestine between the duodenum and the ileum [Latin] **jejunal** *adj*
Jekyll and Hyde *n* a person with two distinct personalities, one good and the other evil [after the character in a novel by R. L. Stevenson]
jell *vb* **1** to take on a definite form: *the changes have had little time to jell* **2** same as **gel** (sense 2) [from *jelly*]
jellaba *n* a loose robe with a hood, worn by some Arab men [Arabic *jallabah*]
jellied *adj* prepared in a jelly: *jellied eels*
jelly *n, pl* **-lies 1** a fruit-flavoured dessert set with gelatine **2** a food made from fruit juice boiled with sugar until the mixture sets, used for spreading on bread **3** a savoury food preparation set with gelatine [Latin *gelare* to freeze] **jelly-like** *adj*
jellyfish *n, pl* **-fish** a small sea creature with a jelly-like umbrella-shaped body and trailing tentacles
jemmy *or US* **jimmy** *n, pl* **-mies** a short steel crowbar, used by burglars to prise open doors and windows [from short form of *James*]
jenny *n, pl* **-nies** a female donkey, ass, or wren [from the name *Jenny*]
jeopardize *or* **-dise** *vb* **-dizing, -dized** *or* **-dising, -dised** to put (something) at risk: *the escalating violence that is jeopardizing current peace moves*
jeopardy *n* danger of harm, loss, or death: *the survival of public hospitals is in jeopardy* [Old French *jeu parti*, literally: divided game, hence uncertain issue]
jerboa *n* a small rodent of Asia and N Africa with long hind legs used for jumping [Arabic *yarbū'*]
jeremiad *n* a long mournful complaint [French *jérémiade*, referring to the Lamentations of Jeremiah in the Bible]
jerepigo (jer-ree-pee-go) *n S African* a sweet fortified wine similar to port [Portuguese *jeropiga*]
jerk *vb* **1** to move with an irregular or spasmodic motion **2** to pull or push (something) abruptly or spasmodically ▷ *n* **3** an abrupt or spasmodic movement **4** an irregular jolting motion: *the irritating jerk that heralded a gear change* **5** *slang, chiefly US & Canad* a stupid or ignorant person [probably variant of *yerk* to pull stitches tight]
jerkin *n* a short jacket [origin unknown]
jerky *adj* **jerkier, jerkiest** having an irregular jolting motion: *avoid any sudden or jerky movements* **jerkily** *adv* **jerkiness** *n*
Jerry *n old-fashioned Brit slang* **1** *pl* **-ries** a German, esp. a German soldier **2** Germans collectively
jerry-built *adj* (of houses) built badly with cheap materials
jerry can *n* a flat-sided can used for carrying petrol or water [from *Jerry* German soldier]
jersey *n* **1** a knitted garment covering the upper part of the body **2** a soft, slightly stretchy, machine-knitted fabric [originally referring to a type of woollen fabric made in *Jersey*]
Jersey *n* a breed of reddish-brown dairy cattle that produces milk with a high butterfat content [after *Jersey*, island in the English Channel]
Jerusalem artichoke *n* a small yellowish-white vegetable that grows underground [altered from Italian *girasole* sunflower]
jest *n* **1** something done or said to amuse people **2 in jest** as a joke: *many a true word is spoken in jest* ▷ *vb* **3** to do or say something to amuse people [variant of *gest* exploit]
jester *n* a professional clown employed by a king or nobleman during the Middle Ages
Jesuit (jezz-yew-it) *n* a member of the Society of Jesus, a Roman Catholic religious order [New Latin *Jesuita*] **Jesuitical** *adj*
Jesus *n* **1** the founder of Christianity, believed by Christians to be the Son of God ▷ *interj* **2** *taboo slang* an oath expressing intense anger or shock
jet[1] *n* **1** an aircraft driven by jet propulsion **2** a thin stream of liquid or gas forced out of a small hole **3** an outlet or nozzle through which a stream of liquid or gas is forced ▷ *vb* **jetting, jetted 4** to travel by jet aircraft [Old French *jeter* to throw]
jet[2] *n* a hard black mineral that is polished and used in jewellery [Old French *jaiet*]
jet-black *adj* deep black
jetboat *n* a motorboat propelled by a jet of water
jet engine *n* an aircraft engine that uses jet propulsion for forward motion
jet lag *n* a feeling of fatigue and disorientation often experienced by air passengers who have crossed several time zones in a short space of time
jet-propelled *adj* driven by jet propulsion
jet propulsion *n* a method of propulsion by which an aircraft is moved forward by the force of the exhaust gases ejected from the rear
jetsam *n* **1** goods thrown overboard to lighten a ship during a storm **2 flotsam and jetsam** See **flotsam** (sense 2) [from *jettison*]
jet set *n* rich and fashionable people who travel widely for pleasure **jet-setter** *n* **jet-setting** *adj*
jet ski *n* a small self-propelled vehicle resembling a scooter, which skims across water on a flat keel **jet skiing** *n*
jettison *vb* **1** to abandon or give up: *jettisoning democracy in favour of fascism* **2** to throw overboard [Latin *jactatio* a tossing about]
jetty *n, pl* **-ties 1** a landing pier or dock **2** a structure built from a shore out into the water to protect a harbour [Old French *jetee* projecting part]
Jew *n* **1** a person whose religion is Judaism **2** a descendant of the ancient Hebrews [Hebrew *yehūdāh* Judah]
jewel *n* **1** a precious or semiprecious stone **2** a person or thing regarded as precious or special: *a fantastic little car, a real little jewel* **3** a gemstone used as part of the machinery of a watch [Old French *jouel*]
jewelled *or US* **jeweled** *adj* decorated with jewels
jeweller *or US* **jeweler** *n* a person who buys, sells, and repairs jewellery
jewellery *or US* **jewelry** *n* objects such as rings, necklaces, and bracelets, worn for decoration
Jewess *n often offensive* a woman whose religion is Judaism
jewfish *n Austral* a freshwater catfish

Jewish *adj* of Jews or Judaism
Jewry *n* Jews collectively
jew's-harp *n* a small musical instrument held between the teeth and played by plucking a metal strip with the finger
Jezebel *n derogatory* a woman considered wicked or shameless [after the wife of Ahab, in the Bible]
jib[1] *n* **1** *naut* a triangular sail set in front of the foremast **2 the cut of someone's jib** a person's manner or style [origin unknown]
jib[2] *vb* **jibbing, jibbed** *chiefly Brit* **1** (of an animal) to stop short and refuse to go forwards: *my animal jibbed three times* **2 jib at** to object to: *he jibs at any suggestion that his side are the underdogs* [origin unknown]
jib[3] *n* the projecting arm of a crane [probably from *gibbet*]
jibe[1] *n* **1** an insulting or taunting remark ▷ *vb* **jibing, jibed 2** to make insulting or taunting remarks
jibe[2] *vb* **jibing, jibed** *informal* to be in accord or be consistent: *their apparent devotion hardly jibed with what he had heard about them*
jibe[3] *vb* **jibing, jibed,** *n naut* same as **gybe**
jiffy *n, pl* **jiffies** *informal* a very short time: *won't be a jiffy!* [origin unknown]
Jiffy bag *n trademark* a large padded envelope
jig *n* **1** a lively folk dance **2** music for this dance **3** a mechanical device that holds and locates a part during machining ▷ *vb* **jigging, jigged 4** to dance a jig **5** to move with quick jerky movements [origin unknown]
jigger *n* a small whisky glass
jiggered *adj old-fashioned, informal* damned or blowed: *well, I'm jiggered, so that's where it went!* [probably euphemism for *buggered*]
jiggery-pokery *n informal, chiefly Brit* dishonest behaviour; cheating [Scots dialect *joukery-pawkery*]
jiggle *vb* **-gling, -gled** to move with quick jerky movements [frequentative of *jig*]
jigsaw *n* **1** Also called: **jigsaw puzzle** a puzzle in which the player has to put together a picture that has been cut into irregularly shaped interlocking pieces **2** a mechanical saw with a fine steel blade for cutting along curved or irregular lines in sheets of material [*jig* (to jerk up and down) + SAW[1]]
jihad *n* an Islamic holy war against unbelievers
jihadi *n* a person who takes part in a jihad
jilt *vb* to leave or reject (a lover) abruptly or callously [dialect *jillet* flighty girl]
Jim Crow *n US history* **1** the policy or practice of segregating Black people **2** *offensive* a Black person [from name of song]
jingle *n* **1** a short catchy song used to advertise a product **2** a light ringing sound ▷ *vb* **-gling, -gled 3** to make a light ringing sound [probably imitative]
jingoism *n* excessive and aggressive patriotism [after the use of *by Jingo!* in a 19th-century song] **jingoistic** *or* **jingoist** *adj*
jink *vb* to move quickly or jerkily in order to dodge someone: *she jinked free and won a race to the line to level the scores* [Scots]
jinks *pl n* **high jinks** boisterous or mischievous behaviour [origin unknown]
jinni *or* **djinni** *n, pl* **jinn** *or* **djinn** (in Islamic belief) a being or spirit that can take on human or animal form [Arabic]
jinx *n* **1** someone or something believed to bring bad luck ▷ *vb* **2** to bring bad luck to [perhaps from Greek *iunx* wryneck, a bird used in magic]
jitterbug *n* **1** a fast jerky American dance that was popular in the 1940s ▷ *vb* **-bugging, -bugged 2** to dance the jitterbug
jitters *pl n* **the jitters** *informal* a feeling of extreme nervousness experienced before an important event: *I had a case of the jitters before my first two speeches* [origin unknown]
jittery *adj* nervous
jive *n* **1** a lively jerky dance that was popular in the 1940s and 1950s ▷ *vb* **jiving, jived 2** to dance the jive [origin unknown] **jiver** *n*
Jnr Junior
job *n* **1** a person's occupation or paid employment **2** a piece of work; task **3** the performance of a task: *he made a good job of the repair* **4** *informal* a difficult task: *they are having a job to fill his shoes* **5** *Brit, Austral & NZ informal* a crime, esp. a robbery **6 just the job** *informal* exactly what is required **7 make the best of a bad job** to cope as well as possible in unsatisfactory circumstances [origin unknown]
jobbing *adj* doing individual jobs for payment: *a jobbing gardener*
jobless *adj* **1** unemployed ▷ *pl n* **2** people who are unemployed: *the young jobless*
job lot *n* a miscellaneous collection of articles sold together
Job's comforter *n* a person who adds to someone else's distress while pretending to be sympathetic [after *Job* in the Bible]
jobseeker's allowance *n* (in Britain) a social-security payment for unemployed people
job sharing *n* an arrangement by which a job is shared by two part-time workers
jockey *n* **1** a person who rides horses in races as a profession ▷ *vb* **2 jockey for position** to try to obtain an advantage by skilful manoeuvring [from the name *Jock*]
jockstrap *n* an elasticated belt with a pouch to support the genitals, worn by male athletes. Also called: **athletic support** [slang *jock* penis]
jocose (joke-kohss) *adj old-fashioned* playful or humorous [Latin *jocus* joke] **jocosely** *adv*
jocular *adj* **1** (of a person) often joking; good-humoured **2** (of a remark) meant lightly or humorously [Latin *joculus* little joke] **jocularity** *n* **jocularly** *adv*
jocund (jok-kund) *adj literary* cheerful or merry [Latin *jucundus* pleasant]
jodhpurs *pl n* trousers worn for riding, which are loose-fitting around the thighs and tight-fitting below the knees [from *Jodhpur*, town in NW India]
joey *n Austral* a young kangaroo
jog *vb* **jogging, jogged 1** to run at a gentle pace for exercise **2** to nudge slightly **3 jog along** to continue in a plodding way: *many people jog along in second gear for the whole of their lives* **4 jog someone's memory** to remind someone of something ▷ *n* **5** a slow run as a form of exercise [probably variant of *shog* to shake] **jogger** *n* **jogging** *n*

joggle *vb* **-gling, -gled** to shake or move with a slightly jolting motion [frequentative of *jog*]

jog trot *n* an easy bouncy pace, midway between a walk and a trot

john *n slang, chiefly US & Canad* a toilet [special use of the name]

John Bull *n* England represented as a man

johnny *n, pl* **-nies** *Brit old-fashioned, informal* a chap: *you legal johnnies*

Johnny Canuck (kan-nuk) *n Canad informal* Canada personified as a man

joie de vivre (zhwah de **veev**-ra) *n* enjoyment of life [French, literally: joy of living]

join *vb* **1** to become a member of (a club or organization) **2** to become part of (a queue or list) **3** to meet (someone) as a companion: *join me for a cup of coffee* **4** to take part in (an activity): *join the relief effort* **5** (of two roads or rivers) to meet and come together **6** to bring into contact: *join hands* **7 join forces** to combine efforts with someone ▷ *n* **8** a place where two things are joined together ▷ See also **join in, join up** [Latin *jungere* to yoke]

joined-up *adj* integrated by an overall strategy: *joined-up government*

j

joiner *n* a person whose job is making finished woodwork, such as window frames and stairs

joinery *n* the skill or work of a joiner

join in *vb* to take part in (an activity)

joint *adj* **1** shared by or belonging to two or more parties: *the two countries have issued a joint statement* ▷ *n* **2** *anatomy* the junction between two or more bones: *a hip joint* **3** a junction of two or more parts or objects: *a mortar joint* **4** a piece of meat suitable for roasting **5** *slang* a building or place of entertainment: *fast-food joints* **6** *slang* a cannabis cigarette **7 out of joint** **A** *informal* out of order or out of keeping: *they find their routine lives out of joint with their training* **B** (of a bone) knocked out of its normal position **8 put someone's nose out of joint** See **nose** (sense 10) ▷ *vb* **9** to provide a joint or joints **10** to cut or divide (meat) into joints **jointed** *adj* **jointly** *adv*

joint-stock company *n Brit* a business firm whose capital is owned jointly by shareholders

join up *vb* to become a member of a military organization

joist *n* a beam made of timber, steel, or concrete, used as a support in the construction of floors and roofs [Old French *giste*]

jojoba (hoe-**hoe**-ba) *n* a shrub whose seeds contain an oil used in cosmetics [Mexican Spanish]

joke *n* **1** something that is said or done to amuse people **2** someone or something that is ridiculous: *the country's inexperienced leaders are regarded as something of a joke* **3 no joke** *informal* a serious or difficult matter: *getting over mountain passes at ten thousand feet is no joke* ▷ *vb* **joking, joked** **4** to say or do something to amuse people [Latin *jocus*] **jokey** *adj* **jokingly** *adv*

joker *n* **1** a person who jokes a lot **2** *slang* a person regarded without respect: *waiting for the next jokers to sign up* **3** an extra playing card in a pack, which can replace any other card in some games **4** *Austral & NZ informal* a chap

jol (joll) *S African slang* ▷ *n* **1** a party ▷ *vb* **jolling, jolled** **2** to have a good time [Dutch]

jollification *n* a merry festivity

jollity *n* the condition of being jolly

jolly *adj* **-lier, -liest** **1** full of good humour **2** involving a lot of fun: *big jolly birthday parties* ▷ *adv* **3** *Brit informal* very: *I'm going to have a jolly good try* ▷ *vb* **-lies, -lying, -lied** **4 jolly along** *informal* to try to keep (someone) cheerful by flattery or cheerful chat [Old French *jolif*]

Jolly Roger *n* the traditional pirate flag, depicting a white skull and crossbones on a black background

jolt *n* **1** a severe shock **2** a sudden violent movement ▷ *vb* **3** to surprise or shock: *he was momentarily jolted by the news* **4** to bump against (someone or something) with a sudden violent movement **5** to move in a jerking manner [origin unknown]

Jonah *n* a person believed to bring bad luck to those around him or her [after *Jonah* in the Bible]

jonquil *n* a narcissus with sweet-smelling yellow or white flowers [French *jonquille*]

Jordanian *adj* **1** of Jordan ▷ *n* **2** a person from Jordan

josh *vb slang* to joke or tease [origin unknown]

joss stick *n* a stick of incense, giving off a sweet smell when burnt [*joss* (a Chinese idol) from Portuguese *deos* god]

jostle *vb* **-tling, -tled** **1** to bump or push roughly: *television crews filming the scene were jostled by police* **2** to compete with someone: *jostling for power* [Old French *jouster* to joust]

jot *vb* **jotting, jotted** **1 jot down** to write a brief note of: *quickly jot down the answers to these questions* ▷ *n* **2** the least bit: *it makes not one jot of difference* [Greek *iōta* iota, smallest letter]

jotter *n* a small notebook

jottings *pl n* notes jotted down

joual (zhwahl) *n* a nonstandard variety of Canadian French [French]

joule (jool) *n physics* the SI unit of work or energy [after J. P. *Joule*, physicist]

journal *n* **1** a newspaper or magazine **2** a daily record of events [Latin *diurnalis* daily]

journalese *n* a superficial style of writing regarded as typical of newspapers and magazines

journalism *n* the profession of collecting, writing, and publishing news through newspapers and magazines or by radio, television, and other media

journalist *n* a person who writes or edits news items for a newspaper or magazine or for radio, television, or other media **journalistic** *adj*

journey *n* **1** the process of travelling from one place to another **2** the time taken or distance travelled on a journey ▷ *vb* **3** to make a journey [Old French *journee* a day, a day's travelling]

journeyman *n, pl* **-men** a qualified craftsman who works for an employer [*journey* (in obsolete sense: a day's work)]

joust *history* ▷ *n* **1** a combat with lances between two mounted knights ▷ *vb* **2** to take part in such a tournament [Old French *jouster*]

Jove *n* **1** Jupiter (the god) **2 by Jove** *old-fashioned* an exclamation of surprise or for emphasis

jovial *adj* happy and cheerful [Latin *jovialis* of (the planet) Jupiter] **joviality** *n* **jovially** *adv*
jowl[1] *n* **1** the lower jaw **2 cheek by jowl** See **cheek** (sense 4) **3 jowls** cheeks [Old English *ceafl* jaw] **jowled** *adj*
jowl[2] *n* fatty flesh hanging from the lower jaw [Old English *ceole* throat]
joy *n* **1** deep happiness and contentment **2** something that brings deep happiness: *a thing of beauty is a joy for ever* **3** *informal* success or satisfaction: *we checked ports and airports without any joy* [Latin *gaudium*]
joyful *adj* feeling or bringing great joy: *joyful crowds; a joyful event* **joyfully** *adv*
joyless *adj* feeling or bringing no joy
joyous *adj* extremely happy and enthusiastic **joyously** *adv*
joyride *n* a drive in a car one has stolen **joyriding** *n* **joyrider** *n*
joystick *n* the control lever of an aircraft or a computer
JP (in Britain) Justice of the Peace
JPEG (jay-peg) *n computers* **A** a standard compressed file format used for pictures **B** a picture held in this file format
Jr Junior
JSA jobseeker's allowance: in Britain, a payment made to unemployed people
jube *n Austral & NZ informal* same as **jujube**
jubilant *adj* feeling great joy [Latin *jubilare* to give a joyful cry] **jubilantly** *adv*
jubilation *n* a feeling of great joy and celebration
jubilee *n* a special anniversary, esp. a 25th (**silver jubilee**) or 50th one (**golden jubilee**) [Old French *jubile*, ultimately from Hebrew *yōbhēl* ram's horn, used for proclamation]
Judaic *adj* of Jews or Judaism
Judaism *n* the religion of the Jews, based on the Old Testament and the Talmud
Judas *n* a person who betrays a friend [after *Judas* Iscariot in the Bible]
judder *vb informal, chiefly Brit* to shake or vibrate violently: *the van juddered before it moved away* [probably blend of *jar* (jolt) + *shudder*]
judder bar *n NZ* a raised strip across a road designed to slow down vehicles
judge *n* **1** a public official with authority to hear cases and pass sentences in a court of law **2** a person appointed to determine the result of a competition **3** a person whose opinion on a particular subject is usually reliable: *a fine judge of character* ▷ *vb* **judging, judged 4** to determine the result of (a competition) **5** to appraise critically: *she hopes people judge her on her work rather than her appearance* **6** to decide (something) after inquiry: *we use a means test to judge the most needy cases* **7** to believe or consider: *doctors judged that the benefits of such treatment outweighed the risk* [Latin *judex*]
judgment *or* **judgement** *n* **1** a decision formed after careful consideration: *the editorials reserve their judgment about the new political plan* **2** the verdict pronounced by a court of law **3** the ability to make critical distinctions and achieve a balanced viewpoint: *their judgment was unsound on foreign and defence issues* **4** the formal decision of the judge of a competition **5 against one's better judgment** contrary to what one thinks is sensible: *against my better judgment, I applied to study law* **6 pass judgment** to give one's opinion, usually a critical one, on a matter
judgmental *or* **judgemental** *adj* making judgments, esp. critical ones, about other people's conduct
Judgment Day *n Christianity* the occasion of the Last Judgment by God at the end of the world
judicial *adj* **1** of judges or the administration of justice **2** showing or using good judgment: *judicial self-restraint* [Latin *judicium* judgment] **judicially** *adv*
judiciary *n* the branch of the central authority in a country that administers justice
judicious *adj* having or showing good judgment: *the judicious use of herbal remedies* **judiciously** *adv*
judo *n* a sport derived from jujitsu, in which the two opponents try to throw or force each other on to the ground [Japanese *jū* gentleness + *dō* way]
jug *n* a container with a handle and a small spout, used for holding and pouring liquids [origin unknown]
jugged hare *n* hare stewed in an earthenware pot
juggernaut *n* **1** *Brit* a very large heavy lorry **2** any terrible force that demands complete self-sacrifice [Hindi *Jagannath* lord of the world]
juggle *vb* **-gling, -gled 1** to throw and catch several objects continuously so that most are in the air at the same time **2** to keep (several activities) in progress at the same time: *women who are adept at juggling priorities* **3** to manipulate (facts or figures) to suit one's purpose [Old French *jogler* to perform as a jester] **juggler** *n*
jugular *n* a large vein in the neck that carries blood to the heart from the head. Also called: **jugular vein** [Latin *jugulum* throat]
juice *n* **1** a drink made from the liquid part of a fruit or vegetable: *grapefruit juice* **2** *informal* **A** petrol **B** electricity **3 juices A** the fluids in a person's or animal's body: *digestive juices* **B** the liquid that comes out of meat when it is cooked [Old French *jus*]
juicy *adj* **juicier, juiciest 1** full of juice **2** *informal* interesting and exciting: *juicy details*
jujitsu *n* the traditional Japanese system of unarmed self-defence [Japanese *jū* gentleness + *jutsu* art]
juju *n* **1** a magic charm or fetish used by some tribes in W Africa **2** the power associated with a juju [probably from W African *djudju* evil spirit, fetish]
jujube *n* a chewy sweet made of flavoured gelatine [Medieval Latin *jujuba*]
jukebox *n* a machine that plays music when a payment is made [*juke* (from a Black American language) bawdy]
jukskei *n S African* a game in which a peg is thrown over a fixed distance at a stake fixed into the ground [Afrikaans *juk* yoke + *skei* pin]
Jul. July
julep *n* a sweet alcoholic drink, usually garnished with sprigs of mint
Julian calendar *n* the calendar introduced by Julius Caesar, in which leap years occur every fourth year and in every centenary year

julienne *adj* **1** (of vegetables or meat) cut into thin shreds ▷ *n* **2** a clear soup containing thinly shredded vegetables [French]

July *n, pl* **-lies** the seventh month of the year [after *Julius* Caesar]

jumble *n* **1** a disordered mass or state **2** articles donated for a jumble sale ▷ *vb* **-bling, -bled 3** to mix up [origin unknown]

jumble sale *n* a sale, usually of second-hand articles, often in aid of charity

jumbo *adj Brit, Austral & NZ informal* very large: *jumbo prawns* [after a famous elephant exhibited by P. T. Barnum]

jumbuck *n Austral old-fashioned slang* sheep [from a native Australian language]

jump *vb* **1** to move suddenly up into the air by using the muscles in the legs and feet **2** to move quickly: *he jumps on a No. 6 bus* **3** to jerk with astonishment or shock: *he jumped when he heard a loud noise* **4** (of prices) to rise suddenly or abruptly **5** to change quickly from one subject to another: *any other comments before I jump on to the next section?* **6** *informal* to attack without warning: *the officer was jumped by three prisoners who broke his jaw* **7** **jump down someone's throat** *informal* to speak sharply to someone **8** **jump the gun** See **gun** (sense 3) **9** **jump the queue** **A** to take a place in a queue ahead of people who are already queuing **B** to have an unfair advantage over other people: *squatters should not be able to jump the queue for housing* **10** **jump to it** *informal* to begin doing something immediately ▷ *n* **11** the act or an instance of jumping **12** *sport* any of several contests that involve jumping: *the long jump* **13** a sudden rise: *a 78% jump in taxable profits* **14** a sudden change from one subject to another: *stunning jumps from thought to thought* **15** a step or degree: *one jump ahead of the competition* **16** **take a running jump** *informal* a contemptuous expression of dismissal ▷ See also **jump at, jump on** [probably imitative]

jump at *vb* to accept eagerly: *I jumped at the chance to return to English county cricket*

jumped-up *adj informal* having suddenly risen in significance and appearing arrogant: *a jumped-up bunch of ex-student-leaders*

jumper[1] *n* **1** *Brit & Austral* a knitted garment covering the upper part of the body **2** *US & Canad* a pinafore dress [obsolete *jump* man's loose jacket]

jumper[2] *n* a person or animal that jumps

jump jet *n informal* a fixed-wing jet aircraft that can land and take off vertically

jump leads *pl n* two heavy cables used to start a motor vehicle with a flat battery by connecting the flat battery to the battery of another vehicle

jump on *vb informal* to make a sudden physical or verbal attack on: *the press really jumped on him*

jump-start *vb* **1** to start the engine of (a motor vehicle) by pushing or rolling it and then engaging the gears ▷ *n* **2** the act of starting a motor vehicle in this way

jump suit *n* a one-piece garment combining trousers and top

jumpy *adj* **jumpier, jumpiest** nervous or apprehensive

Jun. **1** June **2** Junior

junction *n* a place where roads or railway lines meet, link, or cross each other [Latin *junctio* a joining]

juncture *n* a point in time, esp. a critical one: *trade has been halted at a crucial juncture*

June *n* the sixth month of the year [probably from Latin *Junius* of the goddess Juno]

jungle *n* **1** a forest area in a hot country with luxuriant vegetation **2** a confused or confusing situation: *the administrative jungle* **3** a situation where there is an intense struggle for survival: *the economic jungle* [Hindi *jangal*]

junior *adj* **1** lower in rank or position: *junior officers* **2** younger: *world junior champion* **3** (in England and Wales) of school children between the ages of 7 and 11 approximately **4** *US* of the third year of a four-year course at college or high school ▷ *n* **5** a person holding a low rank or position **6** a person who is younger than another person: *the man she is to marry is 20 years her junior* **7** (in England and Wales) a junior school child **8** *US* a junior student [Latin: younger]

Junior *adj* the younger of two: usually used after a name to distinguish between two people of the same name: *Harry Connick Junior*

junior lightweight *n* a professional boxer weighing up to 130 pounds (59 kg)

juniper *n* an evergreen shrub with purple berries which are used to make gin [Latin *juniperus*]

junk[1] *n* **1** old or unwanted objects **2** *informal* rubbish: *the sheer junk written about astrology* **3** *slang* narcotic drugs, esp. heroin [Middle English *jonke* old useless rope]

junk[2] *n* a Chinese sailing boat with a flat bottom and square sails [Portuguese *junco*, from Javanese *jon*]

junk bond *n finance* a security that offers a high yield but often involves a high risk of default

junket *n* **1** an excursion made by a public official and paid for out of public funds **2** a sweet dessert made of flavoured milk set with rennet **3** a feast [Middle English: rush basket, hence custard served on rushes] **junketing** *n*

junk food *n* food with a low nutritional value

junkie *n informal* a drug addict

junk mail *n* unsolicited mail advertising goods or services

Juno *n* the queen of the Roman gods

junta *n* a group of military officers holding the power in a country after a revolution [Spanish: council]

Jupiter *n* **1** the king of the Roman gods **2** the largest planet

Jurassic *adj geol* of the geological period about 180 million years ago, during which dinosaurs flourished [after the *Jura* (Mountains) in W central Europe]

juridical *adj* of law or the administration of justice [Latin *jus* law + *dicere* to say]

jurisdiction *n* **1** the right or power to administer justice and to apply laws **2** the exercise or extent of such a right or power **3** authority in general: *under the jurisdiction of the referee* [Latin *jurisdictio*]

jurisprudence *n* the science or philosophy of law [Latin *juris prudentia*]

jurist *n* a person who is an expert on law [French *juriste*]

juror *n* a member of a jury [Old French *jurer* to take an oath]

jury *n, pl* **-ries 1** a group of, usually, twelve people, sworn to deliver a true verdict according to the evidence upon a case presented in a court of law **2** a group of people appointed to judge a competition [Old French *jurer* to swear]

jury box *n* an enclosure where the jury sits in a court of law

jury-rigged *adj chiefly naut* set up in a makeshift manner [origin unknown]

just *adv* **1** very recently: *the results have just been published* **2** at this very instant or in the very near future: *news is just coming in of a nuclear explosion* **3** no more than; only: *nothing fancy, just solid German fare* **4** exactly: *just the opposite* **5** barely: *the swimmers arrived just in time for the opening ceremony* **6 just about** practically or virtually: *just about everyone* **7 just about to** very soon going to: *it was just about to explode* **8 just a moment** *or* **second** *or* **minute** an expression requesting someone to wait for a short time **9 just now A** a short time ago: *as you said just now* **B** at the present time: *he needs all the support he can get just now* **C** *S African informal* in a little while **10 just so** arranged with precision: *a cottage with the gardens and rooms all just so* ▷ *adj* **11** fair and right: *a just war* [Latin *jus* justice]
justly *adv* **justness** *n*

> **USAGE** The use of *just* with *exactly* (*it's just exactly what they want*) is redundant and should be avoided: *it's exactly what they want*.

justice *n* **1** the quality of being just **2** the administration of law according to prescribed and accepted principles **3** a judge **4 bring to justice** to capture, try, and punish (a criminal) **5 do justice to** to show to full advantage: *the choir was not able to do justice to Handel's music* [Latin *justitia*]

justice of the peace *n* **1** (in Britain) a magistrate who is authorized to act as a judge in a local court of law **2** (in New Zealand) a person authorized to act in a limited judicial capacity

justifiable *adj* having a good cause or reason: *I reacted with justifiable indignation* **justifiably** *adv*

justify *vb* **-fies, -fying, -fied 1** to prove (something) to be just or valid: *the idea of the end justifying the means* **2** to defend (an action) as being warranted: *an essay justifying his conversion to Catholicism* **3** to arrange (text) when typing or printing so that both margins are straight [Latin *justificare*] **justification** *n*

jute *n* a fibre that comes from the bark of an Asian plant, used in making rope, sacks, and mats [Bengali *jhuto*]

jut out *vb* **jutting, jutted** to stick out [variant of JET[1]]

juvenile *adj* **1** young; not fully adult: *juvenile offenders* **2** of or for young people: *juvenile court* **3** immature in behaviour ▷ *n* **4** a young person [Latin *juvenilis*]

juvenile delinquent *n* a young person who is guilty of a crime **juvenile delinquency** *n*

juvenilia *pl n* works produced in an artist's youth

juxtapose *vb* **-posing, -posed** to place (two objects or ideas) close together or side by side [Latin *juxta* next to + POSITION] **juxtaposition** *n*

Kk

K **1** kelvin(s) **2** *chess* king **3** *chem* potassium **4** one thousand **5** *computers* a unit of 1024 words, bits, or bytes
kabaddi *n* a game in which players try to touch opposing players but avoid being captured by them
kabloona *n* a person who is not of Inuit ancestry, esp. a white person
Kaddish *n, pl* **Kaddishim** *Judaism* an ancient Jewish liturgical prayer, recited esp. by mourners [Aramaic *qaddīsh* holy]
Kaffir (**kaf**-fer) *n S African taboo, offensive* a Black African [Arabic *kāfir* infidel]
kaftan *or* **caftan** *n* **1** a long loose garment worn in the Middle East **2** a dress resembling this [Turkish *qaftān*]
k
kahawai *n* a food and game fish of New Zealand [Māori]
kai *n NZ informal* food [Māori]
kail *n* same as **kale**
kaiser (**kize**-er) *n history* a German or Austro-Hungarian emperor [German, from Latin *Caesar* emperor]
kak (**kuck**) *n S African taboo* **1** faeces **2** rubbish [Afrikaans]
kaka *n* a parrot of New Zealand [Māori]
kakapo *n, pl* **-pos** a ground-living nocturnal New Zealand parrot that resembles an owl [Māori]
Kalashnikov *n* a Russian-made automatic rifle [after M *Kalashnikov*, its designer]
kale *n* a type of cabbage with crinkled leaves [Old English *cāl*]
kaleidoscope *n* **1** a tube-shaped toy lined with angled mirrors and containing loose pieces of coloured paper that form intricate patterns when viewed through a hole in the end **2** any complicated or rapidly changing set of colours, circumstances, etc.: *a kaleidoscope of shifting political groups and alliances* [Greek *kalos* beautiful + *eidos* form + *skopein* to look at] **kaleidoscopic** *adj*
kalends *pl n* same as **calends**
kaleyard *n Scot* a vegetable garden [literally: cabbage garden]
Kamasutra (kah-ma-**soo**-tra) *n* **the Kamasutra** an ancient Hindu text on sex [Sanskrit *kāma* love + *sūtra* thread, rule]
kamik *n* a traditional Inuit boot made of caribou hide or sealskin
kamikaze (kam-mee-**kah**-zee) *n* **1** (in World War II) a Japanese pilot who performed a suicidal mission ▹ *adj* **2** (of an action) undertaken in the knowledge that it will result in the death or injury of the person performing it: *a kamikaze attack* [Japanese *kami* divine + *kaze* wind]
Kamloops trout *n* a bright silvery rainbow trout common in British Columbia, Canada
kangaroo *n, pl* **-roos** a large Australian marsupial with powerful hind legs used for leaping [probably Aboriginal]
kangaroo court *n* an unofficial court set up by a group to discipline its members
kangaroo paw *n* an Australian plant with green-and-red flowers
kaolin *n* a fine white clay used in making porcelain and in some medicines [*Kaoling*, Chinese mountain where supplies for Europe were first obtained]
kapa haka *n NZ* the traditional Māori performing arts, often performed competitively [Māori]
ka pai *interj NZ* good! well done! [Māori]
kapok *n* a fluffy fibre from a tropical tree, used for stuffing pillows and padding sleeping bags [Malay]
kaput (kap-**poot**) *adj informal* ruined or broken: *the chronometer, incidentally, is kaput* [German *kaputt*]
karakul *n* **1** a sheep of central Asia, the lambs of which have soft curled dark hair **2** the fur prepared from these lambs [Russian]
karaoke *n* a form of entertainment in which members of the public sing well-known songs over a prerecorded backing tape [Japanese *kara* empty + *ōkesutora* orchestra]
karate *n* a Japanese system of unarmed combat, in which punches, chops, and kicks are made with the hands, feet, elbows, and legs [Japanese: empty hand]
karma *n Hinduism & Buddhism* a person's actions affecting his or her fate in the next incarnation [Sanskrit: action, effect]
karoo *or* **karroo** *n, pl* **-roos** *S African* an arid semidesert plateau of Southern Africa [Khoikhoi *karo* dry]
kaross (ka-**ross**) *n S African* a blanket made of animal skins sewn together [Khoikhoi *karos* animal-skin blanket]
karri *n, pl* **-ris** **1** an Australian eucalypt **2** its wood, used for building
kart *n* same as **go-kart**
kasbah *n* same as **casbah**
katipo *n, pl* **-pos** a small venomous New Zealand spider, commonly black with a red or orange stripe on the abdomen [Māori]
katydid *n* a large green grasshopper of North America [imitative]
kauri *n* a large New Zealand conifer grown for its valuable wood and resin [Māori]
kayak *n* **1** an Inuit canoe-like boat consisting of a frame covered with animal skins **2** a fibreglass or canvas-covered canoe of similar design [Inuktitut]
kazoo *n, pl* **-zoos** a cigar-shaped metal musical instrument that produces a buzzing sound when the player hums into it [probably imitative]
KBE (in Britain) Knight (Commander of the Order) of the British Empire
kbps *computers* kilobits per second
kbyte *computers* kilobyte
kcal kilocalorie
KCB (in Britain) Knight Commander of the Bath
kea *n* a large brown-green parrot of New Zealand [Māori]
kebab *n* a dish consisting of small pieces of meat and vegetables, usually threaded onto skewers and grilled [Arabic *kabāb* roast meat]

kecks *or* **keks** *pl n N English dialect* trousers [from dialect *kicks* breeches]

kedge *naut* ▹ *vb* **kedging, kedged 1** to move (a ship) along by hauling in on the cable of a light anchor ▹ *n* **2** a light anchor used for kedging [Middle English *caggen* to fasten]

kedgeree *n chiefly Brit* a dish consisting of rice, fish, and eggs [Hindi *khicarī*]

keek *vb, n Scot* same as **peep**[1] [probably from Middle Dutch *kīken* to look]

keel *n* **1** one of the main lengthways steel or timber pieces along the base of a ship, to which the frames are fastened **2 on an even keel** working or progressing smoothly without any sudden changes [Old Norse *kjölr*]

keelhaul *vb* **1** to reprimand (someone) harshly **2** *history* to drag (someone) under the keel of a ship as a punishment

keel over *vb* **1** (of an object) to turn upside down **2** *informal* (of a person) to collapse suddenly

keelson *or* **kelson** *n* a lengthways beam fastened to the keel of a ship for strength [probably from Low German *kielswin* keel swine]

keen[1] *adj* **1** eager or enthusiastic: *a keen gardener* **2** intense or strong: *a keen interest in environmental issues* **3** intelligent, quick, and perceptive: *a keen sense of humour* **4** (of sight, smell, or hearing) capable of recognizing fine distinctions **5** (of a knife or blade) having a sharp cutting edge **6** very strong and cold: *a keen wind* **7** very competitive: *keen prices* **8 keen on** fond of; devoted to: *he is very keen on sport* [Old English *cēne*] **keenly** *adv* **keenness** *n*

keen[2] *vb* **1** to lament the dead ▹ *n* **2** a lament for the dead [Irish Gaelic *caoine*]

keep *vb* **keeping, kept 1** to have or retain possession of (something) **2** to have temporary charge of: *he'd kept my broken beads in his pocket for me all evening* **3** to store in a customary place: *I keep it at the back of the drawer with my journal* **4** to remain or cause (someone or something) to remain in a specified state or condition: *keep still* **5** to continue or cause (someone) to continue: *keep going straight on* **6** to stay (in, on, or at a place or position): *keep to the paths* **7** to have as part of normal stock: *they keep a small stock of first-class German wines* **8** to support (someone) financially **9** to detain (someone) **10** to be faithful to (something): *to keep a promise* **11** (of food) to stay in good condition for a certain time: *fish doesn't keep very well* **12** to observe (a religious festival) with rites or ceremonies **13** to maintain by writing regular records in: *I keep a nature diary in my spare time* **14** to look after or maintain for use, pleasure, or profit: *an old man who kept goats and cows* **15** to associate with: *she has started keeping bad company* **16 how are you keeping?** are you well? **17 keep in with** to stay friendly with a person as they may be useful to one ▹ *n* **18** the cost of food and other everyday expenses: *I have to earn my keep* **19** the main tower within the walls of a medieval castle or fortress **20 for keeps** *informal* permanently ▹ See also **keep at, keep away** *etc.* [Old English *cēpan* to observe]

keep at *vb* **1** to persist in (an activity) **2** to compel (a person) to continue doing (a task)

keep away *vb* (often foll. by *from*) to prevent (someone) from going (somewhere)

keep back *vb* to refuse to reveal (something)

keep down *vb* **1** to hold (a group of people) under control **2** to cause (numbers or costs) not to increase **3** to lie low **4** to cause (food) to stay in the stomach; not vomit

keeper *n* **1** a person in charge of animals in a zoo **2** a person in charge of a museum, collection, or section of a museum **3** a person who supervises a person or thing: *the self-appointed keeper of the village conscience* **4** short for **gamekeeper, goalkeeper** or **wicketkeeper**

keep fit *n* exercises designed to promote physical fitness if performed regularly

keep from *vb* **1** to restrain (oneself or someone else) from (doing something) **2** to preserve or protect (someone) from (something): *this will keep you from falling asleep*

keeping *n* **1 in keeping with** suitable or appropriate to or for **2 out of keeping with** unsuitable or inappropriate to or for

keep off *vb* **1** to stay or cause (someone) to stay at a distance (from) **2** to avoid or cause to avoid (something): *to keep off alcohol; to keep babies off sugar* **3** to avoid or cause (someone) to avoid (a topic)

keep on *vb* **1** to persist in (doing something): *petrol consumption keeps on rising* **2** to continue to employ: *a skeleton staff of 20 is being kept on* **3 keep on about** to persist in talking about **4 keep on at** to nag (a person)

keep out *vb* **1** to remain or cause (someone) to remain outside **2 keep out of A** to cause (someone) to remain unexposed to (an unpleasant situation) **B** to avoid: *to keep out of trouble*

keepsake *n* a gift kept in memory of the giver

keep to *vb* **1** to do exactly what was expected of one: *he kept to his normal schedule* **2** to be confined to: *she kept to her bed until her flu had cleared up* **3 keep oneself to oneself** to avoid the company of others **4 keep to oneself A** to avoid the company of others **B** to avoid giving away (information)

keep up *vb* **1** to maintain at the present level **2** to maintain in good condition **3 keep up with A** to maintain a pace set by (someone) **B** to remain informed about: *he liked to think he kept up with current musical trends* **C** to remain in contact with (someone) **4 keep up with the Joneses** *informal* to compete with one's friends or neighbours in material possessions

keg *n* a small barrel in which beer is transported and stored [Scandinavian]

kelp *n* a large brown seaweed rich in iodine and potash [origin unknown]

kelpie *n* **1** (in Scottish folklore) a water spirit in the form of a horse **2** an Australian sheepdog with a smooth coat and upright ears [origin unknown]

kelson *n* same as **keelson**

kelt *n* a salmon that has recently spawned [origin unknown]

Kelt *n* same as **Celt**

kelvin *n physics* the basic SI unit of thermodynamic temperature [after W. T. *Kelvin*, physicist]

Kelvin scale *n physics* a thermodynamic temperature scale starting at absolute zero

ken *n* **1 beyond one's ken** beyond one's range of knowledge ▹ *vb* **kenning, kenned** *or* **kent 2** *Scot & N English dialect* to know [Old English *cennan*]
kendo *n* the Japanese sport of fencing using wooden staves [Japanese]
kennel *n* **1** a hutlike shelter for a dog **2 kennels** a place where dogs are bred, trained, or boarded ▹ *vb* **-nelling, -nelled** *or US* **-neling, -neled 3** to keep (a dog) in a kennel [Latin *canis* dog]
Kenyan *adj* **1** from Kenya ▹ *n* **2** a person from Kenya
kepi *n* a French military cap with a flat top and a horizontal peak [French]
kept *vb* **1** the past of **keep 2 kept woman** *or* **man** a person who is financially supported by a sexual partner
keratin *n* a fibrous protein found in the hair and nails
kerb *or US & Canad* **curb** *n* a line of stone or concrete forming an edge between a pavement and a roadway [Old French *courbe* bent]
kerb crawling *n Brit* the act of driving slowly beside a kerb to pick up a prostitute
kerb crawler *n*
kerbstone *or US & Canad* **curbstone** *n* one of a series of stones that form a kerb
kerchief *n* a piece of cloth worn over the head or round the neck [Old French *cuevrechef*]
kerfuffle *n informal* a noisy and disorderly incident [Scots *curfuffle, carfuffle*]
kermes (**kur**-meez) *n* the dried bodies of female scale insects, used as a red dyestuff [Arabic *qirmiz*]
kernel *n* **1** the edible seed of a nut or fruit within the shell or stone **2** the grain of a cereal, such as wheat, consisting of the seed in a hard husk **3** the central or essential part of something: *there is a kernel of truth in these remarks* [Old English *cyrnel* a little seed]
kerosene *n US, Canad, Austral & NZ* same as **paraffin** (sense 1) [Greek *kēros* wax]
Kerry *n, pl* **-ries** a small black breed of dairy cattle, originally from Ireland [after *Kerry*, county in SW Ireland]
kestrel *n* a small falcon that feeds on small animals such as mice [Old French *cresserele*]
ketch *n* a two-masted sailing ship [Middle English *cache*]
ketchup *n* a thick cold sauce, usually made of tomatoes [Chinese *kōetsiap* brine of pickled fish]
ketone (**kee**-tone) *n chem* any of a class of compounds with the general formula R´COR, where R and R´ are alkyl or aryl groups [German *Keton*, from *Aketon* acetone]
kettle *n* **1** a metal container with a handle and spout, for boiling water **2** any of various metal containers for heating liquid, cooking, etc. **3 a different kettle of fish** a different matter entirely **4 a fine kettle of fish** a difficult or awkward situation ▹ *vb* **-tling, -tled 5** (of police) to force (demonstrators) into an enclosed space [Old Norse *ketill*]
kettledrum *n* a large bowl-shaped metal drum that can be tuned to play specific notes
key[1] *n* **1** a specially shaped metal instrument for moving the bolt of a lock so as to lock or unlock a door, suitcase, etc. **2** an instrument that is turned to operate a valve, clock winding mechanism, etc. **3** any of a set of levers pressed to operate a computer, typewriter, or musical keyboard instrument **4** a scale of musical notes that starts at one specific note **5** something that is crucial in providing an explanation or interpretation **6** a means of achieving a desired end: *education is the key to success in most walks of life today* **7** a list of explanations of symbols, codes, or abbreviations **8** pitch: *he spoke in a low key* ▹ *adj* **9** of great importance: *key prosecution witnesses have been giving evidence* ▹ *vb* **10** to harmonize with: *training and educational programmes uniquely keyed for local needs* **11** to adjust or fasten (something) with a key or some similar device **12** to enter (information or instructions) into a computer by means of a keyboard ▹ See also **key in** [Old English *cǣg*]
key[2] *n* same as **cay**
keyboard *n* **1** a set of keys on a computer, typewriter, or piano **2** a musical instrument played using a keyboard
key card *n* an electronic card that is used for unlocking a door
keyed up *adj* very excited or nervous
key grip *n* the person in charge of moving and setting up camera tracks and scenery in a film or television studio
keyhole *n* an opening for inserting a key into a lock
keyhole surgery *n* surgery carried out using very small instruments, performed through a narrow hole cut in the body rather than through a major incision
key in *vb* to enter (information or instructions) into a computer by means of a keyboard
key money *n Brit* a sum of money required from a new tenant of a house or flat before he or she moves in
Keynesian (**kane**-zee-an) *adj* of the economic theories of J M Keynes, who argued that governments should fund public works to maintain full employment, accepting if necessary the consequence of inflation
keynote *n* **1** a central or dominant idea in a speech or literary work **2** the note on which a scale or key is based ▹ *adj* **3** central or dominating: *his keynote speech to the party conference*
keypad *n* a small panel with a set of buttons for operating an electronic device
keyring *n* a metal ring, often decorative, for keeping keys on
key signature *n music* a group of sharps or flats at the beginning of each stave line to indicate the key
keystone *n* **1** the most important part of a process, organization, etc.: *the keystone of the government's economic policy* **2** the central stone at the top of an arch
keyword *n* a word or phrase that a computer will search for in order to locate the information or file that the computer user has requested
key worker *n chiefly Brit* **1** a social worker, mental health worker, or nursery nurse assigned to an individual case, patient, or child **2** (in Britain) a worker in a profession considered by the government to be essential to society

kg kilogram

KG (in Britain) Knight of the Order of the Garter

KGB (formerly) the Soviet secret police [Russian *Komitet Gosudarstvennoi Bezopasnosti* State Security Committee]

khaki *adj* **1** dull yellowish-brown ▷ *n* **2** a hard-wearing fabric of this colour, used for military uniforms [Urdu, from Persian: dusty]

khan *n* a title of respect in Afghanistan and central Asia [Turkish]

Khoikhoi *n* **1** a race of indigenous people of South Africa which is now almost extinct **2** a member of this race **3** the language of this race

kHz kilohertz

kia ora *interj* NZ a Māori greeting [Māori]

kibbutz *n, pl* **kibbutzim** a farm, factory, or other workplace in Israel, owned and run communally by its members [Modern Hebrew *qibbūs* gathering]

kibosh *n* **put the kibosh on** *slang* to put a stop to [origin unknown]

kick *vb* **1** to drive, push, or hit with the foot or feet **2** to strike out with the feet, as in swimming **3** to raise a leg high, as in dancing **4** *rugby* to score (a conversion, drop kick, or penalty) with a kick: *he kicked his third penalty* **5** (of a firearm) to recoil when fired **6** *informal* to object or resist: *school uniforms give children something to kick against* **7** *informal* to free oneself of (an addiction): *smokers who want to kick the habit* **8** **alive and kicking** *informal* active and in good health **9** **kick someone upstairs** to promote someone to a higher but effectively powerless position ▷ *n* **10** a thrust or blow with the foot **11** any of certain rhythmic leg movements used in swimming **12** the recoil of a firearm **13** *informal* an exciting effect: *I always get a kick out of decorating the Christmas cake* **14** *informal* the intoxicating effect of an alcoholic drink: *a cocktail with a kick in it* **15** **kick in the teeth** *slang* a humiliating rebuff ▷ See also **kick about**, **kick in** *etc.* [Middle English *kiken*]

kick about *or* **kick around** *vb informal* **1** to treat (someone) harshly **2** to discuss (ideas) informally **3** to lie neglected or forgotten: *there's a copy of that book kicking about somewhere*

kickback *n* **1** part of an income paid to a person in return for an opportunity to make a profit, esp. in an illegal arrangement **2** a strong reaction

kick in *vb* to start or become activated

kick off *vb* **1** to start play in a game of football by kicking the ball from the centre of the field **2** *informal* to commence (a discussion, event, etc.) ▷ *n* **kick-off** **3** **A** the kick that officially starts a game of football **B** the time when the first kick is due to take place **4** *informal* the time when an event is due to begin

kick out *vb informal* to dismiss (someone) or throw (someone) out forcefully

kickstand *n* a short metal bar on a motorcycle, which when kicked into a vertical position holds the cycle upright when stationary

kick-start *n* **1** Also: **kick-starter** a pedal on a motorcycle that is kicked downwards to start the engine **2** an action or event that reactivates something ▷ *vb* **3** to start (a motorcycle) with a kick-start **4** to do something bold or drastic in order to begin or improve the performance of something: *to kick-start the economy*

kick up *vb informal* to cause (trouble)

kid¹ *n* **1** *informal* a young person; child **2** a young goat **3** soft smooth leather made from the hide of a kid ▷ *adj* **4** younger: *my kid sister* ▷ *vb* **kidding, kidded** **5** (of a goat) to give birth to (young) [from Old Norse]

kid² *vb* **kidding, kidded** *informal* **1** to tease or deceive (someone) for fun **2** to fool (oneself) into believing something: *don't kid yourself that no-one else knows* [probably from KID¹] **kidder** *n*

kiddie *n informal* a child

kid gloves *pl n* **handle someone with kid gloves** to treat someone with great tact in order not to upset them

kidnap *vb* **-napping, -napped** *or US* **-naping, -naped** to capture and hold (a person), usually for ransom [KID¹ + obsolete *nap* to steal] **kidnapper** *or US* **-naper** *n* **kidnapping** *or US* **-naping** *n*

kidney *n* **1** either of two bean-shaped organs at the back of the abdominal cavity. They filter waste products from the blood, which are excreted as urine **2** the kidneys of certain animals used as food [origin unknown]

kidney bean *n* a reddish-brown kidney-shaped bean, edible when cooked

kidney machine *n* a machine carrying out the functions of damaged human kidneys

kidology *n informal* the practice of bluffing or deception in order to gain a psychological advantage over someone

kill *vb* **1** to cause the death of (a person or animal) **2** *informal* to cause (someone) pain or discomfort: *my feet are killing me* **3** to put an end to: *his obsession with work has killed his marriage* **4** *informal* to quash or veto: *the main opposition party tried to kill the bill* **5** *informal* to overwhelm (someone) completely with laughter, attraction, or surprise: *her jokes really kill me* **6** **kill oneself** *informal* to overexert oneself **7** **kill time** to spend time on something unimportant or trivial while waiting for something: *I'm just killing time until I can talk to the other witnesses* **8** **kill two birds with one stone** to achieve two results with one action ▷ *n* **9** the act of causing death at the end of a hunt or bullfight **10** the animal or animals killed during a hunt **11** **in at the kill** present when something comes to a dramatic end with unpleasant results for someone else [Middle English *cullen*] **killer** *n*

killer whale *n* a black-and-white toothed whale, most common in cold seas

killing *adj* **1** *informal* very tiring: *a killing pace* **2** *informal* extremely funny **3** causing death; fatal ▷ *n* **4** the act of causing death; slaying **5** **make a killing** *informal* to have a sudden financial success

killjoy *n* a person who spoils other people's pleasure

kiln *n* a large oven for burning, drying, or processing pottery, bricks, etc. [Latin *culina* kitchen]

kilo *n, pl* **kilos** short for **kilogram** or **kilometre**

kilo- *combining form* **1** denoting one thousand (10^3): *kilometre* **2** (in computers) denoting 2^{10} (1024): *kilobyte*. In computer usage, *kilo-* is restricted to sizes of storage (eg *kilobit*) when it means 1024: in

other computer contexts it retains its usual meaning of 1000 [Greek *khilioi* thousand]
kilobit *n computers* 1024 bits
kilobyte *n computers* 1024 bytes
kilocalorie *n* one thousand calories
kilocycle *n* an old word for **kilohertz**
kilogram *or* **kilogramme** *n* **1** one thousand grams **2** the basic SI unit of mass
kilohertz *n, pl* **kilohertz** one thousand hertz; one thousand cycles per second
kilojoule *n* one thousand joules
kilolitre *or US* **kiloliter** *n* a measure of volume equivalent to one thousand litres
kilometre *or US* **kilometer** *n* a unit of length equal to one thousand metres
kiloton *n* **1** one thousand tons **2** an explosive power, esp. of a nuclear weapon, equal to the power of 1000 tons of TNT
kilovolt *n* one thousand volts
kilowatt *n* one thousand watts
kilowatt-hour *n* a unit of energy equal to the work done by a power of 1000 watts in one hour
kilt *n* **1** a knee-length pleated tartan skirt-like garment, worn by men in Highland dress and by women and girls ▷ *vb* **2** to put pleats in (cloth) [Scandinavian] **kilted** *adj*
k
kimono (kim-**moan**-no) *n, pl* **-nos** **1** a loose wide-sleeved Japanese robe, fastened with a sash **2** a European dressing gown resembling this [Japanese: clothing]
kin *n* **1** a person's relatives collectively **2** See **next of kin** [Old English *cyn*]
kind¹ *adj* **1** considerate, friendly, and helpful: *a good, kind man; a few kind words* **2** cordial; courteous: *reprinted by kind permission* [Old English *gecynde* natural, native]
kind² *n* **1** a class or group having characteristics in common: *what kind of music do you like?* **2** essential nature or character: *differences of degree rather than of kind* **3** **in kind** **A** (of payment) in goods or services rather than in money **B** with something of the same sort: *the government threatened to retaliate in kind to any act of hostility* **4** **kind of** to a certain extent; loosely: *kind of hard; a kind of socialist* **5** **of a kind** of a poorer quality or standard than is wanted or expected: *a few farmers wrest subsistence of a kind from the thin topsoil* [Old English *gecynd* nature]

> **USAGE** The mixture of plural and singular constructions, although often used informally with *kind* and *sort*, should be avoided in serious writing: *children enjoy those kinds* (not *those kind*) *of stories; these sorts* (not *these sort*) *of distinctions are becoming blurred.*

kindergarten *n* a class or school for children under six years old [from German, literally: children's garden]
kind-hearted *adj* considerate and sympathetic
kindle *vb* **-dling, -dled** **1** to set (a fire) alight or (of a fire) to start to burn **2** to arouse or be aroused: *his passions were kindled as quickly as her own* [Old Norse *kynda*]
kindling *n* material for starting a fire, such as dry wood or straw
kindly *adj* **-lier, -liest** **1** having a warm-hearted and caring nature **2** pleasant or agreeable: *a kindly climate* ▷ *adv* **3** in a considerate or humane way **4** please: *will you kindly stop prattling on about it!* **5** **not take kindly to** to react unfavourably towards **kindliness** *n*
kindness *n* **1** the quality of being kind **2** a kind or helpful act
kindred *adj* **1** having similar qualities: *cholera, and other kindred diseases* **2** related by blood or marriage **3** **kindred spirit** a person with whom one has something in common ▷ *n* **4** relationship by blood or marriage **5** similarity in character **6** a person's relatives collectively [Middle English *kinred*]
kindy *or* **kindie** *n, pl* **-dies** *Austral & NZ informal* a kindergarten
kine *pl n archaic* cows or cattle [Old English *cȳna* of cows]
kinematics (kin-nim-**mat**-iks) *n physics* the study of the motion of bodies without reference to mass or force [Greek *kinēma* movement] **kinematic** *adj*
kinetic (kin-**net**-ik) *adj* relating to or caused by motion [Greek *kinein* to move] **kinetically** *adv*
kinetic art *n* art, such as sculpture, that moves or has moving parts
kinetic energy *n physics* the energy of motion of a body equal to the work it would do if it were brought to rest
kinetics *n physics* the branch of mechanics concerned with the study of bodies in motion
king *n* **1** a male ruler of a country who has inherited the throne from his parents **2** a ruler or chief: *the king of the fairies* **3** a person, animal, or thing considered as the best or most important of its kind: *the king of rock and roll* **4** a playing card with a picture of a king on it **5** a chess piece, able to move one square in any direction: the object of the game is to checkmate one's opponent's king **6** *draughts* a piece which has moved entirely across the board and been crowned and which may therefore move backwards as well as forwards [Old English *cyning*] **kingship** *n*
kingcup *n Brit* a yellow-flowered plant; marsh marigold
kingdom *n* **1** a territory or state ruled by a king or queen **2** any of the three groups into which natural objects may be divided: the animal, plant, and mineral kingdoms **3** a place or area considered to be under the total power and control of a person, organization, or thing: *the kingdom of God*
kingfisher *n* a fish-eating bird with a greenish-blue and orange plumage [originally *king's fisher*]
kingklip *n* an edible eel-like marine fish of S Africa [Afrikaans]
king-of-arms *n, pl* **kings-of-arms** a person holding the highest rank of heraldic office
kingpin *n* **1** the most important person in an organization: *a kingpin of global finance* **2** a pivot pin that provides a steering joint in a motor vehicle
king post *n building* a vertical post connecting the apex of a triangular roof truss to the tie beam
king prawn *n* a large prawn, fished commercially in Australian waters
king-size *or* **king-sized** *adj* larger than a standard size
kink *n* **1** a twist or bend in something such as a rope or hair **2** *informal* a flaw or quirk in someone's

personality ▷ *vb* **3** to form or cause to form a kink [Dutch]
kinky *adj* **kinkier, kinkiest 1** *slang* given to unusual sexual practices **2** tightly looped or curled
kinsfolk *pl n* one's family or relatives
kinship *n* **1** blood relationship **2** the state of having common characteristics
kinsman *or fem* **kinswoman** *n, pl* **-men** *or* **-women** a relation by blood or marriage
kiosk *n* a small booth from which cigarettes, newspapers, and sweets are sold [French *kiosque* bandstand, from Persian *kūshk* pavilion]
kip *Brit slang* ▷ *n* **1** sleep: *a couple of hours' kip* **2** a bed ▷ *vb* **kipping, kipped 3** to sleep or take a nap **4 kip down** to sleep in a makeshift bed [origin unknown]
kipper *n* **1** a herring that has been cleaned, salted, and smoked ▷ *vb* **2** to cure (a herring) by salting and smoking it [Old English *cypera*]
kirk *n Scot* a church [Old Norse *kirkja*]
Kirsch *or* **Kirschwasser** *n* a brandy distilled from black cherries [German *Kirschwasser* cherry water]
kismet *n* fate or destiny [Persian *qismat*]
kiss *vb* **1** to touch with the lips as an expression of love, greeting, or respect **2** to join lips with another person as an act of love or desire **3** *literary* to touch lightly: *a long high free kick that kissed the top of the crossbar* ▷ *n* **4** a caress with the lips **5** a light touch [Old English *cyssan*] **kissable** *adj*
kissagram *n Brit, Austral & NZ* a greetings service in which a person is employed to present greetings by kissing the person celebrating
kiss curl *n* a circular curl of hair pressed flat against the cheek or forehead
kisser *n slang* the mouth or face
kissing crust *n NZ* the soft end of a loaf of bread where two loaves have been separated
kiss of life *n* **the kiss of life** mouth-to-mouth resuscitation in which a person blows gently into the mouth of an unconscious person
kist *n Scot & S African* a large wooden chest
kit[1] *n* **1** a set of tools or supplies for use together or for a purpose: *a first-aid kit* **2** the container for such a set **3** a set of parts sold ready to be assembled: *a model aircraft kit* **4** a basket or box for holding fish **5** clothing and other personal effects, such as those of a soldier: *a complete set of school team kit* ▷ See also **kit out** [Middle Dutch *kitte* tankard]
kit[2] *n NZ* a flax basket [Māori *kete*]
kitbag *n* a canvas or other bag for a soldier's kit
kitchen *n* a room equipped for preparing and cooking food [Late Latin *coquina*]
kitchenette *n* a small kitchen or part of a room equipped for use as a kitchen
kitchen garden *n* a garden for growing vegetables, herbs, etc.
kitchen tea *n Austral & NZ* a party held before a wedding to which guests bring kitchen equipment as presents
kite *n* **1** a light frame covered with a thin material flown in the wind at the end of a length of string **2** a bird of prey with a long forked tail and large wings **3** a four-sided geometrical shape in which each side is equal in length to one of the sides joining it [Old English *cȳta*]
Kite mark *n Brit* the official mark in the form of a kite on articles approved by the British Standards Institution
kith *n* **kith and kin** *old-fashioned* one's friends and relations [Old English *cȳthth*]
kit out *or* **kit up** *vb* **kitting, kitted** *chiefly Brit* to provide with clothes or equipment needed for a particular activity
kitsch *n* tawdry or sentimental art or literature [from German] **kitschy** *adj*
kitten *n* **1** a young cat **2 have kittens** *informal* to react with disapproval or anxiety: *she had kittens when she discovered the price* [Old French *caton*]
kittenish *adj* lively and flirtatious
kittiwake *n* a type of seagull with pale grey black-tipped wings and a square-cut tail [imitative]
kitty[1] *n, pl* **-ties** a diminutive or affectionate name for a **kitten** or **cat**
kitty[2] *n, pl* **-ties 1** any shared fund of money **2** the pool in certain gambling games [probably from KIT[1]]
kiwi *n, pl* **kiwis 1** a flightless bird of New Zealand with a long beak, stout legs, and no tail **2** *informal* a New Zealander [Māori]
kiwi fruit *n* an edible fruit with a fuzzy brown skin and green flesh
kJ kilojoule(s)
kl kilolitre(s)
klaxon *n* a type of loud horn used on fire engines and ambulances as a warning signal [former trademark]
kleinhuisie (**klayn**-hay-see) *n S African* an outside toilet [Afrikaans, literally: little house]
kleptomania *n psychol* a strong impulse to steal [Greek *kleptein* to steal + *mania* madness] **kleptomaniac** *n*
klipspringer *n* a small agile antelope of rocky regions of Africa south of the Sahara [Afrikaans: rock jumper]
kloof *n S African* a mountain pass or gorge [Afrikaans]
km kilometre(s)
km/h kilometres per hour
knack *n* **1** a skilful way of doing something **2** an ability to do something difficult with apparent ease [probably from Middle English *knak* sharp knock]
knacker *n Brit* a person who buys up old horses for slaughter [origin unknown]
knackered *adj slang* **1** extremely tired: *they'd been marching for three hours and were absolutely knackered* **2** broken or no longer functioning: *a knackered TV set*
knapsack *n* a canvas or leather bag carried strapped on the back or shoulder [Low German *knappen* to eat + *sack* bag]
knapweed *n* a plant with purplish thistle-like flowers [Middle English *knopwed*]
knave *n* **1** *cards* the jack **2** *archaic* a dishonest man [Old English *cnafa*] **knavish** *adj*
knavery *n, pl* **-eries** *old-fashioned* dishonest behaviour
knead *vb* **1** to work and press (a soft substance, such as dough) into a smooth mixture with the

hands **2** to squeeze or press with the hands [Old English *cnedan*] **kneader** *n*

knee *n* **1** the joint of the leg between the thigh and the lower leg **2** the area around this joint **3** the upper surface of a sitting person's thigh: *a little girl being cuddled on her father's knee* **4** the part of a garment that covers the knee **5 bring someone to his** *or* **her knees** to force someone into submission ▷ *vb* **kneeing, kneed 6** to strike, nudge, or push with the knee [Old English *cnēow*]

kneecap *n* **1** *anatomy* a small flat triangular bone in front of and protecting the knee ▷ *vb* **-capping, -capped 2** (of terrorists) to shoot (a person) in the kneecap

knee-deep *adj* **1** so deep as to reach or cover the knees **2 A** sunk to the knees: *knee-deep in mud* **B** deeply involved: *knee-deep in work*

knee-high *adj* as high as the knee

knee-jerk *n* **1** *physiol* a sudden involuntary kick of the lower leg caused by a sharp tap on the tendon just below the kneecap ▷ *adj* **kneejerk 2** made or occurring as a predictable and automatic response: *a kneejerk reaction*

kneel *vb* **kneeling, knelt** *or* **kneeled 1** to rest, fall, or support oneself on one's knees ▷ *n* **2** the act or position of kneeling [Old English *cnēowlian*]

knees-up *n Brit informal* a party

knell *n* **1** the sound of a bell rung to announce a death or a funeral **2** something that indicates death or destruction ▷ *vb* **3** to ring a knell **4** to proclaim by a tolling bell [Old English *cnyll*]

knelt *vb* the past of **kneel**

knew *vb* the past tense of **know**

knickerbockers *pl n* loose-fitting short trousers gathered in at the knee or calf [after Diedrich *Knickerbocker*, fictitious author of Washington Irving's *History of New York*]

knickers *pl n* a woman's or girl's undergarment covering the lower trunk and having separate legs or leg-holes [contraction of *knickerbockers*]

knick-knack *n* a small ornament or trinket [reduplication of obsolete *knack* a toy]

knife *n, pl* **knives 1** a cutting instrument or weapon consisting of a sharp-edged blade of metal fitted into a handle ▷ *vb* **knifing, knifed 2** to stab or kill with a knife [Old English *cnīf*] **knifelike** *adj*

knife edge *n* **1** the sharp cutting edge of a knife **2** a critical point in the development of a situation: *and at this point the election result is still poised on a knife edge*

knight *n* **1** a man who has been given a knighthood in recognition of his achievements **2 A** (in medieval Europe) a person who served his lord as a mounted and heavily armed soldier **B** (in medieval Europe) a devoted male admirer of a noblewoman, esp. her champion in a jousting tournament **3** a chess piece shaped like a horse's head, able to move either two squares horizontally and one square vertically or two squares vertically and one square horizontally ▷ *vb* **4** to make (a man) a knight [Old English *cniht* servant]

knight errant *n, pl* **knights errant** (esp. in medieval romance) a knight who wanders in search of deeds of courage, chivalry, etc. **knight errantry** *n*

knighthood *n* an honorary title given to a man by the British sovereign in recognition of his achievements

knightly *adj* of, resembling, or appropriate for a knight **knightliness** *n*

knit *vb* **knitting, knitted** *or* **knit 1** to make (a garment) by looping (wool) using long eyeless needles or a knitting machine **2** to join together closely **3** to draw (one's eyebrows) together ▷ *n* **4** a fabric made by knitting [Old English *cnyttan* to tie in] **knitter** *n*

knitting *n* knitted work or the process of producing it

knitwear *n* knitted clothes, such as sweaters

knives *n* the plural of **knife**

knob *n* **1** a rounded projection from a surface, such as a rotating switch on a radio **2** a rounded handle of a door or drawer **3** a small amount of butter or margarine [Middle Low German *knobbe* knot in wood] **knoblike** *adj*

knobbly *adj* having or covered with small bumps: *a curious knobbly root vegetable*

knobkerrie *n S African* a club or a stick with a rounded end [Khoikhoi *kirri* stick]

knock *vb* **1** to give a blow or push to **2** to rap sharply with the knuckles: *he knocked on the door of the guest room* **3** to make by striking: *he knocked a hole in the wall* **4** to collide (with) **5** to bring into a certain condition by hitting: *he was knocked unconscious in a collision* **6** *informal* to criticize adversely **7** to emit a regular banging sound as a result of a fault: *the engine was knocking badly* **8 knock on the head** to prevent the further development of (a plan) ▷ *n* **9 A** a blow, push, or rap: *he gave the table a knock* **B** the sound so caused **10** the sound of knocking in an engine or bearing **11** *informal* a misfortune, rejection, or setback **12** *informal* criticism ▷ See also **knock about, knock back** *etc.* [Old English *cnocian*]

knock about *or* **knock around** *vb* **1** to wander or travel about: *I have knocked about the world through three continents* **2** (foll. by *with*) to associate **3** to treat brutally: *they used to knock me about a bit and try and make me cry* **4** to consider or discuss informally ▷ *adj* **knockabout 5** (of comedy) lively, boisterous, and physical

knock back *vb informal* **1** to drink quickly: *he fell over after knocking back eight pints of lager* **2** to cost: *lunch for two here will knock you back a small fortune* **3** to reject or refuse: *I don't know any man who'd knock back an offer like that* ▷ *n* **knockback 4** *slang* a refusal or rejection

knock down *vb* **1** to strike to the ground with a blow, such as in boxing **2** (in auctions) to declare an article sold **3** to demolish **4** *informal* to reduce (a price) ▷ *adj* **knockdown 5** powerful: *a knockdown argument* **6** *chiefly Brit* (of a price) very cheap **7** easily dismantled: *knockdown furniture*

knocker *n* **1** a metal object attached to a door by a hinge and used for knocking **2 knockers** *vulgar slang* a woman's breasts

knock-knees *pl n* legs that are bent inwards at the knees **knock-kneed** *adj*

knock off *vb* **1** *informal* to finish work: *around ten, the day shift knocked off* **2** *informal* to make or do hastily or easily: *she knocked off 600 books in all during* *her long life* **3** *informal* to take (an amount) off the price of (an article): *I'll knock off 10% if you pay cash* **4** *Brit, Austral & NZ informal* to steal **5** *slang* to kill **6** *slang* to stop doing something; used as a command: *knock it off!*

knock-on *rugby* ▷ *n* **1** the foul of playing the ball forward with the hand or arm ▷ *vb* **knock on 2** to play (the ball) forward with the hand or arm

knock-on effect *n* the indirect result of an action or decision

knockout *n* **1** the act of rendering someone unconscious **2** *boxing* a blow that renders an opponent unable to continue after the referee has counted to ten **3** a competition in which competitors are eliminated progressively **4** *informal* a person or thing that is very impressive or attractive: *at my youngest sister's wedding she was a knockout in navy and scarlet* ▷ *vb* **knock out 5** to render (someone) unconscious **6** *boxing* to defeat (an opponent) by a knockout **7** to destroy: *communications in many areas were knocked out by the earthquake* **8** to eliminate from a knockout competition **9** *informal* to amaze: *the fantastic audience reaction knocked me out*

knock up *vb* **1** Also: **knock together** *informal* to make or assemble quickly: *my boyfriend can knock up a wonderful lasagne* **2** *Brit informal* to waken: *to knock someone up early* **3** *slang* to make pregnant **4** to practise before a game of tennis, squash, or badminton ▷ *n* **knock-up 5** a practice session at tennis, squash, or badminton

knoll *n* a small rounded hill [Old English *cnoll*]

knot *n* **1** a fastening formed by looping and tying pieces of rope, cord, or string **2** a tangle, such as in hair **3** a decorative bow, such as of ribbon **4** a small cluster or huddled group: *a knot of passengers gathered on the platform* **5** a bond: *to tie the knot of friendship* **6 A** a hard mass of wood where a branch joins the trunk of a tree **B** a cross section of this, visible in timber **7** a feeling of tightness, caused by tension or nervousness: *a dull knot of anxiety that sat in the pit of her stomach* **8** a unit of speed used by ships and aircraft, equal to one nautical mile per hour **9 at a rate of knots** very fast **10 tie someone in knots** to confuse someone completely ▷ *vb* **knotting, knotted 11** to tie or fasten in a knot **12** to form into a knot **13** to entangle or become entangled [Old English *cnotta*] **knotted** *adj* **knotless** *adj*

knothole *n* a hole in a piece of wood where a knot has been

knotty *adj* **-tier, -tiest 1** full of knots **2** extremely difficult or puzzling: *a knotty problem*

know *vb* **knowing, knew, known 1** to be or feel certain of the truth or accuracy of (a fact, answer, or piece of information) **2** to be acquainted with: *I'd known him for many years, since I was seventeen* **3** to have a grasp of or understand (a skill or language) **4** to understand or be aware of (something, or how to do or be something): *she knew how to get on with people* **5** to experience: *you had to have known poverty before you could give money its true value, he claimed* **6** to be intelligent, informed, or sensible enough (to do something): *how did he know to send the letter in the first place?* **7** to be able to distinguish: *I don't know one flower from another* **8 know what's what** to know how one thing or things in general work **9 you never know** things are uncertain ▷ *n* **10 in the know** *informal* aware or informed [Old English *gecnāwan*] **knowable** *adj*

know-all *n informal, derogatory* a person who pretends or appears to know a lot more than other people

know-how *n informal* the ability to do something that is difficult or technical

knowing *adj* **1** suggesting secret knowledge: *Paul saw the knowing look that passed between them* **2** cunning or shrewd **3** deliberate **knowingly** *adv* **knowingness** *n*

knowledge *n* **1** the facts or experiences known by a person or group of people **2** the state of knowing **3** specific information about a subject **4 to my knowledge** as I understand it

knowledgeable *or* **knowledgable** *adj* intelligent or well-informed **knowledgeably** *or* **knowledgably** *adv*

known *vb* **1** the past participle of **know** ▷ *adj* **2** identified: *consorting with known criminals*

knuckle *n* **1** a joint of a finger **2** the knee joint of a calf or pig **3 near the knuckle** *informal* likely to offend people because of frankness or rudeness ▷ See also **knuckle down, knuckle under** [Middle English]

knuckle down *vb* **-ling, -led** *informal* to apply oneself conscientiously: *he's never been able to knuckle down and study anything for long*

knuckle-duster *n* a metal appliance worn over the knuckles to add force to a blow

knuckle under *vb* **-ling, -led** to give way under pressure or authority

knurl *n* a small ridge, often one of a series [probably from *knur* a knot in wood]

KO *or* **k.o.** *vb* **KO'ing, KO'd** *or* **k.o.'ing, k.o.'d 1** to knock out ▷ *n, pl* **KO's** *or* **k.o.'s 2** a knockout

koala *or* **koala bear** *n* a tree-dwelling Australian marsupial with dense grey fur [Aboriginal]

Kobe beef (koh-bi) *n* a grade of beef from cattle raised in Kobe, Japan, which is extremely tender and full-flavoured

koeksister (kook-sist-er) *n S African* a plaited doughnut deep-fried and soaked in syrup [Afrikaans]

kohanga reo *or* **kohanga** *n NZ* an infant class where children are taught in Māori [Māori: language nest]

kohl *n* a cosmetic powder used to darken the area around the eyes [Arabic]

kohlrabi (kole-rah-bee) *n, pl* **-bies** a type of cabbage with an edible stem [Italian *cavolo* cabbage + *rapa* turnip]

kokanee (koh-kan-ee) *n* a freshwater salmon of lakes and rivers in W North America [after *Kokanee* Creek, in British Columbia]

kola *n* same as **cola**

kolkhoz (kol-hawz) *n* (formerly) a collective farm in the Soviet Union [Russian]

komatik (koh-ma-tik) *n Canad* a sledge with wooden runners and crossbars bound with animal hides [Inuktitut]

kook *n US & Canad informal* an eccentric or foolish person [probably from *cuckoo*] **kooky** *or* **kookie** *adj*

kookaburra *n* a large Australian kingfisher with a cackling cry [Aboriginal]

koori *n, pl* **-ris** *Austral* a member of an Aboriginal people

kopeck *n* a former Russian monetary unit worth one hundredth of a rouble [Russian *kopeika*]

kopje *or* **koppie** (**kop**-ee) *n S African* a small isolated hill [Afrikaans]

Koran *n* the sacred book of Islam, believed by Muslims to be the infallible word of God dictated to Mohammed [Arabic *qur'ān* reading, book] **Koranic** *adj*

Korean *adj* **1** of Korea ▷ *n* **2** a person from Korea **3** the official language of North and South Korea

korma *n* a type of mild Indian dish consisting of meat or vegetables cooked in water, yoghurt, or cream [from Urdu]

kosher (**koh**-sher) *adj* **1** *Judaism* **A** conforming to religious law **B** (of food) prepared in accordance with the dietary laws **2** *informal* legitimate, genuine, or proper ▷ *n* **3** kosher food [Yiddish]

kowhai (**koh**-wye, **koh**-fye) *n* a small tree of New Zealand and Chile with clusters of yellow flowers [Māori]

kowtow *vb* **1** to be humble and very respectful (towards): *the senior editors accused each other of kowtowing to his demands* **2** to touch the forehead to the ground in deference ▷ *n* **3** the act of kowtowing [Chinese *k'o* to strike, knock + *t'ou* head]

k

kph kilometres per hour

Kr *chem* krypton

kraal *n* **1** a Southern African hut village surrounded by a strong fence **2** *S African* an enclosure for livestock [Afrikaans, from Portuguese *curral* enclosure]

kraken *n* a legendary sea monster [Norwegian]

krans (**krahnss**) *n S African* a sheer rock face [Afrikaans]

kremlin *n* the citadel of any Russian city [Russian *kreml*]

Kremlin *n* the central government of Russia and, formerly, the Soviet Union

krill *n, pl* **krill** a small shrimplike crustacean [Norwegian *kril* young fish]

Krishna *n* a Hindu god, the incarnation of Vishnu

krona *n, pl* **-nor** the standard monetary unit of Sweden [Swedish, from Latin *corona* crown]

krone (**kroh**-na) *n, pl* **-ner** (-ner) the standard monetary unit of Norway and Denmark [Danish or Norwegian, from Latin *corona* crown]

Krugerrand *n* a one-ounce gold coin minted in South Africa [Paul *Kruger*, Boer statesman + *rand*]

krypton *n chem* an inert gaseous element occurring in trace amounts in air and used in fluorescent lights and lasers. Symbol: **Kr** [Greek *kruptos* hidden]

KS Kansas

Kt Knight

KT (in Britain) Knight of the Order of the Thistle

kt. kiloton

kudos (**kew**-doss) *n* personal fame or glory [Greek]

kudu *or* **koodoo** *n* a spiral-horned African antelope [Afrikaans, from Khoikhoi]

kugel (**koog**-el) *n S African derogatory* a rich, fashion-conscious, materialistic young Jewish woman [from Yiddish *kugel*, a type of savoury pudding popular in Jewish cookery]

Ku Klux Klan *n* a secret organization of White Protestant Americans who use violence against black and Jewish people [probably based on Greek *kuklos* circle + CLAN] **Ku Klux Klanner** *n*

kukri *n* a heavy, curved knife used by Gurkhas [Hindi]

kulak *n* (formerly) a property-owning Russian peasant [Russian]

kumera *or* **kumara** (**koo**-ma-ra) *n NZ* a tropical root vegetable with yellow flesh [Māori]

kümmel *n* a German liqueur flavoured with aniseed and cumin [from German]

kumquat (**kumm**-kwott) *n* a citrus fruit resembling a tiny orange [Cantonese Chinese *kam kwat* golden orange]

kung fu *n* any of various Chinese systems of martial art, esp. unarmed combat in which punches, chops, and kicks are made with the hands and feet; certain styles involve the use of weapons [Chinese: skill; accomplishment]

kura kaupapa Māori *n NZ* a primary school where the teaching is done in Māori

kurrajong *n* an Australian tree or shrub with tough fibrous bark [from a native Australian language]

kV kilovolt

kvetch *vb slang, chiefly US* to complain or grumble [Yiddish]

kW kilowatt

Kwanzaa *n* an African-American festival held from December 26 until January 1 [from Swahili *(matunda ya) kwanza* first (fruits)]

kwashiorkor *n* severe malnutrition of young children, caused by not eating enough protein [native word in Ghana]

kwela *n* a type of music popular among the Black communities of South Africa [Zulu: jump up]

kWh kilowatt-hour

KWIC *computers* keyword in context

KWOC *computers* keyword out of context

KY Kentucky

kyle *n Scot* a narrow strait or channel: *Kyle of Lochalsh* [Gaelic *caol* narrow]

Ll

l litre(s)

L **1** large **2** Latin **3** learner driver **4** usually written: **£** pound **5** the Roman numeral for 50

L. *or* **l.** **1** lake **2** left **3** length **4** *pl* **LL** *or* **ll** line

la *n music* same as **lah**

La *chem* lanthanum

LA **1** Los Angeles **2** Louisiana

laager *n* (in Africa) a camp defended by a circular formation of wagons [Afrikaans *lager*]

lab *n informal* short for **laboratory**

Lab *politics* Labour

label *n* **1** a piece of card or other material attached to an object to show its contents, ownership, use, or destination **2** a brief descriptive term given to a person, group, or school of thought: *we would need a handy label to explain the new company* ▷ *vb* **-belling, -belled** *or US* **-beling, -beled** **3** to attach a label to **4** to describe or classify in a word or phrase [Old French: ribbon]

labial (lay-bee-al) *adj* **1** of or near the lips **2** *phonetics* relating to a speech sound made using the lips ▷ *n* **3** *phonetics* a speech sound such as English *p* or *m*, that involves the lips [Latin *labium* lip]

labiate (lay-bee-it) *n* **1** any of a family of plants with square stems, aromatic leaves, and a two-lipped flower, such as mint or thyme ▷ *adj* **2** of this family [Latin *labium* lip]

labium (lay-bee-um) *n, pl* **-bia** (-bee-a) **1** a lip or liplike structure **2** any one of the four lip-shaped folds of the vulva [Latin: lip]

labor *n US, Austral & sometimes Canad* same as **labour**

laboratory *n, pl* **-ries** a building or room equipped for conducting scientific research or for teaching practical science [Latin *laborare* to work]

Labor Day *n* **1** (in the US and Canada) a public holiday in honour of labour, held on the first Monday in September **2** (in Australia) a public holiday observed on different days in different states

laborious *adj* involving great exertion or prolonged effort **laboriously** *adv*

Labor Party *n* the main left-wing political party in Australia

labour *or US, Austral & sometimes Canad* **labor** *n* **1** productive work, esp. physical work done for wages **2** the people involved in this, as opposed to management **3** the final stage of pregnancy, leading to childbirth **4** difficult work or a difficult job ▷ *vb* **5** to do physical work: *the girls were labouring madly on it* **6** to work hard (for something) **7** to make one's way with difficulty: *she was now labouring down the return length* **8** to emphasize too persistently: *I have laboured the point* **9** (usually foll. by *under*) to be at a disadvantage because of a mistake or false belief: *she laboured under the illusion that I understood her* [Latin *labor*]

Labour Day *n* **1** a public holiday in honour of work, held in Britain on May 1 **2** (in New Zealand) a public holiday commemorating the introduction of the eight-hour day, held on the fourth Monday in October

laboured *or US, Austral & sometimes Canad* **labored** *adj* undertaken with difficulty: *laboured breathing*

labourer *or US, Austral & sometimes Canad* **laborer** *n* a person engaged in physical work

Labour Party *n* the main left-wing political party in a number of countries including Britain and New Zealand

labour-saving *adj* (of a method or piece of equipment) reducing the amount of work or effort needed to carry out a task

Labrador *or* **Labrador retriever** *n* a powerfully built dog with short dense black, brown, or golden hair

laburnum *n* a small ornamental tree that has clusters of yellow drooping flowers. It is highly poisonous [Latin]

labyrinth (lab-er-inth) *n* **1** a mazelike network of tunnels or paths, either natural or man-made **2** any complex or confusing system **3** the interconnecting cavities of the internal ear [Greek *laburinthos*] **labyrinthine** *adj*

lac *n* a resinous substance secreted by certain insects (**lac insects**), used in the manufacture of shellac [Hindi *lākh* resin]

lace *n* **1** a delicate decorative fabric made from threads woven in an open web of patterns **2** a cord or string drawn through eyelets to fasten a shoe or garment ▷ *vb* **lacing, laced** **3** to fasten (shoes) with a lace **4** to draw (a cord or thread) through holes as when tying shoes **5** to add a small amount of alcohol, a drug, or poison to (food or drink) **6** to intertwine; interlace [Latin *laqueus* noose]

lacerate (lass-er-rate) *vb* **-ating, -ated** **1** to tear (the flesh) jaggedly **2** to hurt (the feelings): *it would only lacerate an overburdened conscience* [Latin *lacerare* to tear] **laceration** *n*

lace up *vb* **1** to fasten (clothes or footwear) with laces ▷ *adj* **lace-up** **2** (of footwear) to be fastened with laces ▷ *n* **lace-up** **3** a shoe or boot which fastens with a lace

lachrymal *adj* same as **lacrimal**

lachrymose *adj* **1** given to weeping; tearful **2** mournful; sad [Latin *lacrima* a tear]

lack *n* **1** shortage or absence of something required or desired: *a lack of confidence* ▷ *vb* **2** (often foll. by *in*) to be short (of) or have need (of): *lacking in sparkle* [related to Middle Dutch *laken* to be wanting]

lackadaisical *adj* **1** lacking vitality and purpose **2** lazy and careless in a dreamy way [earlier *lackadaisy*]

lackey *n* **1** a servile follower; hanger-on **2** a liveried male servant or valet [Catalan *lacayo*, *alacayo*]

lacklustre *or US* **lackluster** *adj* lacking brilliance, force, or vitality

laconic *adj* (of a person's speech) using few words [Greek *Lakōnikos* Spartan; referring to the Spartans' terseness of speech] **laconically** *adv*

lacquer *n* **1** a hard glossy coating made by dissolving natural or synthetic resins in a solvent that evaporates quickly **2** a black resin, obtained from certain trees, used to give a hard glossy finish to wooden furniture **3** a clear sticky substance for spraying onto the hair to hold a style in place [Portuguese *laca* lac]
lacquered *adj* coated with lacquer
lacrimal *or* **lachrymal** (lack-rim-al) *adj* of tears or the glands that secrete tears [Latin *lacrima* a tear]
lacrosse *n* a sport in which two teams try to propel a ball into each other's goal using long-handled sticks with a pouched net at the end [Canadian French: the hooked stick]
lactate¹ *vb* **-tating, -tated** (of mammals) to secrete milk
lactate² *n* an ester or salt of lactic acid
lactation *n* **1** the secretion of milk from the mammary glands **2** the period during which milk is secreted
lacteal *adj* **1** of or like milk **2** (of lymphatic vessels) conveying or containing chyle ▷ *n* **3** any of the lymphatic vessels that convey chyle from the small intestine to the blood [Latin *lacteus* of milk]
lactic *adj* relating to or derived from milk [Latin *lac* milk]
lactic acid *n* a colourless syrupy acid found in sour milk and used as a preservative (**E270**) for foodstuffs
lactose *n* a white crystalline sugar occurring in milk
lacuna (lak-**kew**-na) *n, pl* **-nae** (-nee) a gap or space in a book or manuscript [Latin: pool, cavity]
lacy *adj* **lacier, laciest** of or like lace
lad *n* **1** a boy or young man **2** *informal* any male **3 the lads** *informal* a group of males [perhaps from Old Norse]
ladder *n* **1** a portable frame consisting of two long parallel supports connected by steps, for climbing up or down **2** any system thought of as having a series of ascending stages: *the career ladder* **3** *chiefly Brit* a line of connected stitches that have come undone in tights or stockings ▷ *vb* **4** *chiefly Brit* to have or cause to have a line of undone stitches [Old English *hlǣdder*]
ladder back *n* a chair in which the back is made of horizontal slats between two uprights
laddish *adj Brit, Austral & NZ informal, often derogatory* characteristic of young men, esp. by being rowdy or immature
lade *vb* **lading, laded, laden** *or* **laded 1** to put cargo on board (a ship) or (of a ship) to take on cargo **2** (foll. by *with*) to burden or load [Old English *hladen* to load]
laden *adj* **1** loaded **2** burdened
la-di-da *or* **lah-di-dah** *adj informal* affected or pretentious in speech or manners [mockingly imitative of affected speech]
ladies *or* **ladies' room** *n informal* a women's public toilet
lading *n* a load; cargo; freight
ladle *n* **1** a long-handled spoon with a deep bowl for serving soup, stew, etc. ▷ *vb* **-dling, -dled 2** to serve out as with a ladle [Old English *hlædel*]
ladle out *vb informal* to distribute (money, gifts, etc.) generously
lad mag *n* a magazine aimed at or appealing to men, focusing on fashion, gadgets, and often featuring scantily dressed women
lady *n, pl* **-dies 1** a woman regarded as having the characteristics of a good family, such as dignified manners **2** a polite name for a woman ▷ *adj* **3** female: *a lady chef* [Old English *hlǣfdīge*]
Lady *n, pl* **-dies 1** (in Britain) a title borne by various classes of women of the peerage **2 Our Lady** a title of the Virgin Mary
ladybird *n* a small red beetle with black spots [after Our *Lady,* the Virgin Mary]
ladyboy *n informal* a transvestite or a transsexual or transgender woman, esp. in Thailand
Lady Day *n* March 25, the feast of the Annunciation of the Virgin Mary: a quarter day in England, Wales, and Ireland
lady-in-waiting *n, pl* **ladies-in-waiting** a woman who attends a queen or princess
lady-killer *n informal* a man who is, or believes he is, irresistible to women
ladylike *adj* (of a woman) refined and fastidious
Ladyship *n* (preceded by *Your* or *Her*) a title used to address or refer to any peeress except a duchess
lady's-slipper *n* an orchid with reddish or purple flowers
lag¹ *vb* **lagging, lagged 1** (often foll. by *behind*) to hang (back) or fall (behind) in movement, progress, or development **2** to fall away in strength or intensity ▷ *n* **3** a slowing down or falling behind **4** the interval of time between two events, esp. between an action and its effect: *the time lag between mobilization and combat* [origin unknown]
lag² *vb* **lagging, lagged 1** to wrap (a pipe, cylinder, or boiler) with insulating material to prevent heat loss ▷ *n* **2** the insulating casing of a steam cylinder or boiler [Scandinavian]
lag³ *n* **old lag** *Brit, Austral & NZ slang* a convict or ex-convict [origin unknown]
lager *n* a light-bodied effervescent beer, fermented in a closed vessel using yeasts that sink to the bottom of the brew [German *Lagerbier* beer for storing]
laggard *n* a person who lags behind
lagging *n* insulating material wrapped around pipes, boilers, or tanks to prevent loss of heat
lagoon *n* a body of water cut off from the open sea by coral reefs or sand bars [Latin *lacuna* pool]
lah *n music* (in tonic sol-fa) the sixth note of any ascending major scale
laid *vb* the past of **lay¹**
laid-back *adj* relaxed in style or character
laid paper *n* paper with a regular pattern of lines impressed upon it
lain *vb* the past participle of **lie²**
lair *n* **1** the resting place of a wild animal **2** *informal* a place of seclusion or hiding [Old English *leger*]
laird *n Scot* a landowner, esp. of a large estate [Scots variant of *lord*]
laissez faire *or* **laisser faire** (less-ay **fair**) *n* the policy of nonintervention, esp. by a government in commerce [French, literally: let (them) act]

laity (lay-it-ee) *n* **1** people who are not members of the clergy **2** all the people who do not belong to a specific profession [from LAY[3]]
lake[1] *n* an expanse of water entirely surrounded by land [Latin *lacus*]
lake[2] *n* **1** a bright pigment produced by combining organic colouring matter with an inorganic compound **2** a red dye obtained by combining a metallic compound with cochineal [variant of *lac*]
Lake District *n* a region of lakes and mountains in NW England. Also called: **Lakeland, the Lakes**
lake trout *n* a yellow-spotted trout of the Great Lakes region of Canada
lakh (lahk) *n* (in India) 100 000, esp. referring to this sum of rupees [Hindi *lākh*]
lam[1] *vb* **lamming, lammed** *slang* to attack vigorously [Scandinavian]
lam[2] *n* **on the lam** *US & Canad slang* **A** making an escape **B** in hiding [origin unknown]
lama *n* a Buddhist priest or monk in Mongolia or Tibet [Tibetan *blama*]
lamb *n* **1** the young of a sheep **2** the meat of a young sheep eaten as food **3** someone who is innocent, gentle, and good ▷ *vb* **4** (of a ewe) to give birth [Old English]
Lamb *n* **the Lamb** *Christianity* a title given to Christ
lambast *or* **lambaste** *vb* **1** to beat severely **2** to reprimand severely [LAM[1] + BASTE[3]]
lambent *adj* **1** (of a flame or light) flickering softly over a surface **2** (of wit or humour) light or brilliant [Latin *lambere* to lick] **lambency** *n*
lambing *n* **1** the birth of lambs at the end of winter **2** the shepherd's work of tending the ewes and newborn lambs at this time
lamb's fry *n Austral & NZ* lamb's liver for cooking
lambskin *n* the skin of a lamb, usually with the wool still on, used to make coats, slippers, etc.
lame *adj* **1** unable to walk properly because of an injury or illness affecting the legs or feet **2** weak; unconvincing: *lame arguments* ▷ *vb* **laming, lamed** **3** to make lame [Old English *lama*] **lamely** *adv* **lameness** *n*
lamé (lah-may) *n* a fabric interwoven with gold or silver threads [Old French *lame* gold or silver thread]
lame duck *n* a person who is unable to cope without the help of other people
lament *vb* **1** to feel or express sorrow or regret (for or over) ▷ *n* **2** an expression of sorrow **3** a poem or song in which a death is lamented [Latin *lamentum*] **lamentation** *n*
lamentable *adj* very unfortunate or disappointing **lamentably** *adv*
lamented *adj* grieved for: usually said of someone dead
lamina *n, pl* **-nae** a thin plate, esp. of bone or mineral [Latin: thin plate] **laminar** *adj*
laminate *vb* **-nating, -nated** **1** to make (material in sheet form) by sticking together thin sheets **2** to cover with a thin sheet of material **3** to split or be split into thin sheets ▷ *n* **4** a material made by sticking sheets together ▷ *adj* **5** composed of lamina; laminated **lamination** *n*
laminated *adj* **1** composed of many layers stuck together **2** covered with a thin protective layer of plastic
lamington *n Austral & NZ* a sponge cake covered with a sweet coating
Lammas *n* August 1, formerly observed in England as a harvest festival: a quarter day in Scotland [Old English *hlāfmæsse* loaf mass]
lamp *n* **1** a device that produces light: *an electric lamp; a gas lamp; an oil lamp* **2** a device that produces radiation, esp. for therapeutic purposes: *an ultraviolet lamp* [Greek *lampein* to shine]
lampblack *n* a fine black soot used as a pigment in paint and ink
lampoon *n* **1** a piece of writing ridiculing a person ▷ *vb* **2** to ridicule and criticize (someone) in a lampoon [French *lampon*] **lampooner** *or* **lampoonist** *n*
lamppost *n* a metal or concrete pole supporting a lamp in a street
lamprey *n* an eel-like fish with a round sucking mouth [Late Latin *lampreda*]
LAN *computers* local area network
Lancastrian *n* **1** a person from Lancashire or Lancaster **2** a supporter of the house of Lancaster in the Wars of the Roses (1455–85) ▷ *adj* **3** of Lancashire or Lancaster **4** of the house of Lancaster
lance *n* **1** a long weapon with a pointed head used by horsemen ▷ *vb* **lancing, lanced** **2** to pierce (an abscess or boil) with a lancet **3** to pierce with or as with a lance [Latin *lancea*]
lance corporal *n* a noncommissioned officer of the lowest rank
lanceolate *adj* narrow and tapering to a point at each end, like some leaves [Latin *lanceola* small lance]
lancer *n* (formerly) a cavalryman armed with a lance
lancet *n* **1** a pointed surgical knife with two sharp edges **2** short for **lancet arch** or **lancet window** [Old French *lancette* small lance]
lancet arch *n* a narrow acutely pointed arch
lancet window *n* a narrow window with a lancet arch
lancewood *n* a New Zealand tree with slender leaves
Lancs Lancashire
land *n* **1** the solid part of the surface of the earth as distinct from seas and lakes. Related adjective: **terrestrial** **2** ground, esp. with reference to its use or quality: *agricultural land* **3** rural or agricultural areas: *he couldn't leave the land* **4** *law* ground owned as property **5** a country, region, or area: *to bring peace and riches to your land* ▷ *vb* **6** to come down or bring (something) down to earth after a flight or jump **7** to transfer (something) or go from a ship to the shore: *sacks of malt were landed from barges* **8** to come to or touch shore **9** *informal* to obtain: *he landed a handsomely paid job in a bank* **10** *angling* to retrieve (a hooked fish) from the water **11** *informal* to deliver (a blow or punch) ▷ See also **land up** [Old English] **landless** *adj*
land agent *n* a person in charge of a landed estate
landau (lan-daw) *n* a four-wheeled horse-drawn carriage with two folding hoods [after *Landau*, a town in Germany, where first made]

landed *adj* **1** owning land: *landed gentry* **2** consisting of land: *landed property*
landfall *n* the act of sighting or nearing land, esp. from the sea
landfill *n* disposing of waste material by covering it with earth
land girl *n* a girl or woman who does farm work, esp. in wartime
land-holder *n* a person who owns or occupies land **land-holding** *adj, n*
landing *n* **1** the floor area at the top of a flight of stairs **2** the act of coming to land, esp. after a flight or sea voyage **3** a place of disembarkation
landing field *n* an area of land on which aircraft land and from which they take off
landing gear *n* the undercarriage of an aircraft
landlady *n, pl* **-dies 1** a woman who owns and leases property **2** a woman who owns or runs a lodging house or pub
land line *n* a telecommunications wire or cable laid over land
landlocked *adj* (of a country) completely surrounded by land
landlord *n* **1** a man who owns and leases property **2** a man who owns or runs a lodging house or pub
landlubber *n naut* any person without experience at sea
landmark *n* **1** a prominent object in or feature of a particular landscape **2** an important or unique event or development: *a landmark in scientific progress*
landmass *n* a large continuous area of land
land mine *n military* an explosive device placed in the ground, usually detonated when someone steps on it or drives over it
landowner *n* a person who owns land **landowning** *n, adj*
landscape *n* **1** an extensive area of land regarded as being visually distinct **2** a painting, drawing, or photograph depicting natural scenery ▷ *vb* **-scaping, -scaped 3** to improve the natural features of (an area of land) ▷ *adj* **4** (of a page or screen) having greater width than height [Middle Dutch *lantscap* region]
landscape gardening *n* the art of laying out grounds in imitation of natural scenery **landscape gardener** *n*
landside *n* the part of an airport farthest from the aircraft
landslide *n* **1** Also called: **landslip A** the sliding of a large mass of rocks and soil down the side of a mountain or cliff **B** the material dislodged in this way **2** an overwhelming electoral victory
land up *vb* to arrive at a final point or condition
landward *adj* **1** lying, facing, or moving towards land **2** in the direction of the land ▷ *adv also* **landwards 3** towards land
lane *n* **1** a narrow road, esp. in the country **2** one of the parallel strips into which the carriageway of a major road or motorway is divided **3** any well-defined route or course, such as for ships or aircraft **4** one of the parallel strips into which a running track or swimming pool is divided for races [Old English *lane, lanu*]
lang. language
language *n* **1** a system of spoken sounds or conventional symbols for communicating thought **2** the language of a particular nation or people **3** the ability to use words to communicate **4** any other means of communicating: *body language* **5** the specialized vocabulary used by a particular group: *legal language* **6** a particular style of verbal expression: *rough language* **7** *computers* See **programming language** [Latin *lingua* tongue]
languid *adj* lacking energy; dreamy and inactive [Latin *languere* to languish] **languidly** *adv*
languish *vb literary* **1** to suffer deprivation, hardship, or neglect: *she won't languish in jail for it* **2** to lose or diminish in strength or energy: *the design languished into oblivion* **3** (often foll. by *for*) to be listless with desire; pine [Latin *languere*] **languishing** *adj*
languor (**lang**-ger) *n literary* a pleasant state of dreamy relaxation [Latin *languere* to languish] **languorous** *adj*
lank *adj* **1** (of hair) straight and limp **2** thin or gaunt: *a tall, lank, lean man* [Old English *hlanc* loose]
lanky *adj* **lankier, lankiest** ungracefully tall and thin **lankiness** *n*
lanolin *n* a yellowish sticky substance extracted from wool: used in some ointments [Latin *lana* wool + *oleum* oil]
lantana (lan-**tay**-na) *n* a shrub with orange or yellow flowers, considered a weed in Australia
lantern *n* **1** a light with a transparent protective case **2** a raised part on top of a dome or roof which lets in light or air **3** the upper part of a lighthouse that houses the light [Greek *lampein* to shine]
lantern jaw *n* a long hollow jaw that gives the face a drawn appearance **lantern-jawed** *adj*
lanthanide series *n chem* a class of 15 chemically related elements (**lanthanides**) with atomic numbers from 57 (lanthanum) to 71 (lutetium)
lanthanum *n chem* a silvery-white metallic element of the lanthanide series: used in electronic devices and glass manufacture. Symbol: **La** [Greek *lanthanein* to lie unseen]
lanyard *n* **1** a cord worn round the neck to hold a whistle, identity card, etc. **2** *naut* a line for extending or tightening rigging [Old French *lasne* strap]
laodicean (lay-oh-**diss**-see-an) *adj* indifferent, esp. in religious matters [referring to the early Christians of Laodicea (Revelation 3:14–16)]
lap[1] *n* **1** the area formed by the upper surface of the thighs of a seated person **2** a protected place or environment: *in the lap of luxury* **3** the part of a person's clothing that covers the lap **4 drop in someone's lap** to give someone the responsibility of [Old English *læppa* flap]
lap[2] *n* **1** one circuit of a racecourse or track **2** a stage or part of a journey **3 A** an overlapping part **B** the extent of overlap ▷ *vb* **lapping, lapped 4** to overtake (an opponent) in a race so as to be one or more circuits ahead **5** to enfold or wrap around **6** to place or lie partly or completely over, or project beyond: *deep-pile carpet that lapped against his ankles* **7** to envelop or surround with comfort,

love, or peace: *she was lapped by the luxury of Seymour House* [probably same as LAP¹]

lap³ *vb* **lapping, lapped 1** (of small waves) to wash against (the shore or a boat) with light splashing sounds **2** (often foll. by *up*) (esp. of animals) to scoop (a liquid) into the mouth with the tongue ▷ *n* **3** the act or sound of lapping ▷ See also **lap up** [Old English *lapian*]

laparoscopy *n, pl* **-pies** an investigative surgical procedure in which an optical instrument is inserted through a small incision in the abdomen [Greek *lapara* flank + *skopein* to look at] **laparoscopic** *adj*

lap dancing *n* a form of entertainment in which scantily dressed women dance erotically for individual members of the audience

lapdog *n* a small pet dog

lapel (lap-**pel**) *n* the part on the front of a jacket or coat that folds back towards the shoulders [from LAP¹]

lapidary *n, pl* **-daries 1** a person who cuts, polishes, sets, or deals in gemstones ▷ *adj* **2** of or relating to gemstones or the work of a lapidary [Latin *lapidarius*, from *lapis* stone]

lapis lazuli (lap-iss **lazz**-yew-lie) *n* a brilliant blue mineral used as a gemstone [Latin *lapis* stone + Medieval Latin *lazulum* azure]

lap joint *n* a joint made by fastening together overlapping parts

lap of honour *n* a ceremonial circuit of a racing track by the winner of a race

Lapp *sometimes offensive n* **1** a member of the indigenous people of Lapland **2** the language of this people ▷ *adj* **3** of this people or their language. Preferred term: **Sami**

lappet *n* **1** a small hanging flap or piece of lace **2** *zool* a flap of flesh or membrane, such as the ear lobe or a bird's wattle [LAP¹ + *-et* (diminutive suffix)]

lapse *n* **1** a temporary drop in standard as a result of forgetfulness or lack of concentration **2** a moment or instance of bad behaviour, esp. by someone who is usually well-behaved **3** a period of time sufficient for a change to take place: *we returned after a lapse of two years* **4** a gradual decline to a lower degree, condition, or state: *its lapse from the tradition of Disraeli* **5** *law* the loss of some right by neglecting to exercise or renew it ▷ *vb* **lapsing, lapsed 6** to drop in standard or fail to maintain a standard **7** to decline gradually in status, condition, or degree **8** to allow to end or become no longer valid, esp. through negligence: *a bid that lapsed last July* **9** (usually foll. by *into*) to drift (into a condition): *she appeared to lapse into a brief reverie* **10** (often foll. by *from*) to turn away (from beliefs or standards) **11** (of time) to slip away [Latin *lapsus* error] **lapsed** *adj*

laptop *adj* **1** (of a computer) small and light enough to be held on the user's lap ▷ *n* **2** a personal computer that is small and light enough to be held on the user's lap

lap up *vb* **1** to eat or drink **2** to accept (information or attention) eagerly: *the public are lapping up the scandal*

lapwing *n* a bird of the plover family with a crested head. Also called: **peewit** [Old English *hlēapewince* plover]

larboard *n naut* an old word for **port²** (sense 1) [Middle English *laddeborde*]

larceny *n, pl* **-nies** *law* theft [Old French *larcin*] **larcenist** *n*

larch *n* **1** a coniferous tree with deciduous needle-like leaves and egg-shaped cones **2** the wood of this tree [Latin *larix*]

lard *n* **1** the soft white fat obtained from pigs and prepared for use in cooking ▷ *vb* **2** to prepare (lean meat or poultry) by inserting small strips of bacon or fat before cooking **3** to add unnecessary material to (speech or writing) [Latin *laridum* bacon fat]

larder *n* a room or cupboard used for storing food [Old French *lardier*]

lardy cake *n Brit* a sweet cake made of bread dough, lard, sugar, and dried fruit

large *adj* **1** having a relatively great size, quantity, or extent; big **2** of wide or broad scope, capacity, or range; comprehensive: *a large effect* ▷ *n* **3 at large A** as a whole; in general: *both the Navy and the country at large* **B** (of a dangerous criminal or wild animal) out of captivity; free **C** in full detail ▷ *vb* **larging, larged 4 large it** *Brit slang* to enjoy oneself or celebrate in an extravagant way [Latin *largus* ample] **largeness** *n*

large intestine *n* the part of the alimentary canal consisting of the caecum, colon, and rectum

largely *adv* principally; to a great extent

large-scale *adj* **1** wide-ranging or extensive **2** (of maps and models) constructed or drawn to a big scale

largesse *or* **largess** (lar-**jess**) *n* the generous giving of gifts, favours, or money [Old French]

largish *adj* fairly large

largo *music* ▷ *adv* **1** in a slow and stately manner ▷ *n, pl* **-gos 2** a piece or passage to be performed in a slow and stately manner [Italian]

lariat *n US & Canad* **1** a lasso **2** a rope for tethering animals [Spanish *la reata* the lasso]

lark¹ *n* a small brown songbird, esp. the skylark [Old English *lāwerce, lǣwerce*]

lark² *informal* ▷ *n* **1** a carefree adventure or frolic **2** a harmless piece of mischief **3** an activity or job viewed with disrespect ▷ *vb* **4 lark about** to have a good time frolicking or playing pranks [origin unknown] **larky** *adj*

larkspur *n* a plant with blue, pink, or white flowers with slender spikes at the base [LARK¹ + SPUR]

larrikin *n Austral & NZ old-fashioned slang* a mischievous or unruly person

larva *n, pl* **-vae** the immature form of many insects before it develops into its adult form [New Latin] **larval** *adj*

laryngeal *adj* of or relating to the larynx

laryngitis *n* inflammation of the larynx, causing huskiness or loss of voice

larynx (**lar**-rinks) *n, pl* **larynges** (lar-**rin**-jeez) *or* **larynxes** a hollow organ forming part of the air passage to the lungs: it contains the vocal cords [Greek *larunx*]

lasagne *or* **lasagna** (laz-**zan**-ya) *n* **1** a form of pasta in wide flat sheets **2** a dish made from layers of lasagne, meat, and cheese [Italian, from Latin *lasanum* cooking pot]

lascivious (lass-iv-ee-uss) *adj* showing or producing sexual desire; lustful [Latin *lascivia* wantonness] **lasciviously** *adv*

laser (lay-zer) *n* **1** a device that produces a very narrow intense beam of light, which is used for cutting very hard materials and in surgery, etc. ▷ *vb* **2** to use a laser on (something), esp. as part of medical treatment **3** Also: **laser off** to remove (a tattoo, fat, etc.) with laser treatment [from *l*ight *a*mplification by *s*timulated *e*mission of *r*adiation]

laser printer *n* a computer printer that uses a laser beam to produce characters which are then transferred to paper

lash[1] *n* **1** an eyelash **2** a sharp cutting blow from a whip **3** the flexible end of a whip ▷ *vb* **4** to hit (a person or thing) sharply with a whip, esp. formerly as punishment **5** (of rain or waves) to beat forcefully against **6** to attack (someone) with words of ridicule or scolding **7** to flick or wave sharply to and fro: *his tail lashing in irritation* **8** to urge as with a whip: *to lash the audience into a violent mood* ▷ See also **lash out** [perhaps imitative]

lash[2] *vb* to bind or secure with rope, string, or cord [Latin *laqueus* noose]

lashing[1] *n* **1** a flogging **2** a scolding

lashing[2] *n* rope, string, or cord used for binding or securing

lashings *pl n old-fashioned, informal* large amounts; lots: *lashings of cream*

lash out *vb* **1** to make a sudden verbal or physical attack **2** *informal* to spend extravagantly

lass *n* a girl or young woman [origin unknown]

Lassa fever *n* a serious viral disease of Central West Africa, characterized by high fever and muscular pains [after *Lassa*, the Nigerian village where it was first identified]

lassie *n Scot & N English informal* a little lass; girl

lassitude *n* physical or mental weariness [Latin *lassus* tired]

lasso (lass-oo) *n, pl* **-sos** *or* **-soes** **1** a long rope with a noose at one end used for catching horses and cattle ▷ *vb* **-soing, -soed** **2** to catch as with a lasso [Spanish, from Latin *laqueus* noose] **lassoer** *n*

last[1] *adj* **1** being, happening, or coming at the end or after all others **2** most recent: *last April* **3** only remaining: *that's the last one* **4** most extreme; utmost **5** least suitable or likely: *it's the last place on earth I would have expected to be recognized* ▷ *adv* **6** after all others **7** most recently: *we last saw him on Thursday night* **8** as the last or latest item ▷ *n* **9 the last** **A** a person or thing that is last **B** the final moment; end **10** the final appearance, mention, or occurrence: *the last of this season's visitors* **11 at last** in the end; finally **12 at long last** finally, after difficulty or delay [variant of Old English *latest*, *lætest*]

> **USAGE** Since *last* can mean either *after all others* or *most recent*, it is better to avoid using this word where ambiguity might arise, as in *her last novel*. *Final* or *latest* should be used in such contexts to avoid ambiguity.

last[2] *vb* **1** to continue to exist for a length of time: *the soccer war lasted 100 hours* **2** to be sufficient for the needs of (a person) for a length of time: *I shall make a couple of bottles to last me until next summer* **3** to remain fresh, uninjured, or unaltered for a certain time: *the flowers haven't lasted well* ▷ See also **last out** [Old English *lǣstan*]

last[3] *n* the wooden or metal form on which a shoe or boot is made or repaired [Old English *lāst* footprint]

last-ditch *adj* done as a final resort: *a last-ditch attempt*

lasting *adj* existing or remaining effective for a long time

Last Judgment *n* **the Last Judgment** *theol* God's verdict on the destinies of all human beings at the end of the world

lastly *adv* **1** at the end or at the last point **2** finally

last-minute *adj* given or done at the latest possible time: *last-minute changes*

last name *n* same as **surname**

last out *vb* **1** to be sufficient for one's needs: *if the energy supply lasts out* **2** to endure or survive: *I might not last out my hours of duty*

last post *n military* **1** a bugle call used to signal the time to retire at night **2** a similar call sounded at military funerals

last rites *pl n Christianity* religious rites for those close to death

last straw *n* a small incident, irritation, or setback that coming after others is too much to cope with

Last Supper *n* **the Last Supper** *Christianity* the meal eaten by Christ with his disciples on the night before his Crucifixion

lat. latitude

Lat. Latin

latch *n* **1** a fastening for a gate or door that consists of a bar that may be slid or lowered into a groove, hole, or notch **2** a spring-loaded door lock that can only be opened by a key from outside ▷ *vb* **3** to fasten, fit, or be fitted with a latch [Old English *læccan* to seize]

latchkey child *n Brit, Austral & NZ* a child who has to let himself or herself in after school, as there is no adult at home then

latch on *vb informal* **1** (often foll. by *to*) to attach oneself (to): *he should latch on to a man with a deal to do* **2** to understand: *it took a while to latch on to what he was trying to say*

late *adj* **1** occurring or arriving after the correct or expected time: *the plane will be late* **2** towards or near the end: *the late afternoon* **3** occurring or being at a relatively advanced time: *a late starter, his first novel was effectively his last* **4** at an advanced time in the evening or at night: *it's late, I have to get back* **5** having died recently: *her late father* **6** recent: *recollect the late defeats which your enemies have experienced* **7** former: *the late manager of the team* **8 of late** recently ▷ *adv* **9** after the correct or expected time: *Leela arrived late* **10** at a relatively advanced age: *coming late to motherhood* **11** recently: *as late as in 1983, only 9 per cent of that labour force was unionized* **12 late in the day** **A** at a late or advanced stage **B** too late [Old English *læt*] **lateness** *n*

> **USAGE** Since *late* can mean *deceased*, many people think it is better to avoid using this word to refer to the person who held a post or position before its present holder: *the previous* (not *the late*) *editor of The Times*.

lateen *adj naut* denoting a rig with a triangular sail bent to a yard hoisted to the head of a low mast [French *voile latine* Latin sail]
Late Greek *n* the Greek language from about the 3rd to the 8th centuries AD
Late Latin *n* the form of written Latin used from the 3rd to the 7th centuries AD
lately *adv* in recent times; of late
latent *adj* lying hidden and not yet developed within a person or thing [Latin *latere* to lie hidden] **latency** *n*
later *adj, adv* **1** the comparative of **late** ▷ *adv* **2** afterwards
lateral (lat-ter-al) *adj* of or relating to the side or sides [Latin *latus* side] **laterally** *adv*
lateral thinking *n* a way of solving problems by apparently illogical methods
latest *adj, adv* **1** the superlative of **late** ▷ *adj* **2** most recent, modern, or new: *the latest fashions* ▷ *n* **3 at the latest** no later than the time specified
latex *n* a milky fluid produced by many plants: latex from the rubber plant is used in the manufacture of rubber [Latin: liquid]
lath *n* one of several thin narrow strips of wood used as a supporting framework for plaster or tiles [Old English *lætt*]
lathe *n* a machine for shaping metal or wood by turning it against a fixed tool [perhaps from Old Norse]
lather *n* **1** foam formed by soap or detergent in water **2** foamy sweat, as produced by a horse **3** *informal* a state of agitation ▷ *vb* **4** to coat or become coated with lather **5** to form a lather **6** *informal* to beat; flog [Old English *lēathor* soap] **lathery** *adj*
Latin *n* **1** the language of ancient Rome and the Roman Empire **2** a member of any of those peoples whose languages are derived from Latin ▷ *adj* **3** of the Latin language **4** of those peoples whose languages are derived from Latin **5** of the Roman Catholic Church [Latin *Latinus* of Latium]
Latin America *n* those areas of South and Central America whose official languages are Spanish and Portuguese **Latin American** *adj, n*
latish *adj, adv* rather late
latitude *n* **1 A** an angular distance measured in degrees north or south of the equator **B** (*often pl*) a region considered with regard to its distance from the equator **2** scope for freedom of action and thought [Latin *latus* broad] **latitudinal** *adj*
latitudinarian *adj* **1** liberal, esp. in religious matters ▷ *n* **2** a person with latitudinarian views
latrine *n* a toilet in a barracks or camp [Latin *lavatrina* bath]
latte (lat-tay) *n* a drink of strong coffee mixed with hot milk [Italian (*caffè e*) *latte* coffee and milk]
latter *n* **1 the latter** the second or second mentioned of two ▷ *adj* **2** near or nearer the end: *the latter half of the season* **3** more advanced in time or sequence; later [Old English *lætra*]

> **USAGE** *The latter* should only be used to refer to the second of two items: *many people choose to go by hovercraft rather than use the ferry, but I prefer the latter.* The last of three or more items can be referred to as *the last-named.*

latter-day *adj* present-day; modern
latterly *adv* recently; lately
lattice (lat-iss) *n* **1** Also called: **latticework** a framework of strips of wood or metal interlaced in a diagonal pattern **2** a gate, screen, or fence formed of such a framework **3** an array of atoms, ions, or molecules in a crystal, or an array of points indicating their positions in space ▷ *vb* **-ticing, -ticed 4** to make, adorn, or supply with a lattice [Old French *latte* lath] **latticed** *adj*
Latvian *adj* **1** from Latvia ▷ *n* **2** a person from Latvia **3** the language of Latvia
laud *literary* ▷ *vb* **1** to praise or glorify ▷ *n* **2** praise or glorification [Latin *laudare* to praise]
laudable *adj* deserving praise; commendable **laudability** *n* **laudably** *adv*
laudanum (lawd-a-num) *n* a sedative extracted from opium [New Latin]
laudatory *adj* (of speech or writing) expressing praise
laugh *vb* **1** to express amusement or happiness by producing a series of inarticulate sounds **2** to utter or express with laughter: *he laughed his derision at the play* **3** to bring or force (oneself) into a certain condition by laughter: *laughing herself silly* **4 laugh at** to make fun of; jeer at **5 laugh up one's sleeve** to laugh secretly ▷ *n* **6** the act or an instance of laughing **7** *informal* a person or thing that causes laughter: *he's a laugh, that one* **8 the last laugh** final success after previous defeat ▷ See also **laugh off** [Old English *læhan, hliehhen*] **laughingly** *adv*
laughable *adj* ridiculous because so obviously inadequate or unsuccessful
laughing gas *n* nitrous oxide used as an anaesthetic: it may cause laughter and exhilaration when inhaled
laughing stock *n* a person or thing that is treated with ridicule
laugh off *vb* to treat (something serious or difficult) lightly
laughter *n* the action or noise of laughing [Old English *hleahtor*]
launch[1] *vb* **1** to move (a vessel) into the water, esp. for the first time **2 A** to start off or set in motion: *to launch an appeal* **B** to put (a new product) on the market **3** to set (a rocket, missile, or spacecraft) into motion **4** to involve (oneself) totally and enthusiastically: *Francis launched himself into the transfer market with gusto* **5 launch into** to start talking or writing (about) **6** (usually foll. by *out*) to start (out) on a new enterprise ▷ *n* **7** an act or instance of launching [Late Latin *lanceare* to use a lance, hence to set in motion] **launcher** *n*
launch[2] *n* an open motorboat [Malay *lancharan* boat, from *lanchar* speed]
launch pad *or* **launching pad** *n* a platform from which a spacecraft, rocket, or missile is launched
launder *vb* **1** to wash and iron (clothes and linen) **2** to make (money illegally obtained) appear to be legally gained by passing it through foreign banks or legitimate enterprises [Latin *lavare* to wash]
Launderette *n Brit, Austral & NZ trademark* an establishment where clothes can be washed and

dried, using coin-operated machines. Also called (US, Canad, Austral, NZ): **Laundromat**

laundry *n, pl* **-dries** **1** the clothes or linen to be laundered or that have been laundered **2** a place where clothes and linen are washed and ironed

laundry list *n US & Canad* a list of items perceived as being long

laureate (lor-ee-at) *adj* **1** *literary* crowned with laurel leaves as a sign of honour ▷ *n* **2** short for **poet laureate** [Latin *laurea* laurel] **laureateship** *n*

laurel *n* **1** a small Mediterranean evergreen tree with glossy leaves **2 laurels** a wreath of laurel, worn on the head as an emblem of victory or honour in classical times **3 laurels** honour, distinction, or fame **4 look to one's laurels** to be on guard against one's rivals **5 rest on one's laurels** to be satisfied with what one has already achieved and stop striving for further success [Latin *laurus*]

lav *n Brit informal* short for **lavatory**

lava *n* **1** molten rock discharged by volcanoes **2** any rock formed by the solidification of lava [Latin *lavare* to wash]

lavatorial *adj* characterized by frequent reference to excretion: *lavatorial humour*

lavatory *n, pl* **-ries** same as **toilet** [Latin *lavare* to wash]

lavender *n* **1** a plant grown for its bluish-purple flowers and as the source of a sweet-smelling oil **2** its dried flowers, used to perfume clothes ▷ *adj* **3** pale bluish-purple [Medieval Latin *lavendula*]

lavender water *n* a light perfume made from lavender

lavish *adj* **1** great in quantity or richness: *lavish banquets* **2** very generous in giving **3** extravagant; wasteful: *lavish spending habits* ▷ *vb* **4** to give or spend very generously or in great quantities [Old French *lavasse* torrent] **lavishly** *adv*

law *n* **1** a rule or set of rules regulating what may or may not be done by members of a society or community **2** a rule or body of rules made by the legislature or other authority. Related adjectives: **legal, judicial, juridical** **3** the control enforced by such rules: *scant respect for the rule of law* **4 the law** **A** the legal or judicial system **B** the profession or practice of law **C** *informal* the police or a police officer **5 law and order** the policy of strict enforcement of the law, esp. against crime and violence **6** a rule of behaviour: *an unwritten law that teacher knows best* **7** Also called: **law of nature** a generalization based on a recurring fact or event **8** the science or knowledge of law; jurisprudence **9** a general principle, formula, or rule in mathematics, science, or philosophy: *the law of gravity* **10 the Law** the laws contained in the first five books of the Old Testament **11 go to law** to resort to legal proceedings on some matter **12 lay down the law** to speak in an authoritative manner [Old English *lagu*]

law-abiding *adj* obeying the laws: *a law-abiding citizen*

lawbreaker *n* a person who breaks the law **lawbreaking** *n, adj*

lawful *adj* allowed, recognized, or sanctioned by law; legal **lawfully** *adv*

lawgiver *n* **1** the giver of a code of laws **2** Also called: **lawmaker** a maker of laws **lawgiving** *n, adj*

lawless *adj* **1** breaking the law, esp. in a wild or violent way: *lawless butchery* **2** not having laws **lawlessness** *n*

Law Lords *pl n* (in Britain) members of the House of Lords who sit as the highest court of appeal

lawn[1] *n* an area of cultivated and mown grass [Old French *lande*]

lawn[2] *n* a fine linen or cotton fabric [probably from *Laon*, town in France where made]

lawn mower *n* a hand-operated or power-operated machine for cutting grass

lawn tennis *n* **1** tennis played on a grass court **2** same as **tennis**

lawrencium *n chem* an element artificially produced from californium. Symbol: **Lr** [after E. O. *Lawrence*, physicist]

lawsuit *n* a case in a court of law brought by one person or group against another

lawyer *n* a member of the legal profession who can advise clients about the law and represent them in court

lax *adj* lacking firmness; not strict [Latin *laxus* loose] **laxity** *n*

laxative *n* **1** a medicine that induces the emptying of the bowels ▷ *adj* **2** easing the emptying of the bowels [Latin *laxare* to loosen]

lay[1] *vb* **lays, laying, laid** **1** to put in a low or horizontal position; cause to lie: *Mary laid a clean square of white towelling carefully on the grass* **2** to establish as a basis: *ready to lay your new fashion foundations?* **3** to place in a particular state or position: *he laid a finger in his lips* **4** to regard as the responsibility of: *ridiculous attempts to lay the loss at the door of the Admiralty* **5** to put forward: *ruses by which we lay claim on one another* **6** to arrange or prepare: *she would lay her plans* **7** to place in position: *he laid a wreath* **8** (of birds, esp. the domestic hen) to produce (eggs) **9** to make (a bet) with (someone): *I'll lay money he's already gone home* **10** to arrange (a table) for a meal **11** to prepare (a fire) by arranging fuel in the grate **12** *taboo slang* to have sexual intercourse with **13 lay bare** to reveal or explain: *a century of neurophysiology has now laid bare the structures of the brain* **14 lay hold of** to seize or grasp **15 lay oneself open** to make oneself vulnerable (to criticism or attack) **16 lay open** to reveal or disclose **17 lay waste** to destroy completely ▷ *n* **18** the manner or position in which something lies or is placed **19** *taboo slang* **A** an act of sexual intercourse **B** a sexual partner ▷ See also **lay aside, lay down** *etc.* [Old English *lecgan*]

> **USAGE** In standard English, the verb *lay* can only be used with an object, and *lie* can only be used without one: *the Queen laid a wreath; he was lying on the floor.*

lay[2] *vb* the past tense of **lie**[2]

lay[3] *adj* **1** of or involving people who are not members of the clergy **2** nonprofessional or nonspecialist [Greek *laos* people]

lay[4] *n* a short narrative poem intended to be sung [Old French *lai*]

layabout *n* a lazy person

lay aside *vb* **1** to abandon or reject **2** to put aside (one thing) in order to take up another **3** to store or reserve for future use

lay-by *n* **1** *Brit* a place where drivers can stop by the side of a main road **2** *Austral & NZ* a system of payment whereby a buyer pays a deposit on an article, which is reserved for him or her until he or she has paid the full price

lay down *vb* **1** to place on the ground or a surface **2** to sacrifice: *willing to lay down their lives for the truth* **3** to formulate (a rule or principle) **4** to record (plans) on paper **5** to store or stock: *the speed with which we lay down extra, unwanted fat*

layer *n* **1** a single thickness of something, such as a cover or a coating on a surface **2** a laying hen **3** *horticulture* a shoot that forms its own root while still attached to the parent plant ▷ *vb* **4** to form or make a layer or layers [from LAY¹]

layette *n* a complete set of clothing, bedclothes, and other accessories for a newborn baby [Middle Dutch *laege* box]

lay figure *n* **1** an artist's jointed dummy, used esp. for studying effects of drapery **2** a person considered to be subservient or unimportant [Dutch *leeman*, literally: joint-man]

lay in *vb* to accumulate and store: *they've already laid in five hundred bottles of great vintages*

lay into *vb informal* to attack or scold severely

layman *or fem* **laywoman** *n, pl* **-men** *or* **-women** **1** a person who is not a member of the clergy **2** a person who does not have specialized knowledge of a subject: *the layman's guide to nuclear power*

lay off *vb* **1** to suspend (staff) during a slack period at work **2** *informal* to leave (a person, thing, or activity) alone: *'Lay off the defence counsel bit!' he snapped* ▷ *n* **lay-off** **3** a period of imposed unemployment

lay on *vb* **1** to provide or supply: *they laid on a treat for the entourage* **2** **lay it on thick** *slang* to exaggerate, esp. when flattering

lay out *vb* **1** to arrange or spread out **2** to plan or design: *the main streets were laid out on a grid system* **3** to prepare (a corpse) for burial or cremation **4** *informal* to spend (money), esp. lavishly **5** *informal* to knock (someone) unconscious ▷ *n* **layout** **6** the arrangement or plan of something, such as a building **7** the arrangement of printed material

lay reader *n* **1** *Church of England* a person licensed to conduct religious services other than the Eucharist **2** *RC Church* a lay person chosen to read the epistle at Mass

lay up *vb* **1** *informal* to confine through illness: *laid up with a bad cold* **2** to store for future use

laze *vb* **lazing, lazed** **1** to be idle or lazy **2** (often foll. by *away*) to spend (time) in idleness ▷ *n* **3** time spent lazing [from *lazy*]

lazy *adj* **lazier, laziest** **1** not inclined to work or exert oneself **2** done in a relaxed manner with little effort **3** moving in a sluggish manner: *the lazy drift of the bubbles* [origin unknown] **lazily** *adv* **laziness** *n*

lazybones *n informal* a lazy person

lb **1** pound (weight) **2** *cricket* leg bye

lbw *cricket* leg before wicket

lc **1** in the place cited **2** *printing* lower case [(sense 1) Latin *loco citato*]

LCD **1** liquid-crystal display **2** Also: **lcd** lowest common denominator

lcm *or* **LCM** lowest common multiple

lea *n* **1** *poetic* a meadow or field **2** grassland [Old English *lēah*]

LEA (in Britain) Local Education Authority

leach *vb* **1** to remove or be removed from a substance by a liquid passing through it **2** to lose soluble substances by the action of a liquid passing through [perhaps Old English *leccan* to water]

lead¹ (rhymes with **seed**) *vb* **leading, led** **1** to show the way to (an individual or a group) by going with or ahead: *he led her into the house* **2** to guide, control, or direct: *he dismounted and led his horse back* **3** to influence someone to act, think, or behave in a certain way: *researching our family history has led her to correspond with relatives abroad* **4** to have the principal part in (something): *planners led the development of policy* **5** to go at the head of or have the top position in (something): *the pair led the field by almost two minutes* **6** (of a road or way) to be the means of reaching a place: *the footbridge leads on to a fine promenade* **7** to pass or spend: *I've led a happy life* **8** to guide or be guided by physical means: *she took him firmly by the arm and led him home* **9** to direct the course of (water, a rope, or wire) along, or as if along, a channel **10** (foll. by *with*) to have as the most important item: *the Review leads with a critique of A Place of Greater Safety* **11** *Brit music* to play first violin in (an orchestra) **12** to begin a round of cards by putting down the first card ▷ *n* **13** the first or most prominent place **14** example or leadership: *some of his children followed his lead* **15** an advantage over others: *Essex have a lead of 24 points* **16** an indication; clue: *we've got a lead on how the body got into the water* **17** a length of leather, nylon, or chain used to walk or control a dog **18** the principal role in a play, film, or other production, or the person playing such a role **19** the most important news story in a newspaper: *the shooting makes the lead in The Times* **20** the act of playing the first card in a round of cards or the card so played **21** a wire, cable, or other conductor for making an electrical connection ▷ *adj* **22** acting as a leader or lead: *lead singer* ▷ See also **lead off**, **lead on** *etc.* [Old English *lǣdan*]

lead² (rhymes with **bed**) *n* **1** a heavy toxic bluish-white metallic element: used in alloys, cable sheaths, paints, and as a radiation shield. Symbol: **Pb** **2** **A** graphite used for drawing **B** a thin stick of this as the core of a pencil **3** a lead weight suspended on a line, used to take soundings of the depth of water **4** lead weights or shot, as used in cartridges or fishing lines **5** a thin strip of lead for holding small panes of glass or pieces of stained glass **6** **leads** **A** thin sheets or strips of lead used as a roof covering **B** a roof covered with such sheets **7** Also called: **leading** *printing* a thin strip of metal, formerly used for spacing between lines of type ▷ *adj* **8** of, relating to, or containing lead ▷ *vb* **9** to surround, cover, or secure with lead or leads [Old English *lēad*]

leaded *adj* **1** (of petrol) containing tetraethyl lead in order to improve combustion **2** (of windows) made from many small panes of glass held together by lead strips

leaden *adj* **1** heavy or sluggish: *my limbs felt leaden* **2** of a dull greyish colour: *leaden November sky* **3** made of lead **4** gloomy, spiritless, or lifeless: *hollow characters and leaden dialogue*

leader *n* **1** a person who rules, guides, or inspires others; head **2** Also: **leading article** *Brit & Austral* the leading editorial in a newspaper **3** *music* the principal first violinist of an orchestra who acts as the conductor's deputy **4** the person or animal who is leading in a race **5** the best or the most successful of its kind: *the company is a world leader in its field* **6** the leading horse or dog in a team **7** *botany* any of the long slender shoots that grow from the stem or branch of a tree **leadership** *n*

leaderboard *n* a board displaying the current scores of the leading competitors, esp. in a golf tournament

lead-in *n* an introduction to a subject

leading *adj* **1** principal or primary: *the leading designers* **2** in the first position: *the leading driver*

leading aircraftman *or fem* **leading aircraftwoman** *n* the rank above aircraftman in the Royal Air Force

leading light *n* an important and influential person in an organization or campaign

leading question *n* a question worded to suggest the desired answer, such as *What do you think of the horrible effects of pollution?*

leading rating *n* a rank in the Royal Navy comparable to a corporal in the army

lead off *vb* to begin

lead on *vb* to trick (someone) into believing or doing something wrong

lead pencil *n* a pencil containing a thin stick of a graphite compound

lead poisoning *n* acute or chronic poisoning by lead

lead time *n* *manufacturing* the time between the design of a product and its production

lead up to *vb* **1** to act as a preliminary or introduction to **2** to approach (a topic) gradually or cautiously

leaf *n, pl* **leaves** **1** one of the flat usually green blades attached to the stem of a plant **2** the foliage of a tree or plant: *shrubs have been planted for their leaf interest* **3** **in leaf** (of shrubs or trees) with all its leaves fully opened **4** a very thin sheet of metal **5** one of the sheets of paper in a book **6** a hinged, sliding, or detachable part, such as an extension to a table **7** **take a leaf out of someone's book** to imitate someone in a particular course of action **8** **turn over a new leaf** to begin a new and improved course of behaviour ▷ *vb* **9** (usually foll. by *through*) to turn pages casually or hurriedly without reading them **10** (of plants) to produce leaves [Old English *lēaf*] **leafless** *adj*

leafage *n* the leaves of plants

leaflet *n* **1** a sheet of printed matter distributed, usually free, for advertising or information **2** any small leaf **3** one of the divisions of a compound leaf ▷ *vb* **-leting, -leted** **4** to distribute leaflets (to)

leaf mould *n* a rich soil consisting of decayed leaves

leafy *adj* **leafier, leafiest** **1** covered with leaves **2** having many trees or shrubs: *a leafy suburb*

league[1] *n* **1** an association of people or nations formed to promote the interests of its members **2** an association of sporting clubs that organizes matches between member teams **3** *informal* a class or level: *the guy is not even in the same league* **4** **in league (with)** working or planning together with ▷ *vb* **leaguing, leagued** **5** to form or be formed into a league [Latin *ligare* to bind]

league[2] *n* an obsolete unit of distance of varying length: commonly equal to 3 miles (4.8 km) [Late Latin *leuga, leuca*]

leak *n* **1** **A** a crack or hole that allows the accidental escape or entrance of liquid, gas, radiation, etc. **B** such escaping or entering liquid, etc. **2** a disclosure of secret information **3** the loss of current from an electrical conductor because of faulty insulation **4** the act or an instance of leaking **5** *slang* urination ▷ *vb* **6** to enter or escape, or allow to enter or escape, through a crack or hole **7** to make (secret information) public, esp. deliberately [from Old Norse] **leaky** *adj*

leakage *n* the act, an instance, or the result of leaking: *the leakage of 60 tonnes of oil*

lean[1] *vb* **leaning, leaned** *or* **leant** **1** (foll. by *against, on* or *upon*) to rest or put (something) so that it rests against a support **2** to bend or make (something) bend from an upright position **3** (foll. by *to* or *towards*) to have or express a tendency or preference ▷ *n* **4** the condition of bending from an upright position ▷ See also **lean on** [Old English *hleonian, hlinian*]

lean[2] *adj* **1** (esp. of a person) having a trim body with no surplus flesh **2** (of meat) having little or no fat **3** (of a period) sparse, difficult, or causing hardship: *we've been through some lean times in recent years* ▷ *n* **4** the part of meat that contains little or no fat [Old English *hlǣne*] **leanness** *n*

leaning *n* a tendency or inclination

lean on *vb* **1** *informal* to try to influence (someone) by using threats **2** to depend on (someone) for help and advice

leant *vb* a past of **lean**[1]

lean-to *n, pl* **-tos** a building with a sloping roof attached to another building or a wall

leap *vb* **leaping, leapt** *or* **leaped** **1** to jump suddenly from one place to another **2** (often foll. by *at*) to move or react quickly **3** to jump over ▷ *n* **4** the act of jumping **5** an abrupt or important change or increase: *it's been a huge leap to the Premiership from where I started with Wigan* **6** **a leap in the dark** an action performed without knowledge of the consequences **7** **by leaps and bounds** with unexpectedly rapid progress [Old English *hlēapan*]

leapfrog *n* **1** a children's game in which each player in turn leaps over the others' bent backs ▷ *vb* **-frogging, -frogged** **2** **A** to play leapfrog **B** to leap over (something) **3** to advance by jumps or stages

leap year *n* a calendar year of 366 days, February 29 (**leap day**) being the additional day, that occurs every four years

learn *vb* **learning, learned** *or* **learnt** **1** to gain knowledge (of something) or acquire skill in (some art or practice) **2** to memorize (something)

3 to gain by experience, example, or practice: *I learned everything the hard way* **4** (often foll. by *of* or *about*) to become informed; find out: *Captain Nelson learned of the disaster from his wireless* [Old English *leornian*] **learnable** *adj* **learner** *n*

learned (**lurn**-id) *adj* **1** having great knowledge **2** involving or characterized by scholarship: *your learned paper on the subject*

learning *n* knowledge gained by studying

learning difficulties *pl n* difficulty experienced in reaching the average standard of people of the same age group in intellectual and cognitive skills

lease *n* **1** a contract by which an owner rents buildings or land to another person for a specified period **2 a new lease of life** a prospect of renewed energy, health, or happiness ▷ *vb* **leasing, leased 3** to let or rent (land or buildings) by lease [Old French *laissier* to let go]

leasehold *n* **1** land or property held under a lease **2** the holding of such property under lease **leaseholder** *n*

leash *n* **1** a dog's lead **2 straining at the leash** eagerly impatient to begin something ▷ *vb* **3** to put a leash on [Old French *laissier* to loose (hence to let a dog run on a leash)]

least *adj, adv* **1 the least** the superlative of **little**: *without encountering the least sign of civilization; the least talented player on the team* ▷ *adj* **2** of very little importance **3** smallest ▷ *adv* **4 at least** if nothing else: *at least I wrote* **5 at the least** at the minimum: *at the very least you should have some self-respect* **6 not in the least** not at all: *you're not detaining me, not in the least* [Old English *lǣst*, superlative of *lǣssa* less]

leastways *or US & Canad* **leastwise** *adv informal* at least; anyway

leather *n* **1** the skin of an animal made smooth and flexible by tanning and removing the hair **2 leathers** leather clothes, esp. as worn by motorcyclists ▷ *adj* **3** made of leather ▷ *vb* **4** to whip as if with a leather strap **5** to dress in leather [Old English *lether-* (in compound words)]

leatherjacket *n* **1** any of various tropical fishes having a leathery skin **2** the tough-skinned larva of certain craneflies, which destroy the roots of grasses

leathery *adj* looking or feeling like leather, esp. in toughness

leave[1] *vb* **leaving, left 1** to go away (from a person or place) **2** to cause to remain behind, often by mistake, in a place: *I left the paper under the table* **3** to cause to be or remain in a specified state: *the poll leaves the parties neck-and-neck* **4** to stop attending or belonging to a particular organization or institution: *at seventeen she left the convent* **5** to not eat something or not deal with something: *he left a half-eaten lunch* **6** to result in; cause: *I have been terribly hurt by past partners, it leaves indelible marks* **7** to allow (someone) to do something without interfering: *the governor left them to it for a further few hours* **8** to be survived by (members of one's family): *he leaves a widow and one daughter* **9** to bequeath: *her adored son left his millions to an unknown half-sister* **10** to have as a remainder: *37 - 14 leaves 23* **11 leave (someone) alone** **A** to stop annoying (someone) **B** to permit to stay or be alone ▷ See also **leave off**, **leave out** [Old English *lǣfan*]

leave[2] *n* **1** permission to be absent, for instance from work: *so I asked for leave* **2** the length of such absence: *weekend leave* **3** permission to do something: *they were refused leave to appeal* **4 on leave** officially excused from work or duty **5 take (one's) leave of** to say farewell to [Old English *lēaf*]

leaven (**lev**-ven) *n also* **leavening 1** any substance, such as yeast, that produces fermentation in dough and makes it rise **2** an influence that produces a gradual change ▷ *vb* **3** to cause fermentation in (dough) **4** to spread through, causing a gradual change [Latin *levare* to raise]

leave off *vb* **1** to stop; cease **2** to stop wearing or using

leave out *vb* to omit or exclude: *leave out everything not necessary to living*

leaves *n* the plural of **leaf**

leave-taking *n* a departing; a farewell

leavings *pl n* things left behind unwanted, such as food on a plate

Lebanese *adj* **1** from the Lebanon ▷ *n, pl* **-nese 2** a person from the Lebanon

Lebensraum (**lay**-benz-rowm) *n* territory claimed by a nation or state because it is necessary for survival or growth [German: living space]

lecherous (**letch**-er-uss) *adj* having or showing strong and uncontrolled sexual desire [Old French *lechier* to lick] **lecher** *n* **lechery** *n*

lecithin (**less**-sith-in) *n biochem* a yellow-brown compound found in plant and animal tissues, esp. egg yolk: used in making cosmetics and inks, and as an emulsifier and stabilizer (**E322**) in foods [Greek *lekithos* egg yolk]

lectern *n* a sloping reading desk, esp. in a church [Latin *legere* to read]

lecture *n* **1** a talk on a particular subject delivered to an audience **2** a lengthy scolding ▷ *vb* **-turing, -tured 3** to deliver a lecture (to an audience or class) **4** to scold (someone) at length [Latin *legere* to read] **lecturer** *n* **lectureship** *n*

led *vb* the past of **lead**[1]

LED *electronics* light-emitting diode: a semiconductor that gives out light when an electric current is applied to it

ledge *n* **1** a narrow horizontal surface that projects from a wall or window **2** a narrow shelflike projection on a cliff or mountain [perhaps Middle English *leggen* to lay]

ledger *n accounting* the principal book in which the commercial transactions of a company are recorded [perhaps Middle English *leggen* to lay (because kept in a specific place)]

ledger line *n music* a short line above or below the staff used to indicate the pitch of notes higher or lower than the range of the staff

lee *n* **1** a sheltered part or side; the side away from the direction from which the wind is blowing ▷ *adj* **2** *naut* on, at, or towards the side away from the wind: *her lee rail was awash* [Old English *hlēow* shelter]

leech *n* **1** a worm which has a sucker at each end of the body and feeds on the blood or tissues of other animals **2** a person who lives off another person; parasite [Old English *lǣce*]

leek *n* a vegetable of the onion family with a slender white bulb and broad flat green overlapping leaves: the national emblem of Wales [Old English *lēac*]

leer *vb* **1** to give a sneering or suggestive look or grin ▷ *n* **2** such a look [Old English *hlēor* cheek]

leery *adj* **leerier, leeriest 1** *slang* (foll. by *of*) suspicious or wary **2** *chiefly dialect* knowing or sly [perhaps obsolete sense (to look askance) of *leer*]

lees *pl n* the sediment from an alcoholic drink [plural of obsolete *lee*, from Old French]

leet *n Scot* a list of candidates for an office [perhaps Anglo-French *litte*, variant of LIST[1]]

leeward *chiefly naut* ▷ *adj* **1** of, in, or moving in the direction towards which the wind blows ▷ *n* **2** the side towards the lee ▷ *adv* **3** towards the lee

leeway *n* **1** flexibility of action or expenditure: *he gave me a lot of leeway in the work I did* **2** sideways drift of a boat or aircraft

left[1] *adj* **1** denoting the side of something or someone that faces west when the front is turned towards the north **2** on the left side of the body: *I grabbed it with my left hand* **3** liberal, radical, or socialist ▷ *adv* **4** on or in the direction of the left ▷ *n* **5** a left side, direction, position, area, or part **6 the left** the people in a political party or society who have more socialist or liberal views: *the biggest party of the French Left* **7** *boxing* **A** a blow with the left hand **B** the left hand [Old English: idle, weak]

left[2] *vb* the past of **leave**[1]

left field *n* **1** *baseball* **A** the area of the outfield to the batter's left **B** the fielder who covers this area **2 out of left field** unexpected or surprising: *Their proposal came out of left field* ▷ *adj* **left-field 3** *US & Canad informal* unconventional or outside the mainstream

left-hand *adj* **1** of, on, or towards the left **2** for the left hand

left-handed *adj* **1** better at using the left hand than the right **2** done with the left hand **3** designed for use by the left hand **4** awkward or clumsy **5** ambiguous or insincere: *a left-handed compliment* **6** turning from right to left; anticlockwise ▷ *adv* **7** with the left hand: *I write left-handed* **left-hander** *n*

leftist *adj* **1** of or relating to the political left or its principles ▷ *n* **2** a person who supports the political left **leftism** *n*

left-luggage office *n Brit* a place at a railway station or airport where luggage may be left for a small charge

leftover *n* **1** (*often pl*) an unused portion, esp. of cooked food ▷ *adj* **2** left as an unused portion

leftward *adj, adv also* **leftwards** on or towards the left

left-wing *adj* **1** socialist or radical: *the party ditched many of its more left-wing policies* **2** belonging to the more radical part of a political party: *a group of left-wing Conservatives* ▷ *n* **left wing 3** the more radical or progressive section, esp. of a political party: *the left wing of the Labour Party* **4** *sport* **A** the left-hand side of the field of play **B** a player positioned in this area in certain games **left-winger** *n*

lefty *n, pl* **lefties** *informal* **1** *Brit, Austral & NZ* a left-winger **2** *chiefly US & Canad* a left-handed person

leg *n* **1** either of the two lower limbs in humans, or any similar structure in animals, that is used for movement or support **2** the part of a garment that covers the leg **3** a lower limb of an animal, esp. the thigh, used for food: *leg of lamb* **4** something similar to a leg in appearance or function, such as one of the supports of a chair **5** a section of a journey **6** a single stage, lap, or length in a relay race **7** one of a series of games, matches, or parts of games **8** *cricket* the side of the field to the left of a right-handed batsman as he faces the bowler **9 not have a leg to stand on** *informal* to have no reasonable basis for an opinion or argument **10 on one's last legs** worn out or exhausted **11 pull someone's leg** *informal* to tease or make fun of someone **12 shake a leg** *informal* to hurry up **13 stretch one's legs** to stand up or walk around, esp. after sitting for some time ▷ *vb* **legging, legged 14 leg it** *informal* to walk, run, or hurry [Old Norse *leggr*]

legacy *n, pl* **-cies 1** money or personal property left to someone by a will **2** something handed down to a successor [Medieval Latin *legatia* commission]

legal *adj* **1** established by or permitted by law; lawful **2** of or relating to law **3** relating to or characteristic of lawyers [Latin *legalis*] **legally** *adv*

legal aid *n* financial assistance available to people who are unable to meet the full cost of legal proceedings

legalese *n* the conventional language in which legal documents are written

legalism *n* strict adherence to the letter of the law **legalist** *n, adj* **legalistic** *adj*

legality *n, pl* **-ties** the state or quality of being legal or lawful

legalize *or* **-lise** *vb* **-lizing, -lized** *or* **-lising, -lised** to make lawful or legal **legalization** *or* **-lisation** *n*

legal tender *n* currency that a creditor must by law accept to pay a debt

legate *n* a messenger, esp. one representing the Pope [Latin *legare* to delegate]

legatee *n* the recipient of a legacy

legation *n* **1** a diplomatic mission headed by a minister **2** the official residence and office of a diplomatic minister

legato (leg-**ah**-toe) *music* ▷ *adv* **1** smoothly and evenly ▷ *n, pl* **-tos 2** a style of playing with no gaps between notes [Italian]

leg before wicket *n cricket* a dismissal on the grounds that a batsman has been struck on the leg by a bowled ball that otherwise would have hit the wicket. Abbrev: **lbw**

leg break *n cricket* a bowled ball that spins from leg to off on pitching

leg bye *n cricket* a run scored after the ball has hit the batsman's leg or some other part of his body, except his hand, without touching the bat. Abbrev: **lb**

legend *n* **1** a popular story handed down from earlier times which may or may not be true **2** such stories collectively **3** a person whose fame makes him or her seem exceptional: *he is a living legend* **4** modern stories about a famous person which may or may not be true: *no Garland fan could complain about sordid revelations tarnishing the legend* **5** words written on something to explain it: *a pub mirror spelling out the legend 'Saloon Bar'* **6** an explanation on a table, map, or chart, of the symbols used [Medieval Latin *legenda* passages to be read]

legendary *adj* **1** very famous: *the legendary beauty of the Alps* **2** of or relating to legend **3** described in legend: *the legendary birthplace of Aphrodite*

legerdemain (lej-er-de-**main**) *n* **1** same as **sleight of hand** **2** cunning deception [Old French: light of hand]

leger line *n* same as **ledger line**

leggings *pl n* **1** an extra outer covering for the lower legs **2** close-fitting trousers for women or children

leggy *adj* **1** having unusually long legs **2** (of a plant) having a long weak stem

leghorn *n* **1** a type of Italian wheat straw that is woven into hats **2** any hat made from this straw [English name for *Livorno*, in Italy]

Leghorn (leg-**gorn**) *n* a breed of domestic fowl

legible *adj* (of handwriting) able to be read [Latin *legere* to read] **legibility** *n* **legibly** *adv*

legion *n* **1** any large military force: *the French Foreign Legion* **2** *(often pl)* any very large number **3** an infantry unit in the ancient Roman army of three to six thousand men **4** an association of veterans [Latin *legio*] **legionary** *adj, n*

legionnaire *n (often cap)* a member of a legion

Legionnaire's disease *n* a serious bacterial infection, with symptoms similar to pneumonia [after the outbreak at a meeting of the American Legion in Philadelphia in 1976]

legislate *vb* **-lating, -lated** **1** to make or pass laws **2** to bring into effect by legislation [Latin *lex, legis* law + *latus*, past participle of *ferre* to bring] **legislator** *n*

legislation *n* **1** the act or process of making laws **2** the laws so made

legislative *adj* **1** of or relating to the process of making laws **2** having the power or function of making laws: *the House of Lords is one of the largest legislative assemblies in the world*

legislature *n* a body of people authorized to make, amend, and repeal laws

legit *adj informal* short for **legitimate**

legitimate *adj* **1** authorized by or in accordance with law: *legitimate accounting practices* **2** based on correct or acceptable principles of reasoning: *a legitimate argument* **3** (of a child) born of parents legally married to each other **4** of, relating to, or ruling by hereditary right: *under their legitimate ruling house* **5** of or relating to serious drama as distinct from films, television, or vaudeville ▷ *vb* **-mating, -mated** **6** to make, pronounce, or show to be legitimate [Medieval Latin *legitimatus* made legal] **legitimacy** *n* **legitimately** *adv*

legitimize *or* **-mise** *vb* **-mizing, -mized** *or* **-mising, -mised** to make legitimate; legalize **legitimization** *or* **-misation** *n*

legless *adj* **1** without legs **2** *slang* very drunk

Lego *n trademark* a brand of construction toy consisting of plastic bricks and other components that fit together [Danish *leg godt* play well]

leg-pull *n Brit informal* a practical joke

legroom *n* space to move one's legs comfortably, as in a car

leguaan *n* a large amphibious S African lizard [Dutch, from French *l'iguane* the iguana]

legume *n* **1** the pod of a plant of the pea or bean family **2** the seed from such pods, esp. beans or peas [Latin *legere* to pick (a crop)]

leguminous *adj* of or relating to any family of flowering plants having pods (or legumes) as fruits

lei *n* (in Hawaii) a garland of flowers, worn around the neck [Hawaiian]

Leics Leicestershire

leisure *n* **1** time or opportunity for relaxation or hobbies **2 at leisure** **a** having free time **b** not occupied **3 at one's leisure** when one has free time [Old French *leisir*] **leisured** *adj*

leisure centre *n* a building providing facilities, such as a swimming pool, gym, and café, for a range of leisure pursuits

leisurely *adj* **1** unhurried; relaxed ▷ *adv* **2** in a relaxed way **leisureliness** *n*

leitmotif *or* **leitmotiv** (**lite**-mote-eef) *n* **1** *music* a recurring melodic phrase used to suggest a character, thing, or idea **2** an often repeated image in a literary work [German: leading motif]

lekgotla (leh-**hot**-luh) *or* **kgotla** (**hot**-luh) *n S African* **1** a meeting place for village assemblies, court cases, and meetings of village leaders **2** a conference or business meeting [Sotho, Tswana]

lekker *adj S African slang* pleasing, enjoyable, or tasty [Afrikaans, from Dutch]

lemming *n* **1** a small rodent of northern and arctic regions, reputed to rush into the sea in large groups and drown **2** a member of any group following an unthinking course towards destruction [Norwegian]

lemon *n* **1** a yellow oval edible fruit with juicy acidic flesh that grows on an evergreen tree in warm and tropical regions **2** *slang* a person or thing considered to be useless or defective ▷ *adj* **3** light yellow [Arabic *laymūn*] **lemony** *adj*

lemonade *n* a drink made from lemon juice, sugar, and water, or from carbonated water, citric acid, and sweetener

lemon sole *n* an edible European flatfish

lemur *n* a nocturnal animal, related to the monkey, with a foxy face and long tail, found on Madagascar [Latin *lemures* ghosts]

lend *vb* **lending, lent** **1** to permit the temporary use of **2** to provide (money) temporarily, often at interest **3** to contribute (some abstract quality): *a painted trellis lends a classical air to any garden* **4 lend an ear** to listen **5 lend oneself** *or* **itself** to be appropriate for: *the building lends itself to loft conversion* [Old English *lǣnan*] **lender** *n*

length *n* **1** the extent or measurement of something from end to end **2** a specified distance, esp. between two positions: *the length of a cricket pitch* **3** a period of time, as between specified limits or moments **4** the quality, state, or fact of being long rather than short **5** a piece of something, usually longer than it is wide: *a length of twine* **6** *(usually pl)* the amount of trouble taken in doing something: *to go to great lengths*

7 *prosody & phonetics* the duration of a vowel or syllable **8 at length A** after a long interval or period of time **B** in great detail [Old English *lengthu*]

lengthen *vb* to make or become longer

lengthways *or* **lengthwise** *adv, adj* in, according to, or along the direction of length

lengthy *adj* **lengthier, lengthiest** very long or tiresome **lengthily** *adv* **lengthiness** *n*

lenient (lee-nee-ent) *adj* tolerant, not strict or severe [Latin *lenis* soft] **leniency** *n* **leniently** *adv*

lenity *n, pl* **-ties** mercy or clemency

lens *n* **1** a piece of glass or other transparent material with a curved surface or surfaces, used to bring together or spread rays of light passing through it: used in cameras, telescopes, and spectacles **2** *anatomy* a transparent structure in the eye, behind the iris, that focuses images on the retina [Latin: lentil]

lent *vb* the past of **lend**

Lent *n Christianity* the period from Ash Wednesday to Easter Saturday, during which some Christians give up doing something they enjoy [Old English *lencten, lengten* spring, literally: lengthening (of hours of daylight)] **Lenten** *adj*

lentil *n* any of the small edible seeds of a leguminous Asian plant [Latin *lens*]

lento *music* ▷ *adv* **1** slowly ▷ *n, pl* **-tos 2** a movement or passage performed slowly [Italian]

Leo *n astrol* the fifth sign of the zodiac; the Lion [Latin]

leonine *adj* of or like a lion [Latin *leo* lion]

leopard *or fem* **leopardess** *n* a large African and Asian mammal of the cat family, which has a tawny yellow coat with black spots. Also called: **panther** [Greek *leōn* lion + *pardos* panther]

leotard *n* a tight-fitting garment covering the body from the shoulders to the thighs and worn by acrobats, ballet dancers, and people doing exercises [after Jules *Léotard*, acrobat]

leper *n* **1** *offensive* a person who has leprosy **2** a person who is avoided [Greek *lepros* scaly]

> **USAGE** The use of *leper* can be offensive and should be avoided. Instead you should talk about *a person with leprosy*.

lepidopteran *n, pl* **-terans** *or* **-tera 1** an insect that has two pairs of fragile wings and develops from a caterpillar; a butterfly or moth ▷ *adj also* **lepidopterous 2** denoting such an insect [Greek *lepis* scale + *pteron* wing]

lepidopterist *n* a person who studies or collects moths and butterflies

leprechaun *n* (in Irish folklore) a mischievous elf [Irish Gaelic *leipreachān*]

leprosy *n pathol* a chronic infectious disease, characterized by painful inflamed lumps beneath the skin and disfigurement and wasting away of affected parts **leprous** *adj*

lepton *n physics* any of a group of elementary particles with weak interactions [Greek *leptos* thin]

lesbian *n* **1** a female homosexual ▷ *adj* **2** of or characteristic of lesbians [*Lesbos*, Greek Aegean island] **lesbianism** *n*

lese-majesty (lezz-maj-ist-ee) *n* **1** an offence against the sovereign power in a state; treason **2** an act of disrespect towards authority [from Latin *laesa majestas* wounded majesty]

lesion *n* **1** any structural change in an organ or tissue resulting from injury or disease **2** an injury or wound [Late Latin *laesio* injury]

less *adj* **1** the comparative of **little**: *less fibre* **2** *not standard* fewer ▷ *adv* **3** the comparative of **little**: *eat less* **4 less of** to a smaller extent or degree: *it would become less of a problem* **5 no less** *sometimes humorous* used to indicate admiration or surprise: *sculpted by a famous Frenchman, Rodin no less* ▷ *prep* **6** minus: *a two pounds-a-week rise (less tax)* [Old English *lǣssa, lǣs*]

> **USAGE** *Less* should not be confused with *fewer*. *Less* refers strictly only to quantity and not to number: *there is less water than before*. *Fewer* means smaller in number: *there are fewer people than before*.

lessee *n* a person to whom a lease is granted [Old French *lesser* to lease]

lessen *vb* to make or become less

lesser *adj* not as great in quantity, size, or worth

lesson *n* **1 A** a single period of instruction in a subject **B** the content of such a period **2** material assigned for individual study **3** something from which useful knowledge or principles can be learned: *one could still learn an important lesson from these masters* **4** an experience that serves as a warning or example: *the experience will prove a sobering lesson for the military* **5** a passage of Scripture read during a church service [Old French *leçon*]

lessor *n* a person who grants a lease of property

lest *conj* **1** so as to prevent any possibility that: *one grabbed it lest a neighbour got there first* **2** for fear that: *his anxiety lest anything mar the family event* [Old English *thȳ lǣs the*, literally: whereby less that]

let¹ *vb* **letting, let 1** to allow: *a child lets a friend play with his favourite toy* **2 A** an auxiliary expressing a request, proposal, or command, or conveying a warning or threat: *well, let's try it; just let me catch you here again!* **B** an auxiliary expressing an assumption or hypothesis: *let 'a' equal 'b'* **C** an auxiliary used to convey resigned acceptance of the inevitable: *let the worst happen* **3** to allow someone to rent (property or accommodation) **4** to cause the movement of (something) in a specified direction: *he let the air out of the tire* **5 let alone** not to mention: *I could hardly think, let alone find words to say* **6 let alone** *or* **be** stop annoying or interfering with: *let the poor cat alone* **7 let go** to relax one's hold (on) **8 let loose A** to allow (a person or animal) to leave or escape **B** *informal* to make (a sound) suddenly: *he let loose a laugh* **C** *informal* to fire (ammunition) from a gun ▷ *n* **9** *Brit & Austral* the act of letting property or accommodation ▷ See also **let down, let off** *etc.* [Old English *lǣtan* to permit]

let² *n* **1** *tennis & squash* a minor infringement or obstruction of the ball, requiring a point to be replayed **2 without let or hindrance** without obstruction [Old English *lettan* to hinder]

let down *vb* **1** to fail to satisfy the expectations of (someone); disappoint **2** to lower **3** to lengthen a garment by decreasing the hem **4** to deflate: *to let down a tyre* ▷ *n* **letdown 5** a disappointment

lethal *adj* capable of causing death [Latin *letum* death] **lethally** *adv*

lethargy *n, pl* **-gies 1** sluggishness or dullness **2** an abnormal lack of energy [Greek *lēthargos* drowsy] **lethargic** *adj* **lethargically** *adv*

let off *vb* **1** to excuse from (work or duties): *I'll let you off homework for a week* **2** to spare (someone) the expected punishment: *lots were let off because they couldn't be bothered to prosecute anybody* **3** to explode or fire (a bomb, gun, or firework) **4** to release (liquid, air, or steam)

let on *vb informal* **1** to reveal (a secret) **2** to pretend: *he let on that he was a pilgrim*

let out *vb* **1** to emit: *he let out a scream* **2** to allow to leave; release **3** to make (property) available for people to rent **4** to make (a garment) wider by reducing the seams **5** to reveal (a secret) ▷ *n* **let-out 6** a chance to escape

letter *n* **1** a written or printed message, usually enclosed in an envelope and sent by post **2** any of a set of conventional symbols used in writing or printing a language: character of the alphabet **3** the strict meaning of an agreement or document; exact wording: *the letter of the law* **4 to the letter** precisely: *you have to follow treatment to the letter for it to be effective* ▷ *vb* **5** to write or mark letters on (a sign) [Latin *littera* letter of the alphabet] **lettering** *n*

letter bomb *n* an explosive device in an envelope or parcel that explodes when the envelope or parcel is opened

letter box *n chiefly Brit* **1** a slot in a door through which letters are delivered **2** Also called: **pillar box, postbox** a public box into which letters and postcards are put for collection

lettered *adj* **1** well educated **2** printed or marked with letters

letterhead *n* a printed heading on stationery giving the name and address of the sender

letter of credit *n* a letter issued by a bank entitling the bearer to draw money from other banks

letterpress *n* a method of printing in which ink is transferred from raised surfaces to paper by pressure

letters *pl n* **1** literary knowledge or ability: *a man of letters* **2** literary culture in general

letters patent *pl n* See **patent** (senses 1, 3)

lettuce *n* a plant cultivated for its large edible leaves, which are used in salads [Latin *lactuca*, from *lac* milk, because of its milky juice]

let up *vb* **1** to diminish or stop **2** (foll. by *on*) *informal* to be less harsh (towards someone) ▷ *n* **let-up 3** *informal* a lessening: *there has been no let-up in the war*

leucocyte (loo-koh-site) *n* any of the various large white cells in the blood of vertebrates [Greek *leukos* white + *kutos* vessel]

leukaemia *or esp US* **leukemia** (loo-kee-mee-a) *n* an acute or chronic disease characterized by extreme overproduction of white blood cells [Greek *leukos* white + *haima* blood]

levee[1] *n US* **1** a natural or artificial river embankment **2** a quay [French, from Latin *levare* to raise]

levee[2] *n* a formal reception held by a sovereign just after rising from bed [French, from Latin *levare* to raise]

level *adj* **1** on a horizontal plane **2** having an even surface **3** being of the same height as something else: *the floor of the lean-to was level with the patio* **4** equal to or even with (something or someone else): *Johnson was level with the overnight leader* **5** not exceeding the upper edge of (a spoon, etc.) **6** consistent or regular: *a level pulse* **7 one's level best** the best one can do ▷ *vb* **-velling, -velled** *or US* **-veling, -veled 8** (sometimes foll. by *off*) to make horizontal or even **9** to make equal in position or status **10** to direct (an accusation or criticism) emphatically at someone **11** to focus (a look) directly at someone **12** to aim (a weapon) horizontally **13** to demolish completely ▷ *n* **14** a horizontal line or plane **15** a device, such as a spirit level, for determining whether a surface is horizontal **16** position or status in a scale of values: *a high-level delegation* **17** stage or degree of progress: *primary-school level* **18** a specified vertical position: *floor level* **19** the topmost horizontal line or plane from which the height of something is calculated: *sea level* **20** a flat even surface or area of land **21** a degree or intensity reached on a measurable or notional scale: *noise level* **22 on the level** *informal* sincere or genuine [Latin *libella*, diminutive of *libra* scales]

level crossing *n Brit, Austral & NZ* a point at which a railway line and a road cross

level-headed *adj* calm and sensible

lever *n* **1** a handle used to operate machinery **2** a bar used to move a heavy object or to prise something open **3** a rigid bar that turns on a fixed support (fulcrum) to transfer effort and motion, for instance to move a load **4** a means of exerting pressure in order to achieve an aim: *using the hostages as a lever to gain concessions from the government* ▷ *vb* **5** to open or move with a lever [Latin *levare* to raise]

leverage *n* **1** the mechanical advantage gained by using a lever **2** the ability to influence people or events: *information gives leverage*

leveraged buyout *n* a takeover bid in which a small company uses its assets, and those of the target company, to raise the loans required to finance the takeover

leveret (lev-ver-it) *n* a young hare [Latin *lepus* hare]

leviathan (lev-vie-ath-an) *n* any huge or powerful thing [Hebrew *liwyāthān*, a Biblical sea monster]

Levis *pl n trademark* denim jeans

levitate *vb* **-tating, -tated** to rise or cause to rise, suspended, in the air [Latin *levis* light] **levitation** *n*

levity *n, pl* **-ties** a frivolous or too light-hearted attitude to serious matters [Latin *levis* light]

levy (lev-vee) *vb* **levies, levying, levied 1** to impose and collect (a tax, tariff, or fine) **2** to conscript troops for service ▷ *n, pl* **levies 3 A** the imposition and collection of taxes, tariffs, or fines **B** the money so raised **4** troops conscripted for service [Latin *levare* to raise]

lewd *adj* indecently vulgar; obscene [Old English *lǣwde* lay, ignorant] **lewdly** *adv* **lewdness** *n*

lexical *adj* **1** relating to the vocabulary of a language **2** relating to a lexicon **lexically** *adv*

l

lexicography *n* the process or profession of compiling dictionaries **lexicographer** *n*
lexicon *n* **1** a dictionary, esp. one of an ancient language such as Greek **2** the vocabulary of a language or of an individual [Greek *lexis* word]
ley *n* land temporarily under grass [variant of *lea*]
Leyden jar (**lide**-en) *n physics* an early type of capacitor consisting of a glass jar with the lower part of the inside and outside coated with tinfoil [from *Leiden*, city in the Netherlands]
LGBT lesbian, gay, bisexual, and transgender
LGBTQ lesbian, gay, bisexual, transgender, and questioning
LGV (in Britain) large goods vehicle
Li *chem* lithium
liability *n, pl* **-ties 1** someone or something that is a problem or embarrassment **2** the state of being legally responsible **3** (*often pl*) sums of money owed by an organization
liable *adj* **1** probable or likely: *weak and liable to give way* **2** commonly suffering a condition: *he's liable to colds in the chest* **3** legally obliged or responsible; answerable [Old French *lier* to bind]

> **USAGE** The use of *liable to* to mean *probable or likely* was formerly considered incorrect, but is now acceptable.

liaise *vb* **-aising, -aised** (usually foll. by *with*) to communicate and maintain contact with
liaison *n* **1** communication and cooperative contact between groups **2** a secretive or adulterous sexual relationship [Old French *lier* to bind]
liana *n* a woody climbing and twining plant of tropical forests [French]
liar *n* a person who tells lies
lib *n informal* liberation: used in the name of certain movements: *women's lib; gay lib*
Lib *Brit, Austral & S African politics* Liberal
libation (lie-**bay**-shun) *n* **A** the pouring out of wine in honour of a deity **B** the wine so poured out [Latin *libare* to pour an offering of drink]
libel *n* **1** *law* the publication of something false which damages a person's reputation **2** any damaging or unflattering representation or statement ▷ *vb* **-belling, -belled** *or US* **-beling, -beled 3** *law* to make or publish a false damaging statement or representation about (a person) [Latin *libellus* a little book] **libellous** *or US* **libelous** *adj*
liberal *adj* **1** having social and political views that favour progress and reform **2** generous in temperament or behaviour **3** tolerant of other people **4** using or existing in large quantities; lavish: *the world's finest gadgetry, in liberal quantities* **5** not rigid; free: *a more liberal interpretation* **6** (of an education) designed to develop general cultural interests and intellectual ability **7 Liberal** of or relating to a Liberal Party ▷ *n* **8** a person who has liberal ideas or opinions [Latin *liber* free] **liberalism** *n* **liberally** *adv*
Liberal Democrat *n* a member or supporter of the Liberal Democrats, a British centrist political party that advocates proportional representation
liberality *n, pl* **-ties 1** generosity **2** the quality of being broad-minded
liberalize *or* **-lise** *vb* **-lizing, -lized** *or* **-lising, -ised** to make (a law) less strict **liberalization** *or* **-lisation** *n*
Liberal Party *n* **1** *history* a British non-Socialist political party which advocated progress and reform **2** any similar party in various other countries **3** the main right-wing political party in Australia
liberate *vb* **-rating, -rated 1** to free (someone) from social prejudices or injustices **2** to give liberty to; make free **3** to release (a country) from enemy occupation **liberation** *n* **liberator** *n*
liberated *adj* **1** not bound by traditional sexual and social roles: *a liberated woman* **2** given liberty **3** released from enemy occupation
libertarian *n* **1** a person who believes in freedom of thought and action ▷ *adj* **2** believing in freedom of thought and action
libertine (**lib**-er-teen) *n* **1** a person who is promiscuous and unscrupulous ▷ *adj* **2** promiscuous and unscrupulous [Latin *libertus* freed]
liberty *n, pl* **-ties 1** the freedom to choose, think, and act for oneself **2** the right of unrestricted movement and access; freedom **3** (*often pl*) a social action regarded as being forward or improper **4 at liberty** free or unconfined **5 at liberty to** unrestricted or authorized: *I am not at liberty to divulge his name* **6 take liberties (with)** to be overfamiliar (towards someone) [Latin *libertas*]
libidinous *adj* characterized by excessive sexual desire **libidinously** *adv*
libido (lib-**ee**-doe) *n, pl* **-dos 1** *psychoanalysis* psychic energy from the id **2** sexual urge or desire [Latin: desire] **libidinal** *adj*
Libra *n astrol* the seventh sign of the zodiac; the Scales [Latin]
librarian *n* a person in charge of or assisting in a library **librarianship** *n*
library *n, pl* **-braries 1** a room or building where books and other literary materials are kept **2** a collection of literary materials, films, CDs, toys, etc., kept for borrowing or reference **3** the building or institution that houses such a collection **4** a set of books published as a series, often in a similar format **5** *computers* a collection of standard programs, usually stored on disk [Latin *liber* book]
libretto *n, pl* **-tos** *or* **-ti** a text written for an opera [Italian: little book] **librettist** *n*
Libyan *adj* **1** from Libya ▷ *n* **2** a person from Libya
lice *n* the plural of **louse**
licence *or US* **license** *n* **1** a document giving official permission to do, use, or own something **2** formal permission or exemption **3** intentional disregard of conventional rules to achieve a certain effect: *poetic licence* **4** excessive freedom [Latin *licet* it is allowed]
license *vb* **-censing, -censed 1** to grant a licence to or for **2** to give permission to or for **licensable** *adj*
licensee *n* a person who holds a licence, esp. one to sell alcoholic drink
license plate *n* the US and Canadian term for **numberplate**
licentiate *n* a person who holds a certificate of competence to practise a certain profession
licentious *adj* sexually unrestrained or promiscuous [Latin *licentia* licence] **licentiousness** *n*

lichee *n* same as **lychee**

lichen *n* any of various small mossy plants that grow in patches on tree trunks, bare ground, rocks, and stone walls [Greek *leikhein* to lick]

lich gate *n* same as **lych gate**

licit *adj formal* lawful; permitted [Latin *licere* to be permitted]

lick *vb* **1** to pass the tongue over in order to taste, wet, or clean **2** to flicker over or round (something): *flames licked the gutters* **3** *informal* **A** to defeat **B** to thrash **4 lick into shape** to put into a satisfactory condition **5 lick one's wounds** to retire after a defeat ▷ *n* **6** an instance of passing the tongue over something **7** a small amount: *a lick of paint* **8** *informal* a blow **9** *informal* a fast pace: *a pulsating rhythm taken at a lick* **10 a lick and a promise** something hastily done, esp. a hurried wash [Old English *liccian*]

licorice *n US & Canad* same as **liquorice**

lid *n* **1** a removable or hinged cover: *a saucepan lid* **2** short for **eyelid 3 put the (tin) lid on** *informal* to put an end to [Old English *hlid*] **lidded** *adj*

lido (lee-doe) *n, pl* **-dos** *Brit* an open-air swimming pool or a part of a beach used by the public for swimming and sunbathing [*Lido,* island bathing beach near Venice]

lie[1] *vb* **lying, lied 1** to speak untruthfully with the intention of deceiving **2** to convey a false impression: *the camera cannot lie* ▷ *n* **3** an untrue statement deliberately used to mislead **4** something that is deliberately intended to deceive **5 give the lie to A** to disprove **B** to accuse of lying [Old English *lyge, lēogan*]

lie[2] *vb* **lying, lay, lain 1** (often foll. by *down*) to place oneself or be in a horizontal position **2** to be situated: *I left the money lying on the table; Nepal became the only country lying between China and India* **3** to be and remain (in a particular state or condition): *others of their species lie asleep* **4** to stretch or extend: *an enormous task lies ahead* **5** (usually foll. by *in*) to exist or comprise: *her charm lies in her inner beauty* **6** (foll. by *with*) to rest (with): *the fault lies with them* ▷ *n* **7** the manner, place, or style in which something is situated **8** an animal's lair **9 lie of the land** the way in which a situation is developing ▷ See also **lie down, lie in** [Old English *licgan*]

USAGE See at **lay**[1].

Liebfraumilch (leeb-frow-milk) *n* a sweet white wine from the German Rhine [German: from *Liebfrau* the Virgin Mary + *Milch* milk]

lied (leed) *n, pl* **lieder** *music* a musical setting for solo voice and piano of a romantic or lyrical poem [German: song]

lie detector *n informal* a device used to measure any increase in blood pressure, pulse rate, etc., of someone being questioned, which is thought to indicate that the person is lying

lie down *vb* **1** to place oneself or be in a horizontal position in order to rest **2** to yield to: *never take any attack on your candidate lying down* ▷ *n* **lie-down 3** a rest

liege (leej) *adj* **1** (of a lord) owed feudal allegiance: *their liege lord* **2** (of a vassal or subject) owing feudal allegiance: *a liege subject* **3** faithful; loyal ▷ *n* **4** a liege lord **5** a subject [Old French *lige*]

lie in *vb* **1** to remain in bed late into the morning ▷ *n* **lie-in 2** a long stay in bed in the morning

lien *n law* a right to retain possession of someone else's property until a debt is paid [Latin *ligamen* bond]

lieu (lyew) *n* **in lieu of** instead of [Old French]

Lieut. lieutenant

lieutenant (lef-ten-ant, loo-ten-ant) *n* **1** a junior officer in the army, navy, or the US police force **2** a person who acts as principal assistant [Old French, literally: place-holding] **lieutenancy** *n*

lieutenant colonel *n* an officer in an army, air force, or marine corps immediately junior to a colonel

lieutenant commander *n* an officer in a navy immediately junior to a commander

lieutenant general *n* a senior officer in an army, air force, or marine corps

lieutenant governor *n* **1** a deputy governor **2** (in Canada) the representative of the Crown in a province

life *n, pl* **lives 1** the state or quality that identifies living beings, characterized chiefly by growth, reproduction, and response to stimuli **2** the period between birth and death or between birth and the present time **3** a living person or being: *riots which claimed 22 lives* **4** the remainder or extent of one's life: *in that house for the rest of her life* **5** the process of living: *rituals gave his life stability* **6** *informal* a sentence of life imprisonment, usually approximating to fifteen years **7** a characteristic state or mode of existence: *country life is best* **8** the length of time that something is active or functioning: *the life of a battery* **9** a present condition or mode of existence: *they are leading a joyous life* **10** a biography **11** the sum or course of human events and activities **12** liveliness or high spirits: *full of life* **13** a source of strength, animation, or vitality: *he was the life of the show* **14** all living things collectively: *there is no life on Mars; marine life* **15 a matter of life and death** a matter of extreme urgency **16 as large as life** *informal* real and living **17 not on your life** *informal* certainly not **18 to the life** (of a copy of a painting or drawing) resembling the original exactly **19 true to life** faithful to reality [Old English *līf*]

life assurance *n* insurance that provides for a sum of money to be paid to the insured person at a certain age, or to the spouse or children on the death of the insured. Also called: **life insurance**

life belt *n* an inflatable ring used to keep a person afloat when in danger of drowning

lifeblood *n* **1** the blood vital to life **2** something that is essential for existence, development, or success

lifeboat *n* a boat used for rescuing people at sea

life buoy *n* a buoyant device to keep people afloat in an emergency

life coach *n* a person whose job it is to improve the quality of his or her client's life, by offering advice on professional and personal matters, such as careers, health, personal relationships, etc.

life cycle *n* the series of changes occurring in each generation of an animal or plant

lifeguard *n* a person at a beach or pool whose job is to rescue people in danger of drowning
life jacket *n* an inflatable sleeveless jacket worn to keep a person afloat when in danger of drowning
lifeless *adj* **1** inanimate; dead **2** lacking liveliness or animation **3** unconscious
lifelike *adj* closely resembling or representing life
lifeline *n* **1** a single means of contact or support on which a person or an area relies **2** a rope used for life-saving
lifelong *adj* lasting for a lifetime
life peer *n Brit* a peer whose title ceases at his or her death
life preserver *n* **1** *Brit* a bludgeon kept for self-defence **2** *US & Canad* a life belt or life jacket
lifer *n informal* a prisoner sentenced to life imprisonment
life raft *n* a raft for emergency use at sea
life-saver *n* **1** same as **lifeguard** **2** *informal* a person or thing that gives help in time of need **life-saving** *adj, n*
life science *n* any of the sciences concerned with the structure and behaviour of living organisms, such as biology, botany, or zoology
life-size *or* **life-sized** *adj* representing actual size
lifespan *n* **1** the period of time for which a creature normally lives **2** the period of time for which a product normally functions
lifestyle *n* a set of attitudes, habits, and possessions regarded as typical of a particular group or an individual
life-support *adj* (of equipment or treatment) necessary to sustain life
lifetime *n* **1** the length of time a person is alive **2 of a lifetime** (of an opportunity or experience) the most important or memorable
lift *vb* **1** to rise or raise upwards to a higher place: *the breakdown truck was lifting the lorry* **2** to move upwards: *he slowly lifted his hand* **3** to raise in status or estimation: *lifted from poverty* **4** to revoke or cancel: *the government lifted its restrictions on imported beef* **5** to remove (plants or underground crops) from the ground for harvesting **6** to disappear or disperse: *the tension lifted* **7** *informal* to plagiarize (music or writing) ▹ *n* **8 A** a compartment raised or lowered in a vertical shaft to transport people or goods to another floor in a building **B** See **chairlift, ski lift** **9** a ride in a car or other vehicle as a passenger **10** a rise in morale or feeling of cheerfulness **11** the act of lifting **12** the force that lifts airborne objects [from Old Norse]
liftoff *n* the initial movement of a rocket as it leaves its launch pad
lig *Brit slang* ▹ *n* **1** (esp. in the media) a function with free entertainment and refreshments ▹ *vb* **ligging, ligged** **2** to attend such a function **ligger** *n* **ligging** *n*
ligament *n anatomy* a band of tough tissue that connects various bones or cartilage [Latin *ligare* to bind]
ligature *n* **1** a link, bond, or tie **2** *printing* a character of two or more joined letters, such as ff **3** *music* a slur or the group of notes connected by it ▹ *vb* **-turing, -tured** **4** to bind with a ligature [Latin *ligare* to bind]
light¹ *n* **1** the natural medium, electromagnetic radiation, that makes sight possible **2** anything that illuminates, such as a lamp or candle **3** See **traffic light** **4** a particular type of light: *dim yellow light* **5 A** daylight **B** daybreak; dawn **6** anything that lets in light, such as a window **7** an aspect or view: *we have seen the world in a new light* **8** mental understanding or spiritual insight: *suddenly he saw the light* **9** an outstanding person: *a leading light of the movement* **10** brightness of countenance, esp. a sparkle in the eyes **11 A** something that ignites, such as a spark or flame **B** something used for igniting, such as a match **12** See **lighthouse** **13 come to light** to become known or visible **14 in (the) light of** taking into account **15 see the light** to understand **16 see the light (of day) A** to come into being **B** to come to public notice ▹ *adj* **17** full of light **18** (of a colour) pale: *light blue* ▹ *vb* **lighting, lighted** *or* **lit** **19** to ignite **20** (often foll. by *up*) to illuminate or cause to illuminate **21** to guide by light ▹ See also **light up** [Old English *lēoht*] **lightish** *adj*
light² *adj* **1** not heavy; weighing relatively little **2** relatively low in density, strength, amount, degree, etc.: *light oil; light alloy* **3** lacking sufficient weight **4** not bulky or clumsy: *light bedclothes* **5** not serious or difficult to understand; entertaining: *light music* **6** graceful or agile: *light movements* **7** without strong emphasis or serious meaning: *he gazed about with a light inattentive smile* **8** easily digested: *a light lunch* **9** relatively low in alcohol: *a light wine* **10** without burdens, difficulties, or problems: *a light heart lives longest* **11** dizzy or unclear: *a light head* **12** (of bread or cake) spongy or well risen **13 A** (of transport) designed to carry light loads **B** (of a vessel, aircraft, or other transport) not loaded **14** carrying light arms or equipment: *light infantry* **15** (of an industry) producing small consumer goods using light machinery **16 make light of** to treat as insignificant or unimportant ▹ *adv* **17** with little equipment or luggage: *travelling light* ▹ *vb* **lighting, lighted** *or* **lit** **18** (esp. of birds) to settle or land after flight **19** (foll. by *on* or *upon*) to discover by chance ▹ See also **lights** [Old English *lēoht*] **lightish** *adj* **lightly** *adv* **lightness** *n*
light bulb *n* a hollow rounded glass fitting containing a gas and a thin metal filament that gives out light when an electric current is passed through it
lighten¹ *vb* **1** to make less dark **2** to shine; glow **3** (of lightning) to flash
lighten² *vb* **1** to make or become less heavy **2** to make or become less burdensome **3** to make or become more cheerful or lively
lighter¹ *n* a small portable device for lighting cigarettes, etc.
lighter² *n* a flat-bottomed barge used in loading or unloading a ship [probably from Middle Dutch]
light-fingered *adj* skilful at thieving, esp. by picking pockets
light flyweight *n* a professional boxer weighing up to 108 pounds (49 kg) or an amateur boxer weighing up to 48 kg
light-footed *adj* having a light tread

light-headed *adj* giddy; feeling faint
light-hearted *adj* cheerful or carefree in mood or disposition **light-heartedly** *adv*
light heavyweight *n* a professional boxer weighing up to 175 pounds (79.5 kg) or an amateur weighing up to 81 kg
lighthouse *n* a tower with a light to guide ships and warn of obstructions
lighting *n* **1** the apparatus for and design of artificial light effects to a stage, film, or television set **2** the act or quality of illumination
lighting-up time *n* the time when vehicles are required by law to have their lights on
light middleweight *n* a professional boxer weighing up to 154 pounds (70 kg) or an amateur boxer weighing up to 71 kg
lightning *n* **1** a flash of light in the sky caused by a discharge of electricity ▹ *adj* **2** fast and sudden: *a lightning attack* [variant of *lightening*]
lightning conductor *or* **lightning rod** *n* a metal rod attached to the highest part of a building to divert lightning safely to earth
light pen *n* a penlike photoelectric device that in conjunction with a computer can be used to draw lines or identify symbols on a VDU screen
light pollution *n* the glow from the lighting in streets and buildings that obscures the night sky
light rail *n* a transport system using small trains or trams
lights *pl n* the lungs of sheep, bullocks, and pigs, used for feeding pets [because of the light weight of the lungs]
lightship *n* a moored ship equipped as a lighthouse
lights out *n* the time when residents of an institution are expected to retire to bed
light up *vb* **1** to illuminate **2** to make or become cheerful or animated: *their faces lit up and one dug the other in the ribs* **3** to light a cigarette or pipe
lightweight *adj* **1** not serious **2** of relatively light weight ▹ *n* **3** *informal* a person of little importance or influence **4** a person or animal of relatively light weight **5** a professional boxer weighing up to 135 pounds (61 kg) or an amateur weighing up to 60 kg
light welterweight *n* a professional or an amateur boxer weighing up to 140 pounds (63.5 kg)
light year *n astron* the distance travelled by light in one mean solar year, i.e. 9.4607×10^{15} metres
ligneous *adj* of or like wood [Latin *lignum* wood]
lignite (lig-nite) *n* a brown sedimentary rock with a woody texture: used as a fuel
lignum vitae (lig-num **vite**-ee) *n* a tropical American tree with heavy resinous wood [Late Latin, literally: wood of life]
like¹ *adj* **1** resembling ▹ *prep* **2** in the manner of; similar to: *she was like a child; it looks like a traffic cone* **3** such as: *a modern material, like carbon fibre* **4** characteristic of ▹ *adv* **5** in the manner of: *cheering like mad* **6** *dialect* likely ▹ *conj* **7** *not standard* as though; as if: *I don't want to make it seem like I had this bad childhood* **8** in the same way that: *she doesn't dance like you do* ▹ *n* **9** the equal or counterpart of a person or thing **10** **the like** similar things: *magic, supernormal powers and the like* **11** **the likes** *or* **like of** people or things similar to (someone or something specified): *the theatre was not meant for the likes of him* [Old English *gelīc*]

> **USAGE** The use of *like* to mean *such as* was formerly thought to be undesirable in formal writing, but has now become acceptable. It was also thought that *as* rather than *like* should be used to mean *in the same way that*, but now both *as* and *like* are acceptable: *they hunt and catch fish as/like their ancestors used to.* The use of *look like* and *seem like* before a clause, although very common, is thought by many people to be incorrect or nonstandard: *it looks as though he won't come* (not *it looks like he won't come*).

like² *vb* **liking, liked** **1** to find enjoyable **2** to be fond of **3** to prefer or choose: *I'd like to go home* **4** to feel disposed or inclined; choose; wish: *do as you like* **5** to indicate approval of (an item posted on a social media site) ▹ *n* **6** (*usually pl*) a favourable feeling, desire, or preference: *tell me your likes and dislikes* **7** an indication of approval for an item posted on a social media site [Old English *līcian*] **likeable** *or* **likable** *adj*
likelihood *n* chance; probability
likely *adj* **1** tending or inclined: *likely to win* **2** probable: *the likely effects of the tunnel* **3** appropriate for a purpose or activity: *a likely candidate* ▹ *adv* **4** probably or presumably **5** **not likely** *informal* definitely not [Old Norse *līkligr*]

> **USAGE** *Likely* as an adverb is preceded by another, intensifying adverb, as in *it will very likely rain* or *it will most likely rain.* Its use without an intensifier, as in *it will likely rain,* is regarded as unacceptable by most users of British English, though it is common in colloquial US English.

like-minded *adj* sharing similar opinions
liken *vb* to compare
likeness *n* **1** resemblance **2** portrait **3** an imitative appearance; semblance: *in the likeness of a dragon*
likewise *adv* **1** in addition; also **2** similarly
liking *n* **1** fondness **2** what one likes or prefers: *if it's not to your liking, do let me know*
lilac *n* **1** a small tree with large sprays of purple or white sweet-smelling flowers ▹ *adj* **2** pale purple [Persian *nīlak* bluish]
Lilliputian (lil-lip-**pew**-shun) *n* **1** a tiny person or being ▹ *adj* **2** tiny; very small [from *Lilliput*, an imaginary country of tiny people in Swift's *Gulliver's Travels*]
Lilo *n, pl* **-los** *trademark* a type of inflatable plastic mattress
lilt *n* **1** a pleasing musical quality in a speaking voice **2** (in music) a jaunty rhythm **3** a graceful rhythmic motion ▹ *vb* **4** (of a voice, tune, or song) to rise and fall in a pleasant way **5** to move gracefully and rhythmically [origin unknown] **lilting** *adj*
lily *n, pl* **lilies** **1** a perennial plant, such as the tiger lily, with scaly bulbs and showy white or coloured flowers **2** a water lily [Latin *lilium*]
lily-livered *adj old-fashioned* cowardly
lily of the valley *n, pl* **lilies of the valley** a small plant with spikes of sweet-smelling white bell-shaped flowers

l

limb[1] *n* **1** an arm, leg, or wing **2** any of the main branches of a tree **3 out on a limb** **A** in a precarious or questionable position **B** *Brit & NZ* isolated, esp. because of unpopular opinions [Old English *lim*] **limbless** *adj*

limb[2] *n* the apparent outer edge of the sun, a moon, or a planet [Latin *limbus* edge]

limber[1] *adj* **1** pliant; supple **2** able to move or bend the body freely; agile [origin unknown]

limber[2] *n* **1** part of a gun carriage, consisting of an axle, pole, and two wheels ▷ *vb* **2** to attach the limber (to a gun) [Middle English *lymour* shaft of a gun carriage]

limber up *vb* to loosen stiff muscles by exercise

limbo[1] *n, pl* **-bos** **1** (*often cap*) RC Church (formerly) the supposed region intermediate between heaven and hell for the unbaptized **2 in limbo** not knowing the result or next stage of something and powerless to influence it [Medieval Latin *in limbo* on the border (of hell)]

limbo[2] *n, pl* **-bos** a West Indian dance in which dancers lean backwards and pass under a horizontal bar which is gradually lowered [origin unknown]

lime[1] *n agriculture* **1** calcium hydroxide spread as a dressing on acidic land ▷ *vb* **liming, limed** **2** to spread a calcium compound upon (land) [Old English *līm*]

lime[2] *n* the green oval fruit of a small Asian citrus tree with acid fleshy pulp rich in vitamin C [Arabic *līmah*]

lime[3] *n* a European linden tree planted for ornament [Old English *lind* linden]

lime-green *adj* light yellowish-green

limekiln *n* a kiln in which calcium carbonate is burned to produce quicklime

limelight *n* **1 the limelight** glare of publicity: *this issue will remain in the limelight* **2** **A** a type of lamp, formerly used in stage lighting, in which lime is heated to white heat **B** brilliant white light produced in this way

limerick (lim-mer-ik) *n* a form of comic verse consisting of five lines [allegedly from *will you come up to Limerick?* a refrain sung between nonsense verses at a party]

limestone *n* rock consisting mainly of calcium carbonate: used as a building stone and in making cement

limey *n US, Canad & Austral slang* **1** a British person **2** a British sailor or ship [from *lime-juicer*, because British sailors drank lime juice as a protection against scurvy]

limit *n* **1** (*sometimes pl*) the ultimate extent or amount of something: *each soloist was stretched to his or her limit by the demands of the vocal writing* **2** (*often pl*) the boundary of a specific area: *beyond the city limits* **3** the largest quantity or amount allowed **4 the limit** *informal* a person or thing that is intolerably exasperating ▷ *vb* **-iting, -ited** **5** to restrict [Latin *limes* boundary] **limitable** *adj*

limitation *n* **1** a restriction or controlling of quantity, quality, or achievement **2 limitations** the limit or extent of an ability to achieve something: *learn your own limitations*

limited *adj* **1** having a limit; restricted **2** without fullness or scope; narrow **3** (of governing powers or sovereignty) restricted by a constitution, laws, or an assembly: *limited government* **4** *Brit & NZ* (of a business enterprise) owned by shareholders whose liability for the enterprise's debts is restricted

limited edition *n* an edition of something, such as a book, which has been restricted to a particular number of copies

limn *vb old-fashioned* to represent in drawing or painting [Latin *inluminare* to brighten]

limousine *n* any large luxurious car [French, literally: cloak]

limp[1] *vb* **1** to walk with an uneven step, esp. with a weak or injured leg **2** to advance in a labouring or faltering manner ▷ *n* **3** an uneven walk or progress [Old English *lempheal*t lame] **limping** *adj, n*

limp[2] *adj* **1** lacking firmness or stiffness **2** not energetic or vital **3** (of the binding of a book) paperback [probably Scandinavian] **limply** *adv*

limpet *n* **1** a conical shellfish that clings tightly to rocks with its muscular foot ▷ *adj* **2** denoting certain weapons that are magnetically attached to their targets and resist removal: *limpet mines* [Old English *lempedu*]

limpid *adj* **1** clear or transparent **2** (of speech or writing) clear and easy to understand [Latin *limpidus* clear] **limpidity** *n*

limy[1] *adj* **limier, limiest** of, like, or smeared with birdlime

limy[2] *adj* **limier, limiest** of or tasting of lime (the fruit)

linage *n* **1** the number of lines in written or printed matter **2** payment according to the number of lines

linchpin *or* **lynchpin** *n* **1** a pin inserted through an axle to keep a wheel in position **2** an essential person or thing: *she was the linchpin of the experiment* [Old English *lynis*]

Lincs Lincolnshire

linctus *n, pl* **-tuses** a soothing syrupy cough mixture [Latin *lingere* to lick]

linden *n* a large tree with heart-shaped leaves and fragrant yellowish flowers. See also **lime**[3] [Old English *linde* lime tree]

line[1] *n* **1** a narrow continuous mark, such as one made by a pencil or brush **2** a thin indented mark or wrinkle on skin **3** a continuous length without breadth **4** a boundary: *the United Nations established a provisional demarcation line* **5** *sport* **A** a white band indicating a division on a field or track **B** a mark or imaginary mark at which a race begins or ends **6** a boundary or limit: *there's a thin dividing line between confidence and arrogance* **7** the edge or contour of a shape: *the shoulder line* **8** a wire or string with a particular function: *a long washing line* **9** a telephone connection: *it was a very bad line* **10** a conducting wire, cable, or circuit for electric-power transmission or telecommunications **11** a system of travel or transportation: *a shipping line* **12** a route between two points on a railway **13** a railway track **14** a course or direction of movement: *the birds' line of flight* **15** a course of action or behaviour: *to adopt a more aggressive line* **16** a policy or prescribed way of thinking: *city commentators supported the CBI line*

17 a field of interest or activity: *computer gaming – that's their line* **18** straight or orderly alignment: *stand in line* **19** one kind of product or article: *a line of smart suits* **20** a row of people or things **21** a row of printed or written words **22** a unit of verse consisting of words in a single row **23** one of a number of narrow horizontal bands forming a television picture **24** *music* any of the five horizontal marks that make up the stave **25** the most forward defensive position: *the front line* **26** a formation of ships or soldiers abreast of each other **27** the combatant forces of certain armies and navies **28** *US & Canad* a queue **29 all along the line** at every stage in a series **30 draw the line (at)** to object (to) or set a limit (on): *I'm not a killer, I draw the line at that* **31 drop someone a line** to send someone a short note **32 get a line on** *informal* to obtain information about **33 in line for** likely to receive: *high achievers are in line for cash bonuses* **34 in line with** conforming to **35 lay** *or* **put on the line** **A** to speak frankly and directly **B** to risk (one's career or reputation) on something ▷ *vb* **lining, lined 36** to mark with a line or lines **37** to be or form a border: *the square was lined with stalls selling snacks* **38** to place in or form a row, series, or alignment ▷ See also **lines, line-up** [Old French *ligne* + Old English *līn*] **lined** *adj*

line² *vb* **lining, lined 1** to attach an inside layer to **2** to cover the inside of: *the works of Shakespeare lined his walls* **3 line one's pockets** to make a lot of money, esp. dishonestly [Latin *linum* flax]

lineage (lin-ee-ij) *n* direct descent from an ancestor

lineal *adj* **1** being in a direct line of descent from an ancestor **2** of or derived from direct descent **3** linear [Latin *linea* line]

lineament *n* (*often pl*) a facial outline or feature [Latin *lineare* to draw a line]

linear (lin-ee-er) *adj* **1** of or in lines **2** of or relating to length **3** represented by a line or lines **linearity** *n*

linear measure *n* a unit or system of units for the measurement of length

lineation (lin-ee-ay-shun) *n* **1** the act of marking with lines **2** an arrangement of lines

line dancing *n* a form of dancing performed by rows of people to country and western music

line drawing *n* a drawing formed with lines only

linen *n* **1** a hard-wearing fabric woven from the spun fibres of flax **2** articles, such as sheets or tablecloths, made from linen cloth or from cotton [Latin *linum* flax]

line of fire *n* the flight path of a bullet discharged from a firearm

liner¹ *n* **1** a passenger ship or aircraft, esp. one that is part of a commercial fleet **2** Also called: **eyeliner** a cosmetic used to outline the eyes

liner² *n* something used as a lining: *a plastic bin liner*

lines *pl n* **1** the words of a theatrical role: *shaky sets, fluffed lines, and wooden plots* **2** *informal, chiefly Brit* a marriage certificate: *marriage lines* **3** a school punishment of writing out the same sentence or phrase a specified number of times **4 read between the lines** to find an implicit meaning in addition to the obvious one

linesman *n, pl* **-men 1** an official who helps the referee or umpire in various sports, by indicating when the ball has gone out of play **2** a person who maintains railway, electricity, or telephone lines

line-up *n* **1** people or things assembled for a particular purpose: *Christmas TV line-up* **2** the members of such an assembly ▷ *vb* **line up 3** to form or organize a line-up

ling¹ *n, pl* **ling** *or* **lings** a fish with a long slender body [probably Low German]

ling² *n* heather [Old Norse *lyng*]

linger *vb* **1** to delay or prolong departure **2** to survive in a weakened condition for some time before death **3** to spend a long time doing or considering something [Old English *lengan* prolong] **lingering** *adj*

lingerie (lan-zher-ee) *n* women's underwear and nightwear [French, from Latin *lineus* linen]

lingo *n, pl* **-goes** *informal* any foreign or unfamiliar language or jargon [perhaps from LINGUA FRANCA]

lingua franca *n, pl* **lingua francas** *or* **linguae francae 1** a language used for communication among people of different mother tongues **2** any system of communication providing mutual understanding [Italian: Frankish tongue]

lingual *adj* **1** *anatomy* of the tongue **2** articulated with the tongue **3** *rare* of language or languages **lingually** *adv*

linguist *n* **1** a person who is skilled in foreign languages **2** a person who studies linguistics [Latin *lingua* tongue]

linguistic *adj* **1** of language **2** of linguistics **linguistically** *adv*

linguistics *n* the scientific study of language

liniment *n* a medicated oily liquid applied to the skin to relieve pain or stiffness [Latin *linere* to smear]

lining *n* **1** material used to line a garment or curtain **2** any interior covering: *the lining of the womb*

link *n* **1** any of the separate rings that form a chain **2** an emotional or logical relationship between people or things; association **3** a connecting part or episode **4** a type of communications connection: *a rail link*; *radio link* **5** short for **hyperlink** (sense 1) ▷ *vb* **6** (often foll. by *up*) to connect with or as if with links **7** to connect by association [from Old Norse]

linkage *n* **1** the act of linking or the state of being linked **2** a system of links

linkman *n, pl* **-men** a presenter of a television or radio programme consisting of a number of items broadcast from different locations

links *pl n* a golf course beside the sea [Old English *hlincas*, plural of *hlinc* ridge]

link-up *n* a joining together of two systems or groups

linnet *n* a brownish finch: the male has a red breast and forehead [Old French *linotte*, from Latin *līnum* flax (because the bird feeds on flaxseeds)]

lino *n* short for **linoleum**

linocut *n* **1** a design cut in relief in linoleum mounted on a block of wood **2** a print made from such a block

linoleum *n* a floor covering made of hessian or jute with a smooth decorative coating of powdered cork [Latin *linum* flax + *oleum* oil]

linseed *n* the seed of the flax plant [Old English *līn* flax + *sǣd* seed]

linseed oil *n* a yellow oil extracted from flax seeds and used in making paints, inks, linoleum, and varnish

lint *n* **1** an absorbent material with raised fibres on one side, used to dress wounds **2** tiny shreds of yarn or cloth; fluff [probably Latin *linteus* made of linen, from *linum* flax]

lintel *n* a horizontal beam over a door or window [probably ultimately from Latin *limes* boundary]

lion *or fem* **lioness** *n* **1** a large animal of the cat family found in Africa and India, with a tawny yellow coat and, in the male, a shaggy mane **2** a courageous and strong person **3 the lion's share** the largest portion [Latin *leo*]

lion-hearted *adj* very brave; courageous

lionize *or* **-nise** *vb* **-nizing, -nized** *or* **-nising, -nised** to treat as a celebrity

lip *n* **1** *anatomy* either of the two fleshy folds surrounding the mouth **2** any structure resembling a lip, such as the rim of a jug **3** *slang* impudent talk or backchat **4 bite one's lip** to avoid showing feelings of anger or distress **5 keep a stiff upper lip** to maintain one's composure during a time of trouble **6 lick** *or* **smack one's lips** to anticipate or recall something with glee or relish [Old English *lippa*]

lipase *n* *biochem* any of a group of enzymes that digest fat and are produced in the stomach and pancreas and occur in seeds

lipid *n* *biochem* any of a group of organic compounds including fats, oils, waxes, and sterols [Greek *lipos* fat]

lipo *n* *informal* short for **liposuction**

lipogram *n* a piece of writing in which all words containing a particular letter have been deliberately omitted

liposuction *n* a cosmetic surgical operation in which fat is removed from the body by suction

lippy *n* *informal* lipstick

lip-read *vb* **-reading, -read** to interpret speech by lip-reading

lip-reading *n* a method used by deaf people to understand spoken words by interpreting movements of the speaker's lips **lip-reader** *n*

lip service *n* **pay lip service to** to appear to support or obey something publicly while actually disregarding it

lipstick *n* a cosmetic in the form of a stick, for colouring the lips

liquefy *vb* **-fies, -fying, -fied** (esp. of a gas) to make or become liquid [Latin *liquefacere* to make liquid] **liquefaction** *n*

liqueur (lik-**cure**) *n* a highly flavoured sweetened alcoholic spirit, intended to be drunk after a meal [French]

liquid *n* **1** a substance in a physical state which can change shape but not size ▷ *adj* **2** of or being a liquid: *liquid medicines* **3** shining and clear: *liquid sunlight days* **4** flowing, fluent, or smooth **5** (of assets) in the form of money or easily convertible into money [Latin *liquere* to be fluid]

liquidate *vb* **-dating, -dated 1** to settle or pay off (a debt or claim) **2** to dissolve (a company) and divide its assets among creditors **3** to convert (assets) into cash **4** to eliminate or kill

liquidation *n* **1 A** the dissolving of a company by selling its assets to pay off its debts **B go into liquidation** (of a business firm) to have its affairs so terminated **2** destruction; elimination

liquidator *n* an official appointed to liquidate a business

liquid-crystal display *n* a display of information on a screen, using cells containing a liquid with crystalline properties, that change their reflectivity when an electric field is applied to them

liquidity *n* the state of being able to meet financial obligations

liquidize *or* **-dise** *vb* **-dizing, -dized** *or* **-dising, -dised 1** to make or become liquid; liquefy **2** to process (food) in a liquidizer to make it liquid

liquidizer *or* **-diser** *n* a kitchen appliance with blades for liquidizing food

liquid measure *n* a unit or system of units for measuring volumes of liquids or their containers

liquid oxygen *n* oxygen liquefied by cooling: used in rocket fuels

liquid paraffin *n* an oily liquid obtained by petroleum distillation and used as a laxative

liquor *n* **1** spirits or other alcoholic drinks **2** any liquid in which food has been cooked [Latin *liquere* to be liquid]

liquorice *or US & Canad* **licorice** (**lik**-ker-iss) *n* **1** a chewy black sweet with a strong flavour **2** the dried black root of a Mediterranean plant, used as a laxative and in confectionery [Greek *glukus* sweet + *rhiza* root]

lira *n, pl* **lire** *or* **liras 1** a former monetary unit of Italy **2** the standard monetary unit of Turkey [Italian, from Latin *libra* pound]

lisle (rhymes with **mile**) *n* a strong fine cotton thread or fabric, formerly used to make stockings [after *Lisle* (now Lille), in France]

lisp *n* **1** a speech defect in which *s* and *z* are pronounced like the *th* sounds in English *thin* and *then* respectively ▷ *vb* **2** to speak with a lisp [Old English *wlisp* lisping (imitative)]

LISP *n* a high-level computer programming language suitable for work in artificial intelligence [*lis(t) p(rocessing)*]

lissom *or* **lissome** *adj* slim and graceful and agile in movement [variant of *lithesome*, from *lithe* + *-some* of a specific nature]

list[1] *n* **1** an item-by-item record of names or things, usually written one below the other ▷ *vb* **2** to make a list of **3** to include in a list [Old English *līste*]

list[2] *vb* **1** (esp. of ships) to lean to one side ▷ *n* **2** a leaning to one side: *developed a list to starboard* [origin unknown]

listed building *n* (in Britain, Australia, and New Zealand) a building protected from demolition or alteration because of its special historical or architectural interest

listen *vb* **1** to concentrate on hearing something **2** to take heed or pay attention: *listen, let me explain* [Old English *hlysnan*] **listener** *n*

listen in *vb* (often foll. by *on* or *to*) to listen secretly to; eavesdrop
listeriosis *n* a serious form of food poisoning, caused by bacteria of the genus *Listeria* [after Joseph *Lister*, surgeon]
listing *n* **1** a list or an entry in a list **2 listings** lists of films, concerts, etc. printed in newspapers and magazines, and showing details such as times and venues
listless *adj* lacking interest or energy [obsolete *list* desire] **listlessly** *adv*
list price *n* the selling price of merchandise as quoted in a catalogue or advertisement
lists *pl n* **1** *history* the enclosed field of combat at a tournament **2 enter the lists** to engage in a conflict or controversy [plural of Old English *līste* border]
lit *vb* a past of **light¹** or **light²**
lit. 1 literal(ly) **2** literary **3** literature
litany *n, pl* **-nies 1** *Christianity* a prayer consisting of a series of invocations, each followed by the same response **2** any tedious recital: *a litany of complaints* [Late Greek *litaneia* prayer]
litchi *n* same as **lychee**
lite *adj* **1** (of food or drink) containing few calories or little alcohol or fat **2** denoting a less extreme version of a person or thing: *reggae lite* [variant spelling of LIGHT²]
liter *n US* same as **litre**
literacy *n* **1** the ability to read and write **2** the ability to use language effectively
literal *adj* **1** in exact accordance with the explicit meaning of a word or text **2** word for word: *a literal translation* **3** dull or unimaginative: *she's very, very literal and flat in how she interprets what she sees* **4** true; actual ▷ *n* **5** a misprint or misspelling in a text [Latin *littera* letter] **literally** *adv*

> **USAGE** The use of *literally* as an intensifier is common, especially in informal contexts. In some cases, it provides emphasis without adding to the meaning: *the house was literally only five minutes walk away*. Often, however, its careless use results in absurdity: *the news was literally an eye-opener to me*.

literalism *n* the tendency to take words and statements in their literal sense **literalist** *n*
literary *adj* **1** of or characteristic of literature: *literary criticism* **2** knowledgeable about literature **3** (of a word) used chiefly in written work; not colloquial [Latin *litterarius* concerning reading and writing] **literariness** *n*
literate *adj* **1** able to read and write **2** educated ▷ *n* **3** a literate person [Latin *litteratus* learned]
literati *pl n* literary or scholarly people [Latin]
literature *n* **1** written material such as poetry, novels, or essays **2** the body of written work of a particular culture, people, or era: *Elizabethan literature* **3** written or printed matter of a particular type or genre: *medical literature* **4** the art or profession of a writer **5** *informal* printed matter on any subject [Latin *litteratura* writing]
lithe *adj* attractively graceful and supple in movement [Old English *līthe* (in the sense: gentle; later: supple)]
lithium *n chem* a soft silvery element of the alkali metal series: the lightest known metal. Symbol: **Li** [Greek *lithos* stone]
litho *n, pl* **-thos**, *adj, adv* short for **lithography** or **lithograph**
lithograph *n* **1** a print made by lithography ▷ *vb* **2** to reproduce (pictures or text) by lithography **lithographic** *adj* **lithographically** *adv*
lithography (lith-og-ra-fee) *n* a method of printing from a metal or stone surface on which the printing areas are made ink-receptive [Greek *lithos* stone + *graphein* to write] **lithographer** *n*
Lithuanian *adj* **1** from Lithuania ▷ *n* **2** a person from Lithuania **3** the language of Lithuania
litigant *n* a person involved in a lawsuit
litigate *vb* **-gating, -gated 1** to bring or contest a lawsuit **2** to engage in legal proceedings [Latin *lis, lit-* lawsuit + *agere* to carry on] **litigator** *n*
litigation *n* the process of bringing or contesting a lawsuit
litigious (lit-ij-uss) *adj* frequently going to law
litmus *n* a soluble powder obtained from lichens, which is turned red by acids and blue by alkalis. Paper treated with it (**litmus paper**) is used as an indicator in chemistry [perhaps Scandinavian]
litmus test *n* something which is regarded as a simple and accurate test of a particular thing, such as a person's attitude to an issue
litotes *n, pl* **-tes** understatement used for effect, for example 'She was not a little upset' meaning 'She was extremely upset' [Greek *litos* small]
litre *or US* **liter** *n* a measure of volume equivalent to 1 cubic decimetre [Greek *litra* a unit of weight]
litter *n* **1** small items of rubbish carelessly dropped in public places **2** a disordered or untidy collection of objects **3** a group of animals produced at one birth **4** straw or hay used as bedding for animals **5** dry material used to line a receptacle in which a domestic cat can urinate and defecate **6** (esp. formerly) a bed or seat held between parallel poles and used for carrying people ▷ *vb* **7** to strew with litter **8** to scatter or be scattered in an untidy fashion **9** (of animals) to give birth to offspring **10** to provide (an animal) with straw or hay for bedding [Latin *lectus* bed]
litter lout *Brit or US, Canad, Austral & NZ* **litterbug** ▷ *n slang* a person who drops refuse in public places
little *adj* **1** of small or less than average size **2** young: *a little boy* **3** endearingly familiar: *he was a sweet little man* **4** contemptible, mean, or disagreeable: *he was an arrogant little squirt* **5** of small quantity, extent, or duration: *there was little money circulating; I could see little evidence of it* ▷ *adv* **6** (usually preceded by *a*) to a small extent or degree; not a lot: *to sleep a little* **7** not at all, or hardly: *army life varied little as the years passed* **8** not much or often: *we go there very little now* **9 little by little** by small degrees ▷ *n* **10 make little of** to treat as insignificant: *one episode in their history is made little of in the guide books* **11 think little of** to have a low opinion of ▷ See also **less, lesser, least** [Old English *lȳtel*]
little people *pl n folklore* small supernatural beings, such as elves
littoral *adj* **1** of or by the shore ▷ *n* **2** a coastal region [Latin *litus* shore]

liturgy *n, pl* **-gies** the forms of public services officially prescribed by a Church [Greek *leitourgia*] **liturgical** *adj*
livable *or* **liveable** *adj* (foll. by *with*) tolerable or pleasant to live (with)
live[1] (rhymes with **give**) *vb* **living, lived 1** to show the characteristics of life; be alive **2** to remain alive or in existence **3** to exist in a specified way: *to live at ease* **4** to have one's home: *he went to live in Switzerland* **5** to continue or last: *his childhood had always lived inside him* **6** (foll. by *on, upon* or *by*) to support one's style of life: *forest dwellers who live by extracting rubber* **7** (foll. by *with*) to endure the effects (of a crime or mistake); tolerate **8** to pass or spend (one's life) **9** to enjoy life to the full: *he likes to live every day to the full* **10** to put into practice in one's daily life: *the freedom to live his own life as he chooses* **11 live and let live** to be tolerant ▷ See also **live down, live in** *etc.* [Old English *libban, lifian*]
live[2] (rhymes with **hive**) *adj* **1** alive; living **2** *radio & television* transmitted at the time of performance, rather than being prerecorded: *a live broadcast* **3** actual: *I was able to speak to a real live Hurricane pilot* **4** (of a recording) recorded during a performance **5** connected to a source of electric power: *a live cable* **6** of current interest; controversial: *the document has become a live political issue* **7** loaded or capable of exploding: *a live firing exercise with a 4.5in gun* **8** (of a coal or ember) glowing or burning ▷ *adv* **9** during, at, or in the form of a live performance [shortened from *on live* alive]
liveblog *vb* **liveblogging, liveblogged** to report (an event) on one's blog as it happens
live down *vb* to withstand people's reactions to a crime or mistake until they forget it
live in *vb* **1** to have one's home at the place where one works ▷ *adj* **live-in 2** resident: *a live-in nanny is a must; her live-in girlfriend*
livelihood *n* one's job or other source of income
livelong (liv-long) *adj chiefly poetic* long or seemingly long: *all the livelong day*
lively *adj* **-lier, -liest 1** full of life or vigour **2** vivacious or animated **3** vivid **liveliness** *n*
liven *vb* (usually foll. by *up*) to make or become lively; enliven
liver[1] *n* **1** a large glandular organ which secretes bile, balances nutrients, and removes certain poisons from the body **2** the liver of certain animals used as food [Old English *lifer*]
liver[2] *n* a person who lives in a specified way: *a fast liver*
liveried *adj* wearing livery
liverish *adj* **1** *informal* having a disorder of the liver **2** feeling disagreeable and slightly irritable
livermorium *n chem* a synthetic element. Symbol: **Lv** [after the Lawrence *Livermore* National Laboratory in California]
Liverpudlian *adj* **1** of Liverpool, a city in NW England ▷ *n* **2** a person from Liverpool
liver sausage *n* a sausage containing liver
liverwort *n* a plant growing in wet places and resembling green seaweeds or leafy mosses [late Old English *liferwyrt*]
livery *n, pl* **-eries 1** the identifying uniform of a servant **2** distinctive dress or outward appearance **3** the stabling, keeping, or hiring out of horses for money [Old French *livrée* allocation]
lives *n* the plural of **life**
livestock *n* animals kept on a farm
live together *vb* (of an unmarried couple) to live in the same house; cohabit
live up to *vb* to fulfil (an expectation, obligation, or principle)
live wire *n* **1** *informal* an energetic person **2** a wire carrying an electric current
livid *adj* **1** *informal* extremely angry **2** of a dark grey or purple colour: *livid bruises* [Latin *livere* to be black and blue]
living *adj* **1** possessing life; not dead or inanimate **2** currently in use or valid: *a living alliance* **3** seeming to be real: *a living doll* **4** (of people or animals) existing in the present age **5** very: *the living image* **6** of or like everyday life: *living costs* **7** of or involving those now alive: *one of our greatest living actors* ▷ *n* **8** the condition of being alive **9** the manner of one's life: *high living* **10** one's financial means **11** *Church of England* a benefice
living room *n* a room in a private house or flat used for relaxation and entertainment
living wage *n* a wage adequate for a worker to live on and support a family in reasonable comfort
living will *n* a document that states that a person who becomes terminally ill does not want his or her life to be prolonged by artificial means
lizard *n* a reptile with an elongated body, four limbs, and a long tail [Latin *lacerta*]
ll. lines (of written matter)
llama *n* a South American mammal of the camel family, that is used as a beast of burden and is valued for its woolly fleece [from a Native American language]
LLB Bachelor of Laws [Latin *Legum Baccalaureus*]
LLD Doctor of Laws [Latin *Legum Doctor*]
LLM Master of Laws [Latin *Legum Magister*]
lo *interj old-fashioned* look! see!: *lo and behold* [Old English *lā*]
loach *n* a freshwater fish with a long narrow body and barbels around the mouth [Old French *loche*]
load *n* **1** something to be borne or conveyed; weight **2** the amount borne or conveyed **3** something that weighs down or burdens: *I have enough of a load to carry right now* **4** *electronics* the power delivered by a machine, generator, or circuit **5** an external force applied to a component or mechanism **6 a load of** *informal* a quantity of: *a load of half-truths* **7 get a load of** *informal* to pay attention to ▷ *vb* **8** to place cargo or goods upon (a ship or vehicle) **9** to burden or oppress **10** to supply in abundance: *other treats are loaded with fat* **11** to cause to be biased: *the dice are loaded* **12** to put ammunition into (a firearm) **13** *photog* to insert film in (a camera) **14** to weight or bias (a roulette wheel or dice) **15** *computers* to transfer (a program) to a memory ▷ See also **loads** [Old English *lād* course; in meaning, influenced by LADE] **loader** *n*
loaded *adj* **1** carrying a load **2** charged with ammunition **3** (of a question or statement)

containing a hidden trap or implication **4** (of dice or a roulette wheel) weighted or otherwise biased **5** *slang* wealthy **6** *slang, chiefly US & Canad* drunk

loads *pl n informal* (often foll. by *of*) a lot

load shedding *n Austral, S African & Indian* the practice of temporarily reducing the supply of electricity to an area to avoid overloading generators

loadstar *n* same as **lodestar**

loadstone *n* same as **lodestone**

loaf[1] *n, pl* **loaves** **1** a shaped mass of baked bread **2** any shaped or moulded mass of food, such as cooked meat **3** *slang* the head; common sense: *use your loaf!* [Old English *hlāf*]

loaf[2] *vb* to loiter or lounge around in an idle way [perhaps from *loafer*]

loafer *n* **1** a person who avoids work; idler **2** a moccasin-like shoe [perhaps German *Landläufer* vagabond]

loam *n* fertile soil consisting of sand, clay, and decaying organic material [Old English *lām*] **loamy** *adj*

loan *n* **1** money lent at interest for a fixed period of time **2** the act of lending: *I am grateful to her for the loan of her book* **3** property lent **4** **on loan** lent out; borrowed ▷ *vb* **5** to lend (something, esp. money) [Old Norse *lān*]

loan shark *n* a person who lends money at an extremely high interest rate, esp. illegally

loath *or* **loth** (rhymes with **both**) *adj* (usually foll. by *to*) reluctant or unwilling [Old English *lāth* (in the sense: hostile)]

loathe *vb* **loathing, loathed** to feel strong disgust for [Old English *lāthiān*]

loathing *n* strong disgust

loathsome *adj* causing loathing

loaves *n* the plural of **loaf**[1]

lob *sport* ▷ *n* **1** a ball struck or bowled in a high arc ▷ *vb* **lobbing, lobbed** **2** to hit or kick (a ball) in a high arc **3** *informal* to throw [probably Low German]

lobar (**loh**-ber) *adj* of or affecting a lobe

lobate *adj* with or like lobes

lobby *n, pl* **-bies** **1** a room or corridor used as an entrance-hall or vestibule **2** a group which attempts to influence legislators on behalf of a particular interest **3** *chiefly Brit* a hall in a legislative building used for meetings between legislators and members of the public **4** *chiefly Brit* one of two corridors in a legislative building in which members vote ▷ *vb* **-bies, -bying, -bied** **5** to attempt to influence (legislators) in the formulation of policy [Old High German *lauba* arbor]

lobbyist *n* a person who lobbies on behalf of a particular interest

lobe *n* **1** any rounded projection **2** the fleshy lower part of the external ear **3** any subdivision of a bodily organ [Greek *lobos* lobe of the ear or of the liver]

lobelia *n* a plant with blue, red, white, or yellow five-lobed flowers [Matthias de *Lobel*, botanist]

lobola *n S African* (in southern Africa) an African custom by which a bridegroom's family makes a payment in cattle or cash to the bride's family shortly before the marriage [Nguni (language group of southern Africa) *ukulobola* to give bride price]

lobotomy *n, pl* **-mies** the surgical cutting of nerves in the frontal lobe of the brain, formerly performed to treat severe mental disorders [Greek *lobos* lobe + *tomē* a cutting]

lobscouse *n* a sailor's stew of meat, vegetables, and hardtack [perhaps dialect *lob* to boil + *scouse* broth]

lobster *n, pl* **-sters** *or* **-ster** **1** a large edible crustacean with large pincers and a long tail, which turns red when boiled **2** its edible flesh **3** *Austral informal* a $20 note [Old English *loppestre*, from *loppe* spider]

lobster pot *n* a round basket made of open slats, used to catch lobsters

local *adj* **1** of or concerning a particular area **2** restricted to a particular place **3** *med* of, affecting, or confined to a limited area or part: *a local anaesthetic* **4** (of a train or bus) stopping at all stations or stops ▷ *n* **5** an inhabitant of a specified locality: *we swim, sunbathe, meet the locals, unwind* **6** *Brit informal* a pub close to one's home [Latin *locus* place] **locally** *adv*

local anaesthetic *n med* See **anaesthesia**

local authority *n* the governing body of a county, district, or region

locale (loh-**kahl**) *n* the place where something happens or has happened [French, from Latin *locus* place]

local government *n* the government of the affairs of counties, towns, and districts by locally elected political bodies

locality *n, pl* **-ties** **1** a neighbourhood or area **2** the site or scene of an event

localize *or* **-lise** *vb* **-lizing, -lized** *or* **-lising, -lised** to restrict (something) to a particular place

locate *vb* **-cating, -cated** **1** to discover the whereabouts of; find **2** to situate or build: *located around the corner from the church* **3** to become established or settled

location *n* **1** a site or position; situation **2** the act of locating or the state of being located: *make their location and rescue a top priority* **3** a place outside a studio where filming is done: *shot on location* **4** (in South Africa) a Black African or Coloured township [Latin *locare* to place]

loc. cit. (in textual annotation) in the place cited [Latin *loco citato*]

loch *n Scot* **1** a lake **2** a long narrow arm of the sea [Gaelic]

loci (**loh**-sigh) *n* the plural of **locus**

lock[1] *n* **1** a device for fastening a door, drawer, lid, etc., and preventing unauthorized access **2** a section of a canal or river closed off by gates between which the water level can be altered to aid boats moving from one level to the next **3** *Brit & NZ* the extent to which a vehicle's front wheels will turn: *they adopted more steering lock* **4** the interlocking of parts **5** a mechanism that fires a gun **6** **lock, stock, and barrel** completely; entirely **7** a wrestling hold **8** Also called: **lock forward** *rugby* a player in the second row of the scrum ▷ *vb* **9** to fasten or become fastened to prevent entry or exit **10** to secure (a building) by locking all doors and windows **11** to fix or become fixed together securely **12** to become or cause to become immovable: *just before your knees lock* **13** to clasp or entangle in a struggle or embrace ▷ See also **lock out, lock up** [Old English *loc*]

lock² *n* **1** a strand or curl of hair **2 locks** *chiefly literary* hair [Old English *loc*]

locker *n* a small compartment with a lock, used for temporarily storing clothes, valuables, or luggage

locket *n* a small hinged ornamental pendant that holds a picture or keepsake [French *loquet* latch]

lockjaw *n pathol* a nontechnical name for **trismus** or **tetanus**

lock out *vb* **1** to prevent from entering by locking a door **2** to prevent (employees) from working during an industrial dispute, by shutting them out of the premises ▷ *n* **lockout 3** the closing of a place of employment by an employer, in order to force employees to accept terms

locksmith *n* a person who makes or repairs locks

lock up *vb* **1** to imprison **2** to secure a building by locking all the doors and windows ▷ *n* **lockup 3** a jail **4** *Brit* a garage or store separate from the main premises **5** *Brit* a small shop with no attached quarters for the owner ▷ *adj* **lock-up 6** *Brit & NZ* (of premises) without living quarters: *a lock-up garage*

l

loco¹ *n informal* a locomotive

loco² *adj slang, chiefly US* mad [Spanish: crazy]

locomotion *n* the act or power of moving [Latin *loco* from a place + MOTION]

locomotive *n* **1** a self-propelled engine for pulling trains ▷ *adj* **2** of locomotion

locum *n* a person who stands in temporarily for a doctor or a member of the clergy [Medieval Latin *locum tenens* (someone) holding the place (of another)]

locus (loh-kuss) *n, pl* **loci 1** an area or place where something happens **2** *maths* a set of points or lines whose location satisfies, or is determined by, one or more specified conditions: *the locus of points equidistant from a given point is a circle* [Latin]

locust *n* **1** an African insect, related to the grasshopper, which travels in vast swarms, stripping large areas of vegetation **2** a North American leguminous tree with prickly branches; the carob tree [Latin *locusta*]

locution *n* **1** manner or style of speech **2** a word, phrase, or expression [Latin *locutio* an utterance]

lode *n* a vein of metallic ore [Old English *lād* course]

lodestar *n* **1** a star, esp. the North Star, used in navigation or astronomy as a point of reference **2** something that serves as a guide

lodestone *n* **1 A** magnetic iron ore **B** a piece of this, used as a magnet **2** a person or thing regarded as a focus of attraction

lodge *n* **1** *chiefly Brit* the gatekeeper's house at the entrance to the grounds of a country mansion **2** a house or cabin used occasionally by hunters, skiers, etc.: *a hunting lodge* **3** *chiefly Brit* a room used by porters in a university or college **4** a local branch of certain societies **5** a beaver's home ▷ *vb* **lodging, lodged 6** to provide or be provided with rented accommodation **7** to live temporarily in rented accommodation **8** to embed or be embedded: *the bullet lodged in his brain* **9** to leave for safety or storage: *he lodged his wages in the bank* **10** to bring (a charge or accusation) against someone: *the Brazilians lodged a complaint* **11** (often foll. by *in* or *with*) to place (authority or power) in the control (of someone) [Old French *loge*]

lodger *n* a person who pays rent in return for accommodation in someone else's home

lodging *n* **1** a temporary residence: *where might I find a night's lodging?* **2 lodgings** a rented room or rooms in another person's home

loess (loh-iss) *n* a fine-grained soil, found mainly in river valleys, originally deposited by the wind [Swiss German *lösch* loose]

loft *n* **1** the space inside a roof **2** a gallery in a church **3** a room over a stable used to store hay **4** a raised house or coop in which pigeons are kept **5** *golf* **A** the angle of the face of the club used to elevate a ball **B** the height reached by a struck ball ▷ *vb* **6** *sport* to strike or kick (a ball) high in the air [Old Norse *lopt* air, ceiling]

lofty *adj* **loftier, loftiest 1** of majestic or imposing height **2** morally admirable: *lofty ideals* **3** unpleasantly superior: *a lofty contempt* **loftily** *adv* **loftiness** *n*

log¹ *n* **1** a section of a felled tree stripped of branches **2 A** a detailed record of a voyage of a ship or aircraft **B** a record of the hours flown by pilots and aircrews **C** a book in which these records are made; logbook **3** a device consisting of a float with an attached line, formerly used to measure the speed of a ship **4 sleep like a log** to sleep without stirring ▷ *vb* **logging, logged 5** to saw logs from (trees) **6** to enter (a distance or event) in a logbook or log ▷ See also **log in, log out** [origin unknown]

log² *n* short for **logarithm**

loganberry *n, pl* **-ries** a purplish-red fruit, similar to a raspberry, that grows on a trailing prickly plant [after J. H. *Logan*, who first grew it]

logarithm *n* the exponent indicating the power to which a fixed number, the base, must be raised to obtain a given number or variable [Greek *logos* ratio + *arithmos* number] **logarithmic** *adj*

logbook *n* **1** a book containing the official record of trips made by a ship or aircraft **2** *Brit informal* the registration document of a car

loggerhead *n* **1** a large-headed turtle occurring in most seas **2 at loggerheads** engaged in dispute or confrontation [probably dialect *logger* wooden block + HEAD]

loggia (loj-ya) *n* a covered gallery on the side of a building [Italian]

logging *n* the work of felling, trimming, and transporting timber **logger** *n*

logic *n* **1** the branch of philosophy that analyses the patterns of reasoning **2** a particular system of reasoning **3** reasoned thought or argument, as distinguished from irrationality **4** the interdependence of a series of events or facts **5** *electronics & computers* the principles underlying the units in a computer system that produce results from data [Greek *logikos* concerning speech or reasoning]

logical *adj* **1** relating to or characteristic of logic **2** using or deduced from the principles of logic: *a logical conclusion* **3** capable of or using clear and valid reasoning **4** reasonable because of facts or events: *the logical choice* **logically** *adv*

logic gate *n electronics* same as **gate** (sense 4)

logician *n* a person who specializes in or is skilled at logic

log in *or* **log on** *vb* to gain entrance to a computer system by keying in a special command

logistics *n* the detailed planning and organization of a large complex operation, such as a military campaign [French *loger* to lodge] **logistical** *or* **logistic** *adj* **logistically** *adv*

log jam *n chiefly US & Canad* **1** a blockage caused by the crowding together of logs floating in a river **2** a deadlock

logo (loh-go) *n, pl* **-os** a special design that identifies a company or an organization and appears on all its products, printed material, etc. [shortened from *logotype* badge, symbol]

log out *vb* to exit from a computer system by keying in a special command

-logy *combining form* **1** indicating the science or study of: *musicology* **2** indicating writing or discourse: *trilogy; phraseology* [Greek *logos* word] **-logical** *or* **-logic** *combining form* **-logist** *combining form*

loin *n* **1** the part of the body between the pelvis and the ribs **2** a cut of meat from this part of an animal ▷ See also **loins** [Old French *loigne*]

loincloth *n* a piece of cloth covering only the loins

loins *pl n* **1** the hips and the inner surface of the legs where they join the body **2** *euphemistic* the genitals

loiter *vb* to stand or wait aimlessly or idly [perhaps Middle Dutch *löteren* to wobble]

Lolita (low-lee-ta) *n* a sexually precocious young girl [after the character in Nabokov's novel *Lolita*]

loll *vb* **1** to lounge in a lazy manner **2** to hang loosely: *a wet lolling tongue; his head lolled back and forth* [perhaps imitative]

lollipop *n* **1** a boiled sweet stuck on a small wooden stick **2** *Brit* an ice lolly [perhaps dialect *lolly* the tongue + POP²]

lollipop man *or* **lollipop lady** *n Brit informal* a person holding a circular sign on a pole who stops traffic to enable children to cross the road safely

lollop *vb chiefly Brit* to walk or run with a clumsy or relaxed bouncing movement [probably *loll* + *-op*, as in *gallop*]

lolly *n, pl* **-lies** **1** *informal* a lollipop **2** *Brit* short for **ice lolly** **3** *Brit, Austral & NZ slang* money **4** *Austral & NZ informal* a sweet [shortened from *lollipop*]

Londoner *n* a person from London

London pride *n* a rock plant with a rosette of leaves and pink flowers

lone *adj* **1** solitary: *a lone figure* **2** isolated: *a lone isle guarded by the great Atlantic swell* **3** *Brit* having no partner: *a lone parent* [from the mistaken division of *alone* into *a lone*]

lonely *adj* **-lier, -liest** **1** unhappy as a result of solitude **2** resulting from the state of being alone: *command can be a lonely business* **3** isolated and not much visited by people: *a lonely beach* **loneliness** *n*

lonely hearts *adj* of or for people seeking a congenial companion or romantic partner: *lonely hearts ads*

loner *n informal* a person who prefers to be alone

lonesome *adj* **1** *chiefly US & Canad* lonely **2** causing feelings of loneliness: *it was lonesome up here on the mountain*

long¹ *adj* **1** having relatively great length in space or time **2** having greater than the average or expected range, extent, or duration: *a long session of talks* **3** seeming to occupy a greater time than is really so: *she was quiet a long moment* **4** of a specified extent or duration: *trimmed to about two cms long* **5** consisting of a large number of parts: *a long list* **6** *phonetics & prosody* (of a vowel) of relatively considerable duration **7** from end to end; lengthwise **8** *finance* having large holdings of securities or commodities in anticipation of rising prices **9** **in the long run** ultimately; after or over a period of time **10** **long on** *informal* plentifully supplied or endowed with: *long on showbiz gossip* ▷ *adv* **11** for a certain time or period: *how long have we got?* **12** for or during an extensive period of time: *to talk long into the night* **13** a considerable amount of time: *long after I met you; long ago* **14** **as** *or* **so long as** **A** for or during the same length of time that **B** provided that; if ▷ *n* **15** anything that is long **16** **before long** soon **17** **for long** for a long time **18** **the long and the short of it** the essential points or facts [Old English *lang*] **longish** *adj*

long² *vb* to have a strong desire for something or to do something: *I longed for a baby; the more I think of him the more I long to see him* [Old English *langian*]

long. longitude

long- *adv (in combination)* for or lasting a long time: *long-established; long-lasting*

longboat *n* **1** the largest boat carried aboard a commercial ship **2** same as **longship**

longbow *n* a large powerful hand-drawn bow

long-distance *adj* **1** covering relatively long distances: *a long-distance race* **2** (of a telephone call) connecting points relatively far apart

longevity (lon-jev-it-ee) *n* long life [Latin *longus* long + *aevum* age]

long face *n* a glum expression

longhand *n* ordinary handwriting, as opposed to typing or shorthand

longhorn *n* a British breed of beef cattle with long curved horns

longing *n* **1** a strong feeling of wanting something one is unlikely ever to have ▷ *adj* **2** having or showing desire: *longing glances* **longingly** *adv*

longitude *n* distance in degrees east or west of the prime meridian at 0° [Latin *longitudo* length]

longitudinal *adj* **1** of longitude or length **2** placed or extended lengthways

long johns *pl n informal* long underpants

long jump *n* an athletic contest of jumping the greatest length from a fixed mark

long-life *adj* (of milk, batteries, etc.) lasting longer than the regular kind

long-lived *adj* living or lasting for a long time
long-range *adj* **1** of or extending into the future: *a long-range economic forecast* **2** (of vehicles, aircraft, or weapons) capable of covering great distances
longship *n* a narrow open boat with oars and a square sail, used by the Vikings
longshore drift *n* the movement of material along a beach, due to waves approaching the shore at an oblique angle
longshoreman *n, pl* **-men** *US & Canad* a docker
long shot *n* **1** an undertaking, guess, or possibility with little chance of success **2** a bet against heavy odds **3 not by a long shot** not by any means: *she wasn't beaten, not by a long shot*
long-sighted *adj* **1** able to see only distant objects in focus **2** far-sighted
long-standing *adj* existing for a long time
long-suffering *adj* enduring trouble or unhappiness without complaint
long-term *adj* **1** lasting or extending over a long time: *a long-term commitment* ▷ *n* **long term 2 in the long term** over a long period of time: *in the long term the cost of energy will have to go up*
longtime *adj* of long standing: *his longtime colleague; his longtime relationship with Sue*
long wave *n* a radio wave with a wavelength greater than 1000 metres
longways *or US & Canad* **longwise** *adv* lengthways
long-winded *adj* tiresomely long **long-windedness** *n*
loo *n, pl* **loos** *Brit & NZ informal* a toilet [perhaps from French *lieux d'aisance* water closet]
loofah *n* a long rough-textured bath sponge made from the dried pod of a gourd [Arabic *lūf*]
look *vb* **1** (often foll. by *at*) to direct the eyes (towards): *he turned to look at her* **2** (often foll. by *at*) to consider: *let's look at the issues involved* **3** to give the impression of being; seem: *Luxembourg's timetable looks a winner* **4** to face in a particular direction: *Morgan's Rock looks south* **5** (foll. by *for*) to search or seek: *the department looks for reputable firms* **6** (foll. by *into*) to carry out an investigation **7** to direct a look at (someone) in a specified way: *she looks at Teresina suspiciously* **8** to match in appearance with (something): *looking your best* **9** to expect or hope (to do something): *we would look to derive a procedure that would account for most cases* **10 look alive** *or* **lively** *or* **sharp** *or* **smart** to hurry up; get busy **11 look here** an expression used to attract someone's attention or add emphasis to a statement ▷ *n* **12** an instance of looking: *a look of icy contempt* **13** a view or sight (of something): *take a look at my view* **14** (*often pl*) appearance to the eye or mind; aspect: *I'm not happy with the look of things here; better than you by the looks of it* **15** style or fashion: *the look made famous by the great Russian* ▷ *conj* **16** an expression demanding attention or showing annoyance: *look, I won't be coming back* ▷ See also **look after, look back** *etc.* [Old English *lōcian*] **looker** *n*

USAGE See at **like**[1].

look after *vb* to take care of
lookalike *n* a person or thing that is the double of another, often well-known, person or thing
look back *vb* **1** to think about the past **2 never looked back** was extremely successful: *he became the station's first major signing and never looked back*
look down *vb* (foll. by *on* or *upon*) to treat as inferior or unimportant
look forward to *vb* to anticipate with pleasure
look-in *informal* ▷ *n* **1** a chance to be chosen or participate: *before anyone else gets a look-in* ▷ *vb* **look in 2** to pay a short visit
looking glass *n* a mirror
look on *vb* **1** to be a spectator **2** to consider or regard: *I just looked on her as a friend* **looker-on** *n*
lookout *n* **1** the act of watching for danger or for an opportunity: *on the lookout for attack* **2** a person or people keeping such a watch **3** a viewpoint from which a watch is kept **4** *informal* worry or concern: *that is my lookout rather than theirs* **5** *chiefly Brit* chances or prospect: *it's a bad lookout for Europe* ▷ *vb* **look out 6** to be careful **7** to watch out for: *look out particularly for oils that have been flavoured* **8** to find and take out: *little time to look out clothes that she might need* **9** (foll. by *on* or *over*) to face in a particular direction: *looking out over the courtyard*
look over *vb* **1** to inspect or examine ▷ *n* **look-over 2** an inspection
look-see *n slang* a brief inspection
look up *vb* **1** to discover or confirm by checking in a reference book **2** to improve: *things were looking up* **3 look up to** to have respect for: *she looked up to him as a kind of father* **4** to visit (a person): *I'll look you up when I'm in town*
loom[1] *n* a machine for weaving yarn into cloth [variant of Old English *gelōma* tool]
loom[2] *vb* **1** to appear indistinctly, esp. as a tall and threatening shape **2** (of an event) to seem ominously close [perhaps East Frisian *lomen* to move slowly]
loon[1] *n US & Canad* same as **diver** (sense 3) [Scandinavian]
loon[2] *n informal* an unintelligent person
loonie *n Canad slang* **1** a Canadian dollar coin with a loon bird on one of its faces **2** the Canadian currency
loony *slang* ▷ *adj* **loonier, looniest 1** *offensive* insane **2** foolish or ridiculous ▷ *n, pl* **loonies 3** *offensive* an insane person **4** a foolish person [shortened from *lunatic*]
loop *n* **1** the rounded shape formed by a curved line that crosses itself: *a loop of the highway* **2** any round or oval-shaped thing that is closed or nearly closed **3** *electronics* a closed circuit through which a signal can circulate **4** a flight manoeuvre in which an aircraft flies vertically in a complete circle **5** a continuous strip of film or tape **6** *computers* a series of instructions in a program, performed repeatedly until some specified condition is satisfied ▷ *vb* **7** to make into a loop **8** to fasten or encircle with a loop **9** Also: **loop the loop** to fly or be flown vertically in a complete circle [origin unknown]
loophole *n* an ambiguity or omission in the law, which enables one to evade it
loopy *adj* **loopier, loopiest** *informal* slightly unbalanced mentally
loose *adj* **1** (of clothing) not close-fitting: *the jacket loose and unbuttoned* **2** free or released from

confinement or restraint **3** not tight, fastened, fixed, or tense **4** not bundled, fastened, or put in a container: *loose tobacco* **5** inexact or imprecise: *a loose translation* **6** (of cash) accessible: *a lot of the loose money is floating around the city* **7** *old-fashioned* sexually promiscuous **8** lacking a sense of propriety: *loose talk* **9** **at a loose end** bored because one has nothing to do ▹ *n* **10** **on the loose** free from confinement or restraint **11** **the loose** *rugby* the part of play when the forwards close round the ball in a ruck or loose scrum ▹ *adv* **12** in a loose manner; loosely ▹ *vb* **loosing, loosed** **13** to free or release from restraint or obligation: *he loosed the dogs* **14** to unfasten or untie: *the guards loosed his arms* **15** to make or become less strict, tight, firmly attached, or compact **16** to let fly (a bullet, arrow, or other missile) [Old Norse *lauss* free] **loosely** *adv* **looseness** *n*

loosebox *n* an enclosed stall with a door in which an animal can be kept

loose cannon *n* a person or thing, with the potential to cause considerable damage, that appears to be out of control

loose-jointed *adj* supple and lithe

loose-leaf *adj* (of a binder) allowing the removal and addition of pages

loosen *vb* **1** to make or become less tight: *loosen and relax the ankle* **2** (often foll. by *up*) to make or become less firm, compact, or rigid: *massage is used first to loosen up the muscles* **3** to untie **4** (often foll. by *up*) to make or become less strict: *the churches loosen up on sexual teachings*

loot *n* **1** goods stolen in wartime or during riots; plunder **2** *informal* money ▹ *vb* **3** to plunder (a city) during war or riots **4** to steal (money or goods) during war or riots [Hindi *lūt*] **looter** *n*

lop *vb* **lopping, lopped** (usually foll. by *off*) **1** to cut (parts) off a tree or body **2** to cut out or eliminate any unnecessary parts: *some parts of the legislature were lopped off* [Middle English *loppe* branches cut off]

lope *vb* **loping, loped** **1** to move or run with a long easy stride ▹ *n* **2** a long steady gait or stride [Old Norse *hlaupa* to leap]

lop-eared *adj* (of animals) having ears that droop

lopsided *adj* greater in weight, height, or size on one side

loquacious *adj* talkative [Latin *loqui* to speak] **loquacity** *n*

lord *n* **1** a person with power or authority over others, such as a monarch or master **2** a male member of the nobility **3** (in medieval Europe) a feudal superior **4** **my lord** a respectful form of address used to a judge, bishop, or nobleman ▹ *vb* **5** **lord it over someone** to act in a superior manner towards someone [Old English *hlāford* bread keeper]

Lord *n* **1** *Christianity* a title given to God or Jesus Christ **2** *Brit* a title given to certain male peers **3** *Brit* a title given to certain high officials and judges ▹ *interj* **4** an exclamation of dismay or surprise: *Good Lord!*

Lord Chancellor *n* *Brit government* the cabinet minister who is head of the judiciary and Speaker of the House of Lords

Lord Chief Justice *n* (in England and Wales) the judge who is second only to the Lord Chancellor and president of one division of the High Court of Justice

Lord Lieutenant *n* **1** (in Britain) the representative of the Crown in a county **2** (formerly) the British viceroy in Ireland

lordly *adj* **-lier, -liest** **1** haughty or arrogant **2** of or suitable to a lord **lordliness** *n*

Lord Mayor *n* the mayor in the City of London, in certain other English boroughs, and in some Australian cities

Lord Privy Seal *n* (in Britain) the senior cabinet minister without official duties

Lords *n* **the Lords** short for **House of Lords**

lordship *n* the position or authority of a lord

Lordship *n* (preceded by *Your* or *His*) *Brit* a title used to address or refer to a bishop, a judge of the high court, or any peer except a duke

Lord's Prayer *n* **the Lord's Prayer** *Christianity* the prayer taught by Jesus Christ to his disciples

Lords Spiritual *pl n* (in Britain) the Anglican archbishops and senior bishops who are members of the House of Lords

Lord's Supper *n* **the Lord's Supper** same as **Holy Communion**

Lords Temporal *pl n* (in Britain) the peers other than bishops in their capacity as members of the House of Lords

lore *n* collective knowledge or wisdom on a particular subject [Old English *lār*]

lorgnette (lor-**nyet**) *n* a pair of spectacles or opera glasses mounted on a long handle [French, from *lorgner* to squint]

lorikeet *n* a small brightly coloured Australian parrot

lorry *n, pl* **-ries** *Brit & S African* a large motor vehicle for transporting heavy loads [perhaps dialect *lurry* to pull]

lose *vb* **losing, lost** **1** to come to be without, through carelessness or by accident or theft **2** to fail to keep or maintain: *to lose control* **3** to suffer the loss of: *he will lose his redundancy money* **4** to get rid of: *I've lost a stone this summer* **5** to fail to get or make use of: *Lysenko never lost a chance to show his erudition* **6** to be defeated in a fight or competition **7** to fail to see, hear, or understand: *she lost sight of him* **8** to waste: *so I'd lost a fortune* **9** to go astray from: *psychologists lose the trail* **10** to allow to go astray or out of sight: *he lost, at the Gare de Lyon, a case with most of his early manuscripts* **11** to cause the loss of: *I came in to have the gear attended to, which lost me a lap* **12** to absorb or engross: *lost in thought* **13** to die or cause the death of: *two lost as yacht sinks in storm* **14** to outdistance or escape from: *there's some satisfaction in knowing that they've lost us* **15** (of a timepiece) to run slow (by a specified amount) [Old English *losian* to perish]

lose out *vb informal* **1** to be defeated or unsuccessful **2** **lose out on** to fail to secure or make use of: *the yard has already lost out on a number of valuable orders this year*

loser *n* **1** a person or thing that loses **2** *informal* a person or thing that seems destined to fail: *he's a bit of a loser*

losing *adj* unprofitable or failing: *a losing streak that cost him millions*

loss *n* **1** the act or an instance of losing **2** the person, thing, or amount lost: *the only loss was a sleeping bag* **3** the disadvantage or deprivation resulting from losing: *a loss of sovereignty* **4 at a loss** **A** uncertain what to do; bewildered **B** with income less than outlay: *they cannot afford to run branches at a loss* [Old English *lōsian* to be destroyed]

loss leader *n* an article offered at a low price to attract customers

lost *vb* **1** the past of **lose** ▷ *adj* **2** unable to find one's way **3** unable to be found or recovered **4** confused or bewildered: *she seemed a bit lost* **5** (sometimes foll. by *on*) not used, noticed, or understood by: *not that the propaganda value of the game was lost on the authorities* **6** no longer possessed or existing: *lost credit* **7** (foll. by *in*) engrossed (in): *he remained lost in his own thoughts* **8** *old-fashioned* morally ruined **9** damned: *a lost soul*

lost cause *n* something with no chance of success

lot *pron* **1 a lot** a great number or quantity: *not that there was a lot to tell; a lot of people* ▷ *n* **2** a collection of things or people: *your lot have wasted enough time* **3** destiny or fortune: *helping the less well-off to improve their lot* **4** any object, such as a straw or slip of paper, drawn from others at random to make a selection or choice: *they could only be split by the drawing of lots; the casting by lots* **5** the use of lots in making a choice: *chosen by lot* **6** an item or set of items for sale in an auction **7** *US, Canad, Austral & NZ* an area of land: *to the parking lot* **8 a bad lot** an unpleasant or disreputable person **9 cast** *or* **throw in one's lot with someone** to join with voluntarily and share the fortunes of someone **10 the lot** the entire amount or number ▷ *adv* **11** (preceded by *a*) *informal* to a considerable extent, degree, or amount: *steroids are used a lot in weightlifting* ▷ See also **lots** [Old English *hlot*]

loth (rhymes with **both**) *adj* same as **loath**

Lothario (loh-**thah**-ree-oh) *n, pl* **-os** a seducer [after a character in a play]

lotion *n* a liquid preparation having a soothing, cleansing, or antiseptic action, applied to the skin [Latin *lotio* a washing]

lots *informal* ▷ *pl n* **1** (often foll. by *of*) great numbers or quantities: *lots of friends; you can read lots into Nostradamus* ▷ *adv* **2** a great deal

lottery *n, pl* **-teries 1** a method of raising money by selling tickets by which a winner is selected at random **2** a venture whose outcome is a matter of luck: *hospital treatment is a lottery* [Middle Dutch *loterije*]

lotto *n* **1** a game of chance similar to bingo **2 Lotto** (in certain countries) the national lottery [Italian]

lotus *n* **1** (in Greek mythology) a fruit that induces dreamy forgetfulness in those who eat it **2** any of several water lilies of tropical Africa and Asia, regarded as sacred **3** a symbolic representation of such a plant [Greek *lōtos*]

lotus-eater *n* a person who lives in lazy forgetfulness

lotus position *n* a seated cross-legged position with each foot on top of the opposite thigh, used in yoga and meditation

loud *adj* **1** (of sound) relatively great in volume: *loud applause* **2** making or able to make sounds of relatively great volume: *a loud voice* **3** insistent and emphatic: *loud appeals* **4** (of colours or patterns) harsh to look at **5** noisy, vulgar, and offensive ▷ *adv* **6** in a loud manner **7 out loud** audibly [Old English *hlud*] **loudly** *adv* **loudness** *n*

loud-hailer *n* a portable loudspeaker with a built-in amplifier and microphone

loudmouth *n* a person who talks too much, esp. in a boastful or indiscreet way **loudmouthed** *adj*

loudspeaker *n* a device for converting electrical signals into sounds

lough *n Irish* **1** a lake **2** a long narrow arm of the sea [Irish *loch* lake]

lounge *n* **1** a living room in a private house **2** same as **lounge bar** **3** a communal room in a hotel, ship, or airport, used for waiting or relaxing in **4** the act of lounging ▷ *vb* **lounging, lounged** **5** (often foll. by *about* or *around*) to sit or lie in a relaxed manner **6** to pass time lazily or idly [origin unknown]

lounge bar *n* a more expensive and comfortable bar in a pub or hotel

lounge suit *n* a man's suit for daytime wear

lour *vb* same as **lower**[2]

lourie (rhymes with **dowry**) *or* **loerie** *n* a type of African bird with either crimson or grey plumage [Afrikaans, from Malay]

louse *n* **1** *pl* **lice** a wingless blood-sucking insect which feeds off humans and some animals **2** *pl* **louses** *slang* an unpleasant or dishonourable person [Old English *lūs*]

louse up *vb* **lousing, loused** *slang* to ruin or spoil

lousy *adj* **lousier, lousiest 1** *slang* very mean or unpleasant **2** *slang* inferior or bad **3** *slang* ill or unwell **4** infested with lice

lout *n* a crude or oafish person; boor [perhaps Old English *lūtan* to stoop] **loutish** *adj*

louvre *or US* **louver** (**loo**-ver) *n* **A** any of a set of horizontal slats in a door or window, slanted to admit air but not rain **B** the slats and frame supporting them [Old French *lovier*] **louvred** *or US* **louvered** *adj*

lovage *n* a European herb with greenish-white flowers [Old French *luvesche*, from Latin *ligusticum*, literally: Ligurian (plant)]

love *vb* **loving, loved 1** to have a great affection for a person or thing **2** to have passionate desire for someone **3** to like (to do something) very much ▷ *n* **4** an intense emotion of affection towards a person or thing **5** a deep feeling of sexual attraction **6** wholehearted liking for or pleasure in something **7** a beloved person: often used as an endearment **8** *Brit informal* a commonplace term of address, not necessarily restricted to people one knows or has regard for **9** (in tennis, squash, etc.) a score of zero **10 fall in love** to become in love **11 for love or money** in any circumstances **12 in love** feeling a strong emotional and sexual attraction **13 make love to** **A** to have sexual intercourse with **B** *archaic* to court [Old English *lufu*] **lovable** *or* **loveable** *adj*

love affair *n* a romantic or sexual relationship between two people who are not married to each other

lovebird *n* any of several small African parrots often kept as cage birds
lovebite *n* a temporary red mark left on a person's skin by a partner biting or sucking it during lovemaking
love child *n euphemistic* a child whose parents have not been married to each other
loveless *adj* without love: *a loveless marriage*
love-lies-bleeding *n* a plant with drooping spikes of small red flowers
love life *n* a person's romantic or sexual relationships
lovelorn *adj* miserable because of unreturned love or unhappiness in love
lovely *adj* **-lier, -liest 1** very attractive or beautiful **2** highly pleasing or enjoyable: *thanks for a lovely evening* ▷ *n, pl* **-lies 3** *slang* an attractive woman: *suntanned lovelies* **loveliness** *n*
lovemaking *n* **1** sexual play and activity between lovers, including sexual intercourse **2** *archaic* courtship
lover *n* **1** a person having a sexual relationship with another person outside marriage **2** (*often pl*) either of the people involved in a love affair **3** someone who loves a specified person or thing: *an animal-lover*
lovesick *adj* pining or languishing because of love **lovesickness** *n*
lovey-dovey *adj* making a sentimental or showy display of affection
loving *adj* feeling or showing love and affection **lovingly** *adv*
loving cup *n* a large two-handled cup out of which people drink in turn
low[1] *adj* **1** having a relatively small distance from base to top: *a low wall* **2** of less than usual amount, degree, quality, or cost: *low score*; *low inflation* **3** situated at a relatively short distance above the ground, sea level, or the horizon: *heavy weather with low driving cloud* **4** (of numbers) small **5** involving or containing a relatively small amount of something: *low-fat cheese and crackers* **6** having little value or quality: *it sounds as if your self-confidence is low* **7** coarse or vulgar: *low comedy* **8** unworthy or contemptible: *that's a low trick, Justin* **9** inferior in culture or status **10** in a weakened physical or mental state **11** with a hushed tone: *in a low, scared voice* **12** low-necked: *a low evening gown* **13** *music* of or having a relatively low pitch **14** (of latitudes) situated not far north or south of the equator **15** having little or no money **16** unfavourable: *he has a low opinion of Ford* **17** deep: *a low bow* **18** (of a gear) providing a relatively low speed ▷ *adv* **19** in a low position, level, or degree: *the pilot flew low over the area* **20** at a low pitch; deeply: *he's singing very low* **21** cheaply: *the bank is having to buy high and sell low* **22 lay low A** to make (someone) fall by a blow **B** to overcome or destroy **23 lie low** to keep or be concealed or quiet ▷ *n* **24** a low position, level, or degree: *shares hit new low* **25** an area of low atmospheric pressure; depression [Old Norse *lāgr*] **lowness** *n*
low[2] *n* **1** Also: **lowing** the sound uttered by cattle; moo ▷ *vb* **2** to make a mooing sound [Old English *hlōwan*]

low-alcohol *adj* (of beer or wine) containing only a small amount of alcohol
lowborn *adj rare* of ignoble or common parentage
lowbrow *derogatory* ▷ *n* **1** a person with uncultivated or nonintellectual tastes ▷ *adj* **2** of or for such a person
Low Church *n* a section of the Church of England which stresses evangelical beliefs and practices **Low-Church** *adj*
low comedy *n* comedy characterized by slapstick and physical action
Low Countries *pl n* Belgium, Luxembourg, and the Netherlands
low-down *informal* ▷ *adj* **1** mean, underhand, and dishonest ▷ *n* **lowdown 2 the lowdown** information
lower[1] (rhymes with **goer**) *adj* **1** being below one or more other things: *the lower branches* **2** reduced in amount or value: *lower rates* **3 Lower** *geol* denoting the early part of a period or formation ▷ *vb* **4** to cause or allow to move down: *she lowered her head* **5** to behave in a way that damages one's respect: *she'd never lowered herself enough to make a call* **6** to lessen or become less: *the cholesterol was lowered by medication* **7** to make quieter or reduce the pitch of
lower[2] *or* **lour** (rhymes with **sour**) *vb* (of the sky or weather) to be overcast and menacing [Middle English *louren* to scowl] **lowering** *or* **louring** *adj*
lower case *n* (in printing) small letters, as opposed to capital letters **lower-case** *adj*
lower class *n* the class with the lowest position in society **lower-class** *adj*
lower house *n* one of the houses of a parliament that has two chambers: usually the larger and more representative
lowest common denominator *n maths* the smallest integer or polynomial that is exactly divisible by each denominator of a set of fractions
lowest common multiple *n maths* the smallest number or quantity that is exactly divisible by each member of a set of numbers or quantities
low frequency *n* any radio frequency lying between 300 and 30 kilohertz
Low German *n* a language of N Germany, spoken in rural areas
low-key *or* **low-keyed** *adj* **1** restrained or subdued **2** having a low intensity or tone
lowland *n* **1** relatively low ground **2** (*often pl*) a low generally flat region ▷ *adj* **3** of a lowland or lowlands **lowlander** *n*
Lowland *adj* of the Lowlands or the dialects of English spoken there **Lowlander** *n*
Lowlands *pl n* a low generally flat region of S Central Scotland
lowlight *n* **1** an unenjoyable or unpleasant part of an event **2** (*usually pl*) a streak of darker colour artificially applied to the hair
lowly *adj* **-lier, -liest 1** humble in position or status **2** simple and unpretentious **lowliness** *n*
Low Mass *n* a simplified form of Mass that is spoken rather than sung
low-minded *adj* having a vulgar or crude mind **low-mindedness** *n*

low-pitched *adj* **1** pitched low in tone **2** (of a roof) with a shallow slope
low profile *n* a deliberate shunning of publicity: *he kept a low profile* **low-profile** *adj*
low-spirited *adj* depressed or dejected
low-tech *adj* **1** of or using low technology **2** in the style of interior design that uses items associated with low technology
low technology *n* unsophisticated technology that is limited to the production of basic necessities
low tide *n* the tide at its lowest level or the time at which it reaches this
low water *n* **1** low tide **2** the lowest level which a stretch of water reaches
loyal *adj* **1** faithful to one's friends, country, or government **2** of or expressing loyalty: *the loyal toast* [Latin *legalis* legal] **loyally** *adv*
loyalist *n* a patriotic supporter of the sovereign or government **loyalism** *n*
Loyalist *n* (in Northern Ireland) a Protestant wishing to retain Northern Ireland's link with Britain
loyalty *n, pl* **-ties** **1** the quality of being loyal **2** a feeling of friendship or duty towards someone or something
loyalty card *n* a swipe card issued by a supermarket or chain store to a customer, used to record credit points awarded for money spent in the store
lozenge *n* **1** *med* a medicated tablet held in the mouth until it has dissolved **2** *geom* a rhombus [Old French *losange*]
L-plate *n Brit & Austral* a letter 'L' on a square piece of plastic attached to a motor vehicle to indicate that the driver is a learner
Lr *chem* lawrencium
LSD *n* lysergic acid diethylamide; an illegal hallucinogenic drug
L.S.D., £.s.d. *or* **l.s.d.** pounds, shillings, pence [Latin *librae, solidi, denarii*]
Lt Lieutenant
Ltd *Brit* Limited (Liability)
Lu *chem* lutetium
lubber *n* **1** a big, awkward, or stupid person **2** short for **landlubber** [probably from Old Norse] **lubberly** *adj, adv* **lubberliness** *n*
lubricant *n* a lubricating substance, such as oil
lubricate (loo-brik-ate) *vb* **-cating, -cated** **1** to cover with an oily substance to lessen friction **2** to make greasy, slippery, or smooth [Latin *lubricare* to make slippery] **lubrication** *n*
lubricious (loo-**brish**-uss) *adj formal or literary* lewd [Latin *lubricus* slippery]
lucerne *n Brit & Austral* same as **alfalfa**
lucid *adj* **1** clear and easily understood **2** capable of clear thought, particularly between periods of mental illness or confusion **3** shining or glowing [Latin *lucidus* full of light] **lucidity** *n* **lucidly** *adv*
Lucifer *n* Satan [Latin: light-bearer, from *lux* light + *ferre* to bear]
luck *n* **1** events that are subject to chance; fortune, good or bad **2** success or good fortune **3** **down on one's luck** lacking good fortune to the extent of suffering hardship **4** **no such luck** *informal* unfortunately not **5** **try one's luck** to attempt something that is uncertain [Middle Dutch *luc*]
luckless *adj* unfortunate or unlucky
lucky *adj* **luckier, luckiest** **1** having or bringing good fortune **2** happening by chance, esp. as desired **luckily** *adv*
lucky dip *n Brit, Austral & NZ* a box filled with sawdust containing small prizes for which children search
lucrative *adj* profitable
lucre (**loo**-ker) *n usually facetious* money or wealth: *filthy lucre* [Latin *lucrum* gain]
Luddite *Brit history* ▷ *n* **1** any of the textile workers opposed to mechanization, who organized machine-breaking between 1811 and 1816 **2** any opponent of industrial change or innovation ▷ *adj* **3** of the Luddites [after Ned *Ludd*, who destroyed machinery]
luderick *n* an Australian fish, usually black or dark brown in colour
ludicrous *adj* absurd or ridiculous [Latin *ludus* game] **ludicrously** *adv*
ludo *n Brit & Austral* a simple board game in which players move counters forward by throwing dice [Latin: I play]
luff *vb* **1** *naut* to sail (a ship) into the wind **2** to move the jib of a crane in order to shift a load [Old French *lof*]
lug[1] *vb* **lugging, lugged** to carry or drag with great effort [probably from Old Norse]
lug[2] *n* **1** a projecting piece by which something is connected, supported, or lifted **2** *informal Scot* an ear [Scots: ear]
luggage *n* suitcases, trunks, and bags [perhaps LUG[1] + *-age*, as in *baggage*]
lugger *n* *naut* a small working boat with an oblong sail [origin unknown]
lugubrious (loo-**goo**-bree-uss) *adj* mournful or gloomy [Latin *lugere* to grieve]
lugworm *n* a large worm which lives in burrows on sandy shores and is often used as bait by fishermen [origin unknown]
lukewarm *adj* **1** (of a liquid) moderately warm; tepid **2** lacking enthusiasm or conviction [probably from Old English *hlēow* warm]
lull *vb* **1** to soothe (a person or animal) by soft sounds or motions **2** to calm (fears or suspicions) by deception ▷ *n* **3** a short period of calm [perhaps imitative of crooning sounds]
lullaby *n, pl* **-bies** a quiet song to lull a child to sleep [perhaps a blend of *lull* + *goodbye*]
lumbago (lum-**bay**-go) *n* pain in the lower back; low backache [Latin *lumbus* loin]
lumbar *adj* relating to the lower back [Latin *lumbus* loin]
lumbar puncture *n* *med* insertion of a hollow needle into the lower spinal cord to withdraw fluid for diagnosis
lumber[1] *n* **1** *Brit* unwanted disused household articles **2** *chiefly US & Canad* logs; sawn timber ▷ *vb* **3** *informal* to burden with something unpleasant: *somebody gets lumbered with the extra costs* **4** to fill up with useless household articles **5** *chiefly US & Canad* to convert trees into marketable timber [perhaps from LUMBER[2]]

lumber² *vb* to move awkwardly and heavily [Middle English *lomeren*] **lumbering** *adj*

lumberjack *n* (esp. in North America) a person who fells trees and prepares the timber for transport

luminary *n, pl* **-naries 1 A** a famous person **B** an expert in a particular subject **2** *literary* something, such as the sun or moon, that gives off light

luminescence *n physics* the emission of light at low temperatures by any process other than burning **luminescent** *adj*

luminous *adj* **1** reflecting or giving off light: *luminous colours* **2** *not in technical use* luminescent: *luminous sparklers* **3** enlightening or wise [Latin *lumen* light] **luminosity** *n*

lump¹ *n* **1** a small solid mass without definite shape **2** *pathol* any small swelling or tumour **3** *informal* an awkward, heavy, or stupid person **4 a lump in one's throat** a tight dry feeling in one's throat, usually caused by great emotion **5 the lump** *Brit* self-employed workers in the building trade considered collectively ▷ *adj* **6** in the form of a lump or lumps: *lump sugar* ▷ *vb* **7** (often foll. by *together*) to consider as a single group, often without justification **8** to grow into lumps or become lumpy [probably related to Scandinavian dialect: block]

lump² *vb* **lump it** *informal* to accept something irrespective of personal preference: *if you don't like it, you can lump it* [origin unknown]

lumpectomy *n, pl* **-mies** surgical removal of a tumour in a breast [*lump* + Greek *tomē* a cutting]

lumpish *adj* stupid, clumsy, or heavy **lumpishness** *n*

lump sum *n* a relatively large sum of money, paid at one time

lumpy *adj* **lumpier, lumpiest** full of or having lumps **lumpiness** *n*

lunacy *n, pl* **-cies 1** foolishness **2** (formerly) any severe mental illness

lunar *adj* relating to the moon: *lunar eclipse* [Latin *luna* the moon]

lunatic *adj* **1** foolish; eccentric **2** *archaic* mentally ill ▷ *n* **3** a foolish or annoying person **4** *archaic* a mentally ill person [Latin *luna* moon]

lunatic asylum *n archaic* a home or hospital for severely mentally ill people

lunatic fringe *n* the members of a group who adopt views regarded as extreme

lunch *n* **1** a meal eaten during the middle of the day ▷ *vb* **2** to eat lunch [shortened from *luncheon*]

luncheon *n* a lunch, often a formal one [probably variant of *nuncheon*, from Middle English *none* noon + *schench* drink]

luncheon meat *n* a ground mixture of meat (often pork) and cereal, usually tinned

luncheon voucher *n Brit* a voucher for a specified amount issued to employees and accepted by some restaurants as payment for food

lunchroom *n US & Canad* a room where lunch is served or where students or employees may eat lunches they bring

lung *n* the part of the body that allows an animal or bird to breathe air. Humans have two lungs, contained within the chest cavity [Old English *lungen*]

lunge *n* **1** a sudden forward motion **2** *fencing* a thrust made by advancing the front foot and straightening the back leg ▷ *vb* **lunging, lunged 3** to move with a lunge **4** *fencing* to make a lunge [French *allonger* to stretch out (one's arm)]

lungfish *n, pl* **-fish** *or* **-fishes** a freshwater fish with an air-breathing lung

lupin *n* a garden plant with large spikes of brightly coloured flowers and flattened pods [Latin *lupinus* wolfish; from the belief that it ravenously exhausted the soil]

lupine *adj* of or like a wolf [Latin *lupus* wolf]

lupus *n* an ulcerous skin disease [Latin: wolf; so called because it rapidly eats away the affected part]

> **USAGE** In current usage the word *lupus* alone is generally understood to signify *lupus vulgaris*. *Lupus erythematosus* is normally referred to in full or by the abbreviation *LE*.

lurch¹ *vb* **1** to lean or tilt suddenly to one side **2** to stagger ▷ *n* **3** a lurching movement [origin unknown]

lurch² *n* **leave someone in the lurch** to abandon someone in trouble [French *lourche*, a game similar to backgammon]

lure *vb* **luring, lured 1** (sometimes foll. by *away* or *into*) to tempt or attract by the promise of reward ▷ *n* **2** a person or thing that lures **3** *angling* a brightly coloured artificial spinning bait **4** *falconry* a feathered decoy to which small pieces of meat can be attached [Old French *loirre* falconer's lure]

lurid *adj* **1** vivid in shocking detail; sensational: *magazines whose lurid covers sickened him* **2** glaring in colour: *a lurid red tartan* **3** horrible in savagery or violence: *reporting lurid crimes* [Latin *luridus* pale yellow] **luridly** *adv*

lurk *vb* **1** to move stealthily or be concealed, esp. for evil purposes **2** to be present in an unobtrusive way; be latent [probably frequentative of *lour*]

lurking *adj* lingering but almost unacknowledged: *it confirms a lurking suspicion*

luscious (lush-uss) *adj* **1** extremely pleasurable to taste or smell **2** very attractive [perhaps short for *delicious*]

lush¹ *adj* **1** (of vegetation) growing thickly and healthily **2** luxurious, elaborate, or opulent **3** *slang* very attractive or pleasing [Latin *laxus* loose]

lush² *n slang* an alcoholic [origin unknown]

lust *n* **1** a strong sexual desire **2** a strong desire or drive: *a lust for power* ▷ *vb* **3** (often foll. by *after* or *for*) to have a passionate desire (for) [Old English] **lustful** *adj* **lustfully** *adv*

lustre *or US* **luster** *n* **1** soft shining light reflected from a surface; sheen **2** great splendour or glory **3** a shiny metallic surface on some pottery and porcelain [Latin *lustrare* to make bright] **lustrous** *adj*

lusty *adj* **lustier, lustiest 1** healthy and full of strength and energy **2** strong or invigorating **lustily** *adv* **lustiness** *n*

lute *n* an ancient plucked stringed instrument with a long fingerboard and a body shaped like a half pear [Arabic *al 'ūd*, literally: the wood]

lutetium (loo-tee-shee-um) *n chem* a silvery-white metallic element of the lanthanide series. Symbol: **Lu** [*Lutetia*, ancient name of Paris]

Lutheran *n* **1** a follower of Martin Luther (1483–1546), German leader of the Reformation, or a member of a Lutheran Church ▷ *adj* **2** of or relating to Luther, his doctrines, or any of the Churches that follow these doctrines **Lutheranism** *n*

luvvie *or* **luvvy** *n, pl* **-vies** *facetious* a person who is involved in acting or the theatre

lux *n, pl* **lux** the SI unit of illumination [Latin: light]

luxe *n* See **de luxe**

Luxembourger *n* a person from Luxembourg

luxuriant *adj* **1** rich and abundant; lush: *luxuriant foliage* **2** very elaborate or ornate [Latin *luxuriare* to abound to excess] **luxuriance** *n* **luxuriantly** *adv*

USAGE See at **luxurious.**

luxuriate *vb* **-ating, -ated 1 luxuriate in** to take self-indulgent pleasure in; revel in **2** to flourish profusely

luxurious *adj* **1** characterized by luxury **2** enjoying or devoted to luxury **luxuriously** *adv*

USAGE *Luxurious* is sometimes wrongly used where *luxuriant* is meant: *he had a luxuriant* (not *luxurious*) *moustache; the walls were covered with a luxuriant growth of wisteria.*

luxury *n, pl* **-ries 1** indulgence in rich and sumptuous living **2** something considered an indulgence rather than a necessity ▷ *adj* **3** relating to, indicating, or supplying luxury: *a luxury hotel* [Latin *luxuria* excess]

Lv livermorium

LV (in Britain) luncheon voucher

lx lux

lyceum *n* (now chiefly in the names of buildings) a public building for events such as concerts and lectures [Latin: a school in ancient Athens]

lychee (lie-chee) *n* a Chinese fruit with a whitish juicy pulp [Cantonese *lai chi*]

lych gate *or* **lich gate** *n* a roofed gate to a churchyard, formerly used as a temporary shelter for a coffin [Old English *līc* corpse]

Lycra *n trademark* a synthetic elastic fabric used for tight-fitting garments, such as swimsuits

lye *n* **1** a caustic solution obtained from wood ash **2** a concentrated solution of sodium hydroxide or potassium hydroxide [Old English *lēag*]

lying *vb* the present participle of **lie¹** or **lie²**

lying-in *n, pl* **lyings-in** *old-fashioned* confinement in childbirth

lymph *n* the almost colourless body fluid containing chiefly white blood cells [Latin *lympha* water] **lymphatic** *adj*

lymphatic system *n* a network of fine vessels by which lymph circulates throughout the body

lymph node *n* any of many bean-shaped masses of tissue in the lymphatic system that help to protect against infection

lymphocyte *n* a type of white blood cell [*lymph* + Greek *kutos* vessel]

lynch *vb* (of a mob) to kill (a person) for some supposed offence without a trial [after Captain William *Lynch* of Virginia, US] **lynching** *n*

lynchpin *n* same as **linchpin**

lynx *n, pl* **lynxes** *or* **lynx** a mammal of the cat family, with grey-brown mottled fur, tufted ears, and a short tail [Greek *lunx*]

lynx-eyed *adj* having keen sight

lyre *n* an ancient Greek U-shaped stringed instrument, similar to a harp but plucked with a plectrum [Greek *lura*]

lyrebird *n* an Australian bird, the male of which spreads its tail into the shape of a lyre during courtship

lyric *adj* **1 A** (of poetry) expressing the writer's personal feelings **B** (of poetry) having the form and manner of a song **2** of or relating to such poetry **3** (of a singing voice) light and melodic ▷ *n* **4** a short poem of songlike quality **5 lyrics** the words of a popular song: *Cole invests all her lyrics with a touch of drama* [Greek *lura* lyre]

lyrical *adj* **1** same as **lyric** (senses 1, 2) **2** enthusiastic or effusive **lyrically** *adv*

lyricism *n* **1** the quality or style of lyric poetry **2** emotional outpouring

lyricist *n* a person who writes the words for a song, opera, or musical

Mm

m **1** metre(s) **2** mile(s) **3** milli- **4** million **5** minute(s)
M **1** mach **2** medium **3** mega- **4** (in Britain) motorway **5** the Roman numeral for 1000
m. **1** male **2** married **3** masculine **4** meridian **5** month
M. **1** Majesty **2** Master **3** (in titles) Member **4** *pl* **MM.** *or* **MM** Monsieur
ma *n* an informal word for mother
MA **1** Massachusetts **2** Master of Arts
ma'am *n* short for **madam** (sense 1)
maas (mahs) *n S African* thick soured milk [Nguni (language group of southern Africa) *amasi* milk]
mac *or* **mack** *n Brit informal* a mackintosh
Mac *n chiefly US & Canad* an informal term of address to a man [Gaelic *mac* son of]
macabre (mak-**kahb**-ra) *adj* strange and horrible; gruesome [French]
macadam *n* a road surface made of compressed layers of small broken stones, esp. one bound together with tar or asphalt [after John *McAdam*, engineer]
macadamia (mak-a-**day**-mee-a) *n* an Australian tree with edible nuts [after John *Macadam*, Australian chemist]
macadamize *or* **-ise** *vb* **-izing, -ized** *or* **-ising, -ised** to pave a road with macadam
macaque (mak-**kahk**) *n* any of various Asian and African monkeys with cheek pouches and either a short tail or no tail [W African *makaku*]
macaroni *n, pl* **-nis** *or* **-nies** **1** pasta tubes made from wheat flour **2** (in 18th-century Britain) a man who was excessively concerned with his clothes and appearance [Italian (dialect) *maccarone*]
macaroon *n* a sweet biscuit made of ground almonds [French *macaron*]
macaw *n* a large tropical American parrot with a long tail and brightly coloured feathers [Portuguese *macau*]
mace[1] *n* **1** a ceremonial staff carried by certain officials **2** a club with a spiked metal head used in the Middle Ages [probably Vulgar Latin *mattea*]
mace[2] *n* a spice made from the dried outer casing of the nutmeg [Latin *macir*]
macebearer *n* a person who carries a mace in processions or ceremonies
macerate (**mass**-er-ate) *vb* **-ating, -ated** to soften or be softened by soaking [Latin *macerare* to soften] **macerated** *adj* **maceration** *n*
Mach (mak) *n* a unit for expressing the speed of an aircraft as a multiple of the speed of sound: *an airliner capable of cruising at Mach 2*. See also **Mach number**
machete (mash-**ett**-ee) *n* a broad heavy knife used for cutting or as a weapon [Spanish]
Machiavellian (mak-ee-a-**vel**-yan) *adj* cleverly deceitful and unscrupulous [after *Machiavelli*, political philosopher] **Machiavellianism** *n*
machinations (mak-in-**nay**-shuns) *pl n* cunning schemes or plots to gain power or harm an opponent: *the machinations of a power-hungry institution* [Latin *machinari* to plan]
machine *n* **1** an assembly of components arranged so as to perform a particular task and usually powered by electricity **2** a vehicle, such as a car or aircraft **3** a system within an organization that controls activities and policies: *the party machine* ▷ *vb* **-chining, -chined** **4** to shape, cut, or make something using a machine [Latin *machina*] **machinable** *adj*
machine code *or* **machine language** *n* instructions for a computer in binary or hexadecimal code that require no conversion or translation by the computer
machine gun *n* **1** a rapid-firing automatic gun, using small-arms ammunition ▷ *vb* **machine-gun, -gunning, -gunned** **2** to shoot or fire at with a machine gun
machine-readable *adj* in a form suitable for processing by a computer
machinery *n, pl* **-eries** **1** machines, machine parts, or machine systems collectively **2** the mechanism of a machine **3** the organization and procedures by which a system functions: *the machinery of international politics*
machine shop *n* a workshop in which machine tools are operated
machine tool *n* a power-driven machine, such as a lathe, for cutting and shaping metal, wood, or plastic
machinist *n* **1** a person who operates machines to cut or process materials **2** a maker or repairer of machines
machismo (mak-**izz**-moh) *n* strong or exaggerated masculinity [Mexican Spanish *macho* male]
Mach number (mak) *n* the ratio of the speed of a body in a particular medium to the speed of sound in that medium [after Ernst *Mach*, physicist]
macho (**match**-oh) *adj* **1** strongly or exaggeratedly masculine ▷ *n* **2** strong or exaggerated masculinity [from *machismo*]
mack *n Brit informal* same as **mac**
mackerel *n, pl* **-rel** *or* **-rels** an edible sea fish [Old French *maquerel*]
mackinaw *n chiefly US & Canad* a thick short double-breasted plaid coat [from a variant of *Mackinac*, an island in N Michigan]
mackintosh *or* **macintosh** *n Brit* **1** a raincoat made of rubberized cloth **2** any raincoat [after Charles *Macintosh*, who invented it]
macramé (mak-**rah**-mee) *n* **1** the art of knotting and weaving coarse thread into patterns **2** ornaments made in this way [Turkish *makrama* towel]
macro- *or before a vowel* **macr-** *combining form* large, long, or great: *macroscopic* [Greek *makros*]

macrobiotics *n* a dietary system which advocates whole grains and vegetables grown without chemical additives [Greek *makros* long + *biōtikos* relating to life] **macrobiotic** *adj*

macrocarpa *n* a large Californian coniferous tree, used in New Zealand and elsewhere as a windbreak on farms and for rough timber [Greek *makros* large + *karpos* fruit]

macrocosm *n* a complex structure, such as the universe or society, regarded as a whole [Greek *makros kosmos* great world]

macroeconomics *n* the branch of economics concerned with the relationships between aggregates, such as consumption and investment, in a large economic system **macroeconomic** *adj*

macromolecule *n* any very large molecule, such as a protein or synthetic polymer

macron *n* a mark (¯) placed over a letter to represent a long vowel [Greek *makros* long]

macroscopic *adj* **1** large enough to be visible to the naked eye **2** concerned with large units [Greek *makros* large + *skopein* to look at]

macula (mak-kew-la) *n, pl* **-ulae** (-yew-lee) *anatomy* a small spot or area of distinct colour, such as a freckle [Latin]

mad *adj* **madder, maddest 1** *informal* insane **2** extremely foolish; senseless: *that was a mad thing to do!* **3** *informal* angry or annoyed: *he's mad at her for the unjust accusation* **4** extremely excited or confused: *a mad rush* **5 A** (of animals) unusually ferocious: *a mad bear* **B** (of animals) afflicted with rabies **6 like mad** *informal* with great energy, enthusiasm, or haste **7 mad about** *or* **on** *or* **over** wildly enthusiastic about or fond of [Old English *gemǣded* made insane] **madness** *n*

madam *n, pl* **madams 1** *pl* **mesdames** a polite term of address for a woman **2** a woman who runs a brothel **3** *Brit & Austral informal* a spoilt or pert girl: *she is a thoroughly precocious little madam if ever there was one* [Old French *ma dame* my lady]

madame (mad-dam) *n, pl* **mesdames** (may-dam) a French form of address equivalent to *Mrs*

madcap *adj* **1** impulsive, reckless, or unlikely to succeed: *a madcap expansion of council bureaucracy* ▷ *n* **2** an impulsive or reckless person

mad cow disease *n informal* same as **BSE**

madden *vb* to make or become mad or angry **maddening** *adj*

madder *n* **1** a plant with small yellow flowers and a red fleshy root **2** a dark reddish-purple dye formerly obtained from its root **3** an artificial pigment of this colour [Old English *mædere*]

made *vb* **1** the past of **make** ▷ *adj* **2** (*in combination*) produced or shaped as specified: *handmade* **3 get** *or* **have it made** *informal* to be assured of success

Madeira (mad-deer-a) *n* a fortified white wine from Madeira, an island in the N Atlantic

Madeira cake *n* a type of rich sponge cake

mademoiselle (mad-mwah-zel) *n, pl* **mesdemoiselles** (maid-mwah-zel) **1** a French form of address equivalent to *Miss* **2** a French teacher or governess

made-to-measure *adj* (of a piece of clothing) made specifically to fit the person who has ordered it

made-up *adj* **1** invented or fictitious **2** wearing make-up **3** put together: *some made-up carpet shampoo* **4** (of a road) surfaced with tarmac or concrete

madhouse *n informal* **1** a state of uproar or confusion **2** *old-fashioned* a psychiatric hospital

madly *adv* **1** in an crazy or foolish manner: *I yelled and waved madly* **2** with great speed and energy **3** *informal* extremely or excessively: *she was madly in love with him*

madman *or fem* **madwoman** *n, pl* **-men** *or* **-women 1** a person who behaves recklessly **2** *offensive* a person who is insane

Madonna *n* **1** *chiefly RC Church* the Virgin Mary **2** a picture or statue of the Virgin Mary [Italian: my lady]

madras *n* a medium-hot curry: *chicken madras* [after the *Madras* area of India]

madrigal *n* a type of 16th- or 17th-century part song for unaccompanied voices [Medieval Latin *matricale* primitive] **madrigalist** *n*

maelstrom (male-strom) *n* **1** a large powerful whirlpool **2** any confused, violent, and destructive turmoil: *a maelstrom of adulterous passion* [Old Dutch *malen* to whirl round + *stroom* stream]

maenad (mean-ad) *n* **1** *classical history* a female disciple of Dionysus, the Greek god of wine **2** a frenzied woman [Greek *mainas* madwoman]

maestro (my-stroh) *n, pl* **-tri** *or* **-tros 1** a distinguished musician or conductor **2** any master of an art: *Milan's maestro of minimalism* [Italian: master]

Mafia *n* **the Mafia** a secret criminal organization founded in Sicily, and carried to the US by Italian immigrants [Sicilian dialect, literally: hostility to the law]

mafioso (maf-fee-oh-so) *n, pl* **-sos** *or* **-si** (-see) a member of the Mafia

mag *n* short for **magazine** (sense 1)

magazine *n* **1** a periodic publication containing written pieces and illustrations, usually on a particular subject **2** a television or radio programme made up of short nonfictional items **3** a metal case holding several cartridges used in some firearms **4** a rack for automatically feeding slides through a projector **5** a place for storing weapons, explosives, or military equipment [Arabic *makhāzin* storehouses]

magenta (maj-jen-ta) *adj* deep purplish-red [after *Magenta*, Italy]

maggot *n* the limbless larva of various insects, esp. the housefly and blowfly [earlier *mathek*] **maggoty** *adj*

magi (maje-eye) *pl n, sing* **magus** (may-guss) **1** See **magus 2 the three Magi** *Christianity* the wise men from the East who came to worship the infant Jesus (Matthew 2:1–12) [see MAGUS]

magic *n* **1** the supposed power to make things happen by using supernatural means **2** tricks done to entertain; conjuring **3** any mysterious or extraordinary quality or power: *the magic of Placido Domingo* **4 like magic** very quickly ▷ *adj also* **magical 5** of magic **6** possessing or considered to possess mysterious powers **7** unaccountably enchanting **8** *informal* wonderful or marvellous ▷ *vb* **-gicking, -gicked 9** to transform or produce

as if by magic: *he had magicked up a gourmet meal at a moment's notice* [Greek *magikē* witchcraft] **magically** *adv*
magic away *vb* to cause to disappear as if by magic: *to magic away pollution*
magic carpet *n* (in fairy stories) a carpet which can carry people through the air
magician *n* **1** a conjuror **2** a person with magic powers
magic lantern *n* an early type of slide projector
magisterial *adj* **1** commanding and authoritative **2** of a magistrate [Latin *magister* master] **magisterially** *adv*
magistracy *n, pl* **-cies** **1** the office or function of a magistrate **2** magistrates collectively
magistrate *n* **1** a public officer concerned with the administration of law **2** same as **justice of the peace** **3** *Austral & NZ* a former name for **district court judge** [Latin *magister* master]
magistrates' court *n* (in England) a court that deals with minor crimes, certain civil actions, and preliminary hearings
magma *n, pl* **-mas** *or* **-mata** hot molten rock within the earth's crust which sometimes finds its way to the surface where it solidifies to form igneous rock [Greek: salve made by kneading]
Magna Carta *n English history* the charter granted by King John at Runnymede in 1215, recognizing the rights and privileges of the barons, church, and freemen [Medieval Latin: great charter]
magnanimous *adj* generous and forgiving, esp. towards a defeated enemy [Latin *magnanimus* great-souled] **magnanimity** *n* **magnanimously** *adv*
magnate *n* an influential or wealthy person, esp. in industry [Late Latin *magnates* great men]
magnesia *n* a white tasteless substance used as an antacid and laxative; magnesium oxide [Greek *Magnēsia* of *Magnēs*, ancient mineral-rich region]
magnesium *n chem* a light silvery-white metallic element that burns with a very bright white flame. Symbol: **Mg** [from *magnesia*]
magnet *n* **1** a piece of iron, steel, or lodestone that has the property of attracting iron to it **2** a person or thing that exerts a great attraction: *these woods are a magnet for bird watchers* [Greek *magnēs*]
magnetic *adj* **1** of, producing, or operated by means of magnetism **2** of or like a magnet **3** capable of being made into a magnet **4** exerting a powerful attraction: *political leaders of magnetic appeal* **magnetically** *adv*
magnetic disk *n* a computer storage disk
magnetic field *n* an area around a magnet in which its power of attraction is felt
magnetic mine *n* a mine which detonates when a magnetic field, such as that generated by the metal of a ship's hull, is detected
magnetic needle *n* a slender magnetized rod used in certain instruments, such as the magnetic compass, for indicating the direction of a magnetic field
magnetic north *n* the direction in which a compass needle points, at an angle from the direction of true (geographic) north
magnetic pole *n* either of two variable points on the earth's surface towards which a magnetic needle points
magnetic storm *n* a sudden severe disturbance of the earth's magnetic field, caused by emission of charged particles from the sun
magnetic tape *n* a long plastic strip coated with a magnetic substance, used to record sound or video signals or to store information in computers
magnetism *n* **1** the property of attraction displayed by magnets **2** powerful personal charm **3** the branch of physics concerned with magnetic phenomena
magnetite *n* a black magnetizable mineral that is an important source of iron
magnetize *or* **-tise** *vb* **-tizing, -tized** *or* **-tising, -tised** **1** to make a substance or object magnetic **2** to attract strongly: *he was magnetized by her smile* **magnetizable** *or* **-tisable** *adj* **magnetization** *or* **-tisation** *n*
magneto (mag-nee-toe) *n, pl* **-tos** a small electric generator in which the magnetic field is produced by a permanent magnet, esp. one used to provide the spark in an internal-combustion engine [short for *magnetoelectric generator*]
magnetron *n* an electronic valve used with a magnetic field to generate microwave oscillations, used. esp. in radar [*magnet + electron*]
Magnificat *n Christianity* the hymn of the Virgin Mary (Luke 1:46–55), used as a canticle [from its opening word]
magnification *n* **1** the act of magnifying or the state of being magnified **2** the degree to which something is magnified **3** a magnified copy of something
magnificent *adj* **1** splendid or impressive in appearance **2** superb or very fine: *a magnificent performance* [Latin *magnificus* great in deeds] **magnificence** *n* **magnificently** *adv*
magnify *vb* **-fies, -fying, -fied** **1** to make something look bigger than it really is, for instance by using a lens or microscope **2** to make something seem more important than it really is; exaggerate: *you are magnifying the problem out of all proportion* **3** to make something sound louder than it really is: *the stethoscope magnifies internal body sounds* **4** *archaic* to glorify or praise [Latin *magnificare* to praise] **magnified** *adj*
magnifying glass *or* **magnifier** *n* a convex lens used to produce an enlarged image of an object
magniloquent *adj* (of speech) excessively grand, literary, and pompous [Latin *magnus* great + *loqui* to speak] **magniloquence** *n*
magnitude *n* **1** relative importance: *an evil of the first magnitude* **2** relative size or extent **3** *astron* the apparent brightness of a celestial body expressed on a numerical scale on which bright stars have a low value [Latin *magnitudo* size]
magnolia *n* an Asian and North American tree or shrub with white, pink, purple, or yellow showy flowers [after Pierre *Magnol*, botanist]
magnox *n* an alloy composed mainly of magnesium, used in fuel elements of some nuclear reactors (**magnox reactors**) [from *mag(nesium) n(o) ox(idation)*]

m

magnum *n, pl* **-nums** a wine bottle of twice the normal size, holding 1.5 litres [Latin: a big thing]
magnum opus *n* a great work of art or literature, esp. the greatest single work of an artist [Latin]
magpie *n* **1** a bird of the crow family with black-and-white plumage, a long tail, and a chattering call **2** any of various similar Australian birds, eg the butcherbird **3** *Brit* a person who hoards small objects [from *Mag*, diminutive of *Margaret* + *pie*, obsolete name for the magpie]
magus (may-guss) *n, pl* **magi** (maje-eye) **1** a Zoroastrian priest **2** an astrologer or magician of ancient times [Old Persian: magician]
Magyar *n* **1** a member of the main ethnic group of Hungary **2** the Hungarian language ▷ *adj* **3** of the Magyars
maharaja *or* **maharajah** *n* the head of one of the royal families which formerly ruled parts of India [Hindi: great raja]
maharani *or* **maharanee** *n* the wife of a maharaja [Hindi: great rani]
maharishi *n Hinduism* a teacher of religious and mystical knowledge [Hindi: great sage]
mahatma *n* a person revered for his holiness or wisdom: often used as a title or form of address: *Mahatma Gandhi* [Sanskrit *mahā* great + *ātman* soul]
mah jong *or* **mah-jongg** *n* a game of Chinese origin, played using tiles bearing various designs, in which the players try to obtain a winning combination of tiles [Chinese, literally: sparrows]
mahogany *n, pl* **-nies 1** the hard reddish-brown wood of any of several tropical trees ▷ *adj* **2** reddish-brown: *wonderful mahogany tones* [origin unknown]
mahout (ma-**howt**) *n* (in India) an elephant driver or keeper [Hindi *mahāut*]
maid *n* **1** a female servant **2** *archaic or literary* a young unmarried girl; maiden [form of *maiden*]
maiden *n* **1** *archaic or literary* a young unmarried girl, esp. a virgin **2** *horse racing* a horse that has never won a race ▷ *adj* **3** unmarried: *a maiden aunt* **4** first or earliest: *maiden voyage* [Old English *mægden*] **maidenhood** *n* **maidenly** *adj*
maidenhair fern *n* a fern with delicate hairlike fronds of small pale green leaflets
maidenhead *n* **1** the hymen **2** virginity or maidenhood
maiden name *n* a woman's surname before marriage
maiden over *n cricket* an over in which no runs are scored
maid of honour *n* **1** an unmarried woman attending a queen or princess **2** *US & Canad* the principal unmarried attendant of a bride
maidservant *n* a female servant
mail[1] *n* **1** letters and packages transported and delivered by the post office **2** the postal system **3** a single collection or delivery of mail **4** a train, ship, or aircraft that carries mail **5** short for **email** ▷ *vb* **6** *chiefly US & Canad* to send by mail **7** to contact or send by email [Old French *male* bag]
mail[2] *n* flexible armour made of riveted metal rings or links [Old French *maille* mesh] **mailed** *adj*
mailbag *n* a large bag for transporting or delivering mail
mailbox *n* **1** *US, Canad & Austral* a box outside a house into which the postman puts letters for the occupiers of the house **2** (on a computer) the directory in which email messages are stored
mail coach *n history* a fast stagecoach designed primarily for carrying mail
mailing list *n* a register of names and addresses to which information or advertising matter is sent by post or email
mailman *n, pl* **-men** *US & Canad* a postman
mail merge *n computers* a word-processing facility that can produce personalized letters by combining data from two different files
mail order *n* a system of buying and selling goods by post
mailshot *n* a posting of circulars, leaflets, or other advertising to a selected large number of people at once
maim *vb* to injure badly or cruelly, with some permanent damage resulting [Old French *mahaignier* to wound]
main *adj* **1** chief or principal ▷ *n* **2** a principal pipe or line in a system used to distribute water, electricity, or gas **3 mains** the main distribution network for water, gas, or electricity **4** great strength or force: *with might and main* **5** *literary* the open ocean **6 in the main** on the whole [Old English *mægen* strength]
mainbrace *n naut* **1** the rope that controls the movement of the spar of a ship's mainsail **2 splice the mainbrace** See **splice**
main clause *n grammar* a clause that can stand alone as a sentence
mainframe *n* a high-speed, general-purpose computer, with a large storage capacity
mainland *n* the main part of a land mass as opposed to an island
main line *n* **1** *railways* the chief route between two points, usually fed by branch lines ▷ *vb* **mainline** **2** *slang* to inject a drug into a vein
mainly *adv* for the most part; principally
mainmast *n naut* the chief mast of a sailing vessel with two or more masts
mainsail *n naut* the largest and lowermost sail on the mainmast
mainspring *n* **1** the chief cause or motive of something: *the mainspring of a dynamic economy* **2** the chief spring of a watch or clock
mainstay *n* **1** a chief support **2** *naut* a rope securing a mainmast
mainstream *n* **1** the people or things representing the most common or generally accepted ideas and styles in a society, art form, etc.: *the mainstream of academic life* **2** the main current of a river ▷ *adj* **3** belonging to the social or cultural mainstream: *mainstream American movies*
mainstream media *n* newspapers, magazines, television, and radio, as opposed to social media
mainstreeting *n Canad* the practice of a politician walking about a town or city to try to gain votes
maintain *vb* **1** to continue or keep in existence: *we must maintain good relations with them* **2** to keep in

proper or good condition: *an expensive car to maintain* **3** to sustain or keep up a particular level or speed: *he set off at a high speed, but couldn't maintain it all the way* **4** to enable a person to have the money, food and other things he or she needs to live: *the money maintained us for a month* **5** to assert: *he had always maintained that he never wanted children* **6** to defend against contradiction: *he maintained his innocence* [from Latin *manu tenere* to hold in the hand]

maintenance *n* **1** the act of maintaining or the state of being maintained **2** the process of keeping a car, building, etc. in good condition **3** *law* financial provision ordered to be made by way of periodical payments or a lump sum, usually for a separated or divorced spouse

maisonette *n Brit & S African* a flat with more than one floor [French, diminutive of *maison* house]

maitre d'hotel (met-ra dote-**tell**) *n, pl* **maitres d'hotel** a head waiter [French]

maize *n* a type of corn grown for its large yellow edible grains, which are used for food and as a source of oil. See also **sweet corn** [Spanish *maiz*]

Maj. Major

majestic *adj* beautiful, dignified, and impressive **majestically** *adv*

majesty *n* **1** great dignity and grandeur **2** supreme power or authority [Latin *majestas*]

Majesty *n, pl* **-ties** (preceded by *Your, His, Her* or *Their*) a title used to address or refer to a sovereign or the wife or widow of a sovereign

Maj. Gen. Major General

majolica *or* **maiolica** *n* a type of porous pottery glazed with bright metallic oxides. It was extensively made in Renaissance Italy [Italian, from Late Latin *Majorica* Majorca]

major *adj* **1** greater in size, frequency, or importance than others of the same kind: *the major political parties* **2** very serious or significant: *a major investigation* **3** main or principal: *a major road* **4** *music* **A** (of a scale) having notes separated by a whole tone, except for the third and fourth notes, and seventh and eighth notes, which are separated by a semitone **B** of or based on the major scale: *the key of D major* ▷ *n* **5** a middle-ranking military officer **6** *music* a major key, chord, mode, or scale **7** a person who has reached the age of legal majority **8** *US, Canad, S African, Austral & NZ* the principal field of study of a student ▷ *vb* **9** *US, Canad, S African, Austral & NZ* to study as one's principal subject: *he majored in economics* [Latin: greater]

major-domo *n, pl* **-mos** the chief steward or butler of a great household [Medieval Latin *major domus* head of the household]

majorette *n* one of a group of girls who practise formation marching and baton twirling

major general *n* a senior military officer

majority *n, pl* **-ties** **1** the greater number or part of something **2** (in an election) the number of votes or seats by which the strongest party or candidate beats the combined opposition or the runner-up **3** the largest party or group that votes together in a meeting, council or parliament **4** the age at which a person legally becomes an adult **5** **in the majority** forming or part of the group of people or things made up of more than half of a larger group [Medieval Latin *majoritas*]

> **USAGE** *The majority of* can only refer to a number of things or people. When talking about an amount, *most of* should be used: *most of* (not *the majority of*) *the harvest was saved.*

make *vb* **making, made** **1** to create, construct, establish, or draw up; bring into being: *houses made of stone; he will have to make a will* **2** to cause to do or be; compel or induce: *please make her go away* **3** to bring about or produce: *don't make a noise* **4** to carry out or perform: *he made his first trip to China in 1987; she made an obscene gesture* **5** to appoint: *they made him caretaker manager* **6** to come into a specified state or condition: *to make merry* **7** to become: *she will make a good diplomat* **8** to cause or ensure the success of: *that news has made my day* **9** to amount to: *5 and 5 make 10* **10** to earn or be paid: *they must be making a fortune* **11** to have the qualities of or be suitable for: *what makes this book such a good read?* **12** to prepare for use: *she forgot to make her bed* **13** to be the essential element in: *confidence makes a good salesperson* **14** to use for a specified purpose: *they will make this town their base* **15** to deliver: *he made a very good speech* **16** to consider to be: *what time do you make it?* **17** to cause to seem or represent as being: *her girlish pigtails made her look younger than she was; she made the experience sound most unpleasant* **18** to acquire: *she doesn't make friends easily* **19** to engage in: *they made war on the Turks* **20** to travel a certain distance or to a certain place: *we can make at least three miles before it gets dark* **21** to arrive in time for: *he didn't make the first act of the play* **22** to win or score: *he made a break of 125* **23** *informal* to gain a place or position on or in: *to make the headlines* **24** **make a day** *or* **night of it** to cause an activity to last a day or night **25** **make eyes at** *old-fashioned* to flirt with or ogle **26** **make it** *informal* **A** to be able to attend: *I'm afraid I can't make it to your party* **B** to be successful **27** **make like** *slang, chiefly US & Canad* **A** to imitate **B** to pretend **28** **make to** *or* **as if to** *or* **as though to** to act with the intention or with a show of doing something: *she made as if to hit him* ▷ *n* **29** manufacturer; brand: *what make of car is that?* **30** the way in which something is made **31** **on the make** *slang* out for profit or conquest ▷ See also **make away, make for** etc. [Old English *macian*] **maker** *n*

make away *vb* **1** to depart in haste **2** **make away with** **A** to steal **B** to kill or get rid of

make believe *vb* **1** to pretend ▷ *n* **make-believe** **2** a fantasy or pretence

make do *vb* to manage with an inferior alternative

make for *vb* **1** to head towards **2** to prepare to attack **3** to help bring about: *this will make for a spectacular race*

make of *vb* to interpret as the meaning of: *what did she make of it all?*

make off *vb* **1** to go or run away in haste **2** **make off with** to steal or abduct

make out *vb* **1** to manage to see or hear **2** to understand **3** to write out: *how shall I make out the cheque?* **4** to attempt to establish or prove: *she made me out to be a crook* **5** to pretend: *he made out*

that he could play the piano **6** to manage or get on: *how did you make out in the exam?*
make over *vb* **1** to renovate or remodel: *she made over the dress to fit her sister* ▷ *n* **makeover** **2** a complete remodelling **3** a series of alterations, including beauty treatments and new clothes, intended to make an improvement to someone's appearance
Maker *n* a title given to God
makeshift *adj* serving as a temporary substitute
make-up *n* **1** cosmetics, such as powder or lipstick **2** the cosmetics used by an actor to adapt his or her appearance **3** the arrangement of the parts of something **4** mental or physical constitution ▷ *vb* **make up** **5** to form or constitute: *these arguments make up the case for the defence* **6** to devise or compose, sometimes with the intent to deceive: *she was well known for making up stories about herself* **7** to supply what is lacking in; complete: *I'll make up the difference* **8** Also: **make it up** to settle differences amicably **9** **make up for** to compensate for: *one good year can make up for several bad ones* **10** to apply cosmetics to the face **11** **make up to** *informal* **A** to make friendly overtures to **B** to flirt with
makeweight *n* an unimportant person or thing added to make up a lack
making *n* **1** the act or process of producing something **2** **be the making of** to cause the success of **3** **in the making** in the process of becoming or being made
makings *pl n* **have the makings of** to have the potentials, qualities, or materials necessary to make or become something: *it had the makings of a classic showdown*
mako *n, pl* **makos** a powerful shark of the Atlantic and Pacific Oceans [Māori]
mal- *combining form* bad or badly; wrong or wrongly: *maladjusted; malfunction* [Latin *malus* bad, *male* badly]
malachite (mal-a-kite) *n* a green mineral used as a source of copper, and for making ornaments [Greek *molokhitis*]
maladjustment *n psychol* a failure to meet the demands of society, such as coping with problems and social relationships **maladjusted** *adj*
maladminister *vb* to administer badly, inefficiently, or dishonestly **maladministration** *n*
maladroit (mal-a-**droyt**) *adj* clumsy, awkward, or tactless [French *mal* badly + ADROIT] **maladroitly** *adv* **maladroitness** *n*
malady (mal-a-dee) *n, pl* **-dies** *old-fashioned* any disease or illness [Vulgar Latin *male habitus* in poor condition]
malaise (mal-**laze**) *n* **1** a vague feeling of unease, illness, or depression **2** a complex of problems affecting a country, economy, etc.: *decades of political malaise* [Old French *mal* bad + *aise* ease]
malapropism *n* the comic misuse of a word by confusion with one which sounds similar, for example *under the affluence of alcohol* [after Mrs *Malaprop* in Sheridan's play *The Rivals*]
malaria *n* a disease with recurring attacks of fever, caused by the bite of some types of mosquito [Italian *mala aria* bad air] **malarial** *adj*
malarkey *n slang* nonsense or rubbish [origin unknown]
Malay *n* **1** a member of a people living chiefly in Malaysia and Indonesia **2** the language of this people ▷ *adj* **3** of the Malays or their language
Malayan *adj* **1** of Malaya ▷ *n* **2** a person from Malaya
Malaysian *adj* **1** of Malaysia ▷ *n* **2** a person from Malaysia
malcontent *n* a person who is discontented with the existing situation [Old French]
male *adj* **1** of the sex that can fertilize female reproductive cells **2** of or characteristic of a man **3** for or composed of men or boys: *a male choir* **4** (of flowers) bearing stamens but lacking a pistil **5** *electronics & engineering* having a projecting part or parts that fit into a hollow counterpart: *a male plug* ▷ *n* **6** a male person, animal, or plant [Latin *masculus* masculine] **maleness** *n*
male chauvinism *n* the belief, held by some men, that men are better and more important than women **male chauvinist** *n, adj*
malediction (mal-lid-**dik**-shun) *n* the utterance of a curse against someone or something [Latin *maledictio* a reviling] **maledictory** *adj*
malefactor (**mal**-if-act-or) *n* a criminal or wrongdoer [Latin *malefacere* to do evil] **malefaction** *n*
malevolent (mal-**lev**-a-lent) *adj* wishing evil to others; malicious [Latin *malevolens*] **malevolence** *n* **malevolently** *adv*
malfeasance (mal-**fee**-zanss) *n law* wrongful or illegal behaviour, esp. by a public official [Old French *mal faisant* evil-doing]
malformation *n* **1** the condition of being faulty or abnormal in form or shape **2** *pathol* a deformity, esp. when congenital **malformed** *adj*
malfunction *vb* **1** to fail to function properly or fail to function at all ▷ *n* **2** failure to function properly or failure to function at all
malice (**mal**-iss) *n* the desire to do harm or cause mischief to others [Latin *malus* evil] **malicious** *adj* **maliciously** *adv*
malice aforethought *n law* a deliberate intention to do something unlawful
malign (mal-**line**) *vb* **1** to say unpleasant and untrue things about someone; slander ▷ *adj* **2** evil in influence or effect [Latin *malignus* spiteful]
malignant (mal-**lig**-nant) *adj* **1** seeking to harm others **2** tending to cause great harm; injurious **3** *pathol* (of a tumour) uncontrollable or resistant to therapy [Late Latin *malignare* to behave spitefully] **malignancy** *n*
malignity (mal-**lig**-nit-ee) *n* the condition of being malign or deadly
malinger (mal-**ling**-ger) *vb* to pretend to be ill, or exaggerate how ill one is, to avoid work [French *malingre* sickly] **malingerer** *n*
mall (mawl) *n* **1** *US, Canad, Austral & NZ* short for **shopping mall** **2** a shaded avenue, esp. one open to the public [after *the Mall*, an avenue in St James's Park, London]
mallard *n, pl* **-lard** *or* **-lards** a common N hemisphere duck, the male of which has a dark green head [Old French *mallart*]

malleable (**mal**-lee-a-bl) *adj* **1** (esp. of metal) capable of being hammered or pressed into shape without breaking **2** able to be influenced [Medieval Latin *malleabilis*] **malleability** *n* **malleably** *adv*

mallee *n* a low-growing eucalypt found in dry regions of Australia

mallet *n* **1** a hammer with a large wooden head **2** a long stick with a head like a hammer used to strike the ball in croquet or polo [Old French *maillet* wooden hammer]

mallow *n* any of a group of plants, with purple, pink, or white flowers [Latin *malva*]

malnourished *adj* physically weak due to lack of healthy food

malnutrition *n* physical weakness resulting from insufficient food or an unbalanced diet

malodorous (mal-**lode**-or-uss) *adj* having an unpleasant smell: *the malodorous sludge of Boston harbour*

malpractice *n* illegal, unethical, or negligent professional conduct

malt *n* **1** grain, such as barley, that is kiln-dried after it has been germinated by soaking in water **2** See **malt whisky** ▷ *vb* **3** to make into or become malt **4** to make from malt or to add malt to [Old English *mealt*] **malted** *adj* **malty** *adj*

Maltese *adj* **1** of Malta ▷ *n* **2** *pl* **-tese** a person from Malta **3** the language of Malta

Maltese cross *n* a cross with triangular arms that taper towards the centre, sometimes with the outer sides curving in

Malthusian (malth-**yew**-zee-an) *adj* of the theory stating that increases in population tend to exceed increases in the food supply and that therefore sexual restraint should be exercised [after T. R. *Malthus*, economist]

maltose *n* a sugar formed by the action of enzymes on starch [*malt* + *-ose* indicating a sugar]

maltreat *vb* to treat badly, cruelly, or violently [French *maltraiter*] **maltreatment** *n*

malt whisky *n* whisky made from malted barley

malversation *n rare* professional or public misconduct [French *malverser* to behave badly]

malware *n* a computer program designed specifically to damage or disrupt a system, such as a virus

mam *n informal or dialect* same as **mother**

mama *or esp US* **mamma** (mam-**mah**) *n old-fashioned, informal* same as **mother** [reduplication of childish syllable *ma*]

mamba *n* a very poisonous tree snake found in tropical and Southern Africa [Zulu *im-amba*]

mambo *n, pl* **-bos** a Latin American dance resembling the rumba [American Spanish]

mammal *n* a warm-blooded animal, such as a human being, dog or whale, the female of which produces milk to feed her babies [Latin *mamma* breast] **mammalian** *adj, n*

mammary *adj* of the breasts or milk-producing glands [Latin *mamma* breast]

mammary gland *n* any of the milk-producing glands in mammals, such as a woman's breast or a cow's udder

mammon *n* wealth regarded as a source of evil and corruption, personified in the New Testament as a false god (**Mammon**) [New Testament Greek *mammōnas* wealth]

mammoth *n* **1** a large extinct elephant with a hairy coat and long curved tusks ▷ *adj* **2** gigantic [Russian *mamot*]

mammy *n, pl* **-mies** *informal or dialect* same as **mother**

mampara *n S African derogatory, informal* a foolish or stupid person [origin unknown]

man *n, pl* **men** **1** an adult male human being **2** a human being of either sex; person: *all men are born equal* **3** human beings collectively; mankind. Related adjective: **anthropoid** **4** a human being regarded as representative of a particular period or category: *Neanderthal man* **5** an adult male human being with qualities traditionally regarded as masculine **6** an employee, servant, or representative **7** a member of the armed forces who is not an officer **8** a male member of a group or team **9** a husband, boyfriend, or male lover **10** a movable piece in various games, such as draughts **11** *S African slang* any person: used as a term of address **12** **as one man** with unanimous action or response **13** **he's your man** he's the person needed **14** **man and boy** from childhood **15** **sort out the men from the boys** to discover who can cope with difficult or dangerous situations and who cannot **16** **to a man** without exception ▷ *vb* **manning, manned** **17** to provide with sufficient people for operation or defence **18** to take one's place at or near in readiness for action [Old English *mann*] **manhood** *n*

> **USAGE** The use of words ending in *-man* is avoided as implying a male in job advertisements, where sexual discrimination is illegal, and in many other contexts where a term that is not gender-specific is available, such as *salesperson, barperson, camera operator.*

Man. Manitoba

mana *n NZ* authority, influence and prestige

manacle (**man**-a-kl) *n* **1** a metal ring or chain put round the wrists or ankles, used to restrict the movements of a prisoner or convict ▷ *vb* **-cling, -cled** **2** to put manacles on [Latin *manus* hand]

manage *vb* **-naging, -naged** **1** to succeed in doing something: *we finally managed to sell our old house* **2** to be in charge of; administer: *the company is badly managed* **3** to have room or time for: *can you manage lunch tomorrow?* **4** to keep under control: *she disapproved of taking drugs to manage stress* **5** to struggle on despite difficulties, esp. financial ones: *most people cannot manage on a cleaner's salary* [Italian *maneggiare* to train (esp. horses)] **manageable** *adj*

management *n* **1** the people responsible for running an organization or business **2** managers or employers collectively **3** the technique or practice of managing or controlling

manager *n* **1** a person who manages an organization or business **2** a person in charge of a sports team **3** a person who controls the business affairs of an actor or entertainer **manageress** *fem n*

managerial *adj* of a manager or management
managing director *n* the senior director of a company, who has overall responsibility for the way it is run
mañana (man-**yah**-na) *n, adv* **A** tomorrow **B** some other and later time [Spanish]
man-at-arms *n, pl* **men-at-arms** a soldier, esp. a medieval soldier
manatee *n* a large plant-eating mammal occurring in tropical coastal waters of the Atlantic [Carib *Manattouï*]
Manchu *n, pl* **-chus** *or* **-chu** a member of a Mongoloid people of Manchuria, a region of NE China, who conquered China in the 17th century, ruling until 1912
Mancunian (man-**kew**-nee-an) *adj* **1** of Manchester, a city in NW England ▷ *n* **2** a person from Manchester [Medieval Latin *Mancunium* Manchester]
mandala *n Buddhist art* a circular design symbolizing the universe [Sanskrit: circle]
mandarin *n* **1** (in the Chinese Empire) a member of a senior grade of the bureaucracy **2** a high-ranking official with extensive powers **3** a person of standing and influence, esp. in literary or intellectual circles **4** a small citrus fruit resembling the tangerine [Sanskrit *mantrin* counsellor]
Mandarin Chinese *or* **Mandarin** *n* the official language of China since 1917
mandate *n* **1** an official or authoritative command to carry out a particular task: *the UN force's mandate does not allow it to intervene* **2** *politics* the political authority given to a government or an elected representative through an electoral victory **3** Also: **mandated territory** (formerly) a territory administered by one country on behalf of an international body ▷ *vb* **-dating, -dated** **4** to delegate authority to **5** to assign territory to a nation under a mandate [Latin *mandare* to command]
mandatory *adj* **1** obligatory; compulsory **2** having the nature or powers of a mandate **mandatorily** *adv*
mandible *n* **1** the lower jawbone of a vertebrate **2** either of the jawlike mouthparts of an insect **3** either part of the bill of a bird, esp. the lower part [Late Latin *mandibula* jaw]
mandolin *n* a musical instrument with four pairs of strings stretched over a small light body, usually played with a plectrum [Italian *mandolino* small lute]
mandrake *n* a plant with a forked root. It was formerly thought to have magic powers and a narcotic was prepared from its root [Latin *mandragoras*]
mandrel *or* **mandril** *n* **1** a spindle on which the object being worked on is supported in a lathe **2** a shaft on which a machining tool is mounted [perhaps from French *mandrin* lathe]
mandrill *n* a monkey of W Africa. The male has red and blue markings on its face and buttocks [*man* + *drill* an Old-World monkey]
mane *n* **1** the long hair that grows from the neck in such mammals as the lion and horse **2** long thick human hair [Old English *manu*] **maned** *adj*

m

manège (man-**nayzh**) *n* **1** the art of training horses and riders **2** a riding school [Italian *maneggiare* to manage].
maneuver *n, vb US* same as **manoeuvre**
man Friday *n* a loyal male servant or assistant [after a character in *Robinson Crusoe*]
manful *adj* determined and brave **manfully** *adv*
manganese *n chem* a brittle greyish-white metallic element used in making steel. Symbol: **Mn** [probably altered form of Medieval Latin *magnesia*]
mange *n* a skin disease of domestic animals, characterized by itching and loss of hair [Old French *mangeue* itch]
mangelwurzel *n* a variety of beet with a large yellowish root [German *Mangold* beet + *Wurzel* root]
manger *n* a trough in a stable or barn from which horses or cattle feed [Old French *maingeure*]
mangetout (**mawnzh**-too) *n* a variety of garden pea with an edible pod [French: eat all]
mangle[1] *vb* **-gling, -gled** **1** to destroy or damage by crushing and twisting **2** to spoil [Norman French *mangler*] **mangled** *adj*
mangle[2] *n* **1** a machine for pressing or squeezing water out of washed clothes, consisting of two heavy rollers between which the clothes are passed ▷ *vb* **-gling, -gled** **2** to put through a mangle [Dutch *mangel*]
mango *n, pl* **-goes** *or* **-gos** the egg-shaped edible fruit of a tropical Asian tree, with a smooth rind and sweet juicy flesh [Malay *mangā*]
mangrove *n* a tropical evergreen tree or shrub with intertwining aerial roots that forms dense thickets along coasts [older *mangrow* (changed through influence of *grove*), from Portuguese *mangue*]
mangy *adj* **-gier, -giest** **1** having mange **2** scruffy or shabby **mangily** *adv* **manginess** *n*
manhandle *vb* **-handling, -handled** **1** to handle or push someone about roughly **2** to move something by manpower rather than by machinery
manhole *n* a hole with a detachable cover, through which a person can enter a sewer or pipe to inspect or repair it
man-hour *n* a unit of work in industry, equal to the work done by one person in one hour
manhunt *n* an organized search, usually by police, for a wanted man or fugitive
mania *n* **1** an obsessional enthusiasm or liking **2** a mental disorder characterized by great or violent excitement [Greek: madness]
-mania *combining form* indicating extreme or abnormal excitement aroused by something: *kleptomania*
maniac *n* **1** a wild disorderly person **2** a person who has a great craving or enthusiasm for something [Late Latin *maniacus* belonging to madness] **maniacal** (man-**eye**-ak-kl) *adj*
manic *adj* **1** extremely excited or energetic; frenzied: *manic, cavorting dancers* **2** of, involving, or affected by mania: *deep depression broken by periods of manic excitement*

manic-depressive *old-fashioned* ▹ *adj* **1** relating to or having bipolar disorder ▹ *n* **2** a person with bipolar disorder

manicure *n* **1** cosmetic care of the hands and fingernails ▹ *vb* **-curing, -cured 2** to care for the fingernails and hands [Latin *manus* hand + *cura* care] **manicurist** *n*

manifest *adj* **1** easily noticed, obvious ▹ *vb* **2** to reveal or display: *an additional symptom now manifested itself* **3** to show by the way one behaves: *he manifested great personal bravery* **4** (of a disembodied spirit) to appear in visible form ▹ *n* **5** a customs document containing particulars of a ship and its cargo **6** a list of the cargo and passengers on an aeroplane [Latin *manifestus* plain] **manifestation** *n*

manifesto *n, pl* **-tos** *or* **-toes** a public declaration of intent or policy issued by a group of people, for instance by a political party [Italian]

manifold *adj formal* **1** numerous and varied: *her talents are manifold* ▹ *n* **2** a pipe with a number of inlets or outlets, esp. one in a car engine [Old English *manigfeald*]

manikin *n* **1** a little man; dwarf or child **2** a model of the human body [Dutch *manneken*]

manila *or* **manilla** *n* a strong usually brown paper used to make envelopes [after *Manila*, in the Philippines]

man in the street *n* the average person

manioc *n* same as **cassava** [indigenous S American word *mandioca*]

manipulate *vb* **-lating, -lated 1** to handle or use skilfully **2** to control something or someone cleverly or deviously [Latin *manipulus* handful] **manipulation** *n* **manipulator** *n* **manipulative** *adj*

mankind *n* **1** human beings collectively **2** men collectively

> **USAGE** Many people object to the use of *mankind* and *man* to refer to human beings collectively. Gender-neutral alternatives include *human beings*, *people*, and *humankind*.

manly *adj* **-lier, -liest 1** possessing qualities, such as vigour or courage, traditionally regarded as appropriate to a man; masculine **2** characteristic of a man **manliness** *n*

man-made *adj* made by humans; artificial

manna *n* **1** *Bible* the miraculous food which sustained the Israelites in the wilderness (Exodus 16:14–36) **2** a windfall: *manna from heaven* [Hebrew *mān*]

manned *adj* having a human staff or crew: *the hazards of manned space flight*

mannequin *n* **1** a woman who wears the clothes displayed at a fashion show; model **2** a life-size dummy of the human body used to fit or display clothes [French]

manner *n* **1** the way a thing happens or is done **2** a person's bearing and behaviour **3** the style or customary way of doing something: *sculpture in the Greek manner* **4** type or kind **5 in a manner of speaking** in a way; so to speak **6 to the manner born** naturally fitted to a specified role or activity [Old French *maniere*]

mannered *adj* **1** (of speech or behaviour) unnaturally formal and put on to impress others **2** having manners as specified: *ill-mannered*

mannerism *n* **1** a distinctive and individual gesture or way of speaking **2** excessive use of a distinctive or affected manner, esp. in art or literature

mannerly *adj* well-mannered and polite **mannerliness** *n*

manners *pl n* **1** a person's social conduct viewed in the light of whether it is regarded as polite or acceptable or not: *his manners leave something to be desired; shockingly bad manners* **2** a socially acceptable way of behaving: *it's not manners to point*

mannish *adj* (of a woman) displaying an appearance or qualities regarded as typical of a man

manoeuvre *or US* **maneuver** (man-noo-ver) *vb* **-vring, -vred** *or* **-vering, -vered 1** to move or do something with dexterity and skill: *she manoeuvred the car easily into the parking space* **2** to manipulate a situation in order to gain some advantage **3** to perform a manoeuvre or manoeuvres ▹ *n* **4** a movement or action requiring dexterity and skill **5** a contrived, complicated, and possibly deceptive plan or action **6 manoeuvres** military or naval exercises, usually on a large scale **7** a change in course of a ship or aircraft, esp. a complicated one **8 room for manoeuvre** the possibility of changing one's plans or behaviour if it becomes necessary or desirable [French, from Medieval Latin *manuopera* manual work] **manoeuvrable** *or US* **maneuverable** *adj* **manoeuvrability** *or US* **maneuverability** *n*

manoeuvring *or US* **maneuvering** *n* the skilful manipulation of a situation to gain some advantage

man-of-war *n, pl* **men-of-war 1** a warship **2** short for **Portuguese man-of-war**

manor *n* **1** (in medieval Europe) the lands and property controlled by a lord **2** *Brit* a large country house and its lands **3** *Brit slang* an area of operation, esp. of a local police force [Old French *manoir* dwelling] **manorial** *adj*

manor house *n chiefly Brit* a large country house, esp. one that was originally part of a medieval manor

manpower *n* the number of people needed or available for a job

manqué (mong-kay) *adj* unfulfilled; would-be: *an actor manqué* [French, literally: having missed]

mansard *n* a roof with two slopes on both sides and both ends, the lower slopes being steeper than the upper [after François *Mansart*, architect]

manse *n* the house provided for a minister of some Christian denominations [Medieval Latin *mansus* dwelling]

manservant *n, pl* **menservants** a male servant, esp. a valet

mansion *n* **1** a large and imposing house **2 Mansions** *Brit* a name given to some blocks of flats as part of their address: *18 Wilton Mansions* [Latin *mansio* a remaining]

manslaughter *n law* the unlawful but not deliberately planned killing of one human being by another

mantel *n* a wooden, stone, or iron frame around a fireplace [variant of *mantle*]

mantelpiece *n* a shelf above a fireplace often forming part of the mantel. Also: **mantel shelf**, **chimneypiece**

manticore *n* a mythical beast with a lion's body, a scorpion's tail, and a man's head with three rows of teeth [Persian *mardkhora* man-eater]

mantilla *n* a woman's lace or silk scarf covering the shoulders and head, worn esp. in Spain [Spanish *manta* cloak]

mantis *n, pl* **-tises** *or* **-tes** a carnivorous insect resembling a grasshopper, that rests with the first pair of legs raised as if in prayer. Also: **praying mantis** [Greek: prophet]

mantissa *n* the part of a common logarithm consisting of the decimal point and the figures following it: *the mantissa of 2.4771 is .4771* [Latin: something added]

mantle *n* **1** *old-fashioned* a loose wrap or cloak **2** anything that covers completely or envelops: *a mantle of snow covered the ground* **3** the responsibilities and duties which go with a particular job or position: *he refuses to accept the mantle of leader* **4** a small mesh dome used to increase illumination in a gas or oil lamp by becoming incandescent **5** *geol* the part of the earth between the crust and the core ▷ *vb* **-tling, -tled 6** to spread over or become spread over: *mountains mantled in lush vegetation* [Latin *mantellum* little cloak]

m

man-to-man *adj* characterized by frankness and sincerity: *a man-to-man discussion*

mantra *n* **1** *Hinduism & Buddhism* any sacred word or syllable used as an object of concentration **2** *Hinduism* a Vedic psalm of praise **3** any phrase that is consciously repeated because it is believed to contain an important truth [Sanskrit: speech, instrument of thought]

manual *adj* **1** of a hand or hands: *manual dexterity* **2** physical as opposed to mental: *manual labour* **3** operated or done by human labour rather than automatic or computer-aided means: *a manual gearbox* ▷ *n* **4** a book of instructions or information **5** *music* one of the keyboards on an organ [Latin *manus* hand] **manually** *adv*

manufacture *vb* **-turing, -tured 1** to process or make goods on a large scale, esp. using machinery **2** to invent or concoct evidence, an excuse, etc. ▷ *n* **3** the production of goods, esp. by industrial processes [Latin *manus* hand + *facere* to make] **manufacturer** *n* **manufacturing** *n, adj*

manuka (mah-nook-a) *n* a New Zealand tree with strong elastic wood and aromatic leaves [Māori]

manuka honey *n* honey from the nectar of the manuka tree; its antibacterial agent is used for medicinal purposes

manumit (man-new-**mit**) *vb* **-mitting, -mitted** to free from slavery [Latin *manumittere* to release] **manumission** *n*

manure *n* **1** animal excrement used as a fertilizer ▷ *vb* **-nuring, -nured 2** to spread manure upon fields or soil [Anglo-French *mainoverer*]

manuscript *n* **1** a book or other document written by hand **2** the original handwritten or typed version of a book or article submitted by an author for publication [Medieval Latin *manuscriptus* handwritten]

Manx *adj* **1** of the Isle of Man ▷ *n* **2** an almost extinct Celtic language of the Isle of Man ▷ *pl n* **3 the Manx** the people of the Isle of Man [Scandinavian] **Manxman** *or fem* **Manxwoman** *n*

Manx cat *n* a short-haired breed of cat without a tail

many *adj* **1** a large number of; numerous: *many times; many people think the government is incompetent* ▷ *pron* **2** a number of people or things, esp. a large one: *many are seated already; have as many as you want* **3 many a** each of a considerable number of: *many a man* ▷ *n* **4 the many** the majority of mankind, esp. ordinary people [Old English *manig*]

Maoism *n* Communism as interpreted in the theories and policies of Mao Zedong (1893–1976), Chinese statesman **Maoist** *n, adj*

Māori *n* **1** *pl* **-ri** *or* **-ris** a member of the Polynesian people living in New Zealand since before the arrival of European settlers **2** the language of this people ▷ *adj* **3** of this people or their language

map *n* **1** a diagrammatic representation of the earth's surface or part of it, showing the geographical distributions or positions of features such as roads, towns, relief, and rainfall **2** a diagrammatic representation of the stars or of the surface of a celestial body **3** *maths* same as **function 4 put on the map** to make (a town or company) well-known: *William Morris put Kelmscott on the map* ▷ *vb* **mapping, mapped 5** to make a map of **6** *maths* to represent or transform (a function, figure, or set) ▷ See also **map out** [Latin *mappa* cloth]

maple *n* **1** any of various trees or shrubs with five-pointed leaves and winged seeds borne in pairs **2** the hard wood of any of these trees ▷ See also **sugar maple** [Old English *mapeltrēow* maple tree]

maple leaf *n* the leaf of the maple tree, the national emblem of Canada

maple syrup *n* a very sweet syrup made from the sap of the sugar maple

map out *vb* to plan or design

mapping *n* *maths* same as **function**

maquis (mah-**kee**) *n, pl* **-quis** (**-kee**) **1** the French underground movement that fought against the German occupying forces in World War II **2** a type of shrubby, mostly evergreen, vegetation found in coastal regions of the Mediterranean area [French]

mar *vb* **marring, marred** to spoil or be the one bad feature of: *the coastline is marred by high-rise hotels* [Old English *merran*]

Mar. March

marabou *n* **1** a large black-and-white African stork **2** the soft white down of this bird, used to trim hats, etc. [Arabic *murābit* holy man]

maraca (mar-**rak**-a) *n* a shaken percussion instrument, usually one of a pair, consisting of a gourd or plastic shell filled with dried seeds or pebbles [Brazilian Portuguese]

marae (mar-**rye**) *n NZ* **1** an enclosed space in front of a Māori meeting house **2** a Māori meeting house and its buildings [Māori]

maraschino (mar-rass-**kee**-no) *n* a liqueur made from a type of sour cherry having a taste like bitter almonds [Italian]
maraschino cherry *n* a cherry preserved in maraschino
marathon *n* **1** a race on foot of 26 miles 385 yards (42.195 kilometres) **2** any long or arduous task or event ▷ *adj* **3** of or relating to a race on foot of 26 miles 385 yards (42.195 kilometres): *marathon runners* **4** long and arduous: *a marathon nine hour meeting* [referring to the feat of the messenger said to have run 26 miles from Marathon to Athens to bring the news of victory in 490 BC]
maraud *vb* to wander or raid in search of plunder [French *marauder* to prowl] **marauder** *n* **marauding** *adj*
marble *n* **1** a hard limestone rock, which usually has a mottled appearance and can be given a high polish **2** a block of marble or work of art made of marble **3** a small round glass ball used in playing marbles ▷ *vb* **-bling, -bled 4** to mottle with variegated streaks in imitation of marble [Greek *marmaros*] **marbled** *adj*
marbles *n* a game in which marbles are rolled at one another
marbling *n* **1** a mottled effect or pattern resembling marble **2** the streaks of fat in lean meat
marc *n* **1** the remains of grapes or other fruit that have been pressed for wine-making **2** a brandy distilled from these [French]
marcasite *n* **1** a pale yellow form of iron pyrites used in jewellery **2** a cut and polished form of steel used for making jewellery [Arabic *marqashītā*]
march¹ *vb* **1** to walk with very regular steps, like a soldier **2** to walk in a quick and determined manner, esp. when angry: *he marched into the kitchen without knocking* **3** to make a person or group proceed: *he was marched back to his cell* **4** (of an army, procession, etc.) to walk as an organized group: *the demonstrators marched down the main street* **5** to advance or progress steadily: *time marches on* ▷ *n* **6** a regular stride **7** a long or exhausting walk **8** the steady development or progress of something: *the continuous march of industrial development* **9** a distance covered by marching **10** an organized protest in which a large group of people walk somewhere together: *a march against racial violence* **11** a piece of music suitable for marching to **12 steal a march on** to gain an advantage over, esp. by a trick [Old French *marchier* to tread] **marcher** *n* **marching** *adj*
march² *n* **1** a border or boundary **2** the land lying along a border or boundary, often of disputed ownership [Old French *marche*]
March *n* the third month of the year [Latin *Martius* (month) of Mars]
March hare *n* a hare during its breeding season in March, noted for its leaping, chasing, and boxing
marching girl *n Austral & NZ* a girl who does team formation marching as a sport
marching orders *pl n* **1** *informal* dismissal, esp. from employment **2** military orders, giving instructions about a march
marchioness (**marsh**-on-**ness**) *n* **1** a woman who holds the rank of marquis or marquess **2** the wife or widow of a marquis or marquess [Medieval Latin *marchionissa*]
marchpane *n archaic* marzipan [French]
Mardi Gras (**mar**-dee **grah**) *n* the festival of Shrove Tuesday, celebrated in some cities with great revelry [French: fat Tuesday]
mare¹ *n* the adult female of a horse or zebra [Old English *mere*]
mare² (**mar**-ray) *n, pl* **maria** one of many huge dry plains on the surface of the moon or Mars, visible as dark markings [Latin: sea]
mare's-nest *n* a discovery imagined to be important but proving to be worthless
margarine *n* a butter substitute made from vegetable and animal fats [Greek *margaron* pearl]
marge *n Brit & Austral informal* margarine
margin *n* **1** an edge, rim, or border: *we came to the margin of the wood; people on the margin of society* **2** the blank space surrounding the text on a page **3** an additional amount or one beyond the minimum necessary: *the margin of victory was seven lengths; a small margin of error* **4** *chiefly Austral* a payment made in addition to a basic wage, esp. for special skill or responsibility **5** a limit beyond which something can no longer exist or function: *the margin of physical survival* **6** *econ* the minimum return below which an enterprise becomes unprofitable [Latin *margo* border]
marginal *adj* **1** of, in, on, or forming a margin **2** not important; insignificant: *he remained a rather marginal political figure* **3** close to a limit, esp. a lower limit: *marginal legal ability* **4** *econ* relating to goods or services produced and sold at the margin of profitability: *marginal cost* **5** *politics* of or designating a constituency in which elections tend to be won by small margins: *a marginal seat* **6** designating agricultural land on the edge of fertile areas ▷ *n* **7** *politics, chiefly Brit & NZ* a marginal constituency **marginally** *adv*
marginalia *pl n* notes in the margin of a book, manuscript, or letter
margrave *n* (formerly) a German nobleman ranking above a count [Middle Dutch *markgrave* count of the frontier]
marguerite *n* a garden plant with flowers resembling large daisies [French: daisy]
marigold *n* any of various plants cultivated for their yellow or orange flowers [from *Mary* (the Virgin) + *gold*]
marijuana *or* **marihuana** (mar-ree-**wah**-na) *n* the dried leaves and flowers of the hemp plant, used as a drug, esp. in cigarettes [Mexican Spanish]
marimba *n* a percussion instrument consisting of a set of hardwood plates placed over tuned metal resonators, played with soft-headed sticks [West African]
marina *n* a harbour for yachts and other pleasure boats [Latin: marine]
marinade *n* **1** a mixture of oil, wine, vinegar, etc., in which meat or fish is soaked before cooking ▷ *vb* **-nading, -naded 2** same as **marinate** [French]

m

marinate *vb* **-nating, -nated** to soak in marinade [Italian *marinare* to pickle] **marinated** *adj*
marine *adj* **1** of, found in, or relating to the sea **2** of shipping or navigation **3** used or adapted for use at sea ▷ *n* **4** (esp. in Britain and the US) a soldier trained for land and sea combat **5** a country's shipping or navy collectively: *the merchant marine* [Latin *marinus* of the sea]
mariner (mar-in-er) *n* a sailor
marionette *n* a puppet whose limbs are moved by strings [French, from the name *Marion*]
marital *adj* of or relating to marriage [Latin *maritus* married] **maritally** *adv*
maritime *adj* **1** of or relating to shipping **2** of, near, or living near the sea [Latin *maritimus* of the sea]
marjoram *n* a plant with sweet-scented leaves, used for seasoning food and in salads [Medieval Latin *marjorana*]
mark[1] *n* **1** a visible impression on a surface, such as a spot or scratch **2** a sign, symbol, or other indication that distinguishes something **3** a written or printed symbol, as used for punctuation **4** a letter, number, or percentage used to grade academic work **5** a thing that indicates position; marker **6** an indication of some quality: *a mark of respect* **7** a target or goal **8** impression or influence: *this book displays the mark of its author's admiration of Kafka* **9** (in trade names) a particular model or type of a vehicle, machine, etc.: *a Spitfire Mark XI* **10** one of the temperature settings at which a gas oven can work: *bake at gas mark 5 for thirty minutes* **11 make one's mark** to achieve recognition **12 on your mark** *or* **marks** a command given to runners in a race to prepare themselves at the starting line **13 up to the mark** meeting the desired standard ▷ *vb* **14** to make a visible impression, trace, or stain on **15** to have a tendency to become dirty, scratched, or damaged: *this material marks easily* **16** to characterize or distinguish: *the gritty determination that has marked his career* **17** to designate someone as a particular type of person: *she would now be marked as a troublemaker* **18** to label, esp. to indicate price **19** to celebrate or commemorate an occasion or its anniversary: *events marking the anniversary of Shakespeare's birth* **20** to pay attention to: *mark my words* **21** to observe or notice **22** to grade or evaluate academic work **23** *sport* to stay close to an opponent to hamper his or her play **24 mark off** *or* **out** to set boundaries or limits on **25 mark time** A to move the feet alternately as in marching but without advancing B to wait for something more interesting to happen ▷ See also **markdown**, **mark-up** [Old English *mearc*]
mark[2] *n* See **Deutschmark** [Old English *marc* unit of weight of precious metal]
markdown *n* **1** a price reduction ▷ *vb* **mark down** **2** to reduce in price **3** to make a written note of: *she marked down the number of the getaway car*
marked *adj* **1** obvious or noticeable: *a marked improvement* **2** singled out, esp. as the target of attack: *a marked man* **markedly** (mark-id-lee) *adv*
marker *n* **1** an object used to show the position of something **2** Also called: **marker pen** a thick felt-tipped pen used for drawing and colouring
market *n* **1** an occasion at which people meet to buy and sell merchandise **2** a place at which a market is held **3** the buying and selling of goods and services, esp. when unrestrained by political or social considerations: *the market has been brought into health care* **4** the trading opportunities provided by a particular group of people: *the youth market* **5** demand for a particular product **6** short for **stock market** **7 be in the market for** to wish to buy **8 on the market** available for purchase **9 seller's** *or* **buyer's market** a market characterized by excess demand (or supply) and thus favourable to sellers (or buyers) ▷ *adj* **10** of, relating to, or controlled by the buying and selling of goods and services, esp. when unrestrained by political or social considerations: *a market economy* ▷ *vb* **-keting, -keted** **11** to offer or produce for sale [Latin *mercari* to trade] **marketable** *adj*
market forces *pl n* the effect of supply and demand on trading within a free market
market garden *n chiefly Brit & NZ* a place where fruit and vegetables are grown for sale **market gardener** *n*
marketing *n* the part of a business which controls the way that goods or services are sold
market maker *n* a dealer in securities on the London Stock Exchange who can also deal with the public as a broker
marketplace *n* **1** a place where a public market is held **2** the commercial world of buying and selling
market price *n* the prevailing price at which goods may be bought or sold
market research *n* the study of customers' wants and purchases, and of the forces influencing them
market-test *vb* to put (a section of a public-sector service) out to tender, often before full privatization
market town *n chiefly Brit* the main town in an agricultural area, usually one where a market is regularly held
marking *n* **1** the arrangement of colours on an animal or plant **2** the assessment and correction of pupils' or students' written work by teachers
marksman *n, pl* **-men** a person skilled in shooting **marksmanship** *n*
mark-up *n* **1** an amount added to the cost of something to provide the seller with a profit ▷ *vb* **mark up** **2** to increase the cost of something by an amount or percentage in order to make a profit
marl *n* a fine-grained rock consisting of clay, limestone, and silt used as a fertilizer [Late Latin *margila*] **marly** *adj*
marlin *n, pl* **-lin** *or* **-lins** a large fish with a long spear-like upper jaw, found in warm and tropical seas [after *marlinspike* (because of its long jaw)]
marlinspike *or* **marlinespike** (mar-lin-spike) *n naut* a pointed metal tool used in separating strands of rope [Dutch *marlijn* light rope + SPIKE]
marmalade *n* a jam made from citrus fruits, esp. oranges [Portuguese *marmelo* quince]
marmoreal (mar-more-ee-al) *adj* of or like marble [Latin *marmoreus*]

m

marmoset *n* a small South American monkey with a long bushy tail [Old French *marmouset* grotesque figure]

marmot *n* any of various burrowing rodents of Europe, Asia, and North America. They are heavily built and have coarse fur [French *marmotte*]

maroon[1] *vb* **1** to abandon someone in a deserted area, esp. on an island **2** to isolate in a helpless situation: *we're marooned here until the snow stops* [American Spanish *cimarrón* wild] **marooned** *adj*

maroon[2] *adj* **1** dark purplish-red ▷ *n* **2** an exploding firework or flare used as a warning signal [French: chestnut]

marque (**mark**) *n* a brand of product, esp. of a car [French]

marquee *n* a large tent used for a party, exhibition, etc. [invented singular form of MARQUISE]

marquess (mar-kwiss) *n* **1** (in the British Isles) a nobleman ranking between a duke and an earl **2** See **marquis**

marquetry *n, pl* **-quetries** a pattern of inlaid veneers of wood or metal used chiefly as ornamentation in furniture [Old French *marqueter* to inlay]

marquis *n, pl* **-quises** *or* **-quis** (in various countries) a nobleman ranking above a count, corresponding to a British marquess [Old French *marchis* count of the frontier]

marquise (mar-**keez**) *n* **1** (in various countries) a marchioness **2** a gemstone cut in a pointed oval shape [French]

marram grass *n* a grass that grows on sandy shores: often planted to stabilize sand dunes [Old Norse *marálmr*]

marriage *n* **1** the state or relationship of being married: *the institution of marriage* **2** the contract made by two people to live together in a partnership. Related adjectives: **connubial**, **nuptial** **3** the ceremony formalizing this union; wedding **4** a close union or relationship: *the marriage of scientific knowledge and industry*

marriageable *adj* suitable for marriage, usually with reference to age

marriage guidance *n* advice given by trained counsellors to couples who have problems in their married life

married *adj* **1** having a husband or wife **2** of marriage or married people: *married life* ▷ *n* **3** **marrieds** married people: *young marrieds*

marrow *n* **1** the fatty tissue that fills the cavities of bones **2** short for **vegetable marrow** [Old English *mærg*]

marrowfat pea *or* **marrow pea** *n* a variety of large pea

marry[1] *vb* **-ries, -rying, -ried** **1** to take (someone) as one's partner in marriage **2** to join or give in marriage **3** Also: **marry up** to fit together or unite; join: *their playing marries Irish traditional music and rock* [Latin *maritare*]

marry[2] *interj archaic* an exclamation of surprise or anger [euphemistic for the Virgin *Mary*]

Mars *n* **1** the Roman god of war **2** the fourth planet from the sun

Marseillaise (mar-say-**yaze**) *n* **the Marseillaise** the French national anthem [French *(chanson) marseillaise* (song) of Marseilles (first sung in Paris by the battalion of Marseilles)]

marsh *n* low poorly drained land that is wet, muddy, and sometimes flooded [Old English *merisc*] **marshy** *adj*

marshal *n* **1** (in some armies and air forces) an officer of the highest rank: *Field Marshall* **2** an officer who organizes or controls ceremonies or public events **3** *US* the chief police or fire officer in some states **4** (formerly in England) an officer of the royal family or court ▷ *vb* **-shalling, -shalled** *or US* **-shaling, -shaled** **5** to arrange in order: *she marshalled her facts and came to a conclusion* **6** to assemble and organize people or vehicles in readiness for onward movement **7** to guide or lead, esp. in a ceremonious way: *she marshalled them towards the lecture theatre* [Old French *mareschal*] **marshalcy** *n*

marshalling yard *n railways* a place where railway wagons are shunted and made up into trains

Marshal of the Royal Air Force *n* the highest rank in the Royal Air Force

marsh gas *n* a gas largely composed of methane formed when plants decay in the absence of air

marshland *n* land consisting of marshes

marshmallow *n* a spongy pink or white sweet

marsh mallow *n* a plant that grows in salt marshes and has pale pink flowers. It was formerly used to make marshmallows

marsupial (mar-**soop**-ee-al) *n* **1** a mammal, such as a kangaroo or an opossum, the female of which carries her babies in a pouch at the front of her body until they reach a mature state ▷ *adj* **2** of or like a marsupial [Latin *marsupium* purse]

mart *n* a market or trading centre [Middle Dutch: market]

Martello tower *n* a round tower used for coastal defence, formerly much used in Europe [after Cape *Mortella* in Corsica]

marten *n, pl* **-tens** *or* **-ten** **1** any of several agile weasel-like mammals with bushy tails and golden-brown to blackish fur **2** the fur of these animals [Middle Dutch *martren*]

martial *adj* of or characteristic of war, soldiers, or the military life: *martial music* [Latin *martialis* of Mars, god of war]

martial art *n* any of various philosophies and techniques of self-defence originating in China, Japan, and Korea, such as judo or karate

martial law *n* rule of law maintained by military forces in the absence of civil law

Martian (marsh-an) *adj* **1** of the planet Mars ▷ *n* **2** an inhabitant of Mars, in science fiction

martin *n* a bird of the swallow family with a square or slightly forked tail [probably after St *Martin*, because the birds were believed to migrate at Martinmas]

martinet *n* a person who maintains strict discipline [after General *Martinet*, drillmaster under Louis XIV]

martingale *n* a strap from the reins to the girth of a horse, preventing it from carrying its head too high [French]

martini *n* **1** *(often cap) trademark* an Italian vermouth **2** a cocktail of gin and vermouth

Martinmas *n* the feast of St Martin on November 11: a quarter day in Scotland

martyr *n* **1** a person who chooses to die rather than renounce his or her religious beliefs **2** a person who suffers greatly or dies for a cause or belief **3 a martyr to** suffering constantly from: *a martyr to arthritis* ▷ *vb* **4** to make a martyr of [Late Greek *martur-* witness] **martyrdom** *n*

marvel *vb* **-velling, -velled** *or US* **-veling, -veled** **1** to be filled with surprise or wonder ▷ *n* **2** something that causes wonder [Old French *merveille*]

marvellous *or US* **marvelous** *adj* **1** excellent or splendid: *a marvellous idea* **2** causing great wonder or surprise; extraordinary: *electricity is a marvellous thing* **marvellously** *or US* **marvelously** *adv*

Marxism *n* the economic and political theories of Karl Marx (1818–83), German political philosopher, which argue that class struggle is the basic agency of historical change, and that capitalism will be superseded by communism **Marxist** *n, adj*

marzipan *n* a mixture made from ground almonds, sugar, and egg whites that is put on top of cakes or used to make sweets [Italian *marzapane*]

masala *n Indian cookery* a mixture of spices ground into a paste [from Urdu *masalah*, from Arabic *masalih* ingredients]

m

masc. masculine

mascara *n* a cosmetic for darkening the eyelashes [Spanish: mask]

mascarpone (mass-car-**po**-nee) *n* a soft Italian cream cheese [from Italian dialect *mascherpa* ricotta]

mascot *n* a person, animal, or thing considered to bring good luck [French *mascotte*]

masculine *adj* **1** possessing qualities or characteristics considered typical of or appropriate to a man **2** of men **3** *grammar* denoting a gender of nouns that includes some male animate things **4** *prosody* denoting a rhyme between pairs of single final stressed syllables [Latin *masculinus*] **masculinity** *n*

maser *n* a device for amplifying microwaves, working on the same principle as a laser [*m(icrowave) a(mplification by) s(timulated) e(mission of) r(adiation)*]

mash *n* **1** a soft pulpy mass **2** *agriculture* bran, meal, or malt mixed with warm water and used as food for horses, cattle, or poultry **3** *Brit informal* mashed potatoes ▷ *vb* **4** to beat or crush into a mash [Old English *mǣsc-*] **mashed** *adj*

mashup *n* a mixture of several contrasting elements

mask *n* **1** any covering for the whole or a part of the face worn for amusement, protection, or disguise **2** behaviour that hides one's true feelings: *his mask of detachment* **3** *surgery* a sterile gauze covering for the nose and mouth worn to minimize the spread of germs **4** a device placed over the nose and mouth to facilitate or prevent inhalation of a gas **5** a moulded likeness of a face or head, such as a death mask **6** the face or head of an animal such as a fox ▷ *vb* **7** to cover with or put on a mask **8** to hide or disguise: *a high brick wall that masked the front of the building* **9** to cover so as to protect [Arabic *maskharah* clown] **masked** *adj*

masking tape *n* an adhesive tape used to protect surfaces surrounding an area to be painted

masochism (**mass**-oh-kiz-zum) *n* **1** *psychiatry* a condition in which pleasure, esp. sexual pleasure, is obtained from feeling pain or from being humiliated **2** a tendency to take pleasure from one's own suffering [after Leopold von Sacher *Masoch*, novelist] **masochist** *n, adj* **masochistic** *adj*

mason *n* a person skilled in building with stone [Old French *masson*]

Mason *n* a Freemason

Masonic *adj* of Freemasons or Freemasonry

masonry *n* **1** stonework or brickwork **2** the craft of a mason

Masonry *n* Freemasonry

masque (**mask**) *n* a dramatic entertainment of the 16th to 17th centuries, consisting of dancing, dialogue, and song [variant of *mask*] **masquer** *n*

masquerade (mask-er-**aid**) *vb* **-ading, -aded** **1** to pretend to be someone or something else ▷ *n* **2** an attempt to keep secret the real identity or nature of something: *he was unable to keep up his masquerade as the war's victor* **3** a party at which the guests wear masks and costumes [Spanish *mascara* mask]

mass *n* **1** a large body of something without a definite shape **2** a collection of the component parts of something: *a mass of fibres* **3** a large amount or number, as of people **4** the main part or majority **5** the size of a body; bulk **6** *physics* a physical quantity expressing the amount of matter in a body **7** (in painting or drawing) an area of unified colour, shade, or intensity ▷ *adj* **8** done or occurring on a large scale: *mass hysteria* **9** consisting of a mass or large number, esp. of people: *a mass meeting* ▷ *vb* **10** to join together into a mass ▷ See also **masses** [Latin *massa*] **massed** *adj*

Mass *n* **1** (in the Roman Catholic Church and certain other Christian churches) a service in which bread and wine are consecrated to represent the body and blood of Christ **2** a musical setting of parts of this service [Church Latin *missa*]

massacre (**mass**-a-ker) *n* **1** the wanton or savage killing of large numbers of people **2** *informal* an overwhelming defeat ▷ *vb* **-cring, -cred** **3** to kill people indiscriminately in large numbers **4** *informal* to defeat overwhelmingly [Old French]

massage (**mass**-ahzh) *n* **1** the kneading or rubbing of parts of the body to reduce pain or stiffness or help relaxation ▷ *vb* **-saging, -saged** **2** to give a massage to **3** to manipulate statistics or evidence to produce a desired result [French *masser* to rub]

massage parlour *n* **1** a commercial establishment providing massages **2** *euphemistic* a place where men pay to have sex with prostitutes

massasauga (mass-a-**saw**-ga) *n* a North American venomous snake with a horny rattle at the end of the tail [after the *Missisauga* River, Ontario, Canada]
masses *pl n* **1 the masses** ordinary people as a group **2 masses of** *informal, chiefly Brit* a great number or quantity of: *masses of food*
masseur (mass-**ur**) *or fem* **masseuse** (mass-**uhz**) *n* a person who gives massages
massif (mass-**seef**) *n* a series of connected masses of rock forming a mountain range [French]
massive *adj* **1** (of objects) large, bulky, heavy, and usually solid **2** impressive or imposing **3** intensive or considerable: *a massive overdose* [French *massif*] **massively** *adv*
mass-market *adj* of, for, or appealing to a large number of people; popular: *mass-market newspapers*
mass media *pl n* the means of communication that reach large numbers of people, such as television, newspapers, and radio
mass noun *n* a noun that refers to an extended substance rather than to each of a set of objects, eg, *water* as opposed to *lake*
mass number *n* the total number of protons and neutrons in the nucleus of an atom
mass-produce *vb* **-producing, -produced** to manufacture standardized goods on a large scale by extensive use of machinery **mass-produced** *adj* **mass-production** *n*
mass spectrometer *n* an instrument for analysing the composition of a sample of material, in which ions, produced from the sample, are separated by electric or magnetic fields according to their ratios of charge to mass
mast[1] *n* **1** *naut* a vertical pole for supporting sails, radar equipment, etc., above the deck of a ship **2** a tall upright pole used as an aerial for radio or television broadcasting: *a television mast* **3 before the mast** *naut* as an apprentice seaman [Old English *mæst*]
mast[2] *n* the fruit of forest trees, such as beech or oak, used as food for pigs [Old English *mæst*]
mastaba *n* a mud-brick superstructure above tombs in ancient Egypt [Arabic: bench]
mastectomy (mass-**tek**-tom-ee) *n, pl* **-mies** surgical removal of a breast [Greek *mastos* breast + *ek* out + *tomē* a cutting]
master *n* **1** the man who has authority over others, such as the head of a household, the employer of servants, or the owner of animals or, formerly, slaves **2** a person with exceptional skill at a certain thing: *a master of her craft* **3** a person who has complete control of a situation: *the master of his portfolio* **4** an original copy or tape from which duplicates are made **5** a craftsman fully qualified to practise his trade and to train others **6** a player of a game, esp. chess or bridge, who has won a specified number of tournament games **7** a highly regarded teacher or leader **8** a graduate holding a master's degree **9** the chief officer aboard a merchant ship **10** *chiefly Brit* a male teacher **11** the superior person or side in a contest **12** the heir apparent of a Scottish viscount or baron: *the Master of Ballantrae* ▷ *adj* **13** (of a craftsman) fully qualified to practise and to train others **14** overall or controlling: *master plan* **15** designating a mechanism that controls others: *master switch* **16** main or principal: *master bedroom* ▷ *vb* **17** to become thoroughly proficient in **18** to overcome or defeat [Latin *magister* teacher]
Master *n* a title of address for a boy who is not old enough to be called *Mr*
master aircrew *n* a rank in the Royal Air Force, equal to warrant officer
masterful *adj* **1** showing great skill **2** domineering or authoritarian **masterfully** *adv*
master key *n* a key that opens all the locks of a set; passkey
masterly *adj* showing great skill; expert
mastermind *vb* **1** to plan and direct a complex task or project ▷ *n* **2** a person who plans and directs a complex task or project
Master of Arts *n* a degree, usually postgraduate in a nonscientific subject, or a person holding this degree
master of ceremonies *n* a person who presides over a public ceremony, formal dinner, or entertainment, introducing the events and performers
Master of Science *n* a degree, usually postgraduate in a scientific subject, or a person holding this degree
Master of the Rolls *n* (in England and Wales) the judge who presides over the Court of Appeal's Civil Division and who was formerly Keeper of the Records at the Public Record Office
masterpiece *or* **masterwork** *n* **1** an outstanding work or performance **2** the most outstanding piece of work of an artist or craftsman
masterstroke *n* an outstanding piece of strategy, skill, or talent
mastery *n, pl* **-teries 1** outstanding skill or expertise **2** complete power or control: *he had complete mastery over the country*
masthead *n* **1** *naut* the highest part of a mast **2** the name of a newspaper or periodical printed at the top of the front page
mastic *n* **1** an aromatic resin obtained from a Mediterranean tree and used to make varnishes and lacquers **2** any of several putty-like substances used as a filler, adhesive, or seal [Greek *mastikhē*]
masticate *vb* **-cating, -cated** to chew food [Greek *mastikhan* to grind the teeth] **mastication** *n*
mastiff *n* a large powerful short-haired dog, usually fawn or brown with dark streaks [Latin *mansuetus* tame]
mastitis *n* inflammation of the breast
mastodon *n* an extinct elephant-like mammal [New Latin, literally: breast-tooth, referring to the nipple-shaped projections on the teeth]
mastoid *adj* **1** shaped like a nipple or breast ▷ *n* **2** a nipple-like projection of bone behind the ear **3** *informal* mastoiditis [Greek *mastos* breast]
mastoiditis *n* inflammation of the mastoid
masturbate *vb* **-bating, -bated** to fondle one's own genitals, or those of someone else, to cause sexual pleasure [Latin *masturbari*] **masturbation** *n*
mat[1] *n* **1** a thick flat piece of fabric used as a floor covering, a place to wipe one's shoes, etc. **2** a small pad of material used to protect a surface

from heat or scratches from an object placed upon it **3** a large piece of thick padded material put on the floor as a surface for wrestling, gymnastics, etc. ▹ *vb* **matting, matted 4** to tangle or become tangled into a dense mass [Old English *matte*]

mat² *adj* same as **matt** [French, literally: dead]

matador *n* the bullfighter armed with a sword, who attempts to kill the bull [Spanish, from *matar* to kill]

matai *n* a New Zealand tree, the wood of which is used for timber for building [Māori]

match¹ *n* **1** a formal game or sports event in which people or teams compete **2** a person or thing able to provide competition for another: *he has met his match* **3** a person or thing that resembles, harmonizes with, or is equivalent to another: *the colours aren't a perfect match, but they're close enough*; *white wine is not a good match for steak* **4** a person or thing that is an exact copy or equal of another **5** a partnership between two people, as in marriage **6** a person regarded as a possible partner in marriage: *for any number of men she would have been a good match* ▹ *vb* **7** to fit parts together **8** to resemble, harmonize with, or equal one another or something else: *our bedroom curtains match the bedspread*; *she walked at a speed that he could barely match* **9** to find a match for **10 match with** *or* **against A** to compare in order to determine which is the superior **B** to arrange a competition between [Old English *gemæcca* spouse] **matching** *adj*

m

match² *n* **1** a thin strip of wood or cardboard tipped with a chemical that ignites when scraped against a rough or specially treated surface **2** a fuse used to fire cannons' explosives [Old French *meiche*]

matchbox *n* a small box for holding matches

match-fit *adj sport* in good physical condition for competing in a match

matchless *adj* unequalled

matchmaker *n* a person who introduces people in the hope that they will form a couple **matchmaking** *n, adj*

match play *n golf* scoring according to the number of holes won and lost

match point *n sport* the final point needed to win a match

matchstick *n* **1** the wooden part of a match ▹ *adj* **2** (esp. of drawn figures) thin and straight: *little matchstick men*

matchwood *n* **1** wood suitable for making matches **2** splinters

mate¹ *n* **1 A** *informal, chiefly Brit, Austral & NZ* a friend: often used as a term of address between males: *I spotted my mate Jimmy McCrae at the other end of the bar*; *that's all right, mate* **B** an associate or colleague: *a classmate*; *the governor's running mate* **2** the sexual partner of an animal **3** a marriage partner **4** *naut* any officer below the master on a commercial ship **5** (in some trades) an assistant: *a plumber's mate* **6** one of a pair of matching items ▹ *vb* **mating, mated 7** to pair (a male and female animal) or (of animals) to pair for breeding **8** to marry **9** to join as a pair [Low German]

mate² *n, vb* **mating, mated** *chess* same as **checkmate**

mater *n Brit humorous* mother: often used facetiously [Latin]

material *n* **1** the substance of which a thing is made **2** cloth **3** ideas or notes that a finished work may be based on: *the material of the story resembles an incident in his own life* ▹ *adj* **4** concerned with or composed of physical matter or substance; not relating to spiritual or abstract things: *the material universe* **5** of or affecting economic or physical wellbeing: *material prosperity* **6** relevant or pertinent: *material evidence* ▹ See also **materials** [Latin *materia* matter]

materialism *n* **1** excessive interest in and desire for money or possessions **2** the belief that only the material world exists **materialist** *n, adj* **materialistic** *adj*

materialize *or* **-lise** *vb* **-lizing, -lized** *or* **-lising, -lised 1** to become fact; actually happen: *the promised pay rise never materialized* **2** to appear after being invisible: *trees materialized out of the gloom* **3** to take shape: *after hours of talks, a plan began to materialize* **materialization** *or* **-lisation** *n*

materially *adv* to a significant extent: *we were not materially affected*

materials *pl n* the equipment necessary for a particular activity: *building materials*

materiel (mat-ear-ee-**ell**) *n* the materials and equipment of an organization, esp. of a military force [French]

maternal *adj* **1** of or characteristic of a mother **2** related through the mother's side of the family: *his maternal uncle* [Latin *mater* mother] **maternally** *adv*

maternity *n* **1** motherhood **2** motherliness ▹ *adj* **3** relating to women during pregnancy or childbirth: *maternity leave*

mate's rates *pl n informal* reduced charges offered to a friend or colleague

matey *adj Brit informal* friendly or intimate

math *n US & Canad informal* short for **mathematics**

mathematical *adj* **1** using, used in, or relating to mathematics **2** having the precision of mathematics **mathematically** *adv*

mathematician *n* an expert or specialist in mathematics

mathematics *n* **1** a group of related sciences, including algebra, geometry, and calculus, which use a specialized notation to study number, quantity, shape, and space **2** numerical calculations involved in the solution of a problem [Greek *mathēma* a science]

maths *n Brit & Austral informal* short for **mathematics**

matinee (**mat**-in-nay) *n* an afternoon performance of a play or film [French]

matins *n* an early morning service in various Christian Churches [Latin *matutinus* of the morning]

matriarch (**mate**-ree-ark) *n* the female head of a tribe or family [Latin *mater* mother + Greek *arkhein* to rule] **matriarchal** *adj*

matriarchy *n, pl* **-chies** a form of social organization in which a female is head of the family or society, and descent and kinship are traced through the female line

matrices (may-triss-seez) *n* a plural of **matrix**
matricide *n* **1** the act of killing one's mother **2** a person who kills his or her mother [Latin *mater* mother + *caedere* to kill] **matricidal** *adj*
matriculate *vb* **-lating, -lated** to enrol or be enrolled in a college or university [Medieval Latin *matriculare* to register] **matriculation** *n*
matrilineal (mat-rill-in-ee-al) *adj* relating to descent through the female line
matrimony *n* the state of being married [Latin *matrimonium* wedlock] **matrimonial** *adj*
matrix (may-trix) *n, pl* **-trices** *or* **matrixes 1** the context or framework in which something is formed or develops: *a highly complex matrix of overlapping interests* **2** the rock in which fossils or pebbles are embedded **3** a mould, esp. one used in printing **4** *maths* a rectangular array of elements set out in rows and columns [Latin: womb]
matron *n* **1** a staid or dignified married woman **2** a woman in charge of the domestic or medical arrangements in an institution **3** *Brit* (formerly) the administrative head of the nursing staff in a hospital [Latin *matrona*] **matronly** *adj*
matron of honour *n, pl* **matrons of honour** a married woman attending a bride
matt *or* **matte** *adj* having a dull surface rather than a shiny one
matted *adj* tangled into a thick mass
matter *n* **1** the substance of which something, esp. a physical object, is made; material **2** substance that occupies space and has mass, as distinguished from substance that is mental or spiritual **3** substance of a specified type: *vegetable matter* **4** an event, situation, or subject: *a matter of taste; the break-in is a matter for the police* **5** a quantity or amount: *a matter of a few pounds* **6** the content of written or verbal material as distinct from its style or form **7** written material in general: *advertising matter* **8** a secretion or discharge, such as pus **9 for that matter** as regards that **10 no matter** regardless of; irrespective of: *you have to leave, no matter what she thinks* **11 the matter** wrong; the trouble: *there's nothing the matter* ▷ *vb* **12** to be of importance ▷ *interj* **no matter 13** it is unimportant [Latin *materia* cause, substance]
matter of fact *n* **1 as a matter of fact** actually; in fact ▷ *adj* **matter-of-fact 2** unimaginative or emotionless: *he conducted the executions in a completely matter-of-fact manner*
matting *n* a coarsely woven fabric used as a floor covering
mattock *n* a type of large pick that has one flat, horizontal end to its blade, used for loosening soil [Old English *mattuc*]
mattress *n* a large flat cushion with a strong cover, filled with cotton, foam rubber, etc., and often including coiled springs, used as a bed [Arabic *almatrah* place where something is thrown]
maturation *n* the process of becoming mature
mature *adj* **1** fully developed physically or mentally; grown-up **2** (of plans or theories) fully considered and thought-out **3** sensible and balanced in personality and emotional behaviour **4** due or payable: *a mature insurance policy* **5** (of fruit, wine, or cheese) ripe or fully aged ▷ *vb* **-turing, -tured 6** to make or become mature **7** (of bills or bonds) to become due for payment or repayment [Latin *maturus* early, developed] **maturity** *n*
matzo *n, pl* **matzos** a large very thin biscuit of unleavened bread, traditionally eaten by Jews during Passover [Hebrew *matsāh*]
maudlin *adj* foolishly or tearfully sentimental, esp. as a result of drinking [Middle English *Maudelen* Mary Magdalene, often shown weeping]
maul *vb* **1** to tear with the claws: *she was badly mauled by a lion* **2** to criticize a play, performance, etc., severely: *the film was mauled by the critics* **3** to handle roughly or clumsily ▷ *n* **4** *rugby* a loose scrum [Latin *malleus* hammer]
maunder *vb* to move, talk, or act aimlessly or idly [origin unknown]
Maundy Thursday *n* *Christianity* the Thursday before Easter observed as a commemoration of the Last Supper [Latin *mandatum* commandment]
mausoleum (maw-so-lee-um) *n* a large stately tomb [Greek *mausōleion* the tomb of king *Mausolus*]
mauve *adj* light purple [Latin *malva* mallow]
maverick *n* **1** a person of independent or unorthodox views **2** (in the US and Canada) an unbranded stray calf ▷ *adj* **3** (of a person or his or her views) independent and unorthodox [after Samuel A. *Maverick*, Texas rancher]
maw *n* the mouth, throat, or stomach of an animal [Old English *maga*]
mawkish *adj* foolishly or embarrassingly sentimental [obsolete *mawk* maggot] **mawkishness** *n*
max *n informal* **1** the most significant or greatest thing **2 to the max** to the ultimate extent
max. maximum
maxi *adj* **1** (of a garment) very long **2** large or considerable [from *maximum*]
maxilla *n, pl* **-lae 1** the upper jawbone of a vertebrate **2** any part of the mouth in insects and other arthropods [Latin: jaw] **maxillary** *adj*
maxim *n* a brief expression of a general truth, principle, or rule of conduct [Latin *maxima*, in the phrase *maxima propositio* basic axiom]
maximal *adj* of or being a maximum; the greatest possible
maximize *or* **-mise** *vb* **-mizing, -mized** *or* **-mising, -mised** to make as high or great as possible; increase to a maximum **maximization** *or* **-misation** *n*
maximum *n, pl* **-mums** *or* **-ma 1** the greatest possible amount or degree: *he gave the police the maximum of cooperation* **2** the greatest amount recorded, allowed, or reached: *keep to a maximum of two drinks a day* ▷ *adj* **3** of, being, or showing a maximum or maximums: *maximum speed* [Latin: greatest]
maxwell *n* the cgs unit of magnetic flux [after J. C. *Maxwell*, physicist]
may[1] *vb, past tense* **might 1** used as an auxiliary to indicate that permission is requested by or granted to someone: *she may leave* **2** used as an auxiliary to indicate the possibility that something could happen: *problems which may well*

have tragic consequences **3** used as an auxiliary to indicate ability or capacity, esp. in questions: *may I help you?* **4** used as an auxiliary to indicate a strong wish: *long may she reign* [Old English *mæg*, from *magan* to be able]

> **USAGE** It was formerly considered correct to use *may* rather than *can* when referring to permission as in: *you may use the laboratory for your experiments*, but this use of *may* is now almost entirely restricted to polite questions such as: *may I open the window?* The use of *may* with *if* in constructions such as *your analysis may have been more credible if...* is generally regarded as incorrect, *might* being preferred: *your analysis might have been more credible if...*

may² *or* **may tree** *n Brit* same as **hawthorn** [from *May*]
May *n* the fifth month of the year [probably from *Maia*, Roman goddess]
Maya *n* **1** *pl* **-ya** *or* **-yas** a member of an indigenous people of Central America, who once had an advanced civilization **2** the language of this people **Mayan** *n, adj*
maybe *adv* perhaps
Mayday *n* the international radio distress signal [phonetic spelling of French *m'aidez* help me]
May Day *n* the first day of May, traditionally a celebration of the coming of spring: in some countries now a holiday in honour of workers
mayfly *n, pl* **-flies** a short-lived insect with large transparent wings
mayhem *n* **1** any violent destruction or confusion: *a driver caused motorway mayhem* **2** *law* the maiming of a person [Anglo-French *mahem* injury]
mayn't may not
mayo *n informal* short for **mayonnaise**
mayonnaise *n* a thick creamy sauce made from egg yolks, oil, and vinegar [French]
mayor *n* the civic head of a municipal council in many countries [Latin *maior* greater] **mayoral** *adj*
mayoralty *n, pl* **-ties** the office or term of office of a mayor
mayoress *n* **1** *chiefly Brit* the wife of a mayor **2** a female mayor
maypole *n* a tall pole around which people dance during May-Day celebrations
May queen *n* a girl chosen to preside over May-Day celebrations
maze *n* **1** a complex network of paths or passages designed to puzzle people who try and find their way through or out of it **2** a puzzle in which the player must trace a path through a complex network of lines without touching or crossing any of them **3** any confusing network or system: *a maze of regulations* [from *amaze*]
mazurka *n* **1** a lively Polish dance in triple time **2** music for this dance [Polish]
mb millibar
Mb *computers* megabyte
MB **1** Bachelor of Medicine **2** Manitoba
MBE (in Britain) Member of the Order of the British Empire
Mc moscovium
MC **1** Master of Ceremonies **2** (in the US) Member of Congress **3** (in Britain) Military Cross
MCC (in Britain) Marylebone Cricket Club
MCh Master of Surgery [Latin *Magister Chirurgiae*]
Md *chem* mendelevium
MD **1** Doctor of Medicine **2** Managing Director **3** Maryland
MDF medium density fibreboard: a wood-substitute material used in interior decoration
MDMA methylenedioxymethamphetamine: the chemical name for the drug ecstasy
MDT (in the US and Canada) Mountain Daylight Time
me¹ *pron (objective)* **1** refers to the speaker or writer: *that hurts me* ▷ *n* **2** *informal* the personality of the speaker or writer or something that expresses it: *the real me* [Old English *mē*]

> **USAGE** It was formerly regarded as correct to use *I, he, she*, etc. rather than *me, him, her*, after the verb *to be*, as in: *it is I who told him.* Since both I and *me* can sound strange in a sentence like this, it is better to use a different construction: *I am the one who told him.* The use of a possessive before an *-ing* form of a verb was formerly thought to be preferable to using *me*, etc., but now both forms are acceptable: *he didn't like my/me having a job of my own.*

me² *or* **mi** *n music* (in tonic sol-fa) the third note of any ascending major scale
ME **1** Maine **2** Middle English **3** myalgic encephalomyelitis: see **chronic fatigue syndrome**
mea culpa (may-ah **cool**-pah) an acknowledgment of guilt [Latin, literally: my fault]
mead¹ *n* a wine-like alcoholic drink made from honey, often with spices added [Old English *meodu*]
mead² *n archaic or poetic* a meadow [Old English *mǣd*]
meadow *n* **1** a grassy field used for hay or for grazing animals **2** a low-lying piece of grassland, often near a river [Old English *mædwe*]
meadowsweet *n* a plant with dense heads of small fragrant cream-coloured flowers
meagre *or US* **meager** *adj* **1** not enough in amount or extent: *meagre wages* **2** thin or emaciated [Old French *maigre*]
meal¹ *n* **1** any of the regular occasions, such as breakfast or dinner, when food is served and eaten **2** the food served and eaten **3 make a meal of** *informal* to perform a task with unnecessarily great effort [Old English *mǣl* measure, set time, meal]
meal² *n* **1** the edible part of a grain or bean pulse (excluding wheat) ground to a coarse powder **2** *Scot* oatmeal **3** *chiefly US* maize flour [Old English *melu*] **mealy** *adj*
mealie *or* **mielie** *n (often pl) S African* same as **maize** [Afrikaans, from Latin *milium* millet]
meals-on-wheels *n* a service taking hot meals to elderly or disabled people in their own homes
meal ticket *n slang* a person or situation providing a source of livelihood or income [from original US sense of ticket entitling holder to a meal]

mealy-mouthed *adj* unwilling or afraid to speak plainly

mean¹ *vb* **meaning, meant 1** to intend to convey or express: *what do you mean by that?* **2** to denote, represent, or signify: *a red light means 'stop!'; 'gravid' is a technical term meaning 'pregnant'* **3** to intend: *I meant to phone you earlier, but didn't have time* **4** to say or do in all seriousness: *the boss means what she says* **5** to have the importance specified: *music means everything to him* **6** to destine or design for a certain person or purpose: *those sweets weren't meant for you* **7** to produce, cause, or result in: *major road works will mean long traffic delays* **8** to foretell: *those black clouds mean rain* **9 mean well** to have good intentions [Old English *mǣnan*]

> **USAGE** In standard English *mean* should not be followed by *for* when expressing intention: *I didn't mean this to happen* (not *I didn't mean for this to happen*).

mean² *adj* **1** not willing to give or use much of something, esp. money: *she was noticeably mean; don't be mean with the butter* **2** unkind or spiteful: *a mean trick* **3** *informal* ashamed: *she felt mean about not letting the children stay out late* **4** *informal, chiefly US, Canad & Austral* bad-tempered or vicious **5** shabby and poor: *a mean little room* **6** *slang* excellent or skilful: *he plays a mean trumpet* **7 no mean A** of high quality: *no mean player* **B** difficult: *no mean feat* [Old English *gemǣne* common] **meanly** *adv* **meanness** *n*

mean³ *n* **1** the middle point, state, or course between limits or extremes **2** *maths* **A** the mid-point between the highest and lowest number in a set **B** the average ▷ *adj* **3** intermediate in size or quantity **4** occurring halfway between extremes or limits; average [Late Latin *medianus* median]

meander (mee-and-er) *vb* **1** (of a river, road, etc.) to follow a winding course **2** to wander without definite aim or direction ▷ *n* **3** a curve or bend, as in a river **4** a winding course or movement [Greek *Maiandros* the River Maeander]

mean deviation *n* *statistics* the difference between an observed value of a variable and its mean

meanie *or* **meany** *n informal* **1** *chiefly Brit* a miserly person **2** *chiefly US* a nasty ill-tempered person

meaning *n* **1** the sense or significance of a word, sentence, or symbol **2** the inner, symbolic, or true interpretation or message: *the meaning of the New Testament*

meaningful *adj* **1** serious and important: *a meaningful relationship* **2** intended to express a feeling or opinion: *a meaningful pause*

meaningless *adj* having no meaning or purpose; futile

means *n* **1** the medium, method, or instrument used to obtain a result or achieve an end: *a means of transport* ▷ *pl n* **2** income: *a man of means* **3 by all means** without hesitation or doubt; certainly **4 by means of** with the use or help of **5 by no** *or* **not by any means** on no account; in no way

means test *n* the checking of a person's income to determine whether he or she qualifies for financial aid **means-tested** *adj*

meant *vb* the past of **mean¹**

meantime *n* **1** the intervening period: *in the meantime* ▷ *adv* **2** same as **meanwhile**

mean time *or* **mean solar time** *n* the times, at a particular place, measured so as to give 24-hour days (mean solar days) throughout a year

meanwhile *adv* **1** during the intervening period **2** at the same time, esp. in another place

meany *n, pl* **meanies** same as **meanie**

measles *n* a highly contagious viral disease common in children, characterized by fever and a rash of small red spots. See also **German measles** [Low German *masele* spot on the skin]

measly *adj* **-slier, -sliest 1** *informal* too small in quantity or value **2** having or relating to measles

measure *n* **1** the size, quantity, or degree of something, as discovered by measurement or calculation **2** a device for measuring distance, volume, etc., such as a graduated scale or container **3** a system or unit of measurement: *the joule is a measure of energy* **4** an amount of alcoholic drink, esp. that served as standard in a bar **5** degree or extent: *a measure of success* **6** a particular action intended to achieve an effect: *radical measures are needed to cut unemployment* **7** a legislative bill, act, or resolution **8** *music* same as **bar¹** (sense 9) **9** *prosody* poetic rhythm or metre **10** *prosody* a metrical foot **11** *old-fashioned* a dance **12 for good measure** as an extra precaution or beyond requirements ▷ *vb* **-suring, -sured 13** to determine the size, amount, etc., of by measurement: *he measured the room for a new carpet* **14** to indicate or record the size, speed, force, etc., of: *this dial measures the pressure in the pipe* **15** to have the size, quantity, etc., specified: *the room measures six feet* **16** to estimate or assess: *you cannot measure intelligence purely by exam results* **17** to function as a measurement of: *the ohm measures electrical resistance* **18** to bring into competition or conflict with: *he measured his strength against that of his opponent* ▷ See also **measure out, measures, measure up** [Latin *mensura*] **measurable** *adj*

measured *adj* **1** slow or stately **2** carefully considered; deliberate

measurement *n* **1** the act or process of measuring **2** an amount, extent, or size determined by measuring **3** a system or unit used for measuring: *the kilometre is the standard measurement of distance in most countries* **4 measurements** the size of a person's waist, chest, hips, etc., used when buying clothes

measure out *vb* to carefully pour or put the required amount of (something) into a container: *she measured out a large whisky*

measures *pl n* rock strata that contain a particular type of deposit: *coal measures*

measure up *vb* **1** to take the measurement of (an area): *we went round and measured up for curtains* **2 measure up to** to fulfil (expectations or standards)

measuring *adj* used to measure quantities, esp. in cooking: *a measuring jug*

meat *n* **1** the flesh of animals used as food **2** the essence or gist: *get to the meat of your lecture as quickly as possible* [Old English *mete*] **meatless** *adj*

meatball *n* minced beef, shaped into a ball before cooking

m

meaty *adj* **meatier, meatiest 1** of, like, or full of meat **2** heavily built; fleshy or brawny **3** full of import or interest: *a meaty historical drama*
Mecca *n* **1** the holy city of Islam **2** a place that attracts many visitors
mech. 1 mechanical **2** mechanics
mechanic *n* a person skilled in maintaining or operating machinery or motors [Greek *mēkhanē* machine]
mechanical *adj* **1** made, performed, or operated by machinery **2** able to understand how machines work and how to repair or maintain them **3 A** (of an action) done without thought or feeling **B** (of a task) not requiring any thought; routine or repetitive **4** of or involving the science of mechanics **mechanically** *adv*
mechanical drawing *n* a drawing to scale of a machine or architectural plan from which dimensions can be taken
mechanical engineering *n* the branch of engineering concerned with the design, construction, and operation of machines
mechanics *n* **1** the scientific study of motion and force **2** the science of designing, constructing, and operating machines ▷ *pl n* **3** the technical aspects of something
mechanism *n* **1** a system of moving parts that performs some function, esp. in a machine **2** any mechanical device or part of such a device **3** a process or technique: *the body's defence mechanisms* **mechanistic** *adj*

m

mechanize *or* **-nise** *vb* **-nizing, -nized** *or* **-nising, -nised 1** to equip a factory or industry with machinery **2** to make mechanical or automatic **3** *military* to equip an army with armoured vehicles **mechanization** *or* **-nisation** *n*
MEd Master of Education
med. 1 medical **2** medicine **3** medieval **4** medium
medal *n* a small flat piece of metal bearing an inscription or image, given as an award or in commemoration of some outstanding event [French *médaille*]
medallion *n* **1** a disc-shaped ornament worn on a chain round the neck **2** a large medal **3** a circular decorative device used in architecture [Italian *medaglia* medal]
medallist *or US* **medalist** *n* *chiefly sport* a winner of a medal or medals
meddle *vb* **-dling, -dled** to interfere annoyingly [Old French *medler*] **meddler** *n* **meddlesome** *adj*
media *n* **1** a plural of **medium 2 the media** the mass media collectively ▷ *adj* **3** of or relating to the mass media: *media hype*

> **USAGE** When *media* refers to the mass media, it is sometimes treated as a singular form, as in: *the media has shown great interest in these events.* Some people think this use is incorrect and that *media* should always be treated as a plural form: *the media have shown great interest in these events.*

mediaeval (med-ee-**eve**-al) *adj* same as **medieval**
media event *n* an event that is staged for or exploited by the mass media
medial (**mee**-dee-al) *adj* of or situated in the middle [Latin *medius* middle] **medially** *adv*
median *n* **1** a middle point, plane, or part **2** *geom* a straight line joining one corner of a triangle to the midpoint of the opposite side **3** *statistics* the middle value in a frequency distribution, below and above which lie values with equal total frequencies [Latin *medius* middle]
median strip *n US, Canad & NZ* the strip that separates the two sides of a motorway or dual carriageway
mediate (**mee**-dee-ate) *vb* **-ating, -ated 1** to intervene between people or in a dispute in order to bring about agreement **2** to resolve differences by mediation **3** to be changed slightly by (an experience or event): *clients' attitudes to social workers have often been mediated by their past experiences* [Late Latin *mediare* to be in the middle] **mediation** *n* **mediator** *n*
medic *n informal* a doctor, medical orderly, or medical student [from MEDICAL]
medical *adj* **1** of or relating to the science of medicine or to the treatment of patients without surgery ▷ *n* **2** *informal* a medical examination [Latin *medicus* physician] **medically** *adv*
medical certificate *n* **1** a doctor's certificate giving evidence of a person's unfitness for work **2** a document stating the result of a satisfactory medical examination
medicament (mid-**dik**-a-ment) *n* a medicine
medicate *vb* **-cating, -cated 1** to treat a patient with a medicine **2** to add a medication to a bandage, shampoo, etc. [Latin *medicare* to heal] **medicative** *adj*
medication *n* **1** treatment with drugs or remedies **2** a drug or remedy
medicinal (mid-**diss**-in-al) *adj* relating to or having therapeutic properties **medicinally** *adv*
medicine *n* **1** any substance used in treating or alleviating the symptoms of disease **2** the science of preventing, diagnosing, or curing disease **3** any nonsurgical branch of medical science **4 take one's medicine** to accept a deserved punishment [Latin *medicina (ars)* (art) of healing]
medicine man *n* (among certain peoples) a person believed to have supernatural powers of healing
medico *n, pl* **-cos** *informal* a doctor or medical student
medieval *or* **mediaeval** (med-ee-**eve**-al) *adj* **1** of, relating to, or in the style of the Middle Ages **2** *informal* old-fashioned or primitive [New Latin *medium aevum* the middle age] **medievalist** *or* **mediaevalist** *n*
Medieval Greek *n* the Greek language from the 7th to 13th century AD
Medieval Latin *n* the Latin language as used throughout Europe in the Middle Ages
mediocre (mee-dee-**oak**-er) *adj* not very high quality; average or second rate [Latin *mediocris* moderate] **mediocrity** (mee-dee-**ok**-rit-ee) *n*
meditate *vb* **-tating, -tated 1** to think about something deeply: *he meditated on the problem* **2** to reflect deeply on spiritual matters **3** to plan, consider, or think of doing something [Latin *meditari* to reflect upon] **meditative** *adj* **meditator** *n*

meditation *n* **1** the act of meditating; reflection **2** contemplation of spiritual matters, esp. as a religious practice

Mediterranean *adj* of the Mediterranean Sea, lying between S Europe, N Africa, and SW Asia, or the surrounding region [Latin *medius* middle + *terra* land]

medium *adj* **1** midway between extremes of size, amount, or degree: *fry over a medium heat; a man of medium height* ▷ *n, pl* **-dia** *or* **-diums 2** a middle state, degree, or condition: *the happy medium* **3** a substance which has a particular effect or can be used for a particular purpose: *linseed oil is used as a thinning medium for oil paint* **4** a means for communicating information or news to the public **5** a person who can supposedly communicate with the dead **6** the substance or surroundings in which an organism naturally lives or grows **7** *art* the category of a work of art, as determined by its materials: *his works in the photographic medium* [Latin *medius* middle]

USAGE See at **media**.

medium wave *n* a radio wave with a wavelength between 100 and 1000 metres

medlar *n* the apple-like fruit of a small Eurasian tree, which is not edible until it has begun to decay [Old French *medlier*]

medley *n* **1** a mixture of various elements **2** a musical composition consisting of various tunes arranged as a continuous whole **3** *swimming* a race in which a different stroke is used for each length [Old French, from *medler* to mix, quarrel]

medulla (mid-**dull**-la) *n, pl* **-las** *or* **-lae** (-lee) **1** *anatomy* the innermost part of an organ or structure **2** *anatomy* the lower stalklike section of the brain **3** *botany* the central pith of a plant stem [Latin: marrow] **medullary** *adj*

medusa (mid-**dew**-za) *n, pl* **-sas** *or* **-sae** (-zee) jellyfish [*Medusa*, in Greek mythology, who had snakes for hair]

meek *adj* quiet, and ready to do what other people say [related to Old Norse *mjūkr* amenable] **meekly** *adv*

meerkat *n* a South African mongoose [Dutch: sea-cat]

meerschaum (**meer**-shum) *n* **1** a white, heat-resistant, claylike mineral **2** a tobacco pipe with a bowl made of this mineral [German *Meerschaum*, literally: sea foam]

meet[1] *vb* **meeting, met 1** to be in or come to the same place at the same time as, either by arrangement or by accident: *I met him in town* **2** to come into contact with something or each other: *his head met the ground with a crack; the town where the Rhine and the Moselle meet* **3** to come to or be at the place of arrival of: *he met his train at noon* **4** to make the acquaintance of, or be introduced to, someone or each other **5** (of people) to gather together for a purpose: *the board meets once a week* **6** to compete, play, or fight against **7** to cope with effectively; satisfy: *they were unable to meet his demands* **8** to pay for (something): *it is difficult to meet the cost of medical insurance* **9** Also: **meet with** to experience or suffer: *he met his death at the Somme* **10 there is more to this than meets the eye** there is more involved in this than appears ▷ *n* **11** a sports meeting **12** *chiefly Brit* the assembly of hounds and huntsmen prior to a hunt [Old English *mētan*]

meet[2] *adj archaic* proper, fitting, or correct: *meet and proper* [Old English *gemǣte*]

meeting *n* **1** an act of coming together: *a meeting was fixed for the following day* **2** an assembly or gathering of people: *the meeting voted in favour* **3** a sporting competition, as of athletes, or of horse racing

meg *n computers informal* short for **megabyte**

mega *adj slang* extremely good, great, or successful

mega- *combining form* **1** denoting 10^6: *megawatt* **2** (in computer technology) denoting 2^{20} (1 048 576): *megabyte* **3** large or great: *megalith* **4** *informal* very great: *megastar* [Greek *megas* huge, powerful]

megabyte *n computers* 2^{20} or 1 048 576 bytes

megadeath *n* the death of a million people, esp. in a nuclear war or attack

megahertz *n, pl* **megahertz** one million hertz; one million cycles per second

megajoule *n* one million joules

megalith *n* a very large stone, esp. one forming part of a prehistoric monument **megalithic** *adj*

megalomania *n* **1** an obsessional delusion of power and importance **2** *informal* a craving for power [Greek *megas* great + *mania* madness] **megalomaniac** *adj, n*

megaphone *n* a funnel-shaped instrument used to make someone's voice sound louder, esp. out of doors

megapixel *n* one million pixels: used to describe the resolution of digital images

megapode *n* any of various ground-living birds of Australia, New Guinea, and adjacent islands. Their eggs incubate in mounds of sand or rotting vegetation [Greek *megas* great + *-podos* -footed]

megaton *n* **1** one million tons **2** an explosive power, esp. of a nuclear weapon, equal to the power of one million tons of TNT

megavolt *n* one million volts

megawatt *n* one million watts

meiosis (my-**oh**-siss) *n, pl* **-ses** (-seez) a type of cell division in which reproductive cells are produced, each containing half the chromosome number of the parent nucleus [Greek *meiōn* less]

meitnerium *n chem* an element artificially produced in small quantities by high-energy ion bombardment. Symbol: **Mt** [after Lise *Meitner*, physicist]

melaleuca (mel-a-**loo**-ka) *n* an Australian shrub or tree with a white trunk and black branches [Greek *melas* black + *leukos* white]

melamine *n* a colourless crystalline compound used in making synthetic resins [German *Melamin*]

melancholia (mel-an-**kole**-lee-a) *n* an old name for **depression** (sense 1)

melancholy (**mel**-an-kol-lee) *n, pl* **-cholies 1** a tendency to gloominess or depression **2** a sad, thoughtful state of mind ▷ *adj* **3** characterized by, causing, or expressing sadness [Greek *melas* black + *kholē* bile] **melancholic** *adj, n*

melange (may-**lahnzh**) *n* a mixture or assortment: *a melange of historical facts and legends* [French *mêler* to mix]

m

melanin *n* a black pigment present in the hair, skin, and eyes of humans and animals [Greek *melas* black]
melanoma *n, pl* **-mas** *or* **-mata** *pathol* a tumour composed of dark-coloured cells, occurring in some skin cancers [Greek *melas* black + *-oma*, modelled on *carcinoma*]
Melba toast *n* very thin crisp toast [after Dame Nellie *Melba*, singer]
meld *vb* to merge or blend [blend of *melt* + *weld*]
melee (mel-lay) *n* a noisy riotous fight or crowd [French, from *mêler* to mix]
mellifluous (mel-lif-flew-uss) *adj* (of sound) smooth and sweet [Latin *mel* honey + *fluere* to flow]
mellow *adj* **1** (esp. of colours, light, or sounds) soft or rich: *the mellow stillness of a sunny Sunday morning* **2** kind-hearted, esp. through maturity or old age **3** genial and relaxed, for instance through the effects of alcohol or good food **4** (esp. of fruits) sweet, ripe, and full-flavoured **5** (esp. of wine or cheese) having developed a full smooth flavour as a result of maturing **6** (of soil) soft and loamy ▷ *vb* **7** to make or become mellow **8** (foll. by *out*) to make or become calm and relaxed [origin unknown]
melodeon *n* **1** a small accordion **2** a keyboard instrument like a harmonium [German *Melodie* melody]
melodic (mel-lod-ik) *adj* **1** of or relating to melody **2** tuneful and pleasant to the ear; melodious **melodically** *adv*
melodious (mel-lode-ee-uss) *adj* **1** pleasant to the ear: *he gave a melodious chuckle* **2** tuneful and melodic **melodiousness** *n*
melodrama *n* **1** a play or film full of extravagant action and emotion **2** overdramatic emotion or behaviour [Greek *melos* song + *drama* drama] **melodramatic** *adj* **melodramatics** *pl n*
melody *n, pl* **-dies** **1** *music* a succession of notes forming a distinctive sequence; tune **2** sounds that are pleasant because of their tone or arrangement, esp. words of poetry [Greek *melōidia*]
melon *n* any of various large edible fruits which have a hard rind and juicy flesh [Greek *mēlon* apple]
Melpomene (mel-pom-in-nee) *n Greek myth* the Muse of tragedy
melt *vb* **1** to change from a solid into a liquid as a result of the action of heat **2** to dissolve: *these sweets melt in the mouth* **3** Also: **melt away** to diminish and finally disappear; fade away: *he felt his inner doubts melt away* **4** to blend so that it is impossible to tell where one thing ends and another begins: *they melted into the trees until the gamekeeper had passed* **5** to make or become emotional or sentimental; soften: *she melted into tears* ▷ *n* **6** a quantity of a melted substance **7** *US & Canad* a sandwich containing and melted cheese: *a tuna melt* [Old English *meltan* to digest] **meltingly** *adv*
meltdown *n* **1** (in a nuclear reactor) the melting of the fuel rods, with the possible escape of radioactivity **2** *informal* a sudden disastrous failure **3** *informal* a process of irreversible decline
melting point *n* the temperature at which a solid turns into a liquid
melting pot *n* a place or situation in which many races, ideas, etc., are mixed
meltwater *n* melted snow or ice
member *n* **1** a person who belongs to a group or organization such as a club or political party **2** any part of a plant or animal, such as a limb or petal **3** a Member of Parliament: *the member for Glasgow Central* ▷ *adj* **4** (of a country or group) belonging to an organization or alliance: *a summit of the member countries' heads of state is due* [Latin *membrum* limb, part]
Member of Parliament *n* a person who has been elected to the House of Commons or the equivalent assembly in another country
membership *n* **1** the members of an organization collectively **2** the number of members **3** the state of being a member
membrane *n* a thin flexible tissue that covers, lines, or connects plant and animal organs or cells [Latin *membrana* skin covering a part of the body] **membranous** *adj*
meme *n* a video, photo, or story that is spread widely on the internet, often altered by users for humorous effect [perhaps from *mimic*, on the model of *gene*]
memento *n, pl* **-tos** *or* **-toes** something that reminds one of past events; a souvenir [Latin, imperative of *meminisse* to remember]
memento mori *n, pl* **memento mori** an object intended to remind people of death [Latin: remember you must die]
memo *n, pl* **memos** short for **memorandum**
memoir (mem-wahr) *n* a biography or historical account based on personal knowledge [Latin *memoria* memory]
memoirs *pl n* **1** a collection of reminiscences about a period or series of events, written from personal experience **2** an autobiography
memorabilia *pl n, sing* **-rabile** objects connected with famous people or events
memorable *adj* worth remembering or easily remembered because it is very special or important [Latin *memorare* to remember] **memorably** *adv*
memorandum *n, pl* **-dums** *or* **-da** **1** a note sent by one person or department to another within a business organization **2** a note of things to be remembered **3** *law* a short written summary of the terms of a transaction [Latin: (something) to be remembered]
memorial *n* **1** something, such as a statue, built or displayed to preserve the memory of someone or something: *a war memorial* ▷ *adj* **2** in memory of someone or something: *a memorial service* [Late Latin *memoriale* a reminder]
memorize *or* **-rise** *vb* **-rizing, -rized** *or* **-rising, -rised** to commit to memory; learn by heart
memory *n, pl* **-ries** **1** the ability of the mind to store and recall past sensations, thoughts, and knowledge: *she can do it from memory* **2** the sum of everything retained by the mind **3** a particular recollection of an event or person: *he started awake with a sudden memory* **4** the length of time one can remember: *my memory doesn't go that far back*

5 commemoration: *in memory of our leader* **6** a person's reputation after death: *a conductor of fond memory* **7** a part of a computer in which information is stored [Latin *memoria*]

memory card *n* a small removable data storage device, used in mobile phones, digital cameras, etc.

Memory Stick *n computers* **1** *trademark* a standard format for memory cards **2 memory stick** also: **USB memory stick** same as **USB drive**

memsahib *n* (formerly, in India) a term of respect used for a European married woman [*ma'am + sahib*]

men *n* the plural of **man**

menace *vb* **-acing, -aced 1** to threaten with violence or danger ▷ *n* **2** a threat; a source of danger **3** *informal* an annoying person or thing; nuisance [Latin *minax* threatening] **menacing** *adj*

ménage (may-**nahzh**) *n* a household [French]

ménage à trois (ah **trwah**) *n, pl* **ménages à trois** a sexual arrangement involving a married couple and the lover of one of them [French, literally: household of three]

menagerie (min-**naj**-er-ee) *n* a collection of wild animals kept for exhibition [French]

mend *vb* **1** to repair something broken or not working **2** to heal or recover: *a wound like that will take a while to mend* **3** (esp. of behaviour) to improve; make or become better: *if you don't mend your ways you'll be in serious trouble* ▷ *n* **4** a mended area, esp. on a garment **5 on the mend** regaining one's health [from *amend*]

mendacity *n* the tendency to be untruthful [Latin *mendax* untruthful] **mendacious** *adj*

mendelevium *n chem* an artificially produced radioactive element. Symbol: **Md** [after D. I. *Mendeleyev*, chemist]

Mendel's laws *pl n* the principles of heredity proposed by Gregor Mendel (1822–84), Austrian monk and botanist **Mendelism** *n*

mendicant *adj* **1** begging **2** (of a monk, nun, etc.) dependent on charity for food ▷ *n* **3** a mendicant friar **4** a beggar [Latin *mendicus* beggar]

menfolk *pl n* men collectively, esp. the men of a particular family

menhir (**men**-hear) *n* a single standing stone, dating from prehistoric times [Breton *men* stone + *hir* long]

menial (**mean**-nee-al) *adj* **1** involving or doing boring work of low status ▷ *n* **2** a domestic servant [Old French *meinie* household]

meninges (min-**in**-jeez) *pl n, sing* **meninx** (**mean**-inks) the three membranes that surround the brain and spinal cord [Greek, plural of *meninx* membrane]

meningitis (men-in-**jite**-iss) *n* inflammation of the meninges, caused by infection and causing severe headache, fever, and rigidity of the neck muscles

meniscus *n, pl* **-nisci** *or* **-niscuses 1** the curved upper surface of a liquid standing in a tube, produced by the surface tension **2** a crescent-shaped lens [Greek *mēniskos* crescent]

menopause *n* the period during which a woman's menstrual cycle ceases, normally at an age of 45 to 50 [Greek *mēn* month + *pausis* halt] **menopausal** *adj*

menorah (min-**or**-a) *n Judaism* a seven-branched candelabrum used as an emblem of Judaism [Hebrew: candlestick]

menses (**men**-seez) *n* same as **menstruation** [Latin, plural of *mensis* month]

menstrual *adj* of or relating to menstruation: *the menstrual cycle*

menstruate *vb* **-ating, -ated** to undergo menstruation [Latin *menstruare*, from *mensis* month]

menstruation *n* the approximately monthly discharge of blood from the womb in women of childbearing age who are not pregnant

mensuration *n* **1** the study of the measurement of geometric magnitudes such as length **2** the act or process of measuring [Latin *mensura* measure]

menswear *n* clothing for men

mental *adj* **1** of, done by, or involving the mind: *mental alertness* **2** done in the mind without using speech or writing: *mental arithmetic* **3** affected by mental health problems: *a mental patient* **4** concerned with the care of people with mental health problems: *a mental hospital* **5** *slang* extremely foolish or eccentric [Latin *mens* mind] **mentally** *adv*

> **USAGE** When talking about mental health problems, the term *psychiatric* is preferred: *a psychiatric hospital*.

mental age *n* the age which a person is considered to have reached in thinking ability, judged by comparing his or her ability with the average for people of various ages

mental handicap *n old-fashioned, offensive* any intellectual disability resulting from injury to or abnormal development of the brain **mentally handicapped** *adj*

mental illness *n* any of various disorders in which a person's thoughts, emotions, or behaviour are disordered and can cause suffering to himself, herself, or other people

mentality *n, pl* **-ties** a particular attitude or way of thinking: *the traditional civil service mentality*

menthol *n* an organic compound found in peppermint oil and used as an antiseptic, decongestant, and painkiller [Latin *mentha* mint] **mentholated** *adj*

mention *vb* **1** to refer to or speak about briefly or incidentally **2** to include in a report, list, etc., because of high standards or an outstanding achievement: *the hotel is mentioned in all the guidebooks; he was twice mentioned in dispatches during the war* **3 not to mention (something)** to say nothing of (something too obvious to mention) ▷ *n* **4** a slight reference or allusion **5** a recognition or acknowledgment of high quality or an outstanding achievement [Latin *mentio* a calling to mind]

mentor *n* an adviser or guide [*Mentor*, adviser of Telemachus in Homer's *Odyssey*]

menu *n* **1** a list of dishes served at a meal or that can be ordered in a restaurant **2** a list of options displayed on a visual display unit from which the operator can choose [French: small, detailed (list)]

meow or **miaow** (mee-ow) *n* **1** the characteristic high-pitched cry of a cat; mew ▷ *vb* **2** to make such a sound

MEP Member of the European Parliament

Mephistopheles (mef-iss-**stoff**-ill-eez) *n* a devil in medieval mythology to whom Faust sold his soul **Mephistophelean** *adj*

mercantile *adj* of trade or traders; commercial [Italian *mercànte* merchant]

Mercator projection (mer-**kate**-er) *n* a way of drawing maps in which latitude and longitude form a rectangular grid, scale being exaggerated with increasing distance from the equator [after G. *Mercator*, cartographer]

mercenary *n, pl* **-naries 1** a soldier who fights for a foreign army for money ▷ *adj* **2** motivated by greed or the desire for gain: *calculating and mercenary businesspeople* **3** of or relating to a mercenary or mercenaries [Latin *merces* wages]

mercerized or **-rised** *adj* (of cotton) treated with an alkali to make it strong and shiny [after John *Mercer*, maker of textiles]

merchandise *n* **1** goods for buying, selling, or trading with; commodities ▷ *vb* **-dising, -dised 2** to engage in the commercial purchase and sale of goods or services; trade

merchandising *n* **1** the selection and display of goods in a retail outlet **2** commercial goods, esp. ones issued to exploit the popularity of a pop group, sporting event, etc.

m

merchant *n* **1** a person who buys and sells goods in large quantities and usually of one type: *a wine merchant* **2** *chiefly Scot, US & Canad* a person engaged in retail trade; shopkeeper **3** *slang* a person dealing in something undesirable: *a gossip merchant* ▷ *adj* **4** of ships involved in commercial trade or their crews: *a merchant sailor; the British merchant fleet* [Latin *mercari* to trade]

merchant bank *n* a financial institution that deals primarily with foreign trade and business finance **merchant banker** *n*

merchantman *n, pl* **-men** a merchant ship

merchant navy *n* the ships or crew engaged in a nation's commercial shipping

merciful *adj* **1** (of an act or event) giving relief from pain or suffering: *after months of illness, death came as a merciful release* **2** showing or giving mercy; compassionate **mercifully** *adv*

merciless *adj* without mercy; pitiless, cruel, or heartless **mercilessly** *adv*

mercurial (mer-**cure**-ee-al) *adj* **1** lively and unpredictable: *a mercurial and temperamental chess player* **2** of or containing mercury [Latin *mercurialis*]

mercuric *adj* of or containing mercury in the divalent state

mercurous *adj* of or containing mercury in the monovalent state

mercury *n, pl* **-ries** *chem* a silvery toxic metal, the only element liquid at normal temperatures, used in thermometers, barometers, lamps, and dental amalgams. Symbol: **Hg** [Latin *Mercurius*, messenger of Jupiter]

Mercury *n* **1** *Roman myth* the messenger of the gods **2** the second smallest planet and the one nearest the sun

mercy *n, pl* **-cies 1** compassionate treatment of, or attitude towards, an offender or enemy who is in one's power **2** the power to show mercy: *they threw themselves on the King's mercy* **3** a relieving or welcome occurrence or act: *it was a mercy you turned up when you did* **4 at the mercy of** in the power of ▷ *adj* **5** done or undertaken in an attempt to relieve suffering or bring help: *a mercy mission* [Latin *merces* recompense]

mercy killing *n* same as **euthanasia**

mere[1] *adj* nothing more than: *the election in Slovenia seems a mere formality* [Latin *merus* pure] **merely** *adv*

mere[2] *n Brit dialect or archaic* a lake [Old English: sea, lake]

meretricious *adj* superficially or garishly attractive but of no real value [Latin *meretrix* prostitute]

merganser (mer-**gan**-ser) *n, pl* **-sers** or **-ser** a large crested marine diving duck [Latin *mergere* to plunge + *anser* goose]

merge *vb* **merging, merged 1** to combine, esp. so as to become part of a larger whole: *the two airlines merged in 1983* **2** to blend gradually, without any sudden change being apparent: *late afternoon merged imperceptibly into early evening* [Latin *mergere* to plunge]

merger *n* the act of merging, esp. the combination of two or more companies

meridian *n* **1** one of the imaginary lines joining the north and south poles at right angles to the equator, designated by degrees of longitude from 0° at Greenwich to 180° **2** (in acupuncture, etc.) any of various channels through which vital energy is believed to circulate round the body [Latin *meridies* midday]

meridional *adj* **1** of or along a meridian **2** of or in the south, esp. the south of Europe

meringue (mer-**rang**) *n* **1** stiffly beaten egg whites mixed with sugar and baked **2** a small cake made from this mixture [French]

merino *n, pl* **-nos 1** a sheep with long fine wool, originally reared in Spain **2** the yarn made from this wool [Spanish]

merit *n* **1** worth or superior quality; excellence: *the film had two sequels, neither of much merit* **2** an admirable or advantageous quality: *the relative merits of film and video as a medium of communication* **3 have the merit of** to have a positive feature or advantage that the alternatives do not have: *the first version has the merit of being short* **4 on its merits** on its intrinsic qualities or virtues ▷ *vb* **-riting, -rited 5** to be worthy of; deserve: *the issue merits much fuller discussion* [Latin *meritum* reward]

meritocracy (mer-it-**tok**-rass-ee) *n, pl* **-cies** a social system in which power is held by the most talented or intelligent people **meritocrat** *n* **meritocratic** *adj*

meritorious *adj* deserving praise for being good or worthwhile [Latin *meritorius* earning money]

merlin *n* a small falcon with dark plumage [Old French *esmerillon*]

mermaid *n* an imaginary sea creature with a woman's head and upper body and a fish's tail [*mere* sea + *maid*] **merman** *masc n*

merry *adj* **-rier, -riest 1** cheerful and jolly **2** *Brit & Austral informal* slightly drunk **3 make merry** to

take part in noisy cheerful celebrations or fun [Old English *merige* agreeable] **merrily** *adv* **merriment** *n*
merry-go-round *n* **1** a fairground roundabout **2** a whirl of activity
merrymaking *n* noisy cheerful celebrations or fun **merrymaker** *n*
mesa *n* a flat-topped hill found in arid regions [Spanish: table]
mésalliance (mez-**zal**-ee-anss) *n* a marriage with a person of lower social status [French]
mescal (mess-**kal**) *n* **1** a globe-shaped cactus without spines found in Mexico and the southwestern US **2** a Mexican alcoholic spirit similar to tequila [Mexican Indian *mexcalli*]
mescaline *n* a hallucinogenic drug derived from the button-like top of the mescal cactus
mesdames (may-**dam**) *n* the plural of **madame**, **madam** (sense 1)
mesdemoiselles (maid-mwah-**zel**) *n* the plural of **mademoiselle**
mesembryanthemum *n* a low-growing plant with fleshy leaves and bright daisy-like flowers [Greek *mesēmbria* noon + *anthemon* flower]
mesh *n* **1** a material resembling a net made from intersecting strands with a space between each strand **2** an open space between the strands of a net or network: *the minimum permitted size of fishing net mesh* **3** (*often pl*) the strands surrounding these spaces **4** anything that ensnares or holds like a net ▷ *adj* **5** made from mesh: *a wire mesh fence* ▷ *vb* **6** to entangle or become entangled **7** (of gear teeth) to engage or interlock **8** to fit together closely or work in harmony: *she schedules her holidays to mesh with theirs* [probably Dutch *maesche*]
mesmerize *or* **-ise** *vb* **-izing, -ized** *or* **-ising, -ised** **1** to fascinate and hold spellbound: *his voice had the entire audience mesmerized* **2** *archaic* to hypnotize **mesmerism** *n* **mesmerizing** *adj*
Mesolithic (mess-oh-**lith**-ik) *adj* of the middle period of the Stone Age, in Europe from about 12 000 to 3000 BC [Greek *mesos* middle + *lithos* stone]
mesomorph *n physiol* a person with a muscular body build. See also **ectomorph, endomorph** [Greek *mesos* middle + *morphē* shape] **mesomorphic** *adj*
meson (**mee**-zon) *n physics* any of a group of elementary particles that has a mass between those of an electron and a proton [Greek *mesos* middle + *-on*, indicating an elementary particle]
mesosphere (**mess**-oh-sfeer) *n* the atmospheric layer above the stratosphere
Mesozoic (mess-oh-**zoh**-ik) *adj geol* of the geological era that began 225 million years ago and lasted about 155 million years, during which the dinosaurs emerged, flourished, then became extinct [Greek *mesos* middle + *zōion* animal]
mess *n* **1** a state of untidiness or confusion, esp. a dirty or unpleasant one: *the house was in a mess* **2** a confused and difficult situation; muddle: *the firm is in a terrible financial mess* **3** *informal* a dirty or untidy person or thing: *there was a nasty burnt mess in the saucepan* **4** a building providing catering, and sometimes recreation, facilities for service personnel **5** a group of service personnel who regularly eat together **6** *old-fashioned* a portion of soft or runny food: *a mess of pottage* ▷ *vb* **7** (of service personnel) to eat in a group ▷ See also **mess about, mess up, mess with** [Old French *mes* dish of food]
mess about *or* **mess around** *vb* **1** to pass the time doing trivial or silly things without any particular purpose or plan: *messing about in boats* **2** to interfere or meddle: *you have no business messing around here* **3** *chiefly US* to engage in adultery
message *n* **1** a communication from one person or group to another **2** an implicit meaning or moral, as in a work of art **3** a religious or political belief that someone attempts to communicate to others: *paintings with a fierce feminist message* **4 get the message** *informal* to understand [Old French, from Latin *mittere* to send]
message board *n* an internet discussion forum
messages *pl n Scot & Irish dialect* household shopping
messaging *n* the sending of a message by any form of electronic communication: *text messaging*
messenger *n* a person who takes messages from one person or group to another [Old French *messagier*]
Messiah *n* **1** *Judaism* the awaited king of the Jews, who will be sent by God to free them **2** *Christianity* Jesus Christ, when regarded in this role **3** a liberator of a country or people [Hebrew *māshīach* anointed]
Messianic *adj* **1** of or relating to a Messiah, or the arrival on Earth of a Messiah **2 messianic** of or relating to the belief that someone or something will bring about a complete transformation of the existing social order: *a messianic zeal for the free market*
messieurs (may-**syuh**) *n* the plural of **monsieur**
mess jacket *n* a waist-length jacket, worn by officers in the mess for formal dinners
mess kit *n* a soldier's eating utensils for use in the field
Messrs (**mess**-erz) *n* the plural of **Mr**
mess up *vb informal* **1** to make untidy or dirty **2** to spoil something, or do something badly: *he messed up his driving test*
mess with *vb informal, chiefly US* to interfere in, or become involved with, a dangerous person, thing, or situation: *he had started messing with drugs*
messy *adj* **messier, messiest** **1** untidy **2** dirty **3** unpleasantly confused or complicated: *the messy, uncontrollable world of real life* **messily** *adv* **messiness** *n*
met *vb* the past of **meet**¹
Met *adj* **1** Meteorological: *the Met Office* ▷ *n* **2 the Met** the Metropolitan Police, who operate in London
metabolic syndrome *n* a condition associated with obesity, which increases the risk of cardiovascular disease and diabetes
metabolism (met-**tab**-ol-liz-zum) *n* the chemical processes that occur in living organisms, resulting in growth, production of energy, and elimination of waste [Greek *metaballein* to change] **metabolic** *adj*
metabolize *or* **-lise** *vb* **-lizing, -lized** *or* **-lising, -lised** to produce or be produced by metabolism

m

metacarpus *n, pl* **-pi** the set of five long bones in the hand between the wrist and the fingers [Greek *meta* after + *karpos* wrist] **metacarpal** *adj, n*
metal *n* **1** **A** *chem* a chemical element, such as iron or copper, that reflects light and can be shaped, forms positive ions, and is a good conductor of heat and electricity **B** an alloy, such as brass or steel, containing one or more of these elements **2** short for **road metal** **3** *informal* short for **heavy metal** **4** **metals** the rails of a railway ▷ *adj* **5** made of metal [Greek *metallon* mine]
metalanguage *n* the language or system of symbols used to discuss another language or system
metalled *or US* **metaled** *adj* (of a road) surfaced with crushed rock or small stones: *a metalled driveway*
metallic *adj* **1** of or consisting of metal **2** sounding like two pieces of metal hitting each other: *a metallic click* **3** (of a voice) harsh, unpleasant, and unemotional **4** shining like metal: *metallic paint* **5** (of a taste) unpleasantly harsh and bitter
metalliferous *adj* containing a metallic element [Latin *metallum* metal + *ferre* to bear]
metallography *n* the study of the composition and structure of metals
metalloid *n* *chem* a nonmetallic element, such as arsenic or silicon, that has some of the properties of a metal
metallurgy *n* the scientific study of the structure, properties, extraction, and refining of metals [*metal* + Greek *-urgia*, from *ergon* work] **metallurgical** *adj* **metallurgist** *n*
metal road *n NZ* an unsealed road covered in gravel
metalwork *n* **1** the craft of making articles from metal **2** articles made from metal **3** the metal part of something **metalworker** *n*
metamorphic *adj* **1** (of rocks) altered considerably from the original structure and composition by pressure and heat **2** of metamorphosis or metamorphism
metamorphism *n* the process by which metamorphic rocks are formed
metamorphose *vb* **-phosing, -phosed** to change from one state or thing into something different: *laughter which metamorphosed into sobs*
metamorphosis (met-a-mor-foss-is) *n, pl* **-ses** (-seez) **1** a complete change of physical form or substance **2** a complete change of character or appearance **3** *zool* the change of form that accompanies transformation into an adult in certain animals, for example the butterfly or frog [Greek: transformation, from *meta* after + *morphē* form]
metaphor *n* a figure of speech in which a word or phrase is applied to an object or action that it does not literally apply to in order to imply a resemblance, for example *he is a lion in battle* [Greek *metapherein* to transfer] **metaphorical** *adj* **metaphorically** *adv*
metaphysical *adj* **1** of metaphysics **2** abstract, abstruse, or unduly theoretical
Metaphysical *adj* denoting certain 17th-century poets who combined intense feeling with elaborate imagery
metaphysics *n* **1** the philosophical study of the nature of reality **2** abstract or subtle discussion or reasoning [Greek *ta meta ta phusika* the things after the physics, from the arrangement of subjects treated in the works of Aristotle]
metastasis (mit-tass-tiss-iss) *n, pl* **-ses** (-seez) **1** *pathol* the spreading of a disease, esp. cancer, from one part of the body to another **2** the spreading of a problem into new areas [Greek: transition] **metastasize** *or* **-sise** *vb*
metatarsus *n, pl* **-si** the set of five long bones in the foot between the toes and the ankle [Greek *meta* after + *tarsos* instep] **metatarsal** *adj, n*
metathesis (mit-tath-iss-iss) *n, pl* **-ses** (-seez) the transposition of two sounds or letters in a word [Greek *metatithenai* to transpose]
metazoan (met-a-zoh-an) *n* **1** any animal having a body composed of many cells: includes all animals except sponges and protozoans ▷ *adj* **2** of the metazoans [New Latin *Metazoa*]
meteor *n* **1** a small piece of rock or metal that has entered the earth's atmosphere from space **2** Also: **shooting star** the bright streak of light appearing in the sky due to a piece of rock or metal burning up because of friction as it falls through the atmosphere [Greek *meteōros* lofty]
meteoric (meet-ee-or-rik) *adj* **1** of or relating to meteors **2** brilliant and very rapid: *his meteoric rise to power* **meteorically** *adv*
meteorite *n* the rocklike remains of a meteoroid that has collided with the earth
meteoroid *n* any of the small celestial bodies that are thought to orbit the sun. When they enter the earth's atmosphere, they become visible as meteors
meteorol. *or* **meteor.** **1** meteorological **2** meteorology
meteorology *n* the study of the earth's atmosphere and weather-forming processes, esp. for weather forecasting **meteorological** *adj* **meteorologist** *n*
mete out *vb* **meting, meted** to impose or deal out something, usually something unpleasant: *the sentence meted out to him has proved controversial* [Old English *metan* to measure]
meter[1] *n* **1** any device that measures and records the quantity or number of units of something that was used during a specified period or is being used at that moment: *a gas meter* **2** short for **parking meter** **3** short for **taximeter** ▷ *vb* **4** to measure the amount of something used, or a rate of flow, with a meter [Old English *metan* to measure]
meter[2] *n US* same as **metre**[1] or **metre**[2]
-meter *combining form* **1** indicating an instrument for measuring: *barometer* **2** *prosody* indicating a verse having a specified number of feet: *pentameter* [Greek *metron* measure]
meth *n informal* short for **methamphetamine**
methadone *n* a drug similar to morphine, sometimes prescribed as a heroin substitute [*(di)meth(yl)* + *a(mino)* + *d(iphenyl)* + *-one*, indicating a ketone]
methamphetamine *n* a variety of amphetamine used for its stimulant action

methanal *n* same as **formaldehyde**
methane *n* a colourless odourless flammable gas, the main constituent of natural gas [*meth(yl)* + *-ane*, indicating an alkane]
methane series *n chem* a series of saturated hydrocarbons with the general formula C_nH_{2n+2}
methanol *n* a colourless poisonous liquid used as a solvent and fuel. Also: **methyl alcohol** [*methane* + *-ol*, indicating alcohol]
methicillin *n* a semisynthetic penicillin used to treat various infections
methinks *vb, past tense* **methought** *archaic* it seems to me that
method *n* **1** a way of doing something, esp. a systematic or regular one **2** orderliness of thought or action **3** the techniques of a particular field or subject [Greek *methodos*, literally: a going after]
Method *n* an acting technique in which the actor bases his or her role on the inner motivation of the character played
methodical *adj* careful, well-organized, and systematic **methodically** *adv*
Methodist *n* **1** a member of any of the Christian Nonconformist denominations that derive from the beliefs and practices of John Wesley and his followers ▷ *adj* **2** of or relating to Methodists or their Church **Methodism** *n*
methodology *n, pl* **-gies 1** the system of methods and principles used in a particular discipline **2** the philosophical study of method **methodological** *adj*
methought *vb archaic* the past tense of **methinks**
meths *n Brit, Austral & NZ informal* methylated spirits
methyl *adj* of or containing the monovalent saturated hydrocarbon group of atoms CH_3: *methyl mercury* [from *methylene*]
methyl alcohol *n* same as **methanol**
methylate *vb* **-ating, -ated** to mix with methanol
methylated spirits *n* alcohol that has been rendered undrinkable by the addition of methanol and a violet dye, used as a solvent or as a fuel for small lamps or heaters. Also: **methylated spirit**
methylene *adj* of, consisting of, or containing the divalent group of atoms $-CH_2-$: *a methylene group or radical* [Greek *methu* wine + *hulē* wood + *-ene*, indicating a double bond]
meticulous *adj* very precise about details; careful and thorough [Latin *meticulosus* fearful] **meticulously** *adv* **meticulousness** *n*
métier (met-ee-ay) *n* **1** a profession or trade **2** a person's strong point or speciality [French]
Métis (met-teess) *n, pl* **-tis** (-teess, -teez) a person of mixed parentage, esp. the offspring of a Native American and a French Canadian [French] **Métisse** *fem n*
metonymy (mit-on-im-ee) *n, pl* **-mies** a figure of speech in which one thing is replaced by another associated with it, for instance the use of *Downing Street* to mean *the British government* [Greek *meta-*, indicating change + *onoma* name]
metre¹ *or US* **meter** *n* the basic SI unit of length, equal to 100 centimetres (39.37 inches): *the majority of people are between one and a half and two metres tall* [same as METRE²]
metre² *or US* **meter** *n* **1** *prosody* the rhythmic arrangement of syllables in verse, usually according to the number and kind of feet in a line **2** *music, chiefly US* the rhythmic arrangement of the beat in a piece of music [Greek *metron* measure]
metre-kilogram-second *n* See **mks units**
metric *adj* of or relating to the metre or metric system: *use either all metric or all imperial measurements*
metrical *or* **metric** *adj* **1** of or relating to measurement **2** of or in poetic metre **metrically** *adv*
metricate *vb* **-cating, -cated** to convert a measuring system or instrument to metric units **metrication** *n*
metric system *n* any decimal system of units based on the metre. For scientific purposes SI units are used
metric ton *n* (not in technical use) a tonne
metro *n, pl* **-ros** an urban, usually underground, railway system in certain cities, such as Paris [French, from *chemin de fer métropolitain* metropolitan railway]
metronome *n* a device which indicates the speed music should be played at by producing a clicking sound from a pendulum with an adjustable period of swing [Greek *metron* measure + *nomos* law]
metropolis (mit-trop-oh-liss) *n* the main city of a country or region [Greek *mētēr* mother + *polis* city]
metropolitan *adj* **1** of or characteristic of a metropolis **2** of or consisting of a city and its suburbs: *the Tokyo metropolitan region* **3** of or belonging to the home territories of a country, as opposed to overseas territories: *metropolitan France* ▷ *n* **4** *Christianity* the senior member of the clergy, esp. an archbishop, in charge of an ecclesiastical province **5** an inhabitant of a large city
metrosexual *n informal* a heterosexual man who spends a lot of time and money on his appearance
-metry *combining form* indicating the process or science of measuring: *geometry* [Greek *metron* measure] **-metric** *combining form*
mettle *n* **1** courage or spirit: *the lack of mettle evident among politicians* **2** character or abilities: *the mettle saints are made of* **3 on one's mettle** roused to making one's best efforts [variant of *metal*]
MeV million electronvolts (10^6 electronvolts)
mew¹ *n* **1** the characteristic high-pitched cry of a cat; meow ▷ *vb* **2** to make such a sound [imitative]
mew² *n* a seagull [Old English *mǣw*]
mewl *vb* **1** (esp. of a baby) to cry weakly; whimper ▷ *n* **2** a weak or whimpering cry [imitative]
mews *n chiefly Brit* **1** a yard or street lined by buildings originally used as stables but now often converted into dwellings ▷ *adj* **2** (of a flat or house) located in a mews: *a mews cottage* [plural of *mew*, originally referring to royal stables built on the site of hawks' mews (cages)]
Mex. **1** Mexican **2** Mexico
Mexican *adj* **1** of Mexico ▷ *n* **2** a person from Mexico

m

Mexican wave *n* the rippling effect produced when the spectators in successive sections of a sports stadium stand up while raising their arms and then sit down [first seen at the World Cup finals in *Mexico* in 1986]

mezzanine (mez-zan-**een**) *n* an intermediate storey, esp. one between the ground and first floor [Italian *mezzano* middle]

mezzo (**met**-so) *adv* **1** *music* moderately; quite: *mezzo-forte* ▷ *n, pl* **-zos 2** short for **mezzo-soprano** [Italian: half]

mezzo-soprano *n, pl* **-nos 1** a female voice lower than soprano but higher than contralto **2** a singer with such a voice

mezzotint (**met**-so-tint) *n* **1** a method of engraving done by scraping and burnishing the roughened surface of a copper plate **2** a print made from a plate so treated [Italian *mezzotinto* half tint]

mg milligram

Mg *chem* magnesium

M. Glam Mid Glamorgan

Mgr 1 manager **2** monseigneur **3** monsignor

MHz megahertz

mi *n* *music* same as **me²**

MI Michigan

MI5 (formerly, and still in popular use) Military Intelligence, section five; the part of the British security services which combats spying and subversion in Britain. Official name: **the Security Service**

m

MI6 (formerly, and still in popular use) Military Intelligence, section six; the part of the British security services which spies on other countries. Official name: **Secret Intelligence Service**

miasma (mee-**azz**-ma) *n, pl* **-mata** *or* **-mas** an unwholesome or foreboding atmosphere [Greek: defilement]

mica (**my**-ka) *n* any of a group of minerals consisting of flakelike crystals of aluminium or potassium silicates. They have a high resistance to electricity and heat [Latin: crumb]

mice *n* the plural of **mouse**

Michaelmas (**mik**-kl-mass) *n* Sept 29, the feast of St Michael the archangel: one of the four quarter days in England, Ireland, and Wales

Michaelmas daisy *n* *Brit* a garden plant with small daisy-shaped purple, pink, or white flowers in autumn

Mick *n offensive slang* an Irishman [nickname for *Michael*]

mickey *n* **take the mickey (out of)** *informal* to tease (someone) [origin unknown]

Mickey Finn *n slang* a drink containing a drug to make the drinker unconscious [origin unknown]

Mickey Mouse *adj slang* trivial, insignificant, or amateurish: *a Mickey Mouse survey* [after the cartoon character created by Walt Disney]

mickle *or* **muckle** *archaic or Scot & N English dialect* ▷ *adj* **1** large or abundant ▷ *adv* **2** much; greatly ▷ *n* **3** a great amount [Old Norse *mikell*]

micro *n, pl* **micros** short for **microcomputer** or **microprocessor**

micro- *or* **micr-** *combining form* **1** small or minute: *microdot* **2** involving the use of a microscope: *microscopy* **3** denoting 10^{-6}: *microsecond* [Greek *mikros* small]

microbe *n* any microscopic organism, esp. a disease-causing bacterium [MICRO- + Greek *bios* life] **microbial** *or* **microbic** *adj*

microbiology *n* the branch of biology involving the study of microorganisms

microblog *n* a blog in which there is a limitation on the length of individual postings **microblogger** *n* **microblogging** *n*

microchemistry *n* chemical experimentation with minute quantities of material

microchip *n* a tiny wafer of semiconductor material, such as silicon, containing an integrated circuit. Often shortened to: **chip**

microcircuit *n* a miniature electronic circuit in which a number of permanently connected components are contained in one small chip of semiconducting material

microcomputer *n* a compact computer built around a central processing unit on a single microchip

microcosm *n* **1** a miniature representation of something: *this area is a microcosm of France as a whole* **2** humankind regarded as epitomizing the universe **3 in microcosm** on a small scale [Greek *mikros kosmos* little world] **microcosmic** *adj*

microdot *n* a greatly reduced photographic copy (about the size of a pinhead) of a document, used esp in espionage

microeconomics *n* the branch of economics concerned with particular commodities, firms, or individuals and the relationships between them

microelectronics *n* the branch of electronics concerned with microcircuits

microfiche (**my**-kroh-feesh) *n* a small sheet of film on which writing or other information is stored, greatly reduced in size [French, from MICRO- + *fiche* small card]

microfilm *n* **1** a strip of film on which books or documents can be recorded in miniaturized form ▷ *vb* **2** to photograph a page or document on microfilm

microlight *or* **microlite** *n* a very small, light aircraft

micrometer (my-**krom**-it-er) *n* an instrument for the accurate measurement of small distances or angles

microminiaturization *or* **-risation** *n* the production and use of very small electronic components

micron (**my**-kron) *n* a unit of length equal to one millionth of a metre [Greek *mikros* small]

microorganism *n* any organism of microscopic size, such as a virus or bacterium

microphone *n* a device for converting sound into electrical energy

microprocessor *n* *computers* a single integrated circuit which acts as the central processing unit in a small computer

microscope *n* **1** an optical instrument that uses a lens or combination of lenses to produce a greatly magnified image of a small close object **2** any instrument, such as the electron microscope, for producing a greatly magnified visual image of a small object

microscopic *adj* **1** too small to be seen except with a microscope **2** very small; minute **3** of or using a microscope **microscopically** *adv*
microscopy *n* the use of microscopes
microsecond *n* one millionth of a second
microstructure *n* a structure on a microscopic scale, such as that of a metal or a cell
microsurgery *n* intricate surgery performed using a special microscope and miniature precision instruments
microwave *n* **1** an electromagnetic wave with a wavelength of between 0.3 and 0.001 metres: used in radar and cooking **2** short for **microwave oven** ▷ *vb* **-waving, -waved 3** to cook in a microwave oven
microwave detector *n* a device used by police for recording the speed of a motorist
microwave oven *n* a type of cooker which uses microwaves to cook food quickly
micturate *vb* **-rating, -rated** to urinate [Latin *micturire* to desire to urinate] **micturition** *n*
mid[1] *n archaic* the middle [Old English]
mid[2] *or* **'mid** *prep poetic* amid
mid- *combining form* indicating a middle part, point, time, or position: *midday; mid-June; mid-Victorian*
midair *n* some point above ground level, in the air
midday *n* **1** twelve o'clock in the day; noon **2** the middle part of the day, from late morning to early afternoon: *the midday sun*
midden *n Brit & Austral* a dunghill or pile of refuse [from Old Norse]
middle *n* **1** an area or point equal in distance from the ends or edges of a place: *a hotel in the middle of town* **2** the time between the first part and last part of an event or period of time: *the middle of June; the film got a bit boring in the middle* **3** the part of the body around the stomach; waist **4 in the middle of** busy doing something: *I'm in the middle of washing the dishes* ▷ *adj* **5** equally distant from the ends or outer edges of something; central: *the middle finger* **6** having an equal number of elder and younger brothers and sisters: *he was the middle child of three* **7** intermediate in status or situation: *middle management* **8** avoiding extremes; moderate: *we must find a middle course between authoritarianism and anarchy* [Old English *middel*]
middle age *n* the period of life between youth and old age, usually considered to occur between the ages of 40 and 60 **middle-aged** *adj*
Middle Ages *n European history* **1** (broadly) the period from the fall of the W Roman Empire in 476 AD to the Italian Renaissance **2** (narrowly) the period from about 1000 AD to the 15th century
middle-age spread *or* **middle-aged spread** *n* the fat that appears round many people's waists when they become middle-aged
Middle America *n* the US middle class, esp. those groups that are politically conservative
middlebrow *derogatory* ▷ *n* **1** a person with conventional tastes and limited cultural appreciation ▷ *adj* **2** of or appealing to middlebrows
middle C *n music* the note written on the first ledger line below the treble staff or the first ledger line above the bass staff. On a piano it is near the middle of the keyboard
middle class *n* **1** the social class between the working and upper classes. It consists of business and professional people ▷ *adj* **middle-class 2** of or characteristic of the middle class
middle-distance *adj* **1** *athletics* of or being a race of a length between the sprints and the distance events, esp. the 800 or 1500 metres: *a middle-distance runner* ▷ *n* **middle distance 2** the part of a painting between the foreground and the far distance
middle ear *n* the sound-conducting part of the ear immediately inside the eardrum
Middle East *n* the area around the E Mediterranean, esp. Israel and the Arab countries from Turkey to North Africa and eastwards to Iran **Middle Eastern** *adj*
Middle England *n* a characterization of a predominantly middle-class, middle-income section of British society, living mainly in suburban and rural England
Middle English *n* the English language from about 1100 to about 1450
Middle High German *n* High German from about 1200 to about 1500
Middle Low German *n* Low German from about 1200 to about 1500
middleman *n, pl* **-men 1** a trader who buys from the producer and sells to the consumer **2** an intermediary or go-between
middle name *n* **1** a name between a person's first name and surname **2** a characteristic quality for which a person is known: *danger is my middle name*
middle-of-the-road *adj* **1** not extreme, esp. in political views; moderate **2** of or denoting popular music of wide general appeal
middle school *n* (in England and Wales) a school for children aged between 8 or 9 and 12 or 13
middleweight *n* a professional boxer weighing up to 160 pounds (72.5 kg) or an amateur weighing up to 75 kg
middling *adj* **1** neither very good nor very bad **2** moderate in size **3 fair to middling** neither good nor bad, esp. in health ▷ *adv* **4** *informal* moderately: *middling well*
Middx Middlesex
midfield *n soccer* the area between the two opposing defences
midge *n* a small mosquito-like biting insect occurring in swarms, esp. near water [Old English *mycge*]
midget *n old-fashioned, offensive* **1** a dwarf whose skeleton and features are of normal proportions ▷ *adj* **2** much smaller than normal: *a midget submarine* [*midge* + *-et* small]
MIDI *n* a system for transmitting information to electronic musical instruments [*m(usical) i(nstrument) d(igital) i(nterface)*]
midi- *combining form* of medium or middle size or length: *a midi-skirt*
midi system *n* a complete set of compact hi-fi sound equipment designed as a single unit
midland *n* the central or inland part of a country

m

Midlands *n* **1 the Midlands** the central counties of England ▷ *adj* **2** of, in, or from the central counties of England: *a Midlands engineering firm*

midmost *adj, adv* in the middle or midst

midnight *n* **1** the middle of the night; 12 o'clock at night ▷ *adj* **2** happening or apparent at midnight or in the middle of the night: *midnight Mass* **3 burn the midnight oil** to work or study late into the night

midnight sun *n* the sun visible at midnight during the summer inside the Arctic and Antarctic circles

mid-off *n cricket* the fielding position on the off side closest to the bowler

mid-on *n cricket* the fielding position on the on side closest to the bowler

midpoint *n* **1** the point on a line equally distant from either end **2** a point in time halfway between the beginning and end of an event

midriff *n* **1** the middle part of the human body between waist and chest **2** *anatomy* same as **diaphragm** (sense 1) [Old English *midhrif* mid belly]

midshipman *n, pl* **-men** a naval officer of the lowest commissioned rank

midships *adv, adj naut* See **amidships**

midst *n* **1 in our midst** among us **2 in the midst of A** surrounded by **B** at a point during

midsummer *n* **1** the middle or height of summer **2** same as **summer solstice**

Midsummer's Day *or* **Midsummer Day** *n* June 24, the feast of St John the Baptist: one of the four quarter days in England, Ireland, and Wales

midtown *n US & Canad* the centre of a town

midway *adj* **1** in or at the middle of the distance; halfway: *the midway point* ▷ *adv* **2** to the middle of the distance

midweek *n* the middle of the week

Midwest *n* the N central part of the US **Midwestern** *adj*

mid-wicket *n cricket* the fielding position on the on side, roughly the same distance from both wickets, and halfway towards the boundary

midwife *n, pl* **-wives** a person qualified to deliver babies and to care for women before, during, and after childbirth [Old English *mid* with + *wīf* woman] **midwifery** (mid-wiff-fer-ree) *n*

midwinter *n* **1** the middle or depth of winter **2** same as **winter solstice**

mien (mean) *n literary* a person's manner, bearing, or appearance [probably from obsolete *demean* appearance]

mifepristone (mi-fep-riss-tone) *n* a technical name for **abortion pill**

miffed *adj informal* offended or upset [perhaps imitative of bad temper]

might[1] *vb* **1** the past tense or subjunctive mood of **may**[1]: *he might have come* **2** (used as an auxiliary) expressing possibility: *he might well have gone already*. See **may**[1] (sense 2) [Old English *mihte*]

USAGE See at **may**[1].

might[2] *n* **1** great power, strength, or vigour **2 with all one's might** using all one's strength and energy **3 (with) might and main** See **main** [Old English *miht*]

mighty *adj* **mightier, mightiest 1** powerful or strong **2** very great in extent or importance ▷ *adv* **3** *informal, chiefly US, Canad & Austral* very: *mighty hungry* **mightily** *adv* **mightiness** *n*

mignonette (min-yon-net) *n* a plant with spikes of small fragrant greenish-white flowers [French, diminutive of *mignon* dainty]

migraine (mee-grain, mye-grain) *n* a throbbing headache usually affecting only one side of the head and commonly accompanied by nausea and visual disturbances [French, from Greek *hēmi* half + *kranion* skull]

migrant *n* **1** a person or animal that moves from one place to another ▷ *adj* **2** moving from one place to another: *migrant farm labourers*

migrate *vb* **-grating, -grated 1** to go from one place to settle in another, esp. in a foreign country **2** (of living creatures, esp. birds) to journey between different habitats at specific times of the year [Latin *migrare* to change one's abode] **migration** *n* **migratory** *adj*

mikado *n, pl* **-dos** *archaic* the Japanese emperor [Japanese]

mike *n informal* a microphone

mil *n photog* short for **millimetre**: *35-mil film* [Latin *millesimus* thousandth]

milady *n, pl* **-dies** (formerly) a continental title for an English gentlewoman

milch (miltch) *adj chiefly Brit* (esp. of cattle) kept for milk [Old English *-milce* (in compounds)]

mild *adj* **1** (of a taste or sensation) not strong; bland **2** gentle or temperate in character, climate, or behaviour **3** not extreme; moderate: *mild criticism of senior officers* **4** feeble; unassertive: *a mild protest* ▷ *n* **5** *Brit* a dark beer flavoured with fewer hops than bitter [Old English *milde*]

mildew *n* **1** a disease of plants caused by a parasitic fungus **2** same as **mould**[2] ▷ *vb* **3** to affect or become affected with mildew [Old English *mildēaw* honey dew] **mildewy** *adj*

mild steel *n* strong tough steel containing a small quantity of carbon

mile *n* **1** Also: **statute mile** a unit of length used in the UK, the US and certain other countries, equal to 1760 yards. 1 mile is equivalent to 1.60934 kilometres **2** See **nautical mile 3** Also: **miles** *informal* a great distance; great deal: *he missed by miles* **4** a race extending over a mile ▷ *adv* **5 miles** very much: *it's miles better than their first album* [Latin *milia (passuum)* a thousand (paces)]

mileage *n* **1** a distance expressed in miles **2** the total number of miles that a motor vehicle has travelled **3** the number of miles a motor vehicle will travel on one gallon of fuel **4** *informal* the usefulness or benefit of something: *the opposition is trying to make political mileage out of the issue*

mileometer *or* **milometer** (mile-om-it-er) *n Brit* a device that records the number of miles that a vehicle has travelled

milepost *n chiefly US & Canad* a signpost that shows the distance in miles to or from a place

miler *n* an athlete, horse, etc., that specializes in races of one mile

milestone *n* **1** a stone pillar that shows the distance in miles to or from a place **2** a significant event

in a life or history: *a milestone in Turkish-Bulgarian relations*
milfoil *n* same as **yarrow** [Latin *mille* thousand + *folium* leaf]
milieu (**meal**-yuh) *n, pl* **milieux** *or* **milieus** (**meal**-yuhz) the social and cultural environment in which a person or thing exists: *the film takes for its milieu an apparently wholesome small town* [French]
militant *adj* **1** very active or aggressive in the support of a cause **2** *formal* warring; engaged in warfare ▷ *n* **3** a militant person [Latin *militare* to be a soldier] **militancy** *n* **militantly** *adv*
militarism *n* the pursuit of policies intended to create and maintain aggressive and influential armed forces **militarist** *n, adj* **militaristic** *adj*
militarized *or* **-rised** *adj* occupied by armed forces: *one of the most heavily militarized borders in the world* **militarization** *or* **-risation** *n*
military *adj* **1** of or relating to the armed forces or war **2** of or characteristic of soldiers ▷ *n* **3 the military** the armed services, esp. the army [Latin *miles* soldier] **militarily** *adv*
military police *n* a corps within an army that performs police duties
militate *vb* **-tating, -tated** (of facts or events) to have a strong influence or effect: *our position militated against counter-attacks*
USAGE See at **mitigate.**
militia (mill-**ish**-a) *n* a military force of trained civilians enlisted for use in emergency only [Latin: soldiery] **militiaman** *n*
milk *n* **1 A** a whitish fluid secreted by the mammary glands of mature female mammals and used for feeding their young **B** the milk of cows, goats, etc., used by humans as a food and to make cheese, butter, and yogurt **2** any similar fluid, such as the juice of a coconut ▷ *vb* **3** to draw milk from the udder of a cow or other animal **4** to extract as much money, help, or value as possible from: *he was accused of milking the situation for his own ends* [Old English *milc*] **milker** *n* **milkiness** *n* **milky** *adj*
milk-and-water *adj* weak, feeble, or insipid
milk bar *n* (formerly) a snack bar at which milk drinks and light refreshments are served
milk chocolate *n* chocolate that has been made with milk, having a creamy taste
milk float *n Brit* a small electrically powered vehicle used to deliver milk to houses
milkmaid *n* a girl or woman who milks cows
milkman *n, pl* **-men** *Brit, Austral & NZ* a man who delivers milk to people's houses
milk of magnesia *n* a suspension of magnesium hydroxide in water, used as an antacid and laxative
milk pudding *n* a pudding made by cooking milk with a grain, esp. rice
milk round *n* **1** *Brit & NZ* a route along which a milkman regularly delivers milk **2** *Brit* a regular series of visits made by recruitment officers from industry to colleges
milk shake *n* a cold frothy drink made of milk, flavouring, and sometimes ice cream, whisked or beaten together
milksop *n* a feeble or ineffectual man or youth
milk tooth *n* any of the first set of teeth in young children
Milky Way *n* **1** the diffuse band of light stretching across the night sky that consists of millions of distant stars in our galaxy **2** the galaxy in which the Earth is situated [translation of Latin *via lactea*]
mill *n* **1** a building where grain is crushed and ground to make flour **2** a factory, esp. one which processes raw materials: *a steel mill* **3** any of various processing or manufacturing machines, esp. one that grinds, presses, or rolls **4** a small device for grinding solids: *a pepper mill* **5 go** *or* **be put through the mill** to have an unpleasant experience or ordeal ▷ *vb* **6** to grind, press, or process in or as if in a mill **7** to groove or flute the edge of a coin **8** to move about in a confused manner: *the corridor was full of people milling about* [Latin *molere* to grind]
milled *adj* **1** crushed or ground in a mill: *freshly milled black pepper* **2** (of a coin) having a grooved and often raised edge
millennial (mill-**en**-nee-al) *adj* **1** of or relating to a millennium ▷ *n* **2** a member of the generation who became adults in the early 21st century
millennium (mill-**en**-nee-um) *n, pl* **-nia** (-nee-a) *or* **-niums 1** a period of one thousand years **2 the Millennium** *Christianity* the period of a thousand years of Christ's awaited reign upon earth **3** a future period of peace and happiness [Latin *mille* thousand + *annus* year]
millepede *n* same as **millipede**
miller *n history* a person who owns or operates a mill, esp. a corn mill
miller's thumb *n* a small freshwater European fish with a flattened body [from the alleged likeness of the fish's head to a thumb]
millesimal (mill-**less**-im-al) *adj* **1** denoting or consisting of a thousandth ▷ *n* **2** a thousandth part of something [Latin *millesimus*]
millet *n* a cereal grass cultivated for its edible grain and as animal fodder [Latin *milium*]
milli- *combining form* denoting 10^{-3}: *millimetre* [Latin *mille* thousand]
milliard *n Brit* (no longer in technical use) a thousand million [French]
millibar *n* a unit of atmospheric pressure equal to 100 newtons per square metre
milligram *or* **milligramme** *n* one thousandth of a gram [French]
millilitre *or US* **milliliter** *n* a measure of volume equivalent to one thousandth of a litre
millimetre *or US* **millimeter** *n* a unit of length equal to one thousandth of a metre
milliner *n* a person who makes or sells women's hats [originally *Milaner* a native of *Milan*, once famous for its fancy goods] **millinery** *n*
million *n, pl* **-lions** *or* **-lion 1** the number equal to one thousand thousands: 1 000 000 or 10^6 **2** (*often pl*) *informal* an extremely large but unspecified number: *I've got a million things to do today* [early Italian *millione*] **millionth** *n, adj*
millionaire *n* a person who has money or property worth at least a million pounds, dollars, etc. **millionairess** *fem n*

millipede *or* **millepede** *n* a small crawling animal with a cylindrical many-segmented body, each segment of which bears two pairs of legs [Latin *mille* thousand + *pes* foot]

millisecond *n* one thousandth of a second

millpond *n* a pool which provides water to turn a millwheel

millrace *n* the current of water that turns a millwheel

millstone *n* **1** one of a pair of heavy flat stones that are rotated one against the other to grind grain **2** a heavy burden of responsibility or obligation: *the debt had become a millstone round his neck*

millstream *n* a stream of water used to turn a millwheel

millwheel *n* a water wheel that drives a mill

milometer (mile-om-it-er) *n* same as **mileometer**

milord *n* (formerly) a continental title used for an English gentleman [from *my lord*]

milt *n* the male reproductive gland, sperm, or semen of a fish [Old English *milte* spleen]

mime *n* **1** a style of acting using only gesture and bodily movement and not words **2** a performer specializing in this **3** a performance in this style ▷ *vb* **miming, mimed 4** to express or describe something in actions or gestures without using speech **5** (of musicians) to pretend to be singing or playing music that is actually prerecorded [Greek *mimos* imitator] **mimer** *n*

mimetic (mim-met-ik) *adj* **1** imitating or representing something: *most photographs are mimetic representations of the real world* **2** *biol* of or showing mimicry [Greek *mimeisthai* to imitate]

mimic *vb* **-icking, -icked 1** to imitate a person or a way of acting or speaking, esp. to entertain or make fun of **2** to take on the appearance of: *certain flies mimic wasps* **3** to copy closely or in a servile manner: *social climbers in the colonies began to mimic their conquerors* ▷ *n* **4** a person or an animal, such as a parrot, that is clever at mimicking [Greek *mimikos*]

mimicry *n, pl* **-ries 1** the act or art of copying or imitating closely **2** *biol* the resemblance shown by one animal species to another dangerous or inedible one, which protects it from predators

mimosa *n* a tropical shrub with ball-like clusters of yellow flowers and leaves sensitive to touch and light [Latin *mimus* mime, because the plant's sensitivity to touch imitates the similar reaction of animals]

min. 1 minimum **2** minute *or* minutes

Min. 1 Minister **2** Ministry

minaret *n* a slender tower of a mosque with one or more balconies [Arabic *manārat* lamp]

minatory *adj* threatening or menacing [Latin *minari* to threaten]

mince *vb* **mincing, minced 1** to chop, grind, or cut into very small pieces **2** to walk or speak in an affected dainty manner **3 not mince one's words** to be direct and to the point rather than making an effort to avoid upsetting people ▷ *n* **4** *chiefly Brit & NZ* minced meat [Old French *mincier*, from Late Latin *minutia* smallness] **minced** *adj* **mincer** *n*

mincemeat *n* **1** a mixture of dried fruit and spices used for filling pies **2 make mincemeat of** *informal* to defeat completely

mince pie *n* a small round pastry tart filled with mincemeat

mincing *adj* (of a person or their style of walking or speaking) affectedly elegant

mind *n* **1** the part of a person responsible for thought, feelings, and intention. Related adjective: **mental 2** intelligence as opposed to feelings or wishes **3** memory or recollection: *his name didn't spring to mind immediately* **4** a person considered as an intellectual being: *one of Europe's greatest minds* **5** the condition or state of a person's feelings or thoughts: *a confused state of mind* **6** an intention or desire: *I have a mind to go* **7** attention or thoughts: *keep your mind on the job* **8** a sound mental state; sanity: *he's out of his mind* **9 change one's mind** to alter one's decision or opinion **10 give someone a piece of one's mind** to scold someone severely **11 in two minds** undecided or wavering **12 make up one's mind** to reach a decision **13 on one's mind** in one's thoughts **14 to my mind** in my opinion ▷ *vb* **15** to take offence at: *do you mind if I open a window?* **16** to pay attention to: *to mind one's own business* **17** to make certain; ensure: *mind you tell him* **18** to take care of: *mind the shop* **19** to be cautious or careful about: *mind how you go* **20** *dialect* to remember ▷ See also **mind out** [Old English *gemynd*]

mind-boggling *adj* so large, complicated, or surprising that it causes surprise and shock: *mind-boggling wealth*

minded *adj* having a mind or inclination as specified: *commercially minded*

minder *n* **1** *slang* an aide or assistant, esp. one employed as a bodyguard or public relations officer for someone **2** short for **child minder**

mindful *adj* **mindful of** being aware of and taking into account: *the company is ever mindful of the need to find new markets*

mindfulness *n* **1** the state of being mindful **2** the practice of giving complete, non-judgmental attention to one's present experience, used as a method to reduce stress

mindless *adj* **1** stupid or careless **2** requiring little or no intellectual effort **3** heedless: *mindless of the risks involved* **mindlessly** *adv* **mindlessness** *n*

Mind Map *n trademark* a method of representing ideas in a diagram, with related concepts arranged around a core concept

mind out *vb* to be careful or pay attention

mind-reader *n* a person seemingly able to make out the thoughts of another

mind's eye *n* **in one's mind's eye** in one's imagination

mine¹ *pron* **1** something or someone belonging to or associated with me: *it's a great favourite of mine* **2 of mine** belonging to or associated with me ▷ *adj.* **3** *archaic* same as **my**: *mine eyes; mine host* [Old English *mīn*]

mine² *n* **1** a place where minerals, esp. coal, ores, or precious stones, are dug from the ground **2** a type of bomb placed in water or under the ground, and designed to destroy ships, vehicles, or people passing over or near it **3** a profitable source or abundant supply: *a mine of information* ▷ *vb* **mining, mined 4** to dig minerals from the ground: *lead has been mined here for over three centuries* **5** to dig a hole or tunnel, esp. in order to obtain minerals **6** to place explosive mines in or on: *the retreating troops had mined the bridge* [Old French]

mine dump *n S African* a large mound of waste material from gold-mining operations

minefield *n* **1** an area of ground or water containing explosive mines **2** a subject or situation full of hidden problems

minelayer *n* a warship or aircraft for carrying and laying mines

miner *n* a person who works in a mine, esp. a coal mine

mineral *n* **1** a naturally occurring solid inorganic substance with a characteristic chemical composition and structure **2** any inorganic matter **3** any substance obtained by mining, esp. a metal ore **4** *Brit* a soft drink containing carbonated water and flavourings ▷ *adj* **5** of, containing, or resembling minerals [Medieval Latin *minera* mine, ore]

mineralogy (min-er-al-a-jee) *n* the scientific study of minerals **mineralogical** *adj* **mineralogist** *n*

mineral water *n* water containing dissolved mineral salts or gases

Minerva *n* the Roman goddess of wisdom

minestrone (min-ness-**strone**-ee) *n* a soup made from a variety of vegetables and pasta [Italian, from *minestrare* to serve]

minesweeper *n* a naval vessel equipped to clear mines

Ming *adj* of or relating to Chinese porcelain from the time of the Ming dynasty, which ruled China from 1368 to 1644

minger *n Brit informal* an unattractive person

minging *n Brit informal* unattractive or unpleasant

mingle *vb* **-gling, -gled 1** to mix or blend **2** to associate or mix with a group of people: *the performers mingled with the audience after the show* [Old English *mengan* to mix]

mingy *adj* **-gier, -giest** *Brit & NZ informal* mean or miserly [probably a blend of *mean* + *stingy*]

mini *adj* **1** small; miniature **2** (of a skirt or dress) very short ▷ *n, pl* **minis 3** something very small of its kind, esp. a miniskirt

mini- *combining form* smaller or shorter than the standard size: *minibus; miniseries* [from *miniature* + *minimum*]

miniature *n* **1** a model or representation on a very small scale **2** a very small painting, esp. a portrait **3** a very small bottle of whisky or other spirits, which can hold 50 millilitres **4 in miniature** on a small scale ▷ *adj* **5** much smaller than usual; small-scale [Medieval Latin *miniare* to paint red (in illuminating manuscripts), from *minium* red lead] **miniaturist** *n*

miniaturize *or* **-rise** *vb* **-rizing, -rized** *or* **-rising, -rised** to make a very small version of something, esp. electronic components **miniaturization** *or* **-risation** *n*

minibus *n* a small bus

minicab *n Brit* an ordinary car used as a taxi

minicomputer *n* a small computer which is more powerful than a microcomputer

minidisc *n* a small recordable compact disc

minim *n* **1** a unit of fluid measure equal to one sixtieth of a drachm **2** *music* a note with the time value of half a semibreve [Latin *minimus* smallest]

minimal *adj* of the least possible quantity or degree

minimalism *n* **1** a type of music based on the repetition of simple elements **2** a design or style using the simplest and fewest elements to create the maximum effect **minimalist** *adj, n*

minimize *or* **-mise** *vb* **-mizing, -mized** *or* **-mising, -mised 1** to reduce to the lowest possible degree or amount: *these measures should help minimize our costs* **2** to regard or treat as less important than it really is; belittle: *I don't want to minimize the importance of her contribution*

minimum *n, pl* **-mums** *or* **-ma 1** the least possible amount, degree, or quantity: *fry the burgers in the minimum of oil* **2** the least amount recorded, allowed, or reached: *soak the beans for a minimum of eight hours* ▷ *adj* **3** of, being, or showing a minimum or minimums: *the minimum age* [Latin *minimus* least]

minimum lending rate *n* (formerly) the minimum rate at which the Bank of England would lend money: replaced in 1981 by the base rate

minimum wage *n* the lowest wage that an employer is permitted to pay by law or union contract

mining *n* **1** the act, process, or industry of extracting coal or ores from the earth **2** *military* the process of laying mines

minion *n* a servile assistant [French *mignon* darling]

miniseries *n, pl* **-series** a television programme in several parts that is shown on consecutive days over a short period

miniskirt *n* a very short skirt

minister *n* **1** (esp. in Presbyterian and some Nonconformist Churches) a member of the clergy **2** a head of a government department **3** a diplomat with a lower rank than an ambassador ▷ *vb* **4 minister to** to attend to the needs of [Latin: servant] **ministerial** *adj*

minister of state *n* (in the British Parliament) a minister, usually below cabinet rank, appointed to assist a senior minister

Minister of the Crown *n Brit* any Government minister of cabinet rank

ministrations *pl n* the giving of help or service: *the ministrations of the chaplain* [Latin *ministrare* to wait upon]

ministry *n, pl* **-tries 1** the profession or duties of a minister of religion **2** ministers considered as a group **3 A** a government department headed by a minister **B** the buildings of such a department

mink *n, pl* **mink** *or* **minks 1** a mammal of Europe, Asia, and North America, resembling a large stoat **2** its highly valued fur **3** a garment made of this, esp. a woman's coat or stole [Scandinavian]

minneola *n* a juicy citrus fruit that is a cross between a tangerine and a grapefruit

m

minnow *n, pl* **-nows** *or* **-now** a small slender European freshwater fish [Old English *myne*]
Minoan (min-no-an) *adj* of or denoting the Bronze Age culture of Crete from about 3000 BC to about 1100 BC [*Minos*, in Greek mythology, king of Crete]
minor *adj* **1** lesser or secondary in size, frequency, or importance than others of the same kind: *a minor poet* **2** not very serious or significant: *minor injuries* **3** *music* **A** (of a scale) having a semitone between the second and third and fifth and sixth notes (**natural minor**) **B** of or based on the minor scale: *his quintet in C minor; a minor third* ▷ *n* **4** a person below the age of legal majority **5** *US, Canad & Austral education* a subsidiary subject **6** *music* a minor key, chord, mode, or scale ▷ *vb* **7** **minor in** *US & Canad education* to study as a subsidiary subject: *to minor in politics* [Latin: less, smaller]
minority *n, pl* **-ties** **1** the smaller of two parts, factions, or groups **2** a group that is different, esp. racially or politically, from a larger group of which it is a part **3** **in the minority** forming or part of the group of people or things made up of less than half of a larger group ▷ *adj* **4** relating to or being a minority: *a minority sport*
Minotaur *n Greek myth* a monster with the head of a bull and the body of a man [Greek *Minōtauros*]
minster *n Brit* any of certain cathedrals and large churches, usually originally connected to a monastery [Church Latin *monasterium* monastery]
minstrel *n* **1** a medieval singer and musician **2** a performer in a minstrel show [Old French *menestral*]
minstrel show *n* (formerly) a theatrical entertainment consisting of songs and dances performed by actors wearing black face make-up
mint[1] *n* **1** any of various plants with aromatic leaves used for seasoning and flavouring **2** a sweet flavoured with mint [Greek *minthē*] **minty** *adj*
mint[2] *n* **1** a factory where the official coins of a country are made **2** a very large amount of money ▷ *adj* **3** **in mint condition** in perfect condition; as if new ▷ *vb* **4** to make coins by stamping metal **5** to invent or create: *no-one knows who first minted the term 'yuppie'* [Latin *moneta* money, mint]
minuet (min-new-et) *n* **1** a stately court dance of the 17th and 18th centuries in triple time **2** music for this dance [French *menuet* dainty]
minus *prep* **1** reduced by the subtraction of: *six minus two equals four* **2** *informal* without or lacking: *he returned minus his jacket* ▷ *adj* **3** indicating or involving subtraction: *a minus sign* **4** Also: **negative** less than zero: *it's minus eight degrees in Montreal today* **5** *education* slightly below the standard of a particular grade: *a C minus for maths* ▷ *n* **6** short for **minus sign** **7** a negative quantity **8** *informal* something detrimental or negative [Latin, neuter of *minor* less]
minuscule (min-niss-skyool) *adj* very small [Latin *(littera) minuscula* very small (letter)]
minus sign *n* the symbol -, indicating subtraction, a negative quantity, or a negative electrical charge

minute[1] *n* **1** 60 seconds; one sixtieth of an hour **2** any very short period of time; moment: *I'll be with you in a minute* **3** the distance that can be travelled in a minute: *it's about ten minutes away* **4** a measure of angle equal to one sixtieth of a degree **5** **up to the minute** the very latest or newest ▷ *vb* **-nuting, -nuted** **6** to record in minutes: *the decision was minuted in 1990* ▷ See also **minutes** [Medieval Latin *minuta*, noun use of Latin *minutus* minute (small)]
minute[2] *adj* **1** very small; tiny **2** precise or detailed: *a minute examination* [Latin *minutus*, past participle of *minuere* to diminish] **minutely** *adv*
minutes *pl n* an official record of the proceedings of a meeting or conference
minute steak *n* a small piece of steak that can be cooked quickly
minutiae (my-**new**-shee-eye) *pl n, sing* **-tia** trifling or precise details [Late Latin, plural of *minutia* smallness]
minx *n* a bold or flirtatious girl [origin unknown]
Miocene (my-oh-seen) *adj geol* of the epoch of geological time about 25 million years ago [Greek *meiōn* less + *kainos* new]
miracle *n* **1** an event contrary to the laws of nature and attributed to a supernatural cause **2** any amazing and fortunate event: *it's a miracle that no-one was killed in the accident* **3** a marvellous example of something: *a miracle of organization* [Latin *mirari* to wonder at]
miracle play *n* a medieval play based on a biblical story or the life of a saint
miraculous *adj* **1** like a miracle **2** surprising or remarkable
mirage (mir-**rahzh**) *n* **1** an image of a distant object or sheet of water, often inverted or distorted, caused by atmospheric refraction by hot air **2** something illusory: *the mirage of economic recovery* [French, from *(se) mirer* to be reflected]
mire *n* **1** a boggy or marshy area **2** mud, muck, or dirt **3** an unpleasant or difficult situation that is difficult to get out of: *the country sank deeper into the economic mire* ▷ *vb* **miring, mired** **4** to sink or be stuck in a mire: *the company has been mired in financial scandal* [Old Norse *mȳrr*]
mirror *n* **1** a sheet of glass with a metal coating on its back, that reflects an image of an object placed in front of it **2** a thing that reflects or depicts something else ▷ *vb* **3** to reflect or represent faithfully: *the book inevitably mirrors my own interests* [Latin *mirari* to wonder at]
mirror ball *n* a large revolving ball covered with small pieces of mirror glass so that it reflects light in changing patterns: used in discos and ballrooms
mirror image *n* an image or object that has left and right reversed as if seen in a mirror
mirth *n* laughter, gaiety, or merriment [Old English *myrgth*] **mirthful** *adj* **mirthless** *adj*
MIRV multiple independently targeted re-entry vehicle: a missile that has several warheads, each one being aimed at a different target
mis- *prefix* **1** wrong or bad; wrongly or badly: *misunderstanding; mislead* **2** lack of; not: *mistrust* [Old English *mis(se)-*]

misadventure *n* **1** an unlucky event; misfortune **2** *law* accidental death not due to crime or negligence

misaligned *adj* not properly aligned; out of true **misalignment** *n*

misalliance *n* an unsuitable alliance or marriage

misanthrope (miz-zan-thrope) *or* **misanthropist** (miz-zan-throp-ist) *n* a person who dislikes or distrusts people in general [Greek *misos* hatred + *anthrōpos* man] **misanthropic** (miz-zan-**throp**-ik) *adj* **misanthropy** (miz-**zan**-throp-ee) *n*

misapply *vb* **-plies, -plying, -plied** to use something for a purpose for which it is not intended or is not suited **misapplication** *n*

misapprehend *vb* to misunderstand **misapprehension** *n*

misappropriate *vb* **-ating, -ated** to take and use money dishonestly **misappropriation** *n*

misbegotten *adj* **1** planned or designed badly or with dishonourable motives or aims **2** *literary or dialect* illegitimate; bastard

misbehave *vb* **-having, -haved** to behave badly **misbehaviour** *or US* **misbehavior** *n*

miscalculate *vb* **-lating, -lated** to calculate or judge wrongly: *we miscalculated the strength of the opposition* **miscalculation** *n*

miscall *vb* to call by the wrong name

miscarriage *n* **1** spontaneous premature expulsion of a fetus from the womb, esp. before the 20th week of pregnancy **2** an act of mismanagement or failure: *a miscarriage of justice*

miscarry *vb* **-ries, -rying, -ried 1** to expel a fetus prematurely from the womb **2** to fail

miscast *vb* **-casting, -cast** to cast a role or an actor in a play or film inappropriately: *the role of the avaricious boss was miscast; she was miscast as Cassandra*

miscegenation (miss-ij-in-**nay**-shun) *n* *old-fashioned* interbreeding of races, esp. where differences of colour are involved [Latin *miscere* to mingle + *genus* race]

miscellaneous (miss-sel-**lane**-ee-uss) *adj* composed of or containing a variety of things; mixed or assorted [Latin *miscere* to mix]

miscellany (miss-**sell**-a-nee) *n, pl* **-nies** a mixed assortment of items

mischance *n* **1** bad luck **2** an unlucky event or accident

mischief *n* **1** annoying but not malicious behaviour that causes trouble or irritation **2** an inclination to tease **3** injury or harm caused by a person or thing [Old French *meschief*, from *mes-* mis- + *chef* end]

mischief-maker *n* someone who deliberately causes trouble **mischief-making** *n*

mischievous (miss-chiv-uss) *adj* **1** full of mischief **2** teasing; slightly malicious **3** intended to cause harm: *a purveyor of mischievous disinformation* **mischievously** *adv*

miscible (miss-sib-bl) *adj* able to be mixed: *miscible with water* [Latin *miscere* to mix] **miscibility** *n*

miscommunicate *vb* **-cating, -cated** to communicate inaccurately **miscommunication** *n*

misconceived *adj* false, mistaken, or badly thought-out: *a misconceived conception of loyalty*

misconception *n* a false or mistaken view, idea, or belief

misconduct *n* behaviour, such as adultery or professional negligence, that is regarded as immoral or unethical

misconstrue *vb* **-struing, -strued** to interpret mistakenly **misconstruction** *n*

miscreant (miss-kree-ant) *n* a wrongdoer or villain [Old French *mescreant* unbelieving]

misdeal *vb* **-dealing, -dealt 1** to deal out cards incorrectly ▷ *n* **2** a faulty deal

misdeed *n* an evil or illegal action

misdemeanour *or US* **misdemeanor** *n* **1** a minor wrongdoing **2** *criminal law* (formerly) an offence less serious than a felony

misdirect *vb* to give someone wrong directions or instructions **misdirection** *n*

mise en scène (meez on sane) *n* **1** the stage setting and scenery in a play **2** the environment of an event [French]

miser *n* a person who hoards money and hates spending it: *I'm married to a miser* [Latin: wretched] **miserly** *adj*

miserable *adj* **1** unhappy or depressed; wretched **2** causing misery or discomfort: *a miserable existence* **3** sordid or squalid: *miserable living conditions* **4** mean or ungenerous: *a miserable pension* [Latin *miserabilis*] **miserableness** *n* **miserably** *adv*

misericord *n* a ledge projecting from the underside of the hinged seat of a choir stall in a church, which the occupant can rest against while standing [Latin *miserere* to pity + *cor* heart]

misery *n, pl* **-eries 1** intense unhappiness or suffering **2** something which causes such unhappiness **3** squalid or poverty-stricken conditions **4** *Brit informal* a person who is habitually depressed: *he is such a misery* [Latin *miser* wretched]

misfire *vb* **-firing, -fired 1** (of a firearm) to fail to fire as expected **2** (of a motor engine or vehicle) to fail to fire at the appropriate time **3** to fail to have the intended result; go wrong: *he was injured when a practical joke misfired* ▷ *n* **4** the act or an instance of misfiring

misfit *n* a person who is not suited to the role, social group, etc., he or she finds himself or herself in

misfortune *n* **1** bad luck **2** an unfortunate event

misgivings *pl n* feelings of uncertainty, fear, or doubt

misgovern *vb* to govern badly **misgovernment** *n*

misguided *adj* mistaken or unwise

mishandle *vb* **-dling, -dled** to handle or treat badly or inefficiently

mishap *n* a minor accident

mishear *vb* **-hearing, -heard** to fail to hear what someone says correctly

mishit *sport* ▷ *n* **1** a faulty shot, kick, or stroke ▷ *vb* **-hitting, -hit 2** to hit or kick a ball with a faulty stroke

mishmash *n* a confused collection or mixture [reduplication of *mash*]

misinform *vb* to give incorrect information to **misinformation** *n*

m

misinterpret *vb* to understand or represent something wrongly: *the press misinterpreted the President's remarks* **misinterpretation** *n*
misjudge *vb* **-judging, -judged** to judge wrongly or unfairly **misjudgment** *or* **misjudgement** *n*
mislay *vb* **-lays, -laying, -laid** to lose something temporarily, esp. by forgetting where it is
mislead *vb* **-leading, -led** to give false or confusing information to
misleading *adj* giving a false or confusing impression: *misleading use of statistical data*
mismanage *vb* **-naging, -naged** to organize or run something badly **mismanagement** *n*
mismatch *vb* **1** to form an unsuitable partner, opponent, or set ▷ *n* **2** an unsuitable match **mismatched** *adj*
misnamed *adj* having an inappropriate or misleading name: *the grotesquely misnamed Freedom Party*
misnomer (miss-**no**-mer) *n* **1** an incorrect or unsuitable name for a person or thing **2** the use of the wrong name [Old French *mesnommer* to misname]
misogyny (miss-**oj**-in-ee) *n* hatred of women [Greek *misos* hatred + *gunē* woman] **misogynist** *n* **misogynous** *adj*
misplace *vb* **-placing, -placed 1** to lose something temporarily by forgetting where it was placed **2** to put something in the wrong place
misplaced *adj* **1** (of an emotion or action) directed towards a person or thing that does not deserve it: *misplaced optimism* **2** put in the wrong place: *a scrappy game dominated by misplaced kicking*
misprint *n* **1** an error in printing ▷ *vb* **2** to print a letter incorrectly
misprision *n law* the concealment of the commission of a felony or an act of treason [Old French *mesprision* error]
mispronounce *vb* **-nouncing, -nounced** to pronounce a word or name wrongly **mispronunciation** *n*
misquote *vb* **-quoting, -quoted** to quote inaccurately **misquotation** *n*
misread *vb* **-reading, -read 1** to misinterpret or misunderstand: *he misread her politeness as approval* **2** to read incorrectly
misrepresent *vb* to represent wrongly or inaccurately **misrepresentation** *n*
misrule *vb* **-ruling, -ruled 1** to govern inefficiently or without justice ▷ *n* **2** inefficient or unjust government **3** disorder or lawlessness
miss[1] *vb* **1** to fail to notice, see, or hear: *it's right at the top of the hill, so you can't miss it; I missed what he said because I was talking at the time* **2** to fail to hit something aimed at: *he threw the ball at the stumps but missed* **3** to fail to achieve or reach: *they narrowly missed promotion last season* **4** to fail to take advantage of: *he never missed a chance to make money* **5** to fail or be unable to be present: *he had missed the last three meetings* **6** to be too late for: *we missed the bus and had to walk* **7** to discover or regret the loss or absence of: *the boys miss their father when he's away on business* **8** to escape or avoid narrowly: *it missed the helicopter's rotors by inches* ▷ *n* **9** a failure to hit, reach, etc.: *an easy miss in the second frame gave his opponent the advantage* **10 give something a miss** to decide not to do, go to, or take part in something: *I'll give the pub a miss and have a quiet night in* ▷ See also **miss out** [Old English *missan*]
miss[2] *n informal* an unmarried woman or girl [from *mistress*]
Miss *n* a title of a girl or unmarried woman, usually used before the surname: *Miss Brown to you*
missal *n RC Church* a book containing the prayers and rites of the Masses for a complete year [Church Latin *missale*, from *missa* Mass]
misshapen *adj* badly shaped; deformed
missile *n* **1** a rocket with an exploding warhead, used as a weapon **2** an object or weapon that is thrown, launched, or fired at a target [Latin *mittere* to send]
missing *adj* **1** not in its proper or usual place and unable to be found **2** not able to be traced and not known to be dead: *seven men were reported missing after the raid* **3** not included in something although it perhaps should have been: *two things are missing from the report*
missing link *n* **1** any missing section or part in a series **2 the missing link** a hypothetical extinct animal, formerly thought to be intermediate between the apes and man
mission *n* **1** a specific task or duty assigned to a person or group of people **2** a task or duty that a person believes he or she must achieve; vocation: *he felt it was his mission to pass on his knowledge to other people* **3** a group of people representing or working for a particular country or organization in a foreign country: *the UN peacekeeping mission* **4** a group of people sent by a church to a foreign country to do religious and social work **5** the place in which a church or government mission is based **6** the dispatch of aircraft or spacecraft to achieve a particular task **7** a charitable centre that offers shelter or aid to poor or needy people **8** *S African* a long and difficult process [Latin *mittere* to send]
missionary *n, pl* **-naries 1** a person sent abroad by a church to do religious and social work ▷ *adj* **2** of or relating to missionaries: *missionary work* **3** resulting from a desire to convert people to one's own beliefs: *missionary zeal*
mission statement *n* an official statement of the aims and objectives of a business or other organization
missive *n* a formal or official letter [Latin *mittere* to send]
miss out *vb* **1** to leave out or overlook **2 miss out on** to fail to take part in (something enjoyable or beneficial): *she'd missed out on going to university*
misspell *vb* **-spelling, -spelt** *or* **-spelled** to spell a word wrongly **misspelling** *n*
misspend *vb* **-spending, -spent** to waste or spend unwisely **misspent** *adj*
missus *or* **missis** *n* **1** *Brit, Austral & NZ informal* one's wife or the wife of the person addressed or referred to: *the missus is a teacher* **2** an informal term of address for a woman [spoken version of *mistress*]

m

missy *n, pl* **missies** *informal* an affectionate or disparaging form of address to a girl

mist *n* **1** a thin fog **2** a fine spray of liquid, such as that produced by an aerosol container **3** condensed water vapour on a surface **4** something that causes haziness or lack of clarity, such as a film of tears ▷ *vb* **5** to cover or be covered with mist: *the windscreen has misted up again; his eyes misted over and he shook with rage* [Old English] **misty** *adj* **mistiness** *n*

mistake *n* **1** an error or blunder **2** a misconception or misunderstanding ▷ *vb* **-taking, -took, -taken** **3** to misunderstand or misinterpret: *the chaplain quite mistook her meaning* **4** to confuse a person or thing with another: *they saw the HMS Sheffield and mistook her for the Bismarck* **5** to choose badly or incorrectly: *he mistook his path* [Old Norse *mistaka* to take erroneously]

mistaken *adj* **1** wrong in opinion or judgment **2** arising from error in opinion or judgment: *a mistaken viewpoint*

mister *n* an informal form of address for a man [variant of *master*]

Mister *n* the full form of **Mr**

mistime *vb* **-timing, -timed** to do or say at the wrong time

mistle thrush *or* **missel thrush** *n* a large European thrush with a brown back and spotted breast [Old English *mistel* mistletoe]

mistletoe *n* a Eurasian evergreen shrub with waxy white berries, which grows as a parasite on various trees [Old English *misteltān*, from *mistel* mistletoe + *tān* twig]

mistook *vb* the past tense of **mistake**

mistral *n* a strong cold dry northerly wind of S France [Provençal, from Latin *magistralis* masterful]

mistreat *vb* to treat badly **mistreatment** *n*

mistress *n* **1** a woman who has a continuing sexual relationship with a man who is usually married to somebody else **2** a woman in a position of authority, ownership, or control **3** a woman having control over something specified: *she is a mistress of disguise* **4** *chiefly Brit* a female teacher [Old French *maistresse*]

mistrial *n law* a trial which is invalid because of some error

mistrust *vb* **1** to have doubts or suspicions about ▷ *n* **2** lack of trust **mistrustful** *adj* **mistrustfully** *adv*

misunderstand *vb* **-standing, -stood** to fail to understand properly

misunderstanding *n* **1** a failure to understand properly **2** a disagreement

misunderstood *adj* not properly or sympathetically understood: *a misunderstood adolescent*

misuse *n* **1** incorrect, improper, or careless use: *misuse of drugs* **2** cruel or inhumane treatment ▷ *vb* **-using, -used** **3** to use wrongly **4** to treat badly or harshly

mite¹ *n* any of numerous very small creatures of the spider family, some of which live as parasites [Old English *mīte*]

mite² *n* **1** a very small creature or thing **2** a very small sum of money **3** **a mite** *informal* somewhat: *the main course was a mite bland* [Middle Dutch *mīte*]

mitigate *vb* **-gating, -gated** to make less severe or harsh [Latin *mitis* mild + *agere* to make] **mitigating** *adj* **mitigation** *n*

> **USAGE** *Mitigate* is sometimes wrongly used where *militate* is meant: *his behaviour militates (not mitigates) against his chances of promotion.*

mitochondrion *n, pl* **-dria** *biol* a small spherical or rodlike body found in the cytoplasm of most cells [Greek *mitos* thread + *khondrion* grain]

mitosis *n* a type of cell division in which the nucleus divides into two nuclei each containing the same number of chromosomes as the parent nucleus [Greek *mitos* thread]

mitre *or US* **miter** (my-ter) *n* **1** *Christianity* the headdress of a bishop or abbot, consisting of a tall pointed cleft cap **2** Also: **mitre joint** a corner joint formed by cutting bevels of equal angles at the ends of each piece of material ▷ *vb* **-tring, -tred** *or* **-tering, -tered** **3** to join with a mitre joint [Greek *mitra* turban]

mitt *n* **1** a glovelike hand covering that does not cover the fingers **2** short for **mitten** **3** *slang* a hand **4** a baseball glove [from *mitten*]

mitten *n* a glove with one section for the thumb and a single section for the fingers [Old French *mitaine*]

mix *vb* **1** to combine or blend into one mass or substance: *mix the water, yeast, and flour into a smooth dough* **2** to be able to combine into one substance: *oil and water do not mix* **3** to form by combining different substances: *to mix cement* **4** to do at the same time: *to mix business and pleasure* **5** to be outgoing in social situations: *he mixed well* **6** *music* to balance and adjust individual performers' parts to make an overall sound by electronic means ▷ *n* **7** something produced by mixing; mixture **8** a mixture of ingredients, esp. one commercially prepared for making a cake **9** *music* the sound produced by mixing ▷ See also **mix-up** [Latin *miscere*] **mixed** *adj*

mixed bag *n informal* something made up of different elements, characteristics, or people

mixed blessing *n* an event or situation with both advantages and disadvantages

mixed doubles *n tennis & badminton* a doubles game with a man and a woman as partners on each side

mixed economy *n* an economy in which some companies are privately owned and others are owned by the government

mixed farming *n* farming involving both the growing of crops and the keeping of livestock **mixed farm** *n*

mixed grill *n* a dish of several kinds of grilled meat, tomatoes, and mushrooms

mixed marriage *n* a marriage between people of different races or religions

mixed metaphor *n* a combination of incongruous metaphors, such as *when the Nazi jackboots sing their swan song*

mixed-up *adj* in a state of mental confusion

mixer *n* **1** a kitchen appliance, usually electrical, used for mixing foods **2** any of various other devices or machines used for mixing things: *a cement mixer* **3** a nonalcoholic drink such as tonic water or ginger ale that is mixed with an alcoholic drink **4** *informal* a person considered in relation to his or her ability to mix socially: *he's not a good mixer*

mixture *n* **1** something produced by blending or combining other things: *top with the cheese and breadcrumb mixture* **2** a combination of different things, such as feelings: *he speaks of her with a mixture of loyalty and regret* **3** *chem* a substance consisting of two or more substances mixed together without any chemical bonding between them

mix-up *n* **1** a confused condition or situation ▷ *vb* **mix up 2** to make into a mixture **3** to confuse: *he mixes Ryan up with Lee* **4 mixed up in** involved in (an activity or group, esp. one that is illegal): *she's mixed up in a drugs racket*

mizzenmast *n naut* (on a vessel with three or more masts) the third mast from the bow [Italian *mezzano* middle + MAST]

MJ megajoule

Mk (in trade names) mark: *a VW Golf Mk 3*

mks units *pl n* a metric system of units based on the metre, kilogram, and second: it forms the basis of the SI units

ml 1 millilitre(s) **2** mile(s)

ML Medieval Latin

MLA (in Northern Ireland and Australia) Member of the Legislative Assembly

MLitt Master of Letters [Latin *Magister Litterarum*]

Mlle *or* **Mlle.** *pl* **Mlles** *or* **Mlles.** the French equivalent of *Miss* [from *Mademoiselle*]

m

MLR minimum lending rate

mm millimetre(s)

Mme *pl* **Mmes** the French equivalent of *Mrs* [from *Madame, Mesdames*]

MMORPG (more-peg) massive(ly) multi-player online role-playing game: an internet-based computer game set in a virtual world, where many people can play at the same time and interact with each other

MMR a combined vaccine against measles, mumps, and rubella, given to very young children

MMus Master of Music

Mn *chem* manganese

MN Minnesota

mnemonic (nim-on-ik) *n* **1** something, for instance a verse, intended to help the memory ▷ *adj* **2** aiding or meant to aid one's memory [Greek *mnēmōn* mindful] **mnemonically** *adv*

mo *n informal, chiefly Brit* short for **moment** (sense 1)

Mo *chem* molybdenum

MO 1 Medical Officer **2** Missouri

m.o. *or* **MO 1** mail order **2** money order

moa *n* a recently extinct large flightless bird of New Zealand that resembled the ostrich [Māori]

moan *n* **1** a low prolonged cry of pain or suffering **2** any similar sound, esp. that made by the wind **3** *informal* a grumble or complaint ▷ *vb* **4** to make a low cry of, or talk in a way suggesting, pain or suffering: *he moaned in pain* **5** to make a sound like a moan: *the wind moaned through the trees* **6** *informal* to grumble or complain [Old English *mǣnan* to grieve over] **moaner** *n*

moat *n* a wide ditch, originally filled with water, surrounding a fortified place such as a castle [Old French *motte* mound]

mob *n* **1** a riotous or disorderly crowd of people **2** *informal* any group of people **3** the masses **4** *slang* a gang of criminals ▷ *vb* **mobbing, mobbed 5** to attack in a group resembling a mob **6** to surround in a crowd to acclaim or attack: *she was mobbed by her fans when she left the theatre* [shortened from Latin *mobile vulgus* the fickle populace]

mobcap *n* a woman's 18th-century cotton cap with a pouched crown [obsolete *mob* woman, esp. loose-living + CAP]

mobile *adj* **1** able to move or be moved: *mobile toilets* **2** changing quickly in expression: *a mobile face* **3** *sociol* (of individuals or social groups) moving within and between classes, occupations, and localities ▷ *n* **4** a light structure suspended in midair with delicately balanced parts that are set in motion by air currents **5** short for **mobile phone** [Latin *mobilis*] **mobility** *n*

mobile home *n* a large caravan, usually staying in one place, which people live in permanently

mobile phone *n* a portable telephone powered by batteries

mobilize *or* **-lise** *vb* **-lizing, -lized** *or* **-lising, -lised 1** to prepare for war or another emergency by organizing resources and the armed services **2** to organize for a purpose: *we must mobilize local residents behind our campaign* **mobilization** *or* **-lisation** *n*

mobster *n US* a member of a criminal organization; gangster

moccasin *n* **1** a type of soft leather shoe traditionally worn by some Native American peoples **2** a soft leather shoe with a raised seam at the front above the toe [Native American word]

mocha (mock-a) *n* **1** a dark brown coffee originally imported from the port of Mocha in Arabia **2** a flavouring made from coffee and chocolate

mock *vb* **1** to behave with scorn or contempt towards a person or thing: *her husband mocked her attempts to educate herself* **2** to imitate or mimic, esp. in fun **3** to defy or frustrate: *the team mocked the visitors' attempts to score* ▷ *n* **4 mocks** *informal* (in England and Wales) school examinations taken as practice before public exams ▷ *adj* **5** sham or imitation: *mock Georgian windows* **6** serving as an imitation or substitute, esp. for practice purposes: *a mock battle* ▷ See also **mock-up** [Old French *mocquer*] **mocking** *n, adj*

mockers *pl n* **put the mockers on** *Brit, Austral & NZ informal* to ruin the chances of success of [perhaps from *mock*]

mockery *n, pl* **-eries 1** ridicule, contempt, or derision **2** a person, thing, or action that is so worthless that it seems like a parody: *the interview was a mockery from start to finish* **3 make a mockery of something** to make something appear worthless or foolish: *the judge's decision makes a mockery of the law*

mock-heroic *adj* (of a literary work, esp. a poem) imitating the style of heroic poetry in order to satirize an unheroic subject

mockingbird *n* an American songbird which can mimic the song of other birds

mock orange *n* a shrub with white fragrant flowers like those of the orange
mock-up *n* a working full-scale model of a machine or apparatus for test or research purposes
mod[1] *n Brit* a member of a group of teenagers, originally in the mid-1960s, who were very clothes-conscious and rode motor scooters [from *modernist*]
mod[2] *n* an annual Highland Gaelic meeting with musical and literary competitions [Gaelic *mōd* assembly]
MOD (in Britain) Ministry of Defence
mod. **1** moderate **2** modern
modal (mode-al) *adj* **1** of or relating to mode or manner **2** *grammar* (of a verb form or auxiliary verb) expressing possibility, intention, or necessity rather than actuality: 'can', 'might', and 'will' are examples of modal verbs in English **3** *music* of or relating to a mode **modality** *n*
mod cons *pl n informal* modern conveniences, such as hot water and heating
mode *n* **1** a manner or way of doing, acting, or existing **2** a particular fashion or style **3** *music* any of the various scales of notes within one octave **4** *maths* the most frequently occurring of a range of values [Latin *modus* manner]
model *n* **1** a three-dimensional representation, usually on a smaller scale, of a device or structure: *an architect's model of the proposed new housing estate* **2** an example or pattern that people might want to follow: *her success makes her an excellent role model for other young Black women* **3** an outstanding example of its kind: *the report is a model of clarity* **4** a person who poses for a sculptor, painter, or photographer **5** a person who wears clothes to display them to prospective buyers; mannequin **6** a design or style of a particular product: *the cheapest model of this car has a 1300cc engine* **7** a theoretical description of the way a system or process works: *a working model of the human immune system* ▷ *adj* **8** excellent or perfect: *a model husband* **9** being a small-scale representation of: *a model aeroplane* ▷ *vb* **-elling, -elled** *or US* **-eling, -eled** **10** to make a model of: *he modelled a plane out of balsa wood* **11** to plan or create according to a model or models: *it had a constitution modelled on that of the United States* **12** to display (clothing and accessories) as a mannequin **13** to pose for a sculptor, painter, or photographer [Latin *modulus*, diminutive of *modus* mode]
modem (mode-em) *n computers* a device for transmitting information between two computers by a telephone line, consisting of a modulator that converts computer signals into audio signals and a corresponding demodulator [from *mo(dulator) dem(odulator)*]
moderate *adj* **1** not extreme or excessive: *a man of moderate views; moderate consumption of alcohol* **2** (of a size, rate, intensity, etc.) towards the middle of the range of possible values: *a moderate-sized garden; a moderate breeze* **3** of average quality or extent: *moderate success* ▷ *n* **4** a person who holds moderate views, esp. in politics ▷ *vb* **-rating, -rated** **5** to make or become less extreme or violent: *he has moderated his opinions since then* **6** to preside over a meeting, discussion, etc. [Latin *moderari* to restrain] **moderately** *adv*
moderation *n* **1** the quality of being moderate **2** the act of moderating **3** **in moderation** within moderate or reasonable limits
moderato (mod-er-**ah**-toe) *adv music* **1** at a moderate speed **2** with restraint: *allegro moderato* [Italian]
moderator *n* **1** *Presbyterian Church* a minister appointed to preside over a Church court, synod, or general assembly **2** a person who presides over a public or legislative assembly **3** a material, such as heavy water, used for slowing down neutrons in nuclear reactors
modern *adj* **1** of the present or a recent time; contemporary: *there have been very few outbreaks of the disease in modern times* **2** using the latest techniques, equipment, etc.; up-to-date: *modern and efficient railways* **3** of contemporary styles or schools of art, literature, and music, esp. those of an experimental kind ▷ *n* **4** a contemporary person [Late Latin *modernus*, from *modus* mode] **modernity** *n*
Modern English *n* the English language since about 1450
modernism *n* an early- and mid-twentieth century movement in art, literature, and music that rejected traditional styles and techniques **modernist** *n, adj*
modernize *or* **-nise** *vb* **-nizing, -nized** *or* **-nising, -nised** **1** to make modern in style, methods, or equipment: *a commitment to modernizing industry* **2** to adopt modern ways or ideas **modernization** *or* **-nisation** *n*
modern languages *n* the languages spoken in present-day Europe, with the exception of English
modern pentathlon *n* an athletic contest consisting of five different events: horse riding with jumps, fencing with electric épée, freestyle swimming, pistol shooting, and cross-country running
modest *adj* **1** having a humble opinion of oneself or one's accomplishments **2** not extreme or excessive: *a modest increase in inflation* **3** not ostentatious or pretentious: *a modest flat in the suburbs* **4** shy or easily embarrassed **5** *old-fashioned* (esp. of clothes) not revealing much of the body: *a modest dress* [Latin *modestus* moderate] **modestly** *adv* **modesty** *n*
modicum *n* a small amount [Latin: a little way]
modifier *n grammar* a word or phrase that makes the sense of another word more specific: for example, the noun *garage* is a modifier of *door* in *garage door*
modify *vb* **-fies, -fying, -fied** **1** to change or alter slightly **2** to make less extreme or uncompromising **3** *grammar* (of a word or phrase) to act as a modifier to another word or phrase [Latin *modus* measure + *facere* to make] **modification** *n*
modish (mode-ish) *adj* in the current fashion or style **modishly** *adv*
modiste (mode-east) *n* a fashionable dressmaker or milliner [French]

m

modulate *vb* **-lating, -lated 1** to change the tone, pitch, or volume of (one's voice) **2** to adjust or regulate the degree of: *the hormone which modulates the development of the sexual organs* **3** *music* to change from one key to another **4** *physics & electronics* to superimpose the amplitude, frequency, or phase of a wave or signal onto another wave or signal [Latin *modulari* to modulate] **modulation** *n* **modulator** *n*

module *n* **1** a standard self-contained unit, such as an assembly of electronic components or a standardized piece of furniture, that can be used in combination with other units **2** *astronautics* a self-contained separable unit making up a spacecraft **3** *education* a short course of study that together with other such courses counts towards a qualification [Latin *modulus*, diminutive of *modus* mode] **modular** *adj*

modulus *n, pl* **-li** *physics* a coefficient expressing a specified property, for instance elasticity, of a specified substance [Latin]

modus operandi (mode-uss op-er-an-die) *n, pl* **modi operandi** (mode-eye) method of operating [Latin]

modus vivendi (mode-uss viv-venn-die) *n, pl* **modi vivendi** (mode-eye) a working arrangement between conflicting interests [Latin: way of living]

moggy *or* **mog** *n, pl* **moggies** *or* **mogs** *Brit, Austral & NZ slang* a cat [dialect *mog*, originally a pet name for a cow]

m

mogul (moh-gl) *n* an important or powerful person

Mogul *adj* of or relating to a Muslim dynasty of Indian emperors established in 1526 [Persian *mughul* Mongolian]

MOH (in Britain) Medical Officer of Health

mohair *n* **1** the long soft silky hair of the Angora goat **2** a fabric made from yarn of this hair and cotton or wool [Arabic *mukhayyar*, literally: choice]

Mohammed *or* **Muhammad** *n* the prophet who founded Islam

Mohawk *n* **1** a member of a Native American people formerly living along the Mohawk river **2** the language of this people

mohican *n* a punk hairstyle in which the head is shaved at the sides and the remaining strip of hair is worn stiffly erect and often brightly coloured [after the *Mohicans*]

Mohican *n* **1** *pl* **-cans** *or* **-can** a member of a Native American people formerly living along the Hudson river **2** the language of this people

moiety (moy-it-ee) *n, pl* **-ties** *archaic* **1** a half **2** one of two parts or divisions of something [Old French *moitié*]

moire (mwahr) *n* a fabric, usually silk, with a watered effect [French]

moiré (mwahr-ray) *adj* **1** having a watered or wavelike pattern ▷ *n* **2** such a pattern, impressed on fabrics **3** a fabric, usually silk, with such a pattern **4** Also: **moiré pattern** a pattern seen when two geometrical patterns, such as grids, are visually superimposed [French]

moist *adj* slightly damp or wet [Old French]

moisten *vb* to make or become moist

moisture *n* water diffused as vapour or condensed on or in objects

moisturize *or* **-rise** *vb* **-rizing, -rized** *or* **-rising, -rised** to add moisture to the air or the skin **moisturizer** *or* **-riser** *n*

mojo *n, pl* **mojos** *or* **mojoes** *US slang* **1** a charm or magic spell **2** the art of casting magic spells **3** uncanny personal power or influence, esp. the power to attract sexually [from West African]

moke *n* **1** *Brit slang* a donkey **2** *Austral & NZ* a horse of inferior quality [origin unknown]

mol *chem* mole

mol. **1** molecular **2** molecule

molar *n* **1** a large back tooth specialized for crushing and chewing food ▷ *adj* **2** of any of these teeth [Latin *mola* millstone]

molasses *n* **1** the thick brown bitter syrup obtained from sugar during refining **2** *US & Canad* same as **treacle** [Portuguese *melaço*]

mold *n, vb US* same as **mould**[1]

mole[1] *n* a small dark raised spot on the skin

mole[2] *n* **1** a small burrowing mammal with velvety dark fur and forelimbs specialized for digging **2** *informal* a spy who has infiltrated an organization and become a trusted member of it [Middle Dutch *mol*]

mole[3] *n* *chem* the basic SI unit of amount of substance: the amount that contains as many elementary entities as there are atoms in 0.012 kilogram of carbon-12 [German *Mol*, short for *Molekül* molecule]

mole[4] *n* **1** a breakwater **2** a harbour protected by a breakwater [Latin *moles* mass]

molecular (mol-lek-yew-lar) *adj* of or relating to molecules

molecular formula *n* *chem* a chemical formula indicating the number and type of atoms in a molecule, but not its structure: NH_3 *is the molecular formula of ammonia*

molecular weight *n* *chem* the sum of all the atomic weights of the atoms in a molecule

molecule (mol-lik-kyool) *n* **1** the simplest unit of a chemical compound that can exist, consisting of two or more atoms held together by chemical bonds **2** a very small particle [New Latin *molecula*, diminutive of Latin *moles* mass]

molehill *n* **1** the small mound of earth thrown up by a burrowing mole **2** **make a mountain out of a molehill** to exaggerate an unimportant matter out of all proportion

molest *vb* **1** to accost or attack someone, esp. a woman or child, with the intention of assaulting her or him sexually **2** to disturb or injure, esp. by using or threatening violence: *killing, capturing, or molesting the local wildlife was strictly forbidden* [Latin *molestare* to annoy] **molestation** *n* **molester** *n*

moll *n slang* a gangster's female accomplice or girlfriend [from *Moll*, familiar form of *Mary*]

mollify *vb* **-fies, -fying, -fied** to make someone less angry or upset; soothe: *he sought to mollify his critics* [Latin *mollis* soft + *facere* to make] **mollification** *n*

mollusc *or US* **mollusk** *n* an invertebrate with a soft unsegmented body and often a shell, such as a snail, mussel, or octopus [Latin *molluscus*]

mollycoddle *vb* **-coddling, -coddled** to give an excessive amount of care and protection to [from *Molly*, girl's name + *coddle*]
Molotov cocktail *n* a simple bomb made from a bottle filled with petrol and a cloth wick; petrol bomb [after V. M. *Molotov*, Soviet statesman]
molt *vb, n US* same as **moult**
molten *adj* so hot that it has melted and formed a liquid: *molten metal*
molto *adv music* very: *allegro molto; molto adagio* [Italian]
molybdenum (mol-lib-din-um) *n chem* a very hard silvery-white metallic element used in alloys, esp. to harden and strengthen steels. Symbol: **Mo** [Greek *molubdos* lead]
mom *n informal, chiefly US, Canad & S African* same as **mother**
moment *n* **1** a short period of time **2** a specific instant or point in time: *at that moment the phone rang* **3 the moment** the present point of time: *for the moment he is out of prison* **4** importance, significance, or value: *a matter of greatest moment* **5** *physics* **A** a tendency to produce motion, esp. rotation about a point or axis **B** the product of a physical quantity, such as force or mass, and its distance from a fixed reference point [Latin *momentum* movement]
momentary *adj* lasting for only a moment; temporary **momentarily** *adv*
moment of truth *n* a moment when a person or thing is put to the test
momentous (moh-men-tuss) *adj* of great significance **momentousness** *n*
momentum (moh-men-tum) *n* **1** the impetus to go forward, develop, or get stronger: *the campaign steadily gathered support and momentum* **2** the impetus of a moving body: *the sledge gathered momentum as it slid ever faster down the slope* **3** *physics* the product of a body's mass and its velocity [Latin: movement]
momma *n chiefly US* an informal or childish word for **mother**
Mon. Monday
mon- *combining form* See **mono-**
monad *n* **1** *philosophy* any fundamental singular metaphysical entity **2** a single-celled organism **3** an atom, ion, or radical with a valency of one [Greek *monas* unit]
monandrous *adj* **1** *biol* having only one stamen in each flower **2** having only one male sexual partner over a period of time [Greek *monos* sole + *anēr* man]
monarch *n* a sovereign head of state, esp. a king, queen, or emperor, who rules by hereditary right [Greek *monos* sole + *arkhos* ruler] **monarchical** *or* **monarchic** *adj*
monarchism *n* the belief that a country should have a hereditary ruler, such as a king, rather than an elected one **monarchist** *n, adj*
monarchy *n, pl* **-chies** **1** a form of government in which supreme authority is held by a single hereditary ruler, such as a king **2** a country reigned over by a monarch
monastery *n, pl* **-teries** the building or group of buildings where a community of monks lives [Greek *monazein* to live alone]
monastic *adj* **1** of or relating to monasteries, monks, or nuns **2** (of a way of life) simple and austere; ascetic **monasticism** *n*
monatomic *adj chem* **1** (of an element) consisting of single atoms **2** (of a compound or molecule) having only one atom or group that can be replaced in a reaction
Monday *n* the second day of the week, and the first day of the working week [Old English *mōnandæg* moon's day]
monetarism *n* **1** the theory that inflation is caused by an excess quantity of money in an economy **2** an economic policy based on this theory and a belief in the efficiency of free market forces **monetarist** *n, adj*
monetary *adj* of money or currency [Latin *moneta* money]
money *n* **1** a means of payment and measure of value: *some cultures used to use shells as money* **2** the official currency, in the form of banknotes or coins, issued by a government **3 moneys** *or* **monies** *law old-fashioned* a financial sum or income **4** an unspecified amount of wealth: *money to lend* **5** *informal* a rich person or rich people: *he married money* **6 for my money** in my opinion **7 one's money's worth** full value for the money one has paid for something **8 put money on** to place a bet on. ▷ Related adjective: **pecuniary** [Latin *moneta*]
moneybags *n informal* a very rich person
moneychanger *n* a person engaged in the business of exchanging currencies or money
moneyed *or* **monied** *adj* having a great deal of money; rich
money-grubbing *adj informal* seeking greedily to obtain money **money-grubber** *n*
moneylender *n* a person who lends money at interest as a living
moneymaker *n* **1** a person whose chief concern is to make money **2** a person or thing that is or might be profitable **moneymaking** *adj, n*
money-spinner *n informal* an enterprise, idea, or thing that is a source of wealth
-monger *combining form* **1** indicating a trader or dealer: *an ironmonger* **2** indicating a promoter of something: *a warmonger* [Old English *mangere*]
mongol *n old-fashioned, offensive* (not in technical use) a person with Down's syndrome **mongoloid** *n, adj*
Mongolian *adj* **1** of Mongolia ▷ *n* **2** a person from Mongolia **3** the language of Mongolia
mongolism *n old-fashioned, offensive* a former name (not in technical use) for **Down's syndrome**
Mongoloid *adj* of a major racial group of mankind, characterized by yellowish skin, straight black hair, and slanting eyes: includes most of the people of SE Asia, E Asia, and the Arctic area of N America
mongoose *n, pl* **-gooses** a small long-tailed predatory mammal of Asia and Africa that kills snakes [from Marathi (a language of India) *mangūs*]
mongrel *n* **1** a dog of mixed breeding **2** something made up of things from a variety of sources: *despite using components from three other cars,*

m

this new model is no mongrel ▷ *adj* **3** of mixed breeding or origin: *a mongrel race* [from obsolete *mong* mixture]

monied *adj* same as **moneyed**

monies *n law old-fashioned* a plural of **money**

moniker *or* **monicker** *n slang* a person's name or nickname [Shelta *munnik*, altered from Irish Gaelic *ainm* name]

monism *n philosophy* the doctrine that reality consists of only one basic substance or element, such as mind or matter [Greek *monos* sole] **monist** *n, adj*

monition *n* a warning or caution [Latin *monere* to warn]

monitor *n* **1** a person or device that warns, checks, controls, or keeps a continuous record of something **2** *Brit, Austral & NZ* a pupil assisting a teacher with various duties **3** a screen used to display certain kinds of information, for example in airports or television studios **4** a large predatory lizard inhabiting warm regions of Africa, Asia, and Australia ▷ *vb* **5** to act as a monitor of **6** to observe or record the condition or performance of a person or thing **7** to check a broadcast for acceptable quality or content [Latin *monere* to advise] **monitorial** *adj*

monitory *adj* acting as or giving a warning

monk *n* a male member of a religious community bound by vows of poverty, chastity, and obedience. Related adjective: **monastic** [Greek *monos* alone] **monkish** *adj*

m

monkey *n* **1** any long-tailed primate that is not a lemur or tarsier **2** (loosely) any primate that is not a human **3** a naughty or mischievous child **4** *slang* £500 or $500 **5** **give a monkey's** *Brit slang* to care about or regard as important: *who gives a monkey's what he thinks?* ▷ *vb* **6** **monkey around** *or* **about with** to meddle or tinker with [origin unknown]

monkey business *n informal* mischievous or dishonest behaviour or acts

monkey nut *n Brit* a peanut

monkey puzzle *n* a South American coniferous tree with branches shaped like a candelabrum and stiff sharp leaves

monkey tricks *or US* **monkey shines** *pl n informal* mischievous behaviour or acts

monkey wrench *n chiefly Brit* a wrench with adjustable jaws

monkshood *n* a poisonous plant with hooded blue-purple flowers

mono *adj* **1** short for **monophonic** ▷ *n* **2** monophonic sound

mono- *or before a vowel* **mon-** *combining form* **1** one; single: *monorail; monolingual* **2** *chem* indicating that a chemical compound contains a single specified atom or group: *monoxide* [Greek *monos* alone]

monobasic *adj chem* (of an acid, such as hydrogen chloride) having only one replaceable hydrogen atom per molecule

monochromatic *adj* (of light or other electromagnetic radiation) having only one wavelength

monochrome *adj* **1** *photog & television* black-and-white ▷ *n* **2** a painting or drawing done in a range of tones of a single colour [Greek *monokhrōmos* of one colour]

monocle (mon-a-kl) *n* (formerly) a lens worn for correcting defective sight in one eye only, held in position by the facial muscles [MONO- + Latin *oculus* eye] **monocled** *adj*

monocline *n* a fold in stratified rocks in which the strata are inclined in the same direction from the horizontal [MONO- + Greek *klinein* to lean] **monoclinal** *adj, n*

monoclinic *adj crystallog* of the crystal system characterized by three unequal axes, one pair of which are not at right angles to each other

monoclonal antibody *n* an antibody produced from a single clone of cells grown in a culture

monocoque (mon-a-cock) *n* a vehicle body moulded from a single piece of material with no separate load-bearing parts [French]

monocotyledon (mon-no-kot-ill-**leed**-on) *n* any flowering plant with a single embryonic seed leaf, such as the grasses, lilies, palms, and orchids

monocular *adj* having or intended for the use of only one eye [Late Latin *monoculus* one-eyed]

monoculture *n* the continuous growing of one type of crop

monody *n, pl* **-dies** **1** (in Greek tragedy) an ode sung by a single actor **2** *music* a style of composition consisting of a single vocal part, usually with accompaniment [MONO- + Greek *aeidein* to sing] **monodist** *n*

monoecious (mon-**ee**-shuss) *adj* **1** (of some flowering plants) having the male and female reproductive organs in separate flowers on the same plant **2** (of some animals and lower plants) hermaphrodite [MONO- + Greek *oikos* house]

monogamy *n* the state or practice of having only one husband or wife at a time [MONO- + Greek *gamos* marriage] **monogamous** *adj*

monogram *n* a design of one or more letters, esp. initials, on clothing, stationery, etc. [Greek *monogrammatos* consisting of one letter]

monograph *n* a paper, book, or other work concerned with a single subject or aspect of a subject

monolingual *adj* knowing or expressed in only one language

monolith *n* **1** a large block of stone **2** a statue, obelisk, or column cut from one block of stone **3** something which can be regarded as forming one large, single, whole: *the Christian religion should not be thought of as a monolith* [Greek *monolithos* made from a single stone] **monolithic** *adj*

monologue *n* **1** a long speech made by one actor in a play or film; soliloquy **2** a dramatic piece for a single performer **3** any long speech by one person, esp. one which prevents other people talking or expressing their views [Greek *monólogos* speaking alone]

USAGE See at **soliloquy**.

monomania *n* an obsession with one thing or idea **monomaniac** *n, adj*

monomer *n chem* a compound whose molecules can join together to form a polymer

monomial *n maths* an expression consisting of a single term, such as $5ax$ [MONO- + (BIN)OMIAL]

mononucleosis (mon-oh-new-klee-**oh**-siss) *n* **infectious mononucleosis** same as **glandular fever**
monophonic *adj* (of a system of broadcasting, recording, or reproducing sound) using only one channel between source and loudspeaker. Short form: **mono**
monoplane *n* an aeroplane with only one pair of wings
monopolize *or* **-lise** *vb* **-lizing, -lized** *or* **-lising, -lised 1** to have full control or use of, to the exclusion of others **2** to hold exclusive control of a market or supply
monopoly *n, pl* **-lies 1** exclusive control of the market supply of a product or service **2 A** an enterprise exercising this control **B** the product or service so controlled **3** *law* the exclusive right granted to a person or company by the state to trade in a specified commodity or area **4** exclusive control, possession, or use of something [MONO- + Greek *pōlein* to sell] **monopolist** *n* **monopolistic** *adj*
Monopoly *n trademark* a board game for two to six players who deal in 'property' as they move tokens around the board
monorail *n* a single-rail railway
monosaccharide *n* a simple sugar, such as glucose, that cannot be broken down into other sugars
monosodium glutamate *n* a substance which enhances protein flavours: used as a food additive
monosyllable *n* a word of one syllable **monosyllabic** *adj*
monotheism *n* the belief or doctrine that there is only one God **monotheist** *n, adj* **monotheistic** *adj*
monotone *n* **1** a single unvaried pitch level in speech or sound **2** a way of speaking which lacks variety of pitch or expression: *he rambled on in a dull monotone* **3** lack of variety in style or expression ▷ *adj* **4** unvarying
monotonous *adj* tedious because of lack of variety **monotonously** *adv*
monotony *n, pl* **-nies 1** wearisome routine; dullness **2** lack of variety in pitch or tone
monounsaturated *adj* of a group of vegetable oils, such as olive oil, that have a neutral effect on cholesterol in the body
monovalent *adj chem* **1** having a valency of one **2** having only one valency **monovalence** *or* **monovalency** *n*
monoxide *n* an oxide that contains one oxygen atom per molecule
Monseigneur (mon-sen-**nyur**) *n, pl* **Messeigneurs** (may-sen-**nyur**) a title given to French prelates and princes [French, literally: my lord]
monsieur (muss-**syuh**) *n, pl* **messieurs** (may-**syuh**) a French form of address equivalent to *sir* or *Mr* [French, literally: my lord]
Monsignor *n, pl* **Monsignors** *or* **Monsignori** *RC Church* a title given to certain senior clergymen [Italian]
monsoon *n* **1** a seasonal wind of S Asia which blows from the southwest in summer and from the northeast in winter **2** the rainy season when the SW monsoon blows, from about April to October [Arabic *mawsim* season]
monsoon bucket *n NZ* a large container for water carried by helicopter and used to extinguish bush and scrub fires
mons pubis (monz **pew**-biss) *n, pl* **montes pubis** (**mon**-teez) the fatty flesh in human males over the junction of the pubic bones [New Latin: hill of the pubes]
monster *n* **1** an imaginary beast, usually frightening in appearance **2** a very large person, animal, or thing **3** an exceptionally cruel or wicked person **4** a person, animal, or plant with a marked deformity [Latin *monstrum* portent]
monstrance *n RC Church* a vessel in which the consecrated Host is exposed for adoration [Latin *monstrare* to show]
monstrosity *n, pl* **-ties 1** an outrageous or ugly person or thing **2** the state or quality of being monstrous
monstrous *adj* **1** hideous or unnatural in size or character **2** atrocious, unjust, or shocking: *the President described the invasion as monstrous* **3** huge **4** of or like a monster **5** (of plants and animals) abnormal in structure **monstrously** *adv*
mons veneris (monz **ven**-er-iss) *n, pl* **montes veneris** (**mon**-teez) the fatty flesh in human females over the junction of the pubic bones [New Latin: hill of Venus]
montage (mon-**tahzh**) *n* **1** a picture made by combining material from various sources, such as other pictures or photographs **2** the technique of producing pictures in this way **3** a method of film editing by juxtaposition or partial superimposition of several shots to form a single image **4** a film sequence of this kind [French]
month *n* **1** one of the twelve divisions (**calendar months**) of the calendar year **2** a period of time extending from one date to a corresponding date in the next calendar month **3** a period of four weeks or of 30 days [Old English *mōnath*]
monthly *adj* **1** happening or payable once every month: *a monthly magazine* **2** lasting or valid for a month: *a monthly travel pass* ▷ *adv* **3** once a month ▷ *n, pl* **-lies 4** a magazine published once a month
monument *n* **1** something, such as a statue or building, erected in commemoration of a person or event **2** an ancient building which is regarded as an important part of a country's history **3** an exceptional example of the results of something: *the whole town is a monument to bad sixties' architecture* [Latin *monumentum*]
monumental *adj* **1** large, impressive, or likely to last or be remembered for a long time: *a monumental three-volume biography* **2** of or being a monument **3** *informal* extreme: *a monumental gamble*
moo *n* **1** the characteristic deep long sound made by a cow ▷ *vb* **2** to make this sound; low
mooch *vb slang* **1** to loiter or walk aimlessly **2** to cadge or scrounge [perhaps Old French *muchier* to skulk]
mood[1] *n* **1** a temporary state of mind or temper: *a happy mood* **2** a sullen or gloomy state of mind, esp. when temporary: *she's in a mood* **3** a prevailing

atmosphere or feeling: *the current mood of disenchantment with politics* **4 in the mood** inclined to do or have (something) [Old English *mōd* mind, feeling]
mood² *n grammar* a form of a verb indicating whether the verb expresses a fact (indicative mood), a wish or supposition (subjunctive mood), or a command (imperative mood) [same as MOOD¹]
moody *adj* **moodier, moodiest 1** sullen, sulky, or gloomy **2** temperamental or changeable **moodily** *adv* **moodiness** *n*
mooi *adj S African slang* pleasing or nice [Afrikaans]
moolah *n slang* money [origin unknown]
mooli *n* a type of large white radish [E African native name]
moon *n* **1** the natural satellite of the earth. Related adjective: **lunar 2** this satellite as it is seen during its revolution around the earth, esp. at one of its phases: *new moon*; *full moon* **3** any natural satellite of a planet **4** a month **5 over the moon** *informal* extremely happy; ecstatic ▷ *vb* **6 moon about** *or* **around** to be idle in a listless or dreamy way [Old English *mōna*] **moonless** *adj*
moonbeam *n* a ray of moonlight
moon-faced *adj* having a round face
moonlight *n* **1** light from the sun received on earth after reflection by the moon ▷ *adj* **2** illuminated by the moon: *a moonlight walk* ▷ *vb* **-lighting, -lighted 3** *informal* to work at a secondary job, esp. illegally **moonlighter** *n*
moonlight flit *n Brit & Austral informal* a hurried departure at night to avoid paying rent
moonlit *adj* illuminated by the moon
moonscape *n* the surface of the moon or a picture or model of it
moonshine *n* **1** *US & Canad* illegally distilled or smuggled whisky **2** foolish or nonsensical talk or thought
moonshot *n* the launching of a spacecraft to the moon
moonstone *n* a white translucent form of feldspar, used as a gem
moonstruck *adj* slightly mad or odd, as if affected by the moon
moony *adj* **moonier, mooniest** *Brit, Austral & NZ informal* dreamy or listless
moor¹ *n Brit* an expanse of open uncultivated ground covered with heather, coarse grass, and bracken [Old English *mōr*]
moor² *vb* to secure a ship or boat with cables, ropes, or anchors so that it remains in one place [Germanic] **moorage** *n*
Moor *n* a member of a Muslim people of North Africa who ruled much of Spain and Portugal between the 8th and 15th centuries [Greek *Mauros*]
moorhen *n* a waterfowl with black plumage and a red bill
mooring *n* a place where a ship or boat can be tied up or anchored
moorings *pl n naut* the ropes and anchors used in mooring a vessel
Moorish *adj* **1** of or relating to the Moors **2** of a style of architecture used in Spain from the 8th to the 15th centuries, characterized by the horseshoe arch
moorland *n Brit* an area of moor
moose *n, pl* **moose** a large North American deer with large flattened antlers; the American elk [from a Native American language]
moot *adj* **1** subject or open to debate: *a moot point* ▷ *vb* **2** to suggest or bring up for debate: *a compromise proposal, involving building fewer flats, was mooted* ▷ *n* **3** (in Anglo-Saxon England) a local administrative assembly [Old English *gemōt*]
mop *n* **1** a tool with a head made of twists of cotton or sponge and a long handle used for washing or polishing floors **2** a similar tool, except smaller and without a long handle, used to wash dishes **3** a thick untidy mass of hair ▷ *vb* **mopping, mopped 4** to clean or soak up with or as if with a mop: *she mopped her brow with a handkerchief* ▷ See also **mop up** [Latin *mappa* napkin]
mope *vb* **moping, moped 1** to be gloomy or apathetic **2** to walk around in a gloomy and aimless manner [perhaps from obsolete *mope* fool]
moped *n* a light motorcycle not over 50cc [*motor + pedal*]
mopes *pl n* **the mopes** low spirits
mopoke *n* **1** a small spotted owl of Australia and New Zealand **2** *Austral slang* a slow or lugubrious person [imitative of the bird's cry]
moppet *n* same as **poppet** [obsolete *mop* rag doll]
mop up *vb* **1** to clean with a mop **2** *informal* to complete the last remaining stages of a job **3** *military* to clear remaining enemy forces after a battle, by killing them or taking them prisoner
moquette *n* a thick velvety fabric used for carpets and upholstery [French]
moraine *n* a ridge or mound formed from debris deposited by a glacier [French]
moral *adj* **1** concerned with or relating to the distinction between good and bad or right and wrong behaviour: *moral sense* **2** based on a sense of right and wrong according to conscience: *moral duty* **3** displaying a sense of right and wrong; (of support or a victory) psychological rather than practical ▷ *n* **4** a lesson about right or wrong behaviour that is shown in a fable or event **5 morals** principles of behaviour in accordance with standards of right and wrong [Latin *moralis* relating to morals or customs] **morally** *adv*
morale (mor-**rahl**) *n* the degree of confidence or optimism of a person or group [French]
moralist *n* **1** a person who has a strong sense of right and wrong **2** someone who criticizes other people for not doing what he or she thinks is morally correct **moralistic** *adj*
morality *n, pl* **-ties 1** good moral conduct **2** the degree to which something is morally acceptable: *we discussed the morality of fox-hunting* **3** a system of moral principles
morality play *n* a medieval type of drama concerned with the conflict between personified virtues and vices
moralize *or* **-lise** *vb* **-lizing, -lized** *or* **-lising, -lised 1** to discuss or consider something in the light of one's own moral beliefs, esp. with disapproval

2 to interpret or explain in a moral sense 3 to improve the morals of
moral philosophy *n* the branch of philosophy dealing with ethics
morass *n* 1 a tract of swampy low-lying land 2 a disordered, confusing, or muddled state of affairs [Old French *marais* marsh]
moratorium *n, pl* **-ria** *or* **-riums** 1 a legally authorized postponement of the payment of a debt 2 an agreed suspension of activity [Latin *mora* delay]
moray *n* a large marine eel marked with brilliant colours [Greek *muraina*]
morbid *adj* 1 having an unusual interest in death or unpleasant events 2 *med* relating to or characterized by disease [Latin *morbus* illness] **morbidity** *n* **morbidly** *adv*
mordant *adj* 1 sarcastic or caustic: *mordant wit* ▷ *n* 2 a substance used in dyeing to fix colours 3 an acid or other corrosive fluid used to etch lines on a printing plate [Latin *mordere* to bite]
more *adj* 1 the comparative of **much** or **many**: *more joy than you know; even more are leaving the country* 2 additional or further: *no more apples* 3 **more of** to a greater extent or degree: *more of a nuisance* ▷ *adv* 4 used to form the comparative of some adjectives and adverbs: *more quickly* 5 the comparative of **much**: *people listen to the radio more now* 6 **more or less** A as an estimate; approximately B to an unspecified extent or degree: *the film was a disaster, more or less* [Old English *māra*]
USAGE See at **most**.
moreish *or* **morish** *adj informal* (of food) causing a desire for more
morel *n* an edible mushroom with a pitted cap [French *morille*]
morello *n, pl* **-los** a variety of small very dark sour cherry [Italian: blackish]
moreover *adv* in addition to what has already been said
morepork *n chiefly* NZ same as **mopoke**
mores (more-rayz) *pl n* the customs and conventions embodying the fundamental values of a community [Latin: customs]
Moreton Bay bug *n* an Australian flattish edible shellfish [after *Moreton Bay*, Queensland]
morganatic *adj* of or designating a marriage between a person of high rank and a person of low rank, by which the latter is not elevated to the higher rank and any children have no rights to inherit the higher party's titles or property [Medieval Latin *morganaticum* morning-gift after consummation representing the husband's only liability]
morgue *n* 1 a mortuary 2 *informal* a store of clippings and back numbers used for reference in a newspaper [French]
moribund *adj* 1 near death 2 no longer performing effectively or usefully: *a moribund economy* [Latin *mori* to die]
morish *adj* same as **moreish**
Mormon *n* 1 a member of the Church of Jesus Christ of Latter-day Saints, founded in 1830 in New York by Joseph Smith ▷ *adj* 2 of the Mormons, their Church, or their beliefs **Mormonism** *n*
morn *n poetic or Austral* morning [Old English *morgen*]
mornay *adj* served with a cheese sauce: *haddock mornay* [after Philippe de *Mornay*, Huguenot leader]
morning *n* 1 the first part of the day, ending at noon 2 daybreak; dawn 3 **the morning after** *informal* the aftereffects of excess, esp. a hangover ▷ *adj* 4 of or in the morning: *morning coffee* [from *morn*, on the model of *evening*]
morning dress *n* formal daytime dress for men, consisting of a frock coat with the front cut away (**morning coat**), usually with grey trousers and top hat
morning-glory *n, pl* **-ries** a tropical climbing plant with trumpet-shaped blue, pink, or white flowers, which close in late afternoon
mornings *adv informal* in the morning, esp. regularly, or during every morning
morning sickness *n* nausea occurring shortly after rising in early pregnancy
morning star *n* a planet, usually Venus, seen just before sunrise
Moroccan *adj* 1 of Morocco ▷ *n* 2 a person from Morocco
morocco *n* a fine soft leather made from goatskins [after *Morocco*, where it was originally made]
moron *n* 1 *informal, derogatory* a foolish or stupid person 2 *not in technical use, offensive* a person having an intelligence quotient of between 50 and 70 [Greek *mōros* foolish] **moronic** *adj*
morose (mor-rohss) *adj* ill-tempered, sullen, and unwilling to talk very much [Latin *morosus* peevish] **morosely** *adv*
morpheme *n linguistics* a speech element having a meaning or grammatical function that cannot be subdivided into further such elements
morphine *or* **morphia** *n* a drug extracted from opium: used in medicine as an anaesthetic and sedative [*Morpheus*, in Greek mythology, the god of sleep and dreams]
morphing *n* a computer technique used for graphics and in films, in which one image is gradually transformed into another image without individual changes being noticeable in the process [from METAMORPHOSIS]
morphology *n* the science of forms and structures of organisms or words **morphological** *adj*
morris dance *n* an old English folk dance performed by men (**morris men**) who wear a traditional costume decorated with bells [Middle English *moreys daunce* Moorish dance]
morrow *n* **the morrow** *old-fashioned or poetic* 1 the next day 2 the morning [Old English *morgen* morning]
Morse code *n* a code formerly used internationally for transmitting messages, in which letters and numbers are represented by groups of dots and dashes, or by shorter and longer sounds [after Samuel *Morse*, inventor]
morsel *n* a small piece of something, esp. of food [Old French *mors* a bite]
mortal *adj* 1 (of living beings, esp. humans) destined to die sometime rather than living forever 2 causing death; fatal: *a mortal wound*

3 deadly or unrelenting: *he is my mortal enemy* **4** of or resulting from the fear of death: *mortal terror* **5** of or involving life or the world: *the hangman's noose ended his mortal existence* **6** great or very intense: *mortal pain* **7** *informal* conceivable or possible: *there was no mortal reason to leave* **8** *slang* long and tedious: *for three mortal hours* ▷ *n* **9** a human being [Latin *mors* death] **mortally** *adv*

mortality *n, pl* **-ties 1** the condition of being mortal **2** great loss of life, as in war or disaster **3** the number of deaths in a given period

mortal sin *n Christianity* a sin that will lead to damnation unless repented of

mortar *n* **1** a small cannon that fires shells in high arcs **2** a mixture of cement or lime or both with sand and water, used to hold bricks or stones together **3** a vessel, usually bowl-shaped, in which substances are crushed with a pestle ▷ *vb* **4** to fire on with mortars **5** to join bricks or stones with mortar [Latin *mortarium* basin in which mortar is mixed]

mortarboard *n* **1** a black tasselled academic cap with a flat square top **2** a small square board with a handle on the underside for carrying mortar

mortgage *n* **1** an agreement under which a person borrows money to buy property, esp. a house, and the lender can take possession of the property if the borrower fails to repay the money **2** a loan obtained under such an agreement: *a mortgage of three times one's income* **3** a regular repayment of money borrowed under such an agreement: *the monthly mortgage on the building* ▷ *vb* **-gaging, -gaged 4** to pledge a house or other property as security for the repayment of a loan ▷ *adj* **5** of or relating to a mortgage: *a mortgage payment* [Old French, literally: dead pledge]

mortgagee *n* the person or organization who lends money in a mortgage agreement

mortgagor *or* **-ger** *n* the person who borrows money in a mortgage agreement

mortice *or* **mortise** (mor-tiss) *n* **1** a slot or recess cut into a piece of wood or stone to receive a matching projection (tenon) on another piece, or a mortice lock ▷ *vb* **-ticing, -ticed** *or* **-tising, -tised 2** to cut a slot or recess in a piece of wood or stone **3** to join two pieces of wood or stone by means of a mortice and tenon [Old French *mortoise*]

mortice lock *n* a lock set into the edge of a door so that the mechanism of the lock is enclosed by the door

mortician *n chiefly US* same as **undertaker**

mortify *vb* **-fies, -fying, -fied 1** to make someone feel ashamed or embarrassed **2** *Christianity* to subdue one's emotions, the body, etc., by self-denial **3** (of flesh) to become gangrenous [Latin *mors* death + *facere* to do] **mortification** *n* **mortifying** *adj*

mortuary *n, pl* **-aries** a building or room where dead bodies are kept before cremation or burial [Latin *mortuarius* of the dead]

mosaic (moh-zay-ik) *n* a design or decoration made up of small pieces of coloured glass or stone [Greek *mouseios* of the Muses]

Mosaic *adj* of or relating to Moses or the laws and traditions ascribed to him

moscovium *n chem* a synthetic radioactive element produced in small quantities. Symbol: **Mc** [after *Moscow*, where it was first synthesized]

moselle *n* a German white wine from the valley of the river Moselle

mosey *vb* **mosey along** *or* **on** *informal* to walk slowly and casually; amble [origin unknown]

Moslem *n, pl* **-lems** *or* **-lem**, *adj* same as **Muslim**

mosque *n* a Muslim place of worship [Arabic *masjid* temple]

mosquito *n, pl* **-toes** *or* **-tos** a two-winged insect, the females of which pierce the skin of humans and animals to suck their blood [Spanish, diminutive of *mosca* fly]

mosquito net *n* a fine curtain or net to keep mosquitoes away, esp. hung over a bed

moss *n* **1** a very small flowerless plant typically growing in dense mats on trees, rocks, or moist ground **2** *Scot & N English* a peat bog or marsh [Old English *mos* swamp] **mossy** *adj*

mossie *n S African* the common sparrow [Afrikaans]

moss rose *n* a variety of rose that has a mossy stem and fragrant pink flowers

most *n* **1** the greatest number or degree: *the most I can ever remember being paid* **2** the majority: *most of his records are dreadful* **3 at (the) most** at the maximum: *she is fifteen at the most* **4 make the most of** to use to the best advantage: *they made the most of their chances* ▷ *adj* **5** of or being the majority of a group of things or people or the largest part of something: *most people don't share your views* **6 the most** the superlative of **many** or **much**: *he has the most talent* ▷ *adv* **7 the most** used to form the superlative of some adjectives and adverbs: *the most beautiful women in the world* **8** the superlative of **much**: *what do you like most about your job?* **9** very; exceedingly: *a most unfortunate accident* [Old English *māst* or *mǣst*]

> **USAGE** *More* and *most* should be distinguished when used in comparisons. *More* applies to cases involving two people, objects, etc., *most* to cases involving three or more: *John is the more intelligent of the two; he is the most intelligent of the students.*

mostly *adv* **1** almost entirely; generally: *the men at the party were mostly young* **2** on many or most occasions; usually: *rattlesnakes mostly hunt at night*.

Most Reverend *n* (in Britain) a courtesy title applied to archbishops

mot (moh) *n* short for **bon mot** [French: word]

MOT 1 *Brit* short for **MOT test 2** *Brit* the certificate showing that a vehicle has passed its MOT test **3** *NZ* Ministry of Transport

mote *n* a tiny speck [Old English *mot*]

motel *n* a roadside hotel for motorists [*mo(tor)* + *(ho)tel*]

motet (moh-tet) *n* a religious song for a choir in which several voices, usually unaccompanied, sing contrasting parts simultaneously [Old French, diminutive of *mot* word]

moth *n* any of numerous chiefly nocturnal insects resembling butterflies, that typically have stout bodies and do not have club-shaped antennae [Old English *moththe*]

mothball *n* **1** a small ball of camphor or naphthalene placed in stored clothing to repel clothes moths **2** **put in mothballs** to postpone work on ▷ *vb* **3** to take something out of operation but maintain it for future use **4** to postpone work on

moth-eaten *adj* **1** decayed or scruffy **2** eaten away by or as if by moths: *a moth-eaten suit*

mother *n* **1** a female who has given birth to offspring **2** a person's own mother **3** a title given to certain members of female religious orders **4** motherly qualities, such as maternal affection: *it appealed to the mother in her* **5** **the mother of** a female or thing that creates, founds, or protects something: *the mother of modern feminism; necessity is the mother of invention* **6** **the mother of all** *informal* the greatest example of its kind: *the mother of all parties* ▷ *adj* **7** of or relating to a female or thing that creates, founds, or protects something: *our mother company is in New York* **8** native or innate: *mother wit* ▷ *vb* **9** to give birth to or produce **10** to nurture or protect [Old English *mōdor*] **motherless** *adj* **motherly** *adj*

motherboard *n* *electronics* a printed circuit board through which signals between all other boards are routed

Mother Carey's chicken *n* same as **stormy petrel** [origin unknown]

mother country *n* **1** the original country of colonists or settlers **2** a person's native country

motherhood *n* the state of being a mother

Mothering Sunday *n* **1** (in Britain and S Africa) the fourth Sunday in Lent, when mothers traditionally receive presents from their children **2** (in Australia) the second Sunday in May, when mothers traditionally receive presents from their children. Also called: **Mother's Day**

mother-in-law *n, pl* **mothers-in-law** the mother of one's wife or husband

motherland *n* a person's native country

mother-of-pearl *n* a hard iridescent substance that forms the inner layer of the shells of certain molluscs, such as the oyster

Mother's Day *n* **1** See **Mothering Sunday** **2** *US & Canad* the second Sunday in May, observed as a day in honour of mothers

mother superior *n, pl* **mother superiors** *or* **mothers superior** the head of a community of nuns

mother tongue *n* the language first learned by a child

mothproof *adj* **1** (esp. of clothes) chemically treated so as to repel clothes moths ▷ *vb* **2** to make mothproof

motif (moh-**teef**) *n* **1** a distinctive idea, esp. a theme elaborated on in a piece of music or literature **2** a recurring shape in a design **3** a single decoration, such as a symbol or name on a piece of clothing [French]

motile *adj* capable of independent movement [Latin *movere* to move] **motility** *n*

motion *n* **1** the process of continual change in the position of an object; movement: *the motion of the earth round the sun*. Related adjective: **kinetic** **2** a movement or gesture: *he made stabbing motions with the spear* **3** a way or style of moving: *massage the back with steady circular motions* **4** a formal proposal to be discussed and voted on in a debate or meeting **5** *Brit* **A** the evacuation of the bowels **B** excrement **6** **go through the motions** to do something mechanically or without sincerity **7** **set in motion** to make operational or start functioning ▷ *vb* **8** to signal or direct a person by a movement or gesture: *she motioned to me to sit down* [Latin *movere* to move] **motionless** *adj*

motion picture *n* *US & Canad* a film; movie

motivate *vb* **-vating, -vated** **1** to give a reason or inspiration for a course of action to someone: *he was motivated purely by greed* **2** to inspire and encourage someone to do something: *a good teacher must motivate her pupils* **motivation** *n*

motive *n* **1** the reason, whether conscious or unconscious, for a certain course of action **2** same as **motif** (sense 2) ▷ *adj* **3** of or causing motion: *a motive force* [Late Latin *motivus* moving]

motive power *n* **1** any source of energy used to produce motion **2** the means of supplying power to an engine or vehicle

mot juste (moh **zhoost**) *n, pl* **mots justes** the appropriate word or expression [French]

motley *adj* **1** made up of people or things of different types: *a motley assortment of mules, donkeys, and camels* **2** multicoloured ▷ *n* **3** *history* the costume of a jester [perhaps Old English *mot* speck]

motocross *n* the sport of motorcycle racing across rough ground [*moto(r) + cross(-country)*]

motor *n* **1** the engine, esp. an internal-combustion engine, of a vehicle **2** a machine that converts energy, esp. electrical energy, into mechanical energy **3** *chiefly Brit informal* a car ▷ *adj* **4** *chiefly Brit* of or relating to cars and other vehicles powered by petrol or diesel engines: *the motor industry* **5** powered by or relating to a motor: *a new synthetic motor oil* **6** *physiol* producing or causing motion ▷ *vb* **7** to travel by car **8** *informal* to move fast [Latin *movere* to move] **motorized** *or* **-ised** *adj*

motorbicycle *n* **1** a motorcycle **2** a moped

motorbike *n informal* a motorcycle

motorboat *n* any boat powered by a motor

motorcade *n* a procession of cars carrying an important person or people [*motor + (caval)cade*]

motorcar *n* a more formal word for **car**

motorcycle *n* a two-wheeled vehicle driven by an engine **motorcyclist** *n*

motorist *n* a driver of a car

motorman *n, pl* **-men** *Brit, Austral & NZ* the driver of an electric train

motor scooter *n* a light motorcycle with small wheels and an enclosed engine

motor vehicle *n* a road vehicle driven by an engine

motorway *n Brit, Austral & NZ* a dual carriageway for fast-moving traffic, with no stopping permitted and no crossroads

Motown *n trademark* music combining rhythm and blues and pop [*Mo(tor) Town*, nickname for Detroit]

motte *n history* a mound on which a castle was built [Old French]

MOT test *n* (in Britain) a compulsory annual test of the roadworthiness of motor vehicles over 3 years old

mottled *adj* coloured with streaks or blotches of different shades [from *motley*] **mottling** *n*

motto *n, pl* **-toes** *or* **-tos** **1** a short saying expressing the guiding maxim or ideal of a family or organization, esp. when part of a coat of arms **2** a verse or maxim contained in a paper cracker **3** a quotation prefacing a book or chapter of a book [Italian]

mould[1] *or US* **mold** *n* **1** a shaped hollow container into which a liquid material is poured so that it can set in a particular shape: *pour the mixture into a buttered mould, cover, and steam for two hours* **2** a shape, nature, or type: *an orthodox Communist in the Stalinist mould* **3** a framework around which something is constructed or shaped: *the heated glass is shaped round a mould inside a kiln* **4** something, esp. a food, made in or on a mould: *salmon mould* ▷ *vb* **5** to make in a mould **6** to shape or form: *a figure moulded out of clay* **7** to influence or direct: *cultural factors moulding our everyday life* [Latin *modulus* a small measure]

mould[2] *or US* **mold** *n* a coating or discoloration caused by various fungi that develop in a damp atmosphere on food, fabrics, and walls [Northern English dialect *mowlde* mouldy]

mould[3] *or US* **mold** *n* loose soil, esp. when rich in organic matter: *leaf mould* [Old English *molde*]

mouldboard *or US* **moldboard** *n* the curved blade of a plough, which turns over the furrow

moulder *or US* **molder** *vb* to crumble or cause to crumble, as through decay: *John Brown's body lies mouldering in the grave* [from MOULD[3]]

moulding *or US* **molding** *n* a shaped ornamental edging

mouldy *or US* **moldy** *adj* **-dier, -diest** **1** covered with mould **2** stale or musty, esp. from age or lack of use **3** *slang* dull or boring

moult *or US* **molt** *vb* **1** (of birds and animals) to shed feathers, hair, or skin so that they can be replaced by a new growth ▷ *n* **2** the periodic process of moulting [Latin *mutare* to change]

mound *n* **1** a heap of earth, debris, etc. **2** any heap or pile **3** a small natural hill [origin unknown]

mount[1] *vb* **1** to climb or ascend: *he mounted the stairs to his flat* **2** to get up on a horse, a platform, etc. **3** Also: **mount up** to increase or accumulate: *costs do mount up; the tension mounted* **4** to fix onto a backing, setting, or support: *sensors mounted on motorway bridges* **5** to organize and stage a campaign, play, etc.: *the Allies mounted a counter attack on the eastern front* ▷ *n* **6** a backing, setting, or support onto which something is fixed: *a diamond set in a gold mount* **7** a horse for riding: *none of his mounts at yesterday's race meeting finished better than third* [same as MOUNT[2]]

mount[2] *n* a mountain or hill: used in literature and (when cap.) in proper names: *Mount Etna* [Latin *mons* mountain]

mountain *n* **1** a very large, high, and steep hill: *the highest mountain in the Alps* **2** a huge heap or mass: *a mountain of papers* **3** a surplus of a commodity, esp. in the European Union: *a butter mountain* ▷ *adj* **4** of, found on, or for use on a mountain or mountains: *a mountain village* [Latin *mons*]

mountain ash *n* a tree with clusters of small white flowers and bright red berries; rowan

mountain bike *n* a type of bicycle with straight handlebars and heavy-duty tyres, originally designed for use over rough hilly ground

mountain cat *n* any of various wild animals of the cat family, such as the bobcat, lynx, or puma

mountaineer *n* **1** a person who climbs mountains ▷ *vb* **2** to climb mountains **mountaineering** *n*

mountain goat *n* a wild goat inhabiting mountainous regions

mountain lion *n* a puma

mountainous *adj* **1** having many mountains: *a mountainous region* **2** like a mountain or mountains, esp. in size: *mountainous waves*

mountain oyster *n NZ informal* a sheep's testicle eaten as food

mountain sickness *n* nausea, headache, and shortness of breath caused by climbing to high altitudes

mountebank *n* **1** (formerly) a person who sold quack medicines in public places **2** a charlatan or fake [Italian *montambanco* a climber on a bench]

mounted *adj* riding horses: *mounted police*

Mountie *or* **Mounty** *n, pl* **Mounties** *informal* a member of the Royal Canadian Mounted Police [from *mounted*]

mounting *n* same as **mount**[1] (sense 6)

mourn *vb* to feel or express sadness for the death or loss of someone or something [Old English *murnan*] **mourner** *n*

mournful *adj* **1** feeling or expressing grief and sadness: *he stood by, a mournful expression on his face* **2** (of a sound) suggestive or reminiscent of grief or sadness: *the locomotive gave a mournful bellow* **mournfully** *adv*

mourning *n* **1** sorrow or grief, esp. over a death **2** the conventional symbols of grief for a death, such as the wearing of black **3** the period of time during which a death is officially mourned ▷ *adj* **4** of or relating to mourning

mouse *n, pl* **mice** **1** a small long-tailed rodent similar to but smaller than a rat **2** a quiet, timid, or cowardly person **3** a hand-held device used to control cursor movements and computing functions without using a keyboard ▷ *vb* **mousing, moused** **4** *rare* to stalk and catch mice [Old English *mūs*]

mouser *n* a cat or other animal that is used to catch mice

mousetrap *n* **1** a spring-loaded trap for killing mice **2** *Brit informal* cheese of mediocre quality

moussaka *n* a dish originating in the Balkan States, consisting of meat, aubergines, and tomatoes, topped with cheese sauce [Modern Greek]

mousse *n* **1** a light creamy dessert made with eggs, cream, and fruit set with gelatine **2** a similar dish made from fish or meat **3** short for **styling mousse** [French: froth]

moustache *or US* **mustache** *n* unshaved hair growing on the upper lip [French, from Italian *mostaccio*]

mousy *or* **mousey** *adj* **mousier, mousiest 1** (of hair) dull light brown in colour **2** shy or ineffectual **mousiness** *n*

mouth *n, pl* **mouths 1** the opening through which many animals take in food and issue sounds **2** the visible part of the mouth; lips **3** a person regarded as a consumer of food: *three mouths to feed* **4** a particular manner of speaking: *a foul mouth* **5** *informal* boastful, rude, or excessive talk: *she is all mouth* **6** the point where a river issues into a sea or lake **7** an opening, such as that of a bottle, tunnel, or gun **8 down in the mouth** in low spirits ▷ *vb* **9** to form words with movements of the lips but without speaking **10** to speak or say something insincerely, esp. in public: *ministers mouthing platitudes* [Old English *mūth*]

mouthful *n, pl* **-fuls 1** the amount of food or drink put into the mouth at any one time when eating or drinking **2** a long word, phrase, or name that is difficult to say **3** *Brit informal* an abusive response: *I asked him to move and he just gave me a mouthful*

mouth organ *n* same as **harmonica**

mouthpiece *n* **1** the part of a wind instrument into which the player blows **2** the part of a telephone receiver into which a person speaks **3** a person or publication expressing the views of an organization

mouthwash *n* a medicated solution for gargling and cleansing the mouth

mouthwatering *adj* (of food) making one want to eat it, because it looks or smells delicious

movable *or* **moveable** *adj* **1** able to be moved; not fixed **2** (of a festival, esp. Easter) varying in date from year to year ▷ *n* **3 movables** movable articles, esp. furniture

move *vb* **moving, moved 1** to go or take from one place to another; change in position: *I moved your books off the table* **2** to start to live or work in a different place: *I moved to Brighton from Bristol last year* **3** to be or cause to be in motion: *the trees were moving in the wind; the car moved slowly down the road* **4** to act or begin to act: *the government plans to move to reduce crime* **5** to cause or prompt to do something: *public opinion moved the President to act* **6** to change the time when something is scheduled to happen: *can I move the appointment to Friday afternoon, please?* **7** to arouse affection, pity, or compassion in; touch: *her story moved me to tears* **8** to change, progress, or develop in a specified way: *the conversation moved to more personal matters* **9** to suggest a proposal formally, as in a debate: *to move a motion* **10** to spend most of one's time with a specified social group: *they both move in theatrical, arty circles* **11** (in board games) to change the position of a piece **12** (of machines) to work or operate **13 A** (of the bowels) to excrete waste **B** to cause the bowels to excrete waste **14** (of merchandise) to be disposed of by being bought **15** to travel quickly: *this car can really move* **16 move heaven and earth** to do everything possible to achieve a result ▷ *n* **17** the act of moving; movement **18** one of a sequence of actions, usually part of a plan: *the first real move towards disarmament* **19** the act of moving one's home or place of business **20 A** (in a boardgame) a player's turn to move his piece **B** (in a boardgame) a manoeuvre of a piece **21 get a move on** *informal* to hurry up **22 make a move** *informal* **A** to prepare or begin to leave a place to go somewhere else: *we'd better make a move if we want to be home before dark* **B** to do something which will produce a response: *neither of us wanted to make the first move* **23 on the move** travelling from place to place [Latin *movere*]

move in *vb* **1** Also: **move into** to start to live in a different house or flat **2** to start to live in the same house or flat as: *he moved in with his girlfriend* **3** to attack a person or place, or try to gain influence or control over a person or activity: *the police moved in to break up the demonstration*

movement *n* **1** the act, process, or an instance of moving **2** the manner of moving: *their movement is jerky* **3 A** a group of people with a common ideology **B** the organized action and campaigning of such a group: *a successful movement to abolish child labour* **4** a trend or tendency: *a movement towards shorter working hours* **5** *finance* a change in the price or value of shares, a currency, etc.: *adverse currency movements* **6** *music* a principal self-contained section of a large-scale work, such as a symphony **7 movements** a person's location and activities during a specific time: *police were trying to piece together the recent movements of the two men* **8 A** the evacuation of the bowels **B** the matter evacuated **9** the mechanism which drives and regulates a watch or clock

move on *vb* **1** to leave one place in order to go elsewhere: *we spent three days in Perth before moving on towards Inverness* **2** to order (someone) to leave and go elsewhere: *we were moved on by the police* **3** to finish one thing and turn one's attention to something else: *can we move on to the next question?*

move over *vb* **1** to change one's position in order to make room for someone else: *if you moved over there'd be room for us both on the couch* **2** to leave one's job so that someone else can have it: *she decided to move over to let someone younger onto the board*

mover *n* **1** a person or animal that moves in a particular way: *a slow mover* **2** the person who first puts forward a proposal **3** *US & Canad* a removal firm or a person who works for one

movie *n* **1** *informal* a cinema film **2 the movies** the cinema: *I want to go to the movies tonight*

moving *adj* **1** arousing or touching the emotions: *a moving account of her son's death* **2** changing or capable of changing position: *a moving target* **movingly** *adv*

moving staircase *or* **moving stairway** *n* an escalator

mow *vb* **mowing, mowed, mowed** *or* **mown 1** to cut down grass or crops: *a tractor chugged along, mowing hay* **2** to cut the growing vegetation of a field or lawn: *to mow a meadow* [Old English *māwan*] **mower** *n*

mow down *vb* to kill in large numbers, esp. by gunfire

mown *vb* the past participle of **mow**

mozzarella (mot-sa-rel-la) *n* a moist white curd cheese originally made in Italy from buffalo milk [Italian]

m

MP **1** Member of Parliament **2** Military Police **3** Mounted Police
MP3 *n* a format for processing a digital audio file so as to remove unneeded data and produce a smaller file for transmission on the internet, for use in portable players, etc. [from *MPEG-1 Audio Layer-3*]
MP3 player *n* a small portable digital audio player capable of storing and playing files downloaded from the internet or transferred from a CD
MPEG (em-peg) *n computers* **A** a standard compressed file format used for audio and video files **B** a file in this format [from *Motion Picture Experts Group*]
mpg miles per gallon
mph miles per hour
MPhil Master of Philosophy
MPV multipurpose vehicle
Mr *n, pl* **Messrs** a title used before a man's name or before some office that he holds: *Mr Pickwick; Mr President* [from *mister*]
MRI *med* magnetic resonance imaging: a diagnostic scanning technique which gives detailed images of internal tissue by analysing its response to being bombarded with high-frequency radio waves within a strong magnetic field
Mrs *n, pl* **Mrs** *or* **Mesdames** a title used before the name of a married woman [from *mistress*]
ms millisecond(s)
Ms (mizz) *n* a title used before the name of a woman to avoid indicating whether she is married or not
MS **1** Mississippi **2** multiple sclerosis
MS. *or* **ms.** *pl* **MSS.** *or* **mss.** manuscript
MSc Master of Science
MSD (in New Zealand) Ministry of Social Development
MSG monosodium glutamate
MSM mainstream media
MSP (in Britain) Member of the Scottish Parliament
MST Mountain Standard Time
mt megaton
Mt¹ Mount: *Mt Everest*
Mt² *chem* meitnerium
MT Montana
mt. megaton
MTech (in the US) Master of Technology
much *adj* **more, most** **1** a large amount or degree of: *there isn't much wine left* ▷ *n* **2** a large amount or degree **3** **a bit much** *informal* rather excessive **4** **make much of** **A** to make sense of: *he couldn't make much of her letter* **B** to give importance to: *the press made much of the story* **5** **not much of** not to any appreciable degree or extent: *he's not much of a cook* **6** **not up to much** *informal* of a low standard: *this beer is not up to much* ▷ *adv* **7** considerably: *I'm much better now* **8** practically or nearly: *it's much the same* **9** often or a great deal: *that doesn't happen much these days* **10** **(as) much as** even though; although: *much as I'd like to, I can't come* ▷ See also **more, most** [Old English *mycel*]
muchness *n* **much of a muchness** *Brit & NZ* very similar
mucilage (mew-sill-ij) *n* **1** a sticky substance used as an adhesive, such as gum or glue **2** a glutinous substance secreted by certain plants [Late Latin *mucilago* mouldy juice] **mucilaginous** *adj*
muck *n* **1** dirt or filth **2** farmyard dung or decaying vegetable matter **3** *slang, chiefly Brit & NZ* something of poor quality; rubbish: *I don't want to eat this muck* **4** **make a muck of** *slang, chiefly Brit & NZ* to ruin or spoil ▷ *vb* **5** to spread manure upon ▷ See also **muck about, muck in** *etc.* [probably Old Norse]
muck about *or* **muck around** *vb slang* **1** to waste time by misbehaving or being silly **2** **muck about with** to interfere with, annoy, or waste the time of
muck in *vb Brit & NZ slang* to share duties or work with other people
muck out *vb* to clean (a barn, stable, etc.)
muckraking *n* seeking out and exposing scandal relating to well-known people **muckraker** *n*
mucksweat *n Brit informal* profuse sweat
muck up *vb informal* to ruin, spoil, or do very badly: *I mucked up my driving test*
mucky *adj* **1** dirty or muddy: *don't come in here with your mucky boots on!* **2** sexually explicit; obscene: *a mucky book*
mucosa *n* same as **mucous membrane** [Latin *mucosus* slimy] **mucosal** *adj*
mucous membrane *n* a mucus-secreting tissue that lines body cavities or passages
mucus (mew-kuss) *n* the slimy protective secretion of the mucous membranes [Latin: nasal secretions] **mucosity** *n* **mucous** *adj*
mud *n* **1** soft wet earth, as found on the ground after rain or at the bottom of ponds **2** **(someone's) name is mud** *informal* (someone) is disgraced **3** **throw mud at** *informal* to slander or vilify ▷ *adj* **4** made from mud or dried mud: *a mud hut* [probably Low German *mudde*]
mud bath *n* **1** a medicinal bath in heated mud **2** a dirty or muddy place, occasion, or state: *heavy rain turned the pitch into a mud bath*
muddle *n* **1** a state of untidiness or confusion: *the files are in a terrible muddle* **2** a state of mental confusion or uncertainty: *the government are in a muddle over the economy* ▷ *vb* **-dling, -dled** **3** Also: **muddle up** to mix up or confuse (objects or items): *you've got your books all muddled up with mine* **4** to make (someone) confused: *don't muddle her with too many suggestions* [perhaps Middle Dutch *moddelen* to make muddy] **muddled** *adj*
muddleheaded *adj* mentally confused or vague
muddle through *vb* to succeed in spite of lack of organization
muddy *adj* **-dier, -diest** **1** covered or filled with mud **2** not clear or bright: *muddy colours* **3** cloudy: *a muddy liquid* **4** (esp. of thoughts) confused or vague ▷ *vb* **-dies, -dying, -died** **5** to make muddy **6** to make a situation or issue less clear: *the allegations of sexual misconduct only serve to muddy the issue* **muddily** *adv*
mud flat *n* an area of low muddy land that is covered at high tide but not at low tide
mud flow *n* the rapid downhill movement of a mass of mud, typically in the shape of a tongue
mudguard *n* a curved part of a bicycle or other vehicle attached above the wheels to reduce the amount of water or mud thrown up by them

mudpack *n* a cosmetic paste applied to the face to improve the complexion
mudpie *n* a mass of mud moulded into a pielike shape by a child
mudslinging *n* the making of malicious personal attacks on an opponent, esp. in politics **mudslinger** *n*
muesli (mewz-lee) *n* a mixture of rolled oats, nuts, and dried fruit, usually eaten with milk [Swiss German]
muezzin (moo-**ezz**-in) *n Islam* the official of a mosque who calls the faithful to prayer from the minaret [Arabic *mu'adhdhin*]
muff[1] *n* a tube of fur or cloth into which the hands are placed for warmth [probably Dutch *mof*]
muff[2] *vb* **1** to do (something) badly: *I muffed my chance to make a good impression* **2** to bungle (a shot or catch) [origin unknown]
muffin *n* **1** a small cup-shaped sweet bread roll, usually eaten hot with butter **2** a thick round baked yeast roll, usually toasted and served with butter [origin unknown]
muffle *vb* **-fling, -fled 1** to deaden (a sound or noise), esp. by wrapping the source of it in something: *the sound was muffled by the double glazing* **2** to wrap up in a scarf or coat for warmth **3** to censor or restrict: *an attempt to muffle criticism* [probably Old French *moufle* mitten] **muffled** *adj*
muffler *n* **1** *Brit* a thick scarf worn for warmth **2** *US & Canad* a device to deaden sound, esp. one on a car exhaust; silencer
mufti *n* civilian clothes worn by a person who normally wears a military uniform [from *Mufti*, Muslim religious leader]
mug[1] *n* **1** a large drinking cup with a handle **2** the quantity held by a mug or its contents: *a mug of coffee* [probably Scandinavian]
mug[2] *n* **1** *slang* a person's face or mouth: *keep your ugly mug out of this* **2** *slang* a gullible person, esp. one who is swindled easily **3 a mug's game** a worthless activity [perhaps same as MUG[1]]
mug[3] *vb* **mugging, mugged** to attack someone in order to rob them **mugger** *n* **mugging** *n*
muggins *n slang* **A** a stupid or gullible person **B** a title used humorously to refer to oneself [probably from surname *Muggins*]
muggy *adj* **-gier, -giest** (of weather or air) unpleasantly warm and humid [dialect *mug* drizzle] **mugginess** *n*
mug shot *n informal* a photograph of a person's face, esp. one resembling a police-file picture
mug up *vb Brit slang* to study a subject hard, esp. for an exam [origin unknown]
Muhammad *n* same as **Mohammed**
mujaheddin *or* **mujahedeen** (moo-ja-hed-**deen**) *pl n* fundamentalist Muslim guerrillas [Arabic *mujāhidīn* fighters]
mukluk *n* a soft boot, usually of sealskin, worn in the American Arctic [Yupik (native language of Siberia and Alaska) *muklok* large seal]
mulatto (mew-**lat**-toe) *n, pl* **-tos** *or* **-toes** *old-fashioned, offensive* a person with one Black and one White parent [Spanish *mulato* young mule]
mulberry *n, pl* **-ries 1** a tree with edible blackberry-like fruit, the leaves of which are used to feed silkworms **2** the fruit of any of these trees ▷ *adj* **3** dark purple [Latin *morum*]
mulch *n* **1** a mixture of half-rotten vegetable matter and peat used to protect the roots of plants or enrich the soil ▷ *vb* **2** to cover soil with mulch [obsolete *mulch* soft]
mule[1] *n* **1** the sterile offspring of a male donkey and a female horse **2** a machine that spins cotton into yarn [Latin *mulus*]
mule[2] *n* a backless shoe or slipper [Latin *mulleus* a magistrate's shoe]
muleteer *n* a person who drives mules
mulga *n* **1** an Australian acacia shrub growing in desert regions **2** *Austral* the outback [Aboriginal]
mulish *adj* stubborn; obstinate
mull *n Scot* a promontory or headland: *the Mull of Galloway* [probably Gaelic *maol*]
mullah *n* (formerly) a Muslim scholar, teacher, or religious leader [Arabic *mawlā* master]
mulled *adj* (of wine or ale) flavoured with sugar and spices and served hot [origin unknown]
mullet *n, pl* **mullets** *or* **mullet** any of various marine food fishes [Greek *mullos*]
mulligatawny *n* a curry-flavoured soup of Anglo-Indian origin [Tamil *milakutanni* pepper water]
mullion *n* a slender vertical bar between the casements or panes of a window [Old French *moinel*] **mullioned** *adj*
mull over *vb* to study or ponder: *he mulled over the arrangements* [probably from *muddle*]
mulloway *n* a large Australian sea fish, valued for sport and food
multi- *combining form* **1** many or much: *multimillion* **2** more than one: *multistorey* [Latin *multus* much, many]
multicoloured *adj* having many colours: *multicoloured balls of wool*
multicultural *adj* of or for the cultures of several different races
multifarious (mull-tee-**fare**-ee-uss) *adj* many and varied: *multifarious religious movements and political divisions sprang up around this time* [Late Latin *multifarius* manifold]
multiflora rose *n* a climbing rose with clusters of small fragrant flowers
multiform *adj* having many shapes or forms
multilateral *adj* of or involving more than two nations or parties: *multilateral trade negotiations*
multilingual *adj* **1** able to speak more than two languages **2** written or expressed in more than two languages: *a multilingual leaflet*
multimedia *pl n* **1** the combined use of media such as television and slides ▷ *adj* **2** *computers* of or relating to systems that can manipulate data in a variety of forms, such as sound, graphics, or text
multimillionaire *n* a person who has money or property worth several million pounds, dollars, etc.
multinational *adj* **1** (of a large business company) operating in several countries **2** involving people from several countries: *a multinational peacekeeping force* ▷ *n* **3** a large company operating in several countries
multiparous (mull-**tip**-a-russ) *adj* producing many offspring at one birth [New Latin *multiparus*]

m

multiple *adj* **1** having or involving more than one part, individual, or element ▹ *n* **2** a number or polynomial which can be divided by another specified one an exact number of times: *6 is a multiple of 2* [Latin *multiplus*] **multiply** *adv*
multiple-choice *adj* (of a test or question) giving a number of possible answers out of which the correct one must be chosen
multiple sclerosis *n* a chronic progressive disease of the central nervous system, resulting in speech and visual disorders, tremor, muscular incoordination, and partial paralysis
multiplex *n, pl* **-plexes** **1** a purpose-built complex containing several cinemas and usually restaurants and bars ▹ *adj* **2** having many elements; complex [Latin: having many folds]
multiplicand *n* a number to be multiplied by another number (the **multiplier**)
multiplication *n* **1** a mathematical operation, equivalent to adding a number to itself a specified number of times. For instance, 4 multiplied by 3 equals 12 (i.e. 4+4+4) **2** the act of multiplying or state of being multiplied
multiplication sign *n* the symbol ×, placed between numbers to be multiplied
multiplication table *n* a table giving the results of multiplying two numbers together
multiplicity *n, pl* **-ties** **1** a large number or great variety **2** the state of being multiple
multiplier *n* a number by which another number (the **multiplicand**) is multiplied
m
multiply *vb* **-plies, -plying, -plied** **1** to increase or cause to increase in number, quantity, or degree **2** to combine numbers or quantities by multiplication **3** to increase in number by reproduction [Latin *multiplicare*]
multipurpose *adj* having many uses: *a giant multipurpose enterprise*
multipurpose vehicle *n* a large car, similar to a van, designed to carry up to eight passengers
multiracial *adj* consisting of or involving people of many races: *a multiracial society* **multiracialism** *n*
multistage *adj* (of a rocket or missile) having several stages, each of which can be jettisoned after it has burnt out
multistorey *adj* (of a building) having many storeys
multitrack *adj* (in sound recording) using tape containing two or more tracks
multitude *n* **1** a large number of people or things: *a multitude of different pressure groups* **2 the multitude** ordinary people collectively [Latin *multitudo*] **multitudinous** *adj*
multi-user *adj* (of a computer) capable of being used by several people at once
mum[1] *n chiefly Brit informal* same as **mother** [a child's word]
mum[2] *adj* **1 keep mum** remain silent **2 mum's the word** keep quiet (about something) [suggestive of closed lips]
mumble *vb* **-bling, -bled** **1** to speak or say something indistinctly, with the mouth partly closed: *I could hear him mumbling under his breath* ▹ *n* **2** an indistinct or low utterance or sound [Middle English *momelen*, from MUM[2]]
mumbo jumbo *n* **1** meaningless language; nonsense or gibberish **2** foolish religious ritual or incantation [probably from West African *mama dyumbo*, name of a tribal god]
mummer *n* one of a group of masked performers in a folk play or mime [Old French *momer* to mime]
mummery *n, pl* **-meries** **1** a performance by mummers **2** hypocritical or ostentatious ceremony
mummified *adj* (of a body) preserved as a mummy **mummification** *n*
mummy[1] *n, pl* **-mies** *chiefly Brit* an embalmed body as prepared for burial in ancient Egypt [Persian *mūm* wax]
mummy[2] *n, pl* **-mies** a child's word for **mother** [variant of MUM[1]]
mumps *n* an infectious viral disease in which the glands below the ear become swollen and painful [obsolete *mump* to grimace]
munch *vb* to chew noisily and steadily [imitative]
mundane *adj* **1** everyday, ordinary, and therefore not very interesting **2** relating to the world or worldly matters [Latin *mundus* world]
mung bean *n* an E Asian bean plant grown for its edible seeds which are used as a source of bean sprouts [Tamil *mūngu*]
municipal *adj* of or relating to a town or city or its local government [Latin *municipium* a free town]
municipality *n, pl* **-ties** **1** a city, town, or district enjoying local self-government **2** the governing body of such a unit
munificent (mew-**niff**-fiss-sent) *adj* very generous [Latin *munus* gift + *facere* to make] **munificence** *n*
muniments (**mew**-nim-ments) *pl n law* the title deeds and other documentary evidence relating to the title to land [Latin *munire* to defend]
munitions (mew-**nish**-unz) *pl n* military equipment and stores, esp. ammunition
munted *adj NZ slang* **1** destroyed or ruined **2** abnormal or peculiar
muon (**mew**-on) *n* a positive or negative elementary particle with a mass 207 times that of an electron [short for *mu meson*]
mural (**myoor**-al) *n* **1** a large painting on a wall ▹ *adj* **2** of or relating to a wall [Latin *murus* wall] **muralist** *n*
murder *n* **1** the unlawful intentional killing of one human being by another **2** *informal* something dangerous, difficult, or unpleasant: *shopping on Christmas Eve is murder* **3 cry blue murder** *informal* to make an outcry **4 get away with murder** *informal* to do as one pleases without ever being punished ▹ *vb* **5** to kill someone intentionally and unlawfully **6** *informal* to ruin a piece of music or drama by performing it very badly: *he absolutely murdered that song* **7** *informal* to beat decisively [Old English *morthor*] **murderer** *or fem* **murderess** *n* **murderous** *adj*
murk *n* thick gloomy darkness [Old Norse *myrkr* darkness]
murky *adj* **murkier, murkiest** **1** gloomy or dark **2** cloudy or hard to see through: *a murky stagnant pond* **3** obscure and suspicious; shady: *murky goings-on; his murky past* **murkily** *adv* **murkiness** *n*

murmur *vb* **1** to speak or say in a quiet indistinct way **2** to complain ▷ *n* **3** a continuous low indistinct sound, such as that of a distant conversation **4** an indistinct utterance: *a murmur of protest* **5** a complaint or grumble: *he left without a murmur* **6** *med* any abnormal soft blowing sound heard usually over the chest: *a heart murmur* [Latin *murmurare* to rumble] **murmuring** *n, adj* **murmurous** *adj*

Murphy's Law *n* same as **Sod's Law**

murrain (murr-rin) *n* any plaguelike disease in cattle [Old French *morir* to die]

mus. 1 museum **2** music **3** musical

MusB *or* **MusBac** Bachelor of Music

muscle *n* **1** a tissue in the body composed of bundles of elongated cells which produce movement in an organ or part by contracting or relaxing **2** an organ composed of muscle tissue: *the heart is essentially just another muscle* **3** strength or force: *we do not have the political muscle to force through these reforms* ▷ *vb* **-cling, -cled 4 muscle in** to force one's way into a situation; intrude: *I don't like the way he's trying to muscle in here* [Medical Latin *musculus* little mouse]

muscle-bound *adj* having overdeveloped and inelastic muscles

muscleman *n, pl* **-men 1** a man with highly developed muscles **2** a henchman employed to intimidate or use violence upon victims

Muscovite *adj* **1** of Moscow, a city in Russia ▷ *n* **2** a person from Moscow

muscular *adj* **1** having well-developed muscles; brawny **2** of or consisting of muscle: *great muscular effort is needed* **3** forceful or powerful: *a muscular account of Schumann's Fourth Symphony* **muscularity** *n*

muscular dystrophy *n* a hereditary disease in which the muscles gradually weaken and waste away

musculature *n* the arrangement of muscles in an organ, part, or organism

musculoskeletal *adj* of or relating to the skeleton and musculature taken together

MusD *or* **MusDoc** Doctor of Music

muse[1] *vb* **musing, mused** to think deeply and at length about: *she mused unhappily on how right her sister had been* [Old French *muser*]

muse[2] *n* a force or person, esp. a woman, that inspires a creative artist [Greek *Mousa* a Muse]

Muses *pl n* *Greek myth* the nine sister goddesses, each of whom was the protector of a different art or science

museum *n* a building where objects of historical, artistic, or scientific interest are exhibited and preserved [Greek *Mouseion* home of the Muses]

museum piece *n informal* a very old or old-fashioned object or building

mush[1] *n* **1** a soft pulpy mass **2** *informal* cloying sentimentality [obsolete *moose* porridge]

mush[2] *Canad* ▷ *interj* **1** an order to dogs in a sled team to start up or go faster ▷ *vb* **2** to travel by or drive a dogsled [perhaps from imperative of French *marcher* to advance]

mushroom *n* **1** an edible fungus consisting of a cap at the end of a stem **2** something resembling a mushroom in shape or rapid growth ▷ *vb* **3** to grow rapidly: *the deficit has mushroomed* [Late Latin *mussirio*]

mushroom cloud *n* the large mushroom-shaped cloud produced by a nuclear explosion

mushy *adj* **mushier, mushiest 1** soft and pulpy **2** *informal* excessively sentimental

music *n* **1** an art form consisting of sequences of sounds organized melodically, harmonically, and rhythmically **2** such sounds, esp. when produced by singing or musical instruments **3** any written or printed representation of musical sounds: *I can't read music* **4** any sequence of sounds perceived as pleasing or harmonious **5 face the music** *informal* to confront the consequences of one's actions **6 music to one's ears** something, such as a piece of news, that one is pleased to hear [Greek *mousikē (tekhnē)* (art) in the protection of the Muses]

musical *adj* **1** of or used in music **2** talented in or fond of music **3** pleasant-sounding; harmonious: *musical laughter* **4** involving or set to music: *a musical biography of Judy Garland* ▷ *n* **5** a play or film that has dialogue interspersed with songs and dances **musicality** *n* **musically** *adv*

musical box *n* a box containing a mechanical instrument that plays tunes when the box is opened

musical chairs *n* **1** a game in which the players run round a row of chairs while music plays. There is one more player than there are chairs, and when the music stops the player who cannot find a chair to sit on is out **2** any situation involving a number of people in a series of interrelated changes: *the dismissal of the Chancellor started a game of musical chairs in the Cabinet*

music centre *n Brit* a single hi-fi unit containing a turntable, radio, compact disc player, and cassette player

music hall *n chiefly Brit* **1** (formerly) a variety entertainment consisting of songs and comic turns **2** a theatre at which such entertainments were staged

musician *n* a person who plays or composes music, esp. as a profession

musicianship *n* the technical and interpretive skills involved in singing or playing music: *the piano part is simple but performed with great musicianship*

musicology *n* the scholarly study of music **musicologist** *n*

musk *n* **1** a strong-smelling glandular secretion of the male musk deer, used in perfumery **2** any similar substance produced by animals or plants, or manufactured synthetically [Persian *mushk*]

musk deer *n* a small central Asian mountain deer

muskeg *n chiefly Canad* an area of undrained boggy land [Native American: grassy swamp]

musket *n* a long-barrelled muzzle-loading gun fired from the shoulder, a forerunner of the rifle [Italian *moschetto* arrow, earlier: sparrow hawk] **musketeer** *n*

muskmelon *n* any of several varieties of melon, such as the cantaloupe and honeydew

musk ox *n* a large ox, which has a dark shaggy coat, downward-curving horns, and emits a musky smell

m

muskrat *n, pl* **-rats** *or* **-rat** 1 a North American beaver-like amphibious rodent 2 the brown fur of this animal
musk rose *n* a Mediterranean rose, cultivated for its white musk-scented flowers
musky *adj* **muskier, muskiest** having a heady sweet smell **muskiness** *n*
Muslim *or* **Moslem** *n, pl* **-lims** *or* **-lim** 1 a follower of the religion of Islam ▷ *adj* 2 of or relating to Islam [Arabic, literally: one who surrenders]
muslin *n* a very fine plain-weave cotton fabric [French *mousseline*]
musquash *n* muskrat fur [from a Native American language]
muss *vb US & Canad informal* to make untidy; rumple: *watch you don't muss up my hair!* [probably a blend of *mess* + *fuss*]
mussel *n* an edible shellfish, with a dark slightly elongated hinged shell, which lives attached to rocks [Latin *musculus*, diminutive of *mus* mouse]
must[1] *vb* 1 used as an auxiliary to express or indicate the need or necessity to do something: *I must go to the shops* 2 used as an auxiliary to express or indicate obligation or requirement: *you must not smoke in here* 3 used as an auxiliary to express or indicate the probable correctness of a statement: *he must be finished by now* 4 used as an auxiliary to express or indicate inevitability: *all good things must come to an end* 5 used as an auxiliary to express or indicate determination: *I must try and finish this* 6 used as an auxiliary to express or indicate conviction or certainty on the part of the speaker: *you must be kidding!* ▷ *n* 7 an essential or necessary thing: *strong boots are a must for hill walking* [Old English *mōste*, past tense of *mōtan* to be allowed or obliged]
must[2] *n* the pressed juice of grapes or other fruit ready for fermentation [Latin *mustum* new wine]
mustache *n US* same as **moustache**
mustachio *n, pl* **-chios** *often humorous* a moustache, esp. a bushy or elaborate one [Italian *mostaccio*] **mustachioed** *adj*
mustang *n* a small breed of horse, often wild or half wild, found in the southwestern US [Mexican Spanish *mestengo*]
mustard *n* 1 a hot, spicy paste made from the powdered seeds of any of a family of plants 2 any of these plants, which have yellow flowers and slender pods ▷ *adj* 3 brownish-yellow [Old French *moustarde*]
mustard and cress *n* seedlings of white mustard and garden cress, used in salads and as a garnish
mustard gas *n* an oily liquid with poisonous vapour used in chemical warfare, esp. in World War I, which can cause blindness, burns, and sometimes death
mustard plaster *n med* a mixture of powdered black mustard seeds applied to the skin
muster *vb* 1 to summon or gather: *I put as much disbelief in my expression as I could muster* 2 to call or be called together for duty or inspection: *the battalion mustered on the bank of the river* ▷ *n* 3 an assembly of military personnel for duty or inspection 4 a collection, assembly, or gathering 5 **pass muster** to be acceptable [Latin *monstrare* to show]
musty *adj* **-tier, -tiest** 1 smelling or tasting old, stale, or mouldy 2 old-fashioned, dull, or hackneyed: *musty ideas* [perhaps variant of obsolete *moisty*] **mustily** *adv* **mustiness** *n*
mutable (mew-tab-bl) *adj* able to or tending to change [Latin *mutare* to change] **mutability** *n*
mutagen (mew-ta-jen) *n* any substance that can induce genetic mutation [MUTATION + *-gen* (suffix) producing] **mutagenic** *adj*
mutagenesis (mew-ta-jen-iss-iss) *n* the origin and development of a genetic mutation [MUTATION + GENESIS]
mutant (mew-tant) *n* 1 an animal, organism, or gene that has undergone mutation ▷ *adj* 2 of or resulting from mutation
mutate (mew-tate) *vb* **-tating, -tated** to undergo or cause to undergo mutation [Latin *mutare* to change]
mutation (mew-tay-shun) *n* 1 a change or alteration 2 a change in the chromosomes or genes of a cell which may affect the structure and development of the resultant offspring 3 a physical characteristic in an organism resulting from this type of chromosomal change
mute *adj* 1 not giving out sound or speech; silent 2 *old-fashioned, offensive* unable to speak 3 unspoken or unexpressed: *she shot him a look of mute entreaty* 4 (of a letter in a word) silent: *the 'k' in 'know' is mute* ▷ *n* 5 *old-fashioned, offensive* a person who is unable to speak 6 any of various devices used to soften the tone of stringed or brass instruments ▷ *vb* **muting, muted** 7 to reduce the volume or soften the tone of a musical instrument by means of a mute or soft pedal 8 to reduce the volume of a sound: *the double glazing muted the noise* [Latin *mutus* silent] **mutely** *adv* **muteness** *n*
muted *adj* 1 (of a sound or colour) softened: *a muted pink shirt* 2 (of an emotion or action) subdued or restrained: *his response was muted* 3 (of a musical instrument) being played while fitted with a mute: *muted trumpet*
mute swan *n* the swan most commonly seen in Britain, which has a pure white plumage and an orange-red bill
muti (moo-tee) *n S African* medicine, esp. herbal [Zulu]
mutilate (mew-till-ate) *vb* **-lating, -lated** 1 to injure by tearing or cutting off a limb or essential part; maim 2 to damage a book or text so as to render it unintelligible 3 to spoil or damage severely [Latin *mutilare* to cut off] **mutilated** *adj* **mutilation** *n* **mutilator** *n*
mutineer *n* a person who mutinies
mutinous *adj* 1 openly rebellious 2 characteristic or indicative of mutiny
mutiny (mew-tin-ee) *n, pl* **-nies** 1 open rebellion against authority, esp. by sailors or soldiers against their officers ▷ *vb* **-nies, -nying, -nied** 2 to engage in mutiny: *soldiers who had mutinied and taken control* [Old French *mutin* rebellious]
mutt *n slang* 1 a foolish or stupid person 2 a mongrel dog [from *muttonhead*]
mutter *vb* 1 to say something or speak in a low and indistinct tone: *he muttered an excuse* 2 to grumble ▷ *n* 3 a muttered sound or complaint [Middle English *moteren*] **muttering** *n, adj*

mutton *n* **1** the flesh of mature sheep, used as food **2 mutton dressed as lamb** *derogatory* an older woman dressed up to look young [Medieval Latin *multo* sheep]

mutton bird *n* **1** *Austral* a migratory sea bird with dark plumage **2** NZ any of a number of migratory sea birds, the young of which are a Māori delicacy

muttonchops *pl n* side whiskers trimmed in the shape of chops

mutual (**mew**-chew-al) *adj* **1** experienced or expressed by each of two or more people about the other; reciprocal: *mutual respect* **2** common to or shared by two or more people: *a mutual friend* **3** denoting an organization, such as an insurance company, in which the policyholders or investors share the profits and expenses and there are no shareholders [Latin *mutuus* reciprocal] **mutuality** *n* **mutually** *adv*

> **USAGE** The use of *mutual* to mean *common to or shared by two or more people* was formerly considered incorrect, but is now acceptable. Tautologous use of *mutual* should be avoided: *cooperation* (not *mutual cooperation*) *between the two countries.*

mutual fund *n US & Canad* an investment trust that issues units for public sale and invests the money in many different businesses

Muzak *n trademark* recorded light music played in places such as restaurants and shops

muzzle *n* **1** the projecting part of an animal's face, usually the jaws and nose **2** a guard, made of plastic or strap of strong material, fitted over an animal's nose and jaws to prevent it biting or eating **3** the front end of a gun barrel ▷ *vb* **-zling, -zled 4** to prevent from being heard or noticed: *an attempt to muzzle the press* **5** to put a muzzle on an animal [Old French *muse* snout]

muzzy *adj* **-zier, -ziest 1** confused and groggy: *he felt muzzy and hung over* **2** blurred or hazy: *the picture was muzzy and out of focus* [origin unknown] **muzzily** *adv* **muzziness** *n*

MV megavolt

MW 1 megawatt **2** *radio* medium wave

mwah *interj* a representation of the sound of a kiss

Mx *physics* maxwell

my *adj* **1** of, belonging to, or associated with the speaker or writer (me): *my own way of doing things* **2** used in various forms of address: *my lord* ▷ *interj* **3** an exclamation of surprise or awe: *my, how you've grown!* [variant of Old English *mīn*]

> **USAGE** See at **me'**.

myall *n* an Australian acacia with hard scented wood [Aboriginal]

mycelium (mice-**eel**-lee-um) *n, pl* **-lia** (-lee-a) the mass forming the body of a fungus [Greek *mukēs* mushroom + *hēlos* nail]

Mycenaean (mice-in-**ee**-an) *adj* of or relating to the Aegean civilization of Mycenae, a city in S Greece (1400–1100 BC)

mycology *n* the study of fungi [Greek *mukēs* mushroom + -LOGY]

myelin (**my**-ill-in) *n* a white tissue forming an insulating sheath around certain nerve fibres [Greek *muelos* marrow]

myeloma (my-ill-**oh**-ma) *n, pl* **-mas** *or* **-mata** (-ma-ta) a tumour of the bone marrow [Greek *muelos* marrow + *-oma*, modelled on *carcinoma*]

mynah *or* **myna** *n* a tropical Asian starling which can mimic human speech [Hindi *mainā*]

Mynheer (min-**near**) *n* a Dutch title of address equivalent to *Sir* or *Mr* [Dutch *mijnheer* my lord]

myocardium *n, pl* **-dia** the muscular tissue of the heart [Greek *mus* muscle + *kardia* heart] **myocardial** *adj*

myopia (my-**oh**-pee-a) *n* inability to see distant objects clearly because the images are focused in front of the retina; short-sightedness [Greek *muōps* short-sighted] **myopic** (my-**op**-ik) *adj*

myriad (**mir**-ree-ad) *adj* **1** innumerable: *the myriad demands of the modern world* ▷ *n* **2** a large indefinite number: *myriads of tiny yellow flowers* [Greek *murias* ten thousand]

myriapod *n* an invertebrate with a long segmented body and many legs, such as a centipede [Greek *murias* ten thousand + *pous* foot]

myrmidon *n* a follower or henchman [after the followers of Achilles in Greek myth]

myrrh (**mur**) *n* the aromatic resin of an African or Asian shrub or tree, used in perfume, incense, and medicine [Greek *murrha*]

myrtle (**mur**-tl) *n* an evergreen shrub with pink or white flowers and aromatic blue-black berries [Greek *murtos*]

myself *pron* **1** the reflexive form of I or *me*: *I really enjoyed myself at the party* **2** I or me in person, as distinct from anyone else: *I myself know of no answer* **3** my usual self: *I'm not myself today*

mysterious *adj* **1** of unknown cause or nature: *a mysterious illness* **2** creating a feeling of strangeness, curiosity, or wonder: *a fascinating and mysterious old woman* **mysteriously** *adv*

mystery *n, pl* **-teries 1** an unexplained or inexplicable event or phenomenon **2** a person or thing that arouses curiosity or suspense because of an unknown, obscure, or enigmatic quality **3** a story or film which arouses suspense and curiosity because of facts concealed **4** a religious rite, such as the Eucharist in Christianity [Greek *mustērion* secret rites]

mystery play *n* (in the Middle Ages) a type of drama based on the life of Christ

mystery tour *n* an excursion to an unspecified destination

mystic *n* **1** a person who achieves mystical experience ▷ *adj* **2** same as **mystical** [Greek *mustēs* one who has been initiated]

mystical *adj* **1** relating to or characteristic of mysticism **2** *Christianity* having a sacred significance that is beyond human understanding **3** having occult or metaphysical significance **mystically** *adv*

mysticism *n* **1** belief in or experience of a reality beyond normal human understanding or experience **2** the use of prayer and meditation in an attempt to achieve direct intuitive experience of the divine

mystify *vb* **-fies, -fying, -fied 1** to confuse, bewilder, or puzzle: *his success mystifies many in the fashion industry* **2** to make obscure: *it is important for us not to mystify the function of the scientist* **mystification** *n* **mystifying** *adj*

m

mystique (miss-**steek**) *n* an aura of mystery, power, and awe that surrounds a person or thing

myth *n* **1 A** a story about superhuman beings of an earlier age, usually of how natural phenomena or social customs came into existence **B** same as **mythology** (senses 1, 2) **2 A** an idea or explanation which is widely held but untrue or unproven: *the myth that the USA is a classless society* **B** a person or thing whose existence is fictional or unproven: *the Loch Ness Monster is a myth* [Greek *muthos* fable]

myth. 1 mythological **2** mythology

mythical *or* **mythic** *adj* **1** of or relating to myth **2** imaginary or fictitious **mythically** *adv*

mythology *n, pl* **-gies 1** myths collectively, esp. those associated with a particular culture or person **2** a body of stories about a person, institution, etc. **3** the study of myths **mythological** *adj*

myxoedema *or US* **myxedema** (mix-id-**deem**-a) *n* a disease caused by an underactive thyroid gland, characterized by puffy eyes, face, and hands, and mental sluggishness [Greek *muxa* mucus + *oidēma* swelling]

myxomatosis (mix-a-mat-**oh**-siss) *n* an infectious and usually fatal viral disease of rabbits causing swellings and tumours [Greek *muxa* mucus + *-ōma* denoting tumour + *-osis* denoting disease]

m

Nn

n¹ 1 nano- 2 neutron
n² *n* 1 *maths* a number whose value is not stated: *two to the power n* ▷ *adj* 2 an indefinite number of: *there are n objects in the box* **nth** *adj*
N 1 *chess* knight 2 *chem* nitrogen 3 *physics* newton(s) 4 North(ern) 5 nuclear: *N plant*
n. 1 neuter 2 noun 3 number
N. 1 National(ist) 2 Navy 3 New 4 Norse
Na *chem* sodium [Latin *natrium*]
NA North America
n/a not applicable: used to indicate that a question on a form is not relevant to the person filling it in
Naafi *n* 1 *Brit* Navy, Army, and Air Force Institutes 2 a canteen or shop run by this organization, esp. for military personnel
naan *n* same as **nan bread**
naartjie (nahr-chee) *n S African* a tangerine [Afrikaans]
nab *vb* **nabbing, nabbed** *informal* 1 to arrest (someone) 2 to catch (someone) doing something wrong [perhaps Scandinavian]
nabob (nay-bob) *n informal* a rich or important person [Hindi *nawwāb*; see NAWAB]
nacelle (nah-sell) *n* a streamlined enclosure on an aircraft, esp. one housing an engine [French: small boat]
nacho *n, pl* **nachos** *Mexican cookery* a snack of a piece of tortilla topped with cheese, peppers, etc.
nacre (nay-ker) *n* mother-of-pearl [Arabic *naqqārah* shell, drum] **nacreous** *adj*
nadir *n* 1 the point in the sky directly below an observer and opposite the zenith 2 the lowest or worst point of anything: *I had touched the very nadir of despair* [Arabic *nazīr as-samt*, literally: opposite the zenith]
naevus *or US* **nevus** (nee-vuss) *n, pl* **-vi** a birthmark or mole [Latin]
naff *adj Brit slang* in poor taste: *naff frocks and trouser suits* [perhaps back slang from *fan*, short for FANNY] **naffness** *n*
nag¹ *vb* **nagging, nagged** 1 to scold or find fault constantly 2 **nag at** to be a constant source of discomfort or worry to ▷ *n* 3 a person who nags [Scandinavian] **nagging** *adj, n*
nag² *n* 1 *often derogatory* an old horse 2 a small riding horse [Germanic]
naiad (nye-ad) *n, pl* **naiads** *or* **naiades** (nye-ad-deez) *Greek myth* a water nymph [Greek *nāias*]
nail *n* 1 a piece of metal with a point at one end and a head at the other, hit with a hammer to join two objects together 2 the hard covering of the upper tips of the fingers and toes 3 **hit the nail on the head** to say something exactly correct or accurate 4 **on the nail** at once: *he paid always in cash, always on the nail* ▷ *vb* 5 to attach (something) with nails 6 *informal* to arrest or catch (someone) 7 *informal* to execute (an act or performance) to the highest level: *you nailed that song!* [Old English *nægl*]
nail down *vb* 1 to secure or fasten down with nails or as if with nails 2 to force an agreement from 3 to settle in a definite way: *a compromise was agreed in principle but has not yet been nailed down*
nailfile *n* a small metal file used to shape and smooth the nails
nail varnish *or* **nail polish** *n* a thick liquid applied to the nails as a cosmetic
naive *or* **naïve** (nye-eev) *adj* 1 innocent and gullible 2 simple and lacking sophistication: *naive art* [French, from Latin *nativus* native] **naively** *adv*
naivety (nye-eev-tee) *or* **naïveté** *n* the state or quality of being naive
naked *adj* 1 without clothes 2 not concealed: *naked aggression* 3 without any covering: *it was dimly lit by naked bulbs* 4 **the naked eye** the eye unassisted by any optical instrument: *difficult to spot with the naked eye* [Old English *nacod*] **nakedly** *adv* **nakedness** *n*
namby-pamby *adj Brit, Austral & NZ* excessively sentimental or prim [nickname of Ambrose Phillips, 18th-century pastoral poet]
name *n* 1 a word or term by which a person or thing is known. Related adjective: **nominal** 2 reputation, esp. a good one: *he was making a name for himself* 3 a famous person: *she's a big name now* 4 **call someone names** *or* **a name** to insult someone by using rude words to describe him or her 5 **in name only** not possessing the powers or status implied by one's title: *a leadership in name only* 6 **in the name of** A for the sake of: *in the name of decency* B by the authority of: *in the name of the law* 7 **name of the game** the most significant or important aspect of something: *survival is the name of the game in wartime* 8 **to one's name** in one's possession: *she hasn't a penny to her name* ▷ *vb* **naming, named** 9 to give a name to 10 to refer to by name: *he refused to name his source* 11 to fix or specify: *he named a time for the meeting* 12 to appoint: *she was named Journalist of the Year* 13 to ban (an MP) from the House of Commons by mentioning him or her formally by name as being guilty of disorderly conduct 14 **name names** to cite people in order to blame or accuse them [Old English *nama*]
namecheck *vb* 1 to mention (someone) by name ▷ *n* 2 a mention of someone's name, for example on a radio programme
name day *n RC Church* the feast day of a saint whose name one bears
name-dropping *n informal* the practice of referring to famous people as though they were friends, in order to impress others
nameless *adj* 1 without a name 2 unspecified: *the individual concerned had better remain nameless* 3 too horrible to speak about: *the nameless dread*
namely *adv* that is to say
nameplate *n* a small sign on or next to a door giving the occupant's name and, sometimes, profession
namesake *n* a person or thing with the same name as another [probably originally *for the name's sake*]

nan bread *or* **naan** *n* a slightly leavened Indian bread in a large flat leaf shape [Hindi]

nancy *n, pl* **-cies** *Brit, Austral & NZ offensive slang* an effeminate or homosexual boy or man. Also called: **nancy boy** [from the girl's name]

nanny *n, pl* **-nies 1** a person whose job is looking after young children ▷ *vb* **nannies, nannying, nannied 2** to nurse or look after someone else's children **3** to be too protective towards (someone) [child's name for a nurse]

nanny goat *n* a female goat

nano- *combining form* denoting one thousand millionth (10^{-9}): *nanosecond* [Latin *nanus* dwarf]

nanometre *n* one thousand-millionth of a metre. Symbol: **nm**

nanotechnology *n* a branch of technology dealing with the manufacture of objects with dimensions of less than 100 nanometres and the manipulation of individual molecules and atoms

nap¹ *n* **1** a short sleep ▷ *vb* **napping, napped 2** to have a short sleep **3 catch someone napping** to catch someone unprepared: *they don't want to be caught napping when the army moves again* [Old English *hnappian*]

nap² *n* the raised fibres of velvet or similar cloth [probably Middle Dutch *noppe*]

nap³ *n* **1** a card game similar to whist **2** *horse racing* a tipster's choice for a certain winner ▷ *vb* **napping, napped 3** *horse racing* to name (a horse) as a likely winner [shortened from *Napoleon*]

napalm *n* **1** a highly inflammable jellied petrol, used in firebombs and flame-throwers ▷ *vb* **2** to attack (people or places) with napalm [*na(phthene)* + *palm(itate)* salt of palmitic acid]

nape *n* the back of the neck [origin unknown]

naphtha *n chem* a liquid mixture distilled from coal tar or petroleum: used as a solvent and in petrol [Greek]

naphthalene *n chem* a white crystalline substance distilled from coal tar or petroleum, used in mothballs, dyes, and explosives [*naphtha* + *al(cohol)* + *-ene*]

napkin *n* **1** a piece of cloth or paper for wiping the mouth or protecting the clothes while eating **2** same as **sanitary towel** [Latin *mappa* cloth]

nappy *n, pl* **-pies** *Brit & NZ* a piece of soft absorbent material, usually disposable, wrapped around the waist and between the legs of a baby to absorb its urine and excrement [from *napkin*]

narcissism *n* an exceptional interest in or admiration for oneself [after *Narcissus*, a youth in Greek mythology, who fell in love with his reflection] **narcissistic** *adj*

narcissus (nahr-siss-uss) *n, pl* **-cissi** (-siss-eye) a yellow, orange, or white flower related to the daffodil [Greek *narkissos*, perhaps from *narkē* numbness, because of narcotic properties attributed to the plant]

narcosis *n* unconsciousness caused by a narcotic or general anaesthetic [Greek *narkē* numbness]

narcotic *n* **1** a drug, such as opium or morphine, that produces numbness and drowsiness, used medicinally but addictive ▷ *adj* **2** of narcotics or narcosis [Greek *narkē* numbness]

nark *slang* ▷ *vb* **1** to annoy ▷ *n* **2** an informer or spy: *copper's nark* **3** *Brit* someone who complains in an irritating or whining manner [probably from Romany *nāk* nose]

narky *adj* **narkier, narkiest** *slang* irritable, complaining, or sarcastic

narrate *vb* **-rating, -rated 1** to tell (a story); relate **2** to speak the words accompanying and telling what is happening in a film or TV programme [Latin *narrare* to recount] **narrator** *n*

narration *n* **1** a narrating **2** a narrated account or story

narrative *n* **1** an account of events **2** the part of a literary work that relates events ▷ *adj* **3** telling a story: *a narrative account of the main events* **4** of narration: *narrative clarity*

narrow *adj* **1** small in breadth in comparison to length **2** limited in range, extent, or outlook: *a narrow circle of academics* **3** with little margin: *a narrow advantage* ▷ *vb* **4** to make or become narrow **5 narrow down** to restrict or limit: *the search can be narrowed down to a single room* ▷ See also **narrows** [Old English *nearu*] **narrowly** *adv* **narrowness** *n*

narrow boat *n Brit* a long bargelike canal boat

narrow gauge *n* **1** a railway track with less than 56½ inches (1.435 metres) between the lines ▷ *adj* **narrow-gauge 2** denoting a railway with a narrow gauge

narrow-minded *adj* bigoted, intolerant, or prejudiced **narrow-mindedness** *n*

narrows *pl n* a narrow part of a strait, river, or current

narwhal *n* an arctic whale with a long spiral tusk [Old Norse *nāhvalr*, from *nār* corpse + *hvalr* whale]

NASA (in the US) National Aeronautics and Space Administration

nasal *adj* **1** of the nose **2** (of a sound) pronounced with air passing through the nose **3** (of a voice) characterized by nasal sounds [Latin *nasus* nose] **nasally** *adv*

nascent *adj formal* starting to grow or develop [Latin *nasci* to be born]

NASDAQ (in the US) National Association of Securities Dealers Automated Quotations (System)

nasturtium *n* a plant with yellow, red, or orange trumpet-shaped flowers [Latin: kind of cress]

nasty *adj* **-tier, -tiest 1** unpleasant: *a nasty odour* **2** dangerous or painful: *a nasty burn* **3** (of a person) spiteful or ill-natured ▷ *n, pl* **-ties 4** something unpleasant: *free from chemical nasties* [probably related to Dutch *nestig* dirty] **nastily** *adv* **nastiness** *n*

nat. 1 national **2** nationalist

natal (nay-tl) *adj* of or relating to birth [Latin *natalis* of one's birth]

nation *n* a large body of people of one or more cultures or races, organized into a single state: *a major industrialized nation* [Latin *natio* birth, tribe]

national *adj* **1** of or serving a nation as a whole **2** characteristic of a particular nation: *the national character* ▷ *n* **3** a citizen of a particular country: *Belgian nationals* **4** a national newspaper **nationally** *adv*

national anthem *n* a patriotic song adopted by a nation for use on public occasions

National Curriculum *n* (in England and Wales) the curriculum of subjects taught in state schools since 1989

national debt *n* the total outstanding borrowings of a nation's central government
national grid *n Brit & NZ* **1** a network of high-voltage power lines linking major electric power stations **2** the arrangement of vertical and horizontal lines on an ordnance survey map
National Health Service *n* (in Britain) the system of national medical services financed mainly by taxation
national hunt *n Brit (often cap)* horse racing over courses with fences
national insurance *n* (in Britain) state insurance based on contributions from employees and employers, providing payments to unemployed, sick, and retired people
nationalism *n* **1** a policy of national independence **2** patriotism, sometimes to an excessive degree **nationalist** *n, adj* **nationalistic** *adj*
nationality *n, pl* **-ties 1** the fact of being a citizen of a particular nation **2** a group of people of the same race: *young men of all nationalities*
nationalize *or* **-lise** *vb* **-lizing, -lized** *or* **-lising, -lised** to put (an industry or a company) under state control **nationalization** *or* **-lisation** *n*
national park *n* an area of countryside protected by a national government for its scenic or environmental importance and visited by the public
national service *n chiefly Brit* compulsory military service
National Socialism *n German history* the doctrines and practices of the Nazis, involving the supremacy of Hitler, anti-Semitism, state control of the economy, and national expansion **National Socialist** *n, adj*
national superannuation *n NZ* a government pension paid to people of 65 years and over; retirement pension
National Trust *n* (in Britain) an organization concerned with the preservation of historic buildings and areas of natural beauty
nationwide *adj* covering or available to the whole of a nation
native *adj* **1** relating to a place where a person was born: *native land* **2** born in a specified place: *a native New Yorker* **3 native to** originating in: *a plant native to alpine regions* **4** natural or inborn: *native genius* **5** relating to the original inhabitants of a country: *archaeology may uncover magnificent native artefacts* **6 go native** (of a settler) to adopt the lifestyle of the local population ▷ *n* **7** a person born in a specified place: *a native of Palermo* **8** an indigenous animal or plant: *the saffron crocus is a native of Asia Minor* **9** a member of the original race of a country, as opposed to colonial immigrants [Latin *nativus* innate, natural, from *nasci* to be born]

> **USAGE** Because of its potentially offensive and colonial overtones, *native* as a noun without qualification is best avoided. It is, however, acceptable when modified, as in *natives of Edinburgh* or *a native of North Carolina*.

Native American *n* **1** a member of any of the original peoples of North America ▷ *adj* **2** of any of these peoples
native bear *n Austral* same as **koala**
native companion *n Austral* same as **brolga**
native dog *n Austral* same as **dingo**
nativity *n, pl* **-ties** birth or origin [Late Latin *nativitas* birth]
Nativity *n Christianity* **1** the birth of Jesus Christ **2** the feast of Christmas celebrating this
NATO *or* **Nato** North Atlantic Treaty Organization: an international organization established for purposes of collective security
natter *Brit & NZ informal* ▷ *vb* **1** to talk idly and at length ▷ *n* **2** a long idle chat [dialect *gnatter* to grumble, imitative]
natterjack *n* a greyish-brown toad with reddish warty lumps [origin unknown]
natty *adj* **-tier, -tiest** *informal* smart and spruce [dialect *net* neat] **nattily** *adv*
natural *adj* **1** as is normal or to be expected: *the natural consequence* **2** genuine or spontaneous: *talking in a relaxed, natural manner* **3** of, according to, existing in, or produced by nature: *natural disasters* **4** not acquired; inborn: *their natural enthusiasm* **5** not created by human beings **6** not synthetic: *natural fibres such as wool* **7** (of a parent) not adoptive **8** *music* not sharp or flat: F *natural* ▷ *n* **9** *informal* a person with an inborn talent or skill: *she's a natural at bridge* **10** *music* a note that is neither sharp nor flat **naturalness** *n*
natural gas *n* a gaseous mixture, consisting mainly of methane, found below ground; used widely as a fuel
natural history *n* the study of animals and plants in the wild
naturalism *n* a movement in art and literature advocating detailed realism **naturalistic** *adj*
naturalist *n* **1** a student of natural history **2** a person who advocates or practises naturalism
naturalize *or* **-lise** *vb* **-lizing, -lized** *or* **-lising, -lised 1** to give citizenship to (a person born in another country) **2** to introduce (a plant or animal) into another region **3** to cause (a foreign word or custom) to be adopted **naturalization** *or* **-lisation** *n*
natural logarithm *n* a logarithm which has the irrational number *e* as a base
naturally *adv* **1** of course; surely **2** in a natural or normal way **3** instinctively
natural number *n* a positive integer, such as 1, 2, 3, 4, etc.
natural philosophy *n old-fashioned* physics
natural resources *pl n* naturally occurring materials such as coal, oil, and minerals
natural science *n* any of the sciences dealing with the study of the physical world, such as biology, physics, chemistry, and geology
natural selection *n* a process by which only those creatures and plants well adapted to their environment survive
natural wastage *n chiefly Brit* a reduction in the number of employees through not replacing those who leave, rather than by dismissing employees or making them redundant
nature *n* **1** the whole system of the existence, forces, and events of the physical world that are not controlled by human beings **2** fundamental or essential qualities: *the theory and nature of science*

n

3 kind or sort: *problems of a financial nature* 4 temperament or personality: *an amiable and pleasant nature* 5 **by nature** essentially: *he was by nature a cautious man* 6 **in the nature of** essentially; by way of: *it was in the nature of a debate rather than an argument* [Latin *natura*, from *nasci* to be born]

nature reserve *n* an area of land that is preserved and managed in order to protect its animal and plant life

nature study *n* the study of animals and plants by direct observation

nature trail *n* a path through countryside, signposted to draw attention to natural features of interest

naturism *n* the practice of not wearing clothes; nudism **naturist** *n, adj*

naught *n* 1 *archaic or literary* nothing 2 *chiefly US* the figure 0 ▹ *adv* 3 *archaic or literary* not at all: I *care naught* [Old English *nāwiht*]

naughty *adj* **-tier, -tiest** 1 (of children) mischievous or disobedient 2 mildly indecent: *naughty lingerie* [(originally: needy, poor) from *naught*] **naughtily** *adv* **naughtiness** *n*

nausea (naw-zee-a) *n* 1 the feeling of being about to vomit 2 disgust [Greek: seasickness, from *naus* ship]

nauseate *vb* **-ating, -ated** 1 to cause (someone) to feel sick 2 to arouse feelings of disgust in (someone) **nauseating** *adj*

nauseous *adj* 1 as if about to be sick: *he felt nauseous* 2 sickening

nautical *adj* of the sea, ships, or navigation [Greek *nautikos*, from *naus* ship]

nautical mile *n* a unit of length, used in navigation, standardized as 6080 feet

nautilus *n, pl* **-luses** *or* **-li** a sea creature with a shell and tentacles [Greek *nautilos* sailor]

naval *adj* of or relating to a navy or ships [Latin *navis* ship]

nave¹ *n* the long central part of a church [Latin *navis* ship, from the similarity in shape]

nave² *n* the hub of a wheel [Old English *nafu*, *nafa*]

navel *n* the slight hollow in the centre of the abdomen, where the umbilical cord was attached [Old English *nafela*]

navel orange *n* a sweet orange that has a navel-like hollow at the top

navigable *adj* 1 wide, deep, or safe enough to be sailed through: *the navigable portion of the Nile* 2 able to be steered: *the boat has to be watertight and navigable*

navigate *vb* **-gating, -gated** 1 to direct or plot the course or position of a ship or aircraft 2 to travel over or through safely: *your cousin, who's just navigated the Amazon* 3 *informal* to direct (oneself) carefully or safely: *he navigated his unsteady way to the bar* 4 (of a passenger in a vehicle) to read the map and give directions to the driver [Latin *navis* ship + *agere* to drive] **navigation** *n* **navigational** *adj* **navigator** *n*

navvy *n, pl* **-vies** *Brit & Austral informal* a labourer on a building site or road [from *navigator* builder of a *navigation* (in the sense: canal)]

navy *n, pl* **-vies** 1 the branch of a country's armed services comprising warships with their crews, and all their supporting services 2 the warships of a nation ▹ *adj* 3 short for **navy-blue** [Latin *navis* ship]

navy-blue *adj* very dark blue [from the colour of the British naval uniform]

nawab (na-**wahb**) *n* (formerly) a Muslim ruler or powerful landowner in India [Hindi *nawwāb*, from Arabic *nuwwāb*, plural of *na'ib* viceroy]

nay *interj* 1 *old-fashioned* no ▹ *n* 2 a person who votes against a motion ▹ *adv* 3 used for emphasis: *I want, nay, need to know* [Old Norse *nei*]

Nazarene *n* 1 **the Nazarene** *Christianity* Jesus Christ 2 *old-fashioned* a Christian 3 a person from Nazareth, a town in N Israel ▹ *adj* 4 of Nazareth

Nazi *n, pl* **-zis** 1 a member of the fascist National Socialist German Workers' Party, which came to power in Germany in 1933 under Adolf Hitler ▹ *adj* 2 of or relating to the Nazis [German, phonetic spelling of the first two syllables of *Nationalsozialist* National Socialist] **Nazism** *n*

nb *cricket* no-ball

Nb *chem* niobium

NB 1 New Brunswick 2 note well [(sense 2) Latin *nota bene*]

NC 1 North Carolina 2 *Brit education* National Curriculum

NCO noncommissioned officer

Nd *chem* neodymium

ND North Dakota

NDT Newfoundland Daylight Time

Ne *chem* neon

NE 1 Nebraska 2 northeast(ern)

ne- *combining form* same as **neo-**: *Nearctic*

Neanderthal (nee-ann-der-tahl) *adj* 1 of a type of primitive human that lived in Europe before 12 000 BC 2 *informal* having or characterized by excessively conservative views: *his notoriously Neanderthal attitude to women* [after *Neandertal*, a valley in Germany]

neap *n* short for **neap tide** [Old English, as in *nēpflōd* neap tide]

Neapolitan *adj* 1 of Naples, a city in SW Italy ▹ *n* 2 a person from Naples [Greek *Neapolis* new town]

neap tide *n* a tide that occurs at the first and last quarter of the moon when there is the smallest rise and fall in tidal level

near *prep* 1 at or to a place or time not far away from ▹ *adv* 2 at or to a place or time not far away 3 short for **nearly**: *the pain damn near crippled him* ▹ *adj* 4 at or in a place or time not far away: *in the near future* 5 closely connected or intimate: *a near relation* 6 almost being the thing specified: *a mood of near rebellion* ▹ *vb* 7 to draw close (to): *the participants are nearing agreement* [Old English *nēar*, comparative of *nēah* close] **nearness** *n*

nearby *adj* 1 not far away: *a nearby village* ▹ *adv* 2 close at hand: *I live nearby*

Near East *n* same as **Middle East**

nearly *adv* 1 almost 2 **not nearly** nowhere near: *it's not nearly as easy as it looks*

near miss *n* 1 any attempt that just fails to succeed 2 an incident in which two aircraft or vehicles narrowly avoid collision 3 a bomb or shot that does not quite hit the target

nearside *n* 1 *chiefly Brit* the side of a vehicle that is nearer the kerb 2 the left side of an animal

near-sighted *adj* same as **short-sighted**
near thing *n informal* an event whose outcome is nearly a failure or a disaster, or only just a success
neat *adj* **1** clean and tidy **2** smoothly or competently done: *a neat answer* **3** (of alcoholic drinks) undiluted **4** *slang, chiefly US & Canad* admirable; excellent [Latin *nitidus* clean]
neatly *adv* **neatness** *n*
neaten *vb* to make neat
neath *prep archaic* short for **beneath**
neb *n archaic or dialect* the beak of a bird or the nose of an animal [Old English *nebb*]
nebula (neb-yew-la) *n, pl* **-lae** (-lee) *astron* a hazy cloud of particles and gases [Latin: mist, cloud]
nebular *adj*
nebulize *or* **-lise** *vb* **-lizing, -lized** *or* **-lising, -lised** to turn (a liquid) into a fine spray
nebulizer *or* **-liser** *n* a device which turns a drug from a liquid into a fine spray which can be inhaled
nebulous *adj* vague and unclear: *a nebulous concept*
NEC (in Britain) National Executive Committee
necessaries *pl n* essential items: *the necessaries and comforts of life*
necessarily *adv* **1** as a certainty: *the factors were not necessarily connected with one another* **2** inevitably: *tourism is an industry that has a necessarily close connection with governments*
necessary *adj* **1** needed in order to obtain the desired result: *the necessary skills* **2** certain or unavoidable: *the necessary consequences* ▷ *n* **3 do the necessary** *informal* to do something that is necessary in a particular situation **4 the necessary** *informal* the money required for a particular purpose ▷ See also **necessaries** [Latin *necessarius* indispensable]
necessitate *vb* **-tating, -tated** to compel or require
necessitous *adj literary* very needy
necessity *n, pl* **-ties 1** a set of circumstances that inevitably requires a certain result: *the necessity to maintain safety standards* **2** something needed: *the daily necessities* **3** great poverty **4 of necessity** inevitably
neck *n* **1** the part of the body connecting the head with the rest of the body **2** the part of a garment around the neck **3** the long narrow part of a bottle or violin **4** the length of a horse's head and neck taken as the distance by which one horse beats another in a race: *to win by a neck* **5** *informal* impudence **6 by a neck** by a very small margin: *beaten only by a neck* **7 get it in the neck** *informal* to be reprimanded or punished severely **8 neck and neck** absolutely level in a race or competition **9 neck of the woods** *informal* a particular area: *how did they get to this neck of the woods?* **10 stick one's neck out** *informal* to risk criticism or ridicule by speaking one's mind **11 up to one's neck in** *informal* to be deeply involved in: *he was up to his neck in the scandal* ▷ *vb* **12** *slang* to swallow quickly **13** *informal* (of two people) to kiss each other passionately [Old English *hnecca*]
neckband *n* a band around the neck of a garment
neckerchief *n* a piece of cloth worn tied round the neck [*neck* + *kerchief*]
necklace *n* a decorative piece of jewellery worn round the neck
neckline *n* the shape or position of the upper edge of a dress or top
necktie *n US* same as **tie** (sense 5)
necromancy (neck-rome-man-see) *n* **1** communication with the dead **2** sorcery [Greek *nekros* corpse + *mantis* prophet]
necromancer *n*
necrophilia *n* sexual attraction for or sexual intercourse with dead bodies [Greek *nekros* corpse + *philos* loving]
necropolis (neck-rop-pol-liss) *n* a cemetery [Greek *nekros* dead + *polis* city]
necrosis *n* **1** *biol & med* the death of cells in the body, as from an interruption of the blood supply **2** *botany* death of plant tissue due to disease or frost [Greek *nekros* corpse] **necrotic** *adj*
nectar *n* **1** a sugary fluid produced by flowers and collected by bees **2** *classical myth* the drink of the gods **3** any delicious drink [Greek *nektar*]
nectarine *n* a smooth-skinned variety of peach [apparently from *nectar*]
ned *n Scot slang* a hooligan [origin unknown]
née *prep* indicating the maiden name of a married woman: *Jane Gray (née Blandish)* [French, past participle (feminine) of *naître* to be born]
need *vb* **1** to require or be in want of: *they desperately need success* **2** to be obliged: *the government may need to impose a statutory levy* **3** used to express necessity or obligation and does not add -s when used with singular nouns or pronouns: *need he go?* ▷ *n* **4** the condition of lacking something: *he has need of a new coat* **5** a requirement: *the need for closer economic co-operation* **6** necessity: *there was no need for an explanation* **7** poverty or destitution: *the money will go to those areas where need is greatest* **8** distress: *help has been given to those in need* ▷ See also **needs** [Old English *nēad, nied*]
needful *adj* **1** necessary or required ▷ *n* **2 the needful** *informal* what is necessary, usually money
needle *n* **1** a pointed slender piece of metal with a hole in it through which thread is passed for sewing **2** a long pointed rod used in knitting **3** same as **stylus 4** *med* the long hollow pointed part of a hypodermic syringe, which is inserted into the body **5** a pointer on the scale of a measuring instrument **6** a long narrow stiff leaf: *pine needles* **7** *Brit informal* intense rivalry or ill-feeling in a sports match **8** short for **magnetic needle 9 have** *or* **get the needle** *Brit informal* to be or become annoyed ▷ *vb* **-dling, -dled 10** *informal* to goad or provoke [Old English *nǣdl*]
needlecord *n* a fine-ribbed corduroy fabric
needlepoint *n* **1** embroidery done on canvas **2** lace made by needles on a paper pattern
needless *adj* not required; unnecessary
needlessly *adv*
needlewoman *n, pl* **-women** a woman who does needlework
needlework *n* sewing and embroidery
needs *adv* **1** necessarily: *they must needs be admired* ▷ *pl n* **2** what is required: *he provides them with their needs*

n

needy *adj* **needier, neediest** in need of financial support
ne'er *adv poetic* never
ne'er-do-well *n* **1** an irresponsible or lazy person ▷ *adj* **2** useless; worthless: *his ne'er-do-well brother*
nefarious (nif-**fair**-ee-uss) *adj literary* evil; wicked [Latin *ne* not + *fas* divine law]
neg. negative
negate *vb* **-gating, -gated 1** to cause to have no value or effect: *his prejudices largely negate his accomplishments* **2** to deny the existence of [Latin *negare*]
negation *n* **1** the opposite or absence of something **2** a negative thing or condition **3** the act of negating
negative *adj* **1** expressing a refusal or denial: *a negative response* **2** lacking positive qualities, such as enthusiasm or optimism **3** *med* indicating absence of the condition for which a test was made **4** *physics* **A** (of an electric charge) having the same electrical charge as an electron **B** (of a body or system) having a negative electric charge; having an excess of electrons **5** same as **minus** (sense 4) **6** measured in a direction opposite to that regarded as positive **7** short for **electronegative 8** of a photographic negative ▷ *n* **9** a statement or act of denial or refusal **10** *photog* a piece of photographic film, exposed and developed, bearing an image with a reversal of tones or colours, from which positive prints are made **11** a word or expression with a negative meaning, such as *not* **12** a quantity less than zero **13 in the negative** indicating denial or refusal **negatively** *adv*
negative equity *n* the holding of a property of fallen value which is worth less than the amount of mortgage still unpaid
negativism *n* a tendency to be unconstructively critical **negativist** *n, adj*
neglect *vb* **1** to fail to give due care or attention to: *she had neglected her child* **2** to fail (to do something) through carelessness: *he neglected to greet his guests* **3** to disregard: *he neglected his duty* ▷ *n* **4** lack of due care or attention: *the city had a look of shabbiness and neglect* **5** the state of being neglected [Latin *neglegere*]
neglectful *adj* not paying enough care or attention: *abusive and neglectful parents*
negligee (**neg**-lee-zhay) *n* a woman's light, usually lace-trimmed dressing gown [French]
negligence *n* neglect or carelessness **negligent** *adj* **negligently** *adv*
negligible *adj* so small or unimportant as to be not worth considering
negotiable *adj* **1** able to be changed or agreed by discussion: *the prices were negotiable* **2** (of a bill of exchange or promissory note) legally transferable
negotiate *vb* **-ating, -ated 1** to talk with others in order to reach (an agreement) **2** to succeed in passing round or over (a place or a problem) [Latin *negotium* business, from *nec* not + *otium* leisure] **negotiation** *n* **negotiator** *n*
Negro *old-fashioned, offensive* ▷ *n, pl* **-groes 1** a member of any of the dark-skinned peoples originating in Africa ▷ *adj* **2** of Black people [Latin *niger* black]
Negroid *adj old-fashioned, offensive* of or relating to the dark-skinned peoples originating in Africa
neigh *n* **1** the high-pitched sound made by a horse ▷ *vb* **2** to make this sound [Old English *hnǣgan*]
neighbour *or US* **neighbor** *n* **1** a person who lives near or next to another **2** a person, thing, or country near or next to another [Old English *nēah* near + *būr, gebūr* dweller]
neighbourhood *or US* **neighborhood** *n* **1** a district where people live **2** the immediate environment; surroundings **3** the people in a district **4 in the neighbourhood of** approximately ▷ *adj* **5** in and for a district: *our neighbourhood cinema*
neighbouring *or US* **neighboring** *adj* situated nearby: *the neighbouring island*
neighbourly *or US* **neighborly** *adj* kind, friendly, and helpful
neither *adj* **1** not one nor the other (of two): *neither enterprise went well* ▷ *pron* **2** not one nor the other (of two): *neither completed the full term* ▷ *conj* **3 A** used preceding alternatives joined by *nor*; not: *sparing neither strength nor courage* **B** same as **nor** (sense 2) ▷ *adv* **4** *not standard* same as **either** (sense 4) [Old English *nāwther*]

> **USAGE** A verb following a compound subject that uses *neither ...(nor)* should be in the singular if both subjects are in the singular: *neither Jack nor Aisha has done the work.*

nelson *n* a wrestling hold in which a wrestler places his or her arm or arms under the opponent's arm or arms from behind and exerts pressure with his or her palms on the back of the opponent's neck [from a proper name]
nematode *n* a slender unsegmented cylindrical worm [Greek *nēma* thread + *eidos* shape]
nemesis (**nem**-miss-iss) *n, pl* **-ses** (-seez) a means of retribution or vengeance [Greek *nemein* to distribute what is due]
neo- *combining form* new, recent, or a modern form of: *neoclassicism; neo-Nazi* [Greek *neos* new]
neoclassicism *n* a late 18th- and early 19th-century style of art and architecture, based on ancient Roman and Greek models **neoclassical** *adj*
neocolonialism *n* political control wielded by one country over another through control of its economy **neocolonial** *adj*
neocon *n, adj chiefly US* short for **neoconservative**
neoconservative *adj* **1** favouring a return to a set of established (esp. political) conservative values which have been updated to suit current conditions ▷ *n* **2** a person subscribing to neoconservative philosophy
neodymium *n chem* a toxic silvery-white metallic element of the lanthanide series. Symbol: **Nd** [NEO- + *didymium*, a compound originally thought to be an element]
neoliberalism *n* a modern political and economic theory that promotes free trade, privatization, reduced public expenditure, and limited control of business **neoliberal** *n, adj*
Neolithic *adj* of the period that lasted in Europe from about 4000 to 2400 BC, characterized by primitive farming and the use of polished stone and flint tools and weapons [NEO- + Greek *lithos* stone]

n

neologism (nee-**ol**-a-jiz-zum) *n* a newly coined word, or an established word used in a new sense [NEO- + Greek *logos* word]

neon *n* **1** *chem* a colourless odourless rare gas, used in illuminated signs and lights. Symbol: **Ne** ▷ *adj* **2** of or illuminated by neon: *a flashing neon sign* [Greek: new]

neonatal *adj* relating to the first few weeks of a baby's life **neonate** *n*

neo-Nazi *n, pl* **-zis 1** a member of a modern organization with policies similar to those of the German Nazi party ▷ *adj* **2** of or relating to neo-Nazis **neo-Nazism** *n*

neon light *n* a glass tube containing neon, which gives a pink or red glow when a voltage is applied

neophyte *n formal* **1** a beginner **2** a person newly converted to a religious faith **3** a novice in a religious order [Greek *neos* new + *phuton* a plant]

Nepali (nip-**paw**-lee) *or* **Nepalese** (nep-pal-**leez**) *adj* **1** of Nepal ▷ *n* **2** *pl* **-pali, -palis** *or* **-palese** a person from Nepal **3** the language of Nepal

nephew *n* a son of one's sister or brother [Latin *nepos*]

nephritis (nif-**frite**-tiss) *n* inflammation of the kidney [Greek *nephros* kidney]

nepotism (**nep**-a-tiz-zum) *n* favouritism shown to relatives and friends by those with power [Italian *nepote* nephew]

Neptune *n* **1** the Roman god of the sea **2** the eighth planet from the sun

neptunium *n chem* a silvery metallic element synthesized in the production of plutonium. Symbol: **Np** [after *Neptune*, the planet]

nerd *or* **nurd** *n slang* **1** a boring or unpopular person, esp. one who is obsessed with a particular subject: *a computer nerd* **2** a stupid and feeble person [origin unknown] **nerdish, nurdish, nerdy** *or* **nurdy** *adj*

nervate *adj* (of leaves) with veins

nerve *n* **1** a cordlike bundle of fibres that conducts impulses between the brain and other parts of the body **2** bravery and determination **3** *informal* impudence: *you've got a nerve!* **4 lose one's nerve** to lose self-confidence and become afraid about what one is doing **5 strain every nerve** to make every effort (to do something) ▷ *vb* **nerving, nerved 6 nerve oneself** to prepare oneself (to do something difficult or unpleasant) ▷ See also **nerves** [Latin *nervus*]

nerve cell *n* same as **neuron**

nerve centre *n* **1** a place from which a system or organization is controlled: *an underground nerve centre of intelligence* **2** a group of nerve cells associated with a specific function

nerve gas *n* a poisonous gas which affects the nervous system

nerveless *adj* **1** (of fingers or hands) without feeling; numb **2** (of a person) fearless

nerve-racking *or* **nerve-wracking** *adj* very distressing or harrowing

nerves *pl n informal* **1** anxiety or tension: *nerves can often be the cause of wedding-day hitches* **2** the ability or inability to remain calm in a difficult situation: *his nerves are in a shocking state* **3 get on someone's nerves** to irritate someone

nervous *adj* **1** apprehensive or worried **2** excitable; highly strung **3** of or relating to the nerves: *the nervous system* **nervously** *adv* **nervousness** *n*

nervous breakdown *n* a mental illness in which the sufferer ceases to function properly, and experiences symptoms including tiredness, anxiety, and deep depression

nervous system *n* the brain, spinal column, and nerves, which together control thought, feeling, and movement. See **neuron**

nervy *adj* **nervier, nerviest** *Brit & Austral informal* excitable or nervous

ness *n Brit* a headland or cape [Old English *næs*]

-ness *n suffix* indicating state, condition, or quality: *greatness; selfishness* [Old English *-nes*]

nest *n* **1** a place or structure in which birds or other animals lay eggs or give birth to young **2** a cosy or secluded place **3** a set of things of graduated sizes designed to fit together: *a nest of tables* ▷ *vb* **4** to make or inhabit a nest **5** (of a set of objects) to fit one inside another **6** *computers* to position (data) within other data at different ranks or levels [Old English]

nest egg *n* a fund of money kept in reserve

nestle *vb* **-tling, -tled 1** to snuggle or cuddle closely **2** to be in a sheltered position: *honey-coloured stone villages nestling in wooded valleys* [Old English *nestlian*]

nestling *n* a young bird not yet able to fly

net¹ *n* **1** a very fine fabric made from intersecting strands of material with a space between each strand **2** a piece of net, used to protect or hold things or to trap animals **3** (in certain sports) a strip of net over which the ball or shuttlecock must be hit **4** the goal in soccer or hockey **5** a strategy intended to trap people: *innocent fans were caught in the police net* **6** *informal* short for **internet** ▷ *vb* **netting, netted 7** to catch (a fish or other animal) in a net [Old English *net(t)*]

net² *or* **nett** *adj* **1** remaining after all deductions, as for taxes and expenses: *net income* **2** (of weight) excluding the weight of wrapping or container **3** final or conclusive: *the net effect* ▷ *vb* **netting, netted 4** to yield or earn as a clear profit [French: neat]

netball *n* a team game, usually played by women, in which a ball has to be thrown through a net hanging from a ring at the top of a pole

nether *adj old-fashioned* lower or under: *nether regions* [Old English *nithera*, literally: further down]

nethermost *adj* lowest

nether world *n* **1** the underworld **2** hell. Also called: **nether regions**

net profit *n* gross profit minus all operating expenses such as wages and overheads

nett *adj, vb* same as **net²**

netting *n* a fabric or structure made of net

nettle *n* **1** a plant with stinging hairs on the leaves **2 grasp the nettle** to attempt something unpleasant with boldness and courage [Old English *netele*]

nettled *adj* irritated or annoyed

nettle rash *n* a skin condition, usually caused by an allergy, in which itchy red or white raised patches appear

network *n* **1** a system of intersecting lines, roads, veins, etc. **2** an interconnecting group or system: *a network of sympathizers and safe-houses* **3** *radio & television* a group of broadcasting stations that all transmit the same programme at the same time **4** *electronics & computers* a system of interconnected components or circuits ▷ *vb* **5** *radio & television* to broadcast (a programme) over a network **6** to form business contacts through informal social meetings

neural *adj* of a nerve or the nervous system

neuralgia *n* severe pain along a nerve **neuralgic** *adj*

neuritis (nyoor-rite-tiss) *n* inflammation of a nerve or nerves, often causing pain and loss of function in the affected part

neurology *n med* the scientific study of the nervous system **neurological** *adj* **neurologist** *n*

neuron *or* **neurone** *n* a cell specialized to conduct nerve impulses [Greek]

neurosis (nyoor-oh-siss) *n, pl* **-ses** (-seez) a mental disorder producing hysteria, anxiety, depression, or obsessive behaviour

neurosurgery *n med* the branch of surgery concerned with the nervous system **neurosurgeon** *n* **neurosurgical** *adj*

neurotic *adj* **1** tending to be emotionally unstable **2** affected by neurosis ▷ *n* **3** a person with a neurosis or tending to be emotionally unstable

neurotransmitter *n biochem* a chemical by which a nerve cell communicates with another nerve cell or with a muscle

n

neuter *adj* **1** *grammar* denoting a gender of nouns which are neither male nor female **2** (of animals and plants) sexually underdeveloped ▷ *n* **3** *grammar* **A** the neuter gender **B** a neuter noun **4** a sexually underdeveloped female insect, such as a worker bee **5** a castrated animal ▷ *vb* **6** to castrate (an animal) [Latin *ne* not + *uter* either (of two)]

neutral *adj* **1** not taking any side in a war or dispute **2** of or belonging to a neutral party or country **3** not displaying any emotions or opinions **4** (of a colour) not definite or striking **5** *chem* neither acidic nor alkaline **6** *physics* having zero charge or potential ▷ *n* **7** a neutral person or nation **8** the position of the controls of a gearbox that leaves the gears unconnected to the engine [Latin *neutralis* of neuter gender] **neutrality** *n*

neutralize *or* **-lise** *vb* **-lizing, -lized** *or* **-lising, -lised 1** to make electrically or chemically neutral **2** to make ineffective by counteracting **3** to make (a country) neutral by international agreement: *the great powers neutralized Belgium in the 19th century* **neutralization** *or* **-lisation** *n*

neutrino (new-tree-no) *n, pl* **-nos** *physics* an elementary particle with no mass or electrical charge [Italian diminutive of *neutrone* neutron]

neutron *n physics* a neutral elementary particle of about the same mass as a proton [from *neutral*, on the model of *electron*]

neutron bomb *n* a nuclear weapon designed to kill people and animals while leaving buildings virtually undamaged

never *adv* **1** at no time; not ever **2** certainly not; not at all **3** Also: **well I never!** surely not! [Old English *nǣfre*]

> **USAGE** In informal speech and writing, *never* can be used instead of *not* with the simple past tenses of certain verbs, for emphasis (*I never said that; I never realized how clever he was*), but this usage should be avoided in serious writing.

never-ending *adj* long and boring

nevermore *adv literary* never again

never-never *n* **the never-never** *informal* hire-purchase: *they are buying it on the never-never*

never-never land *n* an imaginary idyllic place

nevertheless *adv* in spite of that

new *adj* **1** recently made, brought into being, or acquired: *a new car* **2** of a kind never before existing; novel: *a new approach to monetary policy* **3** recently discovered: *testing new drugs* **4** recently introduced to or inexperienced in a place or situation: *new to this game* **5** fresh; additional: *you can acquire new skills* **6** unknown: *this is new to me* **7** (of a cycle) beginning again: *a new era* **8** (of crops) harvested early: *new potatoes* **9** changed for the better: *she returned a new woman* ▷ *adv* **10** recently, newly: *new-laid eggs* ▷ See also **news** [Old English *nīowe*] **newish** *adj* **newness** *n*

New Age *n* **1** a philosophy, originating in the late 1980s, characterized by a belief in alternative medicine, astrology, and spiritualism ▷ *adj* **2** of the New Age: *New Age therapies* **New Ager** *n*

New Age Music *n* a type of gentle melodic largely instrumental popular music originating in the USA in the late 1980s

New Australian *n Austral* a recent immigrant

newbie *n informal* a person new to a job, club, etc.

newborn *adj* recently or just born

New Canadian *n Canad* a recent immigrant to Canada

newcomer *n* a recent arrival or participant

newel *n* **1** Also called: **newel post** the post at the top or bottom of a flight of stairs that supports the handrail **2** the central pillar of a winding staircase [Old French *nouel* knob]

newfangled *adj* objectionably or unnecessarily modern [Middle English *newefangel* liking new things]

new-found *adj* newly or recently discovered: *new-found confidence*

New Jerusalem *n Christianity* heaven

New Latin *n* the form of Latin used since the Renaissance, mainly for scientific names

newly *adv* **1** recently **2** again; anew: *newly interpreted*

newlyweds *pl n* a recently married couple

New Man *n* **the New Man** *chiefly Brit* a type of modern man who allows the caring side of his nature to show by being supportive and by sharing childcare and housework

new maths *n Brit* an approach to mathematics in which basic set theory is introduced at an elementary level

new moon *n* the moon when it appears as a narrow crescent at the beginning of its cycle

news *n* **1** important or interesting new happenings **2** information about such events, reported in the mass media **3** **the news** a

television or radio programme presenting such information **4** interesting or important new information: *it's news to me* **5** a person or thing widely reported in the mass media: *reggae is suddenly big news again*
news agency *n* an organization that collects news reports and sells them to newspapers, magazines, and TV and radio stations
newsagent *n Brit* a shopkeeper who sells newspapers and magazines
newscast *n* a radio or television broadcast of the news [*news + (broad)cast*] **newscaster** *n*
news conference *n* same as **press conference**
newsflash *n* a brief item of important news, which interrupts a radio or television programme
newsgroup *n computers* a forum where subscribers exchange information about a specific subject
newsletter *n* a periodical bulletin issued to members of a group
newspaper *n* a weekly or daily publication consisting of folded sheets and containing news, features, and advertisements
newspeak *n* the language of politicians and officials regarded as deliberately ambiguous and misleading [from the novel *1984* by George Orwell]
newsprint *n* an inexpensive wood-pulp paper used for newspapers
newsreader *n* a news announcer on radio or television
newsreel *n* a short film with a commentary which presents current events
newsroom *n* a room in a newspaper office or radio or television station where news is received and prepared for publication or broadcasting: *a journalist who was in the newsroom at the time*
newsstand *n* a portable stand from which newspapers are sold
New Style *n* the present method of reckoning dates using the Gregorian calendar
newsworthy *adj* sufficiently interesting to be reported as news
newsy *adj* **newsier, newsiest** (of a letter) full of news
newt *n* a small amphibious creature with a long slender body and tail and short legs [mistaken division of *an ewt*; *ewt* from Old English *efeta*]
New Testament *n* the second part of the Christian Bible, dealing with the life and teachings of Christ and his followers
newton *n* the SI unit of force that gives an acceleration of 1 metre per second per second to a mass of 1 kilogram [after Sir Isaac *Newton*, scientist]
new town *n* (in Britain) a town planned as a complete unit and built with government sponsorship
new wave *n* a movement in politics, the arts, or music that consciously breaks with traditional values
New World *n* **the New World** the western hemisphere of the world, esp. the Americas
New Year *n* the first day or days of the year in various calendars, usually a holiday
New Year's Day *n* January 1, celebrated as a holiday in many countries
New Year's Eve *n* December 31
New Zealander *n* a person from New Zealand
next *adj* **1** immediately following: *the next generation* **2** immediately adjoining: *in the next room* **3** closest to in degree: *the next-best thing* ▷ *adv* **4** at a time immediately to follow: *the patient to be examined next* **5** **next to** **A** adjacent to: *the house next to ours* **B** following in degree: *next to my wife, I love you most* **C** almost: *the evidence is next to totally useless* [Old English *nēhst*, superlative of *nēah* near]
next door *adj, adv* in, at, or to the adjacent house or flat: *the Cabinet retired next door*; *the people next door*
next of kin *n* a person's closest relative
nexus *n, pl* **nexus** **1** a connection or link **2** a connected group or series [Latin, from *nectere* to bind]
NF Newfoundland
Nfld. Newfoundland
ngati (nah-tee) *n, pl* **ngati** NZ (occurring as part of the tribe name) a tribe or clan [Māori]
Nh nihonium
NH New Hampshire
NHS (in Britain) National Health Service
Ni *chem* nickel
NI **1** (in Britain) National Insurance **2** Northern Ireland
niacin *n* a vitamin of the B complex that occurs in milk, liver, and yeast. Also called: **nicotinic acid** [from *ni(cotinic) ac(id)* + *-in* denoting a chemical substance]
nib *n* the writing point of a pen [origin unknown]
nibble *vb* **-bling, -bled** **1** to take little bites (of) **2** to bite gently: *she nibbled at her lower lip* ▷ *n* **3** a little bite **4** a light hurried meal [related to Low German *nibbelen*]
nibs *n* **his** *or* **her nibs** *slang* a mock title used of an important or self-important person [origin unknown]
NICAM near-instantaneous companding system: a technique for coding audio signals into digital form
nice *adj* **1** pleasant **2** kind: *it's really nice of you to worry about me* **3** good or satisfactory: *a nice clean operation* **4** subtle: *a nice distinction* [Latin *nescius* ignorant] **nicely** *adv* **niceness** *n*
nicety *n, pl* **-ties** **1** a subtle point: *the niceties of our arguments* **2** a refinement or delicacy: *social niceties* **3** **to a nicety** precisely
niche (neesh) *n* **1** a recess in a wall for a statue or ornament **2** a position exactly suitable for the person occupying it: *perhaps I will find my niche in a desk job* ▷ *adj* **3** of or aimed at a specialist group or market: *niche retailing ventures* [Old French *nichier* to nest]
nick *vb* **1** to make a small cut in **2** *chiefly Brit slang* to steal **3** *chiefly Brit slang* to arrest ▷ *n* **4** a small notch or cut **5** *slang* a prison or police station **6** *informal* condition: *in good nick* **7** **in the nick of time** just in time [perhaps Middle English *nocke* nock]
nickel *n* **1** *chem* a silvery-white metallic element that is often used in alloys. Symbol: **Ni** **2** a US or Canadian coin worth five cents [German *Kupfernickel* nickel ore, literally: copper demon; it was mistakenly thought to contain copper]

n

nickelodeon *n US* an early type of jukebox [*nickel* + *(mel)odeon*]
nickel silver *n* an alloy containing copper, zinc, and nickel
nicker *n, pl* **nicker** *Brit slang* a pound sterling [origin unknown]
nick-nack *n* same as **knick-knack**
nickname *n* **1** a familiar, pet, or derisory name given to a person or place ▷ *vb* **-naming, -named 2** to call (a person or place) by a nickname: *Gaius Caesar Augustus Germanicus, nicknamed Caligula* [mistaken division of *an ekename* an additional name]
nicotine *n* a poisonous alkaloid found in tobacco [after J. *Nicot*, who introduced tobacco into France] **nicotinic** *adj*
nictitating membrane *n* (in reptiles, birds, and some mammals) a thin fold of skin under the eyelid that can be drawn across the eye
niece *n* a daughter of one's sister or brother [Latin *neptis* granddaughter]
niff *Brit slang* ▷ *n* **1** a stink ▷ *vb* **2** to stink [perhaps from *sniff*] **niffy** *adj*
nifty *adj* **-tier, -tiest** *informal* neat or smart [origin unknown]
Nigerian *adj* **1** of Nigeria ▷ *n* **2** a person from Nigeria
niggard *n* a stingy person [perhaps from Old Norse]
niggardly *adj* not generous: *it pays its staff on a niggardly scale* **niggardliness** *n*
nigger *n offensive, taboo* a Black person [Spanish *negro*]
niggle *vb* **-gling, -gled 1** to worry slightly **2** to find fault continually ▷ *n* **3** a small worry or doubt **4** a trivial objection or complaint [Scandinavian] **niggling** *adj*
nigh *archaic, poetic* ▷ *adv* **1** nearly ▷ *adj* **2** near ▷ *prep* **3** close to [Old English *nēah, nēh*]
night *n* **1** the period of darkness that occurs each 24 hours, between sunset and sunrise. Related adjective: **nocturnal 2** the period between sunset and bedtime; evening **3** the time between bedtime and morning **4** nightfall or dusk **5** an evening designated for a specific activity: *opening night* **6 make a night of it** to celebrate the whole evening ▷ *adj* **7** of, occurring, or working at night: *the night sky* ▷ See also **nights** [Old English *niht*]
nightcap *n* **1** a drink taken just before bedtime **2** a soft cap formerly worn in bed
nightclub *n* a place of entertainment open until late at night, that offers drink and dancing
nightdress *n* a loose dress worn in bed by women or girls
nightfall *n* the approach of darkness; dusk
nightgown *n* same as **nightdress**
nightie *n informal* short for **nightdress**
nightingale *n* a small bird with a musical song, usually heard at night [Old English *nihtegale*, literally: night singer]
nightjar *n* a nocturnal bird with a harsh cry [*night* + JAR² (so called from its discordant cry)]
nightlife *n* the entertainment and social activities available at night in a town or city: *New York nightlife*
night-light *n* a dim light left on overnight
nightlong *adj, adv* throughout the night
nightly *adj* **1** happening each night ▷ *adv* **2** each night
nightmare *n* **1** a terrifying or deeply distressing dream **2** a terrifying or unpleasant experience **3** a thing that is feared: *wheels and loose straps are a baggage handler's nightmare* [*night* + Old English *mare, mære* evil spirit] **nightmarish** *adj*
nights *adv informal* at night or on most nights: *he works nights*
night safe *n* a safe built into the outside wall of a bank, in which customers can deposit money when the bank is closed
night school *n* an educational institution that holds classes in the evening
nightshade *n* a plant which produces poisonous berries with bell-shaped flowers [Old English *nihtscada*]
nightshirt *n* a long loose shirtlike garment worn in bed
night soil *n archaic* human excrement collected at night from cesspools or privies
nightspot *n informal* a nightclub
night-time *n* the time from sunset to sunrise
night watch *n* **1** a watch or guard kept at night for security **2** the period of time this watch is kept
night watchman *n* a person who keeps guard at night on a factory or other building
nihilism (nye-ill-liz-zum) *n* a total rejection of all established authority and institutions [Latin *nihil* nothing] **nihilist** *n, adj* **nihilistic** *adj*
nihonium *n chem* a synthetic radioactive element produced in small quantities. Symbol: **Nh** [Japanese *Nihon* Japan]
-nik *suffix forming nouns* indicating a person associated with a particular state or quality: *refusenik* [Russian]
nil *n* nothing: esp. as a score in games [Latin]
nimble *adj* **1** agile and quick in movement **2** mentally alert or acute [Old English *nǣmel* quick to grasp + *numol* quick at seizing] **nimbly** *adv*
nimbus *n, pl* **-bi** *or* **-buses 1** a dark grey rain cloud **2** a halo [Latin: cloud]
NIMBY not in my back yard: used of people who are opposed to any building or changes that will affect them directly
nincompoop *n informal* a stupid person [origin unknown]
nine *n* **1** the cardinal number that is the sum of one and eight **2** a numeral, 9 or IX, representing this number **3** something representing or consisting of nine units **4 dressed up to the nines** *informal* elaborately dressed **5 999** (in Britain) the telephone number of the emergency services ▷ *adj* **6** amounting to nine: *nine men* [Old English *nigon*] **ninth** *adj, n*
nine-days wonder *n* something that arouses great interest, but only for a short period
nine-eleven, 9-11 *or* **9/11** *n* the 11th of September 2001, the day on which the twin towers of the World Trade Center in New York were flown into and destroyed by aeroplanes hijacked by Islamic fundamentalists. Also called: **September eleven**

[from the US custom of expressing dates in figures, the day of the month following the number of the month]

ninefold *adj* **1** having nine times as many or as much **2** having nine parts ▷ *adv* **3** by nine times as much or as many

ninepins *n* the game of skittles

nineteen *n* **1** the cardinal number that is the sum of ten and nine **2** a numeral, 19 or XIX, representing this number **3** something representing or consisting of nineteen units **4 talk nineteen to the dozen** to talk very fast ▷ *adj* **5** amounting to nineteen: *nineteen years* **nineteenth** *adj, n*

nineteenth hole *n golf slang* the bar in a golf clubhouse [from its being the next objective after a standard 18-hole round]

ninety *n, pl* **-ties 1** the cardinal number that is the product of ten and nine **2** a numeral, 90 or XC, representing this number **3** something representing or consisting of ninety units ▷ *adj* **4** amounting to ninety: *ninety degrees* **ninetieth** *adj, n*

ninja *n, pl* **-ja** *or* **-jas** a person skilled in ninjutsu, a Japanese martial art characterized by stealthy movement and camouflage [Japanese]

ninny *n, pl* **-nies** a stupid person [perhaps from *an innocent*]

niobium *n chem* a white superconductive metallic element. Symbol: **Nb** [Latin after *Niobe* (daughter of Tantalus); because it occurred in tantalite]

nip[1] *vb* **nipping, nipped 1** *informal* to hurry **2** to pinch or squeeze **3** to bite lightly **4** (of the cold) to affect (someone) with a stinging sensation **5** to check the growth of (something): *a trite script nips all hope in the bud* ▷ *n* **6** a pinch or light bite **7** sharp coldness: *a nip in the air* [perhaps from Old Norse]

nip[2] *n* a small drink of spirits [from *nipperkin* a vessel holding a half-pint or less]

nipper *n Brit, Austral & NZ informal* a small child

nipple *n* **1** the small projection in the centre of each breast, which in females contains the outlet of the milk ducts **2** a small projection through which oil or grease can be put into a machine or component [perhaps from *neb* peak, tip]

nippy *adj* **-pier, -piest 1** (of weather) frosty or chilly **2** *informal* quick or nimble **3** (of a motor vehicle) small and relatively powerful

niqab *n* a veil of lightweight opaque fabric, covering all the face except the eyes, worn by some Muslim women [Arabic]

nirvana (near-**vah**-na) *n Buddhism & Hinduism* the ultimate state of spiritual enlightenment and bliss attained by extinction of all desires and individual existence [Sanskrit: extinction]

nisi (**nye**-sigh) *adj* See **decree nisi**

Nissen hut *n chiefly Brit* a tunnel-shaped military shelter made of corrugated steel [after Lt Col. Peter *Nissen*, mining engineer]

nit[1] *n* the egg or larva of a louse [Old English *hnitu*]

nit[2] *n informal* short for **nitwit**

nit-picking *informal* ▷ *n* **1** a concern with insignificant details, usually with the intention of finding fault ▷ *adj* **2** showing such concern

nitrate *chem* ▷ *n* **1** a salt or ester of nitric acid **2** a fertilizer containing nitrate salts ▷ *vb* **-trating, -trated 3** to treat with nitric acid or a nitrate **4** to convert or be converted into a nitrate **nitration** *n*

nitre *or US* **niter** *n chem* same as **potassium nitrate** [Latin *nitrum*]

nitric *adj chem* of or containing nitrogen

nitric acid *n chem* a colourless corrosive liquid widely used in industry

nitride *n chem* a compound of nitrogen with a more electropositive element

nitrify *vb* **-fies, -fying, -fied** *chem* **1** to treat (a substance) or cause (a substance) to react with nitrogen **2** to treat (soil) with nitrates **3** to convert (ammonium compounds) into nitrates by oxidation **nitrification** *n*

nitrite *n chem* a salt or ester of nitrous acid

nitro- *or before a vowel* **nitr-** *combining form* **1** indicating that a chemical compound contains the univalent group, $-NO_2$: *nitrobenzene* **2** indicating that a chemical compound is a nitrate ester: *nitrocellulose* [Greek *nitron* nitre]

nitrogen (**nite**-roj-jen) *n chem* a colourless odourless gas that forms four-fifths of the air and is an essential part of all animal and plant life. Symbol: **N nitrogenous** *adj*

nitrogen cycle *n* the natural cycle by which nitrates in the soil, derived from dead organic matter, are absorbed by plants and reduced to nitrates again when the plants and the animals feeding on them die and decay

nitrogen fixation *n* the conversion of atmospheric nitrogen into nitrogen compounds by soil bacteria

nitroglycerine *or* **nitroglycerin** *n chem* a thick pale yellow explosive liquid made from glycerol and nitric and sulphuric acids

nitrous *adj chem* derived from or containing nitrogen in a low valency state

nitrous acid *n chem* a weak acid known only in solution and in the form of nitrite salts

nitrous oxide *n chem* a colourless gas used as an anaesthetic

nitty-gritty *n* **the nitty-gritty** *informal* the basic facts of a matter or situation [perhaps rhyming compound from *grit*]

nitwit *n informal* a stupid person [perhaps NIT[1] + WIT[1]]

NJ New Jersey

nkosi (ing-**koss**-ee) *n S African* a term of address to a superior; master; chief [Nguni (language group of southern Africa) *inkosi* chief, lord]

nm nanometre

NM New Mexico

no[1] *interj* **1** used to express denial, disagreement, or refusal ▷ *n, pl* **noes** *or* **nos 2** an answer or vote of no **3** a person who answers or votes no [Old English *nā*]

no[2] *adj* **1** not any, not a, or not one: *I have no money; no comment* **2** not at all: *he's no exception* **3** not: *no taller than a child* **4 no way!** an expression of emphatic refusal or denial [Old English *nān* none]

No[1] *or* **Noh** *n, pl* **No** *or* **Noh** the stylized classical drama of Japan, using music and dancing [Japanese *nō* talent]

No[2] *chem* nobelium

n

No. *or* **no.** *pl* **Nos.** *or* **nos.** number [French *numéro*]
n.o. *cricket* not out
nob *n chiefly Brit old-fashioned slang* a person of wealth or social distinction [origin unknown]
no-ball *n cricket* an improperly bowled ball, for which the batting side scores a run. Abbrev: **nb**
nobble *vb* **-bling, -bled** *chiefly Brit, Austral & NZ slang* **1** to bribe or threaten **2** to disable (a racehorse) to stop it from winning **3** to steal [*a nobbler*, a false division of *an hobbler* one who hobbles horses]
nobelium *n chem* a radioactive element produced artificially from curium. Symbol: **No** [after *Nobel* Institute, Stockholm, where it was discovered]
Nobel prize (no-**bell**) *n* a prize for outstanding contributions to chemistry, physics, physiology and medicine, literature, economics, and peace that may be awarded annually [after Alfred *Nobel*, chemist & philanthropist]
nobility *n* **1** the quality of being noble; dignity **2** the class of people who hold titles and high social rank
noble *adj* **1** having or showing high moral qualities: *a noble cause* **2** belonging to a class of people who hold titles and high social rank **3** impressive and magnificent: *a noble beast* **4** *chem* (of certain metals) resisting oxidation ▷ *n* **5** a person who holds a title and high social rank [Latin *nobilis*, originally capable of being known, hence well-known] **nobly** *adv*
noble gas *n* any of the unreactive gases helium, neon, argon, krypton, xenon, and radon
nobleman *or fem* **noblewoman** *n, pl* **-men** *or* **-women** a person of noble rank
noblesse oblige (no-**bless** oh-**bleezh**) *n often humorous* the supposed obligation of the nobility to be honourable and generous [French, lit: nobility obliges]
nobody *pron* **1** no person; no-one ▷ *n, pl* **-bodies** **2** a person of no importance
USAGE See at **everyone**.
no-brainer *n slang* something that requires little or no mental effort
nock *n* **1** a notch on an arrow that fits on the bowstring **2** a groove at either end of a bow that holds the bowstring [related to Swedish *nock* tip]
no-claims bonus *or* **no-claim bonus** *n* a reduction in the cost of an insurance policy made if no claims have been made in a specified period
nocturnal *adj* **1** of the night **2** (of animals) active at night [Latin *nox* night]
nocturne *n* a short dreamy piece of music
nod *vb* **nodding, nodded** **1** to lower and raise (one's head) briefly, to express agreement or greeting **2** to express by nodding: *he nodded his approval* **3** to sway or bend forwards and back **4** to let one's head fall forward with sleep **5** **nodding acquaintance** a slight knowledge (of a subject or person) ▷ *n* **6** a quick down-and-up movement of the head, in agreement **7** **land of Nod** an imaginary land of sleep [origin unknown]
noddle *n chiefly Brit informal* the head or brains [origin unknown]
noddy *n, pl* **-dies** **1** a tropical tern with a dark plumage **2** a fool [perhaps from obsolete *noddy* foolish, drowsy]
node *n* **1** *botany* the point on a plant stem from which the leaves grow **2** *maths* a point at which a curve crosses itself **3** a knot or knob **4** *physics* a point in a vibrating body at which there is practically no vibration **5** *anatomy* any natural bulge or swelling: *lymph node* **6** *astron* either of the two points at which the orbit of a body intersects the path of the sun or the orbit of another body [Latin *nodus* knot] **nodal** *adj*
nod off *vb informal* to fall asleep
nodule *n* **1** a small rounded lump, knot, or node **2** a rounded mineral growth on the root of a plant such as clover [Latin *nodulus*] **nodular** *adj*
Noel *or* **Noël** *n* same as **Christmas** [French, from Latin *natalis* a birthday]
nog *n* an alcoholic drink containing beaten egg [origin unknown]
noggin *n* **1** *informal* the head **2** a small quantity of spirits [origin unknown]
no-go area *n* a district that is barricaded off so that the police or army can enter only by force
noise *n* **1** a sound, usually a loud or disturbing one **2** loud shouting; din **3** an undesired electrical disturbance in a signal **4** unwanted or irrelevant elements in a visual image: *removing noise from pictures* **5** **noises** conventional utterances conveying a reaction: *he made the appropriate noises* ▷ *vb* **noising, noised** **6** **be noised abroad** (of news or gossip) to be spread [Latin *nausea* seasickness]
noiseless *adj* making little or no sound **noiselessly** *adv*
noise pollution *n* annoying or harmful noise in an environment
noisette (nwah-**zett**) *n* a hazelnut chocolate [French]
noisome *adj formal* **1** (of smells) offensive **2** extremely unpleasant [obsolete *noy*, variant of *annoy*]
noisy *adj* **noisier, noisiest** **1** making a lot of noise **2** (of a place) full of noise **noisily** *adv*
nomad *n* **1** a member of a tribe who move from place to place to find pasture and food **2** a wanderer [Greek *nomas* wandering for pasture] **nomadic** *adj*
no-man's-land *n* land between boundaries, esp. an unoccupied zone between opposing forces
nom de plume *n, pl* **noms de plume** same as **pen name** [French]
nomenclature (no-**men**-klatch-er) *n formal* the system of names used in a particular subject [Latin *nomenclatura* list of names]
nominal *adj* **1** in name only: *nominal independence* **2** very small in comparison with real worth: *a nominal amount of aid* [Latin *nomen* name] **nominally** *adv*
nominalism *n* the philosophical theory that a general word, such as *dog*, is merely a name and does not denote a real object **nominalist** *n*
nominal value *n* same as **par value**
nominate *vb* **-nating, -nated** **1** to propose (someone) as a candidate **2** to appoint (someone) to an office or position [Latin *nomen* name] **nomination** *n*
nominative *n grammar* a grammatical case in some languages that identifies the subject of a verb [Latin *nominativus* belonging to naming]

nominee *n* a person who is nominated to an office or as a candidate
non- *prefix* **1** indicating negation: *nonexistent* **2** indicating refusal or failure: *noncooperation* **3** indicating exclusion from a specified class: *nonfiction* **4** indicating lack or absence: *nonevent* [Latin *non* not]
nonaddictive *adj* not causing addiction
nonage *n* **1** *law* the state of being under full legal age for various actions **2** a period of immaturity
nonagenarian *n* a person who is from 90 to 99 years old [Latin *nonaginta* ninety]
nonaggression *n* the policy of not attacking other countries
nonagon *n* *geom* a figure with nine sides **nonagonal** *adj*
nonalcoholic *adj* containing no alcohol
nonaligned *adj* (of a country) not part of a major alliance or power bloc **nonalignment** *n*
nonbeliever *n* a person who does not follow a particular religious movement
nonbelligerent *adj* (of a country) not taking part in a war
nonce *n* **for the nonce** for the present [a mistaken division of *for then anes*, for the once]
nonce word *n* a word coined for a single occasion
nonchalant (non-shall-ant) *adj* casually unconcerned or indifferent [French, from *nonchaloir* to lack warmth] **nonchalance** *n* **nonchalantly** *adv*
non-com *n* short for **noncommissioned officer**
noncombatant *n* a member of the armed forces whose duties do not include fighting, such as a chaplain or surgeon
noncombustible *adj* not capable of igniting and burning
noncommissioned officer *n* (in the armed forces) a person who is appointed as a subordinate officer, from the lower ranks, rather than by a commission
noncommittal *adj* not committing oneself to any particular opinion
noncompliance *n* failure or refusal to do as requested
non compos mentis *adj* of unsound mind [Latin: not in control of one's mind]
nonconductor *n* a substance that is a poor conductor of heat, electricity, or sound
nonconformist *n* **1** a person who does not conform to generally accepted patterns of behaviour or thought ▷ *adj* **2** (of behaviour or ideas) not conforming to accepted patterns: *people who pride themselves on their nonconformist past* **nonconformity** *n*
Nonconformist *n* **1** a member of a Protestant group separated from the Church of England ▷ *adj* **2** of or relating to Nonconformists
noncontributory *adj Brit* denoting a pension scheme for employees, the premiums of which are paid entirely by the employer
non-cooperation *n* the refusal to do more than is legally or contractually required of one
noncustodial *adj* not involving imprisonment: *a noncustodial sentence*
nondescript *adj* lacking outstanding features [NON- + Latin *descriptus*, past participle of *describere* to copy]
non-domicile *n Brit* a UK resident who claims another country as his or her permanent home, esp. to escape certain taxes. Also shortened to: **non-dom non-domiciled** *adj*
nondrinker *n* a person who does not drink alcohol
none *pron* **1** not any: *none of the men was represented by a lawyer; none of it meant anything to him* **2** no-one; nobody: *none could deny it* **3** **none the** in no degree: *her parents were none the wiser* [Old English *nān*, literally: not one]

> **USAGE** *None* is a singular pronoun and should be used with a singular form of a verb: *none of the students has* (not *have*) *a car.*

nonentity (non-enn-tit-tee) *n, pl* **-ties** an insignificant person or thing
non-essential *adj* not absolutely necessary
nonetheless *adv* despite that; however
nonevent *n* a disappointing or insignificant occurrence which was expected to be important
nonexistent *adj* not existing in a particular place **nonexistence** *n*
nonferrous *adj* **1** denoting a metal other than iron **2** not containing iron
nonfiction *n* writing that deals with facts or real events
nonflammable *adj* not easily set on fire
nonfunctional *adj* having no practical function
nonintervention *n* refusal to intervene in the affairs of others
noniron *adj* not requiring ironing
nonmember *n* a person who is not a member of a particular club or organization
nonmetal *n chem* a chemical element that forms acidic oxides and is a poor conductor of heat and electricity **nonmetallic** *adj*
nonmoral *adj* not involving morality; neither moral nor immoral
non-native *adj* not originating in a particular place
non-nuclear *adj* not involving or using nuclear power or weapons
no-nonsense *adj* sensible, practical, and straightforward: *a no-nonsense approach to crime*
nonpareil (non-par-rail) *n* a person or thing that is unsurpassed [French, from NON- + *pareil* similar]
non-partisan *adj* not supporting any single political party
non-payment *n* failure to pay money owed
nonplussed *or US* **nonplused** *adj* perplexed [Latin *non plus* no further]
nonprofessional *adj* not earning a living at a specified occupation: *nonprofessional investors*
non-profit-making *adj* not intended to make a profit
nonproliferation *n* limitation of the production or spread of something such as nuclear or chemical weapons
nonrepresentational *adj art* same as **abstract**
nonresident *n* a person who does not live in a particular country or place
nonsectarian *adj* not confined to any specific subdivision of a religious group
nonsense *n* **1** something that has or makes no sense **2** unintelligible language **3** foolish behaviour: *she'll stand no nonsense* **nonsensical** *adj*

non sequitur (sek-wit-tur) *n* a statement having little or no relation to what preceded it [Latin: it does not follow]
nonslip *adj* designed to prevent slipping: *a nonslip mat*
nonsmoker *n* **1** a person who does not smoke **2** a train carriage or compartment in which smoking is forbidden
nonsmoking *or* **no-smoking** *adj* denoting an area in which smoking is forbidden
nonstandard *adj* denoting words, expressions, or pronunciations that are not regarded as correct
nonstarter *n* a person or an idea that has little chance of success
nonstick *adj* (of cooking utensils) coated with a substance that food will not stick to when cooked
nonstop *adj* **1** without a stop: *two weeks of nonstop rain* ▹ *adv* **2** without a stop: *most days his phone rings nonstop*
nontoxic *adj* not poisonous
non-U *adj Brit informal* (of language or behaviour) not characteristic of the upper classes
nonunion *adj* **1** (of a company) not employing trade union members: *a nonunion shop* **2** (of a person) not belonging to a trade union
nonverbal *adj* not involving the use of language
non-violent *adj* using peaceful methods to bring about change **nonviolence** *n*
nonvoting *adj finance* (of shares in a company) not entitling the holder to vote at company meetings
non-White *adj* **1** belonging to a race of people not European in origin ▹ *n* **2** a member of one of these races
noodle *n* a foolish or unintelligent person [perhaps from NODDLE]
noodles *pl n* ribbon-like strips of pasta [German *Nudeln*]
nook *n* **1** a corner or recess **2** a secluded or sheltered place [origin unknown]
noon *n* the middle of the day; 12 o'clock [Latin *nona (hora)* ninth hour (originally 3 pm, the ninth hour from sunrise)]
noonday *adj* happening or appearing at noon
no-one *or* **no one** *pron* no person; nobody
USAGE See at **everyone**.
noose *n* a loop in the end of a rope, tied with a slipknot, such as one used to hang people [Latin *nodus* knot]
nope *interj informal* no
nor *conj* **1** used to join alternatives, the first of which is preceded by *neither*; and not: *neither willing nor able* **2** and not … either: *he had not arrived yet, nor had any of the models* [contraction of Old English *nōther*]
nordic *adj skiing* of competitions in cross-country racing and ski-jumping
Nordic *adj* of Scandinavia or its typically tall, blond, and blue-eyed people [French *nordique* of the north]
norm *n* a standard that is required or regarded as normal [Latin *norma* carpenter's square]
normal *adj* **1** usual, regular, or typical: *the study of normal behaviour* **2** free from serious mental or physical health problems **3** *geom* same as **perpendicular** (sense 1) ▹ *n* **4** the usual, regular, or typical state, degree, or form **5** *geom* a perpendicular line or plane [Latin *normalis* conforming to the carpenter's square] **normality** *or esp US* **normalcy** *n*
normalize *or* **-lise** *vb* **-lizing, -lized** *or* **-lising, -lised** **1** to make or become normal **2** to bring into conformity with a standard **normalization** *or* **-lisation** *n*
normally *adv* **1** as a rule; usually **2** in a normal manner
Norman *n* **1** a person from Normandy in N France, esp. one of the people who conquered England in 1066 **2** same as **Norman French** ▹ *adj* **3** of the Normans or their dialect of French **4** of Normandy **5** of a style of architecture used in Britain from the Norman Conquest until the 12th century, with rounded arches and massive masonry walls
Norman French *n* the medieval Norman and English dialect of Old French
normative *adj* of or establishing a norm or standard: *a normative model*
Norn *n Norse myth* any of the three virgin goddesses of fate [Old Norse]
Norse *adj* **1** of ancient and medieval Scandinavia **2** of Norway ▹ *n* **3** **A** the N group of Germanic languages spoken in Scandinavia **B** any one of these languages, esp. in their ancient or medieval forms
Norseman *n, pl* **-men** same as **Viking**
north *n* **1** one of the four cardinal points of the compass, at 0° or 360° **2** the direction along a meridian towards the North Pole **3** the direction in which a compass needle points; magnetic north **4** **the north** any area lying in or towards the north ▹ *adj* **5** in or towards the north **6** (esp. of the wind) from the north ▹ *adv* **7** in, to, or towards the north [Old English]
North *n* **1** **the North** **A** the northern part of England, generally regarded as reaching the southern boundaries of Yorkshire, Derbyshire, and Cheshire **B** (in the US) the states north of the Mason-Dixon Line that were known as the Free States during the Civil War **C** the economically and technically advanced countries of the world ▹ *adj* **2** of or denoting the northern part of a country or area
Northants Northamptonshire
northbound *adj* going towards the north
North Country *n* **the North Country** same as **North** (sense 1a)
northeast *n* **1** the direction midway between north and east **2** **the northeast** any area lying in or towards the northeast ▹ *adj also* **northeastern** **3** (*sometimes cap*) of or denoting that part of a country or area which lies in the northeast **4** situated in, moving towards, or facing the northeast **5** (esp. of the wind) from the northeast ▹ *adv* **6** in, to, or towards the northeast **northeasterly** *adj, adv, n*
Northeast *n* **the Northeast** the northeastern part of England, esp. Northumberland and Durham
northeaster *n* a strong wind or storm from the northeast

northerly *adj* **1** of or in the north ▷ *adv, adj* **2** towards the north **3** from the north: *a cold northerly wind*
northern *adj* **1** situated in or towards the north **2** facing or moving towards the north **3** (*sometimes cap*) of or characteristic of the north or North **northernmost** *adj*
Northerner *n* a person from the north of a country or area, esp. England
northern hemisphere *n* that half of the globe lying north of the equator
northern lights *pl n* same as **aurora borealis**
northings *pl n* a series of numbers in a grid reference indicating the distance northwards from a given latitude
Northman *n, pl* **-men** same as **Viking**
North Pole *n* the northernmost point on the earth's axis, at a latitude of 90°N, which has very low temperatures
North Star *n* **the North Star** same as **Pole Star**
Northumb. Northumberland
northward *adj, adv also* **northwards** **1** towards the north ▷ *n* **2** the northward part or direction
northwest *n* **1** the direction midway between north and west **2** **the northwest** any area lying in or towards the northwest ▷ *adj also* **northwestern** **3** (*sometimes cap*) of or denoting that part of a country or area which lies in the northwest **4** situated in, moving towards, or facing the northwest **5** (esp. of the wind) from the northwest ▷ *adv* **6** in, to, or towards the northwest **northwesterly** *adj, adv, n*
Northwest *n* **the Northwest** the northwestern part of England, esp. Lancashire and the Lake District
northwester *n* a strong wind or storm from the northwest
Norwegian *adj* **1** of Norway ▷ *n* **2** a person from Norway **3** the language of Norway
nor'wester *n NZ* a hot dry wind
Nos. *or* **nos.** numbers
nose *n* **1** the organ situated above the mouth, used for smelling and breathing **2** the sense of smell **3** the front part of a vehicle **4** the distinctive smell of a wine or perfume **5** instinctive skill in finding something: *he had a nose for media events* **6** **get up someone's nose** *informal* to annoy someone **7** **keep one's nose clean** to stay out of trouble **8** **look down one's nose at** *informal* to be haughty towards **9** **pay through the nose** *informal* to pay a high price **10** **put someone's nose out of joint** *informal* to make someone envious by doing what he or she would have liked to do or had expected to do **11** **rub someone's nose in it** *informal* to remind someone unkindly of a failing or error **12** **turn up one's nose at** *informal* to show contempt for **13** **win by a nose** to win by a narrow margin ▷ *vb* **nosing, nosed** **14** to move forward slowly and carefully: *a motorboat nosed out of the mist* **15** to pry or snoop **16** **nose out** to discover by searching or prying [Old English *nosu*]
nosebag *n* a bag containing feed, fastened around the head of a horse
noseband *n* the part of a horse's bridle that goes around the nose
nosebleed *n* bleeding from the nose
nose cone *n* the cone-shaped front section of a missile or spacecraft
nose dive *n* **1** (of an aircraft) a sudden plunge with the nose pointing downwards **2** *informal* a sudden drop: *when we fail our self-confidence takes a nose dive* ▷ *vb* **nose-dive, -diving, -dived** **3** to take a nose dive
nosegay *n* a small bunch of flowers [*nose* + *gay* (archaic) toy]
nosey *or* **nosy** *adj* **nosier, nosiest** *informal* prying or inquisitive **nosiness** *n*
nosey parker *n Brit & S African informal* a prying person [arbitrary use of surname *Parker*]
nosh *Brit, Austral & NZ slang* ▷ *n* **1** food ▷ *vb* **2** to eat [Yiddish]
nosh-up *n Brit slang* a large meal
nostalgia *n* **1** a sentimental yearning for the past **2** homesickness [Greek *nostos* a return home + *algos* pain] **nostalgic** *adj* **nostalgically** *adv*
nostril *n* either of the two openings at the end of the nose [Old English *nosu* nose + *thyrel* hole]
nostrum *n* **1** a quack medicine **2** a favourite remedy [Latin: our own (make)]
nosy *adj* **nosier, nosiest** same as **nosey**
not *adv* **1** used to negate the sentence, phrase, or word that it modifies: *I will not stand for it* **2** **not that** which is not to say that: *not that I've ever heard him complain* [Old English *nāwiht*, from *nā* no + *wiht* creature, thing]
nota bene (note-a ben-nay) note well; take note. Abbrev: **NB** [Latin]
notable (note-a-bl) *adj* **1** worthy of being noted; remarkable ▷ *n* **2** a person of distinction [Latin *notare* to note] **notability** *n* **notably** *adv*
notary *or* **notary public** (note-a-ree) *n, pl* **notaries** *or* **notaries public** a public official, usually a solicitor, who is legally authorized to attest and certify documents [Latin *notarius* one who makes notes, a clerk]
notation (no-tay-shun) *n* **1** representation of numbers or quantities in a system by a series of symbols **2** a set of such symbols [Latin *notare* to note]
notch *n* **1** a V-shaped cut **2** *informal* a step or level: *the economy moved up another notch* ▷ *vb* **3** to cut a notch in **4** **notch up** *informal* to score or achieve: *he notched up a hat trick of wins* [mistaken division of *an otch*, from Old French *oche* notch]
note *n* **1** a brief informal letter **2** a brief record in writing for future reference **3** a critical comment or explanation in a book **4** an official written communication, as from a government or from a doctor **5** short for **banknote** **6** *Brit & NZ* a musical sound of a particular pitch **7** a written symbol representing the pitch and duration of a musical sound **8** *chiefly Brit* a key on a piano, organ, or other keyboard instrument **9** a particular feeling or atmosphere: *an optimistic note* **10** a distinctive vocal sound, as of a type of animal **11** a sound used as a signal or warning: *the note to retreat was sounded* **12** short for **promissory note** **13** **of note** **A** distinguished or famous **B** important: *nothing of note* **14** **strike the right note** to behave appropriately **15** **take note of** to pay attention to ▷ *vb* **noting, noted** **16** to notice;

pay attention to: *such criticism should be noted* **17** to make a written note of: *he noted it in his diary* **18** to remark upon: *I note that you do not wear shoes* [Latin *nota* sign]

notebook *n* a book for writing in

notebook computer *n* a portable computer approximately the size of a sheet of A4 paper

notecase *n* same as **wallet**

noted *adj* well-known: *a noted scholar*

notelet *n* a folded card with a printed design on the front, for writing informal letters

notepad *n* a number of sheets of paper fastened together along one edge, used for writing notes or letters on

notepaper *n* paper used for writing letters

noteworthy *adj* worth noting; remarkable

nothing *pron* **1** not anything: *I felt nothing* **2** a matter of no importance: *don't worry, it's nothing* **3** absence of meaning, value, or worth: *the industry shrank to almost nothing* **4** the figure 0 **5 have** *or* **be nothing to do with** to have no connection with **6 nothing but** not something other than; only **7 nothing doing** *informal* an expression of dismissal or refusal **8 nothing less than** downright: *nothing less than complete withdrawal* **9 think nothing of something** to regard something as easy or natural ▷ *adv* **10** not at all: *he looked nothing like his brother* ▷ *n* **11** *informal* a person or thing of no importance or significance [Old English *nāthing, nān thing*]

> **USAGE** *Nothing* normally takes a singular verb, but when *nothing but* is followed by a plural form of a noun, a plural verb is usually used: *it was a large room where nothing but souvenirs were sold.*

n

nothingness *n* **1** nonexistence **2** total insignificance

notice *n* **1** observation or attention: *to attract notice* **2** a displayed placard or announcement giving information **3** advance notification of something such as intention to end a contract of employment: *she handed in her notice* **4** a theatrical or literary review: *the film reaped ecstatic notices* **5 at short notice** with very little notification **6 take no notice of** to ignore or disregard **7 take notice** to pay attention ▷ *vb* **-ticing, -ticed 8** to become aware (of) **9** to point out or remark upon [Latin *notus* known]

noticeable *adj* easily seen or detected **noticeably** *adv*

notice board *n* a board on which notices are displayed

notifiable *adj* having to be reported to the authorities: *a notifiable disease*

notification *n* **1** the act of notifying someone of something **2** a formal announcement

notify *vb* **-fies, -fying, -fied** to inform: *notify gas and electricity companies of your moving date* [Latin *notus* known + *facere* to make]

notion *n* **1** an idea or opinion **2** a whim [Latin *notio* a becoming acquainted (with)]

notional *adj* hypothetical, imaginary, or unreal: *a notional dividend payment*

notorious *adj* well known for some bad reason [Medieval Latin *notorius* well-known] **notoriety** *n* **notoriously** *adv*

not proven *adj* a verdict in Scottish courts, given when there is insufficient evidence to convict the accused

no-trump *cards* ▷ *n* **1** a bid or hand without trumps ▷ *adj* **2** (of a hand) suitable for playing without trumps

Notts Nottinghamshire

notwithstanding *prep* **1** in spite of ▷ *adv* **2** nevertheless

nougat *n* a hard chewy pink or white sweet containing chopped nuts [French, from Latin *nux* nut]

nought *n* **1** the figure 0 ▷ *n, adv* **2** same as **naught** [Old English *nōwiht*, from *ne* not, no + *ōwiht* something]

noughties *pl n informal* the decade from 2000 to 2009

noughts and crosses *n Brit* a game in which two players, one using a nought, the other a cross, alternately mark squares formed by two pairs of crossed lines, the winner being the first to get three of his or her symbols in a row

noun *n* a word that refers to a person, place, or thing [Latin *nomen* name]

nourish *vb* **1** to provide with the food necessary for life and growth **2** to encourage or foster (an idea or feeling) [Latin *nutrire* to feed] **nourishing** *adj*

nourishment *n* the food needed to nourish the body

nous *n old-fashioned slang* common sense [Greek: mind]

nouveau riche (noo-voh **reesh**) *n, pl* **nouveaux riches** (noo-voh **reesh**) a person who has become wealthy recently and is regarded as vulgar [French: new rich]

nouvelle cuisine (noo-vell kwee-**zeen**) *n* a style of preparing and presenting food with light sauces and unusual combinations of flavours [French: new cooking]

Nov. November

nova *n, pl* **-vae** *or* **-vas** a star that undergoes an explosion and fast increase of brightness, then gradually decreases to its original brightness [New Latin *nova (stella)* new (star)]

novel[1] *n* a long fictional story in book form [Latin *novella (narratio)* new (story)]

novel[2] *adj* fresh, new, or original: *a novel approach* [Latin *novus* new]

novelette *n* a short novel, usually one regarded as trivial or sentimental

novelist *n* a writer of novels

novella *n, pl* **-las** a short narrative tale or short novel [Italian]

novelty *n, pl* **-ties 1** the quality of being new and interesting **2** a new or unusual experience or thing **3** a small cheap toy or trinket

November *n* the eleventh month of the year [Latin: ninth month]

novena (no-**vee**-na) *n, pl* **-nas** *or* **-nae** (-nee) *RC Church* a set of prayers or services on nine consecutive days [Latin *novem* nine]

novice (**nov**-viss) *n* **1** a beginner **2** a person who has entered a religious order but has not yet taken vows [Latin *novus* new]

novitiate *or* **noviciate** *n* **1** the period of being a novice **2** the part of a monastery or convent where the novices live

now *adv* **1** at or for the present time **2** immediately: *bring it now* **3** in these times; nowadays **4** given the present circumstances: *now do you understand why?* **5 A** used as a hesitation word: *now, I can't really say* **B** used for emphasis: *now listen to this* **C** used at the end of a command: *run along now* **6 just now A** very recently: *he left just now* **B** very soon: *I'm going just now* **7 now and again** *or* **then** occasionally **8 now now!** an exclamation used to tell someone off or to calm someone ▷ *conj* **9** Also: **now that** seeing that: *now you're here, you can help me* ▷ *n* **10** the present time: *now is the time to go* [Old English *nū*]

nowadays *adv* in these times: *nowadays his work is regarded as out-of-date*

Nowell *n* same as **Noel**

nowhere *adv* **1** in, at, or to no place **2 getting nowhere** *informal* making no progress **3 nowhere near** far from: *the stadium is nowhere near completion* ▷ *n* **4 in the middle of nowhere** (of a place) completely isolated

no-win *adj* with no possibility of a favourable outcome: *a no-win situation*

nowt *n N English dialect* nothing [from *naught*]

noxious *adj* **1** poisonous or harmful **2** extremely unpleasant [Latin *noxius* harmful]

nozzle *n* a projecting spout from which fluid is discharged [diminutive of *nose*]

Np *chem* neptunium

nr near

NS 1 New Style (method of reckoning dates) **2** Nova Scotia

NSPCC (in Britain) National Society for the Prevention of Cruelty to Children

NST Newfoundland Standard Time

NSW New South Wales

NT 1 (in Britain) National Trust **2** New Testament **3** Northern Territory **4** Nunavut

-n't not: added to *be* or *have*, or auxiliary verbs: *can't; don't; isn't*

nth *adj* See **n²**

nuance (new-ahnss) *n* a subtle difference, as in colour, meaning, or tone [French]

nub *n* the point or gist: *this is the nub of his theory* [Middle Low German *knubbe* knob]

nubble *n* a small lump [from *nub*] **nubbly** *adj*

nubile (new-bile) *adj* **1** (of a young woman) sexually attractive **2** (of a young woman) old enough or mature enough for marriage [Latin *nubere* to marry]

nubuck (new-buk) *n* (*sometimes cap*) leather that has been rubbed on the flesh side of the skin to give it a fine, velvet-like finish

nuclear *adj* **1** of nuclear weapons or energy **2** of an atomic nucleus: *nuclear fission*

nuclear bomb *n* a bomb whose force is due to uncontrolled nuclear fusion or fission

nuclear energy *n* energy released during a nuclear reaction as a result of fission or fusion

nuclear family *n sociol & anthropol* a family consisting only of parents and their offspring

nuclear fission *n physics* the splitting of an atomic nucleus, either spontaneously or by bombardment by a neutron: used in atomic bombs and nuclear power plants

nuclear-free *adj* (of an area) barred, esp. by local authorities, from being supplied with nuclear-generated electricity and from storing nuclear waste or weapons

nuclear fusion *n physics* the combination of two nuclei to form a heavier nucleus with the release of energy: used in hydrogen bombs

nuclear physics *n* the branch of physics concerned with the structure of the nucleus and the behaviour of its particles

nuclear power *n* power produced by a nuclear reactor

nuclear reaction *n physics* a process in which the structure and energy content of an atomic nucleus is changed by interaction with another nucleus or particle

nuclear reactor *n* a device in which a nuclear reaction is maintained and controlled to produce nuclear energy

nuclear winter *n* a theoretical period of low temperatures and little light that has been suggested would occur after a nuclear war

nucleate *adj* **1** having a nucleus ▷ *vb* **-ating, -ated 2** to form a nucleus

nuclei (new-klee-eye) *n* the plural of **nucleus**

nucleic acid *n biochem* a complex compound, such as DNA or RNA, found in all living cells

nucleon *n physics* a proton or neutron

nucleonics *n* the branch of physics concerned with the applications of nuclear energy **nucleonic** *adj*

nucleus *n, pl* **-clei 1** *physics* the positively charged centre of an atom, made of protons and neutrons, about which electrons orbit **2** a central thing around which others are grouped **3** a centre of growth or development: *the nucleus of a new relationship* **4** *biol* the part of a cell that contains the chromosomes and associated molecules that control the characteristics and growth of the cell **5** *chem* a fundamental group of atoms in a molecule serving as the base structure for related compounds [Latin: kernel]

nude *adj* **1** completely undressed ▷ *n* **2** a naked figure in painting, sculpture, or photography **3 in the nude** naked [Latin *nudus*] **nudity** *n*

nudge *vb* **nudging, nudged 1** to push (someone) gently with the elbow to get attention **2** to push (something or someone) lightly: *the dog nudged the stick with its nose* **3** to persuade (someone) gently ▷ *n* **4** a gentle poke or push [origin unknown]

nudism *n* the practice of not wearing clothes, esp. on beaches or in camps set aside for this purpose **nudist** *n, adj*

nugatory (new-gat-tree) *adj formal* **1** of little value **2** not valid: *their rejection rendered the treaty nugatory* [Latin *nugae* trifling things]

nugget *n* **1** a small lump of gold in its natural state **2** something small but valuable: *a nugget of useful knowledge* ▷ *vb* **-geting, -geted 3** NZ to polish footwear [origin unknown]

nuisance *n* **1** a person or thing that causes annoyance or bother ▷ *adj* **2** causing annoyance or bother: *nuisance calls* [Old French *nuire* to injure]

NUJ (in Britain) National Union of Journalists

nuke *slang* ▷ *vb* **nuking, nuked 1** to attack with nuclear weapons ▷ *n* **2** a nuclear bomb

null *adj* **1 null and void** not legally valid **2 null set** *maths* a set with no members [Latin *nullus* none] **nullity** *n*

nulla-nulla *n* a wooden stick used by Australian Aboriginal people for hunting, digging, fighting, and for ceremonial purposes

nullify *vb* **-fies, -fying, -fied 1** to make (something) ineffective **2** to make (something) legally void [Latin *nullus* of no account + *facere* to make] **nullification** *n*

NUM (in Britain & S Africa) National Union of Mineworkers

numb *adj* **1** deprived of feeling through cold, shock, or fear **2** unable to move; paralysed ▷ *vb* **3** to make numb [Middle English *nomen*, literally: taken (with paralysis)] **numbly** *adv* **numbness** *n*

numbat *n* a small Australian marsupial with a long snout and tongue

number *n* **1** a concept of quantity that is or can be derived from a single unit, a sum of units, or zero **2** the word or symbol used to represent a number **3** a numeral or string of numerals used to identify a person or thing: *an account number* **4** the person or thing so identified: *he was seeded number two* **5** sum or quantity: *a very large number of people have telephoned* **6** one of a series, as of a magazine **7** a self-contained piece of pop or jazz music **8** a group of people: *one of their number might be willing* **9** *informal* an admired article: *that little number is by Dior* **10** *grammar* classification of words depending on how many people or things are referred to **11 any number of** many **12 beyond** *or* **without number** innumerable **13 have someone's number** *informal* to have discovered someone's true character or intentions **14 one's number is up** *Brit & Austral informal* one is about to die ▷ *vb* **15** to count **16** to assign a number to: *numbered seats* **17** to add up to: *the illustrations numbered well over fifty* **18** to include in a group: *he numbered several Americans among his friends* **19 one's days are numbered** something unpleasant, such as death, is likely to happen to one soon [Latin *numerus*]

number crunching *n informal* the large-scale processing of numerical data **number cruncher** *n*

numberless *adj* too many to be counted

number one *n* **1** *informal* oneself: *he looks after number one* **2** *informal* the bestselling pop record in any one week ▷ *adj* **3** first in importance, urgency, or quality: *he's their number one suspect*

numberplate *n* a plate on a motor vehicle showing the registration number

Number Ten *n* 10 Downing Street, the British prime minister's official London residence

numbskull *or* **numskull** *n informal, derogatory* a stupid person

numeral *n* a word or symbol used to express a sum or quantity [Latin *numerus* number]

numerate *adj* able to do basic arithmetic **numeracy** *n*

numeration *n* **1** the act or process of numbering or counting **2** a system of numbering

numerator *n maths* the number above the line in a fraction

numerical *or* **numeric** *adj* measured or expressed in numbers: *record the severity of your symptoms in numerical form* **numerically** *adv*

numerology *n* the study of numbers and of their supposed influence on human affairs

numerous *adj* **1** many: *they carried out numerous bombings* **2** consisting of a large number of people or things: *the cast is not as numerous as one might suppose*

numinous *adj formal* **1** arousing spiritual or religious emotions **2** mysterious or awe-inspiring [Latin *numen* divine will]

numismatics *n* the study or collection of coins or medals [Greek *nomisma* piece of currency] **numismatist** *n*

numskull *n* same as **numbskull**

nun *n* a female member of a religious order [Late Latin *nonna*]

nuncio *n, pl* **-cios** *RC Church* a papal ambassador [Latin *nuntius* messenger]

nunnery *n, pl* **-neries** a convent

nunny bag *n Canad* (in Newfoundland) a small sealskin knapsack [probably from Scots dialect *noony* lunch]

nuptial *adj* relating to marriage: *a nuptial blessing* [Latin *nuptiae* marriage]

nuptials *pl n* a wedding

nurd *n slang* same as **nerd**

nurse *n* **1** a person trained to look after sick people, usually in a hospital **2** short for **nursemaid** ▷ *vb* **nursing, nursed 3** to look after (a sick person) **4** to breast-feed (a baby) **5** (of a baby) to feed at its mother's breast **6** to try to cure (an ailment) **7** to harbour or foster (a feeling) **8** to clasp fondly: *she nursed her drink* [Latin *nutrire* to nourish] **nursing** *n, adj*

nursemaid *or* **nurserymaid** *n* a woman employed to look after children

nursery *n, pl* **-ries 1** a room in a house where children sleep or play **2** a place providing care for children during the working day **3** a place where plants and young trees are grown for sale

nurseryman *n, pl* **-men** a person who raises plants and trees for sale

nursery nurse *n* a person trained to look after children of pre-school age

nursery rhyme *n* a short traditional verse or song for children

nursery school *n* a school for young children from three to five years old

nursery slopes *pl n* gentle slopes used by beginners in skiing

nursery stakes *pl n* a race for two-year-old horses

nursing home *n* a private hospital or home for people who are old or ill

nursing officer *n* (in Britain) the administrative head of the nursing staff of a hospital

nurture *n* **1** the act or process of promoting the development of a child or young plant ▷ *vb* **-turing, -tured 2** to promote or encourage the development of [Latin *nutrire* to nourish]

nut *n* **1** a dry one-seeded fruit that grows inside a hard shell **2** the edible inner part of such a fruit **3** a small piece of metal with a hole in it, that screws on to a bolt **4** *slang* a foolish or eccentric person **5** *offensive* a person with a mental illness **6** *slang* an enthusiast: *a health nut* **7** *slang* the head **8** *Brit* a small piece of coal **9 a hard** *or* **tough nut to crack** a person or thing that presents difficulties **10 do one's nut** *Brit & Austral slang* to be very angry ▷ See also **nuts** [Old English *hnutu*]

NUT (in Britain) National Union of Teachers

nutcase *n slang* **1** a foolish or eccentric person **2** *offensive* a person with a mental illness
nutcracker *n* a device for cracking the shells of nuts. Also: **nutcrackers**
nuthatch *n* a songbird that feeds on insects, seeds, and nuts [Middle English *notehache* nut hatchet, from its habit of splitting nuts]
nutmeg *n* a spice made from the seed of a tropical tree [Old French *nois muguede* musk-scented nut]
nutraceutical *n* See **functional food**
nutria (new-tree-a) *n* the fur of the coypu [Latin *lutra* otter]
nutrient (new-tree-ent) *n* **1** a substance that provides nourishment: *their only source of nutrient* ▹ *adj* **2** providing nourishment [Latin *nutrire* to nourish]
nutriment (new-tree-ment) *n* the food or nourishment required by all living things to grow and stay healthy [Latin *nutrimentum*]
nutrition (new-trish-un) *n* **1** the process of taking in and absorbing nutrients **2** the process of being nourished **3** the study of nutrition [Latin *nutrire* to nourish] **nutritional** *adj* **nutritionist** *n*
nutritious *adj* providing nourishment [Latin *nutrix* nurse]
nutritive *adj* of nutrition; nutritious
nuts *adj slang* **1** foolish or eccentric **2** *offensive* mentally ill **3 nuts about** very fond of or enthusiastic about
nuts and bolts *pl n informal* the essential or practical details: *the nuts and bolts of photography*
nutshell *n* **in a nutshell** in essence; briefly
nutter *n Brit & NZ slang* **1** a foolish or eccentric person **2** *offensive* a person with a mental illness
nutty *adj* **-tier, -tiest 1** containing or resembling nuts **2** *slang* foolish or eccentric **nuttiness** *n*
nux vomica *n* the seed of a tree, containing strychnine [Medieval Latin: vomiting nut]
nuzzle *vb* **-zling, -zled** to push or rub gently with the nose or snout [from *nose*]
NV Nevada
nvCJD new-variant Creutzfeldt-Jakob disease
NW northwest(ern)
NWT Northwest Territories (of Canada)
NY *or* **N.Y.** New York
NYC New York City
nylon *n* a synthetic material used for clothing and many other products [originally a trademark]
nylons *pl n* stockings made of nylon
nymph *n* **1** *myth* a spirit of nature, represented as a beautiful young woman **2** the larva of certain insects, resembling the adult form **3** *chiefly poetic* a beautiful young woman [Greek *numphē*]
nymphet *n* a girl who is attractive and sexually precocious
nympho *n, pl* **-phos** *informal* short for **nymphomaniac**
nymphomaniac *n* a woman with an abnormally intense sexual desire [Greek *numphē* nymph + *mania* madness] **nymphomania** *n*
NZ *or* **N.Z.** New Zealand
NZE New Zealand English
NZRFU New Zealand Rugby Football Union
NZX 50 Index New Zealand Stock Exchange 50 Index

Oo

O¹ **1** *chem* oxygen **2** Old **3** same as **nought**
O² *interj* same as **oh**
o. *or* **O.** old
o' *prep informal or old-fashioned* of: *a cup o' tea*
OA Order of Australia
oaf *n* a stupid or clumsy person [variant of Old English *ælf* elf] **oafish** *adj*
oak *n* **1** a large forest tree with hard wood, acorns as fruits, and leaves with rounded projections **2** the wood of this tree, used as building timber and for making furniture [Old English *āc*] **oaken** *adj*
oak apple *or* **oak gall** *n* a brownish round lump or ball produced on oak trees by certain wasps
Oaks *n* **the Oaks** an annual horse race for three-year-old fillies, run at Epsom [named after an estate near Epsom]
oakum *n* loose fibre obtained by unravelling old rope, used for filling cracks in wooden ships [Old English *ācumba*, literally: off-combings]
OAM Medal of the Order of Australia
OAP (in Britain) old age pensioner
oar *n* **1** a long pole with a broad blade, used for rowing a boat **2** **put** *or* **stick one's oar in** to interfere or interrupt [Old English *ār*]
oarsman *or fem* **oarswoman** *n, pl* **-men** *or* **-women** a person who rows **oarsmanship** *n*
oasis *n, pl* **-ses** **1** a fertile patch in a desert **2** a place or situation offering relief in the midst of difficulty [Greek]
oast *n chiefly Brit* an oven for drying hops [Old English *āst*]
oast house *n chiefly Brit* a building containing ovens for drying hops
oat *n* **1** a hard cereal grown as food **2** **oats** the edible grain of this cereal **3** **sow one's wild oats** to have casual sexual relationships while young [Old English *āte*] **oaten** *adj*
oatcake *n* a thin unsweetened biscuit made of oatmeal
oath *n, pl* **oaths** **1** a solemn promise, esp. to tell the truth in a court of law **2** an offensive or blasphemous expression; a swearword **3** **on** *or* **under oath** having made a solemn promise to tell the truth, esp. in a court of law [Old English *āth*]
oatmeal *n* **1** a coarse flour made by grinding oats ▷ *adj* **2** greyish-yellow
ob. (on tombstones) he *or* she died [Latin *obiit*]
obbligato (ob-lig-**gah**-toe) *music* ▷ *adj* **1** not to be omitted in performance ▷ *n, pl* **-tos** **2** an essential part or accompaniment: *an aria with bassoon obbligato* [Italian]
obdurate *adj* not to be persuaded; hardhearted or obstinate [Latin *obdurare* to make hard] **obduracy** *n*
OBE (in Britain) Officer of the Order of the British Empire
obedient *adj* obeying or willing to obey [Latin *oboediens*] **obedience** *n* **obediently** *adv*
obeisance (oh-**bay**-sanss) *n formal* **1** an attitude of respect or humble obedience **2** a bow or curtsy showing this attitude [Old French *obéissant* obeying] **obeisant** *adj*
obelisk (**ob**-bill-isk) *n* **1** a four-sided stone pillar that tapers to a pyramid at the top **2** *printing* same as **dagger** (sense 2) [Greek *obeliskos* a little spit]
obese (oh-**beess**) *adj* very fat [Latin *obesus*] **obesity** *n*
obey *vb* **1** to carry out instructions or orders; be obedient **2** to act in accordance with one's feelings, an impulse, etc.: *I had obeyed the impulse to open the gate and had walked up the drive* [Latin *oboedire*]
obfuscate *vb* **-cating, -cated** *formal* to make something unnecessarily difficult to understand [Latin *ob-* (intensive) + *fuscare* to blacken] **obfuscation** *n* **obfuscatory** *adj*
obituary *n, pl* **-aries** a published announcement of a death, usually with a short biography of the dead person [Latin *obitus* death] **obituarist** *n*
obj. **1** objection **2** *grammar* object(ive)
object¹ *n* **1** a thing that can be touched or seen **2** a person or thing seen as a focus for feelings, actions, or thought: *she had become for him an object of compassion* **3** an aim or purpose: *the main object of the exercise* **4** *philosophy* that which can be perceived by the mind, as contrasted with the thinking subject **5** *grammar* a noun, pronoun, or noun phrase that receives the action of a verb or is governed by a preposition, such as *the bottle* in *she threw the bottle* **6** **no object** not a hindrance or obstacle: *money's no object* [Late Latin *objectus* something thrown before (the mind)]
object² *vb* **1** to express disapproval or opposition: *my colleagues objected strongly to further delays* **2** to state as one's reason for opposing: *he objected that his small staff would be unable to handle the added work* [Latin *ob-* against + *jacere* to throw] **objector** *n*
objection *n* **1** an expression or feeling of opposition or disapproval **2** a reason for opposing something: *the planning officer had raised no objection to the proposals*
objectionable *adj* offensive or unacceptable
objective *n* **1** an aim or purpose: *the objective is to highlight the environmental threat to the planet* **2** *grammar* a grammatical case in some languages that identifies the direct object of a verb or preposition **3** *optics* the lens nearest to the object observed in an optical instrument ▷ *adj* **4** not distorted by personal feelings or bias: *I have tried to be as objective as possible in my presentation* **5** of or relating to actual facts as opposed to thoughts or feelings: *stand back and try to take a more objective view of your life as a whole* **6** existing independently of the mind; real **objectival** *adj* **objectively** *adv* **objectivity** *n*
object lesson *n* a practical demonstration of some principle or ideal
objet d'art (ob-zhay **dahr**) *n, pl* **objets d'art** (ob-zhay **dahr**) a small object considered to be of artistic worth [French: object of art]

oblate *adj geom* (of a sphere) flattened at the poles: *the oblate spheroid of the earth* [New Latin *oblatus* lengthened]
oblation *n* **1** *Christianity* the offering of bread and wine to God at Communion **2** any offering made for religious purposes [Medieval Latin *oblatus* offered] **oblational** *adj*
obligated *adj* being morally or legally bound to do something: *they are obligated to provide temporary accommodation* **obligative** *adj*
obligation *n* **1** a moral or legal duty **2** the binding power of such a duty: *I feel under some obligation to help you with your education* **3** a sense of being in debt because of a service or favour: *I don't want him marrying me out of obligation*
obligatory *adj* required or compulsory because of custom or law
oblige *vb* **obliging, obliged 1** to compel someone by legal, moral, or physical means to do something **2** to make (someone) indebted or grateful for a favour: *I am obliged to you for your help* **3** to do a favour to someone: *she obliged the guests with a song* [Latin *ob-* towards + *ligare* to bind]
obliging *adj* willing to be helpful **obligingly** *adv*
oblique (oh-**bleak**) *adj* **1** at an angle; slanting **2** *geom* (of lines or planes) neither perpendicular nor parallel to one another **3** indirect or evasive: *only oblique references have been made to the anti-government unrest* ▷ *n* **4** same as **solidus** [Latin *obliquus*] **obliquely** *adv* **obliqueness** *n*
oblique angle *n* an angle that is not a right angle or any multiple of a right angle
obliterate *vb* **-rating, -rated** to destroy every trace of; wipe out completely [Latin *oblitterare* to erase] **obliteration** *n*
oblivion *n* **1** the condition of being forgotten or disregarded: *the Marxist-Leninist wing of the party looks set to sink into oblivion* **2** the state of being unaware or unconscious: *guests seemed to feel a social obligation to drink themselves into oblivion* [Latin *oblivio* forgetfulness]
oblivious *adj* unaware or unconscious: *oblivious of her soaking clothes; I was oblivious to the beauty* **obliviousness** *n*
oblong *adj* **1** having an elongated, rectangular shape ▷ *n* **2** a figure or object having this shape [Latin *oblongus*]
obloquy (**ob**-lock-wee) *n, pl* **-quies** *formal* **1** abusive statements or blame: *the British press was held up to moral obloquy* **2** disgrace brought about by this: *the punishment of lifelong public obloquy and private embarrassment* [Latin *obloquium* contradiction]
obnoxious *adj* extremely unpleasant [Latin *obnoxius*] **obnoxiousness** *n*
oboe *n* a double-reeded woodwind instrument with a penetrating nasal tone [French *haut bois*, literally: high wood (referring to its pitch)] **oboist** *n*
obs. obsolete
obscene *adj* **1** offensive to accepted standards of decency or modesty **2** *law* tending to deprave or corrupt: *an obscene publication* **3** disgusting: *a great dark obscene pool of blood* [Latin *obscenus* inauspicious] **obscenity** *n*
obscure *adj* **1** not well-known: *the concerts feature several obscure artists* **2** not easily understood: *the contracts are written in obscure language* **3** unclear or indistinct ▷ *vb* **-scuring, -scured 4** to make unclear or vague; hide: *no amount of bluster could obscure the fact that the prime minister had run out of excuses* **5** to cover or cloud over [Latin *obscurus* dark] **obscuration** *n* **obscurity** *n*
obsequies (**ob**-sick-weez) *pl n, sing* **-quy** *formal* funeral rites [Medieval Latin *obsequiae*]
obsequious (ob-**seek**-wee-uss) *adj* being overattentive in order to gain favour [Latin *obsequiosus* compliant] **obsequiousness** *n*
observance *n* **1** the observing of a law or custom **2** a ritual, ceremony, or practice, esp. of a religion
observant *adj* quick to notice details around one; sharp-eyed
observation *n* **1** the act of watching or the state of being watched **2** a comment or remark **3** detailed examination of something before analysis, diagnosis, or interpretation: *you may be admitted to hospital for observation and rest* **4** the facts learned from observing **5** the ability to notice things: *she has good powers of observation* **observational** *adj*
observatory *n, pl* **-ries** a building specially designed and equipped for studying the weather and the stars
observe *vb* **-serving, -served 1** to see or notice: *after some hours I observed a change in the animal's behaviour* **2** to watch (something) carefully **3** to make scientific examinations of **4** to remark: *the speaker observed that times had changed* **5** to keep (a law or custom) [Latin *observare*] **observable** *adj* **observer** *n*
obsess *vb* **1** to be constantly in the thoughts of (someone): *maps obsess Tim* **2** (foll. by *about* or *over*) to be constantly worried: *I tend to obsess about my work* [Latin *obsidere* to besiege] **obsessive** *adj, n*
obsessed *adj* thinking about someone or something all the time: *he had become obsessed with her* [Latin *obsessus* besieged]
obsession *n* **1** something that preoccupies a person to the exclusion of other things: *his principal obsession was with trying to economize* **2** *psychiatry* a persistent idea or impulse, often associated with anxiety and mental illness **obsessional** *adj*
obsidian *n* a dark glassy volcanic rock [after *Obsius*, the discoverer of a stone resembling obsidian]
obsolescent *adj* becoming obsolete or out of date **obsolescence** *n*
obsolete *adj* no longer used; out of date [Latin *obsoletus* worn out]

> **USAGE** The word *obsoleteness* is hardly ever used, *obsolescence* standing as the noun form for both *obsolete* and *obsolescent*.

obstacle *n* **1** a situation or event that prevents something being done: *there are obstacles which could slow the development of a vaccine* **2** a person or thing that hinders movement [Latin *obstaculum*, from *ob-* against + *stare* to stand]
obstetrician *n* a doctor who specializes in obstetrics
obstetrics *n* the branch of medicine concerned with pregnancy and childbirth [Latin *obstetrix* a midwife] **obstetric** *adj*

O

obstinate *adj* **1** keeping stubbornly to a particular opinion or course of action **2** difficult to treat or deal with: *obstinate weeds* [Latin *obstinatus*] **obstinacy** *n* **obstinately** *adv*

obstreperous *adj* noisy and difficult to control: *her obstreperous teenage son* [Latin *ob-* against + *strepere* to roar]

obstruct *vb* **1** to block a way with an obstacle **2** to make progress or activity difficult: *this government will never obstruct the course of justice* **3** to block a clear view of [Latin *obstructus* built against]

obstruction *n* **1** a person or thing that obstructs **2** the act of obstructing or being obstructed **3** *sport* the act of unfairly impeding an opposing player

obstructionist *n* a person who deliberately obstructs legal or parliamentary business **obstructionism** *n*

obstructive *adj* deliberately causing difficulties or delays **obstructively** *adv* **obstructiveness** *n*

obtain *vb* **1** to gain possession of; get **2** *formal* to be customary or accepted: *silence obtains from eight in the evening* [Latin *obtinere* to take hold of] **obtainable** *adj*

obtrude *vb* **-truding, -truded 1** to push oneself or one's opinions on others in an unwelcome way **2** to be or make unpleasantly noticeable [Latin *obtrudere*] **obtrusion** *n*

obtrusive *adj* unpleasantly noticeable: *the music should fit your mood, it shouldn't be too obtrusive* **obtrusiveness** *n*

obtuse *adj* **1** mentally slow or emotionally insensitive **2** *maths* (of an angle) between 90° and 180° **3** not sharp or pointed; blunt [Latin *obtusus* dulled] **obtuseness** *n*

O

obverse *n* **1** a counterpart or opposite: *his true personality being the obverse of his outer image* **2** the side of a coin that bears the main design **3** the front, top, or main surface of anything [Latin *obversus* turned towards]

obviate *vb* **-ating, -ated** *formal* to avoid or prevent (a need or difficulty): *a mediator will obviate the need for independent legal advice* [Latin *obviare*]

> **USAGE** Only things which have not yet occurred can be *obviated*. For example, one can *obviate* a possible future difficulty, but not one which already exists.

obvious *adj* **1** easy to see or understand ▷ *n* **2 state the obvious** to say something that is unnecessary or already known: *he is prone to stating the obvious* [Latin *obvius*] **obviously** *adv* **obviousness** *n*

ocarina *n* a small egg-shaped wind instrument with a mouthpiece and finger holes [Italian: little goose]

occasion *n* **1** a particular event or the time at which it happens **2** a need or reason to do or be something: *we barely knew him and never had occasion to speak of him* **3** a suitable time or opportunity to do something **4** a special event, time, or celebration: *a wedding day is a truly special occasion* **5 on occasion** every so often **6 rise to the occasion** to meet the special demands of a situation ▷ *vb* **7** *formal* to cause, esp. incidentally [Latin *occasio* a falling down]

occasional *adj* happening from time to time; not frequent or regular **occasionally** *adv*

occasional table *n* a small table with no regular use

Occident *n* the western hemisphere, esp. Europe and America [Latin *occidere* to fall (with reference to the setting sun)] **Occidental** *adj*

occiput (ox-sip-putt) *n anatomy* the back of the head or skull [Latin *ob-* at the back of + *caput* head] **occipital** *adj*

occlude *vb* **-cluding, -cluded** *formal* **1** to block or stop up (a passage or opening): *the arteries are occluded by deposits of plaque* **2** to shut in or out: *slowly occluding him from Nash's vision* **3** *chem* (of a solid) to absorb and retain (a gas or other substance) [Latin *occludere*] **occlusion** *n*

occluded front *n meteorol* the front formed when the cold front of a depression overtakes a warm front, raising the warm air from ground level

occult *adj* **1** involving mystical or supernatural phenomena or powers **2** beyond ordinary human understanding **3** secret or mysterious ▷ *n* **4 the occult** the knowledge and study of occult phenomena and powers [Latin *occultus* hidden, secret]

occupancy *n, pl* **-cies 1** the act of occupying a property **2** the period of time during which one is an occupant of a property

occupant *n* a person occupying a property, position, or place

occupation *n* **1** a person's job or profession **2** any activity on which someone's time is spent: *a pleasant and rewarding occupation* **3** the control of a country by a foreign military power **4** the act of occupying or the state of being occupied: *the occupation of Kuwait* **occupational** *adj*

occupational hazard *n* something unpleasant that occurs due to one's job: *frequent colds are an occupational hazard in teaching*

occupational therapy *n* treatment of people with physical, emotional, or social problems using purposeful activity to help them overcome or learn to accept their problems

occupier *n Brit* the person who lives in a particular house, whether as owner or tenant

occupy *vb* **-pies, -pying, -pied 1** to live, stay, or work in (a house, flat, or office) **2** to keep (someone or someone's mind) busy **3** to take up (time or space) **4** to move in and take control of (a country or other place): *soldiers have occupied the country's television station* **5** to fill or hold (a position or office) [Latin *occupare* to seize hold of]

occur *vb* **-curring, -curred 1** to happen **2** to be found or be present; exist **3 occur to** to come into the mind of [Latin *occurrere* to run up to]

> **USAGE** It is usually regarded as incorrect to talk of pre-arranged events *occurring* or *happening*: *the wedding took place* (not *occurred* or *happened*) *in the afternoon*.

occurrence *n* **1** something that happens **2** the fact of occurring: *the likelihood of its occurrence increases with age*

OCD *n* obsessive-compulsive disorder: a condition that causes people to feel anxiety and repeat certain acts over and over again

ocean *n* **1** the vast area of salt water covering about 70 per cent of the earth's surface **2** one of the five principal divisions of this: the Atlantic, Pacific, Indian, Arctic, and Antarctic **3** *informal* a huge quantity or expanse: *oceans of replies* **4** *literary* the sea [from *Oceanus*, Greek god of the stream believed to flow round the earth] **oceanic** *adj*
ocean-going *adj* (of a ship or boat) suited for travel on the open ocean
oceanography *n* the study of oceans and their environment **oceanographer** *n* **oceanographic** *adj*
ocelot (**oss**-ill-lot) *n* a large cat of Central and South America with a dark-spotted yellow-grey coat [Mexican Indian *ocelotl* jaguar]
och *interj Scot & Irish* an expression of surprise, annoyance, or disagreement
oche (**ok**-kee) *n darts* a mark on the floor behind which a player must stand when throwing a dart [origin unknown]
ochre *or US* **ocher** (**oak**-er) *n* **1** a yellow or reddish-brown earth used in paints or dyes ▷ *adj* **2** moderate yellow-orange to orange [Greek *ōkhros* pale yellow]
o'clock *adv* used after a number between one and twelve to specify an hour: *five o'clock in the morning*
OCR optical character recognition: the ability (through a computer device) for letters and numbers to be optically scanned and input to a storage device
Oct. October
octagon *n* a geometric figure with eight sides [Greek *oktagōnos* having eight angles] **octagonal** *adj*
octahedron (ok-ta-**heed**-ron) *n, pl* **-drons** *or* **-dra** a solid figure with eight plane faces
octane *n* a liquid hydrocarbon found in petroleum
octane number *or* **octane rating** *n* a number indicating the quality of a petrol
octave *n* **1** **A** the musical interval between the first note and the eighth note of a major or minor scale **B** the higher of these two notes **C** the series of notes filling this interval **2** *prosody* a rhythmic group of eight lines of verse [Latin *octo* eight]
octavo *n, pl* **-vos** **1** a book size resulting from folding a sheet of paper of a standard size to form eight leaves **2** a book or sheet of this size [New Latin *in octavo* in an eighth (of a sheet)]
octet *n* **1** a group of eight instrumentalists or singers **2** a piece of music for eight performers [Latin *octo* eight]
October *n* the tenth month of the year [Latin *octo* eight, since it was originally the eighth month in Roman reckoning]
octogenarian *n* **1** a person between 80 and 89 years old ▷ *adj* **2** between 80 and 89 years old [Latin *octogenarius* containing eighty]
octopus *n, pl* **-puses** a sea creature with a soft oval body and eight long tentacles with suckers [Greek *oktōpous* having eight feet]
ocular *adj* of or relating to the eyes or sight [Latin *oculus* eye]
oculist *n old-fashioned* an ophthalmologist
OD *informal* ▷ *n* **1** an overdose of a drug ▷ *vb* **OD'ing, OD'd** **2** to take an overdose of a drug
odalisque (**ode**-a-lisk) *n history* a female slave in a harem [Turkish *ōdalik*]
odd *adj* **1** unusual or peculiar: *his increasingly odd behaviour* **2** occasional or incidental: *the odd letter from a friend abroad, the occasional postcard from a chum* **3** leftover or additional: *we use up odd pieces of fabric to make up jerseys in wild designs* **4** (of a number) not divisible by two **5** being part of a pair or set when the other or others are missing: *the drawer was full of odd socks* **6** somewhat more than the round number specified: *I had known him for the past twenty-odd years* **7** **odd man** *or* **one out** a person or thing excluded from others forming a group or unit ▷ See also **odds** [Old Norse *oddi* angle, point, third or odd number] **oddly** *adv* **oddness** *n*
oddball *n informal* a strange or eccentric person
oddity *n, pl* **-ties** **1** an odd person or thing **2** a peculiar characteristic **3** the quality of being or appearing unusual or strange
odd-man rush *n ice hockey* an attacking move when the defence is outnumbered by the opposing team
oddments *pl n* odd pieces or things; leftovers: *oddments of wool*
odds *pl n* **1** the probability, expressed as a ratio, that something will or will not happen: *the odds against an acquittal had stabilized at six to four* **2** the difference, expressed as a ratio, between the money placed on a bet and the amount that would be received as winning payment: *the current odds are ten to one* **3** the likelihood that a certain state of affairs will be so: *the odds are that you are going to fail* **4** the advantage that one contender is judged to have over another: *the odds are in his favour* **5** **at odds** **A** on bad terms **B** at variance **6** **it makes no odds** *Brit & Austral* it does not matter **7** **over the odds** more than is expected or necessary
odds and ends *pl n* small, usually unimportant, objects, jobs to be done, etc.: *I have brought a few odds and ends with me*
odds-on *adj* having a better than even chance of winning
ode *n* a lyric poem, usually addressed to a particular subject, with lines of varying lengths and metres [Greek *ōidē* song]
Odin *n* the chief god in Norse mythology
odious *adj* offensive or hateful: *I steeled myself for the odious task* [see ODIUM] **odiousness** *n*
odium (**oh**-dee-um) *n formal* widespread dislike or disapproval of a person or action [Latin]
odometer (odd-**om**-it-er) *n US & Canad* same as **mileometer** [Greek *hodos* way + -METER]
odoriferous *adj formal* having or giving off a pleasant smell
odour *or US* **odor** *n* a particular and distinctive scent or smell [Latin *odor*] **odorous** *adj* **odourless** *adj*
odyssey (**odd**-iss-ee) *n* a long eventful journey
OE *NZ informal* overseas experience: *he's away on his OE*
OECD Organization for Economic Cooperation and Development
oedema *or* **edema** (id-**deem**-a) *n, pl* **-mata** *pathol* an abnormal accumulation of fluid in the tissues of the body, causing swelling [Greek *oidēma* swelling]

Oedipus complex (ee-dip-puss) *n psychoanalysis* the usually unconscious sexual desire of a child, esp. a male child, for the parent of the opposite sex **oedipal** *adj*

o'er *prep, adv poetic* over

oesophagus *or US* **esophagus** (ee-soff-a-guss) *n, pl* **-gi** (-guy) the tube through which food travels from the throat to the stomach; gullet [Greek *oisophagos*] **oesophageal** *or US* **esophageal** *adj*

oestrogen *or US* **estrogen** (ee-stra-jen) *n* a female sex hormone that controls the reproductive cycle, and prepares the body for pregnancy [from *oestrus* + *-gen* (suffix) producing]

oestrus *or US* **estrus** (ee-struss) *n* a regularly occurring period of fertility and sexual receptivity in the reproductive cycle of most female mammals, except humans; heat [Greek *oistros* gadfly, hence frenzy]

of *prep* **1** belonging to; situated in or coming from; because of: *the inhabitants of former East Germany; I saw five people die of chronic hepatitis* **2** used after words or phrases expressing quantities: *a pint of milk* **3** specifying an amount or value: *we had to release the bombs at a height of 400 metres* **4** made up of, containing, or characterized by: *a length of rope; she was a woman of strong character* **5** used to link a verbal noun with a following noun or noun phrase that is either the subject or the object of the verb: *the sudden slipping of the plates of the Earth's crust; the bombing of civilian targets* **6** at a given distance or space of time from: *you can still find wood within a mile of the village; he had been within hours of leaving for Romania* **7** used to specify or give more information about: *the city of Glasgow; a meeting on the subject of regional security* **8** about or concerning: *speaking of boycotts* **9** US before the hour of: *about quarter of eight in the evening* [Old English]

USAGE See at **off**.

Ofcom *n* (in Britain) Office of Communications: a government body regulating the broadcasting and telecommunications industries

off *prep* **1** so as to be no longer in contact with: *take the wok off the heat* **2** so as to be no longer attached to or associated with: *to take the tax off children's clothes* **3** away from: *he was driven off the road* **4** situated near to or leading away from: *they were laying out a bombing range off the coast* **5** no longer having a liking for: *she's gone off you lately* **6** no longer using: *he was off heroin for a year* ▷ *adv* **7** so as to deactivate or disengage: *turn off the gas supply* **8** **A** so as to get rid of: *he was flying at midnight so he had to sleep off his hangover* **B** as a reduction in price: *she took 20% off* **9** spent away from work or other duties: *it was the assistant manager's day off* **10** away; at a distance: *the men dashed back to their car and sped off* **11** away in the future: *the date was six weeks off* **12** so as to be no longer taking place: *the investigation was hastily called off* **13** removed from contact with something: *he took the jacket off* **14** **off and on** occasionally; not regularly or continuously: *we lived together off and on* ▷ *adj* **15** not on; no longer operating: *her bedroom light was off* **16** cancelled or postponed: *the deal is off and your deposit will be returned in full* **17** in a specified condition, esp. regarding money or provisions: *I'd be better off without this job; how are you off for money?* **18** not up to the usual standard: *an off year for good wine* **19** no longer on the menu: *haddock is off* **20** (of food or drink) having gone bad or sour: *this milk is off* ▷ *n* **21** *cricket* the side of the field to the right of a right-handed batsman when he is facing the bowler [variant of *of*]

USAGE In standard English, *off* is not followed by *of*: *he stepped off* (not *off of*) *the platform*.

offal *n* the edible internal parts of an animal, such as the heart or liver [*off* + *fall*, referring to parts cut off]

offal pit *or* **offal hole** *n NZ* a place on a farm for the disposal of animal offal

offbeat *adj* unusual, unconventional, or eccentric

off-break *n cricket* a bowled ball that spins from off to leg on pitching

off colour *adj* **1** slightly ill; unwell **2** slightly indecent: *an off-colour joke*

offcut *n* a piece of paper, wood, or fabric remaining after the main pieces have been cut; remnant

offence *or US* **offense** *n* **1** a breaking of a law or rule; crime **2** annoyance or anger **3** a cause of annoyance or anger **4** **give offence** to cause to feel upset or angry **5** **take offence** to feel hurt or offended

offend *vb* **1** to hurt the feelings of (a person); insult **2** to be disagreeable to; disgust: *she was offended by what she saw* **3** to commit a crime [Latin *offendere*] **offender** *n* **offending** *adj*

offensive *adj* **1** unpleasant or disgusting to the senses: *there was an offensive smell of beer* **2** causing annoyance or anger; insulting **3** for the purpose of attack rather than defence ▷ *n* **4** an attitude or position of aggression: *to go on the offensive* **5** an attack or hostile action: *troops had launched a major offensive against the rebel forces* **offensively** *adv*

offer *vb* **1** to present for acceptance or rejection: *I offered her a lift* **2** to provide: *this department offers a wide range of courses* **3** to present itself: *if an opportunity should offer* **4** to be willing (to do something): *his father offered to pay his tuition* **5** to put forward (a proposal, information, or opinion) for consideration: *may I offer a different view?* **6** to present for sale **7** to propose as payment; bid **8** to present (a prayer or sacrifice) as an act of worship **9** to show readiness for: *to offer resistance* ▷ *n* **10** something that is offered **11** the act of offering [Latin *offerre* to present]

offering *n* **1** something that is offered **2** a contribution to the funds of a religious organization **3** a sacrifice to a god

offertory *n, pl* **-tories** *Christianity* **1** the part of a church service when the bread and wine for communion are offered for consecration **2** the collection of money at this service **3** the prayers said or sung while the worshippers' offerings are being brought to the altar

off-grid *adj* not involving or requiring the use of mainstream sources of energy

offhand *adj also* **offhanded** **1** curt or casual in manner: *I felt calm enough to adopt a casual offhand manner* ▷ *adv* **2** without preparation: *I don't know offhand why that should be so* **offhandedly** *adv* **offhandedness** *n*

office *n* **1** a room, set of rooms, or building in which business, professional duties, or clerical work are carried out **2** a department of an organization dealing with particular business: *Zoe worked in the store's cash office for 18 months* **3** the group of people working in an office: *she assured him that the office was running smoothly* **4** a government department or agency: *Serious Fraud Office* **5** a position of trust or authority, as in a government: *he would not seek a second term of office* **6** a place where tickets, information, or some service can be obtained: *why don't you give the ticket office a ring?* **7** *Christianity* a religious ceremony or service **8 good offices** the help given by someone to someone else: *Syria's good offices finally led to the release of two Western hostages* **9 in** *or* **out of office** (of a government) in *or* out of power [Latin *officium* service, duty]

officer *n* **1** a person in the armed services, or on a non-naval ship, who holds a position of authority **2** a policeman or policewoman **3** a person holding a position of authority in a government or organization

official *adj* **1** of an office or position of authority: *I'm not here in any official capacity* **2** approved by or derived from authority: *there has been no official announcement* **3** formal or ceremonial: *he was speaking at an official dinner in Warsaw* ▹ *n* **4** a person holding a position of authority **officially** *adv*

officialdom *n* officials or bureaucrats collectively

officialese *n* language typical of official documents, esp. when wordy or pompous

Official Receiver *n Brit* an officer appointed by the government to deal with the affairs of a bankrupt person or company

officiate *vb* **-ating, -ated 1** to perform the duties of an office; act in an official capacity: *the referee will officiate at the match* **2** to conduct a religious or other ceremony: *the priest officiated at the wedding* **officiation** *n* **officiator** *n*

officious *adj* offering unwanted advice or services; interfering [Latin *officiosus* kindly] **officiousness** *n*

offing *n* **1** the part of the sea that can be seen from the shore **2 in the offing** *Brit, Austral & NZ* not far off; likely to occur soon

off key *music* ▹ *adj* **1** out of tune: *an off-key rendition* ▹ *adv* **2** out of tune: *he sings off key*

off-licence *n Brit* a shop or a counter in a shop where alcoholic drink is sold for drinking elsewhere

offline *adj* **1** disconnected from a computer or the internet ▹ *adv* **2** while not connected to a computer or the internet

off-load *vb* to get rid of (something unpleasant), usually by giving it to someone else: *you take all the credit and off-load all the blame*

off-peak *adj* (of services) used at times other than those of greatest demand

off-putting *adj informal* rather unpleasant or disturbing: *we were being stared at by everyone, which was a little off-putting*

off-road *adj* (of a motor vehicle) designed for use away from public roads

off-roader *n* a motor vehicle designed for use away from public roads

offset *vb* **-setting, -set 1** to cancel out or compensate for **2** to print (something) using the offset process ▹ *n* **3** a printing method in which the impression is made onto a surface, such as a rubber roller, which transfers it to the paper **4** *botany* a short runner in certain plants that produces roots and shoots at the tip

offshoot *n* **1** a shoot growing from the main stem of a plant **2** something that has developed from something else

offshore *adj, adv* **1** away from or at some distance from the shore ▹ *adj* **2** sited or conducted at sea: *he reversed his position on offshore drilling*

offside *adj, adv* **1** *sport* (of a player) in a position illegally ahead of the ball when it is played ▹ *n* **2** *chiefly Brit* the side of a vehicle nearest the centre of the road

off spin *n cricket* a method of spin bowling delivery in which the ball spins from off to leg after bouncing **off-spinner** *n*

offspring *n* **1** the immediate descendant or descendants of a person or animal **2** a product, outcome, or result: *the women's liberation movement was the offspring of the 1960s*

off-the-peg *adj* (of clothing) ready to wear; not produced especially for the person buying

Ofgem *n* (in Britain) Office of Gas and Electricity Markets: the body which regulates the power supply industries

Ofsted *n* Office for Standards in Education: the body which assesses the educational standards of schools in England

oft *adv old-fashioned or poetic* short for **often** [Old English]

often *adv* **1** frequently; much of the time **2 as often as not** quite frequently **3 every so often** occasionally **4 more often than not** in more than half the instances [Middle English variant of *oft*]

Ofwat *n* (in Britain) Office of Water Services: the body which regulates the activities of the water companies in England and Wales

Og oganesson

oganesson *n chem* a synthetic radioactive element produced in small quantities. Symbol: **Og** [after Y. *Oganessian*, physicist]

ogee arch (**oh**-jee) *n* a pointed arch made with an S-shaped curve on each side [probably from Old French]

ogle *vb* **ogling, ogled** to stare at (someone) lustfully [probably from Low German *oegeln*]

O grade *n* **1** (formerly) the basic level of the Scottish Certificate of Education **2** a pass in a particular subject at O grade: *she has eight O grades*

ogre *n* **1** (in folklore) a giant that eats human flesh **2** any monstrous or cruel person [French] **ogreish** *adj* **ogress** *fem n*

oh *interj* an exclamation of surprise, pain, pleasure, fear, or annoyance

OH Ohio

ohm *n* the SI unit of electrical resistance [after Georg Simon *Ohm*, physicist]

OHMS (in Britain and the Commonwealth) On Her (*or* His) Majesty's Service

oil *n* **1** any of a number of viscous liquids with a smooth sticky feel, which are usually flammable, insoluble in water, and are obtained from plants, animals, or mineral deposits by synthesis **2** same as **petroleum** **3** a substance derived from petroleum and used for lubrication **4** *Brit* paraffin as a domestic fuel **5** oil colour or paint **6** an oil painting ▷ *vb* **7** to lubricate with oil or apply oil to **8** **oil the wheels** to make things run smoothly [Latin *oleum* (olive) oil]

oilcloth *n* a cotton fabric treated with oil or a synthetic resin to make it waterproof, formerly used esp. for tablecloths

oilfield *n* an area containing reserves of oil

oilfired *adj* using oil as fuel

oil paint *n* a thick paint made of pigment ground in linseed oil

oil painting *n* **1** a picture painted with oil paints **2** the art of painting with oil paints

oil rig *n* a structure used as a base when drilling an oil well

oil-seed rape *n* same as **rape²**

oilskin *n* **1** a thick cotton fabric treated with oil to make it waterproof **2** a protective outer garment made of this fabric

oil slick *n* a mass of floating oil covering an area of water

oil well *n* a well bored into the earth or sea bed to a supply of oil

oily *adj* **oilier, oiliest** **1** soaked or covered with oil **2** of, containing, or like oil **3** attempting to gain favour by insincere behaviour and flattery **oiliness** *n*

oink *n* the grunt of a pig or an imitation of this

ointment *n* a smooth greasy substance applied to the skin to heal or protect, or as a cosmetic: *home-made creams and ointments* [Latin *unguentum* unguent]

O

OK Oklahoma

O.K. *informal* ▷ *interj* **1** an expression of approval or agreement ▷ *adj* **2** in good or satisfactory condition ▷ *adv* **3** reasonably well or in a satisfactory manner ▷ *vb* **O.K.ing, O.K.ed** **4** to approve or endorse ▷ *n, pl* **O.K.s** **5** approval or agreement [perhaps from *o(ll) k(orrect)*, jocular alteration of *all correct*]

okapi (oh-**kah**-pee) *n, pl* **-pis** *or* **-pi** an African mammal related to the giraffe, but with a shorter neck, a reddish coat, and white stripes on the legs [from a Central African word]

okay *interj, adj, adv, vb, n* same as **O.K.**

okra *n* a tall plant with long green pods that are used as food [West African]

old *adj* **1** having lived or existed for a long time: *the old woman; burning witches is one old custom I've no desire to see revived* **2** of or relating to advanced years or a long life: *I twisted my knee as I tried to squat and cursed old age* **3** worn with age or use: *the old bathroom fittings* **4** having lived or existed for a specified period: *he is 60 years old* **5** the earlier or earliest of two or more things with the same name: *the old edition; the Old Testament* **6** designating the form of a language in which the earliest known records are written: *Old English* **7** familiar through long acquaintance or repetition: *an old acquaintance; the legalization argument is an old and familiar one* **8** dear: used as a term of affection or familiarity: *always rely on old Tom to turn out* **9** out of date; unfashionable **10** former or previous: *my old housekeeper lent me some money* **11** of long standing: *he's an old and respected member of staff* **12** **good old days** an earlier period of time regarded as better than the present ▷ *n* **13** an earlier or past time: *in days of old* [Old English *eald*] **oldish** *adj*

old age pension *n* a former name for **retirement pension** **old age pensioner** *n*

Old Bailey *n* the Central Criminal Court of England

old boy *n* **1** a male ex-pupil of a school **2** *informal, chiefly Brit* **A** a familiar form of address used to refer to a man **B** an old man

old country *n* the country of origin of an immigrant or an immigrant's ancestors

olde *adj facetious* quaint [from the former spelling of old]

olden *adj archaic or poetic* old: *the steam trains of olden times*

Old English *n* the English language of the Anglo-Saxons, spoken from the fifth century AD to about 1100. Also called: **Anglo-Saxon**

Old English sheepdog *n* a large sheepdog with thick shaggy hair

old-fashioned *adj* **1** in the style of a previous period; outdated: *she wore her hair in a strangely old-fashioned tight hairdo* **2** favouring or denoting the styles or ideas of a former time: *old-fashioned values*

old flame *n informal, old-fashioned* a person with whom one once had a romantic relationship

Old French *n* the French language in its earliest forms, from about the 9th century up to about 1400

old girl *n* **1** a female ex-pupil of a school **2** *informal, chiefly Brit* **A** an affectionate form of address used to a woman **B** an old woman

old guard *n* a group of people in an organization who have traditional values: *the company's old guard is making way for a new, more youthful team* [after Napoleon's imperial guard]

old hand *n* a skilled or experienced person

old hat *adj* old-fashioned or dull

Old High German *n* a group of West Germanic dialects that developed into modern German; High German up to about 1200

old identity *n NZ* a well-known local person who has lived in an area for a long time

oldie *n informal* an old song, film, or person

old lady *n informal* one's mother or wife

old maid *n sometimes offensive* a woman regarded as unlikely ever to marry; spinster

old man *n* **1** *informal* one's father **2** *informal* one's husband **3** an affectionate form of address used to a man

old master *n* **1** one of the great European painters of the period 1500 to 1800 **2** a painting by one of these

old moon *n* a phase of the moon between last quarter and new moon, when it appears as a waning crescent

Old Nick *n informal* Satan

old school *n* a group of people favouring traditional or conservative ideas or practices

old school tie *n* the system of mutual help supposed to operate among the former pupils of independent schools
Old Style *n* the former method of reckoning dates using the Julian calendar
Old Testament *n* the first part of the Christian Bible, containing the sacred Scriptures of the Hebrews
old-time *adj* of or relating to a former time; old-fashioned: *an old-time waltz*
old wives' tale *n* a belief, usually superstitious or foolish, passed on by word of mouth as a piece of traditional wisdom
old woman *n* **1** *informal* one's mother **2** *informal* one's wife **3** *derogatory* a timid, fussy, or cautious person **old-womanish** *adj*
Old World *n* that part of the world that was known to Europeans before the discovery of the Americas; the eastern hemisphere
old-world *adj* of or characteristic of former times; quaint or traditional
oleaginous (oh-lee-**aj**-in-uss) *adj* like or producing oil; oily [Latin *oleaginus*]
oleander (oh-lee-**ann**-der) *n* an evergreen Mediterranean shrub with fragrant white, pink, or purple flowers [Medieval Latin]
O level *n* **1** (formerly, in Britain) the basic level of the General Certificate of Education **2** a pass in a particular subject at O level: *a very intelligent young woman with ten O levels*
olfactory *adj* of the sense of smell [Latin *olere* to smell + *facere* to make]
oligarch (**ol**-lee-gark) *n* a member of a small group of powerful people
oligarchy (**ol**-lee-gark-ee) *n, pl* **-chies** **1** government by a small group of people **2** a state governed this way **3** a small group of people governing such a state [Greek *oligos* few + *arkhein* to rule] **oligarchic** *or* **oligarchical** *adj*
Oligocene (**ol**-lig-go-seen) *adj geol* of the epoch of geological time about 35 million years ago [Greek *oligos* little + *kainos* new]
oligopoly *n, pl* **-lies** *econ* a market situation in which control over the supply of a commodity is held by a small number of producers [Greek *oligos* few + *pōlein* to sell]
olive *n* **1** an evergreen Mediterranean tree **2** the small green or black fruit of this tree ▹ *adj* **3** short for **olive-green** [Latin *oliva*]
olive branch *n* a peace offering: *I should offer some kind of olive branch and get in touch with them*
olive-green *adj* deep yellowish-green
olive oil *n* a yellowish-green oil pressed from ripe olives and used in cooking and medicines
oloroso (ol-ler-**roh**-so) *n* a golden-coloured sweet sherry [Spanish: fragrant]
Olympiad *n trademark* **1** a staging of the modern Olympic Games **2** an international contest in chess or other games
Olympian *adj* **1** of Mount Olympus or the classical Greek gods **2** majestic or godlike ▹ *n* **3** a competitor in the Olympic Games **4** a god of Mount Olympus
Olympic *adj* of the Olympic Games
Olympic Games *n* **1** an ancient Greek festival, held every fourth year in honour of Zeus, consisting of games and festivities **2** Also called: **the Olympics** *trademark* the modern revival of these games, consisting of international athletic and sporting contests held every four years in a selected country
OM (in Britain) Order of Merit
ombudsman *n, pl* **-men** an official who investigates citizens' complaints against the government or its servants [Swedish: commissioner]
omega *n* **1** the 24th and last letter of the Greek alphabet (Ω, ω) **2** the ending or last of a series
omega-3 *n* an unsaturated fatty acid that occurs naturally in fish oil, valuable in reducing blood cholesterol
omelette *or esp US* **omelet** *n* a dish of beaten eggs cooked in a flat pan and often folded round a savoury filling [French]
omen *n* **1** a thing or occurrence regarded as a sign of future happiness or disaster **2** prophetic significance: *birds of ill omen* [Latin]
OMG Oh my God!: used esp. in emails, text messages, etc.
ominous *adj* warning of evil [Latin *ominosus*] **ominously** *adv*
omission *n* **1** something that has been left out or passed over **2** an act of missing out or failing to do something: *we regret the omission of these and the names of the other fine artists*
omit *vb* **omitting, omitted** **1** to fail to include; leave out **2** to fail (to do something) [Latin *omittere*]
omnibus *n, pl* **-buses** **1** a collection of works by one author or several works on a similar topic, reprinted in one volume **2** Also called: **omnibus edition** a television or radio programme consisting of two or more episodes of a serial broadcast earlier in the week **3** *old-fashioned* a bus ▹ *adj* **4** consisting of or dealing with several different things at once: *this year's version of an omnibus crime bill* [Latin, literally: for all]
omnipotent (om-**nip**-a-tent) *adj* having very great or unlimited power [Latin *omnipotens* all-powerful] **omnipotence** *n*
omnipresent *adj* (esp. of a god) present in all places at the same time [Latin *omnis* all + *praesens* present] **omnipresence** *n*
omniscient (om-**niss**-ee-ent) *adj* knowing or seeming to know everything [Latin *omnis* all + *scire* to know] **omniscience** *n*
omnivore (**om**-niv-vore) *n* an animal that eats any type of food
omnivorous (om-**niv**-or-uss) *adj* **1** eating any type of food **2** taking in everything indiscriminately: *he was an omnivorous reader* [Latin *omnivorus* all-devouring]
on *prep* **1** in contact with or at the surface of: *let the cakes stand in the tins on a wire rack; she had dirt on her dress* **2** attached to: *a piece of paper on a clipboard* **3** carried with: *the message found on her* **4** near to or along the side of: *the hotel is on the coast* **5** within the time limits of (a day or date): *they returned to Moscow on 22nd September* **6** being performed upon or relayed through the medium of: *a construction of refined sounds played on special musical instruments; what's on television?* **7** at the occasion of: *she had*

O

received numerous letters congratulating her on her election **8** immediately after or at the same time as: *check with the tourist office on arrival* **9** through the use of: *an extraordinarily vigorous man who thrives on physical activity; the program runs on the Unix operating system* **10** regularly taking (a drug): *she's on the pill* **11** by means of (a mode of transport): *his only way up the hill had to be on foot; they get around on bicycles* **12** in the process or course of: *he is away on a climbing expedition; the miners went on strike* **13** concerned with or relating to: *an emotional documentary on homelessness among war veterans* **14** (of a statement or action) having as basis or grounds: *I have it on good authority* **15** charged to: *all drinks are on the house for the rest of the evening* **16** staked as a bet: *I'll have a bet on the favourite* ▷ *adv* **17** in operation; functioning: *the lights had been left on all night* **18** attached to, surrounding, or placed in contact with something: *they escaped with nothing on except sleeveless shirts and shorts* **19** taking place: *what do you have on tonight?* **20** continuously or persistently: *the crisis must not be allowed to drag on indefinitely* **21** forwards or further: *they trudged on* **22 on and off** occasionally; not regularly or continuously **23 on and on** without ceasing; continually ▷ *adj* **24** *informal* performing: *who's on next?* **25** *informal* definitely taking place: *is the party still on?* **26** *informal* tolerable, practicable, or acceptable: *that's just not on* **27 on at** *informal* nagging: *he was always on at her to stop smoking* ▷ *n* **28** *cricket* the side of the field to the left of a right-handed batsman when he is facing the bowler [Old English *an, on*]

ON Ontario

onager *n, pl* **-gri** *or* **-gers** a wild ass of Persia [Greek *onagros*]

O

onanism *n* **1** withdrawal in sexual intercourse before ejaculation **2** masturbation [after *Onan*: see Genesis 38:9]

ONC (formerly in Britain) Ordinary National Certificate

once *adv* **1** one time; on one occasion only **2** at some past time, but no longer: *I was in love once* **3** by one degree (of relationship): *he was Deirdre's cousin once removed* **4 once and for all** conclusively; for the last time **5 once in a while** occasionally; now and then **6 once or twice** a few times **7 once upon a time** used to begin fairy tales and children's stories ▷ *conj* **8** as soon as: *once you have learned good grammar you can leave it to nature and forget it* ▷ *n* **9** one occasion or case: *once is enough* **10 all at once** **A** suddenly **B** simultaneously **11 at once** **A** immediately **B** simultaneously **12 for once** this time, even if at no other time [Middle English *ones, anes*]

once-over *n informal* a quick examination or appraisal

oncogene (ong-koh-jean) *n* a gene present in all cells, that when abnormally activated can cause cancer [Greek *onkos* tumour + *-gen* (suffix) producing]

oncology *n* the branch of medicine concerned with cancerous tumours **oncologist** *n*

oncoming *adj* coming nearer in space or time; approaching: *oncoming traffic*

OND (formerly in Britain) Ordinary National Diploma

one *adj, n* **1** single or lone (person or thing); not two or more: *one civilian has died and thirty-three have been injured* **2** only or unique (person or thing): *he is the one to make correct judgments and influence the public; she was unique, inimitable, one of a kind* **3** a specified (person or thing) as distinct from another or others of its kind: *place one hand under the knee and the other under the ankle; which one is correct?* **4 one or two** a few ▷ *adj* **5** a certain, indefinite, or unspecified (time): *one day he would learn the truth about her* **6** *informal, emphatic* a: *we're on to one hell of a story* ▷ *pron* **7** an indefinite person regarded as typical of every person: *one can always hope that there won't be an accident* **8** any indefinite person: *one can catch fine trout in this stream* **9** I or me: *one only wonders what he has against the dogs* ▷ *n* **10** the smallest natural number and first cardinal number **11** a numeral, 1 or I, representing this number **12** something representing or consisting of one unit **13** *informal* a joke or story: *have you heard the one about the actress and the bishop?* **14 (all) in one** combined or united **15 all one** of no consequence: *leave if you want to, it's all one to me* **16 at one with** in agreement or harmony with **17 one and all** everyone, without exception **18 one by one** one at a time; individually [Old English *ān*]

one another *pron* each other: *they seem to genuinely care for one another*

one-armed bandit *n informal* a fruit machine operated by pulling down a lever at one side

one-dimensional *adj* **1** having one dimension **2** completely lacking in depth or complexity: *the production staging is one-dimensional and the direction rigid*

one-horse *adj informal* small or insignificant: *a dusty one-horse town in the foothills of the Karakoram mountain range*

one-liner *n informal* a short joke or witty remark

oneness *n* **1** agreement **2** uniqueness **3** sameness

one-night stand *n* **1** *informal* a sexual encounter lasting only one evening or night **2** a performance given only once at any one place

one-off *n* something that happens or is made only once

onerous (own-er-uss) *adj* (of a task) difficult to carry out [Latin *onus* load] **onerousness** *n*

oneself *pron* **1** the reflexive form of *one* **2** one's normal or usual self: *one doesn't feel oneself after such an experience*

one-sided *adj* **1** considering or favouring only one side of a matter: *a one-sided version of events* **2** having all the advantage on one side: *it was a one-sided match with Brazil missing a succession of chances*

onesie (wonn-zee) *n* a one-piece garment consisting of a long-sleeved top with trousers, which zips up the front

one-stop *adj* having or providing a range of services or goods in one place: *one-stop shopping*

One Thousand Guineas *n* **the One Thousand Guineas** an annual horse race for three-year-old fillies, run at Newmarket

one-time *adj* at some time in the past; former

one-to-one *adj* **1** (of two or more things)

corresponding exactly **2** denoting a relationship or encounter in which someone is involved with only one other person: *one-to-one meetings* **3** *maths* involving the pairing of each member of one set with only one member of another set, without remainder

one-track *adj informal* obsessed with one idea or subject: *she's got a one-track mind*

one-up *adj informal* having an advantage or lead over someone else

one-upmanship *n informal* behaviour that is designed to make other people feel inferior

one-way *adj* **1** moving or allowing travel in one direction only: *the town centre has a baffling one-way system* **2** involving no reciprocal obligation or action: *he does not get anything back out of the one-way relationship*

ongoing *adj* in progress; continuing: *there are still ongoing discussions about the future role of NATO*

onion *n* **1** a vegetable with an edible bulb with a strong smell and taste **2 know one's onions** *Brit & NZ slang* to be fully acquainted with a subject [Latin *unio*] **oniony** *adj*

online *adj* **1** connected to a computer or the internet ▷ *adv* **2** while connected to a computer or the internet

onlooker *n* a person who observes without taking part **onlooking** *adj*

only *adj* **1** alone of its or their kind: *I will be talking to the only journalist to have been inside the prison* **2** (of a child) having no brothers or sisters **3** unique by virtue of superiority; best: *first class is the only way to travel* **4 one and only** incomparable: *the one and only Usain Bolt* ▷ *adv* **5** without anyone or anything else being included; alone: *only you can decide if you can abide by this compromise* **6** merely or just: *it's only Henry* **7** no more or no greater than: *I was talking to a priest only a minute ago* **8** merely: *they had only to turn up to win the competition* **9** not earlier than; not until: *I've only found out today why you wouldn't come* **10 if only** *or* **if ... only** used to introduce a wish or hope **11 only too** extremely: *they were only too willing to do anything to help* ▷ *conj* **12** but or however: *those countries are going through the same cycle, only a little later than us* [Old English *ānlīc*]

> **USAGE** In informal English, *only* is often used as a sentence connector: *I would have phoned you, only I didn't know your number.* This use should be avoided in formal writing: *I would have phoned you if I'd known your number.* In formal speech and writing, *only* is placed directly before the word or words that it modifies: *she could interview only three applicants in the morning.* In all but the most formal contexts, however, it is generally regarded as acceptable to put *only* before the verb: *she could only interview three applicants in the morning.* Care must be taken not to create ambiguity, esp. in written English, in which intonation will not, as it does in speech, help to show to which item in the sentence *only* applies. A sentence such as *she only drinks tea in the afternoon* is capable of two interpretations and is therefore better rephrased either as *she drinks only tea in the afternoon* (i.e. no other drink) or *she drinks tea only in the afternoon* (i.e. at no other time).

o.n.o. or near(est) offer

onomatopoeia (on-a-mat-a-**pee**-a) *n* use of a word which imitates the sound it represents, such as *hiss* [Greek *onoma* name + *poiein* to make] **onomatopoeic** *or* **onomatopoetic** *adj*

onrush *n* a forceful forward rush or flow; surge

onset *n* a start; beginning

onshore *adj, adv* **1** towards the land: *a stiff onshore wind* **2** on land; not at sea

onside *adj, adv* **1** *sport* (of a player) in a legal position, for example, behind the ball or with a required number of opponents between oneself and the opposing team's goal line **2** in a position of support or sympathy: *phoning shareholders in an attempt to bring them onside*

onslaught *n* a violent attack [Middle Dutch *aenslag*]

Ont. Ontario

onto *or* **on to** *prep* **1** to a position that is on: *step onto the train* **2** having discovered or become aware of: *the police are onto us* **3** into contact with: *get onto the factory*

> **USAGE** *Onto* is now generally accepted as a word in its own right. *On to* is still used, however, where *on* is considered to be part of the verb: *he moved on to a different town* as contrasted with *he jumped onto the stage.*

ontology *n philosophy* the study of the nature of being [Greek *ōn* being + -LOGY] **ontological** *adj*

onus (**own**-uss) *n, pl* **onuses** a responsibility, task, or burden: *the courts put the onus on parents* [Latin: burden]

onward *adj* **1** directed or moving forward ▷ *adv also* **onwards** **2** continuing; progressing

onyx *n* a kind of quartz with alternating coloured layers, used as a gemstone [Greek: fingernail (so called from its veined appearance)]

oodles *pl n informal* great quantities: *he has shown he can raise oodles of cash* [origin unknown]

oolite (**oh**-a-lite) *n* a limestone made up of tiny grains of calcium carbonate [New Latin *oolites*, literally: egg stone] **oolitic** *adj*

oom *n S African* a title of respect used to refer to an elderly man [Afrikaans, literally: uncle]

oomiak *or* **oomiac** *n* same as **umiak**

oompah *n* a representation of the sound made by a deep brass instrument, esp. in brass band music

oomph *n informal* enthusiasm, vigour, or energy [origin unknown]

oops *interj* an exclamation of surprise or of apology when someone has a slight accident or makes a mistake

OOS occupational overuse syndrome: pain caused by repeated awkward movements while at work

ooze[1] *vb* **oozing, oozed** **1** to flow or leak out slowly; seep **2** (of a substance) to discharge moisture **3** to overflow with (a feeling or quality): *he oozes confidence* ▷ *n* **4** a slow flowing or leaking [Old English *wōs* juice] **oozy** *adj*

ooze[2] *n* a soft thin mud, such as that found at the bottom of a lake, river, or sea [Old English *wāse* mud]

op. opus

opacity (ohp-**ass**-it-tee) *n, pl* **-ties** **1** the state or quality of being opaque **2** the quality of being difficult to understand; unintelligibility

opal *n* a precious stone, usually milky or bluish in colour, with shimmering changing reflections [Greek *opallios*]

opalescent *adj* having shimmering changing reflections, like opal **opalescence** *n*

opaque *adj* **1** not able to be seen through; not transparent or translucent **2** hard to understand; unintelligible [Latin *opacus* shady]

op. cit. (op sit) (in textual annotations) in the work cited [Latin *opere citato*]

OPEC Organization of Petroleum-Exporting Countries

open *adj* **1** not closed, fastened, or blocked up: *the doctor's office was open* **2** not enclosed, covered, or wrapped: *the parcel was open* **3** extended, expanded, or unfolded: *an open flower* **4** ready for business: *some of the crafts rooms and photography shops are open all night* **5** (of a job) available: *all the positions on the council should be open to women* **6** unobstructed by buildings or trees: *we lived in a small market town surrounded by open countryside* **7** free to all to join in, enter, or use: *there was an open competition and I was appointed* **8** (of a season or period) not restricted for purposes of hunting game of various kinds **9** not decided or finalized: *the legality of these sales is still an open question* **10** ready to consider new ideas: *I was able to approach their problem with an open mind* **11** honest and frank **12** generous: *she has given me love and the open hand* **13** exposed to view; blatant: *there has never been such sustained and open criticism of the President* **14** unprotected; susceptible: *a change of policy which would leave vulnerable youths open to exploitation* **15** having spaces or gaps: *open ranks; an open texture* **16** *computers* designed to an internationally agreed standard to allow communication between computers irrespective of size or manufacturer **17** *music* **A** (of a string) not stopped with the finger **B** (of a note) played on such a string **18** *sport* (of a goal or court) unguarded or relatively unprotected **19** (of a wound) exposed to the air ▷ *vb* **20** to make or become open: *it was easy to open the back door and to slip noiselessly outside; she knelt and tried to open the drawer* **21** to set or be set in action; start: *the US will have to open talks on Palestinian rights; I want to open a dress shop* **22** to arrange for (a bank account), usually by making an initial deposit **23** to declare open ceremonially or officially ▷ *n* **24** *sport* a competition which anyone may enter **25 the open** any wide or unobstructed area [Old English] **opener** *n* **openly** *adv* **openness** *n*

open air *n* the place or space where the air is unenclosed; outdoors

open-and-shut *adj* easily decided or solved; obvious: *an open-and-shut case*

opencast mining *n* mining by excavating from the surface [*open* + archaic *cast* ditch, cutting]

open day *n* a special occasion on which a school, university, or other institution is open for the public to visit

open-ended *adj* **1** without definite limits; unrestricted: *the schedule is open-ended* **2** (of an activity) done without the aim of attaining a particular result or decision: *the dangers of open-ended military involvement*

open-eyed *adj* **1** with the eyes wide open, as in amazement **2** watchful; alert

open-handed *adj* generous

open-hearted *adj* **1** kind or generous **2** willing to speak one's mind; candid

open-heart surgery *n* surgical repair of the heart during which the heart is exposed and the blood circulation is maintained mechanically

open house *n* a situation in which people allow friends or visitors to come to their house whenever they want to

opening *n* **1** the beginning or first part of something **2** the first performance of a theatrical production **3** a chance or opportunity: *an opening into show business* **4** a hole or gap

opening time *n Brit & Austral* the time at which public houses can legally open for business

open letter *n* a letter, esp. one of protest, addressed to an individual but published in a newspaper or magazine for all to read

open market *n* a process by which prices are decided by supply and demand and goods are sold anywhere

open-minded *adj* willing to consider new ideas; unprejudiced

open-mouthed *adj* gaping in surprise

open-plan *adj* having no or few dividing walls between areas: *the house includes an open-plan living room and dining area*

open prison *n* a prison in which the prisoners are not locked up, thus extending the range of work they can do

open secret *n* something that is supposed to be secret but is widely known

open source *n* **1** intellectual property, esp. computer source code, made freely available to the public by its creators ▷ *adj* **open-source** **2** relating to this code: *open-source software*

Open University *n* (in Britain) a university teaching by means of broadcasts, online materials, correspondence courses, and summer schools

open up *vb* **1** to make or become accessible: *the Berlin Wall came down and opened up new territory for dramatists* **2** to speak freely or without self-restraint **3** to start firing a gun or guns **4** *informal* to increase the speed of (a vehicle)

open verdict *n* a finding by a coroner's jury of death, without stating the cause

opera[1] *n* **1** a dramatic work in which most or all of the text is sung to orchestral accompaniment **2** the branch of music or drama relating to operas **3** a group that produces or performs operas **4** a theatre where opera is performed [Latin: work]

opera[2] *n* a plural of **opus**

operable *adj* **1** capable of being treated by a surgical operation **2** capable of being operated or put into practice **operability** *n*

opera glasses *pl n* small low-powered binoculars used by audiences in theatres

opera house *n* a theatre specially designed for the performance of operas

operand *n maths* a quantity, variable, or function upon which an operation is performed

operate *vb* **-ating, -ated 1** to work **2** to control the working of (a machine) **3** to manage, direct, or run (a business or system) **4** to perform a surgical operation (upon a person or animal) **5** to conduct military or naval operations [Latin *operari* to work]

operatic *adj* **1** of or relating to opera **2** overdramatic or exaggerated: *he was about to go out with his operatic strut*

operating system *n* the software controlling a computer

operating theatre *or US* **operating room** *n* a room in which surgical operations are performed

operation *n* **1** the act or method of operating **2** the condition of being in action: *there are 20 teleworking centres in operation around the country* **3** an action or series of actions done to produce a particular result: *a large-scale police operation has been in place to manage the heavy traffic* **4** *surgery* a surgical procedure carried out to remove, replace, or repair a diseased or damaged part of the body **5** a military or naval manoeuvre **6** *maths* any procedure, such as addition, in which a number is derived from another number or numbers by applying specific rules

operational *adj* **1** in working order and ready for use **2** of or relating to an action done to produce a particular result

operations research *n* the analysis of problems in business and industry. Also called: **operational research**

operative (op-rat-tiv) *adj* **1** in force, effect, or operation: *these pension provisions became operative from 1978* **2** (of a word) particularly relevant or significant: *'if' is the operative word* **3** of or relating to a surgical operation ▷ *n* **4** a worker with a special skill

operator *n* **1** a person who operates a machine or instrument, esp. a telephone switchboard **2** a person who runs a business: *your tour operator will arrange a visa for you* **3** *informal* a person who manipulates affairs and other people: *she considered him a shrewd operator who only liked to appear to be simple* **4** *maths* any symbol, term, or letter used to indicate or express a specific operation or process

operculum (oh-**perk**-yew-lum) *n, pl* **-la** (-la) *or* **-lums** a covering flap or lidlike structure in animals or plants [Latin: lid]

operetta *n* a type of comic or light-hearted opera

ophthalmia *n* inflammation of the eyeball or conjunctiva [Greek *ophthalmos* eye]

ophthalmic *adj* of or relating to the eye

ophthalmic optician *n* See **optician** (sense 1)

ophthalmology *n* the branch of medicine concerned with the eye and its diseases **ophthalmologist** *n*

ophthalmoscope *n* an instrument for examining the interior of the eye

opiate (oh-pee-it) *n* **1** a narcotic or sedative drug containing opium **2** something that causes mental dullness or inactivity

opine *vb* **opining, opined** *formal* to hold or express an opinion: *he opined that the navy would have to start again from the beginning* [Latin *opinari*]

opinion *n* **1** belief not founded on certainty or proof but on what seems probable **2** evaluation or estimation of a person or thing: *they seemed to share my high opinion of her* **3** a judgment given by an expert: *medical opinion* **4 a matter of opinion** a point open to question [Latin *opinio* belief]

opinionated *adj* holding very strong opinions which one is convinced are right

opinion poll *n* same as **poll** (sense 1)

opium (oh-pee-um) *n* an addictive narcotic drug made from the seed capsules of the opium poppy and used in medicine as a painkiller and sedative [Latin: poppy juice]

opossum *n, pl* **-sums** *or* **-sum 1** a thick-furred American marsupial, with a long snout and a hairless prehensile tail **2** *Austral & NZ* a similar Australian animal, such as a phalanger [Native American *aposoum*]

opponent *n* a person who opposes another in a contest, battle, or argument [Latin *opponere* to oppose]

opportune *adj formal* **1** happening at a time that is suitable or advantageous: *there was an opportune knock at the door* **2** (of time) suitable for a particular purpose: *I have arrived at a very opportune moment* [Latin *opportunus*, from *ob-* to + *portus* harbour (originally: coming to the harbour, obtaining timely protection)]

opportunist *n* **1** a person who adapts his or her actions to take advantage of opportunities and circumstances without regard for principles ▷ *adj* **2** taking advantage of opportunities and circumstances in this way **opportunism** *n* **opportunistic** *adj*

opportunity *n, pl* **-ties 1** a favourable combination of circumstances **2** a good chance or prospect

opportunity shop *n Austral & NZ* a shop selling second-hand clothes, sometimes for charity. Sometimes shortened to: **op-shop**

opposable *adj zool* (of the thumb) capable of touching the tip of all the other fingers

oppose *vb* **-posing, -posed 1** Also: **be opposed to** to be against (something or someone) in speech or action **2 as opposed to** in strong contrast with: *I'm a realist as opposed to a theorist* [Latin *opponere*] **opposing** *adj*

opposite *adj* **1** situated on the other or further side **2** facing or going in contrary directions: *he saw another small craft heading the opposite way* **3** completely different: *I have a different, in fact, opposite view on this subject* **4** *maths* (of a side in a triangle) facing a specified angle ▷ *n* **5** a person or thing that is opposite; antithesis ▷ *prep* **6** facing; across from ▷ *adv* **7** in an opposite position: *fragments smashed through the windows of the house opposite*

opposite number *n* a person holding an equivalent position in another group or organization: *a ritual exchange of insults with an opposite number*

opposition *n* **1** the act of opposing or being opposed **2** hostility, resistance, or disagreement **3** a person or group antagonistic or opposed to another **4** a political party or group opposed to the ruling party or government **5** *astrol* a

O

diametrically opposite position of two heavenly bodies

oppress *vb* **1** to put down or control by cruelty or force **2** to make anxious or uncomfortable [Latin *ob-* against + *premere* to press] **oppression** *n* **oppressor** *n*

oppressive *adj* **1** cruel, harsh, or tyrannical **2** uncomfortable or depressing: *a small flat can become rather oppressive* **3** (of weather) hot and humid **oppressiveness** *n*

opprobrium (op-**probe**-ree-um) *n formal* **1** the state of being abused or scornfully criticized **2** a cause of disgrace or shame [Latin *ob-* against + *probrum* a shameful act] **opprobrious** *adj*

oppugn (op-**pewn**) *vb formal* to call into question; dispute [Latin *ob-* against + *pugnare* to fight]

op-shop *n Austral & NZ* short for **opportunity shop**

opt *vb* to show preference (for) or choose (to do something) [Latin *optare* to choose]

optic *adj* of the eye or vision [Greek *optos* visible]

optical *adj* **1** of or involving light or optics **2** of the eye or the sense of sight; optic **3** (of a lens) helping vision

optical fibre *n* a thin flexible glass fibre used in fibre optics to transmit information

optician *n* **1** Also called: **ophthalmic optician** a person who is qualified to examine the eyes and prescribe and supply spectacles and contact lenses **2** Also called: **dispensing optician** a person who supplies and fits spectacle frames and lenses, but is not qualified to prescribe lenses

optic nerve *n* a cranial nerve of vertebrates that conducts nerve impulses from the retina of the eye to the brain

O

optics *n* the science dealing with light and vision

optimal *adj* best or most favourable

optimism *n* **1** the tendency to take the most hopeful view in all matters **2** *philosophy* the doctrine of the ultimate triumph of good over evil [Latin *optimus* best] **optimist** *n* **optimistic** *adj* **optimistically** *adv*

optimize *or* **-mise** *vb* **-mizing, -mized** *or* **-mising, -mised** to make the most of

optimum *n, pl* **-ma** *or* **-mums 1** the most favourable conditions or best compromise possible ▷ *adj* **2** most favourable or advantageous; best: *balance is a critical part of an optimum diet* [Latin: the best (thing)]

option *n* **1** the power or liberty to choose: *we have no option other than to fully comply* **2** something that is or may be chosen: *the menu includes a vegetarian option* **3** an exclusive right, usually for a limited period, to buy or sell something at a future date: *a producer could extend his option on the material for another six months* **4 keep** *or* **leave one's options open** not to commit oneself **5 soft option** an easy alternative ▷ *vb* **6** to obtain or grant an option on: *the film rights are optioned by an international film director* [Latin *optare* to choose]

optional *adj* possible but not compulsory; open to choice

optometrist (op-**tom**-met-trist) *n* a person qualified to examine the eyes and prescribe and supply spectacles and contact lenses **optometry** *n*

opt out *vb* **1** (often foll. by *of*) to choose not to be involved (in) or part (of), used esp. of schools and hospitals that leave the public sector ▷ *n* **opt-out 2** the act of opting out, esp. of a local authority administration

opulent (**op**-pew-lent) *adj* **1** having or indicating wealth **2** abundant or plentiful [Latin *opulens*] **opulence** *n*

opus (**oh**-puss) *n, pl* **opuses** *or* **opera** an artistic creation, esp. a musical work by a particular composer, numbered in order of publication: *Beethoven's opus 61* [Latin: a work]

or *conj* **1** used to join alternatives: *do you want to go out or stay at home?* **2** used to join rephrasings of the same thing: *twelve, or a dozen* [Middle English contraction of *other*]

OR Oregon

oracle *n* **1** a shrine in ancient Greece or Rome at which gods were consulted through the medium of a priest or priestess for advice or prophecy **2** a prophecy or statement made by an oracle **3** any person believed to indicate future action with infallible authority [Latin *oraculum*]

oracular *adj* **1** of or like an oracle **2** wise and prophetic **3** mysterious or ambiguous

oral *adj* **1** spoken or verbal; using spoken words **2** of or for use in the mouth: *an oral thermometer* **3** (of a drug) to be taken by mouth: *an oral contraceptive* ▷ *n* **4** an examination in which the questions and answers are spoken rather than written [Latin *os, oris* mouth] **orally** *adv*

orange *n* **1** a round reddish-yellow juicy citrus fruit **2** the evergreen tree on which it grows **3** a colour between red and yellow; the colour of an orange ▷ *adj* **4** of a colour between red and yellow [Arabic *nāranj*]

orangeade *n Brit* a usually fizzy orange-flavoured drink

orange blossom *n* the flowers of the orange tree, traditionally worn by brides

Orangeman *n, pl* **-men** a member of a political society founded in Ireland in 1795 to uphold Protestantism [after William, prince of *Orange*, later William III]

orangery *n, pl* **-eries** a conservatory or greenhouse in which orange trees are grown in cooler climates

orangey *adj* slightly orange

orang-utan *or* **orang-utang** *n* a large ape of the forests of Sumatra and Borneo, with shaggy reddish-brown hair and long arms [Malay *ōrang* man + *hūtan* forest]

oration *n* a formal or ceremonial public speech [Latin *oratio*]

orator (**or**-rat-tor) *n* a person who gives an oration, esp. one skilled in persuasive public speaking

oratorio (or-rat-**tor**-ee-oh) *n, pl* **-rios** a musical composition for soloists, chorus, and orchestra, based on a religious theme [Italian]

oratory[1] (**or**-rat-tree) *n* the art or skill of public speaking [Latin *(ars) oratoria* (the art of) public speaking]

oratory[2] *n, pl* **-ries** a small room or building set apart for private prayer [Latin *orare* to pray]

orb *n* **1** an ornamental sphere with a cross on top, carried by a king or queen in important ceremonies

2 a sphere; globe **3** *poetic* the eye **4** *obsolete or poetic* a heavenly body, such as the sun [Latin *orbis* circle, disc]

orbit *n* **1** the curved path followed by something, such as a heavenly body or spacecraft, in its motion around another body **2** a range or sphere of action or influence **3** *anatomy* the eye socket ▹ *vb* **-biting, -bited 4** to move around (a heavenly body) in an orbit **5** to send (a satellite or spacecraft) into orbit [Latin *orbis* circle] **orbital** *adj*

Orcadian *n* **1** a person from Orkney ▹ *adj* **2** of Orkney [Latin *Orcades* the Orkney Islands]

orchard *n* an area of land on which fruit trees are grown [Old English *orceard*]

orchestra *n* **1** a large group of musicians whose members play a variety of different instruments **2** Also called: **orchestra pit** the space, in front of or under the stage, reserved for musicians in a theatre [Greek: the space in the theatre for the chorus] **orchestral** *adj*

orchestrate *vb* **-trating, -trated 1** to score or arrange (a piece of music) for orchestra **2** to arrange (something) in order to produce a particular result: *he had orchestrated today's meeting* **orchestration** *n*

orchid *n* a plant having flowers of unusual shapes and beautiful colours, usually with one lip-shaped petal which is larger than the other two [Greek *orkhis* testicle, because of the shape of its roots]

ordain *vb* **1** to make (someone) a member of the clergy **2** *formal* to decree or order with authority [Late Latin *ordinare*] **ordainment** *n*

ordeal *n* **1** a severe or trying experience **2** *history* a method of trial in which the accused person was subjected to physical danger [Old English *ordāl*, *ordēl* verdict]

order *n* **1** an instruction that must be obeyed; command **2** a state in which everything is arranged logically, comprehensibly, or naturally: *she strove to keep more order in the house* **3** an arrangement of things in succession; sequence: *group them by letter and then put them in numerical order* **4** an established or customary system of society: *there is an opportunity here for a new world order* **5** a peaceful or harmonious condition of society: *riot police were called in to restore order* **6 A** an instruction to supply something in return for payment: *the waitress came to take their order* **B** the thing or things supplied **7** a written instruction to pay money: *post the coupon below with a cheque or postal order* **8** a social class: *the result will be harmful to society as a whole and to the lower orders in particular* **9** *biol* one of the groups into which a class is divided, containing one or more families **10** kind or sort: *the orchestra played superbly and the singing was of the highest order* **11** Also called: **religious order** a religious community of monks or nuns **12** a group of people who have been awarded a particular honour: *the Order of the Garter* **13** the office or rank of a Christian minister: *he studied for the priesthood as a young man, but never took Holy Orders* **14** the procedure and rules followed by an assembly or meeting: *a point of order* **15** one of the five major classical styles of architecture, classified by the type of columns used **16 a tall order** something difficult or demanding **17 in order A** in sequence **B** properly arranged: *everything is in order for your trip* **C** appropriate or fitting **18 in order that** so that **19 in order to** so that it is possible to: *a healthy diet is necessary in order to keep fit* **20 in** *or* **of the order of** amounting approximately to: *summer temperatures are usually in the order of 35°* **21 keep order** to ensure that people obey the law or behave in an acceptable manner **22 on order** having been ordered but not yet delivered **23 out of order A** not in sequence **B** not working: *the lift was out of order, so we had to use the stairs* **C** not following the rules or customary procedure: *the chairperson ruled the motion out of order* **24 to order** according to a buyer's specifications ▹ *vb* **25** to command or instruct (to do something): *she ordered her son to wash the dishes; the police ordered her into the house* **26** to request (something) to be supplied in return for payment: *I ordered a new car three weeks ago, but it hasn't been delivered yet* **27** to arrange (things) methodically or in their proper places ▹ *interj* **28** an exclamation demanding that orderly behaviour be restored [Latin *ordo*]

order around *or* **order about** *vb* to repeatedly tell (someone) what to do in a bossy or unsympathetic way: *it was intolerable that those two could order her around*

orderly *adj* **1** tidy or well-organized: *they evacuated the building in an orderly manner* **2** well-behaved; law-abiding ▹ *n, pl* **-lies 3** *med* a male hospital attendant **4** *military* a soldier whose duty is to carry out orders or perform minor tasks for a more senior officer **orderliness** *n*

Order of Merit *n Brit* an order awarded for outstanding achievement in any field

order paper *n* (in Britain) a list indicating the order of business, esp. in Parliament

ordinal number *n* a number indicating position in a sequence, such as *first, second, third*

ordinance *n* an official rule or order [Latin *ordinare* to set in order]

ordinarily *adv* in ordinary or usual practice; usually; normally

ordinary *adj* **1** usual or normal: *it was an ordinary working day for them* **2** not special or different in any way: *her campaign speech dwells on the problems faced by ordinary Americans* **3** dull or unexciting: *the restaurant charged very high prices for very ordinary cooking* ▹ *n, pl* **-naries 4** *RC Church* the parts of the Mass that do not vary from day to day **5 out of the ordinary** unusual [Latin *ordinarius* orderly]

Ordinary level *n* (in Britain) the formal name for **O level**

ordinary rating *n* a rank in the Royal Navy equivalent to that of a private in the army

ordinary seaman *n Brit, Austral & NZ* a seaman of the lowest rank

ordinary shares *pl n Brit & Austral* shares issued by a company entitling their holders to a dividend according to the profits of the company and to a claim on net assets

ordinate *n maths* the vertical coordinate of a point in a two-dimensional system of coordinates [Latin *ordinare* to arrange in order]

ordination *n* the act or ceremony of making someone a member of the clergy

ordnance *n* **1** weapons and other military supplies **2 the ordnance** a government department dealing with military supplies [variant of *ordinance*]

Ordnance Survey *n* the British government organization that produces detailed maps of Britain and Ireland

Ordovician (or-doe-**vish**-ee-an) *adj geol* of the period of geological time about 500 million years ago [Latin *Ordovices*, ancient Celtic tribe in N Wales]

ordure *n* excrement; dung [Old French *ord* dirty]

ore *n* rock or mineral from which valuable substances such as metals can be extracted [Old English *ār*, *ōra*]

oregano (or-rig-**gah**-no) *n* a sweet-smelling herb used as seasoning [Greek *origanon* an aromatic herb]

organ *n* **1** a part in animals and plants that is adapted to perform a particular function, for example the heart or lungs **2 A** a musical keyboard instrument which produces sound by forcing air through pipes of a variety of lengths **B** Also called: **electric organ** a keyboard instrument which produces similar sounds electronically **3** a means of communication, such as a newspaper issued by a specialist group or party **4** *euphemistic* a penis [Greek *organon* tool]

organdie *n* a fine, slightly stiff cotton fabric [French *organdi*]

organ-grinder *n* (formerly) an entertainer who played a barrel organ in the streets

organic *adj* **1** of, produced by, or found in plants or animals: *the rocks were carefully searched for organic remains* **2** not using, or grown without, artificial fertilizers or pesticides: *organic vegetables; an organic farm* **3** *chem* of or belonging to the class of chemical compounds that are formed from carbon **4** (of change or development) gradual and natural rather than sudden or forced **5** made up of many different parts which contribute to the way in which the whole society or structure works: *an organic whole* **organically** *adv*

organic chemistry *n chem* the branch of chemistry dealing with carbon compounds

organism *n* **1** an animal or plant **2** anything resembling a living creature in structure, behaviour, or complexity: *cities are more complicated organisms than farming villages*

organist *n* a person who plays the organ

organization *or* **-nisation** *n* **1** an organized group of people, such as a club, society, union, or business **2** the act of organizing: *setting up the European tour took a lot of organization* **3** the structure and arrangement of the different parts of something: *the report recommended radical changes in the organization of the social services department* **4** the state of being organized: *the material in this essay lacks any sort of organization* **organizational** *or* **-isational** *adj*

organize *or* **-nise** *vb* **-nizing, -nized** *or* **-nising, -nised 1** to plan and arrange (something): *we organized a protest meeting in the village hall* **2** to arrange systematically: *the files are organized in alphabetical order and by date* **3** to form, join, or recruit (people) into a trade union: *the seasonal nature of tourism makes it difficult for hotel workers to organize* [Medieval Latin *organizare*] **organizer** *or* **-niser** *n*

organized *or* **-nised** *adj* **1** planned and controlled on a large scale and involving many people: *organized crime* **2** orderly and efficient: *a highly organized campaign* **3** (of the workers in a factory or office) belonging to a trade union: *socialism is especially popular among organized labour*

organza *n* a thin stiff fabric of silk, cotton, or synthetic fibre [origin unknown]

orgasm *n* the most intense point of pleasure and excitement during sexual activity [Greek *orgasmos*] **orgasmic** *adj*

orgy *n, pl* **-gies 1** a wild party involving promiscuous sexual activity and excessive drinking **2** an act of immoderate or frenzied indulgence: *the rioters were engaged in an orgy of destruction* [Greek *orgia* secret rites] **orgiastic** *adj*

oriel window *or* **oriel** *n* a window built out from the wall of a house at an upper level [Old French *oriol* gallery]

orient *vb* **1** to position or set (for example, a map or chart) with relation to the points of the compass or other specific directions **2 orient oneself** to adjust or align oneself or one's ideas according to new surroundings or circumstances: *new employees can take some time to orient themselves to the company's procedures* **3 be oriented to** *or* **towards** to work or act with a particular aim, idea, or person in mind: *training programmes that are oriented towards older people* ▷ *n* **4** *poetic* the east [Latin *oriens* rising (sun)]

Orient *n* **the Orient** *old-fashioned* East Asia

oriental *adj* eastern

Oriental *adj* **1** *old-fashioned* of East Asia ▷ *n* **2** *offensive* a person from East Asia

orientate *vb* **-tating, -tated** same as **orient**

-orientated *or* **-oriented** *combining form* interested in or directed towards the thing specified: *career-orientated people*

orientation *n* **1** the activities and aims that a person or organization is interested in: *the course has a practical rather than theoretical orientation* **2** the position of an object with relation to the points of the compass or other specific directions: *the room's southerly orientation means that it receives a lot of light* ▷ *adj* **3** of or providing information or training needed to understand a new situation or environment: *nearly every college has an orientation programme*

orienteering *n* a sport in which contestants race on foot over a cross-country course consisting of checkpoints found with the aid of a map and compass [Swedish *orientering*]

orifice (or-rif-fiss) *n* an opening or hole through which something can pass, esp. one in the body such as the mouth or anus [Latin *os* mouth + *facere* to make]

orig. **1** origin **2** original(ly)

origami (or-rig-**gah**-mee) *n* the art, originally Japanese, of folding paper intricately into decorative shapes [Japanese *ori* a fold + *kami* paper]

origin *n* **1** the point, source, or event from which something develops: *the origin of the term 'jazz' is obscure; the war had its origin in the clash between rival*

O

nationalists **2** the country, race, or social class of a person's parents or ancestors: *an Australian of Greek origin; he was proud of his working-class origins* **3** *maths* the point at which the horizontal and vertical axes intersect [Latin *origo* beginning]

original *adj* **1** first or earliest: *the dining room also has attractive original beams* **2** fresh and unusual; not copied from or based on something else: *the composer's work has created some original and attractive choreography* **3** able to think of or carry out new ideas or concepts: *he is an excitingly original writer* **4** being the first and genuine form of something, from which a copy or translation is made: *all French recipes were translated from the original abridged versions* ▷ *n* **5** the first and genuine form of something, from which others are copied or translated: *the original is in the British Museum* **6** a person or thing used as a model in art or literature: *she claimed to be the original on whom Lawrence based Lady Chatterley* **originality** *n* **originally** *adv*

original sin *n* a state of sin believed by some Christians to be inborn in all human beings as a result of Adam's disobedience

originate *vb* **-nating, -nated** to come or bring (something) into existence: *humans probably originated in East Africa* **origination** *n* **originator** *n*

oriole *n* a songbird with a long pointed bill and a mostly yellow-and-black plumage [Latin *aureolus* golden]

ormolu *n* a gold-coloured alloy of copper, tin, or zinc, used to decorate furniture and other articles [French *or moulu* ground gold]

ornament *n* **1** anything that adorns someone or something; decoration: *the room's only ornament was a dim, oily picture of the Holy Family* **2** decorations collectively: *he had no watch, nor ornament of any kind* **3** a small decorative object: *I hit a garden ornament while parking* **4** a person whose character or talent makes them an asset to society or the group to which they belong: *an ornament of the firm* **5** *music* a note or group of notes which embellishes the melody but is not an integral part of it, for instance a trill ▷ *vb* **6** to decorate or adorn: *the hall had a high ceiling, ornamented with plaster fruits and flowers* [Latin *ornamentum*] **ornamental** *adj* **ornamentation** *n* **ornamented** *adj*

ornate *adj* **1** heavily or elaborately decorated: *an ornate ceiling painted with allegorical figures* **2** (of style in writing) overelaborate; using many literary expressions [Latin *ornare* to decorate] **ornately** *adv*

ornithology *n* the study of birds [Greek *ornis* bird] **ornithological** *adj* **ornithologist** *n*

orotund *adj* **1** (of the voice) resonant and booming **2** (of speech or writing) pompous; containing many long or formal words [Latin *ore rotundo* with rounded mouth]

orphan *n* **1** a child whose parents are dead ▷ *vb* **2** to cause (someone) to become an orphan: *she was orphaned at 16 when her parents died in a car crash* [Greek *orphanos*]

orphanage *n* a children's home for orphans and abandoned children

orphaned *adj* having no living parents

orrery *n, pl* **-ries** a mechanical model of the solar system in which the planets can be moved around the sun [originally made for the Earl of *Orrery*]

orris *n* **1** a kind of iris that has fragrant roots **2** Also: **orrisroot** the root of this plant prepared and used as perfume [variant of *iris*]

orthodontics *n* the branch of dentistry concerned with correcting irregularities of the teeth [Greek *orthos* straight + *odōn* tooth] **orthodontic** *adj* **orthodontist** *n*

orthodox *adj* conforming to traditional or established standards in religion, behaviour, or attitudes: *orthodox medicine; the concerto has a more orthodox structure than is usual for this composer* [Greek *orthos* correct + *doxa* belief] **orthodoxy** *n*

Orthodox *adj* **1** of the Orthodox Church of Eastern Europe **2** of or being the form of Judaism characterized by traditional interpretation of and strict adherence to Mosaic Law: *an Orthodox Jew*

Orthodox Church *n* the Christian Church dominant in Greece, Russia, and some Eastern European countries, which has the Greek Patriarch of Constantinople as its head

orthography *n* **1** spelling considered to be correct: *British and American orthography is different in many cases* **2** the study of spelling [Greek *orthos* correct + *graphein* to write] **orthographic** *adj*

orthopaedics *or US* **orthopedics** *n* the branch of surgery concerned with disorders of the bones and joints [Greek *orthos* straight + *pais* child] **orthopaedic** *or US* **orthopedic** *adj* **orthopaedist** *or US* **orthopedist** *n*

ortolan *n* a small European songbird, formerly eaten as a delicacy [Latin *hortulus* a little garden]

oryx *n* any of various large straight-horned African antelopes

Os *chem* osmium

OS **1** (in Britain) Ordnance Survey **2** outsize(d)

Oscar *n* an award in the form of a small gold statuette awarded annually in the US for outstanding achievements in various aspects of the film industry: *he won an Oscar for Best Supporting Actor in 1974* [said to have been named after a remark made by an official that it reminded her of her uncle Oscar]

oscillate (oss-ill-late) *vb* **-lating, -lated** **1** to swing repeatedly back and forth: *its wings oscillate up and down many times a second* **2** to waver between two extremes of opinion, attitude, or behaviour: *the government oscillates between a desire for reform and a desire to keep its powers intact* **3** *physics* (of an electric current) to vary between minimum and maximum values [Latin *oscillare* to swing] **oscillation** *n* **oscillator** *n*

oscilloscope (oss-sill-oh-scope) *n* an instrument that produces a visual representation of an oscillating electric current on the screen of a cathode-ray tube

osier (oh-zee-er) *n* **1** a willow tree whose flexible branches or twigs are used for making baskets and furniture **2** a twig or branch from this tree [Old French]

Osiris *n* an Egyptian god of the underworld

osmium *n* *chem* a very hard brittle bluish-white metal, the heaviest known element. Symbol: **Os** [Greek *osmē* smell, from its penetrating odour]

osmoregulation *n* *zool* the adjustment of the osmotic pressure of a cell or organism in relation to the surrounding fluid

osmosis *n* **1** the diffusion of liquids through a membrane until they are mixed **2** the process by which people or ideas influence each other gradually and subtly [Greek *ōsmos* push] **osmotic** *adj*

osprey *n* a large fish-eating bird of prey, with a dark back and whitish head and underparts [Old French *ospres*, apparently from Latin *ossifraga*, literally: bone-breaker]

osseous *adj* consisting of or like bone [Latin *os* bone]

ossify *vb* **-fies, -fying, -fied 1** to change into bone; harden **2** to become rigid, inflexible, or unprogressive: *ossified traditions* [Latin *os* bone + *facere* to make] **ossification** *n*

ostensible *adj* apparent or seeming; alleged: *our ostensible common interest is boats* [Latin *ostendere* to show] **ostensibly** *adv*

ostensive *adj* directly showing or pointing out: *he gave ostensive definitions to things* [Latin *ostendere* to show]

ostentation *n* pretentious, showy, or vulgar display: *she felt the gold taps in the bathroom were tasteless ostentation* **ostentatious** *adj* **ostentatiously** *adv*

osteoarthritis (ost-ee-oh-arth-rite-iss) *n* chronic inflammation of the joints, causing pain and stiffness [Greek *osteon* bone + ARTHRITIS] **osteoarthritic** *adj*

osteopathy *n* a system of healing based on the manipulation of bones or muscle [Greek *osteon* bone + *patheia* suffering] **osteopath** *n*

osteoporosis (ost-ee-oh-pore-**oh**-siss) *n* brittleness of the bones, caused by lack of calcium [Greek *osteon* bone + *poros* passage]

ostinato *n, pl* **-tos** *music* a persistently repeated phrase or rhythm [Italian, from Latin *obstinatus* obstinate]

ostler *n* (formerly) a stableman at an inn [variant of *hostler*, from *hostel*]

ostracize *or* **-cise** *vb* **-cizing, -cized** *or* **-cising, -cised** to exclude or banish (a person) from a particular group or from society: *he was ostracized from his family when his affair became known* [Greek *ostrakizein* to select someone for banishment by voting on potsherds] **ostracism** *n*

ostrich *n* **1** a large African bird which runs fast but cannot fly, and has a long neck, long legs, and soft dark feathers **2** a person who refuses to recognize an unpleasant truth: *he accused the Minister of being 'an ostrich with its head stuck in the sand, while all around him unemployment soars'* [Greek *strouthion*]

OT Old Testament

OTC (in Britain) Officers' Training Corps

OTE *chiefly Brit* (esp. in job adverts) on-target earnings: the minimum amount of money a salesperson is expected to make

other *adj* **1** remaining (one or ones) in a group of which one or some have been specified: *she wasn't getting on with the other children* **2** being a different one or ones from the one or ones already specified or understood: *other people might not be so tolerant of your behaviour; are you sure it's not in your other pocket?* **3** refers to a place or time which is not the one the speaker or writer is in: *results in other countries have been most encouraging* **4** additional; further: *there is one other thing for the government to do* **5 every other** every alternate: *the doctor sees me every other week* **6 other than A** apart from: *he knew little of the country other than it was Muslim* **B** different from: *treatment other than a hearing aid will be possible for those with inner ear deafness* **7 or other** used to add vagueness to the preceding word or phrase: *she could take some evening course or other which could lead to an extra qualification; he was called away from the house on some pretext or other* **8 the other day** a few days ago ▹ *n* **9** an additional person or thing: *show me one other* **10 others** people apart from the person who is being spoken or written about: *she devoted her entire life to helping others* **11 the others** the people or things remaining in a group of which one or some have been specified: *I can't speak for the others* ▹ *adv* **12** otherwise; differently: *they couldn't behave other than they do* [Old English *ōther*] **otherness** *n*

USAGE See at **otherwise**.

other ranks *pl n Brit & Austral* (in the armed forces) all those who do not hold a commissioned rank

otherwise *conj* **1** or else; if not, then: *you need to leave by ten o'clock, otherwise you'll be late* ▹ *adv* **2** differently: *it was fruitless to pretend or to hope otherwise* **3** in other respects: *shrewd psychological twists perk up an otherwise predictable storyline* ▹ *adj* **4** different: *circumstances beyond our control dictated that it should be otherwise* ▹ *pron* **5 or otherwise** or not; or the opposite: *he didn't want company, talkative or otherwise*

USAGE The expression *otherwise than* means *in any other way than* and should not be followed by an adjective: *no-one taught by this method can be other than* (not *otherwise than*) *successful; you are not allowed to use the building otherwise than as a private dwelling.*

otherworldly *adj* **1** concerned with spiritual rather than practical matters: *his otherworldly manner concealed a ruthless business mind* **2** mystical or supernatural: *this part of Italy has an otherworldly beauty*

otiose (oh-tee-oze) *adj* serving no useful purpose: *such a strike is almost otiose* [Latin *otiosus* leisured]

OTT *slang* over the top

otter *n* a small freshwater fish-eating animal with smooth brown fur, a streamlined body, and webbed feet [Old English *otor*]

ottoman *n, pl* **-mans** a storage chest with a padded lid for use as a seat [French *ottomane*, feminine of *Ottoman*]

Ottoman *adj* **1** *history* of the Ottomans or the Ottoman Empire, the Turkish empire which lasted from the late 13th century until the end of World War I, and at its height included the Balkans and much of N Africa ▹ *n, pl* **-mans 2** a member of a Turkish people who formed the basis of this empire [Arabic *Othmānī*]

ou (oh) *n S African slang* a man, bloke, or chap [Afrikaans]

OU 1 the Open University **2** Oxford University

oubaas (oh-bahss) *n S African* a man in authority [Afrikaans *ou* man + *baas* boss]

oubliette (oo-blee-ett) *n history* a dungeon, the only entrance to which is a trapdoor in the ceiling [French *oublier* to forget]

ouch *interj* an exclamation of sharp sudden pain
ought *vb* **1** used to express duty or obligation: *she ought to tell this to the police* **2** used to express advisability: *we ought to get the roof repaired before the attics get any damper* **3** used to express probability or expectation: *a good lawyer ought to be able to fix it for you* **4** used to express a desire on the part of the speaker: *you ought to have a good breakfast before you hit the road* [Old English *āhte*, past tense of *āgan* to owe]

> **USAGE** In correct English, *ought* is not used with *did* or *had*. *I ought not to do it*, not *I didn't ought to do it*; *I ought not to have done it*, not *I hadn't ought to have done it*.

oughtn't ought not
Ouija board *or* **Ouija** (**weej**-a) *n trademark* a board on which are marked the letters of the alphabet. Answers to questions are spelt out by a pointer, which is supposedly guided by spirits [French *oui* yes + German *ja* yes]
ouma (**oh**-mah) *n S African* **1** grandmother, often as a title with a surname **2** *slang* any elderly woman [Afrikaans]
ounce *n* **1** a unit of weight equal to one sixteenth of a pound or 28.4 grams **2** short for **fluid ounce** **3** a small amount: *you haven't got one ounce of control over her* [Latin *uncia* a twelfth]
oupa (**oh**-pah) *n S African* **1** grandfather, often as a title with a surname **2** *slang* any elderly man [Afrikaans]
our *adj* **1** of, belonging to, or associated with us: *our daughter* **2** a formal word for *my* used by monarchs [Old English *ūre*]
Our Father *n* same as the **Lord's Prayer**
ours *pron* **1** something belonging to us: *our son has blue eyes while ours are brown; the money is ours* **2 of ours** belonging to or associated with us: *my wife and a friend of ours had both deserted me*
ourself *pron archaic* a formal word for *myself* used by monarchs
ourselves *pron* **1 A** the reflexive form of *we* or *us*: *we humiliated ourselves* **B** used for emphasis: *we ourselves will finish it* **2** our usual selves: *we've not been feeling quite ourselves since the accident* **3** *not standard* used instead of *we* or *us* in compound noun phrases: *other people and ourselves*
ousel *n* same as **ouzel**
oust *vb* to force (someone) out of a position; expel: *the coup which ousted the President* [Anglo-Norman *ouster*]
ouster *n US* an act or instance of forcing someone out of a position: *the demonstrators called for the ouster of the police chief*
out *adv, adj* **1** away from the inside of a place: *she took her purse out; inspection of the eggs should be done when the hen is out of the nest* **2** away from one's home or place of work for a short time: *I called earlier but you were out; a search party is out looking for survivors* **3** no longer burning, shining, or functioning: *he switched the light out; the living-room fire went out while we were next door eating* **4** used up; not having any more of: *their supplies ran out after two weeks; we're out of milk* **5** public; revealed: *our dirty little secret is out* **6** available to the public: *her biography will be out in December* **7** (of the sun, stars, or moon) visible **8** in bloom: *the roses are out early this year* **9** not in fashion or current usage: *'skinny' is out* **10** excluded from consideration: *pricey ski holidays are out* **11** not allowed: *smoking on duty is out* **12 out for** *or* **to** wanting or intent on (something or doing something): *the young soldiers were out for revenge; they're out to get me* **13** *sport* (of a player in a sport like cricket or baseball) no longer batting because he or she has been dismissed by being caught, bowled, etc. **14** on strike **15** in or into a state of unconsciousness: *he went outside and passed out in an alley* **16** used to indicate a burst of activity as indicated by a verb: *war broke out in the Gulf* **17** out of existence: *the mistakes were scored out* **18** to the fullest extent: *spread out* **19** loudly; clearly: *he cried out in shock and pain* **20** to a conclusion; completely: *she'd worked it out for herself* **21** existing: *the friendliest dog out* **22** inaccurate or incorrect: *the estimate was out by £60* **23** not in office or authority: *she was finally voted out as party leader* **24** (of a period of time) completed: *before the year is out* **25** having made it known that one is not heterosexual: *I came out as a lesbian when I was still in my teens* **26** *old-fashioned* (of a young woman) in or into upper-class society life: *Lucinda had a large party when she came out* **27 out of A** at or to a point outside: *the train pulled out of the station* **B** away from; not in: *they're out of touch with reality; out of focus* **C** because of; motivated by: *out of jealousy* **D** from (a material or source): *made out of plastic* **E** no longer in a specified state or condition: *out of work; out of practice* ▷ *adj* **28** *informal* not concealing one's homosexuality ▷ *prep* **29** *US or not standard* out of; out through: *he ran out the door* ▷ *interj* **30 A** an exclamation of dismissal **B** (in signalling and radio) an expression used to signal that the speaker is signing off: *over and out!* ▷ *vb informal* **31** to name (a person, esp. a public figure) as being not heterosexual, often against their will **32** to reveal something embarrassing or unknown about (a person): *he was outed as a talented goal scorer* [Old English *ūt*]

> **USAGE** The use of *out* as a preposition, though common in American English, is regarded as incorrect in standard British English: *he climbed out of* (not *out*) *a window; he went out through* (not *out*) *the door*.

out- *prefix* **1** excelling or surpassing in a particular action: *outlast; outlive* **2** at or from a point away, outside: *outpost; outpatient* **3** going away, outward: *outcrop; outgrowth*
outage *n* a period of power failure
out and about *adj* regularly going out of the house to work, take part in social activity, etc., esp. after an illness
out-and-out *adj* absolute; thorough: *it's an out-and-out lie*
outback *n* the remote bush country of Australia
outbid *vb* **-bidding, -bidded** *or* **-bid** to offer a higher price than (another person)
outboard motor *n* a portable petrol engine that can be attached externally to the stern of a boat to propel it
outbox *n* a folder in a computer mailbox in which outgoing messages are stored
outbreak *n* a sudden occurrence of disease or war
outbuilding *n* same as **outhouse**

outburst *n* **1** a sudden strong expression of emotion, esp. of anger: *such emotional outbursts do nothing to help calm discussion of the matter* **2** a sudden period of violent activity: *this sudden outburst of violence has come as a shock*
outcast *n* a person who is rejected or excluded from a particular group or from society
outclass *vb* to surpass (someone) in performance or quality
outcome *n* the result or consequence of something
outcrop *n* part of a rock formation that sticks out of the earth
outcry *n, pl* **-cries** a widespread or vehement protest: *there was great popular outcry against the plan for a dual carriageway*
outdated *adj* old-fashioned or obsolete
outdistance *vb* **-tancing, -tanced 1** to surpass (someone) in a particular activity **2** to leave (other competitors) behind in a race
outdo *vb* **-does, -doing, -did, -done** to be more successful or better than (someone or something) in performance: *this car easily outdoes its rivals when it comes to comfort*
outdoor *adj* **1** taking place, existing, or intended for use in the open air: *have a swim at the beach or outdoor pool; she was just taking off her outdoor clothing* **2** fond of the outdoors: *Paul was a butch outdoor type*
outdoors *adv* **1** in the open air; outside: *he hardly ever went outdoors* ▷ *n* **2** the world outside or far away from buildings; the open air: *he'd forgotten his fear of the outdoors*
outer *adj* **1** on the outside; external: *the building's outer walls were painted pale pink* **2** further from the middle: *the outer suburbs* ▷ *n* **3** *archery* **A** the white outermost ring on a target **B** a shot that hits this ring
outermost *adj* furthest from the centre or middle
outer space *n* space beyond the atmosphere of the earth
outface *vb* **-facing, -faced** to subdue or disconcert (someone) by staring
outfall *n Brit, Austral & NZ* the mouth of a river, drain, or pipe: *the survey measured pollution levels near sewer outfalls*
outfield *n* **1** *cricket* the area of the field far from the pitch **2** *baseball* the area of the playing field beyond the lines connecting first, second, and third bases **outfielder** *n*
outfit *n* **1** a set of clothes worn together **2** *informal* a group of people working together as a unit **3** a set of equipment for a particular task; kit: *a complete anti-snakebite outfit*
outfitter *n old-fashioned* a shop or person that sells men's clothes
outflank *vb* **1** to go around and beyond the side of (an enemy army) **2** to get the better of (someone)
outflow *n* **1** anything that flows out, such as liquid or money **2** the amount that flows out
outfox *vb* to defeat or foil (someone) by being more cunning; outsmart
outgoing *adj* **1** leaving: *some members of the outgoing government continued to attend the peace talks* **2** friendly and sociable
outgoings *pl n* expenses
outgrow *vb* **-growing, -grew, -grown 1** to grow too large for (clothes or shoes): *it's amazing how quickly children outgrow their clothes* **2** to lose (a way of behaving or thinking) in the course of becoming more mature: *most teenagers outgrow their moodiness as they near adulthood* **3** to grow larger or faster than (someone or something): *the weeds threatened to outgrow and choke the rice plants*
outgrowth *n* **1** a natural development or consequence: *he argued that religion was an outgrowth of magic* **2** a thing growing out of a main body; offshoot
outhouse *n* a building near to, but separate from, a main building
outing *n* **1** a trip or excursion **2** *informal* the naming of people as being not heterosexual, often against their will
outlandish *adj* extremely unconventional; bizarre
outlast *vb* to last longer than
outlaw *n* **1** *history* a criminal who has been deprived of legal protection and rights ▷ *vb* **2** to make (something) illegal: *racial discrimination was formally outlawed* **3** *history* to make (someone) an outlaw **outlawed** *adj*
outlay *n* the money, effort, or time spent on something
outlet *n* **1** a means of expressing one's feelings: *the shock would give her an outlet for her own grief* **2** **A** a market for a product: *there is a huge sales outlet for personal computers* **B** a shop or organization selling the goods of a particular producer or wholesaler or manufacturer: *her own brand is now sold to outlets throughout the world* **3** an opening permitting escape or release: *make sure the exhaust outlet is not blocked*
outline *n* **1** a general explanation or description of something, which does not give all the details: *the course gave a brief outline of twentieth-century music* **2** **outlines** the important features of something: *the outlines of his theory are correct, we just need to fill in the details* **3** the general shape of something, esp. when only the profile and not the details are visible: *it was still light enough to see the outline of the distant mountains* **4** a drawing showing only the external lines of an object ▷ *vb* **-lining, -lined** **5** to give the main features or general idea of (something): *I outlined what we had done and what we had still to do* **6** to show the general shape of an object but not its details, as light does coming from behind an object: *we could see the towers of the city outlined against the night sky*
outlive *vb* **-living, -lived 1** to live longer than (someone): *she only outlived her husband by a few months* **2** to live beyond (a date or period): *the sparrow outlived the winter* **3** **outlive its usefulness** to be no longer useful or necessary: *some argued that the organization had outlived its usefulness*
outlook *n* **1** a general attitude to life: *my whole outlook on life had changed* **2** the probable condition or outcome of something: *the economic outlook is not good* **3** the weather forecast for the next few days: *the outlook for the weekend* **4** the view from a place: *a dreary outlook of chimneys and smoke*
outlying *adj* far away from the main area
outmanoeuvre *or US* **outmaneuver** *vb* **-vring, -vred** *or* **-vering, -vered** to gain an advantage over (someone) by skilful dealing: *the management outmanoeuvred us into accepting redundancies*

O

outmatch *vb* to surpass or outdo (someone)
outmoded *adj* no longer fashionable or accepted
outnumber *vb* to exceed in number: *they were outnumbered by fifty to one*
out of bounds *adj, adv* **1** (often foll. by *to*) not to be entered (by): *the area has been out of bounds to foreign journalists and closed to tourists* **2** (in a sport such as golf) outside the boundaries of the course or playing area
out-of-date *adj, adv* old-fashioned; outmoded
out of doors *adv* in the open air; outside
out of pocket *adj* having lost or spent money: *I was £10 out of pocket after paying for their drinks*
out-of-the-way *adj* remote and isolated: *an out-of-the-way village in the Bavarian Forest*
out-of-work *adj* unemployed: *an out-of-work engineer*
outpace *vb* **-pacing, -paced 1** to go faster than (someone) **2** to surpass or outdo (someone or something) in growth, development, etc.: *the increase in the number of households is outpacing the number of houses being built*
outpatient *n* a patient who visits a hospital for treatment but does not stay there overnight
outport *n Canad* an isolated fishing village, esp. in Newfoundland
outpost *n* a small settlement in a distant part of the country or in a foreign country, which is used for military or trading purposes
outpouring *n* **1** a great amount of something that is produced very rapidly: *a prolific outpouring of ideas and energy* **2** a passionate outburst: *the hysterical outpourings of fanatics*
output *n* **1** the amount of something that is made or produced: *our weekly output has increased by 240 tonnes* **2** *electronics* the power, voltage, or current delivered by a circuit or component **3** *computers* the information produced by a computer ▷ *vb* **-putting, -putted** *or* **-put 4** *computers* to produce (data) at the end of a process
outrage *n* **1** deep indignation, anger, or resentment: *she felt a sense of outrage that he should abandon her like that* **2** an extremely vicious or cruel act; gross violation of decency, morality, or honour: *there have been reports of another bombing outrage in the capital* ▷ *vb* **-raging, -raged 3** to cause deep indignation, anger, or resentment in (someone): *they were outraged by the news of the assassination* [French *outré* beyond]
outrageous *adj* **1** unusual and shocking: *his sense of humour made him say and do the most outrageous things* **2** shocking and socially or morally unacceptable: *I will fight these outrageous accusations of corruption in the courts if necessary* **outrageously** *adv*
outrank *vb* to be of higher rank than (someone)
outré (oo-tray) *adj* eccentric and rather shocking [French: having gone beyond]
outrider *n* a person who rides a motorcycle or horse in front of or beside an official vehicle as an attendant or guard
outrigger *n* **1** a stabilizing framework projecting from the side of a boat or canoe **2** a boat or canoe equipped with such a framework
outright *adj* **1** complete; total: *he is close to an outright victory* **2** straightforward and direct: *outright hostility* ▷ *adv* **3** completely: *the film was banned outright* **4** instantly: *my driver was killed outright* **5** openly: *ask her outright why she treated you as she did*
outrun *vb* **-running, -ran, -run 1** to run faster or further than (someone) **2** to develop faster than (something): *the population of the city is in danger of outrunning the supply of houses*
outsell *vb* **-selling, -sold** to be sold in greater quantities than: *her last novel outsold all last year's Booker shortlist put together*
outset *n* a start; beginning: *we never really hit it off from the outset*
outshine *vb* **-shining, -shone** to be better than (someone) at something: *by university she had begun to outshine me in sports*
outside *prep* **1** on or to the exterior of: *a crowd gathered outside the court* **2** beyond the limits of: *it was outside my experience and beyond my ability* **3** apart from; other than: *no-one knows outside us* ▷ *adj* **4** on or of the outside: *an outside light is also a good idea* **5** remote; unlikely: *I still had an outside chance of the title* **6** coming from outside a particular group or organization: *the patient had been subjected to outside influences* **7** of or being the lane in a road which is further from the side than other lanes going in the same direction: *he was doing 120 in the outside lane* ▷ *adv* **8** outside a thing or place; out of doors: *we went outside to get some fresh air* **9** *slang* not in prison ▷ *n* **10** the external side or surface of something **11 at the outside** *informal* at the very most: *I'll be away four days at the outside*

> **USAGE** In British English, the use of *outside of* and *inside of*, although fairly common, is generally thought to be incorrect or non-standard: *she waits outside* (not *outside of*) *the school.*

outside broadcast *n radio & television* a broadcast not made from a studio
outsider *n* **1** a person excluded from a group **2** a contestant thought unlikely to win
outsize *adj* **1** Also: **outsized** very large or larger than normal ▷ *n* **2** an outsize garment
outskirts *pl n* the parts of a town or city that are furthest from the centre: *an office in the northernmost outskirts of Glasgow*
outsmart *vb* same as **outwit**
outsource *vb* **1** to subcontract (work) to another company **2** to buy (components for a product) rather than manufacture them
outspan *S African* ▷ *n* **1** an area on a farm kept available for travellers to rest and refresh their animals ▷ *vb* **-spanning, -spanned 2** to unharness or unyoke (animals) **3** to relax [Afrikaans uit out + *spannen* to stretch]
outspoken *adj* **1** saying exactly what one thinks: *an outspoken critic of human rights abuses* **2** spoken candidly: *she is known for her outspoken views* **outspokenness** *n*
outspread *adj* spread or stretched out as far as possible: *a gull glided by with outspread wings*
outstanding *adj* **1** very good; excellent: *an outstanding performance* **2** still to be dealt with or paid: *outstanding bills; a few outstanding problems have to be put right* **3** very obvious or important: *there are significant exceptions, of which oil is the outstanding example* **outstandingly** *adv*
outstation *n* a station or post in a remote region

outstay *vb* same as **overstay**
outstretched *adj* extended or stretched out as far as possible: *he pushed a wad of drachma notes into the young man's outstretched hand*
outstrip *vb* **-stripping, -stripped 1** to surpass (someone) in a particular activity: *his newspapers outstrip all others in vulgarity* **2** to go faster than (someone)
outtake *n* an unreleased take from a recording session, film, or television programme
out there *adj slang* unconventional or eccentric
out-tray *n* a shallow basket in an office for collecting letters and documents that are to be sent out
outvote *vb* **-voting, -voted** to defeat (someone) by getting more votes than him or her
outward *adj* **1** apparent or superficial: *to outward appearances the house is largely unchanged today* **2** of or relating to the outside: *outward shape* **3** (of a journey) away from a place to which one intends to return ▷ *adv also* **outwards 4** in an outward direction; towards the outside **outwardly** *adv*
outweigh *vb* **1** to be more important, significant, or influential than: *these niggles are outweighed by the excellent cooking and service* **2** to be heavier than
outwit *vb* **-witting, -witted** to gain an advantage over (someone) by cunning or ingenuity
outworks *pl n military* defences which lie outside the main fortifications of a fort, etc.
outworn *adj* (of a belief or custom) old-fashioned and no longer of any use or relevance: *there is no point in pandering to outworn superstition*
ouzel *or* **ousel** (ooze-el) *n* same as **dipper** (sense 2) [Old English *ōsle*]
ouzo (ooze-oh) *n, pl* **ouzos** a strong aniseed-flavoured alcoholic drink from Greece [Modern Greek *ouzon*]
ova *n* the plural of **ovum**
oval *adj* **1** egg-shaped ▷ *n* **2** anything that is oval in shape, such as a sports ground [Latin *ovum* egg]
ovary *n, pl* **-ries 1** a reproductive organ in women and female animals in which eggs are produced **2** *botany* the lower part of a pistil, containing the ovules [Latin *ovum* egg] **ovarian** *adj*
ovate *adj* shaped like an egg: *the tree has bluish-green, ovate leaves* [Latin *ovatus* egg-shaped]
ovation *n* an enthusiastic round of applause [Latin *ovatio* rejoicing]
oven *n* **1** an enclosed heated compartment or container for baking or roasting food, or for drying or firing ceramics ▷ *vb* **2** to cook in an oven [Old English *ofen*]
over *prep* **1** directly above; across the top or upper surface of: *set the frying pan over a low heat* **2** on or to the other side of: *the pilot flew over the Channel* **3** during or throughout (a period of time): *over the next few months it became clear what was happening* **4** throughout the whole extent of: *the effects are being felt all over the country now* **5** by means of (an instrument of telecommunication): *there was an announcement over the Tannoy system* **6** more than: *she had met him over a year ago* **7** concerning; about: *there has been much argument over these figures* **8** while occupied in: *I'll tell you over dinner tonight* **9** having recovered from the effects of: *he appeared to be over his niggling injury problems* **10 all over someone** *informal* extremely affectionate or attentive towards someone **11 over and above** added to; in addition to ▷ *adv* **12** in a state, condition, or position over something: *to climb over* **13** onto its side: *the jug toppled over* **14** at or to a point across an intervening space: *she carried him over to the other side of the river* **15** covering the whole area: *there's poverty the world over* **16** from beginning to end: *to read a document over* **17 all over A** finished **B** over one's entire body **C** typically: *that's him all over* **18 over again** once more **19 over and over (again)** repeatedly ▷ *interj* **20** (in signalling and radio) it is now your turn to speak ▷ *adj* **21** finished; no longer in progress: *the second round of voting is over* ▷ *adj, adv* **22** remaining: *there wasn't any money left over* ▷ *n* **23** *cricket* **A** a series of six balls bowled by a bowler from the same end of the pitch **B** the play during this [Old English *ofer*]
over- *prefix* **1** excessive or excessively: *overcharge; overdue* **2** superior in rank: *overlord* **3** indicating location or movement above: *overhang* **4** indicating movement downwards: *overthrow*
overabundance *n* more than is really needed; excess
overact *vb* to act in an exaggerated way
overactive *adj* more active than is normal or desirable: *an overactive thyroid gland*
overall *adj* **1** from one end to the other: *the overall length* **2** including everything; total: *the overall cost* ▷ *adv* **3** in general; on the whole: *overall, I think this is the better car* ▷ *n* **4** *Brit & NZ* a coat-shaped work garment worn over ordinary clothes as a protection against dirt **5 overalls** work trousers with a bib and braces or jacket attached, worn over ordinary clothes as a protection against dirt and wear
overambitious *adj* attempting more than one has the ability to do well: *good plain cookery marred by overambitious sauces*
overarching *adj* overall or all-encompassing: *an overarching concept*
overarm *sport* ▷ *adj* **1** bowled, thrown, or performed with the arm raised above the shoulder ▷ *adv* **2** with the arm raised above the shoulder
overawe *vb* **-awing, -awed** to affect (someone) with an overpowering sense of awe: *he was overawed by the prospect of meeting the Prime Minister*
overbalance *vb* **-lancing, -lanced** to lose one's balance
overbearing *adj* **1** imposing one's views in an unpleasant or forceful manner **2** of particular or overriding importance: *an overbearing need*
overblown *adj* inflated or excessive: *humiliation comes from having overblown expectations for yourself*
overboard *adv* **1** from a boat or ship into the water: *many passengers drowned when they jumped overboard to escape the flames* **2 go overboard** *informal* **A** to be extremely enthusiastic **B** to go to extremes **3 throw overboard** to reject or abandon (an idea or a plan)
overburden *vb* to cause to have more of something than it is possible to cope with: *the city's streets are already overburdened by rush-hour motorists*
overcast *adj* (of the sky or weather) cloudy

overcharge *vb* **-charging, -charged** to charge too high a price
overcoat *n* a warm heavy coat worn in cold weather
overcome *vb* **-coming, -came, -come 1** to deal successfully with or control (a problem or feeling): *once I'd overcome my initial nerves I discovered hang-gliding was great fun* **2** (of an emotion or a feeling) to affect (someone) strongly or make (someone) powerless: *he was overcome by a sudden surge of jealousy* **3** to defeat (someone) in a conflict
overcompensate *vb* **-sating, -sated** to attempt to make up for or cancel out (something) to an unnecessary degree: *when bookings dropped slightly, the company overcompensated by slashing the price of its holidays by 50%*
overconfident *adj* having more belief in one's abilities than is justified
overcook *vb* to spoil food by cooking it for too long
overcrowded *adj* containing more people or things than is desirable: *overcrowded commuter trains*
overcrowding *n* the cramming of too many people into too small a space: *prison overcrowding and poor conditions*
overdo *vb* **-does, -doing, -did, -done 1** to do (something) to excess **2** to exaggerate (something) **3** to cook (something) too long **4 overdo it** *or* **things** to do something to a greater degree than is advisable or healthy
overdose *n* **1** a larger dose of a drug than is safe: *she tried to kill herself with an overdose of alcohol and drugs* ▷ *vb* **-dosing, -dosed 2** to take more of a drug than is safe, either accidentally or deliberately: *this drug is rarely prescribed because it is easy to overdose fatally on it*
overdraft *n* **1** the withdrawal of more money from a bank account than there is in it **2** the amount of money withdrawn thus
overdraw *vb* **-drawing, -drew, -drawn** to withdraw more money from a bank account than is in it
overdrawn *adj* **1** having overdrawn one's bank account **2** (of an account) in debit
overdressed *adj* wearing clothes which are too elaborate or formal for the occasion
overdrive *n* **1** a very high gear in a motor vehicle, used at high speeds to reduce wear **2** a state of great activity or excitement: *the government propaganda machine went into overdrive to try to play down the Minister's comments*
overdub *vb* **-dubbing, -dubbed 1** to add (new sounds) to a recording in such a way that the old and the new sounds can be heard ▷ *n* **2** a sound or series of sounds added by this method
overdue *adj* **1** not having arrived or happened by the time expected or desired: *a reassessment of policy on this issue is long overdue* **2** (of money) not having been paid by the required date: *by this time his rent was three weeks overdue* **3** (of a library book) not having been returned to the library by the required date
overeat *vb* **-eating, -ate, -eaten** to eat more than is necessary or healthy
overemphasize *or* **-sise** *vb* **-sizing, -sized** *or* **-sising, -sised** to give (something) more importance than is necessary or appropriate
overestimate *vb* **-mating, -mated** to believe something or someone to be bigger, more important, or better than is the case **overestimation** *n*
overexcited *adj* excessively enthusiastic or agitated
overexert *vb* to exhaust or injure oneself by doing too much **overexertion** *n*
overexposed *adj* (of a photograph) too light in colour because the film has been exposed to light for too long
overfeed *vb* **-feeding, -fed** to give (a person, plant, or animal) more food than is necessary or healthy
overfill *vb* to put more into (something) than there is room for
overflow *vb* **-flowing, -flowed** *or* (formerly) **-flown 1** to flow over (a brim) **2** to be filled beyond capacity so as to spill over **3 overflow with** to be filled with (an emotion): *a letter overflowing with passion and ardour* ▷ *n* **4** something that overflows, usually a liquid **5** an outlet that enables surplus liquid to be drained off **6** the amount by which a limit or capacity is exceeded ▷ *adj* **7** of or being a subsidiary thing for use when there is no room left in the main one: *an overflow car park*
overgraze *vb* **-grazing, -grazed** to graze (land) too intensively so that it is damaged and no longer provides nourishment
overgrown *adj* covered over with plants or weeds: *they headed up the overgrown and winding trail*
overhang *vb* **-hanging, -hung 1** to project or hang over beyond (something) ▷ *n* **2** an overhanging part or object
overhaul *vb* **1** to examine (a system or an idea) carefully for faults **2** to make repairs or adjustments to (a vehicle or machine) **3** to overtake (a vehicle or person) ▷ *n* **4** a thorough examination and repair
overhead *adj* **1** situated or operating above head height: *overhead compartments* ▷ *adv* **2** over or above head height: *the missile streaked overhead*
overhead projector *n* a projector that throws an enlarged image of a transparency onto a surface above and behind the person using it
overheads *pl n* the general costs of running a business, such as rent, electricity, and stationery
overhear *vb* **-hearing, -heard** to hear (a speaker or remark) unintentionally or without the knowledge of the speaker
overheat *vb* **1** to make or become too hot **2** to cause (an economy) to tend towards inflation **3 become overheated** (of a person, discussion, etc.) to become angry or agitated: *the Colonel becomes overheated if he sees the term 'Ms' in the newspaper*
overindulge *vb* **-dulging, -dulged** to do too much of something pleasant, such as eating or drinking: *nobody ever wants a hangover, but we all overindulge occasionally* **overindulgence** *n*
overjoyed *adj* extremely pleased
overkill *n* any treatment that is greater than that required: *the overkill in negative propaganda resulted in this upsurge*
overlap *vb* **-lapping, -lapped 1** (of two things) to share part of the same space as or lie partly over

(each other): *slice the meat and lay it in overlapping slices in a serving dish* **2** to coincide partly in time or subject: *their careers have overlapped for the last ten years* ▷ *n* **3** a part that overlaps **4** the amount or length of something overlapping

overlay *vb* **-laying, -laid 1** to cover (a surface) with an applied decoration: *a woollen cloth overlaid with gold and silver embroidery* ▷ *n* **2** something that is laid over something else; a covering **3** an applied decoration or layer, for example of gold leaf

overleaf *adv* on the other side of the page

overlie *vb* **-lying, -lay, -lain** to lie on or cover (something or someone): *a thin layer of black dust overlay everything*

overload *vb* **1** to put too large a load on or in (something): *the aircraft was dangerously overloaded* **2** to cause (a transport system) to be unable to function properly because too many people or vehicles are using it: *Heathrow Airport was already overloaded by 1972* **3** to try to put more electricity through a system than the system can cope with ▷ *n* **4** an excessive load

overlook *vb* **1** to fail to notice (something) **2** to disregard or ignore (misbehaviour or a fault): *I'm prepared to overlook your failure, but don't do it again* **3** to give a view of (something) from above: *a cliff overlooking the Atlantic*

overlord *n* a supreme lord or master

overly *adv* too; excessively

overman *vb* **-manning, -manned** to provide with too many staff **overmanned** *adj* **overmanning** *n*

overmuch *adv, adj* too much; very much

overnight *adv* **1** during the night **2** in or as if in the course of one night; suddenly: *we are not saying that a change like this would happen overnight* ▷ *adj* **3** done in, occurring in, or lasting the night: *the army has ordered an overnight curfew* **4** staying for one night: *overnight guests* **5** for use during a single night: *should I pack an overnight case?* **6** happening very quickly; sudden: *he doesn't expect the programme to be an overnight success*

overpaid *adj* earning more money than one deserves

overpass *n* same as **flyover**

overplay *vb* **1** to overemphasize (something) **2 overplay one's hand** to overestimate the worth or strength of one's position

overpopulated *adj* (of a town or country) having more people living in it than it can support

overpopulation *n* the state of being overpopulated

overpower *vb* **1** to conquer or subdue (someone) by superior force **2** to have such a strong effect on (someone) as to make him or her helpless or ineffective: *I was so appalled, so overpowered by my guilt and my shame that I was unable to speak* **overpowering** *adj*

overpriced *adj* costing more than it is thought to be worth

overprint *vb* **1** to print (additional matter or another colour) onto (something already printed) ▷ *n* **2** additional matter or another colour printed onto something already printed

overqualified *adj* having more professional or academic qualifications than are required for a job

O

overrate *vb* to have too high an opinion of: *the director's role was seriously overrated*

overreach *vb* **overreach oneself** to fail by trying to be too clever or achieve too much: *he built up a successful media empire before he overreached himself and lost much of his fortune*

overreact *vb* to react more strongly or forcefully than is necessary: *allergies happen when the body overreacts to a harmless substance* **overreaction** *n*

override *vb* **-riding, -rode, -ridden 1** to set aside or disregard (a person or a person's decisions) by having superior authority or power: *the managing director can override any decision he doesn't like* **2** to be more important than or replace (something): *unsurprisingly the day-to-day struggle for survival overrode all moral considerations* **overriding** *adj*

overripe *adj* (of a fruit or vegetable) so ripe that it has started to decay or go soft

overrule *vb* **-ruling, -ruled 1** to reverse the decision of (a person or organization with less power): *the President overruled the hardliners in the party who wanted to use force* **2** to rule or decide against (an argument or decision): *the initial judgment was overruled by the Supreme Court*

overrun *vb* **-running, -ran, -run 1** to conquer (territory) rapidly by force of numbers **2** to spread over (a place) rapidly: *dirty tenements, overrun by lice, rats, and roaches* **3** to extend or run beyond a set limit: *Tuesday's lunch overran by three-quarters of an hour*

overseas *adv* **1** across the sea; abroad ▷ *adj* **2** of, to, from, or in a distant country or countries ▷ *n* **3** *informal* a foreign country or foreign countries collectively

oversee *vb* **-seeing, -saw, -seen** to watch over and direct (someone or something); supervise **overseer** *n*

oversell *vb* **-selling, -sold** to exaggerate the merits or abilities of

oversew *vb* **-sewing, -sewed, -sewn** *or* **-sewed** to sew (two edges) with stitches that pass over them both

oversexed *adj* more interested in sex than is thought decent

overshadow *vb* **1** to make (someone or something) seem insignificant or less important by comparison **2** to sadden the atmosphere of: *news of their team-mate's injury overshadowed the victory celebrations*

overshoe *n* a protective shoe worn over an ordinary shoe

overshoot *vb* **-shooting, -shot** to go beyond (a mark or target): *the plane overshot the main runway*

overshot *adj* (of a water wheel) driven by a flow of water that passes over the wheel

oversight *n* a mistake caused by not noticing something

oversimplify *vb* **-fies, -fying, -fied** to make something seem simpler than it really is: *the Nationalists' analysis oversimplifies the problems facing the country today*

oversized *adj* much larger than the usual size

oversleep *vb* **-sleeping, -slept** to sleep beyond the intended time for getting up

overspend *vb* **-spending, -spent** to spend more than one can afford

overspill *n Brit* the rehousing of people from crowded cities in smaller towns
overstate *vb* **-stating, -stated** to state (something) too strongly; overemphasize **overstatement** *n*
overstay *vb* **overstay one's welcome** to stay as a guest longer than one's host or hostess would like
overstayer *n* a person who remains in a country after his or her permit has expired
overstep *vb* **-stepping, -stepped 1** to go beyond the limits of what is thought acceptable: *he had overstepped his authority by acting without consulting his superiors* **2 overstep the mark** to go too far and behave in an unacceptable way
overstretch *vb* **1** to attempt to do more than there is time or capability for: *for the first time in her career she may have overstretched her talents* **2** to damage (something) by stretching it further than it can safely go: *he overstretched his Achilles tendon* **overstretched** *adj*
overstrung *adj* too highly strung; tense
overt *adj* done or shown in an open and obvious way: *jurors were now looking at the defendant with overt hostility* [Old French] **overtly** *adv*
overtake *vb* **-taking, -took, -taken 1** *chiefly Brit* to move past (another vehicle or person) travelling in the same direction **2** to do better than (someone) after catching up with him or her **3** to come upon (someone) suddenly or unexpectedly: *a mortal tiredness overtook him*
overtax *vb* **1** to impose too great a strain on: *a singer who had overtaxed her voice* **2** to tax (people) too heavily
over-the-top *adj slang* excessive; beyond the usual or acceptable bounds of behaviour
overthink *vb* **-thinking, -thought** to think about (something) for longer than is necessary or productive
overthrow *vb* **-throwing, -threw, -thrown 1** to defeat and replace (a ruler or government) by force **2** to replace (standards or values) ▷ *n* **3** downfall or destruction: *the overthrow of the US-backed dictatorship*
overtime *n* **1** work at a regular job done in addition to regular working hours **2** pay for such work ▷ *adv* **3** in addition to one's regular working hours: *she had been working overtime and she fell asleep at the wheel*
overtone *n* **1** an additional meaning or hint: *I don't want to deny that from time to time there are political overtones* **2** *music & acoustics* any of the tones, with the exception of the principal or lowest one, that make up a musical sound
overture *n* **1** *music* **A** a piece of orchestral music played at the beginning of an opera, oratorio, ballet, musical comedy, or film, often containing the main musical themes of the work **B** a one-movement orchestral piece, usually having a descriptive or evocative title: *the 1812 Overture* **2 overtures** opening moves towards a new relationship or agreement: *the German government made a variety of friendly overtures towards the French* [Late Latin *apertura* opening]
overturn *vb* **1** to turn over or upside down **2** to overrule or reverse (a legal decision) **3** to overthrow or destroy (a government)
overuse *vb* **1** to use excessively ▷ *n* **2** excessive use
overvalue *vb* **-valuing, -valued** to regard (someone or something) as much more important or valuable than is the case: *his approach overvalues hard work and undervalues true skill* **overvalued** *adj*
overview *n* a general survey
overweening *adj* (of opinions or qualities) excessive or immoderate: *your modesty is a cover for your overweening conceit* [obsolete *ween* to think]
overweight *adj* **1** (of a person) weighing more than is healthy **2** weighing more than is usual or permitted
overwhelm *vb* **1** to overpower the thoughts, emotions, or senses of (someone): *we were overwhelmed with grief* **2** to overcome (people) with irresistible force: *gang violence has overwhelmed an ailing police force* **overwhelming** *adj* **overwhelmingly** *adv*
overwork *vb* **1** to work too hard or too long **2** to use (something) too much: *anti-communism was already being overworked by others* ▷ *n* **3** excessive work
overwrite *vb* **-writing, -wrote, -written 1** to record on a storage medium, such as a magnetic disk, thus destroying what was originally recorded there **2** to write (something) in an excessively ornate style
overwrought *adj* tense, nervous, and agitated
oviduct *n anatomy* the tube through which eggs are conveyed from an ovary [Latin *ovum* egg + *ducere* to lead]
oviform *adj biol* shaped like an egg [Latin *ovum* egg + *forma* shape]
ovine *adj* of or like a sheep [Latin *ovis* sheep]
oviparous (oh-vip-par-uss) *adj zool* producing eggs that hatch outside the body of the mother [Latin *ovum* egg + *-parus* bearing]
ovoid (oh-void) *adj* egg-shaped
ovulate (ov-yew-late) *vb* **-lating, -lated** *biol* to produce or release eggs from an ovary **ovulation** *n*
ovule *n* **1** *botany* the part of a plant that contains the egg cell and develops into the seed after fertilization **2** *zool* an immature ovum [Latin *ovum* egg]
ovum (oh-vum) *n, pl* **ova** an unfertilized female egg cell [Latin: egg]
owe *vb* **owing, owed 1** to be under an obligation to pay an amount of money to (someone): *he owes me a lot of money* **2** to feel an obligation to do or give: *I think I owe you an apology* **3 owe something to** to have something as a result of: *many serving officers owe their present position to the former president* [Old English *āgan* to have]
owing *adj* **1** not yet paid; due: *the bailiffs seized goods worth far more than the amount owing* **2 owing to** because of; as a result of: *the flight was delayed owing to fog*
owl *n* a bird of prey which has a flat face, large eyes, and a small hooked beak, and which is active at night [Old English *ūle*] **owlish** *adj*
own *adj (preceded by a possessive)* **1** used to emphasize that something belongs to a particular person: *rely on your own instincts* ▷ *pron (preceded by a possessive)* **2** the one or ones belonging to a particular

person: *I had one of my own* **3** the people that someone feels loyalty to, esp. relations: *we all look after our own around here* **4 come into one's own** to fulfil one's potential **5 hold one's own** to have the necessary ability to deal successfully with a situation: *he chose a partner who could hold her own with the best* **6 on one's own A** without help: *you'll never manage to lift that on your own* **B** by oneself; alone: *he lives on his own in a flat in town* ▷ *vb* **7** to have (something) as one's possession: *he owns homes in four countries* **8** Also: **own up to** to confess or admit: *I own I could not bear to think of it; I thought she was going to own up to an affair* [Old English *āgen*] **owner** *n* **ownership** *n*

owner-occupier *n* someone who owns the house in which he or she lives

ownership flat *n NZ* a flat owned by the occupier

own goal *n* **1** *sport* a goal scored by a player accidentally playing the ball into his or her own team's net **2** *informal* any action that results in disadvantage to the person who took it or to his or her associates: *the minister's admission was the latest in a series of own goals by the government*

ox *n, pl* **oxen** a castrated bull used for pulling heavy loads and for meat [Old English *oxa*]

oxalic acid *n* a colourless poisonous acid found in many plants [Latin *oxalis* garden sorrel]

oxbow lake *n* a crescent-shaped lake on the flood plain of a river and constituting the remnant of a former meander

Oxbridge *n Brit* the universities of Oxford and Cambridge considered together

oxen *n* the plural of **ox**

Oxfam Oxford Committee for Famine Relief

oxidation *n* the act or process of oxidizing

oxide *n chem* a compound of oxygen with another element [French]

oxidize *or* **-dise** *vb* **-dizing, -dized** *or* **-dising, -dised** to react chemically with oxygen, as in burning or rusting **oxidization** *or* **-disation** *n*

Oxon Oxfordshire

Oxon. (in degree titles) of Oxford University [Latin *Oxoniensis*]

oxtail *n* the tail of an ox, used in soups and stews

oxyacetylene *n* a mixture of oxygen and acetylene, used in blowlamps for cutting or welding metals at high temperatures

oxygen *n chem* a colourless, odourless gaseous element essential to life processes and to combustion. Symbol: **O** [Greek *oxus* sharp + *-genēs* producing: from former belief that all acids contained oxygen]

oxygenate *vb* **-nating, -nated** to add oxygen to: *to oxygenate blood*

oxygen mask *n* a small bowl-shaped object which is connected via a pipe to a cylinder of oxygen and can be placed over a person's nose and mouth to help him or her breathe

oxygen tent *n med* a transparent enclosure covering a bedridden patient, into which oxygen is released to aid breathing

oxymoron (ox-see-**more**-on) *n* a figure of speech that combines two apparently contradictory terms, for example *cruel kindness* [Greek *oxus* sharp + *mōros* stupid]

oyez *or* **oyes** *interj* a cry usually uttered three times by a public crier or court official calling for silence and attention [Old French *oiez!* hear!]

oyster *n* **1** an edible shellfish, some types of which produce pearls **2 the world is your oyster** you are in a position where there is every possible chance of personal advancement and satisfaction ▷ *adj* **3** greyish-white [Greek *ostreon*]

oystercatcher *n* a wading bird with black-and-white plumage and a long stout red bill

oz *or* **oz.** ounce [Italian *onza*]

Oz *n slang* Australia

ozone *n* **1** a form of oxygen with a strong odour, formed by an electric discharge in the atmosphere **2** *informal* clean bracing air, as found at the seaside [Greek *ozein* to smell]

ozone layer *n* a layer of ozone in the upper atmosphere that absorbs harmful ultraviolet rays from the sun

Pp

p *or* **P** *n, pl* **p's**, **P's** *or* **Ps** **1** the 16th letter of the English alphabet **2** **mind one's p's and q's** to be careful to behave correctly and use polite language

p **1** *Brit, Austral & NZ* penny **2** *Brit* pence

P **1** *chem* phosphorus **2** (on road signs) parking **3** *chess* pawn

p. **1** *pl* **pp.** page **2** per

pa[1] *n informal* father

pa[2] *n* NZ (formerly) a fortified Māori settlement

Pa **1** *chem* protactinium **2** *physics* pascal

PA **1** Pennsylvania **2** personal assistant **3** public-address system

p.a. yearly [Latin *per annum*]

pace[1] *n* **1** **A** a single step in walking **B** the length of a step **2** speed of walking or running **3** speed of doing some other activity: *efforts to accelerate the pace of change are unlikely to succeed* **4** manner of walking **5** **keep pace with** to advance at the same speed as **6** **put someone through his** *or* **her paces** to test someone's ability **7** **set the pace** to determine the speed at which a group advances ▷ *vb* **pacing, paced** **8** to walk with regular steps, often in anxiety or impatience: *he paced up and down the foyer impatiently* **9** to set the speed for (the competitors) in a race **10** **pace out** to measure by paces [Latin *passus* step]

pace[2] (pah-chay) *prep* with due respect to: used to express polite disagreement [Latin, from *pax* peace]

pacemaker *n* **1** an electronic device positioned in the body, next to the heart, to regulate the heartbeat **2** a competitor who, by leading a race, causes it to be run at a particular speed

pachyderm (pak-ee-durm) *n* a large thick-skinned mammal, such as an elephant or rhinoceros [Greek *pakhus* thick + *derma* skin]

pacific *adj formal* tending to bring peace; non-aggressive; peaceful [Latin *pax* peace + *facere* to make]

Pacific *adj* of the Pacific Ocean, the world's largest and deepest ocean, lying between Asia and Australia and America, or its islands

pacifier *n US & Canad* a baby's dummy

pacifist *n* a person who is totally opposed to violence and refuses to take part in war **pacifism** *n*

pacify *vb* **-fies, -fying, -fied** to soothe or calm [Old French *pacifier;* see PACIFIC] **pacification** *n*

pack[1] *n* **1** a bundle or load carried on the back **2** *Brit & NZ* a complete set of playing cards **3** a group of animals that hunt together: *a pack of hounds* **4** *rugby* the forwards of a team **5** any collection of people or things: *a pack of lies* **6** *chiefly US & Canad* same as **packet** (sense 1) **7** an organized group of Cub Scouts or Brownie Guides **8** same as **rucksack** or **backpack** **9** Also called: **face pack** a cream treatment that cleanses and tones the skin ▷ *vb* **10** to put (articles) in a case or container for moving **11** to roll (articles) up into a bundle **12** to press tightly together; cram: *thousands of people packed into the city's main square* **13** (foll. by *off*) to send away hastily: *their young son came in to say good night and was packed off to bed* **14** *slang* to be able to deliver a specified amount of unexpected or violent force or power: *the film's unexpected ending packs quite a punch* **15** *US informal* to carry (a gun) habitually **16** **send someone packing** *informal* to dismiss someone abruptly ▷ See also **pack in, pack up** [origin unknown]

pack[2] *vb* to fill (a committee, jury, or audience) with one's own supporters [perhaps from *pact*]

package *n* **1** a small parcel **2** Also: **package deal** a deal in which separate items are presented together as a unit **3** *US & Canad* same as **packet** (sense 1) ▷ *vb* **-aging, -aged** **4** to put (something) into a package **packaging** *n*

package holiday *n* a holiday in which everything is arranged by one company for a fixed price

packet *n* **1** a container, together with its contents: *a packet of crisps* **2** a small parcel **3** Also: **packet boat** a boat that transports mail, passengers, or goods on a fixed short route **4** *slang* a large sum of money: *she was paid a packet* **5** *computers* a unit into which a larger piece of data is broken down for more efficient transmission [Old French *pacquet*]

packhorse *n* a horse used to carry goods

pack ice *n* a large area of floating ice, consisting of pieces that have become massed together

pack in *vb informal* to stop doing (something): *I'm going to pack it in and resign*

packing *n* material, such as paper or plastic, used to protect packed goods

packsack *n* the US and Canadian word for **haversack**

packthread *n* a strong thread for sewing or tying up packages

pack up *vb* **1** to put (articles) in a bag or case before leaving **2** to stop doing (something) **3** (of a machine) to break down

pact *n* a formal agreement between two or more parties [Latin *pactum*]

pad[1] *n* **1** a thick piece of soft material used for comfort, shape, protection, or absorption **2** a number of sheets of paper fastened together along one edge **3** the fleshy cushioned underpart of an animal's paw **4** a level area or flat-topped structure, from which rockets are launched or helicopters take off **5** the floating leaf of the water lily **6** *informal* a person's residence ▷ *vb* **padding, padded** **7** to fill (something) out with soft material for comfort, shape, or protection **8** **pad out** to lengthen (a speech or piece of writing) with unnecessary words or pieces of information [origin unknown]

pad[2] *vb* **padding, padded** **1** to walk with a soft or muffled step **2** to travel (a route) on foot: *men padding the streets in cheap sneakers* [Middle Dutch *pad* path]

padded cell *n* a room with padded walls in a psychiatric hospital, in which patients who are likely to injure themselves are placed

padding *n* **1** any soft material used to pad something **2** unnecessary information put into a speech or written work to make it longer

paddle¹ *n* **1** a short light oar with a flat blade at one or both ends **2** a paddle wheel used to move a boat **3** a blade of a water wheel or paddle wheel ▷ *vb* **-dling, -dled 4** to move (a boat) with a paddle **5** to swim with short rapid strokes, like a dog **6** *US & Canad informal* to spank [origin unknown]

paddle² *vb* **-dling, -dled 1** to walk barefoot in shallow water **2** to dabble (one's fingers, hands, or feet) in water ▷ *n* **3** the act of paddling in water [origin unknown]

paddle steamer *n* a ship propelled by paddle wheels turned by a steam engine

paddle wheel *n* a large wheel fitted with paddles, turned by an engine to propel a ship

paddock *n* **1** a small enclosed field for horses **2** (in horse racing) the enclosure in which horses are paraded and mounted before a race **3** *Austral & NZ* any area of fenced land [Old English *pearruc* enclosure]

paddy¹ *n, pl* **-dies 1** Also: **paddy field** a field planted with rice **2** rice as a growing crop or when harvested but not yet milled [Malay *pādī*]

paddy² *n, pl* **-dies** *Brit & NZ informal* a fit of temper [from *Paddy*, stereotypical name for an Irishman]

pademelon *or* **paddymelon** (pad-ee-mel-an) *n* a small Australian wallaby [from an Aboriginal word]

padkos (pudd-koss) *n S African* snacks and provisions for a journey [Afrikaans, literally: road food]

padlock *n* **1** a detachable lock with a hinged hoop fastened through a ring on the object to be secured ▷ *vb* **2** to fasten (something) with a padlock [origin unknown]

padre (pah-dray) *n informal* a chaplain to the armed forces [via Spanish or Italian from Latin *pater* father]

paean (pee-an) *n literary* an expression of praise or joy [Greek *paian* hymn to Apollo]

paediatrician *or US* **pediatrician** *n* a doctor who specializes in children's diseases

paediatrics *or US* **pediatrics** *n* the branch of medicine concerned with children and their diseases [Greek *pais, paid-* child + *iatros* physician] **paediatric** *or US* **pediatric** *adj*

paedophile *or US* **pedophile** *n* a person who is sexually attracted to children

paedophilia *or US* **pedophilia** *n* the condition of being sexually attracted to children [Greek *pais, paid-* child + *philos* loving]

paella (pie-ell-a) *n* a Spanish dish made from rice, shellfish, chicken, and vegetables [Catalan]

pagan *adj* **1** having, being, or relating to religious beliefs, esp. ancient ones, which are not part of any of the world's major religions: *this was the site of a pagan temple to the sun* **2** irreligious ▷ *n* **3** a person who does not belong to any of the world's major religions **4** a person without any religion [Church Latin *paganus* civilian (hence not a soldier of Christ)] **paganism** *n*

page¹ *n* **1** one side of one of the leaves of a book, newspaper, or magazine **2** one of the leaves of a book, newspaper, or magazine **3** *literary* a period or event: *a new page in the country's political history* **4** a screenful of information from a website or teletext service [Latin *pagina*]

page² *n* **1** a small boy who attends a bride at a wedding **2** a youth employed to run errands for the guests in a hotel or club **3** *medieval history* a boy in training for knighthood ▷ *vb* **paging, paged 4** to summon (a person), by bleeper or loudspeaker, in order to pass on a message [Greek *pais* child]

pageant *n* **1** an outdoor show portraying scenes from history **2** any magnificent display or procession [perhaps from Latin *pagina* scene of a play]

pageantry *n* spectacular display or ceremony

pageboy *n* **1** a hairstyle in which the hair is smooth and the same medium length with the ends curled under **2** same as **page²** (senses 1, 2)

pagination *n* the numbering in sequence of the pages of a book or manuscript **paginate** *vb*

pagoda *n* a pyramid-shaped Asian temple or tower [Portuguese *pagode*]

paid *vb* **1** past of **pay 2 put paid to** to end or destroy: *a knee injury put paid to his promising sporting career*

pail *n* **1** a bucket **2** Also called: **pailful** the amount contained in a pail: *a pail of water* [Old English *pægel*]

pain *n* **1** physical hurt or discomfort caused by injury or illness **2** emotional suffering **3** Also called: **pain in the neck** *informal* a person or thing that is annoying or irritating **4 on pain of** subject to the penalty of: *orders which their soldiers were bound to follow on pain of death* ▷ *vb* **5** to cause (a person) physical or mental suffering **6** *informal* to annoy; irritate ▷ See also **pains** [Latin *poena* punishment] **painless** *adj*

pained *adj* having or suggesting pain or distress: *a pained look*

painful *adj* **1** causing pain or distress: *painful inflammation of the joints; he began the painful task of making funeral arrangements* **2** affected with pain: *the symptoms include fever and painful joints* **3** tedious or difficult: *the hours passed with painful slowness* **4** *informal* extremely bad: *a painful so-called comedy* **painfully** *adv*

painkiller *n* a drug that relieves pain

pains *pl n* care or trouble: *they are at great pains to appear realistic and responsible*

painstaking *adj* extremely careful and thorough **painstakingly** *adv*

paint *n* **1** a coloured substance, spread on a surface with a brush or a roller, that forms a hard coating **2** a dry film of paint on a surface **3** *informal* face make-up ▷ *vb* **4** to apply paint to paper or canvas to make a picture of **5** to coat (a surface) with paint **6** to describe vividly in words: *the survey paints a dismal picture of growing hunger and disease* **7** to apply make-up to (the face) **8** to apply (liquid) to (a surface): *paint the varnish on and leave it to dry for at least four hours* **9 paint the town red** *informal* to celebrate in a lively way [Latin *pingere* to paint]

paintbrush *n* a brush used to apply paint
painted lady *n* a butterfly with pale brownish-red mottled wings
painter[1] *n* **1** an artist who paints pictures **2** a person who paints surfaces of buildings as a trade
painter[2] *n* a rope attached to the bow of a boat for tying it up [probably from Old French *penteur* strong rope]
painting *n* **1** a picture produced by using paint **2** the art of producing pictures by applying paints to paper or canvas **3** the act of applying paint to a surface
paintwork *n* the covering of paint on parts of a vehicle, building, etc.: *someone had damaged the Porsche by scraping a key along its paintwork*
pair *n* **1** two identical or similar things matched for use together: *a pair of shoes* **2** two people, animals, or things used or grouped together: *a pair of tickets* **3** an object consisting of two identical or similar parts joined together: *a pair of jeans* **4** a male and a female animal of the same species kept for breeding purposes **5** *parliament* two opposed members who both agree not to vote on a specified motion **6** two playing cards of the same denomination **7** one member of a matching pair: *I can't find the pair to this glove* ▷ *vb* **8** to group (people or things) in twos **9** **pair off** to separate into groups of two [Latin *par* equal]

USAGE Like other collective nouns, *pair* takes a singular or a plural verb according to whether it is seen as a unit or as a collection of two things: *the pair are said to dislike each other; a pair of good shoes is essential.*

paisley pattern *or* **paisley** *n* a detailed pattern of small curving shapes, used in fabric [after *Paisley*, town in Scotland]
pajamas *pl n US* pyjamas
pakeha (pah-kee-hah) *n, pl* **pakeha** *or* **pakehas** NZ a person of European descent, as distinct from a Māori [Māori]
Paki *Brit slang, offensive* ▷ *n* **1** a Pakistani or person of Pakistani descent ▷ *adj* **2** Pakistani or of Pakistani descent
Pakistani *adj* **1** of Pakistan ▷ *n* **2** a person from Pakistan
pal *informal* ▷ *n* **1** a close friend ▷ *vb* **palling, palled** **2** **pal up with** to become friends with [Romany: brother]
palace *n* **1** the official residence of a king, queen, president, or archbishop **2** a large and richly furnished building [Latin *Palatium* Palatine, the site of the palace of the emperors in Rome]
paladin *n* **1** one of the legendary twelve peers of Charlemagne's court **2** (formerly) a knight who did battle for a king or queen [Italian *paladino*]
palaeo- *or US* **paleo-** *combining form* old, ancient, or prehistoric: *palaeobotany*
Palaeocene *or US* **Paleocene** (pal-ee-oh-seen) *adj geol* of the epoch of geological time about 65 million years ago [Greek *palaeo-* ancient + *kainos* new]
palaeography *or US* **paleography** (pal-ee-og-ra-fee) *n* the study of ancient handwriting [Greek *palaeo-* ancient + -GRAPHY]
Palaeolithic *or US* **Paleolithic** (pal-ee-oh-lith-ik) *adj* of the period from about 2.5 to 3 million years ago until about 12,000 BC, during which primitive humans emerged and unpolished chipped stone tools were made [Greek *palaeo-* ancient + *lithos* stone]
palaeontology *or US* **paleontology** (pal-ee-on-tol-a-jee) *n* the study of past geological periods and fossils [Greek *palaeo-* ancient + *ōn, ont-* being + -LOGY] **palaeontologist** *or US* **paleontologist** *n*
Palaeozoic *or US* **Paleozoic** (pal-ee-oh-zoh-ik) *adj geol* of the geological era that lasted from about 600 million years ago to 230 million years ago [Greek *palaeo-* ancient + *zōion* animal]
Palagi (pa-lang-gee) *n, pl* **-gis** NZ the Samoan name for a Pakeha
palanquin (pal-an-keen) *n* (formerly, in E Asia) a covered bed in which someone could be carried on the shoulders of four bearers [Portuguese *palanquim*]
palatable *adj* **1** (of food or drink) pleasant to taste **2** (of an experience or idea) acceptable or satisfactory
palate *n* **1** the roof of the mouth **2** the sense of taste: *a range of dishes to tempt every palate* [Latin *palatum*]

USAGE Avoid confusion with **palette** or **pallet**[1].

palatial *adj* like a palace; magnificent: *his palatial home*
palatinate *n* a territory ruled by a palatine prince or noble or a count palatine
palatine *adj* possessing royal prerogatives: *a count palatine* [Latin *palatium* palace]
palaver (pal-lah-ver) *n* time-consuming fuss: *all the palaver involved in obtaining a visa* [Portuguese *palavra* talk]
palazzo pants *pl n* women's trousers with very wide legs [Italian *palazzo* palace]
pale[1] *adj* **1** (of a colour) whitish and not very strong: *pale yellow* **2** (of a complexion) having a whitish appearance, usually because of illness, shock, or fear **3** lacking brightness or colour: *the pale, chill light of an October afternoon* ▷ *vb* **paling, paled** **4** to become pale or paler: *the girl paled at the news* [Latin *pallidus*] **paleness** *n*
pale[2] *n* **1** a wooden post used in fences **2** **A** a fence made of pales **B** a boundary **3** **beyond the pale** outside the limits of social convention: *the destruction of forests is beyond the pale* [Latin *palus* stake]
paleface *n* an offensive term for a White person, said to have been used by Native Americans of N America
Palestinian *adj* **1** of Palestine, an area in the Middle East between the Jordan River and the Mediterranean ▷ *n* **2** an Arab from this area, esp. one living in Israel or Israeli-occupied territory or as a refugee
palette *n* **1** a flat board used by artists to mix paints **2** the range of colours characteristic of a particular artist or school of painting: *he uses a cool palette with no strong red* **3** the range of colours or patterns that can be displayed on the visual display unit of a computer [French]

USAGE Avoid confusion with **palate** or **pallet**[1].

palette knife *n* a spatula with a thin flexible blade used in painting or cookery

palindrome *n* a word or phrase that reads the same backwards or forwards, such as *able was I ere I saw Elba* [Greek *palindromos* running back again]

paling *n* **1** a fence made of pales **2** pales collectively **3** a single pale

palisade *n* **1** a fence made of stakes driven into the ground **2** one of the stakes used in such a fence [Latin *palus* stake]

pall[1] *n* **1** a cloth spread over a coffin **2** a coffin at a funeral ceremony **3** a dark heavy covering: *a pall of smoke and dust hung in the air* **4** a depressing atmosphere: *a pall hung on them all after his death* [Latin *pallium* cloak]

pall[2] *vb* to become boring or uninteresting, esp. by continuing for too long: *any pleasure had palled long before the two-hour programme was over* [variant of *appal*]

Palladian *adj* of a style of architecture characterized by symmetry and the revival and development of ancient Roman styles [after Andrea *Palladio*, Italian architect]

palladium *n chem* a rare silvery-white element of the platinum metal group, used in jewellery. Symbol: **Pd** [after the asteroid *Pallas*]

pallbearer *n* a person who helps to carry or who escorts the coffin at a funeral

pallet[1] *n* a straw-filled mattress or bed [Latin *palea* straw]

pallet[2] *n* **1** a tool with a flat, sometimes flexible, blade used for shaping pottery **2** a portable platform for storing and moving goods [Latin *pala* spade]

> **USAGE** Avoid confusion with **palate** or **palette**.

palliasse *n* a straw-filled mattress; pallet [French *paillasse*]

P

palliate *vb* **-ating, -ated 1** to lessen the severity of (pain or disease) without curing it **2** to cause (an offence) to seem less serious [Latin *pallium* a cloak]

palliative *adj* **1** relieving without curing ▷ *n* **2** something that palliates, such as a sedative drug **3** something that alleviates or lessens a problem: *equal pay was a palliative for the growing unrest among women*

pallid *adj* **1** lacking colour, brightness, or vigour: *a pallid autumn sun* **2** lacking energy or vitality; insipid: *many militants find the party's socialism too pallid* [Latin *pallidus*]

pallor *n* paleness of complexion, usually because of illness, shock, or fear [Latin: whiteness]

pally *adj* **-lier, -liest** *informal* on friendly terms

palm[1] *n* **1** the inner surface of the hand from the wrist to the base of the fingers **2** the part of a glove that covers the palm **3 in the palm of one's hand** at one's mercy or command: *he had the jury in the palm of his hand* ▷ *vb* **4** to hide (something) in the hand: *he palmed the key* ▷ See also **palm off** [Latin *palma*]

palm[2] *or* **palm tree** *n* a tropical or subtropical tree with a straight unbranched trunk crowned with long pointed leaves [Latin *palma*, from the likeness of its spreading fronds to a hand]

palmate *adj* shaped like an open hand: *palmate leaves*

palmetto *n, pl* **-tos** a small palm tree with fan-shaped leaves [Spanish *palmito* a little palm]

palmistry *n* fortune-telling by examining the lines and bumps of the hand **palmist** *n*

palm off *vb* **1** to get rid of (someone or something) by passing it on to another: *the risk has to be shared with subcontractors, not simply palmed off on them* **2** to divert (someone) by a lie or excuse: *Mark was palmed off with a series of excuses*

palm oil *n* an oil obtained from the fruit of certain palm trees, used as an edible fat and in soap

Palm Sunday *n Christianity* the Sunday before Easter

palmtop *adj* **1** (of a computer) small enough to be held in the hand ▷ *n* **2** a personal computer that is small enough to be held in the hand

palmy *adj* **palmier, palmiest 1** successful, prosperous and happy: *the palmy days of youth* **2** covered with palm trees: *palmy beaches*

palomino *n, pl* **-nos** a golden or cream horse with a white mane and tail [Spanish: dovelike]

palpable *adj* **1** obvious: *palpable nonsense* **2** (of a feeling or an atmosphere) so intense that it seems capable of being touched: *an air of palpable gloom hung over him* [Latin *palpare* to touch] **palpably** *adv*

palpate *vb* **-pating, -pated** *med* to examine (an area of the body) by touching [Latin *palpare* to stroke] **palpation** *n*

palpitate *vb* **-tating, -tated 1** (of the heart) to beat rapidly **2** to flutter or tremble [Latin *palpitare*] **palpitation** *n*

palsy (**pawl**-zee) *n pathol* paralysis of a specified type: *cerebral palsy* [Old French *paralisie*] **palsied** *adj*

paltry *adj* **-trier, -triest** insignificant [Low Germanic *palter*, *paltrig* ragged]

pampas *n* the extensive grassy plains of South America [Native American *bamba* plain]

pampas grass *n* a South American grass with large feathery silver-coloured flower branches

pamper *vb* to treat (someone) with excessive indulgence or care; spoil [Germanic]

pamphlet *n* a thin paper-covered booklet, often on a subject of current interest [Medieval Latin *Pamphilus*, title of a poem]

pamphleteer *n* a person who writes or issues pamphlets

pan[1] *n* **1** a wide long-handled metal container used in cooking **2** any of various similar containers used in industry, etc. **3** either of the two dishes on a set of scales **4** *Brit* the bowl of a lavatory **5** a natural or artificial hollow in the ground: *a saltpan* ▷ *vb* **panning, panned 6** to sift gold from (a river) in a shallow pan **7** *informal* to criticize harshly: *his first film was panned by the critics* ▷ See also **pan out** [Old English *panne*]

pan[2] *vb* **panning, panned 1** to move (a film camera) or (of a film camera) to be moved to follow a moving object or to take in a whole scene ▷ *n* **2** the act of panning [from *panoramic*]

pan- *combining form* including or relating to all parts or members: *Pan-American* [Greek]

panacea (pan-a-**see**-a) *n* a remedy for all diseases or problems [Greek *pan-* all + *akos* remedy]

panache (pan-**ash**) *n* a confident and stylish manner: *the orchestra played with great panache* [Old Italian *pennacchio* feather]
panama hat *or* **panama** *n* a straw hat with a rounded crown and a wide brim
Pan-American *adj* of North, South, and Central America collectively
panatella *n* a long slender cigar [American Spanish *panetela* long thin biscuit]
pancake *n* **1** a thin flat circle of fried batter **2** Also called: **pancake landing** an aircraft landing made by levelling out a few feet from the ground and then dropping onto it
Pancake Day *n* Shrove Tuesday, when people traditionally eat pancakes
panchromatic *adj photog* (of an emulsion or film) sensitive to light of all colours
pancreas (**pang**-kree-ass) *n* a large gland behind the stomach, that produces insulin and aids digestion [Greek *pan-* all + *kreas* flesh]
pancreatic *adj*
panda *n* **1** Also called: **giant panda** a large black-and-white bearlike animal from the high mountain bamboo forests of China **2** Also called: **lesser panda, red panda** a raccoon-like animal of the mountain forests of S Asia, with a reddish-brown coat and ringed tail [Nepalese]
panda car *n Brit* a police patrol car
pandemic *adj* (of a disease) occurring over a wide geographical area [Greek *pandēmos* general]
pandemonium *n* wild confusion; uproar [Greek *pan-* all + *daimōn* demon]
pander *vb* **1** (foll. by *to*) to indulge (a person or his or her desires): *he pandered to popular fears* ▷ *n* **2** *chiefly archaic* a person who procures a sexual partner for someone [after *Pandarus*, in legend, the procurer of Cressida for Troilus]
pandit *n Hinduism* same as **pundit** (sense 2)
Pandora's box *n* a source of many unforeseen difficulties [a box, in Greek myth, from which all human problems were released]
p & p *Brit* postage and packing
pane *n* a sheet of glass in a window or door [Latin *pannus* rag]
panegyric (pan-ee-**jirr**-rik) *n* a formal speech or piece of writing that praises a person or event [Greek *panēguris* public gathering]
panel *n* **1** a distinct section of a larger surface area, such as that in a door **2** any distinct section of something formed from a sheet of material, such as part of a car body **3** a piece of material inserted in a garment **4** a group of people acting as a team, such as in a quiz or a discussion before an audience **5** *law* **A** a list of jurors **B** the people on a jury **6** short for **instrument panel** ▷ *adj* **7** of a group acting as a panel: *a panel game* ▷ *vb* **-elling, -elled** *or US* **-eling, -eled** **8** to cover or decorate with panels [Old French: portion]
panel beater *n* a person who repairs damage to car bodies
panelling *or US* **paneling** *n* panels collectively, such as on a wall or ceiling
panellist *or US* **panelist** *n* a member of a panel, usually on radio or television
panel van *n Austral & NZ* a small van
pang *n* a sudden sharp feeling of pain or sadness [Germanic]
pangolin *n* an animal of tropical countries with a scaly body and a long snout for feeding on ants and termites. Also called: **scaly anteater** [Malay *peng-gōling*]
panic *n* **1** a sudden overwhelming feeling of terror or anxiety, sometimes affecting a whole group of people ▷ *adj* **2** of or resulting from such terror: *panic measures* ▷ *vb* **-nicking, -nicked** **3** to feel or cause to feel panic [Greek *panikos* emanating from *Pan*, god of the fields]
panicky *adj*
panicle *n botany* a loose, irregularly branched cluster of flowers, such as in the oat [Latin *panicula* tuft]
panic-stricken *adj* affected by panic
panini *n, pl* **-ni** *or* **-nis** a type of Italian bread usually served grilled with a variety of fillings
panjandrum *n* a pompous self-important official [after a character in a nonsense work]
pannier *n* **1** one of a pair of bags fixed on either side of the back wheel of a bicycle or motorcycle **2** one of a pair of large baskets slung over a beast of burden [Old French *panier*]
panoply (**pan**-a-plee) *n* a magnificent array: *ambassadors equipped with the full panoply of diplomatic bags, codes and ciphers* [Greek *pan-* all + *hopla* armour]
panorama *n* **1** a wide unbroken view in all directions: *the beautiful panorama of the Cornish coast* **2** a wide or comprehensive survey of a subject: *the panorama of American life* **3** a picture of a scene unrolled before spectators a part at a time so as to appear continuous [Greek *pan-* all + *horama* view]
panoramic *adj*
pan out *vb* **1** *informal* to work out; result: *Parker's research did not pan out too well* **2** (of gravel) to yield gold by panning
panpipes *pl n* a musical wind instrument made of tubes of decreasing lengths joined together
pansy *n, pl* **-sies** **1** a garden plant whose flowers have rounded white, yellow, or purple velvety petals **2** *offensive slang* an effeminate or homosexual man or boy [Old French *pensée* thought]
pant *vb* **1** to breathe with noisy gasps after exertion **2** to say (something) while breathing in this way **3** (foll. by *for*) to have a frantic desire for ▷ *n* **4** the act of panting [Greek *phantasioun* to have visions]
pantaloons *pl n* baggy trousers gathered at the ankles [French *pantalon* trousers]
pantechnicon *n Brit* a large van used for furniture removals [Greek *pan-* all + *tekhnē* art; originally a London bazaar later used as a furniture warehouse]
pantheism *n* **1** the belief that God is present in everything **2** readiness to worship all gods
pantheist *n* **pantheistic** *adj*
pantheon *n* **1** (in ancient Greece or Rome) a temple built to honour all the gods **2** all the gods of a particular creed: *the Celtic pantheon of horse gods* **3** a group of very important people: *he deserves a place in the pantheon of social reformers* [Greek *pan-* all + *theos* god]

P

panther *n* a leopard, usually a black one [Greek]
panties *pl n* women's or children's underpants
pantihose *pl n US & Austral* women's tights
pantile *n* a roofing tile, with an S-shaped cross section [PAN[1] + *tile*]
panto *n, pl* **-tos** *Brit informal* short for **pantomime** (sense 1)
pantograph *n* **1** an instrument for copying drawings or maps to any scale **2** a device on the roof of an electric train to carry the current from an overhead wire [Greek *pant-* all + *graphein* to write]
pantomime *n* **1** (in Britain) a play based on a fairy tale and performed at Christmas time **2** a theatrical entertainment in which words are replaced by gestures and bodily actions **3** *informal, chiefly Brit* a confused or farcical situation [Greek *pantomīmos*]
pantry *n, pl* **-tries** a small room or large cupboard in which food is kept [Latin *panis* bread]
pants *pl n* **1** *Brit* an undergarment with two leg holes, covering the body from the waist or hips to the thighs **2** *US, Canad, Austral & NZ* trousers or shorts **3** **bore** *or* **scare the pants off someone** *informal* to bore or scare someone very much [shortened from *pantaloons*]
pantyhose *pl n Austral & NZ* women's tights
pap[1] *n* **1** a soft food for babies or invalids **2** worthless or oversimplified entertainment or information **3** *S African* maize porridge [Latin *pappare* to eat]
pap[2] *n old-fashioned Scot & N English dialect* a nipple or teat [from Old Norse]
papa (pap-**pah**) *n old-fashioned, informal* father [French]
papacy (**pay**-pa-see) *n, pl* **-cies** **1** the office or term of office of a Pope **2** the system of government in the Roman Catholic Church that has the Pope as its head [Medieval Latin *papa* Pope]
papal *adj* of the Pope or the papacy
paparazzo (pap-a-**rat**-so) *n, pl* **-razzi** (-**rat**-see) a freelance photographer who specializes in taking shots of famous people without their knowledge or consent [Italian]
papaya (pap-**pie**-a) *n* a large green fruit with sweet yellow flesh, that grows in the West Indies [Spanish]
paper *n* **1** a flexible material made in sheets from wood pulp or other fibres and used for writing on, decorating walls, or wrapping parcels **2** short for **newspaper** or **wallpaper** **3** **papers** documents, such as a passport, which can identify the bearer **4** a set of examination questions **5** **papers** the collected diaries or letters of someone's private or public life **6** a lecture or an essay on a specific subject **7** **on paper** in theory, as opposed to fact: *countless ideas which look good on paper just don't work in practice* ▹ *adj* **8** made of paper: *paper towels; a paper bag* **9** recorded on paper but not yet existing in practice: *a paper profit of more than $50 million* ▹ *vb* **10** to cover (walls) with wallpaper ▹ See also **paper over** [Latin *papyrus*] **papery** *adj*
paperback *n* **1** a book with covers made of flexible card ▹ *adj* **2** of a paperback or publication of paperbacks: *a paperback novel*
paperboy *or* **papergirl** *n* a boy or girl employed to deliver newspapers to people's homes
paper chase *n* a former type of cross-country run in which a runner lays a trail of paper for others to follow
paperclip *n* a bent wire clip for holding sheets of paper together
paperhanger *n* a person who hangs wallpaper as an occupation
paperknife *n, pl* **-knives** a knife-shaped object with a blunt blade for opening sealed envelopes
paper money *n* banknotes, rather than coins
paper over *vb* to conceal (something unpleasant or difficult)
paperweight *n* a small heavy object placed on top of loose papers to prevent them from scattering
paperwork *n* clerical work, such as the writing of reports or letters
papier-mâché (pap-yay **mash**-ay) *n* **1** a hard substance made of layers of paper mixed with paste and moulded when moist ▹ *adj* **2** made of papier-mâché [French, literally: chewed paper]
papilla (pap-**pill**-a) *n, pl* **-lae** (-lee) *biol* a small projection of tissue at the base of a hair, tooth, or feather [Latin: nipple] **papillary** *adj*
papist *n, adj offensive* same as **Roman Catholic** [Church Latin *papa* Pope]
papoose *n* a Native American baby [Native American *papoos*]
paprika *n* a mild powdered seasoning made from red peppers [Hungarian]
Pap test *or* **Pap smear** *n med* same as **cervical smear** [after George *Papanicolaou*, anatomist]
papyrus (pap-**ire**-uss) *n, pl* **-ri** (-rye) *or* **-ruses** **1** a tall water plant of Africa **2** a kind of paper made from the stem of this plant, used by the ancient Egyptians, Greeks, and Romans **3** an ancient document written on this paper [Greek *papuros* reed]
par *n* **1** the usual or average condition: *I feel slightly below par most of the time* **2** *golf* a standard score for a hole or course that a good player should make: *four under par with two holes to play* **3** *finance* the established value of the unit of one national currency in terms of the unit of another **4** *commerce* short for **par value** **5** **on a par with** equal or equivalent to: *an environmental disaster on a par with Chernobyl* **6** **par for the course** to be expected: *random acts of violence were par for the course in the capital* [Latin: equal]
par. **1** paragraph **2** parenthesis
para *n informal* **1** a paratrooper **2** a paragraph
para- *or before a vowel* **par-** *prefix* **1** beside or near: *parameter* **2** beyond: *parapsychology* **3** resembling: *paratyphoid fever* [Greek]
parable *n* a short story that uses familiar situations to illustrate a religious or moral point [Greek *parabolē* analogy]
parabola (par-**ab**-bol-a) *n geom* an open plane curve formed by the intersection of a cone by a plane parallel to its side [Greek *parabolē* a setting alongside] **parabolic** *adj*
paracetamol *n* a mild pain-relieving drug [from *para-acetamidophenol*]

P

parachute *n* **1** a large fabric canopy connected by a harness, that slows the descent of a person or package from an aircraft ▷ *vb* **-chuting, -chuted** **2** to land or to drop (supplies or troops) by parachute from an aircraft [French] **parachutist** *n*

parade *n* **1** an ordered march or procession **2** a public promenade or street of shops **3** a blatant but sometimes insincere display: *a man who made a parade of liking his own company best* ▷ *vb* **-rading, -raded** **4** to exhibit or flaunt: *he neither paraded nor disguised his devout faith* **5** to walk or march, esp. in a procession [French: a making ready]

parade ground *n* a place where soldiers assemble regularly for inspection or display

paradigm (par-a-dime) *n* a model or example: *his experience is a paradigm for the young artist* [Greek *paradeigma* pattern]

paradise *n* **1** heaven; where the good go after death **2** the Garden of Eden **3** any place or condition that fulfils a person's desires [Greek *paradeisos* garden]

paradise duck *n* a New Zealand duck with bright feathers

paradox *n* **1** a statement that seems self-contradictory but may be true: *it's a strange paradox that a musician must practise improvising to become a good improviser* **2** a self-contradictory proposition, such as *I always tell lies* **3** a person or thing that is made up of contradictory elements [Greek *paradoxos* opposed to existing notions] **paradoxical** *adj* **paradoxically** *adv*

paraffin *n* **1** *Brit* a liquid mixture distilled from petroleum or shale and used as a fuel or solvent **2** *chem* the former name for **alkane** [Latin *parum* too little + *affinis* adjacent; so called from its chemical inertia]

paraffin wax *n* a white waxlike substance distilled from petroleum and used to make candles and as a sealing agent

paragon *n* a model of perfection: *a paragon of female integrity and determination* [Old Italian *paragone* comparison]

paragraph *n* **1** a section of a piece of writing, usually devoted to one idea, which begins on a new line and is often indented **2** *printing* the character ¶, used to indicate the beginning of a new paragraph ▷ *vb* **3** to put (a piece of writing) into paragraphs [Greek *paragraphos* line drawing attention to part of a text]

parakeet *n* a small colourful parrot with a long tail [Spanish *periquito* parrot]

paralegal *n* a person trained to assist lawyers but not qualified to practise law

parallax *n* an apparent change in an object's position due to a change in the observer's position [Greek *parallaxis* change]

parallel *adj* **1** separated by an equal distance at every point: *parallel lines; a path parallel to the main road* **2** precisely corresponding: *we decide our salaries by comparison with parallel jobs in other charities* **3** *computers* operating on several items of information or instructions at the same time ▷ *n* **4** *maths* one of a set of parallel lines or planes **5** something with similar features to another **6** a comparison; similarity between two things: *she attempted to excuse herself by drawing a parallel between her behaviour and ours* **7** Also called: **parallel of latitude** any of the imaginary lines around the earth parallel to the equator, marking degrees of latitude **8** *printing* the character ‖, used as a reference mark ▷ *vb* **9** to correspond to: *the increase in smoking is paralleled by an increase in lung cancer* [Greek *parallēlos* alongside one another]

parallel bars *pl n* *gymnastics* a pair of wooden bars on upright posts used for various exercises

parallelepiped (par-a-lel-ee-**pipe**-ed) *n* *geom* a solid shape whose six faces are parallelograms [Greek *parallēlos* parallel + *epipedon* plane surface]

parallelism *n* **1** the state of being parallel **2** a close likeness

parallelogram *n* *geom* a plane figure whose opposite sides are parallel and equal in length [Greek *parallēlos* parallel + *grammē* line]

paralyse *or US* **-lyze** *vb* **-lysing, -lysed** *or* **-lyzing, -lyzed** **1** *pathol* to affect with paralysis **2** to make immobile: *he was paralysed by fear* [French *paralyser*]

paralysis *n* **1** *pathol* inability to move all or part of the body due to damage to the nervous system **2** a state of inactivity: *the economic chaos and political paralysis into which the country has sunk* [Greek *paralusis*, from *para-* beyond + *lusis* a loosening]

paralytic *adj* **1** of or relating to paralysis **2** *Brit informal* very drunk ▷ *n* **3** a person who is paralysed

paramecium (par-a-**mee**-see-um) *n, pl* **-cia** (-see-a) a single-celled animal which lives in ponds, puddles, and sewage filters and swims by means of cilia

paramedic *n* a person, such as a member of an ambulance crew, whose work supplements that of the medical profession **paramedical** *adj*

parameter (par-**am**-it-er) *n* **1** *maths* an arbitrary constant that determines the specific form of a mathematical expression, such as *a* and *b* in $y = ax^2 + b$ **2** *informal* any limiting factor: *exchange rates are allowed to fluctuate only within designated parameters* [Greek *para* beside + *metron* measure]

paramilitary *adj* denoting a group of people organized on military lines

paramount *adj* of the greatest importance [Old French *par* by + *-amont* above]

paramour *n* *old-fashioned* someone's lover [Old French, literally: through love]

paranoia *n* **1** a mental disorder which causes delusions of grandeur or of persecution **2** *informal* intense fear or suspicion, usually unfounded [Greek *para-* beyond + *noos* mind] **paranoid** *or* **paranoiac** *adj, n*

paranormal *adj* **1** beyond normal scientific explanation ▷ *n* **2** **the paranormal** paranormal happenings or matters generally

parapet *n* **1** a low wall or railing along the edge of a balcony or roof **2** *military* a mound of sandbags in front of a trench to conceal and protect troops from fire [Italian *parapetto*]

paraphernalia *n* various articles or bits of equipment [Greek *para-* beyond + *phernē* dowry]

paraphrase *n* **1** an expression of a statement or text in other words ▷ *vb* **-phrasing, -phrased** **2** to put (a statement or text) into other words [Greek *paraphrazein* to recount]

paraplegia (par-a-**pleej**-ya) *n pathol* paralysis of the lower half of the body [Greek: a blow on one side] **paraplegic** *adj, n*
parapsychology *n* the study of mental phenomena such as telepathy
Paraquat *n trademark* an extremely poisonous weedkiller
parasite *n* **1** an animal or plant that lives in or on another from which it obtains nourishment **2** a person who habitually lives at the expense of others; sponger [Greek *para-* beside + *sitos* grain] **parasitic** *adj*
parasol *n* an umbrella-like sunshade [French]
paratrooper *n* a member of the paratroops
paratroops *pl n* troops trained to be dropped by parachute into a battle area
paratyphoid fever *n* a disease resembling but less severe than typhoid fever
parboil *vb* to boil (food) until partially cooked [Late Latin *perbullire* to boil thoroughly; modern meaning due to confusion of *par-* with *part*]
parcel *n* **1** something wrapped up; a package **2** a group of people or things sharing something in common: *a parcel of fools* **3** a distinct portion of land: *he was the recipient of a substantial parcel of land* ▹ *vb* **-celling, -celled** *or US* **-celing, -celed** **4** (often foll. by *up*) to wrap (something) up into a parcel **5** (foll. by *out*) to divide (something) into portions: *the children were parcelled out to relatives* [Old French *parcelle*]
parch *vb* **1** to deprive (something) of water; dry up: *the summer sun parched the hills* **2** to make (someone) very thirsty: *I'm parched. Have we got any lemonade?* [origin unknown]
parchment *n* **1** a thick smooth material made from animal skin and used for writing on **2** a manuscript made of this material **3** a stiff yellowish paper resembling parchment [Greek *pergamēnē*, from *Pergamēnos* of Pergamum (where parchment was made)]

P

pardon *vb* **1** to forgive or excuse (a person) for (an offence, mistake, etc.): *I hope you'll pardon the wait* ▹ *n* **2** forgiveness **3** official release from punishment for a crime ▹ *interj* **4** Also: **pardon me, I beg your pardon** **A** sorry; excuse me **B** what did you say? [Medieval Latin *perdonare* to forgive freely] **pardonable** *adj*
pare *vb* **paring, pared** **1** to peel (the outer layer) from (something): *thinly pare the rind from the grapefruit* **2** to trim or cut the edge of **3** to decrease bit by bit: *the government is prepared to pare down the armed forces* [Latin *parare* to make ready]
parent *n* **1** a father or mother **2** a person acting as a father or mother; guardian **3** a plant or animal that has produced one or more plants or animals [Latin *parens*, from *parere* to bring forth] **parental** *adj* **parenthood** *n*
parentage *n* ancestry or family
parent company *n* a company that owns a number of smaller companies
parenthesis (par-**en**-thiss-iss) *n, pl* **-ses** (-seez) **1** a word or phrase inserted into a passage, and marked off by brackets or dashes **2** Also called: **bracket** either of a pair of characters ( ), used to enclose such a phrase [Greek: something placed in besides] **parenthetical** *adj* **parenthetically** *adv*
parenting *n* the activity of bringing up children
parent teacher association *n* an organization consisting of the parents and teachers of school pupils formed to organize activities on behalf of the school
par excellence *adv* beyond comparison: *this book justifies its claim to be a reference work par excellence* [French]
parfait (par-**fay**) *n* a dessert consisting of layers of ice cream, fruit, and sauce, topped with whipped cream, and served in a tall glass: *a blackberry and apricot parfait* [French: perfect]
pariah (par-**rye**-a) *n* a social outcast: *the man they regard as a pariah* [Tamil *paraiyan* drummer]
parietal (par-**rye**-it-al) *adj anatomy & biol* of or forming the walls of a body cavity: *the parietal bones of the skull* [Latin *paries* wall]
paring *n* something that has been cut off something
parish *n* **1** an area that has its own church and a priest or pastor. Related adjective: **parochial** **2** the people who live in a parish **3** (in England and, formerly, Wales) the smallest unit of local government [Greek *paroikos* neighbour]
parish clerk *n* an official who performs various (esp. administrative) duties for a church or civil parish
parish council *n* (in England and, formerly, Wales) the administrative body of a parish. See **parish** (sense 3)
parishioner *n* a person who lives in a particular parish
parish register *n* a book in which the births, baptisms, marriages, and deaths in a parish are recorded
parity *n* **1** equality, for example of rank or pay **2** close or exact equivalence: *the company maintained parity with the competition* **3** *finance* equivalence between the units of currency of two countries [Latin *par* equal]
park *n* **1** a large area of open land for recreational use by the public **2** a piece of open land for public recreation in a town **3** *Brit* a large area of private land surrounding a country house **4** an area designed to accommodate a number of related enterprises: *a science park* **5** *US & Canad* a playing field or sports stadium **6** **the park** *Brit informal* the pitch in soccer ▹ *vb* **7** to stop and leave (a vehicle) temporarily: *I parked between the two cars already outside; police vans were parked on every street corner* **8** *informal* to leave or put (someone or something) somewhere: *she parked herself on the sofa and stayed there all evening* [Germanic] **parking** *n*
parka *n* a long jacket with a quilted lining and a fur-trimmed hood [from Aleutian (language of Aleutian Islands, off Alaska): skin]
parkade *n Canad* a building used as a car park
park and ride *n* a transportation scheme in which drivers park some distance away from a city centre, tourist attraction, etc. and complete their journey by public transport
parkette *n Canad* a small public car park
parkin *n Brit* a moist spicy ginger cake usually containing oatmeal [origin unknown]
parking lot *n US & Canad* area or building where vehicles may be left for a time

parking meter *n* a coin-operated device beside a parking space that indicates how long a vehicle may be left parked

parking ticket *n* the notice of a fine served on a motorist for a parking offence

Parkinson's disease *or* **Parkinsonism** *n* a progressive disorder of the central nervous system which causes tremor, rigidity, and impaired muscular coordination [after J. *Parkinson*, surgeon]

Parkinson's law *n* the notion that work expands to fill the time available for its completion [after C. N. *Parkinson*, historian and writer]

parkland *n* grassland with scattered trees

parkour (pah-**koor**) *n* the sport of running through urban areas while performing various gymnastic manoeuvres over man-made obstacles [French *parcour* obstacle course]

parky *adj* **parkier, parkiest** *Brit informal* (of the weather) chilly [origin unknown]

parlance *n* the manner of speaking associated with a particular group or subject: *he had, in Marxist parlance, a 'petit bourgeois' mentality* [French *parler* to talk]

parley *old-fashioned* ▷ *n* **1** a discussion between members of opposing sides to decide terms of agreement ▷ *vb* **2** to have a parley [French *parler* to talk]

parliament *n* a law-making assembly of a country [Old French *parlement*, from *parler* to speak]

Parliament *n* **1** the highest law-making authority in Britain, consisting of the House of Commons, the House of Lords, and the sovereign **2** the equivalent law-making authority in another country

parliamentarian *n* an expert in parliamentary procedures

parliamentary *adj* **1** of or from a parliament: *parliamentary elections* **2** conforming to the procedures of a parliament: *parliamentary language*

parlour *or US* **parlor** *n* **1** *old-fashioned* a living room for receiving visitors **2** a room or shop equipped as a place of business: *an ice-cream parlour* [Old French *parler* to speak]

parlous *adj archaic or humorous* dangerously bad; dire: *the parlous state of the economy* [variant of *perilous*]

parma *n Austral informal* a dish of chicken in breadcrumbs, topped with Parmesan cheese and a tomato sauce, and served with ham or bacon

Parmesan (par-miz-**zan**) *n* a hard strong-flavoured cheese used grated on pasta dishes and soups [Italian *parmegiano* of Parma, Italy]

parochial *adj* **1** narrow in outlook; provincial **2** of or relating to a parish [see PARISH]
parochialism *n*

parody *n, pl* **-dies 1** a piece of music or literature that mimics the style of another composer or author in a humorous way **2** something done so badly that it seems like an intentional mockery ▷ *vb* **-dies, -dying, -died 3** to make a parody of [Greek *paroidia* satirical poem] **parodist** *n*

parole *n* **1** the freeing of a prisoner before his or her sentence has run out, on condition that he or she behaves well **2** a promise given by a prisoner to behave well if granted liberty or partial liberty **3 on parole** conditionally released from prison ▷ *vb* **-roling, -roled 4** to place (a person) on parole [Old French *parole d'honneur* word of honour]

parotid gland *n anatomy* either of a pair of salivary glands in front of and below the ears [Greek *para-* near + *ous* ear]

paroxysm *n* **1** an uncontrollable outburst of emotion: *a paroxysm of grief* **2** *pathol* **A** a sudden attack or recurrence of a disease **B** a fit or convulsion [Greek *paroxunein* to goad]
paroxysmal *adj*

parquet (**par**-kay) *n* **1** a floor covering made of blocks of wood ▷ *vb* **2** to cover (a floor) with parquetry [Old French: small enclosure]

parquetry (**par**-kit-tree) *n* pieces of wood arranged in a geometric pattern, used to cover floors

parr *n* a salmon up to two years of age [origin unknown]

parricide *n* **1** a person who kills one of his or her parents **2** the act of killing either of one's parents [Latin *parricidium* murder of a parent or relative] **parricidal** *adj*

parrot *n* **1** a tropical bird with a short hooked beak, bright plumage, and an ability to mimic human speech **2** a person who repeats or imitates someone else's words **3 sick as a parrot** *usually facetious* extremely disappointed ▷ *vb* **-roting, -roted 4** to repeat or imitate (someone else's words) without understanding them [probably from French *paroquet*]

parrot fever *n* same as **psittacosis**

parrotfish *n* a brightly coloured sea fish

parry *vb* **-ries, -rying, -ried 1** to ward off (an attack) **2** to avoid answering (questions) in a clever way ▷ *n, pl* **-ries 3** an instance of parrying **4** a skilful evasion of a question [French *parer* to ward off]

parse (**parz**) *vb* **parsing, parsed** to analyse (a sentence or the words in a sentence) grammatically [Latin *pars (orationis)* part (of speech)]

parsec *n* a unit of astronomical distance equivalent to 3.0857×10^{16} metres or 3.262 light years [*parallax* + *second* (of time)]

parsimony *n formal* extreme caution in spending [Latin *parcimonia*] **parsimonious** *adj*

parsley *n* a herb with curled pleasant-smelling leaves, used for seasoning and garnishing food [Middle English *persely*]

parsnip *n* a long tapering cream-coloured root vegetable [Latin *pastinaca*]

parson *n* **1** a parish priest in the Church of England **2** any member of the clergy **3** NZ a nonconformist minister [Latin *persona* personage]

parsonage *n* the residence of a parson, provided by the parish

parson's nose *n* the rump of a fowl when cooked

part *n* **1** a piece or portion **2** one of several equal divisions: *a salad dressing made with two parts oil to one part vinegar* **3** an actor's role in a play **4** a person's duty: *his ancestors had done their part nobly and well at Bannockburn* **5** an involvement in or contribution to something: *he was jailed for his part in the fraud* **6** a region or area: *he's well known in these parts;*

P

the weather in this part of the country is extreme **7** *anatomy* an area of the body **8** a component that can be replaced in a vehicle or machine **9** *US, Canad & Austral* same as **parting** (sense 2) **10** *music* a melodic line assigned to one or more instrumentalists or singers **11 for my part** as far as I am concerned **12 for the most part** generally **13 in part** to some degree; partly **14 on the part of** on behalf of **15 part and parcel of** an essential ingredient of **16 play a part** A to pretend to be what one is not B (foll. by *in*) to have something to do with: *examinations play a large part in education and in schools* **17 take part in** to participate in **18 take someone's part** to support someone, for example in an argument **19 take something in good part** to respond to (teasing or criticism) with good humour ▷ *vb* **20** to divide or separate from one another: *her lips parted in laughter; the cord parted with a pop* **21** to go away from one another: *we parted with handshakes all round* **22** to split: *the path parts here* **23** to arrange (the hair) in such a way that a line of scalp is left showing **24 part from** to cause (someone) to give up: *I was astonished at the way Henry parted his audience from their money* **25 part with** to give up: *check carefully before you part with your cash* ▷ *adv* **26** to some extent; partly: *this book is part history, part travelogue* ▷ See also **parts** [Latin *pars* a part]

partake *vb* **-taking, -took, -taken 1 partake in** to take part in **2 partake of** to take (food or drink) [from earlier *part taker*]

> **USAGE** *Partake of* is sometimes wrongly used as if it were a synonym of *eat* or *drink*. Correctly, one can only *partake of* food or drink which is available for several people to share.

parterre *n* **1** a formally patterned flower garden **2** the pit of a theatre [French]

P

Parthian shot *n* a hostile remark or gesture delivered while departing [from the custom of archers from Parthia, an ancient Asian empire, who shot their arrows backwards while retreating]

partial *adj* **1** relating to only a part; not complete: *partial deafness* **2** biased: *religious programmes can be as partial as they like* **3 be partial to** to have a particular liking for [Latin *pars* part] **partiality** *n* **partially** *adv*

> **USAGE** See at **partly**.

participate *vb* **-pating, -pated** > **participate in** to become actively involved in [Latin *pars* part + *capere* to take] **participant** *n* **participation** *n* **participatory** *adj*

participle *n grammar* a form of a verb that is used in compound tenses or as an adjective. See also **present participle**, **past participle** [Latin *pars* part + *capere* to take] **participial** *adj*

particle *n* **1** an extremely small piece or amount: *clean thoroughly to remove all particles of dirt* **2** *grammar* an uninflected part of speech, such as an interjection or preposition **3** *physics* a minute piece of matter, such as an electron or proton [Latin *pars* part]

parti-coloured *or US* **particolored** *adj* having different colours in different parts [from obsolete *party* of more than one colour]

particular *adj* **1** of, belonging to, or being one person or thing; specific: *the particular type of tuition on offer* **2** exceptional or special: *the report voices particular concern over the state of the country's manufacturing industry* **3** providing specific details or circumstances: *a particular account* **4** difficult to please; fussy ▷ *n* **5** a separate distinct item as opposed to a generalization: *moving from the general to the particular* **6** an item of information; detail: *she refused to go into particulars* **7 in particular** especially or exactly: *three painters in particular were responsible for these developments* [Latin *particula* a small part] **particularly** *adv*

particularity *n, pl* **-ties 1** great attentiveness to detail **2** the state of being particular as opposed to general; individuality

particularize *or* **-rise** *vb* **-rizing, -rized** *or* **-rising, -rised** to give details about (something) **particularization** *or* **-risation** *n*

parting *n* **1** a departure or leave-taking **2** *Brit & NZ* the line of scalp showing when sections of hair are combed in opposite directions **3** the act of dividing (something): *the parting of the Red Sea*

parting shot *n* a hostile remark or gesture delivered while departing

partisan *n* **1** a person who supports a particular cause or party **2** a member of an armed resistance group within occupied territory ▷ *adj* **3** prejudiced or one-sided [Old Italian *partigiano*] **partisanship** *n*

partition *n* **1** a large screen or thin wall that divides a room **2** the division of a country into two or more independent countries ▷ *vb* **3** to separate (a room) into sections: *the shower is partitioned off from the rest of the bathroom* **4** to divide (a country) into separate self-governing parts: *the subcontinent was partitioned into India and Pakistan* [Latin *partire* to divide]

partitive *grammar* ▷ *adj* **1** (of a noun) referring to part of something. The phrase *some of the butter* is a partitive construction ▷ *n* **2** a partitive word, such as *some* or *any* [Latin *partire* to divide]

partly *adv* not completely

> **USAGE** *Partly* and *partially* are to some extent interchangeable, but *partly* should be used when referring to a part or parts of something: *the building is partly* (not *partially*) *of stone*, while *partially* is preferred for the meaning *to some extent: his mother is partially* (not *partly*) *sighted*.

partner *n* **1** either member of a couple in a relationship **2** a member of a business partnership **3** one of a pair of dancers or of players on the same side in a game: *her bridge partner* **4** an ally or companion: *the country's main European trading partner* ▷ *vb* **5** to be the partner of (someone) [Middle English *parcener* joint inheritor]

partnership *n* **1** a relationship in which two or more people or organizations work together in a business venture **2** the condition of being a partner

part of speech *n grammar* a class of words, such as a noun, verb, or adjective, sharing important syntactic or semantic features

partook *vb* the past tense of **partake**

partridge *n, pl* **-tridges** *or* **-tridge** a game bird with an orange-brown head, greyish neck, and a short rust-coloured tail [Latin *perdix*]

parts *pl n literary* abilities or talents: *a man of many parts*

part song *n* a song composed in harmonized parts

part-time *adj* **1** for less than the normal full working time: *a part-time job* ▷ *adv* **part time 2** on a part-time basis: *he works part time* **part-timer** *n*

parturient *adj formal* giving birth [Latin *parturire* to be in labour]

parturition *n formal* the process of giving birth [Latin *parturire* to be in labour]

party *n, pl* **-ties 1** a social gathering for pleasure **2** a group of people involved in the same activity: *a search party* **3** a group of people sharing a common political aim **4** the person or people who take part in or are involved in something, esp. a legal action or dispute: *a judge will decide who the guilty party is* **5** *informal, humorous* a person: *he's an odd old party* ▷ *vb* **-ties, -tying, -tied 6** *informal* to celebrate; have a good time [Old French *partie* part]

party line *n* **1** the policies of a political party **2** a telephone line shared by two or more subscribers

party wall *n property law* a common wall separating two properties

par value *n* the value printed on a share certificate or bond at the time of its issue

parvenu *or fem* **parvenue** (par-ven-new) *n* a person newly risen to a position of power or wealth who is considered to lack culture or education [French]

pascal *n* the SI unit of pressure; the pressure exerted on an area of 1 square metre by a force of 1 newton [after B. *Pascal*, mathematician and scientist]

Pascal *n* a high-level computer programming language developed as a teaching language [after B. *Pascal*, mathematician and scientist]

paschal (pask-l) *adj* **1** *Judaism* of or relating to the Passover **2** *Christianity* of or relating to Easter [Hebrew *pesah* Passover]

pas de deux (pah de duh) *n, pl* **pas de deux** *ballet* a dance for two people [French: step for two]

pash *Austral & NZ slang* ▷ *vb* **1** to kiss or embrace passionately ▷ *n* **2** a passionate kiss or embrace [from PASSION]

pasha *n* (formerly) a high official of the Ottoman Empire: placed after a name when used as a title [Turkish *paşa*]

pashmina (pash-mee-na) *n* a type of cashmere scarf or shawl made from the underfur of Tibetan goats [Persian *pashm* wool]

Pasifika *Austral & NZ* ▷ *pl n* **1** people from the islands of the South Pacific and their descendants ▷ *adj* **2** relating to the people or culture of the South Pacific islands

paso doble (pass-so dobe-lay) *n* **1** a modern ballroom dance in fast duple time **2** music for this dance [Spanish: double step]

pas op (pass op) *interj S African* beware [Afrikaans]

paspalum (pass-pale-um) *n Austral & NZ* a type of grass with wide leaves

pasqueflower *n* a small purple-flowered plant of Europe and Asia [French *passefleur*, changed to *pasqueflower* Easter flower, because it blooms at Easter]

pass *vb* **1** to go by or past (a person or thing) **2** to continue or extend in a particular direction: *the road to Camerino passes through some fine scenery* **3** to go through or cause (something) to go through (an obstacle or barrier): *the bullet passed through his head* **4** to be successful in (a test or examination) **5** to spend (time) or (of time) go by: *the time passed surprisingly quickly* **6** to hand over or be handed over: *she passed me her glass* **7** to be inherited by: *his mother's small estate had passed to him after her death* **8** *sport* to hit, kick, or throw (the ball) to another player **9** (of a law-making body) to agree to (a law or proposal): *the bill was passed by parliament last week* **10** to pronounce (judgment): *the court is expected to pass sentence later today* **11** to move onwards or over: *a flicker of amusement passed over his face* **12** to exceed: *Australia's population has just passed the 25 million mark* **13** to go without comment: *the insult passed unnoticed* **14** to choose not to answer a question or not to make a bid or a play in card games **15** to discharge (urine, etc.) from the body **16** to come to an end or disappear: *today's jitters will soon pass* **17** (foll. by *for* or *as*) to be likely to be mistaken for (someone or something else): *the few sunny days that pass for summer in this country* **18** *old-fashioned* to take place: *what passed at the meeting?* **19 pass away** *or* **on** *euphemistic* to die ▷ *n* **20** a successful result in an examination or test **21** *sport* the transfer of a ball from one player to another **22** a route through a range of mountains where there is a gap between peaks **23** a permit or licence **24** *military* a document authorizing leave of absence **25** *bridge etc.* an instance of choosing not to answer a question or not to make a bid or a play in card games **26 a pretty pass** a bad state of affairs **27 make a pass at** *informal* to try to persuade (someone) to have sex: *he made a pass at his colleague* ▷ See also **pass off, pass out** *etc.* [Latin *passus* step]

> **USAGE** The past participle of *pass* is sometimes wrongly spelt *past*: *the time for recriminations has passed* (not *past*).

pass. passive

passable *adj* **1** adequate or acceptable: *passable if hardly faultless German* **2** (of a road, path, etc.) capable of being travelled along: *most main roads are passable with care despite the snow* **passably** *adv*

passage *n* **1** a channel or opening providing a way through **2** a hall or corridor **3** a section of a written work, speech, or piece of music **4** a journey by ship **5** the act of passing from one place or condition to another: *Ireland faced a tough passage to qualify for the World Cup finals* **6** the right or freedom to pass: *the aid convoys were guaranteed safe passage through rebel-held areas* **7** the establishing of a law by a law-making body [Old French *passer* to pass]

passageway *n* a corridor or passage

passbook *n* **1** a book issued by a bank or building society for recording deposits and withdrawals **2** *S African* (formerly) an official identity document

P

passé (**pas**-say) *adj* out-of-date: *smoking is a bit passé these days* [French]
passenger *n* **1** a person travelling in a vehicle driven by someone else **2** *Brit & NZ* a member of a team who does not take an equal share of the work: *you'll have to pull your weight – we can't afford passengers* [Old French *passager* passing]
passer-by *n, pl* **passers-by** a person who is walking past someone or something
passerine *adj* **1** belonging to an order of perching birds that includes the larks, finches, and starlings ▹ *n* **2** any bird of this order [Latin *passer* sparrow]
passim *adv* throughout: used to indicate that what is referred to occurs frequently in a particular piece of writing [Latin]
passing *adj* **1** momentary or short-lived: *a passing fad* **2** casual or superficial: *a passing resemblance* ▹ *n* **3** *euphemistic* death **4** the ending of something: *the passing of the old order in Eastern Europe* **5** **in passing** briefly and without going into detail; incidentally: *this fact is only noted in passing*
passion *n* **1** intense sexual love **2** any strongly felt emotion **3** a strong enthusiasm for something: *a passion for football* **4** the object of an intense desire or enthusiasm: *flying is his abiding passion* [Latin *pati* to suffer] **passionless** *adj*
Passion *n* *Christianity* the sufferings of Christ from the Last Supper to his death on the cross
passionate *adj* **1** showing intense sexual desire **2** capable of or revealing intense emotion: *a passionate speech* **passionately** *adv*
passionflower *n* a tropical plant with brightly coloured showy flowers [parts of the flowers are said to resemble the instruments of the Crucifixion]
passion fruit *n* the edible egg-shaped fruit of the passionflower
Passion play *n* a play about the Passion of Christ
passive *adj* **1** not taking an active part **2** submissive and receptive to outside forces **3** *grammar* denoting a form of verbs used to indicate that the subject is the recipient of the action, as *was broken* in *The glass was broken by that boy over there* **4** *chem* (of a substance) chemically unreactive ▹ *n* **5** *grammar* the passive form of a verb [Latin *passivus* capable of suffering] **passively** *adv* **passivity** *n*
passive-aggressive *adj* *psychol* of or relating to a personality that harbours aggressive emotions while behaving in a calm or detached manner
passive resistance *n* resistance to a government or the law by nonviolent acts such as fasting, peaceful demonstrations, or refusing to cooperate
passive smoking *n* the unwilling inhalation of smoke from other people's cigarettes by a nonsmoker
passkey *n* **1** a private key **2** same as **master key** or **skeleton key**
pass law *n* (formerly in South Africa) a law restricting the movement of Black Africans
pass off *vb* **1** to present (something or oneself) under false pretences: *he passed the fake diamonds off as real* **2** to come to a gradual end: *the effects of the gas passed off relatively peacefully* **3** to take place: *the main demonstration passed off peacefully*
pass out *vb* **1** *informal* to become unconscious; faint **2** *Brit* (of an officer cadet) to qualify for a military commission
Passover *n* an eight-day Jewish festival commemorating the sparing of the Israelites in Egypt [*pass over*, translation of Hebrew *pesah*]
pass over *vb* **1** to take no notice of; disregard: *she claims she had been passed over for promotion because she is a woman* **2** to ignore or not discuss: *this disaster cannot be passed over lightly*
passport *n* **1** an official document issued by a government, which identifies the holder and grants him or her permission to travel abroad **2** an asset that gains a person admission or acceptance: *good qualifications are no automatic passport to a job* [French *passer* to pass + *port* port]
pass up *vb informal* to let (something) go by; disregard: *am I passing up my one chance to be really happy?*
password *n* a secret word or phrase that ensures admission by proving identity or membership
past *adj* **1** of the time before the present: *the past history of the world* **2** no longer in existence: *past happiness* **3** immediately previous: *the past year* **4** former: *a past president* **5** *grammar* indicating a tense of verbs used to describe actions that have been begun or completed at the time of speaking ▹ *n* **6** **the past** the period of time before the present: *a familiar face from the past* **7** the history of a person or nation **8** an earlier disreputable period of someone's life: *a man with a bit of a past* **9** *grammar* **A** the past tense **B** a verb in the past tense ▹ *adv* **10** on or onwards: *I called but he just walked past* **11** at a time before the present; ago: *three years past* ▹ *prep* **12** beyond in time: *it's past midnight* **13** beyond in place: *a procession of mourners filed past the coffin* **14** beyond the limit of: *riches past his wildest dreams* **15** **not put it past someone** to consider someone capable of (a particular action): *I wouldn't put it past him to double-cross us* **16** **past it** *informal* unable to do the things one could do when younger [from *pass*]
pasta *n* a type of food, such as spaghetti, that is made from a dough of flour and water and formed into different shapes [Italian]
paste *n* **1** a soft moist mixture, such as toothpaste **2** an adhesive made from water and flour or starch, for use with paper **3** a smooth creamy preparation of fish, meat, or vegetables for spreading on bread: *sausage paste* **4** *Brit & NZ* dough for making pastry **5** a hard shiny glass used to make imitation gems ▹ *vb* **pasting, pasted** **6** to attach by paste: *she bought a scrapbook and carefully pasted in it all her clippings* **7** *slang* to beat or defeat (someone) [Greek *pastē* barley porridge]
pasteboard *n* a stiff board made by pasting layers of paper together
pastel *n* **1** **A** a crayon made of ground pigment bound with gum **B** a picture drawn with such crayons **2** a pale delicate colour ▹ *adj* **3** (of a colour) pale and delicate: *pastel pink* [Latin *pasta* paste]
pastern *n* the part of a horse's foot between the fetlock and the hoof [Old French *pasture* a tether]

paste-up *n* a document or artwork prepared for copying or printing by pasting a number of different sections on a board

pasteurize *or* **-rise** *vb* **-rizing, -rized** *or* **-rising, -rised** to destroy bacteria (in beverages or solid foods) by a special heating process [after Louis *Pasteur,* chemist] **pasteurization** *or* **-risation** *n*

pastiche (past-**eesh**) *n* a work of art that mixes styles or copies the style of another artist [French]

pastille *n* a small fruit-flavoured and sometimes medicated sweet [Latin *pastillus* small loaf]

pastime *n* an activity which makes time pass pleasantly

pasting *n* **1** *slang* a thrashing or heavy defeat **2** *informal* strong criticism

past master *n* a person with a talent for or experience in a particular activity: *a past master at manipulating the media*

pastor *n* a member of the Christian clergy in charge of a congregation [Latin: shepherd]

pastoral *adj* **1** of or depicting country life or scenery **2** (of land) used for pasture **3** of or relating to a member of the Christian clergy or his or her duties **4** of or relating to shepherds or their work ▷ *n* **5** a literary work, picture, or piece of music portraying country life **6** *Christianity* a letter from a bishop to the clergy or people of his diocese [Latin *pastor* shepherd]

pastorale (past-or-**ahl**) *n, pl* **-rales** a musical composition that suggests country life [Italian]

pastoralism *n* a system of agriculture in dry grassland regions based on raising stock such as cattle, sheep, or goats **pastoralist** *n*

past participle *n grammar* a form of verb used to form compound past tenses and passive forms of the verb and to modify nouns: *spoken is the past participle of speak*

pastrami *n* highly seasoned smoked beef [Yiddish]

pastry *n* **1** a dough of flour, water, and fat **2** *pl* **-tries** an individual cake or pie **3** baked foods, such as tarts, made with this dough [from *paste*]

pasturage *n* **1** the business of grazing cattle **2** same as **pasture**

pasture *n* **1** land covered with grass, suitable for grazing by farm animals **2** the grass growing on this land [Latin *pascere* to feed]

pasty[1] (**pay**-stee) *adj* **pastier, pastiest** (of the complexion) pale and unhealthy-looking

pasty[2] (**past**-ee) *n, pl* **pasties** a round of pastry folded over a filling of meat and vegetables [Old French *pastée*]

pat[1] *vb* **patting, patted 1** to tap (someone or something) lightly with the hand **2** to shape (something) with a flat instrument or the palm of the hand **3 pat someone on the back** *informal* to congratulate someone ▷ *n* **4** a gentle tap or stroke **5** a small shaped lump of something soft, such as butter **6 pat on the back** *informal* an indication of approval [probably imitative]

pat[2] *adv* **1** Also: **off pat** thoroughly learned: *he had all his answers off pat* **2 stand pat** *chiefly US & Canad* to stick firmly to a belief or decision ▷ *adj* **3** quick, ready, or glib: *a pat generalization* [perhaps adverbial use ('with a light stroke') of PAT[1]]

patch *n* **1** a piece of material used to cover a hole in a garment **2** a small contrasting section: *there was a bald patch on the top of his head* **3** a small plot of land **4** *med* a protective covering for an injured eye **5** a scrap or remnant **6** the area under someone's supervision, such as a police officer or social worker **7 a bad patch** a difficult time **8 not a patch on** not nearly as good as ▷ *vb* **9** to mend (a garment) with a patch **10 patch together** to produce (something) by piecing parts together hurriedly or carelessly **11 patch up A** to mend (something) hurriedly or carelessly **B** to make up (a quarrel) [perhaps from French *pieche* piece]

patchwork *n* **1** needlework done by sewing together pieces of different materials **2** something made up of various parts

patchy *adj* **patchier, patchiest 1** of uneven quality or intensity: *since then her career has been patchy* **2** having or forming patches

pate *n old-fashioned or humorous* the head or the crown of the head [origin unknown]

pâté (**pat**-ay) *n* a spread of finely minced meat, fish, or vegetables often served as a starter [French]

pâté de foie gras (de fwah **grah**) *n* a smooth rich paste made from the liver of specially fattened geese [French: pâté of fat liver]

patella (pat-**tell**-a) *n, pl* **-lae** (-lee) *anatomy* kneecap [Latin] **patellar** *adj*

paten (**pat**-in) *n Christianity* a plate, usually made of silver or gold, used for the bread at Communion [Latin *patina* pan]

patent *n* **1 A** an official document granting the exclusive right to make, use, and sell an invention for a limited period **B** the right granted by such a document **2** an invention protected by a patent ▷ *adj* **3** open or available for inspection: *letters patent* **4** obvious: *their scorn was patent to everyone* **5** concerning protection of or appointment by a patent **6** (of food, drugs, etc.) made or held under a patent ▷ *vb* **7** to obtain a patent for (an invention) [Latin *patere* to lie open]

> **USAGE** The pronunciation **pat**-tunt is heard in *letters patent* and *Patent Office* and is the usual US pronunciation for all senses. In Britain **pat**-tunt is sometimes heard for senses 1, 2 and 3, but **pay**-tunt is commoner and is regularly used in collocations like *patent leather.*

patent leather *n* leather processed with lacquer to give a hard glossy surface

patently *adv* clearly and obviously: *an outdated and patently absurd promise*

patent medicine *n* a medicine with a patent, available without a prescription

Patent Office *n* a government department that issues patents

pater *n Brit humorous* father [Latin]

paternal *adj* **1** fatherly: *paternal authority* **2** related through one's father: *his paternal grandmother* [Latin *pater* father] **paternally** *adv*

paternalism *n* authority exercised in a way that limits individual responsibility [Latin *pater* father] **paternalistic** *adj*

paternity *n* **1** the fact or state of being a father **2** descent or derivation from a father

paternity suit *n* legal proceedings, usually brought by an unmarried mother, in order to gain legal recognition that a particular man is the father of her child

Paternoster *n* *RC Church* the Lord's Prayer [Latin *pater noster* our father]

path *n, pl* **paths** **1** a road or way, often a narrow trodden track **2** a surfaced walk, such as through a garden **3** the course or direction in which something moves: *his car skidded into the path of an oncoming lorry* **4** a course of conduct: *the path of reconciliation and forgiveness* [Old English *pæth*]

pathetic *adj* **1** arousing pity or sympathy **2** distressingly inadequate: *his pathetic attempt to maintain a stiff upper lip failed* [Greek *pathos* suffering] **pathetically** *adv*

pathetic fallacy *n* (in literature) the presentation of inanimate objects in nature as possessing human feelings

pathname *n* *computers* the name of a file or directory together with its position in relation to other directories

pathogen *n* any agent, such as a bacterium, that can cause disease [Greek *pathos* suffering + *-gen* (suffix) producing] **pathogenic** *adj*

pathological *adj* **1** of or relating to pathology **2** *informal* compulsively motivated: *pathological jealousy*

pathology *n* the branch of medicine that studies diseases [Greek *pathos* suffering + -LOGY] **pathologist** *n*

pathos *n* the power, for example in literature, of arousing feelings of pity or sorrow [Greek: suffering]

P

pathway *n* a path

patience *n* **1** the capacity for calmly enduring difficult situations: *the endless patience of the nurses* **2** the ability to wait calmly for something to happen without complaining or giving up: *he urged the international community to have patience to allow sanctions to work* **3** *Brit & NZ* a card game for one player only [Latin *pati* to suffer]

patient *adj* **1** enduring difficult situations with an even temper **2** persevering or diligent: *his years of patient work may finally pay off* ▷ *n* **3** a person who is receiving medical care **patiently** *adv*

patina *n* **1** a film formed on the surface of a metal **2** the sheen on the surface of an old object, caused by age and much handling [Italian: coating]

patio *n, pl* **-tios** **1** a paved area adjoining a house: *a barbecue on the patio* **2** an open inner courtyard in a Spanish or Spanish-American house [Spanish: courtyard]

patisserie (pat-eess-er-ee) *n* **1** a shop where fancy pastries are sold **2** such pastries [French]

patois (pat-wah) *n, pl* **patois** (pat-wahz) **1** a regional dialect of a language **2** the jargon of a particular group [Old French: rustic speech]

patrial *n* (in Britain, formerly) a person with a right by statute to live in the United Kingdom, and so not subject to immigration control [Latin *patria* native land]

patriarch *n* **1** the male head of a tribe or family **2** *Bible* any of the men regarded as the fathers of the human race or of the Hebrew people **3** **A** *RC Church* the pope **B** *Eastern Orthodox Church* a highest-ranking bishop **4** an old man who is respected [Church Latin *patriarcha*] **patriarchal** *adj*

patriarchate *n* the office, jurisdiction, or residence of a patriarch

patriarchy *n* **1** a form of social organization in which males hold most of the power **2** *pl* **-chies** a society governed by such a system

patrician *n* **1** a member of the nobility of ancient Rome **2** an aristocrat **3** a person of refined conduct and tastes ▷ *adj* **4** (in ancient Rome) of or relating to patricians **5** aristocratic [Latin *patricius* noble]

patricide *n* **1** the act of killing one's father **2** a person who kills his or her father [Latin *pater* father + *caedere* to kill] **patricidal** *adj*

patrimony *n, pl* **-nies** an inheritance from one's father or other ancestor [Latin *patrimonium* paternal inheritance]

patriot *n* a person who loves his or her country and passionately supports its interests [Greek *patris* native land] **patriotic** *adj* **patriotically** *adv* **patriotism** *n*

patrol *n* **1** the action of going round an area or building at regular intervals for purposes of security or observation **2** a person or group that carries out such an action **3** a group of soldiers or ships involved in patrolling a particular area **4** a division of a troop of Scouts or Guides ▷ *vb* **-trolling, -trolled** **5** to engage in a patrol of (a place): *peacekeepers patrolled several areas of the city* [French *patrouiller*]

patrol car *n* a police car used for patrolling streets

patron *n* **1** a person who financially supports artists, writers, musicians, or charities **2** a regular customer of a shop, hotel, etc. [Latin *patronus* protector]

patronage *n* **1** the support or custom given by a patron **2** (in politics) the ability or power to appoint people to jobs **3** a condescending manner

patronize *or* **-nise** *vb* **-nizing, -nized** *or* **-nising, -nised** **1** to treat (someone) in a condescending way **2** to be a patron of **patronizing** *or* **-nising** *adj* **patronizingly** *or* **-nisingly** *adv*

patron saint *n* a saint regarded as the particular guardian of a country or a group of people

patronymic *n* a name derived from one's father's or a male ancestor's [Greek *patēr* father + *onoma* name]

patter[1] *vb* **1** to make repeated light tapping sounds **2** to walk with quick soft steps ▷ *n* **3** a quick succession of light tapping sounds, such as by feet: *the steady patter of rain against the window* [from PAT[1]]

patter[2] *n* **1** the glib rapid speech of comedians or salespeople **2** chatter **3** the jargon of a particular group ▷ *vb* **4** to speak glibly and rapidly [Latin *pater* in *Pater Noster* Our Father]

pattern *n* **1** an arrangement of repeated parts or decorative designs **2** a regular recognizable way that something is done: *I followed a normal eating pattern* **3** a plan or diagram used as a guide to making something: *a knitting pattern* **4** a model worthy of imitation: *a pattern of kindness* **5** a representative sample ▷ *vb* **6** (foll. by *after* or *on*) to model: *an orchestra patterned after Count Basie's* [Medieval Latin *patronus* example]

patterned *adj* having a decorative pattern on it: *a selection of plain and patterned fabrics*

patty *n, pl* **-ties 1** a small flattened cake of minced food **2** a small round pie filled with meat or vegetables [French *pâté*]

paua (pah-ooh-uh) *n* an edible shellfish of New Zealand, which has a pearly shell used for jewellery [Māori]

paucity *n formal* **1** scarcity **2** smallness of amount or number [Latin *paucus* few]

paunch *n* a protruding belly or abdomen [Latin *pantices* bowels] **paunchy** *adj*

pauper *n* **1** a person who is extremely poor **2** (formerly) a person supported by public charity [Latin: poor]

pause *vb* **pausing, paused 1** to stop doing (something) for a short time **2** to hesitate: *she answered him without pausing* ▷ *n* **3** a temporary stop or rest in speech or action **4** *music* a continuation of a note or rest beyond its normal length **5 give someone pause** to cause someone to hesitate: *it gave him pause for reflection* [Greek *pausis*]

pavane (pav-van) *n* **1** a slow and stately dance of the 16th and 17th centuries **2** music for this dance [Spanish *pavana*]

pave *vb* **paving, paved 1** to cover (a road or area of ground) with a firm surface to make it suitable for walking or travelling on **2 pave the way for** to prepare or make easier: *the arrests paved the way for the biggest-ever Mafia trial* [Old French *paver*]

pavement *n* **1** a hard-surfaced path for pedestrians, alongside and a little higher than a road **2** the material used in paving **3** *US* the surface of a road [Latin *pavimentum* hard floor]

pavilion *n* **1** a building at a sports ground, esp. a cricket pitch, in which players can wash and change **2** an open building or temporary structure used for exhibitions **3** a summerhouse or other decorative shelter **4** a large ornate tent [Latin *papilio* butterfly, tent]

paving *n* **1** a paved surface **2** material used for a pavement

pavlova *n* a meringue cake topped with whipped cream and fruit [after Anna *Pavlova*, ballerina]

paw *n* **1** a four-legged mammal's foot with claws and pads **2** *informal* a hand ▷ *vb* **3** to scrape or hit with the paws **4** *informal* to touch or caress (someone) in a rough or overfamiliar manner [Germanic]

pawl *n* a pivoted lever shaped to engage with a ratchet to prevent motion in a particular direction [Dutch *pal*]

pawn¹ *vb* **1** to deposit (an article) as security for money borrowed **2** to stake or risk: *I will pawn my honour on this matter* ▷ *n* **3** an article deposited as security **4** the condition of being so deposited: *in pawn* [Old French *pan* security]

pawn² *n* **1** a chessman of the lowest value, usually able to move only one square forward at a time **2** a person or thing manipulated by someone else: *our city is just a pawn in their power games* [Anglo-Norman *poun*, from Medieval Latin *pedo* infantryman]

pawnbroker *n* a person licensed to lend money on goods deposited **pawnbroking** *n*

Pawnee *n, pl* **Pawnees** *or* **Pawnee 1** a member of a group of Native American peoples, formerly living in Nebraska and Kansas, now chiefly in Oklahoma **2** the language of these peoples

pawnshop *n* the premises of a pawnbroker

pawpaw (paw-paw) *n* same as **papaya**

pax *n* **1** *chiefly RC Church* the kiss of peace ▷ *interj* **2** *Brit children's slang* a call signalling a desire to end hostilities [Latin: peace]

pay *vb* **pays, paying, paid 1** to give (money) in return for goods or services: *Willie paid for the drinks; nurses are not very well paid* **2** to settle (a debt or obligation) by giving or doing something: *he has paid his debt to society* **3** to suffer: *she paid dearly for her mistake* **4** to give (a compliment, regards, attention, etc.) **5** to profit or benefit (someone): *it doesn't always pay to be honest* **6** to make (a visit or call) **7** to yield a return of: *the account pays 5% interest* **8 pay one's way A** to contribute one's share of expenses **B** to remain solvent without outside help ▷ *n* **9** money given in return for work or services; a salary or wage **10 in the pay of** employed by ▷ See also **pay back, pay for** *etc.* [Latin *pacare* to appease]

payable *adj* **1** (often foll. by *on*) due to be paid: *the instalments are payable on the third of each month* **2** that is capable of being paid: *pensions are payable to those disabled during the wars*

pay back *vb* **1** to repay (a loan) **2** to make (someone) suffer for a wrong he or she has done you: *I want to pay him back for all the suffering he's caused me*

payday *n* the day on which wages or salaries are paid

payday lender *n* a person or company that offers short-term loans, in advance of payday, at high rates of interest

PAYE (in Britain, Australia, and New Zealand) pay as you earn; a system by which income tax is deducted by employers and paid directly to the government

payee *n* the person to whom a cheque or money order is made out

pay for *vb* **1** to make payment for **2** to suffer or be punished for (a mistake)

paying guest *n euphemistic* a lodger

payload *n* **1** the amount of passengers, cargo, or bombs which an aircraft can carry **2** the part of a cargo which earns revenue **3** the explosive power of a warhead or bomb carried by a missile or aircraft

paymaster *n* an official responsible for the payment of wages and salaries

payment *n* **1** the act of paying **2** a sum of money paid **3** something given in return; punishment or reward

pay off *vb* **1** to pay the complete amount of (a debt) **2** to pay (someone) all that is due in wages and dismiss him or her from employment **3** to turn out successfully: *her persistence finally paid off*

P

4 *informal* to give a bribe to ▷ *n* **payoff 5** *informal* the climax or outcome of events **6** *informal* a bribe **7** the final payment of a debt **8** the final settlement, esp. in retribution: *the payoff came when the gang besieged the squealer's house*

payola *n informal* a bribe to secure special treatment, esp. to promote a commercial product

pay out *vb* **1** to spend (money) on a particular thing **2** to release (a rope) gradually, bit by bit ▷ *n* **payout 3** a sum of money paid out

pay-per-view *n* a television broadcasting system where a charge is made for receiving a specific programme

payphone *n* a telephone operated by coins or a prepaid card

payroll *n* a list of employees, giving the salary or wage of each

payslip *n* a note given to an employee stating his or her salary or wage and detailing the deductions

pay up *vb* to pay (money) promptly or in full

paywall *n* a system preventing a user from accessing certain information on a website unless a fee is paid

Pb *chem* lead [New Latin *plumbum*]

pc 1 per cent **2** postcard

PC 1 personal computer **2** (in Britain) Police Constable **3** politically correct **4** (in Britain) Privy Council *or* Counsellor **5** (in Canada) Progressive Conservative

PCOS polycystic ovary syndrome

PCV (in Britain) passenger carrying vehicle

pd paid

Pd *chem* palladium

PDA personal digital assistant

PDF portable document format: a format in which electronic documents may be viewed

P

PDSA (in Britain) People's Dispensary for Sick Animals

PDT Pacific Daylight Time

PE 1 physical education **2** Prince Edward Island

pea *n* **1** an annual climbing plant with green pods containing green seeds **2** the seed of this plant, eaten as a vegetable [from *pease* (incorrectly assumed to be a plural)]

peace *n* **1** stillness or silence **2** absence of mental anxiety: *peace of mind* **3** absence of war **4** harmony between people or groups **5** a treaty marking the end of a war **6** law and order within a state: *a breach of the peace* **7 at peace** **A** dead: *the woman is at peace now* **B** in a state of harmony or serenity **8 hold** *or* **keep one's peace** to keep silent **9 keep the peace** to maintain law and order [Latin *pax*]

peaceable *adj* **1** inclined towards peace **2** tranquil or calm

peace dividend *n* additional money available to a government from cuts in defence expenditure because of the end of a period of hostilities

peaceful *adj* **1** not in a state of war or disagreement **2** calm or tranquil **peacefully** *adv*

peacemaker *n* a person who brings about peace, esp. between others

peace offering *n* something given or said in order to restore peace: *I bought Mum some flowers as a peace offering*

peace pipe *n* a long decorated pipe smoked by Native Americans, esp. as a token of peace

peacetime *n* a period without war

peach *n* **1** a soft juicy fruit with a downy skin, yellowish-orange sweet flesh, and a single stone **2** *informal* a person or thing that is especially pleasing: *a peach of a goal* ▷ *adj* **3** pale pinkish-orange [Latin *Persicum malum* Persian apple]

peach melba *n* a dessert made of halved peaches, vanilla ice cream, and raspberries [after Dame Nellie *Melba*, singer]

peachy *adj* **peachier, peachiest** of or like a peach, esp. in colour or texture

peacock *n, pl* **-cocks** *or* **-cock 1** a large male bird of the pheasant family with a crested head and a very large fanlike tail with blue and green eyelike spots **2** a vain strutting person [Latin *pavo* peacock + COCK] **peahen** *fem n*

peafowl *n* a peacock or peahen

peak *n* **1** a pointed tip or projection: *the peak of the roof* **2 A** the pointed summit of a mountain **B** a mountain with a pointed summit **3** the point of greatest success or achievement: *the peak of his career* **4** a projecting piece on the front of some caps ▷ *vb* **5** to form or reach a peak ▷ *adj* **6** of or relating to a period of greatest demand: *hotels are generally dearer in peak season* [perhaps from *pike* (the weapon)]

peaked *adj* having a peak

peak load *n* the maximum load on an electrical power-supply system

peaky *adj* **peakier, peakiest** pale and sickly [origin unknown]

peal *n* **1** a long loud echoing sound, such as of bells or thunder ▷ *vb* **2** to sound with a peal or peals [Middle English *pele*]

peanut *n* a plant with edible nutlike seeds which ripen underground. See also **peanuts**

peanut butter *n* a brownish oily paste made from peanuts

peanuts *n slang* a trifling amount of money

pear *n* **1** a sweet juicy fruit with a narrow top and a rounded base **2 go pear-shaped** *informal* to go wrong: *the plan started to go pear-shaped* [Latin *pirum*]

pearl *n* **1** a hard smooth greyish-white rounded object found inside the shell of a clam or oyster and much valued as a gem **2** See **mother-of-pearl 3** a person or thing that is like a pearl in beauty or value ▷ *adj* **4** of, made of, or set with pearl or mother-of-pearl ▷ *vb* **5** to set with or as if with pearls **6** to shape into or assume a pearl-like form or colour **7** to dive for pearls [Latin *perna* sea mussel]

pearl barley *n* barley ground into small round grains, used in soups and stews

pearly *adj* **pearlier, pearliest 1** resembling a pearl, esp. in lustre **2** decorated with pearls or mother-of-pearl

Pearly Gates *pl n informal* the entrance to heaven

pearly king *or fem* **pearly queen** *n* the London barrow vendor whose ceremonial clothes display the most lavish collection of pearl buttons

peasant *n* **1** (in some countries) a person employed in agricultural labour **2** *derogatory* an uncouth or uncultured person [Old French *païsant*]

peasantry *n* peasants as a class

pease *n, pl* **pease** *archaic or dialect* same as **pea** [Old English *pise, peose*]

pease pudding *n* (esp. in Britain) a dish of split peas that have been soaked and boiled

peasouper *n informal, chiefly Brit* thick dirty yellowish fog

peat *n* decaying vegetable matter found in uplands and bogs and used as a fuel (when dried) and as a fertilizer [perhaps Celtic]

pebble *n* **1** a small smooth rounded stone, esp. one worn by the action of water ▷ *vb* **-bling, -bled** **2** to cover with pebbles [Old English *papolstān* pebble stone] **pebbly** *adj*

pebble dash *n Brit & Austral* a finish for external walls consisting of small stones set in plaster

pec *n informal* a pectoral muscle: *Marvin tore off his shirt to reveal his rippling pecs*

pecan (**pee**-kan) *n* a smooth oval nut with a sweet oily kernel that grows on hickory trees in the Southern US [Native American *paccan*]

peccadillo *n, pl* **-loes** *or* **-los** a trivial misdeed [Spanish *pecadillo*, from Latin *peccare* to sin]

peccary *n, pl* **-ries** *or* **-ry** a piglike animal native to American forests [Carib]

peck¹ *vb* **1** to strike or pick up with the beak **2** *informal* to kiss (a person) quickly and lightly **3** **peck at** to eat slowly and reluctantly: *pecking away at your lunch* ▷ *n* **4** a quick light blow from a bird's beak **5** a mark made by such a blow **6** *informal* a quick light kiss [origin unknown]

peck² *n* an obsolete unit of liquid measure equal to one quarter of a bushel or 2 gallons (9.1 litres) [Anglo-Norman]

pecker *n* **keep one's pecker up** *Brit & NZ slang* to remain cheerful

pecking order *n* the order of seniority or power in a group: *she came from a family low in the social pecking order*

peckish *adj informal* feeling slightly hungry

pectin *n biochem* a water-soluble carbohydrate that occurs in ripe fruit: used in the manufacture of jams because of its ability to gel [Greek *pēktos* congealed]

pectoral *adj* **1** of or relating to the chest, breast, or thorax: *pectoral fins* **2** worn on the breast or chest: *a pectoral cross* ▷ *n* **3** a pectoral organ or part, esp. a muscle or fin [Latin *pectus* breast]

pectoral fin *n* a fin, just behind the head in fishes, that helps to control the direction of movement

peculate *vb* **-lating, -lated** *literary* to embezzle (public money) [Latin *peculari*] **peculation** *n*

peculiar *adj* **1** strange or odd: *a peculiar idea* **2** distinct or special **3** (foll. by *to*) belonging exclusively (to): *a fish peculiar to these waters* [Latin *peculiaris* concerning private property]

peculiarity *n, pl* **-ties** **1** a strange or unusual habit; eccentricity **2** a distinguishing trait **3** the state or quality of being peculiar

pecuniary *adj* **1** of or relating to money **2** *law* (of an offence) involving a monetary penalty [Latin *pecunia* money]

pedagogue *or sometimes US* **pedagog** *n* a teacher, esp. a pedantic one [Greek *pais* boy + *agōgos* leader] **pedagogic** *adj*

pedagogy (**ped**-a-goj-ee) *n* the principles, practice, or profession of teaching

pedal¹ *n* **1** a foot-operated lever used to control a vehicle or machine, or to modify the tone of a musical instrument ▷ *vb* **-dalling, -dalled** *or US* **-daling, -daled** **2** to propel (a bicycle) by operating the pedals **3** to operate the pedals of an organ or piano [Latin *pedalis*, from *pes* foot]

pedal² (**peed**-al) *adj* of or relating to the foot or the feet [Latin *pedalis*, from *pes* foot]

pedant *n* a person who is concerned chiefly with insignificant detail or who relies too much on academic learning [Italian *pedante* teacher] **pedantic** *adj* **pedantically** *adv*

pedantry *n, pl* **-ries** the practice of being a pedant, esp. in the minute observance of petty rules or details

peddle *vb* **-dling, -dled** **1** to sell (goods) from place to place **2** to sell (illegal drugs) **3** to advocate (an idea or information) persistently: *the version of events being peddled by his opponents* [from *pedlar*]

pederast *or* **paederast** *n* a man who has homosexual relations with boys [Greek *pais* boy + *erastēs* lover] **pederasty** *or* **paederasty** *n*

pedestal *n* **1** a base that supports something, such as a statue **2** **put someone on a pedestal** to admire someone very much [Old Italian *piedestallo*]

pedestrian *n* **1** a person who travels on foot ▷ *adj* **2** dull or commonplace: *a pedestrian performance* [Latin *pes* foot]

pedestrian crossing *n Brit & Austral* a path across a road marked as a crossing for pedestrians

pedestrianize *or* **-nise** *vb* **-nizing, -nized** *or* **-nising, -nised** to convert (a street or shopping area) into an area for pedestrians only

pedestrian precinct *n Brit* an area of a town for pedestrians only, esp. an area of shops

pedicure *n* medical or cosmetic treatment of the feet [Latin *pes* foot + *curare* to care for]

pedigree *n* **1** the line of descent of a purebred animal **2** a document recording this **3** a genealogical table, esp. one indicating pure ancestry [Old French *pie de grue* crane's foot, alluding to the spreading lines used in a genealogical chart]

pediment *n* a triangular part over a door, as used in classical architecture [obsolete *periment*, perhaps workman's corruption of *pyramid*]

pedlar *or esp US* **peddler** *n* a person who peddles [Middle English *ped* basket]

pedometer (pid-**dom**-it-er) *n* a device that measures the distance walked by recording the number of steps taken [Latin *pes* foot + METER]

peduncle *n* **1** *botany* a plant stalk bearing a flower cluster or solitary flower **2** *anatomy & pathol* any stalklike structure [Latin *pediculus* little foot] **peduncular** *adj*

pee *informal* ▷ *vb* **peeing, peed** **1** to urinate ▷ *n* **2** urine **3** the act of urinating [euphemistic for *piss*]

peek *vb* **1** to glance quickly or secretly ▷ *n* **2** such a glance [Middle English *pike*]

peel *vb* **1** to remove the skin or rind of (a fruit or vegetable) **2** to come off in flakes **3** (of a person or part of the body) to shed skin in flakes as a

P

result of sunburn ▷ *n* **4** the skin or rind of a fruit, etc. ▷ See also **peel off** [Latin *pilare* to make bald]

peelings *pl n* strips of skin or rind that have been peeled off: *potato peelings*

peel off *vb* **1** to remove or be removed by peeling: *this softens the paint, which can then be peeled off* **2** *slang* to take off one's clothes or a piece of clothing **3** to leave a group of moving people, vehicles, etc. by taking a course that curves away to one side: *two aircraft peeled off to attack the enemy bombers*

peen *n* the end of a hammer head opposite the striking face, often rounded or wedge-shaped [origin unknown]

peep[1] *vb* **1** to look slyly or quickly, such as through a small opening or from a hidden place **2** to appear partially or briefly: *the sun peeped through the clouds* ▷ *n* **3** a quick or sly look **4** the first appearance: *the peep of dawn* [variant of *peek*]

peep[2] *vb* **1** (esp. of young birds) to make small shrill noises ▷ *n* **2** a peeping sound [imitative]

Peeping Tom *n* a man who furtively observes people undressing [after the tailor who, according to legend, peeped at Lady Godiva when she rode naked through Coventry]

peepshow *n* a box containing a series of pictures that can be seen through a small hole

peer[1] *n* **1** a member of a nobility **2** a person who holds any of the five grades of the British nobility: duke, marquess, earl, viscount, and baron **3** a person of equal social standing, rank, age, etc.: *he is greatly respected by his peers in the arts world* [Latin *par* equal]

peer[2] *vb* **1** to look intently or as if with difficulty: *Amir peered anxiously at his father's face* **2** to appear dimly: *the sun peered through the fog* [Flemish *pieren* to look with narrowed eyes]

P

peerage *Brit* ▷ *n* **1** the whole body of peers; aristocracy **2** the position, rank, or title of a peer

peeress *n* **1** (in Britain) a woman holding the rank of a peer **2** the wife or widow of a peer

peer group *n* a social group composed of people of similar age and status

peerless *adj* having no equals; unsurpassed

peer pressure *n* influence from one's peer group

peeve *informal* ▷ *vb* **peeving, peeved 1** to irritate or annoy: *the way he looked at her peeved her* ▷ *n* **2** something that irritates: *my pet peeve* [from *peevish*] **peeved** *adj*

peevish *adj* fretful or irritable [origin unknown] **peevishly** *adv*

peewee *n* a black-and-white Australian bird [imitative of its call]

peewit *or* **pewit** *n* same as **lapwing** [imitative of its call]

peg *n* **1** a small pin or bolt used to join two parts together, to fasten, or to mark **2** a hook or knob for hanging things on **3** *music* a pin on a stringed instrument which can be turned to tune the string wound around it **4** Also called: **clothes peg** a split or hinged pin for fastening wet clothes to a line to dry **5** *Brit* a small drink of spirits **6** an opportunity or pretext for doing something: *the play's subject matter provides a perfect peg for a discussion of issues like morality and faith* **7 bring** *or* **take (someone) down a peg** to lower the pride of (someone) **8 off the peg** *Brit & NZ* (of clothes) ready-to-wear, as opposed to tailor-made ▷ *vb* **pegging, pegged 9** to insert a peg into **10** to secure with pegs: *the balloon was pegged down to stop it drifting away* **11** to mark (a score) with pegs, as in some card games **12** *chiefly Brit* to work steadily: *he pegged away at his job for years* **13** to fix or maintain something, such as prices, at a particular level or value: *a fixed-rate mortgage, pegged at 4.6 per cent* ▷ See also **peg out** [Low Germanic *pegge*]

pegboard *n* **1** a board with a pattern of holes into which small pegs can be fitted, used for playing certain games or keeping a score **2** hardboard with rows of holes from which articles may be hung for display

peggy square *n NZ* a small hand-knitted square [from Peggy Huse, who popularized them]

peg leg *n informal* **1** an artificial leg **2** a person with an artificial leg

peg out *vb* **1** *informal* to collapse or die **2** to mark or secure with pegs: *the scientists pegged out a hectare of land in order to study every plant in it*

PEI Prince Edward Island

peignoir (**pay**-nwahr) *n* a woman's light dressing gown [French]

pejorative (pij-**jor**-a-tiv) *adj* **1** (of a word or expression) having an insulting or critical sense ▷ *n* **2** a pejorative word or expression [Late Latin *pejorare* to make worse]

peke *n informal* a Pekingese dog

Pekingese *or* **Pekinese** *n* **1** *pl* **-ese** a small dog with a long straight coat, curled plumed tail, and short wrinkled muzzle **2** the dialect of Mandarin Chinese spoken in Beijing

pelargonium *n* a plant with circular leaves and red, pink, or white flowers: includes many cultivated geraniums [Greek *pelargos* stork]

pelf *n derogatory* money or wealth [Old French *pelfre* booty]

pelican *n* a large water bird with a pouch beneath its long bill for holding fish [Greek *pelekan*]

pelican crossing *n* (in Britain) a type of road crossing with a pedestrian-operated traffic-light system [from *pe(destrian) li(ght) con(trolled) crossing*, with *-con* adapted to *-can* of *pelican*]

pelisse (pel-**leess**) *n* a cloak or loose coat which is usually fur-trimmed [Old French, from Latin *pellis* skin]

pellagra *n pathol* a disease caused by a diet lacking in vitamin B, which results in scaling of the skin, diarrhoea and mental disorder [Italian, from *pelle* skin + Greek *agra* paroxysm]

pellet *n* **1** a small round ball, esp. of compressed matter **2 A** an imitation bullet used in toy guns **B** a piece of small shot **3** a small pill [Latin *pila* ball]

pell-mell *adv* **1** in a confused headlong rush: *the hounds ran pell-mell into the yard* **2** in a disorderly manner: *the things were piled pell-mell in the room* [Old French *pesle-mesle*]

pellucid *adj literary* **1** transparent or translucent **2** extremely clear in style and meaning [Latin *pellucidus*]

pelmet *n* a board or piece of fabric used to conceal the curtain rail [probably from French *palmette* palm-leaf decoration on cornice moulding]

pelota *n* a game played by two players who use a basket strapped to their wrists or a wooden racket to propel a ball against a specially marked wall [Spanish: ball]

pelt[1] *vb* **1** to throw (missiles) at **2** (foll. by *along* etc.) to hurry **3** to rain heavily ▹ *n* **4** a blow **5 at full pelt** very quickly: *she ran down the street at full pelt* [origin unknown]

pelt[2] *n* the skin or fur of an animal, esp. as material for clothing or rugs: *the lucrative international trade in beaver pelts* [probably from Latin *pellis* skin]

pelvis *n, pl* **-vises** *or* **-ves 1** the framework of bones at the base of the spine, to which the hips are attached **2** the bones that form this structure [Latin: basin] **pelvic** *adj*

pen[1] *n* **1** an instrument for writing or drawing using ink. See also **ballpoint, fountain pen 2 the pen** writing as an occupation ▹ *vb* **penning, penned 3** to write or compose [Latin *penna* feather]

pen[2] *n* **1** an enclosure in which domestic animals are kept **2** any place of confinement ▹ *vb* **penning, penned** *or* **pent 3** to enclose (animals) in a pen **4 penned in** being or feeling trapped or confined: *she stood penned in by bodies at the front of the crowd* [Old English *penn*]

pen[3] *n US & Canad informal* short for **penitentiary** (sense 1)

pen[4] *n* a female swan [origin unknown]

Pen. Peninsula

penal (pee-nal) *adj* **1** of or relating to punishment **2** used as a place of punishment: *a penal colony* [Latin *poena* penalty] **penally** *adv*

penal code *n* the body of laws relating to crime and punishment

penalize *or* **-ise** *vb* **-izing, -ized** *or* **-ising, -ised 1** to impose a penalty on (someone) for breaking a law or rule **2** to inflict a disadvantage on: *why should I be penalized just because I'm a woman?* **penalization** *or* **-isation** *n*

penalty *n, pl* **-ties 1** a legal punishment for a crime or offence **2** loss or suffering as a result of one's own action: *we are now paying the penalty for neglecting to keep our equipment up to date* **3** *sport & games etc.* a handicap awarded against a player or team for illegal play, such as a free shot at goal by the opposing team [Latin *poena*]

penalty box *n* **1** Also called: **penalty area** *soccer* a rectangular area in front of the goal, within which a penalty is awarded for a serious foul by the defending team **2** *ice hockey* a bench for players serving time penalties

penalty corner *n hockey* a free hit from the goal line taken by the attacking side

penalty shoot-out *n sport* a method of deciding the winner of a drawn match, in which players from each team attempt to score with a penalty shot

penance *n* **1** voluntary self-punishment to make amends for a sin **2** *RC Church* a sacrament in which repentant sinners are forgiven provided they confess their sins to a priest and perform a penance [Latin *paenitentia* repentance]

pence *n* a plural of **penny**

> **USAGE** Since the decimalization of British currency and the introduction of the abbreviation *p*, as in *10p, 85p*, etc., the abbreviation has tended to replace *pence* in speech, as in *4p, 12p*, etc.

penchant (pon-shon) *n* strong inclination or liking: *a stylish woman with a penchant for dark glasses* [French]

pencil *n* **1** a rod of graphite encased in wood which is used for writing or drawing ▹ *vb* **-cilling, -cilled** *or US* **-ciling, -ciled 2** to draw, colour, write, or mark with a pencil **3 pencil in** to note, arrange, or include provisionally or tentatively [Latin *penicillus* painter's brush]

pendant *n* **A** an ornament worn on a chain round the neck: *a beautiful pearl pendant* **B** an ornament that hangs from a piece of jewellery [Latin *pendere* to hang down]

pendent *adj literary* **1** dangling **2** jutting [see PENDANT]

pending *prep* **1** while waiting for ▹ *adj* **2** not yet decided or settled **3** imminent: *these developments have been pending for some time*

pendulous *adj literary* hanging downwards and swinging freely [Latin *pendere* to hang down]

pendulum *n* **1** a weight suspended so it swings freely under the influence of gravity **2** such a device used to regulate a clock mechanism **3** a movement from one attitude or belief towards its opposite: *the pendulum has swung back to more punitive measures*

penetrate *vb* **-trating, -trated 1** to find or force a way into or through **2** to diffuse through; permeate: *the smell of cooking penetrated through to the sitting room* **3** to see through: *the sunlight did not penetrate the thick canopy of leaves* **4** (of a man) to insert the penis into the vagina or anus of (a person) **5** to grasp the meaning of (a principle, etc.) [Latin *penetrare*] **penetrable** *adj* **penetrative** *adj*

penetrating *adj* tending to or able to penetrate: *a penetrating mind; a penetrating voice*

penetration *n* **1** the act or an instance of penetrating **2** the ability or power to penetrate **3** keen insight or perception

pen friend *n* a person with whom one exchanges letters, often a person in another country whom one has not met

penguin *n* a flightless black-and-white sea bird with webbed feet and wings modified as flippers for swimming [perhaps from Welsh *pen* head + *gwyn* white]

penicillin *n* an antibiotic used to treat diseases caused by bacteria [Latin *penicillus* tuft of hairs]

peninsula *n* a narrow strip of land projecting from the mainland into a sea or lake [Latin, literally: almost an island] **peninsular** *adj*

> **USAGE** The noun *peninsula* is sometimes confused with the adjective *peninsular: the Iberian peninsula* (not *peninsular*).

penis *n, pl* **-nises** *or* **-nes** the organ of copulation in higher vertebrates, also used for urinating in many mammals [Latin] **penile** *adj*

penitent *adj* **1** feeling regret for one's sins; repentant ▹ *n* **2** a person who is penitent [Church Latin *paenitens* regretting] **penitence** *n*

penitential *adj* of, showing, or as a penance
penitentiary *n, pl* **-ries** **1** (in the US and Canada) a state or federal prison ▷ *adj* **2** of or for penance **3** used for punishment and reformation: *the penitentiary system* [Latin *paenitens* penitent]
penknife *n, pl* **-knives** a small knife with one or more blades that fold into the handle
penmanship *n formal* style or technique of writing by hand
pen name *n* a name used by a writer instead of his or her real name; nom de plume
pennant *n* **1** a long narrow flag, esp. one used by ships as identification or for signalling **2** *chiefly US, Canad & Austral* a flag indicating the winning of a championship in certain sports [probably a blend of *pendant* + *pennon*]
penniless *adj* very poor
pennon *n* **1** a long flag, often tapering and divided at the end, originally a knight's personal flag **2** a small tapering or triangular flag flown by a ship or boat [Latin *penna* feather]
penny *n, pl* **pennies** *or* **pence** **1** a British bronze coin worth one hundredth of a pound **2** a former British and Australian coin worth one twelfth of a shilling **3** *pl* **pennies** *US & Canad* a cent **4** *informal, chiefly Brit* the least amount of money: *I don't have a penny* **5** **a pretty penny** *informal* a considerable sum of money **6** **spend a penny** *Brit & NZ informal* to urinate **7** **the penny dropped** *informal* the explanation of something was finally understood [Old English *penig, pening*]
Penny Black *n* the first adhesive postage stamp, issued in Britain in 1840
penny-dreadful *n Brit informal* a cheap, often lurid book or magazine
penny-farthing *n Brit* an early type of bicycle with a large front wheel and a small rear wheel
penny-pinching *adj* **1** excessively careful with money; miserly ▷ *n* **2** miserliness **penny-pincher** *n*
pennyroyal *n* a Eurasian plant with hairy leaves and small mauve flowers, which provides an aromatic oil used in medicine [Old French *pouliol* pennyroyal + *real* royal]
penny-wise *adj* **penny-wise and pound-foolish** careful or thrifty in small matters but wasteful in large ventures
pennywort *n* a Eurasian rock plant with whitish-green tubular flowers and rounded leaves
pennyworth *n* **1** the amount that can be bought for a penny **2** a small or insignificant amount of something: *they'd thrown in their pennyworth of opinion*
penology (pee-**nol**-a-jee) *n* the study of the punishment of criminals and of prison management [Greek *poinē* punishment]
pen pal *n informal* same as **pen friend**
penpusher *n* a person whose work involves a lot of boring paperwork **penpushing** *adj, n*
pension[1] *n* **1** a regular payment made by the state or a former employer to a person who has retired or to a widowed or disabled person ▷ *vb* **2** to grant a pension to ▷ See also **pension off** [Latin *pensio* a payment] **pensionable** *adj* **pensioner** *n*
pension[2] (pon-syon) *n* (in France and some other countries) a relatively cheap boarding house [French: extended meaning of *pension* grant]
pension off *vb* to cause (someone) to retire from a job and pay him or her a pension
pensive *adj* deeply thoughtful, often with a tinge of sadness [Latin *pensare* to consider] **pensively** *adv*
pent *vb* a past of **pen**[2]
penta- *combining form* five: *pentagon; pentameter* [Greek *pente*]
pentacle *n* same as **pentagram** [Italian *pentacolo* something having five corners]
pentagon *n geom* a figure with five sides **pentagonal** *adj*
Pentagon *n* a five-sided building in Washington DC that houses the headquarters of the US Department of Defense
pentagram *n* a star-shaped figure with five points
pentameter (pen-**tam**-it-er) *n* a line of poetry consisting of five metrical feet
Pentateuch (**pent**-a-tyuke) *n* the first five books of the Old Testament [Greek *pente* five + *teukhos* scroll case] **Pentateuchal** *adj*
pentathlon *n* an athletic contest consisting of five different events. See also **modern pentathlon** [Greek *pente* five + *athlon* contest]
pentatonic scale *n music* a scale consisting of five notes
pentavalent *adj chem* having a valency of five
Pentecost *n* a Christian festival occurring on Whit Sunday celebrating the descent of the Holy Ghost to the apostles [Greek *pentēkostē* fiftieth (day after the Resurrection)]
Pentecostal *adj* relating to any of the Christian groups that have a charismatic and fundamentalist approach to Christianity
penthouse *n* a luxurious flat built on the top floor or roof of a building [Middle English *pentis*, later *penthouse*, from Latin *appendere* to hang from]
pent-up *adj* not released; repressed: *full of pent-up emotional violence*
penultimate *adj* second last
penumbra *n, pl* **-brae** *or* **-bras** **1** the partially shadowed region which surrounds the full shadow in an eclipse **2** *literary* a partial shadow [Latin *paene* almost + *umbra* shadow] **penumbral** *adj*
penurious *adj formal* **1** niggardly with money **2** lacking money or means
penury *n formal* **1** extreme poverty **2** extreme scarcity [Latin *penuria*]
peon *n* a Spanish-American farm labourer or unskilled worker [Spanish]
peony *n, pl* **-nies** a garden plant with showy pink, red, white, or yellow flowers [Greek *paiōnia*]
people *pl n* **1** persons collectively or in general **2** a group of persons considered together: *old people have anaemia more often than younger people do* **3** *pl* **-ples** the persons living in a particular country: *the American people* **4** one's family or ancestors: *her people originally came from Skye* **5** **the people** **A** the mass of ordinary persons without rank or privileges **B** the body of persons in a country who are entitled to vote ▷ *vb* **-pling, -pled** **6** to provide with inhabitants: *the centre of the continent is sparsely peopled* [Latin *populus*]
USAGE See at **person**.

people carrier *n* same as **multipurpose vehicle**
people mover *n Brit, Austral & NZ* same as **multipurpose vehicle**
pep *n* **1** high spirits, energy, or vitality ▷ *vb* **pepping, pepped 2 pep up** to make more lively or interesting: *the company has spent thousands trying to pep up its image* [short for *pepper*]
peplum *n, pl* **-lums** *or* **-la** a flared ruffle attached to the waist of a garment [Greek *peplos* shawl]
pepper *n* **1** a sharp hot condiment obtained from the fruit of an Asian climbing plant **2** Also called: **capsicum** a colourful tropical fruit used as a vegetable and a condiment ▷ *vb* **3** to season with pepper **4** to sprinkle liberally: *his speech is heavily peppered with Americanisms* **5** to pelt with small missiles [Greek *peperi*]
pepper-and-salt *adj* **1** (of a fabric) marked with a fine mixture of black and white **2** (of hair) streaked with grey
peppercorn *n* the small dried berry of the pepper plant
peppercorn rent *n Brit* a rent that is very low or nominal
pepper mill *n* a small hand mill used to grind peppercorns
peppermint *n* **1** a mint plant which produces a pungent oil, used as a flavouring **2** a sweet flavoured with peppermint
pepperoni *n* a dry sausage of pork and beef spiced with pepper [Italian *peperoni* peppers]
pepper spray *n* a defence spray agent derived from hot cayenne peppers, which causes temporary blindness and breathing difficulty
peppery *adj* **1** tasting of pepper **2** irritable
pep pill *n informal* a tablet containing a stimulant drug
pepsin *n* an enzyme produced in the stomach, which, when activated by acid, breaks down proteins [Greek *peptein* to digest]
pep talk *n informal* a talk designed to increase confidence and enthusiasm
peptic *adj* **1** of or relating to digestion **2** of or caused by pepsin or the action of the digestive juices: *a peptic ulcer* [Greek *peptein* to digest]
peptic ulcer *n* an ulcer in the stomach or duodenum
peptide *n chem* a compound consisting of two or more amino acids linked by chemical bonding between the amino group of one and the carboxyl group of another
per *prep* **1** for every: *three pence per pound; 30 pounds per week* **2** by; through **3 as per** according to: *proceed as per the instructions* **4 as per usual** *or* **as per normal** *informal* as usual [Latin: by, for each]
peradventure *archaic* ▷ *adv* **1** by chance; perhaps ▷ *n* **2** chance or doubt [Old French *par aventure* by chance]
perambulate *vb* **-lating, -lated** *formal* to walk about (a place) [Latin *per-* through + *ambulare* to walk] **perambulation** *n*
perambulator *n formal* same as **pram**
per annum *adv* in each year [Latin]
per capita *adj, adv* of or for each person: *the average per capita wage has increased* [Latin, literally: according to heads]
perceive *vb* **-ceiving, -ceived 1** to become aware of (something) through the senses **2** to understand or grasp [Latin *percipere* to seize entirely] **perceivable** *adj*
per cent *adv* **1** in each hundred. Symbol: **%** ▷ *n also* **percent 2** a percentage or proportion [Medieval Latin *per centum* out of every hundred]
percentage *n* **1** proportion or rate per hundred parts **2** any proportion in relation to the whole: *a small percentage of the population* **3** *informal* profit or advantage
percentile *n* one of 99 actual or notional values of a variable dividing its distribution into 100 groups with equal frequencies
perceptible *adj* able to be perceived; recognizable **perceptibly** *adv*
perception *n* **1** the act of perceiving **2** insight or intuition: *his acute perception of other people's emotions* **3** the ability to perceive **4** way of viewing: *advertising affects the customer's perception of a product* [Latin *perceptio* comprehension] **perceptual** *adj*
perceptive *adj* **1** observant **2** able to perceive **perceptively** *adv* **perceptiveness** *n*
perch[1] *n* **1** a branch or other resting place above ground for a bird **2** any raised resting place: *from his perch on the bar stool* ▷ *vb* **3** (of birds) to alight or rest on a perch: *it fluttered to the branch and perched there for a moment* **4** to place or position precariously: *he was perched uneasily on the edge of his chair* [Latin *pertica* long staff]
perch[2] *n, pl* **perch** *or* **perches 1** a spiny-finned edible freshwater fish of Europe and North America **2** any of various similar or related fishes [Greek *perkē*]
perchance *adv archaic or poetic* **1** perhaps **2** by chance [Anglo-French *par chance*]
percipient *adj formal* quick at perceiving; observant [Latin *percipiens* observing] **percipience** *n*
percolate *vb* **-lating, -lated 1** to pass or filter through very small holes: *the light percolating through the stained-glass windows cast coloured patterns on the floor* **2** to spread gradually: *his theories percolated through the academic community* **3** to make (coffee) or (of coffee) to be made in a percolator [Latin *per-* through + *colare* to strain] **percolation** *n*
percolator *n* a coffee pot in which boiling water is forced up through a tube and filters down through the coffee grounds into a container
percussion *n* **1** the striking of one thing against another **2** *music* percussion instruments collectively [Latin *percutere* to hit] **percussive** *adj*
percussion cap *n* a detonator which contains material that explodes when struck
percussion instrument *n* a musical instrument, such as the drums, that produces a sound when struck directly
percussionist *n music* a person who plays percussion instruments
perdition *n* **1** *Christianity* final and unalterable spiritual ruin; damnation **2** same as **hell** [Late Latin *perditio* ruin]
peregrinate *vb* **-nating, -nated** *formal* to travel or wander about from place to place [Latin *peregrinari* to travel] **peregrination** *n*

peregrine falcon *n* a European falcon with dark plumage on the back and wings and lighter underparts [Latin *peregrinus* foreign]

peremptory *adj* **1** urgent or commanding: *a peremptory knock on the door* **2** expecting immediate obedience without any discussion: *he gave peremptory instructions to his son* **3** dogmatic [Latin *peremptorius* decisive] **peremptorily** *adv*

perennial *adj* **1** lasting throughout the year or through many years ▹ *n* **2** a plant that continues its growth for at least three years [Latin *per-* through + *annus* year]

perestroika *n* (in the late 1980s) the policy of restructuring the Soviet economy and political system [Russian: reconstruction]

perfect *adj* **1** having all essential elements **2** faultless: *a perfect circle* **3** correct or precise: *perfect timing* **4** utter or absolute: *a perfect stranger* **5** excellent in all respects: *a perfect day* **6** *maths* exactly divisible into equal integral or polynomial roots: *36 is a perfect square* **7** *grammar* denoting a tense of verbs used to describe a completed action ▹ *n* **8** *grammar* the perfect tense ▹ *vb* **9** to improve to one's satisfaction: *he is in Paris to perfect his French* **10** to make fully accomplished: *he perfected the system* [Latin *perficere* to complete] **perfectly** *adv*

> **USAGE** For most of its meanings, the adjective *perfect* describes an absolute state, i.e. one that cannot be qualified; thus something is either *perfect* or *not perfect*, and cannot be *more perfect* or *less perfect*. However, when *perfect* means excellent in all respects, a comparative can be used with it without absurdity: *the next day the weather was even more perfect.*

P

perfectible *adj* capable of becoming or being made perfect **perfectibility** *n*

perfection *n* the state or quality of being perfect [Latin *perfectio* a completing]

perfectionism *n* the demand for the highest standard of excellence **perfectionist** *n, adj*

perfect pitch *n* same as **absolute pitch**

perfect storm *n* a combination of events which produce a disastrous outcome

perfidious *adj literary* treacherous or deceitful [Latin *perfidus*] **perfidy** *n*

perforate *vb* **-rating, -rated 1** to make a hole or holes in **2** to punch rows of holes between (stamps) for ease of separation [Latin *per-* through + *forare* to pierce] **perforable** *adj* **perforator** *n*

perforation *n* **1** a hole or holes made in something **2** a series of punched holes, such as that between individual stamps

perforce *adv formal* of necessity [Old French *par force*]

perform *vb* **1** to carry out (an action): *the hospital performs more than a hundred such operations each year* **2** to present (a play or concert): *he performed a couple of songs from his new album* **3** to fulfil: *you have performed the first of two conditions* [Old French *parfournir*] **performable** *adj* **performer** *n*

performance *n* **1** the act or process of performing **2** an artistic or dramatic production: *the concert includes the first performance of a new trumpet concerto* **3** manner or quality of functioning: *the car's overall performance is excellent* **4** *informal* conduct or behaviour, esp. when distasteful: *what did you mean by that performance at the restaurant?*

perfume *n* **1** a liquid cosmetic worn for its pleasant smell **2** a fragrant smell ▹ *vb* **-fuming, -fumed 3** to impart a perfume to [French *parfum*, from Latin *per* through + *fumare* to smoke] **perfumed** *adj*

perfumer *n* a person who makes or sells perfume **perfumery** *n*

perfunctory *adj formal* done only as a matter of routine: *he gave his wife a perfunctory kiss* [Late Latin *perfunctorius* negligent] **perfunctorily** *adv* **perfunctoriness** *n*

perfuse *vb* **-fusing, -fused 1** to permeate (a liquid, colour, etc.) through or over (something) **2** *surgery* to pass (a fluid) through tissue

pergola *n* an arched trellis or framework that supports climbing plants [Italian]

perhaps *adv* **1** possibly; maybe **2** approximately; roughly: *it would have taken perhaps three or four minutes* [earlier *perhappes*, from *per* by + *happes* chance]

perianth *n botany* the outer part of a flower [Greek *peri-* around + *anthos* flower]

pericardium *n, pl* **-dia** the membranous sac enclosing the heart [Greek *peri-* around + *kardia* heart] **pericardial** *adj*

pericarp *n botany* the part of a fruit enclosing the seed that develops from the wall of the ovary [Greek *peri-* around + *karpos* fruit]

perigee *n astron* the point in its orbit around the earth when the moon or a satellite is nearest the earth [Greek *peri-* near + *gē* earth]

perihelion *n, pl* **-lia** *astron* the point in its orbit around the sun when a planet or comet is nearest the sun [Greek *peri-* near + *hēlios* sun]

peril *n* great danger or jeopardy [Latin *periculum*] **perilous** *adj*

perimeter (per-**rim**-it-er) *n* **1** *maths* **A** the curve or line enclosing a plane area **B** the length of this curve or line **2** any boundary around something [Latin *perimetros*]

perinatal *adj* of or occurring in the period from about three months before to one month after birth [Greek *peri-* around + Latin *natus* born]

perineum (per-rin-**nee**-um) *n, pl* **-nea** (-**nee**-a) *anatomy* the region of the body between the anus and the genitals [Greek *perinaion*] **perineal** *adj*

period *n* **1** a portion of time: *six inches of rain fell in a 24-hour period* **2** a portion of time specified in some way: *the President's first period of office* **3** an occurrence of menstruation **4** *geol* a unit of geological time during which a system of rocks is formed: *the Jurassic period* **5** a division of time at school, college, or university when a particular subject is taught **6** *physics & maths* the time taken to complete one cycle of a regularly recurring phenomenon **7** *chem* one of the horizontal rows of elements in the periodic table **8** *chiefly US & Canad* same as **full stop** ▹ *adj* **9** dating from or in the style of an earlier time: *a performance on period instruments* [Greek *periodos* circuit]

periodic *adj* recurring at intervals **periodically** *adv* **periodicity** *n*

periodical *n* **1** a publication issued at regular intervals, usually monthly or weekly ▷ *adj* **2** of or relating to such publications **3** periodic or occasional

periodic law *n chem* the principle that the chemical properties of the elements are periodic functions of their atomic numbers

periodic table *n chem* a table of the elements, arranged in order of increasing atomic number, based on the periodic law

peripatetic (per-rip-a-**tet**-ik) *adj* **1** travelling from place to place **2** *Brit* employed in two or more educational establishments and travelling from one to another: *a peripatetic violin teacher* ▷ *n* **3** a peripatetic person [Greek *peripatein* to pace to and fro]

peripheral (per-**if**-er-al) *adj* **1** not relating to the most important part of something; incidental **2** of or relating to a periphery ▷ *n* **3** *computers* any device, such as a printer, that can be connected to a computer

periphery (per-**if**-er-ee) *n, pl* **-eries** **1** the boundary or edge of an area or group: *slums sprouted up on the periphery of the city* **2** fringes of a field of activity: *less developed countries on the periphery of the capitalist system* [Greek *peri-* around + *pherein* to bear]

periphrasis (per-**if**-ra-siss) *n, pl* **-rases** (-ra-seez) a roundabout way of expressing something; circumlocution [Greek *peri-* around + *phrazein* to declare]

periscope *n* an optical instrument used, esp. in submarines, to give a view of objects on a different level [Greek *periskopein* to look around]

perish *vb* **1** to be destroyed or die **2** to cause to suffer: *we were perished with cold* **3** to rot or cause to rot: *to prevent your swimsuit from perishing, rinse it in clean water before it dries* [Latin *perire* to pass away entirely]

perishable *adj* **1** liable to rot ▷ *n* **2** (*often pl*) a perishable article, esp. food

perishing *adj* **1** *informal* (of weather) extremely cold **2** *slang* confounded or blasted: *get rid of the perishing lot!*

peristalsis (per-riss-**tal**-siss) *n, pl* **-ses** (-seez) *physiol* the wavelike involuntary muscular contractions of the walls of the digestive tract [Greek *peri-* around + *stalsis* compression] **peristaltic** *adj*

peritoneum (per-rit-toe-**nee**-um) *n, pl* **-nea** (**-nee**-a) *or* **-neums** a serous sac that lines the walls of the abdominal cavity and covers the abdominal organs [Greek *peritonos* stretched around] **peritoneal** *adj*

peritonitis (per-rit-tone-**ite**-iss) *n* inflammation of the peritoneum, causing severe abdominal pain

periwig *n obsolete* a wig formerly worn by men [French *perruque*]

periwinkle[1] *n* same as **winkle** (sense 1) [origin unknown]

periwinkle[2] *n* a Eurasian evergreen plant with trailing stems and blue flowers [Old English *perwince*]

perjure *vb* **-juring, -jured** > **perjure oneself** *criminal law* to deliberately give false evidence while under oath [Latin *perjurare*] **perjurer** *n*

perjury (**per**-jer-ee) *n, pl* **-juries** *criminal law* the act of deliberately giving false evidence while under oath [Latin *perjurium* a false oath]

perk[1] *n informal* an incidental benefit gained from a job, such as a company car [short for *perquisite*]

perk[2] *vb informal* short for **percolate** (sense 3)

perk up *vb* **1** to make or become more cheerful **2** to rise or cause to rise briskly: *the dog's ears perked up suddenly* [origin unknown]

perky *adj* **perkier, perkiest** **1** jaunty or lively **2** confident or spirited

Perl *n* a computer programming language that is used for text manipulation, esp. on the internet [practical extraction and report language]

perlemoen (**per**-la-moon) *n S African* same as **abalone** [Afrikaans, from Dutch]

perm[1] *n* **1** a hairstyle with long-lasting waves or curls produced by treating the hair with chemicals ▷ *vb* **2** to give a perm to (hair)

perm[2] *n informal* short for **permutation** (sense 4)

permafrost *n* ground that is permanently frozen [*perma(nent)* + *frost*]

permanent *adj* **1** existing or intended to exist forever: *a permanent solution* **2** not expected to change: *a permanent condition* [Latin *permanens* continuing] **permanence** *n* **permanently** *adv*

permanent wave *n* same as **perm**[1] (sense 1)

permanent way *n chiefly Brit* the track of a railway, including the sleepers and rails

permanganate *n* a salt of an acid containing manganese, used as a disinfectant

permeable *adj* capable of being permeated, esp. by liquids **permeability** *n*

permeate *vb* **-ating, -ated** **1** to penetrate or spread throughout (something): *his mystical philosophy permeates everything he creates* **2** to pass through or cause to pass through by osmosis or diffusion: *the rain permeated her anorak* [Latin *permeare*] **permeation** *n*

Permian *adj geol* of the period of geological time about 280 million years ago [after *Perm*, Russian port]

permissible *adj* permitted or allowable **permissibility** *n*

permission *n* authorization to do something

permissive *adj* tolerant or lenient, esp. in sexual matters: *the so-called permissive society* **permissiveness** *n*

permit *vb* **-mitting, -mitted** **1** to allow (something) to be done or to happen: *smoking is not permitted in the office* **2** to allow (someone) to do something: *her father does not permit her to eat sweets* **3** to allow the possibility (of): *they saw each other as often as time and circumstances permitted* ▷ *n* **4** an official document granting permission to do something [Latin *permittere*]

permutate *vb* **-tating, -tated** to alter the sequence or arrangement (of): *endlessly permutating three basic designs*

permutation *n* **1** *maths* an ordered arrangement of the numbers or terms of a set into specified groups: *the permutations of a, b, and c, taken two at a time, are ab, ba, ac, ca, bc, cb* **2** a combination of items made by reordering **3** a transformation **4** a fixed combination for selections of results on football pools [Latin *permutare* to change thoroughly]

P

pernicious *adj formal* **1** wicked or malicious: *pernicious lies* **2** causing grave harm; deadly [Latin *pernicies* ruin]

pernicious anaemia *n* a severe form of anaemia resulting in a reduction of the red blood cells, weakness, and a sore tongue

pernickety *adj informal* **1** excessively fussy about details **2** (of a task) requiring close attention [origin unknown]

peroration *n formal* the concluding part of a speech which sums up the points made previously [Latin *peroratio*]

peroxide *n* **1** hydrogen peroxide used as a hair bleach **2** any of a class of metallic oxides, such as sodium peroxide, Na_2O_2 ▷ *adj* **3** bleached with or resembling peroxide: *a peroxide blonde* ▷ *vb* **-iding, -ided 4** to bleach (the hair) with peroxide

perp *n US & Canad informal* a person who has committed a crime [short for *perpetrator*]

perpendicular *adj* **1** at right angles to a given line or surface **2** upright; vertical **3** denoting a style of English Gothic architecture characterized by vertical lines ▷ *n* **4** *geom* a line or plane perpendicular to another [Latin *perpendiculum* a plumb line] **perpendicularity** *n*

perpetrate *vb* **-trating, -trated** to perform or be responsible for (a deception or crime) [Latin *perpetrare*] **perpetration** *n* **perpetrator** *n*

> **USAGE** *Perpetrate* and *perpetuate* are sometimes confused: *he must answer for the crimes he has perpetrated* (not *perpetuated*); *the book helped to perpetuate* (not *perpetrate*) *some of the myths surrounding his early life.*

perpetual *adj* **1** never ending or never changing: *Mexico's colourful scenery and nearly perpetual sunshine* **2** continually repeated: *his mother's perpetual worries about his health* [Latin *perpetualis*] **perpetually** *adv*

P

perpetual motion *n* motion of a hypothetical mechanism that continues indefinitely without any external source of energy

perpetuate *vb* **-ating, -ated** to cause to continue: *we must not perpetuate the divisions of the past* [Latin *perpetuare* to continue without interruption] **perpetuation** *n*

> **USAGE** See at **perpetrate.**

perpetuity *n, pl* **-ties 1** eternity **2** the state of being perpetual **3** something perpetual, such as a pension that is payable indefinitely **4 in perpetuity** forever [Latin *perpetuitas* continuity]

perplex *vb* **1** to puzzle or bewilder **2** to complicate: *this merely perplexes the issue* [Latin *perplexus* entangled] **perplexing** *adj*

perplexity *n, pl* **-ties 1** the state of being perplexed **2** something that perplexes

perquisite *n formal* same as **perk**[1] [Latin *perquirere* to seek earnestly for something]

perry *n, pl* **-ries** an alcoholic drink made from fermented pear juice [Old French *peré*]

per se (per **say**) *adv* in itself [Latin]

persecute *vb* **-cuting, -cuted 1** to oppress or maltreat (someone), because of race or religion **2** to harass (someone) persistently [Latin *persequi* to take vengeance upon] **persecution** *n* **persecutor** *n*

perseverance *n* continued steady belief or efforts; persistence

persevere *vb* **-severing, -severed** (often foll. by *with* or *in*) to continue to make an effort despite difficulties [Latin *perseverus* very strict]

Persian *adj* **1** of ancient Persia or modern Iran ▷ *n* **2** a person from Persia (now Iran) **3** the language of Iran or of Persia

Persian carpet *n* a hand-made carpet or rug with flowing or geometric designs in rich colours

Persian cat *n* a long-haired variety of domestic cat

Persian lamb *n* **1** a black loosely curled fur from the karakul lamb **2** a karakul lamb

persiflage (per-sif-flahzh) *n literary* light frivolous conversation or writing [French]

persimmon *n* a sweet red tropical fruit [from a Native American language]

persist *vb* **1** to continue without interruption: *if the symptoms persist, see your doctor* **2** (often foll. by *in* or *with*) to continue obstinately despite opposition: *she persisted in using these controversial methods* [Latin *persistere*]

persistent *adj* **1** unrelenting: *persistent rain* **2** showing persistence: *she was a persistent woman* **persistence** *n* **persistently** *adv*

persistent vegetative state *n med* an irreversible condition, resulting from brain damage, characterized by lack of consciousness, thought, and feeling, although reflex activities continue

person *n, pl* **people** *or* **persons 1** an individual human being **2** the body of a human being: *he was found to have a knife concealed about his person* **3** *grammar* a category into which pronouns and forms of verbs are subdivided to show whether they refer to the speaker, the person addressed, or some other individual or thing **4 in person** actually doing something or being somewhere oneself: *I had the chance to hear her speak in person* [Latin *persona* mask]

> **USAGE** *People* is the word usually used to refer to more than one individual: *there were a hundred people at the reception. Persons* is rarely used, except in official English: *several persons were interviewed.*

-person *combining form* sometimes used instead of *man* and *woman*: *chairperson*

> **USAGE** See at **man.**

persona (per-**soh**-na) *n, pl* **-nae** (-nee) the personality that a person adopts and presents to other people [Latin: mask]

personable *adj* pleasant in appearance and personality

personage *n* **1** an important or distinguished person **2** any person

personal *adj* **1** of the private aspects of a person's life: *redundancy can put an enormous strain on personal relationships* **2** of a person's body: *personal hygiene* **3** belonging to, or for the sole use of, a particular individual: *he disappeared, leaving his passport, diary and other personal belongings in his flat* **4** undertaken by an individual: *the sponsorship deal requires him to make a number of personal appearances for publicity purposes* **5** offensive in respect of an individual's personality or intimate affairs: *he has suffered a lifetime of personal remarks about his weight* **6** having the attributes of an individual conscious being:

a personal God **7** *grammar* of person **8** *law* of movable property, such as money

personal assistant *n* a person who is employed to help someone with his or her work, esp. the secretarial and administrative aspects of it

personal column *n* a newspaper column containing personal messages and advertisements

personal computer *n* a computer that is used by one person at a time in a business or school or at home

personality *n, pl* **-ties 1** *psychol* the distinctive characteristics which make an individual unique **2** the distinctive character of a person which makes him or her socially attractive: *some people find him lacking in personality and a bit colourless* **3** a well-known person in a certain field; celebrity **4** a remarkable person: *she is a personality to be reckoned with* **5** (*often pl*) an offensive personal remark: *the argument never degenerated into personalities*

personalize *or* **-lise** *vb* **-lizing, -lized** *or* **-lising, -lised 1** to base (an argument or discussion) around people's characters rather than on abstract arguments **2** to mark (stationery or clothing) with a person's initials or name **3** same as **personify**

personally *adv* **1** without the help of others: *she had seen to it personally that permission was granted* **2** in one's own opinion: *personally, I think it's overrated* **3** as if referring to oneself: *yes, he was rather rude but it's not worth taking it personally* **4** as a person: *I don't like him personally, but he's fine to work with*

personal organizer *n* **1** a diary for storing personal records, appointments, etc. **2** a pocket-sized electronic device that performs the same functions

personal pronoun *n* a pronoun such as *I, you, he, she, it, we,* and *they* that represents a definite person or thing

personal stereo *n chiefly Brit* a small portable cassette or CD player used with lightweight headphones

persona non grata (non grah-ta) *n, pl* **personae non gratae** (grah-tee) an unacceptable person [Latin]

personate *vb* **-ating, -ated** *criminal law* to assume the identity of (another person) with intent to deceive **personation** *n*

personify *vb* **-fies, -fying, -fied 1** to give human characteristics to (a thing or abstraction) **2** to represent (an abstract quality) in human or animal form **3** (of a person or thing) to represent (an abstract quality), as in art **4** to be the embodiment of: *she can be charm personified* **personification** *n*

personnel *n* **1** the people employed in an organization or for a service **2** the department in an organization that appoints or keeps records of employees **3** (in the armed forces) people, as opposed to machinery or equipment [French]

perspective *n* **1** a way of regarding situations or facts and judging their relative importance: *the female perspective on sex and love* **2** objectivity: *Kiara's problems helped me put my minor worries into perspective* **3** a method of drawing that gives the effect of solidity and relative distances and sizes **4** the appearance of objects or buildings relative to each other, determined by their distance from the viewer [Latin *perspicere* to inspect carefully]

Perspex *n trademark* a clear acrylic resin used as a substitute for glass

perspicacious *adj formal* acutely perceptive or discerning [Latin *perspicax*] **perspicacity** *n*

perspicuous *adj literary* (of speech or writing) easily understood; lucid [Latin *perspicuus* transparent] **perspicuity** *n*

perspiration *n* **1** the salty fluid secreted by the sweat glands of the skin; sweat **2** the act of sweating

perspire *vb* **-spiring, -spired** to sweat [Latin *per-* through + *spirare* to breathe]

persuade *vb* **-suading, -suaded 1** to make (someone) do something by reason or charm: *we tried to persuade him not to come up the mountain with us* **2** to cause to believe; convince: *persuading people of the need for enforced environmental protection may be difficult* [Latin *persuadere*] **persuadable** *adj*

persuasion *n* **1** the act of persuading **2** the power to persuade **3** a set of beliefs; creed: *the Roman Catholic persuasion; literary intellectuals of the modernist persuasion*

persuasive *adj* able to persuade: *a persuasive argument* **persuasively** *adv*

pert *adj* **1** saucy or impudent **2** attractive in a neat way: *pert buttocks* [Latin *apertus* open]

pertain *vb* (often foll. by *to*) **1** to have reference or relevance: *the notes pertaining to the case* **2** to be appropriate: *the product pertains to real user needs* **3** to belong (to) or be a part (of) [Latin *pertinere*]

pertinacious *adj* **1** doggedly resolute in purpose or belief **2** stubbornly persistent [Latin *per-* (intensive) + *tenax* clinging] **pertinacity** *n*

pertinent *adj* relating to the matter at hand; relevant [Latin *pertinens*] **pertinence** *n*

perturb *vb* **1** to disturb the composure of **2** to throw into disorder [Latin *perturbare* to confuse]

perturbation *n literary* anxiety or worry

peruke *n obsolete* a wig for men worn in the 17th and 18th centuries [French *perruque*]

peruse *vb* **-rusing, -rused 1** to read or examine with care **2** to browse or read in a leisurely way [*per-* (intensive) + *use*] **perusal** *n*

pervade *vb* **-vading, -vaded** to spread through or throughout (something) [Latin *per-* through + *vadere* to go] **pervasion** *n* **pervasive** *adj*

perverse *adj* **1** deliberately acting in a way different from what is regarded as normal or proper **2** wayward or contrary; obstinate [Latin *perversus* turned the wrong way] **perversely** *adv* **perversity** *n*

perversion *n* **1** any means of obtaining sexual satisfaction that is considered abnormal or unacceptable **2** the act of perverting

pervert *vb* **1** to use wrongly or badly **2** to interpret wrongly or badly; distort **3** to lead (someone) into abnormal behaviour, esp. sexually; corrupt **4** to debase ▷ *n* **5** a person who practises sexual perversion [Latin *pervertere* to turn the wrong way] **perverted** *adj*

pervious *adj* **1** able to be penetrated; permeable: *the thin walls were pervious to the slightest sound*

2 receptive to new ideas; open-minded [Latin *per-* through + *via* a way]

Pesach *or* **Pesah** (**pay**-sahk) *n* same as **Passover**

peseta (pess-**say**-ta) *n* a former monetary unit of Spain [Spanish]

pesky *adj* **peskier, peskiest** *informal, chiefly US & Canad* troublesome [probably changed from *pesty*]

peso (**pay**-so) *n, pl* **-sos** the standard monetary unit of Chile, Colombia, Cuba, the Dominican Republic, Mexico, the Philippines, and Uruguay [Spanish: weight]

pessary *n, pl* **-ries** *med* **1** a device worn in the vagina, either as a support for the uterus or as a contraceptive **2** a vaginal suppository [Greek *pessos* plug]

pessimism *n* **1** the tendency to expect the worst in all things **2** the doctrine of the ultimate triumph of evil over good [Latin *pessimus* worst] **pessimist** *n* **pessimistic** *adj* **pessimistically** *adv*

pest *n* **1** an annoying person or thing; nuisance **2** any organism that damages crops, or injures or irritates livestock or humans [Latin *pestis* plague]

pester *vb* to annoy or nag continually [Old French *empestrer* to hobble (a horse)]

pesticide *n* a chemical used to destroy pests, esp. insects [*pest* + Latin *caedere* to kill]

pestilence *n literary* any deadly epidemic disease, such as the plague

pestilent *adj* **1** annoying or irritating **2** highly destructive morally or physically **3** likely to cause infectious disease [Latin *pestis* plague] **pestilential** *adj*

pestle *n* a club-shaped instrument for grinding or pounding substances in a mortar [Old French *pestel*]

pet¹ *n* **1** a tame animal kept for companionship or pleasure **2** a person who is favoured or indulged: *teacher's pet* ▷ *adj* **3** kept as a pet: *a pet hamster* **4** of or for pet animals: *pet food* **5** strongly felt or particularly cherished: *my pet hate*; *he would not stand by and let his pet project be abandoned* ▷ *vb* **petting, petted 6** to treat as a pet; pamper **7** to pat or stroke affectionately **8** *informal* (of two people) to caress each other in an erotic manner [origin unknown]

pet² *n* a fit of sulkiness [origin unknown]

petal *n* any of the brightly coloured leaflike parts which form the head of a flower [Greek *petalon* leaf] **petalled** *adj*

petard *n* **1** (formerly) a device containing explosives used to break through a wall or door **2 hoist with one's own petard** being the victim of one's own schemes [French: firework]

peter out *vb* to come gradually to an end: *the road petered out into a rutted track* [origin unknown]

Peter Pan *n* a youthful or immature man [after the main character in *Peter Pan*, a play]

pethidine (**peth**-id-een) *n* a white crystalline water-soluble drug used to relieve pain [perhaps a blend of *piperidine* + *ethyl*]

petiole *n botany* the stalk which attaches a leaf to a plant [Latin *petiolus* little foot]

petit bourgeois (pet-ee **boor**-zhwah) *n, pl* **petits bourgeois** (pet-ee **boor**-zhwahz) the lower middle class [French]

petite (pit-**eat**) *adj* (of a woman) small and dainty [French]

petit four (pet-ee **four**) *n, pl* **petits fours** (pet-ee **fours**) a very small fancy cake or biscuit [French, literally: little oven]

petition *n* **1** a written document signed by a large number of people demanding some form of action from a government or other authority **2** any formal request to a higher authority **3** *law* a formal application in writing made to a court asking for some specific judicial action: *she filed a petition for divorce* ▷ *vb* **4** to address or present a petition to (a government or to someone in authority): *he petitioned the Crown for mercy* **5** (foll. by *for*) to seek by petition: *the firm's creditors petitioned for liquidation* [Latin *petere* to seek] **petitioner** *n*

petit mal (pet-ee **mal**) *n* a mild form of epilepsy in which there are periods of loss of consciousness for up to 30 seconds [French: little illness]

petit point (pet-ee **point**) *n* **1** a small diagonal needlepoint stitch used for fine detail **2** work done with such stitches [French: small point]

pet name *n* an affectionate nickname for a close friend or family member

petrel *n* a sea bird with a hooked bill and tubular nostrils, such as the albatross, storm petrel, or shearwater [variant of earlier *pitteral*]

Petri dish (**pet**-ree) *n* a shallow dish used in laboratories, esp. for producing cultures of bacteria [after J. R. *Petri*, bacteriologist]

petrify *vb* **-fies, -fying, -fied 1** to stun or daze with fear: *he was petrified of going to jail* **2** (of organic material) to turn to stone **3** to make or become unable to change or develop: *a society petrified by outmoded conventions* [Greek *petra* stone] **petrification** *n*

petrochemical *n* a substance, such as acetone, obtained from petroleum **petrochemistry** *n*

petrodollar *n* money earned by a country by exporting petroleum

petrol *n* a volatile flammable liquid obtained from petroleum and used as a fuel for internal-combustion engines [see PETROLEUM]

petrolatum (pet-rol-**late**-um) *n* a translucent jelly-like substance obtained from petroleum: used as a lubricant and in medicine as an ointment base

petrol bomb *n* a simple grenade consisting of a bottle filled with petrol. A piece of cloth is put in the neck of the bottle and set alight just before the bomb is thrown

petroleum *n* a dark-coloured thick flammable crude oil occurring in sedimentary rocks, consisting mainly of hydrocarbons: the source of petrol and paraffin [Latin *petra* stone + *oleum* oil]

petroleum jelly *n* same as **petrolatum**

petrol station *n Brit* same as **filling station**

petticoat *n* a woman's underskirt [from *petty* + *coat*]

pettifogging *adj old-fashioned* excessively concerned with unimportant detail [origin unknown] **pettifogger** *n*

pettish *adj* peevish or fretful [from PET²] **pettishness** *n*

petty *adj* **-tier, -tiest 1** trivial or unimportant: *petty details* **2** small-minded: *petty spite* **3** low in importance: *petty criminals* [French *petit* little] **pettily** *adv* **pettiness** *n*

petty cash *n* a small cash fund for minor incidental expenses

petty officer *n* a noncommissioned officer in the navy

petulant *adj* unreasonably irritable or peevish [Latin *petulans* bold] **petulance** *n* **petulantly** *adv*

petunia *n* a tropical American plant with pink, white, or purple funnel-shaped flowers [obsolete French *petun* variety of tobacco]

pew *n* **1 A** (in a church) a long benchlike seat with a back, used by the congregation **B** (in a church) an enclosed compartment reserved for the use of a family or group **2 take a pew** *informal* take a seat [Greek *pous* foot]

pewter *n* **1** an alloy containing tin, lead, and sometimes copper and antimony **2** dishes or kitchen utensils made from pewter [Old French *peaultre*]

pfennig (**fen**-ig) *n* a former German monetary unit worth one hundredth of a mark [German: penny]

PG indicating a film certified for viewing by anyone, but which contains scenes that may be unsuitable for children, for whom parental guidance is necessary

pH *n* potential of hydrogen; a measure of the acidity or alkalinity of a solution

phaeton (**fate**-on) *n* a light four-wheeled horse-drawn carriage with or without a top [from French, after *Phaëthon*, character in Greek myth]

phagocyte (**fag**-go-site) *n* a cell or protozoan that engulfs particles, such as microorganisms [Greek *phagein* to eat + *kutos* vessel]

phalanger *n* an Australian marsupial with dense fur and a long tail [Greek *phalaggion* spider's web, referring to its webbed hind toes]

phalanx (**fal**-lanks) *n, pl* **phalanxes** *or* **phalanges** (fal-**lan**-jeez) **1** any closely grouped mass of people: *a solid phalanx of reporters and photographers* **2** a number of people united for a common purpose **3** an ancient Greek battle formation of infantry in close ranks [Greek]

phallic *adj* of or resembling a phallus: *a phallic symbol*

phallus (**fal**-luss) *n, pl* **-luses** *or* **-li** (-lie) **1** same as **penis 2** an image of the penis as a symbol of reproductive power [Greek *phallos*]

phantasm *n* **1** a phantom **2** an unreal vision; illusion [Greek *phantasma*] **phantasmal** *adj*

phantasmagoria *n psychol* a shifting medley of dreamlike figures [probably from French *fantasmagorie* production of phantoms] **phantasmagoric** *adj*

phantasy *n, pl* **-sies** *archaic* same as **fantasy**

phantom *n* **1** an apparition or spectre **2** the visible representation of something abstract, such as in a dream or hallucination: *the phantom of liberty* ▷ *adj* **3** deceptive or unreal: *she regularly took days off for what her bosses considered phantom illnesses* [Latin *phantasma*]

Pharaoh (**fare**-oh) *n* the title of the ancient Egyptian kings [Egyptian *pr-'o* great house]

Pharisee *n* **1** a member of an ancient Jewish sect teaching strict observance of Jewish traditions **2** (*often not cap*) a self-righteous or hypocritical person [Hebrew *pārūsh* separated] **Pharisaic** *adj*

pharmaceutical *adj* of or relating to drugs or pharmacy

pharmaceutics *n* same as **pharmacy** (sense 1)

pharmacist *n* a person qualified to prepare and dispense drugs

pharmacology *n* the science or study of drugs **pharmacological** *adj* **pharmacologist** *n*

pharmacopoeia (far-ma-koh-**pee**-a) *n* an authoritative book containing a list of medicinal drugs along with their uses, preparation, and dosages [Greek *pharmakopoiia* art of preparing drugs]

pharmacy *n* **1** the preparation and dispensing of drugs **2** *pl* **-cies** a dispensary [Greek *pharmakon* drug]

pharyngitis (far-rin-**jite**-iss) *n* inflammation of the pharynx, causing a sore throat

pharynx (**far**-rinks) *n, pl* **pharynges** (far-**rin**-jeez) *or* **pharynxes** the part of the alimentary canal between the mouth and the oesophagus [Greek *pharunx* throat] **pharyngeal** *adj*

phase *n* **1** any distinct or characteristic stage in a sequence of events: *these two songs sum up two distinct phases in the singer's career* **2** *astron* one of the recurring shapes of the portion of the moon, Mercury, or Venus illuminated by the sun **3** *physics* a particular stage in a periodic process or phenomenon **4** *physics* **in** *or* **out of phase** (of two waves or signals) reaching or not reaching corresponding phases at the same time ▷ *vb* **phasing, phased 5** to do or introduce gradually: *the redundancies will be phased over two years* ▷ See also **phase in, phase out** [Greek *phasis* aspect]

phase in *vb* to introduce in a gradual or cautious manner: *the scheme was phased in over seven years*

phase out *vb* to discontinue gradually: *rent subsidies are being phased out*

PhD Doctor of Philosophy

pheasant *n* a long-tailed bird with a brightly coloured plumage in the male: native to Asia but introduced elsewhere [Latin *phasianus*]

phenobarbitone *or* **phenobarbital** *n* a sedative used to treat insomnia and epilepsy

phenol *n* a white crystalline derivative of benzene, used as an antiseptic and disinfectant and in the manufacture of resins, explosives, and pharmaceutical substances [Greek *phaino-* shining; because originally prepared from illuminating gas]

phenomena *n* a plural of **phenomenon**

phenomenal *adj* **1** extraordinary or outstanding: *a phenomenal success* **2** of or relating to a phenomenon **phenomenally** *adv*

phenomenalism *n philosophy* the doctrine that all knowledge comes from sense perception **phenomenalist** *n, adj*

phenomenon *n, pl* **-ena** *or* **-enons 1** anything that can be perceived as an occurrence or fact

P

2 any remarkable occurrence or person [Greek *phainomenon*, from *phainesthai* to appear]

> **USAGE** Although *phenomena* is often treated as if it were singular, correct usage is to employ *phenomenon* with a singular construction and *phenomena* with a plural: *that is an interesting phenomenon* (not *phenomena*); *several new phenomena were recorded in his notes.*

phenotype *n* the physical form of an organism as determined by the interaction of its genetic make-up and its environment

phenyl (**fee**-nile) *adj* of, containing, or consisting of the monovalent group C_6H_5, derived from benzene: *a phenyl group*

phew *interj* an exclamation of relief, surprise, disbelief, or weariness

phial *n* a small bottle for liquid medicine [Greek *phialē* wide shallow vessel]

phil. **1** philharmonic **2** philosophy

philadelphus *n* a shrub grown for its strongly scented showy flowers [Greek *philadelphon*, literally: loving one's brother]

philander *vb* (of a man) to flirt or have many casual love affairs [Greek *philandros* fond of men, used as a name for a lover in literary works] **philanderer** *n* **philandering** *adj, n*

philanthropy *n, pl* **-pies** **1** the practice of helping people less well-off than oneself **2** love of mankind in general [Greek *philanthrōpia* love of mankind] **philanthropic** *adj* **philanthropist** *n*

philately (fill-**lat**-a-lee) *n* the collection and study of postage stamps [Greek *philos* loving + *ateleia* exemption from tax] **philatelist** *n*

philharmonic *adj* **1** fond of music ▷ *n* **2** a specific choir, orchestra, or musical society: *the Vienna Philharmonic* [French *philharmonique*]

philippic *n* a bitter verbal attack [after the orations of Demosthenes against Philip of Macedon]

Philippine *adj, n* same as **Filipino**

philistine *n* **1** a person who is hostile towards culture and the arts ▷ *adj* **2** boorishly uncultured **philistinism** *n*

Philistine *n* a member of the non-Semitic people who inhabited ancient Palestine

philology *n* the science of the structure and development of languages [Greek *philologia* love of language] **philological** *adj* **philologist** *n*

philosopher *n* **1** a person who studies philosophy **2** a person who remains calm and stoical in the face of difficulties or disappointments

philosopher's stone *n* a substance thought by alchemists to be capable of changing base metals into gold

philosophical *or* **philosophic** *adj* **1** of or relating to philosophy or philosophers **2** calm and stoical in the face of difficulties or disappointments **philosophically** *adv*

philosophize *or* **-phise** *vb* **-phizing, -phized** *or* **-phising, -phised** to discuss in a philosophical manner **philosophizer** *or* **-phiser** *n*

philosophy *n, pl* **-phies** **1** the academic study of knowledge, thought, and the meaning of life **2** the particular doctrines of a specific individual or school relating to these issues: *the philosophy of John Locke* **3** any system of beliefs or values **4** a personal outlook or viewpoint [Greek *philosophia* love of wisdom]

philtre *or US* **philter** *n* a drink supposed to arouse desire [Greek *philtron* love potion]

phishing *n* the practice of using fraudulent emails and copies of legitimate websites to extract financial data from computer users for criminal purposes

phlebitis (fleb-**bite**-iss) *n* inflammation of a vein, usually in the legs [Greek *phleps* vein] **phlebitic** *adj*

phlegm (**flem**) *n* **1** the thick yellowish substance secreted by the walls of the respiratory tract **2** apathy or stolidity **3** calmness [Greek *phlegma*] **phlegmy** *adj*

phlegmatic (fleg-**mat**-ik) *adj* having an unemotional disposition

phloem (**flow**-em) *n botany* the plant tissue that acts as a path for the distribution of food substances to all parts of the plant [Greek *phloos* bark]

phlox *n, pl* **phlox** *or* **phloxes** a plant with clusters of white, red, or purple flowers [Greek, literally: flame]

phobia *n psychiatry* an intense and irrational fear of a given situation or thing [Greek *phobos* fear] **phobic** *adj, n*

Phoenician (fon-**nee**-shun) *adj* **1** of Phoenicia, an ancient E Mediterranean country ▷ *n* **2** a person from Phoenicia

phoenix *n* a legendary Arabian bird said to set fire to itself and rise anew from the ashes every 500 years [Greek *phoinix*]

phone *n, vb* **phoning, phoned** short for **telephone**

phone-in *n* a radio or television programme in which telephone questions or comments from the public are broadcast live as part of a discussion

phoneme *n linguistics* one of the set of speech sounds in any given language that serve to distinguish one word from another [Greek *phōnēma* sound, speech] **phonemic** *adj*

phonemics *n* the classification and analysis of the phonemes of a language

phonetic *adj* **1** of phonetics **2** denoting any perceptible distinction between one speech sound and another **3** conforming to pronunciation: *phonetic spelling* [Greek *phōnein* to make sounds, speak] **phonetically** *adv*

phonetics *n* the study of speech processes, including the production, perception, and analysis of speech sounds

phoney *or esp US* **phony** *informal* ▷ *adj* **-nier, -niest** **1** not genuine: *a phoney two-pound coin* **2** (of a person) insincere or pretentious ▷ *n, pl* **-neys** *or esp US* **-nies** **3** an insincere or pretentious person **4** something that is not genuine [origin unknown]

phonograph *n* **1** an early form of record player capable of recording and reproducing sound on wax cylinders **2** *US & Canad* a record player [Greek *phonē* sound + *graphein* to write]

phonology *n, pl* **-gies** **1** the study of the sound system in a language **2** such a sound system [Greek *phonē* sound, voice + -LOGY] **phonological** *adj*

phooey *interj informal* an exclamation of scorn or contempt [probably variant of *phew*]
phosgene (**foz**-jean) *n* a poisonous gas used in warfare [Greek *phōs* light + *-genēs* born]
phosphate *n* **1** any salt or ester of any phosphoric acid **2** (*often pl*) chemical fertilizer containing phosphorous compounds **phosphatic** *adj*
phosphor *n* a substance capable of emitting light when irradiated with particles of electromagnetic radiation [Greek *phōsphoros* phosphorus]
phosphoresce *vb* **-rescing, -resced** to exhibit phosphorescence
phosphorescence *n* **1** *physics* a fluorescence that persists after the bombarding radiation producing it has stopped **2** the light emitted in phosphorescence **phosphorescent** *adj*
phosphoric *adj* of or containing phosphorus in the pentavalent state
phosphorous *adj* of or containing phosphorus in the trivalent state
phosphorus *n chem* a toxic flammable nonmetallic element which appears luminous in the dark. It exists in two forms, white and red. Symbol: **P** [Greek *phōsphoros* light-bringing]
photo *n, pl* **-tos** short for **photograph**
photo- *combining form* **1** of or produced by light: *photosynthesis* **2** indicating a photographic process: *photolithography* [Greek *phōs, phōt-* light]
photobomb *vb* to intrude into the background of a photograph without the subject's knowledge
photocell *n* a cell which produces a current or voltage when exposed to light or other electromagnetic radiation
photocopier *n* a machine using light-sensitive photographic materials to reproduce written, printed, or graphic work
photocopy *n, pl* **-copies 1** a photographic reproduction of written, printed, or graphic work ▷ *vb* **-copies, -copying, -copied 2** to reproduce on photographic material
photoelectric *adj* of or concerned with electric or electronic effects caused by light or other electromagnetic radiation **photoelectricity** *n*
photoengraving *n* **1** a photomechanical process for producing letterpress printing plates **2** a print made from such a plate **photoengrave** *vb*
photo finish *n* a finish of a race in which contestants are so close that a photograph is needed to decide the result
Photofit *n trademark* a picture of someone wanted by the police which has been made by combining photographs of different facial features resembling those of the wanted person
photoflood *n* a highly incandescent electric lamp used for indoor photography and television
photogenic *adj* **1** (esp. of a person) always looking attractive in photographs **2** *biol* producing or emitting light
photograph *n* **1** a picture made using a camera, either by the chemical action of light on sensitive film or by the creation of a digital image ▷ *vb* **2** to take a photograph of
photographic *adj* **1** of or like photography or a photograph **2** (of a person's memory) able to retain facts or appearances in precise detail **photographically** *adv*
photography *n* **1** the process of recording images either on sensitized material by the action of light or by equipment which enables images to be stored digitally and viewed on a screen **2** the practice of taking photographs **photographer** *n*
photogravure *n* a process, used esp. in art reproduction, in which an image from a photographic negative is transferred to a metal plate and etched in [PHOTO- + French *gravure* engraving]
photolithography *n* **1** a lithographic printing process using photographically made plates **2** a process used in the manufacture of semiconductors and printed circuits, in which a photographically produced pattern acts as a mask during an etching or diffusion process **photolithographer** *n*
photometer (foe-**tom**-it-er) *n* an instrument used to measure the intensity of light
photometry (foe-**tom**-it-tree) *n* the branch of physics concerned with the measurement of the intensity of light **photometrist** *n*
photomontage (foe-toe-mon-**tahzh**) *n* **1** the combination of several photographs to produce one picture **2** a picture produced in this way
photon *n physics* a quantum of electromagnetic radiation energy, such as light, having both particle and wave behaviour
photosensitive *adj* sensitive to electromagnetic radiation, esp. light
Photoshop *n* **1** *trademark* a software application for managing and editing digital images ▷ *vb* **-shopping, -shopped 2** *informal* to alter (a digital image) using Photoshop or a similar application
photostat *n* **1** a type of photocopying machine or process **2** any copy made by such a machine ▷ *vb* **-statting, -statted** *or* **-stating, -stated 3** to make a photostat copy (of)
photosynthesis *n* (in plants) the process by which a green plant uses sunlight to build up carbohydrate reserves **photosynthesize** *or* **-sise** *vb* **photosynthetic** *adj*
phototropism (foe-toe-**trope**-iz-zum) *n* the growth of plants towards a source of light [PHOTO- + Greek *tropos* turn] **phototropic** *adj*
phrasal verb *n* a phrase that consists of a verb plus an adverb or preposition, esp. one whose meaning cannot be deduced from its parts, such as *take in* meaning *deceive*
phrase *n* **1** a group of words forming a unit of meaning in a sentence **2** an idiomatic or original expression **3** *music* a small group of notes forming a coherent unit of melody ▷ *vb* **phrasing, phrased 4** to express orally or in a phrase: *I could have phrased that better* **5** *music* to divide (a melodic line or part) into musical phrases, esp. in performance [Greek *phrasis* speech] **phrasal** *adj*
phrase book *n* a book containing frequently used expressions and their equivalent in a foreign language
phraseology (fray-zee-**ol**-a-jee) *n, pl* **-gies** the manner in which words or phrases are used

P

phrasing *n* **1** the exact words used to say or write something **2** the way in which someone who is performing a piece of music or reading aloud divides up the work being performed by pausing slightly in appropriate places

phrenology *n* (formerly) the study of the shape and size of the skull as a means of finding out a person's character and mental ability [Greek *phrēn* mind + -LOGY] **phrenological** *adj* **phrenologist** *n*

phut *informal* ▷ *n* **1** a representation of a muffled explosive sound ▷ *adv* **2 go phut** to break down or collapse [imitative]

phylactery *n, pl* **-teries** *Judaism* either of the pair of square cases containing biblical passages, worn by Jewish men on the left arm and head during weekday morning prayers [Greek *phulaktērion* safeguard]

phylum *n, pl* **-la** *biol* one of the major groups into which the animal and plant kingdoms are divided, containing one or more classes [Greek *phulon* race]

physical *adj* **1** of the body, as distinguished from the mind or spirit **2** of material things or nature: *the physical world* **3** of or concerned with matter and energy **4** of or relating to physics **physically** *adv*

physical education *n* training and practice in sports and gymnastics

physical geography *n* the branch of geography that deals with the natural features of the earth's surface

physical jerks *pl n Brit & Austral informal* repetitive keep-fit exercises

physical science *n* any of the sciences concerned with nonliving matter, such as physics, chemistry, astronomy, and geology

P

physician *n* **1** a medical doctor **2** *archaic* a healer [Greek *phusis* nature]

physicist *n* a person versed in or studying physics

physics *n* **1** the branch of science concerned with the properties of matter and energy and the relationships between them **2** physical properties of behaviour: *the physics of the electron* [translation of Greek *ta phusika* natural things]

physio *n* **1** short for **physiotherapy** **2** *pl* **physios** short for **physiotherapist**

physiognomy (fiz-ee-**on**-om-ee) *n formal* **1** a person's face considered as an indication of personality **2** the outward appearance of something: *the changed physiognomy of the forests* [Greek *phusis* nature + *gnōmōn* judge]

physiography *n* same as **physical geography** [Greek *phusis* nature + -GRAPHY]

physiology *n* **1** the branch of science concerned with the functioning of organisms **2** the processes and functions of all or part of an organism [Greek *phusis* nature + -LOGY] **physiologist** *n* **physiological** *adj*

physiotherapy *n* the treatment of disease or injury by physical means, such as massage or exercises, rather than by drugs [*physio-* (prefix) physical + *therapy*] **physiotherapist** *n*

physique *n* person's bodily build and muscular development [French]

pi *n, pl* **pis** **1** the 16th letter in the Greek alphabet (Π, π) **2** *maths* a number that is the ratio of the circumference of a circle to its diameter; approximate value: 3.141592.... Symbol: π

pianissimo *adj, adv music* to be performed very quietly [Italian]

pianist *n* a person who plays the piano

piano¹ *n, pl* **-anos** a musical instrument played by depressing keys that cause hammers to strike strings and produce audible vibrations [short for *pianoforte*]

piano² *adj, adv music* to be performed softly [Italian]

piano accordion *n* an accordion in which the right hand plays a piano-like keyboard **piano accordionist** *n*

pianoforte (pee-**ann**-oh-**for**-tee) *n* the full name for **piano¹** [Italian *piano e forte* soft and loud]

Pianola (pee-an-**oh**-la) *n trademark* a type of mechanical piano, the music for which is encoded in perforations in a paper roll

piazza *n* **1** a large open square in an Italian town **2** *chiefly Brit* a covered passageway or gallery [Italian: marketplace]

pibroch (**pee**-brok) *n* a form of music for Scottish bagpipes, consisting of a theme and variations [Gaelic *piobaireachd*]

pic *n, pl* **pics** *or* **pix** *informal* a photograph or illustration

pica (**pie**-ka) *n* **1** a size of printer's type giving six lines to the inch **2** a size of typewriter type that has ten characters to the inch [Latin *pica* magpie; sense connection obscure]

picador *n bullfighting* a horseman who wounds the bull with a lance to weaken it [Spanish]

picaresque *adj literary* of or relating to a type of fiction in which the hero, a rogue, goes through a series of episodic adventures [Spanish *pícaro* a rogue]

picayune (pick-a-**yoon**) *US & Canad informal* ▷ *adj* **1** of small value or importance **2** mean or petty ▷ *n* **3** any coin of little value, such as a five-cent piece **4** an unimportant person or thing [French *picaillon* coin from Piedmont]

piccalilli *n* a pickle of mixed vegetables in a mustard sauce [origin unknown]

piccanin *n S African offensive* a Black African child [variant of *piccaninny*]

piccaninny *or esp US* **pickaninny** *n, pl* **-nies** *offensive* a small Black or Aboriginal child [perhaps from Portuguese *pequenino* tiny one]

piccolo *n, pl* **-los** a woodwind instrument an octave higher than the flute [Italian: small]

pick¹ *vb* **1** to choose or select **2** to gather (fruit, berries, or crops) from (a tree, bush, or field) **3** to remove loose particles from: *she picked some bits of fluff off her sleeve* **4** (foll. by *at*) to nibble (at) without appetite **5** to provoke (an argument or fight) deliberately **6** to separate (strands or fibres), as in weaving **7** to steal from (someone's pocket) **8** to open (a lock) with an instrument other than a key **9** to make (one's way) carefully on foot: *they picked their way through the rubble* **10 pick and choose** to select fastidiously or fussily ▷ *n* **11** choice: *take your pick* **12** the best: *the pick of the country's young cricketers* ▷ See also **pick off, pick on** *etc.* [Middle English *piken*]

pick² *n* **1** a tool with a handle and a long curved steel head, used for loosening soil or breaking rocks **2** any tool used for picking, such as an ice pick or toothpick **3** a plectrum ▷ *vb* **4** to pierce or break up (a hard surface) with a pick [perhaps a variant of PIKE²]
pickaback *n, adv, adj* same as **piggyback**
pickaxe *or US* **pickax** *n* a large pick
picket *n* **1** a person or group standing outside a workplace to dissuade strikebreakers from entering **2** a small unit of troops posted to give early warning of attack **3** a pointed stake that is driven into the ground to support a fence ▷ *vb* **-eting, -eted 4** to act as pickets outside (a workplace) [Old French *piquer* to prick]
picket fence *n* a fence consisting of pickets driven into the ground
picket line *n* a line of people acting as pickets
pickings *pl n* money or profits acquired easily
pickle *n* **1** (*often pl*) food, esp. vegetables preserved in vinegar or brine **2** a liquid or marinade, such as spiced vinegar, for preserving vegetables, meat, or fish **3** *informal* an awkward or difficult situation: *to be in a pickle; they are in a pickle over what to do with toxic waste* ▷ *vb* **-ling, -led 4** to preserve or treat in a pickling liquid [probably Middle Dutch *pekel*]
pickled *adj* **1** (of food) preserved in a pickling liquid **2** *informal* drunk
pick-me-up *n informal* a tonic, esp. a special drink taken as a stimulant
pick off *vb* to aim at and shoot (people or things) one by one
pick on *vb* to continually treat someone unfairly
pick out *vb* **1** to select for use or special consideration: *she picked out a wide gold wedding ring* **2** to distinguish (an object from its surroundings), such as in painting: *the wall panels are light brown, with their edges picked out in gold* **3** to recognize (a person or thing): *she picked the man out in a police identity parade* **4** to play (a tune) tentatively, as by ear
pickpocket *n* a person who steals from the pockets of others in public places
pick up *vb* **1** to lift or raise: *he picked up his glass* **2** to obtain or purchase: *a couple of pictures she had picked up in a flea market in Paris* **3** to improve in health or condition: *business had picked up after a difficult first quarter* **4** to learn as one goes along: *she had a good ear and picked up languages quickly* **5** to raise (oneself) after a fall or setback: *she picked herself up and got on with her life* **6** to resume; return to **7** to accept the responsibility for paying (a bill) **8** to collect or give a lift to (passengers or goods) **9** *informal* to become acquainted with for a sexual purpose **10** *informal* to arrest **11** to receive (sounds or signals)
pick-up *n* **1** a small truck with an open body used for light deliveries **2** *informal* a casual acquaintance made for a sexual purpose **3** *informal* **A** a stop to collect passengers or goods **B** the people or things collected **4** a device which converts vibrations into electrical signals, such as that to which a record player stylus is attached
picky *adj* **pickier, pickiest** *Brit, Austral & NZ informal* fussy; finicky
picnic *n* **1** an excursion on which people bring food to be eaten in the open air **2** an informal meal eaten out-of-doors **3 no picnic** *informal* a hard or disagreeable task ▷ *vb* **-nicking, -nicked 4** to eat or take part in a picnic [French *piquenique*] **picnicker** *n*
pico- *combining form* denoting 10^{-12}: *picofarad* [Spanish *pico* small quantity]
picot (peek-oh) *n* any of a pattern of small loops, for example on lace
Pict *n* a member of any of the peoples who lived in N Britain in the first to the fourth centuries AD [Late Latin *Picti* painted men] **Pictish** *adj*
pictograph *n* **1** a picture or symbol standing for a word or group of words, as in written Chinese **2** Also called: **pictogram** a chart on which symbols are used to represent values [Latin *pingere* to paint] **pictographic** *adj*
pictorial *adj* **1** relating to or expressed by pictures ▷ *n* **2** a periodical containing many pictures [Latin *pingere* to paint]
picture *n* **1** a visual representation produced on a surface, such as in a photograph or painting **2** a mental image: *neither had any clear picture of whom they were looking for* **3** a description or account of a situation considered as an observable scene: *the reports do not provide an accurate picture of the spread of AIDS* **4** a person or thing resembling another: *he is the picture of a perfect host* **5** a person or scene typifying a particular state: *his face was a picture of dejection* **6** the image on a television screen **7** a cinema film **8 in the picture** informed about a situation **9 the pictures** a cinema or film show ▷ *vb* **-turing, -tured 10** to visualize or imagine **11** to describe or depict vividly: *a documentary that had pictured the police as good-natured dolts* **12** to put in a picture or make a picture of: *the women pictured above are all the same age* [Latin *pingere* to paint]
picture rail *n* the rail near the top of a wall from which pictures are hung
picturesque *adj* **1** visually pleasing, as in being striking or quaint: *a small picturesque harbour* **2** (of language) graphic or vivid [French *pittoresque*]
picture window *n* a large window with a single pane of glass, usually facing a view
piddle *vb* **-dling, -dled** *informal* **1** to urinate **2 piddle about** *or* **around** *or* **away** to spend (one's time) aimlessly: *we have been piddling around for seven months* [origin unknown]
piddling *adj informal* petty or trivial: *piddling amounts of money*
pidgin *n* a language made up of elements of two or more languages and used between the speakers of the languages involved [supposed Chinese pronunciation of *business*]
pidgin English *n* a pidgin in which one of the languages involved is English
pie *n* **1** a sweet or savoury filling baked in pastry **2 pie in the sky** illusory hope or promise of some future good [origin unknown]
piebald *adj* **1** marked in two colours, esp. black and white ▷ *n* **2** a black-and-white horse [dialect *pie* magpie + BALD]
piece *n* **1** a separate bit or part **2** an instance or occurrence: *a piece of luck* **3** an example or specimen of a style or type: *each piece of furniture is*

crafted from native red pine by traditional methods **4** a literary, musical, or artistic composition **5** a coin: *a fifty-pence piece* **6** a firearm or cannon **7** a small object used in playing various games: *a chess piece* **8 go to pieces** (of a person) to lose control of oneself; have a breakdown ▷ *vb* **piecing, pieced 9** (often foll. by *together*) to fit or assemble bit by bit **10** (often foll. by *up*) to patch or make up (a garment) by adding pieces [Middle English *pece*]

pièce de résistance (pyess de ray-**zeest**-onss) *n* the most outstanding item in a series [French]

piece goods *pl n* goods, esp. fabrics, made in standard widths and lengths

piecemeal *adv* **1** bit by bit; gradually ▷ *adj* **2** fragmentary or unsystematic: *a piecemeal approach* [Middle English *pece* piece + *-mele* a measure]

piece of eight *n, pl* **pieces of eight** a former Spanish coin worth eight reals

piecework *n* work paid for according to the quantity produced

pie chart *n* a circular graph divided into sectors proportional to the sizes of the quantities represented

pied *adj* having markings of two or more colours [dialect *pie* magpie]

pied-à-terre (**pyay-da-tair**) *n, pl* **pieds-à-terre** (**pyay-da-tair**) a flat or other lodging for occasional use [French, literally: foot on (the) ground]

pie-eyed *adj slang* drunk

pier *n* **1** a structure with a deck that is built out over water and used as a landing place or promenade **2** a pillar or support that bears heavy loads **3** the part of a wall between two adjacent openings [Middle English *per*]

P

pierce *vb* **piercing, pierced 1** to make a hole in (something) with a sharp point **2** to force (a way) through (something) **3** (of light) to shine through (darkness) **4** (of sounds or cries) to sound sharply through (the silence) **5** to penetrate: *the cold pierced the air* [Old French *percer*]

piercing *adj* **1** (of a sound) unpleasantly loud and sharp: *a piercing scream* **2** very intense: *a piercing stare* ▷ *n* **3** a hole made in the body so that an item of jewellery can be inserted into it: *a nose piercing*

pier glass *n* a tall narrow mirror, designed to hang on the wall between windows

Pierrot (**pier**-roe) *n* a male character from French pantomime with a whitened face, white costume, and pointed hat

pietism *n rare* exaggerated piety

piety *n, pl* **-ties 1** dutiful devotion to God and observance of religious principles **2** the quality of being pious **3** a pious action or saying [Latin *pietas*]

piezoelectric effect (pie-eez-oh-ill-**ek**-trik) *or* **piezoelectricity** *n physics* **A** the production of electricity by applying a mechanical stress to certain crystals **B** the converse effect in which stress is produced in a crystal as a result of an applied voltage [Greek *piezein* to press]

piffle *n informal* nonsense [origin unknown]

piffling *adj informal* worthless; trivial

pig *n* **1** a mammal with a long head, a snout, and bristle-covered skin, which is kept and killed for pork, ham, and bacon. Related adjective: **porcine 2** *informal* a dirty, greedy, or bad-mannered person **3** *offensive slang* a police officer **4** a mass of metal cast into a simple shape **5** *Brit informal* something that is difficult or unpleasant: *the coast is a pig for little boats* **6 a pig in a poke** something bought or received without previous sight or knowledge **7 make a pig of oneself** *informal* to overeat ▷ *vb* **pigging, pigged 8** (of a sow) to give birth **9** (often foll. by *out*) *slang* to eat greedily or to excess: *she had pigged out on pizza before the show* [Middle English *pigge*]

pigeon¹ *n* **1** a bird which has a heavy body, small head, and short legs, and is usually grey in colour **2** *slang* a victim or dupe [Old French *pijon* young dove]

pigeon² *n informal* concern or responsibility: *this is our pigeon – there's nothing to keep you* [from *pidgin*]

pigeonhole *n* **1** a small compartment, such as in a bureau, for filing papers ▷ *vb* **-holing, -holed 2** to classify or categorize **3** to put aside

pigeon-toed *adj* with the toes or feet turned inwards

piggery *n, pl* **-geries** a place where pigs are kept

piggish *adj* **1** like a pig in appetite or manners **2** stubborn **piggishness** *n*

piggy *n, pl* **-gies 1** a child's word for a **pig** ▷ *adj* **-gier, -giest 2** same as **piggish**

piggyback *or* **pickaback** *n* **1** a ride on the back and shoulders of another person ▷ *adv, adj* **2** on the back and shoulders of another person

piggy bank *n* a child's money box shaped like a pig with a slot for coins

pig-headed *adj* stupidly stubborn

pig iron *n* crude iron produced in a blast furnace and poured into moulds

piglet *n* a young pig

pigment *n* **1** any substance which gives colour to paint or dye **2** a substance which occurs in plant or animal tissue and produces a characteristic colour [Latin *pigmentum*] **pigmentary** *adj*

pigmentation *n* colouring in plants, animals, or humans, caused by the presence of pigments

Pigmy *n, pl* **-mies** same as **Pygmy**

pigskin *n* **1** the skin of the domestic pig **2** leather made of this skin **3** *US & Canad informal* a football

pigsty *or US & Canad* **pigpen** *n, pl* **-sties 1** a pen for pigs **2** an untidy place

pigswill *n* waste food or other edible matter fed to pigs

pigtail *n* a plait of hair or one of two plaits on either side of the face

pike¹ *n, pl* **pike** *or* **pikes** a large predatory freshwater fish with a broad flat snout, strong teeth, and a long body covered with small scales [Old English *pīc* point, from the shape of its jaw]

pike² *n* a medieval weapon consisting of a metal spearhead on a long pole [Old English *pīc* point] **pikeman** *n*

pikelet *n* a small thick pancake [from Welsh *bara pyglyd* pitchy bread]

piker *n Austral & NZ slang* a shirker

pikestaff *n* **1** the wooden handle of a pike **2 plain as a pikestaff** very obvious or noticeable

pikey *n Brit slang, derogatory* **1** a traveller or vagrant **2** a person perceived to be of low social class

pilaster *n* a shallow rectangular column attached to the face of a wall [Latin *pila* pillar] **pilastered** *adj*

Pilates (pil-lah-teez) *n* a system of gentle exercises that stretch and lengthen the muscles, designed to improve posture and flexibility [after J. *Pilates*, fitness instructor]

pilau *or* **pilaf** *n* a Middle Eastern dish, consisting of rice flavoured with spices and cooked in stock, to which meat, poultry, or fish may be added [Turkish *pilāw*]

pilchard *n* a small edible sea fish of the herring family, with a rounded body covered with large scales [origin unknown]

pile[1] *n* **1** a collection of objects laid on top of one another **2** *informal* a large amount: *boxing has made him a pile of money; I've got piles of work to do* **3** same as **pyre** **4** a large building or group of buildings **5** *physics* a nuclear reactor ▷ *vb* **piling, piled** **6** (often foll. by *up*) to collect or be collected into a pile: *snow piled up in the drive* **7** (foll. by *in*, *into*, *off* or *out* etc.) to move in a group, often in a hurried manner: *the crew piled into the van* **8** **pile it on** *informal* to exaggerate ▷ See also **pile up** [Latin *pila* stone pier]

pile[2] *n* a long heavy beam driven into the ground as a foundation for a structure [Latin *pilum*]

pile[3] *n* the fibres in a fabric that stand up or out from the weave, such as in carpeting or velvet [Latin *pilus* hair]

pile-driver *n* a machine that drives piles into the ground

piles *pl n* swollen veins in the rectum; haemorrhoids [Latin *pilae* balls]

pile up *vb* **1** to gather or be gathered in a pile ▷ *n* **pile-up** **2** *informal* a traffic accident involving several vehicles

pilfer *vb* to steal (minor items) in small quantities [Old French *pelfre* booty]

pilgrim *n* **1** a person who journeys to a holy place **2** any wayfarer [Latin *peregrinus* foreign]

pilgrimage *n* **1** a journey to a shrine or other holy place **2** a journey or long search made for sentimental reasons: *a pilgrimage to the poet's birthplace*

Pilgrim Fathers *pl n* the English Puritans who founded Plymouth Colony in SE Massachusetts (1620)

pill *n* **1** a small mass of medicine intended to be swallowed whole **2** **the pill** *informal* an oral contraceptive taken by a woman **3** something unpleasant that must be endured: *her reinstatement was a bitter pill to swallow; the pill was sweetened by a reduction in interest* [Latin *pilula* a little ball]

pillage *vb* **-laging, -laged** **1** to steal property violently, often in war ▷ *n* **2** the act of pillaging **3** something obtained by pillaging; booty [Old French *piller* to despoil]

pillar *n* **1** an upright support of stone, brick, or metal; column **2** something resembling this: *a pillar of smoke* **3** a prominent supporter or member: *a pillar of society* **4** **from pillar to post** from one place to another [Latin *pila*]

pillar box *n* (in Britain) a red pillar-shaped public letter box situated in the street

pillbox *n* **1** a box for pills **2** a small enclosed fort of reinforced concrete **3** a small round hat

pillion *n* **1** a seat for a passenger behind the rider of a motorcycle or horse ▷ *adv* **2** on a pillion: *the motorbike on which he was riding pillion* [from Gaelic]

pillock *n slang* a stupid or annoying person [Scandinavian dialect *pillicock* penis]

pillory *n, pl* **-ries** **1** (formerly) a wooden frame in which offenders were locked by the neck and wrists and exposed to public abuse and ridicule ▷ *vb* **-ries, -rying, -ried** **2** to expose to public ridicule **3** (formerly) to punish by putting in a pillory [Old French *pilori*]

pillow *n* **1** a cloth bag stuffed with feathers, polyester fibre, or pieces of foam rubber used to support the head in bed ▷ *vb* **2** to rest (one's head) on or as if on a pillow: *he pillowed his head in her lap* [Old English *pylwe*]

pillowcase *or* **pillowslip** *n* a removable washable cover for a pillow

pilot *n* **1** a person who is qualified to fly an aircraft or spacecraft **2** a person employed to steer a ship into or out of a port **3** a person who acts as a guide ▷ *adj* **4** serving as a test or trial: *a pilot scheme* **5** serving as a guide: *a pilot beacon* ▷ *vb* **-loting, -loted** **6** to act as pilot of **7** to guide or lead (a project or people): *the legislation was piloted through its committee stage* [French *pilote*]

pilot light *n* a small flame that lights the main burner of a gas appliance

pilot officer *n* the most junior commissioned rank in certain air forces

pimento *n, pl* **-tos** same as **allspice** or **pimiento** [Spanish *pimiento* pepper plant]

pimiento (pim-yen-toe) *n, pl* **-tos** a Spanish pepper with a red fruit used as a vegetable [variant of PIMENTO]

pimp *n* **1** a man who obtains customers for a prostitute, in return for a share of his or her earnings ▷ *vb* **2** to act as a pimp **3** *informal* (often foll. by *up* or *out*) to make (someone or something, esp. a car) more extravagantly decorated, as with flashy accessories, etc. [origin unknown]

pimpernel *n* a plant, such as the scarlet pimpernel, typically having small star-shaped flowers [Old French *pimpernelle*]

pimple *n* a small swollen infected spot on the skin [Middle English] **pimpled** *adj* **pimply** *adj*

pin *n* **1** a short stiff straight piece of wire with a pointed end and a rounded head: used mainly for fastening **2** short for **cotter pin, hairpin, rolling pin** or **safety pin** **3** a wooden or metal peg **4** a pin-shaped brooch **5** (in various bowling games) a club-shaped wooden object set up in groups as a target **6** a clip that prevents a hand grenade from exploding until it is removed or released **7** *golf* the flagpole marking the hole on a green **8** *informal* a leg ▷ *vb* **pinning, pinned** **9** to fasten with a pin or pins **10** to seize and hold fast: *they pinned his arms behind his back* **11** **pin something on someone** *informal* to place the blame for something on someone: *corruption charges are the easiest to pin on former dictators* ▷ See also **pin down** [Old English *pinn*]

P

PIN Personal Identification Number: a secret number used to gain access an automated system, for example to authorize a financial transaction

pinafore *n* **1** *chiefly Brit* an apron with a bib **2** a dress with a sleeveless bodice or bib top, worn over a jumper or blouse [*pin* + *afore* in front]

pinball *n* an electrically operated table game in which the player shoots a small ball through several hazards

pince-nez (panss-nay) *n, pl* **pince-nez** glasses that are held in place only by means of a clip over the bridge of the nose [French, literally: pinch-nose]

pincers *pl n* **1** a gripping tool consisting of two hinged arms and curved jaws **2** the jointed grasping arms of crabs and lobsters [Old French *pincier* to pinch]

pinch *vb* **1** to squeeze (something, esp. flesh) between a finger and thumb **2** to squeeze by being too tight: *shoes that pinch* **3** to cause stinging pain to: *the cold pinched his face* **4** to make thin or drawn-looking, such as from grief or cold **5** *informal* to steal **6** *informal* to arrest **7** (usually foll. by *out* or *back*) to remove the tips of (a plant shoot) to correct or encourage growth ▷ *n* **8** a squeeze or sustained nip **9** the quantity that can be taken up between a thumb and finger: *a pinch of ground ginger* **10** extreme stress or need: *most companies are feeling the pinch of recession* **11 at a pinch** if absolutely necessary **12 feel the pinch** to be forced to economize [probably from Old French]

pinchbeck *n* **1** an alloy of copper and zinc, used as imitation gold ▷ *adj* **2** sham or cheap [after C. *Pinchbeck*, watchmaker who invented the alloy]

pincushion *n* a small cushion in which pins are stuck ready for use

P

pin down *vb* **1** to force (someone) to make a decision or carry out a promise **2** to define clearly: *the courts have found it difficult to pin down what exactly obscenity is*

pine¹ *n* **1** an evergreen tree with long needle-shaped leaves and brown cones **2** the light-coloured wood of this tree [Latin *pinus*]

pine² *vb* **pining, pined 1** (often foll. by *for*) to feel great longing (for) **2** (often foll. by *away*) to become ill or thin through grief or longing [Old English *pīnian* to torture]

pineal gland *or* **pineal body** (pin-ee-al) *n* a small cone-shaped gland at the base of the brain [Latin *pinea* pine cone]

pineapple *n* a large tropical fruit with juicy flesh and a thick hard skin [Middle English *pinappel* pine cone]

pine cone *n* the woody seed case of a pine tree

pine marten *n* a mammal of N European and Asian coniferous woods, with dark brown fur and a creamy-yellow patch on the throat

ping *n* **1** a short high-pitched sound, such as of a bullet striking metal ▷ *vb* **2** to make such a noise [imitative]

pinger *n* a device that makes a pinging sound, esp. a timer

ping-pong *n* same as **table tennis**

pinhead *n* **1** the head of a pin **2** *informal* a stupid person **pinheaded** *adj*

pinhole *n* a small hole made with or as if with a pin

pinion¹ *n* **1** *chiefly poetic* a bird's wing **2** the outer part of a bird's wing including the flight feathers ▷ *vb* **3** to immobilize (someone) by holding or tying his or her arms **4** to confine [Latin *pinna* wing]

pinion² *n* a cogwheel that engages with a larger wheel or rack [French *pignon*]

pink¹ *n* **1** a colour between red and white **2** anything pink, such as pink paint or pink clothing: *packaged in pink* **3** a garden plant with pink, red, or white fragrant flowers **4 in the pink** in good health ▷ *adj* **5** of a colour between red and white **6** *informal* having mild left-wing sympathies **7** *informal* relating to homosexuals or homosexuality: *the pink vote* ▷ *vb* **8** same as **knock** (sense 7) [origin unknown] **pinkish** *or* **pinky** *adj*

pink² *vb* to cut with pinking shears [perhaps from Low German]

pinkie *or* **pinky** *n, pl* **-ies** *Scot, US, Canad & NZ* the little finger [Dutch *pinkje*]

pinking shears *pl n* scissors with a serrated edge that give a wavy edge to material cut and so prevent fraying

pin money *n* a small amount of extra money earned to buy small luxuries

pinna *n, pl* **-nae** *or* **-nas** *anatomy* the external part of the ear

pinnace *n* a ship's boat [French *pinace*]

pinnacle *n* **1** the highest point of fame or success **2** a towering peak of a mountain **3** a slender spire [Latin *pinna* wing]

pinnate *adj botany* (of compound leaves) having leaflets growing opposite each other in pairs [Latin *pinna* feather]

pinny *n, pl* **-nies** an informal or child's name for **pinafore** (sense 1)

pinotage (pin-oh-tazh) *n* a red wine blended from the Pinot Noir and Hermitage grapes that is unique to South Africa

pinpoint *vb* **1** to locate or identify exactly: *we've pinpointed the fault* ▷ *adj* **2** exact: *pinpoint accuracy*

pinprick *n* a small irritation or annoyance

pins and needles *n informal* a tingling sensation in a part of the body

pinstripe *n* (in textiles) a very narrow stripe in fabric or the fabric itself

pint *n* **1** *Brit* a unit of liquid measure equal to one eighth of an imperial gallon (0.568 litre) **2** *US* a unit of liquid measure equal to one eighth of a US gallon (0.473 litre) **3** *Brit informal* a pint of beer [Old French *pinte*]

pintail *n, pl* **-tails** *or* **-tail** a greyish-brown duck with a pointed tail

pintle *n* a pin or bolt forming the pivot of a hinge [Old English *pintel* penis]

pinto *US & Canad* ▷ *adj* **1** marked with patches of white; piebald ▷ *n, pl* **-tos 2** a pinto horse [American Spanish]

pint-size *or* **pint-sized** *adj informal* very small

pin tuck *n* a narrow, ornamental fold used on shirt fronts and dress bodices

pin-up *n* **1** *informal* a picture of a sexually attractive person, often partially or totally undressed **2** *slang* a person who has appeared in such a picture: *your favourite pin-up* **3** a photograph of a famous personality

pinwheel *n* same as **Catherine wheel**

Pinyin *n* a system of spelling used to represent Chinese in Roman letters

pion *or* **pi meson** *n physics* any of three subatomic particles which are classified as mesons

pioneer *n* **1** an explorer or settler of a new land or region **2** an originator or developer of something new ▷ *vb* **3** to be a pioneer (in or of) **4** to initiate or develop: *the new technique was pioneered in France* [Old French *paonier* infantryman]

pious *adj* **1** religious or devout **2** insincerely reverent; sanctimonious [Latin *pius*] **piousness** *n*

pip¹ *n* the seed of a fleshy fruit, such as an apple or pear [short for *pippin*]

pip² *n* **1** a short high-pitched sound used as a time signal on radio **2** any of the spots on a playing card, dice, or domino **3** *informal* the emblem worn on the shoulder by junior officers in the British Army, indicating their rank [imitative]

pip³ *n* **1** a contagious disease of poultry **2** *facetious slang* a minor human ailment **3** **get** *or* **have the pip** NZ *slang* to sulk **4** **give someone the pip** *Brit, NZ & S African slang* to annoy someone: *it really gives me the pip* [Middle Dutch *pippe*]

pip⁴ *vb* **pipping, pipped** > **pip someone at the post** *Brit & NZ slang* to defeat someone whose success seems certain [probably from PIP²]

pipe *n* **1** a long tube for conveying water, oil, or gas **2** **A** a tube with a small bowl at the end for smoking tobacco **B** the amount of tobacco that fills the bowl of a pipe **3** *zool & botany* any of various hollow organs, such as the respiratory passage of certain animals **4** **A** a tubular instrument in which air vibrates and produces a musical sound **B** any of the tubular devices on an organ **5** a boatswain's whistle **6** **put that in your pipe and smoke it** *informal* accept that fact if you can **7** **the pipes** See **bagpipes** ▷ *vb* **piping, piped** **8** to play (music) on a pipe or on bagpipes **9** to summon or lead by a pipe: *to pipe in the haggis* **10** **A** to signal orders to (the crew) by a boatswain's pipe **B** to signal the arrival or departure of: *he piped his entire ship's company on deck* **11** to utter in a shrill tone **12** to convey (water, oil, or gas) by pipe **13** to force (cream or icing) through a shaped nozzle to decorate food ▷ See also **pipe down, pipe up** [Old English *pīpe*]

pipeclay *n* a fine white pure clay, used in tobacco pipes and pottery and to whiten leather and similar materials

pipe cleaner *n* a short length of wire covered with tiny tufts of yarn: used to clean the stem of a tobacco pipe

piped music *n* light music played as background music in public places

pipe down *vb informal* to stop talking or making noise

pipe dream *n* a fanciful or impossible plan or hope [alluding to dreams produced by smoking an opium pipe]

pipeline *n* **1** a long pipe for transporting oil, water, or gas **2** a means of communication **3** **in the pipeline** in preparation

pipe organ *n* same as **organ** (sense 2a)

piper *n* a person who plays a pipe or bagpipes

pipette *n* a slender glass tube for transferring or measuring out liquids [French: little pipe]

pipe up *vb* to speak up unexpectedly

pipi *n, pl* **pipi** *or* **pipis** *Austral & NZ* an edible mollusc of Australia and New Zealand [Māori]

piping *n* **1** a system of pipes **2** a string of icing or cream used to decorate cakes and desserts **3** a thin strip of covered cord or material, used to edge hems or cushions **4** the sound of a pipe or bagpipes **5** a shrill voice or whistling sound: *a dove's cool piping* ▷ *adj* **6** making a shrill sound ▷ *adv* **7** **piping hot** extremely hot

pipistrelle *n* a type of small brownish bat found throughout the world [Italian *pipistrello*]

pipit *n* a small songbird with a brownish speckled plumage and a long tail [probably imitative]

pippin *n* a type of eating apple [Old French *pepin*]

pipsqueak *n informal* an insignificant or contemptible person

piquant (**pee**-kant) *adj* **1** having a spicy taste **2** stimulating to the mind: *love was a forbidden piquant secret* [French, literally: prickling] **piquancy** *n*

pique (**peek**) *n* **1** a feeling of resentment or irritation, such as from hurt pride ▷ *vb* **piquing, piqued** **2** to hurt (someone's) pride **3** to excite (curiosity or interest) [French *piquer* to prick]

piqué (**pee**-kay) *n* a stiff ribbed fabric of cotton, silk, or spun rayon [French: pricked]

piquet (pik-**ket**) *n* a card game for two people played with a reduced pack [French]

piracy *n, pl* **-cies** **1** robbery on the seas **2** a crime, such as hijacking, committed aboard a ship or aircraft **3** the unauthorized use of patented or copyrighted material

piranha *n* a small fierce freshwater fish of tropical America, with strong jaws and sharp teeth [indigenous S American word: fish with teeth]

pirate *n* **1** a person who commits piracy **2** a vessel used by pirates **3** a person who illegally sells or publishes someone else's literary or artistic work **4** a person or group of people who broadcast illegally ▷ *vb* **-rating, -rated** **5** to sell or reproduce (artistic work, ideas, etc.) illegally [Greek *peira* an attack] **piratical** *adj*

piri-piri *n* a hot sauce, of Portuguese colonial origin, made from red chilli peppers [from a Bantu language: pepper]

pirouette *n* **1** a body spin performed on the toes or the ball of the foot ▷ *vb* **-etting, -etted** **2** to perform a pirouette [French]

piscatorial *adj formal* of or relating to fish, fishing, or fishermen [Latin *piscatorius*]

Pisces *n astrol* the twelfth sign of the zodiac; the Fishes [Latin]

pisciculture (**piss**-ee-cult-cher) *n formal* the rearing and breeding of fish under controlled conditions [Latin *piscis* fish]

piscine (**piss**-sign) *adj* of or resembling a fish [Latin *piscis* fish]

piss *vulgar* ▷ *vb* **1** to urinate **2** to discharge as or in one's urine: *to piss blood* ▷ *n* **3** an act of urinating **4** urine **5** **take the piss** to make fun of or mock someone ▷ See also **piss down, piss off** [probably imitative]

P

pissant *US derogatory slang* ▷ *n* **1** an insignificant or contemptible person ▷ *adj* **2** insignificant or contemptible [from PISS + ANT]

piss down *vb vulgar slang* to rain heavily

pissed *adj vulgar slang* **1** *Brit, Austral, S African & NZ* drunk **2** *US & Canad* angry

piss off *vb vulgar slang* **1** to annoy or disappoint **2** to go away: often used to dismiss a person

pistachio *n, pl* **-chios** a Mediterranean nut with a hard shell and an edible green kernel [Persian *pistah*]

piste (**peest**) *n* a slope or course for skiing [French]

pistil *n* the seed-bearing part of a flower [Latin *pistillum* pestle]

pistillate *adj botany* (of plants) having pistils

pistol *n* a short-barrelled handgun [Czech *pišťala*]

pistol-whip *vb* **-whipping, -whipped** *US* to beat or strike with a pistol barrel

piston *n* a cylindrical part that slides to and fro in a hollow cylinder: in an engine it is attached by a rod to other parts, thus its movement causes the other parts to move [Old Italian *pistone*]

pit[1] *n* **1** a large deep opening in the ground **2** a coal mine **3** *anatomy* **A** a small natural depression on the surface of a body or organ **B** the floor of any natural bodily cavity: *the pit of the stomach* **4** *pathol* a pockmark **5** a concealed danger or difficulty **6** an area at the side of a motor-racing track for servicing or refuelling vehicles **7** the area occupied by the orchestra in a theatre **8** *Brit history* an enclosure for fighting animals or birds **9** the back of the ground floor of a theatre **10** same as **pitfall** (sense 2) **11 the pit** hell ▷ *vb* **pitting, pitted 12** (often foll. by *against*) to match in opposition, esp. as antagonists: *sister pitted against sister* **13** to mark with small dents or scars **14** to place or bury in a pit **15 pit one's wits against** to compete against in a test or contest ▷ See also **pits** [Old English *pytt*]

pit[2] *chiefly US & Canad* ▷ *n* **1** the stone of various fruits ▷ *vb* **pitting, pitted 2** to remove the stone from (a fruit) [Dutch: kernel]

pitapat *adv* **1** with quick light taps ▷ *n* **2** such taps [imitative]

pit bull terrier *n* a strong muscular terrier with a short coat

pitch[1] *vb* **1** to hurl or throw **2** to set up (a tent or camp) **3** to slope or fall forwards or downwards: *she pitched forwards like a diver* **4** (of a ship or plane) to dip and raise its back and front alternately **5** to set the level or tone of: *his ambitions were pitched too high* **6** to aim to sell (a product) to a specified market or on a specified basis **7** *music* to sing or play (a note or interval) accurately ▷ *n* **8** *chiefly Brit* (in many sports) the field of play **9** a level of emotion: *children can wind their parents up to a pitch of anger and guilt* **10** the degree or angle of slope **11** the distance between corresponding points or adjacent threads on a screw thread **12** the pitching motion of a ship or plane **13** *music* the highness or lowness of a note in relation to other notes: *low pitch* **14** the act or manner of pitching a ball **15** *chiefly Brit* the place where a street or market trader regularly sells **16** *slang* a persuasive sales talk, esp. one routinely repeated ▷ See also **pitch in, pitch into** [Middle English *picchen*]

pitch[2] *n* **1** a thick sticky substance formed from coal tar and used for paving or waterproofing **2** any similar substance, such as asphalt, occurring as a natural deposit ▷ *vb* **3** to apply pitch to [Old English *pic*]

pitch-black *adj* extremely dark; unlit: *it was a wild night, pitch-black, with howling gales*

pitchblende *n* a blackish mineral which is the principal source of uranium and radium [German *Pechblende*]

pitch-dark *adj* extremely or completely dark

pitched battle *n* a fierce fight

pitcher[1] *n* a large jug, usually rounded with a narrow neck [Old French *pichier*]

pitcher[2] *n baseball* the player on the fielding team who throws the ball to the batter

pitcher plant *n* a plant with pitcher-like leaves that attract and trap insects, which are then digested

pitchfork *n* **1** a long-handled fork with two or three long curved prongs for tossing hay ▷ *vb* **2** to use a pitchfork on (something)

pitch in *vb* to cooperate or contribute

pitch into *vb informal* to attack (someone) physically or verbally

pitch pine *n* a pine tree of North America: a source of turpentine and pitch

pitch pipe *n* a small pipe that sounds a note to establish the correct starting note for unaccompanied singing

piteous *adj* arousing or deserving pity: *the piteous mewing of an injured kitten* **piteousness** *n*

pitfall *n* **1** an unsuspected difficulty or danger **2** a trap in the form of a concealed pit, designed to catch people or wild animals [Old English *pytt* pit + *fealle* trap]

pith *n* **1** the soft white lining inside the rind of fruits such as the orange **2** the essential part: *policy, though, isn't the pith of what happened yesterday* **3** the soft spongy tissue in the centre of the stem of certain plants [Old English *pitha*]

pithead *n* the top of a mine shaft and the buildings and hoisting gear around it

pith helmet *n* a lightweight hat made of the pith of the sola, an E Indian swamp plant, that is worn for protection from the sun

pithy *adj* **pithier, pithiest 1** terse and full of meaning **2** of, resembling, or full of pith **pithiness** *n*

pitiable *adj* arousing or deserving pity or contempt **pitiableness** *n*

pitiful *adj* arousing or deserving great pity or contempt **pitifully** *adv* **pitifulness** *n*

pitiless *adj* feeling no pity or mercy **pitilessly** *adv*

piton (**peet-on**) *n mountaineering* a metal spike that may be driven into a crack and used to secure a rope [French]

pits *pl n* **the pits** *slang* the worst possible person, place, or thing [perhaps from *armpits*]

pit stop *n* **1** *motor racing* a brief stop made at a pit by a racing car for repairs, refuelling, etc. **2** *informal* any stop made during a car journey for refreshment, rest, or refuelling

P

pitta bread *or* **pitta** *n* a flat rounded slightly leavened bread, originally from the Middle East [Modern Greek *pitta* a cake]
pittance *n* a very small amount of money [Old French *pietance* ration]
pitter-patter *n* **1** the sound of light rapid taps or pats, such as of raindrops ▷ *vb* **2** to make such a sound
pituitary *or* **pituitary gland** *n* the gland at the base of the brain which secretes hormones that affect skeletal growth, development of the sex glands, and other functions of the body [Late Latin *pituitarius* slimy]
pity *n, pl* **pities 1** sorrow felt for the sufferings of others **2** a cause of regret: *it's a great pity he did not live longer* **3 have** *or* **take pity on** to have sympathy or show mercy for ▷ *vb* **pities, pitying, pitied 4** to feel pity for [Latin *pietas* duty] **pitying** *adj*
pivot *n* **1** a central shaft around which something turns **2** the central person or thing necessary for progress or success ▷ *vb* **-oting, -oted 3** to turn on or provide with a pivot [Old French]
pivotal *adj* **1** of crucial importance **2** of or acting as a pivot
pix *n informal* a plural of **pic**
pixel *n* the smallest constituent unit of an image, as on a computer screen [from *pix* pictures + *el(ement)*]
pixelate *or* **pixellate** *vb* **-lating, -lated** to blur (a video image) by overlaying it with a grid of squares, often to disguise the identity of a person **pixelation** *or* **pixellation** *n*
pixie *or* **pixy** *n, pl* **pixies** (in folklore) a fairy or elf
pizza *n* a dish of Italian origin consisting of a baked disc of dough covered with a wide variety of savoury toppings [Italian]
pizzazz *or* **pizazz** *n informal* an attractive combination of energy and style [origin obscure]
pizzicato (pit-see-**kah**-toe) *adj, adv music* (in music for the violin family) to be plucked with the finger [Italian: pinched]
Pl. (in street names) Place
plaas *n S African* a farm [Afrikaans]
placard *n* **1** a notice that is paraded in public ▷ *vb* **2** to attach placards to [Old French *plaquart*]
placate *vb* **-cating, -cated** to calm (someone) to stop him or her feeling angry or upset [Latin *placare*] **placatory** *adj*
place *n* **1** a particular part of a space or of a surface **2** a geographical point, such as a town or city **3** a position or rank in a sequence or order **4** an open square lined with houses in a city or town **5** space or room **6** a house or living quarters: *he's buying his own place* **7** any building or area set aside for a specific purpose **8** the point reached in reading or speaking: *her finger was pressed to the page as if marking her place* **9** right or duty: *it's not my place to do their job for them* **10** appointment, position, or job: *she won a place at university* **11** position, condition, or state: *you know what your place in the world is* **12** a space or seat, as at a dining table **13** *maths* the relative position of a digit in a number **14 all over the place** in disorder or disarray **15 go places** *informal* to become successful **16 in** *or* **out of place** in or out of the proper or customary position **17 in place of A** instead of: *leeks can be used in place of the broccoli* **B** in exchange for: *he gave her it in place of her ring* **18 know one's place** to be aware of one's inferior position **19 put someone in his** *or* **her place** to humble someone who is arrogant, conceited, etc. **20 take place** to happen or occur **21 take the place of** to be a substitute for ▷ *vb* **placing, placed 22** to put in a particular or appropriate place **23** to find or indicate the place of: *I bet you the media couldn't have placed Neath on the map before the by-election* **24** to identify or classify by linking with an appropriate context: *I felt I should know him, but could not quite place him* **25** to make (an order or bet) **26** to find a home or job for (someone) **27** (often foll. by *with*) to put under the care (of) **28** (of a racehorse, greyhound, athlete, etc.) to arrive in first, second, third, or sometimes fourth place [Latin *platea* courtyard]
placebo (plas-**see**-bo) *n, pl* **-bos** *or* **-boes** *med* an inactive substance given to a patient usually to compare its effects with those of a real drug but sometimes for the psychological benefit gained by the patient through believing that he or she is receiving treatment [Latin: I shall please]
place kick *n rugby & American football etc.* a kick in which the ball is placed in position before it is kicked
placement *n* **1** arrangement or position **2** a temporary job which someone is given as part of a training course: *many pupils have been on work placements with local businesses* **3** the act or an instance of finding someone a job or a home: *the main task of the adoption agency is to find the best family placement for each child*
placenta (plass-**ent**-a) *n, pl* **-tas** *or* **-tae** the organ formed in the womb of most mammals during pregnancy, providing oxygen and nutrients for the fetus [Latin, from Greek *plakoeis* flat cake] **placental** *adj*
place setting *n* the cutlery, crockery, and glassware laid for one person at a dining table
placid *adj* having a calm appearance or nature: *placid waters; a placid temperament* [Latin *placidus* peaceful] **placidity** *or* **placidness** *n* **placidly** *adv*
placket *n dressmaking* an opening at the waist of a dress or skirt for buttons or zips or for access to a pocket [perhaps from Medieval Dutch *plackaet* breastplate]
plagiarize *or* **-rise** (**play**-jer-ize) *vb* **-rizing, -rized** *or* **-rising, -rised** to steal ideas or passages from (another's work) and present them as one's own [Latin *plagium* kidnapping] **plagiarism** *n* **plagiarizer** *or* **-riser** *n*
plague *n* **1** any widespread and usually highly contagious disease with a high fatality rate **2** an infectious disease of rodents transmitted to humans by the bite of the rat flea; bubonic plague **3** something that afflicts or harasses: *a plague of locusts* **4** *informal* a nuisance ▷ *vb* **plaguing, plagued 5** to afflict or harass: *a playing career plagued by injury* **6** *informal* to annoy or pester [Latin *plaga* a blow]
plaice *n, pl* **plaice** *or* **plaices** an edible European flatfish with a brown body marked with red or orange spots [Greek *platus* flat]

P

plaid *n* **1** a long piece of tartan cloth worn over the shoulder as part of Highland costume **2** a crisscross weave or cloth [Scottish Gaelic *plaide*]

Plaid Cymru (plide **kumm**-ree) *n* the Welsh nationalist party [Welsh: Party of Wales]

plain *adj* **1** flat or smooth **2** easily understood: *he made it plain what he wanted from me* **3** honest or blunt: *the plain fact is that my mother has no time for me* **4** without adornment: *a plain brown envelope* **5** not good-looking **6** (of fabric) without pattern or of simple weave **7** lowly, esp. in social rank or education: *the plain people of the town* **8** *knitting* of or done in plain stitch ▷ *n* **9** a level stretch of country **10** a simple stitch in knitting made by passing the wool round the front of the needle ▷ *adv* **11** clearly or simply: *that's just plain stupid!* [Latin *planus* level, clear] **plainly** *adv* **plainness** *n*

plainchant *n* same as **plainsong**

plain chocolate *n Brit* chocolate with a slightly bitter flavour and dark colour

plain clothes *pl n* ordinary clothes, as opposed to uniform, worn by a detective on duty

plain flour *n* flour to which no raising agent has been added

plain sailing *n* **1** *informal* smooth or easy progress **2** *naut* sailing in a body of water that is unobstructed; clear sailing

plainsong *n* the style of unaccompanied choral music used in the medieval Church, esp. in Gregorian chant [translation of Medieval Latin *cantus planus*]

plain speaking *n* saying exactly what one thinks **plain-spoken** *adj*

plaint *n* **1** *archaic* a complaint or lamentation **2** *law* a statement in writing of grounds of complaint made to a court of law [Old French *plainte*]

P

plaintiff *n* a person who sues in a court of law [Old French *plaintif* complaining]

plaintive *adj* sad and mournful [Old French *plaintif* grieving] **plaintively** *adv*

plait (platt) *n* **1** a length of hair that has been plaited ▷ *vb* **2** to intertwine (strands or strips) in a pattern [Latin *plicare* to fold]

plan *n* **1** a method thought out for doing or achieving something **2** a detailed drawing to scale of a horizontal section through a building **3** an outline or sketch ▷ *vb* **planning, planned** **4** to form a plan (for) **5** to make a plan of (a building) **6** to intend [Latin *planus* flat]

planchette *n* a device on which messages are written under supposed spirit guidance [French: little board]

plane[1] *n* **1** an aeroplane **2** *maths* a flat surface in which a straight line joining any two of its points lies entirely on that surface **3** a level surface: *an inclined plane* **4** a level of existence or attainment: *her ambition was set on a higher plane than pulling pints in a pub* ▷ *adj* **5** level or flat **6** *maths* lying entirely in one plane ▷ *vb* **planing, planed** **7** to glide or skim: *they planed over the ice* [Latin *planum* level surface]

plane[2] *n* **1** a tool with a steel blade for smoothing timber ▷ *vb* **planing, planed** **2** to smooth (timber) using a plane **3** (often foll. by *away* or *off*) to remove using a plane [Latin *planare* to level]

planet *n* any of the eight celestial bodies, Mercury, Venus, Earth, Mars, Jupiter, Saturn, Uranus, or Neptune, that revolve around the sun in oval-shaped orbits [Greek *planaein* to wander] **planetary** *adj*

planetarium *n, pl* **-riums** *or* **-ria** **1** an instrument for projecting images of the sun, moon, stars, and planets onto a domed ceiling **2** a building in which such an instrument is housed

planetoid (**plan**-it-oid) *n* See **asteroid**

plane tree *or* **plane** *n* a tree with rounded heads of fruit and leaves with pointed lobes [Greek *platus* wide (because of its broad leaves)]

plangent (**plan**-jent) *adj* (of sounds) mournful and resounding

plank *n* **1** a long flat piece of sawn timber **2** one of the policies in a political party's programme **3** **walk the plank** to be forced by sailors to walk to one's death off the end of a plank jutting out from the side of a ship [Late Latin *planca* board]

planking *n* a number of planks

plankton *n* the small drifting plants and animals on the surface layer of a sea or lake [Greek *planktos* wandering]

planner *n* **1** a person who makes plans, esp. for the development of a town, building, etc. **2** a chart for recording future appointments, etc.

planning permission *n* formal permission granted by a local authority for the construction, alteration, or change of use of a building

plant *n* **1** a living organism that grows in the ground and lacks the power of movement **2** the land, building, and equipment used in an industry or business **3** a factory or workshop **4** mobile mechanical equipment for construction or road-making **5** *informal* a thing positioned secretly for discovery by someone else, often in order to incriminate an innocent person ▷ *vb* **6** to set (seeds or crops) into the ground to grow: *it's the wrong time of year for planting roses* **7** to place firmly in position: *I planted my chair beside hers* **8** to introduce into someone's mind: *once Wendy had planted the idea in the minds of the owners, they quite fancied selling* **9** *slang* to deliver (a blow or kiss) **10** *informal* to position or hide (someone) in order to deceive or observe **11** *informal* to hide or secrete (something), usually for some illegal purpose or in order to incriminate someone [Old English]

plantain[1] *n* a plant with a rosette of broad leaves and a slender spike of small greenish flowers [Latin *planta* sole of the foot]

plantain[2] *n* **1** a large tropical fruit like a green-skinned banana **2** the tree on which this fruit grows [Spanish *platano*]

plantation *n* **1** an estate, esp. in tropical countries, where cash crops such as rubber or coffee are grown on a large scale **2** a group of cultivated trees or plants **3** (formerly) a colony of settlers

planter *n* **1** the owner or manager of a plantation **2** a decorative pot for house plants

plantigrade *adj* walking on the entire sole of the foot, as humans and bears do [Latin *planta* sole of the foot + *gradus* a step]

plaque *n* **1** a commemorative inscribed stone or metal plate **2** Also called: **dental plaque** a filmy deposit on teeth consisting of mucus, bacteria, and food, that causes decay [French]

plasma *n* **1** the clear yellowish fluid portion of blood which contains the corpuscles and cells **2** a sterilized preparation of such fluid, taken from the blood, for use in transfusions **3** a former name for **protoplasm** **4** *physics* a hot ionized gas containing positive ions and free electrons [Greek: something moulded]

plasma screen *n* a type of flat television or computer screen that produces high-quality images

plaster *n* **1** a mixture of lime, sand, and water that is applied to a wall or ceiling as a soft paste and dries as a hard coating **2** *Brit, Austral & NZ* an adhesive strip of material for dressing a cut or wound **3** short for **mustard plaster** or **plaster of Paris** ▹ *vb* **4** to coat (a wall or ceiling) with plaster **5** to apply like plaster: *he plastered his face with shaving cream* **6** to cause to lie flat or to adhere: *his hair was plastered to his forehead* [Greek *emplastron* healing dressing] **plasterer** *n*

plasterboard *n* a thin rigid board, made of plaster compressed between two layers of fibreboard, used to form or cover interior walls

plastered *adj slang* drunk

plaster of Paris *n* a white powder that sets to a hard solid when mixed with water, used for making sculptures and casts for setting broken limbs

plastic *n* **1** any of a large number of synthetic materials that can be moulded when soft and then set **2** *informal* Also called: **plastic money** credit cards, etc. as opposed to cash ▹ *adj* **3** made of plastic **4** easily influenced **5** capable of being moulded or formed **6** of moulding or modelling: *the plastic arts* **7** *slang* superficially attractive yet artificial or false: *glamorous models with plastic smiles* [Greek *plastikos* mouldable] **plasticity** *n*

plastic bullet *n* a solid PVC cylinder fired by the police in riot control

plastic explosive *n* an adhesive jelly-like explosive substance

Plasticine *n trademark* a soft coloured material used, esp. by children, for modelling

plasticize *or* **-cise** *vb* **-cizing, -cized** *or* **-cising, -cised** to make or become plastic

plasticizer *or* **-ciser** *n* a substance added to a plastic material to soften it and improve flexibility

plastic surgery *n* the branch of surgery concerned with the repair or reconstruction of missing, injured, or malformed tissues or parts **plastic surgeon** *n*

plate *n* **1** a shallow dish made of porcelain, earthenware, glass, etc., on which food is served **2** Also called: **plateful** the contents of a plate **3** a shallow dish for receiving a collection in church **4** flat metal of even thickness obtained by rolling **5** a thin coating of metal usually on another metal **6** dishes or cutlery made of gold or silver **7** a sheet of metal, plastic, or rubber having a printing surface produced by a process such as stereotyping **8** a print taken from such a sheet or from a woodcut **9** a thin flat sheet of a substance, such as glass **10** a small piece of metal or plastic with an inscription, fixed to another surface: *a brass name plate* **11** *photog* a sheet of glass coated with photographic emulsion on which an image can be formed by exposure to light **12** *informal* same as **denture** **13** *anatomy* any flat platelike structure **14** a cup awarded to the winner of a sporting contest, esp. a horse race **15** any of the rigid layers of the earth's crust **16 have a lot on one's plate** to have many pressing things to deal with **17 on a plate** acquired without trouble: *he got the job handed to him on a plate* ▹ *vb* **plating, plated** **18** to coat (a metal surface) with a thin layer of another metal **19** to cover with metal plates, usually for protection **20** to form (metal) into plate, usually by rolling [Old French: something flat]

plateau (**plat**-oh) *n, pl* **-teaus** *or* **-teaux** (-ohs) **1** a wide level area of high land **2** a relatively long period of stability: *the body temperature rises to a plateau that it keeps until shortly before bedtime* ▹ *vb* **3** to remain stable for a long period [French]

plated *adj* coated with a layer of metal

plate glass *n* glass produced in thin sheets, used for windows and mirrors

platelayer *n Brit* a workman who lays and maintains railway track

platelet *n* a minute particle occurring in the blood of vertebrates and involved in the clotting of the blood

platen *n* **1** the roller on a typewriter, against which the keys strike **2** a flat plate in a printing press that presses the paper against the type [Old French *platine*]

platform *n* **1** a raised floor **2** a raised area at a railway station where passengers get on or off the trains **3** See **drilling platform** **4** the declared aims of a political party **5** the thick raised sole of some shoes **6** a type of computer hardware or operating system [French *plat* flat + *forme* layout]

platform game *n* a type of computer game that is played by moving a figure on the screen through a series of obstacles

platform ticket *n* (formerly) a ticket for admission to railway platforms but not for travel

plating *n* **1** a coating of metal **2** a layer or covering of metal plates

platinum *n* a silvery-white metallic element, very resistant to heat and chemicals: used in jewellery, laboratory apparatus, electrical contacts, dentistry, electroplating, and as a catalyst. Symbol: **Pt** [Spanish *platina* silvery element]

platinum blonde *n* a girl or woman with silvery-blonde hair

platitude *n* a trite or unoriginal remark: *it's a platitude, but people need people* [French: flatness] **platitudinous** *adj*

platonic *adj* friendly or affectionate but without physical desire: *platonic love*

Platonic *adj* of the philosopher Plato or his teachings

Platonism (**plate**-on-iz-zum) *n* the teachings of Plato (?427–?347 BC), Greek philosopher, and his followers **Platonist** *n*

platoon *n military* a subunit of a company, usually comprising three sections of ten to twelve men [French *peloton* little ball, group of men]

P

platteland *n* **the platteland** (in South Africa) the country districts or rural areas [Afrikaans]
platter *n* a large shallow, usually oval, dish [Anglo-Norman *plater*]
platypus *or* **duck-billed platypus** *n, pl* **-puses** an Australian egg-laying amphibious mammal, with dense fur, webbed feet, and a ducklike bill [Greek *platus* flat + *pous* foot]
plaudit *n (usually pl)* an expression of enthusiastic approval [Latin *plaudite* applaud!]
plausible *adj* **1** apparently reasonable or true: *a plausible excuse* **2** apparently trustworthy or believable: *he is an extraordinarily plausible liar* [Latin *plausibilis* worthy of applause] **plausibility** *n* **plausibly** *adv*
play *vb* **1** to occupy oneself in (a sport or recreation) **2** to compete against (someone) in a sport or game: *I saw Brazil play Argentina recently* **3** to fulfil (a particular role) in a team game: *he usually plays in midfield* **4** (often foll. by *about* or *around*) to behave carelessly: *he's only playing with your affections, you know* **5** to act the part (of) in a dramatic piece: *he has played Hamlet to packed Broadway houses* **6** to perform (a dramatic piece) **7** **A** to perform (music) on a musical instrument **B** to be able to perform on (a musical instrument): *she plays the bassoon* **8** to send out (water) or cause to send out (water): *they played a hose across the wrecked building* **9** to cause (a radio, etc.) to emit sound **10** to move freely or quickly: *the light played across the water* **11** *Stock Exchange* to speculate for gain in (a market) **12** *angling* to tire (a hooked fish) by alternately letting out and reeling in the line **13** to put (a card) into play **14** to gamble **15** **play fair** *or* **false with** to act fairly *or* unfairly with **16** **play for time** to gain time to one's advantage by the use of delaying tactics **17** **play into the hands of** to act unwittingly to the advantage of (an opponent) **18** **play politics** **A** to negotiate politically **B** to exploit an important issue merely for political gain **C** to make something into a political issue ▷ *n* **19** **A** a dramatic piece written for performance by actors **B** the performance of such a piece **20** games or other activity undertaken for pleasure **21** the playing of a game or the time during which a game is in progress: *rain stopped play* **22** conduct: *fair play* **23** gambling **24** activity or operation: *radio allows full play to your imagination* **25** scope for freedom of movement: *there was a lot of play in the rope* **26** free or rapidly shifting motion: *the play of light on the water* **27** fun or jest: *I used to throw cushions at her in play* **28** **in** *or* **out of play** (of a ball in a game) in *or* not in a position for continuing play according to the rules **29** **make a play for** *informal* to make an obvious attempt to gain (something) ▷ See also **play along**, **playback** *etc.* [Old English *plega*, *plegan*] **playable** *adj*
play along *vb* to cooperate (with) temporarily: *I'll play along with them for the moment*
playback *n* **1** the action of listening to or watching something recorded ▷ *vb* **play back** **2** to listen to or watch (something recorded)
playbill *n* a poster or bill advertising a play
playboy *n* a rich man who devotes himself to such pleasures as nightclubs and female company
playcentre *n NZ* a centre for preschool children run by parents
playdate *n* an arrangement for children from different families to meet and play
play down *vb* to minimize the importance of: *she played down the problems of the company*
player *n* **1** a person who takes part in a game or sport **2** a person who plays a musical instrument **3** *informal* a leading participant in a particular field or activity: *one of the key players in Chinese politics* **4** an actor
player piano *n* a mechanical piano; Pianola
playful *adj* **1** good-natured and humorous: *a playful remark* **2** full of high spirits and fun: *a playful child* **playfully** *adv*
playgoer *n* a person who goes often to the theatre
playground *n* **1** an outdoor area for children's play, either with swings and slides, or adjoining a school **2** a place or activity enjoyed by a specified person or group: *they oppose turning the island into a tourist playground*
playgroup *n* a regular meeting of infants for supervised creative play
playhouse *n* a theatre
playing field *n (sometimes pl) Brit & NZ* a field or open space used for sport
playlist *n* a list of songs chosen for playing, such as on a radio station
play-lunch *n Austral & NZ* a child's mid-morning snack at school
playmaker *n sport* a player who creates scoring opportunities for his or her team-mates
playmate *n* a companion in play
play off *vb* **1** to set (two people) against each other for one's own ends: *she delighted in playing one parent off against the other* **2** to take part in a play-off ▷ *n* **play-off** **3** *sport* an extra contest to decide the winner when there is a tie **4** *chiefly US & Canad* a contest or series of games to determine a championship
play on *vb* to exploit (the feelings or weakness of another): *he played on my sympathy*
play on words *n* same as **pun**
playpen *n* a small portable enclosure in which a young child can safely be left to play
playschool *n* a nursery group for preschool children
PlayStation *n trademark* a type of games console
plaything *n* **1** a toy **2** a person regarded or treated as a toy
playtime *n* a time for play or recreation, such as a school break
play up *vb* **1** to highlight: *the temptation is to play up the sensational aspects of the story* **2** *Brit & Austral informal* to behave in an unruly way **3** to give (one) trouble or not be working properly: *my back's playing me up again; the photocopier's started to play up* **4** **play up to** to try to please by flattery
playwright *n* a person who writes plays
plaza *n* **1** an open public square, usually in Spain **2** *chiefly US & Canad* a modern shopping complex [Spanish]
PLC *or* **plc** (in Britain) Public Limited Company
plea *n* **1** an emotional appeal **2** *law* a statement by or on behalf of a defendant **3** an excuse: *his*

P

plea of poverty rings a little hollow [Anglo-Norman *plai*]

plead *vb* **pleading, pleaded, plead** *or esp Scot & US* **pled 1** (sometimes foll. by *with*) to ask with deep feeling **2** to give as an excuse: *whenever she invites him to dinner, he pleads a prior engagement* **3** *law* to declare oneself to be (guilty or not guilty) of the charge made against one **4** *law* to present (a case) in a court of law [Latin *placere* to please]

pleadings *pl n law* the formal written statements presented by the plaintiff and defendant in a lawsuit

pleasant *adj* **1** pleasing or enjoyable: *what a pleasant surprise* **2** having pleasing manners or appearance: *he was a pleasant boy* [Old French *plaisant*] **pleasantly** *adv*

pleasantry *n, pl* **-ries 1** (*often pl*) a polite or jocular remark: *we exchanged pleasantries about the weather* **2** agreeable jocularity [French *plaisanterie*]

please *vb* **pleasing, pleased 1** to give pleasure or satisfaction to (a person) **2** to regard as suitable or satisfying: *he can get almost anyone he pleases to work with him* **3 if you please** if you wish, sometimes used in ironic exclamation **4 pleased with** happy because of **5 please oneself** to do as one likes ▷ *adv* **6** used in making polite requests or pleading: *please sit down* **7 yes please** a polite phrase used to accept an offer or invitation [Latin *placere*] **pleased** *adj*

pleasing *adj* giving pleasure

pleasurable *adj* enjoyable or agreeable **pleasurably** *adv*

pleasure *n* **1** a feeling of happiness and contentment: *the pleasure of hearing good music* **2** something that gives enjoyment: *his garden was his only pleasure* **3** the activity of enjoying oneself: *business before pleasure* **4** *euphemistic* sexual gratification: *he took his pleasure of her* **5** a person's preference [Old French *plaisir*]

pleat *n* **1** a fold formed by doubling back fabric and pressing or stitching into place ▷ *vb* **2** to arrange (material) in pleats [variant of *plait*]

pleb *n Brit informal, often offensive* a common vulgar person

plebeian (pleb-ee-an) *adj* **1** of the lower social classes **2** unrefined: *plebeian tastes* ▷ *n* **3** one of the common people, usually of ancient Rome **4** a coarse or unrefined person [Latin *plebs* the common people of ancient Rome]

plebiscite (pleb-iss-ite) *n* a direct vote by all the electorate on an issue of national importance [Latin *plebiscitum* decree of the people]

plectrum *n, pl* **-trums** *or* **-tra** an implement for plucking the strings of a guitar or similar instrument [Greek *plektron*]

pled *vb US & Scot* a past (esp. in legal usage) of **plead**

pledge *n* **1** a solemn promise **2 A** something valuable given as a guarantee that a promise will be kept or a debt paid **B** the condition of being used as security: *in pledge* **3** a token: *a pledge of good faith* **4** an assurance of support or goodwill, given by drinking a toast: *we drank a pledge to their success* **5 take** *or* **sign the pledge** to vow not to drink alcohol ▷ *vb* **pledging, pledged 6** to promise solemnly **7** to promise to give (money to charity, etc.) **8** to bind by or as if by a pledge: *I was pledged to secrecy* **9** to give (one's word or property) as a guarantee **10** to drink a toast to (a person or cause) [Old French *plege*]

Pleiocene *adj, n* same as **Pliocene**

Pleistocene (ply-stow-seen) *adj geol* of the epoch of geological time from about 1.6 million to 10 000 years ago [Greek *pleistos* most + *kainos* recent]

plenary *adj* **1** (of an assembly) attended by all the members **2** full or complete: *plenary powers* [Latin *plenus* full]

plenipotentiary *adj* **1** (usually of a diplomat) invested with full authority ▷ *n, pl* **-aries 2** a diplomat or representative who has full authority to transact business [Latin *plenus* full + *potentia* power]

plenitude *n literary* **1** abundance **2** fullness or completeness [Latin *plenus* full]

plenteous *adj literary* **1** abundant: *a plenteous supply* **2** producing abundantly: *a plenteous harvest*

plentiful *adj* existing in large amounts or numbers **plentifully** *adv*

plenty *n, pl* **-ties 1** (often foll. by *of*) a great number or amount: *plenty of time* **2** abundance: *an age of plenty* ▷ *adj* **3** very many: *there's plenty more fish in the sea* ▷ *adv* **4** *informal* more than adequately: *that's plenty fast enough for me* [Latin *plenus* full]

pleonasm *n rhetoric* **1** the use of more words than necessary, such as *a tiny little child* **2** an unnecessary word or phrase [Greek *pleonasmos* excess] **pleonastic** *adj*

plethora *n* an excess [Greek *plēthōra* fullness]

pleura (ploor-a) *n, pl* **pleurae** (ploor-ee) *anatomy* the thin transparent membrane enveloping the lungs [Greek: side, rib] **pleural** *adj*

pleurisy *n* inflammation of the pleura, making breathing painful **pleuritic** *adj, n*

plexus *n, pl* **-uses** *or* **-us** a complex network of nerves or blood vessels [Latin *plectere* to braid]

pliable *adj* **1** easily bent: *pliable branches* **2** easily influenced: *his easy and pliable nature* **pliability** *n*

pliant *adj* **1** easily bent; supple: *pliant young willow and hazel twigs* **2** easily influenced: *he was a far more pliant subordinate than his predecessor* [Old French *plier* to fold] **pliancy** *n*

pliers *pl n* a gripping tool consisting of two hinged arms usually with serrated jaws [from PLY[1]]

plight[1] *n* a dangerous or difficult situation: *the plight of the British hostages* [Old French *pleit* fold, and probably influenced by Old English *pliht* peril]

plight[2] *vb* **plight one's troth** *old-fashioned* to make a promise to marry [Old English *pliht* peril]

Plimsoll line *n* a line on the hull of a ship showing the level that the water should reach if the ship is properly loaded [after Samuel Plimsoll, who advocated its adoption]

plimsolls *pl n Brit* light rubber-soled canvas sports shoes [from the resemblance of the sole to a Plimsoll line]

plinth *n* **1** a base on which a statue stands **2** the slab that forms the base of a column or pedestal [Greek *plinthos* brick]

Pliocene *or* **Pleiocene** (ply-oh-seen) *adj geol* of the epoch of geological time about 10 million years ago [Greek *pleiōn* more + *kainos* recent]

P

PLO Palestine Liberation Organization
plod *vb* **plodding, plodded 1** to walk with heavy slow steps **2** to work slowly and steadily ▹ *n* **3** the act of plodding **4** *Brit slang* a police officer [imitative] **plodder** *n*
plonk[1] *vb* **1** to put down heavily and carelessly: *he plonked himself down on the sofa* ▹ *n* **2** the act or sound of plonking [variant of *plunk*]
plonk[2] *n informal* cheap inferior wine [origin unknown]
plonker *n Brit slang* a stupid person [origin unknown]
plop *n* **1** the sound made by an object dropping into water without a splash ▹ *vb* **plopping, plopped 2** to drop with such a sound: *a tear rolled down his cheek and plopped into his soup* **3** to fall or be placed heavily or carelessly: *we plopped down on the bed and went straight to sleep* [imitative]
plosive *phonetics* ▹ *adj* **1** pronounced with a sudden release of breath ▹ *n* **2** a plosive consonant [French *explosif* explosive]
plot[1] *n* **1** a secret plan for an illegal purpose **2** the story of a play, novel, or film ▹ *vb* **plotting, plotted 3** to plan secretly; conspire **4** to mark (a course) on a map **5** to make a plan or map of **6 a** to locate (points) on a graph by means of coordinates **b** to draw (a curve) through these points **7** to construct the plot of (a play, novel, or film) [from PLOT[2], influenced by obsolete *complot* conspiracy] **plotter** *n*
plot[2] *n* a small piece of land: *there was a small vegetable plot in the garden* [Old English]
plough *or US* **plow** *n* **1** an agricultural tool for cutting or turning over the earth **2** a similar tool used for clearing snow ▹ *vb* **3** to turn over (the soil) with a plough **4** to make (furrows or grooves) in (something) with or as if with a plough **5** (sometimes foll. by *through*) to move (through something) in the manner of a plough: *the ship ploughed through the water* **6** (foll. by *through*) to work at slowly or perseveringly **7** to invest (money): *he ploughed the profits back into the business* **8 plough into** (of a vehicle, plane, etc.) to go out of control and crash into (something): *the aircraft ploughed into a motorway embankment* [Old English *plōg* plough land]
Plough *n* **the Plough** the group of the seven brightest stars in the constellation Ursa Major
ploughman *or US* **plowman** *n, pl* **-men** a man who ploughs
ploughman's lunch *n* a snack lunch consisting of bread and cheese with pickle
ploughshare *or esp US* **plowshare** *n* the cutting blade of a plough
plover *n* a shore bird with a round head, straight bill, and long pointed wings [Old French *plovier* rainbird]
plow *n, vb US* same as **plough**
ploy *n* a manoeuvre designed to gain an advantage in a situation: *a cheap political ploy* [from obsolete noun sense of *employ*, meaning an occupation]
pluck *vb* **1** to pull or pick off **2** to pull out the feathers of (a bird for cooking) **3** (foll. by *off* or *away* etc.) to pull (something) forcibly or violently (from something or someone) **4** to sound the strings of (a musical instrument) with the fingers or a plectrum ▹ *n* **5** courage **6** a pull or tug ▹ See also **pluck up** [Old English *pluccian*]
pluck up *vb* to summon up (courage)
plucky *adj* **pluckier, pluckiest** courageous **pluckily** *adv* **pluckiness** *n*
plug *n* **1** an object used to block up holes or waste pipes **2** a device with one or more pins which connects an appliance to an electricity supply **3** *informal* a favourable mention of a product, etc., for example on television, to encourage people to buy it **4** See **spark plug 5** a piece of tobacco for chewing ▹ *vb* **plugging, plugged 6** to block or seal (a hole or gap) with a plug **7** *informal* to make frequent favourable mentions of (a product, etc.), for example on television **8** *slang* to shoot: *he lifted the rifle and plugged the deer* **9** *slang* to punch **10** (foll. by *along* or *away* etc.) *informal* to work steadily ▹ See also **plug in** [Middle Dutch *plugge*]
plug in *vb* to connect (an electrical appliance) to a power source by pushing a plug into a socket
plum *n* **1** an oval dark red or yellow fruit with a stone in the middle, that grows on a small tree **2** a raisin, as used in a cake or pudding **3** *informal* something of a superior or desirable kind ▹ *adj* **4** made from plums: *plum cake* **5** dark reddish-purple **6** very desirable: *plum targets for attack* [Old English *plūme*]
plumage *n* the feathers of a bird [Old French *plume* feather]
plumb *vb* **1** to understand (something obscure): *to plumb a mystery* **2** to test the alignment of or make vertical with a plumb line **3** (foll. by *in* or *into*) to connect (an appliance or fixture) to a water pipe or drainage system: *the shower should be plumbed in professionally* **4 plumb the depths** (usually foll. by *of*) to experience the worst extremes (of something): *to plumb the depths of despair* ▹ *n* **5** a lead weight hanging at the end of a string and used to test the depth of water or to test whether something is vertical **6 out of plumb** not vertical ▹ *adv* **7** vertical or perpendicular **8** *informal, chiefly US* utterly: *plumb stupid* **9** *informal* exactly: *plumb in the centre* [Latin *plumbum* lead]
plumber *n* a person who fits and repairs pipes and fixtures for water, drainage, or gas systems [Old French *plommier* worker in lead]
plumbing *n* **1** the pipes and fixtures used in a water, drainage, or gas system **2** the trade or work of a plumber
plumb line *n* a string with a metal weight at one end, used to test the depth of water or to test whether something is vertical
plume *n* **1** a large ornamental feather **2** a group of feathers worn as a badge or ornament on a hat **3** something like a plume: *a plume of smoke* ▹ *vb* **pluming, plumed 4** to adorn with plumes **5** (of a bird) to preen (its feathers) **6 plume oneself** (foll. by *on* or *upon*) to be proud of oneself or one's achievements, esp. unjustifiably: *she was pluming herself on her figure* [Old French]
plummet *vb* **-meting, -meted 1** to drop down; plunge ▹ *n* **2** the weight on a plumb line or fishing line [Old French *plommet* ball of lead]
plummy *adj* **-mier, -miest 1** of, full of, or like plums: *a red wine full of ripe plummy fruit* **2** *Brit*

informal (of a voice) deep, rich, and usually upper-class in accent: *his plummy condescending voice* **3** *Brit informal* desirable: *they lived plummy lives in the hills of Tuscany*

plump[1] *adj* **1** full or rounded: *until puberty I was really quite plump* ▹ *vb* **2** (often foll. by *up* or *out*) to make (something) fuller or rounded: *she plumped up the cushions on the couch* [Middle Dutch *plomp* blunt] **plumpness** *n*

plump[2] *vb* **1** (often foll. by *down* or *into* etc.) to drop or sit suddenly and heavily: *he plumped down on the seat* **2 plump for** to choose (one) from a selection ▹ *n* **3** a heavy abrupt fall or the sound of this ▹ *adv* **4** suddenly or heavily **5** directly: *the plane landed plump in the middle of the field* [probably imitative]

plum pudding *n* a boiled or steamed pudding made with flour, suet, and dried fruit

plumy *adj* **plumier, plumiest 1** like a feather **2** covered or adorned with feathers

plunder *vb* **1** to seize (valuables or goods) from (a place) by force, usually in wartime; loot ▹ *n* **2** anything plundered; booty **3** the act of plundering; pillage [probably from Dutch *plunderen*]

plunge *vb* **plunging, plunged 1** (usually foll. by *into*) to thrust or throw (something or oneself) forcibly or suddenly: *they plunged into the sea*; *he plunged the knife in to the hilt* **2** to throw or be thrown into a certain condition: *the room was plunged into darkness* **3** (usually foll. by *into*) to involve or become involved deeply (in) **4** to move swiftly or impetuously **5** to descend very suddenly or steeply: *temperatures were plunging* ▹ *n* **6** a leap or dive **7** *informal* a swim **8** a pitching motion **9 take the plunge** *informal* to make a risky decision which cannot be reversed later [Old French *plongier*]

plunger *n* **1** a rubber suction cup used to clear blocked drains **2** a device with a plunging motion; piston

plunk *vb* **1** to pluck the strings of (an instrument) to produce a twanging sound **2** (often foll. by *down*) to drop or be dropped heavily ▹ *n* **3** the act or sound of plunking [imitative]

Plunket baby *n NZ* a baby brought up according to the principles of the Plunket Society

Plunket nurse *n NZ* a nurse working for the Plunket Society

Plunket Society *n NZ* an organization for the care of mothers and babies

pluperfect *grammar* ▹ *adj* **1** denoting a tense of verbs used to describe an action completed before a past time. In English this is a compound tense formed with *had* plus the past participle ▹ *n* **2** the pluperfect tense [Latin *plus quam perfectum* more than perfect]

plural *adj* **1** of or consisting of more than one **2** *grammar* denoting a word indicating more than one ▹ *n* **3** *grammar* **A** the plural number **B** a plural form [Latin *plus* more]

pluralism *n* **1** the existence and toleration in a society of a variety of groups of different ethnic origins, cultures, or religions **2** the holding of more than one office by a person **pluralist** *n, adj* **pluralistic** *adj*

plurality *n, pl* **-ties 1** the state of being plural **2** *maths* a number greater than one **3** a large number **4** a majority

pluralize *or* **-ise** *vb* **-izing, -ized** *or* **-ising, -ised** to make or become plural

plus *prep* **1** increased by the addition of: *four plus two* **2** with the addition of: *a good salary, plus a company car* ▹ *adj* **3** indicating addition: *a plus sign* **4** *maths* same as **positive** (sense 7) **5** on the positive part of a scale **6** indicating the positive side of an electrical circuit **7** involving advantage: *a plus factor* **8** *informal* having a value above the value stated: *it must be worth a thousand pounds plus* **9** slightly above a specified standard: *he received a B plus for his essay* ▹ *n* **10** a plus sign (+), indicating addition **11** a positive quantity **12** *informal* something positive or an advantage **13** a gain, surplus, or advantage [Latin: more]

> **USAGE** *Plus, together with,* and *along with* do not create compound subjects in the way that *and* does: the number of the verb depends on that of the subject to which *plus, together with,* or *along with* is added: *this task, plus all the others, was* (not *were*) *undertaken by the government; the doctor, together with the nurses, was* (not *were*) *waiting for the patient.*

plus fours *pl n* men's baggy knickerbockers gathered in at the knee, now only worn for hunting or golf [because made with four inches of material to hang over at the knee]

plush *n* **1** a velvety fabric with a long soft pile, used for furniture coverings ▹ *adj* **2** Also: **plushy** *informal* luxurious [French *pluche*]

plus-one *n informal* someone who accompanies an invited person to a social function

Pluto *n* **1** *classical myth* the god of the underworld **2** a dwarf planet in the solar system, classified as a planet until 2006

plutocracy *n, pl* **-cies 1** government by the wealthy **2** a state ruled by the wealthy **3** a group that exercises power on account of its wealth [Greek *ploutos* wealth + *-kratia* rule] **plutocratic** *adj*

plutocrat *n* a person who is powerful because of being very rich

plutonic *adj* (of igneous rocks) formed from molten rock that has cooled and solidified below the earth's surface [after the Greek god *Pluto*]

plutonium *n chem* a toxic radioactive metallic element, used in nuclear reactors and weapons. Symbol: **Pu** [after *Pluto*, because Pluto lies beyond Neptune and plutonium was discovered soon after neptunium]

pluvial *adj geog & geol* of or due to the action of rain [Latin *pluvia* rain]

ply[1] *vb* **plies, plying, plied 1** to work at (a job or trade) **2** to use (a tool) **3** (usually foll. by *with*) to provide (with) or subject (to) persistently: *he plied us with drink; he plied me with questions* **4** to work steadily **5** (of a ship) to travel regularly along (a route): *to ply the trade routes* [Middle English *plye*, short for *aplye* to apply]

ply[2] *n, pl* **plies 1** a layer or thickness, such as of fabric or wood **2** one of the strands twisted together to make rope or yarn [Old French *pli* fold]

Plymouth Brethren *pl n* a Puritanical religious sect with no organized ministry

P

plywood *n* a board made of thin layers of wood glued together under pressure, with the grain of one layer at right angles to the grain of the next
Pm *chem* promethium
PM **1** Prime Minister **2** Postmaster **3** Paymaster **4** project manager
p.m. **1** after noon **2** postmortem (examination)
PMG **1** Postmaster General **2** Paymaster General
PMS premenstrual syndrome
PMT premenstrual tension
pneumatic *adj* **1** operated by compressed air: *pneumatic drill* **2** containing compressed air: *a pneumatic tyre* **3** of or concerned with air, gases, or wind [Greek *pneuma* breath, wind]
pneumatics *n* the branch of physics concerned with the mechanical properties of air and other gases
pneumonia *n* inflammation of one or both lungs [Greek *pneumōn* lung]
po *n, pl* **pos** *Brit old-fashioned, informal* a chamber pot [from POT[1]]
Po *chem* polonium
PO **1** Also: **p.o.** *Brit* postal order **2** Post Office **3** petty officer **4** Pilot Officer
poach¹ *vb* **1** to catch (game or fish) illegally on someone else's land **2** **A** to encroach on (someone's rights or duties) **B** to steal (an idea, employee, or player) [Old French *pocher*] **poacher** *n*
poach² *vb* to simmer (food) very gently in liquid [Old French *pochier* to enclose in a bag]
pock *n* **1** a pus-filled blister resulting from smallpox **2** a pockmark [Old English *pocc*]
pocket *n* **1** a small pouch sewn into clothing for carrying small articles **2** any pouchlike container, esp. for catching balls at the edge of a snooker table **3** a small isolated area or group: *a pocket of resistance* **4** a cavity in the earth, such as one containing ore **5** **in one's pocket** under one's control **6** **out of pocket** having made a loss ▷ *vb* **-eting, -eted** **7** to put into one's pocket **8** to take secretly or dishonestly **9** *billiards etc.* to drive (a ball) into a pocket **10** to conceal or suppress: *he pocketed his pride and asked for help* ▷ *adj* **11** small: *a pocket edition* [Anglo-Norman *poket* a little bag]

P

pocketbook *n chiefly US* a small case for money and papers
pocket borough *n* (before the Reform Act of 1832) an English borough constituency controlled by one person or family
pocketful *n, pl* **-fuls** as much as a pocket will hold
pocketknife *n, pl* **-knives** a small knife with one or more blades that fold into the handle; penknife
pocket money *n* **1** a small weekly sum of money given to children by parents **2** money for small personal expenses
pockmarked *adj* **1** (of the skin) marked with pitted scars after the healing of smallpox **2** (of a surface) covered in many small hollows: *the building is pockmarked with bullet holes* **pockmark** *n*
pod *n* **1** **A** a long narrow seedcase containing peas, beans, etc. **B** the seedcase as distinct from the seeds ▷ *vb* **podding, podded** **2** to remove the pod from [origin unknown]
podcast *n* **1** an audio file similar to a radio broadcast, which can be downloaded and listened to on a computer, mobile electronic device, etc. ▷ *vb* **-casts, -casting, -cast** *or* **-casted** **2** to create such files and make them available for downloading **3** to make (music, interviews, etc.) available using this format [blend of *iPod* and *broadcast*] **podcaster** *n* **podcasting** *n*
podgy *adj* **podgier, podgiest** short and fat [from *podge* a short plump person] **podginess** *n*
podiatry (pod-eye-a-tree) *n* another word for **chiropody** **podiatrist** *n*
podium *n, pl* **-diums** *or* **-dia** **1** a small raised platform used by conductors or speakers **2** a plinth that supports a colonnade or wall [Latin: platform]
poem *n* **1** a literary work, often in verse, usually dealing with emotional or descriptive themes in a rhythmic form **2** a literary work that is not in verse but deals with emotional or descriptive themes in a rhythmic form: *a prose poem* **3** anything like a poem in beauty or effect: *his painting is a poem on creation* [Greek *poiēma* something created]
poep (poop) *n S African taboo* **1** an emission of intestinal gas from the anus **2** a mean or despicable person [Afrikaans]
poesy *n archaic* poetry
poet *n* **1** a writer of poetry **2** a person with great imagination and creativity [Greek *poiētēs* maker, poet]
poetaster *n* a writer of inferior verse
poetic *or* **poetical** *adj* **1** like poetry, by being expressive or imaginative **2** of poetry or poets **3** recounted in verse
poetic justice *n* an appropriate punishment or reward for previous actions
poetic licence *n* freedom from the normal rules of language or truth, as in poetry
poet laureate *n, pl* **poets laureate** *Brit* the poet selected by the British sovereign to write poems on important occasions
poetry *n* **1** poems in general **2** the art or craft of writing poems **3** a poetic quality that prompts an emotional response: *her acting was full of poetry* [Latin *poeta* poet]
po-faced *adj* wearing a disapproving stern expression [perhaps from PO + POKER-FACED]
pogey *or* **pogy** (pohg-ee) *n, pl* **pogeys** *or* **pogies** *Canad slang* **1** financial or other relief given to unemployed people by the government; dole **2** unemployment insurance [from earlier *pogie* workhouse]
pogo stick *n* a pole with steps for the feet and a spring at the bottom, so that the user can bounce up, down, and along on it [origin unknown]
pogrom *n* an organized persecution and massacre [Russian: destruction]
poi *n NZ* a ball of woven flax swung rhythmically by Māori women during poi dances [Māori]
poi dance *n NZ* a women's formation dance that involves singing and twirling a poi
poignant *adj* **1** sharply painful to the feelings: *a poignant reminder* **2** cutting: *poignant wit* **3** pertinent in mental appeal: *a poignant subject* [Latin *pungens* pricking] **poignancy** *n*

poinsettia *n* a shrub of Mexico and Central America, widely grown for its showy scarlet bracts, which resemble petals [after J. P. *Poinsett*, US Minister to Mexico]

point *n* **1** the essential idea in an argument or discussion: *I agreed with the point he made* **2** a reason or aim: *what is the point of this exercise?* **3** a detail or item **4** a characteristic: *he has his good points* **5** a location or position **6** a dot or tiny mark **7** a dot used as a decimal point or a full stop **8** the sharp tip of anything: *the point of the spear* **9** a headland: *the soaring cliffs at Dwerja Point in the southwest of the island* **10** *maths* a geometric element having a position located by coordinates, but no magnitude **11** a specific condition or degree: *freezing point* **12** a moment: *at that point he left* **13** (*often pl*) any of the extremities, such as the tail, ears, or feet, of a domestic animal **14** (*often pl*) *ballet* the tip of the toes **15** a single unit for measuring something such as value, or of scoring in a game **16** *printing* a unit of measurement equal to one twelfth of a pica **17** *naut* one of the 32 direction marks on the compass **18** *cricket* a fielding position at right angles to the batsman on the off side **19** either of the two electrical contacts that make or break the circuit in the distributor of a motor vehicle **20** *Brit, Austral & NZ* (*often pl*) a movable section of railway track used to direct a train from one line to another **21** *Brit* short for **power point** **22** *boxing* a mark awarded for a scoring blow or knockdown **23** **beside the point** irrelevant **24** **make a point of** **A** to make a habit of (something) **B** to do (something) because one thinks it important **25** **on** *or* **at the point of** about to; on the verge of: *on the point of leaving* **26** **to the point** relevant **27** **up to a point** not completely ▷ *vb* **28** (usually foll. by *at* or *to*) to show the position or direction of something by extending a finger or other pointed object towards it **29** (usually foll. by *at* or *to*) to single out one person or thing from among several: *all the symptoms pointed to epilepsy* **30** to direct or face in a specific direction: *point me in the right direction* **31** to finish or repair the joints in brickwork with mortar or cement **32** (of a gun dog) to show where game is lying by standing rigidly with the muzzle turned towards it ▷ See also **point out** [Latin *pungere* to pierce]

point-blank *adj* **1** fired at a very close target **2** plain or blunt: *a point-blank refusal to discuss the matter* ▷ *adv* **3** directly or bluntly: *the Minister was asked point-blank if he intended to resign* [*point* + *blank* (centre spot of an archery target)]

point duty *n* the control of traffic by a police officer at a road junction

pointed *adj* **1** having a sharp tip **2** cutting or incisive: *pointed wit* **3** obviously directed at a particular person: *a pointed remark* **4** emphasized or obvious: *pointed ignorance* **pointedly** *adv*

pointer *n* **1** something that is a helpful indicator of how a situation has arisen or may turn out: *a significant pointer to the likely resumption of talks* **2** an indicator on a measuring instrument **3** a long stick used by teachers, to point out particular features on a map, chart, etc. **4** a large smooth-coated gun dog

pointillism (pwan-till-iz-zum) *n* a technique used by some impressionist painters, in which dots of colour are placed side by side so that they merge when seen from a distance [French] **pointillist** *n, adj*

pointing *n* the insertion of mortar between the joints in brickwork

pointless *adj* without meaning or purpose

point of no return *n* a point at which one is committed to continuing with an action

point of order *n, pl* **points of order** an objection in a meeting to the departure from the proper procedure

point of view *n, pl* **points of view** **1** a mental viewpoint or attitude: *she refuses to see the other person's point of view* **2** a way of considering something: *a scientific point of view*

point out *vb* to draw someone's attention to

point-to-point *n Brit* a steeplechase organized by a hunt

poise *n* **1** dignified manner **2** physical balance: *the poise of a natural model* **3** mental balance: *he recovered his poise* ▷ *vb* **poising, poised** **4** to be balanced or suspended **5** to hold in readiness: *to poise a lance* [Old French *pois* weight]

poised *adj* **1** absolutely ready **2** behaving with or showing poise

poison *n* **1** a substance that causes death or injury when swallowed or absorbed **2** something that destroys or corrupts: *the poison of Nazism* ▷ *vb* **3** to give poison to someone **4** to add poison to (something) **5** to have a harmful or evil effect on **6** (foll. by *against*) to turn (a person's mind) against: *he poisoned her mind against me* [Latin *potio* a drink, esp. a poisonous one] **poisoner** *n*

poison ivy *n* a North American climbing plant that causes an itching rash if it touches the skin

poisonous *adj* **1** of or like a poison **2** malicious

poison-pen letter *n* a malicious anonymous letter

poke[1] *vb* **poking, poked** **1** to jab or prod with an elbow, finger, etc. **2** to make a hole by poking **3** (sometimes foll. by *at*) to thrust (at): *she poked at the food with her fork* **4** (usually foll. by *in* or *through* etc.) to thrust forward or out: *yellow hair poked from beneath his cap* **5** to stir (a fire) by poking **6** (often foll. by *about* or *around*) to search or pry **7** **poke one's nose into** to meddle in ▷ *n* **8** a jab or prod [Low German & Middle Dutch *poken*]

poke[2] *n* **1** *dialect* a pocket or bag **2** **a pig in a poke** See **pig** [Old French *poque*]

poker[1] *n* a metal rod with a handle for stirring a fire

poker[2] *n* a card game of bluff and skill in which players bet on the hands dealt [origin unknown]

poker face *n informal* an expressionless face, such as that of a poker player trying to hide the value of his or her cards **poker-faced** *adj*

pokerwork *n* the art of producing pictures or designs on wood by burning it with a heated metal point

poky *adj* **pokier, pokiest** (of a room) small and cramped **pokiness** *n*

pol. **1** political **2** politics

P

polar *adj* **1** of or near either of the earth's poles or the area inside the Arctic or Antarctic Circles **2** of or having a pole or polarity **3** directly opposite in tendency or nature: *polar opposites*

polar bear *n* a white bear of coastal regions of the North Pole

polar circle *n* the Arctic or Antarctic Circle

polarity *n, pl* **-ties 1** the state of having two directly opposite tendencies or opinions **2** the condition of a body which has opposing physical properties, usually magnetic poles or electric charge **3** the particular state of a part with polarity: *an electrode with positive polarity*

polarization *or* **-risation** *n* **1** the condition of having or giving polarity **2** *physics* the condition in which waves of light or other radiation are restricted to certain directions of vibration

polarize *or* **-rise** *vb* **-rizing, -rized** *or* **-rising, -rised 1** to cause people to adopt directly opposite opinions: *political opinion had polarized since the restoration of democracy* **2** to have or give polarity or polarization

Polaroid *n trademark* **1** a type of plastic that polarizes light: used in sunglasses to eliminate glare **2 Polaroid camera** a camera that produces a finished print by developing and processing it inside the camera within a few seconds **3 Polaroids** sunglasses with Polaroid plastic lenses

polder *n* a stretch of land reclaimed from the sea [Middle Dutch *polre*]

pole[1] *n* **1** a long slender rounded piece of wood, metal, or other material **2 up the pole** *Brit, Austral & NZ informal* **A** slightly mad **B** in a predicament [Latin *palus* a stake]

pole[2] *n* **1** either end of the earth's axis of rotation. See also **North Pole, South Pole 2** *physics* **A** either of the opposite forces of a magnet **B** either of two points at which there are opposite electric charges **3** either of two directly opposite tendencies or opinions **4 poles apart** having widely divergent opinions or tastes [Greek *polos* pivot]

Pole *n* a person from Poland

poleaxe *or US* **poleax** *vb* **-axing, -axed 1** to hit or stun with a heavy blow ▹ *n* **2** an axe formerly used in battle or used by a butcher [Middle English *pollax* battle-axe]

polecat *n, pl* **-cats** *or* **-cat 1** a dark brown mammal like a weasel that gives off a foul smell **2** US a skunk [origin unknown]

pole dancing *n* a form of entertainment in which a scantily dressed woman dances erotically, turning on and posing against a vertically fixed pole on stage **pole dancer** *n*

polemic (pol-em-ik) *n* **1** a fierce attack on or defence of a particular opinion, belief, etc.: *anti-capitalist polemic* ▹ *adj also* **polemical 2** of or involving dispute or controversy [Greek *polemos* war] **polemicist** *n*

polemics *n* the art of dispute

pole position *n* **1** (in motor racing) the starting position on the inside of the front row, generally considered the best one **2** an advantageous starting position

pole star *n* a guiding principle or rule

Pole Star *n* **the Pole Star** the star closest to the northern celestial pole

pole vault *n* **1 the pole vault** a field event in which competitors try to clear a high bar with the aid of a very flexible long pole ▹ *vb* **pole-vault 2** to perform or compete in the pole vault **pole-vaulter** *n*

police *n* **1** (often preceded by *the*) the organized civil force in a state which keeps law and order **2** the men and women who are members of such a force **3** an organized body with a similar function: *security police* ▹ *vb* **-licing, -liced 4** to maintain order or control by means of a police force or similar body [French, from Latin *politia* administration]

police dog *n* a dog trained to help the police

policeman *or fem* **policewoman** *n, pl* **-men** *or* **-women** a member of a police force

police procedural *n* a novel, film, or television drama that deals with police work

police state *n* a state in which a government controls people's freedom through the police

police station *n* the office of the police force of a district

policy[1] *n, pl* **-cies 1** a plan of action adopted by a person, group, or government **2** *archaic* wisdom or prudence [Old French *policie*, from Latin *politia* administration]

policy[2] *n, pl* **-cies** a document containing an insurance contract [Old French *police* certificate] **policyholder** *n*

polio *n* short for **poliomyelitis**

poliomyelitis (pole-ee-oh-my-el-lite-iss) *n* a viral disease which affects the brain and spinal cord, often causing paralysis [Greek *polios* grey + *muelos* marrow]

polish *vb* **1** to make smooth and shiny by rubbing **2** to perfect or complete: *media experts he had hired to polish his image* **3** to make or become elegant or refined: *not having polished his accent didn't help his career* ▹ *n* **4** a substance used for polishing **5** a shine or gloss **6** elegance or refinement ▹ See also **polish off, polish up** [Latin *polire* to polish]

Polish *adj* **1** of Poland ▹ *n* **2** the language of Poland

polished *adj* **1** accomplished: *a polished actor* **2** done or performed well or professionally: *a polished performance*

polish off *vb informal* **1** to finish completely **2** to dispose of or kill

polish up *vb* **1** to make smooth and shiny by polishing **2** to improve (a skill or ability) by working at it: *I'm going to evening classes to polish up my German*

Politburo *n* (formerly) the chief decision-making committee of a Communist country [Russian]

polite *adj* **1** having good manners; courteous **2** cultivated or refined: *polite society* **3** socially correct but insincere: *he smiled a polite response and stifled an urge to scream* [Latin *politus* polished] **politely** *adv* **politeness** *n*

politic *adj* **1** wise or possibly advantageous: *I didn't feel it was politic to mention it* **2** artful or shrewd: *a politic manager* **3** crafty; cunning: *a politic old* *scoundrel* **4** *archaic* political. See also **body politic** [Old French *politique*, from Greek *polis* city]

political *adj* **1** of the state, government, or public administration **2** relating to or interested in politics: *she was always a very political person* **3** of the parties and the partisan aspects of politics: *the government blames political opponents for fanning the unrest* **politically** *adv*

politically correct *adj* displaying progressive attitudes, esp. in using vocabulary which is intended to avoid any implied prejudice **political correctness** *n*

political prisoner *n* a person imprisoned for holding particular political beliefs

political science *n* the study of the state, government, and politics **political scientist** *n*

politician *n* a person actively engaged in politics, esp. a member of parliament

politicize or **-cise** *vb* **-cizing, -cized** or **-cising, -cised 1** to make political or politically aware **2** to take part in political discussion or activity **politicization** or **-cisation** *n*

politics *n* **1** (*functioning as sing*) the art and science of government **2** (*functioning as pl*) political opinions or sympathies: *his conservative politics* **3** (*functioning as pl*) political activities or affairs: *party politics* **4** (*functioning as sing*) the business or profession of politics **5** (*functioning as sing or pl*) any activity concerned with the acquisition of power: *company politics are often vicious*

polity *n, pl* **-ties** *formal* **1** a politically organized state, church, or society **2** a form of government of a state, church, or society [Greek *politeia* citizenship, from *polis* city]

polka *n* **1** a lively 19th-century dance **2** music for this dance ▷ *vb* **-kaing, -kaed 3** to dance a polka [Czech *pulka* half-step]

polka dots *pl n* a regular pattern of small bold spots on a fabric

poll *n* **1** Also called: **opinion poll** the questioning of a random sample of people to find out the general opinion **2** the casting, recording, or counting of votes in an election **3** the result of such a voting: *a marginal poll* **4** the head ▷ *vb* **5** to receive (a certain number of votes) **6** to record the votes of: *he polled the whole town* **7** to question (a person, etc.) as part of an opinion poll **8** to vote in an election **9** to clip or shear **10** to remove or cut short the horns of (cattle) [Middle Low German *polle* hair, head, top of a tree]

pollack or **pollock** *n, pl* **-lacks, -lack** or **-locks, -lock** a food fish related to the cod, found in northern seas [origin unknown]

pollard *n* **1** an animal that has shed its horns or has had them removed **2** a tree with its top cut off to encourage a more bushy growth ▷ *vb* **3** to cut off the top of (a tree) to make it grow bushy [see POLL] **pollarded** *adj*

pollen *n* a fine powder produced by flowers to fertilize other flowers of the same species [Latin: powder]

pollen count *n* a measure of the amount of pollen in the air over a 24-hour period, often published as a warning to people with hay fever

pollinate *vb* **-nating, -nated** to fertilize by the transfer of pollen **pollination** *n*

polling booth *n* a compartment in which a voter can mark his or her ballot paper in private during an election

polling station *n* a building where voters go during an election to cast their votes

pollock *n* same as **pollack**

pollster *n* a person who conducts opinion polls

poll tax *n* any tax levied equally on each member of the adult population

pollutant *n* a substance that pollutes, usually the chemical waste of an industrial process

pollute *vb* **-luting, -luted 1** to contaminate with poisonous or harmful substances **2** to corrupt morally [Latin *polluere* to defile] **pollution** *n*

polo *n* **1** a game like hockey played on horseback with long-handled mallets and a wooden ball **2** short for **water polo** [Tibetan *pulu* ball]

polonaise *n* **1** a stately Polish dance **2** music for this dance [French *danse polonaise* Polish dance]

polo neck *n* a sweater with a high tight turned-over collar

polonium *n chem* a rare radioactive element found in trace amounts in uranium ores. Symbol: **Po** [Medieval Latin *Polonia* Poland; in honour of the nationality of its discoverer, Marie Curie]

polo shirt *n* a cotton short-sleeved shirt with a collar and three-button opening at the neck

poltergeist *n* a spirit believed to be responsible for noises and acts of mischief, such as throwing objects about [German *poltern* to be noisy + *Geist* ghost]

poltroon *n obsolete* a complete coward [Old Italian *poltrone* lazy good-for-nothing]

poly *n, pl* **polys** *informal* short for **polytechnic**

poly- *combining form* many or much: *polyhedron*; *polysyllabic* [Greek *polus*]

polyandry *n* the practice of having more than one husband at the same time [Greek *polus* many + *anēr* man] **polyandrous** *adj*

polyanthus *n, pl* **-thuses** a hybrid garden primrose with brightly coloured flowers [Greek: having many flowers]

polychromatic *adj* **1** having many colours **2** (of radiation) containing more than one wavelength

polycystic ovary syndrome *n* a hormonal disorder preventing ovulation, leading to reduced fertility, hirsutism, and weight gain

polyester *n* a synthetic material used to make plastics and textile fibres

polyethylene *n* same as **polythene**

polygamy (pol-**ig**-a-mee) *n* the practice of having more than one wife or husband at the same time [Greek *polus* many + *gamos* marriage] **polygamist** *n* **polygamous** *adj*

polyglot *adj* **1** able to speak many languages **2** written in or using many languages ▷ *n* **3** a person who can speak many languages [Greek *poluglōttos* many-tongued]

polygon *n* a geometrical figure with three or more sides and angles [Greek *polugōnon* figure with many angles] **polygonal** *adj*

polygraph *n* an instrument for recording pulse rate and perspiration, often used as a lie detector [Greek *polugraphos* writing copiously]

polygyny *n* the practice of having more than one wife at the same time [Greek *polus* many + *gunē* woman] **polygynous** *adj*

polyhedron *n, pl* **-drons** *or* **-dra** a solid figure with four or more sides [Greek *polus* many + *hedron* side] **polyhedral** *adj*

Polyhymnia *n Greek myth* the muse of singing, mime, and sacred dance

polymath *n* a person of great and varied learning [Greek *polumathēs* having much knowledge]

polymer *n* a natural or synthetic compound with large molecules made up of simple molecules of the same kind

polymeric *adj* of or being a polymer: *polymeric materials such as PVC* [Greek *polumerēs* having many parts]

polymerization *or* **-isation** *n* the process of forming a polymer **polymerize** *or* **-ise** *vb*

polymorphous *or* **polymorphic** *adj* having, or passing through many different forms or stages [Greek *polus* many + *morphē* form]

Polynesian *adj* **1** of Polynesia ▷ *n* **2** a person from Polynesia **3** any of the languages of Polynesia

polynomial *maths* ▷ *adj* **1** consisting of two or more terms ▷ *n* **2** an algebraic expression consisting of the sum of a number of terms

polyp *n* **1** *zool* a small sea creature that has a hollow cylindrical body with a ring of tentacles around the mouth **2** *pathol* a small growth on the surface of a mucous membrane [Greek *polupous* having many feet]

polyphonic *adj music* consisting of several melodies played together

polyphony (pol-if-on-ee) *n, pl* **-nies** a polyphonic style of composition or a piece of music using it [Greek *poluphōnia* diversity of tones]

polysaccharide *n* a carbohydrate which consists of a number of linked sugar molecules, such as starch or cellulose

polystyrene *n* a synthetic material used esp. as white rigid foam for insulating and packing

polysyllable *n* a word having more than two syllables **polysyllabic** *adj*

polytechnic *n* **1** (in New Zealand and formerly in Britain) a college offering courses in many subjects at and below degree level ▷ *adj* **2** of or relating to technical instruction [Greek *polutekhnos* skilled in many arts]

polytheism *n* belief in more than one god **polytheistic** *adj* **polytheist** *n*

polythene *n* a light plastic material made from ethylene, usually made into thin sheets or bags

polyunsaturated *adj* of a group of fats that are less likely to contribute to the build-up of cholesterol in the body

polyurethane *n* a synthetic material used esp. in paints

polyvinyl chloride *n* See **PVC**

pom *n Austral & NZ slang* same as **pommy**

pomace (pumm-iss) *n* apple pulp left after pressing for juice [Latin *pomum* apple]

pomade *n* a perfumed oil put on the hair to make it smooth and shiny, esp. formerly [French *pommade*]

pomander *n* **1** a mixture of sweet-smelling substances in a container, used to perfume drawers or cupboards **2** a container for such a mixture [Medieval Latin *pomum ambrae* apple of amber]

pomegranate *n* a round tropical fruit with a tough reddish rind containing many seeds in a juicy red pulp [Latin *pomum* apple + *granatus* full of seeds]

pomelo (pom-ill-oh) *n, pl* **-los** the edible yellow fruit, like a grapefruit, of a tropical tree [Dutch *pompelmoes*]

Pomeranian *n* a toy dog with a long straight silky coat [after *Pomerania*, region of N central Europe]

pomfret (pum-frit) *or* **pomfret-cake** *n* a small black rounded liquorice sweet [from *Pomfret*, earlier form of *Pontefract*, Yorks., where originally made]

pommel *n* **1** the raised part on the front of a saddle **2** a knob at the top of a sword handle ▷ *vb* **-melling, -melled** *or US* **-meling, -meled 3** same as **pummel** [Old French *pomel* knob]

pommy *n, pl* **-mies** *(sometimes cap) slang* a word used by Australians and New Zealanders for a British person. Sometimes shortened to: **pom** [origin unknown]

pomp *n* **1** stately display or ceremony **2** ostentatious display [Greek *pompē* procession]

pompom *n* **1** a decorative ball of tufted silk or wool **2** the small round flower head of some dahlias and chrysanthemums [French]

pompous *adj* **1** foolishly dignified or self-important **2** foolishly grand in style: *a pompous speech* **pomposity** *n* **pompously** *adv*

ponce *offensive slang, chiefly Brit* ▷ *n* **1** an effeminate man **2** same as **pimp** ▷ *vb* **poncing, ponced 3** (often foll. by *around* or *about*) *Brit & Austral* to act stupidly or waste time [from Polari, an English slang derived from the lingua franca of the Mediterranean ports]

poncho *n, pl* **-chos** a type of cloak made of a piece of cloth with a hole in the middle for the head [American Spanish]

pond *n* a pool of still water [Middle English *ponde* enclosure]

ponder *vb* (sometimes foll. by *on* or *over*) to consider thoroughly or deeply [Latin *ponderare* to weigh, consider] **ponderable** *adj*

ponderous *adj* **1** serious and dull: *much of the film is ponderous and pretentious* **2** heavy or huge **3** (of movement) slow and clumsy [Latin *ponderosus* of great weight]

pondok *or* **pondokkie** *n* (in southern Africa) a crudely made house or shack [Malay *pondók* leaf house]

pondweed *n* a plant which grows in ponds and slow streams

pong *Brit & Austral informal* ▷ *n* **1** a strong unpleasant smell ▷ *vb* **2** to give off a strong unpleasant smell [origin unknown] **pongy** *adj*

ponga (pong-a) *n* a tall New Zealand tree fern with large leathery leaves [Māori]

poniard (pon-yerd) *n* a small slender dagger [Old French *poignard*]

pontiff *n* the Pope [Latin *pontifex* high priest]

pontifical *adj* **1** of a pontiff **2** pompous or dogmatic in manner
pontificate *vb* **-cating, -cated 1** to speak in a dogmatic manner **2** to officiate as a pontiff ▷ *n* **3** the term of office of a Pope
pontoon¹ *n* a floating platform used to support a bridge [Latin *ponto* punt]
pontoon² *n* a card game in which players try to obtain sets of cards worth 21 points [probably an alteration of French *vingt-et-un* twenty-one]
pony *n, pl* **-nies** a breed of small horse [Scots *powney,* perhaps from Latin *pullus* young animal, foal]
ponytail *n* a hairstyle in which the hair is tied in a bunch at the back of the head and hangs down like a tail
pony trekking *n* the pastime of riding ponies cross-country
poodle *n* a dog with curly hair, which is sometimes clipped [German *Pudel*]
poof *n Brit, Austral & NZ offensive slang* a homosexual man [French *pouffe* puff] **poofy** *adj*
pooh *interj* an exclamation of disdain, scorn, or disgust
pooh-pooh *vb* to express disdain or scorn for
pool¹ *n* **1** a small body of still water **2** a small body of spilt liquid: *a pool of blood* **3** See **swimming pool 4** a deep part of a stream or river [Old English *pōl*]
pool² *n* **1** a shared fund of resources or workers: *a typing pool* **2** a billiard game in which all the balls are potted with the cue ball **3** the combined stakes of those betting in many gambling games **4** *commerce* a group of producers who agree to maintain output levels and high prices ▷ *vb* **5** to put into a common fund [French *poule,* literally: hen used to signify stakes in a card game]
pools *pl n* **the pools** *chiefly Brit* a nationwide mainly postal form of gambling which bets on the results of football matches
poop *n naut* a raised part at the back of a sailing ship [Latin *puppis*]
pooped *adj US, Canad, Austral & NZ slang* exhausted or tired: *if I wasn't so pooped I'd run and have a look at it* [Middle English *poupen* to blow]
poor *adj* **1** having little money and few possessions **2** less than is necessary or expected: *it was a poor reward for all his effort* **3** (sometimes foll. by *in*) lacking in (something): *a food which is rich in energy but poor in vitamins* **4** inferior: *poor quality* **5** disappointing or disagreeable: *a poor play* **6** pitiable; unlucky: *poor John is ill* **7 poor man's (something)** a cheaper substitute for (something): *pewter, sometimes known as poor man's silver* [Latin *pauper*]
poorhouse *n* same as **workhouse**
poor law *n English history* a law providing for support of poor people from parish funds
poorly *adv* **1** badly ▷ *adj* **2** *informal* rather ill
poor White *n often offensive* a poverty-stricken White person, usually in the southern US or South Africa
pop¹ *vb* **popping, popped 1** to make or cause to make a small explosive sound **2** (often foll. by *in* or *out* etc.) *informal* to enter or leave briefly or suddenly: *his mother popped out to buy him an ice cream* **3** to place suddenly or unexpectedly: *Benny popped a sweet into his mouth* **4** to burst with a small explosive sound **5** (of the eyes) to protrude **6** *informal* to pawn **7 pop the question** *informal* to propose marriage ▷ *n* **8** a light sharp explosive sound **9** *Brit informal* a nonalcoholic fizzy drink ▷ *adv* **10** with a pop ▷ See also **pop off** [imitative]
pop² *n* **1** music of general appeal, esp. to young people, that usually has a strong rhythm and uses electrical amplification ▷ *adj* **2** relating to pop music: *a pop concert* **3** *informal* short for **popular**
pop³ *n informal* **1** father **2** an old man
POP 1 point of presence: a device that enables access to the internet **2** post office protocol: a protocol which brings email to and from a mail server
pop. 1 population **2** popular(ly)
pop art *n* a movement in modern art that uses the methods, styles, and themes of popular culture and mass media
popcorn *n* grains of maize heated until they puff up and burst
Pope *n* the bishop of Rome as head of the Roman Catholic Church [Greek *pappas* father]
popery (pope-er-ee) *n offensive* Roman Catholicism
popeyed *adj* **1** staring in astonishment **2** having bulging eyes
popgun *n* a toy gun that fires a pellet or cork by means of compressed air
popinjay *n* a conceited, foppish, or overly talkative person [Arabic *babaghā* parrot]
popish (pope-ish) *adj offensive* relating to Roman Catholicism
poplar *n* a tall slender tree with light soft wood, triangular leaves, and catkins [Latin *populus*]
poplin *n* a strong plain-woven fabric, usually of cotton, with fine ribbing [French *papeline*]
pop off *vb informal* **1** to depart suddenly **2** to die suddenly
poppadom *or* **poppadum** *n* a thin round crisp fried Indian bread [Hindi]
popper *n Brit informal* a press stud
poppet *n* a term of affection for a small child or one's romantic partner [variant of *puppet*]
popping crease *n cricket* a line in front of and parallel with the wicket where the batsman stands [from obsolete *pop* to hit]
poppy *n, pl* **-pies 1** a plant with showy red, orange, or white flowers **2** a drug, such as opium, obtained from these plants **3** an artificial red poppy worn to mark Remembrance Sunday and in New Zealand to mark Anzac Day ▷ *adj* **4** reddish-orange [Old English *popæg*]
poppycock *n informal* nonsense [Dutch dialect *pappekak,* literally: soft excrement]
Poppy Day *n informal* Remembrance Sunday
Popsicle *n trademark* the US and Canadian term for **ice lolly**
populace *n* the ordinary people; masses [Latin *populus*]
popular *adj* **1** widely liked or admired **2** (often foll. by *with*) liked by a particular person or group: *the bay is popular with windsurfers and water-skiers*

P

3 common among the general public: *the groundswell of popular feeling* **4** designed to appeal to a mass audience: *an attack on him in the popular press* [Latin *popularis* of the people] **popularity** *n* **popularly** *adv*

popular front *n* a left-wing group or party opposed to fascism

popularize *or* **-rise** *vb* **-rizing, -rized** *or* **-rising, -rised 1** to make popular **2** to make easily understandable **popularization** *or* **-risation** *n*

populate *vb* **-lating, -lated 1** (*often passive*) to live in: *a mountainous region populated mainly by Armenians* **2** to provide with inhabitants [Latin *populus* people] **populated** *adj*

population *n* **1** all the inhabitants of a place **2** the number of such inhabitants **3** all the people of a particular class in a place: *the bulk of the rural population lives in poverty* **4** *ecology* a group of individuals of the same species inhabiting a given area: *a population of grey seals*

populism *n* a political strategy based on a calculated appeal to the interests or prejudices of ordinary people: *they preach a heady message of populism and religion* **populist** *adj, n*

populous *adj* containing many inhabitants

pop-up *adj* **1** (of an appliance) characterized by or having a mechanism that pops up **2** (of a book) having pages that rise when opened, to simulate a three-dimensional form **3** *computers* (of a menu on a computer screen, etc.) suddenly appearing when an option is selected **4** (of a shop, restaurant, etc.) intentionally trading for a short time only: *a pop-up boutique* ▷ *n* **5** *computers* something that appears over or above the open window on a computer screen

porangi (pore-ang-ee) *adj NZ informal* crazy; mad [Māori]

porbeagle *n* a large shark of the N Atlantic and Mediterranean [Cornish *porgh-bugel*]

porcelain *n* **1** a delicate type of china **2** an object or objects made of this [French *porcelaine*, from Italian *porcellana* cowrie shell]

porch *n* a covered approach to the entrance of a building [French *porche*]

porcine *adj* of or like a pig [Latin *porcus* a pig]

porcupine *n* a large rodent covered with long pointed quills [Middle English *porc despyne* pig with spines]

pore¹ *vb* **poring, pored** > **pore over** to examine or study intently: *I pored over account books and ledgers all day* [Middle English *pouren*]

USAGE See at **pour**.

pore² *n* **1** a small opening in the skin or surface of an animal or plant **2** any small hole, such as a tiny gap in a rock [Greek *poros* passage, pore]

poriferan (por-riff-er-an) *n biol* a sponge [from New Latin *porifer* bearing pores]

pork *n* the flesh of pigs used as food [Latin *porcus* pig]

porker *n* a pig fattened for food

pork pie *n* a pie with a minced pork filling

porky *adj* **porkier, porkiest 1** of or like pork **2** *informal* fat or obese

porn *or* **porno** *n, adj informal* short for **pornography** or **pornographic**

pornography *n* writings, pictures, or films designed to be sexually exciting [Greek *pornographos* writing of prostitutes] **pornographer** *n* **pornographic** *adj*

porous *adj* **1** allowing air and liquids to be absorbed **2** *biol & geol* having pores [Late Latin *porus* passage, pore] **porosity** *n*

porphyry (por-fir-ee) *n, pl* **-ries** a reddish-purple rock with large crystals of feldspar in it [Greek *porphuros* purple] **porphyritic** *adj*

porpoise *n, pl* **-poises** *or* **-poise** a small mammal of the whale family with a blunt snout [Latin *porcus* pig + *piscis* fish]

porridge *n* **1** a dish made of oatmeal or other cereal, cooked in water or milk **2** *chiefly Brit slang* a term of imprisonment [variant of *pottage*]

porringer *n* a small dish, often with a handle, used esp. formerly for soup or porridge [Middle English *potinger*]

port¹ *n* a town with a harbour where ships can load and unload [Latin *portus*]

port² *n* **1** the left side of an aircraft or ship when facing the front of it ▷ *vb* **2** to turn or be turned towards the port [origin unknown]

port³ *n* a strong sweet fortified wine, usually dark red [after *Oporto*, Portugal, from where it came originally]

port⁴ *n* **1** *naut* **A** an opening with a watertight door in the side of a ship, used for loading, etc. **B** See **porthole 2** a location on a computer where peripherals and other components can be plugged in [Latin *porta* gate]

port⁵ *vb computers* to change (programs) from one system to another [probably from PORT⁴]

portable *adj* **1** easily carried ▷ *n* **2** an article designed to be easily carried, such as a television or a games console [Latin *portare* to carry] **portability** *n*

portage *n* **1** the transporting of boats and supplies overland between navigable waterways **2** the route used for such transport ▷ *vb* **-taging, -taged 3** to transport (boats and supplies) in this way [French]

portal *n* **1** *literary* a large and impressive gateway or doorway **2** *computers* an internet site providing links to other sites [Latin *porta* gate]

portcullis *n* an iron grating suspended in a castle gateway, that can be lowered to bar the entrance [Old French *porte coleïce* sliding gate]

portend *vb* to be an omen of: *the 0.5% increase certainly portends higher inflation ahead* [Latin *portendere* to indicate]

portent *n* **1** a sign of a future event **2** great or ominous significance: *matters of great portent* **3** a marvel [Latin *portentum* sign]

portentous *adj* **1** of great or ominous significance **2** self-important or pompous: *there was nothing portentous or solemn about him*

porter¹ *n* **1** a person employed to carry luggage at a railway station or hotel **2** a hospital worker who transfers patients from one part of the hospital to another [Latin *portare* to carry] **porterage** *n*

porter² *n chiefly Brit* a doorman or gatekeeper of a building [Latin *porta* door]

porter³ *n Brit* a dark sweet ale brewed from black malt [short for *porter's ale*]

porterhouse *n* a thick, choice beef steak. Also called: **porterhouse steak** [formerly, a place that served porter, beer, and sometimes meals]

portfolio *n, pl* **-os** **1** a flat case for carrying maps, drawings, or papers **2** selected examples, such as drawings or photographs, that show an artist's recent work **3** the area of responsibility of the head of a government department: *the defence portfolio* **4** a list of investments held by an investor **5 Minister without portfolio** a cabinet minister without responsibility for a government department [Italian *portafoglio*]

porthole *n* a small round window in a ship or aircraft

portico *n, pl* **-coes** *or* **-cos** a porch or covered walkway with columns supporting the roof [Italian, from Latin *porticus*]

portion *n* **1** a part of a whole **2** a part belonging to a person or group **3** a helping of food served to one person **4** *law* a dowry **5** *literary* someone's fate or destiny: *utter disaster was my portion* ▷ *vb* **6** to divide (something) into shares [Latin *portio*]

portly *adj* **-lier, -liest** stout or rather fat [from *port* (in the sense: deportment)]

portmanteau *n, pl* **-teaus** *or* **-teaux** *old-fashioned* a large suitcase made of stiff leather that opens out into two compartments [French: cloak carrier]

portmanteau word *n* a word made by joining together the beginning and end of two other words, such as *brunch*. Also called: **blend**

portrait *n* **1** a painting, drawing, or photograph of a person, often only of the face **2** a description ▷ *adj* **3** (of a page or screen) having greater height than width [French] **portraitist** *n*

portraiture *n* **1** the art of making portraits **2** a description **3 A** a portrait **B** portraits collectively

portray *vb* to describe or represent (someone) by artistic means, such as in writing or on film [Old French *portraire* to depict] **portrayal** *n*

Portuguese *adj* **1** of Portugal ▷ *n* **2** *pl* **-guese** a person from Portugal **3** the language of Portugal and Brazil

Portuguese man-of-war *n* a large sea creature like a jellyfish, with long stinging tentacles

pose *vb* **posing, posed** **1** to take up a particular position to be photographed or drawn **2** to behave in an affected way in order to impress others **3** (often foll. by *as*) to pretend to be (someone one is not) **4** to create or be (a problem, threat, etc.): *dressing complicated wounds has always posed a problem for doctors* **5** to put forward or ask: *the question you posed earlier* ▷ *n* **6** a position taken up for an artist or photographer **7** behaviour adopted for effect [Old French *poser* to set in place]

Poseidon *n* *Greek myth* the god of the sea

poser[1] *n* **1** *Brit, Austral & NZ informal* a person who likes to be seen in trendsetting clothes in fashionable bars, clubs, etc. **2** a person who poses

poser[2] *n* a baffling question

poseur *n* a person who behaves in an affected way in order to impress others [French]

posh *adj informal, chiefly Brit* **1** smart or elegant **2** upper-class [probably from obsolete slang *posh* a dandy]

posit (pozz-it) *vb* **-iting, -ited** to lay down as a basis for argument: *the archetypes posited by modern psychology* [Latin *ponere* to place]

position *n* **1** place or location: *the hotel is in an elevated position above the River Wye* **2** the proper or usual place **3** the way in which a person or thing is placed or arranged: *an upright position* **4** point of view; attitude: *the Catholic Church's position on contraception* **5** social status, esp. high social standing **6** a job; appointment **7** *sport* a player's allotted role or place in the playing area **8** *military* a place occupied for tactical reasons **9 in a position to** able to: *you were not in a position to repay the money* ▷ *vb* **10** to put in the proper or usual place; locate [Latin *ponere* to place] **positional** *adj*

positive *adj* **1** expressing certainty: *a positive answer* **2** definite or certain: *are you absolutely positive about the date?* **3** tending to emphasize what is good; constructive: *positive thinking* **4** tending towards progress or improvement: *investment that could have a positive impact on the company's fortunes* **5** *philosophy* constructive rather than sceptical **6** *informal* complete; downright: *a positive delight* **7** *maths* having a value greater than zero: *a positive number* **8** *grammar* denoting the unmodified form of an adjective as opposed to its comparative or superlative form **9** *physics* (of an electric charge) having an opposite charge to that of an electron **10** *physics* short for **electropositive** **11** *med* (of the result of an examination or test) indicating the presence of a suspected condition or organism ▷ *n* **12** something positive **13** *maths* a quantity greater than zero **14** *photog* a print showing an image whose colours and tones correspond to those of the original subject **15** *grammar* the positive degree of an adjective or adverb **16** a positive object, such as a terminal in a voltaic cell [Late Latin *positivus*] **positively** *adv* **positiveness** *or* **positivity** *n*

positive discrimination *n* the provision of special opportunities for a disadvantaged group

positive vetting *n Brit* the thorough checking of all aspects of a person's life to ensure his or her suitability for a position that may involve national security

positivism *n* a system of philosophy that accepts only things that can be seen or proved **positivist** *n, adj*

positron *n* *physics* the antiparticle of the electron, having the same mass but an equal and opposite charge [*posi(tive)* + *(elec)tron*]

poss. **1** possible **2** possession **3** possessive **4** possibly

posse (poss-ee) *n* **1** *US* a selected group of men on whom the sheriff may call for assistance **2** *informal* a group of friends or associates: *a posse of reporters* **3** (in W Canada) a troop of horses and riders who perform at rodeos [Latin: to be able]

possess *vb* **1** to have as one's property; own **2** to have as a quality or attribute: *he possessed an innate elegance, authority, and wit on screen* **3** to gain control over or dominate: *absolute terror possessed her* [Latin *possidere*] **possessor** *n*

possessed *adj* **1** (foll. by *of*) owning or having: *he is possessed of a calm maturity far beyond his years*

P

2 under the influence of a powerful force, such as a spirit or strong emotion: *possessed by the devil; she was possessed by a frenzied urge to get out of Moscow*

possession *n* **1** the state of possessing; ownership: *how had this compromising picture come into the possession of the press?* **2** anything that is possessed **3 possessions** wealth or property **4** the state of being controlled by or as if by evil spirits **5** the occupancy of land or property: *troops had taken possession of the airport* **6** a territory subject to a foreign state **7** the criminal offence of having something illegal on one's person: *arrested for drug dealing and possession* **8** *sport* control of the ball by a team or player: *City had most of the possession, but couldn't score*

possessive *adj* **1** of possession **2** desiring excessively to possess, control, or dominate: *a possessive partner* **3** *grammar* denoting a form of a noun or pronoun used to convey possession, as *my* or *Harry's*: *a possessive pronoun* ▷ *n* **4** *grammar* **A** the possessive case **B** a word in the possessive case **possessiveness** *n*

possibility *n, pl* **-ties 1** the state of being possible **2** anything that is possible **3** a competitor or candidate with a chance of success **4** a future prospect or potential: *all sorts of possibilities began to open up*

possible *adj* **1** capable of existing, happening, or proving true: *the earliest possible moment* **2** capable of being done: *I am grateful to the library staff for making this work possible* **3** having potential: *a possible buyer* **4** feasible but less than probable: *it's possible that's what he meant, but I doubt it* ▷ *n* **5** same as **possibility** (sense 3) [Latin *possibilis*]

> **USAGE** Although it is very common to talk about something being *very possible* or *more possible*, these uses are generally thought to be incorrect, since *possible* describes an absolute state, and therefore something can only be *possible* or *not possible*: *it is very likely* (not *very possible*) *that he will resign; it has now become easier* (not *more possible*) *to obtain an entry visa.*

P

possibly *adv* **1** perhaps or maybe **2** by any means; at all: *he can't possibly come*

possum *n* **1** *informal* an opossum **2** *Austral & NZ* a phalanger **3 play possum** to pretend to be dead, ignorant, or asleep in order to deceive an opponent

post[1] *n* **1** an official system of mail delivery **2** letters or packages that are transported and delivered by the Post Office; mail **3** a single collection or delivery of mail **4** a postbox or post office: *take this to the post* **5** *computers* a blog or message made publicly available ▷ *vb* **6** to send by post **7** *computers* to make (a blog or message) publicly available **8** *accounting* **A** to enter (an item) in a ledger **B** (often foll. by *up*) to enter all paper items in (a ledger) **9 keep someone posted** to inform someone regularly of the latest news [Latin *posita* something placed]

post[2] *n* **1** a length of wood, metal, or concrete fixed upright to support or mark something **2** *horse racing* **A** either of two upright poles marking the beginning and end of a racecourse **B** the finish of a horse race ▷ *vb* **3** (sometimes foll. by *up*) to put up (a notice) in a public place **4** to publish (a name) on a list [Latin *postis*]

post[3] *n* **1** a position to which a person is appointed; job **2** a position to which a soldier or guard is assigned for duty **3** a permanent military establishment **4** *Brit* either of two military bugle calls (**first post** and **last post**) giving notice of the time to retire for the night ▷ *vb* **5** *Brit & Austral* to send (someone) to a new place to work **6** to assign to or station at a particular place or position: *guards were posted at the doors* [French *poste*, from Latin *ponere* to place]

post- *prefix* **1** after in time: *postgraduate* **2** behind: *postorbital* [Latin]

postage *n* the charge for sending a piece of mail by post

postage stamp *n* same as **stamp** (sense 1)

postal *adj* of a post office or the mail-delivery service

postal order *n* a written money order sent by post and cashed at a post office by the person who receives it

postbag *n* **1** *chiefly Brit* a mailbag **2** the mail received by a magazine, radio programme, or public figure

postbox *n* same as **letter box** (sense 2)

postcard *n* a card, often with a picture on one side, for sending a message by post without an envelope

post chaise (**shaze**) *n* a four-wheeled horse-drawn coach formerly used as a rapid means of carrying mail and passengers

postcode *n* a system of letters and numbers used to aid the sorting of mail

post-consumer *adj* (of a consumer item) discarded for disposal or recovery having been recycled: *made from 75% post-consumer waste*

postdate *vb* **-dating, -dated 1** to write a future date on (a cheque or document) **2** to occur at a later date than **3** to assign a date to (an event or period) that is later than its previously assigned date

poster *n* **1** a large notice displayed in a public place as an advertisement **2** a large printed picture

poste restante *n* a post-office department where mail is kept until it is called for [French, literally: mail remaining]

posterior *n* **1** *formal or humorous* the buttocks ▷ *adj* **2** at the back of or behind something: *posterior leg muscles* **3** coming after in a series or time [Latin: latter]

posterity *n* **1** future generations **2** all of one's descendants [Latin *posterus* coming after]

postern *n* a small back door or gate [Old French *posterne*]

post-free *adv, adj* **1** *Brit & Austral* with the postage prepaid **2** free of postal charge

postgraduate *n* **1** a person who is studying for a more advanced qualification after obtaining a degree ▷ *adj* **2** of or for postgraduates

posthaste *adv* with great speed

posthumous (**poss**-tume-uss) *adj* **1** happening after one's death **2** born after the death of one's father **3** (of a book) published after the author's death [Latin *postumus* the last] **posthumously** *adv*

postie *n Scot, Austral & NZ informal* a postman
postilion *or* **postillion** *n* (esp. formerly) a person who rides one of a pair of horses drawing a coach [French *postillon*]
postimpressionism *n* a movement in painting in France at the end of the 19th century which rejected Impressionism but adapted its use of pure colour to paint with greater subjective emotion **postimpressionist** *n, adj*
posting *n* **1** a job to which someone is assigned by his or her employer, which involves moving to a particular town or country: *Bonn was his third posting overseas* **2** *computers* a message that is publicly available
postman *or fem* **postwoman** *n, pl* **-men** *or fem* **-women** a person who collects and delivers mail as a profession
postmark *n* **1** an official mark stamped on mail, showing the place and date of posting ▷ *vb* **2** to put such a mark on (mail)
postmaster *n* **1** Also (fem): **postmistress** an official in charge of a post office **2** a person who is responsible for managing the email system in an organization
postmaster general *n, pl* **postmasters general** the executive head of the postal service
postmeridian *adj* occurring after noon [Latin *postmeridianus*]
postmortem *n* **1** In full: **postmortem examination** medical examination of a dead body to discover the cause of death **2** analysis of a recent event: *a postmortem on the party's recent appalling by-election results* ▷ *adj* **3** occurring after death [Latin, literally: after death]
postnatal *adj* occurring after childbirth: *postnatal depression*
post office *n* a building where stamps are sold and postal business is conducted
Post Office *n* a government department responsible for postal services
postoperative *adj* of or occurring in the period after a surgical operation
postpaid *adv, adj* with the postage prepaid
postpone *vb* **-poning, -poned** to put off until a future time [Latin *postponere* to put after] **postponement** *n*
postpositive *adj grammar* (of an adjective) placed after the word it modifies
postprandial *adj formal* after dinner [Latin *post-* after + *prandium* midday meal]
postscript *n* a message added at the end of a letter, after the signature [Late Latin *postscribere* to write after]
post-traumatic stress disorder *n* a psychological condition, characterized by anxiety, withdrawal, and a proneness to physical illness, that may follow a traumatic experience
postulant *n* an applicant for admission to a religious order [Latin *postulare* to ask]
postulate *formal* ▷ *vb* **-lating, -lated 1** to assume to be true as the basis of an argument or theory **2** to ask, demand, or claim ▷ *n* **3** something postulated [Latin *postulare* to ask for] **postulation** *n*
posture *n* **1** a position or way in which a person stands, walks, etc.: *good posture* **2** a mental attitude: *a cooperative posture* **3** an affected attitude: *an intellectual posture* ▷ *vb* **-turing, -tured 4** to behave in an exaggerated way to attract attention **5** to assume an affected attitude [Latin *positura*] **postural** *adj*
postviral fatigue syndrome *or* **postviral syndrome** *n* same as **chronic fatigue syndrome**
postwar *adj* occurring or existing after a war
posy *n, pl* **-sies** a small bunch of flowers [variant of *poesy*]
pot[1] *n* **1** a round deep container, often with a handle and lid, used for cooking **2** the amount that a pot will hold **3** short for **flowerpot** or **teapot 4** a handmade piece of pottery **5** *billiards etc.* a shot by which a ball is pocketed **6** a chamber pot **7** the money in the pool in gambling games **8** *(often pl) informal* a large sum of money **9** *informal* a cup or other trophy **10** See **potbelly 11 go to pot** *informal* to go to ruin ▷ *vb* **potting, potted 12** to put (a plant) in soil in a flowerpot **13** *billiards etc.* to pocket (a ball) **14** to preserve (food) in a pot **15** to shoot (game) for food rather than for sport **16** to shoot casually or without careful aim **17** *informal* to capture or win [Old English *pott*]
pot[2] *n slang* cannabis [perhaps from Mexican Indian *potiguaya*]
potable (pote-a-bl) *adj formal* drinkable [Latin *potare* to drink]
potage (po-tahzh) *n* thick soup [French]
potash *n* **1** potassium carbonate, used as fertilizer **2** a compound containing potassium: *permanganate of potash* [from *pot ashes*, because originally obtained by evaporating the lye of wood ashes in pots]
potassium *n chem* a light silvery element of the alkali metal group. Symbol: **K** [New Latin *potassa* potash]
potassium nitrate *n* a crystalline compound used in gunpowders, fertilizers, and as a preservative for foods (**E252**)
potation *n formal* **1** the act of drinking **2** a drink, usually alcoholic [Latin *potare* to drink]
potato *n, pl* **-toes 1** a starchy vegetable that grows underground **2** the plant from which this vegetable is obtained [Spanish *patata*, from a Native American language]
potato beetle *n* same as **Colorado beetle**
potato chip *n* the US and Canadian term for **crisp** (sense 7)
potato crisp *n* same as **crisp** (sense 7)
potbelly *n, pl* **-lies 1** a bulging belly **2** a person with such a belly
potboiler *n informal* an inferior work of art produced quickly to make money
pot-bound *adj* (of a pot plant) having roots too big for its pot, so that it is unable to grow further
poteen *or* **poitín** *n* (in Ireland) illegally made alcoholic drink [Irish *poitín* little pot]
potent *adj* **1** having great power or influence **2** (of arguments) persuasive or forceful **3** highly effective: *a potent poison* **4** (of a male) capable of having sexual intercourse [Latin *potens* able] **potency** *n*
potentate *n* a ruler or monarch [Latin *potens* powerful]

P

potential *adj* **1 A** possible but not yet actual: *potential buyers* **B** capable of being or becoming; latent: *potential danger* ▹ *n* **2** ability or talent not yet in full use: *she has great potential as a painter* **3** In full: **electric potential** the work required to transfer a unit positive electric charge from an infinite distance to a given point [Latin *potentia* power] **potentially** *adv*

potential difference *n* the difference in electric potential between two points in an electric field, measured in volts

potential energy *n* the energy which an object has stored up because of its position in an electric, magnetic, or gravitational field

potentiality *n, pl* **-ties** latent capacity for becoming or developing

pother (rhymes with **bother**) *n literary* a fuss or commotion [origin unknown]

potherb *n* a plant whose leaves, flowers, or stems are used in cooking

pothole *n* **1** a hole in the surface of a road **2** a deep hole in a limestone area

potholing *n* the sport of exploring underground caves **potholer** *n*

pothook *n* **1** an S-shaped hook for suspending a pot over a fire **2** an S-shaped mark in handwriting

potion *n* a drink of medicine, poison, or some supposedly magic liquid [Latin *potio* a drink, esp. a poisonous one]

pot luck *n* **take pot luck** *informal* to accept whatever happens to be available: *we'll take pot luck at whatever restaurant might still be open*

potoroo *n, pl* **-roos** an Australian leaping rodent [from a native Australian language]

potpourri (po-poor-ee) *n, pl* **-ris 1** a fragrant mixture of dried flower petals **2** an assortment or medley [French, literally: rotten pot]

pot roast *n* meat cooked slowly in a covered pot with very little liquid

potsherd *n* a broken piece of pottery [*pot* + *schoord* piece of broken crockery]

pot shot *n* **1** a shot taken without careful aim **2** a shot fired at an animal within easy range

pottage *n* a thick soup or stew [Old French *potage* contents of a pot]

potted *adj* **1** grown in a pot: *potted plant* **2** cooked or preserved in a pot: *potted shrimps* **3** *informal* shortened or abridged: *a potted history*

potter[1] *n* a person who makes pottery

potter[2] *or esp US & Canad* **putter** *vb* **1** to move with little energy or direction: *I saw him pottering off to see to his canaries* **2 potter about** *or* **around** *or* **away** to be busy in a pleasant but aimless way: *he potters away doing God knows what all day* [Old English *potian* to thrust]

Potteries *n* **the Potteries** a region of W central England, in Staffordshire, where many china industries are situated

potter's wheel *n* a flat spinning disc on which clay is shaped by hand

pottery *n, pl* **-teries 1** articles made from baked clay **2** a place where such articles are made **3** the craft of making such articles

potting shed *n* a garden hut in which plants are put in flowerpots and potting materials are stored

potty[1] *adj* **-tier, -tiest** *informal* **1** foolish or slightly crazy **2** trivial or insignificant **3** (foll. by *about*) very keen (on) [origin unknown] **pottiness** *n*

potty[2] *n, pl* **-ties** a bowl used as a toilet by a small child

pouch *n* **1** a small bag **2** a baglike pocket in various animals, such as the cheek fold in hamsters ▹ *vb* **3** to place in or as if in a pouch **4** to make or be made into a pouch [Old French *poche* bag]

pouf *or* **pouffe** (**poof**) *n* a large solid cushion used as a seat [French]

poulterer *n Brit* a person who sells poultry

poultice (pole-tiss) *n med* a moist dressing, often heated, applied to painful and swollen parts of the body [Latin *puls* a thick porridge]

poultry *n* domestic fowls [Old French *pouletrie*]

pounce *vb* **pouncing, pounced 1** (often foll. by *on* or *upon*) to spring upon suddenly to attack or capture ▹ *n* **2** the act of pouncing; a spring or swoop [origin unknown]

pound[1] *n* **1** the standard monetary unit of the United Kingdom and some other countries, made up of 100 pence. Official name: **pound sterling 2** the standard monetary unit of various other countries, such as Cyprus and Malta **3** a unit of weight made up of 16 ounces and equal to 0.454 kilograms [Old English *pund*]

pound[2] *vb* **1** (sometimes foll. by *on* or *at*) to hit heavily and repeatedly **2** to crush to pieces or to powder **3** (foll. by *out*) to produce, by typing heavily **4** (of the heart) to throb heavily **5** to run with heavy steps [Old English *pūnian*]

pound[3] *n* an enclosure for stray dogs or officially removed vehicles [Old English *pund-*]

poundage *n* **1** a charge of so much per pound of weight **2** a charge of so much per pound sterling

-pounder *combining form* **1** something weighing a specified number of pounds: *a 200-pounder* **2** something worth a specified number of pounds: *a ten-pounder* **3** a gun that discharges a shell weighing a specified number of pounds: *a two-pounder*

pour *vb* **1** to flow or cause to flow out in a stream **2** to rain heavily **3** to be given or obtained in large amounts: *suggestions are pouring in* **4** to move together in large numbers: *the fans poured onto the pitch* [origin unknown]

> **USAGE** The verbs *pour* and *pore* are sometimes confused: *she poured cream over her strudel; she pored (not poured) over the manuscript.*

pout *vb* **1** to thrust out (the lips) sullenly or provocatively ▹ *n* **2** a pouting [origin unknown]

pouter *n* a breed of domestic pigeon that can puff out its crop

poutine (poo-**teen**) *n Canad* a dish of chipped potatoes topped with curd cheese and gravy [Canadian French]

poverty *n* **1** the state of lacking adequate food or money **2** lack or scarcity: *a poverty of information* **3** inferior quality or inadequacy: *the poverty of political debate in this country* [Old French *poverté*]

poverty-stricken *adj* extremely poor

poverty trap *n* the situation of being unable to raise one's living standard because any extra

P

income would result in state benefits being reduced or withdrawn
pow *interj* an exclamation to indicate that a collision or explosion has taken place
POW prisoner of war
powder *n* **1** a substance in the form of tiny loose particles **2** a medicine or cosmetic in this form ▷ *vb* **3** to cover or sprinkle with powder [Old French *poldre*, from Latin *pulvis* dust]
powdery *adj*
powdered *adj* **1** sold in the form of a powder, esp. one which has been formed by grinding or drying the original material: *powdered milk* **2** covered or made up with a cosmetic in the form of a powder: *liveried footmen in powdered wigs*
powder keg *n* **1** a potential source of violence or disaster: *a political powder keg* **2** a small barrel for holding gunpowder
powder puff *n* a soft pad used to apply cosmetic powder to the skin
powder room *n* *euphemistic* a women's cloakroom or toilet
power *n* **1** ability to do something **2** (*often pl*) a specific ability or faculty **3** political, financial, or social force or authority: *the strong have power over the weak; economic power is the bedrock of political power* **4** a position of control, esp. over the running of a country: *he seized power in a coup in 1966* **5** a state with political, industrial, or military strength **6** a person or group having authority **7** a prerogative or privilege: *the power of veto* **8** official or legal authority **9** *maths* the value of a number or quantity raised to some exponent **10** *physics & engineering* a measure of the rate of doing work expressed as the work done per unit of time **11** the rate at which electrical energy is fed into or taken from a device or system, measured in watts **12** mechanical energy as opposed to manual labour **13** a particular form of energy: *nuclear power* **14** the magnifying capacity of a lens or optical system **15** *informal* a great deal: *a power of good* **16** **the powers that be** established authority ▷ *vb* **17** to supply with power ▷ *adj* **18** producing or using electrical energy: *a large selection of power tools* [Anglo-Norman *poer*]
powerboat *n* a fast powerful motorboat
power cut *n* a temporary interruption in the supply of electricity
powerful *adj* **1** having great power or influence **2** having great physical strength **3** extremely effective: *a powerful drug* **powerfully** *adv* **powerfulness** *n*
powerhouse *n* **1** *informal* a forceful person or thing **2** an electrical generating station
powerless *adj* without power or authority; unable to act **powerlessly** *adv* **powerlessness** *n*
power of attorney *n* **1** legal authority to act for another person **2** the document conferring such authority
power plant *n* another name for **power station**
power play *n* **1** behaviour or tactics intended to magnify a person's influence or power **2** the use of brute strength or force of numbers in order to achieve an objective
power point *n* an electrical socket fitted into a wall for plugging in electrical appliances
power pole *n* *Austral & NZ* a pole carrying an overhead power line
power-sharing *n* a political arrangement in which opposing groups in a society participate in government
power station *n* an installation for generating and distributing electricity
power steering *n* a type of steering in vehicles in which the turning of the steering wheel is assisted by power from the engine
powwow *n* **1** a talk or meeting **2** a meeting of Native Americans ▷ *vb* **3** to hold a powwow [from a Native American language]
pox *n* **1** a disease in which pus-filled blisters or pimples form on the skin **2** **the pox** *informal* syphilis [changed from *pocks*, plural of *pock*]
pp **1** past participle **2** (in signing documents on behalf of someone else) by delegation to [Latin *per procurationem*]

> **USAGE** In formal correspondence, when Brenda Smith is signing on behalf of Peter Jones, she should write *Peter Jones pp* (or *per pro*) *Brenda Smith*, not the other way about.

pp. pages
PPS **1** parliamentary private secretary **2** additional postscript [Latin *post postscriptum*]
PPTA (in New Zealand) Post Primary Teachers' Association
PQ **1** Province of Quebec **2** (in Canada) Parti Québecois
PQE *or* **Pqe** post-qualification experience
pr *pl* **prs** pair
Pr *chem* praseodymium
PR **1** proportional representation **2** public relations
pr. **1** price **2** pronoun
practicable *adj* **1** capable of being done **2** usable [French *praticable*] **practicability** *n*

> **USAGE** See at **practical**.

practical *adj* **1** involving experience or actual use rather than theory **2** concerned with everyday matters: *the kind of practical and emotional upheaval that divorce can bring* **3** sensible, useful, and effective rather than fashionable or attractive: *it's a marvellous design, because it's comfortable, it's practical, and it actually looks good* **4** involving the simple basics: *practical skills* **5** being very close to (a state); virtual: *it's a practical certainty* ▷ *n* **6** an examination or lesson in which something has to be made or done [Greek *praktikos*, from *prassein* to experience] **practicality** *n* **practically** *adv*

> **USAGE** A distinction is usually made between *practical* and *practicable*. *Practical* refers to a person, idea, project, etc., as being more concerned with or relevant to practice than theory: *he is a very practical person; the idea had no practical application*. *Practicable* refers to a project or idea as being capable of being done or put into effect: *the plan was expensive, yet practicable*.

practical joke *n* a trick intended to make someone look foolish **practical joker** *n*
practice *n* **1** something done regularly or repeatedly **2** repetition of an activity in order to gain skill: *regular practice is essential if you want to play an instrument well* **3** the business or surgery of a doctor or lawyer **4** the act of doing something:

P

I'm not sure how effective these methods will be when put into practice **5 in practice** **A** what actually happens as distinct from what is supposed to happen: *many ideas which look good on paper just don't work in practice* **B** skilled in something through having had a lot of regular recent experience at it: *I still go shooting, just to keep in practice* **6 out of practice** not having had much regular recent experience at an activity: *although out of practice, I still love playing my violin* [Greek *praktikē* practical work]

practise *or US* **practice** *vb* **-tising, -tised** *or* **-ticing, -ticed 1** to do repeatedly in order to gain skill **2** to take part in or follow (a religion, etc.): *none of them practise Islam* **3** to work at (a profession): *he originally intended to practise medicine* **4** to do regularly: *they practise meditation* [Greek *prattein* to do]

practised *or US* **practiced** *adj* expert or skilled because of long experience in a skill or field: *the doctor answered with a practised smoothness*

practising *or US* **practicing** *adj* taking part in an activity or career on a regular basis: *a practising barrister*

practitioner *n* a person who practises a profession

praetor (**pree**-tor) *n* (in ancient Rome) a senior magistrate ranking just below the consuls [Latin] **praetorian** *adj, n*

pragmatic *adj* **1** concerned with practical consequences rather than theory **2** *philosophy* of pragmatism [Greek *pragmatikos*] **pragmatically** *adv*

pragmatism *n* **1** policy dictated by practical consequences rather than by theory **2** *philosophy* the doctrine that the content of a concept consists only in its practical applicability **pragmatist** *n, adj*

prairie *n* (*often pl*) a large treeless area of grassland of North America [French, from Latin *pratum* meadow]

P

prairie dog *n* a rodent that lives in burrows in the N American prairies

praise *vb* **praising, praised 1** to express admiration or approval for **2** to express thanks and worship to (one's God) ▷ *n* **3** the expression of admiration or approval **4 sing someone's praises** to praise someone highly [Latin *pretium* prize]

praiseworthy *adj* deserving praise; commendable

praline (**prah**-leen) *n* a sweet made of nuts with caramelized sugar [French]

pram *n* a four-wheeled carriage for a baby, pushed by a person on foot [altered from *perambulator*]

prance *vb* **prancing, pranced 1** to walk with exaggerated movements **2** (of an animal) to move with high springing steps ▷ *n* **3** the act of prancing [origin unknown]

prang *Brit & Austral slang* ▷ *n* **1** a crash in an aircraft or car ▷ *vb* **2** to crash or damage (an aircraft or car) [perhaps imitative]

prank *n* a mischievous trick [origin unknown] **prankster** *n*

praseodymium (pray-zee-oh-**dim**-ee-um) *n* *chem* a silvery-white element of the lanthanide series of metals. Symbol: **Pr** [New Latin]

prat *n* *Brit, Austral & NZ slang* an incompetent or ineffectual person [probably special use of earlier *prat* buttocks, origin unknown]

prate *vb* **prating, prated 1** to talk idly and at length ▷ *n* **2** chatter [Germanic]

prattle *vb* **-tling, -tled 1** to chatter in a foolish or childish way ▷ *n* **2** foolish or childish talk [Middle Low German *pratelen* to chatter]

prawn *n* a small edible shellfish [origin unknown]

praxis *n* **1** practice as opposed to the theory **2** accepted practice or custom [Greek: deed, action]

pray *vb* **1** to say prayers (to one's God) **2** to ask earnestly; beg ▷ *adv* **3** *archaic* I beg you; please: *pray, leave us alone* [Latin *precari* to implore]

prayer[1] *n* **1** a thanksgiving or an appeal spoken to one's God **2** a set form of words used in praying: *the Lord's Prayer* **3** an earnest request **4** the practice of praying: *call the faithful to prayer* **5** (*often pl*) a form of devotion spent mainly praying: *morning prayers* **6** something prayed for

prayer[2] *n* a person who prays

prayer book *n* a book of prayers used in church or at home

prayer mat *or* **prayer rug** *n* the small carpet on which a Muslim performs his or her daily prayers

prayer wheel *n* *Buddhism* (in Tibet) a cylinder inscribed with prayers, each turning of which is counted as an uttered prayer

praying mantis *n* same as **mantis**

pre- *prefix* before in time or position: *predate; pre-eminent* [Latin *prae*]

preach *vb* **1** to talk on a religious theme as part of a church service **2** to speak in support of (something) in a moralizing way [Latin *praedicare* to proclaim]

preacher *n* a person who preaches

preamble *n* an introduction that comes before something spoken or written [Latin *prae* before + *ambulare* to walk]

prearranged *adj* arranged beforehand **prearrangement** *n*

prebend *n* **1** the allowance paid by a cathedral or collegiate church to a canon or member of the chapter **2** the land or tithe from which this is paid [Old French *prébende*] **prebendal** *adj*

prebendary *n, pl* **-daries** a member of the clergy who is a member of the chapter of a cathedral

Precambrian *or* **Pre-Cambrian** *adj* *geol* of the earliest geological era, lasting from about 4500 million years ago to 600 million years ago

precancerous *adj* relating to cells that show signs that they may develop cancer

precarious *adj* (of a position or situation) dangerous or insecure [Latin *precarius* obtained by begging] **precariously** *adv*

precaution *n* an action taken in advance to prevent an undesirable event [Latin *prae* before + *cavere* to beware] **precautionary** *adj*

precede *vb* **-ceding, -ceded** to go or be before (someone or something) in time, place, or rank [Latin *praecedere*]

precedence (**press**-i-denss) *n* formal order of rank or position

precedent *n* **1** a previous occurrence used to justify taking the same action in later similar situations **2** *law* a judicial decision that serves as an authority for deciding a later case ▷ *adj* **3** preceding
precentor *n* a person who leads the singing in church services [Latin *prae* before + *canere* to sing]
precept *n* **1** a rule of conduct **2** a rule for morals **3** *law* a writ or warrant [Latin *praeceptum*] **preceptive** *adj*
preceptor *n rare* an instructor **preceptorial** *adj*
precession *n* **1** the act of preceding **2** the motion of a spinning body, in which the axis of rotation sweeps out a cone **3** **precession of the equinoxes** the slightly earlier occurrence of the equinoxes each year [Latin *praecedere* to precede]
precinct *n* **1** *Brit, Austral & S African* an area in a town closed to traffic: *a shopping precinct* **2** *Brit, Austral & S African* an enclosed area around a building **3** *US* an administrative area of a city [Latin *praecingere* to surround]
precincts *pl n* the surrounding region
preciosity (presh-ee-**oss**-it-ee) *n, pl* **-ties** affectation
precious *adj* **1** very costly or valuable: *precious jewellery* **2** loved and treasured **3** very affected in speech, manners, or behaviour ▷ *adv* **4** *informal* very: *there's precious little to do in this town* [Latin *pretiosus* valuable]
precious metal *n* gold, silver, or platinum
precious stone *n* a rare mineral, such as diamond, ruby, or opal, that is highly valued as a gem
precipice *n* the very steep face of a cliff [Latin *praecipitium* steep place]
precipitant *adj* **1** hasty or rash **2** rushing or falling rapidly ▷ *n* **3** something which helps bring about an event or condition: *stressful events are often the precipitant for a manic attack*
precipitate *vb* **-tating, -tated** **1** to cause to happen earlier than expected: *the scandal could bring the government down, precipitating a general election* **2** to condense or cause to condense and fall as snow or rain **3** *chem* to cause to be deposited in solid form from a solution **4** to throw from a height: *the encircled soldiers chose to precipitate themselves into the ocean* ▷ *adj* **5** done rashly or hastily **6** rushing ahead ▷ *n* **7** *chem* a precipitated solid [Latin *praecipitare* to throw down headlong]
precipitation *n* **1** the formation of a chemical precipitate **2** *meteorol* **A** rain, hail, snow, or sleet formed by condensation of water vapour in the atmosphere **B** the falling of these **3** rash haste: *they decamped with the utmost precipitation*
precipitous *adj* **1** very steep: *precipitous cliffs* **2** very quick and severe: *a precipitous decline* **3** rapid and unplanned; hasty: *European governments urged the Americans not to make a precipitous decision*

USAGE The use of *precipitous* to mean *hasty* is thought by some people to be incorrect.

précis (**pray**-see) *n, pl* **précis** **1** a short summary of a longer text ▷ *vb* **2** to make a précis of [French]
precise *adj* **1** particular or exact: *this precise moment* **2** strictly correct in amount or value: *precise measurements* **3** working with total accuracy: *precise instruments* **4** strict in observing rules or standards [Latin *prae* before + *caedere* to cut] **precisely** *adv*
precision *n* **1** the quality of being precise ▷ *adj* **2** accurate: *precision engineering*
preclude *vb* **-cluding, -cluded** *formal* to make impossible to happen [Latin *prae* before + *claudere* to close]
precocious *adj* having developed or matured early or too soon [Latin *prae* early + *coquere* to ripen] **precocity** *n*
precognition *n psychol* the alleged ability to foresee future events [Latin *praecognoscere* to foresee]
preconceived *adj* (of ideas, etc.) formed without real experience or reliable information **preconception** *n*
precondition *n* something that is necessary before something else can come about
precursor *n* **1** something that comes before and signals something to follow; a forerunner **2** a predecessor [Latin *praecursor* one who runs in front]
pred. predicate
predacious *adj* (of animals) habitually hunting and killing other animals for food [Latin *praeda* plunder]
predate *vb* **-dating, -dated** **1** to occur at an earlier date than **2** to write a date on (a document) that is earlier than the actual date
predator *n* an animal that kills and eats other animals
predatory (**pred**-a-tree) *adj* **1** (of animals) habitually hunting and killing other animals for food **2** eager to gain at the expense of others [Latin *praedari* to pillage]
predecease *vb* **-ceasing, -ceased** to die before (someone else)
predecessor *n* **1** a person who precedes another in an office or position **2** an ancestor **3** something that precedes something else: *the library will be more extravagant than its predecessors* [Latin *prae* before + *decedere* to go away]
predestination *n Christian theol* the belief that future events have already been decided by God
predestined *adj Christian theol* determined in advance by God [Latin *praedestinare* to resolve beforehand]
predetermine *vb* **-mining, -mined** **1** to determine beforehand **2** to influence or bias **predetermined** *adj*
predicable *adj* capable of being predicated
predicament *n* an embarrassing or difficult situation [see PREDICATE]
predicant (**pred**-ik-ant) *adj* **1** of preaching ▷ *n* **2** a member of a religious order founded for preaching, usually a Dominican [Latin *praedicans* preaching]
predicate *n* **1** *grammar* the part of a sentence in which something is said about the subject **2** *logic* something that is asserted about the subject of a proposition ▷ *vb* **-cating, -cated** **3** to base or found: *political aims which are predicated upon a feminist view of women's oppression* **4** to declare or assert: *it has been predicated that the consequence of the budget will be immediate recession* **5** *logic* to assert (something)

P

about the subject of a proposition [Latin *praedicare* to assert publicly] **predication** *n* **predicative** *adj*

predict *vb* to tell about in advance; prophesy [Latin *praedicere*] **predictable** *adj* **predictably** *adv* **predictor** *n*

prediction *n* **1** the act of forecasting in advance **2** something that is forecast in advance

predictive *adj* **1** relating to or able to make predictions **2** (of mobile phone technology) enabling mobile phones to predict the word being entered in a text message from the first few letters: *predictive text*

predikant (pred-ik-**ant**) *n* a minister in the Dutch Reformed Church in South Africa [Dutch]

predilection *n formal* a preference or liking [French *prédilection*]

predispose *vb* **-posing, -posed** (often foll. by *to*) **1** to influence (someone) in favour of something: *some scientists' social class background predisposes them to view the natural world in a certain way* **2** to make (someone) susceptible to something: *a high-fat diet appears to predispose men towards heart disease* **predisposition** *n*

predominant *adj* being more important or noticeable than others: *improved living conditions probably played the predominant role in reducing disease in the nineteenth century* **predominance** *n* **predominantly** *adv*

predominate *vb* **-nating, -nated 1** to be the most important or controlling aspect or part: *the image of brutal repression that has tended to predominate since the protests were crushed* **2** to form the greatest part or be most common: *women predominate in this gathering* [Latin *prae* before + *dominari* to rule]

pre-eminent *adj* outstanding **pre-eminence** *n*

pre-empt *vb* to prevent an action by doing something which makes it pointless or impossible: *he pre-empted his expulsion from the party by resigning*

pre-emption *n law* the purchase of or right to buy property in advance of others [Medieval Latin *praeemere* to buy beforehand]

pre-emptive *adj military* designed to damage or destroy an enemy's attacking strength before it can be used: *a pre-emptive strike*

preen *vb* **1** (of birds) to clean or trim (feathers) with the beak **2** to smarten (oneself) carefully **3 preen oneself** (often foll. by *on*) to be self-satisfied [Middle English *preinen*]

pref. **1** preface **2** prefatory **3** preference **4** preferred **5** prefix

prefab *n* a prefabricated house

prefabricated *adj* (of a building) made in shaped sections for quick assembly

preface (**pref**-iss) *n* **1** an introduction to a book, usually explaining its intention or content **2** anything introductory ▹ *vb* **-facing, -faced 3** to say or do something before proceeding to the main part **4** to act as a preface to [Latin *praefari* to say in advance]

prefatory *adj* concerning a preface [Latin *praefari* to say in advance]

prefect *n* **1** *Brit, Austral & NZ* a senior pupil in a school with limited power over the behaviour of other pupils **2** (in some countries) the chief administrative officer in a department [Latin *praefectus* one put in charge]

prefecture *n* the office or area of authority of a prefect

prefer *vb* **-ferring, -ferred 1** to like better: *most people prefer television to reading books* **2** *law* to put (charges) before a court for judgment **3** (*often passive*) to promote over another or others [Latin *praeferre* to carry in front, prefer]

> **USAGE** Normally, *to* is used after *prefer* and *preferable*, not *than*: *I prefer Brahms to Tchaikovsky; a small income is preferable to no income at all*, but *than* or *rather than* should be used to link infinitives: *I prefer to walk than/rather than to catch the train.*

preferable *adj* more desirable or suitable **preferably** *adv*

> **USAGE** Since *preferable* already means *more desirable*, you should not say something is *more preferable* or *most preferable*. See also at **prefer**.

preference *n* **1** a liking for one thing above the rest **2** a person or thing preferred

preference shares *pl n* shares issued by a company which give their holders a priority over ordinary shareholders to payment of dividend

preferential *adj* **1** showing preference: *preferential treatment* **2** indicating a special favourable status in business affairs: *the President is to renew China's preferential trading status* **3** indicating a voting system which allows voters to rank candidates in order of preference: *a multi-option referendum with preferential voting*

preferment *n* promotion to a higher position

prefigure *vb* **-guring, -gured 1** to represent or suggest in advance **2** to imagine beforehand

prefix *n* **1** *grammar* a letter or group of letters put at the beginning of a word to make a new word, such as *un-* in *unhappy* **2** a title put before a name, such as *Mr* ▹ *vb* **3** *grammar* to add (a letter or group of letters) as a prefix to the beginning of a word **4** to put before

pregnant *adj* **1** carrying a fetus or fetuses within the womb **2** full of meaning or significance: *a pregnant pause* [Latin *praegnans*] **pregnancy** *n*

prehensile *adj* capable of curling round objects and grasping them: *a prehensile tail* [Latin *prehendere* to grasp]

prehistoric *adj* of human development before the appearance of the written word **prehistory** *n*

preindustrial *adj* of a time before the mechanization of industry

prejudge *vb* **-judging, -judged** to judge before knowing all the facts

prejudice *n* **1** an unreasonable or unfair dislike or preference **2** intolerance of or dislike for people because they belong to a specific race, religion, or group: *class prejudice* **3** the act or condition of holding such opinions **4** harm or detriment: *conduct to the prejudice of good order and military discipline* **5 without prejudice** *law* without harm to an existing right or claim ▹ *vb* **-dicing, -diced 6** to cause (someone) to have a prejudice **7** to harm: *the incident prejudiced his campaign* [Latin *prae* before + *judicium* sentence]

prejudicial *adj* harmful; damaging

prelacy *n, pl* **-cies** **1** **A** the office or status of a prelate **B** prelates collectively **2** *often offensive* government of the Church by prelates
prelate (prel-it) *n* a high-ranking member of the clergy, such as a bishop [Church Latin *praelatus*, from Latin *praeferre* to hold in special esteem]
preliminaries *pl n* same as **prelims**
preliminary *adj* **1** occurring before or in preparation; introductory ▷ *n, pl* **-naries** **2** an action or event occurring before or in preparation for an activity: *the discussions are a preliminary to the main negotiations* **3** a qualifying contest held before a main competition [Latin *prae* before + *limen* threshold]
prelims *pl n* **1** the pages of a book, such as the title page and contents, which come before the main text **2** the first public examinations in some universities [a contraction of *preliminaries*]
prelude (prel-yewd) *n* **1** **A** an introductory movement in music **B** a short piece of music for piano or organ **2** an event introducing or preceding the main event ▷ *vb* **-luding, -luded** **3** to act as a prelude to (something) **4** to introduce by a prelude [Latin *prae* before + *ludere* to play]
premarital *adj* occurring before marriage: *premarital sex*
premature *adj* **1** happening or done before the normal or expected time: *premature ageing* **2** impulsive or hasty: *a premature judgment* **3** (of a baby) born weeks before the date when it was due to be born [Latin *prae* in advance + *maturus* ripe] **prematurely** *adv*
premedication *n surgery* any drugs given to prepare a patient for a general anaesthetic
premeditated *adj* planned in advance **premeditation** *n*
premenstrual *adj* occurring or experienced before a menstrual period
premenstrual syndrome *or* **premenstrual tension** *n* symptoms, such as nervous tension, that may be experienced because of hormonal changes in the days before a menstrual period starts
premier *n* **1** a prime minister **2** a head of government of a Canadian province or Australian state ▷ *adj* **3** first in importance or rank: *Torbay, Devon's premier resort* **4** first in occurrence [Latin *primus* first] **premiership** *n*
premiere *n* **1** the first public performance of a film, play, or opera ▷ *vb* **-ering, -ered** **2** to give, or (of a film, play, or opera) be, a premiere: *the play was premiered last year in Johannesburg; the movie premieres tomorrow* [French, feminine of *premier* first]
premise *or* **premiss** *n logic* a statement that is assumed to be true and is used as a basis for an argument [Medieval Latin *praemissa* sent on before]
premises *pl n* **1** a piece of land together with its buildings **2** *law* (in a deed) the matters referred to previously
premium *n* **1** an extra sum of money added to a standard rate, price, or wage: *the superior taste persuades me to pay the premium for bottled water* **2** the (regular) amount paid for an insurance policy **3** the amount above the usual value at which something sells: *some even pay a premium of up to 15% for the privilege* **4** great value or regard: *we do put a very high premium on common sense* **5** **at a premium** **A** in great demand, usually because of scarcity **B** at a higher price than usual [Latin *praemium* prize]
Premium Savings Bonds *pl n* (in Britain) savings certificates issued by the government, on which no interest is paid, but there is a monthly draw for cash prizes. Also called: **premium bonds**
premolar *n* a tooth between the canine and first molar in adult humans
premonition *n* a feeling that something unpleasant is going to happen; foreboding [Latin *prae* before + *monere* to warn] **premonitory** *adj*
prenatal *adj* before birth; during pregnancy
preoccupy *vb* **-pies, -pying, -pied** to fill the thoughts or mind of (someone) to the exclusion of other things [Latin *praeoccupare* to capture in advance] **preoccupation** *n*
preordained *adj* decreed or determined in advance
preowned *adj* already used; second-hand
prep *vb* **prepping, prepped** **1** *chiefly US informal* to prepare ▷ *n* **2** *Brit* short for **preparation** (sense 4)
prep. **1** preparation **2** preparatory **3** preposition
prepacked *adj* (of goods) sold already wrapped
prepaid *adj* paid for in advance
preparation *n* **1** the act of preparing or being prepared **2** (*often pl*) something done in order to prepare for something else: *to make preparations for a wedding* **3** something that is prepared, such as a medicine **4** *Brit old-fashioned* **A** homework **B** the period reserved for this
preparatory (prip-par-a-tree) *adj* **1** preparing for: *a preparatory meeting to organize the negotiations* **2** introductory **3** **preparatory to** before: *Imran cleared his throat preparatory to speaking*
preparatory school *n* **1** *Brit & S African* a private school for children between the ages of 6 and 13, generally preparing pupils for public school **2** (in the US) a private secondary school preparing pupils for college
prepare *vb* **-paring, -pared** **1** to make or get ready: *the army prepared for battle* **2** to put together using parts or ingredients: *he had spent most of the afternoon preparing the meal* **3** to equip or outfit, as for an expedition **4** **be prepared to** to be willing and able to: *I'm not prepared to say* [Latin *prae* before + *parare* to make ready]
prepay *vb* **-paying, -paid** to pay for in advance **prepayment** *n*
preponderant *adj* greater in amount, force, or influence **preponderance** *n*
preponderate *vb* **-ating, -ated** to be more powerful, important, or numerous (than): *the good preponderate over the bad* [Late Latin *praeponderare* to be of greater weight]
preposition *n* a word used before a noun or pronoun to relate it to the other words, for example *in* in *he is in the car* [Latin *praepositio* a putting before] **prepositional** *adj*

> **USAGE** The practice of ending a sentence with a preposition (*Venice is a place I should like to go to*) was formerly regarded as incorrect, but is now acceptable and is the preferred form in many contexts.

P

prepossess *vb* **1** to make a favourable impression in advance **2** to preoccupy or engross mentally **prepossession** *n*

prepossessing *adj* making a favourable impression; attractive

preposterous *adj* utterly absurd [Latin *praeposterus* reversed]

prep school *n informal* See **preparatory school**

prepuce (pree-pyewss) *n* **1** the retractable fold of skin covering the tip of the penis; foreskin **2** the retractable fold of skin covering the tip of the clitoris [Latin *praeputium*]

prequel *n* a film, novel, or play that portrays events that occurred before the events of an existing work [from PRE- + (SE)QUEL]

Pre-Raphaelite (pree-raff-a-lite) *n* **1** a member of a group of painters in the nineteenth century who revived the style considered typical of Italian painting before Raphael ▷ *adj* **2** of or in the manner of Pre-Raphaelite painting and painters

prerecord *vb* to record (music or a programme) in advance so that it can be played or broadcast later **prerecorded** *adj*

prerequisite *n* **1** something that is required before something else is possible ▷ *adj* **2** required before something else is possible

prerogative *n* a special privilege or right [Latin *praerogativa* privilege]

pres. **1** present (time) **2** presidential

Pres. President

presage (press-ij) *vb* **-aging, -aged** **1** to be a warning or sign of something about to happen: *the windless air presaged disaster* ▷ *n* **2** an omen **3** a misgiving [Latin *praesagire* to perceive beforehand]

presbyopia *n med* a gradual inability of the eye to focus on nearby objects [Greek *presbus* old man + *ōps* eye]

presbyter *n* **1** (in some episcopal Churches) an official with administrative and priestly duties **2** (in the Presbyterian Church) an elder [Greek *presbuteros* an older man] **presbyterial** *adj*

presbyterian *adj* **1** of or designating Church government by lay elders ▷ *n* **2** someone who supports this type of Church government **presbyterianism** *n*

Presbyterian *adj* **1** of any of the Protestant Churches governed by lay elders ▷ *n* **2** a member of a Presbyterian Church **Presbyterianism** *n*

presbytery *n, pl* **-teries** **1** *Presbyterian Church* a local Church court **2** *RC Church* the residence of a parish priest **3** elders collectively **4** the part of a church east of the choir; a sanctuary [see PRESBYTER]

preschool *adj* of or for children below the age of five: *a preschool playgroup*

prescience (press-ee-enss) *n formal* knowledge of events before they happen [Latin *praescire* to know beforehand] **prescient** *adj*

prescribe *vb* **-scribing, -scribed** **1** *med* to recommend the use of (a medicine or other remedy) **2** to lay down as a rule [Latin *praescribere* to write previously]

prescript *n* something laid down or prescribed

prescription *n* **1** **A** written instructions from a doctor for the preparation and use of a medicine **B** the medicine prescribed **2** written instructions from an optician specifying the lenses needed to correct bad eyesight **3** a prescribing [Legal Latin *praescriptio* an order]

prescriptive *adj* **1** laying down rules **2** based on tradition

presence *n* **1** the fact of being in a specified place: *the test detects the presence of sugar in the urine* **2** impressive personal appearance or bearing: *a person of dignified and commanding presence* **3** the company or nearness of a person: *she seemed completely unaware of my presence* **4** *military* a force stationed in another country: *the American-led military presence in the Gulf* **5** an invisible spirit felt to be nearby: *I felt a presence in the room* [Latin *praesentia* a being before]

presence of mind *n* the ability to stay calm and act sensibly in a crisis

present¹ *adj* **1** being in a specified place: *he had been present at the birth of his son* **2** existing or happening now **3** current: *the present exchange rate* **4** *grammar* of a verb tense used when the action described is happening now ▷ *n* **5** *grammar* the present tense **6** **at present** now **7** **for the present** for now; temporarily **8** **the present** the time being; now ▷ See also **presents** [Latin *praesens*]

present² *n* (prez-int) **1** a gift ▷ *vb* (pri-**zent**) **2** to introduce (a person) formally to another **3** to introduce to the public: *the Museum of Modern Art is presenting a retrospective of his work* **4** to introduce and compere (a radio or television show) **5** to show or exhibit: *they took advantage of every tax dodge that presented itself* **6** to bring about: *the case presented a large number of legal difficulties* **7** to put forward or submit: *they presented a petition to the Prime Minister* **8** to give or offer formally: *he was presented with a watch to celebrate his twenty-five years with the company* **9** to hand over for action or payment: *to present a bill* **10** to portray in a particular way: *her lawyer presented her as a naive woman who had got into bad company* **11** to aim (a weapon) **12** **present arms** to salute with one's weapon [Latin *praesentare* to exhibit]

presentable *adj* **1** fit to be seen by or introduced to other people **2** acceptable: *the team reached a presentable total* **presentability** *n*

presentation *n* **1** the act of presenting or being presented **2** the manner of presenting **3** a talk or lecture; the manner of presenting **4** a formal ceremony in which an award is made **5** a public performance, such as a play or a ballet

present-day *adj* of the modern day; current: *even by present-day standards these were large aircraft*

presenter *n* a person who introduces a radio or television show and links the items in it

presentiment (priz-zen-tim-ent) *n* a sense that something unpleasant is about to happen; premonition [obsolete French *pressentir* to sense beforehand]

presently *adv* **1** soon: *you will understand presently* **2** *chiefly Scot, US & Canad* at the moment: *these methods are presently being developed*

present participle *n grammar* a form of verb, ending in *-ing*, which is used to describe action that is happening at the same time as that of the main verb

present perfect *adj, n grammar* same as **perfect** (senses 7, 8)

presents *pl n law* used in a deed or document to refer to itself: *know all men by these presents*

preservative *n* **1** a chemical added to foods to prevent decay ▷ *adj* **2** preventing decay

preserve *vb* **-serving, -served 1** to keep safe from change or extinction; protect: *we are interested in preserving world peace* **2** to protect from decay or damage: *the carefully preserved village of Cregneish* **3** to treat (food) in order to prevent it from decaying **4** to maintain; keep up: *the 1.2% increase in earnings needed to preserve living standards* ▷ *n* **5** an area of interest restricted to a particular person or group: *tattoos were once the preserve of sailors* **6** (*usually pl*) fruit preserved by cooking in sugar **7** an area where game is kept for private hunting or fishing [Latin *prae* before + *servare* to keep safe] **preservation** *n*

preset *vb* **-setting, -set 1** to set the timer on a piece of equipment so that it starts to work at a specific time ▷ *adj* **2** (of equipment) with the controls set in advance

preshrunk *adj* (of fabric or a garment) having been shrunk during manufacture so that further shrinkage will not occur when washed

preside *vb* **-siding, -sided 1** to chair a meeting **2** to exercise authority: *he presided over the burning of the books* [Latin *praesidere* to superintend]

presidency *n, pl* **-cies** the office or term of a president

president *n* **1** the head of state of a republic, such as the US **2** the head of a company, society, or institution **3** a person who presides over a meeting **4** the head of certain establishments of higher education [Late Latin *praesidens* ruler] **presidential** *adj*

presidium *n* (in Communist countries) a permanent administrative committee [Russian *prezidium*]

press¹ *vb* **1** to apply weight or force to: *he pressed the button on the camera* **2** to squeeze: *she pressed his hand* **3** to compress to alter in shape **4** to smooth out creases by applying pressure or heat **5** to make (objects) from soft material by pressing with a mould **6** to crush to force out (juice) **7** to urge (someone) insistently: *they pressed for an answer* **8** to force or compel: *I was pressed into playing rugby at school* **9** to plead or put forward strongly: *they intend to press their claim for damages in the courts* **10** to be urgent: *time presses* **11** (sometimes foll. by *on* or *forward*) to continue in a determined way: *they pressed on with their journey* **12** to crowd; push: *shoppers press along the pavements* **13 pressed for** short of: *pressed for time* ▷ *n* **14** any machine that exerts pressure to form or cut materials or to extract liquids or compress solids **15** See **printing press 16** the art or process of printing **17** the opinions and reviews in the newspapers: *the government is not receiving a good press at the moment* **18** the act of pressing or state of being pressed: *at the press of a button* **19** a crowd: *a press of people at the exit* **20** a cupboard for storing clothes or linen **21 go to press** to go to be printed: *when is this book going to press?* **22 the press A** news media collectively, esp. newspapers **B** journalists collectively [Old French *presser*]

press² *vb* **1** to recruit (men) forcibly for military service **2** to use for a purpose other than intended: *press into service* [from *prest* to recruit soldiers]

press agent *n* a person employed to obtain favourable publicity for an individual or organization

press box *n* a room at a sports ground reserved for reporters

press conference *n* an interview for reporters given by a prominent person

press gallery *n* an area for newspaper reporters, esp. in a parliament

press gang *n* **1** (formerly) a group of men used to capture men and boys and force them to join the navy ▷ *vb* **press-gang 2** to force (a person) to join the navy by a press gang **3** to persuade (someone) to do something that he or she does not want to do: *he was press-ganged into joining the family business*

pressie *or* **prezzie** *n informal* a present

pressing *adj* demanding immediate attention

press release *n* an official announcement or account of a news item circulated to the press

press stud *n Brit* a fastener in which one part with a projecting knob snaps into a hole on another part

press-up *n* an exercise in which the body is raised from and lowered to the floor by straightening and bending the arms

pressure *n* **1** the state of pressing or being pressed **2** the application of force by one body on the surface of another **3** urgent claims or demands: *to work under pressure* **4** a condition that is hard to bear: *the pressure of grief* **5** *physics* the force applied to a unit area of a surface **6 bring pressure to bear on** to use influence or authority to persuade ▷ *vb* **-suring, -sured 7** to persuade forcefully: *he was pressured into resignation* [Late Latin *pressura* a pressing, from Latin *premere* to press]

pressure cooker *n* an airtight pot which cooks food quickly by steam under pressure **pressure-cook** *vb*

pressure group *n* a group that tries to influence policies or public opinion

pressurize *or* **-rise** *vb* **-rizing, -rized** *or* **-rising, -rised 1** to increase the pressure in (an aircraft cabin, etc.) in order to maintain approximately atmospheric pressure when the external pressure is low **2** to make insistent demands of (someone): *do not be pressurized into making a decision* **pressurization** *or* **-risation** *n*

prestidigitation *n formal* same as **sleight of hand** [French] **prestidigitator** *n*

prestige *n* **1** high status or respect resulting from success or achievements: *a symbol of French power and prestige* **2** the power to impress: *a humdrum family car with no prestige* [Latin *praestigiae* tricks] **prestigious** *adj*

presto *music* ▷ *adv, adj* **1** very fast ▷ *n, pl* **-tos 2** a passage to be played very quickly [Italian]

presumably *adv* one supposes or guesses; probably: *he emerged from what was presumably the kitchen carrying a tray*

presume *vb* **-suming, -sumed 1** to take (something) for granted: *I presume he's dead*

P

2 to dare (to): *I would not presume to lecture you on medical matters, Dr Jacobs* **3** (foll. by *on* or *upon*) to rely or depend: *don't presume on his agreement* **4** (foll. by *on* or *upon*) to take advantage (of): *I'm afraid I presumed on Aunt Ginny's generosity* [Latin *praesumere* to take in advance] **presumedly** *adv* **presuming** *adj*

presumption *n* **1** the act of presuming **2** a basis on which an assumption is made **3** bold insolent behaviour **4** a belief or assumption based on reasonable evidence **presumptive** *adj*

presumptuous *adj* bold and insolent

presuppose *vb* **-posing, -posed 1** to require as a previous condition in order to be true: *the idea of integration presupposes a disintegrated state* **2** to take for granted **presupposition** *n*

preteen *n* a boy or girl approaching his or her teens

pretence *or US* **pretense** *n* **1** an action or claim that could mislead people into believing something which is not true: *the pretence that many unemployed people are on 'training schemes'* **2** a false display; affectation: *she abandoned all pretence of work and watched me* **3** a claim, esp. a false one, to a right, title, or distinction **4** make-believe **5** a pretext: *they were placed in a ghetto on the pretence that they would be safe there*

pretend *vb* **1** to claim or give the appearance of (something untrue): *he pretended to be asleep* **2** to make believe: *the children pretended to be pop stars* **3** (foll. by *to*) to present a claim, esp. a doubtful one: *to pretend to the throne* [Latin *praetendere* to stretch forth, feign]

pretender *n* a person who makes a false or disputed claim to a throne or title

pretension *n* **1** (*often pl*) a false claim to merit or importance **2** the quality of being pretentious

pretentious *adj* **1** making (unjustified) claims to special merit or importance: *many critics thought her work and ideas pretentious and empty* **2** vulgarly showy; ostentatious: *a family restaurant with no pretentious furnishing*

preterite *or esp US* **preterit** (pret-er-it) *grammar* ▷ *n* **1** a past tense of verbs, such as *jumped, swam* **2** a verb in this tense ▷ *adj* **3** expressing such a past tense [Late Latin *praeteritum (tempus)* past (time)]

preternatural *adj* beyond what is natural; supernatural [Latin *praeter naturam* beyond the scope of nature]

pretext *n* a false reason given to hide the real one: *delivering the book had been a good pretext for seeing her again* [Latin *praetextum* disguise, from *praetexere* to weave in front]

prettify *vb* **-fies, -fying, -fied** to make pretty

pretty *adj* **-tier, -tiest 1** attractive in a delicate or graceful way **2** pleasant to look at **3** *informal, often humorous* excellent or fine: *well, this is a pretty state of affairs to have got into* ▷ *adv* **4** *informal* fairly: *I think he and Nicholas got on pretty well* **5 sitting pretty** *informal* in a favourable state [Old English *prættig* clever] **prettily** *adv* **prettiness** *n*

pretty-pretty *adj informal* excessively pretty

pretzel *n* a brittle salted biscuit in the shape of a knot [from German]

prevail *vb* **1** (often foll. by *over* or *against*) to prove superior; gain mastery: *moderate nationalists have until now prevailed over the radicals* **2** to be the most important feature: *a casual good-natured mood prevailed* **3** to be generally established: *this attitude has prevailed for many years* **4 prevail on** *or* **upon** to succeed in persuading: *he had easily been prevailed upon to accept a lift* [Latin *praevalere* to be superior in strength]

prevailing *adj* **1** widespread: *the prevailing mood* **2** most usual: *the prevailing wind is from the west*

prevalent *adj* widespread or common **prevalence** *n*

prevaricate *vb* **-cating, -cated** to avoid giving a direct or truthful answer [Latin *praevaricari* to walk crookedly] **prevarication** *n* **prevaricator** *n*

prevent *vb* **1** to keep from happening: *vitamin C prevented scurvy* **2** (often foll. by *from*) to keep (someone from doing something): *circumstances prevented her from coming* [Latin *praevenire*] **preventable** *adj* **prevention** *n*

preventive *adj* **1** intended to prevent or hinder **2** *med* tending to prevent disease ▷ *n* **3** something that serves to prevent **4** *med* any drug or agent that tends to prevent disease. Also: **preventative**

preview *n* **1** an opportunity to see a film, exhibition, or play before it is shown to the public ▷ *vb* **2** to view in advance

previous *adj* **1** coming or happening before **2** *informal* happening too soon; premature: *such criticism is a bit previous because no definite decision has yet been taken* **3 previous to** before [Latin *praevius* leading the way] **previously** *adv*

prewar *adj* relating to the period before a war, esp. before World War I or II

prey *n* **1** an animal hunted and killed for food by another animal **2** the victim of a hostile person, influence, emotion, or illness: *children are falling prey to the disease* **3 bird** *or* **beast of prey** a bird or animal that kills and eats other birds or animals ▷ *vb* (often foll. by *on* or *upon*) **4** to hunt and kill for food **5** to worry or obsess: *it preyed on his conscience* **6** to make a victim (of others), by profiting at their expense [Old French *preie*]

price *n* **1** the amount of money for which a thing is bought or sold **2** the cost at which something is obtained: *the price of making the wrong decision* **3** *gambling* odds **4 at any price** whatever the price or cost **5 at a price** at a high price **6 what price (something)?** what are the chances of (something) happening now? ▷ *vb* **pricing, priced 7** to fix the price of **8** to discover the price of [Latin *pretium*]

price-fixing *n* the setting of prices by agreement among producers and distributors

priceless *adj* **1** extremely valuable **2** *informal* extremely amusing

pricey *adj* **pricier, priciest** *informal* expensive

prick *vb* **1** to pierce lightly with a sharp point **2** to cause a piercing sensation (in): *a needle pricked her finger* **3** to cause a sharp emotional pain (in): *the film pricked our consciences about the plight of the Afghan refugees* **4 prick up one's ears A** (of a dog) to make the ears stand erect **B** (of a person) to listen attentively ▷ *n* **5** a sudden sharp pain caused by pricking **6** a mark made by a sharp point **7** a sharp emotional pain: *a prick of conscience* **8** *taboo* *slang* a penis **9** *offensive slang* a man who provokes contempt [Old English *prica* point, puncture]

prickle *n* **1** *botany* a thorn or spike on a plant **2** a pricking or stinging sensation ▷ *vb* **-ling, -led** **3** to feel a stinging sensation [Old English *pricel*]

prickly *adj* **-lier, -liest** **1** having prickles **2** tingling or stinging: *he had a prickly feeling down his back* **3** touchy or irritable: *you know how prickly they can be about the issue*

prickly heat *n* an itchy rash that occurs in very hot moist weather

prickly pear *n* **1** a tropical cactus with edible oval fruit **2** the fruit of this plant

pride *n* **1** satisfaction in one's own or another's success or achievements: *his obvious pride in his son's achievements* **2** an excessively high opinion of oneself **3** a sense of dignity and self-respect: *he must swallow his pride and ally himself with his political enemies* **4** one of the better or most admirable parts of something: *the pride of the main courses is the Japanese fish and vegetable tempura* **5** a group of lions **6** **pride and joy** the main source of pride: *the car was his pride and joy* **7** **pride of place** the most important position ▷ *vb* **priding, prided** **8** (foll. by *on* or *upon*) to take pride in (oneself) for [Old English *prȳde*]

prie-dieu (pree-**dyuh**) *n* an upright frame with a ledge for kneeling upon, for use when praying [French *prier* to pray + *Dieu* God]

priest *or fem* **priestess** *n* **1** (in the Christian Church) a person ordained to administer the sacraments and preach **2** a minister of any religion **3** an official who performs religious ceremonies [Old English *prēost*, apparently from *presbyter*] **priesthood** *n* **priestly** *adj*

prig *n* a person who is smugly self-righteous and narrow-minded [origin unknown] **priggish** *adj* **priggishness** *n*

prim *adj* **primmer, primmest** affectedly proper, or formal, and rather prudish [origin unknown] **primly** *adv*

prima ballerina *n* a leading female ballet dancer [Italian: first ballerina]

primacy *n, pl* **-cies** **1** the state of being first in rank, grade, or order **2** *Christianity* the office of an archbishop

prima donna *n, pl* **prima donnas** **1** a leading female opera singer **2** *informal* a temperamental person [Italian: first lady]

primaeval *adj* same as **primeval**

prima facie (prime-a **fay**-shee) *adj, adv* as it seems at first [Latin]

primal *adj* **1** of basic causes or origins **2** chief or most important [Latin *primus* first]

primarily *adv* **1** chiefly or mainly **2** originally

primary *adj* **1** first in importance **2** first in position or time, as in a series: *he argued that the country was only in the primary stage of socialism* **3** fundamental or basic: *the new policy will put the emphasis on primary health care rather than hospital care* **4** being the first stage; elementary: *all new recruits participated in the same primary training courses* **5** relating to the education of children up to the age of 11 or 12 **6** (of an industry) involving the obtaining of raw materials **7** (of the flight feathers of a bird's wing) outer and longest **8** being the part of an electric circuit in which a changing current causes a current in a neighbouring circuit: *a primary coil* ▷ *n, pl* **-ries** **9** a person or thing that is first in position, time, or importance **10** (in the US) an election in which the voters of a state choose a candidate for office. Full name: **primary election** **11** a primary school **12** a primary colour **13** any of the outer and longest flight feathers of a bird's wing **14** a primary part of an electric circuit [Latin *primarius* principal]

primary accent *or* **primary stress** *n* *linguistics* the strongest accent in a word

primary colours *pl n* **1** *physics* the colours red, green, and blue from which all other colours can be obtained by mixing **2** *art* the colours red, yellow, and blue from which all other colours can be obtained by mixing

primary school *n* **1** (in England and Wales) a school for children between the ages of 5 and 11 **2** (in Scotland, Australia and New Zealand) a school for children between the ages of 5 and 12 **3** (in the US and Canada) a school equivalent to the first three or four grades of elementary school

primate[1] *n* a mammal with flexible hands and feet and a highly developed brain, such as a monkey, an ape, or a human being

primate[2] *n* an archbishop [Latin *primas* principal]

prime *adj* **1** first in importance: *the prime aim* **2** of the highest quality: *prime beef* **3** typical: *a prime example* ▷ *n* **4** the time when a thing is at its best **5** a period of power, vigour, and activity: *he was in the prime of life* **6** *maths* short for **prime number** ▷ *vb* **priming, primed** **7** to give (someone) information in advance to prepare him or her **8** to prepare (a surface) for painting **9** to prepare (a gun or mine) before detonating or firing **10** to fill (a pump) with its working fluid, to expel air from it before starting **11** to prepare (something) [Latin *primus* first]

prime meridian *n* the 0° meridian from which the other meridians are worked out, usually taken to pass through Greenwich

Prime Minister *n* the leader of a government

prime mover *n* a person or thing which was important in helping create an idea, situation, etc.: *he was the prime mover behind the coup*

prime number *n* an integer that cannot be divided into other integers but is only divisible by itself or 1, such as 2, 3, 5, 7, and 11

primer[1] *n* **1** a substance applied to a surface as a base coat or sealer **2** a device for detonating the main charge in a gun or mine [see PRIME (verb)]

primer[2] *n* an introductory text, such as a school textbook [Medieval Latin *primarius (liber)* a first (book)]

prime stock *n* NZ livestock in peak condition and ready for killing

primeval (prime-**ee**-val) *adj* of the earliest age of the world [Latin *primus* first + *aevum* age]

primitive *adj* **1** of or belonging to the beginning **2** *biol* of an early stage in development: *primitive amphibians* **3** characteristic of an early simple state, esp. in being crude or basic: *a primitive dwelling* ▷ *n* **4** a primitive person or thing **5** a painter of

P

any era whose work appears childlike or untrained **6** a work by such an artist [Latin *primitivus* earliest of its kind]

primogeniture *n* **1** *formal* the state of being the first-born child **2** *law* the right of an eldest son to inherit all the property of his parents [Medieval Latin *primogenitura* birth of a first child]

primordial *adj formal* existing at or from the beginning [Late Latin *primordialis* original]

primp *vb* to tidy (one's hair or clothes) fussily [probably from *prim*]

primrose *n* **1** a wild plant which has pale yellow flowers in spring ▷ *adj* **2** Also: **primrose yellow** pale yellow **3** of primroses [Medieval Latin *prima rosa* first rose]

primrose path *n* (often preceded by *the*) a pleasurable way of life

primula *n* a type of primrose with brightly coloured funnel-shaped flowers [Medieval Latin *primula (veris)* little first one (of the spring)]

Primus *n trademark* a portable paraffin cooking stove, used esp. by campers

prince *n* **1** a male member of a royal family, esp. the son of the king or queen **2** the male ruler of a small country **3** an outstanding member of a specified group: *Dryden, that prince of poets* [Latin *princeps* first man, ruler]

prince consort *n* the husband of a queen, who is himself a prince

princely *adj* **-lier, -liest 1** of or characteristic of a prince **2** generous or lavish

Prince of Wales *n* the eldest son of the British sovereign

princess *n* **1** a female member of a royal family, esp. the daughter of the king or queen **2** the wife of a prince

Princess Royal *n* a title sometimes given to the eldest daughter of the British sovereign

principal *adj* **1** first in importance, rank, or value: *salt is the principal source of sodium in our diets; the Republic's two principal parties* ▷ *n* **2** the head of a school or other educational institution **3** a person who holds one of the most important positions in an organization: *she became a principal in the home finance department* **4** the leading actor in a play **5** *law* **A** a person who engages another to act as his or her agent **B** a person who takes an active part in a crime **C** the person held responsible for fulfilling an obligation **6** *finance* **A** capital or property, as contrasted with income **B** the original amount of a debt on which interest is calculated [Latin *principalis* chief]
principally *adv*

USAGE See at **principle.**

principal boy *n Brit* the leading male role in a pantomime, traditionally played by a woman

principality *n, pl* **-ties** a territory ruled by a prince

principal parts *pl n grammar* the main verb forms, from which all other verb forms may be deduced

principle *n* **1** a moral rule guiding personal conduct: *he'd stoop to anything – he has no principles* **2** a set of such moral rules: *a man of principle* **3** a basic or general truth: *the principle of freedom of expression* **4** a basic law or rule underlying a particular theory or philosophy: *the government has been deceitful and has violated basic principles of democracy* **5** a general law in science: *the principle of the conservation of mass* **6** *chem* a constituent of a substance that determines its characteristics **7 in principle** in theory though not always in practice **8 on principle** because of one's beliefs [Latin *principium* beginning, basic tenet]

USAGE *Principle* and *principal* are often confused: *the principal* (not *principle*) *reason for his departure; the plan was approved in principle* (not *in principal*).

principled *adj* (of a person or action) guided by moral rules: *principled opposition to the war*

prink *vb* **1** to dress (oneself) finely **2** to preen oneself [probably changed from *prank* to adorn]

print *vb* **1** to reproduce (a newspaper, book, etc.) in large quantities by mechanical or electronic means **2** to reproduce (text or pictures) by applying ink to paper **3** to write in letters that are not joined up **4** to stamp (fabric) with a design **5** to produce (a photograph) from a negative **6** to fix in the mind or memory ▷ *n* **7** printed content, such as newsprint **8** a printed publication, such as a book **9** a picture printed from an engraved plate or wood block **10** printed text, with regard to the typeface: *italic print* **11** a photograph produced from a negative **12** a fabric with a printed design **13** a mark made by pressing something onto a surface **14** See **fingerprint 15 in print A** in printed or published form **B** (of a book) available from a publisher **16 out of print** no longer available from a publisher ▷ See also **print out** [Old French *preindre* to make an impression]

printed circuit *n* an electronic circuit in which the wiring is a metallic coating printed on a thin insulating board

printer *n* **1** a person or business engaged in printing **2** a machine that prints **3** a machine connected to a computer that makes copies on paper of documents or other information held by the computer

printing *n* **1** the process of producing printed matter **2** printed text **3** all the copies of a book printed at one time **4** a form of writing in which the letters are not joined together

printing press *n* a machine used for printing

print out *vb* **1** *computers* to produce (printed information) ▷ *n* **print-out, printout 2** printed information from a computer

prior[1] *adj* **1** previous: *prior knowledge* **2 prior to** before [Latin: previous]

prior[2] *n* **1** the head monk in a priory **2** the abbot's deputy in a monastery [Late Latin: head]
prioress *fem n*

priority *n, pl* **-ties 1** the most important thing that must be dealt with first **2** the right to be or go before others

priory *n, pl* **-ories** a religious house where certain orders of monks or nuns live

prise *or* **prize** *vb* **prising, prised** *or* **prizing, prized** to force open or out by levering [Old French *prise* a taking]

prism *n* **1** a transparent block, often with triangular ends and rectangular sides, used to disperse light into a spectrum or refract it in optical instruments **2** *maths* a polyhedron with parallel bases and sides that are parallelograms [Greek *prisma* something shaped by sawing]

prismatic *adj* **1** of or shaped like a prism **2** exhibiting bright spectral colours; rainbow-like: *prismatic light*

prison *n* **1** a public building used to hold convicted criminals and accused people awaiting trial **2** any place of confinement [Old French *prisun*, from Latin *prensio* a capturing]

prisoner *n* **1** a person kept in prison as a punishment for a crime, or while awaiting trial **2** a person confined by any restraints: *he's a prisoner of his own past* **3 take (someone) prisoner** to capture and hold (someone) as a prisoner

prisoner of war *n* a member of the armed forces captured by an enemy in wartime

prissy *adj* **-sier, -siest** prim and prudish [probably from *prim* + *sissy*] **prissily** *adv*

pristine *adj* **1** completely new, clean, and pure: *pristine white plates* **2** of or involving the original, unchanged, and unspoilt period or state: *the viewing of wild game in its pristine natural state* [Latin *pristinus* primitive]

privacy *n* **1** the condition of being private **2** secrecy

private *adj* **1** not for general or public use: *a private bathroom* **2** confidential or secret: *a private conversation* **3** involving someone's domestic and personal life rather than his or her work or business: *what I do in my private life is none of your business* **4** owned or paid for by individuals rather than by the government: *private enterprise* **5** not publicly known: *they had private reasons for the decision* **6** having no public office, rank, or position: *the Red Cross received donations from private citizens* **7** (of a place) quiet and secluded: *the garden is completely private* **8** (of a person) quiet and retiring: *she was private – her life was her own* ▹ *n* **9** a soldier of the lowest rank in the army **10 in private** in secret [Latin *privatus* belonging to one individual, withdrawn from public life]
privately *adv*

private bill *n* a bill presented to Parliament on behalf of a private individual or corporation

private company *n* a limited company that does not issue shares for public subscription

private detective *n* a person hired by a client to do detective work

privateer *n* **1** a privately owned armed vessel authorized by the government to take part in a war **2** a captain of such a ship

private eye *n informal* a private detective

private income *n* income from sources other than employment, such as investment

private member *n* a Member of Parliament who is not a government minister

private member's bill *n* a law proposed by a Member of Parliament who is not a government minister

private parts *or* **privates** *pl n euphemistic* the genitals

private school *n* a school controlled by a private body, accepting mostly fee-paying pupils

private sector *n* the part of a country's economy that consists of privately owned enterprises

privation *n formal* loss or lack of the necessities of life [Latin *privatio* deprivation]

privative (priv-a-tiv) *adj* **1** causing privation **2** *grammar* expressing lack or absence, for example *-less* and *un-*

privatize *or* **-tise** *vb* **-tizing, -tized** *or* **-tising, -tised** to sell (a state-owned company) to individuals or a private company **privatization** *or* **-tisation** *n*

privet *n* a bushy evergreen shrub used for hedges [origin unknown]

privilege *n* **1** a benefit or advantage granted only to certain people: *a privilege of rank* **2** the opportunity to do something which gives you great satisfaction and which most people never have the chance to do: *I had the privilege of meeting the Queen when she visited our school* **3** the power and advantages that come with great wealth or high social class: *the use of violence to protect class privilege and thwart popular democracy* [Latin *privilegium* law relevant to rights of an individual]

privileged *adj* enjoying a special right or immunity

privy *adj* **privier, priviest 1** *archaic* secret **2 privy to** sharing in the knowledge of something secret ▹ *n, pl* **privies 3** *obsolete* a toilet, esp. an outside one [Old French *privé* something private]

Privy Council *n* **1** the private council of the British king or queen **2** (in Canada) a formal body of advisers of the governor general
Privy Counsellor *n*

privy purse *n* an allowance voted by Parliament for the private expenses of the British king or queen

privy seal *n* (in Britain) a seal affixed to certain documents of state

prize[1] *n* **1** something of value, such as a trophy, given to the winner of a contest or game **2** something given to the winner of any game of chance, lottery, etc. **3** something striven for ▹ *adj* **4** winning or likely to win a prize: *a prize bull* [Old French *prise* a capture]

prize[2] *vb* **prizing, prized** to value highly [Old French *preisier* to praise]

prizefight *n* a boxing match for a prize or purse
prizefighter *n*

pro[1] *adv* **1** in favour of a motion, etc. ▹ *prep* **2** in favour of ▹ *n, pl* **pros 3** (*usually pl*) an argument or vote in favour of a proposal or motion ▹ See also **pros and cons** [Latin: in favour of]

pro[2] *informal* ▹ *adj* **1** short for **professional** (senses 2, 4) ▹ *n, pl* **pros 2** short for **professional** (sense 5) **3** a prostitute

PRO public relations officer

pro-[1] *prefix* **1** in favour of; supporting: *pro-Chinese* **2** acting as a substitute for: *pronoun* [Latin]

pro-[2] *prefix* before in time or position: *proboscis* [Greek]

proactive *adj* tending to initiate change rather than reacting to events

probability *n, pl* **-ties 1** the condition of being probable **2** an event or other thing that is likely to happen or be true **3** *statistics* a measure of the likelihood of an event happening

probable *adj* **1** likely to happen or be true **2** most likely: *the probable cause of the accident* ▹ *n* **3** a person who is likely to be chosen for a team, event, etc. [Latin *probabilis* that may be proved]

probably *adv* in all likelihood or probability: *the wedding's probably going to be in late August*

probate *n* **1** the process of officially proving the validity of a will **2** the official certificate stating that a will is genuine [Latin *probare* to inspect]

probation *n* **1** a system of dealing with offenders, esp. juvenile ones, by placing them under supervision **2 on probation A** under the supervision of a probation officer **B** undergoing a test or trial period, such as at the start of a new job [Latin *probare* to test] **probationary** *adj*

probationer *n* **1** a person on a trial period in a job **2** a person under the supervision of a probation officer

probation officer *n* an officer of a court who supervises offenders placed on probation

probe *vb* **probing, probed 1** to investigate, or look into, closely **2** to poke or examine (something) with or as if with a probe: *he probed carefully with his fingertips* ▷ *n* **3** *surgery* a slender instrument for exploring a wound, etc. **4** a thorough inquiry, such as one into corrupt practices **5** See **space probe** [Latin *probare* to test]

probiotic *n* **1** a bacterium that protects the body from harmful bacteria ▷ *adj* **2** of or relating to probiotics: *probiotic yogurts*

probity *n formal* honesty; integrity [Latin *probitas* honesty]

problem *n* **1** something or someone that is difficult to deal with **2** a puzzle or question set for solving **3** *maths* a statement requiring a solution usually by means of several operations ▷ *adj* **4** of a literary work that deals with difficult moral questions: *a problem play* **5** difficult to deal with or creating difficulties for others: *a problem child* [Greek *problēma* something put forward]

problematic *or* **problematical** *adj* difficult to solve or deal with

proboscis (pro-**boss**-iss) *n* **1** a long flexible trunk or snout, such as an elephant's **2** the elongated mouthpart of certain insects [Greek *proboskis* trunk of an elephant]

procedure *n* **1** a way of doing something, esp. an established method **2** the established form of conducting the business of a legislature **procedural** *adj*

proceed *vb* **1** to advance or carry on, esp. after stopping **2** (often foll. by *with*) to start or continue doing: *he proceeded to pour himself a cup of tea* **3** *formal* to walk or go **4** (often foll. by *against*) to start a legal action **5** *formal* to arise (from): *their mutual dislike proceeded from differences of political opinion* [Latin *procedere* to advance]

proceeding *n* **1** an act or course of action **2 proceedings** the events of an occasion: *millions watched the proceedings on television* **3 proceedings** the minutes of the meetings of a society **4 proceedings** legal action

proceeds *pl n* the amount of money obtained from an event or activity

process[1] *n* **1** a series of actions or changes: *a process of genuine national reconciliation* **2** a series of natural developments which result in an overall change: *the ageing process* **3** a method of doing or producing something: *the various production processes use up huge amounts of water* **4 A** a summons to appear in court **B** an action at law **5** a natural outgrowth or projection of a part or organism **6 in the process of** during or in the course of ▷ *vb* **7** to handle or prepare by a special method of manufacture **8** *computers* to perform operations on (data) in order to obtain the required information [Latin *processus* an advancing]

process[2] *vb* to move in an orderly or ceremonial group: *the cult members processed through the streets to the music of tambourines*

processed *adj* (of food) treated by adding colouring, preservatives, etc., to improve its appearance or the period it will stay edible: *processed cheese*

procession *n* **1** a line of people or vehicles moving forwards in an orderly or ceremonial manner **2** the act of proceeding in a regular formation [Latin *processio* a marching forwards]

processional *adj* **1** of or suitable for a procession: *the processional route* ▷ *n* **2** *Christianity* a hymn sung as the clergy enter church

processor *n* **1** *computers* same as **central processing unit 2** a person or thing that carries out a process

proclaim *vb* **1** to announce publicly; declare: *Greece was proclaimed an independent kingdom in 1832* **2** to indicate plainly: *the sharp hard glint in the eye proclaimed her determination* [Latin *proclamare* to shout aloud] **proclamation** *n*

proclivity *n, pl* **-ties** *formal* a tendency or inclination [Latin *proclivitas*]

procrastinate *vb* **-nating, -nated** to put off (an action) until later; delay [Latin *procrastinare* to postpone until tomorrow] **procrastination** *n* **procrastinator** *n*

procreate *vb* **-ating, -ated** *formal* to produce (offspring) [Latin *procreare*] **procreative** *adj* **procreation** *n*

Procrustean *adj* ruthlessly enforcing uniformity [after *Procrustes*, robber in Greek myth who fitted travellers into his bed by stretching or lopping off their limbs]

proctor *n* a member of the staff of certain universities having duties including the enforcement of discipline [syncopated variant of *procurator*] **proctorial** *adj*

procurator fiscal *n* (in Scotland) a legal officer who acts as public prosecutor and coroner

procure *vb* **-curing, -cured 1** to get or provide: *it remained very difficult to procure food and fuel* **2** to obtain (people) to act as prostitutes [Latin *procurare* to look after] **procurement** *n*

procurer *n* a person who obtains people to act as prostitutes

prod *vb* **prodding, prodded 1** to poke with a pointed object **2** to rouse (someone) to action ▷ *n* **3** the act of prodding **4** a reminder [origin unknown]

prodigal *adj* **1** recklessly wasteful or extravagant **2 prodigal of** lavish with: *you are prodigal of both your toil and your talent* ▷ *n* **3** a person who squanders money [Latin *prodigere* to squander] **prodigality** *n*

P

prodigious *adj* **1** very large or immense **2** wonderful or amazing [Latin *prodigiosus* marvellous]

prodigy *n, pl* **-gies 1** a person, esp. a child, with marvellous talent **2** anything that is a cause of wonder [Latin *prodigium* an unnatural happening]

produce *vb* **-ducing, -duced 1** to bring (something) into existence **2** to present to view: *he produced his passport* **3** to make: *this area produces much of Spain's best wine* **4** to give birth to **5** to present on stage, film, or television: *the girls and boys write and produce their own plays* **6** to act as producer of ▷ *n* **7** food grown for sale: *farm produce* **8** something produced [Latin *producere* to bring forward] **producible** *adj*

producer *n* **1** a person with the financial and administrative responsibility for a film or television programme **2** a person responsible for the artistic direction of a play **3** a person who supervises the arrangement, performance, and mixing of a recording **4** a person or thing that produces

product *n* **1** something produced **2** a consequence: *their skill was the product of hours of training* **3** *maths* the result achieved by multiplication

production *n* **1** the act of producing **2** anything that is produced **3** the amount produced or the rate at which it is produced **4** *econ* the creation or manufacture of goods and services **5** any work created as a result of literary or artistic effort **6** the presentation of a play, opera, etc. **7** the artistic direction of a play **8** the overall sound of a recording

production line *n* a system in a factory in which an item being manufactured is moved from machine to machine by conveyor belt, and each machine carries out one step in the manufacture of the item

productive *adj* **1** producing or having the power to produce **2** yielding favourable results **3** *econ* producing goods and services that have exchange value: *the country's productive capacity* **4** (foll. by *of*) resulting in: *a period highly productive of books and ideas* **productivity** *n*

product placement *n* the practice of a company of paying for its product to appear prominently in a film or television programme

proem (pro-em) *n formal* an introduction or preface [Greek *pro-* before + *oimē* song]

Prof. Professor

profane *adj* **1** showing disrespect for religion or something sacred **2** secular **3** coarse or blasphemous: *profane language* ▷ *vb* **-faning, -faned 4** to treat (something sacred) with irreverence **5** to put to an unworthy use [Latin *profanus* outside the temple] **profanation** *n*

profanity *n, pl* **-ties 1** the quality of being profane **2** coarse or blasphemous action or speech

profess *vb* **1** to claim (something as true), often falsely: *he professes not to want the job of Prime Minister* **2** to acknowledge openly: *he professed great relief at getting some rest* **3** to have as one's belief or religion: *most Indonesians profess the Islamic faith* [Latin *profiteri* to confess openly] **professed** *adj*

profession *n* **1** a type of work that requires special training, such as in law or medicine **2** the people employed in such an occupation **3** a declaration of a belief or feeling: *a profession of faith* [Latin *professio* public acknowledgment]

professional *adj* **1** of a profession **2** taking part in an activity, such as sport or music, as a means of livelihood **3** displaying a high level of competence or skill: *a professional and polished performance* **4** undertaken or performed by people who are paid: *professional golf* ▷ *n* **5** a professional person **professionalism** *n* **professionally** *adv*

professor *n* **1** the highest rank of teacher in a university **2** *chiefly US & Canad* any teacher in a university or college **3** *rare* a person who professes his or her opinions or beliefs [Latin: a public teacher] **professorial** *adj* **professorship** *n*

proffer *vb formal* to offer for acceptance [Old French *proffrir*]

proficient *adj* skilled; expert [Latin *proficere* to make progress] **proficiency** *n*

profile *n* **1** an outline, esp. of the human face, as seen from the side **2** a short biographical sketch **3** an area of a social media site containing a person's name, picture, and personal information [Italian *profilo*]

profiling *n* the practice of categorizing people and predicting their behaviour according to particular characteristics such as race or age

profit *n* **1** (*often pl*) money gained in business or trade **2** a benefit or advantage ▷ *vb* **-iting, -ited 3** to gain a profit or advantage: *we do not want to profit from someone else's problems* [Latin *proficere* to make progress]

profitable *adj* making money or gaining an advantage or benefit **profitability** *n* **profitably** *adv*

profit and loss *n accounting* an account showing the year's income and expense items and indicating gross and net profit or loss

profiteer *n* **1** a person who makes excessive profits at the expense of the public ▷ *vb* **2** to make excessive profits **profiteering** *n*

profit-sharing *n* a system in which a portion of the net profit of a business is shared among its employees

profligate *adj* **1** recklessly extravagant **2** shamelessly immoral ▷ *n* **3** a profligate person [Latin *profligatus* corrupt] **profligacy** *n*

pro forma *adj* **1** laying down a set form ▷ *adv* **2** performed in a set manner [Latin: for form's sake]

profound *adj* **1** showing or needing great knowledge: *a profound knowledge of Greek literature* **2** strongly felt; intense: *profound relief* **3** extensive: *profound changes* **4** situated at or having a great depth [Latin *profundus* deep] **profoundly** *adv* **profundity** *n*

profuse *adj* **1** plentiful or abundant: *he broke out in a profuse sweat* **2** (often foll. by *in*) generous in the giving (of): *he was profuse in his apologies* [Latin *profundere* to pour lavishly] **profusely** *adv* **profusion** *n*

progenitor (pro-**jen**-it-er) *n* **1** a direct ancestor **2** an originator or founder [Latin: ancestor]

progeny (**proj**-in-ee) *n, pl* **-nies 1** offspring; descendants **2** an outcome [Latin *progenies* lineage]

P

progesterone *n* a hormone, produced in the ovary, that prepares the womb for pregnancy and prevents further ovulation [PRO-¹ + *ge(station)* + *ster(ol)* + *-one*]
prognathous *adj* having a projecting lower jaw
prognosis *n, pl* **-noses 1** *med* a forecast about the course or outcome of an illness **2** any forecast [Greek: knowledge beforehand]
prognosticate *vb* **-cating, -cated 1** to foretell (future events) **2** to indicate or suggest beforehand [Medieval Latin *prognosticare* to predict] **prognostication** *n* **prognosticator** *n*
program *n* **1** a sequence of coded instructions which enables a computer to perform various tasks ▷ *vb* **-gramming, -grammed 2** to arrange (data) so that it can be processed by a computer **3** to feed a program into (a computer) **programmer** *n*
programmable *or* **programable** *adj* capable of being programmed for computer processing
programme *or US* **program** *n* **1** a planned series of events **2** a broadcast on radio or television **3** a printed list of items or performers in an entertainment ▷ *vb* **-gramming, -grammed** *or US* **-graming, -gramed 4** to schedule (something) as a programme [Greek *programma* written public notice] **programmatic** *adj*
programming language *n* a language system by which instructions to a computer are coded, that is understood by both user and computer
progress *n* **1** improvement or development **2** movement forward or advance **3 in progress** taking place ▷ *vb* **4** to become more advanced or skilful **5** to move forwards [Latin *progressus* a going forwards]
progression *n* **1** the act of progressing; advancement **2** the act or an instance of moving from one thing in a sequence to the next **3** *maths* a sequence of numbers in which each term differs from the succeeding term by a fixed ratio
progressive *adj* **1** favouring political or social reform **2** happening gradually: *a progressive illness* **3** (of a dance, card game, etc.) involving a regular change of partners ▷ *n* **4** a person who favours political or social reform **progressively** *adv*
prohibit *vb* **-biting, -bited 1** to forbid by law or other authority **2** to hinder or prevent: *the paucity of information prohibits us from drawing reliable conclusions* [Latin *prohibere* to prevent] **prohibitor** *n*
prohibition *n* **1** the act of forbidding **2** a legal ban on the sale or drinking of alcohol **3** an order or decree that forbids **prohibitionist** *n*
Prohibition *n* the period (1920–33) when making, selling, and transporting alcohol was banned in the US **Prohibitionist** *n*
prohibitive *adj* **1** (esp. of prices) too high to be affordable **2** prohibiting or tending to prohibit: *a prohibitive distance*
project *n* **1** a proposal or plan **2** a detailed study of a particular subject ▷ *vb* **3** to make a prediction based on known data and observations **4** to cause (an image) to appear on a surface **5** to communicate (an impression): *he wants to project an image of a deep-thinking articulate gentleman* **6** to jut out **7** to cause (one's voice) to be heard clearly at a distance **8** to transport in the imagination: *it's hard to project oneself into his situation* [Latin *proicere* to throw down]
projectile *n* **1** an object thrown as a weapon or fired from a gun ▷ *adj* **2** designed to be thrown forwards **3** projecting forwards [New Latin *projectilis* jutting forwards]
projection *n* **1** a part that juts out **2** a forecast based on known data **3** the process of showing film on a screen **4** the representation on a flat surface of a three-dimensional figure or curved line
projectionist *n* a person who operates a film projector
projector *n* an apparatus for projecting photographic images, film, or slides onto a screen
prolapse *pathol* ▷ *n* **1** Also: **prolapsus** the slipping down of an internal organ of the body from its normal position ▷ *vb* **-lapsing, -lapsed 2** (of an internal organ) to slip from its normal position [Latin *prolabi* to slide along]
prolapsed *adj pathol* (of an internal organ) having slipped from its normal position
prolate *adj geom* having a polar diameter which is longer than the equatorial diameter [Latin *prolatus* enlarged]
prole *n chiefly Brit offensive slang* a proletarian
proletarian (pro-lit-**air**-ee-an) *adj* **1** of the proletariat ▷ *n* **2** a member of the proletariat
proletariat (pro-lit-**air**-ee-at) *n* the working class [Latin *proletarius* one whose only contribution to the state was his offspring]
proliferate *vb* **-rating, -rated 1** to increase rapidly in numbers **2** to grow or reproduce (new parts, such as cells) rapidly [Latin *proles* offspring + *ferre* to bear] **proliferation** *n*
prolific *adj* **1** producing a constant creative output: *a prolific author* **2** producing fruit or offspring in abundance **3** (often foll. by *in* or *of*) rich or fruitful [Latin *proles* offspring] **prolifically** *adv*
prolix *adj* (of a speech or piece of writing) overlong and boring [Latin *prolixus* stretched out widely] **prolixity** *n*
prologue *or often US* **prolog** *n* **1** an introduction to a play or book **2** an event that comes before another: *this success was a happy prologue to their transatlantic tour* [Greek *pro-* before + *logos* discourse]
prolong *vb* to make (something) last longer [Late Latin *prolongare*] **prolongation** *n*
prom *n* **1** *Brit* short for **promenade** (sense 1) or **promenade concert 2** *informal* a formal dance held at a high school or college
PROM *n computers* Programmable Read Only Memory
promenade *n* **1** *chiefly Brit* a paved walkway along the seafront at a holiday resort **2** *old-fashioned* a leisurely walk for pleasure or display ▷ *vb* **-nading, -naded 3** *old-fashioned* to take a leisurely walk [French]
promenade concert *n* a concert at which some of the audience stand rather than sit
promethium (pro-**meeth**-ee-um) *n chem* an artificial radioactive element of the lanthanide series. Symbol: **Pm** [from *Prometheus*, in Greek mythology, the Titan who gave fire to mankind]

prominent *adj* **1** standing out from the surroundings; noticeable **2** widely known; famous **3** jutting or projecting outwards: *prominent eyes* [Latin *prominere* to jut out] **prominence** *n* **prominently** *adv*

promiscuous *adj* **1** taking part in many casual sexual relationships **2** *formal* consisting of different elements mingled indiscriminately [Latin *promiscuus* indiscriminate] **promiscuity** *n*

promise *vb* **-mising, -mised 1** to say that one will definitely do or not do something: *I promise I'll have it finished by the end of the week* **2** to undertake to give (something to someone): *he promised me a car for my birthday* **3** to show signs of; seem likely: *she promises to be a fine singer* **4** to assure (someone) of the certainty of something: *everything's fine, I promise you* ▹ *n* **5** an undertaking to do or not do something **6** indication of future success: *a young player who shows great promise* [Latin *promissum* a promise]

Promised Land *n* **1** *Bible* the land of Canaan **2** any longed-for place where one expects to find greater happiness

promising *adj* likely to succeed or turn out well

promissory note *n* *commerce, chiefly US* a written promise to pay a stated sum of money to a particular person on a certain date or on demand

promo *n, pl* **-mos** *informal* an item produced to promote a product, esp. a video used to promote a pop record

promontory *n, pl* **-ries** a point of high land that juts out into the sea [Latin *promunturium* headland]

promote *vb* **-moting, -moted 1** to encourage the progress or success of: *all attempts to promote a lasting ceasefire have failed* **2** to raise to a higher rank or position **3** to encourage the sale of (a product) by advertising **4** to work for: *he actively promoted reform* [Latin *promovere* to push onwards] **promotion** *n* **promotional** *adj*

promoter *n* **1** a person who helps to organize and finance an event, esp. a sports one **2** a person or thing that encourages the progress or success of: *a promoter of peace*

prompt *vb* **1** to cause (an action); bring about: *the killings prompted an anti-Mafia crackdown* **2** to motivate or cause someone to do something: *I still don't know what prompted me to go* **3** to remind (an actor) of lines forgotten during a performance **4** to refresh the memory of ▹ *adj* **5** done without delay **6** quick to act ▹ *adv* **7** *informal* punctually: *at 8 o'clock prompt* ▹ *n* **8** anything that serves to remind [Latin *promptus* evident] **promptly** *adv* **promptness** *n*

prompter *n* **A** a person offstage who reminds the actors of forgotten lines **B** a device which performs a similar function for public speakers, TV presenters, etc

promulgate *vb* **-gating, -gated 1** to put (a law or decree) into effect by announcing it officially **2** to make widely known [Latin *promulgare*] **promulgation** *n* **promulgator** *n*

pron. 1 pronoun **2** pronunciation

prone *adj* **1** having a tendency to be affected by or do something: *I am prone to indigestion* **2** lying face downwards; prostrate [Latin *pronus* bent forward]

prong *n* a long pointed projection from an instrument or tool such as a fork [Middle English]

pronominal *adj* relating to or playing the part of a pronoun

pronoun *n* a word, such as *she* or *it*, that replaces a noun or noun phrase that has already been or is about to be mentioned [Latin *pronomen*]

pronounce *vb* **-nouncing, -nounced 1** to speak (a sound or sounds), esp. clearly or in a certain way **2** to announce or declare officially: *I now pronounce you man and wife* **3** to declare as one's judgment: *he pronounced the wine drinkable* [Latin *pronuntiare* to announce] **pronounceable** *adj*

pronounced *adj* very noticeable: *he speaks with a pronounced lisp*

pronouncement *n* a formal announcement

pronto *adv informal* at once [Spanish: quick]

pronunciation *n* **1** the recognized way to pronounce sounds in a given language **2** the way in which someone pronounces words

proof *n* **1** any evidence that confirms that something is true or exists **2** *law* the total evidence upon which a court bases its verdict **3** *maths & logic* a sequence of steps or statements that establishes the truth of a proposition **4** the act of testing the truth of something **5** an early copy of printed matter for checking before final production **6** *photog* a trial print from a negative **7** (esp. formerly) a defined level of alcoholic content used as a standard measure for comparing the alcoholic strength of other liquids: *Moldavian ruby port, 17° proof* ▹ *adj* **8** (foll. by *against*) able to withstand: *proof against tears* **9** (esp. formerly) having a level of alcoholic content used as a standard measure for comparing the alcoholic strength of other liquids ▹ *vb* **10** to take a proof from (type matter) **11** to render (something) proof, esp. to waterproof [Old French *preuve* a test]

proofread *vb* **-reading, -read** to read and correct (printers' proofs) **proofreader** *n*

proof spirit *n* (in Britain) an alcoholic beverage that contains a standard percentage of alcohol

prop[1] *vb* **propping, propped** (often foll. by *up*) **1** to support (something or someone) in an upright position: *she was propped up by pillows* **2** to sustain or support: *the type of measures necessary to prop up the sagging economy* **3** (often foll. by *against*) to place or lean ▹ *n* **4** something that gives rigid support, such as a pole **5** a person or thing giving moral support [perhaps from Middle Dutch *proppe*]

prop[2] *n* a movable object used on the set of a film or play

prop[3] *n informal* a propeller

prop. 1 proper(ly) **2** property **3** proposition **4** proprietor

propaganda *n* **1** the organized promotion of information to assist or damage the cause of a government or movement **2** such information [Italian] **propagandist** *n, adj*

propagate *vb* **-gating, -gated 1** to spread (information or ideas) **2** *biol* to reproduce or breed **3** *horticulture* to produce (plants) **4** *physics* to transmit, esp. in the form of a wave: *the electrical signal is propagated through a specialized group of conducting fibres*

P

[Latin *propagare* to increase (plants) by cuttings] **propagation** *n* **propagator** *n*

propane *n* a flammable gas found in petroleum and used as a fuel [from *propionic (acid)*]

propel *vb* **-pelling, -pelled** to cause to move forwards [Latin *propellere*] **propellant** *n, adj*

propeller *n* a revolving shaft with blades to drive a ship or aircraft

propene *n* same as **propylene**

propensity *n, pl* **-ties** *formal* a natural tendency: *his problem had always been a propensity to live beyond his means* [Latin *propensus* inclined to]

proper *adj* **1** real or genuine: *a proper home* **2** appropriate or usual: *good wine must have the proper balance of sugar and acid* **3** suited to a particular purpose: *they set out without any proper climbing gear* **4** correct in behaviour: *in those days, it was not considered proper for a woman to be on the stage* **5** excessively moral: *she was very strait-laced and proper* **6** being or forming the main or central part of something: *a suburb some miles west of the city proper* **7** *Brit, Austral & NZ informal* complete: *you made him look a proper fool* [Latin *proprius* special] **properly** *adv*

proper fraction *n* a fraction in which the numerator has a lower absolute value than the denominator, for example $1/2$

proper noun *or* **proper name** *n* the name of a person or place, for example *Iceland* or *Patrick*

property *n, pl* **-ties 1** something owned **2** *law* the right to possess, use, and dispose of anything **3** possessions collectively **4** land or buildings owned by someone **5** a quality or attribute: *the oils have healing properties* **6** same as **prop²** [Latin *proprius* one's own]

prophecy *n, pl* **-cies 1** a prediction **2 A** a message revealing God's will **B** the act of uttering such a message **3** the function or activity of a prophet

P

prophesy *vb* **-sies, -sying, -sied** to foretell

prophet *n* **1** a person supposedly chosen by God to pass on His message **2** a person who predicts the future: *a prophet of doom* **3** a spokesman for, or advocate of, some cause: *a prophet of revolution* [Greek *prophētēs* one who declares the divine will] **prophetess** *fem n*

Prophet *n* **the** the main name used of Mohammed, the founder of Islam

prophetic *adj* **1** foretelling what will happen **2** of the nature of a prophecy **prophetically** *adv*

prophylactic *adj* **1** preventing disease ▷ *n* **2** a drug or device that prevents disease **3** *chiefly US* a condom [Greek *prophulassein* to guard by taking advance measures]

propinquity *n formal* nearness in time, place, or relationship [Latin *propinquus* near]

propitiate *vb* **-ating, -ated** to appease (someone, esp. a god or spirit); make well disposed [Latin *propitiare*] **propitiable** *adj* **propitiation** *n* **propitiator** *n* **propitiatory** *adj*

propitious *adj* **1** favourable or auspicious: *a propitious moment* **2** likely to prove favourable; advantageous: *his origins were not propitious for a literary career* [Latin *propitius* well disposed]

proponent *n* a person who argues in favour of something [Latin *proponere* to propose]

proportion *n* **1** relative size or extent: *a large proportion of our revenue comes from advertisements* **2** correct relationship between parts **3** a part considered with respect to the whole: *the proportion of women in the total workforce* **4 proportions** dimensions or size: *a building of vast proportions* **5** *maths* a relationship between four numbers in which the ratio of the first pair equals the ratio of the second pair **6 in proportion A** comparable in size, rate of increase, etc. **B** without exaggerating ▷ *vb* **7** to adjust in relative amount or size: *the size of the crops are very rarely proportioned to the wants of the inhabitants* **8** to cause to be harmonious in relationship of parts [Latin *pro portione*, literally: for (its, one's) portion]

proportional *adj* **1** being in proportion ▷ *n* **2** *maths* an unknown term in a proportion, for example in $a/b = c/x$, x is the fourth proportional **proportionally** *adv*

proportional representation *n* the representation of political parties in parliament in proportion to the votes they win

proportionate *adj* being in proper proportion **proportionately** *adv*

proposal *n* **1** the act of proposing **2** a suggestion put forward for consideration **3** an offer of marriage

propose *vb* **-posing, -posed 1** to put forward (a plan) for consideration **2** to nominate (someone) for a position **3** to intend (to do something): *I don't propose to waste any more time discussing it* **4** to ask people to drink (a toast) **5** (often foll. by *to*) to make an offer of marriage [Old French *proposer*, from Latin *proponere* to display]

proposition *n* **1** a proposal or offer **2** *logic* a statement that affirms or denies something and is capable of being true or false **3** *maths* a statement or theorem, usually containing its proof **4** *informal* a person or matter to be dealt with: *even among experienced climbers the mountain is considered a tough proposition* **5** *informal* an invitation to engage in sexual intercourse ▷ *vb* **6** *informal* to invite (someone) to engage in sexual intercourse [Latin *propositio* a setting forth]

propound *vb* to put forward for consideration [Latin *proponere* to set forth]

proprietary *adj* **1** denoting a product manufactured and distributed under a trade name **2** possessive: *she watched them with a proprietary eye* **3** privately owned and controlled [Late Latin *proprietarius* an owner]

proprietor *n* an owner of a business establishment **proprietress** *fem n* **proprietorial** *adj*

propriety *n, pl* **-ties 1** the quality or state of being appropriate or fitting **2** correct conduct **3 the proprieties** the standards of behaviour considered correct by polite society [Old French *propriété*, from Latin *proprius* one's own]

propulsion *n* **1** a force that moves (something) forward **2** the act of propelling or the state of being propelled [Latin *propellere* to propel] **propulsive** *adj*

propylene *or* **propene** *n* a gas found in petroleum and used to produce many organic compounds [from *propionic (acid)*]

pro rata *adv, adj* in proportion [Medieval Latin]
prorogue *vb* **-roguing, -rogued** to suspend (Parliament) without dissolving it [Latin *prorogare*, literally: to ask publicly] **prorogation** *n*
prosaic (pro-**zay**-ik) *adj* **1** lacking imagination; dull **2** having the characteristics of prose **prosaically** *adv*
pros and cons *pl n* the advantages and disadvantages of a situation [Latin *pro* for + *con(tra)* against]
proscenium (proh-**see**-nee-um) *n, pl* **-nia** *or* **-niums** the arch in a theatre separating the stage from the auditorium [Greek *pro* before + *skēnē* scene]
proscribe *vb* **-scribing, -scribed 1** to prohibit (something) **2** to condemn (something); outlaw or banish [Latin *proscribere* to put up a public notice] **proscription** *n* **proscriptive** *adj*
prose *n* **1** ordinary spoken or written language in contrast to poetry **2** a passage set for translation into a foreign language **3** commonplace or dull talk [Latin *prosa oratio* straightforward speech]
Prosecco *n* a sparkling Italian white wine, usually dry [from *Prosecco*, a town near Trieste]
prosecute *vb* **-cuting, -cuted 1** to bring a criminal charge against (someone) **2** to continue to do (something): *the business of prosecuting a cold war through propaganda* **3 A** to seek redress by legal proceedings **B** to institute or conduct a prosecution [Latin *prosequi* to follow] **prosecutor** *n*
prosecution *n* **1** the act of bringing criminal charges against someone **2** the institution and conduct of legal proceedings against a person **3** the lawyers acting for the Crown to put the case against a person **4** the carrying out of something begun
proselyte (**pross**-ill-ite) *n* a recent convert [Greek *prosēlutos* recent arrival, convert] **proselytism** *n*
proselytize *or* **-tise** (**pross**-ill-it-ize) *vb* **-tizing, -tized** *or* **-tising, -tised** to attempt to convert (someone)
prosody (**pross**-a-dee) *n* **1** the study of poetic metre and techniques **2** the vocal patterns in a language [Greek *prosōidia* song set to music] **prosodic** *adj* **prosodist** *n*
prospect *n* **1** (*pl*) chances or opportunities for future success: *a job with impossible workloads and poor career prospects* **2** expectation, or something anticipated: *she was terrified at the prospect of bringing up two babies on her own* **3** *old-fashioned* a view or scene: *a prospect of spires, domes, and towers* ▷ *vb* **4** (sometimes foll. by *for*) to search for gold or other valuable minerals [Latin *prospectus* distant view]
prospective *adj* **1** future: *prospective customers* **2** expected or likely: *the prospective loss* **prospectively** *adv*
prospector *n* a person who searches for gold or other valuable minerals
prospectus *n, pl* **-tuses** a booklet produced by a university, company, etc., giving details about it and its activities
prosper *vb* to be successful [Latin *prosperare* to succeed]
prosperity *n* success and wealth
prosperous *adj* wealthy and successful
prostate *n* a gland in male mammals that surrounds the neck of the bladder. Also called: **prostate gland** [Greek *prostatēs* something standing in front (of the bladder)]
prosthesis (pross-**theess**-iss) *n, pl* **-ses** (-seez) *surgery* **A** the replacement of a missing body part with an artificial substitute **B** an artificial body part such as a limb, eye, or tooth [Greek: an addition] **prosthetic** *adj*
prostitute *n* **1** a person who offers sexual intercourse in return for payment ▷ *vb* **-tuting, -tuted 2** to offer (oneself or another) in sexual intercourse for money **3** to offer (oneself or one's talent) for unworthy purposes [Latin *pro-* in public + *statuere* to cause to stand] **prostitution** *n*
prostrate *adj* **1** lying face downwards **2** physically or emotionally exhausted ▷ *vb* **-trating, -trated 3 prostrate oneself** to cast (oneself) face downwards, as in submission **4** to exhaust physically or emotionally [Latin *prosternere* to throw to the ground] **prostration** *n*
prosy *adj* **prosier, prosiest** dull and long-winded **prosily** *adv*
Prot. 1 Protectorate **2** Protestant
protactinium *n chem* a toxic radioactive metallic element. Symbol: **Pa**
protagonist *n* **1** a supporter of a cause: *a great protagonist of the ideas and principles of mutuality* **2** the leading character in a play or story [Greek *prōtos* first + *agōnistēs* actor]
protea (**pro**-tee-a) *n* an African shrub with showy heads of flowers [after *Proteus*, a sea god who could take many shapes]
protean (pro-**tee**-an) *adj* capable of constantly changing shape or form: *he is a protean stylist who can move from blues to ballads with consummate ease* [after *Proteus*; see PROTEA]
protect *vb* **1** to defend from trouble, harm, or loss **2** *econ* to assist (domestic industries) by taxing imports [Latin *protegere* to cover before]
protection *n* **1** the act of protecting or the condition of being protected **2** something that keeps one safe **3 A** the charging of taxes on imports, to protect domestic industries **B** Also called: **protectionism** the policy of such taxation **4** *informal* Also called: **protection money** money paid to gangsters to avoid attack or damage **protectionism** *n* **protectionist** *n, adj*
protective *adj* **1** giving protection: *protective clothing* **2** tending or wishing to protect someone **protectively** *adv* **protectiveness** *n*
protector *n* **1** a person or thing that protects **2** *history* a person who acts for the king or queen during his or her childhood, absence, or incapacity **protectress** *fem n*
protectorate *n* **1** a territory largely controlled by a stronger state **2** the office or term of office of a protector
protégé *or fem* **protégée** (**pro**-tizh-ay) *n* a person who is protected and helped by another [French *protéger* to protect]
protein *n* any of a large group of nitrogenous compounds that are essential for life [Greek *prōteios* primary]

pro tempore *adv, adj* for the time being. Often shortened to: **pro tem**

protest *n* **1** public, often organized, demonstration of objection **2** a strong objection **3** a formal statement declaring that a debtor has dishonoured a bill **4** the act of protesting ▷ *vb* **5** to take part in a public demonstration to express one's support for or disapproval of an action, proposal, etc.: *the workers marched through the city to protest against the closure of their factory* **6** to disagree or object: *'I'm OK,' she protested* **7** to assert in a formal or solemn manner: *all three repeatedly protested their innocence* **8** *US & NZ* to object forcefully to: *students and teachers have protested the budget reductions* [Latin *protestari* to make a formal declaration] **protestant** *adj, n* **protester** *n*

Protestant *n* **1** a follower of any of the Christian Churches that separated from the Roman Catholic Church in the 16th century ▷ *adj* **2** of or relating to any of these Churches or their followers **Protestantism** *n*

protestation *n formal* a strong declaration

protium *n* the most common isotope of hydrogen, with a mass number of 1 [from Greek *prōtos* first]

proto- *or sometimes before a vowel* **prot-** *combining form* **1** first: *protomartyr* **2** original: *prototype* [Greek *prōtos* first]

protocol *n* **1** the rules of behaviour for formal occasions **2** a record of an agreement in international negotiations **3** *computers* a standardized format for exchanging data, esp. between different computer systems [Late Greek *prōtokollon* sheet glued to the front of a manuscript]

proton (pro-ton) *n* a positively charged elementary particle, found in the nucleus of an atom [Greek *prōtos* first]

protoplasm *n biol* a complex colourless substance forming the living contents of a cell [Greek *prōtos* first + *plasma* form] **protoplasmic** *adj*

prototype *n* **1** an early model of a product, which is tested so that the design can be changed if necessary **2** a person or thing that serves as an example of a type

protozoan (pro-toe-zoe-an) *n, pl* **-zoa** a very tiny single-celled invertebrate, such as an amoeba. Also: **protozoon** [Greek *prōtos* first + *zoion* animal]

protract *vb* to lengthen or extend (a situation, etc.) [Latin *protrahere* to prolong] **protracted** *adj* **protraction** *n*

protractor *n* an instrument for measuring angles, usually a flat semicircular piece of plastic

protrude *vb* **-truding, -truded** to stick out or project [PRO-² + Latin *trudere* to thrust] **protrusion** *n* **protrusive** *adj*

protuberant *adj* swelling out; bulging [Late Latin *protuberare* to swell] **protuberance** *n*

proud *adj* **1** feeling pleasure or satisfaction: *she was proud of her daughter's success* **2** feeling honoured **3** haughty or arrogant **4** causing pride: *the city's proud history* **5** dignified: *too proud to accept charity* **6** (of a surface or edge) projecting or protruding ▷ *adv* **7 do someone proud** to entertain someone on a grand scale: *Mum did us all proud last Christmas* [Old French *prud, prod* brave] **proudly** *adv*

proud flesh *n* a mass of tissue formed around a healing wound

prove *vb* **proving, proved, proved** *or* **proven 1** to establish the truth or validity of: *such a claim is difficult to prove scientifically* **2** *law* to establish the genuineness of (a will) **3** to show (oneself) to be: *he proved equal to the task* **4** to be found to be: *it proved to be a trap* **5** (of dough) to rise in a warm place before baking [Latin *probare* to test] **provable** *adj*

proven *vb* **1** a past participle of **prove 2** See **not proven** ▷ *adj* **3** known from experience to work: *a proven ability to make money*

provenance (prov-in-anss) *n* a place of origin [French]

Provençal (prov-on-**sahl**) *adj* **1** of Provence, in SE France ▷ *n* **2** a language of Provence **3** a person from Provence

provender *n old-fashioned* fodder for livestock [Old French *provendre*]

proverb *n* a short memorable saying that expresses a truth or gives a warning, for example *half a loaf is better than no bread* [Latin *proverbium*]

proverbial *adj* **1** well-known because commonly or traditionally referred to **2** of a proverb **proverbially** *adv*

provide *vb* **-viding, -vided 1** to make available **2** to afford; yield: *social activities providing the opportunity to meet new people* **3** (often foll. by *for* or *against*) to take careful precautions: *we provide for the possibility of illness in the examination regulations* **4** (foll. by *for*) to support financially: *both parents should be expected to provide for their children* **5 provide for** *formal* (of a law, treaty, etc.) to make possible: *a bill providing for stiffer penalties for racial discrimination* [Latin *providere* to provide for] **provider** *n*

providence *n* **1** God or nature seen as a protective force that oversees people's lives **2** the foresight shown by a person in the management of his or her affairs

Providence *n Christianity* God, esp. as showing foreseeing care of His creatures

provident *adj* **1** thrifty **2** showing foresight [Latin *providens* foreseeing]

providential *adj* fortunate, as if through divine involvement

provident society *n* same as **friendly society**

providing *or* **provided** *conj* on condition (that): *the deal is on, providing he passes his medical*

province *n* **1** a territory governed as a unit of a country or empire **2** an area of learning, activity, etc. **3 the provinces** those parts of a country lying outside the capital [Latin *provincia* conquered territory]

provincewide *Canad* ▷ *adj* **1** relating to the whole of a province: *a provincewide referendum* ▷ *adv* **2** throughout a province: *an advertising campaign to go provincewide*

provincial *adj* **1** of a province **2** unsophisticated or narrow-minded **3** *NZ* denoting a football team representing a province ▷ *n* **4** an unsophisticated person **5** a person from a province or the provinces **provincialism** *n*

provision *n* **1** the act of supplying something **2** something supplied **3 provisions** food and other necessities **4** a condition incorporated in

a document **5 make provision for** to make arrangements for beforehand: *the company has made provision for future losses* ▷ *vb* **6** to supply with provisions [Latin *provisio* a providing]
provisional *adj* temporary or conditional: *a provisional diagnosis* **provisionally** *adv*
Provisional *n* a member of the Provisional IRA or Sinn Féin
proviso (pro-**vize**-oh) *n, pl* **-sos** *or* **-soes** a condition or stipulation [Medieval Latin *proviso quod* it being provided that] **provisory** *adj*
provocation *n* **1** the act of provoking or inciting **2** something that causes indignation or anger
provocative *adj* provoking or inciting, esp. to anger or sexual desire: *a provocative remark* **provocatively** *adv*
provoke *vb* **-voking, -voked 1** to deliberately act in a way intended to anger someone: *waving a red cape, Delgado provoked the animal into charging* **2** to incite or stimulate: *the army seems to have provoked this latest confrontation* **3** (often foll. by *into*) to cause a person to react in a particular, often angry, way: *keeping your true motives hidden may provoke others into being just as two-faced with you* **4** to bring about: *the case has provoked furious public debate* [Latin *provocare* to call forth] **provoking** *adj*
provost *n* **1** the head of certain university colleges or schools **2** the chief councillor of a Scottish town [Old English *profost*]
provost marshal *n* the officer in charge of military police in a camp or city
prow *n* the bow of a vessel [Greek *prōra*]
prowess *n* **1** superior skill or ability **2** bravery or fearlessness [Old French *proesce*]
prowl *vb* **1** (sometimes foll. by *around* or *about*) to move stealthily around (a place) as if in search of prey or plunder ▷ *n* **2** the act of prowling **3 on the prowl** moving around stealthily [origin unknown] **prowler** *n*
prox. proximo (next month)
proximate *adj* **1** next or nearest in space or time **2** very near **3** immediately coming before or following in a series **4** approximate [Latin *proximus* next]
proximity *n* **1** nearness in space or time **2** nearness or closeness in a series [Latin *proximitas* closeness]
proxy *n, pl* **proxies 1** a person authorized to act on behalf of someone else: *the firm's creditors can vote either in person or by proxy* **2** the authority to act on behalf of someone else [Latin *procuratio* procuration]
proxy server *n computers* a computer that acts as an intermediary between a client machine and a server, caching information to save access time
Prozac *n trademark* an antidepressant drug
prude *n* a person who is excessively modest or prim, esp. regarding sex [Old French *prode femme* respectable woman] **prudery** *n* **prudish** *adj*
prudent *adj* **1** sensible and careful **2** discreet or cautious **3** exercising good judgment [Latin *prudens* far-sighted] **prudence** *n* **prudently** *adv*
prudential *adj old-fashioned* showing prudence: *prudential reasons* **prudentially** *adv*
prune[1] *n* a purplish-black partially dried plum [Latin *prunum* plum]
prune[2] *vb* **pruning, pruned 1** to cut off dead or surplus branches of (a tree or shrub) **2** to shorten or reduce [Old French *proignier* to clip]
prurient *adj* **1** excessively interested in sexual matters **2** exciting lustfulness [Latin *prurire* to lust after, itch] **prurience** *n*
Prussian *adj* **1** of Prussia, a former German state ▷ *n* **2** a person from Prussia
prussic acid *n* the extremely poisonous solution of hydrogen cyanide [French *acide prussique* Prussian acid]
pry *vb* **pries, prying, pried** (often foll. by *into*) to make an impertinent or uninvited inquiry (about a private matter) [origin unknown]
PS 1 Also: **ps** postscript **2** private secretary
PSA (in New Zealand) Public Service Association
psalm *n* (*often cap*) any of the sacred songs that make up a book (Psalms) of the Old Testament [Greek *psalmos* song accompanied on the harp]
psalmist *n* a writer of psalms
psalmody *n, pl* **-dies** the singing of sacred music
Psalter *n* **1** the Book of Psalms **2** a book containing a version of Psalms [Greek *psaltērion* stringed instrument]
psaltery *n, pl* **-teries** an ancient musical instrument played by plucking strings
PSBR (in Britain) public sector borrowing requirement: the money needed by the public sector of the economy for items not paid for by income
psephology (sef-**fol**-a-jee) *n* the statistical and sociological study of elections [Greek *psephos* pebble, vote + -LOGY] **psephologist** *n*
pseud *n informal* a pretentious person
pseudo *adj informal* not genuine
pseudo- *or sometimes before a vowel* **pseud-** *combining form* false, pretending, or unauthentic: *pseudo-intellectual* [Greek *pseudēs* false]
pseudonym *n* a fictitious name adopted, esp. by an author [Greek *pseudēs* false + *onoma* name] **pseudonymity** *n* **pseudonymous** *adj*
psittacosis *n* a viral disease of parrots that can be passed on to humans [Greek *psittakos* a parrot]
psoriasis (so-**rye**-a-siss) *n* a skin disease with reddish spots and patches covered with silvery scales [Greek: itching disease]
psst *interj* a sound made to attract someone's attention, esp. without others noticing
PST Pacific Standard Time
PSV (in Britain, formerly) public service vehicle
psyche *n* the human mind or soul [Greek *psukhē* breath, soul]
psychedelic *adj* **1** denoting a drug that causes hallucinations **2** *informal* having vivid colours and complex patterns similar to those experienced during hallucinations [Greek *psukhē* mind + *delos* visible]
psychiatry *n* the branch of medicine concerned with the study and treatment of mental disorders **psychiatric** *adj* **psychiatrist** *n*
psychic *adj* **1** relating to or having powers (esp. mental powers) which cannot be explained by natural laws **2** relating to the mind ▷ *n* **3** a person who has psychic powers **psychical** *adj*
psycho *informal* ▷ *n, pl* **-chos 1** same as **psychopath** ▷ *adj* **2** same as **psychopathic**

psycho- *or sometimes before a vowel* **psych-** *combining form* indicating the mind or mental processes: *psychology; psychosomatic* [Greek *psukhē* spirit, breath]
psychoactive *adj* capable of affecting mental activity: *a psychoactive drug*
psychoanalyse *or US* **-lyze** *vb* **-lysing, -lysed** *or* **-lyzing, -lyzed** to examine or treat (a person) by psychoanalysis
psychoanalysis *n* a method of treating mental and emotional disorders by discussion and analysis of the patient's thoughts and feelings **psychoanalyst** *n* **psychoanalytical** *or* **psychoanalytic** *adj*
psychogenic *adj psychol* (esp. of disorders or symptoms) of mental, rather than organic, origin
psychological *adj* **1** relating to the mind or mental activity **2** relating to psychology **3** having its origin in the mind: *his backaches are purely psychological* **psychologically** *adv*
psychological moment *n* the best time for achieving the desired response or effect
psychological warfare *n* the military application of psychology, esp. to influence morale in time of war
psychology *n, pl* **-gies 1** the scientific study of all forms of human and animal behaviour **2** *informal* the mental make-up of a person **psychologist** *n*
psychopath *n* a person with a personality disorder which causes him or her to commit antisocial and sometimes violent acts **psychopathic** *adj*
psychopathology *n* the scientific study of mental disorders
psychopathy (sike-**op**-ath-ee) *n* any mental disorder or disease
P
psychosis (sike-**oh**-siss) *n, pl* **-ses** (-seez) a severe mental disorder in which the individual's contact with reality becomes highly distorted: *a classic case of psychosis* **psychotic** *adj*
psychosomatic *adj* (of a physical disorder) thought to have psychological causes, such as stress
psychotherapy *n* the treatment of nervous disorders by psychological methods **psychotherapeutic** *adj* **psychotherapist** *n*
psych up *vb* to prepare (oneself or another) mentally for a contest or task
pt 1 part **2** past tense **3** point **4** port **5** pro tempore
Pt *chem* platinum
PT *old-fashioned* physical training
pt. pint
PTA Parent Teacher Association
ptarmigan (**tar**-mig-an) *n* a bird of the grouse family that turns white in winter
Pte. *military* private
pterodactyl (terr-roe-**dak**-til) *n* an extinct flying reptile with batlike wings [Greek *pteron* wing + *daktulos* finger]
PTO *or* **pto** please turn over
Ptolemaic (tol-lim-**may**-ik) *adj* relating to Ptolemy, the 2nd-century AD Greek astronomer, or to his belief that the earth was in the centre of the universe
ptomaine *or* **ptomain** (**toe**-main) *n* any of a group of poisonous alkaloids found in decaying matter [Greek *ptoma* corpse]
PTSD post-traumatic stress disorder
Pty *Austral & S African* Proprietary
Pu *chem* plutonium
pub *n* **1** *chiefly Brit* a building with a licensed bar where alcoholic drinks may be bought and drunk **2** *Austral & NZ* a hotel
pub. 1 public **2** publication **3** published **4** publisher **5** publishing
pub-crawl *n informal* a drinking tour of a number of pubs
puberty (**pew**-ber-tee) *n* the beginning of sexual maturity [Latin *pubertas* maturity] **pubertal** *adj*
pubes *n, pl* **pubes 1** the region above the genitals **2** the plural of **pubis** ▷ *pl n informal* **3** pubic hair [Latin]
pubescent *adj* **1** arriving or arrived at puberty **2** covered with down, as some plants and animals [Latin *pubescere* to reach manhood] **pubescence** *n*
pubic (**pew**-bik) *adj* of or relating to the pubes or pubis: *pubic hair*
pubis *n, pl* **-bes** one of the three sections of the hipbone that forms part of the pelvis [New Latin *os pubis* bone of the pubes]
public *adj* **1** relating to the people as a whole **2** provided by the government: *public service* **3** open to all: *public gardens* **4** well-known: *a public figure* **5** performed or made openly: *a public proclamation* **6** maintained by and for the community: *a public library* **7** open, acknowledged, or notorious: *a public scandal* **8 go public A** (of a private company) to offer shares for sale to the public: *few German firms have gone public in recent years* **B** to make information, plans, etc., known: *the group would not have gone public with its suspicions unless it was fully convinced of them* ▷ *n* **9** the community or people in general **10** a particular section of the community: *the racing public* [Latin *publicus*] **publicly** *adv*
public-address system *n* a system of microphones, amplifiers, and loudspeakers for increasing the sound level of speech or music at public gatherings
publican *n Brit, Austral & NZ* a person who owns or runs a pub
publication *n* **1** the publishing of a printed work **2** any printed work offered for sale **3** the act of making information known to the public
public bar *n* a bar in a hotel or pub which is cheaper and more basically furnished than the lounge or saloon bar
public company *or* **public limited company** *n* a limited company whose shares may be purchased by the public
public convenience *n formal* a public toilet
public enemy *n* a notorious person who is considered a danger to the public
public house *n* **1** *Brit* a pub **2** *US & Canad* an inn or small hotel
publicist *n* a person, such as a press agent or journalist, who publicizes something
publicity *n* **1** the process or information used to arouse public attention **2** the public interest so aroused

publicize *or* **-cise** *vb* **-cizing, -cized** *or* **-cising, -cised** to bring to public attention
public lending right *n* the right of authors to receive payment when their books are borrowed from public libraries
public prosecutor *n law* an official in charge of prosecuting important cases
Public Protector *n* (in South Africa) an official with powers to investigate irregular government transactions
public relations *n* the practice of gaining the public's goodwill and approval for an organization
public school *n* **1** (in England and Wales) a private independent fee-paying secondary school **2** (in certain Canadian provinces) a public elementary school as distinguished from a separate school **3** (in the US) any school that is part of a free local educational system
public sector *n* the part of a country's economy that consists of state-owned industries and services
public servant *n* **1** an elected or appointed holder of a public office **2** *Austral & NZ* a civil servant
public service *n Austral & NZ* the civil service
public-spirited *adj* having or showing an active interest in the good of the community
public utility *n* an organization that supplies water, gas, or electricity to the public
publish *vb* **1** to produce and issue (printed matter) for sale **2** to have one's written work issued for publication **3** to announce formally or in public [Latin *publicare* to make public] **publishing** *n*
publisher *n* **1** a company or person that publishes books, periodicals, music, etc. **2** *US & Canad* the proprietor of a newspaper
puce *adj* dark brownish-purple: *his face suddenly turned puce with futile rage* [French *couleur puce* flea colour]
puck¹ *n* a small disc of hard rubber used in ice hockey [origin unknown]
puck² *n* a mischievous or evil spirit [Old English *pūca*] **puckish** *adj*
pucker *vb* **1** to gather into wrinkles ▹ *n* **2** a wrinkle or crease [origin unknown]
pudding *n* **1** a dessert, esp. a cooked one served hot **2** a savoury dish with pastry or batter: *steak-and-kidney pudding* **3** a sausage-like mass of meat: *black pudding* [Middle English *poding*]
puddle *n* **1** a small pool of water, esp. of rain **2** a worked mixture of wet clay and sand that is impervious to water ▹ *vb* **-dling, -dled 3** to make (clay, etc.) into puddle [Middle English *podel*] **puddly** *adj*
pudenda *pl n* the human genitals, esp. of a female [Latin: the shameful (parts)]
pudgy *adj* **pudgier, pudgiest** *chiefly US* podgy [origin unknown] **pudginess** *n*
puerile *adj* silly and childish [Latin *puer* a boy] **puerility** *n*
puerperal (pew-er-per-al) *adj* concerning the period following childbirth [Latin *puerperium* childbirth]
puerperal fever *n* a serious, formerly widespread, form of blood poisoning caused by infection during childbirth
puerperium (pure-peer-ee-um) *n* the period after childbirth
puff *n* **1** a short quick blast of breath, wind, or smoke **2** the amount of wind or smoke released in a puff **3** the sound made by a puff **4** an act of inhaling and expelling cigarette smoke **5** a light pastry usually filled with cream and jam **6 out of puff** out of breath: *by the third flight of stairs she was out of puff* ▹ *vb* **7** to blow or breathe in short quick blasts **8** (often foll. by *out*) to cause to be out of breath **9** to take draws at (a cigarette) **10** to move with or by the emission of puffs: *the steam train puffed up the incline* **11** (often foll. by *up* or *out*) to swell [Old English *pyffan*] **puffy** *adj*
puff adder *n* a large venomous African viper whose body swells when alarmed
puffball *n* a ball-shaped fungus that sends out a cloud of brown spores when mature
puffin *n* a black-and-white sea bird with a brightly coloured beak [origin unknown]
puff pastry *or US* **puff paste** *n* a light flaky pastry
pug *n* a small dog with a smooth coat, lightly curled tail, and a short wrinkled nose [origin unknown]
pugilist (pew-jil-ist) *n* a boxer [Latin *pugil* a boxer] **pugilism** *n* **pugilistic** *adj*
pugnacious *adj formal* ready and eager to fight [Latin *pugnax*] **pugnacity** *n*
pug nose *n* a short stubby upturned nose [from *pug* (the dog)] **pug-nosed** *adj*
puissance *n* a showjumping competition that tests a horse's ability to jump large obstacles [see PUISSANT]
puissant (pew-iss-sant) *adj archaic or poetic* powerful [Old French, from Latin *potens* mighty]
puke *slang* ▹ *vb* **puking, puked 1** to vomit ▹ *n* **2** the act of vomiting **3** the matter vomited [probably imitative]
pukeko (poo-kek-oh) *n, pl* **-kos** a brightly coloured New Zealand wading bird [Māori]
pukka *adj Brit old-fashioned* **1** properly done, constructed, etc. **2** genuine or real [Hindi *pakkā* firm]
pulchritude *n formal or literary* physical beauty [Latin *pulchritudo*] **pulchritudinous** *adj*
pule *vb* **puling, puled** *literary* to whine or whimper [imitative]
pull *vb* **1** to exert force on (an object) to draw it towards the source of the force **2** to strain or stretch **3** to remove or extract: *he pulled a crumpled handkerchief from his pocket* **4** *informal* to draw out (a weapon) for use: *he pulled a knife on his attacker* **5** *informal* to attract: *the game is expected to pull a large crowd* **6** *Brit slang* to attract a sexual partner **7** (usually foll. by *on* or *at*) to drink or inhale deeply: *he pulled on his pipe* **8** to possess or exercise the power to move: *this car doesn't pull well on hills* **9** to withdraw or remove: *the board pulled their support* **10** *printing* to take (a proof) from type **11** *golf & baseball etc.* to hit (the ball) in the direction of one's follow-through **12** *cricket* to hit (a ball) to the leg side **13** to row (a boat) or take a stroke of (an oar) in rowing **14 pull a face** to make a grimace **15 pull a fast one** *slang* (often foll. by *on*) to play a sly trick **16 pull apart**

or **to pieces** to criticize harshly **17 pull (one's) punches** to limit the force of one's criticisms or blows ▷ *n* **18** the act of pulling **19** the force used in pulling: *the pull of the moon affects the tides* **20** the act of taking in drink or smoke **21** *printing* a proof taken from type **22** something used for pulling, such as a handle **23** *informal* power or influence: *his uncle is chairman of the company, so he has quite a lot of pull* **24** *informal* the power to attract attention or support **25** a single stroke of an oar in rowing **26** the act of pulling the ball in golf, cricket, etc. ▷ See also **pull down, pull in** *etc.* [Old English *pullian*]

pull down *vb* to destroy or demolish: *the old houses were pulled down*

pullet *n* a hen less than one year old [Old French *poulet* chicken]

pulley *n* a wheel with a grooved rim in which a belt, chain, or piece of rope runs in order to lift weights by a downward pull [Old French *polie*]

pull in *vb* **1** Also: **pull over** (of a motor vehicle) to draw in to the side of the road **2** (often foll. by *to*) to reach a destination: *the train pulled in to the station* **3** to attract: *his appearance will pull in the crowds* **4** *Brit, Austral & NZ slang* to arrest **5** to earn (money): *he pulls in at least thirty thousand a year*

Pullman *n, pl* **-mans** *chiefly Brit* a luxurious railway coach [after G. M. *Pullman*, its inventor]

pull off *vb informal* to succeed in accomplishing (something difficult): *superheroes who pull off the impossible*

pull out *vb* **1** **A** (of a motor vehicle) to draw away from the side of the road **B** (of a motor vehicle) to move out from behind another vehicle to overtake **2** to depart: *the train pulled out of the station* **3** to withdraw: *several companies have pulled out of the student market* **4** to remove by pulling **5** to abandon a situation

pullover *n* a sweater that is pulled on over the head

pull through *vb* to survive or recover, esp. after a serious illness

pull together *vb* **1** to cooperate or work in harmony **2 pull oneself together** *informal* to regain one's self-control

pull up *vb* **1** (of a motor vehicle) to stop **2** to remove by the roots **3** to rebuke

pulmonary *adj* **1** of or affecting the lungs **2** having lungs or lunglike organs [Latin *pulmo* a lung]

pulp *n* **1** a soft wet substance made from matter which has been crushed or beaten: *mash the strawberries to a pulp* **2** the soft fleshy part of a fruit or vegetable: *halve the tomatoes then scoop the seeds and pulp into a bowl* **3** printed or recorded material with little depth or designed to shock: *a music player churned out disco pulp* ▷ *vb* **4** to reduce (a material) to pulp: *he began to pulp the orange in his fingers* [Latin *pulpa*] **pulpy** *adj*

pulpit *n* **1** a raised platform in churches used for preaching **2** (usually preceded by *the*) preaching or the clergy [Latin *pulpitum* a platform]

pulpwood *n* pine, spruce, or any other soft wood used to make paper

pulsar *n* a very small star which emits regular pulses of radio waves [from *puls(ating st)ar*]

pulsate *vb* **-sating, -sated 1** to expand and contract rhythmically, like a heartbeat **2** to quiver or vibrate: *the images pulsate with energy and light* **3** *physics* to vary in intensity or magnitude [Latin *pulsare* to push] **pulsation** *n*

pulse[1] *n* **1** *physiol* **A** the regular beating of blood through the arteries at each heartbeat **B** a single such beat **2** *physics & electronics* a sudden change in a quantity, such as a voltage, that is normally constant in a system **3** a regular beat or vibration **4** bustle or excitement: *the lively pulse of a city* **5** the feelings or thoughts of a group as they can be measured: *the political pulse of the capital* ▷ *vb* **pulsing, pulsed 6** to beat, throb, or vibrate [Latin *pulsus* a beating]

pulse[2] *n* the edible seeds of pod-bearing plants, such as peas, beans, and lentils [Latin *puls* pottage of pulse]

pulverize *or* **-rise** *vb* **-rizing, -rized** *or* **-rising, -rised 1** to reduce to fine particles by crushing or grinding **2** to destroy completely [Latin *pulvis* dust] **pulverization** *or* **-risation** *n*

puma *n* a large American wild cat with a plain greyish-brown coat and a long tail [indigenous S American word]

pumice (pumm-iss) *n* a light porous stone used for scouring and for removing hard skin. Also called: **pumice stone** [Old French *pomis*]

pummel *vb* **-melling, -melled** *or US* **-meling, -meled** to strike repeatedly with the fists [see POMMEL]

pump[1] *n* **1** a device to force a gas or liquid to move in a particular direction ▷ *vb* **2** (sometimes foll. by *from* or *out* etc.) to raise or drive (air, liquid, etc.) with a pump, esp. into or from something **3** (usually foll. by *in* or *into*) to supply in large amounts: *pumping money into the economy* **4** to operate (a handle, etc.) in the manner of a pump: *he was warmly applauded, and his hand was pumped by well-wishers* **5** to obtain information from (someone) by persistent questioning **6 pump iron** *slang* to exercise with weights; do body-building exercises [Middle Dutch *pumpe* pipe]

pump[2] *n* **1** *chiefly Brit* a shoe with a rubber sole, used in games such as tennis; plimsoll **2** *chiefly US* a woman's flat-heeled shoe that does not cover the top part of the foot [origin unknown]

pumpernickel *n* a slightly sour black bread made of coarse rye flour [from German]

pumpkin *n* **1** a large round fruit with a thick orange rind, pulpy flesh, and many seeds **2** the creeping plant that bears this fruit [Greek *pepōn* ripe]

pun *n* **1** the use of words to exploit double meanings for humorous effect, for example *my dog's a champion boxer* ▷ *vb* **punning, punned 2** to make puns [origin unknown]

punch[1] *vb* **1** to strike at with a clenched fist ▷ *n* **2** a blow with the fist **3** *informal* point or vigour: *the jokes are mildly amusing but lack any real punch* [probably variant of *pounce* to stamp]

punch[2] *n* **1** a tool or machine for shaping, piercing, or engraving ▷ *vb* **2** to pierce, cut, stamp, shape, or drive with a punch [Latin *pungere* to prick]

P

punch³ *n* a mixed drink containing fruit juice and, usually, wine or spirits, generally hot and spiced [origin unknown]
Punch *n* the main male character in the children's puppet show, Punch and Judy
punchbag *n* a stuffed or inflated bag suspended by a flexible rod, that is punched for exercise, esp. boxing training
punchball *n* a stuffed or inflated ball supported by a flexible rod, that is punched for exercise, esp. boxing training
punchbowl *n* a large bowl for serving punch
punch-drunk *adj* dazed and confused through suffering repeated blows to the head
punched card *or esp US* **punch card** *n computers* a card on which data can be coded in the form of punched holes
Punchinello *n, pl* **-los** *or* **-loes** a clown from Italian puppet shows, the origin of Punch [Italian *Polecenella*]
punch line *n* the last line of a joke or funny story that gives it its point
punch-up *n informal* a fight or brawl
punchy *adj* **punchier, punchiest** *informal* effective or forceful: *learn to compose short concise punchy letters*
punctilious *adj formal* **1** paying careful attention to correct social behaviour **2** attentive to detail [Latin *punctum* a point] **punctiliously** *adv*
punctual *adj* **1** arriving or taking place at an arranged time **2** (of a person) always keeping exactly to arranged times [Medieval Latin *punctualis* concerning detail] **punctuality** *n* **punctually** *adv*
punctuate *vb* **-ating, -ated 1** to insert punctuation marks into (a written text) **2** to interrupt at frequent intervals: *the meeting was punctuated by heckling* **3** to emphasize: *he punctuated the question by pressing the muzzle into the pilot's neck* [Latin *pungere* to puncture]
punctuation *n* **1** the use of symbols, such as commas, to indicate speech patterns and meaning not otherwise shown by the written language **2** the symbols used for this purpose
punctuation mark *n* any of the signs used in punctuation, such as a comma
puncture *n* **1** a small hole made by a sharp object **2** a tear and loss of pressure in a tyre **3** the act of puncturing or perforating ▷ *vb* **-turing, -tured 4** to pierce a hole in (something) with a sharp object **5** to cause (a tyre, etc.) to lose pressure by piercing [Latin *pungere* to prick]
pundit *n* **1** an expert on a subject who often speaks or writes about it for a non-specialist audience: *Spain's leading sports pundit, who hosts two TV programmes* **2** a Hindu scholar learned in Sanskrit, religion, philosophy, or law [Hindi *pandit*]
pungent *adj* **1** having a strong sharp bitter smell or taste **2** (of speech or writing) biting; critical [Latin *pungens* piercing] **pungency** *n*
punish *vb* **1** to force (someone) to undergo a penalty for some crime or misbehaviour **2** to inflict punishment for (some crime or misbehaviour) **3** to treat harshly, esp. by overexertion: *he continued to punish himself in the gym* [Latin *punire*] **punishable** *adj* **punishing** *adj*
punishment *n* **1** a penalty for a crime or offence **2** the act of punishing or state of being punished **3** *informal* rough physical treatment: *the boxer's face could not withstand further punishment*
punitive (pew-nit-tiv) *adj* relating to punishment: *punitive measures*
punk *n* **1** *US informal* a worthless person **2** a youth movement of the late 1970s, characterized by anti-Establishment slogans, short spiky hair, and the wearing of worthless articles such as safety pins for decoration **3** short for **punk rock** **4** a follower of the punk movement or of punk rock ▷ *adj* **5** relating to the punk youth movement of the late 1970s: *a punk band* **6** *US informal* worthless or insignificant [origin unknown]
punkah *or* **punka** *n* (in India) a ceiling fan made of a cloth stretched over a rectangular frame [Hindi *pankhā*]
punk rock *n* rock music of the punk youth movement of the late 1970s, characterized by energy and aggressive lyrics and performance **punk rocker** *n*
punnet *n* a small basket for fruit [origin unknown]
punster *n* a person who is fond of making puns
punt¹ *n* **1** an open flat-bottomed boat, propelled by a pole ▷ *vb* **2** to propel (a punt) by pushing with a pole on the bottom of a river [Latin *ponto*]
punt² *n* **1** a kick in certain sports, such as rugby, in which the ball is dropped and kicked before it hits the ground ▷ *vb* **2** to kick (a ball) using a punt [origin unknown]
punt³ *chiefly Brit* ▷ *vb* **1** to gamble or bet ▷ *n* **2** a gamble or bet, esp. against the bank, such as in roulette **3 take a punt at** *Austral & NZ* to make an attempt at [French *ponter*]
punt⁴ *n* a former monetary unit of the Republic of Ireland
punter *n* **1** a person who places a bet **2** *Brit, Austral & NZ informal* any member of the public, esp. when a customer: *the punters are flocking into the sales*
puny *adj* **-nier, -niest** small and weakly [Old French *puisné* born later]
pup *n* **1 A** a young dog; puppy **B** the young of various other animals, such as the seal ▷ *vb* **pupping, pupped 2** (of dogs, seals, etc.) to give birth to pups
pupa (pew-pa) *n, pl* **-pae** (-pee) *or* **-pas** an insect at the stage of development between larva and adult [Latin: a doll] **pupal** *adj*
pupil¹ *n* a student who is taught by a teacher [Latin *pupus* a child]
pupil² *n* the dark circular opening at the centre of the iris of the eye [Latin *pupilla*, diminutive of *pupa* doll; from the tiny reflections in the eye]
puppet *n* **1** a small doll or figure moved by strings attached to its limbs or by the hand inserted in its cloth body **2** a person or state that appears independent but is controlled by another: *the former cabinet ministers have denied that they are puppets of a foreign government* [Latin *pupa* doll]
puppeteer *n* a person who operates puppets
puppy *n, pl* **-pies 1** a young dog **2** *informal, derogatory* a brash or conceited young man [Old French *popée* doll] **puppyish** *adj*

P

puppy fat *n* fatty tissue that develops in childhood or adolescence and usually disappears with maturity

purblind *adj* **1** partly or nearly blind **2** lacking in understanding [*pure* (that is, utterly) *blind*]

purchase *vb* **-chasing, -chased 1** to obtain (goods) by payment **2** to obtain by effort or sacrifice: *he had purchased his freedom at the expense of his principles* ▷ *n* **3** something that is bought **4** the act of buying **5** the mechanical advantage achieved by a lever **6** a firm leverage or grip [Old French *porchacier* to strive to obtain] **purchaser** *n*

purdah *n* the custom in some Muslim and Hindu communities of keeping women in seclusion, with clothing that conceals them completely when they go out [Hindi *parda* veil]

pure *adj* **1** not mixed with any other materials or elements: *pure wool* **2** free from tainting or polluting matter: *pure water* **3** innocent: *pure love* **4** complete: *Pamela's presence on that particular flight was pure chance* **5** (of a subject) studied in its theoretical aspects rather than for its practical applications: *pure mathematics* **6** of unmixed descent: *a pure Dalmatian* [Latin *purus* unstained] **purely** *adv* **pureness** *n*

purebred *adj* denoting a pure strain obtained through many generations of controlled breeding

puree (pure-ray) *n* **1** a smooth thick pulp of sieved fruit, vegetables, meat, or fish ▷ *vb* **-reeing, -reed 2** to make (foods) into a puree [French]

purgative *med* ▷ *n* **1** a medicine for emptying the bowels ▷ *adj* **2** causing emptying of the bowels

purgatory *n* **1** *chiefly RC Church* a place in which the souls of those who have died undergo limited suffering for their sins on earth before they go to heaven **2** a situation of temporary suffering or torment: *it was purgatory living in the same house as him* [Latin *purgare* to purify] **purgatorial** *adj*

purge *vb* **purging, purged 1** to rid (something) of undesirable qualities **2** to rid (an organization, etc.) of undesirable people: *the party was purged* **3 A** to empty (the bowels) **B** to cause (a person) to empty his or her bowels **4 A** *law* to clear (a person) of a charge **B** to free (oneself) of guilt by showing repentance **5** to be purified ▷ *n* **6** the act or process of purging **7** the removal of undesirables from a state, organization, or political party **8** a medicine that empties the bowels [Latin *purgare* to purify]

purify *vb* **-fies, -fying, -fied 1** to free (something) of harmful or inferior matter **2** to free (a person) from sin or guilt **3** to make clean, for example in a religious ceremony [Latin *purus* pure + *facere* to make] **purification** *n*

purism *n* strict insistence on the correct usage or style, such as in grammar or art **purist** *adj, n* **puristic** *adj*

puritan *n* **1** a person who follows strict moral or religious principles ▷ *adj* **2** of or like a puritan: *he maintained a streak of puritan self-denial* [Late Latin *puritas* purity] **puritanism** *n*

Puritan *history* ▷ *n* **1** a member of the extreme English Protestants who wished to strip the Church of England of most of its rituals ▷ *adj* **2** of or relating to the Puritans **Puritanism** *n*

puritanical *adj* **1** *usually derogatory* strict in moral or religious outlook **2** (*sometimes cap*) of or relating to a puritan or the Puritans **puritanically** *adv*

purity *n* the state or quality of being pure

purl[1] *n* **1** a knitting stitch made by doing a plain stitch backwards **2** a decorative border, such as of lace ▷ *vb* **3** to knit in purl stitch [dialect *pirl* to twist into a cord]

purl[2] *vb literary* (of a stream) to flow with a gentle movement and a murmuring sound [probably imitative]

purlieu (per-lyoo) *n* **1** *English history* land on the edge of a royal forest **2** (*usually pl*) *literary* a neighbouring area; outskirts **3** (*often pl*) *literary* a place one frequents: *the committee was the purlieu of civil servants* [Anglo-French *puralé* a going through]

purlin *or* **purline** *n* a horizontal beam that supports the rafters of a roof [origin unknown]

purloin *vb formal* to steal [Old French *porloigner* to put at a distance]

purple *n* **1** a colour between red and blue **2** cloth of this colour, often used to symbolize royalty or nobility **3** the official robe of a cardinal **4** anything purple, such as purple paint or purple clothing: *dressed in purple* ▷ *adj* **5** of a colour between red and blue **6** (of writing) excessively elaborate: *purple prose* [Greek *porphura* the purple fish (murex)] **purplish** *adj*

purple heart *n informal, chiefly Brit* a heart-shaped purple tablet consisting mainly of amphetamine

Purple Heart *n* a decoration awarded to members of the US armed forces wounded in action

purport *vb* **1** to claim to be or do something, esp. falsely: *painkillers may actually cause the headaches they purport to cure* **2** (of speech or writing) to signify or imply ▷ *n* **3** meaning or significance [Old French *porporter* to convey]

purpose *n* **1** the reason for which anything is done, created, or exists **2** a fixed design or idea that is the object of an action **3** determination: *his easy manner only lightly conceals a clear sense of purpose* **4** practical advantage or use: *we debated senseless points of dogma for hours to no fruitful purpose* **5 on purpose** intentionally ▷ *vb* **-posing, -posed 6** to intend or determine to do (something) [Old French *porposer* to plan]

purpose-built *adj* made to serve a specific purpose

purposeful *adj* with a fixed and definite purpose; determined **purposefully** *adv*

> **USAGE** *Purposefully* is sometimes wrongly used where *purposely* is meant: *he had purposely (not purposefully) left the door unlocked.*

purposely *adv* on purpose

> **USAGE** See at **purposeful.**

purposive *adj formal* **1** having or showing a definite intention: *the establishment of the camps lacks a purposive trend towards a solution* **2** useful

purr *vb* **1** (esp. of cats) to make a low vibrant sound, usually considered as expressing pleasure **2** to express (pleasure) by this sound or by a sound suggestive of purring ▷ *n* **3** a purring sound [imitative]

purse *n* **1** a small pouch for carrying money **2** *US, Canad, Austral & NZ* a woman's handbag **3** wealth or resources: *the public purse appeared bottomless* **4** a sum of money that is offered as a prize ▷ *vb* **pursing, pursed 5** to pull (the lips) into a small rounded shape [Old English *purs*]

purser *n* an officer aboard a ship who keeps the accounts

purse strings *pl n* **hold the purse strings** to control the spending of a particular family, group, etc.

pursuance *n formal* the carrying out of an action or plan: *the pursuance of duty had taken him abroad*

pursue *vb* **-suing, -sued 1** to follow (a person, vehicle, or animal) in order to capture or overtake **2** to try hard to achieve (some desire or aim) **3** to follow the guidelines of (a plan or policy) **4** to apply oneself to (studies or interests) **5** to follow persistently or seek to become acquainted with: *his desire to pursue and marry Carol* **6** to continue to discuss or argue (a point or subject) [Old French *poursivre*] **pursuer** *n*

pursuit *n* **1** the act of pursuing **2** an occupation or pastime

pursuivant (**purse**-iv-ant) *n* the lowest rank of heraldic officer [Old French]

purulent (**pure**-yew-lent) *adj* of, relating to, or containing pus [Latin *purulentus*] **purulence** *n*

purvey *vb* **1** to sell or provide (foodstuffs) **2** to provide or make available: *the foreign ministry used him to purvey sensitive items of diplomatic news* [Old French *porveeir* to provide] **purveyor** *n*

purview *n* **1** scope of operation: *each designation falls under the purview of a different ministry* **2** breadth or range of outlook: *he hopes that the purview of science will be widened* [Anglo-Norman *purveu*]

pus *n* the yellowish fluid that comes from inflamed or infected tissue [Latin]

push *vb* **1** (sometimes foll. by *off* or *away* etc.) to apply steady force to in order to move **2** to thrust (one's way) through something, such as a crowd **3** (sometimes foll. by *for*) to be an advocate or promoter (of): *there are many groups you can join to push for change* **4** to spur or drive (oneself or another person) in order to achieve more effort or better results: *you must be careful not to push your children too hard* **5** *informal* to sell (narcotic drugs) illegally ▷ *n* **6** the act of pushing; thrust **7** *informal* drive or determination: *everything depends on him having the push to obtain the money* **8** *informal* a special effort to achieve something: *when this push spent itself it was obvious the bid had failed* **9 the push** *Brit & NZ informal* dismissal from employment ▷ See also **push about, push off** *etc.* [Latin *pulsare*]

push about *or* **push around** *vb informal* to bully: *don't let them push you around*

push-bike *n Brit, Austral & NZ informal* a bicycle

push button *n* **1** an electrical switch operated by pressing a button ▷ *adj* **push-button 2** operated by a push button: *a push-button radio*

pushchair *n Brit* a small folding chair on wheels in which a small child can be wheeled around: *escalators are difficult with pushchairs*

pushed *adj* (often foll. by *for*) *informal* short of: *pushed for time*

pusher *n informal* a person who sells illegal drugs

pushing *prep* **1** almost or nearly (a certain age, speed, etc.): *pushing fifty* ▷ *adj* **2** aggressively ambitious

push off *vb informal* to go away; leave

pushover *n informal* **1** something that is easily achieved **2** a person, team, etc., that is easily taken advantage of or defeated

push-start *vb* **1** to start (a motor vehicle) by pushing it, thus turning the engine ▷ *n* **2** the act or process of push-starting a vehicle

push through *vb* to force to accept: *the President wants to push through his economic package*

pushy *adj* **pushier, pushiest** *informal* offensively assertive or ambitious

pusillanimous *adj formal* timid and cowardly: *pusillanimous behaviour* [Latin *pusillus* weak + *animus* courage] **pusillanimity** *n*

puss *n* **1** *informal* a cat **2** *slang* a girl or woman [probably Low German]

pussy[1] *n, pl* **pussies 1** Also called: **pussycat** *informal* a cat **2** *vulgar slang* the female genitals [from *puss*]

pussy[2] *adj* **-sier, -siest** containing or full of pus

pussyfoot *vb informal* **1** to move about stealthily **2** to avoid committing oneself: *don't let's pussyfoot about naming the hit man*

pussy willow *n* a willow tree with silvery silky catkins

pustulate *vb* **-lating, -lated** to form into pustules

pustule *n* a small inflamed raised area of skin containing pus [Latin *pustula* a blister] **pustular** *adj*

put *vb* **putting, put 1** to cause to be (in a position or place): *he put the book on the table* **2** to cause to be (in a state or condition): *what can be done to put things right?* **3** to lay (blame, emphasis, etc.) on a person or thing: *don't try to put the blame on someone else!* **4** to set or commit (to an action, task, or duty), esp. by force: *she put him to work weeding the garden* **5** to estimate or judge: *I wouldn't put him in the same class as Verdi as a composer* **6** (foll. by *to*) to utilize: *he put his culinary skills to good use when he opened a restaurant* **7** to express: *he didn't put it quite as crudely as that* **8** to make (an end or limit): *opponents claim the scheme will put an end to much of the sailing and boating in the area* **9** to present for consideration; propose: *he put the question to the committee* **10** to invest (money) in or expend (time or energy) on: *they put a lot of money into the sport* **11** to throw or cast: *put the shot* ▷ *n* **12** a throw, esp. in putting the shot ▷ See also **put about, put across** *etc.* [Middle English *puten* to push]

put about *vb* **1** to make widely known: *a rumour was put about that he had been drunk* **2** *naut* to change course

put across *vb* to communicate successfully: *he's not very good at putting his ideas across*

put aside *vb* **1** to save: *try to put some money aside in case of emergencies* **2** to disregard: *put aside adolescent fantasies of romance*

putative (**pew**-tat-iv) *adj formal* **1** commonly regarded as being: *the desire of the putative father to establish his possible paternity* **2** considered to exist or have existed; inferred: *a putative earlier form* [Latin *putare* to consider]

put away *vb* **1** to save: *it takes a lot of discipline to put away something for your old age* **2** *informal* to lock up in a prison, mental institution, etc.: *we have enough evidence to put him away for life* **3** *informal* to eat or drink in large amounts: *she would happily put away two bacon sandwiches for breakfast*

put back *vb* **1** to return to its former place **2** to move to a later time: *the finals could be put back until Monday*
put down *vb* **1** to make a written record of **2** to repress: *the rising was put down with revolting cruelty* **3** to consider: *I'd put him down as a complete fool* **4** to attribute: *the government's defeat in the election can be put down to a general desire for change* **5** to put (an animal) to death **6** *slang* to belittle or humiliate ▹ *n* **put-down 7** *informal* a cruelly crushing remark
put forward *vb* **1** to propose or suggest **2** to offer the name of; nominate
put in *vb* **1** to devote (time or effort): *the competitors who did best were the ones who had put in some practice* **2** (often foll. by *for*) to apply (for a job) **3** to submit: *they have put in an official complaint* **4** *naut* to bring a vessel into port
put off *vb* **1** to postpone: *ministers have put off making a decision until next month* **2** to evade (a person) by delay: *they tried to put him off, but he came anyway* **3** to cause dislike in: *he was put off by her appearance* **4** to cause to lose interest in: *the accident put him off sailing* **5** to distract: *a swerving cyclist may have put off the driver*
put on *vb* **1** to dress oneself in **2** to adopt (an attitude or feeling) insincerely: *I don't see why you have to put on that fake American accent* **3** to present (a play or show) **4** to add: *I've put on nearly a stone since September* **5** to cause (an electrical device) to function: *she put on the light* **6** to bet (money) on a horse race or game **7** to impose: *the government has put a tax on gas*
put out *vb* **1 A** to annoy or anger **B** to disturb or confuse **2** to extinguish (a fire, light, etc.) **3** to inconvenience (someone): *I hope I'm not putting you out* **4** to select or lay out for use: *she put out two clean cloths in the kitchen* **5** to publish or broadcast: *she put out a statement denying the rumours* **6** to dislocate: *he put his back out digging the garden*
put over *vb informal* to communicate (facts or information)
putrefy *vb* **-fies, -fying, -fied** *formal* (of organic matter) to rot and produce an offensive smell [Latin *putrefacere*] **putrefaction** *n*
putrescent *adj formal* becoming putrid; rotting: *putrescent toadstools* [Latin *putrescere* to become rotten] **putrescence** *n*
putrid *adj* **1** (of organic matter) rotting: *putrid meat* **2** sickening or foul: *a putrid stench* **3** *informal* deficient in quality or value: *a penchant for putrid puns* **4** morally corrupt [Latin *putrere* to be rotten] **putridity** *n*
putsch *n* a violent and sudden political revolt: *an attempted putsch against the general* [from German]
putt *golf* ▹ *n* **1** a stroke on the green with a putter to roll the ball into or near the hole ▹ *vb* **2** to strike (the ball) in this way [Scot]
puttee *n* (*usually pl*) (esp. as part of a military uniform) a strip of cloth worn wound around the leg from the ankle to the knee [Hindi *paṭṭī*]
putter *n golf* a club, usually with a short shaft, for putting
put through *vb* **1** to connect by telephone: *I'm sorry, you've been put through to the wrong extension* **2** to carry out to a conclusion
putting green *n* (on a golf course) the area of closely mown grass around the hole
putty *n, pl* **-ties 1** a stiff paste used to fix glass into frames and fill cracks in woodwork ▹ *vb* **-ties, -tying, -tied 2** to fix or fill with putty [French *potée* a potful]
put up *vb* **1** to build or erect: *I want to put up a fence round the garden* **2** to display (a poster, sign, etc.) **3** to accommodate or be accommodated at: *can you put me up for tonight?* **4** to increase (prices) **5** to submit (a plan, case, etc.) **6** to offer: *the factory is being put up for sale* **7** to give: *they put up a good fight* **8** to provide (money) for: *they put up 35% of the film's budget* **9** to nominate or be nominated as a candidate: *the party have yet to decide whether to put up a candidate* **10 put up to** to incite to: *I wonder who put them up to it?* **11 put up with** *informal* to endure or tolerate ▹ *adj* **put-up 12** *informal* dishonestly or craftily prearranged: *a put-up job*
put upon *vb* to take advantage of (someone): *he's always being put upon*
putz *n US slang* a despicable or stupid person [Yiddish *puts* ornament]
puzzle *vb* **-zling, -zled 1** to baffle or bewilder **2 puzzle out** to solve (a problem) by mental effort **3 puzzle over** to think deeply about in an attempt to understand: *he puzzled over the squiggles and curves on the paper* ▹ *n* **4** a problem that cannot be easily solved **5** a toy, game, or question presenting a problem that requires skill or ingenuity for its solution [origin unknown] **puzzlement** *n* **puzzled** *adj* **puzzler** *n* **puzzling** *adj*
PVC polyvinyl chloride
PVS persistent vegetative state
PWR pressurized-water reactor
pyaemia *or* **pyemia** *n med* blood poisoning with pus-forming microorganisms in the blood [Greek *puon* pus + *haima* blood]
pye-dog *or* **pi-dog** *n* a half-wild Asian dog with no owner [Hindi *pāhī* outsider]
pygmy *n, pl* **-mies 1** something that is a very small example of its type **2** an abnormally undersized person **3** a person of little importance or significance ▹ *adj* **4** very small: *the pygmy anteater* [Greek *pugmaios* undersized]
Pygmy *n, pl* **-mies** a member of one of the very short peoples of Equatorial Africa
pyjamas *or US* **pajamas** *pl n* a loose-fitting jacket or top and trousers worn to sleep in [Persian *pai* leg + *jāma* garment]
pylon *n* **1** *chiefly Brit* a large vertical steel tower-like structure supporting high-tension electrical cables **2** *US & Canad* a plastic cone used to demarcate areas, esp. on public roads [Greek *pulōn* a gateway]
pyorrhoea *or esp US* **pyorrhea** (pire-ree-a) *n med* a discharge of pus, esp. in diseases of the gums or tooth sockets [Greek *puon* pus + *rhein* to flow]
pyramid *n* **1** a huge stone building with a square base and four sloping triangular sides meeting in a point, such as the royal tombs built by the ancient Egyptians **2** *maths* a solid figure with a polygonal base and triangular sides that meet in a common vertex [Greek *puramis*] **pyramidal** *adj*
pyramid selling *n* the practice of selling distributors batches of goods which they then

P

subdivide and sell to other distributors, this process continuing until the final distributors are left with a stock that is unsaleable except at a loss

pyre *n* a pile of wood for cremating a corpse [Greek *pur* fire]

pyrethrum (pie-**reeth**-rum) *n* **1** a Eurasian chrysanthemum with white, pink, red, or purple flowers **2** an insecticide prepared from dried pyrethrum flowers [Greek *purethron*]

pyretic (pie-**ret**-ik) *adj pathol* of, relating to, or characterized by fever [Greek *puretos* fever]

Pyrex *n trademark* a variety of heat-resistant glassware used in cookery and chemical apparatus

pyrite (**pie**-rite) *n* a yellow mineral consisting of iron sulphide in cubic crystalline form. Formula: FeS_2 [Latin *pyrites* flint]

pyrites (pie-**rite**-eez) *n, pl* **-tes 1** same as **pyrite 2** a disulphide of a metal, esp. of copper and tin

pyromania *n psychiatry* the uncontrollable impulse and practice of setting things on fire [Greek *pur* fire + *mania* madness] **pyromaniac** *n, adj*

pyrotechnics *n* **1** the art of making fireworks **2** a firework display **3** a brilliant display of skill: *all those courtroom pyrotechnics* [Greek *pur* fire + *tekhnē* art] **pyrotechnic** *adj*

Pyrrhic victory (**pir**-ik) *n* a victory in which the victor's losses are as great as those of the defeated [after *Pyrrhus*, who defeated the Romans in 279 BC but suffered heavy losses]

Pythagoras' theorem (pie-**thag**-or-ass) *n* the theorem that in a right-angled triangle the square of the length of the hypotenuse equals the sum of the squares of the other two sides [after *Pythagoras*, Greek philosopher and mathematician]

python *n* a large nonpoisonous snake of Australia, Africa, and S Asia which kills its prey by crushing it with its body [after *Python*, a dragon killed by Apollo]

pyx *n Christianity* any receptacle in which the bread used in Holy Communion is kept [Latin *pyxis* small box]

Qq

Q **1** *chess* queen **2** question
q. **1** quart **2** quarter **3** question **4** quire
Q. **1** Queen **2** question
QC **1** Queen's Counsel **2** Quebec
QED which was to be shown or proved [Latin *quod erat demonstrandum*]
QLD *or* **Qld** Queensland
QM Quartermaster
qr. *pl* **qrs** **1** quarter **2** quire
QR code *n* a type of bar code that can be read both horizontally and vertically [Q(*uick*) R(*esponse*) *code*]
qt *pl* **qt** *or* **qts** quart
q.t. *n* **on the q.t.** *informal* secretly
qua (kwah) *prep* in the capacity of; by virtue of being [Latin]
quack[1] *vb* **1** (of a duck) to utter a harsh guttural sound **2** to make a noise like a duck ▹ *n* **3** the sound made by a duck [imitative]
quack[2] *n* **1** an unqualified person who claims medical knowledge **2** *Brit, Austral & NZ informal* a doctor [short for *quacksalver*, from Dutch]
quackery *n*
quad[1] *n* short for **quadrangle** (sense 1)
quad[2] *n informal* a quadruplet
quad[3] *n* **1** quadraphonics ▹ *adj* **2** quadraphonic
quad bike *or* **quad** *n* a vehicle like a small motorcycle, with four large wheels, designed for agricultural and sporting uses
quadrangle *n* **1** a rectangular courtyard with buildings on all four sides **2** *geom* a figure consisting of four points connected by four lines [Late Latin *quadrangulum*] **quadrangular** *adj*
quadrant *n* **1** *geom* **A** a quarter of the circumference of a circle **B** the area enclosed by two perpendicular radii of a circle **2** a piece of a mechanism in the form of a quarter circle **3** an instrument formerly used in astronomy and navigation for measuring the altitudes of stars [Latin *quadrans* a quarter]
quadraphonic *adj* using four independent channels to reproduce or record sound
quadraphonics *n*
quadrate *n* **1** a cube or square, or a square or cubelike object ▹ *vb* **-rating, -rated** **2** to make square or rectangular [Latin *quadrare* to make square]
quadratic *maths* ▹ *n* **1** Also called: **quadratic equation** an equation in which the variable is raised to the power of two, but nowhere raised to a higher power: *solve the quadratic equation* $2x^2-3x-6=3$ ▹ *adj* **2** of or relating to the second power
quadrennial *adj* **1** occurring every four years **2** lasting four years
quadri- *or before a vowel* **quadr-** *combining form* four: *quadrilateral* [Latin]
quadriceps *n anatomy* a muscle at the front of the thigh [New Latin]
quadrilateral *adj* **1** having four sides ▹ *n* **2** a polygon with four sides
quadrille *n* **1** a square dance for four couples **2** music for this dance [Spanish *cuadrilla*]
quadrillion *n, pl* **-lions** *or* **-lion** **1** the number represented as one followed by 15 zeros (10^{15}) **2** (in Britain, originally) the number represented as one followed by 24 zeros (10^{24}) [French *quadrillon*]
quadriplegia (kwod-rip-**pleej**-ya) *n* paralysis of all four limbs [QUADRI- + Greek *plēssein* to strike]
quadriplegic *adj, n*
quadruped (**kwod**-roo-ped) *n* an animal, esp. a mammal, that has four legs [Latin *quadru-* four + *pes* foot]
quadruple *vb* **-pling, -pled** **1** to multiply by four ▹ *adj* **2** four times as much or as many **3** consisting of four parts **4** *music* having four beats in each bar ▹ *n* **5** a quantity or number four times as great as another [Latin *quadru-* four + *-plus* -fold]
quadruplet *n* one of four children born at one birth
quadruplicate *adj* **1** fourfold or quadruple ▹ *vb* **-cating, -cated** **2** to multiply or be multiplied by four [Latin *quadruplicare* to increase fourfold]
quaff (**kwoff**) *vb old-fashioned* to drink heartily or in one draught [perhaps imitative]
quagga *n, pl* **-gas** *or* **-ga** a recently extinct zebra, striped only on the head and shoulders [Khoikhoi *quăgga*]
quagmire (**kwog**-mire) *n* a soft wet area of land that gives way under the feet; bog [from *quag* bog + *mire*]
quail[1] *n, pl* **quails** *or* **quail** a small game bird of the partridge family [Old French *quaille*]
quail[2] *vb* to shrink back with fear; cower [origin unknown]
quaint *adj* attractively unusual, esp. in an old-fashioned style [Old French *cointe*, from Latin *cognitus* known]
quake *vb* **quaking, quaked** **1** to shake or tremble with or as if with fear **2** to shudder because of instability ▹ *n* **3** *informal* an earthquake [Old English *cwacian*]
Quaker *n* a member of a Christian sect, the Religious Society of Friends [originally an offensive nickname] **Quakerism** *n*
qualification *n* **1** an official record of achievement awarded on the successful completion of a course of training or passing of an examination **2** an ability, quality, or attribute, esp. one that fits a person to perform a particular job or task **3** a condition that modifies or limits; restriction **4** the act of qualifying or being qualified
qualified *adj* **1** having successfully completed a training course or passed the exams necessary in order to be entitled to work in a particular profession: *a qualified lawyer* **2** having the abilities, qualities, or attributes necessary to perform a particular job or task **3** having completed a training or degree course and gained the relevant certificates **4** limited or restricted; not wholehearted: *the mission was only a qualified success*

qualify *vb* **-fies, -fying, -fied 1** to have the abilities or attributes required in order to do or have something, such as a job: *he qualified as a teacher; she did not qualify for a State pension at that time* **2** to moderate or restrict (a statement one has made) **3** to describe or be described as having a particular quality: *it was neither witty nor subtle enough to qualify as a spoof* **4** to be successful in one stage of a competition and as a result progress to the next stage: *Lewis failed to qualify for the semi-final* **5** *grammar* to modify the sense of (a word) [Latin *qualis* of what kind + *facere* to make] **qualifier** *n*

qualitative *adj* involving or relating to distinctions based on quality

qualitative analysis *n chem* analysis of a substance to determine its constituents

quality *n, pl* **-ties 1** degree or standard of excellence **2** a distinguishing characteristic or attribute **3** the basic character or nature of something **4** a feature of personality **5** (formerly) high social status ▹ *adj* **6** excellent or superior: *a quality product* [Latin *qualis* of what sort]

quality assurance *n commerce* the process of verifying that a product conforms to required standards, often performed by an independent assessor

quality control *n* checking of the relative quality of a manufactured product, usually by testing samples

qualm (kwahm) *n* **1** a pang of conscience; scruple **2** a sudden sensation of misgiving **3** a sudden feeling of sickness or nausea [Old English *cwealm* death or plague]

quandary *n, pl* **-ries** a situation in which it is difficult to decide what to do; predicament; dilemma [origin unknown]

quandong (kwon-dong) *n* **1** a small Australian tree with edible fruit and nuts used in preserves **2** an Australian tree with pale timber

quango *n, pl* **-gos** a semipublic government-financed administrative body whose members are appointed by the government [*qu(asi-)a(utonomous) n(on)g(overnmental) o(rganization)*]

quantify *vb* **-fies, -fying, -fied** to discover or express the quantity of [Latin *quantus* how much + *facere* to make] **quantifiable** *adj* **quantification** *n*

quantitative *adj* **1** involving considerations of amount or size **2** capable of being measured

quantitative analysis *n chem* analysis of a substance to determine the proportions of its constituents

quantitative easing *or* **quantitive easing** *n* the practice of increasing the supply of money in order to stimulate economic activity

quantity *n, pl* **-ties 1** a specified or definite amount or number **2** the aspect of anything that can be measured, weighed, or counted **3** a large amount **4** *maths* an entity having a magnitude that may be denoted by a numerical expression [Latin *quantus* how much]

> **USAGE** The use of a plural noun after *quantity of* as in *a large quantity of bananas* was formerly considered incorrect, but is now acceptable.

quantity surveyor *n* a person who estimates the cost of the materials and labour necessary for a construction job

quantum *n, pl* **-ta 1** an amount or quantity, esp. a specific amount **2** *physics* the smallest quantity of some physical property that a system can possess ▹ *adj* **3** of or designating a major breakthrough or sudden advance: *a quantum leap in business computing* [Latin *quantus* how much]

quantum theory *n* a theory concerning the behaviour of physical systems based on the idea that they can only possess certain properties, such as energy and angular momentum, in discrete amounts (quanta)

quarantine *n* **1** a period of isolation, esp. of people or animals arriving from abroad, to prevent the spread of disease ▹ *vb* **-tining, -tined 2** to isolate in or as if in quarantine [Italian *quarantina* period of forty days]

quark *n physics* the hypothetical elementary particle supposed to be a fundamental unit of all baryons and mesons [special use of a word coined by James Joyce in the novel *Finnegans Wake*]

quarrel *n* **1** an angry disagreement; argument **2** a cause of dispute; grievance ▹ *vb* **-relling, -relled** *or US* **-reling, -reled** (often foll. by *with*) **3** to engage in a disagreement or dispute; argue **4** to find fault; complain [Latin *querella* complaint]

quarrelsome *adj* inclined to quarrel or disagree

quarry[1] *n, pl* **-ries 1** a place where stone is dug from the surface of the earth ▹ *vb* **-ries, -rying, -ried 2** to extract (stone) from a quarry [Old French *quarriere*]

quarry[2] *n, pl* **-ries 1** an animal that is being hunted; prey **2** anything pursued [Middle English *quirre* entrails offered to the hounds]

quarry tile *n* an unglazed floor tile

quart *n* a unit of liquid measure equal to one quarter of a gallon or two pints (1.136 litres) [Latin *quartus* fourth]

quarter *n* **1** one of four equal parts of something such as an object or quantity **2** the fraction equal to one divided by four ($^1/_4$) **3** a fourth part of a year; three months **4** *Brit informal* a unit of weight equal to four ounces (113.4 grams) **5** a region or district of a town or city: *the French quarter of New Orleans* **6** a region, direction, or point of the compass **7** *US & Canad* a coin worth 25 cents **8** short for **quarter-hour 9** *astron* **A** one fourth of the moon's period of revolution around the earth **B** either of two phases of the moon when half of the lighted surface is visible **10** (*sometimes pl*) an unspecified person or group of people: *it met stiff opposition in some quarters* **11** mercy or pity shown to a defeated opponent: *no quarter was asked or given* **12** any of the four limbs of a quadruped ▹ *vb* **13** to divide into four equal parts **14** (formerly) to dismember (a human body) **15** to billet or be billeted in lodgings **16** *heraldry* to divide (a shield) into four separate bearings ▹ *adj* **17** being or consisting of one of four equal parts ▹ See also **quarters** [Latin *quartus* fourth]

quarterback *n* a player in American football who directs attacking play

quarter day *n Brit* any of four days in the year when certain payments become due

quarterdeck *n naut* the rear part of the upper deck of a ship, traditionally for official or ceremonial use

quarter-final *n* the round before the semi-final in a competition

quarter-hour *n* **1** a period of 15 minutes **2** either of the points of time 15 minutes before or after the hour

quarterlight *n Brit* a small pivoted window in the door of a car for ventilation

quarterly *adj* **1** occurring, done, due, or issued at intervals of three months ▷ *n, pl* **-lies 2** a periodical issued every three months ▷ *adv* **3** once every three months

quartermaster *n* **1** a military officer responsible for accommodation, food, and equipment **2** a naval officer responsible for navigation

quarters *pl n* accommodation, esp. as provided for military personnel

quarter sessions *n* (formerly) a court with limited jurisdiction, held four times a year

quarterstaff *n, pl* **-staves** a stout iron-tipped wooden staff about 6ft long, formerly used as a weapon [origin unknown]

quartet *n* **1** a group of four singers or instrumentalists **2** a piece of music for four performers **3** any group of four [Italian *quarto* fourth]

quartile *n* **1** one of three values of a variable dividing its distribution into four groups with equal frequencies ▷ *adj* **2** of a quartile

quarto *n, pl* **-tos** a book size resulting from folding a sheet of paper into four leaves or eight pages [New Latin *in quarto* in quarter]

quartz *n* a hard glossy mineral consisting of crystalline silicon dioxide [German *Quarz*]

quartz clock *or* **quartz watch** *n* a very accurate clock or watch that is operated by a vibrating quartz crystal

quartz crystal *n* a thin plate or rod cut from a piece of quartz and ground so that it vibrates at a particular frequency

quasar (kway-zar) *n* any of a class of extremely distant starlike objects that are powerful sources of radio waves and other forms of energy [*quas(i-stell)ar (radio source)*]

quash *vb* **1** to officially reject (something, such as a judgment or decision) as invalid **2** to defeat or suppress forcefully and completely [Latin *quassare* to shake]

quasi- (**kway**-zie) *combining form* **1** almost but not really; seemingly: *a quasi-religious cult* **2** resembling but not actually being; so-called: *a quasi-scholar* [Latin: as if]

quassia (**kwosh**-a) *n* **1** a tropical American tree with bitter bark and wood **2** the wood of this tree or a bitter compound extracted from it, used in insecticides [after Graman *Quassi*, who discovered its medicinal value]

quaternary *adj* consisting of four parts [Latin *quaterni* by fours]

Quaternary *adj geol* of the most recent period of geological time, which started about one million years ago

quatrain *n* a stanza or poem of four lines [French, from Latin *quattuor* four]

quatrefoil *n* **1** a leaf composed of four leaflets **2** *archit* a carved ornament of four arcs about a common centre [Old French *quatre* four + *-foil* leaflet]

quattrocento (kwat-roe-**chen**-toe) *n* the 15th century, esp. in reference to Renaissance Italian art [Italian: four hundred (short for fourteen hundred)]

quaver *vb* **1** (esp. of the voice) to quiver or tremble **2** to say or sing (something) with a trembling voice ▷ *n* **3** *music* a note having the time value of an eighth of a semibreve **4** a tremulous sound or note [Germanic] **quavering** *adj*

quay (**kee**) *n* a wharf built parallel to the shoreline [Old French *kai*]

Que. Quebec

queasy *adj* **-sier, -siest 1** having the feeling that one is about to vomit; nauseous **2** feeling or causing uneasiness [origin unknown] **queasily** *adv* **queasiness** *n*

queen *n* **1** a female sovereign who is the official ruler or head of state **2** the wife of a king **3** a woman, thing, or place considered the best or most important of her or its kind: *the rose is considered the queen of garden flowers* **4** *offensive slang* an effeminate homosexual man **5** the only fertile female in a colony of bees, wasps, or ants **6** a playing card with a picture of a queen on it **7** a chess piece, able to move in a straight line in any direction ▷ *vb* **8** *chess* to promote (a pawn) to a queen when it reaches the eighth rank **9 queen it** *informal* to behave in an overbearing manner: *she is more beautiful than ever and still queening it over everybody* [Old English *cwēn*] **queenly** *adj*

Queen Anne *adj* **1** of or in an 18th-century style of furniture characterized by the use of curves **2** of or in an early 18th-century English architectural style characterized by the use of red bricks and classical ornamentation

queen consort *n* the wife of a reigning king

queen mother *n* the widow of a former king who is also the mother of the reigning sovereign

queen post *n building* one of a pair of vertical posts that connect the tie beam of a truss to the principal rafters of a roof

Queen's Bench *n* (in Britain) one of the divisions of the High Court of Justice

Queensberry rules *pl n* **1** the code of rules followed in modern boxing **2** *informal* gentlemanly conduct, esp. in a dispute [after the ninth Marquess of *Queensberry*, who originated the rules]

Queen's Counsel *n* **1** (in Britain, Australia and New Zealand) a barrister or advocate appointed Counsel to the Crown **2** (in Canada and New Zealand) an honorary title bestowed on lawyers with long experience

Queen's English *n* the version of spoken and written British English that is widely regarded as standard and correct

queen's evidence *n English law* evidence given for the Crown against former associates in crime by an accomplice

Queen's Guide *or* **Queen's Scout** *n* a Guide or Scout who has passed the highest tests of proficiency

queen's highway *n* **1** (in Britain) any public road or right of way **2** (in Canada) a main road maintained by the provincial government

queer *adj* **1** not normal or usual; odd or strange **2** dubious; shady **3** *Brit* faint, giddy, or queasy **4** *informal, sometimes offensive* homosexual **5** *informal* eccentric or slightly mad ▷ *n* **6** *informal, sometimes offensive* a homosexual ▷ *vb* **7 queer someone's pitch** *informal* to spoil or thwart someone's chances of something [origin unknown]

> **USAGE** Although the term *queer* meaning homosexual is considered offensive when used by people outside the gay community, it is used by gay people as a positive term, as in *queer politics, queer cinema*. *Queer* has also come to refer to any person who does not conform with traditional notions of sexuality and gender, and it is used positively by many people who identify themselves this way.

queer street *n* **in queer street** *informal* in a difficult financial situation, esp. debt or bankruptcy

quell *vb* **1** to suppress (rebellion or unrest); subdue **2** to overcome or allay [Old English *cwellan* to kill]

quench *vb* **1** to satisfy (one's thirst) **2** to put out; extinguish **3** to suppress or subdue **4** *metallurgy* to cool (hot metal) by plunging it into cold water [Old English *ācwencan* to extinguish]

quern *n* a stone hand mill for grinding corn [Old English *cweorn*]

querulous (**kwer**-yew-luss) *adj* complaining; whining or peevish [Latin *queri* to complain] **querulously** *adv*

query *n, pl* **-ries 1** a question, esp. one expressing doubt **2** a question mark ▷ *vb* **-ries, -rying, -ried 3** to express uncertainty, doubt, or an objection concerning (something) **4** to express as a query; ask [Latin *quaere* ask!]

quesadilla *n Mexican cookery* a toasted tortilla filled with cheese and sometimes other ingredients [Spanish, diminutive of *queso* cheese]

quest *n* **1** a looking for or seeking; search **2** the object of a search; a goal or target ▷ *vb* **3 quest for** to go in search of **4** (of dogs) to search for game [Old French *queste*]

question *n* **1** a form of words addressed to a person in order to obtain an answer; interrogative sentence **2** a point at issue: *they were silent on the question of social justice* **3** a difficulty or uncertainty **4 A** an act of asking **B** an investigation into some problem **5** a motion presented for debate **6 beyond (all) question** beyond (any) doubt **7 call something into question A** to make something the subject of disagreement **B** to cast doubt upon the validity or truth of something **8 in question** under discussion: *the area in question was not contaminated* **9 out of the question** beyond consideration; impossible ▷ *vb* **10** to put a question or questions to (a person); interrogate **11** to make (something) the subject of dispute **12** to express uncertainty; doubt [Latin *quaestio*]

> **USAGE** *The question whether* should be used rather than *the question of whether* or *the question as to whether: this leaves open the question whether he acted correctly.*

questionable *adj* **1** (esp. of a person's morality or honesty) doubtful **2** of disputable value or authority **questionably** *adv*

questioner *n* a person who asks a question

questioning *adj* **1** proceeding from or characterized by doubt or uncertainty **2** intellectually inquisitive: *a questioning mind* ▷ *n* **3** interrogation

question mark *n* **1** the punctuation mark (?), used at the end of questions **2** a doubt or uncertainty: *a question mark still hangs over their success*

question master *n Brit* the person chairing a radio or television quiz or panel game

questionnaire *n* a set of questions on a form, used to collect statistical information or opinions from people

question time *n* (in parliamentary bodies of the British type) the time set aside each day for questions to government ministers

queue *n* **1** a line of people or vehicles waiting for something ▷ *vb* **queuing** *or* **queueing, queued 2** (often foll. by *up*) to form or remain in a line while waiting [Latin *cauda* tail]

quibble *vb* **-bling, -bled 1** to make trivial objections ▷ *n* **2** a trivial objection or equivocation, esp. one used to avoid an issue **3** *archaic* a pun [origin unknown]

quiche (**keesh**) *n* a savoury flan with an egg custard filling to which cheese, bacon, or vegetables are added [French]

quick *adj* **1** characterized by rapidity of movement or action; fast **2** lasting or taking a short time **3** immediate or prompt: *her quick action minimized the damage* **4** eager or ready to perform (an action): *quick to condemn* **5** responsive to stimulation; alert; lively: *they were impressed by his quick mind* **6** easily excited or aroused: *he is impulsive and has a quick temper* **7** nimble in one's movements or actions; deft: *she has quick hands* ▷ *n* **8** any area of sensitive flesh, esp. that under a nail **9 cut someone to the quick** to hurt someone's feelings deeply **10 the quick** *archaic* living people ▷ *adv* **11** in a rapid manner; swiftly [Old English *cwicu* living] **quickly** *adv* **quickness** *n*

quick-change artist *n* an actor or entertainer who undertakes several rapid changes of costume during a performance

quicken *vb* **1** to make or become faster; accelerate **2** to impart to or receive vigour or enthusiasm: *science quickens the imagination* **3 A** (of a fetus) to begin to show signs of life **B** (of a pregnant woman) to reach the stage of pregnancy at which movements of the fetus can be felt

quick-freeze *vb* **-freezing, -froze, -frozen** to preserve (food) by subjecting it to rapid refrigeration

quickie *informal* ▷ *n* **1** anything made or done rapidly ▷ *adj* **2** made or done rapidly: *a quickie divorce*

quicklime *n* a white caustic solid, mainly composed of calcium oxide, used in the manufacture of glass and steel

quicksand *n* a deep mass of loose wet sand that submerges anything on top of it

quickset *chiefly Brit* ▷ *adj* **1** (of plants or cuttings) planted so as to form a hedge ▷ *n* **2** a hedge composed of such plants

q

quicksilver *n* the metal mercury

quickstep *n* **1** a modern ballroom dance in rapid quadruple time **2** music for this dance

quick-tempered *adj* easy to anger

quick-witted *adj* having a keenly alert mind **quick-wittedness** *n*

quid[1] *n, pl* **quid** *Brit slang* **1** a pound (sterling) **2 be quids in** to be in a very favourable or advantageous position [origin unknown]

quid[2] *n* a piece of tobacco for chewing [Old English *cwidu* chewing resin]

quiddity *n, pl* **-ties 1** the essential nature of something **2** a petty or trifling distinction [Latin *quid* what]

quid pro quo *n, pl* **quid pro quos** one thing, esp. an advantage or object, given in exchange for another [Latin: something for something]

quiescent (kwee-ess-ent) *adj formal* quiet, inactive, or dormant [Latin *quiescere* to rest] **quiescence** *n*

quiet *adj* **1** characterized by an absence of noise **2** calm or tranquil: *the sea is quiet today* **3** untroubled: *a quiet life* **4** not busy: *business is quiet this morning* **5** private or secret: *I had a quiet word with her* **6** free from anger, impatience, or other extreme emotion **7** not showy: *quiet colours; a quiet wedding* **8** modest or reserved: *quiet humour* ▷ *n* **9** the state of being silent, peaceful, or untroubled **10 on the quiet** without other people knowing ▷ *vb* **11** to make or become calm or silent [Latin *quies* repose] **quietly** *adv* **quietness** *n*

quieten *vb Brit & NZ* **1** (often foll. by *down*) to make or become calm or silent **2** to allay (fear or doubts)

quietism *n formal* passivity and calmness of mind towards external events **quietist** *n, adj*

quietude *n formal* quietness, peace, or tranquillity

quietus *n, pl* **-tuses 1** *literary* a release from life; death **2** the discharge or settlement of debts or duties [Latin *quietus est*, literally: he is at rest]

quiff *n Brit* a tuft of hair brushed up above the forehead [origin unknown]

quill *n* **1** Also called: **quill pen** a feather made into a pen **2 A** any of the large stiff feathers of the wing or tail of a bird **B** the hollow stem of a feather **3** any of the stiff hollow spines of a porcupine or hedgehog [origin unknown]

quilt *n* **1** a cover for a bed, consisting of a soft filling sewn between two layers of material, usually with crisscross seams **2** a continental quilt; duvet ▷ *vb* **3** to stitch together two layers of (fabric) with padding between them [Old French *coilte* mattress] **quilted** *adj*

quin *n* a quintuplet

quince *n* the acid-tasting pear-shaped fruit of an Asian tree, used in preserves [Greek *kudōnion*]

quincunx *n* a group of five objects arranged in the shape of a rectangle with one at each corner and the fifth in the centre [Latin: five twelfths; in ancient Rome, this was a coin marked with five spots]

quinine *n* a bitter drug extracted from cinchona bark, used as a tonic and formerly in malaria therapy [Spanish *quina* cinchona bark]

quinquennial *adj* occurring once every five years or over a period of five years

quinquereme *n* an ancient Roman galley with five banks of oars [Latin *quinque* five + *remus* oar]

quinsy *n* inflammation of the tonsils and throat, with abscesses [Greek *kuōn* dog + *ankhein* to strangle]

quint *n US & Canad* a quintuplet

quintal *n* **1** a unit of weight equal to (esp. in Britain) 112 pounds (50.85 kg) or (esp. in US) 100 pounds (45.36 kg) **2** a unit of weight equal to 100 kilograms [Arabic *qintār*]

quintessence *n* **1** the perfect representation of a quality or state **2** an extract of a substance containing its central nature in its most concentrated form [Medieval Latin *quinta essentia* the fifth essence] **quintessential** *adj*

quintet *n* **1** a group of five singers or instrumentalists **2** a piece of music for five performers **3** any group of five [Italian *quintetto*]

quintillion *n, pl* **-lions** *or* **-lion 1** the number represented as one followed by 18 zeros (10^{18}) **2** (in Britain, originally) the number represented as one followed by 30 zeros (10^{30}) [Latin *quintus* fifth]

quintuple *vb* **-pling, -pled 1** to multiply by five ▷ *adj* **2** five times as much or as many **3** consisting of five parts ▷ *n* **4** a quantity or number five times as great as another [Latin *quintus* fifth + *-plus* -fold]

quintuplet *n* one of five children born at one birth

quip *n* **1** a witty saying ▷ *vb* **quipping, quipped 2** to make a quip [probably from Latin *quippe* indeed, to be sure]

quire *n* a set of 24 or 25 sheets of paper [Old French *quaier*]

quirk *n* **1** a peculiarity of character; mannerism or foible **2** an unexpected twist or turn: *a strange quirk of fate* [origin unknown] **quirky** *adj*

quisling *n* a traitor who aids an occupying enemy force; collaborator [after Vidkun *Quisling*, Norwegian collaborator with the Nazis]

quit *vb* **quitting, quit 1** to stop (doing something) **2** to resign (from): *the Prime Minister's decision to quit; he quit his job as a salesman* **3** to leave (a place) [Old French *quitter*] **quitter** *n*

quitch *or* **quitch grass** *n* same as **couch grass**

quite *adv* **1** (*not used with a negative*) to a greater than average extent; somewhat: *he found her quite attractive* **2** absolutely: *you're quite right* **3** in actuality; truly **4 quite a** *or* **an** of an exceptional kind: *she is quite a girl* **5 quite something** a remarkable thing or person ▷ *interj* **6** an expression used to indicate agreement [adverbial use of *quite* (adjective) quit, free of]

USAGE See at **very**.

quits *adj informal* **1** on an equal footing **2 call it quits** to end a dispute or contest, agreeing that honours are even

quittance *n* **1** release from debt or other obligation **2** a document certifying this [Old French *quitter* to release from obligation]

quiver[1] *vb* **1** to shake with a tremulous movement; tremble ▷ *n* **2** a shaking or trembling [obsolete *cwiver* quick, nimble] **quivering** *adj*

quiver[2] *n* a case for holding or carrying arrows [Old French *cuivre*]

quixotic (kwik-**sot**-ik) *adj* unrealistically optimistic or chivalrous [after Don *Quixote* in Cervantes' romance] **quixotically** *adv*

quiz *n, pl* **quizzes 1** an entertainment in which the knowledge of the players is tested by a series of questions **2** any set of quick questions designed to test knowledge **3** an investigation by close questioning ▷ *vb* **quizzing, quizzed 4** to investigate by close questioning; interrogate [origin unknown]

quizzical *adj* questioning and mocking or supercilious: *the question elicits a quizzical expression* **quizzically** *adv*

quoin *n* **1** an external corner of a wall **2** the stone forming the outer corner of a wall; a cornerstone **3** a wedge [variant of *coin* (in former sense of corner)]

quoit *n* a large ring used in the game of quoits [origin unknown]

quoits *n* a game in which quoits are tossed at a stake in the ground in attempts to encircle it

quokka *n* a small Australian wallaby [from a native Australian language]

quondam *adj formal* of an earlier time; former: *her quondam employers* [Latin]

quorate *adj* having or being a quorum: *the meeting is now quorate*

Quorn *n trademark* a vegetable protein used as a meat substitute

quorum *n* the minimum number of members required to be present in a meeting or assembly before any business can be transacted [Latin, literally: of whom]

quota *n* **1** the share that is due from, due to, or allocated to a person or group **2** the prescribed number or quantity allowed, required, or admitted [Latin *quotus* of what number]

quotation *n* **1** a written or spoken passage repeated exactly in a later work, speech, or conversation, usually with an acknowledgment of its source **2** the act of quoting **3** an estimate of costs submitted by a contractor to a prospective client

quotation marks *pl n* the punctuation marks used to begin and end a quotation, either " and " or ' and '

quote *vb* **quoting, quoted 1** to repeat (words) exactly from (an earlier work, speech, or conversation), usually with an acknowledgment of their source **2** to state a price for goods or a job of work **3** to put quotation marks round (words) ▷ *n* **4** *informal* a quotation **5 quotes** *informal* quotation marks ▷ *interj* **6** an expression used to indicate that the words that follow are a quotation [Medieval Latin *quotare* to assign reference numbers to passages] **quotable** *adj*

quoth *vb archaic* (foll. by I, *he* or *she*) said [Old English *cwæth*]

quotidian *adj* **1** daily **2** *literary* commonplace **3** (esp. of fever) recurring daily [Latin *quotidianus*]

quotient *n* the result of the division of one number or quantity by another [Latin *quotiens* how often]

Quran (koo-**rahn**) *n* same as **Koran**

q.v. (denoting a cross-reference) which (word, item, etc.) see [New Latin *quod vide*]

qwerty *or* **QWERTY keyboard** *n* the standard English-language computer or typewriter keyboard with the characters q, w, e, r, t, and y at the top left of the keyboard

Rr

r **1** radius **2** ratio **3** right **4** *cricket* run(s)
R **1** *chem* radical **2** Regina **3** Registered Trademark **4** *physics & electronics* resistance **5** Rex **6** River **7** *chess* rook
Ra *chem* radium
RA **1** rear admiral **2** (in Britain) Royal Academy **3** (in Britain) Royal Artillery
RAAF Royal Australian Air Force
rabbi (rab-bye) *n, pl* **-bis** **1** the spiritual leader of a Jewish congregation **2** an expert in or teacher of Jewish Law [Hebrew: my master] **rabbinical** *adj*
rabbit *n, pl* **-bits** *or* **-bit** **1** a common burrowing mammal with long ears and a short fluffy tail ▷ *vb* **-biting, -bited** **2** *informal* to talk too much: *he keeps rabbiting on about interrogation* [origin unknown]
rabbit ears *pl n Austral & NZ old-fashioned* an indoor television aerial
rabbit fence *n* a fence to prevent the spread of rabbits
rabbiting *n* **go rabbiting** to hunt rabbits
rabbit punch *n* a short sharp blow to the back of the neck
rabble *n* **1** a disorderly crowd of noisy people **2** **the rabble** *derogatory* ordinary people collectively [origin unknown]
rabble-rouser *n* a person who stirs up the feelings of the mob **rabble-rousing** *adj, n*
Rabelaisian *adj* characterized by broad, often bawdy humour and sharp satire [after the work of the French writer, François *Rabelais*]
rabid *adj* **1** fanatical: *a rabid separatist* **2** having rabies [Latin *rabidus* frenzied] **rabidity** *n*
rabies (ray-beez) *n* *pathol* a fatal infectious viral disease of the nervous system transmitted by dogs and certain other animals [Latin: madness]
RAC (in Britain) Royal Automobile Club
raccoon *or* **racoon** *n, pl* **-coons** *or* **-coon** a small American mammal with a long striped tail [from a Native American language]
race¹ *n* **1** a contest of speed **2** any competition or rivalry: *the arms race* **3** a rapid current of water **4** a channel of a stream: *a mill race* **5** *Austral & NZ* a narrow passage through which sheep pass individually, as to a sheep dip ▷ *vb* **racing, raced** **6** to take part in a contest of speed with (someone) **7** to enter (an animal or vehicle) in a race: *to race greyhounds* **8** to travel as fast as possible **9** (of an engine) to run faster than normal **10** (of the heart) to beat faster than normal ▷ See also **races** [Old Norse *rās* running] **racer** *n* **racing** *adj, n*
race² *n* **1** a group of people of common ancestry with distinguishing physical features, such as skin colour or build **2** **the human race** human beings collectively **3** a group of animals or plants having common characteristics that distinguish them from other members of the same species [Italian *razza*]
race caller *n* a professional horse-racing commentator
racecourse *n* a long broad track on which horses are raced
racehorse *n* a horse specially bred for racing
raceme (rass-**eem**) *n* *botany* a cluster of flowers along a central stem, as in the foxglove [Latin *racemus* bunch of grapes]
race meeting *n* a series of horse or greyhound races held at the same place
race relations *pl n* the relations between members of two or more races within a single community
race riot *n* a riot involving violence between people of different races
races *pl n* **the races** a series of contests of speed between horses or greyhounds over a fixed course
racetrack *n* **1** a circuit used for races between cars, bicycles, or runners **2** *US & Canad* a racecourse
racial *adj* **1** relating to the division of the human species into races **2** typically associated with any such group **racially** *adv*
racism *or* **racialism** *n* **1** hostile or oppressive behaviour towards people because they belong to a different race **2** the belief that some races are innately superior to others because of hereditary characteristics **racist** *or* **racialist** *n, adj*
rack¹ *n* **1** a framework for holding particular articles, such as coats or luggage **2** a straight bar with teeth on its edge, to work with a cogwheel **3** **the rack** *history* an instrument of torture that stretched the body of the victim ▷ *vb* **4** to cause great suffering to: *Italy was racked by internal disputes* **5** **rack one's brains** to try very hard to think of something [probably from Middle Dutch *rec* framework]

USAGE See at **wrack¹**.

rack² *n* **go to rack and ruin** to be destroyed through neglect [variant of WRACK¹]
rack³ *vb* to clear (wine or beer) by siphoning it off from the dregs
rack⁴ *n* the neck or rib part of a joint of meat
rack-and-pinion *n* a device for converting rotary into linear motion and vice versa, in which a gearwheel (the pinion) engages with a flat toothed bar (the rack)
racket¹ *n* **1** a noisy disturbance **2** an illegal activity done to make money **3** *slang* a business or occupation: *I've been in the racket since I was sixteen* ▷ *vb* **-eting, -eted** **4** to make a commotion [probably imitative] **rackety** *adj*
racket² *or* **racquet** *n* a bat consisting of an oval frame surrounding a mesh of strings, with a handle, used in tennis, badminton, and squash. See also **rackets** [French *raquette*]
racketeer *n* a person who makes money from illegal activities **racketeering** *n*
rackets *n* a game similar to squash, played by two or four people
rack-rent *n* an extortionate rent
raclette *n* a Swiss dish of melted cheese, usually served on boiled potatoes [French]

raconteur (rak-on-**tur**) *n* a person skilled in telling stories [French]
racoon *n, pl* **-coons** *or* **-coon** same as **raccoon**
racquet *n* same as **racket**[2]
racy *adj* **racier, raciest 1** slightly shocking: *a racy comedy* **2** spirited or lively: *a racy literary style* **racily** *adv* **raciness** *n*
rad radian
RADA (in Britain) Royal Academy of Dramatic Art
radar *n* **1** a method of detecting the position and velocity of a distant object by bouncing a narrow beam of extremely high-frequency radio pulses off it **2** the equipment used in this [*ra(dio) d(etecting) a(nd) r(anging)*]
radar trap *n* a device which uses radar to detect motorists who break the speed limit
raddle *vb Austral & NZ* to mark (sheep) for identification
raddled *adj* (of a person) untidy or rundown in appearance [from *rud* red ochre]
radial *adj* **1** spreading out from a common central point **2** of a radius or ray **3** short for **radial-ply** ▷ *n* **4** a radial-ply tyre **radially** *adv*
radial-ply *adj* (of a tyre) having the fabric cords in the outer casing running radially to enable the sidewalls to be flexible
radian *n* an SI unit of plane angle; the angle between two radii of a circle that cut off on the circumference an arc equal in length to the radius
radiant *adj* **1** characterized by health and happiness: *radiant good looks* **2** shining **3** emitted as radiation: *radiant heat* **4** sending out heat by radiation: *radiant heaters* [Latin *radiare* to shine] **radiance** *n*
radiant energy *n* energy that is emitted or propagated in the form of particles or electromagnetic radiation
radiate *vb* **-ating, -ated 1** to spread out from a central point **2** to show (an emotion or quality) to a great degree: *she radiated competence and composure* **3** to emit or be emitted as radiation ▷ *adj* **4** having rays or a radial structure [Latin *radiare* to emit rays]
radiation *n* **1** *physics* **A** the emission of energy as particles, electromagnetic waves or sound **B** the particles or waves emitted **2** the process of radiating
radiation sickness *n* illness caused by overexposure to radioactive material or X-rays
radiator *n* **1** *Brit* a device for heating a room or building, consisting of a series of pipes containing hot water **2** a device for cooling an internal-combustion engine, consisting of thin-walled tubes containing water **3** *Austral & NZ* an electric fire
radical *adj* **1** favouring fundamental change in political or social conditions: *a radical student movement* **2** of the essential nature of a person or thing; fundamental: *a radical fault* **3** searching or thorough: *a radical interpretation* **4** *maths* of or containing roots of numbers or quantities ▷ *n* **5** a person who favours fundamental change in existing institutions or in political, social, or economic conditions **6** *maths* a root of a number or quantity, such as $\sqrt[3]{5}$, $\sqrt{x}$ **7** *chem* an atom or group of atoms that acts as a unit during chemical reactions [Latin *radix* a root] **radicalism** *n* **radically** *adv*
radicalize *or* **-lise** *vb* **-lizing, -lized** *or* **-lising, -lised** to make (a person, group, or situation) radical or more radical: *the feelings of its own radicalized population*
radical sign *n* the symbol $\sqrt{}$ placed before a number or quantity to indicate the extraction of a root, esp. a square root. The value of a higher root is indicated by a raised digit in front of the symbol, as in $\sqrt[3]{}$
radicchio (rad-**deek**-ee-oh) *n, pl* **-chios** an Italian variety of chicory, with purple leaves streaked with white that are eaten raw in salads [Italian]
radicle *n botany* **A** the part of the embryo of seed-bearing plants that develops into the main root **B** a very small root or rootlike part [Latin *radix* root]
radii *n* a plural of **radius**
radio *n, pl* **-dios 1** the use of electromagnetic waves for broadcasting or two-way communication without the use of linking wires **2** an electronic device for converting radio signals into sounds **3** a communications device for sending and receiving messages using radio waves **4** sound broadcasting ▷ *vb* **5** to transmit (a message) by radio ▷ *adj* **6** of, relating to, or using radio broadcasting or radio signals: *a radio interview* **7** using or producing electromagnetic waves in the range used for radio signals: *radio astronomy* [Latin *radius* ray]
radio- *combining form* **1** (denoting) radio **2** (denoting) radioactivity or radiation: *radiocarbon*
radioactive *adj* showing or using radioactivity
radioactivity *n* the spontaneous emission of radiation from atomic nuclei. The radiation can consist of alpha or beta particles, or gamma rays
radio astronomy *n* astronomy using a radio telescope to analyse signals received from radio sources in space
radiocarbon *n* a radioactive isotope of carbon, esp. carbon-14
radiocarbon dating *n* same as **carbon dating**
radiochemistry *n* the chemistry of radioactive substances
radio-controlled *adj* controlled by signals sent by radio
radio frequency *n* any electromagnetic frequency that lies in the range 10 kilohertz to 300 000 megahertz and can be used for broadcasting
radiogram *n Brit* (formerly) a combined radio and record player built into a cabinet
radiograph *n* an image produced on a special photographic film or plate by radiation, usually by X-rays
radiography (ray-dee-**og**-ra-fee) *n* the production of radiographs for use in medicine or industry **radiographer** *n*
radioisotope *n* a radioactive isotope
radiology (ray-dee-**ol**-a-jee) *n* the use of X-rays and radioactive substances in the diagnosis and treatment of disease **radiologist** *n*
radioscopy (ray-dee-**oss**-kop-ee) *n* examination of a person or object by means of a fluorescent screen and an X-ray source

radiosonde *n* an airborne instrument to send meteorological information back to earth by radio [RADIO- + French *sonde* sounding line]
radiotelegraphy *n* telegraphy in which messages are transmitted by radio waves
radiotelephone *n* a telephone which sends and receives messages using radio waves rather than wires **radiotelephony** *n*
radio telescope *n* an instrument used in radio astronomy to pick up and analyse radio waves from space
radiotherapy *n* the treatment of disease, esp. cancer, by radiation
radio wave *n* an electromagnetic wave of radio frequency
radish *n* a small hot-flavoured red root vegetable eaten raw in salads [Latin *radix* root]
radium *n chem* a highly radioactive luminescent metallic element, found in pitchblende. Symbol: **Ra** [Latin *radius* ray]
radius (ray-dee-uss) *n, pl* **-dii** (-dee-eye) *or* **-diuses** **1** a straight line joining the centre of a circle to any point on the circumference **2** the length of this line **3** *anatomy* the outer, slightly shorter of the two bones of the forearm **4** a circular area of a specified size round a central point: *within a seven-mile radius of the club* [Latin: ray, spoke]
radon (ray-don) *n chem* a colourless radioactive element of the noble gas group. Symbol: **Rn** [from *radium*]
RAF (in Britain) Royal Air Force
Rafferty *or* **Rafferty's rules** *pl n Austral & NZ slang* no rules at all [origin unknown]
raffia *n* a fibre obtained from the leaves of a palm tree, used for weaving [Malagasy]
raffish *adj* unconventional or slightly disreputable [obsolete *raff* rubbish]
raffle *n* **1** a lottery, often to raise money for charity, in which the prizes are goods rather than money ▷ *vb* **-fling, -fled** **2** to offer as a prize in a raffle [Old French]
raft *n* a floating platform of logs or planks tied together [Old Norse *raptr* rafter]
rafter *n* any of the parallel sloping beams that form the framework of a roof [Old English]
rag[1] *n* **1** a small piece of cloth **2** *Brit, Austral & NZ informal* a newspaper **3** **rags** old tattered clothing **4** **from rags to riches** from being extremely poor to being extremely wealthy [probably formed from *ragged*, from Old English *raggig*]
rag[2] *Brit* ▷ *vb* **ragging, ragged** **1** to tease **2** to play rough practical jokes on ▷ *n* **3** a boisterous practical joke ▷ *adj* **4** (in British universities and colleges) of various events organized to raise money for charity: *a rag week* [origin unknown]
rag[3] *n* a piece of ragtime music
ragamuffin *n* **1** a ragged dirty child **2** same as **ragga** [probably from RAG[1]]
rag-and-bone man *n Brit* a man who goes from street to street buying old clothes and furniture
ragbag *n* a confused mixture: *the traditional ragbag of art traders*
rage *n* **1** intense anger or passion **2** a fashion or craze: *the dance was the rage of Europe* **3** aggressive behaviour associated with a specified activity or environment: *road rage; school rage* **4** **all the rage** *informal* very popular **5** *Austral & NZ informal* a dance or party ▷ *vb* **raging, raged** **6** to feel or show intense anger **7** to proceed violently and without restraint: *the argument was still raging* [Latin *rabies* madness]
ragga *n* a dance-oriented style of reggae [from RAGAMUFFIN]
ragged (rag-gid) *adj* **1** dressed in shabby or torn clothes **2** (of clothes) tattered and torn **3** having a rough or uneven surface or edge **4** neglected or untidy: *the ragged stone-built village*
ragged robin *n* a plant that has pink or white flowers with ragged petals
raglan *adj* **1** (of a sleeve) joined to the garment by diagonal seams from the collar to the underarm **2** (of a garment) with this style of sleeve [after Lord *Raglan*, soldier and diplomat]
ragout (rag-goo) *n* a richly seasoned stew of meat and vegetables [French]
ragtag *n* **ragtag and bobtail** *derogatory* ordinary people
ragtime *n* a style of jazz piano music with a syncopated melody [probably *ragged time*]
rag trade *n informal* the clothing business
ragwort *n* a plant with ragged leaves and yellow flowers
raid *n* **1** a sudden surprise attack: *a bombing raid* **2** a surprise visit by police searching for people or goods: *a drugs raid* ▷ *vb* **3** to make a raid on **4** to sneak into (a place) in order to steal [Old English *rād* military expedition] **raider** *n*
rail[1] *n* **1** a horizontal bar supported by vertical posts, used as a fence or barrier **2** a horizontal bar on which to hang things: *a curtain rail* **3** one of a pair of parallel bars that serve as a running surface for the wheels of a train **4** railway: *by car or by rail* **5** **go off the rails** to start behaving improperly or eccentrically ▷ *vb* **6** to fence (an area) with rails [Old French *raille* rod]
rail[2] *vb* **rail against** *or* **at** to complain bitterly or loudly about [Old French *railler* to mock]
rail[3] *n* a small wading marsh bird [Old French *raale*]
railcard *n Brit* an identity card, which pensioners or young people can buy, entitling them to cheaper rail travel
railhead *n* **1** a terminal of a railway **2** the farthest point reached by completed track on an unfinished railway
railing *n* a fence made of rails supported by posts
raillery *n, pl* **-leries** good-natured teasing [French *railler* to tease]
railroad *n* **1** *US* a railway ▷ *vb* **2** *informal* to force (a person) into an action with haste or by unfair means
railway *n* **1** a track composed of a line of parallel metal rails fixed to sleepers, on which trains run **2** any track on which the wheels of a vehicle may run: *a cable railway* **3** the rolling stock, buildings, and tracks used in such a transport system **4** the organization responsible for operating a railway network
raiment *n archaic or poetic* clothing [from *arrayment*]
rain *n* **1** A water falling from the sky in drops formed by the condensation of water vapour in the atmosphere B a fall of rain. ▷ Related adjective:

pluvial **2** a large quantity of anything falling rapidly: *a rain of stones descended on the police* **3 (come) rain or shine** regardless of circumstances **4 right as rain** *informal* perfectly all right ▷ *vb* **5** to fall as rain: *it's raining back home* **6** to fall rapidly and in large quantities: *steel rungs and sawdust raining down* **7 rained off** cancelled or postponed because of rain. US and Canad term: **rained out** ▷ See also **rains** [Old English *regn*] **rainy** *adj*

rainbird *n S African* a common name for **Burchell's coucal**, a bird whose call is believed to be a sign of impending rain

rainbow *n* an arched display in the sky of the colours of the spectrum, caused by the refraction and reflection of the sun's rays through rain

rainbow nation *n* the South African nation

rainbow trout *n* a freshwater trout with black spots and two red stripes

rain check *n* **take a rain check** *informal* to request or accept the postponement of an offer

raincoat *n* a coat made of a waterproof material

rainfall *n* the amount of rain, hail, or snow in a specified place and time

rainforest *n* dense forest found in tropical areas of heavy rainfall

rains *pl n* **the rains** the season in the tropics when there is a lot of rain

rainstorm *n* a storm with heavy rain

rainwater *n* water from rain

rainy day *n* a future time of need, esp. financial need

raise *vb* **raising, raised 1** to lift to a higher position or level **2** to place in an upright position **3** to increase in amount, quality, or intensity: *to raise interest rates* **4** to collect or gather together: *to raise additional capital; to raise an army* **5** to cause to be expressed: *to raise a smile* **6** to stir up **7** to bring up: *to raise a family* **8** to grow: *to raise a crop* **9** to put forward for consideration: *they raised controversial issues* **10** to arouse from sleep or death **11** to build: *to raise a barn* **12** to bring to an end: *to raise a siege* **13** to establish radio communications with: *we raised Moscow last night* **14** to advance in rank; promote **15** *maths* to multiply (a number) by itself a specified number of times: *8 is 2 raised to the power 3* **16** to cause (dough) to rise, as by the addition of yeast **17** *cards* to bet more than (the previous player) **18 raise Cain A** to create a disturbance **B** to protest vehemently ▷ *n* **19** *US, Canad & NZ* an increase in pay [Old Norse *reisa*]

raised *adj* higher than the surrounding area: *a small raised platform*

raisin *n* a dried grape [Old French: grape]

raison d'être (ray-zon **det**-ra) *n, pl* **raisons d'être** (ray-zon **det**-ra) reason or justification for existence [French]

raita (**rye**-ta) *n* an Indian dish of chopped cucumber, mint, etc., in yogurt, served with curry [Hindi]

Raj *n* **the Raj** the British government in India before 1947 [Hindi]

raja *or* **rajah** *n history* an Indian prince or ruler [Hindi]

rake[1] *n* **1** a farm or garden tool consisting of a row of teeth set in a headpiece attached to a long shaft and used for gathering leaves or straw, or for smoothing loose earth **2** any of various implements similar in shape or function ▷ *vb* **raking, raked 3** to scrape or gather with a rake **4** to smooth (a surface) with a rake **5** Also: **rake out** to clear (ashes) from (a fire) **6 rake together** *or* **up** to gather (items or people) with difficulty, as from a limited supply **7** to search or examine carefully: *raking over the past is not always popular* **8** to direct (gunfire) along the length of (a target): *the machine guns raked up and down their line* **9** to scrape or graze: *he raked the tip of his shoe across the pavement* ▷ See also **rake in, rake-off** *etc.* [Old English *raca*]

rake[2] *n* an immoral man [short for *rakehell*]

rake[3] *n* **1** the degree to which an object slopes ▷ *vb* **raking, raked 2** to slope from the vertical, esp. (of a ship's mast) towards the stern **3** to construct with a backward slope [origin unknown]

raked *adj* (of a surface) sloping so that it is higher at the back than at the front

rake in *vb informal* to acquire (money) in large amounts

rake-off *n slang* a share of profits, esp. an illegal one

rake up *vb* to bring back memories of (a forgotten unpleasant event): *she doesn't want to rake up the past*

rakish[1] (**ray**-kish) *adj* dashing or jaunty: *a hat which he wore at a rakish angle* [probably from RAKE[3]]

rakish[2] *adj* immoral: *a rakish life of drinking and womanizing* [from RAKE[2]] **rakishly** *adv*

rallentando *music* ▷ *adj, adv* **1** becoming slower ▷ *n* **2** a passage in which the music becomes slower [Italian]

rally[1] *n, pl* **-lies 1** a large gathering of people for a meeting **2** a marked recovery of strength, as during illness **3** *Stock Exchange* a sharp increase in price or trading activity after a decline **4** *tennis & squash etc.* an exchange of several shots before one player wins the point **5** a car-driving competition on public roads ▷ *vb* **-lies, -lying, -lied 6** to bring or come together after being dispersed **7** to bring or come together for a common cause **8** to summon up (one's strength or spirits) **9** to recover (sometimes only temporarily) from an illness **10** *Stock Exchange* to increase sharply after a decline [Old French *rallier*]

rally[2] *vb* **-lies, -lying, -lied** *old-fashioned* to mock or tease (someone) in a good-natured way [Old French *railler* to tease]

rally round *vb* to group together to help someone

ram *n* **1** an uncastrated adult male sheep **2** a hydraulically or pneumatically driven piston **3** the falling weight of a pile driver **4** short for **battering ram** ▷ *vb* **ramming, rammed 5** to strike against with force **6** to force or drive: *he rammed his sword into the man's belly* **7** to stuff or cram **8 ram something home** to make something clear or obvious: *to ram home the message* **9 ram something down someone's throat** to put forward or emphasize an argument or idea with excessive force [Old English *ramm*]

RAM *computers* random access memory: a temporary storage space which loses its contents when the computer is switched off

Rama *n* a Hindu god, the incarnation of Vishnu

Ramadan *n* **1** the ninth month of the Muslim year, 29 or 30 days long, during which strict fasting is observed from dawn to sunset **2** the fast itself

ramble *vb* **-bling, -bled 1** to walk for relaxation, sometimes with no particular direction **2** to speak or write in a confused style **3** to grow or develop in a random fashion ▷ *n* **4** a walk, esp. in the countryside [Middle English *romblen*]

rambler *n* **1** a person who takes country walks **2** a climbing rose

rambling *adj* **1** long and irregularly shaped: *a rambling fourteenth-century church* **2** (of speech or writing) confused and long-winded ▷ *n* **3** the activity of going for long walks in the country

RAMC (in Britain) Royal Army Medical Corps

ramekin (ram-ik-in) *n* a small container for baking and serving one portion of food [French *ramequin*]

ramification *n* **1 ramifications** the consequences or complications resulting from an action **2** a structure of branching parts

ramify *vb* **-fies, -fying, -fied 1** to become complex **2** to spread in branches; subdivide [French *ramifier*]

ramjet *n* **A** a type of jet engine in which fuel is burned in a duct using air compressed by the forward speed of the aircraft **B** an aircraft powered by such an engine

ramp *n* **1** a slope that joins two surfaces at different levels **2** a place where the level of a road surface changes because of roadworks **3** a movable stairway by which passengers enter and leave an aircraft **4** *Brit* a small hump on a road to make traffic slow down [Old French *ramper* to crawl, rear]

rampage *vb* **-paging, -paged 1** to rush about violently ▷ *n* **2 on the rampage** behaving violently or destructively [Scots]

rampant *adj* **1** growing or spreading uncontrollably **2** *heraldry* (of a beast) standing on the hind legs, the right foreleg raised above the left: *a lion rampant* [Old French *ramper* to crawl, rear]

rampart *n* a mound of earth or a wall built to protect a fort or city [Old French]

rampike *n chiefly Canad* a tall tree that has been burned bare of branches

ramp up *vb* **1** to increase or cause to increase **2** to increase the effort involved in a process

ram raid *n Brit, Austral & NZ informal* a raid on a shop in which a stolen car is driven into the window **ram raider** *n*

ramrod *n* **1** a long thin rod for cleaning the barrel of a gun or forcing gunpowder into an old-fashioned gun ▷ *adj* **2** (of someone's posture) very straight and upright

ramshackle *adj* badly made or cared for: *a curious ramshackle building* [obsolete *ransackle* to ransack]

ran *vb* the past tense of **run**

RAN Royal Australian Navy

ranch *n* **1** a large cattle farm in the American West **2** *chiefly US & Canad* a large farm for the rearing of a particular kind of livestock or crop: *they owned a sheep ranch in Montana* ▷ *vb* **3** to run a ranch [Mexican Spanish *rancho* small farm] **rancher** *n*

ranchslider *n NZ* a glazed sliding door usually opening onto an outside terrace

rancid *adj* (of fatty foods) stale and having an offensive smell [Latin *rancidus*] **rancidity** *n*

rancour *or US* **rancor** *n* deep bitter hate [Old French] **rancorous** *adj*

rand *n* the standard monetary unit of the Republic of South Africa [from *Witwatersrand*, S Transvaal, referring to the gold-mining there]

R & B rhythm and blues

R & D research and development

random *adj* **1** lacking any definite plan or prearranged order: *a random sample* **2** *informal* unknown or unspecified: *some random guy* ▷ *n* **3** *informal* an unknown or unspecified person **4 at random** not following any prearranged order [Old French *randir* to gallop] **randomly** *adv* **randomness** *n*

random access *n* a method of reading data from a computer file without having to read through the file from the beginning

randy *adj* **randier, randiest** *informal* sexually aroused [probably from obsolete *rand* to rant] **randily** *adv* **randiness** *n*

ranee *n* same as **rani**

rang *vb* the past tense of **ring'**

USAGE See at **ring'**.

rangatira (rung-a-teer-a) *n NZ* a Māori chief of either sex [Māori]

range *n* **1** the limits within which a person or thing can function effectively: *academic ability range* **2 A** the maximum effective distance of a projectile fired from a weapon **B** the distance between a target and a weapon **3** the total distance which a ship, aircraft, or vehicle can travel without taking on fresh fuel **4** the difference in pitch between the highest and lowest note of a voice or musical instrument **5** a whole set of related things: *a range of treatments was available* **6** the total products of a manufacturer, designer, or stockist: *the latest skin-care range* **7** the limits within which something can lie: *a range of prices* **8** *US & Canad* an extensive tract of open land on which livestock can graze **9** a chain of mountains **10** an area set aside for shooting practice or rocket testing **11** a large cooking stove with one or more ovens **12** *maths* the set of values that a function or variable can take ▷ *vb* **ranging, ranged 13** to vary between one point and another **14** to cover a specified period or specified things: *attitudes ranged from sympathy to indifference* **15** to roam (over) **16** to establish or be situated in a line or series **17** to put into a specific category: *they ranged themselves with the opposition* [Old French: row]

rangefinder *n* an instrument for finding how far away an object is

ranger *n* **1** an official in charge of a park or nature reserve **2** *US* an armed trooper employed to police a State or district: *a Texas ranger*

Ranger *or* **Ranger Guide** *n Brit & Austral* a member of the senior branch of the Guides

rangy (rain-jee) *adj* **rangier, rangiest** having long slender limbs

r

rani *or* **ranee** *n* the wife or widow of a raja [Hindi]
rank[1] *n* **1** a position within a social organization: *the rank of superintendent* **2** high social or other standing: *accusations were made against people of high rank* **3** a person's social class: *it was too grand for someone of his lowly rank* **4** the position of an item in any ordering or sequence **5** a line or row of people or things **6** a place where taxis wait to be hired **7** a line of people, esp. soldiers, positioned one beside the other **8** any of the eight horizontal rows of squares on a chessboard **9 close ranks** to maintain solidarity **10 pull rank** to get one's own way by virtue of one's superior position **11 rank and file** the ordinary people or members of a group **12 the ranks** ordinary soldiers ▷ *vb* **13** to give or hold a specific position in an organization or group **14** to arrange in rows or lines **15** to arrange in sequence: *to rank students according to their grades* **16** to be important: *the legendary coronation stone ranks high in the hearts of patriots* [Old French *ranc*]
rank[2] *adj* **1** complete or absolute: *rank incompetence* **2** smelling offensively strong **3** growing too quickly: *rank weeds* [Old English *ranc* straight, proud]
rankle *vb* **-kling, -kled** to continue to cause resentment or bitterness [Old French *draoncle* ulcer]
ransack *vb* **1** to search through every part of (a place or thing) **2** to plunder or pillage [Old Norse *rann* house + *saka* to search]
ransom *n* **1** the money demanded in return for the release of someone who has been kidnapped **2 hold to ransom** **A** to keep (a prisoner) in confinement until payment is received **B** to attempt to force (a person) to do something ▷ *vb* **3** to pay money to obtain the release of (a prisoner) **4** to set free (a prisoner) in return for money [Old French *ransoun*] **ransomer** *n*
ransomware *n* illegal software that disables a computer or blocks access to data until a payment is received
rant *vb* **1** to talk in a loud and excited way ▷ *n* **2** loud excited speech [Dutch *ranten* to rave] **ranting** *adj, n*
ranunculus *n, pl* **-luses** *or* **-li** a genus of plants including the buttercup [Latin *rana* frog]
rap *vb* **rapping, rapped 1** to hit with a sharp quick blow **2** to knock loudly and sharply **3 rap out** to utter in sharp rapid speech: *he rapped out his address* **4** to perform a rhythmic monologue with musical backing **5** *slang* to talk in a relaxed and friendly way **6** to rebuke or criticize sharply **7 rap over the knuckles** to reprimand ▷ *n* **8** a sharp quick blow or the sound produced by it **9** a fast rhythmic monologue over a musical backing **10** a sharp rebuke or criticism **11** *slang* a legal charge: *a murder rap* **12 take the rap** *slang* to suffer the punishment for a crime, whether guilty or not [probably from Old Norse] **rapper** *n*
rapacious *adj* **1** greedy or grasping **2** (of animals or birds) living by catching prey [Latin *rapax*] **rapacity** *n*
rape[1] *vb* **raping, raped 1** to commit the offence of rape upon (a person) ▷ *n* **2** the offence of forcing a person to submit to sexual intercourse against that person's will **3** any violation or abuse: *the rape of the country's natural resources* [Latin *rapere* to seize] **rapist** *n*
rape[2] *n* a yellow-flowered plant cultivated for its seeds, **rapeseed**, which yield a useful oil, **rape oil**, and as a fodder plant [Latin *rapum* turnip]
rapid *adj* **1** (of an action) taking or lasting a short time **2** acting or moving quickly: *a rapid advance* [Latin *rapidus*] **rapidly** *adv* **rapidity** *n*
rapid eye movement *n* the movement of the eyeballs while a person is dreaming
rapids *pl n* part of a river where the water is very fast and turbulent
rapier (ray-pyer) *n* a long narrow two-edged sword [Old French *espee rapiere* rasping sword]
rapine (rap-pine) *n* pillage or plundering [Latin *rapina*]
rapport (rap-pore) *n* a sympathetic relationship or understanding [French]
rapprochement (rap-**prosh**-mong) *n* a re-establishment of friendly relations: *diplomatic rapprochement with North Korea* [French]
rapscallion *n old-fashioned* a rascal or rogue [earlier *rascallion*]
rap sheet *n chiefly US & Canad informal* a police record of an individual's criminal history
rapt *adj* **1** totally engrossed: *rapt attention* **2** arising from or showing rapture: *with a rapt look on his face* [Latin *raptus* carried away]
raptor *n* any bird of prey [Latin: robber] **raptorial** *adj*
rapture *n* **1** extreme happiness or delight **2 raptures** ecstatic joy: *they will be in raptures over the rugged scenery* [Latin *raptus* carried away] **rapturous** *adj*
rare[1] *adj* **1** uncommon or unusual: *a rare plant* **2** not happening or done very often: *a rare appearance in London* **3** of uncommonly high quality: *a rare beauty* **4** (of air at high altitudes) having low density; thin [Latin *rarus* sparse]
rare[2] *adj* (of meat) very lightly cooked [Old English *hrēr*]
rarebit *n* short for **Welsh rarebit**
rare earth *n chem* **1** any oxide of a lanthanide **2** Also called: **rare-earth element** any element of the lanthanide series
rarefied (rare-if-ide) *adj* **1** highly specialized: *the rarefied world of classical ballet* **2** (of air) thin **3** exalted in character: *the rarefied heights of academic excellence*
rarely *adv* **1** hardly ever **2** to an unusual degree; exceptionally

> **USAGE** Since *rarely* means *hardly ever*, one should not say something *rarely ever* happens.

raring *adj* **raring to do something** keen and willing to do something [*rare*, variant of REAR[2]]
rarity *n, pl* **-ties 1** something that is valuable because it is unusual **2** the state of being rare
rascal *n* **1** a scoundrel or rogue **2** a mischievous child [Old French *rascaille* rabble] **rascally** *adj*
rase *vb* **rasing, rased** same as **raze**
rash[1] *adj* acting or done without proper thought or consideration; hasty: *rash actions* [Old High German *rasc* hurried, clever] **rashly** *adv* **rashness** *n*
rash[2] *n* **1** an outbreak of spots or patches on the skin, caused by illness or allergy **2** an outbreak of occurrences: *a rash of censorship trials* [Old French *rasche*]

r

rasher *n* a thin slice of bacon [origin unknown]

rasp *n* **1** a harsh grating noise **2** a coarse file with rows of raised teeth ▷ *vb* **3** to say or speak in a grating voice **4** to make a harsh grating noise **5** to scrape or rub (something) roughly **6** to irritate (one's nerves) [Old French *raspe*]

raspberry *n, pl* **-ries** **1** the red fruit of a prickly shrub of Europe and North America **2** *informal* a spluttering noise made with the tongue and lips to express contempt: *she blew a loud raspberry* [origin unknown]

Rastafarian *or* **Rasta** *n* **1** a believer in a religion of Jamaican origin that regards Ras Tafari, the former emperor of Ethiopia, Haile Selassie, as God ▷ *adj* **2** of Rastafarians

raster *n* **1** an image consisting of rows of pixel information, such as a JPEG, GIF, etc. **2** a pattern of horizontal scanning lines traced by an electron beam, esp. on a television screen [from German *Raster* screen]

rat *n* **1** a long-tailed rodent, similar to but larger than a mouse **2** *informal* someone who is disloyal or treacherous **3** **smell a rat** to detect something suspicious ▷ *vb* **ratting, ratted** **4** **rat on** **A** to betray (someone): *good friends don't rat on each other* **B** to go back on (an agreement): *his ex-wife claims he ratted on their divorce settlement* **5** to hunt and kill rats [Old English *ræt*]

ratafia (rat-a-**fee**-a) *n* **1** a liqueur made from fruit **2** an almond-flavoured biscuit [West Indian Creole French]

rat-arsed *adj Brit & Austral slang* drunk

rat-a-tat *or* **rat-a-tat-tat** *n* a repeated knocking or tapping sound

ratatouille (rat-a-**twee**) *n* a vegetable casserole made of stewed tomatoes, aubergines, etc. [French]

ratbag *n slang* an eccentric, stupid, or unreliable person

ratchet *n* **1** a device in which a toothed rack or wheel is engaged by a pivoted lever which permits motion in one direction only **2** the toothed rack or wheel in such a device **3** to operate using a ratchet **4** (usually foll. by *up* or *down*) to increase or decrease, esp. irreversibly: *Hitchcock ratchets up the tension once again* [French *rochet*]

rate¹ *n* **1** a quantity or amount considered in relation to or measured against another quantity or amount: *he was publishing at the rate of about 10 books a year* **2** a price or charge with reference to a standard or scale: *an exchange rate* **3** the speed of progress or change: *crime is increasing at an alarming rate* **4** a charge made per unit for a commodity or service **5** See **rates** **6** relative quality: *a third-rate power* **7** **at any rate** in any case ▷ *vb* **rating, rated** **8** to assign a position on a scale of relative values: *he is rated as one of the top caterers in the country* **9** to estimate the value of: *we rate your services highly* **10** to consider or regard: *it could hardly be rated a success* **11** to be worthy of: *it barely rates a mention* **12** *informal* to have a high opinion of: *the cognoscenti have always rated his political skills* [Medieval Latin *rata*]

rate² *vb* **rating, rated** to scold or criticize severely [origin unknown]

rateable *adj* **1** able to be rated or evaluated **2** liable to payment of rates

rateable value *n* (in Britain) a fixed value assigned to a property, used to assess the rates due on it

ratepayer *n* a person who pays local rates on a building

rates *pl n* (in some countries) a tax on property levied by a local authority

rather *adv* **1** fairly: *that was a rather narrow escape* **2** to a limited extent: *I rather thought that was the case* **3** more truly or appropriately: *they tend to be cat rather than dog people* **4** more willingly: *I would rather go straight home* ▷ *interj* **5** an expression of strong affirmation: *Is it worth seeing? — Rather!* [Old English *hrathor*, comparative of *hrathe* ready, quick]

> **USAGE** Both *would* and *had* are used with *rather* in sentences such as *I would rather* (or *had rather*) *go to the film than to the play. Had rather* is less common and now widely regarded as slightly old-fashioned.

ratify *vb* **-fies, -fying, -fied** to give formal approval to: *they ratified the treaty* [Latin *ratus* fixed + *facere* to make] **ratification** *n*

rating *n* **1** a valuation or assessment **2** a classification according to order or grade **3** a noncommissioned sailor **4** **ratings** the size of the audience for a TV or radio programme

ratio *n, pl* **-tios** **1** the relationship between two numbers or amounts expressed as a proportion: *a ratio of one instructor to every five pupils* **2** *maths* a quotient of two numbers or quantities [Latin: a reckoning]

ration *n* **1** a fixed allowance of something that is scarce, such as food or petrol in wartime **2** **rations** a fixed daily allowance of food, such as that given to a soldier ▷ *vb* **3** to restrict the distribution of (something): *the government has rationed petrol* **4** to distribute a fixed amount of (something) to each person in a group [Latin *ratio* reckoning] **rationing** *n*

rational *adj* **1** reasonable or sensible **2** using reason or logic in thinking out a problem **3** capable of reasoning: *man is a rational being* **4** sane: *rational behaviour* **5** *maths* able to be expressed as a ratio of two integers: *a rational number* [Latin *rationalis*] **rationality** *n* **rationally** *adv*

rationale (rash-a-**nahl**) *n* the reason for an action or belief

rationalism *n* the philosophy that regards reason as the only basis for beliefs or actions **rationalist** *n* **rationalistic** *adj*

rationalize *or* **-ise** *vb* **-izing, -ized** *or* **-ising, -ised** **1** to find reasons to justify or explain (one's actions) **2** to apply logic or reason to (something) **3** to get rid of unnecessary equipment or staff to make (a business) more efficient **rationalization** *or* **-isation** *n*

rational number *n* any real number that can be expressed in the form *a/b*, where *a* and *b* are integers and *b* is not zero, as 7 or 7/3

ratpack *n slang* the members of the press who pursue celebrities and give wide coverage of their private lives: *the royal ratpack*

rat race *n* a continual routine of hectic competitive activity: *get out of the rat race for a while*
rattan *n* a climbing palm with tough stems used for wickerwork and canes [Malay *rōtan*]
ratter *n* a dog or cat that catches and kills rats
rattle *vb* **-tling, -tled 1** to make a rapid succession of short sharp sounds, such as when loose pellets are shaken in a container **2** to send, move, or drive with such a sound: *rain rattled against the window* **3** to shake briskly causing sharp sounds **4** *informal* to frighten or confuse **5 rattle off** *or* **out** to recite perfunctorily or rapidly **6 rattle on** *or* **away** to talk quickly and at length about something unimportant **7 rattle through** to do (something) very quickly: *she rattled through a translation* ▷ *n* **8** a rapid succession of short sharp sounds **9** a baby's toy filled with small pellets that rattle when shaken [Middle Dutch *ratelen*] **rattly** *adj*
rattlesnake *n* a poisonous snake with loose horny segments on the tail that make a rattling sound
rattling *adv informal, old-fashioned* very: *a rattling good yarn*
ratty *adj* **-tier, -tiest** *informal* **1** cross and irritable **2** (of the hair) straggly and greasy **rattily** *adv* **rattiness** *n*
raucous *adj* loud and harsh [Latin *raucus*]
raunchy *adj* **-chier, -chiest** *slang* sexy or earthy [origin unknown]
ravage *vb* **-vaging, -vaged 1** to cause extensive damage to ▷ *n* **2 ravages** the damaging effects: *the ravages of weather and pollution* [Old French *ravir* to snatch away]
rave *vb* **raving, raved 1** to talk in a wild or incoherent manner **2** *informal* to write or speak (about) with great enthusiasm ▷ *n* **3** *informal* an enthusiastically favourable review **4** *slang* a professionally organized large-scale party with electronic dance music **5** a name given to various types of dance music, such as techno, that feature a fast electronic rhythm [probably from Old French *resver* to wander]
ravel *vb* **-velling, -velled** *or US* **-veling, -veled 1** to tangle or become entangled **2** (of a fabric) to fray out in loose ends; unravel [Middle Dutch *ravelen*]
raven *n* **1** a large bird of the crow family with shiny black feathers ▷ *adj* **2** (of hair) shiny black [Old English *hrǣfn*]
ravening *adj* (of animals) hungrily searching for prey
ravenous *adj* **1** very hungry **2** ravening [Old French *ravineux*] **ravenously** *adv*
raver *n slang* **1** *Brit, Austral & S African* a person who leads a wild or uninhibited social life **2** a person who enjoys rave music and goes to raves
ravine (rav-**veen**) *n* a deep narrow steep-sided valley worn by a stream [Old French: torrent]
raving *adj* **1** delirious **2** *informal* great or exceptional: *a raving beauty* ▷ *adv* **3** to an excessive degree: *raving mad* ▷ *n* **4 ravings** frenzied or wildly extravagant talk
ravioli *pl n* small squares of pasta with a savoury filling, such as meat or cheese [Italian]
ravish *vb* **1** to enrapture or delight: *tourists ravished by our brilliant costumes* **2** *literary* to rape [Latin *rapere* to seize] **ravishment** *n*
ravishing *adj* lovely or delightful **ravishingly** *adv*
raw *adj* **1** (of food) not cooked **2** in an unfinished or unrefined state: *raw sewage* **3** not selected or modified: *raw data* **4** (of the skin or a wound) painful, with the surface scraped away **5** untrained or inexperienced: *a raw recruit* **6** (of the weather) harshly cold and damp **7** frank or realistic: *a raw reality* **8 raw deal** *informal* unfair or dishonest treatment ▷ *n* **9 in the raw A** *informal* naked **B** in a natural and uncivilized state: *to see life in the raw* [Old English *hrēaw*]
rawboned *adj* having a lean bony physique
rawhide *n* **1** untanned hide **2** a whip or rope made of strips of this
Rawlplug *n trademark* a short fibre or plastic tube used to provide a fixing in a wall for a screw
ray[1] *n* **1** a narrow beam of light **2** any of a set of lines spreading from a central point **3** a slight indication: *a ray of hope* **4** *maths* a straight line extending from a point **5** a thin beam of electromagnetic radiation or particles **6** any of the spines that support the fin of a fish [Old French *rai*]
ray[2] *n* a sea fish related to the sharks, with a flattened body and a long whiplike tail [Old French *raie*]
ray[3] *n music* (in tonic sol-fa) the second note of any ascending major scale
rayon *n* a textile fibre or fabric made from cellulose [French]
raze *or* **rase** *vb* **razing, razed** *or* **rasing, rased** to destroy (buildings or a town) completely [Old French *raser*]
razoo *n, pl* **-zoos** *Austral & NZ informal* an imaginary coin: *we haven't got a brass razoo* [origin unknown]
razor *n* an implement with a sharp blade, used for shaving [Old French *raseor*]
razorbill *n* a black-and-white sea bird with a stout sideways flattened bill
razor shell *n* **1** a burrowing shellfish with a long narrow shell **2** this shell
razor wire *n* strong wire with pieces of sharp metal set across it at intervals
razzle-dazzle *or* **razzmatazz** *n slang* **1** noisy or showy fuss or activity **2** a spree or frolic [rhyming compound from *dazzle*]
Rb *chem* rubidium
RC 1 Red Cross **2** Roman Catholic
Rd road
re[1] *prep* with reference to [Latin *res* thing]
re[2] *n music* same as **ray**[3]
Re *chem* rhenium
RE (in Britain) **1** Religious Education **2** Royal Engineers
re- *prefix* **1** (used with many main words to mean) repetition of an action: *remarry* **2** (used with many main words to mean) return to a previous condition: *renew* [Latin]
reach *vb* **1** to arrive at or get to (a place) **2** to make a movement (towards), as if to grasp or touch: *she reached for her bag* **3** to succeed in touching: *I can't reach that shelf unless I stand on a chair* **4** to make contact or communication with: *to reach a wider audience* **5** to extend as far as (a point or place): *to reach the ceiling* **6** to come to (a certain condition or situation): *to reach a compromise* **7** to arrive at or

r

amount to (an amount or value): *temperatures in Greece reached 35° yesterday* **8** *informal* to give (something to a person) with the outstretched hand ▷ *n* **9** the extent or distance of reaching: *within easy reach* **10** the range of influence or power: *it symbolized America's global reach* **11 reaches** a section of river, land, or sky: *the quieter reaches of the upper Thames* [Old English *rǣcan*] **reachable** *adj*

reach-me-down *adj Brit informal* cheap and ready-made or second-hand: *a reach-me-down suit*

reacquaint *vb* **reacquaint oneself with** *or* **become reacquainted with** to get to know (someone or something) again

react *vb* **1** (of a person or thing) to act in response to another person, a stimulus, or a situation **2 react against** to act in an opposing or contrary manner **3** *chem* to undergo a chemical reaction **4** *physics* to exert an equal force in the opposite direction to an acting force [Late Latin *reagere*]

reactance *n electronics* the resistance to the flow of an alternating current caused by the inductance or capacitance of the circuit

reactant *n* a substance that participates in a chemical reaction

reaction *n* **1** a physical or emotional response to a stimulus **2** any action resisting another **3** opposition to change **4** *med* any effect produced by a drug or by a substance (allergen) to which a person is allergic **5** *chem* a process that involves changes in the structure and energy content of atoms, molecules, or ions **6** the equal and opposite force that acts on a body whenever it exerts a force on another body **7 reactions** someone's ability to act in response to something that happens

reactionary *adj* **1** opposed to political or social change ▷ *n, pl* **-aries 2** a person opposed to radical change

reactivate *vb* **-vating, -vated** to make (something) active again **reactivation** *n*

reactive *adj* **1** readily taking part in chemical reactions: *ozone is a highly reactive form of oxygen gas* **2** of or having a reactance **3** responsive to stimulus **reactively** *adv* **reactivity** *n*

reactor *n* short for **nuclear reactor**

read *vb* **reading, read 1** to look at and understand or take in (written or printed matter) **2** to look at and say aloud **3** to have a certain wording: *the memorandum read as follows* **4** to interpret in a specified way: *it can be read as satire* **5** to interpret the significance or meaning of: *an astrologer who reads Tarot* **6** to register or show: *the meter reads 100* **7** to make out the true nature or mood of: *she had read his thoughts* **8** to interpret (signs, characters, etc.) other than by visual means: *to read Braille* **9** to have sufficient knowledge of (a language) to understand the written word **10** to undertake a course of study in (a subject): *to read economics* **11** to gain knowledge by reading: *he read about the war* **12** to hear and understand, esp. when using a two-way radio: *we are reading you loud and clear* **13** *computers* to obtain (data) from a storage device, such as magnetic tape ▷ *n* **14** matter suitable for reading: *this book is a very good read* **15** a spell of reading ▷ See also **read into, read out** *etc.* [Old English *rǣdan* to advise, explain]

readable *adj* **1** enjoyable to read **2** (of handwriting or print) legible

reader *n* **1** a person who reads **2** a person who reads aloud in public **3** a person who reads and judges manuscripts sent to a publisher **4** a book of texts for those learning a foreign language **5** *Brit* a member of staff below a professor but above a senior lecturer at a university **6** a proofreader **7** short for **lay reader**

readership *n* all the readers collectively of a publication or author: *a new format would alienate its readership*

reading *n* **1** the act of reading **2** ability to read: *disputes over methods of teaching reading* **3** material for reading **4** a public recital of a literary work **5** a measurement indicated by a gauge or dial **6** one of the three stages in the passage of a bill through a legislative assembly **7** the form of a particular word or passage in a given text **8** an interpretation of a situation or something said ▷ *adj* **9** of or for reading: *reading glasses*

read into *vb* to discover in a statement (meanings not intended by the speaker or writer): *one of the implications we must read into the work*

readjust *vb* to adapt to a new situation **readjustment** *n*

readmit *vb* **-mitting, -mitted** to let (a person or country) back into a place or organization **readmission** *n*

read out *vb* **1** to read (something) aloud **2** to retrieve (information) from a computer memory ▷ *n* **read-out 3** the information retrieved from a computer memory

read up *vb* to read intensively about (a subject) in order to get information: *he had read up on the cases*

read-write *adj computers* allowing existing data to be read and new data to be added

ready *adj* **readier, readiest 1** prepared for use or action **2** prompt or eager: *the ready use of corporal punishment* **3** quick or intelligent: *a ready wit* **4 ready to** on the point of or liable to: *ready to pounce* **5** easily available: *his ready tears* ▷ *n* **6** *informal* same as **ready money 7 at the ready** poised for use: *with pen at the ready* ▷ *vb* **readies, readying, readied 8** to make ready; prepare [Old English *(ge)rǣde*] **readily** *adv* **readiness** *n*

ready-made *adj* **1** for immediate use by any customer **2** extremely convenient or ideally suited: *a ready-made audience*

ready money *n* cash for immediate use. Also: **the ready, the readies**

reaffirm *vb* to state again **reaffirmation** *n*

reafforest *vb* to plant new trees in (an area that was formerly forested) **reafforestation** *n*

reagent (ree-age-ent) *n* a chemical substance that reacts with another, used to detect the presence of the other

real[1] *adj* **1** existing or occurring in the physical world **2** actual: *the real agenda* **3** important or serious: *the real challenge* **4** rightly so called: *a real friend* **5** genuine: *the council has no real authority* **6** (of food or drink) made in a traditional way to ensure the best flavour **7** *maths* involving or containing real numbers alone **8** relating to immovable property such as land or buildings: *real estate* **9** *econ* (of prices or incomes) considered in terms of purchasing power rather than nominal currency value **10 the real thing** the genuine article, not a substitute or imitation [Latin *res* thing]

real² *n* a former small Spanish or Spanish-American silver coin [Spanish, literally: royal]

real ale *n chiefly Brit* beer that has fermented in the barrel

real estate *n* immovable property, esp. land and houses

realignment (ree-a-line-ment) *n* a new arrangement or organization: *there will be a realignment of party allegiances*

realism *n* **1** awareness or acceptance of things as they are, as opposed to the abstract or ideal **2** a style in art or literature that attempts to show the world as it really is **3** *philosophy* the theory that physical objects continue to exist whether they are perceived or not **realist** *n* **realistic** *adj* **realistically** *adv*

reality *n, pl* **-ties 1** the state of things as they are or appear to be, rather than as one might wish them to be **2** something that is real **3** the state of being real **4 in reality** in fact

reality TV *n* television programmes focusing on members of the public living in conditions created especially by the programme makers

realize *or* **-lise** *vb* **-lizing, -lized** *or* **-lising, -lised 1** to be aware of or grasp the significance of **2** to achieve (a plan or ambition) **3** to convert (property or goods) into cash **4** (of goods or property) to sell for (a certain sum): *this table realized a large sum at auction* **5** to produce (a complete work of art) from an idea or draft **realizable** *or* **-lisable** *adj* **realization** *or* **-lisation** *n*

really *adv* **1** truly: *really boring* **2** in reality: *it's really quite harmless* ▷ *interj* **3** an exclamation of dismay, doubt, or surprise

USAGE See at **very**.

realm *n* **1** a kingdom **2** a field of interest or study: *the realm of science* [Old French *reialme*]

real number *n* any rational or irrational number

real tennis *n* an ancient form of tennis played in a four-walled indoor court

real-time *adj* (of a computer system) processing data as it is received

realtor *n US & Canad* an estate agent [from a trademark]

realty *n* same as **real estate**

ream *n* **1** a number of sheets of paper, now equal to 500 or 516 sheets (20 quires) **2 reams** *informal* a large quantity (of written material): *reams of verse* [Arabic *rizmah* bale]

reap *vb* **1** to cut and gather (a harvest) **2** to receive as the result of a previous activity: *reap the benefits of our efforts* [Old English *riopan*]

reaper *n* **1** a person who reaps or a machine for reaping **2 the grim reaper** death

reappear *vb* to come back into view **reappearance** *n*

reappraise *vb* **-praising, -praised** to consider or review (something) to see if changes are needed **reappraisal** *n*

rear¹ *n* **1** the back part **2** the area or position that lies at the back **3** *informal* the buttocks **4 bring up the rear** to come last ▷ *adj* **5** of or in the rear: *the rear carriage* [Old French *rer*]

rear² *vb* **1** to care for and educate (children) until maturity **2** to breed (animals) or grow (plants) **3** (of a horse) to lift the front legs in the air and stand nearly upright **4** to place or lift (something) upright [Old English *rǣran*]

rear admiral *n* a high-ranking naval officer

rearguard *n* **1** the troops who protect the rear of a military formation ▷ *adj* **2 rearguard action** an effort to prevent or postpone something that is unavoidable

rear light *or* **rear lamp** *n* a red light, usually one of a pair, attached to the rear of a vehicle. Also called: **tail-light, tail lamp**

rearm *vb* **1** to arm again **2** to equip with better weapons **rearmament** *n*

rearmost *adj* nearest the back

rearrange *vb* **-ranging, -ranged** to organize differently **rearrangement** *n*

rear-view mirror *n* a mirror on a motor vehicle enabling the driver to see the traffic behind

rearward *adj* **1** in the rear ▷ *adv also* **rearwards 2** towards the rear

reason *n* **1** a cause or motive for a belief or action: *he had two reasons for his dark mood* **2** the ability to think or argue rationally **3** an argument in favour of or a justification for something: *there is every reason to encourage people to keep fit* **4** sanity **5 by reason of** because of **6 within reason** within moderate or justifiable bounds **7 it stands to reason** it is logical or obvious ▷ *vb* **8** to think logically in forming conclusions **9 reason with** to persuade by logical arguments into doing something **10 reason out** to work out (a problem) by reasoning [Latin *reri* to think]

USAGE The expression *the reason is because...* should be avoided. Instead one should say either *this is because...* or *the reason is that...*

reasonable *adj* **1** sensible **2** not making unfair demands **3** logical: *a reasonable explanation* **4** moderate in price **5** average: *a reasonable amount of luck* **reasonably** *adv* **reasonableness** *n*

reasoned *adj* well thought out or well presented: *a reasoned explanation*

reasoning *n* **1** the process of drawing conclusions from facts or evidence **2** the conclusions reached in this way

reassemble *vb* **-bling, -bled** to put back together again

reassert *vb* **1** to state or declare again **2 reassert oneself** to become significant or noticeable again: *reality had reasserted itself*

reassess *vb* to reconsider the value or importance of **reassessment** *n*

reassure *vb* **-assuring, -assured** to relieve (someone) of anxieties **reassurance** *n* **reassuring** *adj*

rebate¹ *n* a refund or discount [Old French *rabattre* to beat down]

rebate² *or* **rabbet** *n* **1** a groove cut into a piece of timber into which another piece fits ▷ *vb* **-bating, -bated** *or* **-beting, -beted 2** to cut a rebate in **3** to join (pieces of timber) with a rebate [Old French *rabattre* to beat down]

rebel *vb* **-belling, -belled 1** to fight against the ruling power **2** to reject accepted conventions of behaviour ▷ *n* **3** a person who rebels **4** a person who rejects accepted conventions of behaviour ▷ *adj* **5** rebelling: *rebel councillors* [Latin *re-* again + *bellum* war]

rebellion *n* **1** organized opposition to a government or other authority involving the use of violence **2** nonviolent opposition to a government or other authority: *a Tory backbenchers' rebellion* **3** rejection of accepted conventions of behaviour [Latin *rebellio*]

rebellious *adj* rebelling or showing a tendency towards rebellion **rebelliously** *adv*

rebirth *n* a revival or renaissance: *the rebirth of their nation*

reboot *vb* **1** to shut down and then restart (a computer system) ▷ *n* **2** an instance of shutting down and restarting a computer system **3** *informal* a new version of something

rebore *or* **reboring** *n* the boring of a cylinder to restore its true shape

reborn *adj* active again after a period of inactivity

rebound *vb* **1** to spring back from a sudden impact **2** (of a plan or action) to misfire so as to hurt the person responsible ▷ *n* **3** the act of rebounding **4 on the rebound** *informal* while recovering from rejection: *she married him on the rebound*

rebrand *vb* to change or update the image of (an organization or product)

rebuff *vb* **1** to snub and reject an offer or suggestion ▷ *n* **2** a blunt refusal; snub [Old French *rebuffer*]

rebuild *vb* **-building, -built 1** to build (a building or town) again, after severe damage **2** to develop (something such as a business or relationship) again after destruction or damage

rebuke *vb* **-buking, -buked 1** to scold sternly ▷ *n* **2** a stern scolding [Old French *rebuker*]

rebus (ree-buss) *n, pl* **-buses** a puzzle consisting of pictures and symbols representing syllables and words [Latin: by things]

rebut *vb* **-butting, -butted** to prove that (a claim) is untrue [Old French *reboter*] **rebuttal** *n*

rec *n* short for **recreation**

recalcitrant *adj* wilfully disobedient [Latin *re-* again + *calcitrare* to kick] **recalcitrance** *n*

recall *vb* **1** to bring back to mind **2** to order to return **3** to annul or cancel ▷ *n* **4** the ability to remember things **5** an order to return

recant *vb* to take back (a former belief or statement) publicly [Latin *re-* again + *cantare* to sing] **recantation** *n*

recap *informal* ▷ *vb* **-capping, -capped 1** to recapitulate ▷ *n* **2** a recapitulation

recapitulate *vb* **-lating, -lated** to restate the main points of (an argument or speech) [Late Latin *recapitulare*, literally: to put back under headings]

recapitulation *n* **1** the act of recapitulating **2** *music* the repeating of earlier themes, esp. in the final section of a movement

recapture *vb* **-turing, -tured 1** to relive vividly (a former experience or sensation): *recaptured some of those first feelings* **2** to capture again ▷ *n* **3** the act of recapturing

recast *vb* **-casting, -cast 1** to give a new form or shape to: *he found the organization wholly recast* **2** to change the actors or singers in (a play, musical, or opera) **3** to rework (a piece of writing or music): *she has recast most of my book*

recce *chiefly Brit slang* ▷ *vb* **-ceing, -ced** *or* **-ceed 1** to reconnoitre ▷ *n* **2** reconnaissance

recede *vb* **-ceding, -ceded 1** to withdraw from a point or limit: *the tide had receded* **2** to become more distant: *the threat of intervention had receded* **3** (of a man's hair) to stop growing at the temples and above the forehead **4** to slope backwards: *a receding chin* [Latin *recedere* to go back]

receipt *n* **1** a written acknowledgment that money or goods have been received **2** the act of receiving **3 receipts** money taken in over a particular period by a shop or business [Old French *receite*]

receive *vb* **-ceiving, -ceived 1** to get (something offered or sent to one) **2** to experience: *he received a knife wound* **3** to greet (guests) **4** to have (an honour) bestowed: *he received the Order of the Garter* **5** to admit (a person) to a society or condition: *he was received into the Church* **6** to convert (incoming radio or television signals) into sounds or pictures **7** to be informed of (news) **8** to react to: *the article was well received* **9** to support or sustain (the weight of something) **10** *tennis etc.* to play at the other end from the server **11** *Brit, Austral & NZ* to buy and sell stolen goods [Latin *recipere*]

received *adj* generally accepted or believed: *contrary to received wisdom*

Received Pronunciation *n* the accent of standard Southern British English

receiver *n* **1** the detachable part of a telephone that is held to the ear **2** the equipment in a telephone, radio, or television that converts the incoming signals into sound or pictures **3** a person appointed by a court to manage property of a bankrupt **4** a person who receives stolen goods knowing they have been stolen

receivership *n law* the state of being administered by a receiver: *the company went into receivership*

recent *adj* **1** having happened lately **2** new [Latin *recens* fresh] **recently** *adv*

Recent *adj* same as **Holocene**

receptacle *n* **1** an object used to contain something **2** *botany* the enlarged or modified tip of the flower stalk that bears the flower [Latin *receptaculum* store-place]

reception *n* **1** an area in an office, hotel, etc., where visitors are received or reservations dealt with **2** a formal party for guests, esp. after a wedding **3** the manner in which something is received: *an enthusiastic reception* **4** the act of formally welcoming **5** *radio & television* the quality of a received broadcast: *the reception was poor*

receptionist *n* a person employed to receive guests or clients and deal with reservations and appointments

reception room *n* a room in a private house suitable for entertaining guests

receptive *adj* willing to consider and accept new ideas or suggestions **receptivity** *or* **receptiveness** *n*

receptor *n physiol* a sensory nerve ending that changes specific stimuli into nerve impulses

recess *n* **1** a space, such as an alcove, set back in a wall **2** a holiday between sessions of work **3 recesses** secret hidden places: *the recesses of her brain* **4** *US & Canad* a break between classes at a school [Latin *recessus* a retreat]

recessed *adj* hidden or placed in a recess

recession *n* **1** a period of economic difficulty when little is being bought or sold **2** the act of receding

recessional *n* a hymn sung as the clergy and choir withdraw after a church service

recessive *adj* **1** tending to recede **2** *genetics* (in a pair of genes) designating a gene that has a characteristic which will only be passed on if the other gene has the same characteristic

recharge *vb* **-charging, -charged** to cause (a battery) to take in and store electricity again **rechargeable** *adj*

recherché (rish-air-shay) *adj* **1** studiedly refined or elegant **2** known only to connoisseurs [French: thoroughly sought after]

recidivism *n* habitual relapse into crime [Latin *recidivus* falling back] **recidivist** *n, adj*

recipe *n* **1** a list of ingredients and directions for making a particular dish **2** a method for achieving something: *a recipe for industrial chaos* [Latin, literally: take (it)!]

recipient *n* a person who receives something

reciprocal (ris-sip-pro-kl) *adj* **1** done or felt by each of two people or groups to or about the other: *a reciprocal agreement* **2** given or done in return: *a reciprocal invitation* **3** *grammar* (of a pronoun) indicating that action is given and received by each subject, for example, *each other* in *they started to shout at each other* ▷ *n* **4** Also called: **inverse** *maths* a number or quantity that when multiplied by a given number or quantity gives a product of one: *the reciprocal of 2 is 0.5* [Latin *reciprocus* alternating] **reciprocally** *adv*

reciprocate *vb* **-cating, -cated 1** to give or feel in return: *not everyone reciprocated his enthusiasm* **2** (of a machine part) to move backwards and forwards **reciprocation** *n*

reciprocity *n* **1** reciprocal action or relation **2** a mutual exchange of commercial or other privileges

recital (ris-**site**-al) *n* **1** a musical performance by a soloist or soloists **2** the act of reciting something learned or prepared **3** a narration or description: *she plagued her with the recital of constant ailments and illnesses*

recitation *n* **1** the act of reciting poetry or prose from memory **2** something recited

recitative (ress-it-a-**teev**) *n* a narrative passage in an opera or oratorio, reflecting the natural rhythms of speech [Italian *recitativo*]

recite *vb* **-citing, -cited 1** to repeat (a poem or passage) aloud from memory before an audience **2** to give a detailed account of [Latin *recitare*]

reckless *adj* having no regard for danger or consequences: *reckless driving* [Old English *recceleās*]

reckon *vb* **1** *informal* to be of the opinion: *she reckoned she could find them* **2** to consider: *he reckoned himself a failure* **3** to calculate or compute **4** to expect **5 reckon with** to take into account: *there is this ancestral hatred to reckon with* **6 reckon without** to fail to take into account **7 reckon on** *or* **upon** to rely on or expect: *they can't reckon on your automatic support* [Old English *(ge)recenian* recount]

reckoning *n* **1** counting or calculating: *by his reckoning, he owed him money* **2** retribution for one's actions: *the moment of reckoning came* **3** settlement of an account or bill

reclaim *vb* **1** to get back possession of: *the club is now trying to reclaim the money from the blockaders* **2** to convert (unusable or submerged land) into land suitable for farming or building on **3** to recover (useful substances) from waste products [Latin *reclamare* to cry out] **reclamation** *n*

recline *vb* **-clining, -clined** to rest in a leaning position [Latin *reclinare*]

reclining *adj* (of a seat) with a back that can be adjusted to slope at various angles

recluse *n* a person who lives alone and avoids people [Late Latin *recludere* to shut away] **reclusive** *adj*

recognition *n* **1** the act of recognizing **2** acceptance or acknowledgment **3** formal acknowledgment of a government or of the independence of a country **4 in recognition of** as a token of thanks for

recognizance *or* **recognisance** (rik-og-nizz-anss) *n law* **A** an undertaking made before a court or magistrate to do something specified, such as to appear in court on a stated day **B** a sum of money promised as a guarantee of this undertaking [Old French *reconoissance*]

recognize *or* **-nise** *vb* **-nizing, -nized** *or* **-nising, -nised 1** to identify (a person or thing) as someone or something already known **2** to accept or be aware of (a fact or problem): *to recognize change* **3** to acknowledge formally the status or legality of (something or someone): *an organization recognized by the UN* **4** to show approval or appreciation of (something) **5** to make formal acknowledgment of (a claim or duty): *I must ask for her to be recognized as a hostile witness* [Latin *re-* again + *cognoscere* to know] **recognizable** *or* **-nisable** *adj*

recoil *vb* **1** to jerk or spring back **2** to draw back in fear or horror **3** (of an action) to go wrong so as to hurt the person responsible ▷ *n* **4** the backward movement of a gun when fired **5** the act of recoiling [Old French *reculer*]

recollect *vb* to remember [Latin *recolligere* to gather again] **recollection** *n*

recombinant (ree-**kom**-bin-ant) *adj genetics* produced by the combining of genetic material from more than one origin

recommend *vb* **1** to advise as the best course or choice **2** to praise or commend: *I would wholeheartedly recommend his books* **3** to make attractive or advisable: *she has everything to recommend her* [Latin *re-* again + *commendare* to commend] **recommendation** *n*

recompense *vb* **-pensing, -pensed 1** to pay or reward for work or help **2** to compensate or make up for loss or injury ▷ *n* **3** compensation for loss or injury **4** reward or repayment [Latin *re-* again + *compensare* to balance]

reconcile *vb* **-ciling, -ciled 1** to make (two apparently conflicting things) compatible or consistent with each other: *in many cases science and*

r

religion are reconciled **2** to re-establish friendly relations with (a person or people) or between (people) **3** to accept or cause to accept an unpleasant situation: *we reconciled ourselves to a change* [Latin *reconciliare*]

reconciliation *n* **1** the state of being reconciled **2** the act of reconciling people or groups **3** *S African* a political term emphasizing the need to acknowledge the wrongs of the past

recondite *adj formal* **1** requiring special knowledge **2** dealing with abstruse or profound subjects [Latin *reconditus* hidden away]

recondition *vb* to restore to good condition or working order: *a reconditioned engine*
reconditioned *adj*

reconfigure *vb* **-guring, -gured** *computers* to rearrange the elements or settings of (a system, device, etc.)

reconnaissance (rik-kon-iss-anss) *n* **1** the process of obtaining information about the position and movements of an enemy **2** a preliminary inspection [French]

reconnoitre *or US* **reconnoiter** (rek-a-noy-ter) *vb* to make a reconnaissance of [obsolete French *reconnoître*]

reconsider *vb* to think about again, with a view to changing one's policy or course of action
reconsideration *n*

reconstitute *vb* **-tuting, -tuted 1** to reorganize in a slightly different form **2** to restore (dried food) to its former state by adding water
reconstitution *n*

reconstruct *vb* **1** to build again **2** to reorganize: *three works proved useful in reconstructing the training routine* **3** to form a picture of (a past event, esp. a crime) by piecing together evidence
reconstruction *n*

reconvene *vb* to gather together again after an interval: *we reconvene tomorrow*

record *n* (**rek**-ord) **1** a document or other thing that preserves information **2 records** information or data on a subject collected over a long period: *dental records* **3** a thin disc of a plastic material upon which sound has been recorded in a continuous spiral groove on each side **4** the best recorded achievement in some field: *her score set a Games record* **5** the known facts about a person's achievements **6** a list of crimes of which an accused person has previously been convicted **7** anything serving as evidence or as a memorial: *the First World War is a record of human folly* **8** *computers* a group of data or piece of information preserved as a unit in machine-readable form **9 for the record** for the sake of strict factual accuracy **10 go on record** to state one's views publicly **11 have a record** to have previous criminal convictions **12 off the record** not for publication **13 on record A** stated in a public document **B** publicly known ▷ *adj* **14** being the highest or lowest, or best or worst ever achieved: *record losses* ▷ *vb* (rik-**kord**) **15** to put in writing to preserve the true facts: *to record the minutes of a meeting* **16** to preserve (sound, TV programmes, etc.) on plastic disc, magnetic tape, etc., for reproduction on a playback device **17** to show or register [Latin *recordari* to remember]

recorded delivery *n Brit* a postal service by which an official receipt is obtained for the posting and delivery of a letter or parcel

recorder *n* **1** a person who keeps records **2** a device for recording sound, data, or pictures **3** *music* a wind instrument, blown through the end, with finger-holes and a reedlike tone **4** (in England and Wales) a barrister or solicitor appointed to sit as a part-time judge in the crown court

recording *n* **1** something that has been recorded **2** the process of storing sounds or visual signals for later use

record player *n* a device for reproducing the sounds stored on a record

recount *vb* to tell the story or details of [Old French *reconter*]

re-count *vb* **1** to count again ▷ *n* **2** a second or further count, esp. of votes in an election

recoup (rik-**koop**) *vb* **1** to regain or make good (a loss) **2** to reimburse or compensate (someone) for a loss [Old French *recouper* to cut back]
recoupment *n*

recourse *n* **1 have recourse to** to turn to a source of help or course of action **2** a source of help or course of action that is turned to when in difficulty [Latin *re-* back + *currere* to run]

recover *vb* **1** (of a person) to regain health, spirits, or composure **2** to regain a former and better condition: *real wages have recovered from the recession* **3** to find again or obtain the return of (something lost) **4** to get back or make good (expense or loss) **5** to obtain (useful substances) from waste **6** *law* to gain (something) by the judgment of a court: *it should be possible to recover damages* [Latin *recuperare*] **recoverable** *adj*

recovery *n, pl* **-veries 1** the act of recovering from sickness, a shock, or a setback **2** restoration to a former and better condition **3** the regaining of something lost **4** the extraction of useful substances from waste

re-create *vb* **-creating, -created** to make happen or exist again **re-creation** *n*

recreation *n* an activity done for pleasure or relaxation [Latin *recreare* to refresh]
recreational *adj*

recreation ground *n* an area of publicly owned land where sports and games may be played

recrimination *n* accusations made by two people or groups about each other: *bitter recrimination* [Latin *re-* back + *criminari* to accuse]
recriminatory *adj*

recrudescence *n literary* an outbreak of trouble or a disease after a period of quiet [Latin *re-* again + *crudus* bloody, raw]

recruit *vb* **1** to enlist (people) for military service **2** to enrol or obtain (members or support) ▷ *n* **3** a newly joined member of a military service **4** a new member or supporter [French *recrute* new growth] **recruitment** *n*

rectal *adj* of the rectum

rectangle *n* an oblong shape with four straight sides and four right angles [Latin *rectus* straight + *angulus* angle] **rectangular** *adj*

rectify *vb* **-fies, -fying, -fied 1** to put right; correct **2** *chem* to separate (a substance) from a mixture by distillation **3** *electronics* to convert (alternating current) into direct current [Latin *rectus* straight + *facere* to make] **rectification** *n* **rectifier** *n*

rectilinear (rek-tee-lin-ee-er) *adj formal* **1** in a straight line **2** bounded by or formed of straight lines

rectitude *n* moral or religious correctness: *a model of rectitude* [Latin *rectus* right]

recto *n, pl* **-tos** **1** the right-hand page of a book **2** the front of a sheet of printed paper [Latin: on the right]

rector *n* **1** *Church of England* a member of the clergy in charge of a parish **2** *RC Church* a cleric in charge of a college or congregation **3** *chiefly Brit* the head of certain academic institutions **4** (in Scotland) a high-ranking official in a university, elected by the students [Latin: director] **rectorship** *n*

rectory *n, pl* **-ries** the house of a rector

rectum *n, pl* **-tums** *or* **-ta** the lower part of the alimentary canal, ending in the anus [Latin: straight]

recumbent *adj* lying down [Latin *recumbere* to lie back]

recuperate *vb* **-rating, -rated** to recover from illness or exhaustion [Latin *recuperare*] **recuperation** *n* **recuperative** *adj*

recur *vb* **-curring, -curred** **1** to happen or occur again **2** (of a thought or feeling) to come back to the mind [Latin *re-* again + *currere* to run] **recurrence** *n* **recurrent** *adj* **recurring** *adj*

recurring decimal *n* a rational number that contains a pattern of digits repeated indefinitely after the decimal point: *1 divided by 11 gives the recurring decimal 0.09090909...*

recusant (rek-yew-zant) *n* **1** *history* a Roman Catholic who did not attend the services of the Church of England **2** a person who refuses to obey authority [Latin *recusans* refusing] **recusancy** *n*

recycle *vb* **-cling, -cled** **1** to reprocess (something already used) for further use: *public demand for recycled paper* **2** to pass (a substance) through a system again for further use **recyclable** *adj*

red *adj* **redder, reddest** **1** of a colour varying from crimson to orange; of the colour of blood **2** reddish in colour or having parts or marks that are reddish: *red deer* **3** flushed in the face from anger or shame **4** (of the eyes) bloodshot **5** (of wine) made from black grapes and coloured by their skins ▷ *n* **6** the colour red; the colour of blood **7** anything red, such as red clothing or red paint: *she had dressed in red* **8** **in the red** *informal* in debt **9** **see red** *informal* to become very angry [Old English *rēad*] **redness** *n* **reddish** *adj*

Red *informal* ▷ *n* **1** a Communist or socialist ▷ *adj* **2** Communist or socialist

red admiral *n* a butterfly with black wings with red and white markings

redback spider *n* a small venomous Australian spider with a red stripe on the back of the abdomen

red blood cell *n* same as **erythrocyte**

red-blooded *adj informal* vigorous or virile

redbreast *n* a robin

redbrick *adj* (of a British university) founded in the late 19th or early 20th century

red card *soccer* ▷ *n* **1** a piece of red pasteboard raised by a referee to indicate that a player has been sent off ▷ *vb* **red-card** **2** to send off (a player)

red carpet *n* very special treatment given to an important guest

redcoat *n* **1** *history* a British soldier **2** *Canad informal* a Mountie

Red Crescent *n* the name and symbol used by the Red Cross in Muslim countries

Red Cross *n* an international organization (**Red Cross Society**) which helps victims of war or natural disaster

redcurrant *n* a very small red edible fruit that grows in bunches on a bush

red deer *n* a large deer of Europe and Asia, which has a reddish-brown coat and a short tail

redden *vb* **1** to make or become red or redder **2** to blush

redecorate *vb* to paint or wallpaper (a room) again **redecoration** *n*

redeem *vb* **1** to make up for **2** to reinstate (oneself) in someone's good opinion: *he missed a penalty but redeemed himself by setting up the winning goal* **3** *Christianity* (of Christ as Saviour) to free (humanity) from sin by death on the Cross **4** to buy back: *she didn't have the money to redeem it* **5** to pay off (a loan or debt) **6** to convert (bonds or shares) into cash **7** to exchange (coupons) for goods **8** to fulfil (a promise): *I vowed to abide by the bill and have redeemed my pledge* [Latin *re-* back + *emere* to buy] **redeemable** *adj* **redeemer** *n*

Redeemer *n* **the Redeemer** *Christianity* Jesus Christ

redeeming *adj* making up for faults or deficiencies: *the soundtrack is the film's only redeeming feature*

redemption *n* **1** the act of redeeming **2** the state of being redeemed **3** *Christianity* deliverance from sin through the incarnation and death of Christ **redemptive** *adj*

redeploy *vb* to assign (people) to new positions or tasks **redeployment** *n*

redevelop *vb* to rebuild or renovate (an area or building) **redeveloper** *n* **redevelopment** *n*

redfish *n, pl* **-fish** *or* **-fishes** *Canad* same as **kokanee**

red flag *n* **1** a symbol of revolution **2** a warning of danger

red-handed *adj* **catch someone red-handed** to catch someone in the act of doing something wrong or illegal

red hat *n* the broad-brimmed crimson hat given to cardinals as the symbol of their rank

redhead *n* a person with reddish hair **redheaded** *adj*

red herring *n* something which diverts attention from the main issue

red-hot *adj* **1** (of metal) glowing hot **2** extremely hot **3** very keen or excited **4** furious: *one of those red-hot blazes of temper* **5** very recent or topical: *red-hot information*

red-hot poker *n* a garden plant with spikes of red or yellow flowers

Red Indian *n, adj offensive* Native American

redirect *vb* **1** to send in a new direction or course **2** to send (mail) to a different address

redistribute *vb* **-uting, -uted** to share out in a different way: *to redistribute the world's wealth*

redistribution *n* **1** the act of redistributing **2** a revision of the number of seats that each province has in the Canadian House of Commons, made every ten years
red lead *n* a bright-red poisonous insoluble oxide of lead
red-letter day *n* a memorably important or happy occasion [from the red letters in ecclesiastical calendars to indicate saints' days]
red light *n* **1** a traffic signal to stop **2** a danger signal
red-light district *n* an area where many prostitutes work
red meat *n* meat, such as beef or lamb, that is dark brown when cooked
redo *vb* **-doing, -did, -done 1** to do over again in order to improve **2** *informal* to redecorate: *we should consider redoing some of the rooms*
redolent *adj* **redolent of** *or* **with 1** reminiscent or suggestive of: *a castle redolent of historical novels* **2** smelling of: *the warm heavy air was redolent of sea and flowers* [Latin *redolens*] **redolence** *n*
redouble *vb* **-bling, -bled 1** to make or become much greater: *the party will have to redouble its efforts* **2** *bridge* to double (an opponent's double)
redoubt *n* **1** a small fort defending a hill top or pass **2** a stronghold [French *redoute*]
redoubtable *adj* to be feared and respected: *the redoubtable Mr Brooks* [Old French *redouter* to dread] **redoubtably** *adv*
redound *vb* **1 redound to** to have an advantageous or disadvantageous effect on: *individual rights redound to the common good* **2 redound on** *or* **upon** to recoil or rebound on [Latin *redundare* to stream over]
redox *n* a chemical reaction between two substances, in which one is oxidized and the other reduced
red pepper *n* **1** the red ripe fruit of the sweet pepper, eaten as a vegetable **2** same as **cayenne pepper**
r
redraft *vb* to write a second copy of (a letter, proposal, essay, etc.)
red rag *n* something that infuriates or provokes: *a red rag to environmentalists* [so called because red objects supposedly infuriate bulls]
redress *vb* **1** to make amends for **2** to adjust in order to make fair or equal: *to redress the balance* ▷ *n* **3** compensation or reparation **4** the setting right of a wrong [Old French *redrecier* to set up again]
red salmon *n* a salmon with reddish flesh
redshank *n* a large common European sandpiper with red legs
red shift *n* the appearance of lines in the spectrum of distant stars nearer the red end of the spectrum than on earth: used to calculate the velocity of objects in relation to the earth
redskin *n informal, offensive* a Native American [so called because one now extinct tribe painted themselves with red ochre]
red squirrel *n* a reddish-brown squirrel of Europe and Asia
redstart *n* **1** a European songbird of the thrush family, the male of which has an orange-brown tail and breast **2** a North American warbler [Old English *rēad* red + *steort* tail]
red tape *n* time-consuming official rules or procedure [from the red tape used to bind official government documents]
reduce *vb* **-ducing, -duced 1** to bring down or lower: *monitoring could reduce the number of perinatal deaths* **2** to weaken or lessen: *vegetarian diets reduce cancer risk* **3** to bring by force or necessity to some state or action: *it reduced her to helpless laughter* **4** to slim **5** to set out systematically as an aid to understanding: *reducing the problem to three main issues* **6** *cookery* to thicken (a sauce) by boiling away some of its liquid **7** to impoverish: *to be in reduced circumstances* **8** *chem* **A** to undergo a chemical reaction with hydrogen **B** to lose oxygen atoms **C** to increase the number of electrons **9** *maths* to simplify the form of (an expression or equation), esp. by substitution of one term by another [Latin *reducere* to bring back] **reducible** *adj*
reduction *n* **1** the act of reducing **2** the amount by which something is reduced **3** a reduced form of an original, such as a copy of a document on a smaller scale **reductive** *adj*
redundant *adj* **1** deprived of one's job because it is no longer necessary or sufficiently profitable **2** surplus to requirements [Latin *redundans* overflowing] **redundancy** *n*
reduplicate *vb* **-cating, -cated** to make double; repeat
redwood *n* a giant Californian conifer with reddish bark
re-echo *vb* **-oing, -oed** to echo over and over again
reed *n* **1** a tall grass that grows in swamps and shallow water **2** a straight hollow stem of this plant **3** *music* **A** a thin piece of cane or metal in certain wind instruments, which vibrates producing a musical note when the instrument is blown **B** a wind instrument or organ pipe that sounds by means of a reed [Old English *hrēod*]
reedy *adj* **reedier, reediest 1** harsh or thin in tone: *his reedy, hesitant voice* **2** (of a place) full of reeds **reedily** *adv* **reediness** *n*
reef[1] *n* **1** a ridge of rock, sand, or coral, lying just beneath the surface of the sea: *a coral reef* **2** a vein of ore [Middle Dutch *ref*]
reef[2] *naut* ▷ *n* **1** the part of a sail which can be rolled up to reduce its area ▷ *vb* **2** to reduce the area of (sail) by taking in a reef [Middle Dutch *rif*]
reefer *n* **1** Also called: **reefer jacket** a man's short heavy double-breasted woollen jacket **2** *old-fashioned slang* a hand-rolled cigarette containing cannabis [from the cigarette's resemblance to the rolled reef of a sail]
reef knot *n* a knot consisting of two overhand knots turned opposite ways
reek *vb* **1** to give off a strong unpleasant smell **2 reek of** to give a strong suggestion of: *the scene had reeked of insincerity* **3** *dialect* to give off smoke or fumes ▷ *n* **4** a strong unpleasant smell **5** *dialect* smoke or steam [Old English *rēocan*]
reel[1] *n* **1** a cylindrical object or frame that turns on an axis and onto which film, tape, wire, or thread is wound **2** a winding device attached to a fishing rod, used for casting and winding in the line **3** a roll of film for projection ▷ *vb* **4 reel in** to wind or draw in on a reel [Old English *hrēol*]

reel² *vb* **1** to move unsteadily or spin round, as if about to fall **2** to be in a state of confusion or stress: *my mind was still reeling* [probably from REEL¹]

reel³ *n* **1** a lively Scottish dance **2** music for this dance [from REEL²]

re-elect *vb* to vote for (someone) to retain his or her position, for example as a Member of Parliament **re-election** *n*

reel off *vb* to recite or write fluently or quickly

re-enact *vb* to act out (a previous event) again **re-enactment** *n*

re-enter *vb* **1** to come back into (a place, esp. a country) **2** (of a spacecraft) to return into (the earth's atmosphere) **re-entry** *n*

re-equip *vb* **-equipping, -equipped** to provide with fresh supplies, components, etc.

re-establish *vb* to create or set up (an organization, link, etc.) again **re-establishment** *n*

reeve *n* **1** *English history* the local representative of the king in a shire until the early 11th century **2** (in medieval England) a steward who supervised the daily affairs of a manor **3** *Canad government* (in some provinces) a president of a local council [Old English *gerēfa*]

re-examine *vb* **-examining, -examined** to inspect or investigate again **re-examination** *n*

ref *n informal* the referee in a sport

refectory *n, pl* **-ries** a dining hall in a religious or academic institution [Latin *refectus* refreshed]

refectory table *n* a long narrow dining table supported by two trestles

refer *vb* **-ferring, -ferred** > **refer to 1** to mention or allude to **2** to be relevant or relate (to): *the word cancer refers to many quite specific different diseases* **3** to seek information (from): *he referred to his notes* **4** to direct the attention of (someone) for information: *the reader is referred to the introduction* **5** to direct (a patient or client) to another doctor or agency: *her GP referred her to a specialist* **6** to hand over for consideration or decision: *to refer a complaint to another department* [Latin *re-* back + *ferre* to carry] **referable** *or* **referrable** *adj* **referral** *n*

> **USAGE** The common practice of adding *back* to *refer* is tautologous, since this meaning is already contained in the *re-* of *refer: this refers to* (not *back to*) *what has already been said*. However, when *refer* is used in the sense of passing a document or question for further consideration to the person from whom it was received, it may be appropriate to say *he referred the matter back*.

referee *n* **1** the umpire in various sports, such as football and boxing **2** a person who is willing to provide a reference for someone for a job **3** a person referred to for a decision or opinion in a dispute ▷ *vb* **-reeing, -reed 4** to act as a referee

reference *n* **1** the act of referring **2** a mention: *this book contains several references to the Civil War* **3** direction to a passage elsewhere in a book or to another book **4** a book or passage referred to **5** a written testimonial regarding one's character or capabilities **6** a person referred to for such a testimonial **7** relation or restriction, esp. to or by membership of a specific group: *without reference to sex or age* **8 with reference to** concerning ▷ *adj* **9** containing information or facts: *reference books* **referential** *adj*

referendum *n, pl* **-dums** *or* **-da** a direct vote of the electorate on a question of importance [Latin: something to be carried back]

refill *vb* **1** to fill (something) again ▷ *n* **2** a second or subsequent filling: *I held out my glass for a refill* **3** a replacement supply of something in a permanent container **refillable** *adj*

refine *vb* **-fining, -fined 1** to make free from impurities; purify **2** to improve: *surgical techniques are constantly being refined* **3** to separate (a mixture) into pure constituents: *molasses is a residual syrup obtained during sugar refining*

refined *adj* **1** cultured or polite **2** freed from impurities **3** highly developed and effective: *refined intelligence tests*

refinement *n* **1** an improvement to something, such as a piece of equipment **2** fineness of taste or manners **3** a subtle point or distinction **4** the act of refining

refinery *n, pl* **-neries** a factory for purifying a raw material, such as sugar or oil

refit *vb* **-fitting, -fitted 1** to make (a ship) ready for use again by repairing or re-equipping ▷ *n* **2** a repair or re-equipping for further use

reflation *n* an increase in the supply of money and credit designed to encourage economic activity [RE- + *-flation*, as in *inflation*] **reflate** *vb* **reflationary** *adj*

reflect *vb* **1** (of a surface or object) to throw back (light, heat, or sound) **2** (of a mirror) to form an image of (something) by reflection **3** to show: *many of her books reflect her obsession with fine art* **4** to consider carefully **5 reflect on** *or* **upon** to cause to be regarded in a specified way: *the incident reflects very badly on me* **6** to bring as a consequence: *the programme reflected great credit on the technicians* [Latin *re-* back + *flectere* to bend]

reflecting telescope *n* a telescope in which the initial image is formed by a concave mirror

reflection *n* **1** the act of reflecting **2** the return of rays of light, heat, or sound **3** an image of an object given back in a mirror **4** careful or long consideration **5 on reflection** after careful consideration or reconsideration **6** discredit or blame: *it's a sad reflection on modern morality* **7** *maths* a transformation of a shape in which right and left, or top and bottom, are reversed

reflective *adj* **1** characterized by quiet thought or contemplation **2** capable of reflecting: *a reflective coating*

reflector *n* **1** a polished surface for reflecting light **2** a reflecting telescope

reflex *n* **1** an immediate involuntary response to a given stimulus **2** a mechanical response to a particular situation, involving no conscious decision **3** an image produced by reflection ▷ *adj* **4** of or caused by a reflex: *a reflex action* **5** reflected **6** *maths* (of an angle) between 180° and 360° [Latin *reflexus* bent back]

reflex camera *n* a camera which uses a mirror to channel light from a lens to the viewfinder, so that the image seen is the same as the image photographed

r

reflexive *adj* **1** *grammar* denoting a pronoun that refers back to the subject of a sentence or clause. Thus, in *that man thinks a great deal of himself*, the pronoun *himself* is reflexive **2** *grammar* denoting a verb used with a reflexive pronoun as its direct object, as in *to dress oneself* **3** *physiol* of or relating to a reflex ▷ *n* **4** a reflexive pronoun or verb

reflexology *n* foot massage as a therapy in alternative medicine **reflexologist** *n*

reform *n* **1** correction of abuses or malpractices: *a programme of economic reforms* **2** improvement of morals or behaviour ▷ *vb* **3** to improve (a law or institution) by correcting abuses **4** to give up or cause to give up a bad habit or way of life [Latin *reformare* to form again] **reformative** *adj* **reformer** *n*

reformation (ref-fer-**may**-shun) *n* **1** a reforming **2 the Reformation** a religious movement in 16th-century Europe that began as an attempt to reform the Roman Catholic Church and resulted in the establishment of the Protestant Churches

reformatory *n, pl* **-ries** (formerly) a place where young offenders were sent to be reformed

Reformed *adj* of a Protestant Church, esp. a Calvinist one

reformist *adj* **1** advocating reform rather than abolition, esp. of a religion or a political movement ▷ *n* **2** a person advocating reform

refract *vb* to cause light, heat, or sound to undergo refraction [Latin *re-* back + *frangere* to break] **refractive** *adj* **refractor** *n*

refracting telescope *n* a type of telescope in which the image is formed by a set of lenses. Also called: **refractor**

refraction *n physics* **1** the change in direction of a wave, such as light or sound, in passing from one medium to another in which it has a different velocity **2** the amount by which a wave is refracted

refractory *adj* **1** *formal* stubborn or rebellious **2** *med* not responding to treatment **3** (of a material) able to withstand high temperatures without fusion or decomposition

refrain[1] *vb* **refrain from** to keep oneself from doing [Latin *refrenare* to check with a bridle]

refrain[2] *n* **1** a frequently repeated part of a song **2** a much repeated saying or idea [Latin *refringere* to break into pieces]

refrangible *adj* capable of being refracted

refresh *vb* **1** to revive or reinvigorate, for example through rest, drink, or food **2** to stimulate (the memory) [Old French *refreschir*] **refresher** *n*

refresher course *n* a course designed to improve or update a person's knowledge of a subject

refreshing *adj* **1** having a reviving effect **2** pleasantly different or new: *refreshing candour*

refreshment *n* **1** the act of refreshing **2 refreshments** snacks and drinks served as a light meal

refrigerant *n* **1** a fluid capable of vaporizing at low temperatures, used in refrigerators ▷ *adj* **2** causing cooling or freezing

refrigerate *vb* **-rating, -rated** to chill or freeze in order to preserve [Latin *refrigerare* to make cold] **refrigeration** *n*

refrigerator *n* the full name for **fridge**

refuel *vb* **-elling, -elled** *or US* **-eling, -eled** to supply or be supplied with fresh fuel

refuge *n* **1** shelter or protection from danger or hardship **2** a place, person, or thing that offers protection or help [Latin *re-* back + *fugere* to escape]

refugee *n* a person who has fled from some danger, such as war or political persecution

refulgent *adj literary* shining brightly [Latin *refulgere* to reflect] **refulgence** *n*

refund *vb* **1** to give back (money) **2** to pay back (a person) ▷ *n* **3** return of money to a purchaser or the amount returned [Latin *re-* back + *fundere* to pour] **refundable** *adj*

refurbish *vb* to renovate and brighten up **refurbishment** *n*

refusal *n* **1** the act of refusing **2** the opportunity to reject or accept: *he was given first refusal on all three scripts*

refuse[1] (rif-**yooz**) *vb* **-fusing, -fused 1** to be determined not (to do something): *he refuses to consider it* **2** to decline to give or allow (something) to (someone): *if the judge refuses bail, he'll appeal* **3** to decline to accept (something offered): *he refused the captaincy* **4** (of a horse) to be unwilling to jump a fence [Latin *refundere* to pour back]

refuse[2] (**ref**-yoos) *n* anything thrown away; rubbish [Old French *refuser* to refuse]

refusenik *n* **1** (formerly) a Jew in the USSR who was refused permission to emigrate **2** a person who refuses to obey a law or cooperate with the government because of strong beliefs

refute *vb* **-futing, -futed** to prove (a statement or theory) to be false or incorrect [Latin *refutare*] **refutation** *n*

USAGE The use of *refute* to mean *deny* is thought by many people to be incorrect.

regain *vb* **1** to get back or recover **2** to reach again: *to regain the shore*

regal *adj* **1** of or fit for a king or queen **2** splendid and dignified; magnificent: *a luxury cruise liner on her serene and regal way around the better ports* [Latin *regalis*] **regality** *n* **regally** *adv*

regale *vb* **-galing, -galed 1** to give delight or amusement to: *she would regale her friends with stories* **2** to provide with abundant food or drink [French *régaler*]

regalia *n* the ceremonial emblems or robes of royalty or high office [Medieval Latin: royal privileges]

regard *vb* **1** to look upon or think of in a specified way: *angina can therefore be regarded as heart cramp* **2** to look closely or attentively at (something or someone) **3** to take notice of: *he has never regarded the conventions* **4 as regards** on the subject of ▷ *n* **5** respect or affection: *you haven't a high regard for her opinion* **6** attention: *he eats what he wants with no regard to health* **7** a gaze or look **8** reference or connection: *with regard to my complaint* **9 regards** an expression of goodwill: *give her my regards* [Old French *regarder* to look at, care about]

regardful *adj* **regardful of** paying attention to

regarding *prep* on the subject of; relating to

regardless *adj* **1 regardless of** taking no notice of: *the illness can affect anyone regardless of their social*

r

class ▷ *adv* **2** in spite of everything: *I carried on regardless*

regatta *n* a series of races of boats or yachts [obsolete Italian *rigatta* contest]

regency *n, pl* **-cies** **1** government by a regent **2** the status of a regent **3** a period when a regent is in power [Latin *regere* to rule]

Regency *adj* of the regency (1811–20) of the Prince of Wales (later George IV) or the styles of architecture or furniture produced during it

regenerate *vb* (ri-**jen**-er-ate) **-rating, -rated** **1** to undergo or cause to undergo physical, economic, or spiritual renewal **2** to come or bring into existence once again **3** to replace (lost or damaged tissues or organs) by new growth ▷ *adj* (ri-**jen**-er-it) **4** physically, economically, or spiritually renewed **regeneration** *n* **regenerative** *adj*

regent *n* **1** the ruler of a country during the childhood, absence, or illness of its monarch **2** *US & Canad* a member of the governing board of certain schools and colleges ▷ *adj* **3** acting as a regent: *the Prince Regent* [Latin *regere* to rule]

reggae *n* a type of popular music of Jamaican origin with a strong beat [West Indian]

regicide *n* **1** the killing of a king **2** a person who kills a king [Latin *rex* king + *caedere* to kill]

regifting *n* the practice of giving an unwanted gift to another person

regime (ray-**zheem**) *n* **1** a system of government **2** a particular administration: *the corrupt regime* **3** *med* a regimen [French]

regimen *n* a prescribed system of diet and exercise [Latin: guidance]

regiment *n* **1** an organized body of troops as a unit in the army **2** a large number or group [Late Latin *regimentum* government] **regimental** *adj*

regimentals *pl n* **1** the uniform and insignia of a regiment **2** military uniform

regimental sergeant major *n military* the senior warrant officer in a regiment or battalion

regimented *adj* very strictly controlled: *the regimented confines of the school* **regimentation** *n*

Regina *n* queen: now used chiefly in documents and inscriptions [Latin]

region *n* **1** an administrative division of a country **2** an area considered as a unit for geographical or social reasons **3** a sphere of activity or interest **4** a part of the body: *the lumbar region* **5 in the region of** approximately: *in the region of 100 000 troops* **6 the regions** the parts of a country away from the capital: *discord between Moscow and the regions* [Latin *regio*] **regional** *adj*

regionalism *n* **1** the division of a country or organization into geographical regions each having some autonomy **2** loyalty to one's home region

register *n* **1** an official list recording names, events, or transactions **2** the book in which such a list is written **3** a device that records data, totals sums of money, etc.: *a cash register* **4** a style of speaking or writing, such as slang, used in particular circumstances or social situations **5** *music* **A** the timbre characteristic of a certain manner of voice production **B** any of the stops on an organ in respect of its tonal quality: *the flute register* ▷ *vb* **6** to enter (an event, person's name, ownership, etc.) in a register **7** to show on a scale or other measuring instrument **8** to show in a person's face or bearing: *his face registered surprise* **9** *informal* to have an effect or make an impression: *the news did not register at first* [Medieval Latin *registrum*] **registration** *n*

register office *n Brit* a government office where civil marriages are performed and births, marriages, and deaths are recorded

registrar *n* **1** a person who keeps official records **2** an official responsible for student records and enrolment in a college **3** *Brit, Austral & S African* a hospital doctor senior to a houseman but junior to a consultant **4** an organization that administers the reservation of internet domain names

registration document *n Brit & Austral* a document giving identification details of a vehicle, including its owner's name

registration number *n Brit* a sequence of letters and numbers given to a motor vehicle when it is registered, displayed on numberplates at the front and rear

registry *n, pl* **-tries** **1** a place where official records are kept **2** the registration of a ship's country of origin: *a ship of Liberian registry*

registry office *n Brit & NZ* same as **register office**

Regius professor (**reej**-yuss) *n Brit* a person appointed by the Crown to a university chair founded by a royal patron [Latin *regius* royal]

regress *vb* **1** to return to a former and worse condition ▷ *n* **2** a return to a former and worse condition [Latin *regredi* to go back] **regressive** *adj*

regression *n* **1** the act of regressing **2** *psychol* the use by an adult of behaviour more appropriate to a child

regret *vb* **-gretting, -gretted** **1** to feel sorry or upset about **2** to express apology or distress about: *we regret any misunderstanding caused* ▷ *n* **3** a feeling of repentance, guilt, or sorrow **4 regrets** a polite expression of refusal: *she had sent her regrets* [Old French *regreter*] **regretful** *adj* **regretfully** *adv* **regrettable** *adj* **regrettably** *adv*

> **USAGE** *Regretful* and *regretfully* are sometimes wrongly used where *regrettable* and *regrettably* are meant: *he gave a regretful smile; he smiled regretfully; this is a regrettable* (not *regretful*) *mistake; regrettably* (not *regretfully*), *I shall be unable to attend.*

regroup *vb* **1** to reorganize (military forces) after an attack or a defeat **2** to rearrange into a new grouping

regular *adj* **1** normal, customary, or usual **2** symmetrical or even: *regular features* **3** according to a uniform principle, arrangement, or order **4** occurring at fixed or prearranged intervals: *we run regular advertisements in the press* **5** following a set rule or normal practice **6** *grammar* following the usual pattern of formation in a language: *regular verbs* **7** of or serving in the permanent military services: *the regular armed forces* **8** *maths* (of a polygon) having all its sides and angles the same **9** officially qualified or recognized: *he's not a regular doctor* **10** *informal* not constipated: *eating fresh vegetables helps keep you regular* **11** *US & Canad* *informal* likeable: *a regular guy* **12** complete or utter: *a regular fool* **13** subject to the rule of an established religious community: *canons regular* ▷ *n* **14** a professional long-term soldier in a military unit **15** *informal* a frequent customer or visitor [Latin *regula* ruler, model] **regularity** *n* **regularize** *or* **-rise** *vb* **regularly** *adv*

regulate *vb* **-lating, -lated 1** to control by means of rules: *a code of practice to regulate advertising by schools* **2** to adjust slightly: *he had to take drugs to regulate his heartbeat* [Late Latin *regulare* to control] **regulatory** *adj*

regulation *n* **1** a rule that governs procedure or behaviour **2** the act of regulating ▷ *adj* **3** in accordance with rules or conventions: *dressed in the orchestra's regulation black tie*

regulator *n* **1** a mechanism that automatically controls pressure, temperature, etc. **2** the mechanism by which the speed of a clock is regulated

regurgitate *vb* **-tating, -tated 1** to vomit **2** (of some birds and animals) to bring back (partly digested food) to the mouth to feed the young **3** to reproduce (ideas or facts) without understanding them [Medieval Latin *re-* back + *gurgitare* to flood] **regurgitation** *n*

rehabilitate *vb* **-tating, -tated 1** to help (a person) to readapt to society after illness or imprisonment **2** to restore to a former position or rank **3** to restore the good reputation of [Medieval Latin *rehabilitare* to restore] **rehabilitation** *n*

rehash *vb* **1** to use (old or already used ideas) in a slightly different form without real improvement ▷ *n* **2** old ideas presented in a new form [*re-* again + *hash* to chop into pieces]

rehearse *vb* **-hearsing, -hearsed 1** to practise (a play, concert, etc.) for public performance **2** to repeat aloud: *he rehearsed his familiar views on the press* **3** to train (a person) for public performance [Old French *rehercier* to harrow a second time] **rehearsal** *n* **rehearser** *n*

rehouse *vb* **-housing, -housed** to provide with a new and better home

Reich (rike) *n* the former German state, esp. the Nazi dictatorship in Germany from 1933–45 (**Third Reich**) [German: kingdom]

reign *n* **1** the period during which a monarch is the official ruler of a country **2** a period during which a person or thing is dominant: *a reign of terror* ▷ *vb* **3** to rule (a country) **4** to be supreme: *a sense of confusion reigns in the capital* [Old French *reigne*]

> **USAGE** *Reign* is sometimes wrongly written for *rein* in certain phrases: *he gave full rein* (not *reign*) *to his feelings; it will be necessary to rein in* (not *reign in*) *public spending.*

reigning *adj* currently holding a title or championship: *the reigning world champion*

reimburse *vb* **-bursing, -bursed** to repay (someone) for (expenses or losses) [Medieval Latin *imbursare* to put in a moneybag] **reimbursement** *n*

rein *n* **1 reins A** long narrow straps attached to a bit to control a horse **B** narrow straps attached to a harness to control a young child **C** means of control: *to take up the reins of government* **2 give (a) free rein** to allow a considerable amount of freedom **3 keep a tight rein on** to control carefully: *we have to keep a tight rein on expenditure* ▷ *vb* **4** to restrain or halt with reins **5** to control or limit: *reining her thoughts, she tried to be objective* ▷ See also **rein in** [Old French *resne*]

> **USAGE** See at **reign**.

reincarnate *vb* **-nating, -nated** (*often passive*) to be born again in a different body: *souls may be reincarnated in human forms*

reincarnation *n* **1** the belief that after death the soul is reborn in another body **2** an instance of rebirth in another body **3** reappearance in a new form of a principle or idea: *he was the reincarnation of the old Republican Party isolationist*

reindeer *n, pl* **-deer** *or* **-deers** a deer with large branched antlers that lives in the arctic regions [Old Norse *hreindýri*]

reinforce *vb* **-inforcing, -inforced 1** to give added emphasis to (an idea or feeling): *his tired face reinforced his own weariness* **2** to make physically stronger or harder: *the plastic panels were reinforced with carbon fibre* **3** to give added support to (a military force) by providing more men or equipment: *the army garrison had been reinforced with helicopters* [French *renforcer*] **reinforcement** *n*

reinforced concrete *n* concrete with steel bars or mesh embedded in it to strengthen it

rein in *vb* **1** to stop (a horse) by pulling on the reins **2** to restrict or stop: *either prices or wage packets had to be reined in*

reinstate *vb* **-stating, -stated 1** to restore to a former rank or status **2** to cause to exist or be important again: *reinstate some semblance of order* **reinstatement** *n*

reinvigorate *vb* to give renewed energy to; refresh

reissue *n* **1** a book, music recording, etc., that is published or released again after being unavailable for a time ▷ *vb* **2** to publish or release (a book, music recording, etc.) again after a period of unavailability

reiterate *vb* **-rating, -rated** *formal* to repeat again and again [Latin *reiterare*] **reiteration** *n*

reject *vb* **1** to refuse to accept, use, or believe **2** to deny to (a person) the feelings hoped for: *the boy had been rejected by his mother* **3** to pass over or throw out as useless **4** (of an organism) to fail to accept (a tissue graft or organ transplant) ▷ *n* **5** a person or thing rejected as not up to standard [Latin *reicere* to throw back] **rejection** *n*

rejig *vb* **-jigging, -jigged 1** to re-equip (a factory or plant) **2** *informal* to rearrange or manipulate, sometimes in an unscrupulous way: *the promoter hastily rejigged the running order*

rejoice *vb* **-joicing, -joiced** to feel or express great happiness [Old French *resjoir*] **rejoicing** *n*

rejoin[1] *vb* to come together with (someone or something) again

rejoin[2] *vb* to reply in a sharp or witty way [Old French *rejoindre*]

rejoinder *n* a sharp or witty reply

rejuvenate *vb* **-nating, -nated** to give back youth or vitality to [Latin *re-* again + *juvenis* young] **rejuvenation** *n*

rekindle *vb* **-dling, -dled** to arouse (former emotions or interests)

relapse *vb* **-lapsing, -lapsed 1** to fall back into bad habits or illness ▷ *n* **2** the act of relapsing **3** the return of ill health after an apparent or partial recovery [Latin *re-* back + *labi* to slip]

relate *vb* **-lating, -lated 1** to establish a relation between **2** to have reference or relation to **3** to have an understanding (of people or ideas): *the inability to relate to others* **4** to tell (a story) or describe (an event) [Latin *relatus* brought back]

related *adj* **1** linked by kinship or marriage **2** connected or associated: *salts and related compounds*

relation *n* **1** the connection between things or people **2** a person who is connected by blood or marriage **3** connection by blood or marriage **4** an account or narrative **5 in** *or* **with relation to** with reference to: *an inquiry into export controls in relation to Iraq*

relations *pl n* **1** social or political dealings between individuals or groups **2** family or relatives **3** *euphemistic* sexual intercourse

relationship *n* **1** the dealings and feelings that exist between people or groups **2** an emotional or sexual affair **3** the connection between two things: *the relationship between exercise and mental health* **4** association by blood or marriage

relative *adj* **1** true to a certain degree or extent: *a zone of relative affluence* **2** having significance only in relation to something else: *time is relative* **3 relative to** in proportion to: *it will benefit from high growth in earnings relative to prices* **4** respective: *the relative qualities of speed and accuracy* **5** relevant: *the facts relative to the enquiry* **6** *grammar* of a clause (**relative clause**) that modifies a noun or pronoun occurring earlier in the sentence **7** *grammar* of or belonging to a class of words, such as *who*, *which*, or *that*, which function as conjunctions introducing relative clauses ▷ *n* **8** a person who is related by blood or marriage **relatively** *adv*

relative atomic mass *n* same as **atomic weight**

relativity *n* **1** either of two theories developed by Albert Einstein, the **special theory of relativity**, which requires that the laws of physics shall be the same as seen by any two different observers in uniform relative motion, and the **general theory of relativity**, which considers observers with relative acceleration and leads to a theory of gravitation **2** the state of being relative

relax *vb* **1** to make or become less tense, looser, or less rigid **2** to ease up from effort or attention **3** to make (rules or discipline) less strict **4** to become more friendly **5** to lessen the intensity of: *he relaxed his vigilance in the lulls between attacks* [Latin *relaxare* to loosen] **relaxed** *adj*

relaxation *n* **1** rest after work or effort **2** a form of recreation: *his favoured form of relaxation was walking on the local moors* **3** the act of relaxing

relay *n* **1** a fresh set of people or animals relieving others **2** short for **relay race 3** an automatic device that controls a valve or switch, esp. one in which a small change in current or voltage controls the switching on or off of circuits **4** *radio* a combination of a receiver and transmitter designed to receive radio signals and retransmit them ▷ *vb* **5** to pass on (a message) **6** to retransmit (a signal) by means of a relay **7** *Brit* to broadcast (a performance or event) as it happens [Old French *relaier* to leave behind]

relay race *n* a race between teams in which each contestant covers a specified portion of the distance

release *vb* **-leasing, -leased 1** to free (a person or animal) from captivity or imprisonment **2** to free (someone) from obligation or duty **3** to free (something) from (one's grip) **4** to allow (news or information) to be made public or available **5** to allow (something) to move freely: *she released the handbrake* **6** to issue (a music recording, film, or book) for sale or public showing: *When was the film originally released?* **7** to give out (heat, energy, radiation, etc.): *the explosion released a cloud of toxic gas* ▷ *n* **8** the act of freeing or state of being freed **9** a statement to the press **10** the act of issuing for sale or publication **11** something issued for sale or public showing [Old French *relesser*]

relegate *vb* **-gating, -gated 1** to put in a less important position **2** to demote (a sports team) to a lower division: *four clubs were relegated from the first division* [Latin *re-* back + *legare* to send] **relegation** *n*

relent *vb* **1** to change one's mind about some decision **2** to become milder or less severe: *the weather relented* [Latin *re-* back + *lentare* to bend]

relentless *adj* **1** never stopping or reducing in severity: *relentless deterioration in standards* **2** (of a person) determined and pitiless

relevant *adj* to do with the matter in hand [Medieval Latin *relevans*] **relevance** *n*

reliable *adj* able to be trusted **reliability** *n* **reliably** *adv*

reliance *n* the state of relying on or trusting (a person or thing) **reliant** *adj*

relic *n* **1** an object or custom that has survived from the past **2** something valued for its past associations **3 relics** remaining parts or traces **4** *RC Church & Eastern churches* a body part or possession of a saint, venerated as holy [Latin *reliquiae* remains]

relict *n* **1** a group of animals or plants that exists as a remnant of a formerly widely distributed group in an environment different from that in which it originated **2** *archaic* anything that is left behind from an earlier time [Latin *relictus* left behind]

relief *n* **1** a feeling of cheerfulness that follows the removal of anxiety, pain, or distress **2** a temporary pause in anxiety, pain, or distress **3** money, food, or clothing given to people in special need: *disaster relief* **4** the act of freeing a besieged town or fortress: *the relief of Mafeking* **5** a person who replaces another at some task or duty **6** a bus, plane, etc., that carries additional passengers when a scheduled service is full **7** Also called: **relievo** *sculpture & archit* the projection of a carved design from the surface **8** any vivid effect resulting from contrast: *a welcome relief* **9** the difference between the highest and lowest level: *study the map of relief and the rainfall map* **10 on relief** *US & Canad* (of people) in receipt of government aid because of personal need [Old French *relever* to relieve]

r

relief map *n* a map showing the shape and height of the land surface by contours and shading

relieve *vb* **-lieving, -lieved 1** to lessen (pain, distress, boredom, etc.) **2** to bring assistance to (someone in need): *a plan to relieve those facing hunger* **3** to free (someone) from an obligation: *a further attempt to relieve the taxpayers of their burdens* **4** to take over the duties of (someone): *the night nurse came in to relieve her* **5** to free (a besieged town or fort) **6 relieve oneself** to urinate or defecate **7** to set off by contrast: *painted walls are marginally relieved by some abstract prints* **8** *informal* to take from: *the prince had relieved him of his duties* [Latin *re-* again + *levare* to lighten] **relieved** *adj*

religion *n* **1** belief in or worship of a supernatural power or powers considered to be divine or to have control of human destiny **2** any formal expression of such belief: *the Christian religion* **3** *chiefly RC Church* the way of life entered upon by monks and nuns: *to enter religion* [Latin *religio*]

religious *adj* **1** of religion **2** pious or devout **3** scrupulous or conscientious: *religious attention to detail* **4** *Christianity* relating to the way of life of monks and nuns ▷ *n* **5** *Christianity* a monk or nun **religiously** *adv*

relinquish *vb formal* **1** to give up: *that hope has to be relinquished* **2** to renounce (a claim or right) **3** to release one's hold on [Latin *relinquere*] **relinquishment** *n*

reliquary (rel-lik-wer-ee) *n, pl* **-quaries** a container for relics of saints

relish *vb* **1** to savour or enjoy (an experience) to the full **2** to anticipate eagerly ▷ *n* **3** liking or enjoyment: *he has an enormous relish for life* **4** pleasurable anticipation: *his early relish for a new challenge* **5** an appetizing or spicy food, such as a pickle, added to a main dish to improve its flavour **6** a zestful quality: *he tells stories with great relish* [earlier *reles* aftertaste]

relive *vb* **-living, -lived** to experience (a sensation or event) again, esp. in the imagination

reload *vb* to put fresh ammunition into (a firearm)

relocate *vb* **-cating, -cated** to move or be moved to a new place of work **relocation** *n*

reluctance *n* **1** unwillingness to do something **2** *physics* a measure of the resistance of a closed magnetic circuit to a magnetic flux [Latin *reluctari* to resist]

reluctant *adj* unwilling or disinclined **reluctantly** *adv*

rely *vb* **-lies, -lying, -lied** > **rely on** *or* **upon A** to be dependent on: *the organization relies on voluntary contributions* **B** to have trust or confidence in: *you can rely on his judgment* [Old French *relier* to fasten together]

REM rapid eye movement

remain *vb* **1** to continue to be: *the situation remains alarming* **2** to stay behind or in the same place: *to remain at home* **3** to be left after use or the passage of time **4** to be left to be done, said, etc.: *whether this will be a long-term trend remains to be seen* [Latin *remanere*]

remainder *n* **1** a part or portion that is left after use or the passage of time: *we ate some biscuits and the remainder of the jam* **2** *maths* **A** the amount left over when one quantity cannot be exactly divided by another: *for 10 ÷ 3, the remainder is 1* **B** the amount left over when one quantity is subtracted from another **3** a number of copies of a book sold cheaply because it has been impossible to sell them at full price ▷ *vb* **4** to sell (copies of a book) as a remainder

remains *pl n* **1** parts left over from something after use or the passage of time: *the remains of the old Roman fortress* **2** a corpse

remake *vb* **-making, -made 1** to make again in a different way ▷ *n* **2** a new version of an old film

remand *vb* **1** *law* to send (a prisoner or accused person) back into custody or put on bail before trial ▷ *n* **2** the sending of a person back into custody or putting on bail before trial **3 on remand** in custody or on bail awaiting trial [Latin *re-* back + *mandare* to command]

remand centre *n* a place where accused people are detained while awaiting trial

remark *vb* **1** to pass a casual comment (about) **2** to say **3** to observe or notice ▷ *n* **4** a brief casually expressed thought or opinion [Old French *remarquer* to observe]

remarkable *adj* **1** worthy of note or attention: *a remarkable career* **2** striking or extraordinary: *a thing of remarkable beauty* **remarkably** *adv*

remarry *vb* **-ries, -rying, -ried** to marry again following a divorce or the death of one's previous spouse **remarriage** *n*

remedial *adj* **1** providing or intended as a remedy **2** of special teaching for slow learners: *remedial classes* **remedially** *adv*

remedy *n, pl* **-edies 1** a drug or treatment for curing pain or disease **2** a way of solving a problem: *every statesman promised a remedy for unemployment* ▷ *vb* **-edies, -edying, -edied 3** to put right or improve [Latin *remedium* a cure] **remediable** *adj*

remember *vb* **1** to become aware of (something forgotten) again **2** to keep (an idea, intention, etc.) in one's mind: *remember to write* **3** to give money to (someone), as in a will or in tipping **4 remember to** to mention (a person's name) to another person, by way of greeting: *remember me to her* **5** to commemorate: *we are here to remember the dead* [Latin *re-* again + *memor* mindful]

remembrance *n* **1** a memory **2** a memento or keepsake **3** the act of honouring some past event or person

Remembrance Day *n* **1** (in Britain) Remembrance Sunday **2** (in Canada and Australia) a statutory holiday observed on November 11 in memory of the dead of both World Wars

Remembrance Sunday *n* (in Britain) the Sunday closest to November 11, on which the dead of both World Wars are commemorated

remind *vb* **1** to cause to remember: *remind her that she was on duty* **2** to put in mind (of someone or something): *you remind me of Alice in Wonderland*

reminder *n* **1** something that recalls the past **2** a note to remind a person of something not done

reminisce *vb* **-niscing, -nisced** to talk or write about old times or past experiences

reminiscence *n* **1** the act of recalling or narrating past experiences **2** something remembered from the past **3 reminiscences** stories about a person's life, often presented in a book

reminiscent *adj* **1 reminiscent of** reminding or suggestive of **2** characterized by reminiscence [Latin *reminisci* to call to mind]

remiss *adj formal* careless in attention to duty or responsibility [Latin *remissus*]

remission *n* **1** a reduction in the length of a prison term **2** forgiveness for sin **3** easing of intensity of the symptoms of a disease **4** a release from an obligation

remit *vb* (rim-**mitt**) **-mitting, -mitted 1** to send (money) for goods or services **2** to cancel (a punishment or debt) **3** *law* to send back (a case) to a lower court for further consideration **4** to slacken or ease off **5** *archaic* to forgive (crime or sins) ▷ *n* (**ree**-mitt) **6** area of authority: *within the review body's remit* [Latin *re-* back + *mittere* to send]

remittance *n* money sent as payment

remittent *adj* (of a disease) periodically less severe

remix *vb* **1** to change the relative prominence of each performer's part of (a recording) ▷ *n* **2** a remixed version of a recording

remnant *n* **1** a part left over **2** a piece of material from the end of a roll **3** a surviving trace or vestige: *the authorities drafted in the military to crush any remnant of protest* [Old French *remenant* remaining]

remodel *vb* **-delling, -delled** *or US* **-eling, -eled** to give a different shape or form to: *a renaissance of boutiques and remodelled apartments; the country is planning to remodel its armed forces*

remonstrance *n formal* a strong protest about something

remonstrate *vb* **-strating, -strated** *formal* to argue in protest or objection: *the player remonstrated loudly with the official* [Latin *re-* again + *monstrare* to show] **remonstration** *n*

remorse *n* a sense of deep regret and guilt for something one did [Medieval Latin *remorsus* a gnawing] **remorseful** *adj*

remorseless *adj* **1** constantly unkind and lacking pity: *remorseless fate* **2** continually intense: *the superintendent's remorseless gaze*

remote *adj* **1** far away **2** far from civilization **3** distant in time **4** not relevant: *the issues seem remote from the general population* **5** (of a person's manner) aloof or abstracted **6** slight or faint: *a remote possibility* **7** operated from a distance; remote-controlled: *a remote manipulator arm* [Latin *remotus* far removed] **remotely** *adv*

remote control *n* control of an apparatus from a distance by radio or electrical signals **remote-controlled** *adj*

remould *vb* **1** to change completely: *to remould the country* **2** *Brit* to bond a new tread onto the casing of (a worn pneumatic tyre) ▷ *n* **3** *Brit* a tyre made by this process

removable *adj* capable of being removed from a place or released from another object: *a farmer's truck with removable wooden sides*

removal *n* **1** the act of removing or state of being removed **2** the process of moving one's possessions from a previous address to a new one

remove *vb* **-moving, -moved 1** to take away and place elsewhere **2** to take (clothing) off **3** to get rid of **4** to dismiss (someone) from office **5** *formal* to change the location of one's home or place of business ▷ *n* **6** the degree of difference: *one remove away from complete rebuttal* **7** *Brit* (in certain schools) a class or form designed to prepare pupils for senior classes [Old French *removoir*]

removed *adj* **1** very different or distant: *madness seemed far removed from the sunny order of things* **2** separated by a degree of descent: *the child of a person's first cousin is their first cousin once removed*

remunerate *vb* **-rating, -rated** *formal* to reward or pay for work or service [Latin *remunerari*] **remuneration** *n* **remunerative** *adj*

renaissance *n* a renewal of interest or creativity in an area: *a complete renaissance in maze building* [French]

Renaissance *n* **1 the Renaissance** the great revival of art, literature, and learning in Europe in the 14th, 15th, and 16th centuries ▷ *adj* **2** of or from the Renaissance

renal (**ree**-nal) *adj* of the kidneys [Latin *renes* kidneys]

renascent *adj literary* becoming active or vigorous again: *renascent nationalism* [Latin *renasci* to be born again] **renascence** *n*

rend *vb* **rending, rent** *literary* **1** to tear violently **2** (of a sound) to break (the silence) with a shrill or piercing tone [Old English *rendan*]

render *vb* **1** to cause to become: *he was rendered unconscious by his wound* **2** to give or provide (aid, a service, etc.) **3** *formal* to present or submit (a bill) **4** to translate **5** to represent in painting, music, or acting **6** to yield or give: *he rendered up his soul to God* **7** to cover with plaster **8** to melt down (fat) [Old French *rendre*] **rendering** *n*

rendezvous (**ron**-day-voo) *n, pl* **-vous** (-vooz) **1** an appointment to meet at a specified time and place **2** a place where people meet ▷ *vb* **3** to meet at a specified time or place [French]

rendition *n formal* **1** a performance of a piece of music or a dramatic role **2** a translation

renegade *n* a person who deserts a cause for another [Spanish *renegado*]

renege (rin-**nayg**) *vb* **-neging, -neged** to go back (on an agreement or promise): *the politicians reneged on every promise* [Medieval Latin *renegare* to renounce]

renew *vb* **1** to begin again **2** to take up again after a break: *they wanted to renew diplomatic ties* **3** to make valid again: *we didn't renew the lease* **4** to grow again **5** to restore to a new or fresh condition **6** to replace (an old or worn-out part or piece) **7** to restate or reaffirm (a promise) **renewal** *n*

renewable *adj* **1** able to be renewed **2** (of energy or an energy source) inexhaustible or capable of being perpetually replenished ▷ *pl n* **renewables 3** renewable energy sources, such as wind and wave power

rennet *n* a substance prepared from the stomachs of calves and used for curdling milk to make cheese [Old English *gerinnan* to curdle]

renounce *vb* **-nouncing, -nounced 1** to give up (a belief or habit) voluntarily **2** to give up formally

r

(a claim or right): *he would renounce his rights to the throne* [Latin *renuntiare*]

renovate *vb* **-vating, -vated** to restore to good condition [Latin *re-* again + *novare* to make new] **renovation** *n* **renovator** *n*

renown *n* widespread good reputation [Old French *renom*]

renowned *adj* famous

rent¹ *vb* **1** to give or have use of (land, a building, a machine, etc.) in return for periodic payments ▷ *n* **2** a payment made periodically for the use of land, a building, a machine, etc. [Old French *rente* revenue]

rent² *n* **1** a slit made by tearing ▷ *vb* **2** the past of **rend**

rental *n* **1** the amount paid or received as rent ▷ *adj* **2** of or relating to rent

rent boy *n* a young male prostitute

rentier (ron-tee-ay) *n* a person who lives off unearned income such as rents or interest

renunciation *n* **1** the act or an instance of renouncing **2** a formal declaration renouncing something

reo *n* NZ a language [Māori]

reopen *vb* to open again after a period of being closed or suspended: *the Supreme Court has agreed to reopen the case*

reorder *vb* to change the order of; organize differently

reorganize *or* **-nise** *vb* **-nizing, -nized** *or* **-nising, -nised** to organize in a new and more efficient way **reorganization** *or* **-nisation** *n*

rep¹ *n theatre* short for **repertory company**

rep² *n* **1** a sales representative **2** someone elected to represent a group of people: *the union rep* **3** NZ *informal* a rugby player selected to represent his district

repair¹ *vb* **1** to restore (something damaged or broken) to good condition or working order **2** to make up for (a mistake or injury) **3** to heal (a breach or division) in (something): *he is attempting to repair his country's relations with America* ▷ *n* **4** the act, task, or process of repairing **5** a part that has been repaired **6** state or condition: *many museums may have to close because they are in such bad repair* [Latin *re-* again + *parare* to make ready] **repairable** *adj*

repair² *vb* **repair to** *formal* to go to (a place) [Latin *re-* back + *patria* fatherland]

reparable (rep-rab-bl) *adj* able to be repaired or remedied

reparation *n* **1** the act of making up for loss or injury **2** **reparations** compensation paid by a defeated nation after a war for the damage and injuries it caused [Latin *reparare* to repair]

repartee *n* **1** conversation consisting of witty remarks **2** a sharp witty remark made as a reply [French *repartie*]

repast *n literary* a meal [Old French *repaistre* to feed]

repatriate *vb* **-ating, -ated** **1** to send back (a person) to the country of his or her birth or citizenship ▷ *n* **2** a person who has been repatriated: *Algerian repatriates* [Latin *re-* back + *patria* fatherland] **repatriation** *n*

repay *vb* **-paying, -paid** **1** to refund or reimburse **2** to make a return for (something): *to repay hospitality* **repayable** *adj* **repayment** *n*

repeal *vb* **1** to cancel (a law) officially ▷ *n* **2** the act of repealing: *the repeal of repressive legislation* [Old French *repeler*] **repealable** *adj*

repeat *vb* **1** to say, write, or do again **2** to tell to another person (the secrets told to one by someone else) **3** to recite (a poem, etc.) from memory **4** to occur more than once: *this pattern repeats itself many times* **5** (of food) to be tasted again after eating as the result of belching **6** to say (the words or sounds) uttered by someone else; echo ▷ *n* **7** the act or an instance of repeating **8** a word, action, pattern, etc., that is repeated **9** *radio & television* a broadcast of a programme which has been broadcast before **10** *music* a passage that is an exact restatement of the passage preceding it [Latin *repetere* to seek again] **repeated** *adj* **repeatedly** *adv* **repeatable** *adj*

> **USAGE** Since *again* is part of the meaning of *repeat*, one should not say something is *repeated again*.

repeater *n* **1** a gun capable of firing several shots without reloading **2** a clock or watch which strikes the hour or quarter-hour just past, when a spring is pressed

repel *vb* **-pelling, -pelled** **1** to cause (someone) to feel disgusted **2** to force or drive back (someone or something) **3** to be effective in keeping away or controlling: *these buzzers are claimed to repel female mosquitoes* **4** to fail to mix with or absorb: *water and oil repel each other* **5** to reject or spurn: *she repelled his advances* [Latin *re-* back + *pellere* to push]

> **USAGE** See at **repulse**.

repellent *adj* **1** disgusting or distasteful **2** resisting water, etc. ▷ *n* **3** a chemical used to keep insects or other creatures away

repent *vb* to feel regret for (something bad one has done) [Old French *repentir*] **repentance** *n* **repentant** *adj*

repercussion *n* **1** **repercussions** results or consequences of an action or event **2** an echo or reverberation [Latin *repercutere* to strike back]

repertoire *n* **1** all the works that a company or performer can perform **2** the entire stock of skills or techniques that someone or something, such as a computer, is capable of: *a superb repertoire of shots* [French]

repertory *n, pl* **-ries** **1** same as **repertoire** (sense 2) **2** short for **repertory company** [Late Latin *repertorium* storehouse]

repertory company *n* a permanent theatre company producing a succession of plays

repetition *n* **1** the act of repeating **2** a thing that is repeated **3** a replica or copy **repetitious** *adj* **repetitive** *adj*

rephrase *vb* **-phrasing, -phrased** to express in different words **rephrasing** *n*

repine *vb* **-pining, -pined** *literary* to be worried or discontented [RE- + PINE²]

replace *vb* **-placing, -placed** **1** to take the place of **2** to substitute a person or thing for (another): *we need to replace that chair* **3** to put (something) back in its rightful place

replacement *n* **1** the act or process of replacing **2** a person or thing that replaces another

replay *n* **1** a showing again of a sequence of action immediately after it happens **2** a second sports match played because an earlier game was drawn ▷ *vb* **3** to play (a recording, match, etc.) again

replenish *vb* to make full or complete again by supplying what has been used up [Old French *replenir*] **replenishment** *n*

replete *adj* **1** pleasantly full of food and drink **2** well supplied: *a world replete with true horror* [Latin *repletus*] **repletion** *n*

replica *n* an exact copy [Italian, literally: a reply]

replicate *vb* **-cating, -cated** to make or be an exact copy of; reproduce [Latin *replicatus* bent back] **replication** *n*

reply *vb* **-plies, -plying, -plied 1** to make answer (to) in words or writing or by an action **2** to say (something) in answer: *she replied that she did not believe him* ▷ *n, pl* **-plies 3** an answer or response [Old French *replier* to fold again]

report *vb* **1** to give an account (of) **2** to give an account of the results of an investigation (into): *the commission is to report on global warming* **3** to make a formal report on (a subject) **4** to make a formal complaint about **5** to present (oneself) at an appointed place or for a specific purpose: *report to the manager's office* **6 report to** to be responsible to and under the authority of **7** to act as a reporter ▷ *n* **8** an account prepared after investigation and published or broadcast **9** an account of the discussions of a committee or other group of people: *I have the report of the mining union* **10** a story for which there is no absolute proof: *according to report, he is not dead* **11** a statement on the progress of a school child **12** a loud bang made by a gun or explosion **13** comment on a person's character or actions: *he is of good report here* [Latin *re-* back + *portare* to carry] **reportedly** *adv*

reported speech *n* a report of what someone said that gives the content of the speech without repeating the exact words

reporter *n* a person who gathers news for a newspaper or broadcasting organization

repose¹ *n* **1** a state of quiet restfulness **2** calmness or composure **3** sleep ▷ *vb* **-posing, -posed 4** to lie or lay down at rest **5** to lie when dead [Old French *reposer*]

repose² *vb* **-posing, -posed** to put (trust) in a person or thing [Latin *reponere* to store up]

reposition *vb* to place in a different position

repository *n, pl* **-ries 1** a place or container in which things can be stored for safety: *a repository for national treasures* **2** a person to whom a secret is entrusted [Latin *repositorium*]

repossess *vb* (of a lender) to take back (property) from a customer who is behind with payments, for example mortgage repayments **repossession** *n*

reprehend *vb* to find fault with [Latin *reprehendere*]

reprehensible *adj* deserving criticism: *Willie's reprehensible behaviour*

represent *vb* **1** to act as the authorized delegate for (a person, country, etc.): *she represented her country at the Olympic Games* **2** to act as a substitute (for) **3** to stand as an equivalent of **4** to be a means of expressing: *the lights are relit to represent resurrection* **5** to display the characteristics of: *romanticism in music is represented by Liszt* **6** to describe as having a specified character or quality: *the magical bird was often represented as having two heads* **7** to state or explain **8** to present an image of through a picture or sculpture **9** to bring clearly before the mind [Latin *repraesentare* to exhibit]

representation *n* **1** the state of being represented **2** anything that represents, such as a pictorial portrait **3 representations** formal statements made to an official body by a person making a complaint **representational** *adj*

representative *n* **1** a person chosen to act for or represent a group **2** a person who tries to sell the products or services of a firm **3** a typical example ▷ *adj* **4** typical of a class or kind **5** representing **6** including examples of all the interests or types in a group **7** acting as deputy for another **8** of a political system in which people choose a person to make decisions on their behalf

repress *vb* **1** to keep (feelings) under control **2** to restrict the freedom of: *he continued to repress his people* **3** *psychol* to banish (unpleasant thoughts) from one's conscious mind [Latin *reprimere* to press back] **repression** *n* **repressive** *adj*

reprieve *vb* **-prieving, -prieved 1** to postpone the execution of (a condemned person) **2** to give temporary relief to ▷ *n* **3** a postponement or cancellation of a punishment **4** a warrant granting a postponement or cancellation **5** a temporary relief from pain or harm [Old French *repris* (something) taken back]

reprimand *vb* **1** to blame (someone) officially for a fault ▷ *n* **2** an instance of blaming someone officially [French *réprimande*]

reprint *vb* **1** to print further copies of (a book) ▷ *n* **2** a reprinted copy

reprisal *n* an act of taking revenge: *many residents say they are living in fear of reprisals by the army* [Old French *reprisaille*]

reprise (rip-preez) *music* ▷ *n* **1** the repeating of an earlier theme ▷ *vb* **-prising, -prised 2** to repeat an earlier theme

reproach *n* **1** blame or rebuke **2** a scolding **3 beyond reproach** beyond criticism ▷ *vb* **4** to express disapproval of (someone's actions) [Old French *reprochier*] **reproachful** *adj*

reprobate (rep-roh-bate) *n* **1** an unprincipled bad person ▷ *adj* **2** morally unprincipled [Late Latin *reprobatus* held in disfavour]

reprobation *n literary* disapproval or blame

reproduce *vb* **-ducing, -duced 1** to make a copy or representation of **2** *biol* to produce offspring **3** to re-create **reproducible** *adj*

reproduction *n* **1** *biol* a process by which an animal or plant produces one or more individuals similar to itself **2** a copy of a work of art **3** the quality of sound from an audio system **4** the act or process of reproducing ▷ *adj* **5** made in imitation of an earlier style: *reproduction furniture* **reproductive** *adj*

reproof *n* a severe blaming of someone for a fault

reprove *vb* **-proving, -proved** to speak severely to (someone) about a fault [Old French *reprover*] **reprovingly** *adv*

reptile *n* **1** a cold-blooded animal, such as a tortoise, snake, or crocodile, that has an outer covering of horny scales or plates and lays eggs **2** a contemptible grovelling person [Late Latin *reptilis* creeping] **reptilian** *adj*

republic *n* **1** a form of government in which the people or their elected representatives possess the supreme power **2** a country in which the head of state is an elected or nominated president [Latin *respublica*, literally: the public thing]

republican *adj* **1** of or supporting a republic ▷ *n* **2** a person who supports or advocates a republic **republicanism** *n*

Republican *adj* **1** belonging to the Republican Party, the more conservative of the two main political parties in the US **2** advocating a united Ireland ▷ *n* **3** a member or supporter of the Republican Party in the US **4** an advocate of a united Ireland **Republicanism** *n*

repudiate (rip-pew-dee-ate) *vb* **-ating, -ated** **1** to reject the authority or validity of **2** to disown (a person) **3** to refuse to acknowledge or pay (a debt) [Latin *repudium* divorce] **repudiation** *n*

repugnant *adj* offensive or disgusting [Latin *repugnans* resisting] **repugnance** *n*

repulse *vb* **-pulsing, -pulsed** **1** to be disgusting to: *this act of feminist rage repulsed as many as it delighted* **2** to drive (an army) back **3** to reject with coldness or discourtesy: *she repulsed his advances* ▷ *n* **4** a driving back **5** a cold discourteous rejection or refusal [Latin *repellere*]

> **USAGE** Some people think that the use of *repulse* in sentences such as *he was repulsed by what he saw* is incorrect and that the correct word is *repel*.

repulsion *n* **1** a feeling of disgust or aversion **2** *physics* a force separating two objects, such as the force between two like electric charges

repulsive *adj* **1** disgusting or distasteful **2** *physics* of repulsion **repulsively** *adv*

reputable (rep-pew-tab-bl) *adj* trustworthy or respectable **reputably** *adv*

reputation *n* **1** the opinion generally held of a person or thing **2** a high opinion generally held about a person or thing **3** notoriety or fame, esp. for some specified characteristic [Latin *reputatio*]

repute *n* good reputation: *a sculptor of international repute* [Latin *reputare* to think over]

reputed *adj* supposed or rumoured: *the island was reputed to have held a Roman temple; the reputed murderess* **reputedly** *adv*

request *vb* **1** to ask for or politely demand: *we requested a formal meeting with the committee* ▷ *n* **2** the act or an instance of asking for something: *a polite request* **3** something asked for **4** **on request** if asked for: *most companies will send samples on request* [Old French *requeste*]

Requiem (rek-wee-em) *n* **1** *RC Church* a Mass celebrated for the dead **2** a musical setting of this Mass [Latin *requies* rest]

require *vb* **-quiring, -quired** **1** to need **2** to impose as a necessary condition: *the decision requires a logical common-sense approach* **3** to insist upon **4** to order or command: *family doctors are required to produce annual reports* [Latin *requirere* to seek to know]

> **USAGE** The use of *require to* as in *I require to see the manager* or *you require to complete a special form* is thought by many people to be incorrect: *I need to see the manager; you are required to complete a special form.*

requirement *n* **1** something demanded or imposed as an obligation **2** a specific need or want

requisite (rek-wizz-it) *adj* **1** absolutely essential ▷ *n* **2** something essential [Latin *requisitus* sought after]

requisition *vb* **1** to demand and take for use, esp. for military or public use ▷ *n* **2** a formal request or demand for the use of something **3** the act of taking something over, esp. for military or public use **4** a formal written demand

requite *vb* **-quiting, -quited** to return to someone (the same treatment or feeling as received): *an Australian who requites her love* [*re-* back + obsolete *quite* to repay] **requital** *n*

reredos (rear-doss) *n* a screen or wall decoration at the back of an altar [Old French *arere* behind + *dos* back]

reroute *vb* **-routing, -routed** to send or direct by a different route

rerun *n* **1** a film or programme that is broadcast again **2** a race that is run again ▷ *vb* **-running, -ran, -run** **3** to put on (a film or programme) again **4** to run (a race) again

resale *n* the selling again of something purchased

reschedule *vb* **-duling, -duled** **1** to change the time, date, or schedule of: *the show has been rescheduled for August* **2** to arrange a revised schedule for repayment of (a debt)

rescind *vb* to annul or repeal [Latin *rescindere* to cut off] **rescission** *n*

rescue *vb* **-cuing, -cued** **1** to bring (someone or something) out of danger or trouble ▷ *n* **2** the act or an instance of rescuing [Old French *rescourre*] **rescuer** *n*

reseal *vb* to close or secure tightly again

research *n* **1** systematic investigation to establish facts or collect information on a subject ▷ *vb* **2** to carry out investigations into (a subject) [Old French *recercher* to search again] **researcher** *n*

resemble *vb* **-bling, -bled** to be or look like [Old French *resembler*] **resemblance** *n*

resent *vb* to feel bitter or indignant about [French *ressentir*] **resentful** *adj* **resentment** *n*

reservation *n* **1** a doubt: *his only reservation was, did he have the stamina?* **2** an exception or limitation that prevents one's wholehearted acceptance: *work I admire without reservation* **3** a seat, room, etc. that has been reserved **4** (esp. in the US) an area of land set aside for Native American peoples: *the Cherokee reservation* **5** Brit short for **central reservation**

reserve *vb* **-serving, -served** **1** to keep back or set aside for future use **2** to obtain by arranging beforehand: *I phoned to reserve two tickets* **3** to keep for oneself: *the association reserves the right to charge a fee* **4** to delay announcing (a legal judgment) ▷ *n* **5** something kept back or set aside for future use **6** the state or condition of being reserved:

we're keeping these two in reserve **7** *sport* a substitute **8** a protected area for wildlife: *an elephant reserve* **9** the hiding of one's feelings and personality **10** the part of a nation's armed services not in active service **11 reserves** *finance* money or assets held by a bank or business to meet future expenses **12** *Canad* a reservation for an indigenous people [Latin *reservare* to keep]

reserved *adj* **1** not showing one's feelings **2** set aside for use by a particular person

reserve price *n* the minimum price acceptable to the owner of property being auctioned or sold

reservist *n* a member of a nation's military reserve

reservoir *n* **1** a natural or artificial lake for storing water for community use **2** a large supply of something: *a vast reservoir of youthful enthusiasm* [French *réservoir*]

resettle *vb* **-tling, -tled** to settle to live in a different place **resettlement** *n*

reshuffle *n* **1** a reorganization of jobs in a government or company ▷ *vb* **-fling, -fled 2** to reorganize jobs or duties in a government or company

reside *vb* **-siding, -sided** *formal* **1** to live permanently (in a place): *my daughter resides in Europe* **2** to be present (in): *desire resides in the unconscious* [Latin *residere* to sit back]

residence *n* **1** a person's home or house **2** a large imposing house **3** the fact of residing in a place **4** a period of residing in a place **5 in residence** **A** living in a particular place: *the Monarch was not in residence* **B** (of an artist) working for a set period at a college, gallery, etc.: *composer in residence*

resident *n* **1** a person who lives in a place **2** a bird or animal that does not migrate ▷ *adj* **3** living in a place **4** living at a place in order to carry out a job: *a resident custodian* **5** employed for one's specialized abilities: *the Museum's resident expert on seventeenth-century Dutch art* **6** (of birds and animals) not in the habit of migrating

residential *adj* **1** (of a part of a town) consisting mainly of houses **2** providing living accommodation: *residential clubs for homeless boys*

residential school *n* **1** any educational establishment providing living accommodation for its students or pupils **2** a government boarding school in N Canada for Native Canadian and Inuit students

residual *adj* **1** of or being a remainder ▷ *n* **2** something left over as a residue

residue *n* **1** what is left over after something has been removed **2** *law* what is left of an estate after the discharge of debts and distribution of specific gifts [Latin *residuus* remaining over]

residuum *n, pl* **-ua** same as **residue**

resign *vb* **1** to give up office or a job **2** to accept (an unpleasant fact): *he resigned himself to the inevitable* **3** to give up (a right or claim) [Latin *resignare* to unseal, destroy]

resignation *n* **1** the act of resigning **2** a formal document stating one's intention to resign **3** passive endurance of difficulties: *full of quiet resignation*

resigned *adj* content to endure something unpleasant **resignedly** *adv*

resilient *adj* **1** (of a person) recovering easily and quickly from misfortune or illness **2** (of an object) capable of regaining its original shape or position after bending or stretching [Latin *resilire* to jump back] **resilience** *n*

resin (rezz-in) *n* **1** a solid or semisolid substance obtained from certain plants: *cannabis resin* **2** a similar substance produced synthetically [Latin *resina*] **resinous** *adj*

resist *vb* **1** to stand firm against or oppose: *the party's old guard continue to resist economic reform* **2** to refrain from in spite of temptation: *I couldn't resist a huge portion of almond cake* **3** to refuse to comply with: *to resist arrest* **4** to be proof against: *airport design should be strengthened to help resist explosion* [Latin *resistere*] **resistible** *adj*

resistance *n* **1** the act of resisting **2** the capacity to withstand something, esp. the body's natural capacity to withstand disease **3** *electronics* the opposition to a flow of electric current through a circuit, component, or substance **4** any force that slows or hampers movement: *wind resistance* **5 line of least resistance** the easiest, but not necessarily the best, course of action **resistant** *adj, n*

Resistance *n* **the Resistance** an illegal organization fighting for national liberty in a country under enemy occupation

resistor *n* an electrical component designed to introduce a known value of resistance into a circuit

resit *vb* **-sitting, -sat 1** to sit (an examination) again ▷ *n* **2** an examination which one must sit again

reskill *vb* to train (workers) to acquire new skills **reskilling** *n*

resolute *adj* firm in purpose or belief [Latin *resolutus*] **resolutely** *adv*

resolution *n* **1** firmness or determination **2** a decision to do something **3** a formal expression of opinion by a meeting **4** the act of resolving **5** *music* the process in harmony whereby a dissonant note or chord is followed by a consonant one **6** the ability of a television, camera, etc. to reproduce fine detail **7** *physics* Also called: **resolving power** the ability of a telescope or microscope to produce separate images of closely placed objects

resolvable *or* **resoluble** *adj* able to be resolved or analysed

resolve *vb* **-solving, -solved 1** to decide or determine firmly **2** to express (an opinion) formally by a vote **3** to separate or cause to separate into (constituent parts) **4** to find the answer or solution to **5** to explain away or dispel: *to resolve the controversy* **6** *music* to follow (a dissonant note or chord) by one producing a consonance **7** *physics* to distinguish between (separate parts) of (an image) as in a microscope, telescope, or other optical instrument ▷ *n* **8** absolute determination: *he spoke of his resolve to deal with the problem of terrorism* [Latin *resolvere* to unfasten, reveal]

resolved *adj* determined

resonance *n* **1** the condition or quality of being resonant **2** sound produced by a body vibrating in sympathy with a neighbouring source of sound [Latin *resonare* to resound]

r

resonant *adj* **1** resounding or re-echoing **2** producing resonance: *the resonant cavities of the mouth* **3** full of resonance: *his voice is a resonant baritone*

resonate *vb* **-nating, -nated** to resound or cause to resound **resonator** *n*

resort *vb* **1 resort to** to have recourse to for help, use, etc.: *some people have resorted to begging for food* **2** to go, esp. often or habitually: *to resort to the beach* ▷ *n* **3** a place to which many people go for holidays **4** the use of something as a means or aid **5 last resort** the last possible course of action open to a person [Old French *resortir* to come out again]

resound (riz-**zownd**) *vb* **1** to ring or echo with sound **2** (of sounds) to echo or ring **3** to be widely known: *his fame resounded throughout India* [Latin *resonare* to sound again]

resounding *adj* **1** echoing **2** clear and emphatic: *he won a resounding victory* **resoundingly** *adv*

resource *n* **1 resources** sources of economic wealth, esp. of a country or business enterprise: *mineral resources* **2 resources** money available for use **3** something resorted to for aid or support: *he saw the university as a resource for the community* **4** the ability to deal with problems: *a man of resource* **5** a means of doing something: *resistance was their only resource* [Old French *resourdre* to spring up again]

resourceful *adj* capable and full of initiative **resourcefulness** *n*

respect *n* **1** consideration: *respect for my feelings* **2** an attitude of deference or esteem **3** the state of being honoured or esteemed **4** a detail or characteristic: *in virtually all respects boys develop more slowly than girls* **5 in respect of** *or* **with respect to** in reference or relation to **6 respects** polite greetings: *he paid his respects to her and left* ▷ *vb* **7** to have an attitude of esteem towards: *she is the person I most respect and wish to emulate* **8** to pay proper attention or consideration to: *he called on rebel groups to respect a cease-fire* [Latin *respicere* to pay attention to] **respecter** *n*

respectable *adj* **1** worthy of respect **2** having good social standing or reputation **3** relatively or fairly good: *they obtained respectable results* **4** fit to be seen by other people **respectability** *n* **respectably** *adv*

respectful *adj* full of or showing respect **respectfully** *adv*

respecting *prep* on the subject of

respective *adj* relating separately to each of several people or things: *the culprits will be repatriated to their respective countries*

respectively *adv* (in listing things that refer to another list) separately in the order given: *Diotema and Mantinea were tutors to Pythagoras and Socrates respectively*

respiration (ress-per-**ray**-shun) *n* **1** breathing **2** the process in living organisms of taking in oxygen and giving out carbon dioxide **3** the breakdown of complex organic substances that takes place in the cells of animals and plants, producing energy and carbon dioxide **respiratory** *adj*

respirator *n* **1** a device worn over the mouth and nose to prevent the breathing in of poisonous fumes **2** an apparatus for providing artificial respiration

respire *vb* **-spiring, -spired 1** to breathe **2** to undergo respiration [Latin *respirare* to exhale]

respite *n* **1** an interval of rest: *I allowed myself a six month respite to enjoy my family* **2** a temporary delay [Old French *respit*]

resplendent *adj* **1** brilliant or splendid in appearance **2** shining [Latin *re-* again + *splendere* to shine] **resplendence** *n*

respond *vb* **1** to state or utter (something) in reply **2** to act in reply: *the government must respond accordingly to our recommendations* **3** to react favourably: *most headaches will respond to the use of relaxants* [Old French *respondre*]

respondent *n law* a person against whom a petition is brought

response *n* **1** the act of responding **2** a reply or reaction **3** a reaction to stimulation of the nervous system **4 responses** *Christianity* the words recited or sung in reply to the priest at a church service

responsibility *n, pl* **-ties 1** the state of being responsible **2** a person or thing for which one is responsible

responsible *adj* **1 responsible for** having control or authority over **2** being the agent or cause (of some action): *only a small number of students were responsible for the disturbances* **3 responsible to** being accountable for one's actions and decisions to: *management should be made more responsible to shareholders* **4** rational and accountable for one's own actions **5** (of a position or duty) involving decision and accountability [Latin *respondere* to respond] **responsibly** *adv*

responsive *adj* reacting quickly or favourably to something **responsiveness** *n*

respray *n* a new coat of paint applied to a vehicle

rest[1] *n* **1** relaxation from exertion or labour **2** a period of inactivity **3** relief or refreshment **4** calm **5** death regarded as repose: *now he has gone to his eternal rest* **6 at rest A** not moving **B** calm **C** dead **D** asleep **7** a pause or interval **8** a mark in a musical score indicating a pause lasting a specific time **9** a thing or place on which to put something for support or to steady it **10 lay to rest** to bury (a dead person) ▷ *vb* **11** to become or make refreshed **12** to position (oneself, etc.) for rest or relaxation **13** to place for support or steadying: *he slumped forward to rest his head on his forearms* **14** to depend or rely: *his presidency rested on the outcome of the crisis* **15** to direct (one's eyes) or (of one's eyes) to be directed: *she rested her gaze on the face of the statue* **16** to be at ease **17** to cease or cause to cease from motion or exertion **18** to remain without further attention or action: *she refused to let the matter rest* **19** *law* to finish the introduction of evidence in (a case) **20** to put (pastry) in a cool place to allow the gluten to contract [Old English *ræst, reste*]

rest[2] *n* **1 the rest A** something left; remainder **B** the others: *the rest of the world* ▷ *vb* **2** to continue to be (as specified): *your conscience can rest easy* [Old French *rester* to remain]

rest area *n Austral & NZ* a motorist's stopping place off a highway, equipped with tables and seats

restart *vb* to commence (something) or set (something) in motion again
restate *vb* to state or affirm (something) again or in a different way **restatement** *n*
restaurant *n* a place where meals are prepared and served to customers [French]
restaurant car *n* a railway coach in which meals are served
restaurateur (rest-er-a-**tur**) *n* a person who owns or runs a restaurant
rest-cure *n* a rest taken as part of a course of medical treatment
restful *adj* relaxing or soothing
restitution *n* **1** the act of giving back something that has been lost or stolen **2** *law* compensation for loss or injury [Latin *restituere* to rebuild]
restive *adj* **1** restless or uneasy **2** impatient of control or authority [Old French *restif* balky]
restless *adj* **1** bored or dissatisfied **2** unable to stay still or quiet **3** not restful: *a restless sleep* **restlessly** *adv* **restlessness** *n*
restoration *n* **1** the act of restoring to a former or original condition, place, etc. **2** the giving back of something lost or stolen **3** something restored, replaced, or reconstructed **4** a model or representation of a ruin or extinct animal **5 the Restoration** *Brit* the re-establishment of the monarchy in 1660 or the reign of Charles II (1660–85)
restorative (rist-or-a-tiv) *adj* **1** giving back health or good spirits ▷ *n* **2** a food or medicine that gives back health or good spirits
restore *vb* **-storing, -stored 1** to return (something) to its original or former condition **2** to bring back to health or good spirits **3** to return (something lost or stolen) to its owner **4** to re-enforce or re-establish: *he must restore confidence in himself and his government; they worked to restore the monarchy* **5** to reconstruct (a ruin, extinct animal, etc.) [Latin *restaurare* to rebuild] **restorer** *n*
restrain *vb* **1** to hold (someone) back from some action **2** to limit or restrict: *restrain any tendency to impulse-buy* **3** to deprive (someone) of liberty [Latin *re-* back + *stringere* to draw]
restrained *adj* not displaying emotion
restraint *n* **1** something that restrains **2** the ability to control one's impulses or passions **3** a restraining or being restrained
restrict *vb* to confine or keep within certain limits [Latin *restrictus* bound up] **restrictive** *adj*
restriction *n* a rule or situation that limits or controls something or someone: *operating under severe financial restrictions*
restrictive practice *n* **1** a trading agreement against the public interest **2** a practice of a union or other group tending to limit the freedom of other workers or employers
rest room *n US, Canad & Austral* a toilet in a public building
restructure *vb* **-turing, -tured** to organize in a different way: *to restructure the world economy*
result *n* **1** the outcome or consequence of an action, policy, etc. **2** the final score of a sporting contest **3** a number or value obtained by solving a mathematical problem **4** a favourable result, esp. a victory or success: *the best chance of a result is at Cheltenham* **5 results** the marks or grades obtained in an examination ▷ *vb* **6 result from** to be the outcome or consequence of: *poverty resulting from high unemployment* **7 result in** to end in (a specified way): *negotiations which resulted in the Treaty of Paris* [Latin *resultare* to spring from]
resultant *adj* **1** arising as a result: *the resultant publicity* ▷ *n* **2** *maths & physics* a single vector that is the vector sum of two or more other vectors, such as a force which results from two other forces acting on a single point
resume *vb* **-suming, -sumed 1** to begin again or go on with (something interrupted) **2** to occupy again or recover: *he will resume his party post today* [Latin *resumere*]
résumé (rezz-yew-may) *n* **1** a short descriptive summary **2** *US, Canad & Austral* a curriculum vitae [French]
resumption *n* the act of resuming or beginning again
resurgence *n* a rising again to vigour: *worldwide religious resurgence* [Latin *resurgere* to rise again] **resurgent** *adj*
resurrect *vb* **1** to bring or be brought back to life from death **2** to bring back into use or activity
resurrection *n* **1** a return to life by a dead person **2** revival or renewal **3 the Resurrection** *Christian theol* **A** the rising again of Christ from the tomb three days after his death **B** the rising again from the dead of all people at the Last Judgment [Latin *resurgere* to rise again]
resuscitate (ris-suss-it-tate) *vb* **-tating, -tated** to restore to consciousness [Latin *re-* again + *suscitare* to raise] **resuscitation** *n*
retail *n* **1** the sale of goods individually or in small quantities to the public ▷ *adj* **2** of or engaged in such selling: *auctioneers have been successful in cornering the retail market* ▷ *adv* **3** in small amounts or at a retail price ▷ *vb* **4** to sell or be sold in small quantities to the public **5** to relate (gossip or scandal) in detail: *he gleefully retailed the story* [Old French *re-* again + *taillier* to cut] **retailer** *n*
retail therapy *n humorous* the action of shopping for clothes, etc., esp. to cheer oneself up
retain *vb* **1** to keep in one's possession **2** to be able to hold or contain: *with this method the salmon retains its flavour and texture* **3** *law* to engage the services of (a barrister) by payment of a preliminary fee **4** (of a person) to be able to remember (something) without difficulty **5** to hold in position [Latin *retinere* to hold back]
retainer *n* **1** a fee paid in advance to engage someone's services **2** *Brit, Austral & NZ* a reduced rent paid for a room or flat to reserve it for future use **3** a servant who has been with a family for a long time
retaining wall *n* a wall constructed to hold back earth, loose rock, etc.
retake *vb* **-taking, -took, -taken 1** to recapture: *they retook Kuwait* **2** to take something, such as an examination or vote, again ▷ *n* **3** *films* a rephotographed scene
retaliate *vb* **-ating, -ated 1** to repay some injury or wrong in kind **2** to cast (accusations) back

r

upon a person [Latin *re-* back + *talis* of such kind] **retaliation** *n* **retaliatory** *adj*

retard *vb* to delay or slow down (the progress or development) of (something) [Latin *retardare*] **retardant** *n, adj* **retardation** *n*

retarded *adj old-fashioned, offensive* underdeveloped mentally

retch *vb* **1** to undergo spasms of the stomach as if one is vomiting ▷ *n* **2** an involuntary spasm of the stomach [Old English *hrǣcan*]

retention *n* **1** the act of retaining or state of being retained **2** the capacity to remember **3** *pathol* the abnormal holding of something within the body, esp. fluid **retentive** *adj*

rethink *vb* **-thinking, -thought 1** to think about (something) again with a view to changing one's tactics ▷ *n* **2** the act or an instance of thinking again

reticent *adj* not willing to say or tell much [Latin *reticere* to keep silent] **reticence** *n*

reticulate *adj* in the form of a network or having a network of parts: *a reticulate leaf* [Late Latin *reticulatus* like a net] **reticulation** *n*

retina *n, pl* **-nas** *or* **-nae** the light-sensitive inner lining of the back of the eyeball [Medieval Latin] **retinal** *adj*

retinopathy *n* any of various noninflammatory diseases of the retina, which may have serious effects on vision

retinue *n* a band of attendants accompanying an important person [Old French *retenue*]

retire *vb* **-tiring, -tired 1** to give up or to cause (a person) to give up work, esp. on reaching pensionable age **2** to go away into seclusion **3** to go to bed **4** to withdraw from a sporting contest, esp. because of injury **5** to pull back (troops) from battle or (of troops) to fall back [French *retirer*] **retired** *adj* **retirement** *n*

retirement pension *n Brit* a regular payment made by the state or a former employee to a retired person over a specified age

retiring *adj* very shy

retort[1] *vb* **1** to reply quickly, wittily, or angrily **2** to use (an argument) against its originator ▷ *n* **3** a sharp, angry, or witty reply **4** an argument used against its originator [Latin *re-* back + *torquere* to twist, wrench]

retort[2] *n* **1** a glass vessel with a long tapering neck that is bent down, used for distillation **2** a vessel used for heating ores in the production of metals or heating coal to produce gas [see RETORT[1]]

retouch *vb* to restore or improve (a painting or photograph) with new touches

retrace *vb* **-tracing, -traced 1** to go back over (one's steps or a route) **2** to go over (a story) from the beginning

retract *vb* **1** to withdraw (a statement, charge, etc.) as invalid or unjustified **2** to go back on (a promise or agreement) **3** to draw in (a part or appendage): *the rear wheels are retracted for tight spaces* [Latin *retractare* to withdraw] **retraction** *n*

retractile *adj* capable of being drawn in: *the retractile claws of a cat*

retrain *vb* to train to do a new or different job **retraining** *n*

retread *vb* **-treading, -treaded 1** to bond a new tread onto (a worn tyre) ▷ *n* **2** a remoulded tyre

retreat *vb* **1** *military* to withdraw or retire in the face of or from action with an enemy **2** to retire or withdraw to seclusion or shelter **3** to alter one's opinion about something ▷ *n* **4** the act of retreating or withdrawing **5** *military* **A** a withdrawal or retirement in the face of the enemy **B** a bugle call signifying withdrawal or retirement **6** a place to which one may retire, esp. for religious contemplation **7** a period of seclusion, esp. for religious contemplation **8** the act of altering one's opinion about something [Old French *retret*]

retrench *vb* to reduce expenditure [Old French *re-* off + *trenchier* to cut] **retrenchment** *n*

retrial *n* a second trial of a defendant in a court of law

retribution *n* punishment or vengeance for evil deeds [Latin *re-* back + *tribuere* to pay] **retributive** *adj*

retrieve *vb* **-trieving, -trieved 1** to get or fetch back again **2** to bring back to a more satisfactory state: *his attempt to retrieve the situation* **3** to rescue or save **4** to recover (stored information) from a computer system **5** (of dogs) to find and fetch (shot birds and animals) **6** to remember ▷ *n* **7** the chance of being retrieved: *beyond retrieve* [Old French *retrover*] **retrievable** *adj* **retrieval** *n*

retriever *n* a dog trained to retrieve shot birds and animals

retro *adj* associated with or revived from the past: *swap sandals for heeled mules to complete the retro look*

retro- *prefix* **1** back or backwards: *retroactive* **2** located behind: *retrochoir* [Latin]

retroactive *adj* effective from a date in the past: *justice through retroactive legislation is never justice*

retrograde *adj* **1** tending towards an earlier worse condition **2** moving or bending backwards **3** (esp. of order) reverse or inverse ▷ *vb* **-grading, -graded 4** to go backwards or deteriorate [Latin *retro-* backwards + *gradi* to walk]

retrogress *vb* to go back to an earlier worse condition [Latin *retrogressus* having moved backwards] **retrogression** *n* **retrogressive** *adj*

retrorocket *n* a small rocket on a larger rocket or a spacecraft, that produces thrust in the opposite direction to the direction of flight in order to slow down

retrospect *n* **in retrospect** when looking back on the past [Latin *retrospicere* to look back]

retrospective *adj* **1** looking back in time **2** applying from a date in the past: *retrospective legislation* ▷ *n* **3** an exhibition of an artist's life's work

retroussé (rit-troo-say) *adj* (of a nose) turned upwards [French]

retsina *n* a Greek wine flavoured with resin [Modern Greek]

return *vb* **1** to come back to a former place or state **2** to give, put, or send back **3** to repay with something of equivalent value: *she returned the compliment* **4** to hit, throw, or play (a ball) back **5** to recur or reappear: *as he relaxed his appetite returned* **6** to come back or revert in thought or speech: *let's return to what he said* **7** to earn or yield (profit or interest) **8** to answer or reply **9** to vote into office **10** *law* (of a jury) to deliver (a verdict) ▷ *n* **11** the act or an instance of coming back **12** the act of being returned **13** replacement or restoration: *the return of law and order* **14** something that is given or sent back **15** *sport* the act of playing or throwing a ball back **16** a recurrence or reappearance: *the return of tuberculosis* **17** the yield or profit from an investment or venture **18** a statement of one's taxable income (a **tax return**) **19** an answer or reply **20** *Brit, Austral & NZ* short for **return ticket** **21** **in return** in exchange **22** **returns** statement of the votes counted at an election **23** **by return (of post)** *Brit* by the next post back to the sender **24** **many happy returns (of the day)** a conventional birthday greeting ▷ *adj* **25** of or being a return: *the team is keen on a return match* [Old French *retorner*] **returnable** *adj*

returning officer *n* an official in charge of conducting an election in a constituency

return ticket *n* a ticket allowing a passenger to travel to a place and back

retweet *vb* to post (another Twitter user's post) for one's own followers

reunify *vb* **-fies, -fying, -fied** to bring together again something previously divided **reunification** *n*

reunion *n* **1** a gathering of people who have been apart **2** the act of coming together again

reunite *vb* **-niting, -nited** to bring or come together again after a separation

reuse *n* **1** the act of using something again ▷ *vb* **-using, -used** **2** to use again **reusable** *adj*

rev *informal* ▷ *n* **1** revolution per minute (of an engine) ▷ *vb* **revving, revved** **2** to increase the speed of revolution of (an engine)

rev. **1** revise(d) **2** revision

Rev. Reverend

revalue *vb* **-valuing, -valued** to adjust the exchange value of (a currency) upwards **revaluation** *n*

revamp *vb* to patch up or renovate

Revd. Reverend

reveal *vb* **1** to disclose or divulge (a secret) **2** to expose to view or show (something concealed) **3** (of God) to disclose (divine truths) [Latin *revelare* to unveil]

revealing *adj* **1** disclosing information that one did not know: *she made several revealing remarks during the interview* **2** (of clothes) showing more of the body than is usual

reveille (riv-val-ee) *n* a signal given by a bugle or drum to awaken soldiers or sailors in the morning [French *réveillez!* awake!]

revel *vb* **-velling, -velled** *or US* **-veling, -veled** **1** **revel in** to take pleasure or wallow in: *he would revel in his victory* **2** to take part in noisy festivities ▷ *n* **3** **revels** noisy merrymaking [Old French *reveler*] **reveller** *n*

revelation *n* **1** the act of making known a truth which was previously secret **2** a fact newly made known **3** a person or experience that proves to be different from expectations: *New York State could prove a revelation to first-time visitors* **4** *Christianity* God's disclosure of his own nature and his purpose for mankind

Revelation *or* **Revelations** *n informal* the last book of the New Testament, containing visionary descriptions of heaven, and of the end of the world

revelry *n, pl* **-ries** noisy or unrestrained merrymaking

revenge *n* **1** vengeance for wrongs or injury received **2** something done as a means of vengeance ▷ *vb* **-venging, -venged** **3** to inflict equivalent injury or damage for (injury received) **4** to take vengeance for (oneself or another) [Old French *revenger*] **revengeful** *adj*

revenge porn *n* a pornographic image or images posted on the internet without the consent of a participant, for vindictive or malicious reasons

revenue *n* **1** income, esp. that obtained by a government from taxation **2** a government department responsible for collecting taxes [Old French *revenir* to return]

reverberate *vb* **-rating, -rated** **1** to resound or re-echo **2** to reflect or be reflected many times [Latin *re-* again + *verberare* to beat] **reverberation** *n*

revere *vb* **-vering, -vered** to be in awe of and respect deeply [Latin *revereri*]

reverence *n* profound respect **reverential** *adj*

Reverence *n* **Your** *or* **His Reverence** a title sometimes used for a Roman Catholic priest

reverend *adj* **1** worthy of reverence **2** relating to or designating a member of the clergy ▷ *n* **3** *informal* a member of the clergy

Reverend *adj* a title of respect for a member of the clergy

> **USAGE** *Reverend* with a surname alone (*Reverend Smith*), as a term of address (*'Yes, Reverend'*), or in the greeting of a letter (*Dear Rev. Mr Smith*) are all generally considered to be wrong usage. Preferred are (*the*) *Reverend John Smith* or *Reverend Mr Smith* and *Dear Mr Smith*.

reverent *adj* feeling or expressing reverence

reverie *n* an absent-minded daydream [Old French *resverie* wildness]

revers (riv-veer) *n, pl* **-vers** the turned-back lining of part of a garment, such as the lapel or cuff [French]

reverse *vb* **-versing, -versed** **1** to turn or set in an opposite direction, order, or position **2** to change into something different or contrary: *the cabinet intends to reverse the trend of recent polls* **3** to move backwards or in an opposite direction: *as he started to reverse the car, the bomb exploded* **4** to run (machinery) in the opposite direction to normal **5** to turn inside out **6** *law* to revoke or set aside (a judgment or decree) **7** **reverse the charges** *Brit* to make a telephone call at the recipient's expense ▷ *n* **8** the opposite or contrary of something **9** the back or rear side of something **10** a change to an opposite position, state, or direction **11** a change for the worse **12** the gear by which a motor vehicle can be made to go backwards **13** the side of a coin bearing a secondary design **14** **in reverse** in an opposite or backward direction **15** **the reverse of** not at all: *the result was the reverse of his expectations* ▷ *adj* **16** opposite or contrary in direction, position, etc. **17** denoting the gear by which a motor vehicle can be made to go backwards [Latin *reversus* turned back] **reversal** *n*

reversible *adj* **1** capable of being reversed: *the effect of the operation may not be reversible* **2** (of a garment) made so that either side may be used as the outer side

reversing lights *pl n* a pair of lights on the rear of a motor vehicle that go on when the vehicle is moving backwards

reversion *n* **1** a return to an earlier condition, practice, or belief **2** *biol* the return of individuals or organs to a more primitive condition or type **3** the rightful passing of property to the owner or designated heir

revert *vb* **1** to go back to a former state **2** *biol* (of individuals or organs) to return to a more primitive, earlier, or simpler condition or type **3** to come back to a subject **4** *property law* (of an estate) to return to its former owner [Latin *revertere*]

> **USAGE** Since *back* is part of the meaning of *revert*, one should not say that someone *reverts back* to a certain type of behaviour.

review *n* **1** a critical assessment of a book, film, etc. **2** a publication containing such articles **3** a general survey or report: *the new curriculum is to be set up a year after the conclusions of the review are due* **4** a formal or official inspection **5** the act or an instance of reviewing **6** a second consideration; re-examination **7** a retrospective survey **8** *law* a re-examination of a case ▹ *vb* **9** to hold or write a review of **10** to examine again: *the committee will review the ban in the summer* **11** to look back upon (a period of time or sequence of events): *he reviewed his achievements with pride* **12** to inspect formally or officially: *when he reviewed the troops they cheered him* **13** *law* to re-examine (a decision) judicially [Latin *re-* again + *videre* to see]

reviewer *n* a person who writes reviews of books, films, etc.

revile *vb* **-viling, -viled** to be abusively scornful of: *his works were reviled and admired in equal measure* [Old French *reviler*]

revise *vb* **-vising, -vised 1** to change or alter: *he grudgingly revised his opinion* **2** to prepare a new edition of (a previously printed work) **3** to read (something) several times in order to learn it in preparation for an examination [Latin *re-* again + *visere* to inspect]

Revised Version *n* a revision of the Authorized Version of the Bible published between 1881 and 1885

revision *n* **1** the act or process of revising **2** a corrected or new version of a book, article, etc.

revisionism *n* **1** (in Marxist ideology) any significant departure from Marx's teachings **2** the advocacy of revision of some political theory **revisionist** *n, adj*

revisory *adj* of or having the power of revision

revitalize *or* **-lise** *vb* **-lizing, -lized** *or* **-lising, -lised** to make more lively or active

revival *n* **1** a reviving or being revived **2** a reawakening of religious faith **3** a new production of a play that has not been recently performed **4** a renewed use or interest in: *there has been an Art Deco revival*

revivalism *n* a movement that seeks to revive religious faith **revivalist** *n, adj*

revive *vb* **-viving, -vived 1** to make or become lively or active again **2** to bring or be brought back to life, consciousness, or strength: *revived by a drop of whisky* **3** *theatre* to put on a new production of (an old play) [Latin *re-* again + *vivere* to live]

revivify *vb* **-fies, -fying, -fied** to give new life to **revivification** *n*

revoke *vb* **-voking, -voked 1** to take back or cancel (an agreement, will, etc.) **2** *cards* to break a rule by failing to follow suit when able to do so ▹ *n* **3** *cards* the act of revoking [Latin *revocare* to call back] **revocation** *n*

revolt *n* **1** a rebellion or uprising against authority **2 in revolt** in the state of rebelling ▹ *vb* **3** to rise up in rebellion against authority **4** to cause to feel disgust [French *révolter*]

revolting *adj* horrible and disgusting

revolution *n* **1** the overthrow of a regime or political system by the governed **2** (in Marxist theory) the transition from one system of production in a society to the next **3** a far-reaching and drastic change **4 A** movement in or as if in a circle **B** one complete turn in a circle: *33 revolutions per minute* [Latin *revolvere* to revolve]

revolutionary *adj* **1** of or like a revolution **2** advocating or engaged in revolution **3** radically new or different: *they have designed revolutionary new materials to build power stations* ▹ *n, pl* **-aries 4** a person who advocates or engages in revolution

revolutionize *or* **-nise** *vb* **-nizing, -nized** *or* **-nising, -nised** to bring about a radical change in

revolve *vb* **-volving, -volved 1** to move or cause to move around a centre **2 revolve around** to be centred or focused upon: *the campaign revolves around one man* **3** to occur periodically or in cycles **4** to consider or be considered [Latin *revolvere*] **revolvable** *adj*

revolver *n* a pistol with a revolving cylinder that allows several shots to be fired without reloading

revolving door *n* **1** a door with four leaves at right angles to each other, revolving about a vertical axis **2** *informal* a situation in which there is a rapid turnover of staff or members

revue *n* a theatrical entertainment with topical sketches and songs [French]

revulsion *n* a violent feeling of disgust [Latin *revulsio* pulling away]

reward *n* **1** something given in return for a service **2** a sum of money offered for finding a criminal or missing property **3** something received in return for good or evil: *sacrifice provided its own reward* ▹ *vb* **4** to give something to (someone) for a service rendered [Old French *rewarder* to regard]

rewarding *adj* giving personal satisfaction: *my most professionally rewarding experience*

rewarewa (ray-wa-ray-wa) *n* a tall New Zealand tree with reddish wood [Māori]

rewind *vb* **-winding, -wound** to run (a tape or film) back to an earlier point in order to replay

rewire *vb* **-wiring, -wired** to provide (a house, engine, etc.) with new wiring

reword *vb* to alter the wording of

rework *vb* to improve or bring up to date: *they need to rework the system* **reworking** *n*

rewrite *vb* **-writing, -wrote, -written 1** to write again in a different way ▷ *n* **2** something rewritten

Rex *n* king: now used chiefly in documents and inscriptions [Latin]

Rf *chem* rutherfordium

RFC Rugby Football Club

Rg roentgenium

RGN (in Britain, New Zealand, and Australia) Registered General Nurse

Rh 1 *chem* rhodium **2** See **Rh factor**

rhapsodize *or* **-dise** *vb* **-dizing, -dized** *or* **-dising, -dised** to speak or write with extravagant enthusiasm

rhapsody *n, pl* **-dies 1** *music* a freely structured and emotional piece of music **2** an expression of ecstatic enthusiasm [Greek *rhaptein* to sew together + *ōidē* song] **rhapsodic** *adj*

rhea (ree-a) *n* a large fast-running flightless bird of South America, similar to the ostrich [after *Rhea*, mother of Zeus]

rhenium (ree-nee-um) *n chem* a silvery-white metallic element with a high melting point. Symbol: **Re** [Latin *Rhenus* the Rhine]

rheostat *n* a variable resistor in an electrical circuit, such as one used to dim lights [Greek *rheos* flow + *-statēs* stationary] **rheostatic** *adj*

rhesus factor (ree-suss) *n* See **Rh factor**

rhesus monkey *n* a small long-tailed monkey of S Asia [Greek *Rhesos*, mythical Thracian king]

rhetoric (ret-a-rik) *n* **1** the art of using speech or writing to persuade or influence **2** artificial or exaggerated language: *there's been no shortage of soaring rhetoric at this summit* [Greek *rhētorikē (tekhnē)* (art) of rhetoric] **rhetorical** (rit-tor-ik-kl) *adj*

rhetorical question *n* a question to which no answer is required, used for dramatic effect, for example *who knows?*

rheum (room) *n* a watery discharge from the eyes or nose [Greek *rheuma* a flow] **rheumy** *adj*

rheumatic *adj* **1** caused by or affected by rheumatism ▷ *n* **2** a person with rheumatism **rheumatically** *adv*

rheumatic fever *n* a disease with inflammation and pain in the joints

rheumatics *n informal* rheumatism

rheumatism *n* any painful disorder of joints, muscles, or connective tissue [Greek *rheuma* a flow]

rheumatoid *adj* (of symptoms) resembling rheumatism

rheumatoid arthritis *n* a chronic disease causing painful swelling of the joints

Rh factor *n* an antigen commonly found in human blood: the terms **Rh positive** and **Rh negative** are used to indicate its presence or absence [after the rhesus monkey, in which it was first discovered]

rhinestone *n* an imitation diamond made of glass [originally made at Strasbourg, on the Rhine]

rhino *n, pl* **-nos** *or* **-no** a rhinoceros

rhinoceros *n, pl* **-roses** *or* **-ros** a large plant-eating mammal of SE Asia and Africa with one or two horns on the nose and a very thick skin [Greek *rhis* nose + *keras* horn]

rhinovirus *n* any of various viruses that occur in the human respiratory tract and cause diseases, such as the common cold

rhizome *n* a thick horizontal underground stem whose buds develop into new plants [Greek *rhiza* a root]

rhodium *n chem* a hard silvery-white metallic element, used to harden platinum and palladium. Symbol: **Rh** [Greek *rhodon* rose, from the pink colour of its compounds]

rhododendron *n* an evergreen shrub with clusters of showy flowers [Greek *rhodon* rose + *dendron* tree]

rhombohedron (rom-boh-**heed**-ron) *n, pl* **-drons** *or* **-dra** (-dra) a six-sided prism whose sides are parallelograms [RHOMBUS + Greek *-edron* -sided]

rhomboid *n* **1** a parallelogram with adjacent sides of unequal length. It resembles a rectangle but does not have 90° angles ▷ *adj also* **rhomboidal 2** having such a shape [Greek *rhomboeidēs* shaped like a rhombus]

rhombus (rom-buss) *n, pl* **-buses** *or* **-bi** (-bye) a parallelogram with sides of equal length but no right angles [Greek *rhombos* something that spins] **rhombic** *adj*

rhubarb *n* **1** a large-leaved plant with long green and red stalks which can be cooked and eaten **2** a related plant of central Asia, whose root can be dried and used as a laxative or astringent ▷ *interj, n* **3** the noise made by actors to simulate conversation, esp. by repeating the word *rhubarb* [Old French *reubarbe*]

rhyme *n* **1** sameness of the final sounds in lines of verse or in words **2** a word that is identical to another in its final sound: *'while' is a rhyme for 'mile'* **3** a piece of poetry with corresponding sounds at the ends of the lines **4 rhyme or reason** sense or meaning ▷ *vb* **rhyming, rhymed 5** (of a word) to form a rhyme with another word **6** to compose (verse) in a metrical structure [Old French *rime*; spelling influenced by *rhythm*]

rhymester *n* a mediocre poet

rhyming slang *n* slang in which a word is replaced by another word or phrase that rhymes with it, eg *apples and pears* meaning *stairs*

rhythm *n* **1** any regular movement or beat: *the side-effects can cause changes in the rhythm of the heart beat* **2** any regular pattern that occurs over a period of time: *the seasonal rhythm of the agricultural year* **3 A** the arrangement of the durations of and stress on the notes of a piece of music, usually laid out in regular groups (**bars**) of beats **B** any specific arrangement of such groupings: *waltz rhythm* **4** (in poetry) the arrangement of words to form a regular pattern of stresses [Greek *rhuthmos*] **rhythmic** *or* **rhythmical** *adj* **rhythmically** *adv*

rhythm and blues *n* a kind of popular music of Black American origin, derived from and influenced by the blues

rhythm method *n* a method of contraception in which intercourse is avoided at times when conception is most likely

RI Rhode Island

rialto *n, pl* **-tos** a market or exchange [after the *Rialto*, the business centre of medieval Venice]

rib[1] *n* **1** one of the curved bones forming the framework of the upper part of the body and attached to the spinal column **2** a cut of meat including one or more ribs **3** a curved supporting part, such as in the hull of a boat **4** one of a series of raised rows in knitted fabric ▷ *vb* **ribbing, ribbed 5** to provide or support with ribs **6** to knit to form a rib pattern [Old English *ribb*] **ribbed** *adj*

rib[2] *vb* **ribbing, ribbed** *informal* to tease or ridicule [short for *rib-tickle*] **ribbing** *n*

RIBA Royal Institute of British Architects

ribald *adj* coarse or obscene in a humorous or mocking way [Old French *ribauld*] **ribaldry** *n*

riband *or* **ribband** *n* a ribbon awarded for some achievement

ribbing *n* **1** a pattern of ribs in knitted material **2** a framework or structure of ribs

ribbon *n* **1** a narrow strip of fine material used for trimming, tying, etc. **2** a long narrow strip of inked cloth or plastic used to produce print in a typewriter **3** a small strip of coloured cloth worn as a badge or as a symbol of an award **4** a long thin strip: *a ribbon of white water* **5 ribbons** ragged strips or shreds: *his clothes were torn to ribbons; his credibility was shot to ribbons* [Old French *riban*]

ribbon development *n* the building of houses along a main road

ribbonwood *n* a small evergreen tree of New Zealand

ribcage *n* the bony structure formed by the ribs that encloses the lungs

riboflavin (rye-boe-**flay**-vin) *n* a vitamin of the B complex that occurs in green vegetables, milk, fish, eggs, liver, and kidney: used as a yellow or orange food colouring (E101). Also called: **vitamin B_2** [*ribose*, a sugar + Latin *flavus* yellow]

ribonucleic acid *n* the full name of **RNA**

rice *n* **1** the edible grain of an erect grass that grows on wet ground in warm climates ▷ *vb* **ricing, riced 2** *US & Canad* to sieve (potatoes or other vegetables) to a coarse mashed consistency [Greek *orūza*]

rice paper *n* **1** a thin edible paper made from rice straw **2** a thin Chinese paper made from the rice-paper plant, the pith of which is flattened into sheets

rich *adj* **1** owning a lot of money or property **2** well supplied (with a desirable substance or quality): *a country rich with cultural interest* **3** having an abundance of natural resources, minerals, etc.: *a land rich in unexploited minerals* **4** producing abundantly: *the island is a blend of hilly moorland and rich farmland* **5** luxuriant or prolific: *the meadows rich with corn* **6** (of food) containing much fat or sugar **7** having a full-bodied flavour: *a gloriously rich Cabernet-dominated wine* **8** (of colour) intense or vivid: *her hair had a rich auburn tint* **9** (of sound or a voice) full or resonant **10** very amusing or ridiculous: *a rich joke* **11** (of a fuel-air mixture) containing a relatively high proportion of fuel [Old English *rīce* (originally of people, with sense: great, mighty)] **richness** *n*

riches *pl n* valuable possessions or desirable substances: *the unexpected riches of Georgian culture*

richly *adv* **1** in a rich or elaborate manner: *the rooms are richly decorated with a variety of classical motifs* **2** fully and appropriately: *he left the field to a richly deserved standing ovation*

Richter scale *n* a scale for expressing the intensity of an earthquake, ranging from 0 to over 8 [after Charles *Richter*, seismologist]

rick[1] *n* a large stack of hay or straw [Old English *hrēac*]

rick[2] *vb* **1** to wrench or sprain (a joint) ▷ *n* **2** a wrench or sprain of a joint [variant of *wrick*]

rickets *n* a disease of children, caused by a deficiency of vitamin D and characterized by softening of developing bone, and hence bow legs [origin unknown]

rickety *adj* **1** likely to collapse or break: *a rickety wooden table* **2** resembling or having rickets **ricketiness** *n*

rickrack *or* **ricrac** *n* a zigzag braid used for trimming [reduplication of RACK[1]]

rickshaw *or* **ricksha** *n* **1** a small two-wheeled passenger vehicle pulled by one or two people, used in parts of Asia **2** a similar vehicle with three wheels, propelled by a person pedalling [Japanese *jinrikisha*]

ricochet (rik-osh-ay) *vb* **-cheting, -cheted** *or* **-chetting, -chetted 1** (of a bullet) to rebound from a surface ▷ *n* **2** the motion or sound of a rebounding bullet [French]

ricotta *n* a soft white unsalted Italian cheese made from sheep's milk [Italian]

rid *vb* **ridding, rid** *or* **ridded 1 rid of** to relieve (oneself) or make a place free of (something undesirable) **2 get rid of** to relieve or free oneself of (something undesirable) [Old Norse *rythja*]

riddance *n* **good riddance** relief at getting rid of someone or something

ridden *vb* **1** the past participle of **ride** ▷ *adj* **2** afflicted or affected by the thing specified: *the police found three bullet-ridden bodies*

riddle[1] *n* **1** a question, puzzle, or verse phrased so that ingenuity is required to find the answer or meaning **2** a puzzling person or thing ▷ *vb* **-dling, -dled 3** to speak in riddles [Old English *rǣdels(e)*]

riddle[2] *vb* **-dling, -dled 1** to pierce with many holes **2** to put through a sieve ▷ *n* **3** a coarse sieve [Old English *hriddel* a sieve]

riddled *adj* **riddled with** full of (something undesirable): *riddled with mistakes*

ride *vb* **riding, rode, ridden 1** to sit on and control the movements of (a horse or other animal) **2** to sit on and propel (a bicycle or motorcycle) **3** to travel on or in a vehicle: *he rides around in a chauffeur-driven Rolls-Royce* **4** to travel over: *they rode the countryside in search of shelter* **5** to travel through or be carried across (sea, sky, etc.): *the moon was riding high* **6** *US & Canad* to cause to be carried: *to ride someone out of town* **7** (of a vessel) to lie at anchor **8** to tyrannize over or dominate: *she was ridden by fear* **9 be riding on** to be dependent on (something) for success: *a lot is riding on the profits of the film* **10** *informal* to continue undisturbed: *let it ride* **11 riding high** popular and successful ▷ *n*

12 a journey on a bicycle, on horseback, or in a vehicle **13** transport in a vehicle: *most of us have been told not to accept rides from strangers* **14** the type of movement experienced in a vehicle: *a bumpy ride* **15** a path for riding on horseback **16 take for a ride** *informal* to cheat or deceive [Old English *rīdan*]

ride out *vb* to survive (a period of difficulty or danger) successfully

rider *n* **1** a person who rides **2** an extra clause or condition added to a document

ride up *vb* (of a garment) to move up from the proper position

ridge *n* **1** a long narrow raised land formation with sloping sides **2** a long narrow raised strip on a flat surface **3** the top of a roof where the two sloping sides meet **4** *meteorol* an elongated area of high pressure [Old English *hrycg*] **ridged** *adj* **ridgy** *adj*

ridgepole *n* **1** a timber along the ridge of a roof, to which the rafters are attached **2** the horizontal pole at the apex of a tent

ridicule *n* **1** language or behaviour intended to humiliate or mock ▹ *vb* **-culing, -culed 2** to make fun of or mock [Latin *ridere* to laugh]

ridiculous *adj* worthy of or causing ridicule

riding¹ *n* the art or practice of horsemanship

riding² *n* **1 Riding** any of the three former administrative divisions of Yorkshire: North Riding, East Riding, and West Riding **2** *Canad* an electoral constituency [Old English *thriding* a third]

riding crop *n* a short whip with a handle at one end for opening gates

riesling *n* a medium-dry white wine [from German]

rife *adj* **1** widespread or common **2 rife with** full of: *the media is rife with speculation* [Old English *rīfe*]

riff *n* *jazz & rock* a short series of chords [probably from REFRAIN²]

riffle *vb* **-fling, -fled 1** to flick through (papers or pages) quickly: *I riffled through the rest of the memos* ▹ *n* **2** *US & Canad* **A** a rapid in a stream **B** a rocky shoal causing a rapid **C** a ripple on water **3** a riffling [probably from *ruffle*]

riffraff *n* worthless or disreputable people [Old French *rif et raf*]

rifle¹ *n* **1** a firearm having a long barrel with a spirally grooved interior, which gives the bullet a spinning motion and thus greater accuracy over a longer range **2 Rifles** a unit of soldiers equipped with rifles: *the Burma Rifles* ▹ *vb* **-fling, -fled 3** to cut spiral grooves inside the barrel of (a gun) [Old French *rifler* to scratch] **rifled** *adj*

rifle² *vb* **-fling, -fled 1** to search (a house or safe) and steal from it **2** to steal and carry off: *he rifled whatever valuables he could lay his hands on* [Old French *rifler* to plunder, scratch]

rift *n* **1** a break in friendly relations between people or groups of people **2** a gap or space made by splitting [Old Norse]

rift valley *n* a long narrow valley resulting from the subsidence of land between two faults

rig *vb* **rigging, rigged 1** to arrange in a dishonest way, for profit or advantage: *he claimed that the poll was rigged* **2** to set up or prepare (something) hastily ready for use **3** *naut* to equip (a vessel or mast) with (sails or rigging) ▹ *n* **4** an apparatus for drilling for oil and gas **5** *naut* the arrangement of the sails and masts of a vessel **6** apparatus or equipment **7** *informal* an outfit of clothes **8** *US, Canad & Austral* an articulated lorry ▹ See also **rig out, rig up** [Scandinavian]

-rigged *adj* (of a sailing vessel) having a rig of a certain kind: *a square-rigged ship*

rigging *n* the ropes and cables supporting a ship's masts and sails

right *adj* **1** morally or legally acceptable or correct: *his conduct seemed reasonable, even right* **2** correct or true: *the customer is always right* **3** appropriate, suitable, or proper: *there were problems involved in finding the right candidate* **4** most favourable or convenient: *she waited until the right moment to broach the subject* **5** in a satisfactory condition: *things are right again now* **6** accurate: *is that clock right?* **7** correct in opinion or judgment **8** sound in mind or body **9** of or on the side of something or someone that faces east when the front is turned towards the north **10** conservative or reactionary: *it was alleged he was an agent of the right wing* **11** *geom* formed by or containing a line or plane perpendicular to another line or plane: *a right angle* **12** of or on the side of cloth worn or facing outwards **13 in one's right mind** sane **14 she'll be right** *Austral & NZ informal* that's all right; not to worry **15 the right side of A** in favour with: *you'd better stay on the right side of him* **B** younger than: *he's still on the right side of fifty* **16 too right** *informal* an exclamation of agreement ▹ *adv* **17** correctly: *if we change the structure of local government we must do it right* **18** in the appropriate manner: *do it right next time!* **19** straight or directly: *let's go right to bed* **20** in the direction of the east from the point of view of a person or thing facing north **21** all the way: *he drove right up to the gate* **22** without delay: *I'll be right over* **23** exactly or precisely: *right here* **24** fittingly: *it serves him right* **25** to good or favourable advantage: *it all came out right in the end* ▹ *n* **26** a freedom or power that is morally or legally due to a person: *the defendant had an absolute right to a fair trial* **27** anything that accords with the principles of legal or moral justice **28 in the right** the state of being in accordance with reason or truth **29** the right side, direction, or part: *the right of the army* **30 the Right** the supporters or advocates of conservatism or reaction: *the rise of the far Right* **31** *boxing* a punch with the right hand **32 rights** *finance* the privilege of a company's shareholders to subscribe for new issues of the company's shares on advantageous terms **33 by right** *or* **rights** properly: *by rights he should have won* **34 in one's own right** having a claim or title oneself rather than through marriage or other connection **35 to rights** consistent with justice or orderly arrangement: *he put the matter to rights* ▹ *vb* **36** to bring or come back to a normal or correct state **37** to bring or come back to a vertical position: *he slipped and righted himself at once* **38** to compensate for or redress: *there is a wrong to be righted* **39** to make (something) accord with truth or facts ▹ *interj* **40** an expression of agreement or compliance [Old English *riht*]

right angle *n* **1** an angle of 90° or π/2 radians **2 at right angles** perpendicular or perpendicularly **right-angled** *adj*

right-angled triangle *n* a triangle with one angle which is a right angle

right away *adv* without delay

righteous (rye-chuss) *adj* **1** moral, just, or virtuous: *the lieutenant was a righteous cop* **2** morally justifiable or right: *her eyes were blazing with righteous indignation* [Old English *rihtwīs*] **righteousness** *n*

rightful *adj* **1** in accordance with what is right **2** having a legally or morally just claim: *he is the rightful heir to her fortune* **3** held by virtue of a legal or just claim: *these moves will restore them to their rightful homes* **rightfully** *adv* **rightfulness** *n*

right-hand *adj* **1** of, on, or towards the right: *in the top right-hand corner* **2** for the right hand **3 right-hand man** a person's most valuable assistant

right-handed *adj* **1** more adept with the right hand than with the left **2** made for or by the right hand **3** turning from left to right

rightist *adj* **1** of the political right or its principles ▷ *n* **2** a supporter of the political right **rightism** *n*

rightly *adv* **1** in accordance with the true facts or justice **2** with good reason: *he was rightly praised for his constancy*

right-minded *or* **right-thinking** *adj* holding opinions or principles considered acceptable by the speaker

right of way *n, pl* **rights of way 1** the right of one vehicle or ship to go before another **2 A** the legal right of someone to pass over someone else's land **B** the path used by this right

right-on *adj informal* trendy and socially aware or relevant: *the judges were fed up with right-on comedy*

Right Reverend *adj* a title of respect for a bishop

rightward *adj* **1** situated on or directed towards the right ▷ *adv also* **rightwards 2** on or towards the right

right whale *n* a large grey or black whalebone whale with a large head [origin unknown]

right-wing *adj* **1** conservative or reactionary: *there's a very fast-growing right-wing feeling in our country* **2** belonging to the more conservative part of a political party: *a group of right-wing Labour MPs* ▷ *n* **right wing 3** the more conservative or reactionary section, esp. of a political party: *the right wing of the Conservative Party* **4** *sport* **A** the right-hand side of the field of play **B** a player positioned in this area in certain games **right-winger** *n*

rigid *adj* **1** inflexible or strict: *the talks will be general, without a rigid agenda* **2** physically unyielding or stiff: *use only rigid plastic containers* [Latin *rigidus*] **rigidity** *n* **rigidly** *adv*

rigmarole *n* **1** a long complicated procedure **2** a set of incoherent or pointless statements [earlier *ragman roll* a list]

rigor mortis *n* the stiffness of joints and muscles of a dead body [Latin: rigidity of death]

rigorous *adj* **1** harsh, strict, or severe: *rigorous enforcement of the libel laws* **2** severely accurate: *rigorous scientific testing*

rigour *or US* **rigor** *n* **1** a severe or cruel circumstance: *the rigours of forced labour* **2** strictness in judgment or conduct **3** harsh but just treatment [Latin *rigor*]

rig out *vb* **1** to dress: *I was rigged out in my usual green shell suit* **2** to equip: *his car is rigged out with gadgets* ▷ *n* **rigout 3** *informal* a person's clothing or costume

rig up *vb* to set up or build temporarily: *they rigged up a loudspeaker system*

rile *vb* **riling, riled 1** to annoy or anger **2** *US & Canad* to stir up (a liquid) [variant of *roil* to agitate]

rill *n* a small stream [Low German *rille*]

rim *n* **1** the raised edge of an object **2** the outer part of a wheel to which the tyre is attached [Old English *rima*] **rimless** *adj*

rime[1] *literary* ▷ *n* **1** frost formed by the freezing of water droplets in fog onto solid objects ▷ *vb* **riming, rimed 2** to cover with rime or something resembling it [Old English *hrīm*] **rimy** *adj*

rime[2] *n, vb* **riming, rimed** *archaic* same as **rhyme**

rind *n* a hard outer layer on fruits, bacon, or cheese [Old English *rinde*]

ring[1] *vb* **ringing, rang, rung 1** to give out a clear resonant sound, like that of a bell **2** to cause (a bell) to give out a ringing sound or (of a bell) to give out such a sound **3** *chiefly Brit & NZ* to call (a person) by telephone **4 ring for** to call by means of a bell: *ring for the maid* **5** (of a building or place) to be filled with sound: *the church rang with singing* **6** (of the ears) to have the sensation of humming or ringing **7** *slang* to change the identity of (a stolen vehicle) by using the licence plate or serial number of another, usually disused, vehicle **8 ring a bell** to bring something to the mind or memory: *the name doesn't ring a bell* **9 ring down the curtain A** to lower the curtain at the end of a theatrical performance **B ring down the curtain on** to put an end to **10 ring true** *or* **false** to give the impression of being true *or* false ▷ *n* **11** the act of or a sound made by ringing **12** a sound produced by or sounding like a bell **13** *informal, chiefly Brit & NZ* a telephone call **14** an inherent quality: *it has the ring of possibility to it* ▷ See also **ring in, ring off** *etc.* [Old English *hringan*]

> **USAGE** *Rang* and *sang* are the correct forms of the past tenses of *ring* and *sing*, although *rung* and *sung* are still heard informally and dialectally: *he rung (rang) the bell.*

ring[2] *n* **1** a circular band of a precious metal worn on the finger **2** any object or mark that is circular in shape **3** a group of people or things standing or arranged in a circle: *a ring of standing stones* **4** a circular path or course: *crowds of people walking round in a ring* **5** a circular enclosure where circus acts perform or livestock is sold at a market **6** a square raised platform, marked off by ropes, in which contestants box or wrestle **7** a group of people, usually illegal, who control a specified market: *a drugs ring* **8** *chem* a closed loop of atoms in a molecule **9** one of the systems of circular bands orbiting the planets Saturn, Uranus, and Jupiter **10 the ring** the sport of boxing **11 throw one's hat in the ring** to announce one's intention to be a candidate or contestant **12 run rings around** *informal* to outclass completely ▷ *vb* **ringing, ringed 13** to put a ring round **14** to mark (a bird) with a ring or clip for subsequent identification **15** to kill (a tree) by cutting the bark round the trunk **16** to fit a ring in the nose of (a bull, etc.) so that it can be led easily [Old English *hring*] **ringed** *adj*

ring binder *n* a loose-leaf binder with metal rings that can be opened to insert perforated paper

ringdove *n* a wood pigeon

ringer *n informal* **1** Also called: **dead ringer** a person or thing that is almost identical to another **2** a person or thing that is presented under a false identity

ring finger *n* the third finger, esp. of the left hand, on which a wedding ring is worn

ring in *vb chiefly Brit* to report to someone by telephone

ringleader *n* a person who leads others in illegal or mischievous actions

ringlet *n* a lock of hair hanging down in a spiral curl **ringleted** *adj*

ringmaster *n* the master of ceremonies in a circus

ring off *vb chiefly Brit & NZ* to end a telephone conversation by replacing the receiver

ring out *vb* to send out a loud resounding noise: *I heard those shots ring out*

ring road *n chiefly Brit* a main road that bypasses a town or town centre

ringside *n* **1** the row of seats nearest a boxing or wrestling ring ▷ *adj* **2** providing a close uninterrupted view: *a ringside seat for the election*

ringtail *n Austral* a possum with a curling tail used to grip branches while climbing

ringtone *n* a tune or sound played by a mobile phone when it receives a call

ring up *vb* **1** *chiefly Brit* to make a telephone call to **2** to record on a cash register **3 ring up the curtain A** to begin a theatrical performance **B ring up the curtain on** to make a start on

ringworm *n* a fungal infection of the skin producing itchy patches

rink *n* **1** a sheet of ice for skating on, usually indoors **2** an area for roller-skating on **3** a building for ice-skating or roller-skating **4 A** a strip of grass or ice on which a game of bowls or curling is played **B** the players on one side in a game of bowls or curling [Old French *renc* row]

rinkhals (rink-hals) *n, pl* **-hals** *or* **-halses** a highly venomous snake of Southern Africa capable of spitting its venom accurately at its victim's eyes [Afrikaans]

rink rat *n Canad slang* a youth who helps with odd chores at an ice-hockey rink in return for free admission to games

rinse *vb* **rinsing, rinsed 1** to remove soap or shampoo from (clothes, dishes, or hair) by washing it out with clean water **2** to wash lightly, esp. without using soap **3** to cleanse (the mouth) by swirling water or mouthwash in it and then spitting the liquid out **4** to give a light tint to (hair) ▷ *n* **5** the act or an instance of rinsing **6** *hairdressing* a liquid to tint hair: *a blue rinse* [Old French *rincer*]

rioja (ree-**oh**-ha) *n* a red or white Spanish wine with a vanilla bouquet and flavour [*La Rioja*, area in central N Spain]

riot *n* **1** a disturbance made by an unruly mob **2** *Brit, Austral & NZ* an occasion of lively enjoyment **3** a dazzling display: *the pansies provided the essential riot of colour* **4** *slang* a very amusing person or thing **5 read the riot act** to reprimand severely **6 run riot A** to behave without restraint **B** (of plants) to grow profusely ▷ *vb* **7** to take part in a riot [Old French *riote* dispute] **rioter** *n* **rioting** *n*

riotous *adj* **1** unrestrained and excessive: *riotous decadence* **2** unruly or rebellious **3** characterized by unrestrained merriment: *riotous celebration*

riot shield *n* a large shield used by police controlling crowds

rip *vb* **ripping, ripped 1** to tear or be torn violently or roughly **2** to remove hastily or roughly **3** *informal* to move violently or hurriedly **4 let rip** to act or speak without restraint ▷ *n* **5** a tear or split ▷ See also **rip off** [origin unknown]

RIP may he, she, *or* they rest in peace [Latin *requiescat or requiescant in pace*]

riparian (rip-**pair**-ee-an) *adj formal* of or on the bank of a river [Latin *ripa* river bank]

ripcord *n* a cord pulled to open a parachute from its pack

ripe *adj* **1** mature enough to be eaten or used: *a round ripe apple* **2** fully developed in mind or body **3** suitable: *wait until the time is ripe* **4 ripe for** ready or eager to (undertake or undergo an action): *China was ripe for revolution* **5 ripe old age** an elderly but healthy age [Old English *rīpe*]

ripen *vb* **1** to make or become ripe **2** to mature

rip off *slang* ▷ *vb* **1** to cheat by overcharging **2** to steal (something) ▷ *n* **rip-off 3** a grossly overpriced article **4** the act of stealing or cheating

riposte (rip-**posst**) *n* **1** a swift clever reply **2** *fencing* a counterattack made immediately after a successful parry ▷ *vb* **-posting, -posted 3** to make a riposte [French]

ripple *n* **1** a slight wave on the surface of water **2** a slight ruffling of a surface **3** a sound like water flowing gently in ripples: *a ripple of applause* **4** vanilla ice cream with stripes of another ice cream through it: *raspberry ripple* ▷ *vb* **-pling, -pled 5** to form ripples or flow with a waving motion **6** (of sounds) to rise and fall gently [origin unknown] **rippling** *adj*

rip-roaring *adj informal* boisterous and exciting

ripsaw *n* a handsaw for cutting along the grain of timber

rise *vb* **rising, rose, risen 1** to get up from a lying, sitting, or kneeling position **2** to get out of bed, esp. to begin one's day: *she rises at 5 am every day to look after her horse* **3** to move from a lower to a higher position or place **4** to appear above the horizon: *as the sun rises higher the mist disappears* **5** to slope upwards: *the road crossed the valley then rose to a low ridge* **6** to increase in height or level: *the tide rose* **7** to swell up: *dough rises* **8** to increase in strength or degree: *frustration is rising amongst sections of the population* **9** to increase in amount or value: *living costs are rising at an annual rate of nine per cent* **10** *informal* to respond (to a challenge or remark) **11** to revolt: *the people rose against their oppressors* **12** (of a court or parliament) to adjourn **13** to be resurrected **14** to become erect or rigid:

the hairs on his neck rose in fear **15** to originate: *that river rises in the mountains* **16** *angling* (of fish) to come to the surface of the water ▷ *n* **17** the act or an instance of rising **18** a piece of rising ground **19** an increase in wages **20** an increase in amount, cost, or quantity **21** an increase in height **22** an increase in status or position **23** an increase in degree or intensity **24** the vertical height of a step or of a flight of stairs **25 get** *or* **take a rise out of** *slang* to provoke an angry reaction from **26 give rise to** to cause the development of [Old English *rīsan*]

riser *n* **1** a person who rises from bed: *an early riser* **2** the vertical part of a step

risible (riz-zib-bl) *adj formal* ridiculous [Latin *ridere* to laugh]

rising *n* **1** a rebellion ▷ *adj* **2** increasing in rank or maturity

rising damp *n* seepage of moisture from the ground into the walls of buildings

risk *n* **1** the possibility of bringing about misfortune or loss **2** a person or thing considered as a potential hazard: *in parts of the world transfusions carry the risk of infection* **3 at risk** in a dangerous situation **4 take** *or* **run a risk** to act without regard to the danger involved ▷ *vb* **5** to act in spite of the possibility of (injury or loss): *if they clamp down they risk a revolution* **6** to expose to danger or loss [French *risque*] **risky** *adj*

risk assessment *n* an analysis of the level of risk attached to a particular activity

risotto *n, pl* **-tos** a dish of rice cooked in stock with vegetables, meat, etc. [Italian]

risqué (risk-ay) *adj* making slightly rude references to sex: *risqué humour* [French *risquer* to risk]

rissole *n* a mixture of minced cooked meat coated in egg and breadcrumbs and fried [French]

ritardando *adj, adv* same as **rallentando** [Italian]

rite *n* **1** a formal act which forms part of a religious ceremony: *the rite of burial* **2** a custom that is carried out within a particular group: *the barbaric rites of public execution* **3** a particular body of such acts, esp. of a particular Christian Church: *the traditional Anglican rite* [Latin *ritus*]

rite of passage *n* a ceremony or event that marks an important change in a person's life

ritual *n* **1** a religious or other ceremony involving a series of fixed actions performed in a certain order **2** these ceremonies collectively: *people need ritual* **3** a regular repeated action or behaviour **4** stereotyped activity or behaviour ▷ *adj* **5** of or like rituals **ritually** *adv*

ritualism *n* exaggerated emphasis on the importance of rites and ceremonies **ritualistic** *adj* **ritualistically** *adv*

ritzy *adj* **ritzier, ritziest** *slang* luxurious or elegant [after the hotels established by César Ritz]

rival *n* **1** a person or group that competes with another for the same object or in the same field **2** a person or thing that is considered the equal of another: *she is without rival in the field of physics* ▷ *adj* **3** in the position of a rival ▷ *vb* **-valling, -valled** *or US* **-valing, -valed 4** to be the equal or near equal of: *his inarticulateness was rivalled only by that of his brother* **5** to try to equal or surpass [Latin *rivalis*, literally: one who shares the same brook]

rivalry *n, pl* **-ries** active competition between people or groups

riven *adj old-fashioned* **1** split apart: *the party is riven by factions* **2** torn to shreds [Old Norse *rīfa* to tear, rend]

river *n* **1** a large natural stream of fresh water flowing along a definite course into the sea, a lake, or a larger river. Related adjective: **fluvial 2** an abundant stream or flow: *rivers of blood* [Old French *riviere*]

rivet (riv-vit) *n* **1** a short metal pin for fastening metal plates, with a head at one end, the other end being hammered flat after being put through holes in the plates ▷ *vb* **-veting, -veted 2** to join by riveting **3** to cause a person's attention to be fixed in fascination or horror: *he was riveted by the story* [Old French *river* to fasten] **riveter** *n*

riveting *adj* very interesting or exciting

rivulet *n* a small stream [Latin *rivus* stream]

RM (in Britain) **1** Royal Mail **2** Royal Marines

RMT (in Britain) (National Union of) Rail, Maritime and Transport (Workers)

Rn *chem* radon

RN 1 (in Canada and New Zealand) Registered Nurse **2** (in Britain) Royal Navy

RNA *n biochem* ribonucleic acid: any of a group of nucleic acids, present in all living cells, that play an essential role in the synthesis of proteins

RNLI (in Britain) Royal National Lifeboat Institution

RNZ Radio New Zealand

RNZAF Royal New Zealand Air Force

RNZN Royal New Zealand Navy

roach[1] *n, pl* **roaches** *or* **roach** a European freshwater food fish [Old French *roche*]

roach[2] *n chiefly US & Canad* a cockroach

road *n* **1** a route, usually surfaced, used by travellers and vehicles to get from one place to another **2** a street **3** a way or course: *on the road to recovery* **4** *naut* same as **roadstead 5 one for the road** *informal* a last alcoholic drink before leaving **6 on the road** travelling about [Old English *rād*]

roadblock *n* a barrier set up across a road by the police or military, in order to stop and check vehicles

road hog *n informal* a selfish or aggressive driver

roadholding *n* the extent to which a vehicle is stable and does not skid on bends or wet roads

roadhouse *n* a pub or restaurant at the side of a road

roadie *n informal* a person who transports and sets up equipment for a band

road metal *n* crushed rock or broken stone used in building roads

road rage *n* aggressive behaviour by a motorist in response to the actions of another road user

road show *n* **1** *radio* a live broadcast from a radio van taking a particular programme on a tour of the country **2** a group of entertainers on tour

roadside *n* **1** the edge of a road ▷ *adj* **2** by the edge or side of a road: *a roadside café*

roadstead *n naut* a partly sheltered anchorage

roadster *n* an open-top or convertible sports car with two seats

road tax *n* (in Britain) a tax paid on vehicles used on the roads

road test *n* **1** a test of something, such as a vehicle in actual use ▷ *vb* **road-test** **2** to test (a vehicle, etc.) in actual use
roadway *n* the part of a road that is used by vehicles
roadworks *pl n* repairs to a road or cable under a road, esp. when they block part of the road
roadworthy *adj* (of a motor vehicle) mechanically sound **roadworthiness** *n*
roam *vb* to walk about with no fixed purpose or direction [origin unknown]
roaming *n* the act of using a mobile phone in a foreign country
roan *adj* **1** (of a horse) having a brown or black coat sprinkled with white hairs ▷ *n* **2** a horse with such a coat [Spanish *roano*]
roar *vb* **1** (of lions and other animals) to make loud growling cries **2** to shout (something) with a loud deep cry: *'Don't do that!' he roared at me* **3** to make a very loud noise: *the engine roared* **4** to laugh in a loud hearty manner **5** (of a fire) to burn fiercely with a roaring sound ▷ *n* **6** a roaring noise: *there was a roar as the train came in* **7** a loud deep cry, uttered by a person or crowd, esp. in anger or triumph: *a roar of approval came from the crowd* [Old English *rārian*]
roaring *adj* **1** **a roaring trade** a brisk and profitable business ▷ *adv* **2** **roaring drunk** noisily or boisterously drunk
roast *vb* **1** to cook (food) by dry heat in an oven or over a fire **2** to brown or dry (coffee or nuts) by exposure to heat **3** to make or be extremely hot **4** *informal* to criticize severely ▷ *n* **5** a roasted joint of meat ▷ *adj* **6** cooked by roasting: *roast beef* [Old French *rostir*] **roaster** *n*
roasting *informal* ▷ *adj* **1** extremely hot ▷ *n* **2** severe criticism or scolding
rob *vb* **robbing, robbed** **1** to take something from (a person or place) illegally **2** to deprive, esp. of something deserved: *I can't forgive him for robbing me of an Olympic gold* [Old French *rober*] **robber** *n*
robbery *n, pl* **-beries** **1** *criminal law* the stealing of property from a person by using or threatening to use force **2** the act or an instance of robbing
robe *n* **1** a long loose flowing garment **2** a dressing gown or bathrobe ▷ *vb* **robing, robed** **3** to put a robe on [Old French]
robin *n* **1** Also called: **robin redbreast** a small Old World songbird with a brown back and an orange-red breast and face **2** a North American thrush similar to but larger than the Old World robin [arbitrary use of name *Robin*]
robot *n* **1** a machine programmed to perform specific tasks in a human manner, esp. one with a human shape **2** a person of machine-like efficiency **3** *S African* a set of traffic lights [used in R.U.R., a play by a Czech writer, from Czech *robota* work] **robotic** *adj*
robotics *n* the science of designing, building, and using robots
robust *adj* **1** very strong and healthy **2** sturdily built: *the new generation of robust lasers* **3** requiring or displaying physical strength: *robust tackles* [Latin *robur* an oak, strength]
roc *n* (in Arabian legend) a bird of enormous size and power [Persian *rukh*]
rock[1] *n* **1** *geol* the mass of mineral matter that makes up part of the earth's crust; stone **2** a large rugged mass of stone **3** *chiefly US, Canad & Austral* a stone **4** a hard peppermint-flavoured sweet, usually in the shape of a long stick **5** a person or thing on which one can always depend: *your loyalty is a rock* **6** *slang* a precious jewel **7** **on the rocks** **A** (of a marriage) about to end **B** (of an alcoholic drink) served with ice [Old French *roche*]
rock[2] *vb* **1** to move from side to side or backwards and forwards **2** to shake or move (something) violently **3** to feel or cause to feel shock: *key events have rocked both countries* **4** to dance to or play rock music **5** *slang* to be very good ▷ *n* **6** Also called: **rock music** a style of pop music with a heavy beat **7** a rocking motion ▷ *adj* **8** of or relating to rock music [Old English *roccian*]
rockabilly *n* a fast style of White rock music which originated in the mid-1950s in the US South [*rock and roll + hillbilly*]
rock and roll *or* **rock'n'roll** *n* a type of pop music originating in the 1950s as a blend of rhythm and blues and country and western
rock bottom *n* the lowest possible level
rock cake *n* a small fruit cake with a rough surface
rock crystal *n* a pure transparent colourless quartz
rock dove *n* a common dove from which domestic and wild pigeons are descended
rocker *n* **1** a rocking chair **2** either of two curved supports on which a rocking chair stands **3** a rock music performer or fan **4** **off one's rocker** *slang* crazy
rockery *n, pl* **-eries** a garden built of rocks and soil, for growing rock plants
rocket *n* **1** a self-propelling device, usually cylindrical, which produces thrust by expelling through a nozzle the gases produced by burning fuel, such as one used as a firework or distress signal **2** any vehicle propelled by a rocket engine, as a weapon or carrying a spacecraft **3** *informal* a severe reprimand: *my sister gave me a rocket for writing such dangerous nonsense* ▷ *vb* **-eting, -eted** **4** to increase rapidly: *within six years their turnover had rocketed* **5** to attack with rockets [Italian *rochetto* little distaff]
rocketry *n* the science and technology of the design and operation of rockets
rock garden *n* a garden featuring rocks or rockeries
rocking chair *n* a chair set on curving supports so that the sitter may rock backwards and forwards
rocking horse *n* a toy horse mounted on a pair of rocking supports on which a child can rock to and fro
rock melon *n US, Austral & NZ* same as **cantaloupe**
rock pool *n* a small pool between rocks on the seashore
rock salmon *n Brit* a former term for dogfish when used as a food
rock salt *n* common salt as a naturally occurring solid mineral
rock tripe *n Canad* any edible lichen that grows on rocks

rocky[1] *adj* **rockier, rockiest** covered with rocks: *rocky and sandy shores* **rockiness** *n*
rocky[2] *adj* **rockier, rockiest** shaky or unstable: *a rocky relationship* **rockiness** *n*
rococo (rok-**koh**-koh) *adj* **1** relating to an 18th-century style of architecture, decoration, and music characterized by elaborate ornamentation **2** excessively elaborate in style [French]
rod *n* **1** a thin straight pole made of wood or metal **2** a cane used to beat people as a punishment **3** short for **fishing rod** **4** a type of cell in the retina, sensitive to dim light [Old English *rodd*] **rodlike** *adj*
rode *vb* the past tense of **ride**
rodent *n* a small mammal with teeth specialized for gnawing, such as a rat, mouse, or squirrel [Latin *rodere* to gnaw] **rodent-like** *adj*
rodeo *n, pl* **-deos** a display of the skills of cowboys, including bareback riding [Spanish]
rodomontade *n literary* boastful words or behaviour [French]
roe[1] *n* the ovary and eggs of a female fish, sometimes eaten as food [Middle Dutch *roge*]
roe[2] *or* **roe deer** *n* a small graceful deer with short antlers [Old English *rā(ha)*]
roentgen (**ront**-gan) *n* a unit measuring a radiation dose [after the German physicist *Roentgen*, who discovered X-rays]
roentgenium (ront-**gen**-ee-um) *n chem* a synthetic radioactive element produced in small quantities. Symbol: **Rg** [after W.K. *Roentgen*, physicist]
roger *interj* **1** (used in signalling) message received **2** an expression of agreement [from the name *Roger*, representing R for *received*]
rogue *n* **1** a dishonest or unprincipled person **2** a mischievous person **3** a crop plant which is inferior, diseased, or of a different variety **4** an inferior or defective specimen ▷ *adj* **5** (of a wild animal) having a savage temper and living apart from the herd: *a rogue elephant* **6** inferior or defective: *rogue heroin* [origin unknown] **roguish** *adj*
roguery *n, pl* **-gueries** dishonest or immoral behaviour
rogues' gallery *n informal* a collection of photographs of known criminals kept by the police for identification purposes
ROI **1** Republic of Ireland **2** *finance* return on investment
roister *vb old-fashioned* to enjoy oneself noisily and boisterously [Old French *rustre* lout] **roisterer** *n*
role *n* **1** a task or function: *their role in international relations* **2** an actor's part in a production [French]
role model *n* a person regarded by others, esp. younger people, as a good example to follow
roll *vb* **1** to move along by turning over and over **2** to move along on wheels or rollers **3** to curl or make by curling into a ball or tube **4** to move along in an undulating movement **5** to rotate wholly or partially: *he would snort in derision, roll his eyes, and heave a deep sigh* **6** to spread out flat or smooth with a roller or rolling pin: *roll the pastry out thinly* **7** (of a ship or aircraft) to turn from side to side around the longitudinal axis **8** to operate or begin to operate: *the cameras continued to roll as she pulled up to the nightclub* **9** to make a continuous deep reverberating sound: *the thunder rolled* **10** to walk in a swaying manner: *the drunks came rolling home* **11** to appear like a series of waves: *mountain ranges rolling away in every direction* **12** to pass or elapse: *watching the time roll away* **13** (of animals) to turn onto the back and kick **14** to trill or cause to be trilled: *she rolled her r's* **15** to throw (dice) ▷ *n* **16** the act or an instance of rolling **17** anything rolled up into a tube: *a roll of paper towels* **18** a small cake of bread for one person **19** a flat pastry or cake rolled up with a meat, jam, or other filling **20** an official list or register of names: *the electoral roll; the voters' roll* **21** a complete rotation about its longitudinal axis by an aircraft **22** a continuous deep reverberating sound: *the roll of musketry* **23** a swaying or unsteady movement or gait **24** a rounded mass: *rolls of fat* **25** a very rapid beating of the sticks on a drum **26** **on a roll** *slang* experiencing continued good luck or success **27** **strike off the roll** to expel from membership of a professional association ▷ See also **roll in, roll on** *etc.* [Old French *roler*]
roll call *n* the reading aloud of an official list of names, to check who is present
rolled gold *n* a metal, such as brass, coated with a thin layer of gold
roller *n* **1** a rotating cylinder used for smoothing, supporting a thing to be moved, spreading paint, etc. **2** a small tube around which hair may be wound in order to make it curly **3** a long heavy wave of the sea **4** a cylinder fitted on pivots, used to enable heavy objects to be easily moved
Rollerblade *n trademark* a type of roller skate in which the wheels are set in a single straight line under the boot
roller coaster *n* (at a funfair) a narrow railway with open carriages, sharp curves and steep slopes
roller skate *n* **1** a shoe with four small wheels that enable the wearer to glide swiftly over a floor ▷ *vb* **roller-skate, -skating, -skated** **2** to move on roller skates **roller skater** *n*
roller towel *n* **1** a towel with the two ends sewn together, hung on a roller **2** a towel wound inside a roller enabling a clean section to be pulled out when needed
rollicking *adj* boisterously carefree: *a rollicking read* [origin unknown]
roll in *vb* **1** to arrive in large numbers **2** **be rolling in** *slang* to have plenty of (money, etc.)
rolling *adj* **1** having gentle rising and falling slopes: *rolling hills* **2** (of a walk) slow and swaying **3** subject to regular review and updating: *a 10-year rolling programme* **4** progressing by stages or in succession: *a rolling campaign*
rolling mill *n* **1** a factory where metal ingots are passed between rollers to produce sheets or bars of the required shape **2** a machine with rollers for doing this
rolling pin *n* a cylinder with handles at both ends used for rolling pastry
rolling stock *n* the locomotives and coaches of a railway
rolling stone *n* a restless or wandering person

rollmop *n* a herring fillet rolled around onion slices and pickled [German *rollen* to roll + *Mops* pug dog]
rollneck *adj* (of a garment) having a high neck that is worn rolled over
roll of honour *n* a list of those who have died in war for their country
roll on *interj* **1** used to express the wish that an eagerly anticipated event will come quickly: *roll on the next light-hearted romp* ▹ *adj* **roll-on 2** (of a deodorant) applied by means of a revolving ball fitted into the neck of the container
roll-on/roll-off *adj* denoting a ship designed so that vehicles can be driven straight on and straight off
roll over *vb* **1** to overturn **2** to allow (a loan or prize) to continue in force for a further period ▹ *n* **rollover 3** an instance of such a continuance of a loan or prize
roll-top *adj* (of a desk) having a slatted wooden panel that can be pulled down over the writing surface when not in use
roll up *vb* **1** to form into a cylindrical shape: *roll up a length of black material* **2** *informal* to arrive ▹ *n* **roll-up 3** *Brit informal* a cigarette made by the smoker from loose tobacco and cigarette papers
roly-poly *adj* **1** plump or chubby ▹ *n, pl* **-lies 2** *Brit* a strip of suet pastry spread with jam, rolled up, and baked or steamed [probably from *roll*]
ROM *n computers* read only memory: a storage device that holds data permanently and cannot be altered by the programmer
Roma *n, pl* **Roma** *or* **Romas** a member of a people scattered throughout Europe and N America, who have a nomadic way of life in industrialized societies
roman *adj* **1** in or relating to the vertical style of printing type used for most printed matter ▹ *n* **2** roman type [so called because the style of letters is that used in ancient Roman inscriptions]
Roman *adj* **1** of Rome, a city in Italy, or its inhabitants in ancient or modern times **2** of Roman Catholicism or the Roman Catholic Church ▹ *n* **3** a person from ancient or modern Rome
Roman alphabet *n* the alphabet evolved by the ancient Romans for writing Latin, used for writing most of the languages of W Europe, including English
Roman blind *n* a window blind which gathers into horizontal folds from the bottom when drawn up
Roman candle *n* a firework that produces a steady stream of coloured sparks [it originated in Italy]
Roman Catholic *adj* **1** of the Roman Catholic Church ▹ *n* **2** a member of this Church **Roman Catholicism** *n*
Roman Catholic Church *n* the Christian Church over which the pope presides
romance *n* **1** a love affair: *a failed romance* **2** love, esp. romantic love idealized for its purity or beauty **3** a spirit of or inclination for adventure or mystery **4** a mysterious or sentimental quality **5** a story or film dealing with love, usually in an idealized way **6** a story or film dealing with events and characters remote from ordinary life **7** an extravagant, absurd, or fantastic account **8** a medieval narrative dealing with adventures of chivalrous heroes ▹ *vb* **-mancing, -manced 9** to tell extravagant or improbable lies [Old French *romans*]
Romance *adj* of the languages derived from Latin, such as French, Spanish, and Italian
Romanesque *adj* of or in the style of architecture used in Europe from the 9th to the 12th century, characterized by rounded arches and massive walls
Romanian *adj* **1** of Romania ▹ *n* **2** a person from Romania **3** the language of Romania
Roman nose *n* a nose with a high prominent bridge
Roman numerals *pl n* the letters used as numerals by the Romans, used occasionally today: I (= 1), V (= 5), X (= 10), L (= 50), C (= 100), D (= 500), and M (= 1000). VI = 6 (V + I) but IV = 4 (V – I)
romantic *adj* **1** of or dealing with love **2** idealistic but impractical: *a romantic notion* **3** evoking or given to thoughts and feelings of love: *romantic images* **4 Romantic** relating to a movement in European art, music, and literature in the late 18th and early 19th centuries, characterized by an emphasis on feeling and content rather than order and form ▹ *n* **5** a person who is idealistic or amorous **6** a person who likes or produces artistic works in the style of Romanticism **romantically** *adv*
romanticism *n* **1** idealistic but unrealistic thoughts and feelings **2 Romanticism** the spirit and style of the Romantic art, music, and literature of the late 18th and early 19th centuries **romanticist** *n*
romanticize *or* **-cise** *vb* **-cizing, -cized** *or* **-cising, -cised** to describe or regard (something or someone) in an unrealistic and idealized way: *the Victorian legacy of romanticizing family life*
Romany *n* **1** *pl* **-nies** a Roma **2** the language of the Roma [Romany *romani* (adjective) Roma]
Romeo *n, pl* **Romeos** an ardent male lover [after the hero of Shakespeare's *Romeo and Juliet*]
romp *vb* **1** to play or run about wildly or joyfully **2 romp home** *or* **in** to win a race or other competition easily **3 romp through** to do (something) quickly and easily ▹ *n* **4** a noisy or boisterous game or prank [probably from Old French *ramper* to crawl, climb]
rompers *pl n Also called* **romper suit** a one-piece baby garment combining trousers and a top
rondavel *n S African* a small circular building with a cone-shaped roof [origin unknown]
rondeau (ron-doe) *n, pl* **-deaux** (-doe) a poem consisting of 13 or 10 lines with the opening words of the first line used as a refrain [Old French]
rondo *n, pl* **-dos** a piece of music with a leading theme continually returned to: often forms the last movement of a sonata or concerto [Italian]
roo *n, pl* **roos** *Austral informal* a kangaroo
rood *n* **1** *Christianity* the Cross **2** a crucifix [Old English *rōd*]
roof *n, pl* **roofs 1** a structure that covers or forms the top of a building **2** the top covering of a

r

vehicle, oven, or other structure **3** the highest part of the mouth or a cave **4 hit** *or* **go through the roof** *informal* to get extremely angry **5 raise the roof** *informal* to be very noisy ▹ *vb* **6** to put a roof on [Old English *hrōf*]

roof garden *n* a garden on a flat roof of a building

roofing *n* material used to build a roof

roof rack *n* a rack for carrying luggage attached to the roof of a car

rooftree *n* same as **ridgepole**

rooibos (roy-boss) *n S African* a kind of tea made from the leaves of a South African wild shrub. Also called: **rooibos tea, bush tea** [Afrikaans *rooi* red + *bos* bush]

rooinek (roy-neck) *n S African* a contemptuous name for an Englishman [Afrikaans *rooi* red + *nek* neck]

rook[1] *n* **1** a large European black bird of the crow family ▹ *vb* **2** *old-fashioned slang* to cheat or swindle [Old English *hrōc*]

rook[2] *n* a chess piece that may move any number of unoccupied squares in a straight line, horizontally or vertically; castle [Arabic *rukhkh*]

rookery *n, pl* **-eries 1** a group of nesting rooks **2** a colony of penguins or seals

rookie *n informal* a newcomer without much experience [changed from *recruit*]

room *n* **1** an area within a building enclosed by a floor, a ceiling, and walls **2** the people present in a room: *the whole room was laughing* **3** unoccupied or unobstructed space: *there wasn't enough room* **4 room for** opportunity or scope for: *there was no room for acts of heroism* **5 rooms** lodgings ▹ *vb* **6** *US* to occupy or share a rented room: *I roomed with him for five years* [Old English *rūm*]

rooming house *n US* a house with self-contained furnished rooms or flats for renting

roommate *n* a person with whom one shares a room or apartment

room service *n* a service in a hotel providing food and drinks in guests' rooms

roomy *adj* **roomier, roomiest** with plenty of space inside: *a roomy entrance hall* **roominess** *n*

roost *n* **1** a place where birds rest or sleep ▹ *vb* **2** to rest or sleep on a roost **3 come home to roost** to have unfavourable repercussions **4 rule the roost** to have authority over people in a particular place [Old English *hrōst*]

rooster *n* the male of the domestic fowl; a cock

root[1] *n* **1** the part of a plant that anchors the rest of the plant in the ground and absorbs water and mineral salts from the soil **2** a plant with an edible root, such as a carrot **3** *anatomy* the part of a tooth, hair, or nail that is below the skin **4 roots** a person's sense of belonging in a place, esp. the one in which he or she was brought up **5** source or origin **6** the essential part or nature of something: *the root of a problem* **7** *linguistics* the form of a word from which other words and forms are derived **8** *maths* a quantity that when multiplied by itself a certain number of times equals a given quantity: *what is the cube root of a thousand?* **9** Also called: **solution** *maths* a number that when substituted for the variable satisfies a given equation **10** *Austral & NZ slang* sexual intercourse **11 root and branch** entirely or utterly. ▹ Related adjective: **radical** ▹ *vb* **12** Also: **take root** to establish a root and begin to grow **13** Also: **take root** to become established or embedded **14** *Austral & NZ slang* to have sexual intercourse (with) ▹ See also **root out, roots** [Old English *rōt*]

root[2] *vb* **1** *Brit* to dig up the earth in search of food, using the snout: *dogs were rooting in the rushes for bones* **2** *informal* to search vigorously but unsystematically: *she was rooting around in her large untidy purse* [Old English *wrōtan*]

root canal *n* the passage in the root of a tooth through which its nerves and blood vessels enter

root crop *n* a crop, such as potato or turnip, cultivated for its roots

root for *vb informal* to give support to (a team or contestant) [origin unknown]

rootle *vb* **-ling, -led** *Brit* same as **root**[2]

rootless *adj* having no sense of belonging: *a rootless city dweller*

root mean square *n* the square root of the average of the squares of a set of numbers or quantities, for example *the root mean square of* 1, 2, *and* 4 *is* $\sqrt{[(1^2 + 2^2 + 4^2)/3]} = \sqrt{7}$

root out *vb* to get rid of completely: *a major drive to root out corruption*

roots *adj* (of popular music) going back to the origins of a style, esp. in being unpretentious: *roots reggae*

rootstock *n* same as **rhizome**

rope *n* **1** a fairly thick cord made of intertwined fibres or wire **2** a row of objects fastened to form a line: *a twenty-inch rope of pearls* **3 know the ropes** to have a thorough understanding of a particular activity **4 the rope A** a rope noose used for hanging someone **B** death by hanging ▹ *vb* **roping, roped 5** to tie with a rope **6 rope off** to enclose or divide with a rope [Old English *rāp*]

rope in *vb* to persuade to take part in some activity

ropey *or* **ropy** *adj* **ropier, ropiest** *Brit informal* **1** poor or unsatisfactory in quality: *a ropey performance* **2** slightly unwell **ropiness** *n*

Roquefort *n* a strong blue-veined cheese made from ewes' milk [after *Roquefort*, village in S France]

ro-ro *adj* (of a ferry) roll-on/roll-off

rorqual *n* a whalebone whale with a fin on the back [Norwegian *rörhval*]

Rorschach test (ror-shahk) *n psychol* a personality test consisting of a number of unstructured inkblots for interpretation [after H. *Rorschach*, psychiatrist]

rort *Austral informal* ▹ *n* **1** a dishonest scheme ▹ *vb* **2** to take unfair advantage of something

rosaceous *adj* of or belonging to a family of plants typically having five-petalled flowers, which includes the rose, strawberry, and many fruit trees

rosary *n, pl* **-saries** *RC Church* **1** a series of prayers counted on a string of beads **2** a string of beads used to count these prayers as they are recited [Latin *rosarium* rose garden]

rose[1] *n* **1** a shrub or climbing plant with prickly stems and fragrant flowers **2** the flower of any of these plants **3** a plant similar to this, such as the

Christmas rose **4** a perforated cap fitted to a watering can or hose, causing the water to come out in a spray **5 bed of roses** a situation of comfort or ease ▹ *adj* **6** reddish-pink [Latin *rosa*]
rose² *vb* the past tense of **rise**
rosé (roe-zay) *n* a pink wine [French]
roseate (roe-zee-ate) *adj* **1** of the colour rose or pink **2** excessively optimistic
rosebay willowherb *n* a widespread perennial plant that has spikes of deep pink flowers
rosebud *n* a rose that has not yet fully opened
rose-coloured *adj* **1** reddish-pink **2 see through rose-coloured** *or* **rose-tinted glasses** *or* **spectacles** to view in an unrealistically optimistic light
rosehip *n* the berry-like fruit of a rose plant
rosella *n* a type of Australian parrot [from *Rose* Hill, former settlement in New South Wales]
rosemary *n, pl* **-maries** an aromatic European shrub widely cultivated for its grey-green evergreen leaves, which are used in cookery and perfumes [Latin *ros* dew + *marinus* marine]
rosette *n* a rose-shaped decoration, esp. a circular bunch of ribbons
rose-water *n* scented water made by the distillation of rose petals
rose window *n* a circular window with spokes branching out from the centre to form a symmetrical roselike pattern
rosewood *n* a fragrant dark wood used to make furniture
Rosh Hashanah *or* **Rosh Hashana** *n* the festival celebrating the Jewish New Year [Hebrew: beginning of the year]
rosin (rozz-in) *n* **1** a translucent brittle substance produced from turpentine and used for treating the bows of stringed instruments ▹ *vb* **2** to apply rosin to [variant of *resin*]
ROSPA (in Britain) Royal Society for the Prevention of Accidents
roster *n* **1** a list showing the order in which people are to perform a duty ▹ *vb* **2** to place on a roster [Dutch *rooster* grating or list]
rostrum *n, pl* **-trums** *or* **-tra** a platform or stage [Latin: beak]
rosy *adj* **rosier, rosiest 1** of the colour rose or pink: *rosy cheeks* **2** hopeful or promising: *the analysis revealed a far from rosy picture* **rosiness** *n*
rot *vb* **rotting, rotted 1** to decay or cause to decay **2** to deteriorate slowly, mentally and physically: *I thought he was either dead or rotting in a Chinese jail* ▹ *n* **3** the process of rotting or the state of being rotten **4** something decomposed **5** short for **dry rot 6** a plant or animal disease which causes decay of the tissues **7** nonsense [Old English *rotian*]
rota *n* a list of people who take it in turn to do a particular task [Latin: a wheel]
rotary *adj* **1** revolving **2** operating by rotation ▹ *n, pl* **-ries 3** *US & Canad* a traffic roundabout
Rotary Club *n* a club that is part of **Rotary International**, an international association of professionals and businesspeople who raise money for charity **Rotarian** *n, adj*
rotate *vb* **-tating, -tated 1** to turn around a centre or pivot **2** to follow or cause to follow a set sequence **3** to regularly change the type of crop grown on a piece of land in order to preserve the fertility of the soil [Latin *rota* wheel] **rotation** *n* **rotational** *adj*
rotator cuff *n anatomy* the structure around the shoulder joint consisting of the capsule of the joint along with the tendons of the adjacent muscles
Rotavator *n trademark* a mechanical cultivator with rotary blades
rote *adj* **1** done by routine repetition: *rote learning* ▹ *n* **2 by rote** by repetition: *we learned by rote* [origin unknown]
rotgut *n chiefly Brit facetious slang* alcoholic drink of inferior quality
rotisserie *n* a rotating spit on which meat and poultry can be cooked [French]
rotor *n* **1** the rotating part of a machine or device, such as the revolving arm of the distributor of an internal-combustion engine **2** a rotating device with blades projecting from a hub which produces thrust to lift a helicopter
rotten *adj* **1** decomposing or decaying: *rotten vegetables* **2** breaking up through age or hard use: *the window frames are rotten* **3** *informal* very bad: *what rotten luck!* **4** morally corrupt: *this country's politics are rotten and out of date* **5** *informal* miserably unwell: *I had glandular fever and spent that year feeling rotten* **6** *informal* distressed and embarrassed: *I'm feeling rotten as a matter of fact, rotten and guilty* ▹ *adv* **7** *informal* extremely; very much: *men fancy her rotten* [Old Norse *rotinn*]
rotter *n chiefly Brit old-fashioned slang* a despicable person
Rottweiler (rot-vile-er) *n* a large sturdy dog with a smooth black-and-tan coat and a docked tail [*Rottweil*, German city where it was first bred]
rotund (roe-**tund**) *adj* **1** round and plump **2** (of speech) pompous or grand [Latin *rotundus*] **rotundity** *n* **rotundly** *adv*
rotunda *n* a circular building or room, esp. with a dome [Italian *rotonda*]
rouble *or* **ruble** (roo-bl) *n* the standard monetary unit of Russia, Belarus and Transnistria [Russian *rubl*]
roué (roo-ay) *n* a man who leads a sensual and immoral life [French]
rouge *n* **1** a red cosmetic for adding colour to the cheeks ▹ *vb* **rouging, rouged 2** to apply rouge to [French: red]
rough *adj* **1** not smooth; uneven or irregular **2** not using enough care or gentleness **3** difficult or unpleasant: *tomorrow will be a rough day* **4** approximate: *a rough guess* **5** violent or stormy **6** troubled by violence or crime: *he lived in a rough area* **7** incomplete or basic: *a rough draft* **8** lacking refinement: *a rough shelter* **9** (of ground) covered with scrub or rubble **10** harsh or grating to the ear **11** harsh or sharp: *the rough interrogation of my father* **12** unfair: *rough luck* **13** *informal* ill: *if you're feeling rough, you won't be hungry* **14** shaggy or hairy: *the rough wool of her sweater* **15** (of work, etc.) requiring physical rather than mental effort: *wear gloves for any rough work* ▹ *vb* **16** to make rough **17 rough it** *informal* to live without the usual comforts of life ▹ *n* **18** rough ground **19** a sketch or preliminary piece of artwork **20** *informal* a

violent person **21 in rough** in an unfinished or crude state **22 the rough** *golf* the part of the course beside the fairways where the grass is untrimmed **23** the unpleasant side of something: *you have to take the rough with the smooth* ▷ *adv* **24** roughly **25 sleep rough** to spend the night in the open without shelter ▷ See also **rough out, rough up** [Old English *rūh*] **roughly** *adv*

roughage *n* the coarse indigestible constituents of food, which help digestion

rough-and-ready *adj* **1** hastily prepared but adequate for the purpose **2** (of a person) without formality or refinement

rough-and-tumble *n* **1** a playful fight **2** a disorderly situation

roughcast *n* **1** a mixture of plaster and small stones for outside walls ▷ *vb* **-casting, -cast 2** to put roughcast on (a wall)

rough diamond *n* **1** an unpolished diamond **2** a kind or trustworthy person whose manners are not good

roughen *vb* to make or become rough

rough-hewn *adj* roughly shaped or cut without being properly finished

roughhouse *n slang* rough or noisy behaviour

roughneck *n slang* **1** a violent person **2** a worker on an oil rig

rough out *vb* to prepare (a sketch or report) in preliminary form: *he offered to rough out some designs for the sets*

roughshod *adv* **ride roughshod over** to act with complete disregard for

rough up *vb informal* to beat up

roulette *n* a gambling game in which a ball is dropped onto a revolving wheel with numbered coloured slots [French]

round *adj* **1** having a flat circular shape, like a hoop **2** having the shape of a ball **3** curved; not angular **4** involving or using circular motion **5** complete **6** *maths* **A** forming or expressed by a whole number, with no fraction **B** expressed to the nearest ten, hundred, or thousand: *in round figures* ▷ *adv* **7** on all or most sides **8** on or outside the circumference or perimeter: *ponds which are steeply sided all round* **9** in rotation or revolution: *she swung round on me* **10** by a circuitous route: *the road to the farm goes round by the pond* **11** to all members of a group: *handing chocolates round* **12** to a specific place: *the boys invited him round* **13 all year round** throughout the year ▷ *prep* **14** surrounding or encircling: *wrap your sash round the wound* **15** on all or most sides of: *the man turned in a circle, looking all round him* **16** on or outside the circumference or perimeter of **17** from place to place in: *a trip round the island in an ancient bus* **18** reached by making a partial circuit about: *just round the corner* **19** revolving about: *if you have two bodies in orbit, they orbit round their common centre of gravity* ▷ *vb* **20** to move round: *as he rounded the last corner, he raised a fist* ▷ *n* **21** a round shape or object **22** a session: *a round of talks* **23** a series: *the petty round of domestic matters* **24** a series of calls: *a paper round* **25 the daily round** the usual activities of a person's day **26** a playing of all the holes on a golf course **27** a stage of a competition: *the first round of the Portuguese Open* **28** one of a number of periods in a boxing or wrestling match **29** a single turn of play by each player in a card game **30** a number of drinks bought at one time for a group of people **31** a bullet or shell for a gun **32** a single discharge by a gun **33** *music* a part song in which the voices follow each other at equal intervals **34** circular movement **35 A** a single slice of bread **B** a serving of sandwiches made from two complete slices of bread **36** a general outburst: *a round of applause* **37 in the round A** in full detail **B** *theatre* with the audience all round the stage **38 go the rounds** (of information or infection) to be passed around from person to person ▷ See also **round down, round off** *etc.* [Old French *ront*]

USAGE See at **around.**

roundabout *n Brit* **1** a road junction in which traffic moves in one direction around a central island **2** a revolving circular platform, often with seats, on which people ride for amusement ▷ *adj* **3** not straightforward: *the roundabout sea route; she thought of asking about it in a roundabout way* ▷ *adv, prep* **round about 4** approximately: *round about 1900*

round dance *n* **1** a dance in which the dancers form a circle **2** a ballroom dance, such as the waltz, in which couples revolve

round down *vb* to lower (a number) to the nearest whole number or ten, hundred, or thousand below it

roundel *n* **1** a circular identifying mark on military aircraft **2** a small circular object [Old French *rondel* little circle]

roundelay *n* a song in which a line or phrase is repeated as a refrain [Old French *rondelet*]

rounders *n Brit & NZ* a bat and ball game in which players run between posts after hitting the ball

Roundhead *n English history* a supporter of Parliament against Charles I during the Civil War [referring to their short-cut hair]

roundhouse *n US & Canad* a circular building in which railway locomotives are serviced

roundly *adv* bluntly or thoroughly: *the Church roundly criticized the bill*

round off *vb* to complete agreeably or successfully: *our afternoon was rounded off with coffee and biscuits*

round on *vb* to attack or reply to (someone) with sudden irritation or anger

round robin *n* **1** a petition with the signatures in a circle to disguise the order of signing **2** a tournament in which each player plays against every other player

round-shouldered *adj* denoting poor posture with drooping shoulders and a slight forward bending of the back

round table *n* a meeting of people on equal terms for discussion

Round Table *n* **1** (in Arthurian legend) the table of King Arthur, shaped so that his knights could sit around as equals **2** one of an organization of clubs of young business and professional men who meet in order to further charitable work

round-the-clock *adj* throughout the day and night

round trip *n* a journey to a place and back again

round up *vb* **1** to gather together: *the police had rounded up a circle of drug users* **2** to raise (a number) to the nearest whole number or ten, hundred, or thousand above it ▷ *n* **roundup 3** a summary or discussion of news and information **4** the act of gathering together livestock or people

roundworm *n* a worm that is a common intestinal parasite of man

rouse[1] *vb* **rousing, roused 1** to wake up **2** to provoke or excite: *his temper was roused and he had a gun* **3 rouse oneself** to become energetic [origin unknown]

rouse[2] (rhymes with **mouse**) *vb* (foll. by *on*) *Austral* to scold or rebuke

rouseabout *n Austral & NZ* a labourer in a shearing shed

rousing *adj* lively or vigorous: *a rousing speech*

roustabout *n* **1** an unskilled labourer on an oil rig **2** *Austral & NZ* another word for **rouseabout**

rout[1] *n* **1** an overwhelming defeat **2** a disorderly retreat **3** a noisy rabble ▷ *vb* **4** to defeat and put to flight [Anglo-Norman *rute*]

rout[2] *vb* **1** to find by searching **2** to drive out: *the dissidents had been routed out* **3** to dig (something) up [variant of ROOT[2]]

route *n* **1** the choice of roads taken to get to a place **2** a fixed path followed by buses, trains, etc. between two places **3** a chosen way or method: *the route to prosperity* ▷ *vb* **routeing, routed 4** to send by a particular route [Old French *rute*]

> **USAGE** When forming the present participle or verbal noun from the verb *to route* it is preferable to retain the *e* in order to distinguish the word from *routing*, the present participle or verbal noun from *rout*[1], to defeat or *rout*[2], to dig, rummage: *the routeing of buses from the city centre to the suburbs*. The spelling *routing* in this sense is, however, sometimes encountered, esp. in American English.

routemarch *n military* a long training march

router *n computers* a device that allows data to be moved efficiently between two points on a network

routine *n* **1** a usual or regular method of procedure **2** the boring repetition of tasks: *mindless routine* **3** a set sequence of dance steps **4** *computers* a program or part of a program performing a specific function: *an input routine* ▷ *adj* **5** relating to or characteristic of routine [Old French *route* a customary way]

roux (roo) *n* a cooked mixture of fat and flour used as a basis for sauces [French: brownish]

rove *vb* **roving, roved 1** to wander about (a place) **2** (of the eyes) to look around [probably from Old Norse] **rover** *n*

row[1] (rhymes with **know**) *n* **1** an arrangement of people or things in a line: *a row of shops* **2** a line of seats in a cinema or theatre **3** *Brit* a street lined with identical houses **4** *maths* a horizontal line of numbers **5 in a row** in succession: *five championships in a row* [Old English *rāw, rǣw*]

row[2] (rhymes with **know**) *vb* **1** to propel (a boat) by using oars **2** to carry (people or goods) in a rowing boat **3** to take part in the racing of rowing boats as a sport ▷ *n* **4** an act or spell of rowing **5** an excursion in a rowing boat [Old English *rōwan*] **rowing** *n*

row[3] (rhymes with **cow**) *informal* ▷ *n* **1** a noisy quarrel **2** a controversy or dispute: *the row over Europe* **3** a noisy disturbance: *go to the insurance offices and kick up a row about your money* **4** a reprimand ▷ *vb* **5** to quarrel noisily [origin unknown]

rowan *n* a European tree with white flowers and red berries; mountain ash [Scandinavian]

rowdy *adj* **-dier, -diest 1** rough, noisy, or disorderly ▷ *n, pl* **-dies 2** a person like this [origin unknown] **rowdily** *adv*

rowel (rhymes with **towel**) *n* a small spiked wheel at the end of a spur [Old French *roel* a little wheel]

rowing boat *n* a small pleasure boat propelled by oars. Usual US and Canad word: **rowboat**

rowlock (rol-luk) *n* a swivelling device attached to the top of the side of a boat that holds an oar in place

royal *adj* **1** of or relating to a king or queen or a member of his or her family: *the royal yacht* **2 Royal** supported by or in the service of royalty: *the Royal Society of Medicine* **3** very grand: *royal treatment* ▷ *n* **4** *informal* a king or queen or a member of his or her family [Old French *roial*] **royally** *adv*

Royal Air Force *n* the air force of the United Kingdom

royal-blue *adj* deep blue

royalist *n* **1** a supporter of a monarch or monarchy ▷ *adj* **2** of or relating to royalists **royalism** *n*

royal jelly *n* a substance secreted by worker bees and fed to all larvae when very young and to larvae destined to become queens throughout their growth

Royal Marines *pl n Brit* a corps of soldiers specially trained in amphibious warfare

Royal Navy *n* the navy of the United Kingdom

royalty *n, pl* **-ties 1** royal people **2** the rank or power of a king or queen **3** a percentage of the revenue from the sale of a book, performance of a work, use of a patented invention or of land, paid to the author, inventor, or owner

royal warrant *n* an authorization to a tradesman to supply goods to a royal household

RPI (in Britain) retail price index: a measure of the changes in the average level of retail prices of selected goods

rpm revolutions per minute

RR 1 Right Reverend **2** *US & Canad* rural route

RSA 1 Republic of South Africa **2** (in New Zealand) Returned Services Association **3** Royal Scottish Academy **4** Royal Society of Arts

RSI repetitive strain injury: pain in the arm caused by repeated awkward movements, such as in typing

RSM (in Britain) regimental sergeant major

RSPCA (in Britain) Royal Society for the Prevention of Cruelty to Animals

RSS Rich Site Summary *or* Really Simple Syndication: a way of allowing web users to receive updated information from selected websites on their browser

RSVP please reply [French *répondez s'il vous plaît*]

RTA *Brit* road traffic accident

r

Rt Hon. Right Honourable: a title of respect for a Privy Councillor, certain peers, and the Lord Mayor or Lord Provost of certain cities

Ru *chem* ruthenium

RU486 *n* the technical name for **abortion pill**

rub *vb* **rubbing, rubbed 1** to apply pressure and friction to (something) with a circular or backwards-and-forwards movement **2** to move (something) with pressure along or against (a surface) **3** to clean, polish, or dry by rubbing **4** to spread with pressure, esp. so that it can be absorbed: *rub beeswax into all polishable surfaces* **5** to chafe or fray through rubbing **6** to mix (fat) into flour with the fingertips, as in making pastry **7 rub it in** to emphasize an unpleasant fact **8 rub up the wrong way** to annoy ▷ *n* **9** the act of rubbing **10 the rub** the obstacle or difficulty: *there's the rub* ▷ See also **rub along, rub down** *etc.* [origin unknown]

rub along *vb* **1** to have a friendly relationship **2** to continue in spite of difficulties

rubato *music* ▷ *n, pl* **-tos 1** flexibility of tempo in performance: *his playing brought much beautifully felt but never sentimental rubato to the music* ▷ *adj, adv* **2** to be played with a flexible tempo [Italian, literally: robbed]

rubber¹ *n* **1** an elastic material obtained from the latex of certain plants, such as the rubber tree **2** a similar substance produced synthetically **3** a piece of rubber used for erasing something written **4** *US slang* a condom **5 rubbers** *US* rubber-coated waterproof overshoes ▷ *adj* **6** made of or producing rubber [the tree was so named because its product was used for rubbing out writing] **rubbery** *adj*

rubber² *n* **1** *bridge & whist* a match of three games **2** a series of matches or games in various sports [origin unknown]

rubber band *n* a continuous loop of thin rubber, used to hold papers together

rubberize *or* **-ise** *vb* **-izing, -ized** *or* **-ising, -ised** to coat or treat with rubber

rubberneck *slang* ▷ *vb* **1** to stare in a naive or foolish manner ▷ *n* **2** a person who stares inquisitively **3** a sightseer or tourist

rubber plant *n* **1** a large house plant with glossy leathery leaves **2** same as **rubber tree**

rubber stamp *n* **1** a device used for imprinting dates or signatures on forms or invoices **2** automatic authorization of something **3** a person or body that gives official approval to decisions taken elsewhere but has no real power ▷ *vb* **rubber-stamp 4** *informal* to approve automatically

rubber tree *n* a tropical tree cultivated for its latex, which is the major source of commercial rubber

rubbing *n* an impression taken of an engraved or raised design by laying paper over it and rubbing with wax or charcoal

rubbish *n* **1** discarded or waste matter **2** anything worthless or of poor quality: *the rubbish on television* **3** foolish words or speech ▷ *vb* **4** *informal* to criticize [origin unknown] **rubbishy** *adj*

rubble *n* **1** debris from ruined buildings **2** pieces of broken stones or bricks [origin unknown]

rub down *vb* **1** to prepare (a surface) for painting by rubbing it with sandpaper **2** to dry or clean (an animal or person) vigorously, esp. after exercise

rubella (roo-**bell**-a) *n* a mild contagious viral disease characterized by cough, sore throat, and skin rash. Also called: **German measles** [Latin *rubellus* reddish]

Rubicon (**roo**-bik-on) *n* **cross the Rubicon** to commit oneself to a course of action which cannot be altered [a stream in N Italy: by leading his army across it, Julius Caesar caused civil war in Rome in 49 BC]

rubicund (**roo**-bik-kund) *adj old-fashioned* of a reddish colour [Latin *rubicundus*]

rubidium (roo-**bid**-ee-um) *n chem* a soft highly reactive radioactive metallic element used in electronic valves, photocells, and special glass. Symbol: **Rb** [Latin *rubidus* red]

ruble *n* same as **rouble**

rub off *vb* **1** to remove or be removed by rubbing: *rub the skins off the hazelnuts* **2** to have an effect through close association: *glamour can rub off on you by association*

rub out *vb* **1** to remove or be removed with a rubber **2** *US slang* to murder

rubric (**roo**-brik) *n* **1** a set of rules of conduct or procedure, esp. one for the conduct of Christian church services **2** a title or heading in a book [Latin *ruber* red]

ruby *n, pl* **-bies 1** a deep red transparent precious gemstone ▷ *adj* **2** deep red **3** denoting a fortieth anniversary: *a ruby wedding* [Latin *ruber* red]

RUC Royal Ulster Constabulary: a former name for the Police Service of Northern Ireland

ruche (**roosh**) *n* a strip of pleated or frilled lace or ribbon used to decorate clothes [French, literally: beehive]

ruck¹ *n* **1 the ruck** ordinary people, often in a crowd **2** *rugby* a loose scrum that forms around the ball when it is on the ground [probably from Old Norse]

ruck² *n* **1** a wrinkle or crease ▷ *vb* **2** to wrinkle or crease: *the toe of his shoe had rucked up one corner of the pale rug* [Scandinavian]

rucksack *n Brit, Austral & S African* a large bag, with two straps, carried on the back [from German]

ruction *n informal* **1** an uproar **2 ructions** an unpleasant row [origin unknown]

rudder *n* **1** *naut* a vertical hinged piece that projects into the water at the stern, used to steer a boat **2** a vertical control surface attached to the rear of the fin used to steer an aircraft [Old English *rōther*] **rudderless** *adj*

ruddy *adj* **-dier, -diest 1** (of the complexion) having a healthy reddish colour **2** red or pink: *a ruddy glow* ▷ *adv, adj* **3** *informal* bloody: *too ruddy slow; I just went through the ruddy ceiling* [Old English *rudig*]

rude *adj* **1** insulting or impolite **2** vulgar or obscene: *rude words* **3** unexpected and unpleasant: *we received a rude awakening* **4** roughly or crudely made: *the rude hovels* **5** robust or sturdy: *the very picture of rude health* **6** lacking refinement [Latin *rudis*] **rudely** *adv* **rudeness** *n*

rudiment *n* **1 rudiments A** the simplest and most basic stages of a subject: *the rudiments of* *painting* **B** a partially developed version of something: *the rudiments of a democratic society* **2** *biol* an organ or part that is incompletely developed or no longer functions [Latin *rudimentum*] **rudimentary** *adj*

rue¹ *vb* **ruing, rued** *literary* to feel regret for [Old English *hrēowan*]

rue² *n* an aromatic shrub with bitter evergreen leaves formerly used in medicine [Greek *rhutē*]

rueful *adj* feeling or expressing sorrow or regret: *a rueful smile* **ruefully** *adv*

ruff¹ *n* **1** a circular pleated or fluted cloth collar **2** a natural growth of long or coloured hair or feathers around the necks of certain animals or birds **3** a bird of the sandpiper family [from *ruffle*]

ruff² *n, vb cards* same as **trump¹** (senses 1, 2) [Old French *roffle*]

ruffian *n* a violent lawless person [Old French *rufien*]

ruffle *vb* **-fling, -fled 1** to disturb the smoothness of: *the wind was ruffling Dad's hair* **2** to annoy or irritate **3** (of a bird) to erect its feathers in anger or display **4** to flick cards or pages rapidly ▷ *n* **5** a strip of pleated material used as a trim [Germanic]

rufous *adj* (of birds or animals) reddish-brown [Latin *rufus*]

rug *n* **1** a small carpet **2** a thick woollen blanket **3** *slang* a wig **4 pull the rug out from under** to betray or leave defenceless [Scandinavian]

rugby *or* **rugby football** *n* a form of football played with an oval ball in which the handling and carrying of the ball is permitted [after the public school at *Rugby*, where it was first played]

rugby league *n* a form of rugby played between teams of 13 players

rugby union *n* a form of rugby played between teams of 15 players

rugged (rug-gid) *adj* **1** rocky or steep: *the rugged mountains of Sicily's interior* **2** with an uneven or jagged surface **3** (of the face) strong-featured **4** rough, sturdy, or determined in character **5** (of equipment or machines) designed to withstand rough treatment or use in rough conditions [probably from Old Norse]

rugger *n chiefly Brit informal* rugby

rug rat *n informal* a young child not yet walking

ruin *vb* **1** to destroy or spoil completely: *the suit was ruined* **2** to cause (someone) to lose money: *the first war ruined him* ▷ *n* **3** the state of being destroyed or decayed **4** loss of wealth or position **5** a destroyed or decayed building or town **6** something that is severely damaged: *my heart was an aching ruin* [Latin *ruina* a falling down]

ruination *n* **1** the act of ruining or the state of being ruined **2** something that causes ruin

ruinous *adj* **1** causing ruin or destruction **2** more expensive than can reasonably be afforded: *ruinous rates of exchange* **ruinously** *adv*

rule *n* **1** a statement of what is allowed, for example in a game or procedure **2** a customary form or procedure: *he has his own rule: be firm, be clear, but never be rude* **3 the rule** the common order of things: *humanitarian gestures were more the exception than the rule* **4** the exercise of governmental authority or control: *under the rule of the dictator* **5** the period of time in which a monarch or government has power: *four decades of Communist rule* **6** a device with a straight edge for guiding or measuring: *a slide rule* **7** *printing* a long thin line or dash **8** *Christianity* a systematic body of laws and customs followed by members of a religious order **9** *law* an order by a court or judge **10 as a rule** usually ▷ *vb* **ruling, ruled 11** to govern (people or a political unit) **12** to be pre-eminent or superior **13** to be customary or prevalent: *chaos ruled as the scene turned into one of total confusion* **14** to decide authoritatively: *the judges ruled that men could be prosecuted for rape offences against their wives* **15** to mark with straight parallel lines or one straight line **16** to restrain or control [Old French *riule*]

rule of thumb *n* a rough and practical approach, based on experience, rather than theory

rule out *vb* **1** to dismiss from consideration **2** to make impossible

ruler *n* **1** a person who rules or commands **2** a strip of wood, metal, or plastic, with straight edges, used for measuring and drawing straight lines

ruling *adj* **1** controlling or exercising authority **2** predominant ▷ *n* **3** a decision of someone in authority

rum¹ *n* an alcoholic drink made from sugar cane [origin unknown]

rum² *adj* **rummer, rummest** *Brit slang* strange or unusual [origin unknown]

Rumanian *adj, n* same as **Romanian**

rumba *n* **1** a rhythmic and syncopated dance of Cuban origin **2** music for this dance [Spanish]

rumble *vb* **-bling, -bled 1** to make or cause to make a deep echoing sound: *thunder rumbled overhead* **2** to move with such a sound: *a slow freight train rumbled past* **3** *Brit slang* to find out about (someone or something): *his real identity was rumbled* ▷ *n* **4** a deep resonant sound **5** *slang* a gang fight [probably from Middle Dutch *rummelen*] **rumbling** *adj, n*

rumbustious *adj* boisterous or unruly [probably variant of *robustious*]

ruminant *n* **1** a mammal that chews the cud, such as cattle, sheep, deer, goats, and camels ▷ *adj* **2** of ruminants **3** meditating or contemplating in a slow quiet way

ruminate *vb* **-nating, -nated 1** (of ruminants) to chew (the cud) **2** to meditate or ponder [Latin *ruminare* to chew the cud] **rumination** *n* **ruminative** *adj*

rummage *vb* **-maging, -maged 1** to search untidily ▷ *n* **2** an untidy search through a collection of things [Old French *arrumage* to stow cargo]

rummage sale *n US & Canad* a jumble sale

rummy *n* a card game based on collecting sets and sequences [origin unknown]

rumour *or US* **rumor** *n* **1** information, often a mixture of truth and untruth, told by one person to another **2** gossip or common talk ▷ *vb* **3 be rumoured** to be circulated as a rumour: *he is rumoured to have at least 53 yachts* [Latin *rumor*]

rump *n* **1** a person's buttocks **2** the rear part of an animal's or bird's body **3** Also called: **rump steak**

a cut of beef from the rump **4** a small core of members within a group who remain loyal to it: *the rump of the once-influential communist party* [probably from Old Norse]

rumple *vb* **-pling, -pled** to make or become crumpled or dishevelled [Middle Dutch *rompelen*]

rumpus *n, pl* **-puses** a noisy or confused commotion [origin unknown]

rumpy-pumpy *n informal* sexual intercourse

run *vb* **running, ran, run 1** to move on foot at a rapid pace **2** to pass over (a distance or route) in running: *being a man isn't about running the fastest mile* **3** to take part in (a race): *I ran a decent race* **4** to carry out as if by running: *he is running errands for his big brother* **5** to flee **6** to travel somewhere in a vehicle **7** to give a lift to (someone) in a vehicle: *one wet day I ran her down to the service* **8** to drive or maintain and operate (a vehicle) **9** to travel regularly between places on a route: *trains running through the night* **10** to move or pass quickly: *he ran his hand across his forehead* **11** to function or cause to function: *run the video tape backwards* **12** to manage: *she ran a small hotel* **13** to continue in a particular direction or for a particular time or distance: *a road running alongside the Nile; a performing arts festival running in the city for six weeks* **14** *law* to have legal force or effect: *the lease runs for two more years* **15** to be subjected to or affected by: *she ran a high risk of losing her hair* **16** to tend or incline: *he was of medium height and running to fat* **17** to recur persistently or be inherent: *the capacity for infidelity ran in the genes* **18** to flow or cause (liquids) to flow: *sweat ran down her face* **19** to dissolve and spread: *the soles of the shoes peeled off and the colours ran* **20** (of stitches) to unravel **21** to spread or circulate: *rumours ran around quickly* **22** to publish or be published in a newspaper or magazine: *our local newspaper ran a story on the appeal* **23** *chiefly US & Canad* to stand as a candidate for political or other office: *due to announce she is running for president* **24** to get past or through: *the oil tanker was hit as it tried to run the blockade* **25** to smuggle (goods, esp. arms) **26** (of fish) to migrate upstream from the sea, esp. in order to spawn **27** *cricket* to score (a run or number of runs) by hitting the ball and running between the wickets ▷ *n* **28** the act or an instance of running: *he broke into a run* **29** a distance covered by running or a period of running: *it's a short run of about 20 kilometres* **30** a trip in a vehicle, esp. for pleasure: *our only treat is a run in the car to Dartmoor* **31** free and unrestricted access: *he had the run of the house* **32** **A** a period of time during which a machine or computer operates **B** the amount of work performed in such a period **33** a continuous or sustained period: *a run of seven defeats* **34** a continuous sequence of performances: *the play had a long run* **35** *cards* a sequence of winning cards in one suit: *a run of spades* **36** type, class, or category: *he had nothing in common with the usual run of terrorists* **37** a continuous and urgent demand: *a run on the pound* **38** a series of unravelled stitches, esp. in tights **39** a steeply inclined course, esp. a snow-covered one used for skiing **40** an enclosure for domestic fowls or other animals: *the chicken run* **41** (esp. in Australia and New Zealand) a tract of land for grazing livestock **42** the migration of fish upstream in order to spawn **43** *music* a rapid scalelike passage of notes **44** *cricket* a score of one, normally achieved by both batsmen running from one end of the wicket to the other after one of them has hit the ball **45** *baseball* an instance of a batter touching all four bases safely, thereby scoring **46** **a run for one's money** *informal* **A** a close competition **B** pleasure or success from an activity **47** **in the long run** as an eventual outcome **48** **on the run** escaping from arrest **49** **the runs** *slang* diarrhoea ▷ See also **runabout, run across** *etc.* [Old English *runnen*]

runabout *n* **1** a small car used for short journeys ▷ *vb* **run about 2** to move busily from place to place

run across *vb* to meet unexpectedly by chance

run along *vb* to go away

run away *vb* **1** to go away **2** to escape **3** (of a horse) to gallop away uncontrollably: *the horse ran away with him* **4** **run away with A** to abscond or elope with: *I ran away with David* **B** to escape from the control of: *he let his imagination run away with him* **C** to win easily or be certain of victory in (a competition): *the Spaniards at one stage seemed to be running away with the match* ▷ *n* **runaway 5** a person or animal that runs away ▷ *adj* **runaway 6** no longer under control: *a runaway train* **7** (of a race or victory) easily won

run down *vb* **1** to be rude about: *he is busy running us down and insulting other Europeans* **2** to reduce in number or size: *it should be possible to run down the existing hospitals almost entirely* **3** (of a device such as a clock or battery) to lose power gradually and cease to function **4** to hit and knock to the ground with a moving vehicle **5** to pursue and find or capture: *while I was there, Moscow ran me down, convinced I was ready to defect* ▷ *adj* **rundown 6** tired or ill **7** shabby or dilapidated ▷ *n* **rundown 8** a reduction in number or size **9** a brief review or summary

rune *n* **1** any of the characters of the earliest Germanic alphabet **2** an obscure piece of writing using mysterious symbols [Old Norse *rūn* secret] **runic** *adj*

rung[1] *n* **1** one of the bars forming the steps of a ladder **2** a crosspiece between the legs of a chair [Old English *hrung*]

rung[2] *vb* the past participle of **ring**[1]

run-holder *n Austral & NZ* the owner or manager of a sheep or cattle station

run in *vb* **1** to run (an engine) gently, usually when it is new **2** *informal* to arrest ▷ *n* **run-in 3** *informal* an argument or quarrel **4** an approach to the end of an event: *the run-in for the championship*

run into *vb* **1** to be beset by: *the mission has run into difficulty* **2** to meet unexpectedly **3** to extend to: *businessmen denied losses running into the thousands* **4** to collide with

runnel *n literary* a small stream [Old English *rynele*]

runner *n* **1** a competitor in a race **2** a messenger for a firm **3** a person involved in smuggling **4** **A** either of the strips of metal or wood on which a sledge runs **B** the blade of an ice skate **5** *botany* a slender horizontal stem of a plant, such as the strawberry, that grows along the surface of the soil and produces new roots and shoots **6** a long strip of cloth used to decorate a table or as a rug **7** a roller or guide for a sliding component **8 do a runner** *slang* to run away to escape trouble or to avoid paying for something

runner bean *n* the edible pod and seeds of a type of climbing bean plant

runner-up *n, pl* **runners-up** a person who comes second in a competition

running *adj* **1** maintained continuously: *a running battle* **2** without interruption: *for the third day running* **3** **A** flowing: *rinse them under cold running water* **B** supplied through a tap: *there is no electricity, no running water, and no telephone* **4** operating: *running costs* **5** discharging pus: *a running sore* **6** accomplished at a run: *a running jump* **7** moving or slipping easily, as a rope or a knot ▷ *n* **8** the act of moving or flowing quickly **9** management or organization: *the running of the farm* **10** the operation or maintenance of a machine **11 in** *or* **out of the running** having *or* not having a good chance in a competition **12 make the running** to set the pace in a competition or race

running board *n* a foot board along the side of a vehicle, typically a feature of early models of car

running head *n* *printing* a heading printed at the top of every page of a book

running mate *n* **1** *US* a candidate for the lesser of two linked positions, esp. a candidate for the vice-presidency **2** a horse that pairs another in a team

running repairs *pl n* repairs that are done without greatly disrupting operations

runny *adj* **-nier, -niest 1** tending to flow: *a runny egg* **2** producing moisture: *a runny nose*

run off *vb* **1** to leave quickly **2 run off with A** to run away with in order to marry or live with **B** to steal **3** to produce (copies of a document) on a machine **4** to drain (liquid) or (of liquid) to be drained ▷ *n* **run-off 5** an extra race or contest to decide the winner after a tie **6** *NZ* grazing land for cattle

run-of-the-mill *adj* ordinary or average

run on *vb* to continue without interruption

run out *vb* **1** to use up or (of a supply) to be used up: *we soon ran out of gas* **2** to become invalid: *my passport has run out* **3 run out on** *informal* to desert or abandon **4** *cricket* to dismiss (a running batsman) by breaking the wicket with the ball while he or she is running between the wickets ▷ *n* **run-out 5** *cricket* dismissal of a batsman by running him or her out

run over *vb* **1** to knock down (a person) with a moving vehicle **2** to overflow **3** to examine hastily

runt *n* **1** the smallest and weakest young animal in a litter **2** an undersized or inferior person [origin unknown]

run through *vb* **1** to practise or rehearse **2** to pierce with a sword or other weapon ▷ *n* **run-through 3** a practice or rehearsal

run to *vb* **1** to reach an amount or size: *the testimony ran to a million words* **2** to be or have enough money for: *we do not run to these luxuries, I am afraid*

run up *vb* **1** to amass: *running up massive debts* **2** to make by sewing together quickly **3 run up against** to experience (difficulties) ▷ *n* **run-up 4** the time just before an event: *the run-up to the elections*

runway *n* a hard level roadway where aircraft take off and land

rupee *n* the standard monetary unit of a number of countries including India and Pakistan [Hindi *rupaīyā*]

rupture *n* **1** the act of breaking or the state of being broken **2** a breach of peaceful or friendly relations **3** *pathol* a hernia ▷ *vb* **-turing, -tured 4** to break or burst **5** to cause a breach in relations or friendship **6** to affect or be affected with a hernia [Latin *rumpere* to burst forth]

rural *adj* in or of the countryside [Latin *ruralis*]

rural dean *n chiefly Brit* a member of the clergy with authority over a group of parishes

rural route *n US & Canad* a mail service or route in a rural area

ruse (**rooz**) *n* an action or plan intended to mislead someone [Old French]

rush[1] *vb* **1** to move or do very quickly **2** to force (someone) to act hastily **3** to make a sudden attack upon (a person or place): *scores of pubescent girls rushed the stage* **4** to proceed or approach in a reckless manner **5** to come or flow quickly or suddenly: *the water rushed in, and the next instant the boat was swamped* ▷ *n* **6** a sudden quick or violent movement **7** a sudden demand or need **8** a sudden surge towards someone or something: *the gold rush* **9** a sudden surge of sensation **10** a sudden flow of air or liquid **11 rushes** (in film-making) the initial prints of a scene before editing ▷ *adj* **12** done with speed or urgency: *a rush job* [Old French *ruser* to put to flight]

rush[2] *n* a plant which grows in wet places and has a slender pithy stem [Old English *risce, rysce*] **rushy** *adj*

rush hour *n* a period at the beginning and end of the working day when large numbers of people are travelling to or from work

rusk *n* a hard brown crisp biscuit, often used for feeding babies [Spanish or Portuguese *rosca* screw, bread shaped in a twist]

russet *adj* **1** *literary* reddish-brown: *a disarray of russet curls* ▷ *n* **2** an apple with a rough reddish-brown skin [Latin *russus*]

Russian *adj* **1** of Russia ▷ *n* **2** a person from Russia **3** the official language of Russia and, formerly, of the Soviet Union

Russian doll *n* any of a set of hollow wooden figures, each of which splits in half to contain the next smallest figure, down to the smallest

Russian roulette *n* an act of bravado in which a person spins the cylinder of a revolver loaded with only one cartridge and presses the trigger with the barrel against his or her own head

rust *n* **1** a reddish-brown oxide coating formed on iron or steel by the action of oxygen and moisture **2** a fungal disease of plants which produces a reddish-brown discoloration ▷ *adj* **3** reddish-brown ▷ *vb* **4** to become coated with a layer of rust **5** to deteriorate through lack of use: *my brain had rusted up* [Old English *rūst*]

rust belt *n* an area where heavy industry is in decline, esp. in the Midwest of the United States

rustic *adj* **1** of or resembling country people **2** of or living in the country **3** crude, awkward, or uncouth **4** made of untrimmed branches: *rustic furniture* ▷ *n* **5** a person from the country [Latin *rusticus*] **rusticity** *n*

rusticate *vb* **-cating, -cated 1** *Brit* to send (a student) down from university for a specified time as a punishment **2** to retire to the country **3** to make or become rustic [Latin *rus* the country]

rustle¹ *vb* **-tling, -tled 1** to make a low crisp whispering sound: *the leaves rustled in the breeze* ▷ *n* **2** this sound [Old English *hrūxlian*]

rustle² *vb* **-tling, -tled** *chiefly US & Canad* to steal (livestock) [probably from RUSTLE¹ (in the sense: to move with a quiet sound)] **rustler** *n*

rustle up *vb informal* to prepare or find at short notice: *Bob rustled up a meal*

rusty *adj* **rustier, rustiest 1** affected by rust: *a rusty old freighter* **2** reddish-brown **3** out of practice in a skill or subject: *your skills may be a little rusty, but your past experience will more than make up for that* **rustily** *adv* **rustiness** *n*

rut¹ *n* **1** a groove or furrow in a soft road, caused by wheels **2** dull settled habits or way of living: *his career was in a rut* [probably from French *route* road]

rut² *n* **1** a recurrent period of sexual excitement in certain male ruminants ▷ *vb* **rutting, rutted 2** (of male ruminants) to be in a period of sexual excitement [Old French *rut* noise, roar]

rutabaga *n* the US and Canadian term for **swede**

ruthenium *n chem* a rare hard brittle white metallic element. Symbol: **Ru** [Medieval Latin *Ruthenia* Russia, where it was discovered]

rutherfordium *n chem* an artificially produced radioactive element. Symbol: **Rf** [after E. *Rutherford*, physicist]

ruthless *adj* **1** feeling or showing no mercy **2** thorough and forceful, regardless of effect: *the ruthless pursuit of cost-effectiveness* [*ruth* pity] **ruthlessly** *adv* **ruthlessness** *n*

rutted *adj* (of a road) very uneven because of ruts

RV Revised Version (of the Bible)

RVS (in Britain) Royal Voluntary Service

rye *n* **1** a tall grasslike cereal grown for its light brown grain **2** the grain of this plant **3** Also called: **rye whiskey** whisky distilled from rye **4** *US* short for **rye bread** [Old English *ryge*]

rye bread *n* bread made entirely or partly from rye flour

rye-grass *n* any of several grasses grown for fodder

Ss

s second (of time)
S **1** South(ern) **2** *chem* sulphur **3** *physics* siemens
-'s *n suffix* **1** forming the possessive singular of nouns and some pronouns: *woman's*; *one's* **2** forming the possessive plural of nouns whose plurals do not end in *-s*: *children's* **3** forming the plural of numbers, letters, or symbols: *20's* **4** *informal* contraction of *is* or *has*: *it's over* **5** *informal* contraction of *us* with *let*: *let's go*
SA **1** Salvation Army **2** South Africa **3** South America **4** South Australia
SAA South African Airways
Sabbath *n* **1** Saturday, observed by Jews as the day of worship and rest **2** Sunday, observed by Christians as the day of worship and rest [Hebrew *shābath* to rest]
sabbatical *adj* **1** denoting a period of leave granted at intervals to university teachers for rest, study, or travel: *a sabbatical year* ▷ *n* **2** a sabbatical period [see SABBATH]
SABC South African Broadcasting Corporation
sable *n, pl* **-bles** *or* **-ble** **1** a marten of N Asia, N Europe, and America, with dark brown luxuriant fur **2** the highly valued fur of this animal, used to make coats and hats ▷ *adj* **3** dark brown-to-black [Slavic]
sable antelope *n* a large black African antelope with stout backward-curving horns
sabot (**sab**-oh) *n* a heavy wooden or wooden-soled shoe; clog [French]
sabotage *n* **1** the deliberate destruction or damage of equipment, for example by enemy agents or dissatisfied employees **2** deliberate obstruction of or damage to a cause or effort ▷ *vb* **-taging, -taged** **3** to destroy or disrupt by sabotage [French]
saboteur *n* a person who commits sabotage [French]
sabre *or US* **saber** *n* **1** a heavy single-edged cavalry sword with a curved blade **2** a light sword used in fencing, with a narrow V-shaped blade [German (dialect) *Sabel*]
sac *n* a pouch or pouchlike part in an animal or plant [Latin *saccus*]
saccharin *n* an artificial sweetener [Greek *sakkharon* sugar]
saccharine *adj* **1** excessively sweet or sentimental: *saccharine ballads* **2** like or containing sugar or saccharin
sacerdotal *adj formal* of priests or the priesthood [Latin *sacerdos* priest]
sachet *n* **1** a small sealed usually plastic envelope containing a small portion of a substance such as shampoo **2** a small soft bag of perfumed powder, placed in drawers to scent clothing [French]
sack¹ *n* **1** a large bag made of coarse cloth or thick paper and used for carrying or storing goods **2** the amount contained in a sack **3 the sack** *informal* dismissal from employment **4** *slang* bed **5 hit the sack** *slang* to go to bed ▷ *vb* **6** *informal* to dismiss from employment [Greek *sakkos*]
sacklike *adj*
sack² *n* **1** the plundering of a captured town or city by an army or mob ▷ *vb* **2** to plunder and partially destroy (a town or city) [French *mettre à sac* to put (loot) in a sack]
sackbut *n* a medieval form of trombone [French *saqueboute*]
sackcloth *n* **1** same as **sacking** **2** garments made of such cloth, worn formerly to indicate mourning **3 sackcloth and ashes** an exaggerated attempt to apologize or compensate for a mistake or wrongdoing
sacking *n* coarse cloth woven from flax, hemp, or jute, and used to make sacks
sacrament *n* **1** a symbolic religious ceremony in the Christian Church, such as baptism or communion **2** Holy Communion **3** something regarded as sacred [Latin *sacrare* to consecrate]
sacramental *adj*
sacred *adj* **1** exclusively devoted to a god or gods; holy **2** connected with religion or intended for religious use: *sacred music* **3** regarded as too important to be changed or interfered with: *sacred principles of free speech* **4 sacred to** dedicated to: *the site is sacred to Vishnu* [Latin *sacer* holy]
sacred cow *n informal* a person, custom, belief, or institution regarded as being beyond criticism [alluding to the Hindu belief that cattle are sacred]
sacrifice *n* **1** a surrender of something of value in order to gain something more desirable or prevent some evil **2** a ritual killing of a person or animal as an offering to a god **3** a symbolic offering of something to a god **4** the person or animal killed or offered ▷ *vb* **-ficing, -ficed** **5** to make a sacrifice (of) **6** *chess* to permit or force one's opponent to capture (a piece) as a tactical move [Latin *sacer* holy + *facere* to make]
sacrificial *adj*
sacrilege *n* **1** the misuse of or disrespect shown to something sacred **2** disrespect for a person who is widely admired or a belief that is widely accepted: *it is a sacrilege to offend democracy* [Latin *sacrilegus* temple robber] **sacrilegious** *adj*
sacristan *n* a person in charge of the contents of a church; sexton [Latin *sacer* holy]
sacristy *n, pl* **-ties** a room attached to a church or chapel where the sacred objects are kept
sacrosanct *adj* regarded as too important to be criticized or changed: *weekend rest days were considered sacrosanct by staff* [Latin *sacer* holy + *sanctus* hallowed] **sacrosanctity** *n*
sacrum (**say**-krum) *n, pl* **-cra** *anatomy* the large wedge-shaped bone in the lower part of the back [Latin *os sacrum* holy bone, because it was used in sacrifices]
sad *adj* **sadder, saddest** **1** feeling sorrow; unhappy **2** causing, suggesting, or expressing sorrow: *a sad story* **3** deplorably bad: *the garden was in a sad state* **4** regrettable: *it's rather sad he can't be*

with us **5** *Brit informal* ridiculously pathetic: *a sad, boring little wimp* ▷ *n* **6 pack a sad** *NZ slang* to strongly express sadness or displeasure [Old English *sæd* weary] **sadly** *adv* **sadness** *n*

sadden *vb* to make (someone) sad

saddle *n* **1** a seat for a rider, usually made of leather, placed on a horse's back and secured under its belly **2** a similar seat on a bicycle, motorcycle, or tractor **3** a cut of meat, esp. mutton, consisting of both loins **4 in the saddle** in a position of control ▷ *vb* **-dling, -dled 5** to put a saddle on (a horse): *we saddled up at dawn* **6 saddle with** to burden with (a responsibility): *he was also saddled with debt* [Old English *sadol, sadul*]

saddleback *n* **1** an animal with a marking resembling a saddle on its back **2** a hill with a concave outline at the top **saddle-backed** *adj*

saddlebag *n* a pouch or small bag attached to the saddle of a horse, bicycle, or motorcycle

saddle horse *n* a horse trained for riding only

saddler *n* a person who makes, deals in, or repairs saddles and other leather equipment for horses

saddlery *n, pl* **-dleries 1** saddles and harness for horses collectively **2** the work or place of work of a saddler

saddle soap *n* a soft soap used to preserve and clean leather

saddo *n Brit informal* a person perceived as socially inadequate

Sadducee (**sad**-yew-see) *n Judaism* a member of an ancient Jewish sect that denied the resurrection of the dead and accepted only the traditional written law

sadhu (**sah**-doo) *n* a Hindu wandering holy man [Sanskrit]

sadism (**say**-diz-zum) *n* the gaining of pleasure, esp. sexual pleasure, from infliction of suffering on another person [after the Marquis de *Sade*, soldier & writer] **sadist** *n* **sadistic** *adj* **sadistically** *adv*

sadomasochism *n* **1** the combination of sadistic and masochistic elements in one person, characterized by both submissive and aggressive periods in relationships with others **2** a sexual practice in which one partner adopts a masochistic role and the other a sadistic one **sadomasochist** *n* **sadomasochistic** *adj*

S

s.a.e. *Brit, Austral & NZ* stamped addressed envelope

safari *n, pl* **-ris** an overland expedition for hunting or observing animals, esp. in Africa [Swahili: journey]

safari park *n* an enclosed park in which wild animals are kept uncaged in the open and can be viewed by the public from cars or buses

safe *adj* **1** giving security or protection from harm: *a safe environment* **2** free from danger: *she doesn't feel safe* **3** taking or involving no risks: *a safe bet* **4** not dangerous: *the beef is safe to eat* **5 on the safe side** as a precaution ▷ *n* **6** a strong metal container with a secure lock, for storing money or valuables [Old French *salf*] **safely** *adv*

safe-conduct *n* **1** a document giving official permission to travel through a dangerous region, esp. in time of war **2** the protection given by such a document

safe-deposit *or* **safety-deposit** *n* a place or building with facilities for the safe storage of money and valuables

safeguard *vb* **1** to protect (someone or something) from being harmed or destroyed ▷ *n* **2** a person or thing that ensures protection against danger or harm: *safeguards to prevent air collisions*

safekeeping *n* protection from theft or damage: *I put my money in a bank for safekeeping*

safe sex *or* **safer sex** *n* nonpenetrative sex, or intercourse using a condom, intended to prevent the spread of sexually transmitted diseases such as HIV

safety *n, pl* **-ties 1** the quality or state of being free from danger **2** shelter: *they swam to safety*

safety belt *n* same as **seat belt**

safety catch *n* a mechanism on a gun that prevents it from being fired accidentally

safety curtain *n* a fireproof curtain that can be lowered to separate the auditorium from the stage in a theatre to prevent the spread of a fire

safety lamp *n* a miner's oil lamp designed to prevent it from igniting combustible gas

safety match *n* a match that will light only when struck against a specially prepared surface

safety net *n* **1** a large net under a trapeze or high wire to catch performers if they fall **2** something that can be relied on for help in the event of difficulties: *the social security safety net*

safety pin *n* a pin bent back on itself so that it forms a spring, with the point shielded by a guard when closed

safety razor *n* a razor with a guard over the blade or blades to protect the skin from deep cuts

safety valve *n* **1** a valve in a boiler or machine that allows fluid or gases to escape at excess pressure **2** an outlet that allows one to express strong feelings without harming or offending other people: *sport acted as a safety valve for his pent-up frustrations*

safflower *n* a thistle-like plant with orange-yellow flowers, which yields a dye and an oil used in paints, medicines, and cooking [Old French *saffleur*]

saffron *n* **1** a type of crocus with purple or white flowers with orange stigmas **2** the dried orange-coloured stigmas of this plant, used for colouring or flavouring ▷ *adj* **3** orange-yellow [Arabic *za'farān*]

sag *vb* **sagging, sagged 1** to sink in the middle, under weight or pressure: *the bed sagged nearly to the floor* **2** (of courage or spirits) to weaken or tire **3** (of clothes) to hang loosely or unevenly **4** to fall in value: *the stock market sagged* ▷ *n* **5** the act or state of sagging [from Old Norse] **saggy** *adj*

saga (**sah**-ga) *n* **1** a medieval Scandinavian legend telling the adventures of a hero or a family **2** *informal* a long story or series of events: *the long-running saga of the hostage issue* [Old Norse]

sagacious *adj formal* wise or sensible [Latin *sagax*] **sagaciously** *adv* **sagacity** *n*

sage[1] *n* **1** a person, esp. an old man, regarded as being very wise ▷ *adj* **2** very wise or knowledgeable, esp. as the result of age or experience [Latin *sapere* to be sensible]

sage² *n* **1** a Mediterranean plant with grey-green leaves which are used in cooking for flavouring **2** short for **sagebrush** [Latin *salvus* in good health (from its curative properties)]

sagebrush *n* an aromatic plant of W North America, with silver-green leaves and large clusters of small white flowers

Sagittarius *n astrol* the ninth sign of the zodiac; the Archer [Latin]

sago *n* an edible starch from the powdered pith of the sago palm tree, used for puddings and as a thickening agent [Malay *sāgū*]

sahib *n* an Indian term of address equivalent to *sir*, formerly used as a mark of respect to a European man [Urdu]

said *adj* **1** named or mentioned already: *she had heard that the said woman was also a medium* ▷ *vb* **2** the past of **say**

sail *n* **1** a sheet of canvas or other fabric, spread on rigging to catch the wind and move a ship over water **2** a voyage on such a ship: *a relaxing sail across the lake* **3** a ship or ships with sails: *to travel by sail* **4** one of the revolving arms of a windmill **5 set sail** to begin a voyage by water **6 under sail** **A** under way **B** with sail hoisted ▷ *vb* **7** to travel in a boat or ship: *to sail around the world* **8** to begin a voyage: *he hoped to sail at eleven* **9** (of a ship) to move over the water **10** to navigate (a ship): *she sailed the schooner up the channel* **11** to sail over: *he had already sailed the Pacific* **12** to move along smoothly **13 sail into** *informal* to make a violent attack on **14 sail through** to progress quickly or effortlessly: *the top seed sailed through to the second round* [Old English *segl*]

sailboard *n* a board with a mast and a single sail, used for windsurfing

sailcloth *n* **1** the fabric used for making sails **2** a canvas-like cloth used for clothing

sailfish *n, pl* **-fish** *or* **-fishes** a large tropical game fish, with a long sail-like fin on its back

sailor *n* **1** any member of a ship's crew, esp. one below the rank of officer **2** a person considered as liable or not liable to seasickness: *a good sailor*

sainfoin (**san**-foin) *n* a Eurasian plant with pink flowers, widely grown as feed for grazing farm animals [Medieval Latin *sanum faenum* wholesome hay]

saint *n* **1** a person who after death is formally recognized by a Christian Church as deserving special honour because of having lived a very holy life **2** an exceptionally good person [Latin *sanctus* holy] **sainthood** *n* **saintlike** *adj*

Saint Bernard *n* a very large dog with a dense red-and-white coat, formerly used as a mountain-rescue dog

sainted *adj* **1** formally recognized by a Christian Church as a saint **2** having the qualities, such as patience and kindness, of a saint **3** hallowed or holy

Saint John's wort *n* a plant with yellow flowers

saintly *adj* behaving in a very good, patient, or holy way **saintliness** *n*

Saint Vitus's dance *n pathol* a nontechnical name for **chorea**

saithe *n Brit* a dark-coloured food fish found in northern seas [Old Norse *seithr* coalfish]

sake¹ *n* **1 for someone's** *or* **one's own sake** for the benefit or interest of someone *or* oneself **2 for the sake of something** for the purpose of obtaining or achieving something **3 for its own sake** for the enjoyment obtained by doing something **4** used in various exclamations of annoyance, impatience, or urgency: *for God's sake* [Old English *sacu* lawsuit (hence, a cause)]

sake² *or* **saki** (**sah**-kee) *n* a Japanese alcoholic drink made from fermented rice [Japanese]

salaam (sal-**ahm**) *n* **1** a Muslim greeting consisting of a deep bow with the right palm on the forehead **2** a greeting signifying peace ▷ *vb* **3** to make a salaam (to) [Arabic *salām* peace]

salacious *adj* **1** having an excessive interest in sex **2** (of books, films, or jokes) concerned with sex in an unnecessarily detailed way [Latin *salax* fond of leaping] **salaciousness** *n*

salad *n* a dish of raw vegetables, often served with a dressing, eaten as a separate course or as part of a main course [Old French *salade*]

salad days *pl n* a period of youth and inexperience [coined by William Shakespeare]

salad dressing *n* a sauce for salad, such as oil and vinegar or mayonnaise

salamander *n* **1** a tailed amphibian which looks like a lizard **2** a mythical creature supposed to live in fire [Greek *salamandra*]

salami *n* a highly spiced sausage, usually flavoured with garlic [Italian]

salaried *adj* earning or providing a salary: *a salaried employee; a salaried position*

salary *n, pl* **-ries** a fixed regular payment made by an employer, usually monthly, for professional or office work [Latin *salarium* the sum given to Roman soldiers to buy salt]

sale *n* **1** the exchange of goods or property for an agreed sum of money **2** the amount sold **3** an event at which goods are sold at reduced prices **4** an auction **5 sales** the department dealing with selling its company's products [Old English *sala*]

saleable *or US* **salable** *adj* fit for selling or capable of being sold **saleability** *or US* **salability** *n*

sale of work *n* a sale of articles, often handmade, the proceeds of which go to a charity

saleroom *n chiefly Brit* a room where objects are displayed for sale by auction

salesgirl *n* a young woman who sells goods in a shop

salesman *n, pl* **-men** a man who sells goods in a shop or within an assigned area

salesmanship *n* the technique of or skill in selling

salesperson *n, pl* **-people** *or* **-persons** a person who sells goods in a shop or within an assigned area

sales pitch *or* **sales talk** *n* persuasive talk used by a salesperson in persuading a customer to buy something

saleswoman *n, pl* **-women** a woman who sells goods in a shop or within an assigned area

saleyard *n Austral & NZ* an area with pens for holding animals before auction

S

salicylic acid (sal-liss-**ill**-ik) *n* a white crystalline substance used to make aspirin and as a fungicide [Latin *salix* willow]

salient (**say**-lee-ent) *adj* **1** (of points or facts) most important: *the salient points of his speech* ▷ *n* **2** *military* a projection of the forward line of an army into enemy-held territory [Latin *salire* to leap]

saline (**say**-line) *adj* **1** of or containing salt: *a saline flavour* **2** *med* of or relating to a saline: *a saline drip* ▷ *n* **3** *med* a solution of sodium chloride and water [Latin *sal* salt] **salinity** *n*

salinization *or* **-nisation** *n* the process by which salts accumulate in undrained land, damaging its potential for plant growth

saliva (sal-**lie**-va) *n* the watery fluid secreted by glands in the mouth, which aids digestion [Latin] **salivary** *adj*

salivate *vb* **-vating, -vated** to produce saliva, esp. an excessive amount **salivation** *n*

sallee *n Austral* **1** a SE Australian eucalyptus with a pale grey bark **2** an acacia tree

sallow *adj* (of human skin) of an unhealthy pale or yellowish colour [Old English *salu*] **sallowness** *n*

sally *n, pl* **-lies 1** a witty remark **2** a sudden brief attack by troops **3** an excursion ▷ *vb* **-lies, -lying, -lied 4 sally forth A** to set out on a journey **B** to set out in an energetic manner [Latin *salire* to leap]

salmon *n, pl* **-mons** *or* **-mon** a large pink-fleshed fish which is highly valued for food and sport: salmon live in the sea but return to fresh water to spawn [Latin *salmo*]

salmonella (sal-mon-**ell**-a) *n* a kind of bacteria that can cause food poisoning [after Daniel E. *Salmon*, veterinary surgeon]

salmon ladder *n* a series of steps designed to enable salmon to move upstream to their breeding grounds

salon *n* **1** a commercial establishment in which hairdressers or fashion designers carry on their business **2** an elegant room in a large house in which guests are received **3** an informal gathering, esp. in the 18th, 19th, and early 20th centuries, of major literary, artistic, and political figures in a fashionable household **4** an art exhibition [French]

saloon *n* **1** a two-door or four-door car with a fixed roof **2** a comfortable but more expensive bar in a pub or hotel **3** a large public room on a passenger ship **4** *chiefly US & Canad* a place where alcoholic drink is sold and consumed [from *salon*]

salsa *n* **1** a lively Puerto Rican dance **2** big-band music accompanying this dance [Spanish, literally: sauce]

salsify *n, pl* **-fies** a Mediterranean plant with a long white edible root [Italian *sassefrica*]

salt *n* **1** sodium chloride, a white crystalline substance, used for seasoning and preserving food **2** *chem* a crystalline solid compound formed from an acid by replacing its hydrogen with a metal **3** lively wit: *his humour added salt to the discussion* **4 old salt** an experienced sailor **5 rub salt into someone's wounds** to make an unpleasant situation even worse for someone **6 salt of the earth** a person or people regarded as the finest of their kind **7 take something with a pinch of salt** to refuse to believe something is completely true or accurate **8 worth one's salt** worthy of one's pay; efficient ▷ *vb* **9** to season or preserve with salt **10** to scatter salt over (an iced road or path) to melt the ice ▷ *adj* **11** preserved in or tasting of salt: *salt beef* ▷ See also **salt away, salts** [Old English *sealt*] **salted** *adj*

SALT Strategic Arms Limitation Talks *or* Treaty

salt away *vb* to hoard or save (money) for the future

saltbush *n* a shrub that grows in alkaline desert regions

saltcellar *n* a small container for salt used at the table [changed from *salt saler*; *saler* from Old French *saliere* container for salt]

saltire *n* **1** *heraldry* a diagonal cross on a shield **2** the national flag of Scotland, a white diagonal cross on a blue background

salt lick *n* **1** a place where wild animals go to lick salt deposits **2** a block of salt given to domestic animals to lick

saltpetre *or US* **saltpeter** *n* same as **potassium nitrate** [Latin *sal petrae* salt of rock]

salts *pl n* **1** *med* mineral salts used as a medicine **2 like a dose of salts** *informal* very quickly

saltwater *adj* of or inhabiting salt water, esp. the sea: *saltwater fish*

salty *adj* **saltier, saltiest 1** of, tasting of, or containing salt **2** (esp. of humour) sharp and witty **saltiness** *n*

salubrious *adj* favourable to health [Latin *salus* health] **salubrity** *n*

Saluki *n* a tall hound with a smooth coat and long fringes on the ears and tail [from *Saluq*, ancient Arabian city]

salutary *adj* **1** (of an experience) producing a beneficial result despite being unpleasant: *a salutary reminder* **2** promoting health [Latin *salutaris* wholesome]

salutation *n formal* a greeting by words or actions [Latin *salutare* to greet]

salute *vb* **-luting, -luted 1** to greet with friendly words or gestures of respect, such as bowing **2** to acknowledge with praise: *the statement salutes the changes of the past year* **3** *military* to pay formal respect to (someone) by raising the right hand to the forehead ▷ *n* **4** the act of saluting as a formal military gesture of respect **5** the act of firing guns as a military greeting of honour [Latin *salutare* to greet]

salvage *n* **1** the rescue of a ship or its cargo from loss at sea **2** the saving of any goods or property from destruction or waste **3** the goods or property so saved **4** compensation paid for the salvage of a ship or its cargo ▷ *vb* **-vaging, -vaged 5** to save (goods or property) from shipwreck, destruction, or waste **6** to gain (something beneficial) from a failure: *it's too late to salvage anything from the whole dismal display* [Latin *salvare* to save] **salvageable** *adj*

salvation *n* **1** the act of preserving someone or something from harm **2** a person or thing that preserves from harm **3** *Christianity* the fact or state of being saved from the influence or consequences of sin [Latin *salvatus* saved]

Salvation Army *n* a Christian body organized on military lines for working among poor and homeless people and spreading the Christian faith

salve *n* **1** an ointment for wounds **2** anything that heals or soothes ▷ *vb* **salving, salved 3 salve one's conscience** to do something in order to feel less guilty [Old English *sealf*]

salver *n* a tray, usually a silver one, on which something is presented [Spanish *salva* tray from which the king's taster sampled food]

salvia *n* any small plant or shrub of the sage genus [Latin]

salvo *n, pl* **-vos** *or* **-voes 1** a simultaneous discharge of guns in battle or on a ceremonial occasion **2** an outburst of applause or questions [Italian *salva*, from Latin *salve!* greetings!]

sal volatile (**sal** vol-**at**-ill-ee) *n* a solution of ammonium carbonate, used as smelling salts [New Latin: volatile salt]

SAM surface-to-air missile

Samaritan *n* **1** short for **Good Samaritan 2** a member of a voluntary organization (**the Samaritans**) which offers counselling to people in despair, esp. by telephone

samarium *n chem* a silvery metallic element of the rare-earth series. Symbol: **Sm** [after Col. von *Samarski*, Russian inspector of mines]

samba *n, pl* **-bas 1** a lively Brazilian dance **2** music for this dance [Portuguese]

same *adj* (usually preceded by *the*) **1** being the very one: *she is wearing the same hat* **2** being the one previously referred to: *it causes problems for the same reason* **3** alike in kind or quantity: *the same age* **4** unchanged in character or nature: *his attitude is the same as ever* **5 all the same** *or* **just the same** nevertheless; even so **6 be all the same** to be a matter of indifference: *it was all the same to me* ▷ *adv* **7** in the same way; similarly: *I felt much the same* ▷ *n* **8 the same** something that is like something else in kind or quantity: *this is basically much more of the same* [Old Norse *samr*] **sameness** *n*

> **USAGE** The use of *same* exemplified in *if you send us your order for the materials, we will deliver same tomorrow* is common in business and official English. In general English, however, this use of the word is avoided: *may I borrow your book? I'll return it* (not *same*) *tomorrow.*

samizdat *n* (in the former Soviet Union) a system of secret printing and distribution of banned literature [Russian]

samosa *n* (in Indian cookery) a small fried triangular spiced meat or vegetable pasty. Also (in S Africa): **samoosa** [Hindi]

samovar *n* a Russian metal tea urn in which the water is heated by an inner container [Russian]

Samoyed *n* a dog with a thick white coat and a tightly curled tail [Russian *Samoed*]

sampan *n* a small flat-bottomed boat with oars, used esp. in China [Chinese *san* three + *pan* board]

samphire *n* a European plant found on rocks by the seashore, with aromatic leaves sometimes eaten as a vegetable [French *herbe de Saint Pierre* Saint Peter's herb]

sample *n* **1** a small part of anything, taken as being representative of a whole ▷ *vb* **-pling, -pled 2** to take a sample or samples of **3** *music* **A** to take a short extract from (one record) and mix it into a different backing track **B** to record (a sound) and feed it into a computerized synthesizer so that it can be reproduced at any pitch [Latin *exemplum*] **sampling** *n*

sampler *n* **1** a piece of embroidery done to show the embroiderer's skill in using many different stitches **2** *music* a piece of electronic equipment used for sampling

Samson *n* a man of outstanding physical strength [from the biblical character who was renowned for his strength]

samurai *n, pl* **-rai** a member of the aristocratic warrior caste of feudal Japan [Japanese]

sanatorium *or US* **sanitarium** *n, pl* **-riums** *or* **-ria 1** an institution providing medical treatment and rest for invalids or convalescents **2** *Brit* a room in a boarding school where sick pupils may be treated [Latin *sanare* to heal]

sanctify *vb* **-fies, -fying, -fied 1** to make holy **2** to free from sin **3** to approve (an action or practice) as religiously binding: *she is trying to make amends for her marriage not being sanctified* [Latin *sanctus* holy + *facere* to make] **sanctification** *n*

sanctimonious *adj* pretending to be very religious and virtuous [Latin *sanctimonia* sanctity]

sanction *n* **1** permission granted by authority: *official sanction* **2** support or approval: *they could not exist without his sanction* **3** something that gives binding force to a law, such as a penalty for breaking it or a reward for obeying it **4 sanctions** coercive measures, such as boycotts and trade embargoes, taken by one or more states against another guilty of violating international law ▷ *vb* **5** to officially approve of or allow: *they do not want to sanction direct payments* **6** to confirm or ratify [Latin *sancire* to decree]

sanctity *n* the quality of something considered so holy or important it must be respected totally: *the sanctity of the Sabbath; the sanctity of marriage*

sanctuary *n, pl* **-aries 1** a holy place, such as a consecrated building or shrine **2** the part of a church nearest the main altar **3** a place of refuge or protection for someone who is being chased or hunted **4** refuge or safety: *the sanctuary of your own home* **5** a place, protected by law, where animals can live and breed without interference [Latin *sanctus* holy]

sanctum *n, pl* **-tums** *or* **-ta 1** a sacred or holy place **2** a room or place of total privacy [Latin]

sand *n* **1** a powdery substance consisting of very small rock or mineral grains, found on the seashore and in deserts **2 sands** a large sandy area, esp. on the seashore or in a desert ▷ *vb* **3** to smooth or polish the surface of (something) with sandpaper or a sander **4** to fill with sand: *the channel sanded up* [Old English]

sandal *n* a light shoe consisting of a sole held on the foot by thongs or straps [Greek *sandalon*] **sandalled** *or US* **sandaled** *adj*

sandalwood *n* **1** the hard light-coloured wood of a S Asian or Australian tree, which is used for carving and for incense, and which yields an aromatic oil used in perfumes **2** a tree yielding this wood [Sanskrit *candana*]

sandbag *n* **1** a sack filled with sand used to make a temporary defence against gunfire or flood water ▹ *vb* **-bagging, -bagged 2** to protect or strengthen with sandbags

sandbank *or* **sand bar** *n* a bank of sand in a sea or river, that may be exposed at low tide

sandblast *n* **1** a jet of sand blown from a nozzle under air or steam pressure ▹ *vb* **2** to clean or decorate (a surface) with a sandblast
sandblaster *n*

sandboy *n* **happy as a sandboy** *old-fashioned* very happy

sand castle *n* a model of a castle made from sand

sander *n* a power-driven tool for smoothing surfaces, removing layers of paint from walls, etc.

S & M *informal* sadomasochism

sandman *n, pl* **-men** (in folklore) a magical person supposed to put children to sleep by sprinkling sand in their eyes

sand martin *n* a small brown European songbird which nests in tunnels bored in sand or river banks

sandpaper *n* **1** a strong paper coated with sand or other abrasive material for smoothing or polishing a surface ▹ *vb* **2** to smooth or polish (a surface) with sandpaper

sandpiper *n* a wading shore bird with a long bill and slender legs

sandpit *n* a shallow pit or container holding sand for children to play in

sandshoes *pl n* light canvas shoes with rubber soles

sandstone *n* a sedimentary rock consisting mainly of sand grains, much used in building

sandstorm *n* a strong wind that whips up clouds of sand, esp. in a desert

sandwich *n* **1** two or more slices of bread, usually buttered, with a layer of food between them ▹ *vb* **2** to place between two other things: *shops sandwiched between flats* [after 4th Earl of *Sandwich*, who ate sandwiches rather than leave the gambling table for meals]

sandwich board *n* one of two connected boards that are hung over the shoulders in front of and behind a person to display advertisements

sandwich course *n Brit* an educational course consisting of alternate periods of study and industrial work

sandy *adj* **sandier, sandiest 1** resembling, containing, or covered with sand **2** (of hair) reddish-yellow **sandiness** *n*

sane *adj* **1** having a normal healthy mind **2** sensible or well-judged: *sane advice* [Latin *sanus* healthy]

sang *vb* the past tense of **sing**

USAGE See at **ring¹**.

sanger *n Austral informal* a sandwich

sang-froid (sahng-**frwah**) *n* composure and calmness in a difficult situation [French, literally: cold blood]

sangoma (sang-go-ma) *n S African* a witch doctor [Nguni (language group of southern Africa) *isangoma* a diviner]

sangria *n* a Spanish drink of red wine, sugar, spices, and fruit [Spanish: a bleeding]

sanguinary *adj formal* **1** (of a battle or fight) involving much violence and bloodshed **2** (of a person) eager to see violence and bloodshed **3** of or stained with blood [Latin *sanguinarius*]

sanguine *adj* **1** cheerful and confident **2** (of the complexion) ruddy [Latin *sanguineus* bloody]

Sanhedrin (san-id-rin) *n Judaism* the highest court and supreme council of the ancient Jewish nation

sanitary *adj* **1** promoting health by getting rid of dirt and germs **2** free from dirt or germs; hygienic [Latin *sanitas* health]

sanitary towel *or esp US* **sanitary napkin** *n* a pad worn externally by women during menstruation to absorb the flow of blood

sanitation *n* **1** the use of sanitary measures to maintain public health **2** the drainage and disposal of sewage

sanitize *or* **-tise** *vb* **-tizing, -tized** *or* **-tising, -tised** to omit unpleasant details to make (news) more acceptable

sanity *n* **1** the state of having a normal healthy mind **2** good sense or soundness of judgment [Latin *sanitas* health]

sank *vb* the past tense of **sink**

sans-culotte (sanz-kew-**lot**) *n* a revolutionary extremist [French, literally: without knee breeches, because during the French Revolution the revolutionaries wore trousers]

Sanskrit *n* the classical literary language of India, used since ancient times for religious purposes [Sanskrit *samskrta* perfected] **Sanskritic** *adj*

Santa Claus *n* the legendary patron saint of children, who brings presents to children on Christmas Eve, commonly identified with Saint Nicholas

sap¹ *n* **1** a thin liquid that circulates in a plant, carrying food and water **2** *slang* a gullible person ▹ *vb* **sapping, sapped 3** to drain of sap [Old English *sæp*]

sap² *vb* **sapping, sapped 1** to weaken or exhaust the strength or confidence of **2** to undermine (an enemy position) by digging saps ▹ *n* **3** a deep and narrow trench used to approach or undermine an enemy position [Italian *zappa* spade]

sapient (say-pee-ent) *adj often humorous* having great wisdom or sound judgment [Latin *sapere* to taste, know] **sapience** *n*

sapling *n* a young tree

saponify *vb* **-fies, -fying, -fied** *chem* to convert (a fat) into a soap by treatment with alkali [Latin *sapo* soap] **saponification** *n*

sapper *n* **1** a soldier who digs trenches **2** (in the British Army) a private of the Royal Engineers

sapphire *n* **1** a transparent blue precious stone ▹ *adj* **2** deep blue [Greek *sappheiros*]

sappy *adj* **-pier, -piest** (of plants) full of sap

saprophyte *n biol* any plant, such as a fungus, that lives and feeds on dead organic matter [Greek *sapros* rotten + *phuton* plant]

S

sarabande *or* **saraband** *n* **1** a stately slow Spanish dance **2** music for this dance [Spanish *zarabanda*]
Saracen *n* **1** an Arab or Muslim who opposed the Crusades ▹ *adj* **2** of the Saracens [Late Greek *Sarakēnos*]
sarcasm *n* **1** mocking or ironic language intended to insult someone **2** the use or tone of such language [Greek *sarkazein* to rend the flesh]
sarcastic *adj* **1** full of or showing sarcasm **2** tending to use sarcasm: *a sarcastic critic* **sarcastically** *adv*
sarcoma *n pathol* a malignant tumour beginning in connective tissue [Greek *sarkōma* fleshy growth]
sarcophagus (sahr-**koff**-a-guss) *n, pl* **-gi** (-guy) *or* **-guses** a stone or marble coffin or tomb, esp. one bearing sculpture or inscriptions [Greek *sarkophagos* flesh-devouring]
sardine *n, pl* **-dines** *or* **-dine** **1** a small fish of the herring family, often preserved in tightly packed tins **2 like sardines** very closely crowded together [Latin *sardina*]
sardonic *adj* (of behaviour) mocking or scornful [Greek *sardonios*] **sardonically** *adv*
sardonyx *n* a type of gemstone with alternating reddish-brown and white parallel bands [Greek *sardonux*]
sargassum *n* a floating brown seaweed with long stringy fronds containing air sacs [Portuguese *sargaço*]
sarge *n informal* sergeant
sari *or* **saree** *n, pl* **-ris** *or* **-rees** the traditional dress of Hindu women, consisting of a very long piece of cloth swathed around the body with one end over the shoulder [Hindi]
sarking *n Scot, N English, Austral & NZ* flat planking supporting the roof cladding of a building [Scots *sark* shirt]
sarky *adj* **-kier, -kiest** *informal* sarcastic
sarmie *n S African children's slang* a sandwich
sarnie *n S Eng informal* a sandwich
sarong *n* a garment worn by Malaysian men and women, consisting of a long piece of cloth tucked around the waist or under the armpits [Malay]
SARS **1** severe acute respiratory syndrome; a severe and contagious viral infection of the lungs characterized by high fever, a dry cough, and breathing difficulties **2** South African Revenue Service
sarsaparilla *n* a nonalcoholic drink prepared from the roots of a tropical American climbing plant [Spanish *sarzaparrilla*]
sartorial *adj formal* of men's clothes or tailoring: *sartorial elegance* [Latin *sartor* a tailor]
SAS (in Britain) Special Air Service
sash[1] *n* a long piece of cloth worn around the waist or over one shoulder, usually as a symbol of rank [Arabic *shāsh* muslin]
sash[2] *n* **1** a frame that contains the panes of a window or door **2** a complete frame together with panes of glass [French *châssis* a frame]
sashay *vb informal* to move or walk in a casual or a showy manner: *the models sashayed down the catwalk* [French *chassé* a gliding dance step]
sash cord *n* a strong cord connecting a weight to the sliding half of a sash window
sashimi (sah-**shee**-mee) *n* a Japanese dish of thin fillets of raw fish [Japanese *sashi* piercing + *mi* fish]
sash window *n* a window consisting of two sashes placed one above the other so that the window can be opened by sliding one frame over the front of the other
Sask. Saskatchewan
sassafras *n* a tree of North America, with aromatic bark used medicinally and as a flavouring [Spanish *sasafras*]
Sassenach *n Scot & sometimes Irish* an English person [Gaelic *Sassunach*]
sat *vb* the past of **sit**
Sat. Saturday
Satan *n* the Devil [Hebrew: plotter]
satanic *adj* **1** of Satan **2** supremely evil or wicked
Satanism *n* the worship of Satan **Satanist** *n, adj*
satchel *n* a small bag, usually with a shoulder strap [Old French *sachel*]
sate *vb* **sating, sated** to satisfy (a desire or appetite) fully [Old English *sadian*]
satellite *n* **1** a man-made device orbiting the earth or another planet, used in communications or to collect scientific information **2** a heavenly body orbiting a planet or star: *the earth is a satellite of the sun* **3** a country controlled by or dependent on a more powerful one ▹ *adj* **4** of, used in, or relating to the transmission of television signals from a satellite to the home: *satellite* TV; *a satellite dish* [Latin *satelles* an attendant]
satiate (**say**-she-ate) *vb* **-ating, -ated** to provide with more than enough, so as to disgust or weary: *enough cakes to satiate several children* [Latin *satiare*] **satiable** *adj* **satiation** *n*
satiety (sat-**tie**-a-tee) *n formal* the feeling of having had too much
satin *n* **1** a fabric, usually made from silk or rayon, closely woven to give a smooth glossy surface on one side ▹ *adj* **2** like satin in texture: *satin polyurethane varnish* [Arabic *zaitūnī*] **satiny** *adj*
satinwood *n* **1** a hard wood with a satiny texture, used in fine furniture **2** the Asian tree yielding this wood
satire *n* **1** the use of ridicule to expose incompetence, evil, or corruption **2** a play, novel, or poem containing satire [Latin *satira* a mixture] **satirical** *adj*
satirist *n* **1** a writer of satire **2** a person who uses satire
satirize *or* **-rise** *vb* **-rizing, -rized** *or* **-rising, -rised** to ridicule (a person or thing) by means of satire **satirization** *or* **-risation** *n*
satisfaction *n* **1** the pleasure obtained from the fulfilment of a desire **2** something that brings fulfilment: *craft workers get satisfaction from their work* **3** compensation or an apology for a wrong done: *consumers unable to get satisfaction from their gas supplier*
satisfactory *adj* **1** adequate or acceptable **2** giving satisfaction **satisfactorily** *adv*
satisfy *vb* **-fies, -fying, -fied** **1** to fulfil the desires or needs of (a person): *his answer didn't satisfy me* **2** to provide sufficiently for (a need or desire):

S

to satisfy public demand **3** to convince: *that trip did seem to satisfy her that he was dead* **4** to fulfil the requirements of: *unable to satisfy the conditions set by the commission* [Latin *satis* enough + *facere* to make] **satisfiable** *adj* **satisfying** *adj*

satnav *n motoring informal* satellite navigation

satrap *n* (in ancient Persia) a provincial governor or subordinate ruler [Old Persian *khshathrapāvan*, literally: protector of the land]

SATs (in England, Wales, and Northern Ireland) standard assessment tasks

satsuma *n* a small loose-skinned variety of orange with easily separable segments [*Satsuma*, former province of Japan]

saturate *vb* **-rating, -rated 1** to soak completely **2** to fill so completely that no more can be added: *saturating the area with their men* **3** *chem* to combine (a substance) or (of a substance) to be combined with the greatest possible amount of another substance [Latin *saturare*]

saturation *n* **1** the process or state that occurs when one substance is filled so full of another substance that no more can be added **2** *military* the use of very heavy force, esp. bombing, against an area

saturation point *n* **1** the point at which the maximum amount of a substance has been absorbed **2** the point at which some capacity is at its fullest; limit: *the market is close to saturation point*

Saturday *n* the seventh day of the week [Latin *Saturni dies* day of Saturn]

Saturn *n* **1** the Roman god of agriculture and vegetation **2** the sixth planet from the sun, second largest in the solar system, around which revolve concentric rings

Saturnalia *n, pl* **-lia** *or* **-lias 1** the ancient Roman festival of Saturn, renowned for its unrestrained revelry **2 saturnalia** a wild party or orgy [Latin *Saturnalis* relating to Saturn]

saturnine *adj* having a gloomy temperament or appearance [Latin *Saturnus* Saturn, from the gloomy influence attributed to the planet]

satyr *n* **1** *Greek myth* a woodland god represented as having a man's body with the ears, horns, tail, and legs of a goat **2** a man who has strong sexual desires [Greek *saturos*]

sauce *n* **1** a liquid added to food to enhance its flavour **2** anything that adds interest or zest **3** *chiefly Brit informal* impudent language or behaviour [Latin *salsus* salted]

sauce boat *n* a boat-shaped container for serving sauce

saucepan *n* a metal pan with a long handle and often a lid, used for cooking food

saucer *n* **1** a small round dish on which a cup is set **2** something shaped like a saucer [Old French *saussier* container for sauce] **saucerful** *n*

saucy *adj* **saucier, sauciest 1** cheeky or slightly rude in an amusing and light-hearted way **2** jaunty and boldly smart: *a saucy hat* **sauciness** *n*

sauerkraut *n* a German dish of finely shredded pickled cabbage [German *sauer* sour + *Kraut* cabbage]

sault (soo) *n Canad* a waterfall or rapids [French *saut* a leap]

sauna *n* **1** a Finnish-style hot steam bath, usually followed by a cold plunge **2** the place in which such a bath is taken [Finnish]

saunter *vb* **1** to walk in a leisurely manner; stroll ▷ *n* **2** a leisurely pace or stroll [origin unknown]

saurian *adj* of or resembling a lizard [Greek *sauros* lizard]

sausage *n* **1** finely minced meat mixed with fat, cereal, and seasonings, in a tube-shaped casing **2** an object shaped like a sausage **3 not a sausage** *informal* nothing at all [Old French *saussiche*]

sausage dog *n informal* same as **dachshund**

sausage roll *n* a roll of sausage meat in pastry

sausage sizzle *n Austral & NZ* an event at which sausages are barbecued, often to raise money for a school or other organization

sauté (so-tay) *vb* **-téing, -téed 1** to fry (food) quickly in a little fat ▷ *n* **2** a dish of sautéed food ▷ *adj* **3** sautéed until lightly brown: *sauté potatoes* [French: tossed]

Sauternes (so-turn) *n* a sweet white wine produced in the southern Bordeaux district of France

savage *adj* **1** wild and untamed: *savage tigers* **2** fierce and cruel: *savage cries* **3** (of peoples) uncivilized or primitive: *savage tribes* **4** rude, crude, and violent: *savage behaviour on the terraces* **5** (of terrain) wild and uncultivated ▷ *n* **6** a member of an uncivilized or primitive society **7** a fierce or vicious person ▷ *vb* **-vaging, -vaged 8** to attack ferociously and wound: *savaged by a wild dog* **9** to criticize extremely severely: *savaged by the press for incompetence* [Latin *silvaticus* belonging to a wood] **savagely** *adv*

savagery *n, pl* **-ries** viciousness and cruelty

savannah *or* **savanna** *n* open grasslands, usually with scattered bushes or trees, in Africa [Spanish *zavana*]

savant *or fem* **savante** *n* a very wise and knowledgeable person [French]

save[1] *vb* **saving, saved 1** to rescue or preserve (a person or thing) from danger or harm **2** to avoid the spending, waste, or loss of (something): *an appeal on television for the public to save energy* **3** to set aside or reserve (money or goods) for future use: *I'm saving for a vintage Mercedes* **4** to treat with care so as to preserve **5** to give a computer an instruction to store (newly entered data) **6** to prevent the necessity for: *a chance saved him from having to make up his mind* **7** *sport* to prevent (a goal) by stopping (a ball or puck) **8** *Christianity* to free (someone) from the influence or consequences of sin ▷ *n* **9** *sport* the act of saving a goal **10** *computers* the act or process of saving data to a storage location [Old French *salver*] **savable** *or* **saveable** *adj* **saver** *n*

save[2] *old-fashioned* ▷ *prep* **1** (often foll. by *for*) with the exception of: *the stage was empty save for a single chair* ▷ *conj* **2** but [Middle English *sauf*]

save as you earn *n* (in Britain) a savings scheme which offers a tax-free bonus and allows employees to buy shares in the company they work for at a fixed price

saveloy *n Brit, Austral & NZ* a highly seasoned smoked sausage made from salted pork [Italian *cervellato*]

saving *n* **1** preservation from destruction or danger **2** a reduction in the amount of time or money used **3 savings** money saved for future use ▷ *adj* **4** tending to rescue or preserve ▷ *prep* **5** with the exception of

saving grace *n* a good quality in a person that prevents him or her from being entirely bad or worthless

saviour *or US* **savior** *n* a person who rescues another person or a thing from danger or harm [Church Latin *Salvator* the Saviour]

Saviour *or US* **Savior** *n Christianity* Jesus Christ, regarded as the saviour of people from sin

savoir-faire (sav-wahr-**fair**) *n* the ability to say and do the right thing in any situation [French]

savory *n, pl* **-vories** an aromatic plant whose leaves are used in cooking [Latin *satureia*]

savour *or US* **savor** *vb* **1** to enjoy and appreciate (food or drink) slowly **2** to enjoy (a pleasure) for as long as possible: *an experience to be savoured* **3 savour of** **A** to have a suggestion of: *that could savour of ostentation* **B** to possess the taste or smell of: *the vegetables savoured of coriander* ▷ *n* **4** the taste or smell of something **5** a slight but distinctive quality or trace [Latin *sapor* taste]

savoury *or US* **savory** *adj* **1** salty or spicy: *savoury foods* **2** attractive to the sense of taste or smell **3** pleasant or acceptable: *one of the book's less savoury characters* ▷ *n, pl* **-ries 4** *chiefly Brit* a savoury dish served before or after a meal **savouriness** *or US* **savoriness** *n*

savoy *n* a cabbage with a compact head and wrinkled leaves [after the *Savoy* region in France]

savvy *slang* ▷ *vb* **-vies, -vying, -vied 1** to understand ▷ *n* **2** understanding or common sense ▷ *adj* **3** shrewd [corruption of Spanish *sabe (usted)* (you) know]

saw[1] *n* **1** a cutting tool with a toothed metal blade or edge, either operated by hand or powered by electricity ▷ *vb* **sawing, sawed, sawed** *or* **sawn 2** to cut with or as if with a saw **3** to form by sawing **4** to move (an object) from side to side as if moving a saw [Old English *sagu*]

saw[2] *vb* the past tense of **see[1]**

saw[3] *n old-fashioned* a wise saying or proverb [Old English *sagu* a saying]

saw doctor *n NZ* a sawmill specialist who sharpens and services saw blades

sawdust *n* particles of wood formed by sawing

sawfish *n, pl* **-fish** *or* **-fishes** a sharklike ray with a long toothed snout resembling a saw

sawhorse *n Austral & NZ* a structure for supporting wood that is being sawn

sawmill *n* a factory where timber is sawn into planks

sawn *vb* a past participle of **saw[1]**

sawn-off *or esp US* **sawed-off** *adj* (of a shotgun) having the barrel cut short to make concealment of the weapon easier

saw-off *n Canad* **1** a deadlock or stalemate **2** a compromise

sawyer *n* a person who saws timber for a living

sax *n informal* short for **saxophone**

saxifrage *n* an alpine rock plant with small white, yellow, purple, or pink flowers [Late Latin *saxifraga*, literally: rock breaker]

Saxon *n* **1** a member of a West Germanic people who raided and settled parts of Britain in the fifth and sixth centuries AD **2** any of the West Germanic dialects spoken by the ancient Saxons ▷ *adj* **3** of the ancient Saxons or their language [Late Latin *Saxon-*, *Saxo*]

saxophone *n* a brass wind instrument with keys and a curved metal body [after Adolphe *Sax*, who invented it] **saxophonist** *n*

say *vb* **saying, said 1** to speak or utter **2** to express (an idea) in words: *I can't say what I feel* **3** to state (an opinion or fact) positively: *I say you are wrong* **4** to indicate or show: *the clock says ten to nine* **5** to recite: *to say grace* **6** to report or allege: *they say we shall have rain today* **7** to suppose as an example or possibility: *let us say that he is lying* **8** to convey by means of artistic expression: *what does the artist have to say in this picture?* **9** to make a case for: *there is much to be said for it* **10 go without saying** to be so obvious as to need no explanation **11 to say the least** at the very least ▷ *adv* **12** approximately: *there were, say, 20 people present* **13** for example: *choose a number, say, four* ▷ *n* **14** the right or chance to speak: *the opposition has hardly had a say in these affairs* **15** authority, esp. to influence a decision: *he has a lot of say* [Old English *secgan*]

SAYE (in Britain) save as you earn

saying *n* a well-known phrase or sentence expressing a belief or a truth

Sb *chem* antimony [New Latin *stibium*]

Sc *chem* scandium

SC South Carolina

scab *n* **1** the dried crusty surface of a healing skin wound or sore **2** *derogatory* a person who refuses to support a trade union's actions, and continues to work during a strike **3** a contagious disease of sheep, caused by a mite **4** a fungal disease of plants ▷ *vb* **scabbing, scabbed 5** to become covered with a scab **6** *derogatory* to work as a scab [Old English *sceabb*]

scabbard *n* a holder for a sword or dagger [Middle English *scauberc*]

scabby *adj* **-bier, -biest 1** *pathol* covered with scabs **2** *informal* mean or despicable **scabbiness** *n*

scabies (**skay**-beez) *n* a contagious skin infection caused by a mite, characterized by intense itching [Latin *scabere* to scratch]

scabious (**skay**-bee-uss) *n* a plant with showy blue, red, or whitish dome-shaped flower heads [Medieval Latin *scabiosa herba* the scabies plant]

scabrous (**skay**-bruss) *adj* **1** rough and scaly **2** indecent or crude: *scabrous stand-up comedy* [Latin *scaber* rough]

scaffold *n* **1** a temporary framework used to support workmen and materials during the construction or repair of a building **2** a raised wooden platform on which criminals are hanged; gallows [Old French *eschaffaut*]

scaffolding *n* **1** a scaffold or scaffolds **2** the building materials used to make scaffolds

S

scalar *maths* ▷ *n* **1** a quantity, such as time or temperature, that has magnitude but not direction ▷ *adj* **2** having magnitude but not direction [Latin *scala* ladder]

scald *vb* **1** to burn with hot liquid or steam **2** to sterilize with boiling water **3** to heat (a liquid) almost to boiling point ▷ *n* **4** a burn caused by scalding [Late Latin *excaldare* to wash in warm water]

scale[1] *n* **1** one of the thin flat overlapping plates covering the bodies of fishes and reptiles **2** a thin flat piece or flake **3** a coating which sometimes forms in kettles and hot-water pipes in areas where the water is hard **4** tartar formed on the teeth ▷ *vb* **scaling, scaled 5** to remove the scales or coating from **6** to peel off in flakes or scales **7** to cover or become covered with scales [Old French *escale*] **scaly** *adj*

scale[2] *n* **1** (*often pl*) a machine or device for weighing **2** one of the pans of a balance **3 tip the scales** to have a decisive influence **4 tip the scales at** to amount in weight to [Old Norse *skāl* bowl]

scale[3] *n* **1** a sequence of marks at regular intervals, used as a reference in making measurements **2** a measuring instrument with such a scale **3** the ratio between the size of something real and that of a representation of it: *the map has a scale of 1:10 000* **4** a series of degrees or graded system of things: *the Western wage scale for the same work* **5** a relative degree or extent: *growing flowers on a very small scale* **6** *music* a sequence of notes taken in ascending or descending order, esp. within one octave **7** *maths* the notation of a given number system: *the decimal scale* ▷ *vb* **scaling, scaled 8** to climb to the top of (an object or height): *the men scaled a wall* **9 scale up** *or* **down** to increase *or* reduce proportionately in size: *the design can easily be scaled up; after five days the search was scaled down* [Latin *scala* ladder]

scalene *adj* *maths* (of a triangle) having all sides of unequal length [Greek *skalēnos*]

scallion *n* a spring onion [Anglo-French *scalun*]

scallop *n* **1** an edible marine mollusc with two fluted fan-shaped shells **2** a single shell of this mollusc **3** one of a series of small curves along an edge [Old French *escalope* shell] **scalloping** *n*

scalloped *adj* decorated with small curves along the edge

scallywag *n informal* a badly behaved but likeable person; rascal [origin unknown]

scalp *n* **1** *anatomy* the skin and hair covering the top of the head **2** (formerly among Native Americans of N America) a part of this removed as a trophy from a slain enemy ▷ *vb* **3** to cut the scalp from **4** *informal, chiefly US* to buy and resell so as to make a high or quick profit [probably from Old Norse *skālpr* sheath]

scalpel *n* a small surgical knife with a very sharp thin blade [Latin *scalper* a knife]

scam *n slang* a stratagem for gain; a swindle

scamp *n* a mischievous person, esp. a child [probably from Middle Dutch *schampen* to decamp]

scamper *vb* **1** to run about hurriedly or quickly ▷ *n* **2** the act of scampering [see SCAMP]

scampi *n* large prawns, usually eaten fried in breadcrumbs [Italian]

scan *vb* **scanning, scanned 1** to scrutinize carefully **2** to glance over quickly **3** *prosody* to analyse (verse) by examining its rhythmic structure **4** *prosody* (of a line or verse) to be metrically correct **5** to examine or search (an area) by systematically moving a beam of light or electrons, or a radar or sonar beam over it **6** *med* to obtain an image of (a part of the body) by means of ultrasound or a scanner ▷ *n* **7** an instance of scanning **8** *med* **A** the examination of part of the body by means of a scanner **B** the image produced by a scanner [Latin *scandere* to climb]

scandal *n* **1** a disgraceful action or event: *the chairman resigned after a loans scandal* **2** shame or outrage arising from a disgraceful action or event: *the figures were a national scandal* **3** malicious gossip [Greek *skandalon* a trap] **scandalous** *adj* **scandalously** *adv*

scandalize *or* **-ise** *vb* **-izing, -ized** *or* **-ising, -ised** to shock (someone) or be shocked by improper behaviour

scandalmonger *n* a person who spreads or enjoys scandal or gossip

Scandinavian *adj* **1** of Scandinavia (Norway, Sweden, Denmark, and often Finland, Iceland, and the Faeroe Islands) ▷ *n* **2** a person from Scandinavia **3** the northern group of Germanic languages, consisting of Swedish, Danish, Norwegian, Icelandic, and Faeroese

scandium *n chem* a rare silvery-white metallic element. Symbol: **Sc** [Latin *Scandia* Scandinavia, where discovered]

scanner *n* **1** an aerial or similar device designed to transmit or receive signals, esp. radar signals **2** a device used in medical diagnosis to obtain an image of an internal organ or part

scansion *n* the metrical scanning of verse

scant *adj* scarcely sufficient: *some issues will get scant attention* [Old Norse *skamt* short]

scanty *adj* **scantier, scantiest** barely sufficient or not sufficient **scantily** *adv* **scantiness** *n*

scapegoat *n* **1** a person made to bear the blame for others ▷ *vb* **2** to make a scapegoat of [*escape* + *goat*, coined to translate Biblical Hebrew *azāzēl*, probably goat for Azazel, mistakenly thought to mean 'goat that escapes']

scapula (skap-pew-la) *n, pl* **-lae** (-lee) the technical name for **shoulder blade** [Late Latin: shoulder]

scapular *adj* **1** *anatomy* of the scapula ▷ *n* **2** a loose sleeveless garment worn by monks over their habits

scar[1] *n* **1** a mark left on the skin following the healing of a wound **2** a permanent effect on a person's character resulting from emotional distress **3** a mark on a plant where a leaf was formerly attached **4** a mark of damage ▷ *vb* **scarring, scarred 5** to mark or become marked with a scar **6** to permanently effect or be permanently affected by mental trauma: *their divorce will scar those kids for life* [Greek *eskhara* scab]

scar[2] *n* a bare craggy rock formation [Old Norse *sker* low reef]

S

scarab *n* **1** the black dung-beetle, regarded by the ancient Egyptians as divine **2** an image or carving of this beetle [Latin *scarabaeus*]

scarce *adj* **1** insufficient to meet the demand: *scarce water resources* **2** not common; rarely found **3 make oneself scarce** *informal* to go away ▷ *adv* **4** *archaic, literary* scarcely [Old French *scars*]

scarcely *adv* **1** hardly at all **2** *often humorous* probably or definitely not: *that is scarcely justification for your actions*

USAGE See at **hardly**.

scarcity *n, pl* **-ties** an inadequate supply

scare *vb* **scaring, scared 1** to frighten or be frightened **2 scare away** *or* **off** to drive away by frightening ▷ *n* **3** a sudden attack of fear or alarm: *you gave me a scare* **4** a period of general fear or alarm: *the bird flu scare* [Old Norse *skirra*]

scarecrow *n* **1** an object, usually in the shape of a man, made out of sticks and old clothes, to scare birds away from crops **2** *informal* a raggedly dressed person

scaremonger *n* a person who starts or spreads rumours of disaster to frighten people **scaremongering** *n*

scarf[1] *n, pl* **scarves** *or* **scarfs** a piece of material worn around the head, neck, or shoulders [origin unknown]

scarf[2] *n, pl* **scarfs 1** a joint between two pieces of timber made by notching the ends and strapping or gluing the two pieces together ▷ *vb* **2** to join (two pieces of timber) by means of a scarf [probably from Old Norse]

scarify *vb* **-fies, -fying, -fied 1** *surgery* to make slight incisions in (the skin) **2** *agriculture* to break up and loosen (topsoil) **3** to criticize without mercy [Latin *scarifare* to scratch open] **scarification** *n*

USAGE *Scarify* is sometimes wrongly thought to mean the same as *scare*: *a frightening* (not *scarifying*) film.

scarlatina *n* the technical name for **scarlet fever** [Italian *scarlatto* scarlet]

scarlet *adj* bright red [Old French *escarlate* fine cloth]

scarlet fever *n* an acute contagious disease characterized by fever, a sore throat, and a red rash on the body

scarp *n* **1** a steep slope or ridge of rock **2** *fortifications* the side of a ditch cut nearest to a rampart [Italian *scarpa*]

scarper *vb chiefly Brit slang* to run away or escape [origin unknown]

Scart *or* **SCART** *n* *electronics* a plug-and-socket system which carries pictures and sound, used in home entertainment systems

scarves *n* a plural of **scarf**[1]

scary *adj* **scarier, scariest** *informal* quite frightening

scat[1] *vb* **scatting, scatted** *informal* to go away in haste [origin unknown]

scat[2] *n* **1** a type of jazz singing using improvised vocal sounds instead of words ▷ *vb* **scatting, scatted 2** to sing jazz in this way [perhaps imitative]

scathing *adj* harshly critical: *there was a scathing review of the play in the paper* [Old Norse *skathi* harm] **scathingly** *adv*

scatology *n* preoccupation with obscenity, esp. with references to excrement [Greek *skat-* excrement + -LOGY] **scatological** *adj*

scatter *vb* **1** to throw about in various directions: *scatter some oatmeal on top of the cake* **2** to separate and move in various directions; disperse: *the infantry were scattering* ▷ *n* **3** the act of scattering **4** a number of objects scattered about [probably variant of *shatter*]

scatterbrain *n* a person who is incapable of serious thought or concentration **scatterbrained** *adj*

scattershot *adj* wide-ranging but indiscriminate: *a scattershot approach to conservation*

scatty *adj* **-tier, -tiest** *informal* rather absent-minded [from *scatterbrained*] **scattiness** *n*

scavenge *vb* **-enging, -enged** to search for (anything usable) among discarded material

scavenger *n* **1** a person who collects things discarded by others **2** any animal that feeds on discarded or decaying matter [Old French *escauwer* to scrutinize]

SCE Scottish Certificate of Education

scenario *n, pl* **-narios 1** a summary of the plot and characters of a play or film **2** an imagined sequence of future events: *the likeliest scenario is another general election* [Italian]

scene *n* **1** the place where an action or event, real or imaginary, occurs **2** an incident or situation, real or imaginary, esp. as described or represented **3** a division of an act of a play, in which the setting is fixed and the action is continuous **4** *films* a shot or series of shots that constitutes a unit of the action **5** the backcloths or screens used to represent a location in a play or film set **6** the view of a place or landscape **7** a display of emotion or loss of temper in public: *you do not want to cause a scene* **8** *informal* a particular activity or aspect of life, and all the things associated with it: *the club scene* **9 behind the scenes A** backstage **B** in secret or in private [Greek *skēnē* tent, stage]

scenery *n, pl* **-eries 1** the natural features of a landscape **2** *theatre* the painted backcloths or screens used to represent a location in a theatre or studio

scenic *adj* **1** of or having beautiful natural scenery: *untouched scenic areas* **2** of the stage or stage scenery: *scenic artists*

scent *n* **1** a distinctive smell, esp. a pleasant one **2** a smell left in passing, by which a person or animal may be traced **3** a trail or series of clues by which something is followed: *he must have got on to the scent of the story through you* **4** perfume ▷ *vb* **5** to become aware of by smelling **6** to suspect: *he scented the beginnings of irritation in the car* **7** to fill with odour or fragrance [Old French *sentir* to sense] **scented** *adj*

sceptic *or US* **skeptic** (**skep**-tik) *n* **1** a person who habitually doubts generally accepted beliefs **2** a person who doubts the truth of a religion [Greek *skeptikos* one who reflects upon] **sceptical** *or US* **skeptical** *adj* **sceptically** *or US* **skeptically** *adv* **scepticism** *or US* **skepticism** *n*

sceptre *or US* **scepter** *n* an ornamental rod symbolizing royal power [Greek *skeptron* staff] **sceptred** *or US* **sceptered** *adj*

S

Schadenfreude (shah-den-froy-da) *n* one person's delight in another's misfortune [German *Schaden* harm + *Freude* joy]

schedule *n* **1** a timed plan of procedure for a project **2** a list of details or items: *the schedule of priorities* **3** a timetable ▷ *vb* **-uling, -uled 4** to plan and arrange (something) to happen at a certain time **5** to make a schedule or include in a schedule [Latin *scheda* sheet of paper]

schema *n, pl* **-mata** an outline of a plan or theory [Greek: form]

schematic *adj* presented as a diagram or plan **schematically** *adv*

schematize *or* **-tise** *vb* **-tizing, -tized** *or* **-tising, -tised** to form into or arrange in a systematic arrangement or plan

scheme *n* **1** a systematic plan for a course of action **2** a systematic arrangement of parts or features: *colour scheme* **3** a secret plot **4** a chart, diagram, or outline **5** a plan formally adopted by a government or organization: *a pension scheme* ▷ *vb* **scheming, schemed 6** to plan in an underhand manner [Greek *skhēma* form] **schemer** *n* **scheming** *adj, n*

scherzo (skairt-so) *n, pl* **-zos** a quick lively piece of music, often the second or third movement in a sonata or symphony [Italian: joke]

schilling *n* a former monetary unit of Austria [from German: shilling]

schism (skizz-um) *n* the division of a group, esp. a religious group, into opposing factions, due to differences in doctrine [Greek *skhizein* to split] **schismatic** *adj*

schist (skist) *n* a crystalline rock which splits into thin layers [Greek *skhizein* to split]

schistosomiasis (shiss-ta-so-**my**-a-siss) *n* same as **bilharzia**

schizo (skit-so) *offensive* ▷ *adj* **1** schizophrenic ▷ *n, pl* **-os 2** a schizophrenic person

schizoid *adj* **1** *psychol* having a personality disorder characterized by extreme shyness and extreme sensitivity **2** *informal* characterized by conflicting or contradictory ideas or attitudes ▷ *n* **3** *offensive* a person with a schizoid personality

> **USAGE** The use of *schizoid* as a noun can be offensive and should be avoided. Instead you should talk about *a person with a schizoid personality*.

schizophrenia *n* **1** a psychotic disorder characterized by withdrawal from reality, hallucinations, or emotional instability **2** *informal* behaviour that seems to be motivated by contradictory or conflicting principles [Greek *skhizein* to split + *phrēn* mind] **schizophrenic** *adj, n*

schmaltz *n* excessive sentimentality, esp. in music [Yiddish: melted fat] **schmaltzy** *adj*

schnapps *n* a strong dry alcoholic drink distilled from potatoes [German *Schnaps*]

schnitzel *n* a thin slice of meat, esp. veal [German: cutlet]

scholar *n* **1** a person who studies an academic subject **2** a student who has a scholarship **3** a pupil [Latin *schola* school] **scholarly** *adj*

scholarship *n* **1** academic achievement; learning gained by serious study **2** financial aid provided for a scholar because of academic merit

scholastic *adj* **1** of schools, scholars, or education **2** of or relating to scholasticism ▷ *n* **3** a scholarly person **4** a disciple or adherent of scholasticism [Greek *skholastikos* devoted to learning]

scholasticism *n* the system of philosophy, theology, and teaching that dominated medieval Europe and was based on the writings of Aristotle

school[1] *n* **1** a place where children are educated **2** the staff and pupils of a school **3** a regular session of instruction in a school: *we stayed behind after school* **4** a faculty or department specializing in a particular subject: *the dental school* **5** a place or sphere of activity that instructs: *the school of hard knocks* **6** a group of artists, writers, or thinkers, linked by the same style, teachers, or methods **7** *informal* a group assembled for a common purpose, such as gambling: *a card school* ▷ *vb* **8** to educate or train: *she schooled herself to be as ambitious as her sister* [Greek *skholē* leisure spent in the pursuit of knowledge]

school[2] *n* a group of sea-living animals that swim together, such as fish, whales, or dolphins [Old English *scolu* shoal]

schoolboy *n* a boy attending school

schooled *adj* **schooled in** trained or educated in: *well schooled in history*

schoolgirl *n* a girl attending school

schoolhouse *n* **1** a building used as a school **2** a house attached to a school

schoolie *n Austral informal* a schoolteacher or a high-school student

schoolies week *n Austral informal* a week of post-exam celebrations for students who have just completed their final year of high school

schooling *n* the education a person receives at school

schoolmarm *n informal* **1** a woman schoolteacher **2** a woman who is old-fashioned and easily shocked by bad language or references to sex

schoolmaster *or fem* **schoolmistress** *n old-fashioned* a person who teaches in or runs a school

school run *n Brit* a journey to take children to school or to bring them home from school

schoolteacher *n* a person who teaches in a school

school year *n* **1** a twelve-month period, usually of three terms, during which pupils remain in the same class **2** the time during this period when the school is open

schooner *n* **1** a sailing ship with at least two masts, one at the back and one at the front **2** *Brit* a large glass for sherry **3** *US, Canad, Austral & NZ* a large glass for beer [origin unknown]

schottische *n* **1** a 19th-century German dance resembling a slow polka **2** music for this dance [German *der schottische Tanz* the Scottish dance]

schuss (shooss) *n skiing* a straight high-speed downhill run [from German]

sciatic *adj* **1** *anatomy* of the hip or the hipbone **2** of or having sciatica: *a sciatic injury* [Greek *iskhia* hip joint]

sciatica *n* severe pain in the large nerve in the back of the leg

science *n* **1** the study of the nature and behaviour of the physical universe, based on observation, experiment, and measurement **2** the knowledge obtained by these methods **3** any particular branch of this knowledge: *medical science* **4** any body of knowledge organized in a way resembling that of the physical sciences but concerned with other subjects: *political science* [Latin *scientia* knowledge]

science fiction *n* stories and films that make imaginative use of scientific knowledge or theories

science park *n* an area where scientific research and commercial development are carried on in cooperation

scientific *adj* **1** relating to science or a particular science: *scientific discovery* **2** done in a systematic way, using experiments or tests **scientifically** *adv*

scientist *n* a person who studies or practises a science

sci-fi *n* short for **science fiction**

scimitar *n* a curved Asian sword [probably from Persian *shimshīr*]

scintilla (sin-**till**-a) *n* a very small amount; hint or trace [Latin: a spark]

scintillate *vb* **-lating, -lated** to give off (sparks); sparkle [Latin *scintilla* a spark] **scintillation** *n*

scintillating *adj* (of conversation or humour) very lively and amusing

scion (**sy**-on) *n* **1** a descendant or young member of a family **2** a shoot of a plant for grafting onto another plant [Old French *cion*]

scissors *pl n* a cutting instrument held in one hand, with two crossed blades pivoted so that they close together on what is to be cut [Old French *cisoires*]

sclera (**skleer**-a) *n biol* the tough white substance that forms the outer covering of the eyeball [Greek *sklēros* hard]

sclerosis (skleer-**oh**-siss) *n, pl* **-ses** (-seez) *pathol* an abnormal hardening or thickening of body tissues, esp. of the nervous system or the inner wall of arteries [Greek *sklērōsis* a hardening]

sclerotic (skleer-**rot**-ik) *adj* **1** of or relating to the sclera **2** of, relating to, or having sclerosis

scoff[1] *vb* **1** (often foll. by *at*) to speak in a scornful and mocking way about (something) ▷ *n* **2** a mocking expression; jeer [probably from Old Norse] **scoffing** *adj, n*

scoff[2] *vb informal* to eat (food) fast and greedily [variant of *scaff* food]

scold *vb* **1** to find fault with or rebuke (a person) harshly **2** *old-fashioned* to use harsh or abusive language ▷ *n* **3** *old-fashioned* a person, esp. a woman, who constantly scolds [from Old Norse *skāld*] **scolding** *n*

scollop *n, vb* same as **scallop**

sconce *n* a bracket fixed to a wall for holding candles or lights [Late Latin *absconsa* dark lantern]

scone (**skonn, skone**) *n* a small plain cake baked in an oven or on a griddle [Scots]

scoop *n* **1** a spoonlike tool with a deep bowl, used for handling loose or soft materials such as flour or ice cream **2** the deep shovel of a mechanical digger **3** the amount taken up by a scoop **4** the act of scooping or dredging **5** a news story reported in one newspaper before all the others ▷ *vb* **6** (often foll. by *up*) to take up and remove (something) with or as if with a scoop **7 scoop out** to hollow out with or as if with a scoop **8** to beat (rival newspapers) in reporting a news item **9** to win (a prize, a large sum of money, etc.) [Germanic]

scoot *vb* to leave or move quickly [origin unknown]

scooter *n* **1** a child's small cycle which is ridden by pushing the ground with one foot **2** a light motorcycle with a small engine

scope *n* **1** opportunity for using abilities: *ample scope for creative work* **2** range of view or grasp: *that is outside my scope* **3** the area covered by an activity or topic: *the scope of his essay was vast* [Greek *skopos* target]

scorbutic (score-**byewt**-ik) *adj* of or having scurvy [Medieval Latin *scorbutus*]

scorch *vb* **1** to burn or become burnt slightly on the surface **2** to parch or shrivel from heat **3** *informal* to criticize harshly ▷ *n* **4** a slight burn **5** a mark caused by the application of excessive heat [probably from Old Norse *skorpna* to shrivel up] **scorching** *adj*

scorcher *n informal* a very hot day

score *n* **1** the total number of points made by a side or individual in a game **2** the act of scoring a point or points: *there was no score and three minutes remained* **3 the score** *informal* the actual situation: *what's the score on this business?* **4** *old-fashioned* a group or set of twenty: *three score years and ten* **5 scores of** lots of: *we received scores of letters* **6** *music* a written version of a piece of music showing parts for each musician **7** **A** the incidental music for a film or play **B** the songs and music for a stage or film musical **8** a mark or scratch **9** a record of money due: *what's the score for the drinks?* **10** an amount recorded as due **11** a reason: *some objections were made on the score of sentiment* **12** a grievance: *a score to settle* **13 over the score** *informal* excessive or unfair ▷ *vb* **scoring, scored 14** to gain (a point or points) in a game or contest **15** to make a total score of **16** to keep a record of the score (of) **17** to be worth (a certain number of points) in a game: *red aces score twenty* **18** to make cuts or lines in or on **19** *slang* to purchase an illegal drug **20** *slang* to succeed in finding a sexual partner **21** to arrange (a piece of music) for specific instruments or voices **22** to write the music for (a film or play) **23** to achieve (success or an advantage): *your idea scored with the boss* [Old English *scora*]

scoreboard *n sport* a board for displaying the score of a game or match

scorecard *n* **1** a card on which scores are recorded in games such as golf **2** a card identifying the players in a sports match, esp. cricket

score off *vb* to make a clever or insulting reply to what someone has just said: *they spent the evening scoring off each other*

scorer *n* **1** a player of a sport who scores a goal, run, or point: *Ireland's record goal scorer has announced his retirement* **2** a person who keeps note of the score of a match or competition as it is being played

S

scoria (score-ee-a) *n* **1** *geol* a mass of solidified lava containing many cavities **2** refuse left after ore has been smelted [Latin: dross]
scorn *n* **1** open contempt for a person or thing ▷ *vb* **2** to treat with contempt: *she attacked the government for scorning her profession* **3** to refuse to have or do (something) because it is felt to be undesirable or wrong: *youths who scorn traditional morals* [Old French *escharnir*] **scornful** *adj* **scornfully** *adv*
Scorpio *n astrol* the eighth sign of the zodiac; the Scorpion [Latin]
scorpion *n* a small lobster-shaped animal with a sting at the end of a jointed tail [Greek *skorpios*]
Scot *n* a person from Scotland
Scot. **1** Scotland **2** Scottish
scotch *vb* **1** to put an end to: *she had scotched the idea of bingo in the church* **2** to wound without killing [origin unknown]
Scotch[1] *not standard* ▷ *adj* **1** same as **Scottish** ▷ *pl n* **2 the Scotch** the Scots

> **USAGE** In Scotland, *Scotch* is not used outside fixed expressions such as *Scotch whisky*. The use of *Scotch* for *Scots* or *Scottish* is otherwise felt to be incorrect, esp. when applied to people.

Scotch[2] *n* whisky distilled in Scotland from fermented malted barley
Scotch broth *n Brit* a thick soup made from mutton or beef stock, vegetables, and pearl barley
Scotch egg *n* a hard-boiled egg encased in sausage meat and breadcrumbs, and fried
Scotch mist *n* a heavy wet mist or drizzle
scot-free *adv, adj* without harm or punishment: *the real crooks got off scot-free* [obsolete *scot* a tax]
Scotland Yard *n* the headquarters of the police force of metropolitan London
Scots *adj* **1** of Scotland ▷ *n* **2** any of the English dialects spoken or written in Scotland
Scotsman *or fem* **Scotswoman** *n, pl* **-men** *or* **-women** a person from Scotland
Scots pine *n* **1** a coniferous tree found in Europe and Asia, with needle-like leaves and brown cones **2** the wood of this tree
Scottish *adj* of Scotland
scoundrel *n old-fashioned* a person who cheats and deceives [origin unknown]
scour[1] *vb* **1** to clean or polish (a surface) by rubbing with something rough **2** to clear (a channel) by the force of water ▷ *n* **3** the act of scouring [Old French *escurer*] **scourer** *n*
scour[2] *vb* **1** to search thoroughly and energetically: *he had scoured auction salerooms* **2** to move quickly over (land) in search or pursuit [probably from Old Norse *skūr* shower]
scourge *n* **1** a person who or thing that causes affliction or suffering **2** a whip formerly used for punishing people ▷ *vb* **scourging, scourged** **3** to cause severe suffering to **4** to whip [Latin *excoriare* to whip]
Scouse *Brit informal* ▷ *n* **1** Also called: **Scouser** a person from Liverpool **2** the Liverpool dialect ▷ *adj* **3** of Liverpool, its people, or their dialect [from *lobscouse* a sailor's stew]
scout *n* **1** *military* a person sent to find out the position of the enemy **2** same as **talent scout** **3** the act or an instance of scouting ▷ *vb* **4** to examine or observe (something) in order to obtain information **5 scout about** *or* **around** to go in search of something [Old French *ascouter* to listen to]
Scout *or* **scout** *n* a member of the Scout Association, an organization for young people which aims to develop character and promote outdoor activities **Scouting** *n*
scow *n* an unpowered barge used for carrying freight [Low German *schalde*]
scowl *vb* **1** to have an angry or bad-tempered facial expression ▷ *n* **2** an angry or bad-tempered facial expression [probably from Old Norse]
scrabble *vb* **-bling, -bled** **1** to scrape at or grope for something with hands, feet, or claws: *scrabbling with his feet to find a foothold* **2** to move one's hands about in order to find something one cannot see: *scrabbling in her handbag for a comb* [Middle Dutch *schrabbelen*]
Scrabble *n trademark* a board game in which words are formed by placing letter tiles in a pattern similar to a crossword puzzle
scrag *n* **1** the thin end of a neck of veal or mutton **2** a thin or scrawny person or animal [perhaps variant of *crag*]
scraggy *adj* **-gier, -giest** unpleasantly thin and bony **scragginess** *n*
scram[1] *vb* **scramming, scrammed** *informal* to leave very quickly [from *scramble*]
scram[2] *n* **1** an emergency shutdown of a nuclear reactor ▷ *vb* **scramming, scrammed** **2** (of a nuclear reactor) to shut down or be shut down in an emergency [perhaps from SCRAM[1]]
scramble *vb* **-bling, -bled** **1** to climb or crawl hurriedly by using the hands to aid movement **2** to go hurriedly or in a disorderly manner **3** to compete with others in a rough and undignified way: *spectators scrambled for the best seats* **4** to jumble together in a haphazard manner **5** to cook (eggs that have been whisked up with milk) in a pan **6** *military* (of a crew or aircraft) to take off quickly in an emergency **7** to make (transmitted speech) unintelligible by the use of an electronic scrambler ▷ *n* **8** the act of scrambling **9** a climb or trek over difficult ground **10** a rough and undignified struggle to gain possession of something **11** *military* an immediate takeoff of crew or aircraft in an emergency **12** *Brit* a motorcycle race across rough open ground [blend of SCRABBLE + RAMP]
scrambler *n* an electronic device that makes broadcast or telephone messages unintelligible without a special receiver
scramjet *n* **A** a type of ramjet in which the forward motion of the craft forces oxygen to mix with fuel (usually hydrogen) at supersonic speeds within a duct in the engine **B** an aircraft powered by such an engine [from s(*upersonic*) + c(*ombustion*) + RAMJET]
scrap[1] *n* **1** a small piece of something larger; fragment **2** waste material or used articles, often collected and reprocessed **3 scraps** pieces of

leftover food ▹ *vb* **scrapping, scrapped** **4** to discard as useless [Old Norse *skrap*]

scrap² *informal* ▹ *n* **1** a fight or quarrel ▹ *vb* **scrapping, scrapped** **2** to quarrel or fight [perhaps from *scrape*]

scrapbook *n* a book of blank pages in which newspaper cuttings or pictures are stuck

scrape *vb* **scraping, scraped** **1** to move (a rough or sharp object) across (a surface) **2** (often foll. by *away* or *off*) to remove (a layer) by rubbing **3** to produce a grating sound by rubbing against (something else) **4** to injure or damage by scraping: *he had scraped his knees* **5** **scrimp and scrape** See **scrimp** (sense 2) ▹ *n* **6** the act or sound of scraping **7** a scraped place: *a scrape on the car door* **8** *informal* an awkward or embarrassing situation **9** *informal* a conflict or struggle [Old English *scrapian*] **scraper** *n*

scrape through *vb* to succeed in or survive with difficulty: *both teams had scraped through their semi-finals*

scrape together *or* **scrape up** *vb* to collect with difficulty: *he scraped together enough money to travel*

scrapheap *n* **on the scrapheap** (of people or things) no longer required: *I was tossed on the scrapheap at a very early age*

scrappy *adj* **-pier, -piest** badly organized or done: *a scrappy draft of a chapter of my thesis*

scratch *vb* **1** to mark or cut (the surface of something) with a rough or sharp instrument **2** (often foll. by *at* or *out* etc.) to tear or dig with the nails or claws **3** to scrape (the surface of the skin) with the nails to relieve itching **4** to rub against (the skin) causing a slight cut **5** to make or cause to make a grating sound **6** (sometimes foll. by *out*) to erase or cross out **7** to withdraw from a race or (in the US) an election ▹ *n* **8** the act of scratching **9** a slight cut on a person's or an animal's body **10** a mark made by scratching **11** a slight grating sound **12** **from scratch** *informal* from the very beginning **13** **not up to scratch** *informal* not up to standard ▹ *adj* **14** put together at short notice: *a scratch team* **15** *sport* with no handicap allowed: *a scratch golfer* [Germanic] **scratchy** *adj*

scratchcard *n* a ticket that reveals whether or not the holder is eligible for a prize when the surface is removed by scratching

scratchie *n* *Austral informal* a scratchcard

scratching *n* *music* a sound produced when the record groove in contact with the stylus of a record player is moved back and forth by hand

scrawl *vb* **1** to write carelessly or hastily ▹ *n* **2** careless or scribbled writing [perhaps blend of SPRAWL + CRAWL] **scrawly** *adj*

scrawny *adj* **scrawnier, scrawniest** very thin and bony [dialect *scranny*] **scrawniness** *n*

scream *vb* **1** to make a sharp piercing cry or sound because of fear or pain **2** (of a machine) to make a high-pitched noise **3** to laugh wildly **4** to utter with a scream: *he screamed abuse up into the sky* **5** to be unpleasantly conspicuous: *bad news screaming out from the headlines* ▹ *n* **6** a sharp piercing cry or sound, esp. of fear or pain **7** *informal* a very funny person or thing [Germanic]

scree *n* a pile of rock fragments at the foot of a cliff or hill, often forming a sloping heap [Old English *scrīthan* to slip]

screech¹ *n* **1** a shrill or high-pitched sound or cry ▹ *vb* **2** to utter a shrill cry [earlier *scritch*, imitative] **screechy** *adj*

screech² *n* *Canad* a dark rum [origin unknown]

screech owl *n* **1** *Brit* same as **barn owl** **2** a small North American barn owl

screed *n* a long tiresome speech or piece of writing [probably from Old English *scrēade* shred]

screen *n* **1** the blank surface of a television set, computer, or mobile phone, on which a visible image is formed **2** the white surface on which films or slides are projected **3** **the screen** the film industry or films collectively **4** a light movable frame, panel, or partition used to shelter, divide, or conceal **5** anything that shelters, protects, or conceals: *a screen of leaves blocking out the sun* **6** a frame containing a mesh that is used to keep out insects ▹ *vb* **7** (sometimes foll. by *off*) to shelter, protect, or conceal with or as if with a screen **8** to test or check (an individual or group) so as to assess suitability for a task or to detect the presence of a disease or weapons: *women screened for breast cancer* **9** to show (a film) in the cinema or show (a programme) on television [Old French *escren*]

screenplay *n* the script for a film, including instructions for sets and camera work

screen process *n* a method of printing by forcing ink through a fine mesh of silk or nylon, some parts of which have been treated so as not to let the ink pass

screen saver *n* software that produces changing images on a computer screen when the machine is operating but idle

screenshot *n* an image created by copying part or all of the display on a computer screen at a particular moment

screenwriter *n* a person who writes screenplays

screw *n* **1** a metal pin with a spiral ridge along its length, twisted into materials to fasten them together **2** a threaded cylindrical rod that engages with a similarly threaded cylindrical hole **3** a thread in a cylindrical hole corresponding with the one on the screw with which it is designed to engage **4** anything resembling a screw in shape **5** *slang* a prison guard **6** *taboo slang* an act of or partner in sexual intercourse **7** **have a screw loose** *informal* **A** to be eccentric **B** *offensive* to be insane **8** **put the screws on** *slang* to use force on or threatening behaviour against ▹ *vb* **9** to rotate (a screw or bolt) so as to drive it into or draw it out of a material **10** to twist or turn: *she screwed up the sheet of paper* **11** to attach or fasten with or as if with a screw or screws **12** *informal* to take advantage of, esp. illegally: *screwed by big business* **13** *informal* to distort or contort: *his face was screwed up in pain* **14** (often foll. by *out of*) *informal* to force out of; extort **15** *taboo slang* to have sexual intercourse (with) **16** **have one's head screwed on the right way** *informal* to be sensible ▹ See also **screw up** [French *escroe*]

S

screwball *slang, chiefly US & Canad* ▷ *n* **1** an odd or eccentric person ▷ *adj* **2** crazy or eccentric: *a screwball comedy*

screwdriver *n* **1** a tool used for turning screws, consisting of a long thin metal rod with a flattened tip that fits into a slot in the head of the screw **2** a drink consisting of orange juice and vodka

screw top *n* **1** a bottle top that screws onto the bottle, allowing the bottle to be resealed after use **2** a bottle with such a top

screw up *vb* **1** *informal* to mishandle or spoil (something): *that screws up all my arrangements* **2** to twist out of shape or distort **3 screw up one's courage** to force oneself to be brave **screwed-up** *adj*

screwy *adj* **screwier, screwiest** *informal* crazy or eccentric

scribble *vb* **-bling, -bled 1** to write or draw quickly and roughly **2** to make meaningless or illegible marks (on) ▷ *n* **3** something written or drawn quickly or roughly **4** meaningless or illegible marks [Latin *scribere* to write] **scribbler** *n* **scribbly** *adj*

scribe *n* **1** a person who made handwritten copies of manuscripts or documents before the invention of printing **2** *Bible* a recognized scholar and teacher of the Jewish Law [Latin *scriba* clerk]

scrimmage *n* **1** a rough or disorderly struggle ▷ *vb* **-maging, -maged 2** to take part in a scrimmage [earlier *scrimish*]

scrimp *vb* **1** to be very sparing in the use of something: *they were scrimping by on the last of the potatoes* **2 scrimp and save** *or* **scrape** to spend as little money as possible [Scots]

scrip[1] *n* *finance* a certificate representing a claim to shares or stocks [short for *subscription receipt*]

scrip[2] *or* **script** *n informal* a medical prescription [from PRESCRIPTION]

script *n* **1** the text of a play, TV programme, or film for the use of performers **2** an alphabet or system of writing: *Cyrillic script* **3** a candidate's answer paper in an examination **4** handwriting **5** a typeface which looks like handwriting ▷ *vb* **6** to write a script for [Latin *scriptum* something written]

scripture *n* the sacred writings of a religion [Latin *scriptura* written material] **scriptural** *adj*

Scripture *n* *Christianity* the Old and New Testaments

scriptwriter *n* a person who writes scripts, esp. for a film or TV programme **scriptwriting** *n*

scrofula *n not in technical use* tuberculosis of the lymphatic glands [Medieval Latin] **scrofulous** *adj*

scroggin *n NZ* a mixture of nuts and dried fruits

scroll *n* **1** a roll of parchment or paper, usually inscribed with writing **2** an ancient book in the form of a roll of parchment, papyrus, or paper **3** a decorative carving or moulding resembling a scroll ▷ *vb* **4** to move (text) on a computer or phone screen in order to view a section that cannot be fitted into a single display [Middle English *scrowle*]

Scrooge *n* a mean or miserly person [after a character in Dickens' story *A Christmas Carol*]

scrotum *n* the pouch of skin containing the testicles in most male mammals [Latin]

scrounge *vb* **scrounging, scrounged** *informal* to get (something) by asking for it rather than buying it or working for it [dialect *scrunge* to steal] **scrounger** *n*

scrub[1] *vb* **scrubbing, scrubbed 1** to rub (something) hard in order to clean it **2** to remove (dirt) by rubbing with a brush and water **3 scrub up** (of a surgeon) to wash the hands and arms thoroughly before operating **4** *informal* to delete or cancel (an idea or plan) ▷ *n* **5** the act of scrubbing [Middle Low German *schrubben* or Middle Dutch *schrobben*]

scrub[2] *n* **1** vegetation consisting of stunted trees or bushes growing in a dry area **2** an area of dry land covered with such vegetation ▷ *adj* **3** stunted or inferior: *scrub pines* [variant of *shrub*]

scrubber *n* **1** *Brit & Austral offensive slang* a woman who is considered promiscuous **2** a device that removes pollutants from the gases that are produced when coal is burned industrially

scrubby *adj* **-bier, -biest 1** (of land) rough, dry, and covered with scrub **2** (of plants) stunted **3** *Brit informal* shabby or untidy

scrubs *pl n* the hygienic clothing worn by surgeons and other operating-theatre staff during an operation

scruff[1] *n* the nape of the neck: *the sergeant had him by the scruff of the neck* [perhaps from Old Norse *skoft* hair]

scruff[2] *n informal* a very untidy person

scruffy *adj* **scruffier, scruffiest** dirty and untidy in appearance

scrum *n* **1** *rugby* a formation in which players from each side form a tight pack and push against each other in an attempt to get the ball, which is thrown on the ground between them **2** *informal* a disorderly struggle ▷ *vb* **scrumming, scrummed 3** (usually foll. by *down*) *rugby* to form a scrum [from *scrummage*]

scrum half *n* *rugby* a player who puts in the ball at scrums and tries to regain its possession in order to pass it to his team's backs

scrummage *n, vb* **-maging, -maged 1** *rugby* same as **scrum 2** same as **scrimmage** [variant of *scrimmage*]

scrump *vb Brit dialect* to steal (apples) from an orchard or garden [variant of *scrimp*]

scrumptious *adj informal* delicious or very attractive [probably changed from *sumptuous*]

scrumpy *n Brit* a rough dry cider brewed in the West Country of England [dialect *scrump* withered apples]

scrunch *vb* **1** to press or crush noisily or be pressed or crushed noisily ▷ *n* **2** the act or sound of scrunching: *the scrunch of tyres on gravel* [variant of *crunch*]

scrunchie *n* a loop of elastic covered loosely with fabric, used to hold the hair in a ponytail

scruple *n* **1** a doubt or hesitation as to what is morally right in a certain situation: *he had no scruples about the drug trade* ▷ *vb* **-pling, -pled 2** to have doubts (about), esp. on moral grounds [Latin *scrupulus* a small weight]

S

scrupulous *adj* **1** taking great care to do what is fair, honest, or morally right **2** very careful or precise: *scrupulous attention to detail* [Latin *scrupulosus*] **scrupulously** *adv*
scrutinize *or* **-nise** *vb* **-nizing, -nized** *or* **-nising, -nised** to examine carefully or in minute detail
scrutiny *n, pl* **-nies 1** very careful study or observation **2** a searching look [Late Latin *scrutari* to search]
scuba (skew-ba) *n* an apparatus used in skin diving, consisting of cylinders containing compressed air attached to a breathing apparatus [*s(elf-)c(ontained) u(nderwater) b(reathing) a(pparatus)*]
scud *vb* **scudding, scudded 1** (esp. of clouds) to move along quickly **2** *naut* to run before a gale ▷ *n* **3** the act of scudding **4** spray, rain, or clouds driven by the wind [probably Scandinavian]
scuff *vb* **1** to drag (the feet) while walking **2** to scrape (one's shoes) by doing so ▷ *n* **3** a mark caused by scuffing **4** the act or sound of scuffing [probably imitative]
scuffle *vb* **-fling, -fled 1** to fight in a disorderly manner ▷ *n* **2** a short disorganized fight **3** a scuffling sound [Scandinavian]
scull *n* **1** a single oar moved from side to side over the back of a boat **2** one of a pair of small oars, both of which are pulled by one oarsman **3** a racing boat rowed by one oarsman pulling two oars ▷ *vb* **4** to row (a boat) with a scull [origin unknown] **sculler** *n*
scullery *n, pl* **-leries** *chiefly Brit* a small room where washing-up and other kitchen work is done [Anglo-Norman *squillerie*]
scullion *n archaic* a servant employed to do the hard work in a kitchen [Old French *escouillon* cleaning cloth]
sculpt *vb* same as **sculpture**
sculptor *or fem* **sculptress** *n* a person who makes sculptures
sculpture *n* **1** the art of making figures or designs in wood, plaster, stone, or metal **2** works or a work made in this way ▷ *vb* **-turing, -tured 3** to carve (a material) into figures or designs **4** to represent (a person or thing) in sculpture **5** to form or be formed in the manner of sculpture: *limestone sculptured by fast-flowing streams* [Latin *sculptura* a carving] **sculptural** *adj*
scum *n* **1** a layer of impure or waste matter that forms on the surface of a liquid: *the build-up of soap scum* **2** a person or people regarded as worthless or criminal ▷ *vb* **scumming, scummed 3** to remove scum from **4** *rare* to form a layer of or become covered with scum [Germanic] **scummy** *adj*
scumbag *n slang* an offensive or despicable person [perhaps from earlier US sense: condom]
scungy (skun-jee) *adj* **scungier, scungiest** *Austral & NZ slang* miserable, sordid, or dirty [origin unknown]
scunner *dialect, chiefly Scot* ▷ *vb* **1** to produce a feeling of dislike in ▷ *n* **2 take a scunner to** to take a strong dislike to **3** a person or thing that is disliked [Scots *skunner*]
scupper[1] *n naut* a drain or spout in a ship's side allowing water on the deck to flow overboard [origin unknown]
scupper[2] *vb* **1** *Brit & NZ slang* to defeat or ruin: *a deliberate attempt to scupper the peace talks* **2** to sink (one's ship) deliberately [origin unknown]
scurf *n* **1** same as **dandruff 2** any flaky or scaly matter sticking to or peeling off a surface [Old English] **scurfy** *adj*
scurrilous *adj* untrue or unfair, insulting, and designed to damage a person's reputation: *scurrilous allegations* [Latin *scurra* buffoon] **scurrility** *n*
scurry *vb* **-ries, -rying, -ried 1** to run quickly with short steps ▷ *n, pl* **-ries 2** a quick hurrying movement or the sound of this movement **3** a short shower of rain or snow [probably from *hurry-scurry*]
scurvy *n* **1** a disease caused by a lack of vitamin C, resulting in weakness, spongy gums, and bleeding beneath the skin ▷ *adj* **-vier, -viest 2** *old-fashioned* deserving contempt [from *scurf*] **scurviness** *n*
scut *n* the short tail of animals such as the deer and rabbit [probably from Old Norse]
scuttle[1] *n* same as **coal scuttle** [Latin *scutella* bowl]
scuttle[2] *vb* **-tling, -tled 1** to run with short quick steps ▷ *n* **2** a hurried pace or run [probably from *scud*]
scuttle[3] *vb* **-tling, -tled 1** *naut* to cause (a ship) to sink by making holes in the sides or bottom **2** to ruin (hopes or plans) or have them ruined: *a new policy scuttled by popular resistance* ▷ *n* **3** *naut* a small hatch in a ship's deck or side [Spanish *escotilla* a small opening]
Scylla (sill-a) *n* **1** (in classical mythology) a sea monster believed to drown sailors navigating the Straits of Messina **2 between Scylla and Charybdis** in an awkward situation in which avoidance of either of two dangers means exposure to the other
scythe *n* **1** a long-handled tool for cutting grass or grain, with a curved sharpened blade that is swung parallel to the ground ▷ *vb* **scything, scythed 2** to cut (grass or grain) with a scythe [Old English *sigthe*]
SD South Dakota
SDLP (in Northern Ireland) Social Democratic and Labour Party
Se *chem* selenium
SE southeast(ern)
sea *n* **1 the sea** the mass of salt water that covers three-quarters of the earth's surface **2 A** one of the smaller areas of this: *the Irish Sea* **B** a large inland area of water: *the Caspian Sea* **3** the area on or close to the edge of the sea, esp. as a place where holidays are taken: *a day by the sea* **4** strong and uneven swirling movement of waves: *rough seas* **5** anything resembling the sea in size or movement: *a sea of red and yellow flags* **6 at sea A** on the ocean **B** in a state of confusion or uncertainty **7 go to sea** to become a sailor **8 put out to sea** to start a sea voyage [Old English *sǣ*]
sea anchor *n naut* a canvas-covered frame, dragged in the water behind a ship to slow it down or reduce drifting
sea anemone *n* a marine animal with a round body and rings of tentacles which trap food from the water

S

sea bird *n* a bird that lives on or near the sea
seaboard *n* land bordering on the sea
seaborgium *n chem* a synthetic element. Symbol: **Sg** [after Glenn *Seaborg*, physicist and chemist]
seaborne *adj* **1** carried on or by the sea **2** transported by ship: *seaborne reinforcements*
sea breeze *n* a breeze blowing inland from the sea
sea cow *n* **1** a whalelike mammal such as a dugong or manatee **2** *archaic* a walrus
sea dog *n* an experienced or old sailor
seafarer *n* **1** a traveller who goes by sea **2** a sailor
seafaring *adj* **1** travelling by sea **2** working as a sailor ▷ *n* **3** the act of travelling by sea **4** the work of a sailor
seafood *n* edible saltwater fish or shellfish
seafront *n* a built-up area facing the sea
seagoing *adj* built for travelling on the sea
sea-green *adj* bluish-green
seagull *n* same as **gull**
sea horse *n* a small marine fish with a horselike head, which swims upright
sea kale *n* a European coastal plant with broad fleshy leaves and asparagus-like shoots that can be eaten
seal[1] *n* **1** a special design impressed on a piece of wax, lead, or paper, fixed to a letter or document as a mark of authentication **2** a stamp or signet ring engraved with a design to form such an impression **3** a substance placed over an envelope or container, so that it cannot be opened without the seal being broken **4** something that serves as an official confirmation of approval: *seal of approval* **5** any substance or device used to close an opening tightly **6 set the seal on** to confirm: *the experience set the seal on their friendship* ▷ *vb* **7** to close or secure with or as if with a seal: *once the manuscripts were sealed up, they were forgotten about* **8 seal off** to enclose or isolate (a place) completely **9** to close tightly so as to make airtight or watertight **10** to inject a compound around the edges of (something) to make it airtight or watertight **11** to attach a seal to or stamp with a seal **12** to finalize or authorize **13 seal one's fate** to make sure one dies or fails **14 seal one's lips** to promise not to reveal a secret [Latin *signum* a sign] **sealable** *adj*
seal[2] *n* **1** a fish-eating mammal with four flippers, which lives in the sea but comes ashore to breed **2** sealskin ▷ *vb* **3** to hunt seals [Old English *seolh*]
sealant *n* any substance, such as wax, used for sealing, esp. to make airtight or watertight
sea legs *pl n informal* the ability to maintain one's balance on board ship and to avoid being seasick
sea level *n* the average level of the sea's surface in relation to the land
sealing wax *n* a hard material made of shellac and turpentine, which softens when heated and which is used to make a seal
sea lion *n* a type of large seal found in the Pacific Ocean
Sea Lord *n* (in Britain) either of two senior Royal Navy officers on the Admiralty Board of the Ministry of Defence
sealskin *n* the skin or prepared fur of a seal, used to make coats
seam *n* **1** the line along which pieces of fabric are joined by stitching **2** a ridge or line made by joining two edges: *the seam between the old and the new buildings* **3** a long narrow layer of coal, marble, or ore formed between layers of other rocks **4** a mark or line like a seam, such as a wrinkle or scar ▷ *adj* **5** *cricket* of a style of bowling in which the bowler uses the stitched seam round the ball in order to make it swing in flight and after touching the ground: *a seam bowler* ▷ *vb* **6** to join together by or as if by a seam **7** to mark with furrows or wrinkles [Old English *sēam*]
seaman *n, pl* **-men 1** a man ranking below an officer in a navy **2** a sailor
seamanship *n* skill in navigating and operating a ship
seamer *or* **seam bowler** *n cricket* a fast bowler who makes the ball bounce on its seam so that it will change direction
seamless *adj* **1** (of a garment) without seams **2** continuous or flowing: *a seamless performance* **seamlessly** *adv* **seamlessness** *n*
seamstress *n* a woman who sews, esp. professionally
seamy *adj* **seamier, seamiest** involving the sordid and unpleasant aspects of life, such as crime, prostitution, poverty, and violence **seaminess** *n*
seance *or* **séance** (say-onss) *n* a meeting at which a spiritualist attempts to communicate with the spirits of the dead [French]
seaplane *n* an aircraft with skis or floats, designed to land on and take off from water
seaport *n* a town or city with a harbour for boats and ships
sear *vb* **1** to scorch or burn the surface of **2** to cause to wither [Old English *sēarian* to become withered]
search *vb* **1** to look through (a place) thoroughly in order to find someone or something **2** to examine (a person) for hidden objects **3** to look at or examine (something) closely: *I searched my heart for one good thing she had done* **4 search out** to find by searching **5** to make a search **6 search me** *informal* I don't know ▷ *n* **7** an attempt to find something by looking somewhere [Old French *cerchier*]
search engine *n* a service that enables users to search the internet for items of interest
search engine optimization *n* the process of improving a website's page ranking in a search engine
searching *adj* keen or thorough: *a searching analysis* **searchingly** *adv*
searchlight *n* **1** a light with a powerful beam that can be shone in any direction **2** the beam of light produced by this device
search warrant *n* a legal document allowing a police officer to enter and search premises
seascape *n* a drawing, painting, or photograph of a scene at sea
Sea Scout *n* a member of the branch of the Scouts which gives training in seamanship
seashell *n* the empty shell of a marine mollusc

seashore *n* land bordering on the sea
seasick *adj* suffering from nausea and dizziness caused by the movement of a ship at sea **seasickness** *n*
seaside *n* an area, esp. a holiday resort, bordering on the sea
season *n* **1** one of the four divisions of the year (spring, summer, autumn, and winter), each of which has characteristic weather conditions **2** a period of the year characterized by particular conditions or activities: *the typhoon season; the football season* **3** the period during which any particular species of animal, bird, or fish is legally permitted to be caught or killed: *the deer season* **4** any definite or indefinite period: *the busy season* **5** any period during which a show or play is performed at one venue: *the show ran for three seasons* **6** **in season** **A** (of game) permitted to be killed **B** (of fresh food) readily available **C** (of animals) ready to mate ▷ *vb* **7** to add herbs, salt, pepper, or spice to (food) in order to enhance the flavour **8** (in the preparation of timber) to dry and harden **9** to make experienced: *old men seasoned by living* [Latin *satio* a sowing] **seasoned** *adj*
seasonable *adj* **1** suitable for the season: *a seasonable Christmas snow scene* **2** coming or happening just at the right time: *seasonable advice*
seasonal *adj* of or depending on a certain season or seasons of the year: *seasonal employment* **seasonally** *adv*
seasoning *n* something that is added to food to enhance the flavour
season ticket *n* a ticket for a series of events or number of journeys, usually bought at a reduced rate
seat *n* **1** a piece of furniture designed for sitting on, such as a chair **2** the part of a chair or other piece of furniture on which one sits **3** a place to sit in a theatre, esp. one that requires a ticket: *there were two empty front-row seats at the pageant* **4** the buttocks **5** the part of a garment covering the buttocks **6** the part or surface on which an object rests **7** the place or centre in which something is based: *the seat of government* **8** *Brit* a country mansion **9** a membership or the right to membership of a legislative or administrative body: *a seat on the council* **10** *chiefly Brit* a parliamentary constituency **11** the manner in which a rider sits on a horse ▷ *vb* **12** to bring to or place on a seat **13** to provide seats for: *the dining hall seats 150 people* **14** to set firmly in place [Old English *gesete*]
seat belt *n* a strap attached to a car or aircraft seat, worn across the body to prevent a person being thrown forward in the event of a collision
seating *n* **1** seats which are provided somewhere, esp. in a public place: *the grandstand has seating for 10 000; hard plastic seating* ▷ *adj* **2** of or relating to the provision of places to sit: *the delegation leader complained about the seating arrangements*
sea urchin *n* a small sea animal with a round body enclosed in a spiny shell
seaward *adv also* **seawards** **1** towards the sea ▷ *adj* **2** directed or moving towards the sea
seawater *n* salt water from the sea
seaweed *n* any plant growing in the sea or on the seashore
seaworthy *adj* (of a ship) in a fit condition for a sea voyage **seaworthiness** *n*
sebaceous *adj* of, like, or secreting fat [Latin *sebum* tallow]
sebaceous glands *pl n* the small glands in the skin that secrete oil into hair follicles and onto most of the body surface
sebum (**see**-bum) *n* the oily substance secreted by the sebaceous glands [Latin: tallow]
sec[1] *adj* (of wines) dry [French]
sec[2] *n informal* a second (of time): *hang on a sec*
sec[3] secant
sec. **1** second (of time) **2** secondary **3** secretary
secant (**seek**-ant) *n* **1** (in trigonometry) the ratio of the length of the hypotenuse to the length of the adjacent side in a right-angled triangle; the reciprocal of cosine **2** a straight line that intersects a curve [Latin *secare* to cut]
secateurs *pl n* a small pair of gardening shears for pruning [French]
secede *vb* **-ceding, -ceded** to make a formal withdrawal of membership from a political alliance, federation, or group: *it will secede from the federation within six months* [Latin *se-* apart + *cedere* to go]
secession *n* the act of seceding **secessionism** *n* **secessionist** *n, adj*
seclude *vb* **-cluding, -cluded** **1** to remove from contact with others **2** to shut off or screen from view [Latin *secludere*]
secluded *adj* **1** kept apart from the company of others: *a secluded private life* **2** private and sheltered: *a secluded cottage*
seclusion *n* the state of being secluded; privacy: *the seclusion of his winter retreat*
second[1] *adj* **1** coming directly after the first in order **2** rated, graded, or ranked between the first and third levels **3** alternate: *every second Saturday* **4** another of the same kind; additional: *a second chance* **5** resembling or comparable to a person or event from the past: *a second Virgin Mary* **6** of lesser importance or position; inferior **7** denoting the second lowest forward gear in a motor vehicle **8** *music* denoting a musical part, voice, or instrument subordinate to or lower in pitch than another (the first): *the second tenors* **9** **at second hand** by hearsay ▷ *n* **10** a person or thing that is second **11** *Brit education* an honours degree of the second class **12** the second lowest forward gear in a motor vehicle **13** (in boxing or duelling) an attendant who looks after a boxer or duellist **14** **seconds** **A** *informal* a second helping of food or the second course of a meal **B** goods that are sold cheaply because they are slightly faulty ▷ *vb* **15** to give aid or backing to **16** (in boxing or duelling) to act as second to (a boxer or duellist) **17** to express formal support for (a motion proposed in a meeting) ▷ *adv* **18** Also: **secondly** in the second place [Latin *secundus* next in order]
second[2] *n* **1** the basic SI unit of time, equal to $^1/_{60}$ of a minute **2** $^1/_{60}$ of a minute of angle **3** a very short period of time [Latin *pars minuta secunda* the second small part (a minute being the first small part of an hour)]

S

second³ (sik-kond) *vb Brit & NZ* to transfer (a person) temporarily to another job [French *en second* in second rank] **secondment** *n*

secondary *adj* **1** below the first in rank or importance: *a secondary consideration* **2** coming next after the first: *secondary cancers* **3** derived from or depending on what is primary or first: *a secondary source* **4** of or relating to the education of people between the ages of 11 and 18 or, in New Zealand, between 13 and 18: *secondary education* **5** (of an industry) involving the manufacture of goods from raw materials ▷ *n, pl* **-aries 6** a person or thing that is secondary

secondary colour *n* a colour formed by mixing two primary colours

secondary school *n* a school for young people, usually between the ages of 11 and 18

second-best *adj* **1** next to the best ▷ *adv* **second best 2 come off second best** *informal* to fail to win against someone ▷ *n* **second best 3** an inferior alternative

second chamber *n* the upper house of a two-chamber system of government

second class *n* **1** the class or grade next in value, rank, or quality to the first ▷ *adj* **second-class 2** of the class or grade next to the best in value, rank, or quality **3** shoddy or inferior **4** denoting the class of accommodation in a hotel or on a train, aircraft, or ship, lower in quality and price than first class **5** (of mail) sent by a cheaper type of postage and taking slightly longer to arrive than first-class mail ▷ *adv* **6** by second-class mail, transport, etc.

Second Coming *n Christianity* the prophesied return of Christ to earth at the Last Judgment

second cousin *n* the child of one's parent's first cousin

second-degree burn *n* a burn in which blisters appear on the skin

second fiddle *n informal* a person who has a secondary status

second floor *n* the storey of a building immediately above the first and two floors up from the ground

second hand *n* a pointer on the face of a watch or clock that indicates the seconds

second-hand *adj* **1** previously owned or used **2** not from an original source or one's own experience: *second-hand opinions* **3** dealing in or selling goods that are not new: *second-hand furniture shops* ▷ *adv* **4** from a source of previously owned or used goods: *they preferred to buy second-hand* **5** not directly or from one's own experience: *his knowledge had been gleaned second-hand*

second lieutenant *n* an officer holding the lowest commissioned rank in an army or navy

secondly *adv* same as **second¹** (sense 18)

second nature *n* a habit or characteristic practised for so long that it seems to be part of one's character

second person *n* the form of a pronoun or verb used to refer to the person or people being addressed

second-rate *adj* **1** not of the highest quality; mediocre **2** second in importance or rank: *a second-rate citizen*

second sight *n* the supposed ability to foresee the future or see actions taking place elsewhere

second thoughts *pl n* a revised opinion or idea on a matter already considered

second wind *n* **1** the return of comfortable breathing following difficult or strenuous exercise **2** renewed ability to continue in an effort

secrecy *n, pl* **-cies 1** the state of being secret **2** the ability or tendency to keep things secret

secret *adj* **1** kept hidden or separate from the knowledge of all or all but a few others **2** secretive: *she had become a secret drinker* **3** operating without the knowledge of outsiders: *secret organizations* ▷ *n* **4** something kept or to be kept hidden **5** something unrevealed; a mystery: *the secrets of nature* **6** an underlying explanation or reason: *the secret of great-looking hair* **7 in secret** without the knowledge of others [Latin *secretus* concealed] **secretly** *adv*

secret agent *n* a person employed by a government to find out the military and political secrets of other governments

secretaire (sek-rit-air) *n* same as **escritoire**

secretariat *n* **1 A** an office responsible for the secretarial, clerical, and administrative affairs of a legislative body or international organization **B** the staff of such an office or department **2** the premises of a secretariat [French]

secretary *n, pl* **-taries 1** a person who handles correspondence, keeps records, and does general clerical work for an individual or organization **2** the official manager of the day-to-day business of a society, club, or committee **3** (in Britain) a senior civil servant who assists a government minister **4** (in the US) the head of a government administrative department [Medieval Latin *secretarius* someone entrusted with secrets] **secretarial** *adj*

secretary bird *n* a large long-legged African bird of prey

secretary-general *n, pl* **secretaries-general** the chief administrative official of a legislative body or international organization

secretary of state *n* **1** (in Britain) the head of a major government department **2** (in the US) the head of the government department in charge of foreign affairs

secrete¹ *vb* **-creting, -creted** (of a cell, organ, or gland) to produce and release (a substance) **secretory** (sik-reet-or-ee) *adj*

secrete² *vb* **-creting, -creted** to put in a hiding place [variant of obsolete *secret* to hide away]

secretion *n* **1** a substance that is released from a cell, organ, or gland **2** the process involved in producing and releasing such a substance [Latin *secretio* a separation]

secretive *adj* hiding feelings and intentions **secretively** *adv*

secret police *n* a police force that operates secretly to suppress opposition to the government

secret service *n* a government agency or department that conducts intelligence or counterintelligence operations

sect *n* **1** a subdivision of a larger religious or political group, esp. one regarded as extreme in its beliefs or practices **2** a group of people with a common interest or philosophy [Latin *secta* faction]

sectarian *adj* **1** of or belonging to a sect **2** narrow-minded as a result of supporting a particular sect ▷ *n* **3** a member of a sect **sectarianism** *n*

section *n* **1** a part cut off or separated from the main body of something: *a non-smoking section* **2** a part or subdivision of a piece of writing or a book: *the business section* **3** a distinct part of a country or community: *the Arabic section* **4** *surgery* the act or process of cutting or separating by cutting **5** *geom* a plane surface formed by cutting through a solid **6** short for **Caesarean section** **7** NZ a plot of land for building on **8** *Austral & NZ* a fare stage on a bus ▷ *vb* **9** to cut or divide into sections **10** to commit (a person) to a psychiatric hospital under an appropriate section of mental health legislation [Latin *secare* to cut]

sectional *adj* **1** concerned with a particular area or group within a country or community, esp. to the exclusion of others: *narrow sectional interests* **2** made of sections **3** of a section

sector *n* **1** a part or subdivision, esp. of a society or an economy: *the public sector* **2** *geom* either portion of a circle bounded by two radii and the arc cut off by them **3** a portion into which an area is divided for military operations [Latin: a cutter]

secular *adj* **1** relating to worldly as opposed to sacred things **2** not connected with religion or the church **3** (of clerics) not bound by religious vows to a monastic or other order [Late Latin *saecularis*]

secularism *n* the belief that religion should have no place in civil affairs **secularist** *n*, *adj*

secularize *or* **-rise** *vb* **-rizing, -rized** *or* **-rising, -rised** to change (something, such as education) so that it is no longer connected with religion or the Church **secularization** *or* **-risation** *n*

secure *adj* **1** free from danger or damage **2** free from fear, doubt, or care **3** tightly locked or well protected **4** fixed or tied firmly in position **5** able to be relied on: *secure profits* ▷ *vb* **-curing, -cured** **6** to obtain: *to secure a change in German policy* **7** to make or become free from danger or fear **8** to make safe from loss, theft, or attack **9** to attach; make fast or firm **10** to guarantee (payment of a loan) by giving something as security [Latin *securus* free from care] **securely** *adv*

security *n, pl* **-ties** **1** precautions taken to ensure against theft, espionage, or other danger **2** the state of being free from danger, damage, or worry **3** assured freedom from poverty: *the security of a weekly pay cheque* **4** a certificate of ownership, such as a share, stock, or bond **5** something given or pledged to guarantee payment of a loan

security risk *n* someone or something thought to be a threat to state security

sedan *n US, Canad, Austral & NZ* a saloon car [origin unknown]

sedan chair *n* an enclosed chair for one passenger, carried on poles by two bearers, commonly used in the 17th and 18th centuries

sedate[1] *adj* **1** quiet, calm, and dignified **2** slow or unhurried: *a sedate walk to the beach* [Latin *sedare* to soothe] **sedately** *adv*

sedate[2] *vb* **-dating, -dated** to calm down or make sleepy by giving a sedative drug to

sedation *n* **1** a state of calm, esp. when brought about by sedatives **2** the administration of a sedative

sedative *adj* **1** having a soothing or calming effect ▷ *n* **2** *med* a sedative drug or agent that makes people sleep or calm down [Latin *sedatus* assuaged]

sedentary (sed-en-tree) *adj* **1** done sitting down and involving very little exercise: *a sedentary job* **2** tending to sit about without taking much exercise [Latin *sedere* to sit]

sedge *n* a coarse grasslike plant growing on wet ground [Old English *secg*] **sedgy** *adj*

sedge warbler *n* a European songbird living in marshy areas

sediment *n* **1** matter that settles to the bottom of a liquid **2** material that has been deposited by water, ice, or wind [Latin *sedimentum* a settling] **sedimentary** *adj*

sedition *n* speech, writing, or behaviour intended to encourage rebellion or resistance against the government [Latin *seditio* discord] **seditionary** *n*, *adj* **seditious** *adj*

seduce *vb* **-ducing, -duced** **1** to persuade to have sexual intercourse **2** to tempt into wrongdoing [Latin *seducere* to lead apart] **seduction** *n*

seductive *adj* **1** (of a person) sexually attractive **2** very attractive or tempting: *a seductive argument* **seductively** *adv* **seductiveness** *n*

sedulous *adj formal* diligent or painstaking: *a sedulous concern with the achievements of western thought* [Latin *sedulus*] **sedulously** *adv*

sedum *n* a rock plant with thick clusters of white, yellow, or pink flowers [Latin]

see[1] *vb* **seeing, saw, seen** **1** to look at or recognize with the eyes **2** to understand: *I explained the problem but he could not see it* **3** to perceive or be aware of: *she had never seen him so angry* **4** to view, watch, or attend: *we had barely seen a dozen movies in our lives* **5** to foresee: *they could see what their fate was to be* **6** to find out (a fact): *I was ringing to see whether you'd got it* **7** to make sure (of something) or take care (of something): *see that he is never in a position to do these things again; you must see to it* **8** to consider or decide: *see if you can come next week* **9** to have experience of: *he had seen active service in the revolution* **10** to meet or pay a visit to: *I see my specialist every three months* **11** to receive: *the Prime Minister will see the deputation now* **12** to frequent the company of: *we've been seeing each other since then* **13** to accompany: *she saw him to the door* **14** to refer to or look up: *see page 35* **15** (in gambling, esp. in poker) to match (another player's bet) or match the bet of (another player) by staking an equal sum **16** **see fit** to consider it proper (to do something): *I did not see fit to send them home* **17** **see you** *or* **see you later** *or*

S

be seeing you an expression of farewell ▷ See also **see about**, **see into** *etc.* [Old English *sēon*]
see² *n* the diocese of a bishop or the place within it where his or her cathedral is situated [Latin *sedes* a seat]
see about *vb* **1** to take care of: *I'll see about some coffee* **2** to investigate: *to see about a new car*
seed *n* **1** *botany* the mature fertilized grain of a plant, containing an embryo ready for germination. Related adjective: **seminal** **2** such seeds used for sowing **3** the source, beginning, or origin of anything: *the seeds of dissent* **4** *chiefly Bible* descendants; offspring: *the seed of David* **5** *sport* a player ranked according to his or her ability **6** **go** *or* **run to seed** **A** (of plants) to produce and shed seeds after flowering **B** to lose strength or usefulness ▷ *vb* **7** to plant (seeds) in (soil) **8** (of plants) to produce or shed seeds **9** to remove the seeds from (fruit or plants) **10** to scatter silver iodide in (clouds) in order to cause rain **11** to arrange (the draw of a tournament) so that outstanding teams or players will not meet in the early rounds [Old English *sǣd*] **seedless** *adj*
seedbed *n* **1** an area of soil prepared for the growing of seedlings before they are transplanted **2** the place where something develops: *a seedbed of immorality*
seedling *n* a plant produced from a seed, esp. a very young plant
seed pearl *n* a very small pearl
seed pod *n* *botany* a carpel or pistil enclosing the seeds of a plant, esp. a flowering plant
seedy *adj* **seedier, seediest** **1** shabby in appearance: *a seedy cinema* **2** *informal* physically unwell **3** (of a plant) at the stage of producing seeds **seediness** *n*
seeing *n* **1** the sense or faculty of sight ▷ *conj* **2** (often foll. by *that* or *as*) in light of the fact (that)

USAGE The use of *seeing as how* as in *seeing as (how) the bus is always late, I don't see any reason to hurry* is generally thought to be incorrect or non-standard.

S

see into *vb* to discover the true nature of: *he could see into my intentions*
seek *vb* **seeking, sought** **1** to try to find by searching: *to seek employment* **2** to try to obtain: *to seek a diplomatic solution* **3** to try (to do something): *we seek to establish a stable relationship* [Old English *sēcan*]
seek out *vb* to search hard for and find (a specific person or thing): *you should seek out healthy role models*
seem *vb* **1** to appear to the mind or eye; give the impression of: *the car seems to be running well* **2** to appear to be: *there seems no need for all this nonsense* **3** to have the impression: *I seem to remember you were there too* [Old Norse *sōma* to be suitable]

USAGE See at **like¹**.

seeming *adj* apparent but not real: *his seeming willingness to participate* **seemingly** *adv*
seemly *adj* **-lier, -liest** *formal* proper or fitting
seen *vb* the past participle of **see¹**
see off *vb* **1** to be present at the departure of (a person going on a journey): *your sisters came to see you off* **2** *informal* to cause to leave or depart, esp. by force
seep *vb* to leak through slowly; ooze [Old English *sīpian*] **seepage** *n*
seer *n* a person who can supposedly see into the future
seersucker *n* a light cotton fabric with a slightly crinkled surface [Hindi *śīrśakar*]
seesaw *n* **1** a plank balanced in the middle so that two people seated on the ends can ride up and down by pushing on the ground with their feet **2** an up-and-down or back-and-forth movement ▷ *vb* **3** to move up and down or back and forth alternately [reduplication of *saw*, alluding to the movement from side to side, as in sawing]
seethe *vb* **seething, seethed** **1** to be in a state of extreme anger or indignation without publicly showing these feelings **2** (of a liquid) to boil or foam [Old English *sēothan*] **seething** *adj*
see through *vb* **1** to perceive the true nature of: *it was difficult to see through people* **2** to remain with until the end or completion: *not all of them saw it through* **3** to help out in a time of need or trouble: *he helped see her through her divorce* ▷ *adj* **see-through** **4** (of clothing) made of thin cloth so that the wearer's body or underclothes are visible
segment *n* **1** one of several parts or sections into which an object is divided **2** *maths* **A** a part of a circle cut off by an intersecting line **B** a part of a sphere cut off by an intersecting plane or planes ▷ *vb* **3** to cut or divide into segments [Latin *segmentum*] **segmental** *adj* **segmentation** *n*
segregate *vb* **-gating, -gated** **1** to set apart from others or from the main group **2** to impose segregation on (a racial or minority group) [Latin *se-* apart + *grex* a flock]
segregation *n* **1** the practice or policy of creating separate facilities within the same society for the use of a racial or minority group **2** the act of segregating **segregational** *adj* **segregationist** *n*
seigneur *n* a feudal lord, esp. in France [Old French] **seigneurial** *adj*
seine (sane) *n* **1** a large fishing net that hangs vertically in the water by means of floats at the top and weights at the bottom ▷ *vb* **seining, seined** **2** to catch (fish) using this net [Old English *segne*]
seismic *adj* relating to or caused by earthquakes [Greek *seismos* earthquake]
seismograph *n* an instrument that records the intensity and duration of earthquakes [Greek *seismos* earthquake + -GRAPH] **seismographer** *n* **seismography** *n*
seismology *n* the branch of geology concerned with the study of earthquakes [Greek *seismos* earthquake + -LOGY] **seismologist** *n*
seismometer *n* same as **seismograph**
seize *vb* **seizing, seized** **1** to take hold of forcibly or quickly; grab **2** to take immediate advantage of: *real journalists would have seized the opportunity* **3** to take legal possession of **4** (sometimes foll. by *on* or *upon*) to understand quickly: *she immediately seized his idea* **5** to affect or fill the mind of suddenly: *a wild frenzy seized her* **6** to take by force

or capture: *the rebels seized a tank factory* **7** (often foll. by *up*) (of mechanical parts) to become jammed through overheating [Old French *saisir*]

seizure *n* **1** *pathol* a sudden violent attack of an illness, such as an epileptic convulsion **2** the act of seizing: *a seizure of drug traffickers' assets*

seldom *adv* rarely; not often [Old English *seldon*]

select *vb* **1** to choose (someone or something) in preference to another or others ▷ *adj* **2** chosen in preference to others **3** restricted to a particular group; exclusive: *a select audience* [Latin *seligere* to sort] **selector** *n*

select committee *n* a small committee of a legislature, set up to investigate and report on a specified matter

selection *n* **1** a selecting or being selected **2** a thing or number of things that have been selected **3** a range from which something may be selected: *a good selection of reasonably priced wines* **4** *biol* the process by which certain organisms or individuals are reproduced and survive in preference to others

selective *adj* **1** tending to choose carefully or characterized by careful choice: *they were selective in their reading* **2** of or characterized by selection **selectively** *adv* **selectivity** *n*

selenium *n chem* a nonmetallic element used in photocells, solar cells, and in xerography. Symbol: **Se** [Greek *selēnē* moon]

self *n, pl* **selves** **1** the distinct individuality or identity of a person or thing **2** a person's typical bodily make-up or personal characteristics: *back to my old self after the scare* **3** one's own welfare or interests: *he only thinks of self* **4** an individual's consciousness of his or her own identity or being ▷ *pron* **5** *not standard* myself, yourself, himself, or herself: *setting goals for self and others* [Old English]

self- *combining form* **1** (used with many main words to mean) of oneself or itself: *self-defence* **2** (used with many main words to mean) by, to, in, due to, for, or from the self: *self-employed*; *self-respect* **3** (used with many main words to mean) automatic or automatically: *self-propelled*

self-abnegation *n* the denial of one's own interests in favour of the interests of others

self-absorption *n* preoccupation with oneself to the exclusion of others **self-absorbed** *adj*

self-abuse *n old-fashioned* masturbation

self-addressed *adj* addressed for return to the sender

self-aggrandizement *or* **self-aggrandisement** *n* the act of increasing one's own power, wealth, or importance

self-appointed *adj* having assumed authority without the agreement of others: *self-appointed moralists*

self-assertion *n* the act of putting forward one's own opinions or demanding one's rights, esp. in an aggressive or confident manner **self-assertive** *adj*

self-assurance *n* confidence in oneself, one's abilities, or one's judgment **self-assured** *adj*

self-catering *adj* (of accommodation) for tenants providing and preparing their own food

self-centred *or US* **self-centered** *adj* totally preoccupied with one's own concerns

self-certification *n* (in Britain) the completion of a form by a worker stating that his or her absence was due to sickness

self-coloured *or US* **self-colored** *adj* **1** having only a single and uniform colour: *a self-coloured tie* **2** (of cloth or wool) having the natural or original colour

self-confessed *adj* according to one's own admission: *a self-confessed addict*

self-confidence *n* confidence in oneself, one's abilities, or one's judgment **self-confident** *adj*

self-conscious *adj* embarrassed or ill at ease through being unduly aware of oneself as the object of the attention of others **self-consciously** *adv* **self-consciousness** *n*

self-contained *adj* **1** containing within itself all parts necessary for completeness **2** (of a flat) having its own kitchen, bathroom, and toilet not shared by others

self-control *n* the ability to control one's feelings, emotions, or reactions **self-controlled** *adj*

self-deception *or* **self-deceit** *n* the act or an instance of deceiving oneself

self-defence *or US* **self-defense** *n* **1** the act or skill of defending oneself against physical attack **2** the act of defending one's actions, ideas, or rights

self-denial *n* the repression or sacrifice of one's own desires **self-denying** *adj*

self-determination *n* **1** the ability to make a decision for oneself without influence from outside **2** the right of a nation or people to determine its own form of government **self-determined** *adj*

self-discipline *n* the act of controlling or power to control one's own feelings, desires, or behaviour **self-disciplined** *adj*

self-drive *adj* relating to a hired vehicle that is driven by the hirer

self-educated *adj* educated through one's own efforts without formal instruction

self-effacement *n* the act of making oneself or one's actions seem less important than they are because of modesty or timidity **self-effacing** *adj*

self-employed *adj* earning one's living in one's own business, rather than as the employee of another

self-esteem *n* respect for or a favourable opinion of oneself

self-evident *adj* so obvious that no proof or explanation is needed **self-evidently** *adv*

self-explanatory *adj* understandable without explanation

self-expression *n* the expression of one's own personality or feelings, esp. in the creative arts **self-expressive** *adj*

self-government *n* the government of a country, nation, or community by its own people **self-governing** *adj*

self-harm *n* the practice of deliberately wounding oneself

self-help *n* **1** the use of one's own abilities and resources to help oneself without relying on the assistance of others **2** the practice of solving one's problems within a group of people with similar problems

S

selfie *n informal* a photograph taken by pointing the camera at oneself
selfie stick *n informal* a rod on which a camera or mobile phone may be mounted in order to take a photograph of oneself
self-image *n* one's own idea of oneself or sense of one's worth
self-important *adj* having an unduly high opinion of one's own importance **self-importance** *n*
self-improvement *n* the improvement of one's position, skills, or education by one's own efforts
self-indulgent *adj* tending to allow oneself to have or do things that one enjoys **self-indulgence** *n*
self-interest *n* **1** one's personal interest or advantage **2** the pursuit of one's own interest **self-interested** *adj*
selfish *adj* **1** caring too much about oneself and not enough about others **2** (of behaviour or attitude) motivated by self-interest **selfishly** *adv* **selfishness** *n*
selfless *adj* putting other people's interests before one's own **selflessly** *adv* **selflessness** *n*
self-made *adj* having achieved wealth or status by one's own efforts
self-opinionated *adj* clinging stubbornly to one's own opinions
self-pity *n* pity for oneself, esp. when greatly exaggerated **self-pitying** *adj*
self-pollination *n botany* the transfer of pollen from the anthers to the stigma of the same flower
self-possessed *adj* having control of one's emotions or behaviour, esp. in difficult situations **self-possession** *n*
self-preservation *n* the instinctive behaviour that protects one from danger or injury
self-propelled *adj* **1** (of a vehicle) driven by its own engine rather than drawn by a locomotive, horse, etc. **2** (of a rocket launcher or artillery piece) mounted on a motor vehicle **self-propelling** *adj*
self-raising *adj* (of flour) having a raising agent, such as baking powder, already added
self-realization *or* **-isation** *n* the fulfilment of one's own potential or abilities
self-regard *n* **1** concern for one's own interest **2** proper esteem for oneself
self-reliance *n* reliance on oneself or one's own abilities **self-reliant** *adj*
self-reproach *n* the act of finding fault with or blaming oneself
self-respect *n* a feeling of confidence and pride in one's own abilities and worth **self-respecting** *adj*
self-restraint *n* control imposed by oneself on one's own feelings, desires, or actions
self-righteous *adj* thinking oneself more virtuous than others **self-righteousness** *n*
self-sacrifice *n* the giving up of one's own interests for the wellbeing of others **self-sacrificing** *adj*
selfsame *adj* the very same: *this was the selfsame woman I'd met on the train*
self-satisfied *adj* smug and complacently satisfied with oneself or one's own actions **self-satisfaction** *n*
self-sealing *adj* **1** (of an envelope) sealable by pressure alone **2** (of a tyre) automatically sealing small punctures
self-seeking *n* **1** the act or an instance of seeking one's own profit or interests ▷ *adj* **2** inclined to promote only one's own profit or interests: *self-seeking politicians* **self-seeker** *n*
self-service *adj* **1** of or denoting a shop or restaurant where the customers serve themselves and then pay a cashier ▷ *n* **2** the practice of serving oneself and then paying a cashier
self-serving *adj* continually seeking one's own advantage, esp. at the expense of others
self-starter *n* **1** an electric motor used to start an internal-combustion engine **2** a person who is strongly motivated and shows initiative at work
self-styled *adj* using a title or name that one has given oneself, esp. without right or justification; so-called: *the self-styled leader of the rebellion*
self-sufficient *adj* able to provide for or support oneself without the help of others **self-sufficiency** *n*
self-supporting *adj* **1** able to support or maintain oneself without the help of others **2** able to stand up or hold firm without support, props, or attachments
self-willed *adj* stubbornly determined to have one's own way, esp. at the expense of others
self-winding *adj* (of a wristwatch) having a mechanism which winds itself automatically
sell *vb* **selling, sold 1** to exchange (something) for money **2** to deal in (objects or property): *he sells used cars* **3** to give up or surrender for a price or reward: *to sell one's honour* **4 sell for** to have a specified price: *they sell for 10 pence each* **5** to promote the sale of (objects or property): *sporting success sells newspapers* **6** to gain acceptance of: *he'll sell an idea to a producer* **7** to be in demand on the market: *his books did not sell well enough* **8 sell down the river** *informal* to betray **9 sell oneself A** to convince someone else of one's potential or worth **B** to give up one's moral standards for a price or reward **10 sell someone short** *informal* to undervalue someone ▷ *n* **11** the act or an instance of selling: *the hard sell* ▷ See also **sell off, sell out, sell up** [Old English *sellan* to give, deliver] **seller** *n*
sell-by date *n* **1** *Brit* the date printed on packaged food specifying the date after which the food should not be sold **2 past one's sell-by date** beyond one's prime
sell off *vb* to sell (remaining items) at reduced prices
Sellotape *n* **1** *Brit trademark* a type of transparent adhesive tape ▷ *vb* **-taping, -taped 2** to seal or stick using adhesive tape
sell out *vb* **1 A** to dispose of (something) completely by selling **B** (of items for sale) to be bought up completely: *these tickets will sell out in minutes* **2** *informal* to abandon one's principles, standards, etc. **3** *informal* to betray in order to gain an advantage or benefit ▷ *n* **sellout**

4 *informal* a performance of a show, etc. for which all tickets are sold **5** a commercial success **6** *informal* a betrayal
sell up *vb chiefly Brit & Austral* to sell all one's goods or property
selvage *or* **selvedge** *n* a specially woven edge on a length of fabric to prevent it from unravelling [SELF + EDGE] **selvaged** *adj*
selves *n* the plural of **self**
semantic *adj* **1** of or relating to the meanings of words **2** of or relating to semantics [Greek *sēma* a sign]
semantics *n* the branch of linguistics that deals with the study of meaning
semaphore *n* **1** a system of signalling by holding two flags in different positions to represent letters of the alphabet ▷ *vb* **-phoring, -phored** **2** to signal (information) by semaphore [Greek *sēma* a signal + *-phoros* carrying]
semblance *n* outward or superficial appearance: *some semblance of order had been established* [Old French *sembler* to seem]
semen *n* the thick whitish fluid containing spermatozoa that is produced by the male reproductive organs and ejaculated from the penis [Latin: seed]
semester *n* either of two divisions of the academic year [Latin *semestris* half-yearly]
semi *n Brit, Austral & S African informal* short for **semidetached** (sense 2)
semi- *prefix* **1** half: *semicircle* **2** partly or almost: *semiprofessional* **3** occurring twice in a specified period: *semiweekly* [Latin]
semiannual *adj* **1** occurring every half-year **2** lasting for half a year
semiarid *adj* denoting land that lies on the edges of a desert but has a slightly higher rainfall (above 300 mm) so that some farming is possible
semiautomatic *adj* **1** (of a firearm) self-loading but firing only one shot at each pull of the trigger ▷ *n* **2** a semiautomatic firearm
semibreve *n music* a note, now the longest in common use, with a time value that may be divided by any power of 2 to give all other notes
semicircle *n* **1** one half of a circle **2** anything having the shape or form of half a circle **semicircular** *adj*
semicolon *n* the punctuation mark (;) used to separate clauses or items in a list, or to indicate a pause longer than that of a comma and shorter than that of a full stop
semiconductor *n physics* a substance, such as silicon, which has an electrical conductivity that increases with temperature
semiconscious *adj* not fully conscious **semiconsciousness** *n*
semidetached *adj* **1** (of a house) joined to another house on one side by a common wall ▷ *n* **2** *Brit* a semidetached house: *the mock Georgian semidetached*
semi-final *n* the round before the final in a competition **semi-finalist** *n*
seminal *adj* **1** highly original and influential: *seminal thinkers* **2** potentially capable of development **3** of semen: *seminal fluid* **4** *biol* of seed [Latin *semen* seed]
seminar *n* **1** a small group of students meeting regularly under the guidance of a tutor for study and discussion **2** one such meeting [Latin *seminarium* a nursery garden]
seminary *n, pl* **-naries** a college for the training of priests [Latin *seminarium* a nursery garden] **seminarian** *n*
semiotics *n* the study of human communication, esp. communication using signs and symbols [Greek *sēmeion* a sign] **semiotic** *adj*
semipermeable *adj* (of a cell membrane) allowing small molecules to pass through but not large ones
semiprecious *adj* (of certain stones) having less value than a precious stone
semiprofessional *adj* **1** (of a person) engaged in an activity or sport part time for pay **2** (of an activity or sport) engaged in by semiprofessional people ▷ *n* **3** a semiprofessional person
semiquaver *n music* a note having the time value of one-sixteenth of a semibreve
semirigid *adj* (of an airship) maintaining shape by means of a main supporting keel and internal gas pressure
semiskilled *adj* partly skilled or trained but not sufficiently so as to perform specialized work
Semite *n* a member of the group of peoples who speak a Semitic language, such as the Jews and Arabs [New Latin *semita* descendant of Shem, eldest of Noah's sons]
Semitic *n* **1** a group of languages that includes Arabic, Hebrew, and Aramaic ▷ *adj* **2** of this group of languages **3** of any of the peoples speaking a Semitic language, esp. the Jews or the Arabs **4** same as **Jewish**
semitone *n* the smallest interval between two notes in Western music represented on a piano by the difference in pitch between any two adjacent keys **semitonic** *adj*
semitrailer *n Austral* a large truck in two separate sections joined by a pivoted bar. Also called: **semi**
semitropical *adj* bordering on the tropics; nearly tropical **semitropics** *pl n*
semivowel *n phonetics* a vowel-like sound that acts like a consonant, such as the sound *w* in *well*
semolina *n* the large hard grains of wheat left after flour has been milled, used for making puddings and pasta [Italian *semolino*]
Semtex *n* a pliable plastic explosive
SEN (in Britain) State Enrolled Nurse
Sen. *or* **sen.** **1** senate **2** senator **3** senior
senate *n* the main governing body at some universities [Latin *senatus* council of the elders]
Senate *n* the upper chamber of the legislatures of Australia, the US, Canada, and many other countries
senator *n* a member of a Senate **senatorial** *adj*
send *vb* **sending, sent** **1** to cause (a person or thing) to go or be taken or transmitted to another place: *send a cheque or postal order* **2** **send for** to dispatch a request or command for (someone or something): *she had sent for me* **3** to cause to go to a place or point: *the bullet sent him flying into the air* **4** to bring to a state or condition: *his schemes to send her mad* **5** to cause to happen or come: *the*

S

thunderstorm sent by the gods **6** *old-fashioned slang* to move to excitement or rapture: *this music really sends me* [Old English *sendan*] **sender** *n*

send down *vb* **1** *Brit* to expel from a university **2** *informal* to send to prison

sendoff *n* **1** *informal* a show of good wishes to a person about to set off on a journey or start a new career ▷ *vb* **send off** **2** to dispatch (something, such as a letter) **3** *sport* (of a referee) to dismiss (a player) from the field of play for some offence

send up *informal* ▷ *vb* **1** to make fun of by doing an imitation or parody ▷ *n* **send-up** **2** a parody or imitation

senescent *adj formal* growing old [Latin *senescere* to grow old] **senescence** *n*

senile *adj* mentally or physically weak or infirm on account of old age [Latin *senex* an old man] **senility** *n*

senior *adj* **1** higher in rank or length of service **2** older in years: *senior citizens* **3** *education* of or designating more advanced or older pupils or students ▷ *n* **4** a senior person [Latin: older]

Senior *adj chiefly US* being older than someone of the same name: *Joe Yule Senior*

senior aircraftman *n* an ordinary rank in the Royal Air Force

senior citizen *n* an old person, esp. a pensioner

seniority *n, pl* **-ties** **1** the state of being senior **2** degree of power or importance in an organization from length of continuous service

senior service *n Brit* the Royal Navy

senna *n* **1** a tropical plant with yellow flowers and long pods **2** the dried leaves and pods of this plant, used as a laxative [Arabic *sanā*]

señor (sen-**nyor**) *n* a Spanish form of address equivalent to *sir* or *Mr*

señora (sen-**nyor**-a) *n* a Spanish form of address equivalent to *madam* or *Mrs*

señorita (sen-nyor-**ee**-ta) *n* a Spanish form of address equivalent to *madam* or *Miss*

sensation *n* **1** the power of feeling things physically: *I lose all sensation in my hands* **2** a physical feeling: *a burning sensation in the throat* **3** a general feeling or awareness: *a sensation of vague resentment* **4** a state of excitement: *imagine the sensation in Washington!* **5** an exciting person or thing: *you'll be a sensation* [Late Latin *sensatus* endowed with feelings]

sensational *adj* **1** causing intense feelings of shock, anger, or excitement: *sensational allegations* **2** *informal* extremely good: *the views are sensational* **3** of the senses or sensation **sensationally** *adv*

sensationalism *n* the deliberate use of sensational language or subject matter to arouse feelings of shock, anger, or excitement **sensationalist** *adj, n*

sense *n* **1** any of the faculties (sight, hearing, touch, taste, and smell) by which the mind receives information about the external world or the state of the body **2** the ability to perceive **3** a feeling perceived through one of the senses: *a sense of warmth* **4** a mental perception or awareness: *a sense of security* **5** ability to make moral judgments: *a sense of honour* **6** (*usually pl*) sound practical judgment or intelligence: *you must have lost your senses when you bought that* **7** reason or purpose: *no sense in continuing* **8** general meaning: *he couldn't understand every word but he got the sense of what they were saying* **9** specific meaning; definition: *the three senses of the word* **10** **make sense** to be understandable or practical ▷ *vb* **sensing, sensed** **11** to perceive without the evidence of the senses: *he sensed that she was impressed* **12** to perceive through the senses [Latin *sentire* to feel]

senseless *adj* **1** having no meaning or purpose: *a senseless act of violence* **2** unconscious **senselessly** *adv* **senselessness** *n*

sense organ *n* a part of the body that receives stimuli and transmits them as sensations to the brain

sensibility *n, pl* **-ties** **1** (*often pl*) the ability to experience deep feelings **2** (*usually pl*) the tendency to be influenced or offended: *its sheer callousness offended her sensibilities* **3** the ability to perceive or feel

sensible *adj* **1** having or showing good sense or judgment **2** (of clothing and footwear) practical and hard-wearing **3** capable of receiving sensation **4** capable of being perceived by the senses **5** perceptible to the mind **6** *literary* aware: *sensible of your kindness* [Latin *sentire* to feel] **sensibly** *adv*

sensitive *adj* **1** easily hurt; tender **2** responsive to feelings and moods **3** responsive to external stimuli or impressions **4** easily offended or shocked **5** (of a subject or issue) liable to arouse controversy or strong feelings **6** (of an instrument) capable of registering small differences or changes in amounts **7** (of photographic materials) responding readily to the action of light: *a sensitive emulsion* **8** *chiefly US* connected with matters affecting national security [Latin *sentire* to feel] **sensitively** *adv* **sensitivity** *n*

sensitize *or* **-tise** *vb* **-tizing, -tized** *or* **-tising, -tised** to make sensitive **sensitization** *or* **-tisation** *n*

sensor *n* a device that detects or measures a physical property, such as radiation

sensory *adj* relating to the physical senses

sensual *adj* **1** giving pleasure to the body and senses rather than the mind: *soft sensual music* **2** having a strong liking for physical, esp. sexual, pleasures **3** of the body and senses rather than the mind or soul [Latin *sensus* feeling] **sensualist** *n*

sensuality *n* **1** the quality or state of being sensual **2** enjoyment of physical, esp. sexual, pleasures

sensuous *adj* **1** pleasing to the senses of the mind or body: *the sensuous rhythms of the drums* **2** (of a person) appreciating qualities perceived by the senses **sensuously** *adv*

sent *vb* the past of **send**

sentence *n* **1** a sequence of words constituting a statement, question, or a command that begins with a capital letter and ends with a full stop when written down **2** **A** the decision of a law court as to what punishment is passed on a convicted person **B** the punishment passed on a convicted person ▷ *vb* **-tencing, -tenced**

3 to pronounce sentence on (a convicted person) in a law court [Latin *sententia* a way of thinking] **sentential** *adj*

sententious *adj formal* **1** trying to sound wise **2** making pompous remarks about morality [Latin *sententiosus* full of meaning] **sententiously** *adv*

sentient (**sen**-tee-ent, **sen**-shent) *adj* capable of perception and feeling [Latin *sentiens* feeling] **sentience** *n*

sentiment *n* **1** a mental attitude based on a mixture of thoughts and feelings: *anti-American sentiment* **2** (*often pl*) a thought, opinion, or attitude expressed in words: *his sentiments were echoed by subsequent speakers* **3** feelings such as tenderness, romance, and sadness, esp. when exaggerated: *a man without the softness of sentiment* [Latin *sentire* to feel]

sentimental *adj* **1** feeling or expressing tenderness, romance, or sadness to an exaggerated extent **2** appealing to the emotions, esp. to romantic feelings: *she kept the ring for sentimental reasons* **sentimentalism** *n* **sentimentalist** *n* **sentimentality** *n* **sentimentally** *adv*

sentimentalize *or* **-lise** *vb* **-lizing, -lized** *or* **-lising, -lised** to make sentimental or behave sentimentally

sentimental value *n* the value of an article to a particular person because of the emotions it arouses

sentinel *n old-fashioned* a sentry [Old French *sentinelle*]

sentry *n, pl* **-tries** a soldier who keeps watch and guards a camp or building [perhaps from obsolete *centrinel* sentinel]

sentry box *n* a small shelter with an open front in which a sentry stands during bad weather

SEO search engine optimization

sepal *n botany* a leaflike division of the calyx of a flower [New Latin *sepalum*]

separable *adj* able to be separated

separate *vb* **-rating, -rated** **1** to act as a barrier between: *the narrow stretch of water which separates Europe from Asia* **2** to part or be parted from a mass or group **3** to distinguish: *it's what separates the women from the boys* **4** to divide or be divided into component parts **5** to sever or be severed **6** (of a couple) to stop living together ▷ *adj* **7** existing or considered independently: *a separate issue* **8** set apart from the main body or mass **9** distinct or individual [Latin *separare*] **separately** *adv* **separateness** *n* **separator** *n*

separates *pl n Brit, Austral & NZ* clothes, such as skirts, blouses, and trousers, that only cover part of the body and are designed to be worn together or separately

separate school *n* (in certain Canadian provinces) a school for a large religious minority financed by provincial grants in addition to the education tax

separation *n* **1** the act of separating: *the separation of child from mother* **2** *family law* the living apart of a married couple without divorce **3** a mark, line, or object that separates one thing from another

separatist *n* a person who advocates the separation of his or her own group from an organization or country **separatism** *n*

sepia *adj* dark reddish-brown, like the colour of very old photographs [Latin: a cuttlefish]

sepoy *n* (formerly) an Indian soldier in the service of the British [Urdu *sipāhī*]

sepsis *n* poisoning caused by the presence of pus-forming bacteria in the body [Greek: a rotting]

sept *n* a clan, esp. in Ireland or Scotland [perhaps variant of *sect*]

Sept. September

September *n* the ninth month of the year [Latin: the seventh (month)]

septennial *adj* **1** occurring every seven years **2** lasting seven years [Latin *septem* seven + *annus* a year]

septet *n* **1** a group of seven performers **2** a piece of music for seven performers [Latin *septem* seven]

septic *adj* of or caused by harmful bacteria **septicity** *n*

septicaemia *or* **septicemia** (sep-tis-**see**-mee-a) *n* an infection of the blood which develops in a wound [Greek *sēptos* decayed + *haima* blood]

septic tank *n* a tank in which sewage is decomposed by the action of bacteria

septuagenarian *n* **1** a person who is between 70 and 79 years old ▷ *adj* **2** between 70 and 79 years old [Latin *septuaginta* seventy]

Septuagint (**sept**-yew-a-jint) *n* the ancient Greek version of the Old Testament, including the Apocrypha [Latin *septuaginta* seventy]

septum *n, pl* **-ta** *biol & anatomy* a dividing partition between two tissues or cavities, such as in the nose [Latin *saeptum* wall]

septuple *vb* **-pling, -pled** **1** to multiply by seven ▷ *adj* **2** seven times as much or as many **3** consisting of seven parts ▷ *n* **4** a quantity or number seven times as great as another [Latin *septem* seven]

sepulchral (sip-**pulk**-ral) *adj* **1** gloomy and solemn, like a tomb or grave **2** of a sepulchre

sepulchre *or US* **sepulcher** (**sep**-pulk-er) *n* **1** a burial vault, tomb, or grave ▷ *vb* **-chring, -chred** *or US* **-chering, -chered** **2** to bury in a sepulchre [Latin *sepulcrum*]

sepulture (**sep**-pult-cher) *n* the act of placing in a sepulchre

sequel *n* **1** a film, novel, or play that continues the story of an earlier one **2** anything that happens after or as a result of something else: *there was an amusing sequel to this incident* [Latin *sequi* to follow]

sequence *n* **1** an arrangement of two or more things in a successive order **2** the successive order of two or more things: *chronological sequence* **3** an action or event that follows another or others **4** *maths* an ordered set of numbers or other quantities in one-to-one correspondence with the integers 1 to *n* **5** a section of a film forming a single uninterrupted episode ▷ *vb* **6** to arrange in a sequence [Latin *sequi* to follow]

sequential *adj* happening in a fixed order or sequence

sequester *vb* **1** to seclude: *he could sequester himself in his own home* **2** *law* same as **sequestrate** [Late Latin *sequestrare* to surrender for safekeeping]

S

sequestrate *vb* **-trating, -trated** *law* to confiscate (property) temporarily until creditors are satisfied or a court order is complied with **sequestration** *n* **sequestrator** *n*

sequin *n* a small piece of shiny metal foil used to decorate clothes [Italian *zecchino*] **sequined** *adj*

sequoia *n* a giant Californian coniferous tree [after *Sequoya*, a Native American scholar]

seraglio (sir-ah-lee-oh) *n, pl* **-raglios 1** the part of a Muslim house or palace where the owner's wives live **2** a Turkish sultan's palace [Italian *serraglio* animal cage]

seraph *n, pl* **-raphim** *theol* a member of the highest order of angels [from Hebrew] **seraphic** *adj*

Serb *adj, n* same as **Serbian**

Serbian *adj* **1** of Serbia ▷ *n* **2** a person from Serbia **3** the dialect of Serbo-Croat spoken in Serbia

Serbo-Croat *or* **Serbo-Croatian** *n* **1** the chief official language of Serbia and Croatia ▷ *adj* **2** of this language

serenade *n* **1** a piece of music played or sung to a woman by a lover **2** a piece of music suitable for this **3** an orchestral suite for a small ensemble ▷ *vb* **-nading, -naded 4** to sing or play a serenade to (someone) [French]

serendipity *n* the gift of making fortunate discoveries by accident [from the fairy tale *The Three Princes of Serendip*, in which the heroes possess this gift]

serene *adj* **1** peaceful or calm **2** (of the sky) clear or bright [Latin *serenus*] **serenely** *adv* **serenity** *n*

serf *n* (esp. in medieval Europe) a labourer who could not leave the land on which he worked [Latin *servus* a slave] **serfdom** *n*

serge *n* a strong fabric made of wool, cotton, silk, or rayon, used for clothing [Old French *sarge*]

sergeant *n* **1** a noncommissioned officer in the armed forces **2** (in Britain, S Africa, Australia, and NZ) a police officer ranking between constable and inspector [Old French *sergent*]

sergeant at arms *n* a parliamentary or court officer responsible for keeping order

sergeant major *n* a noncommissioned officer of the highest rank in the army

serial *n* **1** a story published or broadcast in instalments at regular intervals **2** a publication that is regularly issued and consecutively numbered ▷ *adj* **3** of, in, or forming a series: *serial pregnancies* **4** published or presented as a serial [Latin *series* series] **serially** *adv*

serialize *or* **-ise** *vb* **-izing, -ized** *or* **-ising, -ised** to publish or present in the form of a serial **serialization** *or* **-isation** *n*

serial killer *n* a person who commits a number of murders

serial monogamy *n* the practice of having a number of long-term romantic or sexual partners in succession

serial number *n* any of the consecutive numbers given to objects in a series for identification

series *n, pl* **-ries 1** a group or succession of related things **2** a set of radio or television programmes dealing with the same subject, esp. one having the same characters but different stories **3** *maths* the sum of a finite or infinite sequence of numbers or quantities **4** *electronics* an arrangement of two or more components connected in a circuit so that the same current flows in turn through each of them: *a number of resistors in series* **5** *geol* a set of layers that represent the rocks formed during an epoch [Latin: a row]

seriocomic (seer-ee-oh-**kom**-ik) *adj* mixing serious and comic elements

serious *adj* **1** giving cause for concern: *the situation is serious* **2** concerned with important matters: *there are some serious questions that need to be answered* **3** not cheerful; grave: *I am a serious person* **4** in earnest; sincere: *he believes we are serious* **5** requiring concentration: *a serious book* **6** *informal* impressive because of its substantial quantity or quality: *serious money* [Latin *serius*] **seriously** *adv* **seriousness** *n*

serjeant *n* same as **sergeant**

sermon *n* **1** a speech on a religious or moral subject given by a member of the clergy as part of a church service **2** *derogatory* a serious talk on behaviour, morals, or duty, esp. a long and tedious one [Latin *sermo* discourse]

seropositive (seer-oh-**poz**-zit-iv) *adj* (of a person whose blood has been tested for a specific disease, such as AIDS) showing a significant level of serum antibodies, indicating the presence of the disease

serotonin (ser-roe-**tone**-in) *n biochem* a compound that occurs in the brain, intestines, and blood platelets and acts as a neurotransmitter

serous (**seer**-uss) *adj* of, containing, or like serum

serpent *n* **1** *literary* a snake **2** a devious person [Latin *serpens* a creeping thing]

serpentine[1] *adj* twisting like a snake

serpentine[2] *n* a soft green or brownish-red mineral [so named from its snakelike patterns]

serrated *adj* having a notched or sawlike edge [Latin *serratus* saw-shaped] **serration** *n*

serried *adj literary* in close formation: *the serried ranks of fans* [Old French *serré* close-packed]

serum (**seer**-um) *n* **1** the yellowish watery fluid left after blood has clotted **2** this fluid from the blood of immunized animals used for inoculation or vaccination **3** *physiol & zool* any clear watery animal fluid [Latin: whey]

serval *n* a slender African wild cat with black-spotted tawny fur

servant *n* **1** a person employed to do household work for another person **2** a person or thing that is useful or provides a service: *a distinguished servant of this country* [Old French: serving]

serve *vb* **serving, served 1** to be of service to (a person, community, or cause); help **2** to perform an official duty or duties: *he served on several university committees* **3** to attend to (customers) in a shop **4** to provide (guests) with food or drink: *he served dinner guests German wine* **5** to provide (food or drink) for customers: *breakfast is served from 7 am* **6** to provide with something needed by the public: *the community served by the school* **7** to work as a servant for (a person) **8** to go through (a period of police or military service, apprenticeship, or imprisonment) **9** to meet the needs of: *they serve a purpose* **10** to perform a function: *the attacks only* *served to strengthen their resolve* **11** (of a male animal) to mate with (a female animal) **12** *tennis & squash etc.* to put (the ball) into play **13** to deliver (a legal document) to (a person) **14** **serve someone right** *informal* to be what someone deserves, esp. for doing something stupid or wrong ▷ *n* **15** *tennis & squash etc.* short for **service** (sense 12) [Latin *servus* a slave]

server *n* **1** a computer or program that supplies data to other machines on a network **2** a person who serves

service *n* **1** an act of help or assistance **2** an organization or system that provides something needed by the public: *a consumer information service* **3** a department of public employment and its employees: *the diplomatic service* **4** the installation or maintenance of goods provided by a dealer after a sale **5** availability for use by the public: *the new plane could be in service within fifteen years* **6** a regular check made on a machine or vehicle in which parts are tested, cleaned, or replaced if worn **7** the serving of guests or customers: *service is included on the wine list* **8** one of the branches of the armed forces **9** the serving of food: *silver service* **10** a set of dishes, cups, and plates for use at table **11** a formal religious ceremony **12** *tennis & squash etc.* **A** the act, manner, or right of serving the ball **B** the game in which a particular player serves: *she dropped only one point on her service* ▷ *adj* **13** of or for the use of servants or employees: *a service elevator* **14** serving the public rather than producing goods: *service industries* ▷ *vb* **-vicing, -viced 15** to provide service or services to **16** to check and repair (a vehicle or machine) **17** (of a male animal) to mate with (a female animal) ▷ See also **services** [Latin *servitium* condition of a slave]

serviceable *adj* **1** performing effectively: *serviceable boots* **2** able or ready to be used: *five remaining serviceable aircraft* **serviceability** *n*

service area *n* a place on a motorway with a garage, restaurants, and toilets

service charge *n* a percentage added to a bill in a hotel or restaurant to pay for service

service flat *n* a flat where domestic services are provided by the management

serviceman *or fem* **servicewoman** *n, pl* **-men** *or* **-women 1** a person in the armed services **2** a person employed to service and maintain equipment

service road *n Brit & Austral* a narrow road running parallel to a main road that provides access to houses and shops situated along its length

services *pl n* **1** work performed in a job: *the OBE for her services to the community* **2** **the services** the armed forces **3** a system of providing the public with something it needs, such as gas or water

service station *n* **1** a place that sells fuel, oil, and spare parts for motor vehicles **2** same as **service area**

serviette *n Brit & Canad* a table napkin [Old French]

servile *adj* **1** too eager to obey people; fawning **2** of or suitable for a slave [Latin *servus* slave] **servility** *n*

serving *n* a portion of food

servitor *n archaic* a servant or attendant

servitude *n formal* **1** slavery or bondage **2** the state or condition of being completely dominated [Latin *servus* a slave]

servomechanism *n* a device which converts a small force into a larger force, used esp. in steering mechanisms

sesame (sess-am-ee) *n* an Asian plant, grown for its seeds and oil, which are used in cooking [Greek]

sesh *n slang* a session

sessile *adj* **1** (of flowers or leaves) having no stalk **2** (of animals such as the barnacle) fixed in one position [Latin *sessilis* concerning sitting]

session *n* **1** any period devoted to a particular activity **2** a meeting of a court, parliament, or council **3** a series or period of such meetings **4** a school or university term or year [Latin *sessio* a sitting] **sessional** *adj*

sestet *n* **1** *prosody* the last six lines of a sonnet **2** same as **sextet** (sense 1) [Italian *sesto* sixth]

set[1] *vb* **setting, set 1** to put in a specified position or state: *I set him free* **2** **set to** *or* **on** to bring (something) into contact with (something else): *three prisoners set fire to their cells* **3** to put into order or make ready: *set the table* **4** to make or become firm or rigid: *before the eggs begin to set* **5** to put (a broken bone) or (of a broken bone) to be put into a normal position for healing **6** to adjust (a clock or other instrument) to a particular position **7** to arrange or establish: *to set a date for diplomatic talks; it set the standards of performance* **8** to prescribe or assign (a task or material for study): *the examiners have set 'Paradise Lost'* **9** to arrange (hair) while wet, so that it dries in position **10** to place a jewel in (a setting): *a ring set with diamonds* **11** to provide music for (a poem or other text to be sung) **12** *printing* **A** to arrange (type) for printing **B** to put (text) into type **13** to arrange (a stage or television studio) with scenery and props **14** **set to** *or* **on** to value (something) at a specified price or worth: *he set a high price on his services* **15** (of the sun or moon) to disappear beneath the horizon **16** (of plants) to produce (fruits or seeds) or (of fruits or seeds) to develop **17** to place (a hen) on (eggs) to incubate them **18** (of a gun dog) to turn in the direction of game birds ▷ *n* **19** the act of setting **20** a condition of firmness or hardness **21** manner of standing; posture: *the set of his shoulders* **22** the scenery and other props used in a play or film **23** same as **sett** ▷ *adj* **24** fixed or established by authority or agreement: *set hours of work* **25** rigid or inflexible: *she is set in her ways* **26** unmoving; fixed: *a set expression on his face* **27** conventional or stereotyped: *she made her apology in set phrases* **28** **set in** (of a scene or story) represented as happening at a certain time or place: *a European film set in Africa* **29** **set on** *or* **upon** determined to (do or achieve something): *why are you so set upon avoiding me?* **30** ready: *all set to go* **31** (of material for study) prescribed for students' preparation for an examination ▷ See also **set about, set against** *etc.* [Old English *settan*]

set[2] *n* **1** a number of objects or people grouped or belonging together: *a set of slides* **2** a group of people who associate with each other or have similar interests: *the tennis set* **3** *maths* a collection of numbers or objects that satisfy a given condition or share a property **4** a television or piece of radio equipment **5** the scenery and other props used in a dramatic production, film, etc. **6** *sport* a group of games or points in a match, of which the winner must win a certain number **7** a series of songs or tunes performed by a musician or group on a given occasion: *the front row spent the rest of the set craning their necks* [Old French *sette*]

set about *vb* **1** to start or begin **2** to attack

set against *vb* **1** to balance or compare **2** to cause to be unfriendly to: *the war set brother against brother*

set aside *vb* **1** to reserve for a special purpose **2** to discard or reject

set back *vb* **1** to delay or hinder **2** *informal* to cost (a person) a specified amount ▷ *n* **setback** **3** anything that delays progress

set down *vb* **1** to record in writing **2** *Brit* to allow (passengers) to get off a bus, etc.

set forth *vb formal, archaic* **1** to state or present (an argument or facts) **2** to start out on a journey: *he set forth on foot*

set in *vb* **1** to begin and continue for some time: *decadence has set in* **2** to insert

set off *vb* **1** to start a journey **2** to cause (a person) to act or do something, such as laugh **3** to cause to explode **4** to act as a contrast to: *blue suits you, sets off the colour of your hair*

set on *or* **set upon** *vb* to attack or cause to attack: *they set the dogs on him*

set out *vb* **1** to present, arrange, or display **2** to give a full account of: *the policy was set out in an interview with the BBC* **3** to begin or embark on an undertaking, esp. a journey

set piece *n* **1** a work of literature, music, or art, intended to create an impressive effect **2** *football & hockey etc.* an attacking move from a corner or free kick

set square *n* a thin flat piece of plastic or metal in the shape of a right-angled triangle, used in technical drawing

S

sett *or* **set** *n* **1** a badger's burrow **2** a small rectangular paving block made of stone [variant of SET[1] (noun)]

settee *n* a seat, for two or more people, with a back and usually with arms; couch [from SETTLE[2]]

setter *n* a large long-haired dog originally bred for hunting

set theory *n maths* the branch of mathematics concerned with the properties and interrelationships of sets

setting *n* **1** the surroundings in which something is set **2** the scenery, properties, or background used to create the location for a stage play or film **3** a piece of music written for the words of a text **4** the decorative metalwork in which a gem is set **5** the plates and cutlery for a single place at a table **6** one of the positions or levels to which the controls of a machine can be adjusted

settle[1] *vb* **-tling, -tled** **1** to put in order: *he settled his affairs before he died* **2** to arrange or be arranged firmly or comfortably: *he settled into his own chair by the fire* **3** to come down to rest: *a bird settled on top of the hedge* **4** to establish or become established as a resident: *they eventually settled in Glasgow* **5** to establish or become established in a way of life or a job **6** to migrate to (a country) and form a community; colonize **7** to make or become quiet, calm, or stable **8** to cause (sediment) to sink to the bottom in a liquid or (of sediment) to sink thus **9** to subside: *the dust settled* **10** (sometimes foll. by *up*) to pay off (a bill or debt) **11** to decide or dispose of: *to settle an argument* **12** (often foll. by *on* or *upon*) to agree or fix: *they settled on an elementary code* **13** (usually foll. by *on* or *upon*) to give (a title or property) to a person by gift or legal deed: *he settled his property on his wife* **14** to decide (a legal dispute) by agreement without court action: *they settled out of court* [Old English *setlan*]

settle[2] *n* a long wooden bench with a high back and arms, sometimes having a storage space under the seat [Old English *setl*]

settle down *vb* **1** to make or become quiet and orderly **2** **settle down to** to remove all distractions and concentrate on: *we settled down to a favourite movie* **3** to adopt an orderly and routine way of life, esp. after marriage

settle for *vb* to accept or agree to in spite of dissatisfaction

settlement *n* **1** an act of settling **2** a place newly settled; colony **3** subsidence of all or part of a building **4** an official agreement ending a dispute **5** *law* **A** an arrangement by which property is transferred to a person's possession **B** the deed transferring such property

settler *n* a person who settles in a new country or a colony

set to *vb* **1** to begin working **2** to start fighting ▷ *n* **set-to** **3** *informal* a brief disagreement or fight

set-top box *n* a device which converts the signals from a digital television broadcast into a form which can be viewed on an analogue television, or that enables satellite, cable, or streaming services to be viewed

set up *vb* **1** to build or construct: *the soldiers had actually set up a munitions factory* **2** to put into a position of power or wealth **3** to begin or enable (someone) to begin (a new venture): *he set up a small shop* **4** to begin or produce: *to set up a nuclear chain reaction* **5** to establish: *Broad set up a world record* **6** *informal* to cause (a person) to be blamed or accused **7** to restore the health of: *a pub lunch set me up nicely* ▷ *n* **setup** **8** *informal* the way in which anything is organized or arranged **9** *slang* an event the result of which is prearranged

seven *n* **1** the cardinal number that is the sum of one and six **2** a numeral, 7 or VII, representing this number **3** something representing or consisting of seven units ▷ *adj* **4** amounting to seven: *seven weeks* [Old English *seofon*] **seventh** *adj, n*

sevenfold *adj* **1** having seven times as many or as much **2** composed of seven parts ▷ *adv* **3** by seven times as many or as much

seven seas *pl n old-fashioned* all the oceans of the world

seventeen *n* **1** the cardinal number that is the sum of ten and seven **2** a numeral, 17 or XVII, representing this number **3** something representing or consisting of seventeen units ▷ *adj* **4** amounting to seventeen: *seventeen children* **seventeenth** *adj, n*

seventh heaven *n* a state of supreme happiness

seventy *n, pl* **-ties 1** the cardinal number that is the product of ten and seven **2** a numeral, 70 or LXX, representing this number **3** something representing or consisting of seventy units ▷ *adj* **4** amounting to seventy: *seventy countries* **seventieth** *adj, n*

sever *vb* **1** to cut right through or cut off (something): *it accidentally severed the electrical cable* **2** to break off (a tie or relationship) [Latin *separare* to separate] **severable** *adj* **severance** *n*

several *adj* **1** more than a few: *I spoke to several doctors* **2** *formal* various or separate: *the members with their several occupations* **3** *formal* distinct or different: *misfortune visited her three several times* [Medieval Latin *separalis*]

severally *adv formal* individually or separately: *the Western nations severally rather than jointly decided that they would have to act without Russia*

severance pay *n* compensation paid by a firm to an employee who has to leave because the job he or she was appointed to do no longer exists

severe *adj* **1** strict or harsh in the treatment of others: *a severe parent* **2** serious in appearance or manner: *a severe look; a severe hairdo* **3** very intense or unpleasant: *severe chest pains; the punishments are severe* **4** causing discomfort by its harshness: *severe frost* **5** hard to perform or accomplish: *a severe challenge* [Latin *severus*] **severely** *adv* **severity** *n*

Seville orange *n* a bitter orange used to make marmalade [after *Seville* in Spain]

Sèvres (sev-ra) *n* a kind of fine French porcelain [after *Sèvres*, near Paris]

sew *vb* **sewing, sewed, sewn** *or* **sewed 1** to join with thread repeatedly passed through with a needle **2** to attach, fasten, or close by sewing ▷ See also **sew up** [Old English *sēowan*]

sewage *n* waste matter or excrement carried away in sewers or drains

sewage farm *n* a place where sewage is treated so that it can be used as manure or disposed of safely

sewer *n* a drain or pipe, usually underground, used to carry away surface water or sewage [Old French *essever* to drain]

sewerage *n* **1** a system of sewers **2** the removal of surface water or sewage by means of sewers

sewing *n* **1** a piece of fabric or an article, that is sewn or to be sewn **2** the act of fastening together (pieces of fabric, etc.) with needle and thread

sewing machine *n* a machine that sews material with a needle driven by an electric motor

sewn *vb* a past participle of **sew**

sew up *vb* **1** to fasten or mend completely by sewing **2** *informal* to complete or negotiate successfully: *the deal was sewn up just before the deadline*

sex *n* **1** the state of being male or female with reference to reproductive function **2** either of the two categories, male or female, into which organisms are divided **3** sexual intercourse **4** feelings or behaviour connected with having sex or the desire to have sex **5** sexual matters in general ▷ *adj* **6** of sexual matters: *sex education* **7** based on or resulting from the difference between the sexes: *sex discrimination* ▷ *vb* **8** to find out the sex of (an animal) [Latin *sexus*]

sexagenarian *n* **1** a person who is between 60 and 69 years old ▷ *adj* **2** between 60 and 69 years old [Latin *sexaginta* sixty]

sex appeal *n* sexual attractiveness

sex chromosome *n* either of the chromosomes that determine the sex of an animal

sexism *n* discrimination against the members of one sex, usually women **sexist** *n, adj*

sexless *adj* **1** neither male nor female **2** having no sexual desires **3** sexually unattractive

sex object *n* someone, esp. a woman, regarded only in terms of physical attractiveness and not as a person

sexology *n* the study of sexual behaviour in human beings **sexologist** *n*

sextant *n* an instrument used in navigation for measuring angular distance, for example between the sun and the horizon, to calculate the position of a ship or aircraft [Latin *sextans* one sixth of a unit]

sextet *n* **1** a group of six performers **2** a piece of music for six performers **3** a group of six people or things [variant of *sestet*]

sexton *n* a person employed to look after a church and its churchyard [Medieval Latin *sacristanus* sacristan]

sextuple *vb* **-pling, -pled 1** to multiply by six ▷ *adj* **2** six times as much or as many **3** consisting of six parts ▷ *n* **4** a quantity or number six times as great as another [Latin *sextus* sixth]

sextuplet *n* one of six children born at one birth

sexual *adj* **1** of or characterized by sex **2** (of reproduction) characterized by the union of male and female reproductive cells **3** of or relating to the differences between males and females **sexuality** *n* **sexually** *adv*

sexual harassment *n* the unwelcome directing of sexual remarks, looks, or advances at a person in the workplace or a social setting

sexual intercourse *n* the sexual act in which, typically, the male's erect penis is inserted into the female's vagina

sex up *vb informal* to make (something) more exciting

sexy *adj* **sexier, sexiest** *informal* **1** sexually exciting or attractive: *a sexy voice* **2** interesting, exciting, or trendy: *a sexy project; a sexy new car* **sexiness** *n*

SF *or* **sf** science fiction

SFA Scottish Football Association

SFO (in Britain and New Zealand) Serious Fraud Office

Sg *chem* seaborgium

S. Glam South Glamorgan

Sgt. Sergeant

S

sh *interj* be quiet!

shabby *adj* **-bier, -biest 1** old and worn in appearance **2** wearing worn and dirty clothes **3** behaving in a mean or unfair way: *shabby manoeuvres* [Old English *sceabb* scab] **shabbily** *adv* **shabbiness** *n*

shack *n* **1** a roughly built hut ▷ *vb* **2 shack up with** *slang* to live with (a lover) [perhaps from dialect *shackly* ramshackle]

shackle *n* **1** one of a pair of metal rings joined by a chain for securing someone's wrists or ankles **2 shackles** anything that confines or restricts freedom: *free from the shackles of its feudal past* **3** a metal loop or link closed by a bolt, used for securing ropes or chains ▷ *vb* **-ling, -led 4** to fasten with shackles **5** to restrict or hamper: *an economy shackled by central control* [Old English *sceacel*]

shad *n, pl* **shad** *or* **shads** a herring-like food fish [Old English *sceadd*]

shade *n* **1** relative darkness produced by blocking out sunlight **2** a place sheltered from the sun by trees, buildings, etc. **3** something used to provide a shield or protection from a direct source of light, such as a lamp shade **4** a shaded area in a painting or drawing **5** any of the different hues of a colour: *a much darker shade of grey* **6** a slight amount: *a shade of reluctance* **7 put someone** *or* **something in the shade** to be so impressive as to make another person or thing seem unimportant by comparison **8** *literary* a ghost ▷ *vb* **shading, shaded 9** to screen or protect from heat or light **10** to make darker or dimmer **11** to represent (a darker area) in (a painting or drawing), by graded areas of tone, lines, or dots **12** to change slightly or by degrees [Old English *sceadu*]

shades *pl n* **1** *slang* sunglasses **2 shades of** a reminder of: *shades of Margaret Thatcher*

shading *n* the graded areas of tone, lines, or dots, indicating light and dark in a painting or drawing

shadow *n* **1** a dark image or shape cast on a surface when something stands between a light and the surface **2** a patch of shade **3** the dark portions of a picture **4** a hint or faint trace: *a shadow of a doubt* **5** a person less powerful or vigorous than his or her former self **6** a threatening influence: *news of the murder cast a shadow over the village* **7** a person who always accompanies another **8** a person who trails another in secret, such as a detective ▷ *adj* **9** *Brit & Austral* designating a member or members of the main opposition party in Parliament who would hold ministerial office if their party were in power: *the shadow chancellor* ▷ *vb* **10** to cast a shade or shadow over **11** to make dark or gloomy **12** to follow or trail secretly [Old English *sceadwe*]

shadow-box *vb* *boxing* to box against an imaginary opponent for practice **shadow-boxing** *n*

shadowy *adj* **1** (of a place) full of shadows; shady **2** faint or dark like a shadow: *a shadowy figure* **3** mysterious or not well known: *the shadowy world of espionage*

shady *adj* **shadier, shadiest 1** full of shade; shaded **2** giving or casting shade **3** *informal* of doubtful honesty or legality: *shady business dealings* **shadiness** *n*

shaft *n* **1 A** a spear or arrow **B** its long narrow stem **2 shaft of wit** *or* **humour** a clever or amusing remark **3** a ray or streak of light **4** the long straight narrow handle of a tool or golf club **5** a revolving rod in a machine that transmits motion or power **6** one of the bars between which an animal is harnessed to a vehicle **7** *archit* the middle part of a column or pier, between the base and the capital **8** a vertical passageway through a building for a lift **9** a vertical passageway into a mine [Old English *sceaft*]

shag[1] *n* **1** coarse shredded tobacco **2** a matted tangle of hair or wool ▷ *adj* **3** (of a carpet) having long thick woollen threads [Old English *sceacga*]

shag[2] *n* a kind of cormorant [special use of SHAG[1] (with reference to its crest)]

shag[3] *vb* **shagging, shagged** *Brit, Austral & NZ slang* **1** *taboo* to have sexual intercourse with (a person) **2 shagged out** exhausted [origin unknown]

shaggy *adj* **-gier, -giest 1** having or covered with rough unkempt fur, hair, or wool: *shaggy cattle* **2** rough and untidy **shagginess** *n*

shagreen *n* **1** the skin of a shark, used as an abrasive **2** a rough grainy leather made from certain animal hides [French *chagrin*]

shah *n* the title of the former monarch of Iran [Persian: king]

shake *vb* **shaking, shook, shaken 1** to move up and down or back and forth with short quick movements **2** to be or make unsteady **3** (of a voice) to tremble because of anger or nervousness **4** to clasp or grasp (the hand) of (a person) in greeting or agreement: *they shook hands* **5 shake on it** *informal* to shake hands in agreement or reconciliation **6** to wave vigorously and angrily: *he shook his fist* **7** (often foll. by *up*) to frighten or unsettle **8** to shock, disturb, or upset: *he was badly shaken but unharmed* **9** to undermine or weaken: *a team whose morale had been badly shaken* **10** *US & Canad informal* to get rid of **11** *music* to perform a trill on (a note) **12 shake one's head** to indicate disagreement or disapproval by moving the head from side to side ▷ *n* **13** the act or an instance of shaking **14** a tremor or vibration **15 the shakes** *informal* a state of uncontrollable trembling **16** *informal* a very short period of time: *in half a shake* **17** *music* same as **trill** (sense 1) **18** short for **milk shake** ▷ See also **shake down, shake off, shake up** [Old English *sceacan*]

shake down *vb* **1** to go to bed, esp. in a makeshift bed ▷ *n* **shakedown 2** a makeshift bed

shake off *vb* **1** to remove or get rid of: *I have been trying to shake off the stigma for some time* **2** to escape from; get away from: *they switched to a blue car in a bid to shake off reporters*

shaker *n* **1** a container used for shaking a powdered substance onto something: *a flour shaker* **2** a container in which the ingredients of alcoholic drinks are shaken together

Shakespearean *or* **Shakespearian** *adj* **1** of William Shakespeare, English dramatist and

S

poet, or his works ▷ *n* **2** a student of or specialist in Shakespeare's works

shake up *vb* **1** to mix by shaking **2** to reorganize drastically **3** *informal* to shock mentally or physically: *the thunderstorm really shook me up* ▷ *n* **shake-up 4** *informal* a radical reorganization, such as the reorganization of employees in a company

shako (**shack**-oh) *n, pl* **shakos** a tall cylindrical peaked military hat with a plume [Hungarian *csákó*]

shaky *adj* **shakier, shakiest 1** weak and unsteady, esp. due to illness or shock **2** uncertain or doubtful: *their prospects are shaky* **3** tending to shake or tremble **shakily** *adv*

shale *n* a flaky sedimentary rock formed by compression of successive layers of clay [Old English *scealu* shell]

shall *vb, past tense* **should 1** (*with 'I' or 'we' as subject*) used as an auxiliary to make the future tense: *we shall see you tomorrow* **2** (*with 'you', 'he', 'she', 'it', 'they', or a noun as subject*) **A** used as an auxiliary to indicate determination on the part of the speaker: *you shall pay for this!* **B** used as an auxiliary to indicate compulsion or obligation, now esp. in official documents **3** (*with 'I' or 'we' as subject*) used as an auxiliary in questions asking for advice or agreement: *what shall we do now?; shall I shut the door?* [Old English *sceal*]

> **USAGE** The usual rule given for the use of *shall* and *will* is that where the meaning is one of simple futurity, *shall* is used for the first person of the verb and *will* for the second and third: *I shall go tomorrow; they will be there now.* Where the meaning involves command, obligation, or determination, the positions are reversed: *it shall be done; I will definitely go.* However, *shall* has come to be largely neglected in favour of *will*, which has become the commonest form of the future in all three persons.

shallot (shal-**lot**) *n* a small, onion-like plant used in cooking for flavouring [Old French *eschaloigne*]

shallow *adj* **1** having little depth **2** not involving sincere feelings or serious thought **3** (of breathing) consisting of short breaths ▷ *n* **4** (*often pl*) a shallow place in a body of water [Middle English *shalow*] **shallowness** *n*

sham *n* **1** anything that is not genuine or is not what it appears to be **2** a person who pretends to be something other than he or she is ▷ *adj* **3** not real or genuine ▷ *vb* **shamming, shammed 4** to fake or feign (something); pretend: *he made a point of shamming nervousness* [origin unknown]

shaman (**sham**-man) *n* **1** a priest of shamanism **2** a medicine man or witch doctor of a similar religion [Russian]

shamanism (**sham**-man-iz-zum) *n* a religion of northern Asia, based on a belief in good and evil spirits who can be influenced or controlled only by the shamans **shamanist** *n, adj*

shamble *vb* **-bling, -bled 1** to walk or move along in an awkward shuffling way ▷ *n* **2** an awkward or shuffling walk [perhaps from *shambles*, referring to legs of a meat vendor's table] **shambling** *adj, n*

shambles *n* **1** a disorderly or badly organized event or place: *the bathroom was a shambles* **2** *chiefly Brit* a butcher's slaughterhouse **3** *old-fashioned* any scene of great slaughter [Middle English *shamble* table used by meat vendors]

shambolic *adj informal* completely disorganized

shame *n* **1** a painful emotion resulting from an awareness of having done something wrong or foolish **2** capacity to feel such an emotion: *have they no shame?* **3** loss of respect; disgrace **4** a person or thing that causes this **5** a cause for regret or disappointment: *it's a shame to rush back* **6 put to shame** to show up as being inferior by comparison: *his essay put mine to shame* ▷ *interj* **7** *S African informal* **A** an expression of sympathy **B** an expression of pleasure or endearment ▷ *vb* **shaming, shamed 8** to cause to feel shame **9** to bring shame on **10** (often foll. by *into*) to force someone to do something by making him or her feel ashamed not to: *he was finally shamed into paying the bill* [Old English *scamu*]

shamefaced *adj* embarrassed or guilty [earlier *shamefast*] **shamefacedly** *adv*

shameful *adj* causing or deserving shame: *a shameful lack of concern* **shamefully** *adv*

shameless *adj* **1** having no sense of shame: *a shameless manipulator* **2** without decency or modesty: *a shameless attempt to stifle democracy* **shamelessly** *adv*

shammy *n, pl* **-mies** *informal* a piece of chamois leather [variant of *chamois*]

shampoo *n* **1** a soapy liquid used to wash the hair **2** a similar liquid for washing carpets or upholstery **3** the process of shampooing ▷ *vb* **-pooing, -pooed 4** to wash (the hair, carpets, or upholstery) with shampoo [Hindi *chāmpo*]

shamrock *n* a small clover-like plant with three round leaves on each stem: the national emblem of Ireland [Irish Gaelic *seamrōg*]

shandy *n, pl* **-dies** a drink made of beer and lemonade [origin unknown]

shanghai *slang* ▷ *vb* **-haiing, -haied 1** to force or trick (someone) into doing something **2** *history* to kidnap (a man) and force him to serve at sea **3** *Austral & NZ* to shoot with a catapult ▷ *n* **4** *Austral & NZ* a catapult [after the city of *Shanghai*; senses 3 and 4 altered from Scots dialect *shangie, shangan* cleft stick]

shank *n* **1** the part of the leg between the knee and the ankle **2** a cut of meat from the top part of an animal's shank **3** the long narrow part of a tool, key, spoon, etc. [Old English *scanca*]

shanks's pony *or US* **shanks's mare** *n informal* one's own legs as a means of transport [from *shank*, the lower part of the leg]

shan't shall not

shantung *n* a heavy Chinese silk with a knobbly surface [after province of NE China]

shanty[1] *n, pl* **-ties** a small rough hut; crude dwelling [Canadian French *chantier* cabin built in a lumber camp]

shanty[2] *or* **chanty** *n, pl* **-ties** a rhythmic song originally sung by sailors when working [French *chanter* to sing]

shantytown *n* a town of poor people living in shanties

S

shape *n* **1** the outward form of an object, produced by its outline **2** the figure or outline of the body of a person **3** organized or definite form: *to preserve the union in its present shape* **4** the specific form that anything takes on: *a gold locket in the shape of a heart* **5** a pattern or mould **6** condition or state of efficiency: *in poor shape* **7 take shape** to assume a definite form ▷ *vb* **shaping, shaped 8** (often foll. by *into* or *up*) to receive or cause to receive shape or form: *spinach shaped into a ball* **9** to mould into a particular pattern or form **10** to devise or develop: *to shape a system of free trade* ▷ See also **shape up** [Old English *gesceap*, literally: that which is created]

shapeless *adj* **1** (of a person or object) lacking a pleasing shape: *a shapeless dress* **2** having no definite shape or form: *a shapeless mound* **shapelessness** *n*

shapely *adj* **-lier, -liest** (esp. of a woman's body or legs) pleasing or attractive in shape **shapeliness** *n*

shape up *vb informal* **1** to progress or develop satisfactorily **2** to develop a definite or proper form **3** to start working efficiently or behaving properly: *shape up or face the sack*

shard *n* a broken piece or fragment of pottery, glass, or metal [Old English *sceard*]

share¹ *n* **1** a part or portion of something that belongs to or is contributed by a person or group **2** (*often pl*) any of the equal parts into which the capital stock of a company is divided ▷ *vb* **sharing, shared 3** (often foll. by *out*) to divide and distribute **4** to receive or contribute a portion of: *we shared a bottle of mineral water* **5** to join with another or others in the use of (something): *a programme about four women sharing a house* **6** to go through (a similar experience) as others: *we have all shared the nightmare of toothache* **7** to tell others about (something) **8** to have the same (beliefs or opinions) as others: *universal values shared by both east and west* [Old English *scearu*]

share² *n* short for **ploughshare** [Old English *scear*]

shareholder *n* the owner of one or more shares in a company

S

share index *n* an index showing the movement of share prices

sharemilker *n NZ* a person who works on a dairy farm belonging to someone else and gets a share of the proceeds from the sale of the milk

sharia *n* the body of doctrines that regulate the lives of Muslims [Arabic]

shark *n* **1** a large, usually predatory fish with a long body, two dorsal fins, and rows of sharp teeth **2** *derogatory* a person who swindles or extorts money from other people [origin unknown]

sharkskin *n* a smooth glossy fabric used for sportswear

sharp *adj* **1** having a keen cutting edge **2** tapering to an edge or point **3** involving a sudden change in direction: *a sharp bend on a road*; *a sharp rise in prices* **4** moving, acting, or reacting quickly: *sharp reflexes* **5** clearly defined: *a sharp contrast* **6** quick to notice or understand things; keen-witted **7** clever in an underhand way: *sharp practices* **8** bitter or harsh: *a sharp response* **9** shrill or penetrating: *a sharp cry of horror* **10** having a bitter or sour taste **11** (of pain or cold) acute or biting: *a sharp gust of wind* **12** *music* **A** (of a note) raised in pitch by one semitone: F *sharp* **B** (of an instrument or voice) out of tune by being too high in pitch **13** *informal* neat and stylish: *a sharp dresser* ▷ *adv* **14** promptly **15** exactly: *at ten o'clock sharp* **16** *music* **A** higher than a standard pitch **B** out of tune by being too high in pitch: *she sings sharp* ▷ *n* **17** *music* **A** an accidental that raises the pitch of a note by one semitone. Symbol: ♯ **B** a note affected by this accidental **18** *informal* a cheat; a cardsharp [Old English *scearp*] **sharpish** *adj* **sharply** *adv* **sharpness** *n*

sharpen *vb* to make or become sharp or sharper **sharpener** *n*

sharper *n* a person who cheats or swindles; fraud

sharpshooter *n* a skilled marksman

sharp-tongued *adj* very critical or sarcastic

sharp-witted *adj* very intelligent and perceptive

shat *vb taboo* a past tense and past participle of **shit**

shatter *vb* **1** to break suddenly into many small pieces **2** to damage badly or destroy: *to shatter American confidence* **3** to upset (someone) greatly: *the whole experience shattered me* [origin unknown] **shattering** *adj*

shattered *adj informal* **1** completely exhausted **2** badly upset: *he was shattered by the separation*

shave *vb* **shaving, shaved, shaved** *or* **shaven 1** to remove (the beard or hair) from (the face, head, or body) by using a razor or shaver **2** to remove thin slices from (wood or other material) with a sharp cutting tool **3** to touch (someone or something) lightly in passing ▷ *n* **4** the act or an instance of shaving **5** the removal of hair from a man's face by a razor **6** a tool for cutting off thin slices **7 close shave** *informal* a narrow escape [Old English *sceafan*]

shaver *n* **1** an electrically powered razor **2** *old-fashioned* a young boy

Shavian (shave-ee-an) *adj* **1** of or like George Bernard Shaw, Irish dramatist noted for his sharp wit, or his works ▷ *n* **2** an admirer of Shaw or his works

shaving *n* **1** a thin slice of something such as wood, which has been shaved off ▷ *adj* **2** used when shaving: *shaving foam*

shawl *n* a piece of woollen cloth worn over the head or shoulders by a woman or wrapped around a baby [Persian *shāl*]

she *pron* **1** (refers to) the female person or animal previously mentioned or in question: *she is my sister* **2** (refers to) something regarded as female, such as a car, ship, or nation ▷ *n* **3** (refers to) a female person or animal [Old English *sīe*]

sheaf *n, pl* **sheaves 1** a bundle of papers tied together **2** a bundle of reaped corn tied together ▷ *vb* **3** to bind or tie into a sheaf [Old English *scēaf*]

shear *vb* **shearing, sheared** *or Austral & NZ sometimes* **shore, sheared** *or* **shorn 1** to remove (the fleece) of (a sheep) by cutting or clipping **2** to cut or cut through (something) with shears or a sharp instrument **3** *engineering* to cause (a part) to break or (of a part) to break through strain or twisting ▷ *n* **4** breakage caused through strain or twisting ▷ See also **shears** [Old English *sceran*] **shearer** *n*

shearing shed *n Austral & NZ* a farm building with equipment for shearing sheep

shears *pl n* **A** large scissors, used for sheep shearing **B** a large scissor-like cutting tool with flat blades, used for cutting hedges

sheath *n, pl* **sheaths 1** a case or covering for the blade of a knife or sword **2** *biol* a structure that encloses or protects **3** *Brit, Austral & NZ* same as **condom 4** a close-fitting dress [Old English *scēath*]

sheathe *vb* **sheathing, sheathed 1** to insert (a knife or sword) into a sheath **2** to cover with a sheath or sheathing

sheathing *n* any material used as an outer layer

sheaves *n* the plural of **sheaf**

shebeen *or* **shebean** *n Scot, Irish & S African* a place where alcoholic drink is sold illegally [Irish Gaelic *sībīn* beer of poor quality]

shed¹ *n* **1** a small, roughly made building used for storing garden tools, etc. **2** a large barnlike building used for various purposes at factories, train stations, etc.: *a locomotive shed* [Old English *sced*]

shed² *vb* **shedding, shed 1** to get rid of: *250 workers shed by the company* **2 shed tears** to cry **3 shed light on** to make (a problem or situation) easier to understand **4** to cast off (skin, hair, or leaves): *the trees were already beginning to shed their leaves* **5** to cause to flow off: *this coat sheds water* **6** to separate or divide (a group of sheep) [Old English *sc(e)ādan*]

sheen *n* a glistening brightness on the surface of something: *grass with a sheen of dew on it* [Old English *sciēne*]

sheep *n, pl* **sheep 1** a cud-chewing mammal with a thick woolly coat, kept for its wool or meat. Related adjective: **ovine 2** a timid person **3 like sheep** (of a group of people) allowing a single person to dictate their actions or beliefs **4 separate the sheep from the goats** to pick out the members of a group who are superior in some respects [Old English *scēap*] **sheeplike** *adj*

sheep-dip *n* **1** a liquid disinfectant and insecticide in which sheep are immersed **2** a deep trough containing such a liquid

sheepdog *n* **1** a dog used for herding sheep **2** a breed of dog reared originally for herding sheep

sheepfold *n* a pen or enclosure for sheep

sheepish *adj* embarrassed because of feeling foolish **sheepishly** *adv*

sheepshank *n* a knot made in a rope to shorten it temporarily

sheepskin *n* the skin of a sheep with the wool still attached, used to make clothing and rugs

sheer¹ *adj* **1** absolute; complete: *sheer amazement* **2** perpendicular; very steep: *the sheer rock face* **3** (of textiles) light, delicate, and see-through ▷ *adv* **4** steeply: *the cliff drops sheer to the sea* [Old English *scīr*]

sheer² *vb* **sheer off** *or* **away (from) A** to change course suddenly **B** to avoid (an unpleasant person, thing, or topic) [origin unknown]

sheet¹ *n* **1** a large rectangular piece of cloth used as an inner bed cover **2** a thin piece of material such as paper or glass, usually rectangular **3** a broad continuous surface or layer: *a sheet of ice* **4** a newspaper ▷ *vb* **5** to provide with, cover, or wrap in a sheet **6** (often foll. by *down*) to rain very heavily [Old English *sciete*]

sheet² *n naut* a line or rope for controlling the position of a sail [Old English *scēata* corner of a sail]

sheet anchor *n* **1** *naut* a large strong anchor for use in an emergency **2** a person or thing that can always be relied on

sheeting *n* any material from which sheets are made

sheet metal *n* metal formed into a thin sheet by rolling or hammering

sheet music *n* music printed on individual sheets of paper

sheikh *or* **sheik** (shake) *n* **A** the head of an Arab tribe, village, or family **B** (in Muslim communities) a religious leader [Arabic *shaykh* old man] **sheikhdom** *or* **sheikdom** *n*

sheila *n Austral & NZ old-fashioned, informal* a girl or woman [from the girl's name *Sheila*]

shekel *n* **1** the monetary unit of Israel **2 shekels** *informal* money [Hebrew *sheqel*]

shelduck *or masc* **sheldrake** *n, pl* **-ducks, -duck** *or* **-drakes, -drake** a large brightly coloured wild duck of Europe and Asia [probably from dialect *sheld* pied]

shelf *n, pl* **shelves 1** a board fixed horizontally against a wall or in a cupboard, for holding things **2** a projecting layer of ice or rock on land or in the sea **3 off the shelf** (of products in shops) sold as standard **4 on the shelf** put aside or abandoned; used esp. of unmarried women considered to be past the age of marriage [Old English *scylfe* ship's deck]

shelf life *n* the length of time a packaged product will remain fresh or usable

shell *n* **1** the protective outer layer of an egg, fruit, or nut **2** the hard outer covering of an animal such as a crab or tortoise **3** any hard outer case **4** the external structure of a building, car, or ship, esp. one that is unfinished or gutted by fire **5** an explosive artillery projectile that can be fired from a large gun **6** a small-arms cartridge **7** *rowing* a very light narrow racing boat **8 come** *or* **bring out of one's shell** to become *or* help to become less shy and reserved ▷ *vb* **9** to remove the shell or husk from **10** to attack with artillery shells ▷ See also **shell out** [Old English *sciell*] **shell-like** *adj*

she'll she will *or* she shall

shellac *n* **1** a yellowish resin used in varnishes and polishes **2** a varnish made by dissolving shellac in alcohol ▷ *vb* **-lacking, -lacked 3** to coat with shellac [*shell* + *lac*]

shellfish *n, pl* **-fish** *or* **-fishes** a sea-living animal, esp. one that can be eaten, having a shell

shell out *vb informal* to pay out or hand over (money)

shell shock *n* a nervous disorder characterized by anxiety and depression that occurs as a result of lengthy exposure to battle conditions **shell-shocked** *adj*

S

shell suit *n Brit* a lightweight tracksuit made of a waterproof nylon layer over a cotton layer

Shelta *n* a secret language based on Gaelic, used by some travelling people in Ireland and Britain [origin unknown]

shelter *n* **1** something that provides cover or protection from weather or danger **2** the protection given by such a cover ▷ *vb* **3** to take cover from bad weather **4** to provide with a place to live or a hiding place: *to shelter refugees* [origin unknown]

sheltered *adj* **1** protected from wind and rain **2** protected from unpleasant or upsetting experiences: *a sheltered childhood* **3** specially designed to provide a safe environment for elderly or disabled people: *sheltered housing*

shelve¹ *vb* **shelving, shelved 1** to put aside or postpone: *to shelve a project* **2** to place (something, such as a book) on a shelf **3** to provide with shelves: *to shelve a cupboard* **4** to dismiss (someone) from active service [from *shelves*, plural of *shelf*]

shelve² *vb* **shelving, shelved** to slope away gradually [origin unknown]

shelves *n* the plural of **shelf**

shelving *n* **1** material for shelves **2** shelves collectively

shenanigans *pl n informal* **1** mischief or nonsense **2** trickery or deception [origin unknown]

shepherd *n* **1** a person employed to tend sheep **2** *Christianity* a member of the clergy when considered as the moral and spiritual guide of the people in the parish ▷ *vb* **3** to guide or watch over (people) [SHEEP + HERD] **shepherdess** *fem n*

shepherd's pie *n* a baked dish of minced meat covered with mashed potato

sherbet *n* **1** *Brit, Austral & NZ* a fruit-flavoured slightly fizzy powder, eaten as a sweet or used to make a drink **2** *US, Canad & S African* same as **sorbet** [Turkish *şerbet*]

sheriff *n* **1** (in the US) the chief elected law-enforcement officer in a county **2** (in Canada) a municipal officer who enforces court orders and escorts convicted criminals to prison **3** (in England and Wales) the chief executive officer of the Crown in a county, having chiefly ceremonial duties **4** (in Scotland) a judge in a sheriff court **5** (in Australia) an officer of the Supreme Court [Old English *scīrgerēfa*]

sheriff court *n* (in Scotland) a court having powers to try all but the most serious crimes and to deal with most civil actions

Sherpa *n, pl* **-pas** *or* **-pa** a member of a Tibetan people living on the southern slopes of the Himalayas

sherry *n, pl* **-ries** a pale or dark brown fortified wine, originally from southern Spain [Spanish *Xeres*, now *Jerez*, in Spain]

Shetland pony *n* a very small sturdy breed of pony with a long shaggy mane and tail

shibboleth *n* **1** a slogan or catch phrase, usually considered outworn, that characterizes a particular party or sect: *the shibboleth of Western strategy* **2** a custom, phrase, or use of language that reliably distinguishes a member of one group or class from another [word used in the Old Testament by the Gileadites as a test word for the Ephraimites, who could not pronounce *sh*]

shickered *adj Austral & NZ old-fashioned slang* drunk [Yiddish *shicker* liquor]

shied *vb* the past of **shy¹** or **shy²**

shield *n* **1** a piece of defensive armour carried in the hand or on the arm to protect the body from blows or missiles **2** any person or thing that protects, hides, or defends: *a wind shield* **3** *heraldry* a representation of a shield used for displaying a coat of arms **4** anything that resembles a shield in shape, such as a trophy in a sports competition ▷ *vb* **5** to protect, hide, or defend (someone or something) from danger or harm: *an industry shielded from competition* [Old English *scield*]

shift *vb* **1** to move from one place or position to another **2** to pass (blame or responsibility) onto someone else: *he was trying to shift the blame to me* **3** to change (gear) in a motor vehicle **4** to remove or be removed: *no detergent can shift these stains* **5** *US* to change for another or others **6** *slang* to move quickly ▷ *n* **7** the act or an instance of shifting **8 A** a group of workers who work during a specific period **B** the period of time worked by such a group **9** a method or scheme **10** a loose-fitting straight underskirt or dress [Old English *sciftan*]

shiftless *adj* lacking in ambition or initiative

shifty *adj* **shiftier, shiftiest** looking deceitful and not to be trusted **shiftiness** *n*

shih-tzu *n* a small dog with a long straight dense coat and a tail curling over its back [Chinese, literally: lion]

shillelagh (shil-lay-lee) *n* (in Ireland) a heavy club [Irish Gaelic *sail* cudgel + *éille* thong]

shilling *n* **1** a former British coin worth one twentieth of a pound, replaced by the 5p piece in 1970 **2** a former Australian coin, worth one twentieth of a pound **3** the standard monetary unit in several E African countries [Old English *scilling*]

shillyshally *vb* **-shallies, -shallying, -shallied** *informal* to be indecisive [*shill I shall I*, reduplication of *shall I*]

shim *n* **1** a thin strip of material placed between two close surfaces to fill a gap ▷ *vb* **shimming, shimmed 2** to fit or fill up with a shim [origin unknown]

shimmer *vb* **1** to shine with a faint unsteady light ▷ *n* **2** a faint unsteady light [Old English *scimerian*] **shimmering** *or* **shimmery** *adj*

shin *n* **1** the front part of the lower leg **2** a cut of beef including the lower foreleg ▷ *vb* **shinning, shinned 3 shin up** to climb (something, such as a rope or pole) by gripping with the hands or arms and the legs and hauling oneself up [Old English *scinu*]

shinbone *n* the nontechnical name for **tibia**

shindig *or* **shindy** *n, pl* **-digs** *or* **-dies** *slang* **1** a noisy party or dance **2** a quarrel or brawl [variant of *shinty*]

shine *vb* **shining, shone 1** to give off or reflect light **2** to direct the light of (a lamp or torch): *I shone a torch at the ceiling* **3** *past tense & past participle* **shined** to make clean and bright by polishing: *they earned money by shining shoes* **4** to be very good at something:

S

she shone in most subjects; she shone at school **5** to appear very bright and clear: *her hair shone like gold* ▷ *n* **6** brightness or lustre **7 take a shine to someone** *informal* to take a liking to someone [Old English *scīnan*]

shiner *n informal* a black eye

shingle¹ *n* **1** a thin rectangular tile laid with others in overlapping rows to cover a roof or a wall **2** a woman's short-cropped hairstyle ▷ *vb* **-gling, -gled 3** to cover (a roof or a wall) with shingles **4** to cut (the hair) in a short-cropped style [Latin *scindere* to split]

shingle² *n* coarse gravel found on beaches [Scandinavian]

shingles *n* a disease causing a rash of small blisters along a nerve [Medieval Latin *cingulum* girdle]

shingle slide *n NZ* the loose stones on a steep slope

Shinto *n* a Japanese religion in which ancestors and nature spirits are worshipped [Japanese: the way of the gods] **Shintoism** *n* **Shintoist** *n, adj*

shinty *n* **1** a game (of Scottish origin) like hockey but with taller goals **2** *pl* **-ties** the stick used in this game [perhaps Scottish Gaelic *sinteag* a pace]

shiny *adj* **shinier, shiniest 1** bright and polished **2** (of clothes or material) worn to a smooth and glossy state by continual wear or rubbing

ship *n* **1** a large seagoing vessel with engines or sails **2** short for **airship** or **spaceship 3 when one's ship comes in** when one has become successful ▷ *vb* **shipping, shipped 4** to send or transport by any carrier, esp. a ship **5** *naut* to take in (water) over the side **6** to bring or go aboard a vessel: *to ship oars* **7** (often foll. by *off*) *informal* to send away: *they were shipped off to foreign countries* **8** to be hired to serve aboard a ship: *I shipped aboard a Liverpool liner* [Old English *scip*]

shipboard *adj* taking place or used aboard a ship: *a shipboard romance*

shipbuilder *n* a person or company that builds ships **shipbuilding** *n*

shipmate *n* a sailor who serves on the same ship as another

shipment *n* **1** goods shipped together as part of the same lot: *a shipment of arms* **2** the act of shipping cargo

shipper *n* a person or company that ships

shipping *n* **1** the business of transporting freight, esp. by ship **2** ships collectively: *all shipping should stay clear of the harbour*

shipshape *adj* **1** neat or orderly ▷ *adv* **2** in a neat and orderly manner

shipwreck *n* **1** the destruction of a ship at sea **2** the remains of a wrecked ship **3** ruin or destruction: *the shipwreck of the old science* ▷ *vb* **4** to wreck or destroy (a ship) **5** to bring to ruin or destruction

shipwright *n* someone, esp. a carpenter, who builds or repairs ships

shipyard *n* a place where ships are built and repaired

shire *n* **1** *Brit* a county **2** *Austral* a rural area with an elected council **3 the Shires** the Midland counties of England [Old English *scīr* office]

shire horse *n* a large powerful breed of working horse

shirk *vb* to avoid doing (work or a duty); to be negligent: *no-one shirks when he's around* [probably from German *Schurke* rogue] **shirker** *n*

shirt *n* **1** an item of clothing worn on the upper part of the body, usually with a collar and sleeves and buttoning up the front **2 keep your shirt on** *informal* keep your temper **3 put one's shirt on something** *informal* to bet all one has on something [Old English *scyrte*]

shirt-lifter *n offensive slang* a homosexual man

shirtsleeve *n* **1** the sleeve of a shirt **2 in one's shirtsleeves** not wearing a jacket

shirt-tail *n* the part of a shirt that extends below the waist

shirtwaister *or US* **shirtwaist** *n* a woman's dress with a tailored bodice resembling a shirt

shirty *adj* **shirtier, shirtiest** *slang* bad-tempered or annoyed

shish kebab *n* a dish of small pieces of meat and vegetables grilled on a skewer [Turkish *şiş kebab*]

shit *taboo* ▷ *vb* **shitting, shitted, shit** *or* **shat 1** to defecate ▷ *n* **2** faeces; excrement **3** *slang* rubbish; nonsense **4** *slang* a worthless person ▷ *interj* **5** *slang* an exclamation of anger or disgust [Old English *scītan* to defecate] **shitty** *adj*

shiver¹ *vb* **1** to tremble from cold or fear ▷ *n* **2** a tremble caused by cold or fear **3 the shivers** a fit of shivering through fear or illness [Middle English *chiveren*] **shivering** *n, adj* **shivery** *adj*

shiver² *vb* **1** to break into fragments ▷ *n* **2** a splintered piece [Germanic]

shoal¹ *n* **1** a large group of fish swimming together **2** a large group of people or things [Old English *scolu*]

shoal² *n* **1** a stretch of shallow water **2** a sandbank or rocky area, esp. one that can be seen at low water ▷ *vb* **3** to make or become shallow [Old English *sceald* shallow]

shock¹ *vb* **1** to cause (someone) to experience extreme horror, disgust, or astonishment: *the similarity shocked me* **2** to cause a state of shock in (a person) ▷ *n* **3** a sudden and violent blow or impact **4 A** a sudden and violent emotional disturbance **B** something causing this **5** *pathol* a condition in which a person's blood cannot flow properly because of severe injury, burns, or fright **6** pain and muscular spasm caused by an electric current passing through a person's body [Old French *choc*] **shocker** *n*

shock² *n* **1** a number of grain sheaves set on end in a field to dry ▷ *vb* **2** to set up (sheaves) in shocks [probably Germanic]

shock³ *n* a thick bushy mass of hair [origin unknown]

shock absorber *n* any device designed to absorb mechanical shock, esp. one fitted to a motor vehicle to reduce the effects of travelling over bumpy surfaces

shocking *adj* **1** *informal* very bad or terrible: *a shocking match at Leicester* **2** causing dismay or disgust: *a shocking lack of concern* **3 shocking pink** (of) a very bright shade of pink

shockproof *adj* capable of absorbing shock without damage

shock tactics *pl n* the use of unexpected or unexpectedly forceful methods to carry out a plan

shock therapy *or* **shock treatment** *n* the treatment of certain mental conditions by passing an electric current through the patient's brain

shock wave *n* **1** an area of very high pressure moving through the air, earth, or water **2** a feeling of shock, horror, surprise, etc. that spreads through a community

shod *vb* the past of **shoe**

shoddy *adj* **-dier, -diest 1** made or done badly or carelessly: *shoddy goods* **2** of poor quality; shabby [origin unknown] **shoddily** *adv* **shoddiness** *n*

shoe *n* **1** one of a matching pair of coverings shaped to fit the foot, made of leather or other strong material and ending below the ankle **2** anything resembling a shoe in shape, function, or position **3** short for **horseshoe** **4 be in a person's shoes** *informal* to be in another person's situation ▷ *vb* **shoeing, shod 5** to fit (a horse) with horseshoes [Old English *scōh*]

shoehorn *n* a smooth curved piece of metal or plastic inserted at the heel of a shoe to ease the foot into it

shoelace *n* a cord for fastening shoes

shoemaker *n* a person who makes or repairs shoes or boots **shoemaking** *n*

shoestring *n* **1** same as **shoelace 2** *informal* a very small amount of money: *the theatre will be run on a shoestring*

shoetree *n* a long piece of metal, plastic, or wood, put into a shoe or boot to keep its shape

shone *vb* a past of **shine**

shonky *adj* **-kier, -kiest** *Austral & NZ informal* unreliable or unsound

shoo *interj* **1** go away!: used to drive away unwanted or annoying animals or people ▷ *vb* **shooing, shooed 2** to drive away by crying 'shoo' [imitative]

shook *vb* the past tense of **shake**

shoot *vb* **shooting, shot 1** to hit, wound, or kill with a missile fired from a weapon **2** to fire (a missile or missiles) from a weapon **3** to fire (a weapon) **4** to hunt game with a gun for sport **5** to send out or be sent out quickly and aggressively: *he shot questions at her* **6** to move very rapidly: *the car shot forward* **7** to go or pass quickly over or through: *he was trying to shoot the white water* **8** to slide or push into or out of a fastening: *she shot the bolt quickly* **9** (of a plant) to sprout (a new growth) **10** to photograph or film (a subject, sequence, etc.) **11** *sport* to hit or kick the ball at goal ▷ *n* **12** the act of shooting **13** a new growth or sprout of a plant **14** *chiefly Brit* a meeting or party organized for hunting game with guns **15** an area where game can be hunted with guns **16** *informal* a photographic assignment: *a fashion shoot in New York* [Old English *sceōtan*]

shooter *n* **1** a person or thing that shoots **2** *slang* a gun

shooting gallery *n* a long narrow room where people practise shooting

shooting star *n informal* a meteor

shooting stick *n* a walking stick with a spike at one end and a folding seat at the other

shoot-out *n* **1** a gunfight **2** short for **penalty shoot-out**

shoot up *vb* **1** to grow or increase rapidly: *crime rates have shot up; as my peers started to shoot up, I stopped growing* **2** *slang* to inject oneself with heroin or another strong drug

shop *n* **1** a place for the sale of goods and services **2** a place where a specified type of work is done; workshop: *a repair shop* **3 all over the shop** *informal* scattered everywhere: *his papers were all over the shop* **4 shut up shop** to close business at the end of the day or permanently **5 talk shop** *informal* to discuss one's business or work on a social occasion ▷ *vb* **shopping, shopped 6** (often foll. by *for*) to visit a shop or shops in order to buy (goods) **7** *Brit, Austral & NZ slang* to inform on (someone), esp. to the police [Old English *sceoppa* stall] **shopper** *n*

shop around *vb informal* **1** to visit a number of shops or stores to compare goods and prices **2** to consider a number of possibilities before making a choice

shop assistant *n* a person who serves in a shop

shop floor *n* **1** the production area of a factory **2** workers, esp. factory workers, as opposed to management

shopkeeper *n* a person who owns or manages a shop **shopkeeping** *n*

shoplifter *n* a customer who steals goods from a shop **shoplifting** *n*

shopping *n* **1** the act of going to shops and buying things **2** things that have been bought in shops

shopping centre *n* **1** a complex of stores, restaurants, and sometimes banks, usually under the same roof **2** the area of a town where most of the shops are situated

shopping list *n* **1** a written list of things to be bought when out shopping **2** any list of things desired or demanded: *a long shopping list of amendments to the treaty*

shopping mall *n* a large enclosed shopping centre

shopping plaza *n* a shopping centre, usually a small group of stores built as a strip

shopsoiled *adj* slightly dirty or faded, from being displayed in a shop

shop steward *n* a trade-union official elected by his or her fellow workers to be their representative in dealing with their employer

shoptalk *n* conversation about one's work, carried on outside working hours

shopwalker *n Brit* (esp. formerly) a person employed by a department store to assist sales personnel and help customers

shore[1] *n* **1** the land along the edge of a sea, lake, or wide river. Related adjective: **littoral 2** land, as opposed to water: *150 yards from shore* **3 shores** a country: *a frequent visitor to these shores* [probably from Middle Low German, Middle Dutch *schōre*]

shore[2] *n* **1** a prop placed under or against something as a support ▷ *vb* **shoring, shored 2 shore up A** to prop up (an unsteady building or wall) with a strong support **B** to strengthen or support (something weak): *lower interest rates to shore up the economy* [Middle Dutch *schōre*]

shoreline *n* the edge of a sea, lake, or wide river

shorn *vb* a past participle of **shear**

short *adj* **1** of little length; not long **2** of little height; not tall **3** not lasting long **4** not enough: *the number of places laid at the table was short by four* **5 short of** *or* **on** lacking in: *short of cash; short on detail* **6** concise: *a short book* **7** (of drinks) consisting chiefly of a spirit, such as whisky **8** (of someone's memory) lacking the ability to retain a lot of facts **9** (of a person's manner) abrupt and rather rude: *Kemp was short with her* **10** (of betting odds) almost even **11** *finance* **A** not possessing at the time of sale the stocks or commodities one sells **B** relating to such sales, which depend on falling prices for profit **12** *phonetics* (of a vowel) of relatively brief duration **13** (of pastry) crumbly in texture **14 in short supply** scarce **15 short and sweet** brief and to the point **16 short for** a shortened form of ▷ *adv* **17** abruptly: *to stop short* **18 be caught short** to have a sudden need to go to the toilet **19 go short** not to have enough **20 short of** except: *they want nothing short of his removal from power* ▷ *n* **21** a drink of spirits **22** a short film shown before the main feature in a cinema **23** same as **short circuit** **24 for short** *informal* as a shortened form: *cystic fibrosis, CF for short* **25 in short** briefly ▷ *vb* **26** to short-circuit ▷ See also **shorts** [Old English *sceort*] **shortness** *n*

shortage *n* not enough of something needed

shortbread *n* a rich crumbly biscuit made with butter

shortcake *n* **1** shortbread **2** a dessert made of layers of biscuit or cake filled with fruit and cream

short-change *vb* **-changing, -changed 1** to give (someone) less than the correct change **2** *slang* to treat (someone), unfairly, esp. by giving less than is expected

short circuit *n* **1** a faulty or accidental connection in an electric circuit, which deflects current through a path of low resistance, usually causing the failure of the circuit ▷ *vb* **short-circuit 2** to develop a short circuit **3** to bypass (a procedure): *she wrote to them direct and short-circuited the job agency* **4** to hinder or frustrate (a plan)

shortcoming *n* a fault or weakness

shortcrust pastry *n* a type of pastry with a crisp but crumbly texture

short cut *n* **1** a route that is shorter than the usual one **2** a way of saving time or effort

shorten *vb* to make or become short or shorter

shortening *n* butter or other fat, used in pastry to make it crumbly

shortfall *n* **1** failure to meet a requirement **2** the amount of such a failure; deficit

shorthand *n* a system of rapid writing using simple strokes and other symbols to represent words or phrases

short-handed *adj* (of a company or organization) lacking enough staff to do the required work

shorthand typist *n* a person skilled in the use of shorthand and in typing

shorthorn *n* a member of a breed of cattle with short horns

short list *n* **1** Also called (Scot): **short leet** a list of suitable candidates for a job or prize, from which the successful candidate will be selected ▷ *vb* **short-list 2** to put (someone) on a short list

short-lived *adj* lasting only for a short time: *his authority was short-lived*

shortly *adv* **1** in a short time; soon **2** spoken in a cross and impatient manner

shorts *pl n* **1** trousers reaching the top of the thigh or partway to the knee **2** *chiefly US & Canad* men's underpants

short shrift *n* brief and unsympathetic treatment

short-sighted *adj* **1** unable to see faraway things clearly **2** not taking likely future developments into account: *a short-sighted approach to the problem* **short-sightedness** *n*

short-tempered *adj* easily angered

short-term *adj* of, for, or lasting a short time

short-termism *n* the tendency to concentrate on short-term gains, often at the expense of long-term success

short wave *n* a radio wave with a wavelength in the range 10–100 metres

short-winded *adj* tending to run out of breath easily

shot[1] *n* **1** the act or an instance of firing a gun or rifle **2** *sport* the act or an instance of hitting, kicking, or throwing the ball **3** small round lead pellets used in shotguns **4** a person with specified skill in shooting: *my father was quite a good shot* **5** *informal* an attempt: *a second shot at writing a better treaty* **6** *informal* a guess **7 A** a single photograph **B** an uninterrupted sequence of film taken by a single camera **8** *informal* an injection of a vaccine or narcotic drug **9** *informal* a drink of spirits **10** the launching of a rocket or spacecraft to a specified destination: *a moon shot* **11** *sport* a heavy metal ball used in the shot put **12 like a shot** without hesitating **13 shot in the arm** *informal* something that brings back energy or confidence **14 shot in the dark** a wild guess [Old English *scot*]

shot[2] *vb* **1** the past of **shoot** ▷ *adj* **2** (of textiles) woven to give a changing colour effect **3** streaked with colour: *dark hair shot with streaks of grey*

shotgun *n* a gun for firing a charge of shot at short range

shot put *n* an athletic event in which contestants hurl a heavy metal ball called a shot as far as possible **shot-putter** *n*

should *vb* the past tense of **shall**: used to indicate that an action is considered by the speaker to be obligatory (*you should go*) or to form the subjunctive mood (*I should like to see you; if I should die; should I be late, start without me*) [Old English *sceolde*]

USAGE *Should* has, as its most common meaning in modern English, the sense *ought* as in *I should go to the graduation, but I don't see how I can.* However, the older sense of the subjunctive of *shall* is often used with *I* or *we* to indicate a more polite form than

S

would: I should like to go, but I can't. In much speech and writing, *should* has been replaced by *would* in contexts of this kind, but it remains in formal English when a conditional subjunctive is used: *should he choose to remain, he would be granted asylum.*

shoulder *n* **1** the part of the body where the arm, wing, or foreleg joins the trunk **2** a cut of meat including the upper part of the foreleg **3** the part of an item of clothing that covers the shoulder **4** the strip of unpaved land that borders a road **5 a shoulder to cry on** a person one turns to for sympathy with one's troubles **6 put one's shoulder to the wheel** *informal* to work very hard **7 rub shoulders with someone** *informal* to mix with someone socially **8 shoulder to shoulder** **A** side by side **B** working together ▷ *vb* **9** to accept (blame or responsibility) **10** to push with one's shoulder: *he shouldered his way through the crowd* **11** to lift or carry on one's shoulders **12 shoulder arms** *military* to bring one's rifle vertically close to one's right side [Old English *sculdor*]

shoulder blade *n* either of two large flat triangular bones, one on each side of the back part of the shoulder

shoulder strap *n* a strap worn over the shoulder to hold up an item of clothing or to support a bag

shouldn't should not

shout *n* **1** a loud call or cry **2** *informal* one's turn to buy a round of drinks ▷ *vb* **3** to cry out loudly **4** *Austral & NZ informal* to treat (someone) to (something, such as a drink) [probably from Old Norse *skūta* taunt]

shout down *vb* to silence (someone) by talking loudly

shoutout *n informal* a public greeting to a named person, esp. via radio or television

shove *vb* **shoving, shoved 1** to give a violent push to **2** to push (one's way) roughly **3** *informal* to put (something) somewhere quickly and carelessly: *shove it into the boot* ▷ *n* **4** a rough push [Old English *scūfan*]

shovel *n* **1** a tool for lifting or moving loose material, consisting of a broad blade attached to a large handle **2** a machine or part of a machine resembling a shovel in function ▷ *vb* **-velling, -velled** *or US* **-veling, -veled 3** to lift or move (loose material) with a shovel **4** to put away large quantities of (something) quickly: *shovelling food into their mouths* [Old English *scofl*]

shove off *vb informal* to go away; depart

show *vb* **showing, showed, shown** *or* **showed 1** to make, be, or become visible or noticeable: *to show an interest; excitement showed on everyone's face* **2** to present for inspection: *someone showed me the plans* **3** to demonstrate or prove: *evidence showed that this was the most economical way* **4** to instruct by demonstration: *she showed me how to feed the pullets* **5** to indicate: *the device shows changes in the pressure* **6** to behave towards (someone) in a particular way: *to show mercy* **7** to exhibit or display works of art, goods, etc.: *three artists are showing at the gallery* **8** to present (a film or play) or (of a film or play) to be presented **9** to guide or escort: *he offered to show me around* **10** *informal* to arrive ▷ *n* **11** a theatrical or other entertainment: *a magic show* **12** a display or exhibition: *a show of paintings* **13** something done to create an impression: *a show of indignation* **14** vain and conspicuous display: *it was nothing but mere show* **15** *slang, chiefly Brit* a thing or affair: *jolly good show* ▷ See also **show off, show up** [Old English *scēawian*]

show business *n* the entertainment industry. Also (informal): **show biz**

showcase *n* **1** a setting in which something is displayed to best advantage: *a showcase for young opera singers* **2** a glass case used to display objects in a museum or shop ▷ *vb* **-casing, -cased 3** to display something to its best advantage: *an exhibition showcasing new manufacturing technology*

showdown *n informal* a major confrontation that settles a dispute

shower *n* **1 A** a kind of bathing in which a person stands upright and is sprayed with water from a nozzle **B** a device, room, or booth for such bathing **2** a brief period of rain, hail, sleet, or snow **3** a sudden fall of many small light objects: *a shower of loose gravel* **4** *Brit slang* a worthless or contemptible group of people **5** *US, Canad, Austral & NZ* a party held to honour and present gifts to a prospective bride or prospective mother ▷ *vb* **6** to take a shower **7** to sprinkle with or as if with a shower: *the walkers were showered by volcanic ash* **8** to present (someone) with things liberally: *he showered her with presents* [Old English *scūr*]
showery *adj*

showing *n* **1** a presentation, exhibition, or display **2** manner of presentation

showjumping *n* the sport of riding horses in competitions to demonstrate skill in jumping
showjumper *n*

showman *n, pl* **-men 1** a person skilled at presenting anything in an effective manner **2** a person who presents or produces a show
showmanship *n*

shown *vb* a past participle of **show**

show off *vb* **1** to exhibit or display (something) so as to invite admiration: *he was eager to show off his new car* **2** *informal* to flaunt skills, knowledge, or looks in order to attract attention or impress people ▷ *n* **show-off 3** *informal* a person who flaunts his or her skills, knowledge, or looks in order to attract attention or impress people

showpiece *n* **1** anything displayed or exhibited **2** something admired as a fine example of its type: *an orchestral showpiece*

showplace *n* a place visited for its beauty or interest

showroom *n* a room in which goods for sale, esp. cars or electrical or gas appliances, are on display

show up *vb* **1** to reveal or be revealed clearly **2** to expose the faults or defects of (someone or something) by comparison **3** *informal* to put (someone) to shame; embarrass **4** *informal* to arrive

showy *adj* **showier, showiest 1** colourful, bright in appearance, and very noticeable, and perhaps rather vulgar: *showy jewellery* **2** making an imposing display **showily** *adv* **showiness** *n*

shrank *vb* a past tense of **shrink**

shrapnel *n* **1** an artillery shell containing a number of small pellets or bullets which it is

S

designed to scatter on explosion **2** fragments from this type of shell [after H. *Shrapnel*, who invented it]

shred *n* **1** a long narrow piece torn off something **2** a very small amount: *not a shred of truth* ▷ *vb* **shredding, shredded** *or* **shred 3** to tear into shreds [Old English *scrēad*] **shredder** *n*

shrew *n* **1** a small mouselike animal with a long snout **2** *derogatory* a bad-tempered nagging woman [Old English *scrēawa*] **shrewish** *adj*

shrewd *adj* intelligent and making good judgments [from *shrew* (obsolete verb) to curse, from *shrew*] **shrewdly** *adv* **shrewdness** *n*

shriek *n* **1** a high-pitched scream ▷ *vb* **2** to utter (words or sounds) in a high-pitched tone [probably from Old Norse *skrǣkja* to screech]

shrift *n* See **short shrift** [Old English *scrift* penance]

shrike *n* a bird with a heavy hooked bill, which kills small animals by dashing them on thorns [Old English *scrīc* thrush]

shrill *adj* **1** (of a sound) sharp and high-pitched ▷ *vb* **2** to utter (words or sounds) in a shrill tone [origin unknown] **shrillness** *n* **shrilly** *adv*

shrimp *n* **1** a small edible shellfish with a long tail and a pair of pincers **2** *informal* a small person ▷ *vb* **3** to fish for shrimps [probably Germanic]

shrine *n* **1** a place of worship associated with a sacred person or object **2** a container for sacred relics **3** the tomb of a saint or other holy person **4** a place that is visited and honoured because of its association with a famous person or event: *he'd come to worship at the shrine of Mozart* [Latin *scrinium* bookcase]

shrink *vb* **shrinking, shrank** *or* **shrunk, shrunk** *or* **shrunken 1** to become or cause to become smaller, sometimes because of wetness, heat, or cold **2 shrink from A** to withdraw or move away through fear: *they didn't shrink from danger* **B** to feel great reluctance (to perform a task or duty) ▷ *n* **3** *slang* a psychiatrist [Old English *scrincan*]

shrinkage *n* **1** the fact of shrinking **2** the amount by which anything decreases in size, value, or weight

shrink-wrap *vb* **-wrapping, -wrapped** to package (a product) in a flexible plastic wrapping which shrinks about its contours to seal it

shrivel *vb* **-velling, -velled** *or US* **-veling, -veled** to become dry and withered [probably Scandinavian]

shroud *n* **1** a piece of cloth used to wrap a dead body **2** anything that hides things: *a shroud of smoke* ▷ *vb* **3** to hide or obscure (something): *shrouded in uncertainty; shrouded by smog* [Old English *scrūd* garment]

Shrove Tuesday *n* the day before Ash Wednesday [Old English *scrīfan* to confess one's sins]

shrub *n* a woody plant, smaller than a tree, with several stems instead of a trunk [Old English *scrybb*] **shrubby** *adj*

shrubbery *n, pl* **-beries 1** an area planted with shrubs **2** shrubs collectively

shrug *vb* **shrugging, shrugged 1** to draw up and drop (the shoulders) as a sign of indifference or doubt ▷ *n* **2** the action of shrugging [origin unknown]

shrug off *vb* **1** to treat (a matter) as unimportant **2** to get rid of (someone)

shrunk *vb* a past tense and past participle of **shrink**

shrunken *vb* **1** a past participle of **shrink** ▷ *adj* **2** reduced in size

shudder *vb* **1** to shake or tremble suddenly and violently from horror or fear **2** (of a machine) to shake violently ▷ *n* **3** a shiver of fear or horror [Middle Low German *schōderen*]

shuffle *vb* **-fling, -fled 1** to walk or move (the feet) with a slow dragging motion **2** to mix together in a jumbled mass: *the chairman shuffled his papers* **3** to mix up (playing cards) so as to change their order ▷ *n* **4** an instance of shuffling **5** a rearrangement: *a shuffle of top management* **6** a dance with short dragging movements of the feet [probably from Low German *schüffeln*]

shufti *n slang, chiefly Brit* a look; peep [from Arabic]

shun *vb* **shunning, shunned** to avoid deliberately [Old English *scunian*]

shunt *vb* **1** to move (objects or people) to a different position **2** *railways* to transfer (engines or carriages) from track to track ▷ *n* **3** the act of shunting **4** a railway point **5** *electronics* a conductor connected in parallel across a part of a circuit to divert a known fraction of the current **6** *informal* a collision where one vehicle runs into the back of another [perhaps from Middle English *shunen* to shun]

shush *interj* **1** be quiet! hush! ▷ *vb* **2** to quiet (someone) by saying 'shush' [imitative]

shut *vb* **shutting, shut 1** to move (something) so as to cover an opening: *shut the door* **2** to close (something) by bringing together the parts: *Ridley shut the folder* **3 shut up** to close or lock the doors of: *let's shut up the shop* **4 shut in** to confine or enclose **5 shut out** to prevent from entering **6** (of a shop or other establishment) to stop operating for the day: *the late-night rush after the pubs shut* ▷ *adj* **7** closed or fastened ▷ See also **shutdown, shut off** *etc.* [Old English *scyttan*]

shutdown *n* **1** the closing of a factory, shop, or other business ▷ *vb* **shut down 2** to discontinue operations permanently

shuteye *n slang* sleep

shut off *vb* **1** to cut off the flow or supply of **2** to turn off and stop working: *I shut off the car engine* **3** to isolate or separate: *ghettoes shut off from the rest of society*

shut out *vb* **1** to keep out or exclude **2** to conceal from sight: *blinds were drawn to shut out the sun*

shutter *n* **1** a hinged doorlike cover, usually one of a pair, for closing off a window **2 put up the shutters** to close business at the end of the day or permanently **3** *photog* a device in a camera that opens to allow light through the lens so as to expose the film when a photograph is taken ▷ *vb* **4** to close or equip with a shutter or shutters

shuttle *n* **1** a bus, train, or aircraft that makes frequent journeys between two places which are fairly near to each other **2** a bobbin-like device used in weaving to pass the weft thread between the warp threads **3** a small bobbin-like device used to hold the thread in a sewing machine ▹ *vb* **-tling, -tled 4** to travel back and forth [Old English *scytel* dart, arrow]

shuttlecock *n* a rounded piece of cork or plastic with feathers stuck in one end, struck to and fro in badminton

shut up *vb* **1** *informal* to stop talking or cause (someone) to stop talking: often used in commands **2** to confine or imprison (someone)

shy[1] *adj* **1** not at ease in the company of others **2** easily frightened; timid **3 shy of** cautious or wary of **4** reluctant or unwilling: *camera-shy; workshy* ▹ *vb* **shies, shying, shied 5** to move back or aside suddenly from fear: *with a terrified whinny the horse shied* **6 shy away from** to draw back from (doing something), through lack of confidence ▹ *n, pl* **shies 7** a sudden movement back or aside from fear [Old English *scēoh*] **shyly** *adv* **shyness** *n*

shy[2] *vb* **shies, shying, shied 1** to throw (something) ▹ *n, pl* **shies 2** a quick throw [Germanic]

Shylock *n* an unsympathetic and demanding person to whom one owes money [after the heartless usurer in Shakespeare's *The Merchant of Venice*]

si *n music* same as **te**

Si *chem* silicon

SI See **SI unit**

Siamese *n, pl* **-mese 1** same as **Siamese cat** ▹ *adj, n, pl* **-mese 2** (formerly) same as **Thai**

Siamese cat *n* a breed of cat with cream fur, dark ears and face, and blue eyes

Siamese twins *pl n* a former name for **conjoined twins**

sibilant *adj* **1** having a hissing sound ▹ *n* **2** *phonetics* a consonant, such as *s* or *z*, that is pronounced with a hissing sound [Latin *sibilare* to hiss]

sibling *n* a brother or sister [Old English: a relative]

sibyl *n* (in ancient Greece and Rome) a prophetess [Greek *Sibulla*] **sibylline** *adj*

sic[1] *adv* thus: inserted in brackets in a text to indicate that an odd spelling or reading is in fact what was written, even though it is or appears to be wrong [Latin]

sic[2] *vb* **sicking, sicked 1** to attack: used only in commands to a dog **2** to urge (a dog) to attack (someone) [dialect variant of *seek*]

sick *adj* **1** vomiting or likely to vomit **2** physically or mentally unwell **3** of or for ill people: *sick pay* **4** deeply affected with mental or spiritual distress: *sick at heart* **5** mentally disturbed **6** *informal* making fun of death, illness, or misfortune: *a sick joke* **7 sick of** *or* **sick and tired of** *informal* disgusted by or weary of: *I'm sick of this town* ▹ *n, vb* **8** *informal* same as **vomit** [Old English *sēoc*]

sickbay *n* a room for the treatment of sick people, for example on a ship

sicken *vb* **1** to make (someone) feel nauseated or disgusted **2 sicken for** to show symptoms of (an illness)

sickening *adj* **1** causing horror or disgust: *sickening scenes of violence* **2** *informal* extremely annoying **sickeningly** *adv*

S

sickie *n informal* a day of sick leave from work

sickle *n* a tool for cutting grass and grain crops, with a curved blade and a short handle [Old English *sicol*]

sick leave *n* leave of absence from work through illness

sickly *adj* **-lier, -liest 1** weak and unhealthy **2** (of a person) looking pale and unwell: *sickly pallor* **3** unpleasant to smell, taste, or look at **4** showing excessive emotion in a weak and rather pathetic way: *a sickly tune* ▹ *adv* **5** suggesting sickness: *sickly pale* **sickliness** *n*

sickness *n* **1** a particular illness or disease: *sleeping sickness* **2** the state of being ill or unhealthy: *absent from work due to sickness* **3** a feeling of queasiness in the stomach followed by vomiting

side *n* **1** a line or surface that borders anything **2** *geom* a line forming part of the perimeter of a plane figure: *a square has four sides* **3** either of two parts into which an object, surface, or area can be divided: *the right side and the left side* **4** either of the two surfaces of a flat object: *write on both sides of the page* **5** the sloping part of a hill or bank **6** either the left or the right half of the body, esp. the area around the waist: *he took a nine millimetre bullet in the side* **7** the area immediately next to a person or thing: *at the side of my bed* **8** a place within an area identified by reference to a central point: *the south side of the island* **9** the area at the edge of something, as opposed to the centre: *the far side of the square* **10** aspect or part: *there is a positive side to truancy* **11** one of two or more contesting groups or teams: *the two sides will meet in the final* **12** a position held in opposition to another in a dispute **13** a line of descent through one parent: *a relative on his father's side* **14** *Brit slang* conceit or cheek: *to put on side* **15 on one side** apart from the rest **16 on the side** in addition to a person's main work: *she did a little public speaking on the side* **17 side by side** close together **18 side by side with** beside or near to **19 take sides** to support one party in a dispute against another ▹ *adj* **20** situated at the side: *the side entrance* **21** less important: *a side issue* ▹ *vb* **siding, sided 22 side with** to support (one party in a dispute) [Old English *sīde*]

sidebar *n* (in a newspaper or website) a short article placed next to the main one and containing additional material

sideboard *n* a piece of furniture for a dining room, with drawers, cupboards, and shelves to hold tableware

sideboards *or esp US & Canad* **sideburns** *pl n* a man's whiskers grown down either side of the face in front of the ears

sidecar *n* a small passenger car attached to the side of a motorcycle

side-effect *n* **1** a usually unwanted effect caused by a drug in addition to its intended one **2** any additional effect, usually an undesirable one: *the unforeseen side-effects of the end of the Cold War*

sidekick *n informal* a close friend or associate

sidelight *n* **1** *Brit* either of two small lights at the front of a motor vehicle **2** either of the two navigational lights used by ships at night

sideline *n* **1** an extra job in addition to one's main job ▷ *vb* **-lining, -lined 2** to prevent (a person) from pursuing a particular activity

sidelines *pl n* **1** *sport* **A** the lines that mark the side boundaries of a playing area **B** the area just outside the playing area, where substitute players sit **2 on the sidelines A** only passively involved: *on the sidelines of the modern world* **B** waiting to join in an activity

sidelong *adj* **1** directed to the side; oblique ▷ *adv* **2** from the side; obliquely

sidereal (side-eer-ee-al) *adj* of or determined with reference to the stars: *the sidereal time* [Latin *sidus* a star]

side-saddle *n* **1** a riding saddle originally designed for women in skirts, allowing the rider to sit with both legs on the same side of the horse ▷ *adv* **2** on a side-saddle

sideshow *n* **1** an event or incident considered less important than another: *a mere sideshow compared to the war on the Russian front* **2** a small show or entertainment offered along with the main show at a circus or fair

side-splitting *adj* causing a great deal of laughter

sidestep *vb* **-stepping, -stepped 1** to step out of the way of (something) **2** to dodge (an issue) ▷ *n* **side step 3** a movement to one side, such as in dancing or boxing

sideswipe *n* **1** an unexpected criticism of someone or something while discussing another subject **2** a glancing blow along or from the side ▷ *vb* **-swiping, -swiped 3** to make a sideswipe

sidetrack *vb* to distract (someone) from a main subject

sidewalk *n US & Canad* a raised space alongside a road, for pedestrians

sideways *adv* **1** moving, facing, or inclining towards one side **2** from one side; obliquely **3** with one side forward ▷ *adj* **4** moving or directed to or from one side

side whiskers *pl n* same as **sideboards**

siding *n* a short stretch of railway track connected to a main line, used for loading and unloading freight and storing engines and carriages

sidle *vb* **-dling, -dled** to walk slowly and carefully, not wanting to be noticed [obsolete *sideling* sideways]

SIDS sudden infant death syndrome; cot death

siege *n* **1** a military operation carried out to capture a place by surrounding and blockading it **2** a similar operation carried out by police, for example to force people out of a place **3 lay siege to** to subject (a place) to a siege [Old French *sege* a seat]

siemens *n, pl* **siemens** the SI unit of electrical conductance [after E. W. von *Siemens*, engineer]

sienna *n* **1** a natural earth used as a reddish-brown or yellowish-brown pigment ▷ *adj* **2 burnt sienna** reddish-brown **3 raw sienna** yellowish-brown [after *Siena*, Italian city]

sierra *n* a range of mountains with jagged peaks in Spain or America [Spanish, literally: saw]

sies (siss) *interj S African informal* same as **sis²**

siesta *n* an afternoon nap, taken in hot countries [Spanish]

sieve (siv) *n* **1** a utensil with a mesh through which a substance is sifted or strained ▷ *vb* **sieving, sieved 2** to sift or strain through a sieve [Old English *sife*]

sift *vb* **1** to sieve (a powdery substance) in order to remove the coarser particles **2** to examine (information or evidence) carefully to select what is important [Old English *siftan*]

sigh *vb* **1** to draw in and audibly let out a deep breath as an expression of sadness, tiredness, longing, or relief **2** to make a sound resembling this **3 sigh for** to long for **4** to say (something) with a sigh ▷ *n* **5** the act or sound of sighing [Old English *sīcan*]

sight *n* **1** the ability to see; vision. Related adjective: **visual 2** an instance of seeing **3** the range of vision: *the cemetery was out of sight* **4** anything that is seen **5** point of view; judgment: *nothing has changed in my sight* **6** *informal* anything unpleasant to see: *she looked a sight in the streetlamps* **7** a device for guiding the eye in aiming a gun or making an observation with an optical instrument **8** an aim or observation made with such a device **9 sights** anything worth seeing: *the great sights of Barcelona* **10 a sight** *informal* a great deal: *it's a sight warmer than in the hall* **11 a sight for sore eyes** a welcome sight **12 catch sight of** to glimpse **13 know someone by sight** to be able to recognize someone without having ever been introduced **14 lose sight of A** to be unable to see (something) any longer **B** to forget: *we lose sight of priorities* **15 on sight** as soon as someone or something is seen **16 set one's sights on** to have (a specified goal) in mind **17 sight unseen** without having seen the object concerned: *he would have taken it sight unseen* ▷ *vb* **18** to see (someone or something) briefly or suddenly: *the two suspicious vessels were sighted* **19** to aim (a firearm) using the sight [Old English *sihth*]

sighted *adj* not blind

sightless *adj* blind

sight-read *vb* **-reading, -read** to sing or play (music in a printed form) without previous preparation **sight-reading** *n*

sightscreen *n cricket* a large white screen placed near the boundary behind the bowler, which helps the batsman see the ball

sightseeing *n informal* visiting famous or interesting sights in a place **sightseer** *n*

sigma *n* **1** the 18th letter in the Greek alphabet (Σ, σ) **2** *maths* the symbol Σ, indicating summation

sign *n* **1** something that indicates a fact or condition that is not immediately or outwardly observable: *a sign of tension* **2** a gesture, mark, or symbol intended to convey an idea or information **3** a board or placard displayed in public and intended to advertise, inform, or warn **4** a conventional mark or symbol that has a specific meaning, for example £ for pounds **5** *maths* **A** any symbol used to indicate an operation: *a minus sign* **B** a symbol used to indicate whether a number or expression is positive or negative **6** a visible indication: *no sign of the enemy* **7** an omen **8** *med* any evidence of the presence of

S

a disease or disorder **9** *astrol* short for **sign of the zodiac** ▷ *vb* **10** to write (one's name) on (a document or letter) to show its authenticity or one's agreement **11** to communicate using sign language **12** to make a sign to someone so as to convey an idea or information **13** to engage or be engaged by signing a contract: *he signed for another team* ▷ See also **sign away, sign in** *etc.* [Latin *signum*]

signal *n* **1** any sign, gesture, sound, or action used to communicate information **2** anything that causes immediate action: *this is the signal for a detailed examination of the risk* **3 A** a variable voltage, current, or electromagnetic wave, by which information is conveyed through an electronic circuit **B** the information so conveyed ▷ *adj* **4** *formal* very important: *a signal triumph for the government* ▷ *vb* **-nalling, -nalled** or *US* **-naling, -naled 5** to communicate (information) by signal [Latin *signum* sign] **signally** *adv*

signal box *n* a building from which railway signals are operated

signalman *n, pl* **-men** a railwayman in charge of the signals and points within a section

signatory (sig-na-tree) *n, pl* **-ries 1** a person, organization, or state that has signed a document such as a treaty ▷ *adj* **2** having signed a document or treaty

signature *n* **1** a person's name written by himself or herself, used in signing something **2** a distinctive characteristic that identifies a person or animal **3** *music* a sign at the beginning of a piece to show key or time **4** *printing* a sheet of paper printed with several pages, which when folded becomes a section of a book [Latin *signare* to sign]

signature tune *n* a piece of music used to introduce a particular television or radio programme

sign away *vb* to give up one's right to (something): *she will sign away all rights to these pictures*

signboard *n* a board carrying a sign or notice, often to advertise a business or product

signet *n* a small seal used to make documents official [Medieval Latin *signetum*]

signet ring *n* a finger ring engraved with an initial or other emblem

significance *n* **1** the effect something is likely to have on other things: *an event of important significance in British history* **2** meaning: *the occult significance of the symbol*

significant *adj* **1** very important **2** having or expressing a meaning **significantly** *adv*

significant figures *pl n maths* **1** the figures of a number that express a magnitude to a specified degree of accuracy: *3.141 59 to four significant figures is 3.142* **2** the number of such figures: *3.142 has four significant figures*

signify *vb* **-fies, -fying, -fied 1** to indicate or suggest **2** to stand as a symbol or sign for: *a blue line on the map signified a river* **3** to be important [Latin *signum* a mark + *facere* to make]

sign in *vb* **1** to sign a register on arrival at a place **2** to admit (a nonmember) to a club or institution as a guest by signing a register on his or her behalf

signing *n* a system of communication using hand and arm movements, such as one used by deaf people. Also called: **sign language**

sign off *vb* to announce the end of a radio or television programme

sign of the zodiac *n astrol* any of the 12 areas into which the zodiac is divided

sign on *vb* **1** *Brit & Austral* to register and report regularly at an unemployment-benefit office **2** to commit oneself to a job or activity by signing a form or contract

signor (see-**nyor**) *n* an Italian form of address equivalent to *sir* or *Mr*

signora (see-**nyor**-a) *n* an Italian form of address equivalent to *madam* or *Mrs*

signorina (see-nyor-**ee**-na) *n* an Italian form of address equivalent to *madam* or *Miss*

sign out *vb* to sign a register to indicate that one is leaving a place

signpost *n* **1** a road sign displaying information, such as the distance to the next town **2** an indication as to how an event is likely to develop or advice on what course of action should be taken ▷ *vb* **3** to mark (the way) with signposts

sign up *vb* **1** to agree to do a job or course by signing a document **2 sign someone up** to hire someone officially to do a job **3** to enlist for military service

sik *adj Austral slang* excellent

Sikh (**seek**) *n* **1** a member of an Indian religion that teaches that there is only one God ▷ *adj* **2** of the Sikhs or their religious beliefs or customs [Hindi: disciple] **Sikhism** *n*

silage (**sile**-ij) *n* a fodder crop harvested while green and partially fermented in a silo

silence *n* **1** the state or quality of being silent **2** the absence of sound **3** refusal or failure to speak or communicate when expected: *he's broken his silence on the issue* ▷ *vb* **-lencing, -lenced 4** to cause (someone or something) to become silent **5** to put a stop to: *a way of silencing criticism*

silencer *n* any device designed to reduce noise, for example one fitted to the exhaust system of a motor vehicle or one fitted to the muzzle of a gun

silent *adj* **1** tending to speak very little **2** failing to speak or communicate when expected: *they remained silent as minutes passed* **3** producing no noise: *the silent room* **4** not spoken: *silent reproach* **5** (of a letter) used in the spelling of a word but not pronounced, such as the *k* in *know* **6** (of a film) having no soundtrack [Latin *silere* to be quiet] **silently** *adv*

silhouette *n* **1** the outline of a dark shape seen against a light background **2** an outline drawing, often a profile portrait, filled in with black ▷ *vb* **-etting, -etted 3** to show (something) in silhouette [after E. de *Silhouette*, politician]

silica *n* a hard glossy mineral, silicon dioxide, which occurs naturally as quartz and is used in the manufacture of glass [Latin *silex* hard stone]

silicate *n mineralogy* a compound of silicon, oxygen, and a metal

silicon *n* **1** *chem* a brittle non-metallic element: used in transistors, solar cells, and alloys. Symbol: **Si** ▷ *adj* **2** denoting an area of a country

that contains much high-technology industry: *the Silicon Glen* [from *silica*]
silicon chip *n* same as **chip** (sense 3)
silicone *n chem* a tough synthetic material made from silicon and used in lubricants, paints, and resins
silicosis *n pathol* a lung disease caused by breathing in silica dust
silk *n* **1** the fine soft fibre produced by a silkworm **2** thread or fabric made from this fibre **3** **silks** clothing made of this **4** *Brit* **A** the gown worn by a Queen's (or King's) Counsel **B** *informal* a Queen's (or King's) Counsel **C** **take silk** to become a Queen's (or King's) Counsel [Old English *sioloc*]
silken *adj* **1** made of silk **2** *literary* smooth and soft: *her silken hair*
silk-screen printing *n* same as **screen process**
silkworm *n* a caterpillar that spins a cocoon of silk
silky *adj* **silkier, silkiest** **1** soft, smooth, and shiny **2** (of a voice or manner) smooth and elegant **silkiness** *n*
sill *n* **1** a shelf at the bottom of a window, either inside or outside a room **2** the lower horizontal part of a window or door frame [Old English *syll*]
silly *adj* **-lier, -liest** **1** behaving in a foolish or childish way **2** *old-fashioned* unable to think sensibly, as if from a blow **3** *cricket* (of a fielding position) near the batsman's wicket: *silly mid-off* ▷ *n, pl* **-lies** **4** *informal* a foolish person [Old English *sǣlig* (unattested) happy] **silliness** *n*
silo *n, pl* **-los** **1** an airtight pit or tower in which silage or grain is made and stored **2** an underground structure in which missile systems are sited for protection [Spanish]
silt *n* **1** a fine sediment of mud or clay deposited by moving water ▷ *vb* **2** **silt up** to fill or choke up with silt: *the channels have been silted up* [probably Old Norse]
Silurian (sile-yoor-ee-an) *adj geol* of the period of geological time about 425 million years ago, during which fishes first appeared [after *Silures*, a Welsh tribe who opposed the Romans]
silvan *adj* same as **sylvan**
silver *n* **1** a precious greyish-white metallic element: used in jewellery, tableware, and coins. Symbol: **Ag** **2** a coin or coins made of silver **3** any household articles made of silver **4** short for **silver medal** ▷ *adj* **5** greyish-white: *silver hair* **6** (of anniversaries) the 25th in a series: *Silver Jubilee*; *silver wedding* ▷ *vb* **7** to coat with silver or a silvery substance: *a company that silvers their own mirrors* **8** to cause (something) to become silvery in colour: *the sun silvered the tarmac* [Old English *siolfor*]
silverbeet *n Austral & NZ* a beet of Australia and New Zealand with edible spinach-like leaves
silver birch *n* a tree with silvery-white peeling bark
silverfish *n, pl* **-fish** *or* **-fishes** **1** a small wingless silver-coloured insect **2** a silver-coloured fish
silver lining *n* a hopeful side of an otherwise desperate or unhappy situation
silver medal *n* a medal of silver awarded to a competitor who comes second in a contest or race
silver plate *n* **1** a thin layer of silver deposited on a base metal **2** articles, such as tableware, made of silver plate **silver-plate** *vb*
silver screen *n informal* films collectively or the film industry
silverside *n* a cut of beef from below the rump and above the leg
silversmith *n* a craftsman who makes or repairs items made of silver
silver thaw *n Canad* **1** a freezing rainstorm **2** same as **glitter** (sense 7)
silverware *n* items, such as tableware, made of or plated with silver
silvery *adj* **1** having the appearance or colour of silver: *her silvery eyes* **2** having a clear ringing sound: *a cascade of silvery notes*
silviculture *n* the cultivation of forest trees [Latin *silva* woodland + CULTURE]
SIM card *n* a small card used in a mobile phone to store data about the network, telephone number, etc. [*S(ubscriber) I(dentity) M(odule) card*]
simian *adj* **1** of or resembling a monkey or ape ▷ *n* **2** a monkey or ape [Latin *simia* an ape]
similar *adj* **1** alike but not identical **2** *geom* (of two or more figures) different in size or position, but with exactly the same shape [Latin *similis*] **similarity** *n* **similarly** *adv*

> **USAGE** *As* should not be used after *similar*: *Wilson held a similar position to Jones* (not *a similar position as Jones*); *the system is similar to the one in France* (not *similar as in France*).

simile (sim-ill-ee) *n* a figure of speech that likens one thing to another of a different category, introduced by *as* or *like* [Latin: something similar]
similitude *n formal* likeness; similarity
simmer *vb* **1** to cook (food) gently at just below boiling point **2** (of violence or conflict) to threaten to break out: *revolt simmering among rural MPs* ▷ *n* **3** the state of simmering [perhaps imitative]
simmer down *vb informal* to calm down after being angry
simnel cake *n Brit* a fruit cake with marzipan, traditionally eaten during Lent or at Easter [Latin *simila* fine flour]
simony (sime-on-ee) *n Christianity* the practice of buying or selling Church benefits such as pardons [after *Simon Magus*, a biblical sorcerer who tried to buy magical powers]
simoom *n* a hot suffocating sand-laden desert wind [Arabic *samūm* poisonous]
simper *vb* **1** to smile in a silly and mannered way **2** to say (something) with a simper ▷ *n* **3** a simpering smile [origin unknown] **simpering** *adj*
simple *adj* **1** easy to understand or do: *in simple English*; *simple exercises* **2** plain and not elaborate: *a simple red skirt*; *a simple answer* **3** not combined or complex: *simple diagnostic equipment* **4** leading an uncomplicated life: *I am a simple man myself* **5** sincere or frank: *a simple apology* **6** of humble background: *the simple country girl* **7** *informal* lacking in intelligence **8** straightforward: *a simple matter of choice* **9** *music* denoting a time where the number of beats per bar may be two, three, or four [Latin *simplex* plain] **simplicity** *n*
simple fraction *n maths* a fraction in which the numerator and denominator are both whole numbers

S

simple fracture *n* a fracture in which the broken bone does not pierce the skin
simple interest *n finance* interest paid only on the original amount of a debt
simple-minded *adj* **1** (of people) naive and unsophisticated **2** (of opinions or explanations) not taking the complexity of an issue or subject into account **simple-mindedness** *n*
simple sentence *n* a sentence consisting of a single main clause
simpleton *n* a foolish or stupid person
simplify *vb* **-fies, -fying, -fied 1** to make (something) less complicated **2** *maths* to reduce (an equation or fraction) to its simplest form [Latin *simplus* simple + *facere* to make] **simplification** *n*
simplistic *adj* (of an opinion or interpretation) too simple or naive
USAGE Since *simplistic* already has *too* as part of its meaning, it is tautologous to talk about something being *too simplistic* or *over-simplistic*.
simply *adv* **1** in a simple manner: *an interesting book, simply written* **2** merely; just: *he's simply too slow* **3** absolutely: *a simply enormous success*
simulate *vb* **-lating, -lated 1** to pretend to feel or perform (an emotion or action); imitate: *I tried to simulate anger* **2** to imitate the conditions of (a situation), as in carrying out an experiment: *we can then simulate global warming* **3** to have the appearance of: *the wood had been painted to simulate stone* [Latin *simulare* to copy] **simulated** *adj* **simulation** *n*
simulator *n* a device that simulates specific conditions for the purposes of research or training: *a flight simulator*
simultaneous *adj* occurring or existing at the same time [Latin *simul* at the same time] **simultaneously** *adv* **simultaneity** *n*
simultaneous equations *pl n maths* a set of equations that are all satisfied by the same values of the variables, the number of variables being equal to the number of equations
sin¹ *n* **1** the breaking of a religious or moral law **2** any offence against a principle or standard **3 live in sin** *old-fashioned, informal* (of an unmarried couple) to live together ▷ *vb* **sinning, sinned 4** to commit a sin [Old English *synn*] **sinner** *n*
sin² *maths* sine
SIN (in Canada) Social Insurance Number
sin bin *n slang* (in ice hockey, etc.) the area in which players must sit for a specified period after committing a serious foul
since *prep* **1** during the period of time after: *one of their worst winters since 1945* ▷ *conj* **2** continuously from the time given: *they've been standing in line ever since she arrived* **3** for the reason that; because ▷ *adv* **4** from that time: *I have often been asked since* [Old English *siththan*]
USAGE See at **ago**.
sincere *adj* genuine and honest: *sincere concern* [Latin *sincerus*] **sincerely** *adv* **sincerity** *n*
sine *n* (in trigonometry) the ratio of the length of the opposite side to that of the hypotenuse in a right-angled triangle [Latin *sinus* a bend]
sinecure (sin-ee-cure) *n* a paid job that involves very little work or responsibility [Latin *sine* without + *cura* care]
sine die (sin-ay dee-ay) *adv* without fixing a day for future action or meeting [Latin, literally: without a day]
sine qua non (sin-ay kwah non) *n* an essential requirement [Latin, literally: without which not]
sinew *n* **1** *anatomy* a tough fibrous cord connecting muscle to bone **2** *literary* physical strength [Old English *sinu, seonu*]
sinewy *adj* lean and muscular
sinful *adj* **1** having committed or tending to commit sin: *I am a sinful man* **2** being a sin; wicked: *sinful acts*
sing *vb* **singing, sang, sung 1** to produce musical sounds with the voice **2** to perform (a song) **3** (of certain birds and insects) to make musical calls **4 sing of** to tell a story in song about: *the minstrels sang of courtly love* **5** to make a humming, ringing, or whistling sound: *the arrow sang past his ear* **6** (of one's ears) to be filled with a continuous ringing sound **7** to bring (someone) to a given state by singing: *I sang him to sleep* **8** *slang, chiefly US* to act as an informer ▷ See also **sing out** [Old English *singan*] **singer** *n* **singing** *adj, n*
USAGE See at **ring¹**.
sing. singular
singe *vb* **singeing, singed 1** to burn slightly without setting alight; scorch: *it singed his sheepskin* ▷ *n* **2** a slight burn [Old English *sengan*]
Singhalese *n, pl* **-lese**, *adj* same as **Sinhalese**
singing telegram *n* **1** a service by which a person is employed to present greetings to someone on a special occasion by singing **2** the greetings presented in this way **3** the person who presents the greetings
single *adj* **1** existing alone; solitary: *the cottage's single chimney* **2** distinct from others of the same kind: *every single housing society* **3** designed for one user: *a single room* **4** unmarried **5** even one: *there was not a single bathroom* **6** (of a flower) having only one circle of petals **7 single combat** a duel or fight involving two individuals ▷ *n* **8** a hotel bedroom for one person **9** a song or recording that is marketed in its own right rather than as part of an album **10** *cricket* a hit from which one run is scored **11** *US & Canad* a dollar bill **12** a ticket valid for a one-way journey only ▷ *vb* **-gling, -gled 13 single out** to select from a group of people or things: *the judge had singled him out for praise* ▷ See also **singles** [Old French *sengle*]
single-breasted *adj* (of a jacket or coat) having the fronts overlapping only slightly and with one row of buttons
single cream *n Brit* cream which has a relatively low fat content and does not thicken when beaten
single-decker *n Brit informal* a bus with only one passenger deck
single entry *n* a book-keeping system in which all transactions are entered in one account only
single file *n* a line of people, one behind the other
single-handed *adj* **1** alone; unaided: *a single-handed raid on the enemy camp* ▷ *adv* **2** unaided

S

or working alone: *she had to take on the world single-handed* **single-handedly** *adv*
single-minded *adj* having one purpose or aim only; dedicated **single-mindedly** *adv* **single-mindedness** *n*
single-parent family *n* a family consisting of one parent and his or her child or children living together, the other parent being dead or permanently absent
singles *pl n sport* a match played with one person on each side
singles bar *n* a bar that is a social meeting place for single people
singlet *n Brit & NZ* a man's sleeveless vest
single ticket *n* same as **single** (sense 12)
singleton *n* **1** a person who is not part of a couple **2** *cards* the only card of a particular suit held by a player
singly *adv* one at a time; one by one
sing out *vb* to call out loudly
sing-song *n* **1** an informal group singing session ▷ *adj* **2** (of a voice) having a repetitive rise and fall in tone
singular *adj* **1** *grammar* (of a word or form) denoting only one person or thing: *a singular noun* **2** remarkable; extraordinary: *one of the singular achievements* **3** unusual; odd: *a lovable but very singular old woman* ▷ *n* **4** *grammar* the singular form of a word [Latin *singularis* single] **singularity** *n* **singularly** *adv*
Sinhalese *or* **Singhalese** *n* **1** *pl* **-lese** a member of a people living mainly in Sri Lanka **2** the language of this people ▷ *adj* **3** of this people ▷ See also **Sri Lankan**
sinister *adj* **1** threatening or suggesting evil or harm: *a sinister conspiracy* **2** *heraldry* of, on, or starting from the bearer's left side [Latin: on the left-hand side, considered by Roman augurs to be the unlucky one]
sink *vb* **sinking, sank, sunk** **1** to submerge (in liquid) **2** to cause (a ship) to submerge by attacking it with bombs, torpedoes, etc. **3** to appear to descend towards or below the horizon **4** to make or become lower in amount or value: *the US dollar sank to a low against the euro* **5** to move or fall into a lower position, esp. due to tiredness or weakness: *she sank back in her chair* **6** **sink into** to pass into a lower state or condition, esp. an unpleasant one: *to sink into debt* **7** (of a voice) to become quieter **8** to become weaker in health **9** to dig (something sharp) into a solid object: *she sank her teeth into the steak* **10** *informal* to drink (a number of alcoholic drinks) **11** to dig, drill, or excavate (a hole or shaft) **12** to drive (a stake) into the ground **13** **sink in** *or* **into** to invest (money) in (a venture) **14** *golf & snooker* to hit (the ball) into the hole or pocket: *she sank the putt* ▷ *n* **15** a fixed basin in a kitchen or bathroom, with a water supply and drainpipe ▷ *adj* **16** *informal* (of a housing estate or school) deprived or having low standards of achievement [Old English *sincan*]
sinker *n* a weight attached to a fishing line or net to cause it to sink in water
sink in *vb* (of a fact) to become fully understood: *the euphoria started to wear off as the implications of it all sank in*
sinking fund *n* a fund set aside to repay a long-term debt
Sinn Féin (shin **fane**) *n* an Irish Republican political movement active in Northern Ireland and the Republic of Ireland [Irish Gaelic: we ourselves]
Sino- *combining form* Chinese: *Sino-European*; *Sinology* [Late Latin *Sinae* the Chinese]
Sinology (sine-**ol**-a-jee) *n* the study of Chinese history, language, and culture **Sinologist** *n*
sinuous *adj literary* **1** full of curves **2** having smooth twisting movements: *sinuous dances* [Latin *sinuosus* winding] **sinuosity** *n*
sinus (**sine**-uss) *n anatomy* a hollow space in bone, such as one in the skull opening into a nasal cavity [Latin: a curve]
sinusitis *n* inflammation of the membrane lining a sinus, esp. a nasal sinus
Sioux (soo) *n* **1** *pl* **Sioux** a member of a group of Native American peoples, formerly living over a wide area from Lake Michigan to the Rocky Mountains **2** any of the languages of these peoples
sip *vb* **sipping, sipped** **1** to drink (a liquid) in small mouthfuls ▷ *n* **2** an amount sipped **3** an instance of sipping [probably from Low German *sippen*]
siphon *or* **syphon** *n* **1** a tube which uses air pressure to draw liquid from a container **2** same as **soda siphon** ▷ *vb* **3** **siphon off** **A** to draw (liquid) off through a siphon **B** to redirect (resources or money), esp. dishonestly, into other projects or bank accounts [Greek]
sir *n* a polite term of address for a man [variant of SIRE]
Sir *n* a title placed before the name of a knight or baronet: *Sir David Attenborough*
sire *n* **1** a male parent of a horse or other domestic animal **2** *archaic* a respectful form of address used to a king ▷ *vb* **siring, sired** **3** to father [Old French]
siren *n* **1** a device that gives out a loud wailing sound as a warning or signal **2** **Siren** *Greek myth* a sea nymph whose singing lured sailors to destruction on the rocks **3** a woman considered attractive but dangerous to men [Greek *seirēn*]
sirloin *n* a prime cut of beef from the upper part of the loin [Old French *surlonge*]
sirocco *n, pl* **-cos** a hot stifling wind blowing from N Africa into S Europe [Italian]
sis[1] *n informal* short for **sister**
sis[2] *or* **sies** (siss) *interj S African informal* an exclamation of disgust [Afrikaans]
sisal (**size**-al) *n* a stiff fibre obtained from a Mexican plant and used for making rope [after *Sisal*, a port in Mexico]
siskin *n* a yellow-and-black finch [Middle Dutch *sīseken*]
sissy *or* **cissy** *n, pl* **-sies** *derogatory* **1** an effeminate or cowardly person ▷ *adj* **2** effeminate or cowardly [from SIS[1]]
sister *n* **1** a woman or girl having the same parents as another person **2** a female fellow member of a group, race, or profession **3** a female nurse in charge of a ward **4** *chiefly RC Church* a nun ▷ *adj* **5** of the same class, origin, or design, as another: *its sister paper* [Old English *sweostor*]

S

sisterhood *n* **1** the state of being sisters or like sisters **2** a religious group of women **3** a group of women united by a common interest or belief

sister-in-law *n, pl* **sisters-in-law 1** the sister of one's husband or wife **2** the wife of one's sibling

sisterly *adj* of or like a sister; affectionate

Siswati *n* a language of Swaziland

sit *vb* **sitting, sat 1** to rest one's body upright on the buttocks: *she had to sit on the ground* **2** to cause (someone) to rest in such a position: *they sat their grandfather in the shade* **3** (of an animal) to rest with the rear part of its body lowered to the ground **4** (of a bird) to perch or roost **5 sit on** (of a bird) to cover its eggs so as to hatch them **6** to be located: *the bank sits in the middle of the village* **7** to pose for a painting or photograph **8** to occupy a seat in some official capacity: *no police representatives will sit on the committee* **9** (of a parliament or court) to be in session **10** to remain unused: *his car sat in the garage* **11** (of clothes) to fit or hang in a certain way: *that dress sits well on you* **12** to take (an examination): *he's sitting his finals* **13** (*in combination*) to look after a specified person or thing for someone else: *is someone going to dog-sit for you?* **14 sit for** *chiefly Brit* to be a candidate for (a qualification): *he sat for a degree in medicine* **15 sit tight** *informal* **A** to wait patiently **B** to maintain one's position firmly ▷ See also **sit back, sit down** *etc.* [Old English *sittan*]

sitar *n* an Indian stringed musical instrument with a long neck and a rounded body [Hindi]

sit back *vb* to relax or be passive when action should be taken: *we can't just sit back and let this dreadful situation continue*

sitcom *n informal* (on television or radio) a comedy series involving the same characters in various everyday situations: *yet another unfunny sitcom set in Liverpool*

sit down *vb* **1** to adopt or cause (someone) to adopt a sitting position **2 sit down under** to suffer (insults or humiliations) without resistance ▷ *n* **sit-down 3** a short rest sitting down ▷ *adj* **sit-down 4** (of a meal) eaten while sitting down at a table

S

sit-down strike *n* a strike in which workers refuse to leave their place of employment until a settlement is reached

site *n* **1** the piece of ground where something was, is, or is intended to be located: *a building site*; *a car park is to be built on the site of a Roman fort* **2** same as **website** ▷ *vb* **siting, sited 3** to locate (something) on a specific site [Latin *situs* position]

sit-in *n* **1** a protest in which the demonstrators sit in a public place and refuse to move ▷ *vb* **sit in 2 sit in for** to stand in as a substitute for (someone) **3 sit in on** to be present at (a meeting) as an observer

sitka spruce *n* a tall North American spruce tree, now often grown in Britain [after *Sitka*, a town in Alaska]

sit on *vb informal* to delay action on: *they are sitting on their information*

sit out *vb* **1** to endure to the end: *just sit it out, and it will pass eventually* **2** to take no part in (a dance or game)

sitter *n* **1** a person posing for his or her portrait or photograph **2** same as **baby-sitter 3** (*in combination*) a person who looks after a specified person or thing for someone else: *a house-sitter*

sitting *n* **1** a continuous period of being seated at some activity: *you may not be able to complete it in one sitting* **2** one of the times when a meal is served, when there is not enough space for everyone to eat at the same time: *the second sitting* **3** a period of posing for a painting or photograph **4** a meeting of an official body to conduct business ▷ *adj* **5** current: *a sitting member of Congress* **6** seated: *a sitting position*

sitting duck *n informal* a person or thing in a defenceless or vulnerable position

sitting room *n* a room in a house or flat where people sit and relax

sitting tenant *n* a tenant occupying a house or flat

situate *vb* **-ating, -ated** *formal* to place [Late Latin *situare* to position]

situation *n* **1 A** state of affairs **B** a complex or critical state of affairs **2** location and surroundings **3** social or financial circumstances **4** a position of employment

> **USAGE** *Situation* is often used in contexts in which it is redundant or imprecise. Typical examples are: *the company is in a crisis situation* or *people in a job situation*. In the first example, *situation* does not add to the meaning and should be omitted. In the second example, it would be clearer and more concise to substitute a phrase such as *people at work*.

situation comedy *n* same as **sitcom**

sit up *vb* **1** to raise oneself from a lying position into a sitting one **2** to remain out of bed until a late hour **3** *informal* to become suddenly interested: *make the world sit up and take notice* ▷ *n* **sit-up 4** a physical exercise in which the body is brought into a sitting position from one of lying on the back

SI unit *n* any of the units (metre, kilogram, second, ampere, kelvin, candela, mole, and those derived from them) adopted for international use under the Système International d'Unités, now employed for all scientific and most technical purposes

Siva *n* a Hindu god, the Destroyer

six *n* **1** the cardinal number that is the sum of one and five **2** a numeral, 6 or VI, representing this number **3** something representing or consisting of six units **4** *cricket* a score of six runs, obtained by hitting the ball so that it crosses the boundary without bouncing **5 at sixes and sevens** in a state of confusion **6 knock someone for six** *informal* to upset or overwhelm someone completely **7 six of one and half a dozen of the other** a situation in which there is no real difference between the alternatives ▷ *adj* **8** amounting to six: *six days* [Old English *siex*] **sixth** *adj, n*

sixfold *adj* **1** having six times as many or as much **2** composed of six parts ▷ *adv* **3** by six times as many or as much

Six Nations Championship *n rugby union* an annual competition involving national sides representing England, France, Ireland, Italy, Scotland, and Wales

six-pack *n informal* **1** a package containing six units, esp. six cans of beer **2** a highly developed set of abdominal muscles in a man

sixpence *n* (formerly) a small British, Australian, and New Zealand coin worth six old pennies, or $2^1/_2$ pence

six-pointer *n informal* a football match between two teams in similar positions in the league table, which gains the winning team three points and denies the losing team three points

six-shooter *n US informal* a revolver that fires six shots without reloading

sixteen *n* **1** the cardinal number that is the sum of ten and six **2** a numeral, 16 or XVI, representing this number **3** something representing or consisting of sixteen units ▹ *adj* **4** amounting to sixteen: *sixteen years* **sixteenth** *adj, n*

sixth form *n* (in England and Wales) the most senior form in a secondary school, in which pupils over sixteen may take A levels or retake GCSEs **sixth-former** *n*

sixth sense *n* the supposed ability of knowing something instinctively without having any evidence for it

sixty *n, pl* **-ties 1** the cardinal number that is the product of ten and six **2** a numeral, 60 or LX, representing this number **3** something representing or consisting of sixty units ▹ *adj* **4** amounting to sixty: *sixty seconds* **sixtieth** *adj, n*

sizable *or* **sizeable** *adj* quite large

size¹ *n* **1** the dimensions, amount, or extent of something **2** large dimensions, amount, or extent: *I was overwhelmed by the sheer size of the city* **3** one of a series of standard measurements for goods: *he takes size 11 shoes* **4** *informal* state of affairs as summarized: *that's about the size of it* ▹ *vb* **sizing, sized 5** to sort (things) according to size [Old French *sise*]

> **USAGE** The use of *-size* and *-sized* after *large* or *small* is redundant, except when describing something which is made in specific sizes: *a large* (not *large-size*) *organization*. Similarly, *in size* is redundant in the expressions *large in size* and *small in size*.

size² *n* **1** a thin gluey substance that is used as a sealer ▹ *vb* **sizing, sized 2** to treat (a surface) with size [origin unknown]

sized *adj* of a specified size: *average-sized*

> **USAGE** See at **size¹**.

size up *vb informal* to make an assessment of (a person or situation)

sizzle *vb* **-zling, -zled 1** to make a hissing sound like the sound of frying fat **2** *informal* to be very hot: *the city was sizzling in a hot summer spell* **3** *informal* to be very angry ▹ *n* **4** a hissing sound [imitative] **sizzling** *adj*

sjambok (sham-bock) *S African* ▹ *n* **1** a whip or riding crop made of hide ▹ *vb* **-bokking, -bokked 2** to beat with a sjambok [Malay *tjambok*]

SK Saskatchewan

skanky *adj* **skankier, skankiest** *slang* **1** dirty or unattractive **2** promiscuous

skate¹ *n* **1** same as **ice skate** or **roller skate 2 get one's skates on** *informal* to hurry ▹ *vb* **skating, skated 3** to glide on or as if on skates **4 skate on thin ice** to place oneself in a dangerous situation [Old French *éschasse* stilt] **skater** *n* **skating** *n*

skate² *n, pl* **skate** *or* **skates** a large edible marine fish with a broad flat body [Old Norse *skata*]

skateboard *n* **1** a narrow board mounted on roller-skate wheels, usually ridden while standing up ▹ *vb* **2** to ride on a skateboard **skateboarding** *n*

skatepark *n* a building or enclosure for skateboarding

skate round *or* **skate over** *vb* to avoid discussing or dealing with (a matter) fully: *friends and admirers skated round the question*

skean-dhu (skee-an-doo) *n* a dagger worn in the sock as part of Highland dress [Gaelic *sgian* knife + *dhu* black]

skedaddle *vb* **-dling, -dled** *informal* to run off hastily [origin unknown]

skein *n* **1** a length of yarn or thread wound in a loose coil **2** a flock of geese in flight [Old French *escaigne*]

skeleton *n* **1** the hard framework of bones that supports and protects the organs and muscles of the body **2** the essential framework of any structure: *a metal skeleton supporting the roof and floors* **3** *informal* an extremely thin person or animal **4** an outline consisting of bare essentials: *the mere skeleton of a script* **5** a small steel-frame sledge for racing down an ice-covered run **6** the sport of racing small steel-frame sledges down an ice-covered run **7 skeleton in the cupboard** *or* **closet** an embarrassing or scandalous fact from the past that is kept secret ▹ *adj* **8** reduced to a minimum: *a skeleton staff* [Greek: something dried up] **skeletal** *adj*

skeleton key *n* a key designed so that it can open many different locks

skelm *n S African informal* a villain or crook [Afrikaans]

skeptic *n US or archaic* same as **sceptic**

skerry *n, pl* **-ries** *Scot* a rocky island or reef [Old Norse *sker*]

sketch *n* **1** a quick rough drawing **2** a brief descriptive piece of writing **3** a short funny piece of acting forming part of a show **4** any brief outline ▹ *vb* **5** to make a quick rough drawing (of) **6 sketch out** to make a brief description of: *they sketched out plans for the invasion* [Greek *skhedios* unprepared]

sketchbook *n* a book of blank pages for sketching on

sketchy *adj* **sketchier, sketchiest** giving only a rough or incomplete description **sketchily** *adv*

skew *adj* **1** having a slanting position ▹ *n* **2** a slanting position ▹ *vb* **3** to take or cause to take a slanting position: *our boat skewed off course* **4** to distort or misrepresent: *the takeover bid has skewed last month's figures* [Old French *escuer* to shun]

skewbald *adj* **1** marked with patches of white and another colour ▹ *n* **2** a horse with this marking [origin unknown]

skewed *adj* distorted or biased because of prejudice or lack of information: *a skewed conception of religion*

skewer *n* **1** a long pin for holding meat together during cooking ▹ *vb* **2** to fasten or pierce with or as if with a skewer [probably from dialect *skiver*]

skewwhiff *adj informal* crooked or slanting

ski *n, pl* **skis** *or* **ski** **1** one of a pair of long runners that are used, fastened to boots, for gliding over snow ▹ *vb* **skiing, skied** *or* **ski'd** **2** to travel on skis [Norwegian] **skier** *n* **skiing** *n*

skid *vb* **skidding, skidded** **1** (of a vehicle or person) to slide sideways while in motion ▹ *n* **2** an instance of skidding [origin unknown]

skidoo *n, pl* **-doos** *Canad* same as **snowmobile** [*Ski-Doo*, originally a trademark]

skid row *n slang, chiefly US & Canad* a poor and neglected area of a city, inhabited by down-and-outs

skiff *n* a small narrow boat for one person [French *esquif*]

ski jump *n* a steep snow-covered slope ending in a horizontal ramp from which skiers compete to make the longest jump

skilful *or US* **skillful** *adj* having or showing skill **skilfully** *or US* **skillfully** *adv*

ski lift *n* a series of chairs hanging from a power-driven cable for carrying skiers up a slope

skill *n* **1** special ability or expertise enabling one to perform an activity very well **2** something, such as a trade, requiring special training or expertise [Old Norse *skil* distinction] **skilled** *adj*

skillet *n* **1** a small frying pan **2** *chiefly Brit* a long-handled cooking pot [origin unknown]

skim *vb* **skimming, skimmed** **1** to remove (floating material) from the surface of (a liquid): *skim any impurities off the surface* **2** to glide smoothly over (a surface) **3** to throw (a flat stone) across a surface, so that it bounces: *two men skimmed stones on the surface of the sea* **4** (often foll. by *through*) to read (a piece of writing) quickly and without taking in the details [Middle English *skimmen*]

skimmed *or* **skim milk** *n* milk from which the cream has been removed

skimp *vb* **1** to be extremely sparing or supply (someone) sparingly **2** to do (something) carelessly or with inadequate materials [perhaps a combination of SCANT + SCRIMP]

skimpy *adj* **skimpier, skimpiest** inadequate in amount or size; scant

skin *n* **1** the tissue forming the outer covering of the body **2** a person's complexion: *sallow skin* **3** any outer layer or covering: *potato skin* **4** a thin solid layer on the surface of a liquid: *custard with a thick skin on it* **5** the outer covering of a furry animal, removed and prepared for use **6** a container for liquids, made from animal skin **7 by the skin of one's teeth** by a narrow margin **8 get under one's skin** *informal* to annoy one **9 no skin off one's nose** *informal* not a matter that concerns one **10 save one's skin** to save one from death or harm **11 skin and bone** extremely thin **12 thick** *or* **thin skin** an insensitive *or* sensitive nature ▹ *vb* **skinning, skinned** **13** to remove the outer covering from (fruit, vegetables, dead animals, etc.) **14** to injure (a part of the body) by scraping some of the skin off: *I had skinned my knuckles* **15** *slang* to swindle [Old Norse *skinn*] **skinless** *adj*

skin-deep *adj* not of real importance; superficial: *beauty is only skin-deep*

skin diving *n* underwater swimming using only light breathing apparatus and without a special diving suit **skin-diver** *n*

skin flick *n slang* a pornographic film

skinflint *n* a very mean person [referring to a person so greedy that he or she would skin (swindle) a flint]

skin graft *n* a piece of skin removed from one part of the body and surgically grafted at the site of a severe burn or other injury

skinhead *n* **1** a member of a group of White youths, noted for their closely cropped hair, aggressive behaviour, and overt racism **2** a closely cropped hairstyle

skinny *adj* **-nier, -niest** extremely thin

skint *adj slang* without money, esp. only temporarily [variant of *skinned*]

skintight *adj* (of garments) fitting tightly over the body; clinging

skip[1] *vb* **skipping, skipped** **1** to move lightly by hopping from one foot to the other **2** to jump over a skipping-rope **3** to cause (a stone) to skim over a surface or (of a stone) to move in this way **4** to pass over or miss out; omit: *I skipped a few paragraphs* **5 skip through** *informal* to read or deal with (something) quickly or without great effort or concentration **6 skip it!** *informal* it doesn't matter! **7** *informal* to miss deliberately: *she skipped the class* **8** *informal, chiefly US, Canad & Austral* to leave (a place) in a hurry: *he skipped town three years later* ▹ *n* **9** a skipping movement or action [probably from Old Norse]

skip[2] *n* **1** *Brit* a large open container for transporting building materials or rubbish **2** a cage used as a lift in mines [variant of *skep* a beehive]

ski pants *pl n* stretch trousers, worn for skiing or leisure, which are kept taut by straps under the feet

skipper *n* **1** the captain of a ship or aircraft **2** the captain of a sporting team ▹ *vb* **3** to be the captain of [Middle Low German, Middle Dutch *schipper* shipper]

skipping *n* the act of jumping over a rope held either by the person jumping or by two other people, as a game or for exercise

skipping-rope *n* a rope that is held in the hands and swung round and down so that the holder or others can jump over it

skirl *Scot & N English dialect* ▹ *n* **1** the sound of bagpipes ▹ *vb* **2** (of bagpipes) to give out a shrill sound [probably from Old Norse]

skirmish *n* **1** a brief or minor fight or argument ▹ *vb* **2** to take part in a skirmish [Old French *eskirmir*]

skirt *n* **1** a woman's or girl's garment hanging from the waist **2** the part of a dress or coat below the waist **3** a circular hanging flap, for example round the base of a hovercraft **4** *Brit & NZ* a cut of beef from the flank **5 bit of skirt** *offensive slang* a girl or woman ▹ *vb* **6** to lie along or form the edge of (something): *a track skirting the foot of the mountain* **7** to go around the outer edge of (something): *we skirted the township* **8** to avoid

dealing with (an issue): *I was skirting around the real issues* [Old Norse *skyrta* shirt]
skirting board *n* a narrow board round the bottom of an interior wall where it joins the floor
ski stick *or* **ski pole** *n* one of a pair of sharp pointed sticks used by skiers to gain speed and maintain balance
skit *n* a short funny or satirical sketch [probably Scandinavian]
skite *Austral & NZ* ▷ *vb* **1** to boast ▷ *n* **2** a boast
ski tow *n* a device for pulling skiers uphill, usually a motor-driven rope grasped by the skier while riding on his or her skis
skittish *adj* **1** playful or lively **2** (of a horse) excitable and easily frightened [probably from Old Norse]
skittle *n* **1** a bottle-shaped object used as a target in a game of skittles **2 skittles** a bowling game in which players knock over as many skittles as possible by rolling a wooden ball at them [origin unknown]
skive *vb* **skiving, skived** (often foll. by *off*) *Brit informal* to avoid work or responsibility [origin unknown] **skiver** *n*
skivvy *chiefly Brit, often derogatory* ▷ *n, pl* **-vies 1** a female servant who does menial work; drudge **2** *Austral & NZ* a garment resembling a sweater with long sleeves and a polo neck ▷ *vb* **-vies, -vying, -vied 3** to work as a skivvy [origin unknown]
skolly *or* **skollie** *n, pl* **-lies** *S African* a hooligan, usually one of a gang [origin unknown]
skookum *adj W Canad* strong or brave [Chinook]
skua *n* a large predatory gull living in cold marine regions [Faeroese *skūgvur*]
skulduggery *or US* **skullduggery** *n informal* underhand dealing to achieve an aim [origin unknown]
skulk *vb* **1** to move stealthily, so as to avoid notice **2** to lie in hiding; lurk [from Old Norse]
skull *n* **1** the bony framework of the head **2** *informal* the head or mind: *that would have penetrated even your thick skull* [probably from Old Norse]
skull and crossbones *n* a picture of the human skull above two crossed bones, formerly on the pirate flag, now used as a warning of danger or death
skullcap *n* a closely fitting brimless cap
skunk *n, pl* **skunks** *or* **skunk 1** a mammal with a black-and-white coat and bushy tail, which gives out a foul-smelling fluid when attacked **2** *informal* an unpleasant or unfair person [from a Native American language]
sky *n, pl* **skies 1** the upper atmosphere as seen from earth **2 praise to the skies** praise rather excessively ▷ *vb* **skies, skying, skied 3** *informal* to hit (a ball) high in the air: *the blond-haired forward skied the ball high over the bar* [Old Norse *skȳ* cloud]
sky-blue *adj* bright clear blue
skydiving *n* the sport of jumping from an aircraft and falling freely or performing manoeuvres before opening the parachute **skydiver** *n*
sky-high *adj, adv* **1** very high: *most firms are no longer willing to pay sky-high prices* **2 blow sky-high** to destroy completely
skyjack *vb* to hijack (an aircraft) [SKY + HIJACK]
skylark *n* **1** a lark that sings while soaring at a great height ▷ *vb* **2** *old-fashioned* to play or frolic
skylight *n* a window placed in a roof or ceiling to let in daylight
skyline *n* **1** the line at which the earth and sky appear to meet **2** the outline of buildings, trees, or hills, seen against the sky
Skype *n trademark* **1** a software application by which users can make voice and video calls over the internet ▷ *vb* **Skyping, Skyped 2** to make a call by Skype or call (someone) by Skype
skyrocket *n* **1** same as **rocket** (sense 1) ▷ *vb* **2** *informal* to rise very quickly
skyscraper *n* a very tall building
skyward *adj* **1** towards the sky ▷ *adv also* **skywards 2** towards the sky
slab *n* **1** a broad flat thick piece of wood, stone, or other material **2** *informal* a package containing 24 cans of beer [origin unknown]
slack[1] *adj* **1** not tight, tense, or taut: *the slack jaw hung open* **2** careless in one's work **3** (esp. of water) moving slowly **4** (of trade) not busy ▷ *n* **5** a part that is slack or hangs loose: *take up the slack* **6** a period of less busy activity ▷ *vb* **7** to neglect one's duty or work in a lazy manner: *stop slacking, you pair!* **8** (often foll. by *off*) to loosen or slacken ▷ See also **slacks** [Old English *slæc, sleac*] **slackness** *n*
slack[2] *n* small pieces of coal with a high ash content [probably Middle Low German *slecke*]
slacken *vb* (often foll. by *off*) **1** to make or become looser **2** to make or become slower or less intense: *to slacken the pace of reform*
slacker *n* a person who evades work or duty; shirker
slacks *pl n old-fashioned* casual trousers
slag *n* **1** the waste material left after metal has been smelted **2** *Brit & NZ derogatory slang* a woman considered sexually immoral ▷ *vb* **slagging, slagged 3** *Brit, Austral & NZ slang* (often foll. by *off*) to criticize in an unpleasant way: *I don't think anyone can slag it off* [Middle Low German *slagge*] **slagging** *n* **slaggy** *adj*
slag heap *n* a pile of waste matter from metal smelting or coal mining
slain *vb* the past participle of **slay**
slake *vb* **slaking, slaked 1** *literary* to satisfy (thirst or desire) **2** to add water to (lime) to produce calcium hydroxide [Old English *slacian*]
slalom *n skiing & rowing* a race over a winding course marked by artificial obstacles [Norwegian]
slam[1] *vb* **slamming, slammed 1** to close violently and noisily **2** to throw (something or someone) down violently **3** *slang* to criticize harshly: *his new proposals were slammed by the opposition* **4** to strike with violent force: *he slammed the ball into the back of the net* ▷ *n* **5** the act or noise of slamming [Scandinavian]
slam[2] *n* the winning of all (**grand slam**) or all but one (**little slam**) of the 13 tricks at bridge [origin unknown]
slam dunk *n* **1** *basketball* a scoring shot in which the player jumps up and forces the ball down through the basket **2** *informal* a task so easy that

success in it is deemed a certainty ▷ *vb* **slam-dunk** **3** *basketball* to jump up and force (a ball) through a basket

slammer *n* **the slammer** *slang* prison

slander *n* **1** *law* a false and damaging statement about a person **2** the crime of making such a statement ▷ *vb* **3** to utter slander (about) [Old French *escandle*] **slanderous** *adj*

slang *n* **1** informal language not used in formal speech or writing and often restricted to a particular social group or profession ▷ *vb* **2** to use insulting language to (someone) [origin unknown] **slangy** *adj*

slanging match *n* an angry quarrel in which people trade insults

slant *vb* **1** to lean at an angle; slope **2** to write or present (information) in a biased way ▷ *n* **3** a sloping line or position **4** a point of view, esp. a biased one: *a right-wing slant on the story* **5** **on a** *or* **the slant** sloping ▷ *adj* **6** oblique; sloping [Scandinavian] **slanting** *adj* **slantwise** *adv*

slap *n* **1** a sharp blow or smack with something flat, such as the open hand **2** the sound made by or as if by such a blow **3** **slap and tickle** *Brit old-fashioned, informal* sexual play **4** **a slap in the face** an unexpected rejection or insult **5** **a slap on the back** congratulations ▷ *vb* **slapping, slapped** **6** to strike sharply with something flat, such as the open hand **7** to bring (something) down forcefully: *he slapped down a fiver* **8** (usually foll. by *against*) to strike (something) with a slapping sound **9** *informal* to cover with quickly or carelessly: *she slapped on some make-up* **10** **slap on the back** to congratulate ▷ *adv informal* **11** exactly: *slap in the middle* **12** **slap into** forcibly or abruptly into: *he ran slap into the guard* [Low German *slapp*]

slap-bang *adv informal* **1** directly or exactly: *he's on holiday in LA and has run slap-bang into a famous face* **2** forcefully and abruptly: *he'd gone and run slap-bang into the watchman*

slapdash *adv* **1** carelessly or hastily ▷ *adj* **2** careless or hasty

slap-happy *adj* **-pier, -piest** *informal* cheerfully careless

slaphead *n slang* a bald person [from SLAP + HEAD]

slapstick *n* rough and high-spirited comedy in which the characters behave childishly

slap-up *adj Brit informal* (esp. of meals) large and expensive

slash *vb* **1** to cut (a person or thing) with sharp sweeping strokes **2** to make large gashes in: *I slashed the tyres of his van* **3** to reduce drastically: *to slash costs* **4** to criticize harshly ▷ *n* **5** a sharp sweeping stroke **6** a cut made by such a stroke **7** same as **solidus** **8** *Brit & Austral slang* the act of urinating [origin unknown]

slasher *n Austral & NZ* a tool or tractor-drawn machine used for cutting scrub or undergrowth in the bush

slat *n* a narrow thin strip of wood or metal, such as used in a Venetian blind [Old French *esclat* splinter]

slate[1] *n* **1** a dark grey rock that can be easily split into thin layers and is used as a roofing material **2** a roofing tile of slate **3** (formerly) a writing tablet of slate **4** *chiefly US & Canad* a list of candidates in an election **5** **wipe the slate clean** forget about past mistakes or failures and start afresh **6** **on the slate** *Brit & Austral informal* on credit ▷ *vb* **slating, slated** **7** to cover (a roof) with slates **8** *chiefly US* to plan or schedule: *another exercise is slated for tomorrow* [Old French *esclate* fragment] **slaty** *adj*

slate[2] *vb* **slating, slated** *informal, chiefly Brit & Austral* to criticize harshly: *the new series was slated by the critics* [probably from Old French *esclate* fragment] **slating** *n*

slattern *n old-fashioned, derogatory* a dirty and untidy woman [probably from dialect *slatter* to slop] **slatternliness** *n* **slatternly** *adj*

slaughter *n* **1** the indiscriminate or brutal killing of large numbers of people **2** the savage killing of a person **3** the killing of animals for food ▷ *vb* **4** to kill indiscriminately or in large numbers **5** to kill brutally **6** to kill (animals) for food **7** *informal* (in sport) to defeat easily [Old English *sleaht*]

slaughterhouse *n* a place where animals are killed for food

Slav *n* a member of any of the peoples of Eastern and Central Europe who speak a Slavonic language [Medieval Latin *Sclavus* a captive Slav]

slave *n* **1** a person legally owned by another for whom he or she has to work without freedom, pay, or rights **2** a person under the domination of another or of some habit or influence: *a slave to party doctrine* **3** *informal* a badly-paid person doing menial tasks ▷ *vb* **slaving, slaved** **4** (often foll. by *away* or *over*) to work very hard for little or no money [Medieval Latin *Sclavus* a Slav (the Slavonic peoples were frequently conquered in the Middle Ages)]

slave-driver *n* **1** a person who makes people work very hard **2** (esp. formerly) a person forcing slaves to work

slaver[1] (slay-ver) *n* **1** (esp. formerly) a dealer in slaves **2** *history* a ship used in the slave trade

slaver[2] (slav-ver) *vb* **1** to dribble saliva **2** (often foll. by *over*) to drool (over someone), making flattering remarks ▷ *n* **3** saliva dribbling from the mouth **4** *informal* nonsense [probably from Low German]

slavery *n* **1** the state or condition of being a slave **2** the practice of owning slaves **3** hard work with little reward

slave trade *n* the buying and selling of slaves, esp. the transportation of Black Africans to America and the Caribbean from the 16th to the 19th centuries

slavish *adj* **1** of or like a slave **2** imitating or copying exactly without any originality: *a slavish adherence to the conventions of Italian opera* **slavishly** *adv*

Slavonic *or esp US* **Slavic** *n* **1** a group of languages including Bulgarian, Russian, Polish, and Czech ▷ *adj* **2** of this group of languages **3** of the people who speak these languages

slay *vb* **slaying, slew, slain** *archaic, literary* to kill, esp. violently [Old English *slēan*] **slayer** *n*

sleaze *n informal* behaviour in public life considered immoral, dishonest, or disreputable: *political sleaze*

sleazy *adj* **-zier, -ziest** dirty, rundown, and not respectable: *a sleazy hotel* [origin unknown] **sleaziness** *n*

sledge[1] *or esp US & Canad* **sled** *n* **1** a vehicle mounted on runners, drawn by horses or dogs, for transporting people or goods over snow **2** a light wooden frame used, esp. by children, for sliding over snow ▷ *vb* **sledging, sledged 3** to travel by sledge [Middle Dutch *sleedse*]

sledge[2] *n* short for **sledgehammer**

sledgehammer *n* **1** a large heavy hammer with a long handle, used for breaking rocks and concrete ▷ *adj* **2** crushingly powerful: *the sledgehammer approach* [Old English *slecg* a large hammer]

sleek *adj* **1** smooth, shiny, and glossy: *sleek blond hair* **2** (of a person) elegantly dressed [variant of *slick*]

sleep *n* **1** a state of rest during which the eyes are closed, the muscles and nerves are relaxed, and the mind is unconscious **2** a period spent sleeping **3** the substance sometimes found in the corner of the eyes after sleep **4** a state of inactivity, like sleep **5** *poetic* death ▷ *vb* **sleeping, slept 6** to be in or as in the state of sleep **7** to be inactive or unaware: *their defence slept as we scored another try* **8** to have sleeping accommodation for (a certain number): *the villa sleeps ten* **9** *poetic* to be dead **10 sleep on it** to delay making a decision about (something) until the next day, in order to think about it ▷ See also **sleep around, sleep in** *etc.* [Old English *slǣpan*]

sleep around *vb informal* to have many sexual partners

sleeper *n* **1** a railway sleeping car or compartment **2** one of the blocks supporting the rails on a railway track **3** a small plain gold ring worn in a pierced ear lobe to prevent the hole from closing up **4** *informal* a person or thing that achieves success after an initial period of obscurity

sleep in *vb* to sleep longer than usual

sleeping bag *n* a large well-padded bag for sleeping in, esp. outdoors

sleeping car *n* a railway carriage with small rooms containing beds for passengers to sleep in

sleeping partner *n* a partner in a business who shares in the financing but does not take part in its management

sleeping pill *n* a pill containing a drug that induces sleep

sleeping policeman *n Brit* a bump built across a road to prevent motorists from driving too fast

sleeping sickness *n* an infectious, usually fatal, African disease transmitted by the bite of the tsetse fly, causing fever and sluggishness

sleepless *adj* **1** (of a night) during which one does not sleep **2** unable to sleep **3** *chiefly poetic* always active **sleeplessness** *n*

sleep off *vb informal* to get rid of by sleeping: *go home and sleep it off*

sleepout *n NZ* a small building for sleeping in

sleep out *vb* to sleep in the open air

sleepover *n* an occasion when a person stays overnight at a friend's house

sleep together *vb* to have sexual intercourse and, usually, spend the night together

sleepwalk *vb* to walk while asleep **sleepwalker** *n* **sleepwalking** *n*

sleep with *vb* to have sexual intercourse and, usually, spend the night with

sleepy *adj* **sleepier, sleepiest 1** tired and ready for sleep **2** (of a place) without activity or excitement: *a sleepy little town* **sleepily** *adv*

sleet *n* **1** partly melted falling snow or hail or (esp. US) partly frozen rain ▷ *vb* **2** to fall as sleet [Germanic]

sleeve *n* **1** the part of a garment covering the arm **2** a tubelike part which fits over or completely encloses another part **3 up one's sleeve** secretly ready: *he has a few more surprises up his sleeve* [Old English *slīefe, slēfe*] **sleeveless** *adj*

sleigh *n* **1** same as **sledge**[1] (sense 1) ▷ *vb* **2** to travel by sleigh [Dutch *slee*]

sleight (**slite**) *n old-fashioned* skill or cunning [Old Norse *slǣgth*]

sleight of hand *n* **1** the skilful use of the hands when performing magic tricks **2** the performance of such tricks

slender *adj* **1** (esp. of a person's figure) slim and graceful **2** of small width relative to length or height **3** small or inadequate in amount or size: *a slender advantage* [origin unknown]

slept *vb* the past of **sleep**

sleuth (rhymes with **tooth**) *n informal* a detective [Old Norse *slōth* a trail]

slew[1] *vb* the past tense of **slay**

slew[2] *or esp US* **slue** *vb* **1** to slide or skid sideways: *the bus slewed across the road* ▷ *n* **2** the act of slewing [origin unknown]

slice *n* **1** a thin flat piece or wedge cut from something: *a slice of tomato* **2** a share or portion: *the biggest slice of their income* **3** a kitchen tool having a broad flat blade: *a fish slice* **4** *sport* a shot that causes the ball to go in the opposite direction from one's follow-through ▷ *vb* **slicing, sliced 5** to cut (something) into slices **6** (usually foll. by *through*) to cut through cleanly and effortlessly, with or as if with a knife **7** (usually foll. by *off, from* or *away*) to cut or be cut from a larger piece **8** *sport* to play (a ball) with a slice [Old French *esclice* a piece split off]

slick *adj* **1** (esp. of speech) easy and persuasive: *a slick answer* **2** skilfully devised or executed: *a slick marketing effort* **3** *informal, chiefly US & Canad* shrewd; sly **4** *informal* well-made and attractive, but superficial: *a slick publication* **5** *chiefly US & Canad* slippery ▷ *n* **6** a slippery area, esp. a patch of oil floating on water ▷ *vb* **7** to make smooth or shiny: *long hair slicked back with gel* [probably from Old Norse]

slide *vb* **sliding, slid 1** to move smoothly along a surface in continual contact with it: *doors that slide open* **2** to slip: *he slid on his back* **3** (usually foll. by *into, out of* or *away from*) to pass or move smoothly and quietly: *she slid out of her seat* **4** (usually foll. by *into*) to go (into a specified condition) gradually: *the republic will slide into political anarchy* **5** (of a currency) to lose value gradually **6 let slide** to allow to change to a worse state by neglect: *past chairmen have undoubtedly let things slide* ▷ *n* **7** the act or an instance of sliding **8** a small glass plate on which specimens are placed for study under a microscope **9** a piece of photographic film on a transparent base, mounted in a frame, that can be viewed by means of a projector **10** a smooth surface, such as ice, for sliding on **11** a structure with a steep smooth slope for sliding down in playgrounds **12** *chiefly Brit* an ornamental clip to hold hair in place **13** the sliding curved tube of a trombone that is moved in and out to allow different notes to be played [Old English *slīdan*]

slide rule *n* a device formerly used to make mathematical calculations consisting of two strips, one sliding along a central groove in the other, each strip graduated in two or more logarithmic scales of numbers

slide show *n* **1** any display in the form of a series of static images, such as photographic transparencies on a slide projector or images on a computer screen ▷ *adj* **slide-show** **2** presented as a series of static images: *slide-show presentation*

sliding scale *n* a variable scale according to which things such as wages or prices alter in response to changes in other factors

slight *adj* **1** small in quantity or extent: *a slight improvement* **2** not very important or lacking in substance: *her political career was honourable but relatively slight* **3** slim and delicate ▷ *vb* **4** to insult (someone) by behaving rudely; snub ▷ *n* **5** an act of snubbing (someone) [Old Norse *slēttr* smooth] **slightly** *adv*

slim *adj* **slimmer, slimmest** **1** (of a person) attractively thin **2** small in width relative to height or length: *a slim book* **3** poor; meagre: *a slim chance of progress* ▷ *vb* **slimming, slimmed** **4** to make or become slim by diets and exercise **5** to reduce in size: *that would slim the overheads* [Dutch: crafty] **slimmer** *n* **slimming** *n*

slime *n* **1** soft runny mud or any sticky substance, esp. when disgusting or unpleasant **2** a thick, sticky substance produced by some fish, slugs, and fungi [Old English *slīm*]

slimy *adj* **slimier, slimiest** **1** of, like, or covered with slime **2** pleasant and friendly in an insincere way

sling[1] *n* **1** *med* a wide piece of cloth suspended from the neck for supporting an injured hand or arm **2** a rope or strap by which something may be lifted **3** a simple weapon consisting of a strap tied to cords, in which a stone is whirled and then released ▷ *vb* **slinging, slung** **4** *informal* to throw **5** to carry or hang loosely from or as if from a sling: *her shoulder bag was slung across her chest* **6** to hurl with or as if with a sling [probably from Old Norse]

sling[2] *n* a sweetened mixed drink with a spirit base: *gin sling* [origin unknown]

slingback *n* a shoe with a strap instead of a complete covering for the heel

sling off at *vb Austral & NZ informal* to mock and jeer

slink *vb* **slinking, slunk** to move or act in a quiet and secretive way from fear or guilt [Old English *slincan*]

slinky *adj* **slinkier, slinkiest** *informal* **1** (of clothes) figure-hugging **2** moving in an alluring way

slip[1] *vb* **slipping, slipped** **1** to lose balance and slide unexpectedly: *he slipped on some leaves* **2** to let loose or be let loose: *the rope slipped from his fingers* **3** to move smoothly and easily: *small enough to slip into a pocket* **4** to place quickly or stealthily: *he slipped the pistol back into his holster* **5** to put on or take off easily or quickly: *we had slipped off our sandals* **6** to pass out of (the mind or memory) **7** to move or pass quickly and without being noticed: *we slipped out of the ballroom* **8** to make a mistake **9** to decline in health or mental ability **10** to become worse or lower: *sales had slipped below the level for June of last year* **11** to dislocate (a disc in the spine) **12** to pass (a stitch) from one needle to another without knitting it **13** **let slip** **A** to allow to escape **B** to say unintentionally ▷ *n* **14** a slipping **15** a mistake or oversight: *one slip in concentration that cost us the game* **16** a woman's sleeveless undergarment, worn under a dress **17** same as **slipway** **18** *cricket* a fielding position a little behind and to the offside of the wicketkeeper **19** **give someone the slip** to escape from someone ▷ See also **slip up** [Middle Low German or Dutch *slippen*]

slip[2] *n* **1** a small piece of paper: *the registration slip* **2** a cutting taken from a plant **3** a young slim person: *a slip of a girl* [probably Middle Low German, Middle Dutch *slippe* to cut]

slip[3] *n* clay mixed with water to a thin paste, used for decorating or patching a ceramic piece [Old English *slyppe* slime]

slipe *n NZ* wool removed from the pelt of a slaughtered sheep by immersion in a chemical bath [Middle English *slype* to skin]

slipknot *n* a nooselike knot tied so that it will slip along the rope round which it is made

slip-on *adj* **1** (of a garment or shoe) without laces or buttons so as to be easily and quickly put on ▷ *n* **2** a slip-on garment or shoe

slipped disc *n pathol* a painful condition in which one of the discs which connects the bones of the spine becomes displaced and presses on a nerve

slipper *n* a light soft shoe for indoor wear **slippered** *adj*

slippery *adj* **1** liable or tending to cause objects to slip: *the road was slippery* **2** liable to slip from one's grasp: *a bar of slippery soap* **3** not to be trusted: *slippery politicians* **slipperiness** *n*

slippy *adj* **-pier, -piest** *informal, dialect* same as **slippery** (senses 1, 2) **slippiness** *n*

slip road *n Brit* a short road connecting a motorway to another road

slipshod *adj* **1** (of an action) done in a careless way without attention to detail: *a slipshod piece of research* **2** (of a person's appearance) untidy and slovenly

slip-slop *n S African* same as **flip-flop**

slipstream *n* the stream of air forced backwards by an aircraft or car

slip up *informal* ▷ *vb* **1** to make a mistake ▷ *n* **slip-up** **2** a mistake

slipway *n* a large ramp that slopes down from the shore into the water, on which a ship is built or repaired and from which it is launched

slit *n* **1** a long narrow cut or opening ▷ *vb* **slitting, slit 2** to make a straight long cut in (something) [Old English *slītan* to slice]

slither *vb* **1** to move or slide unsteadily, such as on a slippery surface **2** to move along the ground in a twisting way: *a snake slithered towards the tree* ▷ *n* **3** a slithering movement [Old English *slid(e)rian*] **slithery** *adj*

sliver (sliv-ver) *n* **1** a small thin piece that is cut or broken off lengthwise ▷ *vb* **2** to cut into slivers [obsolete *sliven* to split]

Sloane Ranger *n informal* (in Britain) a young upper-class woman having a home in London and in the country, characterized as wearing expensive informal clothes [from *Sloane* Square, London + *Lone Ranger*, cowboy hero]

slob *n informal* a lazy and untidy person [Irish Gaelic *slab* mud] **slobbish** *adj*

slobber *vb* **1** to dribble (liquid or saliva) from the mouth **2 slobber over** to behave in an excessively sentimental way towards (someone) ▷ *n* **3** liquid or saliva spilt from the mouth [Middle Low German, Middle Dutch *slubberen*] **slobbery** *adj*

slob ice *n Canad* sludgy masses of floating sea ice

sloe *n* **1** the small sour blue-black fruit of the blackthorn **2** same as **blackthorn** [Old English *slāh*]

sloe-eyed *adj* having dark almond-shaped eyes

slog *vb* **slogging, slogged 1** to work hard and steadily **2** to make one's way with difficulty: *we slogged our way through the snow* **3** to hit hard ▷ *n* **4** long exhausting work **5** a long and difficult walk: *a slog through heather and bracken* **6** a heavy blow [origin unknown]

slogan *n* a catchword or phrase used in politics or advertising [Gaelic *sluagh-ghairm* war cry]

sloop *n* a small sailing ship with a single mast [Dutch *sloep*]

slop *vb* **slopping, slopped 1** (often foll. by *about*) to splash or spill (liquid) **2 slop over** *informal, chiefly US & Canad* to be excessively sentimental ▷ *n* **3** a puddle of spilt liquid **4 slops** liquid refuse and waste food used to feed animals, esp. pigs **5** (*often pl*) *informal* liquid food [Old English *-sloppe*]

slope *n* **1** a stretch of ground where one end is higher than the other **2 slopes** hills or foothills **3** any slanting surface **4** the angle of such a slant ▷ *vb* **sloping, sloped 5** to slant or cause to slant **6** (esp. of natural features) to have one end or part higher than another: *the bank sloped sharply down to the river* **7 slope off** or **away** *informal* to go quietly and quickly in order to avoid something or someone **8 slope arms** *military* (formerly) to hold a rifle in a sloping position against the shoulder [origin unknown]

slop out *vb* (of prisoners) to empty chamber pots and collect water

sloppy *adj* **-pier, -piest 1** *informal* careless or untidy: *sloppy workmanship* **2** *informal* excessively sentimental and romantic **3** wet; slushy **sloppily** *adv* **sloppiness** *n*

slosh *vb* **1** *informal* to throw or pour (liquid) carelessly **2** (often foll. by *about* or *around*) *informal* **A** to shake or stir (something) in a liquid **B** (of a person) to splash (around) in water or mud **3** (usually foll. by *about* or *around*) *informal* to shake (a container of liquid) or (of liquid in a container) to be shaken **4** *Brit slang* to deal a heavy blow to ▷ *n* **5** the sound of splashing liquid **6** slush **7** *Brit slang* a heavy blow [variant of SLUSH] **sloshy** *adj*

sloshed *adj slang, chiefly Brit & Austral* drunk

slot *n* **1** a narrow opening or groove, such as one in a vending machine for inserting a coin **2** *informal* a place in a series or scheme: *the late-night slot when people stop watching TV* ▷ *vb* **slotting, slotted 3** to make a slot or slots in **4** (usually foll. by *in* or *into*) to fit or be fitted into a slot: *I slotted my card into the machine* [Old French *esclot* the depression of the breastbone]

sloth (rhymes with **both**) *n* **1** a slow-moving shaggy-coated animal of Central and South America, which hangs upside down in trees by its long arms and feeds on vegetation **2** *formal* laziness, esp. regarding work [Old English *slǣwth*]

slothful *adj* lazy and unwilling to work

slot machine *n* a machine, esp. for vending food and cigarettes or featuring an electronic game on which to gamble, worked by placing a coin in a slot

slouch *vb* **1** to sit, stand, or move with a drooping posture ▷ *n* **2** a drooping posture **3 be no slouch** *informal* be very good or talented: *he was no slouch himself as a negotiator* [origin unknown]

slouch hat *n* a soft hat with a brim that can be pulled down over the ears

slough[1] (rhymes with **now**) *n* **1** a swamp or marshy area **2** (rhymes with **blue**) *US & Canad* a large hole where water collects **3** despair or hopeless depression [Old English *slōh*]

slough[2] (**sluff**) *n* **1** any outer covering that is shed, such as the dead outer layer of the skin of a snake ▷ *vb* **slough off 2** to shed (an outer covering) or (of an outer covering) to be shed: *the dead cells would slough off* **3** to get rid of (something unwanted or unnecessary): *she tried hard to slough off her old personality* [Germanic]

Slovak *adj* **1** of Slovakia ▷ *n* **2** a person from Slovakia **3** the language of Slovakia

sloven *n* a person who is always untidy or careless in appearance or behaviour [origin unknown]

Slovene *adj* **1** Also: **Slovenian** of Slovenia ▷ *n* **2** a person from Slovenia **3** the language of Slovenia

slovenly *adj* **1** always unclean or untidy **2** negligent and careless: *to write in such a slovenly style* ▷ *adv* **3** in a slovenly manner **slovenliness** *n*

slow *adj* **1** taking a longer time than is usual or expected **2** lacking speed: *slow movements* **3** adapted to or producing slow movement: *the slow lane* **4** (of a clock or watch) showing a time earlier than the correct time **5** not quick to understand: *slow on the uptake* **6** dull or uninteresting: *the play was very slow* **7** not easily aroused: *he is slow to anger* **8** (of business) not busy; slack **9** (of a fire or oven) giving off low heat **10** (of photographic film) requiring a relatively long exposure time: *a slow film* ▷ *adv* **11** in a slow manner ▷ *vb* **12** (often foll. by *up* or *down*) to decrease or cause to decrease in speed or activity [Old English *slāw* sluggish] **slowly** *adv*

S

slowcoach *n informal* a person who moves or works slowly
slow motion *n* **1** *films & television* action that is made to appear slower than normal by filming at a faster rate or by replaying a video recording more slowly ▷ *adj* **slow-motion 2** of or relating to such action **3** moving at considerably less than usual speed
slow virus *n* a type of virus that is present in the body for a long time before it becomes active or infectious
slowworm *n* a legless lizard with a brownish-grey snakelike body
sludge *n* **1** soft mud or snow **2** any muddy or slushy sediment **3** sewage [probably related to SLUSH] **sludgy** *adj*
slug¹ *n* a mollusc like a snail but without a shell [probably from Old Norse]
slug² *n* **1** a bullet **2** *informal* a mouthful of alcoholic drink, esp. spirits: *he poured out a large slug of Scotch* [probably from SLUG¹ (with allusion to the shape of the animal)]
slug³ *vb* **slugging, slugged 1** *chiefly US & Canad* to hit very hard ▷ *n* **2** *US & Canad* a heavy blow [probably from SLUG² (bullet)]
sluggard *n old-fashioned* a very lazy person [Middle English *slogarde*]
sluggish *adj* **1** lacking energy **2** moving or working at slower than the normal rate: *the sluggish waters of the canal*
sluice *n* **1** a channel that carries a rapid current of water, with a sluicegate to control the flow **2** the water controlled by a sluicegate **3** same as **sluicegate 4** *mining* a sloping trough for washing ore ▷ *vb* **sluicing, sluiced 5** to draw off or drain with a sluice **6** to wash with a stream of water **7** (often foll. by *away* or *out*) (of water) to run or flow from or as if from a sluice [Old French *escluse*]
sluicegate *n* a valve or gate fitted to a sluice to control the rate of flow of water
slum *n* **1** an overcrowded and badly maintained house **2** (*often pl*) a poor rundown overpopulated section of a city ▷ *vb* **slumming, slummed 3** to visit slums, esp. for curiosity **4 slum it** to temporarily and deliberately experience poorer places or conditions [origin unknown] **slummy** *adj*
slumber *literary* ▷ *vb* **1** to sleep ▷ *n* **2** sleep [Old English *slūma*] **slumbering** *adj*
slumber party *n chiefly US* an occasion when a group of young friends spend the night together at the home of one of the group
slump *vb* **1** (of commercial activity or prices) to decline suddenly **2** to sink or fall heavily and suddenly: *she slumped back with exhaustion* ▷ *n* **3** a severe decline in commercial activity or prices; depression **4** a sudden or marked decline or failure: *a slump in demand for oil* [probably Scandinavian]
slung *vb* the past of **sling¹**
slunk *vb* the past of **slink**
slur *vb* **slurring, slurred 1** to pronounce or say (words) unclearly **2** to make insulting remarks about **3** *music* to sing or play (successive notes) smoothly by moving from one to the other without a break **4** (often foll. by *over*) to treat hastily or carelessly ▷ *n* **5** an insulting remark intended to damage someone's reputation **6** a slurring of words **7** *music* **A** a slurring of successive notes **B** the curved line (⌒ or ‿) indicating this [probably from Middle Low German]
slurp *informal* ▷ *vb* **1** to eat or drink (something) noisily ▷ *n* **2** a slurping sound [Middle Dutch *slorpen* to sip]
slurry *n, pl* **-ries** a thin watery mixture of something such as cement or mud [Middle English *slory*]
slush *n* **1** any watery muddy substance, esp. melting snow **2** *informal* sloppily sentimental language or writing [origin unknown] **slushy** *adj*
slush fund *n* a fund for financing political or commercial corruption
slut *n derogatory* a woman who is considered promiscuous [origin unknown] **sluttish** *adj*
sly *adj* **slyer, slyest** *or* **slier, sliest 1** (of a person's remarks or gestures) indicating that he or she knows something of which other people may be unaware: *she had the feeling they were poking sly fun at her* **2** secretive and skilled at deception: *a sly trickster* **3** roguish: *sly comedy* ▷ *n* **4 on the sly** secretively: *they were smoking on the sly behind the shed* [Old Norse *slōegr* clever] **slyly** *adv*
Sm *chem* samarium
smack¹ *vb* **1** to slap sharply **2** to strike loudly or to be struck loudly **3** to open and close (the lips) loudly to show pleasure or anticipation ▷ *n* **4** a sharp loud slap, or the sound of such a slap **5** a loud kiss **6** a sharp sound made by the lips in enjoyment **7 smack in the eye** *informal* a snub or rejection ▷ *adv informal* **8** directly; squarely: *smack in the middle* **9** sharply and unexpectedly: *he ran smack into one of the men* [probably imitative]
smack² *n* **1** a slight flavour or suggestion (of something): *the smack of loss of self-control* ▷ *vb* **2 smack of A** to have a slight smell or flavour of (something) **B** to have a suggestion of (something): *it smacks of discrimination* [Old English *smæc*]
smack³ *n* a slang word for **heroin** [perhaps from Yiddish *schmeck*]
smack⁴ *n* a small single-masted fishing vessel [Dutch *smak*]
smacker *n slang* **1** a loud kiss **2** a pound note or dollar bill
small *adj* **1** not large in size or amount **2** of little importance or on a minor scale: *a small detail* **3** mean, ungenerous, or petty: *a small mind* **4** modest or humble: *small beginnings* **5 feel small** to be humiliated **6** (of a child or animal) young; not mature **7** unimportant or trivial: *a small matter* **8** (of a letter) written or printed in lower case rather than as a capital ▷ *adv* **9** into small pieces: *cut it small* ▷ *n* **10** the small narrow part of the back **11 smalls** *informal, chiefly Brit* underwear [Old English *smæl*] **smallish** *adj* **smallness** *n*
small beer *n informal, chiefly Brit* people or things of no importance
small change *n* coins of low value
small fry *pl n* **1** people regarded as unimportant **2** young children

S

small goods *pl n Austral & NZ* meats bought from a delicatessen, such as sausages
smallholding *n* a piece of agricultural land smaller than a farm **smallholder** *n*
small hours *pl n* the early hours of the morning, after midnight and before dawn
small intestine *n anatomy* the narrow, longer part of the alimentary canal, in which digestion is completed
small-minded *adj* having narrow selfish attitudes; petty
smallpox *n* a contagious disease causing fever, a rash, and blisters which usually leave permanent scars
small print *n* details in a contract or document printed in small type, esp. when considered as containing important information that people may regret not reading
small-scale *adj* of limited size or scope
small screen *n* **the small screen** television, esp. in contrast to cinema: *despite his film success, he has achieved little on the small screen*
small talk *n* light conversation for social occasions
small-time *adj informal* operating on a limited scale; minor: *a small-time smuggler*
smarm *vb Brit informal* **1** to bring (oneself) into favour (with) **2** *old-fashioned* (often foll. by *down*) to flatten (the hair) with oil [origin unknown]
smarmy *adj* **smarmier, smarmiest** unpleasantly flattering or polite
smart *adj* **1** clean and neatly dressed **2** intelligent and shrewd **3** quick and witty in speech: *a smart talker* **4** (of places or events) fashionable; chic: *smart restaurants* **5** vigorous or brisk: *a smart pace* **6** causing a sharp stinging pain **7** (of a weapon) containing an electronic device which enables it to be guided to its target: *a smart bomb* ▷ *vb* **8** to feel or cause a sharp stinging physical or mental pain: *I was still smarting from the insult* ▷ *n* **9** a stinging pain or feeling ▷ *adv* **10** in a smart manner ▷ See also **smarts** [Old English *smeortan* be painful] **smartly** *adv* **smartness** *n*
smart alec *n informal* a person who thinks he or she is an expert on every subject; know-all
smart card *n* a plastic card with integrated circuits used for storing and processing computer data
smarten *vb* (usually foll. by *up*) to make or become smart
smartphone *n* a mobile phone that performs many of the functions of a computer, having internet access, a touchscreen interface, and able to run various apps
smarts *pl n slang, chiefly US* know-how, intelligence, or wits: *the street smarts of the old crooks*
smash *vb* **1** to break into pieces violently and noisily **2** (often foll. by *against, through* or *into*) to throw or crash (against) violently, causing shattering: *his head smashed against a window* **3** to hit or collide forcefully and suddenly **4** *sport* to hit (the ball) fast and powerfully with an overhead stroke **5** to defeat or destroy: *the police had smashed a major drug ring* ▷ *n* **6** an act or sound of smashing **7** a violent collision of vehicles **8** *sport* a fast and powerful overhead stroke **9** *informal* a show, record or film which is very popular with the public ▷ *adv* **10** with a smash [probably imitative]
smash-and-grab *adj informal* of a robbery in which a shop window is broken and the contents removed
smasher *n informal, chiefly Brit* a person or thing that is very attractive or outstanding
smashing *adj informal, chiefly Brit* excellent or first-rate
smash-up *informal* ▷ *n* **1** a bad collision or crash involving motor vehicles ▷ *vb* **smash up** **2** to damage to the point of complete destruction: *two men smashed up a bar*
smattering *n* a slight or superficial knowledge: *I knew a smattering of Russian*
smear *vb* **1** to spread with a greasy or sticky substance **2** to apply (a greasy or sticky substance) thickly **3** to rub so as to produce a smudge **4** to spread false and damaging rumours (about) ▷ *n* **5** a dirty mark or smudge **6** a false but damaging rumour spread by a rival or enemy **7** *med* a small amount of a substance smeared onto a glass slide for examination under a microscope [Old English *smeoru* a smear] **smeary** *adj*
smear test *n med* same as **Pap test**
smell *vb* **smelling, smelt** *or* **smelled** **1** to perceive the scent of (a substance) with the nose **2** to have a specified kind of smell: *it smells fruity; your supper smells good* **3** (often foll. by *of*) to emit an odour (of): *the place smells of milk and babies* **4** to give off an unpleasant odour **5** (often foll. by *out*) to detect through instinct: *I smell trouble* **6** to use the sense of smell; sniff **7** **smell of** to indicate or suggest: *anything that smells of devaluation* ▷ *n* **8** the sense by which scents or odours are perceived. Related adjective: **olfactory** **9** an odour or scent **10** the act of smelling [origin unknown]
smelling salts *pl n* a preparation containing crystals of ammonium carbonate, used to revive a person feeling faint
smelly *adj* **smellier, smelliest** having a nasty smell **smelliness** *n*
smelt[1] *vb* to extract (a metal) from (an ore) by heating [Middle Low German, Middle Dutch *smelten*]
smelt[2] *n, pl* **smelt** *or* **smelts** a small silvery food fish [Old English *smylt*]
smelt[3] *vb* a past tense and past participle of **smell**
smelter *n* an industrial plant in which smelting is carried out
smile *n* **1** a facial expression in which the corners of the mouth are turned up, showing amusement or friendliness ▷ *vb* **smiling, smiled** **2** to give a smile **3** **smile at** **A** to look at with a kindly expression **B** to look with amusement at **4** **smile on** *or* **upon** to regard favourably: *fortune smiled on us today* **5** to express by a smile: *he smiled a comrade's greeting* [probably from Old Norse]
smiley *adj* **1** cheerful **2** depicting a smile
smirch *vb* **1** to disgrace **2** to dirty or soil ▷ *n* **3** a disgrace **4** a smear or stain [origin unknown]
smirk *n* **1** a smug smile ▷ *vb* **2** to give such a smile [Old English *smearcian*]

smite *vb* **smiting, smote, smitten** *or* **smit** *archaic* **1** to strike with a heavy blow **2** to affect severely: *hunger smites him again* **3** to burden with an affliction in order to punish: *God smote the enemies of the righteous* **4** **smite on** to strike abruptly and with force: *the sun smote down on him* [Old English *smītan*]

smith *n* **1** a person who works in metal: *goldsmith* **2** See **blacksmith** [Old English]

smithereens *pl n* shattered fragments [Irish Gaelic *smidirīn*]

smithy *n, pl* **smithies** the workshop of a blacksmith; forge

smitten *vb* **1** a past participle of **smite** ▷ *adj* **2** deeply affected by love (for)

smock *n* **1** a loose overall worn to protect the clothes **2** a loose blouselike garment worn by women **3** a loose protective overgarment decorated with smocking, worn formerly by farm workers ▷ *vb* **4** to gather (material) by sewing in a honeycomb pattern [Old English *smocc*]

smocking *n* ornamental needlework used to gather material

smog *n* a mixture of smoke and fog that occurs in some industrial areas [SMOKE + FOG] **smoggy** *adj*

smoke *n* **1** the cloudy mass that rises from something burning **2** the act of smoking tobacco **3** *informal* a cigarette or cigar **4** **go up in smoke** **A** to come to nothing **B** to burn up vigorously ▷ *vb* **smoking, smoked** **5** to give off smoke: *a smoking fireplace* **6** **A** to draw the smoke of (burning tobacco) into the mouth and exhale it again **B** to do this habitually **7** to cure (meat, cheese, or fish) by treating with smoke [Old English *smoca*]

Smoke *n* **the Smoke** *informal* short for **Big Smoke**

smokeless *adj* having or producing little or no smoke: *smokeless fuel*

smokeless zone *n* an area where only smokeless fuels may be used

smoke out *vb* **1** to drive (a person or animal) out of a hiding place by filling it with smoke **2** to bring (someone) out of secrecy and into the open: *they smoked out the plotters*

smoker *n* **1** a person who habitually smokes tobacco **2** a train compartment where smoking is permitted

smoke screen *n* **1** something said or done to hide the truth **2** *military* a cloud of smoke used to provide cover for manoeuvres

smokestack *n* a tall chimney that carries smoke away from a factory

smoko *or* **smokeho** (smoke-oh) *n, pl* **-kos** *or* **-hos** *Austral & NZ informal* **1** a short break from work for tea or a cigarette **2** refreshment taken during this break

smoky *adj* **smokier, smokiest** **1** filled with or giving off smoke, sometimes excessively: *smoky coal or wood fires* **2** having the colour of smoke **3** having the taste or smell of smoke **4** made dirty or hazy by smoke **smokiness** *n*

smolt *n* a young salmon at the stage when it migrates from fresh water to the sea [Scots]

smooch *slang* ▷ *vb* **1** (of two people) to kiss and cuddle **2** *Brit* to dance very slowly with one's arms around another person or (of two people) to dance together in such a way ▷ *n* **3** the act of smooching [dialect *smouch*, imitative]

smoodge *or* **smooge** *vb* **smoodging, smoodged** *or* **smooging, smooged** *Austral & NZ* **1** same as **smooch** (sense 1) **2** to attempt to gain favour through flattery

smooth *adj* **1** having an even surface with no roughness, bumps, or holes **2** without obstructions or difficulties: *smooth progress towards an agreement* **3** without lumps: *a smooth paste* **4** free from jolts and bumps: *a smooth landing* **5** not harsh in taste; mellow: *an excellent smooth wine* **6** charming or persuasive but possibly insincere ▷ *adv* **7** in a smooth manner ▷ *vb* **8** (often foll. by *down*) to make or become even or without roughness **9** (often foll. by *out* or *away*) to remove in order to make smooth: *smoothing out the creases* **10** to make calm; soothe **11** to make easier: *Moscow smoothed the path to democracy* ▷ *n* **12** the smooth part of something **13** the act of smoothing [Old English *smōth*] **smoothly** *adv*

smoothie *n* **1** a smooth thick drink made from fresh fruit and yoghurt, ice cream, or milk **2** *slang* a man who is so confident, well-dressed, and charming that one is suspicious of his motives and doubts his honesty

smooth over *vb* to ease or gloss over: *their fears are now being smoothed over*

smooth-talking *adj* confident and persuasive but not necessarily honest or sincere

smorgasbord *n* a variety of savoury dishes served as hors d'oeuvres or as a buffet meal [Swedish]

smote *vb* the past tense of **smite**

smother *vb* **1** to extinguish (a fire) by covering so as to cut it off from the air **2** to suffocate **3** to surround or overwhelm (with): *she smothered him with her idea of affection* **4** to suppress or stifle: *he smothered an ironic chuckle* **5** to cover over thickly: *ice cream smothered with sauce* [Old English *smorian* to suffocate]

smoulder *or US* **smolder** *vb* **1** to burn slowly without flames, usually giving off smoke **2** (of emotions) to exist in a suppressed state without being released [origin unknown]

SMS short message system: used for sending data to mobile phones

smudge *vb* **smudging, smudged** **1** to make or become smeared or soiled ▷ *n* **2** a smear or dirty mark **3** a blurred form or area: *the dull smudge of a ship* [origin unknown] **smudgy** *adj*

smug *adj* **smugger, smuggest** very pleased with oneself; self-satisfied [Germanic] **smugly** *adv* **smugness** *n*

smuggle *vb* **-gling, -gled** **1** to import or export (goods that are prohibited or subject to taxation) secretly **2** (often foll. by *into* or *out of*) to bring or take secretly: *he was smuggled out of the country unnoticed* [Low German *smukkelen*] **smuggler** *n* **smuggling** *n*

smut *n* **1** stories, pictures, or jokes relating to sex or nudity **2** a speck of soot or a dark mark left by soot **3** a disease of cereals, in which black sooty masses cover the affected parts [Old English *smitte*] **smutty** *adj*

Sn *chem* tin [New Latin *stannum*]

S

snack *n* **1** a light quick meal eaten between or in place of main meals ▹ *vb* **2** to eat a snack [probably from Middle Dutch *snacken*]
snack bar *n* a place where light meals or snacks are sold
snaffle *n* **1** a mouthpiece for controlling a horse ▹ *vb* **-fling, -fled 2** *Brit, Austral & NZ informal* to steal or take **3** to fit or control (a horse) with a snaffle [origin unknown]
snafu (snaf-**foo**) *chiefly military slang* ▹ *n* **1** confusion or chaos regarded as the normal state ▹ *adj* **2** confused or muddled up, as usual [*s(ituation) n(ormal): a(ll) f(ucked) u(p)*]
snag *n* **1** a small problem or difficulty: *one possible snag in his plans* **2** a sharp projecting point that may catch on things **3** a small hole in a fabric caused by a sharp object **4** a tree stump in a river bed that is a danger to navigation **5** *Austral slang* a sausage ▹ *vb* **snagging, snagged 6** to tear or catch on a snag [Scandinavian]
snail *n* a slow-moving mollusc with a spiral shell [Old English *snæg(e)l*]
snail mail *informal* ▹ *n* **1** conventional post, as opposed to email or text messages **2** the conventional postal system ▹ *vb* **snail-mail 3** to send by the conventional postal system, rather than by email or text message
snail's pace *n* a very slow speed
snake *n* **1** a long scaly limbless reptile **2** Also: **snake in the grass** a person, esp. a colleague or friend, who secretly acts against one ▹ *vb* **snaking, snaked 3** to glide or move in a winding course, like a snake [Old English *snaca*]
snakebite *n* **1** the bite of a snake **2** a drink of cider and lager
snake charmer *n* an entertainer who appears to hypnotize snakes by playing music
snakes and ladders *n* a board game in which players move counters along a series of squares by means of dice, going up the ladders to squares nearer the finish and down the snakes to squares nearer the start
snaky *adj* **snakier, snakiest 1** twisting or winding **2** treacherous
snap *vb* **snapping, snapped 1** to break suddenly, esp. with a sharp sound **2** to make or cause to make a sudden sharp cracking sound: *he snapped his fingers* **3** to move or close with a sudden sharp sound: *I snapped the lid shut* **4** to move in a sudden or abrupt way **5** to give way or collapse suddenly under strain: *one day someone's temper will snap* **6** to panic when a situation becomes too difficult to cope with: *he could snap at any moment* **7** (often foll. by *at* or *up*) to seize suddenly or quickly **8** (often foll. by *at*) (of animals) to bite at suddenly **9** to speak (words) sharply and angrily **10** to take a photograph of **11 snap one's fingers at** *informal* to defy or dismiss contemptuously **12 snap out of it** *informal* to recover quickly, esp. from depression or anger ▹ *n* **13** the act of breaking suddenly or the sound of a sudden breakage **14** a sudden sharp sound **15** a clasp or fastener that closes with a snapping sound **16** a sudden grab or bite **17** a thin crisp biscuit: *brandy snaps* **18** *informal* an informal photograph taken with a simple camera **19** See **cold snap 20** *Brit & NZ* a card game in which the word *snap* is called when two similar cards are turned up ▹ *adj* **21** done on the spur of the moment: *snap judgments* ▹ *adv* **22** with a snap ▹ *interj* **23 A** *cards* the word called while playing snap **B** a cry used to draw attention to the similarity of two things ▹ See also **snap up** [Middle Dutch *snappen* to seize]
snapdragon *n* a plant with spikes of colourful flowers that can open and shut like a mouth; antirrhinum
snap fastener *n* same as **press stud**
snapper *n* a food fish of Australia and New Zealand with a pinkish body covered with blue spots
snappy *adj* **-pier, -piest 1** smart and fashionable: *snappy designs* **2** Also: **snappish** (of someone's behaviour) irritable, unfriendly, and cross **3** brisk or lively: *short snappy movements* **4 make it snappy** *slang* hurry up! **snappiness** *n*
snapshot *n* same as **snap** (sense 18)
snap up *vb* to take advantage of eagerly and quickly: *the tickets have been snapped up*
snare¹ *n* **1** a trap for birds or small animals, usually a flexible loop that is drawn tight around the prey **2** anything that traps someone or something unawares ▹ *vb* **snaring, snared 3** to catch in or as if in a snare [Old English *sneare*]
snare² *n music* a set of strings fitted against the lower head of a snare drum, which produces a rattling sound when the drum is beaten [Middle Dutch *snaer* or Middle Low German *snare* string]
snare drum *n music* a small drum fitted with a snare
snarl¹ *vb* **1** (of an animal) to growl fiercely with bared teeth **2** to speak or say (something) fiercely: *he snarled out a command to a subordinate* ▹ *n* **3** a fierce growl or facial expression **4** the act of snarling [Germanic]
snarl² *n* **1** a complicated or confused state **2** a tangled mass ▹ *vb* **3 snarl up** to become, be, or make tangled, confused, or complicated: *the line became snarled up on the propeller; the postal service was snarled up at Christmas* [from Old Norse]
snarl-up *n informal* a confused, disorganized situation such as a traffic jam
snatch *vb* **1** to seize or grasp (something) suddenly: *she snatched the paper* **2** (usually foll. by *at*) to attempt to seize suddenly **3** to take hurriedly: *these players had snatched a few hours sleep* **4** to remove suddenly: *she snatched her hand away* ▹ *n* **5** an act of snatching **6** a small piece or incomplete part: *snatches of song* **7** a brief spell: *snatches of sleep* **8** *slang, chiefly US* an act of kidnapping **9** *Brit slang* a robbery: *a wages snatch* [Middle English *snacchen*]
snazzy *adj* **-zier, -ziest** *informal* (esp. of clothes) stylish and flashy [origin unknown]
sneak *vb* **1** to move quietly, trying not be noticed **2** to behave in a cowardly or underhand manner **3** to bring, take, or put secretly: *we sneaked him over the border* **4** *informal, chiefly Brit & NZ* (esp. in schools) to tell tales ▹ *n* **5** a person who acts in an underhand or cowardly manner ▹ *adj* **6** without warning: *a sneak attack* [Old English *snīcan* to creep] **sneaky** *adj*

S

sneakers *pl n US, Canad, Austral & NZ* canvas shoes with rubber soles
sneaking *adj* **1** slight but nagging: *a sneaking suspicion* **2** secret: *a sneaking admiration* **3** acting in a cowardly and furtive way
sneak thief *n* a burglar who sneaks into houses through open doors and windows
sneer *n* **1** a facial expression showing distaste or contempt, typically with a curled upper lip **2** a remark showing distaste or contempt ▷ *vb* **3** to make a facial expression of scorn or contempt **4** to say (something) in a scornful manner [origin unknown] **sneering** *adj, n*
sneeze *vb* **sneezing, sneezed 1** to expel air from the nose suddenly and without control, esp. as the result of irritation in the nostrils ▷ *n* **2** the act or sound of sneezing [Old English *fnēosan* (unattested)]
sneeze at *vb informal* to ignore or dismiss lightly: *the money's not to be sneezed at*
snib *n Scot & NZ* the catch of a door or window
snick *n* **1** a small cut in something; notch **2** *cricket* a glancing blow off the edge of the bat ▷ *vb* **3** to make a small cut or notch in (something) **4** *cricket* to hit (the ball) with a snick [probably Scandinavian]
snicker *n, vb chiefly US & Canad* same as **snigger** [probably imitative]
snide *or* **snidey** *adj* (of comments) critical in an unfair and nasty way [origin unknown]
sniff *vb* **1** to inhale through the nose in short audible breaths **2** (often foll. by *at*) to smell by sniffing ▷ *n* **3** the act or sound of sniffing [imitative] **sniffer** *n*
sniff at *vb* to express contempt or dislike for
sniffer dog *n* a police dog trained to locate drugs or explosives by smell
sniffle *vb* **-fling, -fled 1** to sniff repeatedly when the nasal passages are blocked up ▷ *n* **2** the act or sound of sniffling
sniffles *or* **snuffles** *pl n* **the sniffles** *informal* a cold in the head
sniff out *vb* to discover after some searching: *they eventually sniffed out a suitable Parliamentary seat for him*
sniffy *adj* **-fier, -fiest** *informal* contemptuous or scornful
snifter *n* **1** *informal* a small quantity of alcoholic drink **2** a pear-shaped brandy glass [origin unknown]
snig *vb* **snigging, snigged** *Austral & NZ* to drag (a felled log) by a chain or cable [English dialect]
snigger *n* **1** a quiet and disrespectful laugh kept to oneself ▷ *vb* **2** to utter such a laugh [variant of *snicker*]
snip *vb* **snipping, snipped 1** to cut with small quick strokes with scissors or shears ▷ *n* **2** *informal, chiefly Brit* a bargain **3** the act or sound of snipping **4** a small piece snipped off **5** a small cut made by snipping [Low German, Dutch *snippen*]
snipe *n, pl* **snipe** *or* **snipes 1** a wading bird with a long straight bill ▷ *vb* **sniping, sniped** (often foll. by *at*) **2** to shoot (someone) from a place of hiding **3** (often foll. by *at*) to make critical remarks about [Old Norse *snīpa*] **sniper** *n*
snippet *n* a small scrap or fragment: *the odd snippet of knowledge*

S

snitch *slang* ▷ *vb* **1** to act as an informer **2** to steal small amounts ▷ *n* **3** an informer [origin unknown]
snitchy *adj* **snitchier, snitchiest** *NZ informal* bad-tempered or irritable
snivel *vb* **-velling, -velled** *or US* **-veling, -veled 1** to cry and sniff in a self-pitying way **2** to say (something) tearfully; whine **3** to have a runny nose ▷ *n* **4** the act of snivelling [Middle English *snivelen*]
snob *n* **1** a person who tries to associate with those of higher social status and who hates those of a lower social status **2** a person who feels smugly superior with regard to his or her tastes or interests: *a cultural snob* [origin unknown] **snobbery** *n* **snobbish** *adj*
snoek (snook) *n* a South African edible marine fish [Afrikaans, from Dutch: pike]
snoep (snoop) *adj S African informal* mean or tight-fisted [Afrikaans: greedy]
snog *Brit, NZ & S African slang* ▷ *vb* **snogging, snogged 1** to kiss and cuddle ▷ *n* **2** the act of kissing and cuddling [origin unknown]
snood *n* a pouchlike hat loosely holding a woman's hair at the back [Old English *snōd*]
snook *n* **cock a snook at** *Brit* **A** to make a rude gesture at (someone) by putting one thumb to the nose with the fingers of the hand outstretched **B** to show contempt for (someone in authority) without fear of punishment [origin unknown]
snooker *n* **1** a game played on a billiard table with 15 red balls, six balls of other colours, and a white cue ball **2** a shot in which the cue ball is left in a position such that another ball blocks the target ball ▷ *vb* **3** to leave (an opponent) in an unfavourable position by playing a snooker **4** to put someone in a position where he or she can do nothing [origin unknown]
snoop *informal* ▷ *vb* **1** (often foll. by *about* or *around*) to pry into the private business of others ▷ *n* **2** the act of snooping **3** a person who snoops [Dutch *snoepen* to eat furtively] **snooper** *n* **snoopy** *adj*
snooty *adj* **snootier, snootiest** *informal* behaving as if superior to other people; snobbish [from *snoot* nose]
snooze *informal* ▷ *vb* **snoozing, snoozed 1** to take a brief light sleep ▷ *n* **2** a nap [origin unknown]
snore *vb* **snoring, snored 1** to breathe with snorting sounds while asleep ▷ *n* **2** the act or sound of snoring [imitative]
snorkel *n* **1** a tube allowing a swimmer to breathe while face down on the surface of the water **2** a device supplying air to a submarine when under water ▷ *vb* **-kelling, -kelled** *or US* **-keling, -keled 3** to swim with a snorkel [German *Schnorchel*]
snort *vb* **1** to exhale air noisily through the nostrils **2** to express contempt or annoyance by snorting **3** to say with a snort **4** *slang* to inhale (a powdered drug) through the nostrils ▷ *n* **5** a loud exhalation of air through the nostrils to express contempt or annoyance: *Clare gave a snort of disgust* [Middle English *snorten*]
snot *n* **1** *informal* mucus from the nose **2** *slang* an annoying or disgusting person [Old English *gesnot*]

snotty *adj* **-tier, -tiest** *informal* **1** dirty with nasal discharge **2** having a proud and superior attitude **3** contemptible; nasty **snottiness** *n*

snout *n* **1** the projecting nose and jaws of an animal **2** anything projecting like a snout: *the snout of a gun* **3** *slang* a person's nose [Germanic]

snow *n* **1** frozen vapour falling from the sky in flakes **2** a layer of snow on the ground **3** a falling of snow **4** *slang* cocaine ▷ *vb* **5** (*with 'it' as subject*) to be the case that snow is falling: *it's snowing today* **6** to fall as or like snow **7 be snowed in** *or* **up** *or* **over** to be covered by or confined with a heavy fall of snow **8 be snowed under** to be overwhelmed, esp. with paperwork [Old English *snāw*] **snowy** *adj*

snowball *n* **1** snow pressed into a ball for throwing ▷ *vb* **2** to increase rapidly in size or importance: *production snowballed between 1950 and 1970* **3** to throw snowballs at

snowberry *n, pl* **-ries** a shrub grown for its white berries

snow-blind *adj* blinded for a short time by the intense reflection of sunlight from snow **snow blindness** *n*

snowboard *n* a shaped board, like a skateboard without wheels, on which a person stands to slide across the snow **snowboarding** *n*

snowbound *adj* shut in or blocked off by snow

snowcap *n* a cap of snow on top of a mountain **snowcapped** *adj*

snowdrift *n* a bank of deep snow driven together by the wind

snowdrop *n* a plant with small drooping white bell-shaped flowers

snowfall *n* **1** a fall of snow **2** *meteorol* the amount of snow that falls in a specified place and time

snowflake *n* a single crystal of snow

snow goose *n* a North American goose with white feathers and black wing tips

snow line *n* (on a mountain) the altitude above which there is permanent snow

snowman *n, pl* **-men** a figure like a person, made of packed snow

snowmobile *n* a motor vehicle for travelling on snow, esp. one with caterpillar tracks and front skis

snowplough *or esp US* **snowplow** *n* a vehicle for clearing away snow

snowshoe *n* a racket-shaped frame with a network of thongs stretched across it, worn on the feet to make walking on snow less difficult

snowstorm *n* a storm with heavy snow

SNP Scottish National Party

Snr *or* **snr** senior

snub *vb* **snubbing, snubbed 1** to insult (someone) deliberately ▷ *n* **2** a deliberately insulting act or remark ▷ *adj* **3** (of a nose) short and turned up [Old Norse *snubba* to scold]

snub-nosed *adj* having a short turned-up nose

snuff[1] *vb* **1** to inhale through the nose **2** (esp. of an animal) to examine by sniffing ▷ *n* **3** a sniff [probably Middle Dutch *snuffen* to snuffle]

snuff[2] *n* finely powdered tobacco for sniffing up the nostrils [Dutch *snuf*]

snuff[3] *vb* **1** (often foll. by *out*) to put out (a candle) **2** to cut off the charred part of (a candle wick) **3** (usually foll. by *out*) *informal* to put an end to **4 snuff it** *Brit & Austral informal* to die ▷ *n* **5** the burned portion of the wick of a candle [origin unknown]

snuffbox *n* a small container for holding snuff

snuffle *vb* **-fling, -fled 1** to breathe noisily or with difficulty **2** to say or speak through the nose **3** to cry and sniff in a self-pitying way ▷ *n* **4** an act or the sound of snuffling [Low German or Dutch *snuffelen*] **snuffly** *adj*

snug *adj* **snugger, snuggest 1** comfortably warm and well protected; cosy: *safe and snug in their homes* **2** small but comfortable: *a snug office* **3** fitting closely and comfortably ▷ *n* **4** (in Britain and Ireland) a small room in a pub [Swedish *snygg* tidy] **snugly** *adv*

snuggery *n, pl* **-geries** a cosy and comfortable place or room

snuggle *vb* **-gling, -gled** to nestle into (a person or thing) for warmth or from affection [from SNUG]

so[1] *adv* **1** to such an extent: *the river is so dirty that it smells* **2** to the same extent as: *she is not so old as you* **3** extremely: *it's so lovely* **4** also: *I can speak Spanish and so can you* **5** thereupon: *and so we ended up in France* **6** in the state or manner expressed or implied: *they're happy and will remain so* **7 and so on** *or* **forth** and continuing similarly **8 or so** approximately: *fifty or so people came to see me* **9 so be it** an expression of agreement or resignation **10 so much A** a certain degree or amount (of) **B** a lot (of): *it's just so much nonsense* **11 so much for A** no more need be said about **B** used to express contempt for something that has failed: *so much for all our plans* ▷ *conj* (often foll. by *that*) **12** in order (that): *to die so that you might live* **13** with the consequence (that): *he was late home, so that there was trouble* **14 so as** in order (to): *to diet so as to lose weight* **15** *not standard* in consequence: *she wasn't needed, so she left* **16 so what!** *informal* that is unimportant ▷ *pron* **17** used to substitute for a clause or sentence, which may be understood: *you'll stop because I said so* ▷ *adj* **18** true: *it can't be so* ▷ *interj* **19** an exclamation of surprise or triumph [Old English *swā*]

> **USAGE** In formal English, *so* is not used as a conjunction to indicate either purpose (*he left by a back door so he could avoid photographers*) or result (*the project was abandoned so his services were no longer needed*). In the former case *to* or *in order to* should be used instead, and in the latter case *and so* or *and therefore* would be more acceptable. The expression *so therefore* should not be used.

so[2] *n* *music* same as **soh**

soak *vb* **1** to put or lie in a liquid so as to become thoroughly wet **2** (usually foll. by *in* or *into*) (of a liquid) to penetrate or permeate **3** (usually foll. by *in* or *up*) to take in; absorb: *white clay soaks up excess oil* ▷ *n* **4** a soaking or being soaked **5** *slang* a person who drinks very heavily [Old English *sōcian*] **soaking** *n, adj*

so-and-so *n, pl* **so-and-sos** *informal* **1** a person whose name is not specified **2** *euphemistic* a person regarded as unpleasant; a name used in place of a swear word: *you're a dirty so-and-so*

S

soap *n* **1** a compound of alkali and fat, used with water as a cleaning agent **2** *informal* short for **soap opera** ▷ *vb* **3** to apply soap to [Old English *sāpe*]
soapbox *n* a crate used as a platform for making speeches
soap opera *n* an on-going television or radio serial about the daily lives of a group of people [so called because manufacturers of soap were typical sponsors]
soapstone *n* a soft mineral used for making table tops and ornaments
soapsuds *pl n* foam or lather produced when soap is mixed with water
soapy *adj* **soapier, soapiest 1** containing or covered with soap: *a soapy liquid* **2** like soap in texture, smell, or taste: *the cheese had a soapy taste* **3** *slang* flattering or persuasive **soapiness** *n*
soar *vb* **1** to rise or fly upwards into the air **2** (of a bird or aircraft) to glide while maintaining altitude **3** to rise or increase suddenly above the usual level: *television ratings soared* [Old French *essorer*]
sob *vb* **sobbing, sobbed 1** to cry noisily, breathing in short gasps **2** to speak with sobs ▷ *n* **3** the act or sound of sobbing [probably from Low German]
sober *adj* **1** not drunk **2** tending to drink only moderate quantities of alcohol **3** serious and thoughtful: *a sober and serious fellow* **4** (of colours) plain and dull **5** free from exaggeration: *a fairly sober version of what happened* ▷ *vb* **6** (usually foll. by *up*) to make or become less drunk [Latin *sobrius*] **sobering** *adj*
sobriety *n* the state of being sober
sobriquet *or* **soubriquet** (so-brik-ay) *n* a nickname [French *soubriquet*]
sob story *n* a tale of personal misfortune or bad luck intended to arouse sympathy
Soc. *or* **soc. 1** socialist **2** society
soca (soak-a) *n* a mixture of soul and calypso music popular in the E Caribbean
so-called *adj* called (in the speaker's opinion, wrongly) by that name: *so-called military experts*
soccer *n* a game in which two teams of eleven players try to kick or head a ball into their opponents' goal, only the goalkeeper on either side being allowed to touch the ball with his hands [*Assoc(iation) Football*]
sociable *adj* **1** friendly and enjoying other people's company **2** (of an occasion) providing the opportunity for relaxed and friendly companionship **sociability** *n* **sociably** *adv*
social *adj* **1** living or preferring to live in a community rather than alone **2** of or relating to human society or organization **3** of the way people live and work together in groups: *social organization* **4** of or for companionship or communal activities: *social clubs* **5** of or engaged in social services: *a social worker* **6** relating to a certain class of society: *social misfits* **7** (of certain species of insects) living together in organized colonies: *social bees* ▷ *n* **8** an informal gathering [Latin *socius* a comrade] **socially** *adv*
social charter *n* a document dealing with welfare and workers' rights in the European Union; it later became enshrined in the social chapter of the Maastricht Treaty (1991)
social climber *n* a person who tries to associate with people from a higher social class in the hope that he or she will be thought also to be upper-class
social contract *or* **social compact** *n* an agreement among individuals to cooperate for greater security, which results in the loss of some personal liberties
social democrat *n* **1** a person who is in favour of a market or mixed economy but believes the State must play an active role in ensuring social justice and equality of opportunity **2** (formerly) a person who believed in the gradual transformation of capitalism into democratic socialism **social democracy** *n*
social exclusion *n sociol* the failure of society to provide certain people with those rights normally available to its members, such as employment, health care, education, etc.
social fund *n* (in Britain) a social security fund from which loans or payments may be made to people in cases of extreme need
social inclusion *n sociol* the provision of certain rights to all people in society, such as employment, health care, education, etc.
social intelligence *n* the ability to form rewarding relationships with other people
socialism *n* a political and economic theory or system in which the means of production, distribution, and exchange are owned by the community collectively, usually through the state **socialist** *n, adj*
socialite *n* a person who goes to many events attended by the rich, famous, and fashionable
socialize *or* **-lise** *vb* **-lizing, -lized** *or* **-lising, -lised 1** to meet others socially **2** to prepare for life in society **3** *chiefly US* to organize along socialist principles **socialization** *or* **-lisation** *n*
social media *n* websites and applications that allow users to interact with each other
social networking *n* social interaction among online communities based around shared interests, experiences, etc.
social science *n* the systematic study of society and of human relationships within society **social scientist** *n*
social security *n* state provision for the welfare of elderly, unemployed, or sick people, through pensions and other financial aid
social services *pl n* welfare services provided by local authorities or a state agency for people with particular social needs
social studies *n* the study of how people live and organize themselves in society
social welfare *n* **1** social services provided by a state for the benefit of its citizens **2** (in New Zealand) a government department concerned with pensions and benefits for elderly people, sick people, etc.
social work *n* social services that give help and advice to elderly people, people with disabilities, and families with problems **social worker** *n*
society *n, pl* **-ties 1** human beings considered as a group **2** a group of people forming a single

community with its own distinctive culture and institutions **3** the structure, culture, and institutions of such a group **4** an organized group of people sharing a common aim or interest: *a dramatic society* **5** the rich and fashionable class of society collectively **6** *old-fashioned* companionship: *I enjoy her society* [Latin *societas*]

Society of Friends *n* the Quakers

Society of Jesus *n* the religious order of the Jesuits

socioeconomic *adj* of or involving economic and social factors

sociology *n* the study of the development, organization, functioning, and classification of human societies **sociological** *adj* **sociologist** *n*

sociopath *n* another name for **psychopath**

sociopolitical *adj* of or involving political and social factors

sock[1] *n* **1** a cloth covering for the foot, reaching to between the ankle and knee and worn inside a shoe **2** **pull one's socks up** *informal* to make a determined effort to improve **3** **put a sock in it** *slang* be quiet! [Greek *sukkhos* a light shoe]

sock[2] *slang* ▹ *vb* **1** to hit hard ▹ *n* **2** a hard blow [origin unknown]

socket *n* **1** a device into which an electric plug can be inserted in order to make a connection in a circuit **2** *anatomy* a bony hollow into which a part or structure fits: *the hip socket* [Anglo-Norman *soket* a little ploughshare]

Socratic *adj* of the Greek philosopher Socrates, or his teachings

Socratic method *n* *philosophy* the method of instruction used by Socrates, in which a series of questions and answers lead to a logical conclusion

sod[1] *n* **1** a piece of grass-covered surface soil; turf **2** *poetic* the ground [Low German]

sod[2] *slang, chiefly Brit* ▹ *n* **1** an unpleasant person **2** *humorous* a person, esp. an unlucky one: *the poor sod hasn't been out for weeks* **3** **sod all** *slang* nothing ▹ *interj* **4** **sod it** an exclamation of annoyance [from *sodomite*] **sodding** *adj*

soda *n* **1** a simple compound of sodium, such as sodium carbonate or sodium bicarbonate **2** same as **soda water** **3** *US & Canad* a sweet fizzy drink [perhaps from Arabic]

soda bread *n* a type of bread raised with sodium bicarbonate

soda fountain *n US & Canad* **1** a counter that serves soft drinks and snacks **2** a device dispensing soda water

soda siphon *n* a sealed bottle containing soda water under pressure, which is forced up a tube when a lever is pressed

soda water *n* a fizzy drink made by charging water with carbon dioxide under pressure

sodden *adj* **1** soaking wet **2** (of someone's senses) dulled, esp. by excessive drinking [*soden*, obsolete past participle of *seethe*]

sodium *n* *chem* a very reactive soft silvery-white metallic element. Symbol: **Na** [from SODA]

sodium bicarbonate *n* a white soluble crystalline compound used in fizzy drinks, baking powder, and in medicine as an antacid

sodium carbonate *n* a colourless or white soluble crystalline compound used in the manufacture of glass, ceramics, soap, and paper, and as a cleansing agent

sodium chlorate *n* a colourless crystalline compound used as a bleaching agent, antiseptic, and weedkiller

sodium chloride *n* common table salt; a soluble colourless crystalline compound widely used as a seasoning and preservative for food and in the manufacture of chemicals, glass, and soap

sodium hydroxide *n* a white strongly alkaline solid used in the manufacture of rayon, paper, aluminium, and soap

sodomite *n* *old-fashioned* a person who practises sodomy

sodomy *n* anal intercourse [after *Sodom*, Biblical city, noted for its depravity]

Sod's Law *n informal* a humorous saying stating that if something can go wrong or turn out inconveniently it will

sofa *n* a long comfortable seat with back and arms for two or more people [Arabic *suffah*]

soft *adj* **1** easy to dent, shape, or cut: *soft material* **2** not hard; giving way easily under pressure: *a soft bed* **3** fine, smooth, or fluffy to the touch: *soft fur* **4** (of music or sounds) quiet and pleasing **5** (of light or colour) not excessively bright or harsh **6** (of a breeze or climate) temperate, mild, or pleasant **7** with smooth curves rather than sharp edges: *soft focus* **8** kind or lenient, often to excess **9** easy to influence or make demands on **10** *informal* feeble or silly; simple: *soft in the head* **11** not strong or able to endure hardship **12** (of a drug) nonaddictive **13** *informal* requiring little effort; easy: *a soft job* **14** *chem* (of water) relatively free of mineral salts and therefore easily able to make soap lather **15** loving and tender: *soft words* **16** *phonetics* denoting the consonants *c* and *g* when they are pronounced sibilantly, as in *cent* and *germ* **17** **soft on** A lenient towards: *he was accused of being soft on criminals* B experiencing romantic love for ▹ *adv* **18** in a soft manner: *to speak soft* ▹ *interj* **19** *archaic* quiet! [Old English *sōfte*] **softly** *adv*

softball *n* a game similar to baseball, played using a larger softer ball

soft-boiled *adj* (of an egg) boiled for a short time so that the yolk is still soft

soft coal *n* same as **bituminous coal**

soft drink *n* a nonalcoholic drink

soften *vb* **1** to make or become soft or softer **2** to make or become more sympathetic and less critical: *the farmers softened their opposition to the legislation* **3** to lessen the severity or difficulty of: *foreign relief softened the hardship of a terrible winter* **softener** *n*

soft furnishings *pl n* curtains, hangings, rugs, and covers

softhearted *adj* kind and sympathetic

softie *or* **softy** *n, pl* **softies** *informal* a person who is easily hurt or upset

soft option *n* the easiest of a number of choices

soft palate *n* the fleshy part at the back of the roof of the mouth

S

soft-pedal *vb* **-dalling, -dalled** *or US* **-daling, -daled 1** to deliberately avoid emphasizing (something): *he was soft-pedalling the question of tax increases* ▷ *n* **soft pedal 2** a pedal on a piano that softens the tone

soft sell *n* a method of selling based on subtle suggestion and gentle persuasion

soft-soap *vb informal* to flatter (a person)

soft-spoken *adj* speaking or said with a soft gentle voice

soft touch *n informal* a person who is easily persuaded to perform favours for, or lend money to, other people

software *n* the programs used by a computer

softwood *n* the wood of coniferous trees

soggy *adj* **-gier, -giest 1** soaked with liquid: *a soggy running track* **2** moist and heavy: *a soggy sandwich* [probably from dialect *sog* marsh] **sogginess** *n*

soh *n music* the fifth note of any ascending major scale

soigné *or fem* **soignée** (swah-nyay) *adj* neat, elegant, and well-dressed: *the soignée deputy editor of Vogue* [French]

soil¹ *n* **1** the top layer of the land surface of the earth **2** a specific type of this material: *sandy soil* **3** land, country, or region: *the first US side to lose on home soil* [Latin *solium* a seat, confused with *solum* the ground]

soil² *vb* **1** to make or become dirty or stained **2** to bring disgrace upon: *he's soiled our reputation* ▷ *n* **3** a soiled spot **4** refuse, manure, or excrement [Old French *soillier*]

soiree (swah-ray) *n* an evening social gathering [French]

sojourn (soj-urn) *literary* ▷ *n* **1** a short stay in a place ▷ *vb* **2** to stay temporarily: *he sojourned in Basle during a short illness* [Old French *sojorner*]

sol¹ *n music* same as **soh**

sol² *n chem* a liquid colloidal solution

solace (sol-iss) *n* **1** comfort in misery or disappointment: *it drove him to seek increasing solace in alcohol* **2** something that gives comfort or consolation: *his music was a solace to me during my illness* ▷ *vb* **-lacing, -laced 3** to give comfort or cheer to (a person) in time of sorrow or distress [Old French *solas*]

solar *adj* **1** of the sun: *a solar eclipse* **2** operating by or using the energy of the sun: *solar cell* [Latin *sol* the sun]

solarium (sol-air-ee-um) *n, pl* **-lariums** *or* **-laria** a place with beds equipped with ultraviolet lights used for giving people an artificial suntan [Latin: a terrace]

solar plexus *n* **1** *anatomy* a network of nerves behind the stomach **2** *not in technical use* the vulnerable part of the stomach beneath the diaphragm

solar system *n* the system containing the sun and the planets, comets, and asteroids that go round it

sold *vb* **1** the past of **sell** ▷ *adj* **2 sold on** *slang* enthusiastic and uncritical about

solder *n* **1** an alloy used for joining two metal surfaces by melting the alloy so that it forms a thin layer between the surfaces ▷ *vb* **2** to join or mend or be joined or mended with solder [Latin *solidare* to strengthen]

soldering iron *n* a hand tool with a copper tip that is heated and used to melt and apply solder

soldier *n* **1 A** a person who serves or has served in an army **B** a person who is not an officer in an army ▷ *vb* **2** to serve as a soldier [Old French *soudier*] **soldierly** *adj*

soldier of fortune *n* a man who seeks money or adventure as a soldier; mercenary

soldier on *vb* to continue one's efforts despite difficulties or pressure

sole¹ *adj* **1** being the only one; only **2** not shared; exclusive: *sole ownership* [Latin *solus* alone]

sole² *n* **1** the underside of the foot **2** the underside of a shoe **3** the lower surface of an object ▷ *vb* **soling, soled 4** to provide (a shoe) with a sole [Latin *solea* sandal]

sole³ *n, pl* **sole** *or* **soles** an edible marine flatfish [Latin *solea* a sandal (from the fish's shape)]

sole charge school *n NZ* a country school with only one teacher

solecism (sol-iss-iz-zum) *n formal* **1** a minor grammatical mistake in speech or writing **2** an action considered not to be good manners [Greek *soloikos* speaking incorrectly] **solecistic** *adj*

solely *adv* **1** only; completely: *an action intended solely to line his own pockets* **2** without others

solemn *adj* **1** very serious; deeply sincere: *my solemn promise* **2** marked by ceremony or formality: *a solemn ritual* **3** serious or glum: *a solemn look on her face* [Latin *sollemnis* appointed] **solemnly** *adv*

solemnity *n, pl* **-ties 1** the state or quality of being solemn **2** a solemn ceremony or ritual

solemnize *or* **-nise** *vb* **-nizing, -nized** *or* **-nising, -nised 1** to celebrate or perform (a ceremony, esp. of marriage) **2** to make solemn or serious **solemnization** *or* **-nisation** *n*

solenoid (sole-in-oid) *n* a coil of wire, usually cylindrical, in which a magnetic field is set up by passing a current through it [French *solénoïde*] **solenoidal** *adj*

sol-fa *n* short for **tonic sol-fa**

solicit *vb* **1** *formal* to seek or request, esp. formally: *she was brushed aside when soliciting his support for the vote* **2** to approach a person with an offer of sex in return for money [Latin *sollicitare* to harass] **solicitation** *n*

solicitor *n Brit, Austral & NZ* a lawyer who advises clients on matters of law, draws up legal documents, and prepares cases for barristers

Solicitor General *n, pl* **Solicitors General** (in Britain) the law officer of the Crown ranking next to the Attorney General (in Scotland to the Lord Advocate) and acting as his or her assistant

solicitous *adj formal* **1** anxious about someone's welfare **2** eager [Latin *sollicitus* anxious] **solicitousness** *n*

solicitude *n formal* anxiety or concern for someone's welfare

solid *adj* **1** (of a substance) in a physical state in which it resists changes in size and shape; not liquid or gaseous **2** consisting of matter all through; not hollow **3** of the same substance all through: *solid gold* **4** firm, strong, or substantial: *the solid door of a farmhouse* **5** proved or provable: *solid evidence* **6** law-abiding and respectable:

S

solid family men **7** (of a meal or food) substantial **8** without interruption; continuous or unbroken: *solid bombardment* **9** financially sound: *a solid institution* **10** strongly united or established: *a solid marriage* **11** *geom* having or relating to three dimensions **12** adequate; sound, but not brilliant: *a solid career* **13** of a single uniform colour or tone ▷ *n* **14** *geom* a three-dimensional shape **15** a solid substance [Latin *solidus* firm] **solidity** *n* **solidly** *adv*

solidarity *n, pl* **-ties** agreement in interests or aims among members of a group; total unity

solid geometry *n* the branch of geometry concerned with three-dimensional figures

solidify *vb* **-fies, -fying, -fied 1** to make or become solid or hard **2** to make or become strong or unlikely to change: *a move that solidified the allegiance of our followers* **solidification** *n*

solid-state *adj* (of an electronic device) using a semiconductor component, such as a transistor or silicon chip, in which current flow is through solid material, rather than a valve or mechanical part, in which current flow is through a vacuum

solidus *n, pl* **-di** a short oblique stroke used in text to separate items, such as *and/or*

soliloquize *or* **-quise** *vb* **-quizing, -quized** *or* **-quising, -quised** to say a soliloquy

soliloquy *n, pl* **-quies** a speech made by a person while alone, esp. in a play [Latin *solus* sole + *loqui* to speak]

> **USAGE** *Soliloquy* is sometimes wrongly used where *monologue* is meant. Both words refer to a long speech by one person, but a *monologue* can be addressed to other people, whereas in a *soliloquy* the speaker is always talking to himself or herself.

solipsism *n philosophy* the doctrine that the self is the only thing known to exist [Latin *solus* alone + *ipse* self] **solipsist** *n*

solitaire *n* **1** a game played by one person, involving moving and taking pegs in a pegboard with the object of being left with only one **2** a gem, esp. a diamond, set alone in a ring **3** *chiefly US* patience (the card game) [French]

solitary *adj* **1** experienced or performed alone: *a solitary dinner* **2** living a life of solitude: *a solitary child* **3** single; alone: *the solitary cigarette in the ashtray* **4** having few friends; lonely **5** (of a place) without people; empty ▷ *n, pl* **-taries 6** a person who lives on his or her own; hermit **7** *informal* short for **solitary confinement**: *I can't put him back in solitary* [Latin *solitarius*] **solitariness** *n*

solitary confinement *n* isolation of a prisoner in a special cell

solitude *n* the state of being alone

solo *n, pl* **-los 1** a piece of music or section of a piece of music for one performer: *a trumpet solo* **2** any performance by an individual without assistance **3** Also: **solo whist** a card game in which each person plays on his or her own ▷ *adj* **4** performed by an individual without assistance: *a solo dance* ▷ *adv* **5** by oneself; alone: *to fly solo across the Atlantic* [Latin *solus* alone] **soloist** *n*

Solomon *n* any person considered to be very wise [after 10th-century BC king of Israel]

Solomon's seal *n* a plant with greenish flowers and long waxy leaves

so long *interj* **1** *informal* farewell; goodbye ▷ *adv* **2** *S African slang* for the time being; meanwhile

solo parent *n NZ* a parent bringing up a child or children alone

solstice *n* either the shortest day of the year (**winter solstice**) or the longest day of the year (**summer solstice**) [Latin *solstitium* the standing still of the sun]

soluble *adj* **1** (of a substance) capable of being dissolved **2** (of a mystery or problem) capable of being solved **solubility** *n*

solute *n chem* the substance in a solution that is dissolved [Latin *solutus* free]

solution *n* **1** a specific answer to or way of answering a problem **2** the act or process of solving a problem **3** *chem* a mixture of two or more substances in which the molecules or atoms of the substances are completely dispersed **4** the act or process of forming a solution **5** the state of being dissolved: *the sugar is held in solution* [Latin *solutio* an unloosing]

solve *vb* **solving, solved** to find the explanation for or solution to (a mystery or problem) [Latin *solvere* to loosen] **solvable** *adj*

solvent *adj* **1** having enough money to pay off one's debts **2** (of a liquid) capable of dissolving other substances ▷ *n* **3** a liquid capable of dissolving other substances [Latin *solvens* releasing] **solvency** *n*

solvent abuse *n* the deliberate inhaling of intoxicating fumes from certain solvents

somatic *adj* of or relating to the body as distinct from the mind: *somatic symptoms* [Greek *sōma* the body]

sombre *or US* **somber** *adj* **1** serious, sad, or gloomy: *a sombre message* **2** (of a place) dim or gloomy **3** (of colour or clothes) dull or dark [Latin *sub* beneath + *umbra* shade] **sombrely** *or US* **somberly** *adv*

sombrero *n, pl* **-ros** a wide-brimmed Mexican hat [Spanish]

some *adj* **1** unknown or unspecified: *some man called for you* **2** an unknown or unspecified quantity or number of: *I've got some money* **3 A** a considerable number or amount of: *he lived some years afterwards* **B** a little: *show some respect* **4** *informal* an impressive or remarkable: *that was some game!* ▷ *pron* **5** certain unknown or unspecified people or things: *some can teach and others can't* **6** an unknown or unspecified quantity of something or number of people or things: *he will sell some in his pub* ▷ *adv* **7** approximately: *some thirty pounds* [Old English *sum*]

somebody *pron* **1** some person; someone ▷ *n, pl* **-bodies 2** a person of great importance: *he was a somebody*

> **USAGE** See at **everyone**.

someday *adv* at some unspecified time in the future

somehow *adv* **1** in some unspecified way **2** for some unknown reason: *somehow I can't do it*

someone *pron* some person; somebody

> **USAGE** See at **everyone**.

S

someplace *adv US & Canad informal* same as **somewhere**

somersault *n* **1** a leap or roll in which the head is placed on the ground and the trunk and legs are turned over it ▷ *vb* **2** to perform a somersault [Old French *soubresault*]

something *pron* **1** an unspecified or unknown thing; some thing: *there was something wrong* **2** an unspecified or unknown amount: *something less than a hundred* **3** an impressive or important person, thing, or event: *isn't that something?* **4 something else** *slang, chiefly US* a remarkable person or thing ▷ *adv* **5** to some degree; somewhat: *he looks something like me*

-something *combining form* a person whose age can be approximately expressed by a specific decade: *twentysomethings* [from the US television series *thirtysomething*]

sometime *adv* **1** at some unspecified point of time ▷ *adj* **2** former: *a sometime actor*

> **USAGE** The form *sometime* should not be used to refer to a fairly long period of time: *he has been away for some time* (not *for sometime*).

sometimes *adv* now and then; from time to time

someway *adv* in some unspecified manner

somewhat *adv* rather; a bit: *somewhat surprising*

somewhere *adv* **1** in, to, or at some unknown or unspecified place, point, or amount: *somewhere down south; somewhere between 35 and 45 per cent* **2 getting somewhere** *informal* making progress

somnambulism *n formal* the condition of walking in one's sleep [Latin *somnus* sleep + *ambulare* to walk] **somnambulist** *n*

somnolent *adj formal* drowsy; sleepy [Latin *somnus* sleep] **somnolence** *n*

son *n* **1** a male offspring **2** a form of address for a man or boy who is younger than the speaker **3** a male who comes from a certain place or one closely connected with a certain thing: *a good son of the church*. ▷ Related adjective: **filial** [Old English *sunu*]

Son *n Christianity* the second member of the Trinity, Jesus Christ

sonar *n* a device that locates objects by the reflection of sound waves: used in underwater navigation and target detection [*so(und) na(vigation and) r(anging)*]

sonata *n* a piece of classical music, usually in three or more movements, for piano or for another instrument with or without piano [Italian]

son et lumière (sonn ay loom-yair) *n* an entertainment staged at night at a famous building or historical site, at which its history is described by a speaker accompanied by lighting effects and music [French, literally: sound and light]

song *n* **1** a piece of music with words, composed for the voice **2** the tuneful call made by certain birds or insects **3** the act or process of singing: *he broke into song* **4 for a song** at a bargain price **5 make a song and dance** *informal* to make an unnecessary fuss [Old English *sang*]

songbird *n* any bird that has a musical call

songololo (song-gol-loll-o) *n, pl* **-los** *S African* a kind of millipede [Nguni (language group of southern Africa) *ukusonga* to roll up]

songstress *n* a female singer of popular songs

song thrush *n* a common thrush that repeats each note of its song

sonic *adj* of, involving, or producing sound [Latin *sonus* sound]

sonic barrier *n* same as **sound barrier**

sonic boom *n* a loud explosive sound caused by the shock wave of an aircraft travelling at supersonic speed

son-in-law *n, pl* **sons-in-law** the husband of one's son or daughter

sonnet *n prosody* a verse form consisting of 14 lines with a fixed rhyme scheme and rhythm pattern [Old Provençal *sonet* a little poem]

sonny *n* a familiar, often patronizing, term of address to a boy or man

sonorous *adj* **1** (of a sound) deep or rich **2** (of speech) using language that is unnecessarily complicated and difficult to understand; pompous [Latin *sonor* a noise] **sonority** *n*

sook *Austral & NZ informal* ▷ *vb* **1** to complain peevishly ▷ *n* **2** a peevish complaint [from SULK] **sooky** *adj*

soon *adv* **1** in or after a short time; before long **2 as soon as** at the very moment that: *as soon as he had closed the door* **3 as soon ... as** used to indicate that the first alternative is slightly preferable to the second: *they'd just as soon die for him as live* [Old English *sōna*]

sooner *adv* **1** the comparative of **soon**: *I only wish I'd been back sooner* **2** rather; in preference: *he would sooner leave the party than break with me* **3 no sooner ... than** immediately after or when: *no sooner had he spoken than the stench drifted up* **4 sooner or later** eventually

> **USAGE** *When* is sometimes used instead of *than* after *no sooner*, but this use is generally regarded as incorrect: *no sooner had he arrived than* (not *when*) *the telephone rang*.

soot *n* a black powder formed by the incomplete burning of organic substances such as coal [Old English *sōt*] **sooty** *adj*

sooth *n* **in sooth** *archaic, poetic* in truth [Old English *sōth*]

soothe *vb* **soothing, soothed 1** to make (a worried or angry person) calm and relaxed **2** (of an ointment or cream) to relieve (pain) [Old English *sōthian* to prove] **soothing** *adj*

soothsayer *n* a person who makes predictions about the future; prophet

sop *n* **1** a small bribe or concession given or made to someone to keep them from causing trouble: *a sop to her conscience* **2** *informal* a stupid or weak person **3 sops** food soaked in a liquid before being eaten ▷ *vb* **sopping, sopped 4 sop up** to soak up or absorb (liquid) [Old English *sopp*]

sophism *n* an argument that seems reasonable but is actually false and misleading [Greek *sophisma* ingenious trick]

sophist *n* a person who uses clever but false arguments [Greek *sophistēs* a wise man] **sophistic** *adj*

sophisticate *vb* **-cating, -cated 1** to make (someone) less natural or innocent, such as by education **2** to make (a machine or method)

more complex or refined ▷ *n* **3** a sophisticated person [Latin *sophisticus* sophistic]
sophistication *n*

sophisticated *adj* **1** having or appealing to fashionable and refined tastes and habits: *a sophisticated restaurant* **2** intelligent, knowledgeable, or able to appreciate culture and the arts: *a sophisticated concert audience* **3** (of machines or methods) complex and using advanced technology

sophistry *n* **1** the practice of using arguments which seem clever but are actually false and misleading **2** *pl* **-ries** an instance of this

sophomore *n chiefly US & Canad* a second-year student at a secondary (high) school or college [probably from earlier *sophum*, variant of *sophism*]

soporific *adj* **1** causing sleep ▷ *n* **2** a drug that causes sleep [Latin *sopor* sleep]

sopping *adj* completely soaked; wet through. Also: **sopping wet**

soppy *adj* **-pier, -piest** *informal* foolishly sentimental: *a soppy love song* **soppily** *adv*

soprano *n, pl* **-pranos** **1** the highest adult female voice **2** the voice of a young boy before puberty **3** a singer with such a voice **4** the highest or second highest instrument in a family of instruments ▷ *adj* **5** denoting a musical instrument that is the highest or second highest pitched in its family: *the soprano saxophone* **6** of or relating to the highest female voice, or the voice of a young boy: *the part is quite possibly the most demanding soprano role Wagner ever wrote* [Italian]

sorbet (**saw**-bay) *n* a flavoured water ice [French, from Arabic *sharbah* a drink]

sorcerer *or fem* **sorceress** *n* a person who uses magic powers; a wizard [Old French *sorcier*]

sorcery *n, pl* **-ceries** witchcraft or magic [Old French *sorcerie*]

sordid *adj* **1** dirty, depressing, and squalid: *a sordid backstreet in a slum area* **2** relating to sex in a crude or unpleasant way: *the sordid details of his affair* **3** involving immoral and selfish behaviour: *the sordid history of the slave trade* [Latin *sordidus*]

sore *adj* **1** (of a wound, injury, etc.) painfully sensitive; tender **2** causing annoyance and resentment: *a sore point* **3** upset and angered: *she's still sore about last night* **4** *literary* urgent; pressing: *in sore need of firm government* ▷ *n* **5** a painful or sensitive wound or injury ▷ *adv* **6** **sore afraid** *archaic* greatly frightened [Old English *sār*]

sorely *adv* greatly: *sorely disappointed*

sorghum *n* a grass grown for grain and as a source of syrup [Italian *sorgo*]

sorority *n, pl* **-ties** *chiefly US* a society of female students [Latin *soror* sister]

sorrel *n* a plant with bitter-tasting leaves which are used in salads and sauces [Old French *surele*]

sorrow *n* **1** deep sadness or regret, associated with death or sympathy for another's misfortune **2** a particular cause of this ▷ *vb* **3** *literary* to feel deep sadness (about death or another's misfortunes); mourn [Old English *sorg*]
sorrowful *adj* **sorrowfully** *adv*

sorry *adj* **-rier, -riest** **1** (often foll. by *for* or *about*) feeling or expressing pity, sympathy, grief, or regret: *I'm sorry about this* **2** in bad mental or physical condition: *a sorry state* **3** poor: *a sorry performance* ▷ *interj* **4** an exclamation expressing apology or asking someone to repeat what he or she has said [Old English *sārig*]

sort *n* **1** a class, group, or kind sharing certain characteristics or qualities **2** *informal* a type of character: *she was a good sort* **3** a more or less adequate example: *a sort of dream machine* **4** **of sorts** *or* **of a sort** **A** of a poorer quality: *she was wearing a uniform of sorts* **B** of a kind not quite as intended or desired: *it was a reward, of sorts, for my efforts* **5** **out of sorts** not in normal good health or temper **6** **sort of** as it were; rather: *I sort of quit; sort of insensitive* ▷ *vb* **7** to arrange (things or people) according to class or type **8** to put (something) into working order; fix **9** to arrange (information on a computer) in an order the user finds convenient [Latin *sors* fate]

USAGE See at **kind²**.

sort code *n* a sequence of numbers printed on a cheque or bank card identifying the branch holding the account

sortie *n* **1** a short or relatively short return trip **2** (of troops) a raid into enemy territory **3** an operational flight made by a military aircraft ▷ *vb* **-tieing, -tied** **4** to make a sortie [French]

sort out *vb* **1** to find a solution to (a problem): *did they sort out the mess?* **2** to take or separate (things or people) from a larger group: *to sort out the wheat from the chaff* **3** to organize (things or people) into an orderly and disciplined group **4** **sort someone out** to deal with a person, esp. an awkward one **5** *informal* to punish or tell off (someone)

SOS *n* **1** an international code signal of distress in which the letters SOS are repeatedly spelt out in Morse code **2** *informal* any call for help

so-so *informal* ▷ *adj* **1** neither good nor bad ▷ *adv* **2** in an average or indifferent way

sot *n* a person who is frequently drunk [Old English *sott*] **sottish** *adj*

sotto voce (sot-toe **voe**-chay) *adv* with a soft voice [Italian]

sou *n* **1** a former French coin of low value **2** *old-fashioned* a very small amount of money: *the tax man never saw a sou from this income* [French]

soubrette (soo-**brett**) *n* a minor female role in comedy, often that of a pert maid [French]

soubriquet *n* same as **sobriquet**

soufflé (**soo**-flay) *n* a light fluffy dish made with beaten egg whites and other ingredients such as cheese or chocolate [French]

sough (rhymes with **now**) *vb literary* (of the wind) to make a sighing sound [Old English *swōgan*]

sought (**sawt**) *vb* the past of **seek**

souk (**sook**) *n* an open-air marketplace in Muslim countries [Arabic *sūq*]

soul *n* **1** the spiritual part of a person, regarded as the centre of personality, intellect, will, and emotions: believed by many to survive the body after death **2** the essential part or fundamental nature of anything: *the soul of contemporary America* **3** deep and sincere feelings: *you've got no soul* **4** Also called: **soul music** a type of music using blues and elements of jazz, gospel, and pop **5** a person regarded as a good example of some

S

quality: *the soul of prudence* **6** a person: *there was hardly a soul there* **7 the life and soul** *informal* a person who is lively, entertaining, and fun to be with: *the life and soul of the campus* [Old English *sāwol*]

soul-destroying *adj* (of an occupation or situation) very boring and repetitive

soul food *n informal* food, such as chitterlings and yams, which is traditionally eaten by African-Americans

soulful *adj* expressing deep feelings: *a soulful performance of one of Tchaikovsky's songs*

soulless *adj* **1** lacking human qualities; mechanical: *soulless materialism* **2** (of a person) lacking in sensitivity or emotion

soul mate *n* a person with whom one gets along well because of having shared interests and experiences

soul-searching *n* deep examination of one's actions and feelings

sound[1] *n* **1** anything that can be heard; noise **2** *physics* mechanical vibrations that travel in waves through the air, water, etc. **3** the sensation produced by such vibrations in the organs of hearing **4** the impression one has of something: *I didn't really like the sound of it* **5 sounds** *slang* music, esp. rock, jazz, or pop ▹ *vb* **6** to make or cause (an instrument, etc.) to make a sound **7** to announce (something) by a sound: *guns sound the end of the two minutes silence* **8** to make a noise with a certain quality: *her voice sounded shrill* **9** to suggest (a particular idea or quality): *his argument sounded false* **10** to pronounce (something) clearly: *to sound one's r's* ▹ See also **sound off** [Latin *sonus*]

sound[2] *adj* **1** free from damage, injury, or decay; in good condition **2** firm or substantial: *sound documentary evidence* **3** financially safe or stable: *a sound investment* **4** showing good judgment or reasoning; wise: *sound advice* **5** morally correct; honest **6** (of sleep) deep and uninterrupted **7** thorough: *a sound defeat* ▹ *adv* **8 sound asleep** in a deep sleep [Old English *sund*] **soundly** *adv*

sound[3] *vb* **1** to measure the depth of (a well, the sea, etc.) **2** *med* to examine (a part of the body) by tapping or with a stethoscope ▹ See also **sound out** [Old French *sonder*]

sound[4] *n* a channel between two larger areas of sea or between an island and the mainland [Old English *sund*]

soundalike *n* a person or thing that sounds like another, often well-known, person or thing

sound barrier *n* a sudden increase in the force of air against an aircraft flying at or above the speed of sound

sound bite *n* a short pithy sentence or phrase extracted from a longer speech for use on television or radio: *complicated political messages cannot be properly reduced to fifteen-second sound bites*

soundcard *n* a printed circuit board inserted into a computer, enabling the output and manipulation of sound

sound effects *pl n* sounds artificially produced to make a play, esp. a radio play, more realistic

sounding board *n* a person or group used to test a new idea or policy

soundings *pl n* **1** measurements of the depth of a river, lake, or sea **2** questions asked of someone in order to find out his or her opinion: *soundings among colleagues had revealed enthusiasm for the plan*

sound off *vb* to speak angrily or loudly

sound out *vb* to question (someone) in order to discover his or her opinion: *you might try sounding him out about his family*

soundproof *adj* **1** (of a room) built so that no sound can get in or out ▹ *vb* **2** to make (a room) soundproof

soundtrack *n* the recorded sound accompaniment to a film

sound wave *n* a wave that carries sound

soup *n* **1** a food made by cooking meat, fish, or vegetables in a stock **2 in the soup** *slang* in trouble or difficulties [Old French *soupe*]
soupy *adj*

soupçon (soop-sonn) *n* a slight amount; dash [French]

souped-up *adj slang* (of a car, motorbike, or engine) adjusted so as to be faster or more powerful than normal

soup kitchen *n* a place where food and drink are served to needy people

sour *adj* **1** having a sharp biting taste like the taste of lemon juice or vinegar **2** made acid or bad, such as when milk ferments **3** (of a person's mood) bad-tempered and unfriendly **4 go** *or* **turn sour** to become less enjoyable or happy: *the dream has turned sour* ▹ *vb* **5** to make or become less enjoyable or friendly: *relations soured shortly after the war* [Old English *sūr*] **sourly** *adv*

source *n* **1** the origin or starting point: *the source of discontent among fishermen* **2** any person, book, or organization that provides information for a news report or for research **3** the area or spring where a river or stream begins ▹ *vb* **4** to establish a supplier of (a product, etc) **5** (foll. by *from*) to originate from [Latin *surgere* to rise]

source code *n computers* the original form of a computer program before it is converted into a machine-readable code

sour cream *n* cream soured by bacteria for use in cooking

sour grapes *n* the attitude of pretending to hate something because one cannot have it oneself

sourpuss *n informal* a person who is always gloomy, pessimistic, or bitter

souse *vb* **sousing, soused 1** to plunge (something) into water or other liquid **2** to drench **3** to steep or cook (food) in a marinade ▹ *n* **4** the liquid used in pickling **5** the act or process of sousing [Old French *sous*]

soused *adj slang* drunk

soutane (soo-tan) *n RC Church* a priest's robe [French]

south *n* **1** one of the four cardinal points of the compass, at 180° from north **2** the direction along a line of latitude towards the South Pole **3 the south** any area lying in or towards the south ▹ *adj* **4** situated in, moving towards, or facing the south **5** (esp. of the wind) from the south ▹ *adv* **6** in, to, or towards the south [Old English *sūth*]

South *n* **1 the South** **A** the southern part of England **B** (in the US) the Southern states that formed the Confederacy during the Civil War

c the countries of the world that are not technically and economically advanced ▷ *adj* **2** of or denoting the southern part of a country, area, etc.

South African *adj* **1** of the Republic of South Africa ▷ *n* **2** a person from the Republic of South Africa

southbound *adj* going towards the south

southeast *n* **1** the direction midway between south and east **2 the southeast** any area lying in or towards the southeast ▷ *adj also* **southeastern** **3** of or denoting that part of a country or area which lies in the southeast **4** situated in, moving towards, or facing the southeast **5** (esp. of the wind) from the southeast ▷ *adv* **6** in, to, or towards the southeast **southeasterly** *adj, adv, n*

Southeast *n* the southeast of Britain, esp. the London area

southeaster *n* a strong wind or storm from the southeast

southerly *adj* **1** of or in the south ▷ *adv, adj* **2** towards the south **3** from the south: *light southerly winds*

southern *adj* **1** situated in or towards the south **2** facing or moving towards the south **3** (*sometimes cap*) of or characteristic of the south or South **southernmost** *adj*

Southerner *n* a person from the south of a country or area, esp. England or the US

southern hemisphere *n* that half of the globe lying south of the equator

southern lights *pl n* same as **aurora australis**

southpaw *informal* ▷ *n* **1** any left-handed person, esp. a boxer ▷ *adj* **2** left-handed

South Pole *n* the southernmost point on the earth's axis, at a latitude of 90°S, which has very low temperatures

South Seas *pl n* the seas south of the equator

southward *adj, adv also* **southwards** **1** towards the south ▷ *n* **2** the southward part or direction

southwest *n* **1** the direction midway between west and south **2 the southwest** any area lying in or towards the southwest ▷ *adj also* **southwestern** **3** of or denoting that part of a country or area which lies in the southwest **4** situated in, moving towards, or facing the southwest **5** (esp. of the wind) from the southwest ▷ *adv* **6** in, to, or towards the southwest **southwesterly** *adj, adv, n*

Southwest *n* the southwestern part of Britain, esp. Cornwall, Devon, and Somerset

southwester *n* a strong wind or storm from the southwest

souvenir *n* an object that reminds one of a certain place, occasion, or person; memento [French]

sou'wester *n* **1** a seaman's hat with a broad brim that covers the back of the neck **2** same as **southwester** [a contraction of SOUTHWESTER]

sovereign *n* **1** the Royal ruler of a country **2** a former British gold coin worth one pound sterling ▷ *adj* **3** independent of outside authority; not governed by another country: *a sovereign nation* **4** supreme in rank or authority: *a sovereign queen* **5** *old-fashioned* excellent or outstanding: *a sovereign remedy for epilepsy* [Old French *soverain*]

sovereignty *n, pl* **-ties** **1** the political power a nation has to govern itself **2** the position or authority of a sovereign

soviet *n* (in the former Soviet Union) an elected government council at the local, regional, and national levels [Russian *sovyet*]

Soviet *adj* **1** of the former Soviet Union ▷ *n* **2** a person from the former Soviet Union

sow[1] *vb* **sowing, sowed, sown** *or* **sowed** **1** to scatter or plant (seed) in or on (the ground) so that it may grow: *sow sweet peas in pots; farmers sow their fields with fewer varieties* **2** to implant or introduce: *to sow confusion among the other members* [Old English *sāwan*]

sow[2] *n* a female adult pig [Old English *sugu*]

soya bean *or US & Canad* **soybean** *n* a plant whose bean is used for food and as a source of oil [Japanese *shōyu*]

soy sauce *n* a salty dark brown sauce made from fermented soya beans, used in Chinese cookery

sozzled *adj Brit, Austral & NZ informal* drunk [origin unknown]

spa *n* a mineral-water spring or a resort where such a spring is found [after *Spa*, a watering place in Belgium]

space *n* **1** the unlimited three-dimensional expanse in which all objects exist **2** an interval of distance or time between two points, objects, or events **3** a blank portion or area **4** unoccupied area or room: *barely enough space to walk around* **5** the region beyond the earth's atmosphere containing other planets, stars, and galaxies; the universe ▷ *vb* **spacing, spaced** **6** (often foll. by *out*) to place or arrange (things) at intervals or with spaces between them [Latin *spatium*]

space age *n* **1** the period in which the exploration of space has become possible ▷ *adj* **space-age** **2** very modern, futuristic, or using the latest technology: *a space-age helmet*

space-bar *n* a bar on a keyboard that is pressed in order to leave a space between words or letters

space capsule *n* the part of a spacecraft in which the crew live and work

spacecraft *n* a vehicle that can be used for travel in space

spaced-out *adj informal* vague and dreamy, as if influenced by drugs

Space Invaders *n trademark* an arcade or computer game in which players try to defend themselves against attacking enemy spacecraft

spaceman *or fem* **spacewoman** *n, pl* **-men** *or* **-women** a person who travels in space

space probe *n* a small vehicle equipped to gather scientific information, normally transmitted back to earth by radio, about a planet or conditions in space

spaceship *n* (in science fiction) a spacecraft used for travel between planets and galaxies

space shuttle *n* a manned reusable spacecraft designed for making regular flights

space station *n* a large manned artificial satellite used as a base for scientific research in space and for people travelling in space

spacesuit *n* a sealed protective suit worn by astronauts

space-time *or* **space-time continuum** *n* *physics* the four-dimensional continuum having three space coordinates and one time coordinate that together completely specify the location of an object or an event

spacious *adj* having or providing a lot of space; roomy **spaciousness** *n*

spade[1] *n* **1** a tool for digging, with a flat steel blade and a long wooden handle **2** **call a spade a spade** to speak plainly and frankly [Old English *spadu*]

spade[2] *n* **1** **A** **spades** the suit of playing cards marked with a black leaf-shaped symbol **B** a card with one or more of these symbols on it **2** *offensive* a Black person **3** **in spades** *informal* in plenty: *all you need is talent in spades* [Italian *spada* sword, used as an emblem on playing cards]

spadework *n* dull or routine work done as preparation for a project or activity

spadix (spade-ix) *n, pl* **spadices** (spade-ice-eez) *botany* a spike of small flowers on a fleshy stem [Greek: torn-off frond]

spaghetti *n* pasta in the form of long strings [Italian]

spaghetti junction *n* a junction between motorways with a large number of intersecting roads [from the nickname of the Gravelly Hill Interchange, Birmingham]

spaghetti western *n* a cowboy film made in Europe by an Italian director, esp in the 1960s

spake *vb archaic* a past tense of **speak**

spam *vb* **spamming, spammed** **1** to send unsolicited messages simultaneously to a typically large number of email addresses ▷ *n* **2** unsolicited messages sent in this way [from the repeated use of the word *Spam* in a popular sketch from the British television show *Monty Python's Flying Circus*]

Spam *n trademark* a cold meat made from pork and spices

span *n* **1** the interval or distance between two points, such as the ends of a bridge **2** the complete extent: *that span of time* **3** short for **wingspan** **4** a unit of length based on the width of a stretched hand, usually taken as nine inches (23 centimetres) ▷ *vb* **spanning, spanned** **5** to stretch or extend across, over, or around: *her career spanned fifty years; to span the Danube* [Old English *spann*]

spangle *n* **1** a small piece of shiny material used as a decoration on clothes or hair; sequin ▷ *vb* **-gling, -gled** **2** to cover or decorate (something) with spangles [Middle English *spange* clasp]

Spaniard *n* a person from Spain

spaniel *n* a dog with long drooping ears and a silky coat [Old French *espaigneul* Spanish (dog)]

Spanish *adj* **1** of Spain ▷ *n* **2** the official language of Spain, Mexico, and most countries of South and Central America ▷ *pl n* **3** **the Spanish** the people of Spain

Spanish fly *n* a beetle, the dried body of which is used in medicine

Spanish Main *n* **1** the N coast of South America **2** the Caribbean Sea, the S part of which was frequented by pirates

spank *vb* **1** to slap (someone) with the open hand, on the buttocks or legs ▷ *n* **2** such a slap [probably imitative]

spanking[1] *n* a series of spanks, usually as a punishment for children

spanking[2] *adj* **1** *informal* outstandingly fine or smart: *spanking new uniforms* **2** very fast: *a spanking pace*

spanner *n* **1** a tool for gripping and turning a nut or bolt **2** **throw a spanner in the works** *informal* to cause a problem that prevents things from running smoothly [German *spannen* to stretch]

spanspek *n S African* a cantaloupe melon [Afrikaans]

spar[1] *n* a pole used as a ship's mast, boom, or yard [Old Norse *sperra* beam]

spar[2] *vb* **sparring, sparred** **1** *boxing & martial arts* to fight using light blows for practice **2** to argue with someone ▷ *n* **3** an argument [Old English]

spar[3] *n* a light-coloured, crystalline, easily split mineral [Middle Low German]

spare *adj* **1** extra to what is needed: *there are some spare chairs at the back* **2** able to be used when needed: *a spare parking space* **3** (of a person) tall and thin **4** (of a style) plain and without unnecessary decoration or details; austere: *a spare but beautiful novel* **5** *Brit slang* frantic with anger or worry: *the boss went spare* ▷ *n* **6** an extra thing kept in case it is needed ▷ *vb* **sparing, spared** **7** to stop from killing, punishing, or injuring (someone) **8** to protect (someone) from (something) unpleasant: *spare me the sermon* **9** to be able to afford or give: *can you spare me a moment to talk?* **10** **not spare oneself** to try one's hardest **11** **to spare** more than is required: *a few hours to spare* [Old English *sparian*]

spare part *n* a replacement piece of mechanical or electrical equipment kept in case the original component becomes damaged or worn

spareribs *pl n* a cut of pork ribs with most of the meat trimmed off

spare tyre *n* **1** an additional tyre kept in a motor vehicle in case of puncture **2** *slang* a roll of fat just above the waist

sparing *adj* (sometimes foll. by *of*) economical (with): *she was mercifully sparing in her use of jargon* **sparingly** *adv*

spark *n* **1** a fiery particle thrown out from a fire or caused by friction **2** a short flash of light followed by a sharp crackling noise, produced by a sudden electrical discharge through the air **3** a trace or hint: *a spark of goodwill* **4** liveliness, enthusiasm, or humour: *that spark in her eye* ▷ *vb* **5** to give off sparks **6** to cause to start; trigger: *the incident sparked off an angry exchange* [Old English *spearca*]

sparkie *n Brit, Austral & NZ informal* electrician

sparkle *vb* **-kling, -kled** **1** to glitter with many bright points of light **2** (of wine or mineral water) to be slightly fizzy **3** to be lively, witty, and intelligent ▷ *n* **4** a small bright point of light **5** liveliness and wit [Middle English *sparklen*] **sparkling** *adj*

sparkler *n* **1** a type of hand-held firework that throws out sparks **2** *informal* a sparkling gem; esp. a diamond

spark plug *n* a device in an internal-combustion engine that ignites the fuel by producing an electric spark

sparring partner *n* **1** a person who practises with a boxer during training **2** a person with whom one has friendly arguments

sparrow *n* a very common small brown or grey bird which feeds on seeds and insects [Old English *spearwa*]

sparrowhawk *n* a small hawk which preys on smaller birds

sparse *adj* small in amount and spread out widely: *a sparse population* [Latin *sparsus*] **sparsely** *adv*

Spartan *adj* **1** of or relating to the ancient Greek city of Sparta **2** (of a way of life) strict or simple and with no luxuries: *Spartan accommodation* ▷ *n* **3** a citizen of Sparta **4** a person who leads a strict or simple life without luxuries

spasm *n* **1** a sudden tightening of the muscles, over which one has no control **2** a sudden burst of activity or feeling: *a spasm of applause*; *sudden spasms of anger* [Greek *spasmos* a cramp]

spasmodic *adj* taking place in sudden short spells: *spasmodic bouts of illness* **spasmodically** *adv*

spastic *n* **1** *old-fashioned, offensive* a person who has cerebral palsy, and therefore has difficulty controlling his or her muscles ▷ *adj* **2** affected by involuntary muscle contractions: *a spastic colon* **3** *old-fashioned, offensive* having cerebral palsy [Greek *spasmos* a cramp]

spat[1] *n* a slight quarrel [probably imitative]

spat[2] *vb* a past of **spit**[1]

spate *n* **1** a large number of things happening within a period of time: *a spate of bombings* **2** a fast flow or outpouring: *an incomprehensible spate of words* **3** **in spate** *chiefly Brit* (of a river) flooded [origin unknown]

spathe *n botany* a large leaf that surrounds the base of a flower cluster [Greek *spathē* a blade]

spatial *adj* of or relating to size, area, or position: *spatial dimensions* **spatially** *adv*

spats *pl n* cloth or leather coverings formerly worn by men over the ankle and instep [obsolete *spatterdash* a long gaiter]

spatter *vb* **1** to scatter or splash (a substance, esp. a liquid) in scattered drops: *spattering mud in all directions* **2** to sprinkle (an object or a surface) with a liquid ▷ *n* **3** the sound of spattering **4** something spattered, such as a spot or splash [imitative]

spatula *n* a utensil with a broad flat blade, used in cooking and by doctors [Latin: a broad piece]

spawn *n* **1** the jelly-like mass of eggs laid by fish, amphibians, or molluscs ▷ *vb* **2** (of fish, amphibians, or molluscs) to lay eggs **3** to cause (something) to be created: *the depressed economy spawned the riots* [Anglo-Norman *espaundre*]

spay *vb* to remove the ovaries from (a female animal) [Old French *espeer* to cut with the sword]

spaza shop *n S African slang* a small informal shop in a township, often run from a private house [from township slang *spaza* camouflaged]

speak *vb* **speaking, spoke, spoken** **1** to say words; talk **2** to communicate or express (something) in words **3** to give a speech or lecture **4** to know how to talk in (a specified language): *I don't speak French* **5** **on speaking terms** on good terms; friendly **6** **so to speak** as it were **7** **speak one's mind** to express one's opinions honestly and plainly **8** **to speak of** of a significant nature: *no licensing laws to speak of* [Old English *specan*]

speakeasy *n, pl* **-easies** *US* a place where alcoholic drink was sold illegally during Prohibition

speaker *n* **1** a person who speaks, esp. someone making a speech **2** a person who speaks a particular language: *a fluent Tibetan and English speaker* **3** same as **loudspeaker**

Speaker *n* the official chairman of a law-making body

speakerphone *n* a telephone that has an external microphone and loudspeaker, allowing several people to participate in a call at the same time

speak for *vb* **1** to speak on behalf of (other people) **2** **speak for itself** to be so obvious that no further comment is necessary: *his work on the convention speaks for itself* **3** **speak for yourself!** *informal* do not presume that other people agree with you!

speak up *or* **speak out** *vb* **1** to state one's beliefs bravely and firmly **2** to speak more loudly and clearly

spear[1] *n* **1** a weapon consisting of a long pole with a sharp point ▷ *vb* **2** to pierce (someone or something) with a spear or other pointed object: *she took her fork and speared an oyster from its shell* [Old English *spere*]

spear[2] *n* **1** a slender shoot, such as of grass **2** a single stalk of broccoli or asparagus [probably variant of *spire*]

spearhead *vb* **1** to lead (an attack or a campaign) ▷ *n* **2** the leading force in an attack or campaign

spearmint *n* a minty flavouring used for sweets and toothpaste, which comes from a purple-flowered plant

spec *n* **on spec** *informal* as a risk or gamble: *I still tend to buy on spec*

special *adj* **1** distinguished from or better than others of its kind: *a special occasion* **2** designed or reserved for a specific purpose: *special equipment* **3** not usual; different from normal: *a special case* **4** particular or primary: *a special interest in gifted children* **5** relating to the education of children with disabilities: *a special school* ▷ *n* **6** a product, TV programme, etc., which is only available or shown at a certain time: *a two-hour Christmas special live from Hollywood* **7** a meal, usually at a low price, in a bar or restaurant **8** short for **special constable** [Latin *specialis*] **specially** *adv*

USAGE See at **especial**.

Special Branch *n* (in Britain and S Africa) the department of the police force that is concerned with political security

special constable *n* a person recruited for occasional police duties, such as in an emergency

special delivery *n* the delivery of a piece of mail outside the time of a scheduled delivery, for an extra fee

special effects *pl n films* techniques used in the production of scenes that cannot be achieved by

S

normal methods: *the special effects and make-up are totally convincing*

specialist *n* **1** a person who is an expert in a particular activity or subject **2** a doctor who concentrates on treating one particular category of diseases or the diseases of one particular part of the body: *an eye specialist* ▷ *adj* **3** particular to or concentrating on one subject or activity: *a specialist comic shop*

speciality *or esp US & Canad* **specialty** *n, pl* **-ties** **1** a special interest or skill **2** a service, product, or type of food specialized in

specialize *or* **-lise** *vb* **-lizing, -lized** *or* **-lising, -lised** **1** (often foll. by *in*) to concentrate all one's efforts on studying a particular subject, occupation, or activity: *an expert who specializes in transport* **2** to modify (something) for a special use or purpose: *plants have evolved and specialized in every type of habitat* **specialization** *or* **-lisation** *n*

special licence *n Brit* a licence allowing a marriage to take place without following all the usual legal procedures

specialty *n, pl* **-ties** *chiefly US & Canad* same as **speciality**

specie *n* coins as distinct from paper money [Latin *in specie* in kind]

species *n, pl* **-cies** *biol* one of the groups into which a genus is divided, the members of which are able to interbreed [Latin: appearance]

specific *adj* **1** particular or definite: *a specific area of economic policy* **2** precise and exact: *try and be more specific* ▷ *n* **3** **specifics** particular qualities or aspects of something: *the specifics of the situation* **4** *med* any drug used to treat a particular disease [Latin *species* kind + *facere* to make] **specifically** *adv* **specificity** *n*

specification *n* **1** a detailed description of features in the design of something: *engines built to racing specification* **2** a requirement or detail which is clearly stated: *the main specification was that a good degree was required* **3** the specifying of something

specific gravity *n physics* the ratio of the density of a substance to the density of water

specific heat capacity *n physics* the quantity of heat required to raise the temperature of unit mass of a substance by one degree centigrade

specify *vb* **-fies, -fying, -fied** **1** to state or describe (something) clearly **2** to state (something) as a condition: *the rules specify the number of prisoners to be kept in each cell* [Medieval Latin *specificare* to describe]

specimen *n* **1** an individual or part regarded as typical of its group or class **2** *med* a sample of tissue, blood, or urine taken for analysis **3** *informal* a person: *I'm quite a healthy specimen* [Latin: mark, proof]

specious (**spee**-shuss) *adj* apparently correct or true, but actually wrong or false [Latin *species* outward appearance]

speck *n* **1** a very small mark or spot **2** a small or tiny piece of something: *a speck of fluff* [Old English *specca*]

speckle *vb* **-ling, -led** **1** to mark (something) with speckles ▷ *n* **2** a small mark or spot, such as on the skin or on an egg [Middle Dutch *spekkel*] **speckled** *adj*

specs *pl n informal* short for **spectacles**

spectacle *n* **1** a strange, interesting, or ridiculous scene **2** an impressive public show: *the opening ceremony of the Olympics was an impressive spectacle* **3** **make a spectacle of oneself** to draw attention to oneself by behaving foolishly [Latin *spectare* to watch]

spectacles *pl n* a pair of glasses for correcting faulty vision

spectacular *adj* **1** impressive, grand, or dramatic ▷ *n* **2** a spectacular show **spectacularly** *adv*

spectate *vb* **-tating, -tated** to be a spectator; watch

spectator *n* a person viewing anything; onlooker [Latin *spectare* to watch]

spectator ion *n chem* an ion which is present in a mixture but plays no part in a reaction

spectre *or US* **specter** *n* **1** a ghost **2** an unpleasant or menacing vision in one's imagination: *the spectre of famine* [Latin *spectrum*] **spectral** *adj*

spectrometer (speck-**trom**-it-er) *n physics* an instrument for producing a spectrum, usually one in which wavelength, energy, or intensity can be measured

spectroscope *n physics* an instrument for forming or recording a spectrum by passing a light ray through a prism or grating

spectrum *n, pl* **-tra** **1** *physics* the distribution of colours produced when white light is dispersed by a prism or grating: violet, indigo, blue, green, yellow, orange, and red **2** *physics* the whole range of electromagnetic radiation with respect to its wavelength or frequency **3** a range or scale of anything such as opinions or emotions [Latin: image]

speculate *vb* **-lating, -lated** **1** to form opinions about something, esp. its future consequences, based on the information available; conjecture: *it is too early to speculate about Jackie getting married* **2** to buy securities or property in the hope of selling them at a profit [Latin *speculari* to spy out] **speculation** *n* **speculative** *adj* **speculator** *n*

sped *vb* a past of **speed**

speech *n* **1** the ability to speak: *the loss of speech* **2** spoken language: *Doran's lack of coherent speech* **3** a talk given to an audience: *a speech to parliament* **4** a person's manner of speaking: *her speech was extremely slow* **5** a national or regional language or dialect: *Canadian speech* [Old English *spēc*]

speech day *n* (in schools) an annual day on which prizes are presented and speeches are made by guest speakers

speechify *vb* **-fies, -fying, -fied** to make a dull or pompous speech

speechless *adj* **1** unable to speak for a short time because of great emotion or shock **2** unable to be expressed in words: *speechless disbelief*

speech therapy *n* the treatment of people with speech problems

speed *n* **1** the quality of acting or moving fast; swiftness **2** the rate at which something moves or happens **3** a gear ratio in a motor vehicle or bicycle: *five-speed gearbox* **4** *photog* a measure of the sensitivity to light of a particular type of film **5** *slang* amphetamine **6 at speed** quickly **7 up to speed** **A** operating at an acceptable level **B** in possession of all the necessary information ▷ *vb* **speeding, sped** *or* **speeded 8** to move or go somewhere quickly **9** to drive a motor vehicle faster than the legal limit ▷ See also **speed up** [Old English *spēd* (originally: success)]

speedboat *n* a high-speed motorboat

speed camera *n* a camera for photographing vehicles breaking the speed limit

speed limit *n* the maximum speed at which a vehicle may legally travel on a particular road

speedo *n, pl* **speedos** *informal* a speedometer

speedometer *n* a dial in a vehicle which shows the speed of travel

speed trap *n* a place on a road where the police check that passing vehicles are not being driven at an illegally high speed

speed up *vb* to accelerate or cause to accelerate

USAGE The past tense and past participle of *speed up* is *speeded up* not *sped up*.

speedway *n* **1** the sport of racing on light powerful motorcycles round cinder tracks **2** *US, Canad & NZ* the track or stadium where such races are held

speedwell *n* a small blue or pinkish-white flower

speedy *adj* **speedier, speediest 1** done without delay **2** (of a vehicle) able to travel fast **speedily** *adv*

speleology *n* the scientific study of caves [Latin *spelaeum* cave]

spell¹ *vb* **spelling, spelt** *or* **spelled 1** to write or name in correct order the letters that make up (a word): *how do you spell that name?* **2** (of letters) to make up (a word): *c-a-t spells cat* **3** to indicate (a particular result): *share price slump spells disaster* ▷ See also **spell out** [Old French *espeller*]

spell² *n* **1** a sequence of words used to perform magic **2** the effect of a spell: *the wizard's spell was broken* **3 under someone's spell** fascinated by someone [Old English *spell* speech]

spell³ *n* **1** a period of time of weather or activity: *the dry spell; a short spell in prison* **2** a period of duty after which one person or group relieves another **3** *Scot, Austral & NZ* a period of rest [Old English *spelian* to take the place of]

spellbinding *adj* so fascinating that nothing else can be thought of: *his spellbinding speeches*

spellbound *adj* completely fascinated; as if in a trance

spellchecker *n* *computers* a program that highlights any word in a word-processed document that is not recognized as being correctly spelt

spelling *n* **1** the way a word is spelt: *the British spelling of 'theatre'* **2** a person's ability to spell: *my spelling used to be excellent*

spell out *vb* **1** to make (something) as easy to understand as possible: *to spell out the implications* **2** to read with difficulty, working out each word letter by letter

spelt *vb* a past of **spell¹**

spend *vb* **spending, spent 1** to pay out (money) **2** to pass (time) in a specific way or place: *I spent a year in Budapest* **3** to concentrate (effort) on an activity: *a lot of energy was spent organizing the holiday* **4** to use up completely: *the hurricane spent its force* [Latin *expendere*] **spending** *n*

spendthrift *n* **1** a person who spends money wastefully ▷ *adj* **2** of or like a spendthrift: *a spendthrift policy*

spent *vb* **1** the past of **spend** ▷ *adj* **2** used up or exhausted

sperm *n* **1** *pl* **sperms** *or* **sperm** one of the male reproductive cells released in the semen during ejaculation **2** same as **semen** [Greek *sperma*]

spermaceti (sper-ma-set-ee) *n* a white waxy substance obtained from the sperm whale [Medieval Latin *sperma ceti* whale's sperm]

spermatozoon (sper-ma-toe-**zoe**-on) *n, pl* **-zoa** same as **sperm** (sense 1) [Greek *sperma* seed + *zōion* animal]

spermicide *n* a substance, esp. a cream or jelly, that kills sperm, used as a means of contraception [SPERM + Latin *caedere* to kill] **spermicidal** *adj*

sperm oil *n* an oil obtained from the head of the sperm whale, used as a lubricant

sperm whale *n* a large whale which is hunted for spermaceti and ambergris [short for SPERMACETI WHALE]

spew *vb* **1** to vomit **2** to send or be sent out in a stream: *the hydrant spewed a tidal wave of water* [Old English *spīwan*]

SPF sun protection factor: an indicator of how a sun cream, lotion, etc. protects the skin from the harmful rays of the sun

sphagnum *n* a moss which is found in bogs and which decays to form peat [Greek *sphagnos*]

sphere *n* **1** *geom* a round solid figure in which every point on the surface is equally distant from the centre **2** an object having this shape, such as a planet **3** a particular field of activity **4** people of the same rank or with shared interests: *a humbler social sphere* [Greek *sphaira*]

spherical *adj* shaped like a sphere

spheroid *n* *geom* a solid figure that is almost but not exactly a sphere

sphincter *n* *anatomy* a ring of muscle surrounding the opening of a hollow organ and contracting to close it [Greek *sphingein* to grip tightly]

sphinx *n* **1** one of the huge statues built by the ancient Egyptians, with the body of a lion and the head of a man **2** a mysterious person

Sphinx *n* **1** the huge statue of a sphinx near the pyramids at El Gîza in Egypt **2** *Greek myth* a monster with a woman's head and a lion's body, who set a riddle for travellers, killing them when they failed to answer it. Oedipus answered the riddle and the Sphinx then killed herself [Greek]

spice *n* **1** **A** an aromatic substance, such as ginger or cinnamon, used as flavouring **B** such substances collectively **2** something that makes life or an activity more exciting ▷ *vb* **spicing, spiced 3** to flavour (food) with spices **4** (often foll. by *up*) to add excitement or interest to (something): *they spiced their letters with pointed demands* [Old French *espice*]

spick-and-span *adj* very neat and clean [obsolete *spick* spike + *span-new* absolutely new, like a freshly cut spike]

spicy *adj* **spicier, spiciest 1** strongly flavoured with spices **2** *informal* slightly scandalous: *spicy new story lines*

spider *n* a small eight-legged creature, many species of which weave webs in which to trap insects for food [Old English *spīthra*] **spidery** *adj*

spider monkey *n* a tree-living monkey with very long legs, a long tail, and a small head

spiel *n* a prepared speech made to persuade someone to buy or do something [German *Spiel* play]

spigot *n* **1** a stopper for the vent hole of a cask **2** a wooden tap fitted to a cask [probably from Latin *spica* a point]

spike[1] *n* **1** a sharp-pointed metal object: *a high fence with iron spikes* **2** anything long and pointed: *a hedgehog bristling with spikes* **3** a long metal nail **4 spikes** sports shoes with metal spikes on the soles for greater grip ▷ *vb* **spiking, spiked 5** to secure or supply (something) with spikes: *spiked shoes* **6** to drive a spike or spikes into **7** to add alcohol to (a drink) [Middle English *spyk*] **spiky** *adj*

spike[2] *n botany* **1** an arrangement of flowers attached at the base to a long stem **2** an ear of grain [Latin *spica* ear of corn]

spikenard *n* **1** a fragrant Indian plant with rose-purple flowers **2** an ointment obtained from this plant [Medieval Latin *spica nardi*]

spill[1] *vb* **spilling, spilt** *or* **spilled 1** to pour from or as from a container by accident **2** (of large numbers of people) to come out of a place: *rival groups spilled out from the station* **3** to shed (blood) **4 spill the beans** *informal* to give away a secret ▷ *n* **5** *informal* a fall from a motorbike, bike, or horse, esp. in a competition **6** an amount of liquid spilt [Old English *spillan* to destroy] **spillage** *n*

spill[2] *n* a splinter of wood or strip of paper for lighting pipes or fires [Germanic]

spillikin *n Brit* a thin strip of wood, cardboard, or plastic used in spillikins

spillikins *n Brit* a game in which players try to pick each spillikin from a heap without moving the others

spin *vb* **spinning, spun 1** to revolve or cause to revolve quickly **2** to draw out and twist (fibres, such as silk or cotton) into thread **3** (of a spider or silkworm) to form (a web or cocoon) from a silky fibre that comes out of the body **4 spin a yarn** to tell an unlikely story **5** *sport* to throw, hit, or kick (a ball) so that it spins and changes direction or changes speed on bouncing **6** same as **spin-dry 7** to grow dizzy: *her head was spinning* **8** *informal* to present information in a way that creates a favourable impression ▷ *n* **9** a fast rotating motion **10** a flight manoeuvre in which an aircraft flies in a downward spiral **11** *sport* a spinning motion given to a ball **12** *informal* a short car drive taken for pleasure **13** *informal* the presenting of information in a way that creates a favourable impression ▷ See also **spin out** [Old English *spinnan*] **spinning** *n*

spina bifida *n* a condition in which part of the spinal cord protrudes through a gap in the backbone, sometimes causing paralysis [New Latin: split spine]

spinach *n* a dark green leafy vegetable [Arabic *isfānākh*]

spinal column *n* same as **spine** (sense 1)

spinal cord *n* the thick cord of nerve tissue within the spine, which connects the brain to the nerves of the body

spin bowler *n cricket* same as **spinner** (sense 1a)

spindle *n* **1** a rotating rod that acts as an axle **2** a rod with a notch in the top for drawing out, twisting and winding the thread in spinning [Old English *spinel*]

spindly *adj* **-dlier, -dliest** tall, thin, and frail

spin doctor *n informal* a person who provides a favourable slant to a news item or policy on behalf of a political personality or party [from the spin given to a ball in sport to make it go in the desired direction]

spindrift *n* spray blown up from the sea [Scots variant of *spoondrift*, from *spoon* to scud + DRIFT]

spin-dry *vb* **-dries, -drying, -dried** to dry (clothes) in a spin-dryer

spin-dryer *n* a device that removes water from washed clothes by spinning them in a perforated drum

spine *n* **1** the row of bony segments that surround and protect the spinal cord **2** the back of a book, record sleeve, or video-tape box **3** a sharp point on the body of an animal or on a plant [Latin *spina* thorn] **spinal** *adj*

spine-chiller *n* a frightening film or story **spine-chilling** *adj*

spineless *adj* **1** behaving in a cowardly way **2** (of an animal) having no spine

spinet *n* a small harpsichord [Italian *spinetta*]

spinifex *n* a coarse spiny Australian grass

spinnaker *n* a large triangular sail on a racing yacht [probably from *spin*, but traditionally from Sphinx, the yacht that first used this type of sail]

spinner *n* **1** *cricket* **A** a bowler who specializes in spinning the ball with his or her fingers to make it change direction when it bounces or strikes the batsman's bat **B** a ball that is bowled with a spinning motion **2** a small round object used in angling to attract fish to the bait by spinning in the water **3** a person who makes thread by spinning

spinneret *n* an organ through which silk threads come out of the body of a spider or insect

spinney *n chiefly Brit* a small wood: *the hollow tree in the spinney* [Old French *espinei*]

spinning jenny *n* an early type of spinning frame with several spindles

spinning wheel *n* a wheel-like machine for spinning at home, having one hand- or foot-operated spindle

spin-off *n* **1** a product or development that unexpectedly results from activities designed to achieve something else: *new energy sources could occur as a spin-off from the space effort* **2** a television series involving some of the characters from an earlier successful series

spin out *vb* **1** to take longer than necessary to do (something) **2** to make (money) last as long as possible

spinster *n old-fashioned* an unmarried woman [Middle English, in the sense a woman who spins] **spinsterish** *adj*

spiny *adj* **spinier, spiniest** (of animals or plants) covered with spines

spiracle (spire-a-kl) *n zool* a small blowhole for breathing through, such as that of a whale [Latin *spiraculum* vent]

spiraea *or esp US* **spirea** (spire-ee-a) *n* a plant with small white or pink flowers [Greek *speiraia*]

spiral *n* **1** *geom* a plane curve formed by a point winding about a fixed point at an ever-increasing distance from it **2** something that follows a winding course or that has a twisting form **3** *econ* a continuous upward or downward movement in economic activity or prices ▹ *adj* **4** having the shape of a spiral: *a spiral staircase* ▹ *vb* **-ralling, -ralled** *or US* **-raling, -raled** **5** to follow a spiral course or be in the shape of a spiral **6** to increase or decrease with steady acceleration: *oil prices continue to spiral* [Latin *spira* a coil] **spirally** *adv*

spire *n* the tall cone-shaped structure on the top of a church [Old English *spīr* blade]

spirit[1] *n* **1** the nonphysical aspect of a person concerned with profound thoughts and emotions **2** the nonphysical part of a person believed to live on after death **3** a shared feeling: *a spirit of fun and adventure* **4** mood or attitude: *fighting spirit* **5** a person's character or temperament: *the indomitable spirit of the Polish people* **6** liveliness shown in what a person does: *it has been undertaken with spirit* **7** the feelings that motivate someone to survive in difficult times or live according to his or her beliefs: *someone had broken his spirit* **8** **spirits** an emotional state: *in good spirits* **9** the way in which something, such as a law or an agreement, was intended to be interpreted: *they acted against the spirit of the treaty* **10** a supernatural being, such as a ghost ▹ *vb* **-riting, -rited** **11** **spirit away** *or* **off** to carry (someone or something) off mysteriously or secretly [Latin *spiritus* breath, spirit]

spirit[2] *n* **1** (*usually pl*) distilled alcoholic liquor, such as whisky or gin **2** *chem* **A** a solution of ethanol obtained by distillation **B** the essence of a substance, extracted as a liquid by distillation **3** *pharmacol* a solution of a volatile oil in alcohol [special use of SPIRIT[1]]

spirited *adj* **1** showing liveliness or courage: *a spirited rendition of Schubert's ninth symphony; a spirited defence of the government's policy* **2** characterized by the mood as specified: *high-spirited; mean-spirited*

spirit gum *n* a solution of gum in ether, used to stick on false hair

spirit lamp *n* a lamp that burns methylated or other spirits instead of oil

spirit level *n* a device for checking whether a surface is level, consisting of a block of wood or metal containing a tube partially filled with liquid set so that the air bubble in it rests between two marks on the tube when the block is level

spiritual *adj* **1** relating to a person's beliefs as opposed to his or her physical or material needs **2** relating to religious beliefs **3** **one's spiritual home** the place where one feels one belongs ▹ *n* **4** Also called: **Negro spiritual** a type of religious folk song originally sung by Black slaves in the American South **spirituality** *n* **spiritually** *adv*

spiritualism *n* the belief that the spirits of the dead can communicate with the living **spiritualist** *n*

spirituous *adj* containing alcohol

spirogyra (spire-oh-jire-a) *n* a green freshwater plant that floats on the surface of ponds and ditches [Greek *speira* a coil + *guros* a circle]

spit[1] *vb* **spitting, spat** *or* **spit** **1** to force saliva out of one's mouth **2** to force (something) out of one's mouth: *he spat tobacco into an old coffee can* **3** (of a fire or hot fat) to throw out sparks or particles violently and explosively **4** to rain very lightly **5** (often foll. by *out*) to say (words) in a violent angry way **6** to show contempt or hatred by spitting **7** **spit it out!** *informal* a command given to someone to say what is on his or her mind ▹ *n* **8** same as **spittle** **9** *informal, chiefly Brit* same as **spitting image** [Old English *spittan*]

spit[2] *n* **1** a pointed rod for skewering and roasting meat over a fire or in an oven **2** a long narrow strip of land jutting out into the sea [Old English *spitu*]

spit and polish *n informal* thorough cleaning and polishing

spite *n* **1** deliberate nastiness **2** **in spite of** regardless of: *he loved them in spite of their shortcomings* ▹ *vb* **spiting, spited** **3** to annoy (someone) deliberately, out of spite: *it was to spite his father* [variant of DESPITE] **spiteful** *adj* **spitefully** *adv*

spitfire *n* a person who is easily angered

spitting image *n informal* a person who looks very like someone else [from *spit* likeness]

spittle *n* the fluid that is produced in the mouth; saliva [Old English *spǣtl* saliva]

spittoon *n* a bowl for people to spit into

spitz *n* a stockily built dog with a pointed face, erect ears, and a tightly curled tail [from German]

spiv *n Brit, Austral & NZ slang* a smartly dressed man who makes a living by underhand dealings; black marketeer [dialect *spiving* smart]

splash *vb* **1** to scatter (liquid) on (something) **2** to cause (liquid) to fall or (of liquid) to be scattered in drops **3** to display (a photograph or story) prominently in a newspaper ▹ *n* **4** a splashing sound **5** an amount splashed **6** a patch (of colour or light) **7** **make a splash** *informal* to attract a lot of attention **8** a small amount of liquid added to a drink [alteration of *plash*]

splashdown *n* **1** the landing of a spacecraft on water at the end of a flight ▹ *vb* **splash down** **2** (of a spacecraft) to make a splashdown

splash out *vb* to spend a lot of money on a treat or luxury: *she planned to splash out on a good holiday*

splatter *vb* **1** to splash (something or someone) with small blobs ▹ *n* **2** a splash of liquid

splay *vb* to spread out, with ends spreading out in different directions: *her hair splayed over the pillow* [short for DISPLAY]

splayfooted *adj* same as **flat-footed**

spleen *n* **1** a spongy organ near the stomach, which filters bacteria from the blood

S

2 spitefulness or bad temper: *we vent our spleen on drug barons* [Greek *splēn*]

spleenwort *n* a kind of fern that grows on walls

splendid *adj* **1** very good: *a splendid match* **2** beautiful or impressive: *a splendid palace* [Latin *splendere* to shine] **splendidly** *adv*

splendiferous *adj facetious, old-fashioned* grand in appearance [Latin *splendor* radiance + *ferre* to bring]

splendour *or US* **splendor** *n* **1** beauty or impressiveness **2** **splendours** the impressive or beautiful features of something: *the splendours of the Emperor's Palace*

splenetic *adj literary* irritable or bad-tempered [from SPLEEN]

splice *vb* **splicing, spliced** **1** to join up the trimmed ends of (two pieces of wire, film, or tape) with an adhesive material **2** to join (two ropes) by interweaving the ends **3** **get spliced** *informal* to get married [probably from Middle Dutch *splissen*]

splint *n* a piece of wood used to support a broken bone [Middle Low German *splinte*]

splinter *n* **1** a small thin sharp piece broken off, esp. from wood ▷ *vb* **2** to break or be broken into small sharp fragments [Middle Dutch]

splinter group *n* a number of members of an organization, who split from the main body and form an independent group of their own

split *vb* **splitting, split** **1** to break or cause (something) to break into separate pieces **2** to separate (a piece) or (of a piece) to be separated from (something) **3** (of a group) to separate into smaller groups, through disagreement: *the council is split over rent increases* **4** (often foll. by *up*) to divide (something) among two or more people **5** *slang* to leave a place **6** **split on** *slang* to betray; inform on: *he didn't tell tales or split on him* **7** **split one's sides** to laugh a great deal ▷ *n* **8** a gap or rift caused by splitting **9** a division in a group or the smaller group resulting from such a division **10** a dessert of sliced fruit and ice cream, covered with whipped cream and nuts: *banana split* ▷ *adj* **11** divided (esp. in opinion, etc.) **12** having a split or splits: *split ends* ▷ See also **splits, split up** [Middle Dutch *splitten*]

split infinitive *n* (in English grammar) an infinitive used with another word between *to* and the verb, as in *to really finish it*. This is often thought to be incorrect

> **USAGE** The traditional rule against placing an adverb between *to* and its verb is gradually disappearing. Although it is true that a split infinitive may result in a clumsy sentence (*he decided to firmly and definitively deal with the problem*), this is not enough to justify the absolute condemnation that this practice has attracted. Indeed, very often the most natural position of the adverb is between *to* and the verb (*he decided to really try next time*) and to change it would result in an artificial and awkward construction (*he decided really to try next time*). The current view is therefore that the split infinitive is not a grammatical error. Nevertheless, many writers prefer to avoid splitting infinitives in formal written English, since readers with a more traditional point of view are likely to interpret this type of construction as incorrect.

split-level *adj* (of a house or room) having the floor level of one part about half a storey above that of the other

split pea *n* a pea dried and split and used in soups or as a vegetable

split personality *n* **1** *informal* the tendency to change mood very quickly **2** a former name for **schizophrenia** (sense 1) **3** a nontechnical name for dissociative identity disorder: a disorder in which a person's mind appears to have separated into two or more personalities

splits *n* (in gymnastics and dancing) the act of sitting with both legs outstretched, pointing in opposite directions, and at right angles to the body

split second *n* **1** an extremely short period of time; instant ▷ *adj* **split-second** **2** made in an extremely short time: *split-second timing*

splitting *adj* (of a headache) extremely painful

split up *vb* **1** to separate (something) into parts; divide **2** (of a couple) to end a relationship or marriage **3** (of a group of people) to go off in different directions ▷ *n* **split-up** **4** the act of separating

splodge *or US* **splotch** *n* **1** a large uneven spot or stain ▷ *vb* **splodging, splodged** **2** to mark (something) with a splodge or splodges [alteration of earlier *splotch*]

splurge *n* **1** a bout of spending money extravagantly ▷ *vb* **splurging, splurged** **2** (foll. by *on*) to spend (money) extravagantly: *they rushed out to splurge their pocket money on chocolate* [origin unknown]

splutter *vb* **1** to spit out (something) from the mouth when choking or laughing **2** to say (words) with spitting sounds when choking or in a rage **3** to throw out or to be thrown out explosively: *sparks spluttered from the fire* ▷ *n* **4** the act or noise of spluttering [variant of SPUTTER]

Spode *n* china or porcelain manufactured by the English potter Josiah Spode or his company

spoil *vb* **spoiling, spoilt** *or* **spoiled** **1** to make (something) less valuable, beautiful, or useful **2** to weaken the character of (a child) by giving it all it wants **3** (of oneself) to indulge one's desires: *go ahead and spoil yourself* **4** (of food) to become unfit for consumption **5** **be spoiling for** to have an aggressive urge for: *he is spoiling for a fight* ▷ See also **spoils** [Latin *spolium* booty]

spoilage *n* an amount of material that has been spoilt: *new ways to reduce spoilage*

spoiler *n* **1** a device fitted to an aircraft wing to increase drag and reduce lift **2** a similar device fitted to a car

spoils *pl n* **1** valuables seized during war **2** the rewards and benefits of having political power

spoilsport *n informal* a person who spoils the enjoyment of other people

spoke[1] *vb* the past tense of **speak**

spoke[2] *n* **1** a bar joining the centre of a wheel to the rim **2** **put a spoke in someone's wheel** *Brit & NZ* to create a difficulty for someone [Old English *spāca*]

S

spoken *vb* **1** the past participle of **speak** ▷ *adj* **2** said in speech: *spoken commands* **3** having speech as specified: *quiet-spoken* **4** **spoken for** engaged or reserved

spokesman, spokesperson *or* **spokeswoman** *n, pl* **-men, -people** *or* **-women** a person chosen to speak on behalf of another person or group

spoliation *n* the act or an instance of plundering: *the spoliation of the countryside* [Latin *spoliare* to plunder]

spondee *n prosody* a metrical foot of two long syllables [Greek *spondē* ritual offering of drink] **spondaic** *adj*

sponge *n* **1** a sea animal with a porous absorbent elastic skeleton **2** the skeleton of a sponge, or a piece of artificial sponge, used for bathing or cleaning **3** a soft absorbent material like a sponge **4** Also called: **sponge cake** a light cake made of eggs, sugar, and flour **5** Also called: **sponge pudding** *Brit & Austral* a light steamed or baked spongy pudding **6** a rub with a wet sponge ▷ *vb* **sponging, sponged 7** (often foll. by *down*) to clean (something) by rubbing it with a wet sponge **8** to remove (marks) by rubbing them with a wet sponge **9** (usually foll. by *off* or *on*) to get (something) from someone by taking advantage of his or her generosity: *stop sponging off the rest of us!* [Greek *spongia*] **spongy** *adj*

sponge bag *n* a small waterproof bag for holding toiletries when travelling

sponger *n informal, derogatory* a person who lives off other people by continually taking advantage of their generosity

sponsor *n* **1** a person or group that promotes another person or group in an activity or the activity itself, either for profit or for charity **2** *chiefly US & Canad* a person or firm that pays the costs of a radio or television programme in return for advertising time **3** a person who presents and supports a proposal or suggestion **4** a person who makes certain promises on behalf of a person being baptized and takes responsibility for his or her Christian upbringing ▷ *vb* **5** to act as a sponsor for (someone or something) [Latin *spondere* to promise solemnly] **sponsored** *adj* **sponsorship** *n*

spontaneous *adj* **1** not planned or arranged; impulsive: *a spontaneous celebration* **2** occurring through natural processes without outside influence: *a spontaneous explosion* [Latin *sponte* voluntarily] **spontaneously** *adv* **spontaneity** *n*

spontaneous combustion *n chem* the bursting into flame of a substance as a result of internal oxidation processes, without heat from an outside source

spoof *informal* ▷ *n* **1** an imitation of a film, TV programme, etc., that exaggerates in an amusing way the most memorable features of the original **2** a good-humoured trick or deception ▷ *vb* **3** to fool (a person) with a trick or deception [made-up word]

spook *informal* ▷ *n* **1** a ghost **2** a strange and frightening person ▷ *vb* **3** to frighten: *it was the wind that spooked her* [Dutch] **spooky** *adj*

spool *n* a cylinder around which film, thread, or tape can be wound [Germanic]

spoon *n* **1** a small shallow bowl attached to a handle, used for eating, stirring, or serving food **2** **be born with a silver spoon in one's mouth** to be born into a very rich and respected family ▷ *vb* **3** to scoop up (food or liquid) with a spoon **4** *old-fashioned slang* to kiss and cuddle [Old English *spōn* splinter]

spoonbill *n* a wading bird with a long flat bill

spoonerism *n* the accidental changing over of the first sounds of a pair of words, often with an amusing result, such as *hush my brat* for *brush my hat* [after W. A. *Spooner*, clergyman]

spoon-feed *vb* **-feeding, -fed 1** to feed (someone, usually a baby) using a spoon **2** to give (someone) too much help

spoor *n* the trail of an animal [Afrikaans]

sporadic *adj* happening at irregular intervals; intermittent: *sporadic bursts of gunfire* [Greek *sporas* scattered] **sporadically** *adv*

spore *n* a reproductive body, produced by nonflowering plants and bacteria, that develops into a new individual [Greek *spora* a sowing]

sporran *n* a large pouch worn hanging from a belt in front of the kilt in Scottish Highland dress [Scottish Gaelic *sporan* purse]

sport *n* **1** an activity for exercise, pleasure, or competition: *your favourite sport* **2** such activities collectively: *the minister for sport* **3** the enjoyment gained from a pastime: *just for the sport of it* **4** playful or good-humoured joking: *I only did it in sport* **5** *informal* a person who accepts defeat or teasing cheerfully **6** **make sport of someone** to make fun of someone **7** an animal or plant that is very different from others of the same species, usually because of a mutation **8** *Austral & NZ informal* a term of address between males ▷ *vb* **9** *informal* to wear proudly: *sporting a pair of bright yellow shorts* ▷ See also **sports** [variant of Middle English *disporten* to disport]

sporting *adj* **1** of sport **2** behaving in a fair and decent way **3** **a sporting chance** reasonable likelihood of happening: *a sporting chance of winning*

sportive *adj* playful or high-spirited

sports *adj* **1** of or used in sports: *a sports arena* ▷ *n* **2** Also called: **sports day** *Brit* a meeting held at a school or college for competitions in athletic events

sports car *n* a fast car with a low body and usually seating only two people

sportscast *n US* a programme of sports news **sportscaster** *n*

sports jacket *n* a man's jacket, resembling a suit jacket. Also called (US, Austral & NZ): **sports coat**

sportsman *n, pl* **-men 1** a man who plays sports **2** a person who plays by the rules, is fair, and accepts defeat with good humour **sportsmanlike** *adj* **sportsmanship** *n*

sportsperson *n* a person who plays sports

sportswear *n* clothes worn for sport or outdoor leisure wear

sportswoman *n, pl* **-women** a woman who plays sports

sporty *adj* **sportier, sportiest 1** (of a person) interested in sport **2** (of clothes) suitable for sport **3** (of a car) small and fast **sportily** *adv* **sportiness** *n*

spot *n* **1** a small mark on a surface, which has a different colour or texture from its surroundings **2** a location: *a spot where they could sit* **3** a small mark or pimple on the skin **4** a feature of something that has the attribute mentioned: *the one bright spot in his whole day; the high spot of our trip* **5** *informal* a small amount: *a spot of bother* **6** *informal* an awkward situation: *I'm sometimes in a spot* **7** a part of a show, TV programme, etc., reserved for a specific performer or type of entertainment **8** short for **spotlight** (sense 1) **9** **in a tight spot** in a difficult situation **10** **knock spots off someone** to be much better than someone **11** **on the spot** **A** immediately: *he decided on the spot to fly down* **B** at the place in question: *the expert weapons man on the spot* **C** in an awkward situation: *the British government will be put on the spot* **12** **soft spot** a special affection for someone: *a soft spot for older men* ▷ *vb* **spotting, spotted** **13** to see (something or someone) suddenly **14** to put stains or spots on (something) **15** (of some fabrics) to be prone to marking by liquids: *silk spots easily* **16** to take note of (the numbers of trains or planes observed) **17** (of scouts, agents, etc.) to look out for (talented but unknown actors, sportspersons, etc.) **18** *Brit* to rain lightly [from German]

spot check *n* a quick unplanned inspection

spotless *adj* **1** perfectly clean **2** free from moral flaws: *a spotless reputation* **spotlessly** *adv*

spotlight *n* **1** a powerful light focused so as to light up a small area **2** **the spotlight** the centre of attention: *the spotlight moved to the president* ▷ *vb* **-lighting, -lit** *or* **-lighted** **3** to direct a spotlight on (something) **4** to focus attention on (something)

spot-on *adj informal* absolutely correct; very accurate: *they're spot-on in terms of style*

spotted *adj* **1** having a pattern of spots **2** marked with stains

spotted dick *n Brit* suet pudding containing dried fruit

spotter *n* a person whose hobby is watching for and noting numbers or types of trains or planes

spotty *adj* **-tier, -tiest** **1** covered with spots or pimples **2** not consistent; irregular in quality: *a rather spotty performance* **spottiness** *n*

S

spouse *n* a person's partner in marriage [Latin *sponsus, sponsa* betrothed man or woman]

spout *vb* **1** (of a liquid or flames) to pour out in a stream or jet **2** *informal* to talk about (something) in a boring way or without much thought ▷ *n* **3** a projecting tube or lip for pouring liquids **4** a stream or jet of liquid: *a spout of steaming water* **5** **up the spout** *slang* **A** ruined or lost: *the motor industry is up the spout* **B** pregnant [Middle English *spouten*]

spouting *n NZ* **A** a rainwater downpipe on the outside of a building **B** such pipes collectively

sprain *vb* **1** to injure (a joint) by a sudden twist ▷ *n* **2** this injury, which causes swelling and temporary disability [origin unknown]

sprang *vb* a past tense of **spring**

sprat *n* a small edible fish like a herring [Old English *sprott*]

sprawl *vb* **1** to sit or lie with one's arms and legs spread out **2** to spread out untidily over a large area: *the pulp mill sprawled over the narrow flats* ▷ *n* **3** the part of a city or town that has not been planned and spreads out untidily over a large area: *the huge Los Angeles sprawl* [Old English *spreawlian*] **sprawling** *adj*

spray¹ *n* **1** fine drops of a liquid **2** **A** a liquid under pressure designed to be discharged in fine drops from an aerosol or atomizer: *hair spray* **B** the aerosol or atomizer itself **3** a number of small objects flying through the air: *a spray of bullets* ▷ *vb* **4** to scatter in fine drops **5** to squirt (a liquid) from an aerosol or atomizer **6** to cover with a spray: *spray the crops* [Middle Dutch *sprāien*] **sprayer** *n*

spray² *n* **1** a sprig or branch with buds, leaves, flowers, or berries **2** an ornament or design like this [Germanic]

spray gun *n* a device for spraying fine drops of paint, etc.

spread *vb* **spreading, spread** **1** to open out or unfold to the fullest width: *spread the material out* **2** to extend over a larger expanse: *the subsequent unrest spread countrywide* **3** to apply as a coating: *spread the paste evenly over your skin* **4** to be displayed to its fullest extent: *the shining bay spread out below* **5** to send or be sent out in all directions or to many people: *the news spread quickly; the sandflies that spread the disease* **6** to distribute or be distributed evenly: *we were advised to spread the workload over the whole year* **7** **spread out** (of people) to increase the distance between one another (to widen the scope of a search, for example) ▷ *n* **8** a spreading; distribution, dispersion, or expansion: *the spread of higher education* **9** *informal* a large meal **10** *informal* the wingspan of an aircraft or bird **11** *informal, chiefly US & Canad* a ranch or other large area of land **12** a soft food which can be spread: *cheese spread* **13** two facing pages in a book or magazine **14** a widening of the hips and waist: *middle-age spread* [Old English *sprǣdan*]

spread-eagled *adj* with arms and legs outstretched

spreadsheet *n* a computer program for manipulating figures, used mainly for financial planning

spree *n* a session of overindulgence, usually in drinking or spending money [Scots *spreath* plundered cattle]

sprig *n* **1** a shoot, twig, or sprout **2** an ornamental device like this **3** *NZ* a stud on the sole of a soccer or rugby boot [Germanic] **sprigged** *adj*

sprightly *adj* **-lier, -liest** lively and active [obsolete *spright*, variant of SPRITE] **sprightliness** *n*

spring *vb* **springing, sprang** *or* **sprung, sprung** **1** to jump suddenly upwards or forwards **2** to return or be returned into natural shape from a forced position by elasticity: *the coil sprang back* **3** to cause (something) to happen unexpectedly: *the national coach sprang a surprise* **4** (usually foll. by *from*) to originate; be descended: *this motivation springs from their inborn curiosity; Truman sprang from ordinary people* **5** (often foll. by *up*) to come into being or appear suddenly: *new courses will spring up* **6** to provide (something, such as a mattress) with springs **7** *informal* to arrange the escape of (someone) from prison ▷ *n* **8** the season between winter and summer **9** a leap or jump **10** a coil which can be compressed, stretched, or bent and then return to its original shape when released **11** a natural pool forming the source of a stream **12** elasticity [Old English *springan*] **springlike** *adj*

spring balance *or esp US* **spring scale** *n* a device that indicates the weight of an object by the extension of a spring to which the object is attached

springboard *n* **1** a flexible board used to gain height or momentum in diving or gymnastics **2** anything that makes it possible for an activity to begin: *the meeting acted as a springboard for future negotiations*

springbok *n, pl* **-bok** *or* **-boks 1** a S African antelope which moves in leaps **2** a person who has represented S Africa in a national sports team [Afrikaans]

spring chicken *n* **1** a young chicken, which is tender for cooking **2 he** *or* **she is no spring chicken** *informal* he *or* she is no longer young

spring-clean *vb* **1** to clean (a house) thoroughly, traditionally at the end of winter ▷ *n* **2** an instance of this **spring-cleaning** *n*

spring onion *n* a small onion with a tiny bulb and long green leaves, eaten in salads

spring roll *n* an E Asian dish consisting of a savoury mixture rolled in a thin pancake and fried

spring tide *n* either of the two tides at or just after new moon and full moon: the greatest rise and fall in tidal level

springtime *n* the season of spring

springy *adj* **springier, springiest** (of an object) having the quality of returning to its original shape after being pressed or pulled **springiness** *n*

sprinkle *vb* **-kling, -kled 1** to scatter (liquid or powder) in tiny drops over (something) **2** to distribute over (something): *a dozen mud huts sprinkled around it* [probably from Middle Dutch *sprenkelen*] **sprinkler** *n*

sprinkling *n* a small quantity or amount: *a sprinkling of diamonds*

sprint *n* **1** *athletics* **A** a short race run at top speed **B** a fast run at the end of a longer race **2** any quick run ▷ *vb* **3** to run or cycle a short distance at top speed [Scandinavian] **sprinter** *n*

sprit *n naut* a light pole set diagonally across a sail to extend it [Old English *sprēot*]

sprite *n* **1** (in folklore) a fairy or elf **2** an icon in a computer game which can be manoeuvred around the screen [Latin *spiritus* spirit]

spritsail *n naut* a sail mounted on a sprit

spritzer *n* a tall drink of wine and soda water [German *spritzen* to splash]

sprocket *n* **1** Also called: **sprocket wheel** a wheel with teeth on the rim, that drives or is driven by a chain **2** a cylindrical wheel with teeth on one or both rims for pulling film through an analogue camera or projector [origin unknown]

sprout *vb* **1** (of a plant or seed) to produce (new leaves or shoots) **2** (often foll. by *up*) to begin to grow or develop ▷ *n* **3** a new shoot or bud **4** same as **Brussels sprout** [Old English *sprūtan*]

spruce[1] *n* **1** an evergreen pyramid-shaped tree with needle-like leaves **2** the light-coloured wood of this tree [obsolete *Spruce* Prussia]

spruce[2] *adj* neat and smart [perhaps from *Spruce leather;* see SPRUCE[1]]

spruce up *vb* **sprucing, spruced** to make neat and smart

sprung *vb* a past tense and the past participle of **spring**

spry *adj* **spryer, spryest** *or* **sprier, spriest** active and lively; nimble [origin unknown]

spud *n informal* a potato [obsolete *spudde* short knife]

spume *n literary* **1** foam or froth on the sea ▷ *vb* **spuming, spumed 2** (of the sea) to foam or froth [Latin *spuma*]

spun *vb* **1** the past of **spin** ▷ *adj* **2** made by spinning: *spun sugar; spun silk*

spunk *n* **1** *old-fashioned, informal* courage or spirit **2** *chiefly Brit vulgar slang* semen **3** *Austral & NZ informal* a sexually attractive person, esp. a male [Scottish Gaelic *spong* tinder, sponge] **spunky** *adj*

spur *n* **1** an incentive to get something done **2** a sharp spiked wheel on the heel of a rider's boot used to urge the horse on **3** a sharp horny part sticking out from a cock's leg **4** a ridge sticking out from a mountain side **5 on the spur of the moment** suddenly and without planning; on impulse **6 win one's spurs** to prove one's ability ▷ *vb* **spurring, spurred 7** (often foll. by *on*) to encourage (someone) [Old English *spura*]

spurge *n* a plant with milky sap and small flowers [Latin *expurgare* to cleanse]

spurious *adj* not genuine or real [Latin *spurius* of illegitimate birth]

spurn *vb* to reject (a person or thing) with contempt [Old English *spurnan*]

spurt *vb* **1** to gush or cause (something) to gush out in a sudden powerful stream or jet **2** to make a sudden effort ▷ *n* **3** a short burst of activity, speed, or energy **4** a sudden powerful stream or jet [origin unknown]

sputnik *n* a Russian artificial satellite [Russian, literally: fellow traveller]

sputter *vb, n* same as **splutter** [Dutch *sputteren*, imitative]

sputum *n, pl* **-ta** saliva, usually mixed with mucus [Latin]

spy *n, pl* **spies 1** a person employed to find out secret information about other countries or organizations **2** a person who secretly keeps watch on others ▷ *vb* **spies, spying, spied 3** (foll. by *on*) to keep a secret watch on someone **4** to work as a spy **5** to catch sight of (someone or something); notice [Old French *espier*]

spyglass *n* a small telescope

spy out *vb* to discover (something) secretly

spyware *n* software surreptitiously installed in a computer via the internet to gather and transmit information about the user

sq. square

SQL *n* a computer programming language that is used for database management [structured query language]

Sqn. Ldr. squadron leader

squab *n, pl* **squabs** *or* **squab** a young bird yet to leave the nest [probably Germanic]

squabble *vb* **-bling, -bled 1** to quarrel over a small matter ▷ *n* **2** a petty quarrel [probably Scandinavian]

S

squad *n* **1** the smallest military formation, usually a dozen soldiers **2** any small group of people working together: *the fraud squad* **3** *sport* a number of players from which a team is to be selected [Old French *esquade*]
squadron *n* the basic unit of an air force [Italian *squadrone* soldiers drawn up in square formation]
squadron leader *n* a fairly senior commissioned officer in some air forces; the rank above flight lieutenant
squalid *adj* **1** dirty, untidy, and in bad condition **2** unpleasant, selfish, and often dishonest: *this squalid affair* [Latin *squalidus*]
squall¹ *n* a sudden strong wind or short violent storm [perhaps a special use of SQUALL²]
squall² *vb* **1** to cry noisily; yell ▷ *n* **2** a noisy cry or yell [probably Scandinavian]
squalor *n* **1** dirty, poor, and untidy physical conditions **2** the condition of being squalid [Latin]
squander *vb* to waste (money or resources) [origin unknown]
square *n* **1** a geometric figure with four equal sides and four right angles **2** anything of this shape **3** an open area in a town bordered by buildings or streets **4** *maths* the number produced when a number is multiplied by itself: *9 is the square of 3, written* 3^2 **5** *informal* a person who is dull or unfashionable **6** **go back to square one** to return to the start because of failure or lack of progress ▷ *adj* **7** being a square in shape **8 A** having the same area as that of a square with sides of a specified length: *2,500 square metres of hillside* **B** denoting a square having a specified length on each side: *a cell of only four square metres* **9** straight or level: *I don't think that painting is square* **10** fair and honest: *a square deal* **11** *informal* dull or unfashionable **12** having all debts or accounts settled: *if I give you a pound, then we'll be square* **13 all square** on equal terms; even in score **14 square peg in a round hole** *informal* a misfit ▷ *vb* **squaring, squared 15** *maths* to multiply (a number or quantity) by itself **16** to position so as to be straight or level: *bravely he squared his shoulders* **17** to settle (a debt or account) **18** to level the score in (a game) **19** to be or cause to be consistent: *it would not have squared with her image* ▷ *adv* **20** *informal* same as **squarely** ▷ See also **square off, square up** [Old French *esquare*]
square-bashing *n Brit military slang* marching and other drill on a parade ground
square bracket *n* either of a pair of characters, [ ], used to separate a section of writing or printing from the main text
square dance *n* a country dance in which the couples are arranged in squares
square leg *n cricket* a fielding position on the on side, at right angles to the batsman
squarely *adv* **1** directly; straight: *he looked her squarely in the eye* **2** in an honest and frank way: *you should face squarely anything that worries you*
square meal *n* a meal which is large enough to leave the eater feeling full: *we gave him his first square meal in days*
square off *vb* to stand up as if ready to start boxing or fighting
square-rigged *adj naut* having sails set at right angles to the keel
square root *n* a number that when multiplied by itself gives a given number: *the square roots of 4 are 2 and -2*
square up *vb* **1** to settle bills or debts **2 square up to** to prepare to confront (a problem or a person)
squash¹ *vb* **1** to press or squeeze (something) so as to flatten it **2** to overcome (a difficult situation), often with force **3 squash in** *or* **into** to push or force (oneself or a thing) into a confined space **4** to humiliate (someone) with a sarcastic reply ▷ *n* **5** *Brit & Austral* a drink made from fruit juice or fruit syrup diluted with water **6** a crowd of people in a confined space **7** Also called: **squash rackets** a game for two players played in an enclosed court with a small rubber ball and long-handled rackets [Old French *esquasser*]
squash² *n, pl* **squashes** *or* **squash** *chiefly US & Canad* a marrow-like vegetable [from a Native American language]
squashy *adj* **squashier, squashiest** soft and easily squashed
squat *vb* **squatting, squatted 1** to crouch with the knees bent and the weight on the feet **2** *law* to occupy an unused building to which one has no legal right ▷ *adj* **3** short and thick ▷ *n* **4** a building occupied by squatters [Old French *esquater*]
squatter *n* an illegal occupier of an unused building
squaw *n offensive* a Native American woman of N America [from a Native American language]
squawk *n* **1** a loud harsh cry, esp. one made by a bird **2** *informal* a loud complaint ▷ *vb* **3** to make a squawk [imitative]
squeak *n* **1** a short high-pitched cry or sound **2 a narrow squeak** *informal* a narrow escape or success ▷ *vb* **3** to make a squeak **4 squeak through** *or* **by** to pass (an examination), but only just [probably Scandinavian] **squeaky** *adj* **squeakiness** *n*
squeaky clean *adj* **1** (of hair) washed so clean that wet strands squeak when rubbed **2** completely clean **3** *informal, derogatory* (of a person) cultivating a virtuous and wholesome image
squeal *n* **1** a long high-pitched yelp ▷ *vb* **2** to make a squeal **3** *slang* to inform on someone to the police **4** *informal, chiefly Brit* to complain loudly [Middle English *squelen*, imitative] **squealer** *n*
squeamish *adj* easily shocked or upset by unpleasant sights or events [Anglo-French *escoymous*]
squeegee *n* a tool with a rubber blade used for wiping away excess water from a surface [probably imitative]
squeeze *vb* **squeezing, squeezed 1** to grip or press (something) firmly **2** to crush or press (something) so as to extract (a liquid): *squeeze the tomato and strain the juice; freshly squeezed lemon juice* **3** to push (oneself or a thing) into a confined space **4** to hug (someone) closely **5** to obtain (something) by great effort or force: *to squeeze the last dollar out of every deal* ▷ *n* **6** a squeezing **7** a hug

S

8 a crush of people in a confined space **9** *chiefly Brit & NZ* a restriction on borrowing made by a government to control price inflation **10** an amount extracted by squeezing: *a squeeze of lime* **11 put the squeeze on someone** *informal* to put pressure on someone in order to obtain something [Old English *cwȳsan*]

squelch *vb* **1** to make a wet sucking noise, such as by walking through mud **2** *informal* to silence (someone) with a sarcastic or wounding reply ▷ *n* **3** a squelching sound [imitative] **squelchy** *adj*

squib *n* **1** a firework that burns with a hissing noise before exploding **2 damp squib** something expected to be exciting or successful but turning out to be a disappointment [probably imitative of a light explosion]

squid *n, pl* **squid** *or* **squids** a sea creature with ten tentacles and a long soft body [origin unknown]

squiffy *adj* **-fier, -fiest** *Brit informal* slightly drunk: *a bit squiffy* [origin unknown]

squiggle *n* a wavy line [perhaps SQUIRM + WIGGLE] **squiggly** *adj*

squill *n* a Mediterranean plant of the lily family [Greek *skilla*]

squint *vb* **1** to have eyes which face in different directions **2** to glance sideways ▷ *n* **3** an eye disorder in which one or both eyes turn inwards or outwards from the nose **4** *informal* a quick look; glance: *take a squint at the map* ▷ *adj* **5** *informal* not straight; crooked [short for *asquint*]

squire *n* **1** a country gentleman in England, usually the main landowner in a country community **2** *informal, chiefly Brit* a term of address used by one man to another **3** *history* a knight's young attendant ▷ *vb* **squiring, squired** **4** *old-fashioned* (of a man) to escort (a woman) [Old French *esquier*]

squirm *vb* **1** to wriggle **2** to feel embarrassed or guilty ▷ *n* **3** a wriggling movement [imitative]

squirrel *n* a small bushy-tailed animal that lives in trees [Greek *skiouros*, from *skia* shadow + *oura* tail]

squirt *vb* **1** to force (a liquid) or (of a liquid) to be forced out of a narrow opening **2** to cover or spatter (a person or thing) with liquid in this way ▷ *n* **3** a jet of liquid **4** a squirting **5** *informal* a small or insignificant person [imitative]

squish *vb* **1** to crush (something) with a soft squelching sound **2** to make a squelching sound ▷ *n* **3** a soft squelching sound [imitative] **squishy** *adj*

Sr **1** (after a name) senior **2** Señor **3** *chem* strontium

Sri Lankan *adj* **1** of Sri Lanka ▷ *n* **2** a person from Sri Lanka

SRN (formerly in Britain) State Registered Nurse

SS **1** an organization in the Nazi Party that provided Hitler's bodyguard, security forces, and concentration-camp guards **2** steamship [(sense 1) German *Schutzstaffel* protection squad]

SSL *computers* secure sockets layer: a protocol for encrypting and transmitting sensitive data securely over the internet

St **1** Saint **2** Street

st. stone

stab *vb* **stabbing, stabbed** **1** to pierce with a sharp pointed instrument **2** (often foll. by *at*) to make a thrust (at); jab **3 stab someone in the back** to do harm to someone by betraying him or her ▷ *n* **4** a stabbing **5** a sudden, usually unpleasant, sensation: *a stab of jealousy* **6** *informal* an attempt: *you've got to have a stab at it* **7 stab in the back** an act of betrayal that harms a person [Middle English *stabbe* stab wound] **stabbing** *n*

stability *n* the quality of being stable: *the security and stability of married life*

stabilize *or* **-lise** *vb* **-lizing, -lized** *or* **-lising, -lised** to make or become stable or more stable **stabilization** *or* **-lisation** *n*

stabilizer *or* **-liser** *n* **1** a device for stabilizing a child's bicycle, an aircraft, or a ship **2** a substance added to food to preserve its texture

stable[1] *n* **1** a building where horses are kept **2** an organization that breeds and trains racehorses **3** an organization that manages or trains several entertainers or athletes ▷ *vb* **-bling, -bled** **4** to put or keep (a horse) in a stable [Latin *stabulum* shed]

stable[2] *adj* **1** steady in position or balance; firm **2** lasting and not likely to experience any sudden changes: *a stable environment* **3** having a calm personality; not moody **4** *physics* (of an elementary particle) not subject to decay **5** *chem* (of a chemical compound) not easily decomposed [Latin *stabilis* steady]

staccato (stak-**ah**-toe) *adj* **1** *music* (of notes) short and separate **2** consisting of short abrupt sounds: *the staccato sound of high-heels on the stairs* ▷ *adv* **3** in a staccato manner [Italian]

stack *n* **1** a pile of things, one on top of the other **2** a large neat pile of hay or straw **3 stacks** a large amount: *there's still stacks for us to do* **4** same as **chimney stack** or **smokestack** **5** an area in a computer memory for temporary storage ▷ *vb* **6** to place (things) in a stack **7** to load or fill (something) up with piles of objects: *Henry was watching her stack the dishwasher* **8** to control (a number of aircraft) waiting to land at an airport so that each flies at a different altitude [Old Norse *stakkr* haystack]

stack up *vb* to compare with someone or something else: *how does this stack up against what you have?*

stadium *n, pl* **-diums** *or* **-dia** a large sports arena with tiered rows of seats for spectators [Greek *stadion*]

staff *n, pl* (for senses 1 and 2) **staffs**, (for senses 3 and 4) **staffs** *or* **staves** **1** the people employed in a company, school, or organization **2** *military* the officers appointed to assist a commander **3** a stick with some special use, such as a walking stick or an emblem of authority **4** *music* a set of five horizontal lines on which music is written and which, along with a clef, indicates pitch ▷ *vb* **5** to provide (a company, school, or organization) with a staff [Old English *stæf*]

staff nurse *n* (in Britain) a qualified nurse ranking just below a sister or charge nurse

Staffs Staffordshire

staff sergeant *n* *military* a noncommissioned officer in an army or in the US Air Force or Marine Corps

stag *n* the adult male of a deer [Old English *stagga*]
stag beetle *n* a beetle with large branched jaws
stage *n* **1** a step or period of development, growth, or progress **2** the platform in a theatre where actors perform **3 the stage** the theatre as a profession **4** the scene of an event or action **5** a part of a journey: *the last stage of his tour around France* **6** short for **stagecoach 7** *Brit & Austral* a division of a bus route for which there is a fixed fare ▷ *vb* **staging, staged 8** to present (a dramatic production) on stage: *to stage 'Hamlet'* **9** to organize and carry out (an event) [Old French *estage* position]
stagecoach *n* a large four-wheeled horse-drawn vehicle formerly used to carry passengers and mail on a regular route
stage direction *n* an instruction to an actor, written into the script of a play
stage door *n* a door at a theatre leading backstage
stage fright *n* feelings of fear and nervousness felt by a person about to appear in front of an audience
stagehand *n* a person who sets the stage and moves props in a theatre
stage-manage *vb* **-managing, -managed** to arrange (an event) from behind the scenes
stage manager *n* a person who supervises the stage arrangements of a production at a theatre
stage-struck *adj* having a great desire to act
stage whisper *n* **1** a loud whisper from an actor, intended to be heard by the audience **2** any loud whisper that is intended to be overheard
stagflation *n* inflation combined with stagnant or falling output and employment [STAGNATION + INFLATION]
stagger *vb* **1** to walk unsteadily **2** to amaze or shock (someone): *it staggered her that there was any liaison between them* **3** to arrange (events) so as not to happen at the same time: *staggered elections* ▷ *n* **4** a staggering [dialect *stacker*] **staggering** *adj* **staggeringly** *adv*
staggers *n* a disease of horses and other domestic animals that causes staggering
staging *n* a temporary support used in building
stagnant *adj* **1** (of water) stale from not moving **2** unsuccessful or dull from lack of change or development [Latin *stagnans*]
stagnate *vb* **-nating, -nated** to become inactive or unchanging: *people in old age only stagnate when they have no interests* **stagnation** *n*
stag night *or* **stag party** *n informal* a party for men only, held for a man who is about to get married
stagy *or US* **stagey** *adj* **stagier, stagiest** too theatrical or dramatic
staid *adj* serious, rather dull, and old-fashioned in behaviour or appearance [obsolete past participle of STAY]
stain *vb* **1** to discolour (something) with marks that are not easily removed **2** to dye (something) with a lasting pigment ▷ *n* **3** a mark or discoloration that is not easily removed **4** an incident in someone's life that has damaged his or her reputation: *a stain on his character* **5** a liquid used to penetrate the surface of a material, such as wood, and colour it without covering up the surface or grain [Middle English *steynen*]
stained glass *n* glass that has been coloured for artistic purposes
stainless steel *n* a type of steel that does not rust, as it contains large amounts of chromium
stair *n* **1** one step in a flight of stairs **2** a series of steps: *he fled down the back stair* ▷ See also **stairs** [Old English *stǣger*]
staircase *n* a flight of stairs, usually with a handrail or banisters
stairs *pl n* a flight of steps going from one level to another, usually indoors
stairway *n* a staircase
stairwell *n* a vertical shaft in a building that contains a staircase
stake[1] *n* **1** a stick or metal bar driven into the ground as part of a fence or as a support or marker **2 be burned at the stake** to be executed by being tied to a stake in the centre of a pile of wood that is then set on fire ▷ *vb* **staking, staked 3** to lay (a claim) to land or rights **4** to support (something, such as a plant) with a stake [Old English *staca* stake, post]
stake[2] *n* **1** the money that a player must risk in order to take part in a gambling game or make a bet **2** an interest, usually financial, held in something: *a 50% stake in a new consortium* **3 at stake** at risk **4 stakes A** the money that a player has available for gambling **B** a prize in a race or contest **C** a horse race in which all owners of competing horses contribute to the prize ▷ *vb* **staking, staked 5** to risk (something, such as money) on a result **6** to give financial support to (a business) [origin unknown]
stakeholder *n* **1** a person or group not owning shares in an enterprise but having an interest in its operations, such as the employees, customers, or local community ▷ *adj* **2** relating to policies intended to allow people to participate in decisions made by enterprises in which they have a stake: *stakeholder economy*
stakeout *n* **1** *slang, chiefly US & Canad* a police surveillance of an area or house ▷ *vb* **stake out 2** *slang, chiefly US & Canad* to keep (an area or house) under surveillance **3** to surround (a piece of land) with stakes
stalactite *n* an icicle-shaped mass of calcium carbonate hanging from the roof of a cave: formed by continually dripping water [Greek *stalaktos* dripping]
stalagmite *n* a large pointed mass of calcium carbonate sticking up from the floor of a cave: formed by continually dripping water from a stalactite [Greek *stalagmos* dripping]
stale *adj* **1** (esp. of food) no longer fresh, having being kept too long **2** (of air) stagnant and having an unpleasant smell **3** lacking in enthusiasm or ideas through overwork or lack of variety **4** uninteresting from having been done or seen too many times: *such achievements now seem stale today* **5** no longer new: *her war had become stale news* [probably from Old French *estale* motionless] **staleness** *n*

stalemate *n* **1** a chess position in which any of a player's moves would place his king in check: in this position the game ends in a draw **2** a situation in which further action by two opposing forces is impossible or will not achieve anything; deadlock [obsolete *stale* standing place + CHECKMATE]

Stalinism *n* the policies associated with Joseph Stalin, general secretary of the Communist Party of the Soviet Union 1922–53, which resulted in rapid industrialization, state terror as a means of political control, and the abolition of collective leadership **Stalinist** *n, adj*

stalk[1] *n* **1** the main stem of a plant **2** a stem that joins a leaf or flower to the main stem of a plant [probably from Old English *stalu* upright piece of wood]

stalk[2] *vb* **1** to follow (an animal or person) quietly and secretly in order to catch or kill them **2** to pursue persistently and, sometimes, attack (a person with whom one is obsessed) **3** to spread over (a place) in a menacing way: *danger stalked the streets* **4** to walk in an angry, arrogant, or stiff way [Old English *bestealcian*] **stalker** *n*

stalking-horse *n* something or someone used to hide a true purpose; pretext

stall[1] *n* **1** a small stand for the display and sale of goods **2** a compartment in a stable or shed for a single animal **3** any small room or compartment: *a shower stall* ▷ *vb* **4** to stop (a motor vehicle or its engine) or (of a motor vehicle or its engine) to stop, by incorrect use of the clutch or incorrect adjustment of the fuel mixture [Old English *steall* a place for standing]

stall[2] *vb* to employ delaying tactics towards (someone); be evasive [Anglo-French *estale* bird used as a decoy]

stallion *n* an uncastrated male horse, usually used for breeding [Old French *estalon*]

stalls *n* **1** the seats on the ground floor of a theatre or cinema **2** (in a church) a row of seats, divided by armrests or a small screen, for the choir or clergy

stalwart (**stawl**-wart) *adj* **1** strong and sturdy **2** loyal and reliable ▷ *n* **3** a hard-working and loyal supporter: *local party stalwarts* [Old English *stǣlwirthe* serviceable]

stamen *n* the part of a flower that produces pollen [Latin: the warp in an upright loom]

stamina *n* energy and strength sustained while performing an activity over a long time [Latin: the threads of life spun out by the Fates, hence energy]

stammer *vb* **1** to speak or say (something) with involuntary pauses or repetition, as a result of a speech disorder or through fear or nervousness ▷ *n* **2** a speech disorder characterized by involuntary repetitions and pauses [Old English *stamerian*]

stamp *n* **1** a printed paper label attached to a piece of mail to show that the required postage has been paid **2** a token issued by a shop or business after a purchase that can be saved and exchanged for other goods sold by that shop or business **3** the action or an act of stamping **4** an instrument for stamping a design or words **5** a design, device, or mark that has been stamped **6** a characteristic feature: *the stamp of inevitability* **7** type or class: *men of his stamp* ▷ *vb* **8** (often foll. by *on*) to bring (one's foot) down heavily **9** to walk with heavy or noisy footsteps **10** to characterize: *a performance that stamped him as a star* **11 stamp on** to subdue or restrain: *all of which have stamped on dissent* **12** to impress or mark (a pattern or sign) on **13** to mark (something) with an official seal or device **14** to have a strong effect on: *a picture vividly stamped on memory* **15** to stick a stamp on (an envelope or parcel) [probably from Old English *stampian*]

stampede *n* **1** a sudden rush of frightened animals or of a crowd ▷ *vb* **-peding, -peded 2** to run away in a stampede [Spanish *estampar* to stamp]

stamping ground *n* a favourite meeting place

stamp out *vb* **1** to put an end to (something) by force; suppress: *an attempt to stamp out democracy* **2** to put out by stamping: *I stamped out my cigarette*

stance *n* **1** an attitude towards a particular matter: *a tough stance in the trade talks* **2** the manner and position in which a person stands **3** *sport* the position taken when about to play the ball [Latin *stare* to stand]

stanch (**stahnch**) *vb* same as **staunch**[2] [Old French *estanchier*]

stanchion *n* a vertical pole or bar used as a support [Old French *estanchon*]

stand *vb* **standing, stood 1** to be upright **2** to rise to an upright position **3** to place (something) upright **4** to be situated: *the property stands in a prime position* **5** to have a specified height when standing: *the structure stands sixty feet above the river* **6** to be in a specified position: *Turkey stands to gain handsomely* **7** to be in a specified state or condition: *how he stands in comparison to others* **8** to remain unchanged or valid: *the Conservatives were forced to let much of the legislation stand* **9 stand at** (of a score or an account) to be in the specified position: *now the total stands at nine* **10** to tolerate or bear: *Christopher can't stand him* **11** to survive: *stand the test of time* **12** (often foll. by *for*) to be a candidate: *to stand for president* **13** *informal* to buy: *to stand someone a drink* **14 stand a chance** to have a chance of succeeding **15 stand one's ground** to maintain a position in the face of opposition **16 stand to reason** to be obvious or logical: *it stands to reason you will play better* **17 stand trial** to be tried in a law court ▷ *n* **18** a stall or counter selling goods: *the hot dog stand* **19** a structure at a sports ground where people can sit or stand **20** the act or an instance of standing **21** a firmly held opinion: *its firm stand on sanctions* **22** *US & Austral* a place in a law court where a witness stands **23** a rack on which coats and hats may be hung **24** a base, support, or piece of furniture in or on which articles may be held or stored: *a guitar stand* **25** an effort to defend oneself or one's beliefs against attack or criticism: *a last stand against superior forces* **26** *cricket* a long period at the wicket by two batsmen **27** See **one-night stand** ▷ See also **stand by, stand down** *etc.* [Old English *standan*]

S

standard *n* **1** a level of quality: *cuisine of a high standard* **2** an accepted example of something against which others are judged or measured: *the work was good by any standard* **3** a moral principle of behaviour **4** a flag of a nation or cause **5** an upright pole or beam used as a support: *a lamp standard* **6** a song that has remained popular for many years ▷ *adj* **7** of a usual, medium, or accepted kind: *a standard cost* **8** of recognized authority: *a standard reference book* **9** denoting pronunciations or grammar regarded as correct and acceptable [Old French *estandart* gathering place]

standard assessment tasks *pl n* (in England, Wales, and Northern Ireland) national standardized tests for assessing school pupils

standard-bearer *n* **1** a leader of a movement or party **2** a person who carries a flag in battle or in a march

Standard English *n linguistics* the style of English that is regarded as correct and acceptable by educated native speakers

standard gauge *n* **1** a railway track with a distance of $56^1/_2$ inches (1.435 m) between the lines: used on most railways ▷ *adj* **standard-gauge** **2** denoting a railway with a standard gauge

standardize *or* **-dise** *vb* **-dizing, -dized** *or* **-dising, -dised** to make (things) standard: *to standardize the preparation process* **standardization** *or* **-disation** *n*

standard lamp *n* a tall electric lamp that has a shade and stands on a base

standard of living *n* the level of comfort and wealth of a person, group, or country

standard time *n* the official local time of a region or country determined by the distance from Greenwich of a line of longitude passing through the area

stand by *vb* **1** to be available and ready to act if needed: *stand by for firing* **2** to be present as an onlooker or without taking any action: *the military police stood by watching idly* **3** to be faithful to: *his wife will stand by him* ▷ *n* **stand-by** **4** a person or thing that is ready for use or can be relied on in an emergency **5** **on stand-by** ready for action or use ▷ *adj* **stand-by** **6** not booked in advance but subject to availability: *stand-by planes*

S

stand down *vb* to resign or withdraw, often in favour of another

stand for *vb* **1** to represent: *AIDS stands for Acquired Immune Deficiency Syndrome* **2** to support and represent (an idea or a belief): *to stand for liberty and truth* **3** *informal* to tolerate or bear: *I won't stand for this!*

stand in *vb* **1** to act as a substitute: *she stood in for her father* ▷ *n* **stand-in** **2** a person who acts as a substitute for another

standing *adj* **1** permanent, fixed, or lasting: *it was a standing joke* **2** used to stand in or on: *standing room only* **3** *athletics* (of a jump or the start of a race) begun from a standing position ▷ *n* **4** social or financial status or reputation: *her international standing* **5** duration: *a friendship of at least ten years' standing*

standing order *n* **1** an instruction to a bank to pay a fixed amount to a person or organization at regular intervals **2** a rule or order governing the procedure of an organization

standoff *n* **1** *US & Canad* the act or an instance of standing off or apart **2** a deadlock or stalemate ▷ *vb* **stand off** **3** to stay at a distance

standoffish *adj* behaving in a formal and unfriendly way

stand out *vb* **1** to be more impressive or important than others of the same kind: *his passing ability stood out in this game* **2** to be noticeable because of looking different: *her long fair hair made her stand out from the rest* **3** to refuse to agree or comply: *a hero who stood out against foreign domination*

standpipe *n chiefly Brit* a temporary vertical pipe installed in a street and supplying water when household water supplies are cut off

standpoint *n* a point of view from which a matter is considered

standstill *n* a complete stoppage or halt: *all traffic came to a standstill*

stand to *vb military* to take up positions in order to defend against attack

stand up *vb* **1** to rise to one's feet **2** *informal* to fail to keep a date with (a boyfriend or girlfriend): *sometimes he would stand me up* **3** to be accepted as satisfactory or true: *the decision would not stand up in court* **4** **stand up for** to support or defend **5** **stand up to** **A** to confront or resist (someone) bravely **B** to withstand and endure (something, such as criticism) ▷ *adj* **stand-up** **6** (of a comedian) telling jokes alone to an audience **7** done while standing: *a stand-up breakfast* **8** (of a fight or row) angry and unrestrained ▷ *n* **stand-up** **9** stand-up comedy or a stand-up comedian

stank *vb* a past tense of **stink**

Stanley knife *n trademark* a type of knife with a thick metal handle with a short, very sharp, replaceable blade [after F. T. *Stanley*, businessman]

stanza *n prosody* a verse of a poem [Italian: halting place]

staphylococcus (staff-ill-oh-**kok**-uss) *n, pl* **-cocci** (-**kok**-eye) a bacterium occurring in clusters and including many species that cause disease [Greek *staphulē* bunch of grapes + *kokkos* berry]

staple[1] *n* **1** a short length of wire bent into a square U-shape, used to fasten papers or secure things ▷ *vb* **-pling, -pled** **2** to secure (things) with staples [Old English *stapol* prop]

staple[2] *adj* **1** of prime importance; principal: *the staple diet of a country* ▷ *n* **2** something that forms a main part of the product, consumption, or trade of a region **3** a main constituent of anything: *the personal reflections which make up the staple of the book* [Middle Dutch *stapel* warehouse]

stapler *n* a device used to fasten things together with a staple

star *n* **1** a planet or meteor visible in the clear night sky as a point of light **2** a hot gaseous mass, such as the sun, that radiates energy as heat and light, or in some cases as radio waves and X-rays. Related adjectives: **astral, sidereal, stellar** **3** **stars** same as **horoscope** (sense 1) **4** an emblem with five or more radiating points, often used as a symbol of rank or an award: *the*

RAC awarded the hotel three stars **5** same as **asterisk** **6** a famous person from the sports, acting, or music professions **7** **see stars** to see flashes of light after a blow on the head ▷ *vb* **starring, starred** **8** to feature (an actor or actress) or (of an actor or actress) to be featured as a star: *he's starred in dozens of films* **9** to mark (something) with a star or stars [Old English *steorra*]

starboard *n* **1** the right side of an aeroplane or ship when facing forwards ▷ *adj* **2** of or on the starboard [Old English *stēorbord*, literally: steering side]

starch *n* **1** a carbohydrate forming the main food element in bread, potatoes, and rice: in solution with water it is used to stiffen fabric **2** food containing a large amount of starch ▷ *vb* **3** to stiffen (cloth) with starch [Old English *sterced* stiffened]

starchy *adj* **starchier, starchiest** **1** of or containing starch **2** (of a person's behaviour) very formal and humourless

star-crossed *adj* (of lovers) destined to misfortune

stardom *n* the status of a star in the entertainment or sport world

stare *vb* **staring, stared** **1** (often foll. by *at*) to look at for a long time **2** **stare one in the face** to be glaringly obvious ▷ *n* **3** a long fixed look [Old English *starian*]

starfish *n, pl* **-fish** *or* **-fishes** a star-shaped sea creature with a flat body and five limbs

star fruit *n* same as **carambola**

stargazer *n informal* an astrologer **stargazing** *n*

stark *adj* **1** harsh, unpleasant, and plain: *a stark choice* **2** grim, desolate, and lacking any beautiful features: *the stark landscapes* **3** utter; absolute: *in stark contrast* ▷ *adv* **4** completely: *stark staring bonkers* [Old English *stearc* stiff] **starkly** *adv* **starkness** *n*

stark-naked *adj* completely naked. Also (informal): **starkers** [Middle English *stert naket*, literally: tail naked]

starlet *n* a young actress who has the potential to become a star

starlight *n* the light that comes from the stars

starling *n* a common songbird with shiny blackish feathers and a short tail [Old English *stærlinc*]

starlit *adj* lit by starlight

Star of David *n* a symbol of Judaism, consisting of a star formed by two interlaced equilateral triangles

starry *adj* **-rier, -riest** **1** (of a sky or night) full of or lit by stars **2** of or like a star or stars: *a starry cast*

starry-eyed *adj* full of unrealistic hopes and dreams; naive

Stars and Stripes *n* the national flag of the United States of America

star sign *n astrol* the sign of the zodiac under which a person was born

Star-Spangled Banner *n* **1** the national anthem of the United States of America **2** same as **Stars and Stripes**

star-studded *adj* featuring many well-known performers: *a star-studded premiere*

start *vb* **1** to begin (something or to do something); come or cause to come into being: *to start a war; this conflict started years ago* **2** to set or be set in motion: *he started the van* **3** to make a sudden involuntary movement from fright or surprise; jump **4** to establish; set up: *to start a state lottery* **5** to support (someone) in the first part of a career or activity **6** *Brit informal* to begin quarrelling or causing a disturbance: *don't start with me* **7** **to start with** in the first place ▷ *n* **8** the first part of something **9** the place or time at which something begins **10** a signal to begin, such as in a race **11** a lead or advantage, either in time or distance, in a competitive activity: *he had an hour's start on me* **12** a slight involuntary movement from fright or surprise: *I awoke with a start* **13** an opportunity to enter a career or begin a project **14** **for a start** in the first place ▷ See also **start off, start on** *etc.* [Old English *styrtan*]

starter *n* **1** *chiefly Brit* the first course of a meal **2** **for starters** *slang* in the first place **3** a device for starting an internal-combustion engine **4** a person who signals the start of a race **5** a competitor in a race or contest **6** **under starter's orders** (of competitors in a race) waiting for the signal to start

startle *vb* **-tling, -tled** to slightly surprise or frighten (someone) [Old English *steartlian* to kick, struggle] **startling** *adj*

start off *vb* **1** to set out on a journey **2** to be or make the first step in (an activity): *beginners should start off with a walking programme* **3** to cause (a person) to do something, such as laugh

start on *vb Brit informal* to pick a quarrel with: *they started on me*

start out *vb* **1** to set out on a journey **2** to take the first steps in a career or on a course of action: *I started out as a beautician; it started out as a joke*

start up *vb* **1** to come or cause (something, such as a business) to come into being; found **2** to set (something) in motion: *she started up the car*

starve *vb* **starving, starved** **1** to die from lack of food **2** to deliberately prevent (a person or animal) from having any food **3** *informal* to be very hungry: *we're both starving* **4** **starve of** to deprive (someone) of something needed: *the heart is starved of oxygen* **5** **starve into** to force someone into a specified state by starving: *an attempt to starve him into submission* [Old English *steorfan* to die] **starvation** *n*

stash *informal* ▷ *vb* **1** (often foll. by *away*) *informal* to store (money or valuables) in a secret place for safekeeping ▷ *n* **2** a secret store, usually of illegal drugs, or the place where this is hidden [origin unknown]

state *n* **1** the condition or circumstances of a person or thing **2** a sovereign political power or community **3** the territory of such a community **4** the sphere of power in such a community: *matters of state* **5** (*often cap*) one of a number of areas or communities having their own governments and forming a federation under a sovereign government, such as in the US or Australia **6** (*often cap*) the government, civil service, and armed forces **7** **in a state** *informal* in an emotional or very worried condition

8 lie in state (of a body) to be placed on public view before burial **9 state of affairs** circumstances or condition: *this wonderful state of affairs* **10** grand and luxurious lifestyle, as enjoyed by royalty, aristocrats, or the wealthy: *living in state* ▷ *adj* **11** controlled or financed by a state: *state ownership* **12** of or concerning the State: *state secrets* **13** involving ceremony: *a state visit* ▷ *vb* **stating, stated 14** to express (something) in words [Latin *stare* to stand]

State Enrolled Nurse *n* (formerly in Britain) a nurse who has completed a two-year training course

statehouse *n NZ* a rented house built by the government

stateless *adj* not belonging to any country: *stateless refugees*

stately *adj* **-lier, -liest** having a dignified, impressive, and graceful appearance or manner: *the Rolls-Royce approached him at a stately speed* **stateliness** *n*

stately home *n Brit* a large old mansion, usually one open to the public

statement *n* **1** something stated, usually a formal prepared announcement or reply **2** *law* a declaration of matters of fact **3** an account prepared by a bank at regular intervals for a client to show all credits and debits and the balance at the end of the period **4** an account containing a summary of bills or invoices and showing the total amount due **5** the act of stating

state of the art *n* **1** the current level of knowledge and development achieved in a technology, science, or art ▷ *adj* **state-of-the-art 2** the most recent and therefore considered the best; up-to-the-minute: *state-of-the-art computers*

State Registered Nurse *n* (formerly in Britain) a nurse who has completed an extensive three-year training course

stateroom *n* **1** a private room on a ship **2** *chiefly Brit* a large room in a palace, etc., used on ceremonial occasions

States *pl n* **the States** *informal* the United States of America

state school *n* a school funded by the state, in which education is free

statesman *n, pl* **-men** an experienced and respected political leader **statesmanship** *n*

static *adj* **1** not active, changing, or moving; stationary **2** *physics* (of a weight, force, or pressure) acting but causing no movement **3** *physics* of forces that do not produce movement ▷ *n* **4** hissing or crackling or a speckled picture caused by interference in the reception of radio or television transmissions **5** electric sparks or crackling produced by friction [Greek *statikos* causing to stand]

static electricity *n* same as **static** (sense 5)

statics *n* the branch of mechanics concerned with the forces producing a state of equilibrium

statin *n med* any of several drugs that inhibit the production of cholesterol

station *n* **1** a place along a route or line at which a bus or train stops to pick up passengers or goods **2** the headquarters of an organization such as the police or fire service **3** a building with special equipment for some particular purpose: *power station; a filling station* **4** a television or radio channel **5** *military* a place of duty **6** position in society: *he had ideas above his station* **7** *Austral & NZ* a large sheep or cattle farm **8** the place or position where a person is assigned to stand: *every man stood at his station* ▷ *vb* **9** to assign (someone) to a station [Latin *statio* a standing still]

stationary *adj* not moving: *a line of stationary traffic* [Latin *stationarius*]

USAGE Avoid confusion with **stationery**.

stationer *n* a person or shop selling stationery [Medieval Latin *stationarius* a person having a regular station, hence a shopkeeper]

stationery *n* writing materials, such as paper, envelopes, and pens

USAGE Avoid confusion with **stationary**.

stationmaster *n* the senior official in charge of a railway station

Stations of the Cross *pl n RC Church* **1** a series of 14 crosses with pictures or carvings, arranged around the walls of a church, to commemorate 14 stages in Christ's journey to Calvary **2** a series of 14 prayers relating to each of these stages

station wagon *n US, Austral & NZ* an estate car

statistic *n* a numerical fact collected and classified systematically **statistical** *adj* **statistically** *adv* **statistician** *n*

statistics *n* **1** the science dealing with the collection, classification, and interpretation of numerical information ▷ *pl n* **2** numerical information which has been collected, classified, and interpreted [originally: science dealing with facts of a state, from New Latin *statisticus* concerning state affairs]

statuary *n* statues collectively

statue *n* a sculpture of a human or animal figure, usually life-size or larger [Latin *statuere* to set up]

statuesque (stat-yoo-**esk**) *adj* (of a woman) tall and well-proportioned; like a classical statue

statuette *n* a small statue

stature *n* **1** the height and size of a person **2** the reputation of a person or their achievements: *a batsman of international stature* **3** moral or intellectual distinction [Latin *stare* to stand]

status *n* **1** a person's position in society **2** the esteem in which people hold a person: *priests feel they have lost some of their status in society* **3** the legal or official standing or classification of a person or country: *the status of refugees; Ireland's non-aligned status* **4** degree of importance [Latin: posture]

status quo *n* the existing state of affairs [literally: the state in which]

status symbol *n* a possession regarded as a mark of social position or wealth

statute *n* **1** a law made by a government and expressed in a formal document **2** a permanent rule made by a company or other institution [Latin *statuere* to set up, decree]

statute law *n* **1** a law made by a government **2** such laws collectively

statutory *adj* **1** required or authorized by law **2** (of an offence) declared by law to be punishable

staunch¹ *adj* strong and loyal: *a staunch supporter* [Old French *estanche*] **staunchly** *adv*

staunch² *or* **stanch** *vb* to stop the flow of (blood) from someone's body

stave *n* **1** one of the long strips of wood joined together to form a barrel or bucket **2** a stick carried as a symbol of office **3** a verse of a poem **4** *music* same as **staff** ▷ *vb* **staving, stove 5 stave in** to burst a hole in (something) [from *staves*, plural of STAFF]

stave off *vb* **staving, staved** to delay (something) for a short time: *to stave off political rebellion*

staves *n* a plural of **staff** or **stave**

stay¹ *vb* **1** to continue or remain in a place, position, or condition: *to stay away; to stay inside* **2** to lodge as a guest or visitor temporarily: *we stay with friends* **3** *Scot & S African* to reside permanently; live **4** to endure (something testing or difficult): *you have stayed the course this long* ▷ *n* **5** the period spent in one place **6** the postponement of an order of a court of law: *a stay of execution* [Old French *ester*]

stay² *n* something that supports or steadies something, such as a prop or buttress [Old French *estaye*]

stay³ *n* a rope or chain supporting a ship's mast or funnel [Old English *stæg*]

stay-at-home *adj* **1** (of a person) enjoying a quiet, settled, and unadventurous life ▷ *n* **2** a stay-at-home person

staycation (stay-kay-shun) *n informal* a holiday in which leisure activities are pursued while staying at one's own home [from STAY¹ + (VA)CATION]

staying power *n* endurance to complete something undertaken; stamina

stays *pl n* old-fashioned corsets with bones in them

staysail *n* a sail fastened on a stay

STD sexually transmitted disease

STD code *n Brit* a code preceding a local telephone number, allowing a caller to dial direct without the operator's help [*s(ubscriber) t(runk) d(ialling)*]

stead *n* **1 stand someone in good stead** to be useful to someone in the future **2** *rare* the function or position that should be taken by another: *I cannot let you rule in my stead* [Old English *stede*]

steadfast *adj* dedicated and unwavering **steadfastly** *adv* **steadfastness** *n*

steady *adj* **steadier, steadiest 1** firm and not shaking **2** without much change or variation: *we're on a steady course* **3** continuous: *a steady decline* **4** not easily excited; sober **5** regular; habitual: *the steady drinking of alcohol* ▷ *vb* **steadies, steadying, steadied 6** to make or become steady ▷ *adv* **7** in a steady manner **8 go steady** *old-fashioned, informal* to date one person regularly ▷ *n, pl* **steadies 9** *informal* one's regular boyfriend or girlfriend ▷ *interj* **10** a warning to keep calm or be careful [from *stead*] **steadily** *adv* **steadiness** *n*

steady state *n physics* the condition of a system when all or most changes or disturbances have been eliminated from it

steak *n* **1** a lean piece of beef for grilling or frying **2** a cut of beef for braising or stewing **3** a thick slice of pork, veal, or fish [Old Norse *steik* roast]

steakhouse *n* a restaurant that specializes in steaks

steal *vb* **stealing, stole, stolen 1** to take (something) from someone without permission or unlawfully **2** to use (someone else's ideas or work) without acknowledgment **3** to move quietly and carefully, not wanting to be noticed: *my father stole up behind her* **4 steal the show** (of a performer) to draw the audience's attention to oneself and away from the other performers **5** to obtain or do (something) stealthily: *I stole a glance behind* ▷ *n* **6** *informal* something acquired easily or at little cost [Old English *stelan*]

stealth *n* **1** moving carefully and quietly, so as to avoid being seen **2** cunning or underhand behaviour ▷ *adj* **3** (of technology) able to render an aircraft almost invisible to radar **4** disguised or hidden [Old English *stelan* to steal] **stealthy** *adj* **stealthily** *adv*

stealth tax *n* an indirect tax, such as a tax on fuel or pension plans, esp. one of which people are unaware or one that is felt to be unfair

steam *n* **1** the vapour into which water changes when boiled **2** the mist formed when such vapour condenses in the atmosphere **3** *informal* power, energy, or speed **4 let off steam** *informal* to release pent-up energy or feelings **5 pick up steam** *informal* to gather momentum ▷ *adj* **6** operated, heated, or powered by steam: *a steam train* ▷ *vb* **7** to give off steam **8** (of a vehicle) to move by steam power **9** *informal* to proceed quickly and often forcefully **10** to cook (food) in steam **11** to treat (something) with steam, such as in cleaning or pressing clothes **12 steam open** *or* **off** to use steam in order to open or remove (something): *let me steam open this letter* ▷ See also **steam up** [Old English *stēam*]

steam engine *n* an engine worked by steam

steamer *n* **1** a boat or ship driven by steam engines **2** a container with holes in the bottom, used to cook food by steam

steam iron *n* an electric iron that uses steam to take creases out of clothes

steamroller *n* **1** a steam-powered vehicle with heavy rollers used for flattening road surfaces during road-making ▷ *vb* **2** to make (someone) do what one wants by overpowering force

steamship *n* a ship powered by steam engines

steam up *vb* **1** to cover (windows or glasses) or (of windows or glasses) to become covered with steam **2 steamed up** *slang* excited or angry

steamy *adj* **steamier, steamiest 1** full of steam **2** *informal* (of books, films, etc.) erotic

steatite (stee-a-tite) *n* same as **soapstone** [Greek *stear* fat]

steed *n archaic, literary* a horse [Old English *stēda* stallion]

steel *n* **1** an alloy of iron and carbon, often with small quantities of other elements **2** a steel rod used for sharpening knives **3** courage and mental toughness ▷ *vb* **4** to prepare (oneself) for coping with something unpleasant: *he had steeled himself to accept the fact* [Old English *stēli*] **steely** *adj*

S

steel band *n music* a band of people playing on metal drums, popular in the West Indies
steel-grey *adj* dark bluish-grey
steel wool *n* a mass of fine steel fibres, used for cleaning metal surfaces
steelworks *n* a factory where steel is made **steelworker** *n*
steep[1] *adj* **1** having a sharp slope **2** *informal* (of a fee, price, or demand) unreasonably high; excessive [Old English *stēap*] **steeply** *adv* **steepness** *n*
steep[2] *vb* **1** to soak or be soaked in a liquid in order to soften or cleanse **2 steeped in** filled with: *an industry steeped in tradition* [Old English *stēpan*]
steepen *vb* to become or cause (something) to become steep or steeper
steeple *n* a tall ornamental tower on a church roof [Old English *stēpel*]
steeplechase *n* **1** a horse race over a course with fences to be jumped **2** a track race in which the runners have to leap hurdles and a water jump ▷ *vb* **-chasing, -chased 3** to race in a steeplechase [so called because it originally took place cross-country, with a church tower serving as a landmark for the riders in the race]
steeplejack *n* a person who repairs steeples and chimneys
steer[1] *vb* **1** to direct the course of (a vehicle or vessel) with a steering wheel or rudder **2** to direct the movements or course of (a person, conversation, or activity) **3** to follow (a specified course): *the Dutch government steered a middle course* **4 steer clear of** to avoid [Old English *stīeran*]
steer[2] *n* a castrated male ox or bull [Old English *stēor*]
steerage *n* **1** the cheapest accommodation on a passenger ship **2** steering
steering committee *n* a committee set up to prepare and arrange topics to be discussed, and the order of business, for a government, etc.
steering wheel *n* a wheel turned by the driver of a vehicle in order to change direction
steersman *n, pl* **-men** the person who steers a vessel
stein (stine) *n* an earthenware beer mug [German *Stein*, literally: stone]
stela (steal-a) *or* **stele** (steal-ee) *n, pl* **stelae** (steal-ee) *or* **steles** an upright stone slab or column decorated with figures or inscriptions, common in prehistoric times [Greek *stēlē*]
stellar *adj* **1** relating to the stars **2** *informal* outstanding or immense: *stellar profits* [Latin *stella* star]
stem[1] *n* **1** the long thin central part of a plant **2** a stalk that bears a flower, fruit, or leaf **3** the long slender part of anything, such as a wineglass **4** *linguistics* the form of a word that remains after removal of all inflectional endings ▷ *vb* **stemming, stemmed 5 stem from** originate from: *this tradition stems from pre-Christian times* [Old English *stemn*]
stem[2] *vb* **stemming, stemmed** to stop or hinder the spread of (something): *to stem the flow of firearms* [Old Norse *stemma*]
stem cell *n histology* an undifferentiated embryonic cell that gives rise to specialized cells, such as blood, bone, etc.
stemmed *adj* having a stem: *long-stemmed roses*
stench *n* a strong and very unpleasant smell [Old English *stenc*]
stencil *n* **1** a thin sheet with a cut-out pattern through which ink or paint passes to form the pattern on the surface below **2** a design or letters made in this way ▷ *vb* **-cilling, -cilled** *or US* **-ciling, -ciled 3** to make (a design or letters) with a stencil [Old French *estenceler* to decorate brightly]
Sten gun *n* a light sub-machine-gun [*S & T* (initials of the inventors) + *-en*, as in *Bren gun*]
stenographer *n US & Canad* a shorthand typist [Greek *stenos* narrow + *graphein* to write]
stent *n* a surgical implant used to keep an artery open
stentorian *adj* (of the voice) very loud: *a stentorian tone* [after *Stentor*, a herald in Greek mythology]
step *n* **1** the act of moving and setting down one's foot, such as when walking **2** the distance covered by such a movement **3** the sound made by such a movement **4** one of a sequence of foot movements that make up a dance **5** one of a sequence of actions taken in order to achieve a goal **6** a degree or rank in a series or scale **7** a flat surface for placing the foot on when going up or down **8** manner of walking: *he moved with a purposeful step* **9 steps A** a flight of stairs, usually out of doors **B** same as **stepladder 10** a short easily travelled distance: *Mexico and Brazil were only a step away* **11 break step** to stop marching in step **12 in step A** marching or dancing in time or at the same pace as other people **B** *informal* in agreement: *in step with public opinion* **13 out of step A** not marching or dancing in time or at the same pace as other people **B** *informal* not in agreement: *out of step with the political mood* **14 step by step** gradually **15 take steps** to do what is necessary (to achieve something) **16 watch one's step A** *informal* to behave with caution **B** to walk carefully ▷ *vb* **stepping, stepped 17** (often foll. by *on*) to move by taking a step, such as in walking **18** to place or press the foot; tread **19** to walk a short distance: *please step this way* **20 step into** to enter (a situation) apparently without difficulty: *she stepped into a life of luxury* ▷ See also **step down, step in** *etc.* [Old English *stepe, stæpe*]
Step *n* **1** a set of aerobic exercises which consists of stepping on and off a special box of adjustable height ▷ *adj* **2** denoting this type of exercise: *Step aerobics*
stepbrother *n* a son of one's stepmother or stepfather
stepchild *n, pl* **-children** a stepson or stepdaughter
stepdaughter *n* a daughter of one's husband or wife by an earlier relationship
step down *vb informal* to resign from a position
stepfather *n* a man who is not one's biological father but is married to one's parent
stephanotis (stef-fan-note-iss) *n* a tropical climbing shrub with sweet-smelling white flowers [Greek: fit for a crown]

step in *vb informal* to intervene (in a quarrel or difficult situation)
stepladder *n* a small folding portable ladder with a supporting frame
stepmother *n* a woman who is not one's biological mother but is married to one's parent
step on *vb* **1** to place or press one's foot on (something): *he stepped on the brakes* **2** *informal* to behave badly towards (a person in a less powerful position) **3 step on it** *informal* to go more quickly; hurry up
step out *vb* **1** to leave a room briefly **2** to walk quickly, taking long strides
step-parent *n* a stepfather or stepmother
steppes *pl n* wide grassy plains without trees, in Siberia or SE Europe [Old Russian *step* lowland]
stepping stone *n* **1** one of a series of stones acting as footrests for crossing a stream **2** a stage in a person's progress towards a goal: *it was a big stepping stone in his career*
stepsister *n* a daughter of one's stepmother or stepfather
stepson *n* a son of one's husband or wife by an earlier relationship
step up *vb* **1** *informal* to increase (something) by stages; accelerate **2 step up to the plate A** *baseball* to move into batting position **B** to come forward and take responsibility for something
stereo *adj* **1** (of a sound system) using two or more separate microphones to feed two or more loudspeakers through separate channels ▷ *n, pl* **stereos 2** a music system in which sound is directed through two speakers **3** sound broadcast or played in stereo
stereophonic *adj* same as **stereo** (sense 1) [Greek *stereos* solid + *phōnē* sound]
stereoscopic *adj* having a three-dimensional effect: *stereoscopic vision*
stereotype *n* **1** a set of characteristics or a fixed idea considered to represent a particular kind of person **2** an idea or convention that has grown stale through fixed usage ▷ *vb* **-typing, -typed 3** to form a standard image or idea of (a type of person) [Greek *stereos* solid + TYPE]
sterile *adj* **1** free from germs **2** unable to produce offspring **3** (of plants) not producing or bearing seeds **4** lacking inspiration or energy; unproductive [Latin *sterilis*] **sterility** *n*
sterilize *or* **-lise** *vb* **-lizing, -lized** *or* **-lising, -lised** to make sterile **sterilization** *or* **-lisation** *n*
sterling *n* **1** British money: *sterling fell against the dollar* ▷ *adj* **2** genuine and reliable: first-class: *he has a reputation for sterling honesty* [probably Old English *steorra* star, referring to a small star on early Norman pennies]
sterling silver *n* **1** an alloy containing at least 92.5 per cent of silver **2** articles made of sterling silver
stern[1] *adj* **1** strict and serious: *he's a very stern taskmaster* **2** difficult and often unpleasant: *the stern demands of the day* **3** (of a facial expression) severe and disapproving [Old English *styrne*] **sternly** *adv*
stern[2] *n* the rear part of a boat or ship [Old Norse *stjōrn* steering]
sternum *n, pl* **-na** *or* **-nums** a long flat bone in the front of the body, to which the collarbone and most of the ribs are attached [Greek *sternon*]
steroid *n biochem* an organic compound containing a carbon ring system, such as sterols and many hormones
sterol *n biochem* a natural insoluble alcohol such as cholesterol and ergosterol [shortened from *cholesterol, ergosterol, etc.*]
stertorous *adj* (of breathing) laboured and noisy [Latin *stertere* to snore]
stet *vb* **stetting, stetted 1** used as an instruction to indicate to a printer that certain deleted matter is to be kept **2** to mark (matter) in this way [Latin, literally: let it stand]
stethoscope *n med* an instrument for listening to the sounds made inside the body, consisting of a hollow disc that transmits the sound through hollow tubes to earpieces [Greek *stēthos* breast + *skopein* to look at]
Stetson *n trademark* a felt hat with a broad brim and high crown, worn mainly by cowboys [after John *Stetson*, American hat maker]
stevedore *n chiefly US* a person employed to load or unload ships [Spanish *estibador* a packer]
stew *n* **1** a dish of meat, fish, or other food, cooked slowly in a closed pot **2 in a stew** *informal* in a troubled or worried state ▷ *vb* **3** to cook by long slow simmering in a closed pot **4** *informal* (of a person) to be too hot **5** to cause (tea) to become bitter or (of tea) to become bitter through infusing for too long **6 stew in one's own juice** to suffer, without help, the results of one's actions [Middle English *stuen* to take a very hot bath]
steward *n* **1** a person who looks after passengers and serves meals on a ship or aircraft **2** an official who helps to supervise a public event, such as a race **3** a person who administers someone else's property **4** a person who manages the eating arrangements, staff, or service at a club or hotel **5** See **shop steward** ▷ *vb* **6** to act as a steward (of) [Old English *stigweard* hall keeper]
stewardess *n* a female steward on an aircraft or ship
stewed *adj* **1** (of food) cooked by stewing **2** *Brit* (of tea) bitter through having been left to infuse for too long **3** *slang* drunk
stick[1] *n* **1** a small thin branch of a tree **2 A** a long thin piece of wood **B** such a piece of wood shaped for a special purpose: *a walking stick; a hockey stick* **3** a piece of something shaped like a stick: *a stick of cinnamon* **4** *slang* verbal abuse, criticism: *they gave me a lot of stick* **5 the sticks** a country area considered backward or unsophisticated: *places out in the sticks* **6 sticks** pieces of furniture: *these few sticks are all I have* **7** *informal* a person: *not a bad old stick* **8 get hold of the wrong end of the stick** to misunderstand a situation or an explanation completely [Old English *sticca*]
stick[2] *vb* **sticking, stuck 1** to push (a pointed object) or (of a pointed object) to be pushed into another object **2** to fasten (something) in position by pins, nails, or glue: *she just stuck the label on* **3** to extend beyond something else;

protrude: *he stuck his head out of the door* **4** *informal* to place (something) in a specified position: *stick it in the oven* **5** to fasten or be fastened by or as if by an adhesive **6** to come or be brought to a standstill: *stuck in a rut; two army lorries stuck behind us* **7** to remain for a long time: *the room that sticks in my mind the most* **8** *slang, chiefly Brit* to tolerate; abide: *you couldn't stick it for more than two days* **9** **be stuck** *informal* to be at a loss for; to be baffled or puzzled: *I'm stuck; stuck for words* ▷ See also **stick around**, **stick by** *etc.* [Old English *stician*]

stick around *vb informal* to remain in a place, often when waiting for something

stick by *vb* to remain faithful to: *she's stuck by me for sixty years*

sticker *n* a small piece of paper with a picture or writing on it that can be stuck to a surface

sticking plaster *n* a piece of adhesive material used for covering slight wounds

stick insect *n* a tropical insect with a long thin body and legs, which looks like a twig

stick-in-the-mud *n informal* a person who is unwilling to try anything new or do anything exciting

stickleback *n* a small fish with sharp spines along its back [Old English *sticel* prick, sting + BACK]

stickler *n* a person who insists on something: *a stickler for punctuality*

stick out *vb* **1** to (cause to) project from something else: *she stuck her tongue out at me* **2** *informal* to endure (something unpleasant): *she would stick it out for a year* **3** **stick out a mile** *or* **like a sore thumb** *informal* to be very obvious **4** **stick out for** to continue to demand (something), refusing to accept anything less

stick to *vb* **1** to adhere or cause (something) to adhere to: *the soil sticks to the blade* **2** to remain faithful to (a person, promise, or rule) **3** not to move away from: *stick to the agreement*

stick-up *n slang, chiefly US* a robbery at gunpoint; hold-up

stick up for *vb informal* to support or defend (oneself, another person, or a principle)

sticky *adj* **stickier, stickiest** **1** covered with a substance that sticks to other things: *sticky little fingers* **2** intended to stick to a surface: *sticky labels* **3** *informal* difficult or painful: *a sticky meeting* **4** (of weather) unpleasantly warm and humid **stickiness** *n*

sticky wicket *n* **on a sticky wicket** *informal* in a difficult situation

stiff *adj* **1** firm and not easily bent **2** moving with pain or difficulty: *stiff and aching joints* **3** not moving easily: *the door is stiff* **4** difficult or severe: *a stiff challenge; stiff penalties* **5** formal and not relaxed **6** fairly firm in consistency; thick **7** powerful: *a stiff breeze* **8** (of a drink) containing a lot of alcohol ▷ *n* **9** *slang* a corpse ▷ *adv* **10** completely or utterly: *I was bored stiff* [Old English *stīf*] **stiffly** *adv* **stiffness** *n*

stiffen *vb* to make or become stiff or stiffer

stiff-necked *adj* proud and stubborn

stifle *vb* **-fling, -fled** **1** to stop oneself from expressing (a yawn or cry) **2** to stop (something) from continuing: *the new leadership stifled all internal debate* **3** to feel discomfort and difficulty in breathing **4** to kill (someone) by preventing him or her from breathing [probably from Old French *estouffer* to smother]

stifling *adj* uncomfortably hot and stuffy

stigma *n, pl* **stigmas** *or* **stigmata** **1** a mark of social disgrace: *a stigma attached to being redundant* **2** *botany* the part of a flower that receives pollen **3** **stigmata** *Christianity* marks resembling the wounds of the crucified Christ, believed to appear on the bodies of certain people [Greek: brand]

stigmatize *or* **-tise** *vb* **-tizing, -tized** *or* **-tising, -tised** to regard as being shameful

stile *n* a set of steps in a wall or fence to allow people, but not animals, to pass over [Old English *stigel*]

stiletto *n, pl* **-tos** **1** Also called: **spike heel, stiletto heel** a high narrow heel on a woman's shoe or a shoe with such a heel **2** a small dagger with a slender tapered blade [Italian: little dagger]

still[1] *adv* **1** continuing now or in the future as in the past: *she still loved the theatre* **2** up to this or that time; yet **3** even or yet: *still more pressure on the government* **4** even then; nevertheless: *the baby has been fed and still cries* **5** quietly or without movement: *keep still* ▷ *adj* **6** motionless; stationary **7** undisturbed; silent and calm **8** (of a soft drink) not fizzy ▷ *n* **9** *poetic* silence or tranquillity: *the still of night* **10** a still photograph from a film ▷ *vb* **11** to make or become quiet or calm **12** to relieve or end: *Fowler stilled his conscience* [Old English *stille*] **stillness** *n*

still[2] *n* an apparatus for distilling spirits [Latin *stilla* a drip]

stillborn *adj* **1** (of a baby) dead at birth **2** (of an idea or plan) completely unsuccessful **stillbirth** *n*

still life *n, pl* **still lifes** **1** a painting or drawing of objects such as fruit or flowers **2** this kind of painting or drawing

still room *n Brit* **1** a room in which distilling is carried out **2** a room for storing food in a large house

stilt *n* **1** either of a pair of long poles with footrests for walking raised from the ground **2** a long post or column used with others to support a building above ground level [Middle English *stilte*]

stilted *adj* (of speech, writing, or behaviour) formal or pompous; not flowing continuously or naturally

Stilton *n trademark* a strong-flavoured blue-veined cheese [named after *Stilton*, Cambridgeshire]

stimulant *n* **1** a drug, food, or drink that makes the body work faster, increases heart rate, and makes sleeping difficult **2** any stimulating thing ▷ *adj* **3** stimulating

stimulate *vb* **-lating, -lated** **1** to encourage to start or progress further: *a cut in interest rates should help stimulate economic recovery* **2** to fill (a person) with ideas or enthusiasm: *books satisfy a part of the intellect that needs to be stimulated* **3** *physiol* to excite (a nerve or organ) with a stimulus [Latin *stimulare*] **stimulation** *n*

stimulating *adj* **1** inspiring new ideas or enthusiasm **2** (of a physical activity) making one feel refreshed and energetic; invigorating

stimulus (**stim**-myew-luss) *n, pl* **-li** (-lie) **1** something that acts as an incentive to (someone) **2** something, such as a drug or electrical impulse, that is capable of causing a response in a person or an animal [Latin: a cattle goad]

sting *vb* **stinging, stung 1** (of certain animals and plants) to inflict a wound on (someone) by the injection of poison **2** to cause (someone) to feel a sharp physical pain: *her hand was stinging* **3** to offend or upset (someone) with a critical remark: *I was stung by what he said* **4** to provoke (a response) by angering: *the consulate would be stung into convulsive action* **5** *informal* to cheat (someone) by overcharging ▷ *n* **6** a skin wound caused by stinging **7** pain caused by or as if by a sting **8** a mental pain: *the sting of memory* **9** the sharp pointed organ of certain animals or plants used to inject poison **10** *slang* a deceptive trick **11** *slang* a trap set up by the police to entice a person to commit a crime, thereby producing evidence [Old English *stingan*] **stinging** *adj*

stinging nettle *n* same as **nettle** (sense 1)

stingray *n* a flat fish with a jagged whiplike tail capable of inflicting painful wounds

stingy *adj* **-gier, -giest** very mean [perhaps from *stinge*, dialect variant of STING] **stinginess** *n*

stink *n* **1** a strong unpleasant smell **2 make** *or* **create** *or* **kick up a stink** *slang* to make a fuss ▷ *vb* **stinking, stank** *or* **stunk, stunk 3** to give off a strong unpleasant smell **4** *slang* to be thoroughly bad or unpleasant: *the script stinks, the casting stinks* [Old English *stincan*] **stinky** *adj*

stink bomb *n* a small glass globe used by practical jokers: it releases a liquid with a strong unpleasant smell when broken

stinker *n slang* a difficult or very unpleasant person or thing

stinking *adj* **1** having a strong unpleasant smell **2** *informal* unpleasant or disgusting ▷ *adv* **3 stinking rich** *informal* very wealthy

stink out *vb* **1** to drive (people) away by a foul smell **2** *Brit & NZ* to cause (a place) to stink: *I won't have it stinking the car out!*

stint *vb* **1** to be miserly with (something): *don't stint on paper napkins* ▷ *n* **2** a given amount of work [Old English *styntan* to blunt]

stipend (**sty**-pend) *n* a regular salary or allowance, esp. that paid to a member of the clergy [Latin *stipendium* tax] **stipendiary** *adj*

stipple *vb* **-pling, -pled** to draw, engrave, or paint (something) using dots or flecks [Dutch *stippelen*]

stipulate *vb* **-lating, -lated** to specify (something) as a condition of an agreement [Latin *stipulari*] **stipulation** *n*

stir[1] *vb* **stirring, stirred 1** to mix up (a liquid) by moving a spoon or stick around in it **2** to move slightly **3 stir from** to depart from (one's usual or preferred place). **4** to get up after sleeping **5** to excite or move (someone) emotionally **6** to move (oneself) quickly or vigorously; exert (oneself) **7** to wake up: *to stir someone from sleep* ▷ *n* **8** a stirring **9** a strong reaction, usually of excitement: *she created a stir wherever she went* ▷ See also **stir up** [Old English *styrian*]

stir[2] *n chiefly US slang* prison: *in stir* [Romany *stariben* prison]

stir-crazy *adj slang* mentally disturbed as a result of being in prison

stir-fry *vb* **-fries, -frying, -fried 1** to cook (food) quickly by stirring it in a wok or frying pan over a high heat ▷ *n, pl* **-fries 2** a dish cooked in this way

stirrer *n informal* a person who deliberately causes trouble

stirring *adj* causing emotion, excitement, and enthusiasm

stirrup *n* a metal loop attached to a saddle for supporting a rider's foot [Old English *stig* step + *rāp* rope]

stirrup cup *n chiefly Brit* a cup containing an alcoholic drink offered to riders before they depart on a journey or hunt

stirrup pump *n* a hand-operated pump, the base of which is placed in a bucket of water: used in fighting fires

stir up *vb* **1** to cause (leaves or dust) to rise up and swirl around **2** to set (something) in motion: *that fact has stirred up resentment*

stitch *n* **1** a link made by drawing a thread through material with a needle **2** a loop of yarn formed around a needle or hook in knitting or crocheting **3** a particular kind of stitch **4** *informal* a link of thread joining the edges of a wound together **5** a sharp pain in the side caused by running or exercising **6 in stitches** *informal* laughing uncontrollably **7 not a stitch** *informal* no clothes at all ▷ *vb* **8** to sew or fasten (something) with stitches [Old English *stice* sting] **stitching** *n*

stitch up *vb* **1** to join by stitching **2** *slang* to incriminate by manufacturing evidence **3** *slang* to prearrange in a clandestine manner ▷ *n* **stitch-up 4** *slang* a matter that has been prearranged clandestinely

St Leger (saint **led**-jer) *n* an annual horse race for three-year-old horses, run at Doncaster

stoat *n* a small brown N European mammal related to the weasel: in winter it has a white coat and is then known as an ermine [origin unknown]

stock *n* **1** the total amount of goods kept on the premises of a shop or business **2** a supply of something stored for future use **3** *finance* **A** the money raised by a company through selling shares entitling their holders to dividends, partial ownership, and usually voting rights **B** the proportion of this money held by an individual shareholder **C** the shares of a specified company or industry **4** farm animals bred and kept for their meat, skins, etc. **5** the original type from which a particular race, family, or group is descended **6** the handle of a rifle, held by the firer against the shoulder **7** a liquid produced by simmering meat, fish, bones, or vegetables, and used to make soups and sauces **8** a kind of plant grown for its brightly coloured flowers **9** *old-fashioned* the degree of status a person has **10** See **laughing stock 11 in stock** stored on the premises or available for sale or use **12 out of stock** not immediately available for sale or use **13 take stock** to think carefully about a situation before making a decision ▷ *adj* **14** staple; standard: *stock sizes in clothes* **15** being a cliché; hackneyed: *the stock answer* ▷ *vb* **16** to keep (goods) for sale **17** to obtain a store of (something) for future use or sale: *to stock up on food* **18** to supply (a farm) with animals or (a lake or stream) with fish ▷ See also **stocks** [Old English *stocc* tree trunk]

stockade *n* an enclosure or barrier of large wooden posts [Spanish *estacada*]

stockbreeder *n* a person who breeds or rears farm animals

stockbroker *n* a person who buys and sells stocks and shares for customers and receives a percentage of their profits **stockbroking** *n*

stock car *n* a car that has been strengthened and modified for a form of racing in which the cars often collide

stock cube *n* a small solid cube made from dried meat or vegetables, used to add flavouring to stew, soup, etc.

stock exchange *n* **1 A** a highly organized market for the purchase and sale of stocks and shares, operated by professional stockbrokers and market makers according to fixed rules **B** a place where stocks and shares are traded **2** the prices or trading activity of a stock exchange: *the stock exchange has been rising*

stockholder *n* an owner of some of a company's stock

stockinette *n* a machine-knitted elastic fabric [perhaps from *stocking-net*]

stocking *n* a long piece of close-fitting nylon or knitted yarn covering the foot and part or all of a woman's leg [dialect *stock* stocking]

stockinged *adj* **in one's stockinged feet** wearing stockings, tights, or socks but no shoes

stocking stitch *n* alternate rows of plain and purl in knitting

stock in trade *n* a person's typical behaviour or usual work: *practicality is the farmer's stock in trade*

stockist *n Brit commerce* a dealer who stocks a particular product

stock market *n* same as **stock exchange**

stockpile *vb* **-piling, -piled 1** to store a large quantity of (something) for future use ▷ *n* **2** a large store gathered for future use

stockpot *n Brit & NZ* a pot in which stock for soup is made

stockroom *n* a room in which a stock of goods is kept in a shop or factory

stock route *n Austral & NZ* a route designated for droving farm animals, so as to avoid traffic

stocks *pl n history* an instrument of punishment consisting of a heavy wooden frame with holes in which the feet, hands, or head of an offender were locked

stock-still *adv* absolutely still; motionlessly

stocktaking *n* **1** the counting and valuing of goods in a shop or business **2** a reassessment of a person's current situation and prospects

stocky *adj* **stockier, stockiest** (of a person) short but well-built **stockily** *adv* **stockiness** *n*

stockyard *n* a large yard with pens or covered buildings where farm animals are sold

stodge *n Brit, Austral & NZ informal* heavy and filling starchy food [perhaps blend of STUFF + *podge* a short plump person]

stodgy *adj* **stodgier, stodgiest 1** (of food) full of starch and very filling **2** (of a person) dull, serious, or excessively formal [from STODGE] **stodginess** *n*

stoep (stoop) *n* (in South Africa) a verandah [Afrikaans]

stoic (stow-ik) *n* **1** a person who suffers great difficulties without showing his or her emotions ▷ *adj* **2** same as **stoical**

Stoic *n* **1** a member of the ancient Greek school of philosophy which believed that virtue and happiness could be achieved only by calmly accepting Fate ▷ *adj* **2** of or relating to the Stoics [Greek *stoa* porch] **Stoicism** *n*

stoical *adj* suffering great difficulties without showing one's feelings **stoically** *adv* **stoicism** (stow-iss-iz-zum) *n*

stoke *vb* **stoking, stoked 1** to feed and tend (a fire or furnace) **2** to excite or encourage (a strong emotion) in oneself or someone else [from STOKER]

stoked *adj slang* extremely excited

stokehold *n naut* the hold for a ship's boilers; fire room

stoker *n* a person employed to tend a furnace on a ship or train powered by steam [Dutch *stoken* to stoke]

stole[1] *vb* the past tense of **steal**

stole[2] *n* a long scarf or shawl, worn by women [Greek *stolē* clothing]

stolen *vb* the past participle of **steal**

stolid *adj* showing little or no emotion or interest in anything [Latin *stolidus* dull] **stolidity** *n* **stolidly** *adv*

stoma (stow-ma) *n, pl* **stomata** (stow-ma-ta) **1** *botany* a pore in a plant leaf that controls the passage of gases into and out of the plant **2** *zool* a mouth or mouthlike part [Greek: mouth]

stomach *n* **1** an organ inside the body in which food is stored until it has been partially digested **2** the front of the body around the waist **3** desire or appetite: *he still has the stomach for a fight* ▷ *vb* **4** to put up with: *liberals could not stomach the rest of the package* [Greek *stoma* mouth]

stomach ache *n* pain in the stomach, such as from indigestion

stomacher *n history* a decorative V-shaped panel of stiff material worn over the chest and stomach mainly by women

stomach pump *n med* a pump with a long tube used for removing the contents of a person's stomach, for instance after he or she has swallowed poison

stomp *vb* to tread or stamp heavily [variant of STAMP]

stompie *n S African slang* **1** a cigarette butt **2** a short man [Afrikaans *stomp* stump]

stone *n* **1** the hard nonmetallic material of which rocks are made **2** a small lump of rock **3** Also called: **gemstone** a precious or semiprecious stone that has been cut and polished **4** a piece of rock used for some particular purpose: *gravestone; millstone* **5** the hard central part of fruits such as the peach or date **6** *pl* **stone** *Brit* a unit of weight equal to 14 pounds or 6.350 kilograms **7** *pathol* a hard deposit formed in the kidney or bladder **8 heart of stone** a hard or unemotional personality **9 leave no stone unturned** to do everything possible to achieve something ▷ *adj* **10** made of stoneware: *the polished stone planter* ▷ *vb* **stoning, stoned 11** to throw stones at (someone), for example as a punishment **12** to remove the stones from (a fruit) [Old English *stān*]

Stone Age *n* a phase of human culture identified by the use of tools made of stone

stonechat *n* a songbird that has black feathers and a reddish-brown breast [from its cry, which sounds like clattering pebbles]

stone-cold *adj* **1** completely cold ▷ *adv* **2 stone-cold sober** completely sober

stoned *adj slang* under the influence of drugs or alcohol

stone-deaf *adj* completely deaf

stone fruit *n* same as **drupe**

stoneground *adj* **1** (of flour) made by crushing grain between two large stones **2** made with stoneground flour: *stoneground wholemeal bread*

stonemason *n* a person who is skilled in preparing stone for building

stone's throw *n* a short distance

stonewall *vb* **1** to deliberately prolong a discussion by being long-winded or evasive **2** *cricket* (of a batsman) to play defensively

stoneware *n* a hard type of pottery, fired at a very high temperature

stonewashed *adj* (of clothes or fabric) given a worn faded look by being washed with many small pieces of stone

stonework *n* any structure or part of a building made of stone

stonkered *adj NZ slang* completely exhausted or beaten; whacked [from *stonker* to beat, of unknown origin]

stony *or* **stoney** *adj* **stonier, stoniest 1** (of ground) rough and covered with stones: *the stony path* **2** (of a face, voice, or attitude) unfriendly and unsympathetic **stonily** *adv*

stony-broke *adj slang* completely without money

stood *vb* the past of **stand**

stooge *n* **1** an actor who feeds lines to a comedian or acts as the butt of his jokes **2** *slang* someone who is taken advantage of by someone in a superior position [origin unknown]

stool *n* **1** a seat with legs but no back **2** waste matter from the bowels [Old English *stōl*]

stool pigeon *n* an informer for the police

stoop¹ *vb* **1** to bend (the body) forward and downward **2** to stand or walk with head and shoulders habitually bent forward **3 stoop to** to lower one's normal standards of behaviour; degrade oneself: *no real journalist would stoop to faking* ▷ *n* **4** the act, position, or habit of stooping [Old English *stūpian*] **stooping** *adj*

stoop² *n US* an open porch or small platform with steps leading up to it at the entrance to a building [Dutch *stoep*]

stop *vb* **stopping, stopped 1** to cease from doing (something); discontinue **2** to cause (something moving) to halt or (of something moving) to come to a halt **3** to prevent the continuance or completion of (something) **4** (often foll. by *from*) to prevent or restrain: *I stopped her from going on any further* **5** to keep back: *no agreement to stop arms supplies* **6 stop up** to block or plug: *to stop up a pipe* **7** to stay or rest: *we stopped at a camp site for a change* **8** to instruct a bank not to honour (a cheque) **9** to deduct (money) from pay **10** *informal* to receive (a blow or hit) **11** *music* to alter the vibrating length of (a string on a violin, guitar, etc.) by pressing down on it at some point with the finger **12 stop at nothing** to be prepared to do anything; be ruthless ▷ *n* **13** prevention of movement or progress: *you can put a stop to it quite easily* **14** the act of stopping or the state of being stopped: *the car lurched to a stop* **15** a place where something halts or pauses: *a bus stop* **16** the act or an instance of blocking or obstructing **17** a device that prevents, limits, or ends the motion of a mechanism or moving part **18** *Brit* a full stop **19** *music* a knob on an organ that is operated to allow sets of pipes to sound **20 pull out all the stops** to make a great effort [Old English *stoppian* (unattested)]

stopbank *n NZ* an embankment to prevent flooding

stopcock *n* a valve used to control or stop the flow of a fluid in a pipe

stopgap *n* a thing that serves as a substitute for a short time until replaced by something more suitable

stop off *vb* (often foll. by *at*) to halt and call somewhere on the way to another place

stopover *n* **1** a break in a journey ▷ *vb* **stop over 2** to make a stopover

stoppage *n* **1** the act of stopping something or the state of being stopped: *a heart stoppage* **2** a deduction of money, such as taxation, from pay **3** an organized stopping of work during industrial action

stoppage time *n chiefly Brit* same as **injury time**

stopper *n* a plug for closing a bottle, pipe, etc.

stop press *n* news items inserted into a newspaper after the printing has been started

stopwatch *n* a watch which can be stopped instantly for exact timing of a sporting event

storage *n* **1** the act of storing or the state of being stored **2** space for storing **3** *computers* the process of storing information in a computer

storage device *n* a piece of computer equipment, such as a disk or memory card, on which information can be stored

storage heater *n* an electric device that accumulates and radiates heat generated by cheap off-peak electricity

store *vb* **storing, stored 1** to keep, set aside, or gather (things) for future use **2** to place (furniture or other possessions) in a warehouse for safekeeping **3** to supply or stock (certain goods) **4** *computers* to enter or keep (information) in a storage device ▷ *n* **5** a shop (in Britain usually a large one) **6** a large supply or stock kept for future use **7** short for **department store**

S

8 a storage place, such as a warehouse **9** *computers, chiefly Brit* same as **memory** (sense 7) **10 in store** about to happen; forthcoming: *you've got a treat in store* **11 set great store by something** to value something as important ▷ See also **stores** [Old French *estor*]

storehouse *n* **1** a building where goods are stored **2** a collection of things or ideas: *a storehouse of memories*

storeroom *n* a room in which things are stored

stores *pl n* a supply or stock of food and other essentials for a journey

storey *or esp US* **story** *n, pl* **-reys** *or* **-ries** a floor or level of a building [Anglo-Latin *historia* picture, probably from the pictures on medieval windows]

stork *n* a large wading bird with very long legs, a long bill, and white-and-black feathers [Old English *storc*]

storm *n* **1** a violent weather condition of strong winds, rain, hail, thunder, lightning, etc. **2** a violent disturbance or quarrel: *a storm of protest from the opposition* **3** (usually foll. by *of*) a heavy discharge of bullets or missiles **4 take a place by storm** **A** to capture or overrun a place by a violent attack **B** to surprise people, but receive their praise, by being extremely successful at something ▷ *vb* **5** to attack or capture (a place) suddenly and violently **6** to shout angrily **7** to move or rush violently or angrily: *she stormed into the study* [Old English]

storm centre *n* **1** the centre of a storm, where pressure is lowest **2** the centre of any disturbance or trouble

storm door *n* an additional door outside an ordinary door, providing extra protection against wind, cold, and rain

storm trooper *n* a member of the paramilitary wing of the Nazi Party

stormy *adj* **stormier, stormiest** **1** (of weather) violent with dark skies, heavy rain or snow, and strong winds **2** involving violent emotions: *a stormy affair*

S

stormy petrel *or* **storm petrel** *n* **1** a small sea bird with dark feathers and paler underparts **2** a person who brings trouble

story¹ *n, pl* **-ries** **1** a description of a chain of events told or written in prose or verse **2** Also called: **short story** a piece of fiction, shorter and usually less detailed than a novel **3** Also called: **story line** the plot of a book or film **4** a news report **5** the event or material for such a report **6** *informal* a lie [Latin *historia*]

story² *n, pl* **-ries** *chiefly US* same as **storey**

storybook *n* **1** a book containing stories for children ▷ *adj* **2** better or happier than in real life: *a storybook romance*

stoup *or* **stoop** (stoop) *n* a small basin in a church for holy water [from Old Norse]

stoush *Austral & NZ slang* ▷ *vb* **1** to hit or punch (someone) ▷ *n* **2** fighting or violence [origin unknown]

stout *adj* **1** solidly built or fat **2** strong and sturdy: *stout footwear* **3** brave or determined: *we met unexpectedly stout resistance* ▷ *n* **4** a kind of strong, black beer [Old French *estout* bold] **stoutly** *adv*

stouthearted *adj old-fashioned* determined or brave

stove¹ *n* **1** same as **cooker** (sense 1) **2** any apparatus for heating, such as a kiln [Old English *stofa* bathroom]

stove² *vb* a past tense and past participle of **stave**

stovepipe *n* a pipe that takes fumes and smoke away from a stove

stow *vb* (often foll. by *away*) to pack or store (something) [Old English *stōwian* to keep]

stowage *n* **1** space, room, or a charge for stowing goods **2** the act of stowing

stowaway *n* **1** a person who hides aboard a ship or aircraft in order to travel free ▷ *vb* **stow away** **2** to travel in such a way: *he stowed away on a ferry*

strabismus *n pathol* same as **squint** (sense 3) [Greek *strabismos*]

straddle *vb* **-dling, -dled** **1** to have one leg or part on each side of (something) **2** *US & Canad informal* to be in favour of both sides of (an issue or argument) [from *stride*]

Stradivarius *n* a violin manufactured in Italy by Antonio Stradivari (?1644–1737) or his family

strafe *vb* **strafing, strafed** to machine-gun (an enemy) from the air [German *strafen* to punish]

straggle *vb* **-gling, -gled** **1** to spread out in an untidy and rambling way: *the town straggled off to the east* **2** to linger behind or wander from a main line or part [origin unknown] **straggler** *n* **straggly** *adj*

straight *adj* **1** continuing in the same direction without bending; not curved or crooked **2** even, level, or upright **3** in keeping with the facts; accurate **4** outright or candid: *a straight rejection* **5** in continuous succession **6** (of an alcoholic drink) undiluted **7** not wavy or curly: *straight hair* **8** in good order **9** (of a play or acting style) straightforward or serious **10** honest, respectable, or reliable **11** heterosexual **12** *slang* conventional in views, customs, or appearance **13** *informal* no longer owing or being owed something: *if you buy the next round we'll be straight* ▷ *adv* **14** in a straight line or direct course **15** immediately; at once: *get straight back here* **16** in a level or upright position: *he sat up straight* **17** continuously; uninterruptedly: *we waited for three hours straight* **18** (often foll. by *out*) frankly; candidly: *she asked me straight out* **19 go straight** *informal* to reform after having been a criminal **20 straight away** *or* **straightaway** at once ▷ *n* **21** a straight line, form, part, or position **22** *Brit* a straight part of a racetrack **23** a heterosexual person [Old English *streccan* to stretch]

straighten *vb* (sometimes foll. by *up* or *out*) **1** to make or become straight **2** to make (something) neat or tidy

straighten out *vb* to make (something) less complicated or confused

straight face *n* a serious facial expression which hides a desire to laugh **straight-faced** *adj*

straight fight *n* a contest between two candidates only

straightforward *adj* **1** (of a person) honest, frank, and open **2** (of a task) easy to do

straight man *n* an actor who acts as the butt of a comedian's jokes

strain[1] *n* **1** tension or tiredness resulting from overwork or worry **2** tension between people or organizations: *there are signs of strain between the economic superpowers* **3** an intense physical or mental effort **4** the damage resulting from excessive physical exertion **5** a great demand on the emotions, strength, or resources **6** a way of speaking: *he would have gone on in this strain for some time* **7** *physics* the change in dimension of a body caused by outside forces **8 strains** *music* a theme, melody, or tune ▷ *vb* **9** to subject (someone) to mental tension or stress **10** to make an intense effort: *the rest were straining to follow the conversation* **11** to use (resources) to, or beyond, their limits **12** to injure or damage (oneself or a part of one's body) by overexertion: *he appeared to have strained a muscle* **13** to pour (a substance) through a sieve or filter **14 strain at** to push, pull, or work with violent effort on (something) **15** to draw (something) taut or be drawn taut [Latin *stringere* to bind tightly]

strain[2] *n* **1** a group of animals or plants within a species or variety, distinguished by one or more minor characteristics **2** a trace or streak: *a strain of ruthlessness in their play* [Old English *strēon*]

strained *adj* **1** (of an action, expression, etc.) not natural or spontaneous **2** (of an atmosphere, relationship, etc.) not relaxed; tense

strainer *n* a sieve used for straining sauces, vegetables, or tea

strait *n* **1** (*often pl*) a narrow channel of the sea linking two larger areas of sea **2 straits** a position of extreme difficulty: *in desperate straits* [Old French *estreit* narrow]

straitened *adj* **in straitened circumstances** not having much money

straitjacket *n* **1** a strong canvas jacket with long sleeves used to bind the arms of a violent person **2** anything which holds back or restricts development or freedom: *exporters are wrapped in a straitjacket of regulations*

strait-laced *or* **straight-laced** *adj* having a strict code of moral standards; puritanical

strand[1] *vb* **1** to leave or drive (ships or fish) ashore **2** to leave (someone) helpless, for example without transport or money ▷ *n* **3** *chiefly poetic* a shore or beach [Old English]

strand[2] *n* **1** one of the individual fibres of string or wire that form a rope, cord, or cable **2** a single length of string, hair, wool, or wire **3** a string of pearls or beads **4** a part of something; element: *the many disparate strands of the Anglican Church* [origin unknown]

stranded *adj* stuck somewhere and unable to leave

strange *adj* **1** odd or unexpected **2** not known, seen, or experienced before; unfamiliar **3 strange to** inexperienced in or unaccustomed to: *they are in some degree strange to it* [Latin *extraneus* foreign] **strangely** *adv* **strangeness** *n*

stranger *n* **1** any person whom one does not know **2** a person who is new to a particular place **3 stranger to** a person who is unfamiliar with or new to something: *Paul is no stranger to lavish spending*

strangle *vb* **-gling, -gled 1** to kill (someone) by pressing his or her windpipe; throttle **2** to prevent the growth or development of: *another attempt at strangling national identity* **3** to stifle (a voice, cry, or laugh) by swallowing suddenly: *the words were strangled by sobs* [Greek *strangalē* a halter] **strangler** *n*

stranglehold *n* **1** a wrestling hold in which a wrestler's arms are pressed against his opponent's windpipe **2** complete power or control over a person or situation

strangulate *vb* **-lating, -lated 1** *pathol* to constrict (a hollow organ or vessel) so as to stop the flow of air or blood through it: *a badly strangulated hernia* **2** same as **strangle** **strangulation** *n*

strap *n* **1** a strip of strong flexible material used for carrying, lifting, fastening, or holding things in place **2** a loop of leather or rubber, hanging from the roof in a bus or train for standing passengers to hold on to **3** short for **shoulder strap** **4 the strap** a beating with a strap as a punishment ▷ *vb* **strapping, strapped 5** to tie or bind (something) with a strap [variant of STROP]

straphanger *n informal* a passenger in a bus or train who has to travel standing and holding on to a strap

strapless *adj* (of women's clothes) without straps over the shoulders

strapped *adj* **strapped for** *slang* badly in need of: *strapped for cash*

strapping *adj* tall, strong, and healthy-looking: *a strapping young lad* [from *strap* (in the archaic sense: to work vigorously)]

strata *n* the plural of **stratum**

> **USAGE** *Strata* is sometimes wrongly used as a singular noun: *this stratum* (not *strata*) *of society is often disregarded.*

stratagem *n* a clever plan to deceive an enemy [Greek *stratēgos* a general]

strategic (strat-**ee**-jik) *adj* **1** planned to achieve an advantage; tactical **2** (of weapons, esp. missiles) directed against an enemy's homeland rather than used on a battlefield **strategically** *adv*

strategy *n, pl* **-gies 1** a long-term plan for success, such as in politics or business **2** the art of the planning and conduct of a war [Greek *stratēgia* function of a general] **strategist** *n*

strath *n Scot* a flat river valley [Scottish & Irish Gaelic *srath*]

strathspey *n* **1** a Scottish dance with gliding steps, slower than a reel **2** music for this dance [after *Strathspey*, valley of the River Spey]

stratified *adj* **1** (of rocks) formed in horizontal layers of different materials **2** *sociol* (of a society) divided into different classes or groups [New Latin *stratificare* to form in layers] **stratification** *n*

stratocumulus (strat-oh-**kew**-myew-luss) *n, pl* **-li** (-lie) *meteorol* an unbroken stretch of dark grey cloud

stratosphere *n* the atmospheric layer between about 15 and 50 km above the earth

stratum (**strah**-tum) *n, pl* **-ta** (-ta) **1** any of the distinct layers into which certain rocks are divided **2** a layer of ocean or atmosphere marked off naturally or decided arbitrarily by man **3** a social class [Latin: something strewn]

S

stratus (stray-tuss) *n, pl* **-ti** (-tie) a grey layer cloud [Latin: strewn]
straw *n* **1** dried stalks of threshed grain, such as wheat or barley **2** a single stalk of straw **3** a long thin hollow paper or plastic tube, used for sucking up liquids into the mouth **4 clutch at straws** to turn in desperation to something with little chance of success **5 draw the short straw** to be the person chosen to perform an unpleasant task ▷ *adj* **6** made of straw: *straw baskets* [Old English *strēaw*]
strawberry *n, pl* **-ries** a sweet fleshy red fruit with small seeds on the outside [Old English *strēawberige*]
strawberry blonde *adj* **1** (of hair) reddish-blonde ▷ *n* **2** a woman with such hair
strawberry mark *n* a red birthmark
straw-coloured *adj* pale yellow: *straw-coloured hair*
straw poll *or* **straw vote** *n* an unofficial poll or vote taken to find out the opinion of a group or the public on some issue
strawweight *n* a professional boxer weighing up to 105 pounds (47 kg). Also called: **mini-flyweight**
stray *vb* **1** to wander away from the correct path or from a given area **2** to move away from the point or lose concentration **3** to fail to live up to certain moral standards: *her man had strayed* ▷ *n* **4** a domestic animal that has wandered away from its home **5** *old-fashioned* a lost or homeless child ▷ *adj* **6** (of a domestic animal) having wandered away from its home **7** random or separated from the main group of things of their kind: *stray bombs and rockets* [Old French *estraier*]
streak *n* **1** a long thin stripe or trace of some contrasting colour **2** (of lightning) a sudden flash **3** a quality or characteristic: *a nasty streak* **4** a short stretch of good or bad luck: *a losing streak* **5** *informal* an instance of running naked through a public place ▷ *vb* **6** to mark (something) with a streak or streaks: *sweat streaking the grime of his face* **7** to move quickly in a straight line **8** *informal* to run naked through a public place [Old English *strica*] **streaked** *or* **streaky** *adj* **streaker** *n*
stream *n* **1** a small river **2** any steady flow of water or other liquid **3** something that resembles a stream in moving continuously in a line or particular direction: *the stream of traffic* **4** a fast and continuous flow of speech: *the constant stream of jargon* **5** *Brit, Austral & NZ* a class of school children grouped together because of similar ability ▷ *vb* **6** to pour in a continuous flow: *rain streamed down her cheeks* **7** (of a crowd of people or traffic or a herd of animals) to move in unbroken succession **8** to send video or audio material over the internet so that the receiving system can play it almost simultaneously **9** to float freely or with a waving motion: *a flimsy pink dress that streamed out behind her* **10** *Brit & NZ* to group (school children) in streams [Old English *strēam*] **streaming** *n* **streamlet** *n*
streamer *n* **1** a long coiled ribbon of coloured paper that unrolls when tossed **2** a long narrow flag
streamline *vb* **-lining, -lined 1** to improve (something) by removing the parts that are least useful or profitable **2** to make (an aircraft, boat, or vehicle) less resistant to flowing air or water by improving its shape **streamlined** *adj*
street *n* **1** a public road that is usually lined with buildings, esp. in a town: *Sauchiehall Street* **2** the part of the road between the pavements, used by vehicles **3** the people living in a particular street **4 on the streets** homeless **5 right up one's street** *informal* just what one knows or likes best **6 streets ahead of** *informal* superior to or more advanced than [Old English *strǣt*]
streetcar *n US & Canad* a tram
street cred *or* **street credibility** *n* a command of the styles, knowledge, etc., associated with urban youngsters who are respected by their contemporaries: *having children was the quickest way to lose your street cred*
street value *n* the price that would be paid for goods, esp. illegal ones such as drugs, by the final user: *cocaine with a street value of £2m was seized at Heathrow airport*
streetwalker *n* a prostitute who tries to find customers in the streets
streetwise *adj* knowing how to survive or succeed in poor and often criminal sections of big cities
strength *n* **1** the state or quality of being physically or mentally strong **2** the ability to withstand great force, stress, or pressure **3** something regarded as valuable or a source of power: *his chief strength is rocketry* **4** potency or effectiveness, such as of a drink or drug **5** power to convince: *the strength of this argument* **6** degree of intensity or concentration of colour, light, sound, or flavour: *a medium-strength cheese* **7** the total number of people in a group: *at full strength; 50 000 men below strength* **8 go from strength to strength** to have ever-increasing success **9 on the strength of** on the basis of or relying upon [Old English *strengthu*]
strengthen *vb* to become stronger or make (something) stronger
strenuous *adj* requiring or involving the use of great energy or effort [Latin *strenuus* brisk] **strenuously** *adv*
streptococcus (strep-toe-**kok**-uss) *n, pl* **-cocci** (-**kok**-eye) a bacterium occurring in chains and including many species that cause disease [Greek *streptos* crooked + *kokkos* berry]
streptomycin *n med* an antibiotic used in the treatment of tuberculosis and other bacterial infections [Greek *streptos* crooked + *mukēs* fungus]
stress *n* **1** mental, emotional, or physical strain or tension **2** special emphasis or significance **3** emphasis placed upon a syllable by pronouncing it more loudly than those that surround it **4** *physics* force producing a change in shape or volume ▷ *vb* **5** to give emphasis to (a point or subject): *she stressed how difficult it had been* **6** to pronounce (a word or syllable) more loudly than those surrounding it [shortened from *distress*] **stressful** *adj*
stressed *or* **stressed-out** *adj informal* suffering from anxiety or tension

S

stretch *vb* **1** **stretch over** *or* **for** to extend or spread over (a specified distance): *the flood barrier stretches for several miles* **2** to draw out or extend (something) or to be drawn out or extended in length or area **3** to distort or lengthen (something) or to be distorted or lengthened permanently **4** to extend (the limbs or body), for example when one has just woken up **5** (often foll. by *out* or *forward, etc.*) to reach or hold out (a part of one's body) **6** to reach or suspend (a rope, etc.) from one place to another **7** to draw (something) tight; tighten **8** (usually foll. by *over*) to extend in time: *a dinner which stretched over three consecutive evenings* **9** to put a great strain upon (one's money or resources) **10** to make do with (limited resources): *the Walkers decided to stretch their budget* **11** to extend (someone) to the limit of his or her abilities **12** to extend (someone) to the limit of his or her tolerance **13** **stretch a point** to make an exception not usually made ▷ *n* **14** the act of stretching **15** a large or continuous expanse or distance: *this stretch of desert* **16** extent in time **17** a term of imprisonment **18** **at a stretch** *chiefly Brit & NZ* **A** with some difficulty; by making a special effort **B** at one time: *for hours at a stretch they had no conversation* ▷ *adj* **19** (of clothes) able to be stretched without permanently losing shape: *a stretch suit* [Old English *streccan*] **stretchy** *adj*

stretcher *n* a frame covered with canvas, on which an ill or injured person is carried

stretcher-bearer *n* a person who helps to carry a stretcher

strew *vb* **strewing, strewed, strewn** to scatter (things) over a surface [Old English *streowian*]

strewth *interj informal* an expression of surprise or alarm [alteration of *God's truth*]

stria (strye-a) *n, pl* **striae** (strye-ee) *geol* a scratch or groove on the surface of a rock crystal [Latin: a groove]

striation *n* **1** an arrangement or pattern of striae **2** same as **stria** **striated** *adj*

stricken *adj* badly affected by disease, pain, grief, etc.: *flood-stricken areas* [past participle of STRIKE]

strict *adj* **1** severely correct in attention to behaviour or morality: *a strict disciplinarian* **2** following carefully and exactly a set of rules: *she is a strict vegetarian* **3** (of a rule or law) very precise and requiring total obedience: *a strict code of practice* **4** (of a meaning) exact: *this is not, in the strictest sense, a biography* **5** (of a punishment, etc.) harsh or severe **6** complete; absolute: *strict obedience* [Latin *strictus* drawn tight] **strictly** *adv* **strictness** *n*

stricture *n formal* a severe criticism [Latin *strictura* contraction]

stride *n* **1** a long step or pace **2** the length of such a step **3** a striding walk **4** progress or development: *he has made great strides in regaining his confidence* **5** a regular pace or rate of progress: *it put me off my stride* **6** **take something in one's stride** to do something without difficulty or effort ▷ *vb* **striding, strode, stridden** **7** to walk with long steps or paces **8** **stride over** *or* **across** to cross (over a space or an obstacle) with a stride [Old English *strīdan*]

strident *adj* **1** (of a voice or sound) loud and harsh **2** loud, persistent, and forceful: *a strident critic of the establishment* [Latin *stridens*] **stridency** *n*

strife *n* angry or violent struggle; conflict [Old French *estrif*]

strike *vb* **striking, struck** **1** (of employees) to stop work collectively as a protest against working conditions, low pay, etc. **2** to hit (someone) **3** to cause (something) to come into sudden or violent contact with something **4** **strike at** to attack (someone or something) **5** to cause (a match) to light by friction **6** to sound (a specific note) on a musical instrument **7** (of a clock) to indicate (a time) by the sound of a bell **8** to affect (someone) deeply in a particular way: *he never struck me as the supportive type* **9** to enter the mind of: *a brilliant thought struck me* **10** (of a poisonous snake) to injure by biting **11** *past participle* **struck** *or* **stricken** to change into (a different state): *struck blind* **12** to be noticed by; catch: *the heavy smell of incense struck my nostrils* **13** to arrive at (something) suddenly or unexpectedly: *to strike on a solution* **14** to afflict (someone) with a disease: *he was struck with polio when he was six* **15** to discover a source of (gold, oil, etc.) **16** to reach (something) by agreement: *to strike a deal* **17** to take up (a posture or an attitude) **18** to take apart or pack up: *to strike camp* **19** to make (a coin) by stamping it **20** **strike home** to achieve the desired effect **21** **strike it rich** *informal* to have an unexpected financial success ▷ *n* **22** a stopping of work, as a protest against working conditions, low pay, etc.: *a one-day strike* **23** an act or instance of striking **24** a military attack, esp. an air attack on a target on land or at sea: *a pre-emptive strike* **25** *baseball* a pitched ball swung at and missed by the batter **26** *tenpin bowling* the knocking down of all the pins with one bowl **27** the discovery of a source of gold, oil, etc. ▷ See also **strike off, strike out, strike up** [Old English *strīcan*]

strikebreaker *n* a person who tries to make a strike fail by working or by taking the place of those on strike

strike off *vb* to remove the name of (a doctor or lawyer who has done something wrong) from an official register, preventing him or her from practising again

strike out *vb* **1** to score out (something written) **2** to start out or begin: *I'm going to strike out for town*

strike pay *n* money paid to strikers by a trade union

striker *n* **1** a person who is on strike **2** *soccer* an attacking player

strike up *vb* **1** to begin (a conversation or friendship) **2** (of a band or an orchestra) to begin to play (a tune)

striking *adj* **1** attracting attention; impressive: *her striking appearance* **2** very noticeable: *a striking difference* **strikingly** *adv*

Strimmer *n trademark* an electrical tool for trimming the edges of lawns

Strine *n* a humorous transliteration of Australian pronunciation, as in *Gloria Soame* for *glorious home* [a jocular rendering of the Australian pronunciation of *Australian*]

string *n* **1** thin cord or twine used for tying, hanging, or binding things **2** a group of objects threaded on a single strand: *a string of pearls* **3** a series of things or events: *a string of wins* **4** a tightly stretched wire or cord on a musical instrument, such as the guitar, violin, or piano, that produces sound when vibrated **5 the strings** *music* **A** violins, violas, cellos, and double basses collectively **B** the section of an orchestra consisting of such instruments **6** a group of characters that can be treated as a unit by a computer program **7 with no strings attached** (of an offer) without complications or conditions **8 pull strings** *informal* to use one's power or influence, esp. secretly or unofficially ▷ *adj* **9** composed of stringlike strands woven in a large mesh: *a string bag* ▷ *vb* **stringing, strung** **10** to hang or stretch (something) from one point to another **11** to provide (something) with a string or strings **12** to thread (beads) on a string **13** to extend in a line or series: *towns strung out along the valley* [Old English *streng*] **stringlike** *adj*

string along *vb informal* **1 string along with** to accompany: *I'll string along with you* **2** to deceive (someone) over a period of time: *she had only been stringing him along*

string bean *n* same as **runner bean**

string course *n archit* an ornamental projecting band along a wall

stringed *adj* (of musical instruments) having strings

stringent (strin-jent) *adj* requiring strict attention to rules or detail: *all have particularly stringent environmental laws* [Latin *stringere* to bind] **stringency** *n*

stringer *n* **1** *archit* a long horizontal timber beam that connects upright posts **2** a journalist employed by a newspaper on a part-time basis to cover a particular town or area

string quartet *n music* **1** a group of musicians consisting of two violins, one viola, and one cello **2** a piece of music composed for such a group

string up *vb informal* to kill (a person) by hanging

stringy *adj* **stringier, stringiest** **1** thin and rough: *stringy hair* **2** (of meat or other food) tough and fibrous

stringy-bark *n* an Australian eucalyptus with a fibrous bark

strip[1] *vb* **stripping, stripped** **1** to take (the covering or clothes) off (oneself, another person, or thing) **2 A** to undress completely **B** to perform a striptease **3** to empty (a building) of all furniture **4** to take something away from (someone): *they were stripped of their possessions* **5** to remove (paint) from (a surface or furniture): *she stripped the plaster from the kitchen walls* **6** (often foll. by *down*) to dismantle (an engine or a mechanism) into individual parts ▷ *n* **7** the act or an instance of undressing or of performing a striptease [Old English *bestrīepan* to plunder]

strip[2] *n* **1** a long narrow piece of something **2** short for **airstrip** **3** *Brit, Austral & NZ* the clothes a sports team plays in [Middle Dutch *strīpe* stripe]

strip cartoon *n* a sequence of drawings in a newspaper or magazine, telling an amusing story or an adventure

strip club *n* a club in which striptease performances take place

stripe[1] *n* **1** a long band of colour that differs from the surrounding material **2** a chevron or band worn on a uniform to indicate rank ▷ *vb* **striping, striped** **3** to mark (something) with stripes [probably from Middle Dutch *strīpe*] **striped, stripy** or **stripey** *adj*

stripe[2] *n* a stroke from a whip, rod, or cane [from Middle Low German *strippe*]

strip lighting *n* a method of electric lighting that uses fluorescent lamps in long glass tubes

stripling *n* a teenage boy or young man

stripper *n* **1** a person who performs a striptease **2** a tool or liquid for removing paint or varnish

strip-search *vb* **1** (of police, customs officials, etc.) to strip (a prisoner or suspect) naked to search him or her for drugs or smuggled goods ▷ *n* **2** a search that involves stripping a person naked

striptease *n* an entertainment in which a person gradually undresses to music

strive *vb* **striving, strove, striven** to make a great effort: *to strive for a peaceful settlement* [Old French *estriver*]

strobe *n* short for **strobe lighting** or **stroboscope**

strobe lighting *n* a flashing beam of very bright light produced by a perforated disc rotating in front of a light source

stroboscope *n* an instrument producing a very bright flashing light which makes moving people appear stationary [Greek *strobos* a whirling + *skopein* to look at]

strode *vb* the past tense of **stride**

stroganoff *n* a dish of sliced beef cooked with onions and mushrooms, served in a sour-cream sauce. Also called: **beef stroganoff** [after Count *Stroganoff*, Russian diplomat]

stroke *vb* **stroking, stroked** **1** to touch or brush lightly or gently ▷ *n* **2** a light touch or caress with the fingers **3** *pathol* rupture of a blood vessel in the brain resulting in loss of consciousness, often followed by paralysis and damage to speech **4** a blow, knock, or hit **5** an action or occurrence of the kind specified: *a fantastic stroke of luck; a stroke of intuition* **6 A** the striking of a clock **B** the hour registered by this: *at the stroke of twelve* **7** a mark made by a pen or paintbrush **8** same as **solidus**: used esp. when dictating or reading aloud **9** the hitting of the ball in sports such as golf or cricket **10** any one of the repeated movements used by a swimmer **11** a particular style of swimming, such as the crawl **12** a single pull on the oars in rowing **13 at a stroke** with one action **14 not a stroke (of work)** no work at all [Old English *strācian*]

stroll *vb* **1** to walk about in a leisurely manner ▷ *n* **2** a leisurely walk [probably from dialect German *strollen*]

stroller *n US & Canad* a chair-shaped carriage for a baby

strong *adj* **stronger, strongest** **1** having physical power **2** not easily broken or injured; solid or robust **3** great in degree or intensity; not faint or feeble: *a strong voice; a strong smell of explosive* **4** (of arguments) supported by evidence; convincing

S

5 concentrated; not weak or diluted **6** having a powerful taste or smell: *strong perfume* **7** (of language) using swear words **8** (of a person) self-confident: *a strong personality* **9** committed or fervent: *a strong believer in free trade* **10** important or having a lot of power or influence: *a strong left-wing tendency within the university* **11** very competent at a particular activity: *they sent a very strong team to the Olympics* **12** containing or having a specified number: *the 700-strong workforce* **13** (of an accent) distinct and indicating where the speaker comes from **14** (of a relationship) stable and likely to last **15** having an extreme or drastic effect: *strong discipline* **16** (of a colour) very bright and intense **17** (of a wind, current, or earthquake) moving fast or intensely **18** (of an economy, an industry, a currency, etc.) growing, successful, or increasing in value ▷ *adv* **19 come on strong** *informal* **A** to show blatantly that one is sexually attracted to someone **B** to make a forceful or exaggerated impression **20 going strong** *informal* working or performing well; thriving [Old English *strang*] **strongly** *adv*

strong-arm *adj informal* involving physical force or violence: *strong-arm tactics*

strongbox *n* a box in which valuables are locked for safety

strong drink *n* alcoholic drink

stronghold *n* **1** an area in which a particular belief is shared by many people: *a Labour stronghold* **2** a place that is well defended; fortress

strong-minded *adj* not easily persuaded to change beliefs or opinions

strong point *n* something at which one is very good: *diplomacy wasn't his strong point*

strongroom *n* a specially designed room in which valuables are locked for safety

strontium *n chem* a soft silvery-white metallic element: the radioactive isotope **strontium-90** is used in nuclear power sources and is a hazardous nuclear fallout product. Symbol: **Sr** [after *Strontian*, in Scotland, where discovered]

strop *n* a leather strap for sharpening razors [Greek *strophos* cord]

stroppy *adj* **-pier, -piest** *informal* bad-tempered or deliberately awkward [from *obstreperous*]

strove *vb* the past tense of **strive**

struck *vb* a past of **strike**

structural *adj* **1** of or having structure or a structure **2** of or forming part of the structure of a building **3** *chem* of or involving the arrangement of atoms in molecules: *a structural formula* **structurally** *adv*

structuralism *n* an approach to social sciences and to literature which sees changes in the subject as caused and organized by a hidden set of universal rules **structuralist** *n, adj*

structure *n* **1** something that has been built or organized **2** the way the individual parts of something are made, built, or organized into a whole **3** the pattern of interrelationships within an organization, society, etc. **4** an organized method of working, thinking, or behaving **5** *chem* the arrangement of atoms in a molecule of a chemical compound **6** *geol* the way in which a rock is made up of its component parts ▷ *vb* **-turing, -tured 7** to arrange (something) into an organized system or pattern: *a structured school curriculum* [Latin *structura*]

strudel *n* a thin sheet of filled dough rolled up and baked: *apple strudel* [from German]

struggle *vb* **-gling, -gled 1** to work or strive: *the old regime struggled for power; he struggled to keep the conversation flowing* **2** to move about violently in an attempt to escape from something restricting **3** to fight with someone, often for possession of something **4** to go or progress with difficulty **5 struggle on** to manage to do something with difficulty ▷ *n* **6** something requiring a lot of exertion or effort to achieve **7** a fight or battle **8 the struggle** *S African* the concerted opposition to apartheid [origin unknown] **struggling** *adj*

strum *vb* **strumming, strummed 1** to play (a stringed instrument) by sweeping the thumb or a plectrum across the strings **2** to play (a tune) in this way [probably imitative]

strumpet *n archaic* a prostitute or promiscuous woman [origin unknown]

strung *vb* the past of **string**

strung up *adj informal* tense or nervous: *you sound a bit strung up*

strut *vb* **strutting, strutted 1** to walk in a stiff proud way with head high and shoulders back; swagger ▷ *n* **2** a piece of wood or metal that forms part of the framework of a structure [Old English *strūtian* to stand stiffly]

strychnine (strik-neen) *n* a very poisonous drug formerly used in small quantities as a stimulant [Greek *strukhnos* nightshade]

Stuart *adj* of or relating to the royal house that ruled Scotland from 1371 to 1714 and England from 1603 to 1714

stub *n* **1** a short piece remaining after something has been used: *a cigarette stub* **2** the section of a ticket or cheque which the purchaser keeps as a receipt ▷ *vb* **stubbing, stubbed 3** to strike (one's toe or foot) painfully against a hard surface **4 stub out** to put out (a cigarette or cigar) by pressing the end against a surface [Old English *stubb*]

stubble *n* **1** the short stalks left in a field where a crop has been harvested **2** the short bristly hair on the chin of a man who has not shaved for a while [Old French *estuble*] **stubbly** *adj*

stubble-jumper *n Canad slang* a prairie grain farmer

stubborn *adj* **1** refusing to agree or give in **2** persistent and determined **3** difficult to handle, treat, or overcome: *the most stubborn dandruff* [origin unknown] **stubbornly** *adv* **stubbornness** *n*

stubby *adj* **-bier, -biest** short and broad

stucco *n* **1** plaster used for coating or decorating outside walls ▷ *vb* **-coing, -coed 2** to apply stucco to (a building) [Italian]

stuck *vb* **1** the past of **stick²** ▷ *adj* **2** *informal* baffled by a problem or unable to find an answer to a question **3 be stuck on** *slang* to feel a strong attraction to; be infatuated with **4 get stuck in** *informal* to perform a task with determination

stuck-up *adj informal* proud or snobbish

S

stud¹ *n* **1** a small piece of metal attached to a surface for decoration **2** a fastener consisting of two discs at either end of a short bar, usually used with clothes **3** one of several small round objects attached to the sole of a football boot to give better grip ▷ *vb* **studding, studded 4** to decorate or cover (something) with or as if with studs: *apartment houses studded with satellite dishes* [Old English *studu*]

stud² *n* **1** a male animal, esp. a stallion kept for breeding **2** Also: **stud farm** a place where animals are bred **3** the state of being kept for breeding purposes **4** *slang* a virile or sexually active man [Old English *stōd*]

student *n* **1** a person following a course of study in a school, college, or university **2** a person who makes a thorough study of a subject: *a keen student of opinion polls* [Latin *studens* diligent]

studied *adj* carefully practised or planned: *studied calm*

studio *n, pl* **-dios 1** a room in which an artist, photographer, or musician works **2** a room used to record television or radio programmes or to make films or records **3 studios** the premises of a radio, television, record, or film company [Italian]

studio couch *n* a backless couch that can be converted into a double bed

studio flat *n Brit* a flat with one main room and, usually, a small kitchen and bathroom. Also called: **studio apartment**

studious (styoo-dee-uss) *adj* **1** serious, thoughtful, and hard-working **2** precise, careful, or deliberate [Latin *studiosus* devoted to] **studiously** *adv*

study *vb* **studies, studying, studied 1** to be engaged in the learning or understanding of (a subject) **2** to investigate or examine (something) by observation and research **3** to look at (something or someone) closely; scrutinize ▷ *n, pl* **studies 4** the act or process of studying **5** a room used for studying, reading, or writing **6** (*often pl*) work relating to a particular area of learning: *environmental studies* **7** an investigation and analysis of a particular subject **8** a paper or book produced as a result of study **9** a work of art, such as a drawing, done for practice or in preparation for another work **10** a musical composition designed to develop playing technique [Latin *studium* zeal]

S

stuff *n* **1** substance or material **2** any collection of unnamed things **3** the raw material of something **4** subject matter, skill, etc.: *this journalist knew his stuff* **5** woollen fabric **6 do one's stuff** *informal* to do what is expected of one ▷ *vb* **7** to pack or fill (something) completely; cram **8** to force, shove, or squeeze (something somewhere): *I stuffed it in my briefcase* **9** to fill (food such as poultry or tomatoes) with a seasoned mixture **10** to fill (a dead animal's skin) with material so as to restore the shape of the live animal **11** *slang* to frustrate or defeat **12 get stuffed!** *Brit, Austral & NZ slang* an exclamation of anger or annoyance with someone **13 stuff oneself** *or* **one's face** to eat a large amount of food [Old French *estoffe*]

stuffed shirt *n informal* a pompous or old-fashioned person

stuffed-up *adj* having the passages of one's nose blocked with mucus

stuffing *n* **1** a mixture of ingredients with which poultry or meat is stuffed before cooking **2** the material used to fill and give shape to soft toys, pillows, furniture, etc.; padding

stuffy *adj* **-ier, -iest 1** lacking fresh air **2** old-fashioned and very formal: *an image of stuffy tradition* **stuffiness** *n*

stultify *vb* **-fies, -fying, -fied** to dull (the mind) by boring routine [Latin *stultus* stupid + *facere* to make] **stultifying** *adj*

stumble *vb* **-bling, -bled 1** to trip and almost fall while walking or running **2** to walk in an unsteady or unsure way **3** to make mistakes or hesitate in speech **4 stumble across** *or* **on** *or* **upon** to encounter or discover (someone or something) by accident ▷ *n* **5** an act of stumbling [Middle English *stomble*]

stumbling block *n* any obstacle that prevents something from taking place or progressing

stump *n* **1** the base of a tree trunk left standing after the tree has been cut down or has fallen **2** the part of something, such as a tooth or limb, that remains after a larger part has been removed **3** *cricket* any of three upright wooden sticks that, with two bails laid across them, form a wicket ▷ *vb* **4** to baffle or confuse (someone) **5** *cricket* to dismiss (a batsman) by breaking his or her wicket with the ball **6** *chiefly US & Canad* to campaign or canvass (an area), by political speech-making **7** to walk with heavy steps; trudge [Middle Low German]

stump up *vb Brit informal* to give (the money required)

stumpy *adj* **stumpier, stumpiest** short and thick like a stump; stubby

stun *vb* **stunning, stunned 1** to shock or astonish (someone) so that he or she is unable to speak or act **2** (of a heavy blow or fall) to make (a person or an animal) unconscious [Old French *estoner* to daze]

stung *vb* the past of **sting**

stunk *vb* a past of **stink**

stunner *n Brit, Austral & NZ informal* a person or thing of great beauty

stunning *adj informal* very attractive or impressive **stunningly** *adv*

stunt¹ *vb* to prevent or slow down (the growth or development of a plant, animal, or person) [Old English: foolish] **stunted** *adj*

stunt² *n* **1** an acrobatic or dangerous piece of action in a film or television programme **2** anything spectacular or unusual done to gain publicity ▷ *adj* **3** of or relating to acrobatic or dangerous pieces of action in films or television programmes: *a stunt man* [origin unknown]

stupefaction *n* the state of being unable to think clearly because of tiredness or boredom

stupefy *vb* **-pefies, -pefying, -pefied 1** to make (someone) feel so bored and tired that he or she is unable to think clearly **2** to confuse or astound (someone) [Old French *stupefier*] **stupefying** *adj*

stupendous *adj* very large or impressive [Latin *stupere* to be amazed] **stupendously** *adv*

stupid *adj* **1** lacking in common sense or intelligence **2** trivial, silly, or childish: *we got into a stupid quarrel* **3** unable to think clearly; dazed: *stupid with tiredness* [Latin *stupidus*] **stupidity** *n* **stupidly** *adv*

stupor *n* a state of near unconsciousness in which a person is unable to behave normally or think clearly [Latin]

sturdy *adj* **-dier, -diest 1** (of a person) healthy, strong, and unlikely to tire or become injured **2** (of a piece of furniture, shoes, etc.) strongly built or made [Old French *estordi* dazed] **sturdily** *adv*

sturgeon *n* a bony fish from which caviar is obtained [Old French *estourgeon*]

stutter *vb* **1** to speak (a word or phrase) with involuntary repetition of initial consonants ▷ *n* **2** the tendency to involuntarily repeat initial consonants while speaking [Middle English *stutten*] **stuttering** *n*

sty *n, pl* **sties** a pen in which pigs are kept [Old English *stīg*]

stye *or* **sty** *n, pl* **styes** *or* **sties** inflammation of a gland at the base of an eyelash [Old English *stīgend* swelling + *ye* eye]

Stygian (stij-jee-an) *adj chiefly literary* dark or gloomy [after the *Styx*, a river in Hades]

style *n* **1** a form of appearance, design, or production: *I like that style of dress* **2** the way in which something is done: *a new style of command* **3** elegance or refinement of manners and dress: *he has bags of style* **4** a distinctive manner of expression in words, music, painting, etc.: *a painting in the Expressionist style* **5** popular fashion in dress and looks: *the old ones had gone out of style* **6** a fashionable or showy way of life: *the newly rich could dine in style* **7** the particular kind of spelling, punctuation, and design followed in a book, journal, or publishing house **8** *botany* the stemlike part of a flower that bears the stigma ▷ *vb* **styling, styled 9** to design, shape, or tailor: *neatly styled hair* **10** to name or call: *Walsh, who styled himself the Memory Man* [Latin *stilus* writing implement]

styling mousse *n* a light foam applied to the hair before styling in order to hold the style

stylish *adj* smart, fashionable, and attracting attention **stylishly** *adv*

stylist *n* **1** a hairdresser who styles hair **2** a person who performs, writes, or acts with great attention to the particular style he or she employs

stylistic *adj* of the techniques used in creating or performing a work of art: *there are many stylistic problems facing the performers of Baroque music* **stylistically** *adv*

stylized *or* **-lised** *adj* conforming to an established stylistic form

stylus *n* a needle-like device in the pick-up arm of a record player that rests in the groove in the record and picks up the sound signals [Latin *stilus* writing implement]

stymie *vb* **-mieing, -mied 1** to hinder or foil (someone): *the President was stymied by a reluctant Congress* ▷ *n, pl* **-mies 2** *golf* (formerly) a situation in which an opponent's ball is blocking the line between the hole and the ball about to be played [origin unknown]

styptic *adj* **1** used to stop bleeding: *a styptic pencil* ▷ *n* **2** a styptic drug [Greek *stuphein* to contract]

suave (swahv) *adj* (esp. of a man) smooth, confident, and sophisticated [Latin *suavis* sweet] **suavely** *adv*

sub *n* **1** short for **subeditor, submarine, subscription** or **substitute 2** *Brit informal* an advance payment of wages or salary. Formal term: **subsistence allowance** ▷ *vb* **subbing, subbed 3** to act as a substitute

sub- *or before r* **sur-** *prefix* **1** situated under or beneath: *subterranean* **2** secondary in rank; subordinate: *sublieutenant* **3** falling short of; less than or imperfectly: *subarctic; subhuman* **4** forming a subdivision or less important part: *subcommittee* [Latin]

subaltern *n* a British army officer below the rank of captain [Latin *sub-* under + *alter* another]

subaqua *adj* of or relating to underwater sport: *subaqua swimming*

subatomic *adj physics* of, relating to, or being one of the particles making up an atom

subcommittee *n* a small committee consisting of members of a larger committee and which is set up to look into a particular matter

subconscious *adj* **1** happening or existing without one's awareness ▷ *n* **2** *psychol* the part of the mind that contains memories and motives of which one is not aware but which can influence one's behaviour **subconsciously** *adv*

subcontinent *n* a large land mass that is a distinct part of a continent, such as India is of Asia

subcontract *n* **1** a secondary contract by which the main contractor for a job puts work out to another company ▷ *vb* **2** to let out (work) on a subcontract **subcontractor** *n*

subculture *n* a group of people within a society or class with a distinct pattern of behaviour, beliefs, and attitudes

subcutaneous (sub-cute-**ayn**-ee-uss) *adj med* beneath the skin

subdivide *vb* **-viding, -vided** to divide (a part of something) into smaller parts **subdivision** *n*

subdue *vb* **-duing, -dued 1** to overcome and bring (a person or people) under control by persuasion or force **2** to make (feelings, colour, or lighting) less intense [Latin *subducere* to remove]

subeditor *n* a person who checks and edits text for a newspaper or other publication

subgroup *n* a small group that is part of a larger group

subheading *n* the heading of a subdivision of a piece of writing

subhuman *adj* lacking the intelligence or decency expected of a human being

subject (**sub**-ject) *n* **1** the person, thing, or topic being dealt with or discussed **2** any branch of learning considered as a course of study **3** a person, object, idea, or scene portrayed in a work of art **4** *grammar* a word or phrase that represents the person or thing performing the action of the verb in a sentence; for example, *the cat* in the sentence *The cat catches mice* **5** a person or thing that undergoes an experiment or treatment **6** a person under the rule of a monarch or government: *Zambian subjects* ▹ *adj* **7** being under the rule of a monarch or government: *a subject race* **8 subject to A** showing a tendency towards: *they are expensive and subject to over-runs in cost and time* **B** exposed or vulnerable to: *subject to ridicule* **C** conditional upon: *pay is subject to negotiation* ▹ *adv* **9 subject to** under the condition that something takes place: *my visit was agreed subject to certain conditions* ▹ *vb* (sub-**ject**) **10 subject to A** to cause (someone) to experience (something unpleasant): *they were subjected to beatings* **B** to bring under the control or authority of: *to subject a soldier to discipline* [Latin *subjectus* brought under] **subjection** *n*

subjective *adj* **1** of or based on a person's emotions or prejudices ▹ *n* **2** *grammar* the grammatical case in certain languages that identifies the subject of a verb **subjectively** *adv*

sub judice (sub **joo**-diss-ee) *adj* before a court of law: *he declined to comment on the case saying it was sub judice* [Latin]

subjugate *vb* **-gating, -gated** to bring (a group of people) under one's control [Latin *sub-* under + *jugum* yoke] **subjugation** *n*

subjunctive *grammar* ▹ *adj* **1** denoting a mood of verbs used when the content of the clause is being doubted, supposed, or feared true, for example *were* in the sentence *I'd be careful if I were you* ▹ *n* **2** the subjunctive mood [Latin *subjungere* to add to]

sublet *vb* **-letting, -let** to rent out (property which one is renting from someone else)

sublieutenant *n* a junior officer in a navy

sublimate *vb* **-mating, -mated** *psychol* to direct the energy of (a strong desire, esp. a sexual one) into activities that are socially more acceptable [Latin *sublimare* to elevate] **sublimation** *n*

sublime *adj* **1** causing deep emotions and feelings of wonder or joy **2** without equal; supreme **3** of great moral, artistic, or spiritual value ▹ *n* **4 the sublime** something that is sublime ▹ *vb* **-liming, -limed 5** *chem & physics* to change directly from a solid to a vapour without first melting [Latin *sublimis* lofty] **sublimely** *adv*

subliminal *adj* resulting from or relating to mental processes of which the individual is not aware: *the subliminal message* [Latin *sub* below + *limen* threshold]

sub-machine-gun *n* a portable automatic or semiautomatic gun with a short barrel

submarine *n* **1** a vessel which can operate below the surface of the sea ▹ *adj* **2** existing or located below the surface of the sea: *submarine cables* **submariner** *n*

submerge *vb* **-merging, -merged 1** to put or go below the surface of water or another liquid **2** to involve totally: *she submerged herself in her work* [Latin *submergere*] **submersion** *n*

submersible *adj* **1** capable of operating under water ▹ *n* **2** a small vessel designed to operate under water

submission *n* **1** an act or instance of capitulation **2** the act of submitting (something) **3** something submitted, such as a proposal **4** the state in which someone has to accept the control of another person

submissive *adj* showing quiet obedience **submissively** *adv* **submissiveness** *n*

submit *vb* **-mitting, -mitted 1** to accept the will of another person or a superior force **2** to send (an application or proposal) to someone for judgment or consideration **3** to be voluntarily subjected (to medical or psychiatric treatment) [Latin *submittere* to place under]

subnormal *adj* **1** less than the normal: *subnormal white blood cells* **2** *not in technical use* having a lower than average intelligence

subordinate *adj* **1** of lesser rank or importance ▹ *n* **2** a person or thing that is of lesser rank or importance ▹ *vb* **-nating, -nated 3** (usually foll. by *to*) to regard (something) as less important than another: *the army's interests were subordinated to those of the air force* [Latin *sub-* lower + *ordo* rank] **subordination** *n*

subordinate clause *n grammar* a clause that functions as an adjective, an adverb, or a noun rather than one that functions as a sentence in its own right

suborn *vb formal* to bribe or incite (a person) to commit a wrongful act [Latin *subornare*]

subplot *n* a secondary plot in a novel, play, or film

subpoena (sub-**pee**-na) *n* **1** a legal document requiring a person to appear before a court of law at a specified time ▹ *vb* **-naing, -naed 2** to summon (someone) with a subpoena [Latin: under penalty]

sub-post office *n* (in Britain) a post office which is run by a self-employed agent for the Post Office

subprime *adj* **1** (of a loan) made to a borrower with a poor credit rating: *subprime mortgage* ▹ *n* **2** such a loan

sub rosa (sub **rose**-a) *adv literary* in secret [Latin, literally: under the rose; in ancient times a rose was hung over a table as a mark of secrecy]

subroutine *n* a section of a computer program that is stored only once but can be used at several different points in the program

subscribe *vb* **-scribing, -scribed 1** (usually foll. by *to*) to pay (money) as a contribution (to a charity, for a magazine, etc.) at regular intervals **2 subscribe to** to give support or approval to: *I do not subscribe to this view* [Latin *subscribere* to write underneath] **subscriber** *n*

subscript *printing* ▹ *adj* **1** (of a character) written or printed below the line ▹ *n* **2** a subscript character

subscription *n* **1** a payment for issues of a publication over a specified period of time **2** money paid or promised, such as to a charity, or the fund raised in this way **3** *Brit, Austral & NZ* the membership fees paid to a society **4** an advance order for a new product

subsection *n* any of the smaller parts into which a section may be divided

subsequent *adj* occurring after; succeeding [Latin *subsequens*] **subsequently** *adv*

subservient *adj* **1** overeager to carry out someone else's wishes **2** of less importance or rank: *a loyal, subservient ally* [Latin *subserviens*] **subservience** *n*

subset *n* a mathematical set contained within a larger set
subside *vb* **-siding, -sided 1** to become less loud, excited, or violent **2** to sink to a lower level **3** (of the surface of the earth) to cave in; collapse [Latin *subsidere* to settle down] **subsidence** *n*
subsidiarity *n* the principle of taking political decisions at the lowest practical level
subsidiary *n, pl* **-aries 1** Also called: **subsidiary company** a company which is at least half owned by another company **2** a person or thing that is of lesser importance ▷ *adj* **3** of lesser importance; subordinate [Latin *subsidiarius* supporting]
subsidize *or* **-dise** *vb* **-dizing, -dized** *or* **-dising, -dised** to aid or support (an industry, a person, a public service, or a venture) with money
subsidy *n, pl* **-dies 1** financial aid supplied by a government, for example to industry, or for public welfare **2** any financial aid, grant, or contribution [Latin *subsidium* assistance]
subsist *vb* **subsist on** to manage to live on: *to subsist on a diet of sausage rolls* [Latin *subsistere* to stand firm] **subsistence** *n*
subsistence farming *n* a type of farming in which most of the produce is consumed by the farmer and his family
subsoil *n* the layer of soil beneath the surface soil
subsonic *adj* being or moving at a speed below that of sound
substance *n* **1** the basic matter of which a thing consists **2** a specific type of matter with definite or fairly definite chemical composition: *a fatty substance* **3** the essential meaning of a speech, thought, or written article **4** important or meaningful quality: *the only evidence of substance against him* **5** material possessions or wealth: *a woman of substance* **6 in substance** with regard to the most important points [Latin *substantia*]
substandard *adj* below an established or required standard
substantial *adj* **1** of a considerable size or value: *a substantial amount of money* **2** (of food or a meal) large and filling **3** solid or strong: *substantial brick pillars* **4** *formal* available to the senses; real: *substantial evidence* **5** of or relating to the basic material substance of a thing **substantially** *adv*
substantiate *vb* **-ating, -ated** to establish (a story) as genuine **substantiation** *n*
substantive *n* **1** *grammar* a noun or pronoun used in place of a noun ▷ *adj* **2** having importance or significance: *substantive negotiations between management and staff* **3** of or being the essential element of a thing [Latin *substare* to stand beneath]
substitute *vb* **-tuting, -tuted 1** (often foll. by *for*) to take the place of or put in place of another person or thing **2** *chem* to replace (an atom or group in a molecule) with (another atom or group) ▷ *n* **3** a person or thing that takes the place of another, such as a player who takes the place of a team-mate [Latin *substituere*] **substitution** *n*

> **USAGE** *Substitute* is sometimes wrongly used where *replace* is meant: *he replaced* (not *substituted*) *the worn tyre with a new one.*

substitution reaction *n chem* the replacing of an atom or group in a molecule by another atom or group
substrate *n biol* the substance upon which an enzyme acts [Latin *substratus* strewn beneath]
substructure *n* **1** a structure that forms a part of anything **2** a structure that forms a foundation or framework for a building
subsume *vb* **-suming, -sumed** *formal* to include (something) under a larger classification or group: *an attempt to subsume fascism and communism under a general concept of totalitarianism* [Latin *sub-* under + *sumere* to take]
subtenant *n* a person who rents property from a tenant **subtenancy** *n*
subtend *vb geom* to be opposite (an angle or side) [Latin *subtendere* to extend beneath]
subterfuge *n* a trick or deception used to achieve an objective [Latin *subterfugere* to escape by stealth]
subterranean *adj* **1** found or operating below the surface of the earth **2** existing or working in a concealed or mysterious way: *the resistance movement worked largely by subterranean methods* [Latin *sub* beneath + *terra* earth]
subtext *n* **1** an underlying theme in a piece of writing **2** a message which is not stated directly but can be inferred
subtitle *n* **1 subtitles** *films* a written translation at the bottom of the picture in a film with foreign dialogue **2** a secondary title given to a book or play ▷ *vb* **-tling, -tled 3** to provide subtitles for (a film) or a subtitle for (a book or play)
subtle *adj* **1** not immediately obvious: *a subtle change in his views* **2** (of a colour, taste, or smell) delicate or faint: *the subtle aroma* **3** using shrewd and indirect methods to achieve an objective **4** having or requiring the ability to make fine distinctions: *a subtle argument* [Latin *subtilis* finely woven] **subtly** *adv*
subtlety *n* **1** *pl* **-ties** a fine distinction **2** the state or quality of being subtle
subtract *vb* **1** *maths* to take (one number or quantity) away from another **2** to remove (a part of something) from the whole [Latin *subtrahere* to draw away from beneath] **subtraction** *n*
subtropical *adj* of the region lying between the tropics and temperate lands
suburb *n* a residential district on the outskirts of a city or town [Latin *sub-* close to + *urbs* a city]
suburban *adj* **1** of, in, or inhabiting a suburb **2** *derogatory* conventional and unexciting
suburbanite *n* a person who lives in a suburb
suburbia *n* suburbs or the people living in them considered as a distinct community or class in society
subvention *n formal* a grant or subsidy, for example one from a government [Late Latin *subventio* assistance]
subversion *n* the act or an instance of attempting to weaken or overthrow a government or an institution
subversive *adj* **1** intended or intending to weaken or overthrow a government or an institution ▷ *n* **2** a person engaged in subversive activities

S

subvert *vb* to bring about the downfall of (something existing by a system of law, such as a government) [Latin *subvertere* to overturn]

subway *n* **1** *Brit & Austral* an underground passage for pedestrians to cross a road or railway **2** an underground railway

subzero *adj* lower than zero: *subzero temperatures*

succeed *vb* **1** to achieve an aim **2** to turn out satisfactorily: *Grandfather's plan succeeded* **3** to do well in a specified field: *how to succeed in show biz* **4** to come next in order after (someone or something): *the first shock had been succeeded by a different kind of gloom* **5** to take over (a position) from (someone): *Henry VIII succeeded to the throne in 1509; he will be succeeded as president by his deputy* [Latin *succedere* to follow after] **succeeding** *adj*

success *n* **1** the achievement of something attempted **2** the attainment of wealth, fame, or position **3** a person or thing that is successful [Latin *successus* an outcome]

successful *adj* **1** having a favourable outcome **2** having attained fame, wealth, or position **successfully** *adv*

succession *n* **1** a number of people or things following one another in order **2** the act or right by which one person succeeds another in a position **3 in succession** one after another: *the third time in succession*

successive *adj* following another or others without interruption: *eleven successive victories* **successively** *adv*

successor *n* a person or thing that follows another, esp. a person who takes over another's job or position

succinct *adj* brief and clear: *a succinct answer to this question* [Latin *succinctus*] **succinctly** *adv*

succour or *US* **succor** *n* **1** help in time of difficulty ▷ *vb* **2** to give aid to (someone in time of difficulty) [Latin *succurrere* to hurry to help]

succubus *n, pl* **-bi** a female demon fabled to have sex with sleeping men [Latin *succubare* to lie beneath]

succulent *adj* **1** (of food) juicy and delicious **2** (of plants) having thick fleshy leaves or stems ▷ *n* **3** a plant that can exist in very dry conditions by using water stored in its fleshy tissues [Latin *sucus* juice] **succulence** *n*

succumb *vb* **succumb to** **A** to give way to the force of or desire for (something) **B** to die of (a disease) [Latin *succumbere*]

such *adj* **1** of the sort specified or understood: *such places* **2** so great or so much: *such a mess* ▷ *adv* **3** extremely: *such a powerful friend* ▷ *pron* **4** a person or thing of the sort specified or understood: *such is the law of the land; fruitcakes and puddings and such* **5 as such** in itself or themselves: *the Nordic countries are not lifting sanctions as such* **6 such as** for example: *other socialist groups, such as the Fabians* [Old English *swilc*]

such and such *adj* **1** specific, but not known or named: *such and such a percentage* ▷ *n* **2** a specific, but not known or named, person or thing: *you have not taken such and such into account*

suchlike *n* **1** such or similar things: *shampoos, talcs, and suchlike* ▷ *adj* **2** of such a kind; similar: *astrology and suchlike nonsense*

suck *vb* **1** to draw (a liquid) into the mouth through pursed lips **2** to take (something) into the mouth and moisten, dissolve, or roll it around with the tongue: *suck a mint* **3** to extract liquid from (a solid food): *he sat sucking orange segments* **4** to draw in (fluid) as if by sucking: *the mussel sucks in water* **5** to drink milk from (a mother's breast); suckle **6** (often foll. by *down* or *in, etc.*) to draw (a thing or person somewhere) with a powerful force **7** *slang* to be contemptible or disgusting ▷ *n* **8** a sucking [Old English *sūcan*]

sucker *n* **1** *slang* a person who is easily deceived or swindled **2** *slang* a person who cannot resist something: *he's a sucker for fast cars* **3** *zool* a part of the body of certain animals that is used for sucking or sticking to a surface **4** a rubber cup-shaped device attached to objects allowing them to stick to a surface by suction **5** *botany* a strong shoot coming from a mature plant's root or the base of its main stem

suck into *vb* to draw (someone) into (a situation) by using a powerful pressure or inducement: *to be sucked into a guerrilla war*

suckle *vb* **-ling, -led** to give (a baby or young animal) milk from the breast or udder or (of a baby or young animal) to suck milk from its mother's breast or udder

suckling *n* a baby or young animal that is still sucking milk from its mother's breast or udder

suck up to *vb informal* to flatter (a person in authority) in order to get something, such as praise or promotion

sucrose (soo-kroze) *n chem* sugar [French *sucre* sugar]

suction *n* **1** the act or process of sucking **2** the force produced by drawing air out of a space to make a vacuum that will suck in a substance from another space [Latin *sugere* to suck]

Sudanese *adj* **1** of Sudan ▷ *n, pl* **-nese** **2** a person from Sudan

sudden *adj* **1** occurring or performed quickly and without warning ▷ *n* **2 all of a sudden** without warning; unexpectedly [Latin *subitus* unexpected] **suddenly** *adv* **suddenness** *n*

sudden death *n sport* an extra period of play to decide the winner of a tied competition: the first player or team to go into the lead is the winner

sudden infant death syndrome *n* same as **cot death**

sudoku (soo-**doh**-koo) *n* a logic puzzle involving the insertion of numbers so that none is repeated in the same row, column, or internal square of a larger square [from Japanese]

sudorific (syoo-dor-**if**-ik) *adj* **1** causing sweating ▷ *n* **2** a drug that causes sweating [Latin *sudor* sweat + *facere* to make]

suds *pl n* the bubbles on the surface of water in which soap or detergent has been dissolved; lather [probably from Middle Dutch *sudse* marsh]

sue *vb* **suing, sued** to start legal proceedings (against): *we want to sue the council; he sued for custody of the three children* [Latin *sequi* to follow]

suede *n* a leather with a fine velvet-like surface on one side [French *gants de Suède*, literally: gloves from Sweden]

S

suet *n* a hard fat obtained from sheep and cattle and used for making pastry and puddings [Old French *seu*]

suffer *vb* **1** to undergo or be subjected to (physical pain or mental distress) **2 suffer from** to be badly affected by (an illness): *he was suffering from depression* **3** to become worse in quality; deteriorate: *his work suffered during their divorce* **4** to tolerate: *he suffers no fools* **5** to be set at a disadvantage: *the strongest of them suffers by comparison* [Latin *sufferre*] **sufferer** *n* **suffering** *n*

sufferance *n* **on sufferance** tolerated with reluctance: *I was there on sufferance and all knew it*

suffice (suf-fice) *vb* **-ficing, -ficed 1** to be enough or satisfactory for a purpose **2 suffice it to say ...** it is enough to say ...: *suffice it to say that the overall result was very good* [Latin *sufficere*]

sufficiency *n, pl* **-cies** an adequate amount

sufficient *adj* enough to meet a need or purpose; adequate [Latin *sufficiens*] **sufficiently** *adv*

suffix *grammar* ▷ *n* **1** a letter or letters added to the end of a word to form another word, such as *-s* and *-ness* in *dogs* and *softness* ▷ *vb* **2** to add (a letter or letters) to the end of a word to form another word [Latin *suffixus* fastened below]

suffocate *vb* **-cating, -cated 1** to kill or die through lack of oxygen, such as by blockage of the air passage **2** to feel uncomfortable from heat and lack of air [Latin *suffocare*] **suffocating** *adj* **suffocation** *n*

suffragan *n* a bishop appointed to assist an archbishop [Medieval Latin *suffragium* assistance]

suffrage *n* the right to vote in public elections [Latin *suffragium*]

suffragette *n* (in Britain at the beginning of the 20th century) a woman who campaigned militantly for women to be given the right to vote in public elections

suffragist *n* (in Britain at the beginning of the 20th century) a person who campaigned for women to be given the right to vote in public elections

suffuse *vb* **-fusing, -fused** to spread through or over (something): *the dawn suffused the sky with a cold grey wash* [Latin *suffusus* overspread with] **suffusion** *n*

sugar *n* **1** a sweet carbohydrate, usually in the form of white or brown crystals, which is found in many plants and is used to sweeten food and drinks **2** *informal, chiefly US & Canad* a term of affection ▷ *vb* **3** to add sugar to (food or drink) to make it sweet **4** to cover with sugar: *sugared almonds* **5 sugar the pill** to make something unpleasant more tolerable by adding something pleasant [Old French *çucre*, from Sanskrit *śarkarā*] **sugared** *adj*

sugar beet *n* a beet grown for the sugar obtained from its roots

sugar cane *n* a tropical grass grown for the sugar obtained from its tall stout canes

sugar daddy *n* an elderly man who gives a young person money and gifts in return for their company

sugar glider *n* a common phalanger that glides from tree to tree feeding on insects and nectar

sugaring off *n Canad* the boiling down of maple sap to produce sugar, traditionally a social event in early spring

sugar loaf *n* a large cone-shaped mass of hard refined sugar

sugar maple *n* a North American maple tree, grown as a source of sugar, which is extracted from the sap

sugary *adj* **1** of, like, or containing sugar: *sugary snacks* **2** (of behaviour or language) very pleasant but probably not sincere: *sugary sentiment* **sugariness** *n*

suggest *vb* **1** to put forward (a plan or an idea) for consideration: *he didn't suggest a meeting* **2** to bring (a person or thing) to the mind by the association of ideas: *a man whose very name suggests blandness* **3** to give a hint of: *her grey eyes suggesting a livelier mood than usual* [Latin *suggerere* to bring up]

suggestible *adj* easily influenced by other people's ideas

suggestion *n* **1** something that is suggested **2** a hint or indication: *the entire castle gave no suggestion of period* **3** *psychol* the process whereby the presentation of an idea to a receptive individual leads to the acceptance of that idea

suggestive *adj* **1** (of remarks or gestures) causing people to think of sex **2 suggestive of** communicating a hint of

suicidal *adj* **1** wanting to die by suicide **2** likely to lead to danger or death: *a suicidal attempt to rescue her son* **3** likely to destroy one's own career or future: *it would be suicidal for them to ignore public opinion*

suicide *n* **1** the act of killing oneself deliberately **2** a person who kills himself or herself intentionally **3** the self-inflicted ruin of one's own career or future: *such a cut would be political suicide* [Latin *sui* of oneself + *caedere* to kill]

suicide bomber *n* a terrorist who carries out a bomb attack, knowing that he or she will be killed in the explosion

suit *n* **1** a set of clothes of the same material designed to be worn together, usually a jacket with matching trousers or skirt **2** an outfit worn for a specific purpose: *a diving suit* **3** a legal action taken against someone; lawsuit **4** any of the four types of card in a pack of playing cards: spades, hearts, diamonds, or clubs **5** *slang* a business executive or white-collar worker **6 follow suit** to act in the same way as someone else **7 strong suit** *or* **strongest suit** something one excels in ▷ *vb* **8** to be fit or appropriate for: *that colour suits you* **9** to be acceptable to (someone) **10 suit oneself** to do what one wants without considering other people [Old French *sieute* set of things] **suited** *adj*

suitable *adj* appropriate for a particular function or occasion; proper **suitability** *n* **suitably** *adv*

suitcase *n* a large portable travelling case for clothing

suite *n* **1** a set of connected rooms in a hotel **2** a matching set of furniture, for example two armchairs and a settee **3** *music* a composition of several movements in the same key [French]

suitor *n* **1** *old-fashioned* a man who wants to marry a woman **2** *law* a person who starts legal proceedings against someone; plaintiff [Latin *secutor* follower]

Sukkoth (**sook**-oat) *n* an eight-day Jewish harvest festival, commemorating the period when the Israelites lived in the wilderness

sulk *vb* **1** to be silent and moody as a way of showing anger or resentment: *I went home and sulked for two days* ▷ *n* **2** a mood in which one shows anger or resentment by being silent and moody: *he was just in a sulk*

sulky *adj* **sulkier, sulkiest** moody or silent because of anger or resentment [perhaps from obsolete *sulke* sluggish] **sulkily** *adv* **sulkiness** *n*

sullen *adj* unwilling to talk or be sociable; sulky [Latin *solus* alone] **sullenly** *adv* **sullenness** *n*

sully *vb* **-lies, -lying, -lied 1** to ruin (someone's reputation) **2** to spoil or make dirty: *the stream had been sullied by the smelter's pollution* [probably from French *souiller* to soil]

sulpha drug *or US* **sulfa drug** *n pharmacol* any of a group of sulphonamides that prevent the growth of bacteria: used to treat bacterial infections

sulphate *or US* **sulfate** *n chem* a salt or ester of sulphuric acid

sulphide *or US* **sulfide** *n chem* a compound of sulphur with another element

sulphite *or US* **sulfite** *n chem* any salt or ester of sulphurous acid

sulphonamide *or US* **sulfonamide** (sulf-**on**-a-mide) *n pharmacol* any of a class of organic compounds that prevent the growth of bacteria

sulphur *or US* **sulfur** *n chem* a light yellow, highly inflammable, nonmetallic element used in the production of sulphuric acid, in the vulcanization of rubber, and in medicine. Symbol: **S** [Latin *sulfur*] **sulphuric** *or US* **sulfuric** *adj*

sulphur dioxide *n chem* a strong-smelling colourless soluble gas, used in the manufacture of sulphuric acid and in the preservation of foodstuffs

sulphureous *or US* **sulfureous** (sulf-**yoor**-ee-uss) *adj* same as **sulphurous** (sense 1)

sulphuric acid *n chem* a colourless dense oily corrosive liquid used in the manufacture of fertilizers and explosives

sulphurize, -rise *or US* **sulfurize** (**sulf**-yoor-rise) *vb* **-rizing, -rized** *or* **-rising, -rised** *chem* to combine with or treat (something) with sulphur or a sulphur compound

sulphurous *or US* **sulfurous** *adj chem* **1** of or resembling sulphur **2** containing sulphur, esp. with a valence of four

sultan *n* the sovereign of a Muslim country [Arabic: rule]

sultana *n* **1** the dried fruit of a small white seedless grape **2** a sultan's wife, mother, daughter, or concubine [Italian]

sultanate *n* **1** the territory ruled by a sultan **2** the office or rank of a sultan

sultry *adj* **-trier, -triest 1** (of weather or climate) very hot and humid **2** suggesting hidden passion: *a sultry brunette* [obsolete *sulter* to swelter]

sum *n* **1** the result of the addition of numbers or quantities **2** one or more columns or rows of numbers to be added, subtracted, multiplied, or divided **3** a quantity of money: *they can win enormous sums* **4 in sum** as a summary; in short: *in sum, it's been a bad week for the government* ▷ *adj* **5** complete or final: *the sum total* ▷ *vb* **summing, summed 6** See **sum up** [Latin *summa* the top, sum]

summarize *or* **-rise** *vb* **-rizing, -rized** *or* **-rising, -rised** to give a short account of (something)

summary *n, pl* **-maries 1** a brief account giving the main points of something ▷ *adj* **2** performed quickly, without formality or attention to details: *a summary judgment* [Latin *summarium*] **summarily** *adv*

summation *n* **1** a summary of what has just been done or said **2** the process of working out a sum; addition **3** the result of such a process

summer *n* **1** the warmest season of the year, between spring and autumn **2** *literary* a time of youth, success, or happiness [Old English *sumor*] **summery** *adj*

summerhouse *n* a small building in a garden, used for shade in the summer

summer school *n* an academic course held during the summer

summer solstice *n* the time at which the sun is at its northernmost point in the sky (southernmost point in the S hemisphere), appearing at noon at its highest altitude above the horizon. It occurs about June 21 (December 22 in the S hemisphere)

summertime *n* the period or season of summer

summing-up *n* **1** a summary of the main points of an argument, speech, or piece of writing **2** concluding statements made by a judge to the jury before they retire to consider their verdict

summit *n* **1** the highest point or part of a mountain or hill **2** the highest possible degree or state; peak or climax: *the summit of success* **3** a meeting of heads of governments or other high officials [Old French *somet*]

summon *vb* **1** to order (someone) to come **2** to send for (someone) to appear in court **3** to call upon (someone) to do something: *the authorities had summoned the relatives to be available* **4** to convene (a meeting) **5** (often foll. by *up*) to call into action (one's strength, courage, etc.); muster [Latin *summonere* to give a discreet reminder]

summons *n, pl* **-monses 1** a call or an order to attend a specified place at a specified time **2** an official order requiring a person to attend court, either to answer a charge or to give evidence ▷ *vb* **3** to order (someone) to appear in court: *three others had been summonsed for questioning*

sumo *n* the national style of wrestling of Japan, in which two contestants of great height and weight attempt to force each other out of the ring [Japanese]

sump *n* **1** a container in an internal-combustion engine into which oil can drain **2** same as **cesspool 3** *mining* a hollow at the bottom of a shaft where water collects [Middle Dutch *somp* marsh]

sumptuary *adj* controlling expenditure or extravagant use of resources [Latin *sumptuarius* concerning expense]

sumptuous *adj* magnificent and very expensive; splendid: *sumptuous decoration* [Latin *sumptuosus* costly]

sum up *vb* **1** to give a short account of (the main points of an argument, speech, or piece of writing) **2** to form a quick opinion of: *how well you have summed me up!*

sun *n* **1** the star that is the source of heat and light for the planets in the solar system. Related adjective: **solar** **2** any star around which a system of planets revolves **3** the heat and light received from the sun; sunshine **4** **catch the sun** to become slightly suntanned **5** **under the sun** on earth; at all: *there are no free lunches under the sun* ▷ *vb* **sunning, sunned** **6** **sun oneself** to lie, sit, or walk in the sunshine on a warm day [Old English *sunne*] **sunless** *adj*

Sun. Sunday

sunbathe *vb* **-bathing, -bathed** to lie or sit in the sunshine, in order to get a suntan **sunbather** *n* **sunbathing** *n*

sunbeam *n* a ray of sunlight

sun block *n* a chemical applied to exposed skin to block out all or almost all of the ultraviolet rays of the sun

sunburn *n* painful reddening of the skin caused by overexposure to the sun **sunburnt** *or* **sunburned** *adj*

sun cream *n* a cream applied to exposed skin to reduce the effect of the ultraviolet rays of the sun

sundae *n* ice cream topped with a sweet sauce, nuts, whipped cream, and fruit [origin unknown]

Sunday *n* the first day of the week and the Christian day of worship [Old English *sunnandæg* day of the sun]

Sunday best *n* a person's best clothes, sometimes regarded as those most suitable for wearing at church

Sunday school *n* a school for teaching children about Christianity, usually held in a church hall on Sunday

sundial *n* a device used for telling the time during the hours of sunlight, consisting of a pointer that casts a shadow onto a surface marked in hours

sundown *n US* sunset

sundries *pl n* several things of various sorts

sundry *adj* **1** several or various; miscellaneous ▷ *pron* **2** **all and sundry** everybody [Old English *syndrig* separate]

sunfish *n, pl* **-fish** *or* **-fishes** a large sea fish with a rounded body

sunflower *n* **1** a very tall plant with large yellow flowers **2** **sunflower seed oil** the oil extracted from sunflower seeds, used as a salad oil and in margarine

sung *vb* the past participle of **sing**

▒ **USAGE** See at **ring**¹.

sunglasses *pl n* glasses with darkened lenses that protect the eyes from bright sunlight

sun-god *n* the sun considered as a god

sunk *vb* a past participle of **sink**

sunken *vb* **1** a past participle of **sink** ▷ *adj* **2** (of a person's cheeks, eyes, or chest) curving inward due to old age or bad health **3** situated at a lower level than the surrounding or usual one: *the sunken garden* **4** situated under water; submerged: *sunken ships*

sun lamp *n* a lamp that gives off ultraviolet rays, used for muscular therapy or for giving people an artificial suntan

sunlight *n* the light that comes from the sun **sunlit** *adj*

sun lounge *or US* **sun parlor** *n* a room with large windows designed to receive as much sunlight as possible

sunnies *pl n informal* sunglasses

sunny *adj* **-nier, -niest** **1** full of or lit up by sunshine **2** cheerful and happy

sunrise *n* **1** the daily appearance of the sun above the horizon **2** the time at which the sun rises

sunrise industry *n* any of the fast-developing high-technology industries, such as electronics

sunroof *n* a panel in the roof of a car that may be opened to let in air or sunshine

sunscreen *n* a cream or lotion applied to exposed skin to reduce the effect of the ultraviolet rays of the sun

sunset *n* **1** the daily disappearance of the sun below the horizon **2** the time at which the sun sets

sunshade *n* anything used to shade people from the sun, such as a parasol or awning

sunshine *n* **1** the light and warmth from the sun **2** *Brit* a light-hearted term of address

sunspot *n* **1** *informal* a sunny holiday resort **2** a dark cool patch on the surface of the sun **3** *Austral* a small area of skin damage caused by exposure to the sun

sunstroke *n* a condition caused by spending too much time exposed to intensely hot sunlight, producing high fever and sometimes loss of consciousness

suntan *n* a brownish colouring of the skin caused by exposure to the sun or a sun lamp **suntanned** *adj*

sun-up *n US & Austral* sunrise

sup¹ *vb* **supping, supped** **1** to take (liquid) by swallowing a little at a time ▷ *n* **2** a sip [Old English *sūpan*]

sup² *vb* **supping, supped** *archaic* to have supper [Old French *soper*]

super *informal* ▷ *adj* **1** very good or very nice: *they had a super holiday* ▷ *n Austral & NZ* **2** superannuation **3** superphosphate [Latin: above]

super- *prefix* **1** above or over: *superscript* **2** outstanding: *superstar* **3** of greater size, extent, or quality: *supermarket* [Latin]

superabundant *adj* existing in very large numbers or amount **superabundance** *n*

superannuated *adj* **1** discharged with a pension, owing to age or illness **2** too old to be useful; obsolete [Medieval Latin *superannatus* aged more than one year]

superannuation *n* **A** a regular payment made by an employee into a pension fund **B** the pension finally paid

superb *adj* extremely good or impressive [Latin *superbus* distinguished] **superbly** *adv*

Super Bowl *n American football* the championship game held annually between the best team of the American Football Conference and that of the National Football Conference

S

superbug *n informal* a bacterium resistant to antibiotics
supercharge *vb* **-charging, -charged 1** to increase the power of (an internal-combustion engine) with a supercharger **2** to charge (the atmosphere, a remark, etc.) with an excess amount of (tension, emotion, etc.) **3** to apply pressure to (a fluid); pressurize
supercharger *n* a device that increases the power of an internal-combustion engine by forcing extra air into it
supercilious *adj* behaving in a superior and arrogant manner [Latin *supercilium* eyebrow] **superciliously** *adv* **superciliousness** *n*
superconductivity *n physics* the ability of certain substances to conduct electric current with almost no resistance at very low temperatures **superconducting** *adj* **superconductor** *n*
supercontinent *n* a huge landmass thought to have existed in the geological past and to have split into smaller landmasses and formed the present continents
superego *n, pl* **-egos** *psychoanalysis* that part of the unconscious mind that governs a person's ideas concerning what is right and wrong
supererogation *n* the act of doing more work than is required [Latin *supererogare* to spend over and above]
superficial *adj* **1** not careful or thorough: *a superficial analysis* **2** only outwardly apparent rather than genuine or actual: *those are merely superficial differences* **3** (of a person) lacking deep emotions or serious interests; shallow **4** of, near, or forming the surface: *the gash was superficial* [Late Latin *superficialis*] **superficiality** *n* **superficially** *adv*
superfluous (soo-**per**-flew-uss) *adj* more than is sufficient or required [Latin *superfluus* overflowing] **superfluity** *n*
superfood *n* a food that is especially nutritious or otherwise beneficial to health
superglue *n* an extremely strong and quick-drying glue
supergrass *n Brit, Austral & NZ* an informer who names a large number of people as terrorists or criminals, esp. one who gives this information in order to avoid being put on trial
super heavyweight *n* an amateur boxer weighing over 201 pounds (91 kg)
superhero *n, pl* **-roes** (in science fiction) a person who uses supernatural powers to fight against evil
superhuman *adj* beyond normal human ability or experience: *a superhuman effort*
superimpose *vb* **-posing, -posed** to set or place (something) on or over something else
superintend *vb* to supervise (a person or an activity) [Latin *super-* above + *intendere* to give attention to]
superintendent *n* **1** a senior police officer **2** a person who directs and manages an organization or office
superior *adj* **1** greater in quality, quantity, or usefulness **2** higher in rank, position, or status: *he was reprimanded by a superior officer* **3** believing oneself to be better than others **4** of very high quality or respectability: *superior merchandise* **5** *formal* placed higher up: *damage to the superior surface of the wing* **6** *printing* (of a character) written or printed above the line ▷ *n* **7** a person of greater rank or status **8** See **mother superior** [Latin *superus* placed above] **superiority** *n*

> **USAGE** *Superior* should not be used with *than*: *he is a better* (not *a superior*) *poet than his brother; his poetry is superior to* (not *superior than*) *his brother's.*

superlative (soo-**per**-lat-iv) *adj* **1** of outstanding quality; supreme **2** *grammar* denoting the form of an adjective or adverb that expresses the highest degree of quality ▷ *n* **3** the highest quality **4** *grammar* the superlative form of an adjective or adverb [Old French *superlatif*]
superman *n, pl* **-men** any man with great physical or mental powers
supermarket *n* a large self-service shop selling food and household goods
supermodel *n* a famous and highly-paid fashion model
supernatural *adj* **1** of or relating to things that cannot be explained by science, such as clairvoyance, ghosts, etc. ▷ *n* **2 the supernatural** forces, occurrences, and beings that cannot be explained by science
supernova *n, pl* **-vae** *or* **-vas** a star that explodes and, for a few days, becomes one hundred million times brighter than the sun
supernumerary *adj* **1** exceeding the required or regular number; extra **2** employed as a substitute or assistant ▷ *n, pl* **-aries 3** a person or thing that exceeds the required or regular number **4** a substitute or assistant **5** an actor who has no lines to say [Latin *super-* above + *numerus* number]
superphosphate *n* a chemical fertilizer, esp. one made by treating rock phosphate with sulphuric acid
superpower *n* a country of very great military and economic power, such as the US
superscript *printing* ▷ *adj* **1** (of a character) written or printed above the line ▷ *n* **2** a superscript character
supersede *vb* **-seding, -seded 1** to take the place of (something old-fashioned or less appropriate): *cavalry was superseded by armoured vehicles* **2** to replace (someone) in function or office [Latin *supersedere* to sit above]
supersize *adj also* **supersized 1** larger than standard size ▷ *vb* **-sizes, -sizing, -sized 2** to increase the size of (something, such as a standard portion of food)
supersonic *adj* being, having, or capable of a speed greater than the speed of sound
superstar *n* an extremely popular and famous entertainer or sportsperson **superstardom** *n*
superstate *n* a large state, esp. one created from a federation of states
superstition *n* **1** irrational belief in magic and the powers that supposedly bring good luck or bad luck **2** a belief or practice based on this [Latin *superstitio*] **superstitious** *adj*
superstore *n* a large supermarket

superstructure *n* **1** any structure or concept built on something else **2** *naut* any structure above the main deck of a ship
supertanker *n* a very large fast tanker
supertax *n* an extra tax on incomes above a certain level
supervene *vb* **-vening, -vened** to happen as an unexpected development [Latin *supervenire* to come upon] **supervention** *n*
supervise *vb* **-vising, -vised 1** to direct the performance or operation of (an activity or a process) **2** to watch over (people) so as to ensure appropriate behaviour [Latin *super-* over + *videre* to see] **supervision** *n* **supervisor** *n* **supervisory** *adj*
supine (soo-pine) *adj formal* lying on one's back [Latin *supinus*]
supper *n* **1** an evening meal **2** a late evening snack [Old French *soper*]
supplant *vb* to take the place of (someone or something) [Latin *supplantare* to trip up]
supple *adj* **1** (of a person) moving and bending easily and gracefully **2** (of a material or object) soft and bending easily without breaking [Latin *supplex* bowed] **suppleness** *n*
supplement *n* **1** an addition designed to make something more adequate **2** a magazine distributed free with a newspaper **3** a section added to a publication to supply further information or correct errors **4** (of money) an additional payment to obtain special services ▷ *vb* **5** to provide an addition to (something), esp. in order to make up for an inadequacy: *she supplements her salary by renting her spare bedroom* [Latin *supplementum*] **supplementary** *adj*
supplicant *n formal* a person who makes a humble request [Latin *supplicans* beseeching]
supplication *n formal* a humble request for help [Latin *supplicare* to beg on one's knees]
supply *vb* **-plies, -plying, -plied 1** to provide with something required: *Nigeria may supply them with oil* ▷ *n, pl* **-plies 2** the act of providing something **3** an amount available for use; stock: *electricity supply* **4 supplies** food and equipment needed for a trip or military campaign **5** *econ* the amount of a commodity that producers are willing and able to offer for sale at a specified price: *supply and demand* **6** a person who acts as a temporary substitute ▷ *adj* **7** acting as a temporary substitute: *supply teachers* [Latin *supplere* to complete] **supplier** *n*
support *vb* **1** to carry the weight of (a thing or person) **2** to provide the necessities of life for (a family or person) **3** to give practical or emotional help to (someone) **4** to give approval to (a cause, idea, or political party) **5** to take an active interest in and be loyal to (a particular football or other sports team) **6** to establish the truthfulness or accuracy of (a theory or statement) by providing new facts **7** to speak in a debate in favour of (a motion) **8** (in a concert) to perform earlier than (the main attraction) **9** *films & theatre* to play a less important role to (the leading actor or actress) ▷ *n* **10** the act of supporting or the condition of being supported **11** a thing that bears the weight of an object from below **12** a person who gives someone practical or emotional help **13** the means of providing the necessities of life for a family or person **14** a band or entertainer not topping the bill [Latin *supportare* to bring] **supportive** *adj*
supporter *n* a person who supports a sports team, politician, etc.
suppose *vb* **-posing, -posed 1** to presume (something) to be true without certain knowledge: *I suppose it will be in the papers* **2** to consider (something) as a possible suggestion for the sake of discussion: *suppose you're arrested on a misdemeanour* **3** (of a theory) to depend on the truth or existence of: *this scenario supposes that he would do so* [Latin *supponere* to substitute]
supposed *adj* **1 supposed to** expected to: *spies aren't supposed to be nice* **2** presumed to be true without certain knowledge; doubtful: *the supposed wonders of drug therapy* **supposedly** *adv*
supposition *n* **1** an idea or a statement believed or assumed to be true **2** the act of supposing: *much of it is based on supposition*
suppositious *adj* deduced from an idea or statement believed or assumed to be true; hypothetical
suppository *n, pl* **-ries** *med* a medicine in solid form that is inserted into the vagina or rectum and left to dissolve [Latin *suppositus* placed beneath]
suppress *vb* **1** to put an end to (something) by physical or legal force **2** to prevent the circulation or publication of (information or books) **3** to hold (an emotion or a response) in check; restrain: *he could barely suppress a groan* **4** *electronics* to reduce or eliminate (interference) in a circuit [Latin *suppressus* held down] **suppression** *n*
suppressant *n* a drug that suppresses an action: *a cough suppressant*
suppurate *vb* **-rating, -rated** *pathol* (of a wound or sore) to produce or leak pus [Latin *suppurare*]
supremacy *n* **1** supreme power; dominance **2** the state or quality of being superior
supreme *adj* **1** of highest status or power: *the Supreme Council* **2** of highest quality or importance: *a supreme player* **3** greatest in degree; extreme: *supreme happiness* [Latin *supremus* highest] **supremely** *adv*
supremo *n, pl* **-mos** *informal* a person in overall authority
sur-[1] *prefix* over; above; beyond: *surcharge*; *surrealism* [Old French]
sur-[2] *prefix* See **sub-**
surcharge *n* **1** a charge in addition to the usual payment or tax **2** an excessive sum charged, often unlawfully ▷ *vb* **-charging, -charged 3** to charge (someone) an additional sum or tax **4** to overcharge (someone) for something
surd *maths* ▷ *n* **1** an irrational number ▷ *adj* **2** of or relating to a surd [Latin *surdus* muffled]
sure *adj* **1** free from doubt or uncertainty (in regard to a belief): *she was sure that she was still at home*; *I am sure he didn't mean it* **2 sure of** having no doubt, such as of the occurrence of a future state or event: *sure of winning the point* **3** reliable or accurate: *a sure sign of dry rot* **4** bound inevitably (to be or do something); certain: *his aggressive style is*

S

sure to please the American fans **5 sure of** *or* **about** happy to put one's trust in (someone): *I'm still not quite sure about her* **6 sure of oneself** confident in one's own abilities and opinions **7** not open to doubt: *sure proof* **8** bound to be or occur; inevitable: *victory is sure* **9** physically secure: *a sure footing* **10 be sure** (usually foll. by *to* or *and*) be careful or certain (to do something): *be sure to label each jar* **11 for sure** without a doubt **12 make sure** to make certain: *make sure there is no-one in the car* **13 sure enough** *informal* in fact: *sure enough, this is happening* **14 to be sure** it has to be acknowledged; admittedly ▷ *adv* **15** *informal, chiefly US & Canad* without question; certainly: *it sure is bad news* ▷ *interj* **16** *informal* willingly; yes [Old French *seur*] **sureness** *n*

sure-fire *adj informal* certain to succeed: *a sure-fire cure*

sure-footed *adj* **1** unlikely to fall, slip, or stumble **2** unlikely to make a mistake

surely *adv* **1** am I not right in thinking that?; I am sure that: *surely you can see that?* **2** without doubt: *without support they will surely fail* **3 slowly but surely** gradually but noticeably ▷ *interj* **4** *chiefly US & Canad* willingly; yes

surety *n, pl* **-ties 1** a person who takes legal responsibility for the fulfilment of another's debt or obligation **2** security given as a guarantee that an obligation will be met [Latin *securitas* security]

surf *n* **1** foam caused by waves breaking on the shore or on a reef ▷ *vb* **2** to take part in surfing **3** to move rapidly through a particular medium: *surfing the internet* **4** *informal* to be carried on top of something: *that guy's surfing the audience* [probably variant of *sough*] **surfer** *n*

surface *n* **1** the outside or top of an object **2** the size of such an area **3** material covering the surface of an object **4** the outward appearance as opposed to the real or hidden nature of something: *on the surface the idea seems attractive* **5** *geom* **A** the complete boundary of a solid figure **B** something that has length and breadth but no thickness **6** the uppermost level of the land or sea **7 come to the surface** to become apparent after being hidden ▷ *vb* **-facing, -faced 8** to become apparent or widely known **9** to rise to the surface of water **10** to give (an area) a particular kind of surface **11** *informal* to get up out of bed [French]

surface tension *n physics* a property of liquids, caused by molecular forces, that leads to the apparent presence of a surface film and to rising and falling in contact with solids

surfboard *n* a long narrow board used in surfing

surfeit *n formal* **1** an excessive amount **2** excessive eating or drinking **3** an uncomfortably full or sickened feeling caused by eating or drinking too much [French *sourfait*]

surfie *n Austral & NZ informal* a young person whose main interest is in surfing

surfing *n* the sport of riding towards shore on the crest of a wave by standing or lying on a surfboard

surge *n* **1** a sudden powerful increase: *a surge in spending* **2** a strong rolling movement of the sea **3** a heavy rolling motion or sound: *a great surge of people* ▷ *vb* **surging, surged 4** to move forward strongly and suddenly **5** to increase quickly and strongly **6** (of the sea) to rise or roll with a heavy swelling motion [Latin *surgere* to rise]

surgeon *n* a medical doctor who specializes in surgery

surgery *n, pl* **-geries 1** medical treatment in which a person's body is cut open by a surgeon in order to treat or remove the problem part **2** *Brit* a place where, or time when, a doctor or dentist can be consulted **3** *Brit* a time when an MP or councillor can be consulted [Greek *kheir* hand + *ergon* work]

surgical *adj* **1** involving or used in surgery **2** (of an action) performed with extreme precision: *a surgical air attack* **surgically** *adv*

surgical spirit *n* methylated spirit used medically for cleaning wounds and sterilizing equipment

surly *adj* **-lier, -liest** bad-tempered and rude [from obsolete *sirly* haughty]

surmise *vb* **-mising, -mised 1** to guess (something) from incomplete or uncertain evidence ▷ *n* **2** a conclusion based on incomplete or uncertain evidence [Old French *surmettre* to accuse]

surmount *vb* **1** to overcome (a problem) **2** to be situated on top of (something): *the island is surmounted by a huge black castle* [Old French *surmonter*] **surmountable** *adj*

surname *n* a family name as opposed to a first or Christian name [Old French *sur-* over + *nom* name]

surpass *vb* **1** to be greater in extent than or superior in achievement to (something or someone) **2 surpass oneself** *or* **expectations** to go beyond the limit of what was expected [French *surpasser*]

surplice *n* a loose knee-length garment with wide sleeves, worn by members of the clergy and choristers [Old French *sourpelis*]

surplus *n* **1** a quantity or amount left over in excess of what is required **2** *accounting* an excess of income over spending ▷ *adj* **3** being in excess; extra: *surplus to requirements* [Old French]

surprise *n* **1** the act of taking someone unawares: *the element of surprise* **2** a sudden or unexpected event, gift, etc.: *this is a nice surprise* **3** the feeling of being surprised; astonishment: *to our great surprise* **4 take someone by surprise** to capture someone unexpectedly or catch someone unprepared ▷ *adj* **5** causing surprise: *a surprise attack* ▷ *vb* **-prising, -prised 6** to cause (someone) to feel amazement or wonder **7** to come upon or discover (someone) unexpectedly or suddenly **8** to capture or attack (someone) suddenly and without warning **9 surprise into** to provoke (someone) to unintended action by a trick or deception [Old French *surprendre* to overtake] **surprised** *adj* **surprising** *adj* **surprisingly** *adv*

surreal *adj* very strange or dreamlike; bizarre

surrealism *n* a movement in art and literature in the 1920s, involving the combination of images that would not normally be found together, as if in a dream [French *surréalisme*] **surrealist** *n, adj* **surrealistic** *adj*

surrender *vb* **1** to give oneself up physically to an enemy after defeat **2** to give (something) up to another, under pressure or on demand: *the rebels surrendered their arms* **3** to give (something) up voluntarily to another: *he was surrendering his own chance for the championship* **4** to give in to a temptation or an influence ▷ *n* **5** the act or instance of surrendering [Old French *surrendre*]

surreptitious *adj* done in secret or without permission: *surreptitious moments of bliss* [Latin *surrepticius* furtive] **surreptitiously** *adv*

surrogate *n* **1** a person or thing acting as a substitute ▷ *adj* **2** acting as a substitute: *a surrogate father* [Latin *surrogare* to substitute]

surrogate mother *n* a woman who gives birth to a child on behalf of a couple who cannot have a baby themselves, usually by artificial insemination **surrogate motherhood** *or* **surrogacy** *n*

surround *vb* **1** to encircle or enclose (something or someone) **2** to exist around (someone or something): *the family members who surround him* ▷ *n* **3** *chiefly Brit* a border, such as the area of uncovered floor between the walls of a room and the carpet [Old French *suronder*] **surrounding** *adj*

surroundings *pl n* the area and environment around a person, place, or thing

surtax *n* an extra tax on incomes above a certain level

surveillance *n* close observation of a person suspected of being a spy or a criminal [French]

survey *vb* **1** to view or consider (something) as a whole: *she surveyed her purchases anxiously* **2** to make a detailed map of (an area of land) by measuring or calculating distances and height **3** *Brit* to inspect (a building) to assess its condition and value **4** to make a detailed investigation of the behaviour, opinions, etc., of (a group of people) ▷ *n* **5** a detailed investigation of the behaviour, opinions, etc., of a group of people **6** the act of making a detailed map of an area of land by measuring or calculating distance and height **7** *Brit* an inspection of a building to assess its condition and value [French *surveoir*] **surveying** *n* **surveyor** *n*

survival *n* **1** the condition of having survived something **2** a person or thing that continues to exist in the present despite being from an earlier time, such as a custom ▷ *adj* **3** of, relating to, or assisting the act of surviving: *survival suits*

survive *vb* **-viving, -vived 1 A** to continue to live or exist **B** to continue to live or exist after (a passage of time or a difficult or dangerous experience) **2** to live after the death of (another) [Old French *sourvivre*] **survivor** *n*

susceptibility *n, pl* **-ties 1** the quality or condition of being easily affected or influenced by something **2 susceptibilities** emotional feelings

susceptible *adj* **1 susceptible to A** giving in easily to: *susceptible to political pressure* **B** vulnerable to (a disease or injury): *susceptible to pneumonia* **2** easily affected emotionally; impressionable [Late Latin *susceptibilis*]

sushi (soo-shee) *n* a Japanese dish consisting of small cakes of cold rice with a topping of raw fish [Japanese]

suspect *vb* **1** to believe (someone) to be guilty without having any proof **2** to think (something) to be false or doubtful: *he suspected her intent* **3** to believe (something) to be the case; think probable: *I suspect he had another reason* ▷ *n* **4** a person who is believed guilty of a specified offence ▷ *adj* **5** not to be trusted or relied upon: *her commitment to the cause has always been suspect* [Latin *suspicere* to mistrust]

suspend *vb* **1** to hang (something) from a high place **2** to cause (something) to remain floating or hanging: *a huge orange sun suspended above the horizon* **3** to cause (something) to stop temporarily: *the discussions have been suspended* **4** to remove (someone) temporarily from a job or position, usually as a punishment [Latin *suspendere*]

suspended animation *n* a state in which the body's functions are slowed down to a minimum for a period of time, such as by freezing or hibernation

suspended sentence *n* a sentence of imprisonment that is not served by an offender unless he or she commits a further offence during a specified time

suspender belt *n* a belt with suspenders hanging from it for holding up women's stockings

suspenders *pl n* **1 A** elastic straps attached to a belt or corset, with fasteners for holding up women's stockings **B** similar fasteners attached to garters for holding up men's socks **2** *US & Canad* a pair of straps worn over the shoulders for holding up the trousers. Also called (Brit): **braces**

suspense *n* **1** a state of anxiety or uncertainty: *Sue and I stared at each other in suspense* **2** excitement felt at the approach of the climax of a book, film, or play: *action and suspense abound in this thriller* [Medieval Latin *suspensum* delay] **suspenseful** *adj*

suspension *n* **1** the delaying or stopping temporarily of something: *the suspension of the talks* **2** temporary removal from a job or position, usually as a punishment **3** the act of suspending or the state of being suspended **4** a system of springs and shock absorbers that supports the body of a vehicle **5** a device, usually a wire or spring, that suspends or supports something, such as the pendulum of a clock **6** *chem* a mixture in which fine solid or liquid particles are suspended in a fluid

suspension bridge *n* a bridge suspended from cables that hang between two towers and are secured at both ends

suspicion *n* **1** the act or an instance of suspecting; belief without sure proof that something is wrong **2** a feeling of mistrust **3** a slight trace: *the merest suspicion of a threat* **4 above suspicion** not possibly guilty of anything, through having a good reputation **5 under suspicion** suspected of doing something wrong [Latin *suspicio* distrust]

suspicious *adj* **1** causing one to suspect something is wrong: *suspicious activities* **2** unwilling to trust: *I'm suspicious of his motives* **suspiciously** *adv*

S

suss out *vb Brit, Austral & NZ slang* to work out (a situation or a person's character), using one's intuition [from *suspect*]

sustain *vb* **1** to maintain or continue for a period of time: *I managed to sustain a conversation* **2** to keep up the strength or energy of (someone): *one mouthful of water to sustain him; the merest drop of comfort to sustain me* **3** to suffer (an injury or loss): *he sustained a spinal injury* **4** to support (something) from below **5** to support or agree with (a decision or statement): *objection sustained* [Latin *sustinere* to hold up] **sustained** *adj*

sustainable *adj* **1** capable of being sustained **2** (of economic development or energy sources) capable of being maintained at a steady level without exhausting natural resources or causing ecological damage: *sustainable development*

sustained-release *adj* (of a pill or tablet) coated with a chemical substance that controls the dosage released into a patient's system

sustenance *n* means of maintaining health or life; food and drink

suture (soo-tcher) *n surgery* a stitch made with catgut or silk thread, to join the edges of a wound together [Latin *suere* to sew]

SUV sport (*or* sports) utility vehicle: a car with off-road features such as four-wheel drive and raised ground clearance

suzerain *n* **1** a state or sovereign that has some degree of control over a dependent state **2** (formerly) a person who had power over many people [French] **suzerainty** *n*

svelte *adj* attractively or gracefully slim; slender [French]

SW **1** southwest(ern) **2** short wave

swab *n* **1** *med* a small piece of cotton wool used for applying medication or cleansing a wound ▷ *vb* **swabbing, swabbed** **2** to clean or apply medication to (a wound) with a swab **3** to clean (the deck of a ship) with a mop [probably from Middle Dutch *swabbe* mop]

swaddle *vb* **-dling, -dled** to wrap (a baby) in swaddling clothes [Old English *swæthel* swaddling clothes]

swaddling clothes *pl n* long strips of cloth formerly wrapped round a newborn baby

swag *n* **1** *slang* stolen property **2** *Austral & NZ informal* (formerly) a swagman's pack containing personal belongings [probably Scandinavian]

swagger *vb* **1** to walk or behave in an arrogant manner ▷ *n* **2** an arrogant walk or manner [probably from *swag*]

swagger stick *n* a short cane carried by army officers

swagman *n, pl* **-men** *Austral & NZ informal* a labourer who carries his personal possessions in a pack while looking for work

Swahili (swah-**heel**-ee) *n* a language of E Africa that is an official language of Kenya and Tanzania [Arabic *sawāhil* coasts]

swain *n archaic or poetic* **1** a male lover or admirer **2** a young man from the countryside [Old English *swān* swineherd]

swallow[1] *vb* **1** to pass (food, drink, etc.) through the mouth and gullet to the stomach **2** *informal* to believe (something) trustingly: *I was supposed to swallow the lie* **3** not to show: *I believe they should swallow their pride* **4** to make a gulping movement in the throat, such as when nervous **5** to put up with (an insult) without answering back **6** **be swallowed up** to be taken into and made a part of something: *the old centre was being swallowed up by new estates* ▷ *n* **7** the act of swallowing **8** the amount swallowed at any single time; mouthful [Old English *swelgan*]

swallow[2] *n* a small migratory bird with long pointed wings and a forked tail [Old English *swealwe*]

swallow dive *n* a dive in which the legs are kept straight and the arms outstretched while in the air, with entry into the water made headfirst

swallowtail *n* **1** a butterfly with a long tail-like part on each hind wing **2** the forked tail of a swallow or similar bird

swam *vb* the past tense of **swim**

swami (**swah**-mee) *n* a Hindu religious teacher [Hindi *svāmī*]

swamp *n* **1** an area of permanently waterlogged land; bog ▷ *vb* **2** *naut* to cause (a boat) to sink or fill with water **3** to overwhelm (a person or place) with more than can be dealt with or accommodated [probably from Middle Dutch *somp*] **swampy** *adj*

swan *n* **1** a large, usually white, water bird with a long neck ▷ *vb* **swanning, swanned** **2** **swan around** *or* **about** *informal* to wander about without purpose, but with an air of superiority [Old English]

swank *informal* ▷ *vb* **1** to show off or boast ▷ *n* **2** showing off or boasting [origin unknown] **swanky** *adj*

swanndri (**swan**-dry) *n trademark NZ* a weatherproof woollen shirt or jacket. Also called: **swannie**

swan song *n* the last public act of a person before retirement or death

swap *or* **swop** *vb* **swapping, swapped** *or* **swopping, swopped** **1** to exchange (something) for something else ▷ *n* **2** an exchange [originally, to shake hands on a bargain, strike: probably imitative]

SWAPO *or* **Swapo** South-West Africa People's Organization

sward *n* a stretch of turf or grass [Old English *sweard* skin]

swarm[1] *n* **1** a group of bees, led by a queen, that has left the hive to make a new home **2** a large mass of insects or other small animals **3** a moving mass of people ▷ *vb* **4** to move quickly and in large numbers **5** to be overrun: *the place is swarming with cops* [Old English *swearm*]

swarm[2] *vb* **swarm up** to climb (a ladder or rope) by gripping it with the hands and feet: *the boys swarmed up the rigging* [origin unknown]

swarthy *adj* **swarthier, swarthiest** having a dark complexion [obsolete *swarty*]

swash (swosh) *n* the rush of water up a beach following each break of the waves [probably imitative]

swashbuckling *adj* having the exciting manner or behaviour of pirates, esp. those depicted in films [obsolete *swash* to make the noise of a sword striking a shield + *buckler* shield] **swashbuckler** *n*

swastika *n* **1** a primitive religious symbol in the shape of a Greek cross with the ends of the arms bent at right angles **2** this symbol with clockwise arms as the emblem of Nazi Germany [Sanskrit *svastika*]

swat *vb* **swatting, swatted 1** to hit sharply: *swatting the ball with confidence* ▷ *n* **2** a sharp blow [dialect variant of *squat*]

swatch *n* **1** a sample of cloth **2** a collection of such samples [origin unknown]

swath (**swawth**) *n* same as **swathe** [Old English *swæth*]

swathe *vb* **swathing, swathed 1** to wrap a bandage, garment, or piece of cloth around (a person or part of the body) ▷ *n* **2** a long strip of cloth wrapped around something **3** the width of one sweep of a scythe or of the blade of a mowing machine **4** the strip cut in one sweep **5** the quantity of cut crops left in one sweep **6** a long narrow strip of land [Old English *swathian*]

sway *vb* **1** to swing to and fro: *red poppies swayed in the faint breeze* **2** to lean to one side and then the other: *entire rows swayed in time* **3** to be unable to decide between two or more opinions **4** to influence (someone) in his or her opinion or judgment ▷ *n* **5** power or influence **6** a swinging or leaning movement **7 hold sway** to have power or influence [probably from Old Norse *sveigja* to bend]

swear *vb* **swearing, swore, sworn 1** to use words considered obscene or blasphemous **2** to promise solemnly on oath; vow: *Sally and Peter swore to love and cherish each other* **3 swear by** to have complete confidence in (something) **4** to state (something) earnestly: *I swear he was all right* **5** to give evidence on oath in a law court [Old English *swerian*]

swear in *vb* to make (someone) take an oath when taking up an official position or entering the witness box to give evidence in court: *a new federal president was sworn in*

swear off *vb* to promise to give up: *I lived with memories of the gooey sundaes I've sworn off*

swearword *n* a word considered rude or blasphemous

sweat *n* **1** the salty liquid that comes out of the skin's pores during strenuous activity in excessive heat or when afraid **2** the state or condition of sweating: *he worked up a sweat* **3** *slang* hard work or effort: *climbing to the crest of Ward Hill was a sweat* **4 in a sweat** *informal* in a state of worry **5 no sweat** *slang* no problem ▷ *vb* **sweating, sweat** *or* **sweated 6** to have sweat come through the skin's pores, as a result of strenuous activity, excessive heat, nervousness, or fear **7** *informal* to suffer anxiety or distress **8 sweat blood** *informal* **A** to work very hard **B** to be filled with anxiety ▷ See also **sweats** [Old English *swǣtan*] **sweaty** *adj*

sweatband *n* a piece of cloth tied around the forehead or around the wrist to absorb sweat during strenuous physical activity

sweater *n* a warm knitted piece of clothing covering the upper part of the body

sweat lodge *n* (among native N American peoples) a structure in which water is poured onto hot stones to make the occupants sweat for religious or medicinal purposes

sweat off *vb informal* to get rid of (weight) by doing exercises

sweat out *vb* **sweat it out** *informal* to endure an unpleasant situation for a time, hoping for an improvement

sweats *pl n* sweatshirts and sweat suit trousers collectively

sweatshirt *n* a long-sleeved casual top made of knitted cotton or cotton mixture

sweatshop *n* a workshop where employees work long hours in poor conditions for low pay

sweat suit *n* a suit worn by athletes for training, consisting of a sweatshirt and trousers made of the same material

swede *n* a round root vegetable with a purplish-brown skin and yellow flesh [introduced from Sweden in the 18th century]

Swede *n* a person from Sweden

Swedish *adj* **1** of Sweden ▷ *n* **2** the language of Sweden

sweep *vb* **sweeping, swept 1** to clean (a floor or chimney) with a brush **2** (often foll. by *up*) to remove or collect (dirt or rubbish) with a brush **3** to move smoothly and quickly: *the car swept into the drive* **4** to spread rapidly across or through (a place): *fire swept through Southern California* **5** to move in a proud and majestic fashion: *the boss himself swept into the hall* **6** to direct (one's eyes, line of fire, etc.) over (a place or target) **7 sweep away** *or* **off** to overwhelm (someone) emotionally: *I've been swept away by my fears* **8** to brush or lightly touch (a surface): *the dress swept along the ground* **9** to clear away or get rid of (something) suddenly or forcefully: *these doubts were quickly swept aside*; *bridges have been swept away by the floods* **10** to stretch out gracefully or majestically, esp. in a wide circle: *the hills swept down into the green valley* **11** to win overwhelmingly: *the umbrella party which swept these elections* **12 sweep the board** to win every event or prize in a contest ▷ *n* **13** the act or an instance of sweeping **14** a swift or steady movement: *the wide sweep of the shoulders* **15** a wide expanse: *the whole sweep of the bay* **16** any curving line or contour, such as a driveway **17** short for **sweepstake 18** *chiefly Brit* same as **chimney sweep 19 make a clean sweep** to win an overwhelming victory [Middle English *swepen*]

sweeper *n* **1** a device used to sweep carpets, consisting of a long handle attached to a revolving brush **2** *soccer* a defensive player usually positioned in front of the goalkeeper

sweeping *adj* **1** affecting many people to a great extent: *sweeping financial reforms* **2** (of a statement) making general assumptions about an issue without considering the details **3** decisive or overwhelming: *to suffer sweeping losses* **4** taking in a wide area: *a sweeping view of the area*

sweepstake *or esp US* **sweepstakes** *n* **1** a lottery in which the stakes of the participants make up the prize **2** a horse race involving such a lottery [originally referring to someone who *sweeps* or takes all the stakes in a game]

S

sweet *adj* **1** tasting of or like sugar **2** kind and charming: *that was really sweet of you* **3** attractive and delightful: *a sweet child* **4** (of a sound) pleasant and tuneful: *sweet music* **5** (of wine) having a high sugar content; not dry **6** fresh, clear, and clean: *sweet water; sweet air* **7 sweet on someone** fond of or infatuated with someone ▷ *n Brit, Austral & NZ* **8** a shaped piece of confectionery consisting mainly of sugar **9** a dessert [Old English *swēte*] **sweetly** *adv* **sweetness** *n*

sweet-and-sour *adj* (of food) cooked in a sauce made from sugar and vinegar and other ingredients

sweetbread *n* the meat obtained from the pancreas of a calf or lamb

sweetbrier *n* a wild rose with sweet-smelling leaves and pink flowers

sweet corn *n* **1** a kind of maize with sweet yellow kernels, eaten as a vegetable when young **2** the sweet kernels removed from the maize cob, cooked as a vegetable

sweeten *vb* **1** to make (food or drink) sweet or sweeter **2** to be nice to (someone) in order to ensure cooperation **3** to make (an offer or a proposal) more acceptable

sweetener *n* **1** a sweetening agent that does not contain sugar **2** *Brit, Austral & NZ slang* an inducement offered to someone in order to persuade them to accept an offer or business deal

sweetheart *n* **1** an affectionate name to call someone **2** *old-fashioned* one's boyfriend or girlfriend **3** *informal* a lovable or generous person

sweetie *n informal* **1** an affectionate name to call someone **2** *Brit & NZ* same as **sweet** (sense 8) **3** *chiefly Brit* a lovable or generous person

sweetmeat *n old-fashioned* a small delicacy preserved in sugar

sweet pea *n* a climbing plant with sweet-smelling pastel-coloured flowers

sweet pepper *n* the large bell-shaped fruit of the pepper plant, which is eaten unripe (**green pepper**) or ripe (**red pepper**) as a vegetable

sweet potato *n* a root vegetable, grown in the tropics, with pinkish-brown skin and yellow flesh

sweet spot *n sport* the centre area of a racquet, club, etc., from which the cleanest shots are made

sweet-talk *informal* ▷ *vb* **1** to persuade (someone) by flattery: *I thought I could sweet-talk you into teaching me* ▷ *n* **sweet talk 2** insincere flattery intended to persuade

sweet tooth *n* a strong liking for sweet foods

sweet william *n* a garden plant with clusters of white, pink, red, or purple flowers

swell *vb* **swelling, swelled, swollen** *or* **swelled 1** (of a part of the body) to grow in size as a result of injury or infection: *his face swelled and became pale* **2** to increase in size as a result of being filled with air or liquid: *a balloon swells if you force in more air* **3** to grow or cause (something) to grow in size, numbers, amount, or degree: *Israel's population is swelling* **4** (of an emotion) to become more intense: *his anger swelled within him* **5** (of the seas) to rise in waves **6** (of a sound) to become gradually louder and then die away ▷ *n* **7** the waving movement of the surface of the open sea **8** an increase in size, numbers, amount, or degree **9** a bulge **10** *old-fashioned, informal* a person who is wealthy, upper class, and fashionably dressed **11** *music* an increase in sound followed by an immediate dying away ▷ *adj* **12** *slang, chiefly US* excellent or fine [Old English *swellan*]

swelling *n* an enlargement of a part of the body as the result of injury or infection

swelter *vb* **1** to feel uncomfortable under extreme heat ▷ *n* **2** a hot and uncomfortable condition: *they left the city swelter for the beach* [Old English *sweltan* to die]

sweltering *adj* uncomfortably hot: *a sweltering summer*

swept *vb* the past of **sweep**

swerve *vb* **swerving, swerved 1** to turn aside from a course sharply or suddenly ▷ *n* **2** the act of swerving [Old English *sweorfan* to scour]

swift *adj* **1** moving or able to move quickly; fast **2** happening or performed quickly or suddenly: *a swift glance this way* **3 swift to** prompt to (do something): *swift to retaliate* ▷ *n* **4** a small fast-flying insect-eating bird with long wings [Old English] **swiftly** *adv* **swiftness** *n*

swig *informal* ▷ *n* **1** a large swallow or deep drink, esp. from a bottle ▷ *vb* **swigging, swigged 2** to drink (some liquid) in large swallows, esp. from a bottle [origin unknown]

swill *vb* **1** to drink large quantities of (an alcoholic drink) **2** (often foll. by *out*) *chiefly Brit & NZ* to rinse (something) in large amounts of water ▷ *n* **3** a liquid mixture containing waste food, fed to pigs **4** a deep drink, esp. of beer [Old English *swilian* to wash out]

swim *vb* **swimming, swam, swum 1** to move along in water by movements of the arms and legs, or (in the case of fish) tail and fins **2** to cover (a stretch of water) in this way: *the first person to swim the Atlantic* **3** to float on a liquid: *flies swimming on the milk* **4** to be affected by dizziness: *his head was swimming* **5** (of the objects in someone's vision) to appear to spin or move around: *the faces of the nurses swam around her* **6** (often foll. by *in* or *with*) to be covered or flooded with liquid: *a steak swimming in gravy* ▷ *n* **7** the act, an instance, or a period of swimming **8 in the swim** *informal* fashionable or active in social or political activities [Old English *swimman*] **swimmer** *n* **swimming** *n*

swimming bath *n* an indoor swimming pool

swimming costume *or* **bathing costume** *n chiefly Brit, Austral & NZ* same as **swimsuit**

swimmingly *adv* successfully, effortlessly, or well: *everything went swimmingly*

swimming pool *n* a large hole in the ground, tiled and filled with water for swimming in

swimsuit *n* a woman's swimming garment that leaves the arms and legs bare

swindle *vb* **-dling, -dled 1** to cheat (someone) out of money **2** to obtain (money) from someone by fraud ▷ *n* **3** an instance of cheating someone out of money [German *schwindeln*] **swindler** *n*

swine *n* **1** a mean or unpleasant person **2** *pl* **swine** same as **pig** [Old English *swīn*] **swinish** *adj*

swine flu *n* a form of influenza occurring in swine caused by a virus capable of spreading to humans

swing *vb* **swinging, swung** **1** to move backwards and forwards; sway **2** to pivot or cause (something) to pivot from a fixed point such as a hinge: *the door swung open* **3** to wave (a weapon, etc.) in a sweeping motion **4** to move in a sweeping curve: *the headlights swung along the street* **5** to alter one's opinion or mood suddenly **6** to hang so as to be able to turn freely **7** *old-fashioned slang* to be hanged: *you'll swing for this!* **8** *informal* to manipulate or influence successfully: *it may help to swing the election* **9** (often foll. by *at*) to hit out with a sweeping motion **10** *old-fashioned* to play (music) in the style of swing **11** *old-fashioned slang* to be lively and modern ▷ *n* **12** the act of swinging **13** a sweeping stroke or punch **14** a seat hanging from two chains or ropes on which a person may swing back and forth **15** popular dance music played by big bands in the 1930s and 1940s **16** *informal* the normal pace at which an activity, such as work, happens: *I'm into the swing of things now* **17** a sudden or extreme change, for example in some business activity or voting pattern **18 go with a swing** to go well; be successful **19 in full swing** at the height of activity [Old English *swingan*]

swing bridge *n* a bridge that can be swung open to let ships pass through

swing by *vb informal* to go somewhere to pay a visit

swingeing (swin-jing) *adj chiefly Brit* severe or causing hardship: *swingeing spending cuts*

swipe *vb* **swiping, swiped** **1** *informal* to try to hit (someone or something) with a sweeping blow: *he swiped at a boy who ran forward* **2** *slang* to steal (something) **3** to pass (a credit or debit card) through a machine which electronically interprets the information stored in the card **4** to activate a function on an electronic device by moving one's finger across a touchscreen ▷ *n* **5** *informal* a hard blow [origin unknown]

swipe card *n* a card with a magnetic strip that holds encoded information that can be interpreted when the card is passed through an electronic device

swirl *vb* **1** to turn round and round with a twisting motion ▷ *n* **2** a twisting or spinning motion **3** a twisting shape [probably from Dutch *zwirrelen*] **swirling** *adj*

swish *vb* **1** to move with or cause (something) to make a whistling or hissing sound ▷ *n* **2** a hissing or rustling sound or movement: *she turned with a swish of her skirt* ▷ *adj* **3** *informal, chiefly Brit, Austral & NZ* smart and fashionable [imitative]

Swiss *adj* **1** of Switzerland ▷ *n, pl* **Swiss** **2** a person from Switzerland

Swiss ball *n* a very large inflatable ball made of strong elastic rubber, used for physical exercise and physiotherapy

swiss roll *n* a sponge cake spread with jam or cream and rolled up

switch *n* **1** a device for opening or closing an electric circuit **2** a sudden quick change **3** an exchange or swap **4** a flexible rod or twig, used for punishment **5** *US & Canad* a pair of movable rails for diverting moving trains from one track to another ▷ *vb* **6** to change quickly and suddenly **7** to exchange (places) or swap (something for something else) **8** *chiefly US & Canad* to transfer (rolling stock) from one railway track to another ▷ See also **switch off, switch on** [probably from Middle Dutch *swijch* twig]

switchback *n* a steep mountain road, railway, or track which rises and falls sharply many times

switchboard *n* the place in a telephone exchange or office building where telephone calls are connected

switch off *vb* **1** to cause (a device) to stop operating by moving a switch or lever: *she switched off the television* **2** *informal* to become bored and stop paying attention: *when the conversation turned to house prices I switched off*

switch on *vb* **1** to cause (a device) to operate by moving a switch or lever **2** *informal* to produce (a certain type of behaviour or emotion) suddenly or automatically: *she was good at switching on the charm*

swither *Scot* ▷ *vb* **1** to hesitate or be indecisive ▷ *n* **2** a state of hesitation or uncertainty [origin unknown]

swivel *vb* **-elling, -elled** *or US* **-eling, -eled** **1** to turn on or swing round on a central point ▷ *n* **2** a coupling device which allows an attached object to turn freely [Old English *swīfan* to turn]

swivel chair *n* a chair, whose seat is joined to the legs by a swivel, enabling it to be spun round

swizz *n Brit, NZ & S African informal* a swindle or disappointment [origin unknown]

swizzle stick *n* a small stick used to stir cocktails

swollen *vb* **1** a past participle of **swell** ▷ *adj* **2** enlarged by swelling

swoon *vb* **1** *literary* to faint because of shock or strong emotion **2** to be deeply affected by passion for (someone): *you've swooned over a string of rotten men* ▷ *n* **3** *literary* a faint [Old English *geswōgen* insensible] **swooning** *adj*

swoop *vb* **1** (usually foll. by *down*) to move quickly through the air in a downward curve: *an owl swooped down from its perch* **2** (usually foll. by *on*) to move suddenly and quickly towards (a place) in order to attack, arrest, or question the people inside: *nine police cars and vans swooped on the premises* ▷ *n* **3** the act of swooping [Old English *swāpan* to sweep]

swoosh *vb* **1** to make a swirling or rustling sound when moving or pouring out ▷ *n* **2** a swirling or rustling sound or movement [imitative]

swop *vb* **swopping, swopped,** *n* same as **swap**

sword *n* **1** a weapon with a long sharp blade and a short handle **2 the sword** **A** military power **B** death; destruction: *we will put them to the sword* **3 cross swords** to have a disagreement with someone [Old English *sweord*]

sword dance *n* a dance in which the performer dances over swords on the ground

swordfish *n, pl* **-fish** *or* **-fishes** a large fish with a very long upper jaw that resembles a sword

Sword of Damocles (dam-a-kleez) *n* a disaster that is about to take place [after a flattering

S

courtier forced by Dionysius, tyrant of ancient Syracuse, to sit under a sword suspended by a hair]

swordplay *n* the action or art of fighting with a sword

swordsman *n, pl* **-men** a person who is skilled in the use of a sword **swordsmanship** *n*

swordstick *n* a hollow walking stick that contains a short sword

swore *vb* the past tense of **swear**

sworn *vb* **1** the past participle of **swear** ▹ *adj* **2** bound by or as if by an oath: *a sworn enemy*

swot[1] *informal* ▹ *vb* **swotting, swotted 1** (often foll. by *up*) to study (a subject) very hard, esp. for an exam; cram ▹ *n* **2** a person who works or studies hard [variant of *sweat*]

swot[2] *vb* **swotting, swotted,** *n* same as **swat**

swum *vb* the past participle of **swim**

swung *vb* the past of **swing**

sybarite (**sib**-bar-ite) *n* **1** a lover of luxury and pleasure ▹ *adj* **2** luxurious or sensuous [after *Sybaris,* ancient Greek colony in S Italy, famed for its luxury] **sybaritic** *adj*

sycamore *n* **1** a tree with five-pointed leaves and two-winged fruits **2** *US & Canad* an American plane tree [Latin *sycomorus*]

sycophant *n* a person who uses flattery to win favour from people with power or influence [Greek *sukophantēs*] **sycophancy** *n* **sycophantic** *adj*

syllabic *adj* of or relating to syllables

syllabify *vb* **-fies, -fying, -fied** to divide (a word) into syllables **syllabification** *n*

syllable *n* **1** a part of a word which is pronounced as a unit, which contains a single vowel sound, and which may or may not contain consonants: for example, 'paper' has two syllables **2** the least mention: *without a syllable about what went on* **3 in words of one syllable** simply and plainly [Greek *sullabē*]

syllabub *n Brit & Austral* a dessert made from milk or cream beaten with sugar, wine, and lemon juice [origin unknown]

syllabus (**sill**-lab-buss) *n, pl* **-buses** *or* **-bi** (-bye) **A** the subjects studied for a particular course **B** a list of these subjects [Late Latin]

S

syllogism *n* a form of reasoning consisting of two premises and a conclusion, for example *some temples are in ruins; all ruins are fascinating; so some temples are fascinating* [Greek *sullogismos*] **syllogistic** *adj*

sylph *n* **1** a slender graceful girl or young woman **2** an imaginary creature believed to live in the air [New Latin *sylphus*] **sylphlike** *adj*

sylvan *or* **silvan** *adj chiefly poetic* of or consisting of woods or forests [Latin *silva* forest]

symbiosis *n* **1** *biol* a close association of two different animal or plant species living together to their mutual benefit **2** a similar relationship between different individuals or groups: *the symbiosis of the coal and railway industries* [Greek: a living together] **symbiotic** *adj*

symbol *n* **1** something that represents or stands for something else, usually an object used to represent something abstract **2** a letter, figure, or sign used in mathematics, music, etc., to represent a quantity, operation, function, etc. [Greek *sumbolon* sign]

symbolic *adj* **1** of or relating to a symbol or symbols **2** being a symbol of something **symbolically** *adv*

symbolism *n* **1** the representation of something by the use of symbols **2** an art movement involving the use of symbols to express mystical or abstract ideas **symbolist** *adj, n*

symbolize *or* **-lise** *vb* **-lizing, -lized** *or* **-lising, -lised 1** to be a symbol of (something) **2** to represent with a symbol **symbolization** *or* **-lisation** *n*

symmetry *n, pl* **-tries 1** the state of having two halves that are mirror images of each other **2** beauty resulting from a balanced arrangement of parts [Greek *summetria* proportion] **symmetrical** *adj* **symmetrically** *adv*

sympathetic *adj* **1** feeling or showing kindness and understanding **2** (of a person) likeable and appealing: *the film's only sympathetic character* **3 sympathetic to** showing agreement with or willing to lend support to: *sympathetic to the movement* **sympathetically** *adv*

sympathize *or* **-thise** *vb* **-thizing, -thized** *or* **-thising, -thised** > **sympathize with A** to feel or express sympathy for: *I sympathized with this fear* **B** to agree with or support: *Pitt sympathized with these objectives* **sympathizer** *or* **-thiser** *n*

sympathy *n, pl* **-thies 1** (often foll. by *for*) understanding of other people's problems; compassion **2 sympathy with** agreement with someone's feelings or interests: *we have every sympathy with how she felt* **3** (*often pl*) feelings of loyalty or support for an idea or a cause: *was this where her sympathies lay?* **4** mutual affection or understanding between two people or a person and an animal [Greek *sympatheia*]

symphony *n, pl* **-nies 1** a large-scale orchestral composition with several movements **2** an orchestral movement in a vocal work such as an oratorio **3** short for **symphony orchestra 4** anything that has a pleasing arrangement of colours or shapes: *the garden was a symphony of coloured bunting* [Greek *sun-* together + *phōnē* sound] **symphonic** *adj*

symphony orchestra *n music* a large orchestra that performs symphonies

symposium *n, pl* **-sia** *or* **-siums 1** a conference at which experts or academics discuss a particular subject **2** a collection of essays on a particular subject [Greek *sumposion* a drinking party]

symptom *n* **1** *med* a sign indicating the presence of an illness or disease **2** anything that is taken as an indication that something is wrong: *a growing symptom of grave social injustice* [Greek *sumptōma* chance] **symptomatic** *adj*

synagogue *n* a building for Jewish religious services and religious instruction [Greek *sunagōgē* a gathering]

synapse *n anatomy* a gap where nerve impulses pass between two nerve cells [Greek *sunapsis* junction]

sync *or* **synch** *films, television & computers informal* ▹ *vb* **1** to synchronize ▹ *n* **2** synchronization: *the film and sound are in sync*

synchromesh *adj* **1** (of a gearbox) having a system of clutches that synchronizes the speeds of the gearwheels before they engage

▷ *n* **2** a gear system having these features [*synchronized mesh*]

synchronism *n* the quality or condition of occurrence at the same time or rate

synchronize *or* **-nise** *vb* **-nizing, -nized** *or* **-nising, -nised 1** (of two or more people) to perform (an action) at the same time: *a synchronized withdrawal of Allied forces* **2** to cause (two or more clocks or watches) to show the same time **3** *films* to match (the soundtrack and the action of a film) precisely **synchronization** *or* **-nisation** *n*

synchronous *adj* occurring at the same time and rate [Greek *sun-* together + *khronos* time] **synchrony** *n*

syncline *n geol* a downward slope of stratified rock in which the layers dip towards each other from either side

syncopate *vb* **-pating, -pated** *music* to stress the weak beats in (a rhythm or a piece of music) instead of the strong beats [Medieval Latin *syncopare* to omit a letter or syllable] **syncopation** *n*

syncope (sing-kop-ee) *n* **1** *med* a faint **2** *linguistics* the omission of sounds or letters from the middle of a word, as in *ne'er* for *never* [Greek *sunkopē* a cutting off]

syndic *n Brit* a business or legal agent of some universities or other institutions [Greek *sundikos* defendant's advocate]

syndicalism *n* a movement advocating seizure of economic and political power by the industrial working class by means of industrial action, esp. general strikes **syndicalist** *n*

syndicate *n* **1** a group of people or firms organized to undertake a joint project **2** an association of individuals who control organized crime **3** a news agency that sells articles and photographs to a number of newspapers for simultaneous publication ▷ *vb* **-cating, -cated 4** to sell (articles and photographs) to several newspapers for simultaneous publication **5** to form a syndicate of (people) [Old French *syndicat*] **syndication** *n*

syndrome *n* **1** *med* a combination of signs and symptoms that indicate a particular disease **2** a set of characteristics indicating the existence of a particular condition or problem [Greek *sundromē*, literally: a running together]

synecdoche (sin-neck-dock-ee) *n* a figure of speech in which a part is substituted for a whole or a whole for a part, as in *50 head of cattle* for *50 cows* [Greek *sunekdokhē*]

synergy *n* the potential ability for individuals or groups to be more successful working together than on their own [Greek *sunergos*]

synod *n* a special church council which meets regularly to discuss church affairs [Greek *sunodos*]

synonym *n* a word that means the same as another word, such as *bucket* and *pail* [Greek *sun-* together + *onoma* name]

synonymous *adj* **1** (often foll. by *with*) having the same meaning (as) **2** (foll. by *with*) closely associated (with): *a family whose name had been synonymous with fine jewellery*

synopsis (sin-op-siss) *n, pl* **-ses** (-seez) a brief review or outline of a subject; summary: *they have sent me a monthly synopsis of the plot* [Greek *sunopsis*]

synoptic *adj* **1** of or relating to a synopsis **2** *Bible* of or relating to the Gospels of Matthew, Mark, and Luke **synoptically** *adv*

synovia (sine-oh-vee-a) *n med* a clear thick fluid that lubricates the body joints [New Latin] **synovial** *adj*

syntax *n* the grammatical rules of a language and the way in which words are arranged to form phrases and sentences [Greek *suntassein* to put in order] **syntactic** *or* **syntactical** *adj*

synthesis (sinth-iss-siss) *n, pl* **-ses** (-seez) **1** the process of combining objects or ideas into a complex whole **2** the combination produced by such a process **3** *chem* the process of producing a compound by one or more chemical reactions, usually from simpler starting materials [Greek *sunthesis*]

synthesize *or* **-sise** *vb* **-sizing, -sized** *or* **-sising, -sised 1** to combine (objects or ideas) into a complex whole **2** to produce (a compound) by synthesis

synthesizer *n* a keyboard instrument in which speech, music, or other sounds are produced electronically

synthetic *adj* **1** (of a substance or material) made artificially by chemical reaction **2** not sincere or genuine: *synthetic compassion* ▷ *n* **3** a synthetic substance or material [Greek *sunthetikos* expert in putting together] **synthetically** *adv*

syphilis *n* a sexually transmitted disease that causes sores on the genitals and eventually on other parts of the body [*Syphilis*, hero of a 16th-century Latin poem] **syphilitic** *adj*

syphon *n, vb* same as **siphon**

Syrian *adj* **1** of Syria ▷ *n* **2** a person from Syria

syringa *n* same as **mock orange** or **lilac** [Greek *surinx* tube (its hollow stems were used for pipes)]

syringe *n* **1** *med* a device used for withdrawing or injecting fluids, consisting of a hollow cylinder of glass or plastic, a tightly fitting piston, and a hollow needle ▷ *vb* **-ringing, -ringed 2** to wash out, inject, or spray with a syringe: *a harmless blue dye is syringed into the uterus* [Greek *surinx* tube]

syrup *n* **1** a solution of sugar dissolved in water and often flavoured with fruit juice: used for sweetening fruit, etc. **2** a thick sweet liquid food made from sugar or molasses: *maple syrup* **3** a liquid medicine containing a sugar solution: *cough syrup* [Arabic *sharāb* a drink]

syrupy *adj* **1** (of a liquid) thick or sweet **2** excessively sentimental: *a soundtrack of syrupy violins*

system *n* **1** a method or set of methods for doing or organizing something: *a new system of production or distribution* **2** orderliness or routine; an ordered manner: *there is no system in his work* **3** the manner in which an institution or aspect of society has been arranged: *the Scottish legal system* **4 the system** the government and state regarded as exploiting, restricting, and repressing individuals **5** the manner in which the parts of something fit or function together; structure: *disruption of the earth's weather system* **6** any scheme or set of rules used to classify, explain, or calculate: *the Newtonian system of physics*

S

7 a network of communications, transportation, or distribution **8** *biol* an animal considered as a whole **9** *biol* a set of organs or structures that together perform some function: *the immune system* **10** one's physical or mental constitution: *the intrusion of the virus into my system; to get the hate out of my system* **11** an assembly of electronic or mechanical parts forming a self-contained unit: *an alarm system* [Greek *sustēma*]

systematic *adj* following a fixed plan and done in an efficient and methodical way: *a systematic approach to teaching* **systematically** *adv*

systematize *or* **-tise** *vb* **-tizing, -tized** *or* **-tising, -tised** to arrange (information) in a system **systematization** *or* **-tisation** *n*

systemic *adj biol* (of a poison, disease, etc.) affecting the entire animal or body **systemically** *adv*

systems analysis *n* the analysis of the requirements of a task and the expression of these in a form that enables a computer to perform the task **systems analyst** *n*

systole (siss-tol-ee) *n physiol* contraction of the heart, during which blood is pumped into the arteries [Greek *sustolē*] **systolic** *adj*

S

Tt

t *or* **T** *n, pl* **t's, T's** *or* **Ts** **1** the 20th letter of the English alphabet **2** **to a T** **A** in every detail: *that's her to a T* **B** perfectly: *that dress suits you to a T*
t tonne(s)
T **1** *chem* tritium **2** tera-
t. **1** temperature **2** ton(s)
ta *interj Brit, Austral & NZ informal* thank you [imitative of baby talk]
Ta *chem* tantalum
TA (in Britain) Territorial Army
tab[1] *n* **1** a small flap of material, esp. one on a garment for decoration or for fastening to a button **2** any similar flap, such as a piece of paper attached to a file for identification **3** *chiefly US & Canad* a bill, esp. for a meal or drinks **4** **keep tabs on** *informal* to keep a watchful eye on [origin unknown]
tab[2] *n* short for **tabulator**
TAB (in Australia and New Zealand) Totalisator Agency Board: an agency for betting on horse and greyhound racing
tabard *n* **1** a sleeveless jacket, esp. one worn by a medieval knight over his armour **2** a short coat bearing the coat of arms of the sovereign, worn by a herald [Old French *tabart*]
Tabasco *n trademark* a very hot sauce made from capsicum peppers [after *Tabasco*, state in Mexico]
tabby *n, pl* **-bies** **1** a cat whose fur has dark stripes or wavy markings on a lighter background ▷ *adj* **2** having dark stripes or wavy markings on a lighter background [from the girl's name *Tabitha*, influenced by *tabby*, old kind of striped silk]
tabernacle *n* **1** **the Tabernacle** *Bible* the portable sanctuary in which the ancient Israelites carried the Ark of the Covenant **2** any place of Christian worship that is not called a church **3** *RC Church* a receptacle in which the Blessed Sacrament is kept [Latin *tabernaculum* a tent]
tabla *n, pl* **-bla** *or* **-blas** one of a pair of Indian drums played with the hands [Hindi, from Arabic: drum]
table *n* **1** a piece of furniture consisting of a flat top supported by legs: *a coffee table* **2** a set of facts or figures arranged in rows and columns: *a league table* **3** a group of people sitting round a table for a meal, game, etc.: *the whole table laughed* **4** *formal* the food provided at a meal or in a particular house: *he keeps a good table* **5** **turn the tables** to cause a complete reversal of circumstances ▷ *vb* **-bling, -bled** **6** *Brit & Austral* to submit (a motion) for discussion by a meeting **7** *US* to suspend discussion of (a proposal) indefinitely [Latin *tabula* a writing tablet]
tableau (tab-loh) *n, pl* **-leaux** (-loh) a silent motionless group of people arranged to represent a scene from history, legend, or literature [French]
tablecloth *n* a cloth for covering the top of a table, esp. during meals
table d'hôte (tah-bla **dote**) *adj* **1** (of a meal) consisting of a set number of courses with a limited choice of dishes offered at a fixed price ▷ *n, pl* **tables d'hôte** (tah-bla **dote**) **2** a table d'hôte meal or menu [French: the host's table]
table football *n Brit* a game based on soccer, played on a table with sets of miniature human figures mounted on rods allowing them to be tilted or spun to strike the ball. US & Canad name: **foosball**
tableland *n* a flat area of high ground; plateau
table licence *n Brit* a licence permitting the sale of alcohol with meals only
tablespoon *n* **1** a spoon, larger than a dessertspoon, used for serving food **2** Also called: **tablespoonful** the amount contained in such a spoon **3** a unit of capacity used in cooking, equal to half a fluid ounce
tablet *n* **1** a pill consisting of a compressed medicinal substance **2** a flattish cake of some substance, such as soap **3** a slab of stone, wood, etc., used for writing on before the invention of paper **4** an inscribed piece of stone, wood, etc., that is fixed to a wall as a memorial: *a tablet in memory of those who died* **5** a handheld personal computer that is operated by touchscreen [Latin *tabula* a board]
table tennis *n* a game resembling a miniature form of tennis played on a table with bats and a small light ball
table wine *n* **1** fairly cheap wine for everyday drinking with meals **2** ordinary wine, as opposed to fortified wine such as sherry or port
tabloid *n* a newspaper with fairly small pages, usually with many photographs and a concise and often sensational style [from *tablet*]
taboo *or* **tabu** *n, pl* **-boos** *or* **-bus** **1** a restriction or prohibition resulting from social or other conventions **2** a ritual prohibition, esp. of something that is considered holy or unclean ▷ *adj* **3** forbidden or disapproved of: *a taboo subject* [Tongan *tapu*]
tabor *n* a small drum used esp. in the Middle Ages, struck with one hand while the other held a pipe [Old French *tabour*]
tabular *adj* arranged in parallel columns so as to form a table [Latin *tabula* a board]
tabulate *vb* **-lating, -lated** to arrange (information) in rows and columns **tabulation** *n*
tabulator *n* a key on a typewriter or word processor that sets stops so that data can be arranged and presented in columns
tachograph *n* a device that measures the speed of a vehicle and the distance that it covers, and produces a record (**tachogram**) of its readings [Greek *takhos* speed + -GRAPH]
tachometer *n* a device for measuring speed, esp. that of a revolving shaft [Greek *takhos* speed + -METER]
tacit (tass-it) *adj* understood or implied without actually being stated: *tacit support* [Latin *tacitus* silent]
taciturn (tass-it-turn) *adj* habitually silent, reserved, or uncommunicative [Latin *tacere* to be silent] **taciturnity** *n*

tack¹ *n* **1** a short sharp-pointed nail with a large flat head **2** *Brit & NZ* a long loose temporary stitch used in dressmaking ▷ *vb* **3** to fasten (something) with a tack or tacks: *the carpet needs to be tacked down* **4** *Brit & NZ* to sew (something) with long loose temporary stitches ▷ See also **tack on** [Middle English *tak* fastening, nail]

tack² *n* **1** *naut* the course of a boat sailing obliquely into the wind, expressed in terms of the side of the boat against which the wind is blowing: *on the port tack* **2** a course of action or a policy: *telling her to get off my back hadn't worked, so I took a different tack* ▷ *vb* **3** *naut* to steer (a boat) on a zigzag course, so as to make progress against the wind [from *tack* rope used to secure a sail]

tack³ *n* riding harness for horses, including saddles and bridles [from *tackle*]

tackies *or* **takkies** *pl n, sing* **tacky** *S African informal* tennis shoes or plimsolls [origin unknown]

tackle *vb* **-ling, -led 1** to deal with (a problem or task) in a determined way **2** to confront (someone) about something: *I intend to tackle both management and union on this issue* **3** to attack and fight (a person or animal) **4** *sport* to attempt to get the ball away from (an opposing player) ▷ *n* **5** *sport* an attempt to get the ball away from an opposing player **6** the equipment required for a particular sport or occupation: *fishing tackle* **7** a set of ropes and pulleys for lifting heavy weights **8** *naut* the ropes and other rigging aboard a ship [Middle English]

tack on *vb* to attach or add (something) to something that is already complete: *an elegant mansion with a modern extension tacked on at the back*

tack room *n* a room in a stable building in which bridles, saddles, etc. are kept

tacky¹ *adj* **tackier, tackiest** slightly sticky [earlier *tack* stickiness] **tackiness** *n*

tacky² *adj* **tackier, tackiest** *informal* **1** vulgar and tasteless: *tacky commercialism* **2** shabby or shoddy: *tacky streets* [origin unknown] **tackiness** *n*

taco (tah-koh) *n, pl* **tacos** *Mexican cookery* a tortilla folded into a roll with a filling and usually fried [from Spanish: literally, a bite to eat]

t

tact *n* **1** a sense of the best and most considerate way to deal with people so as not to upset them **2** skill in handling difficult situations [Latin *tactus* a touching] **tactful** *adj* **tactfully** *adv* **tactless** *adj* **tactlessly** *adv* **tactlessness** *n*

tactic *n* a move or method used to achieve an aim or task: *he has perfected dissent as a tactic to further his career*. See also **tactics**

tactical *adj* **1** of or employing tactics: *a tactical advantage* **2** (of missiles, bombing, etc.) for use in limited military operations **tactically** *adv*

tactical voting *n* (in an election) the practice of voting for a candidate or party one would not normally support in an attempt to prevent an even less acceptable candidate or party being elected

tactics *n* **1** *military* the science of the detailed direction of forces in battle to achieve an aim or task ▷ *pl n* **2** the plans and methods used to achieve a particular short-term aim [Greek *tassein* to arrange] **tactician** *n*

tactile *adj* of or having a sense of touch: *the tactile sense* [Latin *tactilis*]

tadpole *n* the aquatic larva of a frog or toad, which develops from a limbless tailed form with external gills into a form with internal gills, limbs, and a reduced tail [Middle English *tadde* toad + *pol* head]

TAFE (in Australia) Technical and Further Education

taffeta *n* a thin shiny silk or rayon fabric used esp. for women's clothes [Persian *tāftah* spun]

taffrail *n* *naut* a rail at the back of a ship or boat [Dutch *taffereel* panel]

tag¹ *n* **1** a piece of paper, leather, etc., for attaching to something as a mark or label: *the price tag* **2** a point of metal or plastic at the end of a cord or lace **3** a brief trite quotation **4** an electronic device worn by a prisoner under house arrest so that his or her movements can be monitored **5** *slang* a graffito consisting of a nickname or personal symbol ▷ *vb* **tagging, tagged 6** to mark with a tag ▷ See also **tag along, tag on** [origin unknown]

tag² *n* **1** a children's game in which one player chases the others in an attempt to touch one of them, who will then become the chaser ▷ *vb* **tagging, tagged 2** to catch and touch (another child) in the game of tag. Also: **tig** [origin unknown]

Tagalog (tag-**gah**-log) *n* a language spoken in the Philippines

tag along *vb* to accompany someone, esp. when uninvited: *I tagged along behind the gang*

tag end *n* the last part of something: *at the tag end of the Ice Age*

tagetes (taj-**eat**-eez) *n, pl* **-tes** any of a genus of plants with yellow or orange flowers, including the French and African marigolds [Latin *Tages*, a god of ancient Etruria]

tagliatelle (tal-yat-**tell**-ee) *n* a form of pasta made in narrow strips [Italian]

tag on *vb* to add at the end of something: *a throwaway remark, tagged on at the end of a casual conversation*

tahini (tah-**hee**-nee) *n* a paste made from ground sesame seeds, used esp. in Middle Eastern cookery [from Arabic]

t'ai chi (tie **chee**) *n* a Chinese system of exercises and self-defence characterized by slow rhythmic movements [Chinese *t'ai chi ch'uan* great art of boxing]

taiga (**tie**-ga) *n* the belt of coniferous forest extending across much of subarctic North America, Europe, and Asia

taikonaut *n* an astronaut from the People's Republic of China [from Cantonese *taikon(g)* cosmos]

tail¹ *n* **1** the rear part of an animal's body, usually forming a long thin flexible part attached to the trunk. Related adjective: **caudal 2** any long thin part projecting or hanging from the back or end of something: *the waiter produced menus from beneath the tail of his coat* **3** the last part: *the tail of the procession* **4** the rear part of an aircraft **5** *astron* the luminous stream of gas and dust particles driven from the head of a comet when it is close to the sun **6** *informal* a person employed to follow and spy upon another **7 turn tail** to run away **8 with one's tail between one's legs** completely defeated and demoralized ▷ *adj* **9** at the back: *tail feathers* ▷ *vb* **10** *informal* to follow (someone) stealthily ▷ See also **tail off, tails** [Old English *tægel*] **tailless** *adj*

tail² *n law* the limitation of an estate or interest to a person and his or her descendants [Old French *taille* a division]

tailback *n Brit* a queue of traffic stretching back from an obstruction

tailboard *n* a removable or hinged rear board on a lorry or trailer

tail coat *n* a man's black coat which stops at the hips at the front and has a long back split into two below the waist

tailgate *n* **1** same as **tailboard** **2** a door at the rear of a hatchback vehicle ▷ *vb* **3** to drive very close behind (a vehicle) **tailgater** *n*

tail-light *or* **tail lamp** *n* same as **rear light**

tail off *or* **tail away** *vb* **1** to decrease gradually: *orders tailed off* **2** (of someone's voice) to become gradually quieter and then silent

tailor *n* **1** a person who makes, repairs, or alters outer garments, esp. menswear. Related adjective: **sartorial** ▷ *vb* **2** to cut or style (a garment) to satisfy specific requirements **3** to adapt (something) so as to make it suitable: *activities are tailored to participants' capabilities* [Old French *taillier* to cut] **tailored** *adj*

tailorbird *n* a tropical Asian warbler that builds a nest by sewing together large leaves using plant fibres

tailor-made *adj* **1** (of clothing) made by a tailor to fit exactly **2** perfect for a particular purpose: *I'm tailor-made for the role*

tailpiece *n* **1** a piece added at the end of something, for example a report **2** a decorative design at the end of a chapter **3** a piece of wood to which the strings of a stringed musical instrument are attached at its lower end

tailpipe *n* a pipe from which exhaust gases are discharged, esp. in a motor vehicle

tailplane *n* a small horizontal wing at the tail of an aircraft to help keep it stable

tails *pl n* **1** *informal* same as **tail coat** ▷ *interj, adv* **2** with the side of a coin uppermost that does not have a portrait of a head on it

tailspin *n* **1** *aeronautics* same as **spin** (sense 10) **2** *informal* a state of confusion or panic

tailwind *n* a wind blowing from behind an aircraft or vehicle

taint *vb* **1** to spoil or contaminate by an undesirable quality: *tainted by corruption* ▷ *n* **2** a defect or flaw **3** a trace of contamination or infection [Old French *teindre* to dye] **tainted** *adj*

taipan *n* a large poisonous Australian snake [Aboriginal]

take *vb* **taking, took, taken** **1** to remove from a place, usually by grasping with the hand: *he took a fifty-dollar note from his wallet* **2** to accompany or escort: *he took me home* **3** to use as a means of transport: *we took a taxi* **4** to conduct or lead: *that road takes you to Preston* **5** to obtain possession of (something), often dishonestly: *they had taken everything most precious to us* **6** to seize or capture: *her husband had been taken by the rebels* **7** (in games such as chess or cards) to win or capture (a piece, trick, etc.) **8** to choose or select (something to use or buy): *I'll take the green one, please* **9** to put an end to: *he took his own life* **10** to require (time, resources, or ability): *this would have taken years to set up* **11** to use as a particular case: *take a friend of mine for example* **12** to find and make use of (a seat, flat, etc.) **13** to accept the duties of: *the legitimate government will take office* **14** to receive in a specified way: *my mother took it calmly* **15** to receive and make use of: *she took the opportunity to splash her heated face* **16** to eat or drink: *all food substances are toxic if taken in excess* **17** to perform (an action, esp. a beneficial one): *she took a deep breath* **18** to accept (something that is offered or given): *she took a job as a waitress* **19** to put into effect: *taking military action simply* **20** to make (a photograph) **21** to write down or copy: *taking notes* **22** to work at or study: *taking painting lessons* **23** to do or sit (a test, exam, etc.) **24** to begin to experience or feel: *he took an interest in psychoanalysis* **25** to accept (responsibility, blame, or credit) **26** to accept as valid: *I take your point* **27** to stand up to or endure: *I can't take this harassment any more* **28** to wear a particular size of shoes or clothes: *what size of shoes do you take?* **29** to have a capacity of or room for: *the Concert Hall can take about 2500 people* **30** to ascertain by measuring: *she comes after breakfast to take her pulse and temperature* **31** to subtract or deduct: *take seven from eleven* **32** to aim or direct: *he took a few steps towards the door* **33** (of a shop, club, etc.) to make (a specified amount of money) from sales, tickets, etc.: *films that take no money at the box office* **34** to have or produce the intended effect: *the dye hasn't taken on your shoes* **35** (of seedlings) to start growing successfully **36 take account of** *or* **take into account** See **account** (sense 9) **37 take advantage of** See **advantage** (sense 4) **38 take care** See **care** (sense 10) **39 take care of** See **care** (sense 11) **40 take it** to assume or believe: *I take it that means they don't want to leave* **41 take part in** See **part** (sense 17) **42 take place** See **place** (sense 20) **43 take upon oneself** to assume the right or duty (to do something) **44 take your time** use as much time as you need ▷ *n* **45** *films & music* one of a series of recordings from which the best will be selected **46** *informal, chiefly US* a version or interpretation: *Minnelli's bleak take on the story* ▷ See also **take after, take against** *etc.* [Old English *tacan*]

take after *vb* to resemble in appearance or character: *he takes after his grandfather*

take against *vb informal* to start to dislike, esp. for no good reason: *I took against her right from the start*

take apart *vb* **1** to separate (something) into its component parts: *once I'd taken the clock apart I couldn't fit the bits together again* **2** *informal* to criticize severely

take away *vb* **1** to remove or subtract: *the lymph glands are taken away and examined under a microscope* **2** to detract from or lessen the value of (something): *this does not take away from their achievement* ▷ *prep* **3** minus: *six take away two is four*

t

▷ *adj* **takeaway 4** *Brit, Austral & NZ* sold for consumption away from the premises: *takeaway food* ▷ *n* **takeaway** *Brit, Austral & NZ* **5** a shop or restaurant that sells such food **6** a meal sold for consumption away from the premises

take back *vb* **1** to retract or withdraw (something said or promised): *I take back what I said about him* **2** to regain possession of **3** to return for exchange or a refund: *shopkeepers are often reluctant to take back unsatisfactory goods* **4** to accept (someone) back into one's home, affections, etc.: *I'll only take you back if you promise to behave* **5** to remind (one) of the past: *this takes me back to my childhood*

take down *vb* **1** to record in writing **2** to dismantle or remove **3** to reduce (someone) in power or arrogance: *I do think he needed taking down a peg or two*

take for *vb informal* to consider or suppose to be, esp. mistakenly: *what kind of mug do you take me for?*

take-home pay *n* the remainder of one's pay after income tax and other compulsory deductions have been made

take in *vb* **1** to understand: *I was too tired to take in all of what was being said* **2** *informal* to cheat or deceive: *don't be taken in by his charming manner* **3** to include: *this tour takes in the romance and history of Salzburg, Vienna, and Munich* **4** to receive into one's house: *his widowed mother lived by taking in boarders* **5** to make (clothing) smaller by altering the seams **6** to go to: *taking in a movie*

taken *vb* **1** the past participle of **take** ▷ *adj* **2 taken with** enthusiastically impressed by

take off *vb* **1** to remove (a garment) **2** (of an aircraft) to become airborne **3** *informal* to set out on a journey: *taking off for the Highlands* **4** *informal* to become successful or popular: *the record took off after being used in a film* **5** to deduct (an amount) from a price or total **6** to withdraw or put an end to: *the bus service has been taken off because of lack of demand* **7** *informal* to mimic (someone) ▷ *n* **takeoff 8** the act or process of making an aircraft airborne **9** *informal* an act of mimicry

take on *vb* **1** to employ or hire **2** to assume or acquire: *his eyes took on a strange intensity* **3** to agree to do: *he took on the job of treasurer* **4** to compete against: *we must take on our foreign competitors*

t

take out *vb* **1** to remove (something) from a place: *she took a comb out of her bag* **2** to obtain: *she took out American citizenship in 1937* **3** to escort or go out with (someone) on a social trip: *can I take you out for a meal some time?* **4** *informal* to kill, destroy, or maim: *most of the enemy's air defences have been taken out* **5 take it** *or* **a lot out of** *informal* to sap the energy or vitality of **6 take it out on** *informal* to vent one's anger on ▷ *adj, n* **takeout 7** *chiefly US & Canad* same as **take away** (senses 4, 5, 6)

take over *vb* **1** to gain control or management of **2** to become responsible for (a job) after another person has stopped doing it: *I'll take over the driving if you want a break* **3 take over from** to become more successful or important than (something), and eventually replace it: *electronic dance music has taken over from rock* ▷ *n* **takeover 4** the act of gaining control of a company by buying its shares **5** the act of seizing and taking control of something: *the rebel takeover in Ethiopia*

taker *n* a person who agrees to take something that is offered: *there's only one sweet left – any takers?*

take to *vb* **1** to form a liking for **2** to start using or doing (something) as a habit: *I took to studying the published records of his life*

take up *vb* **1** to occupy or fill (space or time): *looking after the baby takes up most of my time* **2** to adopt the study, practice, or activity of: *I took up architecture* **3** to shorten (a garment) **4** to accept (an offer): *I'd like to take up your offer of help* **5 take up on A** to accept what is offered by (someone): *I might just take you up on that offer* **B** to discuss (something) further with (someone): *I'd like to take you up on that last point* **6 take up with A** to discuss (an issue) with (someone): *take up the matter with the District Council more seriously* **B** to begin to be friendly and spend time with (someone): *he'd already taken up with the woman he would marry*

taking *adj* charming, fascinating, or intriguing

takings *pl n* receipts; earnings

talaq *or* **talak** *n* a form of divorce under Islamic law in which the husband repudiates the marriage by saying 'talaq' three times [Arabic]

talc *or* **talcum** *n* **1** same as **talcum powder 2** a soft mineral, consisting of magnesium silicate, used in the manufacture of ceramics, paints, and talcum powder [Persian *talk*]

talcum powder *n* a powder made of purified talc, usually scented, used to dry or perfume the body

tale *n* **1** a report, account, or story: *everyone had their own tale to tell about the flood* **2** a malicious piece of gossip **3 tell tales A** to tell fanciful lies **B** to report malicious stories or trivial complaints, esp. to someone in authority **4 tell a tale** to reveal something important **5 tell its own tale** to be self-evident [Old English *talu*]

talent *n* **1** a natural ability to do something well: *the boy has a real talent for writing* **2** a person or people with such ability: *he is the major talent in Italian fashion* **3** *informal* people regarded as attractive or as potential sexual partners: *there's always lots of talent in that pub* **4** any of various ancient units of weight and money [Greek *talanton* unit of money] **talented** *adj*

talent scout *n* a person whose occupation is the search for talented people, such as sportspeople or performers, for work as professionals

talisman *n, pl* **-mans** a stone or other small object, usually inscribed or carved, believed to protect the wearer from evil influences [Medieval Greek *telesma* ritual] **talismanic** *adj*

talk *vb* **1** to express one's thoughts or feelings by means of spoken words **2** to exchange ideas or opinions about something: *they were talking about where they would go on holiday* **3** to give voice to; utter: *he was talking rubbish* **4** to discuss: *the political leaders were talking peace* **5** to reveal information: *she was ready to talk* **6** to be able to speak (a language or style) in conversation: *the ferry was full of people talking French* **7** to spread rumours or gossip **8** to be effective or persuasive: *money talks* **9** to get into a particular condition or state of mind by talking: *I had talked myself hoarse* **10 now you're talking** *informal* at last you're saying something agreeable **11 you can** *or* **can't talk** *informal* you are in no position to comment or criticize ▷ *n* **12** a speech or lecture: *a talk on local government reform* **13** an exchange of ideas or thoughts: *we had a talk about our holiday plans* **14** idle chatter, gossip, or rumour **15** (*often pl*) a conference, discussion, or negotiation ▷ See also **talk back, talk down** *etc.* [Middle English *talkien*] **talker** *n*

talkative *adj* given to talking a great deal

talkback *n NZ* a broadcast in which telephone comments or questions from the public are transmitted live

talk back *vb* to answer (someone) rudely or cheekily

talk down *vb* **1 talk down to** to speak to (someone) in a patronizing manner **2** to give instructions to (an aircraft) by radio to enable it to land

talkie *n informal* an early film with a soundtrack

Talking Book *n trademark* a recording of a book, designed to be used by blind people

talking head *n* (on television) a person, shown only from the shoulders up, who speaks without illustrative material

talking point *n* something that causes discussion or argument: *his appointment as manager was a major talking point in football circles*

talking-to *n informal* a scolding or telling-off

talk into *vb* to persuade (someone) to do something by talking to him or her: *don't let anyone talk you into buying things you don't want*

talk out *vb* **1** to resolve (a problem) by talking: *we won't reach a compromise unless we can talk out our differences* **2** *Brit* to block (a bill) in parliament by discussing it for so long that there is no time to vote on it **3 talk out of** to dissuade (someone) from doing something by talking to him or her

talk round *vb* **1** to persuade (someone) to agree with one's opinion or suggestion: *he didn't want to go, but I talked him round* **2** to discuss (a subject) without coming to a conclusion

tall *adj* **1** of greater than average height **2** having a specified height: *five feet tall* [Middle English]

tallboy *n Brit* a high chest of drawers made in two sections placed one on top of the other

tall order *n informal* a difficult or unreasonable request

tallow *n* a hard fatty animal fat used in making soap and candles

tall poppy syndrome *n Austral & NZ informal* a tendency to disparage any person who is conspicuously successful

tall ship *n* a large square-rigged sailing ship

tall story *n informal* an unlikely and probably untrue tale

tally *vb* **-lies, -lying, -lied 1** to agree with or be consistent with something else: *this description didn't seem to me to tally with what we saw* **2** to keep score ▷ *n, pl* **-lies 3** any record of debit, credit, the score in a game, etc. **4** an identifying label or mark **5** a stick used (esp. formerly) as a record of the amount of a debt according to the notches cut in it [Latin *talea* a stick]

tally-ho *interj* the cry of a participant at a hunt when the quarry is sighted

Talmud *n Judaism* the primary source of Jewish religious law [Hebrew *talmūdh* instruction] **Talmudic** *adj* **Talmudist** *n*

talon *n* a sharply hooked claw, such as that of a bird of prey [Latin *talus* ankle]

tamarillo *n, pl* **-los** a shrub with a red oval edible fruit [pseudo-Spanish coinage based on *tomato*]

tamarind *n* a tropical evergreen tree with fruit whose acid pulp is used as a food and to make beverages and medicines [Arabic *tamr hindī* Indian date]

tamarisk *n* a tree or shrub of the Mediterranean region and S Asia, with scalelike leaves, slender branches, and feathery flower clusters [Latin *tamarix*]

tambour *n* an embroidery frame, consisting of two hoops over which the fabric is stretched while being worked [French]

tambourine *n music* a percussion instrument consisting of a single drum skin stretched over a circular wooden frame with pairs of metal discs that jingle when it is struck or shaken [from Old French]

tame *adj* **1 A** (of an animal) changed by humans from a wild state into a domesticated state **B** (of an animal) not afraid of or aggressive towards humans **2** (of a person) tending to do what one is told without questioning or criticizing it **3** mild and unexciting: *the love scenes are fairly tame by modern standards* ▷ *vb* **taming, tamed 4** to make (an animal) tame; domesticate **5** to bring under control; make less extreme or dangerous: *many previously deadly diseases have been tamed by antibiotics* [Old English *tam*]

Tamil *n* **1** *pl* **-ils** *or* **-il** a member of a people of S India and Sri Lanka **2** the language of the Tamils ▷ *adj* **3** of the Tamils

tam-o'-shanter *n* a Scottish brimless woollen cap with a bobble in the centre [after the hero of Burns's poem *Tam o' Shanter*]

tamp *vb* to force or pack (something) down by tapping it several times: *he tamped the bowl of his pipe* [probably from obsolete *tampin* plug for gun's muzzle]

tamper *vb* (foll. by *with*) **1** to interfere or meddle with without permission: *someone has been tampering with the locks* **2** to attempt to influence someone, esp. by bribery: *an attempt to tamper with the jury* [alteration of *temper* (verb)]

tampon *n* an absorbent plug of cotton wool inserted into the vagina during menstruation [French]

tan[1] *n* **1** a brown coloration of the skin caused by exposure to ultraviolet rays, esp. those of the sun ▷ *vb* **tanning, tanned 2** (of a person or his or her skin) to go brown after exposure to ultraviolet rays **3** to convert (a skin or hide) into leather by treating it with a tanning agent **4** *slang* to beat or flog ▷ *adj* **5** yellowish-brown [Medieval Latin *tannare*]

tan[2] *maths* tangent

tandem *n* **1** a bicycle with two sets of pedals and two saddles, arranged one behind the other for two riders **2 in tandem** together or in conjunction:

the two drugs work in tandem to combat the disease ▹ *adv* **3** one behind the other: *Jim and Ruth arrived, riding tandem* [Latin *tandem* at length]

tandoor *n* a type of Indian clay oven [Urdu]

tandoori *adj* cooked in a tandoor: *tandoori chicken*

tang *n* **1** a strong sharp taste or smell: *we could already smell the tang of the distant sea* **2** a trace or hint of something: *there was a tang of cloves in the apple pie* **3** the pointed end of a tool, such as a knife or chisel, which fits into the handle [Old Norse *tangi* point] **tangy** *adj*

tangata whenua (tang-ah-tah **fen**-noo-ah) *pl n* NZ **1** the original Polynesian settlers in New Zealand **2** descendants of the original Polynesian settlers [Māori: people of the land]

tangent *n* **1** a line, curve, or plane that touches another curve or surface at one point but does not cross it **2** (in trigonometry) the ratio of the length of the opposite side to that of the adjacent side of a right-angled triangle **3 go off at a tangent** suddenly take a completely different line of thought or action ▹ *adj* **4** of or involving a tangent **5** touching at a single point [Latin *linea tangens* the touching line]

tangential *adj* **1** only having an indirect or superficial relevance: *Hitler's vegetarianism only has a tangential link with the policies of the Nazis* **2** of or being a tangent: *a street tangential to the market square* **tangentially** *adv*

tangerine *n* **1** the small orange-like fruit, with a sweet juicy flesh, of an Asian tree ▹ *adj* **2** reddish-orange [*Tangier*, a port in Morocco]

tangi (**tang**-ee) *n NZ* **1** a Māori funeral ceremony **2** *informal* a lamentation

tangible *adj* **1** able to be touched; material or physical **2** real or substantial: *tangible results* [Latin *tangere* to touch] **tangibility** *n* **tangibly** *adv*

tangle *n* **1** a confused or complicated mass of things, such as hair or fibres, knotted or coiled together: *a tangle of wires* **2** a complicated problem or situation ▹ *vb* **-gling, -gled 3** to twist (things, such as hair or fibres) together in a confused mass **4** to come into conflict: *the last thing she wanted was to tangle with the police* **5** to catch or trap in a net, ropes, etc.: *the string of the kite had got tangled in the branches* [Middle English *tangilen*] **tangled** *adj*

tango *n, pl* **-gos 1** a Latin-American dance characterized by long gliding steps and sudden pauses **2** music for this dance ▹ *vb* **-going, -goed 3** to perform this dance [American Spanish]

taniwha (tun-ee-fah) *n NZ* a mythical Māori monster that lives in rivers and lakes [Māori]

tank *n* **1** a large container for storing liquids or gases **2** an armoured combat vehicle moving on tracks and armed with guns **3** Also called: **tankful** the quantity contained in a tank [Gujarati (language of W India) *tānkh* artificial lake]

tankard *n* a large one-handled beer-mug, sometimes fitted with a hinged lid [Middle English]

tanked up *adj slang, chiefly Brit* very drunk

tanker *n* a ship or lorry for carrying liquid in bulk: *an oil tanker*

tank farming *n* same as **hydroponics** **tank farmer** *n*

tannery *n, pl* **-neries** a place or building where skins and hides are tanned

tannic *adj* of, containing, or produced from tannin or tannic acid

tannie (**tun**-nee) *n S African* a title of respect used to refer to an elderly woman [Afrikaans, literally: aunt]

tannin *n* a yellowish compound found in many plants, such as tea and grapes, and used in tanning and dyeing. Also called: **tannic acid**

Tannoy *n trademark Brit* a type of public-address system

tansy *n, pl* **-sies** a plant with yellow flowers in flat-topped clusters [Greek *athanasia* immortality]

tantalize *or* **-lise** *vb* **-lizing, -lized** *or* **-lising, -lised** to tease or make frustrated, for example by tormenting (someone) with the sight of something that he or she wants but cannot have [after *Tantalus*, a mythological king condemned to stand in water that receded when he tried to drink it and under fruit that moved away when he reached for it] **tantalizing** *or* **-lising** *adj* **tantalizingly** *or* **-lisingly** *adv*

tantalum *n chem* a hard greyish-white metallic element that resists corrosion. Symbol: **Ta** [after *Tantalus* (see TANTALIZE), from the metal's incapacity to absorb acids]

tantalus *n Brit* a case in which bottles of wine and spirits may be locked with their contents tantalizingly visible

tantamount *adj* **tantamount to** equivalent in effect to: *the raid was tantamount to a declaration of war* [Anglo-French *tant amunter* to amount to as much]

tantrum *n* a childish outburst of bad temper [origin unknown]

Taoiseach (**tee**-shack) *n* the Prime Minister of the Irish Republic

Taoism *n* a Chinese system of religion and philosophy advocating a simple honest life and noninterference with the course of natural events **Taoist** *n, adj*

tap¹ *vb* **tapping, tapped 1** to knock lightly and usually repeatedly: *she tapped gently on the door* **2** to make a rhythmic sound with the hands or feet by lightly and repeatedly hitting a surface with them: *he was tapping one foot to the music* ▹ *n* **3** a light blow or knock, or the sound made by it **4** the metal piece attached to the toe or heel of a shoe used for tap-dancing **5** same as **tap-dancing** [Middle English *tappen*]

tap² *n* **1** *Brit, Austral & NZ* a valve by which the flow of a liquid or gas from a pipe can be controlled. Usual US word **faucet 2** a stopper to plug a cask or barrel **3** a concealed listening or recording device connected to a telephone **4** *med* the withdrawal of fluid from a bodily cavity: *a spinal tap* **5 on tap A** *informal* ready for use **B** (of drinks) on draught rather than in bottles ▹ *vb* **tapping, tapped 6** to listen in on (a telephone conversation) secretly by making an illegal connection **7** to obtain something useful or desirable from (something): *a new way of tapping the sun's energy* **8** to withdraw liquid from (something) as if through a tap: *to tap a cask of wine*

9 to cut into (a tree) and draw off sap from it **10** *Brit, Austral & NZ informal* to obtain (money or information) from (someone) **11** *informal* to make an illicit attempt to recruit (a player or employee bound by an existing contract) [Old English *tæppa*]

tapas (**tap**-ass) *pl n* (in Spanish cookery) light snacks or appetizers, usually eaten with drinks [Spanish *tapa* cover, lid]

tap-dancing *n* a style of dancing in which the performer wears shoes with metal plates at the heels and toes that make a rhythmic sound on the stage as he or she dances **tap-dancer** *n* **tap dance** *n*

tape *n* **1** a long thin strip of cotton or linen used for tying or fastening: *a parcel tied with pink tape* **2 A** short for **magnetic tape B** a spool or cassette containing magnetic tape, and used for recording or playing sound or video signals: *he put a tape into his stereo* **C** the music, speech, or pictures which have been recorded on a particular cassette or spool of magnetic tape **3** a narrow strip of plastic which has one side coated with an adhesive substance and is used to stick paper, etc., together: *sticky tape* **4** a string stretched across the track at the end of a race course **5** short for **tape measure** ▷ *vb* **taping, taped 6** Also: **tape-record** to record (speech, music, etc.) on magnetic tape **7** to bind or fasten with tape **8 have a person** *or* **situation taped** *Brit & Austral informal* to have full understanding and control of a person or situation [Old English *tæppe*]

tape deck *n* **1** the part of a tape recorder which supports the spools or cassettes, and contains the motor and the playback, recording, and erasing heads **2** the unit in a hi-fi system which fulfils the same function

tape drive *n* a machine for storing or transferring information from a computer onto tape

tape measure *n* a tape or length of metal marked off in centimetres or inches, used for measuring

taper *vb* **1** to become narrower towards one end **2 taper off** to become gradually less: *treatment should be tapered off gradually* ▷ *n* **3** a long thin fast-burning candle **4** a narrowing [Old English *tapor*]

tape recorder *n* an electrical device used for recording and reproducing sounds on magnetic tape

tape recording *n* **1** the act of recording sounds on magnetic tape **2** the magnetic tape used for this: *a tape recording of the interview* **3** the sounds so recorded

tapestry *n, pl* **-tries 1** a heavy woven fabric, often in the form of a picture, used for wall hangings or furnishings **2** same as **needlepoint** (sense 1) **3** a colourful and complicated situation that is made up of many different kinds of things: *the rich tapestry of Hindustani music* [Old French *tapisserie* carpeting]

tapeworm *n* a long flat parasitic worm that inhabits the intestines of vertebrates, including humans

tapioca *n* a beadlike starch made from cassava root, used in puddings [indigenous S American word *tipioca* pressed-out juice]

tapir (**tape**-er) *n* a piglike mammal of South and Central America and SE Asia, with a long snout, three-toed hind legs, and four-toed forelegs [indigenous S American word *tapiira*]

tappet *n* a short steel rod in an engine which moves up and down transferring movement from one part of the machine to another [from TAP[1]]

taproom *n* a bar or room in which beer and other drinks are available on tap

taproot *n* the main root of plants such as the dandelion, which grows straight down and bears smaller lateral roots

tar[1] *n* **1** a dark sticky substance obtained by distilling organic matter such as coal, wood, or peat **2** same as **coal tar** ▷ *vb* **tarring, tarred 3** to coat with tar **4 tar and feather** to cover (someone) with tar and feathers as a punishment **5 tarred with the same brush** having, or regarded as having, the same faults [Old English *teoru*] **tarry** *adj*

tar[2] *n informal* a seaman [short for *tarpaulin*]

tarakihi (**tarr**-a-kee-hee) *or* **terakihi** (**terr**-a-kee-hee) *n* a common edible sea fish of New Zealand waters [Māori]

taramasalata *n* a creamy pale pink pâté, made from the eggs of fish, esp. smoked cod's roe, and served as an hors d'oeuvre [Modern Greek]

tarantella *n* **1** a peasant dance from S Italy **2** music for this dance [Italian]

tarantula *n* **1** a large hairy spider of tropical America with a poisonous bite **2** a large hairy spider of S Europe [Medieval Latin]

tarboosh *n* a felt or cloth brimless cap, usually red and often with a silk tassel, formerly worn by Muslim men [Arabic *tarbūsh*]

tardy *adj* **-dier, -diest 1** occurring later than it is expected to or than it should: *he spent the weekend writing tardy thank-you letters* **2** slow in progress, growth, etc.: *we made tardy progress across the ice* [Latin *tardus* slow] **tardily** *adv* **tardiness** *n*

tare[1] *n* **1** the weight of the wrapping or container in which goods are packed **2** the weight of a vehicle without its cargo or passengers [Arabic *tarhah* something discarded]

tare[2] *n* **1** any of various vetch plants of Eurasia and N Africa **2** *Bible* a weed, thought to be the darnel [origin unknown]

target *n* **1** the object or person that a weapon, ball, etc., is aimed at: *the station was an easy target for an air attack* **2** an object at which an archer or marksman aims, usually a round flat surface marked with circles **3** a fixed goal or objective: *our sales figures are well below target* **4** a person or thing at which criticism or ridicule is directed: *the Chancellor has been the target of much of the criticism* ▷ *vb* **-geting, -geted 5** to direct: *an advertising campaign targeted at gay men* **6** to aim (a missile) [Old French *targette* a little shield]

tariff *n* **1 A** a tax levied by a government on imports or occasionally exports **B** a list of such taxes **2** a list of fixed prices, for example in a hotel **3** *chiefly Brit* a method of charging for services such as gas and electricity by setting a price per unit [Arabic *ta'rīfa* to inform]

Tarmac *n* **1** *trademark* a paving material made of crushed stone bound with a mixture of tar and bitumen, used for a road or airport runway **2 the tarmac** the area of an airport where planes wait and take off or land: *we had to wait for an hour on the tarmac* ▷ *vb* **tarmac, -macking, -macked 3** to apply Tarmac to (a surface) [TAR + MACADAM]

tarn *n chiefly Brit* a small mountain lake [from Old Norse]

tarnish *vb* **1** (of a metal) to become stained or less bright, esp. by exposure to air or moisture **2** to damage or taint: *the affair could tarnish the reputation of the prime minister* ▷ *n* **3** a tarnished condition, surface, or film on a surface [Old French *ternir* to make dull] **tarnished** *adj*

taro *n, pl* **-ros** a plant with a large edible rootstock [Tahitian & Polynesian]

tarot (tarr-oh) *n* **1** a special pack of cards, now used mainly for fortune-telling **2** a card in a tarot pack with a distinctive symbolic design [French]

tarpaulin *n* **1** a heavy waterproof canvas coated with tar, wax, or paint **2** a sheet of this canvas, used as a waterproof covering [probably from TAR[1] + PALL[1]]

tarragon *n* a European herb with narrow leaves, which are used as seasoning in cooking [Old French *targon*]

tarry *vb* **-ries, -rying, -ried** *old-fashioned* **1** to delay or linger: *I have no plans to tarry longer than necessary* **2** to stay briefly: *most people tarried only a few hours before moving on* [origin unknown]

tarsal *anatomy* ▷ *adj* **1** of the tarsus or tarsi ▷ *n* **2** a tarsal bone

tarseal *n NZ* **1** the bitumen surface of a road **2 the tarseal** the main highway

tarsier *n* a small nocturnal primate of the E Indies, which has very large eyes

tarsus *n, pl* **-si 1** the bones of the ankle and heel collectively **2** the corresponding part in other mammals and in amphibians and reptiles [Greek *tarsos* flat surface, instep]

tart[1] *n* **1** a pastry case, often having no top crust, with a sweet filling, such as jam or custard **2** *chiefly US* a small open pie with a fruit filling [Old French *tarte*]

tart[2] *adj* **1** (of a flavour) sour or bitter **2** sharp and hurtful: *he made a rather tart comment* [Old English *teart* rough] **tartly** *adv* **tartness** *n*

tart[3] *n informal* **1** *derogatory* a woman considered promiscuous **2** *old-fashioned* a prostitute. See also **tart up** [from *sweetheart*]

tartan *n* **1** a design of straight lines, crossing at right angles to give a chequered appearance, esp. one associated with a Scottish clan **2** a fabric with this design [origin unknown]

tartar[1] *n* **1** a hard deposit on the teeth **2** a brownish-red substance deposited in a cask during the fermentation of wine [Medieval Greek *tartaron*]

tartar[2] *n* a fearsome or formidable person [from *Tartar*]

Tartar *or* **Tatar** *n* **1** a member of a Mongoloid people who established a powerful state in central Asia in the 13th century, now scattered throughout Russia and central Asia ▷ *adj* **2** of the Tartars [Persian *Tātār*]

tartaric *adj* of or derived from tartar or tartaric acid

tartaric acid *n* a colourless crystalline acid which is found in many fruits

tartar sauce *n* a mayonnaise sauce mixed with chopped herbs and capers, served with seafood

tartine *n* an open sandwich, esp. one with a rich or elaborate topping [French]

tartrazine (tar-traz-zeen) *n* an artificial yellow dye used as a food additive

tart up *vb Brit informal* **1** to decorate in a cheap and flashy way: *the shops were tarted up for Christmas* **2** to try to make (oneself) look smart and attractive

Tarzan *n informal, often humorous* a man with great physical strength, agility, and virility [after the hero of stories by E. R. Burroughs]

task *n* **1** a specific piece of work required to be done **2** an unpleasant or difficult job or duty **3 take to task** to criticize or rebuke [Old French *tasche*]

taskbar *n* a row of selectable buttons and icons typically running along the bottom of a computer screen, displaying information such as the names of running programs

task force *n* **1** a temporary grouping of military units formed to undertake a specific mission **2** any organization set up to carry out a continuing task

taskmaster *n* a person who enforces hard or continuous work

Tasmanian devil *n* a small flesh-eating marsupial of Tasmania

Tass *n* the principal news agency of Russia and, formerly, the Soviet Union

tassel *n* a tuft of loose threads secured by a knot or knob, used to decorate a cushion, piece of clothing, etc. [Old French]

taste *n* **1** the sense by which the flavour of a substance is distinguished by the taste buds **2** the sensation experienced by means of the taste buds **3** a small amount eaten, sipped, or tried on the tongue **4** a brief experience of something: *a taste of the planter's life* **5** a liking for something: *a taste for puns* **6** the ability to appreciate what is beautiful and excellent: *she's got very good taste in clothes* **7** a person's typical preferences as displayed by what they choose to buy, enjoy, etc.: *the film was good but a bit violent for my taste* **8** the quality of not being offensive or bad-mannered: *that remark was in rather poor taste* ▷ *vb* **tasting, tasted 9** to distinguish the taste of (a substance) by means of the taste buds: *I've got a stinking cold and can't taste anything* **10** to take a small amount of (a food or liquid) into the mouth, esp. in order to test the flavour **11** to have a flavour or taste as specified: *the pizza tastes delicious* **12** to have a brief experience of (something): *they have tasted democracy and they won't let go* [Old French *taster*]

taste bud *n* any of the cells on the surface of the tongue, by means of which the sensation of taste is experienced

tasteful *adj* having or showing good social or aesthetic taste: *tasteful decor* **tastefully** *adv*
tasteless *adj* **1** lacking in flavour: *the canteen serves cold, tasteless pizzas* **2** lacking social or aesthetic taste: *a room full of tasteless ornaments; a tasteless remark* **tastelessly** *adv* **tastelessness** *n*
taster *n* **1** a person employed to test the quality of food or drink by tasting it **2** a sample of something intended to indicate what the entire thing is like: *the entrance hall was filled with flowers, giving a taster of the splendours in the main exhibition*
tasty *adj* **tastier, tastiest** having a pleasant flavour
tat *n Brit* tatty or tasteless articles
ta-ta *interj chiefly Brit informal* goodbye [origin unknown]
Tatar *n, adj* same as **Tartar**
tater *n Brit dialect* a potato
tattered *adj* **1** ragged or torn: *a tattered old book* **2** wearing ragged or torn clothing: *the tattered refugees*
tatters *pl n* **1** torn ragged clothing **2 in tatters** **A** (of clothing) torn in several places **B** (of an argument, plan, etc.) completely destroyed
tatting *n* **1** an intricate type of lace made by looping a thread of cotton or linen with a hand shuttle **2** the work of producing this [origin unknown]
tattle *vb* **-tling, -tled** **1** to gossip or chatter ▷ *n* **2** gossip or chatter [Middle Dutch *tatelen*] **tattler** *n*
tattletale *n chiefly US & Canad* a scandalmonger or gossip
tattoo[1] *n, pl* **-toos** **1** a picture or design made on someone's body by pricking small holes in the skin and filling them with indelible dye ▷ *vb* **-tooing, -tooed** **2** to make pictures or designs on (a person's skin) by pricking and staining it with indelible colours [Tahitian *tatau*] **tattooed** *adj* **tattooist** *n*
tattoo[2] *n, pl* **-toos** **1** (formerly) a signal by drum or bugle ordering soldiers to return to their quarters **2** a military display or pageant **3** any drumming or tapping [Dutch *taptoe*]
tatty *adj* **-tier, -tiest** worn out, shabby, or unkempt [Scots]
taught *vb* the past of **teach**
taunt *vb* **1** to tease or provoke (someone) with jeering remarks ▷ *n* **2** a jeering remark [French *tant pour tant* like for like] **taunting** *adj*
Taurus *n astrol* the second sign of the zodiac; the Bull [Latin]
taut *adj* **1** stretched tight: *the cable must be taut* **2** showing nervous strain: *he was looking taut and anxious* **3** (of a film or piece of writing) having no unnecessary or irrelevant details: *a taut thriller* [Middle English *tought*]
tauten *vb* to make or become taut
tautology *n, pl* **-gies** the use of words which merely repeat something already stated, as in *reverse back* [Greek *tautologia*] **tautological** *or* **tautologous** *adj*
tavern *n* **1** *old-fashioned* a pub **2** *US, Canad, Austral & NZ* a place licensed for the sale and consumption of alcoholic drink [Latin *taberna* hut]
tawdry *adj* **-drier, -driest** cheap, showy, and of poor quality: *tawdry Christmas decorations* [Middle English *seynt Audries lace*, finery sold at the fair of St Audrey]
tawny *adj* brown to brownish-orange [Old French *tané*]
tawny owl *n* a European owl having a reddish-brown plumage and a round head
tawse *n Scot* a leather strap with one end cut into thongs, formerly used by schoolteachers to hit children who had misbehaved [probably plural of obsolete *taw* strip of leather]
tax *n* **1** a compulsory payment to a government to raise revenue, levied on income, property, or goods and services ▷ *vb* **2** to levy a tax on (people, companies, etc.) **3** to make heavy demands on: *the task taxed his ingenuity and patience* **4 tax someone with** to accuse someone of: *he was taxed with parochialism and meanness* [Latin *taxare* to appraise] **taxable** *adj* **taxing** *adj*
taxation *n* the levying of taxes or the condition of being taxed
tax avoidance *n* reduction of tax liability by lawful methods
tax-deductible *adj* legally deductible from income or wealth before tax assessment
tax evasion *n* reduction of tax liability by illegal methods
tax-free *adj* not needing to have tax paid on it: *a tax-free lump sum*
tax haven *n* a country or state having a lower rate of taxation than elsewhere
taxi *n, pl* **taxis** **1** Also called: **cab, taxicab** a car that may be hired, along with its driver, to carry passengers to any specified destination ▷ *vb* **taxiing, taxied** **2** (of an aircraft) to move along the ground, esp. before takeoff and after landing [*taximeter cab*]
taxidermy *n* the art of preparing, stuffing, and mounting animal skins so that they have a lifelike appearance [Greek *taxis* arrangement + *derma* skin] **taxidermist** *n*
taximeter *n* a meter fitted to a taxi to register the fare, based on the length of the journey
taxi rank *n* a place where taxis wait to be hired
taxman *n, pl* **-men** **1** a collector of taxes **2** *informal* a tax-collecting body personified: *he was convicted of conspiring to cheat the taxman*
taxonomy *n* **1** the branch of biology concerned with the classification of plants and animals into groups based on their similarities and differences **2** the science or practice of classification [Greek *taxis* order + *nomia* law] **taxonomic** *adj* **taxonomist** *n*
taxpayer *n* a person or organization that pays taxes
tax relief *n* a reduction in the amount of tax a person or company has to pay
tax return *n* a declaration of personal income used as a basis for assessing an individual's liability for taxation
tax year *n* a period of twelve months used by a government as a basis for calculating taxes
Tb *chem* terbium
TB tuberculosis
tba *or* **TBA** to be arranged
tbc *or* **TBC** to be confirmed

T-bone steak *n* a large choice steak cut from the sirloin of beef, containing a T-shaped bone
tbs. *or* **tbsp.** tablespoon(ful)
Tc *chem* technetium
te *n* *music* (in tonic sol-fa) the seventh note of any ascending major scale
Te *chem* tellurium
tea *n* **1** **A** a drink made by infusing the dried chopped leaves of an Asian shrub in boiling water: *would you like a cup of tea?* **B** the dried chopped leaves of an Asian shrub used to make this drink: *could you get some tea at the grocer's?* **C** the Asian shrub on which these leaves grow **2** *Brit, Austral & NZ* the main evening meal **3** *chiefly Brit* a light meal eaten in mid-afternoon, usually consisting of tea and cakes, sometimes with sandwiches **4** a drink like tea made from other plants: *mint tea* [Ancient Chinese *d'a*]
tea bag *n* a small bag containing tea leaves, infused in boiling water to make tea
teacake *n* *chiefly Brit* a flat bun, usually eaten toasted and buttered
teach *vb* **teaching, taught** **1** to tell or show (someone) how to do something **2** to give instruction or lessons in (a subject) to (students) **3** to cause to learn or understand: *life has taught me to seize the day* **4** **teach someone a lesson** to warn or punish someone: *a bully has to be taught a lesson* [Old English *tǣcan*] **teachable** *adj*
teacher *n* a person whose job is to teach others, esp. children
tea chest *n* a large light wooden box used for exporting tea or storing things in
teaching *n* **1** the art or profession of a teacher **2** **teachings** the ideas and principles taught by a person, school of thought, etc.: *the teachings of the Catholic Church*
teaching hospital *n* a hospital attached to a medical school, in which students are taught and given supervised practical experience
tea cloth *n* same as **tea towel**
tea cosy *n* a covering for a teapot to keep the contents hot
teacup *n* **1** a cup out of which tea may be drunk **2** Also called: **teacupful** the amount a teacup will hold
teahouse *n* a restaurant, esp. in Japan or China, where tea and light refreshments are served
teak *n* the hard yellowish-brown wood of an Asian tree, used for furniture making [Malayalam (a language of S India) *tēkka*]
teal *n, pl* **teals** *or* **teal** a small freshwater duck related to the mallard [Middle English *tele*]
tea leaves *pl n, sing* **tea leaf** the dried and shredded leaves of the tea shrub, esp. those left behind in a cup or teapot after tea has been made and drunk
team *n* **1** a group of players forming one of the sides in a sporting contest **2** a group of people organized to work together: *a team of scientists* **3** two or more animals working together: *a sledge pulled by a team of dogs* ▷ *vb* **4** **team up with** to join with (someone) in order to work together **5** **team with** to match (something) with something else: *navy skirts teamed with various coloured blouses* [Old English *tēam* offspring]
team-mate *n* a fellow member of a team
team spirit *n* willingness to cooperate as part of a team
teamster *n* **1** *US & Canad* a truck driver **2** (formerly) a driver of a team of horses
teamwork *n* the cooperative work done by a team
teapot *n* a container with a lid, spout, and handle, in which tea is made and from which it is served
tear[1] *n* **1** Also called: **teardrop** a drop of salty fluid appearing in and falling from the eye. Related adjective: **lacrimal, lachrymal, lacrymal** **2** **in tears** weeping [Old English *tēar*]
tear[2] *vb* **tearing, tore, torn** **1** to rip a hole in (something): *I tore my jumper on a nail* **2** to pull apart or to pieces: *eagles have powerful beaks for tearing flesh* **3** to hurry or rush **4** to remove or take by force: *the sacred things torn from the temples of Inca worshippers* **5** **tear at someone's heartstrings** to cause someone distress or anguish **6** to injure (a muscle or ligament) by moving or twisting it violently ▷ *n* **7** a hole or split ▷ See also **tear away, tear down, tear into** [Old English *teran*]
tear away *vb* **1** to persuade (oneself or someone else) to leave: *she stood and watched, unable to tear herself away from the room* ▷ *n* **tearaway** **2** *Brit* a wild or unruly person
tear down *vb* to destroy or demolish: *it will be cheaper to tear down the old house and build a new one than to repair it*
tear duct *n* a short tube in the inner corner of the eyelid, through which tears drain into the nose
tearful *adj* weeping or about to weep **tearfully** *adv*
tear gas *n* a gas that stings the eyes and causes temporary blindness, used in warfare and to control riots
tearing *adj* very urgent: *I had been in a tearing hurry to leave the camp*
tear into *vb* *informal* to attack vigorously and damagingly
tear-jerker *n* *informal* an excessively sentimental film or book
tearoom *n* **1** *chiefly Brit* a restaurant where tea and light refreshments are served **2** *NZ* a room in a school or university where hot drinks are served
tease *vb* **teasing, teased** **1** to make fun of (someone) in a provocative and often playful manner **2** to arouse sexual desire in (someone) with no intention of satisfying it **3** to raise the nap of (a fabric) with a teasel ▷ *n* **4** a person who teases **5** a piece of teasing behaviour [Old English *tǣsan*] **teasing** *adj*
teasel, teazel *or* **teazle** *n* **1** a plant of Eurasia and N Africa, with prickly heads of yellow or purple flowers **2** the dried flower head of a teasel, used, esp. formerly, for raising the nap of cloth [Old English *tǣsel*]
tease out *vb* **1** to comb (hair, flax, or wool) so as to remove any tangles **2** to extract information with difficulty: *it's not easy to tease out the differences between anxiety and depression*

t

teaser *n* **1** a difficult question **2** a preliminary advertisement in a campaign that makes people curious to know what product is being advertised

teaspoon *n* **1** a small spoon used for stirring tea or coffee **2** Also called: **teaspoonful** the amount contained in such a spoon **3** a unit of capacity used in cooking, etc., equal to 5 ml

teat *n* **1** the nipple of a breast or udder **2** something resembling a teat such as the rubber mouthpiece of a feeding bottle [Old French *tete*]

tea towel *or* **tea cloth** *n* a towel for drying dishes

tea tree *n* a tree of Australia and New Zealand that yields an oil used as an antiseptic

tech *n informal* a technical college

tech. **1** technical **2** technology

techie *or* **techy** *informal* ▷ *n* **1** a person who is skilled in the use of technological devices, such as computers ▷ *adj* **2** of, relating to, or skilled in the use of such devices

technetium (tek-**neesh**-ee-um) *n chem* a silvery-grey metallic element, produced artificially, esp. by the fission of uranium. Symbol: **Tc** [Greek *tekhnētos* man-made]

technical *adj* **1** of or specializing in industrial, practical, or mechanical arts and applied sciences: *a technical school* **2** skilled in practical activities rather than abstract thinking **3** relating to a particular field of activity: *technical jargon* **4** according to the letter of the law: *a last-minute penalty awarded to the Irish for a technical offence* **5** showing technique: *technical perfection* **technically** *adv*

technical college *n Brit & Austral* an institution for further education that provides courses in art and technical subjects

technical drawing *n* drawing done by a draughtsman with compasses, T-squares, etc.

technicality *n, pl* **-ties** **1** a petty formal point arising from a strict interpretation of the law or a set of rules: *the case was dismissed on a legal technicality* **2** a detail of the method used to do something: *the technicalities of making a recording*

technical knockout *n boxing* a judgment of a knockout given when a boxer is, in the referee's opinion, too badly beaten to continue without risk of serious injury

technician *n* a person skilled in a particular technical field: *oil technicians*

Technicolor *n trademark* a process of producing colour film for the cinema by superimposing synchronized films of the same scene, each having a different colour filter

technikon *n S African* a technical college

technique *n* **1** a method or skill used for a particular task: *modern management techniques* **2** proficiency in a practical or mechanical skill: *he lacks the technique to be a good player* [Greek *tekhnē* skill]

techno *n* a type of very fast disco music, using electronic sounds and having a strong technological influence

techno- *combining form* of or relating to technology: *technocrat* [Greek *tekhnē* skill]

technocracy *n, pl* **-cies** government by scientists, engineers, and other experts [Greek *tekhnē* skill + *kratos* power] **technocrat** *n* **technocratic** *adj*

technology *n, pl* **-gies** **1** the application of practical or mechanical sciences to industry or commerce **2** the scientific methods or devices used in a particular field: *the latest aircraft technology* [Greek *tekhnologia* systematic treatment] **technological** *adj* **technologist** *n*

technophile *n* **1** a person who is enthusiastic about technology ▷ *adj* **2** enthusiastic about technology

technophobia *n* fear of using technological devices, such as computers **technophobe** *n* **technophobic** *adj*

tectonics *n geol* the study of the earth's crust and the forces that produce changes in it [Greek *tektōn* a builder]

ted[1] *vb* **tedding, tedded** to shake out (hay), so as to dry it [Old Norse *tethja*]

ted[2] *n Brit informal* short for **teddy boy**

teddy[1] *n, pl* **-dies** short for **teddy bear**

teddy[2] *n, pl* **-dies** a woman's one-piece undergarment incorporating a camisole top and French knickers [origin unknown]

teddy bear *n* a stuffed toy bear [after *Teddy* (Theodore) Roosevelt, US president]

teddy boy *n* (in Britain, esp. in the mid-1950s) a youth who wore mock Edwardian fashions [*Teddy*, from *Edward*]

Te Deum (tee **dee**-um) *n Christianity* an ancient Latin hymn beginning Te Deum Laudamus (we praise thee, O God)

tedious *adj* boring and uninteresting **tediously** *adv* **tediousness** *n*

tedium *n* the state of being bored or the quality of being boring: *the tedium of a nine-to-five white-collar job* [Latin *taedium*]

tee *n* **1** a support for a golf ball, usually a small wooden or plastic peg, used when teeing off **2** an area on a golf course from which the first stroke of a hole is made **3** a mark used as a target in certain games such as curling and quoits ▷ See also **tee off** [origin unknown]

tee-hee *or* **te-hee** *interj* an exclamation of mocking laughter [imitative]

teem[1] *vb* **teem with** to have a great number of: *the woods were teeming with snakes and bears* [Old English *tēman* to produce offspring]

teem[2] *vb* (of rain) to pour down in torrents [Old Norse *tœma*]

teen *adj informal* same as **teenage**

teenage *adj* **1** (of a person) aged between 13 and 19 **2** typical of or designed for people aged between 13 and 19: *teenage fashions*

teenager *n* a person between the ages of 13 and 19

teens *pl n* **1** the years of a person's life between the ages of 13 and 19 **2** all the numbers that end in *-teen*

teeny *adj* **-nier, -niest** *informal* extremely small [variant of *tiny*]

teenybopper *n old-fashioned slang* a young teenager, usually a girl, who is a keen follower of fashion and pop music [*teeny* teenage + *-bopper* someone who bops]

tee off *vb* **teeing, teed** *golf* to hit (the ball) from a tee at the start of a hole
teepee *n* same as **tepee**
teeter *vb* to wobble or move unsteadily [Middle English *titeren*]
teeth *n* **1** the plural of **tooth** **2** the power to produce a desired effect: *resolution 672 had no teeth* **3** **armed to the teeth** very heavily armed **4** **get one's teeth into** to become engrossed in **5** **in the teeth of** in spite of: *trying to run a business in the teeth of the recession*
teethe *vb* **teething, teethed** (of a baby) to grow his or her first teeth
teething ring *n* a hard ring on which babies may bite while teething
teething troubles *pl n* problems arising during the early stages of a project
teetotal *adj* never drinking alcohol [reduplication of *t* + *total*] **teetotaller** *n*
TEFL Teaching of English as a Foreign Language
Teflon *n trademark* a substance used for nonstick coatings on saucepans, etc.
te-hee *interj* same as **tee-hee**
tel. telephone
tele- *combining form* **1** at or over a distance: *telecommunications* **2** television: *telegenic* **3** via telephone or television: *teleconference* [Greek *tele* far]
telecast *vb* **-casting, -cast** *or* **-casted** **1** to broadcast by television ▷ *n* **2** a television broadcast **telecaster** *n*
telecommunications *n* communications using electronic equipment, such as telephones, radio, and television
telecommuting *n* same as **teleworking**
telegram *n* (formerly) a message transmitted by telegraph
telegraph *n* **1** (formerly) a system by which information could be transmitted over a distance, using electrical signals sent along a cable ▷ *vb* **2** (formerly) to send (a message) by telegraph **3** to give advance notice of (something), esp. unintentionally: *the twist in the plot was telegraphed long in advance* **4** *Canad informal* to cast (a vote) illegally by impersonating a registered voter **telegraphist** *n* **telegraphic** *adj*
telegraphy *n* (formerly) the science or use of a telegraph
telekinesis *n* movement of a body by thought or willpower, without the application of a physical force **telekinetic** *adj*
telemarketing *n* another name for **telesales**
telemetry *n* the use of electronic devices to record or measure a distant event and transmit the data to a receiver **telemetric** *adj*
teleology *n* **1** *philosophy* the doctrine that there is evidence of purpose or design in the universe **2** *biol* the belief that natural phenomena have a predetermined purpose and are not determined by mechanical laws [Greek *telos* end + -LOGY] **teleological** *adj* **teleologist** *n*
telepathy *n* the direct communication of thoughts and feelings between minds without the need to use normal means such as speech, writing, or touch [Greek *tele* far + *pathos* suffering] **telepathic** *adj* **telepathically** *adv*
telephone *n* **1** a piece of equipment for transmitting speech, consisting of a microphone and receiver mounted on a handset: *the telephone was ringing* **2** the worldwide system of communications using telephones: *reports came in by telephone* ▷ *vb* **-phoning, -phoned** **3** to call or talk to (a person) by telephone ▷ *adj* **4** of or using a telephone: *a telephone call* [Greek *tele* far + *phōnē* voice] **telephonic** *adj*
telephone box *n* an enclosure from which a paid telephone call can be made
telephone directory *n* a book listing the names, addresses, and telephone numbers of subscribers in a particular area
telephonist *n* a person who operates a telephone switchboard
telephony *n* a system of telecommunications for the transmission of speech or other sounds
telephoto lens *n* a lens fitted to a camera to produce a magnified image of a distant object
Teleprompter *n trademark* a device for displaying a script under a television camera, so that a speaker can read it while appearing to look at the camera
telesales *n* the selling of a commodity or service by telephone
telescope *n* **1** an optical instrument for making distant objects appear closer by use of a combination of lenses **2** See **radio telescope** ▷ *vb* **-scoping, -scoped** **3** to shorten (something) while still keeping the important parts: *a hundred years of change has been telescoped into five years* [New Latin *telescopium* far-seeing instrument] **telescopic** *adj*
telescopic sight *n* a sight on a rifle, etc., consisting of a telescope, used for aiming at distant objects
televangelist *n US* an evangelical preacher who appears regularly on television, preaching the gospel and appealing for donations from viewers [*tele(vision)* + *(e)vangelist*]
televise *vb* **-vising, -vised** to show (a programme or event) on television
television *n* **1** the system or process of producing a moving image with accompanying sound on a distant screen **2** Also called: **television set** a device for receiving broadcast signals and converting them into sound and pictures **3** the content of television programmes: *some people think that television is too violent nowadays* ▷ *adj* **4** of or relating to television: *a television interview* **televisual** *adj*
teleworking *n* the use of home computers, telephones, etc., to enable a person to work from home while maintaining contact with colleagues or customers **teleworker** *n*
telex *n* **1** an international communication service formerly used to send messages by teleprinter **2** a teleprinter used in such a service **3** a message sent by telex ▷ *vb* **4** to transmit (a message) by telex [*tel(eprinter) ex(change)*]
tell *vb* **telling, told** **1** to make known in words; notify: *I told her what had happened* **2** to order or instruct (someone to do something): *he had been told to wait in the lobby* **3** to give an account (of an event or situation): *the President had been told of the*

developments **4** to communicate by words: *he was woken at 5 am to be told the news* **5** to discover, distinguish, or discern: *she could tell that he was not sorry* **6** to have or produce an impact or effect: *the pressure had begun to tell on him* **7** *informal* to reveal secrets or gossip **8 tell the time** to read the time from a clock **9 you're telling me** *slang* I know that very well [Old English *tellan*]

tell apart *vb* to distinguish between: *they're different colours, otherwise how would you tell them apart?*

teller *n* **1** a narrator **2** a bank cashier **3** a person appointed to count votes

telling *adj* having a marked effect or impact: *to inflict telling damage on the enemy*

tell off *vb informal* to reprimand or scold (someone) **telling-off** *n*

telltale *n* **1** a person who tells tales about others ▷ *adj* **2** giving away information: *examining the hands for telltale signs of age*

tellurian *adj* of the earth [Latin *tellus* the earth]

tellurium *n chem* a brittle silvery-white nonmetallic element. Symbol: **Te** [Latin *tellus* the earth]

telly *n, pl* **-lies** *informal* short for **television**

telomere *n genetics* either of the ends of a chromosome [Greek *telos* end + *meros* part]

temazepam (ti-**maz**-i-pam) *n (sometimes cap)* a sedative in the form of a gel-like capsule, which is taken orally or melted and injected by drug users

temerity (tim-**merr**-it-tee) *n* boldness or audacity [Latin *temere* at random]

temp *Brit informal* ▷ *n* **1** a person, esp. a secretary, employed on a temporary basis ▷ *vb* **2** to work as a temp

temp. **1** temperature **2** temporary

temper *n* **1** a sudden outburst of anger: *she stormed out in a temper* **2** a tendency to have sudden outbursts of anger: *you've got a temper all right* **3** a mental condition of moderation and calm: *he lost his temper* **4** a person's frame of mind: *he was in a bad temper* ▷ *vb* **5** to modify so as to make less extreme or more acceptable: *past militancy has been tempered with compassion and caring* **6** to reduce the brittleness of (a hardened metal) by reheating it and allowing it to cool **7** *music* to adjust the frequency differences between the notes of a scale on (a keyboard instrument) [Latin *temperare* to mix]

tempera *n* a painting medium for powdered pigments, consisting usually of egg yolk and water [Italian *temperare* to mingle]

temperament *n* a person's character or disposition [Latin *temperamentum* a mixing]

temperamental *adj* **1** (of a person) tending to be moody and have sudden outbursts of anger **2** *informal* working erratically and inconsistently; unreliable: *the temperamental microphone* **3** of or relating to a person's temperament: *we discussed temperamental and developmental differences* **temperamentally** *adv*

temperance *n* **1** restraint or moderation, esp. in yielding to one's appetites or desires **2** abstinence from alcoholic drink [Latin *temperare* to regulate]

temperate *adj* **1** of a climate which is never extremely hot or extremely cold **2** mild or moderate in quality or character: *try to be more temperate in your statements* [Latin *temperatus*]

Temperate Zone *n* those parts of the earth's surface lying between the Arctic Circle and the tropic of Cancer and between the Antarctic Circle and the tropic of Capricorn

temperature *n* **1** the hotness or coldness of something, as measured on a scale that has one or more fixed reference points **2** *informal* an abnormally high body temperature **3** the strength of feeling among a group of people: *his remarks are likely to raise the political temperature considerably* [Latin *temperatura* proportion]

tempest *n literary* a violent wind or storm [Latin *tempestas*]

tempestuous *adj* **1** violent or stormy **2** extremely emotional or passionate: *a tempestuous relationship* **tempestuously** *adv*

template *n* a wood or metal pattern, used to help cut out shapes accurately [from *temple* a part in a loom that keeps the cloth stretched]

temple[1] *n* a building or place used for the worship of a god or gods [Latin *templum*]

temple[2] *n* the region on each side of the head in front of the ear and above the cheek bone [Latin *tempus*]

tempo (**tem**-po) *n, pl* **-pi** (-pee) *or* **-pos** **1** rate or pace: *the slow tempo of change in an overwhelmingly rural country* **2** the speed at which a piece of music is played or meant to be played [Italian]

temporal[1] *adj* **1** of or relating to time **2** of secular as opposed to spiritual or religious affairs: *in the Middle Ages the Pope had temporal as well as spiritual power* **3** not permanent or eternal: *a temporal view of drugs as the No. 1 social problem* [Latin *tempus* time]

temporal[2] *adj anatomy* of or near the temple or temples

temporal bone *n* either of two compound bones forming the sides of the skull

temporary *adj* lasting only for a short time; not permanent: *temporary accommodation* [Latin *temporarius*] **temporarily** *adv*

temporize *or* **-rise** *vb* **-rizing, -rized** *or* **-rising, -rised** **1** to delay, act evasively, or protract a negotiation in order to gain time or avoid making a decision: *'Well,' I temporized, 'I'll have to ask your mother'* **2** to adapt oneself to circumstances, as by temporary or apparent agreement [Latin *tempus* time]

tempt *vb* **1** to entice (someone) to do something, esp. something morally wrong or unwise: *can I tempt you to have another whisky?* **2** to allure or attract: *she was tempted by the glamour of a modelling career* **3 be tempted** to want to do something while knowing it would be wrong or inappropriate to do so: *many youngsters are tempted to experiment with drugs* **4 tempt fate** *or* **providence** to take foolish or unnecessary risks [Latin *temptare* to test] **tempter** *or fem* **temptress** *n*

temptation *n* **1** the act of tempting or the state of being tempted **2** a person or thing that tempts

tempting *adj* attractive or inviting: *it's tempting to say I told you so* **temptingly** *adv*

ten *n* **1** the cardinal number that is the sum of one and nine **2** a numeral, 10 or X, representing this number **3** something representing or consisting of ten units ▷ *adj* **4** amounting to ten: *ten years* [Old English tēn] **tenth** *adj, n*

tenable *adj* **1** able to be upheld or maintained: *a tenable strategy* **2** (of a job) intended to be held by a person for a particular length of time: *the post will be tenable for three years in the first instance* [Latin *tenere* to hold] **tenability** *n* **tenably** *adv*

tenacious *adj* **1** holding firmly: *a tenacious grasp* **2** stubborn or persistent: *tenacious support* [Latin *tenere* to hold] **tenaciously** *adv* **tenacity** *n*

tenancy *n, pl* **-cies** **1** the temporary possession or use of lands or property owned by somebody else, in return for payment **2** the period of holding or occupying such property

tenant *n* **1** a person who pays rent for the use of land or property **2** any holder or occupant [Old French: one who is holding]

tenant farmer *n* a person who farms land rented from somebody else

tenantry *n old-fashioned* tenants collectively

tench *n* a European freshwater game fish of the carp family [Old French *tenche*]

Ten Commandments *pl n Bible* the commandments given by God to Moses on Mount Sinai, summarizing the basic obligations of people towards God and their fellow humans

tend[1] *vb* to be inclined (to take a particular kind of action or to be in a particular condition) as a rule: *she tends to be rather absent-minded* [Latin *tendere* to stretch]

tend[2] *vb* **1** to take care of: *it is she who tends his wounds* **2 tend to** to attend to: *excuse me, I have to tend to the other guests* [variant of *attend*]

tendency *n, pl* **-cies** **1** an inclination to act in a particular way **2** the general course or drift of something **3** a faction, esp. within a political party [Latin *tendere* to stretch]

tendentious *adj* expressing a particular viewpoint or opinion, esp. a controversial one, in very strong terms: *a somewhat tendentious reading of French history* **tendentiously** *adv*

tender[1] *adj* **1** (of cooked food) having softened and become easy to chew or cut **2** gentle and kind: *tender loving care* **3** vulnerable or sensitive: *at the tender age of 9* **4** painful when touched: *his wrist was swollen and tender* [Old French *tendre*] **tenderly** *adv* **tenderness** *n*

tender[2] *vb* **1** to present or offer: *he tendered his resignation* **2** to make a formal offer or estimate for a job or contract: *contractors tendering for government work* ▷ *n* **3** a formal offer to supply specified goods or services at a stated cost or rate: *the government invited tenders to run television and radio services* [Latin *tendere* to extend] **tenderer** *n* **tendering** *n*

tender[3] *n* **1** a small boat that brings supplies to larger vessels in a port **2** a wagon attached to the rear of a steam locomotive that carries the fuel and water [variant of *attender*]

tenderfoot *n, pl* **-foots** *or* **-feet** a newcomer to a particular activity

tenderize *or* **-rise** *vb* **-rizing, -rized** *or* **-rising, -rised** to make (meat) tender, by pounding it or adding a substance to break down the fibres **tenderizer** *or* **-riser** *n*

tenderloin *n* a tender cut of pork from between the sirloin and ribs

tendon *n* a band of tough tissue that attaches a muscle to a bone [Medieval Latin *tendo*]

tendril *n* a threadlike leaf or stem by which a climbing plant attaches itself to a support [probably from Old French *tendron*]

tenement *n* a large building divided into several different flats [Latin *tenere* to hold]

tenet (ten-nit) *n* a principle on which a belief or doctrine is based [Latin, literally: he (it) holds]

tenfold *adj* **1** having ten times as many or as much **2** composed of ten parts ▷ *adv* **3** by ten times as many or as much

ten-gallon hat *n* (in the US) a cowboy's broad-brimmed felt hat with a very high crown

tenner *n Brit, Austral & NZ informal* **1** a ten-pound or ten-dollar note **2** the sum of ten pounds or ten dollars: *it's worth a tenner at least*

tennessine *n chem* a synthetic radioactive element produced in small quantities. Symbol: **Ts** [after *Tennessee*, US state]

tennis *n* a game played between two players or pairs of players who use a racket to hit a ball to and fro over a net on a rectangular court. See also **lawn tennis, real tennis, table tennis** [probably from Anglo-French *tenetz* hold!]

tennis elbow *n* inflammation of the elbow, typically caused by exertion in playing tennis

tenon *n* a projecting end of a piece of wood, formed to fit into a corresponding slot in another piece [Old French]

tenor *n* **1 A** the second highest male voice, between alto and baritone **B** a singer with such a voice **C** a saxophone, horn, or other musical instrument between the alto and baritone or bass **2** a general meaning or character: *it was clear from the tenor of the meeting that the chairman's actions are very unpopular* ▷ *adj* **3** denoting a musical instrument between alto and baritone: *a tenor saxophone* **4** of or relating to the second highest male voice: *his voice lacks the range needed for the tenor role* [Old French *tenour*]

tenpin bowling *n* a game in which players try to knock over ten skittles by rolling a ball at them

tense[1] *adj* **1** having, showing, or causing mental or emotional strain: *the tense atmosphere* **2** stretched tight: *tense muscles* ▷ *vb* **tensing, tensed** **3** Also: **tense up** to make or become tense [Latin *tensus* taut] **tensely** *adv* **tenseness** *n*

tense[2] *n grammar* the form of a verb that indicates whether the action referred to in the sentence is located in the past, the present, or the future: *'ate' is the past tense of 'to eat'* [Old French *tens* time]

tensile *adj* of or relating to tension or being stretched: *The posts were linked by high tensile wire.*

tensile strength *n* a measure of the ability of a material to withstand lengthwise stress, expressed as the greatest stress that the material can stand without breaking: *the addition of linseed oil improved the tensile strength of the cricket bat*

tension *n* **1** a situation or condition of hostility, suspense, or uneasiness: *a renewed state of tension between old enemies* **2** mental or emotional strain:

t

nervous tension **3** a force that stretches or the state or degree of being stretched tight: *keep tension on the line until the fish comes within range of the net* **4** *physics* a force that tends to produce an elongation of a body or structure **5** *physics* voltage, electromotive force, or potential difference [Latin *tensio*]

tent *n* **1** a portable shelter made of canvas or other fabric supported on poles, stretched out, and fastened to the ground by pegs and ropes **2** See **oxygen tent** [Old French *tente*]

tentacle *n* **1** a flexible organ that grows near the mouth in many invertebrates and is used for feeding, grasping, etc. **2 tentacles** the unseen methods by which an organization or idea, esp. a sinister one, influences people and events: *the tentacles of the secret police* [Latin *tentare* to feel] **tentacled** *adj*

tentative *adj* **1** provisional or unconfirmed: *a tentative agreement* **2** hesitant, uncertain, or cautious: *their rather tentative approach* [Latin *tentare* to test] **tentatively** *adv* **tentativeness** *n*

tenterhooks *pl n* **on tenterhooks** in a state of tension or suspense [Latin *tentus* stretched + HOOK]

tenth *adj, n* See **ten**

tenuous *adj* insignificant or flimsy: *there is only the most tenuous evidence for it* [Latin *tenuis*] **tenuously** *adv*

tenure *n* **1** the holding of an office or position **2** the length of time an office or position lasts **3** the holding of a teaching position at a university on a permanent basis **4** the legal right to live in a place or to use land or buildings for a period of time [Latin *tenere* to hold]

tepee *or* **teepee** (tee-pee) *n* a cone-shaped tent of animal skins, formerly used by Native Americans [Sioux *tīpī*]

tepid *adj* **1** slightly warm **2** lacking enthusiasm: *tepid applause* [Latin *tepidus*] **tepidity** *n* **tepidly** *adv*

tequila *n* a Mexican alcoholic spirit distilled from the agave plant [after *Tequila*, district in Mexico]

tera- *combining form* denoting one million million (10^{12}): *terameter* [Greek *teras* monster]

teratology (terr-a-**tol**-a-jee) *n* the branch of medicine concerned with the development of physical abnormalities during the fetal or early embryonic stage [Greek *teras* monster + -LOGY]

terbium *n chem* a soft silvery-grey element of the lanthanide series of metals. Symbol: **Tb** [after *Ytterby*, Sweden, where discovered]

tercentenary *or* **tercentennial** *adj* **1** marking a 300th anniversary ▷ *n, pl* **-tenaries** *or* **-tennials** **2** a 300th anniversary [Latin *ter* three times + CENTENARY]

teredo (ter-**ree**-doh) *n, pl* **-dos** *or* **-dines** (-din-eez) a marine mollusc that bores into and destroys submerged timber [Greek *terēdōn* wood-boring worm]

term *n* **1** a word or expression, esp. one used in a specialized field of knowledge: *he coined the term 'inferiority complex'* **2** a period of time: *a four-year prison term* **3** one of the periods of the year when a school, university, or college is open or a lawcourt holds sessions **4** the period of pregnancy when childbirth is imminent **5** *maths* any distinct quantity making up a fraction or proportion, or contained in a sequence, series, etc. **6** *logic* any of the three subjects or predicates occurring in a syllogism **7 full term** the end of a specific period of time: *the agony of carrying the child to full term* ▷ *vb* **8** to name, call, or describe as being: *a musical style that could loosely be termed gospel* ▷ See also **terms** [Latin *terminus* end]

termagant *n literary* an unpleasant, aggressive, and overbearing woman [earlier *Tervagaunt*, after an arrogant character in medieval mystery plays]

terminable *adj* capable of being terminated: *his terminable interest in the property* **terminability** *n*

terminal *adj* **1** (of an illness) ending in death **2** situated at an end, terminus, or boundary: *the terminal joints of the fingers* **3** *informal* extreme or severe: *terminal boredom* ▷ *n* **4** a place where vehicles, passengers, or goods begin or end a journey: *the ferry terminal* **5** a point at which current enters or leaves an electrical device **6** *computers* a device, usually a keyboard and a visual display unit, having input/output links with a computer [Latin *terminus* end] **terminally** *adv*

terminal velocity *n physics* the maximum velocity reached by a body falling under gravity through a liquid or gas, esp. the atmosphere

terminate *vb* **-nating, -nated** **1** to bring or come to an end: *his flying career was terminated by this crash* **2** to put an end to (a pregnancy) by inducing an abortion **3** (of the route of a train, bus, etc.) to stop at a particular place and not go any further: *this train terminates at Leicester* [Latin *terminare* to set boundaries] **termination** *n*

terminology *n, pl* **-gies** the specialized words and expressions relating to a particular subject **terminological** *adj* **terminologist** *n*

terminus (term-in-nuss) *n, pl* **-ni** (-nye) *or* **-nuses** the station or town at one end of a railway line or bus route: *Vienna's Westbahnhof is the terminus for trains to France* [Latin: end]

termite *n* a whitish antlike insect of warm and tropical regions that destroys timber [New Latin *termites* white ants]

terms *pl n* **1** the actual language or mode of presentation used: *the test is carried out in plain non-engineering terms* **2** the conditions of an agreement **3** mutual relationship or standing of a specified nature: *he is on first-name terms with many of the directors* **4 come to terms with** to learn to accept (an unpleasant or difficult situation) **5 in terms of** as expressed by; with regard to: *he is the best cricketer we have got in fact in terms of pure ability*

tern *n* a gull-like sea bird with a forked tail and long narrow wings [Old Norse *therna*]

ternary *adj* **1** consisting of three items or groups of three items **2** *maths* (of a number system) to the base three [Latin *ternarius*]

Terpsichore (turp-**sick**-or-ee) *n Greek myth* the Muse of dance

Terpsichorean (turp-sick-or-**ee**-an) *adj often facetious* of or relating to dancing [from *Terpsichore*, the Muse of dance in Greek mythology]

Terr. **1** terrace **2** territory

t

terrace *n* **1** a row of houses, usually identical and joined together by common dividing walls, or the street onto which they face **2** a paved area alongside a building **3** a horizontal flat area of ground, often one of a series in a slope **4 the terraces** *or* **terracing** *Brit & NZ* a tiered area in a stadium where spectators stand ▷ *vb* **-racing, -raced 5** to make into terraces [Latin *terra* earth]
terraced house *n Brit* a house that is part of a terrace
terracotta *n* **1** a hard unglazed brownish-red earthenware used for pottery ▷ *adj* **2** made of terracotta **3** brownish-orange [Italian, literally: baked earth]
terra firma *n* the ground, as opposed to the sea [Latin]
terraforming *n* (esp in science fiction) planetary engineering designed to enhance the capacity of an extraterrestrial planetary environment to sustain human life [Latin *terra* earth]
terrain *n* an area of ground, esp. with reference to its physical character: *mountainous terrain* [Latin *terra* earth]
terra incognita (terr-a in-**kog**-nit-a) *n* an unexplored region [Latin]
terrapin *n* a small turtle-like reptile of N America that lives in fresh water and on land [from a Native American language]
terrarium *n* **1** an enclosed area or container where small land animals are kept **2** a glass container in which plants are grown [Latin *terra* earth]
terrazzo *n, pl* **-zos** a floor made by setting marble chips into a layer of mortar and polishing the surface [Italian: terrace]
terrestrial *adj* **1** of the planet earth **2** of the land as opposed to the sea or air **3** (of animals and plants) living or growing on the land **4** *television* denoting or using a signal sent over land from a transmitter on land, rather than by satellite [Latin *terra* earth]
terrible *adj* **1** very serious or extreme: *war is a terrible thing* **2** *informal* very bad, unpleasant, or unsatisfactory: *terrible books* **3** causing fear [Latin *terribilis*] **terribly** *adv*
terrier *n* any of several small active breeds of dog, originally trained to hunt animals living underground [Old French *chien terrier* earth dog]
terrific *adj* **1** very great or intense: *a terrific blow on the head* **2** *informal* very good; excellent: *a terrific book* [Latin *terrere* to frighten] **terrifically** *adv*
terrify *vb* **-fies, -fying, -fied** to frighten greatly [Latin *terrificare*] **terrified** *adj* **terrifying** *adj* **terrifyingly** *adv*
terrine (terr-**reen**) *n* **1** an oval earthenware cooking dish with a tightly fitting lid **2** the food cooked or served in such a dish, esp. pâté [French]
territorial *adj* **1** of or relating to a territory or territories **2** of or concerned with the ownership and control of an area of land or water: *a territorial dispute* **3** (of an animal or bird) establishing and defending an area which it will not let other animals or birds into: *the baboon is a territorial species* **4** of or relating to a territorial army **territorially** *adv* **territoriality** *n*

Territorial *n* a member of a Territorial Army
Territorial Army *n* (in Britain) a reserve army, known since 2014 as the **Army Reserve**, whose members are not full-time soldiers but undergo military training in their spare time so that they can be called upon in an emergency
territorial waters *pl n* the part of the sea near to a country's coast, which is under the control of the government of that country
territory *n, pl* **-ries 1** any tract of land; district: *mountainous territory* **2** the geographical area under the control of a particular government: *the islands are Japanese territory* **3** an area inhabited and defended by a particular animal or pair of animals **4** an area of knowledge or experience: *all this is familiar territory to readers of her recent novels* **5** a country or region under the control of a foreign country: *a French Overseas Territory* **6** a region of a country, esp. of a federal state, that enjoys less autonomy and a lower status than most constituent parts of the state [Latin *territorium* land surrounding a town]
terror *n* **1** very great fear, panic, or dread **2** a person or thing that inspires great dread **3** *Brit, Austral & NZ informal* a troublesome person, esp. a child [Latin]
terrorism *n* the systematic use of violence and intimidation to achieve political ends **terrorist** *n, adj*
terrorize *or* **-rise** *vb* **-rizing, -rized** *or* **-rising, -rised 1** to control or force (someone) to do something by violence, fear, threats, etc.: *he was terrorized into withdrawing his accusations* **2** to make (someone) very frightened **terrorization** *or* **-risation** *n* **terrorizer** *or* **-riser** *n*
terry *n* a fabric covered on both sides with small uncut loops, used for towelling and nappies [origin unknown]
terse *adj* **1** neatly brief and concise **2** curt or abrupt [Latin *tersus* precise] **tersely** *adv* **terseness** *n*
tertiary (**tur**-shar-ee) *adj* **1** third in degree, order, etc. **2** (of education) at university or college level **3** (of an industry) involving services, such as transport and financial services, as opposed to manufacture [Latin *tertius*]
Tertiary *adj geol* of the period of geological time lasting from about 65 million years ago to 600 000 years ago
Terylene *n trademark* a synthetic polyester fibre or fabric
TESL Teaching of English as a Second Language
tessellated *adj* paved or inlaid with a mosaic of small tiles [Latin *tessellatus* checked]
tessera *n, pl* **-serae** a small square tile used in mosaics [Latin]
test[1] *vb* **1** to try (something) out to ascertain its worth, safety, or endurance: *the company has never tested its products on animals* **2** to carry out an examination on (a substance, material, or system) in order to discover whether a particular substance, component, or feature is present: *baby foods are regularly tested for pesticides* **3** to put under severe strain: *the long delay tested my patience* **4** to achieve a result in a test which indicates the presence or absence of something: *he tested*

positive for cocaine ▷ *n* **5** a method, practice, or examination designed to test a person or thing **6** a series of questions or problems designed to test a specific skill or knowledge: *a spelling test* **7** a chemical reaction or physical procedure for testing the composition or other qualities of a substance **8** *sport* short for **Test match** **9 put to the test** to use (something) in order to gauge its usefulness or effectiveness [Latin *testum* earthen vessel] **testable** *adj* **testing** *adj*

test² *n* the hard outer covering of certain invertebrates [Latin *testa* shell]

testa (**tess**-ta) *n, pl* **-tae** (-tee) the hard outer layer of a seed [Latin: shell]

testaceous (test-**ay**-shuss) *adj biol* of or having a hard continuous shell [Latin *testacens,* from TESTA]

testament *n* **1** something which provides proof of a fact about someone or something: *the size of the audience was an immediate testament to his appeal* **2** *law* a formal statement of how a person wants his or her property to be disposed of after his or her death: *last will and testament* [Latin *testis* a witness] **testamentary** *adj*

Testament *n* either of the two main parts of the Bible, the Old Testament or the New Testament

testate *law* ▷ *adj* **1** having left a legally valid will at death ▷ *n* **2** a person who dies and leaves a legally valid will [Latin *testari* to make a will] **testacy** *n*

testator (test-**tay**-tor) *or fem* **testatrix** (test-**tay**-triks) *n law* a person who has made a will, esp. one who has died testate

test card *n* a complex pattern used to test the characteristics of a television transmission system

test case *n* a legal action that serves as a precedent in deciding similar succeeding cases

testicle *n* either of the two male reproductive glands, in most mammals enclosed within the scrotum, that produce spermatozoa [Latin *testis* a witness (to masculinity)]

testify *vb* **-fies, -fying, -fied** **1** *law* to declare or give evidence under oath, esp. in court **2 testify to** to be evidence of: *a piece of paper testifying to their educational qualifications* [Latin *testis* witness]

testimonial *n* **1** a recommendation of the character or worth of a person or thing **2** a tribute given for services or achievements ▷ *adj* **3** of a testimony or testimonial: *a testimonial match*

> **USAGE** *Testimonial* is sometimes wrongly used where *testimony* is meant: *his re-election is a testimony* (not *a testimonial*) *to his popularity with his constituents.*

testimony *n, pl* **-nies** **1** a declaration of truth or fact **2** *law* evidence given by a witness, esp. in court under oath **3** evidence proving or supporting something: *that they are still talking is a testimony to their 20-year friendship* [Latin *testimonium*]

testis *n, pl* **-tes** same as **testicle**

Test match *n* (in various sports, esp. cricket) an international match, esp. one of a series

testosterone *n* a steroid male sex hormone secreted by the testes

test paper *n* **1** the question sheet of a test **2** *chem* paper impregnated with an indicator for use in chemical tests

test pilot *n* a pilot who flies aircraft of new design to test their performance in the air

test tube *n* a cylindrical round-bottomed glass tube open at one end, which is used in scientific experiments

test-tube baby *n* **1** a fetus that has developed from an ovum fertilized in an artificial womb **2** a baby conceived by artificial insemination

testy *adj* **-tier, -tiest** irritable or touchy [Anglo-Norman *testif* headstrong] **testily** *adv* **testiness** *n*

tetanus *n* an acute infectious disease in which toxins released from a bacterium cause muscular spasms and convulsions [Greek *tetanos*]

tetchy *adj* **tetchier, tetchiest** cross, irritable, or touchy [probably from obsolete *tetch* defect] **tetchily** *adv* **tetchiness** *n*

tête-à-tête *n, pl* **-têtes** *or* **-tête** **1** a private conversation between two people ▷ *adv* **2** together in private: *they dined tête-à-tête* [French, literally: head to head]

tether *n* **1** a rope or chain for tying an animal to a fence, post, etc., so that it cannot move away from a particular place **2 at the end of one's tether** at the limit of one's patience or endurance ▷ *vb* **3** to tie with a tether [Old Norse *tjōthr*]

tetra- *combining form* four: *tetrapod*

tetrad *n* a group or series of four [Greek *tetras*]

tetraethyl lead *n* a colourless oily insoluble liquid used in petrol to prevent knocking

tetragon *n* a shape with four angles and four sides [Greek *tetragōnon*] **tetragonal** *adj*

tetrahedron (tet-ra-**heed**-ron) *n, pl* **-drons** *or* **-dra** a solid figure with four triangular plane faces [Late Greek *tetraedron*] **tetrahedral** *adj*

tetralogy *n, pl* **-gies** a series of four related books, dramas, operas, etc. [Greek *tetralogia*]

tetrameter (tet-**tram**-it-er) *n* **1** *prosody* a line of verse consisting of four metrical feet **2** verse consisting of such lines [Greek *tetra-* four + METER]

Teuton (**tew**-tun) *n* **1** a member of an ancient Germanic people of N Europe **2** a member of any people speaking a Germanic language, esp. a German ▷ *adj* **3** Teutonic [Latin *Teutoni* the Teutons]

Teutonic (tew-**tonn**-ik) *adj* **1** characteristic of or relating to the Germans **2** of the ancient Teutons

Tex-Mex *adj* **1** combining elements of Texan and Mexican culture ▷ *n* **2** Tex-Mex music or cooking

text *n* **1** the main body of a printed or written work as distinct from items such as notes or illustrations **2** any written material, such as words displayed on a visual display unit **3** the written version of the words of a speech, broadcast, or recording: *an advance text of the remarks the president will deliver tonight* **4** a short passage of the Bible used as a starting point for a sermon **5** a book required as part of a course of study: *shelves full of sociology texts* ▷ *vb* **6** to send (a text message) by mobile phone **7** to contact (a person) by means of a text message [Latin *texere* to compose]

textbook *n* **1** a book of facts about a subject used by someone who is studying that subject ▷ *adj*

2 perfect or exemplary: *a textbook example of an emergency descent*

textile *n* **1** any fabric or cloth, esp. a woven one ▷ *adj* **2** of or relating to fabrics or their production: *the world textile market* [Latin *textilis* woven]

text message *n* **1** a message sent in text form, esp. by means of a mobile phone **2** a message appearing on a computer screen **text messaging** *n*

textual *adj* of, based on, or relating to, a text or texts **textually** *adv*

texture *n* **1** the structure, appearance, and feel of a substance: *curtains of many textures and colours* **2** the overall sound of a piece of music, resulting from the way the different instrumental parts in it are combined: *a big orchestra weaving rich textures* ▷ *vb* **-turing, -tured 3** to give a distinctive texture to (something) [Latin *texere* to weave] **textural** *adj*

TGV *n* (in France) a high-speed passenger train [French *train à grande vitesse*]

Th *chem* thorium

Thai *adj* **1** of Thailand ▷ *n* **2** *pl* **Thais** *or* **Thai** a person from Thailand **3** the main language of Thailand

Thalia *n Greek myth* the Muse of comedy

thalidomide (thal-**lid**-oh-mide) *n* a drug formerly used as a sedative and hypnotic but withdrawn from use when found to cause abnormalities in developing fetuses [*thali(mi)do(glutari)mide*]

thallium *n chem* a soft highly toxic white metallic element. Symbol: **Tl** [Greek *thallos* a green shoot; from the green line in its spectrum]

than *conj, prep* **1** used to introduce the second element of a comparison, the first element of which expresses difference: *I'm less optimistic than I was at first* **2** used to state a number, quantity, or value in approximate terms by contrasting it with another number, quantity, or value: *temperatures lower than 25 degrees* **3** used after the adverbs *rather* and *sooner* to introduce a rejected alternative: *fruit is examined by hand, rather than by machine* [Old English *thanne*]

> **USAGE** In formal English, *than* is usually regarded as a conjunction governing an unexpressed verb: *he does it far better than I (do).* The case of any pronoun therefore depends on whether it is the subject or object of the unexpressed verb: *she likes him more than I (like him); she likes him more than (she likes) me.* However in ordinary speech and writing *than* is usually treated as a preposition and is followed by the object form of a pronoun: *my brother is younger than me.*

thane *n* **1** (in Anglo-Saxon England) a nobleman who held land from the king or from a superior nobleman in return for certain services **2** (in medieval Scotland) a person of rank holding land from the king [Old English *thegn*]

thank *vb* **1** to convey feelings of gratitude to: *he thanked the nursing staff for saving his life* **2** to hold responsible: *he has his father to thank for his familiarity with the film world* **3 thank you** a polite response or expression of gratitude **4 thank goodness** *or* **thank heavens** *or* **thank God** an exclamation of relief [Old English *thancian*]

thankful *adj* grateful and appreciative **thankfully** *adv*

thankless *adj* unrewarding or unappreciated: *she took on the thankless task of organizing the office Xmas lunch* **thanklessly** *adv* **thanklessness** *n*

thanks *pl n* **1** an expression of appreciation or gratitude **2 thanks to** because of: *the birth went very smoothly, thanks to the help of the GHQ medical officer* ▷ *interj* **3** *informal* an exclamation expressing gratitude

thanksgiving *n* a formal public expression of thanks to God

Thanksgiving Day *n* (in North America) an annual holiday celebrated on the fourth Thursday of November in the United States and on the second Monday of October in Canada

that *adj* **1** used preceding a noun that has been mentioned or is already familiar: *he'd have to give up on that idea* **2** used preceding a noun that denotes something more remote: *that book on the top shelf* ▷ *pron* **3** used to denote something already mentioned or understood: *that's right* **4** used to denote a more remote person or thing: *is that him over there?* **5** used to introduce a restrictive relative clause: *a problem that has to be overcome* **6 and all that** *or* **and that** *informal* and similar or related things: *import cutting and all that* **7 that is A** to be precise **B** in other words **8 that's that** there is no more to be said or done ▷ *conj* **9** used to introduce a noun clause: *he denied that the country was suffering from famine* **10** used, usually after *so*, to introduce a clause of purpose: *he turns his face away from her so that she shall not see his tears* **11** used to introduce a clause of result: *a scene so sickening and horrible that it is impossible to describe it* ▷ *adv* **12** Also: **all that** *informal* very or particularly: *the fines imposed have not been that large* [Old English *thæt*]

> **USAGE** Precise writers maintain a distinction between *that* and *which*: *that* is used as a relative pronoun in restrictive clauses and *which* in nonrestrictive clauses. In *the book that is on the table is mine*, the clause *that is on the table* is used to distinguish one particular book (the one on the table) from another or others (which may be anywhere, but not on the table). In *the book, which is on the table, is mine*, the *which* clause is merely descriptive or incidental. The more formal the level of language, the more important it is to preserve the distinction between the two relative pronouns; but in informal or colloquial usage, the words are often used interchangeably.

thatch *n* **1** Also called: **thatching** a roofing material that consists of straw or reeds **2** a roof made of such a material **3** a mass of thick untidy hair on someone's head ▷ *vb* **4** to cover with thatch [Old English *theccan* to cover] **thatched** *adj* **thatcher** *n*

thaw *vb* **1** to melt or cause to melt: *snow thawing in the gutter* **2** (of frozen food) to become or cause to become unfrozen; defrost **3** (of weather) to be warm enough to cause ice or snow to melt: *it's not freezing, it's thawing again* **4** to become more relaxed or friendly: *only with Llewelyn did he thaw, let his*

t

defences down ▷ *n* **5** the act or process of thawing **6** a spell of relatively warm weather, causing snow or ice to melt [Old English *thawian*]

THC tetrahydrocannabidinol: the active ingredient in cannabis which gives it its narcotic effect

the¹ *adj (definite article)* **1** used preceding a noun that has been previously specified or is a matter of common knowledge: *those involved in the search* **2** used to indicate a particular person or object: *the man called Frank turned to look at it* **3** used preceding certain nouns associated with one's culture, society, or community: *to comply with the law* **4** used preceding an adjective that is functioning as a collective noun: *the unemployed* **5** used preceding titles and certain proper nouns: *the Middle East* **6** used preceding an adjective or noun in certain names or titles: *Alexander the Great* **7** used preceding a noun to make it refer to its class as a whole: *cultivation of the coca plant* **8** used instead of *my, your, her*, etc., with parts of the body: *swelling of tissues in the brain* **9** the best or most remarkable: *it's THE place in town for good Mexican food* [Old English *thē*]

the² *adv* used in front of each of two things which are being compared to show how they increase or decrease in relation to each other: *the smaller the baby, the lower its chances of survival* [Old English *thē, thȳ*]

theatre *or US* **theater** *n* **1** a building designed for the performance of plays, operas, etc. **2** a large room or hall with tiered seats for an audience: *a lecture theatre* **3** a room in a hospital equipped for surgical operations **4 the theatre** drama and acting in general **5** a region in which a war or conflict takes place: *a potential theatre of war close to Russian borders* **6** *US, Austral & NZ* same as **cinema** (sense 1) [Greek *theatron*]

theatrical *adj* **1** of or relating to the theatre or dramatic performances **2** exaggerated and affected in manner or behaviour **theatricality** *n* **theatrically** *adv*

theatricals *pl n* dramatic performances, esp. as given by amateurs

thee *pron old-fashioned* the objective form of **thou¹**

theft *n* **1** the act or an instance of stealing: *he reported the theft of his passport* **2** the crime of stealing: *he had a number of convictions for theft* [Old English *thēofth*]

their *adj* of or associated with them: *owning their own land; two girls on their way to school* [Old Norse *theira*]

USAGE See at **they**.

theirs *pron* **1** something or someone belonging to or associated with them: *it was his fault, not theirs* **2 of theirs** belonging to them

theism (**thee**-iz-zum) *n* **1** belief in one God as the creator of everything in the universe **2** belief in the existence of a God or gods [Greek *theos* god] **theist** *n, adj* **theistic** *adj*

them *pron (objective)* refers to things or people other than the speaker or people addressed: *I want you to give this to them* [Old English *thāem*]

USAGE See at **me, they**.

theme *n* **1** the main idea or topic in a discussion or lecture **2** (in literature, music, or art) an idea, image, or motif, repeated or developed throughout a work or throughout an artist's career **3** *music* a group of notes forming a recognizable melodic unit, used as the basis of part or all of a composition **4** a short essay, esp. one set as an exercise for a student [Greek *thema*] **thematic** *adj* **thematically** *adv*

theme park *n* an area planned as a leisure attraction in which all the displays and activities are based on a particular theme, story, or idea: *a Wild West theme park*

theme tune *or* **theme song** *n* a tune or song used to introduce or identify a television or radio programme or performer

themselves *pron* **1 A** the reflexive form of *they* or *them*: *two men barricaded themselves into a cell* **B** used for emphasis: *among the targets were police officers themselves* **2** their normal or usual selves: *they don't seem themselves these days*

then *adv* **1** at that time: *he was then at the height of his sporting career* **2** after that: *let's eat first and then we can explore the town* **3** in that case: *then why did he work for you?* ▷ *pron* **4** that time: *since then the list of grievances has steadily grown* ▷ *adj* **5** existing or functioning at that time: *the then Defence Minister* [Old English *thænne, thanne*]

thence *adv formal* **1** from that place: *the train went south into Switzerland, and thence on to Italy* **2** for that reason; therefore [Middle English *thannes*]

thenceforth *or* **thenceforward** *adv formal* from that time on

theocracy *n, pl* **-cies 1** government by a god or by priests **2** a community under such government [Greek *theos* god + *kratos* power] **theocrat** *n* **theocratic** *adj* **theocratically** *adv*

theodolite (thee-**odd**-oh-lite) *n* an instrument used in surveying for measuring horizontal and vertical angles [origin unknown]

theologian *n* a person versed in the study of theology

theology *n, pl* **-gies 1** the systematic study of religions and religious beliefs **2** a specific system, form, or branch of this study: *Muslim theology* [Greek *theos* god + -LOGY] **theological** *adj* **theologically** *adv*

theorem *n* a proposition, esp. in maths, that can be proved by reasoning from the basic principles of a subject [Greek *theōrein* to view]

theoretical *or* **theoretic** *adj* **1** based on or concerned with the ideas and abstract principles relating to a particular subject rather than its practical uses: *theoretical physics* **2** existing in theory but perhaps not in reality: *the secret service is under the theoretical control of the government* **theoretically** *adv*

theoretician *n* a person who develops or studies the theory of a subject rather than its practical aspects

theorize *or* **-rise** *vb* **-rizing, -rized** *or* **-rising, -rised** to produce or use theories; speculate **theorist** *n*

theory *n, pl* **-ries 1** a set of ideas, based on evidence and careful reasoning, which offers an explanation of how something works or why something happens, but has not been completely proved: *the theory of cosmology* **2** the ideas and abstract knowledge relating to something: *political theory* **3** an idea or opinion: *it's only a theory, admittedly, but I think it's worth pursuing* **4 in theory**

t

in an ideal or hypothetical situation: *in theory, the tax is supposed to limit inflation* [Greek *theōria* a sight]

theosophy *n* a religious or philosophical system claiming to be based on an intuitive insight into the divine nature [Greek *theos* god + *sophia* wisdom] **theosophical** *adj* **theosophist** *n*

therapeutic (ther-rap-**pew**-tik) *adj* of or relating to the treatment and cure of disease [Greek *therapeuein* to minister to] **therapeutically** *adv*

therapeutics *n* the branch of medicine concerned with the treatment of disease

therapy *n, pl* **-pies** the treatment of physical, mental, or social disorders or disease [Greek *therapeia* attendance] **therapist** *n*

there *adv* **1** in, at, or to that place or position: *he won't be there* **2** in that respect: *you're right there* **3 there and then** immediately and without delay: *he walked out there and then* ▷ *adj* **4 not all there** *informal* mentally unsound or silly ▷ *pron* **5** that place: *to return from there* **6** used as a grammatical subject when the true subject follows the verb, esp. the verb 'to be': *there are no children in the house* **7 so there!** an exclamation, used esp. by children, that usually follows a declaration of refusal or defiance: *you can't come, so there!* **8 there you are** *or* **go** **A** an expression used when handing a person something **B** an exclamation of satisfaction or vindication ▷ *interj* **9** an expression of sympathy, for example when consoling a child: *there, there, pet!* [Old English *thǣr*]

> **USAGE** In correct usage, the verb should agree with the number of the subject in such constructions as *there is a man waiting* and *there are several people waiting*. However, where the subject is compound, it is common in speech to use the singular as in *there's a police car and an ambulance outside.*

thereabouts *or US* **thereabout** *adv* near that place, time, amount, etc.: *meet me at three o'clock or thereabouts; Methuselah lived 900 years or thereabouts*

thereafter *adv formal* from that time onwards

thereby *adv formal* by that means or consequently

therefore *adv* for that reason: *the training is long, and therefore expensive*

therein *adv formal* in or into that place or thing

thereof *adv formal* of or concerning that or it

thereto *adv formal* **1** to that or it **2** Also: **thereunto** in addition to that

thereupon *adv formal* immediately after that; at that point

therm *n Brit* a unit of heat equal to 1.055 056 × 10^8 joules [Greek *thermē* heat]

thermal *adj* **1** of, caused by, or generating heat **2** hot or warm: *thermal springs* **3** (of garments) specially made so as to have exceptional heat-retaining qualities: *thermal underwear* ▷ *n* **4** a column of rising air caused by uneven heating of the land surface, and used by gliders and birds to gain height

thermionic valve *or esp US & Canad* **thermionic tube** *n* an electronic valve in which electrons are emitted from a heated rather than a cold cathode

thermistor (therm-**mist**-or) *n physics* a metal-oxide rod whose resistance falls as temperature rises, used in electronic circuits and as a thermometer

thermocouple *n* a device for measuring temperature, consisting of a pair of wires of different metals joined at both ends

thermodynamics *n* the branch of physical science concerned with the relationship between heat and other forms of energy

thermoelectric *or* **thermoelectrical** *adj* of or relating to the conversion of heat energy to electrical energy

thermometer *n* an instrument used to measure temperature, esp. one in which a thin column of liquid, such as mercury, expands and contracts within a sealed tube marked with a temperature scale

thermonuclear *adj* **1** (of a nuclear reaction) involving a nuclear fusion reaction of a type which occurs at very high temperatures **2** (of a weapon) giving off energy as the result of a thermonuclear reaction **3** involving thermonuclear weapons

thermoplastic *adj* **1** (of a material, esp. a synthetic plastic) becoming soft when heated and rehardening on cooling ▷ *n* **2** a synthetic plastic or resin, such as polystyrene

Thermos *or* **Thermos flask** *n trademark* a type of stoppered vacuum flask used to preserve the temperature of its contents

thermosetting *adj* (of a material, esp. a synthetic plastic) hardening permanently after one application of heat and pressure

thermostat *n* a device which automatically regulates the temperature of central heating, an oven, etc., by switching it off or on when it reaches or drops below a particular temperature **thermostatic** *adj* **thermostatically** *adv*

thesaurus (thiss-**sore**-uss) *n, pl* **-ruses** *or* **-ri** a book containing lists of synonyms and related words [Greek *thēsauros* a treasury]

these *adj, pron* the plural of **this**

thesis (**theess**-siss) *n, pl* **-ses** (-seez) **1** a written work resulting from original research, esp. one submitted for a higher degree in a university **2** an opinion supported by reasoned argument: *it is the author's thesis that Britain has yet to come to terms with the loss of its Empire* **3** *logic* an unproved statement put forward as a premise in an argument [Greek: a placing]

Thespian *n* **1** *often facetious* an actor or actress ▷ *adj* **2** of or relating to drama and the theatre [after *Thespis*, a Greek poet]

they *pron (subjective)* **1** refers to people or things other than the speaker or people addressed: *they both giggled* **2** refers to people in general: *they say he adores children* **3** *informal* refers to an individual person, whose sex is either not known or not regarded as important: *someone could have a nasty accident if they tripped over that* [Old Norse *their*]

> **USAGE** It was formerly considered correct to use *he, him,* or *his* after pronouns such as *everyone, no-one, anyone,* or *someone* as in *everyone did his best*, but it is now more common to use *they, them,* or *their,* and this use has become acceptable in all but the most formal contexts: *everyone did their best.*

thiamine *or* **thiamin** *n* vitamin B_1, a vitamin found in the outer coat of rice and other grains, a deficiency of which leads to nervous disorders and to beriberi [Greek *theion* sulphur + VITAMIN]

thick *adj* **1** having a relatively great distance between opposite surfaces: *thick slices* **2** having a specified distance between opposite surfaces: *fifty metres thick* **3** having a dense consistency: *thick fog* **4** consisting of a lot of things grouped closely together: *thick forest* **5** (of clothes) made of heavy cloth or wool: *a thick jumper* **6** *informal* stupid, slow, or insensitive **7** (of an accent) very noticeable: *each word was pronounced in a thick Dutch accent* **8** Also: **thick as thieves** *informal* very friendly **9 a bit thick** *Brit informal* unfair or unreasonable: *£2 an hour, that's a bit thick!* **10 thick with A** covered with a lot of: *glass panels thick with dust* **B** (of a voice) throaty and hard to make out: *his voice was thick with emotion* ▷ *adv* **11** in order to produce something thick: *the machine sliced the potatoes too thick* **12 lay it on thick** *informal* **A** to exaggerate a story **B** to flatter someone excessively **13 thick and fast** quickly and in large numbers: *theories were flying thick and fast* ▷ *n* **14 the thick** the most intense or active part: *in the thick of the fighting* **15 through thick and thin** in good times and bad [Old English *thicce*] **thickly** *adv*

thicken *vb* **1** to make or become thick or thicker **2** to become more complicated: *the plot thickens* **thickener** *n*

thickening *n* **1** something added to a liquid to thicken it **2** a thickened part or piece

thicket *n* a dense growth of small trees or shrubs [Old English *thiccet*]

thickhead *n slang* a stupid or ignorant person **thickheaded** *adj*

thickie *n slang* same as **thicko**

thickness *n* **1** the state or quality of being thick **2** the dimension through an object, as opposed to length or width **3** a layer: *several thicknesses of brown paper*

thicko *n, pl* **thickos** *or* **thickoes** *Brit slang* a slow-witted unintelligent person

thickset *adj* **1** stocky in build **2** planted or placed close together

thick-skinned *adj* insensitive to criticism or hints; not easily upset

thief *n, pl* **thieves** a person who steals something from another [Old English *thēof*] **thievish** *adj*

thieve *vb* **thieving, thieved** to steal other people's possessions [Old English *thēofian*] **thieving** *adj*

thigh *n* the part of the human leg between the hip and the knee [Old English *thēh*]

thighbone *n* same as **femur**

thimble *n* a small metal or plastic cap used to protect the end of the finger from the needle when sewing [Old English *thȳmel* thumbstall]

thin *adj* **thinner, thinnest 1** having a relatively small distance between opposite surfaces: *a thin mattress* **2** much narrower than it is long: *push a thin stick up the pipe in order to clear it* **3** (of a person or animal) having no excess body fat **4** made up of only a few, widely separated, people or things: *thin hair* **5** not dense: *a thin film of dust* **6** unconvincing because badly thought out or badly presented: *the evidence against him was extremely thin* **7** (of a voice) high-pitched and not very loud: *a thin squeaky voice* ▷ *adv* **8** in order to produce something thin: *roll the dough very thin* ▷ *vb* **thinning, thinned 9** to make or become thin or sparse [Old English *thynne*] **thinly** *adv* **thinness** *n*

thine *old-fashioned* ▷ *adj* **1** (*preceding a vowel*) of or associated with you (thou): *if thine eye offend thee, pluck it out!* ▷ *pron* **2** something belonging to you (thou): *the victory shall be thine* [Old English *thīn*]

thing *n* **1** any physical object that is not alive: *there are very few jobs left where people actually make things* **2** an object, fact, circumstance, or concept considered as being a separate entity: *that would be a terrible thing to do* **3** an object or entity that cannot or need not be precisely named: *squares and circles and things* **4** *informal* a person or animal: *pretty little thing, isn't she?* **5** a possession, article of clothing, etc.: *have you brought your swimming things?* **6** *informal* a preoccupation or obsession: *they have this thing about cleaning* **7 do one's own thing** to engage in an activity or mode of behaviour satisfying to one's personality **8 make a thing of** to exaggerate the importance of **9 the thing** the latest fashion [Old English: assembly]

thingumabob *or* **thingamabob** *n informal* a person or thing the name of which is unknown, temporarily forgotten, or deliberately overlooked. Also: **thingumajig, thingamajig, thingummy**

think *vb* **thinking, thought 1** to consider, judge, or believe: *I think that it is scandalous* **2** to make use of the mind, for example in order to make a decision: *I'll need to think about what I'm going to do* **3** to engage in conscious thought: *that made me think* **4** to be considerate enough or remember (to do something): *no other company had thought to bring high tech down to the user* **5 think much** *or* **a lot of** to have a favourable opinion of: *I don't think much of the new design* **6 think of A** to remember or recollect: *I couldn't think of your surname* **B** to conceive of or formulate: *for a long time he couldn't think of a response* **7 think twice** to consider something carefully before making a decision ▷ *n* **8** *informal* a careful open-minded assessment: *she had a long hard think* [Old English *thencan*] **thinker** *n*

thinking *n* **1** opinion or judgment: *contrary to all fashionable thinking* **2** the process of thought ▷ *adj* **3** using intelligent thought: *the thinking man's sport*

think over *vb* to ponder or consider

think-tank *n informal* a group of experts employed to study specific problems

think up *vb* to invent or devise

thinner *n* a solvent, such as turpentine, added to paint or varnish to dilute it

thin-skinned *adj* sensitive to criticism or hints; easily upset

third *adj* **1** of or being number three in a series **2** rated, graded, or ranked below the second level **3** denoting the third from lowest forward gear in a motor vehicle ▷ *n* **4** one of three equal parts of something **5** the fraction equal to one divided by three ($^1/_3$) **6** the third from lowest forward gear in a motor vehicle **7** *Brit* an honours degree of the third and usually the lowest class **8** *music* the interval between one note and the note four semitones (**major third**) or three semitones (**minor third**) higher or lower than it ▷ *adv* **9** Also: **thirdly** in the third place [Old English *thirda*]

third class *n* **1** the class or grade next in value, rank, or quality to the second ▷ *adj* **third-class** **2** of the class or grade next in value, rank, or quality to the second

third degree *n informal* torture or bullying, esp. as used to extort confessions or information

third-degree burn *n* a burn in which both the surface and the underlying layers of the skin are destroyed

third man *n cricket* a fielding position on the off side, near the boundary behind the batsman's wicket

third party *n* **1** a person who is involved in an event, legal proceeding, agreement, or other transaction only by chance or indirectly ▷ *adj* **third-party** **2** *insurance* providing protection against liability caused by accidental injury or death of other people: *third-party cover*

third person *n* the form of a pronoun or verb used to refer to something or someone other than the speaker or the person or people being addressed

third-rate *adj* mediocre or inferior

Third Reich *n* See **Reich**

Third World *n* the developing countries of Africa, Asia, and Latin America collectively

thirst *n* **1** a desire to drink, accompanied by a feeling of dryness in the mouth and throat **2** a craving or yearning: *a thirst for knowledge* ▷ *vb* **3** to feel a thirst [Old English *thurst*]

thirsty *adj* **thirstier, thirstiest** **1** feeling a desire to drink **2** causing thirst: *morris dancing is thirsty work* **3** **thirsty for** feeling an eager desire for: *thirsty for information* **thirstily** *adv*

thirteen *n* **1** the cardinal number that is the sum of ten and three **2** a numeral, 13 or XIII, representing this number **3** something representing or consisting of thirteen units ▷ *adj* **4** amounting to thirteen: *thirteen people* **thirteenth** *adj, n*

t

thirty *n, pl* **-ties** **1** the cardinal number that is the product of ten and three **2** a numeral, 30 or XXX, representing this number **3** something representing or consisting of thirty units ▷ *adj* **4** amounting to thirty: *thirty miles* **thirtieth** *adj, n*

Thirty-nine Articles *pl n* a set of formulas defining the doctrinal position of the Church of England

this *adj* **1** used preceding a noun referring to something or someone that is closer: *on this side of the Channel* **2** used preceding a noun that has just been mentioned or is understood: *this text has two chief goals* **3** used to refer to something about to be mentioned: *NPR's Anne Garrels has this report* **4** used to refer to the present time or occasion: *this week's edition of the newspaper* **5** *informal* used instead of *a* or *the* in telling a story: *the film is about this couple who adopt a child* ▷ *pron* **6** used to denote a person or thing that is relatively close: *black coral like this* **7** used to denote something already mentioned or understood: *this didn't seem fair to me* **8** used to denote something about to be mentioned: *just say this: collect Standish from the top of the fire escape* **9** the present time or occasion: *after this it was impossible to talk to him about his feelings* **10** **this and that** various unspecified and trivial events or facts [Old English *thes, thēos, this* (masculine, feminine, and neuter singular)]

thistle *n* a plant with prickly-edged leaves, dense flower heads, and feathery hairs on the seeds [Old English *thīstel*] **thistly** *adj*

thistledown *n* the mass of feathery plumed seeds produced by a thistle

thither *adv formal* to or towards that place [Old English *thider*]

tho' *or* **tho** *conj, adv US or poetic* same as **though**

thole[1] *or* **tholepin** *n* one of a pair of wooden pins set upright in the gunwale on either side of a rowing boat to serve as a fulcrum in rowing [Old English *tholl*]

thole[2] *vb* **tholing, tholed** *Scot & N English* to bear or put up with

thong *n* **1** a thin strip of leather or other material **2** *US, Canad & Austral* same as **flip-flop** **3** a skimpy article of beachwear consisting of thin strips of leather or cloth attached to a piece of material that covers the genitals while leaving the buttocks bare [Old English *thwang*]

Thor *n Norse myth* the god of thunder

thorax (**thaw**-racks) *n, pl* **thoraxes** *or* **thoraces** (**thaw**-rass-seez) **1** the part of the human body enclosed by the ribs **2** the part of an insect's body between the head and abdomen [Greek: breastplate, chest] **thoracic** *adj*

thorium *n chem* a silvery-white radioactive metallic element. It is used in electronic equipment and as a nuclear power source. Symbol: **Th** [after *Thor*, Norse god of thunder]

thorn *n* **1** a sharp pointed woody projection from a stem or leaf **2** any of various trees or shrubs having thorns, esp. the hawthorn **3** **a thorn in one's side** *or* **flesh** a source of irritation: *he was sufficiently bright at school to become a thorn in the side of his maths teacher* [Old English] **thornless** *adj*

thorny *adj* **thornier, thorniest** **1** covered with thorns **2** difficult or unpleasant: *a thorny issue*

thorough *adj* **1** carried out completely and carefully: *he needs a thorough checkup by the doctor* **2** (of a person) painstakingly careful: *he is very thorough if rather unimaginative* **3** great in extent or degree; utter: *a thorough disgrace* [Old English *thurh* through] **thoroughly** *adv* **thoroughness** *n*

thoroughbred *adj* **1** obtained through successive generations of selective breeding: *thoroughbred horses* ▷ *n* **2** a pedigree animal, esp. a horse

thoroughfare *n* a way through from one place to another: *the great thoroughfare from the Castle to the Palace of Holyrood*

thoroughgoing *adj* **1** extremely thorough **2** absolute or complete: *a thoroughgoing hatred*

those *adj, pron* the plural of **that** [Old English *thās*, plural of *this*]

thou[1] *pron old-fashioned* same as **you** used when talking to one person [Old English *thū*]

thou[2] *n, pl* **thou** *informal* **1** one thousandth of an inch **2** a thousand

though *conj* **1** despite the fact that: *he was smiling with relief and happiness though the tears still flowed down his cheeks* ▷ *adv* **2** nevertheless or however: *he can't dance – he sings well, though* [Old English *thēah*]

thought *vb* **1** the past of **think** ▷ *n* **2** the act or process of thinking **3** a concept or idea **4** ideas typical of a particular time or place: *the development of Western intellectual thought* **5** detailed consideration: *he appeared to give some sort of thought to the question* **6** an intention, hope, or reason for doing something: *his first thought was to call the guard and have the man arrested* [Old English *thōht*]

thoughtful *adj* **1** considerate in the treatment of other people **2** showing careful thought: *a thoughtful and scholarly book* **3** quiet, serious, and deep in thought **thoughtfully** *adv* **thoughtfulness** *n*

thoughtless *adj* not considerate of the feelings of other people **thoughtlessly** *adv* **thoughtlessness** *n*

thousand *n, pl* **-sands** *or* **-sand** **1** the cardinal number that is the product of ten and one hundred **2** a numeral, 1000 or 10^3, representing this number **3** a very large but unspecified number: *thousands of bees swarmed out of the hive* **4** something representing or consisting of 1000 units ▷ *adj* **5** amounting to a thousand: *a thousand members* [Old English *thūsend*] **thousandth** *adj, n*

thrall *n* the state of being completely in the power of, or spellbound by, a person or thing: *he was held in thrall by her almost supernatural beauty* [Old English *thrǣl* slave]

thrash *vb* **1** to beat (someone), esp. with a stick or whip **2** to defeat totally: *the All Blacks thrashed England 24-3* **3** to move about in a wild manner: *his legs stuck and he fell sideways, thrashing about wildly* **4** same as **thresh** ▷ *n* **5** *informal* a party ▷ See also **thrash out** [Old English *therscan*]

thrashing *n* a severe beating

thrash out *vb* to discuss (a problem or difficulty) fully in order to come to an agreement or decision about it: *we must arrange a meeting to thrash out the details of the scheme*

thread *n* **1** a fine strand or fibre of some material **2** a fine cord of twisted yarns, esp. of cotton, used in sewing or weaving **3** something acting as the continuous link or theme of a whole: *the thread of the story* **4** the spiral ridge on a screw, bolt, or nut **5** a very small amount (of something): *there was a thread of nervousness in his voice* **6** a very thin seam of coal or vein of ore ▷ *pl n* **threads** **7** *chiefly US slang* clothes ▷ *vb* **8** to pass thread through the eye of (a needle) before sewing with it **9** to string together: *plastic beads threaded on lengths of nylon line* **10** to make (one's way) through a crowd of people or group of objects: *she threaded and pushed her way through the crowds* [Old English *thrǣd*] **threadlike** *adj*

threadbare *adj* **1** (of cloth, clothing, or a carpet) having the nap worn off so that the threads are exposed **2** having been used or expressed so often as to be no longer interesting: *threadbare ideas* **3** wearing shabby worn-out clothes

threadworm *n* a small threadlike worm that is a parasite of humans

threat *n* **1** a declaration of an intention to inflict harm: *they carried out their threat to kill the hostages* **2** a strong possibility of something dangerous or unpleasant happening: *the wet weather will bring a threat of flooding* **3** a person or thing that is regarded as dangerous and likely to inflict harm: *unemployment is a serious threat to the social order* [Old English *thrēat*]

threaten *vb* **1** to express a threat to (someone): *he threatened John with the sack* **2** to be a threat to: *he was worried about anything that might threaten the health of his child* **3** to be a menacing indication of (something): *the early summer threatened drought* **threatening** *adj* **threateningly** *adv*

three *n* **1** the cardinal number that is the sum of one and two **2** a numeral, 3 or III, representing this number **3** something representing or consisting of three units ▷ *adj* **4** amounting to three: *three days* [Old English *thrēo*]

three-dimensional *or* **3-D** *adj* **1** having three dimensions **2** lifelike or realistic: *all the characters are three-dimensional*

three-decker *n* **1** a warship with guns on three decks **2** anything that has three levels, layers, or tiers

threefold *adj* **1** having three times as many or as much **2** composed of three parts ▷ *adv* **3** by three times as many or as much

three-legged race *n* a race in which pairs of competitors run with their adjacent legs tied together

three-ply *adj* made of three thicknesses, layers, or strands

three-point turn *n* a complete turn of a motor vehicle using forward and reverse gears alternately, and completed after only three movements

three-quarter *adj* **1** amounting to three out of four equal parts of something **2** being three quarters of the normal length: *a three-quarter-length coat* ▷ *n* **3** *rugby* any of the four players between the fullback and the halfbacks

three Rs *pl n* reading, writing, and arithmetic regarded as the three fundamental skills to be taught in primary schools [humorous spelling of *reading, 'riting, and 'rithmetic*]

threescore *adj archaic* sixty

threesome *n* a group of three people

threnody *n, pl* **threnodies** *formal* a lament for the dead [Greek *thrēnōidia*] **threnodic** *adj* **threnodist** *n*

thresh *vb* **1** to beat (stalks of ripe corn, rice, etc.), either with a hand tool or by machine to separate the grain from the husks and straw **2** **thresh about** to toss and turn [Old English *therscan*]

thresher *n* any of a genus of large sharks occurring in tropical and temperate seas. They have a very long whiplike tail

threshold *n* **1** the lower horizontal part of an entrance or doorway, esp. one made of stone or hardwood **2** any doorway or entrance: *he had never been over the threshold of a pub before* **3** the starting point of an experience, event, or venture: *she was on the threshold of a glorious career* **4** the point at which something begins to take effect or be noticeable: *the threshold for basic rate tax; he has a low boredom threshold* [Old English *therscold*]

threw *vb* the past tense of **throw**

thrice *adv literary* **1** three times: *twice or thrice in a lifetime* **2** three times as big, much, etc.: *his vegetables are thrice the size of mine* [Old English *thrīwa, thrīga*]

thrift *n* **1** wisdom and caution with money **2** a low-growing plant of Europe, W Asia, and North America, with narrow leaves and round heads of pink or white flowers [Old Norse: success] **thriftless** *adj*

thrifty *adj* **thriftier, thriftiest** not wasteful with money **thriftily** *adv* **thriftiness** *n*

thrill *n* **1** a sudden sensation of excitement and pleasure: *he felt a thrill of excitement* **2** a situation producing such a sensation: *all the thrills of rafting the meandering Dordogne* **3** a sudden trembling sensation caused by fear or emotional shock ▷ *vb* **4** to feel or cause to feel a thrill **5** to vibrate or quiver [Old English *thȳrlian* to pierce] **thrilling** *adj*

thriller *n* a book, film, or play depicting crime, mystery, or espionage in an atmosphere of excitement and suspense

thrips *n, pl* **thrips** a small slender-bodied insect with piercing mouthparts that feeds on plant sap [Greek: woodworm]

thrive *vb* **thriving, thrived** *or* **throve, thrived** *or* **thriven 1** to do well; be successful: *Munich has thrived as a centre of European commerce* **2** to grow strongly and vigorously: *the vine can thrive in the most unlikely soils* [Old Norse *thrīfask* to grasp for oneself]

thro' *or* **thro** *prep, adv informal* same as **through**

throat *n* **1** the passage from the mouth and nose to the stomach and lungs **2** the front part of the neck **3 at each other's throats** quarrelling or fighting with each other **4 cut one's own throat** to bring about one's own ruin **5 cut someone's throat** to kill someone **6 ram** *or* **force something down someone's throat** to insist that someone listen to or accept something **7 stick in one's throat** to be hard to accept: *his arrogance really sticks in my throat* [Old English *throtu*]

throaty *adj* **throatier, throatiest 1** hoarse and suggestive of a sore throat: *a throaty 40 fags-a-day bark* **2** deep, husky, or guttural: *she gives a deliciously throaty laugh*

t

throb *vb* **throbbing, throbbed 1** to pulsate or beat repeatedly, esp. with abnormally strong force: *her eardrums were throbbing with pain* **2** (of engines, drums, etc.) to have a strong rhythmic vibration or beat ▷ *n* **3** the act or sensation of throbbing: *he felt a throb of fear; the throb of the engines* [imitative] **throbbing** *adj, n*

throes *pl n* **1** violent pangs, pain, or convulsions: *an animal in its death throes* **2 in the throes of** struggling to cope with (something difficult or disruptive): *in the throes of a civil war* [Old English *thrāwu* threat]

thrombosis (throm-**boh**-siss) *n, pl* **-ses** (-seez) coagulation of the blood in the heart or in a blood vessel, forming a blood clot [Greek: curdling] **thrombotic** (throm-**bot**-ik) *adj*

throne *n* **1** the ceremonial seat occupied by a monarch or bishop on occasions of state **2** the rank or power of a monarch: *she came to the throne after her father was murdered* [Greek *thronos*]

throng *n* **1** a great number of people or things crowded together ▷ *vb* **2** to gather in or fill (a place) in large numbers: *streets thronged with shoppers* [Old English *gethrang*]

throstle *n poetic* a song thrush [Old English]

throttle *n* **1** a device that controls the fuel-and-air mixture entering an engine ▷ *vb* **-tling, -tled 2** to kill or injure (someone) by squeezing his or her throat **3** to suppress or censor: *the government is trying to throttle dissent* [Middle English *throtel* throat]

throttle back *vb* to reduce the speed of a vehicle or aircraft by reducing the quantity of fuel entering the engine: *throttling back the engine failed to bring the plane under control*

through *prep* **1** going in at one side and coming out at the other side of: *he drove through the West of the city* **2** occupying or visiting several points scattered around in (an area): *a journey through the Scottish Highlands* **3** as a result of: *she retired through ill health* **4** during: *driving for five hours through the night* **5** for all of (a period): *it rained all through that summer* **6** *chiefly US* up to and including: *from Monday through Saturday* ▷ *adj* **7** finished: *I'm through with history* **8** having completed a specified amount of an activity: *he tried to stop the investigation halfway through* **9** (on a telephone line) connected **10** no longer able to function successfully in some specified capacity: *they are through, they haven't got a chance* **11** (of a train, plane flight, etc.) going directly to a place, so that passengers do not have to change: *the first ever through train between Singapore and Bangkok* ▷ *adv* **12** through a thing, place, or period of time: *the script gives up around halfway through* **13** extremely or absolutely: *I'm soaked through* **14 through and through** to the greatest possible extent: *the boards are rotten through and through* [Old English *thurh*]

throughout *prep* **1** through the whole of (a place or a period of time): *radio stations throughout the UK* ▷ *adv* **2** through the whole of a place or a period of time: *I led both races throughout*

throughput *n* the amount of material processed in a given period, esp. by a computer

throve *vb* a past tense of **thrive**

throw *vb* **throwing, threw, thrown 1** to hurl (something) through the air, esp. with a rapid motion of the arm **2** to put or move suddenly, carelessly, or violently: *she threw her arms round his neck* **3** to bring into a specified state or condition, esp. suddenly: *the invasion threw the region into turmoil* **4** to move (a switch or lever) so as to engage or disengage a mechanism **5** to cause (someone) to fall: *I'm riding the horse that threw me* **6 A** to tip (dice) out onto a flat surface **B** to obtain (a specified number) in this way: *one throws a 3 and the other throws a 5* **7** to shape (clay) on a potter's wheel **8** to give (a party) **9** *informal* to confuse or disconcert: *the question threw me* **10** to direct or cast (a look, light, etc.): *the lamp threw a shadow on the ceiling* **11** to project (the voice) so as to make it appear to come from somewhere else **12** *informal* to lose (a contest) deliberately **13 throw a punch** to strike, or attempt to strike, someone with one's fist **14 throw oneself at** to behave in a way which makes it clear that one is trying to win the affection of (someone) **15 throw oneself into** to involve oneself enthusiastically in **16 throw oneself on** to rely entirely upon (someone's goodwill, etc.): *the president threw himself on the mercy of the American people* ▷ *n* **17** the act or an instance of throwing **18** the distance thrown: *a throw of 90 metres* **19** (in sports such as wrestling or judo) a move which causes one's opponent to fall to the floor **20** a decorative blanket or cover **21 a throw** each: *we drank our way through a couple of bottles of claret at £12.50 a throw* ▷ See also **throwaway**, **throwback** *etc.* [Old English *thrāwan* to turn, torment]

throwaway *adj* **1** said or done incidentally: *a throwaway line* **2** designed to be discarded after use: *throwaway cups* ▷ *vb* **throw away 3** to get rid of or discard: *try to recycle glass bottles instead of simply throwing them away* **4** to fail to make good use of: *she threw away the chance of a brilliant career when she got married*

throwback *n* **1** a person or thing that is like something that existed or was common long ago: *his ideas were a throwback to old colonial attitudes* ▷ *vb* **throw back 2** to remind someone of (something he or she said or did previously) in order to upset him or her: *he threw back at me everything I'd said the week before*

throw in *vb* **1** to add at no additional cost: *he'd got good at bargaining them down, making them throw in variations for free* **2** to contribute (a remark) in a discussion **3 throw in the towel** *informal* to give in; accept defeat ▷ *n* **throw-in 4** *soccer etc.* the act of putting the ball back into play when it has gone over one of the sidelines, by throwing it over one's head with both hands

throw off *vb* **1** to take off (clothing) hurriedly **2** *literary* to free oneself of: *Vietnamese farmers threw off their dependency on European seed potatoes*

throw out *vb* **1** to discard or reject: *the court threw out the case* **2** to expel or dismiss, esp. forcibly: *her parents threw her out when they discovered she was pregnant*

throw over *vb old-fashioned* to leave or reject (a lover)

throw together *vb* **1** to assemble (something) hurriedly **2** (of a set of circumstances) to cause (people) to meet and get to know each other

throw up *vb* **1** *informal* to vomit **2** to give up or abandon: *he would threaten to throw up his job* **3** to construct (a building or structure) hastily **4** to produce: *these links are throwing up fresh opportunities*

thru *prep, adv, adj chiefly US* same as **through**

thrum *vb* **thrumming, thrummed 1** to strum rhythmically but without expression on (a musical instrument) **2** to make a low beating or humming sound: *the air conditioner thrummed* ▷ *n* **3** a repetitive strumming [imitative]

thrush[1] *n* any of a large group of songbirds, esp. one having a brown plumage with a spotted breast, such as the mistle thrush and song thrush [Old English *thrȳsce*]

thrush[2] *n* **1** a fungal disease, esp. of infants, in which whitish spots form on the mouth, throat, and lips **2** a genital infection caused by the same fungus [origin unknown]

thrust *vb* **thrusting, thrust 1** to push (someone or something) with force: *he took him by the arm and thrust him towards the door* **2** to force (someone) into some condition or situation: *unemployed people have been thrust into the front line of politics* **3** to force (one's way) through a crowd, forest, etc.: *Edward thrust his way towards them* **4** to stick out or up: *she thrust out her lower lip* ▷ *n* **5** a forceful drive, push, stab, or lunge: *the thrust of his spear* **6** a force, esp. one that produces motion **7** the propulsive force produced by the pressure of air and gas forced out of a jet engine or rocket engine **8** the essential or most forceful part: *the main thrust of the report* **9** *physics* a continuous pressure exerted by one part of an object against another **10** *informal* intellectual or emotional drive; forcefulness: *thanks to the ingenuity and enterprising thrust of this company* [Old Norse *thrȳsta*]

thrusting *adj* ambitious and having great drive: *a thrusting young executive*

thud *n* **1** a dull heavy sound **2** a blow or fall that causes such a sound ▷ *vb* **thudding, thudded 3** to make or cause to make such a sound [Old English *thyddan* to strike]

thug *n* a tough and violent man, esp. a criminal [Hindi *thag* thief] **thuggery** *n* **thuggish** *adj*

thulium *n chem* a silvery-grey element of the lanthanide series. Symbol: **Tm** [after *Thule*, a region thought by ancient geographers to be northernmost in the world]

thumb *n* **1** the short thick finger of the hand, set apart from the others **2** the part of a glove shaped to fit the thumb **3 all thumbs** very clumsy **4 thumbs down** an indication of refusal or disapproval **5 thumbs up** an indication of encouragement or approval **6 under someone's thumb** completely under someone else's control ▷ *vb* **7** to touch, mark, or move with the thumb: *he thumbed the volume switch to maximum* **8** to attempt to obtain (a lift in a motor vehicle) by signalling with the thumb: *he thumbed a lift to the station* **9 thumb one's nose at** to behave in a way that shows one's contempt or disregard for: *her mother had always thumbed her nose at convention* **10 thumb through** to flip the pages of (a book or magazine) in order to glance at the contents [Old English *thūma*]

thumb index *n* a series of notches cut into the fore-edge of a book to facilitate quick reference

thumbnail *n* **1** the nail of the thumb ▷ *adj* **2** concise and brief: *a thumbnail sketch*

thumbscrew *n* (formerly) an instrument of torture that pinches or crushes the thumbs

thumbtack *n* the US and Canadian term for **drawing pin**

thump *n* **1** the sound of something heavy hitting a comparatively soft surface **2** a heavy blow with the hand ▷ *vb* **3** to place (something) on or bang against (something) with a loud dull sound: *thumping the table is aggressive* **4** to hit or punch (someone): *stop that at once or I'll thump you!* **5** to throb or beat violently: *he could feel his heart thumping* [imitative]

thumping *adj slang* huge or excessive: *a thumping majority*

thunder *n* **1** a loud cracking or deep rumbling noise caused by the rapid expansion of atmospheric gases that are suddenly heated by

lightning **2** any loud booming sound: *the thunder of heavy gunfire* **3** **steal someone's thunder** to lessen the effect of someone's idea or action by anticipating it ▹ *vb* **4** to make a loud noise like thunder: *an explosion thundered through the shaft* **5** to speak in a loud, angry manner: *'Get out of here this instant!' he thundered* **6** to move fast, heavily, and noisily: *a lorry thundered by* [Old English *thunor*]
thundery *adj*

thunderbolt *n* **1** a flash of lightning accompanying thunder **2** something sudden and unexpected: *his career has been no thunderbolt* **3** *myth* a weapon thrown to earth by certain gods **4** *sport* a very fast-moving shot or serve

thunderclap *n* **1** a loud outburst of thunder **2** something as violent or unexpected as a clap of thunder

thundercloud *n* a large dark electrically charged cloud associated with thunderstorms

thundering *old-fashioned slang* ▹ *adj* **1** extreme: *a thundering disgrace* ▹ *adv* **2** extremely: *thundering good music*

thunderous *adj* **1** resembling thunder in loudness: *thunderous applause* **2** threatening or angry: *a thunderous scowl*

thunderstorm *n* a storm with thunder and lightning and usually heavy rain or hail

thunderstruck *adj* amazed or shocked

thurible (thyoor-rib-bl) *n* same as **censer** [Latin *turibulum*]

Thurs. Thursday

Thursday *n* the fifth day of the week [Old English *Thursdæg* Thor's day]

thus *adv* **1** as a result or consequence: *the platforms provided a new floor and thus improved and enlarged the premises* **2** in this manner: *I sat thus for nearly half an hour* **3** to such a degree: *the competition has been almost bereft of surprise thus far* [Old English]

thwack *vb* **1** to beat with something flat ▹ *n* **2** **A** a blow with something flat **B** the sound made by it [imitative]

thwart *vb* **1** to prevent or foil: *they inflicted such severe losses that they thwarted the invasion* ▹ *n* **2** the seat across a boat where the rower sits [Old Norse *thvert* across]

t

thy *adj old-fashioned* belonging to or associated in some way with you (thou): *love thy neighbour* [variant of *thine*]

thyme (time) *n* a small shrub with white, pink, or red flowers and scented leaves used for seasoning food [Greek *thumon*]

thymol *n* a white crystalline substance obtained from thyme, used as a fungicide and an antiseptic

thymus (thigh-muss) *n, pl* **-muses** *or* **-mi** (-my) *anatomy* a small gland situated near the base of the neck [Greek *thumos* sweetbread]

thyroid *anatomy* ▹ *adj* **1** of or relating to the thyroid gland **2** of or relating to the largest cartilage of the larynx, which forms the Adam's apple in men ▹ *n* **3** the thyroid gland [Greek *thureos* oblong shield]

thyroid gland *n anatomy* an endocrine gland that secretes hormones that control metabolism and body growth

thyself *pron old-fashioned* the reflexive form of **thou'**

ti *n music* same as **te**

Ti *chem* titanium

tiara *n* **1** a semicircular jewelled headdress worn by some women on formal occasions **2** the triple-tiered crown sometimes worn by the pope [Greek]

tibia (tib-ee-a) *n, pl* **tibiae** (tib-ee-ee) *or* **tibias** the inner and thicker of the two bones of the human leg below the knee; shinbone [Latin: leg, pipe]
tibial *adj*

tic *n* a spasmodic muscular twitch [French]

tick[1] *n* **1** a mark (✓) used to check off or indicate the correctness of something **2** a recurrent metallic tapping or clicking sound, such as that made by a clock **3** *informal* a moment or instant: *won't be a tick* ▹ *vb* **4** to mark or check with a tick **5** to produce a recurrent tapping sound or indicate by such a sound: *the clock ticked away* **6** **what makes someone tick** *informal* the basic motivation of a person ▹ See also **tick off**, **tick over** [Low German *tikk* touch]

tick[2] *n* a small parasitic creature typically living on the skin of warm-blooded animals and feeding on the blood and tissues of their hosts: *a sheep tick* [Old English *ticca*]

tick[3] *n Brit & NZ informal* account or credit: *a spending spree that was financed on tick* [from *ticket*]

ticker *n slang* the heart

ticker tape *n* (formerly) a continuous paper tape on which current stock quotations were printed by machine

ticket *n* **1** a printed piece of paper or cardboard showing that the holder is entitled to certain rights, such as travel on a train or bus or entry to a place of public entertainment **2** a label or tag attached to an article showing information such as its price and size **3** an official notification of a parking or traffic offence **4** the declared policy of a political party **5** **that's (just) the ticket** *informal* that's the right or appropriate thing ▹ *vb* **-eting, -eted** **6** to issue or attach a ticket or tickets to [Old French *etiquet*]

tickets *pl n S African informal* death or ruin; the end

ticking *n* a strong cotton fabric, often striped, used esp. for mattress and pillow covers [probably from Middle Dutch *tīke*]

tickle *vb* **-ling, -led** **1** to touch or stroke (someone), so as to produce laughter or a twitching sensation **2** to itch or tingle **3** to amuse or please **4** **tickled pink** *or* **to death** *informal* greatly pleased **5** **tickle someone's fancy** to appeal to or amuse someone ▹ *n* **6** a sensation of light stroking or itching: *a tickle in the throat* **7** the act of tickling **8** *Canad* (in the Atlantic Provinces) a narrow strait [Middle English *titelen*]

ticklish *adj* **1** sensitive to being tickled **2** delicate or difficult: *a ticklish problem*

tick off *vb* **1** to mark with a tick, esp. to show that an item on a list has been dealt with **2** *informal* to reprimand or scold (someone)
ticking-off *n*

tick over *vb* **1** (of an engine) to run at low speed with the transmission disengaged **2** to run smoothly without any major changes: *the business is just ticking over*

ticktack *n Brit & Austral* a system of sign language, mainly using the hands, by which bookmakers transmit their odds to each other at race courses
ticktock *n* a ticking sound made by a clock
tidal *adj* **1** (of a river, lake, or sea) having tides **2** of or relating to tides: *a tidal surge*
tidal wave *n* **1** *not in technical use* same as **tsunami** **2** an unusually large incoming wave, often caused by high winds and spring tides **3** a forceful and widespread movement in public opinion, action, etc.: *a tidal wave of scandals and embezzlement*
tiddler *n informal* **1** a very small fish, esp. a stickleback **2** a small child [perhaps from TIDDLY[1]]
tiddly[1] *adj* **-dlier, -dliest** *Brit* very small [childish variant of *little*]
tiddly[2] *adj* **-dlier, -dliest** *informal, chiefly Brit* slightly drunk [origin unknown]
tiddlywinks *n* a game in which players try to flick discs of plastic into a cup [origin unknown]
tide *n* **1** the alternate rise and fall of sea level caused by the gravitational pull of the sun and moon **2** the current caused by these changes in level: *I got caught by the tide and almost drowned* **3** a widespread tendency or movement: *the rising tide of nationalism* **4** *literary or old-fashioned* a season or time: *Yuletide* [Old English *tīd* time]
tideline *n* the mark or line left by the tide when it retreats from its highest point
tidemark *n* **1** a mark left by the highest or lowest point of a tide **2** *chiefly Brit & NZ* a line of dirt left round a bath after the water has been drained away **3** *informal, chiefly Brit* a dirty mark on the skin, indicating the extent to which someone has washed
tide over *vb* **tiding, tided** to help (someone) to get through a period of difficulty or distress: *they need some form of Social Security to tide them over*
tidings *pl n* information or news [Old English *tīdung*]
tidy *adj* **-dier, -diest** **1** neat and orderly **2** *Brit, Austral & NZ informal* quite large: *a tidy sum of money* ▷ *vb* **-dies, -dying, -died** **3** to put (things) in their proper place; make neat: *I've tidied up the toys under the bed* ▷ *n, pl* **-dies** **4** a small container for odds and ends [(originally: timely, excellent) from *tide*] **tidily** *adv* **tidiness** *n*
tie *vb* **tying, tied** **1** to fasten or be fastened with string, rope, etc.: *a parcel tied with string* **2** to make a knot or bow in (something): *hang on while I tie my laces* **3** to restrict or limit: *they had children and were consequently tied to the school holidays* **4** to equal the score of a competitor or fellow candidate: *three players tied for second place* ▷ *n* **5** a long narrow piece of material worn, esp. by men, under the collar of a shirt, tied in a knot close to the throat with the ends hanging down the front **6** a bond or link: *he still has close ties to the town where he grew up* **7** a string, wire, etc., with which something is tied **8** *Brit sport* a match in a knockout competition: *whoever wins the tie will play Australia in the semi-finals* **9** **A** a result in a match or competition in which the scores or times of some of the competitors are the same: *a tie for second place* **B** the match or competition in which the scores or results are equal **10** a regular commitment that limits a person's freedom: *it's a bit of a tie having to visit him every day* **11** something which supports or links parts of a structure **12** *US & Canad* a sleeper on a railway track **13** *music* a curved line connecting two notes of the same pitch indicating that the sound is to be prolonged for their joint time value ▷ See also **tie in, tie up** [Old English *tīgan*]
tie-break *or* **tie-breaker** *n* an extra game or question that decides the result of a contest that has ended in a draw
tied *adj Brit* **1** (of a public house) allowed to sell beer from only one particular brewery **2** (of a house) rented out to the tenant for as long as he or she is employed by the owner
tie-dye, tie-dyed *or* **tie and dye** *adj* (of a garment or fabric) dyed in a pattern by tying sections of the cloth together so that they will not absorb the dye: *a tie-dye T-shirt*
tie in *vb* **1** to have or cause to have a close link or connection: *there's no evidence to tie this killing in with the murder of Mrs McGowan* ▷ *n* **tie-in** **2** a link or connection **3** a book or other product that is linked with a film or TV programme
tiepin *n* an ornamental pin used to pin the two ends of a tie to a shirt
tier *n* one of a set of rows placed one above and behind the other, such as theatre seats [Old French *tire*]
tie up *vb* **1** to bind (someone or something) securely with string or rope **2** to moor (a vessel) **3** to commit (money, etc.) so that it is unavailable for other uses: *people don't want to tie up their savings for a long period* ▷ *n* **tie-up** **4** a link or connection
tiff *n* a minor quarrel [origin unknown]
tiffin *n* (in India) a light meal, esp. at midday [probably from obsolete *tiff* to sip]
tiger *n* **1** a large Asian mammal of the cat family which has a tawny yellow coat with black stripes **2** a dynamic, forceful, or cruel person **3** a country, esp. in E Asia, that is achieving rapid economic growth [Greek *tigris*]
tiger lily *n* a lily of China and Japan with black-spotted orange flowers
tiger moth *n* a moth with conspicuously striped and spotted wings
tiger snake *n* a highly venomous brown-and-yellow Australian snake
tight *adj* **1** stretched or drawn taut: *loosening-up of tight muscles* **2** closely fitting: *wearing a jacket that was too tight for him* **3** made, fixed, or closed firmly and securely: *a tight band* **4** constructed so as to prevent the passage of water, air, etc.: *watertight; airtight* **5** cramped and allowing very little room for movement: *they squeezed him into the tight space* **6** unyielding or stringent: *tight security* **7** (of a situation) difficult or dangerous **8** allowing only the minimum time or money for doing something: *we have been working to a tight schedule* **9** *Brit, Austral & NZ informal* mean or miserly **10** (of a match or game) very close or even **11** *old-fashioned, informal* drunk **12** (of a corner or turn) turning through a large angle in a short distance: *the boat skidded round in a tight turn* ▷ *adv* **13** in a close, firm, or secure way: *they held each*

other tight [Old Norse *thēttr* of close texture] **tightly** *adv* **tightness** *n*

tighten *vb* to make or become tight or tighter

tight-fisted *adj* unwilling to spend money; mean

tightknit *adj* closely integrated: *a tightknit community*

tight-lipped *adj* **1** unwilling to give any information; secretive: *the Minister remained tight-lipped when it came to answering the press's questions* **2** with the lips pressed tightly together, as through anger: *tight-lipped determination*

tightrope *n* a rope stretched taut on which acrobats perform

tights *pl n* a one-piece clinging garment covering the body from the waist to the feet, worn by women and also by acrobats, dancers, etc.

tigress *n* **1** a female tiger **2** a fierce, cruel, or passionate woman

tik *n S African slang* crystal methamphetamine

tike *n* same as **tyke**

tiki (**tee**-kee) *n* a Māori greenstone neck ornament in the form of a fetus [Māori]

tikka *adj Indian cookery* (of meat) marinated in spices and then dry-roasted: *chicken tikka*

tilde *n* a mark (˜) used in some languages to indicate that the letter over which it is placed is pronounced in a certain way, as in Spanish *señor* [Spanish]

tile *n* **1** a thin piece of ceramic, plastic, etc., used with others to cover a surface, such as a floor or wall **2** a rectangular block used as a playing piece in mah jong and other games **3 on the tiles** *informal* out having a good time and drinking a lot ▷ *vb* **tiling, tiled 4** to cover (a surface) with tiles [Latin *tegula*] **tiled** *adj* **tiler** *n*

tiling *n* **1** tiles collectively **2** something made of or surfaced with tiles

till[1] *conj, prep* same as **until** [Old English *til*]

> **USAGE** *Till* is a variant of *until* that is acceptable at all levels of language. *Until* is, however, often preferred at the beginning of a sentence in formal writing: *until his behaviour improves, he cannot become a member.*

till[2] *vb* to cultivate (land) for the raising of crops: *a constant round of sowing, tilling and harvesting* [Old English *tilian* to try, obtain] **tillable** *adj* **tiller** *n*

till[3] *n* a box or drawer into which money taken from customers is put, now usually part of a cash register [origin unknown]

tillage *n* **1** the act, process, or art of tilling **2** tilled land

tiller *n naut* a handle used to turn the rudder when steering a boat [Anglo-French *teiler* beam of a loom]

tilt *vb* **1** to move into a sloping position with one end or side higher than the other: *Dave tilted his chair back on two legs* **2** to move (part of the body) slightly upwards or to the side: *Marie tilted her head back* **3** to become more influenced by a particular idea or group: *the party is tilting more and more to the right* **4** to compete against someone in a jousting contest ▷ *n* **5** a slope or angle: *a tilt to one side* **6** the act of tilting **7 A** a jousting contest, esp. in medieval Europe **B** a thrust with a lance delivered during a medieval tournament **8** an attempt to win a contest: *a tilt at the world title* **9 at full tilt** at full speed or force [Old English *tealtian*]

tilth *n* **1** the tilling of land **2** the condition of land that has been tilled

timber *n* **1** wood as a building material **2** trees collectively **3** a wooden beam in the frame of a house, boat, etc. ▷ *adj* **4** made out of timber: *timber houses* **5** of or involved in the production or sale of wood as a building material: *a timber merchant* [Old English] **timbered** *adj* **timbering** *n*

timber limit *n Canad* **1** the area to which rights of cutting timber, granted by a government licence, are limited **2** same as **timber line**

timber line *n* the geographical limit beyond which trees will not grow

timbre (**tam**-bra) *n* the distinctive quality of sound produced by a particular voice or musical instrument [French]

timbrel *n chiefly Bible* a tambourine [Old French]

Timbuktu *or* **Timbuctoo** (tim-buck-**too**) *n* any distant or outlandish place: *we could run our office from Timbuktu as long as there was a good Wi-Fi connection* [after *Timbuktu*, town in Africa]

time *n* **1** the past, present, and future regarded as a continuous whole. Related adjective: **temporal** **2** *physics* a quantity measuring duration, measured with reference to the rotation of the earth or from the vibrations of certain atoms **3** a specific point in time expressed in hours and minutes: *what time are you going?* **4** a system of reckoning for expressing time: *the deadline is 5:00 Eastern Time today* **5** an unspecified interval; a while: *some recover for a time and then relapse* **6** an instance or occasion: *when was the last time you saw it?* **7** a sufficient interval or period: *I need time to think* **8** an occasion or period of specified quality: *they'd had a lovely time* **9** a suitable moment: *the time has come to make peace* **10** a period or point marked by specific attributes or events: *in Victorian times* **11** *Brit* the time at which licensed premises are required by law to stop selling alcoholic drinks **12** the rate of pay for work done in normal working hours: *you get double time for working on a Sunday* **13 A** the system of combining beats in music into successive groupings by which the rhythm of the music is established **B** a specific system having a specific number of beats in each grouping or bar: *duple time* **14 against time** in an effort to complete something in a limited period **15 ahead of time** before the deadline **16 at one time A** once or formerly **B** simultaneously **17 at the same time A** simultaneously **B** nevertheless or however **18 at times** sometimes **19 beat time** to indicate the tempo of a piece of music by waving a baton, hand, etc. **20 do time** *informal* to serve a term in jail **21 for the time being** for the moment; temporarily **22 from time to time** at intervals; occasionally **23 have no time for** to have no patience with **24 in no time** very quickly **25 in one's own time A** outside paid working hours **B** at the speed of one's choice **26 in time A** early or at the appointed time: *he made it to the hospital in time for the baby's arrival* **B** eventually: *in time, the children of intelligent parents will come to dominate* **C** *music* at a correct metrical or rhythmic pulse **27 make time** to find an opportunity **28 on time** at the expected or scheduled time **29 pass the time** to occupy oneself when there is nothing else to do: *they pass the time watching game shows on television* **30 pass the time of day** to have a short casual conversation (with someone) **31 time and again** frequently **32 time of one's life** a memorably enjoyable time **33 time out of mind** from long before anyone can remember ▷ *vb* **timing, timed 34** to measure the speed or duration of: *my Porsche was timed at 128 mph* **35** to set a time for: *the attack was timed for 6 am* **36** to do (something) at a suitable time: *her entry could not have been better timed* ▷ *adj* **37** operating automatically at or for a set time: *an electrical time switch* ▷ *interj* **38** the word called out by a publican signalling that it is closing time ▷ See also **times** [Old English *tīma*]

time and a half *n* a rate of pay one and a half times the normal rate, often offered for overtime work

time-and-motion study *n* the analysis of work procedures to work out the most efficient methods of operation

time bomb *n* **1** a bomb containing a timing mechanism that is set so that the bomb will explode at a specified time **2** something that will have a large, often damaging, effect at a later date: *the decline of the manufacturing industry is a political time bomb*

time capsule *n* a container holding articles representative of the current age, buried for discovery in the future

time clock *n* a clock with a device for recording the time of arrival or departure of an employee

time-consuming *adj* taking up a great deal of time

time exposure *n* a photograph produced by exposing film for a relatively long period, usually a few seconds

time-honoured *adj* having been used or done for a long time and established by custom

timekeeper *n* **1** a person or thing that keeps or records time, for instance at a sporting event **2** an employee with a record of punctuality as specified: *a poor timekeeper* **timekeeping** *n*

time lag *n* a gap or delay between one event and a related event that happens after it: *the time lag between the development and the marketing of new products*

timeless *adj* **1** unaffected by time or by changes in fashion, society, etc.: *the timeless appeal of tailored wool jackets* **2** eternal and everlasting: *the timeless universal reality behind all religions* **timelessness** *n*

timely *adj* **-lier, -liest**, *adv* at the right or an appropriate time

time-out *n* **1** *sport, chiefly US, Canad & Austral* an interruption in play during which players rest, discuss tactics, etc. **2 take time out** to take a break from a job or activity

timepiece *n* a device, such as a clock or watch, which measures and indicates time

timer *n* a device for measuring time, esp. a switch or regulator that causes a mechanism to operate at a specific time

times *prep* multiplied by: *ten times four is forty*

timescale *n* the period of time within which events occur or are due to occur

time-served *adj* having successfully completed an apprenticeship or period of training: *a time-served electrician*

timeserver *n* a person who changes his or her views in order to gain support or favour

time-share *n* a holiday property that is owned by several people under a time-sharing scheme

time sharing *n* **1** a system of part ownership of a property for use as a holiday home whereby each participant owns the property for a particular period every year **2** a system by which users at different terminals of a computer can communicate with it at the same time

time signature *n music* a sign, usually consisting of two figures placed after the key signature, that indicates the number and length of beats in the bar

timetable *n* **1** a plan of the times when a job or activity should be done: *the timetable for the Royal Visit* **2** a list of departure and arrival times of trains or buses: *a timetable hung on the wall beside the ticket office* **3** a plan of the times when different subjects or classes are taught in a school or college: *a heavy timetable of lectures and practical classes* ▷ *vb* **-tabling, -tabled 4** to set a time when a particular thing should be done: *the meeting is timetabled for 3 o'clock*

time value *n music* the duration of a note relative to other notes in a composition and considered in relation to the basic tempo

time warp *n* an imagined distortion of the progress of time, so that, for instance, events from the past seem to be happening in the present

timeworn *adj* **1** showing the adverse effects of overlong use or of old age: *a timeworn café* **2** having been used so often as to be no longer interesting: *a timeworn cliché*

time zone *n* a region throughout which the same standard time is used

timid *adj* **1** lacking courage or self-confidence: *a timid youth* **2** indicating shyness or fear: *a timid and embarrassed smile* [Latin *timere* to fear] **timidity** *n* **timidly** *adv*

timing *n* the ability to judge when to do or say something so as to make the best effect, for instance in the theatre, in playing an instrument, or in hitting a ball in sport

timorous (tim-mor-uss) *adj literary* lacking courage or self-confidence: *a reclusive timorous creature* [Latin *timor* fear] **timorously** *adv*

timpani *or* **tympani** (tim-pan-ee) *pl n* a set of kettledrums [Italian] **timpanist** *or* **tympanist** *n*

tin *n* **1** a soft silvery-white metallic element. Symbol: **Sn 2** a sealed airtight metal container used for preserving and storing food or drink: *a cupboard full of packets and tins* **3** any metal container: *a tin of paint* **4** the contents of a tin **5** *Brit, Austral & NZ* galvanized iron, used to make roofs ▷ *vb* **tinning, tinned 6** to put (food) into tins [Old English]

tin can *n* a metal food container

tincture *n* a medicine consisting of a small amount of a drug dissolved in alcohol [Latin *tinctura* a dyeing]

tinder *n* dry wood or other easily-burning material used to start a fire [Old English *tynder*] **tindery** *adj*
tinderbox *n* (formerly) a small box for tinder, esp. one fitted with a flint and steel which could be used to make a spark
tine *n* a slender prong of a fork or a deer's antler [Old English *tind*] **tined** *adj*
tinfoil *n* a paper-thin sheet of metal, used for wrapping foodstuffs
ting *n* a high metallic sound such as that made by a small bell [imitative]
ting-a-ling *n* the sound of a small bell
tinge *n* **1** a slight tint or colouring: *his skin had an unhealthy greyish tinge* **2** a very small amount: *both goals had a tinge of fortune* ▷ *vb* **tingeing** *or* **tinging, tinged 3** to colour or tint faintly: *the sunset tinged the lake with pink* **4 tinged with** having a small amount of a particular quality: *the victory was tinged with sadness* [Latin *tingere* to colour]
tingle *vb* **-gling, -gled 1** to feel a mild prickling or stinging sensation, as from cold or excitement ▷ *n* **2** a mild prickling or stinging feeling [probably a variant of *tinkle*] **tingling** *adj* **tingly** *adj*
tin god *n* a self-important person
tinker *n* **1** (esp. formerly) a travelling mender of pots and pans **2** *Scot & Irish, usually derogatory* a traveller **3** a mischievous child ▷ *vb* **4 tinker with** to try to repair or improve (something) by making lots of minor adjustments [origin unknown]
tinker's damn *or* **tinker's cuss** *n* **not give a tinker's damn** *or* **cuss** *slang* not to care at all
tinkle *vb* **-kling, -kled 1** to ring with a high tinny sound like a small bell ▷ *n* **2** a high clear ringing sound **3** *Brit old-fashioned, informal* a telephone call [imitative] **tinkly** *adj*
tinned *adj* (of food) preserved by being sealed in a tin
tinny¹ *adj* **-nier, -niest 1** (of a sound) high, thin, and metallic: *the tinny sound of a transistor radio* **2** cheap or shoddy: *tinny little cars*
tinny² *adj* **-nier, -niest** *Austral & NZ slang* lucky
tin-opener *n* a small tool for opening tins
Tin Pan Alley *n* the popular music industry, esp. the more commercial aspects of it
tin plate *n* thin steel sheet coated with a layer of tin to protect it from corrosion
tinpot *adj informal* worthless or unimportant: *a tinpot dictator*
tinsel *n* **1** a decoration consisting of a piece of metallic thread with thin strips of metal foil attached along its length **2** anything cheap, showy, and gaudy: *all their tinsel and show counts for nothing* ▷ *adj* **3** made of or decorated with tinsel **4** cheap, showy, and gaudy [Latin *scintilla* a spark] **tinselly** *adj*
Tinseltown *n informal* Hollywood, the centre of the US film industry
tinsmith *n* a person who works with tin or tin plate
tint *n* **1** a shade of a colour, esp. a pale one: *his eyes had a yellow tint* **2** a colour that is softened by the addition of white: *a room decorated in pastel tints* **3** a dye for the hair ▷ *vb* **4** to give a tint to (something, such as hair) [Latin *tingere* to colour]
tintinnabulation *n* the ringing or pealing of bells [Latin *tintinnare* to tinkle]
tiny *adj* **tinier, tiniest** very small [origin unknown]
tip¹ *n* **1** a narrow or pointed end of something: *the northern tip of Japan* **2** a small piece attached to the end or bottom of something: *boot tips keep boots from getting scuffed* ▷ *vb* **tipping, tipped 3** to make or form a tip on: *the long strips that hang down are tipped with silver cones* [Old Norse *typpi*] **tipped** *adj*
tip² *n* **1** an amount of money given to someone, such as a waiter, in return for service **2** a helpful hint or warning: *here are some sensible tips to help you avoid sunburn* **3** a piece of inside information, esp. in betting or investing ▷ *vb* **tipping, tipped 4** to give a tip to [origin unknown]
tip³ *vb* **tipping, tipped 1** to tilt: *he tipped back his chair* **2 tip over** to tilt so as to overturn or fall: *the box tipped over and the clothes in it spilled out* **3** *Brit* to dump (rubbish) **4** to pour out (the contents of a container): *he tipped the water from the basin down the sink* ▷ *n* **5** a rubbish dump [origin unknown]
tip-off *n* **1** a warning or hint, esp. one given confidentially and based on inside information ▷ *vb* **tip off 2** to give a hint or warning to: *the police had been tipped off about the robbery*
tippet *n* a scarflike piece of fur, often made from a whole animal skin, worn, esp. formerly, round a woman's shoulders [probably from TIP¹]
tipple *vb* **-pling, -pled 1** to drink alcohol regularly, esp. in small quantities ▷ *n* **2** an alcoholic drink [origin unknown] **tippler** *n*
tipstaff *n* **1** a court official **2** a metal-tipped staff formerly used as a symbol of office
tipster *n* a person who sells tips to people betting on horse races or speculating on the stock market
tipsy *adj* **-sier, -siest** slightly drunk [from TIP³] **tipsiness** *n*
tiptoe *vb* **-toeing, -toed 1** to walk quietly with the heels off the ground ▷ *n* **2 on tiptoe** on the tips of the toes or on the ball of the foot and the toes: *I stood on tiptoe*
tiptop *adj, adv* of the highest quality or condition
tip-up *adj* able to be turned upwards around a hinge or pivot: *tip-up seats*
tirade *n* a long angry speech or denunciation [French]
tire¹ *vb* **tiring, tired 1** to reduce the energy of, as by exertion: *she could still do things that would tire women half her age* **2** to become wearied or bored: *he simply stopped talking when he tired of my questions* [Old English *tēorian*] **tiring** *adj*
tire² *n US* same as **tyre**
tired *adj* **1** weary or exhausted: *they were tired after their long journey* **2** bored with or no longer interested in something: *I'm tired of staying in watching TV every night* **3** having been used so often as to be no longer interesting: *you haven't fallen for that tired old line, have you?* **tiredness** *n*
tireless *adj* energetic and determined: *a tireless worker for charity* **tirelessly** *adv*
tiresome *adj* boring and irritating
'tis *poetic or dialect* it is

tissue *n* **1** a group of cells in an animal or plant with a similar structure and function: *muscular tissue forms 42% of the body tissue* **2** a thin piece of soft absorbent paper used as a disposable handkerchief, towel, etc. **3** short for **tissue paper** **4** an interwoven series: *a tissue of lies* [Old French *tissu* woven cloth]

tissue paper *n* very thin soft delicate paper used esp. to wrap breakable goods

tit[1] *n* any of various small European songbirds, such as the bluetit, that feed on insects and seeds [Middle English *tite* little]

tit[2] *n* **1** *slang* a female breast **2** a teat or nipple [Old English *titt*]

titan *n* a person of great strength, importance, or size: *one of the titans of the computer industry* [after the *Titans*, a family of gods in Greek mythology]

titanic *adj* having or requiring colossal strength: *a titanic struggle*

titanium *n chem* a strong white metallic element used in the manufacture of strong lightweight alloys, esp. aircraft parts. Symbol: **Ti** [from *titan*]

titbit *or esp US* **tidbit** *n* **1** a tasty small piece of food **2** a pleasing scrap of scandal: *an interesting titbit of gossip* [origin unknown]

tit-for-tat *adj* done in return or retaliation for a similar act: *a spate of tit-for-tat killings* [earlier *tip for tap*]

tithe *n* **1** one tenth of one's income or produce paid to the church as a tax **2** a tenth or very small part of anything: *he had accomplished only a tithe of his great dream* ▷ *vb* **tithing, tithed** **3** to demand a tithe from **4** to pay a tithe or tithes [Old English *teogotha*] **tithable** *adj*

Titian (tish-un) *adj* (of hair) reddish-yellow [from *Titian*, Italian painter, because he often used this hair colour in his paintings]

titillate *vb* **-lating, -lated** to arouse or excite pleasurably, esp. in a sexual way [Latin *titillare*] **titillating** *adj* **titillation** *n*

titivate *vb* **-vating, -vated** to make smarter or neater [perhaps from *tidy* + *cultivate*] **titivation** *n*

title *n* **1** the distinctive name of a book, film, record, etc.: *his first album bore the title 'Safe as Milk'* **2** a descriptive name or heading of a section of a book, speech, etc. **3** a book or periodical: *publishers were averaging a total of 500 new titles annually* **4** a name or epithet signifying rank, office, or function: *the job bears the title Assistant Divisional Administrator* **5** a formal designation, such as *Mrs* or *Dr* **6** *sport* a championship: *the Italians have won the title* **7** *law* the legal right to possession of property [Latin *titulus*]

titled *adj* having a title such as 'Lady' or 'Sir' which indicates a high social rank

title deed *n* a document containing evidence of a person's legal right or title to property, esp. a house or land

titleholder *n* a person who holds a title, esp. a sporting championship

title page *n* the page in a book that gives the title, author, publisher, etc.

title role *n* the role of the character after whom a play or film is named

titmouse *n, pl* **-mice** same as **tit**[1] [Middle English *tite* little + MOUSE]

titrate (tite-rate) *vb* **-trating, -trated** *chem* to measure the volume or concentration of (a solution) by titration [French *titrer*]

titration *n chem* an operation in which a measured amount of one solution is added to a known quantity of another solution until the reaction between the two is complete. If the concentration of one solution is known, that of the other can be calculated

titter *vb* **1** to snigger, esp. derisively or in a suppressed way ▷ *n* **2** a suppressed laugh or snigger [imitative]

tittle *n* a very small amount: *it doesn't matter one jot or tittle what you think* [Latin *titulus* title]

tittle-tattle *n* **1** idle chat or gossip ▷ *vb* **-tattling, -tattled** **2** to chatter or gossip

tittup *vb* **-tupping, -tupped** *or US* **-tuping, -tuped** **1** to prance or frolic ▷ *n* **2** a caper [probably imitative]

titular *adj* **1** in name only: *titular head of state* **2** of or having a title

tizzy *n, pl* **-zies** *informal* a state of confusion or excitement [origin unknown]

T-junction *n* a junction where one road joins another at right angles but does not cross it

Tl *chem* thallium

Tm *chem* thulium

TN Tennessee

TNT *n* 2,4,6-trinitrotoluene: a type of powerful explosive

to *prep* **1** used to indicate the destination of the subject or object of an action: *he went to the theatre* **2** used to introduce the indirect object of a verb: *talk to him* **3** used to introduce the infinitive of a verb: *I'm going to lie down* **4** as far as or until: *from September 11 to October 25* **5** used to indicate that two things have an equivalent value: *there are 16 ounces to the pound* **6** against or onto: *I put my ear to the door* **7** before the hour of: *17 minutes to midnight* **8** accompanied by: *dancing to a live band* **9** as compared with: *four goals to nil* **10** used to indicate a resulting condition: *burnt to death* **11** working for or employed by: *Chaplain to the Nigerian Chaplaincy in Britain* **12** in commemoration of: *a memorial to the victims of the disaster* ▷ *adv* **13** towards a closed position: *push the door to* [Old English *tō*]

toad *n* **1** an amphibian which resembles a frog, but has a warty skin and spends more time on dry land **2** a loathsome person [Old English *tādige*]

toadflax *n* a plant with narrow leaves and yellow-orange flowers

toad-in-the-hole *n* a traditional British dish made of sausages baked in a batter

toadstool *n* any of various poisonous funguses consisting of a caplike top on a stem

toady *n, pl* **toadies** **1** a person who flatters and ingratiates himself or herself in a fawning way: *a spineless political toady* ▷ *vb* **toadies, toadying, toadied** **2** to fawn on and flatter (someone) [shortened from *toadeater*, originally a quack's assistant who pretended to eat toads, hence a flatterer] **toadyism** *n*

to and fro *adv, adj also* **to-and-fro** **1** back and forth: *he moved his head to and fro as if dodging blows* **2** from one place to another then back again: *the ferry sailed to and fro across the river* **toing and froing** *n*

toast[1] *n* **1** sliced bread browned by exposure to heat ▷ *vb* **2** to brown (bread) under a grill or over a fire **3** to warm or be warmed: *toasting his feet at the fire* [Latin *tostus* parched]

toast[2] *n* **1** a proposal of health or success given to a person or thing and marked by people raising glasses and drinking together **2** a person or thing that is honoured: *his success made him the toast of the British film industry* ▷ *vb* **3** to propose or drink a toast to (a person or thing) [from the spiced toast formerly put in wine]

toaster *n* an electrical device for toasting bread

toastmaster *n* a person who introduces speakers and proposes toasts at public dinners

tobacco *n, pl* **-cos** *or* **-coes** an American plant with large leaves which are dried for smoking, or chewing, or made into snuff [Spanish *tabaco*]

tobacconist *n Brit & Austral* a person or shop that sells tobacco, cigarettes, pipes, etc.

-to-be *adj* about to be; future: *the bride-to-be*

toboggan *n* **1** a long narrow sledge used for sliding over snow and ice ▷ *vb* **2** to ride on a toboggan [from a Native American language]

toby *n, pl* **-bies** *NZ* a water stopcock at the boundary of a street and house section [origin unknown]

toby jug *n chiefly Brit* a beer mug or jug in the form of a stout seated man wearing a three-cornered hat and smoking a pipe [from the name *Tobias*]

toccata (tok-**kah**-ta) *n* a piece of fast music for the organ, harpsichord, or piano, usually in a rhythmically free style [Italian]

tocsin *n* **1** a warning signal **2** an alarm bell [French]

tod *n* **on one's tod** *Brit slang* by oneself; alone [rhyming slang *Tod Sloan/alone*]

today *n* **1** this day, as distinct from yesterday or tomorrow **2** the present age: *in today's world* ▷ *adv* **3** during or on this day: *I hope you're feeling better today* **4** nowadays: *this is one of the most reliable cars available today* [Old English *tō dæge*, literally: on this day]

toddle *vb* **-dling, -dled 1** to walk with short unsteady steps, like a young child **2 toddle off** *humorous* to depart: *he toddled off to bed* ▷ *n* **3** the act or an instance of walking with short unsteady steps [origin unknown]

toddler *n* a young child who has only just learned how to walk

toddy *n, pl* **-dies** a drink made from spirits, esp. whisky, hot water, sugar, and usually lemon juice [Hindi *tārī* juice of the palmyra palm]

to-do *n, pl* **-dos** *Brit, Austral & NZ* a commotion, fuss, or quarrel

toe *n* **1** any one of the digits of the foot **2** the part of a shoe or sock covering the toes **3 on one's toes** alert **4 tread on someone's toes** to offend a person, esp. by trespassing on his or her field of responsibility ▷ *vb* **toeing, toed 5** to touch or kick with the toe **6 toe the line** to conform to expected attitudes or standards [Old English *tā*]

toecap *n* a reinforced covering for the toe of a boot or shoe

toehold *n* **1** a small space on a rock, mountain, etc., which can be used to support the toe of the foot in climbing **2** any means of gaining access or advantage: *the French car industry has lost its last toehold in America*

toenail *n* a thin hard clear plate covering part of the upper surface of the end of each toe

toerag *n Brit slang* a contemptible or despicable person

toff *n Brit slang* a well-dressed or upper-class person [perhaps from *tuft*, nickname for a titled student at Oxford University wearing a cap with a gold tassel]

toffee *n* **1** a sticky chewy sweet made by boiling sugar with water and butter **2 can't (do something) for toffee** *informal* is not competent or talented at (doing something): *she couldn't dance for toffee* [earlier *taffy*]

toffee-apple *n* an apple fixed on a stick and coated with a thin layer of toffee

toffee-nosed *adj slang* snobbish or conceited

tofu *n* a food with a soft cheeselike consistency made from unfermented soya-bean curd [Japanese]

tog *n* unit for measuring the insulating power of duvets

toga (**toe**-ga) *n* a garment worn by citizens of ancient Rome, consisting of a piece of cloth draped around the body [Latin] **togaed** *adj*

together *adv* **1** with cooperation between people or organizations: *we started a company together* **2** in or into contact with each other: *he clasped his hands together* **3** in or into one place: *the family gets together to talk* **4** at the same time: *'Disgusting,' said Julie and Alice together* **5** considered collectively: *the properties together were worth more as a unit* **6** *old-fashioned* continuously: *working for eight hours together* **7 together with** in addition to ▷ *adj* **8** *slang* self-possessed, competent, and well-organized [Old English *tōgædere*]

USAGE See at **plus**.

togetherness *n* a feeling of closeness to and affection for other people

togged up *adj informal* dressed up in smart clothes. Also: **togged out**

toggle *n* **1** a bar-shaped button inserted through a loop for fastening coats, etc. **2** *computers* a key on a keyboard which, when pressed, will turn a function or feature on if it is currently off, and turn it off if it is currently on **3** short for **toggle switch** (sense 1) [origin unknown]

toggle switch *n* **1** an electric switch with a projecting lever that is moved in a particular way to open or close a circuit **2** same as **toggle** (sense 2)

togs *pl n* **1** *Brit, Austral & NZ informal* clothes **2** *Austral, NZ & Irish* a swimming costume [probably from *toga*]

toheroa (toe-a-**roe**-a) *n* a large edible mollusc of New Zealand with a distinctive flavour [Māori]

tohunga (toe-hung-a) *n NZ* a Māori priest [Māori]

toil *n* **1** hard or exhausting work: *hours of toil beneath the Catalan sun* ▷ *vb* **2** to work hard: *workers toiling in the fields to produce tea for westerners to drink* **3** to move slowly and with difficulty, for instance because of exhaustion or the steepness of a slope: *Joanna toiled up the steps to the church* [Anglo-French *toiler* to struggle]

toilet *n* **1 A** a bowl fitted with a water-flushing device and connected to a drain, for receiving and disposing of urine and faeces **B** a room with such a fitment **2** *old-fashioned* the act of dressing and preparing oneself [French *toilette* dress]

toilet paper *n* thin absorbent paper used for cleaning oneself after defecation or urination

toilet roll *n* a long strip of toilet paper wound around a cardboard tube

toiletry *n, pl* **-ries** an object or cosmetic used in making up, dressing, etc.

toilette (twah-**let**) *n* same as **toilet** (sense 2) [French]

toilet water *n* liquid perfume lighter than cologne

toilsome *adj literary* requiring hard work: *a most toilsome job*

token *n* **1** a symbol, sign, or indication of something: *as a token of respect* **2** a gift voucher that can be used as payment for goods of a specified value **3** a metal or plastic disc, such as a substitute for currency for use in a slot machine **4 by the same token** in the same way as something mentioned previously ▷ *adj* **5** intended to create an impression but having no real importance: *as a token gesture of goodwill* [Old English *tācen*]

tokenism *n* the practice of making only a token effort or doing no more than the minimum, esp. in order to comply with a law **tokenist** *adj*

token strike *n* a brief stoppage of work intended to convey strength of feeling on a disputed issue

told *vb* the past of **tell**

tolerable *adj* **1** able to be put up with; bearable **2** *informal* fairly good **tolerably** *adv*

tolerance *n* **1** the quality of accepting other people's rights to their own opinions, beliefs, or actions **2** capacity to endure something, esp. pain or hardship **3** the ability of a substance to withstand heat, stress, etc., without damage **4** *med* the capacity to endure the effects of a continued or increasing dose of a drug, poison, etc. **5** an acceptable degree of variation in a measurement or value: *the bodywork of the car is precision-engineered with a tolerance of 0.01 millimetres*

tolerant *adj* **1** accepting of the beliefs, actions, etc., of other people **2 tolerant of** able to withstand (heat, stress, etc.) without damage

tolerate *vb* **-ating, -ated 1** to allow something to exist or happen, even though one does not approve of it: *you must learn to tolerate opinions other than your own* **2** to put up with (someone or something): *he found the pain hard to tolerate* [Latin *tolerare* to sustain] **toleration** *n*

toll¹ *vb* **1** to ring (a bell) slowly and regularly **2** to announce by tolling: *the bells tolled the Queen's death* ▷ *n* **3** the slow regular ringing of a bell [origin unknown]

toll² *n* **1** a charge for the use of certain roads and bridges: *the Skye bridge toll* **2** loss or damage from a disaster: *the annual death toll on the roads is about 4500* **3 take a** *or* **its toll** to have a severe and damaging effect: *the continued stress had taken a toll on her health* [Old English *toln*]

tollgate *n* a gate across a toll road or bridge at which travellers must pay

tolu (tol-**loo**) *n* a sweet-smelling balsam obtained from a South American tree, used in medicine and perfume [after *Santiago de Tolu*, Colombia]

toluene *n* a flammable liquid obtained from petroleum and coal tar and used as a solvent and in the manufacture of dyes, explosives, etc. [previously obtained from tolu]

tom *n* **1** a male cat ▷ *adj* **2** (of an animal) male: *a tom turkey* [from *Thomas*]

tomahawk *n* a fighting axe used by the Native Americans of N America [from a Native American language]

tomato *n, pl* **-toes 1** a red fleshy juicy fruit with many edible seeds, eaten in salads, as a vegetable, etc. **2** the plant, originally from South America, on which this fruit grows [indigenous S American word *tomatl*]

tomb *n* **1** a place for the burial of a corpse **2** a monument over a grave **3 the tomb** *poetic* death [Greek *tumbos*]

tombola *n Brit* a type of lottery, in which tickets are drawn from a revolving drum [Italian]

tomboy *n* a girl who behaves or dresses in ways traditionally considered to be like a boy

tombstone *n* a gravestone

tome *n* a large heavy book [Greek *tomos* a slice]

tomfoolery *n* foolish behaviour

Tommy *n, pl* **-mies** *Brit old-fashioned, informal* a private in the British Army [originally *Thomas Atkins*, name used in specimen copies of official forms]

Tommy gun *n* a type of light sub-machine-gun [in full *Thompson sub-machine-gun*, from the name of the manufacturer]

tommyrot *n old-fashioned, informal* utter nonsense

tomorrow *n* **1** the day after today: *tomorrow's meeting has been cancelled* **2** the future: *the struggle to build a better tomorrow* ▷ *adv* **3** on the day after today: *the festival starts tomorrow* **4** at some time in the future: *they live today as millions more will live tomorrow* [Old English *tō morgenne*]

tomtit *n Brit* a small European bird that eats insects and seeds

tom-tom *n* a long narrow drum beaten with the hands [Hindi *tamtam*]

ton¹ *n* **1** *Brit* a unit of weight equal to 2240 pounds or 1016.046 kilograms **2** *US & Canad* a unit of weight equal to 2000 pounds or 907.184 kilograms **3** See **metric ton 4 come down on someone like a ton of bricks** to scold someone very severely ▷ *adv* **5 tons** a lot: *I've got tons of things to do before going on holiday* [variant of *tun*]

ton² *n slang, chiefly Brit* a hundred miles per hour [special use of TON¹]

tonal *adj* **1** *music* written in a key **2** of or relating to tone or tonality

tonality *n, pl* **-ties 1** *music* the presence of a musical key in a composition **2** the overall scheme of colours and tones in a painting

tone *n* **1** sound with reference to its pitch, timbre, or volume **2** *US & Canad* same as **note** (sense 6) **3** *music* an interval of two semitones, such as that between doh and ray in tonic sol-fa **4** the quality or character of a sound: *her tone was angry* **5** general aspect, quality, or style: *the tone of the conversation made him queasy* **6** high quality or style: *my car with*

t

its patches of rust lowered the tone of the neighbourhood **7** the quality of a given colour, as modified by mixture with white or black; shade or tint **8** *physiol* the natural firmness of the tissues and normal functioning of bodily organs in health ▷ *vb* **toning, toned 9** to be of a matching or similar tone **10** to give a tone to or correct the tone of [Greek *tonos*] **toneless** *adj* **tonelessly** *adv*

tone-deaf *adj* unable to distinguish subtle differences in musical pitch

tone down *vb* to moderate in tone: *I sensed some reserve in his manner, so I toned down my enthusiasm*

tone poem *n music* an extended orchestral composition based on nonmusical material, such as a work of literature or a fairy tale

toner *n* **1** a cosmetic applied to the skin to reduce oiliness **2** a powdered chemical that forms the image produced by a photocopier

tone up *vb* to make or become more vigorous, healthy, etc.: *muscle tissue can be toned up*

tong *n* (formerly) a secret society of Chinese Americans [Chinese (Cantonese) *t'ong* meeting place]

tongs *pl n* a tool for grasping or lifting, consisting of two long metal or wooden arms, joined with a hinge or flexible metal strip at one end [Old English *tange*]

tongue *n* **1** a movable mass of muscular tissue attached to the floor of the mouth, used for tasting, eating, and speaking **2** a language, dialect, or idiom: *the Scots tongue* **3** the ability to speak: *taken aback, she could not find her tongue* **4** a manner of speaking: *a sharp tongue* **5** the tongue of certain animals used as food **6** a narrow strip of something that extends outwards: *a narrow tongue of flame* **7** a flap of leather on a shoe **8** the clapper of a bell **9** a projecting strip along an edge of a board that is made to fit a groove in another board **10 hold one's tongue** to keep quiet **11 on the tip of one's tongue** about to come to mind **12 with (one's) tongue in (one's) cheek** with insincere or ironical intent [Old English *tunge*]

tongue-tie *n* a congenital condition in which movement of the tongue is limited as the result of the fold of skin under the tongue extending too close to the front of the tongue

t

tongue-tied *adj* speechless, esp. with embarrassment or shyness

tongue twister *n* a sentence or phrase that is difficult to say clearly and quickly, such as *the sixth sick sheikh's sixth sheep's sick*

tonguing *n* a technique of playing a wind instrument by obstructing and uncovering the air passage through the lips with the tongue

tonic *n* **1** a medicine that improves the functioning of the body or increases the feeling of wellbeing **2** anything that enlivens or strengthens: *his dry humour was a stimulating tonic* **3** Also called: **tonic water** a carbonated beverage containing quinine and often mixed with alcoholic drinks: *gin and tonic* **4** *music* the first note of a major or minor scale and the tonal centre of a piece composed in a particular key ▷ *adj* **5** having an invigorating or refreshing effect: *a tonic bath* **6** *music* of the first note of a major or minor scale [Greek *tonikos* concerning tone]

tonic sol-fa *n* a method of teaching music, by which syllables are used as names for the notes of the major scale in any key

tonight *n* **1** the night or evening of this present day: *tonight's edition* ▷ *adv* **2** in or during the night or evening of this day: *I want to go out dancing tonight* [Old English *tōniht*]

toning table *n* an exercise table, parts of which move mechanically to exercise specific parts of the body of the person lying on it

tonnage *n* **1** the capacity of a merchant ship expressed in tons **2** the weight of the cargo of a merchant ship **3** the total amount of shipping of a port or nation

tonne (tunn) *n* a unit of mass equal to 1000 kg or 2204.6 pounds [French]

tonsil *n* either of two small oval lumps of spongy tissue situated one on each side of the back of the mouth [Latin *tonsillae* tonsils] **tonsillar** *adj*

tonsillectomy *n, pl* **-mies** surgical removal of the tonsils [TONSIL + Greek *tomē* a cutting]

tonsillitis *n* inflammation of the tonsils, causing a sore throat and fever

tonsorial *adj often facetious* of a barber or his trade [Latin *tondere* to shave]

tonsure *n* **1 A** (in certain religions and monastic orders) the shaving of the head or the crown of the head only **B** the part of the head left bare by such shaving ▷ *vb* **-suring, -sured 2** to shave the head of [Latin *tonsura* a clipping] **tonsured** *adj*

too *adv* **1** as well or also: *I'll miss you, too* **2** in or to an excessive degree: *it's too noisy in here* **3** extremely: *you're too kind* **4** *US, Canad & Austral informal* used to emphasize contradiction of a negative statement: *You didn't! – I did too!* [Old English *tō*]

USAGE See at **very**.

took *vb* the past tense of **take**

tool *n* **1 A** an implement, such as a hammer, saw, or spade, that is used by hand to help do a particular type of work **B** a power-driven instrument: *machine tool* **2** the cutting part of such an instrument **3** a person used to perform dishonourable or unpleasant tasks for another: *the government is acting as a tool of big business* **4** any object, skill, etc., used for a particular task or in a particular job: *a skilled therapist can use photographs as tools* ▷ *vb* **5** to work, cut, or form (something) with a tool [Old English *tōl*]

toolbar *n* a row or column of buttons displayed on a computer screen, allowing the user to select a variety of functions

tool-maker *n* a person who specializes in the production or reconditioning of machine tools **tool-making** *n*

tool-pusher *n* a person who supervises drilling operations on an oil rig

toonie *or* **twonie** *n Canad informal* a Canadian two-dollar coin

toot *n* **1** a short hooting sound ▷ *vb* **2** to give or cause to give a short blast, hoot, or whistle: *motorists tooted their car horns* [imitative]

tooth *n, pl* **teeth 1** one of the bonelike projections in the jaws of most vertebrates that are used for biting, tearing, or chewing **2** one of the sharp projections on the edge of a comb, saw, zip, etc.

3 long in the tooth old or ageing **4 a sweet tooth** a liking for sweet food **5 tooth and nail** with great vigour and determination: *the union would oppose compulsory redundancies tooth and nail* ▷ See also **teeth** [Old English *tōth*]

toothache *n* a pain in or near a tooth

toothbrush *n* a small brush with a long handle, for cleaning the teeth

toothless *adj* **1** having no teeth **2** having no real power: *the proposed Commission will not be as toothless as scoffers suggest*

toothpaste *n* a paste used for cleaning the teeth, applied with a toothbrush

toothpick *n* a small wooden or plastic stick used for extracting pieces of food from between the teeth

tooth powder *n* a powder used for cleaning the teeth, applied with a toothbrush

toothsome *adj* delicious or appetizing in appearance, flavour, or smell

toothy *adj* **toothier, toothiest** having or showing numerous, large, or prominent teeth: *a toothy grin*

tootle *vb* **-tling, -tled 1** to hoot softly or repeatedly ▷ *n* **2** a soft hoot or series of hoots

top[1] *n* **1** the highest point or part of anything: *the top of the stairs* **2** the most important or successful position: *at the top of the agenda* **3** a lid or cap that fits on to one end of something, esp. to close it: *he unscrewed the top from a quart of ale* **4** the highest degree or point: *the two people at the top of the Party* **5** the most important person or people in an organization: *the top of the military establishment* **6** the loudest or highest pitch: *she cheered and sang at the top of her voice* **7** a garment, esp. for a woman, that extends from the shoulders to the waist or hips **8** the part of a plant that is above ground: *nettle tops* **9** same as **top gear 10 off the top of one's head** without previous preparation or careful thought **11 on top of A** in addition to: *the average member of staff will get 25% on top of salary* **B** *informal* in complete control of: *we're on top of our costs and expenses and looking for other opportunities* **12 over the top A** lacking restraint or a sense of proportion: *you went over the top when you called her a religious maniac* **B** *military* over the edge of a trench ▷ *adj* **13** at, of, or being the top: *men still hold most of the top jobs in industry* ▷ *vb* **topping, topped 14** to put on top of (something): *top your salad with a mild dressing* **15** to reach or pass the top of **16** to be at the top of: *her biggest hit topped the charts for six weeks* **17** to exceed or surpass: *his estimated fortune tops £2 billion* **18 top and tail A** to trim off the ends of (fruit or vegetables) before cooking **B** to wash only a baby's face and bottom ▷ See also **top off, top out, tops** *etc.* [Old English *topp*]

top[2] *n* **1** a toy that is spun on its pointed base **2 sleep like a top** to sleep very soundly [Old English]

topaz (toe-pazz) *n* a hard glassy yellow, pink, or colourless mineral used in making jewellery [Greek *topazos*]

top brass *pl n* the most important or high-ranking officials or leaders

topcoat *n* **1** an overcoat **2** a final coat of paint applied to a surface

top dog *n informal* the leader or chief of a group

top-drawer *adj informal* of the highest quality or status

top dressing *n* a layer of fertilizer or manure spread on the surface of land **top-dress** *vb*

tope[1] *vb* **toping, toped** to drink (alcohol), usually in large quantities [perhaps from French *toper* to take a bet] **toper** *n*

tope[2] *n* a small grey shark of European coastal waters [origin unknown]

topee *or* **topi** (toe-pee) *n* same as **pith helmet** [Hindi *topī* hat]

top-flight *adj* of very high quality

topgallant *n* **1** a mast or sail above a topmast ▷ *adj* **2** of or relating to a topgallant

top gear *n* the highest forward ratio of a gearbox in a motor vehicle

top hat *n* a man's hat with a tall cylindrical crown and narrow brim, now only worn for some formal occasions

top-heavy *adj* unstable through being overloaded at the top

topiary (tope-yar-ee) *n* **1** the art of trimming trees or bushes into artificial decorative shapes **2** trees or bushes trimmed into decorative shapes ▷ *adj* **3** of or relating to topiary [Latin *topia* decorative garden work] **topiarist** *n*

topic *n* a subject of a speech, book, conversation, etc. [Greek *topos* place]

topical *adj* of or relating to current affairs **topicality** *n* **topically** *adv*

topknot *n* a crest, tuft, decorative bow, etc., on the top of the head

topless *adj* of or relating to women wearing costumes that do not cover the breasts: *topless beaches*

top-level *adj* of, involving, or by those with the highest level of influence or ability: *a top-level meeting*

topmast *n* the mast next above a lower mast on a sailing vessel

topmost *adj* at or nearest the top

top-notch *adj informal* excellent or superb: *top-notch entertainment*

top off *vb* to finish or complete, esp. with some decisive action

topography *n, pl* **-phies 1** the surface features of a region, such as its hills, valleys, or rivers: *the islands are fragile, with a topography constantly changed by wind and wave* **2** the study or description of such surface features **3** the representation of these features on a map [Greek *topos* a place + -GRAPHY] **topographer** *n* **topographical** *adj*

topology *n* a branch of geometry describing the properties of a figure that are unaffected by continuous distortion [Greek *topos* a place + -LOGY] **topological** *adj*

top out *vb* to place the highest stone on (a building)

topper *n informal* a top hat

topping *n* a sauce or garnish for food

topple *vb* **-pling, -pled 1** to fall over or cause (something) to fall over, esp. from a height: *he staggered back against the railing and toppled over into the river* **2** to overthrow or oust: *few believe the scandal will topple the government* [from TOP[1] (verb)]

tops *slang* ▷ *n* **1 the tops** a person or thing of top quality ▷ *adj* **2** excellent: *Pacino's no-holds-barred performance is tops*

topsail *n* a square sail carried on a yard set on a topmast

top-secret *adj* (of military or government information) classified as needing the highest level of secrecy and security

topside *n* a lean cut of beef from the thigh containing no bone

topsoil *n* the surface layer of soil

topsy-turvy *adj* **1** upside down **2** in a state of confusion ▷ *adv* **3** in a topsy-turvy manner [probably *top* + obsolete *tervy* to turn upside down]

top up *vb* **1** to refill (a container), usually to the brim: *I topped up his glass* **2** to add to (an amount) in order to make it sufficient: *the grant can be topped up by a student loan* ▷ *n* **top-up 3** another serving of a drink in the glass that was used for the first one: *anyone want a top-up?* ▷ *adj* **top-up 4** serving to top something up: *a top-up loan*

toque (toke) *n* **1** a woman's small round brimless hat **2** *Canad* same as **tuque** (sense 2) [French]

tor *n chiefly Brit* a high hill, esp. a bare rocky one [Old English *torr*]

Torah *n* the whole body of traditional Jewish teaching, including the Oral Law [Hebrew: precept]

torch *n* **1** a small portable electric lamp powered by batteries **2** a wooden shaft dipped in wax or tallow and set alight **3** anything regarded as a source of enlightenment, guidance, etc.: *a torch of hope* **4 carry a torch for** to be in love with (someone), esp. unrequitedly ▷ *vb* **5** *informal* to deliberately set (a building) on fire [Old French *torche* handful of twisted straw]

tore *vb* the past tense of **tear**[2]

toreador (torr-ee-a-dor) *n* a bullfighter, esp. one on horseback [Spanish]

torero (tor-air-oh) *n, pl* **-ros** a bullfighter, esp. one on foot [Spanish]

torment *vb* **1** to cause (someone) great pain or suffering **2** to tease or pester (a person or animal) in an annoying or cruel way ▷ *n* **3** physical or mental pain **4** a source of pain or suffering [Latin *tormentum*] **tormentor** *n*

t

tormentil *n* a creeping plant with yellow four-petalled flowers [Old French *tormentille*]

torn *vb* **1** the past participle of **tear**[2] ▷ *adj* **2** split or cut **3** divided or undecided, as in preference: *torn between two lovers*

tornado *n, pl* **-dos** *or* **-does** a rapidly whirling column of air, usually characterized by a dark funnel-shaped cloud causing damage along its path [Spanish *tronada* thunderstorm]

torpedo *n, pl* **-does 1** a cylindrical self-propelled weapon carrying explosives that is launched from aircraft, ships, or submarines and follows an underwater path to hit its target ▷ *vb* **-doing, -doed 2** to attack or hit (a ship) with one or a number of torpedoes **3** to destroy or wreck: *the Prime Minister warned his party against torpedoing the bill* [Latin: crampfish (whose electric discharges can cause numbness)]

torpedo boat *n* (formerly) a small high-speed warship for torpedo attacks

torpid *adj* **1** sluggish or dull: *he has a rather torpid intellect* **2** (of a hibernating animal) dormant [Latin *torpere* to be numb]

torpor *n* drowsiness and apathy

torque (tork) *n* **1** a force that causes rotation around a central point such as an axle **2** an ancient Celtic necklace or armband made of twisted metal [Latin *torques* necklace + *torquere* to twist]

torr *n, pl* **torr** a unit of pressure equal to one millimetre of mercury (133.3 newtons per square metre) [after E. *Torricelli*, physicist]

torrent *n* **1** a fast or violent stream, esp. of water **2** a rapid flow of questions, abuse, etc. [Latin *torrens*]

torrential *adj* (of rain) very heavy

torrid *adj* **1** (of weather) so hot and dry as to parch or scorch **2** (of land) arid or parched **3** highly charged emotionally: *a torrid affair* [Latin *torrere* to scorch]

torsion *n* the twisting of a part by equal forces being applied at both ends but in opposite directions [Latin *torquere* to twist] **torsional** *adj*

torso *n, pl* **-sos 1** the trunk of the human body **2** a statue of a nude human trunk, esp. without the head or limbs [Italian: stalk, stump]

tort *n law* a civil wrong or injury, for which an action for damages may be brought [Latin *torquere* to twist]

tortilla *n* (in Mexican cooking) a kind of thin pancake made from corn meal [Spanish: little cake]

tortoise *n* a land reptile with a heavy dome-shaped shell into which it can withdraw its head and legs [Medieval Latin *tortuca*]

tortoiseshell *n* **1** the horny yellow-and-brown mottled shell of a sea turtle, used for making ornaments and jewellery **2** a domestic cat with black, cream, and brownish markings **3** a butterfly which has orange-brown wings with black markings ▷ *adj* **4** made of tortoiseshell

tortuous *adj* **1** twisted or winding: *a tortuous route* **2** devious or cunning: *months of tortuous negotiations*

USAGE See at **torture**.

torture *vb* **-turing, -tured 1** to cause (someone) extreme physical pain, esp. to extract information, etc.: *suspects were regularly tortured and murdered by the secret police* **2** to cause (someone) mental anguish ▷ *n* **3** physical or mental anguish **4** the practice of torturing a person **5** something which causes great mental distress: *she was going through the torture of a collapsing marriage* [Latin *torquere* to twist] **tortured** *adj* **torturer** *n* **torturous** *adj*

USAGE The adjective *torturous* is sometimes confused with *tortuous*. One speaks of a *torturous* experience, i.e. one that involves pain or suffering, but of a *tortuous* road, i.e. one that winds or twists.

Tory *n, pl* **-ries 1** a member or supporter of the Conservative Party in Great Britain or Canada **2** *history* a member of the English political party that supported the Church and Crown and traditional political structures and opposed the Whigs ▷ *adj* **3** of or relating to a Tory or Tories [Irish *tōraidhe* outlaw] **Toryism** *n*

tosa (toe-za) *n* a large reddish dog, originally bred for fighting [after a province on the Japanese island of Shikoku]

toss *vb* **1** to throw (something) lightly **2** to fling or be flung about, esp. in a violent way: *the salty sea breeze tossing the branches of the palms* **3** to coat (food) with a dressing by gentle stirring or mixing: *her technique for tossing Caesar salad* **4** (of a horse) to throw (its rider) **5** to move (one's head) suddenly backwards, as in impatience **6** to throw up (a coin) to decide between alternatives by guessing which side will land uppermost **7 toss and turn** to be restless when trying to sleep ▷ *n* **8** the act or an instance of tossing **9** the act of deciding between alternatives by throwing up a coin and guessing which side will land uppermost: *Essex won the toss and decided to bat first* **10 argue the toss** to waste time and energy arguing about an unimportant point **11 not give a toss** *informal* not to care at all [Scandinavian]

toss off *vb* **1** to do or produce (something) quickly and easily: *the tales my sister tossed off so lightly over the dusting* **2** to finish (a drink) in one swallow

toss up *vb* **1** to spin (a coin) in the air in order to decide between alternatives by guessing which side will land uppermost ▷ *n* **toss-up 2** an instance of tossing up a coin **3** *informal* an even chance or risk: *it's a toss-up whether prices will go up or down over the days ahead*

tot *n* **1** a very young child **2** a small drink of spirits [origin unknown]

total *n* **1** the whole, esp. regarded as the sum of a number of parts **2 in total** overall: *the company employs over 700 people in total* ▷ *adj* **3** complete: *a total ban on alcohol* **4** being or related to a total: *the total number of deaths* ▷ *vb* **-talling, -talled** *or US* **-taling, -taled 5** to amount to: *the firm's losses totalled more than $2 billion* **6** to add up: *purchases are totalled with a pencil and a notepad* [Latin *totus* all] **totally** *adv*

totalitarian *adj* **1** of a political system in which there is only one party, which allows no opposition and attempts to control everything: *a totalitarian state* ▷ *n* **2** a person who is in favour of totalitarian policies **totalitarianism** *n*

totality *n, pl* **-ties 1** the whole amount **2** the state of being total

totalizator, totalizer, totalisator *or* **totaliser** *n* a machine to operate a system of betting on a racecourse in which money is paid out to the winners in proportion to their stakes

tote[1] *vb* **toting, toted** *informal* **1** to carry or wear (a gun) **2** to haul or carry [origin unknown]

tote[2] *n* **the tote** *trademark* short for **totalizator**

tote bag *n* a large handbag or shopping bag

totem *n* **1** (esp. among Native Americans) an object or animal symbolizing a clan or family **2** a representation of such an object [from a Native American language] **totemic** *adj* **totemism** *n*

totem pole *n* a pole carved or painted with totemic figures set up by certain Native Americans as a tribal symbol

totter *vb* **1** to move in an unsteady manner **2** to sway or shake as if about to fall **3** to be failing, unstable, or precarious: *the world was tottering on the edge of war* [origin unknown]

tot up *vb* **totting, totted** to add (numbers) together: *I'll just tot up what you owe me* [from *total*]

toucan *n* a tropical American fruit-eating bird with a large brightly coloured bill [Portuguese *tucano*]

touch *vb* **1** to cause or permit a part of the body to come into contact with (someone or something): *the baking tin is too hot to touch* **2** to tap, feel, or strike (someone or something): *he touched me on the shoulder* **3** to come or bring (something) into contact with (something else): *the plane's wheels touched the runway* **4** to move or disturb by handling: *we shouldn't touch anything before the police arrive* **5** to have an effect on: *millions of people's lives had been touched by the music of the Beatles* **6** to produce an emotional response in: *the painful truth of it touched her* **7** to eat or drink: *she hardly ever touched alcohol* **8** to compare to in quality or attainment; equal or match: *nothing can touch them for scope and detail* **9** *Brit, Austral & NZ slang* to ask (someone) for a loan or gift of money **10** to fondle in a sexual manner: *I wouldn't let him touch me unless I was in the mood* **11** to strike, harm, or molest: *I never touched him!* **12 touch on** *or* **upon** to allude to briefly or in passing: *these two issues may be touched upon during the talks* ▷ *n* **13** the sense by which the texture and other qualities of objects can be experienced when they come in contact with a part of the body surface, esp. the tips of the fingers. Related adjective: **tactile 14** the feel or texture of an object as perceived by this sense: *she enjoyed the touch of the damp grass on her feet* **15** the act or an instance of something coming into contact with the body: *he remembered the touch of her hand* **16** a gentle push, tap, or caress: *the switch takes only the merest touch to operate* **17** a small amount; trace: *a touch of luxury* **18** a particular manner or style of doing something: *his songs always reveal his keen melodic touch* **19** a detail of some work: *final touches were now being put to the plans* **20** a slight attack: *a touch of dysentery* **21** (in sports such as football or rugby) the area outside the lines marking the side of the pitch: *he kicked the ball into touch* **22** the technique of fingering a keyboard instrument **23 a touch** slightly or marginally: *it's nice, but a touch expensive* **24 in touch** **A** regularly speaking to, writing to, or visiting someone **B** having up-to-date knowledge or understanding of a situation or trend **25 lose touch** **A** to gradually stop speaking to, writing to, or visiting someone **B** to stop having up-to-date knowledge or understanding of a situation or trend **26 out of touch** **A** no longer speaking to, writing to, or visiting someone **B** no longer having up-to-date knowledge or understanding of a situation or trend ▷ See also **touchdown, touch off, touch up** [Old French *tochier*]

touch and go *adj* risky or critical: *it was touch and go whether the mission would succeed*

touchdown *n* **1** the moment at which a landing aircraft or spacecraft comes into contact with the landing surface **2** *American football* a scoring move in which an attacking player takes the ball into the area behind his opponents' goal ▷ *vb* **touch down 3** (of an aircraft or spacecraft) to land

t

touché (too-shay) *interj* **1** an acknowledgment that a remark or witty reply has been effective **2** an acknowledgment of a scoring hit in fencing [French, literally: touched]
touched *adj* **1** moved to sympathy or emotion: *I was touched by her understanding* **2** *informal* slightly mad: *she's a bit touched*
touching *adj* **1** arousing tender feelings ▹ *prep* **2** relating to or concerning: *she might talk about matters touching both of them*
touch judge *n* one of the two linesmen in rugby
touchline *n* either of the lines marking the side of the playing area in certain games, such as rugby
touch off *vb* to cause (a disturbance, violence, etc.) to begin: *the death of a teenager in police custody touched off a night of riots*
touchpaper *n* a fuse of dark blue paper on a firework
touchscreen *n* a visual display unit screen that allows the user to give commands to the computer by touching parts of the screen instead of using the keyboard
touchstone *n* a standard by which judgment is made: *this restaurant is the touchstone for genuine Italian cookery in Leeds*
touch-type *vb* **-typing, -typed** to type without looking at the keyboard **touch-typist** *n*
touch up *vb* to enhance, renovate, or falsify (a picture) by adding extra touches to it
touchwood *n* something, esp. dry wood, used as tinder [*touch* (in the sense: to kindle)]
touchy *adj* **touchier, touchiest 1** easily upset or irritated: *he is a touchy and quick-tempered man* **2** requiring careful and tactful handling: *a touchy subject* **touchiness** *n*
touchy-feely *adj informal, sometimes offensive* sensitive and caring
tough *adj* **1** strong and difficult to break, cut, or tear: *this fabric is tough and water-resistant* **2** (of meat or other food) difficult to cut and chew; not tender **3** physically or mentally strong and able to cope with hardship: *a tough uncompromising woman, unwilling to take no for an answer* **4** rough or violent: *a tough and ruthless mercenary* **5** strict and firm: *the country's tough drugs laws* **6** difficult or troublesome to do or deal with: *a tough task* **7 tough luck!** *informal* an expression of lack of sympathy for someone else's problems ▹ *n* **8** a rough, vicious, or violent person ▹ *vb* **9 tough it out** *informal* to endure a difficult situation until it improves: *criticism of his performance has reinforced his desire to tough it out* [Old English *tōh*] **toughness** *n*
toughen *vb* to make or become tough or tougher
toupee (too-pay) *n* a hairpiece worn by men to cover a bald place [French *toupet* forelock]
tour *n* **1** an extended journey visiting places of interest along the route **2** a trip, by a band, theatre company, etc., to perform in several places **3** an overseas trip made by a cricket team, rugby team, etc., to play in several places **4** *military* a period of service, esp. in one place: *the regiment has served several tours in Northern Ireland* ▹ *vb* **5** to make a tour of (a place) [Old French: a turn]
tour de force *n, pl* **tours de force** a masterly or brilliant stroke or achievement [French, literally: feat of skill or strength]
tourism *n* tourist travel, esp. when regarded as an industry
tourist *n* **1** a person who travels for pleasure, usually sightseeing and staying in hotels **2** a member of a sports team which is visiting a country to play a series of matches: *the tourists were bowled out for 135* **3** the lowest class of accommodation on a passenger ship ▹ *adj* **4** of or relating to tourists or tourism: *a popular tourist attraction* **5** of the lowest class of accommodation on a passenger ship or aircraft
touristy *adj informal, often derogatory* full of tourists or tourist attractions
tourmaline *n* a hard crystalline mineral used in jewellery and electrical equipment [German *Turmalin*]
tournament *n* **1** a sporting competition in which contestants play a series of games to determine an overall winner **2** Also: **tourney** *medieval history* a contest in which mounted knights fought for a prize [Old French *torneiement*]
tournedos (**tour**-ned-doh) *n, pl* **-dos** (-doze) a thick round steak of beef [French]
tourniquet (**tour**-nick-kay) *n med* a strip of cloth tied tightly round an arm or leg to stop bleeding from an artery [French]
tourtière (tour-tee-**air**) *n Canad* a type of meat pie [French: plate (referring to the shallow dish in which it is baked)]
tousle (rhymes with **arousal**) *vb* **-sling, -sled** to make (hair or clothes) ruffled and untidy [Low German *tūsen* to shake] **tousled** *adj*
tout (rhymes with **shout**) *vb* **1** to seek (business, customers, etc.) or try to sell (goods), esp. in a persistent or direct manner: *he went from door to door touting for business* **2** to put forward or recommend (a person or thing) as a good or suitable example or candidate: *the plant was once touted as a showcase factory* ▹ *n* **3** a person who sells tickets for a heavily booked event at inflated prices [Old English *tȳtan* to peep]
tow[1] *vb* **1** to pull or drag (a vehicle), esp. by means of a rope or cable ▹ *n* **2** the act or an instance of towing **3 in tow** *informal* in one's company or one's charge or under one's influence: *she had an older man in tow* **4 on tow** (of a vehicle) being towed [Old English *togian*]
tow[2] *n* fibres of hemp, flax, jute, etc., prepared for spinning [Old English *tōw*]
towards *or US* **toward** *prep* **1** in the direction of: *towards the lake* **2** with regard to: *hostility towards the President* **3** as a contribution to: *the profits will go towards three projects* **4** just before: *towards evening*
towbar *n* a rigid metal bar attached to the back of a vehicle, from which a trailer or caravan can be towed
towel *n* **1** a piece of absorbent cloth or paper used for drying things **2 throw in the towel** See **throw in** (sense 3) ▹ *vb* **-elling, -elled** *or US* **-eling, -eled** **3** to dry or wipe with a towel [Old French *toaille*]
towelling *or US* **toweling** *n* a soft, fairly thick fabric used to make towels and dressing gowns
tower *n* **1** a tall, usually square or circular structure, sometimes part of a larger building and usually built for a specific purpose **2 tower of strength** a person who supports or comforts

t

someone else at a time of difficulty ▷ *vb* **3 tower over** to be much taller than: *sheer walls of limestone towered over us* [Latin *turris*]

tower block *n Brit* a very tall building divided into flats or offices

towering *adj* **1** very tall **2** very impressive or important: *his towering presence on stage* **3** very intense: *in a towering rage*

towheaded *adj* having blonde or yellowish hair [*tow* flax]

town *n* **1** a large group of houses, shops, factories, etc., smaller than a city and larger than a village. Related adjective: **urban 2** the nearest town or the chief town of an area: *people from town rarely went out to the farm* **3** the central area of a town where most of the shops and offices are: *we're going to a pub in town tonight* **4** the people of a town: *the town is split over the plans for a bypass* **5** built-up areas in general, as opposed to the countryside: *migration from the country to the town* **6 go to town** to make a supreme or unrestricted effort **7 on the town** visiting nightclubs, restaurants, etc.: *we had a night on the town to celebrate her promotion* [Old English *tūn* village]

town clerk *n* (currently in Australia and in Britain until 1974) the chief administrative officer of a town

town crier *n* (formerly) a person employed to make public announcements in the streets

town hall *n* a large building in a town often containing the council offices and a hall for public meetings

town house *n* **1** a terraced house in an urban area, esp. an up-market one **2** a person's town residence as distinct from his or her country residence

townie *or* **townee** *n chiefly Brit informal, often derogatory* a resident in a town, esp. as distinct from country dwellers

town planning *n* the comprehensive planning of the physical and social development of a town

township *n* **1** a small town **2** (in South Africa) a planned urban settlement of Black people or people of mixed racial descent **3** (in the US and Canada) a small unit of local government, often consisting of a town and the area surrounding it **4** (in Canada) a land-survey area, usually 36 square miles (93 square kilometres)

townsman *or fem* **townswoman** *n, pl* **-men** *or* **-women** an inhabitant of a town

townspeople *or* **townsfolk** *pl n* the people who live in a town

towpath *n* a path beside a canal or river, formerly used by horses pulling barges

towrope *n* a rope or cable used for towing a vehicle or vessel

toxaemia *or US* **toxemia** (tox-**seem**-ya) *n* **1** a form of blood poisoning caused by toxins released by bacteria at a wound or other site of infection **2** a condition in pregnant women characterized by high blood pressure [Latin *toxicum* poison + *haima* blood] **toxaemic** *or US* **toxemic** *adj*

toxic *adj* **1** poisonous: *toxic fumes* **2** caused by poison: *toxic effects* [Greek *toxikon (pharmakon)* (poison) used on arrows] **toxicity** *n*

toxicology *n* the branch of science concerned with poisons and their effects **toxicological** *adj* **toxicologist** *n*

toxin *n* **1** any of various poisonous substances produced by microorganisms and causing certain diseases **2** any other poisonous substance of plant or animal origin

toy *n* **1** an object designed for children to play with, such as a doll or model car **2** an object that adults use for entertainment rather than for a serious purpose: *I do use my computer: it's not just a toy* ▷ *adj* **3** being an imitation or model of something for children to play with: *a toy aeroplane* **4** (of a dog) of a variety much smaller than is normal for that breed: *a toy poodle* [origin unknown]

toy boy *n* the much younger male lover of an older person

toy-toy *or* **toyi-toyi** *S African n* **1** a dance expressing defiance and protest ▷ *vb* **2** to dance in this way [origin uncertain]

toy with *vb* **1** to consider an idea without being serious about it or being able to decide about it: *I've been toying with the idea of setting up my own firm* **2** to keep moving (an object) about with one's fingers, esp. when thinking about something else: *Jessica sat toying with her glass*

trace *vb* **tracing, traced 1** to locate or work out (the cause or source of something): *he traced the trouble to a faulty connection* **2** to find (something or someone that was missing): *the police were unable to trace her missing husband* **3** to discover or describe the progress or development of (something): *throughout the 19th century we can trace the development of more complex machinery* **4** to copy (a design, map, etc.) by putting a piece of transparent paper over it and following the lines which show through the paper with a pencil **5** to make the outline of (a shape or pattern): *his index finger was tracing circles on the arm of the chair* ▷ *n* **6** a mark, footprint, or other sign that shows that a person, animal, or thing has been in a particular place: *the police could find no trace of the missing van* **7** an amount of something so small that it is barely noticeable: *I detected a trace of jealousy in her voice* **8** a remnant of something: *traces of an Iron-Age fort remain visible* **9** a pattern made on a screen or a piece of paper by a device that is measuring or detecting something: *a baffling radar trace* [French *tracier*] **traceable** *adj*

trace element *n* a chemical element that occurs in very small amounts in soil, water, etc. and is essential for healthy growth

tracer *n* **1** a projectile that can be observed when in flight by the burning of chemical substances in its base **2** *med* an element or other substance introduced into the body to study metabolic processes

tracer bullet *n* a round of small-arms ammunition containing a tracer

tracery *n, pl* **-eries 1** a pattern of interlacing lines, esp. one in a stained glass window **2** any fine lacy pattern resembling this

traces *pl n* **1** the two side straps that connect a horse's harness to the vehicle being pulled **2 kick over the traces** to escape or defy control [Old French *trait*]

trachea (track-**kee**-a) *n, pl* **-cheae** (-kee-ee) *anatomy & zool* the tube that carries inhaled air from the throat to the lungs [Greek]

tracheotomy (track-ee-**ot**-a-mee) *n, pl* **-mies** surgical incision into the trachea, as performed when the air passage has been blocked [TRACHEA + Greek *tomē* a cutting]

trachoma (track-**oh**-ma) *n* a chronic contagious disease of the eye characterized by inflammation of the inner surface of the lids and the formation of scar tissue [Greek *trakhōma* roughness]

tracing *n* **1** a copy of something, such as a map, made by tracing **2** a line traced by a recording instrument

track *n* **1** a rough road or path: *a farm track* **2** the mark or trail left by something that has passed by: *the fox didn't leave any tracks* **3** a rail or pair of parallel rails on which a vehicle, such as a train, runs **4** a course for running or racing on: *a running track* **5** a separate song or piece of music on a record, tape, or CD: *Dolphy switches back to bass clarinet for the final track* **6** a course of action, thought, etc.: *I don't think you're on the right track at all* **7** an endless band on the wheels of a tank, bulldozer, etc. to enable it to move across rough ground **8 keep** *or* **lose track of** to follow or fail to follow the course or progress of **9 off the beaten track** in an isolated location: *the village where she lives is a bit off the beaten track* ▷ *vb* **10** to follow the trail of (a person or animal) **11** to follow the flight path of (a satellite, etc.) by picking up signals transmitted or reflected by it **12** *films* to follow (a moving object) while filming ▷ See also **tracks** [Old French *trac*] **tracker** *n*

track down *vb* to find (someone or something) by tracking or pursuing

tracker dog *n* a dog specially trained to search for missing people

track event *n* a competition in athletics, such as sprinting, that takes place on a running track

track record *n informal* the past record of the accomplishments and failures of a person or organization

tracks *pl n* **1** marks, such as footprints, left by someone or something that has passed **2 in one's tracks** on the very spot where one is standing: *those words stopped her in her tracks* **3 make tracks** to leave or depart: *it was time to start making tracks*

track shoe *n* a light running shoe fitted with steel spikes for better grip

tracksuit *n* a warm loose-fitting suit worn by athletes, etc., esp. during training

tract[1] *n* **1** a large area, esp. of land: *an extensive tract of moorland* **2** *anatomy* a system of organs or glands that has a particular function: *the urinary tract* [Latin *tractus* a stretching out]

tract[2] *n* a pamphlet, esp. a religious one [Latin *tractatus*]

tractable *adj formal* easy to control, manage, or deal with: *he could easily manage his tractable and worshipping younger brother* [Latin *tractare* to manage] **tractability** *n*

traction *n* **1** pulling, esp. by engine power: *the increased use of electric traction* **2** *med* the application of a steady pull on an injured limb using a system of weights and pulleys or splints: *he was in traction for weeks following the accident* **3** the grip that the wheels of a vehicle have on the ground: *four-wheel drive gives much better traction in wet or icy conditions* **4** the quality of being influential or popular: *her ideas are gaining traction with the public* [Latin *tractus* dragged]

traction engine *n* a heavy steam-powered vehicle used, esp. formerly, for drawing heavy loads along roads or over rough ground

tractor *n* a motor vehicle with large rear wheels, used to pull heavy loads, esp. farm machinery [Late Latin: one who pulls]

trade *n* **1** the buying and selling of goods and services **2** a person's job, esp. a craft requiring skill: *he's a plumber by trade* **3** the people and practices of an industry, craft, or business **4** amount of custom or commercial dealings: *a brisk trade in second-hand weapons* **5** a specified market or business: *the wool trade* **6 trades** the trade winds ▷ *vb* **trading, traded 7** to buy and sell (goods) **8** to exchange: *he traded a job in New York for a life as a cowboy* **9** to engage in trade **10** to deal or do business (with) [Low German: track, hence a regular business] **tradable** *or* **tradeable** *adj* **trader** *n* **trading** *n*

trade-in *n* **1** a used article given in part payment for the purchase of a new article ▷ *vb* **trade in** **2** to give (a used article) as part payment for a new article

trademark *n* **1 A** the name or other symbol used by a manufacturer to distinguish his or her products from those of competitors **B Registered Trademark** one that is officially registered and legally protected **2** any distinctive sign or mark of a person or thing: *the designer bars which have become the trademark of the city*

trade name *n* **1** the name used by a trade to refer to a product or range of products **2** the name under which a commercial enterprise operates in business

trade-off *n* an exchange, esp. as a compromise: *there is often a trade-off between manpower costs and computer costs*

trade on *vb* to exploit or take advantage of: *a demanding woman who traded on her poor health to get her own way*

tradescantia (trad-dess-**kan**-shee-a) *n* a widely cultivated plant with striped leaves [after John *Tradescant*, botanist]

trade secret *n* a secret formula, technique, or process known and used to advantage by only one manufacturer

tradesman *or fem* **tradeswoman** *n, pl* **-men** *or* **-women 1** a skilled worker, such as an electrician or painter **2** a shopkeeper

Trades Union Congress *n* (in Britain and South Africa) the major association of trade unions, which includes all the larger unions

trade union *or* **trades union** *n* a society of workers formed to protect and improve their working conditions, pay, etc. **trade unionism** *or* **trades unionism** *n* **trade unionist** *or* **trades unionist** *n*

trade wind *n* a wind blowing steadily towards the equator either from the northeast in the N hemisphere or the southeast in the S hemisphere

trading estate *n chiefly Brit* a large area in which a number of commercial or industrial firms are situated
tradition *n* **1** the handing down from generation to generation of customs, beliefs, etc. **2** the unwritten body of beliefs, customs, etc. handed down from generation to generation **3** a custom or practice of long standing **4 in the tradition of** having many features similar to those of a person or thing in the past: *a thriller writer in the tradition of Chandler* [Latin *traditio* a handing down]
traditional *adj* of, relating to, or being a tradition **traditionally** *adv*
traditionalist *n* a person who supports established customs or beliefs **traditionalism** *n*
traduce *vb* **-ducing, -duced** *formal* to speak badly of (someone) [Latin *traducere* to lead over, disgrace] **traducement** *n* **traducer** *n*
traffic *n* **1** the vehicles travelling on roads **2** the movement of vehicles or people in a particular place or for a particular purpose: *air traffic* **3** trade, esp. of an illicit kind: *drug traffic* **4** the exchange of ideas between people or organizations: *a lively traffic in ideas* ▷ *vb* **-ficking, -ficked 5** to carry on trade or business, esp. of an illicit kind: *he confessed to trafficking in gold and ivory* [Old French *trafique*] **trafficker** *n*
traffic island *n* a raised area in the middle of a road designed as a guide for traffic flow and to provide a stopping place for pedestrians crossing
traffic jam *n* a number of vehicles so obstructed that they can scarcely move
traffic light *n* one of a set of coloured lights placed at a junction to control the flow of traffic
traffic warden *n Brit* a person employed to supervise road traffic and report traffic offences
tragedian (traj-jee-dee-an) *or fem* **tragedienne** (traj-jee-dee-**enn**) *n* **1** an actor who specializes in tragic roles **2** a writer of tragedy
tragedy *n, pl* **-dies 1** a shocking or sad event **2** a serious play, film, or opera in which the main character is destroyed by a combination of a personal failing and adverse circumstances [Greek *tragōidia*]
tragic *adj* **1** sad and distressing because it involves death or suffering: *she was blinded in a tragic accident* **2** of or like a tragedy: *a tragic hero* **3** sad or mournful: *a tragic melody* **tragically** *adv*
tragicomedy *n, pl* **-dies** a play or other written work having both comic and tragic elements **tragicomic** *adj*
trail *n* **1** a rough path across open country or through a forest **2** a route along a series of roads or paths that has been specially planned to let people see or do particular things: *a nature trail through the woods* **3** a print, mark, or scent left by a person, animal, or object: *a trail of blood was found down three flights of stairs* **4** something that trails behind: *a vapour trail* **5** a sequence of results from an event: *a trail of mishaps* ▷ *vb* **6** to drag or stream along the ground or through the air behind someone or something: *part of her sari trailed behind her on the floor* **7** to lag behind (a person or thing): *Max had arrived as well, trailing behind the others* **8** to follow or hunt (an animal or person), usually secretly, by following the marks or tracks he, she, or it has made: *the police had trailed him the length and breadth of the country* **9** to be falling behind in a race, match or competition: *they trailed 2-1 at half-time* **10** to move wearily or slowly: *we spent the afternoon trailing round the shops* [Old French *trailler* to tow]
trail away *or* **trail off** *vb* to become fainter, quieter, or weaker: *his voice trailed away*
trailblazer *n* a pioneer in a particular field **trailblazing** *adj, n*
trailer *n* **1** a road vehicle, usually two-wheeled, towed by a motor vehicle and used for carrying goods, transporting boats, etc.: *ahead of us was a tractor, drawing a trailer laden with dung* **2** the rear section of an articulated lorry **3** an extract or series of extracts from a film, TV, or radio programme, used to advertise it **4** *US & Canad* same as **caravan** (sense 1)
trailer trash *n derogatory* poor people living in trailer parks in the US
trailing *adj* (of a plant) having a long stem which spreads over the ground or hangs loosely: *trailing ivy*
train *vb* **1** to instruct (someone) in a skill: *soldiers are trained to obey orders unquestioningly* **2** to learn the skills needed to do a particular job or activity: *she was training to be a computer programmer* **3** to do exercises and prepare for a specific purpose: *he was training for a marathon* **4** to focus on or aim at (something): *the warship kept its guns trained on the trawler* **5** to discipline (an animal) to obey commands or perform tricks **6** to tie or prune (a plant) so that it grows in a particular way: *he had trained the roses to grow up the wall* ▷ *n* **7** a line of railway coaches or wagons coupled together and drawn by a engine **8** a sequence or series: *following an earlier train of thought* **9** the long back section of a dress that trails along the floor **10 in its train** as a consequence: *economic mismanagement brought unemployment and inflation in its train* **11 in train** actually happening or being done: *the programme of reforms set in train by the new government* ▷ *adj* **12** of or by a train: *the long train journey North* [Old French *trahiner*]
trainbearer *n* an attendant who holds up the train of a dignitary's robe or bride's gown
trainee *n* **1** a person undergoing training ▷ *adj* **2** (of a person) undergoing training: *a trainee journalist*
trainer *n* **1** a person who coaches a person or team in a sport **2** a person who trains racehorses **3** an aircraft used for training pilots **4** *Brit* a flat-soled sports shoe of the style used by athletes when training
training *n* the process of bringing a person to an agreed standard of proficiency by practice and instruction
training shoe *n* same as **trainer** (sense 4)
train spotter *n Brit* **1** a person who collects the numbers of railway locomotives **2** *informal* a person who is obsessed with trivial details, esp. of a subject generally considered uninteresting
traipse *informal* ▷ *vb* **traipsing, traipsed 1** to walk heavily or tiredly ▷ *n* **2** a long or tiring walk [origin unknown]
trait *n* a characteristic feature or quality of a person or thing [French]

traitor *n* a person who betrays friends, country, a cause, etc. [Latin *tradere* to hand over] **traitorous** *adj* **traitress** *fem n*

trajectory *n, pl* **-ries** the path described by an object moving in air or space, esp. the curved path of a projectile [Latin *trajectus* cast over]

tram *n* an electrically driven public transport vehicle that runs on rails laid into the road and takes its power from an overhead cable [probably from Low German *traam* beam]

tramlines *pl n* **1** the tracks on which a tram runs **2** the outer markings along the sides of a tennis or badminton court

trammel *vb* **-melling, -melled** *or US* **-meling, -meled 1** to hinder or restrict: *trammelled by family responsibilities* ▷ *n* **2 trammels** things that hinder or restrict someone: *the trammels of social respectability* [Old French *tramail* three-mesh net]

tramp *vb* **1** to walk long and far; hike **2** to walk heavily or firmly across or through (a place): *she tramped slowly up the beach* ▷ *n* **3** a homeless person who travels about on foot, living by begging or doing casual work **4** a long hard walk; hike: *we went for a long tramp over the downs* **5** the sound of heavy regular footsteps: *we could hear the tramp of the marching soldiers* **6** a small cargo ship that does not run on a regular schedule **7** *US, Canad, Austral & NZ derogatory slang* a woman considered promiscuous [probably from Middle Low German *trampen*]

tramping *n NZ* the leisure activity of walking in the bush **tramper** *n*

trample *vb* **-pling, -pled 1** Also: **trample on** to tread on and crush: *three children were trampled to death when the crowd panicked and ran* **2 trample on** to treat (a person or his or her rights or feelings) with disregard or contempt [from *tramp*]

trampoline *n* **1** a tough canvas sheet suspended by springs or cords from a frame, which acrobats, gymnasts, etc., bounce on ▷ *vb* **-lining, -lined 2** to exercise on a trampoline [Italian *trampolino*]

trance *n* **1** a hypnotic state resembling sleep in which a person is unable to move or act of his or her own will **2** a dazed or stunned state [Latin *transire* to go over]

t

tranche (**trahnsh**) *n* an instalment or portion, esp. of a loan or share issue: *the new shares will be offered in four tranches around the world*

trannie *or* **tranny** *n, pl* **-nies** *informal, chiefly Brit* a transistor radio

tranquil *adj* calm, peaceful, or quiet [Latin *tranquillus*] **tranquilly** *adv*

tranquillity *or US sometimes* **tranquility** *n* a state of calmness or peace

tranquillize, -lise *or US* **tranquilize** *vb* **-lizing, -lized** *or* **-lising, -lised 1** to make or become calm or calmer **2** to give (someone) a drug to make them calm or calmer **tranquillization, -lisation** *or US* **tranquilization** *n* **tranquillizing, -lising** *or US* **tranquilizing** *adj*

tranquillizer, -liser *or US* **tranquilizer** *n* a drug that calms someone suffering from anxiety, tension, etc.

trans *adj* short for **transgender**

trans. **1** transitive **2** translated

trans- *prefix* **1** across, beyond, crossing, or on the other side of: *transnational* **2** changing thoroughly: *transliterate* [Latin]

transact *vb* to do, conduct, or negotiate (a business deal) [Latin *transigere* to drive through]

transaction *n* **1** something that is transacted, esp. a business deal **2 transactions** the records of the proceedings of a society, etc.: *an article on land use in the Niagara area taken from the 'Transactions of the Royal Canadian Institute'*

transalpine *adj* beyond the Alps, esp. as viewed from Italy

transatlantic *adj* **1** on or from the other side of the Atlantic **2** crossing the Atlantic

transceiver *n* a device which transmits and receives radio or electronic signals [*trans(mitter)* + *(re)ceiver*]

transcend *vb* **1** to go above or beyond what is expected or normal: *a vital party issue that transcends traditional party loyalties* **2** to overcome or be superior to: *to transcend all difficulties* [Latin *transcendere* to climb over]

transcendent *adj* **1** above or beyond what is expected or normal **2** *theol* (of God) having existence outside the created world **transcendence** *n*

transcendental *adj* **1** above or beyond what is expected or normal **2** *philosophy* based on intuition or innate belief rather than experience **3** supernatural or mystical **transcendentally** *adv*

transcendentalism *n* any system of philosophy that seeks to discover the nature of reality by examining the processes of thought rather than the things thought about, or that emphasizes intuition as a means to knowledge **transcendentalist** *n, adj*

Transcendental Meditation *n* a technique (trademarked in the US), based on Hindu traditions, for relaxing and refreshing the mind and body through the silent repetition of a special formula of words

transcribe *vb* **-scribing, -scribed 1** to write, type, or print out (a text) fully from a speech or notes **2** to make an electrical recording of (a programme or speech) for a later broadcast **3** *music* to rewrite (a piece of music) for an instrument other than that originally intended [Latin *transcribere*] **transcriber** *n*

transcript *n* **1** a written, typed, or printed copy made by transcribing **2** *chiefly US & Canad* an official record of a student's school progress

transcription *n* **1** the act of transcribing **2** something transcribed

transducer *n* any device, such as a microphone or electric motor, that converts one form of energy into another [Latin *transducere* to lead across]

transect *n biol* a sample strip of land used to monitor plant distribution and animal populations within a given area

transept *n* either of the two shorter wings of a cross-shaped church [Latin *trans-* across + *saeptum* enclosure]

transfer *vb* **-ferring, -ferred 1** to change or move from one thing, person, place, etc., to another: *he was transferred from prison to hospital* **2** to move (money or property) from the control of one person or organization to that of another: *the money has been transferred into your account* **3** (of a football club) to sell or release (a player) to another club: *he was transferred to Juventus for a world record fee* **4** to move (a drawing or design) from one surface to another ▷ *n* **5** the act, process, or system of transferring, or the state of being transferred **6** a person or thing that transfers or is transferred **7** a design or drawing that is transferred from one surface to another **8** the moving of (money or property) from the control of one person or organization to that of another [Latin *trans* across + *ferre* to carry] **transferable** *or* **transferrable** *adj* **transference** *n*

transfer station *n NZ* a depot where rubbish is sorted for recycling

transfiguration *n* a transfiguring or being transfigured

Transfiguration *n* **1** *New Testament* the change in the appearance of Christ on the mountain **2** the Church festival held in commemoration of this on August 6

transfigure *vb* **-guring, -gured 1** to change or cause to change in appearance **2** to become or cause to become more exalted [Latin *trans-* beyond + *figura* appearance]

transfix *vb* **-fixing, -fixed** *or* **-fixt 1** to make (someone) motionless, esp. with horror or shock: *they stood transfixed and revolted by what they saw* **2** to pierce (a person or animal) through with a pointed object: *the Pharaoh is shown transfixing enemies with arrows from a moving chariot* [Latin *transfigere* to pierce through]

transform *vb* **1** to change completely in form or function: *the last forty years have seen the country transformed from a peasant economy to a major industrial power* **2** to change so as to make better or more attractive: *most religions claim to be able to transform people's lives* **3** to convert (one form of energy) to another **4** *maths* to change the form of (an equation, expression, etc.) without changing its value **5** to change (an alternating current or voltage) using a transformer [Latin *transformare*]

transformation *n* **1** a change or alteration, esp. a radical one **2** the act of transforming or the state of being transformed **3** *S African* a political slogan for demographic change in the power struggle

transformer *n* a device that transfers an alternating current from one circuit to one or more other circuits, usually with a change of voltage

transfuse *vb* **-fusing, -fused 1** to inject (blood or other fluid) into a blood vessel **2** *literary* to transmit or instil [Latin *transfundere* to pour out]

transfusion *n* **1** the injection of blood, blood plasma, etc., into the blood vessels of a patient **2** the act of transferring something: *a transfusion of new funds*

transgender *adj* having a gender identity that does not fully correspond to the gender assigned to one at birth

transgenic *adj* (of an animal or plant) containing genetic material artificially transferred from another species

transgress *vb formal* **1** to break (a law or rule) **2** to overstep (a limit): *he had never before been known to transgress the very slowest of walks* [Latin *trans* beyond + *gradi* to step] **transgression** *n* **transgressor** *n*

transient *adj* **1** lasting for a short time only: *she had a number of transient relationships with fellow students* **2** (of a person) not remaining in a place for a long time: *the transient population of the inner city* ▷ *n* **3** a transient person or thing [Latin *transiens* going over] **transience** *n*

transistor *n* **1** a semiconductor device used to amplify and control electric currents **2** *informal* a small portable radio containing transistors [*transfer* + *resistor*]

transistorized *or* **-ised** *adj* (of an electronic device) using transistors

transit *n* **1** the moving or carrying of goods or people from one place to another **2** a route or means of transport: *transit by road* **3** *astron* the apparent passage of a celestial body across the meridian **4 in transit** while travelling or being taken from one place to another: *in transit the fruit can be damaged* ▷ *adj* **5** indicating a place or building where people wait or goods are kept between different stages of a journey: *a transit lounge for passengers who are changing planes* [Latin *transitus* a going over]

transit camp *n* a camp in which refugees, soldiers, etc., live temporarily

transition *n* **1** the process of changing from one state or stage to another: *the transition from dictatorship to democracy* **2** *music* a movement from one key to another ▷ *vb* **3** to change from one state or stage to another [Latin *transitio* a going over] **transitional** *adj*

transition element *or* **transition metal** *n chem* any element belonging to one of three series of elements with atomic numbers between 21 and 30, 39 and 48, and 57 and 80 (**transition series**). They tend to have more than one valency and to form complexes

transitive *adj grammar* denoting a verb that requires a direct object: *'to find' is a transitive verb*

transitory *adj* lasting only for a short time

translate *vb* **-lating, -lated 1 A** to change (something spoken or written in one language) into another **B** to be capable of being changed from one language into another: *puns do not translate well* **2** to express (something) in a different way, for instance by using a different measurement system or less technical language: *the temperature is 30° Celsius, or if we translate into Fahrenheit, 86°* **3** to transform or convert, for instance by putting an idea into practice: *cheap crops translate into lower feed prices* **4** to interpret the significance of (a gesture, action, etc.): *I gave him what I hoped would be translated as a thoughtful look* **5** to act as a translator: *I had to translate for a party of visiting Greeks* [Latin *translatus* carried over] **translatable** *adj* **translator** *n*

translation *n* **1** a piece of writing or speech that has been translated into another language **2** the act of translating something **3** the expression of something in a different way or form: *the book's plot was radically altered during its translation to film* **4** *maths* a transformation in which the origin of a

t

coordinate system is moved to another position so that each axis retains the same direction **translational** *adj*

transliterate *vb* **-rating, -rated** to write or spell (a word, etc.) into corresponding letters of another alphabet [Latin *trans-* across + *littera* letter] **transliteration** *n*

translucent *adj* allowing light to pass through, but not transparent [Latin *translucere* to shine through] **translucency** *or* **translucence** *n*

transmigrate *vb* **-grating, -grated** (of a soul) to pass from one body into another at death **transmigration** *n*

transmission *n* **1** the sending or passing of something, such as a message or disease from one place or person to another **2** something that is transmitted, esp. a radio or television broadcast **3** a system of shafts and gears that transmits power from the engine to the driving wheels of a motor vehicle

transmit *vb* **-mitting, -mitted 1** to pass (something, such as a message or disease) from one place or person to another **2 A** to send out (signals) by means of radio waves **B** to broadcast (a radio or television programme) **3** to allow the passage of (particles, energy, etc.): *water transmits sound better than air* **4** to transfer (a force, motion, etc.) from one part of a mechanical system to another: *the chain of the bike transmits the motion of the pedals to the rear wheel* [Latin *transmittere* to send across] **transmittable** *adj*

transmitter *n* **1** a piece of equipment used for broadcasting radio or television programmes **2** a person or thing that transmits something

transmogrify *vb* **-fies, -fying, -fied** *humorous* to change or transform (someone or something) into a different shape or appearance, esp. a grotesque or bizarre one [origin unknown] **transmogrification** *n*

transmute *vb* **-muting, -muted** to change the form or nature of: *self-contempt is transmuted into hatred of others* [Latin *transmutare* to shift] **transmutation** *n*

transom *n* **1** a horizontal bar across a window **2** a horizontal bar that separates a door from a window over it [Old French *traversin*]

t

transparency *n, pl* **-cies 1** the state of being transparent **2** a positive photograph on transparent film, usually mounted in a frame or between glass plates, which can be viewed with the use of a slide projector

transparent *adj* **1** able to be seen through; clear **2** easy to understand or recognize; obvious: *transparent honesty* [Latin *trans-* through + *parere* to appear] **transparently** *adv*

transpire *vb* **-spiring, -spired 1** to come to light; become known **2** *not standard* to happen or occur **3** *physiol* to give off (water or vapour) through the pores of the skin, etc. **4** (of plants) to lose (water vapour) through the stomata [Latin *trans-* through + *spirare* to breathe] **transpiration** *n*

> **USAGE** It is often maintained that *transpire* should not be used to mean happen or occur, as in *the event transpired late in the evening*, and that the word is properly used to mean become known, as in *it transpired later that the thief had been caught*. The word is, however, widely used in the former sense, esp. in spoken English.

transplant *vb* **1** *surgery* to transfer (an organ or tissue) from one part of the body or from one person to another **2** to remove or transfer (esp. a plant) from one place to another ▷ *n* **3** *surgery* **A** the procedure involved in transferring an organ or tissue **B** the organ or tissue transplanted **transplantation** *n*

transponder *n* a type of radio or radar transmitter-receiver that transmits signals automatically when it receives predetermined signals [*transmitter* + *responder*]

transport *vb* **1** to carry or move (people or goods) from one place to another, esp. over some distance **2** *history* to exile (a criminal) to a penal colony **3** to have a strong emotional effect on: *transported by joy* ▷ *n* **4** the business or system of transporting goods or people: *public transport* **5** *Brit* freight vehicles generally **6** a vehicle used to transport troops **7** a transporting or being transported **8** ecstasy or rapture: *transports of delight* [Latin *trans-* across + *portare* to carry] **transportable** *adj*

transportation *n* **1** a means or system of transporting **2** the act of transporting or the state of being transported **3** *history* deportation to a penal colony

transport café *n Brit* an inexpensive eating place on a main road, used mainly by long-distance lorry drivers

transporter *n* a large vehicle used for carrying cars from the factory to garages for sale

transpose *vb* **-posing, -posed 1** to change the order of (letters, words, or sentences) **2** *music* to play (notes, music, etc.) in a different key **3** *maths* to move (a term) from one side of an equation to the other with a corresponding reversal in sign: *transposing 3 in* $x - 3 = 6$ *gives* $x = 6 + 3$ [Old French *transposer*] **transposition** *n*

transsexual *or* **transexual** *n* **1** a person who believes that his or her true identity is of the opposite sex **2** a person who has had medical treatment to alter his or her sexual characteristics to those of the opposite sex

transship *vb* **-shipping, -shipped** to transfer or be transferred from one ship or vehicle to another **transshipment** *n*

transubstantiation *n Christianity* the doctrine that the bread and wine consecrated in Communion changes into the substance of Christ's body and blood [Latin *trans-* over + *substantia* substance]

transuranic (tranz-yoor-**ran**-ik) *adj chem* (of an element) having an atomic number greater than that of uranium

transverse *adj* crossing from side to side: *the transverse arches in the main hall of the college* [Latin *transvertere* to turn across]

transvestite *n* a person, esp. a man, who seeks sexual pleasure from wearing clothes of the opposite sex [Latin *trans-* across + *vestitus* clothed] **transvestism** *n*

trap *n* **1** a device or hole in which something, esp. an animal, is caught: *a fox trap* **2** a plan for tricking a person into being caught unawares **3** a situation from which it is difficult to escape: *caught in the poverty trap* **4** a bend in a pipe that contains standing water to prevent the passage of gases **5** a boxlike stall in which greyhounds are enclosed before the start of a race **6** a device that hurls clay pigeons into the air to be fired at **7** See **trap door** **8** a light two-wheeled carriage: *a pony and trap* **9** *Brit, Austral & NZ slang* the mouth: *shut your trap!* ▷ *vb* **trapping, trapped** **10** to catch (an animal) in a trap **11** to catch (someone) by a trick: *the police trapped the drug dealers by posing as potential customers* **12** to hold or confine in an unpleasant situation from which it is difficult to escape: *trapped in the rubble of collapsed buildings* ▷ See also **trap out** [Old English *træppe*]

trap door *n* a hinged door in a ceiling, floor, or stage

trap-door spider *n* a spider that builds a silk-lined hole in the ground closed by a hinged door of earth and silk

trapeze *n* a horizontal bar suspended from two ropes, used by circus acrobats [French]

trapezium *n, pl* **-ziums** *or* **-zia** **1** a quadrilateral having two parallel sides of unequal length **2** *chiefly US & Canad* a quadrilateral having neither pair of sides parallel [Greek *trapeza* table]
trapezial *adj*

trapezoid (trap-piz-zoid) *n* **1** a quadrilateral having neither pair of sides parallel **2** *US & Canad* same as **trapezium** (sense 1) [Greek *trapeza* table]

trap out *vb* **trapping, trapped** to dress or adorn [Old French *drap* cloth]

trapper *n* a person who traps animals, esp. for their furs or skins

trappings *pl n* **1** the accessories that symbolize a condition, office, etc.: *the trappings of power* **2** ceremonial harness for a horse or other animal [probably from Old French *drap* cloth]

Trappist *n* a member of an order of Christian monks who follow a rule of strict silence

trash *n* **1** foolish ideas or talk; nonsense **2** *US, Canad, NZ & S African* unwanted objects; rubbish **3** *chiefly US, Canad & NZ* a worthless person or group of people ▷ *vb* **4** *slang* to attack or destroy maliciously: *we've never trashed a hotel room* [origin unknown] **trashy** *adj*

trattoria (trat-or-ee-a) *n* an Italian restaurant [Italian]

trauma (traw-ma) *n* **1** *psychol* an emotional shock that may have long-lasting effects **2** *pathol* any bodily injury or wound [Greek: a wound]
traumatic *adj* **traumatically** *adv* **traumatize** *or* **-ise** *vb*

travail *n literary* painful or exceptionally hard work [Old French *travaillier*]

travel *vb* **-elling, -elled** *or US* **-eling, -eled** **1** to go or move from one place to another **2** to go or journey through or across (an area, region, etc.): *Margaret travelled widely when she was in New Zealand* **3** to go at a specified speed or for a specified distance: *the car was travelling at 30 mph* **4** to go from place to place as a salesperson **5** (of perishable goods) to withstand a journey: *not all wines travel well* **6** (of light or sound) to be transmitted or carried from one place to another: *sound travels a long distance in these conditions* **7** (of a machine or part) to move in a fixed path **8** *informal* (of a vehicle) to move rapidly ▷ *n* **9** the act or a means of travelling: *air travel has changed the way people live* **10** a tour or journey: *his travels took him to Dublin* **11** the distance moved by a mechanical part, such as the stroke of a piston [Old French *travaillier* to travail]

travel agency *n* an agency that arranges flights, hotel accommodation, etc., for tourists
travel agent *n*

traveller *or US* **traveler** *n* **1** a person who travels, esp. habitually **2** a travelling salesman **3** a member of a people with a nomadic lifestyle

traveller's cheque *n* a cheque sold by a bank, travel agency, etc., which the buyer signs on purchase and can cash abroad by re-signing it

travelling salesman *n* a person who travels within an assigned area in order to sell goods or get orders for the company he or she represents

travelogue *or US* **travelog** *n* a film or lecture on travels and travelling

travel sickness *n* nausea or vomiting caused by riding in a car or other moving vehicle
travel-sick *adj*

traverse *vb* **-versing, -versed** **1** to move over or back and forth over; cross: *he once traversed San Francisco harbour in a balloon* **2** to reach across **3** to walk, climb, or ski diagonally up or down a slope ▷ *n* **4** something being or lying across, such as a crossbar **5** the act or an instance of traversing or crossing **6** a path or road across ▷ *adj* **7** being or lying across [Latin *transversus* turned across]
traversal *n*

travesty *n, pl* **-ties** **1** a grotesque imitation or mockery: *a travesty of justice* ▷ *vb* **-ties, -tying, -tied** **2** to make or be a travesty of [French *travesti* disguised]

travois (trav-voy) *n, pl* **-vois** (-voyz) *Canad* a sled used for dragging logs [Canadian French]

trawl *n* **1** a large net, usually in the shape of a sock or bag, dragged at deep levels behind a fishing boat ▷ *vb* **2** to fish using such a net [Middle Dutch *traghelen* to drag]

trawler *n* a ship used for trawling

tray *n* **1** a flat board of wood, plastic, or metal, usually with a rim, on which things can be carried **2** an open receptacle for office correspondence [Old English *trieg*]

TRC *n* (in South Africa) Truth and Reconciliation Commission: a commission which encourages people who committed human rights abuses or acts of terror during the apartheid era to reveal the truth about their crimes in return for immunity from prosecution

treacherous *adj* **1** disloyal and untrustworthy: *he was cruel, treacherous, and unscrupulous* **2** unreliable or dangerous, esp. because of sudden changes: *the tides here can be very treacherous* **treacherously** *adv*

treachery *n, pl* **-eries** the act or an instance of wilful betrayal [Old French *trecherie*]

treacle *n* a thick dark syrup obtained during the refining of sugar [Latin *theriaca* antidote to poison] **treacly** *adj*

tread *vb* **treading, trod, trodden** *or* **trod** **1** to set one's foot down on or in something: *he trod on* *some dog's dirt* **2** to crush or squash by treading (on): *treading on a biscuit* **3** to walk along (a path or road) **4** **tread carefully** *or* **warily** to proceed in a delicate or tactful manner **5** **tread water** to stay afloat in an upright position by moving the legs in a walking motion ▷ *n* **6** a way of walking or the sound of walking: *he walked, with a heavy tread, up the stairs* **7** the top surface of a step in a staircase **8** the pattern of grooves in the outer surface of a tyre that helps it grip the road **9** the part of a shoe that is generally in contact with the ground [Old English *tredan*]

treadle (**tred**-dl) *n* a lever operated by the foot to turn a wheel [Old English *tredan* to tread]

treadmill *n* **1** (formerly) an apparatus turned by the weight of men or animals climbing steps on a revolving cylinder or wheel **2** a dreary routine: *they are chained to the treadmill of a job* **3** an exercise machine that consists of a continuous moving belt on which to walk or jog

treason *n* **1** betrayal of one's sovereign or country, esp. by attempting to overthrow the government **2** any treachery or betrayal [Latin *traditio* a handing over] **treasonable** *adj* **treasonous** *adj*

treasure *n* **1** a collection of wealth, esp. in the form of money, precious metals, or gems **2** a valuable painting, ornament, or other object: *the museum has many art treasures* **3** *informal* a person who is highly valued: *she can turn her hand to anything, she's a perfect treasure* ▷ *vb* **-suring, -sured** **4** to cherish (someone or something) [Greek *thēsauros*]

treasure hunt *n* a game in which players act upon successive clues to find a hidden prize

treasurer *n* a person appointed to look after the funds of a society or other organization

treasure-trove *n law* any articles, such as coins or valuable objects found hidden and without any evidence of ownership [Anglo-French *tresor trové* treasure found]

treasury *n, pl* **-uries** **1** a storage place for treasure **2** the revenues or funds of a government or organization

Treasury *n* (in various countries) the government department in charge of finance

treat *vb* **1** to deal with or regard in a certain manner: *her love for a man who treats her abominably* **2** to attempt to cure or lessen the symptoms of (an illness or injury or a person suffering from it): *the drug is prescribed to treat asthma* **3** to subject to a chemical or industrial process: *the wood should be treated with a preservative* **4** to provide (someone) with something as a treat: *I'll treat you to an ice cream* **5** **treat of** to deal with (something) in writing or speaking: *this book treats of a most abstruse subject* ▷ *n* **6** a celebration, entertainment, gift, or meal given for or to someone and paid for by someone else **7** any delightful surprise or specially pleasant occasion [Old French *tretier*] **treatable** *adj*

treatise (**treat**-izz) *n* a formal piece of writing that deals systematically with a particular subject [Anglo-French *tretiz*]

treatment *n* **1** the medical or surgical care given to a patient **2** a way of handling a person or thing: *the party has had unfair treatment in the press*

treaty *n, pl* **-ties** **1** a formal written agreement between two or more states, such as an alliance or trade arrangement: *the Treaty of Rome established the Common Market* **2** an agreement between two parties concerning the purchase of property [Old French *traité*]

treble *adj* **1** three times as much or as many **2** of or denoting a soprano voice or part or a high-pitched instrument **3** of the highest range of musical notes: *these loudspeakers give excellent treble reproduction* ▷ *n* **4** a soprano voice or part or a high-pitched instrument ▷ *vb* **-bling, -bled** **5** to make or become three times as much or as many: *sales have trebled in three years* [Latin *triplus* threefold] **trebly** *adv*

treble chance *n Brit* a method of betting in football pools in which the chances of winning are related to the number of draws and the number of home and away wins forecast by the competitor

treble clef *n music* the clef that establishes G a fifth above middle C as being on the second line of the staff

tree *n* **1** any large woody perennial plant with a distinct trunk and usually having leaves and branches. Related adjective: **arboreal** **2** See **family tree, shoetree** **3** **at the top of the tree** in the highest position of a profession [Old English *trēow*] **treeless** *adj*

tree creeper *n* a small songbird of the N hemisphere that creeps up trees to feed on insects

tree diagram *n maths* a branching diagram showing the probability of various events

tree fern *n* any of numerous large tropical ferns with a trunklike stem

tree kangaroo *n* a tree-living kangaroo of New Guinea and N Australia

tree line *n* same as **timber line**

tree-lined *adj* (of a road) having trees on either side of it: *a pleasant tree-lined avenue in Bristol*

tree surgery *n* the treatment of damaged trees by filling cavities, applying braces, etc. **tree surgeon** *n*

tree tomato *n* same as **tamarillo**

treetop *n* the highest part of a tree, where the leaves and branches are: *monkeys swung through the treetops*

trefoil (**tref**-foil) *n* **1** a plant, such as clover, with leaves divided into three smaller leaves **2** *archit* a carved ornament with a shape like such leaves [Latin *trifolium* three-leaved herb] **trefoiled** *adj*

trek *n* **1** a long and often difficult journey, esp. on foot **2** *S African* a journey or stage of a journey, esp. a migration by ox wagon ▷ *vb* **trekking, trekked** **3** to make a trek [Afrikaans]

trellis *n* a frame made of vertical and horizontal strips of wood, esp. one used to support climbing plants [Old French *treliz* fabric of open texture] **trelliswork** *n*

tremble *vb* **-bling, -bled** **1** to shake with short slight movements: *her hands trembled uncontrollably; he felt the ground trembling beneath him* **2** to experience fear or anxiety: *his parents trembled with apprehension about his future* **3** (of the voice) to sound uncertain or unsteady, for instance through pain or emotion ▷ *n* **4** the act or an instance of trembling [Latin *tremere*] **trembling** *adj*

tremendous *adj* **1** very large or impressive: *a tremendous amount of money* **2** very exciting or unusual: *a tremendous feeling of elation* **3** very good or pleasing: *my wife has given me tremendous support* [Latin *tremendus* terrible] **tremendously** *adv*

tremolo *n, pl* **-los** *music* **1** (in playing the violin or other stringed instrument) the rapid repetition of a note or notes to produce a trembling effect **2** (in singing) a fluctuation in pitch [Italian: quavering]

tremor *n* **1** an involuntary shudder or vibration: *the slight tremor of excitement* **2** a minor earthquake [Latin]

tremulous *adj literary* trembling, as from fear or excitement: *I managed a tremulous smile* [Latin *tremere* to shake] **tremulously** *adv*

trench *n* **1** a long narrow ditch in the ground, such as one for laying a pipe in **2** a long deep ditch used by soldiers for protection in a war: *my grandfather fought in the trenches in the First World War* ▷ *adj* **3** of or involving military trenches: *trench warfare* [Old French *trenche* something cut]

trenchant *adj* **1** keen or incisive: *a trenchant screenplay* **2** vigorous and effective: *the prime minister's trenchant adoption of this issue* [Old French: cutting] **trenchancy** *n*

trench coat *n* a belted raincoat similar in style to a military officer's coat

trencher *n history* a wooden board on which food was served or cut [Old French *trencheoir*]

trencherman *n, pl* **-men** a person who enjoys food; hearty eater

trench warfare *n* a type of warfare in which opposing armies face each other in entrenched positions

trend *n* **1** general tendency or direction: *a trend towards more flexible working hours* **2** fashionable style: *she set a trend for wearing lingerie as outer garments* ▷ *vb* **3** to take a certain trend **4** to be widely discussed on a social media site [Old English *trendan* to turn]

trendsetter *n* a person or thing that creates, or may create, a new fashion **trendsetting** *adj*

trendy *informal* ▷ *adj* **trendier, trendiest** **1** consciously fashionable: *a flat in Glasgow's trendy West End* ▷ *n, pl* **trendies** **2** a trendy person: *a media trendy* **trendily** *adv* **trendiness** *n*

trepidation *n formal* a state of fear or anxiety [Latin *trepidatio*]

trespass *vb* **1** to go onto somebody else's property without permission ▷ *n* **2** the act or an instance of trespassing **3** *old-fashioned* a sin or wrongdoing [Old French *trespas* a passage] **trespasser** *n*

trespass on *or* **trespass upon** *vb formal* to take unfair advantage of (someone's friendship, patience, etc.): *I won't trespass upon your hospitality any longer*

tresses *pl n* a woman's long flowing hair [Old French *trece*]

trestle *n* **1** a support for one end of a table or beam, consisting of two rectangular frameworks or sets of legs which are joined at the top but not the bottom **2** Also called: **trestle table** a table consisting of a board supported by a trestle at each end [Old French *trestel*]

trevally (trih-val-lee) *n, pl* **-lies** *Austral & NZ* any of various food and game fishes [probably alteration of *cavalla*, species of tropical fish]

trews *pl n chiefly Brit* close-fitting trousers of tartan cloth [Scottish Gaelic *triubhas*]

tri- *combining form* **1** three or thrice: *trilingual* **2** occurring every three: *triweekly* [Latin *tres*]

triad *n* **1** a group of three **2** *music* a three-note chord consisting of a note and the third and fifth above it [Greek *trias*] **triadic** *adj*

Triad *n* a Chinese secret society involved in criminal activities, such as drug trafficking

trial *n* **1** *law* an investigation of a case in front of a judge to decide whether a person is innocent or guilty of a crime by questioning him or her and considering the evidence **2** the act or an instance of trying or proving; test or experiment: *the new drug is undergoing clinical trials* **3** an annoying or frustrating person or thing: *young children can be a great trial at times* **4** a motorcycling competition in which the skills of the riders are tested over rough ground **5 trials** a sporting competition for individual people or animals: *horse trials* **6 on trial** **A** undergoing trial, esp. before a court of law **B** being tested, for example before a commitment to purchase: *I only have the car out on trial* ▷ *adj* **7** on a temporary basis while being tried out or tested: *a trial run* ▷ *vb* **trialling, trialled** **8** to test or make experimental use of: *the idea has been trialled in several schools* [Anglo-French *trier* to try]

trial and error *n* a method of discovery based on practical experiment and experience rather than on theory: *raising her children has been a matter of trial and error*

trial balance *n accounting* a statement of all the debit and credit balances in the double-entry ledger

triallist *or* **trialist** *n* **1** a person who takes part in a competition **2** *sport* a person who takes part in a preliminary match or heat held to determine selection for a team or event

triangle *n* **1** a geometric figure with three sides and three angles **2** any object shaped like a triangle: *a triangle of streets running up from the river* **3** *music* a percussion instrument that consists of a metal bar bent into a triangular shape, played by striking it with a metal stick **4** any situation involving three people or points of view: *a torrid sex triangle* [TRI- + Latin *angulus* corner] **triangular** *adj*

triangulate *vb* **-lating, -lated** to survey (an area) by dividing it into triangles

triangulation *n* a method of surveying in which an area is divided into triangles, one side (the base line) and all angles of which are measured and the lengths of the other lines calculated by trigonometry

Triassic *adj geol* of the period of geological time about 230 million years ago [Latin *trias* triad]

triathlon *n* an athletic contest in which each athlete competes in three different events: swimming, cycling, and running [TRI- + Greek *athlon* contest] **triathlete** *n*

tribalism *n* loyalty to a tribe, esp. as opposed to a modern political entity such as a state

t

tribe *n* **1** a group of families or clans believed to have a common ancestor **2** *informal* a group of people who do the same type of thing: *a tribe of German yachtsmen* [Latin *tribus*] **tribal** *adj*

tribesman *n, pl* **-men** a member of a tribe

tribulation *n* great distress: *the tribulations of a deserted wife* [Latin *tribulare* to afflict]

tribunal *n* **1** a special court or committee that is appointed to deal with a particular problem: *an industrial tribunal investigating allegations of unfair dismissal* **2** a court of justice [Latin *tribunus* tribune]

tribune *n* **1** a person who upholds public rights **2** (in ancient Rome) an officer elected by the plebs to protect their interests [Latin *tribunus*]

tributary *n, pl* **-taries 1** a stream or river that flows into a larger one: *Frankfurt lies on the River Main, a tributary of the Rhine* **2** a person, nation, or people that pays tribute ▹ *adj* **3** (of a stream or river) flowing into a larger stream **4** paying tribute: *Egypt was formerly a tributary province of the Turkish Empire*

tribute *n* **1** something given, done, or said as a mark of respect or admiration **2** a payment by one ruler or state to another, usually as an acknowledgment of submission **3** something that shows the merits of a particular quality of a person or thing: *the car's low fuel consumption is a tribute to the quality of its engine* [Latin *tributum*]

tribute band *n* a rock or pop group that plays the music and copies the style of another, much more famous, group

trice *n* **in a trice** in a moment: *she was back in a trice* [originally, at one tug, from *trice* to haul up]

triceps *n* the muscle at the back of the upper arm [Latin]

trichology (trick-ol-a-jee) *n* the branch of medicine concerned with the hair and its diseases [Greek *thrix* hair] **trichologist** *n*

trichromatic *or* **trichromic** *adj* **1** having or involving three colours **2** of or having normal colour vision **trichromatism** *n*

trick *n* **1** a deceitful or cunning action or plan: *she was willing to use any dirty trick to get what she wanted* **2** a joke or prank: *he loves playing tricks on his sister* **3** a clever way of doing something, learned from experience: *an old campers' trick is to use three thin blankets rather than one thick one* **4** an illusory or magical feat or device **5** a simple feat learned by an animal or person **6** a deceptive illusion: *a trick of the light* **7** a habit or mannerism: *she had a trick of saying 'oh dear'* **8** *cards* a batch of cards played in turn and won by the person playing the highest card **9 do the trick** *informal* to produce the desired result **10 how's tricks?** *slang* how are you? ▹ *vb* **11** to defraud, deceive, or cheat (someone) [Old French *trique*] **trickery** *n*

trickle *vb* **-ling, -led 1** to flow or cause to flow in a thin stream or drops: *tears trickled down her cheeks* **2** to move slowly or in small groups: *voters trickled to the polls* ▹ *n* **3** a thin, irregular, or slow flow of something: *a trickle of blood* [probably imitative]

trickle-down *adj* of the theory that granting concessions like tax cuts to the rich will benefit all levels of society by stimulating the economy

trick out *vb* to dress up: *tricked out in chauffeur's rig*

trickster *n* a person who deceives or plays tricks

tricky *adj* **trickier, trickiest 1** involving snags or difficulties: *a tricky task* **2** needing careful handling: *a tricky situation* **3** sly or wily: *a tricky customer* **trickily** *adv* **trickiness** *n*

tricolour *or US* **tricolor** (trick-kol-lor) *n* a flag with three equal stripes in different colours, esp. the French or Irish national flags

tricycle *n* a three-wheeled cycle **tricyclist** *n*

trident *n* a three-pronged spear [Latin *tridens* three-pronged]

tried *vb* the past of **try**

triennial *adj* occurring every three years [TRI- + Latin *annus* year] **triennially** *adv*

trier *n* a person or thing that tries

trifle[1] *n* **1** a thing of little or no value or significance **2** *Brit, Austral & NZ* a cold dessert made of sponge cake spread with jam or fruit, soaked in sherry, covered with custard and cream **3 a trifle** to a small extent or degree; slightly: *he is a trifle eccentric* [Old French *trufle* mockery]

trifle[2] *vb* **trifling, trifled** > **trifle with** to treat (a person or his or her feelings) with disdain or disregard

trifling *adj* insignificant, petty, or frivolous: *a trifling misunderstanding*

trig. trigonometry

trigger *n* **1** a small lever that releases a catch on a gun or machine **2** any event that sets a course of action in motion: *his murder was the trigger for a night of rioting* ▹ *vb* **3** Also: **trigger off** to set (an action or process) in motion: *various factors can trigger off a migraine* [Dutch *trekker*]

trigger-happy *adj informal* too ready or willing to use guns or violence: *trigger-happy border guards*

trigonometry *n* the branch of mathematics concerned with the relations of sides and angles of triangles, which is used in surveying, navigation, etc. [Greek *trigōnon* triangle]

trig point *n* a point on a hilltop, etc., used for triangulation by a surveyor

trike *n informal* a tricycle

trilateral *adj* having three sides

trilby *n, pl* **-bies** a man's soft felt hat with an indented crown [after *Trilby*, the heroine of a novel by George Du Maurier]

trill *n* **1** *music* a rapid alternation between a note and the note above it **2** a shrill warbling sound made by some birds: *the canary's high trills* ▹ *vb* **3** (of a bird) to make a shrill warbling sound **4** (of a person) to talk or laugh in a high-pitched musical voice [Italian *trillo*]

trillion *n* **-lions** *or* **-lion 1** the number represented as one followed by twelve zeros (10^{12}); a million million **2** (in Britain, originally) the number represented as one followed by eighteen zeros (10^{18}); a million million million ▹ *adj* **3** amounting to a trillion: *a trillion dollars* [French] **trillionth** *n, adj*

trillium *n* a plant of Asia and North America that has three leaves at the top of the stem with a single white, pink, or purple three-petalled flower [New Latin]

trilobite (trile-oh-bite) *n* a small prehistoric marine arthropod, found as a fossil [Greek *trilobos* having three lobes]

t

trilogy (trill-a-jee) *n, pl* **-gies** a series of three books, plays, etc., which form a related group but are each complete works in themselves [Greek *trilogia*]

trim *adj* **trimmer, trimmest 1** neat and spruce in appearance: *trim lace curtains* **2** attractively slim: *his body was trim and athletic* ▷ *vb* **trimming, trimmed 3** to make (something) neater by cutting it slightly without changing its basic shape: *his white beard was neatly trimmed* **4** to adorn or decorate (something, such as a garment) with lace, ribbons, etc.: *a cotton camisole neatly trimmed with lace* **5 A** to adjust the balance of (a ship or aircraft) by shifting cargo, etc. **B** to adjust (a ship's sails) to take advantage of the wind **6** to reduce or lower the size of: *the company has trimmed its pretax profits forecast by $2.3 million* **7** to alter (a plan or policy) by removing parts which seem unnecessary or unpopular: *the government would rather trim its policies than lose the election* **8 trim off** *or* **away** to cut so as to remove: *trim off most of the fat before cooking the meat* ▷ *n* **9** a decoration or adornment: *a black suit with scarlet trim* **10** the upholstery and decorative facings of a car's interior **11** good physical condition: *he had always kept himself in trim* **12** a haircut that neatens but does not alter the existing hairstyle [Old English *trymman* to strengthen]

trimaran (trime-a-ran) *n* a boat with one smaller hull on each side of the main hull [*tri-* + *(cata)maran*]

trimming *n* **1** an extra piece added to a garment for decoration: *a pink nightie with lace trimming* **2 trimmings** usual or traditional accompaniments: *bacon and eggs with all the trimmings*

Trinitarian *n* **1** a person who believes in the doctrine of the Trinity ▷ *adj* **2** of or relating to the Trinity **Trinitarianism** *n*

trinitrotoluene *n* the full name for **TNT**

trinity *n, pl* **-ties** a group of three people or things [Latin *trinus* triple]

Trinity *n Christianity* the union of three persons, the Father, Son, and Holy Spirit, in one God

trinket *n* a small or worthless ornament or piece of jewellery [origin unknown]

trio *n, pl* **trios 1** a group of three people or things **2** a group of three instrumentalists or singers **3** a piece of music for three performers [Italian]

trip *n* **1** a journey to a place and back, esp. for pleasure: *they took a coach trip round the island* **2** a false step; stumble **3** the act of causing someone to stumble or fall by catching his or her foot with one's own **4** *informal* a hallucinogenic drug experience **5** a catch on a mechanism that acts as a switch ▷ *vb* **tripping, tripped 6** Also: **trip up** to stumble or cause (someone) to stumble **7** Also: **trip up** to trap or catch (someone) in a mistake **8** to walk lightly and quickly, with a dancelike motion: *I could see Amelia tripping along beside him* **9** *informal* to experience the effects of a hallucinogenic drug [Old French *triper* to tread]

tripartite *adj* involving or composed of three people or parts **tripartism** *n*

tripe *n* **1** the stomach lining of a cow or pig used as a food **2** *Brit, Austral & NZ informal* nonsense or rubbish [Old French]

Tripitaka (trip-it-**tah**-ka) *n* the three collections of books making up the Buddhist scriptures [Pali (an ancient language of India) *tri* three + *pitaka* basket]

triple *adj* **1** made up of three parts or things: *a triple murder* **2** (of musical time or rhythm) having three beats in each bar **3** three times as great or as much: *a triple brandy* ▷ *vb* **-pling, -pled 4** to make or become three times as much or as many: *the company has tripled its sales over the past five years* ▷ *n* **5** something that is, or contains, three times as much as normal **6** a group of three [Latin *triplus*] **triply** *adv*

triple jump *n* an athletic event in which the competitor has to perform a hop, a step, and a jump in a continuous movement

triple point *n chem* the temperature and pressure at which a substance can exist as a solid, liquid, and gas

triplet *n* **1** one of three children born at one birth **2** a group of three musical notes played in the time that two would normally take **3** a group or set of three similar things

triplicate *adj* **1** triple ▷ *vb* **-cating, -cated 2** to multiply or be multiplied by three ▷ *n* **3 in triplicate** written out three times: *my request to interview the commander had to be made in triplicate* [Latin *triplicare* to triple] **triplication** *n*

tripod (**tripe**-pod) *n* **1** a three-legged stand to which a camera can be attached to hold it steady **2** a three-legged stool, table, etc. [TRI- + Greek *pous* a foot]

tripos (**tripe**-poss) *n Brit* the final honours degree examinations at Cambridge University [Latin *tripus* tripod]

tripper *n chiefly Brit* a tourist

triptych (**trip**-tick) *n* a set of three pictures or panels, usually hinged together and often used as an altarpiece [TRI- + Greek *ptux* plate]

trireme (**try**-ream) *n* an ancient Greek warship with three rows of oars on each side [TRI- + Latin *remus* oar]

trismus *n pathol* the state of being unable to open the mouth because of sustained contractions of the jaw muscles, caused by tetanus. Nontechnical name: **lockjaw** [Greek *trismos* a grinding]

triste (treest) *adj old-fashioned* sad [French]

trite *adj* (of a remark or idea) commonplace and unoriginal [Latin *tritus* worn down]

tritium *n* a radioactive isotope of hydrogen. Symbol: **T** or ^{3}**H** [Greek *tritos* third]

triumph *n* **1** the feeling of great happiness resulting from a victory or major achievement **2** an outstanding success, achievement, or victory: *the concert was a musical triumph* **3** (in ancient Rome) a procession held in honour of a victorious general ▷ *vb* **4** to gain control or success: *triumphing over adversity* **5** to rejoice over a victory [Latin *triumphus*] **triumphal** *adj*

triumphant *adj* **1** feeling or displaying triumph: *her smile was triumphant* **2** celebrating a victory or success: *the general's triumphant tour round the city* **triumphantly** *adv*

triumvir (try-**umm**-vir) *n* (esp. in ancient Rome) a member of a triumvirate [Latin]

triumvirate (try-umm-vir-rit) *n* **1** a group of three people in joint control of something: *the triumvirate of great orchestras which dominates classical music in Europe* **2** (in ancient Rome) a board of three officials jointly responsible for some task

trivalent *adj chem* **1** having a valency of three **2** having three valencies **trivalency** *n*

trivet (triv-vit) *n* **1** a three-legged stand for holding a pot, kettle, etc., over a fire **2** a short metal stand on which hot dishes are placed on a table [Old English *trefet*]

trivia *n* petty and unimportant things or details

trivial *adj* of little importance: *a trivial matter* [Latin *trivialis* common] **triviality** *n* **trivially** *adv*

trivialize *or* **-lise** *vb* **-lizing, -lized** *or* **-lising, -lised** to make (something) seem less important or complex than it is

trochee (troke-ee) *n prosody* a metrical foot of one long and one short syllable [Greek *trekhein* to run] **trochaic** *adj*

trod *vb* the past tense and a past participle of **tread**

trodden *vb* a past participle of **tread**

troglodyte *n* a person who lives in a cave [Greek *trōglodutēs* one who enters caves]

troika *n* **1** a Russian coach or sleigh drawn by three horses abreast **2** a group of three people in authority: *a troika of European foreign ministers* [Russian]

Trojan *adj* **1** of ancient Troy or its people ▷ *n* **2** a person from ancient Troy **3** a hard-working person

Trojan Horse *n* **1** *Greek myth* the huge wooden hollow figure of a horse used by the Greeks to enter Troy **2** a trap or trick intended to undermine an enemy

troll[1] *n* (in Scandinavian folklore) a supernatural dwarf or giant that dwells in a cave or mountain [Old Norse: demon]

troll[2] *vb* **1** *angling* to fish by dragging a lure through the water **2** to post deliberately provocative messages on an internet discussion board ▷ *n* **3** a person who posts deliberately provocative messages on an internet discussion board [Old French *troller* to run about]

trolley *n* **1** a small table on casters used for carrying food or drink **2** a wheeled cart or stand used for moving heavy items, such as shopping in a supermarket or luggage at a railway station **3** *Brit* See **trolley bus** **4** *US & Canad* See **trolley car** **5** a device, such as a wheel that collects the current from an overhead wire, to drive the motor of an electric vehicle **6** *Brit & Austral* a low truck running on rails, used in factories, mines, etc. [probably from TROLL[2]]

trolley bus *n* a bus powered by electricity from two overhead wires but not running on rails

trolley car *n US & Canad* same as **tram**

trollop *n derogatory* a woman who is considered promiscuous or slovenly [origin unknown]

trombone *n* a brass musical instrument with a sliding tube which is moved in or out to alter the note played [Italian] **trombonist** *n*

trompe l'oeil (tromp luh-ee) *n, pl* **trompe l'oeils** (tromp luh-ee) **1** a painting, etc. giving a convincing illusion that the objects represented are real **2** an effect of this kind [French, literally: deception of the eye]

troop *n* **1** a large group: *a troop of dogs* **2** **troops** soldiers: *troops have been maintaining an unusually high profile* **3** a subdivision of a cavalry or armoured regiment **4** a large group of Scouts made up of several patrols ▷ *vb* **5** to move in a crowd: *we trooped into the room after her* **6** *military, chiefly Brit & Austral* to parade (a flag or banner) ceremonially: *trooping the colour* [French *troupe*]

trooper *n* **1** a soldier in a cavalry regiment **2** *US & Austral* a mounted police officer **3** *US* a state police officer **4** a cavalry horse **5** *informal, chiefly Brit* a troopship

troopship *n* a ship used to transport military personnel

trope *n* a word or expression used in a figurative sense [Greek *tropos* style, turn]

trophy *n, pl* **-phies** **1** a cup, shield, etc., given as a prize **2** a memento of success, esp. one taken in war or hunting: *stuffed animal heads and other hunting trophies* ▷ *adj* **3** *informal* regarded as a highly desirable symbol of wealth or success: *a trophy wife* [Greek *tropaion*]

tropic *n* **1** either of the lines of latitude at about 23½°N (**tropic of Cancer**) and 23½°S (**tropic of Capricorn**) of the equator **2** **the tropics** that part of the earth's surface between the tropics of Cancer and Capricorn: *the intense heat and humidity of the tropics* [Greek *tropos* a turn; from the belief that the sun turned back at the solstices]

tropical *adj* belonging to, typical of, or located in, the tropics: *tropical rainforests* **tropically** *adv*

tropism *n* the tendency of a plant or animal to turn or curve in response to an external stimulus [Greek *tropos* a turn]

troposphere *n* the lowest layer of the earth's atmosphere, about 18 kilometres (11 miles) thick at the equator to about 6 km (4 miles) at the Poles [Greek *tropos* a turn + SPHERE]

trot *vb* **trotting, trotted** **1** (of a horse) to move in a manner faster than a walk but slower than a gallop, in which diagonally opposite legs come down together **2** (of a person) to move fairly quickly, with small quick steps ▷ *n* **3** a medium-paced gait of a horse, in which diagonally opposite legs come down together **4** a steady brisk pace **5** **on the trot** *informal* one after the other: *ten years on the trot* **6** **the trots** *slang* diarrhoea [Old French]

Trot *n chiefly Brit informal* a follower of Trotsky

troth (rhymes with **growth**) *n archaic* **1** a pledge of fidelity, esp. a betrothal **2** **in troth** truly [Old English *trēowth*]

trot out *vb informal* to repeat (old information or ideas) without fresh thought: *the government trots out the same excuse every time*

Trotskyist *or* **Trotskyite** *adj* **1** of the theories of Leon Trotsky (1879–1940), Russian Communist, which call for a worldwide revolution by the proletariat ▷ *n* **2** a supporter of Trotsky or his theories **Trotskyism** *n*

trotter *n* **1** the foot of a pig **2** a horse that is specially trained to trot fast

troubadour (troo-bad-oor) *n* a travelling poet and singer in S France or N Italy from the 11th to the 13th century who wrote chiefly on courtly love [French]

trouble *n* **1** difficulties or problems: *I'd trouble finding somewhere to park* **2** a cause of distress, disturbance, or pain: *we must be sensitive to the troubles of other people* **3** disease or a problem with one's health: *ear trouble* **4** a state of disorder, ill-feeling, or unrest: *the police had orders to intervene at the first sign of trouble* **5** effort or exertion to do something: *they didn't even take the trouble to see the film before banning it* **6** a personal weakness or cause of annoyance: *his trouble is that he's constitutionally jealous* **7 in trouble** **A** likely to be punished for something one has done: *in trouble with the public prosecutor* **B** *old-fashioned* pregnant when not married **8 more trouble than it's worth** involving a lot of time or effort for very little reward: *making your own pasta is more trouble than it's worth* ▷ *vb* **-bling, -bled 9** to cause trouble to **10** to make an effort or exert oneself: *he dismissed the letters as forgeries without troubling to examine them* **11** to cause inconvenience or discomfort to: *sorry to trouble you!* [Old French *troubler*] **troubled** *adj*

troublemaker *n* a person who causes trouble, esp. between people **troublemaking** *adj, n*

troubleshooter *n* a person employed to locate and deal with faults or problems **troubleshooting** *n, adj*

troublesome *adj* causing trouble

trouble spot *n* a place where there is frequent fighting or violence: *the Balkans have long been one of the major European trouble spots*

troublous *adj literary* unsettled or agitated

trough (troff) *n* **1** a long open container, esp. one for animals' food or water **2** a narrow channel between two waves or ridges **3** a low point in a pattern that has regular high and low points: *the trough of the slump in pupil numbers was in 1985* **4** *meteorol* a long narrow area of low pressure **5** a narrow channel or gutter [Old English *trōh*]

trounce *vb* **trouncing, trounced** to defeat (someone) utterly [origin unknown]

troupe (troop) *n* a company of actors or other performers [French]

trouper *n* **1** a member of a troupe **2** an experienced person: *Bette plays a showbiz trouper*

trouser *adj* **1** of or relating to trousers: *trouser legs* ▷ *vb* **2** *Brit slang* to take (something, esp. money), often surreptitiously or unlawfully

trousers *pl n* a garment that covers the body from the waist to the ankles or knees with a separate tube-shaped section for each leg [Scottish Gaelic *triubhas* trews]

trousseau (troo-so) *n, pl* **-seaux** (-so) the clothes, linen, and other possessions collected by a bride for her marriage [Old French]

trout *n, pl* **trout** *or* **trouts** any of various game fishes related to the salmon and found chiefly in fresh water in northern regions [Old English *trūht*]

trove *n* See **treasure-trove**

trowel *n* **1** a hand tool resembling a small spade with a curved blade, used by gardeners for lifting plants, etc. **2** a similar tool with a flat metal blade, used for spreading cement or plaster on a surface [Latin *trulla* a scoop]

troy weight *or* **troy** *n* a system of weights used for precious metals and gemstones in which one pound equals twelve ounces [after the city of *Troyes*, France, where first used]

truant *n* **1** a pupil who stays away from school without permission **2 play truant** to stay away from school without permission ▷ *adj* **3** being or relating to a truant: *a truant schoolkid* [Old French: vagabond] **truancy** *n*

truce *n* a temporary agreement to stop fighting or quarrelling [plural of Old English *trēow* pledge]

truck[1] *n* **1** *Brit* a railway wagon for carrying freight **2** a large motor vehicle for transporting heavy loads **3** any wheeled vehicle used to move goods ▷ *vb* **4** *chiefly US* to transport goods in a truck [perhaps from *truckle* a small wheel]

truck[2] *n* **1** *history* the payment of wages in goods rather than in money **2 have no truck with** to refuse to be involved with: *the opposition will have no truck with the planned cut in pensions* [Old French *troquer* (unattested) to barter]

trucker *n* a long-distance lorry driver

truckie *n Austral & NZ informal* a truck driver

truckle *vb* **-ling, -led** to yield weakly or give in: *he accused the government of truckling to the right-wing press* [from obsolete *truckle* to sleep in a truckle bed]

truckle bed *n chiefly Brit* a low bed on wheels, stored under a larger bed

truculent (truck-yew-lent) *adj* defiantly aggressive or bad-tempered [Latin *trux* fierce] **truculence** *n* **truculently** *adv*

trudge *vb* **trudging, trudged 1** to walk or plod heavily or wearily ▷ *n* **2** a long tiring walk [origin unknown]

true *adj* **truer, truest 1** in accordance with the truth or facts; factual: *not all of the stories about her are true* **2** real or genuine: *he didn't want to reveal his true feelings* **3** faithful and loyal: *a true friend* **4** accurate or precise: *he looked through the telescopic sight until he was convinced his aim was true* **5** (of a compass bearing) according to the earth's geographical rather than magnetic poles: *true north* **6 come true** to actually happen: *fortunately his gloomy prediction didn't come true* ▷ *n* **7 in** *or* **out of true** in *or* not in correct alignment ▷ *adv* **8** truthfully or rightly: *I'd like to move to Edinburgh, true, but I'd need to get a job there first* [Old English *trīewe*]

true-blue *adj* **1** staunchly loyal ▷ *n* **true blue 2** *chiefly Brit & Austral* a staunch royalist or Conservative

true-life *adj* taken directly from reality: *true-life TV horror stories*

truelove *n* the person that one loves

true north *n* the direction from any point along a meridian towards the North Pole

truffle *n* **1** a round fungus which grows underground and is regarded as a delicacy **2** Also called: **rum truffle** a sweet flavoured with chocolate or rum [French *truffe*]

trug *n Brit* a long shallow basket for carrying garden tools, flowers, etc. [perhaps variant of *trough*]

truism *n* a statement that is clearly true and well known

truly *adv* **1** in a true, just, or faithful manner **2** really: *a truly awful poem*

trump[1] *n* **1** same as **trump card** ▷ *vb* **2** *cards* to beat a card by playing a card which belongs to a suit which outranks it **3** to outdo or surpass: *she trumped his news by announcing that she had been picked for the Olympic team* ▷ See also **trumps** [variant of *triumph*]

trump[2] *n archaic, literary* **1** a trumpet or the sound produced by one **2 the last trump** the final trumpet call on the Day of Judgment [Old French *trompe*]

trump card *n* **1** any card from the suit that ranks higher than any other suit in one particular game **2** an advantage, weapon, etc., that is kept in reserve until needed: *the President hoped to use his experience of foreign affairs as a trump card in the election*. Also called: **trump**

trumped up *adj* (of charges, excuses, etc.) made up in order to deceive

trumpery *n, pl* **-eries 1** something useless or worthless ▷ *adj* **2** useless or worthless [Old French *tromperie* deceit]

trumpet *n* **1** a valved brass musical instrument consisting of a narrow tube ending in a flare **2** a loud sound such as that of a trumpet: *the elephant gave a loud trumpet* **3 blow one's own trumpet** to boast about one's own skills or good qualities ▷ *vb* **-peting, -peted 4** to proclaim or state forcefully: *almost every one of the party's loudly trumpeted election claims is untrue* **5** (of an elephant) to make a loud cry [Old French *trompette*] **trumpeter** *n*

trumps *pl n* **1** *cards* any one of the four suits that outranks all the other suits for the duration of a deal or game **2 turn up trumps** (of a person) to bring about a happy or successful conclusion, esp. unexpectedly

truncate *vb* **-cating, -cated** to shorten by cutting [Latin *truncare*] **truncated** *adj* **truncation** *n*

truncheon *n chiefly Brit* a small club, esp one carried by a police officer [Old French *tronchon* stump]

trundle *vb* **-dling, -dled** to move heavily on or as if on wheels: *a bus trundled along the drive* [Old English *tryndel* circular or spherical object]

t

trundle bed *n US, Canad & NZ* a low bed on wheels, stored under a larger bed

trundler *n* **1** NZ a golf or shopping trolley **2** a child's pushchair

trunk *n* **1** the main stem of a tree **2** a large strong case or box used to contain clothes when travelling and for storage **3** a person's body excluding the head, neck, and limbs; torso **4** the long nose of an elephant **5** US the boot of a car ▷ See also **trunks** [Latin *truncus*]

trunk call *n chiefly Brit & Austral* a long-distance telephone call

trunk line *n* **1** a direct link between two distant telephone exchanges or switchboards **2** the main route or routes on a railway

trunk road *n Brit* a main road, esp. one maintained by the central government

trunks *pl n* shorts worn by a man for swimming

truss *vb* **1** to tie or bind (someone) up **2** to bind the wings and legs of (a fowl) before cooking ▷ *n* **3** *med* a device for holding a hernia in place **4** a framework of wood or metal used to support a roof, bridge, etc. **5** a cluster of flowers or fruit growing at the end of a single stalk [Old French *trousse*]

trust *vb* **1** to believe that (someone) is honest and means no harm: *my father warned me never to trust strangers* **2** to feel that (something) is safe and reliable: *I don't trust those new gadgets* **3** to entrust (someone) with important information or valuables: *she's not somebody I would trust with this sort of secret* **4** to believe that (someone) is likely to do something safely and reliably: *I wouldn't trust anyone else to look after my child properly* **5** to believe (a story, account, etc.) **6** to expect, hope, or suppose: *I trust you've made your brother welcome here* ▷ *n* **7** confidence in the truth, worth, reliability, etc., of a person or thing; faith: *he knew that his father had great trust in him* **8** the obligation of someone in a responsible position: *he was in a position of trust as her substitute father* **9 A** a legal arrangement whereby one person looks after property, money, etc., on another's behalf **B** property that is the subject of such an arrangement **10** (in England and Wales) a self-governing hospital, group of hospitals, or other body that operates as an independent commercial unit within the National Health Service **11** *chiefly US & Canad* a group of companies joined together to control the market for any commodity ▷ *adj* **12** of or relating to a trust or trusts: *trust status* [Old Norse *traust* help, support, confidence]

trustee *n* **1** a person who administers property on someone else's behalf **2** a member of a board that manages the affairs of an institution or organization

trustful *or* **trusting** *adj* characterized by a readiness to trust others **trustfully** *or* **trustingly** *adv*

trust fund *n* money, securities, etc., held in trust

trustworthy *adj* (of a person) honest, reliable, or dependable

trusty *adj* **trustier, trustiest 1** faithful or reliable: *his trusty steed* ▷ *n, pl* **trusties 2** a trustworthy convict to whom special privileges are granted

truth *n* **1** the quality of being true, genuine, or factual: *there is no truth in the allegations* **2** something that is true: *he finally learned the truth about his parents' marriage* **3** a proven or verified fact, principle, etc.: *some profound truths about biology have come to light* [Old English *trīewth*]

truthful *adj* **1** telling the truth; honest **2** true; based on facts: *a truthful answer* **truthfully** *adv* **truthfulness** *n*

try *vb* **tries, trying, tried 1** to make an effort or attempt: *you must try to understand* **2** to sample or test (something) to see how enjoyable, good, or useful it is: *I tried smoking once but didn't like it* **3** to put strain or stress on (someone's patience) **4** to give pain, affliction, or vexation to: *sometimes when I've been sorely tried, my temper gets a little out of hand* **5 A** to investigate (a case) in a court of law **B** to hear evidence in order to determine the guilt or innocence of (a person) ▷ *n, pl* **tries 6** an attempt or effort **7** *rugby* a score made by placing the ball down behind the opposing team's goal line [Old French *trier* to sort]

USAGE The use of *and* instead of *to* after *try* is very common, but should be avoided in formal writing: *we must try to prevent* (not *try and prevent*) *this happening.*

trying *adj* upsetting, difficult, or annoying

try on *vb* **1** to put on (a garment) to find out whether it fits **2** **try it on** *informal* to attempt to deceive or fool someone ▷ *n* **try-on** **3** *Brit informal* something done to test out a person's tolerance, etc.

try out *vb* **1** to test (something), esp. to find out how good it is ▷ *n* **tryout** **2** *chiefly US & Canad* a trial or test, for example of an athlete or actor

trysail *n* a small fore-and-aft sail set on a sailing vessel to help keep her head to the wind in a storm

tryst *n archaic or literary* **1** an arrangement to meet, esp. secretly **2** a meeting, esp. a secret one with a lover, or the place where such a meeting takes place [Old French *triste* lookout post]

Ts tennessine

tsar *or* **czar** (**zahr**) *n* (until 1917) the emperor of Russia. Also: **tzar** [Russian, ultimately from CAESAR] **tsarist** *or* **czarist** *n*

tsarevitch *or* **czarevitch** (zahr-rev-itch) *n* the eldest son of a Russian tsar

tsarina *or* **czarina** (zahr-**een**-a) *n* the wife of a Russian tsar

tsetse fly *or* **tzetze fly** (tset-see) *n* a bloodsucking African fly whose bite transmits disease, esp. sleeping sickness [Tswana (language of southern Africa) *tse tse*]

T-shirt *or* **tee-shirt** *n* a short-sleeved casual shirt or top [T-shape formed when laid flat]

tsotsi (tsot-see) *n S African* a Black street thug or gang member [perhaps from Nguni (language group of southern Africa) *tsotsa* to dress flashily]

tsp. teaspoon

T-square *n* a T-shaped ruler used for drawing horizontal lines and to support set squares when drawing vertical and inclined lines

tsunami *n* a large, often destructive, sea wave, usually caused by an earthquake under the sea [Japanese]

TT **1** teetotal **2** teetotaller **3** tuberculin-tested

tuatara (too-ah-**tah**-rah) *n* a large lizard-like New Zealand reptile [Māori *tua* back + *tara* spine]

tub *n* **1** a low wide, usually round container **2** a small plastic or cardboard container for ice cream, etc. **3** *chiefly US* same as **bath** (sense 1) **4** Also called: **tubful** the amount a tub will hold **5** a slow and uncomfortable boat or ship [Middle Dutch *tubbe*]

tuba (tube-a) *n* a low-pitched brass musical instrument with valves [Latin]

tubby *adj* **-bier, -biest** (of a person) fat and short **tubbiness** *n*

tube *n* **1** a long hollow cylindrical object, used for the passage of fluids or as a container **2** a flexible cylinder of soft metal or plastic closed with a cap, used to hold substances such as toothpaste **3** *anatomy* any hollow cylindrical structure: *the Fallopian tubes* **4** **the Tube** *Brit trademark* the underground railway system in London **5** *electronics* See **cathode-ray tube** **6** *slang, chiefly US* a television set [Latin *tubus*] **tubeless** *adj*

tuber (**tube**-er) *n* a fleshy underground root of a plant such as a potato [Latin: hump]

tubercle (**tube**-er-kl) *n* **1** a small rounded swelling **2** any abnormal hard swelling, esp. one characteristic of tuberculosis [Latin *tuberculum* a little swelling]

tubercular (tube-**berk**-yew-lar) *or* **tuberculous** *adj* **1** of or symptomatic of tuberculosis **2** of or relating to a tubercle

tuberculin (tube-**berk**-yew-lin) *n* a sterile liquid prepared from cultures of the tubercle bacillus and used in the diagnosis of tuberculosis

tuberculin-tested *adj* (of milk) produced by cows that have been certified as free of tuberculosis

tuberculosis (tube-berk-yew-**lohss**-iss) *n* an infectious disease characterized by the formation of tubercles, esp. in the lungs

tuberous (**tube**-er-uss) *adj* (of plants) forming, bearing, or resembling a tuber or tubers

tubing (**tube**-ing) *n* **1** a length of tube **2** a system of tubes

tub-thumper *n* a noisy or ranting public speaker **tub-thumping** *adj, n*

tubular (**tube**-yew-lar) *adj* **1** having the shape of a tube or tubes **2** of or relating to a tube or tubing

tubule (**tube**-yewl) *n* any small tubular structure, esp. in an animal or plant

TUC (in Britain and South Africa) Trades Union Congress

tuck *vb* **1** to push or fold into a small space or between two surfaces: *she tucked the letter into her handbag* **2** to thrust the loose ends or sides of (something) into a confining space, so as to make it neat and secure: *he tucked his shirt back into his trousers* **3** to make a tuck or tucks in (a garment) ▷ *n* **4** a pleat or fold in a part of a garment, usually stitched down **5** *Brit informal* food, esp. cakes and sweets [Old English *tūcian* to torment]

tuck away *vb informal* **1** to eat (a large amount of food) **2** to store (something) in a safe place: *we knew he had some money tucked away somewhere* **3** to have a quiet, rarely disturbed or visited location: *the chapel is tucked away in a side street*

tucker *n* **1** a detachable yoke of lace, linen, etc., formerly worn over the breast of a low-cut dress **2** *Austral & NZ informal* food **3** **one's best bib and tucker** *informal* one's best clothes

tuckered *adj* **tuckered out** *informal, chiefly US & Canad* exhausted

tuck in *vb* **1** to put (someone) to bed and make him or her snug **2** to thrust the loose ends or sides of (something) into a confining space: *tuck in the bedclothes* **3** *informal* to eat, esp. heartily

tuck shop *n chiefly Brit* a shop in or near a school, where cakes and sweets are sold

Tudor *adj* **1** of or in the reign of the English royal house ruling from 1485 to 1603 **2** denoting a style of architecture characterized by half-timbered houses: *a Tudor cottage*

Tues. Tuesday

Tuesday *n* the third day of the week [Old English *tīwesdæg* day of Tyr, Norse god]

t

tufa (tew-fa) *n* a porous rock formed of calcium carbonate deposited from springs [Italian *tufo*]

tuff *n geol* a porous rock formed from volcanic dust or ash [Old French *tuf*]

tuffet *n* a small mound or low seat [from *tuft*]

tuft *n* a bunch of feathers, grass, hair, threads, etc., held together at the base [probably from Old French *tufe*] **tufted** *adj* **tufty** *adj*

tug *vb* **tugging, tugged 1** to pull or drag with a sharp or powerful movement: *she tugged at my arm* **2** to tow (a ship or boat) by means of a tug ▷ *n* **3** a strong pull or jerk **4** Also called: **tugboat** a boat with a powerful engine, used for towing barges, ships, etc. [Middle English *tuggen*]

tug-of-love *n* a conflict over the custody of a child between divorced parents or between the child's natural parents and its foster or adoptive parents

tug-of-war *n* **1** a contest in which two people or teams pull opposite ends of a rope in an attempt to drag the opposition over a central line **2** any hard struggle between two people or two groups

tuition *n* **1** instruction, esp. that received individually or in a small group **2** the payment for instruction, esp. in colleges or universities [Latin *tueri* to watch over]

tuktu *n Canad* another name for **caribou**

tuk-tuk *n* (in Thailand) a three-wheeled motor vehicle used as a taxi

tulip *n* **1** a plant which produces bright cup-shaped flowers in spring **2** the flower or bulb [Turkish *tülbend* turban]

tulip tree *n* a North American tree with tulip-shaped greenish-yellow flowers and long conelike fruits

tulle (tewl) *n* a fine net fabric of silk, rayon, etc., used to make evening dresses [French]

tumble *vb* **-bling, -bled 1** to fall or cause to fall, esp. awkwardly or violently: *chairs tumbled over* **2** to roll or twist, esp. in playing: *they rolled and tumbled as wild beasts* **3** to decrease in value suddenly: *interest rates tumbled* **4** to move in a quick and uncontrolled manner: *the crowd tumbled down the stairs* **5** to disturb, rumple, or toss around: *she was all tumbled by the fall* **6** to perform leaps or somersaults ▷ *n* **7** a fall, esp. an awkward or violent one: *he took a tumble down the stairs* **8** a somersault [Old English *tumbian* dance, jump] **tumbled** *adj*

tumbledown *adj* (of a building) falling to pieces; dilapidated

tumble dryer *or* **tumble drier** *n* an electrically-operated machine that dries wet laundry by rotating it in warmed air inside a metal drum

tumbler *n* **1** A a flat-bottomed drinking glass with no handle or stem B the amount a tumbler will hold **2** a person who performs somersaults and other acrobatic feats **3** a part of the mechanism of a lock

tumble to *vb* to understand or become aware of: *how did he tumble to this?*

tumbril *n* a farm cart that tilts backwards to empty its load, which was used to take condemned prisoners to the guillotine during the French Revolution [Old French *tumberel*]

tumescent (tew-mess-ent) *adj* swollen or becoming swollen

tumid (tew-mid) *adj rare* **1** (of an organ or part of the body) enlarged or swollen **2** pompous or fulsome in style: *a tumid tome* [Latin *tumere* to swell] **tumidity** *n*

tummy *n, pl* **-mies** an informal or childish word for **stomach**

tumour *or US* **tumor** (tew-mer) *n pathol* A any abnormal swelling B a mass of tissue formed by a new growth of cells [Latin *tumere* to swell] **tumorous** *adj*

tumult (tew-mult) *n* **1** a loud confused noise, such as one produced by a crowd **2** a state of confusion and excitement: *a tumult of emotions* [Latin *tumultus*]

tumultuous (tew-mull-tew-uss) *adj* **1** exciting, confused, or turbulent: *this week's tumultuous events* **2** unruly, noisy, or excited: *a tumultuous welcome*

tumulus (tew-myew-luss) *n, pl* **-li** (-lie) *archaeol not in technical use* a burial mound [Latin: a hillock]

tun *n* a large beer cask [Old English *tunne*]

tuna (tune-a) *n, pl* **-na** *or* **-nas 1** a large marine spiny-finned fish **2** the flesh of this fish, often tinned for food [American Spanish]

tundra *n* a vast treeless Arctic region with permanently frozen subsoil [Russian]

tune *n* **1** a melody, esp. one for which harmony is not essential **2** the correct musical pitch: *many of the notes are out of tune* **3 call the tune** to be in control of the proceedings **4 change one's tune** to alter one's attitude or tone of speech **5 in** *or* **out of tune with** in *or* not in agreement or sympathy with: *in tune with public opinion* **6 to the tune of** *informal* to the amount or extent of ▷ *vb* **tuning, tuned 7** to adjust (a musical instrument) so each string, key, etc., produces the right note **8** to make small adjustments to (an engine, machine, etc.) to obtain the proper or desired performance **9** to adjust (a radio or television) to receive a particular station or programme: *the radio was tuned to the local station* [variant of *tone*] **tuner** *n*

tuneful *adj* having a pleasant tune **tunefully** *adv*

tune in *vb* **1** to adjust (a radio or television) to receive (a station or programme) **2 tuned in to** *slang* aware of or knowledgeable about: *tuned in to European cinema*

tuneless *adj* having no melody or tune

tune up *vb* **1** to adjust (a musical instrument) to a particular pitch **2** to adjust the engine of a car, etc., to improve its performance

tungsten *n chem* a hard greyish-white metallic element. Symbol: **W** [Swedish *tung* heavy + *sten* stone]

tunic *n* **1** a close-fitting jacket forming part of some uniforms **2** a loose-fitting knee-length garment [Latin *tunica*]

tuning fork *n* a two-pronged metal fork that when struck produces a pure note of constant specified pitch

tunnel *n* **1** an underground passageway, esp. one for trains or cars **2** any passage or channel through or under something: *the carpal tunnel* ▷ *vb* **-nelling, -nelled** *or US* **-neling, -neled 3** to make one's way through or under (something) by digging a tunnel: *ten men succeeded in tunnelling out of the prisoner-of-war camp* **4** to dig a tunnel (through or under something): *the idea of tunnelling under the English Channel had been around for a long time* [Old French *tonel* cask]

tunnel vision *n* **1** a condition in which a person is unable to see things that are not straight in front **2** narrowness of viewpoint resulting from concentration on only one aspect of a subject or situation

tunny *n, pl* **-nies** *or* **-ny** same as **tuna** [Latin *thunnus*]

tup *n chiefly Brit* a male sheep [origin unknown]

tupik (too-pick) *n* a tent of seal or caribou skin used for shelter by the Inuit in summer [Inuktitut *tupiq*]

tuppence *n Brit* same as **twopence**

tuppenny *adj Brit* worth or costing two pence

tuque (rhymes with **fluke**) *n Canad* **1** a knitted cap with a long tapering end **2** a close-fitting knitted hat often with a tassel or pompom [Canadian French]

turban *n* **1** a head-covering worn by a Muslim, Hindu, or Sikh man, consisting of a long piece of cloth wound round the head **2** any head-covering resembling this [Turkish *tülbend*] **turbaned** *adj*

turbid *adj literary* (of water or air) full of mud or dirt, and frequently swirling around: *the turbid stream of the Loire* [Latin *turbare* to agitate] **turbidity** *n*

turbine *n* a machine in which power is produced by a stream of water, air, etc., that pushes the blades of a wheel and causes it to rotate [Latin *turbo* whirlwind]

turbocharger *n* a device that increases the power of an internal-combustion engine by using the exhaust gases to drive a turbine **turbocharged** *adj*

turbofan *n* a type of engine in which a large fan driven by a turbine forces air rearwards to increase the propulsive thrust

turbojet *n* **1** a gas turbine in which the exhaust gases provide the propulsive thrust to drive an aircraft **2** an aircraft powered by turbojet engines

turboprop *n* an aircraft propulsion unit where the propeller is driven by a gas turbine

turbot *n, pl* **-bot** *or* **-bots** a European flatfish, highly valued as a food fish [Old French *tourbot*]

turbulence *n* **1** a state or condition of confusion, movement, or agitation **2** *meteorol* instability in the atmosphere causing gusty air currents

turbulent *adj* **1** involving a lot of sudden changes and conflicting elements: *the city has had a turbulent history* **2** (of people) wild and unruly: *a harsh mountain land inhabited by a score of turbulent tribes* **3** (of water or air) full of violent unpredictable currents: *the turbulent ocean* [Latin *turba* confusion]

turd *n taboo* **1** a piece of excrement **2** *slang* a contemptible person [Old English *tord*]

tureen *n* a large deep dish with a lid, used for serving soups [French *terrine* earthenware vessel]

turf *n, pl* **turfs** *or* **turves** **1** a layer of thick even grass with roots and soil attached: *a short turf rich in wild flowers* **2** a piece cut from this layer: *we spent the afternoon digging turves* **3** *informal* **A** the area where a person lives and feels at home: *my boyhood turf of east Cork* **B** a person's area of knowledge or influence: *when Kate is at work, she's on her own turf* **4 the turf A** a track where horse races are run **B** horse racing as a sport or industry **5** same as **peat** ▷ *vb* **6** to cover (an area of ground) with pieces of turf [Old English]

turf accountant *n Brit* same as **bookmaker**

turf out *vb informal* to throw (someone or something) out: *the residents fear a new landlord might push up rents and turf them out of their homes*

turgid (tur-jid) *adj* **1** (of language) pompous, boring, and hard to understand **2** (of water or mud) unpleasantly thick and brown [Latin *turgere* to swell] **turgidity** *n*

Turing test *n computers* a test designed to show whether one is communicating with a human or a computer [after A. *Turing*, mathematician]

Turk *n* a person from Turkey

turkey *n, pl* **-keys** *or* **-key** **1** a large bird of North America bred for its meat **2** *informal, chiefly US & Canad* something, esp. a theatrical production, that fails **3 cold turkey** *slang* a method of curing drug addiction by abrupt withdrawal of all doses **4 talk turkey** *informal, chiefly US & Canad* to discuss, esp. business, frankly and practically [used at first of the African guinea fowl (because it was brought through Turkish territory), later applied by mistake to the American bird]

Turkic *n* a family of Asian languages including Turkish and Azerbaijani

Turkish *adj* **1** of Turkey ▷ *n* **2** the language of Turkey

Turkish bath *n* **1** a type of bath in which the bather sweats freely in hot dry air, is then washed, often massaged, and has a cold plunge or shower **2 Turkish baths** an establishment for such baths

Turkish coffee *n* very strong black coffee

Turkish delight *n* a jelly-like sweet flavoured with flower essences, usually cut into cubes and covered in icing sugar

turmeric *n* **1** a tropical Asian plant with yellow flowers and an aromatic underground stem **2** a yellow spice obtained from the root of this plant [Old French *terre merite* meritorious earth]

turmoil *n* disorder, agitation, or confusion: *a period of political turmoil and uncertainty* [origin unknown]

turn *vb* **1** to move to face in another direction **2** to rotate or move round **3** to operate (a switch, key, etc.) by twisting it **4** to aim or point (something) in a particular direction: *they turned their guns on the crowd* **5** to change in course or direction: *the van turned right into Victoria Road* **6** (of a road, river, etc.) to have a bend or curve in it **7** to perform or do (something) with a rotating movement: *a small boy was turning somersaults* **8** to change so as to become: *he turned pale* **9** to reach, pass, or progress beyond in age, time, etc.: *she had just turned fourteen* **10** to find (a particular page) in a book: *turn to page 78* **11** to look at the other side of: *turning the pages of a book* **12** to shape (wood, metal, etc.) on a lathe **13** (of leaves) to change colour in autumn **14** to make or become sour: *the milk is starting to turn* **15** to affect or be affected with nausea or giddiness: *that would turn the strongest stomach* **16** (of the tide) to start coming in or going out **17 turn against** to stop liking (something or someone one previously liked): *people turned against her because she became so dictatorial* **18 turn into** to become or change into: *my mother turned our house into four apartments* **19 turn loose** to set (an animal or a person) free **20 turn someone's head** to affect someone mentally or emotionally **21 turn to A** to direct or apply (one's attention or thoughts) to **B** to stop doing or using one thing and start doing or using (another): *I turned to photography from writing* **C** to appeal or apply to (someone) for help, advice, etc. ▷ *n* **22** the act of turning **23** a movement of complete or partial rotation: *a turn of the dial* **24** a change of direction or position **25** same as **turning** (sense 1) **26** the right or opportunity to do something in an agreed order or succession: *it was her turn to play next* **27** a change in something that is happening or being done: *events took an unhappy turn* **28** a period of action, work, etc. **29** a short walk, ride, or excursion **30** natural inclination: *a liberal turn of mind* **31** distinctive form or style: *she'd a nice turn of phrase* **32** a deed that helps or hinders someone: *I'm trying to do you a good turn* **33** a twist, bend, or distortion in shape **34** a slight attack of an illness: *she's just having one of her turns* **35** *music* a melodic ornament that alternates the main note with the notes above and below it, beginning with the note above, in a variety of sequences **36** a short theatrical act: *tonight's star turn* **37** *informal* a shock or surprise: *you gave me rather a turn* **38 done to a turn** *informal* cooked perfectly **39 turn and turn about** one after another; alternately ▷ See also **turn down, turn in** *etc.* [Old English *tyrnan*] **turner** *n*

turnaround *or* **turnabout** *n* a complete change or reversal: *a prompt economic turnaround*

turncoat *n* a person who deserts one cause or party to join an opposing one

turn down *vb* **1** to reduce (the volume, brightness, or temperature of something): *turn the heat down* **2** to reject or refuse: *the invitation was turned down* **3** to fold down (sheets, etc.)

turn in *vb informal* **1** to go to bed for the night **2** to hand in: *turning in my essay* **3** to hand (a suspect or criminal) over to the police: *his own brother turned him in*

turning *n* **1** a road, river, or path that turns off the main way **2** the point where such a way turns off **3** the process of turning objects on a lathe

turning circle *n* the smallest circle in which a vehicle can turn

turning point *n* a moment when a decisive change occurs

turnip *n* a vegetable with a large yellow or white edible root [Latin *napus*]

turnkey *n old-fashioned* a jailer

turn off *vb* **1** to leave (a road or path): *turning off the main road* **2** (of a road or path) to lead away from (another road or path): *a main street with alleys twisting and turning off it* **3** to cause (something) to stop operating by turning a knob, pushing a button, etc. **4** *informal* to cause disgust or disinterest in (someone): *keeping kids from getting turned off by mathematics* ▷ *n* **turn-off 5** a road or other way branching off from the main thoroughfare **6** *informal* a person or thing that causes dislike

turn on *vb* **1** to cause (something) to operate by turning a knob, pushing a button, etc.: *turn on the radio, please* **2** to attack (someone), esp. without warning: *the Labrador turned on me* **3** *informal* to produce suddenly or automatically: *turning on that bland smile* **4** *slang* to arouse emotionally or sexually **5** to depend or hinge on: *the match turned on a contentious decision* ▷ *n* **turn-on 6** *slang* a person or thing that causes emotional or sexual arousal

turn out *vb* **1** to cause (something, esp. a light) to stop operating by moving a switch **2** to produce or create: *turning out two hits a year* **3** to force (someone) out of a place or position: *turned out of office* **4** to empty the contents of (something): *the police ordered him to turn out his pockets* **5** to be discovered or found (to be or do something): *he turned out to be a Finn* **6** to end up or result: *how interesting to see how it all turned out!* **7** to dress and groom: *she is always very well turned out* **8** to assemble or gather: *crowds turned out to see him* **9 turn out for** *informal* to make an appearance, esp. in a sporting competition: *he was asked to turn out for Liverpool* ▷ *n* **turnout 10** a number of people attending an event: *there has been a high turnout of voters in elections in Bulgaria* **11** the quantity or amount produced

turn over *vb* **1** to change position, esp. so as to reverse top and bottom **2** to shift position, for instance by rolling onto one's side: *he turned over and went straight to sleep* **3** to consider carefully: *as I walked, I turned her story over* **4** to give (something) to someone who has a right to it or to the authorities: *the police ordered him to turn over the files to them* **5** (of an engine) to start or function correctly: *when he pressed the starter button, the engine turned over at once* **6** *slang* to rob: *the house had been turned over while they were out* ▷ *n* **turnover 7 A** the amount of business done by a company during a specified period **B** the rate at which stock in trade is sold and replenished **8** a small pastry case filled with fruit or jam: *an apple turnover* **9** the number of workers employed by a firm in a given period to replace those who have left

turnpike *n* **1** *history* a barrier across a road to prevent vehicles or pedestrians passing until a charge (toll) had been paid **2** *US* a motorway for use of which a toll is charged [*turn + pike* a spike]

turnstile *n* a mechanical barrier with arms that are turned to admit one person at a time

turntable *n* **1** the circular platform in a record player that rotates the record while it is being played **2** a circular platform used for turning locomotives and cars

turn up *vb* **1** to arrive or appear: *few people turned up* **2** to find or discover or be found or discovered: *a medical checkup has only turned up a sinus infection* **3** to increase the flow, volume, etc., of: *he turned up the radio* ▷ *n* **turn-up 4** *Brit* the turned-up fold at the bottom of some trouser legs **5 a turn-up for the books** *informal* an unexpected happening

turpentine *n* **1** a strong-smelling colourless oil distilled from the resin of some coniferous trees, and used for thinning paint, for cleaning, and in medicine **2** a semisolid mixture of resin and oil

t

obtained from various conifers, which is the main source of commercial turpentine **3** *not in technical use* any one of a number of thinners for paints and varnishes, consisting of fractions of petroleum [Latin *terebinthina*]

turpitude *n formal* depravity or wickedness: *newspapers owned by proprietors whose moral turpitude far exceeded anything chronicled in their pages* [Latin *turpitudo* ugliness]

turps *n* short for **turpentine** (senses 1, 3)

turquoise *adj* **1** greenish-blue ▷ *n* **2** a greenish-blue precious stone [Old French *turqueise* Turkish (stone)]

turret *n* **1** a small tower that projects from the wall of a building, esp. a castle **2** (on a tank or warship) a rotating structure on which guns are mounted **3** (on a machine tool) a turret-like steel structure with tools projecting from it that can be rotated to bring each tool to bear on the work [Latin *turris* tower] **turreted** *adj*

turtle *n* **1** an aquatic reptile with a flattened shell enclosing the body and flipper-like limbs adapted for swimming **2 turn turtle** (of a boat) to capsize [French *tortue* tortoise]

turtledove *n* an Old World dove noted for its soft cooing and devotion to its mate [Old English *turtla*]

turtleneck *n* a round high close-fitting neck on a sweater or a sweater with such a neck

Tuscan *adj* of a style of classical architecture characterized by unfluted columns [from *Tuscany*, a region in central Italy]

tusk *n* a long pointed tooth in the elephant, walrus, and certain other mammals [Old English *tūsc*] **tusked** *adj*

tussle *n* **1** an energetic fight, struggle, or argument: *she resigned following a protracted boardroom tussle* ▷ *vb* **-sling, -sled 2** to fight or struggle energetically [Middle English *tusen* to pull]

tussock *n* a dense tuft of grass or other vegetation [origin unknown] **tussocky** *adj*

tut *interj, n, vb* **tutting, tutted** short for **tut-tut**

tutelage (**tew**-till-lij) *n formal* **1** instruction or guidance, esp. by a tutor **2** the state of being supervised by a guardian or tutor [Latin *tueri* to watch over]

tutelary (**tew**-till-lar-ee) *adj literary* **1** having the role of guardian or protector **2** of a guardian

tutor *n* **1** a teacher, usually one instructing individual pupils **2** (at a college or university) a member of staff responsible for the teaching and supervision of a certain number of students ▷ *vb* **3** to act as a tutor to (someone) [Latin: a watcher] **tutorship** *n*

tutorial *n* **1** a period of intensive tuition given by a tutor to an individual student or to a small group of students ▷ *adj* **2** of or relating to a tutor

tutti *adj, adv music* to be performed by the whole orchestra, choir, etc. [Italian]

tutti-frutti *n, pl* **-fruttis** an ice cream or other sweet food containing small pieces of candied or fresh fruits [Italian, literally: all the fruits]

tut-tut *interj* **1** an exclamation of mild reprimand, disapproval, or surprise ▷ *vb* **-tutting, -tutted 2** to express disapproval by the exclamation of 'tut-tut' ▷ *n* **3** the act of tut-tutting: *his bright red tennis shorts provoked a few tut-tuts from the traditionalists*

tutu *n* a very short skirt worn by ballerinas, made of projecting layers of stiffened material [French]

tuxedo *n, pl* **-dos** a dinner jacket [after a country club in *Tuxedo Park*, New York]

TV television

TVEI *Brit* technical and vocational educational initiative: a national educational scheme in which pupils gain practical experience in technology and industry, often through work placement

twaddle *n* **1** silly, trivial, or pretentious talk or writing ▷ *vb* **-dling, -dled 2** to talk or write in a silly or pretentious way [earlier *twattle*]

twain *adj, n archaic* two [Old English *twēgen*]

twang *n* **1** a sharp ringing sound produced by or as if by the plucking of a taut string **2** a strongly nasal quality in a person's speech: *a high-pitched Texas twang* ▷ *vb* **3** to make or cause to make a twang: *a bunch of angels twanging harps* [imitative] **twangy** *adj*

twat *n Brit, Austral & NZ taboo slang* **1** the female genitals **2** a foolish person [origin unknown]

tweak *vb* **1** to twist or pinch with a sharp or sudden movement: *she tweaked his ear* **2** *informal* to make a minor alteration ▷ *n* **3** the act of tweaking **4** *informal* a minor alteration [Old English *twiccian*]

twee *adj informal* excessively sentimental, sweet, or pretty [from *tweet*, affected pronunciation of *sweet*]

tweed *n* **1** a thick woollen cloth produced originally in Scotland **2 tweeds** a suit made of tweed [probably from *tweel*, Scots variant of *twill*]

tweedy *adj* **tweedier, tweediest 1** of, made of, or resembling tweed **2** showing a fondness for a hearty outdoor life, often associated with wearers of tweeds

tweet *n* **1** an imitation of the thin chirping sound made by small birds **2** a short message posted on the Twitter website ▷ *vb* **3** to make this sound **4** to post a short message on the Twitter website [imitative]

tweeter *n* a loudspeaker used in high-fidelity systems for the reproduction of high audio frequencies

tweezers *pl n* a small pincer-like tool used for tasks such as handling small objects or plucking out hairs [obsolete *tweeze* case of instruments]

twelfth *adj* **1** of or being number twelve in a series ▷ *n* **2** number twelve in a series **3** one of twelve equal parts of something

Twelfth Day *n* January 6, the twelfth day after Christmas and the feast of the Epiphany

twelfth man *n* a reserve player in a cricket team

Twelfth Night *n* **A** the evening of January 5, the eve of Twelfth Day **B** the evening of Twelfth Day itself

twelve *n* **1** the cardinal number that is the sum of ten and two **2** a numeral, 12 or XII, representing this number **3** something representing or consisting of twelve units ▷ *adj* **4** amounting to twelve: *twelve months* [Old English *twelf*]

twelvemonth *n archaic, chiefly Brit* a year

twelve-tone *adj* of or denoting the type of serial music which uses as its musical material a sequence of notes containing all 12 semitones of the chromatic scale

twenty *n, pl* **-ties 1** the cardinal number that is the product of ten and two **2** a numeral, 20 or XX, representing this number **3** something representing or consisting of twenty units ▹ *adj* **4** amounting to twenty: *twenty minutes*
twentieth *adj, n*

Twenty20 *n* form of one-day cricket in which each side bats for twenty overs

twenty-four-seven *or* **24/7** *adv informal* constantly or all the time: *consultants would no longer be available 24/7* [from twenty-four hours a day, seven days a week]

twerking *n* a provocative dance performed by moving the hips rapidly back and forth, while pushing the buttocks out

twerp *or* **twirp** *n informal* a silly, stupid, or contemptible person [origin unknown]

twice *adv* **1** two times; on two occasions or in two cases: *I've met her only twice* **2** double in degree or quantity: *twice as big* [Old English *twiwa*]

twiddle *vb* **-dling, -dled 1** to twirl or fiddle, often in an idle way: *twiddling the knobs of a radio* **2 twiddle one's thumbs A** to rotate one's thumbs around one another, when bored or impatient **B** to be bored, with nothing to do ▹ *n* **3** an unnecessary decoration, esp. a curly one [probably *twirl* + *fiddle*]

twig[1] *n* a small branch or shoot of a tree [Old English *twigge*] **twiggy** *adj*

twig[2] *vb* **twigging, twigged** *informal* to realize or understand: *I should have twigged it earlier* [origin unknown]

twilight *n* **1** the soft dim light that occurs when the sun is just below the horizon after sunset **2** the period in which this light occurs: *soon after twilight we started marching again* **3** a period in which strength, importance, etc., is gradually declining: *the twilight of his political career* ▹ *adj* **4** of or relating to the period towards the end of the day: *the twilight shift* **5** of or being a period of decline: *he spent most of his twilight years working on a history of France* **6** denoting irregularity and obscurity: *a twilight existence* [Old English *twi-* half + LIGHT] **twilit** *adj*

twilight zone *n* any indefinite or intermediate condition or area: *the twilight zone between sleep and wakefulness*

twill *n* a fabric woven to produce an effect of parallel diagonal lines or ribs in the cloth [Old English *twilic* having a double thread]

twin *n* **1** one of a pair of people or animals conceived at the same time **2** one of a pair of people or things that are identical or very similar ▹ *vb* **twinning, twinned 3** to pair or be paired together [Old English *twinn*]

twin bed *n* one of a pair of matching single beds

twin-bedded *adj* (of a room in a hotel, etc.) containing two single beds

twine *n* **1** string or cord made by twisting fibres together ▹ *vb* **twining, twined 2** to twist or wind together: *she twined the flowers into a garland* **3 twine round** *or* **around** to twist or wind around: *she twined her arms around her neck* [Old English *twīn*]

twin-engined *adj* (of an aeroplane) having two engines

twinge *n* **1** a sudden brief darting or stabbing pain **2** a sharp emotional pang: *a twinge of conscience* [Old English *twengan* to pinch]

twinkle *vb* **-kling, -kled 1** to shine brightly and intermittently; sparkle **2** (of the eyes) to sparkle, esp. with amusement or delight ▹ *n* **3** a flickering brightness; sparkle [Old English *twinclian*]

twinkling *n* **in the twinkling of an eye** in a very short time

twinset *n* a matching jumper and cardigan

twin town *n* a town that has cultural and social links with a foreign town: *Nuremberg is one of Glasgow's twin towns*

twirl *vb* **1** to move around rapidly and repeatedly in a circle **2** to twist, wind, or twiddle, often idly: *twirling the glass in her hand* ▹ *n* **3** a whirl or twist **4** a written flourish [origin unknown]

twist *vb* **1** to turn one end or part while the other end or parts remain still or turn in the opposite direction: *never twist or wring woollen garments* **2** to distort or be distorted **3** to wind or twine: *the wire had been twisted twice* **4** to force or be forced out of the natural form or position: *I twisted my knee* **5** to change the meaning of; distort: *he'd twisted the truth to make himself look good* **6** to revolve or rotate: *he twisted the switch to turn the radio off* **7** to wrench with a turning action: *he twisted the wheel sharply* **8** to follow a winding course: *the road twisted as it climbed* **9** to dance the twist **10 twist someone's arm** to persuade or coerce someone ▹ *n* **11** the act of twisting: *she gave a dainty little twist to her parasol* **12** something formed by or as if by twisting: *there's a twist in the cable* **13** a decisive change of direction, aim, meaning, or character: *the latest revelations give a new twist to the company's boardroom wranglings* **14** an unexpected development in a story, play, or film **15** a bend: *a twist of the mountain road* **16** a distortion of the original shape or form **17** a jerky pull, wrench, or turn **18 the twist** a dance popular in the 1960s, in which dancers vigorously twist the hips **19 round the twist** *slang* mad or eccentric [Old English] **twisty** *adj*

twisted *adj* (of a person) cruel or perverted

twister *n Brit* a swindling or dishonest person

twit[1] *vb* **twitting, twitted** *Brit* to poke fun at (someone) [Old English *ætwītan*]

twit[2] *n informal* a foolish or stupid person [from TWIT[1]]

twitch *vb* **1** (of a person or part of a person's body) to move in a jerky spasmodic way: *his left eyelid twitched involuntarily* **2** to pull (something) with a quick jerky movement: *she twitched the curtains shut* ▹ *n* **3** a sharp jerking movement, esp. one caused by a nervous condition [Old English *twiccian* to pluck]

twitcher *n Brit informal* a bird-watcher who tries to spot as many rare varieties as possible

twitchy *adj* **twitchier, twitchiest** nervous, worried, and ill-at-ease: *he was twitchy with anticipation*

twitter *vb* **1** (esp. of a bird) to utter a succession of chirping sounds **2** to talk rapidly and nervously in a high-pitched voice: *novelists who twittered about how much they admired him* **3** to post a short message on the Twitter website ▷ *n* **4** the act or sound of twittering **5 in a twitter** in a state of nervous excitement [imitative] **twitterer** *n* **twittering** *n* **twittery** *adj*

Twitter *n trademark* a website where people can post short messages

two *n* **1** the cardinal number that is the sum of one and one **2** a numeral, 2 or II, representing this number **3** something representing or consisting of two units **4 in two** in or into two parts: *cut the cake in two and take a bit each* **5 put two and two together** to reach an obvious conclusion by considering the evidence available **6 that makes two of us** the same applies to me ▷ *adj* **7** amounting to two: *two years* [Old English *twā*]

twoccing *or* **twocking** *n Brit slang* the act of breaking into a motor vehicle and driving it away [from T*(aking)* W*(ithout)* O*(wner's)* C*(onsent)*, the legal offence] **twoccer** *or* **twocker** *n*

two-dimensional *adj* **1** having two dimensions **2** somewhat lacking in depth or complexity: *a modern audience is unable to tolerate two-dimensional characters*

two-edged *adj* **1** (of a remark) having both a favourable and an unfavourable interpretation, such as *she looks nice when she smiles* **2** (of a knife, saw, etc.) having two cutting edges

two-faced *adj* deceitful or hypocritical: *he's a two-faced liar and opportunist*

twofold *adj* **1** having twice as many or as much **2** composed of two parts ▷ *adv* **3** by twice as many or as much

two-four *n Canad informal* a box containing 24 bottles of beer

two-handed *adj* **1** requiring the use of both hands **2** requiring the participation of two people: *a two-handed transatlantic yacht race*

twopence *or* **tuppence** (**tup**-pence) *n Brit* **1** the sum of two pennies **2** the slightest amount: *I don't care twopence who your father is*

twopenny *or* **tuppenny** (**tup**-pen-ee) *adj chiefly Brit* **1** cheap or tawdry **2** worth or costing two pence

two-piece *adj* **1** consisting of two separate parts, usually matching, such as a woman's suit or swimsuit ▷ *n* **2** such an outfit

two-ply *adj* made of two thicknesses, layers, or strands

two-sided *adj* **1** having two sides: *two-sided paper* **2** having two aspects or interpretations: *an ambivalent two-sided event*

twosome *n* a group of two people

two-step *n* **1** an old-time dance in duple time: *the next dance was the Military Two-Step* **2** music for this dance

two-stroke *adj* of an internal-combustion engine whose piston makes two strokes for every explosion

Two Thousand Guineas *n* **the Two Thousand Guineas** an annual horse race for three-year-olds, run at Newmarket

two-time *vb* **-timing, -timed** *informal* to deceive (a lover) by having an affair with someone else **two-timer** *n*

two-way *adj* **1** moving in, or allowing movement in, two opposite directions: *two-way traffic* **2** involving mutual involvement or cooperation: *two-way communication* **3** (of a radio or transmitter) capable of both transmission and reception of messages

TX Texas

tycoon *n* a businessperson of great wealth and power [Japanese *taikun* great ruler]

tyke *or* **tike** *n* **1** *Brit, Austral & NZ informal* a small or cheeky child **2** *Brit dialect* a rough ill-mannered person [Old Norse *tīk* bitch]

tympani *pl n* same as **timpani**

tympanic membrane *n anatomy* the thin membrane separating the external ear from the middle ear; eardrum

tympanum *n, pl* **-nums** *or* **-na** **1** *anatomy* **A** the cavity of the middle ear **B** same as **tympanic membrane** **2** *archit* the recessed space between the arch and the lintel above a door [Greek *tumpanon* drum] **tympanic** *adj*

Tynwald (**tin**-wold) *n* the Parliament of the Isle of Man [Old Norse *thing* assembly + *vollr* field]

type *n* **1** a kind, class, or category of things, all of which have something in common **2** a subdivision of a particular class; sort: *it is more alcoholic than most wines of this type* **3** the general characteristics distinguishing a particular group: *the old-fashioned type of nanny* **4** *informal* a person, esp. of a specified kind: *a seagoing type* **5** a block with a raised character on it used for printing **6** text printed from type; print ▷ *vb* **typing, typed** **7** to write using a typewriter or word processor **8** to be a symbol of or typify **9** to decide the type of; classify [Greek *tupos* image]

typecast *vb* **-casting, -cast** to cast (an actor or actress) in the same kind of role continually

typeface *n* the size and style of printing used in a book, magazine, etc.

typescript *n* any typewritten document

typeset *vb* **-setting, -set** *printing* to set (text for printing) in type

typesetter *n* a person, machine, or company that sets type; compositor

typewriter *n* a machine which prints a letter or other character when the appropriate key is pressed

typewritten *adj* typed on a typewriter or word processor

typhoid *pathol* ▷ *n* **1** short for **typhoid fever** ▷ *adj* **2** of or relating to typhoid fever: *typhoid vaccines*

typhoid fever *n* an acute infectious disease characterized by high fever, spots, abdominal pain, etc. It is spread by contaminated food or water

typhoon *n* a violent tropical storm, esp. one in the China Seas or W Pacific [Chinese *tai fung* great wind]

typhus *n* an acute infectious disease transmitted by lice or mites and characterized by high fever, skin rash, and severe headache [Greek *tuphos* fever]

typical *adj* **1** being or serving as a representative example of a particular type; characteristic: *a typical working day* **2** considered to be an example of some undesirable trait: *it was typical that he*

t

should start talking almost before he was inside the room [Greek *tupos* image] **typically** *adv*

typify *vb* **-fies, -fying, -fied 1** to be typical of or characterize: *the beers made here typify all that is best about the independent brewing sector* **2** to symbolize or represent: *a number of dissident intellectuals, typified by Andrei Sakharov*

typing *n* **1** the work or activity of using a typewriter or word processor **2** the skill of using a typewriter quickly and accurately

typist *n* a person who types letters, reports, etc., esp. for a living

typo *n, pl* **-pos** *informal* a typographical error

typography *n* **1** the art or craft of printing **2** the style or quality of printing and layout in a book, magazine, etc. **typographical** *adj* **typographically** *adv*

tyrannical *adj* of or like a tyrant; unjust and oppressive

tyrannize *or* **-ise** *vb* **-nizing, -nized** *or* **-nising, -nised** to rule or exercise power (over) in a cruel or oppressive manner: *he dominated and tyrannized his younger brother*

tyrannosaurus (tirr-ran-oh-sore-uss) *or* **tyrannosaur** *n* a large two-footed flesh-eating dinosaur common in North America in Cretaceous times [Greek *turannos* tyrant + *sauros* lizard]

tyranny *n, pl* **-nies 1 A** government by a tyrant **B** oppressive and unjust government by more than one person **2** the condition or state of being dominated or controlled by something that makes unpleasant or harsh demands: *the tyranny of fashion drives many women to diet although they are not overweight* **tyrannous** *adj*

tyrant *n* **1** a person who governs oppressively, unjustly, and arbitrarily **2** any person who exercises authority in a tyrannical manner: *a domestic tyrant* [Greek *turannos*]

tyre *or US* **tire** *n* a ring of rubber, usually filled with air but sometimes solid, fitted round the rim of a wheel of a road vehicle to grip the road [earlier *tire*, probably archaic variant of *attire*]

tyro *n, pl* **-ros** a novice or beginner [Latin *tiro* recruit]

tzar *n* same as **tsar**

tzatziki (tsat-see-kee) *n* a Greek dip made from yogurt, chopped cucumber, and mint [Modern Greek]

tzetze fly *n* same as **tsetse fly**

Uu

U **1** (in Britain) universal (used to describe a film certified as suitable for viewing by anyone) **2** *chem* uranium ▷ *adj* **3** *Brit informal* (of language or behaviour) characteristic of the upper class

ubiquitous (yew-**bik**-wit-uss) *adj* being or seeming to be everywhere at once [Latin *ubique* everywhere] **ubiquity** *n*

U-boat *n* a German submarine [German *Unterseeboot* undersea boat]

Ubuntu *n S African* humanity or fellow feeling; kindness [Nguni (language group of southern Africa)]

uc *printing* upper case

UCAS (in Britain) Universities and Colleges Admissions Service

udder *n* the large baglike milk-producing gland of cows, sheep, or goats, with two or more teats [Old English *ūder*]

UDI Unilateral Declaration of Independence

UEFA Union of European Football Associations

UFO unidentified flying object

ugh (uhh) *interj* an exclamation of disgust, annoyance, or dislike

ugly *adj* **uglier, ugliest** **1** so unattractive as to be unpleasant to look at **2** very unpleasant and involving violence or aggression: *an ugly incident in which one man was stabbed* **3** repulsive or displeasing: *ugly rumours* **4** bad-tempered or sullen: *an ugly mood* [Old Norse *uggligr* dreadful] **ugliness** *n*

ugly duckling *n* a person or thing, initially ugly or unpromising, that becomes beautiful or admirable [from *The Ugly Duckling* by Hans Christian Andersen]

UHF *radio* ultrahigh frequency

UHT ultra-heat-treated (milk or cream)

UK United Kingdom

UKAEA United Kingdom Atomic Energy Authority

ukase (yew-**kaze**) *n* (in imperial Russia) a decree from the tsar [Russian *ukaz*]

Ukrainian *adj* **1** of Ukraine ▷ *n* **2** a person from Ukraine **3** the language of Ukraine

ukulele *or* **ukelele** (yew-kal-**lay**-lee) *n* a small four-stringed guitar [Hawaiian, literally: jumping flea]

ulcer *n* an open sore on the surface of the skin or a mucous membrane [Latin *ulcus*]

ulcerated *adj* made or becoming ulcerous **ulceration** *n*

ulcerous *adj* of, like, or characterized by ulcers

ulna *n, pl* **-nae** *or* **-nas** the inner and longer of the two bones of the human forearm or of the forelimb in other vertebrates [Latin: elbow] **ulnar** *adj*

ulster *n* a man's heavy double-breasted overcoat [*Ulster*, the northernmost province of Ireland]

Ulsterman *or fem* **Ulsterwoman** *n, pl* **-men** *or* **-women** a person from Ulster

ult. ultimo

ulterior (ult-**ear**-ee-or) *adj* (of an aim, reason, etc.) concealed or hidden: *an ulterior motive* [Latin: further]

ultimate *adj* **1** final in a series or process: *predictions about the ultimate destination of modern art* **2** highest, supreme, or unchallengeable: *he has the ultimate power to dismiss the Prime Minister* **3** fundamental or essential: *a believer in the ultimate goodness of people* **4** most extreme: *genocide is the ultimate abuse of human rights* **5** final or total: *she should be able to estimate the ultimate cost* ▷ *n* **6 the ultimate in** the best example of: *the ultimate in luxury holidays* [Latin *ultimus* last, distant] **ultimately** *adv*

ultimatum (ult-im-**may**-tum) *n* a final warning to someone that they must agree to certain conditions or requirements, or else action will be taken against them: *Britain declared war after the Nazis rejected the ultimatum to withdraw from Poland*

ultimo *adv* in or during the previous month. It is rare except when abbreviated to ult. in formal correspondence: *your communication of the 1st ultimo* [Latin: on the last]

ultra *n* a person who has extreme or immoderate beliefs or opinions [Latin: beyond]

ultra- *prefix* **1** beyond a specified extent, range, or limit: *ultrasonic* **2** extremely: *ultraleftist* [Latin]

ultraconservative *adj* **1** highly reactionary ▷ *n* **2** a reactionary person

ultrahigh frequency *n* a radio frequency between 3000 and 300 megahertz

ultramarine *n* **1** a blue pigment originally made from lapis lazuli ▷ *adj* **2** vivid blue [Latin *ultra* beyond + *mare* sea; because the lapis lazuli from which the pigment was made was imported from Asia]

ultramodern *adj* extremely modern

ultramontane *adj* **1** on the other side of the mountains, usually the Alps, from the speaker or writer **2** of a movement in the Roman Catholic Church which favours supreme papal authority ▷ *n* **3** a person from beyond the Alps **4** a member of the ultramontane party of the Roman Catholic Church

ultrasonic *adj* of or producing sound waves with higher frequencies than humans can hear **ultrasonically** *adv*

ultrasonics *n* the branch of physics concerned with ultrasonic waves

ultrasound *n* ultrasonic waves, used in echo sounding, medical diagnosis, and therapy

ultrasound scan *n* an examination of an internal bodily structure by the use of ultrasonic waves, esp. for diagnosing abnormality in a fetus

ultraviolet *n* **1** the part of the electromagnetic spectrum with wavelengths shorter than light but longer than X-rays ▷ *adj* **2** of or consisting of radiation lying in the ultraviolet: *ultraviolet light*

ultra vires (ult-ra **vire**-eez) *adv, adj* beyond the legal power of a person or organization [Latin, literally: beyond strength]

ululate (yewl-yew-late) *vb* **-lating, -lated** *literary* to howl or wail [Latin *ululare*] **ululation** *n*

umbel *n* a type of compound flower in which the flowers arise from the same point in the main stem and have stalks of the same length, to give a cluster with the youngest flowers at the centre [Latin *umbella* a sunshade] **umbellate** *adj*

umbelliferous *adj* of or denoting a plant with flowers in umbels, such as fennel, parsley, carrot, or parsnip [Latin *umbella* a sunshade + *ferre* to bear]

umber *n* **1** a type of dark brown earth containing ferric oxide (rust) ▷ *adj* **2** dark brown to reddish-brown [French *(terre d')ombre* or Italian *(terra di) ombra* shadow (earth)]

umbilical (um-bill-ik-kl) *adj* of or like the navel or the umbilical cord

umbilical cord *n* the long flexible cordlike structure that connects a fetus to the placenta

umbilicus (um-bill-ik-kuss) *n anatomy* the navel [Latin: navel, centre]

umbra *n, pl* **-brae** *or* **-bras** a shadow, usually the shadow cast by the moon onto the earth during a solar eclipse [Latin: shade]

umbrage *n* **take umbrage** to take offence [Latin *umbra* shade]

umbrella *n* **1** a portable device used for protection against rain, consisting of a light canopy supported on a collapsible metal frame mounted on a central rod **2** a single organization, idea, etc., that contains or covers many different organizations or ideas **3** anything that has the effect of a protective screen or general cover: *under the umbrella of the Helsinki security conference* ▷ *adj* **4** containing or covering many different organizations, ideas, etc.: *an umbrella group of nationalists and anti-communists* [Italian *ombrella*, from *ombra* shade] **umbrella-like** *adj*

umiak, oomiak *or* **oomiac** (oo-mee-ak) *n* a large open boat made of stretched skins, used by Inuit [Inuktitut]

umlaut (oom-lout) *n* **1** the mark (¨) placed over a vowel, esp. in German, indicating change in its sound **2** (esp. in Germanic languages) the change of a vowel brought about by the influence of a vowel in the next syllable [German, from *um* around + *Laut* sound]

umlungu (oom-loong-goo) *n S African derogatory* a White man: used esp. as a term of address [Nguni (language group of southern Africa)]

umpire *n* **1** an official who ensures that the people taking part in a game follow the rules; referee ▷ *vb* **-piring, -pired** **2** to act as umpire in a game [Old French *nomper* not one of a pair]

umpteen *adj informal* very many: *the centre of umpteen scandals* [*umpty* a great deal + *-teen* ten] **umpteenth** *n, adj*

UN United Nations

un-[1] *prefix (freely used with adjectives, participles, and their derivative adverbs and nouns: less frequently used with certain other nouns)* not; contrary to; opposite of: *uncertain; untidiness; unbelief; untruth* [Old English *on-, un-*]

un-[2] *prefix* **1** denoting reversal of an action or state: *uncover; untie* **2** denoting removal from, release, or deprivation: *unharness* [Old English *un-, on-*]

unabashed *adj* not ashamed or embarrassed

unabated *adv* without any reduction in force: *the storm continued unabated*

unable *adj* **unable to** not having the power, ability, or authority to; not able to

unabridged *adj* (of a book or text) complete and not shortened or condensed

unacceptable *adj* too bad to be accepted; intolerable

unaccompanied *adj* **1** not having anyone with one: *unaccompanied female travellers should take care* **2** (of singing or a musical instrument) not being accompanied by musical instruments

unaccountable *adj* **1** without any sensible explanation: *for some unaccountable reason I got on the wrong bus* **2** not having to justify or answer for one's actions to other people: *the secret service remains unaccountable to the public* **unaccountably** *adv*

unaccounted *adj* **unaccounted for** unable to be found or traced: *four people were killed in the floods, and eleven remain unaccounted for*

unaccustomed *adj* **1 unaccustomed to** not used to: *unaccustomed to such behaviour* **2** not familiar: *moments of unaccustomed freedom*

unacknowledged *adj* **1** ignored or not accepted as true or existing **2** not officially recognized as being important

unacquainted *adj* **unacquainted with** not knowing about; unfamiliar with

unadopted *adj Brit* (of a road) not maintained by a local authority

unadorned *adj* not decorated; plain

unadulterated *adj* **1** completely pure, with nothing added: *fresh unadulterated spring water* **2** (of an emotion) not mixed with anything else: *a look of unadulterated terror*

unadventurous *adj* not taking chances or trying anything new

unaffected[1] *adj* unpretentious, natural, or sincere

unaffected[2] *adj* not influenced or changed

unafraid *adj* not frightened or nervous

unaided *adv* without any help or assistance; independently: *he could not walk unaided for months after the accident*

unalienable *adj law* same as **inalienable**

unalike *adj* not similar; different

unalloyed *adj literary* not spoiled by being mixed with anything else

unalterable *adj* not able to be changed

unambiguous *adj* having a clear meaning which can only be interpreted in one way

un-American *adj* **1** not in accordance with the aims, ideals, or customs of the US **2** against the interests of the US **un-Americanism** *n*

unanimous (yew-nan-im-uss) *adj* **1** in complete agreement **2** characterized by complete agreement: *unanimous approval* [Latin *unus* one + *animus* mind] **unanimity** *n* **unanimously** *adv*

unannounced *adv* without warning: *she turned up unannounced*

unanswerable *adj* **1** having no possible answer **2** so obviously correct that disagreement is impossible

unappealing *adj* unpleasant or off-putting

unappetizing *adj* tasting, looking, or smelling unpleasant to eat

unappreciated *adj* not given the respect or recognition that is deserved
unapproachable *adj* discouraging friendliness; aloof
unarguable *adj* so obviously correct that disagreement is impossible
unarmed *adj* **1** not carrying any weapons: *they were shooting unarmed peasants* **2** not using any weapons: *unarmed combat*
unashamed *adj* not embarrassed, esp. when doing something some people might find offensive: *unashamed greed* **unashamedly** *adv*
unasked *adv* **1** without being asked to do something: *he opened the door unasked* ▹ *adj* **2** (of a question) not asked, although sometimes implied
unassailable *adj* not able to be destroyed or overcome: *an unassailable lead*
unassisted *adj* without help from anyone else
unassuming *adj* modest or unpretentious
unattached *adj* **1** not connected with any specific body or group **2** not engaged or married
unattainable *adj* not able to be achieved; impossible
unattended *adj* not being watched or looked after: *unattended baggage*
unattractive *adj* not attractive or appealing
unauthorized or **-ised** *adj* done or made without official permission
unavailable *adj* not able to be met, obtained, or contacted
unavailing *adj* useless or futile
unavoidable *adj* unable to be avoided or prevented **unavoidably** *adv*
unaware *adj* **1** not aware or conscious: *unaware of my surroundings* ▹ *adv* **2** *not standard* same as **unawares**
unawares *adv* **1** by surprise: *death had taken him unawares* **2** without knowing: *had he passed her, all unawares?*
unbalanced *adj* **1** lacking balance **2** mentally deranged **3** biased; one-sided: *his unbalanced summing-up*
unbearable *adj* not able to be endured **unbearably** *adv*
unbeatable *adj* not able to be bettered
unbecoming *adj* **1** unattractive or unsuitable: *unbecoming garments* **2** not proper or appropriate to a person or position: *acts unbecoming of university students*
unbeknown *adv* (foll. by *to*) without the knowledge of (a person): *unbeknown to her family she had acquired modern ways*. Also (esp. Brit): **unbeknownst** [archaic *beknown* known]
unbelievable *adj* **1** too unlikely to be believed **2** extremely impressive; marvellous **3** *informal* terrible or shocking **unbelievably** *adv*
unbeliever *n* a person who does not believe in a religion
unbend *vb* **-bending, -bent** to become less strict or more informal in one's attitudes or behaviour
unbending *adj* rigid or inflexible: *an unbending routine*
unbiased *adj* not having or showing prejudice or favouritism; impartial
unbidden *adj literary* not ordered or asked; voluntary or spontaneous: *unbidden thoughts came into Catherine's mind*
unbind *vb* **-binding, -bound 1** to set free from bonds or chains **2** to unfasten or untie
unblemished *adj* not spoiled or tarnished: *smooth unblemished skins*
unblinking *adj* looking at something without blinking
unblock *vb* to remove a blockage from; clear or free
unblushing *adj* immodest or shameless
unbolt *vb* to unfasten a bolt of a door
unborn *adj* not yet born
unbosom *vb* to relieve oneself of secrets or feelings by telling someone [UN-² + *bosom* (in the sense: centre of the emotions)]
unbounded *adj* having no boundaries or limits
unbowed *adj* not giving in or submitting: *the battered but as yet unbowed general secretary*
unbreakable *adj* not able to be broken; indestructible
unbridled *adj* (of feelings or behaviour) not restrained or controlled in any way: *unbridled passion*
unbroken *adj* **1** complete or whole **2** continuous: *I slept for eight unbroken hours* **3** not disturbed or upset: *an unbroken night* **4** (of a record) not improved upon **5** (of animals, esp. horses) not tamed
unburden *vb* to relieve one's mind or oneself of a worry or trouble by telling someone about it
uncalled-for *adj* unnecessary or unwarranted: *uncalled-for comments*
uncanny *adj* **1** weird or mysterious: *an uncanny silence* **2** beyond what is normal: *an uncanny eye for detail* **uncannily** *adv* **uncanniness** *n*
uncared-for *adj* not cared for; neglected
uncaring *adj* showing no concern for other people's suffering and hardship
unceasing *adj* continuing without a break; never stopping
unceremonious *adj* **1** relaxed and informal: *she greeted him with unceremonious friendliness* **2** abrupt or rude: *the answer was an unceremonious 'no'* **unceremoniously** *adv*
uncertain *adj* **1** not able to be accurately known or predicted: *an uncertain future* **2** not definitely decided: *they are uncertain about the date* **3** not to be depended upon: *an uncertain career* **4** changeable: *an uncertain sky* **uncertainty** *n*
unchallenged *adj, adv* done or accepted without being challenged: *seventy years of unchallenged rule; her decisions went unchallenged*
unchangeable *adj* not able to be altered
unchanged *adj* remaining the same
uncharacteristic *adj* not typical **uncharacteristically** *adv*
uncharitable *adj* unkind or harsh **uncharitably** *adv*
uncharted *adj* **1** (of an area of sea or land) not having had a map made of it, esp. because it is unexplored **2** unknown or unfamiliar: *a whole uncharted universe of emotions*
unchecked *adj* **1** not prevented from continuing or growing: *unchecked population growth* **2** not examined or inspected ▹ *adv* **3** without being

stopped or hindered: *the virus could spread unchecked* **4** without being examined or inspected: *the drugs passed unchecked through airport security*

unchristian *or* **un-Christian** *adj* not in accordance with Christian principles

uncial (un-see-al) *adj* **1** of or written in letters that resemble modern capitals, as used in Greek and Latin manuscripts of the third to ninth centuries ▷ *n* **2** an uncial letter or manuscript [Late Latin *unciales litterae* letters an inch long]

uncivil *adj* impolite, rude, or bad-mannered **uncivilly** *adv*

uncivilized *or* **-lised** *adj* **1** (of a tribe or people) not yet civilized **2** lacking culture or sophistication

unclassified *adj* **1** not arranged in any specific order or grouping **2** (of official information) not secret

uncle *n* **1** a brother of one's father or mother **2** the husband of one's aunt **3** a child's term of address for a male friend of its parents **4** *slang* a pawnbroker [Latin *avunculus*]

unclean *adj* lacking moral, spiritual, or physical cleanliness

unclear *adj* confusing or hard to understand

Uncle Sam *n* a personification of the government of the United States [apparently a humorous interpretation of the letters stamped on army supply boxes during the War of 1812: US]

Uncle Tom *n informal, offensive* a Black person whose behaviour towards White people is regarded as servile [from *Uncle Tom's Cabin* by H. B. Stowe]

unclothed *adj* not wearing any clothes; naked

uncluttered *adj* not containing anything unnecessary; austere and simple

uncoil *vb* to unwind or untwist

uncomfortable *adj* **1** not physically relaxed: *he was forced to sit in an uncomfortable cross-legged position* **2** not comfortable to be in or use: *an uncomfortable chair* **3** causing discomfort or unease: *the uncomfortable truth* **uncomfortably** *adv*

uncommitted *adj* not bound to a specific opinion, course of action, or cause

uncommon *adj* **1** not happening or encountered often **2** in excess of what is normal: *an uncommon amount of powder*

uncommonly *adv* **1** in an unusual manner or degree **2** extremely: *an uncommonly good humour*

uncommunicative *adj* disinclined to talk or give information

uncomplaining *adj* doing or tolerating something unpleasant or difficult without complaint: *uncomplaining devotion*

uncomplicated *adj* simple and straightforward

uncomplimentary *adj* not expressing respect or praise; insulting

uncomprehending *adj* not understanding what is happening or what has been said

uncompromising *adj* not prepared to compromise; inflexible **uncompromisingly** *adv*

unconcealed *adj* not hidden or disguised: *a look of unconcealed hatred*

unconcern *n* apathy or indifference

unconcerned *adj* **1** not interested in something and not wanting to become involved **2** not worried or troubled **unconcernedly** (un-kon-sern-id-lee) *adv*

unconditional *adj* without conditions or limitations: *an unconditional ceasefire* **unconditionally** *adv*

unconfirmed *adj* not yet proved to be true: *unconfirmed reports of a major accident*

uncongenial *adj* (of a place or condition) unpleasant and unfriendly

unconnected *adj* not linked to each other: *a series of unconnected incidents*

unconscionable *adj* **1** unscrupulous or unprincipled: *an unconscionable charmer* **2** excessive in amount or degree: *unconscionable number of social obligations*

unconscious *adj* **1** unable to notice or respond to things which one would normally be aware of through the senses; insensible or comatose **2** not aware of one's actions or behaviour: *unconscious of his failure* **3** not realized or intended: *unconscious duplicity* **4** coming from or produced by the unconscious: *unconscious mental processes* ▷ *n* **5** *psychoanalysis* the part of the mind containing instincts, impulses, and ideas that are not available for direct examination **unconsciously** *adv* **unconsciousness** *n*

unconstitutional *adj* forbidden by the rules or laws which state how an organization or country must function

uncontrollable *adj* **1** unable to be restrained or prevented: *a fit of uncontrollable giggles* **2** (of a person) wild and unmanageable in behaviour: *he became violent and uncontrollable* **uncontrollably** *adv*

unconventional *adj* not conforming to accepted rules or standards

unconvinced *adj* not certain that something is true or right: *I remained unconvinced by his arguments*

unconvincing *adj* (of a reason, argument, etc.) not good enough to convince people that something is true or right

uncooked *adj* raw

uncooperative *adj* not willing to help other people with what they are trying to do

uncoordinated *adj* **1** not joining or functioning together properly to form a whole **2** (of a person) not able to control his or her movements properly; clumsy

uncork *vb* to remove the cork from a bottle

uncorroborated *adj* not supported by other evidence or proof

uncountable *adj* existing in such large numbers that it is impossible to say how many there are: *uncountable millions*

uncouple *vb* **-pling, -pled** to disconnect or become disconnected

uncouth *adj* lacking in good manners, refinement, or grace [Old English *un-* not + *cūth* familiar]

uncover *vb* **1** to remove the cover or top from **2** to reveal or disclose: *they have uncovered a plot to overthrow the government* **uncovered** *adj*

uncritical *adj* not making a judgment about the merits or morality of something

uncrowned *adj* **1** having the powers, but not the title, of royalty **2** (of a king or queen) not yet crowned

u

unction *n* **1** *chiefly RC Church & Eastern churches* the act of anointing with oil in sacramental ceremonies **2** oily charm **3** an ointment **4** anything soothing [Latin *unguere* to anoint]
unctuous *adj* pretending to be kind and concerned but obviously not sincere [Latin *unctum* ointment]
uncultured *adj* not knowing much about art, literature, etc.
uncut *adj* **1** not shortened or censored **2** not cut **3** (of precious stones) not having shaped and polished surfaces
undamaged *adj* not spoilt or damaged; intact
undaunted *adj* not put off, discouraged, or beaten
undeceive *vb* **-ceiving, -ceived** to reveal the truth to someone previously misled or deceived
undecided *adj* **1** not having made up one's mind **2** (of an issue or problem) not agreed or decided upon
undeclared *adj* not acknowledged for tax purposes
undemanding *adj* not difficult to do or deal with: *an undemanding task*
undemocratic *adj* not organized or run as a democracy
undemonstrative *adj* not showing emotions openly or easily
undeniable *adj* **1** unquestionably true **2** of unquestionable excellence: *of undeniable character* **undeniably** *adv*
under *prep* **1** directly below; on, to, or beneath the underside or base of: *under the bed* **2** less than: *in just under an hour* **3** lower in rank than: *under a general* **4** subject to the supervision, control, or influence of: *under communism for 45 years* **5** in or subject to certain circumstances or conditions: *the bridge is still under construction; under battle conditions* **6** in (a specified category): *he had filed Kafka's 'The Trial' under crime stories* **7** known by: *under their own names* **8** planted with: *a field under corn* **9** powered by: *under sail* ▷ *adv* **10** below; to a position underneath [Old English]
under- *prefix* **1** below or beneath: *underarm; underground* **2** insufficient or insufficiently: *underemployed* **3** of lesser importance or lower rank: *undersecretary* **4** indicating secrecy or deception: *underhand*
underachieve *vb* **-achieving, -achieved** to fail to achieve a performance appropriate to one's age or talents **underachiever** *n*
underactive *adj* less active than is normal or desirable: *an underactive thyroid gland*
underage *adj* below the required or standard age, usually below the legal age for voting or drinking: *underage sex*
underarm *adj* **1** *sport* denoting a style of throwing, bowling, or serving in which the hand is swung below shoulder level **2** below the arm ▷ *adv* **3** in an underarm style
underbelly *n, pl* **-lies 1** the part of an animal's belly nearest the ground **2** a vulnerable or unprotected part, aspect, or region
underbrush *n US, Canad & Austral* same as **undergrowth**
undercarriage *n* **1** the wheels, shock absorbers, and struts that support an aircraft on the ground and enable it to take off and land **2** the framework supporting the body of a vehicle
undercharge *vb* **-charging, -charged** to charge too little for something
underclass *n* a class beneath the usual social scale consisting of the most disadvantaged people, such as the long-term unemployed
underclothes *pl n also called* **underclothing** same as **underwear**
undercoat *n* **1** a coat of paint applied before the top coat **2** *zool* a layer of soft fur beneath the outer fur of animals such as the otter ▷ *vb* **3** to apply an undercoat to a surface
undercook *vb* to cook for too short a time or at too low a temperature
undercover *adj* done or acting in secret: *an undercover investigation*
undercurrent *n* **1** a current that is not apparent at the surface **2** an underlying opinion or emotion
undercut *vb* **-cutting, -cut 1** to charge less than a competitor in order to obtain trade **2** to undermine or render less effective: *the latest fighting undercuts diplomatic attempts to find a peaceful solution* **3** to cut away the under part of something
underdeveloped *adj* **1** immature or undersized **2** (of a country or its economy) lacking the finance, industries, and organization necessary to advance
underdog *n* a person or team in a weak or underprivileged position
underdone *adj* insufficiently or lightly cooked
underemployed *adj* not fully or adequately employed
underestimate *vb* **-mating, -mated 1** to make too low an estimate of: *the trust had underestimated the cost of work* **2** to not be aware or take account of the full abilities or potential of: *the police had underestimated him* ▷ *n* **3** too low an estimate **underestimation** *n*

> **USAGE** *Underestimate* is sometimes wrongly used where *overestimate* is meant: *the importance of his work cannot be overestimated* (not *cannot be underestimated*).

underexpose *vb* **-posing, -posed** *photog* to expose (a film, plate, or paper) for too short a time or with insufficient light **underexposure** *n*
underfed *adj* not getting enough food to be healthy
underfelt *n* thick felt laid under a carpet to increase insulation
underfoot *adv* **1** underneath the feet; on the ground **2 trample** *or* **crush underfoot A** to damage or destroy by stepping on **B** to treat with contempt
undergarment *n* a garment worn under clothes
undergo *vb* **-going, -went, -gone** to experience, endure, or sustain: *he underwent a three-hour operation* [Old English *undergān*]
undergraduate *n* a person studying in a university for a first degree
underground *adv* **1** below ground level: *moles digging underground* **2** secretly: *several political parties had to operate underground for many years* ▷ *adj* **3** beneath the ground: *an underground bunker*

4 secret; clandestine: *an underground organization* 5 (of art, film, music, etc.) avant-garde, experimental, or subversive ▷ *n* 6 a movement dedicated to overthrowing a government or occupation forces 7 (often preceded by *the*) an electric passenger railway operated in underground tunnels

undergrowth *n* small trees and bushes growing beneath taller trees in a wood or forest

underhand *adj also* **underhanded** 1 sly, deceitful, and secretive 2 *sport* same as **underarm** ▷ *adv* 3 in an underhand manner or style

underinsured *adj* not insured for enough money to cover the replacement value of the goods covered

underlay *n* felt or rubber laid under a carpet to increase insulation and resilience

underlie *vb* **-lying, -lay, -lain** 1 to lie or be placed under 2 to be the foundation, cause, or basis of: *the basic unity which underlies all religion*

underline *vb* **-lining, -lined** 1 to put a line under 2 to emphasize

underling *n derogatory* a subordinate

underlying *adj* 1 not obvious but detectable: *the deeper and underlying aim of her travels* 2 fundamental; basic: *an underlying belief* 3 lying under: *the underlying layers of the skin*

undermanned *adj* not having enough staff to function properly

undermentioned *adj* mentioned below or later

undermine *vb* **-mining, -mined** 1 to weaken gradually or insidiously: *morphia had undermined his grasp of reality* 2 (of the sea or wind) to wear away the base of cliffs

underneath *prep* 1 under or beneath: *a table underneath an olive tree* ▷ *adv* 2 under or beneath: *the chest of drawers was scratched underneath* ▷ *adj* 3 lower ▷ *n* 4 a lower part or surface [Old English *underneothan*]

undernourished *adj* lacking the food needed for health and growth **undernourishment** *n*

underpaid *adj* not paid as much as the job deserves

underpants *pl n* a man's undergarment covering the body from the waist or hips to the thighs

underpass *n* 1 a section of a road that passes under another road or a railway line 2 a subway for pedestrians

underpay *vb* **-paying, -paid** to pay someone insufficiently **underpayment** *n*

underpin *vb* **-pinning, -pinned** 1 to give strength or support to: *the principles that underpin his political convictions* 2 to support from beneath with a prop: *to underpin a wall* **underpinning** *n*

underplay *vb* to achieve (an effect) by deliberate lack of emphasis

underprivileged *adj* 1 lacking the rights and advantages of other members of society; deprived ▷ *n* 2 **the underprivileged** underprivileged people regarded as a group

underrate *vb* **-rating, -rated** to not be aware or take account of the full abilities or potential of **underrated** *adj*

underscore *vb* **-scoring, -scored** same as **underline**

undersea *adj, adv* below the surface of the sea

underseal *n* 1 a special coating applied to the underside of a motor vehicle to prevent corrosion ▷ *vb* 2 to apply such a coating to a motor vehicle

undersecretary *n, pl* **-taries** a senior civil servant or junior minister in a government department

undersell *vb* **-selling, -sold** to sell at a price lower than that of another seller

undersexed *adj* having weaker sexual urges than is considered normal

undershirt *n US & Canad* an undergarment covering the body from the shoulders to the hips

undershoot *vb* **-shooting, -shot** *aviation* to land an aircraft short of a runway

underside *n* the bottom or lower surface

undersigned *n* **the undersigned** the person or people who have signed at the foot of a document, statement, or letter

undersized *adj* smaller than normal

underskirt *n* a skirtlike garment worn under a skirt or dress; petticoat

understaffed *adj* not having enough staff to function properly

understand *vb* **-standing, -stood** 1 to know and comprehend the nature or meaning of: *I understand what you are saying* 2 to know what is happening or why it is happening: *in order to understand the problems that can occur* 3 to assume, infer, or believe: *I understand he is based in this town* 4 to know how to translate or read: *don't you understand Russian?* 5 to be sympathetic to or compatible with: *she needed him to understand her completely* [Old English *understandan*] **understandable** *adj* **understandably** *adv*

understanding *n* 1 the ability to learn, judge, or make decisions 2 personal opinion or interpretation of a subject: *my understanding of what he said* 3 a mutual agreement, usually an informal or private one ▷ *adj* 4 kind, sympathetic, or tolerant towards people

understate *vb* **-stating, -stated** 1 to describe or portray something in restrained terms, often to obtain an ironic effect 2 to state that something, such as a number, is less than it is **understatement** *n*

understood *vb* 1 the past of **understand** ▷ *adj* 2 implied or inferred 3 taken for granted

understudy *n, pl* **-studies** 1 an actor who studies a part so as to be able to replace the usual actor if necessary 2 anyone who is trained to take the place of another if necessary ▷ *vb* **-studies, -studying, -studied** 3 to act as an understudy to

undertake *vb* **-taking, -took, -taken** 1 to agree to or commit oneself to something or to do something: *I undertook the worst job in gardening* 2 to promise to do something

undertaker *n* a person whose job is to look after the bodies of people who have died and to organize funerals

undertaking *n* 1 a task or enterprise 2 an agreement to do something 3 *informal* the practice of overtaking on an inner lane a vehicle which is travelling in an outer lane

undertone *n* 1 a quiet tone of voice 2 something which suggests an underlying quality or feeling: *an undertone of anger*

undertow *n* a strong undercurrent flowing in a different direction from the surface current, such as in the sea
undervalue *vb* **-valuing, -valued** to value a person or thing at less than the true worth or importance
underwater *adj* **1** situated, occurring, or for use under the surface of the sea, a lake, or a river ▷ *adv* **2** beneath the surface of the sea, a lake, or a river
under way *adj* **1** in progress; taking place: *this test is already under way* **2** *naut* in motion in the direction headed
underwear *n* clothing worn under other garments, usually next to the skin
underweight *adj* weighing less than is average, expected, or healthy
underwent *vb* the past tense of **undergo**
underworld *n* **1** criminals and their associates **2** *classical myth* the regions below the earth's surface regarded as the abode of the dead
underwrite *vb* **-writing, -wrote, -written 1** to accept financial responsibility for a commercial project or enterprise **2** to sign and issue an insurance policy, thus accepting liability **3** to support **underwriter** *n*
undeserved *adj* not earned or deserved
undesirable *adj* **1** not desirable or pleasant; objectionable ▷ *n* **2** a person considered undesirable
undetected *adj* not having been discovered: *an undetected cancer*
undeterred *adj* not put off or dissuaded
undeveloped *adj* **1** not yet mature or adult **2** (of land) not built on or used for commercial or agricultural purposes
undies *pl n Brit, Austral & NZ informal* women's underwear
undignified *adj* foolish or embarrassing
undiluted *adj* **1** (of a liquid) not having any water added to it; concentrated **2** not mixed with any other feeling or quality: *undiluted hatred*
undiminished *adj* not lessened or decreased: *his admiration for her remained undiminished*
undine (un-dean) *n* a female water spirit [Latin *unda* a wave]
undisciplined *adj* behaving badly, with a lack of self-control
undisclosed *adj* not made known or revealed: *the family business was sold for an undisclosed sum*
undisguised *adj* shown openly; not concealed: *undisguised curiosity*
undismayed *adj* not upset about something; undaunted
undisputed *adj* unquestionably true or accurately described: *Mao became undisputed leader of China*
undistinguished *adj* not particularly good or bad; mediocre
undisturbed *adj* **1** quiet and peaceful: *an undisturbed village* **2** uninterrupted: *three hours' undisturbed work* **3** not touched, moved, or used by anyone: *the wreck has lain undisturbed for centuries*
undivided *adj* **1** total and whole-hearted: *her undivided attention* **2** not separated into different parts or groups
undo *vb* **-doing, -did, -done 1** to open, unwrap or untie **2** to reverse the effects of: *all the work of the congress would be undone* **3** to cause the downfall of
undoing *n* **1** ruin; downfall **2** the cause of someone's downfall: *his confidence was his undoing*
undone[1] *adj* not done or completed; unfinished
undone[2] *adj* **1** ruined; destroyed **2** unfastened; untied
undoubted *adj* beyond doubt; certain or indisputable **undoubtedly** *adv*
undreamed *or* **undreamt** *adj* (often foll. by *of*) not thought of or imagined
undress *vb* **1** to take off the clothes of oneself or another ▷ *n* **2 in a state of undress** naked or nearly naked **3** informal or ordinary working clothes or uniform **undressed** *adj*
undue *adj* greater than is reasonable; excessive: *undue attention*

> **USAGE** The use of *undue* in sentences such as *there is no cause for undue alarm* is redundant and should be avoided.

undulate *vb* **-lating, -lated 1** to move gently and slowly from side to side or up and down **2** to have a wavy shape or appearance [Latin *unda* a wave] **undulation** *n*
unduly *adv* excessively
undying *adj* never ending; eternal
unearned *adj* **1** not deserved **2** not yet earned
unearned income *n* income from property or investments rather than work
unearth *vb* **1** to discover by searching **2** to dig up out of the earth
unearthly *adj* **1** strange, unnatural, or eerie: *unearthly beauty* **2** ridiculous or unreasonable: *the unearthly hour of seven in the morning* **unearthliness** *n*
unease *n* **1** anxiety or nervousness: *my unease grew when she was not back by midnight* **2** dissatisfaction or tension: *unease about the government's handling of the affair*
uneasy *adj* **1** (of a person) anxious or apprehensive **2** (of a condition) precarious or insecure: *an uneasy peace* **3** (of a thought or feeling) disquieting **uneasily** *adv* **uneasiness** *n*
uneatable *adj* (of food) so rotten or unattractive as to be unfit to eat
uneconomic *adj* not producing enough profit
uneconomical *adj* not economical; wasteful
uneducated *adj* not educated well or at all
unemotional *adj* (of a person) not displaying any emotion
unemployable *adj* unable or unfit to keep a job
unemployed *adj* **1** without paid employment; out of work **2** not being used; idle ▷ *pl n* **3** people who are out of work: *the long-term unemployed*
unemployment *n* **1** the condition of being unemployed **2** the number of unemployed workers: *unemployment rose again last month*
unemployment benefit *n* (formerly, in the British National Insurance scheme, and currently, in New Zealand) a regular payment to an unemployed person
unencumbered *adj* not hindered or held back: *unencumbered by the responsibilities of childcare*
unending *adj* not showing any signs of ever stopping
unendurable *adj* too unpleasant to bear

unenthusiastic *adj* not keen about or interested in (something) **unenthusiastically** *adv*
unenviable *adj* (of a task) so difficult, dangerous, or unpleasant that one is glad not to have to do it oneself: *the unenviable task of phoning the parents of the dead child*
unequal *adj* **1** not equal in quantity, size, rank, or value **2** **unequal to** inadequate for: *he felt unequal to the job* **3** not offering all people or groups the same opportunities and privileges: *the unequal distribution of wealth* **4** (of a contest) having competitors of different ability **unequally** *adv*
unequalled *or US* **unequaled** *adj* greater, better, or more extreme than anything else of the same kind
unequivocal *adj* completely clear in meaning; unambiguous **unequivocally** *adv*
unerring *adj* never mistaken; consistently accurate
UNESCO United Nations Educational, Scientific, and Cultural Organization
unethical *adj* morally wrong
uneven *adj* **1** (of a surface) not level or flat **2** not consistent in quality: *an uneven performance* **3** not parallel, straight, or horizontal **4** not fairly matched: *the uneven battle*
uneventful *adj* ordinary, routine, or quiet **uneventfully** *adv*
unexampled *adj* without precedent
unexceptionable *adj* not likely to be criticized or objected to
unexceptional *adj* usual, ordinary, or normal
unexciting *adj* slightly dull and boring
unexpected *adj* surprising or unforeseen **unexpectedly** *adv*
unexplained *adj* strange or unclear because the reason for it is not known
unexpurgated *adj* (of a piece of writing) not censored by having allegedly offensive passages removed
unfailing *adj* continuous or reliable: *his unfailing enthusiasm* **unfailingly** *adv*
unfair *adj* **1** unequal or unjust **2** dishonest or unethical **unfairly** *adv* **unfairness** *n*
unfaithful *adj* **1** having sex with someone other than one's regular partner **2** not true to a promise or vow **unfaithfulness** *n*
unfamiliar *adj* **1** not known; strange: *an unfamiliar American accent* **2** **unfamiliar with** not acquainted with: *anyone who is unfamiliar with the language* **unfamiliarity** *n*
unfashionable *adj* not popular or in vogue
unfasten *vb* to undo, untie, or open or become undone, untied, or opened
unfathomable *adj* too strange or complicated to be understood: *pugs exert a powerful, unfathomable hold over their owners*
unfavourable *or US* **unfavorable** *adj* **1** making a successful or positive outcome unlikely: *unfavourable weather conditions* **2** disapproving: *an unfavourable opinion* **unfavourably** *or US* **unfavorably** *adv*
unfeeling *adj* without sympathy; callous
unfettered *adj* not limited or controlled: *unfettered competition*
unfinished *adj* **1** incomplete or imperfect **2** (of paint) without an applied finish
unfit *adj* **1** unqualified for or incapable of a particular role or task: *an unfit mother; he was unfit to drive* **2** unsuitable: *this meat is unfit for human consumption* **3** in poor physical condition
unfitted *adj* unsuitable: *unused to and unfitted for any form of manual labour*
unflappable *adj informal* (of a person) not easily upset **unflappability** *n*
unfledged *adj* **1** (of a young bird) not having developed adult feathers **2** immature and inexperienced
unflinching *adj* not shrinking from danger or difficulty
unfold *vb* **1** to open or spread out from a folded state **2** to reveal or be revealed: *a terrible truth unfolds* **3** to develop or be developed: *the novel unfolds through their recollections*
unfollow *vb* to stop following (a person) on a social networking site
unforeseen *adj* surprising because not expected
unforgettable *adj* making such a strong impression that it is impossible to forget **unforgettably** *adv*
unforgivable *adj* too bad or cruel to be excused
unforgiving *adj* **1** unwilling to forgive other people's mistakes or wrongdoings **2** (of a machine) allowing little or no opportunity for mistakes to be corrected **3** harsh: *an unforgiving and desolate landscape*
unformed *adj* in an early stage of development; not fully developed or thought out
unforthcoming *adj* not inclined to speak, explain, or communicate
unfortunate *adj* **1** caused or accompanied by bad luck: *an unfortunate coincidence* **2** having bad luck: *my unfortunate daughter* **3** regrettable or unsuitable: *an unfortunate choice of phrase* ▷ *n* **4** an unlucky person **unfortunately** *adv*
unfounded *adj* (of ideas, fears, or allegations) not based on facts or evidence
unfreeze *vb* **-freezing, -froze, -frozen** **1** to thaw or cause to thaw **2** to relax restrictions or controls on (trade, the transfer of money, etc.): *Congress is considering unfreezing US aid to Jordan*
unfriend *vb* to remove (a person) as a friend on a social networking site
unfriendly *adj* **-lier, -liest** not friendly; hostile
unfrock *vb* to deprive (a person in holy orders) of the status of a priest
unfulfilled *adj* not satisfied
unfurl *vb* to unroll or spread out (an umbrella, flag, or sail) or (of an umbrella, flag, or sail) to be unrolled or spread out
unfurnished *adj* not containing any furniture
ungainly *adj* **-lier, -liest** lacking grace when moving [dialect *gainly* graceful] **ungainliness** *n*
ungenerous *adj* **1** mean or overly thrifty **2** (of a remark or thought) unfair or harsh
ungodly *adj* **-lier, -liest** **1** wicked or sinful **2** *informal* unreasonable or outrageous: *at this ungodly hour* **ungodliness** *n*
ungovernable *adj* **1** (of an emotion) not able to be controlled or restrained: *an ungovernable rage* **2** (of a country or area) not able to be effectively

u

governed, esp. because of unrest or violence: *years of religious conflict had made much of the island ungovernable*
ungracious *adj* not polite or friendly, esp. when being offered praise or thanks
ungrammatical *adj* not following the rules of grammar
ungrateful *adj* not showing or offering thanks for a favour or compliment
unguarded *adj* **1** unprotected **2** open or frank: *one unguarded briefing* **3** incautious or careless: *an unguarded moment*
unguent (ung-gwent) *n literary* an ointment [Latin *unguere* to anoint]
ungulate (ung-gyew-lit) *n* a hoofed mammal [Latin *ungula* hoof]
unhallowed *adj* **1** not consecrated or holy: *unhallowed ground* **2** sinful or wicked
unhand *vb old-fashioned or literary* to release from one's grasp
unhappy *adj* **-pier, -piest 1** sad or depressed **2** unfortunate or wretched **unhappily** *adv* **unhappiness** *n*
unharmed *adj* not hurt or damaged in any way
unhealthy *adj* **-healthier, -healthiest 1** likely to cause illness or poor health: *unhealthy foods such as hamburger and chips* **2** not very fit or well **3** caused by or looking as if caused by poor health: *a thin unhealthy look about him* **4** morbid or unwholesome: *an unhealthy interest in computer fraud* **unhealthiness** *n*
unheard *adj* not listened to; unheeded: *all my warnings went unheard*
unheard-of *adj* **1** without precedent: *an unheard-of phenomenon* **2** highly offensive: *unheard-of behaviour*
unheeded *adj* noticed but ignored: *their protests went unheeded*
unhelpful *adj* doing nothing to improve a situation
unheralded *adj* not announced beforehand
unhindered *adj* **1** not prevented or obstructed: *unhindered access* ▷ *adv* **2** without being prevented or obstructed: *he was able to go about his work unhindered*
unhinge *vb* **-hinging, -hinged** to make a person mentally deranged or unbalanced **unhinged** *adj*
unholy *adj* **-lier, -liest 1** immoral or wicked **2** *informal* outrageous or unnatural: *this unholy mess* **unholiness** *n*
unhook *vb* **1** to unfasten the hooks of a garment **2** to remove something from a hook
unhurried *adj* done at a leisurely pace, without any rush or anxiety
unhurt *adj* not injured in an accident, attack, etc.
unhygienic *adj* dirty and likely to cause disease or infection
uni *n Brit, Austral & NZ informal* short for **university**
uni- *combining form* of, consisting of, or having only one: *unilateral* [Latin *unus* one]
unicameral *adj* of or having a single legislative chamber: *Denmark's unicameral parliament, known as the Folketing*
UNICEF United Nations Children's Fund
unicellular *adj* (of organisms) consisting of a single cell
Unicode *n computers* a character set for all languages
unicorn *n* a legendary creature resembling a white horse with one horn growing from its forehead [Latin *unus* one + *cornu* a horn]
unicycle *n* a one-wheeled vehicle driven by pedals, used in a circus **unicyclist** *n*
unidentified *adj* **1** not able to be recognized; unknown: *unidentified gunmen* **2** anonymous or unnamed: *the house of an unidentified Scottish tycoon* **unidentifiable** *adj*
uniform *n* **1** a special identifying set of clothes for the members of an organization, such as soldiers ▷ *adj* **2** regular and even throughout: *the mixture must be beaten to a uniform consistency* **3** alike or like: *uniform green metal filing cabinets* [Latin *unus* one + *forma* shape] **uniformity** *n* **uniformly** *adv*
unify *vb* **-fies, -fying, -fied** to make or become one; unite [Latin *unus* one + *facere* to make] **unification** *n*
unilateral *adj* made or done by only one person or group: *unilateral action* **unilateralism** *n*
unilingual *adj* **1** of or relating to only one language **2** *chiefly Canad* knowing only one language ▷ *n* **3** *chiefly Canad* a person who knows only one language
unimaginable *adj* so unusual, great, or extreme that it is difficult to imagine or understand: *the unimaginable vastness of space*
unimaginative *adj* not having or showing much imagination
unimpeachable *adj* completely honest and reliable
unimpeded *adj* not stopped or disrupted by anything
unimportant *adj* trivial or insignificant
uninhabitable *adj* not able to support human life: *an uninhabitable wasteland*
uninhabited *adj* having no people living in or on it: *an uninhabited island*
uninhibited *adj* behaving freely and naturally, without worrying what other people will think
uninitiated *pl n* **the uninitiated** people who have no special knowledge or experience: *no easy way for the uninitiated to find out what the internet can do*
uninspired *adj* not particularly good or exciting
uninspiring *adj* not likely to make people interested or excited
unintelligible *adj* impossible to make out or understand; incomprehensible: *an unintelligible London accent*
unintended *adj* (of an action or its consequences) not planned or intended: *sometimes drugs have unintended side-effects*
unintentional *adj* (of an action) not done deliberately; accidental: *unintentional discrimination* **unintentionally** *adv*
uninterested *adj* having or showing no interest in someone or something
USAGE See at **disinterested**.
uninteresting *adj* boring or dull
uninterrupted *adj* continuous, with no breaks or interruptions: *uninterrupted applause*
uninvited *adj* **1** not having been asked: *uninvited guests* ▷ *adv* **2** without having been asked: *he sat down uninvited on the side of the bed*
union *n* **1** the act of merging two or more things to become one, or the state of being merged in

such a way **2** short for **trade union** **3** an association of individuals or groups for a common purpose: *the Scripture Union* **4 A** an association or society: *the Students' union* **B** the buildings of such an organization **5** marriage or sexual intercourse **6** *maths* a set containing all the members of two given sets **7** (in 19th-century England) a workhouse maintained by a number of parishes ▷ *adj* **8** of a trade union [Latin *unus* one]

unionism *n* **1** the principles of trade unions **2** adherence to the principles of trade unions **unionist** *n, adj*

Unionist *n* a supporter of union between Britain and Northern Ireland

unionize *or* **-ise** *vb* **-izing, -ized** *or* **-ising, -ised** to organize workers into a trade union **unionization** *or* **-isation** *n*

Union Jack *or* **Union flag** *n* the national flag of the United Kingdom, combining the crosses of Saint George, Saint Andrew, and Saint Patrick

unique (yew-**neek**) *adj* **1** being the only one of a particular type **2 unique to** concerning or belonging to a particular person, thing, or group: *certain dishes are unique to this restaurant* **3** without equal or like **4** *informal* remarkable [Latin *unicus* unparalleled] **uniquely** *adv*

> **USAGE** *Unique* is normally taken to describe an absolute state, i.e. one that cannot be qualified; thus something is either *unique* or *not unique*; it cannot be *rather unique* or *very unique*. However *unique* is sometimes used informally to mean remarkable or unusual, and this makes it possible to use comparatives or intensifiers with it, although many people object to this use.

unisex *adj* (of clothing, a hairstyle, or hairdressers) designed for both sexes

unisexual *adj* **1** of one sex only **2** (of an organism) having either male or female reproductive organs but not both

unison *n* **1 in unison** at the same time as another person or other people: *smiling and nodding in unison* **2** (usually preceded by *in*) complete agreement: *to act in unison* **3** *music* a style, technique, or passage in which all the performers sing or play the same notes at the same time [Latin *unus* one + *sonus* sound]

UNISON *n* a British trade union consisting mainly of council, public sector, and health service workers

unit *n* **1** a single undivided entity or whole **2** a group or individual regarded as a basic element of a larger whole: *the clan was the basic unit of Highland society* **3** a mechanical part or small device that does a particular job: *a waste disposal unit* **4** a team of people that performs a specific function, and often also their buildings and equipment: *a combat unit* **5** a standard amount of a physical quantity, such as length or energy, used to express magnitudes of that quantity: *the year as a unit of time* **6** *maths* the digit or position immediately to the left of the decimal point **7** a piece of furniture designed to be fitted with other similar pieces: *bedroom units* **8** NZ a self-propelled railcar **9** *Austral & NZ* short for **home unit** [from *unity*]

Unitarian *n* **1** a person who believes that God is one being and rejects the Trinity ▷ *adj* **2** of Unitarians or Unitarianism **Unitarianism** *n*

unitary *adj* **1** consisting of a single undivided whole: *a unitary state* **2** of a unit or units

unit cost *n* the actual cost of producing one article

unite *vb* **uniting, united 1** to make or become an integrated whole: *conception occurs when a sperm unites with the egg* **2** to form an association or alliance: *the opposition parties united to fight against privatization* **3** to possess (a combination of qualities) at the same time: *he manages to unite charm and ruthlessness* [Latin *unus* one]

united *adj* **1** produced by two or more people or things in combination: *a united effort* **2** in agreement: *we are united in our opposition to these proposals* **3** in association or alliance

United Kingdom *n* a kingdom of NW Europe, consisting of the island of Great Britain together with Northern Ireland

United Nations *n* an international organization of independent states, formed to promote peace and international security

unit price *n* the price charged per unit

unit trust *n* an investment trust that issues units for public sale and invests the money in many different businesses

unity *n, pl* **-ties 1** the state of being one **2** mutual agreement: *unity of intention* **3** the state of being a single thing that is composed of separate parts, organizations, etc.: *moves towards church unity* **4** *maths* the number or numeral one [Latin *unus* one]

Univ. University

univalent *adj chem* same as **monovalent**

universal *adj* **1** of or relating to everyone in the world or everyone in a particular place or society: *the introduction of universal primary education* **2** of, relating to, or affecting the entire world or universe: *the universal laws of physics* **3** true and relevant at all times and in all situations: *there may be no single universal solution* ▷ *n* **4** something which exists or is true in all places and all situations: *universals such as beauty and justice* **universality** *n* **universally** *adv*

> **USAGE** The use of *more universal* as in *his writings have long been admired by fellow scientists, but his latest book should have more universal appeal* is acceptable in modern English usage.

universal joint *or* **universal coupling** *n* a form of coupling between two rotating shafts allowing freedom of movement in all directions

universe *n* **1** the whole of all existing matter, energy, and space **2** the world [Latin *universum* the whole world]

university *n, pl* **-ties 1** an institution of higher education with authority to award degrees **2** the buildings, members, staff, or campus of a university [Medieval Latin *universitas* group of scholars]

Unix (yew-nicks) *n trademark* an operating system found on many types of computer

unjust *adj* not fair or just

unjustifiable *adj* inexcusably wrong or unfair

unjustified *adj* not necessary or reasonable

unkempt *adj* **1** (of the hair) uncombed or dishevelled **2** untidy or slovenly: *an unkempt appearance* [Old English *uncembed*, from *cemban* to comb]
unkind *adj* unsympathetic or cruel **unkindly** *adv* **unkindness** *n*
unknowing *adj* unaware or ignorant: *unknowing victims of fraud*
unknown *adj* **1** not known, understood, or recognized **2** not famous: *a young and then unknown actor* **3 unknown quantity** a person or thing whose action or effect is unknown or unpredictable ▷ *n* **4** an unknown person, quantity, or thing ▷ *adv* **5 unknown to someone** without someone being aware: *unknown to him, the starboard engine had dropped off*
unlawful *adj* not permitted by law; illegal
unleaded *adj* (of petrol) containing less tetraethyl lead, in order to reduce environmental pollution
unlearn *vb* **-learning, -learned** *or* **-learnt** to try to forget something learnt or to discard accumulated knowledge
unlearned (un-lurn-id) *adj* ignorant or uneducated
unlearnt *or* **unlearned** *adj* **1** denoting knowledge or skills innately present rather than learnt **2** not learnt or taken notice of: *unlearnt lessons*
unleash *vb* to set loose or cause (something bad): *to unleash war*
unleavened (un-lev-vend) *adj* (of bread) made without yeast or leavening
unless *conj* except under the circumstances that; except on the condition that: *you can't get in unless you can prove you're over eighteen*
unlettered *adj* uneducated or illiterate
unlike *adj* **1** not similar; different ▷ *prep* **2** not like or typical of: *unlike his brother, he could not control his weight* **unlikeness** *n*
unlikely *adj* not likely; improbable **unlikeliness** *n*
unlimited *adj* **1** apparently endless: *there was unlimited coffee* **2** not restricted or limited: *unlimited access to the rest of the palace*
unlisted *adj* **1** not entered on a list **2** (of securities) not quoted on a stock exchange **3** *Austral, US & Canad* not listed in a telephone directory by request
unlit *adj* **1** (of a fire, cigarette, etc.) not lit and therefore not burning **2** (of a road) not having any streetlights switched on
unload *vb* **1** to remove cargo from a ship, lorry, or plane **2** to express worries or problems by telling someone about them **3** to remove the ammunition from a gun
unlock *vb* **1** to unfasten a lock or door **2** to release or let loose: *the revelation unlocked a flood of tears*
unlooked-for *adj* unexpected or unforeseen
unloose *or* **unloosen** *vb* **-loosing, -loosed** *or* **-loosening, -loosened** to set free or release
unlovable *adj* too unpleasant or unattractive to be loved
unloved *adj* not loved by anyone
unlovely *adj* unpleasant in appearance or character
unlucky *adj* **1** having bad luck or misfortune: *an unlucky man* **2** caused by bad luck or misfortune: *an unlucky coincidence* **3** regarded as likely to bring about bad luck: *an unlucky number* **unluckily** *adv*
unmade *adj* **1** (of a bed) with the bedclothes not smoothed and tidied **2** (of a road) not surfaced with tarmac **3** not yet made
unmake *vb* **-making, -made** to undo or destroy
unman *vb* **-manning, -manned** **1** to cause to lose courage or nerve **2** to make effeminate
unmanageable *adj* difficult to use, deal with, or control, esp. because it is too big
unmanly *adj* **1** not masculine or virile **2** cowardly or dishonourable
unmanned *adj* **1** having no personnel or crew: *the border posts were unmanned* **2** (of an aircraft or spacecraft) operated by automatic or remote control
unmannerly *adj* lacking manners; discourteous **unmannerliness** *n*
unmarked *adj* **1** having no signs of damage or injury **2** not having any identifying signs or markings: *an unmarked police car*
unmarried *adj* not married
unmask *vb* **1** to remove the mask or disguise from **2** to expose or reveal the true nature or character of
unmatched *adj* **1** not equalled or surpassed: *his pace is unmatched by any other modern player* **2** not coordinated or forming a set with anything else: *three unmatched chairs*
unmentionable *adj* unsuitable as a topic of conversation
unmercifully *adv* excessively and relentlessly: *the young boy is hounded unmercifully*
unmistakable *or* **unmistakeable** *adj* clear or unambiguous **unmistakably** *or* **unmistakeably** *adv*
unmitigated *adj* **1** not reduced or lessened in severity or intensity **2** total and complete: *unmitigated boredom*
unmolested *adv* without disturbance or interference: *the enemy aircraft passed overhead unmolested*
unmoved *adj* not affected by emotion; indifferent
unmoving *adj* still and motionless
unmusical *adj* **1** (of a person) unable to appreciate or play music **2** (of a sound) harsh and unpleasant
unnamed *adj* **1** not mentioned by name; anonymous: *an unnamed government spokesman* **2** not known or described clearly enough to be named: *unnamed fears*
unnatural *adj* **1** strange and slightly frightening because it is not usual; abnormal: *an unnatural silence* **2** not in accordance with accepted standards of behaviour: *an unnatural relationship* **3** affected or forced: *a determined smile which seemed unnatural* **4** inhuman or monstrous: *unnatural evils* **unnaturally** *adv*
unnecessary *adj* not essential, or more than is essential **unnecessarily** *adv*
unnerve *vb* **-nerving, -nerved** to cause to lose courage, confidence, or self-control: *he unnerves me* **unnerving** *adj*
unnoticed *adj* without being seen or noticed
unnumbered *adj* **1** countless; too many to count **2** not counted or given a number

UNO United Nations Organization
unobtainable *adj* impossible to get
unobtrusive *adj* not drawing attention to oneself or itself; inconspicuous
unoccupied *adj* **1** (of a building) without occupants **2** unemployed or idle **3** (of an area or country) not overrun by foreign troops
unofficial *adj* **1** not authorized or approved by the relevant organization or person: *an unofficial strike* **2** not confirmed officially: *unofficial reports of the minister's resignation*
unorganized *or* **-nised** *adj* **1** not arranged into an organized system or structure **2** (of workers) not unionized
unorthodox *adj* **1** (of ideas, methods, etc.) unconventional and not generally accepted **2** (of a person) not conventional in beliefs, behaviour, etc.
unpack *vb* **1** to remove the packed contents of a case **2** to take something out of a packed container
unpaid *adj* **1** without a salary or wage: *unpaid overtime* **2** still to be paid: *unpaid bills*
unpalatable *adj* **1** (of food) unpleasant to taste **2** (of a fact, idea, etc.) unpleasant and hard to accept
unparalleled *adj* not equalled; supreme
unpardonable *adj* unforgivably wrong or rude
unparliamentary *adj* not consistent with parliamentary procedure or practice
unperson *n* a person whose existence is officially denied or ignored
unpick *vb* to undo the stitches of a piece of sewing
unpin *vb* **-pinning, -pinned 1** to remove a pin or pins from **2** to unfasten by removing pins
unplanned *adj* not intentional or deliberate
unplayable *adj sport* **1** (of a ball) thrown too fast or too skilfully to be hit **2** (of a pitch or course) too badly affected by rain or frost to be used
unpleasant *adj* not pleasant or agreeable **unpleasantly** *adv* **unpleasantness** *n*
unplug *vb* **-plugging, -plugged** to disconnect a piece of electrical equipment by taking the plug out of the socket
unplugged *adj* using acoustic rather than electric instruments: *an unplugged version of the song*
unplumbed *adj* **1** not measured **2** not understood in depth
unpolished *adj* **1** not polished **2** not elegant or refined
unpopular *adj* generally disliked or disapproved of **unpopularity** *n*
unpractised *or US* **unpracticed** *adj* not experienced or skilled: *an unpractised surgical technique*
unprecedented *adj* never having happened before: *an unprecedented decision*
unpredictable *adj* not easy to predict or foresee
unprejudiced *adj* free from bias; impartial
unprepared *adj* surprised or put at a disadvantage by something because you are not ready to deal with it
unprepossessing *adj* not very attractive or appealing
unpretentious *adj* modest, unassuming, and down-to-earth
unprincipled *adj* lacking moral principles; unscrupulous
unprintable *adj* unsuitable for printing for reasons of obscenity, libel, or indecency
unproductive *adj* not producing any worthwhile results: *unproductive talks*
unprofessional *adj* not behaving according to the standards expected of a member of a particular profession
unprofitable *adj* **1** not making a profit **2** not producing any worthwhile results: *an unprofitable line of thinking*
unpromising *adj* not likely to turn out well
unprompted *adj* doing without being urged by anyone else; spontaneous
unpronounceable *adj* (of a name or word) too difficult to say
unprotected *adj* not defended or protected from harm
unprovoked *adj* carried out without any cause or reason: *an unprovoked attack*
unpunished *adj* without suffering or resulting in a penalty: *the guilty must not go unpunished; such crimes should not remain unpunished*
unputdownable *adj* (of a book, usually a novel) so gripping that one wants to read it at one sitting
unqualified *adj* **1** lacking the necessary qualifications **2** having no conditions or limitations: *an unqualified denial* **3** total or complete: *unqualified admiration*
unquestionable *adj* not to be doubted; indisputable **unquestionably** *adv*
unquestioned *adj* accepted by everyone without doubt or disagreement: *an engineer of unquestioned genius*
unquestioning *adj* accepting a belief or order without thinking about or doubting it in any way: *unquestioning obedience* **unquestioningly** *adv*
unquiet *adj chiefly literary* anxious or uneasy
unquote *interj* an expression used to indicate the end of a quotation that was introduced with the word 'quote'
unravel *vb* **-velling, -velled** *or US* **-veling, -veled** **1** to separate something knitted or woven into individual strands **2** to become separated into individual strands **3** to explain or solve: *we unravelled the secrets*
unreactive *adj* (of a substance) not readily partaking in chemical reactions
unread *adj* **1** (of a book or article) not yet read **2** (of a person) having read little
unreadable *adj* **1** unable to be read or deciphered; illegible **2** too difficult or dull to read
unreal *adj* **1** existing only in the imagination or giving the impression of doing so: *an unreal quality* **2** insincere or artificial **unreality** *n*
unrealistic *adj* **1** not accepting the facts of a situation and not dealing with them in a practical way: *he had unrealistic expectations of his son* **2** not true to life: *an unrealistic portrayal of Scottish life* **unrealistically** *adv*
unreasonable *adj* **1** unfair and excessive: *an unreasonable request* **2** refusing to listen to reason **unreasonably** *adv*

u

unreasoning *adj* not controlled by reason; irrational
unrecognizable *or* **-nisable** *adj* changed or damaged so much that it is hard to recognize
unrecognized *or* **-nised** *adj* not properly identified or acknowledged: *her talents went unrecognized during her lifetime*
unregenerate *adj* unrepentant or unreformed
unrelated *adj* not connected with each other: *a series of unrelated mishaps*
unrelenting *adj* **1** refusing to relent or take pity **2** not diminishing in determination, effort, or force
unreliable *adj* not able to be trusted or relied on
unremitting *adj* never slackening or stopping
unrepentant *adj* not ashamed of one's beliefs or actions
unrequited *adj* (of love) not returned
unreserved *adj* **1** complete and without holding back any doubts: *unreserved support* **2** open and forthcoming in manner **3** not booked or not able to be booked: *all the seats are unreserved* **unreservedly** (un-riz-**zerv**-id-lee) *adv*
unresolved *adj* not satisfactorily solved or concluded: *the mystery of her death remains unresolved*
unresponsive *adj* not reacting or responding
unrest *n* **1** a rebellious state of discontent **2** an uneasy or troubled state
unrestrained *adj* not controlled or limited: *the unrestrained use of state power*
unrestricted *adj* not limited by any laws or rules
unrewarding *adj* not giving any satisfaction
unrighteous *adj* sinful or wicked
unripe *adj* not fully matured
unrivalled *or US* **unrivaled** *adj* having no equal; matchless
unroll *vb* **1** to open out or unwind: *I unrolled the map* **2** (of a series of events or period of time) to happen or be revealed or remembered one after the other
unruffled *adj* **1** calm and unperturbed **2** smooth and still: *unruffled ponds*
unruly *adj* **-lier, -liest** difficult to control or organize; disobedient or undisciplined **unruliness** *n*
unsaddle *vb* **-dling, -dled 1** to remove the saddle from a horse **2** to cause to fall or dismount from a horse
unsafe *adj* **1** dangerous **2** (of a criminal conviction) based on inadequate or false evidence
unsaid *adj* not said or expressed
unsaleable *adj* unable to be sold
unsatisfactory *adj* not good enough
unsaturated *adj* **1** *chem* (of an organic compound) containing a double or triple bond and therefore capable of combining with other substances **2** (of a fat, esp. a vegetable fat) containing a high proportion of fatty acids with double bonds
unsavoury *or US* **unsavory** *adj* objectionable or distasteful: *an unsavoury divorce*
unscathed *adj* not harmed or injured
unscheduled *adj* not planned or intended
unscramble *vb* **-bling, -bled 1** to sort out something confused or disorderly **2** to restore a scrambled message to an intelligible form **unscrambler** *n*
unscrew *vb* **1** to loosen a screw or lid by turning it **2** to unfasten something by removing the screws which fasten it: *the mirror had been unscrewed and removed*
unscripted *adj* spoken without a previously prepared text
unscrupulous *adj* prepared to act in a dishonest or immoral manner
unseasonable *adj* **1** (of the weather) inappropriate for the season **2** inappropriate or unusual for the time of year: *an unseasonable dip in the sea*
unseat *vb* **1** to throw or displace from a seat or saddle **2** to depose from office or position
unseeded *adj* (of a player in a sport) not given a top player's position in the opening rounds of a tournament
unseeing *adj* not noticing or looking at anything: *staring with unseeing eyes*
unseemly *adj* not according to expected standards of behaviour **unseemliness** *n*
unseen *adj* **1** hidden or invisible: *an unseen organist was practising* **2** mysterious or supernatural: *unseen powers* ▷ *adv* **3** without being seen; unnoticed: *the thief entered unseen* ▷ *n* **4** a passage which is given to students for translation without them having seen it in advance
unselfish *adj* concerned about other people's wishes and needs rather than one's own **unselfishly** *adv* **unselfishness** *n*
unsettle *vb* **-tling, -tled 1** to change or become changed from a fixed or settled condition **2** to confuse or agitate a person or the mind
unsettled *adj* **1** lacking order or stability: *an unsettled time* **2** disturbed and restless: *your child will feel unsettled and insecure* **3** constantly changing or moving from place to place: *his wandering unsettled life* **4** (of an argument or dispute) not resolved **5** (of a debt or bill) not yet paid
unshakable *or* **unshakeable** *adj* (of beliefs) utterly firm and unwavering
unshaken *adj* (of faith or feelings) not having been weakened
unshaven *adj* (of a man who does not have a beard) having stubble on his chin because he has not shaved recently
unsheathe *vb* **-sheathing, -sheathed** to pull a weapon from a sheath
unshockable *adj* not likely to be upset by anything seen, heard, or read
unsightly *adj* unpleasant to look at; ugly **unsightliness** *n*
unsigned *adj* (of a letter, etc.) anonymous
unskilled *adj* not having or requiring any special skill or training
unsociable *adj* (of a person) not fond of the company of other people
unsocial *adj* **1** not fond of the company of other people **2** (of the hours of work of a job) falling outside the normal working day
unsolicited *adj* given or sent without being asked for: *unsolicited advice; unsolicited junk mail*
unsophisticated *adj* **1** (of a person) lacking experience or worldly wisdom **2** lacking refinement or complexity: *unsophisticated fighter aircraft*

unsound *adj* **1** unhealthy or unstable: *of unsound mind* **2** based on faulty ideas: *unsound judgment* **3** not firm: *unsound foundations* **4** not financially reliable: *his business plan was unsound*

unsparing *adj* **1** very generous; lavish **2** harsh or severe **unsparingly** *adv*

unspeakable *adj* **1** incapable of expression in words: *unspeakable gratitude* **2** indescribably bad or evil: *unspeakable atrocities* **unspeakably** *adv*

unspoiled *adj* **1** not damaged or harmed **2** (of a place) attractive and not having changed for a long time

unspoken *adj* not openly expressed: *unspoken fears; an unspoken agreement*

unsporting *adj* not following the principles of fair play

unstable *adj* **1** not firmly fixed and likely to wobble or fall: *an unstable pile of books* **2** likely to change suddenly and create difficulties or danger: *the unstable political climate* **3** (of a person) having abrupt changes of mood or behaviour **4** *chem & physics* readily decomposing

unsteady *adj* **1** not securely fixed: *unsteady metal posts* **2** (of a manner of walking, standing, or holding) shaky or staggering **unsteadily** *adv* **unsteadiness** *n*

unstinting *adj* generous and gladly given: *unstinting praise*

unstoppable *adj* impossible to prevent from continuing or developing

unstrap *vb* **-strapping, -strapped** to undo the straps fastening (something) in position

unstructured *adj* without formal or systematic organization

unstuck *adj* **1** freed from being stuck, glued, or fastened **2 come unstuck** to suffer failure or disaster

unstudied *adj* natural or spontaneous: *her unstudied elegance and grace*

unsubscribe *vb* **-scribing, -scribed** to cancel a subscription, esp. to an online service

unsubstantial *adj* **1** lacking weight or firmness **2** having no material existence

unsubstantiated *adj* not yet confirmed or proved to be true: *unsubstantiated rumours*

unsuccessful *adj* not achieving success

unsuitable *adj* not right or appropriate for a particular purpose

unsuited *adj* **1** not appropriate for a particular task or situation: *a likeable man unsuited to a military career* **2** (of a couple) having different personalities or tastes and unlikely to form a lasting relationship: *they are totally unsuited to each other*

unsung *adj* not appreciated or honoured: *an unsung hero*

unsure *adj* **1** lacking assurance or self-confidence **2** uncertain or undecided: *he was unsure who was really in charge*

unsurpassed *adj* better or greater than anything else of its kind

unsuspected *adj* **1** not known to exist: *an unsuspected talent* **2** not under suspicion

unsuspecting *adj* having no idea of what is happening or about to happen

unsweetened *adj* having no sugar or other sweetener added

unswerving *adj* not turning aside; constant

unsympathetic *adj* **1** not feeling or showing sympathy **2** unpleasant and unlikeable **3** (foll. by *to*) opposed or hostile to

untamed *adj* not brought under human control; wild: *an untamed wilderness*

untangle *vb* **-gling, -gled** to free from tangles or confusion

untapped *adj* not yet used or exploited: *untapped mineral reserves*

untaught *adj* **1** without training or education **2** acquired without instruction

untenable *adj* (of a theory, idea, etc.) impossible to defend in an argument

unthinkable *adj* **1** so shocking or unpleasant that one cannot believe it to be true **2** unimaginable or inconceivable

unthinking *adj* **1** thoughtless and inconsiderate **2** done or happening without careful consideration: *an unthinking reflex* **unthinkingly** *adv*

untidy *adj* **-dier, -diest** not neat; messy and disordered **untidily** *adv* **untidiness** *n*

untie *vb* **-tying, -tied** to unfasten or free something that is tied

until *conj* **1** up to a time that: *he lifted the wire until it was taut* **2** before (a time or event): *until the present crisis, they weren't allowed into the country* ▷ *prep* **3** (often preceded by *up*) in or throughout the period before: *up until then I'd never thought about having kids* **4** before: *Baker does not get to Israel until Sunday* [earlier untill]

> **USAGE** The use of *until such time as* (as in *industrial action will continue until such time as our demands are met*) is unnecessary and should be avoided: *industrial action will continue until our demands are met*. See also at **till**[1].

untimely *adj* **1** occurring before the expected or normal time: *his untimely death* **2** inappropriate to the occasion or time: *an untimely idea to raise at the United Nations* **untimeliness** *n*

unto *prep archaic* to [from Old Norse]

untold *adj* **1** incapable of description: *untold misery* **2** incalculably great in number or quantity: *untold millions* **3** not told

untouchable *adj* **1** above criticism, suspicion or punishment **2** unable to be touched ▷ *n offensive* **3** a member of the lowest class in India, whose touch was formerly regarded as defiling to the four main castes

untouched *adj* **1** not changed, moved, or affected: *a sleepy backwater untouched by mass tourism* **2** not injured or harmed: *the Cathedral survived the war untouched* **3** (of food or drink) not eaten or consumed **4** emotionally unaffected: *he was untouched by the news of his uncle's death*

untoward *adj* **1** causing misfortune or annoyance **2** unfavourable: *untoward reactions* **3** out of the ordinary; out of the way: *nothing untoward had happened*

untrained *adj* without formal or adequate training or education

untrammelled *or US* **untrammeled** *adj* able to act freely and without restrictions

untried *adj* **1** not yet used, done, or tested **2** (of a prisoner) not yet put on trial

untroubled *adj* calm and unworried

untrue *adj* **1** incorrect or false **2** disloyal or unfaithful
untrustworthy *adj* unreliable and not able to be trusted
untruth *n* a statement that is not true; lie
untruthful *adj* **1** (of a person) given to lying **2** (of a statement) not true **untruthfully** *adv*
untutored *adj* **1** without formal education **2** lacking sophistication or refinement
unusable *adj* not in good enough condition to be used
unused *adj* **1** not being or never having been used **2** (foll. by *to*) not accustomed to
unusual *adj* uncommon or extraordinary **unusually** *adv*
unutterable *adj* incapable of being expressed in words **unutterably** *adv*
unvarnished *adj* not elaborated upon; plain: *an unvarnished account of literary life*
unvarying *adj* always staying the same; unchanging
unveil *vb* **1** to ceremonially remove the cover from a new picture, statue, plaque, etc. **2** to make public a secret **3** to remove the veil from one's own or another person's face
unveiling *n* **1** a ceremony involving the removal of a veil covering a statue **2** the presentation of something for the first time
unvoiced *adj* **1** not expressed or spoken **2** *phonetics* voiceless
unwaged *adj* (of a person) not having a paid job
unwanted *adj* not wanted or welcome
unwarranted *adj* not justified or necessary
unwary *adj* not careful or cautious and therefore likely to be harmed **unwarily** *adv* **unwariness** *n*
unwavering *adj* (of a feeling or attitude) remaining firm and never weakening
unwelcome *adj* unpleasant and unwanted
unwell *adj* not healthy; ill
unwept *adj* not wept for or lamented
unwholesome *adj* **1** harmful to the body or mind: *unwholesome food* **2** morally harmful: *unwholesome dreams* **3** unhealthy-looking **4** (of food) of inferior quality
unwieldy *adj* too heavy, large, or awkward to be easily handled
unwilling *adj* **1** reluctant **2** done or said with reluctance **unwillingly** *adv* **unwillingness** *n*
unwind *vb* **-winding, -wound 1** to slacken, undo, or unravel: *Paul started to unwind the bandage* **2** to relax after a busy or tense time: *we go out to unwind after work*
unwise *adj* foolish; not sensible **unwisely** *adv*
unwitting *adj* **1** not intentional **2** not knowing or conscious [Old English *unwitende*] **unwittingly** *adv*
unwonted *adj* out of the ordinary; unusual
unworkable *adj* impractical and certain to fail: *unworkable proposals for reform*
unworldly *adj* **1** not concerned with material values or pursuits **2** lacking sophistication; naive
unworn *adj* **1** not having deteriorated through use or age **2** (of a garment) never having been worn
unworried *adj* not bothered or perturbed
unworthy *adj* **1** not deserving or meriting: *a person deemed unworthy of membership* **2** (often foll. by *of*) beneath the level considered befitting (to): *unworthy of a prime minister* **3** lacking merit or value **unworthiness** *n*
unwrap *vb* **-wrapping, -wrapped** to remove the wrapping from something or (of something wrapped) to have the covering removed
unwritten *adj* **1** not printed or in writing **2** operating only through custom: *an unwritten code of conduct*
unyielding *adj* remaining firm and determined
unzip *vb* **-zipping, -zipped 1** to unfasten the zip of a garment or (of a zip or a garment with a zip) to become unfastened **2** to open (a data file that has been compressed)
up *prep* **1** indicating movement to a higher position: *go up the stairs* **2** at a higher or further level or position in or on: *a shop up the road* ▷ *adv* **3** to an upward, higher, or erect position: *the men straightened up from their digging* **4** indicating readiness for an activity: *up and about* **5** indicating intensity or completion of an action: *he tore up the cheque* **6** to the place referred to or where the speaker is: *a man came up to me* **7 A** to a more important place: *up to the city* **B** to a more northerly place: *pensioners who were going up to Norway* **C** to or at university **8** above the horizon: *the sun came up* **9** appearing for trial: *up before the judge* **10** having gained: *ten pounds up on the deal* **11** higher in price: *beer has gone up again* **12 all up with someone** *informal* over for or hopeless for someone **13 something's up** *informal* something strange is happening **14 up against** having to cope with: *look what we're up against now* **15 up for** being a candidate or applicant for: *he's up for the job* **16 up to A** occupied with; scheming: *she's up to no good* **B** dependent upon: *the decision is up to you* **C** equal to or capable of: *are you up to playing in the final?* **D** as far as: *up to his neck in mud* **E** as many as: *up to two years' credit* **F** comparable with: *not up to my usual standard* **17 what's up?** *informal* **A** what is the matter? **B** what is happening? ▷ *adj* **18** of a high or higher position **19** out of bed: *aren't you up yet?* **20** (of a period of time) over or completed: *the examiner announced that their time was up* **21** of or relating to a train going to a more important place: *the up platform* ▷ *vb* **upping, upped 22** to increase or raise **23 up and** *informal* to do something suddenly: *he upped and left her* ▷ *n* **24** a high point: *when the ups come along you have to enjoy them* **25 on the up and up A** *Brit, Austral & NZ* on an upward trend: *our firm's on the up and up* **B** *US* trustworthy or honest [Old English *upp*]

> **USAGE** The use of *up* before *until* is redundant and should be avoided: *the talks will continue until* (not *up until*) *March 23*.

up-and-coming *adj* likely to be successful in the future; promising
upbeat *adj* **1** *informal* cheerful and optimistic: *the upbeat atmosphere of a thriving metropolis* ▷ *n* **2** *music* **A** an unaccented beat **B** the upward gesture of a conductor's baton indicating this
upbraid *vb* to scold or reproach [Old English *upbrēdan*]
upbringing *n* the education of a person during his or her formative years

upcoming *adj* coming soon: *the upcoming election*
upcountry *adj* **1** of or from the interior of a country ▷ *adv* **2** towards or in the interior of a country
upcycle *vb* **-cycling, -cycled** to recycle a disposable or unwanted object into something of greater value or use
update *vb* **-dating, -dated 1** to bring up to date **2** inform; relay the most recent information to
upend *vb* to turn or set or become turned or set on end
upfront *adj* **1** open and frank **2** (of money) paid at the beginning of a business arrangement ▷ *adv* **up front 3** at the front; (in sport) in attack: *Liverpool's strikers dominated up front* **4** at the beginning of a business arrangement; in advance: *we charge up front*
upgrade *vb* **-grading, -graded 1** to promote a person or job to a higher rank **2** to raise in value, importance, or esteem
upheaval *n* a strong, sudden, or violent disturbance
uphill *adj* **1** sloping or leading upwards **2** requiring a great deal of effort: *an uphill struggle* ▷ *adv* **3** up a slope ▷ *n* **4** *S African* a difficulty
uphold *vb* **-holding, -held 1** to maintain or defend against opposition **2** to give moral support to **upholder** *n*
upholster *vb* to fit chairs or sofas with padding, springs, and covering **upholstered** *adj* **upholsterer** *n*
upholstery *n* the padding, springs, and covering of a chair or sofa
upkeep *n* **1** the act or process of keeping something in good repair **2** the cost of maintenance
upland *adj* of or in an area of high or relatively high ground: *an upland wilderness*
uplands *pl n* an area of high or relatively high ground: *the uplands of Nepal*
uplift *vb* **1** to raise or lift up **2** to raise morally or spiritually **3** *Scot* to collect or pick up ▷ *n* **4** the act or process of bettering moral, social, or cultural conditions ▷ *adj* **5** (of a bra) designed to lift and support the breasts **uplifting** *adj*
upload *vb* **1** to transfer (data or a program) from one computer's memory into that of another ▷ *n* **2** a file transferred in such a way
upmarket *adj* expensive and of superior quality
upon *prep* **1** on **2** up and on: *they climbed upon his lap for comfort* [*up* + *on*]
upper *adj* **1** higher or highest in physical position, wealth, rank, or status **2 Upper** *geol* denoting the late part of a period or formation: *Upper Cretaceous* ▷ *n* **3** the part of a shoe above the sole **4 on one's uppers** *Brit, Austral & NZ* very poor; penniless
upper-case *adj* denoting capital letters as used in printed or typed matter
upper class *n* **1** the highest social class; aristocracy ▷ *adj* **upper-class 2** of the upper class
upper crust *n Brit, Austral & NZ informal* the upper class
uppercut *n* a short swinging upward punch delivered to the chin
upper hand *n* the position of control: *the hardliners have gained the upper hand*
Upper House *n* the smaller and less representative chamber of a two-chamber parliament, for example the House of Lords or a Senate
uppermost *adj* **1** highest in position, power, or importance ▷ *adv* **2** in or into the highest place or position
uppish *adj Brit informal* uppity
uppity *adj informal* snobbish, arrogant, or presumptuous [*up* + fanciful ending]
upright *adj* **1** vertical or erect **2** honest or just ▷ *adv* **3** vertically or in an erect position ▷ *n* **4** a vertical support, such as a post **5** short for **upright piano 6** the state of being vertical **uprightness** *n*
upright piano *n* a piano which has a rectangular vertical case
uprising *n* a revolt or rebellion
up-river *adj, adv* nearer the source of a river: *we sailed slowly up-river; the village of Juffure, four days up-river*
uproar *n* **1** a commotion or disturbance characterized by loud noise and confusion **2** angry public criticism or debates: *the decision to close the railway led to an uproar*
uproarious *adj* **1** very funny **2** (of laughter) loud and boisterous
uproot *vb* **1** to pull up by or as if by the roots **2** to displace (a person or people) from their native or usual surroundings **3** to remove or destroy utterly: *we must uproot all remnants of feudalism*
ups and downs *pl n* alternating periods of good and bad luck or high and low spirits
upscale *informal* ▷ *adj* (**up**-skale) **1** of or for the upper end of an economic or social scale; upmarket ▷ *vb* (up-**skale**) **-scaling, -scaled 2** to increase the scale of
upset *adj* **1** emotionally or physically disturbed or distressed ▷ *vb* **-setting, -set 2** to turn or tip over **3** to disrupt the normal state or progress of: *bad weather upset their plans* **4** to disturb mentally or emotionally **5** to make physically ill: *it still seems to upset my stomach* ▷ *n* **6** an unexpected defeat or reversal, as in a contest or plans **7** a disturbance or disorder of the emotions, mind, or body **upsetting** *adj*
upset price *n chiefly Scot, US & Canad* the lowest price acceptable for something that is for sale by auction, usually a house
upshot *n* the final result or conclusion; outcome [*up* + *shot*]
upside down *adj* **1** with the bottom where the top would normally be; inverted **2** *informal* confused or jumbled ▷ *adv* **3** in an inverted fashion **4** in a chaotic manner or into a chaotic state: *recent events have turned many people's lives upside down* [by folk etymology, from *upsodown*]
upsides *adv informal, chiefly Brit* (foll. by *with*) equal or level with, as through revenge
upstage *adv* **1** on, at, or to the rear of the stage ▷ *adj* **2** at the back half of the stage ▷ *vb* **-staging, -staged 3** to move upstage of another actor, forcing him or her to turn away from the audience **4** *informal* to draw attention to oneself and away from someone else
upstairs *adv* **1** to or on an upper floor of a building **2** *informal* to or into a higher rank or

office ▷ *n* **3** an upper floor ▷ *adj* **4** situated on an upper floor: *an upstairs bedroom*
upstanding *adj* **1** of good character **2** upright and vigorous in build
upstart *n* a person who has risen suddenly to a position of power and behaves arrogantly
upstream *adv, adj* in or towards the higher part of a stream; against the current
upsurge *n* a rapid rise or swell
upswing *n* **1** *econ* a recovery period in the trade cycle **2** any increase or improvement
upsy-daisy *or* **upsadaisy** *interj* an expression of reassurance, usually used to a child, eg when it stumbles or is being lifted up [originally *up-a-daisy*]
uptake *n* **1 quick** *or* **slow on the uptake** *informal* quick *or* slow to understand or learn **2** the use or consumption of something by a machine or part of the body: *the uptake of oxygen into the blood*
upthrust *n* **1** an upward push **2** *geol* a violent upheaval of the earth's surface
uptight *adj informal* **1** nervously tense, irritable, or angry **2** unable to express one's feelings
up-to-date *adj* modern or fashionable: *an up-to-date kitchen*
up-to-the-minute *adj* the latest or most modern possible: *up-to-the-minute news about what's on in town*
uptown *US & Canad* ▷ *adj, adv* **1** towards, in, or relating to some part of a town that is away from the centre ▷ *n* **2** such a part of town, esp. a residential part
upturn *n* **1** an upward trend or improvement ▷ *vb* **2** to turn or cause to turn over or upside down
UPVC unplasticized polyvinyl chloride
upward *adj* **1** directed or moving towards a higher place or level ▷ *adv also* **upwards 2** from a lower to a higher place, level, or condition **3 upward** *or* **upwards of** more than (the stated figure): *a crowd estimated at upward of one hundred thousand people*
upward mobility *n* movement from a lower to a higher economic and social status
upwind *adv* **1** into or against the wind **2** towards or on the side where the wind is blowing ▷ *adj* **3** going against the wind **4** on the windward side
Urania *n Greek myth* the Muse of astronomy
uranium (yew-**rain**-ee-um) *n chem* a radioactive silvery-white metallic element of the actinide series. It is used chiefly as a source of nuclear energy by fission of the radioisotope **uranium 235**. Symbol: **U** [from *Uranus*, from the fact that the element was discovered soon after the planet]
Uranus *n* **1** *Greek myth* a god; the personification of the sky **2** the seventh planet from the sun [Greek *Ouranos* heaven]
urban *adj* **1** of or living in a city or town **2** relating to modern pop music of African-American origin, such as hip-hop [Latin *urbs* city]
urbane *adj* polite, elegant, and sophisticated in manner [Latin *urbanus* of the town]
urbanity *n* the quality of being urbane
urbanize *or* **-nise** *vb* **-nizing, -nized** *or* **-nising, -nised** to make a rural area more industrialized and urban **urbanization** *or* **-nisation** *n*
urchin *n* **1** a mischievous child **2** See **sea urchin** [Latin *ericius* hedgehog]
Urdu (**oor**-doo) *n* an Indic language of the Indo-European family which is an official language of Pakistan and is also spoken in India [Hindustani *(zabāni) urdū* (language of the) camp]
urea (**yew**-ree-a) *n* a white soluble crystalline compound found in urine [Greek *ouron* urine]
ureter (yew-**reet**-er) *n* the tube that carries urine from the kidney to the bladder [Greek *ourein* to urinate]
urethra (yew-**reeth**-ra) *n* the tube that in most mammals carries urine from the bladder out of the body [Greek *ourein* to urinate]
urethritis (yew-rith-**rite**-iss) *n* inflammation of the urethra causing a discharge and painful urination **urethritic** *adj*
urge *n* **1** a strong impulse, inner drive, or yearning ▷ *vb* **urging, urged 2** to plead with or press someone to do something: *he urged his readers to do the same* **3** to advocate earnestly and persistently: *I have long urged this change* **4** (often foll. by *on*) to force or hasten onwards: *something very powerful urged him on* [Latin *urgere*]
urgent *adj* **1** requiring speedy action or attention: *an urgent inquiry* **2** earnest and forceful: *she heard loud urgent voices in the corridor* [Latin *urgere* to urge] **urgency** *n* **urgently** *adv*
uric (**yew**-rik) *adj* of or derived from urine
uric acid *n* a white odourless crystalline acid present in the blood and urine
urinal *n* **1** a sanitary fitting, used by men for urination **2** a room containing urinals
urinary *adj anatomy* of urine or the organs that secrete and pass urine
urinary bladder *n* a membranous sac that can expand in which urine excreted from the kidneys is stored
urinate *vb* **-nating, -nated** to excrete urine **urination** *n*
urine *n* the pale yellow fluid excreted by the kidneys, containing waste products from the blood. It is stored in the bladder and discharged through the urethra [Latin *urina*]
urinogenital (yew-rin-oh-**jen**-it-al) *adj* same as **urogenital**
URL uniform resource locator: a standardized address of a location on the internet
urn *n* **1** a vaselike container, usually with a foot and a rounded body **2** a vase used as a container for the ashes of the dead **3** a large metal container, with a tap, used for making and holding tea or coffee [Latin *urna*]
urogenital (yew-roh-**jen**-it-al) *or* **urinogenital** *adj* of the urinary and genital organs and their functions. Also: **genitourinary**
urology (yew-**rol**-a-jee) *n* the branch of medicine concerned with the urinary system and its diseases
ursine *adj* of or like a bear [Latin *ursus* a bear]
us *pron (objective)* **1** refers to the speaker or writer and another person or other people: *the bond between us* **2** refers to all people or people in general: *this table shows us the tides* **3** *informal* me: *give us a kiss!* **4** *formal* same as **me**[1]: used by monarchs [Old English *ūs*]
USAGE See at **me**[1].
US *or* **U.S.** United States

USA *or* **U.S.A.** United States of America
usable *adj* able to be used **usability** *n*
usage *n* **1** regular or constant use: *a move to reduce pesticide usage* **2** the way in which a word is actually used in a language **3** a particular meaning or use that a word can have [Latin *usus* a use]
USB Universal Serial Bus: a standard for connection sockets on computers and other electronic equipment
USB drive *n computers* a small portable data storage device with a USB connection
use *vb* **using, used 1** to put into service or action; employ for a given purpose: *use a garden fork to mix them together* **2** to choose or employ regularly: *what sort of toothpaste do you use?* **3** to take advantage of; exploit: *I used Jason and he used me* **4** to consume or expend: *a manufacturing plant uses 1000 tonnes of steel a month* ▷ *n* **5** the act or fact of using or being used: *large-scale use of pesticides* **6** the ability or permission to use **7** need or opportunity to use: *the Colombian government had no use for them* **8** usefulness or advantage: *there is no use in complaining* **9** the purpose for which something is used **10 have no use for A** to have no need of **B** to have a contemptuous dislike for **11 make use of A** to employ; use **B** to exploit (a person) ▷ See also **use up** [Latin *usus* having used] **user** *n*
use-by date *n* the date on packaged food after which it should not be sold
used *adj* second-hand: *it was a used car*
used to *adj* **1** accustomed to: *I am used to being a medical guinea pig* ▷ *vb* **2** used as an auxiliary to express habitual or accustomed actions or states taking place in the past but not continuing to be the case in the present: *he used to vanish into his studio for days*

> **USAGE** The most common negative form of *used to* is *didn't used to* (or *didn't use to*), but in formal contexts *used not to* is preferred.

useful *adj* **1** able to be used advantageously or for several purposes **2** *informal* commendable or capable: *a useful hurdler* **usefully** *adv* **usefulness** *n*
useless *adj* **1** having no practical use **2** *informal* ineffectual, weak, or stupid: *I'm useless at most things* **uselessly** *adv* **uselessness** *n*
Usenet *n* a computer network, popular in the early years of the World Wide Web, used for discussions and the sharing of files by means of newsgroups
user-friendly *adj* easy to familiarize oneself with, understand, and use
username *n computers* a name that someone uses for identification purposes when logging onto a computer or certain computer applications
use up *vb* to finish a supply of something completely
U-shaped valley *n* a steep-sided valley caused by glacial erosion
usher *n* **1** an official who shows people to their seats, as in a church **2** a person who acts as doorkeeper in a court of law ▷ *vb* **3** to conduct or escort **4** (foll. by *in*) to happen immediately before something or cause it to happen; herald: *the French Revolution ushered in a new age* [Old French *huissier* doorkeeper]
usherette *n* a woman assistant in a cinema, who shows people to their seats
USP *commerce* unique selling point
USSR Union of Soviet Socialist Republics: a former state in E Europe and N Asia, covering the area now composed of Russia, Ukraine, Kazakhstan and a number of smaller states
usual *adj* **1** of the most normal, frequent, or regular type: *the usual assortment of stories* ▷ *n* **2** ordinary or commonplace events: *the dirt was nothing out of the usual* **3 as usual** as happens normally **4 the usual** *informal* the habitual or usual drink [Latin *usus* use] **usually** *adv*
usurp (yewz-**zurp**) *vb* to seize a position or power without authority [Latin *usurpare* to take into use] **usurpation** *n* **usurper** *n*
usury (**yewz**-yoor-ree) *n, pl* **-ries** *old-fashioned* **1** the practice of loaning money at an exorbitant rate of interest **2** an unlawfully high rate of interest [Latin *usura* usage] **usurer** *n*
UT Utah
ute *n Austral & NZ informal* a utility truck
utensil *n* a tool or container for practical use: *cooking utensils* [Latin *utensilia* necessaries]
uterine *adj* of or affecting the womb
uterus (**yew**-ter-russ) *n, pl* **uteri** (**yew**-ter-rye) *anatomy* a hollow muscular organ in the pelvic cavity of female mammals, which houses the developing fetus; womb [Latin]
utilidor (yew-till-lid-or) *n Canad* above-ground insulated casing for pipes carrying water, sewerage and electricity in permafrost regions [*utility* + *-dor*, from Greek *dōron* gift]
utilitarian *adj* **1** useful rather than beautiful **2** of utilitarianism ▷ *n* **3** an advocate of utilitarianism
utilitarianism *n ethics* the doctrine that the right thing to do is that which brings about the greatest good for the greatest number
utility *n, pl* **-ties 1** usefulness **2** something useful **3** a public service, such as water or electricity ▷ *adj* **4** designed for use rather than beauty: *utility fabrics* [Latin *utilitas* usefulness, from *uti* to use]
utility room *n* a room with equipment for domestic work like washing and ironing
utility truck *n Austral & NZ* a small truck with an open body and low sides
utilize *or* **-lise** *vb* **-lizing, -lized** *or* **-lising, -lised** to make practical or worthwhile use of **utilization** *or* **-lisation** *n*
utmost *adj* **1** of the greatest possible degree or amount: *the utmost seriousness* **2** at the furthest limit: *the utmost point* ▷ *n* **3** the greatest possible degree or amount: *I was doing my utmost to comply* [Old English *ūtemest*]
Utopia (yew-**tope**-ee-a) *n* any real or imaginary society, place, or state considered to be perfect or ideal [coined by Sir Thomas More in 1516 as the title of his book that described an imaginary island representing the perfect society, literally: no place, from Greek *ou* not + *topos* a place] **Utopian** *adj*
utter[1] *vb* **1** to express something in sounds or words: *she hadn't uttered a single word* **2** *criminal law* to put counterfeit money or forged cheques into circulation [Middle Dutch *ūteren* to make known]

U

utter² *adj* total or absolute: *utter amazement* [Old English *ūtera* outer] **utterly** *adv*
utterance *n* **1** something expressed in speech or writing **2** the expression in words of ideas, thoughts, or feelings
uttermost *adj, n* same as **utmost**
U-turn *n* **1** a turn, made by a vehicle, in the shape of a U, resulting in a reversal of direction **2** a complete change in policy
UUP (in Northern Ireland) Ulster Unionist Party
UV ultraviolet
UV-A *or* **UVA** *n* ultraviolet radiation with a range of 320-380 nanometres
UV-B *or* **UVB** *n* ultraviolet radiation with a range of 280-320 nanometres
uvula (yew-view-la) *n* the small fleshy part of the soft palate that hangs in the back of the throat [Medieval Latin, literally: a little grape] **uvular** *adj*
uxorious (ux-or-ee-uss) *adj* excessively fond of or dependent on one's wife [Latin *uxor* wife]

Vv

V **1** *chem* vanadium **2** volt **3** the Roman numeral for five

v. **1** verb **2** verse **3** versus **4** volume

VA Virginia

vac *n Brit informal* short for **vacation**

vacancy *n, pl* **-cies** **1** an unoccupied job or position: *he had heard of a vacancy for a librarian* **2** an unoccupied room in a hotel or guesthouse: *the last hotel we tried had a vacancy* **3** the state of being unoccupied

vacant *adj* **1** (of a toilet, room, etc.) unoccupied or not being used: *I sat down in a vacant chair* **2** (of a job or position) unfilled at the present time **3** having or suggesting a lack of interest or understanding: *he sat there staring at me with a vacant look* **4** (of a period of time) not set aside for any particular activity: *two slots in his programme have been left vacant* [Latin *vacare* to be empty] **vacantly** *adv*

vacate *vb* **-cating, -cated** **1** to cause (something) to be empty by leaving: *do you wish us to vacate the room?* **2** to give up (a job or position)

vacation *n* **1** *Brit & S African* a time of the year when the universities or law courts are closed **2** *US, Canad & Austral* same as **holiday** (sense 2) [Latin *vacatio* freedom]

vaccinate *vb* **-nating, -nated** to inject (someone) with a vaccine in order to protect them against a disease: *children vaccinated against meningitis* **vaccination** *n*

vaccine *n* **1** *med* a substance made from the germs that cause a disease which is given to people to prevent them getting the disease **2** *computers* a piece of software that detects and removes computer viruses from a system [Latin *variolae vaccinae* cowpox (source of the first smallpox vaccine), from *vacca* a cow]

vacillate (vass-ill-late) *vb* **-lating, -lated** to keep changing one's mind or opinions about something: *he vacillated between republican and monarchist sentiments* [Latin *vacillare* to sway] **vacillation** *n*

vacuity *n* an absence of intelligent thought or ideas: *I suggested to one of his advisers that his vacuity was a handicap in these debates*

vacuous *adj* **1** lacking in intelligent ideas **2** showing no sign of intelligence or understanding: *her smile was vacuous but without malice* [Latin *vacuus* empty]

vacuum *n, pl* **vacuums** *or* **vacua** **1** a space which contains no air or other gas **2** a vacant place or position that needs to be filled by someone or something else: *the army moved in to fill the power vacuum* **3** short for **vacuum cleaner** ▷ *vb* **4** to clean (something) with a vacuum cleaner [Latin *vacuus* empty]

vacuum cleaner *n* an electric machine which sucks up dust and dirt from carpets and upholstery **vacuum cleaning** *n*

vacuum flask *n* a double-walled flask with a vacuum between the walls that keeps drinks hot or cold

vacuum-packed *adj* (of food) packed in an airtight container in order to preserve freshness

vacuum tube *or* **vacuum valve** *n* same as **valve** (sense 3)

vade mecum (vah-dee **make**-um) *n* a handbook carried for immediate use when needed [Latin, literally: go with me]

vagabond *n* a person who travels from place to place and has no fixed home or job [Latin *vagari* to roam]

vagary (vaig-a-ree) *n, pl* **-garies** an unpredictable change in a situation or in someone's behaviour: *I was unused to the vagaries of the retailer's world* [probably from Latin *vagari* to roam]

vagina (vaj-**jine**-a) *n* the passage in most female mammals that extends from the neck of the womb to the external genitals [Latin: sheath] **vaginal** *adj*

vagrant (vaig-rant) *n* **1** a person who moves from place to place and has no regular home or job ▷ *adj* **2** wandering about [probably from Old French *waucrant*] **vagrancy** *n*

vague *adj* **1** not expressed or explained clearly: *he thought of his instructions, so vague and imprecise* **2** deliberately withholding information: *she was rather vague about the whole deal* **3** (of a sound or shape) unable to be heard or seen clearly: *he heard some vague sound from downstairs* **4** (of a person) not concentrating or thinking clearly: *she was mumbling to herself in a vague way* **5** not clearly established or known: *it was a vague rumour which would fade away and be forgotten* [Latin *vagus* wandering] **vaguely** *adv* **vagueness** *n*

vain *adj* **1** excessively proud of one's appearance or achievements **2** senseless or unsuccessful: *he made a vain attempt to lighten the atmosphere* ▷ *n* **3** **in vain** without achieving the desired effects or results: *the old man searched in vain for his son* [Latin *vanus*] **vainly** *adv*

vainglorious *adj* boastful or proud: *his vainglorious posturing had earned him numerous powerful enemies*

valance (val-lenss) *n* a short piece of decorative material hung round the edge of a bed or above a window [perhaps after *Valence* in SE France]

vale *n literary* a valley [Latin *vallis* valley]

valediction (val-lid-**dik**-shun) *n* a farewell speech [Latin *vale* farewell + *dicere* to say] **valedictory** *adj*

valence (vale-enss) *n chem* the ability of atoms and chemical groups to form compounds

valency *or esp US & Canad* **valence** *n, pl* **-cies** *or* **-ces** *chem* the number of atoms of hydrogen that an atom or chemical group is able to combine with in forming compounds [Latin *valere* to be strong]

valentine *n* **1** a card sent, often anonymously, as an expression of love on Saint Valentine's Day, February 14 **2** the person to whom one sends such a card [after Saint Valentine]

valerian *n* a plant with small white or pinkish flowers and a medicinal root [Medieval Latin *valeriana (herba)* (herb) of Valerius]

valet *n* **1** a male servant employed to look after another man ▷ *vb* **-eting, -eted 2** to act as a valet (for) **3** to clean the bodywork and interior of (a car) as a professional service [Old French *vaslet* page]

valeta *or* **veleta** (vel-**lee**-ta) *n* an old-time dance in triple time [Spanish *veleta* weather vane]

valetudinarian (val-lit-yew-din-**air**-ee-an) *n* **1** a person who is chronically sick **2** a person who continually worries about his or her health [Latin *valetudo* state of health] **valetudinarianism** *n*

Valhalla *n* *Norse myth* the great hall of Odin where warriors who die as heroes in battle dwell eternally [Old Norse *valr* slain warriors + *höll* hall]

valiant *adj* very brave: *it was a valiant attempt to rescue the struggling victim* [Latin *valere* to be strong] **valiantly** *adv*

valid *adj* **1** based on sound reasoning: *I think that's a very valid question* **2** legally acceptable: *she must produce a valid driving licence* **3** important or serious enough to say or do: *religious broadcasting has a valid purpose* [Latin *validus* robust] **validity** *n*

validate *vb* **-dating, -dated 1** to prove (a claim or statement) to be true or correct **2** to give legal force or official confirmation to **validation** *n*

valise (val-**leez**) *n old-fashioned* a small suitcase [Italian *valigia*]

Valium *n trademark* a drug used as a tranquillizer

Valkyrie (val-**keer**-ee) *n* *Norse myth* any of the beautiful maidens who take the dead heroes to Valhalla [Old Norse *valr* slain warriors + *kyrja* chooser]

valley *n* a long stretch of land between hills, often with a river flowing through it [Latin *vallis*]

valour *or US* **valor** *n literary* great bravery, esp. in battle [Latin *valere* to be strong] **valorous** *adj*

valuable *adj* **1** worth a large amount of money: *his house was furnished with valuable antique furniture* **2** of great use or importance: *the investigations will provide valuable information* ▷ *n* **3 valuables** valuable articles of personal property, such as jewellery

valuation *n* **1** a formal assessment of how much something is worth: *they will arrange a valuation on your house* **2** the price arrived at by the process of valuing

value *n* **1** the desirability of something, often in terms of its usefulness or exchangeability **2** an amount of money considered to be a fair exchange for something: *scrap metal with a value of £100* **3** something worth the money it cost: *the set meal was great value* **4 values** the moral principles and beliefs of a person or group **5** *maths* a particular number or quantity represented by a figure or symbol **6** *music* short for **time value** ▷ *vb* **-uing, -ued 7** to assess the worth or desirability of (something) **8** to hold (someone or something) in high regard [Latin *valere* to be worth] **valued** *adj* **valueless** *adj* **valuer** *n*

value-added tax *n Brit & S African* See **VAT**

value judgment *n* a personal opinion about something based on an individual's beliefs and not on facts which can be checked or proved

valve *n* **1** a part attached to a pipe or tube which controls the flow of gas or liquid **2** *anatomy* a small flap in a hollow organ, such as the heart, that controls the flow and direction of blood **3** a closed tube through which electrons move in a vacuum **4** *zool* one of the hinged shells of an oyster or clam **5** *music* a device on some brass instruments by which the effective length of the tube may be varied [Latin *valva* a folding door]

valvular *adj* of or relating to valves: *valvular heart disease*

vamoose *vb* **-moosing, -moosed** *slang, chiefly US* to leave a place hurriedly [Spanish *vamos* let's go]

vamp¹ *informal* ▷ *n* **1** a sexually attractive woman who seduces men ▷ *vb* **2** (of a woman) to seduce (a man) [short for *vampire*]

vamp² *vb* **vamp up** to make (a story, piece of music, etc.) seem new by inventing additional parts [Old French *avantpié* the front part of a shoe]

vampire *n* (in European folklore) a corpse that rises nightly from its grave to drink the blood of living people [from Magyar]

vampire bat *n* a bat of Central and South America that feeds on the blood of birds and mammals

van¹ *n* **1** a road vehicle with a roof and no side windows used to transport goods **2** *Brit* a closed railway wagon used to transport luggage, goods, or mail [shortened from *caravan*]

van² *n* short for **vanguard**

vanadium *n* *chem* a silvery-white metallic element used to toughen steel. Symbol: **V** [Old Norse *Vanadīs*, epithet of the goddess Freya]

Van Allen belt *n* either of two belts of charged particles which surround the Earth [after J. A. *Van Allen*, physicist]

vandal *n* someone who deliberately causes damage to personal or public property [from the name of a Germanic tribe of the 3rd and 4th centuries AD] **vandalism** *n*

vandalize *or* **-lise** *vb* **-lizing, -lized** *or* **-lising, -lised** to cause damage to (personal or public property) deliberately

Van der Hum *n S African* a liqueur made from tangerines [origin uncertain but possibly derived from the humorous uncertainty of the name, equivalent of *whatshisname*]

Vandyke beard *n* a short pointed beard [after Sir Anthony *Van Dyck*, Flemish painter]

vane *n* **1** one of the blades forming part of the wheel of a windmill, a screw propeller, etc. **2** short for **weather vane** [Old English *fana*]

vanguard *n* **1** the leading division or units of an army **2** the most advanced group or position in scientific research, a movement, etc.: *a distinguished architect in the vanguard of her profession* [Old French *avant-garde* advance guard]

vanilla *n* **1** a flavouring for food such as ice cream, which comes from the pods of a tropical plant **2** a flavouring extract prepared from the beans of this plant and used in cooking ▷ *adj* **3** flavoured with vanilla: *vanilla essence* **4** *slang* ordinary or conventional: *a vanilla kind of guy* [Spanish *vainilla* pod]

vanish *vb* **1** to disappear suddenly: *the choppers vanished from radar screens at dawn yesterday* **2** to cease to exist: *the old landmarks had vanished* [Latin *evanescere* to evaporate]

vanishing cream *n old-fashioned* a cosmetic cream that is colourless once applied
vanishing point *n* the point in the distance where parallel lines appear to meet
vanity *n* **1** a feeling of pride about one's appearance or ability **2** *pl* **-ties** something about which one is vain: *it's one of my vanities that I can guess scents* [Latin *vanitas* emptiness]
vanity case *n* a small bag for holding cosmetics
vanity unit *n* a hand basin built into a surface, usually with a cupboard below it
vanquish *vb literary* to defeat (someone) in a battle, contest, or argument [Latin *vincere*]
vantage *n* a state, position, or opportunity offering advantage [Old French *avantage* advantage]
vantage point *n* a position that gives one an overall view of a scene or situation
vape *vb* **vaping, vaped** *informal* to inhale vapour from an e-cigarette
vapid *adj* dull and uninteresting: *their publications were vapid and amateurish* [Latin *vapidus*] **vapidity** *n*
vapor *n US* same as **vapour**
vaporize *or* **-rise** *vb* **-rizing, -rized** *or* **-rising, -rised** (of a liquid or solid) to change into vapour **vaporization** *or* **-risation** *n*
vaporous *adj* resembling or full of vapour
vapour *or US* **vapor** *n* **1** a mass of tiny drops of water or other liquids in the air, which appear as a mist **2** the gaseous form of a substance that is usually a liquid or a solid **3 the vapours** *old-fashioned* a feeling of faintness, dizziness, and depression [Latin *vapor*]
VAR video assistant referee: an official at a football match who examines important incidents using video replay equipment
variable *adj* **1** likely to change at any time: *variable weather* **2** *maths* having a range of possible values ▷ *n* **3** something that is subject to variation **4** *maths* an expression that can be assigned any of a set of values [Latin *variare* to diversify] **variability** *n* **variably** *adv*
variance *n* **at variance** not in agreement: *the real record is at variance with the public record*
variant *adj* **1** differing from a standard or type: *variant spellings* ▷ *n* **2** something that differs from a standard or type
variation *n* **1** something presented in a slightly different form: *his books are all variations on a basic theme* **2** a change in level, amount, or quantity: *there was a variation in the figures* **3** *music* the repetition of a simple tune with the addition of new harmonies or a change in rhythm: *Variations on a Hussar's Song*
varicoloured *or US* **varicolored** *adj* having many colours
varicose *adj* of or resulting from varicose veins: *a varicose ulcer* [Latin *varix* a swollen vein]
varicose veins *pl n* veins, usually in the legs, which have become knotted, swollen, and sometimes painful
varied *adj* of different types, sizes, or quantities: *these young men and women would be of varied backgrounds*
variegated *adj* having patches or streaks of different colours: *variegated holly* **variegation** *n*
variety *n, pl* **-ties 1** the state of being diverse or various **2** different things of the same kind: *I'm cooking the mince with a variety of vegetables* **3** a particular type of something in the same general category: *this variety of pear is extremely juicy* **4** *taxonomy* a race whose distinct characters do not justify classification as a separate species **5** a type of entertainment consisting of short unrelated acts, such as singing, dancing, and comedy [Latin *varietas*]
varifocal *adj* of a lens that is gradated to permit any length of vision between near and distant
varifocals *pl n* a pair of spectacles with varifocal lenses
various *adj* **1** several different: *there are various possible answers to this question* **2** of different kinds: *the causes of high blood pressure are various and complicated* [Latin *varius* changing] **variously** *adv*

USAGE The use of *different* after *various* should be avoided: *the disease exists in various forms* (not *in various different forms*).

varlet *n old-fashioned* **1** a menial servant **2** a rascal [Old French *vaslet*]
varmint *n informal* an irritating or obnoxious person or animal [dialect variant of *varmin* vermin]
varnish *n* **1** a liquid painted onto a surface to give it a hard glossy finish **2** a smooth surface, coated with or as if with varnish **3** an artificial, superficial, or deceptively pleasing manner or appearance: *those who aspired to become civil servants acquired a varnish of university education* **4** *chiefly Brit* short for **nail varnish** ▷ *vb* **5** to apply varnish to **6** to try to make (something unpleasant) appear more attractive: *when did we start equivocating, camouflaging, varnishing the truth?* [Old French *vernis*]
varsity *n, pl* **-ties** *old-fashioned or informal* short for **university**
vary *vb* **varies, varying, varied 1** to change in appearance, character, or form **2** to be different or cause to be different: *the age of appearance of underarm and body hair varies greatly from person to person* **3** to give variety to: *you can vary the type of exercise you do* **4** to change in accordance with another variable: *an individual's calorie requirement varies with age, sex, and physical activity* [Latin *varius* changing] **varying** *adj*
vas *n, pl* **vasa** *anatomy & zool* a vessel or tube that carries a fluid [Latin: vessel]
vascular *adj biol & anatomy* of or relating to the vessels that conduct and circulate body fluids such as blood or sap [Latin *vas* vessel]
vas deferens *n, pl* **vasa deferentia** *anatomy* either of the two ducts that convey sperm from the testicles to the penis [Latin *vas* vessel + *deferens* carrying away]
vase *n* a glass or pottery jar used as an ornament or for holding cut flowers [Latin *vas* vessel]
vasectomy *n, pl* **-mies** surgical removal of all or part of the vas deferens as a method of contraception [VAS + Greek *tomē* a cutting]
Vaseline *n trademark* petroleum jelly, used as an ointment or a lubricant
vassal *n* **1** (in feudal society) a man who gave military service to a lord in return for protection

V

and often land **2** a person, nation, or state dominated by another [Medieval Latin *vassus* servant] **vassalage** *n*

vast *adj* unusually large in size, degree, or number [Latin *vastus* deserted] **vastly** *adv* **vastness** *n*

vat *n* a large container for holding or storing liquids [Old English *fæt*]

VAT (in Britain and S Africa) value-added tax: a tax levied on the difference between the cost of materials and the selling price of a commodity or service

Vatican *n* **1** the Pope's palace, in Rome **2** the authority of the Pope [Latin *Vaticanus (mons)* Vatican (hill)]

vaudeville *n* variety entertainment consisting of short acts such as song-and-dance routines and comic turns [French]

vault[1] *n* **1** a secure room where money and other valuables are stored safely **2** an underground burial chamber **3** an arched structure that forms a roof or ceiling **4** a cellar for storing wine [Old French *voute, voulte*]

vault[2] *vb* **1** to jump over (something) by resting one's hands on it or by using a long pole ▷ *n* **2** the act of vaulting [Italian *voltare* to turn] **vaulter** *n*

vaulted *adj* being or having an arched roof: *an atmospheric vaulted dining room*

vaulting[1] *n* the arrangement of ceiling vaults in a building

vaulting[2] *adj* excessively confident: *a vaulting ambition for the highest political office*

vaunt *vb* **1** to describe or display (one's success or possessions) boastfully ▷ *n* **2** a boast [Latin *vanus* vain] **vaunted** *adj*

vb verb

VC **1** Vice Chancellor **2** Victoria Cross **3** *history* Vietcong: the Communist-led guerrilla force of South Vietnam

vCJD variant Creutzfeldt-Jakob disease

VD venereal disease

VDU visual display unit

veal *n* the meat from a calf, used as food [Latin *vitulus* calf]

vector *n* **1** *maths* a variable quantity, such as force, that has magnitude and direction **2** *pathol* an animal, usually an insect, that carries a disease-producing microorganism from person to person [Latin: carrier]

Veda (vay-da) *n* any or all of the most ancient sacred writings of Hinduism [Sanskrit: knowledge] **Vedic** *adj*

veer *vb* **1** to change direction suddenly: *the plane veered off the runway and careered through the perimeter fence* **2** to change from one position or opinion to another: *her feelings veered from tenderness to sudden spurts of genuine love* ▷ *n* **3** a change of course or direction [Old French *virer*]

veg *n informal* a vegetable or vegetables

vegan (vee-gan) *n* a person who refrains from using any animal product for food, clothing, or any other purpose

vegeburger *or* **veggieburger** *n* a flat cake of chopped vegetables or pulses that is grilled or fried and served in a roll

vegetable *n* **1** a plant, such as potato or cauliflower, with parts that are used as food **2** *offensive* someone who is unable to move or think, as a result of brain damage ▷ *adj* **3** of or like plants or vegetables [Late Latin *vegetabilis* animating]

vegetable marrow *n* a long green vegetable which can be cooked and eaten

vegetable oil *n* any of a group of oils that are obtained from plants

vegetal *adj* of or relating to plant life

vegetarian *n* **1** a person who does not eat meat or fish ▷ *adj* **2** excluding meat and fish: *a vegetarian diet* **vegetarianism** *n*

vegetate *vb* **-tating, -tated** to live in a dull and boring way with no mental stimulation

vegetation *n* plant life as a whole

vegetative *adj* **1** of or relating to plant life or plant growth **2** (of reproduction) characterized by asexual processes

veggie *informal* ▷ *n* **1** a vegetable **2** a vegetarian ▷ *adj* **3** vegetarian: *a veggie cookbook*

veggieburger *n* same as **vegeburger**

veg out *vb* **vegges, vegging, vegged** *slang* to relax in a passive way

vehement *adj* **1** expressing strong feelings or opinions **2** (of actions or gestures) performed with great force or energy [Latin *vehemens* ardent] **vehemence** *n* **vehemently** *adv*

vehicle *n* **1** a machine such as a bus or car for transporting people or goods **2** something used to achieve a particular purpose or as a means of expression: *the newspaper was a vehicle for explaining government policies* **3** *pharmacol* an inactive substance mixed with the active ingredient in a medicine **4** a liquid, such as oil, in which a pigment is mixed before it is applied to a surface [Latin *vehere* to carry] **vehicular** *adj*

veil *n* **1** a piece of thin cloth, usually as part of a hat or headdress, used to cover a woman's face **2** something that conceals the truth: *a veil of secrecy* **3** **take the veil** to become a nun ▷ *vb* **4** to cover or conceal with or as if with a veil [Latin *velum* a covering]

veiled *adj* (of a comment or remark) presented in a disguised form: *it was a thinly veiled criticism*

vein *n* **1** any of the tubes that carry blood to the heart **2** a thin line in a leaf or in an insect's wing **3** a clearly defined layer of ore or mineral in rock **4** an irregular streak of colour in marble, wood, or cheese **5** a distinctive trait or quality in speech or writing: *critics have exposed a strong vein of moralism in the poem* **6** a temporary mood: *we're in a very humorous vein tonight* [Latin *vena*] **veined** *adj*

Velcro *n trademark* a type of fastening consisting of one piece of fabric with tiny hooked threads and another with a coarse surface that sticks to it

veld *or* **veldt** *n* the open country of South Africa including landscapes which are grassy, bushy, or thinly forested [Afrikaans: field]

veldskoen *or* **velskoen** (felt-skoon) *n S African* a sturdy ankle boot [Afrikaans]

veleta *n* same as **valeta**

vellum *n* **1** a fine calf, kid, or lamb parchment **2** a strong good-quality paper that resembles vellum [Old French *velin* of a calf]

velocipede (vel-**loss**-sip-peed) *n* an early form of bicycle [Latin *velox* swift + *pes* foot]
velocity (vel-**loss**-it-ee) *n, pl* **-ties** the speed at which something is moving in a particular direction [Latin *velox* swift]
velour *or* **velours** (vel-**loor**) *n* a silk or cotton cloth similar to velvet [Latin *villus* shaggy hair]
velouté (vuh-**loo**-tay) *n* a rich white sauce made from stock, eggs, and cream [French, literally: velvety]
velskoen *n* same as **veldskoen**
velvet *n* **1** a fabric with a thick close soft pile on one side **2** the furry covering of the newly formed antlers of a deer ▷ *adj* **3** made of velvet **4** soft or smooth like velvet **5 an iron fist** *or* **hand in a velvet glove** determination concealed by a gentle manner [Old French, from Latin *villus* shaggy hair] **velvety** *adj*
velveteen *n* a cotton fabric that resembles velvet
venal (**vee**-nal) *adj* **1** willing to accept bribes in return for acting dishonestly: *venal politicians* **2** associated with corruption or bribery: *venal greed* [Latin *venum* sale] **venality** *n*
vend *vb* to sell (goods) [Latin *vendere* to sell]
Venda *n* **1** *pl* **-da** *or* **-das** a member of a people of southern Africa, living chiefly in NE South Africa **2** the language of this people
vendetta *n* **1** a long-lasting quarrel between people or organizations in which they attempt to harm each other: *it's an inexplicable vendetta against the firm and its directors* **2** a private feud between families in which members of one family kill members of the other family in revenge for earlier murders [Italian]
vending machine *n* a machine that automatically dispenses food, drinks, etc. when money is inserted
vendor *n* **1** a person who sells goods such as newspapers or hamburgers from a stall or cart **2** *chiefly law* a person who sells property
veneer *n* **1** a thin layer of wood or plastic used to cover the surface of something made of cheaper material **2** a deceptive but convincing appearance: *nobody penetrated his veneer of modest charm* [Old French *fournir* to furnish]
venerable *adj* **1** (of a person) entitled to respect because of great age or wisdom **2** (of an object) impressive because it is old or important historically **3** *RC Church* a title given to a dead person who is going to be declared a saint **4** *Church of England* a title given to an archdeacon [Latin *venerari* to venerate]
venerate *vb* **-ating, -ated** to hold (someone) in deep respect [Latin *venerari*] **venerator** *n*
veneration *n* a feeling of awe or great respect: *George Gershwin is worthy of the veneration accorded his classical counterparts*
venereal (vin-**ear**-ee-al) *adj* **1** transmitted by sexual intercourse: *venereal infections* **2** of the genitals: *venereal warts* [Latin *venus* sexual love]
venereal disease *n* a disease, such as syphilis, transmitted by sexual intercourse
Venetian *adj* **1** of Venice, a port in NE Italy ▷ *n* **2** a person from Venice
Venetian blind *n* a window blind made of thin horizontal slats

V

vengeance *n* **1** the act of killing, injuring, or harming someone for revenge **2 with a vengeance** to a much greater extent or with much greater force than expected: *my career was beginning to take off with a vengeance* [Old French, from Latin *vindicare* to punish]
vengeful *adj* wanting revenge
venial (**veen**-ee-al) *adj* easily excused or forgiven: *venial sins* [Latin *venia* forgiveness]
venison *n* the flesh of a deer, used as food [Old French *venaison*]
Venn diagram *n maths* a drawing which uses circles to show the relationships between different sets [after John *Venn*, logician]
venom *n* **1** a feeling of great bitterness or anger towards someone **2** the poison that certain snakes and scorpions inject when they bite or sting [Latin *venenum* poison, love potion] **venomous** *adj* **venomously** *adv*
venous (**vee**-nuss) *adj* of or relating to veins [Latin *vena* vein]
vent[1] *n* **1** a small opening in something through which fresh air can enter and fumes can be released **2** the shaft of a volcano through which lava and gases erupt **3** the anal opening of a bird or other small animal **4 give vent to** to release (an emotion) in an outburst: *she gave vent to her misery and loneliness* ▷ *vb* **5** to release or express freely: *consumers vented their anger on the group by boycotting its products* **6** to make vents in [Old French *esventer* to blow out]
vent[2] *n* a vertical slit in the lower hem of a jacket [Latin *findere* to cleave]
ventilate *vb* **-lating, -lated 1** to let fresh air into (a room or building) **2** to discuss (ideas or feelings) openly: *people need a safe place to ventilate their feelings* [Latin *ventilare* to fan] **ventilation** *n*
ventilator *n* an opening or device, such as a fan, used to let fresh air into a room or building
ventral *adj* relating to the front part of the body [Latin *venter* abdomen] **ventrally** *adv*
ventricle *n anatomy* **1** a chamber of the heart that pumps blood to the arteries **2** any one of the four main cavities of the brain [Latin *ventriculus*] **ventricular** *adj*
ventriloquism *n* the ability to speak without moving the lips so that the words appear to come from another person or from another part of the room [Latin *venter* belly + *loqui* to speak] **ventriloquist** *n*
venture *n* **1** a project or activity that is risky or of uncertain outcome **2** a business operation in which there is the risk of loss as well as the opportunity for profit ▷ *vb* **-turing, -tured 3** to do something that involves risk or danger: *I thought it wise to venture into foreign trade* **4** to dare to express (an opinion) **5** to go to an unknown or dangerous place **6** to dare (to do something): *you have asked me so often to come to your place that I ventured to drop in* [variant of *adventure*] **venturer** *n*
venture capital *n* money provided for investment in new commercial enterprises **venture capitalist** *n*
Venture Scout *or* **Venturer** *n* a member of the senior branch of the Scouts

venturesome *adj* willing to take risks
venue *n* a place where an organized gathering, such as a concert or a sporting event, is held [Latin *venire* to come]
Venus *n* **1** the Roman goddess of love **2** the planet second nearest to the sun
Venus's flytrap *or* **Venus flytrap** *n* a plant that traps and digests insects between hinged leaves
veracious *adj* habitually truthful [Latin *verus* true]
veracity *n* **1** habitual truthfulness **2** accuracy
verandah *or* **veranda** *n* **1** an open porch attached to a house **2** NZ a continuous overhead canopy outside shops that gives shelter to pedestrians [Portuguese *varanda* railing]
verb *n* a word that is used to indicate the occurrence or performance of an action or the existence of a state, for example *run, make,* or *do* [Latin *verbum* word]
verbal *adj* **1** of or relating to words: *verbal skills* **2** spoken rather than written: *a verbal agreement* **3** *grammar* of or relating to a verb **verbally** *adv*
verbalism *n* an exaggerated emphasis on the importance of words
verbalize *or* **-lise** *vb* **-lizing, -lized** *or* **-lising, -lised** to express (an idea or feeling) in words
verbal noun *n grammar* a noun derived from a verb, for example *dancing* in the sentence *dancing is good for your health*
verbatim (verb-**bait**-im) *adv* **1** using exactly the same words: *I'll repeat it verbatim* ▹ *adj* **2** using exactly the same words: *a verbatim account* [Medieval Latin: word by word]
verbena *n* a plant with red, white, or purple sweet-smelling flowers [Latin: sacred bough used by the priest in religious acts]
verbiage *n* the excessive use of words [Latin *verbum* word]
verbose (verb-**bohss**) *adj* using more words than is necessary **verbosity** *n*
verdant *adj literary* covered with green vegetation [from Latin *viridis* green]
verdict *n* **1** the decision made by a jury about the guilt or innocence of a defendant **2** an opinion formed after examining the facts [Latin *vere dictum* truly spoken]
verdigris (ver-dig-reess) *n* a green or bluish coating which forms on copper, brass, or bronze that has been exposed to damp [Old French *vert de Grice* green of Greece]
verdure *n literary* flourishing green vegetation [from Latin *viridis* green]
verge[1] *n* **1** a grass border along a road **2 on the verge of** having almost reached (a point or condition) **3** an edge or rim ▹ *vb* **verging, verged** **4 verge on** to be near to: *she was verging on hysteria* [Latin *virga* rod]
verge[2] *vb* **verging, verged** to move in a specified direction: *verging towards the Irish Sea* [Latin *vergere*]
verger *n chiefly Church of England* **1** a church official who acts as caretaker **2** an official who carries the rod of office before a bishop or dean in ceremonies and processions [Latin *virga* rod, twig]
verify *vb* **-fies, -fying, -fied** **1** to check the truth of (something) by investigation **2** to prove (something) to be true [Latin *verus* true + *facere* to make] **verifiable** *adj* **verification** *n*
verily *adv literary* truly: *for verily, this was their destiny* [from *very*]
verisimilitude *n* the appearance of truth or reality [Latin *verus* true + *similitudo* similitude]
veritable *adj* rightly called; real: *a veritable mine of information* **veritably** *adv*
verity *n, pl* **-ties** a true statement or principle [Latin *verus* true]
vermicelli (ver-me-**chell**-ee) *n* **1** very fine strands of pasta, used in soups **2** tiny chocolate strands used as a topping for cakes or ice cream [Italian: little worms]
vermiform *adj* shaped like a worm
vermiform appendix *n anatomy* same as **appendix**
vermilion *adj* **1** orange-red ▹ *n* **2** mercuric sulphide, used as an orange-red pigment; cinnabar [Late Latin *vermiculus* insect from which red dye was prepared]
vermin *pl n* **1** small animals collectively, such as insects and rodents, that spread disease and damage crops **2** unpleasant people [Latin *vermis* worm] **verminous** *adj*
vermouth (ver-muth) *n* a wine flavoured with herbs [German *Wermut* wormwood]
vernacular (ver-**nak**-yew-lar) *n* **1** the commonly spoken language or dialect of a particular people or place ▹ *adj* **2** in or using the vernacular [Latin *vernaculus* belonging to a household slave]
vernal *adj* of or occurring in spring [Latin *ver* spring] **vernally** *adv*
vernier (ver-nee-er) *n* a small movable scale in certain measuring instruments such as theodolites, used to obtain a fractional reading of one of the divisions on the main scale [after Paul *Vernier*, mathematician]
veronica *n* a plant with small blue, pink, or white flowers [perhaps from the name *Veronica*]
verruca (ver-**roo**-ka) *n pathol* a wart, usually on the sole of the foot [Latin: wart]
versatile *adj* having many different skills or uses [Latin *versare* to turn] **versatility** *n*
verse *n* **1** a division of a poem or song **2** poetry as distinct from prose **3** one of the short sections into which chapters of the books of the Bible are divided **4** a poem [Latin *versus* furrow, literally: a turning (of the plough)]
versed *adj* **versed in** knowledgeable about or skilled in
versify *vb* **-fies, -fying, -fied** **1** to put (something) into verse **2** to write in verse [Latin *versus* verse + *facere* to make] **versification** *n* **versifier** *n*
version *n* **1** a form of something, such as a piece of writing, with some differences from other forms **2** an account of something from a certain point of view: *so far there's been no official version of the incident* **3** an adaptation, for example of a book or play into a film [Latin *vertere* to turn]
verso *n, pl* **-sos** **1** the left-hand page of a book **2** the back of a sheet of printed paper [New Latin *verso (folio)* (the leaf) having been turned]
versus *prep* **1** (in a sporting competition or lawsuit) against **2** in opposition to or in contrast with: *man versus machine* [Latin: turned (in the direction of), opposite]

vertebra (ver-tib-bra) *n, pl* **-brae** (-bree) one of the bony segments of the spinal column [Latin] **vertebral** *adj*

vertebrate *n* **1** an animal with a backbone, such as a fish, amphibian, reptile, bird, or mammal ▷ *adj* **2** having a backbone

vertex (ver-tex) *n, pl* **-tices** (-tiss-seez) **1** the highest point **2** *maths* **A** the point on a geometric figure where the sides form an angle **B** the highest point of a triangle [Latin: top]

vertical *adj* **1** at right angles to the horizon: *the vertical cliff* **2** straight up and down: *a vertical cut* **3** *econ* of or relating to associated or consecutive, though not identical, stages of industrial activity: *the purchase of a chain of travel agents by a leading tour operator will increase vertical integration in the holiday industry* ▷ *n* **4** a vertical line or direction [from Latin *vertex* top, pole of the sky] **vertically** *adv*

vertiginous *adj* producing dizziness

vertigo *n pathol* a sensation of dizziness felt because one's balance is disturbed, sometimes experienced when looking down from a high place [Latin: a whirling round]

vervain *n* a plant with long slender spikes of purple, blue, or white flowers [Latin *verbena* sacred bough]

verve *n* great enthusiasm or liveliness [Latin *verba* words, chatter]

very *adv* **1** used to add emphasis to adjectives and adverbs that are able to be graded: *I'm very happy; he'll be home very soon* ▷ *adj* **2** used with nouns to give emphasis or exaggerated intensity: *the very end of his visit; the very thing I need* [Old French *verai* true]

> **USAGE** In strict usage adverbs of degree such as *very, too, quite, really,* and *extremely* are used only to qualify adjectives: *he is very happy; she is too sad.* By this rule, these words should not be used to qualify past participles that follow the verb *to be,* since they would then be technically qualifying verbs. With the exception of certain participles, such as *tired* or *disappointed,* that have come to be regarded as adjectives, all other past participles are qualified by adverbs such as *much, greatly, seriously,* or *excessively: he has been much* (not *very*) *inconvenienced; she has been excessively* (not *too*) *criticized.*

very high frequency *n* a radio-frequency band lying between 30 and 300 megahertz

Very light *n* a coloured flare for signalling at night [after Edward W. *Very,* naval ordnance officer]

vesicle *n biol* **1** a small sac or cavity, esp. one filled with fluid **2** a blister [Latin *vesica* bladder, sac]

vespers *n* an evening service in some Christian churches [Latin *vesper* the evening star]

vessel *n* **1** a ship or large boat **2** an object used as a container for liquid **3** *biol* a tubular structure in animals and plants that carries body fluids, such as blood and sap [Latin *vas*]

vest *n* **1** *Brit* an undergarment covering the top half of the body **2** *US, Canad & Austral* a waistcoat ▷ *vb* **3** **vest in** to settle (power or property) on: *by the power vested in me, I pronounce you married* **4** **vest with** to bestow on: *the sponsorship has vested these matches with a new interest* [Latin *vestis* clothing]

vestal *adj* **1** chaste or pure ▷ *n* **2** *archaic, literary* a chaste woman [Latin *Vestalis* virgin priestess of the goddess Vesta]

vestal virgin *n* (in ancient Rome) one of the virgin priestesses dedicated to the goddess Vesta and to maintaining the sacred fire in her temple

vested *adj property law* having an existing right to the immediate or future possession of property

vested interest *n* **1** a strong personal interest someone has in a matter because he or she might benefit from it **2** *property law* an existing right to the immediate or future possession of property

vestibule *n* a small entrance hall [Latin *vestibulum*]

vestige (vest-ij) *n* **1** a small amount or trace **2** *biol* an organ or part that is a small nonfunctional remnant of a functional organ in an ancestor [Latin *vestigium* track]

vestigial (vest-ij-ee-al) *adj* remaining after a larger or more important thing has gone: *a strong seam of vestigial belief*

vestments *pl n* **1** ceremonial clothes worn by the clergy at religious services **2** robes that show authority or rank [Latin *vestire* to clothe]

vestry *n, pl* **-tries** a room in a church used as an office by the priest or minister [probably Old French *vestiarie* wardrobe]

vet[1] *n* **1** short for **veterinary surgeon** ▷ *vb* **vetting, vetted** **2** to make a careful check of (a person or document) for suitability: *guests have to be vetted and vouched for*

vet[2] *n US, Canad, Austral & NZ* short for **veteran**

vetch *n* **1** a climbing plant with blue or purple flowers **2** the beanlike fruit of the vetch, used as fodder [Latin *vicia*]

veteran *n* **1** a person who has given long service in some capacity **2** a soldier who has seen a lot of active service **3** a person who has served in the military forces ▷ *adj* **4** long-serving: *the veteran American politician* [Latin *vetus* old]

veteran car *n Brit & Austral* a car built before 1919, esp. before 1905

veterinarian *n US, Canad & Austral* a veterinary surgeon

veterinary *adj* relating to veterinary science [Latin *veterinae* draught animals]

veterinary medicine *or* **veterinary science** *n* the branch of medicine concerned with the treatment of animals

veterinary surgeon *n Brit* a person qualified to practise veterinary medicine

veto (vee-toe) *n, pl* **-toes** **1** the power to prevent legislation or action proposed by others: *no single state has a veto* **2** the exercise of this power ▷ *vb* **-toing, -toed** **3** to refuse consent to (a proposal, such as a government bill) **4** to prohibit or forbid: *the minister vetoed the appointments* [Latin: I forbid]

vex *vb* to cause (someone) to feel annoyance or irritation [Latin *vexare* to jolt (in carrying)] **vexing** *adj* **vexation** *n*

vexatious *adj* vexing

vexed *adj* **1** annoyed and puzzled **2** much debated: *the vexed question of pay*

VHF *or* **vhf** *radio* very high frequency
VI Vancouver Island
via *prep* **1** by way of; through: *they fled to London via Crete* **2** by means of: *we keep in touch via email* [Latin]
viable *adj* **1** able to be put into practice: *the party has failed to propose a viable alternative* **2** (of seeds or eggs) capable of growth **3** (of a fetus) sufficiently developed to survive outside the uterus [Latin *vita* life] **viability** *n*
viaduct *n* a bridge for carrying a road or railway across a valley [Latin *via* way + *ducere* to bring]
Viagra *n trademark* a drug that allows increased blood flow into the penis, used to treat impotence in men
vial *n* same as **phial** [Greek *phialē* a bowl]
viands *pl n old-fashioned* food [Latin *vivenda* things to be lived on]
viaticum *n, pl* **-ca** *or* **-cums** *Christianity* Holy Communion given to a person dying or in danger of death [Latin *viaticus* belonging to a journey]
vibes *pl n informal* **1** the emotional reactions between people **2** the atmosphere of a place **3** short for **vibraphone**
vibrant (**vibe**-rant) *adj* **1** full of energy and enthusiasm **2** (of a voice) rich and full of emotion **3** (of a colour) strong and bright [Latin *vibrare* to agitate] **vibrancy** *n*
vibraphone *n* a musical instrument with metal bars that resonate electronically when hit
vibrate *vb* **-brating, -brated 1** to move backwards and forwards rapidly **2** to have or produce a quivering or echoing sound **3** *physics* to undergo or cause to undergo vibration [Latin *vibrare*] **vibratory** *adj*
vibration *n* **1** a vibrating **2** *physics* **A** a periodic motion about an equilibrium position, such as in the production of sound **B** a single cycle of such a motion
vibrato *n, pl* **-tos** *music* a slight rapid fluctuation in the pitch of a note
vibrator *n* a device for producing a vibratory motion, used for massage or as a sex aid
viburnum (vie-**burn**-um) *n* a subtropical shrub with white flowers and berry-like fruits [Latin]
Vic. Victoria (Australian state)
vicar *n* **1** *Church of England* a priest who is in charge of a parish **2** *RC Church* a church officer acting as deputy to a bishop [Latin *vicarius* a deputy] **vicarial** *adj*
vicarage *n* the house where a vicar lives
vicar apostolic *n RC Church* a clergyman with authority in missionary countries
vicar general *n, pl* **vicars general** an official appointed to assist the bishop in his administrative duties
vicarious (vik-**air**-ee-uss) *adj* **1** felt indirectly by imagining what another person experiences: *vicarious satisfaction* **2** undergone or done as the substitute for another: *vicarious adventures* **3** delegated: *vicarious power* [Latin *vicarius* substituted] **vicariously** *adv*
Vicar of Christ *n RC Church* the Pope as Christ's representative on earth
vice¹ *n* **1** an immoral or evil habit or action: *greed is only one of their vices* **2** a habit regarded as a weakness in someone's character: *his only vice is an obsession with gadgets* **3** criminal activities involving sex, drugs, or gambling [Latin *vitium* a defect]
vice² *or US* **vise** *n* a tool with a pair of jaws for holding an object while work is done on it [Latin *vitis* vine, plant with spiralling tendrils]
vice³ *adj* serving in the place of; being next in importance to: *the vice chairman* [Latin *vicis* interchange]
vice admiral *n* a senior commissioned officer in certain navies
vice chancellor *n* the chief executive or administrator at a number of universities
vicegerent *n* a person appointed to exercise all or some of the authority of another [VICE³ + Latin *gerere* to manage]
vice president *n* an officer ranking immediately below a president and serving as his or her deputy **vice-presidency** *n*
viceregal *adj* **1** of a viceroy **2** *chiefly Austral & NZ* of a governor or governor general
viceroy *n* a governor of a colony or country who represents the monarch [VICE³ + French *roi* king]
vice squad *n* a police division responsible for the enforcement of gaming and prostitution laws
vice versa *adv* the other way round: *there were attacks on northerners by southerners and vice versa* [Latin: relations being reversed]
Vichy water (**vee**-shee) *n* a natural mineral water from Vichy in France which is supposed to be good for the health
vicinity (viss-**in**-it-ee) *n* the area immediately surrounding a place [Latin *vicinus* neighbouring]
vicious *adj* **1** cruel or violent: *vicious attacks* **2** forceful or ferocious: *she gave the chair a vicious jerk* **3** intended to cause hurt or distress: *vicious letters* **4** (of an animal) fierce or hostile [Latin *vitiosus* full of faults] **viciously** *adv* **viciousness** *n*
vicious circle *n* a situation in which an attempt to resolve one problem creates new problems that recreate the original one
vicissitudes (viss-**iss**-it-yewds) *pl n* changes in circumstance or fortune [Latin *vicis* change]
victim *n* **1** a person or thing that suffers harm or death **2** a person who is tricked or swindled **3** a living person or animal sacrificed in a religious rite [Latin *victima*]
victimize *or* **-mise** *vb* **-mizing, -mized** *or* **-mising, -mised** to punish or discriminate against (someone) selectively or unfairly **victimization** *or* **-misation** *n*
victor *n* **1** a person or nation that has defeated an enemy in war **2** the winner of a contest or struggle [Latin, from *vincere* to conquer]
victoria *n* **1** a large sweet red-and-yellow plum **2** a light four-wheeled horse-drawn carriage with a folding hood [after Queen *Victoria*]
Victoria Cross *n* the highest decoration for bravery in battle awarded to the British and Commonwealth armed forces
Victoria Day *n* the Monday preceding May 24: observed in Canada as a national holiday
Victorian *adj* **1** of or in the reign of Queen Victoria of Great Britain and Ireland (1837–1901) **2** characterized by prudery or hypocrisy **3** of or relating to Victoria (the state or any of the cities)

▷ *n* **4** a person who lived during the reign of Queen Victoria **5** an inhabitant of Victoria (the state or any of the cities)

Victoriana *pl n* objects of the Victorian period

victorious *adj* **1** having defeated an enemy or opponent: *the victorious allies* **2** of or characterized by victory: *a victorious smile*

victory *n, pl* **-ries** **1** the winning of a war or battle **2** success attained in a contest or struggle [Latin *victoria*]

victual *vb* **-tualling, -tualled** *or US* **-tualing, -tualed** *old-fashioned* to supply with or obtain victuals [Latin *victus* sustenance] **victualler** *or US* **-tualer** *n*

victuals (vit-tals) *pl n old-fashioned* food and drink

vicuna (vik-**kew**-na) *n* **1** a S American mammal like the llama **2** the fine cloth made from its wool [Spanish]

vide (**vie**-dee) see: used to direct a reader to a specified place in a text or in another book [Latin]

videlicet (vid-**deal**-ee-set) *adv* namely: used to specify items [Latin]

video *n, pl* **-os** **1** the recording and broadcasting of moving images using digital technology or (esp. formerly) video tape **2** a recording of moving images **3** short for **video cassette** **4** short for **video cassette recorder** ▷ *vb* **videoing, videoed** **5** to record (moving images) ▷ *adj* **6** relating to or used in recording moving images [Latin *videre* to see]

video cassette *n* a cassette containing video tape

video cassette recorder *n* a device for recording and playing back television programmes and films

video game *n* a game that involves moving images on a television or computer screen

video nasty *n* a film, usually specially made for video, that is explicitly horrific and pornographic

video recorder *n* short for **video cassette recorder**

video tape *n* **1** magnetic tape used mainly for recording the video-frequency signals of a television programme or film ▷ *vb* **video-tape, -taping, -taped** **2** to record (a film or programme) on video tape

vie *vb* **vying, vied** to compete (with someone): *the sisters vied with each other to care for her* [probably Old French *envier* to challenge]

V

Vietnamese *adj* **1** of Vietnam ▷ *n* **2** *pl* **-ese** a person from Vietnam **3** the language of Vietnam

view *n* **1** opinion, judgment, or belief: *in my view that doesn't really work* **2** an understanding of or outlook on something: *a specific view of human history* **3** everything that can be seen from a particular place or in a particular direction: *there was a beautiful view from the window* **4** vision or sight, esp. range of vision: *as they turned into the drive, the house came into view* **5** a picture of a scene **6** the act of seeing or observing **7** **in view of** taking into consideration **8** **on view** exhibited to the public **9** **take a dim** *or* **poor view of** to regard (something) unfavourably **10** **with a view to** with the intention of ▷ *vb* **11** to consider in a specified manner: *they viewed the visit with hardly disguised apprehension* **12** to examine or inspect (a house or flat) carefully with a view to buying it **13** to look at **14** to watch (television, videos, etc.) [Latin *videre* to see]

viewer *n* a person who views something, esp. television

viewfinder *n* a device on a camera that lets the user see what will be included in the photograph

viewpoint *n* **1** a person's attitude towards something **2** a place from which one gets a good view

vigil (**vij**-ill) *n* **1** a night-time period of staying awake to look after a sick person, pray, etc. **2** *RC Church & Church of England* the eve of certain major festivals [Latin: alert]

vigilance *n* careful attention

vigilant *adj* on the watch for trouble or danger [Latin *vigilare* to be watchful]

vigilante (vij-ill-**ant**-ee) *n* a person who takes it upon himself or herself to enforce the law [Spanish, from Latin *vigilare* to keep watch]

vignette (vin-**yet**) *n* **1** a short description of the typical features of something **2** a small decorative illustration in a book **3** a photograph or drawing with edges that are shaded off [French, literally: little vine (frequently used to embellish a text)]

vigorous *adj* **1** having physical or mental energy **2** displaying or performed with vigour: *vigorous exercise* **vigorously** *adv*

vigour *or US* **vigor** *n* **1** physical or mental energy: *the vigour of his invective astonished MPs* **2** strong healthy growth [Latin *vigor*]

Viking *n* any of the Scandinavians who raided by sea most of N and W Europe from the 8th to the 11th centuries [Old Norse *vīkingr*]

vile *adj* **1** morally wicked: *a vile regime* **2** disgusting: *the vile smell of the man* **3** unpleasant or bad: *I had a vile day at work* [Latin *vilis* cheap] **vilely** *adv* **vileness** *n*

vilify (**vill**-if-fie) *vb* **-fies, -fying, -fied** to speak very badly of (someone) [Latin *vilis* worthless + *facere* to make] **vilification** *n*

villa *n* **1** a large house with gardens **2** *Brit* a house rented to holiday-makers [Latin: a farmhouse]

village *n* **1** a small group of houses in a country area **2** the inhabitants of such a community [Latin *villa* a farmhouse] **villager** *n*

villain *n* **1** a wicked or evil person **2** the main wicked character in a novel or play [Late Latin *villanus* worker on a country estate]

villainous *adj* of or like a villain

villainy *n, pl* **-lainies** evil or vicious behaviour

villein (**vill**-an) *n* (in medieval Europe) a peasant who was directly subject to his lord, to whom he paid dues and services in return for his land [see VILLAIN] **villeinage** *n*

villus *n, pl* **villi** *zool & anatomy* **1** any of the numerous finger-like projections of the mucous membrane lining the small intestine of many vertebrates **2** any of the finger-like projections formed in the placenta of mammals [from Latin: shaggy hair]

vim *n informal* vigour and energy [Latin *vis* force]

vinaigrette *n* salad dressing made from oil and vinegar with seasonings [French]

vindaloo *n, pl* **-loos** a type of very spicy Indian dish [perhaps from Portuguese *vin d'alho* wine and garlic sauce]

vindicate *vb* **-cating, -cated 1** to clear (someone) of guilt or suspicion **2** to provide justification for: *the arrests may vindicate the strong-arm tactics* [Latin *vindex* claimant] **vindication** *n*

vindictive *adj* **1** maliciously seeking revenge **2** characterized by spite or ill will [Latin *vindicare* to avenge] **vindictively** *adv* **vindictiveness** *n*

vine *n* **1** a plant, such as the grapevine, with long flexible stems that climb by clinging to a support **2** the stem of such a plant [Latin *vinea* vineyard] **viny** *adj*

vinegar *n* **1** a sour-tasting liquid made by fermentation of beer, wine, or cider, used for salad dressing or for pickling **2** bad temper or spitefulness: *the vinegar in her pen is often a welcome seasoning to duller news* [French *vin* wine + *aigre* sour] **vinegary** *adj*

vineyard (vinn-yard) *n* an area of land where grapes are grown [Old English *wīngeard*]

vingt-et-un (van-tay-uhn) *n* same as **pontoon²** [French, literally: twenty-one]

viniculture *n* the process or business of growing grapes and making wine [Latin *vinum* wine + CULTURE] **viniculturist** *n*

vino (vee-noh) *n, pl* **-nos** *informal* wine [Spanish or Italian: wine]

vinous (vine-uss) *adj* of or characteristic of wine [Latin *vinum* wine]

vintage *n* **1** the wine obtained from a particular harvest of grapes **2** the harvest from which such a wine is obtained **3** a time of origin: *an open-necked shirt of uncertain vintage* ▹ *adj* **4** (of wine) of an outstandingly good year **5** representative of the best and most typical: *a vintage Saint Laurent dress* [Latin *vindemia*]

vintage car *n* a car built between 1919 and 1930

vintner *n* a wine merchant [Latin *vinetum* vineyard]

vinyl (vine-ill) *n* **1** any of various strong plastics made by the polymerization of vinyl compounds, such as PVC **2** musical records produced on vinyl discs ▹ *adj* **3** *chem* of or containing the monovalent group of atoms CH_2CH–: *vinyl chloride* **4** of or made of vinyl: *vinyl tiles* [Latin *vinum* wine]

viol (vie-oll) *n* a stringed musical instrument that preceded the violin [Old Provençal *viola*]

viola¹ (vee-**oh**-la) *n* a bowed stringed instrument of the violin family, slightly larger and lower in pitch than the violin [Italian]

viola² (vie-ol-la) *n* a variety of pansy [Latin: violet]

viola da gamba (vee-**oh**-la da **gam**-ba) *n* the second largest and lowest member of the viol family [Italian, literally: viol for the leg]

violate *vb* **-lating, -lated 1** to break (a law or agreement): *he violated export laws* **2** to disturb rudely or improperly: *these men who were violating her privacy* **3** to treat (a sacred place) disrespectfully **4** to rape [Latin *violare* to do violence to] **violation** *n* **violator** *n*

violence *n* **1** the use of physical force, usually intended to cause injury or destruction **2** great force or strength in action, feeling, or expression [Latin *violentus* violent]

violent *adj* **1** using or involving physical force with the intention of causing injury or destruction: *violent clashes with government supporters* **2** very intense: *I took a violent dislike to him* **3** sudden and forceful: *a violent explosion* **violently** *adv*

violet *n* **1** a plant with bluish-purple flowers ▹ *adj* **2** bluish-purple [Latin *viola*]

violin *n* a musical instrument, the highest member of the violin family, with four strings played with a bow [Italian *violino* a little viola]

violinist *n* a person who plays the violin

violist (vee-**oh**-list) *n* a person who plays the viola

violoncello (vie-oll-on-**chell**-oh) *n, pl* **-los** same as **cello** [Italian]

VIP very important person

viper *n* a type of poisonous snake [Latin *vipera*]

virago (vir-**rah**-go) *n, pl* **-goes** *or* **-gos** *archaic* an aggressive woman [Latin: a manlike maiden]

viral (vie-ral) *adj* **1** of or caused by a virus ▹ *adv* **2 go viral** (of an image, video, story, etc.) to spread quickly and widely among internet users ▹ *n* **3** an image, video, story, etc. that is spread quickly and widely via the internet

virgin *n* **1** a person who has never had sexual intercourse **2** a person who is inexperienced in a specified field: *a ski virgin* ▹ *adj* **3** not having had sexual intercourse **4** fresh and unused: *he found a scrap of virgin paper in a sea of memoranda* **5** not yet cultivated, explored, or exploited by people: *virgin territory* [Latin *virgo*]

Virgin *n* **1 the Virgin** same as **Virgin Mary** **2** a statue or picture of the Virgin Mary

virginal¹ *adj* **1** like a virgin **2** extremely pure or fresh

virginal² *n* an early keyboard instrument like a small harpsichord [probably Latin *virginalis* virginal, perhaps because it was played largely by young women]

Virgin Birth *n Christianity* the doctrine that Jesus Christ was conceived solely by the direct intervention of the Holy Spirit so that Mary remained a virgin

Virginia creeper *n* a climbing plant with leaves that turn red in autumn

virginity *n* the condition or fact of being a virgin

Virgin Mary *n* **the Virgin Mary** *Christianity* Mary, the mother of Christ

Virgo *n astrol* the sixth sign of the zodiac; the Virgin [Latin]

virile *adj* **1** having the traditional male characteristics of physical strength and a high sex drive **2** forceful and energetic: *a virile Highland fling* [Latin *virilis* manly] **virility** *n*

virology *n* the branch of medicine concerned with the study of viruses **virological** *adj*

virtual *adj* **1** having the effect but not the appearance or form of: *the investigation has now come to a virtual standstill* **2** *computers* designed so as to extend the potential of a finite system beyond its immediate limits: *virtual memory* **3** of or relating to virtual reality [Latin *virtus* virtue]

virtually *adv* almost or nearly: *he is virtually a prisoner in his own palace*

virtual reality *n* a computer-generated environment that seems real to the user

virtue *n* **1** moral goodness **2** a positive moral quality: *the virtue of humility* **3** an advantage or benefit: *the added virtue of being harmless* **4** chastity, esp. in women **5 by virtue of** by reason of; because of: *they escaped execution by virtue of their high rank* [Latin *virtus* manliness, courage]

virtuoso *n, pl* **-si** *or* **-sos 1** a person with exceptional musical skill **2** a person with exceptional skill in any area ▷ *adj* **3** showing exceptional skill or brilliance: *a virtuoso performance* [Italian: skilled] **virtuosity** *n*

virtuous *adj* morally good **virtuously** *adv*

virulent (vir-yew-lent) *adj* **1** extremely bitter or hostile **2 A** (of a microorganism) very infectious **B** (of a disease) having a violent effect **3** extremely poisonous or harmful: *the most virulent poison known to humanity* [Latin *virulentus* full of poison] **virulence** *n*

virus *n* **1** a microorganism that is smaller than a bacterium and can cause disease in humans, animals, or plants **2** *informal* a disease caused by a virus **3** *computers* an unsanctioned and self-replicating program which, when activated, corrupts a computer's data and disables its operating system [Latin: slime, poisonous liquid]

visa *n* an official stamp in a passport permitting its holder to travel into or through the country of the government issuing it [Latin: things seen]

visage (viz-zij) *n chiefly literary* **1** face **2** appearance [Latin *visus* appearance]

vis-à-vis (veez-ah-vee) *prep* in relation to [French: face-to-face]

viscera (viss-er-a) *pl n anatomy* the large internal organs of the body collectively [Latin: entrails]

visceral *adj* **1** of or affecting the viscera **2** instinctive rather than rational: *visceral hatred of the neighbours*

viscid (viss-id) *adj* sticky [Latin *viscum* mistletoe, birdlime]

viscose *n* **1** a sticky solution obtained by dissolving cellulose **2** rayon made from this material [Latin *viscum* birdlime]

viscosity *n, pl* **-ties 1** the state of being viscous **2** *physics* the extent to which a fluid resists a tendency to flow

viscount (vie-count) *n* (in the British Isles) a nobleman ranking below an earl and above a baron [Old French *visconte*] **viscountcy** *n*

V

viscountess (vie-count-iss) *n* **1** a woman holding the rank of viscount **2** the wife or widow of a viscount

viscous *adj* (of liquids) thick and sticky

vise *n US* same as **vice²**

Vishnu *n* a Hindu god, the Preserver

visibility *n* **1** the range or clarity of vision: *visibility was good, despite rain* **2** the condition of being visible

visible *adj* **1** able to be seen **2** able to be perceived by the mind: *a visible and flagrant act of aggression* [Latin *visibilis*] **visibly** *adv*

vision *n* **1** the ability to see **2** a vivid mental image produced by the imagination: *I kept having visions of her getting lost* **3** a hallucination caused by divine inspiration, madness, or drugs: *visions of angels* **4** great perception of future developments: *what he had instead of charisma was vision* **5** the image on a television screen **6** a person or thing of extraordinary beauty [Latin *visio* sight, from *videre* to see]

visionary *adj* **1** showing foresight: *a visionary leader* **2** idealistic but impractical **3** given to having visions **4** of or like visions ▷ *n, pl* **-naries 5** a visionary person

visit *vb* **-siting, -sited 1** to go or come to see (a person or place) **2** to stay with (someone) as a guest **3** *old-fashioned* (of a disease or disaster) to afflict **4 visit on** *or* **upon** to inflict (punishment) on **5 visit with** *US informal* to chat with (someone) ▷ *n* **6** the act or an instance of visiting **7** a professional or official call **8** a stay as a guest [Latin *visitare* to go to see]

visitant *n* **1** a ghost or apparition **2** a migratory bird temporarily resting in a particular region

visitation *n* **1** an official visit or inspection **2** a punishment or reward from heaven **3** an appearance of a supernatural being

Visitation *n* **A** the visit made by the Virgin Mary to her cousin Elizabeth (Luke 1: 39–56) **B** the Church festival commemorating this, held on July 2

visiting hours *pl n* the times when visitors are allowed to see someone in a hospital or other institution: *many prisoners' wives complain about the short visiting hours*

visitor *n* a person who visits a person or place

visitor's passport *n* a British passport, valid for one year, that grants access to some countries, usually for a restricted period

visor (vize-or) *n* **1** a transparent flap on a helmet that can be pulled down to protect the face **2** a small movable screen attached above the windscreen in a vehicle, used as protection against the glare of the sun **3** a peak on a cap [Old French *vis* face]

vista *n* **1** an extensive view **2** a wide range of possibilities or future events: *the vista of opportunity* [Italian]

visual *adj* **1** done by or used in seeing **2** capable of being seen [Latin *visus* sight] **visually** *adv*

visual aids *pl n* objects to be looked at that help the viewer to understand or remember something

visual display unit *n computers* a device with a screen for displaying data held in a computer

visualize *or* **-lise** *vb* **-lizing, -lized** *or* **-lising, -lised** to form a mental image of (something not at that moment visible) **visualization** *or* **-lisation** *n*

vital *adj* **1** essential or highly important: *marriage isn't such a vital part of his life* **2** energetic or lively: *the epitome of vital youthful manhood* **3** necessary to maintain life: *the vital organs* ▷ *n* **4 vitals** the bodily organs, such as the brain and heart, that are necessary to maintain life [Latin *vita* life] **vitally** *adv*

vitality *n* physical or mental energy

vitalize *or* **-lise** *vb* **-lizing, -lized** *or* **-lising, -lised** to fill with life or vitality **vitalization** *or* **-lisation** *n*

vital statistics *pl n* **1** population statistics, such as the numbers of births, marriages, and deaths **2** *informal* the measurements of a woman's bust, waist, and hips

vitamin *n* one of a group of substances that occur naturally in certain foods and are essential for normal health and growth [from Latin *vita* life + AMINE]

vitiate (vish-ee-ate) *vb* **-ating, -ated 1** to spoil or weaken the effectiveness of (something) **2** to destroy the legal effect of (a contract) [Latin *vitiare* to injure] **vitiation** *n*

viticulture *n* the cultivation of grapevines [Latin *vitis* vine]

vitreous *adj* **1** of or like glass **2** of or relating to the vitreous humour [Latin *vitrum* glass]

vitreous humour *or* **vitreous body** *n* a transparent gelatinous substance that fills the eyeball between the lens and the retina

vitrify *vb* **-fies, -fying, -fied** to change into glass or a glassy substance **vitrification** *n*

vitriol *n* **1** language expressing bitterness and hatred **2** sulphuric acid [Latin *vitrum* glass, referring to the glossy appearance of the sulphates]

vitriolic *adj* (of language) severely bitter or harsh

vituperative (vite-tyew-pra-tiv) *adj* bitterly abusive [Latin *vituperare* to blame] **vituperation** *n*

viva¹ *interj* long live (a specified person or thing) [Italian, literally: may (he or she) live!]

viva² *Brit* ▷ *n* **1** an examination in the form of an interview ▷ *vb* **vivaing, vivaed 2** to examine (a candidate) in a spoken interview [from VIVA VOCE]

vivace (viv-vah-chee) *adj music* to be performed in a lively manner [Italian]

vivacious *adj* full of energy and enthusiasm [Latin *vivax* lively]

vivacity *n* the quality of being vivacious

vivarium *n, pl* **-riums** *or* **-ria** a place where live animals are kept under natural conditions [Latin *vivus* alive]

viva voce (vive-a voh-chee) *adv, adj* **1** by word of mouth ▷ *n* **2** same as **viva²** (sense 1) [Medieval Latin, literally: with living voice]

vivid *adj* **1** very bright: *a vivid blue sky* **2** very clear and detailed: *vivid memories* **3** easily forming lifelike images: *a vivid imagination* [Latin *vividus* animated] **vividly** *adv* **vividness** *n*

vivify *vb* **-fies, -fying, -fied 1** to bring to life **2** to make more vivid or striking [Latin *vivus* alive + *facere* to make]

viviparous (viv-vip-a-russ) *adj* giving birth to living offspring, as most mammals do [Latin *vivus* alive + *parere* to bring forth]

vivisection *n* the performing of experiments on living animals, involving cutting into or dissecting the body [Latin *vivus* living + *sectio* a cutting] **vivisectionist** *n*

vixen *n* **1** a female fox **2** *Brit, Austral & NZ derogatory* a spiteful woman [related to Old English *fyxe*, feminine of *fox*]

viz *adv* namely: used to specify items: *I had only one object, viz, to win the trophy* [abbreviated from Latin *videlicet* namely]

vizier (viz-zeer) *n* a high official in certain Muslim countries [Turkish *vezīr*]

vizor *n* same as **visor**

VLF *or* **vlf** *radio* very low frequency

vlog *n* **1** a video journal uploaded to the internet ▷ *vb* **vlogging, vlogged 2** to create and upload vlogs **vlogger** *n* **vlogging** *n*

V neck *n* **A** a neck on a garment that comes down to a point, like the letter V **B** a sweater with a neck like this **V-neck** *or* **V-necked** *adj*

vocab *n* short for **vocabulary**

vocable *n linguistics* a word regarded simply as a sequence of letters or spoken sounds [Latin *vocare* to call]

vocabulary *n, pl* **-laries 1** all the words that a person knows **2** all the words contained in a language **3** the specialist terms used in a given subject **4** a list of words in another language with their translations **5** a range of symbols or techniques as used in any of the arts or crafts: *the building's vocabulary of materials, textures, and tones* [Latin *vocabulum* vocable]

vocal *adj* **1** of or relating to the voice: *vocal pitch* **2** expressing one's opinions clearly and openly: *a vocal minority with racist views* ▷ *n* **3 vocals** the singing part of a piece of jazz or pop music [Latin *vox* voice] **vocally** *adv*

vocal cords *pl n* either of two pairs of membranous folds in the larynx, of which the lower pair can be made to vibrate and produce sound by forcing air from the lungs over them

vocalist *n* a singer with a pop group

vocalize *or* **-lise** *vb* **-lizing, -lized** *or* **-lising, -lised 1** to express with or use the voice **2** to make vocal or articulate: *vocalize your discontent* **3** *phonetics* to articulate (a speech sound) with voice **vocalization** *or* **-lisation** *n*

vocation *n* **1** a specified profession or trade **2 A** a special urge to a particular calling or career, esp. a religious one **B** such a calling or career [Latin *vocare* to call]

vocational *adj* directed towards a particular profession or trade: *vocational training*

vocative *n grammar* a grammatical case used in some languages when addressing a person or thing [Latin *vocare* to call]

vociferate *vb* **-rating, -rated** to exclaim or cry out about (something) noisily [Latin *vox* voice + *ferre* to bear] **vociferation** *n*

vociferous *adj* loud and forceful: *a vociferous minority* **vociferously** *adv*

VOD video on demand: a system that allows a television viewer to select content and view it at a time of his or her own choosing

vodka *n* a clear alcoholic spirit originating in Russia, made from potatoes or grain [Russian]

voetsak *or* **voetsek** (foot-sak) *interj S African offensive, informal* an expression of dismissal or rejection [Afrikaans, from Dutch *voort se ek* forward, I say, commonly applied to animals]

vogue *n* **1** the popular style at a given time **2 in vogue** fashionable ▷ *adj* **3** fashionable: *a vogue word* [French] **voguish** *adj*

voice *n* **1** the sound made by the vibration of the vocal cords, esp. when modified by the tongue and mouth **2** a distinctive tone of the speech sounds characteristic of a particular person: *he can recognize her voice* **3** the ability to speak or sing: *he had at last found his voice* **4** the condition or quality of a person's voice: *her voice was kind* **5** the musical sound of a singing voice: *what I have is a good voice and a great love of lyrics* **6** the expression of feeling or opinion: *there was a chorus of dissenting voices* **7** a right to express an opinion: *the party should now move towards a system which will give every member an equal voice* **8** *grammar* a category of the verb that expresses whether it is active or passive **9** *phonetics* the sound characterizing the articulation of several speech sounds, that is produced when the vocal cords are vibrated by the breath **10 with one voice** unanimously ▷ *vb* **voicing, voiced 11** to express verbally: *anyone with an objection has a chance to voice it* **12** to articulate (a speech sound) with voice [Latin *vox*]

voiced *adj phonetics* articulated with accompanying vibration of the vocal cords, for example 'b' in English

voiceless *adj* **1** without a voice **2** *phonetics* articulated without accompanying vibration of the vocal cords, for example 'p' in English

voice mail *n* an electronic system for the transfer and storage of telephone messages, which can then be dealt with by the user at his or her convenience

voice-over *n* the voice of an unseen commentator heard during a film

void *n* **1** a feeling or condition of loneliness or deprivation **2** an empty space or area ▷ *adj* **3** having no official value or authority, because the terms have been broken or have not been fulfilled: *the race was declared void and rerun* **4** *old-fashioned or literary* empty: *behold, the tomb is void!* **5 void of** devoid of or without: *the fact of being punished becomes void of all moral significance* ▷ *vb* **6** to make ineffective or invalid **7** to empty **8** to discharge the contents of (the bowels or bladder) [Latin *vacare* to be empty]

voile (voyl) *n* a light semitransparent dress fabric [French: veil]

VoIP *n* Voice over Internet Protocol: a system for converting analogue signals to digital so that telephone calls may be made over the internet

vol. volume

volatile (voll-a-tile) *adj* **1** (of circumstances) liable to sudden change **2** (of people) liable to sudden changes of mood and behaviour **3** (of a substance) changing quickly from a solid or liquid form to a vapour [Latin *volare* to fly] **volatility** *n*

V

volatilize *or* **-lise** *vb* **-lizing, -lized** *or* **-lising, -lised** to change from a solid or liquid to a vapour **volatilization** *or* **-lisation** *n*

vol-au-vent (voll-oh-von) *n* a very light puff pastry case with a savoury filling [French, literally: flight in the wind]

volcanic *adj* **1** of or relating to volcanoes: *volcanic ash* **2** displaying sudden violence or anger: *their boisterous and often volcanic behaviour*

volcano *n, pl* **-noes** *or* **-nos 1** an opening in the earth's crust from which molten lava, ashes, dust, and gases are ejected from below the earth's surface **2** a mountain formed from volcanic material ejected from a vent [Italian, from Latin *Volcanus* Vulcan, Roman god of fire]

vole *n* a small rodent with a stocky body and a short tail [short for *volemouse*, from Old Norse *vollr* field + *mus* mouse]

volition *n* **1** the ability to decide things for oneself **2 of one's own volition** through one's own choice [Latin *volo* I will] **volitional** *adj*

volley *n* **1** the simultaneous firing of several weapons **2** the bullets fired **3** a burst of questions or critical comments **4** *sport* a stroke or kick at a moving ball before it hits the ground ▷ *vb* **5** to fire (weapons) in a volley **6** *sport* to hit or kick (a moving ball) before it hits the ground [French *volée* a flight]

volleyball *n* a game in which two teams hit a large ball backwards and forwards over a high net with their hands

volt *n* the SI unit of electric potential; the potential difference between two points on a conductor carrying a current of 1 ampere, when the power dissipated between these points is 1 watt [after Count Alessandro *Volta*, physicist]

voltage *n* an electromotive force or potential difference expressed in volts

voltaic *adj* same as **galvanic** (sense 1)

volte-face (volt-**fass**) *n, pl* **volte-face** a reversal of opinion [Italian *volta* turn + *faccia* face]

voltmeter *n* an instrument for measuring voltage

voluble *adj* talking easily and at length [Latin *volubilis* turning readily] **volubility** *n* **volubly** *adv*

volume *n* **1** the magnitude of the three-dimensional space enclosed within or occupied by something **2** an amount or total: *the volume of trade between the two countries; the volume of military traffic* **3** loudness of sound **4** the control on a radio, etc. for adjusting the loudness of sound **5** a book: *a slim volume* **6** one of several books that make up a series **7** a set of issues of a magazine over a specified period [Latin *volumen* a roll]

volumetric *adj* of or using measurement by volume: *a simple volumetric measurement*

voluminous *adj* **1** (of clothes) large and roomy **2** (of writings) extensive and detailed

voluntary *adj* **1** done or undertaken by free choice: *voluntary repatriation* **2** done or maintained without payment: *voluntary work* **3** (of muscles) having their action controlled by the will ▷ *n, pl* **-taries 4** *music* a composition, usually for organ, played at the beginning or end of a church service [Latin *voluntarius*] **voluntarily** *adv*

volunteer *n* **1** a person who offers voluntarily to do something **2** a person who freely undertakes military service ▷ *vb* **3** to offer (oneself or one's services) by choice and without being forced **4** to enlist voluntarily for military service **5** to give (information) willingly **6** to offer the services of (another person)

voluptuary *n, pl* **-aries** a person devoted to luxury and sensual pleasures [Latin *voluptas* pleasure]

voluptuous *adj* **1** (of a woman) sexually alluring because of the fullness of her figure **2** pleasing to the senses: *voluptuous yellow peaches* **voluptuously** *adv* **voluptuousness** *n*

volute *n* a spiral or twisting shape or object, such as a carved spiral scroll on an Ionic capital [Latin *volvere* to roll up]

vomit *vb* **-iting, -ited 1** to eject (the contents of the stomach) through the mouth **2** to eject or be ejected forcefully ▷ *n* **3** the partly digested food and drink ejected in vomiting [Latin *vomitare* to vomit repeatedly]

voodoo *n* **1** a religion involving ancestor worship and witchcraft, practised by some people in the West Indies, esp. in Haiti ▷ *adj* **2** of or relating to voodoo: *a voodoo curse* [from West African]

voorkamer (foor-kahm-er) *n S African* the front room of a house [Afrikaans]

voracious *adj* **1** eating or craving great quantities of food **2** very eager or insatiable in some activity: *a voracious collector* [Latin *vorare* to devour] **voraciously** *adv* **voracity** *n*

vortex (vor-tex) *n, pl* **-tices** (-tiss-seez) **1** a whirling mass or motion, such as a whirlpool or whirlwind **2** a situation which draws people into it against their will: *the vortex of other people's problems* [Latin: a whirlpool] **vortical** *adj*

votary *n, pl* **-ries 1** *RC Church & Eastern churches* a person who has dedicated himself or herself to religion by taking vows **2** a person devoted to a cause [Latin *votum* a vow] **votaress** *fem n*

vote *n* **1** a choice made by a participant in a shared decision, esp. in electing a candidate **2** the right to vote **3** the total number of votes cast **4** the opinion of a group of people as determined by voting: *the draft should be put to the vote at a meeting of the Council* **5** a body of votes or voters collectively: *the youth vote* ▷ *vb* **voting, voted 6** to make a choice by vote **7** to authorize or allow by voting: *the organizing committee voted itself controversial new powers* **8** to declare oneself as being (something or in favour of something) by voting: *I've always voted Labour* **9** *informal* to declare by common opinion: *he was voted hotelier of the year for the third time* [Latin *votum* a solemn promise]

vote down *vb* to decide against or defeat in a vote: *a proposed British resolution was voted down*

voter *n* a person who can or does vote

votive *adj* done or given to fulfil a vow [Latin *votivus* promised by a vow]

vouch *vb* **vouch for A** to give personal assurance about: *I can vouch for the man, he's a relative by marriage* **B** to give supporting evidence for or be proof of: *his presence alone vouches for the political nature of the trip* [Latin *vocare* to call]

voucher *n* **1** a ticket or card used instead of money to buy specified goods: *a gift voucher* **2** a document recording a financial transaction [Old French *vo(u)cher* to summon]

vouchsafe *vb* **-safing, -safed 1** *old-fashioned* to give or grant: *she has powers vouchsafed to few* **2** to offer assurances about; guarantee: *he absolutely vouchsafed your integrity* [vouch + safe]

vow *n* **1** a solemn and binding promise **2 take vows** to enter a religious order and commit oneself to its rule of life by the vows of poverty, chastity, and obedience ▷ *vb* **3** to promise or decide solemnly: *she vowed to fight on; I solemnly vowed that some day I would return to live in Europe* [Latin *votum*]

vowel *n* **A** a voiced speech sound made with the mouth open and the stream of breath unobstructed by the tongue, teeth, or lips, for example *a* or *e* **B** a letter representing this [Latin *vocalis (littera)*, from *vox* voice]

vox pop *n Brit* interviews with members of the public on a radio or television programme

vox populi *n* public opinion [Latin: the voice of the people]

voyage *n* **1** a long journey by sea or in space ▷ *vb* **-aging, -aged 2** to go on a voyage: *in this story he voyages to Ireland* [Latin *viaticum* provision for travelling] **voyager** *n*

voyageur (voy-ahzh-ur) *n* **1** (formerly) a French or Métis canoeman who transported furs from trading posts in the North American interior **2** (in Canada) a woodsman, guide, trapper, boatman, or explorer, esp. in the North [French: voyager]

voyeur *n* a person who obtains sexual pleasure from watching people undressing or having sexual intercourse [French, literally: one who sees] **voyeurism** *n* **voyeuristic** *adj*

VPL *humorous* visible panty line

VPN virtual private network: a network that uses the internet to transfer information using secure methods

VR virtual reality

vrou (froh) *n S African* an Afrikaner woman, esp. a married woman [Afrikaans]

vs versus

VSA (in New Zealand) Voluntary Service Abroad

V-sign *n* **1** (in Britain and Australia) an offensive gesture made by sticking up the index and middle fingers with the palm of the hand inwards **2** a similar gesture with the palm outwards meaning victory or peace

VSO (in Britain) Voluntary Service Overseas

VSOP very special (*or* superior) old pale: used of brandy or port

VT Vermont

VTOL vertical takeoff and landing

Vulcan *n* the Roman god of fire

vulcanite *n* a hard black rubber produced by vulcanizing natural rubber with sulphur

vulcanize *or* **-nise** *vb* **-nizing, -nized** *or* **-nising, -nised** to treat (rubber) with sulphur under heat and pressure to improve elasticity and strength [after *Vulcan*, Roman god of fire] **vulcanization** *or* **-nisation** *n*

vulgar *adj* **1** showing lack of good taste, decency, or refinement: *vulgar tabloid sensationalism* **2** denoting a form of a language spoken by the ordinary people, rather than the literary form [Latin *vulgus* the common people] **vulgarly** *adv*

vulgar fraction *n* same as **simple fraction**

vulgarian *n* a vulgar person, usually one who is rich

vulgarism *n* a coarse or obscene word or phrase

vulgarity *n, pl* **-ties 1** the condition of being vulgar **2** a vulgar action or phrase

vulgarize *or* **-rise** *vb* **-rizing, -rized** *or* **-rising, -rised 1** to make vulgar **2** to make (something little known or difficult to understand) popular **vulgarization** *or* **-risation** *n*

Vulgar Latin *n* any of the dialects of Latin spoken in the Roman Empire other than classical Latin

Vulgate *n* the fourth-century Latin version of the Bible

vulnerable *adj* **1** able to be physically or emotionally hurt **2** easily influenced or tempted **3** *military* exposed to attack **4** financially weak and likely to fail: *this company could be vulnerable in a prolonged economic slump* **5** *bridge* (of a side that has won one game towards rubber) subject to increased bonuses or penalties [Latin *vulnus* a wound] **vulnerability** *n*

vulpine *adj* **1** of or like a fox **2** clever and cunning [Latin *vulpes* fox]

vulture *n* **1** a very large bird of prey that feeds on flesh of dead animals **2** a person who profits from the misfortune and weakness of others [Latin *vultur*]

vulva *n* the external genitals of human females [Latin: covering, womb, matrix]

vuvuzela *n S African* an elongated plastic instrument that football fans blow to make a loud trumpeting noise [from Zulu]

vying *vb* the present participle of **vie**

V

Ww

w *cricket* **A** wicket **B** wide
W **1** *chem* tungsten **2** watt **3** West(ern)
WA **1** Washington (state) **2** Western Australia
wacko *informal, chiefly US & Canad* ▷ *adj* **1** mad or eccentric ▷ *n, pl* **wackos** **2** a mad or eccentric person [from WACKY]
wacky *adj* **wackier, wackiest** *slang* odd, eccentric, or crazy: *a wacky idea* [dialect: a fool] **wackiness** *n*
wad *n* **1** a small mass of soft material, such as cotton wool, used for packing or stuffing **2** a roll or bundle of banknotes or papers [Late Latin *wadda*]
wadding *n* a soft material used for padding or stuffing
waddle *vb* **-dling, -dled** **1** to walk with short steps, rocking slightly from side to side ▷ *n* **2** a swaying walk [from *wade*]
waddy *n, pl* **-dies** a heavy wooden club used by Aboriginal Australians
wade *vb* **wading, waded** **1** to walk slowly and with difficulty through water or mud **2** **wade in** *or* **into** to begin doing (something) in an energetic way: *wading into the fray* **3** **wade through** to proceed with difficulty through: *a stack of literature to wade through* [Old English *wadan*]
wader *n* a long-legged bird, such as the heron or stork, that lives near water and feeds on fish. Also called: **wading bird**
waders *pl n* long waterproof boots which completely cover the legs, worn by anglers for standing in water
wadi (wod-dee) *n, pl* **-dies** a river in N Africa or Arabia, which is dry except in the rainy season [Arabic]
wafer *n* **1** a thin crisp sweetened biscuit, often served with ice cream **2** *Christianity* a round thin piece of unleavened bread used at Communion **3** *electronics* a small thin slice of germanium or silicon that is separated into numerous individual components or circuits [Old French *waufre*]
wafer-thin *adj* very thin: *wafer-thin meat*
waffle[1] *n* a square crisp pancake with a gridlike pattern [Dutch *wafel*]
waffle[2] *informal, chiefly Brit, Austral & NZ* ▷ *vb* **-fling, -fled** **1** to speak or write in a vague and wordy manner ▷ *n* **2** vague and wordy speech or writing [origin unknown]
waft *vb* **1** to move gently through the air as if being carried by the wind: *the scent of summer flowers gently wafting through my window* ▷ *n* **2** a scent carried on the air [Middle Dutch *wachter* guard]
wag[1] *vb* **wagging, wagged** **1** to move rapidly and repeatedly from side to side or up and down: *Franklin wagged his tail* ▷ *n* **2** an instance of wagging [Old English *wagian*]
wag[2] *n old-fashioned* a humorous or witty person [origin unknown] **waggish** *adj*
Wag *n informal* the wife or girlfriend of a famous sportsperson [from *w(ives) a(nd) g(irlfriends)*]
wage *n* **1** Also: **wages** the money paid in return for a person's work, esp. when paid weekly or daily rather than monthly: *a campaign for higher wages* ▷ *vb* **waging, waged** **2** to engage in (a campaign or war) [Old French *wagier* to pledge]
wager *n* **1** a bet on the outcome of an event or activity ▷ *vb* **2** to bet (something, esp. money) on the outcome of an event or activity [Old French *wagier* to pledge]
waggle *vb* **-gling, -gled** to move with a rapid shaking or wobbling motion [from WAG[1]]
wagon *or* **waggon** *n* **1** a four-wheeled vehicle used for carrying heavy loads, sometimes pulled by a horse or tractor **2** an open railway freight truck **3** a lorry **4** **on the wagon** *informal* abstaining from alcoholic drink [Dutch *wagen*] **wagoner** *or* **waggoner** *n*
wagtail *n* a small songbird of Eurasia and Africa with a very long tail that wags up and down when it walks
Wagyu (wag-yoo) *n* **1** any of several Japanese breeds of beef cattle, raised to produce Kobe beef **2** another name for **Kobe beef** [Japanese]
wahine (wah-hee-nay) *n NZ* a Māori woman, esp. a wife [Māori]
wahoo *n* a large food and game fish of tropical seas
waif *n* a person, esp. a child, who is, or who looks as if he or she might be, homeless or neglected [Anglo-Norman]
wail *vb* **1** to utter a prolonged high-pitched cry of pain or sorrow ▷ *n* **2** a prolonged high-pitched cry of pain or sorrow [from Old Norse] **wailing** *n, adj*
wain *n poetic* a farm cart [Old English *wægn*]
wainscot *n* a wooden covering on the lower half of the walls of a room. Also: **wainscoting** [Middle Low German *wagenschot*]
waist *n* **1** *anatomy* the narrow part of the body between the ribs and the hips **2** the part of a garment covering the waist [origin unknown]
waistband *n* a band of material sewn on to the waist of a garment to strengthen it
waistcoat *n* a sleeveless upper garment which buttons up the front and is usually worn by men over a shirt and under a jacket
waistline *n* **1** an imaginary line around the body at the narrowest part of the waist **2** the place where the upper and lower part of a garment are joined together
wait *vb* **1** to stay in one place or remain inactive in expectation of something: *the delegates have to wait for a reply* **2** to be temporarily delayed: *the celebrations can wait* **3** (of a thing) to be ready or be in store: *waiting for her on the library table was the latest Jilly Cooper novel* ▷ *n* **4** the act or a period of waiting **5** **lie in wait for** **A** to prepare an ambush for **B** to be ready or be in store for ▷ See also **wait on, wait up** [Old French *waitier*]
Waitangi Day *n* February 6, the national day of New Zealand commemorating the Treaty Of Waitangi in 1840

waiter *n* a man who serves people with food and drink in a restaurant
waiting game *n* **play a waiting game** to postpone taking action or making a decision in order to gain an advantage
waiting list *n* a list of people waiting for something that is not immediately available: *a long waiting list for heart surgery*
waiting room *n* a room in which people can wait, for example at a railway station or doctor's surgery
wait on *vb* **1** to serve (people) with food and drink in a restaurant **2** to look after the needs of: *they were waited on by a manservant* ▷ *interj* **3** NZ stop! hold on! ▷ Also (for senses 1, 2): **wait upon**
waitress *n* **1** a woman who serves people with food and drink in a restaurant ▷ *vb* **2** to work as a waitress
wait up *vb* to delay going to bed in order to wait for someone or something: *when he's late, she waits up for him*
waive *vb* **waiving, waived** to refrain from enforcing or claiming (a rule or right) [Old French *weyver*]
waiver *n* the act or an instance of voluntary giving up a claim or right
waka *n* NZ a Māori canoe
wake[1] *vb* **waking, woke, woken 1** Also: **wake up** to become conscious again or bring (someone) to consciousness again after a sleep **2 wake up** to make (someone) more alert after a period of inactivity **3 wake up to** to become aware of: *the world did not wake up to this tragedy until many people had died* **4 waking hours** the time when a person is awake: *he often used his waking hours to write music* ▷ *n* **5** a watch or vigil held over the body of a dead person during the night before burial [Old English *wacian*]

> **USAGE** Where there is an object and the sense is the literal one *wake (up)* and *waken* are the commonest forms: *I wakened him; I woke him (up)*. Both verbs are also commonly used without an object: *I woke up. Awake* and *awaken* are preferred to other forms of *wake* where the sense is a figurative one: *he awoke to the danger.*

wake[2] *n* **1** the track left by a ship moving through water **2 in the wake of** following soon after: *the arrests come in the wake of the assassination* [Scandinavian]
wakeful *adj* **1** unable to sleep **2** without sleep: *wakeful nights* **3** alert: *wakeful readiness* **wakefulness** *n*
waken *vb* to become conscious again or bring (someone) to consciousness again after a sleep

> **USAGE** See at **wake**[1].

walk *vb* **1** to move on foot at a moderate rate with at least one foot always on the ground **2** to pass through, on, or over on foot: *to walk a short distance* **3** to walk somewhere with (a person or a dog) **4 walking on air** very happy and excited **5 walk the streets** to wander about, esp. when looking for work or when homeless ▷ *n* **6** a short journey on foot, usually for pleasure **7** the action of walking rather than running **8** a manner of walking: *a proud slow walk* **9** a place or route for walking **10 walk of life** social position or profession: *people from all walks of life were drawn to her* ▷ See also **walk into, walk out** *etc.* [Old English *wealcan*] **walker** *n*
walkabout *n* **1** an occasion when royalty, politicians, or other celebrities walk among and meet the public **2 go walkabout** *Austral* **A** to wander through the bush as a nomad **B** *informal* to be lost or misplaced **C** *informal* to lose one's concentration
walkie-talkie *n* a small combined radio transmitter and receiver that can be carried around by one person
walking stick *n* a stick or cane carried in the hand to assist walking
walk into *vb* to encounter unexpectedly: *the troop reinforcements had walked into a trap*
walk-on *adj* (of a part in a film or play) small and not involving speaking
walk out *vb* **1** to leave suddenly and without explanation, usually in anger **2** (of workers) to go on strike **3 walk out on** *informal* to abandon or desert ▷ *n* **walkout 4** a strike by workers
walkover *n* **1** *informal* an easy victory ▷ *vb* **walk over 2** to mistreat or bully; take advantage of: *if you don't make your mark early, people will walk all over you*
walkway *n* **1** a path designed for use by pedestrians **2** a passage or pathway between two buildings
wall *n* **1** a vertical structure made of stone, brick, or wood, with a length and height much greater than its thickness, used to enclose, divide, or support. Related adjective: **mural 2** anything that suggests a wall in function or effect: *a wall of elm trees; a wall of suspicion* **3** *anatomy* any lining or membrane that encloses a bodily cavity or structure: *cell walls* **4 drive someone up the wall** *slang* to make someone angry or irritated **5 go to the wall** *informal* to be financially ruined **6 have one's back to the wall** *informal* to be in a very difficult situation, with no obvious way out of it ▷ *vb* **7** to surround or enclose (an area) with a wall **8 wall in** *or* **up** to enclose (someone or something) completely in a room or place [Old English *weall*] **walled** *adj*
wallaby *n, pl* **-bies** a marsupial of Australia and New Guinea that resembles a small kangaroo [Aboriginal *wolabā*]
wallah (woll-a) *n informal* a person involved with or in charge of a specified thing: *rickshaw wallahs* [Hindi *-wālā*]
wallaroo *n* a large stocky Australian kangaroo of rocky regions
wall bars *pl n* a series of horizontal bars attached to a wall and used in gymnastics
wallet *n* a small folding case, usually of leather, for holding paper money and credit cards [Germanic]
walleye *n* a North American pikeperch with large opaque eyes
walleyed *adj* having eyes with an abnormal amount of white showing because of a squint [Old Norse *vagleygr*]
wallflower *n* **1** a plant grown for its clusters of yellow, orange, red, or purple fragrant flowers

W

2 *informal* a person who does not get involved in dancing or talking at a social event because they are shy
Walloon (wol-**loon**) *n* **1** a French-speaking person from S Belgium or the neighbouring part of France **2** the French dialect of Belgium ▷ *adj* **3** of the Walloons [Germanic]
wallop *informal* ▷ *vb* **1** to hit hard ▷ *n* **2** a hard blow [Old French *waloper* to gallop]
walloping *informal* ▷ *n* **1** a severe physical beating ▷ *adj* **2** large or great: *a walloping amount of sodium*
wallow *vb* **1** to indulge oneself in some emotion: *they wallow in self-pity* **2** to lie or roll about in mud or water for pleasure ▷ *n* **3** the act or an instance of wallowing **4** a muddy place where animals wallow [Old English *wealwian* to roll (in mud)]
wallpaper *n* **1** a printed or embossed paper for covering the walls of a room ▷ *vb* **2** to cover (walls) with wallpaper
wall-to-wall *adj* (of carpeting) completely covering a floor
wally *n, pl* **-lies** *Brit slang* a stupid or foolish person [from the name *Walter*]
walnut *n* **1** an edible nut with a hard, wrinkled, light brown shell **2** a tree on which walnuts grow **3** the light brown wood of a walnut tree, used for making furniture [Old English *walh-hnutu* foreign nut]
walrus *n, pl* **-ruses** *or* **-rus** a mammal of cold northern seas, with two tusks that hang down from the upper jaw, tough thick skin, and coarse whiskers [Dutch: whale horse]
waltz *n* **1** a ballroom dance in triple time in which couples spin round as they progress round the room **2** music for this dance ▷ *vb* **3** to dance a waltz **4** *informal* to move in a relaxed and confident way: *he waltzed over to her table to say hello* [German *Walzer*]
wampum (**wom**-pum) *n* (formerly) money used by Native Americans of N America, made of shells strung or woven together [Native American *wampompeag*]
wan (rhymes with **swan**) *adj* **wanner, wannest** very pale, as a result of illness or unhappiness [Old English *wann* dark] **wanly** *adv*
WAN *computers* wide area network
wand *n* **1** a rod supposed to have magical properties, used to perform conjuring tricks or casting spells **2** a hand-held electronic device which is pointed at or passed over an item to read the data stored there [Old Norse *vǫndr*]
wander *vb* **1** to walk about in a place without any definite purpose or destination **2** (often foll. by *off*) to leave a place where one is supposed to stay: *kids wander off* **3** (of the mind) to lose concentration ▷ *n* **4** the act or an instance of wandering [Old English *wandrian*] **wanderer** *n* **wandering** *adj, n*
wanderlust *n* a great desire to travel
wane *vb* **waning, waned 1** to decrease gradually in size, strength, or power: *the influence of the extremists is waning* **2** (of the moon) to show a gradually decreasing area of brightness from full moon until new moon ▷ *n* **3 on the wane** decreasing in size, strength, or power: *his fame was on the wane* [Old English *wanian*] **waning** *adj*
wangle *vb* **-gling, -gled** *informal* to get (something) by cunning or devious methods: *I've wangled you both an invitation* [origin unknown]
wanigan (**wonn**-ig-an) *n Canad* **1** a watertight box or chest used by canoeists or lumberjacks to hold provisions **2** a sled or boat for carrying camping supplies [from a Native American language]
wank *taboo slang* ▷ *vb* **1** to masturbate ▷ *n* **2** an instance of masturbating [origin unknown]
wanker *n taboo slang* a worthless or stupid person
wannabe *or* **wannabee** *adj* **1** wanting to be, or be like, a particular person or thing: *a wannabe actress* ▷ *n* **2** a person who wants to be, or be like, a particular person or thing
want *vb* **1** to feel a need or longing for: *I want a job* **2** to wish or desire (to do something): *we did not want to get involved* **3** *Brit, Austral & NZ* to have need of or require (doing or being something): *what will you do when it wants cleaning?* **4** should or ought (to do something): *the last person you want to hire is someone who is desperate for a job* **5 want for** to be lacking or deficient in: *they were convinced I was wealthy and wanted for nothing* ▷ *n* **6** something that is needed, desired, or lacked: *attempts to satisfy a number of wants* **7** a lack, shortage, or absence: *for want of opportunity* **8 in want of** needing or lacking: *the Chinese peasant farmer may be in want of a roof, a job, a doctor nearby* [Old Norse *vanta* to be deficient]
wanted *adj* being searched for by the police in connection with a crime that has been committed
wanting *adj* **1** lacking: *I would be wanting in charity if I did not explain the terms* **2** not meeting requirements or expectations: *she compares herself to her sister and finds herself wanting*
wanton *adj* **1** without motive, provocation, or justification: *sheer wanton destruction* **2** (of a person) maliciously and unnecessarily cruel **3** *old-fashioned* (of a woman) sexually unrestrained or immodest ▷ *n* **4** *old-fashioned* a woman considered sexually unrestrained or immodest [Middle English *wantowen* unruly]
WAP *n* Wireless Application Protocol: a system that allows mobile phone users to access the internet and other information services
wapiti (**wop**-pit-tee) *n, pl* **-tis** a large North American deer, now also found in New Zealand [from a Native American language]
war *n* **1** open armed conflict between two or more countries or groups: *this international situation led to war* **2** a particular armed conflict: *the American war in Vietnam* **3** any conflict or contest: *a trade war* **4 have been in the wars** *informal* to look as if one has been in a fight ▷ *adj* **5** relating to war or a war: *the war effort; a war correspondent* ▷ *vb* **warring, warred 6** to conduct a war [Old Northern French *werre*] **warring** *adj*
waratah *n* an Australian shrub with crimson flowers
warble *vb* **-bling, -bled** to sing in a high-pitched trilling voice [Old French *werbler*]
warbler *n* any of various small songbirds
war crime *n* a crime committed in wartime in violation of the accepted customs, such as ill-treatment of prisoners **war criminal** *n*

war cry *n* **1** a rallying cry used by combatants in battle **2** a slogan used to rally support for a cause

ward *n* **1** a room in a hospital for patients requiring similar kinds of care: *the maternity ward* **2** one of the districts into which a town, parish, or other area is divided for administration or elections **3** Also called: **ward of court** *law* a person, esp. a child whose parents are dead, who is placed under the control or protection of a guardian or of a court ▹ See also **ward off** [Old English *weard* protector] **wardship** *n*

-ward *n suffix* **1** *(forming adjectives)* indicating direction towards: *a backward step* **2** *(forming adverbs) chiefly US & Canad* same as **-wards** [Old English *-weard*]

warden *n* **1** a person who is in charge of a building, such as a youth hostel, and its occupants **2** a public official who is responsible for the enforcement of certain regulations: *a game warden* **3** the chief officer in charge of a prison [Old French *wardein*]

warder *or fem* **wardress** *n chiefly Brit* a prison officer [Old French *warder* to guard]

ward off *vb* to prevent (something unpleasant) from happening or from causing harm: *to ward off the pangs of hunger; to ward off cancer cells*

wardrobe *n* **1** a tall cupboard, with a rail or hooks on which to hang clothes **2** the total collection of articles of clothing belonging to one person: *your autumn wardrobe* **3** the collection of costumes belonging to a theatre or theatrical company [Old French *warder* to guard + *robe* robe]

wardrobe mistress *n* the woman in charge of the costumes in a theatre or theatrical company **wardrobe master** *masc n*

wardroom *n* the quarters assigned to the officers of a warship, apart from the captain

-wards *or* **-ward** *suffix forming adverbs* indicating direction towards: *a step backwards* [Old English *-weardes*]

ware *n* articles of the same kind or material: *crystal ware*. See also **wares** [Old English *waru*]

warehouse *n* a place where goods are stored prior to their sale or distribution

wares *pl n* goods for sale

warfare *n* **1** the act of conducting a war **2** a violent or intense conflict of any kind: *class warfare*

war game *n* **1** a tactical exercise for training military commanders, in which no military units are actually deployed **2** a game in which model soldiers are used to create battles in order to study tactics

warhead *n* the front section of a missile or projectile that contains explosives

warhorse *n* **1** (formerly) a horse used in battle **2** *informal* a veteran soldier or politician

warlike *adj* **1** of or relating to war: *warlike stores and equipment* **2** hostile and eager to have a war: *a warlike nation*

warlock *n* a man who practises black magic [Old English *wǣrloga* oath breaker]

warlord *n* a military leader of a nation or part of a nation

warm *adj* **1** feeling or having a moderate degree of heat **2** giving heat: *warm clothing* **3** (of colours) predominantly red or yellow in tone **4** kindly or affectionate: *warm embraces* **5** *informal* near to finding a hidden object or guessing facts, for example in a children's game ▹ *vb* **6** to make warm **7 warm to A** to become fonder of: *I warmed to him when he defended me* **B** to become more excited or enthusiastic about: *he had warmed to his theme* ▹ See also **warm up** [Old English *wearm*] **warmly** *adv* **warmness** *n*

warm-blooded *adj* **1** (of an animal, such as a mammal or a bird) having a constant body temperature, usually higher than the surrounding temperature **2** having a passionate nature **warm-bloodedness** *n*

warm-down *n* light exercises performed to aid recovery from strenuous physical activity

war memorial *n* a monument to people who have died in a war, esp. local people

warm front *n meteorol* the boundary between a warm air mass and the cold air it is replacing

warm-hearted *adj* kind, affectionate, or sympathetic

warming pan *n* a long-handled pan filled with hot coals, formerly pulled over the sheets to warm a bed

warmonger *n* a person who encourages warlike ideas or advocates war **warmongering** *n*

warmth *n* **1** the state of being warm **2** affection or cordiality: *the warmth of their friendship*

warm up *vb* **1** to make or become warm or warmer **2** to prepare for a race, sporting contest, or exercise routine by doing gentle exercises immediately beforehand **3** (of an engine or machine) to be started and left running until the working temperature is reached **4** to become more lively: *wait until things warm up* **5** to reheat (food that has already been cooked) ▹ *n* **warm-up** **6** a preparatory exercise routine

warn *vb* **1** to make (someone) aware of a possible danger or problem **2** to inform (someone) in advance: *you'd better warn your girlfriend that you'll be working at the weekend* **3 warn off** to advise (someone) to go away or not to do something [Old English *wearnian*]

warning *n* **1** a hint, threat, or advance notice of a possible danger or problem **2** advice not to do something ▹ *adj* **3** giving or serving as a warning: *warning signs* **warningly** *adv*

warp *vb* **1** (esp. of wooden objects) to be twisted out of shape, for example by heat or damp **2** to distort or influence in a negative way: *love warps judgment* ▹ *n* **3** a fault or an irregularity in the shape or surface of an object **4** a fault or deviation in someone's character **5** See **time warp** **6** the yarns arranged lengthways on a loom through which the weft yarns are woven [Old English *wearp* a throw] **warped** *adj*

war paint *n* **1** paint applied to the face and body by certain Native Americans before battle **2** *informal* cosmetics

warpath *n* **on the warpath A** preparing to engage in battle **B** *informal* angry and looking for a fight or conflict

warrant *n* **1** an official authorization for some action or decision: *Scotland Yard today issued a warrant for the arrest of this man* **2** a document that certifies or guarantees something, such as a receipt or licence ▷ *vb* **3** to make necessary: *we've no hard evidence to warrant a murder investigation* [Old French *guarant*]

warrant officer *n* an officer in certain armed services with a rank between those of commissioned and noncommissioned officers

Warrant of Fitness *n NZ* a certificate required for a motor vehicle certifying that it is mechanically sound

warrantor *n* a person or company that provides a warranty

warranty *n, pl* **-ties** a guarantee or assurance that goods meet a specified standard or that the facts in a legal document are as stated [Anglo-French *warantie*]

warren *n* **1** a series of interconnected underground tunnels in which rabbits live **2** an overcrowded building or area of a city with many narrow passages or streets: *a mountainous concrete warren of apartments* [Anglo-French *warenne*]

warrigal *Austral* ▷ *n* **1** a dingo ▷ *adj* **2** wild

warrior *n* a person who is engaged in or experienced in war [Old French *werreieor*]

warship *n* a ship designed for naval warfare

wart *n* **1** a firm abnormal growth on the skin caused by a virus **2 warts and all** including faults: *she loves him warts and all* [Old English *weart(e)*] **warty** *adj*

warthog *n* a wild African pig with heavy tusks, wartlike lumps on the face, and a mane of coarse hair

wartime *n* **1** a time of war ▷ *adj* **2** of or in a time of war: *the wartime coalition*

wary (ware-ree) *adj* **warier, wariest** cautious or on one's guard: *be wary of hitchhikers* [Old English *wær* aware, careful] **warily** *adv* **wariness** *n*

was *vb (with 'I', 'he', 'she', 'it', or a singular noun as subject)* the past tense of **be** [Old English *wæs*]

wash *vb* **1** to clean (oneself, part of one's body, or a thing) with soap or detergent and water **2** (of a garment or fabric) to be capable of being washed without damage or loss of colour **3** to move or be moved in a particular direction by water: *houses may be washed away in floods* **4** (of waves) to flow or sweep against or over (a surface or object), often with a lapping sound **5** *informal* to be acceptable or believable: *the masculine pride argument won't wash now when so many women go out to work* ▷ *n* **6** the act or process of washing **7** all the clothes, etc. to be washed together on one occasion **8** a thin layer of paint or ink: *a pale wash of blue* **9** the disturbance in the air or water produced at the rear of an aircraft, boat, or other moving object: *we were hit by the wash of a large vessel* **10 come out in the wash** *informal* to become known or apparent in the course of time ▷ See also **wash down, wash out, wash up** [Old English *wæscan, waxan*] **washable** *adj*

Wash. Washington (state)

washbasin *n* a small sink in a bathroom, used for washing the face and hands. Also: **wash-hand basin**

wash down *vb* **1** to have a drink with or after (food or medicine): *a large steak, washed down with coffee* **2** to wash from top to bottom: *she washed down the staircase*

washed out *adj* **1** exhausted and lacking in energy **2** faded or colourless

washed up *adj informal* no longer as successful or important as previously: *she stands discredited, her career probably washed up*

washer *n* **1** a flat ring of rubber, felt, or metal used to provide a seal under a nut or bolt or in a tap or valve **2** *informal* a washing machine **3** a person who washes things, esp. as a job: *chief cook and bottle washer* **4** *Austral* a small piece of towelling cloth used to wash the face

washerwoman *n, pl* **-women** a woman who washes clothes as a job

washing *n* all the clothes, etc. to be washed together on one occasion

washing machine *n* a machine for washing clothes and bed linen in

washing soda *n* crystalline sodium carbonate, used as a cleansing agent

washing-up *n* the act of washing used dishes and cutlery after a meal

wash out *vb* **1** Also: **wash off** to remove or be removed by washing: *the rain washes the red dye out of the cap* **2** to wash the inside of (a container) ▷ *n* **washout 3** a total failure or disaster **4** NZ a part of a road or railway washed away by floodwaters

washroom *n US & Canad* a toilet

washstand *n* a piece of furniture designed to hold a basin for washing the face and hands in

wash up *vb* **1** to wash used dishes and cutlery after a meal **2** *US & Canad* to wash one's face and hands

washy *adj* **washier, washiest 1** overdiluted or weak **2** lacking intensity of colour: *a washy blend of pale brown and pale grey*

wasn't was not

wasp *n* a common stinging insect with a slender black-and-yellow striped body [Old English *wæsp*]

Wasp *or* **WASP** (in the US and Canada) White Anglo-Saxon Protestant: a person descended from N European, usually Protestant stock, forming a group often considered to be the most dominant and privileged in N American society

waspish *adj* bad-tempered or spiteful: *waspish comments*

wasp waist *n* a very narrow waist **wasp-waisted** *adj*

wassail *n* **1** (formerly) a toast drunk to a person during festivities **2** a festivity involving a lot of drinking **3** hot spiced beer or mulled wine drunk at such a festivity ▷ *vb* **4 go wassailing** to go from house to house singing carols at Christmas [Old Norse *ves heill* be in good health]

wastage *n* **1** the act of wasting something or the state of being wasted: *wastage of raw materials* **2** reduction in the size of a workforce by retirement, redundancy, etc.

> **USAGE** *Waste* and *wastage* are to some extent interchangeable, but many people think that *wastage* should not be used to refer to loss resulting from human carelessness, inefficiency, etc.: *a waste* (not *a wastage*) *of time, money, effort,* etc.

waste *vb* **wasting, wasted 1** to use up thoughtlessly, carelessly, or unsuccessfully

W

2 to fail to take advantage of: *let's not waste an opportunity to see the children* 3 **be wasted on** to be too good for; not be appreciated by: *fine brandy is wasted on you* 4 **waste away** to lose one's strength or health: *wasting away from unrequited love* ▷ *n* 5 the act of wasting something or the state of being wasted: *a waste of time* 6 something that is left over because it is in excess of requirements 7 rubbish: *toxic waste* 8 *physiol* matter discharged from the body as faeces or urine 9 **wastes** a region that is wild or uncultivated ▷ *adj* 10 rejected as being useless, unwanted, or worthless: *waste products* 11 not cultivated or productive: *waste ground* 12 *physiol* discharged from the body as faeces or urine: *waste matter* 13 **lay waste** *or* **lay waste to** to devastate or destroy: *the Bikini atoll, laid waste by nuclear tests* [Latin *vastare* to lay waste]

wasted *adj* 1 unnecessary or unfruitful: *wasted effort* 2 pale, thin, and unhealthy: *the hunched shoulders and the wasted appearance of his body*

wasteful *adj* causing waste: *wasteful expenditure* **wastefully** *adv*

wasteland *n* 1 a barren or desolate area of land 2 something that is considered spiritually, intellectually, or aesthetically barren: *the TV wasteland*

wastepaper basket *n* a container for paper discarded after use

waster *n informal* a lazy or worthless person

wasting *adj* reducing the vitality and strength of the body: *a pernicious wasting illness*

wastrel *n literary* a lazy or worthless person

watap (wat-tahp) *n* a stringy thread made by Native Americans from the roots of conifers [from a Native American language]

watch *vb* 1 to look at or observe closely and attentively 2 to look after (a child or a pet) 3 to maintain a careful interest in or control over: *it reminds me to watch my diet* 4 **watch for** to be keenly alert to or cautious about: *the vigilant night watchman hired to watch for thieves* 5 **watch it!** be careful! ▷ *n* 6 a small portable timepiece worn strapped to the wrist or in a waistcoat pocket 7 the act or an instance of watching 8 *naut* any of the periods, usually of four hours, during which part of a ship's crew are on duty 9 **keep a close watch on** to maintain a careful interest in or control over: *he keeps a close watch on party opinion* 10 **keep watch** to be keenly alert to danger; keep guard 11 **on the watch** on the lookout ▷ See also **watch out, watch over** [Old English *wæccan*] **watcher** *n*

W

watchable *adj* interesting, enjoyable, or entertaining: *watchable films*

watchdog *n* 1 a dog kept to guard property 2 a person or group that acts as a guard against inefficiency or illegality

watchful *adj* 1 carefully observing everything that happens 2 **under the watchful eye of** being closely observed by **watchfully** *adv* **watchfulness** *n*

watchmaker *n* a person who makes or mends watches and clocks

watchman *n, pl* **-men** a man employed to guard buildings or property

watch-night service *n* A (in Protestant churches) a service held on the night of December 24, to mark the arrival of Christmas Day B (in Protestant churches) a service held on the night of December 31, to mark the passing of the old year

watch out *vb* to be careful or on one's guard

watch over *vb* to look after or supervise: *her main ambition is still to watch over the family*

watchstrap *n* a strap attached to a watch for fastening it round the wrist. Also called (US and Canad): **watchband**

watchtower *n* a tower on which a sentry keeps watch

watchword *n* a slogan or motto: *quality, not quantity, is the watchword*

water *n* 1 a clear colourless tasteless liquid that is essential for plant and animal life, that falls as rain, and forms seas, rivers, and lakes. Related adjectives: **aquatic, aqueous** 2 any area of this liquid, such as a sea, river, or lake 3 the surface of such an area of water: *four-fifths of an iceberg's mass lie below water* 4 the level of the tide: *at high water* 5 *physiol* A any fluid discharged from the body, such as sweat, urine, or tears B the fluid surrounding a fetus in the womb 6 **hold water** (of an argument or idea) to be believable or reasonable 7 **of the first water** of the highest quality or the most extreme degree: *he's a scoundrel of the first water* 8 **pass water** to urinate 9 **water under the bridge** events that are past and done with ▷ *vb* 10 to moisten or soak with water: *keep greenhouse plants well watered* 11 to give (an animal) water to drink 12 (of the eyes) to fill with tears: *our eyes were watering from the fumes* 13 (of the mouth) to fill with saliva in anticipation of food ▷ See also **water down** [Old English *wæter*] **waterless** *adj*

water bed *n* a waterproof mattress filled with water

water biscuit *n* a thin crisp unsweetened biscuit, usually eaten with butter or cheese

water buffalo *n* a large black oxlike draught animal of S Asia, with long backward-curving horns

water cannon *n* a machine that pumps a jet of water through a nozzle at high pressure, used to disperse crowds

water chestnut *n* the edible tuber of a Chinese plant, used in E Asian cookery

water closet *n old-fashioned* a toilet. Abbrev: **WC**

watercolour *or US* **watercolor** *n* 1 a kind of paint that is applied with water rather than oil 2 a painting done in watercolours

water-cooled *adj* (of an engine) kept from overheating by a flow of water circulating in a casing

watercourse *n* the channel or bed of a river or stream

watercress *n* a plant that grows in ponds and streams, with strong-tasting leaves that are used in salads and as a garnish

water cycle *n geol* the circulation of the earth's water, in which water from the sea evaporates, forms clouds, falls as rain or snow, and returns to the sea by rivers

water diviner *n* a person who can locate the presence of water underground with a divining rod
water down *vb* **1** to weaken (a drink or food) with water **2** to make (a story, plan, or proposal) weaker and less controversial **watered-down** *adj*
waterfall *n* a cascade of falling water where there is a vertical or almost vertical step in a river
waterfowl *n, pl* **-fowl** a bird that swims on water, such as a duck or swan
waterfront *n* the area of a town or city next to an area of water, such as a harbour or dockyard
waterhole *n* a pond or pool in a desert or other dry area, used by animals as a drinking place
water ice *n* ice cream made from frozen fruit-flavoured syrup
watering can *n* a container with a handle and a spout with a perforated nozzle, used to sprinkle water over plants
watering hole *n facetious slang* a pub
watering place *n* **1** a place where people or animals can find drinking water **2** *Brit* a spa or seaside resort
water jump *n* a ditch or brook over which athletes or horses must jump in a steeplechase
water level *n* **1** the level reached by the surface of an area of water **2** same as **water line**
water lily *n* a plant with large leaves and showy flowers that float on the surface of an area of water
water line *n* the level to which a ship's hull will be immersed when afloat
waterlogged *adj* **1** saturated with water: *waterlogged meadows* **2** (of a boat) having taken in so much water as to be likely to sink
water main *n* a principal supply pipe in an arrangement of pipes for distributing water to houses and other buildings
watermark *n* **1** a mark impressed on paper during manufacture, visible when the paper is held up to the light **2** a line marking the level reached by an area of water
water meadow *n* a meadow that remains fertile by being periodically flooded by a stream
watermelon *n* a large round melon with a hard green rind and sweet watery reddish flesh
water pistol *n* a toy pistol that squirts a stream of water
water polo *n* a game played in water by two teams of seven swimmers in which each side tries to throw a ball into the opponents' goal
water power *n* the power of flowing or falling water to drive machinery or generate electricity
waterproof *adj* **1** not allowing water to pass through: *waterproof trousers* ▷ *n* **2** *chiefly Brit* a waterproof garment, such as a raincoat ▷ *vb* **3** to make waterproof: *the bridge is having its deck waterproofed*
water rat *n* same as **water vole**
water rate *n* a charge made for the public supply of water
water-resistant *adj* (of a fabric or garment) having a finish that resists the absorption of water
watershed *n* **1** the dividing line between two adjacent river systems, such as a ridge **2** an important period or factor that serves as a dividing line: *a watershed in history*
waterside *n* the area of land beside a river or lake
watersider *n NZ* a person employed to load and unload ships
water-ski *n* **1** a type of ski used for gliding over water ▷ *vb* **-skiing, -skied** *or* **-ski'd** **2** to ride over water on water-skis while holding a rope towed by a speedboat **water-skier** *n* **water-skiing** *n*
water softener *n* a device or substance that removes the minerals that make water hard
waterspout *n* a tornado occurring over water, which forms a column of water and mist
water table *n* the level below which the ground is saturated with water
watertight *adj* **1** not letting water through: *watertight compartments* **2** without loopholes or weak points: *a watertight system*
water tower *n* a storage tank mounted on a tower so that water can be distributed at a steady pressure
water vapour *n* water in a gaseous state, esp. when due to evaporation at a temperature below boiling point
water vole *n* a small ratlike animal that can swim and lives on the banks of streams and ponds
waterway *n* a river, canal, or other navigable channel used as a means of travel or transport
water wheel *n* a large wheel with vanes set across its rim, which is turned by flowing water to drive machinery
water wings *pl n* an inflatable rubber device shaped like a pair of wings, which is placed under the arms of a person learning to swim
waterworks *n* **1** an establishment for storing, purifying, and distributing water for community supply ▷ *pl n* **2** *informal, chiefly Brit euphemistic* the urinary system **3** **turn on the waterworks** *informal* to begin to cry deliberately, in order to attract attention or gain sympathy
watery *adj* **1** of, like, or containing water: *a watery discharge* **2** (of eyes) filled with tears **3** insipid, thin, or weak: *a watery sun had appeared*
watt (wott) *n* the SI unit of power, equal to the power dissipated by a current of 1 ampere flowing across a potential difference of 1 volt [after J. *Watt*, engineer]
wattage *n* the amount of electrical power, expressed in watts, that an appliance uses or generates
wattle (wott-tl) *n* **1** a frame of rods or stakes interwoven with twigs or branches used to make fences **2** a loose fold of brightly coloured skin hanging from the throat of certain birds and lizards **3** an Australian acacia tree with dense golden, yellow or cream flowers ▷ *adj* **4** made of, formed by, or covered with wattle: *a wattle fence* [Old English *watol*]
wattle and daub *n* a building material consisting of interwoven twigs plastered with a mixture of clay and water
wave *vb* **waving, waved** **1** to move (one's hand) to and fro as a greeting **2** to direct (someone) to move in a particular direction by waving: *I waved him on* **3** to hold (something) up and move it from side to side in order to attract attention **4** to move freely to and fro: *flowers waving in the wind* ▷ *n* **5** one

of a sequence of ridges or undulations that moves across the surface of the sea or a lake **6** a curve in the hair **7** a sudden rise in the frequency or intensity of something: *a wave of sympathy* **8** a widespread movement that advances in a body: *a new wave of refugees* **9** a prolonged spell of some particular type of weather: *a heat wave* **10** the act or an instance of waving **11** *physics* an energy-carrying disturbance travelling through a medium or space by a series of vibrations without any overall movement of matter **12 make waves** to cause trouble [Old English *wafian*]

waveband *n* a range of wavelengths or frequencies used for a particular type of radio transmission

wave down *vb* to signal to (the driver of a vehicle) to stop

wavelength *n* **1** *physics* the distance between two points of the same phase in consecutive cycles of a wave **2** the wavelength of the carrier wave used by a particular broadcasting station **3 on the same wavelength** *informal* having similar views, feelings, or thoughts

waver *vb* **1** to hesitate between possibilities; be indecisive **2** to swing from one thing to another: *she wavered between annoyance and civility* **3** (of a voice or stare) to become unsteady **4** to move back and forth or one way and another: *the barrel of the gun began to waver* [Old Norse *vafra* to flicker] **wavering** *adj*

wavey *n Canad* a snow goose or other wild goose [from a Native American language]

wavy *adj* **wavier, waviest** having curves: *wavy hair; a wavy line*

wax¹ *n* **1** a solid fatty or oily substance used for making candles and polish, which softens and melts when heated **2** short for **beeswax** or **sealing wax** **3** *physiol* a brownish-yellow waxy substance secreted by glands in the ear ▷ *vb* **4** to coat or polish with wax [Old English *weax*] **waxed** *adj* **waxy** *adj*

wax² *vb* **1** to increase gradually in size, strength, or power: *trading has waxed and waned with the economic cycle* **2** (of the moon) to show a gradually increasing area of brightness from new moon until full moon **3** to become: *he waxed eloquent on the disadvantages of marriage* [Old English *weaxan*]

waxed paper *or* **wax paper** *n* paper treated or coated with wax or paraffin to make it waterproof

waxen *adj* **1** resembling wax in colour or texture: *his face is waxen and pale* **2** made of, treated with, or covered with wax: *a waxen image*

W

waxeye *n* a small New Zealand bird with a white circle round its eye

waxwork *n* a life-size lifelike wax figure of a famous person

waxworks *n* a museum or exhibition of wax figures

way *n* **1** a manner, method, or means: *a new way of life; a tactful way of finding out* **2** a characteristic style or manner: *we are all special in our own way* **3 ways** habits or customs: *he had a liking for British ways* **4** an aspect or detail of something: *the tourist industry is in many ways a success story* **5** a choice or option, for example in a vote: *he thought it could go either way* **6** a route or direction: *the shortest way home* **7** a journey: *you could buy a magazine to read on the way* **8** distance: *they are a long way from Paris* **9** space or room for movement or activity: *you won't be in his way* **10 by the way** incidentally: *by the way, I've decided to leave* **11 by way of** **A** serving as: *by way of explanation* **B** by the route of: *I went by way of my family home* **12 get one's own way** to have things exactly as one wants them to be **13 give way** **A** to collapse or break **B** to yield or concede: *I tried to make him understand but he did not give way an inch* **14 give way to** **A** to be replaced by: *my first feelings of dismay have given way to comparative complacency* **B** to show (an emotion) unrestrainedly **C** to slow down or stop when driving to let (another driver) pass **15 go out of one's way** to take considerable trouble: *he had gone out of his way to reassure me* **16 have it both ways** to enjoy two things that would normally be mutually exclusive **17 in a bad way** *informal* in a poor state of health or a poor financial state **18 in a way** in some respects **19 in no way** not at all **20 make one's way** to proceed or go: *he decided to make his way back in the dark* **21 on the way out** *informal* becoming unfashionable **22 out of the way** **A** removed or dealt with so as to be no longer a hindrance **B** remote **23 under way** having started moving or making progress ▷ *adv* **24** *informal* far or by far: *that is way out of line* [Old English *weg*]

waybill *n* a document stating the nature, origin, and destination of goods being transported

wayfarer *n old-fashioned* a traveller

waylay *vb* **-laying, -laid** **1** to lie in wait for and attack **2** to intercept (someone) unexpectedly

way-out *adj old-fashioned, informal* extremely unconventional

waypoint *n* the co-ordinates of a specific location as defined by a GPS

ways and means *pl n* **1** the methods and resources for accomplishing something **2** the money and the methods of raising the money needed for the functioning of a political unit

wayside *adj* **1** *old-fashioned* situated by the side of a road: *wayside shrines* ▷ *n* **2 fall by the wayside** to be unsuccessful or stop being successful: *thousands of new diets are dreamed up yearly – many fall by the wayside*

wayward *adj* erratic, selfish, or stubborn [AWAY + -WARD] **waywardness** *n*

Wb *physics* weber

WC *or* **wc** *n* a toilet

we *pron (used as the subject of a verb)* **1** the speaker or writer and another person or other people: *we arrived in Calais* **2** all people or people in general: *it's an unfair world we live in* **3** *formal* same as **I¹**: used by monarchs and editors [Old English *wē*]

weak *adj* **1** lacking in physical or mental strength **2** (of a part of the body) not functioning as well as is normal: *a weak heart* **3** liable to collapse or break: *weak bridges* **4** lacking in importance, influence, or strength: *a weak government* **5** (of a currency or shares) falling in price or characterized by falling prices **6** lacking in moral strength; easily influenced **7** not convincing: *weak arguments* **8** lacking strength or power: *his voice was weak* **9** not having a strong flavour: *weak coffee* [Old English *wāc* soft] **weakly** *adv*

weaken *vb* to become or make weak or weaker
weak-kneed *adj informal* lacking strength, courage, or resolution
weakling *n* a person who is lacking in physical or mental strength
weak-minded *adj* **1** lacking willpower **2** of low intelligence; foolish
weakness *n* **1** the state of being weak **2** a failing in a person's character: *his weakness is his impetuosity* **3** a self-indulgent liking: *a weakness for gin*
weal¹ *n* a raised mark on the skin produced by a blow [from Old English *walu* ridge]
weal² *n old-fashioned* prosperity or wellbeing: *the public weal* [Old English *wela*]
wealth *n* **1** the state of being rich **2** a large amount of money and valuable material possessions: *redistribution of wealth* **3** a great amount or number: *a wealth of detail* [Middle English *welthe*]
wealthy *adj* **wealthier, wealthiest 1** having a large amount of money and valuable material possessions **2 wealthy in** having a great amount or number of: *a continent exceptionally wealthy in minerals*
wean *vb* **1** to start giving (a baby or young mammal) food other than its mother's milk **2** to cause (oneself or someone else) to give up a former habit: *they are unable to wean themselves from the tobacco habit* [Old English *wenian* to accustom] **weaning** *n*
weapon *n* **1** an object used in fighting, such as a knife or gun **2** anything used to get the better of an opponent: *having a sense of humour is a weapon of self-defence* [Old English *wǣpen*]
weaponry *n* weapons regarded collectively
wear *vb* **wearing, wore, worn 1** to carry or have (a garment or jewellery) on one's body as clothing or ornament **2** to have (a particular facial expression): *she wore a scowl of frank antagonism* **3** to style (the hair) in a particular way: *she wears her hair in a braid* **4** to deteriorate or cause to deteriorate by constant use or action **5** *informal* to accept: *he won't be given a top job – the Party wouldn't wear it* **6 wear thin** to lessen or become weaker: *his patience began to wear thin* **7 wear well** to remain in good condition for a long time ▷ *n* **8** clothes that are suitable for a particular time or purpose: *evening wear; beach wear* **9** deterioration from constant or normal use **10** the quality of resisting the effects of constant use ▷ See also **wear down, wear off, wear out** [Old English *werian*] **wearable** *adj* **wearer** *n*
wearable *adj* **1** (of a garment) comfortable and practical **2** (of an electronic device) designed to be worn on the body
wear and tear *n* damage or loss resulting from ordinary use
wear down *vb* **1** to make shorter by long or constant wearing or rubbing: *the back of his heels were worn down* **2** to overcome gradually by persistent effort: *to wear down the enemy*
wearing *adj* causing exhaustion and sometimes irritation
wearisome *adj* causing fatigue and irritation
wear off *vb* to have a gradual decrease in effect or intensity: *the novelty began to wear off*
wear out *vb* **1** to make or become unfit for use through wear: *my red trousers are worn out* **2** *informal* to exhaust: *the afternoon's races and games had worn him out*
weary *adj* **-rier, -riest 1** very tired; lacking energy **2** caused by or suggestive of weariness: *he managed a weary smile* **3** causing exhaustion: *a long weary struggle* **4 weary of** discontented or bored with: *he was weary of the war* ▷ *vb* **-ries, -rying, -ried 5** to make weary **6 weary of** to become discontented or bored with: *he seems to have wearied of her possessiveness* [Old English *wērig*] **wearily** *adv* **weariness** *n* **wearying** *adj*
weasel *n, pl* **-sels** *or* **-sel 1** a small meat-eating mammal with reddish-brown fur, a long body and neck, and short legs **2** *informal* a sly or treacherous person [Old English *wesle*]
weather *n* **1** the day-to-day atmospheric conditions, such as temperature, cloudiness, and rainfall, affecting a specific place **2 make heavy weather of** *informal* to carry out (a task) with great difficulty or needless effort **3 under the weather** *informal* feeling slightly ill ▷ *vb* **4** to undergo or cause to undergo changes, such as discoloration, due to the action of the weather **5** to come safely through (a storm, problem, or difficulty) [Old English *weder*]
weather-beaten *adj* **1** tanned by exposure to the weather: *a crumpled weather-beaten face* **2** worn or damaged as a result of exposure to the weather
weatherboard *n* a timber board that is fixed with others in overlapping horizontal rows to form an exterior cladding on a wall or roof **weatherboarded** *adj*
weathercock *n* a weather vane in the shape of a cockerel
weather eye *n* **keep a weather eye on** to keep a careful watch on: *keep a weather eye on your symptoms*
weather girl *n* a woman who forecasts the weather on radio or television
weathering *n* the breakdown of rocks by the action of the weather
weatherman *n, pl* **-men** a man who forecasts the weather on radio or television
weatherproof *adj* able to withstand exposure to weather without deterioration: *a weatherproof roof*
weather vane *n* a metal object on a roof that indicates the direction in which the wind is blowing
weave *vb* **weaving, wove** *or* **weaved, woven** *or* **weaved 1** to form (a fabric) by interlacing yarn on a loom **2** to make (a garment or a blanket) by this process **3** to construct (a basket or fence) by interlacing cane or twigs **4** to compose (a story or plan) by combining separate elements into a whole **5** to move from side to side while going forward: *to weave in and out of lanes* **6 get weaving** *informal* to hurry ▷ *n* **7** the structure or pattern of a woven fabric: *the rough weave of the cloth* [Old English *wefan*] **weaver** *n* **weaving** *n*
web *n* **1** a mesh of fine tough threads built by a spider to trap insects **2** anything that is intricately formed or complex: *a web of relationships* **3** a membrane connecting the toes of some water birds and water-dwelling animals such as frogs **4 the web** (*often cap*) short for **World Wide Web**

▷ *adj* **5** of or situated on the World Wide Web: *a web server; web pages* [Old English *webb*] **webbed** *adj*
Web 2.0 *n* the internet viewed as a medium in which interactive experience plays a more important role than simply accessing information
web address *n* another name for **URL**
webbing *n* a strong fabric that is woven in strips and used under springs in upholstery or for straps
webcam *n* a camera that transmits still or moving images over the internet
webcast *n* a broadcast of an event over the internet
weber (vay-ber) *n* the SI unit of magnetic flux (the strength of a magnetic field over a given area) [after W. E. *Weber*, physicist]
web-footed *or* **web-toed** *adj* (of certain animals or birds) having webbed feet that aid swimming
weblog *n* a person's online journal
webmail *n* an email system that allows account holders to access mail via an internet site rather than by downloading it onto a computer
website *n* a group of connected pages on the World Wide Web situated under a single domain name
wed *vb* **wedding, wedded** *or* **wed 1** *old-fashioned* to take (a person) as a husband or wife; marry **2** to unite closely: *to wed folklore and magic* [Old English *weddian*]
Wed. Wednesday
wedded *adj* **1** of marriage: *wedded bliss* **2** firmly in support of an idea or institution: *wedded to the virtues of capitalism*
wedding *n* **1** a marriage ceremony **2** a special wedding anniversary, esp. the 25th (**silver wedding**) or 50th (**golden wedding**)
wedding breakfast *n* the meal usually served after a wedding ceremony or just before the bride and bridegroom leave for their honeymoon
wedding cake *n* a rich iced fruit cake, with one, two, or more tiers, which is served at a wedding reception
wedding ring *n* a plain ring, usually made of a precious metal, worn to indicate that one is married
wedge *n* **1** a block of solid material, esp. wood or metal, that is shaped like a narrow V in cross section and can be pushed or driven between two objects or parts of an object in order to split or secure them **2** a slice shaped like a wedge: *a wedge of quiche* **3** *golf* a club with a wedge-shaped face, used for bunker or pitch shots **4 drive a wedge between** to cause a split between (people or groups) **5 the thin end of the wedge** anything unimportant in itself that implies the start of something much larger ▷ *vb* **wedging, wedged 6** to secure (something) with a wedge **7** to squeeze into a narrow space: *a book wedged between the bed and the table* [Old English *wecg*]
wedge-tailed eagle *n* a large brown Australian eagle with a wedge-shaped tail
Wedgwood *n trademark* a type of fine pottery with applied decoration in white on a coloured background [after Josiah *Wedgwood*, potter]
wedlock *n* **1** the state of being married **2 born out of wedlock** born when one's parents are not legally married [Old English *wedlāc*]
Wednesday *n* the fourth day of the week [Old English *Wōdnes dæg* Woden's day]
wee¹ *adj Brit, Austral & NZ* small or short [Old English *wǣg* weight]
wee² *informal* ▷ *n* **1** an instance of urinating ▷ *vb* **weeing, weed 2** to urinate. Also: **wee-wee** [origin unknown]
weed *n* **1** any plant that grows wild and profusely, esp. among cultivated plants **2** *slang* **A** marijuana **B the weed** *or* **the evil weed** tobacco **3** *informal* a thin weak person ▷ *vb* **4** to remove weeds from (a garden) [Old English *wēod*]
weedkiller *n* a chemical or hormonal substance used to kill weeds
weed out *vb* to separate out, remove, or eliminate (an unwanted element): *to weed out the thugs*
weedy *adj* **weedier, weediest 1** *informal* thin or weak: *sick and weedy children* **2** full of weeds: *weedy patches of garden*
week *n* **1** a period of seven consecutive days, esp. one beginning with Sunday **2** a period of seven consecutive days from a specified day: *a week from today* **3** the period of time within a week that is spent at work [Old English *wice, wicu*]
weekday *n* any day of the week other than Saturday or Sunday
weekend *n* Saturday and Sunday
weekly *adj* **1** happening once a week or every week: *a weekly column* **2** determined or calculated by the week: *weekly earnings* ▷ *adv* **3** once a week or every week: *report to the police weekly* ▷ *n, pl* **-lies 4** a newspaper or magazine issued every week
weeny *adj* **-nier, -niest** *informal* very small; tiny [from WEE¹]
weep *vb* **weeping, wept 1** to shed tears; cry **2** to ooze liquid: *the skin cracked and wept; the label is weeping black ink in the rain* ▷ *n* **3** a spell of weeping: *together we had a good weep* [Old English *wēpan*]
weeping willow *n* a willow tree with graceful drooping branches
weepy *informal* ▷ *adj* **weepier, weepiest 1** liable or tending to weep ▷ *n, pl* **weepies 2** a sentimental film or book
weevil *n* a beetle with a long snout that feeds on plants [Old English *wifel*]
wee-wee *n, vb* **-weeing, -weed** *informal, chiefly Brit* same as **wee²**
weft *n* the yarns woven across the width of the fabric through the lengthways warp yarns [Old English]
weigh *vb* **1** to have weight as specified: *the tree weighs nearly three tons* **2** to measure the weight of **3** to consider carefully: *the President now has to weigh his options* **4** to be influential: *the authorities did not enter my mind or weigh with me.* **5 weigh anchor** to raise a ship's anchor **6 weigh out** to measure out by weight ▷ See also **weigh down, weigh in** *etc.* [Old English *wegan*]
weighbridge *n* a machine for weighing vehicles by means of a metal plate set into a road
weigh down *vb* **1** (of a heavy load) to impede the movements of **2** (of a problem or difficulty) to worry (someone) a great deal
weigh in *vb* **1** (of a boxer or jockey) to be weighed to check that one is of the correct weight for the

contest **2** *informal* to contribute to a discussion or conversation: *he weighed in with a few sharp comments* ▹ *n* **weigh-in** **3** *sport* the occasion of checking the competitors' weight before a boxing match or a horse race

weigh on *vb* to be oppressive or burdensome to: *public anger weighed heavily on his young mind*

weight *n* **1** the heaviness of an object, substance, or person **2** *physics* the vertical force experienced by a mass as a result of gravitation **3 A** a system of units used to express weight: *metric weight* **B** a unit used to measure weight: *the kilogram is the weight used in the metric system* **4 A** an object of known heaviness used for weighing objects, substances, or people **B** an object of known heaviness used in weight training or weightlifting to strengthen the muscles **5** any heavy load: *with a weight of fish on their backs* **6** force, importance, or influence: *they want their words to carry weight* **7** an oppressive force: *the weight of expectation* **8 pull one's weight** *informal* to do one's full share of a task **9 throw one's weight about** *informal* to act in an aggressive authoritarian manner ▹ *vb* **10** to add weight to; make heavier **11** to slant (a system) so that it favours one side rather than another [Old English *wiht*]

weighting *n Brit* an allowance paid to compensate for higher living costs: *salary includes Inner London weighting*

weightless *adj* **1** seeming to have very little weight or no weight at all **2** seeming not to be affected by gravity, as in the case of astronauts in an orbiting spacecraft **weightlessness** *n*

weightlifting *n* the sport of lifting barbells of specified weights in a prescribed manner **weightlifter** *n*

weight training *n* physical exercise using light or heavy weights in order to strengthen the muscles

weighty *adj* **weightier, weightiest 1** important or serious: *weighty matters* **2** very heavy

weigh up *vb* to make an assessment of (a person or situation)

weir *n* **1** a low dam that is built across a river to divert the water or control its flow **2** a fencelike trap built across a stream for catching fish in [Old English *wer*]

weird *adj* **1** strange or bizarre **2** suggestive of the supernatural; uncanny [Old English *(ge)wyrd* destiny] **weirdly** *adv* **weirdness** *n*

weirdo *n, pl* **-dos** *informal* a person whose behaviour or dress is considered bizarre or eccentric

welch *vb* same as **welsh**

welcome *vb* **-coming, -comed 1** to greet the arrival of (a guest) cordially **2** to receive or accept (something) gladly: *I would welcome a chance to speak to him* ▹ *n* **3** the act of greeting or receiving someone or something in a specified manner: *the President was given a warm welcome* ▹ *adj* **4** gladly received or admitted: *I wouldn't want to stay where I'm not welcome* **5** encouraged or invited: *you are welcome to join us at one of our social events* **6** bringing pleasure: *a welcome change* **7 you're welcome** an expression used to acknowledge someone's thanks [Old English *wilcuma*] **welcoming** *adj*

weld *vb* **1** to join (two pieces of metal or plastic) by softening with heat and hammering or by fusion **2** to unite closely: *the diverse ethnic groups had been welded together by the anti-Fascist cause* ▹ *n* **3** a joint formed by welding [obsolete *well* to melt, weld] **welder** *n*

welfare *n* **1** health, happiness, prosperity, and general wellbeing **2** financial and other assistance given, usually by the government, to people in need [WEL(L)[1] + FARE]

welfare state *n* a system in which the government undertakes responsibility for the wellbeing of its population, through unemployment insurance, retirement pensions, and other social-security measures

well[1] *adv* **better, best 1** satisfactorily or pleasingly: *well proportioned* **2** skilfully: *I played well for the last six holes* **3** thoroughly: *make sure the chicken is well cooked* **4** comfortably or prosperously: *he has lived well from his various nautical exploits* **5** suitably or fittingly: *you can't very well refuse* **6** intimately: *darling Robert, I know him so well* **7** favourably: *it will go down very well with all the people who support him* **8** by a considerable margin: *well over half; she left well before tea* **9** very likely: *the claim may well be true* **10** *informal* extremely: *well cool* **11 all very well** used ironically to express discontent or annoyance: *that's all very well, but I'm left to pick up the pieces* **12 as well A** in addition **B** with equal effect: used to express indifference or reluctance: *I might as well go out* **13 as well as** in addition to **14 just as well** fortunate or appropriate: *it's just as well I didn't spend all my money* ▹ *adj* **15** in good health: *I'm not feeling well* **16** satisfactory or acceptable: *all was well in the aircraft* ▹ *interj* **17 A** an expression of surprise, indignation, or reproof: *well, what a cheek!* **B** an expression of anticipation in waiting for an answer or remark: *well, what do you think?* [Old English *wel*]

well[2] *n* **1** a hole or shaft bored into the earth to tap a supply of water, oil, or gas **2** an open shaft through the floors of a building, used for a staircase ▹ *vb* **3** to flow upwards or outwards: *tears welled up into my eyes* [Old English *wella*]

we'll we will *or* we shall

well-advised *adj* prudent or sensible: *you would be well-advised to cooperate with me*

well-appointed *adj* (of a room or building) equipped or furnished to a high standard

well-balanced *adj* sensible and emotionally stable

well-behaved *adj* having good manners; not causing trouble or mischief

well-being *n* the state of being contented and healthy: *a sense of well-being*

well-born *adj* belonging to a noble or upper-class family

well-bred *adj* having good manners; polite

well-built *adj* strong and well-proportioned

well-connected *adj* having influential or important relatives or friends

well-disposed *adj* inclined to be sympathetic, kindly, or friendly towards a person or idea

well-done *adj* **1** made or accomplished satisfactorily **2** (of food, esp. meat) cooked very thoroughly

W

well-founded *adj* having a sound basis in fact: *a well-founded fear of persecution*
well-groomed *adj* having a smart tidy appearance
well-grounded *adj* having a sound basis in fact: *well-grounded suspicions*
wellhead *n* **1** the source of a well or stream **2** a source, fountainhead, or origin
well-heeled *adj informal* wealthy
wellies *pl n Brit, NZ & Austral informal* Wellington boots
well-informed *adj* knowing a lot about a great variety of subjects or about one particular subject
Wellington boots *or* **wellingtons** *pl n* long rubber boots, worn in wet or muddy conditions [after the 1st Duke of *Wellington*, soldier and statesman]
well-intentioned *adj* having good or kindly intentions, usually with unfortunate results
well-known *adj* widely known; famous
well-meaning *adj* having or indicating good intentions, usually with unfortunate results
well-nigh *adv* almost: *a well-nigh impossible task*
well-off *adj* **1** moderately wealthy **2** in a fortunate position: *some people don't know when they are well-off*
well-preserved *adj* not showing signs of ageing: *amazingly well-preserved for a man of 70*
well-read *adj* having read and learned a lot
well-rounded *adj* **1** desirably varied: *his well-rounded team* **2** rounded in shape or well developed: *a voluptuous well-rounded woman*
well-spoken *adj* having a clear, articulate, and socially acceptable accent and way of speaking
wellspring *n* a source of abundant supply: *the wellspring of truth*
well-thought-of *adj* liked and respected
well-to-do *adj* moderately wealthy
well-versed *adj* knowing a lot about a particular subject
well-wisher *n* a person who shows benevolence or sympathy towards a person or cause
well-worn *adj* **1** (of a word or phrase) having lost its meaning or force through being overused **2** having been used so much as to show signs of wear: *well-worn leather*
welly *n Brit slang* energy or commitment: *give it some welly!*
welsh *or* **welch** *vb* **welsh on** to fail to pay (a debt) or fulfil (an obligation) [origin unknown]
Welsh *adj* **1** of Wales ▷ *n* **2** a Celtic language spoken in some parts of Wales ▷ *pl n* **3 the Welsh** the people of Wales [Old English *Wēlisc, Wǣlisc*]
Welshman *or fem* **Welshwoman** *n, pl* **-men** *or* **-women** a person from Wales
Welsh rarebit *n* melted cheese, sometimes mixed with milk or seasonings, served on hot toast. Also called: **Welsh rabbit**
welt *n* **1** a raised mark on the skin produced by a blow **2** a raised or strengthened seam in a garment [origin unknown]
welter *n* a confused mass or jumble: *a welter of facts* [Middle Low German, Middle Dutch *weltern*]
welterweight *n* a professional boxer weighing up to 147 pounds (66.5 kg) or an amateur boxer weighing up to 67 kg
wen *n pathol* a cyst on the scalp [Old English *wenn*]
wench *n old-fashioned* **1** *facetious* a girl or young woman **2** a prostitute or female servant [Old English *wencel* child]
wend *vb* to make (one's way) in a particular direction: *it's time to wend our way back home* [Old English *wendan*]
Wendy house *n* a small toy house for a child to play in [after *Wendy*, the girl in J. M. Barrie's play *Peter Pan*]
wensleydale *n* a white cheese with a flaky texture [after *Wensleydale*, North Yorkshire]
went *vb* the past tense of **go**
wept *vb* the past of **weep**
were *vb* the form of the past tense of **be**: used after *we, you, they*, or a plural noun, or as a subjunctive in conditional sentences [Old English *wēron, wǣron*]

> **USAGE** *Were*, as a remnant of the past subjunctive in English, is used in formal contexts in clauses expressing hypotheses (*if he were to die, she would inherit everything*), suppositions contrary to fact (*if I were you, I would be careful*), and desire (*I wish he were there now*). In informal speech, however, *was* is often used instead.

we're we are
weren't were not
werewolf *n, pl* **-wolves** (in folklore) a person who can turn into a wolf [Old English *wer* man + *wulf* wolf]
west *n* **1** one of the four cardinal points of the compass, at 270° clockwise from north; the direction along a line of latitude towards the sunset **2 the west** any area lying in or towards the west ▷ *adj* **3** situated in, moving towards, or facing the west **4** (esp. of the wind) from the west ▷ *adv* **5** in, to, or towards the west [Old English]
West *n* **1 the West** **A** the western part of the world contrasted historically and culturally with the East **B** (esp. formerly) the non-Communist countries of Europe and America contrasted with the Communist states of the East ▷ *adj* **2** of or denoting the western part of a country or region
westbound *adj* going towards the west
westerly *adj* **1** of or in the west ▷ *adv, adj* **2** towards the west **3** from the west: *a westerly wind*
western *adj* **1** situated in or towards the west **2** facing or moving towards the west **3** (*sometimes cap*) of or characteristic of the west or West ▷ *n* **4** a film or book about cowboys in the western states of the US in the 19th century **westernmost** *adj*
Western *adj* (esp. formerly) of or characteristic of the Americas and the parts of Europe not under Communist rule
Westerner *n* a person from the west of a country or region
western hemisphere *n* the half of the globe that contains the Americas
westernize *or* **-nise** *vb* **-nizing, -nized** *or* **-nising, -nised** to influence or make familiar with the customs or practices of the West **westernization** *or* **-nisation** *n*

W

West Indian *adj* **1** of the West Indies ▷ *n* **2** a person from the West Indies
Westminster *n* the British Houses of Parliament
westward *adj, adv also* **westwards** **1** towards the west ▷ *n* **2** the westward part or direction
wet *adj* **wetter, wettest** **1** moistened, covered, or soaked with water or some other liquid **2** not yet dry or solid: *wet paint* **3** rainy: *the weather was cold and wet* **4** *Brit & NZ informal* feeble or foolish **5 wet behind the ears** *informal* immature or inexperienced ▷ *n* **6** rainy weather **7** *Brit informal* a feeble or foolish person ▷ *vb* **wetting, wet** *or* **wetted** **8** to make wet: *wet the brush before applying the paint* **9** to urinate in (one's clothes or bed) **10 wet oneself** to urinate in one's clothes [Old English *wǣt*] **wetly** *adv* **wetness** *n*
wet blanket *n informal* a person whose low spirits or lack of enthusiasm have a depressing effect on others
wet dream *n* an erotic dream accompanied by an emission of semen
wether *n* a male sheep, esp. a castrated one [Old English]
wetland *n* an area of marshy land
wet nurse *n* (esp. formerly) a woman hired to breast-feed another woman's baby
wet room *n* a type of waterproofed room with a drain in the floor often serving as an open-plan shower
wet suit *n* a close-fitting rubber suit used by skin-divers and yachtsmen to retain body heat
W. Glam West Glamorgan
whack *vb* **1** to hit hard: *that lad whacked him over the head with a bottle* **2** (usually foll. by *in* or *on*) *informal* to put something onto or into (something else) with force or abandon: *whack on some sunscreen* ▷ *n* **3** a hard blow or the sound of one: *a whack with a blunt instrument* **4** *informal* a share: *he took his whack of that money* **5 have a whack** to make an attempt **6 out of whack** *informal* out of order or out of condition: *my body is just a little out of whack* [imitative]
whacked *adj informal* completely exhausted
whacking *n* **1** *old-fashioned* a severe beating ▷ *adv* **2** *Brit, Austral & NZ informal* extremely: *a whacking great elm*
whale *n* **1** a very large fishlike sea mammal that breathes through a blowhole on the top of its head **2 have a whale of a time** *informal* to enjoy oneself very much [Old English *hwæl*]
whalebone *n* a thin strip of a horny material that hangs from the upper jaw of some whales, formerly used for stiffening corsets
whalebone whale *n* any whale with a double blowhole and strips of whalebone between the jaws instead of teeth, including the right whale and the blue whale
whaler *n* **1** a ship used for hunting whales **2** a person whose job is to hunt whales
whaling *n* the activity of hunting and killing whales for food or oil
wham *interj informal* an expression indicating suddenness or forcefulness: *suddenly, wham! you are caught up right in the middle of it* [imitative]
whammy *n, pl* **-mies** *informal* a devastating setback: *the double whammy of drugs and divorce*
wharepuni (for-rep-poon-ee) *n* NZ (in a Māori community) a tall carved building used as a guesthouse [Māori]
wharf *n, pl* **wharves** *or* **wharfs** a platform along the side of a waterfront for docking, loading, and unloading ships [Old English *hwearf*]
wharfie *n Austral & NZ* a dock labourer
what *pron* **1** used in requesting further information about the identity or categorization of something: *what was he wearing?*; *I knew what would happen* **2** the person, thing, people, or things that: *all was not what it seemed* **3** used in exclamations to add emphasis: *what a creep!* **4 what for?** for what reason? **5 what have you** other similar or related things: *qualifications, interests, profession, what have you* ▷ *adj* **6** used with a noun in requesting further information about the identity or categorization of something: *what difference can it make now?* **7** to any degree or in any amount: *they provided what financial support they could* [Old English *hwæt*]

> **USAGE** The use of *are* in sentences such as *what we need are more doctors* is common, although many people think *is* should be used: *what we need is more doctors.*

whatever *pron* **1** everything or anything that: *I can handle whatever comes up* **2** no matter what: *whatever you do, keep your temper* **3** *informal* other similar or related things: *a block of wood, rock, or whatever* **4** an intensive form of *what*, used in questions: *whatever gave you that impression?* ▷ *adj* **5** an intensive form of *what*: *I can take whatever actions I deem necessary* **6** at all: *there is no foundation whatever for such opinions* ▷ *interj* **7** an expression of indifference
whatnot *n informal* other similar or related things: *groceries, wines, and whatnot*
whatsoever *adj* at all: used for emphasis after a noun phrase that uses words such as *none* or *any*: *there is nothing whatsoever wrong with your heart; it can be used at any time and under any circumstances whatsoever*
wheat *n* **1** a kind of grain used in making flour and pasta **2** the plant from which this grain is obtained [Old English *hwǣte*]
wheatear *n* a small northern songbird with a white rump [from *white* + *arse*]
wheaten *adj* made from the grain or flour of wheat: *wheaten bread*
wheat germ *n* the vitamin-rich middle part of a grain of wheat
wheatmeal *n* a brown flour intermediate between white flour and wholemeal flour
wheedle *vb* **-dling, -dled** **1** to try to persuade (someone) by coaxing or flattery: *wheedling you into giving them their way* **2** to obtain (something) in this way: *she wheedled money out of him* [origin unknown] **wheedling** *adj, n*
wheel *n* **1** a circular object mounted on a shaft around which it can turn, fixed under vehicles to enable them to move **2** anything like a wheel in shape or function: *the steering wheel*; *a spinning wheel* **3** something that is repeated in cycles: *the wheel of fashion would turn, and the clothes would be back in style* **4 at** *or* **behind the wheel** driving a vehicle ▷ *vb* **5** to push (a bicycle, wheelchair, or pram) along

W

6 to turn in a circle **7 wheel and deal** to operate shrewdly and sometimes unscrupulously in order to advance one's own interests **8 wheel round** to change direction or turn round suddenly ▷ See also **wheels** [Old English *hwēol, hweowol*]

wheelbarrow *n* a shallow open box for carrying small loads, with a wheel at the front and two handles

wheelbase *n* the distance between the front and back axles of a motor vehicle

wheelchair *n* a special chair on large wheels, for use by people who cannot walk properly

wheel clamp *n* a device fixed onto one wheel of an illegally parked car to prevent the car being driven off

wheelhouse *n* an enclosed structure on the bridge of a ship from which it is steered

wheelie *n* a manoeuvre on a cycle or skateboard in which the front wheel or wheels are raised off the ground

wheelie bin *n Brit, Austral & NZ* a large container for household rubbish, mounted on wheels so that it can be moved more easily

wheeling and dealing *n* shrewd and sometimes unscrupulous moves made in order to advance one's own interests **wheeler-dealer** *n*

wheels *pl n* **1** *informal* a car **2** the main force and mechanism of an organization or system: *the wheels of the economy* **3 wheels within wheels** a series of intricately connected events or plots

wheelwright *n* a person whose job is to make and mend wheels

wheeze *vb* **wheezing, wheezed 1** to breathe with a rasping or whistling sound ▷ *n* **2** a wheezing breath or sound **3** *Brit old-fashioned slang* a trick or plan: *a money-making wheeze* [probably from Old Norse *hvǣsa* to hiss] **wheezy** *adj*

whelk *n* an edible sea creature with a strong snail-like shell [Old English *weoloc*]

whelp *n* **1** a young wolf or dog **2** *offensive* a youth ▷ *vb* **3** (of an animal) to give birth [Old English *hwelp*]

when *adv* **1** at what time?: *when are they leaving?* ▷ *conj* **2** at the time at which: *he was twenty when the war started* **3** although: *he drives when he could walk* **4** considering the fact that: *how did you pass the exam when you hadn't studied for it?* ▷ *pron* **5** at which time: *she's at the age when girls get interested in boys* [Old English *hwanne, hwænne*]

> **USAGE** *When* should not be used loosely as a substitute for *in which* after a noun which does not refer to a period of time: *paralysis is a condition in which* (not *when*) *parts of the body cannot be moved.*

whence *conj old-fashioned or poetic* from what place, cause, or origin: *he would then ask them whence they came* [Middle English *whannes*]

> **USAGE** The expression *from whence* should be avoided, since *whence* already means from which place: *the tradition whence* (not *from whence*) *such ideas flowed.*

whenever *conj* **1** at every or any time that: *the filly was trained to stop whenever a jockey used a whip* ▷ *adv* **2** no matter when: *I am eager to come whenever you suggest* **3** *informal* at an unknown or unspecified time: *the 16th, 17th, or whenever* **4** an intensive form of *when*, used in questions: *if we can't exercise restraint now, whenever can we?*

where *adv* **1** in, at, or to what place, point, or position?: *where are we going?; I know where he found it* ▷ *pron* **2** in, at, or to which place: *he found a sandwich bar where he could get a snack* ▷ *conj* **3** in the place at which: *he should have stayed where he was doing well* [Old English *hwǣr*]

whereabouts *pl n* **1** the place, esp. the approximate place, where a person or thing is: *the whereabouts of the president are unknown* ▷ *adv* **2** approximately where: *whereabouts will you go?*

whereas *conj* but by contrast: *she was crazy about him, whereas for him it was just another affair*

whereby *pron* by or because of which: *the process whereby pests become resistant to pesticides*

wherefore *n* **1 the whys and wherefores** the reasons or explanation: *the whys and wherefores of the war* ▷ *conj* **2** *old-fashioned, formal* for which reason

wherein *old-fashioned or formal* ▷ *adv* **1** in what place or respect?: *wherein lies the truth?* ▷ *pron* **2** in which place or thing: *the mirror wherein he had been gazing*

whereof *old-fashioned or formal* ▷ *adv* **1** of what or which person or thing? ▷ *pron* **2** of which person or thing: *I know whereof I speak*

whereupon *conj* at which point: *they sentenced him to death, whereupon he fainted*

wherever *pron* **1** at, in, or to every place or point which: *I got a wonderful reception wherever I went* ▷ *conj* **2** in, to, or at whatever place: *wherever they went, the conditions were harsh* ▷ *adv* **3** no matter where: *we're going to find him, wherever he is* **4** *informal* at, in, or to an unknown or unspecified place: *the jungles of Borneo or wherever* **5** an intensive form of *where*, used in questions: *wherever have you been?*

wherewithal *n* **the wherewithal** the necessary funds, resources, or equipment: *the wherewithal for making chemical weapons*

whet *vb* **whetting, whetted 1 whet someone's appetite** to increase someone's desire for or interest in something: *she gave him just enough information to whet his appetite* **2** *old-fashioned* to sharpen (a knife or other tool) [Old English *hwettan*]

whether *conj* **1** used to introduce an indirect question: *he asked him whether he had seen the hunter* **2** used to introduce a clause expressing doubt or choice: *you are entitled to the assistance of a lawyer, whether or not you can afford one; we learn from experience, whether good or bad* [Old English *hwæther*]

whetstone *n* a stone used for sharpening knives or other tools

whew *interj* an exclamation of relief, surprise, disbelief, or weariness

whey (**way**) *n* the watery liquid that separates from the curd when milk is clotted, for example in making cheese [Old English *hwǣg*]

which *adj* **1** used with a noun in requesting that the particular thing being referred to is further identified or distinguished: *which way had he gone?; a questionnaire to find out which shops local consumers use* **2** any out of several: *you have to choose which goods and services you want* ▷ *pron* **3** used in requesting that the particular thing being referred to is

W

further identified or distinguished: *which of these occupations would be suitable for you?* **4** used in relative clauses referring to a thing rather than a person: *a discovery which could have lasting effects* **5** and that: *her books were all over the dining table, which meant we had to eat in the kitchen* [Old English *hwelc*]

USAGE See at **that**.

whichever *adj* **1** any out of several: *choose whichever line you feel more comfortable with* **2** no matter which: *whichever bridge you take, pause mid-stream for a look up and down the river* ▷ *pron* **3** any one or ones out of several: *delete whichever is inapplicable* **4** no matter which one or ones: *whichever you choose, you must be consistent throughout*

whiff *n* **1** a passing odour: *I got a whiff of her perfume* **2** a trace or hint: *the first whiff of jealousy* [imitative]

Whig *n* **1** a member of a British political party of the 18th–19th centuries that sought limited political and social reform and provided the core of the Liberal Party ▷ *adj* **2** of or relating to Whigs [probably from *whiggamore*, one of a group of 17th-century Scottish rebels] **Whiggism** *n*

while *conj* **1** at the same time that: *anti-inflammatory remedies may be used to alleviate the condition while background factors are investigated* **2** at some point during the time that: *her father had died while she was gone* **3** although or whereas: *while she tossed and turned, he fell into a dreamless sleep* ▷ *n* **4** a period of time: *I'd like to stay a while* [Old English *hwīl*]

USAGE It was formerly considered incorrect to use *while* to mean *although* or *whereas*, but these uses have now become acceptable.

while away *vb* **whiling, whiled** to pass (time) idly but pleasantly

whilst *conj chiefly Brit* same as **while**

whim *n* a sudden, passing, and often fanciful idea [origin unknown]

whimper *vb* **1** to cry, complain, or say (something) in a whining plaintive way ▷ *n* **2** a soft plaintive whine [imitative]

whimsical *adj* unusual, playful, and fanciful: *a whimsical story* **whimsically** *adv*

whimsy *n* **1** *pl* **-sies** a fanciful or playful idea: *they thought sparing the rod a foolish whimsy* **2** capricious or playful behaviour: *sudden flights of whimsy* [from *whim*]

whin *n chiefly Brit* same as **gorse** [from Old Norse]

whine *n* **1** a long high-pitched plaintive cry or moan **2** a peevish complaint ▷ *vb* **whining, whined** **3** to whinge or complain **4** to issue a long high-pitched moan [Old English *hwīnan*] **whiner** *n* **whining** *adj, n*

whinge *Brit, Austral & NZ informal* ▷ *vb* **whingeing, whinged** **1** to complain in a moaning manner ▷ *n* **2** a complaint [Old English *hwinsian* to whine] **whinger** *n*

whinny *vb* **-nies, -nying, -nied** **1** (of a horse) to neigh softly or gently ▷ *n, pl* **-nies** **2** a gentle or low-pitched neigh [imitative]

whip *n* **1** a piece of leather or rope attached at one end to a stiff handle, used for hitting people or animals **2 A** a member of a political party who is responsible for urging members to attend Parliament to vote on an important issue **B** a notice sent to members of a political party by the whip, urging them to attend Parliament to vote in a particular way on an important issue **3** a dessert made from egg whites or cream beaten stiff: *raspberry whip* ▷ *vb* **whipping, whipped** **4** to hit with a whip **5** to hit sharply: *strands of hair whipped across her cheeks* **6** *informal* to move or go quickly and suddenly: *machine-gun bullets whipped past him* **7** to beat (cream or eggs) with a whisk or fork until frothy or stiff **8** to rouse (someone) into a particular condition: *politicians have whipped themselves into a panic about never-ending recession* **9** *informal* to steal (something) ▷ See also **whip out, whip-round, whip up** [perhaps from Middle Dutch *wippen* to swing] **whipping** *n*

whip bird *n Austral* a bird with a whistle ending in a whipcrack note

whip hand *n* **the whip hand** an advantage or dominating position: *buyers have the whip hand over estate agents*

whiplash *n* **1** a quick lash of a whip **2** short for **whiplash injury**

whiplash injury *n* an injury to the neck resulting from the head being suddenly thrust forward and then snapped back, for example in a car crash

whip out *or* **whip off** *vb* to take (something) out or off quickly and suddenly: *she whipped off her glasses*

whipper-in *n, pl* **whippers-in** a huntsman's assistant who manages the hounds

whippersnapper *n old-fashioned* a young impertinent overconfident person

whippet *n* a small slender dog similar to a greyhound [perhaps based on *whip it!* move quickly!]

whipping boy *n* a person who is expected to take the blame for other people's mistakes or incompetence

whip-round *n informal* an impromptu collection of money

whipstock *n* the handle of a whip

whip up *vb* **1** to excite or arouse: *to get people all whipped up about something; to whip up enthusiasm* **2** *informal* to prepare quickly: *she had whipped up a rich sauce*

whir *n, vb* **whirring, whirred** same as **whirr**

whirl *vb* **1** to spin or turn round very fast **2** to seem to spin from dizziness or confusion: *my mind whirled with half-formed thoughts* ▷ *n* **3** the act or an instance of whirling: *he grasps her by the waist and gives her a whirl* **4** a round of intense activity: *the social whirl of Paris* **5** a confused state: *my thoughts are in a whirl* **6** **give something a whirl** *informal* to try something new [Old Norse *hvirfla* to turn about]

whirligig *n* **1** a spinning toy, such as a top **2** same as **merry-go-round** **3** anything that whirls

whirlpool *n* a powerful circular current of water, into which objects floating nearby are drawn

whirlwind *n* **1** a column of air whirling violently upwards in a spiral ▷ *adj* **2** done or happening much more quickly than usual: *a whirlwind tour of France*

whirr *or* **whir** *n* **1** a prolonged soft whizz or buzz: *the whirr of the fax machine* ▷ *vb* **whirring, whirred** **2** to produce a prolonged soft whizz or buzz [probably from Old Norse] **whirring** *n, adj*

W

whisk *vb* **1** to move or take somewhere swiftly: *I was whisked away in a police car* **2** to brush away lightly: *the waiter whisked the crumbs away with a napkin* **3** to beat (cream or eggs) with a whisk or fork until frothy or stiff ▷ *n* **4** the act or an instance of whisking: *a whisk of a scaly tail* **5** a utensil for beating cream or eggs until frothy or stiff [Old Norse *visk* wisp]

whisker *n* **1** any of the long stiff hairs that grow out from the sides of the mouth of a cat or other mammal **2** any of the hairs growing on a man's face, esp. on the cheeks or chin **3 by a whisker** by a very small distance or amount: *we missed him by a whisker* [Old Norse *visk* wisp] **whiskered** *or* **whiskery** *adj*

whiskey *n* Irish or American whisky

whisky *n, pl* **-kies** a strong alcoholic drink made by distilling fermented cereals [Scottish Gaelic *uisge beatha* water of life]

whisky-jack *n Canad* same as **Canada jay**

whisper *vb* **1** to speak or say (something) very softly, using the breath instead of the vocal cords **2** to make a low soft rustling sound: *the leaves whispered* ▷ *n* **3** a low soft voice: *her voice sank to a whisper* **4** *informal* a rumour: *I just picked up a whisper on this killing* **5** a low soft rustling sound: *a whisper of breeze in the shrubbery* [Old English *hwisprian*] **whispered** *adj*

whist *n* a card game for two pairs of players [perhaps from *whisk*, referring to the whisking up of the tricks]

whist drive *n* a social gathering where whist is played

whistle *vb* **-tling, -tled 1** to produce a shrill sound by forcing breath between pursed lips **2** to produce (a tune) by making a series of such sounds **3** to signal (to) by whistling or blowing a whistle: *the doorman whistled a cruising cab* **4** to move with a whistling sound: *a shell whistled through the upper air* **5** (of a kettle or train) to produce a shrill sound caused by steam being forced through a small opening **6** (of a bird) to give a shrill cry **7 whistle in the dark** to try to keep up one's confidence in spite of being afraid ▷ *n* **8** the act or sound of whistling: *he gave a whistle of astonishment* **9** a metal instrument that is blown down its end to produce a tune, signal, or alarm: *he played the tin whistle; the referee's whistle* **10** a device in a kettle or a train that makes a shrill sound by means of steam under pressure **11 blow the whistle on** *informal* to reveal and put a stop to (wrongdoing or a wrongdoer): *to blow the whistle on corrupt top-level officials* **12 wet one's whistle** *informal* to have a drink [Old English *hwistlian*]

W

whistle-blower *n informal* a person who informs on someone or puts a stop to something

whistle for *vb informal* to expect in vain: *he could whistle for his vote in the future*

whistle-stop *adj* denoting a tour, esp. a campaign tour by a political candidate, in which short stops are made at many different places

whit *n* **not a whit** not at all: *it does not matter a whit* [probably variant of obsolete *wight* a person]

Whit *n* **1** short for **Whitsuntide** ▷ *adj* **2** of Whitsuntide: *Whit Monday*

white *adj* **1** having no hue, owing to the reflection of all or almost all light; of the colour of snow **2** pale, because of illness, fear, shock, or another emotion: *white with rage* **3** (of hair) having lost its colour, usually from age **4** (of coffee or tea) with milk or cream **5** (of wine) made from pale grapes or from black grapes separated from their skins **6** denoting flour, or bread made from flour, that has had part of the grain removed ▷ *n* **7** the lightest colour; the colour of snow **8** the clear fluid that surrounds the yolk of an egg **9** *anatomy* the white part of the eyeball **10** anything white, such as white paint or white clothing: *a room decorated all in white* ▷ See also **whites** [Old English *hwīt*] **whiteness** *n* **whitish** *adj*

White *n* **1** a member of a light-skinned race ▷ *adj* **2** of or relating to a White or Whites

whitebait *n* **1** the young of herrings, sprats, or pilchards, cooked and eaten whole **2** any of various small silvery fishes of Australia and New Zealand and of North American coastal regions of the Pacific

white blood cell *n* same as **leucocyte**

whitecaps *pl n* waves with white broken crests

white-collar *adj* denoting workers employed in professional and clerical occupations

white dwarf *n* a small, faint, very dense star

white elephant *n* a possession that is unwanted by its owner

white feather *n* a symbol of cowardice

white fish *n* a sea fish with white flesh that is used for food, such as cod or haddock

white flag *n* a signal of surrender or to request a truce

whitefly *n, pl* **-flies** a tiny whitish insect that is harmful to greenhouse plants

White Friar *n* a Carmelite friar

white gold *n* a white lustrous hard-wearing alloy containing gold together with platinum or other metals, used in jewellery

white goods *pl n* large household appliances, such as refrigerators and cookers

white heat *n* **1** intense heat that produces a white light **2** *informal* a state of intense emotion: *the white heat of hate*

white hope *n informal* a person who is expected to accomplish a great deal: *the great white hope of Polish cinema*

white horses *pl n* same as **whitecaps**

white-hot *adj* **1** at such a high temperature that white light is produced **2** *informal* in a state of intense emotion: *white-hot agony*

White House *n* the US president and the executive branch of the US government: *the White House reviewed the report* [after the official home of the US president in Washington DC]

white lie *n* a small lie, usually told to avoid hurting someone's feelings

white light *n* light that contains all the wavelengths of the visible spectrum, as in sunlight

white matter *n* the whitish tissue of the brain and spinal cord, consisting mainly of nerve fibres

white meat *n* meat, such as chicken or pork, that is light in colour when cooked

whiten *vb* to make or become white or whiter **whitener** *n* **whitening** *n*
white noise *n* noise that has a wide range of frequencies of uniform intensity
whiteout *n* an atmospheric condition in which blizzards or low clouds make it very difficult to see
white paper *n* an official government report which sets out the government's policy on a specific matter
white pepper *n* a hot seasoning made from the seeds of the pepper plant with the husks removed
White Russian *adj* **1** (formerly) of Byelorussia, an administrative division of the W Soviet Union: now Belarus ▹ *n* **2** (formerly) a person from Byelorussia **3** (formerly) the language of Byelorussia
whites *pl n* white clothes, as worn for playing cricket
white sauce *n* a thick sauce made from flour, butter, seasonings, and milk or stock
white slave *n old-fashioned* a White woman forced into prostitution, typically one lured to a foreign country for this purpose **white slavery** *n*
white spirit *n* a colourless liquid obtained from petroleum and used as a substitute for turpentine
White supremacy *n* the theory or belief that White people are superior to people of other races **White supremacist** *n, adj*
white tie *n* **1** a white bow tie worn as part of a man's formal evening dress ▹ *adj* **white-tie** **2** denoting an occasion when formal evening dress should be worn: *tickets for the white-tie Shelley Ball*
white trash *n derogatory* poor White people living in the United States, esp. in the South
whitewash *n* **1** a mixture of lime or chalk in water, for whitening walls and other surfaces **2** an attempt to conceal the unpleasant truth: *the report was a whitewash* ▹ *vb* **3** to cover with whitewash **4** to conceal the unpleasant truth about **whitewashed** *adj*
whitewood *n* a light-coloured wood often prepared for staining
whither *conj old-fashioned or poetic* to what place or for what purpose: *they knew not whither they went* [Old English *hwider, hwæder*]
whiting (**white**-ing) *n* **1** a white-fleshed food fish of European seas **2** *Austral* any of several marine food fishes
whitlow *n* an inflamed sore on the end of a finger or toe [originally *white* + *flaw*]
Whitsun *n* **1** short for **Whitsuntide** ▹ *adj* **2** of Whit Sunday or Whitsuntide
Whit Sunday *n* the seventh Sunday after Easter [Old English *hwīta sunnandæg* white Sunday]
Whitsuntide *n* the week that begins with Whit Sunday
whittle *vb* **-tling, -tled** **1** to make (an object) by cutting or shaving pieces from (a piece of wood) with a small knife **2** **whittle down** *or* **away** to reduce in size or effectiveness gradually: *my self-confidence had been whittled away to almost nothing* [Old English *thwītan* to cut]
whizz *or* **whiz** *vb* **whizzing, whizzed** **1** to move with a loud humming or buzzing sound: *the bullets whizzed overhead* **2** *informal* to move or go quickly: *the wind surfers fairly whizzed along the water* ▹ *n, pl* **whizzes** **3** a loud humming or buzzing sound **4** *informal* a person who is extremely good at something: *he's a whizz on finance* **5** *slang* amphetamine [imitative]
whizz kid *or* **whiz kid** *n informal* a person who is outstandingly able and successful for his or her age
who *pron* **1** which person: *who are you?*; *he didn't know who had started it* **2** used at the beginning of a relative clause referring to a person or people already mentioned: *he is a man who can effect change* [Old English *hwā*]

USAGE See at **whom**.

WHO World Health Organization
whoa *interj* a command used to stop horses or to slow down someone who is moving or talking too fast
whodunnit *or* **whodunit** (hoo-**dun**-nit) *n informal* a novel, play, or film about the solving of a murder mystery
whoever *pron* **1** the person or people who: *whoever bought it for you has to make the claim* **2** no matter who: *I pity him, whoever he is* **3** *informal* other similar or related people or person: *your best friend, your neighbours, or whoever* **4** an intensive form of *who*, used in questions: *whoever thought of such a thing?*
whole *adj* **1** constituting or referring to all of something: *I'd spent my whole allowance by Saturday afternoon* **2** unbroken or undamaged ▹ *adv* **3** in an undivided or unbroken piece: *truffles are cooked whole* **4** *informal* completely or entirely: *a whole new theory of treatment* ▹ *n* **5** all there is of a thing: *the whole of my salary* **6** a collection of parts viewed together as a unit: *taking Great Britain as a whole* **7** **on the whole** **A** taking all things into consideration: *on the whole he has worked about one year out of twelve* **B** in general: *on the whole they were not successful* [Old English *hāl*] **wholeness** *n*
wholefood *n* **1** food that has been refined or processed as little as possible ▹ *adj* **2** of or relating to wholefood: *a wholefood diet*
wholehearted *adj* done or given with total sincerity or enthusiasm: *wholehearted support* **wholeheartedly** *adv*
wholemeal *adj Brit & Austral* **1** (of flour) made from the entire wheat kernel **2** made from wholemeal flour: *wholemeal bread*
whole number *n maths* a number that does not contain a fraction, such as 0, 1, or 2
wholesale *n* **1** the business of selling goods in large quantities and at lower prices to retailers for resale **2** relating to such business: *wholesale prices* **3** extensive or indiscriminate: *the wholesale destruction of forests* ▹ *adv* **4** by or through the wholesale business: *we buy beef wholesale* **5** extensively or indiscriminately: *buffalo were slaughtered wholesale* **wholesaler** *n*
wholesome *adj* **1** physically beneficial: *wholesome food* **2** morally beneficial: *a wholesome attitude of the mind* [from *whole* healthy]
whole-wheat *adj US & Canad* same as **wholemeal**
wholly *adv* completely or totally

W

whom *pron* the objective form of *who*: *whom will you tell?; he was devoted to his wife, whom he married in 1960* [Old English *hwām*]

> **USAGE** It was formerly considered correct to use *whom* whenever the objective form of *who* was required. This is no longer thought to be necessary and the objective form *who* is now commonly used, even in formal writing: *there were several people there who he had met before*. *Who* cannot be used directly after a preposition – the preposition is usually displaced, as in *the man (who) he sold his car to*. In formal writing *whom* is preferred in sentences like these: *the man to whom he sold his car*. There are some types of sentence in which *who* cannot be used: *the refugees, many of whom were old and ill, were allowed across the border*.

whomever *pron* the objective form of *whoever*: *this law limits an employer's right to employ whomever he wants*

whoop *vb* **1** to cry out in excitement or joy **2 whoop it up** *informal* to indulge in a noisy celebration ▷ *n* **3** a loud cry of excitement or joy [imitative]

whoopee *old-fashioned, informal* ▷ *interj* **1** an exclamation of joy or excitement ▷ *n* **2 make whoopee A** to indulge in a noisy celebration **B** to make love

whooping cough *n* an acute infectious disease mainly affecting children, that causes coughing spasms ending with a shrill crowing sound on breathing in

whoops *interj* an exclamation of mild surprise or of apology

whopper *n informal* **1** an unusually large or impressive example of something: *Deauville's beach is a whopper* **2** a big lie

whopping *informal* ▷ *adj* **1** unusually large: *a whopping 40 per cent* ▷ *adv* **2** extremely: *it's a whopping great gamble*

whore (hore) *n* a prostitute or promiscuous woman: often a term of abuse [Old English *hōre*]

whorehouse *n informal* a brothel

whorl *n* **1** *botany* a circular arrangement of leaves or flowers round the stem of a plant **2** *zool* a single turn in a spiral shell **3** anything shaped like a coil [probably variant of *whirl*]

who's who is *or* who has

whose *pron* **1** of whom? belonging to whom?: used in direct and indirect questions: *whose idea was it?; I wondered whose it was* **2** of whom or of which: used as a relative pronoun: *Gran had sympathy for anybody whose life had gone wrong* [Old English *hwæs*, genitive of *hwā* who + *hwæt* what]

whosoever *pron old-fashioned or formal* same as **whoever**

why *adv* **1** for what reason?: *why did he marry her?; she avoided asking him why he was there* ▷ *pron* **2** for or because of which: *you can think of all kinds of reasons why you should not believe it* ▷ *n, pl* **whys 3 the whys and wherefores** See **wherefore** (sense 1) ▷ *interj* **4** an exclamation of surprise, indignation, or impatience: *why, I listen to you on the radio twice a week* [Old English *hwȳ, hwī*]

WI 1 Wisconsin **2** *Brit & NZ* Women's Institute

wick *n* **1** a cord through the middle of a candle, through which the fuel reaches the flame **2 get on someone's wick** *Brit & Austral slang* to annoy someone [Old English *wēoce*]

wicked *adj* **1** morally bad: *the wicked queen in 'Snow White'* **2** playfully mischievous or roguish: *let's be wicked and go skinny-dipping* **3** dangerous or unpleasant: *there was a wicked cut over his eye* **4** *slang* very good [Old English *wicca* sorcerer, *wicce* witch] **wickedly** *adv* **wickedness** *n*

wicker *adj* made of wickerwork: *a wicker chair* [from Old Norse]

wickerwork *n* a material consisting of slender flexible twigs woven together

wicket *n cricket* **1** either of two sets of three stumps stuck in the ground with two wooden bails resting on top, at which the batsman stands **2** the playing space between these **3** the act or instance of a batsman being got out [Old French *wiket*]

wicketkeeper *n cricket* the fielder positioned directly behind the wicket

wicking *adj* acting to move moisture by capillary action from the inside to the surface: *wicking fabric*

wide *adj* **1** having a great extent from side to side: *the wide main street* **2** having a specified extent from side to side: *three metres wide* **3** covering or including many different things: *a wide range of services* **4** covering a large distance or extent: *the proposal was voted down by a wide margin* **5** (of eyes) opened fully ▷ *adv* **6** to a large or full extent: *he swung the door wide* **7 far and wide** See **far** (sense 7) ▷ *n* **8** *cricket* a ball bowled outside the batsman's reach, which scores a run for the batting side [Old English *wīd*] **widely** *adv*

wide-angle lens *n* a lens on a camera which can cover a wider angle of view than an ordinary lens

wide-awake *adj* fully awake

wide-eyed *adj* **1** innocent or naive **2** surprised or frightened: *wide-eyed astonishment* ▷ *adv* **3** in a frightened, surprised, or excited manner: *they looked at me wide-eyed*

widen *vb* to make or become wide or wider

wide open *adj* **1** open to the full extent: *the main door was wide open* **2** exposed or vulnerable: *he was leaving himself wide open to problems*

wide-ranging *adj* covering or including many different things or subjects: *a wide-ranging review*

widescreen *adj* (of a television set) having a screen whose width is much greater than its height

widespread *adj* affecting an extensive area or a large number of people: *widespread damage; widespread public support*

widgeon *n* same as **wigeon**

widget *n* **1** *informal* any small device, the name of which is unknown or forgotten **2** a small device in a beer can which, when the can is opened, releases nitrogen gas into the beer, giving it a head **3** (in the graphical user interface of a computer or mobile phone) an element of interaction, such as a scroll bar or button [changed from GADGET]

widow *n* a woman whose spouse has died and who has not remarried [Old English *widewe*] **widowhood** *n*

widowed *adj* denoting a person whose spouse has died and who has not remarried
widower *n* a man whose spouse has died and who has not remarried
widow's weeds *pl n old-fashioned* the black mourning clothes traditionally worn by a widow [from Old English *wǣd* a band worn in mourning]
width *n* **1** the extent or measurement of something from side to side **2** the distance across a rectangular swimming bath, as opposed to its length
wield *vb* **1** to handle or use (a weapon or tool) **2** to exert or maintain (power or influence) [Old English *wieldan, wealdan*]
wife *n, pl* **wives** the woman to whom a person is married [Old English *wīf*] **wifely** *adj*
Wi-Fi *n trademark computers* a system of wireless access to the internet
wig *n* an artificial head of hair [from *periwig*]
wigeon *or* **widgeon** *n* a wild marshland duck [origin unknown]
wigging *n Brit old-fashioned slang* a reprimand [origin unknown]
wiggle *vb* **-gling, -gled 1** to move with jerky movements from side to side or up and down: *she wiggled her toes in the cool water* ▷ *n* **2** a wiggling movement or walk [Middle Low German, Middle Dutch *wiggelen*]
wigwam *n* a Native American's tent, made of animal skins [Native American *wīkwām*]
wiki *computers* ▷ *n* **1** a website, or page within one, whose content can be edited freely by anyone with access to a web browser ▷ *adj* **2** of or relating to the software which facilitates such open editing: *wiki technology* [from Hawaiian *wiki-wiki* quick]
wilco *interj* an expression in signalling and telecommunications, indicating that a message just received will be complied with [abbreviation for *I will comply*]
wild *adj* **1** (of animals or birds) living in natural surroundings; not domesticated or tame **2** (of plants) growing in a natural state; not cultivated **3** uninhabited and desolate: *wild country* **4** living in a savage or uncivilized way: *a wild mountain man* **5** lacking restraint or control: *a wild party* **6** stormy or violent: *a wild windy October morning* **7** in a state of extreme emotional intensity: *wild with excitement* **8** without reason or substance: *wild accusations* **9** **wild about** *informal* very enthusiastic about: *his colleagues aren't all that wild about him* ▷ *adv* **10** **run wild** to behave without restraint: *she was allowed to run completely wild* ▷ *n* **11** **the wild** a free natural state of living: *creatures of the wild* **12** **the wilds** a desolate or uninhabited region: *the wilds of Africa* [Old English *wilde*] **wildly** *adv* **wildness** *n*
wild card *n* **1** *sport* a player or team that is allowed to take part in a competition despite not having met the normal qualifying requirements **2** *computers* a character that can be substituted for any other in a file
wildcat *n, pl* **-cats** *or* **-cat 1** a wild European cat that looks like a domesticated cat but is larger and has a bushy tail **2** *informal* a quick-tempered person ▷ *adj* **3** *chiefly US* risky and financially unsound: *a wildcat operation*
wildcat strike *n* a strike begun by workers spontaneously or without union approval
wildebeest *n, pl* **-beests** *or* **-beest** same as **gnu** [Afrikaans]
wilderness *n* **1** a wild uninhabited uncultivated region **2** a confused mass or tangle: *a wilderness of long grass and wild flowers* **3** a state of being no longer in a prominent position: *a long spell in the political wilderness* [Old English *wildēornes*, from *wildēor* wild beast]
wildfire *n* **spread like wildfire** to spread very quickly or uncontrollably
wild flower *n* any flowering plant that grows in an uncultivated state
wildfowl *pl n* wild birds, such as grouse and pheasants, that are hunted for sport or food
wild-goose chase *n* a search that has little or no chance of success
wildlife *n* wild animals and plants collectively
wild rice *n* the dark-coloured edible grain of a North American grass that grows on wet ground
Wild West *n* the western US during its settlement, esp. with reference to its lawlessness
wiles *pl n* artful or seductive tricks or ploys [from Old Norse *vēl* craft]
wilful *or US* **willful** *adj* **1** determined to do things in one's own way: *a wilful and insubordinate child* **2** deliberate and intentional: *wilful misconduct* **wilfully** *adv*
will¹ *vb, past tense* **would 1** used as an auxiliary to make the future tense: *he will go on trial on October 7* **2** to express resolution: *they will not consider giving up territories* **3** to express a polite request: *will you please calm Mummy and Daddy down* **4** to express ability: *many essential oils will protect clothing from moths* **5** to express probability or expectation: *his followers will be relieved to hear that* **6** to express customary practice: *boys will be boys!* **7** to express desire: *go in very small steps, if you will* [Old English *willan*]

USAGE See at **shall**.

will² *n* **1** a strong determination: *a fierce will to survive* **2** desire or wish: *a referendum to determine the will of the people* **3** a document setting out a person's wishes regarding the disposal of his or her property after death **4** **at will** when and as one chooses: *customers can withdraw money at will* ▷ *vb* **willing, willed 5** to try to make (something) happen by wishing very hard for it: *she willed herself not to cry* **6** to wish or desire: *if he wills it, we will meet again* **7** to leave (property) in one's will: *the farm had been willed to her* [Old English *willa*]
willies *pl n* **give someone the willies** *slang* to make someone nervous or frightened [origin unknown]
willing *adj* **1** favourably disposed or inclined: *I'm willing to hear what you have to say* **2** keen and obliging: *willing volunteers* **willingly** *adv* **willingness** *n*
will-o'-the-wisp *n* **1** someone or something that is elusive or deceptively alluring: *their freedom was just a will-o'-the-wisp* **2** a pale light that is sometimes seen over marshy ground at night [*Will*, short for *William* + *wisp* twist of hay burning as a torch]

W

willow *n* a tree that grows near water, with thin flexible branches used in weaving baskets and wood used for making cricket bats [Old English *welig*]
willowherb *n* a plant with narrow leaves and purplish flowers
willow pattern *n* a pattern in blue on white china, depicting a Chinese landscape with a willow tree, river, bridge, and figures
willowy *adj* slender and graceful
willpower *n* strong self-disciplined determination to do something
willy *n, pl* **-lies** *Brit, Austral & NZ informal* a childish or jocular word for **penis**
willy-nilly *adv* **1** in a haphazard fashion; indiscriminately: *spending taxpayers' money willy-nilly* **2** whether desired or not [Old English *wile hē, nyle hē* will he or will he not]
willy wagtail *n Austral* black-and-white flycatcher
willy-willy *n Austral* a small tropical dust storm [from a native Australian language]
wilt *vb* **1** (of a flower or plant) to become limp or drooping **2** (of a person) to lose strength or confidence [perhaps from obsolete *wilk* to wither]
Wilts Wiltshire
wily *adj* **wilier, wiliest** sly or crafty
wimp *informal* ▷ *n* **1** a feeble ineffective person ▷ *vb* **2 wimp out of** to fail to do (something) through lack of courage [origin unknown] **wimpish** *or* **wimpy** *adj*
WIMP windows, icons, menus (or mice), pointers: denoting a type of user-friendly screen display used on computers
wimple *n* a piece of cloth draped round the head to frame the face, worn by women in the Middle Ages and now by some nuns [Old English *wimpel*]
win *vb* **winning, won 1** to achieve first place in (a competition or race) **2** to gain (a prize or first place) in a competition or race **3** to gain victory in (a battle, argument, or struggle) **4** to gain (sympathy, approval, or support) ▷ *n* **5** *informal* a success, victory, or triumph: *three consecutive wins* ▷ See also **win over** [Old English *winnan*] **winnable** *adj*
wince *vb* **wincing, winced 1** to draw back slightly, as if in sudden pain ▷ *n* **2** the act of wincing [Old French *wencier, guenchir* to avoid]
winch *n* **1** a lifting or hauling device consisting of a rope or chain wound round a barrel or drum ▷ *vb* **2** to haul or lift using a winch: *two men were winched to safety by a helicopter* [Old English *wince* pulley]
wind¹ (rhymes with **pinned**) *n* **1** a current of air moving across the earth's surface **2** a trend or force: *the chill wind of change* **3** the power to breathe normally, esp. during or after physical exercise: *if you feel tired during the exercise, persevere – you'll soon get a second wind* **4** gas in the stomach or intestines **5** *informal* foolish or empty talk: *political language is designed to give an appearance of solidity to pure wind* **6 break wind** to release intestinal gas through the anus **7 get wind of** *informal* to find out about: *the media finally got wind of her disappearance* ▷ *adj* **8** *music* of or relating to wind instruments: *the wind section* ▷ *vb* **winding, winded 9** to cause (someone) to be short of breath: *he fell with a thud that left him winded* **10** to cause (a baby) to bring up wind after feeding [Old English] **windless** *adj*
wind² (rhymes with **pined**) *vb* **winding, wound 1** to twist (something flexible) round some object: *a sweatband was wound round his head* **2** to tighten the spring of (a clock or watch) by turning a key or knob **3** to follow a twisting course: *a narrow path wound through the shrubbery* ▷ See also **wind down, wind up** [Old English *windan*] **winding** *adj, n*
windbag *n slang* a person who talks a lot but says little of interest
windblown *adj* blown about by the wind: *windblown hair*
windbreak *n* a fence or a line of trees that gives protection from the wind by breaking its force
windcheater *n chiefly Brit* a warm jacket with a close-fitting knitted neck, cuffs, and waistband
wind chill *n* the serious chilling effect of wind and low temperature
wind down *vb* **1** to move downwards by turning a handle: *he wound down the rear window* **2** (of a clock or watch) to slow down before stopping completely **3** to relax after a stressful or tiring time: *I have not had a chance to wind down from a busy day* **4** to diminish gradually: *trading wound down for the day*
winded *adj* temporarily out of breath after physical exercise or a blow to the stomach
windfall *n* **1** a piece of unexpected good fortune, esp. financial gain **2** a fruit blown off a tree by the wind
windfall tax *n* a tax levied on profits made from the privatization of public utilities
wind farm *n* a large group of wind-driven generators for electricity supply
wind gauge *n* same as **anemometer**
winding sheet *n* a sheet in which a dead person is wrapped before being buried
wind instrument *n* a musical instrument, such as a flute, that is played by having air blown into it
windjammer *n history* a large merchant sailing ship
windlass *n* a machine for lifting heavy objects by winding a rope or chain round a barrel or drum driven by a motor [Old Norse *vindāss*]
windmill *n* **1** a building containing machinery for grinding corn or for pumping, driven by sails that are turned by the wind **2** *Brit* a toy consisting of a stick with plastic vanes attached, which revolve in the wind
window *n* **1** an opening in a building or a vehicle containing glass within a framework, which lets in light and enables people to see in or out **2** the display area behind a glass window in a shop **3** a transparent area in an envelope which reveals the address on the letter inside **4** an area on a computer screen that can be manipulated separately from the rest of the display area, for example so that two or more files can be displayed at the same time **5** a period of unbooked time in a diary or schedule [Old Norse *vindauga* wind eye]

window box *n* a long narrow box, placed on a windowsill, in which plants are grown

window-dressing *n* **1** the art of arranging goods in shop windows in such a way as to attract customers **2** an attempt to make something seem better than it is by stressing only its attractive features: *do you think that the president's calling for an investigation is window-dressing, or do you think he actually means to do something?* **window-dresser** *n*

windowpane *n* a sheet of glass in a window

window seat *n* **1** a seat below a window **2** a seat beside a window in a bus, train, or aircraft

window-shopping *n* looking at goods in shop windows without intending to buy anything

windowsill *n* a shelf at the bottom of a window, either inside or outside a room

windpipe *n* a nontechnical name for **trachea**

windscreen *n Brit, Austral & NZ* the sheet of glass that forms the front window of a motor vehicle

windscreen wiper *n Brit, Austral & NZ* an electrically operated blade with a rubber edge that wipes a windscreen clear of rain

windshield *n US & Canad* the sheet of glass that forms the front window of a motor vehicle

windshield wiper *n US & Canad* an electrically operated blade with a rubber edge that wipes a windshield clear of rain

windsock *n* a cloth cone mounted on a mast, used esp. at airports to indicate the direction of the wind

windsurfing *n* the sport of riding on water using a surfboard steered and propelled by an attached sail **windsurfer** *n*

windswept *adj* **1** exposed to the wind: *the vast windswept plains* **2** blown about by the wind: *his hair was looking a bit windswept*

wind tunnel *n* a chamber through which a stream of air is forced, in order to test the effects of wind on aircraft, buildings, and vehicles

wind up *vb* **1** to bring to a conclusion: *we want to wind this conflict up as quickly as possible* **2** *informal* to dissolve (a company) and divide its assets among creditors **3** to tighten the spring of (a clockwork mechanism) by turning a key or knob **4** to move (a car window) upwards by turning a handle **5** *informal* to end up: *to wind up in the hospital* **6** *informal* to make nervous or tense: *as crisis after crisis broke, I became increasingly wound up* **7** *Brit, Austral & NZ slang* to tease or annoy: *that really used to wind my old man up something rotten* ▷ *adj* **wind-up** **8** operated by clockwork: *a wind-up toy* ▷ *n* **wind-up** **9** a light-hearted hoax **10** the finish

windward *chiefly naut* ▷ *adj* **1** of or in the direction from which the wind blows ▷ *n* **2** the windward direction ▷ *adv* **3** towards the wind

windy *adj* **windier, windiest 1** denoting a time or conditions in which there is a strong wind: *a windy day* **2** exposed to the wind: *the windy graveyard* **3** long-winded or pompous: *his speeches are long and windy* **4** *old-fashioned slang* frightened

wine *n* **1** **A** an alcoholic drink produced by the fermenting of grapes with water and sugar **B** an alcoholic drink produced in this way from other fruits or flowers: *dandelion wine* ▷ *adj* **2** dark purplish-red ▷ *vb* **wining, wined 3 wine and dine** to entertain (someone) with wine and fine food [Latin *vinum*]

wine bar *n* a bar that specializes in serving wine and usually food

wine box *n* a cubic carton containing wine, with a tap for dispensing

wine cellar *n* **1** a cellar where wine is stored **2** the stock of wines stored there

wineglass *n* a glass for wine, usually with a small bowl on a stem with a flared base

wing *n* **1** one of the limbs or organs of a bird, bat, or insect that are used for flying **2** one of the two winglike supporting parts of an aircraft **3** a projecting part of a building: *converting the unused east wing into a suitable habitation* **4** a faction or group within a political party or other organization: *the youth wing of the African National Congress* **5** *Brit* the part of a car body surrounding the wheels **6** *sport* **A** either of the two sides of the pitch near the touchline **B** same as **winger** **7 wings** *theatre* the space offstage to the right or left of the acting area **8 in the wings** ready to step in when needed **9 on the wing** flying **10 spread one's wings** to make fuller use of one's abilities by trying new experiences: *he increasingly spread his wings abroad* **11 take someone under one's wing** to look after someone **12 take wing** to fly away ▷ *vb* **13** to fly: *a lone bird winging its way from the island* **14** to move through the air: *sending a shower of loose gravel winging towards the house* **15** to shoot or wound in the wing or arm **16** to provide with wings [Old Norse *vængr*] **winged** *adj* **wingless** *adj*

wing chair *n* an easy chair with side pieces extending forward from a high back

wing commander *n* a middle-ranking commissioned officer in an air force

winger *n sport* a player positioned on a wing

wing nut *n* a threaded nut with two flat projections which allow it to be turned by the thumb and forefinger

wingspan *n* the distance between the wing tips of a bird, insect, bat, or aircraft

wink *vb* **1** to close and open one eye quickly as a signal **2** (of a light) to shine brightly and intermittently; twinkle ▷ *n* **3** the act or an instance of winking, esp. as a signal **4** a twinkling of light **5** *informal* the smallest amount of sleep: *I didn't sleep a wink last night* **6 tip someone the wink** *Brit, Austral & NZ informal* to give someone a hint or warning [Old English *wincian*]

winkle *n* **1** an edible shellfish with a spirally coiled shell ▷ *vb* **-kling, -kled 2 winkle out** *informal, chiefly Brit* **A** to obtain (information) from someone who is not willing to provide it: *try to winkle the real problem out of them* **B** to coax or force out: *he somehow managed to winkle him out of his room*

winkle-pickers *pl n* men's shoes with very pointed narrow toes, popular in the 1950s

winner *n* **1** a person or thing that wins **2** *informal* a person or thing that seems sure to be successful

winning *adj* **1** gaining victory: *the winning side* **2** charming or attractive: *her winning smiles*

winnings *pl n* the money won in a competition or in gambling

winnow *vb* **1** to separate (grain) from (chaff) by a current of air **2** (often foll. by *out*) to separate out (an unwanted element): *the committee will need to winnow out the nonsense* [Old English *windwian*]
wino (**wine**-oh) *n, pl* **winos** *informal* a destitute person who habitually drinks cheap wine
win over *vb* to gain the support or consent of: *his robust performance won over his critics*
winsome *adj literary* charming or attractive: *a winsome smile* [Old English *wynsum*]
winter *n* **1** the coldest season of the year, between autumn and spring ▷ *vb* **2** to spend the winter in a specified place: *wintering in Rome* [Old English]
wintergreen *n* an evergreen shrub from which is obtained a pleasant-smelling oil that is used medicinally and for flavouring
winter solstice *n* the time, about December 22, at which the sun is at its southernmost point in the sky
winter sports *pl n* sports held on snow or ice, such as skiing and skating
wintertime *n* the period or season of winter
wintry *adj* **-trier**, **-triest** **1** of or characteristic of winter: *a cold wintry day* **2** cold or unfriendly: *a wintry smile*
win-win *adj* guaranteeing a favourable outcome for everyone involved: *a win-win situation for NATO*
wipe *vb* **wiping**, **wiped** **1** to rub (a surface or object) lightly with a cloth or the hand, in order to remove dirt or liquid from it **2** to remove by wiping: *she made a futile attempt to wipe away her tears* **3** to erase a recording from (a video or audio tape) ▷ *n* **4** the act or an instance of wiping: *a quick wipe* [Old English *wīpian*]
wipe out *vb* to destroy or get rid of completely: *a hail storm wipes out a wheat crop in five minutes*
wiper *n* short for **windscreen wiper** or **windshield wiper**
wire *n* **1** a slender flexible strand of metal **2** a length of this used to carry electric current in a circuit **3** a long continuous piece of wire or cable connecting points in a telephone or telegraph system **4** *old-fashioned, informal* a telegram ▷ *vb* **wiring**, **wired** **5** to fasten with wire **6** to equip (an electrical system, circuit, or component) with wires **7** *informal* to send a telegram to **8** to send by telegraph: *they wired the money for a train ticket* [Old English *wīr*]
wired *adj* **1** *slang* excitable or edgy, usually from stimulant intake: *I don't want coffee, I'm wired enough as it is* **2** using computers to send and receive information, esp. via the internet
wire-haired *adj* (of a dog) having a rough wiry coat
wireless *n* **1** *old-fashioned* same as **radio** ▷ *adj* **2** *computers* communicating without connecting wires: *wireless application protocol*
wire netting *n* a net made of wire, used for fencing
wiretapping *n* the practice of making a connection to a telegraph or telephone wire in order to obtain information secretly
wireworm *n* a destructive wormlike beetle larva
wiring *n* the network of wires used in an electrical system, device, or circuit

W

wiry *adj* **wirier**, **wiriest** **1** (of a person) slim but strong **2** coarse and stiff: *wiry grass*
wisdom *n* **1** the ability to use one's experience and knowledge to make sensible decisions or judgments **2** accumulated knowledge or learning: *the wisdom of Asia and of Africa* [Old English *wīsdōm*]
wisdom tooth *n* any of the four molar teeth, one at the back of each side of the jaw, that are the last of the permanent teeth to come through
wise[1] *adj* **1** possessing or showing wisdom: *a wise move* **2** **none the wiser** knowing no more than before: *I left the conference none the wiser* **3** **wise to** *informal* aware of or informed about: *they'll get wise to our system; he put him wise to the rumour* [Old English *wīs*] **wisely** *adv*
wise[2] *n old-fashioned* way, manner, or respect: *in no wise* [Old English *wīse* manner]
-wise *suffix forming adverbs* **1** indicating direction or manner: *crabwise* **2** with reference to: *moneywise* [Old English *-wisan*]
wiseacre *n* a person who wishes to seem wise [Middle Dutch *wijsseggher* soothsayer]
wisecrack *informal* ▷ *n* **1** a clever, amusing, sometimes unkind, remark ▷ *vb* **2** to make such remarks **wisecracking** *adj*
wise guy *n US informal* a person who likes to give the impression of knowing more than other people
wise up *vb* **wising**, **wised** *slang* (often foll. by *to*) to become aware (of) or informed (about)
wish *vb* **1** to want or desire (something impossible or improbable): *he wished he'd kept quiet* **2** to desire or prefer to be or do something: *the next person who wished to speak* **3** to feel or express a hope concerning the welfare, health, or success of: *we wished him well* **4** to greet as specified: *I wished her a Merry Christmas* ▷ *n* **5** a desire, often for something impossible or improbable: *a desperate wish to succeed as a professional artist* **6** something desired or wished for: *your wishes will come true* **7** the expression of a hope for someone's welfare, health, or success: *give him our best wishes* [Old English *wȳscan*]
wishbone *n* the V-shaped bone above the breastbone of a chicken or turkey
wishful *adj* desirous or longing: *she seemed wishful of prolonging the discussion*
wishful thinking *n* an interpretation of the facts as one would like them to be, rather than as they are: *was it wishful thinking, or had the enemy lost heart?*
wish list *n* a list of things desired by a person or organization: *the government's wish list*
wish on *vb* to want (something unpleasant) to be experienced by: *I wouldn't wish that wretched childhood on anyone*
wishy-washy *adj informal* lacking in character, force, or colour
wisp *n* **1** a thin, delicate, or filmy piece or streak: *little wisps of cloud* **2** a small untidy bundle, tuft, or strand: *a wisp of hair* **3** a slight trace: *a wisp of a smile* [origin unknown]
wispy *adj* **wispier**, **wispiest** thin, fine, or delicate: *grey wispy hair*

wisteria *n* a climbing plant with large drooping clusters of blue, purple, or white flowers [after Caspar *Wistar*, anatomist]

wistful *adj* sadly wishing for something lost or unobtainable **wistfully** *adv* **wistfulness** *n*

wit[1] *n* **1** the ability to use words or ideas in a clever, amusing, and imaginative way **2** a person possessing this ability **3** practical intelligence: *do credit me with some wit* ▷ See also **wits** [Old English *witt*]

wit[2] *vb* **to wit** (used to introduce a statement or explanation) that is to say; namely [Old English *witan*]

witblits (vit-blits) *n S African* an illegally distilled strong alcoholic drink [Afrikaans *wit* white + *blits* lightning]

witch *n* **1** (in former times) a woman believed to possess evil magic powers **2** a person who practises magic or sorcery, esp. black magic **3** an ugly or wicked old woman [Old English *wicce*]

witchcraft *n* the use of magic, esp. for evil purposes

witch doctor *n* a man in certain tribal societies who is believed to possess magical powers, which can be used to cure sickness or to harm people

witchetty grub *n* a wood-boring edible Australian caterpillar

witch hazel *n* a medicinal solution made from the bark and leaves of a N American shrub, which is put on the skin to treat bruises and inflammation

witch-hunt *n* a rigorous campaign to expose and discredit people considered to hold unorthodox views on the pretext of safeguarding the public welfare

with *prep* **1** accompanying; in the company of: *the captain called to the sergeant to come with him* **2** using; by means of: *unlocking the padlock with a key* **3** possessing or having: *a woman with black hair; the patient with angina* **4** concerning or regarding: *be gentle with me* **5** in a manner characterized by: *I know you will handle it with discretion* **6** as a result of: *his voice was hoarse with nervousness* **7** following the line of thought of: *are you with me so far?* **8** having the same opinions as; supporting: *are you with us or against us?* [Old English]

withdraw *vb* **-drawing, -drew, -drawn 1** to take out or remove: *he withdrew an envelope from his pocket* **2** to remove (money) from a bank account or savings account **3** to leave one place to go to another, usually quieter, place: *he withdrew into his bedroom* **4** (of troops) to leave or be pulled back from the battleground **5** to take back (a statement) formally **6 withdraw from** to give up: *they withdrew from the competition* [*with*, in the sense: away from]

withdrawal *n* **1** the act or an instance of withdrawing **2** the period that a drug addict goes through after stopping using drugs, during which he or she may experience symptoms such as tremors, sweating, and vomiting ▷ *adj* **3** of or relating to withdrawal from an addictive drug: *withdrawal symptoms*

withdrawn *vb* **1** the past participle of **withdraw** ▷ *adj* **2** extremely reserved or shy

wither *vb* **1** to make or become dried up or shrivelled: *the leaves had withered but not fallen* **2** to fade or waste: *deprived of the nerve supply the muscles wither* **3** to humiliate (someone) with a scornful look or remark [probably variant of *weather* (verb)] **withered** *adj*

withering *adj* (of a look or remark) extremely scornful

withers *pl n* the highest part of the back of a horse, between the shoulders [earlier *widersones*]

withhold *vb* **-holding, -held** to keep back (information or money)

within *prep* **1** in or inside: *within the hospital grounds* **2** before (a period of time) has passed: *within a month* **3** not beyond: *within the confines of a low budget; he positioned a low table within her reach* ▷ *adv* **4** *formal* inside or internally: *a glimpse of what was hidden within*

without *prep* **1** not accompanied by: *I can't imagine going through life without him* **2** not using: *our Jeep drove without lights* **3** not possessing or having: *four months without a job; a lot of them came across the border without shoes* **4** in a manner showing a lack of: *without reverence* **5** while not or after not: *she sat without speaking for some while* ▷ *adv* **6** *formal* outside: *seated on the graveyard without*

withstand *vb* **-standing, -stood** to resist or endure successfully: *our ability to withstand stress*

witless *adj* **1** *formal* lacking intelligence or sense **2 scared witless** extremely frightened

witness *n* **1** a person who has seen or can give first-hand evidence of some event: *the only witness to a killing* **2** a person who gives evidence in a court of law: *a witness for the defence* **3** a person who confirms the genuineness of a document or signature by adding his or her own signature **4** evidence proving or supporting something: *the Church of England, that historic witness to the power of the Christian faith* **5 bear witness to** to be evidence or proof of: *the high turn-out bore witness to the popularity of the contest* ▷ *vb* **6** to see, be present at, or know at first hand: *I have witnessed many motor-racing accidents* **7** to be the scene or setting of: *the 1970s witnessed an enormous increase in international lending* **8** to confirm the genuineness of (a document or signature) by adding one's own signature **9 witness to** *formal* to confirm: *our aim is to witness to the fact of the empty tomb* [Old English *witnes*]

witness box *or esp US* **witness stand** *n* the place in a court of law where witnesses stand to give evidence

wits *pl n* **1** the ability to think and act quickly: *when he was sober his wits were razor-sharp* **2 at one's wits' end** at a loss to know what to do **3 have one's wits about one** to be able to think and act quickly **4 live by** *or* **on one's wits** to gain a livelihood by craftiness rather than by hard work **5 scared out of one's wits** extremely frightened

witter *vb chiefly Brit informal* to chatter or babble pointlessly or at unnecessary length [origin unknown]

witticism *n* a witty remark

wittingly *adv* intentionally and knowingly

witty *adj* **-tier, -tiest** clever and amusing **wittily** *adv*

wives *n* the plural of **wife**

wizard *n* **1** a man in fairy tales who has magic powers **2** a person who is outstandingly gifted in some specified field: *a financial wizard* [from *wise*]
wizardry *n* **1** magic or sorcery **2** outstanding skill or accomplishment in some specified field: *technological wizardry*
wizened (wiz-zend) *adj* shrivelled, wrinkled, or dried up with age
WMD *n* weapon(s) of mass destruction
woad *n* a blue dye obtained from a European plant, used by the ancient Britons as a body dye [Old English *wād*]
wobbegong *n* an Australian shark with brown-and-white skin
wobble *vb* **-bling, -bled 1** to move or sway unsteadily **2** to shake: *she was having difficulty in controlling her voice, which wobbled about* ▷ *n* **3** a wobbling movement or sound [Low German *wabbeln*]
wobbly *adj* **-blier, -bliest 1** unsteady **2** trembling ▷ *n* **3 throw a wobbly** *Brit slang* to become suddenly angry or upset
wodge *n informal* a thick lump or chunk: *my wodge of Kleenex was a sodden ball* [from *wedge*]
woe *n* **1** *literary* intense grief **2 woes** misfortunes or problems: *economic woes* **3 woe betide someone** someone will or would experience misfortune: *woe betide anyone who got in his way* [Old English *wā, wǣ*]
woebegone *adj* sad in appearance [*woe* + obsolete *bego* to surround]
woeful *adj* **1** extremely sad **2** pitiful or deplorable: *a woeful lack of understanding*
woefully *adv*
wok *n* a large bowl-shaped metal Chinese cooking pot, used for stir-frying [Chinese (Cantonese)]
woke *vb* the past tense of **wake'** ▷ *adj informal* alert to social and political injustice
woken *vb* the past participle of **wake'**
wold *n* a large area of high open rolling country [Old English *weald* wood]
wolf *n, pl* **wolves 1** a predatory doglike wild animal which hunts in packs **2** *old-fashioned, informal* a man who habitually tries to seduce women **3 cry wolf** to give false alarms repeatedly: *if you cry wolf too often, people will take no notice* ▷ *vb* **4 wolf down** to eat quickly or greedily: *they will wolf down kidneys but refuse tongue* [Old English *wulf*]
wolfhound *n* a very large dog, formerly used to hunt wolves
wolf whistle *n* **1** a whistle produced by a man to express admiration of a person's appearance ▷ *vb* **wolf-whistle, -whistling, -whistled 2** to produce such a whistle
wolverine *n* a large meat-eating mammal of Eurasia and North America with very thick dark fur [earlier *wolvering*, from *wolf*]
wolves *n* the plural of **wolf**
woman *n, pl* **women 1** an adult female human being **2** adult female human beings collectively: *the very image of woman pared of the trappings of 'femininity'* **3** an adult female human being with qualities traditionally regarded as feminine **4** *old-fashioned* a female subordinate, servant, or employee **5** *informal* a wife or girlfriend ▷ *adj* **6** female: *a woman doctor* [Old English *wīfmann*]
womanhood *n* **1** the state of being a woman: *young girls approaching womanhood* **2** women collectively: *Asian womanhood*
womanish *adj* (of a man) looking or behaving like a woman
womanizer *or* **-niser** *n* a man who has casual affairs with many women
womanizing *or* **-nising** *n* (of a man) the practice of indulging in casual affairs with women
womankind *n* all women considered as a group
womanly *adj* possessing qualities generally regarded as typical of, or appropriate to, a woman
womb *n* the nontechnical name for **uterus** [Old English *wamb*]
wombat *n* a furry heavily-built plant-eating Australian marsupial [Aboriginal]
women *n* the plural of **woman**
womenfolk *pl n* **1** women collectively **2** a group of women, esp. the female members of one's family
Women's Liberation *n* a movement promoting the removal of inequalities based upon the assumption that men are superior to women. Also called: **women's lib**
won *vb* the past of **win**
wonder *vb* **1** to think about something with curiosity or doubt: *I wonder why she did that* **2** to be amazed: *I did wonder at her leaving valuable china on the shelves* ▷ *n* **3** something that causes surprise or awe: *it's a wonder she isn't speechless with fright* **4** the feeling of surprise or awe caused by something strange: *the wonder of travel* **5 do** *or* **work wonders** to achieve spectacularly good results **6 no** *or* **small wonder** it is not surprising: *no wonder you're going broke* ▷ *adj* **7** causing surprise or awe because of spectacular results achieved: *a new wonder drug for treating migraine* [Old English *wundor*]
wonderingly *adv* **wonderment** *n*
wonderful *adj* **1** extremely fine; excellent: *I've been offered a wonderful job* **2** causing surprise, amazement, or awe: *a strange and wonderful phenomenon* **wonderfully** *adv*
wonderland *n* **1** an imaginary land of marvels or wonders **2** an actual place of great or strange beauty: *the apartment was a wonderland of design and colour*
wondrous *adj old-fashioned or literary* causing surprise or awe; marvellous
wonky *adj* **-kier, -kiest** *Brit, Austral & NZ slang* **1** shaky or unsteady: *wonky wheelbarrows; wonky knees* **2** insecure or unreliable: *his marriage is looking a bit wonky* [dialect *wanky*]
wont (rhymes with **don't**) *old-fashioned* ▷ *adj* **1** accustomed: *most murderers, his police friends were wont to say, were male* ▷ *n* **2** a usual practice: *she waded straight in, as was her wont* [Old English *gewunod*]
won't will not
woo *vb* **wooing, wooed 1** to coax or urge: *it will woo people back into the kitchen* **2** *old-fashioned* to attempt to gain the love of (a woman) [Old English *wōgian*] **wooing** *n*
wood *n* **1** the hard fibrous substance beneath the bark in trees and shrubs, which is used in

building and carpentry and as fuel. Related adjective: **ligneous** **2** an area of trees growing together that is smaller than a forest: *a track leading into a wood*. Related adjective: **sylvan** **3** *golf* a long-shafted club with a wooden head ▷ *adj* **4** made of, using, or for use with wood: *wood fires* ▷ See also **woods** [Old English *widu, wudu*]

wood alcohol *n* same as **methanol**

woodbine *n* a wild honeysuckle with sweet-smelling yellow flowers

woodcarving *n* **1** a work of art produced by carving wood **2** the act or craft of carving wood

woodcock *n* a large game bird with a long straight bill

woodcut *n* a print made from a block of wood with a design cut into it

woodcutter *n* a person who cuts down trees or chops wood

wooded *adj* covered with woods or trees

wooden *adj* **1** made of wood **2** lacking spirit or animation: *the man's expression became wooden* **woodenly** *adv*

wooden spoon *n* a booby prize, esp. in sporting contests

woodland *n* **1** land that is mostly covered with woods or trees ▷ *adj* **2** living in woods: *woodland birds*

woodlouse *n, pl* **-lice** a very small grey creature with many legs that lives in damp places

woodpecker *n* a bird with a strong beak with which it bores into trees for insects

wood pulp *n* pulp made from wood fibre, used to make paper

woodruff *n* a plant with small sweet-smelling white flowers and sweet-smelling leaves [Old English *wudurofe*]

woods *pl n* closely packed trees forming a forest or wood

woodsman *n, pl* **-men** a person who lives in a wood or who is skilled at woodwork or carving

woodwind *music* ▷ *adj* **1** of or denoting a type of wind instrument, such as the oboe ▷ *n* **2** the woodwind instruments of an orchestra

woodwork *n* **1** the parts of a room or house that are made of wood, such as the doors and window frames: *stark white walls and blue woodwork* **2** the art or craft of making objects from wood **3 crawl out of the woodwork** to appear suddenly and in large numbers: *intellectuals and environmentalists crawled out of the woodwork*

woodworm *n* **1** a beetle larva that bores into wooden furniture or beams **2** the damage caused to wood by these larvae

woody *adj* **woodier, woodiest** **1** (of a plant) having a very hard stem **2** (of an area) covered with woods or trees

woof[1] *n* same as **weft** [Old English *ōwef*]

woof[2] *n* an imitation of the bark of a dog

woofer *n* a loudspeaker used in high-fidelity systems for the reproduction of low audio frequencies

wool *n* **1** the soft curly hair of sheep and some other animals **2** yarn spun from this, used in weaving and knitting **3** cloth made from this yarn **4 pull the wool over someone's eyes** to deceive someone [Old English *wull*]

woolgathering *n* idle or absent-minded daydreaming

woollen *or US* **woolen** *adj* **1** made of wool or of a mixture of wool and another material **2** relating to wool: *woollen mills* ▷ *n* **3 woollens** woollen clothes, esp. knitted ones

woolly *or US* **wooly** *adj* **-lier, -liest** **1** made of or like wool **2** confused or indistinct: *woolly ideas* ▷ *n, pl* **-lies** **3** a woollen garment, such as a sweater

woolshed *n Austral & NZ* a large building in which sheep shearing takes place

woomera *n* a notched stick used by Aboriginal Australians to aid the propulsion of a spear

woozy *adj* **woozier, wooziest** *informal* feeling slightly dizzy [origin unknown]

wop-wops *pl n NZ informal* remote rural areas

Worcester sauce (wooss-ter) *or* **Worcestershire sauce** *n* a sharp-tasting sauce, made from soy sauce, vinegar, and spices

Worcs Worcestershire

word *n* **1** the smallest single meaningful unit of speech or writing. Related adjective: **lexical** **2** a brief conversation: *I would like a word with you* **3** a brief statement: *a word of warning* **4** news or information: *let me know if you get word of my wife* **5** a solemn promise: *he had given his word as a rabbi* **6** a command or order: *he had only to say the word and they'd hang him* **7** *computers* a set of bits used to store, transmit, or operate upon an item of information in a computer **8 by word of mouth** by spoken rather than by written means: *their reputation spreads by word of mouth* **9 in a word** briefly or in short: *in a word, we've won* **10 my word!** Also: **upon my word!** *old-fashioned* an exclamation of surprise or amazement **11 take someone at his** *or* **her word** to accept that someone really means what he or she says: *they're willing to take him at his word when he says he'll change* **12 take someone's word for it** to believe what someone says **13 the last word** the closing remark of a conversation or argument, often regarded as settling an issue **14 the last word in** the finest example of: *the last word in comfort* **15 word for word** using exactly the same words: *he repeated almost word for word what had been said* **16 word of honour** a solemn promise ▷ *vb* **17** to state in words: *the questions have to be carefully worded* ▷ See also **words** [Old English]

Word *n* **the Word** the message and teachings contained in the Bible

-word *combining form (preceded by 'the' and an initial letter)* a euphemistic way of referring to a word by its first letter because it is considered to be unmentionable by the user: *the c-word, meaning cancer*

word game *n* any game involving the discovery, formation, or alteration of a word or words

wording *n* the way in which words are used to express something: *the exact wording of the regulation has still not been worked out*

word-perfect *adj* able to repeat from memory the exact words of a text one has learned

word processing *n* the creation, organization, and storage of text on a computer or word processor

word processor *n* a computer program or electronic machine for the creation, organization, and storage of text entered from a keyboard and providing a means for printing out such text

words *pl n* **1** the text of a song, as opposed to the music **2** the text of an actor's part **3 have words** to have an argument or disagreement **4 in other words** expressing the same idea in a different, more understandable, way **5 put into words** to express in speech or writing: *she was reluctant to put her thoughts into words*

wordy *adj* **wordier, wordiest** using too many words, esp. long words: *wordy explanations*

wore *vb* the past tense of **wear**

work *n* **1** physical or mental effort directed to doing or making something **2** paid employment at a job, trade, or profession **3** duties or tasks: *I had to delegate as much work as I could* **4** something done or made as a result of effort: *a work by a major artist* **5** the place where a person is employed: *accidents at work* **6** *physics old-fashioned* the transfer of energy occurring when a force is applied to move a body **7 at work** working or in action: *the social forces at work in society* ▷ *adj* **8** of or for work: *work experience* ▷ *vb* **9** to do work; labour: *no-one worked harder than Arnold* **10** to be employed: *she worked as a waitress* **11** to make (a person or animal) labour **12** to operate (a machine or a piece of equipment) **13** (of a machine or a piece of equipment) to function, esp. effectively: *he doesn't have to know how things work* **14** (of a plan or system) to be successful **15** to cultivate (land) **16** to move gradually into a specific condition or position: *he picked up the shovel, worked it under the ice, and levered* **17** to make (one's way) with effort: *he worked his way to the top* **18** *informal* to manipulate to one's own advantage: *they could see an angle and they'd know how to work it* ▷ See also **work off, works** *etc.* [Old English *weorc*]

workable *adj* **1** able to operate efficiently: *a workable solution* **2** able to be used: *a workable mine*

workaday *adj* commonplace or ordinary: *workaday surroundings*

workaholic *n* a person who is obsessed with work

workbench *n* a heavy table at which a craftsman or mechanic works

worker *n* **1** a person who works in a specified way: *a hard worker* **2** a person who works at a specific job: *a government worker* **3** an employee, as opposed to an employer **4** a sterile female bee, ant, or wasp, that works for the colony

work ethic *n* a belief in the moral value of work

workforce *n* **1** the total number of workers employed by a company **2** the total number of people available for work: *the local workforce*

workhorse *n* a person or thing that does a lot of work, esp. dull or routine work: *this plane is the workhorse of most short-haul airlines*

workhouse *n* (formerly, in England) a public institution where very poor people did work in return for food and accommodation

working *adj* **1** having a job: *the working mother* **2** concerned with, used in, or suitable for work: *working conditions* **3** capable of being operated or used: *a working mechanism* ▷ *n* **4** a part of a mine or quarry that is or has been used **5 workings** the way that something works: *the workings of the human brain*

working capital *n* the amount of capital that a business has available to meet the day-to-day cash requirements of its operations

working class *n* **1** the social group that consists of people who earn wages, esp. as manual workers ▷ *adj* **working-class 2** of or relating to the working class: *a working-class neighbourhood*

working day *or esp US & Canad* **workday** *n* **1** a day when people normally go to work: *the last working day of the week* **2** the part of the day allocated to work: *the long working day of twelve to fourteen hours*

working party *n* a committee established to investigate a problem

workload *n* the amount of work to be done, esp. in a specified period: *a heavy workload*

workman *n, pl* **-men** a man who is employed to do manual work

workmanlike *adj* skilfully done: *a neat workmanlike job*

workmanship *n* the degree of skill with which an object is made: *shoddy workmanship*

workmate *n informal* a person who works with another person; fellow worker

work of art *n* **1** a piece of fine art, such as a painting or sculpture **2** an object or a piece of work that has been exceptionally skilfully made or produced: *the doll was truly a work of art*

work off *vb* to get rid of, usually by effort: *he went along to the tennis club and worked off his pique there*

work on *vb* to try to persuade or influence (someone)

work out *vb* **1** to solve, find out, or plan by reasoning or calculation: *working out a new budget* **2** to happen in a particular way: *he decided to wait and see how things worked out* **3** to be successful or satisfactory: *the dates never worked out* **4** to take part in physical exercise **5 work out at** to be calculated at (a certain amount): *the return on capital works out at 15 per cent* ▷ *n* **workout 6** a session of physical exercise for training or to keep fit

work over *vb slang* to give (someone) a severe beating: *whoever worked her over did a thorough job*

works *n* **1** a place where something is manufactured: *a chemical works* ▷ *pl n* **2** the sum total of a writer's or artist's achievements considered together: *the works of Goethe* **3 the works** *slang* everything associated with a particular subject or thing: *traditional Indian music, sitars, the works*

worksheet *n* a sheet of paper containing exercises to be completed by a student

workshop *n* **1** a room or building where manufacturing or other manual work is carried on **2** a group of people engaged in intensive study or work in a creative or practical field: *a writers' workshop*

workshy *adj* not inclined to work; lazy

work station *n* **1** an area in an office where one person works **2** a component of an electronic office system consisting of a VDU and keyboard

worktable *n* a table at which writing, sewing, or other work may be done

worktop *n* a surface in a kitchen, usually the top of a fitted kitchen unit, which is used for food preparation. Also: **work surface**

work-to-rule *n* a form of industrial action in which employees keep strictly to their employers' rules, with the result of reducing the work rate

work up *vb* **1** to make angry, excited, or upset: *he worked himself up into a rage* **2** to build up or develop: *I'd worked up a thirst* **3** to work on (something) in order to improve it: *there was enough material to be worked up into something publishable* **4 work one's way up** to make progress: *he worked his way up in the catering trade* **5 work up to** to develop gradually towards: *the fete worked up to a climax around lunch time*

world *n* **1** the earth as a planet **2** the human race; people generally: *providing food for the world* **3** any planet or moon, esp. one that might be inhabited **4** a particular group of countries or period of history, or its inhabitants: *the Arab world; the post-Cold War world* **5** an area, sphere, or realm considered as a complete environment: *the art world; the world of nature* **6** the total circumstances and experience of a person that make up his or her life: *there may not ever be a place for us in your world* **7 bring into the world** to deliver or give birth to (a baby) **8 come into the world** to be born **9 for all the world** exactly or very much: *they looked for all the world like a pair of newly-weds* **10 in the world** used to emphasize a statement: *she didn't have a worry in the world* **11 man** *or* **woman of the world** a man *or* woman who is experienced in social or public life **12 worlds apart** very different from each other: *this man and I are worlds apart* ▷ *adj* **13** of or concerning the entire world: *the world championship* [Old English *w(e)orold*]

world-class *adj* being as good as anyone else in the world in a particular field: *he has the makings of a world-class batsman*

World Cup *n* an international competition held between national teams in various sports, most notably association football

worldly *adj* **-lier, -liest 1** not spiritual; earthly or temporal: *as a simple monk he had no interest in politics and other worldly affairs* **2** of or relating to material things: *all his worldly goods* **3** wise in the ways of the world; sophisticated: *a suave, worldly, charming Frenchman* **worldliness** *n*

worldly-wise *adj* wise in the ways of the world; sophisticated

world music *n* popular music of a variety of ethnic origins and styles

world-shaking *adj* of enormous significance; momentous: *world-shaking events*

World War I *n* the war (1914–18) between the Allies (principally France, Russia, Britain, Italy, Australia, Canada, and the US) and the Central Powers (principally Germany, Austria-Hungary, and Turkey). Also: **First World War**

World War II *n* the war (1939–45) between the Allies (Britain, France, Australia, Canada, the US, and the Soviet Union) and the Axis (Germany, Italy, and Japan). Also: **Second World War**

world-weary *adj* no longer finding pleasure in life

worldwide *adj* applying or extending throughout the world

World Wide Web *n computers* a vast network of hypertext files, stored on computers throughout the world, that can provide a computer user with information on a huge variety of subjects

worm *n* **1** a small invertebrate animal with a long thin body and no limbs **2** an insect larva that looks like a worm **3** a despicable or weak person **4** a slight trace: *a worm of doubt* **5** a shaft on which a spiral thread has been cut, for example in a gear arrangement in which such a shaft drives a toothed wheel **6** *computers* a type of virus ▷ *vb* **7** to rid (an animal) of worms in its intestines **8 worm one's way A** to go or move slowly and with difficulty: *I had to worm my way out sideways from the bench* **B** to get oneself into a certain situation or position gradually: *worming your way into my good books* **9 worm out of** to obtain (information) from someone who is not willing to provide it: *it took me weeks to worm the facts out of him* ▷ See also **worms** [Old English *wyrm*]

WORM *n computers* write once read many (times): an optical disk which enables users to store their own data

wormcast *n* a coil of earth or sand that has been excreted by a burrowing worm

worm-eaten *adj* eaten into by worms: *worm-eaten beams*

wormhole *n* a hole made by a worm in timber, plants, or fruit

worms *n* a disease caused by parasitic worms living in the intestines

wormwood *n* a plant from which a bitter oil formerly used in making absinthe is obtained [Old English *wormōd, wermōd*]

wormy *adj* **wormier, wormiest** infested with or eaten by worms

worn *vb* **1** the past participle of **wear** ▷ *adj* **2** showing signs of long use or wear: *the worn soles of his boots* **3** looking tired and ill: *that worn pain-creased face*

worn-out *adj* **1** worn or used until threadbare, valueless, or useless **2** completely exhausted: *worn-out by their exertions*

worried *adj* concerned and anxious about things that may happen **worriedly** *adv*

worrisome *adj old-fashioned* causing worry

worry *vb* **-ries, -rying, -ried 1** to be or cause to be anxious or uneasy **2** to annoy or bother: *don't worry yourself with the details* **3** (of a dog) to frighten (sheep or other animals) by chasing and trying to bite them **4 worry away at** to struggle with or work on (a problem) ▷ *n, pl* **-ries 5** a state or feeling of anxiety: *he was beside himself with worry* **6** a cause for anxiety: *having a premature baby is much less of a worry these days* [Old English *wyrgan*] **worrier** *n*

worry beads *pl n* a string of beads that supposedly relieves nervous tension when fingered or played with

worrying *adj* causing concern and anxiety

worse *adj* **1** the comparative of **bad 2 none the worse for** not harmed by (adverse events or circumstances) **3 the worse for wear** *informal* in a poor condition; not at one's best: *returning the worse for wear from the pub* ▷ *n* **4 for the worse** into a worse condition: *taking a turn for the worse* ▷ *adv*

5 the comparative of **badly 6 worse off** in a worse condition, esp. financially [Old English *wiersa*]

worsen *vb* to make or become worse **worsening** *adj, n*

worship *vb* **-shipping, -shipped** *or US* **-shiping, -shiped 1** to show profound religious devotion to (one's god), for example by praying **2** to have intense love and admiration for (a person) ▷ *n* **3** religious adoration or devotion **4** formal expression of religious adoration, for example by praying **5** intense love or devotion to a person [Old English *weorthscipe*] **worshipper** *n*

Worship *n* **Your** *or* **His** *or* **Her Worship** *chiefly Brit* a title for a mayor or magistrate

worshipful *adj* feeling or showing reverence or adoration

worst *adj, adv* **1** the superlative of **bad** or **badly** ▷ *n* **2** the least good or the most terrible person, thing, or part: *the worst is yet to come* **3 at one's worst** in the worst condition or aspect of a thing or person: *the British male is at his worst in July and August* **4 at worst** in the least favourable interpretation or conditions: *all the questions should ideally be answered 'no', or at worst 'sometimes'* ▷ *vb* **5** *old-fashioned* to defeat or beat [Old English *wierrest*]

worsted (**wooss**-tid) *n* a close-textured woollen fabric used to make jackets and trousers [after *Worstead*, a district in Norfolk]

worth *prep* **1** having a value of: *the fire destroyed property worth $200 million* **2** worthy of; meriting or justifying: *if a job is worth doing, it's worth doing well* **3 worth one's weight in gold** extremely useful or helpful; very highly valued **4 worth one's while** worthy of spending one's time or effort on something: *they needed a wage of at least £140 a week to make it worth their while returning to work* ▷ *n* **5** monetary value: *the corporation's net worth* **6** high quality; value: *the submarine proved its military worth during the Second World War* **7** the amount of something that can be bought for a specified price: *$10 billion worth of property* [Old English *weorth*]

worthless *adj* **1** without value or usefulness: *worthless junk bonds* **2** without merit: *he sees himself as a worthless creature* **worthlessness** *n*

worthwhile *adj* sufficiently important, rewarding, or valuable to justify spending time or effort on it

worthy *adj* **-thier, -thiest 1** deserving of admiration or respect: *motives which were less than worthy* **2 worthy of** deserving of: *he would practise extra hard to be worthy of such an honour* ▷ *n, pl* **-thies 3** *often facetious* an important person **worthily** *adv* **worthiness** *n*

would *vb* **1** used as an auxiliary to form the past tense or subjunctive mood of **will[1]**: *he asked if she would marry him; that would be delightful* **2** to express a polite offer or request: *would you like some lunch?* **3** to describe a habitual past action: *sometimes at lunch time I would choose a painting to go and see*

USAGE See at **should**.

would-be *adj* wanting or pretending to be: *would-be brides*

wouldn't would not

wound[1] *n* **1** an injury to the body such as a cut or a gunshot injury **2** an injury to one's feelings or reputation ▷ *vb* **3** to cause an injury to the body or feelings of [Old English *wund*] **wounding** *adj*

wound[2] *vb* the past of **wind[2]**

wove *vb* a past tense of **weave**

woven *vb* a past participle of **weave**

wow *interj* **1** an exclamation of admiration or amazement ▷ *n* **2** *slang* a person or thing that is amazingly successful: *he would be an absolute wow on the chat shows* ▷ *vb* **3** *slang* to be a great success with: *the new Disney film wowed festival audiences* [Scots]

wowser *n Austral & NZ slang* **1** a fanatically puritanical person **2** a teetotaller [dialect *wow* to complain]

wp word processor

WPC (in Britain, formerly) woman police constable

wpm words per minute

wrack[1] *n* same as **rack[2]** [Old English *wræc* persecution]

USAGE The use of the spelling *wrack* rather than *rack* in sentences such as *she was wracked by grief* or *the country was wracked by civil war* is very common but is thought by many people to be incorrect.

wrack[2] *n* seaweed that is floating in the sea or has been washed ashore [probably from Middle Dutch *wrak* wreckage]

wraith *n literary* a ghost [Scots] **wraithlike** *adj*

wrangle *vb* **-gling, -gled 1** to argue noisily or angrily ▷ *n* **2** a noisy or angry argument [Low German *wrangeln*]

wrap *vb* **wrapping, wrapped 1** to fold a covering round (something) and fasten it securely: *a small package wrapped in brown paper* **2** to fold or wind (something) round a person or thing: *she wrapped a handkerchief around her bleeding palm* **3** to fold, wind, or coil: *she wrapped her arms around her mother* **4** to complete the filming of (a motion picture or television programme) ▷ *n* **5** *old-fashioned* a garment worn wrapped round the shoulders **6** (in the filming of a motion picture or television programme) the end of a day's filming or the completion of filming **7** a type of sandwich consisting of filling rolled up in a flour tortilla **8** *Brit slang* a small packet of an illegal drug in powder form: *a wrap of heroin* **9 keep something under wraps** to keep something secret [origin unknown]

wraparound *adj* **1** (of a skirt) designed to be worn wrapped round the body **2** extending in a curve from the front round to the sides: *wraparound shades*

wrap party *n* a party held by cast and crew to celebrate the completion of filming of a motion picture or television programme

wrapper *n* a paper, foil, or plastic cover in which a product is wrapped: *a single sweet wrapper*

wrapping *n* a piece of paper, foil, or other material used to wrap something in

wrap up *vb* **1** to fold paper, cloth, or other material round (something) **2** to put warm clothes on: *remember to wrap up warmly on cold or windy days* **3** *informal* to finish or settle: *he will need 60 to 90 days to wrap up his current business dealings* **4** *slang* to stop talking **5 wrapped up in** giving all one's attention to: *wrapped up in her new baby*

wrasse *n* a brightly coloured sea fish [Cornish *wrach*]
wrath (roth) *n old-fashioned or literary* intense anger [Old English *wrǣththu*] **wrathful** *adj*
wreak *vb* **1 wreak havoc** to cause chaos or damage: *this Australian sun will wreak havoc with your complexions* **2 wreak vengeance on** to take revenge on [Old English *wrecan*]
USAGE See at **wrought**.
wreath *n, pl* **wreaths 1** a ring of flowers or leaves, placed on a grave as a memorial or worn on the head as a garland or a mark of honour **2** anything circular or spiral: *a wreath of smoke* [Old English *writha*]
wreathe *vb* **wreathing, wreathed** *literary* **1 wreathed in A** surrounded by: *wreathed in pipe smoke* **B** surrounded by a ring of: *wreathed in geraniums* **2 wreathed in smiles** smiling broadly
wreck *vb* **1** to break, spoil, or destroy completely **2** to cause the accidental sinking or destruction of (a ship) at sea ▷ *n* **3** something that has been destroyed or badly damaged, such as a crashed car or aircraft **4** a ship that has been sunk or destroyed at sea **5** a person in a poor mental or physical state [from Old Norse]
wreckage *n* the remains of something that has been destroyed or badly damaged, such as a crashed car or aircraft
wrecker *n* **1** a person who destroys or badly damages something: *a marriage wrecker* **2** (formerly) a person who lured ships on to the rocks in order to plunder them **3** *chiefly US, Canad & NZ* a person whose job is to demolish buildings or dismantle cars **4** *US & Canad* a breakdown van
wreckers *pl n NZ* a business which sells material from demolished cars or buildings
wren *n* a very small brown songbird [Old English *wrenna*]
Wren *n informal* (formerly, in Britain and certain other nations) a member of the former Women's Royal Naval Service [from abbreviation WRNS]
wrench *vb* **1** to twist or pull (something) violently, for example to remove it from something to which it is attached: *he grabbed the cable and wrenched it out of the wall socket* **2** to move or twist away with a sudden violent effort: *she wrenched free of his embrace* **3** to injure (a limb or joint) by a sudden twist ▷ *n* **4** a violent twist or pull **5** an injury to a limb or joint, caused by twisting it **6** a feeling of sadness experienced on leaving a person or place: *it would be a wrench to leave Essex after all these years* **7** a spanner with adjustable jaws [Old English *wrencan*]
wrest *vb* **1** to take (something) away from someone with a violent pull or twist **2** to seize forcibly by violent or unlawful means: *she must begin to wrest control of the army and the police* [Old English *wrǣstan*]
wrestle *vb* **-tling, -tled 1** to fight (someone) by grappling and trying to throw or pin him or her to the ground, often as a sport **2 wrestle with** to struggle hard with (a person, problem, or thing): *I wrestled with my conscience* [Old English *wrǣstlian*] **wrestler** *n*
wrestling *n* a sport in which each contestant tries to overcome the other either by throwing or pinning him or her to the ground or by forcing a submission
wretch *n old-fashioned* **1** a despicable person **2** a person pitied for his or her misfortune [Old English *wrecca*]
wretched (retch-id) *adj* **1** in poor or pitiful circumstances: *a vast wretched slum* **2** feeling very unhappy **3** of poor quality: *the wretched state of the cabbages* **4** *informal* undesirable or displeasing: *what a wretched muddle* **wretchedly** *adv* **wretchedness** *n*
wriggle *vb* **-gling, -gled 1** to twist and turn with quick movements: *he wriggled on the hard seat* **2** to move along by twisting and turning **3 wriggle out of** to avoid (doing something that one does not want to do): *he wriggled out of donating blood* ▷ *n* **4** a wriggling movement or action [Middle Low German *wriggeln*]
wring *vb* **wringing, wrung 1** Also: **wring out** to squeeze water from (a cloth or clothing) by twisting it tightly **2** to twist (a neck) violently **3** to clasp and twist (one's hands) in anguish **4** to grip (someone's hand) vigorously in greeting **5** to obtain by forceful means: *to wring concessions from the army* **6 wring someone's heart** to make someone feel sorrow or pity [Old English *wringan*]
wringer *n* same as **mangle**[1] (sense 2)
wringing *adv* **wringing wet** extremely wet
wrinkle *n* **1** a slight ridge in the smoothness of a surface, such as a crease in the skin as a result of age ▷ *vb* **-kling, -kled 2** to develop or cause to develop wrinkles [Old English *wrinclian* to wind around] **wrinkled** *or* **wrinkly** *adj*
wrist *n* **1** the joint between the forearm and the hand **2** the part of a sleeve that covers the wrist [Old English]
wristwatch *n* a watch worn strapped round the wrist
writ *n* a formal legal document ordering a person to do or not to do something [Old English]
write *vb* **writing, wrote, written 1** to draw or mark (words, letters, or numbers) on paper or a blackboard with a pen, pencil, or chalk **2** to describe or record (something) in writing: *he began to write his memoirs* **3** to be an author: *he still taught writing, but he didn't write* **4** to write a letter to or correspond regularly with someone: *don't forget to write!* **5** *informal, chiefly US & Canad* to write a letter to (someone): *I wrote him several times* **6** to say or communicate in a letter or a book: *in a recent letter a friend wrote that everything costs more in Russia now* **7** to fill in the details for (a cheque or document) **8** *computers* to record (data) in a storage device **9 write down** to record in writing: *write it down if you find it too embarrassing to talk about* [Old English *wrītan*]
write off *vb* **1** *accounting* to cancel (a bad debt) from the accounts **2** to dismiss from consideration: *he wrote her off as a tense woman* **3** to send a written request (for something): *he wrote off for leaflets on the subject* **4** *informal* to damage (a vehicle) beyond repair ▷ *n* **write-off 5** *informal* a vehicle that is damaged beyond repair
write out *vb* **1** to put into writing or reproduce in full form in writing **2** to remove (a character)

W

from a television or radio series: *another actress is to be written out of the BBC soap*
writer *n* **1** a person whose job is writing; author **2** the person who has written something specified: *the writer of this letter is pretty dangerous*
write up *vb* **1** to describe fully, complete, or bring up to date in writing: *she would write up her diary in bed* ▷ *n* **write-up 2** a published account of something, such as a review in a newspaper or magazine: *I see the Herald didn't give you a very good write-up*
writhe *vb* **writhing, writhed** to twist or squirm in pain: *writhing in agony* [Old English *wrīthan*]
writing *n* **1** something that has been written: *the writing on the outer flap was faint* **2** written form: *permission in writing* **3** short for **handwriting 4** a kind or style of writing: *creative writing* **5** the work of a writer: *Wilde never mentioned chess in his writing*
written *vb* **1** the past participle of **write** ▷ *adj* **2** recorded in writing: *written permission*
WRNS (in Britain, formerly) Women's Royal Naval Service
wrong *adj* **1** not correct or accurate: *the wrong answers* **2** acting or judging in error; mistaken: *do correct me if I'm wrong* **3** not in accordance with correct or conventional rules or standards; immoral: *this group argues that even gently slapping a child is wrong* **4** not intended or appropriate: *I ordered the wrong things; you've picked the wrong time to ask such questions* **5** being a problem or trouble: *come on, I know when something's wrong* **6** not functioning properly: *there's something wrong with the temperature sensor* **7** denoting the side of cloth that is worn facing inwards ▷ *adv* **8** in a wrong manner: *I guessed wrong* **9 get someone wrong** to misunderstand someone: *don't get me wrong, I'm not making threats* **10 get something wrong** to make a mistake about something: *he had got his body language wrong* **11 go wrong A** to turn out badly or not as intended **B** to make a mistake **C** (of a machine) to stop functioning properly: *pilots must be able to react instantly if the automatic equipment suddenly goes wrong* ▷ *n* **12** something bad, immoral, or unjust: *how can such a wrong be redressed?* **13 in the wrong** mistaken or guilty ▷ *vb* **14** to treat (someone) unjustly **15** to think or speak unfairly of (someone) [Old English *wrang* injustice] **wrongly** *adv*
wrongdoing *n* immoral or illegal behaviour **wrongdoer** *n*
wrong-foot *vb* **1** *sport* to play a shot in such a way as to catch (an opponent) off-balance: *he constantly wrong-footed his opponent with fine passing* **2** to gain an advantage over (someone) by doing something unexpected: *China wrong-footed Vietnam by supporting the peace plan*
wrongful *adj* unjust or illegal: *wrongful imprisonment* **wrongfully** *adv*
wrong-headed *adj* constantly and stubbornly wrong in judgment
wrote *vb* the past tense of **write**
wroth *adj old-fashioned or literary* angry [Old English *wrāth*]
wrought (rawt) *vb* **1** *old-fashioned* a past of **work** ▷ *adj* **2** *metallurgy* shaped by hammering or beating: *wrought copper and brass*

> **USAGE** *Wrought* is sometimes used as if it were the past tense and past participle of *wreak*, as in *the hurricane wrought havoc in coastal areas*. Many people think this use is incorrect.

wrought iron *n* a pure form of iron with a low carbon content, often used for decorative work
wrung *vb* the past of **wring**
wry *adj* **wrier, wriest** *or* **wryer, wryest 1** drily humorous; sardonic: *wry amusement* **2** (of a facial expression) produced by twisting one's features to denote amusement or displeasure: *a small wry smile twisted the corner of his mouth* [Old English *wrīgian* to turn] **wryly** *adv*
wrybill *n* a New Zealand plover whose bill is bent to one side enabling it to search for food beneath stones
wryneck *n* a woodpecker that has a habit of twisting its neck round
wt. weight
WTO World Trade Organization
wuss (woos) *or* **wussy** *n, pl* **wusses** *or* **wussies** *slang, chiefly US* a feeble or ineffectual person [perhaps from PUSSY[1]]
WV West Virginia
WWI World War One
WWII World War Two
WWW World Wide Web
WY Wyoming
wych-elm *or* **witch-elm** *n* a Eurasian elm with long pointed leaves [Old English *wice*]
WYSIWYG *n, adj computers* what you see is what you get: referring to what is displayed on the screen being the same as what will be printed out

Xx

x *maths* **1** (along with *y* and *z*) an unknown quantity **2** the multiplication symbol

X **1** indicating an error, a choice, or a kiss **2** indicating an unknown, unspecified, or variable factor, person, or thing: *Miss X* **3** the Roman numeral for ten **4** (formerly) indicating a film that may not be publicly shown to anyone under 18: since 1982 replaced by symbol 18

X-chromosome *n* the sex chromosome that occurs in pairs in the females of many animals, including humans, and as one of a pair with the Y-chromosome in males

Xe *chem* xenon

xenon *n chem* a colourless odourless gas found in minute quantities in the air. Symbol: **Xe** [Greek: something strange]

xenophobia (zen-oh-**fobe**-ee-a) *n* hatred or fear of foreigners or strangers [Greek *xenos* foreign + *phobos* fear] **xenophobic** *adj*

xerography (zeer-**og**-ra-fee) *n* a photocopying process in which an image of the written or printed material is electrically charged on a surface and attracts oppositely charged dry ink particles which are then fixed by heating [Greek *xēros* dry + -GRAPHY] **xerographic** *adj*

Xerox (**zeer**-ox) *n trademark* **1** a machine for copying printed material **2** a copy made by a Xerox machine ▷ *vb* **3** to produce a copy of (a document) using such a machine

Xhosa (**kawss**-a) *n* **1** *pl* **-sa** *or* **-sas** a member of a Black people living in the Republic of South Africa **2** the language of this people **Xhosan** *adj*

Xmas (**eks**-mass) *n informal* short for **Christmas** [from the Greek letter *chi* (X), first letter of *Khristos* Christ]

XML extensible markup language: a computer language used in text formatting

X-rated *adj* **1** (formerly, in Britain) (of a film) considered suitable for viewing by adults only **2** *informal* involving bad language, violence, or sex: *an X-rated conversation*

X-ray *or* **x-ray** *n* **1** a stream of electromagnetic radiation of short wavelength that can pass through some solid materials **2** a picture produced by exposing photographic film to X-rays: used in medicine as a diagnostic aid, since parts of the body, such as bones, absorb X-rays and so appear as opaque areas on the picture ▷ *vb* **3** to photograph, treat, or examine using X-rays

X-ray diffraction *n physics* the scattering of X-rays on contact with matter, resulting in changes in radiation intensity, which is used for studying atomic structure

xylem (**zile**-em) *n botany* a plant tissue that conducts water and mineral salts from the roots to all other parts [Greek *xulon* wood]

xylene (**zile**-lean) *n chem* a hydrocarbon existing in three isomeric forms, all three being colourless flammable volatile liquids used as solvents and in the manufacture of synthetic resins, dyes, and insecticides [Greek *xulon* wood]

xylitol *n chem* an artificial sweetener produced from xylose and used esp. in chewing gum

xylophone (**zile**-oh-fone) *n music* a percussion instrument consisting of a set of wooden bars played with hammers [Greek *xulon* wood] **xylophonist** *n*

xylose *n* a white crystalline sugar derived from wood and straw

Yy

y *maths* (along with *x* and *z*) an unknown quantity
Y **1** an unknown, unspecified, or variable factor, number, person, or thing **2** *chem* yttrium
ya *interj S African* yes
yabby *n, pl* **-bies** *Austral* **1** a small freshwater crayfish **2** a marine prawn used as bait [from a native Australian language]
yacht (yott) *n* **1** a large boat with sails or an engine, used for racing or pleasure cruising ▷ *vb* **2** to sail or cruise in a yacht [obsolete Dutch *jaghte*] **yachting** *n, adj*
yachtsman *or fem* **yachtswoman** *n, pl* **-men** *or* **-women** a person who sails a yacht
yack *n, vb* same as **yak²**
yah *interj* **1** *informal* same as **yes** **2** an exclamation of derision or disgust
yahoo *n, pl* **-hoos** a crude, brutish, or obscenely coarse person [after the brutish creatures in *Gulliver's Travels*]
yahweh *or* **yahveh** *n Bible* a personal name of god [Hebrew YHVH, with conjectural vowels]
yak¹ *n* a Tibetan ox with long shaggy hair [Tibetan *gyag*]
yak² *slang* ▷ *n* **1** noisy, continuous, and trivial talk ▷ *vb* **yakking, yakked** **2** to talk continuously about unimportant matters [imitative]
yakka *n Austral & NZ informal* work [from a native Australian language]
Yale lock *n trademark* a type of cylinder lock using a flat serrated key [after L. *Yale*, inventor]
yam *n* **1** a twining plant of tropical and subtropical regions, cultivated for its starchy roots which are eaten as a vegetable **2** the sweet potato [Portuguese *inhame*]
yammer *informal* ▷ *vb* **1** to whine in a complaining manner ▷ *n* **2** a yammering sound **3** nonsense or jabber [Old English *geōmrian* to grumble]
Yang *n* See **Yin and Yang**
yank *vb* **1** to pull (someone or something) with a sharp movement: *I yanked myself out of the water* ▷ *n* **2** a sudden pull or jerk [origin unknown]
Yank *n slang* a person from the United States
Yankee *n* **1** *slang* same as **Yank** **2** a person from the Northern United States ▷ *adj* **3** of or characteristic of Yankees [perhaps from Dutch *Jan Kees* John Cheese, nickname for English colonists]
yap *vb* **yapping, yapped** **1** to bark with a high-pitched sound **2** *informal* to talk at length in an annoying or stupid way ▷ *n* **3** a high-pitched bark **4** *slang* annoying or stupid speech [imitative] **yappy** *adj*
yarborough *n bridge & whist* a hand in which no card is higher than nine [supposedly after the second earl of *Yarborough*, said to have bet a thousand to one against its occurrence]
yard¹ *n* **1** a unit of length equal to 3 feet (0.9144 metre) **2** *naut* a spar slung across a ship's mast to extend the sail [Old English *gierd* rod, twig]
yard² *n* **1** a piece of enclosed ground, often adjoining or surrounded by a building or buildings **2** an enclosed or open area where a particular type of work is done: *a shipbuilding yard* **3** *US, Canad & Austral* the garden of a house **4** *US & Canad* the winter pasture of deer, moose, and similar animals [Old English *geard*]
Yard *n* **the Yard** *Brit informal* short for **Scotland Yard**
yardarm *n naut* the outer end of a ship's yard
yardstick *n* **1** a measure or standard used for comparison: *there's no yardstick for judging a problem of this sort* **2** a graduated measuring stick one yard long
yarmulke (yar-mull-ka) *n* a skullcap worn by Jewish men [Yiddish]
yarn *n* **1** a continuous twisted strand of natural or synthetic fibres, used for knitting or making cloth **2** *informal* a long involved story **3** **spin a yarn** *informal* to tell such a story [Old English *gearn*]
yarrow *n* a wild plant with flat clusters of white flowers [Old English *gearwe*]
yashmak *n* a veil worn by some Muslim women to cover the face in public [Arabic]
yaw *vb* **1** (of an aircraft or ship) to turn to one side or from side to side while moving ▷ *n* **2** the act or movement of yawing [origin unknown]
yawl *n* **1** a two-masted sailing boat **2** a ship's small boat [Dutch *jol* or Middle Low German *jolle*]
yawn *vb* **1** to open one's mouth wide and take in air deeply, often when sleepy or bored **2** to be open wide as if threatening to engulf someone or something: *the doorway yawned blackly open at the end of the hall* ▷ *n* **3** the act or an instance of yawning [Old English *geonian*] **yawning** *adj*
yaws *n* an infectious disease of tropical climates characterized by red skin eruptions [Carib]
Yb *chem* ytterbium
Y-chromosome *n* the sex chromosome that occurs as one of a pair with the X-chromosome in the males of many animals, including humans
yd yard (measure)
ye¹ (yee) *pron old-fashioned or dialect* you [Old English *gē*]
ye² *adj (definite article) old-fashioned or humorous* the: *ye olde Rose and Crown pub* [a misinterpretation of *the*, written with the old letter thorn (þ), representing *th*]
yea *interj* **1** *old-fashioned* yes ▷ *adv* **2** *old-fashioned or literary* indeed or truly: *they wandered about the church, yea, even unto the altar* [Old English *gēa*]
yeah *interj informal* same as **yes**
year *n* **1** the time taken for the earth to make one revolution around the sun, about 365 days **2** the twelve months from January 1 to December 31 **3** a period of twelve months from any specified date **4** a specific period of time, usually occupying a definite part or parts of a twelve-month period, used for some particular activity: *the financial year* **5** a group of people who have started an academic course at the same time **6** **year in, year out** regularly or monotonously, over a long period **7** **years** **a** a long time: *the legal*

case could take years to resolve **B** age, usually old age: *a man of his years* [Old English *gēar*]

USAGE In writing spans of years, it is important to choose a style that avoids ambiguity. The practice adopted in this dictionary is, in four-figure dates, to specify the last two digits of the second date if it falls within the same century as the first: *1801–08; 1850–51; 1899–1901*. In writing three-figure BC dates, it is advisable to give both dates in full: 159–156BC, not 159–56BC unless of course the span referred to consists of 103 years rather than three years. It is also advisable to specify BC or AD in years under 1000 unless the context makes this self-evident.

yearbook *n* a reference book published once a year containing details of events of the previous year

yearling *n* an animal that is between one and two years old

yearly *adj* **1** occurring, done, or appearing once a year or every year **2** lasting or valid for a year: *the yearly cycle* ▷ *adv* **3** once a year

yearn *vb* **1** to have an intense desire or longing: *he often yearned for life in a country town* **2** to feel tenderness or affection: *I yearn for you* [Old English *giernan*] **yearning** *n, adj*

yeast *n* a yellowish fungus used in fermenting alcoholic drinks and in raising dough for bread [Old English *giest*] **yeasty** *adj*

yebo *interj S African informal* yes [Zulu *yebo* yes, I agree]

yell *vb* **1** to shout, scream, or cheer in a loud or piercing way ▷ *n* **2** a loud piercing cry of pain, anger, or fear [Old English *giellan*]

yellow *n* **1** the colour of a lemon or an egg yolk **2** anything yellow, such as yellow clothing or yellow paint: *painted in yellow* ▷ *adj* **3** of the colour yellow; of the colour of a lemon or an egg yolk **4** *informal* cowardly or afraid **5** having a yellowish complexion ▷ *vb* **6** to make or become yellow or yellower [Old English *geolu*] **yellowish** *or* **yellowy** *adj*

yellow-belly *n, pl* **-bellies** *slang* a coward **yellow-bellied** *adj*

yellow card *n soccer* a piece of yellow pasteboard raised by a referee to indicate that a player has been booked for a serious violation of the rules

yellow fever *n* an acute infectious tropical disease causing fever and jaundice, caused by certain mosquitoes

yellowfin tuna *n* a large marine food fish of tropical and subtropical waters

yellowhammer *n* a European songbird with a yellowish head and body [origin unknown]

Yellow Pages *pl n trademark* a telephone directory that lists businesses under the headings of the type of business or service they provide

yellow streak *n informal* a cowardly or weak trait

yelp *vb* **1** to utter a sharp or high-pitched cry of pain ▷ *n* **2** a sharp or high-pitched cry of pain [Old English *gielpan* to boast]

yen[1] *n, pl* **yen** the standard monetary unit of Japan [Japanese *en*]

yen[2] *informal* ▷ *n* **1** a longing or desire ▷ *vb* **yenning, yenned 2** to have a longing [perhaps from Chinese *yän* a craving]

yeoman (yo-man) *n, pl* **-men** *history* a farmer owning and farming his own land [perhaps from *yongman* young man]

yeoman of the guard *n* a member of the ceremonial bodyguard (**Yeomen of the Guard**) of the British monarch

yeomanry *n* **1** yeomen collectively **2** (in Britain) a former volunteer cavalry force

yep *interj informal* same as **yes**

yes *interj* **1** used to express consent, agreement, or approval, or to answer when one is addressed **2** used to signal someone to speak or keep speaking, enter a room, or do something ▷ *n* **3** an answer or vote of *yes* **4** a person who answers or votes *yes* [Old English *gēse*]

yes man *n* a person who always agrees with his or her superior in order to gain favour

yesterday *n* **1** the day before today **2** the recent past ▷ *adv* **3** on or during the day before today **4** in the recent past

yesteryear *formal or literary* ▷ *n* **1** last year or the past in general ▷ *adv* **2** during last year or the past in general

yet *conj* **1** nevertheless or still: *I'm too tired to work, yet I have to go on* ▷ *adv* **2** up until then or now: *this may be her most rewarding book yet* **3** still: *yet more work to do* **4** now (as contrasted with later): *not ready for that yet* **5** eventually in spite of everything: *I'll break your spirit yet!* **6 as yet** up until then or now [Old English *gīeta*]

yeti *n* same as **abominable snowman** [Tibetan]

yew *n* an evergreen tree with needle-like leaves, red berries, and fine-grained elastic wood [Old English *īw*]

YHA (in Britain) Youth Hostels Association

yid *n slang, offensive* a Jew [probably from *Yiddish*]

Yiddish *n* **1** a language derived from High German, spoken by Jews in Europe and elsewhere by Jewish emigrants, and usually written in the Hebrew alphabet ▷ *adj* **2** of this language [German *jüdisch* Jewish]

yield *vb* **1** to produce or bear **2** to give as a return: *some of his policies have yielded large savings* **3** to give up control of; surrender **4** to give way, submit, or surrender, through force or persuasion: *the players finally yielded to the weather* **5** to agree (to): *governments too weak to say no repeatedly yielded to petitions for charters* **6** to grant or allow: *to yield right of way* ▷ *n* **7** the amount produced [Old English *gieldan*]

yielding *adj* **1** compliant or submissive **2** soft or flexible: *he landed on a yielding surface rather than rock or board*

Yin and Yang *n* two complementary principles of Chinese philosophy: Yin is negative, dark, and feminine, Yang is positive, bright, and masculine [Chinese *yin* dark + *yang* bright]

yippee *interj* an exclamation of joy, pleasure, or anticipation

YMCA Young Men's Christian Association

yo *interj* an expression used as a greeting or to attract someone's attention [origin unknown]

yob *or* **yobbo** *n, pl* **yobs** *or* **yobbos** *Brit, Austral & NZ slang* a bad-mannered aggressive youth [perhaps back slang for *boy*] **yobbish** *adj*

yodel *vb* **-delling, -delled** *or US* **-deling, -deled 1** to sing with abrupt changes back and forth between the normal voice and falsetto, as in folk songs of the Swiss Alps ▷ *n* **2** the act or sound of yodelling [German *jodeln* (imitative)] **yodeller** *or US* **yodeler** *n*

yoga *n* **1** a Hindu system of philosophy aiming at spiritual, mental, and physical wellbeing by means of deep meditation, prescribed postures, and controlled breathing **2** a system of exercising involving such meditation, postures, and breathing [Sanskrit: a yoking]

yogi *n* a person who practises or is a master of yoga

yogurt *or* **yoghurt** *n* a slightly sour custard-like food made from milk curdled by bacteria, often sweetened and flavoured with fruit [Turkish]

yoke *n, pl* **yokes** *or* **yoke** **1** a wooden frame with a bar put across the necks of two animals to hold them together so that they can be worked as a team **2** a pair of animals joined by a yoke **3** a frame fitting over a person's shoulders for carrying buckets **4** an oppressive force or burden: *people are still suffering under the yoke of slavery* **5** a fitted part of a garment to which a fuller part is attached ▷ *vb* **yoking, yoked** **6** to put a yoke on **7** to unite or link [Old English *geoc*]

yokel *n derogatory* a person who lives in the country, esp. one who appears simple and old-fashioned [perhaps from dialect *yokel* green woodpecker]

yolk *n* the yellow part in the middle of an egg that provides food for the developing embryo [Old English *geoloca*]

Yom Kippur *n* an annual Jewish holiday celebrated as a day of fasting, with prayers of penitence [Hebrew *yōm* day + *kippūr* atonement]

yon *adj* **1** *chiefly Scot & N English dialect* that: *yon dog* ▷ *adv* **2** yonder: *he flicked glances hither and yon* ▷ *pron* **3** that person or thing: *yon was a pretty sight* [Old English *geon*]

yonder *adv* **1** over there ▷ *adj* **2** situated over there: *a tree at yonder waterfall* [Old English *geond*]

yonks *pl n informal* a very long time: *he must have been planning this for yonks* [origin unknown]

yoo-hoo *interj* a call to attract a person's attention

yore *n* **of yore** a long time ago: *in days of yore* [Old English *geāra*]

yorker *n cricket* a ball bowled so as to pitch just under or just beyond the bat [probably after the *Yorkshire* County Cricket Club]

Yorkist *English history* ▷ *n* **1** a supporter of the royal House of York, esp. during the Wars of the Roses ▷ *adj* **2** of or relating to the supporters or members of the House of York

Yorks. Yorkshire

Yorkshire pudding *n* a baked pudding made from a batter of flour, eggs, and milk, often served with roast beef [from *Yorkshire*, county in NE England]

Y

you *pron* **1** (refers to) the person or people addressed: *can I get you a drink?* **2** (refers to) an unspecified person or people in general: *just keep it simple and you can't go wrong* ▷ *n* **3** *informal* the personality of the person being addressed: *that hat isn't really you* [Old English *ēow*]

USAGE See at **me**[1].

you'd you had *or* you would

you'll you will *or* you shall

young *adj* **1** having lived or existed for a relatively short time **2** having qualities associated with youth: *their innovative approach and young attitude appealed to him* **3** of or relating to youth: *he'd been a terrorist himself in France in his young days* **4** of a group representing the younger members of a larger organization: *Young Conservatives* ▷ *n* **5** young people in general: *that never seems very important to the young* **6** offspring, esp. young animals: *a deer suckling her young* [Old English *geong*] **youngish** *adj*

youngster *n* a young person

your *adj* **1** of, belonging to, or associated with you: *ask your doctor to make the necessary calls* **2** of, belonging to, or associated with an unspecified person or people in general: *it is not right to take another baby to replace your own* **3** *informal* used to indicate all things or people of a certain type: *these characters are not your average housebreakers* [Old English *ēower*]

you're you are

yours *pron* **1** something belonging to you: *my reputation is better than yours* **2** your family: *a blessed Christmas to you and yours* **3** used in closing phrases at the end of a letter: *yours sincerely; yours faithfully* **4 of yours** belonging to you: *that husband of yours*

yourself *pron, pl* **-selves** **1** **A** the reflexive form of *you* **B** used for emphasis: *you've stated publicly that you yourself use drugs* **2** your normal self: *you're not yourself today*

yours truly *pron informal* I *or* me [from the closing phrase of letters]

youth *n* **1** the period between childhood and maturity **2** the quality or condition of being young, immature, or inexperienced: *his youth told against him in the contest* **3** a young man or boy **4** young people collectively: *there is still hope for today's youth* **5** the freshness, vigour, or vitality associated with being young [Old English *geogoth*]

youth club *n* a club that provides leisure activities for young people

youthful *adj* **1** vigorous or active: *the intermediate section was won by a youthful grandmother* **2** of, relating to, possessing, or associated with youth: *youthful good looks* **youthfully** *adv* **youthfulness** *n*

youth hostel *n* an inexpensive lodging place for young people travelling cheaply

YouTube *n* a website on which subscribers can post and watch videos

you've you have

yowl *vb* **1** to produce a loud mournful wail or cry ▷ *n* **2** a wail or howl [Old Norse *gaula*]

yo-yo *n, pl* **-yos** **1** a toy consisting of a spool attached to a string, the end of which is held while it is repeatedly spun out and reeled in ▷ *vb* **yo-yoing, yo-yoed** **2** to change repeatedly from one position to another [originally a trademark for this type of toy]

yrs **1** years **2** yours

YT Yukon Territory

ytterbium (it-terb-ee-um) *n chem* a soft silvery element that is used to improve the mechanical properties of steel. Symbol: **Yb** [after *Ytterby*, Swedish quarry where discovered]

yttrium (it-ree-um) *n chem* a silvery metallic element used in various alloys and in lasers. Symbol: **Y** [see YTTERBIUM]

yuan *n, pl* **-an** the standard monetary unit of the People's Republic of China [Chinese *yüan* round object]

yucca *n* a tropical plant with spiky leaves and white flowers [from a Native American language]

yucky *or* **yukky** *adj* **yuckier, yuckiest** *or* **yukkier, yukkiest** *slang* disgusting or nasty [from *yuck*, exclamation of disgust]

Yule *n literary or old-fashioned* Christmas or the Christmas season: *Yuletide* [Old English *geōla*, originally a pagan feast lasting 12 days]

yummy *slang* ▷ *adj* **-mier, -miest 1** delicious or attractive: *yummy sauces* ▷ *interj* **2** Also: **yum-yum** an exclamation indicating pleasure or delight, as in anticipation of delicious food [*yum-yum* (imitative)]

yuppie *n* **1** a young highly-paid professional person, esp. one who has a fashionable way of life ▷ *adj* **2** typical of or reflecting the values of yuppies: *a yuppie accessory* [*y(oung) u(rban)* or *u(pwardly mobile) p(rofessional)*]

yuppify *vb* **-fies, -fying, -fied** to make yuppie in nature: *Mount Pleasant was being yuppified*
yuppification *n*

YWCA Young Women's Christian Association

Zz

z *or* **Z** *n, pl* **z's, Z's** *or* **Zs 1** the 26th and last letter of the English alphabet **2 from A to Z** See **a** (sense 3)
z *maths* (along with *x* and *y*) an unknown quantity
Z *chem* atomic number
zabaglione (zab-al-**lyoh**-nee) *n* a dessert made of egg yolks, sugar, and wine, whipped together [Italian]
zany (**zane**-ee) *adj* **zanier, zaniest** comical in an endearing way [Italian dialect *Zanni*, nickname for *Giovanni* John; traditional name for a clown]
zap *vb* **zapping, zapped** *slang* **1** to kill, esp. by shooting **2** to change television channels rapidly by remote control **3** to move quickly [imitative]
zeal *n* great enthusiasm or eagerness, esp. for a religious movement [Greek *zēlos*]
zealot (**zel**-lot) *n* a fanatic or an extreme enthusiast **zealotry** *n*
zealous (**zel**-luss) *adj* extremely eager or enthusiastic **zealously** *adv*
zebra *n, pl* **-ras** *or* **-ra** a black-and-white striped African animal of the horse family [Old Spanish: wild ass]
zebra crossing *n Brit* a pedestrian crossing marked by broad black and white stripes: once on the crossing the pedestrian has right of way
zebu (**zee**-boo) *n* a domesticated ox of Africa and Asia, with a humped back and long horns [French]
zed *n* (in most English-speaking countries) the spoken form of the letter *z*
zee *n* (in the US) the spoken form of the letter *z*
zeitgeist (**zite**-guyst) *n* the spirit or general outlook of a specific time or period [German, literally: time spirit]
Zen *n* a Japanese form of Buddhism that concentrates on learning through meditation and intuition
Zend-Avesta *n* the Zoroastrian scriptures (the **Avesta**), together with the traditional interpretive commentary known as the **Zend**
zenith *n* **1** the point in the sky directly above an observer **2** the highest or most successful point of anything: *he was at the zenith of his military career* [Arabic *samt arrās* path over one's head] **zenithal** *adj*
zephyr (**zef**-fer) *n* a soft gentle breeze [Greek *zephuros* the west wind]
Zeppelin *n* a large cylindrical rigid German airship of the early 20th century [after Count von *Zeppelin*, its designer]
zero *n, pl* **-ros** *or* **-roes 1** the cardinal number between +1 and -1 **2** the symbol, 0, representing this number **3** the line or point on a scale of measurement from which the graduations commence **4** the lowest point or degree: *my credibility is down to zero* **5** nothing or nil **6** the temperature, pressure, etc., that registers a reading of zero on a scale ▹ *adj* **7** amounting to zero: *zero inflation* **8** *meteorol* (of visibility) limited to a very short distance ▹ *vb* **-roing, -roed 9** to adjust (an instrument or scale) so as to read zero [Arabic *sifr* empty]
zero gravity *n* the state of weightlessness
zero hour *n* **1** *military* the time set for the start of an operation **2** *informal* a critical time, usually at the beginning of an action
zero in on *vb* **1** to aim a weapon at (a target) **2** to concentrate one's attention on
zero-rated *adj* denoting goods on which the buyer pays no value-added tax
zest *n* **1** invigorating or keen excitement or enjoyment: *she has a zest for life and a quick intellect* **2** added interest, flavour, or charm: *he said that she would provide a new zest for his government* **3** the peel of an orange or lemon, used as flavouring [French *zeste*] **zestful** *adj*
Zeus *n Greek myth* the ruler of the gods
ziggurat *n* (in ancient Mesopotamia) a temple in the shape of a pyramid [Assyrian *ziqqurati* summit]
zigzag *n* **1** a line or course having sharp turns in alternating directions ▹ *adj* **2** formed in or proceeding in a zigzag ▹ *adv* **3** in a zigzag manner ▹ *vb* **-zagging, -zagged 4** to move in a zigzag [German *zickzack*]
Zika virus (**zee**-ka) *n* a virus that causes a mild fever and is associated with birth defects in humans [after the *Zika* Forest in Uganda, where it was first isolated]
zilch *n informal* nothing [origin unknown]
zillion *n, pl* **-lions** *or* **-lion** *(often pl) informal* an extremely large but unspecified number: *there are zillions of beautiful spots to visit* [after *million*]
Zimmer *n trademark* a tubular frame with rubber feet, used as a support to help infirm people walk
zinc *n chem* a brittle bluish-white metallic element that is used in alloys such as brass, to form a protective coating on metals, and in battery electrodes. Symbol: **Zn** [German *Zink*]
zinc ointment *n* a medicinal ointment consisting of zinc oxide, petroleum jelly, and paraffin
zinc oxide *n chem & pharmacol* a white insoluble powder used as a pigment and in making zinc ointment
zing *n* **1** *informal* the quality in something that makes it lively or interesting **2** a short high-pitched buzzing sound, like the sound of a bullet or vibrating string [imitative]
zinnia *n* a plant of tropical and subtropical America, with solitary heads of brightly coloured flowers [after J. G. *Zinn*, botanist]
Zion *n* **1** the hill on which the city of Jerusalem stands **2 A** the modern Jewish nation **B** Israel as the national home of the Jewish people **3** *Christianity* heaven
Zionism *n* a political movement for the establishment and support of a national homeland for Jews in what is now Israel **Zionist** *n, adj*

zip *n* **1** Also called: **zip fastener** a fastener with two parallel rows of metal or plastic teeth, one on either side of a closure, which are interlocked by a sliding tab **2** *informal* energy or vigour **3** a short sharp whizzing sound, like the sound of a passing bullet ▷ *vb* **zipping, zipped 4** (often foll. by *up*) to fasten with a zip **5** to move with a sharp whizzing sound: *bullets zipped and ricocheted all around us* **6** to hurry or rush **7** to compress (a data file) prior to transmission [imitative]
zip code *n* the US equivalent of **postcode** [*z(one) i(mprovement) p(lan)*]
zipline *or* **zipwire** *n* a cable mechanism used for transportation across a river, gorge, etc
zipper *n US & Canad* same as **zip** (sense 1)
zippy *adj* **-pier, -piest** *informal* full of energy
zircon *n mineralogy* a hard mineral consisting of zirconium silicate, used as a gemstone and in industry [German *Zirkon*]
zirconium *n chem* a greyish-white metallic element, occurring chiefly in zircon, that is exceptionally corrosion-resistant. Symbol: **Zr**
zit *n slang* a spot or pimple
zither *n* a musical instrument consisting of numerous strings stretched over a flat box and plucked to produce notes [Greek *kithara*] **zitherist** *n*
zloty *n, pl* **-tys** *or* **-ty** the standard monetary unit of Poland [Polish: golden]
Zn *chem* zinc
zodiac *n* **1** an imaginary belt in the sky within which the sun, moon, and planets appear to move, and which is divided into 12 equal areas called **signs of the zodiac,** each named after the constellation which once lay in it **2** *astrol* a diagram, usually circular, representing this belt [Greek *zōidion* animal sign, from *zōion* animal] **zodiacal** *adj*
zombie *or* **zombi** *n, pl* **-bies** *or* **-bis 1** a person who appears to be lifeless, apathetic, or totally lacking in independent judgment **2** a corpse brought to life by witchcraft [W African *zumbi* good-luck fetish]
zone *n* **1** a region, area, or section characterized by some distinctive feature or quality: *a demilitarized zone* **2** *geog* one of the divisions of the earth's surface according to temperature **3** a section on a transport route **4** *maths* a portion of a sphere between two parallel lines intersecting the sphere **5** NZ a catchment area for a specific school ▷ *vb* **zoning, zoned 6** to divide (a place) into zones for different uses or activities [Greek *zōnē* girdle] **zonal** *adj* **zoning** *n*
zonked *adj Brit, Austral & NZ slang* **1** highly intoxicated with drugs or alcohol **2** exhausted [imitative]
zoo *n, pl* **zoos** a place where live animals are kept, studied, bred, and exhibited to the public [from *zoological garden*]
zooid (**zoh**-oid) *n* **1** any independent animal body, such as an individual of a coral colony **2** a cell or body, produced by an organism and capable of independent motion, such as a gamete [Greek *zōion* animal]
zool. 1 zoological **2** zoology
zoological garden *n* the formal term for **zoo**
zoology *n* the study of animals, including their classification, structure, physiology, and history [Greek *zōion* animal + -LOGY] **zoological** *adj* **zoologist** *n*
zoom *vb* **1** to move very rapidly: *the first rocket zoomed into the sky* **2** to increase or rise rapidly: *stocks zoomed on the American exchange* **3** to move with or make a continuous buzzing or humming sound ▷ *n* **4** the sound or act of zooming **5** a zoom lens [imitative]
zoom in *or* **zoom out** *vb* to increase or decrease rapidly the magnification of an image, esp. by using a zoom lens
zoom lens *n* a lens system that can make the details of a picture larger or smaller while keeping the picture in focus
zoophyte (**zoh**-a-fite) *n* any animal resembling a plant, such as a sea anemone [Greek *zōion* animal + *phuton* plant]
Zoroastrianism (zorr-oh-**ass**-tree-an-iz-zum) *or* **Zoroastrism** *n* the religion founded by the ancient Persian prophet Zoroaster, based on the concept of a continuous struggle between good and evil **Zoroastrian** *adj*
zounds *interj old-fashioned* a mild oath indicating surprise or indignation [euphemistic shortening of *God's wounds*]
Zr *chem* zirconium
zucchetto (tsoo-**ket**-toe) *n, pl* **-tos** *RC Church* a small round skullcap worn by clergymen and varying in colour according to the rank of the wearer [Italian]
zucchini (zoo-**keen**-ee) *n, pl* **-ni** *or* **-nis** *chiefly US, Canad & Austral* a courgette [Italian]
Zulu *n* **1** *pl* **-lus** *or* **-lu** a member of a people of Southern Africa **2** the language of this people
Zumba *n trademark* a system of dance-like exercises performed to Latin American music
zygote *n* the cell resulting from the union of an ovum and a spermatozoon [Greek *zugōtos* yoked]

Z

Common mistakes and controversial issues

Words that are often confused

Homophones

Homophones are words which sound the same but are spelled differently, and it is possible to get them confused:

affect Affect is a *verb*: *How will this new law affect me?*	***effect*** Effect is a *noun*: *What will the effect of the new law be?*
already Already is an *adverb*. If something has already happened, it has happened before the present time: *I've already called an ambulance.*	***all ready*** In the phrase 'all ready', 'all' is a *quantifier* meaning 'the whole of a group or a thing', and 'ready' is an *adjective*: *Are you all ready to go?*
alter Alter is a *verb*, meaning 'to change': *Nothing in the house had altered since 1960.*	***altar*** An altar is the holy table in a church: *The priest stood in front of the altar.*
anyone Anyone is a *pronoun* and always refers to people: *Has anyone seen my hat?*	***any one*** In the phrase 'any one', 'one' is a *pronoun* or a *determiner* that can refer to a person or a thing, depending on the context: *We never spend long in any one place.* *It could have happened to any one of us.*

bare Bare is an *adjective* meaning 'not covered' or 'not wearing any clothes': *We ran along the beach with bare feet.*	***bear*** A bear is a wild animal: *There are bears in the woods.*
board A board is a flat piece of wood: *They nailed a board over the window.*	***bored*** If you are bored, you are not interested by something: *I was so bored at school today.*
coarse Coarse is an *adjective* meaning 'having a rough texture' or 'talking and behaving in a rude way': *The sand was very coarse.* *His manners are coarse.*	***course*** Course is a *noun* with several meanings, including 'a series of lessons' and 'a route or path': *I did a course in art history.* *The plane changed course.*
compliment A compliment is a nice thing that someone says about someone or something. Compliment can also be used as a *verb*: *They paid him a lot of compliments.* *She complimented me on my roses.*	***complement*** If people or things complement each other, they have different qualities that go well together: *The dry wine complements this rich dish perfectly.*
counsellor A counsellor gives people advice, often on personal matters, such as a job: *They went to see a marriage counsellor.*	***councillor*** A councillor is an official in a local council: *She was elected as a councillor last year.*

dependent Dependent is an *adjective*. If you are dependent on someone or something, you rely on them: *Their economy is very dependent on oil.*	***dependant*** Dependant is a *noun*. Your dependants are the people you are financially responsible for: *He has a large income and no dependants.*
discreet If you are discreet, you are careful to avoid attracting attention or revealing private information: *I made a few discreet inquiries about her.*	***discrete*** If things are discrete, they are not joined or connected in any way: *I met him on three discrete occasions.*
draft A draft of a piece of writing is a first, rough version of it: *He showed me the first draft of his story.*	***draught*** A draught is a current of air: *There's a draught coming in through that window.* Note that in American English, this is spelled 'draft'.
draw Draw is a *verb* meaning to make a picture with a pencil: *Shall we draw a picture?*	***drawer*** A drawer is part of a desk, cupboard, etc.: *I put the papers away in a drawer.*
everyone Everyone is a *pronoun* and always refers to people: *Everyone enjoyed the show.*	***every one*** In the phrase 'every one', 'one' is a *pronoun* or a *determiner* that can refer to a person or a thing, depending on the context: *They have talked to every one of my colleagues.* *We have eaten every one of the biscuits.*

hoard If you hoard things such as food or money, you save or store them for yourself: *She hoarded jars of fruit in the cellar.* Hoard can also be a *noun*: *We found a hoard of guns under the floorboards.*	***horde*** A horde is a large crowd of people: *Hordes of shoppers crowded outside the store.*
hole A hole is an opening or a hollow space in something: *There's a hole in my shoe.*	***whole*** Whole is a *quantifier* meaning 'all of something': *He ate the whole loaf.*
its Its means 'belonging to it': *The dog wagged its tail.*	***it's*** It's means 'it is': *It's going to be difficult to fit in all this work.*
led Led is the past participle of the *verb* 'lead': *He led me into a small room.*	***lead*** Lead is a *noun*, meaning 'a soft, grey metal': *The roof is covered with lead.* Lead is also a *verb*, but it has a different pronunciation.
licence Licence is a *noun*: *I showed him my driving licence.*	***license*** License is a *verb*: *We are not licensed to serve alcohol.* Note that in American English, *license* is used for the verb and the noun.

pedal Pedal is a *noun* meaning the part of a bike you press with your foot, or a *verb* meaning to press that part: *Put your foot on the pedal.* *You'll have to pedal harder.*	***peddle*** If you peddle something, you sell it: *He was caught peddling drugs.*
practice Practice is a *noun*: *I did my piano practice.*	***practise*** Practise is a *verb*: *I practised the piano.* Note that in American English, *practice* is used for the verb and the noun.
principle Principle is a *noun* meaning 'a belief about what is right or wrong' or 'a basic rule': *Eating meat is against my principles.* *We learned the basic principles of yoga.*	***principal*** Principal is an *adjective* meaning 'most important': *Bad weather was the principal reason for the failure of the expedition.* Principal can also be a *noun* meaning 'the person in charge of a school or college': *She was sent to the principal's office.*
site A site is an area that is used for a particular purpose or where something happens: *He works on a building site.* *This is the site of the explosion.*	***sight*** Sight is the ability to see, and a sight is something you can see: *She lost her sight in an accident.* *I faint at the sight of blood.*

stationery Stationery is a *noun* meaning 'paper, envelopes, and writing equipment': *Envelopes are kept in the stationery cupboard.*	***stationary*** Stationary is an *adjective* meaning 'not moving': *I drove into a stationary vehicle.*
story A story is something you read in a book: *I bought a book of fairy stories.*	***storey*** A storey is a level of a building: *My office is in a six-storey building.*
whether Whether is a *conjunction* used to talk about a choice between two or more alternatives: *I can't decide whether to have soup or salad.*	***weather*** Weather is a *noun* used to talk about rain, snow, sun, etc.: *The weather was great in Portugal.*
whose Whose is a *pronoun* and a *determiner* used to ask questions about who something belongs to, or to talk about things connected to a particular person: *Whose shoes are these?* *He helped a woman whose face was covered with blood.*	***who's*** Who's means 'who is': *Who's going to do the washing up?*

witch Witch is a *noun*, meaning an evil magic woman: *We painted a witch on a broomstick.*	***which*** Which is a *pronoun* and a *determiner* used to ask questions when there are two or more possible alternatives, or to talk about things connected to a particular person: *Which is your cabin?* *I took the coat which looked warmest.*
your Your is a *pronoun* showing that something belongs to you or relates to you: *Where is your car?*	***you're*** You're means 'you are': *You're late again.*

Other words that are often confused

These words do not sound the same, but they are spelled in quite a similar way, and often cause confusion:

accept Accept is a *verb* and means 'agree to have': *I cannot accept money from you.*	***except*** Except is a *preposition* and a *conjunction* meaning 'not including': *Everyone was invited except Flora.*
adverse Adverse is a formal *adjective* meaning 'bad' or 'negative': *Do not attempt the climb in adverse weather conditions.*	***averse*** If you are averse to something, you do not like it: *I'm not averse to a sing-song now and then.*

advice Advice is a *noun*: *Can you give me some advice about growing roses?*	***advise*** Advise is a *verb*: *I advised him to wait a bit longer.*
beside Beside means 'next to': *Put the chair beside the window.*	***besides*** Besides means 'as well' or 'in addition to': *I don't need any help. Besides, I've nearly finished.* *He designed houses, office blocks, and much else besides.*
censure Censure is a formal *verb*, meaning 'to criticize strongly'. It is also a *noun* meaning the criticism itself: *They were censured for their failure to implement safety measures.* *The company received censure for its poor safety record.*	***censor*** Censor is a *verb* meaning 'to cut out parts of speech or writing'. It is also a *noun* meaning the person who does this: *His letters home from the war were heavily censored.* *Government censors cut out much of what he wrote.*
continual Continual is used to mean that something happens without interruption, and also that something happens repeatedly: *I'm fed up with this continual noise.* *There have been continual demands for action.*	***continuous*** Continuous is only used for things that happen without interruption and do not stop at all: *He has a continuous buzzing sound in his ear.*

definite If something is definite, it is firm and clear and not likely to be changed: *Do we have a definite date for the meeting?*	***definitive*** Something that is definitive provides a firm, unquestionable conclusion: *No one has come up with a definitive answer.*
dessert A dessert is the sweet dish you eat at the end of a meal: *Shall we have a dessert?*	***desert*** A desert is a large, dry sandy area: *We travelled through the Sahara Desert.*
elder Elder is used when you are saying which of two people was born first. It is not used with *than*: *I live with my elder sister.* *He is the elder of the two.*	***older*** Older simply means 'more old', and can be used of people or things, and can be followed by *than*: *My car is older than yours.*
flout If you flout a law or a rule, you do not obey it: *He accused the president of flouting international law.*	***flaunt*** If you flaunt something, you show it off in an obvious way: *I saw her at the party, flaunting her jewellery.*
infer If you infer something, you draw a conclusion from what you have seen, heard, or read: *From his resignation letter, I inferred that he had been forced to leave.*	***imply*** If you imply something, you say it in an indirect way: *She implied that he owed her money.*

lay Lay is a *transitive verb* meaning 'to put something somewhere carefully', and must have an object: *Mothers often lay babies on their backs to sleep.* It is not correct to say 'I'm going to lay down' – you should use *lie* for this. Lay is also the past tense of *lie*: *We lay on the floor.*	***lie*** Lie is an *intransitive verb* meaning 'to be in a horizontal position': *I want to lie down.*
loose Loose is an *adjective* meaning 'not firmly fixed': *The bolts had worked loose.*	***lose*** Lose is a *verb* meaning 'to not have something any more' or 'to be defeated': *I'm always losing my keys.* *I think we're going to lose the match.*
personal Personal is an *adjective* meaning 'private' or 'relating to a particular person': *He asked me some very personal questions.* *She has her own personal helicopter.*	***personnel*** Personnel is a *noun* meaning 'the people who work in an organization': *All military personnel must report to base.*
quite Quite is an *adverb* and used to mean 'very' in a less emphatic way: *It was quite expensive.*	***quiet*** Quiet is an *adjective* and describes things or people that do not make much noise: *She had a very quiet voice.*

These groups of three words are among the most commonly misused words in English.

they're	They're means 'they are': *They're going to come on the train.* *I'll be angry if they're late again.*
their	Their is the possessive pronoun from 'they': *They forgot to bring their coats.* *Their faces were white and tear-stained.*
there	There is a pronoun and adverb used to show position or direction, to show that something exists, and at the beginning of many sentences and phrases: *There's your jacket.* *Can you see the lion over there?* *The old buildings are still there today.* *There must be another way of doing this.* *There are three churches in our town.*
too	Too is used before adjectives to mean 'more than is good': *It's too hot in here.* It also means 'as well': *I want some too.*
to	To is a preposition that is used in many ways, but the main ones are showing direction, showing who receives something, and forming the infinitive: *We went to the zoo.* *I gave it to John.* *I need to buy a new coat.*
two	Two is the number 2: *I have two brothers.*

we're	We're means 'we are': *We're having a party.* *I'll phone you when we're there.*
were	Were is the past tense of *be* when the subject is plural: *We were very happy.* *They were going to tell you.*
where	Where is used to talk about the location of things or to ask questions about the location of things: *Where do you live?* *I left the keys where Kabelo would be sure to find them.*

Words that are often spelled wrongly

These are words which people often misspell.

accidentally	Don't forget *-ally* at the end, not just *-ly*.
accommodation	Double *c* and double *m*. This is one of the most commonly misspelled words in English.
acquire	Don't forget the *c* before the *q*.
advertisement	Don't forget the *e* after the *s*.
apparent	Double *p* but only one *r*.
beautiful	Remember the group of vowels – *eau* – at the beginning.
beginning	Double *n* but only one *g*.
believe	Remember *ie*, not *ei*.
business	Don't forget the *i* in the middle.
Caribbean	Only one *r* but double *b*.
cemetery	This word ends in *-ery*.
committee	Double *m* and double *t*.
conscious	Remember that it's *sc* in the middle.
definite/definitely	Remember that there are two *i*'s and no *a*'s in this word.

different	Double *f* and don't forget the *e* after them.
disappear/disappoint/ disappointing	Single *s* and double *p*. Remember that these words begin with the suffix 'dis-'.
embarrassing	Double *r* and double *s*.
encyclopaedia or ***encyclopedia***	Formerly, British English used the first of these spellings, but the second is now used commonly. American English uses *encyclopedia*.
environment	Don't forget the *n* in the middle of this word.
excerpt	Don't forget the *c* or the *p*.
extrovert	This word begins *extro-*, not *extra-*.
favourite	Don't forget the *u* in the middle of this word. However, in American English, this word is spelled *favorite*.
foreign	Remember *ei* in the second syllable, and don't forget the *g*.
forty	Unlike *four*, there is no *u* in this word.
gauge	Remember that it's *au* in the middle.
government	Don't forget the *n* in the middle of this word. Remember that it comes from the word 'govern'.
grammar	Remember that this word ends *-ar*, not *-er*.

guarantee	Remember the *u* in the first syllable of this word.
independent	Remember that this word ends *-ent*, not *-ant*.
inoculate	Remember that there is only one *n*.
leisure	Remember that in this word, *e* comes before *i*, which is the other way round from the usual rule.
liaise/liaison	Don't forget the second *i*, which comes after the *a*.
library	Don't forget the *r* after the *b*.
manoeuvre	The British spelling of this word (both the noun and the verb) has the complicated set of vowels *oeu* in it. The American English spelling of this word is *maneuver*.
mediaeval or ***medieval***	Formerly, British English used the first of these spellings, but the second is now used commonly. American English uses *medieval*.
millennium	Double *l* and double *n*.
miniature	Don't forget the second *i*.
minuscule	Note that the second vowel is *u*, not i. Try to think of it as beginning with *minus-*, not *mini-*.
occurrence	Double *c* and double *r*.

opportunity	Double *p* and don't forget the *r* before the *t*.
possess/possession	Two lots of double *s*.
privilege	Remember that the middle vowel is *i*, and the last vowel is *e*. There are no *a*'s in this word.
profession/ professional/professor	Remember that there is only one *f* in these words.
pronunciation	Don't be tempted to add an *o* in the second syllable.
questionnaire	Remember to write double *n* in the middle.
receipt	Remember *ei* in the second syllable, and don't forget the silent *p*.
receive	Remember *ei* in the second syllable.
recommend	Only one *c* but double *m*.
relevant	Remember that the second vowel is *e*, not *a*.
restaurant	Remember to write *au* after the first *t*.
seize	Remember *ei* here, not *ie*.
separate	Remember that the second vowel is *a*, not *e*.
truly	Don't be tempted to add an *e* after *tru*.
weird	Remember *ei*, not *ie*.

Controversial issues

The English language arouses strong emotions. Many people have very fixed ideas about what is 'wrong' and what is 'right'.

Several customs of English grammar have come about as a result of people applying the grammar of Latin to English. However, many people are inconsistent about this. For instance, someone who objects to the use of the word *data* as a singular noun (because it is plural in Latin), may be quite happy to use the words *agenda* and *stamina* as singular nouns, even though they are Latin plurals too.

Another important thing to bear in mind is that language changes. The language used by EM Forster writing in the 20th century is very different from that of Shakespeare writing in the 16th century, but nobody would say that Forster's English was incorrect.

New words and phrases come into the language all the time, and even the grammar and structure of our sentences changes. Of course, British English is influenced by American English, and although some people dislike this, others pick up new usages with enthusiasm. For instance when asked '*How are you?*', many British people would now say '*Good, thanks*', or even '*I'm good*', which would not have been heard even five or ten years ago.

In the notes that follow, you will find guidance on what is acceptable and what is not acceptable in current British English. However, there are many issues where people disagree, and as always, it is important to think of your audience. For instance, many people do not care about split infinitives – in fact most people do not know what a split infinitive is! Nevertheless, if your writing is very formal, very important, or will be read by someone you know has very strict views on grammar, it may be best to avoid them.

All right or alright?

Some people consider that *alright* is not a 'real' word, and that *all right* should always be used. However, *alright* is very commonly used, particularly when representing speech. It may be best to avoid it in very formal writing.

Among or amongst?

Some people make the distinction that *among* is used when there is no movement and *amongst* when there is movement:

> *I stood among the crowd.*
> *We walked amongst the sand dunes.*

However, in modern English, is it not usual to make this distinction.

Among or between?

If we are talking, for example, of dividing or sharing things, *between* is usually used when there are only two people or things, and *among* when there are more than two:

> *Noma and Doyin shared the bread between them.*
> *We distributed leaflets among the crowd.*

Between is used after the verb *choose* no matter how many things there are:

> *It is difficult to choose between all the different styles.*

Amount and quantity

In formal writing, it is best to use these nouns only with uncountable or mass nouns:

The project cost a huge amount of money.
We bought a small quantity of gold.

It is not good style in formal writing to say things like: *I've got a huge amount of apples*. For countable nouns, it is best to use *number*, or to re-phrase the sentence, for example: *I've got a lot of apples*.

Comprise

Comprise is a rather formal word, and should not be used with the preposition *of*, even though the similar words *consist* or *be composed* are followed by *of*:

The grounds comprise a large lawn and 20 acres of woodland.
My cold remedy consists of lemon, honey, and garlic.
The committee is composed of members of the legal profession.

Concerning

It is common to see concerning used as an adjective meaning 'worrying'. However, this use of concerning is not shown in most dictionaries, and must be considered non-standard. Concerning should be used only as a preposition:

She wrote to me concerning the new building work.

Could have/should have, etc.

It is a very common error to use *of* after modal verbs such as could, might, should, or would. This is because in speech, it sounds as if that is what we are saying. However, the sound is really a weak form of the verb *have*, and this should always be used in writing:

> *We could have helped you if you had asked.*
> *You should have called for a taxi.*

Dangling participles

Dangling participles occur when the subject of the main clause is not the subject of the modifying clause that contains a participle (usually a word ending in *-ing* or *-ed*).

Look at the following sentence:

> *Coming home from work, my hat blew off.*

Coming is a dangling participle here because its subject is not *my hat*. In formal writing, it would be better to say something like:

> *As I was coming home from work, my hat blew off.*

Here is an example of a dangling past participle:

> *Loathed by his colleagues, we understood why he had been sacked.*

This is incorrect in formal writing, because the subject of the main clause is 'we', but the subject of the participle is 'he'. It would be better to write something like:

> *He was loathed by his colleagues, so we understood why he had been sacked.*

It is fine to use clauses with participles as long as the subject of the main clause matches:

Having seen the play before, I was keen to go again.

Data

Strictly speaking, data is the plural form of the Latin *datum*. Some people insist that it should be used with a plural verb:

The data were collected over several years.

However, data is increasingly being used as a singular noun, and most people would accept that as a valid modern use. There is some logic to this too, since data is often used as a synonym for *information* or *evidence*, which would take singular verbs:

All the data was uploaded to the new server.

Data tends to be used as a plural more commonly in scientific or academic writing. Whether you decide to use a singular or a plural verb with data, make sure that you are consistent throughout your document.

Decimate

This word originated from the Roman custom of killing one in ten of a group of soldiers guilty of crimes such as mutiny. A few people, therefore, prefer to use decimate very specifically to mean 'to reduce by one tenth'.

However, in modern English, decimate is used to mean 'to destroy a large amount or number of something', and this is widely acceptable:

Troops were decimated by illness.

Note that it is best not to use decimate – as many people do – to mean 'to destroy completely'. It is better to use a word like *destroy* or *annihilate* for this.

Different

The safest preposition to use with different is *from*, which is the same use as the related verb *differ from*:

These biscuits taste different from the other ones.

It is also considered acceptable in British, but not American English, to use *to*:

Your circumstances are different to mine.

In American English, but not British English, *than* can be used:

He has a different job than me.

Dilemma

The word dilemma comes from the Greek prefix *di-* meaning 'two'. Therefore, purists argue that it should only be used to describe a situation where there are two alternatives, and not where there is a wider range of alternatives:

To support my husband or my son: that was my dilemma.

In formal writing, dilemma should not be used simply as a synonym of 'problem', but only for situations where some sort of choice or decision is to be made.

Because the original Greek word referred to two unpleasant alternatives, some people also believe that it should still only be used in this way, and not for a choice between two pleasant things.

Disinterested or uninterested?

In formal, modern English, uninterested is used to mean 'not interested' and disinterested to mean 'unbiased' or 'impartial':

The audience seemed completely uninterested in what she had to say.
We need a disinterested person to make a decision for us.

However, in reality, the two words are used so interchangeably that even if you try to make the distinction, it is probably best to avoid 'disinterested' altogether to avoid ambiguity, and use *unbiased* or *impartial* instead.

Double negatives

A double negative is the use of two negative words in the same sentence. These are common in some dialects of spoken English, but should never be used in writing:

I haven't got no money. (double negative)
I haven't got any money. (standard English)
She didn't tell me nothing. (double negative)
She didn't tell me anything. (standard English)

Due to or owing to?

Some people make a distinction between these two because *due* is an adjective and should therefore be used with a noun, and not a verb or a clause, where it is better to use *owing to*. A simple way to remember the difference is that *due to* can be replaced by *caused by* and *owing to* can be replaced by *because of*:

His illness was due to stress at work.
Owing to the weather, the plane could not take off.

Equally

It is common to see sentences such as the following:

> *Their work was equally as good.*
> *His house is equally as large as Ava's.*

However, in formal English, you should not use the word *as* with equally. Equally should come directly before the adjective:

> *Their work was equally good.*
> *His house and Ava's house are equally large.*

Farther/farthest or further/furthest?

The simplest rule is to use further/furthest all the time. A few people prefer to use farther when they are talking about literal distances:

> *We travelled farther into the mountains.*

However, very few people make that distinction nowadays, and further is almost always used in more figurative senses:

> *We agreed to race to the furthest tree.*
> *Let's pause to reflect before going any further with our discussion.*

Fewer or less?

For people who are strict about grammar, fewer should be used with plural forms of countable nouns and less with uncountable nouns:

> *There are fewer pupils in her class than last year.*
> *I hope you'll have fewer problems this time.*
> *I'm trying to use less butter in my cooking.*
> *I had even less information about it than you.*

In formal writing, it is best to stick to this rule, but in more informal contexts it is common to see less used with plural forms of countable nouns:

There were less people there than I expected.
This checkout is for people with 10 items or less.

Hopefully

In current English it is extremely common to see the word hopefully used to mean 'it is hoped', usually at the beginning of a sentence:

Hopefully we won't have to wait long.
Hopefully they'll pay us for the time we spent.

However, some people object to this, saying that hopefully should only be used to mean 'in a hopeful way':

He looked at her hopefully.
We waited hopefully to see if she would appear.

It is best to stick to this second use in very formal writing.

I or me?

You should avoid writing sentences such as *Tim and me cooked a meal*.

When you use two pronouns or a personal name and a pronoun together, think about whether they are the subject or the object of the sentence:

Tom and I went to the football match. (subject)
He asked Jo and me to sweep all the floors. (object)

If you are not sure whether to use I or me, imagine you were only writing about yourself and not the other person. For instance, you would say *I went to the football match*, so that is the form to use when you add the other person too.

Irregardless

This is not a word in standard English, so do not use it in your writing. The word you need is *regardless*.

Lend or borrow?

If you lend someone something, you let them use it for a while. If you borrow something, you take it from someone else to use for a while:

Can you lend me a pen?
Can I borrow your pen?

Literally

This word should be used only to emphasize that what follows is exact fact, and is not being said in an exaggerated or figurative way:

The waves were literally as high as a house.
She was literally penniless.

It is common for literally to be used simply to emphasize what follows, but examples like this should be avoided in formal writing:

I literally jumped out of my skin.
Their eyes were literally out on stalks.

Media

Strictly speaking, media is the plural form of the Latin *medium*. Some people insist that it should be used with a plural verb:

> *The media were guilty of invading her privacy.*

However, media is often used as a singular noun in current English:

> *The media is making the most of this scandal.*

However, if you want to talk about one particular form of communication, you should use the singular *medium*:

> *She is of the view that television is a dangerous medium.*

Off

The preposition off should not be followed by of:

> *It fell off of the table.* (incorrect)
> *It fell off the table.* (correct)

In other cases where 'off of' is used in spoken or non-standard English, the preposition *from* should be used:

> *I got it off of a friend.*
> *I got it from a friend.*

Ought

Unlike with the other modal verbs (can, might, must, etc.), when you make questions and negatives with ought, it is necessary to add *to*. The use of ought in questions and negatives sounds quite formal:

Ought he to have gone?
Oughtn't we to see if he's all right?
You ought not to leave your keys in the door.

Out

The word out is an adverb:

I dropped my bag and all my money fell out.
I'm not going to go out today.

In standard, written English, if you want to use it as a preposition, you have to add *of*:

She threw the bag out of the window.
I walked out of the room.

Phenomena

Remember that phenomena is the plural of phenomenon. Do not use phenomena as a singular:

Lightning is a natural phenomena. (incorrect)
Lightning is a natural phenomenon. (correct)

The reason being

Do not use the verb 'is' after this phrase, because it does not relate grammatically. You should use *that*:

We had to sell the business, the reason being that my husband was ill.

Refute

This word is often used simply to mean 'deny', but this is not correct, standard use. Refute means 'to prove something wrong with evidence'.

With these documents, he was able to refute the allegations.

Sat

Avoid sentences such as *I was sat on the floor*. This is not a grammatically correct tense because we do not use a past participle after *was* or *were*. Instead, you should write:

I was sitting on the floor.

Split infinitives

A split infinitive is where you write an adverb between *to* and a verb, e.g. *to finally agree*.

A lot of people do not like this, although plenty of great writers such as Donne, Eliot, and Browning have used it. In very formal writing, it is best to re-order your words:

We were asked to carefully look inside the box.
(split infinitive)
We were asked to look carefully inside the box.

In a few cases, a split infinitive is necessary to avoid a change in meaning:

He failed to completely understand my point.
(split infinitive, but means that he did not understand everything about the point)

He completely failed to understand my point.
(this has a different meaning – that he was unable to understand the point at all)

He failed to understand my point completely.
(this could have either meaning, and is therefore ambiguous)

Try

In British English, it is acceptable to use *and* or *to* after try, though *and* is slightly less formal:

Try and find the coin.
We will try to help you.

In American English, *try and* is not considered correct.

Used to

Note that when using the negative and question forms with used to, you need to drop the *d* from *used*:

Years ago, children used to be more polite.
I used to hate broccoli, but now I like it.
Children didn't use to have TVs in their bedrooms.
Did you use to play football when you were a child?

In a very formal style, we could write:

I used not to have a car.
I usedn't to need glasses.

While or whilst?

These two words are used in the same way in British English:

I read a book while I was waiting.
Whilst she slept, I cooked a meal.

In American English, *while* is used.

Who or whom?

Who is now commonly used as the object where in the past it was only considered correct to use whom:

Who do you work for?

If you use whom in sentences like this, your writing will sound extremely formal:

For whom do you work?

However, you must use whom directly after a preposition:

The woman to whom I spoke was a local nurse.
There were twenty masked prisoners, many of whom were armed.

multiple modernities 1905 — 1970

This book was published to coincide with the exhibition "Multiple Modernities, 1905–1970," presented at the Centre Pompidou from 23 October 2013 to 26 January 2015.

ISBN: 978-2-84426-653-8
Publisher number: 1559

multiple modernities 1905 — 1970

edited by
Catherine Grenier

from the collections of the National Museum of Modern Art

Centre Pompidou

Centre National d'Art et de Culture Georges Pompidou

The Centre National d'Art et de Culture Georges Pompidou is a French national public establishment under the supervision of the Ministry of Culture (Law 75-1, 3 January 1975).

Exhibition

HEAD CURATOR
Catherine Grenier
assisted by Marion Guibert

ASSOCIATE CURATORS
Clément Chéroux, Cécile Debray, Michel Gauthier, Aurélien Lemonier

WITH THE SUPPORT OF
ART MENTOR FOUNDATION LUCERNE

Exhibition

HEAD CURATOR
Catherine Grenier
assisted by Marion Guibert

ASSOCIATE CURATORS
Clément Chéroux, Cécile Debray,
Michel Gauthier, Aurélien Lemonier

PRODUCTION AND COORDINATION
Dolors Sala Fenés
Architecture: Valentina Moimas,
Anne-Marie Zuchelli

ARCHIVISTS
Mica Gherghescu
with the help of
Agnès Leroux de Bretagne
and Laurence Gueye-Parmentier

EXHIBITION RESEARCHERS
Rita Cusimano, Nathalie Ernoult,
Emmanuelle Etchecopar-Etchart,
Anna Hiddelston, Julie Jones,
Lucie Le Corre, Doïna Lemny,
Yekhan Pinarligil

RESEARCH FELLOWS
Audrey Coudre, Eliza Culea,
Stéphanie Dadour, Fanny Drugeon,
Émeline Jaret, Manolis Karterakis,
Magda Maaoui, Yves Mintoogue,
Hélia Paukner, Natalia Valencia,
Sebastian Vidal.

COLLECTION MANAGERS
Yannick Château
assisted by Rachel Milliez
Jean-Claude Boulet, Catherine Guillon,
Carole Hubert

SCENOGRAPHY
Corinne Marchand
with the help of Julie Boidin

DESIGNERS
Margaret Gray
Christian Beneyton

ADMINISTRATIVE AND FINANCIAL COORDINATOR
Alexia Szumigala

WORKS REGISTRAR
Lora Houssaye

COLLECTIONS REGISTRARS
Xavier Isaia, Éric L'Hospitalier,
Stéphane Lecoq, Benoît Masduraud,
Frank Pequignat

ART CONSERVATION
Clotilde Cooper, Jonathan Girault,
Véronique Landy, Sylvie Lepigeon,
Astrid Lorenzen, Valérie Millot, Rémi
Navarro, Isabelle Prieur, Anne-Catherine
Prud'hom, Chantal Quirot, Sophie Spalek,
Véronique Sorano-Stedman

DIGITALIZATION
Brigitte Vincens
with the help of Elsa Denoux,
Bibliothèque Kandinsky
Bruno Descout, Valérie Leconte,
and Philippe Migeat, Photo Laboratory

MOUNTING AND INSTALLATION OF PAPER DOCUMENTS
James Caritey
assisted by Adeline Bonhomme,
Estelle Peuron, Magali Sanheira,
Agnès Ribault, Zijian Xi

HANDLING MANAGER
Vahid Hamidi
assisted byChristophe Bechter,
Éric Hagopian, Emmanuel Rodoreda

ARTISTIC AND TECHNICAL MANAGER FOR AUDIOVISUAL PRODUCTION
Gérard Chiron

AUDIOVISUAL PRODUCTION COORDINATOR
Murielle Dos Santos
assisted by Pauline Gauthron

MANAGEMENT OF EXHIBITION SPACE
André Toutcheff
assisted byMichel Nait

FRAMING
Daniel Legué, Marion Jahan,
Jean-Gabriel Massardier,
Maria Pasvantis, Gilles Pezzana,
Marion Jahan, Lydia Serio

CARPENTRY
Philippe Delapierre,
workshop coordinator
Pascal Dumont, Raphaëlle Jeandrot,
Patrice Richard

PAINTING
Lamri Bouaoune, Mokhlos Farhat,
Dominique Gentilhomme, Sofiane Saal

LIGHTING TECHNICIAN
Dominique Fasquel

LIGHTING
Philippe Fourrier, Thierry Kouache,
and Jacques Rodriguès

PACKING WORKSHOP
Franck Buisson, Christophe Chomet,
Jérôme Tillaud, Antoine Wallois

TRUCKING UNIT
Philippe Chagnon, Serge Sauvage

PUBLIC INFORMATION AND MEDIATION
Marc Archambault, Margot Boyer,
Stéphanie Chaillou, Chantal Noël,
Marie-José Rodriguez, Pierre Ryngaert
with the help of
Audrey Foucault and Anna Mirsky

Musée National d'Art Moderne-Centre de Création Industrielle

DIRECTOR
Alfred Pacquement (2000–2013)

DEPUTY DIRECTORS
Catherine Grenier (2009–2013)
(Research and Globalization)
Brigitte Leal
(Collections)
Frédéric Migayrou
(Industrial Design)
Didier Ottinger
(Cultural Programming)

ADMINISTRATOR
Catherine Perdrial

BIBLIOTHÈQUE KANDINSKY
Didier Schulmann,
Curator and Head of Department

COLLECTIONS DEPARTMENT
Ariane Coulondre

Department of Cultural Development

DIRECTOR
Bernard Blistène (2009–2013)

DEPUTY DIRECTOR
Roger Rotmann

HEAD OF SPOKEN WORD UNIT
Jean-Pierre Criqui

Production Department

DIRECTOR
Stéphane Guerreiro

DEPUTY DIRECTOR, HEAD OF THE ADMINISTRATIVE AND FINANCIAL UNIT
Anne Poperen

HEAD OF THE EVENTS DEPARTMENT
Yvon Figueras

INTERIM HEAD OF THE ARTWORKS MANAGEMENT UNIT
Marjolaine Beuzard

HEAD OF THE WORKSHOPS AND TECHNICAL UNIT
Gilles Carle

HEAD OF THE ARCHITECTURAL UNIT
Katia Lafitte

PREVENTION
David Martin

Public Programs Department

DIRECTOR
Donald Jenkins (2012–2013)

DEPUTY DIRECTOR
Patrice Chazottes

HEAD OF THE GENERAL INFORMATION UNIT
Benoît Sallustro

HEAD OF THE PUBLIC INFORMATION AND MEDIATION UNIT
Josée Chapelle

Communications and Partnerships Department

DIRECTOR
Françoise Pams (2008–2013)

DEPUTY DIRECTORS
Marc-Antoine Chaumien
Stéphanie Hussonnois-Bouhayati

DELEGATE, INTERNATIONAL RELATIONS
Alexandre Colliex

SPONSORSHIP AND CORPORATE PARTNER
Alix de la Marandais

IMAGE UNIT
Christian Beneyton

PUBLIC RELATIONS UNIT
Lydia Poitevin, Manager

PRESS ATTACHÉ
Céline Janvier

Catalogue

EDITOR
Catherine Grenier
assisted by Marion Guibert

RESEARCH AND DOCUMENTATION
Camille Morando, Évelyne Pomey, Anne Lemonnier

IMAGE LIBRARY
Necha Mamod, Manager
Perrine Renaud, Iconographer

EDITORIAL COORDINATION
Amarante Szidon

COPY EDITOR
Phoebe Green

TRANSLATORS
Phoebe Green
Anna Knight
Caroline Taylor-Bouché

GRAPHIC DESIGN AND LAYOUT
P&J, Laurent Pinon and Aurore Jannin

PRODUCTION
Bernadette Borel Lorie

PHOTOGRAPHERS
Guy Carrard, Valérie Leconte, Georges Meguerditchian, Philippe Migeat, Adam Repzka

Publications Department

DIRECTOR
Nicolas Roche

DEPUTY DIRECTOR, HEAD OF PUBLISHING
Jean-Christophe Claude

EDITORIAL MANAGER
Françoise Marquet

SALES MANAGER
Marie-Sandrine Cadudal

SALES OFFICER
Francesca Baldi

DISPATCH AND STOCK CONTROL
Josiane Peperty

ADMINISTRATIVE AND FINANCIAL MANAGEMENT
HEAD OF LEGAL PROCEDURES AND BUDGETARY CONTROL
Thomas Reby

RECEIPTS
Matthias Battestini

ADMINISTRATIVE ASSISTANTS
Isabelle Charles-Planchet
Philippe Léonard
Danielle Malemanche

IMAGE AND RIGHTS MANAGEMENT
Claudine Guillon
ICONOGRAPHERS
Mai-Lise Benedic
Audrey Klébaner
ASSISTANT
Xavier Delamare

MULTIMEDIA DEPARTMENT
Emmanuelle Bermès, Manager

Acknowledgments

Our warmest thanks go the organizations of friends of the Centre Pompidou for their support of the museum's activities:
Jacques Boissonnas
PRESIDENT OF THE SOCIÉTÉ DES AMIS DU MUSÉE NATIONAL D'ART MODERNE

Steven J. Guttman
PRESIDENT OF THE CENTRE POMPIDOU FOUNDATION

Takeo Obayashi
PRESIDENT OF THE JAPANESE FRIENDS OF THE CENTRE POMPIDOU

We wish to thank all those whose recent and generous gifts have contributed to the enrichment of the collections:
Chris ine Abboud
Marcos Acayaba
Tadao Ando
Rosa Artigas
Antonio Asis
Benetton Group SPA
Helena Benitez
Irma Blank
Bratke Family
Candilis Family
Micheline Catti
Júlio Camargo Artigas
Andrey Chernikhov
Iakov Chernikhov International Foundation
Collection de Pari Amirbayat Radpay, Ghazel
Scott Christopher
Christopher Foundation for the Arts
Mirtha Dermisache †
Erró
Parvaneh Etemadi
Henrique Farina
León Ferrari †
Mitra Goberville-Hananeh
Itsuko Hasegawa
Masaki Hayashi
Mauro Herlitzka
Agustín Hernández
L'Humanité
Enio Iommi †
Arata Isozaki
Foundation of Egill and Evelyn Jacobsen
Jeu de Paume
Anibal Jozami
KA collection art moderne et contemporain
Société Kandinsky
Jacques Karquel
Júlio Roberto Katinsky
Maneli Keykavoussi
Gyula Kosice
Tatsuhiko Kuramoto
Galerie Alex Lachmann
Julio Le Parc
Magnum
Cildo Meireles
MRA+A Arquitecto Mario Roberto Álvarez y associados – Álvarez, Kopiloff, Álvarez, Rivanera, Bernabó, Sabatini
Juan Nicolás Melé
Paulo Archias Mendes da Rocha
Daniel Menkès
François Morellet
Aga Murata
Ruy Ohtake
Masato Otaka
Bernard Plossu
Sidsel Ramson
Pierre Rey
Raj Rewal Associates
Roca-Rey Andreassi Family
Yves Rocher
Diva Sanovicz
Odiléa Helena Setti Toscano
Kuldip Singh
Fernando de Szyszlo
Akiko Takatsuki
Tange Family
Jannick Thiroux
Decio Tozzi
Didier Vallens and the Association des Ayant Droits du Peintre Henry Valensi
Gizella Varga Sinai
Alexander von Vegesack
Fondation Munio Weinraub Gitai
Clarence Westbury Foundation
Kazumasa Yamashita

We particularly wish to thank the embassies that facilitated those gifts:
THE EMBASSY OF ARGENTINA IN FRANCE
Her Excellency Magdalena Faillace, Director of Cultural Affairs for the Ministry of Foreign and Religious Affairs of the Argentine Republic
Carlos Ernesto Manteiga, Minister for the Embassy (Cultural Department)

THE EMBASSY OF FRANCE IN IRAN
His Excellency Bruno Foucher
Henri Lebreton, Cooperation and Cultural Affairs Advisor

THE EMBASSY OF INDIA IN FRANCE
Apoorva Srivastava, Cultural Advisor

THE EMBASSY OF PERU IN FRANCE
Alonso Ruiz-Rosas, Cultural Attaché of Peru in France

We would like to take this opportunity to thank the artists, collectors, foundations, and galleries who have shown such great generosity over the years in enriching the museum's collections.

We wish to thank the institutions that have helped make this new presentation of the collections possible thanks to their generous loans and returns of artworks:

MUSÉE DU QUAI BRANLY, PARIS
Stéphane Martin, President
Karim Mouttalib, Deputy Managing Director
Yves Le Fur, Director
Catherine Duruel, Hélène Joubert, André Delpuech, Philippe Peltier, Julien Rousseau

FONDS NATIONAL D'ART CONTEMPORAIN, PARIS
Richard Lagrange, Director
Françoise Cohen, Head of the Collections Department

CITÉ DE L'ARCHITECTURE ET DU PATRIMOINE, PARIS
Guy Amsellem, President
David Peycéré, Curator, Archives Manager

MUSÉE DE L'ABBAYE SAINTE-CROIX, LES SABLES-D'OLONNE
Gaëlle Rageot-Deshayes, Director

MUSÉE DES ANNÉES 1930/ESPACE LANDOWSKI, BOULOGNE-BILLANCOURT
Frédéric Chappey, Director

MUSÉE DES ARTS DÉCORATIFS, PARIS
Olivier Gabet, Director

MUSÉE D'ART MODERNE ET CONTEMPORAIN DE LA VILLE DE STRASBOURG
Estelle Pietrzyk, Director

MUSÉE D'ART MODERNE ET CONTEMPORAIN LES ABATTOIRS, TOULOUSE
Olivier Michelon, Director

MUSÉE GOYA, MUSÉE D'ART HISPANIQUE, CASTRES
Jean-Louis Augé, Director
Pascal Bugis, Mayor of the city of Castres

MUSÉE D'ART MODERNE LILLE MÉTROPOLE
Sophie Lévy, Director

MUSÉE D'ART MODERNE RICHARD ANACRÉON, GRANVILLE
Brigitte Richart, Director

MUSÉE D'ORSAY, PARIS
Guy Cogeval, President
Caroline Mathieu, Curator

MUSÉE DE GRENOBLE
Guy Tosatto, Director

MUSÉE DES BEAUX-ARTS ET D'ARCHÉOLOGIE DE LIBOURNE
Thierry Saumier, Director

MUSÉE DES BEAUX-ARTS DE BORDEAUX
José de los Llanos, Director

MUSÉE DES BEAUX-ARTS DE LIMOGES
Véronique Notin, Director

MUSÉE DES BEAUX-ARTS DE NANCY
Charles Villeneuve de Janti, Directeur

MUSÉE DES BEAUX-ARTS DE REIMS
David Liot, Directeur
Catherine Delot, Head Curator

MUSÉE FABRE, MONTPELLIER
Michel Hilaire, Director

MUSÉE FRANCO-AMÉRICAIN DU CHÂTEAU DE BLÉRANCOURT
Anne Dopffer, Head Curator

MUSÉE GÉO-CHARLES, ECHIROLLES
Élisabeth Chambon, Curator

MUSÉE GOETZ-BOUMEESTER, VILLEFRANCHE-SUR-MER
Madeleine Servera, Head Curator

MUSÉE GUIMET, PARIS
Caroline Arhuero, Head of the Collections Department and Contemporary Art
Amida Okada, Head Curator, India Department

LA PISCINE, MUSÉE D'ART ET D'INDUSTRIE ANDRÉ DILIGENT, ROUBAIX
Bruno Gaudichon, Head Curator

MUSÉE PICASSO, PARIS
Anne Baldassari, President
Jean-Paul Mercier-Baudrier, Collections and Heritage Manager

BIBLIOTHÈQUE LITTÉRAIRE JACQUES-DOUCET, PARIS
Isabelle Diu, Director
Marie-Dominique Nobécourt-Mutarelli, Head Curator

BIBLIOTHÈQUE PUBLIQUE D'INFORMATION, PARIS
Patrick Bazin, Director

CINÉMATHÈQUE DE LA DANSE, PARIS
Patrick Bensard, Director

As well as their valued associates:
Catherine Assous, Aude Baudet, Stéphane Bayard, Cécile Berthoumieu, Daria Cevoli, Lola Chalou, Ludovic Chauwin, Laetitia Dalet, Laurence Dubaut, Stéphanie Elarbi, Valérie Eyene, Aurélien Gaborit, Stéphanie Fargier, Sarah Frioux Salgas, Nadine Hingot, Lydie Joubert, Anne Laffont, Antoine Leriche, Sylvaine Lestable, Judith Lethier, Hélène Maigret-Philippe, Pauline Marlaud, Magali Melandri, Enora Oulc'hen, Ruth Peer, Philippe Perreaudin, Peggy Podemski, Florence Portallegri, Alexandre Ragois, Dominique Reviller, David Romagnan, Fabrice Sauvagnargues, Alain Segura, Adrien Smette, Aurélie Steding, Ghislaine Varlet, Isabelle Varloteaux

Together with those who helped in a variety of ways to make this event possible:
Pascale Accoyer, Helene Afanasieff, Mario Roberto Álvarez †, Renato Anelli, Élodie Aparicio-Bentz, Teresita Araya-Monge, Ali Bakhtiari, Olivier de Bernon, Raphaële Bianchi, Javier Barreiro Cavestany †, Jean-Michel Bossu, Bernardes Family Véronique Borgeaud, Sylvia Bozan, Laura Buccellato, Sergio J. Campos, Takis Candilis, Anna Carboncini, Aurèle Caudan Vila, Aurélie Champion, Isabelle Daire, Denis Chalard, Max Claudet, Michel Correa da Costa, Patricia Dal Pra, Christine Devos, Christelle Desclouds, Fernando Diez, Stéphanie Doucet, Jean Écochard, Kamran Farman Farmaian, Christian Florès, Julien Fourrey, Anne-Marie Grand, Guedes Family, Abilio Guerra, Laure Guyot, Sönke Hoff, Laurent Juillard, Yvette Langrand, Jean Lathuillière, Nelson Kon, Sergio Krymer, Camille Lenglois, Laure Leprince, David Libeskind, Dominique Liquois, Émilie Lormée, Ana Maria Magalhães, Marlene Milan Acayaba, Rebecca Nelson, Rodrigo Ohtake, Stéphane Paumier, Agostina Pinon, Daniela Pires, Fernando Sabatini, Marcos Urcola, Sangeet Sharma, Justo Solsona, Mahendra Raj, Alvaro Roca-Rey, Rohit Raj Mehndiratta, Maya Ravereau, André Ravéreau, Hélène Rewal, Manu Rewal, Raj Rewal, Annalisa Rimmaudo, Alain Roche, Clelia Taricco, Warchavchik Family, Williams Family, Yuki Yoshikawa, M. et Mme Zenderoudi

We thank the scholars and researchers who supported us in the preparation of this new presentation of the collections:
Rose Corral, Philippe Dagen, Marie Gispert, Rémi Labrusse, Maureen Murphy, and Jacques Leenhardt.
Carolina Ariza, Camila Bechelany, Cecilia Braschi, Sirine Fattouh, Fanny Gillet, Caroline Hancock, Aliocha Imhoff, Émeline Jaret, Cécile Laly, Sarah Ligner, Samira Kaveh, Hélène Meisel, Morad Montazami, Susanna Muston, Sophie Orlando, Kantuta Quiros, Andrea Rodriguez Novoa, Némésis Srour, Akili Tommasino, Aminata Tembély, Elsa Urtizverea et Stéphanie Vergnaud.

We also wish to thank the museum's curators for their varied contributions in shaping the exhibition:

Jean-Paul Ameline, Christian Briend, Olivier Cinqualbre, Angela Lampe, Philippe-Alain Michaud, Didier Schulmann.

And all those who preferred to remain anonymous.

foreword

Today a century separates us from art's avant-gardes, and yet modernity, that formidable worldwide impulse, is more alive and timely than ever. Artists, historians, and critics are looking anew at a period that distance and new modes of thought allow us to reconsider in all its richness, complexity, and worldwide impact. The art history put forward by Western museums—often ethnocentric, even partial (in both senses of the world)—today may and must be revised and brought up to date. The Centre Pompidou contributes to the development of this new vision, both globalized and more open to different forms of artistic expression, with the program initiated in 2010, "Research and Globalization," of which this new presentation of the collections is one of the first demonstrations, welcoming the widest possible public.

Several projects were carried out conjointly by the program team: an in-depth study of the collections, their resources, and their history; research on non-European modernities; and a contextual exploration leading to a new perspective on historical avant-gardes. Catherine Grenier directed both this complex of work and the exhibition embodying it; Clément Chéroux, Cécile Debray, Michel Gauthier, and Aurélien Lemonier were co-curators; Didier Schulmann coordinated the teams and the immense resources of the Kandinsky Library; Olivier Cinqualbre, Christian Briend, Angela Lampe, the restoration team, collections management, and many heritage preservation specialists contributed in various ways to this enterprise.

For the first time, the Centre Pompidou joined forces with a university to conduct its work. The research on art and globalization initiated with this project is the subject of a long-term partnership with Labex (Laboratoire d'excellence) Création Art Patrimoine [Laboratory of Excellence: Creation Art Heritage]. This collaborative dimension is indispensable to the vast work in progress of rewriting art history. It concerns not merely the relationship of museum and university, but also the establishment of a network of scientific collaboration bringing together many French museums in a common effort.

Unprecedented in its aim and scope, the exhibition "Multiple Modernities" is unprecedented as well in its collaborative practice, bringing together all the resources of the Centre Pompidou and many researchers, but also those of institutions whom I must thank for their scientific contribution to this project as well as the loans kindly granted by some among them: the Centre National des Arts Plastiques, the Branly Museum, the Guimet Museum, the Musée d'Orsay, the Cité de l'Architecture et du Patrimoine, and the Musée de Grenoble, as well as various French regional museums which graciously made temporary loans of works entrusted to them from the national collections.

"Multiple Modernities" illustrates various perspectives to which I wished to commit the Centre Pompidou. Setting up a policy of research, integrating regular collaborative practices, intensifying relationships with the museums of France, and taking our place in a diversified international network have been made to serve the idea of a global museum and an ambitious policy of rewriting art history. This is accompanied by a policy of developing the collections and giving new energy to their presentation within the museum, to which all our efforts will henceforth be brought to bear. I am particularly happy to note the commitment and support that this renewal has engendered, and I would like to salute, especially, the artists, artists' families, and collectors who responded so enthusiastically to our appeal and have contributed with their exceptional gifts to the enrichment and diversification of our collections. With this new presentation, we enter fully the new era of cultural globalization, while at the same time renewing the primordial mission of the museum, inspired by the humanist and universalist philosophy of the Age of Enlightenment: to nurture understanding of art and the world; to contribute to developing a common history that transcends borders; and to create a bridge between the past, the present, and the future.

Alain Seban
CHAIRMAN, DIRECTOR & CEO, CENTRE POMPIDOU

preface

Museum visitors pass through room after room of arrangements of artworks and objects, organized according to an order whose intrinsic logic they do not necessarily seek to comprehend. They take for granted, for instance, that in a museum of Classical art, paintings are grouped according to national schools, sculpture is separated from painting, and different phases of the Classical era are arranged according to chronology and geography. Similarly, in a museum of technology, mechanical, electrical, and communications technologies will be separate, each in its own area. The field of modern art is distinctive in that its history may be composed and recomposed in myriad ways. Not that art history has said its final word on past centuries; far from it. But modern art has been the subject of an extremely structured discourse based on certain major figures inscribed within a certain number of well-established movements, the whole comprised in an evolution of art taking place essentially in Western Europe and North America. This history, as such, is not in question: the major figures remain major and their followers often deserve reevaluation. But the field of study continues to expand, including other personalities and new scenes, all heretofore unknown. If Western culture has often seemed the sole point of convergence of avant-gardes, the latter now associate themselves with all sorts of territories. Far from being set in stone, history can thus be added to—sometimes shaken up—bringing to the fore individualities neglected except in their country of origin and aesthetic movements associated with tendencies yesterday considered marginal and which now bring new centers to the center.

This is the project of these "multiple modernities," a rereading of the modern art of the first two-thirds of the 20th century, based essentially upon the collection of the National Museum of Modern Art, supplemented by loans from other French public collections. Although matter of course for contemporary art, which regardless of context no longer allows a purely Western-centered vision, this approach is less so when it comes to a rereading of history. With the help of the very antecedents of our museum, which distinguished, before WWII, between artists living in France and contemporary foreign schools, this presentation explores certain territories and also brings to light works that have been generally forgotten, whose exhibition will tell if time justifies their rehabilitation.

The presentation is organized in a succession of themes, some related to specific historical moments, others concentrating on regional or national scenes. Some people might well be disturbed by an approach excluding certain major figures normally present in our rooms, or by the absence of important chapters of art history. We remind them that this is an experiment by the scientific teams of the National Museum of Modern Art in the interest of advancing research; that it does not mean to proclaim a new *doxa*; and that the expansion it facilitates is meant only to read differently a story which has until now been told in too fragmentary a fashion. Chronology is an inarguable format for ordering the collection, but every now and then it is useful to shake it up in order to address in a different way the succession of avant-gardes; as was done, for instance, with "elles@centrepompidou" four years ago.
This very accomplished work of research has been led by a team of curators, documentarians, and researchers whose remarkable efforts I wish to salute here.
Coordinated by Catherine Grenier, the curatorial team consisted of Clément Chéroux, Cécile Debray, Michel Gauthier, and Aurélien Lemonier. I thank them all for their involvement in this important project, as well as Didier Schulmann and the teams of the Kandinsky Library, Ariane Coulondre and the Collections Department, and all those who contributed in their own ways to the preparation of this exhibition and its accompanying catalogue. Finally, I must thank the French institutions that have lent us artworks, the regional museums that have allowed us temporary possession of the works from national collections entrusted to them, and the artists and donors who have so generously supported our project.

Alfred Pacquement
DIRECTOR, NATIONAL MUSEUM OF MODERN ART–INDUSTRIAL DESIGN CENTER (2000–2013)

Amédée OZENFANT
The Four Races
1928
Gift of the artist, 1953

An Upside-Down World?

Catherine Grenier

"Multiple Modernities" is a presentation of the Centre Pompidou collections based on a critical reinterpretation of the history of art in the 20th century. This exhibition-manifesto, the result of research carried out by a large team of curators and young university academics, is an initial proposal for renewing the conventional approach to modern art. It breaks with long years of consensus on the uniform, linear, and progressive narrative proposed, with slight national differences, by all Western museums. This consensus is now undergoing a crisis; it demands to be brought up to date and re-established on new foundations. We must address two interrelated areas: a critical reinterpretation of Western modernity and the context of globalization. It is vital to challenge mainstream discourse and established hierarchies, to react to the existing scheme's inadequacy in presenting a global history of art. This proposal in the form of an exhibition provides a response and lays down the foundations for a fresh view of history. It is intended as the first milestone in a new way of interpreting the modern art period, revealing it to the public in all its richness and complexity.

A History of Art "in Works"

In a museum, updating the history of art has two aspects: one practical, the other policy-related. What should be shown, how should it be shown, and in what direction should the collection be developed? These three questions are fundamental; the responses provided involve the museum's responsibility in both intellectual and social terms. The main challenge for the museum of the future lies in the appropriateness of these responses to requirements generated by changes in thinking. Inspired by the philosophy of the Enlightenment, the museum was designed from the outset as a place of knowledge, based on a universalist conception of culture, contributing to the emancipation and progress of the individual. An interface between creation and the world, the museum is not only a repository of artistic wealth, but also provides a history of art "in works," for enjoyment and instruction alike. As a place for the interpretation and construction of meaning, as a bridge thrown between past, present, and future, the museum occupies a privileged position in social life. Its role is even more important in our own time, a period of uncertainty and change when the need to understand—to understand art, history, and the world—takes precedence over the search for aesthetic pleasure alone. Even if it seems objective, the history of art deployed on the walls of the museum is an intellectual construction, an account whose legitimacy is upheld by the institution. This legitimacy engages museums of modern art all the more in that they have to produce a history of art "on the spot." Where the first half of the 20th century is concerned, the established account has hitherto been based on a certain conception of modernity where "modern" describes not people belonging to the modern world, but people subscribing to a certain number of values in artistic modernity. The "big picture" of the history of art, as displayed up till now in Western museums, was thus founded on a typology of movements, classified according to criteria of progressiveness, and expressed in a genealogy. It focused on artists whose work corresponded to established canons and who participated in collective history through their involvement in modernist movements. This simplified, teleological, self-referencing concept developed and crystallized in the reconstruction period after World Wars I and II. In the name of artistic radicalism and the concept of rupture, it left aside or played down the importance of numerous individual or collective forms of expression, which were dismissed as hybrid, local, late, or anti-modern. That retrospective organization of the history of art of the first half of the 20th century was both the result of a crisis in Western modernity and the expression of a desire to surmount this crisis by shoring up progressive values. It arose in a political and cultural context radically different from the current context, where these values and the ideologies that conveyed them are now being challenged. The work of historians, like that of the human sciences, has made us aware of the political aspect of writing the history of art, and the close relationship this has with the writing of history. The canonical history presented in museums seems partial and obsolete today. It encompasses neither the many forms of modernity that developed in different parts of the world, nor even the sheer variety and richness of modernity in the West, which has been gradually subjected to simplification and exclusion processes. It is now vital to reform this model, to reintroduce a complexity and diversity that will enrich our understanding of the modern period. The museum should thus develop not merely *a narrative*, but *many narratives*, in order to restore the multiplicity inherent in modernities.

Revising the Canons

Today, our distance from this historical period means that we can see it in a new perspective, informed by research carried out in various fields of knowledge. "Post-colonial" studies, which have flourished since the 1980s, have criticized the Western-centric history of art and reassessed the forms of art practiced in non-Western countries and areas hitherto considered "marginal." "Cultural" and "visual" studies have also played their part in overturning hierarchies and shedding new light on artistic expression previously played down or disregarded: art by women, forms of art relating to the expression of minorities, and marginal or local aesthetics. The impact of these political and theoretical studies on the history of art is considerable and has spawned further research. Numerous art historians throughout the world are cutting a path through territories hitherto unexplored. The challenging of too-exclusive

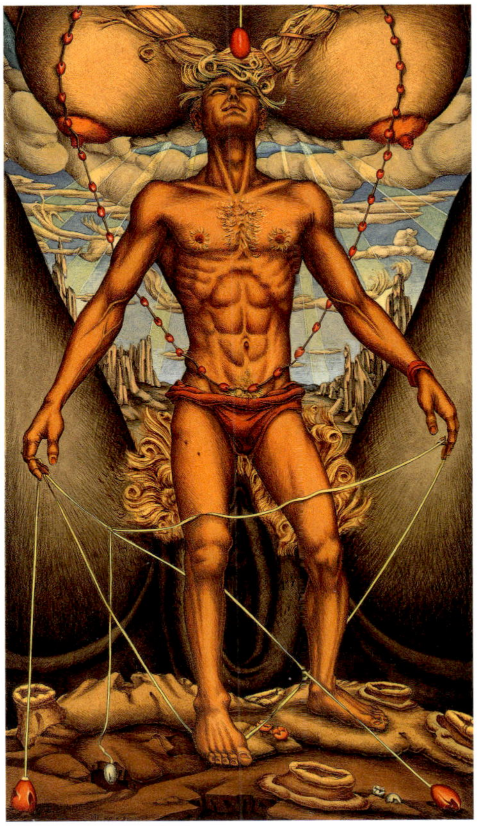

Alfonso-Angel OSSORIO
Red Egg
1942
Donation of Daniel Cordier, 1989

criteria, together with a less ideological, more historical approach, has refreshed thinking on little-known and undervalued forms of art. For example, a new interest in Latin American countries and more in-depth studies on the diversity of Western aesthetics are spotlighting the context of the emergence of aesthetics previously qualified as "anti-modern"—such as the various "Realisms." A history of all this, free from kneejerk condemnation as a "return to order," is only just starting to be written. Asia, Africa, and the Middle East exemplify the tense relationship between modernity and tradition, between Western and non-Western cultures. And lastly, even the artists at the origin of European modernity must be reconsidered in terms of the complexity of their own particular careers. A closer scrutiny of sometimes paradoxical changes in artists' output can thus shed new light on their exploratory work and periods of creation, which are little represented in museums because they diverge from the spirit of the times and the canonical order. An observation of the contemporary artistic scene, where so many works seek to reinterpret and re-perform the actions and signs of the modern period, shows that artists themselves are challenging the established fields of reference and values in what they do. Well before institutions, they have set the example of a different relationship with history and the world, free from frontiers and hierarchies. Museums must follow the lead of artists, historians, and critical studies. Over the next few years, if they fulfil their role properly, they could become spaces uniting and reflecting the research and reassessment carried out on the history of modern and contemporary art. To do so, they must change their paradigm through a "historically effected" hermeneutics of art and the history of art, following Hans-Georg Gadamer's precept of achieving greater self-knowledge by thinking about the Other (the past; otherness), without denying one's own identity. When in 1980 the American critic and exhibition curator Lucy R. Lippard said that "feminism's greatest contribution to the future of art has probably been precisely its *lack* of contribution to modernism,"[1] she opened the way to reconsidering the values of modernism far beyond the art produced by women. When the Pakistani-born British conceptual artist Rasheed Araeen proposed telling "the Other Story": that of "men and women who have defied their 'otherness' to enter the modern space forbidden to them," he emphasized the challenge to the framework of modernism, which the artists concerned wanted to both enter and transform. And he added, "Would it be possible to inscribe the story in question here within the master narrative of the history of modern art?"[2] The implications of such a question are broader than the already considerable undertaking of putting a specific artistic output into political and geopolitical perspective. Such a question involves reconsidering the scope and nature of works to be included when writing the history of art. Seen as part of the world picture, the established methods for classifying and interpreting art in relation to the dominant Western movements are called into question. Qualifying criteria (modern, anti-modern, pioneering, late, major, minor, and so on) are

1. Lucy R. Lippard, "Sweeping Exchanges: The Contribution of Feminism to the Art of the 1970s," *Art Journal*, Fall/Winter 1980.

2. Rasheed Araeen, "Introduction: When Chickens Come Home to Roost," in *The Other Story: Afro-Asian Artists in Post-War Britain*, London, Hayward Gallery, 1989, pp. 9-15.

no longer legitimate. New dynamics are coming into being, ending the disregard of art in "undeveloped" or "provincial" cultural zones. The study of influences gives way to the study of exchanges, transfers, and resistances. Complexity is reintroduced and given value. The hybrid and the disparate are once more considered in positive terms. Historical determinism is seen in perspective; chronological frameworks become more flexible. The borders between "work of art" and "artisanal product" or "tribal art" are seen to be untrustworthy. Even time-honored terms like "modernity," "avant-garde," and "contemporary art" reveal ambiguity and inconsistency.

Towards a New Narrative

Museums' first response to the challenging of the linear view of history was to present their collections thematically. The Museum of Modern Art (MoMA) initiated this movement in 1999, rapidly followed by the Tate Modern, when it opened, and the Centre Pompidou. Some have even permanently adopted the thematic rather than historical approach, like the Tate Modern and the Museo National Centro de Arte Reina Sofía. "Multiple Modernities" draws from these different examples, in particular the experiments carried out previously within the Centre Pompidou with the thematic presentations "Big Bang. Destruction and Creation in 20th Century Art" in 2005, "The Movement of Images" in 2006, and "elles@centrepompidou" in 2009.[3] These three proposals, more like exhibitions than traditional permanent presentations, provided a completely new reading of the collections. "Multiple Modernities" broadens this principle: reading the history of art in a way that is not so much thematic as general and historical. Our aim is to offer the public a new, open, off-center vision of 20th century art. But this vision, which visitors should be aware is by nature partial and linked to the current situation, is in no way intended to become canonical. The development of critical and historical thinking poses questions to museums that are far from being resolved, and whose interest, incidentally, lies more in an interrogatory approach than in the production of new assertions. The critical deconstruction of established history now under way should be followed by reconstruction and the proposal of new premises. However, while a new consensus must be found, it will no longer be based on the definition and imposition of universal criteria, but on shared principles and methods. Over the next few years, the museum will become the focal point for publicly expressing this collective historical project and the new narratives arising from it. New philosophies in terms of presenting and developing collections will result, and this project is the first draft. In the context of a museum, this new, more open view of artistic modernity is developing within specific, constrained parameters: those of a collection that has both riches—some of which are unexplored—and gaps. Within the museum, the rereading of the

Alexandre HOGUE
Oil in the Sandhills
1944
Gift of William A. King, 1962

3. "Big Bang. Destruction et création dans l'art du xxe siècle," 15 June 2005–22 February 2006; "Le mouvement des images," 9 April 2006–27 January 2007; "elles@centrepompidou. Artistes femmes dans la collection du Musée national d'art moderne-Centre de création industrielle," 27 May 2009–16 February 2010.

Antonin PROCHÁZKA
Young Girl
1933
Purchase by the State (Jeu de Paume), 1934

history of art thus depends on the reinterpretation of the collective memory represented by the collection, with the various stages and vagaries of its construction. This was the first stage we undertook: retracing the history of the Centre Pompidou collections and exploring all their components, including works little or never exhibited before. This has enabled us to pinpoint the collective decisions that have hitherto led our predecessors and ourselves to ignore certain works, or not to find a place for them in the collection presentation structure—decisions of an intellectual, ideological, and cultural order, which remind us that the museum, inseparable from the context of its times, provides one of the chief testimonies of the often contradictory forces that shape society and history.

In the Beginning Was the Museum of Contemporary Foreign Schools

An initiative of this kind was made possible only through the exceptional richness of this collection—a richness linked not only with the cosmopolitan art scene of Paris during the modern period, but also a specific historical background. The National Museum of Modern Art collection, now housed in the Centre Pompidou, resulted from the merger of two distinct entities: the Museum of Living Artists and the Museum of Contemporary Foreign Schools. The former, also known as the Musée du Luxembourg, after the building housing it, was created in 1818. It was conceived as a "holding tank," to provide a latency period before various contemporary artists were admitted to the Louvre collections. In 1923, in response to criticism about the scant representation of foreign artists in this collection, a special section devoted to foreign schools was created. Originally part of the Luxembourg, the Museum of Contemporary Foreign Schools became independent in 1932. Up to 1940, the two museums stood next to each other in parallel buildings in the Jardins des Tuileries, which now contain the Musée de l'Orangerie and the Galerie Nationale du Jeu de Paume. The Luxembourg, although dedicated to living art, had links with the academic system and focused on "official" art, almost totally ignoring independent art. Meanwhile, the Museum of Contemporary Foreign Schools, which came to be known as the Jeu de Paume, had an ambivalent position: it was marked by the conservatism imposed by its administrative supervision, but also evinced signs of modernism. This situation was strongly criticized by the intellectual community, which increasingly called for the creation of a single museum of modern art open to all forms of modernism. In 1930, the magazine *Cahiers d'Art* started a campaign to create a "museum of living artists," accompanied by plans for a "museum of unlimited growth" by Le Corbusier. This had no immediate effect, but fed debate on the role of the museum and the national collections. Well aware of the inadequacy of the Museum of Contemporary Foreign Schools' collection in terms of avant-garde movements, its director, André Dezarrois, decided to add a number of major loans from artists and collectors to the presentation of the collection in the opening exhibition at the Jeu de Paume in 1931. Thus works by Amedeo Modigliani, Pablo Picasso, and Kees Van Dongen were presented in a national museum for the first time. The exhibition design, simple

Irma STERN
The Sultan's Palace in Zanzibar
1944
Purchase from the artist, 1949

and modern, was a first in the French environment. Before the introduction of this permanent presentation, the venue had specialized from the early 1920s in hosting exhibitions from different countries throughout the world, staged by both the museum and, in a diplomatic context, the Ministry of Foreign Affairs. After World War I, the idea of a European Union began to emerge, combined with a desire for national promotion that involved countries increasing cultural exchanges.[4] Eager to maintain its position as the capital of the arts, France encouraged these initiatives, and in 1922 created the AFEEA (French Association for Artistic Expansion and Exchanges). This development association was attached to the Ministry of Foreign Affairs, which was also partly involved in running the Museum of Contemporary Foreign Schools. This led to the staging of some thirty exhibitions devoted to the art of different countries at the Jeu de Paume between 1922 and 1940. After 1932, these exhibitions regularly replaced the permanent presentation of collections. There was thus a series of artistic overviews covering a broad period of history, like "Ancient and Modern Dutch Art" (1921), "Ancient and Modern Belgian Art" (1923), "Ancient and Modern Romanian Art" (1925), and "Danish Art from the 17th Century to 1900" (1928). Other exhibitions, including those staged by the museum itself, focused on the contemporary period, such as "Contemporary Swiss Art Since Hodler" (1934), "Italian Art of the 19th and 20th Centuries" (1935),[5] "Exhibition of Works by Contemporary Belgian Artists" (1935), and "Contemporary Spanish Art" (1936). Some were dedicated to artists, like "The Works of James Ensor" in 1932 and "F. Kupka, A. Mucha" in 1936. Dutch, Belgian, Swiss, Romanian, Austrian, Danish, Japanese, Argentinian, Canadian, Swedish, Polish, Chinese, Italian, Spanish, American, Latvian... the art of many countries was featured in these exhibitions. Their cultural goals were twofold: to establish contemporary art in its historical context for educational purposes[6] and to pinpoint the characteristics of a national identity in the artistic output of friendly countries, to enable a comparison with the specific features of French art. The more or less academic nature of the works selected depended on locally-appointed officers.

4. This upsurge in diplomatic exchanges was motivated in large part by a determination to avoid another war. In 1929, Gaston Riou, later to become a Republican deputy for the Ardèche region, published a work entitled *S'unir ou mourir*, Paris, Éditions Valois. In September 1929, Aristide Briand put forward the first project for a European Union before the League of Nations.

5. This exhibition was organized in collaboration with the Mussolini government. In its wake, Senator Borletti, President of the Italia-Francia Committee and member of the Fascist party, presented the museum with a gift of several works.

6. The didactic mission of these exhibitions was corroborated by Léonce Bénédite, head curator at the Luxembourg from 1892 to 1925, in the first catalogue devoted to the collections of the Jeu de Paume (1924). He quoted from his own *Rapport général de l'Exposition universelle de 1900*, written in 1904. The aim was to raise awareness of current developments in the arts among the general public but also to point to national specificities, which would lead to an appreciation of the art of one's own country.

State Purchases: A Contextual Collection

With each new exhibition, the French state began to buy works, which formed most of the Musée des Écoles Étrangères collection. The museum also benefited, though to a lesser degree, from works bought in salons and sometimes in galleries. When it was closed in 1940, it had a collection of 600 paintings and drawings and a hundred-odd sculptures. The Museum of Living Artists had collected a somewhat larger number of works, including nearly a thousand from the 20th century. But taken as a whole, the national collection of contemporary art was not very extensive. It was a very pale reflection of avant-garde movements, in contrast with American museums like the MoMA, whose collections were being swelled by informed collectors. On the other hand, the collection of the Museum of Contemporary Foreign Schools constituted a valuable record of the range of art styles in the Parisian cosmopolitan scene known as the "School of Paris" and the international cultural exchange policy of the time. The acquisitions made after exhibitions were most often inoffensive works favored by a distinctly conventional purchasing commission. But a number of gifts broadened the spectrum of these purchases to include more innovative styles. For example, a study on Belgian art[7] showed that most acquisitions were from artists living in Paris and did not reflect the most decisive advances in modern art; but after exhibitions at the Jeu de Paume, works by James Ensor, George Minne, and Constant Permeke also joined the collection thanks to gifts by a collector and the artists.[8] Independently of exhibitions, the Museum was also enriched, through various purchases and gifts, by several major works by modern artists living in France, including Picasso, Marc Chagall, Jules Pascin, Pablo Gargallo, Vassily Kandinsky, Paul Klee, František Kupka, Salvador Dalí, and Giorgio De Chirico. These were joined by the works of artists having only a minor link with Paris, bought in galleries and at salons. In addition, amongst works commonly described as "inoffensive," there were diverse forms of artistic expression which though not avant-garde were not academic either, and of considerable interest. Most of the works acquired between the wars were by artists living in Paris, and evince the various aesthetics brought together under the term "School of Paris." The collection contained a large number of works by Russian and Central European artists, whose style was often influenced by Expressionism, and numerous works representing the Realist movements that flourished during those years. Two exhibitions devoted to China and an exhibition on Japanese art also resulted in purchases illustrating tradition-based contemporary styles. Thus, as well as Modernist artists, the permanent presentation at the Museum of Contemporary Foreign Schools included a room dedicated to "traditionalist

7. Céline De Potter, "Du temps où les artistes étaient nos 'meilleurs' ambassadeurs: art et politique étrangère dans les relations Belgique-France de 1919 à 1939," *Pyramides. Revue du Centre d'études et de recherches en administration publique*, 2008, available online at http://pyramides.revues org/221.

8. The Jeu de Paume held a solo exhibition of Ensor's works in 1932.

Japanese paintings." These works, and those of Asian artists living in Paris, formed the basis of the modern Asian art collection now at the Centre Pompidou.

The Creation of the National Museum of Modern Art

The 1937 International Exhibition in Paris provided the ideal opportunity for the Popular Front government to implement its plans for a new museum, the National Museum of Modern Art, combining the two existing structures. Jean Cassou was commissioned to design the project and rapidly a made-to-measure museum building was erected, the Palais de Tokyo. The International Exhibition acted as a catalyst, prompting a number of seminal shows both in 1937 and in 1938. In 1937, the launch of the Palais de Tokyo featured a broad spectrum of French art, while the Petit Palais devoted an exhibition to "The Masters of Independent Art"; at the Jeu de Paume, meanwhile, André Dezarrois organized the first-ever official exhibition to display the various trends of Abstract Art and Surrealism, "Origins and Development of Independent International Art." The exhibition called on a committee of artists, one of whose most active members was Kandinsky. Interestingly, alongside the modern works were presented "sculptures and objects from Black Africa," as well as Polynesia, Oceania, and New Zealand, most of them loaned by the artists. A few months earlier, the Jeu de Paume had paid tribute to "Women Artists of Europe" in an exhibition featuring over three hundred women artists, which then traveled to the Metropolitan Museum of Art in New York. Another important event occurred in 1938, the exhibition "Three Centuries of American Art," organized in conjunction with MoMa. This particular exhibition had a powerful symbolic agenda: first mooted in 1933, it had been postponed by the Americans for fear of the volatile political situation in Europe, but then rescheduled despite an even more imminent danger. It included 380 works and comprised not only paintings and sculpture but architecture, the popular arts, photography, and film. Lack of funds meant that these exhibitions did not give rise to any major acquisitions. The war then put a spoke in the wheel of progress and the National Museum of Modern Art, which had been forced to close back in 1938 in order to complete its building work, not only ceased operating but also put an end to its acquisitions policy.[9] These were to start up again, with a new approach and in a new context, in the wake of World War II.

9. The head curator, Jean Cassou, was removed from office as soon as the Vichy government took over. He was only reinstated in 1945, when the museum officially opened to receive the collections of the Museum of Living Artists and the Museum of Contemporary Foreign Schools. It was opened to the public in 1947.

A Collection with a Universal Remit

The Museum of Living Artists and the Museum of Contemporary Foreign Schools, on the fringes of the Louvre, wanted to emulate their role model by setting their sights on building a universal history of the arts.

Azouaou MAMMERI
Moroccan Festival in Marrakesh
1930
Attribution (Jeu de Paume), 1932

The new Museum of Modern Art was the tangible embodiment of this concept and it never reneged on its universal remit, despite the stirrings of nationalism generated by the historical context. It became the beneficiary of all the collections of the Museum of Living Artists and the Museum of Contemporary Foreign Schools, together with a number of foreign works purchased during the same period by the State. Despite its heterogeneous nature, the collection was striking in its remarkable palette of international works. Although the most famous figures were poorly represented, the collection bore the hallmark of artists from all over the world who had moved to Paris either to study or to take up residence. Through this collection and gifts, the Centre Pompidou therefore houses a significant ensemble of works from 1910 to 1940, spanning artists from Brazil (Monteiro, Di Cavalcanti, Lasar Segall, Victor Brecheret, Morgan-Snell), Mexico (Ángel Zárraga, Frida Kahlo), Argentina (Alfredo Gramajo Gutiérrez, Julia Codesido, Emilio Terry), Cuba (Mario Carreño), and Uruguay (José Cuneo, Joaquín Torres-García). In European terms, Central Europe has the best coverage, with 306 artists. Also featured are a number of protagonists of Spanish Realism (Ignacio Zuloaga, Ramón de Zubiaurre, Maria Blanchard, Ismaël de la Serna, Maruja Mallo, José Maria Uzelai), Italian Realism (Gino Severini, Carlo Carrà, Mario Sironi, Fausto Pirandello, Filippo De Pisis, Felice Casorati, Gianfilippo Usellini, and Achille Funi, among others), together with their counterparts from Northern Europe (Per Lasson Krohg, Carl Oscar Kylberg, Eero Snellman). The collection also includes artists from Egypt (Mahmoud Mokhtar, Georges Hanna Sabbagh), Algeria (Azouaou Mammeri), Tunisia (Edmond Küss), Israel (Achiam), South Africa (Irma Stern, Maud Sumner), Russia (Jacovleff, Ivan Babij, Chana Orloff, Boris Grigorieff, Mane-Katz, Jaan Koort, Nicolai and Svetoslav Roerich, etc.), Canada (Alfred Pellan, Albert H. Robinson), and Australia (Rix Nicholas).

The post-World War II drive to encompass leading avant-garde artists meant that the 1910–1940 collection also stood out by virtue of its variety and internationalism. It reflected the extraordinary cosmopolitanism of the Parisian scene[10] and its diversity of co-existing forms of expression. The relaunch of the National Museum of Modern Art in 1947 gave the collection a new lease of life. Despite extremely limited means and the restrictions imposed by the academism of the national purchasing commission, Jean Cassou led a tireless campaign to expand the collection, approaching major avant-garde artists and collectors with a request to donate artworks. Henri Matisse, Georges Braque, Picasso, Fernand Léger, Juan Gris, Chagall, Joan Miró, Marcel Duchamp, and Francis Picabia all contributed major works. From 1960, under the impetus of a young curator, Maurice Besset, the museums also acquired a number of works

10. According to census statistics, over thirty Hungarian artists were living in Paris during this period.

BAYA
Untitled
1966
Purchase by the State, 1969

by hitherto ignored German artists:[11] Ernst Ludwig Kirchner, Max Pechstein, Otto Dix, and Emil Nolde. The major donations made by artists or their heirs took the form of studio collections and these remain one of the museum's distinctive features even today. They included a corpus of exceptional works by French and foreign artists, the latter represented by Chagall, Picasso, Antoine Pevsner, Kupka, Zoltán Kemény, Julio González, and Kandinsky, as well as the entire contents of Brancusi's studio.

The Creation of the Centre Pompidou

As the Palais de Tokyo soon proved too cramped to allow for expansion, new initiatives were called for. In 1959 one particular development caused a stir: Jean Cassou was approached by the Council of Europe to organize a major exhibition, in the form of an overview of twentieth-century art. He called in a bevy of European specialists to draw up a selection of the greatest masterpieces in modern art. In the wake of this project, the International Council of Museums (ICOM) appointed him to write a report on the definition of a museum of modern art, while the French Minister of Culture, André Malraux, asked him to reflect on the possibilities of creating such a museum in France. Following a lengthy gestation period, and a concomitant stagnation in acquisitions, a decision was finally reached—a new model for a museum was formed, culminating in the Centre Pompidou. In 1974, Pontus Hultén, then director of the Moderna Museet in Stockholm, was put in charge of forward planning for the "Centre Beaubourg" as it was then called. The museum was granted budgetary and administrative independence and this paved the way for an ambitious acquisitions policy. An active campaign was launched to fill the gaps in the modern art section and to encompass the younger generation of artists, who had been left on the sidelines until that point. Purchases mainly targeted the major figures of the avant-garde movements, which were still inadequately represented, and post-war American artists, who did not feature at all. When the Centre Pompidou opened on 31 January 1977, it housed 18,530 works. Despite the highly rewarding impetus given to the collection during the 1970s, some forms of expression were nevertheless neglected. Although the Paris art scene between 1950 and 1970 was once again defined by its cosmopolitan nature, this was only minimally reflected in the collection, and its creative output was only acknowledged with hindsight. The "Second School of Paris," for instance, characterized by outmoded Lyrical Abstraction and overtaken by American Abstraction, only received scant attention, and Kineticism, which gave way to the more radical expressions of Minimalism, was equally overlooked. The influx of Latin American artists, forced into exile by dictatorial regimes, together with a convergence

11. The only exhibition of German art to have been planned at the Museum of Contemporary Foreign Schools, as a tribute to Max Liebermann, was finally cancelled due to pressure from veterans' associations.

of artists from North Africa, the Middle East, and Asia, had minimal impact on the collection. These artists did however reap the benefit of the acquisitions made by the Ministry of Culture's Fonds National d'Art Contemporain in the decades following World War II, as part of their campaign to enrich France's artistic heritage. A number of works were attributed to the Centre Pompidou by the Fonds National d'Art Contemporain to expand its collection and the latter's lending policy has also been instrumental in completing the museum's new presentation. The kinetic works, although they met with little success at the time of their creation, were later to become one of the high spots of the collection, thanks to a significant number of purchases and monographic gifts. The 1980s broadened the multi-disciplinary aspect of the collection, which until then had only covered paintings, sculptures, and drawings. The cultural policy set up by the Ministry of Culture in 1981, under the aegis of Jack Lang, lent its support to major institutions and actively encouraged acquisitions,[12] while several sizeable donations reinforced this policy.[13] The photography, film, and video collections gradually gathered strength,[14] and today the photographic collection alone includes over 25,000 works. The video collection, which emphasizes emerging modes of expression and new artistic territories, is outstanding in the amazing geographical diversity of its protagonists. In 1992, the Centre Pompidou also reached out to architecture and design and by virtue of an ambitious acquisitions policy and a sizeable number of donations these are now at the forefront of the collection. Although the international dimension of these art forms remained circumscribed for many years within Europe, the United States, and Japan, it recently opened up its acquisitions policy to include remarkable ensembles of works from Latin America and India.

"Multiple Modernities"

What direction was needed to present the Centre Pompidou collection anew, taking into account the geographical and aesthetic diversity that the latter, once analyzed, could represent? What "tool," what method of introduction was needed to shift our outlook without being artificial or dogmatic? To guide our work and structure the different rooms, we decided to draw on the extraordinary documentary collection of the Centre Pompidou's Kandinsky Library. This heritage, enriched in 2006 by the Paul Destribats collection, provided material for the study program carried out in preparation for this exhibition. In view of the exhibition, it was further enlarged by the purchase of magazines published

12. In 1982, the museum's acquisitions budget was doubled by comparison with 1981. An ambitious policy allowing works to be donated in lieu of tax was upheld by the government.

13. The two donations made by Daniel Cordier in 1989 and 2009 made a significant contribution to the introduction of Art Brut and Art Singulier, together with traditional artifacts of non-Western origin.

14. The photographic collection now comprises 25,000 prints and 50,000 negatives. When the Centre Pompidou opened in 1977, it contained only thirty-odd photographs. That same year, Pontus Hultén asked Peter Kubelka to lay the foundations of a film collection. This collection now numbers 1,500 items.

in Africa, Japan and Latin America. These magazines, often created on the initiative of artists or major "go-betweens" in contemporary art, enabled us to shift our approach and get a picture of the aesthetic spectra promoted by each of these publications in various areas of the world. Similar to microhistory, this study of how certain approaches and artistic clusters grew up in all these different circumstances has brought to light situations that were far more disparate, complex, and indeed globalized than an oversimplified history of art movements had led us to believe. These magazines, which are in any case exceptional documents in terms of content, also provide extremely rich material for an exhibition: their graphic inventiveness and the confrontation of images and references they feature are often extremely intense. This is why we decided to exhibit these sources in two ways: by presenting meaningful examples on display next to the art works, and by incorporating a more documentary system into the rooms in the form of a "wallpaper" of contextual references.

Art Without Borders

Advocating a break with tradition and doing away with the hierarchies between the different categories of objects and images, the avant-gardes incorporated non-Western art, ethnographic objects, popular art, and children's drawings into the modern artistic imagination. Primitivism (which influenced most movements between 1900 and 1920), then Expressionism, Cubism, and Surrealism were all different interpretations of this desire to broaden their outlook and reassess categories hitherto held to be non-artistic or secondary. In magazines and exhibitions alike, these types of works were displayed alongside new creations, setting up dynamic and often stimulating confrontations. "We will place an Egyptian figurine next to a small Zeh, a Chinese work opposite one by Rousseau, a popular image alongside a Picasso and all sorts of things of the same kind!"[15] wrote Kandinsky to Franz Marc in June 1911, at the time they were preparing the *Blaue Reiter Almanach*. This broader attitude and the principle of variety have gradually been forgotten, finding no place within museums, which generally separate objects into typologies. For example, at the time when Louise and Michel Leiris donated the collection of the writer and his brother-in-law Daniel-Henry Kahnweiler to the State, the paintings and sculptures were allocated to the Centre Pompidou, while the ethnographic objects went to join the collection of the Musée de l'Homme. The rooms we are devoting to that great "go-between," Leiris,[16] reunite the two categories of objects for the first time, together with issues of the magazine *Documents*, on which the writer collaborated. They show a highly personal collection based on the human figure, which creates links between Cubism and

15. Excerpt from a letter written by V. Kandinsky to F. Marc on 19 June 1911 and published in F. Marc, *Écrits et correspondances*, Maria Stavrinaki (ed.), Th. de Keyser (trans.), Paris, École Nationale Supérieure des Beaux-Arts, 2006, p. 364.

16. A major exhibition is currently being planned for 2014 by the Centre Pompidou-Metz. Devised by Marie-Laure Bernadac and Agnès de la Beaumelle, it will present the collection for the first time in an extensive and contextualized form.

Ernest PROCTER
The Watchers... Burma
1921
Purchase by the State (Jeu de Paume), 1927

Surrealism, and between the avant-gardes and art from outside Europe. Several sections restore the rapprochements created by the artists themselves. For example, the role played by Kandinsky in broadening the categories and locations of art is highlighted in two places. One room, based on the *Blaue Reiter Almanach*, illustrates the spirit of the Expressionist movement, which advocated rapprochements transcending borders and periods. Another room is also dedicated to the memory of the artist, reproducing the diversity and variety of Nina Kandinsky's donation to the museum. This reconstructs the painter's studio, which contains all sorts of works: his own and his friends' paintings, anonymous works by Bauhaus students, non-European objects, Japanese prints, objects of popular art, children's drawings—all part of a single unified donation to the museum. Lastly, the Surrealist room evokes the activity and insatiable curiosity of André Breton, associating paintings of all kinds from every sort of background in a presentation as dense as his own displays.

The Spread of the Avant-Garde

The desire to devise a universal language, the importance given to collective dynamics, and the development of transnational networks fostered the international dissemination of major modernist ideas. We have endeavored to reflect these exchanges and movements in a section devoted to the spread of the modern avant-garde. Art became globalized to a truly extraordinary degree between 1910 and 1940. Expressionism, Cubism, Futurism, Constructivism, Dadaism, various forms of abstraction and realism, and then Surrealism made waves and were discussed over the world. The intensified movement of information, fostered notably by the creation of countless magazines, artists' travel, and the migrations caused by social and political situations, had a decisive impact on creativity. "Go-betweens"—artists, intellectuals and writers—propagated the modern spirit throughout the world. The various artistic proposals found echoes in different countries and cultures, and generated a variety of highly original local currents. These were often marked by a desire for synthesis between different aesthetics, and between a universal language and local and vernacular elements of identity. For example, the Italian Futurists' admiration of modernity and speed aroused a whole range of reactions. Cubo-Futurism, Simultaneism, Ultraism, Rayonism, Vibrationism, Synthetism, and so on were all aspects of the international wave of a movement that had widened its scope of action to literature, music, and even lifestyles. These developments were generally characterized by a free and personal adaptation, often expressed in hybrid forms. The Futurist aesthetic and its desire to reproduce the sensation of movement is evident in the work of many artists involved with other movements, like Duchamp, Picabia, Amadeo de Souza-Cardoso, and Natalia S. Goncharova. The search for motion crosses paths with the musical inspiration of artists like Henry Valensi and Kupka, whose work lies at the crossroads of Cubism and Futurism. And lastly, even though they did not agree with the Fascist ideology already espoused by Filippo Tommaso Marinetti at the time of his transatlantic voyage, Latin American artists also responded to the injunction to live intensely and to Futurism's work on language. Linked to the social changes brought about by the Soviet revolution, Constructivism was characterized by the desire to extend the effects of art, whether architecture, design, or collective creativity, to all aspects of daily life. We find echoes of this revolutionary goal and the Constructivist aesthetics that accompanied it in most regions of the world. It first of all caused a proliferation of new forms in all Central and Eastern European countries. These are given considerable attention in "Multiple Modernities" through a spotlight on little-known artists and work illustrating the synthesis of different utopian movements in constructed art. Seen from relatively close to, the distinction between the Suprematism of Kazimir Malevich and the Constructivism of Alexander Rodchenko and Vladimir Tatlin is blurred, despite the differences between the two in terms of aesthetics and theories. The magazines of Central Europe, America, and Japan bear witness to the international spread of a Constructivism with enlarged borders, often integrating the forms of De Stijl and Bauhaus, the movements that followed it. In France, the reconciliation of art and the applied arts brought about by Sonia Delaunay and Sophie Taeuber-Arp, together with various developments in Art Deco, also fed a movement to abolish the divide between art and daily life. At this period, architecture and interior design were ways to disseminate modern ideas. While the possibilities for building modern buildings were restricted in Europe, new architectural forms found fertile ground in the USA and Latin America, and in the colonial zones of North Africa and the Middle East. Obliged to adapt to climatic conditions and local lifestyles, the programmed, spare style of modern architecture combined these with local traditional building features and techniques.

Transforming Foreign Intake

In reaction to the avant-gardes, whom they knew well as many of them had spent time in Europe, Latin American artists equated the birth of modernity with a claim to identity as powerful as their desire to belong to the international community. An initiative of a group of poets and artists, the Brazilian Anthropophagy movement promoted a modern revolutionary spirit while claiming visual references and a language that were strictly Amerindian. They thus echoed the various Indigenista movements that sprang up in the wake of the Mexican revolution, advocating the recognition and revival of local pre-colonial cultures. And yet, resisting the pull towards folklore that characterized some of

Gizella VARGA SINAI
Sheep's Head Peddler
1973
Gift by the artist, 2013

these movements, the artists who rallied together around the *Anthopophagic Manifesto* contributed to a fully appropriated dialogue with Western modernity. By using the metaphor of anthropophagy, they harked back to a mythical past while situating themselves in line with a revolutionary future. It is interesting to note that this metaphor of ingestion was also used by the Chinese artist Dong Xiwen to describe the relationship of Asian artists with Western modernity: "We must not only pursue the mastery of the various techniques of Western oil painting, and thus give free rein to the different aspects of oil paint, but also absorb it. We will change our own blood through the digestion process. In other words, we need to transform foreign intake so that it becomes our own national thing, with our own national style."[17] Many Chinese and Japanese artists who settled in France are well-known, like Léonard Foujita and Zao Wou-Ki. But the Centre Pompidou collection also includes a number of other artists, some of whom lived in Paris, some not, whose work can now be exhibited in this presentation. We thus see side by side the modernist forms of artists who adopted the Western style, like Foujita, Takanori Oguiss, Liu Haisu, Pan Yuliang, and Zao Wou-Ki, and those of artists of the traditionalist school who opted for a cultural alternative to this modernity. Among these Chinese and Japanese "ink painting" artists, who adapted tradition to only a few modern characteristics, some are now very famous, like Zhang Daqian, Wang Yachen, Xu Beihong, and Eikyu Teruo Matsuoka, who joined the collection via the Museum of Contemporary Foreign Schools. These works evoke the lively debate in Asian artistic communities on the desire to participate in European modernity versus that of asserting a Pan-Asian identity. This sort of debate also took place in Africa, as witness the metaphor of ingestion that the Nigerian writer Wole Soyinka used to refute Léopold Sédar Senghor's concept of Négritude: "A tiger does not proclaim its tigerness. It leaps onto its prey and devours it."[18] The conflict between the supporters of Westernized techniques and those of a neo-Africanism seeking its inspiration in tradition and local arts and crafts emerged in the 1920s and then took on different configurations according to country and period. For the first time, "Multiple Modernities" includes in a global history of art some of the different forms of artistic expression that developed in Sub-Saharan Africa between 1940 and 1970. These works, whose documented history is still waiting to be written, illustrate the vitality of a very wide-ranging creation in terms of the forms and status of the works produced. Whether they bear witness to the migration of traditional practices towards the field of art—such as funerary or healing art—or the "Africanist" inspiration developed in a number of creative workshops promoted by European figures, or the concept of Négritude formulated by Senghor, or the adoption of Western codes, these works reveal an extremely broad aesthetic spectrum encompassing various forms of abstract and figurative art.

17. Dong Xiwen, "Débat sur les méthodes de représentation picturales appliquées au style de peinture en Chine," *Beaux-Arts*, no. 2, 1962.

18. "Tigritude," a term coined by Wole Soyinka during the African Writers Conference, University of Makerere, Kampala.

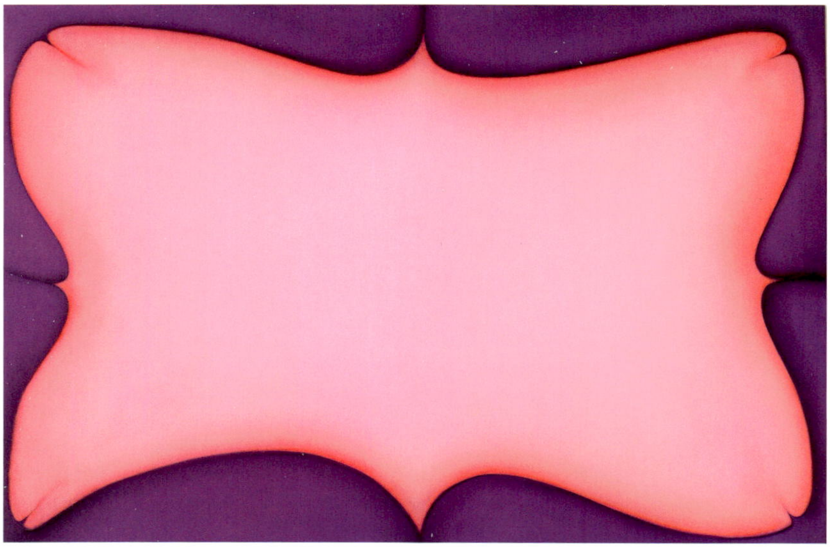

Huguette CALAND
Body Bits
1973
Gift of KA Collection Art Moderne et Contemporain, 2013

A Broader Spectrum

A history of art open to a more numerous forms of artistic expression implies a larger number of women artists. So more than 50 such artists from 19 countries are represented in the various sections of the exhibition. Alongside well-known figures such as Natalia S. Goncharova, Sonia Delaunay, Frida Kahlo, and Georgia O'Keeffe are found important artists who have been forgotten or relegated to the sidelines. And yet several, such as Maria Blanchard, Chana Orloff, Pan Yuliang, and Baya, were recognized during their lifetimes by their peers and had high public profiles. The exhibition also makes it possible to rediscover Suzanne Roger, Louise Janin, Janice Biala, Maruja Mallo, Alicia Penalba, Morgan-Snell, Mirtha Dermisache, Behjat Sadr, Farideh Lashai, and Huguette Caland. It is worth noting that these women artists were often prominent in artistic movements that history has ignored, or in which their role was played down, like Art Deco, Magic Realism, and extensions of international Surrealism. Alongside Surrealism, always highly present on the museum's walls, "Multiple Modernities" shows the development of various forms of Realism—movements that have generally been ignored despite their impact on the rest of the world. A section is notably devoted to Magic Realism, whose international fortunes can be compared with those of Surrealism. The term is borrowed from the art critic Franz Roh, who gave this name in 1925 to the various Realist movements appearing in European art scenes[19]. He described their characteristics: a reaction to the trauma of the war and the pervading sense of dehumanization, these works depict an inexpressive and disturbing world through enigmatic figures and objects. The metaphysical painting of De Chirico, the German New Objectivity and verism, the return to Realism of André Derain and Picasso, like many international artists, thus became grouped together under a term that rapidly spread throughout Latin America via the Spanish translation of Roh's book. The representations of disguise and masquerade found with Picasso and Severini, and with Mallo and Rosario de Velasco as well, recall the ironic and critical aspect of a movement too long confined within the single reading of a "return to order." Bearing witness to the numerous forms of Realist expression, different sections are also dedicated to Naive art, Art Deco, Social Realism, and anti-fascist Realism.

19. Franz Roh, *Nach-Expressionismus. Magischer Realismus. Probleme der neuesten Europaïschen Malerei*, Leipzig, Klinkhardt & Biermann, 1925.

20. Salvador Dalí, *Neo-Cubist Academy (Composition with Three Figures)*, 1926, Museu de Montserrat, Montserrat.

Modernities and Neomodernities

When in 1926 Salvador Dalí entitled a Picasso-inspired composition *Neo-Cubist Academy*,[20] he mockingly expressed the feeling of his generation that they no longer belonged to a modernism now threatening to become academic, which they sought to counteract through quotation. He thus joined Picasso himself, for whom Cubism, from 1915 onwards, was only an aesthetic like any other available to his palette. As a transformation of modernity, Neomodernity developed almost instantaneously in the wake of the avant-gardes. The most obvious sign of the modern break, Abstraction was thus the first model for this practice of quotation, whose radicalism lay in its faithfulness to an obsolete Utopia, rather than in a renewal endorsing renunciation. The period between 1930 and 1970 saw various movements and types of Abstraction developing throughout the world, inspired respectively by geometric and expressive forms. Firstly (neo-)Concrete art and Kinetic art and secondly informal and sign-based abstraction offered themselves as the two universal languages for the contextual and temporal expression of the avant-gardes' formal proposals. Constructed Abstraction, highly developed in Anglo-Saxon Europe, also gained considerable currency with Latin American artists, who promoted neo-Concrete and Kinetic art after World War I. At the same period, the artists of the Maghreb, Middle East, and Asia began to adopt more expressive forms of Abstraction: lyrical abstraction and the aesthetics of the sign, often influenced by vernacular references. As several artists had lived in Paris, these abstract styles were assimilated with those of the "Second School of Paris" although they went largely beyond its framework. Huge sections of the presentation are thus devoted to these "hot" and "cold" forms of Abstraction, considered in all their diversity and international scope.

"Multiple Modernities" starts with two works that we have rediscovered and restored, which illustrate the crisis of modern thinking brought about by the horrors of World War I. *The Four Races* of 1928 [REPR P. 14] is a monumental painting by Amédée Ozenfant, where the representation of a reconciled humanity bears witness to the artist's humanist and pacifist commitment, together with his hope for a new world in whose construction art would play a crucial role. *Europe*, a work painted by Ismaël de la Serna around 1935 [REPR P. 130], during the dark period leading up to the Spanish Civil War, depicts a hallucinatory vision of an enslaved people preyed on by disaster. What defines the modern spirit? What is the role of the artist? Utopia or prophecy? Universality or identity? This new presentation of the collections is vibrant with all these questions, which underlie the art produced in every region of the world throughout the 20th century. Not only are history and the history of art intermingled, but also aesthetics and politics. Modernity is multiple in not only its forms, but also its philosophies. Each transmitter has a particular tone of voice combining numerous harmonics. This is why we wanted above all to pay tribute to the artists with an exhibition that offers over 1,000 works by 400 artists. This is a mobile presentation, which will soon be enriched and transformed by other works, adding new narratives to this undertaking that has no end: writing a globalized, open-spirited history of art.

Translated from the French by Caroline Taylor-Bouché (incorporating some material previously translated by the company 4T [S.A.S.], Montreuil-sous-Bois, France)

A Brief History of Modernism

Michel Gauthier

Modernism is constitutively dualistic. Édouard Manet, *Argenteuil, les canotiers* (1874): at once a painting of modern life and a modern practice of painting. The canvas takes into account the increase in leisure activities and commercial entertainment in the areas surrounding Haussmann's Paris; the chimney spewing smoke in the background bears witness to the industrialization of the landscape; the indigo water of the river is not a quirk on the part of the painter: several kilometers upstream from Argenteuil, dye factories expelled waste that colored the water. It is modern life in its dual determination—industry and leisure—that is captured here in such an exemplary manner. At the same time, the canvas displays signs of self-conscious painterliness: the verticality of the "wall" of water exalts the flatness of the canvas; the piece of tulle that, without concern for perspective, adorns the woman's hat seems to provide an opportunity for the brushstroke to show itself as such—a moment of pure painting. In other words, with a work such as this, the two components of modernism are jointly expressed. Painting here is just as realistic as it is self-reflexive. Manet is the Adamic figure of an age in which modernism was able to assert its fundamental duality.

Throughout its history, modernism has been both the proclamation of this duality and the proof of its progressive impossibility. Charles Harrison has ventured the hypothesis that Claude Monet, from 1869 on, seemed to doubt that the representation of modern life could be reconciled with the requirements inherent in the development of modern painting.[1] Monet, thus, in his views of the banks of the Seine, chose angles that minimized the signs of industrialization, whereas another Impressionist, Camille Pissarro, opted for the opposite approach. The history of Modernism follows the movements of a cursor, in one direction or the other, on a line whose two extremities are participation in the radical changes of modern life and consideration of the nature of art—in short, realism and formalism. In the first half of the 20th century, the Futurists, the Purists, Fernand Léger, or the American Precisionists, to name but a few, sought to keep this dualistic ideal alive: a new and modern form, attuned to the rhythms of industrial society and the sensorial stimuli of the metropolis.

The dialectic relationship between these two poles, which defines modernism, took a decisive turn during the Russian Revolution. The Constructivist contribution to the Modernist movement played out over two main periods. The first, spanning 1920 and 1921, gave rise to a series of works that embodied the result of a way of thinking about art as a mode of production, rather than as a mode of expression: the three monochromes by Alexander Rodchenko, envisaged as the

1. Charles Harrison, "Impressionism, Modernism and Originality," in Francis Frascina et al., *Modernity and Modernism: French Painting in the Nineteenth Century*, New Haven (Conn.)/London, Yale University Press in association with the Open University, 1993, p. 180.

Fernand LÉGER
The Medrano Circus
1918

Henryk BERLEWI
Mécano-facture
1924/1961

ultimate phase of pictorial art, and the necessity for a transition to the third dimension to escape from the unavoidable illusionism of painting. The "Spatial Constructions" shown by Rodchenko, Karl Ioganson, or the Stenberg brothers in May and June 1921 in Moscow were the crowning achievements of this phase. The second Constructivism, which emerged that same spring of 1921, took as its watchword the abandonment of research into the nature of art in favor of a strong influx of artists into the world of production.[2] The Modernist concern for an art in touch with the transformations of the world was here expressed by the transformation of artists into designers or engineers. Manet or Pissarro had represented factories; the Constructivists now wanted to work in them. In other words, Modernism, at each of its two poles, was reaching a radical extreme, arriving in a certain sense at the logical end of the process it had begun: on the one hand, the process of reducing painting and sculpture to their elementary components could go no further; on the other hand, the artists wanted not only to represent modern life, but to construct it.

After the global failure of this productivist watershed, the Modernist project nonetheless quickly got back on track. Rodchenko (who had only designed a few posters for an airline company, in the end) sought a new means of reconciling the two structural tropisms of Modernism. From 1924 onwards, he found this in photography, through the ontological realism of the medium and the formal play of low- and high-angle shots. Rodchenko photographed not only architecture but also athletes, acrobats, clowns, and faces [REPR. P. 81]. As Jacques Rancière has written: "The objectivity of photography is the regime of thought, perception and sensation that makes the love of pure forms coincide with the apprehension of the inexhaustible historicity found at every street corner, in every skin fold, and at every moment of time."[3] Elsewhere, in the *Mitteleuropa* of the same era, other Constructivists resorted to other strategies to preserve the Modernist ideal in its constitutive hybridity. In 1923, in Prague, the Devětsil movement, of which Karel Teige was the dominant figure, organized an exhibition entitled "The Bazaar of Modern Art": paintings, drawings, photographs, but also architectural plans, theater and film sets, and advertising posters were all jumbled in together. More significantly, circus performances and sporting events were held. Prague's version of Constructivism, crossbred with Surrealism, thus seemed to aspire to a bazaar, and even more to a kind of Luna Park. A year later, in Warsaw, exhibitions by the Polish Constructivist Henryk Berlewi, then the avant-garde Polish group Blok to which Władysław Strzemiński and Katarzyna Kobro also belonged, were held on car dealers' premises. It was no longer the works themselves that were manifesting the modernist duality, but the way in which they were exhibited. Geometric constructions in pure colors were shown next to those ultimate exemplars of modern life: cars.

In other words, until the mid-20th century, Modernism was denoted by exchanges between savant culture and popular culture, center and periphery, formal research and social awareness—exchanges to which Clement Greenberg, the great narrator of the following decades' Modernist fable, would no longer give credence. He also has Manet start the story that must result in the triumph of American painting. However, from *Argenteuil, les canotiers*, he retains only the flatness of the indigo wall and the abstract white brushstrokes on the hat, forgetting the factory's smokestack—just as he was to ignore the Constructivist episode. This is because for him Modernism does not

2. See Maria Gough, *The Artist As Producer: Russian Constructivism in Revolution*, Berkeley/London, University of California Press, 2005.

3. Jacques Rancière, *Aisthesis: Scenes from the Aesthetic Regime of Art*, Paul Zakir (trans.), London, Verso, 2013.

reside in duality, but in a "process of self-purification" of art. "It seems to be a law of modernism [...] that the conventions not essential to the viability of a medium be discarded as soon as they are recognized. [...] Painting continues, then, to work out its modernism with unchecked momentum because it still has a relatively long way to go before being reduced to its viable essence."[4] In a Yalta of purification, the exact counterpart of this artistic absolutism was ultra-functionalism: a totally specific and autonomous art, and exclusively functional architecture, that is, architecture devoid of art. Of course, the pure art that Greenberg, a Marxist, was fighting for was not devoid of ideological perspective, since its mission was to preserve itself from any kind of compromise with the industry of spectacle and kitsch. Yet it still signified nothing less than the end of historical Modernism.

4. Clement Greenberg, "'American-Type' Painting" [1958] in *Art and Culture: Critical Essays*, Beacon Press, Boston, 1989, pp. 403-404.

The reformed brand of Modernism needed a champion. This was Jackson Pollock. Why him? Greenberg certainly couldn't have chosen an artist in the tradition that Constructivism and, in broader terms, Geometric Abstraction had borne to such a stage of development that the elected artist's story would have appeared already told. However, nothing had destined Pollock to assume the role that was allocated to him within the great Modernist story. This was the same Pollock who admired the Mexican muralists in the 1930s, and saw José Clemente Orozco and Diego Rivera at work, then collaborated with David Alfaro Siqueiros. The same Pollock who was close to Matta, while refusing to participate in the "First Papers of Surrealism" exhibition that André Breton and Marcel Duchamp organized in New York in 1942. By plucking his hero from among the ranks of the Surrealist enemy, Greenberg accomplished a brilliant coup: with the advent of Abstract Expressionism, Automatism became a footnote. But to have thus become the figurehead of pure painting, and beyond this, an instrument of American propaganda at the height of the Cold War, was, as Peter Wollen has written, "a strange and tragic fate for a great artist, who [...] fought with the cops on demonstrations, haunted the Museum of Natural History in reverent contemplation of the art of Native Americans, scoured the beach for detritus to fling down into his paint-encrusted canvas [...] played Exquisite Corpse in a Surrealist salon, was thrown off the Federal Art Project as a Red."[5] Pollock could have been the protagonist of quite a different story, one that was more sensitive—if I may borrow from Édouard Glissant's lexicon—to the "Creolization" of painting than its self-purification. Beyond the fate of an artist, the consequence of the great Greenbergian narrative was to eliminate from Modernism its original hybridity, its twofold definition—formal and social-minded, savant and popular. Consequently, only Postmodernism—even with its underlying threat of anomie—would be able to restore this hybridity to favor. But that, of course, is another story.

5. See the chapter "The Triumph of American Painting," in Peter Wollen, *Raiding The Icebox: Reflections on Twentieth Century Culture* [1993], London, Verso, 2008, p. 114.

Jackson POLLOCK
The Moon-Woman Cuts the Circle
1943

Translated from the French by Anna Knight

Conceptualizing the World
The Mundaneum Project

Stéphanie Dadour

The technological innovations of the late 19th century contributed to the emergence of new organizations on a global scale. The first World's Fair (London's Crystal Palace Exhibition of 1851), the 1894 Congress in Paris for the revival of the Olympic Games, and the International Peace Conference held in The Hague in 1899 all drew together representatives from different countries testifying to the desire to "bring the world together" in a single place during a certain period. The industrialized countries initiated economic, political, and cultural collaborations in response to progressive outlooks and ideas. In Europe, Socialist doctrines were widely disseminated in the context of the uncertainty brought about by technological progress; they were part of a humanist movement advocating the progressive advent of peace and social justice.

It was in this spirit that Belgians Henri La Fontaine, Socialist senator and fervent supporter of the rights of minorities and women, and Paul Otlet, lawyer and activist, labored for universal peace and international cooperation. Thus, in 1895, they created the Office International de Bibliographie, through which a universal bibliographic index was established (the Universal Decimal Classification, UDC). From then on, books published all over the world were indexed and classified. Knowledge could now truly be shared. This kind of approach, both rationalist and scientific, encouraged its authors to imagine a place in which a museum of the world, a library, international associations, a global university, and exhibitions could all be brought together.

Establishing this site in Western Europe (the cities under consideration were Brussels, Geneva, Rome, and The Hague) was meant to facilitate access and place the continent at the heart of the development of global networks. However, this utopian project—representative of the early 20th century—met a decidedly mixed reception.

For Otlet, this world-museum constituted a "unique universal book," comparable to an encyclopedia. It was not a museum, devoted to preserving or collecting objects, but a site, of an educational and social character, centralizing documentation on civilizations and societies. It would be divided into three sections: the first national and geographic (dealing with questions of territories, topography, natural resources, populations, politics, and laws), the second scientific (focusing on nature, humanity, society, the city as an intellectual hub) and the third historical (considering the development of humanity, revolutionary ideas, industrial progress, colonization, and so forth).

While World War I delayed the materialization of the project, it paradoxically confirmed its necessity: that of avoiding the inevitable through the alliance of representatives and the collection of documents originating from the four corners of the earth. In the pacifist humanism and positivist universalism of its inventors, this "Mundaneum," as they called it from 1920 onwards,[1]

1. At the time of implementation of the United Nations Pact.

Paul OTLET
Mundaneum, Brussels,
Union of International Associations, 1928
LE CORBUSIER FOUNDATION

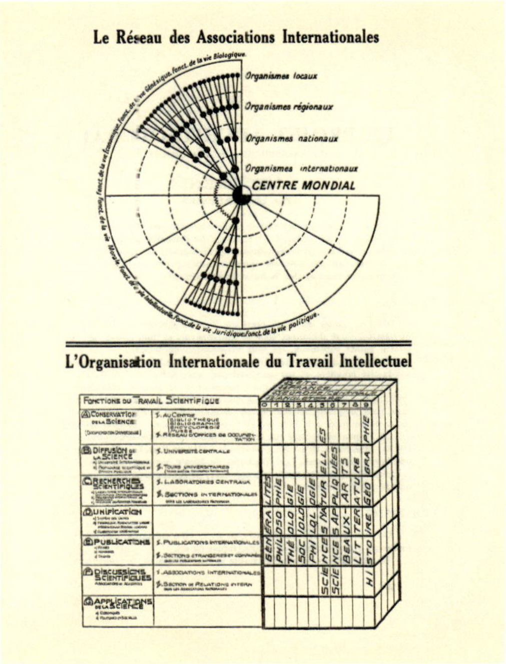

opposed "to the horrors and confusions of crisis, war, and revolution, the ideal and advantage of prosperity, peace, justice, and the ascension of men toward a higher destiny."[2] Physical designs for this site fall within the camp of the many utopian works by architects and town planners. The Cities and Town Planning Exhibition, organized by Patrick Geddes (1911), or the project for a World Center of Communication by Hendrik Christian Andersen and Ernest M. Hébrard (1913) share this utopian bent. But it was to one of the main representatives of the modern movement, Le Corbusier, that Otlet entrusted the project in the late 1920s. Architecture as mediation constituted, in his eyes, the only concrete means of expressing this political utopia. For the commission of the Mundaneum, he insisted on the importance of the use of symbolic references, a request that the architect was to rework in a formal manner.

In 1928, the project designed by Le Corbusier and Pierre Jeanneret for the Geneva site was presented in a brochure entitled *Mundaneum* and in the magazine *L'Architecture vivante*. In a 1929 issue of the same magazine, the architects justified the layout of the buildings through the regulating lines of the project and the use of the Golden Section. A spiral-shaped pyramid was built in the center of the composition, recalling a Ziggurat and harboring an inner Sacrarium (temple of knowledge).

Several different sites were considered for the construction of the Mundaneum, but since the various governments and patrons concerned did not support the project, the necessary funds were never found. It was in the architectural milieu, however, that the very foundations of the project were called into question.

A figurehead of the Russian avant-garde and a journalist on Western architecture, El Lissitzky, published an article in 1928 entitled "Idols and Idol-worshippers,"[3] in which he clearly makes reference to the Corbusian figure, which he attacks.[4] The following year Karel Teige, who was up until then a follower and supporter of Le Corbusier, also sparked a controversy in the Czech architectural magazine *Stavba*.[5] As Jean-Louis Cohen explains, Le Corbusier's trip to Moscow in 1928, the year of the creation of the CIAM [International Congress of Modern Architecture] incited a less unconditional and more assertive attitude[6] among the various factions of the Soviet avant-garde with respect to the Parisian architect, at a time when the latter had just won the competition to build the Centrosojuz building for the Soviet bureaucracy.

Both critics targeted the Mundaneum project's political conception of the world. The installation of an international cooperative in a single place, as a solution to the questions of politics, diplomacy, and state interests was called into question, as was the vision of a unitary and

2. Paul Otlet, *Traité de documentation*, Brussels, Palais Mondial, 1934, p. 64.

3. El Lissitzky, "Idoli i idolopoklonniki," *Stroitel'naja Promyslennost'*, no. 11-12, 1929, pp. 854-858.

4. According to Jean-Louis Cohen, it is highly likely that this was in response to the refusal to publish his text in the 1924 issue of *L'Esprit nouveau*.

5. Karel Teige, "Mundaneum," *Stavba* [Prague], April 1929, pp. 145-155.

6. Jean-Louis Cohen, *Le Corbusier et la mystique de l'URSS. Théories et projets pour Moscou, 1928–1936*, Liège, P. Mardaga, 1995, p. 139.

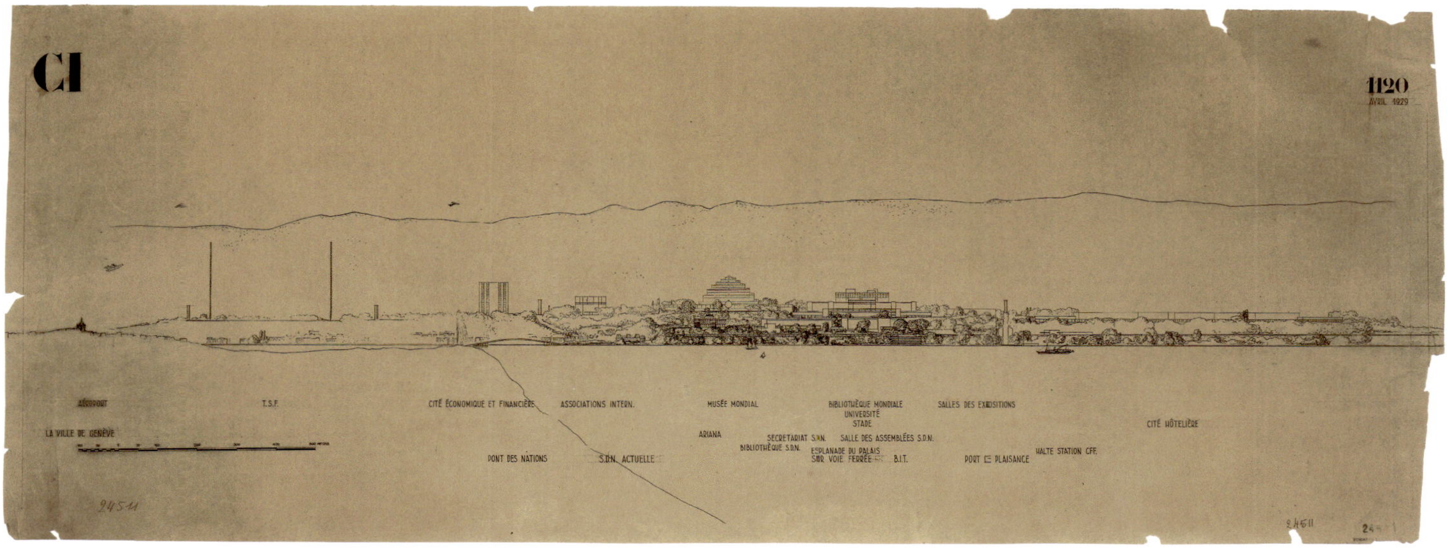

LE CORBUSIER
Overall Elevation Viewed from the Lake With Captions
1929
Heavy tracing paper with black ink and black pencil
55 × 144 cm
LE CORBUSIER FOUNDATION

settled world. The idea of a single regime bore the paradox of an indivisible authority, which, on a global scale, would conflate various types of power. The architecture of this miniature world was also disparaged. The archaic appearance of the pyramid was not justified in the critics' view: the historic and stylistic references inspired by Ancient Egypt or Mexico, the monumentality and the use of the golden ratio all represented factors that contributed to an architectural failure in a context in which Constructivism was rejecting formalist theories, and aesthetics. Moreover, the Mundaneum did not take social and economic needs into account; scientific and rational solutions were absent from this hybrid project, which oscillated between academicism and classicism. For Teige, Le Corbusier thenceforth aspired to making art; he no longer advocated *Sachlichkeit* [objectivity] and broke away from the rigorous functionalism that then prevailed.

Articles by El Lissitzky and Teige denouncing the *composition* and *symbolism* of the Mundaneum led Le Corbusier to broaden his conception of architecture. This polemic provided him with the opportunity, in 1931,[7] to revise his earlier somewhat dogmatic positions. Without entirely abandoning his architecture's scientific and utilitarian rigor, Le Corbusier addressed Teige with a sometimes friendly, sometimes paternalistic tone, and introduced an anecdote about the benefits of aesthetics and the limits of progressive thinking. He thus sought to justify his choice while liberating himself from the limits of supposedly objective architecture. Thus initiated in the early 20th century, the period of the historicist shift, the Mundaneum project began a timid redefinition of

7. Le Corbusier, "Obrana architektury, Odpoved K. Teigovi," *Musaion* [Prague], no. 2, 1931, pp. 42-53. This response in Czech was published in French two years later: Le Corbusier, "Défense de l'architecture," *L'Architecture d'aujourd'hui*, no. 10, 1933, pp. 38-61.

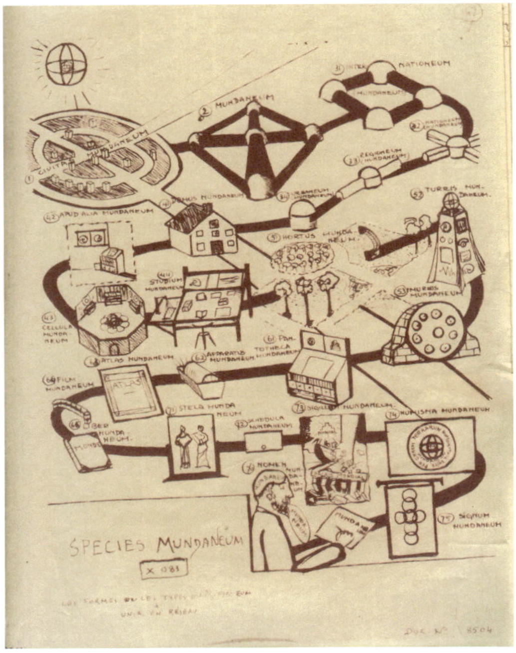

Paul OTLET
Species Mundaneum
n.d.
Transparency from the *Encyclopedia Universalis Mundaneum*, 28 × 21 cm
MUNDANEUM, ARCHIVAL CENTER OF THE WALLOON-BRUSSELS FEDERATION & TEMPORARY EXHIBITION SPACE, MONS

modernity. The Corbusian regulating lines, references, and composition broke away from the principle of an alleged objectivity and revealed an ideological detachment.

Emerging from the need to transcend the limits of a worldview, the Mundaneum gives this conception an active form both visually and spatially[8] through the design of an urban structure. As the center of the world's intelligentsia, it represents the modern ideal, rationalistic and democratic. Remaining no more than a project, it constituted a prefiguration of the World Wide Web, the network representative of post-modernity par excellence. The systematization of knowledge and information on the Web paradoxically implies the dissolution of rationalism and has led to an explosion of references owing to hypertext links. In a world in which information is one of the stakes of power, the immateriality and deterritorialization of the Web has led to political, social, and economic reconfigurations. While the world may appear to be smaller than it once was, its temporal horizon is now increasingly vast. New international geographies are emerging, but, unlike the stability and steadiness inherent to the paper medium, knowledge only has meaning through interactions among its users, in various channels. This information society is questioning the condition of knowledge and taking stock of the collapse of the grand narratives,[9] calling into question the criteria of truth. Recently, the collaboration between Google and the Mundaneum confirmed the latter's relationship to the Web. It bore witness to the disenchantment with respect to a totalizing system and served as the echo of a fragmented society, dissociated from a shared order.

Translated from the French by Anna Knight

8. Jean Davallon, *L'Exposition à l'œuvre. Stratégies de communication et médiation symbolique*, Paris/Montréal, L'Harmattan, 2000. For more exhaustive research on this subject, see Pierre Chabard, "Towers & Globes: Architectural and Epistemological Differences between Patrick Geddes' Outlook Towers and Paul Otlet's Mundaneums," in W. Boyd Rayward (ed.), *European Modernism and the Information Society: Informing the Present, Understanding the Past*, Aldershot, Ashgate, 2008, pp. 105-125.

9. Jean-François Lyotard, *La Condition postmoderne*, Paris, Éditions de Minuit, 1979.

Grids and Networks

The Role of Magazines in the Construction of the Modern Art World

Mica Gherghescu

In July 1922, in a little Lyon-based magazine, *Manomètre* (Pressure Gauge), Émile Malespine published a peculiar alphabet-manifesto declaring, under the auspices of "supranationality," the reign of plurilingualism and multiculturalism: "*Now it's time to begin. Don't delay.* [In English in the original—trans.] No trumpet, no neons. Let's begin very simply. Grammar lesson: class is held at the Terminus Hotel, in Paris, Nice, Madrid, Anvers, London, etc. [...]. To continue the list, learn your geography. The doorman is your phrasebook. A smartly-bound and gold-braided *Wörterbuch*. He emits at will German, English, Spanish, French, Italian, *und so weiter*. [...] The result: a polyglot salad topped with *sauce anglaise* [...] and a language is never immutable. It hardly bears repeating, *common thing* [in English in the original – trans.], *n'est-ce pas?*"[1] This magazine, through the year 1928, became the hub of multiple connections, which constructed a space transcending borders. Gathered together in the eclectic movement of *suridéalisme* forged by Malespine in the wake of Dadaism, texts by Jorge Luis Borges appeared side by side with Lajos Kassák's constructivist manifesto of *Bildarchitektur* and Piet Mondrian's reflections on form. The poems of the Zenithist Ljubomir Micić, the Ultra-ists Guillermo de Torre and Rogelio Buendía, and the Stridentist Manuel Maples Arce erupted beside the texts of Tristan Tzara, Jean Cocteau, Tadeusz Peiper, and Tony Garnier, broken up by the images of Norah Borges, Jozef Peeters, and Jean Arp. *Manomètre* took the pulse, as it beat, of an active, rebellious, mobile modernism.

At the moment of the historic crystallization of avant-gardes, magazines strongly favored the permeability of borders in the name of a cosmopolitan creative spirit opening up towards international distribution. Thanks to their eminently "relational" function, they constituted strategic tools for exploring synchronous intellectual and artistic dynamics made up of superimposed histories and varied ideological inflections. Shifts between the avant-garde's radical discourses and the mutations of artistic modernity took place in complex registers.[2] To analyze correctly this editorial phenomenon, it is necessary to adopt a comparative approach, leafing through the magazine as, effectively, the heterogeneous product of a collective. This is characterized by the diversity of its members, designers, and contributors,[3] artists, gallery owners, and collectors divided between aesthetic considerations and policies of legitimation, publication, and distribution. Moving object, *querschnitt* (section), *kunstblatt* (art sheet), almanac, syncretic *miscellanea*, *cahier d'art* (art notebook), *little review*, *comprimido* (digest), *bibelot*,[4] or *firebrand*, the magazine was the voice of a team and of a linguistic community, either *coterie* (to use the title of a magazine published by Chaman Lall in London in 1919) or *rete*—in reference to

1. [Émile Malespine], "ABCD," *Manomètre*, no. 1 (July 1922): 1-3, unsigned.

2. The historiography of literary and artistic magazines is a fairly recent critical phenomenon, started by Trevor Fawcett and Clive Phillpot's landmark work, *The Art Press: Two Centuries of Art Magazines* (London, The Art Book Company, 1976), and continued with Géza Perneczky's reference study, which gives a cartography of magazines (*The Magazine Network: The Trends of Alternative Art in the Light of Their Periodicals, 1968–1988*, Cologne, Soft Geometry, 1993), both atlas and inventory, an expression of his own relationship to the intellectual dynamic of "mail-artists." More recently, Beatriz Colomina and Craig Buckley published another illustrated atlas on radical architectural publications of the years 1960–1970 as "sites of innovation and debate": *Clip, Stamp, Fold: The Radical Architecture of Little Magazines 196X to 197X*, Barcelona, Actar, 2010. The same time period is covered by Marion von Osten, "Architectures of Decolonization," *Le Journal des laboratoires*, January-April 2011, p. 19-21, available on the websites of Les Laboratoires d'Aubervilliers: www.leslaboratoires.org/sites/leslaboratoires.org/files/jdl_jan-avril_2011_bd_2.pdf. See also the contextual work collected by Peter Brooker and Andrew Thacker in *The Oxford Critical and Cultural History of Modernist Magazines, Vol. I: Britain and Ireland, 1880–1955*, Oxford, Oxford University Press, 2009; as well as Évanghélia Stead and Hélène Védrine, *L'Europe des revues, 1880–1920. Estampes, photographies, illustrations*, Paris, Presses Universitaires de Paris-Sorbonne, 2008; Rossella Froissart Pezone and Yves Chevrefils-Desbiolles (eds.), *Les Revues d'art. Formes, stratégies et réseaux au xxe siècle*, Rennes, Presses Universitaires de Rennes, 2011; or the inventory of the Fonds Paul Destribats, a new addition to the collection of international magazines of the Kandinsky Library. National Museum of Modern Art, Centre Pompidou, Paris (Didier Schulmann, Agnès de Bretagne [eds.], *Le Fonds Paul Destribats. Une collection de revues et de périodiques des avant-gardes internationales à la Bibliothèque Kandinsky*, Paris, Éditions du Centre Pompidou, 2011).

3. The magazine *Ma*, for instance, had contributors in Vienna, Zagreb, Berlin, and Kosice.

4. A chapbook. See Frederick Winthrop Faxon, *Ephemeral Bibelots: A Bibliography of the Modern Chap-Books and their Imitators*, Boston, The Boston Book Company, 1903.

the distended and networked geography conceived by Ardengo Soffici[5] to promote a planetary futurism.
The international dimension advocated by the magazines cannot be understood without taking into account the acute receptivity of these connected creators to "contemporary world events," which they registered with almost seismographic sensibility. One should not ignore, meanwhile, the stance of collective, populist, and pan-humanist ambitions variously expressed under the different forms of pacifism, communism, and fascism. For example, the Europeanism of the Franco-Austrian Richard de Coudenhove-Kalergi or the Hungarian immigrant to Catalonia Oliver Brachfeld and the ecumenical aspirations of Hermann von Keyserling inhabited the unifying space of the magazine cheek by jowl with Leo Frobenius' theory of cultural morphologies, the African art exalted by Carl Einstein in his cult work *Negerplastik*,[6] the poetry of Yvan Goll, Vicente Huidobro, and Blaise Cendrars, and Anatoli Lounatcharski's socialist and Proletkultist internationalism. These phenomena cannot be understood without recognizing the complex coexistence of avowed internationalisms with violent returns to self-centered cultures. The transnational permeability put forward as a postulate was met with deep resistance. The rhetoric of the synthesis of the arts presided over the circulation of texts and ideas, facilitated by technology—typewriter, radio, telegraph, and aerogram. But this world of elastic circulation reproduced by the magazines is often circuitous, shaped by multiple variables relating to the language and translation of manifesto texts; to the tensions engendered by actors' differing political orientations; to beliefs, affinities, and tastes; and importantly enough, to territories varying in their geography and ethnic composition. These modulations also affected the hierarchies established between the centers themselves. They inflect the "complexes" suffered and the regionalisms created by those on the periphery, explain temporal disjunctions, and confront us with the singularity of the careers of actors and mediators. Edited in Berlin by Herwarth Walden from 1910 to 1932, *Der Sturm* [The Storm] served as a nexus for the affirmation and legitimation of expressionisms, futurisms, constructivisms, Dadaism, and many other forms of realisms, in an eclectic synthesis of styles and genres. The members of avant-gardist and modern circles came and went, with more fanfare or less, and rubbed elbows with authors on the German literary scene—such as Lothar Schreyer, August Stramm, Alfred Döblin, Rudolf Blümner, and Kurt Schwitters. Similarly, in the May 1922 issue of the Hungarian activist magazine *Ma* [Today], edited from Vienna by Kassák, there coexisted pictures of De Stijl buildings, Francis Picabia's "cannibalism," and Lázsló Moholy-Nagy's *Nikkelplastika* [Nickel sculpture]. Cendrars shared the page with Gorham Munson, member of the Greenwich Village artistic scene and one of the founders of the magazine *Secession*. Meanwhile *Zenit*, an international magazine published in Zagreb by the poet Micić, presented Zenithism as "the definitive movement for the synthesis of new art" while simultaneously spreading the theory of a virulent and barbaric Balkanization announcing the collapse of the West and the coming of the Balkans as a sixth continent. Finally, we must note that a modernist magazine with an international scope, like *Martin Fierro*, was nonetheless placed under the tutelary figure of a pureblooded gaucho and shaped by debates on Argentinian nationalism and Creolism. In the graphic design of the magazines, the heterogeneity of contributions and cultural circulation was embodied by an ingenious layout: the grid, translating in its elementary form

5. Ardengo Soffici, *Rete Mediterranea* [Mediterranean Network], Florence, Vallechi Editore, 1920.

6. Carl Einstein, *Negerplastik* [Negro Sculpture], Leipzig, Verlag der weißen Bücher, 1915.

Blok. Czasopismo awangardy artystycznej, (Warsaw), no. 6-7 (1924), back cover
Editors: Henryk Stazewski, Teresa Żarnowerówna, Mieczysław Szczuka, Edmund Miller

a network, a "*revue des revues*", a magazine of many magazines. In a literal fashion, the grid reflected the linkage of artistic and publishing circuits, of which it was a graphic epitome, and created a situation of polycentric sociability, both as an economy of recognition and an economy of exchange. Like Marinetti and Kassák, exceptional figures in magazine design and distribution, the globetrotting publisher carried in his suitcases stacks of issues of his editorial expression; the cover redistributed, in a non-hierarchical and tabular form, that intellectual community of innovators in a transnational dynamic, captured in a *nexus*. It is through the lines and squares of the grid that Teresa Żarnowerówna and Mieczysław Szczuka's Polish magazine, *Blok*, "connected" with Roberto Ortelli's Argentinean magazine *Inicial*, with Margaret Anderson's *Little Review*, with the Japanese Constructivists' *Mavo*, or, in Anvers, with Michel Seuphor and Peeters' *Het Overzicht* [Panorama]. In 1925, another magazine, *Integral*, whose watchword was the exaggerated intensification of genius, took up the motif of the synthesis of the arts in the aesthetic of "Integralism," capturing the role of the artistic and cultural press in constructing space for dialogue "with telegraph wires for nerves," stretching "from the Equator to the poles." The editor's note in the first issue proclaimed that only "journalism has intuited the meaning of modern life."[7]

7. Anonymous, "The Integral Man," editorial, *Integral* (Bucharest), no. 1, March 1925.

Translated from the French by Phoebe Green

1. *Manomètre. Mélange les langues, enregistre les idées, indique la pression sur tous les méridiens, est polyglotte et supranational*, Lyon, 1922 Editor: Émile Malespine

2. *Der Sturm. Monatsschrift*, Berlin, 17th year, no. 5, May 1922. Editor: Herwarth Walden Cover: Georges Ribemont-Dessaignes

3. *L'Esprit nouveau. Revue internationale d'esthétique*, Paris, Éditions de l'Esprit Nouveau, no. 1, 1920. Editor: Paul Dermée

4. *Little Review: Quarterly Journal of Art and Letters. Exiles' Number*, New York, Spring 1923 Editors: Margaret Anderson, jh [Jane Heap], Ezra Pound. Cover: Fernand Léger

5. *Klaxon. Mensario de arte moderna*, São Paulo, no. 1, 15 May 1922. Editor: Mário de Andrade

6. *Ma. Aktivista folyóirat*, Budapest/Vienna, no. 5/6, May 1922. Editor: Lajos Kassák Cover: László Moholy-Nagy

7. *Actual. Hoja de vanguardia. Comprimido estridentista de Manuel Maples Arce*, Mexico, no. 1, 1921. Editor: Manuel Maples Arce

8. *Martin Fierro. Periodico quincenal de arte y crítica libre*, Buenos Aires, no. 1, February 1924 Editor: Evar Méndez

9. *Broom: An International Magazine of the Arts Published by Americans in Italy*, Rome/Berlin/New York, no. 4, July 1922. Editors: Harold A. Loeb, Alfred Kreymborg. Cover: Fernand Léger

10. *Cosmópolis. Revista mensual*, Madrid, no. 25, January 1921. Founder: Manuel Allende; editor: Enrique Gómez Carrillo

11. *LEF. Zurnal levogo fronta iskusstv*, Moscow, no. 3, June-July 1923. Editor: Vladimir Mayakovsky Cover: Alexander Rodchenko

12. *V_L tra. Poesia, critica, arte*, Madrid, no. 4, 1921. Editors: Rafael Cansinos-Asséns, Ramón Gómez de la Serna. Cover: Rafael Barradas

13. *Zenit. Internacionalna revija za novu umetnosti kulturu*, Zagreb, no. 11, February 1922 Editor: Ljubomir Micić. Cover: Vladimir Tatlin

14. *Život. Sborník vìtvarného*, Prague, Umělecká Beseda, no. 2, 1922. Editor: Jaromír Krejcar Cover: Karel Teige

15. *Integral. Revistă de sinteză modernă. Organ al mişcării moderne din ţară şi străinătate*, no. 1, March 1925. Bucharest editor: M. H. Maxy; Paris editor: Benjamin Fondane. Cover: M. H. Maxy

16. *Bulletin de l'Effort moderne*, Paris, L'Effort moderne, no. 1, January 1924 Editor: Léonce Rosenberg. Cover: Georges Valmier

17. *Bauhaus. Zeitschrift für Gestaltung*, Dessau, no. 1, 1928. Publisher: Hannes Meyer; editors: Walter Gropius and László Moholy-Nagy Cover: Herbert Bayer

1.

2.

3.

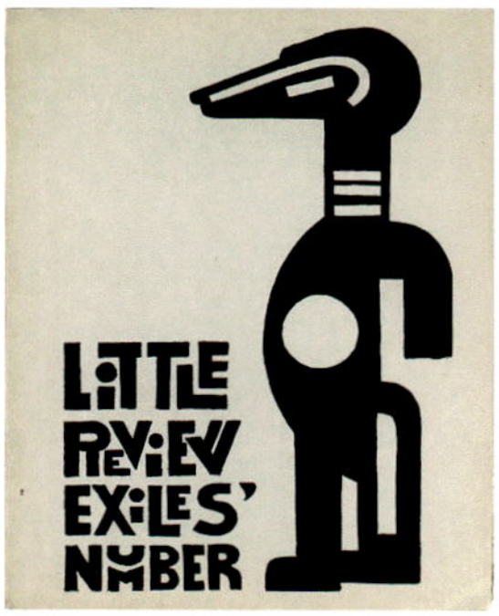

4.

5.

6.

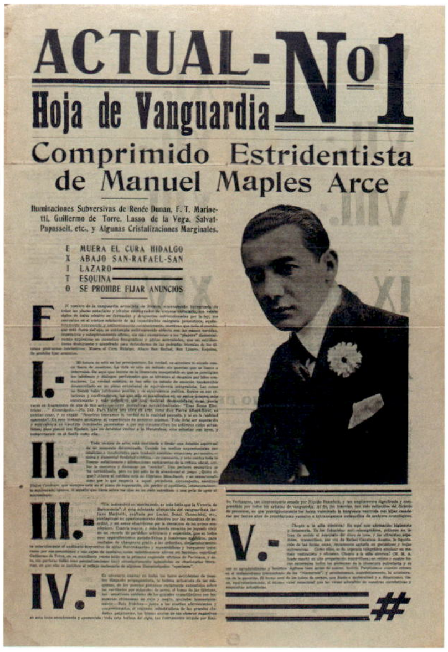

7.

8.

9.

10.

11.

12.

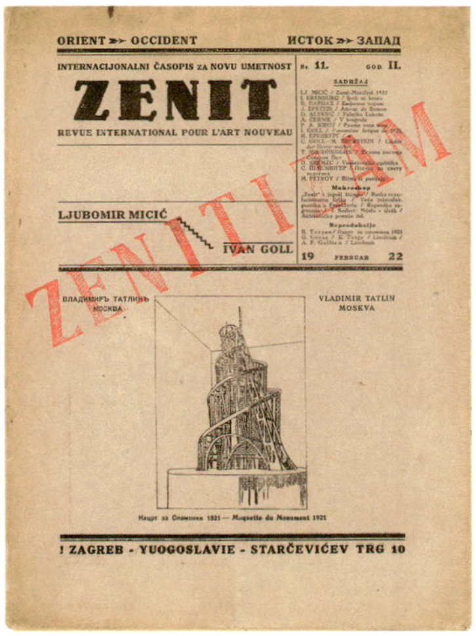

13.

14.

15.

16.

17.

DINAMO
FUTURISTA
Nº2
Periodico mensile illustrato - Rovereto marzo 1933 XI - C. C. Postale - Costa L. 2 - Anno 1°
FUTURISTA

1.

HEBDOMADAIRE -- CINQUIEME ANNÉE, Nº 203 -- SAMEDI 23 AVRIL 1932 -- LE NUMÉRO 1 FR. 50
MONDE
Directeur : HENRI BARBUSSE
RÉDACTEUR EN CHEF : LÉON WERTH
Comité directeur : ALBERT EINSTEIN, P. FIREMAN, M. GORKI, M. KAROLYI, M. MORHARDT, UPTON SINCLAIR, MANUEL UGARTE, MIGUEL DE UNAMUNO
Rédaction, Administration, Publicité : 50, rue Etienne-Marcel, PARIS (2e) Téléphone : Central 14-76 et 18-23
CLINIQUE du Docteur S.D.N
Pas trop près! la langue est chargée !
LE GLOBE

2.

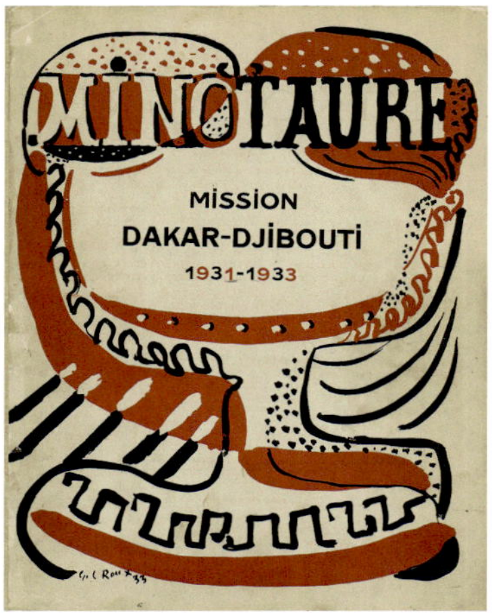
MINOTAURE
MISSION
DAKAR-DJIBOUTI
1931-1933

3.

SOCIAL KUNST
8
FOTOMONTAGE

4.

СССР
НА СТРОЙКЕ
12

5.

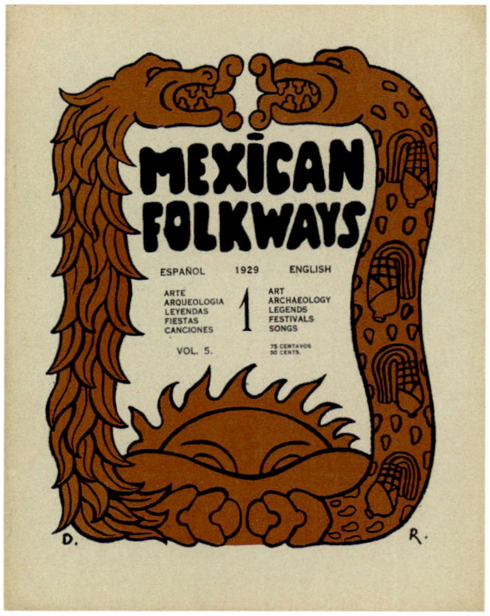
MEXICAN
FOLKWAYS
ESPAÑOL 1929 ENGLISH
ARTE
ARQUEOLOGIA
LEYENDAS
FIESTAS
CANCIONES
1
ART
ARCHAEOLOGY
LEGENDS
FESTIVALS
SONGS
VOL. 5.
D. R.

6.

LÉGITIME
DÉFENSE
Textes de :
étienne léro
rené ménil
jules-marcel monnerot
maurice-sabas quitman
simone yoyotte

7.

8.

9.

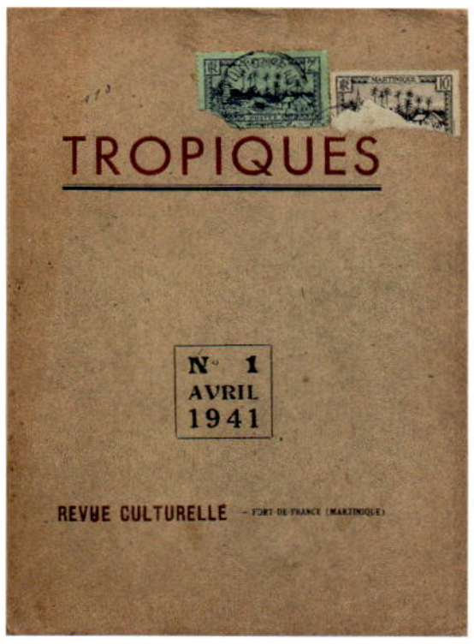

10.

11.

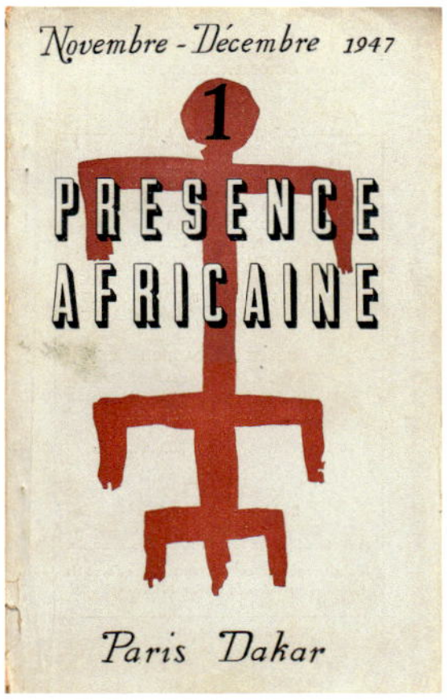

12.

14.

13.

1. *Dinamo futurista*, Roveretto, no. 2, 1933.
Editor: Fortunato Depero. Cover: Fortunato Depero

2. *Monde. Hebdomadaire d'information littéraire, artistique, scientifique, économique et sociale*, Paris, no. 203, 23 April 1932.
Director: Henri Barbusse; editor: Léon Werth
Cover: [Georges] Delaw

3. *Minotaure. Revue artistique et littéraire*, Paris, Éd. Albert Skira, special issue "Mission Dakar–Djibouti," no. 2, 1933.
Administrative director: Albert Skira; artistic director: Émile Tériade. Cover: Gaston-Louis Roux

4. *Social Kunst*, published by Monde Gruppen, Copenhagen, Mondes Forlag, no. 8, special issue on photomontage, 1932. Cover: John Heartfield

5. *S.S.S.R. na Strojke*, Moscow, Ogiz Izogiz -Gosudarstvennoe izdatel'stvo. no. 12, special issue *Parachutte*, 1935. Editors: Maxime Gor'kij [Maxim Gorky], G. Grinko, T. Enukidze.
Design: Alexander Rodchenko and Varvara Stepanova

6. *Mexican Folkways*, Mexico, no. 4, 1929
Editor: Frances Toor. Cover: Diego Rivera

7. *Légitime défense*, Paris, no. 1, 1 June 1932.
Administrator: Étienne Léro

8. *Helhesten. Tidsskrift for Kunst*, Copenhagen, no. 1, 1941. Editor: Robert Dahlmann Olsen
Cover: Henry Heerup

9. *Cendre. Revue de Vou club*, Tokyo, no. 3, 1948
Editor: Kitasono Katue

10. *Tropiques. Revue culturelle*, Fort-de-France, no. 1, April 1941. Editor: Aimé Césaire

11. *Cobra. Bulletin pour la coordination des investigations artistiques*, Brussels/Copenhagen/Amsterdam, no. 1, March 1949.
Editor-in-chief and Belgian editor: Christian Dotremont; Danish editor: Robert Dahlmann Olsen; Dutch editor: Constant Nieuwenhuys [Constant]
Cover: Asger Jorn

12. *Présence africaine*, Paris/Dakar, no. 1, November-December 1947. Editor: Alioune Diop
Cover: Dogon mask, pictogram derived from Marcel Griaule, *Masques dogons*, Paris, 1938

13. *Black Orpheus. A Journal of African and Afro-American Literature*, Ibadan (Nigeria), no. 9, June 1961. Editors: Ulli Beier and Janheinz Jahn
Cover: Suzanne Wenger

14. *Islas. Revista de la universidad central de las villas*, Santa Clara (Cuba), no. 19, 1965
Editor: Samuel Feijóo. Cover: Wifredo Lam

Reproductions

Alicia PENALBA
Homage to César Vallejo
1955/1960

Constantin BRANCUSI
Caryatid
1943–1948

Jacques LIPCHITZ
Figure
1926–1930

Agustín CÁRDENAS
Hello to Earth
1966

ANONYMOUS
Bamileke Anthropomorphic Chambranle Pillar (Cameroon)
n.d.

Ramón de ZUBIAURRE
The Rowers, Winners at Ondarroa
ca. 1914–1915

Natalia S. GONCHAROVA
Planting Potatoes
1908–1909

Sonia DELAUNAY
Finnish Girl
1907

Raoul DUFY
Fisherman with Net
ca. 1914

Marc CHAGALL
The Newspaper Seller
1914

Der Blaue Reiter Almanach

Beyond Divisions

Angela Lampe

"The whole œuvre
that we call art knows neither race
nor border, but only humanity."[1]

The birthdate of *Der Blaue Reiter* [The Blue Rider] is well established. It was 19 June 1911, the day Vassily Kandinsky [REPR. P. 57] revealed his new plan to his friend Franz Marc:
"[...] Well, I have a new idea. Piper must be the publisher and the two of us the editors. A kind of almanac (annual) with reproductions and articles... and a *chronicle!!* that is, reports on exhibitions reviewed by artists and artists alone. In the book, the entire year must be reflected; and a link to the past as wall as a ray to the future must give this mirror its full life [...] We will put an Egyptian work next to a small Zeh [the last name of two talented children], a Chinese work beside a Rousseau, a folk print beside a Picasso and the like! Eventually we will attract poets and musicians. The book

1. Vassily Kandinsky, Franz Marc, drafts for a preface, derived from the posthumous writings of August Macke, October 1911, in *L'Almanach du Blaue Reiter (Le Cavalier bleu)* (1965), presented and annotated by Klaus Lankheit, Paris, Klincksieck, 1987, p. 63.

could be called *Die Kette* [The Chain] or some other title."[2]

The world nonetheless had to wait nearly twelve months before the almanac was released, on 10 May 1912, under the title *Der Blaue Reiter* [REPR. P. 56]. In the meantime, the contributors organized two eponymous group exhibitions in Munich[3] that gave the impression of a collective approach, which was retrospectively contested by Kandinsky. For him, an association or group of artists bearing the name Blaue Reiter never existed.[4] Originally, it was only the title that Marc and he had found to name their editorial project. It was the publication that was at the heart of their enterprise. The hierarchy established by Kandinsky is very clear on this score. As he didn't much appreciate the work of the Expressionist group Die Brücke [The Bridge], he accorded Marc the right to *exhibit* them, but "immortalizing them in the record of our art of today (which is what our journal must be) as a kind of decisive and directive force is an error in my opinion. In any case, I would be against large reproductions [...] the little ones mean: this kind of thing is *also produced today*, the large ones mean: *this* is what we're doing."[5]

This chronicle of contemporary art can also—and especially?—be read through its iconography, which is significant and on a par with its textual discourse. As readers turn the pages, they effectively discover images as diverse as a Japanese wash drawing opposite a bull painted by Marc, Bavarian votive paintings following a canvas by Henri Matisse, or an arrangement of figures from Egyptian shadow theater and popular Russian etchings, without forgetting the reproductions of sculptures from Easter Island or Cameroon, Chinese or Brazilian masks. By delving into this abundant visual dialogue, without borders or classifications, Kandinsky not only wants the reader to "feel many vibrations," but to easily capture the main subject of this synthetic book, which the artist formulates as follows: "The question of art is not a question of form but one of artistic content."[6] Beyond their apparent differences and diverse origins, a fundamental kinship would seem to exist between authentic artworks, sometimes defined by "an inner life" connected to spiritual revival, sometimes by the principle of an "inner necessity."

While the juxtaposition of objects from different cultures and periods was not new, it was having an increasingly strong impact during this period. In his essay on "spiritual properties," Marc evokes the example of El Greco, whose works, recently exhibited by the new general director of Munich's Neue Pinakothek, Hugo von Tschudi, next to paintings by Paul Cézanne, deeply affected Kandinsky and himself and contributed to defining their new conceptions of art. Despite the centuries that separated the two painters, "spiritual affinities" emerged.[7] Marc, who had been

2. Extract from a letter by V. Kandinsky to F. Marc, 19 June 1911, quoted in Klaus Lankheit, *The Blaue Reiter Almanac*, Boston MFA Publications, 1974, p. 15-16.

3. The first exhibition bringing together the main collaborators of the almanac opened on 18 November 1911 at the Thannhauser Gallery. It would then be presented in Cologne, Berlin, Bremen, Hagen, and Frankfurt. The second event, at the Buchhandlung Hans Goltz (12 February–18 March 1912), entirely devoted to the works on paper, once again widened the circle of international artists: Arp, Klee, Picasso, La Fresnaye, Vlaminck, the Russians Malevich, Goncharova, and Larionov, among others.

4. K. Lankheit, "Histoire de l'almanach," in V. Kandinsky, F. Marc, *L'Almanach du Blaue Reiter*, op. cit., p. 6.

5. V. Kandinsky, letter to F. Marc, 2 February 1912, published in Andreas Hüneke (ed.), *Der Blaue Reiter. Eine Geschichte in Dokumenten*, Stuttgart, Reclam, 2011, p. 71. This translation is from the French cited by Paul Vogt, "Der Blaue Reiter [Le Cavalier bleu]", in *Paris-Berlin, 1900–1933*, exh. cat, Paris, Éditions du Centre Pompidou, 1978, p. 86.

6. V. Kandinsky, "Franz Marc," *Cahiers d'Art*, no. 8-10, 1936; cited in German in *Essays über Kunst und Künstler* (1955), edited and commented by Max Bill, Berne, Benteli, 1963, p. 199.

7. F. Marc, "Biens spirituels," in V. Kandinsky, F. Marc, *L'Almanach du Blaue Reiter*, op. cit., p. 77 [our translation]. Marc is referring here to the exhibition of the Hungarian Marczell von Nemes' collection, which Tschudi, several weeks before he died in November 1911, had presented at the Alte Pinakothek in Munich. The almanac is dedicated to Tschudi, the great supporter of Der Blaue Reiter.

collecting Japanese engravings since his trip to Paris in 1903,[8] seemed to be interested in the principle of comparison even before Kandinsky. Hence, a year after the resounding success of the exhibition on Islamic art in Munich in 1910, "Masterpieces of Islamic Art," he regretted not being able to hang "Kandinsky's large composition and many other works next to the Muslim carpets. A comparison would be inevitable and enriching for all of us!"[9] It's not unlikely that his friendship with August Macke [REPR. P. 58] formed the basis for this interest. When Marc invited Macke to participate in the almanac, he alluded to the latter's "old goal" of undertaking a comparative history of art that would finally find its place in this book.[10] We know the enthusiasm that, from 1908, the Rhenish artist brought to the Folkwang Museum in Hagen, which grouped together both modern art and Egyptian, Greek, Indian, Gothic, and Italian art.[11] Its founder, Karl Ernst Osthaus, had assembled one of the very first "global" collections, while closely following contemporary art. From 1909, it presented works by Kandinsky and Alexej von Jawlensky [REPR. P. 59], before presenting the touring Blaue Reiter exhibition in 1912. The example of the Folkwang Museum allows us to capture the extraordinary character of Kandinsky and Marc's project. Despite the variety of its collections, derived from diverse cultures and periods, a presentation in which modern artworks were shown alongside extra-European objects was only put in place as of the fall of 1912. This was not long, then, after the release of the almanac, and Osthaus was one of its patrons. The German museum was thus the first institution in the world to exhibit the avant-garde alongside tribal arts.[12] This evolution is emblematic of a shift in the way in which artists, from Fauvists to Cubists, to the Die Brücke Expressionists, appreciated tribal art. The initial shock that liberated a great and inspiring force was succeeded by a question concerning the existence of common roots and approaches. Thenceforth, the order of the day was to federate the troops, near or far, contemporary or precursors, in order to defeat the curse of materialism through a more spiritual art, going beyond the reproduction of reality. This desire to "bring together the artists of the new age" under the banner of an inner expressiveness found an echo at the 1913 First German Autumn Salon, organized by Herwarth Walden in Berlin. Aided by Marc and Macke, the founder of the Der Sturm gallery not only exhibited the work of seventy-five artists of diverse nationalities, but also, for the first time, Indian paintings belonging to Marc as well as Chinese engravings from Kandinsky's collection, complemented by contemporary Turkish painting and Japanese engravings. Unlike their first two exhibitions, the Blaue Reiter writers were now able to transpose their universal approach into the exhibition space.

8. On this subject, see Brigitte Salmen, "Die Maler des 'Blauen Reiter' und ihre Begegnung mit japanischer Kunst," in *"... diese zärtlichen, geistvollen Phantasien...". Die Maler des 'Blauen Reiter' und Japan*, exh. cat, Murnau, Schlossmuseum, 2011, pp. 69-70. All of the artists from Der Blaue Reiter (Kandinsky, Marc, Macke, Jawlensky, Werefkin, Münter, Klee) were interested in Japanese art in varying degrees.

9. F. Marc, "Au sujet de l'exposition de la Neue Künstler Vereinigung chez Thannhauser," in Maria Stavrinaki (ed.), *Écrits et correspondances*, Th. de Keyser (trans.), Paris, École Nationale des Beaux-Arts, 2006, pp. 101-102 [our translation].

10. F. Marc, letter to August Macke, 8 September 1911, published in *Écrits et correspondances*, op. cit., p. 330. The main comparison is found in the core of the essay "The Masks" that Macke published in the almanac. His conclusion is in complete agreement with a universal idiom: "As though regardless of the European aesthetic, forms speak a solemn language everywhere." (V. Kandinsky, F. Marc, *L'Almanach du Blaue Reiter, op. cit.*, p. 117.)

11. Macke shared his visit to Hagen in a letter to the collector Bernhard Koehler, the uncle of his wife Elisabeth and future principal patron of the almanac. See Mario-Andreas von Lüttichau, "Expressionisten," in Hartwig Fischer, Uwe Schneede (ed.), *"Das schönste Museum der Welt." Museum Folkwang bis 1933*, exh. cat, Göttingen, Folkwang/Steidl, 2010, p. 78.

12. On this subject, see Rainer Stamm, "Weltkunst und Moderne Kunst," in H. Fischer, U. Schneede (eds.), *"Das schönste Museum der Welt." Museum Folkwang bis 1933. Essays zur Geschichte des Museum Folkwang*, Göttingen, Folkwang/Steidl, 2010, pp. 30-35.

The publication of the almanac, hailed as "a courageous and liberating act,"[13] thus marked the start of this fight for a new synthesis of the arts. While the comparison between El Greco and Cézanne suggested by Tschudi served as a model, the Blaue Reiter artists were to go further by confronting the latest productions of the European avant-garde with the artistic expressions of different domains, cultures, and periods. In a provocative and almost violent manner, they put all artistic creations on the same level, independent of their origins and their habitual status. This new fury could be explained by the political context in which the project came to light. Thus it is perhaps not a pure accident if in the phrase preceding the well-known exposé of the almanac project that Kandinsky sent to Marc in June 1911, the Russian artist mentions the response that he made to the pamphlet of the painter Carl Vinnen "Ein Protest deutscher Künstler" [A Protest of German Artists], which was published in the *Süddeutsche Monatshefte*.[14] In his role as representative of the Munich New Artists' Association Kandinsky reacted to the hateful statements of Vinnen, who, with an openly xenophobic tone, violently attacked the keen interest in French art shown by museum directors (particularly Gustav Pauli in Bremen) and German art dealers to the detriment of national art. Kandinsky's reply was most particularly directed at the critic Hans Rosenhagen who had attacked the Russian members of the Munich association. For the future *Blaue Reiter* editor, it was vain to apply limits to the evolution of art, since "the most powerful art, that is, essential art, will still prevail and exercise its influence, in one form or another, over all artistically gifted peoples."[15] In light of these lines, the almanac can be read as a retort meant to curtail this appalling polemic on national priority through what these artists most strongly believed in: the vitality of universal art.

Translated from the French by Anna Knight

13. See Hans Tietze, "Der Blaue Reiter," *Die Kunst für Alle*, no. XXVII, 1911–1912, p. 543 sq.; cited by K. Lankheit, "Histoire de l'Almanach," art. cit., pp. 43-44.

14. Letter from V. Kandinsky to F. Marc, 19 June 1911, cited above (see note 2).

15. V. Kandinsky, cited by M. Stavrinaki in F. Marc, *Écrits et correspondances*, op. cit., p. 121, note 5. On this controversy, see the summary given by Stavrinaki, pp. 118-122.

Paintings by Emil Nolde, *Still Life with Wooden Statuette* and *Still Life with Masks III*, with Oceanic art objects, Museum Folkwang, Hagen, 1912

"We will put an Egyptian work next to a small Zeh, a Chinese work beside a Rousseau, a folk print beside a Picasso and the like!"

LETTER FROM KANDINSKY TO MARC, 19 JUNE 1911

Vassily KANDINSKY, Franz MARC
The Blue Rider Almanac
1914 [2nd edition]

ANONYMOUS
Ponou Mask (Gabon)
1880–1920

Ernst Ludwig KIRCHNER
Toilette. Woman at the Mirror
1913/1920

Vassily KANDINSKY
Impression V (Park)
1911

ANONYMOUS
The Combat of Ruslan the Glorious Riding the Serpent to Rescue the Tsarina Anastasia
1880–1900

ANONYMOUS
Saint Martin
ca. 1810–1850

Robert DELAUNAY
The Towers of Laon
1912

August MACKE
Woman's Head in Orange and Brown
ca. 1911

Le Douanier ROUSSEAU
The Painter and His Model
1900–1905

Pablo PICASSO
The Guitar Player
1910

Henri MATISSE
The Gypsy Woman
1905

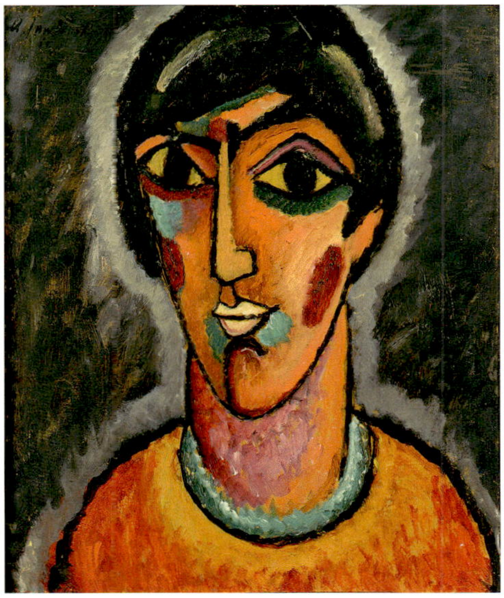

Alexej von JAWLENSKY
Byzantine Woman (Pale Lips)
1913

Max PECHSTEIN
Landscape
1912

FUTURISMO ФУТУРИСТЫ БУДЕТЛЯНЕ HOMMES DU FUTU

Luigi RUSSOLO
Dynamism of a Car
1912–1913

Giacomo BALLA
The Planet Mercury Passes in Front of the Sun
1914

VĚTOVÝ FUTURISMUS FUTURISME MONDIAL SYNTHÉTISME

Jean POUGNY
Chair, Palette, and Violin
ca. 1917-1918

Michel LARIONOV
Stroll. Boulevard Venus
1912-1913

ЛУЧИЗМ LUCIZM RAYONNISME SIMULTANÉISME ВСЕЧЕСТВО

Francis PICABIA
Udnie
1913

František KUPKA
Compliment
1912

TISME ЗАУМЬ ZAUM FUTURYZMU ESTRIDENTISMO ULTRAÍSMO

Raymond DUCHAMP-VILLON
The Big Horse
1914/1955

Marcel DUCHAMP
The Chess Players
1911

Henry VALENSI
Green Symphony
1935

KLAXISMO TACTILISMO ЗЕНИТИЗАМ ZENITIZAM マヴォ

Georges YAKOULOV
Untitled (Abstract Composition)
ca. 1913

Fernand LÉGER
Contrast of Shapes
1913

Amadeo de SOUZA-CARDOSO
Horsemen
1913

O CREACIONISMO IMAGISM VORTICISM VIBRACIONISMO

Virgilio MARCHI
Fantastic City, Building for a Square
1919

Henry VALENSI
Spring Symphony
1936–1960

Sonia DELAUNAY
Cradle Cover
1911

Man RAY
Tapestry
1911

Jean ARP, Sophie TAEUBER-ARP
Pathetic Symmetry
1916–1917

Sophie TAEUBER-ARP
Dada Tapestry
1916

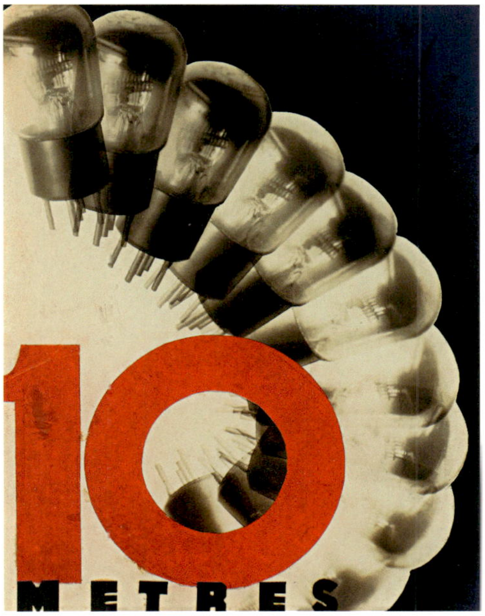

Gaston KARQUEL
"10 Meters." Advertising Sketch for Light Bulbs
ca. 1938

Sonia DELAUNAY
Advertising Sketch for Zenith Watches
1914

Patrick Henry BRUCE
Composition
ca. 1923–1926

Man RAY
Arrangement of Shapes
1917

Walker EVANS
Birmingham Steel Mill and Workers' Houses
1936

Stanton MACDONALD-WRIGHT
Prophecy
1955

Georgia O'KEEFFE
Red, Yellow and Black Streak
1924

Morgan RUSSELL
For the Life of the Material
1925

At the Crossroads of Art, Practice, and Theory

The Kahnweiler-Leiris Collection

Cécile Debray

The collection assembled under the aegis of Daniel-Henry Kahnweiler and Louise and Michel Leiris traces an extraordinary course: it covers three quarters of the 20th century—from 1908 to the early 1970s—building bridges between Western modern art, Cubism in particular, and African, Oceanic, and American art, comparing aesthetic, poetic, ethnographic and anthropological approaches.[1] The fruit of the tastes, interests, and friendships of Pablo Picasso's and Georges Braque's first dealer and Cubism theorist Daniel-Henry Kahnweiler, and those of the writer close to the Surrealists, ethnographer Michel Leiris, the collection notably sheds light on and testifies to debates arising from the discovery of African art and the early days of ethnography in intellectual milieus and modern art circles.

The donation made in 1984 by Louise and Michel Leiris to the National Museum of Modern Art offered a kind of essence of the circle close to Kahnweiler and the Leiris couple and their fields of interest: from the first painters they

1. *Donation Louise et Michel Leiris. Collection Kahnweiler-Leiris*, Paris, Éditions du Centre Pompidou, 1984.

championed as early as 1908—Braque and Picasso [REPR. P. 74]—to the artist friends of Michel Leiris—such as Alberto Giacometti or Francis Bacon [REPR. P. 75]—and finally, the surprising ensemble of extra-occidental works, sculptures from Sub-Saharan Africa [REPR. P. 75], the Americas, or Oceania, acquired by both the elder and the younger, representing a kind of hyphen between two open and curious minds.

This counterpoint of an art today known as "tribal" provides a thematic throughline for this diverse set of paintings, sculptures, and objects, from the questioning of form in Cubist research, to the plurality affirmed by *Documents* magazine, to ethnographic and political practices.

Daniel-Henry Kahnweiler, a young German from Mannheim, destined for a career in finance, arrived in Paris at the turn of the century and, wishing to open a gallery,[2] broached the intellectual and artistic milieus. In 1907, his compatriot Wilhelm Uhde led him to Picasso's studio in the Bateau-Lavoir, where he discovered in the disorder the large painting of the *Demoiselles d'Avignon* and, placed here and there, African sculptures—objects that were in vogue, as the dealer recalls: "Around 1907, a few painters and their friends started to collect, casually, sculptures from Black Africa and Oceania."[3] This interest shared by the first painters championed by Kahnweiler—André Derain, Maurice de Vlaminck, Picasso, and Braque—fueled the development of a type of Cubism that had little to do with the romantic aspiration of a return to origins, as seen in Paul Gauguin's painting or that of the German Expressionists of Die Brücke. Their observation of African statuary accompanied their formal research into a fresh new pictorial form that was more incisive, capable of suggesting movement and involving expressive simplification. "Cubism had assigned to painting the role of plastic text, inventing symbols that signified the outside world instead of imitating it," Kahnweiler wrote many years later.[4] The story of the first objects that Vlaminck and Derain, then Henri Matisse, Picasso, and Guillaume Apollinaire bought and exchanged is well known.[5] Kahnweiler also had a few African and Oceanic pieces that he must have been attached to: these "other" works no doubt enabled him to formulate the basis of his aesthetic questioning.[6] In that respect, he was close to his German or Czech counterparts, who were all Cubist theorists: Vincenc Kramář, Carl Einstein or Wilhelm Uhde.[7] The latter, a great fan of Le Douanier Rousseau's painting [REPR. P. 58], as well as that of Picasso, championed another form of artistic otherness, Naïve art,[8] which Kahnweiler also presented, particularly with the exhibition of Naïve painting "The Unknown" in November 1922, at the Galerie Simon, based on the collections of Fernand Léger, André Lhote, André Malraux, André Masson, and Picasso. Berlin-born intellectual Carl Einstein met Kahnweiler and the Cubist painters in Paris in 1906–1907 and shared the same passion for objects brought back from Africa. Particularly interested in the conception of space, he expressed in his famous book *Negerplastik*[9] the conjunction of the plastic research of painters and the discovery of African works of art. The publication was an initial approach to a history of African sculpture and was funded by the Parisian dealer of

2. He successively opened three galleries in Paris. From 1907 to 1914, he directed the Kahnweiler Gallery at 28 rue Vignon. His assets were seized and confiscated as enemy property during World War I, his artworks sold off cheaply at four auctions held between 1921 and 1923. He opened a second gallery under an associate's name, Simon Gallery, at 29 bis rue d'Astorg, from 1920 to 1940, a gallery that would later be bought back and put under her own name by his daughter-in-law —becoming the Louise Leiris Gallery— during the Occupation while Kahnweiler was under threat as a Jew under the decree of 2 June 1942. The gallery was relocated to new premises at 57 rue de Monceau in 1957.

3. Daniel-Henry Kahnweiler, *Confessions esthétiques*, Paris, Gallimard, 1963, p. 222.

4. D.-H. Kahnweiler, "Avant-propos," in *André Masson*, exh. cat., Lyon, Musée des Beaux-Arts, 1967.

5. William Rubin (ed.), *"Primitivism" in 20th Century Art: Affinity of the Tribal and the Modern*, exh. cat., New York, The Museum of Modern Art, 1984; Colin Rhodes, *Primitivism and Modern Art*, Thames & Hudson, 1994.

6. Most of the African pieces of the donation (34) as well as the three Oceanian objects were bought by Kahnweiler before 1914 (*Donation Louise et Michel Leiris*, op. cit., pp. 230-238.)

7. Wilhelm Uhde wrote *Picasso et la tradition française. Notes sur la peinture actuelle*, Paris, Éditions des Quatre-Chemins, 1928; Vincenc Kramář, a Germanophone Czech and art historian, close to the Berlin and Vienna intellectual milieus, published the book *Kubismus* in 1921 before constituting the modern art collection (featuring Cubist works in particular) at the National Gallery in Prague after World War II. Carl Einstein, besides his articles on numerous artists (Masson, Picasso) and his books on African art, produced a history of the art of the 20th century, *Die Kunst des 20. Jahrhunderts* published in 1931 (cited in Carl Einstein, *Werke*, vol. V, Berlin, Fannei & Walz, 1996).

8. W. Uhde, *Cinq maîtres primitifs. Rousseau, Vivin, Bombois, Bauchant, Séraphine*, A. Ponchont (trans.), Paris, P. Daudy, 1949.

9. C. Einstein, *Negerplastik*, Leipzig, Verlag der Weissen Bücher, 1915.

African and Oceanic art objects, Joseph Brummer. Carl Einstein defined his project as follows: "to have African art works examined from a Cubist perspective," thus enabling him "to identify accomplished examples of Cubist art in Africa." Kahnweiler appreciated the Cubist writer in him, the author of an anti-novel, *Bebuquin oder Die Dilettanten des Wunders* [Bebuquin, or The Dilettantes of the Miracle][10] (1912), in which he reinvents the expression of time and space.[11] A "novel" without a narrator or a story, only a shattering of time into multiple episodes without origins or end. Carl Einstein was very close to Kahnweiler during the war, when the latter, who had sought shelter in Berne, started writing his theoretical book on Cubism, *Der Weg zum Kubismus*.[12] Einstein, with an approach to African art that was both plastic and anthropological (its religious, cultural, and collective dimensions) as well as to the history of art broadly speaking, concurred with the magazine *Documents*, whose subheading "Doctrines, archeology, fine arts, ethnography" announced the shift toward a more open conception of art and the anti-aesthetic position.[13] Alongside Georges Bataille and Georges-Henri Rivière, assistant director and reformer of the Ethnographic Museum of the Trocadéro from April 1929 to January 1931, he edited the 15 issues of this magazine with its deliberately eclectic iconography: popular art, ethnography, modern works by Picasso and Masson, documentary and clinical photography by Jacques-André Boiffard [REPR. P. 75]. Leiris joined the magazine as assistant editor. Close to Masson [REPR. P. 158] and the group of friends (the poet Roland Tual, reader of Sade and Lautréamont, Georges Limbour, Antonin Artaud, Joan Miró, and Bataille, among others) from the rue Blomet, the painter's home, he was part of a dissident group that broke away from Surrealism, founded on a rejection of André Breton's aestheticism and federated through a shared interest in a multidisciplinary approach combining anthropology, scientific naturalism, poetry, and psychoanalysis, and through a fascination for all forms of otherness capable of reformulating the questions of transgression, normality, and identity. Einstein, through his acute analysis of Cubism and African art, his presence among the ranks of the German Jewish intelligentsia, his theoretical and literary talent, emerged as the almost generational link between Kahnweiler and Leiris, his son-in-law.[14] In the same way, Masson, a painter from the Simon Gallery, became one of Leiris' closest friends. For the latter, travel and ethnographic activities sustained an analytical and literary quest, as well as his unique perspective concerning his friends' work.[15] For instance, in an article on Giacometti's sculpture, Leiris suggested a connection with the magical powers of the "fetishes" of Black Africa: "I love Giacometti's sculpture because everything he does is like the petrification of one of these crises, the intensity of an adventure taken by surprise and immediately fixed, the milepost that testifies to it. However, there is nothing dead about this sculpture; on the contrary, it's all there, like the real fetishes that people worship as idols (real fetishes: meaning those that relate to us and represent

10. C. Einstein, *Bebuquin oder die Dilettanten des Wunders. Ein Roman*, Berlin, Verlag der Wochenschrift/Die Aktion, 1912.

11. C. Einstein, D.-H. Kahnweiler, *Correspondance, 1921–1939*, French trans. presented and annotated by L. Meffre, Marseille, A. Dimanche, 1993.

12. Kahnweiler, in exile in Switzerland, spent the war studying art history and philosophy; in particular, he read the Viennese art historian Aloïs Riegl and articulated his interpretation of Cubism based on a Neo-Kantian analysis in *Der Weg zum Kubismus* (Munich, Delphin-Verlag, 1920). He wrote that Cubism revealed the basic geometry of bodies in space, since these geometric forms were the "visual categories" essential to our perception of the world.

13. See Georges Didi-Huberman, *Devant le temps. Histoire de l'art et anachronisme des images*, Paris, Éditions de Minuit, 2000, and "Carl Einstein et les Primitivismes," *Gradhiva*, no. 14, 2011.

14. Michel Leiris married Louise Godon (the natural daughter of Lucie Kahnweiler) in 1926.

15. Since we do not have the space here to summarize all of the various works and activities of Michel Leiris, let us recall his interest in non-Western civilizations, psychoanalysis, and different forms of representations (or disfigurations)—including the portraits of Picasso, Masson, Giacometti or Bacon—as well as his literary work in the form of a self-portrait initiated by *L'Âge d'Homme* (1939) and continued in the four volumes of *La Règle du jeu* (between 1948 and 1976.)

the objectified form of our desire), prodigiously alive, endowed with a charming life and a good dose of humor, a beautiful expression of this sentimental ambivalence, the gentle sphinx that we continue to nourish, more or less secretly, in our heart of hearts." [16]

At the invitation of Marcel Griaule, Leiris' participation in the famous Dakar-Djibouti mission (1931–1933), traversing Sub-Saharan Africa from west to east and thus founding field ethnology, was decisive for his career as an ethnologist. He was also involved in the creation of the Musée de l'Homme, inaugurated in 1938. His travel log, *L'Afrique fantôme* [Phantom Africa], published in 1934, expressed a reflexive and concerned distance with respect to the practices of object collections, and a denunciation of colonialism—a moral and political engagement that underpinned his perception of artworks. Therefore, several studies conducted after his missions—like that of the belief in Zaar spirits in Northern Ethiopia, exploring phenomena relating to possession,[17] or those concerning voodoo rites in the West Indies (Haiti, Guadeloupe, and Martinique) in 1948 and 1952—were in line with the poetic research of the likes of Artaud (who left in 1936 for Mexico to observe theatrical and sacrificial rites) or Bataille, based on hallucination, magic, the face and its theatrical appearances, and the effacing of the subject behind ritual and mask. A large proportion of the objects given to the Musée de l'Homme by Leiris reflect this curiosity:[18] African masks offered to the new Museum of Oceanic and African Arts in 1960,[19] objects from voodoo rituals, fragments of ceramics in the form of human heads from the Taïno culture, collected during his mission with Alfred Métraux to the West Indies in October 1948.[20] Besides the works handed down by bequest,[21] there are around one hundred Chinese paper cutouts, folkloric images brought back by Leiris from his trip to China in 1955.[22] Among this set of objects we thus find a combination of sculptures acquired as works of art or objects "that operate symbolically," craft pieces and collected objects, and the remains of rituals and other social practices.

While the collection of modern artworks that draws together Kahnweiler's painters (including Braque, Picasso, Léger, Juan Gris, Masson, André Beaudin, Eugène de Kermadec, Gaston-Louis Roux, Élie Lascaux, and Paul Klee) and the artists close to Leiris (Miró, Giacometti, Bacon) presents the diversity inherent to the two men's careers over several decades, it nonetheless reveals a striking and surprising coherency through their mutual interest in a form of figuration torn between the formal solutions of Cubism and surrealistic explorations of images with new geometric or hallucinatory possibilities in the perception of space and figures.

Translated from the French by Anna Knight

16. M. Leiris, "Alberto Giacometti," *Documents*, no. 4, September 1929, p. 214.

17. Id., *La Possession et ses aspects théâtraux chez les Éthiopiens de Gondar*, Paris, Plon, 1958.

18. The Leiris collection at the Quai Branly Museum contains 304 objects: 107 fragments of earthenware vases from the Taino culture (known as "postwar Arawak") found in Haiti; 24 polished adzes, terracotta crockery, basketwork, 107 Chinese paper cutouts, and 66 African objects. I would like to thank André Delpuech and Hélène Joubert, curators at the Quai Branly Museum, for their advice.

19. Michel Leiris was a member of the museum's acquisitions committee. Since its closure in 2003, the objects have entered the collection of the Quai Branly Museum (ref. 75.11496 75.11513; 75.11509; 75.11525; 75.11503; 75.11517, etc.).

20. Donation of Alfred Métraux and M. Leiris (archeology of Haiti-Arawak civilization, obtained in October 1948): ceramic fragment (vase); the following description appears on the file from the former Musée de l'Homme: "All of the objects were found on the ground in the place where the current inhabitants live. They call the pottery fragments '*zye la te*,' meaning 'flows of the earth' and the polished stone tools are referred to as 'stones,' while ordinary stones are 'rocks'" (Archives of the Quai Branly Museum). I would like to thank Sarah Frioux-Salgas for giving me access to this information.

21. Note of 19 December 1990 from Francine N'Diaye, from the Black Africa department: "Received from the Americas department: 34 African objects that belonged to Daniel-Henry Kahnweiler and Michel Leiris" (Archives of the Quai Branly Museum).

22. The following description appears in the original file from the Musée de l'Homme: "Gift from M. Leiris, 1955, Chinese ethnography. Peking. Sleeves containing colorful cutout 'Chien Tse' paper images made by block stamping, using chemical colors and guillotine trimming with metal matrices. Price: 2 yen 60 and fine paper colored on both sides. Bought for 2 yen 80 at Wang Fou Tsin, art services on 24.9.55. Peking" (Archives of the Quai Branly Museum). I would like to thank Hélia Paukner and Anna Hiddleston for their assistance.

Pablo PICASSO
Reclining Nude
1936

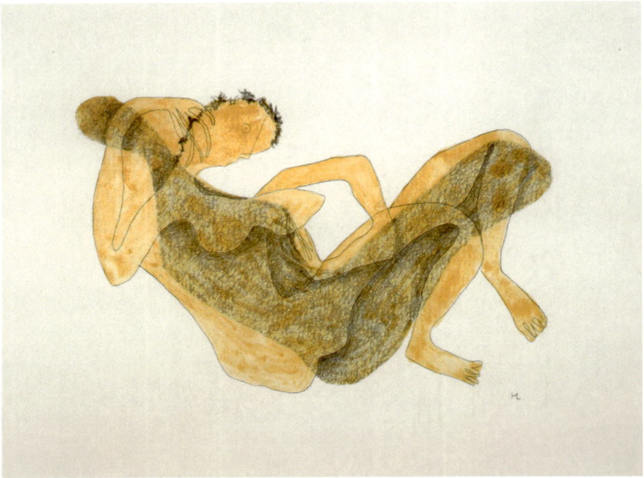

Henri LAURENS
Reclining Woman
1950

Suzanne ROGER
Riot with Knives
1934

Jacques-André BOIFFARD
Untitled (Hooded Man)
1930

ANONYMOUS
Anthropomorphic Face Mask (Dogon)
n.d.

Francis BACON
Study for a Portrait
1978

Vassily KANDINSKY
Yellow-Red-Blue
1925

Marianne BRANDT
Study of Elementary Colors and Shapes
1923–1924

HIROSHIGE
Famous Places of Our Land
Shichirigahama in Sagama Province
19th century

Lyonel FEININGER
Marine
1924

Paul KLEE
KN the Smith
1922

ANONYMOUS
Untitled
n.d.

Vladimir TATLIN
Model of the Monument to the Third International
1919–1920/1979

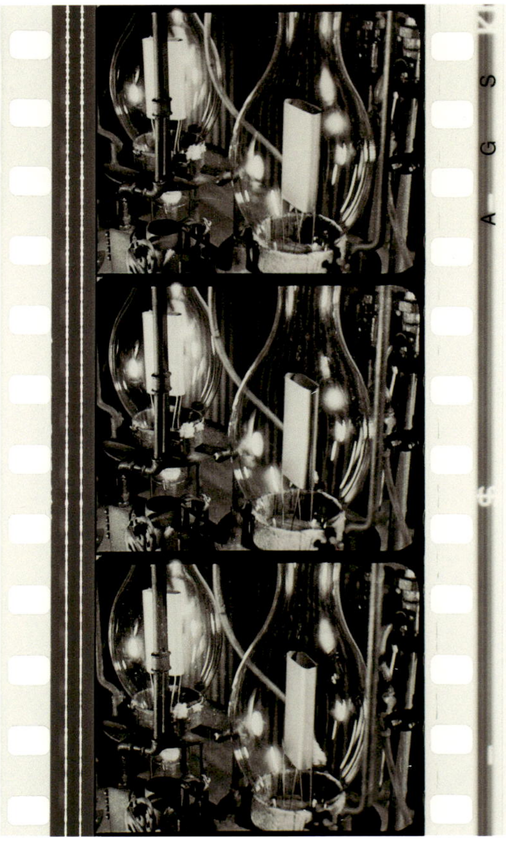

Joris IVENS
Philips Radio (Industrial Symphony)
1931

Kazimir MALEVICH
Black Cross
1915

Antoine PEVSNER
Mask
1923

Vladimir TATLIN
Chair
1927

Vilmos HUSZÁR
Composition-Flowers
1923

Iakov Georgievich CHERNIKHOV
Architectural Fantasies. Composition 3
1933

Paul MANSOUROFF
Sketch for Grandstand III. Design for Red Square Decorations for May Day 1921
1921

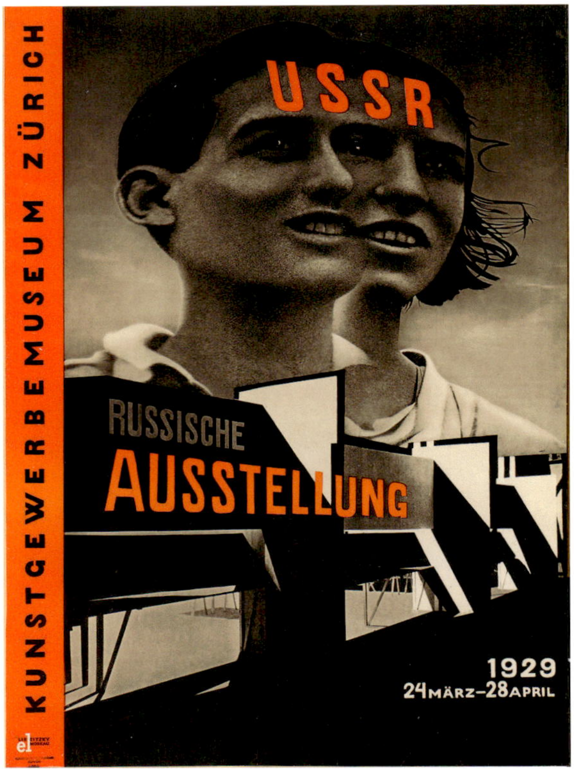

El LISSITZKY
Poster for the 1929 Russian Exhibition at the Zurich Museum of Decorative Arts
1929

Jaroslav RÖSSLER
Eiffel Tower, Paris
1929

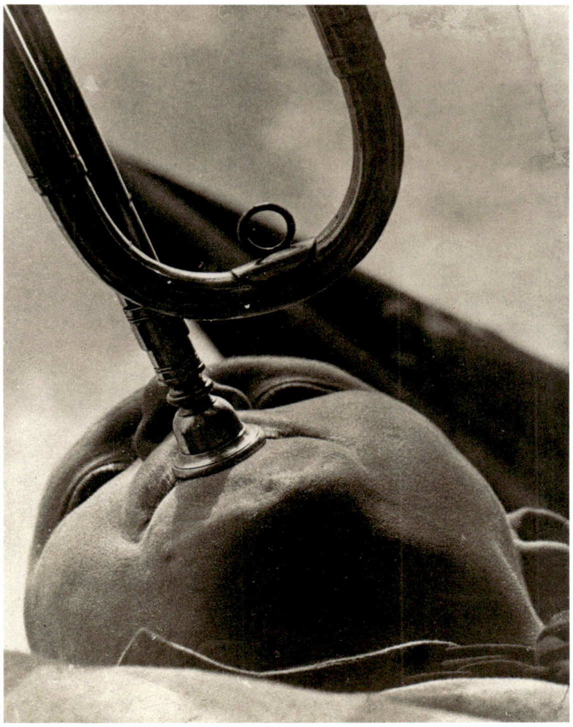

Alexander RODCHENKO
Pioneer Playing the Trumpet
1930

ANONYMOUS
Tobacco Pavilion (architect: Constantin Melnikov); Agriculture and Craft Fair, Moscow
1923

László MOHOLY-NAGY
Composition A.XX
1924

Willi BAUMEISTER
Wall Painting with Circle
1923

Lajos TIHANYI
La Rue de la Glacière
1925

ANDREENKO
Painting
1924

Joaquín TORRES-GARCÍA
Universal Composition
1937

Piet MONDRIAN
Composition in Red, Blue, and White II
1937

Pierre DAURA
Painting
1928–1930

Joaquín TORRES-GARCÍA
Fish
ca. 1942

Auguste HERBIN
Sculpture
1921

Kurt SCHWITTERS
MZ 1926.2. selbst oben
1926

Multiple Realisms

Catherine Grenier

In 1981, the Centre Pompidou held an exhibition devised by Jean Clair and entitled "Realisms." Despite its subtitle, "Between Revolution and Reaction," and the painstaking efforts made by the authors of the catalogue[1] to distinguish between the different categories of works and their ideological leanings, the event failed to lift the leaden weight of the "return to order" that had crushed and indiscriminately collapsed together the entire spectrum of post-World War I figurative artists. By implying that realist works were politically as well as aesthetically biased, the term limited the far-reaching implications of this highly significant international trend, keeping it solely within the bounds of the debate that had taken place on the French art scene during the 1920s. Even today it retains a stigma, despite the fact that other partisans of the reinstatement of the subject, such as the Surrealists, managed to emerge unscathed. From the "return to order" given the seal of approval by Jean Cocteau[2] to the "quarrel of realism" initiated by

1. Jean Clair (ed.), *Les Réalismes, 1919–1939*, exh. cat., Paris, Éditions du Centre Pompidou, 1980.

2. The expression "return to order" was coined by the critic Roger Bissière in 1917 in a review of a Georges Braque exhibition; it was taken up by Jean Cocteau as the title of one of his works, published in 1926. Jean Laude refers to a process of "historical reconstruction" leading to an a-historical, ideological, and unequivocal reading of the 1920–1930 Realisms ("La crise de l'humanisme et la fin des utopies," in *L'Art face à la crise. L'art en Occident, 1929–1939*, the proceedings of a conference on contemporary history of art delivered at the Université de Saint-Étienne [France], 1980). On the same subject, see Annick Lantenois' "Analyse critique d'une formule: retour à l'ordre," *Vingtième Siècle. Revue d'histoire*, 1995, vol. 45, no. 45, pp. 40-53 (available online at http://www.persee.fr/web/revues/home/prescript/article/xxs_0294-1759_1995_num_45_1_3381).

Louis Aragon, the multiplicity of realist artistic expression found itself reduced to a single element, anti-modernism, deemed reprehensible by its very nature. The fact that totalitarianism regimes had chosen and imposed Neoclassic and Naturalist aesthetics was fundamental in creating this univocal reading, contributing to a retrospective interpretation of realisms as anticipation of, or even preparation for, a return to order that would prove to be political rather than aesthetic, coercive rather than voluntary.

To facilitate a more objective and multi-faceted reappraisal of realisms, it might have been better to go beyond Europe and broaden the scope to encompass the entire world, particularly Latin America. In that configuration, both the term "return" and the notion of "order" seem poorly suited to contexts of burgeoning modernity in which avant-garde proclamations frequently conjoined with the realist lexicon. Brazil was a case in point: the conditions that paved the way for artistic modernity opened up a new angle of inquiry which in turn led to a reappraisal of the approach adopted by a number of European realists. To the artists who had rallied to the *Anthropophagic Manifesto* (1928) [REPR. P. 98], the first emblematic sign of militant modernity on Latin American soil, an adherence to Realism neither betrayed an ignorance of the radical avant-gardes nor the abandonment of the utopian remit of art. All the participants were perfectly aware of developments in European art—the most eminent were even living in Paris, having nailed their colors to the avant-garde mast in France before pervading São Paulo with the spirit of modernity. "I did my military service in Cubism," proclaimed one of its leading protagonists, Tarsila [REPR. P. 99]. Although this return to their roots to help lay the foundations of a modern movement took place within the realm of figurative painting, the latter betrayed neither relinquishment nor nostalgia. In fact it was not impervious to the modernist credo, the object of the "ritual feast" celebrated by its modern-day anthropophagic representatives, who incorporated Cubist plastic art into the realist image. The Brazilians, like most of the Mexican, Argentinean, and Peruvian followers of the modern movement, reverted to the sphere of iconography because it was the mode of expression favored by the Resistance. A Resistance with a twofold agenda: to refute any attempt by Europe to impose an artistic language and to counter the colonial legacy by exalting indigenous culture. In Mexico, during the same decade, Diego Rivera [REPR. P. 112] and the Muralists were campaigning in favor of "the spiritual independence of Mexico" and targeting their art at the people.[3] In 1933, José Clemente Orozco declared: "The resurgence of frescoes is the sign of a revolution in artistic methods."[4] When these artists distanced themselves from the modernist lexicon, they were not abandoning Cubism itself but the watered-down version that flourished once the foundational period had passed. By 1928, the year of the *Anthropophagic Manifesto*, it was already thirteen years since figurative painting had found its way back onto Pablo Picasso's palette. Back in 1915, his output of portraits in the classic style [REPR. P. 119] was already pointing toward the declamatory gesture of his vast backdrop for the ballet *Parade* (1917), which was to unleash a scandal in the art world and perplexity among his entourage. In so doing,

3. Quoted by Raquel Tibol, "Le muralisme," in *L'Art d'Amérique Latine, 1911–1968*, exh. cat., Paris, Éditions du Centre Pompidou, 1992, p. 190.

4. Quoted by Serge Fauchereau, "La naissance du muralisme mexicain," in *L'Art d'Amérique Latine, 1911–1968*, op. cit., p. 192.

Picasso was not abandoning Cubism, to which he long remained faithful, but opting for stylistic freedom. Also in 1917, and for the same reason, Rivera triggered outrage among their mutual friends. Condemning the "whimsical" reappropriations of the new proponents of Cubism, Pierre Reverdy wrote of Rivera: "It goes without saying that we cannot condone a portrait created by a Cubist painter."[5] Rivera retorted by slapping Reverdy and the quarrel culminated in a vengeful description published by the poet, in which he portrayed the Mexican painter as an ill-bred, cowardly Indian, whose only way of fighting the revolutionary cause was through words.[6] In Picasso's case, no blows were exchanged and there was no question of being labeled a "foreign upstart" like Rivera. The convergence of these deviations from the orthodoxy of the avant-garde, embodied by the movement's founder and a latecomer on the scene, is nevertheless of considerable significance. As the flame of Cubism died down, following its short-lived revolutionary period, many artists started looking for new and more personal approaches. In rekindling the embers of the avant-garde, the Dada movement had no hesitation in declaring Cubism obsolete,[7] although Dada itself turned out to be only a flash in the pan and petered out after 1922. From 1918, the magazine *Valori plastici*, reflecting the crisis in Futurism, called for a return to the Italian masters. In 1921, Gino Severini [REPR. P. 119] recalled the laws of harmony in his *From Cubism to Classicism*, advocating an "aesthetic of the compass and number."[8] The magazine *L'Esprit nouveau*, launched the preceding year by Amédée Ozenfant and Le Corbusier, suggested overstepping the boundaries of easel paintings through the architectural dimension of mural painting, and allying anthropomorphic reference and constructive form. Fernand Léger epitomized this to perfection in his large compositions at the crossroads of Cubism and Realism [REPR. P. 64]. This exhortation to drive painting into the social arena chimed in with developments in modern architecture, the realm of predilection of a form of architectonic realism, as well as the abstract and figurative gamut of Art Deco. The art scene in France emerged from World War I in a state of turmoil. Veterans whose utopian vision had been shaken to the core by their experience in the front line found themselves mixing with newcomers from every corner of the globe. Even more cosmopolitan than before, Paris became a melting-pot for artists from countries in the newly-formed Soviet Union, Germany, Central Europe, and the United States, but also Latin America, Asia, the Middle and Far East, and South Africa. These artists gleaned their lessons from several sources at once: for those who had come over to study, Academism was still on the curriculum; as for exiles and travelers, they could pick and choose between Modernism and an eclectic range of Realisms. Figurative paintings and sculpture were produced by artists reintegrating the subject into the constructive style, by renegade Modernists, and by artists who had never adhered to avant-garde aesthetics in the first place. Artists' studios were therefore a glorious mix of figurative Modernist stylization,

5. P. Reverdy, "Sur le cubisme," *Nord-Sud*, no. 1, 15 March 1917; reprinted in "Diego Rivera, ou comment ne plus être 'cubiste'" by Christian Derouet, in *L'Art d'Amérique Latine, 1911–1968*, op. cit., p. 62.

6. Ibid., p. 62.

7. Francis Picabia, *Manifeste dada*, read out at the Salon des Indépendants on 5 February 1920: "Cubism represents the dearth of ideas. They cubed primitive paintings, cubed Negro sculptures, cubed violins, cubed guitars, cubed picture magazines, cubed shit and girls' profiles and now they want to cube money!!!"

8. Gino Severini, *From Cubism to Classicism*, Peter Brooke (trans.), London, Francis Boutle Publishers, 2001.

9. Quoted by Jan Walravens, "Rencontre avec Magritte," 1962; reprinted in *Magritte. Écrits complets*, edited and annotated by André Blavier, Paris, Flammarion, 2009, p. 535.

10. During the same period a great "mural cycle of Modern Times" was launched in Mexico. The artists who took part, all adepts of European modernity, advocated an anti-elitist monumental art and developed an eclectic realism.

Neoclassicism after David or Ingres, references to the grand Renaissance or pre-Renaissance masters, and the influences of Seurat and the latest Renoir or Matisse, not to mention the Naïve painters. Their aesthetics, references, and purpose were equally diverse. Both newcomers and young artists found themselves tantalized by a range of aesthetic possibilities. Many of them must have been familiar with the dilemma described by René Magritte: "In 1921, I could not make up my mind whether to paint like the Cubists, the Futurists, traditional, or abstract painters. Their theories were obviously contradictory and held enormous fascination for me."[9] A number therefore opted for interpretation and hybridization. André Lhote's blend of Cubism and figurative art earned worldwide recognition thanks to the success of his academy, attended by artists from a host of strikingly different countries. Art Deco was another manifestation of this desire for synthesis. A hybrid mix of Cubism and Realism that placed Modernist inspiration within a more popular framework this frequently derided style actually had an exceptional impact on a wide range of countries as far afield as Latin America, Asia, and the Middle East. The advent of this "Realist Modernism" also brought major women artists to the forefront of the Paris art scene, namely Marie Laurencin, Maria Blanchard [REPR. P. 123], and Tamara de Lempicka [REPR. P. 123].

Anthropophagy and Indigenismo

The *Anthropophagic Manifesto* represented the culmination of a movement that had been given its initial impetus in the early 1920s.[10] The seminal event was the art festival Semana de Arte Moderna [Modern Art Week], held in São Paulo in 1922. The participants did not stem from a homogenous group and their works were imbued with an eclectic mix of European references, Expressionist, Cubist, and Dadaist. In the wake of this festival, artists from all realms joined forces to steer Brazil into the era of modernity. At the instigation of two poets, Oswald de Andrade and Mário de Andrade, a group was formed. They solicited the artists living in Paris, who left Europe to fire up the São Paulo art scene. In his *Pau-Brasil Manifesto* (1924), Oswald de Andrade outlined their plan of campaign: to create a national art that would promote indigenous cultures and throw off the mantle of colonialist culture while also riding on the crest of modernity. To tempt Tarsila back to her homeland, Mário de Andrade made the following entreaty: "Tarsila, Tarsila, come back to yourself. Abandon Gris and Lhote [...]. Come back to the virgin forest. That is the entreaty made by the world, art, Brazil, and by you."[11] Although she felt at home in Paris—she studied under Lhote, her clothes were designed by Paul Poiret, and she had befriended, among others, Constantin Brancusi, Léger, and Blaise Cendrars (she illustrated his anthology of poems, *Feuilles de route* [Roadmaps] in 1924)—Tarsila gave in and agreed to opt for "Brazilianity." A constellation of artists was thus formed, including Di Cavalcanti (the organizer of Modern Art Week), Monteiro [REPR. P. 100], Tarsila, Candido Portinari [REPR. P. 101] and Lasar Segall [REPR. P. 98], a Lithuanian émigré who melded perfectly into the Brazilian scene. As Oswald de Andrade was to recall, the movement stemmed from an increase in political awareness. When he made his first visit to Paris in 1912, "pacifist Europe" and "la vie de bohème" kept him "at bay

11. Letter from Mário de Andrade to Tarsila, November 1923, quoted by Alfredo Medina, "La fondation de l'art latino-américain," in *L'Art d'Amérique Latine, 1911–1968*, op. cit., p. 35.

from the revolutionary axis of the world."[12] Nevertheless, it was in the context of postwar Paris, and influenced by the deconsecration meted out by the avant-gardes, that in 1924 he called for a reversal of European-New World relations. "The work of the Futurist generation was cyclopean," he explained, "but now that this bridge has been crossed the problem is different."[13] In his view, the aim was now "to be regional and pure in one's era."[14] Four years later, now back in Brazil, he proclaimed in his *Anthropophagic Manifesto* that "We want a Caribbean revolution."[15] The most famous quote from the manifesto, "Tupi or not tupi, that is the question"[16] encapsulates the commitment to indigenous cultures that was to characterize these modern artists and nourish their iconography.[17] The architect Flávio de Carvalho [REPR. P. 165] represented the "anthropophagics" at the 4th Pan-American Congress of Architecture in 1930 with a project that neatly summed up the philosophy of the movement: "The City of the Naked Man aims to resurrect primitive man, released from Western taboos [...], the savage with all his desires and curiosity intact, no longer repressed as in the days of the colonial conquest."[18] The main common denominator between these artists was their description of popular life and in particular that of the indigenous populations. There were also recurrent references to Pre-Columbian art. This commitment to Amerindian culture and the depiction of untamed nature were traits that cropped up on all the Latin American art scenes of the period. They mirrored the Indigenista political movement that had surfaced in the 1910s, in the wake of the Mexican revolution. This Indigenismo left its mark on a range of burgeoning artistic trends and produced politically motivated works and a picturesque genre—"Brazilianizing Brazil",[19] "Let's Peruvianize Peru,"[20] and "Colombianizing Colombia."[21] These artistic slogans, which were launched almost simultaneously, effectively capture the political agenda behind the indigenous references. Coming from artists who had rubbed shoulders with the European avant-gardes, like the "anthropophagics" in Brazil, the Muralists in Mexico, Oswaldo Guyasamin in Ecuador, Alfredo Gramajo Gutiérrez in Argentina [REPR. P. 103], Carlos Mérida in Guatemala, and Julia Codesido in Peru [REPR. P. 103], their nationalist preoccupations and commitment to the Indigenista cause were not incompatible with the feeling that they were taking an active part in the global sea change of modernity. As Andrade put it, however, this had to be a two-way process: "Let us separate: Imported poetry. And Pau-Brasil poetry, which is exported."[22] Brazilian musician Heitor Villa-Lobos gave his take on it, declaring after his first visit to Paris that "I did not go there to learn; I came to show what I had done."[23] Implementing these mission statements turned out to be more complicated, as the Latin American artists' relationship with Europe was usually underscored by a desire for synthesis.

12. Quoted by Mario Carelli, "À Paris, les Brésiliens à l'affût de la modernité," in *Les Réalismes, 1919–1939*, op. cit., p. 95.

13. Oswald de Andrade, "Manifeste de la poésie Pau Brasil" in *L'Art d'Amérique Latine, 1911–1968*, op. cit., p. 129.

14. Ibid.

15. *The Anthropophagic Manifesto* (1928), reprinted in *L'Art d'Amérique Latine, 1911–1968*, op. cit., pp. 130-131.

16. Tupi is one of the indigenous dialects spoken in Brazil.

17. In 1921, David Alfaro Siqueiros published a manifesto in Barcelona. It included illustrations by Joaquín Torres-García, who proclaimed: "All we glean from Europe is wishy-washy influences that poison our youth. [...] Let us go back to the works of the ancient inhabitants of our valleys, the Indian painters and sculptors (Maya, Aztec, Inca, etc.)," quoted by A. Medina, "La fondation de l'art latino-américain," art. cit., p.30.

18. Flávio de Carvalho, "A cidade do homem nu," delivered to the Pan-American Congress of Architects, Rio de Janeiro, 1930. Published in *Diario da noite*, 1 July 1930 and reprinted in Inti Guerrero, "Flávio de Carvalho," *Afterall*, no. 24, summer 2010.

19. The group that was formed around *Verde* magazine in Brazil suggested "Brazilianizing Brazil, at our own risk" (quoted by A. Medina, "La fondation de l'art latino-américain," art. cit., p. 35).

20. "Peruanicemos al Perú" was the title of a piece written by José Carlos Mariátegui in the journal *Mundial*, Lima, 11 September 1925.

21. A suggestion made by the founders of the Colombian avant-garde group Bachué, quoted by A. Medina, "La fondation de l'art latino-américain," art. cit., p. 35.

22. O. de Andrade, "Manifeste de la poésie Pau Brasil," art. cit., pp. 128-129.

23. Quoted by Mario Carelli, "L'avant-garde brésilienne," in *L'Art d'Amérique Latine, 1911–1968*, op. cit., p. 99.

24. In his strident manifesto written in 1921, the Mexican poet Manuel Maples Arce proclaimed: "No creationism, Dadaism, paroxysm, expressionism, sythetism, imaginism, suprematism, cubism, orphism, etc., etc., no vaguely theoreticized or effective 'isms'. We need a quintessential, purifying synthesis." To achieve this, he suggested: "Making art with innate, congenital elements conceived in their own environment. We should not reintegrate values but create them from start to finish" (quoted by A. Medina, "La fondation de l'art latino-américain," art. cit., p. 33).

Indeed this was the term that was used in most of the manifestos and declarations, indicating a stance that was both aesthetic and cultural. Thus interpreted, synthesis did not preclude cultural differences but promoted the expression of specific identities by means of a common language.[24]

Social Realism and Antifascism

A great many artists saw figurative art as a way of depicting the political and social ambience of the period. In Germany, for instance, a commitment to Socialism and the scars left by the war led several Expressionist or Dadaist artists to draw from life and depict the outcasts of the inter-war years and the decadence of society. Otto Dix [REPR. P. 119] and George Grosz [REPR. P. 107] developed a critical and razor-sharp figurative form, halfway between caricature and hyper-objectivity. "No more Futurist romanticism but an impersonal line, like a photographic construction," insisted Grosz.[25] In all the other European countries, not least in France, and in both North and South America, Realist motifs portraying social subjects became all the rage. They showed the workplace as well as tramps and beggars, the misery of daily life but also popular fetes, family homes alongside dives and prostitution. Although they may be overlooked today, the works of Yves Alix [REPR. P. 105], Marcel Gromaire [REPR. P. 104], Constant Permeke [REPR. P. 109], Frans Masereel [REPR. P. 109], Joseph Kutter [REPR. P. 104], Maruja Mallo [REPR. P. 122], Portinari [REPR. P. 101], Monteiro [REPR. P. 100] and Di Cavalcanti [REPR. P. 99] all clearly depict art's preoccupations with society. Artists opted for a style that could be read both as a description and as a protest, a Naturalist figurative form far removed from the Neoclassical remit to aestheticize reality and often rendered more effective and brutal through Cubist-inspired structuralization, which lent it a sculptural aspect. Many of these artists were Communist sympathizers. One could also find subjects with a social connotation, however, in works by artists of a reactionary persuasion. Noucentisme, a Catalan-identified realist movement first propagated by the poet Eugenio d'Ors in 1906, depicted popular life in the name of regionalist cultural values that were not dissimilar from those developed by the Indigenista, even though their political lines were radically different. The Italian members of the Novecento movement, created in the early 1920s by the Fascist art critic Margherita Sarfatti, set about defending Italianism through the portrayal of everyday city and rural life among the people. Despite their ideological message, however, the paintings were stylistically no different from the principal Realist trends of the time and can therefore be compared to both Social and Magic Realism. A number of artists, however, only skirted around these movements, without adhering wholeheartedly to the ideologies they were propounding. Both Joaquín Torres-García and Salvador Dalí went through a period tinged with Noucentism. During the 1930s, the propaganda art of Social Realism and Nazi art imposed a prescriptive realism, demonstratively glorifying the people and borrowing the forms of a nineteenth-century Naturalist aesthetic or a version of Neoclassicism that sometimes verged on pastiche.

The rise of fascism generated a more prolific artistic output than that of World War I, which was relatively modest. The figurative language

25. George Grosz, *Das Kunstblatt*, 5th year, no. 1, quoted in *Les Réalismes, 1919–1939*, op. cit., p. 508.

which made a comeback among a number of artists during the 1920s paved the way for a more bellicose art form. Nazism, then the cruelty meted out by Franco's troops during the Spanish Civil War, gave rise to a multiplicity of works in a range of different modes. Victor Brauner, for instance, used two methods: a caricature of the main Nazi leaders and the metaphor of the dictator, depicted in the guise of a grotesque figure [REPR. P. 131]. German artists, for their part, opted for the violence of monstrous realism and caricature. Broadly speaking, works fell into two categories, the metaphorical and the descriptive. This is borne out, for example, in works by international artists determined to express their indignation at the Spanish Civil War. Even before Picasso's famous *Guernica*, protests and wake-up calls were rife. André Masson was to stigmatize destructive power in his symbolic depiction of death in the bullfighting ring (*The Spurt of Blood*, 1936), Ismaël de la Serna conveyed in hallucinatory style the prophetic vision of a Europe reduced to serfdom [REPR. P. 130], while Edmond Küss produced a detailed, cruel description of torture and murder [REPR. P. 133]. In Latin America, where political art was particularly developed, the anti-fascist movement had a special impact. The process of engraving carried out in collective workshops led to a significant production of works designed for publication in anti-fascist magazines.

Magic Realism

In 1925, Spanish intellectual José Ortega y Gasset created a stir with his work *The Dehumanization of Art.*[26] The author claimed that the West was undergoing a cultural crisis and analyzed the divisions between the new languages of art, which despite their revolutionary tone only reached the ears of the elite, and a society hostile to artistic modernity. Even if his criticism was basically targeting conservative bourgeois culture rather than the modernist expressions themselves, his description of an art devoid of any human figure, dominated by trickery and absurdity, was to trigger a debate in European and Latin American artistic circles, thereby encouraging or legitimizing a widespread return to figurative art. That same year, a book by Franz Roh with the subtitle *Magischer Realismus* [Magic Realism][27] acknowledged an artistic practice that was now predominant in Germany and used the same term to embrace the many different forms of Realism that had emerged in Europe since World War I. While finding common ground and yet distinguishing between right-wing and left-wing realisms, his essay attributed the movements' desire for objectivity to the trauma of the war, although he also stressed its "magic" dimension, the hermetic and melancholic quality of the images produced. The term "Magic Realism" had already been used by Joan Miró to describe the series of works that included *Interior* (*The Farmer's Wife*) (1922–1923). Embracing an essentially heterogeneous reality and overtaken by concepts such as "New Objectivity" and "Surrealism," it was not to last. The Spanish translation of Roh's book in the review edited by Ortega y Gasset brought the term to a Latin American audience, however, and gave it a new lease of life. The work offered the same slant on the metaphysical

26. José Ortega y Gasset, "La Deshumanizacíon del arte e ideas sobre la novela," *Revista de Occidente*, 1925; American edition: *The Dehumanization of Art and Other Essays on Art, Culture and Literature*, Princeton, Princeton University Press, 1968.

27. The full title of this work by Franz Roh is *Nach-Expressionismus. Magischer Realismus. Probleme der neuesten Europäischen Malerei* [After Expressionism. Magic Realism. Problems of the latest European painting.], Leipzig, Klinkhardt & Biermann, 1925. It was abridged and translated into Spanish by Fernando Vela and published in *Revista de Occidente*, edited by Ortega y Gasset, Madrid, in 1927, under the title *Realismo Mágico*.

works of Giorgio De Chirico [REPR. P. 120] and Carlo Carrà, whose "worrying strangeness" heralded the movement, those of the Germans of every realist persuasion, from Otto Dix [REPR. P. 105] to Christian Schad [REPR. P. 121] and Max Ernst [REPR. P. 121] and those of artists living in France who had reverted to figurative art, like Picasso [REPR. P. 119], André Derain [REPR. P. 120], Auguste Herbin [REPR. P. 85] and Balthus [REPR. P. 121]. Many of the cosmopolitan artists from the School of Paris were categorized as belonging to the school of Magic Realism, including Ivan Babij [REPR. P. 120], Léonard Foujita [REPR. P. 138], Johannes Kahrs, and Moïse Kisling. The comparison of two different types of work, inspired by diametrically opposed political views—the left-wing Berliners' Verism and the right-wing Neo-Traditionalism of their Munich counterparts—was strongly contested from the outset. This justifiable ideological distinction cannot, however, disguise the fact that a powerful aesthetic current certainly existed in the 1920s and 1930s, comprising a mix of individuals and expressions far more composite, and even at times ambiguous, than might first appear from the mere political divide.[28] The characteristics of these realisms are mainly of a psychological nature: they encapsulate a disillusioned vision of a society in which the individual is devoid of the slightest heroic dimension and frequently dehumanized or reified. Roh emphasizes the "cold cerebral nature" of these representations, which he sets against both Naturalism and Expressionism. The concept of "Magic Realism" chosen as a means of bringing them together owed as much to the "magic silence" Carrà found in Giotto as to the romanticism of Novalis. A number of common themes spanned these different expressions: reflection and the double portrait, illustrated by several examples in the Centre Pompidou collections (De Chirico, Mario Sironi, Severini [REPR. P. 118], Léger, Schad, Babij, and Felice Casorati [REPR. P. 118]), masquerade and pantomime (Picasso, Maruja Mallo [REPR. P. 122], Derain), the impassivity of bodies, the neutrality of objects, and the suspension of time (Carrà, Léger [REPR. P. 122], Balthus, Herbin, Alfred Courmes, Henri Jannot, Gianfilippo Usellini, Filippo De Pisis). In the turmoil and uncertainty of the inter-war years, this realist vision brought together artists who until that point had been at opposite extremes, not only in terms of their political views—which sometimes underwent drastic transformations—but in their philosophical reflections and artistic affinities. Echoes of Magic Realism even made themselves heard in the United States, through the voices of several artists from the Realist school, including the most famous regionalist painter, Grant Wood, on whom it left a deep impression following his visit to Europe. Lastly, this pictorial movement cannot be divorced from precisionist objectivity and the reification of the world, which also spread to literature and photography. The different pictorial trends that came under the heading of Magic Realism must also be seen in the light of contemporary photographic research, from the New Objectivity taken up by German, Russian, and American photographers to the urban visions of the *"fantastique social"* as described by Pierre Mac Orlan or the poetic realism of Latin American photographers such as Manuel Álvarez Bravo [REPR. P. 163].

28. In the case of Italian art, for example, Fanette Roche-Pézard has clearly demonstrated the difficulty of assimilating political and aesthetic concerns. Even if some *Valori plastici* artists, like Mario Broglio, were anti-Fascist, the movement's members, in upholding Italian traditions and their vision of an ordered world, were heralding the philosophy of the future authoritarian regime. Similarly, the realism of the Novecento—a group composed of artists who had responded to the Fascist call—suspended "in an immobility bordering on dread and indifference," "far removed from the victorious energy" Mussolini was determined to stir up "involuntarily escaped Fascism" (F. Roche-Pézard, "Valori plastici et Novecento," in *Les Réalismes, 1919–1939* op. cit., p. 58).

Art Deco

The International Exhibition of Modern Decorative and Industrial Arts which took place in Paris in 1925, with contributions from twenty-one different countries, consecrated the term "Art Deco" to describe on the one hand an architectural and decorative trend and on the other a plastic aesthetic with an agenda that was more "modernistic" than modernist. In common parlance, the term was therefore not linked to the art of the two figures who featured most prominently in this international exhibition—Sonia Delaunay [REPR. PP. 66, 67], who presented her fashion designs, and Sophie Taeuber-Arp [REPR. P. 67].[29] Although their works abolished the frontier between painting and the decorative arts, these two pioneers had launched their revolution under the aegis of Abstraction and were still attached to the avant-garde ethic. The expression "Art Deco," which did not denote a movement but a style, tended to be applied to artists with a stylized, geometricized figurative approach, the most famous example being Tamara de Lempicka [REPR. P. 125]. This hybrid art form, alternately "too high society" or "too popular" to be considered avant-garde, found itself somewhat overlooked in the history of art. Yet this aesthetic synthesis of Cubism, Futurism, and Realism could not be reduced to a single figure, or to ambitions of a purely decorative and superficial nature, and was also rooted in a complex context. In France, Art Deco emerged in the wake of World War I and reflected the effervescence of the Roaring Twenties in Paris. The discovery of jazz, music-hall entertainment, and the iconoclastic performances of the avant-gardes contributed to the excitement triggered by this new-found freedom. A freedom that took the form of female emancipation, with the emergence of the flapper, immortalized in so many depictions of Art Deco, the cosmopolitanism epitomized by the "Paris Nègre" nightclubs, and not least the success of non-European, particularly Latin American, traditional music. The Art Deco style latched onto the manifestations of this "brave new world." It was represented by several female artists, including Marie Laurencin, Chana Orloff [REPR. P. 127], Lempicka, and also Maria Blanchard [REPR. P. 123], who abandoned her self-imposed Cubist manner in favor of a highly original Cubo-Realism, imbued with fantasy. A number of Cubist sculptors were also attracted to this style, namely Jacques Lipchitz [REPR. P. 48] and Henri Laurens, who found in it a plastic interpretation of synthetic Cubism. The international ramifications of the Cubo-Realist style were another of its hallmarks. The Art Deco style was the first architectural syntax to have such widespread repercussions—its trace can be found beyond Europe and the Americas, in a number of Asian, Middle-Eastern, and North African countries. The same applies to its pictorial style. In Paris, it had a brief but profound effect on Foujita [REPR. P. 138], although he reverted to a more realist style, while other foreign artists studying in France were determined to export this aesthetic to their native countries. Among these was the Yugoslav artist Ivan Meštrović [REPR. P. 128], who was to become a leading figure in his country, and the Egyptian Mahmoud Mokhtar [REPR. P. 129], considered to be the father of modern Egyptian sculpture. The painter Mahmoud Saïd, one of the pioneers of Egyptian modernity, developed a style that vacillated between Realism and Cubo-Realism. From their time

29. Sonia Delaunay set up her fashion boutique in the temporary exhibition installations on the bridge Alexandre-III; Sophie Taeuber-Arp showed her work at the Grand Palais.

in France, the African-American artists of the Harlem Renaissance movement also retained the legacy of a realist style branded with Cubism, which they applied to their depictions of urban life among the black populations. In Latin America, most modern artistic expressions showed a certain affinity with this style, reflecting the syncretic aspirations of the artists. A number of Rivera's works [REPR. P. 112], for example, can be compared to those of Lempicka [REPR. P. 125]. As far as the Brazilians were concerned, Tarsila [REPR. P. 99], Monteiro [REPR. P. 100], Di Cavalcanti [REPR. P. 99], and Morgan-Snell [REPR. P. 126] shared a stylistic kinship with Art Deco, which they adapted to indigenist and often social subjects. Several artists made a brief foray into this style of synthesis, such as Antonio Berni in Argentina or Mario Carreño [REPR. P. 127] in Cuba. The hallmark of this style and the reason for its success can be attributed to its extensive aesthetic spectrum, ranging from the highly decorative, frozen stylization of Jean Dupas [REPR. P. 124] to the syncopated jazz-inspired art of Paul Joostens [REPR. P. 125], and its adaptability to a plethora of diverse figurative registers, from Lempicka's society portraits to Rivera's socially-committed subjects or Mokhtar's archaist figurative sculptures.

International Surrealism

Surrealism cannot be dissociated from other forms of a return to Realism. Although André Breton [REPR. PP. 110-111] saw the movement as following on directly from Dada and refuted any reference to classical art, the artists around him developed a figurative style, with some of them, such as De Chirico [REPR. P. 120], Magritte [REPR. P. 114], Ernst [REPR. P. 112], and Dalí, refusing to go along with the rejection of Realism and the pictorial tradition posited by the theoretician.[30] The attachment to Surrealism shared by such a strikingly disparate group, both in terms of generation and in their plastic modes of expression, was mainly motivated by Breton's intellectually pioneering spirit, underpinned by his inventive personality and charisma. Nevertheless, despite his denials, it was not in their aesthetic that the Surrealists differed from the Realists but in their reference to a reality of a different order, pertaining to the realm of dreams and fantasy, as already depicted in De Chirico's metaphysical paintings.[31] They did not all have the same way of conveying it, but artists such as Miró, Jean Arp [REPR. P. 66], Alberto Giacometti [REPR. P. 114], and Masson [REPR. P. 158], who touched upon the lexicon of the modernist avant-gardes, were few and far between. Most developed an art of the image, often crafted in classic style, which enabled them to conjure up dream-like visions (Yves Tanguy, Brauner [REPR. P. 113], Dalí), a nonsense world (Magritte, Ernst), or the invention of modern myths (Masson, Óscar Dominguez, Wifredo Lam [REPR. P. 159]). Rather than through an aesthetic, however, the specificity of Surrealism was defined by its elaborations of the image—automatism, collage, assemblage—a way of producing visual and semantic shocks, thereby making a valuable contribution to the search for "new intellectual tremors."[32] Breton's boundless energy, his spur-of-the-moment hiring and firing, his constant traveling (to Prague, the Canary Islands, England, Mexico, America, and the Caribbean), the exile of artists during World War II, the dissemination of

30. Breton's positions on this subject were ambiguous: although he distanced himself from Derain in 1921, despite having initially considered him to be "almost a father-figure" (Isabelle Monod-Fontaine, in Agnès de la Beaumelle and I. Monod-Fontaine [eds.], *André Breton. La beauté convulsive*, exh. cat., Paris, Éditions du Centre Pompidou, 1991), he also vaunted his admiration for a number of earlier painters, even the traditionalist Gustave Moreau, lauded Le Douanier Rousseau, hailed Dalí, even though the latter claimed an allegiance with the overblown "style pompier" painters (although he was later to repudiate him for that very reason, among others), and acknowledged the works of Edward Hopper Frida Kahlo, Rivera, etc.

31. A number of Surrealist artists—Ernst, Valentine Hugo, Giacometti, Tanguy—actually took part in the debates set up by Louis Aragon in 1936, under the aegis of the Maison de la Culture, and published in a collection entitled *La Querelle du réalisme* (1936), presented by S. Fauchereau, Paris, Cercle d'Art, 1987.

32. André Breton, quoted in *André Breton*..., op. cit., p. 25

manifestos, magazines and the exponential increase in exhibitions, not to mention the exceptional longevity of a movement that its leader kept alive until the 1960s, all paved the way for the widespread internationalization of Surrealism. It therefore included, or at least influenced, myriad artists from every European country, particularly Central Europe (the Prague group: Joseph Sima [REPR. P. 113], Marie Toyen [REPR. P. 114], Jindřich Štyrský), as well as North Africa, North and South America, Egypt, and the Sudan. Several female artists also participated in the movement, including Dorothea Tanning [REPR. P. 115], Dora Maar, Meret Oppenheim, Toyen, and Frida Kahlo [REPR. P. 112]. The postwar generation welcomed new recruits alongside the "old-timers." These included Romanian Ghérasim Luca [REPR. P. 162], Hungarians Simon Hantaï and Judit Reigl, German Konrad Klapheck, Brazilian Sérgio Lima, Cuban Jorge Camacho, and a young Algerian female artist, Baya [REPR. P. 25].

Breton's trip to Mexico in 1938 provides an insight into the mitigated support of the artists invited to participate in international Surrealist exhibitions. The Surrealists' acceptance of other cultures and their interest in irrational phenomena certainly got an enthusiastic reception from the Latin Americans, but they were keen to distance themselves from the French faction by stressing their cultural identity. This sentiment was described by the photographer Manuel Álvarez Bravo [REPR. P. 163]: "André Breton arrived in Mexico in 1938. He considered my country to be culturally and socially Surrealist but Breton was confusing Surrealism with fantasy. Mexico is more fantastic than Surrealist. Speaking for myself, I am not a Surrealist photographer."[33] Frida Kahlo reacted in similar vein, claiming that it was unfair to rank her alongside the Surrealists. She had never painted dreams, she was depicting reality.[34] It is certainly true that these artists welcomed the concept of "Magic Realism" with as much, if not more, warmth as that of "Surrealism," while continuing to defend their own identity. In the 1930s, Mexico therefore held a more prestigious position in the imagination of the Parisian Surrealists than the reverse. The Surrealists were actually more intrigued by traditional, popular Mexico than by the contemporary art scene; the Muralists, once lauded by Breton and his peers, were now treated with disdain, not so much for resorting to Realism but on account of their nationalism and their commitment to Soviet Communism.[35]

Fragmentation and Synthesis

The blanket term "return to order" thus covered a multitude of highly diverse and even antagonistic practices, in stark contrast to the rallying impetus of the modernist avant-gardes. The various artists involved in this "return" were flanked by others who had never actually joined the modernist ranks, towing their own aesthetic line according to their academic training. The post-World War I European art scene was therefore epitomized by a fragmentation of the

33. Quoted by Olivia Speer in "Manuel Álvarez Bravo et le réalisme magique," online publication, Paris, Galerie Nationale du Jeu de Paume, 2012, http://lemagazine.jeudepaume.org/2013/01/olivia-speer-manuel-alvarez-bravo-et-le-réalisme-magique/.

34. See Carlos Fuentes, introduction to *The Diary of Frida Kahlo*, New York, Harry N. Abrams, 2005. During her visit to Paris at Breton's invitation, the artist was particularly harsh in her criticism of the Surrealists, dismissing them as a "gang of crazy sons of bitches" and writing: "There are so many rotten useless intellectuals here that I can't stand it any more. They're just too much for me."

35. The major exhibition on Mexican art organized in 1952 by Jean Cassou at the National Museum of Modern Art was boycotted by the Surrealists in protest at the Stalinism of the Mexican contributors.

artistic fabric and by a wavering, not to say indifferent, plastic expression that affected the adepts of Realism as much as the Modernists. On a philosophical and psychological level, this was a time of doubt and of reaffirmation of stable, common values, whether reactionary or liberal, nationalist[36] or internationalist. Consequently, commitment to Realism was often circumstantial and very few artists kept it up beyond the 1930s. In countries that had only just rallied to the modern cause, in Latin America for instance, the plastic options that presided over realisms had a collective dimension and stemmed from revolutionary convictions. Artists set an example by showing that a meeting of minds was feasible between the nationalist and culturalist struggle and the desire to belong to the universal community of artistic modernity; a seeming paradox familiar to many European artists, particularly in Central Europe, and also in the cosmopolitan circles of the School of Paris. On a plastic level, despite the range of references cited by the realist artists, the general tendency leaned toward eclecticism and a desire for synthesis. Realisms were rooted in a quintessentially hybrid aesthetic. When non-European artists took up realism, they did so not with reference to a tradition they had not shared, but as a *lingua franca*, a vehicular language that would allow them, according to circumstances, to express their acceptance of or resistance to a modern culture that was now global. Franz Roh's work draws a portrait of a generation that had turned its back on Expressionism, Futurism, and Cubism. The author takes Le Douanier Rousseau as his figurehead [REPR. P. 58], with a reproduction of *The Sleeping Gypsy* (1897) as his frontispiece, just like Vassily Kandinsky in *Der Blaue Reiter Almanach* [The Blue Rider Almanac] [REPR. P. 56], in which he inserted a picture of the Naïve painter. Kandinsky [REPR. P. 57, 76] paid tribute to this figurative artist, who was admired by the avant-garde, for his art that "isolated [the thing] from the practical world and its outcome in order to reveal its interior resonance," claiming him to be the father of the "great new Realism."[37] This analogy shows the complexity of the Realism issue and its relationship to the avant-gardes,[38] opening up a wide field of study that promises to deliver a host of revelations and reappraisals.

Translated from the French by Caroline Taylor-Bouché

36. As in the "return to order" advocated by Bissière, followed by Cocteau (see footnote 1).

37. Vassily Kandinsky, "On the Question of Form," in *The Blue Rider Almanac. The Blue Rider*, Boston, Museum of Fine Arts, 2005.

38. The political and ideological issue is equally complex. Apologias of order and nationalism did not wait for the Realist movements to make themselves heard, as can be seen from the tone adopted by Guillaume Apollinaire in 1914, in defense of Le Douanier Rousseau: "But Rousseau was not merely a decorator, nor was he a dabbler, he was a painter. And this is what makes his works so difficult to understand for some people. He had order, and one can see this not only in his paintings but in his drawings, which are as methodical as Persian miniatures. His art possessed purity, it comprises in its female figures, in the construction of the trees, in the harmonious melody of his color chart, a style that only belongs to French painters and which characterizes them wherever they may be. I am naturally referring here to the canvases of the great masters." (*Les Soirées de Paris*, 15 January 1914).

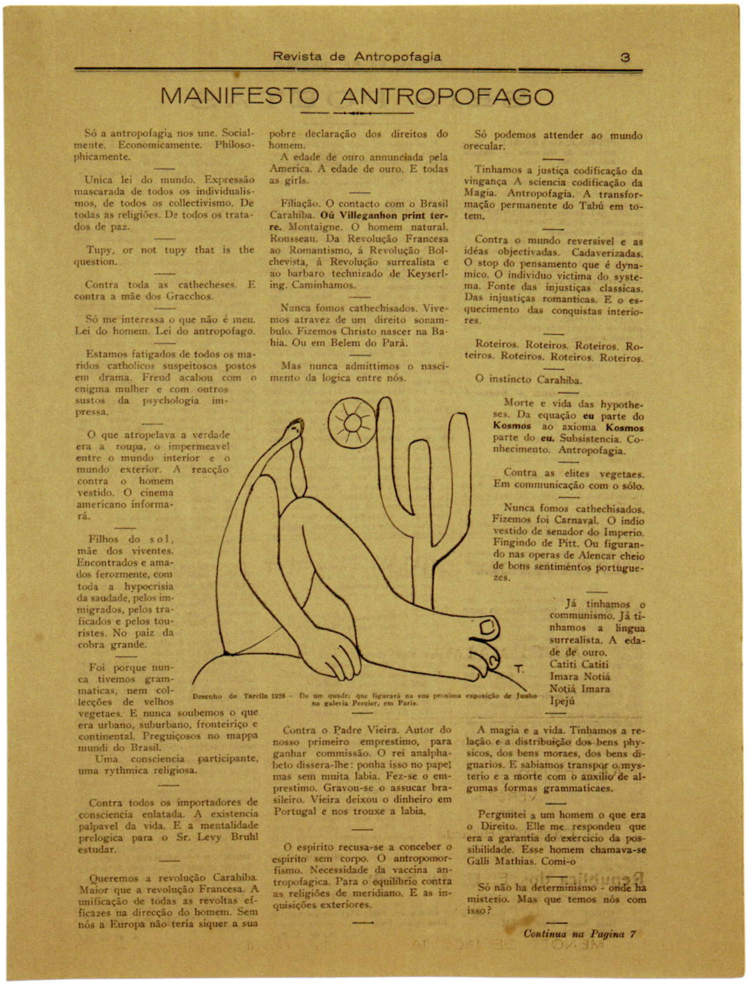

Revista de Antropofagia 3

MANIFESTO ANTROPOFAGO

Só a antropofagia nos une. Socialmente. Economicamente. Philosophicamente.

Unica lei do mundo. Expressão mascarada de todos os individualismos, de todos os collectivismo. De todas as religiões. De todos os tratados de paz.

Tupy, or not tupy that is the question.

Contra toda as cathecheses. E contra a mãe dos Gracchos.

Só me interessa o que não é meu. Lei do homem. Lei do antropofago.

Estamos fatigados de todos os maridos catholicos suspeitosos postos em drama. Freud acabou com o enigma mulher e com outros sustos da psychologia impressa.

O que atropelava a verdade era a roupa, o impermeavel entre o mundo interior e o mundo exterior. A reacção contra o homem vestido. O cinema americano informará.

Filhos do sol, mãe dos viventes. Encontrados e amados ferozmente, com toda a hypocrisia da saudade, pelos immigrados, pelos traficados e pelos touristes. No paiz da cobra grande.

Foi porque nunca tivemos grammaticas, nem collecções de velhos vegetaes. E nunca soubemos o que era urbano, suburbano, fronteiriço e continental. Preguiçosos no mappa mundi do Brasil.

Uma consciencia participante, uma rythmica religiosa.

Contra todos os importadores de consciencia enlatada. A existencia palpavel da vida. E a mentalidade prelogica para o Sr. Levy Bruhl estudar.

Queremos a revolução Carahiba. Maior que a revolução Francesa. A unificação de todas as revoltas efficazes na direcção do homem. Sem nós a Europa não teria siquer a sua pobre declaração dos direitos do homem.

A edade de ouro annunciada pela America. A edade de ouro. E todas as girls.

Filiação. O contacto com o Brasil Carahiba. **Oú Villeganhon print terre.** Montaigne. O homem natural. Rousseau. Da Revolução Francesa ao Romantismo, á Revolução Bolchevista, á Revolução surrealista e ao barbaro technizado de Keyserling. Caminhamos.

Nunca fomos cathechisados. Vivemos atravez de um direito sonambulo. Fizemos Christo nascer na Bahia. Ou em Belem do Pará.

Mas nunca admittimos o nascimento da logica entre nós.

Desenho de Tarsila 1928 – De um quadro que figurará na sua proxima exposição de Junho na galeria Percier, em Paris.

Contra o Padre Vieira. Autor do nosso primeiro emprestimo, para ganhar commissão. O rei analphabeto dissera-lhe: ponha isso no papel mas sem muita labia. Fez-se o emprestimo. Gravou-se o assucar brasileiro. Vieira deixou o dinheiro em Portugal e nos trouxe a labia,

O espirito recusa-se a conceber o espirito sem corpo. O antropomorfismo. Necessidade da vaccina antropofagica. Para o equilibrio contra as religiões de meridiano. E as inquisições exteriores.

Só podemos attender ao mundo orecular.

Tinhamos a justiça codificação da vingança A sciencia codificação da Magia. Antropofagia. A transformação permanente do Tabú em totem.

Contra o mundo reversivel e as idéas objectivadas. Cadaverizadas. O stop do pensamento que é dynamico. O individuo victima do systema. Fonte das injustiças classicas. Das injustiças romanticas. E o esquecimento das conquistas interiores.

Roteiros. Roteiros. Roteiros. Roteiros. Roteiros. Roteiros. Roteiros.

O instincto Carahiba.

Morte e vida das hypotheses. Da equação **eu** parte do **Kosmos** ao axioma **Kosmos** parte do **eu.** Subsistencia. Conhecimento. Antropofagia.

Contra as elites vegetaes. Em communicação com o sólo.

Nunca fomos cathechisados. Fizemos foi Carnaval. O indio vestido de senador do Imperio. Fingindo de Pitt. Ou figurando nas operas de Alencar cheio de bons sentimentos portuguezes.

Já tinhamos o communismo. Já tinhamos a lingua surrealista. A edade de ouro.
Catiti Catiti
Imara Notiá
Notiá Imara
Ipejú

A magia e a vida. Tinhamos a relação e a distribuição dos bens physicos, dos bens moraes, dos bens dignarios. E sabiamos transpor o mysterio e a morte com o auxilio de algumas formas grammaticaes.

Perguntei a um homem o que era o Direito. Elle me respondeu que era a garantia do exercicio da possibilidade. Esse homem chamava-se Galli Mathias. Comi-o

Só não ha determinismo - onde ha misterio. Mas que temos nós com isso?

Continua na Pagina 7

Oswald de ANDRADE
"Anthropophagic Manifesto,"
Revista de antropofagia,
vol. 1, no. 1, May 1928

"Anthropophagy. Devouring the sacred enemy. To transform it into a totem."

OSWALD DE ANDRADE, "ANTHROPOPHAGIC MANIFESTO"

Lasar SEGALL
Lucy (Portrait of Lucy VI
1936

ANONYMOUS FAIRGROUND PHOTOGRAPHER
Brancusi with Oswald de Andrade, Tarsila, Yvette Farkou, Fernand Léger, and Maximilien Gauthier in a boat setting at the Paris Foire du Trône
14 July 1926

DI CAVALCANTI
Brazilian Folk Dance
1937

TARSILA
The Bogeyman
1924

MONTEIRO
The Hunt
1923

Candido PORTINARI
Composition
1945

"Brazilianizing Brazil."

MOVIMENTO VERDE, CATAGUASES, 1927

José CUNEO
Three-Pointed Moon
n.d.

José Antonio TERRY
The Dwarf Chepa and Her Pitcher
1923

"Colombianizing Colombia."

JAIME BARRERA PARRA, *EL TIEMPO*, BOGOTÁ, 1930

Julia CODESIDO
Huanca Women
1931

Amanda de LEON
Bird Vendors
n.d.

"Let's Peruvianize Peru."

JOSÉ CARLOS MARIÁTEGUI, *MUNDIAL*, LIMA, 1925

Alfredo GRAMAJO GUTIÉRREZ
A Burial in My Village
1920

Joseph KUTTER
Man with Cut Finger
1930

Marcel GROMAIRE
The Vagabond
1939

Yves ALIX
The Master of the Harvest
1921

Otto DIX
Memory of the Halls of Mirrors in Brussels
1920

Fausto PIRANDELLO
Morning Interior
1931

George GROSZ
The Way of All Flesh II
1931

Tadeusz MAKOWSKI
The Drinkers
1930

Georges ROUAULT
Laborer (Green Background),
from the *Suburbs* series
1939–1945

Frans MASEREEL
Sailor's Wife
1930

Constant PERMEKE
Head of a Peasant Woman
1925

André BRETON
Wall of André Breton's Studio
1922–1966

Max ERNST
Ubu Imperator
1923

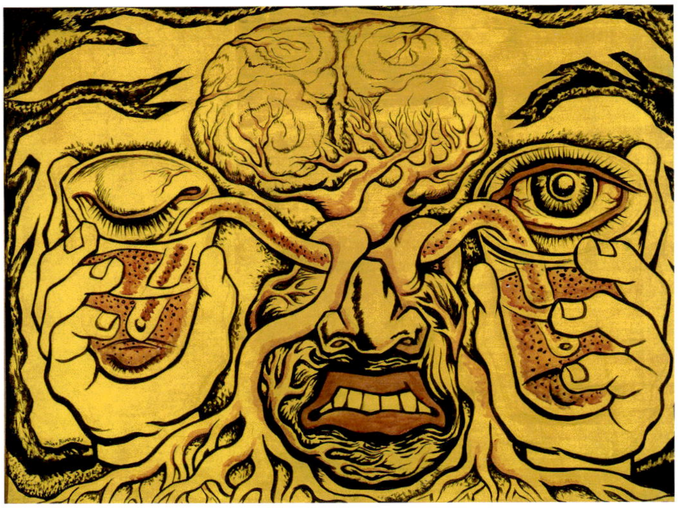

Diego RIVERA
Communicating Vessels
1938

Frida KAHLO
"The Frame"
1938

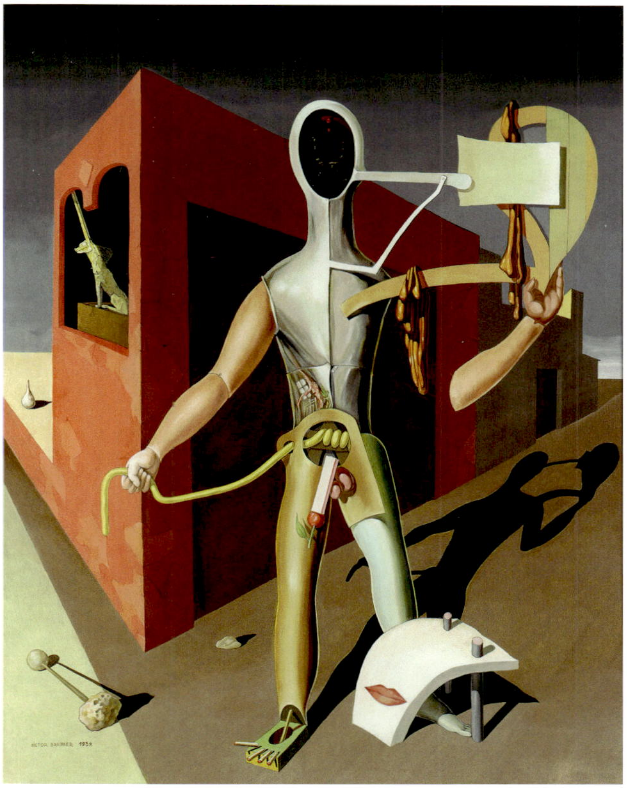

Victor BRAUNER
Prestige of the Air
1934

Jan ZRZAVÝ
The Widow
1923

Joseph SIMA
Double Landscape, Electric Storm
1928

René MAGRITTE
The Red Model
1935

Marie TOYEN
One in the Other
1965

Alberto GIACOMETTI
Disagreeable Object
1931

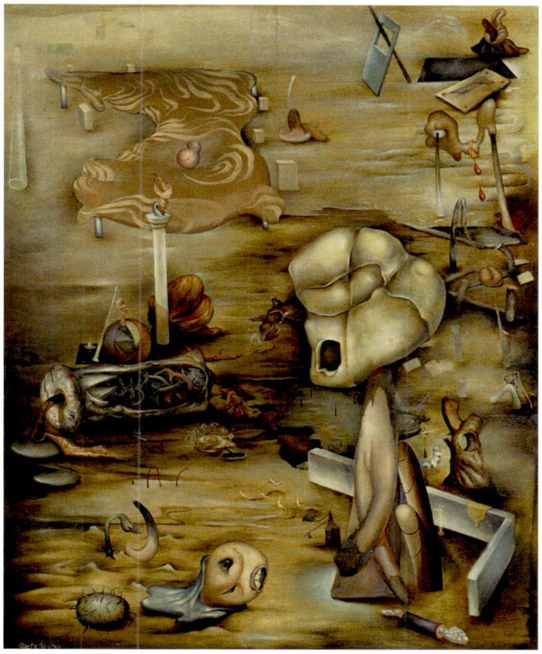

Henri GOETZ
Untitled
1941–1945

Graham SUTHERLAND
Standing Form
1952

Dorothea TANNING
A Very Happy Picture
1947

Aristide CAILLAUD
Venice
n.d.

Séraphine de SENLIS
Red Tree
1928–1930

Germain VAN DER STEEN
Entente cordiale
n.d.

ANONYMOUS
King and Queen
n.d.

Gino SEVERINI
The Artist's Wife and Daughter (Jeanne and Gina)
1934–1935

Felice CASORATI
Portrait of a Young Girl
1932

Otto DIX
Portrait of the Journalist Sylvia von Harden
1926

Pablo PICASSO
Harlequin
1923

André DERAIN
Still Life with Rabbit
1938–1939

Giorgio DE CHIRICO
Premonitory Portrait of Guillaume Apollinaire
1914

Ivan BABIJ
Two Nudes
ca. 1930

BALTHUS
Cathy Dressing
1933

Christian SCHAD
Count St-Genois d'Anneaucourt
1927

Maruja MALLO
Kermesse
1928

Rosario de VELASCO
Carnival
ca. 1936

Maria BLANCHARD
Child with Ice Cream
1925

"Calm, tranquillity, even serenity—that will be the artist's attitude. But such serenity will contain all the pathos of the world."

GIORGIO DE CHIRICO, 1915

Jean DUPAS
Woman in Red
1927

Marc CHAGALL
Bella with a White Collar
1917

Tamara de LEMPICKA
Young Woman in Green
1927–1930

Paul JOOSTENS
To Africa
1920

KOCHAR
Eastern Women
1924

MORGAN-SNELL
The Son of Rhea
1955

Mario CARREÑO
Two Female Nudes
1939

Chana ORLOFF
Crouching Woman
1925

Ivan MEŠTROVIĆ
Woman with Harp
n.d.

Boris LOVET-LORSKI
Unknown God, Head
1927

Mahmoud MOKHTAR
Bride of the Nile
ca. 1929

Joaquín ROCA-REY
Execution of a Villager
1957/1961

Ismaël de la SERNA
Europe
ca. 1935

Francis PICABIA
The Adoration of the Golden Calf
1941–1942

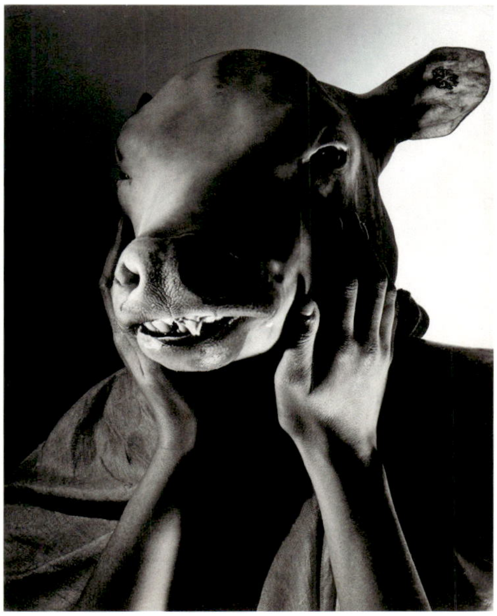

Erwin BLUMENFELD
The Dictator
1937

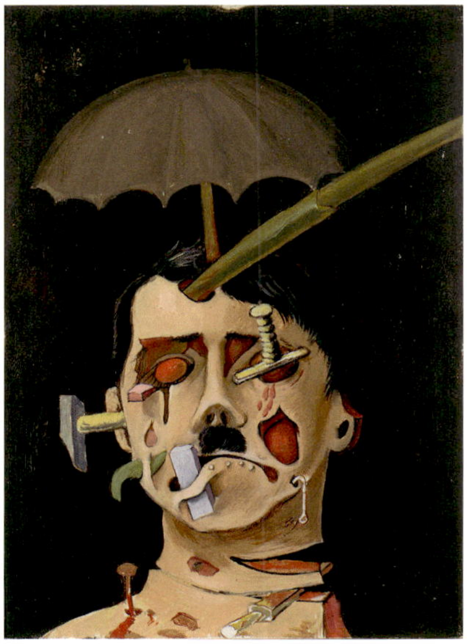

Victor BRAUNER
Hitler
1934

Luis FERNÁNDEZ
Bull's Head
ca. 1939

Demetrio URRUCHÚA
Fighter
1936

Edmond KÜSS
Spain
1937

Multiple Modernities in Japan and China

Jacques Giès

Including an Asian perspective in "Multiple Modernities" is a justified evocation. While only partial, given the limited number of artistic personalities and nations represented (Japan and China), the field it embraces is a significant one: it concerns not only artistic creation, the *modernity of Others* whose history is little known, but also its reception in the West and presence in a modern art museum; what is more, a Parisian art museum—Paris being the city where a page of modernity was written, between the late 19th and mid-20th century, for China and Japan.

The Situation of Modernity

Considered from a generic point of view, the concept of "modernity"—until the advent of globalization, that is, until very recently—reflects the center/periphery schema and the model of a creative present announcing future directions. It implies a break with the past. Historical *Modernity* has been known to arise in one place: one cultural capital (which is sometimes also political)—Kaifeng (China) under the Song Dynasty in the 11th century, Florence under the Medicis in the 15th century; or in one civilization—the India of the Gupta period (5th–7th centuries), the China of the Ming Dynasty (14th–17th centuries). What remains constant throughout History is the idea of a *model*: the characteristic of the contemporary era. This influence is shared well beyond direct and tangible spheres of influence, acting on the level of *ideas*, intellectual representations, as was the case for the *Western model* for Asia since the end of the 19th century. As a model, modernity is always attached to a centralized and hegemonic cultural world. The question of *subalternity* comes into play in a very subtle way. Any other world that does not relate to this *moment* sees itself as though anchored in its traditions and its past, a prisoner of its origins. That is the issue here.

Modernity in Response to the Western Challenge

The *modernity* of art in Asia—or so we think—should not be a mystery to us, as Westerners. We perceive it as an approach by artists who are coming to meet the Western world, in both the literal and figurative senses. We therefore perceive, superficially, the works of Japanese artists such as Rihaku Harada [REPR. P. 142], Léonard Foujita [REPR. P. 138], Kojima Torajiro, and certain Chinese artists such as Chang Shuhong [REPR. P. 139], Yun Gee [REPR. P. 143], Liu Haisu [REPR. P. 143], or Pan Yuliang [REPR. P. 139], by recognizing in each of them the influences of our artistic values. We recognize well-known movements—whether Neo-Impressionism or Realism, these movements are part of a list of identifiable phases on the path leading from *modernity* to *contemporary art*. Finally, we think, this contemporary perspective certainly applies to the approach of the few personalities residing in Paris. These considerations now bring us to the subject at hand, *modernity* in a plural mode, as it is perceived from the Asian perspective, and the problematic that Asian artists have faced. Modernity is a leap into the unknown, in the vein of "never seen *before*" in the fine arts, never heard *before* in music, or written in literature—there is nothing very specific about this. However, when the adverb "before"—which marks the persistence of the action or of a state during this period—happens to be seriously affected by a breakdown in its *essence*, as was the case when Chinese and Japanese artists were confronted with the entirely different mode of Western painting, the problematic of modernity thus finds itself transfigured. Rather than coloring the *order of things* differently, this modernity, *lacking from history* and disconnected from it, actualizes and profoundly expresses an *identity crisis* while at the same time serving as a stimulant, as a new and open pathway that can provide a holistic response. This is how artistic modernity in China and Japan found its feet: by holistically combining many different orders (economic, political, and cultural) on their paths of reform in response to the Western challenge.

In China especially, the proximity of these questions assumed the dramatic character of an identity crisis, concerning the very essence of the culture and the basis of the elite, which was unprecedented in its history.[1] The failure of the traditional Chinese paradigm distinguishing between the essence (*ti*) and the means (*yong*), transposed in the two-pronged sentence "Chinese knowledge as essence and Western knowledge as application," which served as a cultural and political slogan in the face of the Western challenge in the last quarter of the 19th century, was to widen this identity rift. The defeat in the war against Japan (1894–1895) led to a failure that the conservative and partial modernization underway between 1861 and 1894 ("Movement of Self-Reinforcement" and "Movement of Western Affairs") had been unable to prevent. This was followed by the failure of the "Hundred Day Reforms" proposed in 1898 by reformers, who, for the first time, placed Western and Chinese knowledge on an equal footing by laying down the *conditions* of modernity: the abolition of a traditional view of the world with China as its hub, the establishment of a constitutional monarchy and educational institutions inspired by the Western model. After that came the key moment, under the First Republic, of the "Movement of 4 May" in 1919, when all crystallized ideologies came into conflict. This constituted a high point in debates opened up by Chinese intellectuals, from the partisans of the Neo-Confucianist tradition, whereby European civilization was a "materialistic monster," to the liberal thinkers, who advised greater scientificity with a program of "total Westernization."[2] From all of this intensity, discordant but signaling a broad debate of ideas, we retain the annunciatory call for a "New Culture" issued by radical intellectuals in 1915.[3] The syllogism stresses the idea that

1. The phenomena of acculturation that China experienced in the course of the Mongolian (14th century) and Manchurian (17th century) conquests took place in just the opposite manner, since it turned to the advantage of its model.

2. To mention only these opposing groups alongside the nationalists, close to Sun Yatsen and his party the Kuomintang, and Marxists, such as Chen Duxiu and Mao Zedong, whose objective was the advent of the "new man" to wipe the slate of Chinese feudal culture clean, based on a new Socialist identity inspired by Marxism and Leninism.

3. In answer to the fear that President Yuan Shikai would declare himself the new emperor.

Chinese culture—pre-modern, far more than traditional—had been the cause of an unsuitability to the modern world.
Japan, for its part, had a very different response owing to its history: the insularity it had jealously guarded for three centuries. Faced with a challenge of the same nature, it started along the path of serious reforms in the Meiji period, one of the more remarkable feats of voluntary acculturation in history, while preserving the essentials, its tradition.

Asia Facing the Multiple Forms of Modernity

Whether it be the founding of a "new culture" for China, or an "enriching openness" for Japan, the problematic of modernity is not limited to cultural adaptation to the Western model. Among the works presented, the authentic modern research in the practice of ink painting testifies to this, stemming from the two national traditions—Chinese, under the brush of Chen Shuren or Fang Ruo; Japanese, under that of Kansetsu Hashimoto or Kawai Gyokudo. The two countries experienced the establishment of the first fine arts academies and the first national arts courses, resulting from the recognition of the *multiple modernities* that were active at the time. Twinned yet distinct courses were dedicated to teaching ink and oil painting—multiple but unconnected modernities. These art schools determined the personal pathways of the most representative artists, via the two paths of expression. Only a few rare figures like Xu Beihong [REPR. P. 140] and Lin Fengmian attempted, after studies in Europe, to establish a *connection* in their work between the modernities, which they considered to be a *duty* to "regenerate Chinese art." Two very different pedagogical paths of *access* to artistic modernity developed in parallel. The Tokyo University of the Arts, founded in 1887, taught Japanese painting and the cultural values attached to it. Nine years later, in 1896, the "Western Painting Program" was created, and significantly renamed in 1933 the "Oil Painting Program." In China, the Central Academy of Fine Arts was founded in Beijing in 1918. The teaching of Western painting within the department of oil painting was visibly present from the outset. It even seems to have been the argument for creating the college, inspired by the great educator Cai Yuanpei[4] and was part of a vast national program of modernization instigated by the First Republic. Modernity, as it was perceived at the time, actualized a *duality* in pictorial art. Two contemporary pathways, that were nonetheless foreign to one another, were also *established* within painting. On the one hand, ink painting, which undoubtedly had potential for renewal in the modern age; and on the other, Western-style painting that marked a cultural *decentering* that imposed the idea of placing Chinese knowledge and Western knowledge on an equal footing. A conception that did not match so well with the idea of the centrality of China and that, with the upheavals of the modern age, shook up its cultural foundations in a profound way.

4. Cai Yuanpei (1898–1940), admirer of the French system of tertiary education, which he wanted to reproduce. Note with respect to the permanence of this figure in relations between France and China, the very recent Cai Yuanpei program (2013).

A Much Larger Question

What was the modernity of Western painting that was revealed in the eyes of the artists and the intellectual elite in China? First of all, it was oil painting: a technique allowing quasi-infinite reworkings, whereas Chinese ink painting did not allow for second thoughts. Next, it was characterized by special procedures that highlighted the cultural rift: *scientific* protocols of precise representation (human anatomy, axonometric perspective); special treatment of the subjects: objective *landscapes* designed as panoramic views, as they present themselves to "an" observer, *still lifes* made from fragments derived from all of nature "as One" and presented in the studio of "the" artist; finally, and above all, the importance of the human figure. Not the representation of the average human in our relationship to the natural elements, but of a specific human subject, with individual traits—from the psychological "portrait" to compositions on religious or secular subjects, sometimes presenting a kind of social realism that was ahead of its time. This search for "life" under "form," to paraphrase the inherent terms of the Chinese aesthetic theories formulated as of the 11th century—"transcribe the idea" (*xieyi*) and "transcribe life" (*xiesheng*)—was immediately perceptible to modern Chinese artists. Just as the daring exploration of forms could be, among the contemporary approaches adopted by these artists on their visits to Paris: (i.e., in the Cubism movement), from the internal logic of forms to the extreme end of the spectrum of deconstruction with their visual relationship to the subject opening up to the unknown, to the rendering of "life."

In the desire affirmed by certain artists to establish a relationship between Chinese and Western art, had there been a misunderstanding or awareness of bigger stakes? The painter Lin Fengmian, reviving an outmoded slogan from the late 19th century, thus declared in 1926 that it was important "to have recourse to Western art in order to serve Chinese art." Calling into question the *excesses* of one and the other, he recommended a balanced solution, in some sense an *in-between*. Confining Western art, as he did, solely to the "reproduction of the outer appearance of things" and opposing the "purely inner" quality of Chinese painting to it testified to a curious ignorance of both of these arts, for an artist who was trained in Paris. Unless the real meaning of the pamphlet aimed at higher stakes, the "cultural renaissance" of China. Nonetheless, this clumsy procedure reinforced a number of solid prejudices. It was superficial to bring the question back to the purely technical differential of oil painting, both to characterize Western painting and to signify the site of modernity in art.

The Artists and the Works

The question here is of *modernity* as it was posed to the intellectual and artistic elites of China and Japan, confronted by the Western challenge. Few names have been put forward as examples. The reason for this is, besides the fact that there are so many of them,[5] that despite rare exceptions, none of them truly stands out for their artistic personality (a *personality* leading radically towards a new path). Two artists stand out nonetheless: Japanese artist Léonard (Tsuguharu) Foujita [REPR. P. 138] and Chinese artist Zhang Daqian. Without claiming to impose an explanation by way of the *milieus* to which they respectively belong, we can recognize in them an echo of the big questions pertaining to modernity, in Japan, on the one hand, and in China, on the other. In his works from the 1920s, Foujita engaged entirely in a new pictorial language in relation to the modernity of oil painting, through the practice of painting nudes. His fame was first European and Western, well before it became Japanese. Then there is Zhang Daqian, a great and resolutely "Chinese" modern painter, but the appreciation of his genius as an ink painter has not yet passed over to the West.

In conclusion, let us recall the "Exhibition of Contemporary Chinese Art" event at the Jeu de Paume in 1933, which had a major impact in Paris. The French government acquired several works. Despite the personality of one of the curators, the Chinese painter Xu Beihong, then living in Paris, among the two hundred paintings presented in the section devoted to contemporary Chinese painting,[6] none were inspired by Western modernity. All of them, even those (and there were many) by painters trained in the Western style, demonstrated the modern creativity of ink painting. The success of the exhibition was based on the discovery of Chinese painting in its somewhat *intimate* modernity, suited to the process of its pictorial language. After a long period in the shadows, visitors to "Multiple Modernities" have been offered the chance to rediscover the different forms of this Chinese modernity.

Translated from the French by Anna Knight

5. Concerning these Chinese personalities, see the list provided in Éric Lefèvre (ed.), *Artistes chinois à Paris*, exh. cat., Paris, Paris-Musées, 2011.

6. Another section was dedicated to traditional painting.

Léonard FOUJITA
Portrait of the Artist
1928

SANYU
Nude Woman
ca. 1930

PAN Yuliang
After the Bath
1952

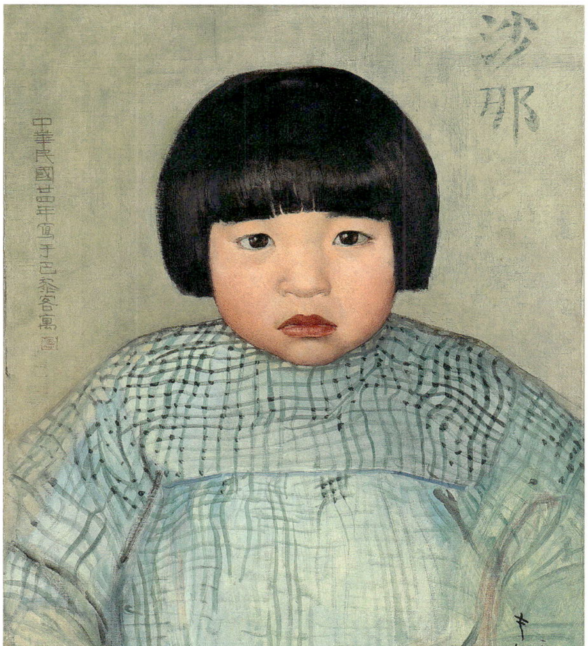

CHANG Shuhong
Portrait of Shana
1935

WANG Yachen
Landscape
1932

XU Beihong
Trees and Figure
1932

Gengetsu YAZAWA
Mountain Lake
n.d.

Ichiyo MATSUMOTO
Princess Chujo in Hibariyama
ca. 1925

Somei YUKI
Raspberry Bush
ca. 1925

Rihaku HARADA
Antwerp Ferry
1937

YUN Gee
M. Pierre Mille
ca. 1930

LIU Haisu
Gushan
ca. 1931

Building a Mediterranean Heritage

The Role of Architectural Reviews

Anne-Marie Zucchelli

It was not until the 1930s that French architectural reviews really turned their attention to contemporary building projects in the countries of the Mediterranean Basin, particularly the colonized territories (Algeria and Libya),[1] those under protectorate (Morocco, Tunisia, Egypt and Palestine), and those under Western mandate (Syria and the Lebanon). Historical and archaeological reviews, together with more broad-based publications, had however been devoting widespread pictorial coverage to these countries since the nineteenth century. A piecemeal cultural heritage was therefore built from scratch, and gradually encompassed the heritage of countries under colonial rule by emphasizing their ancient ruins and encouraging a new attitude to the Orient.[2] By appropriating the emblems of the past and importing the concept of

1. On the subject of Libyan architecture, see Brian L. McLaren, *Architecture and Tourism in Italian Colonial Libya. An Ambivalent Modernism*, Seattle/London, University of Washington Press, 2006, or Donata Pizzi, Giorgio Muratore, *Oltre Mare. Itinerari di Architettura in Libia, Etiopia, Eritrea*, Cagliari, Sirai, 2001.

2. Jean Schmitz, "Territorialisation du savoir et invention de la Méditerranée," *Cahiers d'études africaines*, no. 165, 2002.

3. Nabila Oulebsir, *Les Usages du patrimoine. Monuments, musées et politique coloniale en Algérie, 1830–1930*, Paris, Maison des Sciences de l'Homme, 2004, p. 14.

heritage into cultures where no such concept existed.[3] France was passing off these territories as new creations. This was how the nineteenth-century notion of a Mediterranean identity first emerged. Colonialism became the main vector of north-south relations in the Mediterranean, imposing a simplified perception, in potted history form, of a population mix that was actually still ongoing, and a melting-pot of cultures.[4] Modern architectural achievements in the Mediterranean began to find their way into trade magazines just as a sea change was taking place among their designers, who were determined to overcome the cultural divide and eradicate the tensions between academic and popular culture.[5] Mediterranean modernity could not be measured with the yardstick of Northern European tradition.

Today, as Mediterranean studies are being given a new lease of life and the collections of drawings and scale models held by the National Museum of Modern Art and the French Architecture Institute are widening their historical scope to include the analysis of the architectural image, the collation of invaluable source material such as reviews and essays, which provide a contemporary slant on building and town planning programs, has developed an initial answer to a fundamental question: how the image of modern architecture was perceived in the Mediterranean region in the period between the two World Wars, given the particular strictures of working in a colonized country.

4. Romeo Carabelli, *Héritage architectural récent en Méditerranée. Temporalités et territoires*, Paris, Publibook, 2006.

5. Xavier Malaverti, "Alger, Méditerranée, soleil et modernité", in Maurice Culot and Jean-Marie Thiveaud (eds.), *Architectures françaises outre-mer*, Liège, Mardaga, 1992, p. 30.

Between Antiquity and Orientalism

Ancient ruins represented the first architectural image of its Mediterranean colonies to be disseminated in France itself. Publications such as *La Revue archéologique*, launched in 1844, or *Monuments et mémoires*, in 1894, which reproduced drawings and measured diagrams executed in the course of military and scientific expeditions in Algeria, helped shape a Mediterranean identity that perpetuated the notion among its readers of an ongoing unity. A number of painters also brought back works from their travels, and these inspired a taste for the exotic, illustrated by the Exhibition of Fine Arts Applied to Industry in 1874. The fact that Oriental motifs were inherently simple to reproduce prompted a change in the decorative canon. It was in the 19th century that these motifs first appeared in Parisian architecture, although one had to wait until the early 20th century for them to resurface in the newly-erected buildings of Algeria's main cities.[6] In France, publishing houses began to specialize in Orientalism; Maisonneuve, launched in Paris in 1835, was the first to devote itself to this theme. Within the colonial Empire itself, curators and architects carried out an inventory of monuments and the latest acquisitions of museums, and then published their findings, in the manner of Henri Terrasse, Head of the Service des Monuments Historiques in Morocco and author of *Arts décoratifs au Maroc* (1925).[7] Meanwhile, French Institutes based abroad began issuing scientific bulletins, such as *Syria*, published by the French Archeology Institute of The Near East, and *Hespéris*, by the Moroccan Institute of Higher Education. In Algiers,

6. François Béguin, *Arabisances. Décor architectural et tracé urbain en Afrique du Nord, 1830–1950*, Paris, Dunod, 1983.

7. In similar vein, Louis Hautecœur, Director-General of Fine Arts in Egypt, and Gaston Wiet, Director of the Museum of Islamic Art in Cairo, published *Les Mosquées du Caire* (1932), and architect Albert Laprade his *Croquis* [Sketches] of Asia Minor (1952) and Morocco (1958).

La Revue africaine by the Algerian Historical Society, the *Annales de l'Institut d'études orientales*, and the *Revue d'Alger* all published work by academics carrying out research in the Mediterranean region.

Magazines aimed at the general public, such as *L'Afrique du Nord illustrée* and *Le Maroc du nord au sud*, provided the first tourists with picturesque photographs. Through publications, postcards, stamps, movies, and colonial novels lauding the legacy of "The Other France," France highlighted its "civilizing" effect. International colonial exhibitions also raised awareness of the Empire among the French population—the 1931 Fair in particular brought the expression of Imperial culture to its apogee.

In 1930, to mark the centenary of Algeria, a current state of knowledge was published in twelve *Cahiers*. The *Maison indigène du centenaire* or "Maison mauresque," designed by Léon Claro, director of the architectural faculty of the National School of Fine Arts in Algiers, was a high spot of the festivities, offering the European visitor an astutely conceived experience of traditional architecture and an unprecedented opportunity to cast a critical eye, as Albert Camus recounted.[8]

8. Albert Camus, "La maison mauresque" (1933), *Cahiers Albert Camus*, no. 2; reprinted in Paul Viallaneix (ed.), *Le Premier Camus*, followed by *Albert Camus. Écrits de jeunesse*, Paris, Gallimard, 1973, pp. 207-218.

The New Movement and Its Repercussions

It was the modern movement that first acknowledged the invaluable lessons of local architecture within the colonial Empire, as illustrated by the number and quality of the events it inspired. In 1933, for instance, the Friends of Algiers, under the aegis of the Modern Architects' Society, held an "Exhibition of Town Planning and Modern Architecture in the City of Algiers," attended by the movement's figurehead, Le Corbusier [REPR. P. 150].

It was not the first time the latter had set foot in Algiers. In 1931, he had been invited by one of his former colleagues, Pierre-André Émery, who had been living in Algeria since 1926, and around whom gravitated a whole generation of architects looking for change. During his second visit, Le Corbusier decided to concentrate on producing measured drawings of the Kasbah.[9] He also delivered two lectures, which received coverage in the local press, while his articles entitled "Louange à l'Algérie" [In Praise of Algeria] were published in two Algerian reviews, both of them committed to the quest for a Mediterranean architectural identity: *Le Journal général des travaux publics et du bâtiment* (1926–1947) and *Les Chantiers nord-africains* (1928–1940).

9. Jean de Maisonseul, "Djenan el-Hassan: Relations espace-temps, ou la redécouverte de l'échelle humaine," in Roland Simounet, *Pour une invention de l'espace*, Paris, Electa/Le Moniteur, 1986, pp. 17-21.

The above-mentioned "Exhibition of Town Planning and Modern Architecture in the City of Algiers" raised the possibility of a regional town planning organization, run by the municipality of Algiers. Although Le Corbusier's project, *Bombshell. A Town Planning Project for the City of Algiers* was perceived by the local authorities as a provocation, the Algerian reviews gave particularly wide coverage to the event, publishing the projects and conferences of both Le Corbusier and Pierre Jeanneret, and also of Maurice Rotival and Henri Prost. In *Non!*, the bulletin of Algeria's young socialists, Jean de Maisonseul, a town planner from Algiers, devoted a front-page article to the *Bombshell* project. Back in France, the trade review *La Construction moderne* also covered the event.

A new exhibition, entitled "The Modern City," was held in 1936 to coincide with the fourth Algiers Fair. *Le Journal général des travaux publics et du bâtiment*, *L'Afrique du Nord illustrée*, *Les Chantiers nord-africains* and *Algeria*, the review of the Algerian Office for Action on the Economy and Tourism all published special issues. In March, *L'Architecture d'aujourd'hui* opened with "La Cité moderne," a volume devoted to the large number of works-in-progress in France's overseas territories, and particularly those whose structural rationalism stemmed from the teachings of Auguste Perret. Perret's influence actually struck more of a chord than that of Le Corbusier with young architects working in North Africa.[10] Some of these architects were actually born in North Africa and others had come there especially, on account of the local building boom and receptivity to innovation. A number of them went on to complete their training in Perret's studio in Paris. From 1912 on, Perret Frères, alongside other companies like Hennebique, gave local architects the benefit of their expertise on most of the major projects taking place in Algeria, Morocco and Egypt.[11]

Town Planning Under Question

The early 20th century was characterized by sprawling urbanization throughout the Mediterranean Basin, with the colonial city replacing traditional constructions with European-style buildings and excluding the indigenous population from the city centers. In order to regulate this expansion and keep it in check, Maréchal Lyautey called on the town planner Henri Prost, who planned the layout of Morocco's main cities between 1914 and 1923.[12] In the early 1930s, Prost took over the presidency of the management committee of the International Institute of Colonial Urbanization, created in 1931. In 1932, for the very first time, a publication entitled *Urbanisme* was launched to tackle "this new science that no review in France has ever really bothered to bring to people's attention."[13]

One of the members of the Institute, the surveyor and town planner René Danger, set up in the early 1920s the Planned City Society which was particularly active in Mediterranean countries. His *Cours d'urbanisme* [Lessons on Town Planning], published in 1933, and his articles in *L'Architecture*, *La Construction moderne*, and *Urbanisme* laid down the principles of an "urban monographic survey," which underpinned Michel Écochard's first projects in Syria and the Lebanon,[14] reproduced in March 1936 in *L'Architecture d'aujourd'hui*.

This form of town planning, however, which highlighted specifically chosen landscapes and monuments, went hand in hand with a colonial romanticism that was quickly repudiated in Egypt, where access to professionalization enabled local architects to proclaim an autonomous architecture stemming from an idea of history that was as wary of the pastiche of tradition as it was of borrowings from Europe. This view was upheld by the review *Al-'Emara*,

10. Perret's influence spread as far afield as Palestine, then under British mandate, where a number of architects originating mainly from Eastern Europe, including Al Mansfeld [repr. p. 151], studied under him. It was however mainly in the teachings of Bauhaus that these architects saw their way to fulfilling their aspirations toward a more socially-biased architecture. See for example the special issue of *L'Architecture d'aujourd'hui* devoted to Palestine, September 1937.

11. Jean-Louis Cohen, Joseph Abram and Guy Lambert, *Encyclopédie Perret*, Paris, Éditions du Patrimoine, 2002.

12. Henri Prost, "Le développement de l'urbanisme dans le protectorat du Maroc de 1914 à 1923," in Jean Royer, *L'Urbanisme aux colonies et dans les pays tropicaux. Communications & rapports du Congrès international de l'urbanisme aux colonies et dans les pays de latitude "intertropicale"* [Congress held at the Exposition Coloniale Internationale, Vincennes, 10-15 October 1931], vol. 1, La Charité-sur-Loire/Paris, Delayance/Éditions d'Urbanisme, 1932, pp. 59-105.

12. *Urbanisme*, no. 1, 1932, n.p.

13. Jean-Pierre Gaudin, "L'urbanisme au Levant et le mandat français," in *Architectures françaises outre-mer*, op. cit., p. 181.

14. Mercedes Volait, *L'Architecture moderne en Égypte et la revue al-'Imara, 1939–1959*, Cairo/Paris, Centre d'Études et de Documentation Économique, Juridique et Sociale/ Le Point du Jour, 1988.

edited in Cairo by Saïd Karim.[15] The international press also reported on the new slant on the communal space taken by Egyptian architects such as Hassan Fathy and his "New Gurna."[16] Concepts of place and history put in a brief appearance in the articles published in *L'Architecture d'aujourd'hui*'s special issues devoted to Tunisia (1948) and Morocco (1951), and also in *L'Architecture marocaine*, the review launched by the Order of Architects in 1955. When Écochard took over the running of the protectorate's town planning teams between 1946 and 1953, his notion of a specifically designed habitat for each culture harmonized with that of Vladimir Bodiansky, who in 1951 launched the agency Atbat-Afrique in Casablanca [REPR. P. 150], with architects Georges Candilis [REPR. P. 150] and Shadrach Woods.[17] On the lookout for solutions to help develop a large-scale, low-cost housing project, the team found in the spontaneous nature of traditional town development a way of reviewing their approach to urban forms. With the launch of the Algerian branch of the CIAM—the International Congress of Modern Architecture—in 1952, the town planning section, federated by the personality of Albert Camus, began to look for ways of expressing their attachment to their Mediterranean roots.[18] Roland Simounet and Marcel Gut were therefore put in charge of carrying out a survey of the slums of Mahiedinne; their project for the clearance of these slums was to form the group's contribution to the 1953 CIAM in Aix-en-Provence.[19] They put forward a chart that transgressed the Housing Unit model in its determination to adapt it to the urban space, a research synthesis heralded by their predecessors, Louis Miquel, Pierre Bourlier and José Ferrer-Laloë, in the *Aéro habitat* unit (Algiers, 1943–1954).[20]

A similar method was applied by the Algiers Town Planning Agency, which Pierre Dalloz took over in 1954. It acted as a kind of experimental laboratory on collective space, thereby challenging the model of the vast housing estates advocated by Le Corbusier. Fernand Pouillon and Jean Bossu's suggestions, for instance, added individual variations to traditional urban typologies. In the first issue of *Cahiers d'urbanisme de la Ville d'Alger* (1958), Dalloz defended working methods that placed "Algiers in the vanguard of urban design," to quote the title of one of his articles. In 1955, André Bloc and the architects of the CIAM group sounded the alarm bells in the columns of *L'Architecture d'aujourd'hui. Afrique du Nord*. Attitudes were changing radically. The review set the foundations for a new debate, which was also to touch upon town planning in Europe: "Every time we juxtapose mass-produced serial buildings with examples of primitive constructions the shock is on a par with the contrast. [...] We are seeing here a primitive form of architecture, its spirit in perfect osmosis with spiritual needs."[21] It was no longer a matter of simply diversifying the modern lexicon. In their gradual acknowledgment of the anthropological and social aspect of their work, architects were imposing limits on Western hegemony

15. The publication in France, in 1971, of Hassan Fathy's work, *Construire avec le peuple. Histoire d'un village d'Égypte. Gourna*, originally published in English in 1969 under the more succinct title *Gourna, a Tale of Two Villages* (although his complete works were entitled *An Architecture for People*), had considerable impact in Western academic circles. Fathy combined his reflections on anthropology with his social preoccupations and architectural experience.

16. Atbat was the acronym of the African branch of the Atelier des Bâtisseurs [Builders' Studio], founded just after the war by Le Corbusier, Vladimir Bodiansky and André Wogenscky.

17. Louis Miquel, "Alger, Le Corbusier et le groupe CIAM-Alger," *Techniques et architecture*, no. 329, February 1980, pp. 58-59.

18. Jean-Lucien Bonillo, *Le CIAM-Alger, Albert Camus et Le Corbusier. Modernité et identité*, available on the website of the National School of Architecture Paris-La Villette, June 2012: http://www.paris-lavillette.archi.fr/leseditions11/wp-content/uploads/2012/06/alber_Ind_DEF2_Bonillo_dassedef.pdf

19. Reprinted in 1953 in the issue devoted to Algeria of *Techniques et architecture*.

20. [André Bloc], "Pour un logis humain," *L'Architecture d'aujourd'hui*, no. 60, June 1955, p. 33.

and "universal" methods of town planning. In 1964, the architects who formed part of the modern movement discovered with fascination "vernacular, anonymous, spontaneous, indigenous, rural" constructions on display at Bernard Rudofsky's "Architecture without Architects," at the Museum of Modern Art in New York.

Today, the construction of Europe has reconfigured the concept of a Mediterranean heritage by making it part of the wider picture. The difficulties inherent in defining Mediterranean architecture, halfway between globalization and cultural uniqueness, can perhaps find a dynamic solution through "a living continuity between the intelligence of traditions and the audacity of the future."[22] Experimentation and local variations will then go with the flow, in a "history that is slowly distilled and transformed, often characterized by persistent returns and endlessly recurrent cycles."[23]

Translated from the French by Caroline Taylor-Bouché

21. Bernard Rudofsky, *Architecture Without Architects. A Short Introduction to Non-Pedigreed Architecture*, New York, MoMA/ Doubleday, 1965, n.p.

22. Jean Dethier, *Architectures de terre. Atouts et enjeux d'un matériau de construction méconnu*, exh. cat., Paris, Éditions du Centre Pompidou, 1986.

23. Fernand Braudel, *La Méditerranée et le monde méditerranéen à l'époque de Philippe II* (1949), vol. 1, Paris, Colin, 1990, p. 13.

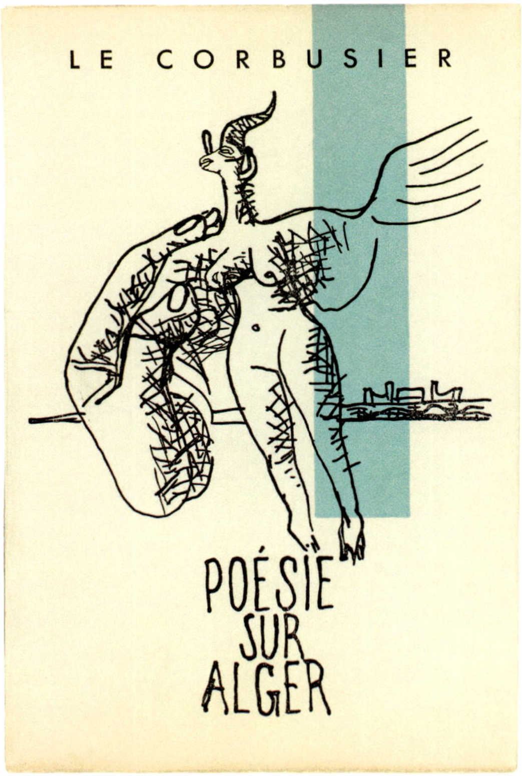

LE CORBUSIER
Poésie sur Alger, Paris, Falaise
1950

Cover of *L'Architecture d'aujourd'hui*, December 1954
Atbat Afrique: Georges Candilis, Shadrach Woods, architects

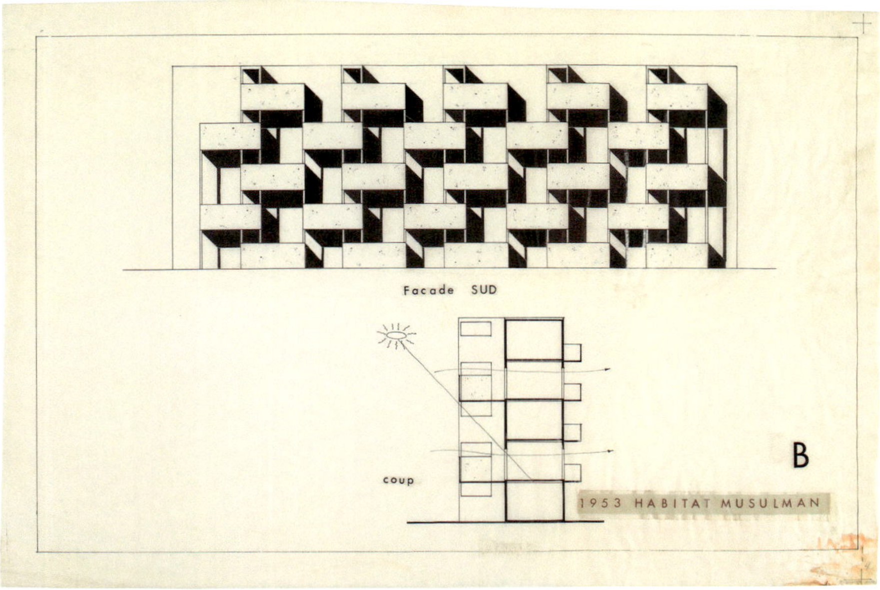

Georges CANDILIS
Islamic Residence, Type B, Southern Elevation
1953

Gabriele BASILICO
T Building, Ramat Hadar, Haifa, 1993
Architects: Weinraub & Mansfeld, 1959–1964

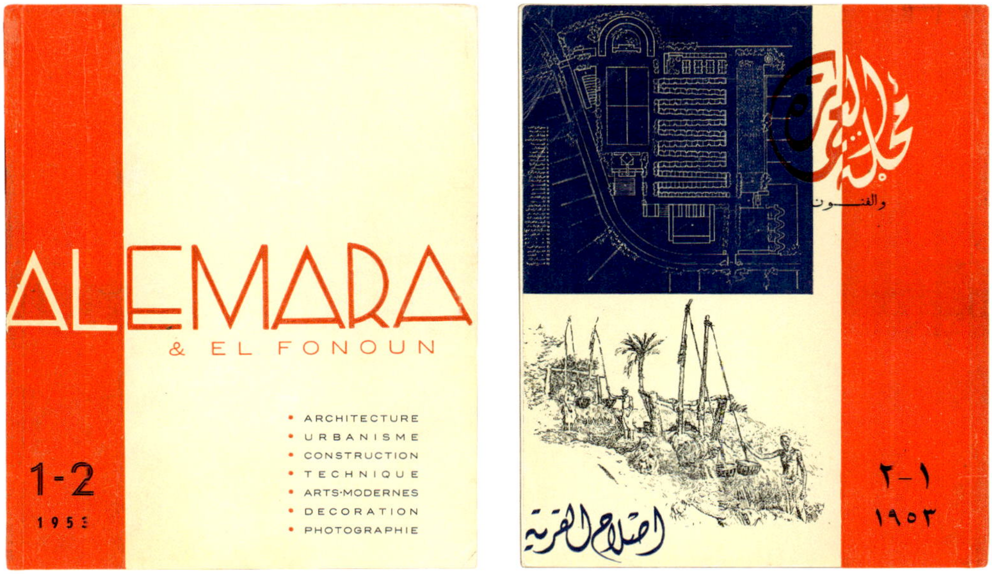

Magazine *Al-'Emara*, Cairo, nos. 1-2, 1953, front and back covers

Marc RIBOUD
Untitled. Referendum Vote on Algerian Self-Determination, Algiers, 1 July 1962
1962

Pierre VERGER
Morro-Naba Celebrant in Ouahigouya, Upper Volta, 3 February 1936
1936

André STEINER
Hanging Laundry, Morocco
1933

Pierre ICHAC
Swordfight, Touareg Warriors
1930

Totemism

Philippe Dagen

In New York, a keen interest in "negro art"—in the vocabulary of the time—closely followed its discovery by the Parisian avant-gardes from 1906 onwards. Initially, it was Alfred Stieglitz and his gallery exhibitions, starting before 1914, that permanently associated Cubism and African statuary in the American mind: the former revealing the latter, the latter decisive in the creation of the former. After World War I, the presence of dealers such as Joseph Brummer, the rising influence of Paul Guillaume, and the activities of collectors such as lawyer John Quinn (whose acquisitions were photographed by Charles Sheeler) contributed to accelerating the movement of recognition. The Museum of Modern Art was its most logical locus, since it had also presented *Les Demoiselles d'Avignon* (1907) and the "African Negro Art" exhibition in 1935. Associating modernity and the arts of Black Africa therefore seemed obvious and was unanimously accepted as such. However, this association was based on an essentially formalist understanding of "negro art" and, in more general terms, of the so-called "primitive" arts. The latter were considered to be large repositories of previously-unknown plastic solutions. These solutions, founded on geometric forms and stylization, replaced the imitation of bodies and faces of the naturalist type that characterized the European tradition, constituting radically new synthetic formulations. This conception of primitivism, which dominated the first book dedicated to the phenomenon,

Primitivism in Modern Painting, published by Robert Goldwater in 1938, was only faintly concerned with the religious, social, or sexual symbolism that were in fact borne by these sculptures. They were seen as objects of beauty much more than as forms charged with expression and spiritual efficacy. Notions such as totemism or magic were kept at bay.

The Surrealists' conception was quite different. André Breton and Paul Éluard celebrated not so much the beauty and originality of the forms as their intensity, what they revealed of an erotic or macabre nature, and their powers of suggestion over the imagination. They had a preference for Oceanic works, at the expense of an Africa that seemed too classical to them, so to speak. In the 1930s, the arts of Pre-Columbian cultures and that of the Eskimos were progressively added. Their "primitivism" was not merely different from the kind that took Cubism as the basis for its formulation, but opposed to it, going so far as attempting to make Africa seem insignificant. This information is necessary for the analysis of what would later occur when Surrealism shifted from Paris to New York, owing to the Nazi occupation and the Vichy regime in France. On 24 March 1941, Breton and Wifredo Lam, but also Claude Lévi-Strauss, left the Port of Marseille, heading for New York. André Masson, Max Ernst, Marcel Duchamp, and Matta joined them there. Yves Tanguy had taken up residence in 1938. This departure had some major consequences. It revolutionized the approach to the so-called "primitive" arts in the United States, and it did so in several ways.

The most immediate was that the presence of Breton or Ernst confronted a generation of young American artists with the words and works of the founders of the movement. Up until then, Surrealism seemed to have been represented in New York through the personality of Salvador Dalí, who gave an image to the movement that was as spectacular as it was limited—Dalí was also, of all the Surrealists, one of the least curious regarding non-Western arts. It was quite a different story when it came to Ernst or Masson, whose Primitivism was both plastic and anthropological, with these two approaches being inseparable.

Following Freud, who set the trend of the term "totem," with the very title of the book, *Totem and Taboo*, in which he paid tribute to the two mythologists James Frazer and Salomon Reinach, Surrealism reread and analyzed myths, whether in the magazine *Documents*, one of whose founders was Georges Bataille, close to Masson, or in the magazines *Minotaure* and *Cahiers d'Art*, in which Breton and Éluard published many texts. *The Labyrinth* (1938) by Masson [REPR. P. 158] could thus be considered to be an exacerbated version of the Greek myth of the Minotaur, but also as the emergence of a wild, part-man part-beast divinity, both macabre and obscene. The painter suggested a no less "wild" interpretation of the figure of Pythia, whom he presents nude, in a trance, possessed by her hallucinations, vastly different from the representations that the Renaissance might have produced. This rereading of Greco-Roman mythologies liberated them from their classical artistic and literary representations. It also served as a reminder that the oldest religions of Europe were haunted by tragedy and fury, fueled by sacrifices and punishments, and that they were therefore just as savage—if not even more cruel—than the religions of the "primitive" peoples that the heirs of this Antiquity now considered barbaric, forgetting the kinds of barbarism they themselves came from.

In addition, American exile determined a shift of interest towards "primitives" who were not African, nor Oceanian, but geographically closer: the Indian populations of the semi-arid zones of Arizona or New Mexico and those of the northwestern coast as far as Alaska. Not that the Hopi, Kwakiutl, or Tlingit were unknown before then. Aby Warburg's journey in 1895–1896 among the Hopi to witness the "snake ritual" would suffice to prove it.

But the Surrealists, through their acquisitions of masks from the inhabitants of the Northwest and of Hopi and Zuñi Kachinas, of which Max Ernst amassed a considerable collection, contributed strongly to the emergence of an "American" form of Primitivism that was not founded on African and Oceanic "negro art" but on native arts. Until then, the latter had not been taken into consideration by the most modern American artists, but thenceforth Jackson Pollock helped them to penetrate within the poetic and plastic "depths" from which *The Moon-Woman Cuts the Circle* (1943) [REPR. P. 34] was derived. Furthermore, we know to what extent he proved attentive to Masson's experiments when the latter introduced sand and squirts of paint into his works, *The Earth* (1939) being in this respect all the more emblematic in that it combined the archaic symbolism of Mother Earth, that of the sexual origins of the world, blood, and an explicit allusion to "sand painting." The fact that Pollock's painting was contemporary with Masson's *Pythia* was therefore no accident. The drip paintings of the following years develop the "dance" aspect to the extreme, that of the gesture by which color is projected onto the surface, a gesture from the whole body, whose magnitude is measured by the dimensions of the canvas, placed on the floor. The drip painting thus emerged as the trace of a pictorial choreography, both a physical and mental form of painting. The call for automatism formulated by Breton in 1924 in the first *Surrealist Manifesto* found the most complete response that it could obtain, although we know that in the execution of drip paintings the automatism was not pure, as Pollock remained concerned with composition and chromatic relationships. This dialectic of the creative subconscious and pictorial art—its norms, history, and even its teaching—likewise structured the work of Arshile Gorky [REPR. P. 161]. The latter became one of the rare American friends of Breton, and his suicide, in 1948, was the cause of a crisis within the Surrealist group, from which Matta was at that time excluded, as he was held partially responsible for the depression that led Gorky to take his own life. *The Homely Protestant (Bust)* (1947–1948) by Robert Motherwell [REPR. P. 160], who was responsible for introducing and translating Dada and Surrealism in the United States, falls within the same context. It is therefore not surprising that we recognize in it the traces of Ernst, Joan Miró, and Paul Klee, and that the artists, who didn't know what title to give to the artwork, chose it at random from a page of James Joyce—a procedure inherited from Dadaism. The New York episode of Surrealism was thus decisive in several respects. For the first time on American soil, artists born in the United States or who had come to live there long before were confronted with major artists from a poetic and artistic European avant-garde that until then they had only encountered in the rooms of the Museum of Modern Art. This avant-garde brought new concepts and practices and, in addition, assimilated Indian cultures that had previously only interested ethnologists and specialized connoisseurs. The contact between artists, the emergence of a milieu of which, in various ways, Peggy Guggenheim and Marcel Duchamp were major figures, the attention paid to little-known "primitive" cultures were decisive factors in the formation of what later came to be known as Abstract Expressionism. Moreover, the passing presence of Surrealism affected Mark Rothko and Barnett Newman just as much as it did Pollock, Gorky, and Motherwell. This aesthetic and historical relationship is well known and is no longer under debate today as it may have been when it seemed important to American curators or critics to minimize the Surrealist and thus European influence in the gestation of Abstract Expressionism. Conversely, it has very often been insufficiently noted that the geography of these artistic and intellectual relationships was not simply a line maintained between the two coasts of the North Atlantic. An appropriate geometric figure would be more of the triangular variety, or would contain several triangles. Although Paris and New York were two of its invariable points, the third would be situated—depending on the time and the artists—in Chile, Argentina, Brazil, Mexico, or Cuba. The Caribbean and Central and South America were directly involved in this cartography, which is also a history, and in several ways. The first is based on the role that the Pre-Columbian civilizations played very early on in the Primitivist movement. Breton, Antonin Artaud, and D.H. Lawrence's journeys to Mexico were obvious signs of this. Claude Lévi-Strauss' travels to Amazonia were even more significant for our purposes in that the author of *Tristes Tropiques* was Breton's companion during the crossing in 1941. Pre-Hispanic civilizations were obviously not a discovery of the interwar period, but the European avant-gardes' perspective was not limited to just curiosity and admiration. The journey to meet the Tarahumara Indians was no less important for Artaud in 1936 than Breton's visit to Frida Kahlo and Diego Rivera [REPR. P. 112] in 1938, even though the latter's main goal was to meet Leon Trotsky. In Mexico, Breton was able to better measure the intensity of an artistic movement that had until then been little discussed in Europe. His hosts, Kahlo and Rivera, were two of the protagonists; David Alfaro Siqueiros and Rufino Tamayo [REPR. P. 160] were others. For the artists of the "South," the call for a political and social revolution that the Parisian Surrealists never ceased to hope for, despite their increasingly strained relations with the French Communist Party, was most often accompanied by a call for the development of a South American modern art rooted in the native and therefore Pre-Hispanic civilizations, and in the contact with a natural world that was still largely preserved at that time from the violations of the mining or forestry industries. A quick perusal of the titles of their artworks corroborates this: *Ancestral Butterfly* (1955) for the Argentinian Alicia Penalba, *Hello to Earth* (1966) for the Cuban Agustín Cárdenas [REPR. P. 49], *Environmental Fragment No. 5* (1973–1974) for the Brazilian Frans Krajcberg. The preference accorded to wood of the Chilean Juana Muller, Cárdenas, and Krajcberg is just as significant: wood calls for direct cuts, and thus for the intervention and physical efforts of the artist's body. Furthermore, wood is obviously the material of "primitive" sculptors, Indians and Africans alike, on a par with stone, which must also be worked on directly and which also belongs to the most ancient history of sculpture. Thus a form of Primitivism extended through to the second half of the 20th century. Its earliest creations, cut from wood, were the divinities that Paul Gauguin sculpted between 1891 and 1893 in Tahiti based on references taken from on site, but also from the cultures of the Marquesas Islands, Easter Island, and the Maori of New Zealand. Its chronological continuity was inseparable from the progressive expansion of its geography, which eventually encompassed the whole of the American continent.

Translated from the French by Anna Knight

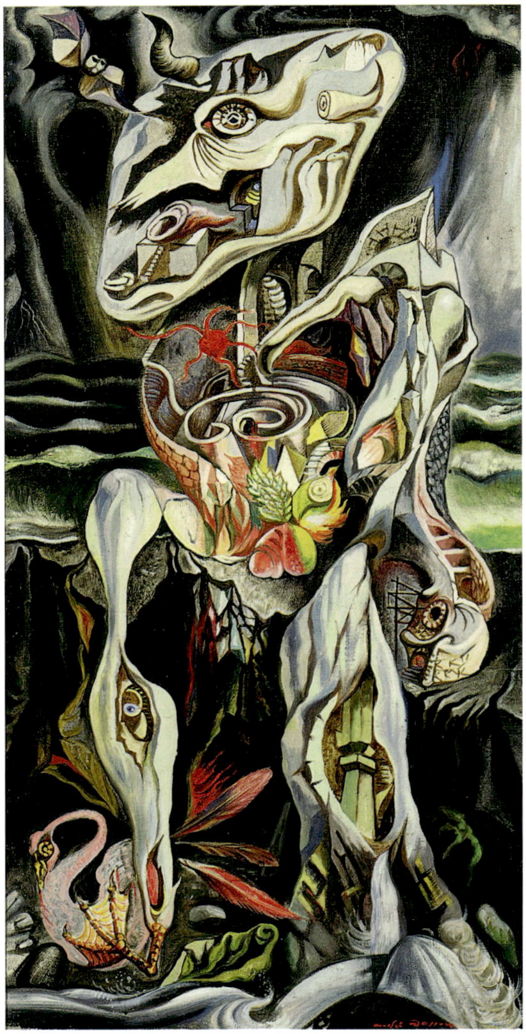

André MASSON
The Labyrinth
1938

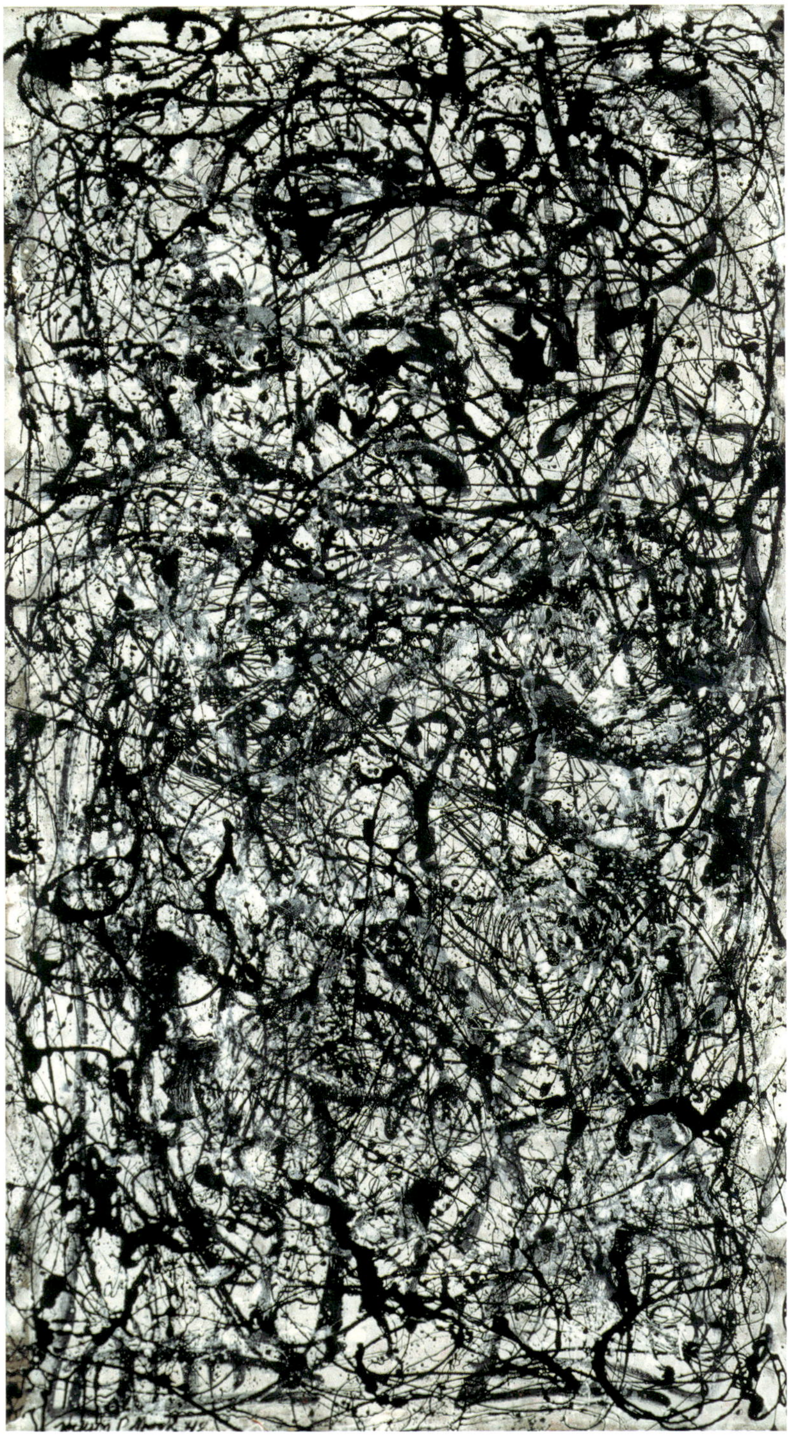

Jackson POLLOCK
Number 26 A, Black and White
1948

Wifredo LAM
Initiation
1950

Carlos PÁEZ VILARÓ
Bull
1956

Rufino TAMAYO
Singing Man
1950

Sesostris VITULLO
Chola
1951

Robert MOTHERWELL
The Homely Protestant (Bust)
1947-1948

MATTA
Xpace and the Ego
1945

Arshile GORKY
Landscape-Table
1945

Ghérasim LUCA
Matto Grosso Indians [from the *Brazil* series]
1960–1970

Gisèle FREUND
Frida Kahlo Next to a Sculpture in Her Courtyard
1951

Susan MEISELAS
Soldiers Searching Bus Passengers, Northern Highway, Salvador
1980

Manuel ÁLVAREZ BRAVO
Good Reputation Sleeping
1938

Manuel CARRILLO
Silvia with a Little Hen (One Eye Seen)
1950–1960

Mathias GOERITZ
Mexican Pyramids
1959

Graciela ITURBIDE
Oaxaca
1973

Flávio de CARVALHO
Portrait of the Soul of Professor Rivet
1952

Modern Architecture in Brazil

A History Being Written

Valentina Moimas

"Architecture isn't the Wild West." That was Lúcio Costa's response to Geraldo Ferraz[1] in 1948, when the latter invited him to reestablish the true history of the origins of modern architecture in Brazil and the identity of its real pioneers: Gregóri Warchavchik and Flávio de Carvalho [REPR. P. 165][2] Although, in his response, Costa recognized that work produced in the late 1920s was the first to open a discussion in Brazil on the topic of modern architecture, he affirmed that an architecture with its own striking singularity and which could truly be called Brazilian did not emerge until a decade later. Oscar Niemeyer, who had derived his knowledge of modernist precepts directly from Le Corbusier [REPR. P. 213], was for Costa one of the movement's greatest representatives, expressing the nation's spirit in his works. It was thus pointless to look for modernism's "pioneers" in the earlier period. Costa, instead, emphasized the "Brazilianity" of the architecture produced by Niemeyer's generation. It is true that at the moment of this polemic,

1. The students responsible for the publication of the portfolio "Arquitetura contemporânea no Brasil" in the magazine *Anteprojeto* (1947) had dedicated it to Costa, whom they considered the master of traditional architecture and the pioneer of contemporary architecture in Brazil. This dedication provoked Ferraz's reaction: see G. Ferraz, "Falta o depoimento de Lúcio Costa," *Diário de São Paulo*, 1 February 1948, and Costa's reply, from which the quote is taken, dated 21 February 1948, published in *O Jornal*, 14 March 1948 [author's translation to French]. These two articles were reprinted in Lúcio Costa, *Lúcio Costa. Sôbre arquitetura. Cartas, entrevistas, manifestações e pronunciamentos*, A. Xavier (ed.), Porto Alegre, Editora UniRitter/Centro Universitário Dos Reis, 1962, pp. 119-128.

2. To explore the two architects' work during this period, which extends to the 1930s, see Cécilia Rodríguez dos Santos, "L'autre phare de Colomb. Origines de l'architecture moderne au Brésil," in *Art d'Amérique Latine, 1911–1968*, exh. cat., Paris, Éditions du Centre Pompidou, 1992, pp. 116-119, and L. Costa, "SPHAN. Serviço do Patrimônio Histórico e Artístico Nacional" (1970), in *Lúcio Costa. Registro de uma Vivência*, São Paulo, Empresa das Artes, 1995, p. 437. The SPHAN, founded January 1937, is Brazil's National Service of Historic and Artistic Heritage.

modern Brazilian architecture was at the forefront of the international scene. The catalogue of the exhibition "Brazil Builds: Architecture New and Old, 1642–1942," organized at the Museum of Modern Art (MoMA) in New York by Philip Goodwin in 1943, contributed enormously to its influence. Rio de Janeiro's Ministry of Education and Health Building, begun in 1937, and the Brazilian pavilion of the 1939 New York World's Fair are generally considered the starting points of this new architecture. Thenceforth, Brazilian architecture was covered by many magazines[3] and exhibitions were organized in several countries. A 1956 book by the Brazilian architect Henrique Mindlin,[4] with a preface by Sigfried Giedion, took up and expanded upon the MoMA catalogue in displaying a panorama of works built between 1937 and 1956. The third reference work on Brazilian architecture was by the Frenchman Yves Bruand.[5] While certainly the most complete, it nevertheless displayed the then-current hegemonic perspective that, under Costa's influence, had guided the earlier publications.[6] According to Costa, Brazilian architecture was, on the one hand, the result of the fusion of European principles and Brazilian national culture, and, on the other, the product of "native genius." In this version of history, Le Corbusier appears as the principal vector for the diffusion of modern ideas from Europe, both through his 1929 lectures, repeated in Brazil in 1936, and through his joint work with a young Brazilian team during the preliminary studies for the Ministry of Health and Education Building project (1936). In reality, Le Corbusier's ideas were disseminated in Brazil in the early 1920s through the magazine *L'Esprit nouveau*, which had subscribers in Brazil. And, in São Paulo in 1925, two architectural manifestos, one signed Rino Levi, the other Gregóri Warchavchik,[7] took up the refrain. In 1926 Fernand Léger and Blaise Cendrars informed Le Corbusier that the construction of the new Brazilian capital, Planaltina (the future Brasilia), specified in the first republican constitution of 1891, was on the agenda, and put him in contact with Paulo Prado. It was thanks to this important sponsorship that Cendrars visited Brazil and Le Corbusier added this new stage to his first South American trip. During the 1929 visit he had the opportunity to tour the houses built by Warchavchik. This visit was followed by a party at the architect's home, attended, notably, by Flávio de Carvalho and the journalist Geraldo Ferraz,[8] who, upon learning of the Swiss architect's arrival, had prepared a questionnaire for him. Le Corbusier went so far as to write a letter to Giedion recommending Warchavchik as a South American delegate to the CIAM. Le Corbusier would never have the opportunity to work on Brasilia, since the 1957 competition to define its pilot plan was strictly national. Lúcio Costa was the winner. The specificity of Brazil's national culture, Costa explained, was that it was rooted in tradition: "In Brazil, in 1922 as in 1936, those who were committed to renovation were the same as

3. In France, see monograph issues of *L'Architecture d'aujourd'hui*, no. 13/14, September 1947; no. 42/43, August 1952; no. 90, June 1960; no. 171, January-February 1974.

4. Henrique Mindlin was one of the Brazilian architects featured in "Brazil Builds." See Henrique E. Mindlin, *Modern Architecture in Brazil*, New York, Reinhold Publishing Corp., 1956.

5. Yves Bruand, *Arquitetura contemporânea no Brasil*, São Paulo, Perspectiva, 1981. This is a Portuguese translation of Bruand's doctoral dissertation, under the supervision of André Chastel, which he defended in 1973.

6. There are numerous reflections on the relationship between Costa and the theses of these three works, and on his role in the construction of the story of modern Brazilian architecture, including: Carlos Alberto Ferreira Martins, "Hay algo de irracional... Apuntes sobre la historiografía de la arquitectura brasileña," *Block*, no. 4, December 1999, pp. 8-22; reprinted in Abílio Guerra (ed.), *Textos fundamentais sobre história da arquitetura moderna brasileira*, vol. II, São Paulo, Romano Guerra, 2010, pp. 131-168; Abílio Guerra, "A construção de um campo historiográfico," in A. Guerra (ed.) *Textos fundamentais sobre história da arquitetura moderna brasileira*, vol. I, São Paulo, Romano Guerra, 2010, pp. 11-22; id., "Lúcio Costa. Modernidade e tradição. Montagem discursiva da arquitetura moderna brasileira," doctoral dissertation, Universidade Estadual de Campinas, Unicamp, 2002.

7. For more information on the two manifestos, see C. Rodríguez dos Santos, "L'autre phare de Colomb. Origines de l'architecture moderne au Brésil," art. cit., p. 127.

8. Geraldo Ferraz, *Warchavchik e a introdução da nova arquitetura no Brasil, 1925 a 1940*, São Paulo, Museu de Arte São Paulo, 1965, p. 29; José Lira, *Warchavchik. Fraturas da vanguarda*, São Paulo, Cosac Naify, 2011, p. 185; Luiz Carlos Daher, *Flávio de Carvalho. Arquitetura e expressionismo*, São Paulo, Projeto, 1982, p. 30.

those who strove for 'preservation,' whereas elsewhere, at that time, people educated in diametrically opposite ways clashed over these goals. In 1922, Mário [de Andrade], Tarsila, Oswald [de Andrade] and the rest, at the same time they were bringing our out-of-date culture up to speed internationally, were also exploring the ancient cities of Minas and the North, in an 'anthropophagic' quest for our roots; in 1936, the architects who struggled to adapt architecture to new construction technologies were the same who worked with Rodrigo M. F. de Andrade to study and preserve forever our authentic past."[9] This tradition, which structured the thought even of those who opposed it, brought the local dimension into consideration. The narrative was nourished as well by the local/global opposition represented by tradition versus modern ideas. In a fundamental text of the 1950s, the writer and critic Antonio Candido studied local/international interaction in Brazilian culture. He maintained that "if it were possible to establish a law of evolution for our spiritual life, we could perhaps consider it to be entirely determined by the dialectic between the local and the cosmopolitan."[10] Candido located the source of the tension between the two concepts "in the ethnic realm, in the condition of the Latin people, culturally of European heritage but ethnically mixed, tropical, influenced by primitive cultures."[11] Furthermore, he posited that Primitivism, as developed in Europe, was in fact better suited to the Brazilian context. Oswald de Andrade, in 1949, had also maintained that in France Primitivism appeared merely as an exoticism, while for Brazilian Modernists it was genuine "Primitivism."[12] This confrontation was capital in Andrade's vision of *Pau-Brasil*: "a quest for synthesis between the multiracial culture of Brazil and a basis of European civilization."[13] Finally, tradition was invoked again by José Lins do Rego in an article in *L'Architecture d'aujourd'hui*, entitled "L'homme et le paysage" [Man and Landscape]: "Modern architects looked for what was vital in ancient houses, what was functional in some of the Portuguese colonists' solutions, and managed to correct monstrous errors by integrating stone, mortar, cement, iron, wood, in fact all construction materials, in the heart of the landscape."[14] This was a tradition unlimited by type, form, or material, based above all on the relationship of human being and landscape. A text by Costa published in the same issue of the magazine illustrated his idea of the native genius of Brazil and its creativity. "Fundamentally, it is the national personality expressed through figures of 'native' artistic genius using the materials, techniques, and artistic vocabulary of our era. [...] It is not a mere quest for 'originality' or a silly obsession with 'daring' or "bizarre' solutions—which would be the very opposite of art—but the legitimate course of innovating, delving to the very depths of the potentialities of new techniques, with the sacred obsession of truly creative artists, to reveal the heretofore unrevealed world of form."[15] This vision, propagated in Brazil and beyond for decades, was here raised to the status of a founding myth. The development and operation of this narrative would be brought into question only by the new historiography,[16] originating with the generation of historians produced by university curricula introduced in the 1970s and early 1980s. The turn between these two decades saw the birth of new specialty magazines (*Projeto*, 1979, and *AU*, 1985)

9. L. Costa, "SPHAN. Serviço do Patrimônio Histórico e Artístico Nacional" (1970), in *Lúcio Costa. Registro de uma vivência*, São Paulo, Empresa das Artes, 1995, p. 437. The SPHAN, founded January 1937, is Brazil's National Service for Historic and Artistic Heritage.

10. Antonio Candido, *Litteratura e sociedade*, São Paulo, Companhia Editora Nacional, 1985, p. 109; quoted in C. A. Ferreira Martins, "Identidade Nacional e Estado no Projeto Modernista. Modernidade, Estado e Tradição," *Óculum*, no. 2, September 1992, pp. 71-76 [author's translation into French].

11. A. Candido, quoted in C. A. Ferreira Martins, "Identidade nacional e estado no projeto modernista. Modernidade, estado e tradição," art. cited, p. 283 [author's translation into French]. In his dissertation "Lúcio Costa...," op. cit., A. Guerra also mentions the contributions of Martins and Candido (p. 120).

12. As reported by Péricles Eugênio da Silva Ramos, *Correio Paulistano*, 26 June 1949, quoted by A. Guerra, "Lúcio Costa...," op. cit., p. 131. This discovery of primitive Brazil, new both to Blaise Cendrars and the Brazilian Modernists who accompanied him, has been well described by José Brito Broca ("Blaise Cendrars no Brasil, em 1924," *A Manhã*, 4 May 1952; quoted in A. Guerra, "Lúcio Costa...," art. cit., p. 122).

13. A. Guerra, "Lúcio Costa...," art. cit., p. 123 [author's translation into French]. "Pau-Brasil" refers to Oswald de Andrade's "Manifesto Pau-Brasil," *Correio da Manhã*, 18 March 1924.

14. José Lins do Rego, "L'homme et le paysage," *L'Architecture d'aujourd'hui*, no. 42-43, August 1952, pp. 8-14.

15. L. Costa, "Imprévu et importance de la contribution des architectes brésiliens au développement actuel de l'architecture contemporaine," *L'Architecture d'aujourd'hui*, no. 42-43, August 1952, pp. 4-7.

16. A. Guerra, "A construção de um campo historiográfico," art. cit., pp. 11-22.

and university magazines (*Gávea*, 1984, and *Óculum*, 1992). We cannot describe here the volume and richness of the historiographic and scientific production of the past thirty years.[17] Nevertheless, in light of the interrogation of the narrative concerning modern Brazilian architecture's origin and characteristics, it is interesting to observe that the relationship to nature and the landscape is still in effect today. The historian Abílio Guerra demonstrated this in the exhibition "Brazilian Architecture. Living in the Forest,"[18] as well as in his writing.[19] With the first issue of the magazine *Klaxon* (1922) [REPR. P. 42], the Modernists seized upon the idea of Graça Aranha,[20] to whom they dedicated the magazine, that tropical nature formed the basis of the natural character. The traveling they did in the 1920s, particularly with Cendrars in 1924, brought them face to face with wild landscapes, simple people, and a past in which they sought elements that would be meaningful in the contemporary world. "The inventory of Brazilian life produced by Mário de Andrade is the foundation of a solid cultural project offering an art inflected by erudition and raised upon a pedestal of popular culture: Tarsila's painting [REPR. P. 99], Oswald's poetry, Villa-Lobos' music, Lúcio Costa's architecture,"[21] recalled Guerra. In the exhibition, the historian traced the connection running from Costa's project for Monlevade (1934) to Tenório Angelo Bucci's beach house (2009) by way of Pampulha (1943) and Oscar Niemeyer's Ibirapuera Park, Oswaldo Arthur Bratke's Vila Serra do Navio (1959), João Batista Vilanova Artigas and Carlos Cascaldi's Faculty of Architecture and Urban Planning (1961), Marcos Acayaba's Baeta House (1994), Ruy Ohtake's Tietê Ecological Park (1970–2012), and Decio Tozzi's Veneza Farm Chapel (2002). Landscape, in all its forms, is at the heart of each of these projects. Bucci and Acayaba's houses have footprints reduced to the minimum, in order to preserve the tropical forest, and are open to the surrounding panorama. The pilings of Costa's Monlevade houses allow residents to go about their lives in the fresh air but sheltered from the sun. The shade of Niemeyer's marquees stretches from one building to another: nature is welcoming rather than threatening, inviting walkers to stroll at their ease. Natural elements become part of the architectural composition, like the water in Tozzi's open air chapel. In his text "The Spirit of South America," Le Corbusier recalled what his friend Blaise Cendrars said about Brazilians: "Whatever they do, with their little urban plans, the landscape will crush them."[22] This woeful prophesy, of course, never came to pass.

Translated from the French by Phoebe Green

17. On principle, the present essay is based exclusively on non-European texts which are often unavailable in French or English.

18. The exhibition was held at the Instituto Tomie Ohtake, São Paulo, 14 June–1 August 2010, then at the Palácio das Artes, Belo Horizonte, 8 April–8 May 2011. See A. Guerra (ed.), *Arquitetura brasileira. Viver na floresta*, exh. cat., São Paulo, Instituto Tomie Ohtake, 2010.

19. A. Guerra, "Lúcio Costa, Gregóri Warchavchik e Roberto Burle Marx. Síntese entre arquitetura e natureza tropical," *Revista USP*, no. 53, March–May 2002, pp. 18-31; cited in *Textos fundamentais sobre história da arquitetura moderna brasileira*, vol. II, pp. 299-325. For more information on this subject, see A. Guerra, "Lúcio Costa..." op. cit., 2002.

20. *Klaxon*, a magazine founded three months after the Semana de Arte Moderna [Modern Art Week] of 1922, a seminal event for Brazilian modernists. The first issue was reserved for the distinguished writer in order to leverage his renown.

21. A. Guerra (ed.), *Arquitetura brasileira. Viver na floresta*, op. cit., p. 23 [author's translation into French].

22. As reported by Le Corbusier in "L'esprit de la Sud-Amérique," an unpublished text by Le Corbusier presented for the first time in Portuguese in Margareth Campos da Silva Pereira, Romão Veriano da Silva Pereira, Cécilia Rodriguez dos Santos, Vasco Caldeira da Silva, *Le Corbusier e o Brasil*, São Paulo, Tessela/Projeto, 1987, p. 71. This text was later published in French *Le Corbusier. Conférences de Rio. Le Corbusier au Brésil*, éd. par Y. Tsiomis, Paris. Flammarion, 2006, p. 187.

Agustín HERNÁNDEZ
Folkloric Ballet School, Mexico City
1965

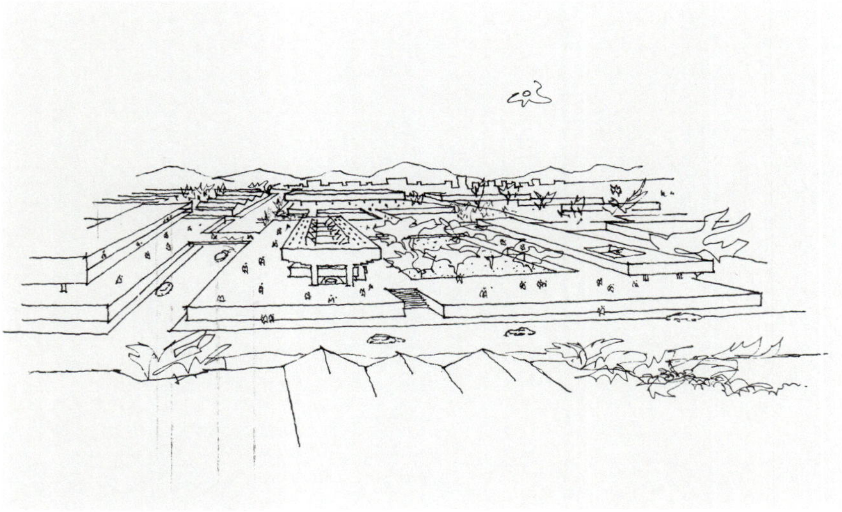

Decio TOZZI, Luiz Carlos RAMOS
Technical and Commercial School, Santos
1963–1965

GRUPO AUSTRAL
Hardoy Chair
1940

Oswaldo Arthur BRATKE
Casa Oswaldo Arthur Bratke in Morumbi, São Paulo
1951–1954

Ruy OHTAKE
Telephone Center, Campos do Jordão
1971–1973

Paulo MENDES DA ROCHA
Gymnasium of the Paulistano Athletic Club,
São Paulo
1958–1961

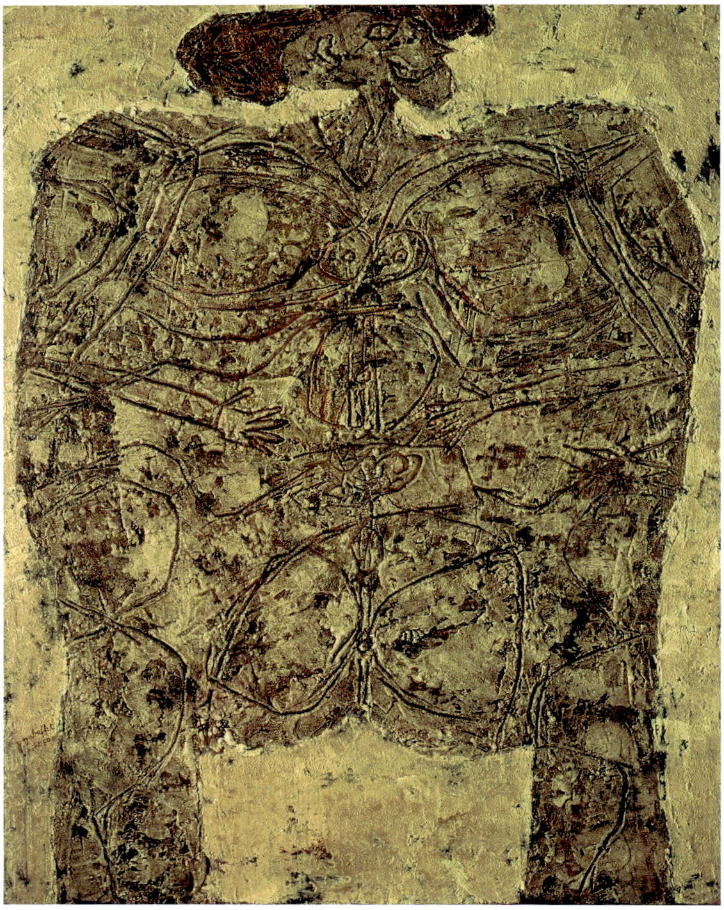

Jean DUBUFFET
Le Métafizyx
1950

Zoltán KEMÉNY
Black Fart
1951

Alfonso-Angel OSSORIO
Knots of Spring
1954

Bernard RÉQUICHOT
House of the Sleeping Carousel
1958-1959

African Modernities

Audrey Coudre

While the contribution of African cultures to European art has been analyzed many times, studies of artistic expression in Africa during the modern period are rare. Contemporary African scenes are much better known in France, particularly since the 1980s and the "Magicians of the Earth" exhibition. But in order to consider African artists of past generations, we are obliged to broach periods that art history has not explored even in their broad outlines: the colonial era and the first decades of independence, a political and historical context playing a crucial role in the emergence of an African art that differentiates itself from traditional practices while remaining connected to local cultures.

To speak of modernity in reference to African art is to deny the essentialism of a "pure" African aesthetic echoing an age-old past, an artistic expression exempt of any external influence. On the contrary, to situate Africa and its artistic productions within the modern context is to place these creations at the heart of a field of political and cultural interactions between Africa and Europe, Africa and the Americas, or even between certain African countries and the countries of the former Communist Bloc. This study demands, similarly, that communications and exchanges within the African continent be taken into consideration. Contrary to what is often implicitly accepted, the colonial era did not result in the disappearance of all original creation in Africa. An overview of the various African countries shows the proliferation of new artistic forms that began in the 1930s, but were particularly active in the 1950s and 1960s. No longer derived from traditional norms and incompatible with international Modernism, these artworks, mainly created for Europeans, have by and large been completely forgotten and discredited. However, an attentive study allows different schools and individual expressions during this period to be identified. Widely diverse artistic forms were developed based on individual or communitarian impulses, or encouraged by a government. These creations proceed by way both of appropriation and reinterpretation and are generally characterized by their syncretism. Thus cultural confrontations and crossovers did not mark the end of creation, but its reinvention.

The arts of Africa cannot therefore be summed up by the traditional/contemporary artistic dichotomy that assumes a seamless transition from collectively-produced to individual creation. During the modern period, ritual artistic practices stemming from funerary or healing traditions and folk art—Senegalese *souwères* (paintings under glass) or Nigerian *batiks* and embroidery—experienced considerable evolutions with the introduction of new media and materials borrowed from the Western world. Other more radical changes were undertaken, caused by the spread to several countries of education advocating the invention of specifically African styles and by contact with certain expressions of European Modernist movements.

Starting in the late 1920s, artists formed a network of relationships, some within missionary schools that encouraged the development of an art relating to craft practices, others in art schools and studios connected to universities and generally established by Europeans. Others remained independent, either by choice or obligation. During the decades 1940–1960, arts education was put in place in most African countries. Many artists left to study abroad, some returned to practice their art or teach in their country of origin, others continued their careers in Europe.

In 1926, the Belgian colonial administrator of the Congo, Georges Thiry, identified the panel painters Djilatendo and Albert Lubaki.[1] He encouraged them to develop a practice as watercolorists and publicized their creations, which were shown shortly afterwards in Belgium. The Congo later became the hotbed for many initiatives. The École Saint-Luc was founded by Brother Marc Stanislas in Gombe-Matadi (1943) and trained sculptors, relaying a traditional practice in the Congo. It was transferred in 1949 to Léopoldville (Kinshasa), where it became the Academy of Fine Arts, the first institution of this kind in Central Africa. Maurice Alhadeff, a businessman and patron, opened a studio in Kinshasa in 1948. The painters, sculptors, and potters that frequented it had access to documentation on European art and were able to market their creations, which were integrated within a number of collections in Europe and the United States. In Elisabethville (Lubumbashi), Pierre-Romain Desfossés' studio or "Academy of Indigenous Art," founded in 1947, and the fine arts and crafts academy instituted by Laurent Moonens in 1951 provided an education that called on the "African interiority" of artists, encouraged to express rhythms and colors in scenes inspired by everyday life. Mwenze Kibwanga was one of the figureheads of this "Lubumbashi school." He produced the mural decorations of the Congolese pavilion at the 1958 World's Fair in Brussels, where the works of Bela and Pilipili Mulongoy were also presented.

In Nigeria, it was the artist Aina Onabolu who, after training as a painter in London and Paris, introduced modern arts teaching. Considered the father of Nigerian modern art, he practiced a realistic academic style that soon became a school, and advocated recourse to European teachers. This was how in 1927 the archaeologist and artist Kenneth C. Murray (who was later to create the first National Museum in Lagos, in 1957) was invited to set up an arts cursus for secondary schools. The curriculum,

1. Georges Thiry, commenting on Lubaki, who was an ivory sculptor and panel painter when he met him in 1929: "I gave him paper and watercolor paints and he started to make very decorative drawings" (G. Thiry, *À la recherche de la peinture nègre*, Liège, Yellow Now, 1982, p. 11). Lubaki's work was first exhibited in 1929 at the Palais des Beaux-Arts de Bruxelles.

founded on the study of pre-colonial culture and craft, refused to imitate European artistic movements and aimed to promote a new Nigerian cultural identity. It encouraged a neo-traditional aesthetic, particularly inspired by the Igbo culture. This position gave rise to a controversy with Onabolu. The latter, who intended through his practice to breach the prejudice whereby African artists were incapable of mastering academic techniques, saw in Murray's approach an extension of the colonial concept of artistic primitivism. Benedict Chuka Enwonwu and Uthman Ibrahim were among Murray's most well-known students. Nigeria became one of the most dynamic African countries in terms of artistic centers, presenting both European models and neo-traditionalist aesthetics. The "rebels" of the Zaria Art Society, created in 1958 at the Nigerian College of Arts, Science, and Technology, advocated a "natural synthesis" between the contemporary art practiced in Europe and traditional art, as well as the cultural traditions of the various Nigerian ethnicities. In 1957, German academic Ulli Beier founded *Black Orpheus* [REPR. P. 184] Africa's first cultural magazine, in which major Nigerian authors such as Chinua Achebe and Wole Soyinka were published, and established the Mbari Cultural Centre in 1962 in Oshogbo, open to all artistic disciplines. Its art studio, launched in 1964 by artist Georgina Betts Beier, was founded on the creative freedom of its participants, often converted artisans.[2] Jimoh Buraimo, Muraina Oyelami and Twins Seven Seven featured among these artists of the "Oshogbo school"; their works were soon shown in Europe and the United States.

In Ghana, in 1937, after having founded an art school in South Africa, German sculptor Herbert Vladimir Meyerowitz joined the College of Achimota, created to train the African elite. He replaced European academic models by an approach based on local culture and crafts, while teaching Western art techniques. In Uganda, Margaret Trowell founded the art department of Makerere University in Kampala in 1939. She also advocated the use of Western techniques to create an "African aesthetic," and a choice of subjects derived from local themes. This department became the training center for all of East Africa. It attracted many artists, including the Tanzanian painters Sam Joseph Ntiro and Elimo Njau, as well as Kenyan sculptor Gregory Maloba. Several among them were to undertake further studies in England. From 1958, Cecil Todd, Trowell's successor, broke away from the latter's teaching and showed her students the modern forms of Western art.

In Mozambique, the Núcleo de Arte in Lourenço Marques (Maputo), an association created in 1922 by young Portuguese-born artists and writers, developed through the patronage of Portuguese architect Pancho Guedes, and was opened up in the late 1950s to Mozambican artists such as Malangatana Valente Ngwenya and Alberto Chissano.

In Rhodesia (Zimbabwe), in 1939, Reverend Canon Paterson offered a program at the Cyrene Mission School that encouraged the creative freedom of African artists. Art historian and artist Frank McEwen, who had frequented Constantin Brancusi and the Cubists during his training in France, was named in 1957 as the director of the new Rhodes National Gallery, where he set up a stone sculpture studio. Directing the artists towards "spiritual" art, he created the school of "Shona sculpture." Tom Blomefield, a South African living near Harare, discovered a deposit of serpentinite stone on his farm and created the Tengenenge Art Community, which allowed this Shona sculpture to develop; these works were presented at the Museum of Modern Art, New York, in 1968 then at the Rodin Museum, Paris, in 1971. In 1951, Pierre Lods founded in Brazzaville, in the Congo, the "Atelier-hangar," commonly known as the "Poto-Poto School," which was an enduring and seminal site. Its teachings advocated a "purely African" style, founded on the method of *"laisser-faire"* (non-interventionism). The artists were Félix Ossali, Jacques Zigoma, François Thango and Nicolas Ondongo [REPR. P. 180], later joined by Marcel Gotène [REPR. P. 181]. They sourced their inspiration from the everyday life and traditions of the Congo, developing a special style characterized by blocks of

2. Jimoh Buraimo reported: "The system of education adopted by Georgina was to allow us to be totally independent. She never showed us an example and never told us what to do. On the contrary, we were supposed to express what we had in mind. Our theater practice helped us a lot. Our first plastic expressions clearly represented an interpretation of music, choreography or theatrical images" (cited in "Oshogbo Art School, from Mbari Experiment to Global Reckoning," *Nigerian Compass*, 21 December 2009).

color edged with black. In 1958, Thango was sent by Lods to Brussels to represent the Poto-Poto School at the World Fair. Several artists from the school would present their works in exhibitions abroad. Gotène travelled to France in 1963, where he frequented the studio of Jean Lurçat and the National Academy of Arts and Crafts of Aubusson. In 1961, at the request of Léopold Sédar Senghor, first president of Senegal, Lods moved to Dakar and became the director of the National School of Fine Arts. The main courses were taught by Senegalese artists Iba N'Diaye [REPR. P. 185] and Papa Ibra Tall, who had both trained in France and returned to Senegal at the time of Independence. While the latter, who created the National Manufacture of Tapestry, taught a Senghor-inspired course on Négritude following the tradition of the Africanizing style of the Poto-Poto School, N'Diaye contested its folkloric character and turned to European models. After organizing the World Festival of Black Arts (1966), he left Senegal in 1967 to move to Paris. In the 1970s, the Agit'Art Laboratory, founded by Hel Sy and Issa Samb (Joe Ouakam) also contested the notion of artistic Négritude.

In Sudan, as in Ethiopia, the pioneer generation comprised artists trained abroad, who were characterized by a style mid-way between European Modernist movements and formal African and Islamic references. The Sudanese Ibrahim El-Salahi, Ahmed Shibrain, and Amir Nour were thus also educated in London, where the former developed a part of his career. El-Salahi and Shibrain integrated calligraphic variations within their Western-inspired works based on verses of the Koran. In Khartoum, the School of Design, created in 1946, taught an art course from which the "Khartoum School" emerged, around the figure of El-Salahi who was a student and later a teacher there. In Ethiopia, major artists such as Afewerk Tekle, Skunder Boghossian, and Gebre Kristos Desta were trained abroad. Some of them would later teach at the Academy of Fine Arts of Addis-Abeba, created in 1958 by Ale Felege Selam.

The art of South Africa is more strongly permeated by Western movements. Most of the pioneers of modern art left to train or reside in Europe. Irma Stern [REPR. P. 20], of German origin, studied at the Weimar Academy, where she frequented the studio of Max Pechstein in 1917, before returning to South Africa. She devoted her life to travel, painting the landscapes and populations of various Sub-Saharan African countries. Maggie Laubser travelled and lived in Europe from 1913 onwards. Like Stern, she was strongly influenced by the Expressionist style, returning to South Africa in 1924. Ernest Mancoba [REPR. P. 194] became famous in 1929 with the representation of a "Bantu Madonna," which caused a scandal. He came to Paris in 1938; after the war he met the artists of the Cobra movement, in which his wife Danish artist Sonja Ferlov participated. He adopted an abstract style, situated at the crossroads of European and African cultures. Gerard Sekoto, the first black South African artist from whom the Johannesburg Art Gallery acquired an artwork, in 1940, went into self-imposed exile, leaving for Paris in 1947. He placed his realist-style painting in service to his commitment to the recognition of a Pan-African culture. A contemporary of Sekoto's, after studying in Germany, the artist John Koenakeefe Mohl opened the first South African school for black artists in the township of Sophiatown, in 1944. The artist Cecil Skotnes later directed the Polly Street Art Centre in Johannesburg from 1952, fostering the emergence of a whole generation of black artists. With the establishment of apartheid in 1948, social subjects devoted to the black proletariat of the townships gave way to the expression of the artists' political demands.

Translated from the French by Anna Knight

ANONYMOUS
Village Market Scene, Nigeria
n.d.

GERA
Untitled
n.d.

ANONYMOUS
Mami Watta
ca. 1950

Aniedi OKON AKPAN
Standing Chief
n.d.

ANONYMOUS
Wrapped Radio
ca. 1940

Nicolas ONDONGO
Market in A.E.F.
1958

Marcel GOTÈNE
Untitled
ca. 1960

Malick SIDIBÉ
Birthday Abib
27 April 1969

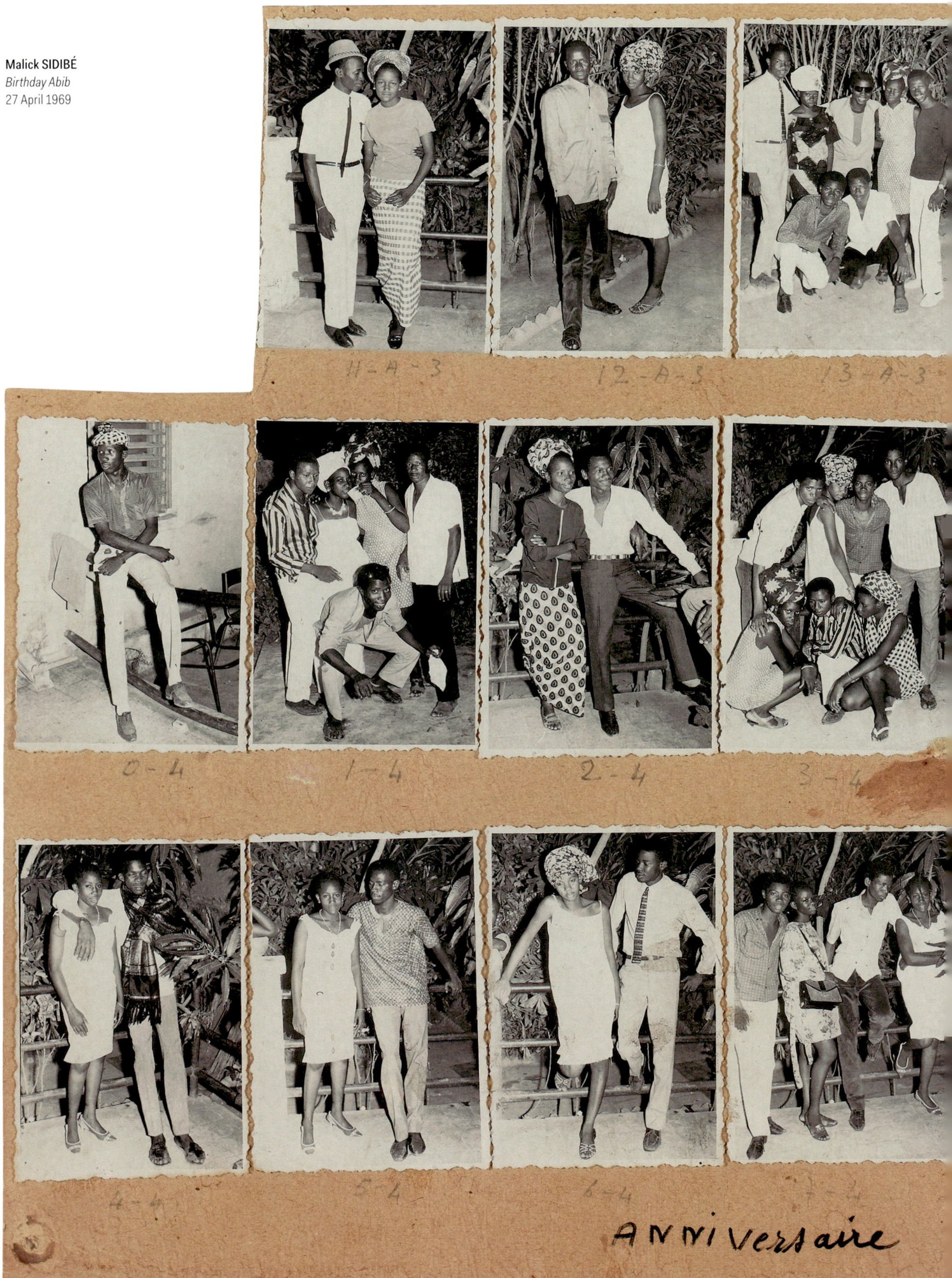

9-4
10-4
11-4
12-4
13-4
14-4
15-4
17-4
16-4
18-4
Abib 27-4-1969

Black Orpheus, Ibadan (Nigeria), no 10, 1962
Editors: Ulli Beier, Janheinz Jahn
Cover: Susanne Wenger

Leandro MBOMIO
Demonstration
1974

Iba N'DIAYE
Untitled
1970

Modernities in the Middle East

Under the Sign of Artistic Plurality

Fanny Drugeon

"Therefore as much as the West itself, the Orient is an idea that has a history and tradition of thought, imagery, and vocabulary that have given it reality and presence in and for the West. The two geographical entities thus support and to an extent reflect each other."[1] In a work both admired and condemned, Edward W. Said thus examined Orientalism, which he described as the West's fantasy of the Orient.[2] Doing so, he also opened the question of modernities, their construction in the Middle East,[3] and the effects of a mutual fascination and interpenetration of cultures. To formulate a unifying consideration of the different countries of the Middle

1. Edward W. Said, *Orientalism*, New York, Vintage Books, 1978, p. 5.

2. See Sophie Orlando, "Decolonizing the Gaze?" in the present work, pp. 238-241.

3. Defining this geographic zone is problematic; this essay will discuss the Arab world and Iran. For the lexical and sociopolitical problems inherent in the term, see the article by Monia Abdallah analyzing the fluctuations of this generic title: "Analyse topique d'une caractérisation artistique. Étude des lieux communs dans l'art contemporain islamique," *Images revues* [online magazine], document 5, uploaded 1 September 2005: http://imagesrevues.revues. org/324.

East would be wasted effort, given the importance of their individual complexities and specificities.[4]

Nevertheless, the examination of modernities in the Middle East takes on a different cast from the perspective of the collections of the National Museum of Modern Art and with the early 20th century as a starting point. The diversity of Oriental modernities arises from the difference of context and references when a form becomes the affirmation of a school rather than a tradition. In this sense, Western domination from the 19th century on played a role not so much by the nature of the models it made available as by their circulation and confrontation with existing artistic tradition, which included both the calligraphic and the figurative—notably the art of the miniature. Exchanges and transfers were intensified both through the residence of Western artists in the Orient and the "Grand Tour" of Oriental artists through Europe to pursue or complete their training, with or without an official scholarship. The creation and institutionalization of art schools had a great influence on the construction of artistic modernities in the Arab world, whether such education was taken as a reference or stringently opposed. So were created the School of Fine Arts in Cairo (1908), another in Tunis (1923), the Lebanese Academy of Fine Arts in Beirut (1937), and a department of painting and sculpture in the Institute of Fine Arts in Baghdad (1939). Careers and influences intersected; artists such as the Lebanese Georges Daoud Corm (1852–1930) became go-betweens. In 1906 the Egyptian Georges Hanna Sabbagh (1877–1951) took up residence in France, where he became familiar with School of Paris painters like Amedeo Modigliani and developed a personal synthesis of Cubist and Oriental influences, in both subject and form. His compatriots Mohamed Naghi (1888–1956) and Mahmoud Mokhtar (1891–1934) [REPR. P. 129] similarly introduced a modern dimension in their work. Naghi, that "Egyptian Impressionist,"[5] entered in contact with Claude Monet, whom he met in 1918, but also with

4. Many monographs have been published, as well as studies of specific countries such as Egypt or Iran. In transnational historiography, several works examine the issue of modernity in the Middle East. See, for example, Wijdan Ali, *Modern Islamic Art: Development and Continuity*, Gainesville, University of Florida Press, 1997; Nada M. Shabout, *Modern Arab Art: Formation of Arab Aesthetics*, Gainesville, University of Florida Press, 2007; Bernard Heyberger, Silvia Naef (eds.), *La Multiplication des images en pays d'Islam. De l'estampe à la télévision, XVIIe-XXIe siècle. Actes du colloque "Images. Fonctions et langages. L'Incursion de l'image moderne dans l'Orient musulman et sa périphérie," Istanbul, Université du Bosphore, 25–27 Mars 1999*, vol. II, Würzburg, Ergon, 2003; Saeb Eigner, *Art of the Middle East: Modern and Contemporary Art of the Arab World and Iran*, London/New York, Merrell Publishers Ltd., 2010; Silvia Naef, *À la recherche d'une modernité arabe. L'évolution des arts plastiques en Égypte au Liban et en Irak*, Geneva, Slatkine, 1996.

5. See Effat Naghi, Christine Roussillon, Alain Roussillon, et al., *Mohamed Naghi (1888–1956). Un impressionniste égyptien* [Cairo], Les Cahiers de Chabramant, [1988]. Naghi's notes evoke his examination of Egyptian and modern art and his main theoretical texts are published in this work.

André Lhote, whose teaching would continue by correspondence and with whom he would remain close until the artist-theorist's arrival in Egypt in the early 1950s. As for Mokhtar, he introduced multiple influences in his sculpture, from reminiscences of ancient Egyptian sculpture to traces of his Paris apprenticeship, combined with a political drive for emancipation in works like *Egypt's Awakening* (1920).[6] Another artistic path, liberated from European references, would be found by the next generation, as demonstrated by the career of the Algerian artist Baya (1931–1998) [REPR. P. 24]. She was discovered at a very young age in Algiers by Aimé Maeght, who in autumn 1947 organized a show for her at his Paris gallery. In the catalogue's preface, André Breton projected on the artist's work an Oriental vision: "Baya, whose mission is to restore the meaning of those beautiful, nostalgic words: Arabia the happy."[7] This modernity was not in line with the experience of Western avant-gardes, in that it did not embody a rupture relative to an existing pictorial tradition; whence, perhaps, the lack of enthusiasm for the forms of modernism and an attachment to traditional references. The complex intertwining of aesthetic and political issues developed in parallel with colonial and post-colonial debates, the militancy of art and its movements growing after the turn of the century. Increasingly, artists would adopt a posture affirming ties with pre-Islamic history, allowing a specifically Arab artistic identity to be constructed. This position disassociated them from both traditional academic art and modernist trends. Several of them took advantage of a heritage of folklore, tradition, and craft, proceeding to a subtle displacement and the integration of practices such as calligraphy. So, before taking up residence in Paris, Charles Hossein Zenderoudi (b. 1937) was in the late 1950s one of the main protagonists of Iran's Saqqa-khaneh School, which gave a decisive launch to modern art in that country.[8] While attempting to create its own identity, this movement drew upon Iran's cultural and folkloric heritage. Zenderoudi pressed for a gestural Oriental writing free of the traditional rules of calligraphy [REPR. P. 194]. The letter became a plastic and rhythmic instrument with a spiritual scope. In the exchanges cultivated between Orient and Occident during this period, the appropriation of a common plastic language, the language of abstraction, favored the development of similar explorations in works emerging from environments as dissimilar as those of Behjat Sadr (1924–2009) [REPR. P. 195], Ahmed Cherkaoui (1934–1967), [REPR. P. 190] and Farid Belkahia (b. 1934) [REPR. P. 193]. When the Lebanese artist Shafic Abboud [REPR. P. 192] arrived in Paris, after WWII, abstraction was the dominant trend. Within it, one tendency, as illustrated for instance by Jean Atlan [REPR. P. 190], was to develop an aesthetic of the sign—partially inspired by Oriental motifs, particularly those borrowed from traditional decorative art—which could be attributed to a new type of Orientalism. The works of Abboud, meanwhile, offered a transposition of sensations evoked by experiencing nature. In the 1960s he would criticize the excessive influence of the aesthetic of the sign and seek to free himself from all domination, whether artistic or national.

6. See Nadia Radwan, "Les arts visuels de l'Égypte moderne, Méthodes de recherches et sources. L'exemple de Mahmud Mukhtar [Mahmoud Mokhtar]," *Quaderns de la Mediterrània*, no. 15, April 2011, pp. 51-61.

7. André Breton, *Derrière le miroir*, no. 6, November 1947 ; reprinted in Ramon Tio Bellido (ed.), *Le xxe Siècle dans l'art algérien*, exh. cat., Paris, AICA Press, 2003, p. 143.

8. Staci Gem Scheiwiller (ed.), *Performing the Iranian State: Visual Culture and Representations of Iranian Identity*, London/New York, Anthem Press, 2013.

As Silvia Naef states: "Western-style modern art (*al-fann al-hadîth*)—constituting a rupture with regional artistic traditions—appears in the context of the movement towards modernization, which questions or redefines a certain number of values."[9] The artistic richness and complexity of the Orient since the early 20th century must free themselves from the question of the interplay of influences and redefine the concepts of modernity, tradition, and circulation.

Translated from the French by Phoebe Green

9. S. Naef, "Figurer le corps féminin," in Philippe Cardinal and Hoda Makram-Ebeid (eds.), *Le Corps découvert*, exh. cat., Paris, Hazan, 2012, p. 95.

Jean ATLAN
The Mirrors of Asia
1953–1954

NEJAD
Celestial Perpetuals (1)
1951–1952

Ahmed CHERKAOUI
The Coronation
1964

Alfred MANESSIER
Neap Tide
1954

Fernando de SZYSZLO
Red Falcon V
1966

Abdelkader GUERMAZ
Untitled
1972-1973

Shafic ABBOUD
Composition
1965

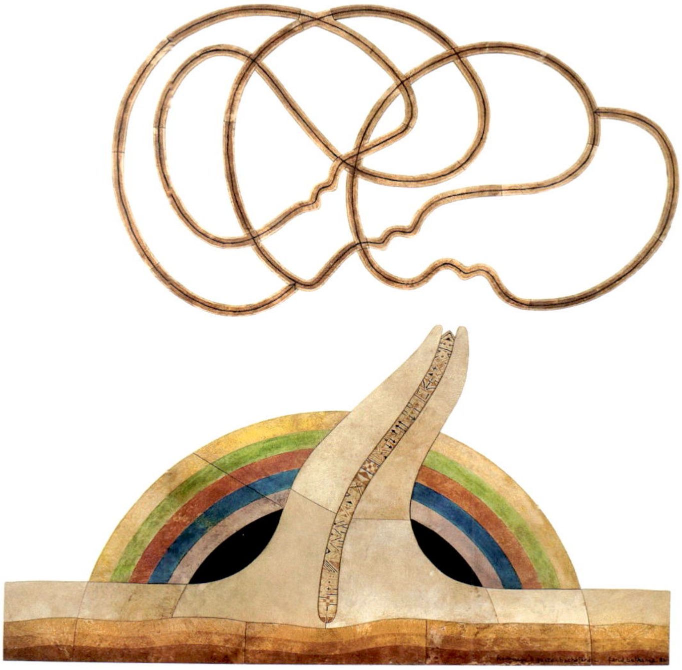

Farid BELKAHIA
Homage to Gaston Bachelard
1984

Farideh LASHAI
Untitled
1967

Charles Hossein ZENDEROUDI
Miuz skfe
1971

Ernest MANCOBA
Painting 1965
1965

Behjat SADR
Untitled
1974

Parvaneh ETEMADI
Untitled
1971

ZAO Wou-Ki
Wind
1954

Jean DEGOTTEX
Writing, 10.2.63
1963

Hisao DOMOTO
Painting
1960

Paul Shusaku FOUJINO
Collage
[after 1962]

Gyula KOSICE
Madí Light Sculpture
1946

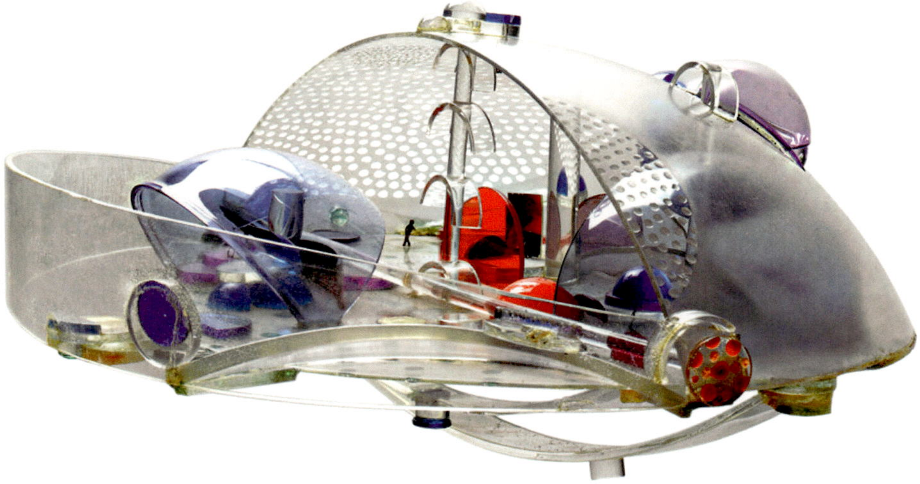

Gyula KOSICE
Model of the Hydrospatial City
1947

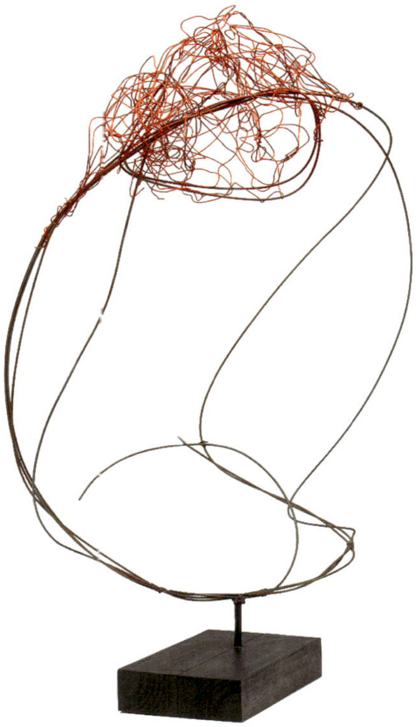

Enio OMMI
Linear Rhythm with Color
1950

Carmelo ARDEN QUIN
Cosmopolis VIII
1946

Juan Nicolás MELÉ
Construction No. 37
1948

Kenneth NOLAND
Air
1964

Sayed Haider RAZA
Bindu
1986

Kumi SUGAÏ
Blue Sun
1969

Esther MAHLANGU
Untitled
1997

"Kineticists of Planet Earth!"[1]

Marion Guibert

1. Lev Nusberg, manifesto of the Dvizheniye group, Moscow, 1966; published [in French] in *Opus International*, no. 4, December 1967, p. 32.

It has long been acknowledged that kinetic-optical art was born in Paris around 1955, the year the Galerie Denise René presented the exhibition "Mouvement." Nonetheless, it is interesting to note that this new aesthetic was created by artists originating in countries that at the time were considered "marginal." Established in the two great cosmopolitan cities of Paris and New York, the movement benefited from a rapid recognition which contributed to its worldwide success throughout the 1960s. Even though today's theoretical studies lead us to analyze the transnational spread of aesthetic forms in terms of transfers rather than influences, kinetic art provides the original example, on an extraordinary scale, of "counter-transference." From the very beginning, it grew explosively. Simultaneously and throughout the world, in the various countries of Western Europe, Eastern Europe, Latin America, the United States, Russia, and Japan, a new generation of artists shared astonishingly similar aesthetic concerns. Beginning in the late 1950s, many exhibitions[2] and massive critical response allowed its aesthetic specificities to be defined. Op Art thus entered very quickly into art history—even though it was harshly condemned by some critics, the most hostile of whom denounced it as an infantilizing "gadget" art. Furthermore, its ramifications spread very rapidly into domains other than the plastic arts: design, fashion, interior decoration.

Kinetic artists, who did not necessarily know each other, nevertheless had in common a search for a new point of departure, an aesthetic course other than the Tachisme and Lyrical Abstraction then in vogue. Defending the concept of a universal art, they did not consider that the geometric tendency of abstract art had been exhausted. On the contrary, they wanted to bring it up to date by developing a visual dynamism using color, geometry, vibration, and movement, harking back to the founders of modernism.[3] "Everything moves, there is no immutability. [...] Stop resisting transformation,"[4] Jean Tinguely affirmed in a tract scattered from a helicopter in the sky above Düsseldorf (1959). As Carlos Cruz-Diez emphasized [REPR. P. 207, 208], even color should not be considered an absolute fact, it is inscribed in the present: "Color has always, even as late as the time of Josef Albers, been conceived as a fixed element [...]. But color is something else entirely! It is an event, it is the perception of the ambiguous and ephemeral. [...] The Pemon people of the Amazon rainforest have another conception of seeing color. If you ask them what color the sky is, they will reply: 'At night? In the evening? In the morning?...' A Westerner will answer without thinking: 'Blue.'"[5] How could real time be integrated into painting? How could one be freed from the fixity of the plastic arts? Kinetic artists escaped from the flat surface of the painting (which became a relief, an installation), painting with light (introducing neon, Plexiglass, lightbulbs), creating an optic vibration (through color, geometry, relief) or a mobile (through mechanical, motorized, or manual movement). With these new artistic expressions they stimulated a different way of looking and offered a new relationship to the work, whose evolutive, tactile, or vibrational nature made it accessible to all, universal.

Why were these artistic studies conducted mainly by artists from regions far from the great art centers? Were they encouraged by a feeling of isolation, giving rise to critical distance and reaction to the art of their era? For some of these artists, it was a matter, at first, of confronting their practice with modern movements of which they knew the great names without having seen their works. For example, it was by traveling in France and Italy that the German Heinz Mack [REPR. P. 211], one of the founders of the ZERO group, discovered modern artworks, living as he did in a culturally annihilated country where for years no books on modern art had been available. Ivan Picelj, one of the founders of the Croatian group EXAT 51, also evoked the isolation of Zagreb, where nothing on Suprematism, De Stijl, or the Bauhaus was available in bookstores, where a work by Piet Mondrian had become part of Belgrade's Narodni Muzej collections in 1932 without ever having been shown or published. The Venezuelan Jesús Rafael Soto [REPR. P. 210] chose exile in Paris, he said, because "That's where I thought I'd find out what had happened to

2. See Serge Lemoine's text outlining the history of these exhibitions: "Créer avec la lumière, inventer du movement," in Serge Lemoine (ed.), *Dynamo. Un siècle de lumière et de mouvement dans l'art*, exh. cat., Paris, Réunion des Musées Nationaux/Grand Palais, 2013, pp. 16-22.

3. Among the historical references they defended were Impressionism, Pointillism, Cubism, Futurism, Constructivism, Suprematism, De Stijl, the Bauhaus, Concrete Art, and Unism.

4. French translation published in *1960, les Nouveaux Réalistes*, exh. cat.., Paris, Paris Musées/Société des Amis du Musée d'Art Moderne de la Ville de Paris, 1986, p. 261.

5. Carlos Cruz-Diez, quoted in Hans Ulrich Obrist, *Conversations*, vol. 1, Paris, Manuella, 2008, p. 143 [our translation].

art between 1918 and 1950. I hadn't had access to that part of art history. I didn't know anything about Mondrian. I didn't even know that abstract art existed[...]."[6] The situation differed, depending on the country; thus, most South American kinetic artists had access to the history of modern art. Joaquín Torres-García [REPR. P. 84, 85], who returned to his country after forty years living in Europe, spread modernist culture throughout Latin America. In Argentina, Julio Le Parc [REPR. P. 211], Francisco Sobrino, Hugo Demarco [REPR. P. 206], Antonio Asis [REPR. P. 207] and Horacio García-Rossi [REPR. P. 209] followed the lessons on the "Psychology of Form and Vision" given by Héctor José Cartier at the Buenos Aires School of Fine Arts. "We did color and balance exercises, we had a very good training in modern art, we know all about constructivism and geometric art,"[7] Asis emphasizes. "In Argentina, Vantongerloo had great influence, he was a sort of spiritual leader to us,"[8] Gregorio Vardanega explains. Major exhibitions were equally influential: that of Victor Vasarely, for instance, presented at the Buenos Aires Museum of Fine Arts in 1958, confirmed these artists in the orientation of their artistic studies. In Brazil, an exhibition of Concrete Art at the Museo de Arte de São Paulo (1951) incited Almir Mavignier to take up residence in Europe to study with Max Bill. When Carlos Raúl Villanueva built the University of Caracas, which included the works of Alexander Calder, Vasarely, Jean Arp, and Antoine Pevsner, Cruz-Diez created models for public works (*Design for an Exterior Wall, Caracas*, 1954 [REPR. P. 207]). Beyond the influence of modern avant-gardes claimed by the artists themselves, who wanted to take their place in a history of Western art, other sources must today be reevaluated. Thus the role of Zdeněk Pešánek, who published his 1941 treaty *Kinetismus* in Prague, deserves deeper study. If the contribution of the *Manifesto Blanco*, published by Lucio Fontana in Buenos Aires (1946), has long been acknowledged, we must remember that it was the debates of the young generation of Argentinian artists that stimulated Fontana to begin this reflection and renew his practice. Similarly, the influence of the Latin American art of the 1940s has been underestimated, particularly that of the groups Arte Concreto-Invención (1945) and Madí (1946) in Buenos Aires. Taking their place in the lineage of Concrete Art, the members of the Madí group (Gyula Kosice [REPR. P. 198], Carmelo Arden Quin [REPR. P. 199], Rhod Rothfuss) nevertheless rejected the static rectangular frame and refuted the idea of a fixed work. Influenced by Calder and Torres-García's jointed toys, Madí liberated art from the traditional frame, conceived jointed structures that could be manipulated by the spectator, introduced new media like water and neon. The Arte Concreto-Invención group, founded under the aegis of Tomás Maldonado, remained faithful to the Zurich Concrete Art practitioners (Max Bill and Richard Paul Lohse) and defended a serial, mathematical art, free of all sentimental expression. These two aesthetic movements had repercussions a few years later in the artistic choices of kinetic artists, some of whom claimed to be followers of Max Bill while others created works in movement, freeing themselves from painting and the flat surface of the canvas. And yet, even though the works of the Madí group were known in Paris as of the late 1940s, when the group exhibited at the Salon des Réalités Nouvelles as well as

6. J. R. Soto, quoted in H. U. Obrist, *Interviews*, Thomas Boutoux ed., vol. II, Milan, Charta, p. 194.

7. Interview with A. Asis, Paris, 3 May 2013.

8. Interview with Martha Boto and G. Vardanega by Maurice Eschapasse, Paris, 8 April 1976, (30 min. 18 sec.), Kandinsky Library, Centre Pompidou, Paris.

in the Galeries Colette Allendy and Denise René, these artists would be absent from the legendary "Mouvement" exhibition. Was this one of the reasons the recognition of their influence has been somewhat neglected? To break their isolation, many kinetic artists formed groups, most often far from the great art centers—in Madrid, Düsseldorf, Padua, Milan, Zagreb, Moscow, and Los Angeles.[9] Favoring a more solitary study, isolated figures emerged such as Agam [REPR. P. 206], Takis, Wen-Ying Tsai, Luis Tomasello, and Cruz-Diez. Although they lived in Paris, the latter refused to participate in the Groupe de Recherche d'Art Visuel (GRAV).[10] These groups made possible a wide distribution of their members' works. These works became part of a vast international network of artists, galleries, critics, and institutions. Far from the Romantic image of the artist alone in his studio, they not only practiced their art, but also curated exhibitions in institutions or galleries, managed artist-run spaces, and published magazines. They created and developed an alternative network in which artists helped each other and shared powerful affinities, going so far, in some cases, as to participate in exhibitions anonymously. Works were signed with the name of the group to which the artist belonged "because we wanted to negate the mythic figure of The Artist," Enzo Mari recalls, adding: "Today, and for thirty years now, I think we were very naïve."[11] Over time, the groups dissolved, letting everyone pursue his optical-kinetic research alone. Rarely did artists abandon this form of expression (as did the Romanian Cadere or the Iranian Sadr [REPR. P. 195]). Without minimizing the role of Paris, the home of many kinetic artists upheld by galleries and critics (and later by institutions), that of other artistic centers was primordial. Thus the "Nouvelles Tendances" movement was formed in Zagreb, rather than a major Western European city. Almir Mavignier explains: "Only Zagreb was ready to offer these young artists a forum for their work, only Zagreb believed in these young artists. Zagreb was eager for any new information and thus was the ideal environment for this art. In the end, it was a coincidence—but Zagreb seized the opportunity when it arose."[12] Moving into the political and social arena, kinetic art postulated building a new world by giving art a radical, universal orientation accessible to all. This utopian approach to art was more likely to develop on marginal artistic scenes, which were quicker to react and eager for novelty. Of all these movements, the Russian group Dvizheniye was certainly the boldest: its manifesto, published in 1966, radical and militant, defined kinetic art as a revolutionary tool contributing to the liberation of humanity. To the criticisms of Jiří Padrta on the subject of this idealism, based on an almost mystical faith, Lev Nusberg replied: "The Russian soul cannot live without faith, nor without enthusiasm."[13] In other countries, on the contrary, kinetic art was very badly received, even by intellectuals. In Iran, both public and critics were very offensive towards Behjat Sadr, who would not be able to sell a single work from her kinetic period.[14] Although Op Artists of widely scattered origins worldwide laid claim to universalism, it would nevertheless be worthwhile to develop a topological reading of their works. By superimposing different readings, this approach would shed light on the singularity of each group of artists by emphasizing the contribution of each of the different countries' traditions.

Translated from the French by Phoebe Green

9. EQUIPO 57 (Madrid, 1957), Gruppo N (Padua, 1959), Gruppo T (Milan, 1960), Dvizheniye (Moscow, 1963), Light and Space (Los Angeles, mid-1960s), and Nove Tendencije (Zagreb 1961) brought together artists from different countries as well as already-formed groups, while ZERO (Düsseldorf, 1957) was an "open" group including many artists, not all of whom were kineticists.

10. GRAV included artists such as García-Rossi, Le Parc, François Morellet, Francisco Sobrino, Joël Stein, and Yvaral.

11. Interview of E. Mari by Ines Bauer and Tobias Hoffmann, 23 May 2006, Milan, in T. Hoffmann and I. Bauer (eds.), *Die neuen Tendenzen. Eine europäische Künstlerbewegung 1961–1973*, exh. cat., Heidelberg, Ed. Braus, 2007, p. 220.

12. Interview of A. Mavignier by T. Hoffmann and Rasmus Kleine, 29 April 2006, in T. Hoffmann and I. Bauer, *Die neuen Tendenzen*, op. cit., p. 211.

13. Jiří Padrta, "Nusberg. Lumière et mouvement," *Opus international*, no. 4, December 1967, p. 30.

14. A work from this series (*Louver and Painting on Canvas*, 1967) is preserved at the Museum of Contemporary Art in Teheran.

AGAM
Moving Assembly
1953

Hugo DEMARCO
Rotation-Reflection
1965

Carlos CRUZ-DIEZ
Design for an Exterior Wall, Caracas
1954

Antonio ASIS
Blue and White Concentric Interferences
1961

Martha BOTO
Swarm of Reflections
1965

Carlos CRUZ-DIEZ
Physichrome No. 506
1970

André CADERE
Untitled
1968–1969

Horacio GARCÍA-ROSSI
Movement
1964–1965

Jesús Rafael SOTO
Extension
1989

Heinz MACK
Light Rotator, Sun of the Sea
1967

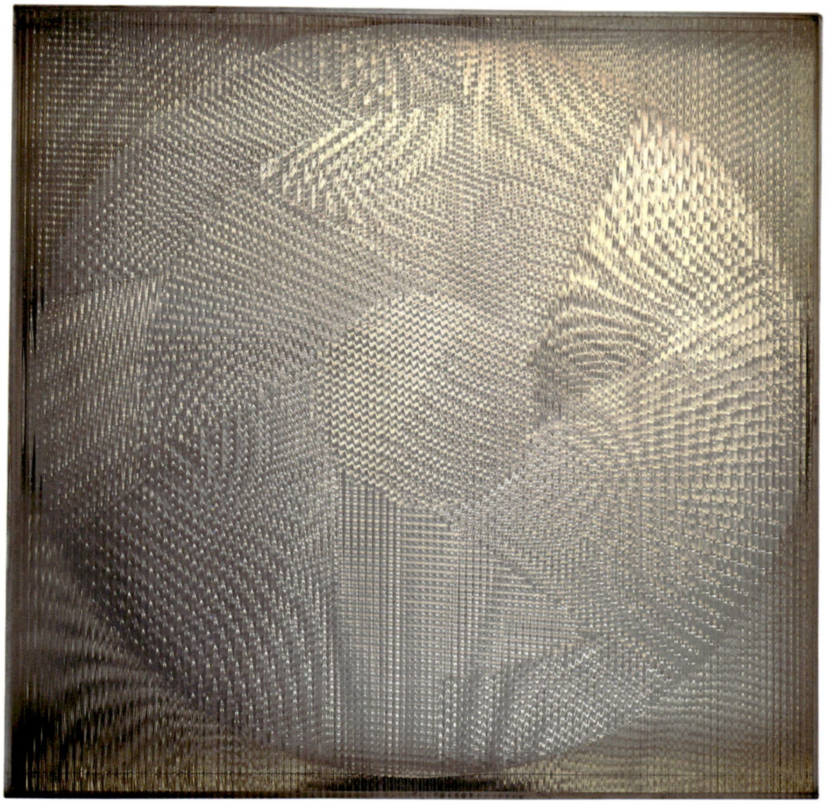

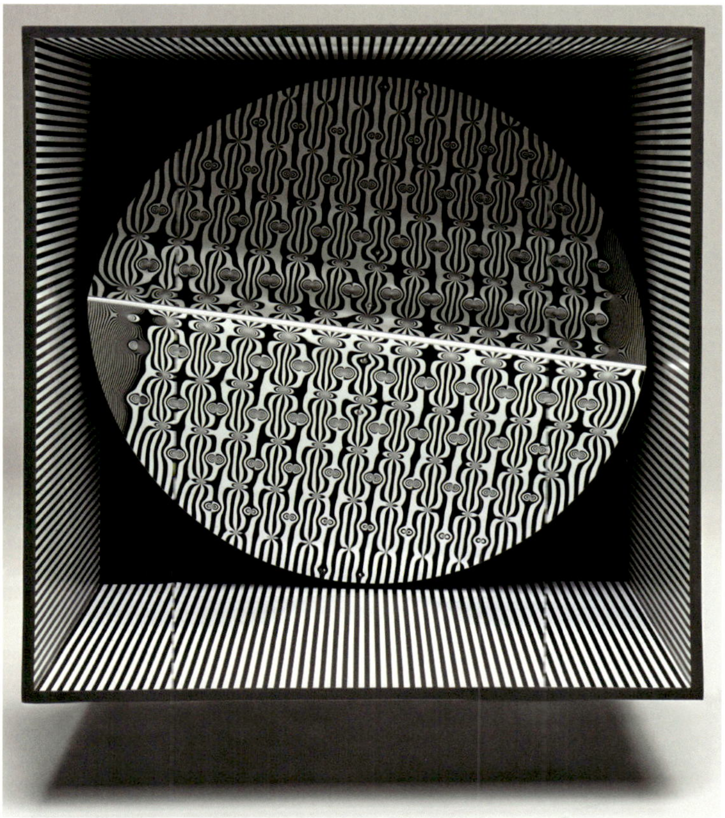

Julio LE PARC
Altered Web
1965

India:
The Age of Cities

Aurélien Lemonier

"What frightens me in Asia is the vision of our own future, which it is already experiencing,"[1] admitted Claude Lévi-Strauss in 1950 while on a UNESCO mission to Pakistan devoted to the teaching of human sciences. In the course of his assignment he traveled throughout Northern India, from Karachi to Calcutta, via Delhi and Agra. In *Tristes Tropiques*, Lévi-Strauss devoted several pages to the description of the chaotic crowds thronging these cities. The origin of his disquiet was twofold: on the one hand, the population shifts caused by the Indian partition and the creation of Pakistan—the exorbitant ransom of Independence that remains a determining factor even today—and on the other, the culmination of a cycle, the dying embers of a process of worldwide urbanization, with the Asian city epitomizing both its beginning and its end. "I could thus see, taking shape before my very eyes, an Asia characterized by workers' dwellings and cheap blocks of flats. This Asia of the future which rejects all

1. Claude Lévi-Strauss, *Tristes Tropiques*, John and Doreen Weightman (trans.), New York, Atheneum, 1975, p. 150.

forms of exoticism, may link up again, after an eclipse of five thousand years, with that dreary yet efficient style of life which the Asiatics [sic] perhaps invented in 3000 BC. It subsequently moved across the earth's surface, making a temporary halt in the New World, so that we tend to think of it as being specifically American; but then, as early as 1850, it resumed its advance westwards, reaching first Japan and now at last its place of origin, after going right round the world."[2]

The stage was set: whereas to his anthropological eye, tropical America reflected an image of small communities on a human scale in which the primitive conditions of social living still persisted—"the reflection, however fleeting it may have now become, of an era when the human species was in proportion to the world it occupied, and when there was still a valid relationship between the enjoyment of freedom and the symbols denoting it"[3]—his travels across the Indian sub-continent triggered contrasting impressions of over-population, of a "martyred continent" and of the wisdom of nothingness. Sixty years on, Indian cities have grown exponentially and are seemingly unable to sustain their growth in population and rural exodus, with resources remaining a pivotal issue (to borrow a recent example from the architect Bernard Kohn, the city of Ahmedabad has seen its population increase sixfold in under fifty years). The study of the architecture of Indian cities therefore stretches beyond the boundaries of history. Its aim is to provide a few pointers regarding the contemporary urban condition: the relationship between the city and its natural environment—the "exhausted territory" as Lévi-Strauss put it—that between its architecture and cultural imprint, and the generalization of industrial economy are all challenges that have been faced head-on by Indian architects since the 1950s. The specificity and multitude of their approaches have contributed to a redefinition of the conventional slant and interpretation of modern architecture, blurring the age-old dichotomy between East and West, modernity and tradition, scientific and vernacular culture, industry and craftsmanship, modernity and spirituality. With this shift in emphasis now pervading the museum space, this seems an appropriate time to examine some of the cornerstones in its history.

2. Ibid., p. 130. The author would like to thank Gwenaël Delhumeau for bringing this passage to his attention.

3. Ibid., p. 150.

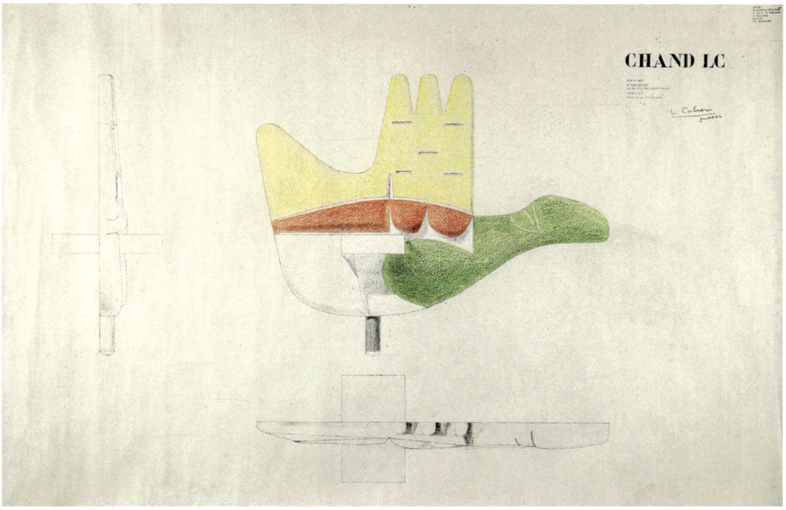

LE CORBUSIER
The Open Hand [Chandigarh]
1964

A City Without Limits

The layout drawn up by Edward Lyutens and Herbert Baker for colonial New Delhi undoubtedly represented a turning point, featuring the cardinal elements of a modern city in the making. Whereas the traditional walled city, modeled on the Northern cities built in the sixteenth and seventeenth centuries under the Mogul Empire, encouraged more densely-packed building, thereby limiting the spread of the city, the plan for the modern city, with its open, less concentrated model, introduced the concept of an "extrovert" city. This change of paradigm, so "foreign to Oriental culture," in sharp contrast to Gandhi's philosophy of a "return" to communal village life, defined the scale of town planning in colonial times. Behind the ostentatious symbols of power, such as the esplanade and monumental avenue leading to the Viceroy's palace, the extension plan for Delhi was underpinned by a system of space distribution rendered by an axial circulation pattern and green vistas (tree-lined thoroughfares set out in a star pattern). Although space was the key resource in the modern city, it was its linear layout, systematically assimilated to vehicular or pedestrian axes, that was to ensure the "hygienic," functional effectiveness of this model in India. It was precisely this strategy that Le Corbusier identified so clearly in Delhi, and then brought to its most radical, generic culmination in Chandigarh:[4] a quadrangular network of sectors measuring 800 × 1200 meters, each one self-sufficient,[5] and a grid whose layout and linkage could be potentially extended into infinity. "The herding together of individuals whose only reason for living is to herd together in millions, whatever the conditions of life may be"[6] as Lévi-Strauss described it, was probably not that different from that which Le Corbusier observed when he was commissioned in 1921 to design the new capital of the Punjab[7]. The architect, however, propagated a totally different image, in the form of a laudatory acclaim of the Athens Charter and the *ex nihilo* creation of a city which was then raised to the ranks of national symbol. Although the media coverage of the Chandigarh project was relayed to a large extent by the political clout of the new democracy, its implementation was an inherent part of the vast program to erect new cities launched by the Indian state in the wake of Independence. The preconceived notion of a country lacking a fully-fledged urban infrastructure during the colonial period is actually inaccurate—the first modern cities emerged in the 1920s, before Independence. The first was Jamshedpur, which was built at the instigation of industrialist Jamsetji Tata,[8] who decided to build a steel plant there. Over a seventy-year period, over one hundred cities were actually designed and built across India.[9] From 1947, however, the urban planning program crossed paths with ongoing industrial development projects, territorial infrastructure designs including roads, dams, and hydroelectric plants, and a political and administrative reorganization of the country based on the creation of regional capitals. The first was Bhubaneswar, the capital of

4. On Chandigarh, see Rémi Papillault, *Chandigarh et Le Corbusier. Création d'une ville en Inde, 1950–1965*, Toulouse, Poësis, 2011.

5. The document produced by the agency, which uses the same scale to compare the layout of New Delhi and Chandigarh, is of particular relevance here. Document published in Jean-Louis Véret, Raj Rewal, Ram Sharma (eds.), *Architecture in India*, exh. cat., ENSBA/Electa Moniteur, Paris, 1985, p. 99.

6. C. Lévi-Strauss, *Tristes Tropiques*, op. cit., p. 134.

7. The Punjab was the northern province most affected by partition; since 1947 its historical capital, Lahore, has been located in Pakistan.

8. Romila Thapar, "Role of the City in Indian Culture. New Contributions to the 'Model of Asian Production'," *Lotus International*, no. 34, 1982, pp. 6-17.

9. See Bijit Ghosh, "New Towns in India. A Home, a Cow, an Acre of Land," *Lotus International*, no. 34, 1982, pp. 19-31.

Orissa, to the east of the country, designed by German architect and town planner Otto Königsberger, who had been living in India since the mid-1930s.[10] Fifty kilometers to the north of Ahmedabad, Ghandinagar, under the aegis of Deepak Mewada, was chosen to become the new administrative capital of Gujarat[11], to the west. There is no end to such examples: the industrial city of Durgapur designed by Joseph Allen Stein (1957–1958), Charles Correa's layout of New Bombay, or the implementation of Aureville's plans by Roger Anger in the late 1960s in the Pondicherry region[12] all emphasize the variety of typological models.

Osmosis

"I like the creative approach, not being tied down to what has been done by our forefathers, but thinking in new terms, of light and air and ground and water and human beings," declared Nehru during a seminar on architecture held in Delhi in 1959, adding that Chandigarh "hits you on the head."[13] This "hit [...] on the head" proved cathartic, as it "provoked and created new ideas," thereby paving the way for a doctrine that qualified the architectural output of the 1950s, implemented by the public works departments, their main brief being to handle national projects, with a postcolonial approach seemingly unaffected by planned economy principles,[14] but also by the minority of self-employed architects (approximately three hundred in 1950).[15] The challenge lay in choosing the planning tools while marking a symbolic break with British rule by creating a new stylistic identity. Chandigarh fulfilled both criteria. Criteria that encapsulated more than any others the link between architecture and national policy in the era immediately following Independence. Nehru's determination to rebuff nationalism and isolationism (the architectural equivalent being Revivalism) in favor of an internationalist philosophy—a hand "open to give and open to receive"—is familiar to all but its relevance here is particularly apt. It was to provide an institutional cornerstone for Indian architecture's extraordinary receptivity to foreign doctrines, which were seasoned and flavored to meet local tastes, and then molded to meet the demands of the country's democratic and economic structures, against a background in which "the spirit of Gandhi and Tagore was still ever-present."[16] "It is unfortunate that we have long been estranged from our own culture and that, consequently, the culture of the West has not been put in its proper perspective. [...] But to say that it is wrong to remain in touch with the latter is to encourage the worst form of provincialism, producing nothing but intellectual poverty. [...] Today's problem is global. No nation can survive by detaching itself from the rest. We must survive together or fall together." This observation by the writer Rabindranath Tagore, quoted by Romain Rolland twenty-three years before Independence,[17] pinpoints the philosophical

10. See Ravi Kalia, *Bhubaneswar. From a Temple Town to a Capital City*, Delhi, Oxford University Press, 1994.

11. See R. Kalia, *Ghandinagar. Building National Identity in Postcolonial India*, Columbia, University of South Carolina Press, 2004.

12. See Anupama Kundoo, *Roger Anger. Research on Beauty, Architecture, 1953–2008*, Berlin, Jovis, 2009.

13. Jon T. Lang, Madhavi Desai, Miki Desai, *Architecture and Independence, the Search for Identity. India, 1880–1980*, Delhi, Oxford University Press, 1997.

14. The first five-year plan, adopted in 1951, related to agriculture, the second, in 1956, was devoted to industry and building development.

15. Raman Kavinde's Calcutta secretariat epitomized this period, see J.T. Lang, Ma. Desai, Mi. Desai, *Architecture and Independence...*, op. cit.

16. See Stephen White, *Building in the Garden: the Architecture of Joseph Allen Stein in India and California*, Delhi/New York, Oxford University Press, 1993.

17. Romain Rolland, "Mahatma Gandhi" [1924]; reprinted in Christine Guyot-Clément and Jean Clément (eds.), *L'Inde. Des rêves, des peuples et des dieux*, Paris, Omnibus, 2007, p. 686 [our translation].

and political issues at stake in building a modern-day India in the wake of British rule: how to achieve modernity and yet draw on the sources of Indian culture, how to revive age-old traditions yet be part of a universal civilization. Such issues reach far beyond the realm of architecture and it would be simplistic to sum them up so literally were it not for the fact that these were precisely the tenets propounded by the architects who helped build the State of India in the decades following Independence. It was the Schools of Architecture in particular that proved to be breeding-grounds for this cultural osmosis. A large majority of architects born in the 1920s and 1930s trained initially in the United States, Great Britain, or France—this was therefore a clear call to increase the number of institutes of higher education devoted to architecture, design and town planning within India itself. Alongside business schools and scientific research centers, a large number of Schools of Architecture were therefore created in the late 1950s, shifting the hub of training and theoretical research from Bombay to Northern India. Apart from Calcutta's historic institution, modeled on the teachings of Claude Batley, and its Delhi counterpart, which put the accent on town planning and heritage studies, the pioneering School of Chandigarh was founded just as building began on the brand-new city.[18] Reflecting the functionalist vision applied by Le Corbusier to every echelon, it owed much to the ten-year presence of Pierre Jeanneret. At the instigation of Richard Neutra, in 1952, Joseph Allen Stein took over the Bengal School of Architecture. In Ahmedabad, Charles and Ray Eames were commissioned in 1958 by the Indian government to devise the curriculum for the future National Institute of Design (NID). Based from the outset on the need to invent a methodology that would combine traditional culture, particularly weaving, and modern production tools, the program aimed to define long-term growth and development strategies. Thanks to the support of the Sarabhai family, the School opened in 1961.[19] The following year, as Louis Kahn was drawing up the initial plans for the Indian Institute of Management (IIM) and pooling a number of architects and students to form a kind of seminar, Balkrishna Doshi (who contributed toward the design of the IIM) and Bernard Kohn set up the Centre for Environment Planning and Technology University (CEPT), which was to become a hotbed of theory and reflection on the subject of Indian architecture.[20]

Tradition—Modernity—Identity

The issue of identity in Indian architecture was a regular feature of the debates launched by the centers for design and production. Indira Gandhi, who came to power in 1966, encouraged the pursuit of the major national projects instigated by Nehru, although she stressed the idea of an architecture that would be both international and dictated by local criteria (vernacular/scholarly, Hindu/Muslim, rural/urban, etc.). Even the term identity, an almost systematic *leitmotiv* of the critical texts of the last twenty years, actually derives, as Bernard Huet suggests, from a synthesis.[21] This synthesis, while

18. Vikramaditya Prakash, *Chandigarh's Le Corbusier. The Struggle for Modernity in Postcolonial India*, Seattle/London, University of Washington Press, 1982.

19. The building was designed by Gautam and Gira Sarabhai, who had worked in Frank Lloyd Wright's Taliesin studio in the 1940s. Wright had also been approached to design a museum in Calico but this never materialized. It is worth recalling that the Sarabhai family run a large number of industries and continue to sponsor a great many cultural and artistic projects.

20. It was at the CEPT that Christopher Alexander really honed the principles of "pattern languages," based on rural Indian architecture.

21. Bernard Huet, "Indira Gandhi National Centre," *Mimar*, March 1987, pp. 37-39. See also *Le Corbusier in India*, a documentary film by Manu Rewal, Duniya Vision, 100 mins, 2001.

Construction of *Permanent Exhibition Complex*
by Raj Rewal, New Delhi, ca. 1970

aiming to overcome cultural specificities, is nevertheless anchored in the formulation or expression of the particular context: a symbiosis between building and climate, a correlation between the architecture and local customs, the updating of cultural and aesthetic references, and a grasp of material and energy sources. In what manner can the collective conscious be conveyed? How can one render the singularity of Indian architecture without turning it into an expression of community identity? The mid-1960s saw increasingly blatant criticism of the waning functionalist model and its excesses, from a territorial point of view (the repetitive and anarchic proliferation of "concrete cubes"), on economic grounds (waste of resources), and as a symbolic reaction (with a refusal to ape the so-called international style). When Raj Rewal [REPR. PP.220-221] returned to Delhi in the 1960s after spending several years in England and in

France—working under town planner Michel Écochard—he campaigned to raise awareness of his country's architectural heritage with a view to shaping the contemporary relevance of modern India's latest projects: "Our generation has been trying to discover the common thread with which the fabric of Indian architecture has been woven in the past and its significance for our times"[22] he wrote in 1985. If one were to follow the architect's comments to the letter (their rhetorical dimension can be measured by the fact that Rewal built most of his designs in Delhi and recently unveiled his Parliamentary library right opposite Baker's monument), this weaving could be read as encompassing in a single span the entire colonial period. In fact, he is putting forward a new fundamental strategy for Indian architecture.

To Rewal and a number of his peers, it is precisely this knot, interweaving memory, tradition and modernity, that provides a plausible stance, a "Third Way." This way unites past and present in a single continuous cycle and is largely derived from a fascination with historical heritage and a review of the refined architecture erected during the Mogul period, such as Fatehpur Sikri, built in the reign of Emperor Akbar, and ranging from the Gujarat stepwells to the Hindu temples in the south of the country, and from the compact city of Jaisalmer to the "poems in stone" of Agra or the tomb of Humâyûn. The architectural designs of Rewal, who introduced Indian architecture into the collections of the National Museum of Modern Art,[23] together with on-site visits of the completed buildings, reveal the architect's signature link between memory and geometry. Rewal rejects any direct references to traditional motifs, turning to the abstract nature of the geometrical layout of classical academic architecture as a way of defining his way of handling space when carrying out his numerous large-scale commissions. He uses the same approach with public buildings as with housing projects, the latter providing fertile ground for research into the typology and economics of constructional modes.[24] This search for the "identity" of Indian architecture might equally be initiated through the use of materials (the reintroduction of stone in conjunction with concrete, for example, and the reappropriation of brick and more recently wood as a means of expression) together with operational techniques that do not overlap with the simplistic categorization of industry versus craftsmanship. Rewal's style stems in fact from a blend of cutting-edge technical expertise, on the cusp of contemporary research, and intermediary implementation techniques, frequently involving a substantial workforce and rudimentary mechanization tools. In this regard, the figure of engineer Mahendra Raj provides the key to understanding sixty years of building in India.[25]

Horizon

Although Indian architecture was only recognized in Europe and the United States in the late 1970s, despite the wide-ranging mobility of its protagonists, one must acknowledge that even today our knowledge remains limited, as the significant number of studies

22. J.-L. Véret, R. Rewal, R. Sharma (eds.), *Architecture in India*, op. cit., p. 12.

23. In December 2012, Raj Rewal gave the National Museum of Modern Art seven scale models and fifty-one drawings, which are currently on display in the museum galleries. I would like to take this opportunity of thanking him for his time and generosity. To find out more about his work, see Giordano Tironi, *Humanisme et architecture. Raj Rewal, Construire pour la ville indienne*, Paris, L'Âge d'Homme, 2013.

24. The shanty town improvement programs initiated by the City and Industrial Development Corporation of Maharashtra (CIDCO), in the Mumbai Region are of particular interest here.

25. Raj began his career by designing the structural system for the Chandigarh Court of Justice and since then has been a key player in almost every emblematic project in contemporary India. See his conference before the Société Française des Architectes, 7 December 2012.

undertaken by Indians themselves are still difficult to find in Europe. It would be therefore simplistic, not to say risky, to reproduce the cursory summaries that are so often propounded, even if these are due to linguistic shortcomings: assimilating the Indian architecture of the 1950s and 1960s, for instance, to a local version of the teachings of architects such as Le Corbusier or Kahn, or reducing certain contemporary doctrines to "critical regionalism." Devoting a room to Indian architecture, it would be all too easy to fall into the trap of univocally transposing Western doctrines to the context of the Subcontinent. Le Corbusier, Louis Kahn, Roger Anger, and Alison Smithson[26] were *transformed* by their approach to Indian culture, rather than governed by some pre-established doctrine—they adapted it, just as Rewal transformed what he learned from Michel Écochard, Doshi from Le Corbusier, and Stein from Wright and Neutra. The culmination of a cycle, in the eyes of Lévi-Strauss, a "birth" given widespread media coverage by Le Corbusier or the continuum of secular humanism advocated by Raj Rewal—even these can be turned into truisms. However sketchy, they nevertheless put forward the hypothesis of a possible escape route from the striking tensions between the unending acceleration of urban sprawl and industrial development and the shifting forms of social and territorial exclusion (poverty, pollution, depleted resources, etc.). We must address this tension and its paradoxes. To what extent do the theoretical and practical viewpoints of the key players in Indian city design allow for alternative models?

As a start, in the complex recent history of Indian architecture, a possible horizon might be envisioned, activated by the continuous two-way flow between East and West that India initiates and absorbs and that someone like Tagore reminds us is still a work-in-progress.

Translated from the French by Caroline Taylor-Bouché

26. Alison Smithson, *Imprint of India*, London, Architectural Association, 1994.

Raj REWAL
State Trading Corporation, New Delhi
1976–1989

Raj REWAL
"Scope" Office Complex, New Delhi
1980–1989

Raj REWAL
Hall of Nations, New Delhi
1970–1972

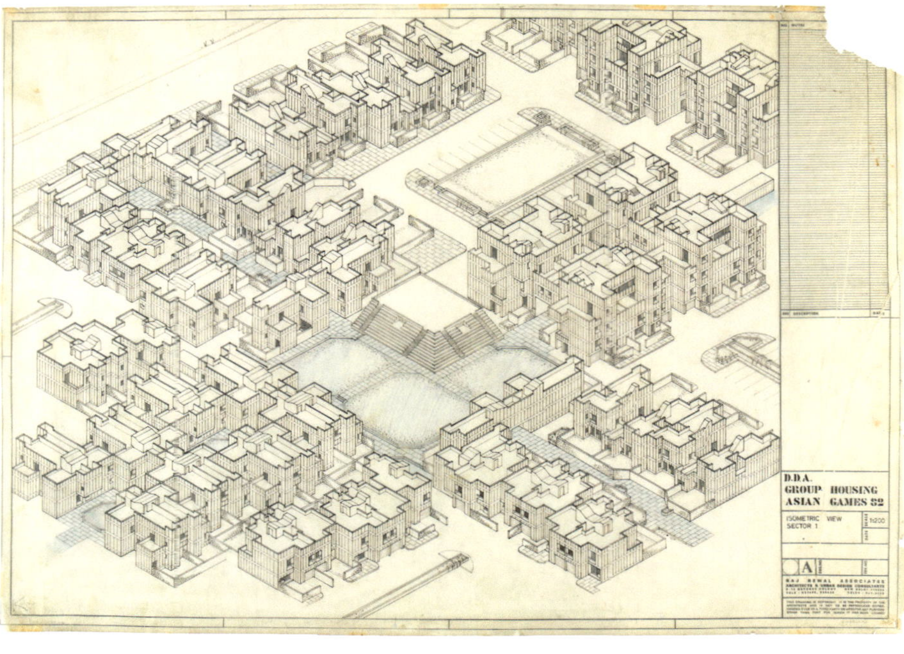

Raj REWAL
Asian Games Village, New Delhi
1980–1982

Kenzo TANGE
Communication Center, Yamanashi Region, Kofu
1961–1966

Masato OTAKA
Sakaide Artificial Ground
1968

Kisho KUROKAWA
Floating City, Kasumigaura
1961

Kazumasa YAMASHITA
Face House, Kyoto
1974

Tadao ANDO
Church of Light, Osaka
1987–1989

Planet Concept

Michel Gauthier

In May 1971, John Perreault wrote in the *Village Voice*: "Conceptual Art is a symptom of globalism and it is the first—Surrealism almost was—international style."[1] The connection, as logical as it is historical, was thus established between Conceptual Art and the phenomenon of globalization, the advent of which had just been proclaimed by Marshall McLuhan. In assuming this position, Conceptualism was perceived as the artistic aspect of the information and communication society then emerging. It could be to this new society what Pop Art was to consumer society. A number of major exhibitions that contributed to consecrating the conceptual phenomenon emphasized this dimension. In the summer of 1970, Kynaston McShine organized "Information" at the MoMA in New York. Beyond the reality of the exhibition—the list of works selected, its display—the title alone sufficed to match conceptual art to the transformation described by McLuhan: information had become the

1. John Perreault, "It's Only Words," *Village Voice*, 20 May 1971; cited in Gregory Battcock (dir.), *Idea Art: A Critical Anthology*, New York, E. P. Dutton, 1973, p. 137-138.

basic commodity; material objects were merely accessory to data flow. That same year, in the same city, the Jewish Museum presented "Software–Information, Technology: Its New Meaning for Art." Jack Burnham, the curator of the exhibition, presented works by conceptual artists such as Joseph Kosuth, Hans Haacke, and Les Levine. The event identified the relationships between the computer systems that the technological art of the time was using and the "dematerializing" tropism of Conceptual Art. Haacke presented *News* (1969): five teleprinters continually delivering a flow of information from several press agencies.
Seth Siegelaub, the New York gallery owner and promoter of Conceptual Art, very quickly affirmed the international vocation of his activities: "My gallery is the world now"; "I have become interested in the broader communications between artists around the world [...]. I am concerned about the artists being able to have their work known no matter where they live—not just artists living in New York."[2] With these declarations Siegelaub became one of the first art world stakeholders to have glimpsed and desired that world's contemporary reality: the globalization of art. The cover of the exhibition catalogue "July, August, September 1969" featured a planisphere. The exhibition was shown in eleven different sites (in the United States, the Netherlands, Canada, Mexico, Germany, England, and France). Conceptual Art, by nature of its methods and "productions," was thought to have de-territorializing properties rendering it independent of both artistic institutions and the geographical centralization of artistic activities.

2. Seth Siegelaub, interview with Patricia Norvell, in Alexander Alberro and Patricial Norvell (dir.), *Recording Conceptual Art*, Berkeley, University of California Press, 2001, p. 38, and S. Siegelaub, "Statement of Condition," 9 May 1969, Seth Siegelaub Archives, New York, box 1, file 3.

In its international ambition, Conceptual Art inherited the ideals of historical modernism. The quest for a universal alphabet never ceased to haunt Geometric Abstraction. Conceptual Art nonetheless seems less a kind of Esperanto than a tool adapted to the global village, to the age of rapid and global transmission of information. Without questioning the sincerity of Siegelaub's internationalism, we may nonetheless note the profound complicity between the strategies of communication and dissemination adopted by the promoter and the process of globalization of industrial, commercial, and financial transactions related to the intensification and liberalization of exchanges. Even if this was not its sole determining principle, Conceptual Art was connected to the movement that, in the Western capitalism of the 1960s, saw publicity and communication overtake production.[3] Given the way in which it was thought of and organized in New York in the late 1960s, it thus appears highly ambivalent. At the same time, as the heir of the historical avant-gardes through its desire to call into question the separation between art and life, its way of deflating the hot air of High Art, and its critical position in its desire to escape institutional frameworks, it seems to be the "natural" aesthetic of postmodern society.
This ambivalence no doubt explains why Conceptual Art, despite its proclaimed globalist vocation, has long been endowed with an ultra-centralized official history focused on New York and a few Western European offshoots. Again, in 1989, an exhibition such as "Conceptual Art: A Perspective" curated by Claude Gintz at the Paris Museum of Modern Art, presented only artists living in the United

3. See A. Alberro, *Conceptual Art and the Politics of Publicity*, Cambridge (MA), The MIT Press, 2003.

States and Western Europe. It took ten years, with "Global Conceptualism: Points of Origin, 1950s–1980s," which Luis Camnitzer, Jane Farver, and Rachel Weiss organized at the Queens Museum of Art (New York), for the specifically international reality of Conceptual Art to come to light. Unlike certain historical avant-gardes, such as Surrealism, Conceptual Art is "global" not because it has spread from a center into other regions of the globe, but because it is essentially multipolar. Of course, the dynamism of the New York scene and Siegelaub's advertising genius played a decisive role in the recognition of Conceptual Art. All the same, it is impossible to assign it a precise birthplace.

We will not take stock here of the geographic plurality of the practices now considered an integral part of Conceptualism and its history. Just a few examples should suffice. At about the same time, in the first half of the 1950s, Mangelos [REPR. P. 231], in Zagreb, presented a frame empty of any paint or transfixed a printed image with a large red cross, and Robert Rauschenberg, in New York, erased a drawing by Willem De Kooning. In 1961, Alberto Greco declared that he had signed the whole city of Buenos Aires as though it was an artwork, and Piero Manzoni, in Denmark, made the planet a work of art by placing it on a pedestal. In 1964, in Japan, Yutaka Matsuzawa produced a small poster, reworking the mandala grid, on which can be read: "A non-sensory painting surrounds you, fills you, enters you;" in Buenos Aires, León Ferrari produced *Cuadro escrito* [Written Painting]—a detailed description of what he would have painted and the way in which he would have painted it if he had chosen the paint; and in Bratislava, Július Koller [REPR. P. 229] inscribed the word "*more*" [sea] on a colored background. In 1966, two years before Siegelaub's exhibition, "Douglas Huebler: November 1968," the catalogue of which was the only material element, the Argentinian Roberto Jacoby also held an exhibition with a catalogue as its only object. In 1968, Robert Filliou, then in Düsseldorf, formulated his principle of equivalency between the "well-made," the "badly-made," and the "not-made." Not long after, Lawrence Weiner defined the three equivalent conditions of existence of his works: the artist can produce the work; the work can be produced by someone other than the artist; the work may not be produced at all. Also in 1969, in Moscow, Ilya Kabakov [REPR. P. 229] began the *Answers of the Experimental Group* that introduced questions regarding the images shown. One last example: both Graciela Carnevale and Robert Barry closed a gallery during an exhibition, with just a few months between the two respective acts of closure. The former, in Rosario, in 1968, locked the door of the space, empty of any art object, once the spectators were inside. The second, in 1969, in three different cities (Amsterdam, Turin, and Los Angeles), left the galleries closed throughout the full duration of the exhibition. It would be possible to multiply these comparisons, not to prove or refute their antecedents or re-establish the correct chronology, but instead, to testify to the singularly multipolar and decentralized character of Conceptual Art.

Indifference to the question of medium—which was at the heart of Modernist preoccupations—tends toward dematerialization. From the rejection of the primacy of form, there follows a valorization of the idea, the protocol, and a privileged recourse to language, to the tools of documentation or to performance. In other words, Conceptualism is to be understood as a complex ensemble of practices whose common denominator is that of being in opposition to the traditional conception of art. Consequently, as soon as here or there, and for such and such a reason—through lack of means of production or exhibition space, the existence of censorship, a desire to explore new distribution channels, an aversion to formalism, etc.—artists do not use the sanctified means of Fine Art, their works fall within this vast Conceptualist current without borders, aesthetics, or geography.

The avant-gardes of the 1960s put Duchamp's *Bottle Rack* (1914/1964) back at center stage [REPR. P. 228] as the work that had brought about the conceptual regime of art. With it, the artwork no longer resided within an object, but in a concept—in this case, the fact of exhibiting a bottle rack as an art object. This change of artistic regime had enormous consequences. For instance, even allowed the bottles that were no longer drying on the readymade to be used. Bottles of beer that, in 1970, in San Francisco, Tom Marioni suggested that people drink. Bottles of Coca-Cola that, in the same year, in Rio de Janeiro, Cildo Meireles, reversing the principle of the readymade, put back into circulation in shops, after having affixed various political slogans to them, such as "*Yankees Go Home*" [REPR. P. 228]. Conceptual Art is Janus-faced. In the end, its crystallization and its success in New York made the supreme and globalizing dream of Capitalism a reality: that anything, anywhere, could become a commodity. But it will have also aided the recognition of practices representing, all over the world, an authentic project of social emancipation and resistance to reification.

Translated from the French by Anna Knight

Marcel DUCHAMP
Bottle Rack
1914/1964

Cildo MEIRELES
Insertions in Ideological Circuits
Coca-Cola Project
1970

Ilya KABAKOV
Who Drove This Nail? I Don't Know
1972

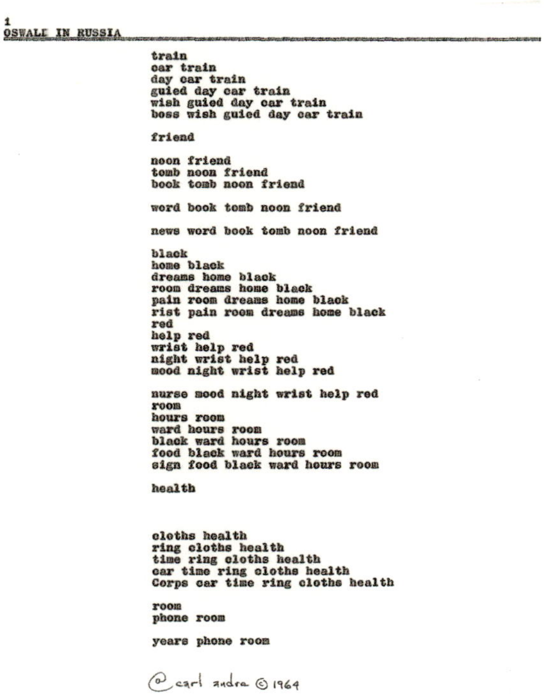
1
OSWALD IN RUSSIA

train
car train
day car train
guied day car train
wish guied day car train
boss wish guied day car train

friend

noon friend
tomb noon friend
book tomb noon friend

word book tomb noon friend

news word book tomb noon friend

black
home black
dreams home black
room dreams home black
pain room dreams home black
rist pain room dreams home black
red
help red
wrist help red
night wrist help red
mood night wrist help red

nurse mood night wrist help red
room
hours room
ward hours room
black ward hours room
food black ward hours room
sign food black ward hours room

health

cloths health
ring cloths health
time ring cloths health
car time ring cloths health
Corps car time ring cloths health

room
phone room

years phone room

@ carl andre © 1964

Július KOLLER
Antihappening
1965

Carl ANDRE
Oswald in Russia
1964

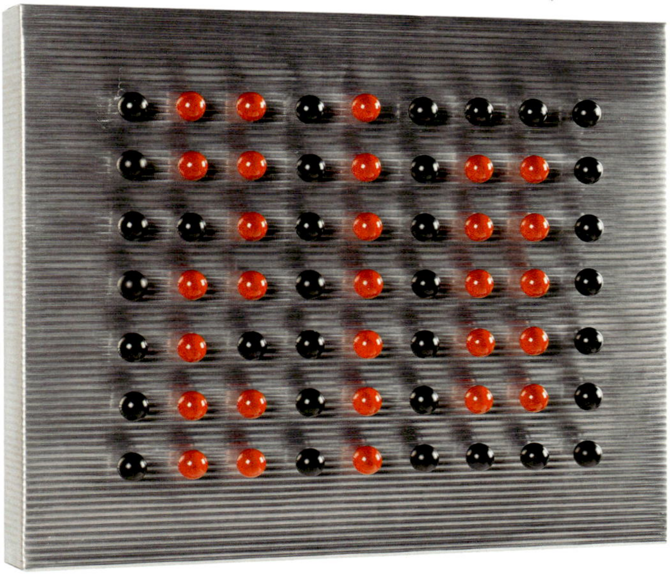

Margarita PAKSA
NO
1976

Nil YALTER
The Headless Woman or the Belly Dance
1974

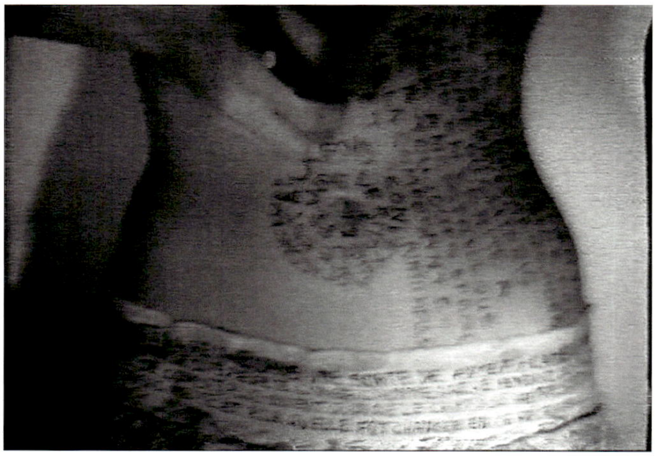

Frédéric BRULY BOUABRÉ
The Weights to Be Weighed [detail]
1988

Braco DIMITRIJEVIĆ
The Casual Passer-By I Met at 11.09 A.M., Paris
1971

MANGELOS
Relations Manifesto, m.4-m.8
1971–1977

The Moving Gaze

Clément Chéroux

Taoism teaches us that the journey itself, not the destination, is the most important thing. Western art historians would do well to set themselves more often to Chinese time. Most studies of 19th and 20th century painters' travels focus on what they found once they'd arrived safe and sound: dear old "local color," exoticism, or at the very least a sense of unfamiliarity. Almost unexamined are the impressions received en route; the experience of the journey itself. Yet, precisely at that time, travel was evolving radically. With the opening to the public of the first railway lines in the 1830s and 1840s, the development of the automobile in the late 19th century, then of aviation in the first decades of the following century, the element of travel represented by *transportation* was deeply transformed, particularly in terms of the visual field. For painters, trains, cars, and then airplanes were like so many new "machines for seeing," offering new and original views of the landscape. Whether lateral in a train compartment, frontal in an automobile, or tilted in an airplane, the *moving gaze* obliged them to rethink perception in its relationship to the three-dimensionality of Euclidian space. In the early 1890s, Edgar Degas thus produced a series of monotypes from his impressions aboard the train. "I stood at the carriage door, and looked out vaguely. That gave me the idea to do some landscapes,"[1] he explained to his friend Ludovic Halévy. Several decades later, Henri Matisse was intrigued by what he saw from his automobile. Pierre Matisse related that in the summer of 1917, while he was following his father on the Villacoublay road, the latter suddenly had the idea to paint the tree-lined pavement from inside the car.[2] The canvas thus produced was entitled *Le Pare-Brise* [The Windshield] and shows the road in perspective, the wheel, a few elements of the dashboard and passenger compartment, and the landscape flying past on either side of the car. Then it was the Futurist painters' turn to become interested in airplane views. On 22 September 1929, Filippo Tommaso Marinetti, Giacomo Balla [REPR. P. 60], Benedetta Cappa, Fortunato Depero, Gerardo Dottori, Fillìa, Enrico Prampolini, Mino Somenzi, and Tato launched the *Manifesto dell'Aeropittura futurista* that glorified "perpetual [...] mobility," "changing perspectives of flight" or "spinning visions," and called for "a new extra-terrestrial plastic spirituality." "The airplane, which glides, dives, or spins upwards, creates an ideal, hypersensitive observatory, suspended entirely within infinity and energized by the awareness of the movement that," they noted "changes the value and rhythm of the minutes and seconds of vision-sensation."[3] Like Albert Einstein, who had the idea for the theory of relativity by observing one moving train from aboard another, painters of the turn of the 20th century intuited that the revolution in transportation profoundly modified their relationship to space and time. They realized, with Lao-Tzu, that the most important thing was the journey itself.

While modern painters very *quickly* understood that trains, cars, and airplanes radically modified the perception of landscape, they did not extend their questions beyond the experimentation evoked above. After the twenty-one monotypes painted from the train window, Degas stopped being interested in landscape per se. Besides another canvas painted in 1917 representing a road in Clamart,[4] Matisse also stopped taking an interest in *car painting*. As for *aeropittura* [aeropainting], while the production of canvases or decorative frescoes was particularly intensive in the 1930s, it did not last for much longer. Far more than painting, it was in fact other faster, more precise media—particularly those resulting from analog recording, in this case cinema and photography—that provided a plastic form for this new moving vision. Less than a year was needed after the invention of the cinematograph by the Lumière brothers for their technicians Constant Girel and Alexandre Promio to come up with the idea of taking a camera on a boat or in a train, thus inventing the *tracking shot*.[5] In the 1920s, avant-garde filmmakers (Dziga Vertov, René Clair, Man Ray, to name but a few) also became enthralled by what they were able

1. Edgar Degas, *Lettres de Degas réunies et annotées par Marcel Guérir*, Paris, Grasset, 1945, p. 278 [English translation: http://www.musee-orsay.fr, accessed 19 November 2013].

2. See Enda Duffy, *The Speed Handbook. Velocity, Pleasure, Modernism*, Durham, Duke University Press, 2009, p. 157-158. The painting is now conserved at the Cleveland Museum of Art.

3. F. T. Marinetti, G. Balla, B. Cappa, F. Depero, G. Dottori, Fillia, E. Prampolini, M. Somenzi, Tato, *Manifesto dell'Aeropittura*, cited in Giovanni Lista, *Futurisme. Manifestes, documents, proclamations*, Lausanne L'Âge d'Homme, 1973, pp. 224-227. On this subject, see also Bruno Mantura, Patrizia Rosazza-Ferraris, Livia Velani (eds.), *Aereo e Pittura. Mostra dell'aria e della sua conquista*, exh. cat., Rome, De Luca Edizioni d'Arte, 1989.

4. Henri Matisse, *Route à Clamart*, 1917, Centre Pompidou, National Museum of Modern Art, Paris.

5. See Jean-Claude Seguin, *Alexandre Promio ou les Énigmes de la lumière*, Paris/Montréal, L'Harmattan, 1998.

to observe from trains, cars, or airplanes. Film offered them the opportunity to capture this turbulent vision, which was both synthetic and compressed. Whereas cinema reproduces and replays the flow of movement faithfully, photography freezes it and breaks it down. In this sense, it is more *analytical*. Constantin Brancusi understood this well. In the mid-1930s, on a train trip, he was, like Paul Verlaine before him, fascinated by the telegraph poles that ran alongside the window of the car, and "whose wires had the strange allure of a parapet."[6] Rhythmically they fell and suddenly rose at each post, following a design that probably reminded him of the rhythm and rhomboidal forms of his *Endless Column* placed horizontally. With a small camera, Brancusi filmed the dance of the telegraph wires from the train window. But once he returned to his studio and developed his film, he felt the need to place the latter under the enlarger in order to extract a few stills from it and print them on photographic paper [REPR. P. 236]. It was as though he wanted to verify this hypothesis from philosopher Henri Bergson, which Brancusi had underlined in black pen in his copy of *Creative Evolution*: "[...] there is no form, since form is immobile and reality is movement. What is real is the continual changing of form: form is only a snapshot of a transition."[7] It was in a photographic snapshot torn from the filmed continuum that the Romanian sculptor recognized the *endless form* that he was looking for. Brancusi was hardly the only artist interested in the moving gaze. Germaine Krull, Pierre Ichac [REPR. P. 237], Walker Evans, then Bernard Plossu [REPR. P. 236], Philippe Durand, and Sophie Ristelhueber [REPR. P. 237]... from the avant-gardes through to the present day, there are legions of artists who have endeavored to take photographs not only from trains, cars, and airplanes, but also from bicycles, buses, kites, or even from a camel's or horse's back or on skis. Mobility has now become a part of our perceptual habits. In the 1980s, the designers of the Mission Photographique de la DATAR, whose ambition was to construct a visual report on French territory in the late 20th century, had to request the photographers they commissioned to focus as much on urban and peri-urban spaces, the countryside, the mountains, and the seashore, as on landscapes seen from the train.[8] In the various registers of subject matter that define our relationship to the landscape, the moving gaze has now become a photographic category in its own right. However, the multiplication of photographic works taken from a mobile point of view cannot be explained solely by the desire to bear witness to an accelerated vision bespeaking modernity. Behind each of these moving gazes, there is always a more personal goal as

6. Paul Verlaine, "La bonne chanson," cited in Marc Baroli, *Le Train dans la littérature française*, Paris, Éditions N. M., 1964, p. 147.

7. Henri Bergson, *L'Évolution créatrice* (1907) Paris, Félix Alcan, 1914, p. 211 [our translation]. Brancusi's personal copy is now preserved at the Kandinsky Library, Centre Pompidou, National Museum of Modern Art, Paris.

8. See Bernard Latarjet, François Hers (eds.), *Paysages, photographies, 1984–1985. En France, les années quatre-vingt*, Paris, Mission Photographique de la DATAR/Crédit Foncier de France/Hazan, 1989.

9. Jacques Henri Lartigue, *Mémoires sans mémoire*, Paris, Robert Laffont, 1975, p. 32 [our translation].

10. Ibid., p. 372.

well, and I would like to advance the hypothesis here that it pertains to a reaction in the face of loss. To understand this, we must return to one of the leading photographers of the 20th century: Jacques Henri Lartigue, who incidentally also took photographs from cars driving at high speed. As a child, Lartigue had invented a strategy that he quaintly called his "eye-trap": "I open my eyes, then close them, then open them again very very wide, and bing! I catch the picture with everything in it: the colors! The real size! What I keep in my mind is something alive that moves and smells,"[9] he wrote in his diary. But noting a few days later that his "fairytale invention" did not retain everything, he started to take photographs. "I take photos," he observed a little later, "in order to tell myself (as much as I possibly can) that I am preserving a bit of my happiness."[10] Photography represents his desperate attempt to preserve his memories. In the third volume of his memoirs, Lartigue also questioned his ability to retain all of the visual sensations that a car ride "at 100 mph" procured him. "What a perpetual waste!" he wrote "[...] which is why, when I was younger, I photographed each tree and little house that passed like an arrow into my stunned eyes and before my powerless memory."[11] For Lartigue, photography responds to anxiety in the face of the transience of the world. It allows him to retain memories that fly by like passing landscapes. It is a tool for the overall safeguarding of his memory. In short, moving photography is to *space* what the memory-image is to *time*: a reaction to programmed disappearance, a memory-trap, and a veritable antidote to melancholy.

Translated from the French by Anna Knight

11. J. H. Lartigue, *L'Œil de la mémoire, 1932–1985. Extraits du Journal de Jacques Henri Lartigue de 1932 à 1985*, Paris, Carrère-Lafon, 1986, p. 78 [our translation].

Constantin BRANCUSI
Romanian Countryside, Seen from the Train
1937–1938

Bernard PLOSSU
Alain Rérat, Lille
1988

Sophie RISTELHUEBER
Fact
1992

Pierre ICHAC
Aerial View, Forest
ca. 1938

Decolonizing the Gaze?

Sophie Orlando

Floral wallpaper and patterned rugs surround a rectangular, almost statuesque figure, seated in front of a Venetian mirror: *Decorative Figure on an Ornamental Background* (winter 1925–1926) offers an insight into the "paradox of the Odalisque"[1] in the paintings of Henri Matisse—a paradox expressed in his contradictory, or at least ambivalent, desire to understand and borrow from the arts of the Middle East[2] and North Africa, particularly the decorative and architectural arts, while continuing to draw on the idealized, mythical imagery of the Orient, as portrayed in both painting and literature since the 19th century. In 1978, Edward W. Said published *Orientalism*[3], a literary critique following on from the way the history of Europe grew out of a need to establish a concept of otherness, and a dichotomy between a modern, forward-looking West and a timeless, mystical Orient—both of which justified political domination and colonial rule.

1. Isabelle Monod-Fontaine, "Le paradoxe de l'Odalisque," in *Le Maroc de Matisse*, exh. cat., Paris, Gallimard, 1999, pp. 115-156.

2. The expression "Middle East" was coined in the early twentieth century to describe a region with indeterminate borders, its definition fluctuating according to one's vantage point. A geopolitical term, it replaced among others that of "Ottoman Empire," and was sometimes juxtaposed with controversial appellations such as "Islamic civilization," "Islamic art," or "Muslim art."

3. Edward W. Said, *Orientalism*, New York, Pantheon Books, 1978.

Said, in the wake of Michel Foucault, points to the constructive nature of the Orient and its inherent contribution to the formulation of a hegemonic testimonial of European identity. The arts of Egypt, India, Iran, and Turkey began to interweave with the European fabric as early as the 11th century and the Crusades. The emergence of the notion of Orientalism in art, however, must be seen from the political and scientific perspective of the Egyptian Campaign, led by Napoleon Bonaparte between 1798 and 1801 to counter Britain's expanding colonial interests in India. During Napoleon's military occupation of Egypt, archaeological research into ancient civilizations was carried out on site, as Dominique Vivant Denon recounts in detail in his *Voyage dans la Basse et la Haute Égypte* [Travels in Lower and Upper Egypt] (1802). This quest for the origins of Antiquity was imbued with the exoticism of an Oriental myth. To the construction of the Romantic Orient was added the development of a supposedly authoritative view of the "genuine" Orient, supported by expanding scientific research." Painters and novelists made the most of these new slants to review their rendering of a subject that had already been broached in the 17th century by Rembrandt and also by the first European translation of *The Arabian Nights* [*Les Mille et Une Nuits*, Antoine Galland (1704–1717)], the publication of Montesquieu's *Persian Letters*, and a host of other travelogues and memoirs. The seventeenth-century tradition of the "Grand Tour," a rite of passage for the elite, who for many years hardly ventured beyond Italy, gradually began to take in more "picturesque" destinations. It was on just such a voyage, in 1832, that Eugène Delacroix first visited North Africa, as illustrated by his *Women of Algiers* (1834).

The nineteenth century saw a proliferation of definitions of Orientalism. Initially the term was used to describe the academic discipline of Oriental Studies; it then came to denote an artistic and literary genre; but it also fulfilled an ideological purpose: by forging an account of its origins that stressed the opposition between Orient and Occident, it condoned the humanist, forward-looking, modern mission of countries in the midst of an industrial revolution.[4]

Decorative Figure on an Ornamental Background belongs to the Orientalist vein that was first given form by John Frederick Lewis (*A Lady Receiving Visitors [The Reception]*, 1873) and Jean-Léon Gérôme (*Turkish* or *Moorish Bath*, 1870). Using drawings, studies and reproductions of objects and elements of architecture originating from Cairo, they created a fictionalized wonderland based on totally anarchic assemblages. Their seemingly authentic nature helped to reinforce the mythology of the Orient, as Linda Nochlin observes with regard to Gérôme's *Snake Charmer* (ca. 1870): "[...] an iconic distillation of the Westerner's notion of the Oriental couched in the language of a would-be transparent naturalism."[5] Matisse's work, however, points to a different legacy, assimilated by Rémi Labrusse to "Islamophilia,"[6] and defined as the appropriation of the arts of the Middle East and North Africa, no longer rendered by means of visual effects, colors and "exoticized" subjects, transplanted into a mimetic depiction of Renaissance painting, but as an aesthetic conception of the void, form, and space, a signature expression of ornamental art. From the second half of the 19th century, the "Islamic Arts"—the nomenclature adopted

4. Ibid., pp. 14-15. Rémi Brague made a study of the quest for identity in Europe during the period of the Maastricht Treaty in *Europe, la voie romaine*, Paris, Critérion, 1992.

5. Linda Nochlin, "The Imaginary Orient," *The Politics of Vision: Essays on Nineteenth-Century Art and Society*, New York, Harper & Row, 1989, p. 35.

6. Rémi Labrusse, *Islamophilies. L'Europe moderne et les arts de l'Islam*, Paris, Lyon, Somogy/Musée des Beaux-Arts de Lyon, 2011.

7. The question of "Orientalism" versus "Islamophilia" epitomizes two major currents which originated with the discovery of Oriental and Middle Eastern lands by European artists; on the one hand, the fictionalization of otherness through the prism of the aesthetic codes of European art, and on the other a calling into question of art history since the Renaissance, with particular emphasis being placed on the use of an aesthetic proper to the decorative arts of the Middle East and Morocco. Matisse's œuvre belongs to this second category.

by the Louvre and taken up by the Museum of Arts and Crafts in Paris—began to feature in the private collections of its adepts. A major exhibition, "Masterpieces of Islamic Art," was held in Munich by Friedrich Sarre in 1910.[7] Colonialism had enabled the acquisitions of artifacts, theoretically aimed at lending scientific credibility to the decorative arts, and there was now fierce competition between the British Museum in England and the Louvre in France to see which of them could show off the wealth of its collections—and by implication its power—to best effect. The decorative arts also became a means of transcending sacred art in favor of the progressive formal art form now advocated by William Morris and the Arts and Crafts movement; while in literature, there was an ever-increasing demand for books on ornamental subjects, such as Owen Jones' *The Grammar of Ornament* (1856) and *Théorie de l'ornement* (1873) by Jules Bourgoin. The interaction between fine arts and decorative arts came to the fore after the Munich Exhibition (1910), and found its expression through Fauvism, the Bloomsbury Group, and the paintings of Vassily Kandinsky [REPR. P. 57, 76]. Matisse saw a way round his aversion to Orientalism through Iznic tiles and Ottoman fabrics, as these released him from the strictures of imitating the real and the faithful depictions of approximations of reality in volume, and overcame the contradiction between figurative and abstract art; his *Red Studio* (1911) is a case in point, as is his work on the Rosary Chapel in Vence and his series of bronzes, *Back[s]*, its final version in 1930 challenging the rift between the anatomical and botanical visions of the human figure initiated by the painters of the Renaissance. Despite this, *Decorative Figure on an Ornamental Background* "paradoxically" depicts one of the protagonists or heroines of Romantic Orientalism, the "Odalisque" or lady's maid, the beauty at the beck and call of the Sultan, or the slave, half-veiled and half-dressed, encapsulated by Matisse in *Odalisque With Red Trousers* in 1921 [REPR. P. 242]. One can perceive here a need for a "return to order," in reaction to the reappraisals and doubts raised by World War I, in other words a return to representational art, in particular the Classic and Neoclassic period, as illustrated by Picasso's *Two Women Running on the Beach* (1922).

In 1907, the Louvre juxtaposed two canvases, *The Great Odalisque* by Ingres (1814) and Manet's *Olympia* (1863). In the early 20th century, Ingres' nudes—*The Turkish Bath* (1862), *Roger Delivering Angelica* (1819), and *The Valpinçon Bather* (1806)—stimulated a debate that was no longer centered on Orientalism and the influence of the decorative arts on the European avant-gardes but on the history of art and its proponents, as well as on the nude and the manifestations of its heritage. Matisse and Picasso frequently revisited the great works of the past, but they were not the only ones—the practice was shared by André Derain, Amedeo Modigliani, Félix Vallotton, and Francis Picabia, not to mention the Surrealists. In 1918, Picasso painted *The Young Ladies of Avignon*, followed by *The Bathers*, but in 1955 his *Nude in a Turkish Cap* [REPR. P. 243] literally returned to the motif of an Odalisque, propped up against a wall, in a direct reference to Matisse. In overblown "style pompier" mode, Henri Ottmann produced a *Sleeping Courtesan* (1920), halfway between Alexandre Cabanel's *Birth of Venus*

(1863) and the lines of Raphael's nudes, which Ingres had studied closely for many years. The reproduction and dissemination of these images created an indiscriminate heritage, in which the Odalisque was confused with the Courtesan, and Olympia with Venus. Brassaï (*Odalisque [Transmutations]*, 1934–1967) and Man Ray (*Ingres' Violin*, 1924, [REPR. P. 245]) turned the pun "violon d'Ingres," which also means hobby in French, into a photographic play on words, with the woman's body acting as a projection screen for cultural history. New reproduction techniques and widespread distribution methods made Ingres' nudes part of a visual heritage, and represented an infinite source of inspiration for Martial Raysse's series *Made in Japan* [REPR. P. 245]. In a true critique of the idea of the untouchable "masterpiece," Raysse created a tongue-in-cheek parody of over sixty nudes by Ingres, depicting them in fluorescent colors. The fashion for putting a new slant on traditional works of art also found favor with Robert Rauschenberg (*Centennial Certificate MMA*, 1969) and also with Erró, who spanned a wide range of artistic registers, associating virile astronauts with Ingres' bathers (*The Turkish Bath*, ca. 1979–1980), and Ghérasim Luca (*Cubomania after Ingres, the Seated Bather*, 1960), who relied on repetition and doubling effects to deconstruct the sign and its manifestations by composing a disconcerting jigsaw puzzle of fragments. Suzanne Valadon, for her part, in response to the question "Who is this Odalisque?" replied "Me." In 1923, in *The Blue Bedroom* [REPR. P. 242], she portrayed herself in striped pajamas, staring into space, a cigarette dangling from her mouth, with books now replacing the bather's drapes and veils. Here she was foiling the eroticized, sexualized portraits of women, composed by and for the male viewer for his sheer visual pleasure—a theory propounded by Laura Mulvey in 1975 in a cinematic context.[8] The deconstruction of this perception was compounded by the development of feminist theories and gender studies, while "race, class and gender," to quote Stuart Hall,[9] evokes a cross-reference between Kochar's *Orientals* (1924) [REPR. P. 126] and Larry Rivers' *I Like Olympia in Black Face* (1970) [REPR. P. 243]. By invoking the relationship between the black servant and the white courtesan, depicted in the matrix of the original *Olympia*, and then turning it on its head, using a double image to lend it even greater impact, Larry Rivers was alluding to the Civil Rights Movement in the United States, while pointing out the limitations of a Manichean political concept, against a background of permeable cultural identity concepts, which Frantz Fanon demonstrated to great effect in *Black Skin, White Masks* (1952).[10] When in her video *Let's Dance* (2003) [REPR. P. 244] Zoulikha Bouabdellah meticulously prepares the superimposition of blue, white and red veils, before launching into a dance to the sound of France's national anthem *La Marseillaise*—transforming the military injunction "March on" into the artistic gesture, "Dance on"—she is giving form to a postcolonial cultural hybridism, the irony of which condenses the historical incongruity of the values of the French Republic, established during the invasion of Algiers, and clinging exotic clichés and attitudes to Orientalism, underlining the pertinence of Edward W. Said's theories in the context of a study of our (de)colonized gaze.

Translated from the French by Caroline Taylor-Bouché

8. Laura Mulvey, "Visual Pleasure and Narrative Cinema," *Screen*, vol. 16, no. 3, 1975, pp. 6-18.

9. Stuart Hall, "New Ethnicities," in David Morley, Kuan-Hsing (eds.), *Stuart Hall: Critical Dialogues in Cultural Studies*, London/New York, Routledge, 1996.

10. Frantz Fanon, *Black Skin, White Masks* (1952), Charles Lam Markmann (trans.), New York, Grove Press, 1967.

Henri MATISSE
Odalisque with Red Trousers
1921

Suzanne VALADON
The Blue Bedroom
1923

Larry RIVERS
I Like Olympia in Black Face
1970

Pablo PICASSO
Nude in a Turkish Cap
1955

Federico BELTRÁN MASSES
Sick Pierrot
1929

Zoulikha BOUABDELLAH
Let's Dance
2003

Martial RAYSSE
Made in Japan. La grande odalisque
1964

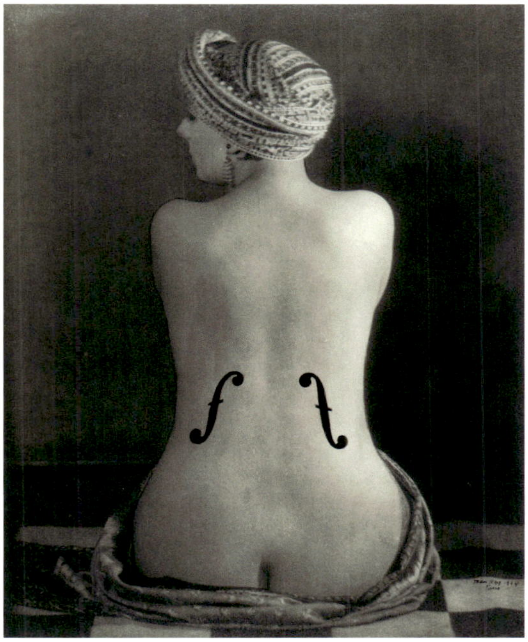

Man RAY
Ingres' Violin
1924

"The Orient was almost a European invention, and had been since Antiquity a place of romance, exotic beings, haunting memories and landscapes, remarkable experiences. Now it was disappearing; in a sense it had happened, its time was over."

EDWARD W. SAID, *ORIENTALISM*, 1978

CHRONOLOGY
History of the collections

Nathalie Ernoult

A short history of the presence of foreign or foreign-born artists in French national museums of modern art before the creation of the Centre Pompidou.
This chronology outlines the history of the presence of foreign or foreign-born artists in the Musée National du Luxembourg (MNL); then in the Département des Écoles Étrangères [Department of Foreign Schools] in the Musée National du Luxembourg; at the Musée du Jeu de Paume (MJP); and finally at the Musée National d'Art Moderne (MNAM) [National Museum of Modern Art], up to the creation of the Centre Pompidou. This period, relatively little known, saw the constitution of a significant gathering of works by artists from all continents. In fact, the majority (59%) of the works that entered the collections of these museums from 1900 to 1969 were by foreign or foreign-born artists.

AFEEA: Association Française d'Expansion et d'Échanges Artistiques [French Association for Artistic Expansion and Exchange], later Association Française d'Action Artistique (AFAA) [French Association for Artistic Action] **MJP:** Département des Écoles Étrangères du Musée National du Luxembourg (1922–1931), Musée National du Jeu de Paume–Écoles Étrangères (1932–1940) **MNAM:** Musée National d'Art Moderne **MNL:** Musée National du Luxembourg **RMN:** Réunion des Musées Nationaux

1818

Creation of the Museum of Living Artists, also called the Musée National du Luxembourg.

1848

The Musée National du Luxembourg enters under the management of the Musées de France.

1878

Creation of the Bureau of Artworks, responsible for commissioning and acquiring artworks from living artists, as well as their distribution among public institutions (museums, embassies, ministries, and so forth). After a deposit and storage period, the works are attributed by the State to museums, which then become their owners. In 1976, the Bureau of Artworks becomes the National Holdings of Contemporary Art.

1892

Léonce Bénédite is named curator of the Musée National du Luxembourg. He will remain there until his death in 1925.

1900–1925

Foundation of numerous associations of foreign artists: Paris Franco-Japanese Society (1900), Franco-Scandinavian Association (1904), Russian Academy (1908), New Society of American Painters in Paris (1908), Polish Literary and Artistic Society (1910), Society of Polish Artists in Paris (1911), Association of Scandinavian Artists-Maison Watteau (1917), Association of Chinese Artists in France (1920), Union of Polish Artists in France (1922), Paris Estonian Association (1925).

1903

Creation of the Autumn Salon, meant to provide an outlet to young artists and be open to a wide public. This show is notable for its pluridisciplinarity, the clarity and elegance of its layout, and the significant presence of foreign artists.

1907

In his report on "The Salons of 1907" published in the *Gazette des Beaux-Arts* (no. 37), the critic André Pératé declares that Fauvists should be considered "foreigners" because he finds them "incoherent, in revolt against the Latin soul."

1908

January Henri Matisse opens a free academy in the former Couvent des Oiseaux on rue de Sèvres in Montparnasse, immediately frequented by many foreign students: German, Scandinavian, American, Hungarian, and others. It closes in 1912.

1912

First Futurist exhibition in Paris, with Gino Severini, Umberto Boccioni, Giacomo Balla, Carlo Carrà, and Luigi Russolo, at the Galerie Bernheim-Jeune, Paris.

1914

3 August France declares war on Germany. Marie Vassilieff, Léonard Foujita, and the latter's friend Riichirô Kawashima sign up as Red Cross nurses. Guillaume Apollinaire, Blaise Cendrars, Moïse Kisling, František Kupka, Alfred Reth, Serge Férat, Otto Gutfreund, and Louis Marcoussis join the Foreign Legion. Chaïm Soutine volunteers, but soon leaves the army for health reasons. Sonia and Robert Delaunay take up residence in Madrid. Jules Pascin flees to New York. Marc Chagall and Vassily Kandinsky return to Russia; Otto Freundlich, to Germany. Pablo Picasso, Constantin Brancusi, and Diego Rivera stay in Montparnasse. Pablo Gargallo tries to enlist but, due to his frail health, is forced to return to Spain.

1916

July To compensate for the closing of other salons during WWI, André Salmon organizes the Salon d'Antin under the sponsorship of couturier Paul Poiret. It features Hayden, Amedeo Modigliani, Giorgio De Chirico, Férat, Severini, Kisling, Pinchus Krémègne, Chana Orloff, Picasso, Kees Van Dongen, Matisse, André Dunoyer de Segonzac, Albert Marquet, and André Derain. Picasso's *Demoiselles d'Avignon* (1907) are exhibited there for the first time. The Paris gallery of the German-born dealer Daniel-Henry Kahnweiler, exiled in Switzerland during the war, is impounded as enemy property. His Cubist paintings, by Picasso, Georges Braque, Fernand Léger, and Derain, among others, are separated and sold cheaply at four Drouot sales in 1921 and 1923.

1919

Inauguration of a policy of exhibiting works by foreign and foreign-born artists from the Musée National du Luxembourg as part of diplomatic agreements for the consolidation of peace in Europe.

April–May "Exhibition of Modern Spanish Painting," organized by the Committee for Franco-Spanish Unity (Musée du Petit Palais, 148 artists, 396 works).

12 April–15 May "Exhibition of Yugoslav Artists," organized by a committee of Yugoslav artists (Musée du Petit Palais, 64 artists, 285 works).

October–November "Exhibition of Artists of the American School," under the patronage of American president Thomas Woodrow Wilson and French president Raymond Poincaré (MNL, 255 works, of which 66 works by 45 artists come from French national collections). Among the artists selected are Marie Laurencin, Romaine Brooks, John Flanagan, Ben Foster, Samuel Halpert, John Hamilton, Mary Cassatt, and James Whistler.

1921

April–May "Dutch Exhibition: Ancient and Modern Paintings, Watercolors, Drawings" (MJP, 40 artists, 211 works). "Exhibition of Russian Artists in Paris, 1921," organized by members and exhibitors of the Mir Iskusstva [World of Art] group at the Galerie La Boétie. Among the artists: Léon Bakst, Natalia S. Goncharova, Alexandre Jacovleff, and George Loukomski.

1922

29 July The foreign collections of the Musée du Luxembourg (MNL) have become too large to be presented at the same time as those of the French School. A transfer is made to the Musée du Jeu de Paume (MJP) in the Tuileries of 420 paintings and drawings and some sixty sculptures by foreign artists. Until 1932, these exhibition rooms will be an annex of the MNL. The permanent collections and temporary exhibitions of foreign and foreign-born artists' works are presented there. Temporary exhibitions are an opportunity for the museum to develop its policy of acquiring works by foreign artists. Creation of the Association Française d'Expansion et d'Échanges Artistiques (AFEEA), which in 1934 will become the Association Française d'Action Artistique (AFAA), to promote French art worldwide.

1923

10 February–11 March Salon des Indépendants. Paul Signac, under pressure from nationalist French artists, decides to arrange artists by nationality rather than, as has been the case since the mid-19th century, by alphabetical order. Kisling, granted French citizenship for his participation in WWI in the Foreign Legion, appears in the French section, while the Bulgarian-born Pascin, an American citizen since 1920, is found among the Americans.

10 May–10 July "Exhibition of Ancient and Modern Belgian Art," organized by Léonce Bénédite under the auspices of the French and Belgian governments (MJP, 47 artists, 172 works and decorative objects).

1924

June–July "Exhibition of 15th–19th Century Swiss Art, from Holbein to Hodler," organized by Bénédite under the auspices of the Swiss and French governments (MJP, 65 artists, 245 works). Robert Rey is named head curator of the Musée du Jeu de Paume.

1925

26 May–1 August "Exhibition of Ancient and Modern Romanian Art," organized with the assistance of H.R.H. Prince Carol and the Society of Friends of Romania (MJP, 47 artists, 185 works).

July First survey by *L'Art vivant*, "For a Museum of Modern Art": 63 responses, 36 in favor 17 against, 10 no opinion. Among the published responses are those of Alfred Flechtheim, Van Dongen, Marcoussis, Waldemar-George, Rolf de Maré, Adolphe Basler, Kisling, and Jean Crotti. The Musée de Lyon decides to acquire several works by modern foreign painters: Henry de Groux, Ramón de Zubiaurre, Anna Boberg, and Anders Zorn. The press criticizes this choice.

1926

March "Exhibition of Argentinian Art," organized by the University of La Plata (MJP, 53 artists, 187 works).

10 April–31 May "Dutch Exhibition: Paintings, Watercolors, Drawings" (MJP, 60 artists, 163 works).

22–31 October Exhibition and auction of works by foreign artists, organized by the newspaper *Paris-Midi* at the Musée Galliera for the defense of the franc, threatened by financial speculation. 14 works by foreign artists are acquired by the State, including Alice Halicka's *Still Life* (pre-1925); Ossip Zadkine's *Man's Head* (1922); and Ángel Zárraga's *The Football Match* (1925).

30 October–15 November "Exhibition of the Paris Group of American Painters and Sculptors" (Galerie Durand-Ruel). Pascin, a naturalized American citizen, is featured in the exhibition.

1927

11 April–11 May "Exhibition of Canadian Art," organized by the Canadian Fine Art Commission and the Musée National du Luxembourg (MJP, 71 artists, 257 works).

15 June–15 August "Exhibition of Austrian Art: The Treasures of Maximilian Lent by the Republic of Austria," organized by the RMN (MJP, 161 works by anonymous artists and decorative objects). A planned MJP show dedicated to the German painter Max Liebermann is cancelled at the last minute for political reasons: the artist called for war against France in 1914

1928

2 May–1 June "Belgian Art Since Impressionism," organized under the auspices of the Association for the Promotion of Belgian Art Abroad (MJP, 71 artists, 229 works).

9 June–8 July "Danish Art from the 17th Century to 1900," organized by the French and Danish governments (MJP, 57 artists, 281 works).

4 November–16 December Autumn Salon. Polish artists fill an entire room. They include Henryk Stażewski and Władysław Strzemiński.

1929

8–20 April "Japanese Artists' Salon," organized by the Association of Japanese Artists under the auspices of the AFEEA (Galerie La Renaissance Paris, 49 artists, 118 works).

19 April–23 May "Swedish Art Since 1880," organized by a French and Swedish committee headed by Prince Eugen of Sweden (MJP, 73 artists, 384 works).

1 June–25 July "Exhibition of Japanese Art (Contemporary Classic School)," organized under the sponsorship of the French and Japanese governments, head curator: *Daimyo* [feudal lord] Moritatsu Hosokawa (MJP, 351 artists, 352 works).

8 November Inauguration of the Museum of Modern Art (MoMA) in New York, Alfred H. Barr, Jr., director.

1930

July *Cahiers d'Art* magazine launches a campaign in favor of the creation of a museum of modern art. Le Corbusier contributes by giving the magazine an architectural design (*Cahiers d'Art*, no. 7, 1930, pp. 337-339).

22 December–30 January 1931 "Polish Exhibition: Poland 1830, 1920, 1930," organized by the Polish and French governments (MJP). On this occasion, International Red Aid distributes a leaflet denouncing fascism in Poland.

1931

6 May–15 November "Paris Colonial Exhibition," Bois de Vincennes. The Surrealists are against the exhibition, considering it a manifestation of colonialism. They publish a leaflet: "Don't Visit the Colonial Exhibition."

June–July "Portuguese Exhibition: From the Era of Great Discoveries to the 20th Century," organized by the Portuguese and French governments (MJP, 181 works of decorative art).

Anne Morgan's gift to the State of the Château de Blérancourt and its collection is the starting point for the National Museum of Franco-American Cooperation, dedicated to the memory of France's participation in the American War of Independence and American solidarity with France during WWI.

1932

8 March Partial reopening of the Jeu de Paume after renovations.

10 June–10 July "The Works of James Ensor," organized by the group L'Art Contemporain, founded in Anvers in 1905 (MJP, 107 works).

23 December Official inauguration of the Museum of Contemporary Foreign Schools at the Musée National du Jeu de Paume with a radically new layout and artificial lighting. Some 500 paintings and 100 sculptures by foreign artists are on display, many borrowed from private collectors to fill in gaps in the museum's collection. Room 14, devoted to School of Paris painters, brings together works by Foujita, Gargallo, Kisling, Modigliani, Pascin, Picasso, Zadkine, and Van Dongen. Since the museum is dependent on an agreement between the Ministry of Foreign Affairs and the Directorate of French Museums, its curator is frequently obligated to host exhibitions organized for diplomatic reasons by the Ministry of Foreign Affairs.

Gift of the Milanese collector Carlo Frua de Angeli: 17 works by Italian artists (including Carrà, Severini, De Chirico).

1933

March "Ivan Meštrović," organized by André Dezarrois with the assistance of the AFEEA (MJP, 92 works).

May–June "Exhibition of Contemporary Chinese Art," curators: Ju Peon [Xu Beihong], painter, professor at National Central University, Nanjing, and Dezarrois (MJP, 74 artists, 191 works).

The plans for the 1937 Exposition Internationale des Arts et Techniques include the construction of a "Museum of Living Artists" bringing together the collections of the Musée du Luxembourg and the Jeu de Paume.

1934

1 February–1 March "Contemporary Swiss Art Since Hodler: Painting and Sculpture," organized with the cooperation of a group of Swiss artists and the Federal Commission of Fine Arts (MJP, 57 artists, 256 works).

22 February Dealer Daniel-Henry Kahnweiler offers the MJP three works by Paul Klee, an artist not represented in its collections. In the end, a single watercolor will be acquired (*Sturm durch die Ebene* [Storm on the Plain], 1930).

14–29 March "Painters and Printmakers of Revolutionary China" (Galerie Billiet-Pierre Vorms, Paris, traveling to Lyon, 14 April–29 May).

December "Exhibition of Monumental Sculptures by José Fioravanti," curator: Dezarrois (MJP, 24 works).

1935

February–March "Exhibition of Works by Contemporary Belgian Artists," organized by the Association of Belgian Newspaper Correspondents in France and the Belgian Ministry of Public Education (MJP, 72 artists, 208 works).

May–July Subsequent to the January 7 signing of the Italo-French agreement by Benito Mussolini and Pierre Laval, two exhibitions of Italian art are organized in Paris: "Italian Art of the 19th and 20th Centuries" (MJP, 104 artists, 318 works) and "Italian Art: From Cimabue to Tiepolo" (Musée du Petit Palais).

Gift of Italian senator Borletti, an industrialist with ties to the Fascist party, president of the Comitato Italia-Francia: 13 works of the 1930s by Italian artists from the "Italian Art of the 19th and 20th Centuries" exhibition.

1936

12 February–March "Contemporary Spanish Art: Painting and Sculpture," co-organized by Madrid's Sociedad de Artistas Ibéricos (MJP, 123 artists, 324 works).

June "F. Kupka, A. Mucha. Exhibited Works" (MJP, 233 works).

Gift of Hermine David and Lucy Krohg: 6 works by Pascin.

1937

February "Women Artists of Europe Exhibit at the Jeu de Paume." 15 countries represented, plus an "international" room with artists from the School of Paris (402 artists, 550 works). 9 works are acquired by the State after the exhibition.

March–April "Catalan Art from the 10th to 15th Centuries," organized by the Generalitat de Catalunya and the French government; Catalan curator: Joaquim M. Folch I Torres, Director General, Museus d'Art de Catalunya; organizer and head curator: Dezarrois (MJP, 110 works).

May–June "Exhibition of Austrian Art," organized by the French and Austrian governments with the assistance of the AFAA (MJP, 178 artists, 615 works).

25 May–25 November Exposition Internationale des Arts et Techniques dans la Vie Moderne, Paris.

June–October "Masters of Independent Art, 1895–1937" (Musée du Petit Palais, 117 artists, 1,526 works). The organizing committee decides to call upon foreign artists resident in Paris since before 1925. This measure allows the works of Picasso and Juan Gris to be displayed for the first time in a museum. De Chirico, Severini, Soutine, Pascin, Modigliani, Max Ernst, Marcoussis, Kisling, and Chagall share Room 20. Maria Blanchard, Picasso, Gris, Gargallo, Orloff, Zadkine, and Jacques Lipchitz, who is awarded first prize, have a room each.

30 July–31 October "Origins and Development of Independent International Art," dedicated to "artists of foreign Schools" (MJP, 68 artists, 172 works, as well as decorative objects and sculptures from Polynesia, Oceania, New Zealand, and Sub-Saharan Africa). Artists in exile, particularly Germans, are numerous. Naum Gabo, César Domela, Kandinsky, and Freundlich are exhibited in a single room. Americans include Alexander Calder and Man Ray. Alberto Magnelli sends two paintings. Klee, Marcoussis, Joan Miró, and Piet Mondrian are exhibited among non-figurative artists; Gris, Picasso, Lipchitz, and Brancusi in the Cubist room; Salvador Dalí, Ernst, De Chirico, and Chagall in the Surrealist room.

The International Exposition is an opportunity for Paris to create two new museums in the newly constructed Palais de Tokyo: a national museum of modern art which will at last unite French and foreign artists, shown separately since 1922, and a museum of modern art for the City of Paris.

9 November The MJP's arts board refuses to buy a work by Picasso (*Still Life*, 1937), provoking an argument with the head curator, Dezarrois.

1938

24 May–24 July "Three Centuries of Art in the United States: Painting, Sculpture, Architecture, Folk Art, Photography, Cinema," in collaboration with New York's MoMA (MJP, 119 painters, 35 sculptors, 8 craftspeople, 36 printmakers, 43 photographers, 380 works).

July–August "Modern German Art: Impressionism, Expressionism, Cubism and Surrealism," New Burlington Galleries, London. Prudence dictates that Dezarrois refuse to bring the exhibition to the MJP.

The collections of the Musée National du Luxembourg and the Musée du Jeu de Paume begin to be transferred to the Palais de Tokyo.

Gift of Foldes: 9 sculptures.

1939

27 January–28 February "The Art of Latvia: Painting, Sculpture, and Folk Art," organized by the French and Latvian governments; curators: Vilhelms Purvītis for Latvia, Dezarrois for France (MJP, 39 artists, 187 works).

March "The Works of Chang Shan-Tse" (MJP, 112 works).

Important donation by Charles Wakefield-Mori (curator of Monaco's National Museum of Fine Arts): Chagall, Alexis Gritchenko, Otakar Kubín, Ismaël de la Serna, Demetrios Galanis, Ubaldo Oppi.

Closing of the Palais de Tokyo until the end of the Occupation.

1940

April Jean Cassou is named head curator of the National Museum of Modern Art. The Vichy government will revoke his nomination in September due to his ties with the Communist Party. He will be restored to his position in 1945 and will head the National Museum of Modern Art until 1965.

Picasso requests French nationality and is refused.

Many foreign artists take refuge in the *zone libre*: Ernst, Victor Brauner, Wols, Kisling, Lipchitz, Hans Hartung, and Julio González (Toulouse and environs), Magnelli, Sonia Delaunay, and Jean Arp (Grasse). Kandinsky, who was naturalized as French in 1939, leaves Paris for the Pyrenees. Nicolas de Staël enlists in the Foreign Legion.

1941

Ernst, Lipchitz, Chagall, and Zadkine manage to escape from France and reach the United States. Kupka takes refuge in Beaugency, on the Loire. Alberto Giacometti and Hayden leave Paris, the first for Geneva, the second for Auvergne. Brancusi and Soutine stay in the capital. The latter, identified as a Jew, is sought by the Germans. He is denounced and forced to hide away in Chinon. Kisling, condemned to death by the Nazis, flees to Portugal, then to the United States.

October-November The Third Reich invites a delegation of French artists to visit Germany.

Charles Despiau, Othon Friesz, Maurice de Vlaminck, Van Dongen, and others accept and visit Weimar.

1-16 November Exhibition of Nazi soldiers' works: "Kunst der Front. Art at the Front," organized by the Luftwaffe (MJP).

1942

15 May-31 July "Arno Breker," an exhibition organized by the Nazi government at the Musée de l'Orangerie (51 works). Jean Cocteau publishes "Hail to Breker" in *Comœdia*, 23 May 1942.

6 August 1942-15 November 1943 The partial opening of the Palais de Tokyo allows the permanent collections to be shown.

October In New York, the Galerie Pierre Matisse organizes "Artists in Exile," an exhibition of 14 artists from many countries, most via Paris: Eugène Berman, André Breton, Chagall, Ernst, Léger, Lipchitz, Matta, André Masson, Mondrian, Amédée Ozenfant, Kurt Seligmann, Yves Tanguy, Paul Tchelitchew, and Zadkine.

1943

May Hundreds of works by Ernst, Kisling, Klee, Léger, Mane-Katz, Miró, Francis Picabia, and Picasso, looted from Jewish collections but not transferred to Germany, are destroyed at the MJP. Works sent to Germany will be recovered after the war. If their rightful owners are not identified, they will be given temporary MNR (National Museums Recovery) reference numbers, entrusted by the Office of Private Property to the care of the Directorate of French Museums (decree of 30 September 1949), and assigned to French national museums.

1944

22 June The G.I. Bill, which finances education and training for veterans of the U.S. Army, makes such American artists eligible for a 75 dollar/month grant to study in France.

October The Autumn Salon celebrates the Liberation with a Picasso retrospective. After the artist joins the Communist Party, some works are defaced and taken down by protesters.

1946

The French government renews its policy of cultural exchange and organizes, under the auspices of the AFAA, many exhibitions of artists from various countries.

15 February-15 March "Art and Resistance," organized by The Friends of French Francs-Tireurs and Partisans in homage to resistance fighters of all origins who combatted the German occupation (Musée d'Art Moderne de la Ville de Paris, 227 artists and 455 works). The exhibition mingles the works of foreign artists (Chagall, Joseph Csaky, Giacometti, Lipchitz, Picasso, Liao Sin Hio, Victor Vasarely) and French artists (Auguste Herbin, Masson, Matisse, and others).

19 March-15 April "Seven Belgian Painters," organized as part of a Franco-Belgian agreement under the auspices of the AFAA (Musée de l'Orangerie, 91 works).

June "Modern British Paintings from the Tate Gallery Exhibited under the Auspices of the British Council" (MJP, 53 artists, 120 works).

18 November-28 December "International Exhibition of Modern Art," organized by UNESCO at the future National Museum of Modern Art [Musée National d'Art Moderne, MNAM]. Countries and sections: Argentina (19 artists and works), Australia (20 artists, 29 works), Belgium (37 artists and works), Bolivia (1 artist, 5 works), Brazil (24 artists, 33 works), British Colonies [West Africa and Nigeria, Oriental Africa, Ceylon] (10 artists, 15 works), British Naïve artists (7 artists, 8 works), Canada (30 artists and works), Central European refugee artists (10 artists, 15 works), Chile (18 artists and works), China (22 artists, 24 works), Czechoslovakia (16 artists, 37 works), Denmark (19 artists, 21 works), Ecuador (11 artists, 19 works), France (86 artists, 88 works), French Overseas Departments and Territories (3 artists and works), Great Britain (28 artists, 60 works), Haiti (28 artists and works), Hungarian artists living in Paris (10 artists and works), Luxembourg (6 artists, 7 works), Netherlands (24 artists, 31 works), Polish artists living in Great Britain (8 artists, 16 works), Polish artists living in Paris (11 artists and works), Spanish School of Paris artists (14 artists and works), Sweden (45 artists, 50 works), Turkey (33 artists, 41 works), United States (68 artists, 84 works), Uruguay (16 artists, 24 works), Venezuela (5 artists, 11 works), and Yugoslavia (16 artists, 18 works).

Donation by gallery owner Paul Rosenberg: 16 works, including 1 Picasso (*Still Life with Antique Head*, 1925).

1947

9 June Official opening of the MNAM, Jean Cassou, director. For the first time, French and foreign artists are shown together. At the request of Jean Cassou, Picasso offers 10 works.

17 October-22 December "Marc Chagall," organized by the RMN (MNAM, 67 works, dating from 1908 to 1947).

26 December 1947-26 January 1948 "Permeke," under the honorary patronage of the Belgian Ministry of Public Education (MNAM, 65 works).

1948

1 February-1 March "Paul Klee," organized with the assistance of the Société Klee (Berne, Switzerland), the Fondation Klee, and D.-H. Kahnweiler (MNAM, 365 works).

16 April-15 May "Laethem-Saint-Martin. Artists' Colony in Flanders, 1890-1940," organized as part of Franco-Belgian cultural agreements (MNAM, 8 artists, 68 works).

23 July-30 August 3rd Salon of New Realities. Exceptionally, foreign artists are grouped in the catalogue according to their national origin. The United States are the best represented with 34 artists.

15 October-15 November "Fritz Wotruba," organized by the RMN (MNAM, 12 paintings).

22 November-19 December "Emile Terry [Emilio Terry], Cuban Architect. Models, Furniture, Drawings" (MNAM, 30 works).

1949

1 January-6 February "Polish Folk Art," organized under the honorary patronage of the French and Polish governments (MNAM, 199 works from the 13th-20th centuries).

26 March-24 May "Contemporary Hungarian Art," organized by the RMN (MNAM, 31 artists, 83 works).

May "The Works of Zadkine," organized by the RMN (MNAM, 73 sculptures).

18 November-31 December "Henry Moore," organized with the British Council as part of Franco-British agreements (MNAM, 57 works).

Gift of Marc and Ida Chagall: 5 paintings.

1950

11 January-12 February "Some Contemporary Walloon Artists," organized as part of Franco-Belgian cultural agreements (MNAM, 176 works).

May-June "Exhibition of Modern Italian Art," organized under the auspices of the AFAA; curator: Paolo D'Ancona, art historian (MNAM, 19 artists, 106 works).

"19 Haitian Painters," traveling exhibition organized by the Stedelijk Museum, Amsterdam (MNAM, 54 works).

1951

February-March "Contemporary Cuban Art," organized by the Cuban cultural delegation to Europe under the auspices of the AFAA (MNAM, 27 artists, 52 works).

April "Norwegian Mural Art, 1920-1950," organized under the auspices of the AFAA; curator: Sigurd Willoch, director of the National Gallery of Norway, Oslo (MNAM, 6 artists, 93 works).

October-November "Carl Cylberg [Carl Oscar Kylberg]," organized under the honorary patronage of the French and Swedish governments by the AFAA (MNAM, 70 works).

November-December "Joseph Kutter," organized under the honorary patronage of the French and Luxembourg governments under the auspices of the AFAA (MNAM, 71 works).

Gift of Léonard Foujita: 4 paintings.

1952

1 February-9 March "Julio González," organized by the RMN (MNAM, 115 works).

May-June "20th Century Works. Paintings-Sculptures," under the auspices of the Congress for Cultural Freedom (MNAM, 44 artists, most of them foreign, 114 works).

May-July "Mexican Art (From the Pre-Columbian to Today)," organized under the auspices of the AFAA; curators: Jean Cassou and Fernando Gamboa, subdirector general, Instituto Nacional de Bellas Artes, Mexico (1,481 works in 4 categories: Pre-Columbian, Colonial, Modern and Contemporary, and Popular).

7 November-14 December "Graham Sutherland," organized by the British Council and the Musées de France (MNAM, 71 works).

December "Vitullo, Argentine Sculptor," organized under the auspices of the AFAA, subsequent to several exhibitions of French art in Argentina (MNAM, 45 works).

Donation by patron and collector Raoul La Roche: 5 works, including 2 Picassos (*The Violin* [1914], *Still Life* [1922]) and 1 Gris (*Still Life on a Chair* [1917]).

Donation by the collectors M. and Mme André Lefèvre: 18 works, including 4 Gris, 1 Klee, 1 Modigliani, and 4 Picassos.

1953

30 January-9 April "Cubism, 1907-1914," organized by the RMN (MNAM, 31 artists including 10 foreign or of foreign origin, 231 works).

April-June "12 Contemporary American Painters and Sculptors," co-organized by the RMN and MoMA, New York, under the auspices of the AFAA (MNAM, 74 works).

Autumn Exhibition of Brazilian architecture organized by the Brazilian Embassy (Musée d'Art Moderne de la Ville de Paris).

17 November-31 January 1954 "Le Corbusier. Plastic Works," organized by the RMN (MNAM, 60 works).

1954

February-April "The Works James Ensor," organized under the auspices of the AFAA as part of Franco-Belgian cultural agreements (MNAM, 294 works).

October-November "Contemporary Drawing in the United States," organized under the auspices of the AFAA; curator: Carl O. Schniewind, curator at the Art Institute of Chicago (MNAM, 49 artists, 139 works).

1955

21 January-21 February "Views on Ben Nicholson," organized by the British Council as part of Franco-British agreements (MNAM, 86 works).

February-March "Pellan [Alfred Pellan]," organized under the auspices of the AFAA (MNAM, 139 works).

April-May "Fifty Years of Art in the United States: The MoMA Collection," organized with the assistance of the AFAA and the cultural relations department of the United States Embassy (MNAM, 211 artists in all disciplines, 552 works).

14 October-13 November "Young Painters," under the auspices of the Congress for Cultural Freedom. Countries represented: Belgium (20 artists and works), England (18 artists and works), France (28 artists and works), Germany (15 artists and works), Italy (35 artists and works), the Netherlands (12 artists and works), Switzerland (17 artists and works), and the United States (18 artists and works).

November-December "Joaquín Torres-García. Montevideo, 18 July 1874-Montevideo, 3 August 1949," organized by the RMN (MNAM, 68 works).

28 November-16 December "Guggenheim Prize 1956," exhibition of works selected by the juries of 19 countries (MNAM, 78 artists, 96 works).

1956

9 January-5 February "Gajin Kôsaka, 1877-1953," organized by the RMN (MNAM, 46 works).

22 February-2 April "Nicolas de Staël, 1914-1955," organized by the RMN (MNAM, 150 works).

21 December 1956-10 March 1957 "Antoine Pevsner," organized by the RMN (MNAM, 81 works).

Gift of Le Corbusier of the model of the Notre-Dame-de-Ronchamp chapel, the first architectural work to enter French national collections.

Bequest of Maurice Meunier: 1 De Chirico, 1 Marcoussis, 1 Miró, 2 Picassos.

1957

Creation of the Ateneo Ibero-Americano de Paris for Portuguese in exile and Latino-American intellectuals residing in Paris. Rafael Alberti, Albert Camus, Pablo Casals, Jean Cassou, Carlos Fuentes, and Alfonso Reyes are members of the honorary committee.

7 February-10 March "Lynn Chadwick" (30 works) and "Ivon Hitchens" (24 works), co-organized with the British Council as part of Franco-British cultural agreements under the patronage of the AFAA (MNAM).

October-November "Rik Wouters," organized as part of Franco-Belgian cultural agreements under the auspices of the AFAA (MNAM, 149 works).

15 November 1957-6 February 1958 "Kandinsky," traveling exhibition of 44 works from the Solomon R. Guggenheim Museum, New York (MNAM).

December 1957-January 1958 "Polish Traditions and Folk Art of the 16th-20th Centuries," co-organized by the Polish Ministry of Culture and Fine Arts and the General Directorate of Cultural and Technical Affairs of the French Ministry of Foreign Affairs under the auspices of the AFAA (MNAM, 147 works).

Constantin Brancusi bequeaths his studio to the French State: 144 sculptures, 33 drawings, and more than 1,600 period photographic prints and nearly 500 negatives. This exceptional photographic ensemble is immediately considered a research collection. It will be integrated into the collections of the MNAM's Photography section when the latter is created in the 1980s.

1958

24 January–23 February "Pougny," organized by the RMN (MNAM, 160 works).

6 March–20 April "Dutch Art Since Van Gogh," organized as part of Franco-Dutch agreements under the auspices of the AFAA (MNAM, 17 artists, 92 works).

Spring "Japanese Art Through the Centuries," a traveling exhibition organized as part of Franco-Japanese cultural agreements under the auspices of the AFAA (MNAM, London, The Hague, Rome, 95 works from all periods).

27 May–13 July "Kupka," organized by the RMN (MNAM, 11_ works).

22 November–21 December "Kenneth Armitage, Stanley William Hayter, William Scott," organized by the British Council and the Directorate of French Museums as part of Franco-British cultural agreements under the auspices of the AFAA (MNAM, 104 works).

1959

16 January–15 February "Jackson Pollock and New American Painting," organized by the International Council at the Museum of Modern Art, New York, under the auspices of the AFAA (MNAM, 17 artists, 139 works).

February–March "Lasar Segall," organized under the auspices of the AFAA; general curator: Pietro Maria Bardi, director of the Museu de Arte de São Paulo (MNAM, 273 works).

20 May–28 June "Jacques Lipchitz," traveling exhibition organized by the Stedelijk Museum, Amsterdam (MNAM, 106 works).

July "The School of Paris in Belgian Collections," organized by the Société des Amis du Musée d'Art Moderne (MNAM, 98 artists, 169 works).

13 November–31 December "Max Ernst," organized by the RMN (MNAM, 175 works).

Gift by Xénia Pougny: 12 paintings by Jean Pougny.

1960

15 January–14 February "Swiss Modern Art from Hodler to Klee," organized by the Fondation Pro Helvetia; curator general: Georg Schmidt, director of the Kunstmuseum, Basel (MNAM, 33 artists, 132 works).

7 April–8 May "Contemporary Israeli Art," organized by the Department of Cultural Relations of the Israeli Ministry of Foreign Affairs under the auspices of the AFAA, curator general: Dr. F. Schiff, director of the Haifa Museum of Art (MNAM, 24 artists, 117 works).

May–June "Russian and Soviet Painting," organized by the Soviet state museums under the auspices of the AFAA (MNAM, 91 artists recognized by the Soviet government, 168 works).

[May–June?] "Pedro Figari," in collaboration with the Sociedad Rioplatense Amigos de Figari (MNAM, 132 works).

4 November 1960–23 January 1961 "The Sources of the 20th Century: The Arts in Europe, 1884–1914," co-organized with the Council of Europe (MNAM, 326 artists, most of them foreign; 1,346 works in three categories: Plastic Arts, Sculpture, Graphic Arts Architecture and Decorative Arts; Literature, Music, Theater, and Film)

Gift of Hans Hartung: 4 drawings.

1961

February–March "Twelve Modern Polish Painters," organized by the Polish Ministry of Culture and Fine Arts under the auspices of the AFAA; curator general: Stanisław Lorentz, art historian (MNAM, 43 works).

19 October–19 November "Drawings from James Ensor to Today," organized as part of Franco-Belgian agreements under the auspices of the AFAA (MNAM, 31 artists, 143 works).

25 October–4 December "Romanian Art from the 19th Century to Today," organized by the People's Republic of Romania under the auspices of the AFAA (MNAM, 42 artists, 188 works).

20 December–28 January "Contemporary Art in Yugoslavia," organized by the Federal People's Republic of Yugoslavia; curator: Aleksa Čelebonović, director of the Permanent Exhibition of Contemporary Yugoslav Art (MNAM, 47 artists, 150 works).

Gift of D.-H. Kahnweiler: 10 drawings by Manolo.

1962

15 May–10 June "August Strindberg: Paintings," traveling exhibition organized by the Moderna Museet, Stockholm (MNAM, 29 works).

June–November "Joan Miró," organized by the RMN (MNAM, 241 works).

November 1962–January 1963 "Le Corbusier," organized by the RMN (MNAM, 299 works).

Gift of Mme Pevsner: 11 works by Antoine Pevsner.

1963

22 March–15 April "Eric Grate, Swedish Sculptor," organized under the auspices of the AFAA (MNAM, 100 works).

23 October–1 December "Three British Artists at the Musée National d'Art Moderne: Robert Adams, Hubert Dalwood, Ceri Richards," organized by the British Council as part of Franco-British agreements under the auspices of the AFAA (MNAM, 85 works).

December 1963–February 1964 "Argentinian Art Today," organized under the honorary patronage of the Argentine and French governments (curator: Gyula Kosice, artist), presenting, among others, Carlos Alonso, Horacio Butler, Lucio Fontana, Antonio Seguí, Luis Tomasello, and Julio Le Parc (MNAM, 59 artists, 154 works). "Vassily Kandinsky. Rétrospective," traveling exhibition organized by the Solomon R. Guggenheim Museum, New York (MNAM, 44 works).

Kupka donation: 52 paintings, 86 drawings.

Donation by Adèle and George Besson (art critic): 420 works in the custody of the Musée de Besançon, including works by Johan Barthold Jongkind, Kubín, Orloff, Pascin, Picasso, and Van Dongen.

1964

3 July–4 October "Louis Marcoussis," organized by the RMN (MNAM, 228 works).

24 April–22 June "Sophie Taeuber-Arp," organized by the RMN (MNAM, 155 works).

González donation: 8 paintings, 121 drawings, 66 sculptures.

Donation by Sonia and Charles Delaunay: 114 works, including 16 paintings and 37 drawings by Sonia Delaunay.

Pevsner donation: 10 works by Antoine Pevsner.

1965

Bernard Dorival is named curator in chief of the MNAM.

Opening of the Cité Internationale des Arts, Paris, providing a residence for professional artists from abroad seeking to develop an artistic work in France.

July–October "Calder," co-organized by the Solomon R. Guggenheim Museum, New York (MNAM, 334 works).

15 January–15 February "Amar Nath Sehgal, Indian Sculptor," organized under the auspices of the AFAA and the cultural services division of the Indian Embassy (MNAM, 40 works).

Bequest by Baroness Eva Gourgaud: 12 works from her collection, including 4 Picassos.

1966

15 January–6 March "French Fauves and German Expressionists," co-organized with the Haus der Kunst, Munich (MNAM, 30 artists, 283 works).

March–April "Paris–Prague, 1906–1930. Prague's Braques and Picassos and Their Czech Contemporaries," organized by the French and Czechoslovakian governments under the auspices of the AFAA (MNAM, 18 artists, 189 works).

15 October–20 November "Vallotton," organized by the RMN (MNAM, 195 works).

22 October–25 December "Zoltán Kemény," co-organized with the Palais des Beaux-Arts, Brussels (MNAM, 100 works).

30 November 1966–30 January 1967 "Dada: 50th Anniversary Exhibition," co-organized with the Kunsthaus, Zurich (MNAM, 45 artists, 292 works).

"Homage to Picasso" (Grand Palais, Paris). The exhibition is enormously popular, the first exhibition by a living artist visited by so many (600,000).

Gift by Calder: 4 works, followed by a gift of 18 works in 1966.

Pougny donation: 54 works, including 5 sculptures, 22 paintings, and 26 drawings.

Bequest by M. and Mme Léon Baratz: 15 works by Russian artists.

1967

6 January–12 February "Willi Baumeister: Paintings, Drawings," organized by the German Fine Arts Council (MNAM, 120 works).

July–October "Gino Severini," organized by the RMN (MNAM, 202 works).

13 October–26 November "Van Dongen," co-organized with the Museum Boijmans Van Beuningen, Rotterdam, as part of Franco-Dutch cultural agreements (MNAM, 164 works).

23 October Creation of the Centre National d'Art Contemporain (CNAC), which will merge with the Centre Pompidou in 1975.

2 December 1967–7 January 1968 "Sonia Delaunay: Retrospective," organized by the RMN (MNAM, 197 works).

Severini donation: 4 paintings, 12 drawings, 7 sculptures.

1968

Jean Leymarie is named curator in chief of the MNAM

12 January–18 February "Canada: Art of Today," organized by the National Gallery of Canada under the auspices of the AFAA (MNAM, 19 artists, 76 works).

26 February–21 April "Magnelli," co-organized with the Kunstforeningen, Copenhagen (MNAM, 173 works).

3 May–2 June "Hayden: Sixty Years of Painting," organized by the Friends of the National Museum of Modern Art (MNAM, 107 works).

7 November–23 December "Joseph Sima," organized by the National Gallery in Prague under the auspices of the AFAA (MNAM, 188 works).

25 September–28 October "Max Beckmann," organized with the Haus der Kunst, Munich (MNAM, 107 works).

Gift of Roberta González: 18 drawings by Julio González.

1969

7 January–24 February "Hartung", organized by the Société des Amis du Musée National d'Art Moderne (MNAM, 152 works).

2 April–22 June "Bauhaus, 1919–1969," co-organized by the Würtembergischer Kunstverein, Stuttgart, and the RMN (MNAM, 94 artists, 1,714 works and documents).

28 June–15 September "Picassos of the Cuttoli-Laugier Donation at the National Museum of Modern Art" (Musée de l'Orangerie, 14 works).

24 September–10 November "Vieira da Silva. Painting, 1935–1969," organized by the CNAC (MNAM, 87 works).

24 October Creation of the Centre de Création Industrielle. On 24 December 1992, the CCI is absorbed into the National Museum of Modern Art; this merger facilitates the creation of the architectural drawing and model collection.

Gift of M. Pierre Gaut, art supplier and film producer, in memory of Marguerite Savary, collector: 5 Picassos.

25 November 1969–15 February 1970 "Paul Klee" organized by the RMN (MNAM, 199 works).

11 December 1969–January 1977 French president Georges Pompidou makes the decision to build a great museum of contemporary art as well as a public library on the Beaubourg Plateau in the center of Paris. In 1970, the government launches a major design competition. An international jury selects a design by a group of three architects, Renzo Piano, Gianfranco Franchini, and Richard Rogers. The building is inaugurated on 31 January 1977. In 1970, Dr. Robert Le Masle bequeaths two period prints by Man Ray, which will be added to the museum inventory in 1974. These are the two first photographs to enter the art collections of the National Museum of Modern Art. In 1973, the Centre Pompidou acquires its first cinematographic works. In 1976, new media become part of the collection. From its opening on, the Centre Pompidou pursues a policy of presenting artists from all over the world by organizing great multidisciplinary exhibitions: "Paris-New York" (1977), "Paris-Berlin" (1978), "Paris-Moscow" (1979), "Italian Identity: Art in Italy from 1959 to Today" (1981), "Architectures of Earth or the Future of a Millenial Tradition" (1981), "Vienna, 1880–1938. The Merry Apocalypse" (1986), "Avant-Garde Japan" (1986), "Magicians of the Earth" (1989), "Latin American Art, 1911–1968" (1992), "Photography of Latin America" (1992), "Japanese Design, 1950–1995" (1996), "Alors la Chine" (2003), "Africa Remix: The Contemporary Art of a Continent" (2005). "Los Angeles, 1955–1985: Birth of an Art Capital" (2006), "The Promises of the Past: A Broken History of Art in the Former Eastern Europe" (2010), "Paris-Delhi-Bombay..." (2011).

Thanks to the Magnelli (1984) and Cordier (2008) donations, the MNAM collection is also enriched by primitive art sculptures.

Translated from the French by Phoebe Green

LIST OF REPRODUCED WORKS

Note: unless otherwise specified, these works are from the collections of the Centre Pompidou, Musée National d'Art Moderne

Shafic ABBOUD
1926 (MHAYDSEH)–2004 (PARIS)
Composition, 1965
Oil on canvas, 146 × 114 cm
GIFT OF CHRISTINE ABBOUD
AM 2013-485
→ **Repr. p. 192**

AGAM
1928 (RISHON LEZION)
Assemblage mouvant
[Moving Assembly], 1953
Painted wood,
25 × 49.5 × 3.5 cm
GIFT OF JEAN-JACQUES LEBEL IN MEMORY OF NINA LEBEL, 2004
AM 2004-421
→ **Repr. p. 206**

Magazine *Al-'Emara*,
Cairo, nos. 1-2, 1953,
front and back covers
KANDINSKY LIBRARY, CENTRE POMPIDOU
→ **Repr. p. 151**

Yves ALIX
1890 (FONTAINEBLEAU)–1969 (PARIS)
Le Maître de moisson
[The Master of the Harvest], 1921
Oil on canvas, 200 × 162 cm
GIFT OF THE ARTIST, 1949
AM 2792 P
→ **Repr. p. 105**

Manuel ÁLVAREZ BRAVO
1902 (MEXICO CITY)–2002 (MEXICO CITY)
La Buena Fama durmiendo
[Good Reputation Sleeping],
1938
Silver gelatin print,
20.6 × 25.2 cm
ACQUIRED BY THE STATE, 1983
ATTRIBUTION, 1988
AM 1988-698
→ **Repr. p. 163**

Tadao ANDO
1941 (OSAKA)
Church of Light, Osaka, Japan,
1987–1989
Executed design
Model, 1987–1989
Concrete, 95.5 × 223 × 101.5 cm
GIFT OF THE ARCHITECT, 2010
AM 2010-2-687
→ **Repr. p. 223**

Oswald DE ANDRADE
1890 (SÃO PAULO)–1954 (SÃO PAULO)
Manifesto Antropofago
[Anthropophagic Manifesto],
Revista de antropofagia, vol. 1,
no. 1, May 1928
BIBLIOTHECA BRASILIANA GUITA E JOSÉ MINDLIN, USP, SÃO PAULO
→ **Repr. p. 98**

Carl ANDRE
1935 (QUINCY, MASSACHUSETTS)
Oswald in Russia, 1964
Carbon copy of typescript
and pencil on letter paper,
27.7 × 21.2 cm
PURCHASE, 1993
AM 1993-155 (2)
→ **Repr. p. 229**

ANDREENKO
1894 (KHERSON)–1982 (PARIS)
Peinture [Painting], 1924
Oil on canvas, 55.6 × 37.9 cm
GIFT OF THE ARTIST, 1982
AM 1982-353
→ **Repr. p. 83**

ANONYMOUS
Anthropomorphic Face Mask (Dogon), n.d.
Mission Dakar-Djibouti
Wood, 45 × 18 × 20 cm
QUAI BRANLY MUSEUM
71.1931.74.1997
→ **Repr. p. 75**

ANONYMOUS
Bamileke Anthropomorphic Chambranle Pillar (Cameroon),
n.d.
Wood, 245 × 28 × 23 cm
QUAI BRANLY MUSEUM
GIFT OF THE FRENCH SECRÉTARIAT D'ÉTAT À LA COOPÉRATION ET À LA FRANCOPHONIE
71.1962.59.5
→ **Repr. p. 49**

ANONYMOUS
Mami Watta, ca. 1950
Reverse glass painting,
glass, adhesive paper,
48.2 × 36.9 × 0.5 cm
QUAI BRANLYMUSEUM
73.1994.4.38
→ **Repr. p. 179**

ANONYMOUS
Ponou Mask (Gabon),
1880–1920
Polychrome wood, kaolin,
34 × 21.5 × 15.5 cm
DONATION OF SUSI MAGNELLI, 1984
AM 1984-346
→ **Repr. p. 56**

ANONYMOUS
Le Roi et la Reine
[King and Queen], n.d.
Gouache on paper cut and
pasted on paper set on
canvas glued to plywood,
209.5 × 166.5 cm
GIFT TO THE STATE, 1953
ATTRIBUTION, 1953
AM 5046 P
→ **Repr. p. 117**

ANONYMOUS
Saint Martin, ca. 1810–1850
Polychrome wood,
75 × 54.5 × 37 cm
BEQUEST OF NINA KANDINSKY, 1981
AM 81-65-1029
→ **Repr. p. 57**

ANONYMOUS
Untitled, n.d.
Oil on canvas, 36.8 × 56.4 cm
BEQUEST OF NINA KANDINSKY, 1981
AM 81-65-884 (1)
→ **Repr. p. 77**

ANONYMOUS
Scène villageoise de marché, Nigeria
[Village Market Scene,
Nigeria], n.d.
Weaving, resist dyeing, cotton,
indigo, 203 × 243 cm
QUAI BRANLY MUSEUM
70.2006.18.168
→ **Repr. p. 178**

ANONYMOUS
The Combat of Ruslan the Glorious Riding the Serpent to Rescue the Tsarina Anastasia,
1880–1900
Lubok [colored print],
35.3 × 44 cm
BEQUEST OF NINA KANDINSKY, 1981
AM 81-65-1034 (1)
→ **Repr. p. 57**

ANONYMOUS
Tobacco Pavilion (architect: Constantin Melnikov); Agriculture and Craft Fair, Moscow, 1923
Silver gelatin print, 12.5 × 11 cm
KANDINSKY LIBRARY, CAHIERS D'ART COLLECTION, 10710
→ **Repr. p. 81**

ANONYMOUS
Wrapped Radio, ca. 1940
Plastic, metal, black cotton
cloth, glass beads on cotton
thread, 38.5 × 30.5 × 11.5 cm
QUAI BRANLY MUSEUM
70.1999.11.210
→ **Repr. p. 180**

ANONYMOUS FAIRGROUND PHOTOGRAPHER
Brancusi with Oswald de Andrade, Tarsila, Yvette Farkou, Fernand Léger, and Maximilien Gauthier in a boat setting at the Paris Foire du Trône, 14 July 1926
Silver gelatin print,
8.9 × 13.9 cm
BEQUEST OF CONSTANTIN BRANCUSI, 1957
PH 1253 B
→ **Repr. p. 98**

Carmelo ARDEN QUIN
1913 (RIVERA)–2010 (PARIS)
Cosmopolis VIII, 1946
Lacquer on wood,
35.5 × 45.5 × 5 cm
CENTRE NATIONAL DES ARTS PLASTIQUES/FONDS NATIONAL D'ART CONTEMPORAIN (PARIS-LA DÉFENSE, FRANCE)
PURCHASE, 1990
90086
→ **Repr. p. 199**

Jean ARP
1886 (STRASBOURG)–1966 (BASEL)
Sophie TAEUBER-ARP
1889 (DAVOS)–1943 (ZURICH)
Symétrie pathétique
[Pathetic Symmetry],
1916–1917
Pattern by Jean Arp
embroidered
by Sophie Taeuber-Arp,
cotton, 76 × 65 cm
GIFT OF MARGUERITE ARP-HAGENBACH, 1967
AM 1248 OA
→ **Repr. p. 66**

Antonio ASIS
1932 (BUENOS AIRES)
Interférences concentriques bleues et blanches
[Blue and White Concentric
Interferences], 1961
Acrylic on wood, 170 × 85 cm
GIFT OF THE ARTIST, 2012
AM 2013-225
→ **Repr. p. 207**

ATBAT-AFRIQUE
Georges Candilis,
Shadrach Woods,
Apartment façades, Nid d'Abeille residence, Casablanca
Cover of *Architecture d'aujourd'hui*, special issue
Habitations collectives, no. 57,
December 1954
KANDINSKY LIBRARY, CENTRE POMPIDOU
→ **Repr. p. 150**

Jean ATLAN
1913 (CONSTANTINE)–1960 (PARIS)
Les Miroirs de l'Asie
[The Mirrors of Asia],
1953–1954
Oil on canvas, 195.5 × 130 cm
PURCHASE, 1980 AM 1980-4
→ **Repr. p. 190**

Ivan BABIJ
1896 (KARKHOV)–1974 (RUSSIA)
Deux nus
[Two Nudes], ca. 1930
Oil on canvas, 92 × 73 cm
PURCHASE BY THE STATE, 1937
ATTRIBUTION, 1937
JP 794 P
→ **Repr. p. 120**

Francis BACON
1909 (DUBLIN)–1992 (MADRID)
Study for a Portrait, 1978
Oil on canvas, 35.5 × 30.5 cm
DONATION OF LOUISE AND MICHEL LEIRIS, 1984
AM 1984-488
→ **Repr. p. 75**

Giacomo BALLA
1871 (TURIN)–1958 (ROME)
Il pianeta Mercurio passa davanti al sole
[The Planet Mercury Passes
in Front of the Sun], 1914
Oil on embossed paper,
61 × 50.5 cm
PURCHASE BY FRENCH MUSÉES NATIONAUX, 1951
AM 3058 P
→ **Repr. p. 60**

BALTHUS
1908 (PARIS)–2001 (ROSSINIÈRE)
La Toilette de Cathy
[Cathy Dressing], 1933
Oil on canvas, 165 × 150 cm
PURCHASE, 1977
AM 1977-196
→ **Repr. p. 121**

Gabriele BASILICO
1944 (MILAN)–2013 (MILAN)
T Building, Ramat Hadar, Haifa, 1993
Architects: Weinraub
& Mansfeld, 1959–1964
Silver gelatin print,
38.3 × 50.4 cm
GIFT OF THE ARTIST, 1998
AM 1998-209
→ **Repr. p. 151**

Willi BAUMEISTER
1889 (STUTTGART)–1955 (STUTTGART)
Mauerbild mit Kreis
[Wall Painting with Circle], 1923
Oil on canvas, plywood,
and oil-painted cardboard glued
to the canvas, 121 × 72 × 3.3 cm
GIFT OF KRISTA GUTBROD-BAUMEISTER AND FELICITAS KARG-BAUMEISTER, 1990
AM 1990-203
→ **Repr. p. 82**

BAYA
1931 (BORDJ EL KIFFAN)–1998 (BLIDA)
Sans titre [Untitled], 1966
Gouache on paper,
100 × 150 cm
CENTRE NATIONAL DES ARTS PLASTIQUES/FONDS NATIONAL D'ART CONTEMPORAIN (PARIS-LA DÉFENSE, FRANCE)
PURCHASE, 1969
FNAC 29675
→ **Repr. p. 25**

Farid BELKAHIA
1934 (MARRAKESH)
Hommage à Gaston Bachelard
[Homage to Gaston Bachelard],
1984
Dye on skin stretched on wood,
320 × 296 cm
PURCHASE, 2013
AM 2013-265
→ **Repr. p. 193**

Federico BELTRÁN MASSES
1885 (GÜIRA DE MELENA)–1949 (BARCELONA)
Pierrot malade [Sick Pierrot],
1929
Oil on canvas, 160 × 180 cm
MODE OF ACQUISITION UNRECORDED, 1933
JP 642 P
→ **Repr. p. 244**

Henryk BERLEWI
1894 (WARSAW)–1967 (PARIS)
Mécano-facture, 1924/1961
Screenprint on paper,
60.9 × 50 cm
GIFT OF THE ARTIST, 1966
AM 10897 GR
→ **Repr. p. 33**

Black Orpheus
A Journal of African and Afro-American Literature,
Ibadan (Nigeria), no. 10, 1962
Editors: Ulli Beier, Janheinz Jahn
Cover: Susanne Wenger
KANDINSKY LIBRARY, CENTRE POMPIDOU
→ **Repr. p. 184**

Maria BLANCHARD
1881 (SANTANDER)–1932 (PARIS)
L'Enfant à la glace
[Child with Ice Cream], 1925
Oil on canvas, 162 × 99.5 cm
PURCHASE, 1953
AM 3274 P
→ **Repr. p. 123**

Erwin BLUMENFELD
1897 (BERLIN)–1969 (ROME)
Le Dictateur [The Dictator], 1937
Silver gelatin print, retouched
by airbrush, 33.7 × 26.7 cm
PURCHASE, 1995
AM 1995-75
→ **Repr. p. 131**

Jacques-André BOIFFARD
1902 (ÉPERNON–1961 (PARIS)
Sans titre (Homme cagoulé)
[Untitled (Hooded Man)], 1930
Silver gelatin print,
22.7 × 16.9 cm
PURCHASE, 1984
AM 1984-154
→ **Repr. p. 75**

Martha BOTO
1925 (BUENOS AIRES)–2004 (PARIS)
Essaim de reflets
[Swarm of Reflections], 1965
Stainless steel, aluminium,
Plexiglas, motor,
152 × 59 × 59 cm
GIFT OF GREGORIO VARDANEGA IN MEMORY OF HIS WIFE, 2006
AM 2006-92
→ **Repr. p. 208**

Zoulikha BOUABDELLAH
1977 (MOSCOW)
Dansons [Let's Dance], 2003
DIGITAL BETACAM VIDEOTAPE, PAL, COLOR, SOUND, 5 MIN.
PURCHASE, 2005
AM 2005-169
→ **Repr. p. 244**

Constantin BRANCUSI
1876 (PESTISANI)–1957 (PARIS)
Campagne roumaine, vue du train [Romanian Countryside,
Seen from the Train], 1937–1938
Photogram, silver gelatin print,
24 × 30 cm
BEQUEST OF CONSTANTIN BRANCUSI, 1957
PH 1074 A
→ **Repr. p. 236**

Constantin BRANCUSI
Cariatide [Caryatid], 1943–1948
Wood, 229 × 45.5 × 43.5 cm
BEQUEST OF CONSTANTIN BRANCUSI, 1957
AM 4002-137
→ **Repr. p. 48**

Marianne BRANDT
1893 (CHEMNITZ)–1983 (KIRCHBERG)
Étude de couleurs et formes élémentaires [Study of
Elementary Colors and Shapes],
1923–1924
Gouache-painted paper glued
on paper, 31.8 × 32 cm
BEQUEST OF NINA KANDINSKY, 1981
AM 81-65-916
→ **Repr. p. 76**

Oswaldo ARTHUR BRATKE
1907 (BOTUCATU)–1997 (SÃO PAULO)
Casa Oswaldo Arthur Bratke in Morumbi, São Paulo, Brazil,
1951–1954
Executed design
Front elevation, 1951–1954
Collage of a print retouched
with pastels, gouaches,
and black ink on black Canson
paper, 29.6 × 56.8 cm
GIFT OF CARLOS BRATKE, ROBERTO BRATKE, MARIA DE LOURDE SILVEIRA BRATKE, 2009
AM 2009-2-329
→ **Repr. p. 171**

Victor BRAUNER
1903 (PIATRA NEAMȚ)–1966 (PARIS)
Hitler, 1934
Oil on cardboard, 22 × 16 cm
GIFT OF AUBE BRETON-ELLÉOUËT, 2003
AM 2003-259
→ **Repr. p. 131**

Victor BRAUNER
Prestige de l'air
[Prestige of the Air], 1934
Oil on canvas, 146 × 113.5 cm
BEQUEST OF JACQUELINE VICTOR BRAUNER, 1986
AM 1987-1200
→ **Repr. p. 113**

André BRETON
1896 (TINCHEBRAY)–1966 (PARIS)
Wall of André Breton's Studio,
1922–1966
Assemblage of 255 objects
and artworks brought
together by André Breton in
the office of his studio on rue
Fontaine (Paris), where he lived
and worked from 1922 until
his death
DATION, 2003
AM 2003-3 (1 TO 257)
→ **Repr. p. 110-111**

Patrick HENRY BRUCE
1881 (CAMPBELL CITY)–1936 (NEW YORK)
Composition, ca. 1923–1926
Oil and pencil on canvas,
64.7 × 80.5 cm
GIFT OF M. AND MME MICHEL SEUPHOR IN 1978
AM 1977-609
→ **Repr. p. 68**

Frédéric BRULY BOUABRÉ
1923 (ZÉPRÉGÜHÉ)
Les Poids à peser [The Weights
to Be Weighed], 1988 [detail]
Assemblage of 9 drawings and
9 texts, arranged 2 by 2
Pencil and ballpoint pen on two
panels of packing cardboard,
14.5 × 9.6 cm each
PURCHASE, 1990
AM 1990-48
→ **Repr. p. 230**

André CADERE
1934 (WARSAW)–1978 (PARIS)
Untitled, 1968–1969
Oil on canvas, 129.5 × 195 cm
GIFT OF THE FRIENDS OF THE NATIONAL MUSEUM OF MODERN ART, 2011
AM 2011-26
→ **Repr. p. 209**

Aristide CAILLAUD
1902 (MAULÉON)–1990 (JAUNAY-CLAN)
Venise [Venice], n.d.
Oil on plywood, 173 × 91 cm
PURCHASE BY THE STATE, 1957
ATTRIBUTION, 1957
AM 3538 P
→ **Repr. p. 116**

Huguette CALAND
1931 (BEIRUT)
Bribes de corps [Body Bits],
1973
Oil on canvas, 90 × 120 cm
GIFT OF KA COLLECTION ART MODERNE ET CONTEMPORAIN, 2013
AM 2014-6
→ **Repr. p. 30**

Georges CANDILIS
1913 (BAKU)–1995 (PARIS)
Islamic Residence, Type B, Southern Elevation, 1953
India ink and adhesive tape
on tracing paper, 39.5 × 59 cm
GIFT OF THE ARTIST, 1996
AM 1996-2-9
→ **Repr. p. 150**

Agustín CÁRDENAS
1927 (MATANZAS)–2001 (HAVANA)
Bonjour à la terre
[Hello to Earth], 1966
Wood, 230 × 35 × 95 cm
CENTRE NATIONAL DES ARTS PLASTIQUES/FONDS NATIONAL D'ART CONTEMPORAIN (PARIS-LA DÉFENSE, FRANCE)
PURCHASE, 1968
FNAC 9598
→ **Repr. p. 49**

Mario CARREÑO
1913 (HAVANA)–1999 (SANTIAGO)
Deux nus féminins
[Two Female Nudes], 1939
Oil on canvas, 92 × 73 cm
MODE OF ACQUISITION UNRECORDED
FORMER COLLECTION OF THE JEU DE PAUME
AM 5055 P
→ **Repr. p. 127**

Manuel CARRILLO
1906 (MEXICO CITY)–1989 (MEXICO CITY)
Silvia con gallinita (se ve un ojo)
[Silvia with a Little Hen
(One Eye Seen)], 1950–1960
Silver gelatin print,
35.5 × 27.7 cm
GIFT OF THE CHRISTOPHER FOUNDATION FOR THE ARTS, 2013
AM 2013-385
→ **Repr. p. 163**

Flávio DE CARVALHO
1899 (AMPARO)–1973 (VALINHOS)
Portrait de l'âme du Professeur Rivet [Portrait of the
Soul of Professor Rivet], 1952
Oil on canvas, 92 × 73 cm
GIFT OF THE ARTIST, 1958
AM 3579 P
→ **Repr. p. 165**

Felice CASORATI
1886 (NOVARA)–1963 (TURIN)
Rittrato di giovanetta
[Portrait of a Young Girl], 1932
Oil on plywood, 72.5 × 56.5 cm
MODE OF ACQUISITION UNRECORDED
JP 865 BIS P
→ **Repr. p. 118**

Marc CHAGALL
1887 (VITEBSK)–1985
(SAINT-PAUL-DE-VENCE)
Bella au col blanc
[Bella with a White Collar], 1917
Oil on linen, 149 × 72 cm
DATION, 1988
AM 1988-61
→ **Repr. p. 124**

Marc CHAGALL
Le Marchand de journaux
[The Newspaper Seller], 1914
Oil on cardboard, 98 × 78.5 cm
DONATION OF IDA CHAGALL, 1984
AM 1984-121
→ **Repr. p. 51**

Chang SHUHONG
1904 (HANGZHOU)–1994 (BEIJING)
Portrait de Shana
[Portrait of Shana], 1935
Oil on canvas, 46 × 38 cm
PURCHASE BY THE STATE, 1936
ATTRIBUTION, 1936
JP 690 BIS P
→ **Repr. p. 139**

Ahmed CHERKAOUI
1934 (BOUJAD)–1967 (CASABLANCA)
Le Couronnement
[The Coronation], 1964
Oil on canvas, 91 × 119 cm
CENTRE NATIONAL DES ARTS PLASTIQUES/FONDS NATIONAL D'ART CONTEMPORAIN (PARIS-LA DÉFENSE, FRANCE)
PURCHASE, 1964
FNAC 28551
→ **Repr. p. 190**

Iakov Georgievich CHERNIKHOV
1889 (PAVLOGRAD)–1951 (MOSCOW)
Architectural Fantasies. Perspective Kompozitsiia 3
[Composition 3], 1933
Gouaches and India ink on
cardboard, 24 × 30 cm
GIFT OF ANDREY CHERNIKHOV AND OF THE IAKOV CHERNIKHOV INTERNATIONAL FOUNDATION, 1996
AM 1997-2-11
→ **Repr. p. 80**

Julia CODESIDO
1892 (LIMA)–1979 (LIMA)
Indias Huancas
[Huanca Women], 1931
Oil on canvas, 106 × 116 cm
PURCHASE BY THE STATE, 1939
ATTRIBUTION, 1939
JP 914 P
→ **Repr. p. 103**

Carlos CRUZ-DIEZ
1923 (CARACAS)
Physichromie no 506
[Physichrome No. 506], 1970
Acrylic paint on PVC strips glued
on plywood, aluminum frame,
180 × 180 cm
PURCHASE BY THE STATE, 1970
ATTRIBUTION, 2008
AM 2009-83
→ **Repr. p. 208**

Carlos CRUZ-DIEZ
Proyecto para un mural exterior, Caracas
[Design for an Exterior Wall,
Caracas], 1954
Painted wood brackets on
plywood, 70.5 × 55.5 × 10.3 cm
PURCHASE, 2004
AM 2004-176
→ **Repr. p. 207**

José CUNEO
1887 (MONTEVIDEO)1977 (BONN)
Luna de tres picos
[Three-Pointed Moon], n.d.
Oil on canvas, 101 × 81.5 cm
MODE OF ACQUISITION UNRECORDED
FORMER COLLECTION OF THE JEU DE PAUME
AM 5062 P
→ **Repr. p. 102**

Pierre DAURA
1896 (MINORCA)–1976
(ROCKBRIDGE BATHS, VIRGINIA)
Peinture [Painting], 1928–1930
Oil on canvas, 24 × 33 cm
GIFT OF MARTHA R. DAURA, 1996
AM 1996-439
→ **Repr. p. 84**

Giorgio DE CHIRICO
1888 (VOLOS)–1978 (ROME)
Portrait prémonitoire de Guillaume Apollinaire
[Premonitory Portrait of Guillaume Apollinaire], 1914
Oil and charcoal on canvas
81.5 × 65 cm
PURCHASE, 1975
AM 1975-52
→ **Repr. p. 120**

Jean DEGOTTEX
1918 (SATHONAY-CAMP)–1988 (PARIS)
Écriture [Writing], 10.2.63, 1963
Oil on canvas, 195 × 129.8 cm
DATION, 1992
AM 1992-77
→ **Repr. p. 196**

Robert DELAUNAY
1885 (PARIS)–1941 (MONTPELLIER)
Les Tours de Laon
[The Towers of Laon], 1912
Oil on canvas, 162 × 130 cm
PURCHASE BY THE STATE, 1935
ATTRIBUTION, 1936
AM 2070 P
→ **Repr. p. 58**

Sonia DELAUNAY
1885 (GRADIZHSK)–1979 (PARIS)
Couverture de berceau
[Cradle Cover], 1911
Cloth sewn on canvas,
111 × 82 cm
DONATION OF SONIA DELAUNAY AND CHARLES DELAUNAY, 1964
AM 1143 OA
→ **Repr. p. 66**

Sonia DELAUNAY
Étude publicitaire pour les montres Zénith
[Advertising Sketch for Zenith Watches], 1914
Draft poster
Colored paper cut and glued on paper, 66 × 81.5 cm
DONATION OF SONIA DELAUNAY AND CHARLES DELAUNAY, 1964
AM 2601 D
→ **Repr. p. 67**

Sonia DELAUNAY
Jeune Finlandaise
[Finnish Girl], 1907
Oil on canvas, 80 × 64 cm
DONATION OF SONIA DELAUNAY AND CHARLES DELAUNAY, 1964
AM 4087 P
→ **Repr. p. 51**

Hugo DEMARCO
1932 (BUENOS AIRES)–1995 (PARIS)
Rotation-réflexion
[Rotation-Reflection], 1965
Wood, UV rays,
185 × 162 × 17 cm
CENTRE NATIONAL DES ARTS PLASTIQUES/FONDS NATIONAL D'ART CONTEMPORAIN (PARIS-LA DÉFENSE, FRANCE)
PURCHASE, 1976
FNAC 1621
→ **Repr. p. 206**

André DERAIN
1880 (CHATOU)–1954 (GARCHES)
Nature morte au lapin
[Still Life with Rabbit], 1938–1939
Oil on canvas, 89.2 × 116.2 cm
DATION, 1982
AM 1982-105
→ **Repr. p. 120**

DI CAVALCANTI
1897 (RIO DE JANEIRO)–1976
(RIO DE JANEIRO)
Danse populaire brésilienne
[Brazilian Folk Dance], 1937
Oil on canvas, 114 × 146 cm
PURCHASE BY THE STATE, 1939
ATTRIBUTION, 1939
JP 899 P
→ **Repr. p. 99**

Braco DIMITRIJEVIĆ
1948 (SARAJEVO)
The Casual Passer-By I Met at 11.09 A.M., Paris, 1971
Bromide emulsion on canvas,
448 × 352 cm
PURCHASE, 1977
Created in 1971 for the Paris Biennale and exhibited in that context on the boulevard Saint-Germain
AM 1978-5 (1)
→ **Repr. p. 231**

Otto DIX
1891 (UNTERMHAUS)–1969 (SINGEN)
Bildnis der Journalistin Sylvia von Harden
[Portrait of the Journalist Sylvia von Harden], 1926
Oil and tempera on wood,
121 × 89 cm
PURCHASE, 1961
AM 3899 P
→ **Repr. p. 119**

Otto DIX
Erinnerungen an die Spiegelsäle von Brüssel
[Memory of the Halls of Mirrors in Brussels], 1920
Oil and glaze on silvered canvas, 124 × 80.4 cm
PURCHASE IN MEMORY OF SIEGFRIED POPPE, 1999
AM 1999-178
→ **Repr. p. 106**

Hisao DOMOTO
1928 (KYOTO)
Peinture
[Painting], 1960
Oil on canvas, 89 × 130 cm
PURCHASE BY THE STATE, 1962
ATTRIBUTION, 1962
AM 4052 P
→ **Repr. p. 197**

Jean DUBUFFET
1901 (LE HAVRE)–1985 (PARIS)
Le Métafizyx, 1950
Oil on canvas, 116 × 89.5 cm
PURCHASE, 1976
AM 1976-12
→ **Repr. p. 172**

Marcel DUCHAMP
1887 (BLAINVILLE-CREVON)–1968
(NEUILLY-SUR-SEINE)
Les Joueurs d'échecs
[The Chess Players], 1911
Oil on canvas, 50 × 61 cm
PURCHASE, 1954
AM 3329 P
→ **Repr. p. 63**

Marcel DUCHAMP
Porte-bouteilles
[Bottle Rack], 1914/1964
Galvanized iron
Height: 64 cm; diameter: 42 cm
PURCHASE, 1986
AM 1986-288
→ **Repr. p. 228**

Raymond DUCHAMP-VILLON
1876 (DAMVILLE)–1918 (CANNES)
Le Grand Cheval
[The Big Horse], 1914/1955
Bronze, 100 × 55 × 95 cm
Cast at Susse Fondeur, Arcueil 1955
PURCHASE WITH THE PARTICIPATION OF MME MARCEL DUCHAMP AND LOUIS CARRÉ, 1976
AM 1976-258
→ **Repr. p. 63**

Raoul DUFY
1877 (LE HAVRE)–1953 (FORCALQUIER)
Pêcheur au filet
[Fisherman with Net], ca. 1914
Oil on canvas, 220.5 × 66 cm
BEQUEST OF MME RAOUL DUFY, 1963
AM 4119 P
→ **Repr. p. 51**

Jean DUPAS
1882 (BORDEAUX)–1964 (PARIS)
Femme en rouge
[Woman in Red], 1927
Oil on wood, 104 × 75 cm
PURCHASE BY THE STATE, 1929
ATTRIBUTION, 1929
ON PERMANENT LOAN TO THE MUSEUM OF DECORATIVE ARTS
LUX 1707 P
→ **Repr. p. 124**

Max ERNST
1891 (BRÜHL)–1976 (PARIS)
Ubu Imperator, 1923
Oil on canvas, 81 × 65 cm
GIFT OF THE FONDATION POUR LA RECHERCHE MÉDICALE IN HONOR OF HÉLÈNE ANAVI, 1984
AM 1984-281
→ **Repr. p. 112**

Parvaneh ETEMADI
1948 (TEHERAN)
Untitled, 1971
Oil on cement, mounted on wooden panel,
70 × 69.5 × 4.5 cm
GIFT OF THE ARTIST
AM 2013-500
→ **Repr. p. 195**

Walker EVANS
1903 (SAINT LOUIS, MISSOURI)–1975 (NEW HAVEN, CONNECTICUT)
Birmingham Steel Mill and Workers' Houses, 1936
Silver gelatin print,
37.62 × 45.7 cm
PURCHASE, 1984
AM 1984-718
→ **Repr. p. 68**

Lyonel FEININGER
1871 (NEW YORK)–1956 (NEW YORK)
Marine, 1924
Oil on canvas, 40 × 42 cm
BEQUEST OF NINA KANDINSKY, 1981
AM 81-65-871
→ **Repr. p. 77**

Luis FERNÁNDEZ
1900 (OVIEDO)–1973 (PARIS)
Tête de taureau
[Bull's Head], ca. 1939
Distemper on canvas,
180 × 251 cm
GIFT TO THE STATE, 1972
ATTRIBUTION, 1977
AM 1979-423
→ **Repr. p. 132**

Paul SHUSAKU FOUJINO
1925 (JAPAN)–1982 (FONTENAY-AUX-ROSES)
Collage [after 1962]
Wallpaper, cut and pasted on cork, mounted on plywood,
160 × 130 cm
FORMER HOLDINGS OF THE MUSÉE NATIONAL D'ART MODERNE
AM 5003 P
→ **Repr. p. 197**

Léonard FOUJITA
1886 (TOKYO)–1968 (ZURICH)
Portrait de l'artiste
[Portrait of the Artist], 1928
Oil and gouache on canvas,
35 × 27 cm
PURCHASE BY THE STATE, 1937
ATTRIBUTION, 1937
JP 848 P
→ **Repr. p. 138**

Gisèle FREUND
1908 (BERLIN)–2000 (PARIS)
Frida Kahlo à côté d'une sculpture dans sa cour, Mexico City
[Frida Kahlo Next to a Sculpture in Her Courtyard], 1951
Silver gelatin print, 30 × 40 cm
DONATION OF THE ARTIST, 1992
AM 1992-306
→ **Repr. p. 162**

Horacio GARCÍA-ROSSI
1929 (BUENOS AIRES)–2012 (PARIS)
Mouvement
[Movement], 1964–1965
Wood, aluminium, Plexiglas, motor, electric bulbs
150 × 150 × 60 cm
CENTRE NATIONAL DES ARTS PLASTIQUES/FONDS NATIONAL D'ART CONTEMPORAIN (PARIS-LA DÉFENSE, FRANCE)
PURCHASE, 1977
ON PERMANENT LOAN TO THE CENTRE POMPIDOU, NATIONAL MUSEUM OF MODERN ART, SINCE 2009
FNAC 1658
→ **Repr. p. 209**

GERA
Sans titre
[Untitled], n.d.
Acrylic paint on canvas, wood,
129.5 × 92 × 1.2 cm
QUAI BRANLY MUSEUM
GIFT OF JACQUES MERCIER
73.1995.2.101
→ **Repr. p. 178**

Alberto GIACOMETTI
1901 (BORGONOVO)–1966 (COIRE)
Objet désagréable
[Disagreeable Object], 1931
Plâtre original,
10.4 × 49.3 × 15 cm
GIFT OF BRUNO AND ODETTE GIACOMETTI AND SILVIO BERTHOUD, 1988
AM 1987-1171
→ **Repr. p. 114**

Mathias GOERITZ
1915 (DANZIG)–1990 (MEXICO CITY)
Pyramides mexicaines
[Mexican Pyramids], 1959
5 elements in partially-painted sheet metal nailed to a wooden core, 279 × 324 × 138 cm
PURCHASE, 1987
AM 1987-1142
→ **Repr. p. 164**

Henri GOETZ
1909 (NEW YORK)–1989 (NICE)
Untitled, 1941–1945
Tempera and oil on paper glued to a wood backing, 77 × 61 cm
GIFT OF THE ARTIST, 1981
AM 1981-632
→ **Repr. p. 115**

Natalia S. GONCHAROVA
1881 (NEGAEVO)–1962 (PARIS)
Plantation de pommes de terre
[Planting Potatoes], 1908–1909
Oil on canvas, 111 × 131 cm
DONATION OF THE SOVIET STATE, 1988
AM 1988-879
→ **Repr. p. 50**

Arshile GORKY
1904 (KHORKOM VARIHAIYOTZ DZOR)–1948 (SHERMAN, CONNECTICUT)
Landscape-Table, 1945
Oil on canvas, 92 × 121 cm
PURCHASE, 1971
AM 1971-151
→ **Repr. p. 161**

Marcel GOTÈNE
CA. 1935 (YABA, BURKINA FASO)–2013
(RABAT, MOROCCO)
Untitled, ca. 1960
Gouache sur toile,
141 × 200 × 2.7 cm
QUAI BRANLY MUSEUM
73.1999.25.1
→ **Repr. p. 181**

Alfredo GRAMAJO GUTIÉRREZ
1893 (MONTEAGUDO)–1961 (OLIVOS)
Un entierro en mi pueblo
[A Burial in My Village], 1920
Oil on cardboard,
58.5 × 78.5 cm
MODE OF ACQUISITION BY THE STATE UNRECORDED, 1926
ENTERED THE JEU DE PAUME MUSEUM AFTER THE "EXHIBITION OF ARGENTINE ART," 1926
JP 389 P
→ **Repr. p. 103**

Marcel GROMAIRE
1892 (NOYELLES-SUR-SAMBRE)–1971 (PARIS)
Le Vagabond
[The Vagabond], 1939
Oil on canvas, 100 × 81 cm
PURCHASE BY THE STATE, 1939
ATTRIBUTION, 1942
AM 2347 P
→ **Repr. p. 104**

George GROSZ
1893 (BERLIN)–1959 (BERLIN)
Weg allen Fleisches II
[The Way of All Flesh II], 1931
Oil on canvas, 100.5 × 81 cm
GIFT OF THÉA STERNHEIM, 1934
JP 700 P
→ **Repr. p. 107**

GRUPO AUSTRAL
1938 (BUENOS AIRES)
Hardoy Chair, 1940
Also known as *BKF*, *AA Chair* and *Butterfly Chair*
Still in production
Lacquered bent steel tubing; leather cover, 83 × 90 × 75 cm
GIFT OF ALEXANDER VON VEGESACK, 1993
AM 1993-1-651
→ **Repr. p. 170**

Abdelkader GUERMAZ
1919 (MASCARA)–1996 (PARIS)
Untitled, 1972–1973
Oil on canvas, 195 × 130 cm
GIFT OF PIERRE REY, 2012
AM 2013-223
→ **Repr. p. 192**

Rihaku HARADA
1890 (TOKYO)–1954 (NIEDERNAI)
Le Bac d'Anvers
[Antwerp Ferry], 1937
Painting on silk, 50 × 63 cm
PURCHASE OF THE STATE, 1938
ATTRIBUTION, 1938
JP 890 P
→ **Repr. p. 142**

Auguste HERBIN
1882 (QUIÉVY)–1960 (PARIS)
Sculpture, 1921
Polychromed wood,
46 × 28.8 × 29 cm
PURCHASE, 1978
AM 1978-21
→ **Repr. p. 85**

Agustín HERNÁNDEZ
1924 (MEXICO CITY)
Folkloric Ballet School, Mexico City, 1965
Executed design
Model, 1965
1/100 scale
Wood, 20.5 × 80.2 × 40.4 cm
GIFT OF THE ARCHITECT, 2011
AM 2011-2-137
→ **Repr. p. 170**

HIROSHIGE
1797 (EDO)–1858 (EDO)
Famous Places of Our Land (Honchô Meisho). Shichirigahama in Sagama Province (Sôshû Shichirigahama), 19th century
Polychrome woodblock print,
23.8 × 37 cm
BEQUEST OF NINA KANDINSKY, 1981
AM 81-65-1252
→ **Repr. p. 76**

Alexandre HOGUE
1898 (MEMPHIS, MISSOURI)–1994
(TULSA, OKLAHOMA)
Oil in the Sandhills, 1944
Oil on canvas, 77 × 107 cm
GIFT OF WILLIAM A. KING, 1962
AM 3956 P
→ **Repr. p. 18**

Vilmos HUSZÁR
1884 (BUDAPEST)–1960 (HIERDEN)
Composition-fleurs
[Composition-Flowers], 1923
Oil on canvas, 60.5 × 55.5 cm
GIFT OF M. AND MME MICHEL SEUPHOR, 1978
AM 1977-607
→ **Repr. p. 79**

Pierre ICHAC
1901 (PARIS)–1978 (PARIS)
Combat au sabre de guerriers touaregs [Swordfight, Touareg Warriors], 1930
Silver gelatin print, 18 × 24.3 cm
PURCHASE SPONSORED BY YVES ROCHER, 2011
FORMERLY PART OF THE CHRISTIAN BOUQUERET COLLECTION
AM 2012-3155
→ **Repr. p. 153**

Pierre ICHAC
Vue aérienne, forêt
[Aerial View, Forest], ca. 1938
Silver gelatin print,
21.9 × 21.9 cm
PURCHASE SPONSORED BY YVES ROCHER, 2011
FORMERLY PART OF THE CHRISTIAN BOUQUERET COLLECTION
AM 2012-3205
→ **Repr. p. 237**

Enio IOMMI
1926 (ROSARIO)–2013 (BUENOS AIRES)
Ritmo linear con color
[Linear Rhythm with Color], 1950
Wood, painted iron,
117.5 × 78.5 × 21.4 cm
GIFT OF THE ARTIST, 2011
AM 2011-124
→ **Repr. p. 199**

Graciela ITURBIDE
1942 (MEXICO CITY)
Oaxaca, 1973
Silver gelatin print,
29.9 × 22.5 cm
PURCHASE, 1983
AM 1983-381
→ **Repr. p. 165**

Joris IVENS
1898 (NIJMEGEN)–1989 (PARIS)
Philips radio (Symphonie industrielle)
[Philips Radio (Industrial Symphony)], 1931
35 mm film, b/w, sound 36 min.
PURCHASE, 1994
AM 1994-F1340
→ **Repr. p. 78**

Alexej von JAWLENSKY
1864 (TORZHOK)–1941 (WIESBADEN)
Byzantinerin (Helle Lippen)
[(Byzantine Woman (Pale Lips)], 1913
Oil on cardboard, 64 × 53.5 cm
DONATION ROBERT HAAS, 1982
AM 1982-44
→ **Repr. p. 59**

Paul JOOSTENS
1889 (ANTWERP)–1960 (ANTWERP)
À l'Afrique [To Africa], 1920
Oil on canvas, 118.5 × 91 cm
GIFT OF M. AND MME MICHEL SEUPHOR, 1978
AM 1977-602
→ **Repr. p. 125**

Ilya KABAKOV
1933 (DNIPROPETROVSK)
Qui a planté ce clou? Je ne sais pas
[Who Drove This Nail? I Don't Know], 1972
Enamel and oil paints, iron nail on Isorel (hardboard),
54.5 × 83.5 × 12 cm
PURCHASE, 1982
AM 1982-38
→ **Repr. p. 229**

Frida KAHLO
1907 (MEXICO CITY)–1954 (MEXICO CITY)
"The Frame," 1938
Oil on aluminum, mounted under glass, painted wood frame,
28.5 × 20.7 cm
PURCHASE BY THE STATE, 1939
ATTRIBUTION, 1939
JP 929 P
→ **Repr. p. 112**

Vassily KANDINSKY
1866 (MOSCOW)–1944
(NEUILLY-SUR-SEINE)
Gelb-Rot-Blau
[Yellow-Red-Blue], 1925
Oil on canvas, 128 × 201.5 cm
DONATION OF NINA KANDINSKY, 1976
AM 1976-856
→ **Repr. p. 76**

Vassily KANDINSKY
Impression V (Parc)
[Impression V (Park)], 1911
Oil on canvas, 106 × 157.5 cm
DONATION OF NINA KANDINSKY, 1976
AM 1976-851
→ **Repr. p. 57**

Vassily KANDINSKY
Franz MARC
1880 (MUNICH)–1916 (BRAQUIS)
Livre-almanach Der Blaue Reiter
[The Blue Rider Almanac], 1914
Bound volume, cardboard cover, color engravings, 22.5 × 23.9 cm
Munich, Piper, 1914
[2nd edition]
BEQUEST OF NINA KANDINSKY, 1981
AM 81-65-1123
→ **Repr. p. 56**

Gaston KARQUEL
1906 (AIX-LES-BAINS)–1971 (?)
"10 mètres." Étude publicitaire pour des ampoules
["10 meters." Advertising Sketch for Light Bulbs], ca. 1938
Photomontage,
35.2 cm × 23.3 cm
GIFT OF JACQUES KARQUEL, 2012
AM 2013-203
→ **Repr. p. 67**

Zoltán KEMÉNY
1907 (BANICA)–1965 (ZURICH)
Pet noir [Black Fart], 1951
Plaster, earth, mica, sawdust on glass, 133.5 × 83.5 cm
GIFT OF MADELEINE KEMÉNY, 1980
AM 1980-361
→ **Repr. p. 172**

Ernst LUDWIG KIRCHNER
1880 (ASCHAFFENBURG)–1938
(FRAUENKIRCH)
Toilette. Frauvordem Spiegel
[Toilette. Woman at the Mirror], 1913/1920
Oil on canvas, 100.5 × 75.5 cm
PURCHASE, 1980
AM 1980-54
→ **Repr. p. 56**

Paul KLEE
1879 (MÜNCHENBUCHSEE)–1940 (LOCARNO)
KN der Schmied [KN the Smith], 1922
Oil, watercolor, and pen on gauze glued to cardboard,
32.8 × 35.6 cm
BEQUEST OF NINA KANDINSKY, 1981
AM 81-65-881
→ **Repr. p. 77**

Július KOLLER
1939 (PIEŠŤANY)–2007 (BRATISLAVA)
Antihappening, 1965
Conceptual card
Green ink stamp on cardboard,
11.4 × 16.2 cm
PURCHASE, 2005
AM 2005-256
→ **Repr. p. 229**

Gyula KOSICE
1924 (KOŠICE)
Escultura luminica Madí
[Madí Light Sculpture], 1946
Neon, 64 × 47 × 17 cm
GIFT OF THE ARTIST, 2012
AM 2013-242
→ **Repr. p. 198**

Gyula KOSICE
Maqueta de la Ciudad Hidroespacial [Model of the Hydrospatial City], 1947
Plexiglas, water,
28 × 56 × 52 cm
GIFT OF THE ARTIST, 2012
AM 2013-2-71
→ **Repr. p. 198**

KOCHAR
1899 (TBILISI)–1979 (EREVAN)
Orientales [Eastern Women], 1924
Oil on canvas, 54 × 81 cm
ANONYMOUS GIFT, 1938
JP 879 P
→ **Repr. p. 126**

František KUPKA
1871 (OPOČNO)–1957 (PUTEAUX)
Compliment, 1912
Oil on canvas, 89 × 108 cm
GIFT OF EUGÉNIE KUPKA, 1963
AM 4175 P
→ **Repr. p. 62**

Kisho KUROKAWA
1934 (NAGOYA)–2007 (TOKYO)
Floating City, Kasumigaura, Japan, 1961
UnExecuted design
Site Plan: Detail, 1961
Graphite on tracing paper,
31 × 30.5 cm
GIFT OF THE ARCHITECT, 1997
AM 1997-2-32
→ **Repr. p. 222**

Edmond KÜSS
1902 (CARTHAGE)–1970 (PARIS)
Espagne [Spain], 1937
Oil on canvas, 116 × 89 cm
PURCHASE BY THE STATE, 1938
ATTRIBUTION, 1938
AM 2158 P
→ **Repr. p. 133**

Joseph KUTTER
1894 (LUXEMBOURG)–1941 (LUXEMBOURG)
L'Homme au doigt coupé
[Man with Cut Finger], 1930
Oil on canvas, 126.5 × 100 cm
PURCHASE, 1952
AM 3119 P
→ **Repr. p. 104**

Wifredo LAM
1902 (SAGUA LA GRANDE)–1982 (PARIS)
Umbral [Initiation], 1950
Oil on canvas, 185 × 170 cm
PURCHASE BY THE STATE, 1969
ATTRIBUTION, 1976
AM 1976-990
→ **Repr. p. 159**

Michel LARIONOV
1881 (TIRASPOL)–1964
(FONTENAY-AUX-ROSES)
Promenade. Vénus de boulevard
[Stroll. Boulevard Venus], 1912–1913
Oil on canvas, 117 × 87 cm
PURCHASE, 1983
AM 1982-436
→ **Repr. p. 61**

Farideh LASHAI
1944 (RASHT)–2013 (TEHERAN)
Untitled, 1967
Oil on canvas, 136 × 99 cm
GIFT OF MME MANELI KEYKAVOUSSI, 2013
AM 2013-497
→ **Repr. p. 193**

Henri LAURENS
1885 (PARIS)–1954 (PARIS)
Femme étendue
[Reclining Woman], 1950
Pencil and gouache on paper,
48.6 × 68.3 cm
DONATION OF LOUISE AND MICHEL LEIRIS, 1964
AM 1984-575
→ **Repr. p. 74**

LE CORBUSIER
1887 (LA CHAUX-DE-FONDS)–1965
(ROQUEBRUNE-CAP-MARTIN)
La Main ouverte
[The Open Hand], 1964
Ink and crayon on paper,
96 × 141.5 cm
FONDS NATIONAL D'ART CONTEMPORAIN ACQUISITION, 1987
ATTRIBUTION, 1987
AM 1987-529
→ **Repr. p. 213**

LE CORBUSIER
Poésie sur Alger
[Poetry on Algiers], Paris, Falaise, 1950
KANDINSKY LIBRARY, CENTRE POMPIDOU
→ **Repr. p. 150**

Fernand LÉGER
1881 (ARGENTAN)–1955 (GIF-SUR-YVETTE)
Le Cirque Médrano
[The Medrano Circus], 1918
Oil on canvas, 58 × 94.5 cm
BEQUEST OF BARONNE EVA GOURGAUD, 1965
AM 4316 P
→ **Repr. p. 32 (unexhibited work)**

Fernand LÉGER
Contraste de formes
[Contrast of Shapes], 1913
Oil on canvas, 100 × 81 cm
DONATION M. AND MME ANDRÉ LEFÈVRE, 1952
AM 3304 P
→ **Repr. p. 64**

Tamara DE LEMPICKA
1898 (WARSAW)–1980 (CUERNAVACA)
Jeune fille en vert
[Young Woman in Green], 1927–1930
Oil on plywood, 61.5 × 45.5 cm
PURCHASE BY THE STATE, 1932
ATTRIBUTION, 1932
JP 557 P
→ **Repr. p. 125**

Amanda DE LEON
1908 (SPAIN)–?
Bird Vendors, n.d.
Oil on canvas, 103.2 × 66.8 cm
GIFT OF M. AND MME EUGEN KILPATRICK PERRY, 1955
ATTRIBUTION, 1955
AM 3378 P
→ **Repr. p. 103**

Julio LE PARC
1928 (MENDOZA)
Trame altérée
[Altered Web], 1965
Wood, metal, screenprint, motor,
60 × 60 × 61 cm
PURCHASE, 2011
AM 2011-157
→ **Repr. p. 211**

Jacques LIPCHITZ
1891 (DRUSKININKAI)–1973 (CAPRI)
Figure, 1926–1930
Painted plaster,
220 × 95 × 75 cm
Pedestal, 14 × 85 × 50 cm
DONATION OF JACQUES AND YULLA LIPCHITZ FOUNDATION, 1976
AM 1976-822
→ **Repr. p. 48**

El LISSITZKY
1890 (POCHINOK)–1941 (SKHODNYA)
Affiche pour l'Exposition russe au Musée des Arts Décoratifs de Zurich en 1929 [Poster for the 1929 Russian Exhibition at the Zurich Museum of Decorative Arts], 1929
Poster, 125 × 90 cm
PURCHASE, 1977
AM 1977-205
→ **Repr. p. 80**

LIU Haisu
1896 (WUJIN)–1994 (SHANGHAI)
Gushan, ca. 1931
Oil on canvas, 60 × 72 cm
MODE OF ACQUISITION UNRECORDED, 1934
FORMER COLLECTION OF THE JEU DE PAUME MUSEUM
ON PERMANENT LOAN TO THE GUIMET MUSEUM, PARIS
AM 5080 P
→ **Repr. p. 143**

Boris LOVET-LORSKI
1891 (RUSSIA)–1973 (NEW YORK CITY)
Dieu inconnu, tête
[Unknown God, Head], 1927
Veined yellow marble,
26.5 × 16.5 × 23.5 cm
Pedestal: 19 × 15 × 15 cm
MODE OF ACQUISITION UNRECORDED, 1936
JP 115 S
→ **Repr. p. 128**

Gherasim LUCA
1913 (BUCHAREST)–1994 (PARIS)
Indiens de Matto Grosso
[de la série *Brésil*]
[Matto Grosso Indians,
from the *Brazil* series], 1960–1970
Printed vignettes glued on silver
gelatin print mounted on cardboard,
22 × 16 cm
GIFT OF MICHELINE CATTI, 2009
AM 2009-295 (6)
→ **Repr. p. 162**

Stanton MACDONALD-WRIGHT
1890 (CHARLOTTESVILLE, VIRGINIA)–
1973 (SANTA MONICA, CALIFORNIA)
La Prophétie [Prophecy], 1955
Oil on canvas, 122 × 91.5 cm
GIFT OF M. AND MME MICHEL SEUPHOR, 1978
AM 1977-610
→ **Repr. p. 69**

Heinz MACK
1931 (LOLLAR)
Lichtrotoren, Sonne des Meeres
[Light Rotator, Sun of the Sea], 1967
Aluminium, 143 × 143 × 17 cm
DONATION OF SOLANGE AND JACQUES DU CLOSEL, 1994
AM 1995-55
→ **Repr. p. 211**

August MACKE
1887 (MESCHEDE)–1914 (PERTHES-LÈS-HURLUS)
Frauenkopf in Orange und Braun
[Woman's Head in Orange and Brown],
ca. 1911
Oil on canvas, 63.5 × 52.5 cm
GIFT OF LA SOCIÉTÉ DES AMIS DU MUSÉE NATIONAL D'ART
MODERNE, 1964
AM 4229 P
→ **Repr. p. 58**

René MAGRITTE
1898 (LESSINES)–1967 (BRUSSELS)
Le Modèle rouge
[The Red Model], 1935
Oil on canvas glued on cardboard,
56 × 46 cm
PURCHASE, 1975
AM 1975-216
→ **Repr. p. 114**

Esther MAHLANGU
1935 (MIDDLEBURG)
Untitled, 1997
Acrylic on canvas, 283.5 × 459 cm
QUAI BRANLYMUSEUM
PAINTINGS COLLECTION, A98.7.1
→ **Repr. p. 201**

Tadeusz MAKOWSKI
1882 (OŚWIĘCIM)–1932 (PARIS)
Les Buveurs
[The Drinkers], 1930
Oil on canvas, 97 × 130.5 cm
GIFT OF HELENA RUBINSTEIN, 1937
JP 850 P
→ **Repr. p. 108**

Kazimir MALEVICH
1878 (KIEV)–1935 (SAINT PETERSBURG)
Croix noire
[Black Cross], 1915
Oil on canvas, 80 × 80 cm
GIFT OF THE SCALER FOUNDATION AND THE BEAUBOURG
FOUNDATION, 1980
AM 1980-1
→ **Repr. p. 79**

Maruja MALLO
1902 (VIVEIRO)–1995 (MADRID)
Kermesse, 1928
Oil on canvas, 120 × 166 cm
PURCHASE BY THE STATE, 1936
ATTRIBUTION, 1936
JP 798 P
→ **Repr. p. 122**

Azouaou MAMMERI
1890 (TAOURIRT-MIMOUN)–1954 (ALGIERS)
Fête marocaine à Marrakech
[Moroccan Festival in Marrakesh],
1930
Gouache on gray paper, 48 × 63 cm
MODE OF ACQUISITION UNRECORDED, 1931
ATTRIBUTION, 1932
AM 1061 D
→ **Repr. p. 24**

Ernest MANCOBA
CA. 1907 (JOHANNESBURG)–2002 (CLAMART)
Peinture 1965
[Painting 1965], 1965
Oil on canvas, 81 × 65 cm
CENTRE NATIONAL DES ARTS PLASTIQUES/FONDS NATIONAL
D'ART CONTEMPORAIN (PARIS-LA DÉFENSE, FRANCE)
PURCHASE, 1976
FNAC 32412
→ **Repr. p. 194**

Alfred MANESSIER
1911 (SAINT-OUEN–1993 (ORLÉANS)
Morte-eau [Neap Tide], 1954
Oil on canvas, 114 × 114 cm
DATION, 2003
AM 2003-350
→ **Repr. p. 191**

MANGELOS
1921 (ŠÍD)–1987 (ZAGREB)
Relations Manifesto, m.4-m.8.
1971–1977
Acrylic on plastic globe, 37 × 26.5 cm
PURCHASE, 1994
AM 1995-4
→ **Repr. p. 231**

Paul MANSOUROFF
1896 (SAINT-PETERSBURG)–1983 (NICE)
Esquisse pour l'édification
d'une tribune III. Projet de décoration
de la Place Rouge pour le 1er mai 1921
[Sketch for Grandstand III.
Design for Red Square Decorations
for May Day 1921], 1921
Graphite, India ink, watercolor,
and gouache on paper, 76 × 49 cm
GIFT OF THE ARTIST, 1972
AM 1972-47
→ **Repr. p. 80**

Virgilio MARCHI
1895 (LIVORNO)–1960 (ROME)
Ville fantastique, édifice
pour une place [Fantastic City,
Building for a Square], 1919
Gouache, watercolor,
and charcoal on paper, 123 × 148 cm
GIFT OF BENETTON GROUP SPA, 2006
AM 2006-2-47
→ **Repr. p. 65**

Frans MASEREEL
1889 (BLANKENBERGE)–1972 (AVIGNON)
Femme de marin
[Sailor's Wife], 1930
Oil on canvas, 116 × 89 cm
PURCHASE BY THE STATE, 1938
ATTRIBUTION, 1938
JP 876 BIS P
→ **Repr. p. 109**

André MASSON
1896 (BALAGNY-SUR-THÉRAIN)–1987 (PARIS)
Le Labyrinthe [The Labyrinth], 1938
Oil on canvas, 120 × 61 cm
GIFT OF BASIL AND ELISA GOULANDRIS, 1982
AM 1982-46
→ **Repr. p. 158**

Henri MATISSE
1869 (CATEAU-CAMBRÉSIS)–1954 (NICE)
La Gitane
[The Gypsy Woman], 1905
Oil on canvas, 55 × 46 cm
BEQUEST OF GEORGES GRAMMONT FOR THE MUSÉE DE
L'ANNONCIADE, SAINT-TROPEZ, 1959
AM 3815 P
→ **Repr. p. 59**

Henri MATISSE
Odalisque à la culotte rouge
[Odalisque with Red Trousers], 1921
Oil on canvas, 65 × 90 cm
PURCHASE BY THE STATE, 1922
ATTRIBUTION, 1923
LUX .0.85 P
→ **Repr. p. 242**

Ichiyo MATSUMOTO
1893 (KYOTO)–1952 (KYOTO)
La Princesse Chujo à Hibariyama
[Princess Chujo at Hibariyama],
ca. 1925
India ink and watercolor on silk,
65.9 × 69.7 cm
PURCHASE BY THE STATE, 1929
ATTRIBUTION, 1931
JP 952 P
→ **Repr. p. 142**

MATTA
1911 (SANTIAGO [CHILI])–2002 (CIVITAVECCHIA)
Xpace and the Ego, 1945
Oil on canvas, 202.2 × 457.2 cm
PURCHASE, 1983
AM 1983-94
→ **Repr. p. 161**

Leandro MBOMIO
1938 (MIKOMESENG)–2012 (MALABO)
Manifestation
[Demonstration], 1974
Bronze, 78 × 53 × 18 cm
CENTRE NATIONAL DES ARTS PLASTIQUES/FONDS NATIONAL
D'ART CONTEMPORAIN (PARIS-LA DÉFENSE, FRANCE)
PURCHASE, 1975
FNAC 9942
→ **Repr. p. 184**

Cildo MEIRELES
1948 (RIO DE JANEIRO)
Inserçoes em circuitos
ideólogicos. Projeto Coca-Cola
[Insertions in Ideological Circuits.
Coca-Cola Project], 1970
Glass, metal; height: 24.5 cm
GIFT OF THE ARTIST, 2006
AM 2006-95
→ **Repr. p. 228**

Susan MEISELAS
1948 (BALTIMORE, MARYLAND)
Soldiers Searching Bus Passengers,
Northern Highway, Salvador, 1980
Second edition of the portfolio
IN OUR TIME. The World as Seen by
Magnum Photographers presented at
the time of the exhibition at the National
Photography Center (Paris), 1989
Silver gelatin print, 58 × 77 cm
GIFT OF THE JEU DE PAUME, WITH THE SUPPORT OF MAGNUM, 2013.
FORMER COLLECTION OF THE NATIONAL PHOTOGRAPHY CENTER
AM 1999-DEP220
→ **Repr. p. 162**

Juan NICOLÁS MELÉ
1923 (BUENOS AIRES)–2012 (BUENOS AIRES)
Construcción no 37
[Construction No. 37],
1948
Oil on wood, 76 × 51 × 3 cm
GIFT OF THE ARTIST, 2012
AM 2012-59
→ **Repr. p. 199**

Paulo MENDES DA ROCHA
1928 (VITÓRIA)
Gymnasium of the Paulistano
Athletic Club, São Paulo, Brazil,
1958–1961
Executed design
Exterior view of the building under
construction, detail of pillars,
1958–1965
B/w photographic print on paper,
18.2 × 23.3 cm
GIFT OF THE ARCHITECT, 2009
→ **Repr. p. 171**

Ivan MEŠTROVIĆ
1883 (VRPOLJE)–1962 (SOUTH BEND
Femme à la harpe
[Woman with Harp], n.d.
Bronze, 198 × 71.05 × 7 cm
PURCHASE BY THE STATE, 1932
ATTRIBUTION, 1932
JP 87 S
→ **Repr. p. 128**

László MOHOLY-NAGY
1895 (BÁCSBORSÓD)–1946 (CHICAGO, ILLINOIS)
Composition A.XX, 1924
Oil on canvas, 135.5 × 115 cm
GIFT OF THE FRIENDS OF THE NATIONAL MUSEUM OF
MODERN ART, 1962
AM 4025 P
→ **Repr. p. 82**

Mahmoud MOKHTAR
1891 (TANBARA)–1934 (CAIRO)
Arous el-Nil
[Bride of the Nile], ca. 1929
Stone, 150 × 36 × 24 cm
PURCHASE BY THE STATE, 1930
ATTRIBUTION, 1930
JP 66 S
→ **Repr. p. 129**

Piet MONDRIAN
1872 (AMERSFOORT)–1944 (NEW YORK CITY)
Composition en rouge,
bleu et blanc II
[Composition in Red, Blue,
and White II], 1937
Oil on canvas, 75 × 60.5 cm
PURCHASE, 1975
AM 1975-53
→ **Repr. p. 84**

MONTEIRO
1899 (RECIFE, BRAZIL)–1970 (RECIFE, BRAZIL)
A Caçada
[The Hunt], 1923
Oil on canvas, 202 × 259.2 cm
PURCHASE BY THE STATE, 1959
ATTRIBUTION, 1959
AM 3672 P
→ **Repr. p. 100**

MORGAN-SNELL
1920 (SÃO PAULO)–2007 (?)
Le Fils de Rhéa
[The Son of Rhea], 1955
Tempera and India ink on paper,
70.2 × 75 cm
MODE OF ACQUISITION UNRECORDED
FORMER HOLDINGS OF THE NATIONAL MUSEUM OF MODERN ART
AM 4650 D
→ **Repr. p. 126**

Robert MOTHERWELL
1915 (ABERDEEN, WASHINGTON)–
1991 (PROVINCETOWN, MASSACHUSETTS)
The Homely Protestant (Bust),
1947–1948
Oil on canvas, 76 × 61 cm
PURCHASE, 2003
AM 2003-337
→ **Repr. p. 160**

N'DIAYE Iba
1928 (SAINT-LOUIS)–2008 (PARIS)
Untitled, 1970
Oil on canvas, 97 × 146 cm
CENTRE NATIONAL DES ARTS PLASTIQUES/FONDS NATIONAL
D'ART CONTEMPORAIN (PARIS-LA DÉFENSE, FRANCE)
PURCHASE, 1971
FNAC 30688
→ **Repr. p. 185**

NEJAD
1923 (ISTANBUL)–1995 (NOWY SĄCZ)
Perpetuales celestes (1)
[Celestial Perpetuals (1)],
1951–1952
Oil on canvas, 162 × 97 cm
GIFT OF THE ARTIST TO THE STATE, 1952
ATTRIBUTION, 1953
AM 3158 P
→ **Repr. p. 190**

Kenneth NOLAND
1924 (ASHEVILLE, NORTH CAROLINA)–
2010 (PORT CLYDE, MAINE)
Air, 1964
Acrylic on canvas,
226.5 × 217.5 cm
GIFT OF BARON AND BARONNE ALAIN DE GUNZBURG, 1981
AM 1981-513
→ **Repr. p. 200**

Ruy OHTAKE
1938 (SÃO PAULO)
Telephone Center,
Campos do Jordão, Brazil, 1971–1973
Executed design
Perspective. General view of building,
1971–1973
India ink on wove paper, 25 × 41.5 cm
GIFT OF THE ARCHITECT, 2011
AM 2011-2-693
→ **Repr. p. 171**

Georgia O'KEEFFE
1887 (SUN PRAIRIE, WISCONSIN)–
1986 (SANTA FE, NEW MEXICO)
Red, Yellow and Black Streak, 1924
Oil on canvas, 101.3 × 81.3 cm
GIFT OF THE GEORGIA O'KEEFFE FOUNDATION, 1995
AM 1995-178
→ **Repr. p. 69**

Aniedi OKON AKPAN
CA. 1916 (?) (NIGERIA)
Chef debout
[Standing Chief], n.d.
Pigment, concrete, 223 × 51 × 30 cm
QUAI BRANLY MUSEUM
73.2012.0.1 D
→ **Repr. p. 179**

Nicolas ONDONGO
1933 (OKOUNGOU)–1990 (?)
Marché en A.E.F.
[Market in A.E.F.
[French Equatorial Africa]], 1958
Oil on canvas, 62.1 × 73.8 × 3 cm
QUAI BRANLYMUSEUM
HISTORY COLLECTION
75.15564.3
→ **Repr. p. 180**

Chana ORLOFF
1888 (KONSTANTINOVKA)1968 (TELAVIV)
Femme accroupie
[Crouching Woman], 1925
Gilded bronze, 116 × 77 × 62 cm
PURCHASE BY THE STATE FROM THE ARTIST, 1939
ATTRIBUTION, 1939
JP 34 S
→ **Repr. p. 127**

Alfonso-Angel OSSORIO
1916 (MANILA)–1990 (EAST HAMPTON, NEW YORK)
Knots of Spring, 1954
Oil on plywood, 76 × 101.5 cm
DONATION OF DANIEL CORDIER, 1989
AM 1989-470
→ **Repr. p. 173**

Alfonso-Angel OSSORIO
Red Egg, 1942
Watercolor and India ink on paper
glued on cardboard, 61.8 × 35 cm
DONATION OF DANIEL CORDIER, 1989
AM 1989-464
→ **Repr. p. 17**

Masato OTAKA
1923 (FUKUSHIMA)
Sakaide Artificial Ground, Japan, 1968
Executed design
Model, 1968
Wood, 24.5 × 116 × 81 cm
1/200 scale
GIFT OF THE ARCHITECT, 2010
AM 2010-2-17
→ **Repr. p. 222**

Amédée OZENFANT
1886 (SAINT-QUENTIN)–1966 (CANNES)
Les Quatre Races
[The Four Races], 1928
Oil on canvas, 332 × 500 cm
GIFT OF THE ARTIST TO THE STATE, 1953
ATTRIBUTION, 1953
AM 3271 P
→ **Repr. p. 14**

Carlos PÁEZ VILARÓ
1923 (MONTEVIDEO)
Toro
[Bull], 1956
Oil on Isorel (hardboard),
100.5 × 61 cm
MODE OF ACQUISITION UNRECORDED
AM 5026 P
→ **Repr. p. 159**

Margarita PAKSA
1936 (BUENOS AIRES)
NO, 1976
Lined zinc sheeting, painted metal,
38 × 46 × 5 cm
PERMANENT LOAN BY THE CENTRE POMPIDOU FOUNDATION,
2010 (GIFT OF MAURO HERLITZKA AND OF HENRIQUE FARIA FINE
ART TO THE CENTRE POMPIDOU FOUNDATION)
AM 2010-DEP 34
→ **Repr. p. 230**

PAN Yuliang
1895 (YANGZHOU)–1977 (PARIS)
Après le bain [After the Bath], 1952
India ink and watercolor on paper,
92 × 59.5 cm
PURCHASE BY THE STATE, 1955
ATTRIBUTION, 1955
ON PERMANENT LOAN TO THE GUIMET, NATIONAL MUSEUM OF
ASIAN ARTS, PARIS
AM 3371 P
→ **Repr. p. 139**

Max PECHSTEIN
1881 (ZWICKAU)–1955 (BERLIN)
Paysage [Landscape], 1912
Oil on canvas, 71 × 80 cm
REGISTERED IN THE STATE'S INVENTORY, 1966
ATTRIBUTION, 1966
AM 4364 P
→ **Repr. p. 59**

Alicia PENALBA
1913 (SAN PEDRO)–1982 (DAX, FRANCE)
Hommage à César Vallejo
[Homage to César Vallejo],
1955/1960
Bronze in three overlaid pieces,
267.5 × 55 × 35 cm
EX. NO. 3/4
PURCHASE, 1980
AM 1980-41
→ **Repr. p. 48**

Constant PERMEKE
1886 (ANTWERP)–1952 (OSTEND)
Tête de paysanne
[Head of a Peasant Woman],
1925
Oil on canvas, 59.5 × 49.9 cm
PURCHASE, 1960
AM 3761 P
→ **Repr. p. 109**

Antoine PEVSNER
1884 (KLIMAVICHY)–1962 (PARIS)
Masque [Mask], 1923
Celluloid and zinc, 33 × 20 × 20 cm
PURCHASE BY THE STATE, 1974
ATTRIBUTION, 1974
AM 1974-24
→ **Repr. p. 79**

Francis PICABIA
1879 (PARIS)–1953 (PARIS)
L'Adoration du veau
[The Adoration of the Golden Calf],
1941–1942
Oil on canvas, 106 × 76.2 cm
PURCHASE WITH THE SUPPORT OF THE FONDS DU PATRIMOINE,
THE CLARENCE WESTBURY FOUNDATION, AND THE FRIENDS OF
THE NATIONAL MUSEUM OF MODERN ART, 2007
AM 2007-198
→ **Repr. p. 131**

Francis PICABIA
Udnie, 1913
Oil on canvas, 290 × 300 cm
PURCHASE BY THE STATE, 1948
ATTRIBUTION, 1949
AM 2874 P
→ **Repr. p. 62**

Pablo PICASSO
1881 (MÁLAGA)–1973 (MOUGINS)
Arlequin
[Harlequin], 1923
Oil on canvas, 130 × 97 cm
BEQUEST OF BARONNE EVA GOURGAUD, 1965
AM 4313 P
→ **Repr. p. 119**

Pablo PICASSO
Femme nue au bonnet turc
[Nude in a Turkish Cap],
1955
Oil on canvas, 116 × 89 cm
DONATION OF LOUISE AND MICHEL LEIRIS, 1984
AM 1984-637
→ **Repr. p. 243**

Pablo PICASSO
Femme nue couchée
[Reclining Nude], 1936
Oil on canvas, 130.6 × 162.5 cm
DONATION OF LOUISE AND MICHEL LEIRIS, 1984
AM 1984-633
→ **Repr. p. 74**

Pablo PICASSO
Le Guitariste
[The Guitar Player], 1910
Oil on canvas, 100 × 73 cm
DONATION M. AND MME ANDRÉ LEFÈVRE, 1952
AM 3970 P
→ **Repr. p. 59**

Fausto PIRANDELLO
1899 (ROME)–1975 (ROME)
Interno di mattina
[Morning Interior], 1931
Oil on canvas, 178 × 151 cm
GIFT OF PIER LUIGI PIRANDELLO, 1979
AM 1979-253
→ **Repr. p. 107**

Bernard PLOSSU
1945 (ĐÀ LAT)
Alain Rérat, Lille, 1988
Silver gelatin print, 40.2 × 30.3 cm
GIFT OF THE ARTIST, 1999
AM 1999-40
→ **Repr. p. 236**

Jackson POLLOCK
1912 (CODY, WYOMING)–
1956 (EAST HAMPTON, NEW YORK)
Number 26 A, Black and White,
1948
Enamel on canvas, 205 × 121.7 cm
DATION, 1984
AM 1984-312
→ **Repr. p. 158**

Jackson POLLOCK
The Moon-Woman Cuts the Circle,
1943
Oil on canvas, 109.5 × 104 cm
GIFT OF FRANK K. LLOYD, 1980
AM 1980-66
→ **Repr. p. 34**

Candido PORTINARI
1903 (BRODOWSKI)–1962 (RIO DE JANEIRO)
Composition, 1945
Oil on canvas, 179 × 150 cm
CENTRE NATIONAL DES ARTS PLASTIQUES/FONDS NATIONAL
D'ART CONTEMPORAIN (PARIS-LA DÉFENSE, FRANCE)
PURCHASE, 1946
FNAC 20015
→ **Repr. p. 101**

Jean POUGNY
1892 (KUOKKALA)–1956 (PARIS)
Chaise, palette et violon
[Chair, Palette, and Violin],
ca. 1917–1918
Oil on canvas, 100 × 73 cm
DONATION OF XÉNIA POLGNY, 1966
AM 4330 P
→ **Repr. p. 61**

Antonin PROCHÁZKA
1882 (VAZANY, CZECH REPUBLIC)–1945 (BRNO)
Divka
[Young Girl], 1933
Oil on canvas, 92.2 × 64.7 cm
PURCHASE BY THE STATE, 1934
ATTRIBUTION, 1934
JP 713 P
→ **Repr. p. 19**

Ernest PROCTER
1886 (TYNEMOUTH)-1935 (TYNEMOUTH)
The Watchers... Burma, 1921
Oil on canvas, 76.5 × 61 cm
PURCHASE BY THE STATE, 1927
ATTRIBUTION, 1928
JP 441 P
→ **Repr. p. 26**

Man RAY
1890 (PHILADELPHIA, PENNSYLVANIA)–1976 (PARIS)
Arrangement de formes
[Arrangement of Shapes], 1917
Oil on cardboard, 88 × 81.5 cm
PURCHASE, 1980
AM 1980-442
→ **Repr. p. 68**

Man RAY
Tapestry, 1911
Wool patchwork on linen canvas,
210 × 151.8 × 2.2 cm
DATION, 1994
AM 1994-296
→ **Repr. p. 66**

Man RAY
Violon d'Ingres [Ingres' Violin], 1924
Silver gelatin print, 31 × 24.7 cm
PURCHASE, 1993
AM 1993-117
→ **Repr. p. 245**

Martial RAYSSE
1936 (GOLFE-JUAN)
Made in Japan.
La grande odalisque, 1964
Acrylic, glass, fly, synthetic fiber
fringe on photograph glued to canvas,
130 × 97 cm
GIFT OF THE SCALER FOUNDATION, 1995
AM 1995-213
→ **Repr. p. 245**

Sayed HAIDER RAZA
1922 (BARBARA)
Bindu, 1986
Diptych
Acrylic on canvas, 200.5 × 99.5 cm
CENTRE NATIONAL DES ARTS PLASTIQUES/FONDS NATIONAL
D'ART CONTEMPORAIN (PARIS-LA DÉFENSE, FRANCE)
PURCHASE, 1987
FNAC 35452
→ **Repr. p. 200**

Bernard RÉQUICHOT
1929 (ASNIÈRES-SUR-VÈGRE)–1961 (PARIS)
Maison du manège endormi
[House of the Sleeping Carousel],
1958–1959
Reliquary: assemblage of painted
objects in a wood and glass case
Oil paint, fragments of painted canvas,
various objects, 110.5 × 79.4 × 56 cm
DONATION OF DANIEL CORDIER, 1989
AM 1989-478
→ **Repr. p. 173**

Raj REWAL
Asian Games Village, New Delhi, India,
1980–1982
Executed design
Isometric View of Sector 1
India ink and blue pencil on tracing
paper, 70.8 × 100.5 cm
1/200 scale
GIFT OF RAJ REWAL ASSOCIATES, 2012
AM 2013-2-40
→ **Repr. p. 221**

Raj REWAL
Hall of Nations, New Delhi, India,
1970–1972
Executed design
Perspective, Interior View 1.
Charcoal on tracing paper,
91 × 200 cm
GIFT OF RAJ REWAL ASSOCIATES, 2012
AM 2013-2-69
→ **Repr. p. 221**

Raj REWAL
1934 (HOSHIARPUR)
"Scope" Office Complex, New Delhi,
India, 1980–1989
Executed design
Model
1 print, plan glued to front of model
Wood, 27 × 124.5 × 94.5 cm
GIFT OF RAJ REWAL ASSOCIATES, 2012
AM 2013-2-23
→ **Repr. p. 220**

Raj REWAL
State Trading Corporation, New Delhi, India, 1976–1989
Executed design
Model with three movable elements
Wood, 110 × 122.5 × 183 cm
GIFT OF RAJ REWAL ASSOCIATES, 2012
AM 2013-2-21
→ **Repr. p. 220**

Marc RIBOUD
1923 (LYON)
Sans titre. Vote du référendum d'autodétermination de l'Algérie, Alger, 1er juillet 1962
[Untitled. Referendum Vote on Algerian Self-Determination, Algiers, 1 July 1962], 1962
Silver gelatin print, 29 × 17.2 cm
DATION, 2011
AM 2011-448
→ **Repr. p. 152**

Sophie RISTELHUEBER
1949 (PARIS)
Fait [Fact], 1992
1/3
Chromogenic color print, 100 × 130 cm
DONATION OF THE CAISSE DES DÉPÔTS, 2006
AM 2006-632
→ **Repr. p. 237**

Diego RIVERA
1886 (GUANAJUATO)–1957 (MEXICO CITY)
Les Vases communicants
[Communicating Vessels], 1938
Gouache on paper glued to canvas, 93 × 121 cm
PURCHASE, 2003
AM 2003-267
→ **Repr. p. 112**

Larry RIVERS
1923 (NEW YORK CITY)–2002 (SOUTHAMPTON, NEW YORK)
I Like Olympia in Black Face, 1970
Oil on wood, oilcloth, plastic, and Plexiglas, 182 × 194 × 120 cm
GIFT OF THE MENIL FOUNDATION IN MEMORY OF JEAN DE MENIL, 1976
AM 1976-1231
→ **Repr. p. 243**

Joaquín ROCA REY
1923 (LIMA)–2004 (ROME)
Fusiliamiento de un comunero
[Execution of a Villager], 1957/1961
Mahogany and iron, 99 × 71 × 37 cm
GIFT OF THE ROCA REY ANDREASSI FAMILY, 2013
AM 2013-482
→ **Repr. p. 130**

Alexander RODCHENKO
1891 (SAINT PETERSBURG)–1956 (MOSCOW)
Pionnier jouant de la trompette
[Pioneer Playing the Trumpet], 1930
Silver gelatin print, 38.5 × 29.5 cm
GIFT OF MOULI RODCHENKO, 1981
AM 1981-584
→ **Repr. p. 81**

Suzanne ROGER
1898 (PARIS)–1986 (PARIS)
L'Émeute aux couteaux
[Riot with Knives], 1934
Oil on canvas, 60 × 73 cm
DONATION OF LOUISE AND MICHEL LEIRIS, 1984
AM 1984-673
→ **Repr. p. 74**

Jaroslav RÖSSLER
1902 (SMILOV)–1990 (PRAGUE)
Tour Eiffel, Paris
[Eiffel Tower, Paris], 1929
Silver gelatin print, 16.7 × 17.5 cm
PURCHASE, 1983
AM 1983-64
→ **Repr. p. 81**

Georges ROUAULT
1871 (PARIS)–1958 (PARIS)
Ouvrier (fond vert)
[de la série *Faubourg*]
[Laborer (Green Background), from the Suburbs series], 1939–1945
Oil, ink, gouache, bronzine on transparent film, 30.5 × 21.3 cm
DONATION OF MME ROUAULT AND HER CHILDREN, 1963
AM 4231 (341)
→ **Repr. p. 108**

Le Douanier ROUSSEAU
1844 (LAVAL)–1910 (PARIS)
Le Peintre et son modèle
[The Painter and His Model], 1900–1905
Oil on canvas, 46.5 × 55.5 cm
BEQUEST OF NINA KANDINSKY, 1981
AM 81-65-861
→ **Repr. p. 58**

Morgan RUSSELL
1886 (NEW YORK CITY)–1953 (BROOMALL, PENNSYLVANIA)
À la vie de la matière
[For the Life of the Material], 1925
Oil on cardboard, 61.5 × 50.5 cm
GIFT OF M. AND MME MICHEL SEUPHOR, 1978
AM 1977-608
→ **Repr. p. 69**

Luigi RUSSOLO
1885 (PORTOGRUARO)–1947 (CERRO DI LAVENO)
Automobile in corsa
[Dynamism of a Car], 1912–1913
Oil on canvas, 106 × 140 cm
GIFT OF SONIA DELAUNAY, 1949
AM 2917 P
→ **Repr. p. 60**

Behjat SADR
1924 (ARAK)–2009 (PORTO-VECCHIO)
Untitled, 1974
Oil and adhesive tape on canvas, 87 × 170 cm
GIFT OF MITRA GOBERVILLE-HANANEH
EC2013-2-CC04
→ **Repr. p. 195**

SANYU
1900 (NANCHONG)–1966 (PARIS)
Femme nue
[Nude Woman], ca. 1930
Ink on paper, 42.5 × 22.5 cm
PURCHASE, 2013
AM 2013-383
→ **Repr. p. 138**

Christian SCHAD
1894 (MIESBACH)–1982 (STUTTGART)
Graf St-Genois d'Anneaucourt
[Count St-Genois d'Anneaucourt], 1927
Oil on wood, 103 × 80.5 cm
PURCHASE IN MEMORY OF SIEGFRIED POPPE, 2000
AM 2000-4
→ **Repr. p. 121**

Kurt SCHWITTERS
1887 (HANOVER)–1948 (KENDAL)
MZ 1926.2. selbst oben, 1926
Cut papers and photograph glued on paper, 33.8 × 27 cm
PURCHASE WITH THE SUPPORT OF FRIEDER BURDA, 2006
AM 2006-31
→ **Repr. p. 85**

Lasar SEGALL
1891 (VILNIUS)–1957 (SÃO PAULO)
Lucy (Retrato de Lucy VI)
[(Lucy (Portrait of Lucy VI)], 1936
Oil on canvas, 58.5 × 40 cm
PURCHASE BY THE STATE, 1938
ATTRIBUTION, 1938
JP 870 P
→ **Repr. p. 98**

Séraphine DE SENLIS
1864 (ARSY)–1942 (CLERMONT-DE-L'OISE)
Arbre rouge [Red Tree], 1928–1930
Oil on canvas, 193 × 130 cm
PURCHASE, 1945
AM 2583 P
→ **Repr. p. 116**

Ismaël DE LA SERNA
1900 (GRENADA)–1968 (PARIS)
Europe, ca. 1935
Oil on canvas, 200.5 × 123.5 cm
PURCHASE BY THE STATE, 1936
ATTRIBUTION, 1936
AM 5019 P
→ **Repr. p. 130**

Gino SEVERINI
1883 (CORTONE)–1966 (PARIS)
La Femme et la Fille de l'artiste (Jeanne et Gina)
[The Artist's Wife and Daughter (Jeanne and Gina)], 1934–1935
Oil on canvas, 147 × 115 cm
PURCHASE, 1935
JP 780 P
→ **Repr. p. 118**

Malick SIDIBÉ
1936 (SOLOBA)
Anniversaire Abib
[Birthday Abib], 27 April 1969
Silver gelatin prints, 32 × 48 cm; 7.4 × 5.6 cm each
Yellow cardboard folder taken from a notebook containing 22 photographs glued by groups of 6 or 7, with the title and date of the reported event
PURCHASE, 2006
AM 2006-768
→ **Repr. p. 182–183**

Joseph SIMA
1891 (JAROMĚŘ)–1971 (PARIS)
Double paysage, tempête électrique
[Double Landscape, Electric Storm], 1928
Oil on canvas, 67 × 137 cm
PURCHASE, 1978
AM 1978-320
→ **Repr. p. 113**

Jesús RAFAEL SOTO
1923 (CIUDAD BOLIVAR)–2005 (PARIS)
Extension, 1989
Formica and painted metal, 50 × 400 × 300 cm
DATION, 2011
AM 2012-117
→ **Repr. p. 210**

Amadeo de SOUZA-CARDOSO
1887 (AMARANTE)–1918 (ESPINHO)
Cavaleiros [Horsemen], 1913
Oil on canvas, 100 × 100 cm
PURCHASE, 1959
AM 3636 P
→ **Repr. p. 64**

André STEINER
1901 (SZÉKESFEHÉRVÁR)1978 (PARIS)
Linge étendu, Maroc
[Hanging Laundry, Morocco], 1933
Silver gelatin print, 23.5 × 17.2 cm
PURCHASE THROUGH THE SPONSORSHIP OF YVES ROCHER, 2011. FORMER CHRISTIAN BOUQUERET COLLECTION
AM 2012-7149
→ **Repr. p. 153**

Irma STERN
1894 (SCHWEIZER-RENEKE)–1966 (CAPE TOWN)
Le Palais du sultan à Zanzibar
[The Sultan's Palace in Zanzibar], 1944
Oil on canvas, 71 × 71 cm
PURCHASE BY THE STATE FROM THE ARTIST, 1949
ATTRIBUTION, 1951
AM 3049 P
→ **Repr. p. 20**

Kumi SUGAÏ
1919 (KOBE)–1996 (KOBE)
Soleil bleu
[Blue Sun], 1969
Acrylic on canvas, 152.5 × 400 × 6.5 cm
GIFT OF MITSUKO SUGAI, 1999
AM 1999-149
→ **Repr. p. 201**

Graham SUTHERLAND
1903 (LONDON)–1980 (LONDON)
Standing Form, 1952
Oil on canvas, 218 × 100 cm
PURCHASE, 1953
AM 3246 P
→ **Repr. p. 115**

Fernando de SZYSZLO
1925 (LIMA)
Puka Wamani V
[Red Falcon V], 1966
Acrylic on built-up wood, 150 × 120 cm
GIFT OF THE ARTIST, 2012
AM 2013-225
→ **Repr. p. 191**

Sophie TAEUBER-ARP
1889 (DAVOS)–1943 (ZURICH)
Tapisserie dada. Composition à triangles, rectangles et parties d'anneaux
[Dada Tapestry. Composition with Triangles, Rectangles, and Parts of Rings], 1916
Wool, 41 × 41 cm
BEQUEST OF RUTH TILLARD-ARP, 2007
AM 2007-153
→ **Repr. p. 67**

Rufino TAMAYO
1899 (OAXACA)–1991 (MEXICO CITY)
L'homme qui chante
[Singing Man], 1950
Oil on canvas, 196 × 130 cm
PURCHASE, 1951
AM 3030 P
→ **Repr. p. 130**

Kenzo TANGE
1913 (IMABARI, JAPAN)–2005 (TOKYO)
Communication Center, Yamanashi Region, Kofu, Japan, 1961–1966
Executed design
Study model, 1961–1966
Dyed wood and cork, 27 × 57 × 48.5 cm
GIFT OF THE ARCHITECT, 1998
AM 1998-2-69
→ **Repr. p. 222**

Dorothea TANNING
1910 (GALESBURG, ILLINOIS)–2012 (NEW YORK CITY)
Un tableau très heureux
[A Very Happy Picture], 1947
Oil on canvas, 91.1 × 122 cm
PURCHASE BY THE STATE, 1968
ATTRIBUTION, 2008
AM 2009-65
→ **Repr. p. 115**

TARSILA
1886 (CAPIVARI)–1973 (SÃO PAULO)
A Cuca [The Bogeyman], 1924
Oil on canvas, 72 × 100 cm
GIFT OF THE ARTIST, 1926
ON PERMANENT LOAN TO THE MUSÉE DE GRENOBLE SINCE 1928
FNAC 9459
→ **Repr. p. 99**

Vladimir TATLIN
1885 (KHARKOV)–1953 (MOSCOW)
Fauteuil [Chair], 1927
Producer: Nikol Internazionale (Italy)
Chromed steel tubing and leather, 78 × 52 × 80 cm
FORMER HOLDINGS OF THE CENTRE DE CRÉATION INDUSTRIELLE
AM 1993-1-835
→ **Repr. p. 79**

Vladimir TATLIN
Model of the Monument to the Third International, 1919–1920/1979
Reconstruction by the Ateliers Longépé, 1979
Wood and metal; height: 420 cm, diameter: 300 cm, base: 80 cm
PURCHASE, 1979
AM 1979-413
→ **Repr. p. 78**

José ANTONIO TERRY
1885 (BUENOS AIRES)–1954 (BUENOS AIRES)
La Enana Chepa con su cantaro
[The Dwarf Chepa and Her Pitcher], 1923
Oil on canvas, 160 × 122 cm
MODE OF ACQUISITION BY THE STATE UNRECORDED, 1924
ENTERED THE MUSÉE DU LUXEMBOURG, 1924
JP 135 P
→ **Repr. p. 102**

Lajos TIHANYI
1885 (BUDAPEST)–1938 (PARIS)
La Rue de la Glacière, 1925
Oil on canvas, 100 × 65 cm
GIFT OF THE REPUBLIC OF HUNGARY, 1970
AM 4515 P
→ **Repr. p. 83**

Joaquín TORRES-GARCÍA
1874 (MONTEVIDEO)–1949 (MONTEVIDEO)
Composition universelle
[Universal Composition], 1937
Oil on cardboard, 108 × 85 cm
GIFT OF THE ARTIST'S FAMILY TO THE STATE, 1956
ATTRIBUTION, 1956
AM 3416 P
→ **Repr. p. 84**

Joaquín TORRES-GARCÍA
Pez [Fish], ca. 1942
Polychrome wood, 61 × 155 cm
PURCHASE BY THE STATE, 1977
ATTRIBUTION, 1981
AM 1982-86
→ **Repr. p. 85**

Marie TOYEN
1902 (PRAGUE)–1980 (PARIS)
L'Un dans l'autre
[One in the Other], 1965
Oil on canvas, 145 × 88 cm
PURCHASE BY THE STATE, 1958
ATTRIBUTION, 2006
AM 2009-66
→ **Repr. p. 114**

Decio TOZZI
1936 (SÃO PAULO)

Luiz CARLOS RAMOS
1932 (BRODOWSKI)–1996 (?)
Technical and Commercial School, Santos, Brazil, 1963–1965
Executed design
Aerial View of the Neighborhood, 2009
Black felt-tip pen on paper, 21 × 29.7 cm
GIFT OF DECIO TOZZI, 2009
AM 2009-2-371 (0001)
→ **Repr. p. 170**

Demetrio URRUCHÚA
1902 (PEHUAJÓ)–1978 (BUENOS AIRES)
Combatiente [Fighter], 1936
Monotype, ink on paper, 52 × 66 cm
GIFT OF ANIBAL JOZAMI, 2013
AM 2013-354
→ **Repr. p. 132**

Suzanne VALADON
1865 (BESSINES-SUR-GARTEMPE)–1938 (PARIS)
La Chambre bleue
[The Blue Bedroom], 1923
Oil on canvas, 90 × 116 cm
PURCHASE BY THE STATE, 1924
ATTRIBUTION, 1924
LUX.1506 P
→ **Repr. p. 242**

Henry VALENSI
1883 (ALGIERS)–1960 (BAILLY)
Symphonie printanière
[Spring Symphony], 1936–1960
35 mm color film, silent, 33 min.
GIFT OF THE ASSOCIATION DES AYANTS DROIT DU PEINTRE HENRY VALENSI [ASSOCIATION OF RIGHTS HOLDERS OF THE PAINTER HENRY VALENSI], 2013
AM 2013-F4
→ **Repr. p. 65**

Henry VALENSI
Symphonie verte
[Green Symphony], 1935
Oil on canvas, 95 × 131 cm
PURCHASE BY THE STATE, 1949
ATTRIBUTION, 1949
AM 2897 P
→ **Repr. p. 63**

Germain VAN DER STEEN
1897 (VERSAILLES)–1985 (PARIS)
Entente cordiale, n.d.
Oil on cardboard, 54 × 65 cm
GIFT TO THE STATE, 1955
ATTRIBUTION, 1955
AM 3366 P
→ **Repr. p. 116**

Gizella VARGA SINAI
1944 (HUNGARY)
Kallepaz [Sheep's Head Peddler], 1973
Mixed media on canvas, 149 × 100 cm
GIFT BY THE ARTIST, 2013
AM 2013-481
→ **Repr. p. 29**

Rosario de VELASCO
1912 (MADRID)–?
Carnaval [Carnival], ca. 1936
Oil on canvas, 115 × 110 cm
PURCHASE BY THE STATE, 1936
ATTRIBUTION, 1936
JP 799 P (R)
→ **Repr. p. 123**

Pierre VERGER
1902 (PARIS)–1996 (SALVADOR [BRÉSIL])
Homme de compagnie du Morro Naba dans la ville de Ouahigouya, Haute Volta
[Morro-Naba Celebrant in Ouahigouya, Upper Volta], 3 February 1936
1936
Silver gelatin print, 25.4 × 20.3 cm
PURCHASE SPONSORED BY YVES ROCHER, 2011. FORMER CHRISTIAN BOUQUERET COLLECTION
AM 2012-7807
→ **Repr. p. 153**

Sesostris VITULLO
1899 (BUENOS AIRES)–1953 (MONTROUGE)
Chola, 1951
Pearwood, 71 × 17 × 14 cm
PURCHASE, 1953
AM 961 S
→ **Repr. p. 160**

WANG Yachen
1893 (ZHEJIANG)–1983 (?)
Paysage
[Landscape], 1932
Ink and watercolor on paper, 136.7 × 34 cm
MODE OF ACQUISITION UNRECORDED, 1933
JP 684 P
ON PERMANENT LOAN TO THE MUSÉE GUIMET, PARIS
→ **Repr. p. 140**

XU Beihong
1896 (YIXING, JIANGSU)1953 (NANJING)
Arbres et personage
[Trees and Figure], 1932
Ink and ink wash on paper, 108.2 × 108.4 cm
MODE OF ACQUISITION UNRECORDED
ATTRIBUTION, 1933
JP 692 P
ON PERMANENT LOAN TO THE MUSÉE GUIMET, PARIS
→ **Repr. p. 140**

Georges YAKOULOV
1882 (TBILISI)–1928 (YEREVAN)
Sans titre (Composition abstraite)
[Untitled (Abstract Composition)], ca. 1913
Oil on split cardboard glued on plywood parquet, 64.5 × 53.5 cm
GIFT OF SONIA DELAUNAY, 1961
AM 3902 P (R)
→ **Repr. p. 64**

Nil YALTER
1938 (CAIRO)
La Femme sans tête
[The Headless Woman]
or La Danse du ventre
[The Belly Dance], 1974
Video, b/w, sound, 24:47
CENTRE NATIONAL DES ARTS PLASTIQUES/FONDS NATIONAL D'ART CONTEMPORAIN (PARIS-LA DÉFENSE, FRANCE)
ON PERMANENT LOAN TO THE NATIONAL MUSEUM OF MODERN ART, 2009
FNAC 07-475
→ **Repr. p. 230**

Kazumasa YAMASHITA
1937 (TOKYO)
Face House, Kyoto, Japan, 1974
Executed design
Model, 1974
Wood, 20 × 14.5 × 14.5 cm
GIFT OF THE ARCHITECT, 2011
AM 2011-2-27
→ **Repr. p. 223**

Gengetsu YAZAWA
1886 (NAGANO)–1956 (?)
Lac de montagne
[Mountain Lake], n.d.
Ink and pastel on paper, 66.8 × 95 cm
MODE OF ACQUISITION UNRECORDED
ATTRIBUTION, 1929
JP 485 P
→ **Repr. p. 141**

Somei YUKI
1875 (TOKYO)–1957 (TOKYO)
Framboisier
[Raspberry Bush], ca. 1925
India ink, watercolor, and gouache on paper, 59.5 × 69 cm
PURCHASE BY THE STATE, 1929
ATTRIBUTION, 1929
JP 479 P
→ **Repr. p. 142**

YUN Gee
1906 (CANTON)–1960 (NEW YORK)
M. Pierre Mille, ca. 1930
Oil on canvas, 91.5 × 73 cm
GIFT OF PIERRE MILLE, 1938
JP 880 P
→ **Repr. p. 143**

ZAO Wou-Ki
1920 (BEIJING)–2013 (NYON, FRANCE)
Vent [Wind], 1954
Oil on canvas, 195 × 96.5 cm
PURCHASE, 1985
AM 1985-20
→ **Repr. p. 196**

Charles Hossein ZENDEROUDI
1937 (TEHERAN)
Miuz skfe, 1971
Oil on canvas, 195 × 195 cm
PURCHASE, 1971
FNAC 30546
→ **Repr. p. 194**

Jan ZRZAVÝ
1890 (OKROUHLICE)–1977 (PRAGUE)
La Veuve [The Widow], 1923
Oil on canvas, 75.2 × 47.5 cm
PURCHASE, 1982
AM 1982-140
→ **Repr. p. 113**

Ramón de ZUBIAURRE
1882 (GARAIOA)–1969 (MADRID)
Los Remeros vencedores de Ondarroa
[The Rowers, Winners at Ondarroa], ca. 1914–1915
Oil on canvas, 200 × 211 cm
PURCHASE BY THE STATE, 1919
ATTRIBUTION, 1920
JP 140 P
→ **Repr. p. 50**

INDEX

Photo credits

© 2013, Musée du Quai Branly • Scala, Florence, p. 201 bottom • photo: Claude Germain, p. 49 r., 75 top r., 178 bottom, 179 l., 180 bottom, 181 • photo: Patrick Gries, p. 180 top • photo: Sylvain Leurent, p. 178 top /photo: Léo Delafontaine, p. 179 r.
© Biblioteca Brasiliana Guita e José Mindlin-USP, São Paulo, SP, Brésil, p. 98 top l.
© Bildarchiv Foto Marburg, photo: Albert Renger-Patzsch, p. 55
© Collection Centre Pompidou, Mnam-CCI, Bibliothèque Kandinsky, Paris, p. 41, 42-43, 44-45, 150 top l., 150 top r., 151 bottom, 184 l. • photo: Jean-Claude Planchet, 81 bottom l.
© Collection Centre Pompidou, dist. RMN-GP: p. 14, 18, 19, 34, 48 middle, 56 bottom l., 56 bottom r., 58 r., 58 bottom l., 59 bottom l., 60 bottom, 61 r., 64, 66 top l., 67 bottom r., 68 r., 69 top r., 74, 77 l., 77 bottom r., 78 r., 79 top, 79 middle r., 82, 84 r., 100, 104 r., 106, 112 top l., 112 bottom l., 113 top l., 115 top r., 115 bottom r., 116 top l., 119 l., 120 top l., 120 r., 121 top, 124 r., 125 r., 133, 158 l., 159 l., 160 top l., 161, 171 bottom, 172 l., 196 l., 197 top, 200 l., 228 l., 229, 230 middle, 242 bottom, 243 bottom, 245 bottom • photo: Christian Bahier and Philippe Migeat, p. 69 bottom r., 164, 165 l. • photo: Henri Faivre, p. 231 top • photo: Béatrice Hatala, p. 17, 173 • photo: Jacqueline Hyde, p. 48 r., 62 bottom, 66 bottom l., 68 top l., 79 bottom, 113 bottom, 115 l., 116 r., 123 bottom • photo: Jacques Faujour, p. 32, 84 top l., 122 • photo: Georges Meguerditchian, p. 19, 23, 29, 33, 50 top, 62 top, 65 top, 67 l., 67 top r., 68 bottom l., 75 top l., 76 bottom r., 80 top r., 80 bottom r., 81 top l., 83, 85 top r., 85 bottom r., 98 bottom l., 98 r., 108 bottom, 119 r., 120 bottom l., 121 bottom, 126 bottom, 130 r., 131 r., 132 bottom, 138 r., 142 l., 142 bottom, 152, 159 r., 160 bottom, 162 bottom, 170 top, 170 middle, 171 top, 171 middle, 190 middle, 191 bottom, 193 r., 195, 207 r., 209 top, 210, 220, 221 top, 223, 229 bottom l., 229 bottom r., 236 top, 237 top, 244 bottom • photo: Philippe Migeat, p. 20, 50 bottom, 51 l., 51 bottom r., 56 top, 59 top r., 59 bottom r., 61 l., 63 top l., 69 l., 76 top, 76 bottom l., 80 l., 85 bottom l., 99 top, 107, 108 top, 109 bottom, 110-111, 124 l., 125 l., 126 top, 127 l., 129, 131 top l., 131 bottom, 141, 142 top r., 150 bottom, 153, 162 top r., 163, 172 r., 182-183, 190 top l., 191 top, 192 l., 196 r., 198, 199 top l., 199 bottom, 201 top, 206 top, 207 l., 208, 209 bottom, 211, 213, 221 bottom, 222 middle, 228 r., 229 top, 230 bottom, 231 bottom, 236 bottom, 237 bottom, 242 top, 243 top, 244 top, 245 top • photo: Jean-Claude Planchet, p. 58 top l., 59 top l., 60 top, 63 bottom, 104 l., 112 r., 118 l., 128 r., 170 bottom, 222 top, 222 bottom • photo: Bertrand Prévost, p. 27, 57 top, 57 bottom l., 75 bottom, 77 top r., 79 middle l., 102, 103, 105, 109 top, 114 r., 116 bottom l., 117, 123 top, 127 r., 128 l., 130 l., 132 top, 138 l., 143 top, 151 top, 160 r., 165 r., 197 bottom, 230 top • photo: Adam Rzepka, p. 48 l., 57 bottom r., 63 top r., 66 r., 78 l., 81 r., 84 bottom l., 114 top l., 114 bottom l., 118 r., 158 r., 162 top l. • photo: Benjamin Soligny and Raphaël Chipault, p. 139 l. • photo: Jean-François Tomasian, p. 51 top r., 113 top r. • photo: Hervé Véronèse, p. 65 bottom
© CNAP, p. 24, 49 l., 194, 200 r., 206 bottom
© CNAP / photo DR, p. 190 bottom
© CNAP / photo: Paris, Galerie Krief, p. 199 top r.
© CNAP / photo: Yves Chenot, Paris, p. 101, 185
© CNAP / photo: Stanislas de Grailly, Paris, p. 184 r.
© Julienne Hsu, p. 30
© Fondation Le Corbusier, Paris, p. 35, 37
© Fouad Maazouz, p. 193 l.
© Mundaneum, centre d'archives, Mons (Belgium), p. 38
© Musée de Grenoble, p. 99 bottom
© Musée Guimet, Paris, dist. RMN-GP, photo: Benjamin Soligny et Raphaël Chipault, p. 139 r., 140, 143 bottom
© Alain Pérus, p. 192 r.
© DR, p. 217

The titles for this book were set in
Euclid BP (Emmanuel Rey, 2013, Swiss Typefaces)
and Fakt Soft Pro (Thomas Thiemich, 2012, Our Type),
the running text in Egyptienne F (Adrian Frutiger, 1956, Linotype)
and the subheads and annexes in Fakt Soft Pro.
Photoengraving Arciel, Paris
First printed on 13 March 2014
Deckers-Snoeck, Ghent, Belgium
Printed in Belgium